境外资本市场重要法律文献译丛 ❽

美洲卷

美国多德-弗兰克华尔街改革与消费者保护法

（中英文对照本）

Dodd-Frank Wall Street Reform and Consumer Protection Act

（下 册）

中国证券监督管理委员会 组织编译

法律出版社
LAW PRESS · CHINA

《美国多德—弗兰克华尔街改革与消费者保护法》

主　编：杨迈军
副主编：刘能元　席志勇
编　委：田　丰　鲍建平　杨　柯　雷晓冰
米　盈　王海洋　颜文俊　张　华
曲蓉晖　张翼飞

致　谢

上海期货交易所对本书的出版给予了大力支持!

译者说明

《多德—弗兰克华尔街改革与消费者保护法》(Dodd-Frank Wall Street Reform and Consumer Protection Act)(以下简称《多德—弗兰克法》)是美国联邦政府为了应对2008年肇始于美国并迅速席卷全球的金融风暴而制定的一部大规模的金融改革法案。综观该法案的制定过程不难看出,美国政府在推行金融监管体制改革、弥补金融体系缺陷方面,可谓步履维艰。

2009年6月17日,奥巴马政府正式发布实施一系列全面彻底的金融监管改革措施,之后各大利益集团之间开始了长达一年多的激烈博弈,国会众议院和参议院分别于2009年12月11日和2010年5月20日通过了各自版本的金融监管法案。为协调立法分歧,两院任命了联席委员会,修改并形成了两院统一版本的《多德—弗兰克法》。2010年7月15日,参议院通过了该法案的最终版本。2010年7月21日,美国总统奥巴马在法案上签字,《多德—弗兰克法》正式生效。

这份鸿篇巨制的金融改革法案,标志着美国完成了历时近两年的金融改革立法,体现了美国对于金融危机爆发的原因的深刻反思,并由此开启了与新自由主义分道扬镳的金融监管路径。该法案不仅是美国在全球范围内率先针对危机中饱受诟病的金融监管体制建立的新规则,更是今后各国进行金融监管改革的新标尺,对美国境内以及全球范围的金融生态产生了深远影响。

一、《多德—弗兰克法》的立法背景

金融监管体制改革向来具有“危机指向”的特征,《多德—弗兰克法》的出台亦是一种事后立法改革的具体举措。

华尔街,这一曾经创造无数荣耀、辉煌与梦想的金融“麦加”圣地,几十年来一直引领着全球金融市场的发展方向,但却在2008年以其贪婪无度与极端不负责为全球金融体系带来了一次沉重打击。单就美国而言,在这场继大萧条以来最糟糕的金融危机中,800万个就业机会付诸东流,企业破产,房价下跌,个人储蓄蒸发……经济衰退的背后是实体经济与虚拟经济比例的严重失衡,是房地产资本泡沫的彻底破灭,是金融衍生工具的过度创新,是金融机构道德风险的肆意泛滥,是信用评级机构剧烈的利益冲突,而这一切的一切,将美国金融监管体制的内生性缺陷暴露无遗。

在金融危机爆发之时,美国“双线多头”的金融监管体制呈现出多种弊端,在这样一种“伞形”的金融监管体系下,监管机构之间的职能既有分工,又有交叉,多个监管机构并存。此种模式在飞速发展的金融市场中,引发了监管重叠、监管真空和监管套利等情况,暴露出了诸多难以胜任市场发展现状的缺陷,如各监管机构之间协调性差,容易出现监管真空地带;各监管机构之间难以统一号令,不可避免地产生摩擦;针对混业经营体制而实行分业监管,容易导致重复监管;多重监管之下易催生监管套利行为;从整体上看,金融监管机构庞大,导致监管成本较高等。

在这种情况下,只有通过一场根本性的重大革新,才能消弭美国金融监管体系的结构性缺陷。而在此过程中,如何在不减损美国金融市场的全球竞争力的同时,重塑行之有效的金融监管机制,同时维持金融市场的稳定并保护金融消费者的合法权益,无疑是一场艰难的平衡。

回顾美国金融监管法律法规的历史变迁,可以发现其经历了一条在"管制与自由之间"、在"金融监管与市场发展之间"不断寻求平衡点的曲折道路,美国的整个金融法制史就是一个"放松管制—加强管制—再放松管制—再次重构管制"的循环过程。

具体来说,在20世纪30年代的大萧条背景之下,罗斯福总统颁布了具有里程碑意义的《格拉斯—斯蒂格尔法》,将投资银行和商业银行分离,逐步形成分业经营、分业监管的格局,美国金融发展逐渐法制化和机构化;此后,面对20世纪70年代开始的产业空心化和滞胀局面,美国国会于1999年通过了《金融服务现代化法》,打破了分业经营的界限,以"效率与竞争"的理念整合了美国的金融法律体系,放松管制成为这一时期的主要趋势;在金融实践的新自由主义舞台上,美国金融机构的经营规模越来越大,金融创新越来越多,在市场份额迅速扩张的乐观局面下,酝酿着不断累积的系统性金融风险,终于在2008年全面爆发。

这场监管放松与金融自由化的"滑铁卢"所带来了巨大灾难,直接催生了《多德—弗兰克法》,其方向直指"重构管制"。

二、《多德—弗兰克法》的主要内容及特点

《多德—弗兰克法》充分体现了后危机时代美国金融监管理念和监管模式的变革方向,篇幅宏大、规定细致,共设16编,1600多条规定,文本多达2300多页。该法案对包括银行、证券、保险、对冲基金、信用评级机构、交易商、投资咨询机构、会计制度、上市公司等在内的金融体系运行规则和监管架构进行了全面改革与修订。

《多德—弗兰克法》的核心宗旨主要体现在以下两方面:其一,改变目前超级金融机构"太大而不能倒"的局面,有效防范系统性风险;其二,保护金融市场中的弱势群体,避免金融消费者受到欺诈。

围绕系统性风险和消费者金融保护两大核心问题,法案从系统性风险、消费者金融保护、重构原有监管机构和监管职能、提高对"具有系统重要性"金融机构的监管标准、填补关于对冲基金等金融行业的监管空白、对证券化及场外衍生品金融市场进行规范和约束、严格银行资本金监管和业务监管、华尔街高管薪酬监管等几个方面对现有监管规则进行了调整和改革。

在金融监管机构方面的改革,主要体现为以下三方面:

其一,设立了金融稳定监督委员会(Financial Stability Oversight Council)。该法案规

定，由财政部部长担任主席，领导10名成员设立金融稳定监督委员会，负责监测和处理危及全美金融稳定的系统风险金融。金融稳定监督委员会有权认定哪些金融机构可能对市场产生系统性冲击，从而在资本金和流动性方面对这些机构提出更加严格的监管要求，并识别、审查具有系统重要性的金融市场服务平台及各类金融活动，促进市场秩序、消除美国金融体系稳定所面临的潜在威胁。

其二，成立了金融研究办公室(Office of Financial Research)。法案规定，在财政部管辖下再成立金融研究办公室，此办公室旨在为金融稳定监督委员会及其附属机构提供行政、技术、预算分析等服务。办公室由数据中心和调查分析中心构成，有权利制定管制措施以及收集报告、数据和信息，无须国会批准。

其三，新建消费者金融保护局(Bureau of Consumer Financial Protection)。在美国联邦储备委员会下新设消费者金融保护局，并赋予其在规划和执行消费者金融产品和服务标准时的广泛的实质性权力。消费者金融保护局负责对提供信用卡、抵押贷款和其他贷款等消费者金融产品及服务的金融机构实施监管，还被授权根据金融产品和服务的特征来制定披露相关信息规则。该局接受美国总审计局的审计，并且每半年得向参议院银行委员会和众议院金融服务委员会汇报。

除了这三个机构的新设之外，《多德—弗兰克法》还对现有的监管机构进行了一系列改革及职能的重新定位，明晰界定各自的职责，以防止出现监管竞次的局面。

在具体内容方面，该法案的修订主要涉及以下几方面：

其一，终结金融机构“太大而不能倒”(too-big-to-fail)现象，停止政府救市。具体措施包括：当金融机构经营失败时，对其采取安全的清算程序；规定新的严格的资本金充足率及流动性要求使金融机构自觉不宜过大；更新美联储的权力，允许其提供系统范围内的支持，但不再扶持个别金融机构；建立更加严格的标准和监督体系以保护美国经济、消费者、投资者和企业的利益。

其二，杜绝不公平、欺诈性的金融产品或金融活动，打击隐蔽费用、条款滥用等欺骗行为，确保消费者获取信用卡公司、房地产抵押贷款经纪人、银行等金融机构提供的有关贷款或其他金融产品的详尽信息，以保护消费者权益。

其三，改进金融监管法规，采纳“沃克尔规则”，限制大金融机构的投机性交易，禁止银行或拥有银行的机构从事违背客户要求的自营交易或投资套利基金，限制银行持有的最大负债额，以保证银行机构资产结构合理和管理制度完善。

其四，强化金融衍生产品交易管理，剥离掉期业务与场外市场场内化。法案对于美国银行设立私募基金、对冲基金，信用卡消费等方面作出了诸多限制以及规定，禁止联邦政府救济任何掉期交易企业或从事任何掉期、证券支持掉期交易或其他交易活动，要求场外金融衍生产品交易通过集中清算系统完成，防止金融体系出现不当风险行为。

其五，改革保险监管，迈向全国集中统一监管模式。法案规定由美国联邦政府对保险业进行集中统一监管，而不再由各州分散监管。法案试图在保险监管的两个领域，即保险市场和再保险市场设立全国统一标准。

其六,规制公司高层薪酬水平,在公司高层薪酬待遇方面,为股东提供发言权,使其对高层薪酬水平和高管解职补偿费等方面取得不具约束力的投票权,进一步完善公司治理。

三、《多德—弗兰克法》的现实意义与启示

《多德—弗兰克法》是美国金融体制立法上的一项历史性革新,通过对该法案具体内容的梳理,可以看出其在重构美国金融监管体系的努力中所遵循的思路,即注重宏观审慎监管、严格金融监管标准、扩大监管覆盖范围以及强调跨机构协调监管。

就宏观层面而言,法案基于对金融市场本质的思考,对金融市场的功能重新进行了定位,推动了金融机构向传统业务的回归。就微观层面而言,法案对金融机构的非审慎行为进行了纠正,强调了将所有具有系统重要性的金融机构纳入宏观审慎的监管框架之下,对有系统性风险的金融机构,提出了更高的资本充足率、杠杆限制和风险集中度要求,还对银行自营交易及高风险的衍生品交易进行了更为严格的限制,并将此前缺乏监管的场外衍生品市场、对冲基金、私募基金等金融市场参与者纳入了监管视野。

事实上,该法案并没有全盘否定20世纪以来的金融自由化思想和放松监管模式,而是透过危机认识到金融监管结构中的弊端和不足,有针对性地调整监管架构和创设监管规则,从而使美国现行的金融监管制度能够适应金融体系的新变化,以防范金融体系中新变化可能带来的风险。的确,绝对依靠监管或绝对信赖市场这两种极端的模式均不能创造出良好的金融体系,只有在金融监管与市场力量中寻找到一个平衡,才能更好地实现金融稳定、风险控制及高效率的金融发展。

《多德—弗兰克法》正是在保留过去30多年金融自由化的基本成果、确认市场化仍是美国金融业未来发展基本方向的前提下,致力于改善和提高金融监管的技术和艺术,并将其尽可能覆盖所有的金融产品和服务、所有的金融市场和所有的金融机构。

当然,我们也应当认识到,《多德—弗兰克法》的立法意图在于维持金融稳定,但这仅仅是进一步实现金融发展的保障与条件,而非最终目的。没有任何一种监管模式可以称得上完美,这次金融体制改革也不例外。具体来说,该法案依然存在种种不足,如没有对真正引起危机的房利美和房地美进行约束,出于对美国房市稳定的考虑,两房问题成为此次改革中的空白区域;而且此法案仅仅确定了改革的框架,其具体实施还有待相关监管当局制定进一步的细则。但是,金融监管具有天生的滞后性,在具体问题暴露出来以后,监管者要对此进行逐步调整和完善,构建出一个比此前的金融监管制度更为适合的整体框架,达到促进金融市场健康、有序发展的基本要求。公允地说,只要在一次改革中能够为上一阶段金融体系新发展所带来的负面效应提供些许有益的解决方案,那么这次改革的价值就不容低估。

华东政法大学国际金融法律学院　罗培新

总译校：

吴志攀，北京大学教授、博士研究生导师，中国法学会副会长，北京大学党委常委、常务副校长、法律总顾问，兼任北京大学亚太研究院院长、北京大学金融法研究中心主任，最高人民法院专家咨询员。北京大学法学博士，美国哈佛大学法学院访问学者，美国艾森豪威尔基金会学者。出版《金融法概论》、《国际金融法》等十余部专著。

审校人员：

罗培新，华东政法大学国际金融法律学院院长、科研处处长，教授、博士研究生导师。北京大学国际金融法专业博士，中国社会科学院法学所博士后，美国耶鲁大学、英国牛津大学访问学者。国家教育部新世纪优秀人才、上海市第三届十大"优秀中青年法学家"。在《中国社会科学》、《中国法学》、《法学研究》发表论文若干篇，出版专著、译著 10 多部。

宋金莹，北京思必锐翻译公司译审。通过全国翻译专业资格英语一级笔译考试。北京外国语大学高级翻译学院翻译硕士、中国人民大学法学学士、南开大学英语语言文学学士。曾就职于司法部司法协助交流中心、司法协助与外事司，担任高级翻译。负责审校《美国多德—弗兰克华尔街改革与消费者保护法》第一章到第八章、第十章到第十六章以及最后的统稿工作。

翻译人员：

瞿乃明，法国巴黎高等翻译学院翻译学硕士、法国巴黎第九大学国际企业管理硕士、台湾大学经济学学士，北京优笔客翻译中心总经理。主要翻译作品有《欧盟金融工具市场指令》、《中国证监会 2011 年年报》、《美国商品交易法》、《美国证券交易委员会自身组织与通用规章》、《欧盟金融监管体制改革法规汇编》、《欧盟证券监管法规汇编》和《欧盟另类投资基金管理人指令》等。

艾飞，北京大学法学院法学学士。2007 年通过中国司法考试，北京优笔客翻译中心质量经理。主要翻译作品有《美国商品交易法》、《美国证券交易委员会自身组织与通用规章》和《欧盟证券监管法规汇编》。

董雷召，天津外国语大学英美文学学士、南开大学法学院法律硕士。2005 年通过中国司法考试，北京优笔客翻译中心专职译者。主要翻译作品有《美国商品交易法》和《欧盟另类投资基金管理人指令》等。

福宇，北京外国语大学英语学士。曾任北京优笔客翻译中心专职译者，现任中国铁建国际集团有限公司专职译者。主要翻译作品有《美国证券交易委员会自身组织与通用规章》。

范一，中国政法大学中美法学院比较法硕士、中国政法大学法学学士。2007 年通过中国司法考试，北京优笔客翻译中心专职译者。主要翻译作品有《美国证券交易委员会自身组织与通用规章》。

冯永杰，烟台师范学院外语系英语学士，华东政法大学法律硕士。2009 年通过中国司法考试，曾任某知名律师事务所翻译部负责人，现任优笔客翻译中心兼职译者。

梁霏，美国纽约大学法学院法学硕士、中国人民大学经济学学士及法学硕士。曾长期执业于国际律师事务所北京及香港分所,并任职诺基亚西门子通信和惠普中国区法律顾问。现任北京市君泰律师事务所合伙人律师。

周舒诞,美国波士顿大学法学院法律博士(J.D.)、上海外国语大学高级翻译学院翻译学硕士、中山大学中文系中国语言文学学士。现任国际律师事务所伦敦总部美国税法律师。主要翻译作品有《欧盟金融工具市场指令》和《美国商品交易法》等。

程宇凡,首都经贸大学法律学士。现任某美国律师事务所专职法律翻译。主要翻译作品有《美国证券交易委员会自身组织与通用规章》、《欧盟金融监管体制改革法规汇编》和《欧盟另类投资基金管理人指令》等。

钱淳,北京语言大学文学学士。北京优笔客翻译中心专职译者。主要翻译作品有《美国证券交易委员会自身组织与通用规章》等。

区欣,波兰什切青大学伊拉斯谟世界(Erasmus Mundus)硕士课程班学习欧盟法和欧盟指令,中山大学西方哲学硕士。北京优笔客翻译中心专职译者。主要翻译作品有《欧盟金融监管体制改革法规汇编》和《欧盟证券监管法规汇编》等。

总　序

中国资本市场是适应我国经济体制改革和对外开放的形势要求逐步建立发展起来的。为了有效借鉴境外成熟市场的制度经验,中国资本市场从成立伊始,就特别注重按照“立足国情,为我所用”的原则,不断学习、消化和吸收境外成熟市场的运行规则和监管制度。目前,中国资本市场现行有效的法律、法规、规章、规范性文件共521件,加上大量的交易所和协会的自律规则,基本形成了我国资本市场的法律制度规范体系。这些制度规范构建起一整套与国际通行原则基本相符的法律框架、交易规则和监管体系,有效维护了市场秩序,保证了市场功能和作用的发挥,保护了投资者的合法权益。

经过20余年的改革发展,我国资本市场进入了创新发展的新阶段。立足于服务实体经济发展的大局需要,重点解决资本市场自身结构不平衡、服务实体经济能力不足、为居民提供投资理财产品相对匮乏等突出现实问题,资本市场现有的以股票公开发行并在交易所上市交易为主的境内市场体系,将逐步发展成为一个公募与私募并重、股票与债券平衡、场内与场外协调发展的资本市场体系。与此相适应,需要进一步发展壮大财富管理行业,立足于功能监管的制度定位,统一资产管理行为规则,放松行政管制,增强创新活力。实现这样的改革目标,需要我们更加重视学习境外成熟市场的制度经验,充分借鉴境外市场有关私募发行、债权融资、资产管理、期货及衍生品等方面的法律制度,在尊重市场规律的前提下,大胆进行制度和机制创新,确保我们的各项制度适应和满足市场改革的实际需要。

坚持对外开放是中国资本市场改革和发展的一贯方针。在经济全球化深入发展的时代背景下,适应我国经济结构调整和经济方式转变和“逐步实现人民币资本项目可兑换”的金融对外开放的总体要求,中国资本市场必须以更加积极的态度参与全球经济竞争,提高在全球范围内配置资源,服务实体经济发展的能力。不论是支持境内企业到境外发行融资,鼓励境内机构和个人到境外进行证券投资,还是畅通境外企业到境内发行融资渠道,平等保护境外机构和个人到境内进行证券投资,都需要在立足国情的前提下,实现制度衔接互通,消除制度壁垒。特别重要的是,市场竞争首先是制度规则的竞争,增强我国资本市场的国际竞争力,一方面要确保我国市场通过制度规则体现法治环境吸引力,另一方面还要增强我国在涉及资本市场对外开放的国际规则的制定中的话语权,增强我国在国际监管合作和跨境执法合作中的主动权。

同时,我们也注意到,2008 年国际金融危机发生后,境外资本市场对监管体制、机制做了较为重大的调整,提出了不少新的监管要求,出台了不少新的法律文件。例如,美国制定了具有金融综合监管性质的《多德—弗兰克华尔街改革与消费者保护法》,英国则将原来集证券、银行、保险于一身的《2000 年金融服务与市场法》修改成《2010 年金融服务法》。对于境外相关法律制度的动态发展,需要及时掌握情况,借鉴有益经验,为进一步完善我国资本市场的基础性制度建设提供参考。

经过长期的努力,中国资本市场的制度借鉴和引进已经越过了概念化、碎片状的发展阶段,进入全面、系统、精细化的更高阶段。由于种种原因,对境外资本市场法律制度的介绍,无论是在法学界、法律界,还是在证券期货行业内,一直以来都存在及时性不够、系统性不足、权威性不强的情况。特别是翻译介绍的质量不高、精品不多,这在客观上影响了对境外经验的学习和借鉴。

为了适应资本市场学习借鉴境外制度经验的形势要求,中国证监会精选了境外资本市场国家和地区的重要法律文献,包括境外主要资本市场的重要法律、监管部门的监管规则、经典的司法判例、最新的资本市场立法成果以及相关法学理论权威著作等,组织翻译出版了这套《境外资本市场重要法律文献译丛》。译丛的翻译出版工作,在系统单位、部门和关心市场发展的专家学者的共同努力下,紧紧抓住保质量、出精品的关键环节,建立了"竞标择优确定翻译人员、知名专家评审保证翻译质量、适当报酬和学术声誉结合激励"的工作机制,落实"精选译题、精细翻译、精心审校、精致出版"的工作要求,是中国证监会打造国人了解国际资本市场法律制度权威平台的有益尝试。为此,愿以本文向参与丛书翻译、审校的国际金融、法律方面的专家和学者表示感谢,并与大家共勉,共同为建设起一个权利公平、机会公平、规则公平的资本市场而努力。

中国证监会

2013 年 2 月

序

党的十八大明确指出，树立社会主义法治理念，增强全社会学法尊法守法用法意识，提高领导干部运用法治思维和法治方式深化改革、推动发展、化解矛盾、维护稳定的能力。对期货与衍生品市场而言，法规就是市场的生命线，因此，加强我国期货与衍生品市场的法制建设，首先就是要学习、研究国际期货与衍生品市场的法规规则。2010年出台的《多德—弗兰克华尔街改革与消费者保护法》(以下简称《多德—弗兰克法》)作为美国20世纪30年代后颁布的最大规模的金融监管改革法案，对全球期货与衍生品市场发展产生了深远影响。因此，对该法案进行翻译与学习对我国期货与衍生品市场发展具有重要意义。

近年来，世界经济正在发生深刻变化，全球经济的一体化进程加快，促使生产要素和金融资本在全球范围内快速流动,商品和各类金融资产价格剧烈波动，经济、金融体系中的不确定因素明显增多，与经济发展密切相关的汇率、能源、金属和农产品等价格大幅波动。在交易电子化与网络化的背景下，期货与衍生品市场交易量快速增长，已成为国际资本市场的重要组成部分。相较境外成熟资本市场，我国期货及衍生品发展不足的问题还很突出。"十二五"时期，中国资本市场应更好地承担起服务经济社会发展大局的历史责任，金融衍生品的发展可以大大拓展资本市场的深度，起到价格发现和风险管理的作用。但是，复杂的衍生品本身隐含风险。2008年肇始于美国华尔街并席卷全球的金融危机，已经让各国政府及监管机构充分认识到金融衍生品的高杠杆、高风险性和迅速的风险传递性。因此，完善金融衍生品市场法规，加强金融衍生品市场的监管是非常必要的。从美国2000年《商品期货交易现代化法》全面放松金融监管，到《多德—弗兰克法》对金融监管的再次重构历程中可以看出，金融衍生品市场的稳步发展需要完善的法律制度支撑和保障。

推动我国期货与衍生品市场由数量扩张向质量提升转变，对于保障我国经济战略安全具有重要意义。我国期货与衍生品市场发展较晚，是在学习、借鉴境外主要期货与衍生品市场经验的基础上建立并发展起来的，期货与衍生品市场法规规则也是在学习、借鉴境外主要期货与衍生品市场经验的基础上建立并发展起来的。因此，学习借鉴《多德—弗兰克法》等国际法规，促进我国期货与衍生品市场的法制建设与业务发展非常必要。

为防范系统性风险同时加大对投资者的保护，《多德—弗兰克法》从总体上加强了对场外衍生品市场的监管力度,抑制过度性投机,立体化拓宽了风险控制制度和措施,同时注重不同风险类型市场间的风险隔离,通过适当放宽市场操纵等市场欺诈行为的认定标准,进一步加大了对欺诈行为的打击力度,多维度加强了对市场安全的维护。这些新的监管思路和措施,对我国进一步发展期货与衍生品市场,完善监管制度有很大的启示意义。

此外,衍生品市场的国际化和电子化也进一步加剧了全球衍生品市场间的竞争,交易电子化越来越普及,几乎在世界任何一个角落都可以交易全球的产品。在交易标的、投资者与影响力等因素全球化的背景下,我国期货与衍生品市场与境外市场已存在被动的竞争关系,亟待通过“走出去”和“引进来”逐步完成期货市场的对外开放。在这个过程中,一方面需要完善相关制度与规则,为境内机构创造条件,使其逐步接近国际市场的运作标准;另一方面需要降低外资进入门槛,分阶段允许境外投资者进入我国期货与衍生品市场交易,积极构建一个稳定、有竞争力的衍生品市场。

为此,我们都要继续加大国内外期货与衍生品法规规则的研究力度,在深刻把握我国期货与衍生品市场发展规律的基础上,不断对我国现有规则、制度、机制进行调整,建立一套适合我国国情又与国际接轨的高效法规规则体系,通过法规规则和制度创新,带动业务发展,夯实我国期货与衍生品市场发展的制度基础。

杨迈军

2013 年 9 月

CONTENTS

目　　录

TITLE XI—FEDERAL RESERVE SYSTEM PROVISIONS 638

TITLE XII—IMPROVING ACCESS TO MAINSTREAM FINANCIAL INSTITUTIONS 674

Dodd-Frank Wall Street Reform and Consumer Protection Act

美国多德—弗兰克华尔街改革与消费者保护法

TITLE IX–INVESTOR PROTECTIONS AND IMPROVEMENTS TO THE REGULATION OF SECURITIES

SEC.901. SHORT TITLE.

This title may be cited as the "Investor Protection and Securities Reform Act of 2010".

Subtitle A—Increasing Investor Protection

SEC.911. INVESTOR ADVISORY COMMITTEE ESTABLISHED.

Title I of the Securities Exchange Act of 1934 (15 U.S.C.78a et seq.) is amended by adding at the end the following:

"SEC.39. INVESTOR ADVISORY COMMITTEE.

"(a) ESTABLISHMENT AND PURPOSE.—

"(1) ESTABLISHMENT. —There is established within the Commission the Investor Advisory Committee (referred to in this section as the 'Committee').

"(2) PURPOSE. —The Committee shall —

"(A) advise and consult with the Commission on —

"(i) regulatory priorities of the Commission;

"(ii) issues relating to the regulation of securities products, trading strategies, and fee structures, and the effectiveness of disclosure;

"(iii) initiatives to protect investor interest; and

"(iv) initiatives to promote investor confidence and the integrity of the securities marketplace; and

"(B) submit to the Commission such findings and recommendations as the Committee determines are appropriate, including recommendations for proposed legislative changes.

"(b) MEMBERSHIP. —

第九编——投资者保护与证券监管的完善

第901条　简称

引述本编时,可简称为《2010年投资者保护与证券改革法》。

第A子编——加强投资者保护

第911条　设立投资者顾问委员会

在《1934年证券交易法》第一编(《美国法典》第十五编第78a节及其后条文)结尾处增加如下内容,作为对该编的修正:

“第39条　投资者顾问委员会

(a)**设立与宗旨**。——

(1)**设立**。——证券交易委员会下设投资者顾问委员会(投资者顾问委员会)。

(2)**宗旨**。——投资者顾问委员会应——

(A)针对如下事项向证券交易委员会提供咨询意见,并与证券交易委员会磋商——

(i)证券交易委员会的监管重点;

(ii)与证券产品、交易策略、收费结构监管相关的事宜,以及与信息披露有效性相关的事宜;

(iii)投资者利益保护计划;及

(iv)提振投资者信心和加强证券市场完整性的计划;并

(B)向证券交易委员会提交其认为适当的认定结论和建议,包括关于立法变动提案的建议。

(b)**成员**。——

"(1) IN GENERAL. —The members of the Committee shall be —

"(A) the Investor Advocate;

"(B) a representative of State securities commissions;

"(C) a representative of the interests of senior citizens; and

"(D) not fewer than 10, and not more than 20, members appointed by the Commission, from among individuals who —

"(i) represent the interests of individual equity and debt investors, including investors in mutual funds;

"(ii) represent the interests of institutional investors, including the interests of pension funds and registered investment companies;

"(iii) are knowledgeable about investment issues and decisions; and

"(iv) have reputations of integrity.

"(2) TERM. —Each member of the Committee appointed under paragraph (1)(B) shall serve for a term of 4 years.

"(3) MEMBERS NOT COMMISSION EMPLOYEES. —Members appointed under paragraph (1)(B) shall not be deemed to be employees or agents of the Commission solely because of membership on the Committee.

"(c) CHAIRMAN; VICE CHAIRMAN; SECRETARY; ASSISTANT SECRETARY. —

"(1) IN GENERAL.—The members of the Committee shall elect, from among the members of the Committee —

"(A) a chairman, who may not be employed by an issuer;

"(B) a vice chairman, who may not be employed by an issuer;

"(C) a secretary; and

"(D) an assistant secretary.

"(2) TERM.—Each member elected under paragraph (1) shall serve for a term of 3 years in the capacity for which the member was elected under paragraph (1).

"(d) MEETINGS. —

"(1) FREQUENCY OF MEETINGS. -The Committee shall meet —

"(A) not less frequently than twice annually, at the call of the chairman of the Committee; and

"(B) from time to time, at the call of the Commission.

"(2) NOTICE.—The chairman of the Committee shall give the members of the Committee written notice of each meeting, not later than 2 weeks before the date of the meeting.

"(e) COMPENSATION AND TRAVEL EXPENSES. —Each member of the Committee who is not a full-time employee of the United States shall —

"(1) be entitled to receive compensation at a rate not to exceed the daily equivalent of

(1)一般规定。——投资者顾问委员会应由如下成员组成——

(A)投资者维权办公室主任;

(B)一名州证券委员会代表;

(C)一名老年公民利益代表;及

(D)证券交易委员会从符合如下条件的人员中任命的10名(含)以上20名(含)以下的成员——

(i)代表股权和债券个人投资者(包括共同基金投资者)的利益;

(ii)代表机构投资者(包括养老基金及注册投资公司)的利益;

(iii)对投资事宜和投资决策具有深入了解;且

(iv)享有良好、诚实的声誉。

(2)**任期**。——根据第(1)(B)款任命的每一名投资者顾问委员会成员的任期均为4年。

(3)**投资者顾问委员会成员不属于证券交易委员会雇员**。——根据第(1)(B)款任命的投资者顾问委员会成员，不得仅因该等成员身份而被视为证券交易委员会的雇员或代理人。

(c)**主席、副主席、秘书、助理秘书**。——

(1)一般规定。——投资者顾问委员会成员应从成员中推选——

(A)一名主席,不得是受雇于发行人的人士;

(B)一名副主席,不得是受雇于发行人的人士;

(C)一名秘书;及

(D)一名助理秘书。

(2)**任期**。——根据第(1)款选举的每名成员担任根据第(1)款被推选担任的职务的任期均为3年。

(d)**会议**。——

(1)**会议频率**。——投资者顾问委员会的会议——

(A)应由投资者顾问委员会主席召集,每年至少举行两次;且

(B)可由证券交易委员会随时召集。

(2)**通知**。——投资者顾问委员会主席应于每次会议举行之前,至少提前两周向投资者顾问委员会成员发出书面会议通知。

(e)薪酬和差旅费。——不属于联邦政府全职雇员的每一投资者顾问委员会成员均应——

(1)有权按照其在投资者顾问委员会的实际履职天数领取报酬,但报酬标准不得

the annual rate of basic pay in effect for a position level V of the Executive Schedule at under section 5316 of title 5, United States Code, for each day during which the member is engaged in the actual performance of the duties of the Committee; and

"(2) while away from the home or regular place of business of the member in the performance of services for the Committee, be allowed travel expenses, including per diem in lieu of subsistence, in the same manner as persons employed intermittently in the Government service are allowed expenses under section 5703(b) of title 5, United States Code.

"(f) STAFF. —The Commission shall make available to the Committee such staff as the chairman of the Committee determines are necessary to carry out this section.

"(g) REVIEW BY COMMISSION. —The Commission shall —

"(1) review the findings and recommendations of the Committee; and

"(2) each time the Committee submits a finding or recommendation to the Commission, promptly issue a public statement —

"(A) assessing the finding or recommendation of the Committee; and

"(B) disclosing the action, if any, the Commission intends to take with respect to the finding or recommendation.

"(h) COMMITTEE FINDINGS.—Nothing in this section shall require the Commission to agree to or act upon any finding or recommendation of the Committee.

"(i) FEDERAL ADVISORY COMMITTEE ACT.—The Federal Advisory Committee Act (5 U.S.C.App.) shall not apply with respect to the Committee and its activities.

"(j) AUTHORIZATION OF APPROPRIATIONS.—There is authorized to be appropriated to the Commission such sums as are necessary to carry out this section.".

SEC.912. CLARIFICATION OF AUTHORITY OF THE COMMISSION TO ENGAGE IN INVESTOR TESTING.

Section 19 of the Securities Act of 1933 (15 U.S.C.77s) is amended by adding at the end the following:

"(e) EVALUATION OF RULES OR PROGRAMS.—For the purpose of evaluating any rule or program of the Commission issued or carried out under any provision of the securities laws, as defined in section 3 of the Securities Exchange Act of 1934 (15 U.S.C.78c), and the purposes of considering, proposing, adopting, or engaging in any such rule or program or developing new rules or programs, the Commission may —

"(1) gather information from and communicate with investors or other members of the public;

"(2) engage in such temporary investor testing programs as the Commission determines are in the public interest or would protect investors; and

高于根据《美国法典》第五编第5316节规定的“高级公务员序列第V级别”职位当时适用的基本年薪折算的日均报酬;且

(2)在为投资者顾问委员会开展工作而离开家庭住所或正常办公场所的差旅期间,与间歇性受雇于政府部门的雇员根据《美国法典》第五编第5703(b)节规定获得差旅费一样,获得差旅费,包括每日津贴。

(f)**工作人员**。——证券交易委员会应为投资者顾问委员会配备投资者顾问委员会主席判定的对于实施本条规定确属必要的工作人员。

(g)**证券交易委员会的审查**。——证券交易委员会应——

(1)审查投资者顾问委员会的认定结论和建议;并

(2)在投资者顾问委员会每次向证券交易委员会提交认定结论或建议时,及时发布公开声明——

(A)对投资者顾问委员会的认定结论或建议进行评估;并

(B)披露证券交易委员会针对该认定结论或建议打算采取的行动(如有)。

(h)**投资者顾问委员会的认定结论**。——本条任何内容均不要求证券交易委员会必须对投资者顾问委员会的任何认定结论或建议表示同意,亦不要求其必须针对该等认定结论或建议采取任何行动。

(i)**《联邦顾问委员会法》**。——《联邦顾问委员会法》(《美国法典》第五编附件)不适用于投资者顾问委员会及其活动。

(j)**拨款授权**。——兹授权向证券交易委员会划拨实施本条规定所需的必要款项。”

第912条　关于证券交易委员会开展投资者测试的权力的说明

在《1933年证券法》第19条(《美国法典》第十五编第77s节)结尾处增加如下内容,作为对该条的修正:

“(e)**对规则或计划的评价**。——为了对证券交易委员会根据证券法律[定义见《1934年证券交易法》第3条(《美国法典》第十五编第78c节)]的任何规定发布或实施的规则或计划进行评价,以及为了探讨、提出、制定或执行该等规则或计划,或者制订新的规则或计划,证券交易委员会可以——

(1)向投资者或其他公众收集信息,并与其开展交流;

(2)开展证券交易委员会判定符合公共利益或有利于投资者保护的临时性投资者测试计划;并

"(3) consult with academics and consultants, as necessary to carry out this subsection.

"(f) RULE OF CONSTRUCTION.—For purposes of the Paperwork Reduction Act (44 U.S.C.3501 et seq.), any action taken under subsection (e) shall not be construed to be a collection of information.".

SEC.913. STUDY AND RULEMAKING REGARDING OBLIGATIONS OF BROKERS, DEALERS, AND INVESTMENT ADVISERS.

(a) DEFINITION.—For purposes of this section, the term "retail customer" means a natural person, or the legal representative of such natural person, who—

(1) receives personalized investment advice about securities from a broker or dealer or investment adviser; and

(2) uses such advice primarily for personal, family, or household purposes.

(b) STUDY.—The Commission shall conduct a study to evaluate—

(1) the effectiveness of existing legal or regulatory standards of care for brokers, dealers, investment advisers, persons associated with brokers or dealers, and persons associated with investment advisers for providing personalized investment advice and recommendations about securities to retail customers imposed by the Commission and a national securities association, and other Federal and State legal or regulatory standards; and

(2) whether there are legal or regulatory gaps, shortcomings, or overlaps in legal or regulatory standards in the protection of retail customers relating to the standards of care for brokers, dealers, investment advisers, persons associated with brokers or dealers, and persons associated with investment advisers for providing personalized investment advice about securities to retail customers that should be addressed by rule or statute.

(c) CONSIDERATIONS.—In conducting the study required under subsection (b), the Commission shall consider—

(1) the effectiveness of existing legal or regulatory standards of care for brokers, dealers, investment advisers, persons associated with brokers or dealers, and persons associated with investment advisers for providing personalized investment advice and recommendations about securities to retail customers imposed by the Commission and a national securities association, and other Federal and State legal or regulatory standards;

(2) whether there are legal or regulatory gaps, shortcomings, or overlaps in legal or regulatory standards in the protection of retail customers relating to the standards of care for brokers, dealers, investment advisers, persons associated with brokers or dealers, and persons associated with investment advisers for providing personalized investment advice about securities to retail customers that should be addressed by rule or statute;

(3) whether retail customers understand that there are different standards of care applicable to brokers, dealers, investment advisers, persons associated with brokers or dealers, and persons associated with investment advisers in the provision of personalized

(3)就本子条的实施与学术界人士及顾问开展必要磋商。

(f)**解释规则**。——就《文书削减法》(《美国法典》第四十四编第3501节及其后条文)而言,根据第(e)子条采取的任何行动均不得被解释为信息收集行为。”

第913条　关于经纪商、自营商及投资顾问所承担义务的研究以及相关规则制定

(a)**定义**。——就本条而言,“零售客户”一词系指符合如下条件的自然人或该等自然人的法律代理人——

(1)接受经纪商、自营商或投资顾问提供的个性化证券投资意见;且

(2)主要出于个人、家庭或共同居住人的目的使用该等意见。

(b)**研究**。——证券交易委员会应开展研究,对以下各项进行评价——

(1)经纪商、自营商、投资顾问以及上述各者的业务相关人向零售客户提供个性化证券投资意见和建议时所应遵守的由证券交易委员会和全国性证券协会设定的现行法定注意标准或监管注意标准的有效性, 以及其他联邦和州法定标准或监管标准的有效性;及

(2)对于与经纪商、自营商、投资顾问以及上述各者的业务相关人向零售客户提供个性化证券投资意见时所应遵守的注意标准, 零售投资者保护法定标准或监管标准是否存在应通过规则或制定法予以解决的漏洞、不足或重叠问题。

(c)**考虑因素**。——在开展第(b)子条规定的研究时,证券交易委员会应考虑如下因素——

(1)经纪商、自营商、投资顾问以及上述各者的业务相关人向零售客户提供个性化证券投资意见和建议时所应遵守的由证券交易委员会和全国性证券协会设定的现行法定注意标准或监管注意标准的有效性,以及其他联邦、州法定标准或监管标准的有效性;及

(2)对于与经纪商、自营商、投资顾问以及上述各者的业务相关人向零售客户提供个性化证券投资意见时所应遵守的注意标准, 零售投资者保护法定标准或监管标准是否存在应通过规则或制定法予以解决的漏洞、不足或重叠问题;

(3)零售客户是否了解,经纪商、自营商、投资顾问以及上述各者的业务相关人向零售客户提供个性化证券投资意见时是否适用不同的注意标准;

investment advice about securities to retail customers;

(4) whether the existence of different standards of care applicable to brokers, dealers, investment advisers, persons associated with brokers or dealers, and persons associated with investment advisers is a source of confusion for retail customers regarding the quality of personalized investment advice that retail customers receive;

(5) the regulatory, examination, and enforcement resources devoted to, and activities of, the Commission, the States, and a national securities association to enforce the standards of care for brokers, dealers, investment advisers, persons associated with brokers or dealers, and persons associated with investment advisers when providing personalized investment advice and recommendations about securities to retail customers, including —

(A) the effectiveness of the examinations of brokers, dealers, and investment advisers in determining compliance with regulations;

(B) the frequency of the examinations; and

(C) the length of time of the examinations;

(6) the substantive differences in the regulation of brokers, dealers, and investment advisers, when providing personalized investment advice and recommendations about securities to retail customers;

(7) the specific instances related to the provision of personalized investment advice about securities in which —

(A) the regulation and oversight of investment advisers provide greater protection to retail customers than the regulation and oversight of brokers and dealers; and

(B) the regulation and oversight of brokers and dealers provide greater protection to retail customers than the regulation and oversight of investment advisers;

(8) the existing legal or regulatory standards of State securities regulators and other regulators intended to protect retail customers;

(9) the potential impact on retail customers, including the potential impact on access of retail customers to the range of products and services offered by brokers and dealers, of imposing upon brokers, dealers, and persons associated with brokers or dealers —

(A) the standard of care applied under the Investment Advisers Act of 1940 (15 U.S.C. 80b–1 et seq.) for providing personalized investment advice about securities to retail customers of investment advisers, as interpreted by the Commission and the courts; and

(B) other requirements of the Investment Advisers Act of 1940 (15 U.S.C.80b–1 et seq.);

(10) the potential impact of eliminating the broker and dealer exclusion from the definition of "investment adviser" under section 202(a)(11)(C) of the Investment Advisers Act of 1940 (15 U.S.C.80b–2(a)(11)(C)), in terms of —

(A) the impact and potential benefits and harm to retail customers that could result from

(4)适用于经纪商、自营商、投资顾问以及上述各者的业务相关人的不同注意标准的存在是否导致零售客户对其获得的个性化投资意见产生质量困惑;

(5)证券交易委员会、各州及全国性证券协会为执行经纪商、自营商、投资顾问以及上述各者的业务相关人在向零售客户提供个性化证券投资意见和建议时所应遵守的注意标准,而开展的活动及投入的监管、检查及执法资源,包括——

(A)针对经纪商、自营商和投资顾问开展的合规检查的成效;

(B)检查频率;及

(C)检查时间长短;

(6)经纪商、自营商及投资顾问向零售客户提供个性化证券投资意见和建议时所受监管的重大差异;

(7)与提供个性化证券投资意见相关的如下具体情形——

(A)相对于对经纪商和自营商进行规制与监管而言,对投资顾问进行规制与监管为零售客户提供更完善的保护具体情形;及

(B)相对于对投资顾问进行规制与监管而言,对经纪商和自营商进行规制与监管为零售客户提供更完善的保护的具体情形;

(8)州证券监管者和其他监管者旨在保护零售客户的现行法定标准或监管标准;

(9)对经纪商、自营商以及上述二者的业务相关人实施如下标准和要求对零售客户造成的潜在影响,包括对零售客户可从经纪商及自营商处获得的产品和服务种类范围造成的潜在影响——

(A)投资顾问在向零售客户提供个性化证券投资意见时根据《1940年投资顾问法》(《美国法典》第十五编第80b-1节及其后条文)应适用的注意标准(以证券交易委员会及法院的解释为准);及

(B)《1940年投资顾问法》(《美国法典》第十五编第80b-1节及其后条文)的其他要求;

(10)因不再将经纪商和自营商排除在《1940年投资顾问法》第202(a)(11)(C)条[《美国法典》第十五编第80b-2(a)(11)(C)节]定义的“投资顾问”范围之外而给以下各项带来的潜在影响——

(A)该等改变可能对零售客户造成的影响,以及可能给零售客户带来的潜在利益

such a change, including any potential impact on access to personalized investment advice and recommendations about securities to retail customers or the availability of such advice and recommendations;

(B) the number of additional entities and individuals that would be required to register under, or become subject to, the Investment Advisers Act of 1940 (15 U.S.C.80b–1 et seq.), and the additional requirements to which brokers, dealers, and persons associated with brokers and dealers would become subject, including —

(i) any potential additional associated person licensing, registration, and examination requirements; and

(ii) the additional costs, if any, to the additional entities and individuals; and

(C) the impact on Commission and State resources to —

(i) conduct examinations of registered investment advisers and the representatives of registered investment advisers, including the impact on the examination cycle; and

(ii) enforce the standard of care and other applicable requirements imposed under the Investment Advisers Act of 1940 (15 U.S.C.80b–1 et seq.);

(11) the varying level of services provided by brokers, dealers, investment advisers, persons associated with brokers or dealers, and persons associated with investment advisers to retail customers and the varying scope and terms of retail customer relationships of brokers, dealers, investment advisers, persons associated with brokers or dealers, and persons associated with investment advisers with such retail customers;

(12) the potential impact upon retail customers that could result from potential changes in the regulatory requirements or legal standards of care affecting brokers, dealers, investment advisers, persons associated with brokers or dealers, and persons associated with investment advisers relating to their obligations to retail customers regarding the provision of investment advice, including any potential impact on —

(A) protection from fraud;

(B) access to personalized investment advice, and recommendations about securities to retail customers; or

(C) the availability of such advice and recommendations;

(13) the potential additional costs and expenses to —

(A) retail customers regarding and the potential impact on the profitability of their investment decisions; and

(B) brokers, dealers, and investment advisers resulting from potential changes in the regulatory requirements or legal standards affecting brokers, dealers, investment advisers, persons associated with brokers or dealers, and persons associated with investment advisers relating to their obligations, including duty of care, to retail customers; and

(14) any other consideration that the Commission considers necessary and appropriate

和导致的潜在损害，包括对零售客户获取个性化证券投资意见和建议机会的任何潜在影响,或对该等意见和建议的可获得性的任何潜在影响;

(B)应根据《1940年投资顾问法》(《美国法典》第十五编第80b-1节及其后条文)进行注册或应受制于该法的新增实体和个人的数量,以及经纪商、自营商以及上述二者的业务相关人将需遵守的额外要求,包括——

(i)关于业务相关人许可、注册及审查的任何潜在的额外要求;及

(ii)新增实体和个人将产生的额外成本(如有);及

(C)对证券交易委员会和各州以下资源的影响——

(i)用以对注册投资顾问及其代表进行检查的资源,包括对审查周期的影响;及

(ii)用以执行《1940年投资顾问法》(《美国法典》第十五编第80b-1节及其后条文)规定的注意标准及其他适用要求的资源;

(11)经纪商、自营商、投资顾问以及上述各者的业务相关人向零售客户所提供服务水平的差异,以及经纪商、自营商、投资顾问以及上述各者的业务相关人的零售客户关系在范围和条款方面的差异;

(12)因经纪商、自营商、投资顾问以及上述各者的业务相关人所应遵守的与其就提供投资意见向零售客户承担的义务相关的监管要求或法定注意标准可能发生的变化而可能对零售客户造成的影响,包括可能对以下各项造成的任何影响——

(A)反欺诈保护;

(B)零售客户获取个性化证券投资意见和建议的机会;或

(C)该等意见和建议的可获得性;

(13)可能发生的如下额外成本和费用——

(A)零售客户作出投资决策时需要支出的额外成本和费用,以及其投资决策的盈利能力可能遭受的影响的额外成本和费用;及

(B)由于经纪商、自营商、投资顾问以及上述各者的业务相关人所应遵守的与其向零售客户承担的义务(包括注意义务)相关的监管要求或法定标准发生的潜在变化而产生的额外成本和费用;及

(14)证券交易委员会在判定是否应根据第(f)子条制定相关规则时认为确属必要

in determining whether to conduct a rulemaking under subsection (f).

(d) REPORT.—

(1) IN GENERAL. -Not later than 6 months after the date of enactment of this Act, the Commission shall submit a report on the study required under subsection (b) to—

(A) the Committee on Banking, Housing, and Urban Affairs of the Senate; and

(B) the Committee on Financial Services of the House of Representatives.

(2) CONTENT REQUIREMENTS. —The report required under paragraph (1) shall describe the findings, conclusions, and recommendations of the Commission from the study required under subsection (b), including—

(A) a description of the considerations, analysis, and public and industry input that the Commission considered, as required under subsection (b), to make such findings, conclusions, and policy recommendations; and

(B) an analysis of whether any identified legal or regulatory gaps, shortcomings, or overlap in legal or regulatory standards in the protection of retail customers relating to the standards of care for brokers, dealers, investment advisers, persons associated with brokers or dealers, and persons associated with investment advisers for providing personalized investment advice about securities to retail customers.

(e) PUBLIC COMMENT.—The Commission shall seek and consider public input, comments, and data in order to prepare the report required under subsection (d).

(f) RULEMAKING.—The Commission may commence a rulemaking, as necessary or appropriate in the public interest and for the protection of retail customers (and such other customers as the Commission may by rule provide), to address the legal or regulatory standards of care for brokers, dealers, investment advisers, persons associated with brokers or dealers, and persons associated with investment advisers for providing personalized investment advice about securities to such retail customers. The Commission shall consider the findings conclusions, and recommendations of the study required under subsection (b).

(g) AUTHORITY TO ESTABLISH A FIDUCIARY DUTY FOR BROKERS AND DEALERS.—

(1) SECURITIES EXCHANGE ACT OF 1934. —Section 15 of the Securities Exchange Act of 1934 (15 U.S.C.78o) is amended by adding at the end the following:

"(k) STANDARD OF CONDUCT.—

"(1) IN GENERAL. —Notwithstanding any other provision of this Act or the Investment Advisers Act of 1940, the Commission may promulgate rules to provide that, with respect to a broker or dealer, when providing personalized investment advice about securities to a retail customer (and such other customers as the Commission may by rule provide), the standard of conduct for such broker or dealer with respect to such customer shall be the same as the standard of conduct applicable to an investment adviser under section 211 of the

且适当的任何其他考虑因素。

(d)**报告**。——

(1)**一般规定**。——证券交易委员会应于本法颁布之日后6个月内就第(b)子条所规定研究向以下委员会提交一份报告——

(A)参议院银行、住房与城市事务委员会;及

(B)众议院金融服务委员会。

(2)**内容要求**。——第(1)款所规定报告应说明证券交易委员会就第(b)子条所规定研究得出的认定、结论和建议,包括——

(A)说明证券交易委员会按照第(b)子条要求作出该等认定、结论和政策建议时所考虑的考虑因素、分析报告以及公众意见和行业意见;及

(B)分析与经纪商、自营商、投资顾问以及上述各者的业务相关人向零售客户提供个性化证券投资意见时所应遵守的注意标准相关的投资者保护法定标准或监管标准是否存在任何已确认的漏洞、不足或重叠问题。

(e)**公众意见**。——证券交易委员会在编制第(d)子条规定的报告时,应寻求并考虑公众意见、公众评论和数据。

(f)**规则制定**。——证券交易委员会可以制定符合公共利益并有利于零售客户(以及证券交易委员会发布的规则所规定的其他客户)保护的必要或适当的规则,以便解决经纪商、自营商、投资顾问以及上述各者的业务相关人向零售客户提供个性化证券投资意见时所应遵守的法定标准或监管标准中存在的问题。证券交易委员会在制定上述规则时,应考虑根据第(b)子条所规定之研究得出的认定、结论和建议。

(g)**为经纪商和自营商设定受信义务的权力**。——

(1)**《1934年证券交易法》**。——在《1934年证券交易法》第15条(《美国法典》第十五编第78o节)结尾处增加如下内容,作为对该条的修正:

"(k)**行为准则**。——

(1)**一般规定**。——无论本法或《1940年投资顾问法》是否存在不同规定,证券交易委员会均可以颁发规则,作出如下规定:经纪商或自营商在向零售客户(以及证券交易委员会发布的规则所规定的其他客户)提供个性化证券投资意见时,适用的行为准则应与《1940年投资顾问法》第211条规定的适用于投资顾问的行为准则相同。经纪商或自营商因出售证券而获得佣金或其他标准报酬的行为本身不得视为违反该等准则的行为。本条任何内容均不要求经纪商、自营商或其注册代表在提供个性化证券投

Investment Advisers Act of 1940. The receipt of compensation based on commission or other standard compensation for the sale of securities shall not, in and of itself, be considered a violation of such standard applied to a broker or dealer. Nothing in this section shall require a broker or dealer or registered representative to have a continuing duty of care or loyalty to the customer after providing personalized investment advice about securities.

"(2) DISCLOSURE OF RANGE OF PRODUCTS OFFERED. —Where a broker or dealer sells only proprietary or other limited range of products, as determined by the Commission, the Commission may by rule require that such broker or dealer provide notice to each retail customer and obtain the consent or acknowledgment of the customer. The sale of only proprietary or other limited range of products by a broker or dealer shall not, in and of itself, be considered a violation of the standard set forth in paragraph (1).

"(l) OTHER MATTERS. —The Commission shall —

"(1) facilitate the provision of simple and clear disclosures to investors regarding the terms of their relationships with brokers, dealers, and investment advisers, including any material conflicts of interest; and

"(2) examine and, where appropriate, promulgate rules prohibiting or restricting certain sales practices, conflicts of interest, and compensation schemes for brokers, dealers, and investment advisers that the Commission deems contrary to the public interest and the protection of investors.".

(2) INVESTMENT ADVISERS ACT OF 1940. —Section 211 of the Investment Advisers Act of 1940, is further amended by adding at the end the following new subsections:

"(g) STANDARD OF CONDUCT. —

"(1) IN GENERAL. —The Commission may promulgate rules to provide that the standard of conduct for all brokers, dealers, and investment advisers, when providing personalized investment advice about securities to retail customers (and such other customers as the Commission may by rule provide), shall be to act in the best interest of the customer without regard to the financial or other interest of the broker, dealer, or investment adviser providing the advice. In accordance with such rules, any material conflicts of interest shall be disclosed and may be consented to by the customer. Such rules shall provide that such standard of conduct shall be no less stringent than the standard applicable to investment advisers under section 206(1) and (2) of this Act when providing personalized investment advice about securities, except the Commission shall not ascribe a meaning to the term 'customer' that would include an investor in a private fund managed by an investment adviser, where such private fund has entered into an advisory contract with such adviser. The receipt of compensation based on commission or fees shall not, in and of itself, be considered a violation of such standard applied to a broker, dealer, or investment adviser.

"(2) RETAIL CUSTOMER DEFINED. —For purposes of this subsection, the term

资意见之后继续对客户负有注意义务或忠诚责任。

(2)**所售产品品种范围披露**。——如果证券交易委员会判定经纪商或自营商仅销售自有产品或其他品种范围有限的产品（范围是否有限取决于证券交易委员会的判定),证券交易委员会可以发布规则,要求该等经纪商或自营商向每一零售客户发出通知,并要求其取得该等客户的同意或确认。经纪商或自营商仅销售自有产品或范围有限的其他产品品种的行为本身不得视为违反第(1)款规定的标准行为。

(l)**其他事项**。——证券交易委员会应——

(1)促进实施经纪商、自营商及投资顾问向投资者简单、明确地披露彼此关系之条款,包括彼此之间存在的任何重大利益冲突;并

(2)对其认为违反公共利益且不利于投资者保护的经纪商、自营商及投资顾问的特定销售做法、利益冲突及薪酬方案进行检查,并在适当情况下颁发规则予以相应禁止或限制。”

(2)**《1940年投资顾问法》**。——在《1940年投资顾问法》第211条结尾处增加如下新子条,作为对该条的进一步修正:

“(g)**行为准则**。——

(1)**一般规定**。——证券交易委员会可以颁发规则,作出如下规定:所有经纪商、自营商和投资顾问在向零售客户（以及证券交易委员会发布的规则所规定的其他客户)提供个性化证券投资意见时,应以符合客户最佳利益的标准行事,而不考虑提供意见的经纪商、自营商或投资顾问的经济利益或其他利益。经纪商、自营商和投资顾问应根据该等规则向客户披露任何重大利益冲突,而客户可予以同意。该等规则应规定，上述行为准则的严格程度不得低于投资顾问在提供个性化证券投资建议时根据本法第206(1)条和第206(2)条所应遵守的标准,但是,如果投资顾问管理的私募基金已与该顾问签订顾问合同,则证券交易委员会在对‘客户’一词进行解释时,不得将该等私募基金的投资者包括在内。收受佣金或手续费此类报酬的行为本身不得视为违反适用于经纪商、自营商或投资顾问的该等准则的行为。

(2)**零售客户的定义**。——就本子条而言,‘零售客户’一词系指符合如下条件的

'retail customer' means a natural person, or the legal representative of such natural person, who —

"(A) receives personalized investment advice about securities from a broker, dealer, or investment adviser; and

"(B) uses such advice primarily for personal, family, or household purposes.

"(h) OTHER MATTERS. —The Commission shall —

"(1) facilitate the provision of simple and clear disclosures to investors regarding the terms of their relationships with brokers, dealers, and investment advisers, including any material conflicts of interest; and

"(2) examine and, where appropriate, promulgate rules prohibiting or restricting certain sales practices, conflicts of interest, and compensation schemes for brokers, dealers, and investment advisers that the Commission deems contrary to the public interest and the protection of investors.".

(h) HARMONIZATION OF ENFORCEMENT. —

(1) SECURITIES EXCHANGE ACT OF 1934.—Section 15 of the Securities Exchange Act of 1934, as amended by subsection (g)(1), is further amended by adding at the end the following new subsection:

"(m) HARMONIZATION OF ENFORCEMENT.—The enforcement authority of the Commission with respect to violations of the standard of conduct applicable to a broker or dealer providing personalized investment advice about securities to a retail customer shall include —

"(1) the enforcement authority of the Commission with respect to such violations provided under this Act; and

"(2) the enforcement authority of the Commission with respect to violations of the standard of conduct applicable to an investment adviser under the Investment Advisers Act of 1940, including the authority to impose sanctions for such violations, and the Commission shall seek to prosecute and sanction violators of the standard of conduct applicable to a broker or dealer providing personalized investment advice about securities to a retail customer under this Act to same extent as the Commission prosecutes and sanctions violators of the standard of conduct applicable to an investment advisor under the Investment Advisers Act of 1940.".

(2) INVESTMENT ADVISERS ACT OF 1940.—Section 211 of the Investment Advisers Act of 1940, as amended by subsection (g)(2), is further amended by adding at the end the following new subsection:

"(i) HARMONIZATION OF ENFORCEMENT.—The enforcement authority of the Commission with respect to violations of the standard of conduct applicable to an investment adviser shall include —

"(1) the enforcement authority of the Commission with respect to such violations

自然人或该等自然人的法律代理人——

(A)接受经纪商、自营商或投资顾问提供的个性化证券投资意见;且

(B)主要出于个人、家庭或共同居住人的目的使用该等意见。

(h)**其他事项**。——证券交易委员会应——

(1)促进实施经纪商、自营商及投资顾问向投资者简单、明确地披露彼此关系之条款,包括彼此之间存在的任何重大利益冲突;并

(2)对其认为违反公共利益且不利于投资者保护的经纪商、自营商及投资顾问的特定销售做法、利益冲突及薪酬方案进行检查,并在适当情况下颁布规则予以相应禁止或限制。"

(h)**执法协调**。——

(1)**《1934年证券交易法》**。——在经第(g)(1)子条修正后的《1934年证券交易法》第15条结尾处增加如下新子条,作为对该条的进一步修正:

"(m)**执法协调**。——对于经纪商或自营商向零售客户提供个性化证券投资意见时违反其应遵守的行为准则的行为,证券交易委员会的执法权应包括——

(1)证券交易委员会对本法规定的该等违规行为享有的执法权;及

(2)证券交易委员会对投资顾问违反投资顾问根据《1940年投资顾问法》应遵守的行为准则的行为享有的执法权,包括对该等违规行为进行处罚的权力,并且如果经纪商或自营商在根据本法向零售客户提供个性化证券投资意见时违反其应遵守的行为准则,证券交易委员会应在寻求对该等经纪商或自营商提起追诉和予以处罚时,力度与其在对违反《1940年投资顾问法》规定的投资顾问应遵守的行为准则的投资顾问提起追诉和予以处罚时保持一致。"

(2)**《1940年投资顾问法》**。——在经第(g)(2)子条修正后的《1940年投资顾问法》第211条结尾处增加如下新子条,作为对该条的进一步修正:

"(i)**执法协调**。——对于投资顾问违反其所应遵守的行为准则的行为,证券交易委员会的执法权应包括——

(1)证券交易委员会对本法规定的该等违规行为享有的执法权;及

provided under this Act; and

"(2) the enforcement authority of the Commission with respect to violations of the standard of conduct applicable to a broker or dealer providing personalized investment advice about securities to a retail customer under the Securities Exchange Act of 1934, including the authority to impose sanctions for such violations, and the Commission shall seek to prosecute and sanction violators of the standard of conduct applicable to an investment adviser under this Act to same extent as the Commission prosecutes and sanctions violators of the standard of conduct applicable to a broker or dealer providing personalized investment advice about securities to a retail customer under the Securities Exchange Act of 1934.".

SEC.914. STUDY ON ENHANCING INVESTMENT ADVISER EXAMINATIONS.

(a) STUDY REQUIRED.—

(1) IN GENERAL.—The Commission shall review and analyze the need for enhanced examination and enforcement resources for investment advisers.

(2) AREAS OF CONSIDERATION.—The study required by this subsection shall examine—

(A) the number and frequency of examinations of investment advisers by the Commission over the 5 years preceding the date of the enactment of this subtitle;

(B) the extent to which having Congress authorize the Commission to designate one or more self–regulatory organizations to augment the Commission's efforts in overseeing investment advisers would improve the frequency of examinations of investment advisers; and

(C) current and potential approaches to examining the investment advisory activities of dually registered broker–dealers and investment advisers or affiliated broker–dealers and investment advisers.

(b) REPORT REQUIRED.—The Commission shall report its findings to the Committee on Financial Services of the House of Representatives and the Committee on Banking, Housing, and Urban Affairs of the Senate, not later than 180 days after the date of enactment of this subtitle, and shall use such findings to revise its rules and regulations, as necessary. The report shall include a discussion of regulatory or legislative steps that are recommended or that may be necessary to address concerns identified in the study.

SEC.915. OFFICE OF THE INVESTOR ADVOCATE.

Section 4 of the Securities Exchange Act of 1934 (15 U.S.C.78d) is amended by adding at the end the following:

"(g) OFFICE OF THE INVESTOR ADVOCATE.—

"(1) OFFICE ESTABLISHED.—There is established within the Commission the Office of the Investor Advocate (in this subsection referred to as the 'Office').

"(2) INVESTOR ADVOCATE.—

(2)证券交易委员会对经纪商或自营商根据《1934年证券交易法》向零售客户提供个性化证券投资意见之时违反其应遵守的行为准则的行为享有的执法权，包括对该等违规行为进行处罚的权力，并且如果投资顾问违反其根据本法应遵守的行为准则,证券交易委员会应在寻求对该等投资顾问提起追诉和予以处罚时,力度与其在对根据《1934年证券交易法》向零售客户提供个性化证券投资意见之时违反经纪商或自营商应遵守的行为准则的经纪商或自营商提起追诉和处以处罚时保持一致。”

第914条　关于加强投资顾问检查工作的研究

(a)**研究要求**。——

(1) **一般规定**。——证券交易委员会应评估并分析是否有必要针对投资顾问的检查和执法工作加大资源投入力度。

(2)**考虑因素**。——根据本子条规定开展研究时,应考察如下因素——

(A)证券交易委员会在本子编颁布之日前5年内对投资顾问开展检查工作的次数和频率;

(B)国会授权证券交易委员会指定一家或一家以上自律组织辅助证券交易委员会开展对投资顾问的监督工作，在多大程度上将能增加对投资顾问开展检查工作的频率;及

(C)对双重注册的经纪自营商、投资顾问或者关联经纪自营商、关联投资顾问的投资顾问活动当前采取的或可能采取的检查方法。

(b)**报告提交要求**。——证券交易委员会应于本子编颁布之日后180天内就其认定结论向众议院金融服务委员会及参议院银行、住房与城市事务委员会提交报告,并基于该等认定结论对其规则和规章进行必要修订。该报告应探讨研究中所建议的监管或立法措施,或对解决研究中提出的问题所需的必要监管或立法措施进行探讨。

第915条　投资者维权办公室

在《1934年证券交易法》第4条(《美国法典》第十五编第78d节)结尾处增加如下内容,作为对该条的修正:

“(g)**投资者维权办公室**。——

(1)**投资者维权办公室的设立**。——证券交易委员会下设投资者维权办公室(‘投资者维权办公室’)。

(2)**投资者维权办公室主任**。——

"(A) IN GENERAL. —The head of the Office shall be the Investor Advocate, who shall—

"(i) report directly to the Chairman; and

"(ii) be appointed by the Chairman, in consultation with the Commission, from among individuals having experience in advocating for the interests of investors in securities and investor protection issues, from the perspective of investors.

"(B) COMPENSATION. —The annual rate of pay for the Investor Advocate shall be equal to the highest rate of annual pay for other senior executives who report to the Chairman of the Commission.

"(C) LIMITATION ON SERVICE. —An individual who serves as the Investor Advocate may not be employed by the Commission —

"(i) during the 2–year period ending on the date of appointment as Investor Advocate; or

"(ii) during the 5–year period beginning on the date on which the person ceases to serve as the Investor Advocate.

"(3) STAFF OF OFFICE. —The Investor Advocate, after consultation with the Chairman of the Commission, may retain or employ independent counsel, research staff, and service staff, as the Investor Advocate deems necessary to carry out the functions, powers, and duties of the Office.

"(4) FUNCTIONS OF THE INVESTOR ADVOCATE. —The Investor Advocate shall —

"(A) assist retail investors in resolving significant problems such investors may have with the Commission or with self–regulatory organizations;

"(B) identify areas in which investors would benefit from changes in the regulations of the Commission or the rules of self–regulatory organizations;

"(C) identify problems that investors have with financial service providers and investment products;

"(D) analyze the potential impact on investors of —

"(i) proposed regulations of the Commission; and

"(ii) proposed rules of self–regulatory organizations registered under this title; and

"(E) to the extent practicable, propose to the Commission changes in the regulations or orders of the Commission and to Congress any legislative, administrative, or personnel changes that may be appropriate to mitigate problems identified under this paragraph and to promote the interests of investors.

"(5) ACCESS TO DOCUMENTS. —The Commission shall ensure that the Investor Advocate has full access to the documents of the Commission and any self–regulatory organization, as necessary to carry out the functions of the Office.

"(6) ANNUAL REPORTS. —

(A)**一般规定**。——投资者维权办公室主任作为投资者维权办公室的负责人,应当——

(i)直接向证券交易委员会主席汇报工作;并

(ii)由证券交易委员会主席任命,但是证券交易委员会主席在与证券交易委员会磋商后,应从投资者角度任命具有证券投资者维权和投资者保护方面经验的个人担任该职务。

(B)**薪酬**。——投资者维权办公室主任的年薪水平应等同于向证券交易委员会主席汇报工作的其他高级公务员的最高年薪水平。

(C)**任职限制**。——在如下期间内,担任投资者维权办公室主任的个人不得受雇于证券交易委员会——

(i)被任命为投资者维权办公室主任之日前2年内;或

(ii)停止担任投资者维权办公室主任之日起5年内。

(3)**投资者维权办公室的工作人员**。——经与证券交易委员会主席磋商后,投资者维权办公室主任可以聘用或雇用其认为必要的独立法律顾问、研究人员和服务人员,以履行投资者维权办公室的职能、权力及职责。

(4)**投资者维权办公室主任的职能**。——投资者维权办公室主任应——

(A)协助零售投资者解决与证券交易委员会或自律组织之间可能存在的重大问题;

(B)确定投资者因证券交易委员会规章或自律组织规则发生变化而将受益的领域;

(C)确定投资者与金融服务提供者及投资产品之间存在的问题;

(D)分析以下提案对投资者的潜在影响——

(i)证券交易委员会提出的规章草案;及

(ii)根据本编注册的自律组织提出的规则草案;及

(E)在可行范围内,针对证券交易委员会发布的规章或命令提出适当的变更提案,并向国会提出任何适当的立法、行政或人事变更提案,以便缓解根据本款识别的问题并促进投资者利益。

(5)**文件查阅权**。——证券交易委员会应确保投资者维权办公室主任对证券交易委员会及任何自律组织文件拥有必要的全面查阅权,以履行投保者维权办公室的职能。

(6)**年度报告**。——

"(A) REPORT ON OBJECTIVES.—

"(i) IN GENERAL.—Not later than June 30 of each year after 2010, the Investor Advocate shall submit to the Committee on Banking, Housing, and Urban Affairs of the Senate and the Committee on Financial Services of the House of Representatives a report on the objectives of the Investor Advocate for the following fiscal year.

"(ii) CONTENTS.—Each report required under clause (i) shall contain full and substantive analysis and explanation.

"(B) REPORT ON ACTIVITIES.—

"(i) IN GENERAL.—Not later than December 31 of each year after 2010, the Investor Advocate shall submit to the Committee on Banking, Housing, and Urban Affairs of the Senate and the Committee on Financial Services of the House of Representatives a report on the activities of the Investor Advocate during the immediately preceding fiscal year.

"(ii) CONTENTS.—Each report required under clause (i) shall include—

"(I) appropriate statistical information and full and substantive analysis;

"(II) information on steps that the Investor Advocate has taken during the reporting period to improve investor services and the responsiveness of the Commission and self–regulatory organizations to investor concerns;

"(III) a summary of the most serious problems encountered by investors during the reporting period;

"(IV) an inventory of the items described in subclause (III) that includes—

"(aa) identification of any action taken by the Commission or the self–regulatory organization and the result of such action;

"(bb) the length of time that each item has remained on such inventory; and

"(cc) for items on which no action has been taken, the reasons for inaction, and an identification of any official who is responsible for such action;

"(V) recommendations for such administrative and legislative actions as may be appropriate to resolve problems encountered by investors; and

"(VI) any other information, as determined appropriate by the Investor Advocate.

"(iii) INDEPENDENCE.—Each report required under this paragraph shall be provided directly to the Committees listed in clause (i) without any prior review or comment from the Commission, any commissioner, any other officer or employee of the Commission, or the Office of Management and Budget.

"(iv) CONFIDENTIALITY.—No report required under clause (i) may contain confidential information.

"(7) REGULATIONS.—The Commission shall, by regulation, establish procedures requiring a formal response to all recommendations submitted to the Commission by the Investor Advocate, not later than 3 months after the date of such submission.".

(A)**目标报告**。——

(i)**一般规定**。——2010年之后,投资者维权办公室主任应于每年6月30日之前就其下一财政年度的目标向参议院银行、住房与城市事务委员会及众议院金融服务委员会提交报告。

(ii)**内容**。——第(i)项规定的每份报告均应包含全面性和实质性分析和解释。

(B)**活动报告**。——

(i)**一般规定**。——2010年之后,投资者维权办公室主任应于每年12月31日之前就其上一财政年度的活动向参议院银行、住房与城市事务委员会及众议院金融服务委员会提交报告。

(ii)**内容**。——第(i)项规定的每份报告均应包含——

(I)适当的统计信息以及全面性和实质性分析;

(II)投资者维权办公室主任为提升证券交易委员会和自律组织的投资者服务水平及回应投资者关切问题的能力在报告期内采取的相关措施;

(III)投资者在报告期内遭遇的最严重问题的汇总;

(IV)第(III)子项所述问题的清单,包括——

(aa)列明证券交易委员会或自律组织所采取的任何行动及该等行动的结果;

(bb)每一问题自列入该清单以来所持续时间长短;及

(cc)对于未采取任何行动的问题而言,说明未采取行动的理由,并指明对此负责的任何官员;

(V)为解决投资者遇到的问题而提出的适当的行政及立法行动建议;及

(VI)投资者维权办公室主任判定确属适当的任何其他信息。

(iii)**独立性**。——本款规定的每份报告均应直接向第(i)项所列委员会提交,而不必提交给证券交易委员会及其任何委员、任何其他官员或职员或者行政管理和预算局进行事先审查,也不必征求上述各者的意见。

(iv)**保密**。——第(i)项规定的报告不得含有任何保密信息。

(7)**规章**——证券交易委员会应发布规章,制定相关程序,要求证券交易委员会在投资者维权办公室主任向其提交建议之日后3个月内,对所有建议作出正式答复。”

SEC.916. STREAMLINING OF FILING PROCEDURES FOR SELF－REGULATORY ORGANIZATIONS.

(a) FILING PROCEDURES. —Section 19(b) of the Securities Exchange Act of 1934 (15 U.S.C.78s (b)) is amended by striking paragraph (2) (including the undesignated matter immediately following subparagraph (B)) and inserting the following:

"(2) APPROVAL PROCESS. —

"(A) APPROVAL PROCESS ESTABLISHED. —

"(i) IN GENERAL. —Except as provided in clause (ii), not later than 45 days after the date of publication of a proposed rule change under paragraph (1), the Commission shall —

"(I) by order, approve or disapprove the proposed rule change; or

"(II) institute proceedings under subparagraph (B) to determine whether the proposed rule change should be disapproved.

"(ii) EXTENSION OF TIME PERIOD. —The Commission may extend the period established under clause (i) by not more than an additional 45 days, if —

"(I) the Commission determines that a longer period is appropriate and publishes the reasons for such determination; or

"(II) the self–regulatory organization that filed the proposed rule change consents to the longer period.

"(B) PROCEEDINGS. —

"(i) NOTICE AND HEARING. —If the Commission does not approve or disapprove a proposed rule change under subparagraph (A), the Commission shall provide to the self–regulatory organization that filed the proposed rule change —

"(I) notice of the grounds for disapproval under consideration; and

"(II) opportunity for hearing, to be concluded not later than 180 days after the date of publication of notice of the filing of the proposed rule change.

"(ii) ORDER OF APPROVAL OR DISAPPROVAL. —

"(I) IN GENERAL. —Except as provided in subclause (II), not later than 180 days after the date of publication under paragraph (1), the Commission shall issue an order approving or disapproving the proposed rule change.

"(II) EXTENSION OF TIME PERIOD. —The Commission may extend the period for issuance under clause (I) by not more than 60 days, if —

"(aa) the Commission determines that a longer period is appropriate and publishes the reasons for such determination; or

"(bb) the self–regulatory organization that filed the proposed rule change consents to the longer period.

"(C) STANDARDS FOR APPROVAL AND DISAPPROVAL. —

"(i) APPROVAL.—The Commission shall approve a proposed rule change of a

第916条 精简自律组织的报批程序

(a)**报批程序**。——删除《1934年证券交易法》第19(b)条[《美国法典》第十五编第78s(b)节]第(2)款[包括紧接第(B)子款之后的无编号内容],替以如下内容,作为对该条的修正:

“(2)**批准程序**。——

(A)**批准程序的设立**。——

(i)**一般规定**。——除第(ii)项规定的情形外,证券交易委员会应于第(1)款规定的规则变更草案公布之日后45天内——

(I)发布命令,批准或否决该规则变更草案;或

(II)启动第(B)子款规定的程序,以判定是否应否决该等规则变更草案。

(ii)**时限延长**。——在下述情形下,证券交易委员会可以将第(i)项规定的期限另行延长不超过45天——

(I)证券交易委员会判定延期确属适当,并公布作出该判定的理由;或

(II)报批该等规则变更草案的自律组织同意延期。

(B)**程序**。——

(i)**通知与听证**。——如果证券交易委员会根据第(A)子款规定的程序,未批准或否决规则变更草案,则证券交易委员会应向报批该规则变更草案的自律组织——

(I)发出通知,说明否决的具体理由;并

(II)提供听证机会,且听证应在规则变更草案报批通知公布之日后180天内完成。

(ii)**批准令或否决令**。——

(I)**一般规定**。——除第(II)子项规定的情形外,证券交易委员会应在第(1)款规定的公布日起180天内针对该等规则变更草案签发批准令或否决令。

(II)**时限延长**。——在下述情形下,证券交易委员会可以将第(I)项规定的命令签发期限延长不超过60天——

(aa)证券交易委员会判定延期确属适当,并公布作出该判定的理由;或

(bb)报批该等规则变更草案的自律组织同意延期。

(C)**批准与否决的标准**。——

(i)**批准**。——如果证券交易委员会认定自律组织的规则变更草案符合本编以及

self–regulatory organization if it finds that such proposed rule change is consistent with the requirements of this title and the rules and regulations issued under this title that are applicable to such organization.

"(ii) DISAPPROVAL. —The Commission shall disapprove a proposed rule change of a self–regulatory organization if it does not make a finding described in clause (i).

"(iii) TIME FOR APPROVAL.—The Commission may not approve a proposed rule change earlier than 30 days after the date of publication under paragraph (1), unless the Commission finds good cause for so doing and publishes the reason for the finding.

"(D) RESULT OF FAILURE TO INSTITUTE OR CONCLUDE PROCEEDINGS. –A proposed rule change shall be deemed to have been approved by the Commission, if —

"(i) the Commission does not approve or disapprove the proposed rule change or begin proceedings under subparagraph (B) within the period described in subparagraph (A); or

"(ii) the Commission does not issue an order approving or disapproving the proposed rule change under subparagraph (B) within the period described in subparagraph (B)(ii).

"(E) PUBLICATION DATE BASED ON FEDERAL REGISTER PUBLISHING. —For purposes of this paragraph, if, after filing a proposed rule change with the Commission pursuant to paragraph (1), a self–regulatory organization publishes a notice of the filing of such proposed rule change, together with the substantive terms of such proposed rule change, on a publicly accessible website, the Commission shall thereafter send the notice to the Federal Register for publication thereof under paragraph (1) within 15 days of the date on which such website publication is made. If the Commission fails to send the notice for publication thereof within such 15 day period, then the date of publication shall be deemed to be the date on which such website publication was made.

"(F) RULEMAKING. —

"(i) IN GENERAL. —Not later than 180 days after the date of enactment of the Investor Protection and Securities Reform Act of 2010, after consultation with other regulatory agencies, the Commission shall promulgate rules setting forth the procedural requirements of the proceedings required under this paragraph.

"(ii) NOTICE AND COMMENT NOT REQUIRED. —The rules promulgated by the Commission under clause (i) are not required to include republication of proposed rule changes or solicitation of public comment.".

(b) CLARIFICATION OF FILING DATE. —

(1) RULE OF CONSTRUCTION. —Section 19 (b) of the Securities Exchange Act of 1934 (15 U.S.C.78s(b)) is amended by adding at the end the following:

"(10) RULE OF CONSTRUCTION RELATING TO FILING DATE OF PROPOSED RULE CHANGES. —

"(A) IN GENERAL.—For purposes of this subsection, the date of filing of a proposed

根据本编发布的规则和规章中适用于该等组织的要求，则证券交易委员会应批准该等规则变更草案。

(ii)**否决**。——如果证券交易委员会未作出第(i)项所述认定,则证券交易委员会应否决自律组织的规则变更草案。

(iii)**批准时限**。——证券交易委员会不得在第(1)款规定的公布日起30天内批准规则变更草案,但证券交易委员会认定其拥有提前批准的正当理由,并公布该等理由的除外。

(D)**未能启动或完结程序的后果**。——在下述情形下,规则变更草案应视为已获得证券交易委员会批准——

(i)证券交易委员会未在第(A)子款所述期限内批准或否决该等规则变更草案,亦未启动第(B)子款规定的程序;或

(ii)证券交易委员会未在第(B)(ii)子款所述期限内根据第(B)子款对该等规则变更草案签发批准令或否决令。

(E)**公布日期以《联邦公报》发布时间为准**。——就本款而言,如果自律组织在根据第(1)款规定向证券交易委员会报批规则变更草案后,通过可公开访问的网站公布了关于该等规则变更草案的报批通知以及该等规则变更草案的实质条款，则证券交易委员会应在自律组织通过上述网站进行公布之日起15天内根据第(1)款规定将该通知发送给《联邦公报》予以公布。如果证券交易委员会未能在上述15天期限内将上述通知发送给《联邦公报》予以公布,则该等通知在上述网站公布的日期应视为其公布日期。

(F)**规则制定**。——

(i)**一般规定**。——证券交易委员会应于《2010年投资者保护与证券改革法》颁布之日后180天内,在与其他监管机关磋商后,颁发规则,对本款规定的程序确立程序性要求。

(ii)**不必发出通知和征求公众意见**。——证券交易委员会根据第(i)项颁发的规则不必规定规则变更草案必须重新公布或征求公众意见。”

(b)**关于报批日期的说明**。——

(1)**解释规则**。——在《1934年证券交易法》第19(b)条[《美国法典》第十五编第78s(b)节]结尾处增加如下内容,作为对该条的修正:

“(10)**与规则变更草案报批日期相关的解释规则**。——

(A)**一般规定**。——就本子条而言,规则变更草案的报批日期应视为证券交易委

rule change shall be deemed to be the date on which the Commission receives the proposed rule change.

"(B) EXCEPTION.—A proposed rule change has not been received by the Commission for purposes of subparagraph (A) if, not later than 7 business days after the date of receipt by the Commission, the Commission notifies the self-regulatory organization that such proposed rule change does not comply with the rules of the Commission relating to the required form of a proposed rule change, except that if the Commission determines that the proposed rule change is unusually lengthy and is complex or raises novel regulatory issues, the Commission shall inform the self-regulatory organization of such determination not later than 7 business days after the date of receipt by the Commission and, for the purposes of subparagraph (A), a proposed rule change has not been received by the Commission, if, not later than 21 days after the date of receipt by the Commission, the Commission notifies the self-regulatory organization that such proposed rule change does not comply with the rules of the Commission relating to the required form of a proposed rule change.".

(2) PUBLICATION. —Section 19 (b)(1) of the Securities Exchange Act of 1934 (15 U.S.C.78s(b)(1)) is amended by striking "upon" and inserting "as soon as practicable after the date of".

(c) EFFECTIVE DATE OF PROPOSED RULES. —Section 19(b)(3) of the Securities Exchange Act of 1934 (15 U.S.C.78s(b)(3)) is amended —

(1) in subparagraph (A) —

(A) by striking "may take effect" and inserting "shall take effect"; and

(B) by inserting "on any person, whether or not the person is a member of the self-regulatory organization" after "charge imposed by the self-regulatory organization"; and

(2) in subparagraph (C) —

(A) by amending the second sentence to read as follows:

"At any time within the 60-day period beginning on the date of filing of such a proposed rule change in accordance with the provisions of paragraph (1), the Commission summarily may temporarily suspend the change in the rules of the self-regulatory organization made thereby, if it appears to the Commission that such action is necessary or appropriate in the public interest, for the protection of investors, or otherwise in furtherance of the purposes of this title.";

(B) by inserting after the second sentence the following:

"If the Commission takes such action, the Commission shall institute proceedings under paragraph(2)(B) to determine whether the proposed rule should be approved or disapproved."; and

(C) in the third sentence, by striking "the preceding sentence" and inserting "this subparagraph".

员会收到规则变更草案之日。

(B)**例外规定**。——如果证券交易委员会在收到规则变更草案之日后7个营业日内通知自律组织该等规则变更草案不符合证券交易委员会的相关格式要求,则就第(A)子款而言,应视为证券交易委员会并未收到该等规则变更草案;但是,如果证券交易委员会判定规则变更草案异常冗长、复杂,或引发了无先例可循的监管问题,则应在收到该等规则变更草案之日后7个营业日内将该判定告知自律组织,在该种情况下,如果证券交易委员会在收到规则变更草案之日后21天内通知自律组织该等规则变更草案不符合证券交易委员会的相关格式要求,则就第(A)子款而言,应视为证券交易委员会并未收到该等规则变更草案。"

(2)**公布**。——《1934年证券交易法》第19(b)(1)条[《美国法典》第十五编第78s(b)(1)节]修正如下:删除"规则变更草案一经报批",替以"在规则变更草案报批日后尽快"。

(c)**规则草案的生效日**。——《1934年证券交易法》第19(b)(3)条[《美国法典》第十五编第78s(b)(3)节]修正如下——

(1)在第(A)子款中——

(A)删除"可生效",替以"应生效";并

(B)删除"自律组织征收的应付款项、费用和其他收费",替以"自律组织向任何主体征收的应付款项、费用和其他收费,不论该主体是否具有自律组织会员身份";及

(2)在第(C)子款中——

(A)第二句修正后如下:

"在按照第(1)款规定报批规则变更草案之日起60天内的任何时候,如果证券交易委员会认为对于促进公共利益、加强投资者保护或实现本编宗旨必要或适当,其可以通过简易程序临时暂停适用自律组织做出的规则变更。";

(B)在第二句之后插入如下内容:

"如果证券交易委员会采取该等行动,则其应根据第(2)(B)款启动相关程序,以判定该等规则变更草案应予以批准还是否决。";并

(C)在第三句中,删除"前一句",替以"本子款"。

(d) CONFORMING CHANGE. —Section 19 (b)(4)(D) of the Securities Exchange Act of 1934 (15 U.S.C.78s(b)(4)(D)) is amended to read as follows:

"(D)(i) The Commission shall order the temporary suspension of any change in the rules of a clearing agency made by a proposed rule change that has taken effect under paragraph (3), if the appropriate regulatory agency for the clearing agency notifies the Commission not later than 30 days after the date on which the proposed rule change was filed of—

"(I) the determination by the appropriate regulatory agency that the rules of such clearing agency, as so changed, may be inconsistent with the safeguarding of securities or funds in the custody or control of such clearing agency or for which it is responsible; and

"(II) the reasons for the determination described in subclause (I).

"(ii) If the Commission takes action under clause (i), the Commission shall institute proceedings under paragraph (2)(B) to determine if the proposed rule change should be approved or disapproved.".

SEC.917. STUDY REGARDING FINANCIAL LITERACY AMONG INVESTORS.

(a) IN GENERAL. —The Commission shall conduct a study to identify —

(1) the existing level of financial literacy among retail investors, including subgroups of investors identified by the Commission;

(2) methods to improve the timing, content, and format of disclosures to investors with respect to financial intermediaries, investment products, and investment services;

(3) the most useful and understandable relevant information that retail investors need to make informed financial decisions before engaging a financial intermediary or purchasing an investment product or service that is typically sold to retail investors, including shares of open–end companies, as that term is defined in section 5 of the Investment Company Act of 1940 (15 U.S.C.80a–5) that are registered under section 8 of that Act;

(4) methods to increase the transparency of expenses and conflicts of interests in transactions involving investment services and products, including shares of open–end companies described in paragraph (3);

(5) the most effective existing private and public efforts to educate investors; and

(6) in consultation with the Financial Literacy and Education Commission, a strategy (including, to the extent practicable, measurable goals and objectives) to increase the financial literacy of investors in order to bring about a positive change in investor behavior.

(b) REPORT. –Not later than 2 years after the date of enactment of this Act, the Commission shall submit a report on the study required under subsection (a) to—

(1) the Committee on Banking, Housing, and Urban Affairs of the Senate; and

(d)一致性修正。——《1934年证券交易法》第19(b)(4)(D)条[《美国法典》第十五编第78s(b)(4)(D)节]修正后全文如下:

“(D)(i)对于结算机构作出的且已根据第(3)款规定生效的规则变更草案,如果该结算机构的相应监管机关在该等规则变更草案报批日起30天内向证券交易委员会发出通知,说明如下内容,则证券交易委员会应命令结算机构临时暂停该等规则变更草案对该结算机构规则作出的任何变更——

(I)相应监管机关判定该结算机构变更后的规则可能不利于该结算机构存管、控制或负责的证券或基金的安全保障;及

(II)作出第(I)子项所述判定的理由。

(ii)证券交易委员会根据第(i)项采取行动的,应根据第(2)(B)款启动相关程序,以判定该等规则变更草案应予以批准还是否决。”

第917条　关于投资者金融素养的研究

(a)**一般规定**。——证券交易委员会应开展研究,以确定——

(1)零售投资者(包括证券交易委员会确定的投资者细分群体)的现有金融素养水平;

(2)改进向投资者披露金融中介机构、投资产品和投资服务相关信息的时间、内容和格式的方法;

(3)在聘用金融中介机构之前,或者在购买通常面向零售投资者出售的投资产品或服务[包括按照《1940年投资公司法》第8条注册的开放式公司(定义见《1940年投资公司法》第5条(《美国法典》第十五编第80a-5节)]的股票)之前,零售投资者作出知情决策所需的最为有用且易于理解的相关信息;

(4)提高投资服务和产品[包括第(3)款所述开放式公司的股票]交易中费用及利益冲突的透明度的方法;

(5)现有最为有效的关于投资者教育的活动,无论是私人部门还是公共部门发起的;及

(6)提高投资者金融素养进而使投资者行为发生积极转化的策略(在可行的范围内,包含可量化的目的和目标)但是在确定该策略时,应与金融扫盲和教育委员会进行磋商。

(b)**报告**。——证券交易委员会应于本法颁布之日后两年内就第(a)子条所规定的研究向下述委员会提交报告——

(1)参议院银行、住房与城市事务委员会;及

(2) the Committee on Financial Services of the House of Representatives.

SEC.918. STUDY REGARDING MUTUAL FUND ADVERTISING.

(a) IN GENERAL. —The Comptroller General of the United States shall conduct a study on mutual fund advertising to identify —

(1) existing and proposed regulatory requirements for open–end investment company advertisements;

(2) current marketing practices for the sale of open–end investment company shares, including the use of past performance data, funds that have merged, and incubator funds;

(3) the impact of such advertising on consumers; and

(4) recommendations to improve investor protections in mutual fund advertising and additional information necessary to ensure that investors can make informed financial decisions when purchasing shares.

(b) REPORT. —Not later than 18 months after the date of enactment of this Act, the Comptroller General of the United States shall submit a report on the results of the study conducted under subsection (a) to —

(1) the Committee on Banking, Housing, and Urban Affairs of the United States Senate; and

(2) the Committee on Financial Services of the House of Representatives.

SEC.919. CLARIFICATION OF COMMISSION AUTHORITY TO REQUIRE INVESTOR DISCLOSURES BEFORE PURCHASE OF INVESTMENT PROD UCTS AND SERVICES.

Section 15 of the Securities Exchange Act of 1934 (15 U.S.C.78o) is amended by adding at the end the following:

"(n) DISCLOSURES TO RETAIL INVESTORS. —

"(1) IN GENERAL.—Notwithstanding any other provision of the securities laws, the Commission may issue rules designating documents or information that shall be provided by a broker or dealer to a retail investor before the purchase of an investment product or service by the retail investor.

"(2) CONSIDERATIONS.—In developing any rules under paragraph(1), the Commission shall consider whether the rules will promote investor protection, efficiency, competition, and capital formation.

"(3) FORM AND CONTENTS OF DOCUMENTS AND INFORMATION. —Any documents or information designated under a rule promulgated under paragraph (1) shall —

"(A) be in a summary format; and

"(B) contain clear and concise information about —

"(i) investment objectives, strategies, costs, and risks; and

"(ii) any compensation or other financial incentive received by a broker, dealer, or other

(2)众议院金融服务委员会。

第918条　关于共同基金广告宣传的研究

(a)**一般规定**。——政府问责办公室主任应针对共同基金广告宣传开展研究,以确定——

(1)针对开放式投资公司广告宣传的现有监管要求以及拟施加的监管要求;

(2)开放式投资公司股份销售的当前营销做法,包括对历史业绩数据、已兼并基金及孵化基金的利用;

(3)该等广告宣传对消费者的影响;及

(4)在共同基金广告宣传中加强投资者保护的建议,以及确保投资者在购买股票时能够作出知情金融决策所需的必要额外信息。

(b)**报告**。——政府问责办公室主任应于本法颁布之日后18个月内就第(a)子条所规定研究的结果向以下委员会提交报告——

(1)参议院银行、住房与城市事务委员会;及

(2)众议院金融服务委员会。

第919条　关于证券交易委员会要求在投资者购买投资产品和服务之前向投资者进行披露的权力的说明

在《1934年证券交易法》第15条(《美国法典》第十五编第78o节)结尾处增加如下内容,作为对该条的修正:

"(n)**向零售投资者进行披露**。——

(1)**一般规定**。——无论证券法律是否存在任何不同规定,证券交易委员会均可以发布规则,指定在零售投资者购买投资产品或服务之前,经纪商自营商应向零售投资者提供的文件或信息。

(2)**考虑因素**。——在根据第(1)款规定任何规则时,证券交易委员会应考虑该等规则是否将加强投资者保护、提高效率,并促进竞争和资本形成。

(3)**文件和信息的格式和内容**。——根据第(1)款规定颁发的规则中指定的任何文件或信息均应——

(A)以摘要形式作出;并

(B)载明关于以下各项的明确、简洁的信息——

(i)投资目标、策略、成本和风险;及

(ii)经纪商、自营商或其他中介机构因投资者购买零售投资产品而获得的任何报

intermediary in connection with the purchase of retail investment products.”.

SEC.919A. STUDY ON CONFLICTS OF INTEREST.

(a) IN GENERAL. —The Comptroller General of the United States shall conduct a study —

(1) to identify and examine potential conflicts of interest that exist between the staffs of the investment banking and equity and fixed income securities analyst functions within the same firm; and

(2) to make recommendations to Congress designed to protect investors in light of such conflicts.

(b) CONSIDERATIONS.—In conducting the study under subsection(a), the Comptroller General shall —

(1) consider —

(A) the potential for investor harm resulting from conflicts, including consideration of the forms of misconduct engaged in by the several securities firms and individuals that entered into the Global Analyst Research Settlements in 2003 (also known as the “Global Settlement”);

(B) the nature and benefits of the undertakings to which those firms agreed in enforcement proceedings, including firewalls between research and investment banking, separate reporting lines, dedicated legal and compliance staffs, allocation of budget, physical separation, compensation, employee performance evaluations, coverage decisions, limitations on soliciting investment banking business, disclosures, transparency, and other measures;

(C) whether any such undertakings should be codified and applied permanently to securities firms, or whether the Commission should adopt rules applying any such undertakings to securities firms; and

(D) whether to recommend regulatory or legislative measures designed to mitigate possible adverse consequences to investors arising from the conflicts of interest or to enhance investor protection or confidence in the integrity of the securities markets; and

(2) consult with State attorneys general, State securities officials, the Commission, the Financial Industry Regulatory Authority (“FINRA”), NYSE Regulation, investor advocates, brokers, dealers, retail investors, institutional investors, and academics.

(c) REPORT. —The Comptroller General shall submit a report on the results of the study required by this section to the Committee on Banking, Housing, and Urban Affairs of the Senate and the Committee on Financial Services of the House of Representatives, not later than 18 months after the date of enactment of this Act.

SEC.919B. STUDY ON IMPROVED INVESTOR ACCESS TO INFORMATION ON INVESTMENT ADVISERS AND BROKER–DEALERS.

(a) STUDY. —

酬或其他财务激励。”

第919A条　关于利益冲突的研究

(a)**一般规定**。——政府问责办公室主任应开展研究,以便——

(1)识别并审查同一家证券公司内部投资银行人员与股权及固定收益证券分析师之间的潜在利益冲突;并

(2)基于该等利益冲突向国会提出旨在保护投资者的建议。

(b)**考虑因素**。——在根据第(a)子条规定开展研究时,政府问责办公室主任应——

(1)考虑如下因素——

(A)利益冲突可能对投资者造成的损害,包括2003年签署《全球分析师研究协议》(亦称《全球分析师协议》)的证券公司和个人所从事的不当行为的形式;

(B)该等公司同意在执法程序中作出的承诺之性质和利益,包括研究部门与投资银行部门之间的隔离墙、投诉专线、专门的法务及合规人员、预算分配、物理隔离、薪酬、员工绩效评价、分析对象范围决策、投资银行业务招揽限制、信息披露、透明度以及其他措施;

(C)是否应将任何上述承诺成文,并正式适用于证券公司,或者证券交易委员会是否应制定规则,将任何上述承诺适用于证券公司;及

(D)是否建议采取监管或立法措施,以缓解利益冲突可能对投资者造成的不利后果,加强投资者保护,或提振投资者对证券市场完整性的信心;并

(2)与州检察长、州证券官员、证券交易委员会、金融业监管局(FINRA)、纽约证券交易所监管部、投资者维权人士、经纪商、自营商、零售投资者、机构投资者及学术界人士进行磋商。

(c)**报告**。——政府问责办公室主任应于本法颁布之日后18个月内就本条所规定研究的结果向参议院银行、住房与城市事务委员会及众议院金融服务委员会提交报告。

第919B条　关于完善投资者获取投资顾问和经纪自营商信息的渠道的研究

(a)**研究**。——

(1) IN GENERAL. —Not later than 6 months after the date of enactment of this Act, the Commission shall complete a study, including recommendations, of ways to improve the access of investors to registration information (including disciplinary actions, regulatory, judicial, and arbitration proceedings, and other information) about registered and previously registered investment advisers, associated persons of investment advisers, brokers and dealers and their associated persons on the existing Central Registration Depository and Investment Adviser Registration Depository systems, as well as identify additional information that should be made publicly available.

(2) CONTENTS. —The study required by subsection (a) shall include an analysis of the advantages and disadvantages of further centralizing access to the information contained in the 2 systems, including —

(A) identification of those data pertinent to investors; and

(B) the identification of the method and format for displaying and publishing such data to enhance accessibility by and utility to investors.

(b) IMPLEMENTATION. —Not later than 18 months after the date of completion of the study required by subsection (a), the Commission shall implement any recommendations of the study.

SEC.919C. STUDY ON FINANCIAL PLANNERS AND THE USE OF FINANCIAL DESIGNATIONS.

(a) IN GENERAL. —The Comptroller General of the United States shall conduct a study to evaluate —

(1) the effectiveness of State and Federal regulations to protect investors and other consumers from individuals who hold themselves out as financial planners through the use of misleading titles, designations, or marketing materials;

(2) current State and Federal oversight structure and regulations for financial planners; and

(3) legal or regulatory gaps in the regulation of financial planners and other individuals who provide or offer to provide financial planning services to consumers.

(b) CONSIDERATIONS. —In conducting the study required under subsection (a), the Comptroller General shall consider —

(1) the role of financial planners in providing advice regarding the management of financial resources, including investment planning, income tax planning, education planning, retirement planning, estate planning, and risk management;

(2) whether current regulations at the State and Federal level provide adequate ethical and professional standards for financial planners;

(3) the possible risk posed to investors and other consumers by individuals who hold themselves out as financial planners or as otherwise providing financial planning services in

(1)**一般规定**。——证券交易委员会应于本法颁布之日后6个月内,针对如何完善投资者通过现有集中注册信息存管系统以及投资顾问注册信息存管系统,获取关于当前和先前注册的投资顾问、经纪商、自营商及其各自的业务相关人的注册信息(包括纪律处分、监管、司法、仲裁程序及其他信息)的渠道,完成一项研究并提出相应建议,同时确定应予公开的额外信息。

(2)**内容**。——根据第(a)子条规定开展研究时,应对进一步统一上述两个系统的信息获取方式进行利弊分析,包括——

(A)识别与投资者相关的数据;并

(B)识别列示和公布该等数据的方法和格式,以使投资者更便利地获取数据和使用该等数据。

(b)**实施**。——证券交易委员会应在完成第(a)子条所规定研究之日后18个月内实施该研究中提出的任何建议。

第919C条　关于金融理财师和金融称号使用的研究

(a)**一般规定**。——政府问责办公室主任应开展研究,以评价——

(1)在保护投资者及其他消费者使其免受通过利用误导性名称、称号或营销材料而以金融理财师身份自居的个人损害方面,州规章和联邦规章的有效性;

(2)当前针对金融理财师的州及联邦监管架构和规章;及

(3)在对金融理财师及向消费者提供或要约金融理财服务的其他个人进行监管方面存在的法律漏洞或监管漏洞。

(b)**考虑因素**。——在开展第(a)子条所规定研究时,政府问责办公室主任应考虑如下因素——

(1)金融理财师在对金融资源管理(包括投资规划、所得税规划、教育规划、退休规划、遗产规划及风险管理)提供咨询意见方面起到的作用;

(2)现行的州规章和联邦规章是否对金融理财师设定了充分的道德和专业标准;

(3)以金融理财师身份自居的个人,或在金融产品(包括保险和证券)销售过程中以金融理财服务提供者身份自居的个人对投资者及其他消费者可能造成的风险;

connection with the sale of financial products, including insurance and securities;

(4) the possible risk posed to investors and other consumers by individuals who otherwise use titles, designations, or marketing materials in a misleading way in connection with the delivery of financial advice;

(6) the ability of investors and other consumers to understand licensing requirements and standards of care that apply to individuals who hold themselves out as financial planners or as otherwise providing financial planning services;

(7) the possible benefits to investors and other consumers of regulation and professional oversight of financial planners; and

(8) any other consideration that the Comptroller General deems necessary or appropriate to effectively execute the study required under subsection (a).

(c) RECOMMENDATIONS. —In providing recommendations for the appropriate regulation of financial planners and other individuals who provide or offer to provide financial planning services, in order to protect investors and other consumers of financial planning services, the Comptroller General shall consider —

(1) the appropriate structure for regulation of financial planners and individuals providing financial planning services; and

(2) the appropriate scope of the regulations needed to protect investors and other consumers, including but not limited to the need to establish competency standards, practice standards, ethical guidelines, disciplinary authority, and transparency to investors and other consumers.

(d) REPORT. —

(1) IN GENERAL. —Not later than 180 days after the date of enactment of this Act, the Comptroller General shall submit a report on the study required under subsection (a) to —

(A) the Committee on Banking, Housing, and Urban Affairs of the Senate;

(B) the Special Committee on Aging of the Senate; and

(C) the Committee on Financial Services of the House of Representatives.

(2) CONTENT REQUIREMENTS. —The report required under paragraph (1)shall describe the findings and determinations made by the Comptroller General in carrying out the study required under subsection(a), including a description of the considerations, analysis, and government, public, industry, nonprofit and consumer input that the Comptroller General considered to make such findings, conclusions, and legislative, regulatory, or other recommendations.

SEC.919D. OMBUDSMAN.

Section 4 (g) of the Securities Exchange Act of 1934, as added by section 914, is amended by adding at the end the following:

"(8) OMBUDSMAN. —

(4)在提供金融咨询意见过程中以误导性方式使用名称、称号或营销材料的个人对投资者及其他消费者可能造成的风险;

(6)对以金融理财师身份自居的个人,或以金融理财服务提供者身份自居的个人而言,投资者及其他消费者对该等人士所应遵守的注册要求和注意标准的理解能力;

(7)对金融理财师的规制和专业监管可能给投资者及其他消费者带来的益处;及

(8)政府问责办公室主任认为对有效开展第(a)子条规定的研究确属必要或适当的任何其他考虑因素。

(c)**建议**。——为了保护投资者及其他金融理财服务消费者,政府问责办公室主任就如何对金融理财师及提供或要约金融理财服务的其他个人进行适当监管提出建议时,应考虑如下因素——

(1)对金融理财师及提供金融理财服务的个人进行规制的适当架构;及

(2)保护投资者及其他消费者所需的规章的适当管辖范围,包括但不限于是否需要制定胜任性标准、执业标准、职业道德指引,以及是否需要设立纪律处分权并确定对投资者及其他消费者的透明度要求。

(d)**报告**。——

(1)**一般规定**。——政府问责办公室主任应于本法颁布之日后180天内就第(a)子条所规定研究向以下委员会提交报告——

(A)参议院银行、住房与城市事务委员会;

(B)参议院老龄问题特别委员会;及

(C)众议院金融服务委员会。

(2)**内容要求**。——第(1)款所规定报告应说明政府问责办公室主任开展第(a)子条所规定研究时作出的认定和判定,包括政府问责办公室主任为作出该等认定、结论以及提出立法建议、监管建议或其他建议所考虑的因素、分析以及政府、公众、行业、非营利组织和消费者的意见。

第919D条 监察专员

在第914条增加的《1934年证券交易法》第4(g)条结尾处增加如下内容,作为对该条的修正:

"(8)**监察专员**。——

"(A) APPOINTMENT. —Not later than 180 days after the date on which the first Investor Advocate is appointed under paragraph (2)(A)(i), the Investor Advocate shall appoint an Ombudsman, who shall report directly to the Investor Advocate.

"(B) DUTIES. —The Ombudsman appointed under subparagraph (A) shall —

"(i) act as a liaison between the Commission and any retail investor in resolving problems that retail investors may have with the Commission or with self–regulatory organizations;

"(ii) review and make recommendations regarding policies and procedures to encourage persons to present questions to the Investor Advocate regarding compliance with the securities laws; and

"(iii) establish safeguards to maintain the confidentiality of communications between the persons described in clause (ii) and the Ombudsman.

"(C) LIMITATION. —In carrying out the duties of the Ombudsman under subparagraph (B), the Ombudsman shall utilize personnel of the Commission to the extent practicable. Nothing in this paragraph shall be construed as replacing, altering, or diminishing the activities of any ombudsman or similar office of any other agency.

"(D) REPORT. —The Ombudsman shall submit a semiannual report to the Investor Advocate that describes the activities and evaluates the effectiveness of the Ombudsman during the preceding year. The Investor Advocate shall include the reports required under this section in the reports required to be submitted by the Inspector Advocate under paragraph (6).".

Subtitle B—Increasing Regulatory Enforcement and Remedies

SEC.921. AUTHORITY TO RESTRICT MANDATORY PRE-DISPUTE ARBITRATION.

(a) AMENDMENT TO SECURITIES EXCHANGE ACT OF 1934.—Section 15 of the Securities Exchange Act of 1934(15 U.S.C.78o), as amended by this title, is further amended by adding at the end the following new subsection:

"(o) AUTHORITY TO RESTRICT MANDATORY PRE–DISPUTE ARBITRATION. — The Commission, by rule, may prohibit, or impose conditions or limitations on the use of, agreements that require customers or clients of any broker, dealer, or municipal securities dealer to arbitrate any future dispute between them arising under the Federal securities laws, the rules and regulations thereunder, or the rules of a self–regulatory organization if it finds that such prohibition, imposition of conditions, or limitations are in the public interest and for

(A)**任命**。——首任投资者维权办公室主任在其根据第(2)(A)(i)款获得任命之日后180天内,应任命一名监察专员。监察专员应直接向投资者维权办公室主任汇报工作。

(B)**职责**。——根据第(A)子款任命的监察专员应——

(i) 在解决任何零售投资者与证券交易委员会或自律组织之间可能存在的问题时,负责担任证券交易委员会与该等零售投资者之间的联络人;

(ii)对鼓励向投资者维权办公室主任提出证券法律合规相关问题的政策和程序进行审查,并提出建议;并

(iii)制定保障措施,以维持第(ii)项所述主体与监察专员之间沟通的保密性。

(C)**限制**。——在履行第(B)子款规定的监察专员职责时,监察专员应在可行的范围内利用证券交易委员会的人力。本款任何内容均不得被解释为替代、改变或削弱任何其他机关的任何监察专员或类似职务人员的工作。

(D)**报告**。——监察专员应向投资者维权办公室主任[1]提交半年度报告,说明监察专员在上一年度开展的工作并评价其工作的成效。投资者维权办公室主任应将本条规定的报告纳入其根据第(6)款应提交的报告之中。”

第B子编——加强监管执法和救济

第921条　对强制性纠纷仲裁前置程序进行限制的权力

(a)**对《1934年证券交易法》的修正**。——在经本编修正后的《1934年证券交易法》第15条(《美国法典》第十五编第78o节)结尾处增加如下新子条,作为对该条的进一步修正:

“(o)**对强制性纠纷仲裁前置程序进行限制的权力**。——任何经纪商、自营商或市政证券自营商与其委托方或客户之间的协议,如果要求必须对双方因联邦证券法律、依据联邦法律制定的规则与规章或者自律组织规则而引发的任何未来纠纷进行仲裁的协议,则证券交易委员会可以发布规则禁止使用该等协议,或对该等协议的使用设定条件或限制,前提是证券交易委员会认定该等禁止、条件设定后限制符合公共利益

1　此处的“Investor Advocate”似应为“Inspector Advocate”,译文中按后者处理。——译者注

the protection of investors.".

(b) AMENDMENT TO INVESTMENT ADVISERS ACT OF 1940. —Section 205 of the Investment Advisers Act of 1940 (15 U.S.C.80b–5) is amended by adding at the end the following new subsection:

"(f) AUTHORITY TO RESTRICT MANDATORY PRE–DISPUTE ARBITRATION. —The Commission, by rule, may prohibit, or impose conditions or limitations on the use of, agreements that require customers or clients of any investment adviser to arbitrate any future dispute between them arising under the Federal securities laws, the rules and regulations thereunder, or the rules of a self–regulatory organization if it finds that such prohibition, imposition of conditions, or limitations are in the public interest and for the protection of investors.".

SEC.922. WHISTLEBLOWER PROTECTION.

(a) IN GENERAL. —The Securities Exchange Act of 1934 (15 U.S.C.78a et seq.) is amended by inserting after section 21E the following:

"SEC.21F. SECURITIES WHISTLEBLOWER INCENTIVES AND PROTECTION.

"(a) DEFINITIONS. —In this section the following definitions shall apply:

"(1) COVERED JUDICIAL OR ADMINISTRATIVE ACTION.—The term 'covered judicial or administrative action' means any judicial or administrative action brought by the Commission under the securities laws that results in monetary sanctions exceeding $1,000,000.

"(2) FUND.—The term 'Fund' means the Securities and Exchange Commission Investor Protection Fund.

"(3) ORIGINAL INFORMATION. —The term 'original information' means information that —

"(A) is derived from the independent knowledge or analysis of a whistleblower;

"(B) is not known to the Commission from any other source, unless the whistleblower is the original source of the information; and

"(C) is not exclusively derived from an allegation made in a judicial or administrative hearing, in a governmental report, hearing, audit, or investigation, or from the news media, unless the whistleblower is a source of the information.

"(4) MONETARY SANCTIONS. —The term 'monetary sanctions', when used with respect to any judicial or administrative action, means —

"(A) any monies, including penalties, disgorgement, and interest, ordered to be paid; and

"(B) any monies deposited into a disgorgement fund or other fund pursuant to section 308(b) of the Sarbanes–Oxley Act of 2002 (15 U.S.C.7246(b)), as a result of such action or any settlement of such action.

并有利于投资者保护。”

(b)**对《1940年投资顾问法》的修正**。——在《1940年投资顾问法》第205条(《美国法典》第十五编第80b-5节)结尾处增加如下新子条,作为对该条的修正:

“(f)**对强制性纠纷仲裁前置程序进行限制的权力**。——如果任何协议要求任何投资顾问的委托方或客户必须对双方因联邦证券法律、依据联邦法律制定的规则与规章或者自律组织规则而引发的任何未来纠纷进行仲裁的,证券交易委员会可以发布规则禁止使用该等协议,或对该等协议的使用设定条件或限制,前提是证券交易委员会认定该等禁止、条件设定或限制符合公共利益并有利于投资者保护。”

第922条　举报人保护

(a)**一般规定**。——在《1934年证券交易法》(《美国法典》第十五编第78a节及其后条文)第21E条之后插入如下内容,作为对该法的修正:

“第21F条 对证券举报人的激励和保护

“(a)**定义**——就本条而言,应适用如下定义:

(1)**所涉司法或行政诉讼**——‘所涉司法或行政诉讼’一词系指证券交易委员会根据证券法律提起的导致100万美元以上金钱制裁的任何司法或行政诉讼。

(2)**基金**——‘基金’一词系指证券交易委员会投资者保护基金。

(3)**原始信息**——‘原始信息’一词系指符合下述条件的信息——

(A)完全因举报人自身掌握的情况或分析而获取的信息;

(B)证券交易委员会并非从任何其他来源获知的信息,但是原始来源为举报人的信息除外;且

(C)并非完全源自司法审理或行政听证、政府报告、听证、审计、调查或新闻媒体的信息,但是源自举报人的信息除外。

(4)**金钱制裁**。——就任何司法或行政诉讼而言,‘金钱制裁’一词系指——

(A)被勒令支付的任何款项,包括罚款、没收款项和利息;及

(B)因上述诉讼或该等诉讼和解而依据《2002年萨班斯—奥克斯利法》第308(b)条[《美国法典》第十五编第7246(b)节]存入没收基金或其他基金的任何款项。

"(5) RELATED ACTION. —The term 'related action', when used with respect to any judicial or administrative action brought by the Commission under the securities laws, means any judicial or administrative action brought by an entity described in subclauses (I) through (IV) of subsection (h)(2)(D)(i) that is based upon the original information provided by a whistleblower pursuant to subsection (a) that led to the successful enforcement of the Commission action.

"(6) WHISTLEBLOWER. —The term 'whistleblower' means any individual who provides, or 2 or more individuals acting jointly who provide, information relating to a violation of the securities laws to the Commission, in a manner established, by rule or regulation, by the Commission.

"(b) AWARDS. —

"(1) IN GENERAL.—In any covered judicial or administrative action, or related action, the Commission, under regulations prescribed by the Commission and subject to subsection (c), shall pay an award or awards to 1 or more whistleblowers who voluntarily provided original information to the Commission that led to the successful enforcement of the covered judicial or administrative action, or related action, in an aggregate amount equal to—

"(A) not less than 10 percent, in total, of what has been collected of the monetary sanctions imposed in the action or related actions; and

"(B) not more than 30 percent, in total, of what has been collected of the monetary sanctions imposed in the action or related actions.

"(2) PAYMENT OF AWARDS. —Any amount paid under paragraph (1) shall be paid from the Fund.

"(c) DETERMINATION OF AMOUNT OF AWARD; DENIAL OF AWARD. —

"(1) DETERMINATION OF AMOUNT OF AWARD. —

"(A) DISCRETION. —The determination of the amount of an award made under subsection (b) shall be in the discretion of the Commission.

"(B) CRITERIA. —In determining the amount of an award made under subsection (b), the Commission —

"(i) shall take into consideration —

"(I) the significance of the information provided by the whistleblower to the success of the covered judicial or administrative action;

"(II) the degree of assistance provided by the whistleblower and any legal representative of the whistleblower in a covered judicial or administrative action;

"(III) the programmatic interest of the Commission in deterring violations of the securities laws by making awards to whistleblowers who provide information that lead to the successful enforcement of such laws; and

"(IV) such additional relevant factors as the Commission may establish by rule or

(5)**关联诉讼**。——就证券交易委员会依据证券法律提起的任何司法或行政诉讼而言,'关联诉讼'一词系指第(h)(2)(D)(i)子条第(I)子项至第(IV)子项所述实体基于举报人依据第(a)子条提供的原始信息提起的任何司法或行政诉讼,且该原始信息导致了证券交易委员会胜诉。

(6)**举报人**。——'举报人'一词系指按证券交易委员会发布的规则或规章所确定的方式向证券交易委员会提供与违反证券法律的行为相关的信息的任何个人,或共同提供上述信息的两名(含)以上的个人。

(b)**奖励**。——

(1)**一般规定**。——在任何所涉司法或行政诉讼或关联诉讼中,对于自愿向证券交易委员会提供原始信息并导致所涉司法诉讼、行政诉讼或关联诉讼胜诉的1名或1名以上举报人,证券交易委员会应根据其所制定的规章并在不违反第(c)子条的前提下向其提供奖励,奖励总额应——

(A)不低于该等诉讼或关联诉讼判处的金钱制裁的10%;且

(B)不高于该等诉讼或关联诉讼判处的金钱制裁的30%。

(2)**奖励支付**。——第(1)款规定的任何金额均应通过基金支付。

(c)**奖励金额的确定;不授予奖励的情形**——

(1)**奖励金额的确定**。——

(A)**自由裁量权**。——第(b)子条规定的奖励金额应由证券交易委员会依其自由裁量权确定。

(B)**标准**。——在确定第(b)子条所规定的奖励金额时,证券交易委员会——

(i)应考虑如下因素——

(I)举报人提供的信息对于所涉司法或行政诉讼能否胜诉的重要性;

(II)举报人及其任何法律代理人在所涉司法或行政诉讼中提供协助的程度;

(III)举报人提供信息帮助证券交易委员会成功执行证券法规定的,证券交易委员会向举报人授予奖励以期威慑违反证券法的行为而获得的战略性效益;及

(IV)证券交易委员会发布的规则或规章所确定的其他相关因素;且

regulation; and

"(ii) shall not take into consideration the balance of the Fund.

"(2) DENIAL OF AWARD. —No award under subsection (b) shall be made —

"(A) to any whistleblower who is, or was at the time the whistleblower acquired the original information submitted to the Commission, a member, officer, or employee of —

"(i) an appropriate regulatory agency;

"(ii) the Department of Justice;

"(iii) a self–regulatory organization;

"(iv) the Public Company Accounting Oversight Board; or

"(v) a law enforcement organization;

"(B) to any whistleblower who is convicted of a criminal violation related to the judicial or administrative action for which the whistleblower otherwise could receive an award under this section;

"(C) to any whistleblower who gains the information through the performance of an audit of financial statements required under the securities laws and for whom such submission would be contrary to the requirements of section 10A of the Securities Exchange Act of 1934 (15 U.S.C.78j–1); or

"(D) to any whistleblower who fails to submit information to the Commission in such form as the Commission may, by rule, require.

"(d) REPRESENTATION. —

"(1) PERMITTED REPRESENTATION. —Any whistleblower who makes a claim for an award under subsection (b) may be represented by counsel.

"(2) REQUIRED REPRESENTATION. —

"(A) IN GENERAL. —Any whistleblower who anonymously makes a claim for an award under subsection (b) shall be represented by counsel if the whistleblower anonymously submits the information upon which the claim is based.

"(B) DISCLOSURE OF IDENTITY.—Prior to the payment of an award, a whistleblower shall disclose the identity of the whistleblower and provide such other information as the Commission may require, directly or through counsel for the whistleblower.

"(e) NO CONTRACT NECESSARY. —No contract with the Commission is necessary for any whistleblower to receive an award under subsection (b), unless otherwise required by the Commission by rule or regulation.

"(f) APPEALS. —Any determination made under this section, including whether, to whom, or in what amount to make awards, shall be in the discretion of the Commission. Any such determination, except the determination of the amount of an award if the award was made

(ii)不得将基金余额作为确定奖励金额的考虑因素。

(2)**不授予奖励的情形**。——在以下情形下,不得向举报人授予第(b)子条规定的奖励——

(A)任何举报人身为下述组织或机关的成员、官员或雇员的举报人,或者,任何举报人在获取提交给证券交易委员会的原始信息时身为下列组织或机构的成员、官员或雇员——

(i)相应的监管机关;

(ii)司法部;

(iii)自律组织;

(iv)公众公司会计监督委员会;或

(v)执法组织;

(B)任何举报人本可以依据本条获得奖励,但在相关司法或行政诉讼中被判犯有刑事违法违规行为;

(C)符号下述条件的任何举报人:按照证券法律的规定开展财务报表审计获得信息,且提交该等信息将违反《1934年证券交易法》第10A条(《美国法典》第十五编第78j-1节)的要求;或

(D)任何举报人未按照证券交易委员会发布的规则所要求的格式向证券交易委员会提交信息。

(d)**代理**。——

(1)**选择性代理**。——依第(b)子条索取奖励的任何举报人可选择聘请律师进行代理。

(2)**强制性代理**。——

(A)**一般规定**。——如果任何举报人匿名提交了其认为可获奖励的信息,则其在根据第(b)子条匿名索取奖励时应由律师代理。

(B)**身份披露**。——在支付奖励之前,举报人应披露其身份,直接地或通过其律师提供证券交易委员会要求的其他信息。

(e)**不必签订合同**。——除非证券交易委员会发布的规则或规章另有要求,否则,举报人根据第(b)子条获得奖励的,不必与证券交易委员会签订合同。

(f)**司法审查请求**。——依据本条作出的所有判定,包括是否给予奖励、奖励对象、奖励金额,均应由证券交易委员会依其自由裁量权作出。除按照第(b)子条作出的有关奖励金额的判定之外,所有其他判定均可在证券交易委员会做出判定后30天内

in accordance with subsection (b), may be appealed to the appropriate court of appeals of the United States not more than 30 days after the determination is issued by the Commission. The court shall review the determination made by the Commission in accordance with section 706 of title 5, United States Code.

"(g) INVESTOR PROTECTION FUND.—

"(1) FUND ESTABLISHED.—There is established in the Treasury of the United States a fund to be known as the 'Securities and Exchange Commission Investor Protection Fund'.

"(2) USE OF FUND.—The Fund shall be available to the Commission, without further appropriation or fiscal year limitation, for—

"(A) paying awards to whistleblowers as provided in subsection (b); and

"(B) funding the activities of the Inspector General of the Commission under section 4 (i).

"(3) DEPOSITS AND CREDITS.—

"(A) IN GENERAL.—There shall be deposited into or credited to the Fund an amount equal to—

"(i) any monetary sanction collected by the Commission in any judicial or administrative action brought by the Commission under the securities laws that is not added to a disgorgement fund or other fund under section 308 of the Sarbanes-Oxley Act of 2002 (15 U.S.C.7246) or otherwise distributed to victims of a violation of the securities laws, or the rules and regulations thereunder, underlying such action, unless the balance of the Fund at the time the monetary sanction is collected exceeds $300,000,000;

"(ii) any monetary sanction added to a disgorgement fund or other fund under section 308 of the Sarbanes-Oxley Act of 2002 (15 U.S.C.7246) that is not distributed to the victims for whom the Fund was established, unless the balance of the disgorgement fund at the time the determination is made not to distribute the monetary sanction to such victims exceeds $200,000,000; and

"(iii) all income from investments made under paragraph (4).

"(B) ADDITIONAL AMOUNTS.—If the amounts deposited into or credited to the Fund under subparagraph (A) are not sufficient to satisfy an award made under subsection (b), there shall be deposited into or credited to the Fund an amount equal to the unsatisfied portion of the award from any monetary sanction collected by the Commission in the covered judicial or administrative action on which the award is based.

"(4) INVESTMENTS.—

"(A) AMOUNTS IN FUND MAY BE INVESTED.—The Commission may request the Secretary of the Treasury to invest the portion of the Fund that is not, in the discretion of the Commission, required to meet the current needs of the Fund.

"(B) ELIGIBLE INVESTMENTS.—Investments shall be made by the Secretary of the

向相应的联邦上诉法院提请司法审查。法院应根据《美国法典》第五编第706节的规定对证券交易委员会的判定进行审查。

(g)**投资者保护基金**。——

(1)**基金的设立**。——美国财政部下设'证券交易委员会投资者保护基金'。

(2)**基金的使用**。——证券交易委员会应当将基金用于如下目的,不受追加拨款或财政年度限制——

(A)按第(b)子条规定向举报人支付奖励;及

(B)为证券交易委员会监察长根据第4(i)条规定开展的工作提供经费。

(3)**存储和贷项**。——

(A)**一般规定**。——下述款项应存入基金或记入基金贷项——

(i)证券交易委员会根据证券法律提起的任何司法或行政诉讼中收取的任何金钱制裁款项中,未记入没收基金或《2002年萨班斯—奥克斯利法》第308条(《美国法典》第十五编第7246节)规定的其他基金,也未向引发该等诉讼的违法违规行为(即违反证券法律或依其发布的规则与规章的行为)的受害人分配的部分,但收取该等金钱制裁款项时基金余额已超过3亿美元的除外;

(ii)已记入没收基金或《2002年萨班斯—奥克斯利法》第308条(《美国法典》第十五编第7246节)规定的其他基金,但未向作为基金保障对象的受害人分配的金钱制裁款项(但作出不向该等受害人分配金钱制裁款项的判定时没收基金余额已超过2亿美元的除外);及

(iii)根据第(4)款进行投资时产生的所有收入。

(B)**补充金额**。——根据第(A)子款存入基金或记入基金贷项的金额不足以支付第(b)子条规定的奖励的,应从证券交易委员会在与该奖励相关的任何司法或行政诉讼中收取的任何金钱制裁款项提取不足的金额存入基金或记入基金贷项。

(4)**投资**。——

(A)**基金内可用于投资的款项**。——对于证券交易委员会依其自由裁量权判断不必用于满足基金当期需求的基金款项,证券交易委员会可要求财政部部长对其进行投资。

(B)**适格投资**。——投资应由财政部部长作出,投资标的应为联邦政府债券,或

Treasury in obligations of the United States or obligations that are guaranteed as to principal and interest by the United States, with maturities suitable to the needs of the Fund as determined by the Commission on the record.

"(C) INTEREST AND PROCEEDS CREDITED. —The interest on, and the proceeds from the sale or redemption of, any obligations held in the Fund shall be credited to the Fund.

"(5) REPORTS TO CONGRESS. —Not later than October 30 of each fiscal year beginning after the date of enactment of this subsection, the Commission shall submit to the Committee on Banking, Housing, and Urban Affairs of the Senate, and the Committee on Financial Services of the House of Representatives a report on —

"(A) the whistleblower award program, established under this section, including —

"(i) a description of the number of awards granted; and

"(ii) the types of cases in which awards were granted during the preceding fiscal year;

"(B) the balance of the Fund at the beginning of the preceding fiscal year;

"(C) the amounts deposited into or credited to the Fund during the preceding fiscal year;

"(D) the amount of earnings on investments made under paragraph (4) during the preceding fiscal year;

"(E) the amount paid from the Fund during the preceding fiscal year to whistleblowers pursuant to subsection (b);

"(F) the balance of the Fund at the end of the preceding fiscal year; and

"(G) a complete set of audited financial statements, including —

"(i) a balance sheet;

"(ii) income statement; and

"(iii) cash flow analysis.

"(h) PROTECTION OF WHISTLEBLOWERS. —

"(1) PROHIBITION AGAINST RETALIATION. —

"(A) IN GENERAL.—No employer may discharge, demote, suspend, threaten, harass, directly or indirectly, or in any other manner discriminate against, a whistleblower in the terms and conditions of employment because of any lawful act done by the whistleblower —

"(i) in providing information to the Commission in accordance with this section;

"(ii) in initiating, testifying in, or assisting in any investigation or judicial or administrative action of the Commission based upon or related to such information; or

"(iii) in making disclosures that are required or protected under the Sarbanes–Oxley Act of 2002 (15 U.S.C.7201 et seq.), the Securities Exchange Act of 1934 (15 U.S.C.78a et seq.), including section 10A(m) of such Act (15 U.S.C.78f(m)), section 1513(e) of title 18, United States Code, and any other law, rule, or regulation subject to the jurisdiction of the Commission.

联邦政府担保本息偿付的债券，债券期限以证券交易委员会在记录在案的基础上判定确属适当的符合基金需求的期限为准。

(C)**记入贷项的利息和卖出或赎回债券所获资金**。——基金所持债券产生的利息以及其卖出或赎回所获资金均应记入基金贷项。

(5)**向国会报告**。——证券交易委员会应于本子条规定颁布之日后的每一财政年度的10月30日之前,向参议院银行、住房与城市事务委员会以及众议院金融服务委员会提交一份报告,说明如下事项——

(A)证券交易委员会依据本条制订的举报人奖励计划,包括——

(i)授予的奖励案件数量;及

(ii)前一财政年度授予奖励的案件类型;

(B)前一财政年度期初基金余额;

(C)前一财政年度存入基金或记入基金贷项的金额;

(D)前一财政年度依照第(4)款进行投资产生的收益金额;

(E)前一财政年度依照第(b)子条从基金拨付并向举报人支付的金额;

(F)前一财政年度期末基金余额;及

(G)整套审计财务报表,包括——

(i)资产负债表;

(ii)损益表;及

(iii)现金流量分析。

(h)**举报人保护**。——

(1)**禁止报复**。——

(A)**一般规定**。——任何雇主均不得因举报人从事下列任何合法行为而对举报人进行直接或间接的解聘、降职、停职、威胁、骚扰,亦不得在雇用条款和条件上对之进行任何其他歧视——

(i)按照本条规定向证券期货交易委员会提供信息;

(ii)为证券交易委员会基于上述信息启动的或与上述信息相关的任何调查行动、司法或行政诉讼提供证明或协助;或

(iii)进行《2002年萨班斯—奥克斯利法》(《美国法典》第十五编第7201节及其后条文)、《1934年证券交易法》(《美国法典》第十五编第78a节及其后条文){包括该法第10A(m)条[《美国法典》第十五编第78f(m)节]}、《美国法典》第十八编第1513(e)节以及证券交易委员会负责实施的任何其他法律、规则或规章所要求或保护的披露。

"(B) ENFORCEMENT.—

"(i) CAUSE OF ACTION. —An individual who alleges discharge or other discrimination in violation of subparagraph (A) may bring an action under this subsection in the appropriate district court of the United States for the relief provided in subparagraph (C).

"(ii) SUBPOENAS. —A subpoena requiring the attendance of a witness at a trial or hearing conducted under this section may be served at any place in the United States.

"(iii) STATUTE OF LIMITATIONS.—

"(I) IN GENERAL. —An action under this subsection may not be brought—

"(aa) more than 6 years after the date on which the violation of subparagraph (A) occurred; or

"(bb) more than 3 years after the date when facts material to the right of action are known or reasonably should have been known by the employee alleging a violation of subparagraph (A).

"(II) REQUIRED ACTION WITHIN 10 YEARS. —Not withstanding subclause (I), an action under this subsection may not in any circumstance be brought more than 10 years after the date on which the violation occurs.

"(C) RELIEF.—Relief for an individual prevailing in an action brought under subparagraph (B) shall include—

"(i) reinstatement with the same seniority status that the individual would have had, but for the discrimination;

"(ii) 2 times the amount of back pay otherwise owed to the individual, with interest; and

"(iii) compensation for litigation costs, expert witness fees, and reasonable attorneys' fees.

"(2) CONFIDENTIALITY.—

"(A) IN GENERAL. —Except as provided in subparagraphs(B) and(C), the Commission and any officer or employee of the Commission shall not disclose any information, including information provided by a whistleblower to the Commission, which could reasonably be expected to reveal the identity of a whistleblower, except in accordance with the provisions of section 552a of title 5, United States Code, unless and until required to be disclosed to a defendant or respondent in connection with a public proceeding instituted by the Commission or any entity described in subparagraph (C). For purposes of section 552 of title 5, United States Code, this paragraph shall be considered a statute described in subsection (b)(3)(B) of such section.

"(B) EXEMPTED STATUTE. —For purposes of section 552 of title 5, United States Code, this paragraph shall be considered a statute described in subsection(b)(3)(B)of such section 552.

"(C) RULE OF CONSTRUCTION. —Nothing in this section is intended to limit, or

（B）**执法**。——

（i）**诉因**。——主张存在违反第（A）子款规定的解聘或其他歧视行为的个人，可以根据本子条向相应的联邦地区法院提起诉讼，请求第（C）子款规定的救济。

（ii）**传票**。——传唤证人出席根据本子条开展的审判或听证的传票，可向美国境内任何地方送达。

（iii）**诉讼时效**。——

（I）**一般规定**。——本子条规定的诉讼必须在如下时间提起——

（aa）违反第（A）子款的行为发生之日后6年内；或

（bb）主张存在违反第（A）子款的行为的雇员知晓或理应知晓成立其诉讼权的主要事实之日后3年内。

（II）**必须在10年内提起诉讼**。——无论第（I）子项如何规定，在任何情况下，根据本子条提起的诉讼均必须在违法违规行为发生后10年内提起。

（C）**救济**。——在根据第（B）子款提起的诉讼中，胜诉方享有的救济应包括——

（i）恢复若未发生歧视其本应享有的雇用年资；

（ii）获得本应向其支付的欠付工资及利息的2倍金额；及

（iii）诉讼成本、专家证人费及合理律师费补偿。

（2）**保密**。——

（A）**一般规定**。——除第（B）子款和第（C）子款规定的情形外，证券交易委员会及其任何官员或职员，除非按照《美国法典》第五编第552a节的规定，否则不得披露据合理预期将导致举报人身份泄露的信息（包括举报人向证券交易委员会提供的信息），但在证券交易委员会或第（C）子款所述任何实体发起的公开程序中按规定向被告或相对人进行披露的除外。就《美国法典》第五编第552节而言，本款规定应视为该第552节第（b）（3）（B）子节所述的制定法。

（B）**豁免制定法**。——就《美国法典》第五编第552节而言，本款规定应视为该第552节第（b）（3）（B）子节所述的制定法。

（C）**解释规则**。——本条任何内容均无意限制，亦不得被解释为限制联邦总检察

shall be construed to limit, the ability of the Attorney General to present such evidence to a grand jury or to share such evidence with potential witnesses or defendants in the course of an ongoing criminal investigation.

"(D) AVAILABILITY TO GOVERNMENT AGENCIES. —

"(i) IN GENERAL. —Without the loss of its status as confidential in the hands of the Commission, all information referred to in subparagraph (A) may, in the discretion of the Commission, when determined by the Commission to be necessary to accomplish the purposes of this Act and to protect investors, be made available to —

"(I) the Attorney General of the United States;

"(II) an appropriate regulatory authority;

"(III) a self-regulatory organization;

"(IV) a State attorney general in connection with any criminal investigation;

"(V) any appropriate State regulatory authority;

"(VI) the Public Company Accounting Over sight Board;

"(VII) a foreign securities authority; and

"(VIII) a foreign law enforcement authority.

"(ii) CONFIDENTIALITY. —

"(I) IN GENERAL. —Each of the entities described in subclauses (I) through (VI) of clause(i)shall maintain such information as confidential in accordance with the requirements established under subparagraph (A).

"(II) FOREIGN AUTHORITIES.—Each of the entities described in subclauses (VII) and (VIII) of clause (i) shall maintain such information in accordance with such assurances of confidentiality as the Commission determines appropriate.

"(3) RIGHTS RETAINED.—Nothing in this section shall be deemed to diminish the rights, privileges, or remedies of any whistleblower under any Federal or State law, or under any collective bargaining agreement.

"(i) PROVISION OF FALSE INFORMATION. —A whistleblower shall not be entitled to an award under this section if the whistleblower —

"(1) knowingly and willfully makes any false, fictitious, or fraudulent statement or representation; or

"(2) uses any false writing or document knowing the writing or document contains any false, fictitious, or fraudulent statement or entry.

"(j) RULEMAKING AUTHORITY. —The Commission shall have the authority to issue such rules and regulations as may be necessary or appropriate to implement the provisions of this section consistent with the purposes of this section.".

(b) PROTECTION FOR EMPLOYEES OF NATIONALLY RECOGNIZED STATISTICAL RATING ORGANIZATIONS. —Section 1514A (a) of title 18, United States Code, is

长在正在进行的刑事调查中将证据呈交大陪审团或提供给潜在证人或被告。

(D)**向政府机关提供保密信息**。——

(i)**一般规定**。——在证券交易委员会维持第(A)子款提及的信息保密状态的前提下，如果证券交易委员会判定将该信息提供给以下机构对实现本法宗旨和保护客户确属必要或适当，并且符合第(ii)项规定，证券交易委员会可以依其自由裁量权将该信息提供给——

(I)联邦总检察长；

(II)相应监管机关；

(III)自律组织；

(IV)州总检察长(如涉及任何刑事调查)；

(V)任何相应的州监管机关；

(VI)公众公司会计监督委员会；

(VII)外国证券监管机构；及

(VIII)外国执法机构。

(ii)**保密**。——

(I)**一般规定**。——第(i)项第(I)子项至第(VI)子项所述任何实体均应按照第(A)子款的要求对该等信息予以保密。

(II)**外国监管机构**。——第(i)项第(VII)子项至第(VIII)子项所述任何实体在持有该等信息时，均应根据证券交易委员会判定确属适当的保密保证予以保密。

(3)**保留权利**。——本条的任何内容均不得视为削弱了任何联邦法律、州法律或任何集体劳动合同赋予任何举报人的权利、特殊待遇或救济。

(i)**提供虚假信息**。——在下述情况下，举报人无权获得本条规定的奖励——

(1)举报人明知且故意作出任何虚假、虚构或欺诈性声明或陈述；或

(2)举报人在明知书面资料或文件包含任何虚假、虚构或欺诈性声明或内容的情况下使用该虚假书面资料或文件。

(j)**规则制定权**。——证券交易委员会有权发布对实施本条规定和实现本条目的确属必要或适当的规则与规章。”

(b)**全国公认统计评级组织雇员的保护**。——《美国法典》第十八编第1514A(a)节修正如下——

amended —

(1) by inserting "or nationally recognized statistical rating organization (as defined in section 3(a) of the Securities Exchange Act of 1934 (15 U.S.C.78c)," after "78o(d)),"; and

(2) by inserting "or nationally recognized statistical rating organization" after "such company".

(c) SECTION 1514A OF TITLE 18, UNITED STATES CODE. —

(1) STATUTE OF LIMITATIONS; JURY TRIAL. —Section 1514A(b)(2) of title 18, United States Code, is amended —

(A) in subparagraph (D) —

(i) by striking "90" and inserting "180"; and

(ii) by striking the period at the end and inserting ", or after the date on which the employee became aware of the violation."; and

(B) by adding at the end the following:

"(E) JURY TRIAL. —A party to an action brought under paragraph (1)(B) shall be entitled to trial by jury.".

(2) PRIVATE SECURITIES LITIGATION WITNESSES; NON-ENFORCEABILITY; INFORMATION. —Section 1514A of title 18, United States Code, is amended by adding at the end the following:

"(e) NONENFORCEABILITY OF CERTAIN PROVISIONS WAIVING RIGHTS AND REMEDIES OR REQUIRING ARBITRATION OF DISPUTES. —

"(1) WAIVER OF RIGHTS AND REMEDIES. —The rights and remedies provided for in this section may not be waived by any agreement, policy form, or condition of employment, including by a predispute arbitration agreement.

"(2) PREDISPUTE ARBITRATION AGREEMENTS. —No predispute arbitration agreement shall be valid or enforceable, if the agreement requires arbitration of a dispute arising under this section.".

(d) STUDY OF WHISTLEBLOWER PROTECTION PROGRAM. —

(1) STUDY. —The Inspector General of the Commission shall conduct a study of the whistleblower protections established under the amendments made by this section, including —

(A) whether the final rules and regulation issued under the amendments made by this section have made the whistleblower protection program (referred to in this subsection as the "program") clearly defined and user-friendly;

(B) whether the program is promoted on the website of the Commission and has been widely publicized;

(C) whether the Commission is prompt in —

(i) responding to —

(I) information provided by whistleblowers; and

(1)在“78o(d)节”之后插入“或全国公认统计评级组织[定义见《1934年证券交易法》第3(a)条(《美国法典》第十五编第78c节)],”;并

(2)在“该等公司”之后插入“或全国公认统计评级组织”。

(c)**《美国法典》第十八编第1514A节**。——

(1)**诉讼时效;陪审团审理**。——《美国法典》第十八编第1514A(b)(2)节修正如下——

(A)在第(D)子款中——

(i)删除“90”,替以“180”;及

(ii)删除结尾处的句号,替以“,或在雇员知晓违法违规行为之日后”;及

(B)在结尾处增加如下内容:

“(E)**陪审团审理**。——根据第(1)(B)款提起诉讼的当事人拥有接受陪审团审判的权利。”

(2)**私人证券诉讼证人;不具强制执行力;信息**。——在《美国法典》第十八编第1514A节结尾处增加如下内容,作为对该节的修正:

“(e)**放弃权利和救济的特定条款或要求通过仲裁解决争议的特定条款不具强制执行力**。——

(1)**放弃权利和救济**。——本条赋予的权利和救济不得通过任何协议、保单或雇用条件(包括争议前缔结的仲裁协议)予以放弃。

(2)**争议前缔结的仲裁协议**。——如果争议前缔结的仲裁协议要求通过仲裁解决由于本条规定而产生的争议,在该等协议一律无效,不具强制执行力。”

(d)**关于举报人保护计划的研究**。——

(1)**研究**。——证券交易委员会监察长应就本条作出的修正所确立的举报人保护开展研究,研究的内容包括——

(A)根据本条作出的修正发布的最终规则和规章是否已使得举报人保护计划(“举报人保护计划”)更加清晰明确且便于操作;

(B)举报人保护计划是否已通过证券交易委员会网站进行推广和广泛宣传;

(C)证券交易委员会——

(i)对以下事项的回应是否及时——

(I)举报人提供的信息;及

(II) applications for awards filed by whistleblowers;

(ii) updating whistleblowers about the status of their applications; and

(iii) otherwise communicating with the interested parties;

(D) whether the minimum and maximum reward levels are adequate to entice whistleblowers to come forward with information and whether the reward levels are so high as to encourage illegitimate whistleblower claims;

(E) whether the appeals process has been unduly burdensome for the Commission;

(F) whether the funding mechanism for the Investor Protection Fund is adequate;

(G) whether, in the interest of protecting investors and identifying and preventing fraud, it would be useful for Congress to consider empowering whistleblowers or other individuals, who have already attempted to pursue the case through the Commission, to have a private right of action to bring suit based on the facts of the same case, on behalf of the Government and themselves, against persons who have committee securities fraud;

(H)(i) whether the exemption under section 552(b)(3) of title 5 (known as the Freedom of Information Act) established in section 21F(h)(2)(A) of the Securities Exchange Act of 1934, as added by this Act, aids whistleblowers in disclosing information to the Commission;

(ii) what impact the exemption described in clause (i) has had on the ability of the public to access information about the regulation and enforcement by the Commission of securities; and

(iii) any recommendations on whether the exemption described in clause(i) should remain in effect; and

(I) such other matters as the Inspector General deems appropriate.

(2) REPORT. —Not later than 30 months after the date of enactment of this Act, the Inspector General shall —

(A) submit a report on the findings of the study required under paragraph(1) to the Committee on Banking, Housing, and Urban Affairs of the Senate and the Committee on Financial Services of the House; and

(B) make the report described in subparagraph (A) available to the public through publication of the report on the website of the Commission.

SEC.923. CONFORMING AMENDMENTS FOR WHISTLEBLOWER PROTECTION.

(a) IN GENERAL. —

(1) SECURITIES ACT OF 1933. —Section 20(d)(3)(A) of the Securities Act of 1933 (15 U.S.C.77t(d)(3)(A)) is amended by inserting "and section 21F of the Securities Exchange Act of 1934" after "the Sarbanes-Oxley Act of 2002".

(II)举报人提出的奖励申请;
(ii)是否已将申请的最新进展情况及时告知举报人;及
(iii)与利害关系人的其他沟通是否及时;
(D)所设定的奖励最低和最高水平是否足以吸引举报人提供信息,或者奖励水平是否过高,以致将诱发不合理的举报情况;

(E)司法审查程序是否已对证券交易委员会造成过度负担;
(F)投资者保护基金的经费筹措机制是否充分;
(G)在举报人或其他个人已经尝试通过证券交易委员会对案件进行追究的情况下,如果国会考虑赋予该等举报人或个人私人诉讼权利,令其基于同一案件事实,以政府和自身名义对作出[1]证券欺诈行为之人提起诉讼,该举措是否有利于投资者保护,并有助于欺诈行为的识别和防范;

(H)(i)本法增加的《1934年证券交易法》第21F(h)(2)(A)条《美国法典》第五编第552(b)(3)节(即《信息自由法》)规定的豁免是否有助于举报人向证券交易委员会披露信息;

(ii)对于公众获取证券交易委员会的证券监管和执法行动相关信息的能力,第(i)项所述豁免将造成何种影响;及

(iii)关于第(i)项所述豁免是否应继续有效的建议;及

(I)监察长认为确属适当的其他事项。
(2)**报告**。——监察长应于本法颁布之日后30个月内——

(A)就第(1)款所规定研究的认定结果向参议院银行、住房与城市事务委员会以及众议院金融服务委员会提交一份报告;并

(B)通过在证券交易委员会网站上发布的方式公开第(A)子款所述报告。

第923条　关于举报人保护的一致性修正

(a)**一般规定**。——
(1)**《1933年证券法》**。——《1933年证券法》第20(d)(3)(A)条[《美国法典》第十五编第77t(d)(3)(A)节]修正如下:在《2002年萨班斯—奥克斯利法》之后插入"及

1　原文中的"committee"一词似乎应为"committed",译文中按后者处理。——译者注

(2) INVESTMENT COMPANY ACT OF 1940. —Section 42 (e) (3) (A)of the Investment Company Act of 1940 (15 U.S.C.80a-41(e)(3)(A)) is amended by inserting "and section 21F of the Securities Exchange Act of 1934" after "the Sarbanes-Oxley Act of 2002".

(3) INVESTMENT ADVISERS ACT OF 1940. —Section 209(e)(3)(A) of the Investment Advisers Act of 1940 (15 U.S.C.80b-9(e)(3)(A)) is amended by inserting "and section 21F of the Securities Exchange Act of 1934" after "the Sarbanes-Oxley Act of 2002".

(b) SECURITIES EXCHANGE ACT. —

(1) SECTION 21. -Section 21(d)(3)(C)(i) of the Securities Exchange Act of 1934 (15 U.S.C.78u(d)(3)(C)(i)) is amended by inserting "and section 21F of this title" after "the Sarbanes-Oxley Act of 2002".

(2) SECTION 21A. —Section 21A of the Securities Exchange Act of 1934 (15 U.S.C. 78u-1) is amended —

(A) in subsection (d)(1) by —

(i) striking "(subject to subsection (e))"; and

(ii) inserting "and section 21F of this title" after "the Sarbanes-Oxley Act of 2002";

(B) by striking subsection (e); and

(C) by redesignating subsections (f) and (g) as subsections (e) and (f), respectively.

SEC.924. IMPLEMENTATION AND TRANSITION PROVISIONS FOR WHISTLEBLOWER PROTECTION.

(a) IMPLEMENTING RULES. —The Commission shall issue final regulations implementing the provisions of section 21F of the Securities Exchange Act of 1934, as added by this subtitle, not later than 270 days after the date of enactment of this Act.

(b) ORIGINAL INFORMATION. —Information provided to the Commission in writing by a whistleblower shall not lose the status of original information (as defined in section 21F (a)(3) of the Securities Exchange Act of 1934, as added by this subtitle) solely because the whistleblower provided the information prior to the effective date of the regulations, if the information is provided by the whistleblower after the date of enactment of this subtitle.

(c) AWARDS. —A whistleblower may receive an award pursuant to section 21F of the Securities Exchange Act of 1934, as added by this subtitle, regardless of whether any violation of a provision of the securities laws, or a rule or regulation thereunder, underlying the judicial or administrative action upon which the award is based, occurred prior to the date of enactment of this subtitle.

(d) ADMINISTRATION AND ENFORCEMENT. —The Securities and Exchange Commission shall establish a separate office within the Commission to administer and enforce the provisions of section 21F of the Securities Exchange Act of 1934 (as add by section 922

《1934年证券交易法》第21F条”。

(2)**《1940年投资公司法》**。——《1940年投资公司法》第42(e)(3)(A)条[《美国法典》第十五编第80a－41(e)(3)(A)节]修正如下:在《2002年萨班斯—奥克斯利法》之后插入“及《1934年证券交易法》第21F条”。

(3)**《1940年投资顾问法》**。——《1940年投资顾问法》第209(e)(3)(A)条[《美国法典》第十五编第80b－9(e)(3)(A)节]修正如下:在《2002年萨班斯—奥克斯利法》之后插入“及《1934年证券交易法》第21F条”。

(b)**《证券交易法》**。——

(1)**第21条**。——《1934年证券交易法》第21(d)(3)(C)(i)条[《美国法典》第十五编第78u(d)(3)(C)(i)节]修正如下:在《2002年萨班斯—奥克斯利法》之后插入“及本编第21F条”。

(2)**第21A条**。——《1934年证券交易法》第21A条(《美国法典》第十五编第78u－1节)修正如下——

(A)在第(d)(1)子条中——

(i)删除“[在不违反第(e)子条的前提下]”;及

(ii)在《2002年萨班斯—奥克斯利法》之后插入“及本编第21F条”;

(B)删除第(e)子条;及

(C)第(f)子条和第(g)子条分别重新编号为第(e)子条和第(f)子条。

第924条　关于举报人保护的实施条款和过渡条款

(a)**实施规则**。——证券交易委员会应于本法颁布之日后270天内,针对本子编增加的《1934年证券交易法》第21F条发布最终实施规章。

(b)**原始信息**。——举报人于本子编颁布之日后向证券交易委员会提供的书面信息,不得仅因该信息提供日早于实施规章的生效日而失去原始信息的性质[“原始信息”的定义见本子编增加的《1934年证券交易法》第21F(a)(3)条]。

(c)**奖励**。——举报人可以按照本子编增加的《1934年证券交易法》第21F条获取奖励。如果举报人的举报促成了相关司法或行政程序的启动,则不论被举报的证券违法违规行为发生在本子编颁布之前或之后,举报人均可以获取奖励。

(d)**管理和执行**。——证券交易委员会应下设一独立办公室,负责实施和执行第922(a)条增加的《1934年证券交易法》第21F条的规定。该办公室应每年向参议院银行、住房与城市事务委员会和众议院金融服务委员会汇报该办公室开展的各项活动、

(a)). Such office shall report annually to the Committee on Banking, Housing, and Urban Affairs of the Senate and the Committee on Financial Services of the House of Representatives on its activities, whistleblower complaints, and the response of the Commission to such complaints.

SEC.925. COLLATERAL BARS.

(a) SECURITIES EXCHANGE ACT OF 1934. —

(1) SECTION 15. —Section 15(b)(6)(A) of the Securities Exchange Act of 1934 (15 U.S.C.78o(b)(6)(A)) is amended by striking "12 months, or bar such person from being associated with a broker or dealer," and inserting "12 months, or bar any such person from being associated with a broker, dealer, investment adviser, municipal securities dealer, municipal advisor, transfer agent, or nationally recognized statistical rating organization,".

(2) SECTION 15B. —Section 15B (c)(4) of the Securities Exchange Act of 1934 (15 U.S.C.78o-4 (c)(4)) is amended by striking "twelve months or bar any such person from being associated with a municipal securities dealer," and inserting "12 months or bar any such person from being associated with a broker, dealer, investment adviser, municipal securities dealer, municipal advisor, transfer agent, or nationally recognized statistical rating organization,".

(3) SECTION 17A. —Section 17A(c)(4)(C) of the Securities Exchange Act of 1934 (15 U.S.C.78q-1(c)(4)(C)) is amended by striking "twelve months or bar any such person from being associated with the transfer agent," and inserting "12 months or bar any such person from being associated with any transfer agent, broker, dealer, investment adviser, municipal securities dealer, municipal advisor, or nationally recognized statistical rating organization,".

(b) INVESTMENT ADVISERS ACT OF 1940. —Section 203 (f) of the Investment Advisers Act of 1940 (15 U.S.C.80b-3(f)) is amended by striking "twelve months or bar any such person from being associated with an investment adviser," and inserting "12 months or bar any such person from being associated with an investment adviser, broker, dealer, municipal securities dealer, municipal advisor, transfer agent, or nationally recognized statistical rating organization,".

SEC.926. DISQUALIFYING FELONS AND OTHER "BAD ACTORS" FROM REGULATION DOFFERINGS.

Not later than 1 year after the date of enactment of this Act, the Commission shall issue rules for the disqualification of offerings and sales of securities made under section 230.506 of title 17, Code of Federal Regulations, that —

(1) are substantially similar to the provisions of section 230.262 of title 17, Code of Federal Regulations, or any successor thereto; and

(2) disqualify any offering or sale of securities by a person that —

举报人的投诉以及证券交易委员会对该等投诉的回应。

第925条　关联禁止

(a)**《1934年证券交易法》**。——

(1)**第15条**。——《1934年证券交易法》第15(b)(6)(A)条[《美国法典》第十五编第78o(b)(6)(A)节]修正如下:删除“12个月,或禁止该人与经纪商或自营商存在业务相关关系,”,替以“12个月,或禁止任何上述人与经纪商、自营商、投资顾问、市政证券自营商、市政顾问、过户代理人或全国公认统计评级组织存在业务相关关系,”。

(2)**第15B条**。——《1934年证券交易法》第15B(c)(4)条[《美国法典》第十五编第78o-4(c)(4)节]修正如下:删除“12个月,或禁止任何上述人与市政证券自营商存在业务相关关系,”,替以“12个月,或禁止任何上述人与经纪商、自营商、投资顾问、市政证券自营商、市政顾问、过户代理人或全国公认统计评级组织存在业务相关关系,”。

(3)**第17A条**。——《1934年证券交易法》第17A(c)(4)(C)条[《美国法典》第十五编第78q-1(c)(4)(C)节]修正如下:删除“12个月,或禁止任何上述人与过户代理人存在业务相关关系,”,替以“12个月,或禁止任何上述人与过户代理人、经纪商、自营商、投资顾问、市政证券自营商、市政顾问或全国公认统计评级组织存在业务相关关系,”。

(b)**《1940年投资顾问法》**。——《1940年投资顾问法》第203(f)条[《美国法典》第十五编第80b-3(f)节]修正如下:删除“12个月,或禁止任何上述人与投资顾问存在业务相关关系,”,替以“12个月,或禁止任何上述人与投资顾问、经纪商、自营商、市政证券自营商、市政顾问、过户代理人或全国公认统计评级组织存在业务相关关系,”。

第926条　取消重罪犯及其他“行为不当者”根据《D管理办法》发行证券的资格

证券交易委员会应于本法颁布之日后1年内针对《联邦规章汇编》第十七编第230.506部分所规定证券发行和出售资格的取消发布规则。该等规则应——

(1)与《联邦规章汇编》第十七编第230.262部分或其后续规定基本类似;并

(2)取消以下主体发行或出售证券的资格——

(A) is subject to a final order of a State securities commission (or an agency or officer of a State performing like functions), a State authority that supervises or examines banks, savings associations, or credit unions, a State insurance commission (or an agency or officer of a State performing like functions), an appropriate Federal banking agency, or the National Credit Union Administration, that —

(i) bars the person from —

(I) association with an entity regulated by such commission, authority, agency, or officer;

(II) engaging in the business of securities, insurance, or banking; or

(III) engaging in savings association or credit union activities; or

(ii) constitutes a final order based on a violation of any law or regulation that prohibits fraudulent, manipulative, or deceptive conduct within the 10–year period ending on the date of the filing of the offer or sale; or

(B) has been convicted of any felony or misdemeanor in connection with the purchase or sale of any security or involving the making of any false filing with the Commission.

SEC.927. EQUAL TREATMENT OF SELF–REGULATORY ORGANIZATION RULES.

Section 29 (a) of the Securities Exchange Act of 1934 (15 U.S.C.78cc (a)) is amended by striking "an exchange required thereby" and inserting "a self–regulatory organization,".

SEC.928. CLARIFICATION THAT SECTION 205 OF THE INVESTMENT ADVISERS ACT OF 1940 DOES NOT APPLY TO STATE–REGISTERED ADVISERS.

Section 205(a) of the Investment Advisers Act of 1940 (15 U.S.C.80b–5(a)) is amended, in the matter preceding paragraph (1) —

(1) by striking ", unless exempt from registration pursuant to section 203(b)," and inserting "registered or required to be registered with the Commission";

(2) by striking "make use of the mails or any means or instrumentality of interstate commerce, directly or indirectly, to"; and

(3) by striking "to" after "in any way".

SEC.929. UNLAWFUL MARGIN LENDING.

Section 7(c)(1)(A) of the Securities Exchange Act of 1934 (15 U.S.C.78g(c)(1)(A)) is amended by striking "; and" and inserting "; or".

SEC.929A. PROTECTION FOR EMPLOYEES OF SUBSIDIARIES AND AFFILIATES OF PUBLICLY TRADED COMPANIES.

Section 1514A of title 18, United States Code, is amended by inserting "including any subsidiary or affiliate whose financial information is included in the consolidated financial

(A)受制于州证券委员会(或州政府内行使类似职能的机关或官员),负责监管或检查银行、储蓄协会或信贷联盟的州监管机构,州保险委员会(或州政府内行使类似职能的机关或官员),相应的联邦银行业监管机关或国家信贷联盟署具有以下特征的最终命令的主体——

(i)禁止该主体——

(I)与受该等委员会、监管机构、机关或官员监管的实体存在业务相关关系;

(II)从事证券、保险或银行业务;或

(III)从事储蓄协会或信贷联盟活动;或

(ii)属于针对证券发行或出售申请文件提交日起10年内出现的违反禁止欺诈、操纵或欺骗行为的任何法律法规的行为发出的最终命令;或

(B)被判在任何证券的买卖过程中犯有任何重罪或轻罪的主体,或被判因涉及向证券交易委员会提交任何虚假信息而犯有任何重罪或轻罪的主体。

第927条　平等对待自律组织的规则

《1934年证券交易法》第29(a)条[《美国法典》第十五编第78cc(a)节]修正如下:删除"本编要求的交易所的规则",替以"自律组织规则,"。

第928条　关于《1940年投资顾问法》第205条不适用于州注册顾问的说明

《1940年投资顾问法》第205(a)条[《美国法典》第十五编第80b-5(a)节]修正如下:在第(1)款之前的内容中——

(1)删除",除非已根据第203(b)条获得注册豁免",替以"已在或应在证券交易委员会注册的";

(2)删除"直接或间接使用邮件或任何州际商业手段或工具以";及

(3)删除"通过任何方式"后的"以"。

第929条　非法保证金贷款

《1934年证券交易法》第7(c)(1)(A)条[《美国法典》第十五编第78g(c)(1)(A)节]修正如下:删除";及",替以";或"。

第929A条　对上市公司子公司和关联公司雇员的保护

《美国法典》第十八编第1514A节修正如下:在"《1934年证券交易法》[《美国法典》第十五编第78o(d)节]"之后插入"包括财务信息被纳入该公司合并财务报表的任何子

statements of such company" after "the Securities Exchange Act of 1934 (15 U.S.C.78o (d))".

SEC.929B. FAIR FUND AMENDMENTS.

Section 308 of the Sarbanes-Oxley Act of 2002 (15 U.S.C.7246(a)) is amended —

(1) by striking subsection (a) and inserting the following:

"(a) CIVIL PENALTIES TO BE USED FOR THE RELIEF OF VICTIMS. — If, in any judicial or administrative action brought by the Commission under the securities laws, the Commission obtains a civil penalty against any person for a violation of such laws, or such person agrees, in settlement of any such action, to such civil penalty, the amount of such civil penalty shall, on the motion or at the direction of the Commission, be added to and become part of a disgorgement fund or other fund established for the benefit of the victims of such violation.";

(2) in subsection (b) —

(A) by striking "for a disgorgement fund described in subsection (a)" and inserting "for a disgorgement fund or other fund described in subsection (a)"; and

(B) by striking "in the disgorgement fund" and inserting "in such fund"; and

(3) by striking subsection (e).

SEC.929C. INCREASING THE BORROWING LIMIT ON TREASURY LOANS.

Section 4(h) of the Securities Investor Protection Act of 1970 (15 U.S.C.78ddd(h)) is amended in the first sentence, by striking "$1,000,000,000" and inserting "$2,500,000,000".

SEC.929D. LOST AND STOLEN SECURITIES.

Section 17(f)(1) of the Securities Exchange Act of 1934 (15 U.S.C.78q(f)(1)) is amended —

(1) in subparagraph (A), by striking "missing, lost, counterfeit, or stolen securities" and inserting "securities that are missing, lost, counterfeit, stolen, or cancelled"; and

(2) in subparagraph (B), by striking "or stolen" and inserting "stolen, cancelled, or reported in such other manner as the Commission, by rule, may prescribe".

SEC.929E. NATIONWIDE SERVICE OF SUBPOENAS.

(a) SECURITIES ACT OF 1933. —Section 22(a) of the Securities Act of 1933 (15 U.S.C.77v(a)) is amended by inserting after the second sentence the following: "In any action or proceeding instituted by the Commission under this title in a United States district court for any judicial district, a subpoena issued to compel the attendance of a witness or the production of documents or tangible things (or both) at a hearing or trial may be served at any place within the United States. Rule 45 (c) (3) (A) (ii) of the Federal Rules of Civil

公司或关联公司”。

第929B条 关于公平基金的修正

《2002年萨班斯—奥克斯利法》第308条[《美国法典》第十五编第7246(a)节]修正如下——

(1)删除第(a)子条,替以如下内容:

“(a)**将民事罚款用于救济受害人**。——如果在证券交易委员会根据证券法律提起的任何司法或行政诉讼中,实施违反证券法律行为的任何人被处以民事罚款,而证券交易委员会获得该民事罚款,或者,在上述诉讼的和解过程中,该人同意交纳民事罚款,则证券交易委员会可提出动议或行使自由裁量权,将该民事罚款纳入没收基金,或纳入为上述违法行为受害人之利益设立的其他基金。”;

(2)在第(b)子条中——

(A)删除“为第(a)子条所述的没收基金”,替以“为没收基金或第(a)子条所述其他基金”;及

(B)删除“存入该没收基金内”,替以“存入该基金内”;及

(3)删除第(e)子条。

第929C条 提高国库贷款上限

《1970年证券投资者保护法》第4(h)条[《美国法典》第十五编第78ddd(h)节]修正如下:在第一句中,删除“10亿美元”,替以“25亿美元”。

第929D条 遗失及失窃证券

《1934年证券交易法》第17(f)(1)条[《美国法典》第十五编第78q(f)(1)节]修正如下——

(1)在第(A)子款中,删除“丢失、遗失、伪造或失窃证券”,替以“丢失、遗失、伪造、失窃或被撤销的证券”;及

(2)在第(B)子款中,删除“或失窃”,替以“失窃、被撤销或按照证券交易委员会发布的规则所规定其他方式上报的”。

第929E条 全国范围内的传票送达

(a)**《1933年证券法》**。——在《1933年证券法》第22(a)条[《美国法典》第十五编第77v(a)节]第二句之后插入如下内容,作为对该条的修正:“在证券交易委员会根据本编规定向任何司法辖区的联邦地区法院提起的任何诉讼或程序中,签发的用以强制证人在听审或审判中作证的传票,或者强制文件和/或实物在听审或审判中出示的传票可向美国境内任何地点送达。《联邦民事诉讼规则》第45(c)(3)(A)(ii)条不适用于根据上一句规定签发的传票。”

Procedure shall not apply to a subpoena issued under the preceding sentence.".

(b) SECURITIES EXCHANGE ACT OF 1934. —Section 27 of the Securities Exchange Act of 1934 (15 U.S.C.78aa) is amended by inserting after the third sentence the following: "In any action or proceeding instituted by the Commission under this title in a United States district court for any judicial district, a subpoena issued to compel the attendance of a witness or the production of documents or tangible things (or both) at a hearing or trial may be served at any place within the United States. Rule 45(c)(3)(A)(ii) of the Federal Rules of Civil Procedure shall not apply to a subpoena issued under the preceding sentence.".

(c) INVESTMENT COMPANY ACT OF 1940. —Section 44 of the Investment Company Act of 1940 (15 U.S.C.80a-43) is amended by inserting after the fourth sentence the following: "In any action or proceeding instituted by the Commission under this title in a United States district court for any judicial district, a subpoena issued to compel the attendance of a witness or the production of documents or tangible things (or both) at a hearing or trial may be served at any place within the United States. Rule 45(c)(3)(A)(ii) of the Federal Rules of Civil Procedure shall not apply to a subpoena issued under the preceding sentence.".

(d) INVESTMENT ADVISERS ACT OF 1940. —Section 214 of the Investment Advisers Act of 1940 (15 U.S.C.80b-14) is amended by inserting after the third sentence the following: "In any action or proceeding instituted by the Commission under this title in a United States district court for any judicial district, a subpoena issued to compel the attendance of a witness or the production of documents or tangible things (or both) at a hearing or trial may be served at any place within the United States. Rule 45(c)(3)(A)(ii) of the Federal Rules of Civil Procedure shall not apply to a subpoena issued under the preceding sentence.".

SEC.929F. FORMERLY ASSOCIATED PERSONS.

(a) MEMBER OR EMPLOYEE OF THE MUNICIPAL SECURITIES RULE-MAKING BOARD. -Section 15B(c)(8) of the Securities Exchange Act of 1934 (15 U.S.C.78o-4(c)(8)) is amended by striking "any member or employee" and inserting "any person who is, or at the time of the alleged violation or abuse was, a member or employee".

(b) PERSON ASSOCIATED WITH A GOVERNMENT SECURITIES BROKER OR DEALER. -Section 15C(c) of the Securities Exchange Act of 1934 (15 U.S.C.78o-5(c)) is amended —

(1) in paragraph (1)(C), by striking "any person associated, or seeking to become associated," and inserting "any person who is, or at the time of the alleged misconduct was, associated or seeking to become associated"; and

(2) in paragraph (2) —

(b)**《1934年证券交易法》**。——在《1934年证券交易法》第27条(《美国法典》第十五编第78aa节)第三句之后插入如下内容,作为对该条的修正:“在证券交易委员会根据本编规定向任何司法辖区联邦地区法院提起的任何诉讼或程序中,签发的用以强制证人在听审或审判中作证的传票,或者强制文件和/或实物在听审或审判中出示的传票可向美国境内任何地点送达。《联邦民事诉讼规则》第45(c)(3)(A)(ii)条不适用于根据上一句规定签发的传票。”

(c)**《1940年投资公司法》**。——在《1940年投资公司法》第44条(《美国法典》第十五编第80a-43节)第四句之后插入如下内容,作为对该条的修正:“在证券交易委员会根据本编规定向任何司法辖区的联邦地区法院提起的任何诉讼或程序中,签发的用以强制证人在听审或审判中作证的传票,或者强制文件和/或实物在听审或审判中出示的传票可向美国境内任何地点送达。《联邦民事诉讼规则》第45(c)(3)(A)(ii)条不适用于根据上一句规定签发的传票。”

(d)**《1940年投资顾问法》**。——在《1940年投资顾问法》第214条(《美国法典》第十五编第80b-14节)第三句之后插入如下内容,作为对该条的修正:“在证券交易委员会根据本编规定向任何司法辖区联邦地区法院提起的任何诉讼或程序中,签发的用以强制证人在听审或审判中作证的传票,或者强制文件和/或实物在听审或审判中出示的传票可向美国境内任何地点送达。《联邦民事诉讼规则》第45(c)(3)(A)(ii)条不适用于根据上一句规定签发的传票。”

第929F条　前业务相关人

(a)**市政证券规则制定委员会的委员或雇员**。——《1934年证券交易法》第15B(c)(8)条[《美国法典》第十五编第78o-4(c)(8)节]修正如下:删除“任何委员或雇员”,替以“当前身为委员或雇员的任何人,或被指控的违法违规或滥用行为发生时身为委员或雇员的任何人”。

(b)**政府证券经纪商或自营商的业务相关人**。——《1934年证券交易法》第15C(c)条[《美国法典》第十五编第78o-5(c)节]修正如下——

(1)在第(1)(C)款中,删除“任何业务相关人或寻求建立业务相关关系的任何人,”,替以“当前的任何业务相关人或正在寻求建立业务相关关系的任何人,或被指控的不当行为发生时的任何业务相关人或当时正在寻求建立业务相关关系的任何人”;及

(2)在第(2)款中——

(A) in subparagraph (A), by inserting ", seeking to become associated, or, at the time of the alleged misconduct, associated or seeking to become associated" after "any person associated"; and

(B) in subparagraph (B), by inserting ", seeking to become associated, or, at the time of the alleged misconduct, associated or seeking to become associated" after "any person associated".

(c) PERSON ASSOCIATED WITH A MEMBER OF A NATIONAL SECURITIES EXCHANGE OR REGISTERED SECURITIES ASSOCIATION. —Section 21(a)(1) of the Securities Exchange Act of 1934 (15 U.S.C.78u(a)(1)) is amended, in the first sentence, by inserting ", or, as to any act or practice, or omission to act, while associated with a member, formerly associated" after "member or a person associated".

(d) PARTICIPANT OF A REGISTERED CLEARING AGENCY. —Section 21(a)(1) of the Securities Exchange Act of 1934 (15 U.S.C.78u(a)(1)) is amended, in the first sentence, by inserting "or, as to any act or practice, or omission to act, while a participant, was a participant," after "in which such person is a participant,".

(e) OFFICER OR DIRECTOR OF A SELF-REGULATORY ORGANIZATION. —Section 19(h)(4) of the Securities Exchange Act of 1934 (15 U.S.C.78s(h)(4)) is amended—

(1) by striking "any officer or director" and inserting "any person who is, or at the time of the alleged misconduct was, an officer or director"; and

(2) by striking "such officer or director" and inserting "such person".

(f) OFFICER OR DIRECTOR OF AN INVESTMENT COMPANY. —Section 36(a) of the Investment Company Act of 1940 (15 U.S.C.80a-35(a)) is amended —

(1) by striking "a person serving or acting" and inserting "a person who is, or at the time of the alleged misconduct was, serving or acting"; and

(2) by striking "such person so serves or acts" and inserting "such person so serves or acts, or at the time of the alleged misconduct, so served or acted".

(g) PERSON ASSOCIATED WITH A PUBLIC ACCOUNTING FIRM. —

(1) SARBANES-OXLEY ACT OF 2002 AMENDMENT. —Section 2(a)(9) of the Sarbanes-Oxley Act of 2002 (15 U.S.C.7201(9)) is amended by adding at the end the following:

"(C) INVESTIGATIVE AND ENFORCEMENT AUTHORITY. — For purposes of sections 3(c), 101(c), 105, and 107(c) and the rules of the Board and Commission issued thereunder, except to the extent specifically excepted by such rules, the terms defined in subparagraph (A) shall include any person associated, seeking to become associated, or formerly associated with a public accounting firm, except that —

(A)第(A)子款在“任何业务相关人”之后插入“,或寻求建立业务相关关系的任何人，或被指控的不当行为发生时的任何业务相关人或当时正在寻求建立业务相关关系的任何人”;及

(B)第(B)子款在“任何业务相关人”之后插入“,或寻求建立业务相关关系的任何人，或被指控的不当行为发生时的任何业务相关人或当时正在寻求建立业务相关关系的任何人”。

(c) **全国性证券交易所会员或注册证券协会会员的业务相关人**。——《1934年证券交易法》第21(a)(1)条[《美国法典》第十五编第78u(a)(1)节]修正如下:第一句中,在“会员或业务相关人”之后插入“,或者对于会员的前业务相关人在业务相关关系存在期间的任何作为、做法或不作为”。

(d)**注册结算机构的参与者**。——《1934年证券交易法》第21(a)(1)条[《美国法典》第十五编第78u(a)(1)节]修正如下:在第一句中,在“违反该人作为参与者参与的注册结算机构的规则”之后插入“,或者对于前参与者在以参与者身份参与注册结算机构期间的任何作为、做法或不作为,”。

(e)**自律组织的管理人员或董事**。——《1934年证券交易法》第19(h)(4)条[《美国法典》第十五编第78s(h)(4)节]修正如下——

(1)删除“任何管理人员或董事”,替以“身为管理人员或董事的任何人,或被指控的不当行为发生时身为管理人员或董事的任何人”;及

(2)删除“该管理人员或董事”,替以“该人”。

(f)**投资公司的管理人员或董事**。——《1940年投资公司法》第36(a)条[《美国法典》第十五编第80a-35(a)节]修正如下——

(1)删除“担任以下一个或一个以上职务或以该等身份行事的人”,替以“当前或在被指控的不当行为发生时担任以下一个或一个以上职务或以该等身份行事的人”;及

(2)删除“担任该等职务或以该等身份行事的人”,替以“当前或在被指控的不当行为发生时担任该等职务或以该等身份行事的人”。

(g)**公共会计师事务所的业务相关人**。——

(1)**对《2002年萨班斯—奥克斯利法》的修正**。——在《2002年萨班斯—奥克斯利法》第2(a)(9)条[《美国法典》第十五编第7201(9)节]结尾处增加如下内容,作为对该条的修正:

“(C)**调查和执法权**。——就第3(c)条、第101(c)条、第105条、第107(c)条以及公众公司会计监督委员会和证券交易委员会根据该等条款发布的规则而言，除非该等规则另有明确规定,否则第(A)子款中所定义的术语应包括公共会计师事务所的任何现有业务相关人及任何前业务相关人以及正在寻求与之建立业务相关关系的任何人,但是——

"(i) the authority to conduct an investigation of such person under section 105(b) shall apply only with respect to any act or practice, or omission to act, by the person while such person was associated or seeking to become associated with a registered public accounting firm; and

"(ii) the authority to commence a disciplinary proceeding under section 105(c)(1), or impose sanctions under section 105(c)(4), against such person shall apply only with respect to—

"(I) conduct occurring while such person was associated or seeking to become associated with a registered public accounting firm; or

"(II) non–cooperation, as described in section 105(b)(3), with respect to a demand in a Board investigation for testimony, documents, or other information relating to a period when such person was associated or seeking to become associated with a registered public accounting firm.".

(2) SECURITIES EXCHANGE ACT OF 1934 AMENDMENT. —Section 21(a)(1) of the Securities Exchange Act of 1934 (15 U.S.C.78u(a)(1)) is amended by striking "or a person associated with such a firm" and inserting ", a person associated with such a firm, or, as to any act, practice, or omission to act, while associated with such firm, a person formerly associated with such a firm".

(h) SUPERVISORY PERSONNEL OF AN AUDIT FIRM. —Section 105(c)(6) of the Sarbanes–Oxley Act of 2002 (15 U.S.C.7215(c)(6)) is amended —

(1) in subparagraph (A), by striking "the supervisory personnel" and inserting "any person who is, or at the time of the alleged failure reasonably to supervise was, a supervisory person"; and

(2) in subparagraph (B) —

(A) by striking "No associated person" and inserting "No current or former supervisory person"; and

(B) by striking "any other person" and inserting "any associated person".

(i) MEMBER OF THE PUBLIC COMPANY ACCOUNTING OVERSIGHT BOARD. —Section 107(d)(3) of the Sarbanes–Oxley Act of 2002 (15 U.S.C.7217(d)(3)) is amended by striking "any member" and inserting "any person who is, or at the time of the alleged misconduct was, a member".

SEC.929G. STREAMLINED HIRING AUTHORITY FOR MARKET SPECIALISTS.

(a) APPOINTMENT AUTHORITY. —Section 3114 of title 5, United States Code, is amended by striking the section heading and all that follows through the end of subsection (a) and inserting the following:

"§ 3114. Appointment of candidates to certain positions in the competitive service by

(i)根据第105(b)条针对该人开展调查时,调查范围仅限于该人作为注册公共会计师事务所的前业务相关人或寻求与之建立业务相关关系期间的任何作为、做法或不作为;且

(ii)根据第105(c)(1)条对该人启动纪律处分程序,或者根据第105(c)(4)条对该人施以处罚时,范围仅限于——

(I)该人作为注册公共会计师事务所前业务相关人或寻求与之建立业务相关关系期间的行为;或

(II) 在公众公司会计监督委员会要求该人在调查中提供其作为注册公共会计师事务所前关联人或寻求与之建立业务相关关系期间的相关证词、文件或其他信息时,该人实施的第105(b)(3)条所述不合作行为。”

(2)**对《1934年证券交易法》的修正**。——《1934年证券交易法》第21(a)(1)条[《美国法典》第十五编第78u(a)(1)节]修正如下:删除“或该事务所的业务相关人”,替以“,该事务所的业务相关人,或者对于该事务所前业务相关人在业务相关关系存在期间的任何作为、做法或不作为”。

(h)**审计事务所的领导监督人员**。——《2002年萨班斯—奥克斯利法》第105(c)(6)条[《美国法典》第十五编第7215(c)(6)节]修正如下——

(1)在第(A)子款中,删除“领导监督人员”,替以“当前身为领导监督人员的任何人,或被指控未合理履行监督职责事件发生时身为领导监督人员的任何人”;及

(2)在第(B)子款中——

(A)删除“任何业务相关人”,替以“任何现任或前任领导监督人员”;及

(B)删除“任何其他人”,替以“任何业务相关人”。

(i)**公众公司会计监督委员会委员**。——《2002年萨班斯—奥克斯利法》第107(d)(3)条[《美国法典》第十五编第7217(d)(3)节]修正如下:删除“任何委员”,替以“当前身为委员的任何人,或被指控的不当行为发生时身为委员的任何人”。

第929G条　对聘用市场专家的权力进行限缩

(a)**任命权**。——《联邦规章汇编》第五编第3114部分修正如下:删除本条标题直至第(a)子条结尾的全部内容,替以如下内容:

“第3114条　由证券交易委员会为某些竞争上岗职位任命候选人

the Securities and Exchange Commission

"(a) APPLICABILITY. —This section applies with respect to any position of accountant, economist, and securities compliance examiner at the Commission that is in the competitive service, and any position at the Commission in the competitive service that requires specialized knowledge of financial and capital market formation or regulation, financial market structures or surveillance, or information technology.".

(b) CLERICAL AMENDMENT. —The table of sections for chapter 31 of title 5, United States Code, is amended by striking the item relating to section 3114 and inserting the following:

"3114. Appointment of candidates to positions in the competitive service by the Securities and Exchange Commission.".

(c) PAY AUTHORITY. —The Commission may set the rate of pay for experts and consultants appointed under the authority of section 3109 of title 5, United States Code, in the same manner in which it sets the rate of pay for employees of the Commission.

SEC.929H. SIPC REFORMS.

(a) INCREASING THE CASH LIMIT OF PROTECTION. —Section 9 of the Securities Investor Protection Act of 1970 (15 U.S.C.78fff-3) is amended —

(1) in subsection (a)(1), by striking "$100,000 for each such customer" and inserting "the standard maximum cash advance amount for each such customer, as determined in accordance with subsection (d)"; and

(2) by adding the following new subsections:

"(d) STANDARD MAXIMUM CASH ADVANCE AMOUNT DEFINED. — For purposes of this section, the term 'standard maximum cash advance amount' means $250,000, as such amount may be adjusted after December 31, 2010, as provided under subsection (e).

"(e) INFLATION ADJUSTMENT. —

"(1) IN GENERAL. —Not later than January 1, 2011, and every 5 years thereafter, and subject to the approval of the Commission as provided under section 3(e)(2), the Board of Directors of SIPC shall determine whether an inflation adjustment to the standard maximum cash advance amount is appropriate. If the Board of Directors of SIPC determines such an adjustment is appropriate, then the standard maximum cash advance amount shall be an amount equal to —

"(A) $250,000 multiplied by —

"(B) the ratio of the annual value of the Personal Consumption Expenditures Chain-Type Price Index (or any successor index thereto), published by the Department of Commerce, for the calendar year preceding the year in which such determination is made, to the published annual value of such index for the calendar year preceding the year in which

(a)**适用范围**。——本条规定适用于证券交易委员会内通过竞争上岗的任何会计师、经济学家和证券合规检查员职位,并适用于证券交易委员会内要求拥有金融和资本市场形成或监管、金融市场结构或监测或信息技术方面专业知识的任何竞争上岗职位。”

(b)**目录修正**。——《联邦规章汇编》第五编第三十一章条款目录修正如下:删除与第3114条部分相关的内容,替以如下内容:

“第3114条 由证券交易委员会为竞争上岗职位任命候选人。”

(c)**薪酬设定权**。——对于根据《美国法典》第五编第3109节的授权任命的专家和顾问,证券交易委员会在为其设定薪酬水平时,可沿用证券交易委员会设定其他雇员薪酬时所采用的方式。

第929H条 证券投资者保护公司的改革

(a)**提高保护现金额上限**。——《1970年证券投资者保护法》第9条(《美国法典》第十五编第78fff-3节)修正如下——

(1)在第(a)(1)子条中,删除“每一上述客户10万美元”,替以“每一上述客户按最高预付标准现金额计算,具体根据第(d)子条确定”;及

(2)增加如下新子条:

“(d)**最高预付标准现金额的定义**。——就本条而言,‘最高预付标准现金额’一词系指25万美元,但是该金额按照第(e)子条的规定可在2010年12月31日后进行调整。

(e)**通胀调整**。——

(1)**一般规定**。——证券投资者保护公司董事会应于2011年1月1日之前判定是否适宜对最高预付标准现金额进行通胀调整,且此后应每5年作出一次判定,但是所有决定均应由证券交易委员会根据第3(e)(2)条进行批准。如果证券投资者保护公司董事会判定进行上述通胀调整确属适当,则最高预付标准现金额应按如下方式计算——

(A)25万美元乘以——

(B)按如下公式计算得出的比率:商务部针对做出上述判定之日历年的上一日历年度所发布的个人消费支出链型物价指数(或任何后续指数)的年度值,除以商务部针对本子条规定颁布之日历年的上一日历年度所发布上述指数的年度值。

this subsection was enacted.

The index values used in calculations under this paragraph shall be, as of the date of the calculation, the values most recently published by the Department of Commerce.

"(2) ROUNDING. —If the standard maximum cash advance amount determined under paragraph (1) for any period is not a multiple of $10,000, the amount so determined shall be rounded down to the nearest $10,000.

"(3) PUBLICATION AND REPORT TO THE CONGRESS. —Not later than April 5 of any calendar year in which a determination is required to be made under paragraph (1)—

"(A) the Commission shall publish in the Federal Register the standard maximum cash advance amount; and

"(B) the Board of Directors of SIPC shall submit a report to the Congress stating the standard maximum cash advance amount.

"(4) IMPLEMENTATION PERIOD. —Any adjustment to the standard maximum cash advance amount shall take effect on January 1 of the year immediately succeeding the calendar year in which such adjustment is made.

"(5) INFLATION ADJUSTMENT CONSIDERATIONS. —In making any determination under paragraph (1) to increase the standard maximum cash advance amount, the Board of Directors of SIPC shall consider—

"(A) the overall state of the fund and the economic conditions affecting members of SIPC;

"(B) the potential problems affecting members of SIPC; and

"(C) such other factors as the Board of Directors of SIPC may determine appropriate.".

(b) LIQUIDATION OF A CARRYING BROKER-DEALER. —Section 5(a)(3) of the Securities Investor Protection Act of 1970 (15 U.S.C.78eee(a)(3)) is amended—

(1) by striking the undesignated matter immediately following subparagraph (B);

(2) in subparagraph (A), by striking "any member of SIPC" and inserting "the member";

(3) in subparagraph (B), by striking the comma at the end and inserting a period;

(4) by striking "If SIPC" and inserting the following:

"(A) IN GENERAL. —SIPC may, upon notice to a member of SIPC, file an application for a protective decree with any court of competent jurisdiction specified in section 21(e) or 27 of the Securities Exchange Act of 1934, except that no such application shall be filed with respect to a member, the only customers of which are persons whose claims could not be satisfied by SIPC advances pursuant to section 9, if SIPC"; and

(5) by adding at the end the following:

"(B) CONSENT REQUIRED. —No member of SIPC that has a customer may enter into an insolvency, receivership, or bankruptcy proceeding, under Federal or State law, without the

根据本款使用各项指数进行计算时，应使用商务部截至开展计算当日所发布的最新数值。

(2)**取整**。——如果按照第(1)款计算得出的任何期间的最高预付标准现金额并非1万美元的整数倍,则该金额应向下取最接近的1万美元的倍数。

(3)**发布信息并向国会报告**。——在按照第(1)款应作出判定的任何日历年度的4月5日之前——

(A)证券交易委员会应在《联邦公报》上发布最高预付标准现金额;且

(B)证券投资者保护公司董事会应向国会提交一份报告,对最高预付标准现金额进行说明。

(4) **实施期间**。——对最高预付标准现金额进行的任何调整应于进行该调整之日历年的下一日历年度的1月1日生效。

(5)**通胀调整考虑因素**。——在按照第(1)款作出上调最高预付标准现金额的任何判定时,证券投资者保护公司董事会应考虑——

(A)基金整体情况和影响证券投资者保护公司会员的经济条件;

(B)可能影响证券投资者保护公司会员的问题;及

(C)证券投资者保护公司董事会判定确属适当的其他因素。”

(b)**代持经纪自营商的清算**。——《1970年证券投资者保护法》第5(a)(3)条[《美国法典》第十五编第78eee(a)(3)节]修正如下——

(1)删除紧接第(B)子款之后的无编号内容;

(2)在第(A)子款中,删除“证券投资者保护公司任何会员”,替以“该会员”;

(3)在第(B)子款中,删除结尾处的句号,替以逗号;

(4)删除“如果证券投资者保护公司”,替以如下内容:

“(A)**一般规定**。——证券投资者保护公司在向其会员发出通知后,可向《1934年证券交易法》第21(e)条或第27条规定的任何有管辖权的法院申请保护令,但是,如果某会员仅有的客户的权利主张无法按照第9条由证券投资者保护公司的预支款予以满足,则证券投资者保护公司不得针对该会员申请上述保护令,前提是证券投资者保护公司”;及

(5)在结尾处增加如下内容:

“(B)**同意要求**。——拥有客户的证券投资者保护公司任何会员在未事先获得证券投资者保护公司特别同意的情况下,不得根据联邦法律或州法律进入资不抵债、接

specific consent of SIPC, except as provided in title II of the Dodd–Frank Wall Street Reform and Consumer Protection Act.".

SEC.929I. PROTECTING CONFIDENTIALITY OF MATERIALS SUBMITTED TO THE COMMISSION.

(a) SECURITIES EXCHANGE ACT OF 1934. —Section 24 of the Securities Exchange Act of 1934 (15 U.S.C.78x) is amended —

(1) in subsection (d), by striking "subsection (e)" and inserting "subsection (f)";

(2) by redesignating subsection (e) as subsection (f); and

(3) by inserting after subsection (d) the following:

"(e) RECORDS OBTAINED FROM REGISTERED PERSONS. —

"(1) IN GENERAL. —Except as provided in subsection (f), the Commission shall not be compelled to disclose records or information obtained pursuant to section 17 (b), or records or information based upon or derived from such records or information, if such records or information have been obtained by the Commission for use in furtherance of the purposes of this title, including surveillance, risk assessments, or other regulatory and oversight activities.

"(2) TREATMENT OF INFORMATION. —For purposes of section 552 of title 5, United States Code, this subsection shall be considered a statute described in subsection (b)(3)(B) of such section 552. Collection of information pursuant to section 17 shall be an administrative action involving an agency against specific individuals or agencies pursuant to section 3518(c)(1) of title 44, United States Code.".

(b) INVESTMENT COMPANY ACT OF 1940. —Section 31 of the Investment Company Act of 1940 (15 U.S.C.80a–30) is amended —

(1) by striking subsection (c) and inserting the following:

"(c) LIMITATIONS ON DISCLOSURE BY COMMISSION. —Notwithstanding any other provision of law, the Commission shall not be compelled to disclose any records or information provided to the Commission under this section, or records or information based upon or derived from such records or information, if such records or information have been obtained by the Commission for use in furtherance of the purposes of this title, including surveillance, risk assessments, or other regulatory and oversight activities. Nothing in this subsection authorizes the Commission to withhold information from the Congress or prevent the Commission from complying with a request for information from any other Federal department or agency requesting the information for purposes within the scope of jurisdiction of that department or agency, or complying with an order of a court of the United States in an action brought by the United States or the Commission. For purposes of section 552 of title 5, United States Code, this section shall be considered a statute described in subsection (b)(3)(B) of such section 552. Collection of information pursuant to section 31 shall be an administrative action involving an agency against specific individuals or agencies pursuant to

管或破产程序,但《多德—弗兰克华尔街改革与消费者保护法》第二编规定的情形除外。”

第929I条　保护向证券交易委员会提交的材料的保密性

(a)**《1934年证券交易法》**。——《1934年证券交易法》第24条(《美国法典》第十五编第78x节)修正如下——

(1)在第(d)子条中,删除“第(e)子条”,替以“第(f)子条”;

(2)第(e)子条重新编号为第(f)子条;及

(3)在第(d)子条之后插入如下内容:

“(e)**从注册人处获取的记录**。——

(1)**一般规定**。——除第(f)子条规定的情形外,对于证券交易委员会根据第17(b)条为促进本编宗旨之实现(包括为开展监测、风险评估或其他规制或监管活动之目的)获取的记录和信息,或基于上述记录或信息而制作或衍生的记录或信息,不得强制证券交易委员会予以披露。

(2)**信息的处理**。——就《美国法典》第五编第552节而言,本子条应视为该第552节第(b)(3)(B)子节所述的制定法。按照第17条进行的信息收集应属于某一机关按照《美国法典》第四十四编第3518(c)(1)节针对具体个人或其他机关开展的行政行动。”

(b)**《1940年投资公司法》**。——《1940年投资公司法》第31条(《美国法典》第十五编第80a－30节)修正如下——

(1)删除第(c)子条,替以如下内容:

“(c)**证券交易委员会的披露限制**。——无论是否存在任何不同法律规定,对于按照本条规定向证券交易委员会提供的任何记录或信息,如证券交易委员会系为促进本编宗旨之实现(包括为开展监测、风险评估或其他规制或监管活动之目的)获取该等记录和信息,则不得强制证券交易委员会披露该等记录和信息或基于该等记录或信息而制作或衍生的记录或信息。但是,证券交易委员会无权依据本子条拒绝向国会提供信息,本条规定也不妨碍证券交易委员会向提出请求的任何其他联邦部门或联邦机关提供相关信息,以便该等部门或机关将该信息用于其管辖范围内的目的,亦不妨碍证券交易委员会在联邦政府或证券交易委员会提起的诉讼程序中按照联邦法院发出的命令提供相关信息。就《美国法典》第五编第552节而言,本条应视为该第552节第(b)(3)(B)子节所述的制定法。按照第31条进行的信息收集应属于某一机关按照《美国法典》第四十四编第3518(c)(1)节针对具体个人或机关开展的行政行动。”;

section 3518(c)(1) of title 44, United States Code.";

(2) by striking subsection (d); and

(3) by redesignating subsections (e) and (f) as subsections (d) and (e), respectively.

(c) INVESTMENT ADVISERS ACT OF 1940. —Section 210 of the Investment Advisers Act of 1940 (15 U.S.C.80b–10) is amended by adding at the end the following:

"(d) LIMITATIONS ON DISCLOSURE BY THE COMMISSION. —Notwithstanding any other provision of law, the Commission shall not be compelled to disclose any records or information provided to the Commission under section 204, or records or information based upon or derived from such records or information, if such records or information have been obtained by the Commission for use in furtherance of the purposes of this title, including surveillance, risk assessments, or other regulatory and oversight activities. Nothing in this subsection authorizes the Commission to withhold information from the Congress or prevent the Commission from complying with a request for information from any other Federal department or agency requesting the information for purposes within the scope of jurisdiction of that department or agency, or complying with an order of a court of the United States in an action brought by the United States or the Commission. For purposes of section 552 of title 5, United States Code, this subsection shall be considered a statute described in subsection (b)(3)(B) of such section 552. Collection of information pursuant to section 204 shall be an administrative action involving an agency against specific individuals or agencies pursuant to section 3518(c)(1) of title 44, United States Code.".

SEC.929J. EXPANSION OF AUDIT INFORMATION TO BE PRODUCED AND EXCHANGED.

Section 106 of the Sarbanes–Oxley Act of 2002 (15 U.S.C.7216) is amended —

(1) by striking subsection (b) and inserting the following:

"(b) PRODUCTION OF DOCUMENTS. —

"(1) PRODUCTION BY FOREIGN FIRMS. —If a foreign public accounting firm performs material services upon which a registered public accounting firm relies in the conduct of an audit or interim review, issues an audit report, performs audit work, or conducts interim reviews, the foreign public accounting firm shall —

"(A) produce the audit work papers of the foreign public accounting firm and all other documents of the firm related to any such audit work or interim review to the Commission or the Board, upon request of the Commission or the Board; and

"(B) be subject to the jurisdiction of the courts of the United States for purposes of enforcement of any request for such documents.

"(2) OTHER PRODUCTION. —Any registered public accounting firm that relies, in whole or in part, on the work of a foreign public accounting firm in issuing an audit report,

(2)删除第(d)子条;及

(3)第(e)子条和第(f)子条分别重新编号为第(d)子条和第(e)子条。

(c)**《1940年投资顾问法》**。——在《1940年投资顾问法》第210条(《美国法典》第十五编第80b-10节)结尾处增加如下内容,作为对该条的修正:

“(d)**证券交易委员会的披露限制**。——无论是否存在任何不同法律规定,对于根据第204条规定向证券交易委员会提供的任何记录或信息,如证券交易委员会系为促进本编宗旨之实现(包括为开展监测、风险评估或其他规制或监管活动)获取该等记录和信息,则不得强制证券交易委员会披露该等记录和信息或基于该等记录或信息而制作或衍生的记录或信息。但是,证券交易委员会无权依据本子条拒绝向国会提供信息,本条规定也不妨碍证券交易委员会向提出请求的任何其他联邦部门或联邦机关提供相关信息,以便该等部门或机关将该信息用于其管辖范围内的目的,亦不妨碍证券交易委员会在由联邦政府或证券交易委员会提起的诉讼程序中按照联邦法院发出的命令提供相关信息。就《美国法典》第五编第552节而言,本子条应视为该第552节第(b)(3)(B)子节所述的制定法。按照第204条进行的信息收集应属于某一机关按照《美国法典》第四十四编第3518(c)(1)节针对具体个人或其他机关开展的行政行动。”

第929J条　扩大应予提供和交换的审计信息范围

《2002年萨班斯—奥克斯利法》第106条(《美国法典》第十五编第7216节)修正如下——

(1)删除第(b)子条,替以如下内容:

“(b)**文件提供**。——

(1)**外国事务所的文件提供**。——如果注册公共会计师事务所进行审计或开展中期审查时利用外国公共会计师事务所提供的重要服务,或者如果外国公共会计师事务所发布审计报告、开展审计工作或进行中期审查,则该等外国公共会计师事务所应——

(A)按照证券交易委员会或公众公司会计监督委员会的要求,向证券交易委员会或公众公司会计监督委员会提供该外国公共会计师事务所的任何该等审计工作底稿以及与任何上述审计工作或中期审查相关的所有其他文件;并

(B)接受联邦法院为强制执行获取上述文件的任何请求而对其实施的管辖。

(2)**其他文件的提供**。——任何注册公共会计师事务所在发布审计报告、开展审计工作或进行中期审查时完全或部分利用外国公共会计师事务所工作的,应——

performing audit work, or conducting an interim review, shall—

"(A) produce the audit work papers of the foreign public accounting firm and all other documents related to any such work in response to a request for production by the Commission or the Board; and

"(B) secure the agreement of any foreign public accounting firm to such production, as a condition of the reliance by the registered public accounting firm on the work of that foreign public accounting firm.";

(2) by redesignating subsection (d) as subsection (g); and

(3) by inserting after subsection (c) the following:

"(d) SERVICE OF REQUESTS OR PROCESS. —

"(1) IN GENERAL. —Any foreign public accounting firm that performs work for a domestic registered public accounting firm shall furnish to the domestic registered public accounting firm a written irrevocable consent and power of attorney that designates the domestic registered public accounting firm as an agent upon whom may be served any request by the Commission or the Board under this section or upon whom may be served any process, pleadings, or other papers in any action brought to enforce this section.

"(2) SPECIFIC AUDIT WORK. —Any foreign public accounting firm that performs material services upon which a registered public accounting firm relies in the conduct of an audit or interim review, issues an audit report, performs audit work, or, performs interim reviews, shall designate to the Commission or the Board an agent in the United States upon whom may be served any request by the Commission or the Board under this section or upon whom may be served any process, pleading, or other papers in any action brought to enforce this section.

"(e) SANCTIONS. —A willful refusal to comply, in whole in or in part, with any request by the Commission or the Board under this section, shall be deemed a violation of this Act.

"(f) OTHER MEANS OF SATISFYING PRODUCTION OBLIGATIONS.—Notwithstanding any other provisions of this section, the staff of the Commission or the Board may allow a foreign public accounting firm that is subject to this section to meet production obligations under this section through alternate means, such as through foreign counterparts of the Commission or the Board.".

SEC.929K. SHARING PRIVILEGED INFORMATION WITH OTHER AUTHORITIES.

Section 24 of the Securities Exchange Act of 1934 (15 U.S.C.78x) is amended —

(1) in subsection (d), as amended by subsection (d)(1)(A), by striking "subsection (f)" and inserting "subsection (g)";

(2) in subsection (e), as added by subsection (d)(1)(C), by striking "subsection (f)" and inserting "subsection (g)";

(A)在证券交易委员会或公众公司会计监督委员会提出要求时,向证券交易委员会或公众公司会计监督委员会提供审计工作底稿以及与任何上述工作相关的所有其他文件;并

(B)就提供上述文件获得该等外国公共会计师事务所的同意,以此作为其利用该等外国公共会计师事务所工作的前提条件。”

(2)第(d)子条重新编号为第(g)子条;及

(3)在第(c)子条之后插入如下内容:

“(d)**请求或程序文件的送达**。——

(1)**一般规定**。——为境内注册公共会计师事务所提供服务的任何外国公共会计师事务所均应向该境内公共会计师事务所提供一份不可撤销的书面同意及授权书,指定该境内注册公共会计师事务所作为其代理人,代为接收证券交易委员会或公众公司会计监督委员会按照本条规定发出的任何要求,或代为接收为执行本条规定所提起任何诉讼中的任何程序文件、诉讼文件或其他文件。

(2)**具体审计工作**。——如果注册公共会计师事务所进行审计或开展中期审查时利用任何外国公共会计师事务所提供的重要服务,或者如果该等外国公共会计师事务所发布审计报告、开展审计工作或进行中期审查,则该等外国公共会计师事务所应向证券交易委员会或公共会计公司监督委员会指定一名美国境内代理人,代为接收证券交易委员会或公众公司会计监督委员会按照本条规定发出的任何要求,或代为接收为执行本条规定所提起的任何诉讼中的任何程序文件、诉讼文件或其他文件。

(e)**处罚**。——对证券交易委员会或公众公司会计监督委员会按照本条规定发出的任何请求故意全部或部分拒绝履行的行为应视为违反本法的行为。

(f)**履行文件提供义务的其他方式**。——无论本条是否存在任何不同规定,证券交易委员会或公众公司会计监督委员会的工作人员均可以允许受制于本条规定的外国公共会计师事务所通过其他方式履行本条规定的文件提供义务,例如,通过其母国的相当于证券交易委员会或公众公司会计监督委员会的机关提供该等文件。”

第929K条　与其他机构共享受保密特权保护的信息

《1934年证券交易法》第24条(《美国法典》第十五编第78x节)修正如下——

(1)在经第(d)(1)(A)子条修正的第(d)子条中,删除“第(f)子条”,替以“第(g)子条”;

(2)在经第(d)(1)(C)子条增加的第(e)子条中,删除“第(f)子条”,替以“第(g)子条”;

(3) by redesignating subsection (f) as subsection (g); and

(4) by inserting after subsection (e) the following:

"(f) SHARING PRIVILEGED INFORMATION WITH OTHER AUTHORITIES.—

"(1) PRIVILEGED INFORMATION PROVIDED BY THE COMMISSION.—The Commission shall not be deemed to have waived any privilege applicable to any information by transferring that information to or permitting that information to be used by—

"(A) any agency (as defined in section 6 of title 18, United States Code);

"(B) the Public Company Accounting Oversight Board;

"(C) any self-regulatory organization;

"(D) any foreign securities authority;

"(E) any foreign law enforcement authority; or

"(F) any State securities or law enforcement authority.

"(2) NONDISCLOSURE OF PRIVILEGED INFORMATION PROVIDED TO THE COMMISSION.—The Commission shall not be compelled to disclose privileged information obtained from any foreign securities authority, or foreign law enforcement authority, if the authority has in good faith determined and represented to the Commission that the information is privileged.

"(3) NONWAIVER OF PRIVILEGED INFORMATION PROVIDED TO THE COMMISSION.—

"(A) IN GENERAL.—Federal agencies, State securities and law enforcement authorities, self-regulatory organizations, and the Public Company Accounting Oversight Board shall not be deemed to have waived any privilege applicable to any information by transferring that information to or permitting that information to be used by the Commission.

"(B) EXCEPTION.—The provisions of subparagraph (A) shall not apply to a self-regulatory organization or the Public Company Accounting Oversight Board with respect to information used by the Commission in an action against such organization.

"(4) DEFINITIONS.—For purposes of this subsection—

"(A) the term 'privilege' includes any work-product privilege, attorney-client privilege, governmental privilege, or other privilege recognized under Federal, State, or foreign law;

"(B) the term 'foreign law enforcement authority' means any foreign authority that is empowered under foreign law to detect, investigate or prosecute potential violations of law; and

"(C) the term 'State securities or law enforcement authority' means the authority of any State or territory that is empowered under State or territory law to detect, investigate, or prosecute potential violations of law.".

(3)第(f)子条重新编号为第(g)子条;及

(4)在第(e)子条之后插入如下内容:

"(f)**与其他机构共享受保密特权保护的信息**。——

(1)**证券交易委员会提供的受保密特权保护的信息**。——证券交易委员会向以下各者提供受保密特权保护的任何信息或允许其使用该等信息的，不得因此而视为证券交易委员会已放弃该等信息的任何保密特权——

(A)任何机关(定义见《美国法典》第十八编第6节);

(B)公众公司会计监督委员会;

(C)任何自律组织;

(D)任何外国证券监管机构;

(E)任何外国执法机构;或

(F)任何州证券监管机构或执法机构。

(2)**不得强制证券交易委员会披露向其提供的受保密特权保护的信息**。——对于证券交易委员会从外国证券监管机构或外国执法机构处获得的受保密特权保护的信息,如果该等外国机构善意判定该等信息属于受保密特权保护的信息,并已告知证券交易委员会该信息受保密特权保护,则不得强制证券交易委员会披露受保密特权保护的该等信息。

(3)**向证券交易委员会提供特许保密信息不构成对保密特权的放弃**。——

(A)**一般规定**。——联邦机关、州证券监管机构和执法机构、自律组织以及公众公司会计监督委员会向证券交易委员会提供受保密特权保护的任何信息或允许证券交易委员会使用该等信息的,不得因此而视为上述各者已放弃该等信息的保密特权。

(B)**例外规定**。——证券交易委员会在针对自律组织或公众公司会计监督委员会提起的诉讼中使用受保密特权保护的信息的,第(A)子款的规定不适用于该等自律组织或公众公司会计监督委员会。

(4)**定义**。——就本子条而言——

(A)'保密特权'一词包括工作成果保密特权、律师—当事人保密特权、政府保密特权或联邦法律、州法律或外国法律认可的其他保密特权;

(B)'外国执法机构'一词系指根据外国法律有权对涉嫌违法行为进行侦查、调查或提起公诉的任何外国监管机构;及

(C)'州证券监管机构或执法机构'一词系指美国任何州或准州内根据该等州或准州的法律有权对涉嫌违法行为进行侦查、调查或提起公诉的部门。"

SEC.929L. ENHANCED APPLICATION OF ANTIFRAUD PROVISIONS.

The Securities Exchange Act of 1934 (15 U.S.C.78a et seq.) is amended —

(1) in section 9 —

(A) by striking "registered on a national securities exchange" each place that term appears and inserting "other than a government security";

(B) in subsection (b), by striking "by use of any facility of a national securities exchange,"; and

(C) in subsection (c), by inserting after "unlawful for any" the following: "broker, dealer, or";

(2) in section 10(a)(1), by striking "registered on a national securities exchange" and inserting "other than a government security"; and

(3) in section 15(c)(1)(A), by striking "otherwise than on a national securities exchange of which it is a member".

SEC.929M. AIDING AND ABETTING AUTHORITY UNDER THE SECURITIES ACT AND THE INVESTMENT COMPANY ACT.

(a) UNDER THE SECURITIES ACT OF 1933. —Section 15 of the Securities Act of 1933 (15 U.S.C.77o) is amended —

(1) by striking "Every person who" and inserting "(a) CONTROLLING PERSONS. — Every person who"; and

(2) by adding at the end the following:

"(b) PROSECUTION OF PERSONS WHO AID AND ABET VIOLATIONS. — For purposes of any action brought by the Commission under subparagraph (b) or (d) of section 20, any person that knowingly or recklessly provides substantial assistance to another person in violation of a provision of this Act, or of any rule or regulation issued under this Act, shall be deemed to be in violation of such provision to the same extent as the person to whom such assistance is provided.".

(b) UNDER THE INVESTMENT COMPANY ACT OF 1940. —Section 48 of the Investment Company Act of 1940(15 U.S.C.80a–48) is amended by redesignating subsection (b) as subsection (c) and inserting after subsection (a) the following:

"(b) For purposes of any action brought by the Commission under subsection (d) or (e) of section 42, any person that knowingly or recklessly provides substantial assistance to another person in violation of a provision of this Act, or of any rule or regulation issued under this Act, shall be deemed to be in violation of such provision to the same extent as the person to whom such assistance is provided.".

SEC.929N. AUTHORITY TO IMPOSE PENALTIES FOR AIDING AND ABETTING VIOLATIONS OF THE INVESTMENT ADVISERS ACT.

Section 209 of the Investment Advisers Act of 1940 (15 U.S.C.80b–9) is amended by

第929L条　加强反欺诈条款的适用

《1934年证券交易法》(《美国法典》第十五编第78a节及其后条文)修正如下——

(1)在第9条中——

(A)删除所有的“在全国性证券交易所注册的”,全部替以“除政府证券之外的”;

(B)第(b)子条删除“通过使用全国性证券交易所的任何设施,”;及

(C)第(c)子条在“全国性证券交易所的任何会员”前插入“经纪商、自营商或”;

(2)第10(a)(1)条删除“在全国性证券交易所注册的”,替以“除政府证券之外的”;及

(3)第15(c)(1)(A)条删除“在其作为会员参与的全国性证券交易所之外”。

第929M条　《证券法》和《投资公司法》关于协同及教唆犯罪的规定

(a)**《1933年证券法》关于协同及教唆犯罪的规定**。——《1933年证券法》第15条(《美国法典》第十五编第77o节)修正如下——

(1)删除“符合以下条件的所有人”,替以“(a)**控制人**。——符合以下条件的所有人”;及

(2)在结尾处增加如下内容:

“(b)**对协同及教唆他人实施犯罪的人提起公诉**。——就证券交易委员会根据第20条第(b)子款或第(d)子款提起的任何诉讼而言,如果任何人在知情的情况下或轻率地为另一人实施违反本法或依据本法发布的任何规则或规章的行为提供实质性协助,则二者均应视为违反了本法或依据本法发布的任何规则或规章且违法违规程度相同。”

(b)**《1940年投资公司法》关于协同及教唆犯罪的规定**。——《1940年投资公司法》第48条(《美国法典》第十五编第80a-48节)修正如下:第(b)子条重新编号为第(c)子条,并在第(a)子条之后插入如下内容:

“(b)就证券交易委员会根据第42条第(d)子条或第(e)子条提起的任何诉讼而言,如果任何人在知情的情况下或轻率地为另一人实施违反本法或依据本法发布的任何规则或规章的行为提供实质性协助,则二者均应视为违反了本法或依据本法发布的任何规则或规章且违法违规程度相同。”

第929N条　对协同及教唆他人实施违反《投资顾问法》行为的人进行处罚的权力

在《1940年投资顾问法》第209条(《美国法典》第十五编第80b-9节)结尾处增加如

inserting at the end the following new subsection:

"(f) AIDING AND ABETTING. —For purposes of any action brought by the Commission under subsection (e), any person that knowingly or recklessly has aided, abetted, counseled, commanded, induced, or procured a violation of any provision of this Act, or of any rule, regulation, or order hereunder, shall be deemed to be in violation of such provision, rule, regulation, or order to the same extent as the person that committed such violation.".

SEC.929O. AIDING AND ABETTING STANDARD OF KNOWLEDGE SATISFIED BY RECKLESSNESS.

Section 20(e) of the Securities Exchange Act of 1934 (15 U.S.C.78t(e)) is amended by inserting "or recklessly" after "knowingly".

SEC.929P. STRENGTHENING ENFORCEMENT BY THE COMMISSION.

(a) AUTHORITY TO IMPOSE CIVIL PENALTIES IN CEASE AND DESIST PROCEEDINGS. —

(1) UNDER THE SECURITIES ACT OF 1933. —Section 8A of the Securities Act of 1933 (15 U.S.C.77h-1) is amended by adding at the end the following new subsection:

"(g) AUTHORITY TO IMPOSE MONEY PENALTIES. —

"(1) GROUNDS. —In any cease-and-desist proceeding under subsection (a), the Commission may impose a civil penalty on a person if the Commission finds, on the record, after notice and opportunity for hearing, that —

"(A) such person —

"(i) is violating or has violated any provision of this title, or any rule or regulation issued under this title; or

"(ii) is or was a cause of the violation of any provision of this title, or any rule or regulation thereunder; and

"(B) such penalty is in the public interest.

"(2) MAXIMUM AMOUNT OF PENALTY. —

"(A) FIRST TIER. —The maximum amount of a penalty for each act or omission described in paragraph (1) shall be $7,500 for a natural person or $75,000 for any other person.

"(B) SECOND TIER. — Notwithstanding subparagraph (A), the maximum amount of penalty for each such act or omission shall be $75,000 for a natural person or $375,000 for any other person, if the act or omission described in paragraph (1) involved fraud, deceit, manipulation, or deliberate or reckless disregard of a regulatory requirement.

"(C) THIRD TIER. — Notwithstanding subparagraphs (A) and (B), the maximum amount of penalty for each such act or omission shall be $150,000 for a natural person or $725,000 for any other person, if —

下新子条,作为对该条的修正:

“(f)**协同与教唆犯罪**。——就证券交易委员会根据第(e)子条提起的任何诉讼而言,如果任何人在知情的情况下或轻率地协同、教唆、指导、指使、引诱或促使他人违反本法任何规定或依据本法发布的任何规则、规章或命令,则二者均应视为违反了该等法律、规则、规章或命令且违法违规程度相同。”

第929O条 犯罪人存在轻率的主观状态的,即可认定为满足协同与教唆犯罪的犯意要求

《1934年证券交易法》第20(e)条[《美国法典》第十五编第78t(e)节]修正如下:在“或轻率地”之后插入“在知情的情况下”。

第929P条 加强证券交易委员会的执法力度

(a)**在制止令程序中处以民事罚款的权力**。——

(1)**根据《1933年证券法》处以民事罚款的权力**。——在《1933年证券法》第8A条(《美国法典》第十五编第77h-1节)结尾处增加如下新子条,作为对该条的修正:

“(g)**处以罚款的权力**。——

(1)**依据**。——在根据第(a)子条提起的任何制止令程序中,如果证券交易委员会在发出通知并提供听证机会的前提下对任何人做出如下记录在案的认定,则证券交易委员会可以对该人处以民事罚款——

(A)该人——

(i)正在违反或已经违反本编的任何规定或依据本编发布的任何规则或规章;或

(ii)导致或曾经导致违反本编任何规定或依据本编发布的任何规则或规章的行为的发生;且

(B)处以上述罚款符合公共利益。

(2)**最高罚款**。——

(A)**第一层次**。——对于第(1)款所述每一作为或不作为,自然人最高应处以7500美元的罚款,其他主体最高应处以7.5万美元的罚款。

(B)**第二层次**。——无论第(A)子款如何规定,如果第(1)款所述作为或不作为涉及欺诈、欺骗、操纵,或者故意无视,或漠视监管要求的行为,则对于每一上述作为或不作为,自然人最高应处以7.5万美元的罚款,其他主体最高应处以37.5万美元的罚款。

(C)**第三层次**。——无论第(A)子款和第(B)子款如何规定,在以下情况下,对于第(1)款所述每一作为或不作为,自然人最高应处以15万美元的罚款,其他主体最高应处以72.5万美元的罚款——

"(i) the act or omission described in paragraph(1) involved fraud, deceit, manipulation, or deliberate or reckless disregard of a regulatory requirement; and

"(ii) such act or omission directly or indirectly resulted in —

"(I) substantial losses or created a significant risk of substantial losses to other persons; or

"(II) substantial pecuniary gain to the person who committed the act or omission.

"(3) EVIDENCE CONCERNING ABILITY TO PAY. — In any proceeding in which the Commission may impose a penalty under this section, a respondent may present evidence of the ability of the respondent to pay such penalty. The Commission may, in its discretion, consider such evidence in determining whether such penalty is in the public interest. Such evidence may relate to the extent of the ability of the respondent to continue in business and the collectability of a penalty, taking into account any other claims of the United States or third parties upon the assets of the respondent and the amount of the assets of the respondent.".

(2) UNDER THE SECURITIES EXCHANGE ACT OF 1934. — Section 21B(a) of the Securities Exchange Act of 1934 (15 U.S.C.78u-2(a)) is amended —

(A) by striking the matter following paragraph (4);

(B) in the matter preceding paragraph (1), by inserting after "opportunity for hearing," the following: "that such penalty is in the public interest and";

(C) by redesignating paragraphs (1) through (4) as subparagraphs (A) through (D), respectively, and adjusting the margins accordingly;

(D) by striking "In any proceeding" and inserting the following:

"(1) IN GENERAL. — In any proceeding"; and

(E) by adding at the end the following:

"(2) CEASE-AND-DESIST PROCEEDINGS. — In any proceeding instituted under section 21C against any person, the Commission may impose a civil penalty, if the Commission finds, on the record after notice and opportunity for hearing, that such person —

"(A) is violating or has violated any provision of this title, or any rule or regulation issued under this title; or

"(B) is or was a cause of the violation of any provision of this title, or any rule or regulation issued under this title.".

(3) UNDER THE INVESTMENT COMPANY ACT OF 1940. — Section 9 (d)(1) of the Investment Company Act of 1940 (15 U.S.C.80a-9(d)(1)) is amended —

(A) by striking the matter following subparagraph (C);

(B) in the matter preceding subparagraph(A), by inserting after "opportunity for hearing," the following: "that such penalty is in the public interest, and";

(C) by redesignating subparagraphs (A) through (C) as clauses (i) through (iii),

(i)上述作为或不作为涉及欺诈、欺骗、操纵,或者故意无视,或漠视监管要求的行为;且

(ii)该等作为或不作为直接或间接地导致——

(I)其他人遭受重大损失,或面临严重的重大损失风险;或

(II)该等作为人或不作为的实施人获得重大金钱收益。

(3)**证明支付能力的证据**。——在证券交易委员会可以根据本条规定处以罚款的任何程序中,相对人可提供证据,证明其具有支付该等罚款的能力。在判断该等罚款是否符合公共利益时,证券交易委员会可以依其自由裁量权对该证据予以考量。相对人提供的证据可在考虑联邦政府或第三方对相对人资产拥有的任何其他权利主张以及相对人的资产数额基础上,说明其在多大程度上能继续开展业务经营,以及是否具有缴纳罚款的能力。"

(2)**根据《1934年证券交易法》处以民事罚款的权力**。——《1934年证券交易法》第21B(a)条[《美国法典》第十五编第78u-2(a)节]修正如下——

(A)删除第(4)款之后的内容;

(B)第(1)款之前的内容在"认定"之后插入"该罚款符合公共利益且";

(C)第(1)款至第(4)款分别重新编号为第(A)子款至第(D)子款,并相应调整缩进距离;

(D)删除"在任何程序中",替以如下内容:

"(1)**一般规定**。——在任何程序中";及

(E)在结尾处增加如下内容:

"(2)**制止令程序**。——在根据第21C条针对任何人提起的程序中,如果证券交易委员会在发出通知并已提供听证机会的前提下作出如下记录在案的认定,则证券交易委员会可以对该人处以民事罚款——

(A)该人正在违反或已经违反本编的任何规定或依据本编发布的任何规则或规章;或

(B)该人导致或曾经导致违反本编任何规定或依据本编发布的任何规则或规章的行为的发生。"

(3)**根据《1940年投资公司法》处以民事罚款的权力**。——《1940年投资公司法》第9(d)(1)条[《美国法典》第十五编第80a-9(d)(1)节]修正如下——

(A)删除第(C)子款之后的内容;

(B)第(A)子款之前的内容在"认定"之后插入"该罚款符合公共利益,且";

(C)第(A)子款至第(C)子款分别重新编号为第(i)项至第(iii)项,并相应调整缩进

respectively, and adjusting the margins accordingly;

(D) by striking "In any proceeding" and inserting the following: "(A) IN GENERAL. –In any proceeding"; and

(E) by adding at the end the following:

"(B) CEASE–AND–DESIST PROCEEDINGS. —In any proceeding instituted pursuant to subsection (f) against any person, the Commission may impose a civil penalty if the Commission finds, on the record, after notice and opportunity for hearing, that such person—

"(i) is violating or has violated any provision of this title, or any rule or regulation issued under this title; or

"(ii) is or was a cause of the violation of any provision of this title, or any rule or regulation issued under this title.".

(4) UNDER THE INVESTMENT ADVISERS ACT OF 1940. —Section 203(i)(1) of the Investment Advisers Act of 1940 (15 U.S.C.80b–3(i)(1)) is amended —

(A) by striking the matter following subparagraph (D);

(B) in the matter preceding subparagraph (A), by inserting after "opportunity for hearing," the following: "that such penalty is in the public interest and";

(C) by redesignating subparagraphs (A) through (D) as clauses (i) through (iv), respectively, and adjusting the margins accordingly;

(D) by striking "In any proceeding" and inserting the following: "(A) IN GENERAL. — In any proceeding"; and

(E) by adding at the end the following new subparagraph:

"(B) CEASE–AND–DESIST PROCEEDINGS. — In any proceeding instituted pursuant to subsection (k) against any person, the Commission may impose a civil penalty if the Commission finds, on the record, after notice and opportunity for hearing, that such person—

"(i) is violating or has violated any provision of this title, or any rule or regulation issued under this title; or

"(ii) is or was a cause of the violation of any provision of this title, or any rule or regulation issued under this title.".

(b) EXTRATERRITORIAL JURISDICTION OF THE ANTIFRAUD PROVISIONS OF THE FEDERAL SECURITIES LAWS. —

(1) UNDER THE SECURITIES ACT OF 1933. — Section 22 of the Securities Act of 1933 (15 U.S.C.77v(a)) is amended by adding at the end the following new subsection:

"(c) EXTRATERRITORIAL JURISDICTION. — The district courts of the United States and the United States courts of any Territory shall have jurisdiction of an action or proceeding brought or instituted by the Commission or the United States alleging a violation of section 17(a) involving —

"(1) conduct within the United States that constitutes significant steps in furtherance of

距离;

(D)删除“在任何程序中”,替以“(A)**一般规定**。——在任何程序中”;及

(E)在结尾处增加如下内容:

“(B)**制止令程序**。——在根据第(f)子条针对任何人提起的程序中,如果证券交易委员会在发出通知并已提供听证机会的前提下作出如下记录在案的认定,则证券交易委员会可以对该人处以民事罚款——

(i)该人正在违反或已经违反本编的任何规定或依据本编发布的任何规则或规章;或

(ii)该人导致或曾经导致违反本编任何规定或依据本编发布的任何规则或规章的行为的发生。”

(4)**根据《1940年投资顾问法》处以民事罚款的权力**。——《1940年投资顾问法》第203(i)(1)条[《美国法典》第十五编第80b-3(i)(1)节]修正如下——

(A)删除第(D)子款之后的内容;

(B)在第(A)子款之前,在“认定”之后插入“该罚款符合公共利益且”;

(C)第(A)子款至第(D)子款分别重新编号为第(i)项至第(iv)项,并相应调整缩进距离;

(D)删除“在任何程序中”,替以“(A)**一般规定**。——在任何程序中”;及

(E)在结尾处增加如下新子款:

“(B)**制止令程序**。——在根据第(k)子条针对任何人提起的程序中,如果证券交易委员会在发出通知并已提供听证机会的前提下作出如下记录在案的认定,则证券交易委员会可以对该人处以民事罚款——

(i)该人正在违反或已经违反本编的任何规定或依据本编发布的任何规则或规章;或

(ii)该人导致或曾经导致违反本编任何规定或依据本编发布的任何规则或规章的行为的发生。”

(b)**联邦证券法律反欺诈条款的域外适用**。——

(1)**《1933年证券法》反欺诈条款的域外适用**。——在《1933年证券法》第22条[《美国法典》第十五编第77v(a)节]结尾处增加如下新子条,作为对该条的修正:

“(c)**域外管辖权**。——对于证券交易委员会或联邦政府针对涉嫌违反第17(a)条并涉及以下行为的涉案人提起的诉讼或程序,联邦地区法院和任何准州的联邦法院均具有管辖权——

(1)在美国境内发生的行为,且该行为属于促成上述违法行为发生的关键因素,

the violation, even if the securities transaction occurs outside the United States and involves only foreign investors; or

"(2) conduct occurring outside the United States that has a foreseeable substantial effect within the United States.".

(2) UNDER THE SECURITIES EXCHANGE ACT OF 1934. — Section 27 of the Securities Exchange Act of 1934 (15 U.S.C.78aa) is amended —

(A) by striking "The district" and inserting the following: "(a) IN GENERAL. — The district"; and

(B) by adding at the end the following new subsection:

"(b) EXTRATERRITORIAL JURISDICTION. — The district courts of the United States and the United States courts of any Territory shall have jurisdiction of an action or proceeding brought or instituted by the Commission or the United States alleging a violation of the antifraud provisions of this title involving —

"(1) conduct within the United States that constitutes significant steps in furtherance of the violation, even if the securities transaction occurs outside the United States and involves only foreign investors; or

"(2) conduct occurring outside the United States that has a foreseeable substantial effect within the United States.".

(3) UNDER THE INVESTMENT ADVISERS ACT OF 1940. — Section 214 of the Investment Advisers Act of 1940 (15 U.S.C.80b-14) is amended —

(A) by striking "The district" and inserting the following:

"(a) IN GENERAL. — The district"; and

(B) by adding at the end the following new subsection:

"(b) EXTRATERRITORIAL JURISDICTION. —The district courts of the United States and the United States courts of any Territory shall have jurisdiction of an action or proceeding brought or instituted by the Commission or the United States alleging a violation of section 206 involving —

"(1) conduct within the United States that constitutes significant steps in furtherance of the violation, even if the violation is committed by a foreign adviser and involves only foreign investors; or

"(2) conduct occurring outside the United States that has a foreseeable substantial effect within the United States.".

(c) CONTROL PERSON LIABILITY UNDER THE SECURITIES EXCHANGE ACT OF 1934. — Section 20(a) of the Securities Exchange Act of 1934 (15 U.S.C.78t(a)) is amended by inserting after "controlled person is liable" the following: "(including to the Commission in any action brought under paragraph (1) or (3) of section 21(d))".

即使证券交易发生在美国境外且仅涉及境外投资者;或

(2)在美国境外发生的对美国境内产生可预见重大影响的行为。”

(2)**《1934年证券交易法》反欺诈条款的域外适用**。——《1934年证券交易法》第27条(《美国法典》第十五编第78aa节)修正如下——

(A)删除“联邦地区法院”,替以“(a)**一般规定**。——联邦地区法院”;及

(B)在结尾处增加如下新子条:

“(b)**域外管辖权**。——对于证券交易委员会或联邦政府针对涉嫌违反本编反欺诈条款并涉及以下行为的涉案人提起的诉讼或程序,联邦地区法院和任何准州的联邦法院均具有管辖权——

(1)在美国境内发生的行为,且该行为属于促成上述违法行为发生的关键因素,即使证券交易发生在美国境外且仅涉及境外投资者;或

(2)在美国境外发生的对美国境内产生可预见重大影响的行为。”

(3)**《1940年投资顾问法》反欺诈条款的域外适用**。——《1940年投资顾问法》第214条(《美国法典》第十五编第80b-14节)修正如下——

(A)删除“联邦地区法院”,替以:

“(a)**一般规定**。——联邦地区法院”;及

(B)在结尾处增加如下新子条:

“(b)**域外管辖权**。——对于证券交易委员会或联邦政府针对涉嫌违反第206条并涉及以下行为的涉案人提起的诉讼或程序,联邦地区法院和任何准州的联邦法院均具有司法管辖权——

(1)在美国境内发生的行为,且该行为属于促成上述违法行为发生的关键因素,即使证券交易发生在美国境外且仅涉及境外投资者;或

(2)在美国境外发生的对美国境内产生可预见重大影响的行为。”

(c)**《1934年证券交易法》中的控制人责任**。——《1934年证券交易法》第20(a)条[《美国法典》第十五编第78t(a)节]修正如下:在“应与被控制人承担相同责任”之后插入“[包括在按照第21(d)条第(1)款或第(3)款提起的诉讼中向证券交易委员会承担责任]”。

SEC.929Q. REVISION TO RECORDKEEPING RULE.

(a) INVESTMENT COMPANY ACT OF 1940 AMENDMENTS. — Section 31 of the Investment Company Act of 1940 (15 U.S.C.80a-30) is amended —

(1) in subsection (a)(1), by adding at the end the following:

"Each person having custody or use of the securities, deposits, or credits of a registered investment company shall maintain and preserve all records that relate to the custody or use by such person of the securities, deposits, or credits of the registered investment company for such period or periods as the Commission, by rule or regulation, may prescribe, as necessary or appropriate in the public interest or for the protection of investors."; and

(2) in subsection (b), by adding at the end the following:

"(4) RECORDS OF PERSONS WITH CUSTODY OR USE. —

"(A)IN GENERAL. — Records of persons having custody or use of the securities, deposits, or credits of a registered investment company that relate to such custody or use, are subject at any time, or from time to time, to such reasonable periodic, special, or other examinations and other information and document requests by representatives of the Commission, as the Commission deems necessary or appropriate in the public interest or for the protection of investors.

"(B) CERTAIN PERSONS SUBJECT TO OTHER REGULATION. —Any person that is subject to regulation and examination by a Federal financial institution regulatory agency (as such term is defined under section 212(c)(2) of title 18, United States Code) may satisfy any examination request, information request, or document request described under subparagraph (A), by providing to the Commission a detailed listing, in writing, of the securities, deposits, or credits of the registered investment company within the custody or use of such person.".

(b)INVESTMENT ADVISERS ACT OF 1940 AMENDMENT. — Section 204 of the Investment Advisers Act of 1940(15 U.S.C.80b-4) is amended by adding at the end the following new subsection:

"(d) RECORDS OF PERSONS WITH CUSTODY OR USE. —

"(1)IN GENERAL. — Records of persons having custody or use of the securities, deposits, or credits of a client, that relate to such custody or use, are subject at any time, or from time to time, to such reasonable periodic, special, or other examinations and other information and document requests by representatives of the Commission, as the Commission deems necessary or appropriate in the public interest or for the protection of investors.

"(2) CERTAIN PERSONS SUBJECT TO OTHER REGULATION. — Any person that is subject to regulation and examination by a Federal financial institution regulatory agency (as such term is defined under section 212(c)(2) of title 18, United States Code) may satisfy any examination request, information request, or document request described under

第929Q条　对记录保存规则的修订

(a)**对《1940年投资公司法》的修正**。——《1940年投资公司法》第31条(《美国法典》第十五编第80a-30节)修正如下——

(1)在第(a)(1)子条结尾处增加如下内容：

"保管或使用注册投资公司的证券、存款或信贷的每一主体均应维持并保存与该等保管或使用相关的所有记录，保存期限以证券交易委员会发布的规则或规章所规定的对维护公共利益或保护投资者确属必要或适当的期限为准"；及

(2)在第(b)子条结尾处增加如下内容：

"(4)**证券存管或使用人的记录**。——

(A)**一般规定**。——存管或使用注册投资公司的证券、存款或信贷的主体，对其拥有的与该等存管和使用相关的记录，应随时或不时地接受证券交易委员会认为对维护公共利益或保护投资者确属必要或适当的合理性定期检查、特别检查或其他检查，并应满足证券交易委员会代表提出的证券交易委员会认为对维护公共利益或保护投资者确属必要或适当的其他信息和文件获取要求。

(B)**受其他机关监管的特定主体**。——受联邦金融机构监管机关[定义见《美国法典》第十八编第212(c)(2)节]监管和检查的任何主体可向证券交易委员会提供一份书面清单，详细列明其存管或使用的该等注册投资公司的证券、存款或信贷，以此满足第(A)子款所述任何检查要求、信息获取要求或文件获取要求。"

(b)**对《1940年投资顾问法》的修正**。——在《1940年投资顾问法》第204条(《美国法典》第十五编第80b-4节)结尾处增加如下新子条，作为对该条的修正：

"(d)**证券存管或使用人的记录**。——

(1)**一般规定**。——存管或使用注册投资公司的证券、存款或信用的主体，对于其拥有的与该等存管和使用相关的记录，应随时或不时地接受证券交易委员会认为对维护公共利益或保护投资者确属必要或适当的合理性定期检查、特别检查或其他检查，并应满足证券交易委员会代表提出的证券交易委员会认为对维护公共利益或保护投资者确属必要或适当的其他信息和文件获取要求。

(2)**受其他机关监管的特定主体**。——受联邦金融机构监管机关[定义见《美国法典》第十八编第212(c)(2)节]监管和检查的任何主体可向证券交易委员会提供一份书面清单，详细列明该人存管或使用的该等注册投资公司的证券、存款或信用，以此满足第(1)款所述任何检查要求、信息获取要求或文件获取要求。"

paragraph (1), by providing the Commission with a detailed listing, in writing, of the securities, deposits, or credits of the client within the custody or use of such person.".

SEC.929R. BENEFICIAL OWNERSHIP AND SHORT-SWING PROFIT REPORTING.

(a) BENEFICIAL OWNERSHIP REPORTING. —Section 13 of the Securities Exchange Act of 1934 (15 U.S.C.78m) is amended —

(1) in subsection (d)(1) —

(A) by inserting after "within ten days after such acquisition" the following: "or within such shorter time as the Commission may establish by rule"; and

(B) by striking "send to the issuer of the security at its principal executive office, by registered or certified mail, send to each exchange where the security is traded, and";

(2) in subsection (d)(2) —

(A) by striking "in the statements to the issuer and the exchange, and"; and

(B) by striking "shall be transmitted to the issuer and the exchange and";

(3) in subsection (g)(1), by striking "shall send to the issuer of the security and"; and

(4) in subsection (g)(2) —

(A) by striking "sent to the issuer and"; and

(B) by striking "shall be transmitted to the issuer and".

(b) SHORT–SWING PROFIT REPORTING.— Section 16(a) of the Securities Exchange Act of 1934 (15 U.S.C.78p(a)) is amended —

(1) in paragraph (1), by striking "(and, if such security is registered on a national securities exchange, also with the exchange)"; and

(2) in paragraph (2)(B), by inserting after "officer" the following: ", or within such shorter time as the Commission may establish by rule".

SEC.929S. FINGERPRINTING.

Section 17 (f)(2) of the Securities Exchange Act of 1934 (15 U.S.C.78q (f)(2)) is amended —

(1) in the first sentence, by striking "and registered clearing agency," and inserting "registered clearing agency, registered securities information processor, national securities exchange, and national securities association"; and

(2) in the second sentence, by striking "or clearing agency," and inserting "clearing agency, securities information processor, national securities exchange, or national securities association,".

SEC.929T. EQUAL TREATMENT OF SELF–REGULATORY ORGANIZATION RULES.

Section 29(a) of the Securities Exchange Act of 1934 (15 U.S.C.78cc(a)) is amended by striking "an exchange required thereby" and inserting "a self–regulatory organization,".

第929R条　受益所有权报告及短线收益报告

(a)**受益所有权报告**。——《1934年证券交易法》第13条(《美国法典》第十五编第78m节)修正如下——

(1)在第(d)(1)子条中——

(A)在"在收购后10天内"之后插入"或在证券交易委员会发布的规则所规定的其他更短的期限内";及

(B)删除"通过挂号或注册邮件向证券发行人的主要办公场所以及交易该证券的每一交易所送达,并";

(2)在第(d)(2)子条中——

(A)删除"提供给发行人和交易所的声明,和";及

(B)删除"应发送给发行人和交易所,并";

(3)在第(g)(1)子条中,删除"应向证券发行人送达,并";及

(4)在第(g)(2)子条中——

(A)删除"向发行人送达,并";及

(B)删除"应发送给发行人及"。

(b)**短线收益报告**。——《1934年证券交易法》第16(a)条[《美国法典》第十五编第78p(a)节]修正如下——

(1)在第(1)款中,删除"(并且,该证券在全国性证券交易所处注册的,还应向该交易所报备说明书)";及

(2)在第(2)(B)款中,在"管理人员"之后插入",或在证券交易委员会发布的规则所规定的其他更短的期限内"。

第929S条　指纹采样

《1934年证券交易法》第17(f)(2)条[《美国法典》第十五编第78q(f)(2)节]修正如下——

(1)在第一句中,删除"及注册结算机构",替以"注册结算机构、注册证券信息处理机构、全国性证券交易所及全国性证券协会";及

(2)在第二句中,删除"或结算机构,",替以"结算机构、证券信息处理机构、全国性证券交易所或全国性证券协会"。

第929T条　平等对待自律组织的规则

《1934年证券交易法》第29(a)条[《美国法典》第十五编第78cc(a)节]修正如下:删除"本编要求的交易所",替以"自律组织"。

SEC.929U. DEADLINE FOR COMPLETING EXAMINATIONS, INSPECTIONS AND ENFORCEMENT ACTIONS.

The Securities Exchange Act of 1934 (15 U.S.C.78a et seq.) is amended by inserting after section 4D the following new section:

"SEC.4E. DEADLINE FOR COMPLETING ENFORCEMENT INVESTIGATIONS AND COMPLIANCE EXAMINATIONS AND INSPECTIONS.

"(a) ENFORCEMENT INVESTIGATIONS.—

"(1) IN GENERAL.—Not later than 180 days after the date on which Commission staff provide a written Wells notification to any person, the Commission staff shall either file an action against such person or provide notice to the Director of the Division of Enforcement of its intent to not file an action.

"(2) EXCEPTIONS FOR CERTAIN COMPLEX ACTIONS.—Notwithstanding paragraph (1), if the Director of the Division of Enforcement of the Commission or the Director's designee determines that a particular enforcement investigation is sufficiently complex such that a determination regarding the filing of an action against a person cannot be completed within the deadline specified in paragraph (1), the Director of the Division of Enforcement of the Commission or the Director's designee may, after providing notice to the Chairman of the Commission, extend such deadline as needed for one additional 180-day period. If after the additional 180-day period the Director of the Division of Enforcement of the Commission or the Director's designee determines that a particular enforcement investigation is sufficiently complex such that a determination regarding the filing of an action against a person cannot be completed within the additional 180-day period, the Director of the Division of Enforcement of the Commission or the Director's designee may, after providing notice to and receiving approval of the Commission, extend such deadline as needed for one or more additional successive 180-day periods.

"(b) COMPLIANCE EXAMINATIONS AND INSPECTIONS.—

"(1) IN GENERAL.— Not later than 180 days after the date on which Commission staff completes the on-site portion of its compliance examination or inspection or receives all records requested from the entity being examined or inspected, whichever is later, Commission staff shall provide the entity being examined or inspected with written notification indicating either that the examination or inspection has concluded, has concluded without findings, or that the staff requests the entity undertake corrective action.

"(2) EXCEPTION FOR CERTAIN COMPLEX ACTIONS.— Notwithstanding paragraph (1), if the head of any division or office within the Commission responsible for compliance examinations and inspections or his designee determines that a particular compliance examination or inspection is sufficiently complex such that a determination regarding concluding the examination or inspection, or regarding the staff requests the entity undertake

第929U条　完成检查、核查和执法行动的期限

《1934年证券交易法》(《美国法典》第十五编第78a节及其后条文)修正如下:在第4D条之后插入如下内容:

"第4E条　完成执法调查、合规检查和核查的期限。

(a)**执法调查**。——

(1)**一般规定**。——证券交易委员会工作人员应在向任何人提供书面韦尔斯通知之日后180天内,针对该人申请采取执法行动,或者将其不申请采取执法行动的意向通知执法部主任。

(2)**特定复杂行动的例外规定**。——无论第(1)款如何规定,如果证券交易委员会执法部主任或其指定人员判定某项执法调查十分复杂,以致无法在第(1)款规定的期限内作出是否申请采取执法行动的判定,则证券交易委员会执法部主任或其指定人员可在通知证券交易委员会主席后,根据需要将该期限延长180天。如果上述180天的延期届满后,证券交易委员会执法部主任或其指定人员判定某项执法调查十分复杂,以致无法在上述180天的延期内作出是否申请采取执法行动的决定,则证券交易委员会执法部主任或其指定人员可在通知证券交易委员会并获其批准后,根据需要将该期限再延长一次或一次以上(每次延长180天)。

(b)**合规检查和审查**。——

(1)**一般规定**。——证券交易委员会工作人员应在完成合规检查或核查的现场环节后180天内,或者在收到受检查或核查实体按证券交易委员会的要求提供的所有记录后180天内(以较晚者为准),向该等实体发出书面通知,说明如下事项:检查或核查已结束;检查或核查已结束但未得出认定结论;或工作人员要求该等实体采取整改措施。

(2)**特定复杂行动的例外规定**。——无论第(1)款如何规定,如果证券交易委员会内负责合规审查和检查的任何部门或办公室的负责人或其指定人员判定某项合规检查或核查工作十分复杂,以致无法在第(1)款规定的期限内作出结束检查或核查工作的判定,或作出要求受检查或核查实体采取整改措施的判定,则证券交易委员会内负责合规审查或检查的部门或办公室的负责人或其指定人员可在通知证券交易委员

corrective action, cannot be completed within the deadline specified in paragraph (1), the head of any division or office within the Commission responsible for compliance examinations and inspections or his designee may, after providing notice to the Chairman of the Commission, extend such deadline as needed for one additional 180–day period.".

SEC.929V. SECURITY INVESTOR PROTECTION ACT AMENDMENTS.

(a) INCREASING THE MINIMUM ASSESSMENT PAID BY SIPC MEMBERS. — Section 4(d)(1)(C) of the Securities Investor Protection Act of 1970 (15 U.S.C.78ddd(d)(1)(C)) is amended by striking "$150 per annum" and inserting the following: "0.02 percent of the gross revenues from the securities business of such member of SIPC".

(b) INCREASING THE FINE FOR PROHIBITED ACTS UNDER SIPA. —Section 14(c) of the Securities Investor Protection Act of 1970 (15 U.S.C.78jjj(c)) is amended—

(1) in paragraph (1), by striking "$50,000" and inserting "$250,000"; and

(2) in paragraph (2), by striking "$50,000" and inserting "$250,000".

(c) PENALTY FOR MISREPRESENTATION OF SIPC MEMBERSHIP OR PROTECTION. — Section 14 of the Securities Investor Protection Act of 1970 (15 U.S.C. 78jjj) is amended by adding at the end the following new subsection:

"(d) MISREPRESENTATION OF SIPC MEMBERSHIP OR PROTECTION. —

"(1) IN GENERAL. — Any person who falsely represents by any means (including, without limitation, through the Internet or any other medium of mass communication), with actual knowledge of the falsity of the representation and with an intent to deceive or cause injury to another, that such person, or another person, is a member of SIPC or that any person or account is protected or is eligible for protection under this Act or by SIPC, shall be liable for any damages caused thereby and shall be fined not more than $250,000 or imprisoned for not more than 5 years.

"(2) INJUNCTIONS. — Any court having jurisdiction of a civil action arising under this Act may grant temporary injunctions and final injunctions on such terms as the court deems reasonable to prevent or restrain any violation of paragraph (1). Any such injunction may be served anywhere in the United States on the person enjoined, shall be operative throughout the United States, and shall be enforceable, by proceedings in contempt or otherwise, by any United States court having jurisdiction over that person. The clerk of the court granting the injunction shall, when requested by any other court in which enforcement of the injunction is sought, transmit promptly to the other court a certified copy of all papers in the case on file in such clerk's office.".

SEC.929W. NOTICE TO MISSING SECURITY HOLDERS.

Section 17A of the Securities Exchange Act of 1934 (15 U.S.C.78q–1) is amended by adding at the end the following new sub section:

会主席后,根据需要将该期限延长180天。”

第929V条　对《证券投资者保护法》的修正

(a)**提高证券投资者保护公司会员的最低计征费金额**。——《1970年证券投资者保护法》第4(d)(1)(C)条[《美国法典》第十五编第78ddd(d)(1)(C)节]修正如下:删除“每年150美元”,替以“该证券投资者保护公司会员证券业务总收入的0.02%”。

(b)**提高针对《证券投资者保护法》所禁止行为的罚款金额**。——《1970年证券投资者保护法》第14(c)条[《美国法典》第十五编第78jjj(c)节]修正如下——

(1)在第(1)款中,删除“5万美元”,替以“25万美元”;及

(2)在第(2)款中,删除“5万美元”,替以“25万美元”。

(c)**针对谎称具有证券投资者保护公司会员资格的行为或谎称有资格获得《证券投资者保护法》保护的行为的处罚**。——在《1970年证券投资者保护法》第14条(《美国法典》第十五编第78jjj节)结尾处增加如下新子条,作为对该条的修正:

“(d)**谎称具有证券投资者保护公司会员资格的行为或谎称有资格获得《证券投资者保护法》保护的行为**。——

(1)**一般规定**。——如果任何人明知所述失实,并出于蓄意欺骗或伤害他人的主观态度,通过任何方式(包括但不限于互联网或任何其他大众传播媒介)谎称自身或任何其他人具有证券投资者保护公司会员身份,或者谎称任何人或账户受或有资格受《证券投资者保护法》或证券投资者保护公司的保护,则该人应对由此造成的损失承担责任,并应处以25万美元以下的罚金或5年以下监禁。

(2)**禁令**。——对依据本法提起的民事诉讼拥有管辖权的任何法院可基于其认为对于防范或限制违反第(1)款的任何行为确属合理的条件,签发临时禁令和最终禁令。任何上述禁令可在美国境内的任何地方向被签发人送达,应在美国全境有效,并应由对该人具有管辖权的任何联邦法院通过藐视法庭程序或其他程序予以强制执行。收到强制执行该禁令请求的任何其他法院提出请求之时,签发该禁令的法院的书记员应立即向上述其他法院提供其办公室内存档的与该案件相关的所有文件的认证复本。”

第929W条　向失去联络的证券持有人发出的通知

在《1934年证券交易法》第17A条(《美国法典》第十五编第78q-1节)结尾处增加如下新子条,作为对该条的修正:

"(g) DUE DILIGENCE FOR THE DELIVERY OF DIVIDENDS, INTEREST, AND OTHER VALUABLE PROPERTY RIGHTS. —

"(1) REVISION OF RULES REQUIRED. — The Commission shall revise its regulations in section 240.17Ad–17 of title 17, Code of Federal Regulations, as in effect on December 8, 1997, to extend the application of such section to brokers and dealers and to provide for the following:

"(A) A requirement that the paying agent provide a single written notification to each missing security holder that the missing security holder has been sent a check that has not yet been negotiated. The written notification may be sent along with a check or other mailing subsequently sent to the missing security holder but must be provided no later than 7 months after the sending of the not yet negotiated check.

"(B) An exclusion for paying agents from the notification requirements when the value of the not yet negotiated check is less than $25.

"(C) A provision clarifying that the requirements described in subparagraph (A) shall have no effect on State escheatment laws.

"(D) For purposes of such revised regulations —

"(i) a security holder shall be considered a 'missing security holder' if a check is sent to the security holder and the check is not negotiated before the earlier of the paying agent sending the next regularly scheduled check or the elapsing of 6 months after the sending of the not yet negotiated check; and

"(ii) the term 'paying agent' includes any issuer, transfer agent, broker, dealer, investment adviser, indenture trustee, custodian, or any other person that accepts payments from the issuer of a security and distributes the payments to the holders of the security.

"(2) RULEMAKING. — The Commission shall adopt such rules, regulations, and orders necessary to implement this subsection no later than 1 year after the date of enactment of this subsection. In proposing such rules, the Commission shall seek to minimize disruptions to current systems used by or on behalf of paying agents to process payment to account holders and avoid requiring multiple paying agents to send written notification to a missing security holder regarding the same not yet negotiated check.".

SEC.929X. SHORT SALE REFORMS.

(a) SHORT SALE DISCLOSURE. — Section 13 (f) of the Securities Exchange Act of 1934 (15 U.S.C.78m(f)) is amended by redesignating paragraphs (2), (3), (4), and (5) as paragraphs (3), (4), (5), and (6), respectively, and inserting after paragraph (1) the following:

"(2) The Commission shall prescribe rules providing for the public disclosure of the name of the issuer and the title, class, CUSIP number, aggregate amount of the number of short sales of each security, and any additional information determined by the Commission

"(g)**对于股息、利息及其他有价财产权的交付的尽职调查**。——

(1)**规则修订要求**。——证券交易委员会应修订《联邦规章汇编》第十七编第240.17Ad－17部分(1997年12月8日有效适用的版本)的规章,将该节适用范围扩大至经纪商和自营商,并作出如下规定:

(A)付款代理人应向失去联络的每一证券持有人发出单个书面通知,说明已向其寄出一张未议付支票。该书面通知可随同支票一并寄出,或随同其后邮寄给该等持有人的其他信函一并寄出,但必须在未议付支票寄出后7个月内提供给该等持有人。

(B)如果上述未议付支票金额小于25美元,则付款代理人不必向遗失证券的原持有人发出上述通知。

(C)对第(A)子款所述要求进行说明的任何规定并不影响各州的充公法。

(D)就上述修订规章而言——

(i)如果支票已寄给证券持有人,而在付款代理人按照正常安排定期寄出下一张支票之前,或者在该未议付支票寄出后届满6个月之前(以较早者为准),该支票仍然未经议付,则该证券持有人应视为'失去联络的证券持有人';且

(ii)'付款代理人'包括任何发行人、过户代理人、经纪商、自营商、投资顾问、契约受托人、存管人或其他接受证券发行人的支付款项并向证券持有人转付的任何人。

(2)**规则制定**。——证券交易委员会应于本子条规定颁布之日后1年内制定必要的规则、规章和命令,以便实施本子条。制定该等规则草案时,证券交易委员会应争取将对付款代理人或其代表用以处理向账户持有人付款的现行制度造成的扰乱减到最低限度,并应争取避免要求多名付款代理人就同一张未议付支票向同一名失去联络的证券持有人发出书面通知。"

第929X条　关于卖空的改革

(a)**关于卖空的披露**。——《1934年证券交易法》第13(f)条[《美国法典》第十五编第78m(f)节]修正如下:第(2)款、第(3)款、第(4)款和第(5)款分别重新编号为第(3)款、第(4)款、第(5)款和第(6)款,并在第(1)款之后插入如下内容:

"(2)证券交易委员会应制定相关规则,规定针对每只证券的卖空交易,应公开披露发行人名称以及证券名称、类别、库斯普编号、总数额以及证券交易委员会在报告期结束后确定的其他额外信息。上述公开披露至少应每月进行一次。"

following the end of the reporting period. At a minimum, such public disclosure shall occur every month.".

(b) SHORT SELLING ENFORCEMENT. — Section 9 of the Securities Exchange Act of 1934 (15 U.S.C.78i) is amended —

(1) by redesignating subsections (d), (e), (f), (g), (h), and (i) as subsections (e), (f), (g), (h), (i), and (j), respectively; and

(2) inserting after subsection (c), the following new subsection:

"(d) TRANSACTIONS RELATING TO SHORT SALES OF SECURITIES. — It shall be unlawful for any person, directly or indirectly, by the use of the mails or any means or instrumentality of interstate commerce, or of any facility of any national securities exchange, or for any member of a national securities exchange to effect, alone or with one or more other persons, a manipulative short sale of any security. The Commission shall issue such other rules as are necessary or appropriate to ensure that the appropriate enforcement options and remedies are available for violations of this subsection in the public interest or for the protection of investors.".

(c) INVESTOR NOTIFICATION. — Section 15 of the Securities Exchange Act of 1934 (15 U.S.C.78o) is amended —

(1) by redesignating subsections (e), (f), (g), (h), and (i) as subsections (f), (g), (h), (i), and (j), respectively; and

(2) inserting after subsection (d) the following new subsection:

"(e) NOTICES TO CUSTOMERS REGARDING SECURITIES LENDING. — Every registered broker or dealer shall provide notice to its customers that they may elect not to allow their fully paid securities to be used in connection with short sales. If a broker or dealer uses a customer's securities in connection with short sales, the broker or dealer shall provide notice to its customer that the broker or dealer may receive compensation in connection with lending the customer's securities. The Commission, by rule, as it deems necessary or appropriate in the public interest and for the protection of investors, may prescribe the form, content, time, and manner of delivery of any notice required under this paragraph.".

SEC.929Y. STUDY ON EXTRATERRITORIAL PRIVATE RIGHTS OF ACTION.

(a) IN GENERAL. — The Securities and Exchange Commission of the United States shall solicit public comment and thereafter conduct a study to determine the extent to which private rights of action under the antifraud provisions of the Securities and Exchange Act of 1934 (15 U.S.C.78u–4) should be extended to cover —

(1) conduct within the United States that constitutes a significant step in the furtherance of the violation, even if the securities transaction occurs outside the United States and involves only foreign investors; and

(b)**关于卖空的执法**。——《1934年证券交易法》第9条(《美国法典》第十五编第78i节)修正如下——

(1)第(d)子条、第(e)子条、第(f)子条、第(g)子条、第(h)子条和第(i)子条分别重新编号为第(e)子条、第(f)子条、第(g)子条、第(h)子条、第(i)子条和第(j)子条;及

(2)在第(c)子条之后插入如下新子条:

"(d)**与证券卖空相关的交易**。——任何人单独或与其他人联合直接或间接使用邮件、任何州际商业手段或工具或任何全国性证券交易所的任何设施对任何证券的卖空交易进行操作的行为,当属违法。全国性证券交易所的任何会员单独或与其他人联合对任何证券的卖空交易进行操作的行为,当属违法。为维护公共利益或保护投资者,证券交易委员会应发布其他必要或适当的规则,确保对于违反本子条规定的行为提供适当的执法选择和救济。"

(c)**向投资者发出通知**。——《1934年证券交易法》第15条(《美国法典》第十五编第78o节)修正如下——

(1)第(e)子条、第(f)子条、第(g)子条、第(h)子条和第(i)子条分别重新编号为第(f)子条、第(g)子条、第(h)子条、第(i)子条和第(j)子条;及

(2)在第(d)子条之后插入以下新子条:

"(e)**向客户发出融券通知**。——所有注册经纪商或自营商均应通知客户其可选择不允许经纪商和自营商将其已全额付款的证券用于卖空交易。如果经纪商或自营商在卖空交易过程中使用客户证券,则该经纪商或自营商应通知该等客户,说明经纪商或自营商可能会因借出该等客户的证券而获得报酬。证券交易委员会可以发布其认为对于维护公共利益和保护投资者确属必要或适当的规则,对本款所规定任何通知的格式、内容、时间和送达方式作出规定。"

第929Y条 关于域外私人诉讼权利的研究

(a)**一般规定**。——证券交易委员会应征求公众意见,并随后开展研究,判定《1934年证券交易法》反欺诈条款(《美国法典》第十五编第78u-4节)赋予的私人诉讼权利在多大程度上应扩展适用于以下行为——

(1)在美国境内发生的行为,且该行为属于促成违法行为发生的关键因素,即使证券交易发生在美国境外且仅涉及境外投资者;及

(2) conduct occurring outside the United States that has a foreseeable substantial effect within the United States.

(b) CONTENTS. — The study shall consider and analyze, among other things —

(1) the scope of such a private right of action, including whether it should extend to all private actors or whether it should be more limited to extend just to institutional investors or otherwise;

(2) what implications such a private right of action would have on international comity;

(3) the economic costs and benefits of extending a private right of action for transnational securities frauds; and

(4) whether a narrower extraterritorial standard should be adopted.

(c) REPORT. — A report of the study shall be submitted and recommendations made to the Committee on Banking, Housing, and Urban Affairs of the Senate and the Committee on Financial Services of the House not later than 18 months after the date of enactment of this Act.

SEC.929Z. GAO STUDY ON SECURITIES LITIGATION.

(a) STUDY. — The Comptroller General of the United States shall conduct a study on the impact of authorizing a private right of action against any person who aids or abets another person in violation of the securities laws. To the extent feasible, this study shall include —

(1) a review of the role of secondary actors in companies issuance of securities;

(2) the courts interpretation of the scope of liability for secondary actors under Federal securities laws after January 14, 2008; and

(3) the types of lawsuits decided under the Private Securities Litigation Act of 1995.

(b) REPORT. — Not later than 1 year after the date of enactment of this Act, the Comptroller General shall submit a report to Congress on the findings of the study required under subsection (a).

Subtitle C—Improvements to the Regulation of Credit Rating Agencies

SEC.931. FINDINGS.

Congress finds the following:

(1) Because of the systemic importance of credit ratings and the reliance placed on credit ratings by individual and institutional investors and financial regulators, the activities and performances of credit rating agencies, including nationally recognized statistical rating organizations, are matters of national public interest, as credit rating agencies are central to capital formation, investor confidence, and the efficient performance of the United States

(2)在美国境外发生的对美国境内产生可预见重大影响的行为。

(b)**内容**。——该研究考察和分析的对象应包括但不限于如下内容——

(1)该私人诉讼权利的范围,包括该私人诉讼权利是否应延伸至所有的私法行为实施人,或该私人诉讼权利是否应缩小适用范围而仅延伸至机构投资者或以其他方式缩小适用范围;

(2)该私人诉讼权利将会对国际礼让产生的影响;

(3)对于跨境证券欺诈行为扩大私人诉讼权利范围将产生的经济成本和收益;及

(4)是否应采用狭义的域外标准。

(c)**报告**。——证券交易委员会应于本法颁布之日后18个月内,将研究报告和建议提交给参议院银行、住房与城市事务委员会及众议院金融服务委员会。

第929Z条　政府问责办公室关于证券诉讼的研究

(a)**研究**。——对于准许对协同或教唆他人从事违反证券法律行为的任何人提起民事诉讼将产生何等影响,政府问责办公室主任应开展研究。在可行的范围内,该项研究应包括如下内容——

(1)评价公司证券发行中次要行为人所发挥的作用;

(2)2008年1月14日之后法院对次要行为人根据联邦证券法律应承担的责任范围进行的解释;及

(3)根据《1995年私人证券诉讼法》裁决的案件类型。

(b)**报告**。——政府问责办公室主任应于本法颁布之日后1年内就第(a)子条所规定研究的认定结论向国会提交报告。

第C子编——完善对信用评级机构的监管

第931条　认定

国会兹作出如下认定:

(1)鉴于信用评级的系统重要性,个人投资者、机构投资者及金融监管者对信用评级的依赖性,以及信用评级机构对资本形成、投资者信心及美国经济的高效运行所具有的核心作用,信用评级机构(包括全国公认统计评级组织)的活动和表现属于事关国家公共利益的事项。

economy.

(2)Credit rating agencies, including nationally recognized statistical rating organizations, play a critical "gatekeeper" role in the debt market that is functionally similar to that of securities analysts, who evaluate the quality of securities in the equity market, and auditors, who review the financial statements of firms. Such role justifies a similar level of public oversight and accountability.

(3) Because credit rating agencies perform evaluative and analytical services on behalf of clients, much as other financial "gatekeepers" do, the activities of credit rating agencies are fundamentally commercial in character and should be subject to the same standards of liability and oversight as apply to auditors, securities analysts, and investment bankers.

(4) In certain activities, particularly in advising arrangers of structured financial products on potential ratings of such products, credit rating agencies face conflicts of interest that need to be carefully monitored and that therefore should be addressed explicitly in legislation in order to give clearer authority to the Securities and Exchange Commission.

(5) In the recent financial crisis, the ratings on structured financial products have proven to be inaccurate. This inaccuracy contributed significantly to the mismanagement of risks by financial institutions and investors, which in turn adversely impacted the health of the economy in the United States and aroundtheworld. Such inaccuracy necessitates increased accountability on the part of credit rating agencies.

SEC.932. ENHANCED REGULATION, ACCOUNTABILITY, AND TRANSPAREN CY OF NATIONALLY RECOGNIZED STATISTICAL RATING ORGANIZATIONS.

(a) IN GENERAL. — Section 15E of the Securities Exchange Act of 1934 (15 U.S.C. 78o-7) is amended —

(1) in subsection (b) —

(A) in paragraph (1)(A), by striking "furnished" and inserting "filed" and by striking "furnishing" and inserting "filing";

(B) in paragraph (1)(B), by striking "furnishing" and inserting "filing"; and

(C) in the first sentence of paragraph (2), by striking "furnish to" and inserting "file with";

(2) in subsection (c) —

(A) in paragraph (2) —

(i) in the second sentence, by inserting "any other provision of this section, or" after "Notwithstanding"; and

(ii) by inserting after the period at the end the following: "Nothing in this paragraph may be construed to afford a defense against any action or proceeding brought by the Commission to enforce the antifraud provisions of the securities laws."; and

(2)信用评级机构(包括全国公认统计评级组织)在债务市场中扮演关键性的“守门员”角色,在职能上与评估股权市场证券质量的证券分析师以及审查公司财务报表的审计师类似。因此,信用评级机构所扮演的上述角色使得有必要让其接受类似水平的公众监督与问责。

(3)与其他金融“守门员”大体类似,信用评级机构为客户提供评估和分析服务,因此,信用评级机构的活动基本属于商业性质,应适用与审计师、证券分析师及投资银行相同的责任和监督标准。

(4)在特定活动中,尤其是在向结构性金融产品策划人提供产品评级建议时,需要对信用评级机构面临的利益冲突进行审慎监控,并应在立法中作出明确规定,从而赋予证券交易委员会更加明确的职权。

(5)近期发生的金融危机证明结构性金融产品的评级有欠准确。该等不准确性在很大程度上导致了金融机构和投资者对风险的管理不善,进而对美国及世界经济的健康发展造成了不利影响。鉴于该等不准确性,有必要加强对信用评级机构的问责管理。

第932条 加强对全国公认统计评级组织的监管、问责并提升其透明度

(a)**一般规定**。——《1934年证券交易法》第15E条(《美国法典》第十五编第78o–7节)修正如下——

(1)在第(b)子条中——

(A)第(1)(A)款删除“提供的”,替以“提交的”,删除“提供”,替以“提交”;

(B)第(1)(B)款删除“提供”,替以“提交”;及

(C)第(2)款第一句删除“提供”,替以“提交”;

(2)在第(c)子条中——

(A)第(2)款——

(i)第二句在“无论”之后插入“本条是否存在任何不同规定,或者”;及

(ii)结尾处的句号之后插入如下内容:“对于证券交易委员会提起的旨在执行证券法律中的反欺诈条款的任何诉讼或程序,本款任何内容均不得被解释为对该等诉讼或程序构成抗辩。”;及

(B) by adding at the end the following:

"(3) INTERNAL CONTROLS OVER PROCESSES FOR DETERMINING CREDIT RATINGS.—

"(A) IN GENERAL.— Each nationally recognized statistical rating organization shall establish, maintain, enforce, and document an effective internal control structure governing the implementation of and adherence to policies, procedures, and methodologies for determining credit ratings, taking into consideration such factors as the Commission may prescribe, by rule.

"(B) ATTESTATION REQUIREMENT.— The Commission shall prescribe rules requiring each nationally recognized statistical rating organization to submit to the Commission an annual internal controls report, which shall contain—

"(i) a description of the responsibility of the management of the nationally recognized statistical rating organization in establishing and maintaining an effective internal control structure under subparagraph (A);

"(ii) an assessment of the effectiveness of the internal control structure of the nationally recognized statistical rating organization; and

"(iii) the attestation of the chief executive officer, or equivalent individual, of the nationally recognized statistical rating organization.";

(3) in subsection (d)—

(A) by inserting after "or revoke the registration of any nationally recognized statistical rating organization" the following: ", or with respect to any person who is associated with, who is seeking to become associated with, or, at the time of the alleged misconduct, who was associated or was seeking to become associated with a nationally recognized statistical rating organization, the Commission, by order, shall censure, place limitations on the activities or functions of such person, suspend for a period not exceeding 1 year, or bar such person from being associated with a nationally recognized statistical rating organization,";

(B) by inserting "bar" after "placing of limitations, suspension,";

(C) in paragraph (2), by striking "furnished to" and inserting "filed with";

(D) in paragraph (2), by redesignating subparagraphs (A) and (B) as clauses (i) and (ii), respectively, and adjusting the clause margins accordingly;

(E) by redesignating paragraphs (1) through (5) as subparagraphs (A) through (E), respectively, and adjusting the subparagraph margins accordingly;

(F) in the matter preceding subparagraph (A), as so redesignated, by striking "The Commission" and inserting the following:

"(1) IN GENERAL.—The Commission";

(G) in subparagraph (D), as so redesignated—

(i) by striking "furnish" and inserting "file"; and

(B)结尾处增加如下内容：

“(3)**针对信用评级确定程序的内部控制**。——

(A)**一般规定**。——每一全国公认统计评级组织均应在考虑证券交易委员会发布的规则中规定的因素基础上，就信用评级确定之政策、程序和方法的实施和遵守，建立、维持和执行有效的内部控制结构，并形成书面文件。

(B)**证明要求**。——证券交易委员会应制定规则，要求每一全国公认统计评级组织向其提交年度内部控制报告。该等报告应包含——

(i)关于全国公认统计评级组织的管理人员在根据第(A)子款规定建立并维持有效内部控制结构时所承担责任的说明；

(ii)关于全国公认统计评级组织内部控制结构有效性的评估；及

(iii)全国公认统计评级组织的首席执行官或同等职位人士作出的证明。”；

(3)在第(d)子条中——

(A)在“或撤销任何全国公认统计评级组织的注册”之后插入如下内容：“，或对于当前具有全国公认统计评级组织业务相关人身份的任何人，或正在寻求与该等组织建立业务相关关系的任何人而言，或者对于在被指控的不当行为发生时，具有全国公认统计评级组织业务相关人身份的任何人，或正在寻求与该等组织建立业务相关关系的任何人而言，证券交易委员会应发布命令予以谴责，对上述人的活动或职能设定限制，暂停其与全国公认统计评级组织的业务相关关系(暂停期不超过一年)，或禁止其与全国公认统计评级组织存在业务相关关系，”；

(B)在“设定限制、暂停、”之后插入“禁止”；

(C)第(2)款删除“向……提供”，替以“向……提交”；

(D)在第(2)款中，第(A)子款和第(B)子款分别重新编号为第(i)项和第(ii)项，并相应调整每项的缩进距离；

(E)第(1)款至第(5)款分别重新编号为第(A)子款至第(E)子款，并相应调整每一子款的缩进距离；

(F)第(A)子款(以重新编号后的序号为准)之前的内容删除“证券交易委员会”，替以如下内容：

“(1)**一般规定**。——证券交易委员会”；

(G)在第(D)子款(以重新编号后的序号为准)中，——

(i)删除“提供”，替以“提交”；及

(ii) by striking "or" at the end.

(H) in subparagraph (E), as so redesignated, by striking the period at the end and inserting a semicolon; and

(I) by adding at the end the following:

"(F) has failed reasonably to supervise, with a view to preventing a violation of the securities laws, an individual who commits such a violation, if the individual is subject to the supervision of that person.

"(2) SUSPENSION OR REVOCATION FOR PARTICULAR CLASS OF SECURITIES. —

"(A) IN GENERAL. — The Commission may temporarily suspend or permanently revoke the registration of a nationally recognized statistical rating organization with respect to a particular class or subclass of securities, if the Commission finds, on the record after notice and opportunity for hearing, that the nationally recognized statistical rating organization does not have adequate financial and managerial resources to consistently produce credit ratings with integrity.

"(B) CONSIDERATIONS. — In making any determination under subparagraph (A), the Commission shall consider —

"(i) whether the nationally recognized statistical rating organization has failed over a sustained period of time, as determined by the Commission, to produce ratings that are accurate for that class or subclass of securities; and

"(ii) such other factors as the Commission may determine.";

(4) in subsection (h), by adding at the end the following:

"(3) SEPARATION OF RATINGS FROM SALES AND MARKETING. —

"(A) RULES REQUIRED. — The Commission shall issue rules to prevent the sales and marketing considerations of a nationally recognized statistical rating organization from influencing the production of ratings by the nationally recognized statistical rating organization.

"(B) CONTENTS OF RULES. — The rules issued under subparagraph (A) shall provide for —

"(i) exceptions for small nationally recognized statistical rating organizations with respect to which the Commission determines that the separation of the production of ratings and sales and marketing activities is not appropriate; and

"(ii) suspension or revocation of the registration of a nationally recognized statistical rating organization, if the Commission finds, on the record, after notice and opportunity for a hearing, that —

"(I) the nationally recognized statistical rating organization has committed a violation of a rule issued under this subsection; and

(ii)删除结尾处的“或”。

(H)在第(E)子款(以重新编号后的序号为准)中,删除结尾处的句号,替以分号;及

(I)在结尾处增加如下内容:

“(F)未能对受其领导监管的个人进行旨在防范违反证券法律行为发生的合理领导监管,以至于该个人实施上述违法行为。

(2)**针对特定类别的证券,暂停或撤销全国公认统计评级组织的注册资格**。——

(A)**一般规定**。——如果证券交易委员会在发出通知并提供听证机会后,在记录在案的基础上认定全国公认统计评级组织缺乏持续进行诚信信用评级的充足财务和管理资源,则证券交易委员会可以针对特定类别或子类别的证券,暂停或永久撤销该全国公认统计评级组织的注册资格。

(B)**考虑因素**。——在根据第(A)子款作出任何判定时,证券交易委员会均应考虑如下因素——

(i)全国公认统计评级组织是否曾在证券交易委员会确定的某一持续期间内,未对该类别或子类别证券作出准确评级;及

(ii)证券交易委员会确定的其他因素。”;

(4)在第(h)子条结尾处增加如下内容:

“(3)**评级与销售和营销的分离**。——

(A)**规则发布要求**。——证券交易委员会应发布规则,防止全国公认统计评级组织的销售及营销考虑因素对其评级行为造成影响。

(B)**规则内容**。——根据第(A)子款发布的规则应作出如下规定——

(i)对于证券交易委员会判定不宜将评级行为与销售营销活动相分离的小型全国公认统计评级组织,应适用例外规定;及

(ii)如果证券交易委员会在发出通知并提供听证机会后,作出如下记录在案的认定,则应暂停或撤销全国公认统计评级组织的注册——

(I)全国公认统计评级组织实施了违反依据本子条所发布规则的行为规则;且

"(II) the violation of a rule issued under this subsection affected a rating.

"(4) LOOK-BACK REQUIREMENT. —

"(A)REVIEW BY THE NATIONALLY RECOGNIZED STATISTICAL RATING ORGANIZATION. —Each nationally recognized statistical rating organization shall establish, maintain, and enforce policies and procedures reasonably designed to ensure that, in any case in which an employee of a person subject to a credit rating of the nationally recognized statistical rating organization or the issuer, underwriter, or sponsor of a security or money m arket instrument subject to a credit rating of the nationally recognized statistical rating organization was employed by the nationally recognized statistical rating organization and participated in any capacity in determining credit ratings for the person or the securities or money market instruments during the 1-year period preceding the date an action was taken with respect to the credit rating, the nationally recognized statistical rating organization shall—

"(i) conduct a review to determine whether any conflicts of interest of the employee influenced the credit rating; and

"(ii) take action to revise the rating if appropriate, in accordance with such rules as the Commission shall prescribe.

"(B) REVIEW BY COMMISSION. —

"(i) IN GENERAL. — The Commission shall conduct periodic reviews of the policies described in subparagraph (A) and the implementation of the policies at each nationally recognized statistical rating organization to ensure they are reasonably designed and implemented to most effectively eliminate conflicts of interest.

"(ii) TIMING OF REVIEWS. — The Commission shall review the code of ethics and conflict of interest policy of each nationally recognized statistical rating organization —

"(I) not less frequently than annually; and

"(II) whenever such policies are materially modified or amended.

"(5) REPORT TO COMMISSION ON CERTAIN EMPLOYMENT TRANSITIONS. —

"(A) REPORT REQUIRED. — Each nationally recognized statistical rating organization shall report to the Commission any case such organization knows or can reasonably be expected to know where a person associated with such organization within the previous 5 years obtains employment with any obligor, issuer, underwriter, or sponsor of a security or money market instrument for which the organization issued a credit rating during the 12-month period prior to such employment, if such employee —

"(i) was a senior officer of such organization;

"(ii) participated in any capacity in determining credit ratings for such obligor, issuer, underwriter, or sponsor; or

"(iii) supervised an employee described in clause (ii).

"(B) PUBLIC DISCLOSURE. — Upon receiving such a report, the Commission shall

(II)违反依据本子条所发布规则的上述行为对评级造成了影响。

(4)**回顾要求**。——

(A)**全国公认统计评级组织的审查**。——每一全国公认统计评级组织均应制定、维持并实施设计合理的政策和程序,以确保:如果被该等全国公认统计评级组织做出信用评级的主体的雇员,或者被该等全国公认统计评级组织做出信用评级的证券或货币市场工具的发行人、承销商或保荐人的雇员,在该等全国公认统计评级组织对上述信用评级采取行动之日前1年内曾被该全国公认统计评级组织所雇用,并曾以任何身份参与对该等主体或者证券或货币市场工具的信用评级,则该等全国公认统计评级组织应——

(i)开展审查,以判定该等雇员引起的任何利益冲突是否对信用评级造成了影响;及

(ii)在适当情况下,按照证券交易委员会制定的规则采取修改评级的行动。

(B)**证券交易委员会的审查**。——

(i)**一般规定**。——证券交易委员会应定期审查第(A)子款所述政策以及每一全国公认统计评级组织对该等政策的实施情况,以确保该等政策的设计和实施具有合理性,可以最有效地消除利益冲突。

(ii)**审查时间**。——证券交易委员会应按照如下规定审查每一全国公认统计评级组织的职业道德准则和利益冲突处理政策——

(I)审查频率不得低于每年一次;且

(II)每当该等政策发生重大修改或修正时均应进行审查。

(5)**向证券交易委员会报告特定雇佣关系转变情形**。——

(A)**报告提交要求**。——如果任何全国公认统计评级组织知晓或据合理预期理应知晓,在过去5年内与其存在业务相关关系的任何人被证券或货币市场工具的任何债务人、发行人、承销商或保荐人所雇佣,而该等组织组织曾在上述雇佣关系发生前12个月内对该等债务人、发行人、承销商或保荐人做出信用评级,并且上述人存在如下情形,则该等组织应向证券交易委员会报告该等情形——

(i)曾担任该等组织的高级管理人员;

(ii)曾以任何身份参与确定该等债务人、发行人、承销商或保荐人的信用评级;或

(iii)曾负责对第(ii)项所述雇员进行领导监督。

(B)**公开披露**。——证券交易委员会应在收到上述报告后公开上述信息。”;

make such information publicly available.";

(5) in subsection (j) —

(A) by striking "Each" and inserting the following:

"(1) IN GENERAL. -Each"; and

(B) by adding at the end the following:

"(2) LIMITATIONS. —

"(A)IN GENERAL. —Except as provided in subparagraph (B), an individual designated under paragraph (1) may not, while serving in the designated capacity —

"(i) perform credit ratings;

"(ii) participate in the development of ratings methodologies or models;

"(iii) perform marketing or sales functions; or

"(iv) participate in establishing compensation levels, other than for employees working for that individual.

"(B)EXCEPTION. — The Commission may exempt a small nationally recognized statistical rating organization from the limitations under this paragraph, if the Commission finds that compliance with such limitations would impose an unreasonable burden on the nationally recognized statistical rating organization.

"(3)OTHER DUTIES. —Each individual designated under paragraph (1) shall establish procedures for the receipt, retention, and treatment of —

"(A) complaints regarding credit ratings, models, methodologies, and compliance with the securities laws and the policies and procedures developed under this section; and

"(B) confidential, anonymous complaints by employees or users of credit ratings.

"(4) COMPENSATION. — The compensation of each compliance officer appointed under paragraph (1) shall not be linked to the financial performance of the nationally recognized statistical rating organization and shall be arranged so as to ensure the independence of the officer's judgment.

"(5) ANNUAL REPORTS REQUIRED. —

"(A) ANNUAL REPORTS REQUIRED. — Each individual designated under paragraph (1) shall submit to the nationally recognized statistical rating organization an annual report on the compliance of the nationally recognized statistical rating organization with the securities laws and the policies and procedures of the nationally recognized statistical rating organization that includes —

"(i) a description of any material changes to the code of ethics and conflict of interest policies of the nationally recognized statistical rating organization; and

"(ii) a certification that the report is accurate and complete.

"(B) SUBMISSION OF REPORTS TO THE COMMISSION. — Each nationally recognized statistical rating organization shall file the reports required under subparagraph

(5)在第(j)子条中——

(A)删除“每一”,替以如下内容:

“(1)**一般规定**。——每一”;及

(B)在结尾处增加如下内容:

“(2)**限制**。——

(A)**一般规定**。——除第(B)子款规定的情形外,根据第(1)款规定指定的个人不得在担任指定职务期间——

(i)进行信用评级;

(ii)参与评级方法或模型的开发;

(iii)履行营销或销售职能;或

(iv)参与薪酬水平(但为其工作的雇员的薪酬水平除外)的设定。

(B)**例外规定**。——如果证券交易委员会认定遵守本款规定的限制将对小型全国公认统计评级组织造成不合理负担,则证券交易委员会可以向该等小型全国公认统计评级组织授予豁免,使其不必遵守该等限制。

(3)**其他职责**。——根据第(1)款指定的每一个人均应制定受理、保留和处理以下投诉的程序——

(A)与信用评级、模型、方法、对证券法律及依据本条制定的政策和程序的遵守情况相关的投诉;及

(B)雇员或信用评级用户的保密性、匿名投诉。

(4)**薪酬**。——根据第(1)款任命的每一名合规官的薪酬均不得与全国公认统计评级组织的财务绩效挂钩,但是应进行相应安排,以确保合规官判断的独立性。

(5)**年度报告提交要求**。——

(A)**年度报告提交要求**。——根据第(1)款指定的每一名个人均应向全国公认统计评级组织提交年度报告,汇报全国公认统计评级组织对证券法律及其自身政策和程序的遵守情况,包括——

(i)关于全国公认统计评级组织的职业道德准则和利益冲突处理政策所发生任何重大变更的说明;及

(ii)关于该等报告准确性和完整性的证明。

(B)**向证券交易委员会提交报告**。——每一全国公认统计评级组织均应提交第(A)子款所规定报告,同时一并提交依本条规定应向证券交易委员会提交的财务

(A) together with the financial report that is required to be submitted to the Commission under this section.";

(6) in subsection (k), by striking "furnish to" and inserting "file with";

(7) in subsection (l)(2)(A)(i), by striking "furnished" and inserting "filed"; and

(8) by striking subsection (p) and inserting the following:

"(p) REGULATION OF NATIONALLY RECOGNIZED STATISTICAL RATING ORGANIZATIONS.—

"(1) ESTABLISHMENT OF OFFICE OF CREDIT RATINGS.—

"(A) OFFICE ESTABLISHED. — The Commission shall establish within the Commission an Office of Credit Ratings (referred to in this subsection as the 'Office') to administer the rules of the Commission —

"(i) with respect to the practices of nationally recognized statistical rating organizations in determining ratings, for the protection of users of credit ratings and in the public interest;

"(ii) to promote accuracy in credit ratings issued by nationally recognized statistical rating organizations; and

"(iii) to ensure that such ratings are not unduly influenced by conflicts of interest.

"(B) DIRECTOR OF THE OFFICE. — The head of the Office shall be the Director, who shall report to the Chairman.

"(2) STAFFING. — The Office established under this subsection shall be staffed sufficiently to carry out fully the requirements of this section. The staff shall include persons with knowledge of and expertise in corporate, municipal, and structured debt finance.

"(3) COMMISSION EXAMINATIONS.—

"(A) ANNUAL EXAMINATIONS REQUIRED.—The Office shall conduct an examination of each nationally recognized statistical rating organization at least annually.

"(B) CONDUCT OF EXAMINATIONS. — Each examination under subparagraph (A) shall include a review of —

"(i) whether the nationally recognized statistical rating organization conducts business in accordance with the policies, procedures, and rating methodologies of the nationally recognized statistical rating organization;

"(ii) the management of conflicts of interest by the nationally recognized statistical rating organization;

"(iii) implementation of ethics policies by the nationally recognized statistical rating organization;

"(iv) the internal supervisory controls of the nationally recognized statistical rating organization;

"(v) the governance of the nationally recognized statistical rating organization;

"(vi) the activities of the individual designated by the nationally recognized statistical

报告。”;

(6)第(k)子条,删除“提供”,替以“提交”;

(7)第(l)(2)(A)(i)子条,删除“提供的”,替以“提交的”;及

(8)删除第(p)子条,替以如下内容:

“(p)**对全国公认统计评级组织的监管**。——

(1)**设立信用评级办公室**。——

(A)**信用评级办公室的设立**。——证券交易委员会应下设信用评级办公室(信用评级办公室),负责出于以下目的实施与全国公认统计评级组织确定评级的惯例相关的证券交易委员会规则——

(i)保护信用评级用户,维护公共利益;

(ii)提高全国公认统计评级组织发布的信用评级的准确性;并

(iii)确保该等评级不会受到利益冲突的不当影响;

(B)**信用评级办公室主任**。——信用评级办公室的负责人应为信用评级办公室主任。信用评级办公室主任应向证券交易委员会主席汇报工作。

(2)**工作人员**。——根据本子条设立的信用评级办公室应配备人数充足的工作人员,以全面实施本条规定。所配备人员中应包含具有企业、市政及结构性债券融资方面的知识和专长的人员。

(3)**证券交易委员会进行的检查**。——

(A)**年度检查要求**。——信用评级办公室应至少每年对每一全国公认统计评级组织开展一次检查工作。

(B)**检查工作的开展**。——第(A)子款所述每次检查应包括对以下各方面的审查——

(i)全国公认统计评级组织开展业务时是否遵循其自有的政策、程序和评级方法;

(ii)全国公认统计评级组织对利益冲突的管理情况;

(iii)全国公认统计评级组织对职业道德政策的实施情况;

(iv)全国公认统计评级组织的内部监督控制;

(v)全国公认统计评级组织的治理;

(vi)全国公认统计评级组织根据第(j)(1)子条指定的个人活动;

rating organization under subsection (j)(1);

"(vii) the processing of complaints by the nationally recognized statistical rating organization; and

"(viii) the policies of the nationally recognized statistical rating organization governing the post–employment activities of former staff of the nationally recognized statistical rating organization.

"(C) INSPECTION REPORTS. — The Commission shall make available to the public, in an easily understandable format, an annual report summarizing —

"(i) the essential findings of all examinations conducted under subparagraph (A), as deemed appropriate by the Commission;

"(ii) the responses by the nationally recognized statistical rating organizations to any material regulatory deficiencies identified by the Commission under clause (i); and

"(iii) whether the nationally recognized statistical rating organizations have appropriately addressed the recommendations of the Commission contained in previous reports under this subparagraph.

"(4) RULEMAKING AUTHORITY. — The Commission shall —

"(A) establish, by rule, fines, and other penalties applicable to any nationally recognized statistical rating organization that violates the requirements of this section and the rules thereunder; and

"(B) issue such rules as may be necessary to carry out this section.

"(q) TRANSPARENCY OF RATINGS PERFORMANCE. —

"(1) RULEMAKING REQUIRED. — The Commission shall, by rule, require that each nationally recognized statistical rating organization publicly disclose information on the initial credit ratings determined by the nationally recognized statistical rating organization for each type of obligor, security, and money market instrument, and any subsequent changes to such credit ratings, for the purpose of allowing users of credit ratings to evaluate the accuracy of ratings and compare the performance of ratings by different nationally recognized statistical rating organizations.

"(2) CONTENT. — The rules of the Commission under this subsection shall require, at a minimum, disclosures that —

"(A) are comparable among nationally recognized statistical rating organizations, to allow users of credit ratings to compare the performance of credit ratings across nationally recognized statistical rating organizations;

"(B) are clear and informative for investors having a wide range of sophistication who use or might use credit ratings;

"(C) include performance information over a range of years and for a variety of types of credit ratings, including for credit ratings withdrawn by the nationally recognized statistical

(vii)全国公认统计评级组织对投诉的处理情况;及

(viii)全国公认统计评级组织对前任工作人员离职后的活动所制定的政策。

(C)**检查报告**。——证券交易委员会应以简明易懂的格式向公众提供一份年度报告,对以下内容作出总结——

(i)根据第(A)子款开展的所有检查得出的证券交易委员会认为确属适当的基本认定结论;

(ii)对于证券交易委员会在根据第(i)项确定的任何重大监管不足,全国公认统计评级组织作出的回应;及

(iii)对于证券交易委员会之前依本子款发布的报告中提出的建议,全国公认统计评级组织是否已进行了适当处理。

(4)**规则制定权**。——证券交易委员会应——

(A)发布规则,针对违反本条规定及依据本条颁发的规则的任何全国公认统计评级组织设定罚款及其他处罚;并

(B)发布必要规则,以实施本条规定。

(q)**评级绩效的透明性**。——

(1)**规则制定要求**。——证券交易委员会应发布规则,要求各全国公认统计评级组织针对其对每类债务人、证券及货币市场工具作出的初始信用评级以及该等信用评级的任何后续变更,公开披露相关信息,以便信用评级用户评估评级的准确性,并对不同全国公认统计评级组织的评级绩效进行比较。

(2)**内容**。——证券交易委员会根据本子条发布规则,要求各全国公认统计评级组织进行披露时,至少应达到如下效果——

(A)使各全国公认统计评级组织进行的披露具有可比性,以便信用评级用户对不同全国公认统计评级组织的信用评级绩效进行比较;

(B)对于使用或可能使用信用评级的经验丰富的投资者而言,披露信息应具有明确性和切实性;

(C)披露信息中应包含多年期间内各类信用评级(包括全国公认统计评级组织已撤销的信用评级)的绩效信息;

rating organization;

"(D) are published and made freely available by the nationally recognized statistical rating organization, on an easily accessible portion of its website, and in writing, when requested;

"(E) are appropriate to the business model of a nationally recognized statistical rating organization; and

"(F) each nationally recognized statistical rating organization include an attestation with any credit rating it issues affirming that no part of the rating was influenced by any other business activities, that the rating was based solely on the merits of the instruments being rated, and that such rating was an independent evaluation of the risks and merits of the instrument.

"(r) CREDIT RATINGS METHODOLOGIES. — The Commission shall prescribe rules, for the protection of investors and in the public interest, with respect to the procedures and methodologies, including qualitative and quantitative data and models, used by nationally recognized statistical rating organizations that require each nationally recognized statistical rating organization —

"(1) to ensure that credit ratings are determined using procedures and methodologies, including qualitative and quantitative data and models, that are —

"(A) approved by the board of the nationally recognized statistical rating organization, a body performing a function similar to that of a board; and

"(B) in accordance with the policies and procedures of the nationally recognized statistical rating organization for the development and modification of credit rating procedures and methodologies;

"(2) to ensure that when material changes to credit rating procedures and methodologies (including changes to qualitative and quantitative data and models) are made, that —

"(A) the changes are applied consistently to all credit ratings to which the changed procedures and methodologies apply;

"(B) to the extent that changes are made to credit rating surveillance procedures and methodologies, the changes are applied to then-current credit ratings by the nationally recognized statistical rating organization within a reasonable time period determined by the Commission, by rule; and

"(C) the nationally recognized statistical rating organization publicly discloses the reason for the change; and

"(3) to notify users of credit ratings —

"(A) of the version of a procedure or methodology, including the qualitative methodology or quantitative inputs, used with respect to a particular credit rating;

(D)披露信息应由全国公认统计评级组织通过其网站中易于访问的网页发布,公众可自由获取,且如公众提出请求,还应以书面形式提供;

(E)披露信息对全国公认统计评级组织的商业模式而言应确属适当;且

(F)每一全国公认统计评级组织均应对其发布的所有信用评级提供证明,确认评级任何部分均未受到任何其他业务活动影响,评级完全基于被评级工具的实质价值而作出,并且该等评级属于对该等工具的风险及实质价值进行的独立评估。

(r)**信用评级方法**。——证券交易委员会应出于保护投资者和维护公共利益的目的,就全国公认统计评级组织使用的程序和方法(包括定性和定量数据及模型)制定规则,要求每一全国公认统计评级组织——

(1)确保其确定信用评级时采用符合如下条件的程序和方法(包括定性和定量数据及模型)——

(A)已获得全国公认统计评级组织董事会或履行董事会类似职能的机构批准;且

(B)符合全国公认统计评级组织关于制定和修改信用评级程序和方法的政策及程序;

(2)确保在对信用评级程序和方法(包括定性和定量数据及模型)作出重大变更时——

(A)变更后的程序和方法统一适用于所有的信用评级;

(B)如果信用评级监测程序和方法发生变更,全国公认统计评级组织在证券交易委员会在其发布的规则中所确定的合理期间内,将该等变更适用于届时有效的信用评级;且

(C)全国公认统计评级组织公开披露变更的原因;并

(3)将下述内容通知信用评级用户,或在下述时间向信用评级用户发出通知——

(A)对于特定信用评级所使用的程序或方法(包括定性方法或定量值输入)的版本;

"(B) when a material change is made to a procedure or methodology, including to a qualitative model or quantitative inputs;

"(C) when a significant error is identified in a procedure or methodology, including a qualitative or quantitative model, that may result in credit rating actions; and

"(D) of the likelihood of a material change described in subparagraph (B) resulting in a change in current credit ratings.

"(s) TRANSPARENCY–OF CREDIT RATING METHODOLOGIES AND INFORMATION REVIEWED. —

"(1) FORM FOR DISCLOSURES. — The Commission shall require, by rule, each nationally recognized statistical rating organization to prescribe a form to accompany the publication of each credit rating that discloses —

"(A) information relating to —

"(i) the assumptions underlying the credit rating procedures and methodologies;

"(ii) the data that was relied on to determine the credit rating; and

"(iii) if applicable, how the nationally recognized statistical rating organization used servicer or remittance reports, and with what frequency, to conduct surveillance of the credit rating; and

"(B) information that can be used by investors and other users of credit ratings to better understand credit ratings in each class of credit rating issued by the nationally recognized statistical rating organization.

"(2) FORMAT. — The form developed under paragraph (1) shall —

"(A) be easy to use and helpful for users of credit ratings to understand the information contained in the report;

"(B) require the nationally recognized statistical rating organization to provide the content described in paragraph (3)(B) in a manner that is directly comparable across types of securities; and

"(C) be made readily available to users of credit ratings, in electronic or paper form, as the Commission may, by rule, determine.

"(3) CONTENT OF FORM. —

"(A) QUALITATIVE CONTENT. — Each nationally recognized statistical rating organization shall disclose on the form developed under paragraph (1) —

"(i) the credit ratings produced by the nationally recognized statistical rating organization;

"(ii) the main assumptions and principles used in constructing procedures and methodologies, including qualitative methodologies and quantitative inputs and assumptions about the correlation of defaults across underlying assets used in rating structured products;

"(iii) the potential limitations of the credit ratings, and the types of risks excluded from

(B)程序或方法(包括定性模型或定量值输入)发生重大变更之时;

(C)程序或方法(包括定性或定量模型)被发现存在可能导致信用评级被采取行动的重大错误之时;及

(D)第(B)子款所述重大变更导致当前信用评级发生变更的可能性。

(s)**信用评级方法及审查信息的透明度**。——

(1)**信息披露的标准格式书表格**。——证券交易委员会应发布规则,要求每一全国公认统计评级组织针对披露以下信息的每一信用评级的发布制定标准格式书——

(A)与以下各项相关的信息——

(i)信用评级程序和方法所基于的假设;

(ii)确定信用评级时所采信的数据;及

(iii)全国公认统计评级组织开展信用评级监测时对服务机构或汇款报告的利用方式及频率(如适用);及

(B)有助于投资者及其他信用评级用户更好地了解全国公认统计评级组织发布的每类信用评级中信用评级的信息。

(2)**格式**。——根据第(1)款制定的标准格式书应——

(A)便于使用,并有助于信用评级用户理解报告中包含的信息;

(B)要求全国公认统计评级组织按照可以对各类证券直接进行对比的方式提供第(3)(B)款所述内容;并

(C)通过电子或纸质形式(具体由证券交易委员会在其发布的规则中确定)向信用评级用户便利地提供。

(3)**标准格式书的内容**。——

(A)**定性内容**。——每一全国公认统计评级组织均应通过根据第(1)款制定的标准格式书披露——

(i)全国公认统计评级组织作出的信用评级;

(ii)构建程序和方法时使用的主要假设和原则,包括定性方法、定量输入以及关于结构性产品评级中使用的各类基础资产之间违约相关性的假设;

(iii)信用评级的潜在限制,以及全国公认统计评级组织未予置评的被排除在信用

the credit ratings that the nationally recognized statistical rating organization does not comment on, including liquidity, market, and other risks;

"(iv) information on the uncertainty of the credit rating, including —

"(I) information on the reliability, accuracy, and quality of the data relied on in determining the credit rating; and

"(II) a statement relating to the extent to which data essential to the determination of the credit rating were reliable or limited, including —

"(aa) any limits on the scope of historical data; and

"(bb) any limits in accessibility to certain documents or other types of information that would have better informed the credit rating;

"(v) whether and to what extent third party due diligence services have been used by the nationally recognized statistical rating organization, a description of the information that such third party reviewed in conducting due diligence services, and a description of the findings or conclusions of such third party;

"(vi) a description of the data about any obligor, issuer, security, or money market instrument that were relied upon for the purpose of determining the credit rating;

"(vii) a statement containing an overall assessment of the quality of information available and considered in producing a rating for an obligor, security, or money market instrument, in relation to the quality of information available to the nationally recognized statistical rating organization in rating similar issuances;

"(viii) information relating to conflicts of interest of the nationally recognized statistical rating organization; and

"(ix) such additional information as the Commission may require.

"(B) QUANTITATIVE CONTENT. —Each nationally recognized statistical rating organization shall disclose on the form developed under this subsection —

"(i) an explanation or measure of the potential volatility of the credit rating, including —

"(I) any factors that might lead to a change in the credit ratings; and

"(II) the magnitude of the change that a user can expect under different market conditions;

"(ii) information on the content of the rating, including —

"(I) the historical performance of the rating; and

"(II) the expected probability of default and the expected loss in the event of default;

"(iii) information on the sensitivity of the rating to assumptions made by the nationally recognized statistical rating organization, including —

"(I) 5 assumptions made in the ratings process that, without accounting for any other factor, would have the greatest impact on a rating if the assumptions were proven false or inaccurate; and

评级之外的风险类型(包括流动性风险、市场风险及其他风险);

(iv)与信用评级不确定性相关的信息,包括——

(I)确定信用评级时所采信的数据之可靠性、准确性和质量的信息;及

(II)关于确定信用评级时所必不可少数据的可靠程度或限制程度的声明,包括——

(aa)历史数据的任何范围限制;及

(bb)本应为信用评级提供更充分依据的特定文件或其他类型信息之可获取性的任何限制;

(v)全国公认统计评级组织是否使用以及在多大范围内使用第三方尽职调查服务、关于该等第三方在开展尽职调查服务中所审查信息的说明、及关于该等第三方所作出认定或结论的说明;

(vi)关于为了确定信用评级之目的而采信的与任何债务人、发行人、证券或货币市场工具相关的数据的说明;

(vii)对债务人、证券或货币市场工具进行评级时所使用并考虑的信息之质量(相对于全国公认统计评级组织在对类似发行进行评级时所使用的信息之质量而言)进行整体评估的声明;

(viii)与全国公认统计评级组织的利益冲突相关的信息;及

(ix)证券交易委员会要求提供的其他信息。

(B)**定量内容**。——每一全国公认统计评级组织均应按照依本子条制定的标准格式书披露——

(i)关于信用评级潜在波动性的说明或指标,包括——

(I)可能导致信用评级发生变化的任何因素;及

(II)用户在不同市场条件下所能够预期的上述变化的幅度;

(ii)关于评级内容的信息,包括——

(I)评级的历史绩效;及

(II)违约的预期可能性以及违约造成的预期损失;

(iii)关于评级是否容易受到全国公认统计评级组织作出的假设影响的信息,包括——

(I)如下所述之评级过程中作出的5种假设:在不考虑任何其他因素的情况下,如果该五种假设被证明为虚假或不准确,将会对评级造成的最大程度影响;及

"(II) an analysis, using specific examples, of how each of the 5 assumptions identified under subclause (I) impacts a rating;

"(iv) such additional information as may be required by the Commission.

"(4) DUE DILIGENCE SERVICES FOR ASSET–BACKED SECURITIES. —

"(A) FINDINGS. —The issuer or underwriter of any asset–backed security shall make publicly available the findings and conclusions of any third–party due diligence report obtained by the issuer or underwriter.

"(B) CERTIFICATION REQUIRED. —In any case in which third–party due diligence services are employed by a nationally recognized statistical rating organization, an issuer, or an underwriter, the person providing the due diligence services shall provide to any nationally recognized statistical rating organization that produces a rating to which such services relate, written certification, as provided in subparagraph (C).

"(C) FORMAT AND CONTENT. —The Commission shall establish the appropriate format and content for the written certifications required under subparagraph (B), to ensure that providers of due diligence services have conducted a thorough review of data, documentation, and other relevant information necessary for a nationally recognized statistical rating organization to provide an accurate rating.

"(D) DISCLOSURE OF CERTIFICATION. —The Commission shall adopt rules requiring a nationally recognized statistical rating organization, at the time at which the nationally recognized statistical rating organization produces a rating, to disclose the certification described in subparagraph (B) to the public in a manner that allows the public to determine the adequacy and level of due diligence services provided by a third party.

"(t) CORPORATE GOVERNANCE, ORGANIZATION, AND MANAGEMENT OF CONFLICTS OF INTEREST. —

"(1) BOARD OF DIRECTORS. —Each nationally recognized statistical rating organization shall have a board of directors.

"(2) INDEPENDENT DIRECTORS. —

"(A) IN GENERAL. —At least 1/2 of the board of directors, but not fewer than 2 of the members thereof, shall be independent of the nationally recognized statistical rating agency. A portion of the independent directors shall include users of ratings from a nationally recognized statistical rating organization.

"(B) INDEPENDENCE DETERMINATION. —In order to be considered independent for purposes of this subsection, a member of the board of directors of a nationally recognized statistical rating organization —

"(i) may not, other than in his or her capacity as a member of the board of directors or any committee thereof —

"(I) accept any consulting, advisory, or other compensatory fee from the nationally

(II)使用具体事例对第(I)子项所确定的5项假设分别对评级造成的影响进行的分析;

(iv)证券交易委员会要求提供的其他信息。

(4)**针对资产支持证券的尽职调查服务**。——

(A)**认定**。——任何资产支持证券的发行人或承销商获得任何第三方尽职调查报告的,均应向公众提供该等报告作出的认定及结论。

(B)**证明要求**。——如果全国公认统计评级组织、发行人或承销商采用第三方尽职调查服务,则该等尽职调查服务提供者应按照第(C)子款规定,向作出与其服务相关的评级的任何全国公认统计评级组织提供书面自查证明。

(C)**格式及内容**。——对于第(B)子款所述书面自查证明,证券交易委员会应规定适当的格式及内容,以确保尽职调查服务提供者已对全国公认统计评级组织做出准确评级所需的必要数据、文件及其他相关信息开展彻底审查。

(D)**自查证明的披露**。——证券交易委员会应制定规则,要求全国公认统计评级组织在作出评级的同时,公开披露第(B)子款所述自查证明,披露的方式应足以使公众判定第三方所提供尽职调查服务的充分性及水平。

(t)**公司治理、组织结构及利益冲突管理**。——

(1)**董事会**。——每一全国公认统计评级组织均应设立董事会。

(2)**独立董事**。——

(A)**一般规定**。——董事会中至少应有1/2成员(但不得少于两名)独立于全国公认统计评级组织。独立董事中应包括使用全国公认统计评级组织评级的用户。

(B)**独立性的判定**。——就本子条而言,全国公认统计评级组织董事会成员必须满足以下条件,始得被视为具有独立性——

(i)在担任董事会或董事会任何委员会的成员职务之外——

(I)不得接受全国公认统计评级组织提供的任何咨询费、顾问费或其他报酬;或

recognized statistical rating organization; or

"(II) be a person associated with the nationally recognized statistical rating organization or with any affiliated company thereof; and

"(ii) shall be disqualified from any deliberation involving a specific rating in which the independent board member has a financial interest in the outcome of the rating.

"(C) COMPENSATION AND TERM. —The compensation of the independent members of the board of directors of a nationally recognized statistical rating organization shall not be linked to the business performance of the nationally recognized statistical rating organization, and shall be arranged so as to ensure the independence of their judgment. The term of office of the independent directors shall be for a pre-agreed fixed period, not to exceed 5 years, and shall not be renewable.

"(3) DUTIES OF BOARD OF DIRECTORS. —In addition to the overall responsibilities of the board of directors, the board shall oversee —

"(A) the establishment, maintenance, and enforcement of policies and procedures for determining credit ratings;

"(B) the establishment, maintenance, and enforcement of policies and procedures to address, manage, and disclose any conflicts of interest;

"(C) the effectiveness of the internal control system with respect to policies and procedures for determining credit ratings; and

"(D) the compensation and promotion policies and practices of the nationally recognized statistical rating organization.

"(4) TREATMENT OF NRSRO SUBSIDIARIES. —If a nationally recognized statistical rating organization is a subsidiary of a parent entity, the board of the directors of the parent entity may satisfy the requirements of this subsection by assigning to a committee of such board of directors the duties under paragraph (3), if —

"(A) at least 1/2 of the members of the committee (including the chairperson of the committee) are independent, as defined in this section; and

"(B) at least 1 member of the committee is a user of ratings from a nationally recognized statistical rating organization.

"(5) EXCEPTION AUTHORITY. —If the Commission finds that compliance with the provisions of this subsection present an unreasonable burden on a small nationally recognized statistical rating organization, the Commission may permit the nationally recognized statistical rating organization to delegate such responsibilities to a committee that includes at least one individual who is a user of ratings of a nationally recognized statistical rating organization.".

(b) CONFORMING AMENDMENT. —Section 3(a)(62) of the Securities Exchange Act of 1934 (15 U.S.C.78c (a) (62)) is amended by striking subparagraph (A) and redesignating subparagraphs (B) and (C) as subparagraphs (A) and (B), respectively.

(II)不得与全国公认统计评级组织或其任何关联公司产生业务相关关系;且

(ii)如果其与特定评级的结果有经济上利害关系,应回避参与该等特定评级的审议。

(C)**薪酬与任期**。——全国公认统计评级组织董事会独立成员的薪酬不得与该组织的业务绩效挂钩,但是应进行相应安排,以确保其判断的独立性。独立董事任期应为事先约定的固定期限,但不得超过5年,也不得连任。

(3)**董事会职责**。——除总体职责外,董事会还负责监督——

(A)信用评级确定政策及程序的制定、维持和实施;

(B)利益冲突处理、管理和披露政策及程序的制定、维持和执行;

(C)信用评级确定政策及程序的内部控制制度的有效性;及

(D)全国公认统计评级组织的薪酬和晋级政策及实践。

(4)**全国公认统计评级组织系子公司的情形的处理**。——如果全国公认统计评级组织属于母公司的一家子公司,则其母实体的董事会可将第(3)款所述职责委派给母公司董事会下属委员会履行,以满足本子条的要求,前提是该下属委员会满足下列条件——

(A)该委员会至少1/2的成员(包括委员会主席在内)具有本条所定义的独立性;且

(B)至少有一名委员会成员是使用全国公认统计评级组织评级的用户。

(5)**例外权力**。——如果证券交易委员会认定遵守本子条规定将对小型全国公认统计评级组织造成不合理负担,证券交易委员会可以允许该等全国公认统计评级组织委托一个委员会履行上述职责,但是该委员会至少应包含一名使用全国公认统计评级组织评级的个人用户。”

(b)**一致性修正**。——《1934年证券交易法》第3(a)(62)条[《美国法典》第十五编第78c(a)(62)节]修正如下:删除第(A)子款,并且第(B)子款和第(C)子款分别重新编号为第(A)子款和第(B)子款。

SEC.933. STATE OF MIND IN PRIVATE ACTIONS.

(a) ACCOUNTABILITY. —Section 15E (m) of the Securities Exchange Act of 1934 (15 U.S.C.78o–7(m)) is amended to read as follows:

"(m) ACCOUNTABILITY. —

"(1) IN GENERAL. —The enforcement and penalty provisions of this title shall apply to statements made by a credit rating agency in the same manner and to the same extent as such provisions apply to statements made by a registered public accounting firm or a securities analyst under the securities laws, and such statements shall not be deemed forward–looking statements for the purposes of section 21E.

"(2) RULEMAKING. —The Commission shall issue such rules as may be necessary to carry out this subsection.".

(b) STATE OF MIND. —Section 21D(b)(2) of the Securities Exchange Act of 1934 (15 U.S.C.78u–4(b)(2)) is amended—

(1) by striking "In any" and inserting the following:

"(A) IN GENERAL. —Except as provided in subparagraph (B), in any"; and

(2) by adding at the end the following:

"(B) EXCEPTION. —In the case of an action for money damages brought against a credit rating agency or a controlling person under this title, it shall be sufficient, for purposes of pleading any required state of mind in relation to such action, that the complaint state with particularity facts giving rise to a strong inference that the credit rating agency knowingly or recklessly failed —

"(i) to conduct a reasonable investigation of the rated security with respect to the factual elements relied upon by its own methodology for evaluating credit risk; or

"(ii) to obtain reasonable verification of such factual elements (which verification may be based on a sampling technique that does not amount to an audit) from other sources that the credit rating agency considered to be competent and that were independent of the issuer and underwriter.".

SEC.934. REFERRING TIPS TO LAW ENFORCEMENT OR REGULATORY AUTHORITIES.

Section 15E of the Securities Exchange Act of 1934 (15 U.S.C.78o–7), as amended by this subtitle, is amended by adding at the end the following:

"(u) DUTY TO REPORT TIPS ALLEGING MATERIAL VIOLATIONS OF LAW. —

"(1) DUTY TO REPORT. —Each nationally recognized statistical rating organization shall refer to the appropriate law enforcement or regulatory authorities any information that the nationally recognized statistical rating organization receives from a third party and finds credible that alleges that an issuer of securities rated by the nationally recognized statistical rating organization has committed or is committing a material violation of law that has not

第933条 私人诉讼中的主观状态

(a)**问责制**。——《1934年证券交易法》第15E(m)条[《美国法典》第十五编第78o-7(m)节]修正后全文如下:

"(m)**问责制**。——

(1)**一般规定**。——本编的执行及处罚规定应适用于信用评级机构做出的声明,适用方式与适用范围均应与注册公共会计师事务所或证券分析师根据证券法律作出的声明相同,并且该等声明不得被视为第21E条意义上的前瞻性声明。

(2)**规则制定**。——证券交易委员会应发布必要规则,以实施本子条规定。"

(b)**主观状态**。——《1934年证券交易法》第21D(b)(2)条[《美国法典》第十五编第78u-4(b)(2)节]修正如下——

(1)删除"在任何",替以如下内容:

"(A)**一般规定**。——除第(B)子款规定的情形外,在任何";及

(2)在结尾处增加如下内容:

"(B)**例外规定**。——在根据本编规定对信用评级机构或控制人提起的金钱损害赔偿诉讼中,只要基于起诉状中提供的详细事实可确切推断出信用评级机构在知情的情况下或轻率地未实施以下行为,即应视为对提起该等诉讼所必需的任何主观状态进行了充分的证明——

(i)针对其内部采用的信用风险评估方法所依赖的事实要素,对被评级证券开展合理调查;或

(ii)通过信用评级机构认为适格并独立于发行人及承销商的其他信息来源,对该等事实要素进行合理的核实(核实可通过不构成审计的抽查技术进行)。"

第934条 向执法或监管机构提交信息线索

在经本子编修正后的《1934年证券交易法》第15E条(《美国法典》第十五编第78o-7节)结尾处增加如下内容,作为对该条的进一步修正:

"(u)**报告重大违法行为线索的职责**。——

(1)**报告职责**。——对于每一全国公认统计评级组织从第三方获得的宣称存在如下事项的其认定确实可信的任何信息,即被该等组织评级的证券的发行人实施了或正在实施联邦法院或州法院尚未裁决过的重大违法行为,则该等组织应向相应执法或监管机构提交该等信息。

been adjudicated by a Federal or State court.

"(2) RULE OF CONSTRUCTION. —Nothing in paragraph(1) may be construed to require a nationally recognized statistical rating organization to verify the accuracy of the information described in paragraph (1).".

SEC.935. CONSIDERATION OF INFORMATION FROM SOURCES OTHER THAN THE ISSUER IN RATING DECISIONS.

Section 15E of the Securities Exchange Act of 1934 (15 U.S.C.78o-7), as amended by this subtitle, is amended by adding at the end the following:

"(v) INFORMATION FROM SOURCES OTHER THAN THE ISSUER. —In producing a credit rating, a nationally recognized statistical rating organization shall consider information about an issuer that the nationally recognized statistical rating organization has, or receives from a source other than the issuer or underwriter, that the nationally recognized statistical rating organization finds credible and potentially significant to a rating decision.".

SEC.936. QUALIFICATION STANDARDS FOR CREDIT RATING ANALYSTS.

Not later than 1 year after the date of enactment of this Act, the Commission shall issue rules that are reasonably designed to ensure that any person employed by a nationally recognized statistical rating organization to perform credit ratings —

(1) meets standards of training, experience, and competence necessary to produce accurate ratings for the categories of issuers whose securities the person rates; and

(2) is tested for knowledge of the credit rating process.

SEC.937. TIMING OF REGULATIONS.

Unless otherwise specifically provided in this subtitle, the Commission shall issue final regulations, as required by this subtitle and the amendments made by this subtitle, not later than 1 year after the date of enactment of this Act.

SEC.938. UNIVERSAL RATINGS SYMBOLS.

(a) RULEMAKING. —The Commission shall require, by rule, each nationally recognized statistical rating organization to establish, maintain, and enforce written policies and procedures that—

(1) assess the probability that an issuer of a security or money market instrument will default, fail to make timely payments, or otherwise not make payments to investors in accordance with the terms of the security or money market instrument;

(2) clearly define and disclose the meaning of any symbol used by the nationally recognized statistical rating organization to denote a credit rating; and

(3) apply any symbol described in paragraph (2) in a manner that is consistent for all types of securities and money market instruments for which the symbol is used.

(b) RULE OF CONSTRUCTION. —Nothing in this section shall prohibit a nationally

(2)**解释规则**。——第(1)款任何内容均不得被解释为要求全国公认统计评级组织核实第(1)款所述信息的准确性。”

第935条 作出评级决定时对来自发行人以外的来源的信息的考虑

在经本子编修正后的《1934年证券交易法》第15E条(《美国法典》第十五编第78o-7节)结尾处增加如下内容,作为对该条的进一步修正:

“(v)**来自发行人以外的来源的信息**。——如果全国公认统计评级组织认定其拥有的或收到的来自发行人或承销商以外的来源的有关该发行人的信息确实可信并可能对评级决定具有重大意义,则该等组织应在作出信用评级时考虑该等信息。”

第936条 信用评级分析师的资格标准

证券交易委员会应于本法颁布之日后1年内发布设计合理规则,以确保全国公认统计评级组织所雇用的开展信用评级工作的任何人均——

(1)符合必要的培训、经验和胜任标准,以便对其所评级的证券的各类发行人作出准确评级;并

(2)已通过信用评级程序方面的知识测试。

第937条 规章发布时限

除非本子编另有明确规定,否则,证券交易委员会应于本法颁布之日后1年内,按本子编及本子编所做修正的要求发布最终规章。

第938条 通用评级标识

(a)**规则制定**。——证券交易委员会应发布规则,要求每一全国公认统计评级组织制定、维持和实施符合如下条件的书面政策和程序——

(1)评估证券或货币市场工具发行人是否可能发生违约、是否可能不按照该证券或货币市场工具的条款向投资人及时支付款项的或是否可能由于其他原因不按照该证券或货币市场工具的条款向投资人支付款项;

(2)明确界定并披露全国公认统计评级组织用以表示信用评级的任何标识的含义;且

(3)将第(2)款所述任何标识以统一的方式适用于所有类型的证券及货币市场工具。

(b)**解释规则**。——本条任何内容均不禁止全国公认统计评级组织对不同类型

recognized statistical rating organization from using distinct sets of symbols to denote credit ratings for different types of securities or money market instruments.

SEC.939. REMOVAL OF STATUTORY REFERENCES TO CREDIT RATINGS.

(a) FEDERAL DEPOSIT INSURANCE ACT. —The Federal Deposit Insurance Act (12 U.S.C.1811 et seq.) is amended —

(1) in section 7 (b)(1)(E)(i), by striking "credit rating entities, and other private economic" and insert "private economic, credit,";

(2) in section 28(d) —

(A) in the subsection heading, by striking "NOT OF INVESTMENT GRADE";

(B) in paragraph (1), by striking "not of investment grade" and inserting "that does not meet standards of credit–worthiness as established by the Corporation";

(C) in paragraph (2), by striking "not of investment grade";

(D) by striking paragraph (3);

(E) by redesignating paragraph (4) as paragraph (3); and

(F) in paragraph (3), as so redesignated —

(i) by striking subparagraph (A);

(ii) by redesignating subparagraphs (B) and (C) as subparagraphs (A) and (B), respectively; and

(iii) in subparagraph (B), as so redesignated, by striking "not of investment grade" and inserting "that does not meet standards of credit–worthiness as established by the Corporation"; and

(3) in section 28(e) —

(A) in the subsection heading, by striking "NOT OF INVESTMENT GRADE";

(B) in paragraph (1), by striking "not of investment grade" and inserting "that does not meet standards of credit–worthiness as established by the Corporation"; and

(C) in paragraphs (2) and (3), by striking "not of investment grade" each place that it appears and inserting "that does not meet standards of credit–worthiness established by the Corporation".

(b) FEDERAL HOUSING ENTERPRISES FINANCIAL SAFETY AND SOUNDNESS ACT OF 1992. —Section 1319 of the Federal Housing Enterprises Financial Safety and Soundness Act of 1992 (12 U.S.C.4519) is amended by striking "that is a nationally recognized statistical rating organization, as such term is defined in section 3 (a) of the Securities Exchange Act of 1934,".

(c) INVESTMENT COMPANY ACT OF 1940. — Section 6 (a) (5) (A) (iv) (I) Investment Company Act of 1940 (15U.S.C.80a–6 (a) (5) (A) (iv) (I)) is amended by striking "is rated investment grade by not less than 1 nationally recognized statistical rating

的证券或货币市场工具的信用评级使用不同系列的标识。

第939条　删除制定法中提及的信用评级

(a)**《联邦存款保险法》**。——《联邦存款保险法》(《美国法典》第十二编第1811节及其后条文)修正如下——

(1)在第7(b)(1)(E)(i)条中，删除“信用评级实体及其他私人经济”，替以“私人经济、信用、”；

(2)在第28(d)条中——

(A)删除子条标题中的“**非投资等级的**”；

(B)第(1)款删除“非投资等级的”，替以“不符合联邦存款保险公司设定的资信标准的”；

(C)第(2)款删除“非投资等级的”；

(D)删除第(3)款；

(E)第(4)款重新编号为第(3)款；及

(F)第(3)款(以重新编号后的序号为准)——

(i)删除第(A)子款；

(ii)第(B)子款和第(C)子款分别重新编号为第(A)子款和第(B)子款；及

(iii)第(B)子款(以重新编号后的序号为准)删除“非投资等级的”，替以“不符合联邦存款保险公司设定的资信标准的”；及

(3)在第28(e)条中——

(A)删除子条标题中的“非投资等级的”；

(B)第(1)款删除“非投资等级的”，替以“不符合联邦存款保险公司设定的资信标准的”；及

(C)第(2)款和第(3)款删除所有的“非投资等级的”，全部替以“不符合联邦存款保险公司设定的资信标准的”。

(b)**《1992年联邦住房企业财务安全和稳健法》**。——《1992年联邦住房企业财务安全和稳健法》第1319条(《美国法典》第十二编第4519节)修正如下：删除“性质属于全国公认统计评级组织[定义见《1934年证券交易法》第3(a)条]的，”。

(c)**《1940年投资公司法》**。——《1940年投资公司法》第6(a)(5)(A)(iv)(I)条[《美国法典》第十五编第80a-6(a)(5)(A)(iv)(I)节]修正如下：删除“被至少一家全国公认统计评级组织评定为投资等级的”，替以“符合证券交易委员会采用的资信标

organization" and inserting "meets such standards of credit-worthiness as the Commission shall adopt".

(d) REVISED STATUTES. —Section 5136A of title LXII of the Revised Statutes of the United States (12 U.S.C.24a) is amended —

(1) in subsection (a) (2) (E), by striking "any applicable rating" and inserting "standards of credit-worthiness established by the Comptroller of the Currency";

(2) in the heading for subsection (a)(3) by striking "RATING OR COMPARABLE REQUIREMENT" and inserting "REQUIREMENT";

(3) subsection (a)(3), by amending subparagraph (A) to read as follows:

"(A) IN GENERAL. —A national bank meets the requirements of this paragraph if the bank is one of the 100 largest insured banks and has not fewer than 1 issue of outstanding debt that meets standards of credit-worthiness or other criteria as the Secretary of the Treasury and the Board of Governors of the Federal Reserve System may jointly establish.".

(4) in the heading for subsection (f), by striking "MAINTAIN PUBLIC RATING OR" and inserting "MEET STANDARDS OF CREDIT-WORTHINESS"; and

(5) in subsection (f)(1), by striking "any applicable rating" and inserting "standards of credit-worthiness established by the Comptroller of the Currency".

(e) SECURITIES EXCHANGE ACT OF 1934. —Section 3(a) Securities Exchange Act of 1934 (15 U.S.C.78a(3)(a)) is amended —

(1) in paragraph(41), by striking "is rated in one of the two highest rating categories by at least one nationally recognized statistical rating organization" and inserting "meets standards of credit-worthiness as established by the Commission"; and

(2) in paragraph(53)(A), by striking "is rated in 1 of the 4 highest rating categories by at least 1 nationally recognized statistical rating organization" and inserting "meets standards of credit-worthiness as established by the Commission".

(f) WORLD BANK DISCUSSIONS. —Section 3(a)(6) of the amendment in the nature of a substitute to the text of H.R. 4645, as ordered reported from the Committee on Banking, Finance and Urban Affairs on September 22, 1988, as enacted into law by section 555 of Public Law 100-461, (22 U.S.C.286hh(a)(6)), is amended by striking "credit rating" and inserting "credit-worthiness".

(g) EFFECTIVE DATE. —The amendments made by this section shall take effect 2 years after the date of enactment of this Act.

(h) STUDY AND REPORT. —

(1) IN GENERAL. —Commission shall undertake a study on the feasability and desirability of —

(A) standardizing credit ratings terminology, so that all credit rating agencies issue credit ratings using identical terms;

准的”。

(d)**《美国制定法汇编》(修订版)**。——《美国制定法汇编》(修订版)第六十二编第5136A条(《美国法典》第十二编第24a节)修正如下——

(1)在第(a)(2)(E)子条中,删除“任何适用评级”,替以“货币监理署署长设定的资信标准”;

(2)删除第(a)(3)子条标题中的“**评级或具有可比性的要求**”,替以“**要求**”;

(3)在第(a)(3)子条中,第(A)子款修正后如下:

“(A)**一般规定**。——如果某一国民银行是100家最大参保银行之一,并且其一种以上发行在外的债务符合财政部部长与联邦储备委员会联合设定的资信标准或其他标准,则该国民银行视为符合本款要求。”

(4)在第(f)子条标题中,删除“**维持公共评级或**”,替以“**符合资信标准**”;及

(5)在第(f)(1)子条中,删除“任何适用评级”,替以“货币监理署署长设定的资信标准”。

(e)**《1934年证券交易法》**。——《1934年证券交易法》第3(a)条[《美国法典》第十五编第78a(3)(a)节]修正如下——

(1)在第(41)款中,删除“被至少一家全国公认统计评级组织评定为两类最高评级之一的”,替以“符合证券交易委员会设定的资信标准的”;及

(2)在第(53)(A)款中,删除“被至少一家全国公认统计评级组织评定为四类最高评级之一的”,替以“符合证券交易委员会设定的资信标准的”。

(f)**世界银行讨论**。——参议院银行、住房与城市事务委员会于1988年9月22日命令该委员会主席向参议院报告,并制定为法律(第100—461号公法第555条)的第4645号众议院法案内容的替代性修正案第3(a)(6)条[《美国法典》第二十二编第286hh(a)(6)节]修正如下:删除“信用评级”,替以“资信”。

(g)**生效日**。——本条作出的修正应于本法颁布之日后届满两年之日生效。

(h)**研究与报告**。——

(1)**一般规定**。——证券交易委员会应针对以下各项的可行性和可取性开展研究——

(A)对信用评级术语进行标准化统一,以便所有信用评级机构使用相同术语发布信用评级;

(B) standardizing the market stress conditions under which ratings are evaluated;

(C) requiring a quantitative correspondence between credit ratings and a range of default probabilities and loss expectations under standardized conditions of economic stress; and

(D) standardizing credit rating terminology across asset classes, so that named ratings correspond to a standard range of default probabilities and expected losses independent of asset class and issuing entity.

(2) REPORT. —Not later than 1 year after the date of enactment of this Act, the Commission shall submit to Congress a report containing the findings of the study under paragraph (1) and the recommendations, if any, of the Commission with respect to the study.

SEC.939A. REVIEW OF RELIANCE ON RATINGS.

(a) AGENCY REVIEW. —Not later than 1 year after the date of the enactment of this subtitle, each Federal agency shall, to the extent applicable, review —

(1) any regulation issued by such agency that requires the use of an assessment of the credit-worthiness of a security or money market instrument; and

(2) any references to or requirements in such regulations regarding credit ratings.

(b) MODIFICATIONS REQUIRED. —Each such agency shall modify any such regulations identified by the review conducted under subsection (a) to remove any reference to or requirement of reliance on credit ratings and to substitute in such regulations such standard of credit-worthiness as each respective agency shall determine as appropriate for such regulations. In making such determination, such agencies shall seek to establish, to the extent feasible, uniform standards of credit-worthiness for use by each such agency, taking into account the entities regulated by each such agency and the purposes for which such entities would rely on such standards of credit-worthiness.

(c) REPORT. —Upon conclusion of the review required under subsection (a), each Federal agency shall transmit a report to Congress containing a description of any modification of any regulation such agency made pursuant to subsection (b).

SEC.939B. ELIMINATION OF EXEMPTION FROM FAIR DISCLOSURE RULE.

Not later than 90 days after the date of enactment of this subtitle, the Securities Exchange Commission shall revise Regulation FD (17 C.F.R. 243.100) to remove from such regulation the exemption for entities whose primary business is the issuance of credit ratings (17 C.F.R. 243.100(b)(2)(iii)).

SEC.939C. SECURITIES AND EXCHANGE COMMISSION STUDY ON STRENGTHENING CREDIT RATING AGENCY INDEPENDENCE.

(a) STUDY. —The Commission shall conduct a study of—

(1) the independence of nationally recognized statistical rating organizations; and

(B)对评级所采用的市场压力条件进行标准化统一;

(C)要求在标准化经济压力条件下实现信用评级与一系列违约可能性及预期损失之间的定量对应;及

(D)对适用于不同资产类别的信用评级术语进行标准化统一,以便所涉各项评级与一系列标准的违约可能性及预期损失范围相对应,不受资产类别及发行实体的影响。

(2) **报告**。——证券交易委员会应于本法颁布之日后1年内向国会提交报告,说明根据第(1)款开展研究所得出的认定结论及其针对研究提出的建议(如有)。

第939A条 审查对评级的依赖情况

(a)**机关审查**。——每一联邦机关均应在本子编颁布之日后1年内,在适用范围内对以下各项进行审查——

(1)该等机关发布的要求使用证券或货币市场工具资信评估的任何规章;及

(2)该等规章中对信用评级的任何提述或关于信用评级的任何要求。

(b)**修改要求**。——每一上述机关在根据第(a)子条开展审查后,应对审查中确定需要修改的规章进行修改,删除对信用评级的任何提述或采用信用评级的要求,并替以各机关判定为适当的资信标准。在做出上述判定时,该等机关应在考虑受每一上述机关监管的实体以及该等实体将会采用前述资信标准的目的基础上,在可行范围内寻求设定统一的资信标准,供每一上述机关使用。

(c)**报告**。——每一联邦机关均应在第(a)子条所规定审查结束后向国会提交一份报告,说明其按照第(b)子条对任何规章作出的任何修改。

第939B条 取消对公平披露规则的豁免

证券交易委员会应于本子编颁布之日后90天内对《FD管理办法》(《联邦规章汇编》第十七编第243.100部分)进行修订,删除其中对主要从事信用评级发布业务的实体授予的豁免[《联邦规章汇编》第十七编第243.100(b)(2)(iii)部分]。

第939C条 证券交易委员会关于加强信用评级机构独立性的研究

(a)**研究**。——证券交易委员会应针对以下事项开展研究——

(1)全国公认统计评级组织的独立性;及

(2) how the independence of nationally recognized statistical rating organizations affects the ratings issued by the nationally recognized statistical rating organizations.

(b) SUBJECTS FOR EVALUATION. —In conducting the study under subsection (a), the Commission shall evaluate —

(1) the management of conflicts of interest raised by a nationally recognized statistical rating organization providing other services, including risk management advisory services, ancillary assistance, or consulting services;

(2) the potential impact of rules prohibiting a nationally recognized statistical rating organization that provides a rating to an issuer from providing other services to the issuer; and

(3) any other issue relating to nationally recognized statistical rating organizations, as the Chairman of the Commission determines is appropriate.

(c) REPORT. —Not later than 3 years after the date of enactment of this Act, the Chairman of the Commission shall submit to the Committee on Banking, Housing, and Urban Affairs of the Senate and the Committee on Financial Services of the House of Representatives a report on the results of the study conducted under subsection (a), including recommendations, if any, for improving the integrity of ratings issued by nationally recognized statistical rating organizations.

SEC.939D. GOVERNMENT ACCOUNTABILITY OFFICE STUDY ON ALTERNATIVE BUSINESS MODELS.

(a) STUDY. —The Comptroller General of the United States shall conduct a study on alternative means for compensating nationally recognized statistical rating organizations in order to create incentives for nationally recognized statistical rating organizations to provide more accurate credit ratings, including any statutory changes that would be required to facilitate the use of an alternative means of compensation.

(b) REPORT. —Not later than 18 months after the date of enactment of this Act, the Comptroller General shall submit to the Committee on Banking, Housing, and Urban Affairs of the Senate and the Committee on Financial Services of the House of Representatives a report on the results of the study conducted under subsection(a), including recommendations, if any, for providing incentives to credit rating agencies to improve the credit rating process.

SEC.939E. GOVERNMENT ACCOUNTABILITY OFFICE STUDY ON THE CREATION OF AN INDEPENDENT PROFESSIONAL ANALYST ORGANIZATION.

(a) STUDY. —The Comptroller General of the United States shall conduct a study on the feasibility and merits of creating an independent professional organization for rating analysts employed by nationally recognized statistical rating organizations that would be responsible for —

(1) establishing independent standards for governing the profession of rating analysts;

（2）全国公认统计评级组织的独立性对其发布的评级的影响。

（b）**评价对象**。——证券交易委员会在根据第（a）子条开展研究时，应评价——

（1）全国公认统计评级组织提供其他服务（包括风险管理顾问服务、辅助性服务或咨询服务）时所引发利益冲突的管理；

（2）旨在禁止为发行人提供评级服务的全国公认统计评级组织向该等发行人提供其他服务的规则可能造成的影响；及

（3）证券交易委员会主席判定的与全国公认统计评级组织相关的确属适当的任何其他事项。

（c）**报告**。——证券交易委员会主席应于本法颁布之日后3年内向参议院银行、住房与城市事务委员会及众议院金融服务委员会提交一份报告，汇报根据第（a）子条所开展研究的结果，包括提高全国公认统计评级组织所发布评级的诚信度的建议（如有）。

第939D条　政府问责办公室关于替代性商业模式的研究

（a）**研究**。——政府问责办公室主任应就向全国公认统计评级组织支付报酬的替代性方式开展研究，以激励全国公认统计评级组织提供更加准确的信用评级，包括为促进替代性报酬支付方式的使用而须在制定法方面进行的任何修改。

（b）**报告**。——政府问责办公室主任应于本法颁布之日后18个月内，向参议院银行、住房与城市事务委员会以及众议院金融服务委员会提交报告，汇报根据第（a）子条所开展研究的结果以及激励信用评级机构完善信用评级工作流程的建议（如有）。

第939E条　政府问责办公室关于为评级分析师设立独立的专业性组织的研究

（a）**研究**。——对于为全国公认统计评级组织雇用的评级分析师组建负责如下事项的独立性专业性组织的可行性和优点，政府问责办公室主任应开展研究——

（1）为评级分析师制定独立的行业标准；

(2) establishing a code of ethical conduct; and

(3) overseeing the profession of rating analysts.

(b) REPORT. —Not later than 1 year after the date of publication of the rules issued by the Commission pursuant to section 936, the Comptroller General shall submit to the Committee on Banking, Housing, and Urban Affairs of the Senate and the Committee on Financial Services of the House of Representatives a report on the results of the study conducted under subsection (a).

SEC.939F. STUDY AND RULEMAKING ON ASSIGNED CREDIT RATINGS.

(a) DEFINITION. —In this section, the term "structured finance product" means an asset–backed security, as defined in section 3(a)(77) of the Securities Exchange Act of 1934, as added by section 941, and any structured product based on an asset–backed security, as determined by the Commission, by rule.

(b) STUDY. —The Commission shall carry out a study of—

(1) the credit rating process for structured finance products and the conflicts of interest associated with the issuer–pay and the subscriber–pay models;

(2) the feasibility of establishing a system in which a public or private utility or a self–regulatory organization assigns nationally recognized statistical rating organizations to determine the credit ratings of structured finance products, including—

(A) an assessment of potential mechanisms for determining fees for the nationally recognized statistical rating organizations;

(B) appropriate methods for paying fees to the nationally recognized statistical rating organizations;

(C) the extent to which the creation of such a system would be viewed as the creation of moral hazard by the Federal Government; and

(D) any constitutional or other issues concerning the establishment of such a system;

(3) the range of metrics that could be used to determine the accuracy of credit ratings; and

(4) alternative means for compensating nationally recognized statistical rating organizations that would create incentives for accurate credit ratings.

(c) REPORT AND RECOMMENDATION. —Not later than 24 months after the date of enactment of this Act, the Commission shall submit to the Committee on Banking, Housing, and Urban Affairs of the Senate and the Committee on Financial Services of the House of Representatives a report that contains—

(1) the findings of the study required under subsection (b); and

(2) any recommendations for regulatory or statutory changes that the Commission determines should be made to implement the findings of the study required under subsection (b).

(2)制定职业道德准则;并

(3)对评级分析师行业进行监督。

(b)**报告**。——政府问责办公室主任应在证券交易委员会按照第936条发布的规则公布后1年内,向参议院银行、住房与城市事务委员会以及众议院金融服务委员会提交报告,汇报根据第(a)子条所开展研究的结果。

第939F条　关于指定信用评级的研究及相关规则制定

(a)**定义**。——就本子条而言,“结构性金融产品”一词系指资产支持证券[定义见本法第941条增加的《1934年证券交易法》第3(a)(77)条],以及证券交易委员会发布的规则所确定的基于资产支持证券的任何结构性产品。

(b)**研究**。——证券交易委员会应针对以下各项开展研究——

(1)结构性金融产品的信用评级流程,以及与发行人付费模式及认购人付费模式相关的利益冲突;

(2)建立以下制度的可行性,即由公共或私人服务平台或者自律组织指定全国公认统计评级组织确定结构性金融产品信用评级的,包括——

(A)对可能采取的确定全国公认统计评级组织的收费金额的机制进行的评估;

(B)向全国公认统计评级组织支付费用的适当方式;

(C)联邦政府将在多大程度上将该等制度的创立视为带来道德风险;及

(D)与建立该等制度相关的任何宪法问题或其他问题;

(3)可用以判定信用评级准确性的指标之范围;及

(4)将激励全国公认统计评级组织提供准确评级的替代性报酬支付方式。

(c)**报告与建议**。——证券交易委员会应于本法颁布之日后24个月内,向参议院银行、住房与城市事务委员会以及众议院金融服务委员会提交一份报告,汇报——

(1)第(b)子条所规定研究得出的认定结论;及

(2)证券交易委员会判定的为实施第(b)子条所规定研究得出的认定结论而应在监管或制定法方面作出的变更的任何建议。

(d) RULEMAKING.—

(1) RULEMAKING.—After submission of the report under subsection (c), the Commission shall, by rule, as the Commission determines is necessary or appropriate in the public interest or for the protection of investors, establish a system for the assignment of nationally recognized statistical rating organizations to determine the initial credit ratings of structured finance products, in a manner that prevents the issuer, sponsor, or underwriter of the structured finance product from selecting the nationally recognized statistical rating organization that will determine the initial credit ratings and monitor such credit ratings. In issuing any rule under this paragraph, the Commission shall give thorough consideration to the provisions of section 15E(w) of the Securities Exchange Act of 1934, as that provision would have been added by section 939D of H.R. 4173 (111th Congress), as passed by the Senate on May 20, 2010, and shall implement the system described in such section 939D unless the Commission determines that an alternative system would better serve the public interest and the protection of investors.

(2) RULE OF CONSTRUCTION.—Nothing in this subsection may be construed to limit or suspend any other rulemaking authority of the Commission.

SEC.939G. EFFECT OF RULE 436(G).

Rule 436 (g), promulgated by the Securities and Exchange Commission under the Securities Act of 1933, shall have no force or effect.

SEC.939H. SENSE OF CONGRESS.

It is the sense of Congress that the Securities and Exchange Commission should exercise the rulemaking authority of the Commission under section 15E(h)(2)(B) of the Securities Exchange Act of 1934 (15 U.S.C.78o-7(h)(2)(B)) to prevent improper conflicts of interest arising from employees of nationally recognized statistical rating organizations providing services to issuers of securities that are unrelated to the issuance of credit ratings, including consulting, advisory, and other services.

Subtitle D—Improvements to the Asset-Backed Securitization Process

SEC.941. REGULATION OF CREDIT RISK RETENTION.

(a) DEFINITION OF ASSET-BACKED SECURITY.—Section 3 (a) of the Securities Exchange Act of 1934 (15 U.S.C.78c(a)) is amended by adding at the end the following:

"(77) ASSET-BACKED SECURITY.—The term 'asset-backed security'—

"(A) means a fixed-income or other security collateralized by any type of self-liquidating financial asset (including a loan, a lease, a mortgage, or a secured or

(d)**规则制定**。——

(1)**规则制定**。——在提交第(c)子条所述报告后,证券交易委员会应发布其判定对于维护公共利益或保护投资者确属必要或适当的规则,建立相关制度,据以指定全国公认统计评级组织为结构性金融产品确定初始信用评级,防止结构性金融产品的发行人、保荐人或承销商自行选择全国公认统计评级组织确定该等产品的最初信用评级,并应同时对该等信用评级进行监控。在根据本款发布任何规则时,证券交易委员会应充分考虑《1934年证券交易法》第15E(w)条的规定[该规定由参议院于2010年5月20日通过的第4173号法案(第111届国会会议)第939D条增加],并应实施该第939D条所述制度,但证券交易委员会判定其他制度将能更好地维护公共利益和保护投资者的除外。

(2)**解释规则**。——本子条任何内容均不得被解释为限制或暂停证券交易委员会的任何其他规则制定权。

第939G条 《436(G)规则》的效力

证券交易委员会根据《1933年证券法》颁发的《436(g)规则》兹予废止。

第939H条 国会态度

国会认为,证券交易委员会应行使《1934年证券交易法》第15E(h)(2)(B)条(《美国法典》第十五编第78o-7(h)(2)(B)节)规定的规则制定权,以防止全国公认统计评级组织雇员在向证券发行人提供与信用评级发布无关的服务(包括咨询、顾问及其他服务)时,引发不当利益冲突。

第D子编——完善资产证券化流程

第941条 对信用风险自留的监管

(a)**资产支持证券的定义**。——在《1934年证券交易法》第3(a)条[《美国法典》第十五编第78c(a)节]结尾处增加如下内容,作为对该条的修正:

“(77)**资产支持证券**。——‘资产支持证券’一词——

(A)系指以任何类型的自偿性金融资产(包括贷款、租赁、抵押贷款或者有担保或无担保应收款项)作为担保的固定收益证券或其他证券,且该等证券的持有人有权获

unsecured receivable) that allows the holder of the security to receive payments that depend primarily on cash flow from the asset, including —

"(i) a collateralized mortgage obligation;

"(ii) a collateralized debt obligation;

"(iii) a collateralized bond obligation;

"(iv) a collateralized debt obligation of asset–backed securities;

"(v) a collateralized debt obligation of collateralized debt obligations; and

"(vi) a security that the Commission, by rule, determines to be an asset–backed security for purposes of this section; and

"(B) does not include a security issued by a finance subsidiary held by the parent company or a company controlled by the parent company, if none of the securities issued by the finance subsidiary are held by an entity that is not controlled by the parent company."

(b) CREDIT RISK RETENTION. —The Securities Exchange Act of 1934 (15 U.S.C. 78a et seq.) is amended by inserting after section 15F, as added by this Act, the following:

"SEC.15G. CREDIT RISK RETENTION.

"(a) DEFINITIONS. —In this section —

"(1) the term 'Federal banking agencies' means the Office of the Comptroller of the Currency, the Board of Governors of the Federal Reserve System, and the Federal Deposit Insurance Corporation;

"(2) the term 'insured depository institution' has the same meaning as in section 3(c) of the Federal Deposit Insurance Act (12 U.S.C.1813(c));

"(3) the term 'securitizer' means —

"(A) an issuer of an asset–backed security; or

"(B) a person who organizes and initiates an asset–backed securities transaction by selling or transferring assets, either directly or indirectly, including through an affiliate, to the issuer; and

"(4) the term 'originator' means a person who —

"(A) through the extension of credit or otherwise, creates a financial asset that collateralizes an asset–backed security; and

"(B) sells an asset directly or indirectly to a securitizer.

"(b) REGULATIONS REQUIRED. —

"(1) IN GENERAL. —Not later than 270 days after the date of enactment of this section, the Federal banking agencies and the Commission shall jointly prescribe regulations to require any securitizer to retain an economic interest in a portion of the credit risk for any asset that the securitizer, through the issuance of an asset–backed security, transfers, sells, or conveys to a third party.

"(2) RESIDENTIAL MORTGAGES. —Not later than 270 days after the date of the

得的款项主要取决于该等资产现金流。上述自偿性金融资产包括——

(i)担保抵押凭证;
(ii)担保债务凭证;
(iii)担保债券凭证;
(iv)基于资产支持证券的担保债务凭证;
(v)双层担保债务凭证;及
(vi)证券交易委员会在其发布规则中判定属于本条意义上的资产支持证券的证券;且
(B)不包括金融子公司发行的由其母公司或其母公司控制的公司持有的证券,前提是金融子公司发行的任何证券均未被其母公司所控制实体以外的实体所持有。"

(b)**信用风险自留**。——在本法增加的《1934年证券交易法》(《美国法典》第十五编第78a节及其后条文)第15F条之后插入如下内容,作为对该法的修正:

"第15G条　信用风险自留

"(a)**定义**。——就本条而言——

(1)"联邦银行业监管机关"一词系指货币监理署、联邦储备委员会以及联邦存款保险公司;

(2)"参保存款机构"一词的含义以《联邦存款保险法》第3(c)条[《美国法典》第十二编第1813(c)节]的定义为准;
(3)'证券化机构'一词系指——
(A)资产支持证券的发行人;或
(B)通过直接或间接向发行人出售或转让资产(包括通过关联方进行该等出售或转让)组织和发起资产支持证券交易的主体;及

(4)'发起人'一词系指从事以下行为的主体——
(A)通过授信或其他方式,创立为资产支持证券提供担保的金融资产;并

(B)直接或间接向证券化机构出售资产。
(b)**规章制定要求**。——
(1)**一般规定**。——联邦银行业监管机关及证券交易委员会应在本条规定颁布之日后270天内联合制定规章,要求任何证券化机构在经济上保留与其通过资产支持证券发行向第三方转让、出售或转移的任何资产的部分信用风险之间的利害关系。

(2)**住房抵押贷款**。——联邦银行业监管机关、证券交易委员会、住房与城市发

enactment of this section, the Federal banking agencies, the Commission, the Secretary of Housing and Urban Development, and the Federal Housing Finance Agency, shall jointly prescribe regulations to require any securitizer to retain an economic interest in a portion of the credit risk for any residential mortgage asset that the securitizer, through the issuance of an asset-backed security, transfers, sells, or conveys to a third party.

"(c) STANDARDS FOR REGULATIONS. —

"(1) STANDARDS. —The regulations prescribed under subsection (b) shall —

"(A) prohibit a securitizer from directly or indirectly hedging or otherwise transferring the credit risk that the securitizer is required to retain with respect to an asset;

"(B) require a securitizer to retain —

"(i) not less than 5 percent of the credit risk for any asset —

"(I) that is not a qualified residential mortgage that is transferred, sold, or conveyed through the issuance of an asset-backed security by the securitizer; or

"(II) that is a qualified residential mortgage that is transferred, sold, or conveyed through the issuance of an asset-backed security by the securitizer, if 1 or more of the assets that collateralize the asset-backed security are not qualified residential mortgages; or

"(ii) less than 5 percent of the credit risk for an asset that is not a qualified residential mortgage that is transferred, sold, or conveyed through the issuance of an asset-backed security by the securitizer, if the originator of the asset meets the underwriting standards prescribed under paragraph (2)(B);

"(C) specify —

"(i) the permissible forms of risk retention for purposes of this section;

"(ii) the minimum duration of the risk retention required under this section; and

"(iii) that a securitizer is not required to retain any part of the credit risk for an asset that is transferred, sold or conveyed through the issuance of an asset-backed security by the securitizer, if all of the assets that collateralize the asset-backed security are qualified residential mortgages;

"(D) apply, regardless of whether the securitizer is an insured depository institution;

"(E) with respect to a commercial mortgage, specify the permissible types, forms, and amounts of risk retention that would meet the requirements of subparagraph (B), which in the determination of the Federal banking agencies and the Commission may include —

"(i) retention of a specified amount or percentage of the total credit risk of the asset;

"(ii) retention of the first-loss position by a third-party purchaser that specifically negotiates for the purchase of such first loss position, holds adequate financial resources to back losses, provides due diligence on all individual assets in the pool before the issuance of the asset-backed securities, and meets the same standards for risk retention as the Federal banking agencies and the Commission require of the securitizer;

展部部长及联邦住房金融局应于本条规定颁布之日后270天内联合制定规章,要求任何证券化机构在经济上保留与其通过资产支持证券发行向第三方转让、出售或转移任何住房抵押贷款资产的部分信用风险之间的利害关系。

(c)**规章标准**。——

(1)**标准**。——根据第(b)子条制定的规章——

(A)应禁止证券化机构直接或间接对冲或以其他方式转让其对于资产应自留的信用风险;

(B)应要求证券化机构——

(i)对于以下资产而言,自留不低于5%的信用风险——

(I)并非证券化机构通过资产支持证券发行而转让、出售或转移的合格住房抵押贷款的资产;或

(II)属于证券化机构通过资产支持证券发行而转让、出售或转移的合格住房抵押贷款的资产,但是为资产支持证券提供抵押的1项或1项以上资产不属于合格住房抵押贷款;或

(ii)对于并非证券化机构通过资产支持证券发行而转让、出售或转移的合格住房抵押贷款的资产而言,如果资产发起人符合第(2)(B)款规定的承销标准,自留该等资产5%以下的信用风险;

(C)应明确规定——

(i)就本条而言,允许采用的风险自留形式;

(ii)本条所规定风险自留的最短期限;及

(iii)如果为资产支持证券提供抵押的所有资产均为合格住房抵押贷款,则证券化机构不必就其通过资产支持证券发行而转让、出售或交割的资产自留任何部分信用风险;

(D)应适用于证券化机构,而不论其是否为一家参保存款机构;

(E)就商业抵押贷款而言,应明确规定风险自留允许采用的符合第(B)子款要求的类型、形式和金额;经联邦银行业监管机关和证券交易委员会判定,该等要求可包括——

(i)要求在资产总信用风险中,自留具体金额或比例的风险;

(ii)要求符合下述条件的第三方购买者保留承担第一损失的证券持仓:对购买承担第一损失的证券持仓开展具体磋商;拥有充足财务资源可承担损失;在资产支持证券发行前对池中所有单项资产提供了尽职调查;达到联邦银行业监管机关及证券交易委员会要求证券化机构达到的同一风险自留标准;

"(iii) a determination by the Federal banking agencies and the Commission that the underwriting standards and controls for the asset are adequate; and

"(iv) provision of adequate representations and warranties and related enforcement mechanisms; and

"(F) establish appropriate standards for retention of an economic interest with respect to collateralized debt obligations, securities collateralized by collateralized debt obligations, and similar instruments collateralized by other asset–backed securities; and

"(G) provide for —

"(i) a total or partial exemption of any securitization, as may be appropriate in the public interest and for the protection of investors;

"(ii) a total or partial exemption for the securitization of an asset issued or guaranteed by the United States, or an agency of the United States, as the Federal banking agencies and the Commission jointly determine appropriate in the public interest and for the protection of investors, except that, for purposes of this clause, the Federal National Mortgage Association and the Federal Home Loan Mortgage Corporation are not agencies of the United States;

"(iii) a total or partial exemption for any asset–backed security that is a security issued or guaranteed by any State of the United States, or by any political subdivision of a State or territory, or by any public instrumentality of a State or territory that is exempt from the registration requirements of the Securities Act of 1933 by reason of section 3(a)(2) of that Act (15 U.S.C.77c(a)(2)), or a security defined as a qualified scholarship funding bond in section 150(d)(2) of the Internal Revenue Code of 1986, as may be appropriate in the public interest and for the protection of investors; and

"(iv) the allocation of risk retention obligations between a securitizer and an originator in the case of a securitizer that purchases assets from an originator, as the Federal banking agencies and the Commission jointly determine appropriate.

"(2) ASSET CLASSES. —

"(A) ASSET CLASSES. —The regulations prescribed under subsection (b) shall establish asset classes with separate rules for securitizers of different classes of assets, including residential mortgages, commercial mortgages, commercial loans, auto loans, and any other class of assets that the Federal banking agencies and the Commission deem appropriate.

"(B) CONTENTS. —For each asset class established under subparagraph(A), the regulations prescribed under subsection (b) shall include underwriting standards established by the Federal banking agencies that specify the terms, conditions, and characteristics of a loan within the asset class that indicate a low credit risk with respect to the loan.

"(d) ORIGINATORS. —In determining how to allocate risk retention obligations between a securitizer and an originator under subsection(c)(1)(E)(iv), the Federal banking agencies and the Commission shall—

(iii) 要求联邦银行业监管机关及证券交易委员会判定资产所适用的承销标准及控制具有充分性;及

(iv)要求提供充分的声明、保证及相关执行机制;并

(F)应对于如何在经济上保留与担保债务凭证、以担保债务凭证为抵押的证券以及以其他资产支持证券为抵押的类似工具之间的利害关系,设定适当的标准;并

(G)应规定——

(i)在对维护公共利益及保护投资者确属适当的情况下,为任何证券化提供完全或部分豁免;

(ii)在联邦银行业监管机关及证券交易委员会共同判定对维护公共利益及保护投资者确属适当的情况下, 为联邦政府发行或担保的或某一联邦政府机关发行或担保的资产的证券化提供完全或部分豁免,但是,就本项规定而言,联邦国民抵押贷款协会以及联邦住房贷款抵押公司不具有联邦政府机关身份;

(iii)在对维护公共利益及保护投资者确属适当的情况下,为性质属于以下证券的任何资产支持证券提供完全或部分豁免:美国任何州、或州或准州的任何下属行政区域、或州或准州的任何公共职能部门所发行或担保的因《1933年证券法》第3(a)(2)条[《美国法典》第十五编第77c(a)(2)节]而豁免于该法注册要求的证券,或者《1986年国内税收法典》第150(d)(2)条定义为合格奖学金融资债券的证券;及

(iv)在证券化机构向发起人购买资产的情况下,按照联邦银行业监管机关和证券交易委员会联合确定的适当比例,在证券化机构与发起人之间分配风险自留义务。

(2)**资产类别**。——

(A)**资产类别**。——根据第(b)子条制定的规章应划定资产类别(包括住房抵押贷款、商业抵押贷款、商业贷款、汽车贷款以及联邦银行业监管机关和证券交易委员会认为确属适当的任何其他类别的资产),并针对不同类别资产的证券化机构制定不同规则。

(B)**内容**。——对于根据第(A)子款划定的每一资产类别而言,根据第(b)子条制定的规章应包括联邦银行业监管机关设定的对如下内容作出具体规定的承销标准,即何等贷款条款、条件和特点可以显示该资产类别内的贷款具有较低信用风险。

(d)**发起人**。——在判定如何根据第(c)(1)(E)(iv)子条分配证券化机构和发起人之间的风险自留义务时,联邦银行业监管机关和证券交易委员会应——

"(1) reduce the percentage of risk retention obligations required of the securitizer by the percentage of risk retention obligations required of the originator; and

"(2) consider —

"(A) whether the assets sold to the securitizer have terms, conditions, and characteristics that reflect low credit risk;

"(B) whether the form or volume of transactions in securitization markets creates incentives for imprudent origination of the type of loan or asset to be sold to the securitizer; and

"(C) the potential impact of the risk retention obligations on the access of consumers and businesses to credit on reasonable terms, which may not include the transfer of credit risk to a third party.

"(e) EXEMPTIONS, EXCEPTIONS, AND ADJUSTMENTS. —

"(1) IN GENERAL. —The Federal banking agencies and the Commission may jointly adopt or issue exemptions, exceptions, or adjustments to the rules issued under this section, including exemptions, exceptions, or adjustments for classes of institutions or assets relating to the risk retention requirement and the prohibition on hedging under subsection (c)(1).

"(2) APPLICABLE STANDARDS. —Any exemption, exception, or adjustment adopted or issued by the Federal banking agencies and the Commission under this paragraph shall —

"(A) help ensure high quality underwriting standards for the securitizers and originators of assets that are securitized or available for securitization; and

"(B) encourage appropriate risk management practices by the securitizers and originators of assets, improve the access of consumers and businesses to credit on reasonable terms, or otherwise be in the public interest and for the protection of investors.

"(3) CERTAIN INSTITUTIONS AND PROGRAMS EXEMPT. —

"(A) FARM CREDIT SYSTEM INSTITUTIONS. —Notwithstanding any other provision of this section, the requirements of this section shall not apply to any loan or other financial asset made, insured, guaranteed, or purchased by any institution that is subject to the supervision of the Farm Credit Administration, including the Federal Agricultural Mortgage Corporation.

"(B) OTHER FEDERAL PROGRAMS. —This section shall not apply to any residential, multifamily, or health care facility mortgage loan asset, or securitization based directly or indirectly on such an asset, which is insured or guaranteed by the United States or an agency of the United States. For purposes of this subsection, the Federal National Mortgage Association, the Federal Home Loan Mortgage Corporation, and the Federal home loan banks shall not be considered an agency of the United States.

"(4) EXEMPTION FOR QUALIFIED RESIDENTIAL MORTGAGES. —

"(A) IN GENERAL. —The Federal banking agencies, the Commission, the Secretary of

(1)降低要求证券化机构承担的风险自留义务比例,降低幅度以要求发起人承担的风险自留义务比例为准;并

(2)考虑如下因素——

(A)向证券化机构出售的资产是否具有显示其信用风险较低的条款、条件及特点;

(B)证券化市场内交易的形式或交易量是否会刺激盲目发起向证券化机构出售的贷款或资产类型的行为;及

(C)风险自留义务对消费者及企业以合理条件(不得包括信用风险向第三方转移)获取信贷的机会造成的潜在影响。

(e)**豁免、例外及调整规定**。——

(1)**一般规定**。——联邦银行业监管机关和证券交易委员会可以针对依据本条发布的规则,联合制定或发布豁免、例外或调整规定,包括针对第(c)(1)子条所述风险自留要求和对冲禁止规定对特定类型的机构或资产类别制定或发布豁免、例外或调整规定。

(2)**适用标准**。——联邦银行业监管机关和证券交易委员会根据本款制定或发布的任何豁免、例外或调整规定均应——

(A)有助于确保对证券化资产或可证券化的资产的证券化机构和发起人适用高质量承销标准;并

(B)鼓励资产证券化机构及资产发起人采取适当的风险管理做法,增加消费者及企业以合理条件获得信贷的机会,或以其他方式维护公共利益并保护投资者。

(3)**特定机构和计划的豁免**。——

(A)**农业信贷系统机构**。——无论本条是否存在任何不同规定,本条规定不适用于受农业信贷管理局监管的任何机构(包括联邦农业抵押贷款公司)所设立、承保、担保或购买的任何贷款或其他金融资产。

(B)**其他联邦计划**。——本条规定不适用于由联邦政府或某一联邦政府机关承保或担保的任何住房、多户家庭或卫生保健设施抵押贷款资产,或者直接或间接基于该等资产进行的证券化。就本子条而言,联邦国民抵押协会、联邦住房贷款抵押公司以及联邦住房贷款银行不得被视为联邦政府机关。

(4)**合格住房抵押贷款的豁免**。——

(A)**一般规定**。——联邦银行业监管机关、证券交易委员会、住房与城市发展部

Housing and Urban Development, and the Director of the Federal Housing Finance Agency shall jointly issue regulations to exempt qualified residential mortgages from the risk retention requirements of this subsection.

"(B) QUALIFIED RESIDENTIAL MORTGAGE. —The Federal banking agencies, the Commission, the Secretary of Housing and Urban Development, and the Director of the Federal Housing Finance Agency shall jointly define the term 'qualified residential mortgage' for purposes of this subsection, taking into consideration underwriting and product features that historical loan performance data indicate result in a lower risk of default, such as —

"(i) documentation and verification of the financial resources relied upon to qualify the mortgagor;

"(ii) standards with respect to —

"(I) the residual income of the mortgagor after all monthly obligations;

"(II) the ratio of the housing payments of the mortgagor to the monthly income of the mortgagor;

"(III) the ratio of total monthly installment payments of the mortgagor to the income of the mortgagor;

"(iii) mitigating the potential for payment shock on adjustable rate mortgages through product features and underwriting standards;

"(iv) mortgage guarantee insurance or other types of insurance or credit enhancement obtained at the time of origination, to the extent such insurance or credit enhancement reduces the risk of default; and

"(v) prohibiting or restricting the use of balloon payments, negative amortization, prepayment penalties, interest–only payments, and other features that have been demonstrated to exhibit a higher risk of borrower default.

"(C) LIMITATION ON DEFINITION. —The Federal banking agencies, the Commission, the Secretary of Housing and Urban Development, and the Director of the Federal Housing Finance Agency in defining the term 'qualified residential mortgage', as required by subparagraph (B), shall define that term to be no broader than the definition 'qualified mortgage' as the term is defined under section 129C (c) (2) of the Truth in Lending Act, as amended by the Consumer Financial Protection Act of 2010, and regulations adopted thereunder.

"(5) CONDITION FOR QUALIFIED RESIDENTIAL MORTGAGE EXEMPTION. — The regulations issued under paragraph (4) shall provide that an asset–backed security that is collateralized by tranches of other asset–backed securities shall not be exempt from the risk retention requirements of this subsection.

"(6) CERTIFICATION. —The Commission shall require an issuer to certify, for each

部长及联邦住房金融局局长应联合发布规章，对合格住房抵押贷款豁免适用本子条的风险自留要求。

(B)**合格住房抵押贷款**。——联邦银行业监管机关、证券交易委员会、住房与城市发展部部长及联邦住房金融局局长应联合对本子条所用‘合格住房抵押贷款’一词进行定义,在进行定义时,应考虑根据历史贷款履约数据,能够降低违约风险的审核和产品方面的特色条款,如——

(i)对获得抵押人资格所利用财务资源的证明和核实；

(ii)关于以下各项的标准——
(I)抵押人支付所有月供后的剩余收入；
(II)抵押人房贷月供和抵押人月收入的比率；

(III)抵押人每月分期付款总额和抵押人收入的比率；

(iii)利用产品特征和审核标准来减轻还款可能对可调利率抵押贷款造成的冲击；

(iv)在发起阶段获得的能够降低违约风险的抵押贷款担保保险,或其他类型的保险或信用增级;及

(v)禁止或限制使用大额尾付、负值摊还本金、提前还款违约金、仅还利息还款以及被证明具有借款人违约较高风险的其他特色条款。

(C)**对定义的限制**。——联邦银行业监管机关、证券交易委员会、住房与城市发展部部长以及联邦住房金融局局长在按照第(B)子款规定对‘合格住房抵押贷款’一词进行定义时,应使该词的定义不超出经《2010年消费者金融保护法》修正后的《公信贷款法》第129C(c)(2)条和依据该条制定的规章对‘合格抵押贷款’所做定义的范围。

(5)**向合格住房抵押贷款授予豁免的条件**。——根据第(4)款发布的规章应规定,以其他资产支持证券系列为抵押的资产支持证券,不得豁免适用本子条的风险自留要求。

(6)**自查证明**。——证券交易委员会应要求发行人证明,对于完全以合格住房抵

issuance of an asset-backed security collateralized exclusively by qualified residential mortgages, that the issuer has evaluated the effectiveness of the internal supervisory controls of the issuer with respect to the process for ensuring that all assets that collateralize the asset-backed security are qualified residential mortgages.

"(f) ENFORCEMENT.—The regulations issued under this section shall be enforced by—

"(1) the appropriate Federal banking agency, with respect to any securitizer that is an insured depository institution; and

"(2) the Commission, with respect to any securitizer that is not an insured depository institution.

"(g) AUTHORITY OF COMMISSION.—The authority of the Commission under this section shall be in addition to the authority of the Commission to otherwise enforce the securities laws.

"(h) AUTHORITY TO COORDINATE ON RULEMAKING.—The Chairperson of the Financial Stability Oversight Council shall coordinate all joint rulemaking required under this section.

"(i) EFFECTIVE DATE OF REGULATIONS.—The regulations issued under this section shall become effective—

"(1) with respect to securitizers and originators of asset-backed securities backed by residential mortgages, 1 year after the date on which final rules under this section are published in the Federal Register; and

"(2) with respect to securitizers and originators of all other classes of asset-backed securities, 2 years after the date on which final rules under this section are published in the Federal Register.".

(c) STUDY ON RISK RETENTION.—

(1) STUDY.—The Board of Governors of the Federal Reserve System, in coordination and consultation with the Comptroller of the Currency, the Director of the Office of Thrift Supervision, the Chairperson of the Federal Deposit Insurance Corporation, and the Securities and Exchange Commission shall conduct a study of the combined impact on each individual class of asset-backed security established under section 15G(c)(2) of the Securities Exchange Act of 1934, as added by subsection (b), of—

(A) the new credit risk retention requirements contained in the amendment made by subsection (b), including the effect credit risk retention requirements have on increasing the market for Federally subsidized loans; and

(B) the Financial Accounting Statements 166 and 167 issued by the Financial Accounting Standards Board.

(2) REPORT.—Not later than 90 days after the date of enactment of this Act, the Board of Governors of the Federal Reserve System shall submit to Congress a report on the

押贷款为抵押的资产支持证券的每次发行，发行人为确保所有为资产支持证券提供抵押的资产均为合格住房抵押贷款，均已对其发行过程内部监督控制的有效性进行自我评价。

(f)**执行**。——根据本条发布的规章应由以下各者实施——

(1)对性质为参保存款机构的任何证券化机构而言,由相应的联邦银行业监管机关实施;及

(2)对非参保存款机构的任何证券化机构而言,由证券交易委员会实施。

(g)**证券交易委员会的权力**。——本条规定的证券交易委员会的权力与证券交易委员会享有的其他证券法律执法权具有并存性,前者不限制后者。

(h)**负责对规则制定进行协调的权力**。——金融稳定监督委员会主席应负责协调依据本条规定联合开展的规则制定行为。

(i)**规章生效日**。——根据本条发布的规章应于以下日期生效——

(1)对于由住房抵押贷款支持的资产支持证券的证券化机构和发起人而言,应于根据本条发布的最终规则在《联邦公报》发布之日后届满1年之日生效;及

(2)对于其他类别资产支持证券的证券化机构和发起人而言,应于根据本条发布的最终规则在《联邦公报》发布之日后届满2年之日生效。”

(c)**风险自留研究**。——

(1)**研究**。——联邦储备委员会应与货币监理署署长、储蓄机构监理局局长、联邦存款保险公司主席及证券交易委员会协调并磋商后,就以下事项对按照第(b)子条增加的《1934年证券交易法》第15G(c)(2)条所划定的每一类资产支持证券的综合影响,开展研究——

(A)第(b)子条所作修正中新规定的信用风险自留要求,包括信用风险自留要求对扩大联邦贴息贷款市场的影响;及

(B)财务会计准则委员会发布的第166号及第167号《财务会计准则公告》。

(2)**报告**。——联邦储备委员会应于本法颁布之日后90天内,针对按照第(1)款开展的研究向国会提交一份报告。该等报告应包括针对以下事项提出的制定法和监

study conducted under paragraph (1). Such report shall include statutory and regulatory recommendations for eliminating any negative impacts on the continued viability of the asset–backed securitization markets and on the availability of credit for new lending identified by the study conducted under paragraph (1).

SEC.942. DISCLOSURES AND REPORTING FOR ASSET-BACKED SECURITIES.

(a) SECURITIES EXCHANGE ACT OF 1934. –Section 15(d) of the Securities Exchange Act of 1934 (15 U.S.C.78o(d)) is amended —

(1) by striking "(d) Each" and inserting the following:

"(d) SUPPLEMENTARY AND PERIODIC INFORMATION. —

"(1) IN GENERAL. —Each";

(2) in the third sentence, by inserting after "securities of each class" the following: "other than any class of asset–backed securities,"; and

(3) by adding at the end the following:

"(2) ASSET–BACKED SECURITIES. —

"(A) SUSPENSION OF DUTY TO FILE. —The Commission may, by rule or regulation, provide for the suspension or termination of the duty to file under this subsection for any class of asset–backed security, on such terms and conditions and for such period or periods as the Commission deems necessary or appropriate in the public interest or for the protection of investors.

"(B) CLASSIFICATION OF ISSUERS. —The Commission may, for purposes of this subsection, classify issuers and prescribe requirements appropriate for each class of issuers of asset–backed securities.".

(b) SECURITIES ACT OF 1933. —Section 7 of the Securities Act of 1933 (15 U.S.C. 77g) is amended by adding at the end the following:

"(c) DISCLOSURE REQUIREMENTS. —

"(1) IN GENERAL. —The Commission shall adopt regulations under this subsection requiring each issuer of an asset–backed security to disclose, for each tranche or class of security, information regarding the assets backing that security.

"(2) CONTENT OF REGULATIONS. —In adopting regulations under this subsection, the Commission shall —

"(A) set standards for the format of the data provided by issuers of an asset–backed security, which shall, to the extent feasible, facilitate comparison of such data across securities in similar types of asset classes; and

"(B) require issuers of asset–backed securities, at a minimum, to disclose asset–level or loan–level data, if such data are necessary for investors to independently perform due diligence, including —

管方面的建议,即消除按照第(1)款开展的研究所发现的资产证券化市场之持续活力以及新贷款信用可获得性遭受的任何不利影响。

第942条　资产支持证券的披露和报告

(a)**《1934年证券交易法》**。——《1934年证券交易法》第15(d)条[《美国法典》第十五编第78o(d)节]修正如下——

(1)删除"(d)每一",替以如下内容:

"(d)**补充和定期信息**。——

(1)**一般规定**。——每一";

(2)在第三句中,在"每类证券"之后插入"(但任何类别的资产支持证券除外),";及

(3)在结尾处增加如下内容:

"(2)**资产支持证券**。——

(A)**暂停提交补充和定期信息的义务**。——证券交易委员会可以发布规则或规章,按照其认为对维护公共利益或保护投资者确属必要或适当的条款、条件及期限,暂停或终止本子条规定的对任何类别资产支持证券提交补充和定期信息的义务。

"(B)发行人分类。——证券交易委员会可以为本子条之目的,对发行人进行分类,并针对每一类资产支持证券发行人制定适当的要求。"

(b)**《1933年证券法》**。——在《1933年证券法》第7条(《美国法典》第十五编第77g节)结尾处增加如下内容,作为对该条的修正:

"(c)**披露要求**。——

(1)**一般规定**。——证券交易委员会应依据本子条制定规章,要求每一资产支持证券发行人针对每一系列或类别的证券,披露支持该等证券的资产的相关信息。

(2)**规章内容**。——在根据本子条制定规章时,证券交易委员会应——

(A)就资产支持证券发行人提供的数据设定格式标准(在可行范围内,该等标准应有助于在类似资产类别的证券之间对该等数据进行比较);并

(B)要求资产支持证券发行人至少披露资产层面或贷款层面的数据,前提是该等数据对投资者独立开展尽职调查具有必要性。该等数据包括——

"(i) data having unique identifiers relating to loan brokers or originators;

"(ii) the nature and extent of the compensation of the broker or originator of the assets backing the security; and

"(iii) the amount of risk retention by the originator and the securitizer of such assets.".

SEC.943. REPRESENTATIONS AND WARRANTIES IN ASSET-BACKED OFFERINGS.

Not later than 180 days after the date of enactment of this Act, the Securities and Exchange Commission shall prescribe regulations on the use of representations and warranties in the market for asset-backed securities (as that term is defined in section 3(a)(77) of the Securities Exchange Act of 1934, as added by this subtitle) that —

(1) require each national recognized statistical rating organization to include in any report accompanying a credit rating a description of —

(A) the representations, warranties, and enforcement mechanisms available to investors; and

(B) how they differ from the representations, warranties, and enforcement mechanisms in issuances of similar securities; and

(2) require any securitizer (as that term is defined in section 15G(a) of the Securities Exchange Act of 1934, as added by this subtitle) to disclose fulfilled and unfulfilled repurchase requests across all trusts aggregated by the securitizer, so that investors may identify asset originators with clear underwriting deficiencies.

SEC.944. EXEMPTED TRANSACTIONS UNDER THE SECURITIES ACT OF 1933.

(a) EXEMPTION ELIMINATED. —Section 4 of the Securities Act of 1933 (15 U.S.C. 77d) is amended —

(1) by striking paragraph (5); and

(2) by striking "(6) transactions" and inserting the following: "(5) transactions".

(b) CONFORMING AMENDMENT. —Section 3(a)(4)(B)(vii)(I) of the Securities Exchange Act of 1934 (15 U.S.C.78c(a)(4)(B)(vii)(I)) is amended by striking "4(6)" and inserting "4(5)".

SEC.945. DUE DILIGENCE ANALYSIS AND DISCLOSURE IN ASSET-BACKED SECURITIES ISSUES.

Section 7 of the Securities Act of 1933(15 U.S.C.77g), as amended by this subtitle, is amended byadding at the end the following:

"(d) REGISTRATION STATEMENT FOR ASSET-BACKED SECURITIES. —Not later than 180 days after the date of enactment of this subsection, the Commission shall issue rules relating to the registration statement required to be filed by any issuer of an

(i)具有贷款经纪人或发起人唯一识别码的与贷款经纪人或发起人相关的数据;
(ii)向为证券提供支持的资产的经纪人或发起人提供的薪酬的性质和额度;及

(iii)该等资产的发起人及证券化机构的自留风险金额。"

第943条　资产支持证券发行中的声明与保证

证券交易委员会应于本法颁布之日后180天内,针对资产支持证券[定义见本子编增加《1934年证券交易法》第3(a)(77)条)]市场中对声明与保证的使用制定相关规章——

(1)要求每一全国公认统计评级组织在信用评级附带的任何报告中说明——

(A)投资者可以获得的声明、保证及强制执行机制;及

(B)该等声明、保证及强制执行机制与类似证券发行过程中使用的声明、保证及强制执行机制有何不同;并

(2)要求任何证券化机构[定义见本子编增加的《1934年证券交易法》第15G(a)条]披露其汇集的全部信托中已实现和未实现的回购请求,以便投资者能够识别存在明显承销缺陷的资产发起人。

第944条　《1933年证券法》规定的豁免交易

(a)**取消豁免**。——《1933年证券法》第4条(《美国法典》第十五编第77d节)修正如下——

(1)删除第(5)款;及

(2)删除"(6)交易",替以:"(5)交易"。

(b)**一致性修正**。——《1934年证券交易法》第3(a)(4)(B)(vii)(I)条[《美国法典》第十五编第78c(a)(4)(B)(vii)(I)节]修正如下:删除"4(6)",替以"4(5)"。

第945条　资产支持证券发行中的尽职调查分析和披露

在经本子编修正后的《1933年证券法》第7条(《美国法典》第十五编第77g节)结尾处增加如下内容,作为对该条的进一步修正:

"(d)**资产支持证券注册说明书**。——证券交易委员会应于本子条规定颁布之日后180天内,针对资产支持证券[定义见《1934年证券交易法》第3(a)(77)条]的任何发行人须提交的注册说明书发布规则,要求资产支持证券任何发行人——

asset-backed security(as that term is defined in section 3(a)(77) of the Securities Exchange Act of 1934) that require any issuer of an asset-backed security —

"(1) to perform a review of the assets underlying the asset-backed security; and

"(2) to disclose the nature of the review under paragraph (1).".

SEC.946. STUDY ON THE MACROECONOMIC EFFECTS OF RISK RETENTION REQUIREMENTS.

(a) STUDY REQUIRED. —The Chairman of the Financial Services Oversight Council shall carry out a study on the macroeconomic effects of the risk retention requirements under this subtitle, and the amendments made by this subtitle, with emphasis placed on potential beneficial effects with respect to stabilizing the real estate market. Such study shall include—

(1) an analysis of the effects of risk retention on real estate asset price bubbles, including a retrospective estimate of what fraction of real estate losses may have been averted had such requirements been in force in recent years;

(2) an analysis of the feasibility of minimizing real estate price bubbles by proactively adjusting the percentage of risk retention that must be borne by creditors and securitizers of real estate debt, as a function of regional or national market conditions;

(3) a comparable analysis for proactively adjusting mortgage origination requirements;

(4) an assessment of whether such proactive adjustments should be made by an independent regulator, or in a formulaic and transparent manner;

(5) an assessment of whether such adjustments should take place independently or in concert with monetary policy; and

(6) recommendations for implementation and enabling legislation.

(b) REPORT. —Not later than the end of the 180-day period beginning on the date of the enactment of this title, the Chairman of the Financial Services Oversight Council shall issue a report to the Congress containing any findings and determinations made in carrying out the study required under subsection (a).

Subtitle E—Accountability and Executive Compensation

SEC.951. SHAREHOLDER VOTE ON EXECUTIVE COMPENSATION DISCLOSURES.

The Securities Exchange Act of 1934(15 U.S.C.78a et seq.) is amended by inserting after section 14 (15 U.S.C.78n) the following:

(1)对资产支持证券的基础资产进行审查;并

(2)披露根据第(1)款所述审查的性质。”

第946条　关于风险自留要求对宏观经济的影响之研究

(a)**研究要求**。——金融服务监督理事会主席应针对本子编以及本子编作出的修正中的风险自留要求对宏观经济的影响开展研究，并以该等要求在稳定不动产市场方面可能产生的积极作用为研究重点。该项研究应包括——

(1)关于风险自留对不动产价格泡沫的影响之分析(包括以下回溯式估值:上述要求已在前几年得以实施的,有多大比例的不动产损失本可以避免);

(2)关于通过以下方式将不动产价格泡沫减少到最低限度的可行性分析:根据地区或全国市场状况，对必须由不动产债务的债权人和证券化机构承担的风险自留百分比进行主动调整;

(3)为对抵押贷款发起要求进行主动调整而开展的可比性分析;

(4)评估该主动调整应由独立的监管者完成,还是应通过公式化、透明的方式完成;

(5)评估该等调整应独立进行,还是应与货币政策共同实施;及

(6)实施风险自留要求的建议和相关立法建议。

(b)**报告**。——金融服务监督理事会主席应于本编颁布之日起180天内,向国会提交一份报告,说明其根据第(a)子条开展研究过程中做出的任何认定及判定。

第E子编——问责制及高级管理人员薪酬

第951条　股东对高级管理人员薪酬披露进行的表决

在《1934年证券交易法》(《美国法典》第十五编第78a节及其后条文)第14条(《美国法典》第十五编第78n节)之后插入如下内容,作为对该法的修正:

"SEC.14A. SHAREHOLDER APPROVAL OF EXECUTIVE COMPENSATION.

"(a) SEPARATE RESOLUTION REQUIRED.—

"(1) IN GENERAL.—Not less frequently than once every 3 years, a proxy or consent or authorization for an annual or other meeting of the shareholders for which the proxy solicitation rules of the Commission require compensation disclosure shall include a separate resolution subject to shareholder vote to approve the compensation of executives, as disclosed pursuant to section 229.402 of title 17, Code of Federal Regulations, or any successor thereto.

"(2) FREQUENCY OF VOTE.—Not less frequently than once every 6 years, a proxy or consent or authorization for an annual or other meeting of the shareholders for which the proxy solicitation rules of the Commission require compensation disclosure shall include a separate resolution subject to shareholder vote to determine whether votes on the resolutions required under paragraph (1) will occur every 1, 2, or 3 years.

"(3) EFFECTIVE DATE.—The proxy or consent or authorization for the first annual or other meeting of the shareholders occurring after the end of the 6-month period beginning on the date of enactment of this section shall include—

"(A) the resolution described in paragraph (1); and

"(B) a separate resolution subject to shareholder vote to determine whether votes on the resolutions required under paragraph (1) will occur every 1, 2, or 3 years.

"(b) SHAREHOLDER APPROVAL OF GOLDEN PARACHUTE COMPENSATION.—

"(1) DISCLOSURE.—In any proxy or consent solicitation material (the solicitation of which is subject to the rules of the Commission pursuant to subsection (a)) for a meeting of the shareholders occurring after the end of the 6-month period beginning on the date of enactment of this section, at which shareholders are asked to approve an acquisition, merger, consolidation, or proposed sale or other disposition of all or substantially all the assets of an issuer, the person making such solicitation shall disclose in the proxy or consent solicitation material, in a clear and simple form in accordance with regulations to be promulgated by the Commission, any agreements or understandings that such person has with any named executive officers of such issuer (or of the acquiring issuer, if such issuer is not the acquiring issuer) concerning any type of compensation (whether present, deferred, or contingent) that is based on or otherwise relates to the acquisition, merger, consolidation, sale, or other disposition of all or substantially all of the assets of the issuer and the aggregate total of all such compensation that may (and the conditions upon which it may) be paid or become payable to or on behalf of such executive officer.

"(2) SHAREHOLDER APPROVAL.—Any proxy or consent or authorization relating to the proxy or consent solicitation material containing the disclosure required by paragraph (1) shall include a separate resolution subject to shareholder vote to approve such agreements or understandings and compensation as disclosed, unless such agreements or

“第14A条　股东对高级管理人员薪酬的批准

(a)**单独决议要求**。——

(1)**一般规定**。——如果证券交易委员会代理权征集规则要求，签发股东年会或其他股东会议的代理委托书、代理同意书或授权书时，必须对高管薪酬进行披露，则该等代理委托书、代理同意书或授权书应至少每3年含有1项关于高管薪酬的单独决议，该决议须由股东表决通过并按《联邦规章汇编》第十七编第229.402部分(或其后续规定)披露。

(2)**表决的频率**。——如果证券交易委员会代理权征集规则要求，签发股东年会或其他股东会议的代理委托书、代理同意书或授权书时，必须对高管薪酬进行披露，则该等代理委托书、代理同意书或授权书应至少每6年含有1项须有股东表决通过的旨在确定第(1)款所规定决议表决频率(每1年、每两年或每3年表决1次)的单独决议。

(3)**生效日**。——对于在本条规定颁布之日起6个月之后首次举行的股东年会或其他股东会议而言，其代理委托书、代理同意书或授权书中应包括——

(A)第(1)款所述决议；及

(B)一项须有股东表决通过的旨在确定第(1)款所规定决议表决频率(每1年、每2年或每3年1次)的单独决议。

(b)**股东对黄金降落伞薪酬的批准**。——

(1)**披露**。——对于在本条规定颁布之日起6个月之后召开的股东会议而言，如果股东需要在该会议上批准对某一发行人的收购、兼并、合并，或批准对该发行人全部或基本全部资产的出售或其他处置，且根据第(a)子条，在不违反证券交易委员会规则的前提下发出代理权或代理同意书征集材料的人，与该发行人或收购发行人(如发行人与收购发行人并非同一主体)的具名高级管理人员达成了关于任何类型的薪酬(无论是当前薪酬、递延薪酬还是或有薪酬)的协议或谅解文件，且该等薪酬系基于上述收购、兼并、合并或发行人全部或基本全部资产的出售或其他处置或与之相关，则该征集人应根据证券交易委员会颁发的规章，在该代理权或代理同意书征集材料中以清楚、简明的格式披露上述协议和谅解文件、可能需要向上述高级管理人员支付的或应向其支付的(或可能需要代表上述高级管理人员支付的或应付的)薪酬总额以及付款条件。

(2)**股东批准**。——如果代理权或代理同意书征集材料中含有第(1)款规定的披露信息，则与该等征集材料相关的任何代理委托书、代理同意书或授权书中应包含一份须经股东表决通过旨在批准所披露协议或谅解文件及薪酬的单独决议，但该等协议或谅解文件已根据第(a)子条由股东表决通过的除外。

understandings have been subject to a shareholder vote under subsection (a).

"(c) RULE OF CONSTRUCTION. —The shareholder vote referred to in subsections (a) and (b) shall not be binding on the issuer or the board of directors of an issuer, and may not be construed —

"(1) as overruling a decision by such issuer or board of directors;

"(2) to create or imply any change to the fiduciary duties of such issuer or board of directors;

"(3) to create or imply any additional fiduciary duties for such issuer or board of directors; or

"(4) to restrict or limit the ability of shareholders to make proposals for inclusion in proxy materials related to executive compensation.

"(d) DISCLOSURE OF VOTES. —Every institutional investment manager subject to section 13(f) shall report at least annually how it voted on any shareholder vote pursuant to subsections (a) and (b), unless such vote is otherwise required to be reported publicly by rule or regulation of the Commission.

"(e) EXEMPTION. —The Commission may, by rule or order, exempt an issuer or class of issuers from the requirement under subsection (a) or (b). In determining whether to make an exemption under this subsection, the Commission shall take into account, among other considerations, whether the requirements under subsections (a) and (b) disproportionately burdens small issuers.".

SEC.952. COMPENSATION COMMITTEE INDEPENDENCE.

(a) IN GENERAL. —The Securities Exchange Act of 1934 (15 U.S.C.78 et seq.) is amended by inserting after section 10B, as added by section 753, the following:

"SEC.10C. COMPENSATION COMMITTEES.

"(a) INDEPENDENCE OF COMPENSATION COMMITTEES. —

"(1) LISTING STANDARDS. —The Commission shall, by rule, direct the national securities exchanges and national securities associations to prohibit the listing of any equity security of an issuer, other than an issuer that is a controlled company, limited partnership, company in bankruptcy proceedings, open–ended management investment company that is registered under the Investment Company Act of 1940, or a foreign private issuer that provides annual disclosures to shareholders of the reasons that the foreign private issuer does not have an independent compensation committee, that does not comply with the requirements of this subsection.

"(2) INDEPENDENCE OF COMPENSATION COMMITTEES. —The rules of the Commission under paragraph (1) shall require that each member of the compensation committee of the board of directors of an issuer be —

"(A) a member of the board of directors of the issuer; and

(c)**解释规则**。——第(a)子条和第(b)子条所述股东表决对发行人或发行人的董事会不应具有约束力,且不得被解释为——

(1)推翻了发行人或董事会作出的决定;

(2)对发行人或董事会的受信义务造成任何改变或暗示发行人或董事会的受信义务发生任何改变;

(3)针对发行人或董事会创设任何额外受信义务或暗示为发行人或董事会带来任何额外受信义务;或

(4)约束或限制股东在代理材料中纳入与高级管理人员薪酬相关提议的能力。

(d)**表决的披露**。——每一受制于第13(f)条的机构投资管理人均应至少每年汇报一次其如何根据第(a)子条和第(b)子条对任何须经股东表决通过的决议进行表决,但该证券交易委员会的规则或规章对该等表决的公开报告另有规定的除外。

(e)**豁免**。——证券交易委员会有权发布规则或命令,向某一发行人或某类发行人授予豁免,使其不必遵守第(a)子条或第(b)子条规定的限制。证券交易委员会在判定是否应根据本子条授予豁免时,应考虑第(a)子条和第(b)子条的规定是否会对小规模发行人造成与其规模不成比例的负担以及其他因素。"

第952条　薪酬委员会的独立性

(a)**一般规定**。——在第753条增加的《1934年证券交易法》(《美国法典》第十五编第78节及其后条文)第10B条之后插入如下内容,作为对该法的修正:

"第10C条　薪酬委员会

(a)**薪酬委员会的独立性**。——

(1)**上市标准**。——证券交易委员会应发布规则,指令全国性证券交易所和全国性证券协会禁止对不符合本子条规定的发行人的任何股权证券进行上市交易,但具有以下身份的发行人除外:受控公司、有限合伙、已进入破产程序的公司、已根据《1940年投资公司法》注册的开放性管理型投资公司,或每年向股东披露未设立独立薪酬委员会之原因的外国私募发行人。

(2)**薪酬委员会的独立性**。——第(1)款所述证券交易委员会规则应要求发行人董事会下设的薪酬委员会的每名成员均应——

(A)身为该发行人董事会成员;并

"(B) independent.

"(3) INDEPENDENCE. —The rules of the Commission under paragraph (1) shall require that, in determining the definition of the term 'independence' for purposes of paragraph (2), the national securities exchanges and the national securities associations shall consider relevant factors, including —

"(A) the source of compensation of a member of the board of directors of an issuer, including any consulting, advisory, or other compensatory fee paid by the issuer to such member of the board of directors; and

"(B) whether a member of the board of directors of an issuer is affiliated with the issuer, a subsidiary of the issuer, or an affiliate of a subsidiary of the issuer.

"(4) EXEMPTION AUTHORITY. —The rules of the Commission under paragraph (1) shall permit a national securities exchange or a national securities association to exempt a particular relationship from the requirements of paragraph (2), with respect to the members of a compensation committee, as the national securities exchange or national securities association determines is appropriate, taking into consideration the size of an issuer and any other relevant factors.

"(b) INDEPENDENCE OF COMPENSATION CONSULTANTS AND OTHER COMPENSATION COMMITTEE ADVISERS. —

"(1) IN GENERAL. —The compensation committee of an issuer may only select a compensation consultant, legal counsel, or other adviser to the compensation committee after taking into consideration the factors identified by the Commission under paragraph (2).

"(2) RULES. —The Commission shall identify factors that affect the independence of a compensation consultant, legal counsel, or other adviser to a compensation committee of an issuer. Such factors shall be competitively neutral among categories of consultants, legal counsel, or other advisers and preserve the ability of compensation committees to retain the services of members of any such category, and shall include —

"(A) the provision of other services to the issuer by the person that employs the compensation consultant, legal counsel, or other adviser;

"(B) the amount of fees received from the issuer by the person that employs the compensation consultant, legal counsel, or other adviser, as a percentage of the total revenue of the person that employs the compensation consultant, legal counsel, or other adviser;

"(C) the policies and procedures of the person that employs the compensation consultant, legal counsel, or other adviser that are designed to prevent conflicts of interest;

"(D) any business or personal relationship of the compensation consultant, legal counsel, or other adviser with a member of the compensation committee; and

"(E) any stock of the issuer owned by the compensation consultant, legal counsel, or other adviser.

(B)具有独立性。

(3)**独立性**。——第(1)款所述证券交易委员会规则应要求全国性证券交易所和全国性证券协会在确定第(2)款所述“独立性”一词的定义时,应考虑相关因素,包括——

(A)发行人董事会成员薪酬的来源,包括该发行人向董事会成员支付的任何咨询费、顾问费或其他报酬;及

(B)发行人董事会成员是否与该发行人、其子公司或者该发行人子公司的关联方存在关联关系。

(4)**豁免权**。——第(1)款所述证券交易委员会规则应允许全国性证券交易所或全国性证券协会在考虑发行人规模和任何其他相关因素的基础上,对薪酬委员会成员的特定关系授予其判定确属适当的豁免,使其不必受第(2)款要求的限制。

(b)**薪酬顾问和薪酬委员会其他顾问的独立性**。——

(1)**一般规定**。——发行人薪酬委员会可以在考虑证券交易委员会根据第(2)款所确定的其他因素之后,为薪酬委员会仅选定一名薪酬顾问、法律顾问或其他顾问。

(2)**规则**。——证券交易委员会应确定影响发行人薪酬委员会薪酬顾问、法律顾问或其他顾问独立性的因素。对于不同类别的咨询顾问、法律顾问或其他顾问而言,该等因素不得导致某一类别的顾问获得竞争优势或劣势,并应使薪酬委员会能够继续聘用上述任何类别的顾问为其提供服务;该等考虑因素应包括——

(A)该等薪酬顾问、法律顾问或其他顾问的雇主为该等发行人提供的其他服务;

(B)该等薪酬顾问、法律顾问或其他顾问的雇主从该等发行人处收到的费用金额在该等雇主收入总额中所占百分比;

(C)该等薪酬顾问、法律顾问或其他顾问的雇主为防范利益冲突而制定的政策和程序;

(D)该等薪酬顾问、法律顾问或其他顾问与薪酬委员会成员间的任何业务关系或私人关系;及

(E)该等薪酬顾问、法律顾问或其他顾问拥有的该等发行人的任何股票。

"(c) COMPENSATION COMMITTEE AUTHORITY RELATING TO COMPENSATION CONSULTANTS.—

"(1) AUTHORITY TO RETAIN COMPENSATION CONSULTANT.—

"(A) IN GENERAL.—The compensation committee of an issuer, in its capacity as a committee of the board of directors, may, in its sole discretion, retain or obtain the advice of a compensation consultant.

"(B) DIRECT RESPONSIBILITY OF COMPENSATION COMMITTEE.—The compensation committee of an issuer shall be directly responsible for the appointment, compensation, and oversight of the work of a compensation consultant.

"(C) RULE OF CONSTRUCTION.—This paragraph may not be construed—

"(i) to require the compensation committee to implement or act consistently with the advice or recommendations of the compensation consultant; or

"(ii) to affect the ability or obligation of a compensation committee to exercise its own judgment in fulfillment of the duties of the compensation committee.

"(2) DISCLOSURE.—In any proxy or consent solicitation material for an annual meeting of the shareholders (or a special meeting in lieu of the annual meeting) occurring on or after the date that is 1 year after the date of enactment of this section, each issuer shall disclose in the proxy or consent material, in accordance with regulations of the Commission, whether—

"(A) the compensation committee of the issuer retained or obtained the advice of a compensation consultant; and

"(B) the work of the compensation consultant has raised any conflict of interest and, if so, the nature of the conflict and how the conflict is being addressed.

"(d) AUTHORITY TO ENGAGE INDEPENDENT LEGAL COUNSEL AND OTHER ADVISERS.—

"(1) IN GENERAL.—The compensation committee of an issuer, in its capacity as a committee of the board of directors, may, in its sole discretion, retain and obtain the advice of independent legal counsel and other advisers.

"(2) DIRECT RESPONSIBILITY OF COMPENSATION COMMITTEE.—The compensation committee of an issuer shall be directly responsible for the appointment, compensation, and oversight of the work of independent legal counsel and other advisers.

"(3) RULE OF CONSTRUCTION.—This subsection may not be construed—

"(A) to require a compensation committee to implement or act consistently with the advice or recommendations of independent legal counsel or other advisers under this subsection; or

"(B) to affect the ability or obligation of a compensation committee to exercise its own judgment in fulfillment of the duties of the compensation committee.

(c)**薪酬委员会拥有的与薪酬顾问相关的权力**。——

(1)**聘用薪酬顾问的权力**。——

(A)**一般规定**。——发行人薪酬委员会,作为董事会下属委员会,可以完全依其自由裁量权聘用薪酬顾问或获取薪酬顾问提供的顾问服务。

(B)**薪酬委员会的直接责任**。——发行人薪酬委员会应直接负责薪酬顾问的任命、薪酬和对其工作的监督。

(C)**解释规则**。——本款不得被解释为——

(i)要求薪酬委员会实施薪酬顾问的意见或建议,或按照该等意见或建议行事;或

(ii)影响薪酬委员会履行职责过程中作出独立判断的能力或义务。

(2)**披露**。——对于在本条规定颁布之日后届满1年之日或之后召开的股东年会(或代替年度会议的特别会议)而言,每一发行人应在相关的任何代理权或代理同意书征集材料中,根据证券交易委员会的规章对以下情况进行披露——

(A)该发行人的薪酬委员会是否聘用了薪酬顾问,或获取了薪酬顾问提供的顾问服务;及

(B)该薪酬顾问的工作是否引发了任何利益冲突;如是,则应披露该等冲突的性质以及处理方式。

(d)**聘用独立法律顾问和其他顾问的权力**。——

(1)**一般规定**。——发行人薪酬委员会,作为董事会的下属委员会,可以完全依其自由裁量权聘用独立法律顾问和其他顾问,或获取独立法律顾问和其他顾问提供的顾问服务。

(2)**薪酬委员会的直接责任**。——发行人薪酬委员会应直接负责独立法律顾问和其他顾问的任命、薪酬和对其工作的监督。

(3)**解释规则**。——本子条不得被解释为——

(A)要求薪酬委员会实施本子条所述独立法律顾问和其他顾问的意见或建议,或按照该等意见或建议行事;或

(B)影响薪酬委员会在履行职责过程中作出独立判断的能力或义务。

"(e) COMPENSATION OF COMPENSATION CONSULTANTS, INDEPENDENT LEGAL COUNSEL, AND OTHER ADVISERS. —Each issuer shall provide for appropriate funding, as determined by the compensation committee in its capacity as a committee of the board of directors, for payment of reasonable compensation —

"(1) to a compensation consultant; and

"(2) to independent legal counsel or any other adviser to the compensation committee.

"(f) COMMISSION RULES. —

"(1) IN GENERAL. —Not later than 360 days after the date of enactment of this section, the Commission shall, by rule, direct the national securities exchanges and national securities associations to prohibit the listing of any security of an issuer that is not in compliance with the requirements of this section.

"(2) OPPORTUNITY TO CURE DEFECTS. —The rules of the Commission under paragraph (1) shall provide for appropriate procedures for an issuer to have a reasonable opportunity to cure any defects that would be the basis for the prohibition under paragraph (1), before the imposition of such prohibition.

"(3) EXEMPTION AUTHORITY. —

"(A) IN GENERAL. —The rules of the Commission under paragraph (1) shall permit a national securities exchange or a national securities association to exempt a category of issuers from the requirements under this section, as the national securities exchange or the national securities association determines is appropriate.

"(B) CONSIDERATIONS. — In determining appropriate exemptions under subparagraph (A), the national securities exchange or the national securities association shall take into account the potential impact of the requirements of this section on smaller reporting issuers.

"(g) CONTROLLED COMPANY EXEMPTION. —

"(1) IN GENERAL. —This section shall not apply to any controlled company.

"(2) DEFINITION. —For purposes of this section, the term 'controlled company' means an issuer —

"(A) that is listed on a national securities exchange or by a national securities association; and

"(B) that holds an election for the board of directors of the issuer in which more than 50 percent of the voting power is held by an individual, a group, or another issuer.".

(b) STUDY AND REPORT. —

(1) STUDY. —The Securities and Exchange Commission shall conduct a study and review of the use of compensation consultants and the effects of such use.

(2) REPORT. —Not later than 2 years after the date of the enactment of this Act, the Commission shall submit a report to Congress on the results of the study and review required

（e）**薪酬顾问、独立法律顾问和其他顾问的薪酬**。——每一发行人均应按照薪酬委员会以董事会下属委员会身份判定确属适当的金额，为薪酬委员会提供经费，以便向以下顾问支付合理报酬——

（1）薪酬顾问；及

（2）薪酬委员会的独立法律顾问或任何其他顾问。

（f）**证券交易委员会规则**。——

（1）**一般规定**。——证券交易委员会应于本条规定颁布之日后360天内发布规则，指令全国性证券交易所和全国性证券协会禁止不符合本条规定的发行人的任何证券进行上市交易。

（2）**缺陷补救机会**。——第（1）款所述证券交易委员会规则应规定适当的程序，为存在缺陷的发行人在第（1）款所述相关禁止规定实施前，提供合理的补救机会。

（3）**豁免权**。——

（A）**一般规定**。——第（1）款所述证券交易委员会规则应允许全国性证券交易所或全国性证券协会对其判定确属适当的某类发行人授予豁免，使其不必受本条要求的限制。

（B）**考虑因素**。——全国性证券交易所或全国性证券协会在根据第（A）子款判定豁免是否适当时，应考虑本条要求可能对负有报告义务的小规模发行人产生的影响。

（g）**对受控公司的豁免**。——

（1）**一般规定**。——本条规定不适用于任何受控公司。

（2）**定义**。——就本条而言，‘受控公司’一词系指具有以下特征的发行人——

（A）在全国性证券交易所上市，或由全国性证券协会完成上市；且

（B）选举产生的董事会50%以上的表决权由某一个人、集团或其他发行人拥有。”

（b）**研究及报告**。——

（1）**研究**。——证券交易委员会应针对薪酬顾问的使用及使用薪酬顾问产生的影响开展研究和评价。

（2）**报告**。——证券交易委员会应于本法颁布之日后2年内，就本子条所规定研究和评价的结果向国会提交一份报告。

by this subsection.

SEC.953. EXECUTIVE COMPENSATION DISCLOSURES.

(a) DISCLOSURE OF PAY VERSUS PERFORMANCE. —Section 14 of the Securities Exchange Act of 1934 (15 U.S.C.78n), as amended by this title, is amended by adding at the end the following:

"(i) DISCLOSURE OF PAY VERSUS PERFORMANCE. —The Commission shall, by rule, require each issuer to disclose in any proxy or consent solicitation material for an annual meeting of the shareholders of the issuer a clear description of any compensation required to be disclosed by the issuer under section 229.402 of title 17, Code of Federal Regulations (or any successor thereto), including information that shows the relationship between executive compensation actually paid and the financial performance of the issuer, taking into account any change in the value of the shares of stock and dividends of the issuer and any distributions. The disclosure under this subsection may include a graphic representation of the information required to be disclosed.".

(b) ADDITIONAL DISCLOSURE REQUIREMENTS. —

(1) IN GENERAL. —The Commission shall amend section 229.402 of title 17, Code of Federal Regulations, to require each issuer to disclose in any filing of the issuer described in section 229.10(a) of title 17, Code of Federal Regulations (or any successor thereto) —

(A) the median of the annual total compensation of all employees of the issuer, except the chief executive officer (or any equivalent position) of the issuer;

(B) the annual total compensation of the chief executive officer (or any equivalent position) of the issuer; and

(C) the ratio of the amount described in subparagraph(A) to the amount described in subparagraph (B).

(2) TOTAL COMPENSATION. —For purposes of this subsection, the total compensation of an employee of an issuer shall be determined in accordance with section 229.402(c)(2)(x) of title 17, Code of Federal Regulations, as in effect on the day before the date of enactment of this Act.

SEC.954. RECOVERY OF ERRONEOUSLY AWARDED COMPENSATION.

The Securities Exchange Act of 1934 is amended by inserting after section 10C, as added by section 952, the following:

"SEC.10D. RECOVERY OF ERRONEOUSLY AWARDED COMPENSATION POLICY.

"(a) LISTING STANDARDS. —The Commission shall, by rule, direct the national securities exchanges and national securities associations to prohibit the listing of any security of an issuer that does not comply with the requirements of this section.

"(b) RECOVERY OF FUNDS. —The rules of the Commission under subsection (a)

第953条　高级管理人员的薪酬披露

(a)**薪酬支付与财务绩效披露**。——在经本编修正后的《1934年证券交易法》第14条(《美国法典》第十五编第78n节)结尾处增加如下内容,作为对该条的进一步修正:

"(i)**薪酬支付与财务绩效披露**。——证券交易委员会应发布规则,要求每一发行人在考虑股份价值、股息发生的任何变化以及任何股息分配的基础上,在其股东年会的任何代理权或代理同意书征集材料中清楚说明根据《联邦规章汇编》第十七编第229.402部分(或其后续规定)发行人应予披露的任何薪酬,包括实际支付的高级管理人员薪酬与该等发行人的财务绩效之间的关系。根据本子条进行的披露中可包含一份图示,对要求披露的信息予以说明。"

(b)**补充披露要求**。——

(1)**一般规定**。——证券交易委员会应对《联邦规章汇编》第十七编第229.402部分进行修正,以便要求每一发行人在其根据《联邦规章汇编》第十七编第229.10(a)部分(或其后续规定)提交的任何材料中披露——

(A)除首席执行官(或任何同等职位管理人员)以外该等发行人全体雇员年薪总额的中间值;

(B)该等发行人首席执行官(或任何同等职位管理人员)的年薪总额;及

(C)第(A)子款所述金额和第(B)子款所述金额的比率。

(2)**薪酬总额**。——就本子条而言,发行人雇员的薪酬总额应根据本法颁布之日前1天有效适用的《联邦规章汇编》第十七编第229.402(c)(2)(x)部分进行确定。

第954条　错付薪酬的追索

在经第952条增加的《1934年证券交易法》第10C条之后插入如下内容,作为对该法的修正:

"第10D条　错付薪酬追索政策

(a)**上市标准**。——证券交易委员会应发布规则,指令全国性证券交易所和全国性证券协会禁止对不符合本条规定的发行人的任何证券进行上市交易。

(b)**资金的追索**。——第(a)子条所述证券交易委员会规则应要求每一发行人制

shall require each issuer to develop and implement a policy providing —

"(1) for disclosure of the policy of the issuer on incentive–based compensation that is based on financial information required to be reported under the securities laws; and

"(2) that, in the event that the issuer is required to prepare an accounting restatement due to the material noncompliance of the issuer with any financial reporting requirement under the securities laws, the issuer will recover from any current or former executive officer of the issuer who received incentive–based compensation (including stock options awarded as compensation) during the 3–year period preceding the date on which the issuer is required to prepare an accounting restatement, based on the erroneous data, in excess of what would have been paid to the executive officer under the accounting restatement.".

SEC.955. DISCLOSURE REGARDING EMPLOYEE AND DIRECTOR HEDGING.

Section 14 of the Securities Exchange Act of 1934(15 U.S.C.78n), as amended by this title, is amended by adding at the end the following:

"(j) DISCLOSURE OF HEDGING BY EMPLOYEES AND DIRECTORS. — The Commission shall, by rule, require each issuer to disclose in any proxy or consent solicitation material for an annual meeting of the shareholders of the issuer whether any employee or member of the board of directors of the issuer, or any designee of such employee or member, is permitted to purchase financial instruments(including prepaid variable forward contracts, equity swaps, collars, and exchange funds) that are designed to hedge or offset any decrease in the market value of equity securities —

"(1) granted to the employee or member of the board of directors by the issuer as part of the compensation of the employee or member of the board of directors; or

"(2) held, directly or indirectly, by the employee or member of the board of directors.".

SEC.956. ENHANCED COMPENSATION STRUCTURE REPORTING.

(a) ENHANCED DISCLOSURE AND REPORTING OF COMPENSATION ARRANGEMENTS. —

(1) IN GENERAL. —Not later than 9 months after the date of enactment of this title, the appropriate Federal regulators jointly shall prescribe regulations or guidelines to require each covered financial institution to disclose to the appropriate Federal regulator the structures of all incentive–based compensation arrangements offered by such covered financial institutions sufficient to determine whether the compensation structure —

(A) provides an executive officer, employee, director, or principal shareholder of the covered financial institution with excessive compensation, fees, or benefits; or

(B) could lead to material financial loss to the covered financial institution.

(2) RULES OF CONSTRUCTION. —Nothing in this section shall be construed as requiring the reporting of the actual compensation of particular individuals. Nothing in this

定并实施作出如下规定的政策——

(1)对于该等发行人基于根据证券法律应予以报告的财务信息而制定的激励性薪酬政策,该等发行人应予以披露;且

(2)如果该等发行人因存在严重违反证券法律中财务报告要求的行为而被要求对会计报表进行重述,且在该等发行人被要求对财务报表进行重述之日前3年内,该等发行人的任何现任或前任高级管理人员已基于错误数据获得了超过根据重述的会计报表将向其支付的薪酬金额的激励性薪酬(包括作为薪酬授予的股票期权),则该等发行人将向上述高级管理人员进行追索超额支付的薪酬。”

第955条　关于雇员和董事套期保值行为的披露

在经本编修正后的《1934年证券交易法》第14条(《美国法典》第十五编第78n节)结尾处增加如下内容,作为对该条的进一步修正:

“(j)**关于雇员和董事套期保值行为的披露**。——证券交易委员会应发布规则,要求每一发行人在其股东年会的任何代理权或代理同意书征集材料中披露如下信息:该等发行人的任何雇员或董事会成员,或该等雇员或董事会成员的任何指定人员是否被允许购买旨在为以下股权证券的市场价值提供套期保值或抵销其市场价值下滑的金融工具(包括预付可变远期合约、股权互换、保护性封顶保底期权以及交换基金)——

(1)该等发行人授予该等雇员或董事会成员的作为该等雇员或董事会成员薪酬组成部分的股权证券;或

(2)该等雇员或董事会成员直接或间接持有的股权证券。”

第956条　加强薪酬结构报告

(a)**加强对薪酬安排的披露和报告**。——

(1)**一般规定**。——相应的联邦监管者应于本编颁布之日后9个月内,联合制定规章或指引,要求每一所涉金融机构向相应的联邦监管者充分披露其所提供全部激励性薪酬安排的结构,以便该等监管者判定该等薪酬结构——

(A)向该等所涉金融机构的高级管理人员、职员、董事或主要股东提供的薪酬、费用或福利是否过高;或

(B)是否能够导致该等所涉金融机构遭受重大财务损失。

(2)**解释规则**。——本条的任何规定均不得被解释为要求对特定个人的实际薪酬进行报告,亦不得被解释为要求不存在任何激励性报酬安排的所涉金融机构进行

section shall be construed to require a covered financial institution that does not have an incentive-based payment arrangement to make the disclosures required under this subsection.

(b) PROHIBITION ON CERTAIN COMPENSATION ARRANGEMENTS. — Not later than 9 months after the date of enactment of this title, the appropriate Federal regulators shall jointly prescribe regulations or guidelines that prohibit any types of incentive-based payment arrangement, or any feature of any such arrangement, that the regulators determine encourages inappropriate risks by covered financial institutions —

(1) by providing an executive officer, employee, director, or principal shareholder of the covered financial institution with excessive compensation, fees, or benefits; or

(2) that could lead to material financial loss to the covered financial institution.

(c) STANDARDS. —The appropriate Federal regulators shall —

(1) ensure that any standards for compensation established under subsections(a) or (b) are comparable to the standards established under section of the Federal Deposit Insurance Act (12 U.S.C.2 1831p-1) for insured depository institutions; and

(2) in establishing such standards under such subsections, take into consideration the compensation standards described in section 39(c) of the Federal Deposit Insurance Act (12 U.S.C.1831p- 9 1(c)).

(d) ENFORCEMENT. —The provisions of this section and the regulations issued under this section shall be enforced under section 505 of the Gramm-Leach-Bliley Act and, for purposes of such section, a violation of this section or such regulations shall be treated as a violation of subtitle A of title V of such Act.

(e) DEFINITIONS. —As used in this section —

(1) the term "appropriate Federal regulator" means the Board of Governors of the Federal Reserve System, the Office of the Comptroller of the Currency, the Board of Directors of the Federal Deposit Insurance Corporation, the Director of the Office of Thrift Supervision, the National Credit Union Administration Board, the Securities and Exchange Commission, the Federal Housing Finance Agency; and

(2) the term "covered financial institution" means —

(A) a depository institution or depository institution holding company, as such terms are defined in section 3 of the Federal Deposit Insurance Act (12 U.S.C.1813);

(B) a broker-dealer registered under section 15 of the Securities Exchange Act of 1934 (15 U.S.C.78o);

(C) a credit union, as described in section 19(b)(1)(A)(iv) of the Federal Reserve Act;

本子条所规定的披露。

(b)**关于特定薪酬安排的禁止性规定**。——相应的联邦监管者应于本编颁布之日后9个月内,联合制定规章或指引,以禁止订立该等监管者判定的具有如下情形的任何类型激励性报酬安排,或禁止该等安排具有如下情形的任何特征——

(1)鼓励所涉金融机构通过向其高级管理人员、职员、董事,或主要股东提供过高薪酬、费用或福利的方式承担不当风险;或

(2)鼓励所涉金融机构承担可能会导致其遭受重大财务损失的不当风险。

(c)**标准**。——相应的联邦监管者应——

(1)确保根据第(a)子条或第(b)子条制定的任何薪酬标准与根据《联邦存款保险法》(《美国法典》第十二编第 1831p-1节[1])制定的针对参保存款机构的标准具有可比性;并

(2)在制定该等标准时,考虑《联邦存款保险法》第39(c)条[《美国法典》第十二编第1831p-9 1(c)节]所述薪酬标准。

(d)**实施**。——本条规定以及根据本条发布的规章均应根据《格雷姆—里奇—比利雷法》第505条进行实施,且就第505条而言,违反本条或根据本条发布的规章的行为即应视为违反《格雷姆—里奇—比利雷法》第五编第A子编的行为。

(e)**定义**。——就本条而言——

(1)"相应的联邦监管者"一词系指联邦储备委员会、货币监理署、联邦存款保险公司董事会、储蓄机构监理局局长、国家信贷联盟署委员会、证券交易委员会和联邦住房金融局;且

(2)"所涉金融机构"一词系指——

(A)存款机构或存款机构控股公司["存款机构"及"存款机构控股公司"的定义见《联邦存款保险法》第3条(《美国法典》第十二编第1813节)];

(B)根据《1934年证券交易法》第15条(《美国法典》第十五编第78o节)注册的经纪自营商;

(C)《联邦储备法》第19(b)(1)(A)(iv)条所述信贷联盟;

1 该索引与本项目其他地方的索引格式不一致,据查证《美国法典》原文,"2"为多余,译文中将其删除。——译者注

(D) an investment advisor, as such term is defined in section 202(a)(11) of the Investment Advisers Act of 1940 (15 U.S.C.80b–2(a)(11));

(E) the Federal National Mortgage Association;

(F) the Federal Home Loan Mortgage Corporation; and

(G) any other financial institution that the appropriate Federal regulators, jointly, by rule, determine should be treated as a covered financial institution for purposes of this section.

(f) EXEMPTION FOR CERTAIN FINANCIAL INSTITUTIONS. —The requirements of this section shall not apply to covered financial institutions with assets of less than $1,000,000,000.

SEC.957. VOTING BY BROKERS.

Section 6(b) of the Securities Exchange Act of 1934 (15 U.S.C.78f(b)) is amended —

(1) in paragraph (9) —

(A) in subparagraph (A), by redesignating clauses (i) through (v) as subclauses (I) through (V), respectively, and adjusting the margins accordingly;

(B) by redesignating subparagraphs (A) through (D) as clauses (i) through (iv), respectively, and adjusting the margins accordingly;

(C) by inserting "(A)" after "(9)"; and

(D) in the matter immediately following clause (iv), as so redesignated, by striking "As used" and inserting the following:

"(B) As used".

(2) by adding at the end the following:

"(10)(A) The rules of the exchange prohibit any member that is not the beneficial owner of a security registered under section 12 from granting a proxy to vote the security in connection with a shareholder vote described in subparagraph (B), unless the beneficial owner of the security has instructed the member to vote the proxy in accordance with the voting instructions of the beneficial owner.

"(B) A shareholder vote described in this subparagraph is a shareholder vote with respect to the election of a member of the board of directors of an issuer, executive compensation, or any other significant matter, as determined by the Commission, by rule, and does not include a vote with respect to the uncontested election of a member of the board of directors of any investment company registered under the Investment Company Act of 1940 (15 U.S.C.80b–1 et seq.).

"(C) Nothing in this paragraph shall be construed to prohibit a national securities exchange from prohibiting a member that is not the beneficial owner of a security registered under section 12 from granting a proxy to vote the security in connection with a shareholder vote not described in subparagraph (A).".

(D)投资顾问(定义见《1940年投资顾问法》第202(a)(11)条[《美国法典》第十五编第80b-2(a)(11)节)];

(E)联邦国民住房贷款协会;

(F)联邦住房贷款抵押公司;及

(G)相应的联邦监管者联合发布规则确定的应视为本条意义上的所涉金融机构的任何其他金融机构。

(f)**对特定金融机构的豁免**。——资产不足10亿美元的所涉金融机构不适用本条规定。

第957条 经纪商的表决

《1934年证券交易法》第6(b)条[《美国法典》第十五编第78f(b)节]修正如下——

(1)在第(9)款中——

(A)第(A)子款第(i)项至第(v)项分别重新编号为第(I)子项至第(V)子项,并相应调整缩进距离;

(B)第(A)子款至第(D)子款分别重新编号为第(i)项至第(iv)项,并相应调整缩进距离;

(C)在"(9)"之后插入"(A)";及

(D)在紧接第(iv)项(以重新编号后的序号为准)之后的内容中,删除"就本款而言",替以:

"(B)就本款而言"。

(2)在该条结尾处增加如下内容:

"(10)(A)如果任何成员并非根据第12条注册的证券的受益所有人,则根据交易所规则,在进行第(B)子款所述股东表决之时,该等成员不得就该等证券授予代理表决权,但该证券的受益所有人已指示该等成员根据该受益所有人的指示进行代理表决的除外。

(B)本子款所述股东表决是针对发行人董事会成员选举、高级管理人员薪酬或证券交易委员会发布的规则所确定的其他重大事项的股东表决,而不包括根据《1940年投资公司法》(《美国法典》第十五编第80b-1节及其后条文)注册的任何投资公司进行的针对董事会成员非竞争性选举的表决。

(C)本款中的任何规定均不得被解释为禁止全国性证券交易所禁止身份并非根据第12条所注册证券之受益所有人的成员在进行第(A)子款所述之外的股东表决时就该等证券授予代理表决权。"

Subtitle F—Improvements to the Management of the Securities and Exchange Commission

SEC.961. REPORT AND CERTIFICATION OF INTERNAL SUPERVISORY CONTROLS.

(a) ANNUAL REPORTS AND CERTIFICATION. —Not later than 90 days after the end of each fiscal year, the Commission shall submit a report to the Committee on Banking, Housing, and Urban Affairs of the Senate and the Committee on Financial Services of the House of Representatives on the conduct by the Commission of examinations of registered entities, enforcement investigations, and review of corporate financial securities filings.

(b) CONTENTS OF REPORTS. —Each report under subsection (a) shall contain —

(1) an assessment, as of the end of the most recent fiscal year, of the effectiveness of —

(A) the internal supervisory controls of the Commission; and

(B) the procedures of the Commission applicable to the staff of the Commission who perform examinations of registered entities, enforcement investigations, and reviews of corporate financial securities filings;

(2) a certification that the Commission has adequate internal supervisory controls to carry out the duties of the Commission described in paragraph (1)(B); and

(3) a summary by the Comptroller General of the United States of the review carried out under subsection (d).

(c) CERTIFICATION. —

(1) SIGNATURE. —The certification under subsection(b)(2) shall be signed by the Director of the Division of Enforcement, the Director of the Division of Corporation Finance, and the Director of the Office of Compliance Inspections and Examinations(or the head of any successor division or office).

(2) CONTENT OF CERTIFICATION. —Each individual described in paragraph (1) shall certify that the individual —

(A) is directly responsible for establishing and maintaining the internal supervisory controls of the Division or Office of which the individual is the head;

(B) is knowledgeable about the internal supervisory controls of the Division or Office of which the individual is the head;

(C) has evaluated the effectiveness of the internal supervisory controls during the 90-day period ending on the final day of the fiscal year to which the report relates; and

(D) has disclosed to the Commission any significant deficiencies in the design or

第F子编——完善证券交易委员会的管理

第961条　内部监督控制报告及证明

(a)**年度报告与自查证明**。——证券交易委员会应于每一财政年度结束后90天内,就其对注册实体的检查工作、执法调查工作以及对与公司融资之证券相关的提交材料审查工作向参议院银行、住房与城市事务委员会和众议院金融服务委员会提交一份报告。

(b)**报告内容**。——第(a)子条所述每份报告均应——

(1)评估截至最近一财政年度年末,以下工作及程序的成效——

(A)证券交易委员会内部监督控制工作;及

(B)对于负责检查注册实体、实施执法调查、审查公司金融证券提交材料的证券交易委员会工作人员,证券交易委员会适用的程序;

(2)证明证券交易委员会具有充分的内部监督控制机制,足以履行第(1)(B)款所述各项职责;及

(3)政府问责办公室主任对其根据第(d)子条实施的审查作出的总结。

(c)**自查证明**。——

(1)**签字**。——第(b)(2)子条所述证明须经执法部主任、公司融资部主任、合规检查及核查办公室主任(或上述部门或办公室的继任部门或办公室的负责人)签字确认。

(2)**证明内容**。——第(1)款所述每名人员均应证明其——

(A)直接负责建立和维持其主管的部门或办公室的内部监督控制机制;

(B)对其主管的部门或办公室的内部监督控制机制有深入了解;

(C)在该报告所覆盖财政年度结束前90天内,已完成对上述内部监督控制机制成效的评价;且

(D)已向证券交易委员会披露内部监督控制机制在设计或运行方面可能会对该

operation of internal supervisory controls that could adversely affect the ability of the Division or Office to consistently conduct inspections, or investigations, or reviews of filings with professional competence and integrity.

(d) NEW DIRECTOR OR ACTING DIRECTOR. —Notwithstanding subsection(a), if the Director of the Division of Enforcement, the Director of the Division of Corporate Finance, or the Director of the Office of Compliance Inspections and Examinations has served as Director of the Division or Office for less than 90 days on the date on which a report is required to be submitted under subsection (a), the Commission may submit the report on the date on which the Director has served as Director for 90 days. If there is no Director of the Division of Enforcement, the Division of Corporate Finance, or the Office of Compliance Inspections and Examinations, on the date on which a report is required to be submitted under subsection (a), the Acting Director of the Division or Office may make the certification required under subsection (c).

(e) REVIEW BY THE COMPTROLLER GENERAL. —

(1) REPORT. —The Comptroller General of the United States shall submit to the Committee on Banking, Housing, and Urban Affairs of the Senate and the Committee on Financial Services of the House of Representatives a report that contains a review of the adequacy and effectiveness of the internal supervisory control structure and procedures described in subsection (b)(1), not less frequently than once every 3 years, at a time to coincide with the publication of the reports of the Commission under this section.

(2) AUTHORITY TO HIRE EXPERTS. —The Comptroller General of the United States may hire independent consultants with specialized expertise in any area relevant to the duties of the Comptroller General described in this section, in order to assist the Comptroller General in carrying out such duties.

SEC.962. TRIENNIAL REPORT ON PERSONNEL MANAGEMENT.

(a) TRIENNIAL REPORT REQUIRED. —Once every 3 years, the Comptroller General of the United States shall submit a report to the Committee on Banking, Housing, and Urban Affairs of the Senate and the Committee on Financial Services of the House of Representatives on the quality of personnel management by the Commission.

(b) CONTENTS OF REPORT. —Each report under subsection (a) shall include —

(1) an evaluation of —

(A) the effectiveness of supervisors in using the skills, talents, and motivation of the employees of the Commission to achieve the goals of the Commission;

(B) the criteria for promoting employees of the Commission to supervisory positions;

(C) the fairness of the application of the promotion criteria to the decisions of the Commission;

(D) the competence of the professional staff of the Commission;

部门或办公室始终以专业和诚信的精神开展检查、调查或提交资料审查工作的能力造成不利影响的任何重大缺陷。

(d)**新任主任或代理主任**。——无论第(a)子条如何规定,如果截至根据第(a)子条应提交报告之日,执法部主任、公司融资部主任、合规检查及核查办公室主任担任上述部门或办公室主任的时间尚不足90天,则证券交易委员会可以在上述主任任职满90天之日提交该报告。如果在按第(a)子条应提交报告之日,上述部门或办公室暂无主任,则上述部门或办公室的代理主任可以提供第(c)子条所规定的证明。

(e)**政府问责办公室主任的审查**。——

(1)**报告**。——政府问责办公室主任应至少每3年向参议院银行、住房与城市事务委员会和众议院金融服务委员会提交一份报告,说明针对第(b)(1)子条所述内部监督控制结构和程序之充分性和有效性的审查结果;报告提交时间应与证券交易委员会根据本条规定公布报告的时间同步。

(2)**聘用专家的权力**。——政府问责办公室主任在履行本条所述职责时,可以聘用在任何相关领域具有专业知识的独立顾问,以协助其履行职责。

第962条 每3年提交一次人事管理报告

(a)每3年提交一次报告。——政府问责办公室主任应就证券交易委员会的人事管理质量,每3年向参议院银行、住房与城市事务委员会以及众议院金融服务委员会提交一份报告。

(b)**报告内容**。——第(a)子条所述每份报告均应——

(1)对以下各项进行评价——

(A)主管人员在发挥证券交易委员会雇员技能、才能和主动性实现证券交易委员会各项目标方面的工作成效;

(B)证券交易委员会雇员晋升主管职位的标准;

(C)证券交易委员会作出决定时是否公平地适用职位晋升;

(D)证券交易委员会专业工作人员的胜任能力;

(E) the efficiency of communication between the units of the Commission regarding the work of the Commission (including communication between divisions and between subunits of a division) and the efforts by the Commission to promote such communication;

(F) the turnover within subunits of the Commission, including the consideration of supervisors whose subordinates have an unusually high rate of turnover;

(G) whether there are excessive numbers of low–level, mid–level, or senior–level managers;

(H) any initiatives of the Commission that increase the competence of the staff of the Commission;

(I) the actions taken by the Commission regarding employees of the Commission who have failed to perform their duties and circumstances under which the Commission has issued to employees a notice of termination; and

(J) such other factors relating to the management of the Commission as the Comptroller General determines are appropriate;

(2) an evaluation of any improvements made with respect to the areas described in paragraph (1) since the date of submission of the previous report; and

(3) recommendations for how the Commission can use the human resources of the Commission more effectively and efficiently to carry out the mission of the Commission.

(c) CONSULTATION. —In preparing the report under subsection (a), the Comptroller General shall consult with current employees of the Commission, retired employees and other former employees of the Commission, the Inspector General of the Commission, persons that have business before the Commission, any union representing the employees of the Commission, private management consultants, academics, and any other source that the Comptroller General deems appropriate.

(d) REPORT BY COMMISSION. —Not later than 90 days after the date on which the Comptroller General submits each report under subsection (a), the Commission shall submit to the Committee on Banking, Housing, and Urban Affairs of the Senate and the Committee on Financial Services of the House of Representatives a report describing the actions taken by the Commission in response to the recommendations contained in the report under subsection (a).

(e) REIMBURSEMENTS FOR COST OF REPORTS. —

(1) REIMBURSEMENTS REQUIRED. —The Commission shall reimburse the Government Accountability Office for the full cost of making the reports under this section, as billed therefor by the Comptroller General.

(2) CREDITING AND USE OF REIMBURSEMENTS. —Such reimbursements shall —

(A) be credited to the appropriation account "Salaries and Expenses, Government Accountability Office" current when the payment is received; and

(E)证券交易委员会各部门间开展工作沟通(包括部门间以及部门的子部门间的沟通)的效率,以及证券交易委员会为促进该等沟通所做的工作;

(F)证券交易委员会各子部门的人员流动情况,包括对下属人员流动率率异常偏高的主管进行的考量;

(G)低层、中层或高层管理人员的数量是否过高;

(H)证券交易委员会旨在提高其工作人员任职能力所的任何计划;

(I)证券交易委员会针对失职雇员采取的行动,以及证券交易委员会向雇员发出解聘通知的情形;及

(J)政府问责办公室主任判定的与证券交易委员会的管理工作相关的其他适当因素;

(2)评价自上一份报告提交之日起在第(1)款所述各个方面作出的任何改进;及

(3)针对证券交易委员会如何能够更加高成效、高效率地利用其人力资源实现证券交易委员会宗旨而提出的建议。

(c)**磋商**。——政府问责办公室主任在编制第(a)子条所述报告时,应与证券交易委员会的现任雇员、退休雇员及其他前任雇员、证券交易委员会监察长、在证券交易委员会办理业务的人、代表证券交易委员会雇员的任何工会、私人管理顾问、学术界人士以及政府问责办公室主任认为确属适当的任何其他人员进行磋商。

(d)**证券交易委员会报告**。——证券交易委员会应在政府问责办公室主任提交第(a)子条规定的每份报告之日后90天内,向参议院银行、住房与城市事务委员会以及众议院金融服务委员会提交一份报告,说明针对第(a)子条所述报告中提出的各项建议,证券交易委员会采取的行动。

(e)**报销报告编制费用**。——

(1)**报销要求**。——对于政府问责办公室因编制本条所述报告而发生的费用,证券交易委员会应根据政府问责办公室主任开具的账单予以全额报销。

(2)**报销款项的贷记和使用**。——该等报销款项应——

(A)贷记至政府问责办公室收到款项时有效开立的“政府问责办公室工资及费用”拨款账户;且

(B) remain available until expended.

(f) AUTHORITY TO HIRE EXPERTS. —The Comptroller General of the United States may hire independent consultants with specialized expertise in any area relevant to the duties of the Comptroller General described in this section, in order to assist the Comptroller General in carrying out such duties.

SEC.963. ANNUAL FINANCIAL CONTROLS AUDIT.

(a) REPORTS OF COMMISSION. —

(1) ANNUAL REPORTS REQUIRED. —Not later than 6 months after the end of each fiscal year, the Commission shall publish and submit to Congress a report that —

(A) describes the responsibility of the management of the Commission for establishing and maintaining an adequate internal control structure and procedures for financial reporting; and

(B) contains an assessment of the effectiveness of the internal control structure and procedures for financial reporting of the Commission during that fiscal year.

(2) ATTESTATION. —The reports required under paragraph (1) shall be attested to by the Chairman and chief financial officer of the Commission.

(b) REPORT BY COMPTROLLER GENERAL. —

(1) REPORT REQUIRED. —Not later than 6 months after the end of the first fiscal year after the date of enactment of this Act, the Comptroller General of the United States shall submit a report to Congress that assesses —

(A) the effectiveness of the internal control structure and procedures of the Commission for financial reporting; and

(B) the assessment of the Commission under subsection (a)(1)(B).

(2) ATTESTATION. —The Comptroller General shall attest to, and report on, the assessment made by the Commission under subsection (a).

(c) REIMBURSEMENTS FOR COST OF REPORTS. —

(1) REIMBURSEMENTS REQUIRED. —The Commission shall reimburse the Government Accountability Office for the full cost of making the reports under subsection (b), as billed therefor by the Comptroller General.

(2) CREDITING AND USE OF REIMBURSEMENTS. —Such reimbursements shall—

(A) be credited to the appropriation account "Salaries and Expenses, Government Accountability Office" current when the payment is received; and

(B) remain available until expended.

SEC.964. REPORT ON OVERSIGHT OF NATIONAL SECURITIES ASSOCIATIONS.

(a) REPORT REQUIRED. —Not later than 2 years after the date of enactment of this Act, and every 3 years thereafter, the Comptroller General of the United States shall submit to

(B)在支出前不得转作他用。

(f)**聘用专家的权限**。——政府问责办公室主任在履行本条所述职责时,可以聘用在任何相关领域具有专业知识的独立顾问,以协助其履行职责。

第963条 关于财务控制工作的年度审计

(a)**证券交易委员会报告**。——

(1)**年度报告提交要求**。——证券交易委员会应于每一财政年度结束后6个月内,发布并向国会提交一份报告。该报告应——

(A)说明证券交易委员会管理人员担负的建立并维持充分的内部控制结构和财务报告程序的责任;并

(B)评估在该财政年度内证券交易委员会内部控制结构和财务报告程序的有效性。

(2)**鉴证**。——第(1)款规定的报告应由证券交易委员会主席和首席财务官进行鉴证。

(b)**政府问责办公室主任的报告**。——

(1)**报告提交要求**。——政府问责办公室主任应于本法颁布之日后第一个财政年度结束后6个月内,向国会提交一份报告,对以下各项进行评估——

(A)证券交易委员会内部控制结构和财务报告程序的有效性;及

(B)第(a)(1)(B)子条所述针对证券交易委员会的评估。

(2)**鉴证**。——政府问责办公室主任应对证券交易委员会根据第(a)子条作出的评估进行鉴证,并提供一份报告。

(c)**报销报告编制费用**。——

(1)**报销要求**。——对于政府问责办公室因编制第(b)子条所述报告而发生的费用,证券交易委员会应根据政府问责办公室主任开具的账单予以全额报销。

(2)**报销款项的贷记和使用**。——该等报销款项应——

(A)贷记至政府问责办公室收到款项时有效开立的“政府问责办公室工资及费用”拨款账户;且

(B)在支出前不得转作他用。

第964条 关于全国性证券协会监管的报告

(a)**报告提交要求**。——政府问责办公室主任应于本法颁布之日后2年内,向参议院银行、住房与城市事务委员会以及众议院金融服务委员会提交一份报告(并在首次

the Committee on Banking, Housing, and Urban Affairs of the Senate and the Committee on Financial Services of the House of Representatives a report that includes an evaluation of the oversight by the Commission of national securities associations registered under section 15A of the Securities Exchange Act of 1934 (15 U.S.C.78o-3) with respect to —

(1) the governance of such national securities associations, including the identification and management of conflicts of interest by such national securities associations, together with an analysis of the impact of any conflicts of interest on the regulatory enforcement or rulemaking by such national securities associations;

(2) the examinations carried out by the national securities associations, including the expertise of the examiners;

(3) the executive compensation practices of such national securities associations;

(4) the arbitration services provided by the national securities associations;

(5) the review performed by national securities associations of advertising by the members of the national securities associations;

(6) the cooperation with and assistance to State securities administrators by the national securities associations to promote investor protection;

(7) how the funding of national securities associations is used to support the mission of the national securities associations, including —

(A) the methods of funding;

(B) the sufficiency of funds;

(C) how funds are invested by the national securities association pending use; and

(D) the impact of the methods, sufficiency, and investment of funds on regulatory enforcement by the national securities associations;

(8) the policies regarding the employment of former employees of national securities associations by regulated entities;

(9) the ongoing effectiveness of the rules of the national securities associations in achieving the goals of the rules;

(10) the transparency of governance and activities of the national securities associations; and

(11) any other issue that has an impact, as determined by the Comptroller General, on the effectiveness of such national securities associations in performing their mission and in dealing fairly with investors and members;

(b) REIMBURSEMENTS FOR COST OF REPORTS. —

(1) REIMBURSEMENTS REQUIRED. —The Commission shall reimburse the Government Accountability Office for the full cost of making the reports under subsection (a), as billed therefor by the Comptroller General.

(2) CREDITING AND USE OF REIMBURSEMENTS. —Such reimbursements shall —

提交后,每3年提交一次),评价证券交易委员会在以下方面对根据《1934年证券交易法》第15A条(《美国法典》第十五编第78o-3节)注册的全国性证券协会开展的监管——

(1)该等全国性证券协会的治理工作,包括该等全国性证券协会对利益冲突的识别和管理,以及关于该等全国性证券协会引发的任何利益冲突对监管执法或规则制定所造成影响的分析;

(2)该等全国性证券协会开展的检查工作,包括检查人员的专业知识;

(3)该等全国性证券协会关于高级管理人员薪酬的做法;
(4)该等全国性证券协会提供的仲裁服务;
(5)该等全国性证券协会对其会员广告宣传活动的审查;

(6)该等全国性证券协会为加强投资者保护与州证券管理者开展的合作以及向州证券管理者提供的协助;
(7)该等全国性证券协会的经费用于帮助实现其宗旨的方式,包括——

(A)经费筹集方式;
(B)经费的充足性;
(C)该等全国性证券协会对尚未使用的经费进行投资的方式;及
(D)该等全国性证券协会经费来源方式、经费充足性及其投资情况对监管执法的影响;
(8)关于受监管实体雇用该等全国性证券协会前任雇员的政策;

(9)该等全国性证券协会制定的规则在实现该等规则宗旨方面的持续有效性;

(10)该等全国性证券协会的治理和活动的透明度;及

(11)政府问责办公室主任判定影响该等全国性证券协会有效实现其宗旨并公平对待投资者及其会员的任何其他问题;

(b)**报销报告编制费用**。——
(1)**报销要求**。——对于政府问责办公室因编制第(a)子条所述报告而发生的费用,证券交易委员会应根据政府问责办公室主任开具的账单予以全额报销。

(2)**报销款项的贷记和使用**。——该等报销款项应——

(A) be credited to the appropriation account "Salaries and Expenses, Government Accountability Office" current when the payment is received; and

(B) remain available until expended.

SEC.965. COMPLIANCE EXAMINERS.

Section 4 of the Securities Exchange Act of 1934 (15 U.S.C.78d) is amended by adding at the end the following:

"(h) EXAMINERS. —

"(1) DIVISION OF TRADING AND MARKETS. —The Division of Trading and Markets of the Commission, or any successor organizational unit, shall have a staff of examiners who shall —

"(A) perform compliance inspections and examinations of entities under the jurisdiction of that Division; and

"(B) report to the Director of that Division.

"(2) DIVISION OF INVESTMENT MANAGEMENT. —The Division of Investment Management of the Commission, or any successor organizational unit, shall have a staff of examiners who shall —

"(A) perform compliance inspections and examinations of entities under the jurisdiction of that Division; and

"(B) report to the Director of that Division.".

SEC.966. SUGGESTION PROGRAM FOR EMPLOYEES OF THE COMMISSION.

The Securities Exchange Act of 1934 (15 U.S.C.78a et seq.) is amended by inserting after section 4C (15 U.S.C.78d-3) the following:

"SEC.4D. ADDITIONAL DUTIES OF INSPECTOR GENERAL.

"(a) SUGGESTION SUBMISSIONS BY COMMISSION EMPLOYEES. —

"(1) HOTLINE ESTABLISHED. —The Inspector General of the Commission shall establish and maintain a telephone hotline or other electronic means for the receipt of —

"(A) suggestions by employees of the Commission for improvements in the work efficiency, effectiveness, and productivity, and the use of the resources, of the Commission; and

"(B) allegations by employees of the Commission of waste, abuse, misconduct, or mismanagement within the Commission.

"(2) CONFIDENTIALITY. —The Inspector General shall maintain as confidential —

"(A) the identity of any individual who provides information by the means established under paragraph (1), unless the individual requests otherwise, in writing; and

"(B) at the request of any such individual, any specific information provided by the individual.

(A)贷记至政府问责办公室主任收到款项时有效开立的“政府问责办公室工资及费用”拨款账户;且

(B)在支出前不得转作他用。

第965条 合规检查员

在《1934年证券交易法》第4条(《美国法典》第十五编第78d节)结尾处增加如下内容,作为对该条的修正:

“(h)**检查员**。——

(1)**交易和市场部**。——证券交易委员会交易和市场部或该部门的继任部门应配备担任检查员的工作人员,负责——

(A)针对受该部门管辖的实体开展合规检查和核查;并

(B)向该部门负责人汇报工作。

(2)**投资管理部**。——证券交易委员会投资管理部或该部门的继任部门应配备担任检查员的工作人员,负责——

(A)针对受该部门管辖的实体开展合规检查和核查;并

(B)向该部门负责人汇报工作。”

第966条 证券交易委员会的雇员建议和举报计划

在《1934年证券交易法》(《美国法典》第十五编第78a节及其后条文)第4C条(《美国法典》第十五编第78d-3节)之后插入如下内容,作为对该法的修正:

“第4D条 监察长的补充职责

(a)**证券交易委员会雇员提交的建议**。——

(1)**开通热线**。——证券交易委员会监察长应开通并维持电话热线或其他电子方式,以接收如下信息——

(A)证券交易委员会雇员对于证券交易委员会工作效率、成效、生产效率和资源使用情况提出的改进建议;及

(B)证券交易委员会雇员关于证券交易委员会内部浪费、滥用行为、不当行为或管理不善的举报。

(2)**保密**。——监察长应维持以下信息的保密性——

(A)通过第(1)款所述方式提供信息的任何个人的身份,但该人书面请求不予保密的除外;及

(B)任何上述人提供的并请求予以保密的任何具体信息。

"(b) CONSIDERATION OF REPORTS. —The Inspector General shall consider any suggestions or allegations received by the means established under subsection (a)(1), and shall recommend appropriate action in relation to such suggestions or allegations.

"(c) RECOGNITION. —The Inspector General may recognize any employee who makes a suggestion under subsection (a)(1) (or by other means) that would or does —

"(1) increase the work efficiency, effectiveness, or productivity of the Commission; or

"(2) reduce waste, abuse, misconduct, or mismanagement within the Commission.

"(d) REPORT. —The Inspector General of the Commission shall submit to Congress an annual report containing a description of —

"(1) the nature, number, and potential benefits of any suggestions received under subsection (a);

"(2) the nature, number, and seriousness of any allegations received under subsection (a);

"(3) any recommendations made or actions taken by the Inspector General in response to substantiated allegations received under subsection (a); and

"(4) any action the Commission has taken in response to suggestions or allegations received under subsection (a).

"(e) FUNDING. —The activities of the Inspector General under this subsection shall be funded by the Securities and Exchange Commission Investor Protection Fund established under section 21F.".

SEC.967. COMMISSION ORGANIZATIONAL STUDY AND REFORM.

(a) STUDY REQUIRED. —

(1) IN GENERAL. —Not later than the end of the 90-day period beginning on the date of the enactment of this subtitle, the Securities and Exchange Commission (hereinafter in this section referred to as the "SEC") shall hire an independent consultant of high caliber and with expertise in organizational restructuring and the operations of capital markets to examine the internal operations, structure, funding, and the need for comprehensive reform of the SEC, as well as the SEC's relationship with and the reliance on self-regulatory organizations and other entities relevant to the regulation of securities and the protection of securities investors that are under the SEC's oversight.

(2) SPECIFIC AREAS FOR STUDY. —The study required under paragraph (1) shall, at a minimum, include the study of —

(A) the possible elimination of unnecessary or redundant units at the SEC;

(B) improving communications between SEC offices and divisions;

(C) the need to put in place a clear chain-of-command structure, particularly for enforcement examinations and compliance inspections;

(b)**对建议或举报的考虑**。——监察长应对通过第(a)(1)子条所述方式接收的任何建议或举报进行考虑,并针对该等建议或举报提出适当的行动建议。

(c)**表彰**。——对于通过第(a)(1)子条所述方式(或通过其他方式)提供建议的任何雇员,如果该等建议将产生如下效果或确实产生了如下效果,监察长可以对该等雇员表彰——

(1)提高证券交易委员会工作效率、成效或生产效率;或

(2)减少证券交易委员会的内部浪费、滥用行为、不当行为或管理不善情况。

(d)**报告**。——监察长应每年向国会提交一份报告,说明——

(1)通过第(a)子条所述方式收到的任何建议之性质、数量以及可能带来的利益;

(2)通过第(a)子条所述方式收到的任何举报之性质、数量及严重程度;

(3)监察长针对通过第(a)子条所述方式收到的有事实依据的举报提出的任何建议或采取的行动;及

“(4)证券交易委员会针对通过第(a)子条所述方式收到的建议或举报采取的任何行动。

(e)**经费来源**。——根据第21F条设立的证券交易委员会投资者保护基金应作为本子条所述监察长各项活动的经费来源。”

第967条 证券交易委员会组织结构研究及改革

(a)**研究要求**。——

(1)**一般规定**。——证券交易委员会应于本法颁布之日起90天内,聘用一位在组织重构和资本市场运作方面具有专长的高资质独立顾问,对证券交易委员会的内部运营、结构、经费来源以及全面改革的必要性进行研究,并对证券交易委员会与受其监管的与证券监管和证券投资者保护相关的自律组织和其他实体之间的关系,以及证券交易委员会对该等组织和实体的依赖程度进行研究。

(2)**需要研究的特定领域**。——第(1)款所规定研究至少应包括对以下问题的研究——

(A)撤销证券交易委员会非必要或冗余部门的可能性;

(B)改进证券交易委员会办公室及部门之间沟通的方式;

(C)建立清晰的指令链结构的必要性(尤其是针对执法核查及合规检查工作而言);

(D) the effect of high-frequency trading and other technological advances on the market and what the SEC requires to monitor the effect of such trading and advances on the market;

(E) the SEC's hiring authorities, workplace policies, and personal practices, including—

(i) whether there is a need to further streamline hiring authorities for those who are not lawyers, accountants, compliance examiners, or economists;

(ii) whether there is a need for further pay reforms;

(iii) the diversity of skill sets of SEC employees and whether the present skill set diversity efficiently and effectively fosters the SEC's mission of investor protection; and

(iv) the application of civil service laws by the SEC;

(F) whether the SEC's oversight and reliance on self-regulatory organizations promotes efficient and effective governance for the securities markets; and

(G) whether adjusting the SEC's reliance on self-regulatory organizations is necessary to promote more efficient and effective governance for the securities markets.

(b) CONSULTANT REPORT. —Not later than the end of the 150-day period after being retained, the independent consultant hired pursuant to subsection (a)(1) shall issue a report to the SEC and the Congress containing —

(1) a detailed description of any findings and conclusions made while carrying out the study required under subsection (a)(1); and

(2) recommendations for legislative, regulatory, or administrative action that the consultant determines appropriate to enable the SEC and other entities on which the consultant reports to perform their statutorily or otherwise mandated missions.

(c) SEC REPORT. —Not later than the end of the 6-month period beginning on the date the consultant issues the report under subsection (b), and every 6-months thereafter during the 2-year period following the date on which the consultant issues such report, the SEC shall issue a report to the Committee on Financial Services of the House of Representatives and the Committee on Banking, Housing, and Urban Affairs of the Senate describing the SEC's implementation of the regulatory and administrative recommendations contained in the consultant's report.

SEC.968. STUDY ON SEC REVOLVING DOOR.

(a) GOVERNMENT ACCOUNTABILITY OFFICE STUDY. —The Comptroller General of the United States shall conduct a study that will —

(1) review the number of employees who leave the Securities and Exchange Commission to work for financial institutions regulated by such Commission;

(2) determine how many employees who leave the Securities and Exchange Commission worked on cases that involved financial institutions regulated by such Commission;

(3) review the length of time employees work for the Securities and Exchange Commission before leaving to be employed by financial institutions regulated by such

(D)高频交易及其他技术进步对市场的影响,以及证券交易委员会对该等影响实施监控应开展的工作;

(E)证券交易委员会的雇用权力、工作场所政策以及人事惯例,包括——

(i)是否有必要对雇用不具有律师、会计师、合规检查员或经济学家身份的人员的权力进行进一步精简;

(ii)是否有必要推行进一步的工资改革;

(iii)证券交易委员会雇员技能组合的多元性,以及当前的技能组合多元性是否能高效率、高成效地促进证券交易委员会实现保护投资者的宗旨;及

(iv)证券交易委员会适用公务员法的情况;

(F)证券交易委员会对自律组织的监管和依赖是否能促进对证券市场进行更加高效率、高成效的治理;及

(G)是否证券交易委员会对自律组织的依赖程度是否有必要进行调整,以便促进对证券市场进行更加高效率、高成效的治理。

(b)**顾问报告**。——证券交易委员会根据第(a)(1)子条聘用的独立顾问应在其受聘后150天内,向证券交易委员会和国会提交一份报告,说明以下内容——

(1)关于开展第(a)(1)子条所述研究过程中得出的任何认定与结论的详细情况;及

(2)该顾问判定的使证券交易委员会及该顾问报告所涉其他实体能够实现其法定宗旨或其他强制性宗旨的确属适当的立法、监管或行政行动建议。

(c)**证券交易委员会的报告**。——证券交易委员会应于上述顾问提交第(b)子条所述报告之日起6个月内,向众议院金融服务委员会和参议院银行、住房与城市事务委员会提交一份报告,说明证券交易委员会对该顾问报告中提出的监管和行政建议的实施情况。证券交易委员会应在该顾问提交报告之日后2年内,每6个月提交一份上述报告。

第968条　关于证券交易委员会离职人员重新进入金融机构工作问题的研究

(a)**政府问责办公室的研究**。——政府问责办公室主任应开展研究,以便——

(1)对证券交易委员会原雇员离职后进入受证券交易委员会监管的金融机构任职的人数进行审查;

(2)确定离职后转而处理涉及受证券交易委员会监管的金融机构的案件的证券交易委员会原雇员人数;

(3)对证券交易委员会原雇员受聘于受证券交易委员会监管的金融机构之前在证券交易委员会的任职时间进行审查;

Commission;

(4) review existing internal controls and make recommendations on strengthening such controls to ensure that employees of the Securities and Exchange Commission who are later employed by financial institutions did not assist such institutions in violating any rules or regulations of the Commission during the course of their employment with such Commission;

(5) determine if greater post-employment restrictions are necessary to prevent employees of the Securities and Exchange Commission from being employed by financial institutions after employment with such Commission;

(6) determine if the volume of employees of the Securities and Exchange Commission who are later employed by financial institutions has led to inefficiencies in enforcement;

(7) determine if employees of the Securities and Exchange Commission who are later employed by financial institutions assisted such institutions in circumventing Federal rules and regulations while employed by such Commission;

(8) review any information that may address the volume of employees of the Securities and Exchange Commission who are later employed by financial institutions, and make recommendations to Congress; and

(9) review other additional issues as may be raised during the course of the study conducted under this subsection.

(b) REPORT. —Not later than 1 year after the date of the enactment of this subtitle, the Comptroller General of the United States shall submit to the Committee on Financial Services of the House of Representatives and the Committee on Banking, Housing, and Urban Affairs of the Senate a report on the results of the study required by subsection (a).

Subtitle G—Strengthening Corporate Governance

SEC.971. PROXY ACCESS.

(a) PROXY ACCESS. —Section 14(a) of the Securities Exchange Act of 1934 (15 U.S.C.78n(a)) is amended —

(1) by inserting "(1)" after "(a)"; and

(2) by adding at the end the following:

"(2) The rules and regulations prescribed by the Commission under paragraph (1) may include —

"(A) a requirement that a solicitation of proxy, consent, or authorization by(or on behalf of) an issuer include a nominee submitted by a shareholder to serve on the board of directors of the issuer; and

(4)对证券交易委员会现有内部控制机制进行审查,并提出加强该等内部控制机制的建议，以确保受雇于金融机构的证券交易委员会原雇员在证券交易委员会任职期间未曾协助该等金融机构违反证券交易委员会的任何规则或规章;

(5)判定否有必要对雇员离职后活动实施更加严格的限制,以防范证券交易委员会雇员在结束与证券交易委员会的雇佣关系后受雇于金融机构;

(6)判定受聘于金融机构的证券交易委员会原雇员的人数是否导致了证券交易委员会执法效率低下;

(7)判定受聘于金融机构的证券交易委员会原雇员是否曾在证券交易委员会任职期间协助该等金融机构规避联邦规则和规章;

(8)审查与受聘于金融机构的证券交易委员会原雇员的人数相关的任何信息,并向国会提出建议;并

(9)对其在根据本子条开展该项研究过程中可能提出的其他问题进行审查。

(b)**报告**。——政府问责办公室主任应于本子编颁布之日后1年内,针对第(a)子条所述研究的结果向众议院金融服务委员会和参议院银行、住房与城市事务委员会提交一份报告。

第G子编——加强公司治理

第971条　征集代理权的条件

(a)**征集代理权的条件**。——《1934年证券交易法》第14(a)条[《美国法典》第十五编第78n(a)节]修正如下——

(1)在“(a)”之后插入“(1)”;及

(2)在该条结尾处增加如下内容:

“(2)证券交易委员会根据第(1)款制定的规则及规章可要求——

(A)发行人或其代表提供的代理权、代理同意书或授权书征集材料中应包含股东提名的一名发行人董事会成员候选人;及

"(B) a requirement that an issuer follow a certain procedure in relation to a solicitation described in subparagraph (A).".

(b) REGULATIONS. —The Commission may issue rules permitting the use by a shareholder of proxy solicitation materials supplied by an issuer of securities for the purpose of nominating individuals to membership on the board of directors of the issuer, under such terms and conditions as the Commission determines are in the interests of shareholders and for the protection of investors.

(c) EXEMPTIONS. —The Commission may, by rule or order, exempt an issuer or class of issuers from the requirement made by this section or an amendment made by this section. In determining whether to make an exemption under this subsection, the Commission shall take into account, among other considerations, whether the requirement in the amendment made by subsection (a) disproportionately burdens small issuers.

SEC.972. DISCLOSURES REGARDING CHAIRMAN AND CEO STRUCTURES.

The Securities Exchange Act of 1934(15 U.S. C. 78a et seq.) is amended by inserting after section 14A, as added by this title, the following:

"SEC.14B. CORPORATE GOVERNANCE.

"Not later than 180 days after the date of enactment of this subsection, the Commission shall issue rules that require an issuer to disclose in the annual proxy sent to investors the reasons why the issuer has chosen —

"(1) the same person to serve as chairman of the board of directors and chief executive officer (or in equivalent positions); or

"(2) different individuals to serve as chairman of the board of directors and chief executive officer (or in equivalent positions of the issuer).".

Subtitle H—Municipal Securities

SEC.975. REGULATION OF MUNICIPAL SECURITIES AND CHANGES TO THE BOARD OF THE MSRB.

(a) REGISTRATION OF MUNICIPAL SECURITIES DEALERS AND MUNICIPAL ADVISORS. —Section 15B (a) of the Securities Exchange Act of 1934 (15 U.S.C.78o-4 (a)) is amended —

(1) in paragraph (1) —

(A) by inserting "(A)" after "(1)"; and

(B) by adding at the end the following:

(B)发行人在提供第(A)子款所述征集材料时应遵守特定程序。”

(b)**规章**。——证券交易委员会可以发布规则,准许股东根据证券交易委员会判定的符合股东利益并有助于保护投资者的条款和条件使用证券发行人提供的代理权征集材料,提名发行人董事会成员的候选人。

(c)**豁免**。——证券交易委员会可以发布规则或命令,向某一或某类发行人授予豁免,使其不必遵守本条规定或本条作出的做修正中的规定。证券交易委员会在判定是否应根据本子条规定授予豁免时应考虑第(a)子条作出的修正中的规定是否会对小规模发行人造成与其规模不成比例的负担以及其他因素。

第972条　关于董事长和首席执行官架构的披露

在经本编增加的《1934年证券交易法》(《美国法典》第十五编第78a节及其后条文)第14A条之后插入如下内容,作为对该法的进一步修正:

“第14B条　公司治理

证券交易委员会应于本子条规定颁布之日后180天内发布规则,要求发行人在发送给投资者的年度代理委托书中披露其做出以下行为的原因——

(1)选择同一人担任董事长和首席执行官(或同等职位的管理人员);或

(2)选择不同的人担任董事长和首席执行官(或该发行人内部同等职位的管理人员)。”

第H子编——市政证券

第975条　市政证券监管及市政证券规则制定委员会委员组成的变动

(a)**市政证券自营商和市政顾问的注册**。——《1934年证券交易法》第15B(a)条[《美国法典》第十五编第78o-4(a)节]修正如下——

(1)在第(1)款中——
(A)在“(1)”之后插入“(A)”;及
(B)在结尾处增加如下内容:

"(B) It shall be unlawful for a municipal advisor to provide advice to or on behalf of a municipal entity or obligated person with respect to municipal financial products or the issuance of municipal securities, or to undertake a solicitation of a municipal entity or obligated person, unless the municipal advisor is registered in accordance with this subsection.";

(2) in paragraph (2), by inserting "or municipal advisor" after "municipal securities dealer" each place that term appears;

(3) in paragraph (3), by inserting "or municipal advisor" after "municipal securities dealer" each place that term appears;

(4) in paragraph (4), by striking "dealer, or municipal securities dealer or class of brokers, dealers, or municipal securities dealers" and inserting "dealer, municipal securities dealer, or municipal advisor, or class of brokers, dealers, municipal securities dealers, or municipal advisors"; and

(5) by adding at the end the following:

"(5) No municipal advisor shall make use of the mails or any means or instrumentality of interstate commerce to provide advice to or on behalf of a municipal entity or obligated person with respect to municipal financial products, the issuance of municipal securities, or to undertake a solicitation of a municipal entity or obligated person, in connection with which such municipal advisor engages in any fraudulent, deceptive, or manipulative act or practice.".

(b) MUNICIPAL SECURITIES RULEMAKING BOARD. —Section15B (b)of the Securities Exchange Act of 1934 (15 U.S.C.78o–4(b)) is amended —

(1) in paragraph (1) —

(A) in the first sentence, by striking "Not later than" and all that follows through "appointed by the Commission" and inserting "The Municipal Securities Rulemaking Board shall be composed of 15 members, or such other number of members as specified by rules of the Board pursuant to paragraph (2)(B),";

(B) by striking the second sentence and inserting the following: "The members of the Board shall serve as members for a term of 3 years or for such other terms as specified by rules of the Board pursuant to paragraph (2)(B), and shall consist of (A) 8 individuals who are independent of any municipal securities broker, municipal securities dealer, or municipal advisor, at least 1 of whom shall be representative of institutional or retail investors in municipal securities, at least 1 of whom shall be representative of municipal entities, and at least 1 of whom shall be a member of the public with knowledge of or experience in the municipal industry (which members are hereinafter referred to as 'public representatives'); and (B) 7 individuals who are associated with a broker, dealer, municipal securities dealer, or municipal advisor, including at least 1 individual who is associated with and representative

“(B)除非市政顾问已根据本子条办理注册,否则其就市政金融产品或市政证券发行向市政实体或市政证券义务人提供建议，或代表市政实体或市政证券义务人提供建议,或者向市政实体或市政证券义务人招揽业务的行为,当属非法。”;

(2)在第(2)款所有的“市政证券自营商”之后插入“或市政顾问”;

(3)在第(3)款所有的“市政证券自营商”之后插入“或市政顾问”;

(4)在第(4)款中,删除“自营商或市政证券自营商,或某类经纪商、自营商或市政证券自营商”,替以“自营商、市政证券自营商或市政顾问,或某类经纪商、自营商、市政证券自营商或市政顾问”;及

(5)在结尾处增加如下内容:

“(5)任何市政顾问均不得使用邮件或任何州际商业手段和工具,在就市政金融产品、市政证券发行向市政实体或市政证券义务人提供建议,或代表市政实体或市政证券义务人提供建议，或者向市政实体或市政证券义务人招揽业务的过程中有任何欺诈、欺骗或操纵性的行为或做法。”

(b)**市政证券规则制定委员会**。——《1934年证券交易法》第15B(b)条[《美国法典》第十五编第78o-4(b)节]修正如下——

(1)在第(1)款中——

(A)第一句删除“在《1975年证券修正法案》颁布之日(即1975年6月4日)后120天内”及其后直至“由证券交易委员会任命的15名委员组成”的全部内容,替以“市政证券规则制定委员会应由15名委员组成,或由市政证券规则制定委员会根据第(2)(B)款发布的规则所规定的其他人数的委员组成,”;

(B)删除第二句,替以如下内容:“市政证券规则制定委员会的委员任期应为3年或该委员会根据第(2)(B)款发布的规则所规定的其他时间,并由如下人员组成:(A)8名独立于市政证券经纪商、市政证券自营商或市政顾问的个人,其中至少一人应为市政证券机构或零售投资者的代表,至少一人应为市政实体的代表,至少一人应为具有市政行业知识或经验的社会人士(以下简称公众代表);以及(B)7名与经纪商、自营商、市政证券自营商或市政顾问存在业务相关关系的个人,其中至少一人应为代表不具有银行或银行子公司、部门或单位身份的经纪商、自营商或市政自营商,并与之存在业务相关关系的个人(以下简称经纪自营商代表),至少一人应为代表具有银行或银行子公司、部门或单位身份的市政自营商,并与之存在业务相关关系的个人(以下简称银行代表),且至少一人应为与市政顾问存在业务相关关系的个人(以下简称为

of brokers, dealers, or municipal securities dealers that are not banks or subsidiaries or departments or divisions of banks(which members are hereinafter referred to as 'broker–dealer representatives'), at least 1 individual who is associated with and representative of municipal securities dealers which are banks or subsidiaries or departments or divisions of banks (which members are hereinafter referred to as 'bank representatives'), and at least 1 individual who is associated with a municipal advisor (which members are hereinafter referred to as 'advisor representatives' and, together with the broker–dealer representatives and the bank representatives, are referred to as 'regulated representatives'). Each member of the board shall be knowledgeable of matters related to the municipal securities markets."; and

(C) in the third sentence, by striking "initial";

(2) in paragraph (2)—

(A) in the matter preceding subparagraph (A)—

(i) by inserting before the period at the end of the first sentence the following: "and advice provided to or on behalf of municipal entities or obligated persons by brokers, dealers, municipal securities dealers, and municipal advisors with respect to municipal financial products, the issuance of municipal securities, and solicitations of municipal entities or obligated persons undertaken by brokers, dealers, municipal securities dealers, and municipal advisors"; and

(ii) by striking the second sentence;

(B) in subparagraph (A)—

(i) in the matter preceding clause (i)—

(I) by inserting ", and no broker, dealer, municipal securities dealer, or municipal advisor shall provide advice to or on behalf of a municipal entity or obligated person with respect to municipal financial products or the issuance of municipal securities," after "sale of, any municipal security"; and

(II) by inserting "and municipal entities or obligated persons" after "protection of investors";

(ii) in clause(i), by striking "municipal securities brokers and municipal securities dealers" each place that term appears and inserting "municipal securities brokers, municipal securities dealers, and municipal advisors";

(iii) in clause (ii), by adding "and" at the end;

(iv) in clause (iii), by striking "; and" and inserting a period; and

(v) by striking clause (iv);

(C) by amending subparagraph (B) to read as follows:

"(B) establish fair procedures for the nomination and election of members of the Board and assure fair representation in such nominations and elections of public representatives,

顾问代表,并与经纪自营商代表和银行代表合称为受监管代表)。市政证券规则制定委员会的每名委员均应对市政证券市场的相关问题有深刻了解。";及

(C)第三句删除"首届";

(2)在第(2)款中——

(A)第(A)子款之前的内容中——

(i)在第一句结尾处的句号前插入如下内容:"以及经纪商、自营商、市政证券自营商及市政顾问就市政金融产品和市政证券发行向市政实体或市政证券义务人提供的建议,或代表市政实体或市政证券义务人提供的建议,或者针对市政实体或市政证券义务人开展的业务招揽活动";及

(ii)删除第二句;

(B)第(A)子款——

(i)第(i)项之前的内容——

(I)在"任何市政证券的购买或出售"之后插入",且任何经纪商、自营商、市政证券自营商或市政顾问均不得就市政金融产品和市政证券的发行向市政实体或市政证券义务人提供建议,或代表市政实体或市政证券义务人提供建议";及

(II)删除"投资者保护",替以"投资者以及市政实体或市政证券义务人的保护";

(ii)第(i)项删除所有的"市政证券经纪商和市政证券自营商",替以"市政证券经纪商、市政证券自营商和市政顾问";

(iii)第(ii)项结尾处增加"及";

(iv)第(iii)项删除";及",替以句号;及

(v)删除第(iv)项;

(C)第(B)子款修正后全文如下:

"(B)制定公平的市政证券规则制定委员会委员提名及选任程序,确保公众代表、经纪自营商代表、银行代表以及顾问代表的提名和选任能够实现公平的代表。该等

broker dealer representatives, bank representatives, and advisor representatives. Such rules—

"(i) shall provide that the number of public representatives of the Board shall at all times exceed the total number of regulated representatives and that the membership shall at all times be as evenly divided in number as possible between public representatives and regulated representatives;

"(ii) shall specify the length or lengths of terms members shall serve;

"(iii) may increase the number of members which shall constitute the whole Board, provided that such number is an odd number; and

"(iv) shall establish requirements regarding the independence of public representatives.".

(D) in subparagraph (C)—

(i) by inserting "and municipal financial products" after "municipal securities" the first two times that term appears;

(ii) by inserting ", municipal entities, obligated persons," before "and the public interest";

(iii) by striking "between" and inserting "among";

(iv) by striking "issuers, municipal securities brokers, or municipal securities dealers, to fix" and inserting "municipal entities, obligated persons, municipal securities brokers, municipal securities dealers, or municipal advisors, to fix"; and

(v) by striking "brokers or municipal securities dealers, to regulate" and inserting "brokers, municipal securities dealers, or municipal advisors, to regulate";

(E) in subparagraph (D)—

(i) by inserting "and advice concerning municipal financial products" after "transactions in municipal securities";

(ii) by striking "That no" and inserting "that no";

(iii) by inserting "municipal advisor," before "or person associated"; and

(iv) by striking "a municipal securities broker or municipal securities dealer may be compelled" and inserting "a municipal securities broker, municipal securities dealer, or municipal advisor may be compelled";

(F) in subparagraph (E)—

(i) by striking "municipal securities brokers and municipal securities dealers" and inserting "municipal securities brokers, municipal securities dealers, and municipal advisors"; and

(ii) by striking "municipal securities broker or municipal securities dealer" and inserting "municipal securities broker, municipal securities dealer, or municipal advisor";

(G) in subparagraph (G), by striking "municipal securities brokers and municipal securities dealers" and inserting "municipal securities brokers, municipal securities dealers,

规则——

(i)应规定无论何时,市政证券规则制定委员会中公众代表人数均应超过受监管代表的总人数,且公众代表和受监管代表的人数应始终尽可能均衡地分配;

(ii)应明确规定委员的任期时长;

(iii)可增加市政证券规则制定委员会全体委员的人数,但是总人数应为奇数;并

(iv)应制定关于公众代表独立性的要求。”

(D)第(C)子款——

(i)在第一次和第二次出现的“市政证券”之后插入“及市政金融产品”;

(ii)在“以及公共利益”前插入“,市政实体、市政证券义务人”;

(iii)删除“二者间”,替以“各者之间”;

(iv)删除“不得对客户、发行人、市政证券经纪商或市政证券自营商进行不公平的歧视,不得设定”,替以“不得对客户、市政实体、市政证券义务人、市政证券经纪商、市政证券自营商或市政顾问进行不公平的歧视,不得设定”;及

(v)删除“不得就市政证券经纪商或市政证券自营商收取的佣金、折扣”,替以“不得就市政证券经纪商、市政证券自营商或市政顾问收取的佣金、折扣”;

(E)第(D)子款——

(i)在“市政证券交易”之后插入“以及有关市政金融产品的建议”;

(ii)删除首字母大写的“That no”,替以首字母小写的“that no”;

(iii)在“或业务相关人”前插入“市政顾问”;及

(iv)删除“不可强迫除市政证券经纪商、市政证券自营商或者以上二者的业务相关人以外的人接受该等仲裁”,替以“不可强迫除市政证券经纪商、市政证券自营商、市政顾问或者上述各者的业务相关人以外的人接受该等仲裁”;

(F)第(E)子款——

(i)删除“市政证券经纪商和市政证券自营商”,替以“市政证券经纪商、市政证券自营商及市政顾问”;及

(ii)删除“市政证券经纪商或市政证券自营商”,替以“市政证券经纪商、市政证券自营商或市政顾问”;

(G)第(G)子款删除“市政证券经纪商和市政证券自营商”,替以“市政证券经纪商、市政证券自营商及市政顾问”;

and municipal advisors";

(H) in subparagraph (J)—

(i) by striking "municipal securities broker and each municipal securities dealer" and inserting "municipal securities broker, municipal securities dealer, and municipal advisor"; and

(ii) by striking the period at the end of the second sentence and inserting ", which may include charges for failure to submit to the Board, or to any information system operated by the Board, within the prescribed timeframes, any items of information or documents required to be submitted under any rule issued by the Board.";

(I) in subparagraph (K)—

(i) by inserting "broker, dealer, or" before "municipal securities dealer" each place that term appears; and

(ii) by striking "municipal securities investment portfolio" and inserting "related account of a broker, dealer, or municipal securities dealer"; and

(J) by adding at the end the following:

"(L) with respect to municipal advisors—

"(i) prescribe means reasonably designed to prevent acts, practices, and courses of business as are not consistent with a municipal advisor's fiduciary duty to its clients;

"(ii) provide continuing education requirements for municipal advisors;

"(iii) provide professional standards; and

"(iv) not impose a regulatory burden on small municipal advisors that is not necessary or appropriate in the public interest and for the protection of investors, municipal entities, and obligated persons, provided that there is robust protection of investors against fraud.";

(3) by redesignating paragraph (3) as paragraph (7); and

(4) by inserting after paragraph (2) the following:

"(3) The Board, in conjunction with or on behalf of any Federal financial regulator or self-regulatory organization, may—

"(A) establish information systems; and

"(B) assess such reasonable fees and charges for the submission of information to, or the receipt of information from, such systems from any persons which systems may be developed for the purposes of serving as a repository of information from municipal market participants or otherwise in furtherance of the purposes of the Board, a Federal financial regulator, or a self-regulatory organization, except that the Board—

"(i) may not charge a fee to municipal entities or obligated persons to submit documents or other information to the Board or charge a fee to any person to obtain, directly from the Internet site of the Board, documents or information submitted by municipal entities, obligated persons, brokers, dealers, municipal securities dealers, or municipal advisors,

(H)第(J)子款——

(i)删除“市政证券经纪商和每一市政证券自营商”,替以“市政证券经纪商、市政证券自营商及市政顾问”;及

(ii)删除第二句结尾处的句号,替以“,可包括因未在规定时限内按市政证券规则制定委员会发布的任何规则向该委员会或该委员会运行的信息系统提交信息或文件,而向其收取的费用。”;

(I)第(K)子款——

(i)在所有的“市政证券自营商”前插入“经纪商、自营商或”;及

(ii)删除“市政证券投资组合”,替以“经纪商、自营商或市政证券自营商的相关账户”;及

(J)在结尾处增加如下内容:

“(L)就市政顾问而言——

(i)规定旨在防范发生违反市政顾问对客户承担的受信义务的行为、做法及业务运作的合理方式;

(ii)规定针对市政顾问的继续教育要求;

(iii)规定专业标准;并

(iv)不得向小型市政顾问施加对于维护公共利益和保护投资者、市政实体及市政证券义务人而言并非必要或适当的监管负担,但是须为投资者提供稳健的保护,使之免受欺诈。”;

(3)第(3)款重新编号为第(7)款;且

(4)在第(2)款之后插入如下内容:

“(3)市政证券规则制定委员会可以协同或代表任何联邦金融监管者或自律组织或与之共同——

(A)建立信息系统;并

(B)在任何人向该等系统提交信息或从该等系统获取信息时,向其计征合理费用及收费;开发该等系统的目的可以是存储市政市场参与者提供的信息,或以其他方式促进市政证券规则制定委员会、联邦金融监管者或自律组织目标的实现,但是,市政证券规则制定委员会——

(i)不得对向市政证券规则制定委员会提交文件或其他信息的市政实体或市政证券义务人收取费用,也不得在任何人从市政证券规则制定委员会互联网网站上直接获取由市政实体、市政证券义务人、经纪商、自营商、市政证券自营商或市政顾问提交的文件或信息(包括根据证券交易委员会的规则或市政证券规则制定委员会的规则

including documents submitted under the rules of the Board or the Commission; and

"(ii) shall not be prohibited from charging commercially reasonable fees for automated subscription–based feeds or similar services, or for charging for other data or document–based services customized upon request of any person, made available to commercial enterprises, municipal securities market professionals, or the general public, whether delivered through the Internet or any other means, that contain all or part of the documents or information, subject to approval of the fees by the Commission under section 19(b).

"(4) The Board may provide guidance and assistance in the enforcement of, and examination for, compliance with the rules of the Board to the Commission, a registered securities association under section 15A, or any other appropriate regulatory agency, as applicable.

"(5) The Board, the Commission, and a registered securities association under section 15A, or the designees of the Board, the Commission, or such association, shall meet not less frequently than 2 times a year —

"(A) to describe the work of the Board, the Commission, and the registered securities association involving the regulation of municipal securities; and

"(B) to share information about —

"(i) the interpretation of the Board, the Commission, and the registered securities association of Board rules; and

"(ii) examination and enforcement of compliance with Board rules.".

(c) DISCIPLINE OF BROKERS, DEALERS, MUNICIPAL SECURITIES DEALERS AND MUNICIPAL ADVISORS; FIDUCIARY DUTY OF MUNICIPAL ADVISORS. –Section 15B(c) of the Securities Exchange Act of 1934 (15 U.S.C.78o–4(c)) is amended—

(1) in paragraph (1), by inserting ", and no broker, dealer, municipal securities dealer, or municipal advisor shall make use of the mails or any means or instrumentality of interstate commerce to provide advice to or on behalf of a municipal entity or obligated person with respect to municipal financial products, the issuance of municipal securities, or to undertake a solicitation of a municipal entity or obligated person," after "any municipal security";

(2) by adding at the end of paragraph (1) the following:

"A municipal advisor and any person associated with such municipal advisor shall be deemed to have a fiduciary duty to any municipal entity for whom such municipal advisor acts as a municipal advisor, and no municipal advisor may engage in any act, practice, or course of business which is not consistent with a municipal advisor's fiduciary duty or that is in contravention of any rule of the Board.".

(3) in paragraph (2), by inserting "or municipal advisor" after "municipal securities dealer" each place that term appears;

提交的文件)时,向其收取费用;并

(ii)不得被禁止就其向商业企业、市政证券市场专业人员或一般公众提供的以下服务向上述各者收取商业上合理的费用:提供的自动订阅信息馈送服务或类似服务,或应任何人之请求定制的基于数据或文件的服务(无论该等服务是通过因特网还是任何其他方式提供),但是收取该等费用须按照第19(b)条的规定获得证券交易委员会的批准。

(4)市政证券规则制定委员会在实施其规则或检查其规则是否得到遵守之时,可以向证券交易委员会、根据第15A条注册的证券协会或任何其他相应的监管机关(视具体情况而定)提供指导和协助。

(5)市政证券规则制定委员会、证券交易委员会及根据第15A条注册的证券协会,或上述各者的指定人员,每年应至少召开两次会议——

(A)介绍证券规则制定委员会、证券交易委员会以及该等注册证券协会开展的涉及市政证券监管的工作;并

(B)共享与以下各项相关的信息——

(i)市政证券规则制定委员会、证券交易委员会以及该等注册证券协会对市政证券规则制定委员会规则的解释;及

(ii)针对市政证券规则制定委员会规则是否得以遵守开展的检查以及市政证券规则制定委员会规则的实施情况。"

(c)**对经纪商、自营商、市政证券自营商以及市政顾问的纪律处分;市政顾问的受信义务**。——《1934年证券交易法》第15B(c)条[《美国法典》第十五编第78o-4(c)节]修正如下——

(1)在第(1)款中,在"任何市政证券"之后插入",任何经纪商、自营商、市政证券自营商或市政顾问均不得使用邮件或任何州际商业手段和工具,就市政金融产品和市政证券发行向市政实体或市政证券义务人提供建议,或代表市政实体或市政证券义务人提供建议,或者向市政实体或市政证券义务人招揽业务";

(2)在第(1)款结尾处增加如下内容:

"市政顾问以及该市政顾问的任何业务相关人均应视为对接受其市政顾问服务的市政实体负有受信义务,且任何市政顾问均不得有任何违反市政顾问受信义务或市政证券规则制定委员会规则的行为、做法或业务运作。"

(3)在第(2)款所有的"市政证券自营商"之后插入"或市政顾问";

(4) in paragraph (3) —

(A) by inserting "or municipal entities or obligated person" after "protection of investors" each place that term appears; and

(B) by inserting "or municipal advisor" after "municipal securities dealer" each place that term appears;

(5) in paragraph (4), by inserting "or municipal advisor" after "municipal securities dealer or obligated person" each place that term appears;

(6) in paragraph (6)(B), by inserting "or municipal entities or obligated person" after "protection of investors";

(7) in paragraph (7) —

(A) in subparagraph (A) —

(i) in clause (i), by striking "; and" and inserting a semicolon;

(ii) in clause (ii), by striking the period and inserting "; and"; and

(iii) by adding at the end the following:

"(iii) the Commission, or its designee, in the case of municipal advisors.".

(B) in subparagraph (B), by inserting "or municipal entities or obligated person" after "protection of investors"; and

(8) by adding at the end the following:

"(9)(A) Fines collected by the Commission for violations of the rules of the Board shall be equally divided between the Commission and the Board.

"(B) Fines collected by a registered securities association under section 15A(7) with respect to violations of the rules of the Board shall be accounted for by such registered securities association separately from other fines collected under section 15A(7) and shall be allocated between such registered securities association and the Board, and such allocation shall require the registered securities association to pay to the Board 1/3 of all fines collected by the registered securities association reasonably allocable to violations of the rules of the Board, or such other portion of such fines as may be directed by the Commission upon agreement between the registered securities association and the Board.".

(d) ISSUANCE OF MUNICIPAL SECURITIES. —Section 15B(d)(2) of the Securities Exchange Act of 1934 (15 U.S.C.78o–4(d)) is amended —

(1) by striking "through a municipal securities broker or municipal securities dealer or otherwise" and inserting "through a municipal securities broker, municipal securities dealer, municipal advisor, or otherwise"; and

(2) by inserting "or municipal advisors" before "to furnish".

(e) DEFINITIONS. –Section 15B of the Securities Exchange Act of 1934 (15 U.S.C. 78o–4) is amended by adding at the end the following:

"(e) DEFINITIONS. –For purposes of this section —

(4)在第(3)款中——

(A)删除所有的“投资者保护”,全部替以“投资者或市政实体或市政证券义务人的保护”;及

(B)在所有的“市政证券自营商”之后插入“或市政顾问”;

(5)第(4)款所有的“市政证券自营商或市政证券义务人”之后插入“或市政顾问”;

(6)第(6)(B)款删除“投资者保护”,替以“投资者、市政实体或市政证券义务人的保护”;

(7)第(7)款——

(A)第(A)子款——

(i)第(i)项删除“;及”,替以分号;

(ii)第(ii)项删除句号,替以“;及”;并

(iii)在该子款结尾处增加如下内容:

“(iii)证券交易委员会或其指定人员(对于市政顾问而言)。”

(B)第(B)子款删除“投资者保护”,替以“投资者、市政实体或市政证券义务人的保护”;及

(8)在该条结尾处增加如下内容:

“(9)(A)证券交易委员会针对违反市政证券规则制定委员会规则的行为收缴的罚款应在证券交易委员会和市政证券规则制定委员会之间平均分配。

(B)注册证券协会根据第15A(7)条针对违反市政证券规则制定委员会规则的行为收缴的罚款应与其根据第15A(7)条收缴的其他罚款分开核算,并应在该等注册证券协会和市政证券规则制定委员会之间分配;在分配时,注册证券协会须将其收缴可合理划归为针对违反市政证券规则制定委员会规则的行为的全部罚款中的1/3支付给市政证券规则制定委员会,或在该等注册证券协会与市政证券规则制定委员会达成协议后,按证券交易委员会指示的其他比例将罚款支付给市政证券规则制定委员会。”

(d)**市政证券的发行**。——《1934年证券交易法》第15B(d)(2)条[《美国法典》第十五编第78o-4(d)节]修正如下——

(1)删除“通过市政证券经纪商或市政证券自营商或以其他方式”,替以“通过市政证券经纪商、市政证券自营商、市政顾问或以其他方式”;及

(2)在“向市政证券规则制定委员会或该等证券的买方或潜在买方提供”前插入“或市政顾问,”。

(e)**定义**。——在《1934年证券交易法》第15B条(《美国法典》第十五编第78o-4节)结尾处增加如下内容,作为对该条的修正:

“(e)**定义**。——就本条而言——

"(1) the term 'Board' means the Municipal Securities Rule making Board established under subsection (b)(1);

"(2) the term 'guaranteed investment contract' includes any investment that has specified withdrawal or reinvestment provisions and a specifically negotiated or bid interest rate, and also includes any agreement to supply investments on 2 or more future dates, such as a forward supply contract;

"(3) the term 'investment strategies' includes plans or programs for the investment of the proceeds of municipal securities that are not municipal derivatives, guaranteed investment contracts, and the recommendation of and brokerage of municipal escrow investments;

"(4) the term 'municipal advisor'—

"(A) means a person (who is not a municipal entity or an employee of a municipal entity) that—

"(i) provides advice to or on behalf of a municipal entity or obligated person with respect to municipal financial products or the issuance of municipal securities, including advice with respect to the structure, timing, terms, and other similar matters concerning such financial products or issues; or

"(ii) undertakes a solicitation of a municipal entity;

"(B) includes financial advisors, guaranteed investment contract brokers, third-party marketers, placement agents, solicitors, finders, and swap advisors, if such persons are described in any of clauses (i) through (iii) of subparagraph (A); and

"(C) does not include a broker, dealer, or municipal securities dealer serving as an underwriter (as defined in section 2(a)(11) of the Securities Act of 1933) (15 U.S.C.77b (a)(11)), any investment adviser registered under the Investment Advisers Act of 1940, or persons associated with such investment advisers who are providing investment advice, any commodity trading advisor registered under the Commodity Exchange Act or persons associated with a commodity trading advisor who are providing advice related to swaps, attorneys offering legal advice or providing services that are of a traditional legal nature, or engineers providing engineering advice;

"(5) the term 'municipal financial product' means municipal derivatives, guaranteed investment contracts, and investment strategies;

"(6) the term 'rules of the Board' means the rules proposed and adopted by the Board under subsection (b)(2);

"(7) the term 'person associated with a municipal advisor' or 'associated person of an advisor' means—

"(A) any partner, officer, director, or branch manager of such municipal advisor (or any person occupying a similar status or performing similar functions);

"(B) any other employee of such municipal advisor who is engaged in the management,

(1)‘市政证券规则制定委员会’一词系指根据第(b)(1)子条成立的市政证券规则制定委员会;

(2)‘担保投资合约’一词包括含有明确撤销投资条款或再投资条款,以及具体协商利率或竞价利率的所有投资,也包括在未来两个或两个以上的日期提供投资的协议,如:远期供应合约;

(3)‘投资策略’一词包括市政衍生品、担保投资合约以外的市政证券募集资金的投资方案或计划,以及市政代管投资的建议和经纪业务;

(4)‘市政顾问’一词——

(A)系指具有以下特征且不属于市政实体或市政实体雇员的人——

(i)针对市政金融产品或市政证券发行向市政实体或市政证券义务人提供建议,或代表市政实体或市政证券义务人提供建议,包括针对该等金融产品或发行的结构、时间、条款及其他类似事项提供建议;或

(ii)向市政实体招揽业务;

(B)包括金融顾问、担保投资合约经纪商、第三方营销商、配售代理人、事务律师、居间人以及互换顾问,前提是上述人属于第(A)子款第(i)项至第(iii)项所述之人;且

(C)不包括如下主体:作为承销商[定义见《1933年证券法》第2(a)(11)条(《美国法典》第十五编第77b(a)(11)节)]开展承销业务的经纪商、自营商或市政证券自营商;根据《1940年投资顾问法》注册的任何投资顾问,或提供投资顾问服务的该等投资顾问的业务相关人;根据《商品交易法》注册的任何商品交易顾问,或提供与互换相关的顾问服务的商品交易顾问业务相关人;提供法律意见或传统法律服务的律师;或提供工程顾问服务的工程师;

(5)‘市政金融产品’一词系指市政衍生品、担保投资合约以及投资策略;

(6)‘市政证券规则制定委员会规则’一词系指市政证券规则制定委员会根据第(b)(2)子条拟定并正式通过的规则;

(7)‘市政顾问的业务相关人’或‘顾问的业务相关人’一词系指——

(A)该等市政顾问的任何合伙人、高级管理人员、董事或分支机构经理(或担任类似职位或履行类似职能的任何人);

(B)负责管理、领导、监督或执行与以下建议相关的任何活动的任何其他雇员:就

direction, supervision, or performance of any activities relating to the provision of advice to or on behalf of a municipal entity or obligated person with respect to municipal financial products or the issuance of municipal securities; and

"(C) any person directly or indirectly controlling, controlled by, or under common control with such municipal advisor;

"(8) the term 'municipal entity' means any State, political subdivision of a State, or municipal corporate instrumentality of a State, including —

"(A) any agency, authority, or instrumentality of the State, political subdivision, or municipal corporate instrumentality;

"(B) any plan, program, or pool of assets sponsored or established by the State, political subdivision, or municipal corporate instrumentality or any agency, authority, or instrumentality thereof; and

"(C) any other issuer of municipal securities;

"(9) the term 'solicitation of a municipal entity or obligated person' means a direct or indirect communication with a municipal entity or obligated person made by a person, for direct or indirect compensation, on behalf of a broker, dealer, municipal securities dealer, municipal advisor, or investment adviser(as defined in section 202 of the Investment Advisers Act of 1940) that does not control, is not controlled by, or is not under common control with the person undertaking such solicitation for the purpose of obtaining or retaining an engagement by a municipal entity or obligated person of a broker, dealer, municipal securities dealer, or municipal advisor for or in connection with municipal financial products, the issuance of municipal securities, or of an investment adviser to provide investment advisory services to or on behalf of a municipal entity; and

"(10) the term 'obligated person' means any person, including an issuer of municipal securities, who is either generally or through an enterprise, fund, or account of such person, committed by contract or other arrangement to support the payment of all or part of the obligations on the municipal securities to be sold in an offering of municipal securities.".

(f) REGISTERED SECURITIES ASSOCIATION. —Section 15A(b) of the Securities Exchange Act of 1934 (15 U.S.C.78o-3(b)) is amended by adding at the end the following:

"(15) The rules of the association provide that the association shall —

"(A) request guidance from the Municipal Securities Rulemaking Board in interpretation of the rules of the Municipal Securities Rulemaking Board; and

"(B) provide information to the Municipal Securities Rulemaking Board about the enforcement actions and examinations of the association under section 15B(b)(2)(E), so that the Municipal Securities Rulemaking Board may —

"(i) assist in such enforcement actions and examinations; and

"(ii) evaluate the ongoing effectiveness of the rules of the Board.".

市政金融产品以及市政证券发行向市政实体或市政证券义务人提供的建议,或就市政金融产品以及市政证券发行代表市政实体或市政证券义务人提供的建议;及

(C)直接或间接控制该市政顾问的任何人、被该市政顾问控制的任何人或与该市政顾问受同一控制的任何人;

(8)'市政实体'一词系指任何州、州下属行政区域或任何州的市政法人职能机构,包括——

(A)该州的任何机关、监管机构、职能机构、行政区域或市政法人职能机构;

(B)该州、州下属行政区域、市政法人职能机构或其任何机关、部门或职能机构发起或制定的任何方案、计划或资产池;及

(C)任何其他市政证券发行人;

(9)'向市政实体或市政证券义务人招揽业务'一词系指:某人为了取得直接或间接的报酬,代表经纪商、自营商、市政证券自营商、市政顾问或投资顾问(定义见《1940年投资顾问法》第202条)直接或间接与市政实体或市政证券义务人沟通,以期市政实体或市政证券义务人聘用或继续聘用经纪商、自营商、市政证券自营商或市政顾问,就市政金融产品及市政证券发行提供服务或提供与市政金融产品及市政证券发行相关的服务,或聘用或继续聘用投资顾问向市政实体提供或代表市政实体提供投资顾问服务,且该经纪商、自营商、市政证券自营商、市政顾问或投资顾问并未直接或间接控制从事上述招揽业务之人,亦未被该人控制或与之受同一控制;且

(10)'市政证券义务人'一词系指具有以下特征的任何人(包括市政证券发行人):该人通过合约或其他安排,承诺对将在市政证券发行中出售的市政证券上的全部或部分义务提供一般性的偿付支持,或通过该人的企业、基金或账户提供偿付支持。"

(f)**注册证券协会**。——在《1934年证券交易法》第15A(b)条[《美国法典》第十五编第78o-3(b)节]结尾处增加如下内容,作为对该条的修正:

"(15)根据该协会的规则,该协会应——

(A)请求市政证券规则制定委员会就市政证券规则制定委员规则的解释提供指导;并

(B)将该协会根据第15B(b)(2)(E)条开展的执法行动和检查工作的相关信息提供给市政证券规则制定委员会,以便市政证券规则制定委员会能够——

(i)为该等执法行动及检查工作提供协助;并

(ii)对市政证券规则制定委员会规则的持续有效性进行评价。"

(g) REGISTRATION AND REGULATION OF BROKERS AND DEALERS. —Section 15 of the Securities Exchange Act of 1934 is amended —

(1) in subsection (b)(4), by inserting "municipal advisor," after "municipal securities dealer" each place that term appears; and

(2) in subsection (c), by inserting "broker, dealer, or" before "municipal securities dealer" each place that term appears.

(h) ACCOUNTS AND RECORDS, REPORTS, EXAMINATIONS OF EXCHANGES, MEMBERS, AND OTHERS. —Section 17(a)(1) of the Securities Exchange Act of 1934 is amended by inserting "municipal advisor," after "municipal securities dealer".

(i) EFFECTIVE DATE. —This section, and the amendments made by this section, shall take effect on October 1, 2010.

SEC.976. GOVERNMENT ACCOUNTABILITY OFFICE STUDY OF INCREASED DISCLOSURE TO INVESTORS.

(a) STUDY. —The Comptroller General of the United States shall conduct a study and review of the disclosure required to be made by issuers of municipal securities.

(b) SUBJECTS FOR EVALUATION. —In conducting the study under subsection (a), the Comptroller General of the United States shall —

(1) broadly describe —

(A) the size of the municipal securities markets and the issuers and investors; and

(B) the disclosures provided by issuers to investors;

(2) compare the amount, frequency, and quality of disclosures that issuers of municipal securities are required by law to provide for the benefit of municipal securities holders, including the amount of and frequency of disclosures actually provided by issuers of municipal securities, with the amount of and frequency of disclosures that issuers of corporate securities provide for the benefit of corporate securities holders, taking into account the differences between issuers of municipal securities and issuers of corporate securities;

(3) evaluate the costs and benefits to various types of issuers of municipal securities of requiring issuers of municipal bonds to provide additional financial disclosures for the benefit of investors;

(4) evaluate the potential benefit to investors from additional financial disclosures by issuers of municipal bonds; and

(5) make recommendations relating to disclosure requirements for municipal issuers, including the advisability of the repeal or retention of section 15B (d) of the Securities Exchange Act of 1934(15 U.S.C.78o-4(d))(commonly known as the "Tower Amendment").

(c) REPORT. —Not later than 24 months after the date of enactment of this Act, the Comptroller General of the United States shall submit a report to Congress on the results of the study conducted under subsection (a), including recommendations for how to improve

(g)**经纪商和自营商的注册与监管**。——《1934年证券交易法》第15条修正如下——

(1)在第(b)(4)子条中,在所有的“市政证券自营商”之后插入“、市政顾问”;及

(2)在第(c)子条中,在所有的“市政证券自营商”前插入“经纪商、自营商或”。

(h)**交易所、会员及其他主体的账簿、记录、报告及检查资料**。——《1934年证券交易法》第17(a)(1)条修正如下:在“市政证券自营商”之后插入“、市政顾问”。

(i)**生效日**。——本条以及本条作出的各项修正应于2010年10月1日生效。

第976条　政府问责办公室关于加强向投资者进行披露的研究

(a)**研究**。——政府问责办公室主任应针对市政证券发行人应作出的披露开展研究和评估。

(b)**评估对象**。——在根据第(a)子条开展研究时,政府问责办公室主任应——

(1)总体说明——

(A)市政证券市场、发行人和投资者的规模;及

(B)发行人向投资者提供的披露信息;

(2)在考虑市政证券发行人与公司证券发行人差别的基础上,对市政证券发行人为了市政证券持有人的利益依法应提供的披露信息的数量、质量及披露频率(包括市政证券发行人实际提供的披露信息的数量和披露频率),与公司证券发行人为了公司证券持有人的利益提供的披露信息的数量和披露频率进行对比。

(3)评估如果要求市政债券发行人为了投资者利益披露额外的财务信息,该要求将导致各类市政证券发行人承担的费用以及为其带来的收益;

(4)评估市政债券发行人披露额外财务信息将可能为投资者带来的利益;并

(5)针对市政证券发行人的信息披露要求提供建议,包括针对废止或保留《1934年证券交易法》第15B(d)条[《美国法典》第十五编第78o-4(d)节](通常称为堡垒修正)是否适当提出建议。

(c)**报告**。——政府问责办公室主任应于本法颁布之日后24个月内,就其根据第(a)子条所开展研究的结果(包括关于如何完善市政证券发行人信息披露工作的建议)向国会提交一份报告。

disclosure by issuers of municipal securities.

SEC.977. GOVERNMENT ACCOUNTABILITY OFFICE STUDY ON THE MUNICIPAL SECURITIES MARKETS.

(a) STUDY. —The Comptroller General of the United States shall conduct a study of the municipal securities markets.

(b) REPORT. —Not later than 18 months after the date of enactment of this Act, the Comptroller General of the United States shall submit a report to the Committee on Banking, Housing, and Urban Affairs of the Senate, and the Committee on Financial Services of the House of Representatives, with copies to the Special Committee on Aging of the Senate and the Commission, on the results of the study conducted under subsection (a), including —

(1) an analysis of the mechanisms for trading, quality of trade executions, market transparency, trade reporting, price discovery, settlement clearing, and credit enhancements;

(2) the needs of the markets and investors and the impact of recent innovations;

(3) recommendations for how to improve the transparency, efficiency, fairness, and liquidity of trading in the municipal securities markets, including with reference to items listed in paragraph (1); and

(4) potential uses of derivatives in the municipal securities markets.

(c) RESPONSES. —Not later than 180 days after receipt of the report required under subsection (b), the Commission shall submit a response to the Committee on Banking, Housing, and Urban Affairs of the Senate, and the Committee on Financial Services of the House of Representatives, with a copy to the Special Committee on Aging of the Senate, stating the actions the Commission has taken in response to the recommendations contained in such report.

SEC.978. FUNDING FOR GOVERNMENTAL ACCOUNTING STANDARDS BOARD.

(a) AMENDMENT TO THE SECURITIES ACT OF 1933. —Section 19 of the Securities Act of 1933 (15 U.S.C.77s), as amended by section 912, is further amended by adding at the end the following:

"(g) FUNDING FOR THE GASB. —

"(1) IN GENERAL. —The Commission may, subject to the limitations imposed by section 15B of the Securities Exchange Act of 1934 (15 U.S.C.78o–4), require a national securities association registered under the Securities Exchange Act of 1934 to establish —

"(A) a reasonable annual accounting support fee to adequately fund the annual budget of the Governmental Accounting Standards Board (referred to in this subsection as the 'GASB'); and

"(B) rules and procedures, in consultation with the principal organizations representing State governors, legislators, local elected officials, and State and local finance officers, to

第977条　政府问责办公室关于市政证券市场的研究

(a)**研究**。——政府问责办公室主任应对市政证券市场开展研究。

(b)**报告**。——政府问责办公室主任应于本法颁布之日后18个月内,针对根据第(a)子条所开展研究的结果向参议院银行、住房与城市事务委员会及众议院金融服务委员会提交一份报告,并同时抄送给参议院老龄问题特别委员会和证券交易委员会。该报告的内容应包括——

(1)关于交易机制、交易执行的质量、市场透明度、交易报告、价格发现、清算结算和信用增级的分析;

(2)市场和投资者的需求及近期创新工作带来的影响;

(3)关于如何提高市政证券市场交易透明度、效率、公平性和流动性的建议,包括关于第(1)款所列各项内容的建议;及

(4)市政证券市场采用衍生品的可能性。

(c)**答复**。——证券交易委员会应于收到第(b)子条规定的报告后180天内,向参议院银行、住房与城市事务委员会及众议院金融服务委员会提交一份答复,对证券交易委员会针对该报告中提出的建议已采取的行动进行说明,并同时抄送给参议院老龄问题特别委员会。

第978条　政府会计标准委员会的经费来源

(a)**对《1933年证券法》的修正**。——在经第912条修正后的《1933年证券法》第19条(《美国法典》第十五编第77s节)结尾处增加如下内容,作为对该条的进一步修正:

“(g)**政府会计标准委员会的经费来源**。——

(1)**一般规定**。——在不违反《1934年证券交易法》第15B条(《美国法典》第十五编第78o-4节)施加的限制条件的前提下,证券交易委员会可要求根据《1934年证券交易法》注册的全国性证券协会——

(A)设定合理的年度会计支持费,以便为政府会计标准委员会(本子条中英文简称GASB)的年度预算提供充足资金;并

(B)在与代表各州州长、立法委员、地方选举产生的官员以及州和地方财政官员的主要机构磋商后,制定相关规则和程序,以便公平分配、摊派并向协会会员征收根

provide for the equitable allocation, assessment, and collection of the accounting support fee established under subparagraph (A) from the members of the association, and the remittance of all such accounting support fees to the Financial Accounting Foundation.

"(2) ANNUAL BUDGET. —For purposes of this subsection, the annual budget of the GASB is the annual budget reviewed and approved according to the internal procedures of the Financial Accounting Foundation.

"(3) USE OF FUNDS. —Any fees or funds collected under this subsection shall be used to support the efforts of the GASB to establish standards of financial accounting and reporting recognized as generally accepted accounting principles applicable to State and local governments of the United States.

"(4) LIMITATION ON FEE. —The annual accounting support fees collected under this subsection for a fiscal year shall not exceed the recoverable annual budgeted expenses of the GASB (which may include operating expenses, capital, and accrued items).

"(5) RULES OF CONSTRUCTION. —

"(A) FEES NOT PUBLIC MONIES. —Accounting support fees collected under this subsection and other receipts of the GASB shall not be considered public monies of the United States.

"(B) LIMITATION ON AUTHORITY OF THE COMMISSION. —Nothing in this subsection shall be construed to —

"(i) provide the Commission or any national securities association direct or indirect oversight of the budget or technical agenda of the GASB; or

"(ii) affect the setting of generally accepted accounting principles by the GASB.

"(C) NONINTERFERENCE WITH STATES. —Nothing in this subsection shall be construed to impair or limit the authority of a State or local government to establish accounting and financial reporting standards.".

(b) STUDY OF FUNDING FOR GOVERNMENTAL ACCOUNTING STANDARDS BOARD. —

(1) STUDY. —The Comptroller General of the United States shall conduct a study that evaluates —

(A) the role and importance of the Governmental Accounting Standards Board in the municipal securities markets; and

(B) the manner and the level at which the Governmental Accounting Standards Board has been funded.

(2) CONSULTATION. —In conducting the study required under paragraph (1), the Comptroller General shall consult with the principal organizations representing State governors, legislators, local elected officials, and State and local finance officers.

(3) REPORT. —Not later than 180 days after the date of enactment of this Act, the

据上文第(A)子款设定的会计支持费,并将所有该等会计支持费汇入财务会计基金会。

(2)**年度预算**。——就本子条而言,政府会计标准委员会的年度预算系指按照财务会计基金会的内部程序获得审批的年度预算。

(3)**资金的用途**。——根据本子条征收的任何费用或资金均应用于支持政府会计标准委员会的财务会计和财务报告标准制定工作,该等标准应作为公认会计原则适用于美国各州和地方政府。

(4)**会计支持费的金额限制**。——根据本子条在某一财政年度征收的年度会计支持费不得超过政府会计标准委员会的可摊派年度预算内开支(可包括运营开支、资本和应计项目)。

(5)**解释规则**。——

(A)**会计支持费不视为公共资金**。——根据本子条征收的会计支持费以及政府会计标准委员会的其他收入不得视为联邦公共资金。

(B)**证券交易委员会的权力限制**。——本子条任何内容均不得被解释为——

(i)证券交易委员会或任何全国性证券协会可以政府会计标准委员会的预算或技术议程实施直接或间接的监督;或

(ii)影响政府会计标准委员会的公认会计原则制定工作。

(C)**不干涉各州权力**。——本子条任何内容均不得被解释为削弱或限制州政府或地方政府制定会计和财务报告标准的权力。”

(b)**关于政府会计标准委员会经费来源的研究**。——

(1)**研究**。——政府问责办公室主任应开展研究,对以下事项进行评价——

(A)政府会计标准委员会在市政证券市场中的作用和重要性;及

(B)政府会计标准委员会获取经费的方式和水平。

(2)**磋商**。——在开展第(1)款规定的研究时,政府问责办公室主任应与代表各州州长、立法委员、地方选举产生的官员以及州和地方财政官员的主要机构磋商。

(3)**报告**。——政府问责办公室主任应于本法颁布之日后180天内,针对第(1)款

Comptroller General shall submit to the Committee on Banking, Housing, and Urban Affairs of the Senate and the Committee on Financial Services of the House of Representatives a report on the study required under paragraph (1).

SEC.979. COMMISSION OFFICE OF MUNICIPAL SECURITIES.

(a) IN GENERAL. —There shall be in the Commission an Office of Municipal Securities, which shall —

(1) administer the rules of the Commission with respect to the practices of municipal securities brokers and dealers, municipal securities advisors, municipal securities investors, and municipal securities issuers; and

(2) coordinate with the Municipal Securities Rulemaking Board for rulemaking and enforcement actions as required by law.

(b) DIRECTOR OF THE OFFICE. —The head of the Office of Municipal Securities shall be the Director, who shall report to the Chairman.

(c) STAFFING. —

(1) IN GENERAL. —The Office of Municipal Securities shall be staffed sufficiently to carry out the requirements of this section.

(2) REQUIREMENT. —The staff of the Office of Municipal Securities shall include individuals with knowledge of and expertise in municipal finance.

Subtitle I—Public Company Accounting Oversight Board, Portfolio Margining, and Other Matters

SEC.981. AUTHORITY TO SHARE CERTAIN INFORMATION WITH FOREIGN AUTHORITIES.

(a) DEFINITION. —Section 2(a) of the Sarbanes-Oxley Act of 2002 (15 U.S.C.7201 (a)) is amended by adding at the end the following:

"(17) FOREIGN AUDITOR OVERSIGHT AUTHORITY. —The term 'foreign auditor oversight authority' means any governmental body or other entity empowered by a foreign government to conduct inspections of public accounting firms or otherwise to administer or enforce laws related to the regulation of public accounting firms.".

(b) AVAILABILITY TO SHARE INFORMATION. —Section 105 (b) (5) of the Sarbanes-Oxley Act of 2002(15 U.S.C.7215(b)(5)) is amended by adding at the end the following:

"(C) AVAILABILITY TO FOREIGN OVERSIGHT AUTHORITIES. — Without the loss of its status as confidential and privileged in the hands of the Board, all information

规定的研究向参议院银行、住房与城市事务委员会及众议院金融服务委员会提交一份报告。

第979条 证券交易委员会的市政证券办公室

(a)**一般规定**。——证券交易委员会应下设市政证券办公室,负责——

(1)实施证券交易委员会关于市政证券经纪商、市政证券自营商、市政证券顾问、市政证券投资者和市政证券发行人的业务活动的规则;并

(2)与市政证券规则制定委员会协调,按法律要求开展规则制定和执法行动。

(b)**办公室主任**。——市政证券办公室的负责人应为办公室主任;办公室主任应向证券交易委员会主席汇报工作。

(c)**人员配备**。——

(1)**一般规定**。——市政证券办公室应当配备人数充足的工作人员,以实施本条规定。

(2)**要求**。——市政证券办公室的工作人员中应包含具备市政金融方面知识和专长的个人。

第I子编——公众公司会计监督委员会、投资组合保证金制度及其他事项

第981条 与外国监管机构共享特定信息的权力

(a)**定义**。——在《2002年萨班斯—奥克斯利法》第2(a)条[《美国法典》第十五编第7201(a)节]结尾处增加如下内容,作为对该条的修正:

"(17)**外国审计师监管机构**。——'外国审计师监管机构'一词系指经外国政府授权对公共会计师事务所进行检查,或者以其他方式实施或强制执行与公共会计师事务所监管相关的法律的任何政府机构或其他实体。"

(b)**信息共享条件**。——在《2002年萨班斯—奥克斯利法》第105(b)(5)条[《美国法典》第十五编第7215(b)(5)节]结尾处增加如下内容,作为对该条的修正:

"(C)**与外国监管机构共享信息的条件**。——对于第(A)子款提及的与作为外国政府授权的外国审计师监管机构的检查或执法对象的公共会计师事务所相关的所有

referred to in subparagraph (A) that relates to a public accounting firm that a foreign government has empowered a foreign auditor oversight authority to inspect or otherwise enforce laws with respect to, may, at the discretion of the Board, be made available to the foreign auditor oversight authority, if—

"(i) the Board finds that it is necessary to accomplish the purposes of this Act or to protect investors;

"(ii) the foreign auditor oversight authority provides—

"(I) such assurances of confidentiality as the Board may request;

"(II) a description of the applicable information systems and controls of the foreign auditor oversight authority; and

"(III) a description of the laws and regulations of the foreign government of the foreign auditor oversight authority that are relevant to information access; and

"(iii) the Board determines that it is appropriate to share such information.".

(c) CONFORMING AMENDMENT. —Section 105(b)(5)(A) of the Sarbanes–Oxley Act of 2002 (15 U.S.C.7215(b)(5)(A)) is amended by striking "subparagraph (B)" and inserting "subparagraphs (B) and (C)".

SEC.982. OVERSIGHT OF BROKERS AND DEALERS.

(a) DEFINITIONS. —

(1) DEFINITIONS AMENDED. —Title I of the Sarbanes–Oxley Act of 2002 (15 U.S. C.7201 et seq.) is amended by adding at the end the following new section:

"SEC.110. DEFINITIONS.

"For the purposes of this title, the following definitions shall apply:

"(1) AUDIT. —The term 'audit' means an examination of the financial statements, reports, documents, procedures, controls, or notices of any issuer, broker, or dealer by an independent public accounting firm in accordance with the rules of the Board or the Commission, for the purpose of expressing an opinion on the financial statements or providing an audit report.

"(2) AUDIT REPORT. —The term 'audit report' means a document, report, notice, or other record —

"(A) prepared following an audit performed for purposes of compliance by an issuer, broker, or dealer with the requirements of the securities laws; and

"(B) in which a public accounting firm either —

"(i) sets forth the opinion of that firm regarding a financial statement, report, notice, or other document, procedures, or controls; or

"(ii) asserts that no such opinion can be expressed.

"(3) BROKER. —The term 'broker' means a broker (as such term is defined in section

信息，公众公司会计监督委员会可在该等信息的保密和受保密特权保护的状态不丧失的情况下,依其自由裁量权该等信息提供给该外国审计师监管机构,前提是——

(i)公众公司会计监督委员会认定为实现本法宗旨或者保护投资者而有必要提供该等信息;

(ii)外国审计师监管机构——

(I)提供了公众公司会计监督委员会要求的保密保证;

(II)提供了关于外国审计师监管机构相关信息系统和控制措施的说明;并

(III)提供了外国审计师监管机构所属外国政府与信息查询权相关的法律法规的说明;且

(iii)公众公司会计监督委员会判定与外国审计师监管机构共享信息确属适当。”

(c)**一致性修正**。——《2002年萨班斯—奥克斯利法》第105(b)(5)(A)条[《美国法典》第十五编第7215(b)(5)(A)节]修正如下:删除“第(B)子款”,替以“第(B)子款和第(C)子款”。

第982条　对经纪商和自营商的监督

(a)**定义**。——

(1)**定义修正**。——在《2002年萨班斯—奥克斯利法》第一编(《美国法典》第十五编第7201节及其后条文)结尾处增加如下新条文,作为对该编的修正:

“第110条　定义

就本编而言,应适用如下定义:

(1)**审计**。——‘审计’一词系指独立的公共会计师事务所为了对任何发行人、经纪商或自营商财务报表出具意见或者提供审计报告，按照公众公司会计监督委员会或证券交易委员会的规则对该发行人、经纪商或自营商的财务报表、报告、文件、程序、控制措施或公告进行核验的活动。

(2)**审计报告**。——‘审计报告’一词系指符合下列条件的文件、报告、公告或其他记录——

(A)在审计发行人、经纪商或自营商对证券法律的遵守情况之后编制;且

(B)公共会计师事务所在其中——

(i)出具了关于财务报表、报告、公告、其他文件、程序或控制措施的意见;或

(ii)声明其无法出具上述意见。

(3)**经纪商**。——‘经纪商’一词系指根据《1934年证券交易法》第17(e)(1)(A)条

3(a)(4) of the Securities Exchange Act of 1934 (15 U.S.C.78c(a)(4))) that is required to file a balance sheet, income statement, or other financial statement under section 17 (e)(1)(A) of such Act (15 U.S.C.78q(e)(1)(A)), where such balance sheet, income statement, or financial statement is required to be certified by a registered public accounting firm.

"(4) DEALER. —The term 'dealer' means a dealer (as such term is defined in section 3(a)(5) of the Securities Exchange Act of 1934 (15 U.S.C.78c(a)(5))) that is required to file a balance sheet, income statement, or other financial statement under section 17(e)(1)(A) of such Act (15 U.S.C.78q(e)(1)(A)), where such balance sheet, income statement, or financial statement is required to be certified by a registered public accounting firm.

"(5) PROFESSIONAL STANDARDS. —The term 'professional standards' means —

"(A) accounting principles that are—

"(i) established by the standard setting body described in section 19 (b) of the Securities Act of 1933, as amended by this Act, or prescribed by the Commission under section 19(a) of that Act (15 U.S.C.17a(s)) or section 13(b) of the Securities Exchange Act of 1934 (15 U.S.C.78a(m)); and

"(ii) relevant to audit reports for particular issuers, brokers, or dealers, or dealt with in the quality control system of a particular registered public accounting firm; and

"(B) auditing standards, standards for attestation engagements, quality control policies and procedures, ethical and competency standards, and independence standards (including rules implementing title II) that the Board or the Commission determines —

"(i) relate to the preparation or issuance of audit reports for issuers, brokers, or dealers; and

"(ii) are established or adopted by the Board under section 103(a), or are promulgated as rules of the Commission.

"(6) SELF–REGULATORY ORGANIZATION . — The term ' self–regulatory organization' has the same meaning as in section 3(a) of the Securities Exchange Act of 1934 (15 U.S.C.78c(a)).".

(2) CONFORMING AMENDMENT. —Section 2(a) of the Sar–banes–Oxley Act of 2002 (15 U.S.C.7201(a)) is amended in the matter preceding paragraph (1), by striking "In this" and inserting "Except as otherwise specifically provided in this Act, in this".

(b) ESTABLISHMENT AND ADMINISTRATION OF THE PUBLIC COMPANY ACCOUNTING OVERSIGHT BOARD. —Section 101 of the Sarbanes–Oxley Act of 2002 (15 U.S.C.7211) is amended —

(1) by striking "issuers" each place that term appears and inserting "issuers, brokers, and dealers"; and

(2) in subsection (a) —

(A) by striking "public companies" and inserting "companies"; and

[《美国法典》第十五编第78q(e)(1)(A)节]应提交须经注册公共会计师事务核证的资产负债表、损益表或其他财务报表的经纪商[定义见《1934年证券交易法》第3(a)(4)条][《美国法典》第78c(a)(4)节]。

(4)**自营商**。——‘自营商’一词系指根据《1934年证券交易法》第17(e)(1)(A)条[《美国法典》第十五编第78q(e)(1)(A)节]应提交须经注册公共会计师事务核证的资产负债表、损益表或其他财务报表的自营商[定义见《1934年证券交易法》第3(a)(5)条][《美国法典》第78c(a)(5)节]。

(5)**专业标准**。——‘专业标准’一词系指——

(A)符合下列条件的会计原则——

(i)由经本法修正后的《1933年证券法》第19(b)条所述标准制定机构制定,或者由证券交易委员会根据该法第19(a)条[《美国法典》第十五编第17a(s)节]或者《1934年证券交易法》第13(b)条[《美国法典》第十五编第78a(m)节]所规定;且

(ii)与特定发行人、经纪商或自营商的审计报告相关,或者涉及特定注册公共会计师事务所的质量控制制度;及

(B)公众公司会计监督委员会或证券交易委员会判定符合下列条件的审计标准、鉴证委托服务标准、质量控制政策和程序、职业道德和胜任能力标准以及独立性标准(包括第二编实施规则)——

(i)与发行人、经纪商或自营商的审计报告编制或出具相关;且

(ii)由公众公司会计监督委员会根据第103(a)条制定或正式通过,或者已作为证券交易委员会的规则颁发。

(6)**自律组织**。——‘自律组织’一词的含义以《1934年证券交易法》第3(a)条[《美国法典》第十五编第78c(a)节]的定义为准。”

(2)**一致性修正**。——《2002年萨班斯—奥克斯利法》第2(a)条[《美国法典》第十五编第7201(a)节]修正如下:在第(1)款之前的内容中,删除“就本法而言”,替以“除本法另有明确规定的情形外,就本法而言”。

(b)**公众公司会计监督委员会的成立和管理**。——《2002年萨班斯—奥克斯利法》第101条(《美国法典》第十五编第7211节)修正如下——

(1)删除所有“发行人”,全部替以“发行人、经纪商和自营商”;及

(2)在第(a)子条中——

(A)删除“公众公司”,替以“公司”;及

(B) by striking "for companies the securities of which are sold to, and held by and for, public investors".

(c) REGISTRATION WITH THE BOARD. —Section 102 of the Sarbanes–Oxley Act of 2002 (15 U.S.C.7212) is amended —

(1) in subsection (a) —

(A) by striking "Beginning 180" and all that follows through "101(d), it" and inserting "It"; and

(B) by striking "issuer" and inserting "issuer, broker, or dealer";

(2) in subsection (b) —

(A) in paragraph (2)(A), by striking "issuers" and inserting "issuers, brokers, and dealers"; and

(B) by striking "issuer" each place that term appears and inserting "issuer, broker, or dealer".

(d) AUDITING AND INDEPENDENCE. —Section 103(a) of the Sarbanes–Oxley Act of 2002 (15 U.S.C.7213(a)) is amended —

(1) in paragraph (1), by striking "and such ethics standards" and inserting "such ethics standards, and such independence standards";

(2) in paragraph (2)(A)(iii), by striking "describe in each audit report" and inserting "in each audit report for an issuer, describe"; and

(3) in paragraph (2)(B)(i), by striking "issuers" and inserting "issuers, brokers, and dealers".

(e) INSPECTIONS OF REGISTERED PUBLIC ACCOUNTING FIRMS. —

(1) AMENDMENTS. —Section 104(a) of the Sarbanes–Oxley Act of 2002 (15 U.S.C. 7214(a)) is amended —

(A) by striking "The Board shall" and inserting the following:

"(1) INSPECTIONS GENERALLY. —The Board shall"; and

(B) by adding at the end the following:

"(2) INSPECTIONS OF AUDIT REPORTS FOR BROKERS AND DEALERS. —

"(A) The Board may, by rule, conduct and require a program of inspection in accordance with paragraph (1), on a basis to be determined by the Board, of registered public accounting firms that provide one or more audit reports for a broker or dealer. The Board, in establishing such a program, may allow for differentiation among classes of brokers and dealers, as appropriate.

"(B) If the Board determines to establish a program of inspection pursuant to subparagraph (A), the Board shall consider in establishing any inspection schedules whether differing schedules would be appropriate with respect to registered public accounting firms that issue audit reports only for one or more brokers or dealers that do not receive, handle, or

(B)删除"向公众投资者出售证券的公司,以及证券为公众投资者或其代表所持有的公司"。

(c)**在公众公司会计监督委员会注册**。——《2002年萨班斯—奥克斯利法》第102条(《美国法典》第十五编第7212节)修正如下——

(1)在第(a)子条中——

(A)删除"自证券交易委员会根据第101(d)条作出判定后届满180天之日始",并

(B)删除"发行人",替以"发行人、经纪商或自营商",

(2)在第(b)子条中——

(A)第(2)(A)款删除"发行人",替以"发行人、经纪商和自营商";及

(B)删除所有"发行人",全部替以"发行人、经纪商或自营商"。

(d)**审计和独立性**。——《2002年萨班斯—奥克斯利法》第103(a)条[《美国法典》第十五编第7213(a)节]修正如下——

(1)在第(1)款中,删除"及该等道德标准",替以"该等道德标准及独立性标准";

(2)在第(2)(A)(iii)款中,删除"在每份审计报告中说明",替以"在发行人的每份审计报告中说明";及

(3)在第(2)(B)(i)款中,删除"发行人",替以"发行人、经纪商及自营商"。

(e)**对注册公共会计师事务所的检查**。——

(1)**修正**。——《2002年萨班斯—奥克斯利法》第104(a)条[《美国法典》第十五编第7214(a)节]修正如下——

(A)删除"公众公司会计监督委员会应",替以如下内容:

"(1)**总体检查**。——公众公司会计监督委员会应";及

(B)在结尾处增加如下内容:

"(2)**对经纪商和自营商审计报告的检查**。——

(A)公众公司会计监督委员会可以发布规则,针对为经纪商或自营商提供一份或一份以上审计报告的注册公共会计师事务所,按照公众公司会计监督委员会确定的基础和第(1)款的规定开展一项检查计划并要求对等会计师事务所开展该项检查计划。在制订该项检查计划时,公众公司会计监督委员会可以允许对不同类别的经纪商和自营商进行适当的差异化处理。

(B)如果公众公司会计监督委员会决定根据第(A)子款制定检查计划,其在确定检查安排时应考虑,如果注册公共会计师事务仅为一个或一个以上的经纪商或自营商出具审计报告,而该等经纪商或自营商并不接收、处理或持有客户证券或现金,也非证券投资者保护公司会员,对该等注册公共会计师事务所采用不同的检查安排是

hold customer securities or cash or are not a member of the Securities Investor Protection Corporation.

"(C) Any rules of the Board pursuant to this paragraph shall be subject to prior approval by the Commission pursuant to section 107(b) before the rules become effective, including an opportunity for public notice and comment.

"(D) Notwithstanding anything to the contrary in section 102 of this Act, a public accounting firm shall not be required to register with the Board if the public accounting firm is exempt from the inspection program which may be established by the Board under subparagraph (A).".

(2) CONFORMING AMENDMENT. —Section 17 (e) (1) (A) of the Securities Exchange Act of 1934 (15 U.S.C.78q(e)(1)(A)) is amended by striking "registered public accounting firm" and inserting "independent public accounting firm, or by a registered public accounting firm if the firm is required to be registered under the Sarbanes–Oxley Act of 2002,".

(f) INVESTIGATIONS AND DISCIPLINARY PROCEEDINGS. —Section 105(c)(7)(B) of the Sarbanes–Oxley Act of 2002 (15 U.S.C.7215(c)(7)(B)) is amended —

(1) in the subparagraph heading, by inserting ", BROKER, OR DEALER" after "ISSUER";

(2) by striking "any issuer" each place that term appears and inserting "any issuer, broker, or dealer"; and

(3) by striking "an issuer under this subsection" and inserting "a registered public accounting firm under this subsection".

(g) FOREIGN PUBLIC ACCOUNTING FIRMS. —Section 106(a) of the Sarbanes–Oxley Act of 2002 (15 U.S.C.7216(a)) is amended —

(1) in paragraph (1), by striking "issuer" and inserting "issuer, broker, or dealer"; and

(2) in paragraph (2), by striking "issuers" and inserting "issuers, brokers, or dealers".

(h) FUNDING. —Section 109 of the Sarbanes–Oxley Act of 2002 (15 U.S.C.7219) is amended —

(1) in subsection (c)(2), by striking "subsection (i)" and inserting "subsection (j)";

(2) in subsection (d) —

(A) in paragraph (2), by striking "allowing for differentiation among classes of issuers, as appropriate" and inserting "and among brokers and dealers, in accordance with subsection (h), and allowing for differentiation among classes of issuers, brokers and dealers, as appropriate"; and

(B) by adding at the end the following:

"(3) BROKERS AND DEALERS. —The Board shall begin the allocation, assessment, and collection of fees under paragraph (2) with respect to brokers and dealers with the

否适当。

(C)公众公司会计监督委员会根据本款制定的任何规则均应在生效前,由证券交易委员会根据第107(b)条进行事先批准,包括进行公布并征求公众意见。

(D)无论本法第102条是否存在任何相反规定,如果公共会计师事务所获得豁免,不必适用公众公司会计监督委员会根据第(A)子款制定的检查计划,则不应要求该等公共会计师事务所在公众公司会计监督委员会办理注册。”

(2)**一致性修正**。——《1934年证券交易法》第17(e)(1)(A)条[《美国法典》第十五编第78q(e)(1)(A)节]修正如下:删除“注册公共会计师事务所核证的”,替以“独立公共会计师事务所核证的,或注册公共会计师事务所核证的(如果根据《2002年萨班斯—奥克斯利法》该事务所需要进行注册),”。

(f)**调查和纪律处分程序**。——《2002年萨班斯—奥克斯利法》第105(c)(7)(B)条[《美国法典》第十五编第7215(c)(7)(B)节]修正如下——

(1)在子款标题中,在“发行人”之后插入“,**经纪商或自营商**”;

(2)删除所有的“任何发行人”,全部替以“任何发行人、经纪商或自营商”;及

(3)删除“本子条规定的发行人”,替以“本子条规定的注册公共会计师事务所”。

(g)**外国公共会计师事务所**。——《2002年萨班斯—奥克斯利法》第106(a)条[《美国法典》第十五编第7216(a)节]修正如下——

(1)在第(1)款中,删除“发行人”,替以“发行人、经纪商或自营商”;及

(2)在第(2)款中,删除“发行人”,替以“发行人、经纪商或自营商”。

(h)**经费来源**。——《2002年萨班斯—奥克斯利法》第109条(《美国法典》第十五编第7219节)修正如下——

(1)在第(c)(2)子条中,删除“第(i)子条”,替以“第(j)子条”;

(2)在第(d)子条中——

(A)第(2)款删除“允许对不同类别的发行人进行适当的差异化处理”,替以“允许对不同类别的发行人、经纪商和自营商进行适当的差异化处理”;及

(B)在结尾处增加如下内容:

“(3)**经纪商和自营商**。——公众公司会计监督委员会应开始根据第(2)款规定对经纪商和自营商进行费用分配、摊派和征收,为《2010年投资者保护与证券改革法》

payment of support fees to fund the first full fiscal year beginning after the date of enactment of the Investor Protection and Securities Reform Act of 2010.";

(3) by redesignating subsections (h), (i), and (j) as subsections (i), (j), and (k), respectively; and

(4) by inserting after subsection (g) the following:

"(h) ALLOCATION OF ACCOUNTING SUPPORT FEES AMONG BROKERS AND DEALERS. —

"(1) OBLIGATION TO PAY. —Each broker or dealer shall pay to the Board the annual accounting support fee allocated to such broker or dealer under this section.

"(2) ALLOCATION. —Any amount due from a broker or dealer (or from a particular class of brokers and dealers) under this section shall be allocated among brokers and dealers and payable by the broker or dealer (or the brokers and dealers in the particular class, as applicable).

"(3) PROPORTIONALITY. —The amount due from a broker or dealer shall be in proportion to the net capital of the broker or dealer (before or after any adjustments), compared to the total net capital of all brokers and dealers (before or after any adjustments), in accordance with rules issued by the Board.".

(i) REFERRAL OF INVESTIGATIONS TO A SELF-REGULATORY ORGANIZATION. — Section 105(b)(4)(B) of the Sarbanes-Oxley Act of 2002 (15 U.S.C.7215(b)(4)(B)) is amended —

(1) by redesignating clauses (ii) and (iii) as clauses (iii) and (iv), respectively; and

(2) by inserting after clause (i) the following:

"(ii) to a self-regulatory organization, in the case of an investigation that concerns an audit report for a broker or dealer that is under the jurisdiction of such self-regulatory organization;".

(j) USE OF DOCUMENTS RELATED TO AN INSPECTION OR INVESTIGATION. —

Section 105(b)(5)(B)(ii) of the Sarbanes-Oxley Act of 2002 (15 U.S.C.7215(b)(5)(B)(ii)) is amended —

(1) in subclause (III), by striking "and" at the end;

(2) in subclause (IV), by striking the comma and inserting "; and"; and

(3) by inserting after subclause (IV) the following:

"(V) a self-regulatory organization, with respect to an audit report for a broker or dealer that is under the jurisdiction of such self-regulatory organization,".

SEC.983. PORTFOLIO MARGINING.

(a) ADVANCES. —Section 9(a)(1) of the Securities Investor Protection Act of 1970 (15 U.S.C.78fff3 (a) (1)) is amended by inserting "or options on commodity futures contracts" after "claim for securities".

颁布之日后的首个完整财政年度提供支持经费。”;

(3)第(h)子条、第(i)子条和第(j)子条分别重新编号为第(i)子条、第(j)子条和第(k)子条;及

(4)在第(g)子条之后插入如下内容:

“(h)**在经纪商和自营商之间分摊会计支持费**。——

(1)**支付义务**。——每一经纪商或自营商均应按照本条规定的分摊金额,向公众公司会计监督委员会支付年度会计支持费。

(2)**分摊**。——经纪商或自营商(或特定类别的经纪商及自营商)按照本条规定应付任何款项均应在经纪商和自营商之间进行分摊,并由该等经纪商或自营商(或特定类别的经纪商和自营商,视具体情况而定)支付。

(3)**比例**。——按照公众公司会计监督委员会发布的规则,经纪商或自营商的应付款项应根据其净资本额(指进行任何调整之前或之后的净资本额)在全体经纪商及自营商净资本总额(指进行任何调整之前或之后的净资本额)中的比例进行计算。”

(i)**移交自律组织开展调查**。——《2002年萨班斯—奥克斯利法》第105(b)(4)(B)条[《美国法典》第十五编第7215(b)(4)(B)节]修正如下——

(1)第(ii)项和第(iii)项分别重新编号为第(iii)项和第(iv)项;及

(2)在第(i)项之后插入如下内容:

“(ii)转交自律组织,如果该调查涉及自律组织所管辖的经纪商或自营商的审计报告;”。

(j)**检查或调查相关文件的使用**。——《2002年萨班斯—奥克斯利法》第105(b)(5)(B)(ii)条[《美国法典》第十五编第7215(b)(5)(B)(ii)节]修正如下——

(1)在第(III)子项中,删除结尾处的“及”;

(2)在第(IV)子项中,删除逗号,替以“;及”;并

(3)在第(IV)子项之后插入如下内容:

“(V) 提供给自律组织(就该自律组织所管辖的经纪商或自营商的审计报告而言),”。

第983条 投资组合保证金制度

(a)**预付款**。——《1970年证券投资者保护法》第9(a)(1)条[《美国法典》第十五编第78fff3(a)(1)节]修正如下:在“证券权利主张”之后插入“或商品期货合约期权”。

(b) DEFINITIONS. —Section 16 of the Securities Investor Protection Act of 1970 (15 U.S.C.78lll) is amended —

(1) by striking paragraph (2) and inserting the following:

"(2) CUSTOMER. —

"(A) IN GENERAL. —The term 'customer' of a debtor means any person (including any person with whom the debtor deals as principal or agent) who has a claim on account of securities received, acquired, or held by the debtor in the ordinary course of its business as a broker or dealer from or for the securities accounts of such person for safekeeping, with a view to sale, to cover consummated sales, pursuant to purchases, as collateral, security, or for purposes of effecting transfer.

"(B) INCLUDED PERSONS. —The term 'customer' includes —

"(i) any person who has deposited cash with the debtor for the purpose of purchasing securities;

"(ii) any person who has a claim against the debtor for cash, securities, futures contracts, or options on futures contracts received, acquired, or held in a portfolio margining account carried as a securities account pursuant to a portfolio margining program approved by the Commission; and

"(iii) any person who has a claim against the debtor arising out of sales or conversions of such securities.

"(C) EXCLUDED PERSONS. —The term 'customer' does not include any person, to the extent that —

"(i) the claim of such person arises out of transactions with a foreign subsidiary of a member of SIPC; or

"(ii) such person has a claim for cash or securities which by contract, agreement, or understanding, or by operation of law, is part of the capital of the debtor, or is subordinated to the claims of any or all creditors of the debtor, notwithstanding that some ground exists for declaring such contract, agreement, or understanding void or voidable in a suit between the claimant and the debtor.";

(2) in paragraph (4) —

(A) in subparagraph (C), by striking "and" at the end;

(B) by redesignating subparagraph (D) as subparagraph (E); and

(C) by inserting after subparagraph (C) the following:

"(D) in the case of a portfolio margining account of a customer that is carried as a securities account pursuant to a portfolio margining program approved by the Commission, a futures contract or an option on a futures contract received, acquired, or held by or for the account of a debtor from or for such portfolio margining account, and the proceeds thereof; and";

（b）**定义**。——《1970年证券投资者保护法》第16条（《美国法典》第15编第78lll节）修正如下——

（1）删除第（2）款，替以如下内容：

"（2）**客户**。——

（A）**一般规定**。——债务人的"客户"系指因以下证券而对债务人拥有权利主张的任何人（包括债务人以委托人或代理人身份与之进行交易的任何人）：债务人在作为经纪商或自营商开展正常业务运作过程中，出于保管、出售、就已完成销售支付对价之目的，或者因购买，或者作为抵押、担保，或为了实施转让，而通过或为了该人的证券账户而收到、获取或持有的证券。

（B）**包含的主体**。——'客户'一词包括——

（i）为购买证券而向债务人交存现金的任何人；

（ii）根据证券交易委员会批准的投资组合保证金计划，针对作为证券账户而持有的投资组合保证金账户中所收到、获取或持有的现金、证券、期货合约或期货合约期权，对债务人享有权利主张的任何人；及

（iii）因该等证券的出售或转换而对债务人享有权利主张的任何人。

（C）**排除在外的主体**。——'客户'一词不包括以下存在下列情形的任何人——

（i）因与证券投资者保护公司会员的外国子公司进行交易而享有权利主张；或

（ii）根据合同、协议、谅解或法律规定，该人对现金或证券所享有的权利主张属于债务人资本的一部分，或者优先顺序次于该债务人的所有债权人的权利主张，不论权利主张人与债务人之间的诉讼中是否存在可使该等合同、协议或谅解归于无效或可撤销的理由。"；

（2）在第（4）款中——

（A）第（C）子款删除结尾处的"及"；

（B）第（D）子款重新编号为第（E）子款；及

（C）在第（C）子款之后插入如下内容：

"（D）债务人账户通过或为了客户投资组合保证金账户而收到、获取或持有的期货合约或期货合约的期权，以及该等账户产生的收益（前提是根据证券交易委员会批准的投资组合保证金计划，客户的投资组合保证金账户作为证券账户持有）；及"；

(3) in paragraph (9), in the matter following subparagraph (L), by inserting after "Such term" the following: "includes revenues earned by a broker or dealer in connection with a transaction in the portfolio margining account of a customer carried as securities accounts pursuant to a portfolio margining program approved by the Commission. Such term"; and

(4) in paragraph (11)—

(A) in subparagraph (A)—

(i) by striking "filing date, all" and all that follows through the end of the subparagraph and inserting the following: "filing date—

"(i) all securities positions of such customer (other than customer name securities reclaimed by such customer); and

"(ii) all positions in futures contracts and options on futures contracts held in a portfolio margining account carried as a securities account pursuant to a portfolio margining program approved by the Commission, including all property collateralizing such positions, to the extent that such property is not otherwise included herein; minus"; and

(B) in the matter following subparagraph (C), by striking "In determining" and inserting the following: "A claim for a commodity futures contract received, acquired, or held in a portfolio margining account pursuant to a portfolio margining program approved by the Commission or a claim for a security futures contract, shall be deemed to be a claim with respect to such contract as of the filing date, and such claim shall be treated as a claim for cash. In determining".

SEC.984. LOAN OR BORROWING OF SECURITIES.

(a) RULEMAKING AUTHORITY.—Section 10 of the Securities Exchange Act of 1934 (15 U.S.C.78j) is amended by adding at the end the following:

"(c)(1) To effect, accept, or facilitate a transaction involving the loan or borrowing of securities in contravention of such rules and regulations as the Commission may prescribe as necessary or appropriate in the public interest or for the protection of investors.

"(2) Nothing in paragraph (1) may be construed to limit the authority of the appropriate Federal banking agency (as defined in section 3(q) of the Federal Deposit Insurance Act (12 U.S.C.1813(q))), the National Credit Union Administration, or any other Federal department or agency having a responsibility under Federal law to prescribe rules or regulations restricting transactions involving the loan or borrowing of securities in order to protect the safety and soundness of a financial institution or to protect the financial system from systemic risk.".

(b) RULEMAKING REQUIRED.—Not later than 2 years after the date of enactment of this Act, the Commission shall promulgate rules that are designed to increase the transparency of information available to brokers, dealers, and investors, with respect to the

(3)第(9)款第(L)子款之后的内容在“该词”之后插入:“包括经纪商或自营商按照证券交易委员会批准的投资组合保证金计划通过作为证券账户持有的客户投资组合保证金账户开展交易所获取的收益。该词”;及

(4)在第(11)款中——

(A)第(A)子款——

(i)删除“如果在申报日期,债务人已通过购买或销售清算了所有”直至该子款结尾处的全部内容,替以如下内容:“如果在申报日期,债务人已通过购买或销售清算了——

“(i)该客户的所有证券持仓(但该客户收回的客户名下证券除外);及

“(ii)根据证券交易委员会批准的投资组合保证金计划,作为证券账户持有的客户投资组合保证金账户中持有的所有期货合约持仓及期货合约期权持仓,包括为该等持仓提供担保的所有财产(前提是该等财产由于其他原因未被计入上述账户);减去”;及

(B)第(C)子款之后的内容删除“在确定”,替以:“针对按照证券交易委员会批准的投资组合保证金计划在客户投资组合保证金账户所收到、获取或持有的商品期货合约提出的权利主张,或者针对证券期货合约提出的权利主张,应视为对截至申报之日提出的该等合约的权利主张,且应作为现金权利主张处理。在确定”。

第984条　融券

(a)**规则制定权**。——在《1934年证券交易法》第10条(《美国法典》第十五编第78j节)结尾处增加如下内容,作为对该条的修正:

“(c)(1)违反证券交易委员会为维护公共利益或保护投资者而制定的必要或适当的规则和规章,实施、受理融券交易或者为之提供便利。

(2)第(1)款的任何内容均不得被解释为对以下各者的权力构成限制:相应的联邦银行业监管机关{定义见《联邦存款保险法》第3(q)条[《美国法典》第十二编第1813(q)节]}、国家信贷联盟署或根据联邦法律负有如下责任的任何其他联邦部门或机关,即为保护金融机构的安全性和稳健性或保护金融系统不受系统性风险影响制定限制融券交易的规则或规章的责任。”

(b)**规则制定要求**。——证券交易委员会应于本法颁布之日后2年内颁发规则,以提高经纪商、自营商和投资者可获得的与融券相关的信息的透明度。

loan or borrowing of securities.

SEC.985. TECHNICAL CORRECTIONS TO FEDERAL SECURITIES LAWS.

(a) SECURITIES ACT OF 1933. —The Securities Act of 1933 (15 U.S.C.77a et seq.) is amended—

(1) in section 3(a)(4) (15 U.S.C.77c(a)(4)), by striking "individual;" and inserting "individual,";

(2) in section 18 (15 U.S.C.77r) —

(A) in subsection (b)(1)(C), by striking "is a security" and inserting "a security"; and

(B) in subsection (c)(2)(B)(i), by striking "State, or" and inserting "State or";

(3) in section 19(d)(6)(A) (15 U.S.C.77s(d)(6)(A)), by striking "in paragraph (1) of (3)" and inserting "in paragraph (1) or (3)"; and

(4) in section 27A(c)(1)(B)(ii) (15 U.S.C.77z-2(c)(1)(B)(ii)), by striking "business entity;" and inserting "business entity,".

(b) SECURITIES EXCHANGE ACT OF 1934. —The Securities Exchange Act of 1934 (15 U.S.C.78a et seq.) is amended —

(1) in section 2 (15 U.S.C.78b), by striking "affected" and inserting "effected";

(2) in section 3 (15 U.S.C.78c) —

(A) in subsection (a)(55)(A), by striking "section 3(a)(12) of the Securities Exchange Act of 1934" and inserting "section 3(a)(12) of this title"; and

(B) in subsection (g), by striking "company, account person, or entity" and inserting "company, account, person, or entity";

(3) in section 10A(i)(1)(B) (15 U.S.C.78j-1(i)(1)(B)) —

(A) in the subparagraph heading, by striking "MINIMUS" and inserting "MINIMIS"; and

(B) in clause (i), by striking "nonaudit" and inserting "non-audit";

(4) in section 13(b)(1) (15 U.S.C.78m(b)(1)), by striking "earning statement" and inserting "earnings statement";

(5) in section 15 (15 U.S.C.78o) —

(A) in subsection (b)(1) —

(i) in subparagraph (B), by striking "The order granting" and all that follows through "from such membership."; and

(ii) in the undesignated matter immediately following subparagraph (B), by inserting after the first sentence the following: "The order granting registration shall not be effective until such broker or dealer has become a member of a registered securities association, or

第985条　对联邦证券法律的技术性修正

(a)**《1933年证券法》**。——《1933年证券法》(《美国法典》第十五编第77a节及其后条文)修正如下——

(1)在第3(a)(4)条[《美国法典》第十五编第77c(a)(4)节]中,删除“个人;”,替以“个人,”;

(2)在第18条(《美国法典》第十五编第77r节)中——

(A)第(b)(1)(C)子条删除“属于证券”,替以“证券”;及

(B)第(c)(2)(B)(i)子条删除“州,或”,替以“州或”;

(3)第19(d)(6)(A)条[《美国法典》第十五编第77s(d)(6)(A)节]删除“在第(3)款的第(1)款中”,替以“在第(1)款或第(3)款中”;及

(4)在第27A(c)(1)(B)(ii)条[《美国法典》第十五编第77z-2(c)(1)(B)(ii)节]中,删除“业务实体;”,替以“业务实体,”。

(b)**《1934年证券交易法》**。——《1934年证券交易法》(《美国法典》第十五编第78a节及其后条文)修正如下——

(1)在第2条(《美国法典》第十五编第78b节)中,删除“有效实施”的错误拼写“affected”,替以正确拼写“effected”;

(2)在第3条(《美国法典》第十五编第78c节)中——

(A)第(a)(55)(A)子条删除“《1934年证券交易法》第3(a)(12)条”,替以“本编第3(a)(12)条”;及

(B)第(g)子条删除“公司、账户人员或实体”,替以“公司、账户、人员或实体”;

(3)第10A(i)(1)(B)条[《美国法典》第15编第78j-1(i)(1)(B)节]——

(A)删除子款标题中的“微量”的错误拼写“**MINIMUS**”,替以正确拼写“**MINIMIS**”;及

(B)第(i)项删除“非审计”的错误拼写“nonaudit”,替以正确拼写“non-audit”;

(4)第13(b)(1)条[《美国法典》第十五编第78m(b)(1)节]删除“损益表”的错误拼写“earning statement”,替以正确拼写“earnings statement”;

(5)在第15条(《美国法典》第十五编第78o节)中——

(A)第(b)(1)子条——

(i)第(B)子款删除“准予注册令”直至“向该等经纪商或自营商授予会员资格豁免的除外。”的全部内容;及

(ii)紧接第(B)子款之后的无编号内容在第一句之后插入如下内容:“准予注册令在该等经纪商或自营商成为注册证券协会的会员或全国性证券交易所的会员(前提是该等经纪商或自营商仅通过该交易所开展交易)之前,不得生效,但证券交易委员

until such broker or dealer has become a member of a national securities exchange, if such broker or dealer effects transactions solely on that exchange, unless the Commission has exempted such broker or dealer, by rule or order, from such membership.";

(6) in section 15C(a)(2) (15 U.S.C.78o–5(a)(2))—

(A) by redesignating clauses (i) and (ii) as subparagraphs (A) and (B), respectively, and adjusting the subparagraph margins accordingly;

(B) in subparagraph (B), as so redesignated, by striking "The order granting" and all that follows through "from such membership."; and

(C) in the matter following subparagraph (B), as so redesignated, by inserting after the first sentence the following: "The order granting registration shall not be effective until such government securities broker or government securities dealer has become a member of a national securities exchange registered under section 6 of this title, or a securities association registered under section 15A of this title, unless the Commission has exempted such government securities broker or government securities dealer, by rule or order, from such membership.";

(7) in section 17(b)(1)(B) (15 U.S.C.78q(b)(1)(B)), by striking "15A(k) gives" and inserting "15A(k), give"; and

(8) in section 21C (c) (2) (15 U.S.C.78u–3 (c) (2)), by striking "paragraph (1) subsection" and inserting "Paragraph (1)".

(c) TRUST INDENTURE ACT OF 1939. —The Trust Indenture Act of 1939 (15 U.S.C.77aaa et seq.) is amended—

(1) in section 304(b) (15 U.S.C.77ddd(b)), by striking "section 2 of such Act" and inserting "section 2(a) of such Act"; and

(2) in section 317 (a) (1) (15 U.S.C.77qqq (a) (1)), by striking ", in the" and inserting "in the".

(d) INVESTMENT COMPANY ACT OF 1940. —The Investment Company Act of 1940 (15 U.S.C.80a–1 et seq.) is amended—

(1) in section 2(a)(19) (15 U.S.C.80a–2(a)(19)), in the matter following subparagraph (B)(vii)—

(A) by striking "clause (vi)" each place that term appears and inserting "clause (vii)"; and

(B) in each of subparagraphs (A)(vi) and (B)(vi), by adding "and" at the end of subclause (III);

(2) in section 9(b)(4)(B) (15 U.S.C.80a–9(b)(4)(B)), by adding "or" after the semicolon at the end;

(3) in section 12(d)(1)(J) (15 U.S.C.80a–12(d)(1)(J)), by striking "any provision of this subsection" and inserting "any provision of this paragraph";

会已发布规则或命令,向该等经纪商或自营商授予会员资格豁免的除外。”;

(6)在第15C(a)(2)条[《美国法典》第十五编第78o-5(a)(2)节]中——

(A)第(i)项和第(ii)项分别重新编号为第(A)子款和第(B)子款,并相应调整缩进距离;

(B)第(B)子款(以重新编号后的序号为准)删除“准予注册令”直至“向该等经纪商或自营商授予会员资格豁免的除外。”的全部内容;及

(C)第(B)子款(以重新编号后的序号为准)之后的内容在第一句之后插入如下内容:“准予注册令在该等政府证券经纪商或政府证券自营商成为根据本编第6条注册的全国性证券交易所的会员或根据本编第15A条注册的证券协会的会员之前,不得生效,但证券交易委员会已发布规则或命令,向该等政府证券经纪商或政府证券自营商授予会员资格豁免的除外。”;

(7)在第17(b)(1)(B)条[《美国法典》第十五编第78q(b)(1)(B)节]中,删除“15A(k)gives”,替以“15A(k),give”;及

(8)在第21C(c)(2)条[《美国法典》第十五编第78u-3(c)(2)节]中,删除“第(1)款子条”,替以“第(1)款”。

(c)**《1939年信托契约法》**。——《1939年信托契约法》(《美国法典》第十五编第77aaa节及其后条文)修正如下——

(1)在第304(b)条[《美国法典》第十五编第77ddd(b)节]中,删除“该法第2条”,替以“该法第2(a)条”;及

(2)在第317(a)(1)条[《美国法典》第十五编第77qqq(a)(1)节]中,删除“,in the”,替以“in the”。

(d)**《1940年投资公司法》**。——《1940年投资公司法》(《美国法典》第十五编第80a-1节及其后条文)修正如下——

(1)在第2(a)(19)条[《美国法典》第十五编第80a-2(a)(19)节]中,在第(B)(vii)子款之后的内容中——

(A)删除所有的“第(vi)项”,全部替以“第(vii)项”;及

(B)分别在第(A)(vi)子款和第(B)(vi)子款的第(III)子项结尾处增加“及”;

(2)在第9(b)(4)(B)条[《美国法典》第十五编第80a-9(b)(4)(B)节]结尾处分号之后增加“或”;

(3)在第12(d)(1)(J)条[《美国法典》第十五编第80a-12(d)(1)(J)节]中,删除“本子条任何规定”,替以“本款任何规定”;

(4) in section 17(f) (15 U.S.C.80a–17(f))—

(A) in paragraph (4), by striking "No such member" and inserting "No member of a national securities exchange"; and

(B) in paragraph (6), by striking "company may serve" and inserting "company, may serve"; and

(5) in section 61(a)(3)(B)(iii) (15 U.S.C.80a–60(a)(3)(B)(iii)) —

(A) by striking "paragraph (1) of section 205" and inserting "section 205(a)(1)"; and

(B) by striking "clause (A) or (B) of that section" and inserting "paragraph (1) or (2) of section 205(b)".

(e) INVESTMENT ADVISERS ACT OF 1940. —The Investment Advisers Act of 1940 (15 U.S.C.80b–1 et seq.) is amended —

(1) in section 203 (15 U.S.C.80b–3) —

(A) in subsection (c)(1)(A), by striking "principal business office and" and inserting "principal office, principal place of business, and"; and

(B) in subsection (k)(4)(B), in the matter following clause (ii), by striking "principal place of business" and inserting "principal office or place of business";

(2) in section 206(3) (15 U.S.C.80b–6(3)), by adding "or" after the semicolon at the end;

(3) in section 213(a) (15 U.S.C.80b–13(a)), by striking "principal place of business" and inserting "principal office or place of business"; and

(4) in section 222 (15 U.S.C.80b–18a), by striking "principal place of business" each place that term appears and inserting "principal office and place of business".

SEC.986. CONFORMING AMENDMENTS RELATING TO REPEAL OF THE PUBLIC UTILITY HOLDING COMPANY ACT OF 1935.

(a) SECURITIES EXCHANGE ACT OF 1934. —The Securities Exchange Act of 1934 (15 U.S.C.78 et seq.) is amended —

(1) in section 3(a)(47) (15 U.S.C.78c(a)(47)), by striking "the Public Utility Holding Company Act of 1935 (15 U.S.C.79a et seq.),";

(2) in section 12(k) (15 U.S.C.78l(k)), by amending paragraph (7) to read as follows:

"(7) DEFINITION. —For purposes of this subsection, the term 'emergency' means —

"(A) a major market disturbance characterized by or constituting —

"(i) sudden and excessive fluctuations of securities prices generally, or a substantial threat thereof, that threaten fair and orderly markets; or

（4）在第17（f）条［《美国法典》第十五编第80a-17（f）节］中——

（A）第（4）款删除“任何会员均不得”，替以“任何全国性证券交易所的会员均不得”；及

（B）第（6）款删除“作为注册管理公司的关联人、发起人、组建人、保荐人或主承销商可担任”，替以“作为注册管理公司的关联人、发起人、组建人、保荐人或主承销商，可担任”；及

（5）在第61（a）（3）（B）（iii）条［《美国法典》第十五编第80a-60（a）（3）（B）（iii）节］中——

（A）删除“第205条第（1）款”，替以“第205（a）（1）条”；及

（B）删除“该条第（A）项或第（B）项”，替以“第205（b）条第（1）款或第（2）款”。

（e）**《1940年投资顾问法》**。——《1940年投资顾问法》（《美国法典》第十五编第80b-1节及其后条文）修正如下——

（1）在第203条（《美国法典》第十五编第80b-3节）中——

（A）第（c）（1）（A）子条删除“主要营业场所及”，替以“主要办公场所、主要营业地及”；并

（B）第（k）（4）（B）子条在第（ii）项之后的内容删除“主要营业地”，替以“主要办公场所或主要营业地”；

（2）在第206（3）条［《美国法典》第十五编第80b-6（3）节］结尾处分号之后增加“或”；

（3）在第213（a）条［《美国法典》第十五编第80b-13（a）节］中，删除“主要营业地”，替以“主要办公场所或主要营业地”；及

（4）在第222条（《美国法典》第十五编第80b-18a节）中，删除所有的“主要营业地”，全部替以“主要办公场所和主要营业地”。

第986条　与废止《1935年公用事业控股公司法》相关的一致性修正

（a）**《1934年证券交易法》**。——《1934年证券交易法》（《美国法典》第十五编第78节及其后条文）修正如下——

（1）在第3（a）（47）条［《美国法典》第十五编第78c（a）（47）节］中，删除“《1935年公用事业控股公司法》（《美国法典》第十五编第79a节及其后条文），”；

（2）在第12（k）条［《美国法典》第十五编第78l（k）节］中，第（7）款修正后全文如下：

“（7）**定义**。——就本子条而言，‘紧急情况’一词系指——

（A）具有如下特征或情形的重大市场干扰——

（i）由于证券整体价格出现突然和过度波动，或者存在该等价格突然和过度波动的严重威胁，市场的公平、有序运行遭受威胁；或

"(ii) a substantial disruption of the safe or efficient operation of the national system for clearance and settlement of transactions in securities, or a substantial threat thereof; or

"(B) a major disturbance that substantially disrupts, or threatens to substantially disrupt —

"(i) the functioning of securities markets, investment companies, or any other significant portion or segment of the securities markets; or

"(ii) the transmission or processing of securities transactions."; and

(3) in section 21(h)(2)(15 U.S.C.78u(h)(2)), by striking "section 18(c) of the Public Utility Holding Company Act of 1935,".

(b) TRUST INDENTURE ACT OF 1939. —The Trust Indenture Act of 1939 (15 U.S. C.77aaa et seq.) is amended —

(1) in section 303(15 U.S.C.77ccc), by striking paragraph (17) and inserting the following:

"(17) The terms 'Securities Act of 1933' and 'Securities Exchange Act of 1934' shall be deemed to refer, respectively, to such Acts, as amended, whether amended prior to or after the enactment of this title.";

(2) in section 308 (15 U.S.C.77hhh), by striking "Securities Act of 1933, the Securities Exchange Act of 1934, or the Public Utility Holding Company Act of 1935" each place that term appears and inserting "Securities Act of 1933 or the Securities Exchange Act of 1934";

(3) in section 310 (15 U.S.C.77jjj), by striking subsection (c);

(4) in section 311 (15 U.S.C.77kkk), by striking subsection (c);

(5) in section 323(b) (15 U.S.C.77www(b)), by striking "Securities Act of 1933, or the Securities Exchange Act of 1934, or the Public Utility Holding Company Act of 1935" and inserting "Securities Act of 1933 or the Securities Exchange Act of 1934"; and

(6) in section 326 (15 U.S.C.77zzz), by striking "Securities Act of 1933, or the Securities Exchange Act of 1934, or the Public Utility Holding Company Act of 1935," and inserting "Securities Act of 1933 or the Securities Exchange Act of 1934".

(c) INVESTMENT COMPANY ACT OF 1940. —The Investment Company Act of 1940 (15 U.S.C.80a–1 et seq.) is amended —

(1) in section 2(a)(44) (15 U.S.C.80a–2(a)(44)), by striking " 'Public Utility Holding Company Act of 1935',";

(2) in section 3(c) (15 U.S.C.80a–3(c)), by striking paragraph(8) and inserting the following:

"(8) [Repealed]";

(3) in section 38(b) (15 U.S.C.80a–37(b)), by striking "the Public Utility Holding Company Act of 1935,"; and

(ii)全国性证券交易清算和结算系统的安全和有效运行遭受重大扰乱,或者存在遭受该等干扰的严重威胁;或

(B)对以下各项造成严重扰乱或可能造成严重扰乱的重大干扰——

(i)证券市场、投资公司或证券市场任何其他重要部分或环节的运行;或

'(ii)证券交易的传输或处理。';并

(3)在第21(h)(2)条[《美国法典》第十五编第78u(h)(2)节]中,删除'《1935年公用事业控股公司法》第18(c)条,'。

(b)**《1939年信托契约法》**。——《1939年信托契约法》(《美国法典》第十五编第77aaa节及其后条文)修正如下——

(1)在第303条(《美国法典》第十五编第77ccc节)中,删除第(17)款,替以如下内容:

(17)'《1933年证券法》'或'《1934年证券交易法》'均应视为系指该等法修正后的版本,而不论修正的时间在本编颁布之前或之后。"

(2)在第308条(《美国法典》第十五编第77hhh节)中,删除所有"《1933年证券法》、《1934年证券交易法》或《1935年公用事业控股公司法》",全部替以"《1933年证券法》或《1934年证券交易法》";

(3)在第310条(《美国法典》第十五编第77jjj节)中,删除第(c)子条;

(4)在第311条(《美国法典》第十五编第77kkk节)中,删除第(c)子条;

(5)在第323(b)条[《美国法典》第十五编第77www(b)节]中,删除"《1933年证券法》、《1934年证券交易法》或《1935年公用事业控股公司法》",替以"《1933年证券法》或《1934年证券交易法》";及

(6)在第326条(《美国法典》第十五编第77zzz节)中,删除"《1933年证券法》、《1934年证券交易法》或《1935年公用事业控股公司法》",替以"《1933年证券法》或《1934年证券交易法》"。

(c)**《1940年投资公司法》**。——《1940年投资公司法》(《美国法典》第十五编第80a-1节及其后条文)修正如下——

(1)在第2(a)(44)条[《美国法典》第十五编第80a-2(a)(44)节]中,删除"《1935年公用事业控股公司法》,";

(2)在第3(c)条[《美国法典》第十五编第80a-3(c)节]中,删除第(8)款,替以如下内容:

"(8)[已废止]";

(3)在第38(b)条(《美国法典》第十五编第80a-37(b)节)中,删除"《1935年公用事业控股公司法》,";及

(4) in section 50 (15 U.S.C.80a–49), by striking "the Public Utility Holding Company Act of 1935,".

(d) INVESTMENT ADVISERS ACT OF 1940. —Section 202(a)(21) of the Investment Advisers Act of 1940 (15 U.S.C.80b–2(a)(21)) is amended by striking " 'Public Utility Holding Company Act of 1935',".

SEC.987. AMENDMENT TO DEFINITION OF MATERIAL LOSS AND NON–MATERIAL LOSSES TO THE DEPOSIT INSURANCE FUND FOR PURPOSES OF INSPECTOR GENERAL REVIEWS.

(a) IN GENERAL. —Section 38 (k) of the Federal Deposit Insurance Act (U.S.C. 1831o(k)) is amended —

(1) in paragraph (2), by striking subparagraph (B) and inserting the following:

"(B) MATERIAL LOSS DEFINED. —The term 'material loss' means any estimated loss in excess of —

"(i) $200,000,000, if the loss occurs during the period beginning on January 1, 2010, and ending on December 31, 2011;

"(ii) $150,000,000, if the loss occurs during the period beginning on January 1, 2012, and ending on December 31, 2013; and

"(iii) $50,000,000, if the loss occurs on or after January 1, 2014, provided that if the inspector general of a Federal banking agency certifies to the Committee on Banking, Housing, and Urban Affairs of the Senate and the Committee on Financial Services of the House of Representatives that the number of projected failures of depository institutions that would require material loss reviews for the following 12 months will be greater than 30 and would hinder the effectiveness of its oversight functions, then the definition of 'material loss' shall be $75,000,000 for a duration of 1 year from the date of the certification.";

(2) in paragraph (4)(A) by striking "the report" and inserting "any report on losses required under this subsection,";

(3) by striking paragraph (6);

(4) by redesignating paragraph (5) as paragraph (6); and

(5) by inserting after paragraph (4) the following:

"(5) LOSSES THAT ARE NOT MATERIAL. —

"(A) SEMIANNUAL REPORT. —For the 6–month period ending on March 31, 2010, and each 6–month period thereafter, the Inspector General of each Federal banking agency shall —

"(i) identify losses that the Inspector General estimates have been incurred by the Deposit Insurance Fund during that 6–month period, with respect to the insured depository institutions supervised by the Federal banking agency;

"(ii) for each loss incurred by the Deposit Insurance Fund that is not a material loss,

(4)在第50条(《美国法典》第十五编第80a-49节)中,删除"《1935年公用事业控股公司法》,"。

(d)**《1940年投资顾问法》**。——《1940年投资顾问法》第202(a)(21)条[《美国法典》第十五编第80b-2(a)(21)节]修正如下:删除"《1935年公用事业控股公司法》,"。

第987条 对监察长开展审查时适用的存款保险基金重大损失及非重大损失定义之修正

(a)**一般规定**。——《联邦存款保险法》第38(k)条[《美国法典》1831o(k)节]修正如下——

(1)在第(2)款中,删除第(B)子款,替以如下内容:

"(B)**重大损失定义**。——'重大损失'一词系指预计将超过以下金额的任何损失——

(i)2亿美元,前提是损失发生于2010年1月1日至2011年12月31日期间;

(ii)1.5亿美元,前提是损失发生于2012年1月1日至2013年12月31日期间;及

(iii)5000万美元,前提是损失发生于2014年1月1日或之后,但是,如果联邦银行业监管机关的监察长向参议院银行、住房与城市事务委员会及众议院金融服务委员会证明,在未来12个月内出现预计经营失败须进行重大损失审查的存款机构数量将超过30家,并且将妨碍联邦银行业监管机关监管职能的有效行使,则于证明之日后一年内,"重大损失"应定义为7500万美元。";

(2)在第(4)(A)款中,删除"该报告",替以"本子条所规定的任何损失报告,";

(3)删除第(6)款;

(4)第(5)款重新编号为第(6)款;及

(5)在第(4)款之后插入如下内容:

"(5)**非重大损失**。——

(A)**半年度报告**。——在截至2010年3月31日的6个月内及此后的每6个月内,每一联邦银行业监管机关的监察长均应——

(i)确定其预计存款保险基金将在上述6个月内发生的与受该等联邦银行业监管机关监管的参保存款机构相关的损失;

(ii)对于存款保险基金发生的每项非重大损失而言,判定——

determine —

"(I) the grounds identified by the Federal banking agency or State bank supervisor for appointing the Corporation as receiver under section 11(c)(5); and

"(II) whether any unusual circumstances exist that might warrant an in–depth review of the loss; and

"(iii) prepare and submit a written report to the appropriate Federal banking agency and to Congress on the results of any determination by the Inspector General, including —

"(I) an identification of any loss that warrants an in–depth review, together with the reasons why such review is warranted, or, if the Inspector General determines that no review is warranted, an explanation of such determination; and

"(II) for each loss identified under subclause (I) that warrants an in–depth review, the date by which such review, and a report on such review prepared in a manner consistent with reports under paragraph (1)(A), will be completed and submitted to the Federal banking agency and Congress.

"(B) DEADLINE FOR SEMIANNUAL REPORT. —The Inspector General of each Federal banking agency shall —

"(i) submit each report required under paragraph (A) expeditiously, and not later than 90 days after the end of the 6–month period covered by the report; and

"(ii) provide a copy of the report required under paragraph (A) to any Member of Congress, upon request.".

(b) TECHNICAL AND CONFORMING AMENDMENT. —The heading for subsection (k) of section 38 of the Federal Deposit Insurance Act (U.S.C.1831o(k)) is amended to read as follows:

"(k) REVIEWS REQUIRED WHEN DEPOSIT INSURANCE FUND INCURS LOSSES. —".

SEC.988. AMENDMENT TO DEFINITION OF MATERIAL LOSS AND NON–MATERIAL LOSSES TO THE NATIONAL CREDIT UNION SHARE INSURANCE FUND FOR PURPOSES OF INSPECTOR GENERAL REVIEWS.

(a) IN GENERAL. —Section 216(j) of the Federal Credit Union Act (12 U.S.C.1790d (j)) is amended to read as follows:

"(j) REVIEWS REQUIRED WHEN SHARE INSURANCE FUND EXPERIENCES LOSSES. —

"(1) IN GENERAL. —If the Fund incurs a material loss with respect to an insured credit union, the Inspector General of the Board shall —

"(A) submit to the Board a written report reviewing the supervision of the credit union by the Administration (including the implementation of this section by the Administration), which shall include —

(Ⅰ)该等联邦银行业监管机关或州银行监管者所确定的根据第11(c)(5)条指定联邦存款保险公司担任接管人的理由;及

(Ⅱ)是否存在有必要对该等损失进行深入审查的任何异常情形;并

(iii)针对其所作出任何判定的结果编制一份书面报告,并将其提交给向相应的联邦银行监管机关和国会,在该报告中——

(Ⅰ)指明有必要进行深入审查的任何损失,并说明理由,或者如果监察长判定不必进行任何审查,对该判定进行说明;并

(Ⅱ)对于根据第(Ⅰ)子项确定的有必要进行深入审查的每项损失而言,应说明完成该等审查的日期,以及按照与第(1)(A)款所述报告一致的方式编制的关于该等审查的报告完成编制并提交给相应的联邦银行业监管机关和国会的日期。

(B)**半年度报告的最后期限**。——每一联邦银行业监管机关的监察长均应——

(i)在报告所涉6个月期间结束后90天内及时提交第(A)款所规定每份报告;并

(ii)按照任何国会议员的要求向其提交第(A)款所规定报告的复本。”

(b)**技术性和一致性修正**。——《联邦存款保险法》第38条第(k)子条[《美国法典》第1831o(k)节]标题修正后全文如下:

“(k)**存款保险基金发生损失时须开展的审查**。——”

第988条 对监察长开展审查时适用的国家信贷联盟股份保险基金重大损失及非重大损失定义的修正

(a)**一般规定**。——《联邦信贷联盟法》第216(j)条[《美国法典》第十二编第1790d(j)节]修正后全文如下:

“(j)**国家信贷联盟股份保险基金发生损失时须开展的审查**。——

(1)**一般规定**。——如果国家信贷联盟股份保险基金发生与参保信贷联盟相关的重大损失,国家信贷联盟署委员会的监察长应——

(A)就国家信贷联盟署对信贷联盟的监管(包括国家信贷联盟署对本条的实施情况)向国家信贷联盟署委员会提交一份书面审查报告,该报告应——

"(i) a description of the reasons why the problems of the credit union resulted in a material loss to the Fund; and

"(ii) recommendations for preventing any such loss in the future; and

"(B) submit a copy of the report under subparagraph (A) to—

"(i) the Comptroller General of the United States;

"(ii) the Corporation;

"(iii) in the case of a report relating to a State credit union, the appropriate State supervisor; and

"(iv) to any Member of Congress, upon request.

"(2) MATERIAL LOSS DEFINED.—For purposes of determining whether the Fund has incurred a material loss with respect to an insured credit union, a loss is material if it exceeds the sum of—

"(A) $25,000,000; and

"(B) an amount equal to 10 percent of the total assets of the credit union on the date on which the Board initiated assistance under section 208 or was appointed liquidating agent.

"(3) PUBLIC DISCLOSURE REQUIRED.—

"(A) IN GENERAL.—The Board shall disclose a report under this subsection, upon request under section 552 of title 5, United States Code, without excising—

"(i) any portion under section 552(b)(5) of title 5, United States Code; or

"(ii) any information about the insured credit union (other than trade secrets) under section 552(b)(8) of title 5, United States Code.

"(B) RULE OF CONSTRUCTION.—Subparagraph (A) may not be construed as requiring the agency to disclose the name of any customer of the insured credit union (other than an institution-affiliated party), or information from which the identity of such customer could reasonably be ascertained.

"(4) LOSSES THAT ARE NOT MATERIAL.—

"(A) SEMIANNUAL REPORT.—For the 6-month period ending on March 31, 2010, and each 6-month period thereafter, the Inspector General of the Board shall—

"(i) identify any losses that the Inspector General estimates were incurred by the Fund during such 6-month period, with respect to insured credit unions;

"(ii) for each loss to the Fund that is not a material loss, determine—

"(I) the grounds identified by the Board or the State official having jurisdiction over a State credit union for appointing the Board as the liquidating agent for any Federal or State credit union; and

"(II) whether any unusual circumstances exist that might warrant an in-depth review of the loss; and

"(iii) prepare and submit a written report to the Board and to Congress on the results of

(i)说明该等信贷联盟的问题导致国家信贷联盟股份保险基金发生重大损失的原因;并

(ii)针对如何防范将来发生任何上述损失提出建议;并

(B)向以下各者提交第(A)子款所述报告的复本——

(i)政府问责办公室主任;

(ii)联邦存款保险公司;

(iii)相应的州监管者(如报告与州信贷联盟相关);及

(iv)任何提出要求的国会议员。

(2)**重大损失定义**。——在判定国家信贷联盟股份保险基金是否已经发生与参保信贷联盟相关的重大损失时,如果损失高于以下金额的总和,即构成重大损失——

(A)2500万美元;及

(B)国家信贷联盟署委员会根据第208条开始提供协助或者被指定为清算代理人当日,该信贷联盟资产总额的10%。

(3)**公开披露要求**。——

(A)**一般规定**。——国家信贷联盟署委员会应在不删除以下内容的情况下,根据《美国法典》第五编第552节要求披露本子条所述报告的内容——

(i)《美国法典》第五编第552(b)(5)节规定的任何内容;或

(ii)《美国法典》第五编第552(b)(8)节规定的与参保信贷联盟相关的任何信息(但商业秘密除外)。

(B)**解释规则**。——第(A)子款规定不得被解释为要求国家信贷联盟署委员会披露参保信贷联盟任何客户(但机构关联方除外)的名称或者能够合理确定该等客户身份的信息。

(4)**非重大损失**。——

(A)**半年度报告**。——在截至2010年3月31日的6个月内及此后的每6个月内,联邦储备委员会的监察长均应——

(i)确定其预计国家信贷联盟股份保险基金在上述6个月内发生的与参保信贷联盟相关的损失;

(ii)对于国家信贷联盟股份保险基金发生的每项非重大损失而言,判定——

(I)国家信贷联盟署委员会或对州信贷联盟有管辖权的州政府官员指定国家信贷联盟署委员会担任任何联邦信贷联盟或州信贷联盟清算的代理人的理由;及

(II)是否存在有必要对该损失进行深入审查的任何异常情形;并

(iii)针对其所作出判定的结果编制一份书面报告,并将其提交给国家信贷联盟署

the determinations of the Inspector General that includes —

"(I) an identification of any loss that warrants an in–depth review, and the reasons such review is warranted, or if the Inspector General determines that no review is warranted, an explanation of such determination; and

"(II) for each loss identified in subclause (I) that warrants an in–depth review, the date by which such review, and a report on the review prepared in a manner consistent with reports under paragraph (1)(A), will be completed.

"(B) DEADLINE FOR SEMIANNUAL REPORT. —The Inspector General of the Board shall —

"(i) submit each report required under subparagraph (A) expeditiously, and not later than 90 days after the end of the 6–month period covered by the report; and

"(ii) provide a copy of the report required under subparagraph (A) to any Member of Congress, upon request.

"(5) GAO REVIEW. —The Comptroller General of the United States shall, under such conditions as the Comptroller General determines to be appropriate —

"(A) review each report made under paragraph (1), including the extent to which the Inspector General of the Board complied with the requirements under section 8L of the Inspector General Act of 1978 (5 U.S.C.App.) with respect to each such report; and

"(B) recommend improvements to the supervision of insured credit unions (including improvements relating to the implementation of this section).".

SEC.989. GOVERNMENT ACCOUNTABILITY OFFICE STUDY ON PROPRIETARY TRADING.

(a) DEFINITIONS. —In this section —

(1) the term "covered entity" means —

(A) an insured depository institution, an affiliate of an insured depository institution, a bank holding company, a financial holding company, or a subsidiary of a bank holding company or a financial holding company, as those terms are defined in the Bank Holding Company Act of 1956 (12 U.S.C.1841 et seq.); and

(B) any other entity, as the Comptroller General of the United States may determine; and

(2) the term "proprietary trading" means the act of a covered entity investing as a principal in securities, commodities, derivatives, hedge funds, private equity firms, or such other financial products or entities as the Comptroller General may determine.

(b) STUDY. —

(1) IN GENERAL. —The Comptroller General of the United States shall conduct a study regarding the risks and conflicts associated with proprietary trading by and within covered entities, including an evaluation of —

委员会和国会,在该报告中——

(I)指明有必要进行深入审查的任何损失,并说明理由,或者如果监察长判定不必进行任何审查,对该判定进行说明;并

(II)对于根据第(I)子项确定的有必要进行深入审查的每项损失而言,应说明完成该等审查的日期,以及按照与第(1)(A)款所述报告一致的方式编制的关于该等审查的报告完成编制的日期。

(B)**半年度报告的最后期限**。——国家信贷联盟署委员会监察长应——

(i)在报告所涉6个月期间结束后90天内及时提交第(A)子款所述每项报告,且提交时间不得迟于;并

(ii)按照任何国会议员的要求向其提交第(A)子款所规定报告的复本。

(5)**政府问责办公室的审查**。——政府问责办公室主任应在其判定确属适当的条件下——

(A)审查根据第(1)款提交的每份报告,包括国家信贷联盟署委员会监察长在编制每份上述报告时对《1978年监察长法》第8L条(《美国法典》第五编附件)的遵守程度;并

(B)提出完善参保信贷联盟监管的建议(包括改善本条实施情况的建议)。"

第989条　政府问责办公室关于自营交易的研究

(a)**定义**。——就本条而言——

(1)"所涉实体"一词系指——

(A)参保存款机构、参保存款机构的关联方、银行控股公司、金融控股公司、银行控股公司或金融控股公司的子公司［上述词语的定义见《1956年银行控股公司法》(《美国法典》第十二编第1841节及其后条文)］;及

(B)政府问责办公室主任确定的任何其他实体;且

(2)"自营交易"一词系指所涉实体以委托人身份对证券、商品、衍生品、对冲基金、私募股权公司或政府问责办公室主任确定的其他金融产品或实体进行投资的行为。

(b)**研究**。——

(1)**一般规定**。——政府问责办公室主任应就所涉实体从事以及内部开展自营交易所带来的风险和利益冲突开展研究,包括对以下各项进行评估——

(A) whether proprietary trading presents a material systemic risk to the stability of the United States financial system, and if so, the costs and benefits of options for mitigating such systemic risk;

(B) whether proprietary trading presents material risks to the safety and soundness of the covered entities that engage in such activities, and if so, the costs and benefits of options for mitigating such risks;

(C) whether proprietary trading presents material conflicts of interest between covered entities that engage in proprietary trading and the clients of the institutions who use the firm to execute trades or who rely on the firm to manage assets, and if so, the costs and benefits of options for mitigating such conflicts of interest;

(D) whether adequate disclosure regarding the risks and conflicts of proprietary trading is provided to the depositors, trading and asset management clients, and investors of covered entities that engage in proprietary trading, and if not, the costs and benefits of options for the improvement of such disclosure; and

(E) whether the banking, securities, and commodities regulators of institutions that engage in proprietary trading have in place adequate systems and controls to monitor and contain any risks and conflicts of interest related to proprietary trading, and if not, the costs and benefits of options for the improvement of such systems and controls.

(2) CONSIDERATIONS. —In carrying out the study required under paragraph (1), the Comptroller General shall consider —

(A) current practice relating to proprietary trading;

(B) the advisability of a complete ban on proprietary trading;

(C) limitations on the scope of activities that covered entities may engage in with respect to proprietary trading;

(D) the advisability of additional capital requirements for covered entities that engage in proprietary trading;

(E) enhanced restrictions on transactions between affiliates related to proprietary trading;

(F) enhanced accounting disclosures relating to proprietary trading;

(G) enhanced public disclosure relating to proprietary trading; and

(H) any other options the Comptroller General deems appropriate.

(c) REPORT TO CONGRESS. —Not later than 15 months after the date of enactment of this Act, the Comptroller General shall submit a report to Congress on the results of the study conducted under subsection (b).

(d) ACCESS BY COMPTROLLER GENERAL. —For purposes of conducting the study required under subsection (b), the Comptroller General shall have access, upon request, to any information, data, schedules, books, accounts, financial records, reports, files, electronic

(A)对美国金融系统的稳定而言,自营交易是否构成重大系统性风险(如果构成重大系统性风险,应评估化解该等系统性风险的各项选择方案的成本和收益);

(B)对从事该等活动的所涉实体的安全性和稳健性而言,自营交易是否构成重大风险(如果构成重大风险,应评估缓释该等风险的各项选择方案的成本和收益);

(C)自营交易是否在从事自营交易的所涉实体与通过上述公司执行交易或管理资产的机构的客户之间造成重大利益冲突(如果造成重大利益冲突,应评估缓释该等风险的各项选择方案的成本和收益);

(D)对于从事自营交易的实体的存款人、交易和资产管理客户以及投资者而言,就自营交易带来的风险和利益冲突进行的披露是否充分(如果未进行充分披露,还应评估完善该等披露的各项选择方案的成本和收益);及

(E)自营交易机构的银行、证券和商品监管者是否拥有充分的制度和控制措施,足以监控和制止与自营交易相关的风险和利益冲突(如果尚不具备充分的制度和控制措施,应评估完成该等制度和控制措施的各项选择方案的成本和收益)。

(2)**考虑因素**。——在开展第(1)款所规定研究时,政府问责办公室主任应考虑——

(A)当前与自营交易相关的做法;
(B)完全禁止自营交易是否可取;
(C)所涉实体从事自营交易的活动范围限制;

(D)对从事自营交易的所涉实体施加附加资本要求是否可取;

(E)加强对与自营交易相关的关联交易的限制;

(F)加强与自营交易相关的会计信息披露;
(G)加强与自营交易相关的公开披露;及
(H)政府问责办公室主任认为确属适当的任何其他因素。
(c)**向国会报告**。——政府问责办公室主任应于本法颁布之日后15个月内,就其根据第(b)子条规定所开展研究的结果向国会提交一份报告。

(d)**政府问责办公室主任的查阅和接触权**。——为了开展第(b)子条所规定的研究,政府问责办公室主任应在提出要求后,有权在其要求的合理时间,查阅从事自营交易的所涉实体拥有或正在使用的任何信息、数据、计划表、账簿、账目、财务记录、报

communications, or other papers, things, or property belonging to or in use by a covered entity that engages in proprietary trading, and to the officers, directors, employees, independent public accountants, financial advisors, staff, and agents and representatives of a covered entity (as related to the activities of the agent or representative on behalf of the covered entity), at such reasonable times as the Comptroller General may request. The Comptroller General may make and retain copies of books, records, accounts, and other records, as the Comptroller General deems appropriate.

(e) CONFIDENTIALITY OF REPORTS. —

(1) IN GENERAL. — Except as provided in paragraph (2), the Comptroller General may not disclose information regarding —

(A) any proprietary trading activity of a covered entity, unless such information is disclosed at a level of generality that does not reveal the investment or trading position or strategy of the covered entity for any specific security, commodity, derivative, or other investment or financial product; or

(B) any individual interviewed by the Comptroller General for purposes of the study under subsection (b), unless such information is disclosed at a level of generality that does not reveal —

(i) the name of or identifying details relating to such individual; or

(ii) in the case of an individual who is an employee of a third party that provides professional services to a covered entity believed to be engaged in proprietary trading, the name of or any identifying details relating to such third party.

(2) EXCEPTIONS. — The Comptroller General may disclose the information described in paragraph (1) —

(A) to a department, agency, or official of the Federal Government, for official use, upon request;

(B) to a committee of Congress, upon request; and

(C) to a court, upon an order of such court.

SEC. 989A. SENIOR INVESTOR PROTECTIONS.

(a) DEFINITIONS. — As used in this section —

(1) the term "eligible entity" means —

(A) a securities commission (or any agency or office performing like functions) of a State that the Office determines has adopted rules on the appropriate use of designations in the offer or sale of securities or the provision of investment advice that meet or exceed the minimum requirements of the NASAA Model Rule on the Use of Senior-Specific Certifications and Professional Designations (or any successor thereto);

(B) the insurance commission (or any agency or office performing like functions) of any State that the Office determines has —

告、文档、电子通信或其他文件、物品或财产,并有权接触所涉实体的管理人员、董事、职员、独立公共会计师、金融顾问、工作人员以及代理人和代表(以与代表所涉实体行事的代理人或代表的活动相关为限)。政府问责办公室主任可以制作并保留其认为确属适当的账簿、记录、账目及其他记录的副本。

(e)**报告的保密性**。——

(1)**一般规定**。——除第(2)款规定的情形外,政府问责办公室主任不得披露如下信息——

(A)与所涉实体的任何自营交易活动相关的信息,除非披露仅具一般性,且未透露所涉实体对任何具体证券、商品、衍生品或其他投资或金融产品的投资、交易持仓或策略;或

(B)与政府问责办公室主任为了开展第(b)子条所规定研究而采访的任何个人相关的信息,除非披露仅具一般性,且未透露——

(i)上述个人的姓名或身份性信息;或

(ii)向被认为从事自营交易的所涉实体提供专业服务的第三方的名称或身份性信息(如果受访个人是该等第三方的雇员)。

(2)**例外规定**。——政府问责办公室主任可以按如下规定披露第(1)款所述信息——

(A)在联邦政府部门、机关或官员提出要求后,向其披露上述信息,以供其为了公务目的使用上述信息;

(B)在国会下属委员会提出要求后,向其披露上述信息;及

(C)在法院下达命令后,向其披露上述信息。

第989A条　老年投资者保护

(a)**定义**。——就本条而言——

(1)“适格实体”一词系指——

(A)州证券委员会(或履行类似职能的任何机关或办公室),前提是金融扫盲办公室判定该等州证券委员会已制定规则,对证券要约、销售或者投资意见提供过程中所用专业称号的适当使用进行规范,且该等规则符合或超出《北美证券管理者协会关于面向老年人的认证和专业称号的使用示范规则》(或其任何后续规则)的最低要求;

(B)任何州的保险委员会(或履行类似职能的任何机关或办公室),前提是金融扫盲办公室判定该等保险委员会——

(i) adopted rules on the appropriate use of designations in the sale of insurance products that, to the extent practicable, conform to the minimum requirements of the National Association of Insurance Commissioners Model Regulation on the Use of Senior–Specific Certifications and Professional Designations in the Sale of Life Insurance and Annuities (or any successor thereto); and

(ii) adopted rules with respect to fiduciary or suitability requirements in the sale of annuities that meet or exceed the minimum requirements established by the Suitability in Annuity Transactions Model Regulation of the National Association of Insurance Commissioners (or any successor thereto); or

(C) a consumer protection agency of any State, if —

(i) the securities commission (or any agency or office performing like functions) of the State is eligible under subparagraph (A); or

(ii) the insurance commission (or any agency or office performing like functions) of the State is eligible under subparagraph (B);

(2) the term "financial product" means a security, an insurance product (including an insurance product that pays a return, whether fixed or variable), a bank product, and a loan product;

(3) the term "misleading designation" —

(A) means a certification, professional designation, or other purported credential that indicates or implies that a salesperson or adviser has special certification or training in advising or servicing seniors; and

(B) does not include a certification, professional designation, license, or other credential that —

(i) was issued by or obtained from an academic institution having regional accreditation;

(ii) meets the standards for certifications and professional designations outlined by the NASAA Model Rule on the Use of Senior–Specific Certifications and Professional Designations (or any successor thereto) or by the Model Regulations on the Use of Senior–Specific Certifications and Professional Designations in the Sale of Life Insurance and Annuities, adopted by the National Association of Insurance Commissioners (or any successor thereto); or

(iii) was issued by or obtained from a State;

(4) the term "misleading or fraudulent marketing" means the use of a misleading designation by a person that sells to or advises a senior in connection with the sale of a financial product;

(5) the term "NASAA" means the North American Securities Administrators Association;

(i)已制定规则,对保险产品销售中所用专业称号的适当使用进行规范,且该等规则在可行范围内符合《美国保险监督官协会关于在人寿保险和年金销售中面向老年人的认证和专业称号的使用示范管理办法》(或其任何后续管理办法)的最低要求;且

(ii)已针对年金销售中的受信义务或适当性要求制定规则,且该等规则符合或超出《美国保险监督官协会年金交易适当性示范管理办法》(或其任何后续管理办法)的最低要求;或

(C)任何州的消费者保护监管机关,前提是——

(i)该州的证券委员会(或履行类似职能的任何机关或办公室)根据第(A)子款具有适格性;或

(ii)该州的保险委员会(或履行类似职能的任何机关或办公室)根据第(B)子款具有适格性;

(2)"金融产品"一词系指证券、保险产品(包括给予固定或可变收益的保险产品)、银行产品及贷款产品;

(3)"误导性称号"一词——

(A)系指明示或暗示销售人员或顾问在向老年人提供咨询或服务方面具有特殊认证或接受过培训的认证、专业称号或其他证书;且

(B)不包括符合如下条件的认证、专业称号、执照或其他证书——

(i)由拥有区域认证资格的学术机构颁发或授予;

(ii)符合《北美证券管理者协会关于面向老年人的认证和专业称号的使用示范规则》(或其任何后续规则)或者《美国保险监督官协会关于在人寿保险和年金销售中面向老年人的认证和专业称号的使用示范管理办法》(或其任何后续管理办法)所概述的认证和专业称号标准;或

(iii)由各州颁发或授予;

(4)"误导性或欺诈性营销"一词系指向老年人销售金融产品之人或向老年人提供与金融产品销售相关的咨询意见之人使用误导性称号的行为;

(5)"NASAA"一词系指北美证券管理者协会;

(6) the term "Office" means the Office of Financial Literacy of the Bureau;

(7) the term "senior" means any individual who has attained the age of 62 years or older; and

(8) the term "State" has the same meaning as in section 3 of the Securities Exchange Act of 1934 (15 U.S.C.78c(a)).

(b) GRANTS TO STATES FOR ENHANCED PROTECTION OF SENIORS FROM BEING MISLED BY FALSE DESIGNATIONS. —The Office shall establish a program under which the Office may make grants to States or eligible entities —

(1) to hire staff to identify, investigate, and prosecute (through civil, administrative, or criminal enforcement actions) cases involving misleading or fraudulent marketing;

(2) to fund technology, equipment, and training for regulators, prosecutors, and law enforcement officers, in order to identify salespersons and advisers who target seniors through the use of misleading designations;

(3) to fund technology, equipment, and training for prosecutors to increase the successful prosecution of salespersons and advisers who target seniors with the use of misleading designations;

(4) to provide educational materials and training to regulators on the appropriateness of the use of designations by salespersons and advisers in connection with the sale and marketing of financial products;

(5) to provide educational materials and training to seniors to increase awareness and understanding of misleading or fraudulent marketing;

(6) to develop comprehensive plans to combat misleading or fraudulent marketing of financial products to seniors; and

(7) to enhance provisions of State law to provide protection for seniors against misleading or fraudulent marketing.

(c) APPLICATIONS. —A State or eligible entity desiring a grant under this section shall submit an application to the Office, in such form and in such a manner as the Office may determine, that includes —

(1) a proposal for activities to protect seniors from misleading or fraudulent marketing that are proposed to be funded using a grant under this section, including —

(A) an identification of the scope of the problem of misleading or fraudulent marketing in the State;

(B) a description of how the proposed activities would —

(i) protect seniors from misleading or fraudulent marketing in the sale of financial products, including by proactively identifying victims of misleading and fraudulent marketing who are seniors;

(ii) assist in the investigation and prosecution of those using misleading or fraudulent

(6)“金融扫盲办公室”一词系指消费者金融保护局金融扫盲办公室；

(7)“老年人”一词系指年满62周岁的任何个人；及

(8)“州”一词的含义以《1934年证券交易法》第3条[《美国法典》第十五编第78c(a)节]的定义为准。

(b)**向各州提供补助金用于更好地保护老年人免受虚假称号误导**。——金融扫盲办公室应制订计划，向各州或适格实体发放补助金，用于——

(1)聘用工作人员对误导性或欺诈性营销案件进行识别、调查和起诉(通过民事、行政或刑事诉讼方式起诉)；

(2)为监管者、检察官和执法人员识别以老年人为目标使用误导性称号的销售人员和顾问所需技术、设备和培训提供资金支持；

(3)在技术、设备和培训方面为检察官提供资金支持，以便其对更多地以老年人为目标使用误导性称号的销售人员和顾问成功提起公诉；

(4)针对销售人员和顾问在金融产品销售和营销过程中所用专业称号的适当性，向监管者提供教材和培训；

(5)向老年人提供教材和培训，提高其对误导性或欺诈性营销的防范意识和理解；

(6)制订全面计划，打击面向老年人的误导性或欺诈性金融产品营销活动；并

(7)完善州法律规定，保护老年人免受误导性或欺诈性营销行为侵害。

(c)**申请**。——希望根据本条获得补助金的各州或适格实体，应按照金融扫盲办公室确定的格式和方式提交申请，其中应包括——

(1)拟通过使用本条所规定补助金开展旨在保护老年人免受误导性或欺诈性营销行为侵害的活动的计划书，包括——

(A)确定本州误导性或欺诈性营销问题的范围；

(B)说明计划开展的活动将如何实现以下目标——

(i)保护老年人免受金融产品销售中误导性或欺诈性营销行为的侵害，包括主动查明受误导性或欺诈性营销活动侵害的老年受害人；

(ii)协助调查和起诉从事误导性或欺诈性营销行为的人；及

marketing; and

(iii) discourage and reduce cases of misleading or fraudulent marketing; and

(C) a description of how the proposed activities would be coordinated with other State efforts; and

(2) any other information, as the Office determines is appropriate.

(d) PERFORMANCE OBJECTIVES AND REPORTING REQUIREMENTS. —The Office may establish such performance objectives and reporting requirements for States and eligible entities receiving a grant under this section as the Office determines are necessary to carry out and assess the effectiveness of the program under this section.

(e) MAXIMUM AMOUNT. —The amount of a grant under this section may not exceed—

(1) $500,000 for each of 3 consecutive fiscal years, if the recipient is a State, or an eligible entity of a State, that has adopted rules —

(A) on the appropriate use of designations in the offer or sale of securities or investment advice that meet or exceed the minimum requirements of the NASAA Model Rule on the Use of Senior–Specific Certifications and Professional Designations (or any successor thereto);

(B) on the appropriate use of designations in the sale of insurance products that, to the extent practicable, conform to the minimum requirements of the National Association of Insurance Commissioners Model Regulation on the Use of Senior–Specific Certifications and Professional Designations in the Sale of Life Insurance and Annuities (or any successor thereto); and

(C) with respect to fiduciary or suitability requirements in the sale of annuities that meet or exceed the minimum requirements established by the Suitability in Annuity Transactions Model Regulation of the National Association of Insurance Commissioners (or any successor thereto); and

(2) $100,000 for each of 3 consecutive fiscal years, if the recipient is a State, or an eligible entity of a State, that has adopted —

(A) rules on the appropriate use of designations in the offer or sale of securities or investment advice that meet or exceed the minimum requirements of the NASAA Model Rule on the Use of Senior–Specific Certifications and Professional Designations (or any successor thereto); or

(B) rules —

(i) on the appropriate use of designations in the sale of insurance products that, to the extent practicable, conform to the minimum requirements of the National Association of Insurance Commissioners Model Regulation on the Use of Senior–Specific Certifications and Professional Designations in the Sale of Life Insurance and Annuities (or any successor thereto); and

(ii) with respect to fiduciary or suitability requirements in the sale of annuities that meet

(iii)阻止并减少误导性或欺诈性营销案件的发生;并

(C)说明计划开展的活动将如何与本州的其他工作相协调;及

(2)金融扫盲办公室判定确属适当的任何其他信息。

(d)**绩效目标和报告提交要求**。——金融扫盲办公室可以为根据本条获得补助金的各州及适格实体制定其判定为开展本条所述计划并评估其有效性确属必要的绩效目标和报告提交要求。

(e)**最高金额**。——本条所述补助金的最高金额如下——

(1)对于已制定如下规则的州或适格实体而言,3个连续财政年度中,每一财政年度不得超过50万美元——

(A)对证券要约、销售或者投资意见提供过程中所用专业称号的适当使用进行规范的规则,且该等规则符合或超出《北美证券管理者协会关于面向老年人的认证和专业称号的使用示范规则》(或其任何后续规则)的最低要求;

(B)对保险产品销售中所用专业称号的适当使用进行规范的规则,且该等规则在可行的范围内符合《美国保险监督官协会关于在人寿保险和年金销售中面向老年人的认证和专业称号的使用示范管理办法》(或其任何后续管理办法)的最低要求;及

(C)关于年金销售中的受信义务或适当性要求的规则,且该等规则符合或超出《美国保险监督官协会年金交易适当性示范管理办法》(或其任何后续管理办法)的最低要求;且

(2)对于已制定如下规则的州或适格实体而言,3个连续财政年度中,每一财政年度不得超过10万美元——

(A)对证券要约、销售或者投资意见提供过程中所用专业称号的适当使用进行规范的规则,且该等规则符合或超出《北美证券管理者协会关于面向老年人的认证和专业称号的使用示范规则》(或其任何后续规则)的最低要求;或

(B)如下规则——

(i)对保险产品销售中所用专业称号的适当使用进行规范的规则,且该等规则在可行的范围内符合《美国保险监督官协会关于在人寿保险和年金销售中面向老年人的认证和专业称号的使用示范管理办法》(或其任何后续管理办法)的最低要求;及

(ii)关于年金销售中的受信义务或适当性要求的规则,且该等规则符合或超出

or exceed the minimum requirements established by the Suitability in Annuity Transactions Model Regulation of the National Association of Insurance Commissioners (or any successor thereto).

(f) SUBGRANTS. —A State or eligible entity that receives a grant under this section may make a subgrant, as the State or eligible entity determines is necessary to carry out the activities funded using a grant under this section.

(g) REAPPLICATION. —A State or eligible entity that receives a grant under this section may reapply for a grant under this section, notwithstanding the limitations on grant amounts under subsection (e).

(h) AUTHORIZATION OF APPROPRIATIONS. —There are authorized to be appropriated to carry out this section, $8,000,000 for each of fiscal years 2011 through 2015.

SEC.989B. DESIGNATED FEDERAL ENTITY INSPECTORS GENERAL INDEPENDENCE.

Section 8G of the Inspector General Act of 1978 (5 U.S.C.App.) is amended —

(1) in subsection (a)(4) —

(A) in the matter preceding subparagraph (A), by inserting "the board or commission of the designated Federal entity, or in the event the designated Federal entity does not have a board or commission," after "means";

(B) in subparagraph (A), by striking "and" after the semicolon; and

(C) by adding after subparagraph (B) the following:

"(C) with respect to the Federal Labor Relations Authority, such term means the members of the Authority (described under section 7104 of title 5, United States Code);

"(D) with respect to the National Archives and Records Administration, such term means the Archivist of the United States;

"(E) with respect to the National Credit Union Administration, such term means the National Credit Union Administration Board (described under section 102 of the Federal Credit Union Act (12 U.S.C.1752a));

"(F) with respect to the National Endowment of the Arts, such term means the National Council on the Arts;

"(G) with respect to the National Endowment for the Humanities, such term means the National Council on the Humanities; and

"(H) with respect to the Peace Corps, such term means the Director of the Peace Corps;"; and

(2) in subsection (h), by inserting "if the designated Federal entity is not a board or commission, include" after "designated Federal entities and".

SEC.989C. STRENGTHENING INSPECTOR GENERAL ACCOUNTABILITY.

Section 5(a) of the Inspector General Act of 1978 (5 U.S.C.App.) is amended—

《美国保险监督官协会年金交易适当性示范管理办法》(或其任何后续管理办法)的最低要求。

(f)**补助金分发**。——根据本条获取补助金的州或适格实体可以对补助金进行该州或适格实体判定确属必要的分发,以借助本条规定的补助金开展活动。

(g)**再申请**。——尽管第(e)子条对补助金金额作出了限制,根据本条获取补助金的州或适格实体仍可以根据本条规定再申请补助金。

(h)**授权拨款金额**。——2011年至2015年,用于实施本条规定的授权拨款金额为每一财政年度800万美元。

第989B条 指定联邦实体监察长的独立性

《1978年监察长法》第8G条(《美国法典》第五编附件)修正如下——

(1)在第(a)(4)子条中——

(A)第(A)子款之前的内容在"指"之后插入"指定联邦实体的董事会或委员会;如果指定联邦实体未设董事会或委员会,则指";

(B)第(A)子款删除分号之后的"及";并

(C)在第(B)子款之后增加如下内容:

"(C)就联邦劳动关系局而言,该词指联邦劳动关系局成员(见《美国法典》第五编第7104节的规定);

(D)就国家档案和记录管理局而言,该词指美国国家档案馆馆长;

(E)就国家信贷联盟署而言,该词指国家信贷联盟署委员会(见《联邦信贷联盟法》第102条[《美国法典》第十二编第1752a节)的规定];

(F)就全国艺术基金会而言,该词指全国艺术理事会;

(G)就全国人文基金会而言,该词指全国人文理事会;及

(H)就和平队而言,该词指和平队队长;";及

(2)在第(h)子条中,在"指定联邦实体,且"之后插入"如果指定联邦实体并非某一理事会或委员会,包括"。

第989C条 加强对监察长的问责

《1978年监察长法》第5(a)条(《美国法典》第五编附件)修正如下——

(1) in paragraph (12), by striking "and" after the semicolon;

(2) in paragraph (13), by striking the period and inserting a semicolon; and

(3) by adding at the end the following:

"(14)(A) an appendix containing the results of any peer review conducted by another Office of Inspector General during the reporting period; or

"(B) if no peer review was conducted within that reporting period, a statement identifying the date of the last peer review conducted by another Office of Inspector General;

"(15) a list of any outstanding recommendations from any peer review conducted by another Office of Inspector General that have not been fully implemented, including a statement describing the status of the implementation and why implementation is not complete; and

"(16) a list of any peer reviews conducted by the Inspector General of another Office of the Inspector General during the reporting period, including a list of any outstanding recommendations made from any previous peer review (including any peer review conducted before the reporting period) that remain outstanding or have not been fully implemented.".

SEC.989D. REMOVAL OF INSPECTORS GENERAL OF DESIGNATED FEDERAL ENTITIES.

Section 8G(e) of the Inspector General Act of 1978 (5 U.S.C.App.) is amended —

(1) by redesignating the sentences following "(e)" as paragraph (2); and

(2) by striking "(e)" and inserting the following:

"(e)(1) In the case of a designated Federal entity for which a board or commission is the head of the designated Federal entity, a removal under this subsection may only be made upon the written concurrence of a 2/3 majority of the board or commission.".

SEC.989E. ADDITIONAL OVERSIGHT OF FINANCIAL REGULATORY SYSTEM.

(a) COUNCIL OF INSPECTORS GENERAL ON FINANCIAL OVERSIGHT. —

(1) ESTABLISHMENT AND MEMBERSHIP. —There is established a Council of Inspectors General on Financial Oversight (in this section referred to as the "Council of Inspectors General") chaired by the Inspector General of the Department of the Treasury and composed of the inspectors general of the following:

(A) The Board of Governors of the Federal Reserve System.

(B) The Commodity Futures Trading Commission.

(C) The Department of Housing and Urban Development.

(D) The Department of the Treasury.

(E) The Federal Deposit Insurance Corporation.

(F) The Federal Housing Finance Agency.

(G) The National Credit Union Administration.

(1)在第(12)款中,删除分号之后的“及”;

(2)在第(13)款中,删除句号,替以分号;及

(3)在结尾处增加如下内容:

“(14)(A)一份含有其他监察长办公室于报告期间所开展任何同行审评的结果的附件;或

(B)如果报告期间内未开展任何同行审评,则应提交一份声明,指明其他监察长办公室开展的最近一次同行审评的日期;

(15)其他监察长办公室开展的任何同行审评中提出但尚未得到充分实施的任何未决建议的清单,包括一份对该等建议的实施情况及未该等建议未得到充分实施的原因进行说明的声明;及

(16)其他监察长办公室于报告期间内所开展任何同行审评的清单,包括以往同行审评(包括于报告期间之前开展的任何同行审评)中提出但仍然处于未决状态或尚未得到充分实施的未决建议之清单。”

第989D条　指定联邦实体监察长的免职

《1978年监察长法》第8G(e)条(《美国法典》第五编附件)修正如下——

(1)将编号“(e)”之后的内容编号为第(2)款;及

(2)删除“(e)”,替以如下内容:

“(e)(1)如果指定联邦实体的领导机构为董事会或委员会,本子条规定的免职须经该董事会或委员会2/3以上成员书面同意方可通过。”

第989E条　对金融监管系统的补充监督

(a)**金融监督监察长委员会**。——

(1)**组建和成员**。——兹成立金融监督监察长委员会(本条以下简称监察长委员会),由财政部监察长担任主席,成员由以下各者的监察长组成:

(A)联邦储备委员会;

(B)商品期货交易委员会;

(C)住房与城市发展部;

(D)财政部;

(E)联邦存款保险公司;

(F)联邦住房金融局;

(G)国家信贷联盟署;及

(H) The Securities and Exchange Commission.

(I) The Troubled Asset Relief Program (until the termination of the authority of the Special Inspector General for such program under section 121 (k) of the Emergency Economic Stabilization Act of 2008 (12 U.S.C.5231(k))).

(2) DUTIES. —

(A) MEETINGS. —The Council of Inspectors General shall meet not less than once each quarter, or more frequently if the chair considers it appropriate, to facilitate the sharing of information among inspectors general and to discuss the ongoing work of each inspector general who is a member of the Council of Inspectors General, with a focus on concerns that may apply to the broader financial sector and ways to improve financial oversight.

(B) ANNUAL REPORT. —Each year the Council of Inspectors General shall submit to the Council and to Congress a report including —

(i) for each inspector general who is a member of the Council of Inspectors General, a section within the exclusive editorial control of such inspector general that highlights the concerns and recommendations of such inspector general in such inspector general's ongoing and completed work, with a focus on issues that may apply to the broader financial sector; and

(ii) a summary of the general observations of the Council of Inspectors General based on the views expressed by each inspector general as required by clause (i), with a focus on measures that should be taken to improve financial oversight.

(3) WORKING GROUPS TO EVALUATE COUNCIL. —

(A) CONVENING A WORKING GROUP. —The Council of Inspectors General may, by majority vote, convene a Council of Inspectors General Working Group to evaluate the effectiveness and internal operations of the Council.

(B) PERSONNEL AND RESOURCES. —The inspectors general who are members of the Council of Inspectors General may detail staff and resources to a Council of Inspectors General Working Group established under this paragraph to enable it to carry out its duties.

(C) REPORTS. —A Council of Inspectors General Working Group established under this paragraph shall submit regular reports to the Council and to Congress on its evaluations pursuant to this paragraph.

(b) RESPONSE TO REPORT BY COUNCIL. —The Council shall respond to the concerns raised in the report of the Council of Inspectors General under subsection (a)(2)(B) for such year.

SEC.989F. GAO STUDY OF PERSON TO PERSON LENDING.

(a) STUDY. —

(1) IN GENERAL. —The Comptroller General of the United States shall conduct a study of person to person lending to determine the optimal Federal regulatory structure.

(2) CONSULTATION. —In conducting the study required under paragraph (1), the

(H)证券交易委员会。

(I)问题资产救助计划{直至该计划的特别监察长的职权根据《2008年紧急经济稳定法》第121(k)条[《美国法典》第十二编第5231(k)节]的规定终止}。

(2)**职责**。——

(A)**会议**。——监察长委员会至少应每季度举行一次会议,如果主席认为适当,可提高会议举行频率,以促进各位监察长之间的信息共享,并讨论担任监察长委员会成员的每一名监察长的当前工作,尤其是可能涉及更广泛金融领域的问题以及改善金融监督的方式。

(B)**年度报告**。——监察长委员会应每年向金融稳定监督委员会和国会提交一份报告。该报告中应包括——

(i)担任监察长委员会成员的每一监察长完全独立地编辑的章节,其中应强调该监察长关于其当前工作和已完成工作的问题和建议,尤其是可能涉及更广泛金融领域的事宜;及

(ii)监察长委员会基于各监察长根据第(i)项规定表达的观点而得出的总体意见概要,尤其是应采取的改善金融监督的举措。

(3)**对金融稳定监督委员会工作进行评价的工作小组**。——

(A)**工作小组的召集**。——经过半数以上成员表决同意,监察长委员会可以召集监察长委员会工作小组,评价金融稳定监督委员会的成效和内部运行。

(B)**人力和资源**。——担任监察长委员会成员的监察长可以向根据本款组建的监察长委员会工作小组分派人力和资源,确保其能够履行职责。

(C)**报告**。——根据本款规定成立的监察长委员会工作小组应就根据本款开展的评价工作定期向金融稳定监督委员会和国会提交报告。

(b)**金融稳定监督委员会对报告的回应**。——金融稳定监督委员会应对监察长委员会根据第(a)(2)(B)子条在年度报告中提出的问题作出回应。

第989F条　政府问责办公室关于民间个人借贷的研究

(a)**研究**。——

(1)**一般规定**。——政府问责办公室主任应就民间个人借贷开展研究,以确定最佳的联邦监管架构。

(2)**磋商**。——在开展第(1)款所规定研究时,政府问责办公室主任应与联邦银

Comptroller General shall consult with Federal banking agencies, the Commission, consumer groups, outside experts, and the person to person lending industry.

(3) CONTENT OF STUDY. —The study required under paragraph (1) shall include an examination of—

(A) the regulatory structure as it exists on the date of enactment of this Act, as determined by the Commission, with particular attention to —

(i) the application of the Securities Act of 1933 to person to person lending platforms;

(ii) the posting of consumer loan information on the EDGAR database of the Commission; and

(iii) the treatment of privately held person to person lending platforms as public companies;

(B) the State and other Federal regulators responsible for the oversight and regulation of person to person lending markets;

(C) any Federal, State, or local government or private studies of person to person lending completed or in progress on the date of enactment of this Act;

(D) consumer privacy and data protections, minimum credit standards, anti-money laundering and risk management in the regulatory structure as it exists on the date of enactment of this Act, and whether additional or alternative safeguards are needed; and

(E) the uses of person to person lending.

(b) REPORT. —

(1) IN GENERAL. —Not later than 1 year after the date of enactment of this Act, the Comptroller General shall submit a report on the study required under subsection (a) to the Committee on Banking, Housing, and Urban Affairs of the Senate and the Committee on Financial Services of the House of Representatives.

(2) CONTENT OF REPORT. —The report required under paragraph (1) shall include alternative regulatory options, including —

(A) the involvement of other Federal agencies; and

(B) alternative approaches by the Commission and recommendations on whether the alternative approaches are effective.

SEC.989G. EXEMPTION FOR NONACCELERATED FILERS.

(a) EXEMPTION. —Section 404 of the Sarbanes-Oxley Act of 2002 is amended by adding at the end the following:

"(c) EXEMPTION FOR SMALLER ISSUERS. —Subsection (b) shall not apply with respect to any audit report prepared for an issuer that is neither a 'large accelerated filer' nor an 'accelerated filer' as those terms are defined in Rule 12b-2 of the Commission (17 C.F. R. 240.12b-2).".

(b) STUDY. —The Securities and Exchange Commission shall conduct a study to

行业监管机关、证券交易委员会、消费者群体、外部专家以及民间个人借贷行业磋商。

(3)**研究内容**。——第(1)款所规定研究应包括对如下事项的审查——

(A)证券交易委员会确定的截至本法颁布之日现存的监管架构,尤其是如下事项——

(i)《1933年证券法》对民间个人借贷平台的适用情况;

(ii)通过证券交易委员会EDGAR(埃德加)数据库发布消费者贷款信息的情况;及

(iii)将私人持有的民间个人借贷平台作为公众公司处理的情况;

(B)对民间个人借贷市场负有监管与规制责任的州监管者和其他联邦监管者;

(C)截至本法颁布之日,任何联邦、州或地方政府或者私人已经完成的或正在进行的民间个人借贷研究;

(D)在截至本法颁布之日存在的监管架构下,消费者隐私和数据保护、最低信用标准、反洗钱及风险管理情况,以及是否需要实施额外或替代性的保障措施;及

(E)民间个人借贷的使用情况。

(b)**报告**。——

(1)**一般规定**。——政府问责办公室主任应于本法颁布之日后一年内,就根据第(a)子条所规定研究向参议院银行、住房与城市事务委员会及众议院金融服务委员会提交一份报告。

(2)**报告内容**。——第(1)款所规定报告应包含替代性监管方案,包括——

(A)借助其他联邦机关的力量进行监管;及

(B)证券交易委员会可以采用的替代性方法,以及针对该等替代性方法是否有效提出建议。

第989G条　对于非加速报告人的豁免

(a)**豁免**。——在《2002年萨班斯—奥克斯利法》第404条结尾处增加如下内容,作为对该条的修正:

"(c)**对小规模发行人的豁免**。——如果发行人既非"大型加速报告人"亦非"加速报告人"[定义见证券交易委员会的《12b-2规则》(《联邦规章汇编》第十七编第240.12b-2部分)],则为其编制的任何审计报告均不得适用第(b)子条的规定。"

(b)**研究**。——证券交易委员会应开展研究,以确定对于在相关报告期间市值介

determine how the Commission could reduce the burden of complying with section 404(b) of the Sarbanes–Oxley Act of 2002 for companies whose market capitalization is between $75,000,000 and $250,000,000 for the relevant reporting period while maintaining investor protections for such companies. The study shall also consider whether any such methods of reducing the compliance burden or a complete exemption for such companies from compliance with such section would encourage companies to list on exchanges in the United States in their initial public offerings. Not later than 9 months after the date of the enactment of this subtitle, the Commission shall transmit a report of such study to Congress.

SEC.989H. CORRECTIVE RESPONSES BY HEADS OF CERTAIN ESTABLISHMENTS TO DEFICIENCIES IDENTIFIED BY INSPECTORS GENERAL.

The Chairman of the Board of Governors of the Federal Reserve System, the Chairman of the Commodity Futures Trading Commission, the Chairman of the National Credit Union Administration, the Director of the Pension Benefit Guaranty Corporation, and the Chairman of the Securities and Exchange Commission shall each —

(1) take action to address deficiencies identified by a report or investigation of the Inspector General of the establishment concerned; or

(2) certify to both Houses of Congress that no action is necessary or appropriate in connection with a deficiency described in paragraph (1).

SEC.989I. GAO STUDY REGARDING EXEMPTION FOR SMALLER ISSUERS.

(a) STUDY REGARDING EXEMPTION FOR SMALLER ISSUERS. —The Comptroller General of the United States shall carry out a study on the impact of the amendments made by this Act to section 404(b) of the Sarbanes–Oxley Act of 2002 (15 U.S.C.7262(b)), which shall include an analysis of —

(1) whether issuers that are exempt from such section 404(b) have fewer or more restatements of published accounting statements than issuers that are required to comply with such section 404(b);

(2) the cost of capital for issuers that are exempt from such section 404(b) compared to the cost of capital for issuers that are required to comply with such section 404(b);

(3) whether there is any difference in the confidence of investors in the integrity of financial statements of issuers that comply with such section 404(b) and issuers that are exempt from compliance with such section 404(b);

(4) whether issuers that do not receive the attestation for internal controls required under such section 404(b) should be required to disclose the lack of such attestation to investors; and

(5) the costs and benefits to issuers that are exempt from such section 404(b) that

于7500万美元至2.5亿美元之间的公司而言，如何在保证投资者保护的同时减轻其遵守《2002年萨班斯—奥克斯利法》第404(b)条的合规负担。研究亦应考虑,采用减轻该等公司的合规负担的方法或者完全使其豁免适用该条规定是否将鼓励公司在首次公开发行时在美国境内交易所上市。证券交易委员会应于本编颁布之日后9个月内就该项研究向国会提交一份报告。

第989H条　特定机构负责人针对监察长发现的缺陷采取的整改措施

联邦储备委员会主席、商品期货交易委员会主席、国家信贷联盟署署长、联邦养老金担保公司总裁以及证券交易委员会主席应分别——

(1)采取行动,解决各自的监察长在报告中指出或通过调查发现的缺陷;或

(2)向国会两院证明,对于第(1)款所述缺陷,既不必也不宜采取任何行动。

第989I条　政府问责办公室关于小规模发行人豁免的研究

(a)**关于小规模发行人豁免的研究**。——政府问责办公室主任应就本法对《2002年萨班斯—奥克斯利法》第404(b)条[《美国法典》第十五编第7262(b)节]所做修正带来的影响展开研究。该项研究应包括对以下各项进行分析——

(1)相对于应遵守上述第404(b)条规定的发行人而言,获得豁免不必遵守该条规定的发行人对已公布会计报表进行重述的比例更高还是更低;

(2)应遵守上述第404(b)条规定的发行人与获得豁免不必遵守该条规定的发行人在资本成本上的比较;

(3)对于应遵守上述第404(b)条规定的发行人和获得豁免不必遵守该条规定的发行人,投资者对于其财务报表完整性的信心是否存在任何区别;

(4)对于未按照上述第404(b)条规定获得内部控制鉴证的发行人,是否应要求其向投资者披露该等情况;及

(5)获得豁免不必遵守上述第404(b)条规定的发行人主动获得独立审计师鉴证

voluntarily have obtained the attestation of an independent auditor.

(b) REPORT. —Not later than 3 years after the date of enactment of this Act, the Comptroller General shall submit to the Committee on Banking, Housing, and Urban Affairs of the Senate and the Committee on Financial Services of the House of Representatives a report on the results of the study required under subsection (a).

SEC.989J. FURTHER PROMOTING THE ADOPTION OF THE NAIC MODEL REGULATIONS THAT ENHANCE PROTECTION OF SENIORS AND OTHER CONSUMERS.

(a) IN GENERAL. —The Commission shall treat as exempt securities described under section 3(a)(8) of the Securities Act of 1933 (15 U.S.C.77c(a)(8)) any insurance or endowment policy or annuity contract or optional annuity contract —

(1) the value of which does not vary according to the performance of a separate account;

(2) that —

(A) satisfies standard nonforfeiture laws or similar requirements of the applicable State at the time of issue; or

(B) in the absence of applicable standard nonforfeiture laws or requirements, satisfies the Model Standard Nonforfeiture Law for Life Insurance or Model Standard Nonforfeiture Law for Individual Deferred Annuities, or any successor model law, as published by the National Association of Insurance Commissioners; and

(3) that is issued —

(A) on and after June 16, 2013, in a State, or issued by an insurance company that is domiciled in a State, that —

(i) adopts rules that govern suitability requirements in the sale of an insurance or endowment policy or annuity contract or optional annuity contract, which shall substantially meet or exceed the minimum requirements established by the Suitability in Annuity Transactions Model Regulation adopted by the National Association of Insurance Commissioners in March 2010; and

(ii) adopts rules that substantially meet or exceed the minimum requirements of any successor modifications to the model regulations described in subparagraph (A) within 5 years of the adoption by the Association of any further successors thereto; or

(B) by an insurance company that adopts and implements practices on a nationwide basis for the sale of any insurance or endowment policy or annuity contract or optional annuity contract that meet or exceed the minimum requirements established by the National Associat-ion of Insurance Commissioners Suitability in Annuity Transactions Model Regulation (Model 275), and any successor thereto, and is therefore subject to examination by the State of domicile of the insurance company, or by any other State where the insurance company conducts sales of such products, for the purpose of monitoring compliance under this section.

所产生的成本和收益。

(b)**报告**。——政府问责办公室主任应于本法颁布之日后3年内,就根据第(a)子条所规定研究的结果向参议院银行、住房与城市事务委员会及众议院金融服务委员会提交一份报告。

第989J条 进一步促进美国保险监督官协会示范规章的制定,加强对老年人和其他消费者的保护

(a)**一般规定**。——对于符合如下条件的任何保险单、人寿定期保险单、年金合同或选择性年金合同,证券交易委员会应将其视为《1933年证券法》第3(a)(8)条[《美国法典》第十五编第77c(a)(8)节]所述豁免证券处理——

(1)其价值不会随某一独立账户的业绩表现而波动;

(2)满足如下要求——

(A)保单签发时相关州的标准不丧失价值法[1]或类似要求;或

(B)美国保险监督官协会发布的《人寿保险示范标准不丧失价值法》或《个人递延年金示范标准丧失价值法》或其任何后续示范法律(如不存在适用的标准不丧失价值法或要求);且

(3)系按照如下规定签发——

(A)于2013年6月16日或之后,在符合如下条件的州内签发,或由位于该等州的保险公司签发——

(i)制定对保险单、人寿定期保险单、年金合同或选择性年金合同销售中的适当性要求进行规范的规则,且该等规则应基本上符合或超出美国保险监督官协会于2010年3月制定的《年金交易适当性示范管理办法》的最低要求;且

(ii)在美国保险监督官协会制定第(A)子款所述示范规章的任何后续规章后5年内,制定基本上符合或超出上述规章的后续修正中最低要求的规则;或

(B)由保险公司签发,且对于保险单、人寿定期保险单、年金合同或选择性年金合同,该保险公司采取并实施了全国统一的做法,而该等做法符合或超出《美国保险监督官协会年金交易适当性示范管理办法》(第275号)及其任何后续管理办法的最低要求,同时该保险公司因此须接受其所在州或开展该等产品销售活动所在的任何其他州的检查,以便该等州监控保险公司对本条规定的合规情况。

---

1 根据不丧失价值法,在保单持有人停止缴纳保费的情况下,寿险公司应退还保单现金值,存在若干种不同的退还方式,由保单持有人自行选择。——译者注

(b) RULE OF CONSTRUCTION. —Nothing in this section shall be construed to affect whether any insurance or endowment policy or annuity contract or optional annuity contract that is not described in this section is or is not an exempt security under section 3 (a)(8) of the Securities Act of 1933 (15 U.S.C.77c(a)(8)).

Subtitle J—Securities and Exchange Commission Match Funding

SEC.991. SECURITIES AND EXCHANGE COMMISSION MATCH FUNDING.

(a) MATCH FUNDING AUTHORITY. —

(1) AMENDMENTS. —Section 31 of the Securities Exchange Act of 1934 (15 U.S.C. 78ee) is amended —

(A) by striking subsection (a) and inserting the following:

"(a) RECOVERY OF COSTS OF ANNUAL APPROPRIATION. —The Commission shall, in accordance with this section, collect transaction fees and assessments that are designed to recover the costs to the Government of the annual appropriation to the Commission by Congress.";

(B) in subsection (e)(2), by striking "September 30" and inserting "September 25";

(C) in subsection (g), by striking "April 30 of the fiscal year preceding the fiscal year to which such rate applies" and inserting "30 days after the date on which an Act making a regular appropriation to the Commission for such fiscal year is enacted";

(D) by striking subsection (j) and inserting the following:

"(j) ADJUSTMENTS TO FEE RATES. —

"(1) ANNUAL ADJUSTMENT. —Subject to subsections (i)(1)(B) and (k), for each fiscal year, the Commission shall by order adjust each of the rates applicable under subsections (b) and (c) for such fiscal year to a uniform adjusted rate that, when applied to the baseline estimate of the aggregate dollar amount of sales for such fiscal year, is reasonably likely to produce aggregate fee collections under this section (including assessments collected under subsection (d) of this section) that are equal to the regular appropriation to the Commission by Congress for such fiscal year.

"(2) MID-YEAR ADJUSTMENT. —Subject to subsections (i)(1)(B) and (k), for each fiscal year, the Commission shall determine, by March 1 of such fiscal year, whether, based on the actual aggregate dollar volume of sales during the first 5 months of such fiscal year, the baseline estimate of the aggregate dollar volume of sales used under paragraph (1) for such fiscal year is reasonably likely to be 10 percent (or more) greater or less than the

(b)**解释规则**。——本条任何内容均不得被解释为对本条所述之外的任何保险单、人寿定期保险单、年金合同或选择性年金合同是否属于《1933年证券法》第3(a)(8)条[《美国法典》第十五编第77c(a)(8)节]所述豁免证券造成影响。

第J子编——证券交易委员会的对等筹资

第991条　证券交易委员会的对等筹资

(a)**对等筹资权**。——

(1)**修正**。——《1934年证券交易法》第31条(《美国法典》第十五编第78ee节)修正如下——

(A)删除第(a)子条,替以如下内容:

"(a)**年度拨款产生费用的收回**。——证券交易委员会应按照本条规定收取交易手续费和计征费，以收回联邦政府因国会对证券交易委员会进行年度拨款而产生的费用。";

(B)在第(e)(2)子条中,删除"9月30日",替以"9月25日";

(C)在第(g)子条中,删除"适用该等费率的财政年度的前一财政年度的4月30日",替以"规定在该财政年度向证券交易委员会提供常规拨款的法律颁布之日后30天内";

(D)删除第(j)子条,替以如下内容:

"(j)**费率调整**。——

(1)**年度调整**。——在不违反第(i)(1)(B)子条和第(k)子条规定的前提下,证券交易委员会应于每一财政年度发布命令,将根据第(b)子条和第(c)子条该财政年度适用的费率调整为统一费率,调整后的费率应达到如下效果:将该统一费率适用于该财政年度的基准估算销售总金额后,根据合理预期可能使按照本条收取的费用总额[包括根据本条第(d)子条收取的摊派费用]等于国会在该财政年度向证券交易委员会提供的常规拨款金额。

(2)**年中调整**。——在不违反第(i)(1)(B)子条和第(k)子条规定的前提下,证券交易委员会应于每一财政年度的3月1日之前判定,基于该财政年度前5个月的实际销售总金额,根据第(1)款适用的该财政年度的基准估算销售总金额与该财政年度实际销售总金额的偏离根据合理预期是否可能超过10%(或更高百分比)。如果证券交易委员会判定确实存在上述比例的偏离,其应于3月1日之前发布命令,将根据第(b)子条

actual aggregate dollar volume of sales for such fiscal year. If the Commission so determines, the Commission shall by order, no later than March 1, adjust each of the rates applicable under subsections (b) and (c) for such fiscal year to a uniform adjusted rate that, when applied to the revised estimate of the aggregate dollar amount of sales for the remainder of such fiscal year, is reasonably likely to produce aggregate fee collections under this section (including fees collected during such five–month period and assessments collected under subsection (d) of this section) that are equal to the regular appropriation to the Commission by Congress for such fiscal year. In making such revised estimate, the Commission shall, after consultation with the Congressional Budget Office and the Office of Management and Budget, use the same methodology required by subsection (1).

"(3) REVIEW. —In exercising its authority under this subsection, the Commission shall not be required to comply with the provisions of section 553 of title 5, United States Code. An adjusted rate prescribed under paragraph (1) or (2) and published under subsection (g) shall not be subject to judicial review.

"(4) EFFECTIVE DATE. —

"(A) ANNUAL ADJUSTMENT. —Subject to subsections (i)(1)(B) and (k), an adjusted rate prescribed under paragraph (1) shall take effect on the later of —

"(i) the first day of the fiscal year to which such rate applies; or

"(ii) 60 days after the date on which an Act making a regular appropriation to the Commission for such fiscal year is enacted.

"(B) MID–YEAR ADJUSTMENT. —An adjusted rate prescribed under paragraph (2) shall take effect on April 1 of the fiscal year to which such rate applies.";

(E) in subsection (k), by striking "30 days" and inserting "60 days"; and

(F) in subsection (1), by striking "DEFINITIONS. —" and all that follows through "SALES. —The baseline" and inserting "BASELINE ESTIMATE OF THE AGGREGATE DOLLAR AMOUNT OF SALES. —The baseline".

(2) EFFECTIVE DATE. —The amendments made by this subsection shall take effect on the later of—

(A) October 1, 2011; or

(B) the date of enactment of an Act making a regular appropriation to the Commission for fiscal year 2012.

(b) AMENDMENTS TO REGISTRATION FEE PROVISIONS. —

(1) SECTION 6 (b) OF THE SECURITIES ACT OF 1933. —Section 6 (b) of the Securities Act of 1933 (15 U.S.C.77f(b)) is amended —

(A) by striking "offsetting" each place that term appears and inserting "fee";

(B) by striking paragraphs (1), (3), (4), (6), (8), and (9);

(C) by redesignating paragraph (2) as paragraph (1);

和第(c)子条该财政年度适用的所有费率调整为统一费率,调整后的费率应达到如下效果:将该经统一调整的费率适用于该财政年度剩余期间的修正后的估算销售总金额后,根据合理预期可能使按照本条收取的费用总额(包括上述5个月期间收取的手续费以及根据本条第(d)子条收取的摊派费用)等于国会在该财政年度向证券交易委员会提供的常规拨款金额。在对估算进行修正时,证券交易委员会应与国会预算办公室及行政管理和预算办公室磋商后,使用第(I)子条规定的同一种方法。

(3)**审查**。——在根据本子条行使权力时,证券交易委员会不必遵守《美国法典》第五编第553节的规定。根据第(1)款或第(2)款规定调整并根据第(g)子条发布的任何费率不得成为司法审查的对象。

(4)**生效日**。——

(A)**年度调整**。——在不违反第(i)(1)(B)子条和第(k)子条规定的前提下,第(1)款所规定经调整的费率应于如下日期(以较晚者为准)生效——

(i)适用该费率的财政年度的第一天;或

(ii)规定在该财政年度向证券交易委员会提供常规拨款的法律颁布之日后第60天。

(B)**年中调整**。——第(2)款规定的调整费率应于适用该费率的财政年度的4月1日生效。";

(E)在第(k)子条中,删除"30天",替以"60天";及

(F)在第(l)子条中,删除"**定义**。——"直至"销售额。——基准"的全部内容,替以"**基准估算销售总金额**。——基准"。

(2)**生效日**。——根据本子条做出的修正应于如下日期(以较晚者为准)生效——

(A)2011年10月1日;或

(B)规定在2012财政年度向证券交易委员会提供常规拨款的法律颁布之日。

(b)**对注册费规定的修正**。——

(1)**《1933年证券法》第6(b)条**。——《1933年证券法》第6(b)条[《美国法典》第十五编第77f(b)节]修正如下——

(A)删除所有的"抵销",全部替以"收费";

(B)删除第(1)款、第(3)款、第(4)款、第(6)款、第(8)款和第(9)款;及

(C)第(2)款重新编号为第(1)款;

(D) by redesignating paragraph (5) as paragraph (2);

(E) by redesignating paragraph (7) as paragraph (3);

(F) by redesignating paragraph (10) as paragraph (5);

(G) by redesignating paragraph (11) as paragraph (6);

(H) in paragraph (1), as so redesignated, by striking "paragraph (5) or (6)." and inserting "paragraph (2).";

(I) in paragraph (2), as so redesignated —

(i) by striking "of the fiscal years 2003 through 2011" and inserting "fiscal year"; and

(ii) by striking "paragraph (2)" and inserting "paragraph (1)";

(J) by inserting after paragraph (3), as so redesignated, the following:

"(4) REVIEW AND EFFECTIVE DATE. —In exercising its authority under this subsection, the Commission shall not be required to comply with the provisions of section 553 of title 5, United States Code. An adjusted rate prescribed under paragraph (2) and published under paragraph (5) shall not be subject to judicial review. An adjusted rate prescribed under paragraph (2) shall take effect on the first day of the fiscal year to which such rate applies.";

(K) in paragraph (5), as redesignated, by striking "April 30" and inserting "August 31";

(L) in paragraph (6), as so redesignated —

(i) by striking "of the fiscal years 2002 through 2011" and inserting "fiscal year"; and

(ii) by inserting at the end of the table in subparagraph (A) the following:

"2012	$425,000,000
2013	$455,000,000
2014	$485,000,000
2015	$515,000,000
2016	$550,000,000
2017	$585,000,000
2018	$620,000,000
2019	$660,000,000
2020	$705,000,000

2021 and each fiscal year thereafter An amount that is equal to the target fee collection amount for the prior fiscal year, adjusted by the rate of inflation.".

(2) SECTION 13(e) OF THE SECURITIES EXCHANGE ACT OF 1934. —Section 13(e) of the Securities Exchange Act of 1934 (15 U.S.C.78m(e)) is amended —

(A) in paragraph (3), by striking "paragraphs (5) and (6)" and inserting "paragraph (4)";

(B) by striking paragraphs (4), (5), and (6);

(D)第(5)款重新编号为第(2)款;

(E)第(7)款重新编号为第(3)款;

(F)第(10)款重新编号为第(5)款;

(G)第(11)款重新编号为第(6)款;

(H)在第(1)款(以重新编号后的序号为准)中,删除"第(5)款或第(6)款",替以"第(2)款。";

(I)在第(2)款(以重新编号后的序号为准)中——

(i)删除"2003财政年度至2011财政年度",替以"财政年度";及

(ii)删除"第(2)款",替以"第(1)款";

(J)在第(3)款(以重新编号后的序号为准)之后插入如下内容:

"(4)**审查和生效日**。——在根据本子条行使权力时,证券交易委员会不必遵守《美国法典》第五编第553节的规定。按第(2)款规定调整并根据第(5)款发布的费率不得成为司法审查的对象。第(2)款规定的经调整的费率应于适用该费率的财政年度的第一天生效。";

(K)在第(5)款(以重新编号后的序号为准)中,删除"4月30日",替以"8月31日";

(L)在第(6)款(以重新编号后的序号为准)中——

(i)删除"2002财政年度至2011财政年度",替以"财政年度";及

(ii)在第(A)子款表格结尾处插入如下内容:

"2012年	4.25亿美元
2013年	4.55亿美元
2014年	4.85亿美元
2015年	5.15亿美元
2016年	5.5亿美元
2017年	5.85亿美元
2018年	6.2亿美元
2019年	6.6亿美元
2020年	7.05亿美元
2021年以及之后的每一财政年度	以上一财政年度的目标收费金额进行通胀调整后的金额为准。"

(2)《1934年证券交易法》第13(e)条。——《1934年证券交易法》第13(e)条[《美国法典》第十五编第78m(e)节]修正如下——

(A)第(3)款删除"第(5)款和第(6)款",替以"第(4)款";

(B)删除第(4)款、第(5)款和第(6)款;

(C) by inserting after paragraph (3) the following:

"(4) ANNUAL ADJUSTMENT. —For each fiscal year, the Commission shall by order adjust the rate required by paragraph (3) for such fiscal year to a rate that is equal to the rate (expressed in dollars per million) that is applicable under section 6(b) of the Securities Act of 1933 for such fiscal year.

"(5) FEE COLLECTIONS. —Fees collected pursuant to this subsection for fiscal year 2012 and each fiscal year thereafter shall be deposited and credited as general revenue of the Treasury and shall not be available for obligation.

"(6) EFFECTIVE DATE; PUBLICATION. —In exercising its authority under this subsection, the Commission shall not be required to comply with the provisions of section 553 of title 5, United States Code. An adjusted rate prescribed under paragraph (4) shall be published and take effect in accordance with section 6(b) of the Securities Act of 1933 (15 U.S.C.77f(b))."; and

(D) by striking paragraphs (8), (9), and (10).

(3) SECTION 14 (g) OF THE SECURITIES EXCHANGE ACT OF 1934. —Section 14(g) of the Securities Exchange Act of 1934 (15 U.S.C.78n(g)) is amended —

(A) in paragraph (1), by striking "paragraphs (5) and (6)" each time that term appears and inserting "paragraph (4)";

(B) in paragraph (3), by striking "paragraphs (5) and (6)" and inserting "paragraph (4)";

(C) by striking paragraphs (4), (5), and (6);

(D) by inserting after paragraph (3) the following:

"(4) ANNUAL ADJUSTMENT. —For each fiscal year, the Commission shall by order adjust the rate required by paragraphs (1) and (3) for such fiscal year to a rate that is equal to the rate (expressed in dollars per million) that is applicable under section 6 (b) of the Securities Act of 1933 (15 U.S.C.77f(b)) for such fiscal year.

"(5) FEE COLLECTION. —Fees collected pursuant to this subsection for fiscal year 2012 and each fiscal year thereafter shall be deposited and credited as general revenue of the Treasury and shall not be available for obligation.

"(6) REVIEW; EFFECTIVE DATE; PUBLICATION. —In exercising its authority under this subsection, the Commission shall not be required to comply with the provisions of section 553 of title 5, United States Code. An adjusted rate prescribed under paragraph (4) shall be published and take effect in accordance with section 6 (b) of the Securities Act of 1933 (15 U.S.C.77f(b)).";

(E) by striking paragraphs (8), (9), and (10); and

(F) by redesignating paragraph (11) as paragraph (8).

(4) EFFECTIVE DATE. —The amendments made by this subsection shall take effect

(C)在第(3)款之后插入如下内容:

"(4)**年度调整**。——证券交易委员会应于每一财政年度发布命令,对该财政年度适用的第(3)款规定的费率进行调整,调整后的费率应与根据《1933年证券法》第6(b)条该财政年度适用的费率(以百万美元为单位)相同。

(5)**费用收取**。——根据本条规定于2012财政年度以及之后的每一财政年度收取的费用均应作为财政部一般收入交存和入账,不得用于偿还债务。

(6)**生效日;发布**。——在根据本子条行使权力时,证券交易委员会不必遵守《美国法典》第五编第553节的规定。第(4)款规定的调整费率应按照《1933年证券法》第6(b)条[《美国法典》第十五编第77f(b)节]的规定发布并生效。";及

(D)删除第(8)款、第(9)款及第(10)款。

(3)**《1934年证券交易法》第14(g)条**。——《1934年证券交易法》第14(g)条[《美国法典》第十五编第78n(g)节]修正如下——

(A)在第(1)款中,删除所有的"第(5)款和第(6)款",全部替以"第(4)款";

(B)在第(3)款中,删除所有的"第(5)款和第(6)款",全部替以"第(4)款";

(C)删除第(4)款、第(5)款和第(6)款;

(D)在第(3)款之后插入如下内容:

"(4)**年度调整**。——证券交易委员会应于每一财政年度发布命令,对该财政年度适用的第(1)款和第(3)款规定的费率进行调整,调整后的费率应与根据《1933年证券法》第6(b)条[《美国法典》第十五编第77f(b)节]该财政年度适用的费率(以百万美元为单位)相同。

(5)**费用收取**。——根据本条规定于2012年财政年度以及之后的每一财政年度所收取的费用均应作为财政部一般收入交存和入账,不得用于偿还债务。

(6)**审查;生效日;发布**。——在根据本子条行使权力时,证券交易委员会不必遵守《美国法典》第五编第553节的规定。第(4)款规定的调整费率应按照《1933年证券法》第6(b)条[《美国法典》第十五编第77f(b)节]的规定发布并生效。";

(E)删除第(8)款、第(9)款和第(10)款;及

(F)第(11)款重新编号为第(8)款。

(4)**生效日**。——本子条所做修正应于2011年10月1日生效。证券交易委员会应

on October 1, 2011, except that for fiscal year 2012, the Commission shall publish the rate established under section 6(b) of the Securities Act of 1933 (15 U.S.C.77f(b)), as amended by this Act, on August 31, 2011.

(c) AUTHORIZATION OF APPROPRIATIONS. —Section 35 of the Securities Exchange Act of 1934 (15 U.S.C.78kk) is amended to read as follows:

"SEC.35. AUTHORIZATION OF APPROPRIATIONS.

"In addition to any other funds authorized to be appropriated to the Commission, there are authorized to be appropriated to carry out the functions, powers, and duties of the Commission —

"(1) for fiscal year 2011, $1,300,000,000;

"(2) for fiscal year 2012, $1,500,000,000;

"(3) for fiscal year 2013, $1,750,000,000;

"(4) for fiscal year 2014, $2,000,000,000; and

"(5) for fiscal year 2015, $2,250,000,000.".

(d) TRANSMITTAL OF BUDGET REQUESTS. —

(1) AMENDMENT. —Section 31 of the Securities Exchange Act of 1934 (15 U.S.C. 78ee) is amended by adding at the end the following:

"(m) TRANSMITTAL OF COMMISSION BUDGET REQUESTS. —

"(1) BUDGET REQUIRED. —For fiscal year 2012, and each fiscal year thereafter, the Commission shall prepare and submit a budget to the President. Whenever the Commission submits a budget estimate or request to the President or the Office of Management and Budget, the Commission shall concurrently transmit copies of the estimate or request to the Committee on Appropriations of the Senate, the Committee on Appropriations of the House of Representatives, the Committee on Banking, Housing, and Urban Affairs of the Senate, and the Committee on Financial Services of the House of Representatives.

"(2) SUBMISSION TO CONGRESS. —The President shall submit each budget submitted under paragraph (1) to Congress, in unaltered form, together with the annual budget for the Administration submitted by the President.

"(3) CONTENTS. —The Commission shall include in each budget submitted under paragraph (1) —

"(A) an itemization of the amount of funds necessary to carry out the functions of the Commission.

"(B) an amount to be designated as contingency funding to be used by the Commission to address unanticipated needs; and

"(C) a designation of any activities of the Commission for which multi–year budget authority would be suitable.".

(2) BUDGET OF THE PRESIDENT. —For fiscal year 2012, and each fiscal year

于2011年8月31日公布根据经本法修正后的《1933年证券法》第6(b)条[《美国法典》第十五编第77f(b)节]设定的费率(但2012财政年度的费率除外)。

(c)**拨款授权**。——《1934年证券交易法》第35条(《美国法典》第十五编第78kk节)修正后全文如下:

"第35条　拨款授权

在已批准向证券交易委员会划拨的任何其他资金之外，兹授权向证券交易委员会进行如下拨款,用于履行其职能、权力和职责——

(1)2011财政年度,13亿美元;

(2)2012财政年度,15亿美元;

(3)2013财政年度,17.5亿美元;

(4)2014财政年度,20亿美元;及

(5)2015财政年度,22.5亿美元。"

(d)**提交预算申请**。——

(1)**修正**。——在《1934年证券交易法》第31条(《美国法典》第十五编第78ee节)结尾处增加如下内容,作为对该条的修正:

"(m)**提交证券交易委员会预算申请**。——

(1)**预算要求**。——对于2012财政年度以及之后的每一财政年度,证券交易委员会均应编制并向总统提交一份预算。证券交易委员会向总统或行政管理和预算办公室提交概算或预算申请时,证券交易委员会应同时向参议院拨款委员会、众议院拨款委员会、参议院银行、住房与城市事务委员会以及众议院金融服务委员会提交该等概算或预算申请的复本。

(2)**向国会提交预算**。——对于根据第(1)款提交的每份预算,总统均应保留其原有形式,并与总统提交的联邦政府年度预算一并向国会提交。

(3)**内容**。——证券交易委员会应在根据第(1)款提交的所有预算中——

(A)逐项列明履行证券交易委员会职能所需必要资金的金额。

(B)说明证券交易委员会用于应对意外需求的应急资金金额;及

(C)说明需要批准跨年度预算的任何证券交易委员会活动。"

(2)**总统预算**。——对于2012财政年度及之后的每一财政年度,总统向国会提交

thereafter, the annual budget for the Administration submitted by the President to Congress shall reflect the amendments made by this section.

(e) SECURITIES AND EXCHANGE COMMISSION RESERVE FUND.—

(1) AMENDMENT.—Section 4 of the Securities Exchange Act of 1934 (15 U.S.C. 78d), as amended by this Act, is amended by adding at the end the following:

"(i) SECURITIES AND EXCHANGE COMMISSION RESERVE FUND.—

"(1) RESERVE FUND ESTABLISHED.—There is established in the Treasury of the United States a separate fund, to be known as the 'Securities and Exchange Commission Reserve Fund' (referred to in this subsection as the 'Reserve Fund').

"(2) RESERVE FUND AMOUNTS.—

"(A) IN GENERAL.—Except as provided in subparagraph (B), any registration fees collected by the Commission under section 6(b) of the Securities Act of 1933 (15 U.S.C.77f(b)) or section 24(f) of the Investment Company Act of 1940 (15 U.S.C.80a-24(f)) shall be deposited into the Reserve Fund.

"(B) LIMITATIONS.—For any 1 fiscal year—

"(i) the amount deposited in the Fund may not exceed $50,000,000; and

"(ii) the balance in the Fund may not exceed $100,000,000.

"(C) EXCESS FEES.—Any amounts in excess of the limitations described in subparagraph (B) that the Commission collects from registration fees under section 6(b) of the Securities Act of 1933 (15 U.S.C.77f(b)) or section 24(f) of the Investment Company Act of 1940 (15 U.S.C.80a-24(f)) shall be deposited in the General Fund of the Treasury of the United States and shall not be available for obligation by the Commission.

"(3) USE OF AMOUNTS IN RESERVE FUND.—The Commission may obligate amounts in the Reserve Fund, not to exceed a total of $100,000,000 in any 1 fiscal year, as the Commission determines is necessary to carry out the functions of the Commission. Any amounts in the reserve fund shall remain available until expended. Not later than 10 days after the date on which the Commission obligates amounts under this paragraph, the Commission shall notify Congress of the date, amount, and purpose of the obligation.

"(4) RULE OF CONSTRUCTION.—Amounts collected and deposited in the Reserve Fund shall not be construed to be Government funds or appropriated monies and shall not be subject to apportionment for the purpose of chapter 15 of title 31, United States Code, or under any other authority.".

(2) EFFECTIVE DATE.—The amendment made by this subsection shall take effect on October 1, 2011.

的政府年度预算均应反映本条作出的修正。

(e)**证券交易委员会储备基金**。——

(1)**修正**。——在经本法修正后的《1934年证券交易法》第4条(《美国法典》第十五编第78d节)结尾处增加如下内容,作为对该条的进一步修正:

“(i)**证券交易委员会储备基金**。——

(1)**设立储备基金**。——美国财政部下设名为‘证券交易委员会储备基金’的独立基金(本子条以下简称储备基金)。

(2)**储备基金金额**。——

(A)**一般规定**。——除第(B)子款规定的情形外,证券交易委员会根据《1933年证券法》第6(b)条[《美国法典》第十五编第77f(b)节]或《1940年投资公司法》第24(f)条[《美国法典》第十五编第80a-24(f)节]收取的任何注册费用均应存入储备基金。

(B)**限制**。——对于任何一个财政年度而言——

(i)存入储备基金的金额均不得超过5000万美元;且

(ii)储备基金内的余额不得超过1亿美元。

(C)**超额收费**。——证券交易委员会根据《1933年证券法》第6(b)条[《美国法典》第十五编第77f(b)节]或《1940年投资公司法》第24(f)条[《美国法典》第十五编第80a-24(f)节]从注册费用中收取的超出第(B)子款所述限额的任何款项均应存入美国财政部一般基金。证券交易委员会不得将该等款项用于偿还债务。

(3)**储备基金款项的使用**。——证券交易委员会可以在任何一个财政年度,将其判定对于履行其职能确属必要的储备基金款项指定用于既定用途,但是总额不得超过1亿美元。储备基金的任何款项均应随时处于可支用状态,不得另作他用。证券交易委员会应在根据本款将储备基金款项指定用于既定用途之日后10内,通知国会指定使用储备基金款项的日期、金额和目的。

(4)解释规则。——收取并存入储备基金的款项不得被视为属于政府资金或拨款,也不得根据《美国法典》第三十一编第十五章或任何其他法律规定进行分配。”

(2)生效日。——本子条所做修正应于2011年10月1日生效。

TITLE X — BUREAU OF CONSUMER FINANCIAL PROTECTION

SEC. 1001. SHORT TITLE.

This title may be cited as the "Consumer Financial Protection Act of 2010".

SEC. 1002. DEFINITIONS.

Except as otherwise provided in this title, for purposes of this title, the following definitions shall apply:

(1) AFFILIATE. — The term "affiliate" means any person that controls, is controlled by, or is under common control with another person.

(2) BUREAU. — The term "Bureau" means the Bureau of Consumer Financial Protection.

(3) BUSINESS OF INSURANCE. — The term "business of insurance" means the writing of insurance or the reinsuring of risks by an insurer, including all acts necessary to such writing or reinsuring and the activities relating to the writing of insurance or the reinsuring of risks conducted by persons who act as, or are, officers, directors, agents, or employees of insurers or who are other persons authorized to act on behalf of such persons.

(4) CONSUMER. — The term "consumer" means an individual or an agent, trustee, or representative acting on behalf of an individual.

(5) CONSUMER FINANCIAL PRODUCT OR SERVICE. — The term "consumer financial product or service" means any financial product or service that is described in one or more categories under —

(A) paragraph (15) and is offered or provided for use by consumers primarily for personal, family, or household purposes; or

(B) clause (i), (iii), (ix), or (x) of paragraph (15)(A), and is delivered, offered, or provided inconnection with a consumer financial product or service referred to in subparagraph (A).

(6) COVERED PERSON. — The term "covered person" means —

(A) any person that engages in offering or providing a consumer financial product or

第十编——消费者金融保护局

第1001条　简称

引述本编时,可简称《2010年消费者金融保护法》。

第1002条　定义

就本编而言,除本编另有规定的情形外,下列术语应适用如下定义:

(1)**关联方**。——“关联方”一词系指控制另一主体的任何主体、被另一主体控制的任何主体或与另一主体受同一控制的任何主体。

(2)**消费者金融保护局**。——“消费者金融保护局”一词系指美国消费者金融保护局。

(3)**保险业务**。——“保险业务”一词系指保险公司承保保险或对风险进行再保险的行为,包括对于开展该等承保或再保险活动而言确属必要的所有相关行为;以及保险公司管理人员、董事、代理人或职员,或者以该等身份行事的人,或者该等人员的授权代表开展的与该等保险承保或风险再保险业务相关的活动。

(4)**消费者**。——“消费者”一词系指个人或代表个人行事的代理人、受托人或代表。

(5)**消费者金融产品或服务**。——“消费者金融产品或服务”一词系指属于如下某一类别或多个类别的任何金融产品或服务——

(A)第(15)款规定的主要供消费者个人、家庭或共同居住人使用而要约或提供的金融产品或服务;或

(B)第(15)(A)款第(i)项、第(iii)项、第(ix)项或第(x)项规定的就第(A)子款所述消费者金融产品或服务而交付、要约或提供的相关金融产品或服务。

(6)**所涉主体**。——“所涉主体”一词系指——

(A)要约或提供消费者金融产品或服务的任何主体;及

service; and

(B) any affiliate of a person described in subparagraph (A) if such affiliate acts as a service provider to such person.

(7) CREDIT. — The term "credit" means the right granted by a person to a consumer to defer payment of a debt, incur debt and defer its payment, or purchase property or services and defer payment for such purchase.

(8) DEPOSIT-TAKING ACTIVITY. — The term "deposit-taking activity" means —

(A) the acceptance of deposits, maintenance of deposit accounts, or the provision of services related to the acceptance of deposits or the maintenance of deposit accounts;

(B) the acceptance of funds, the provision of other services related to the acceptance of funds, or the maintenance of member share accounts by a credit union; or

(C) the receipt of funds or the equivalent thereof, as the Bureau may determine by rule or order, received or held by a covered person (or an agent for a covered person) for the purpose of facilitating a payment or transferring funds or value of funds between a consumer and a third party.

(9) DESIGNATED TRANSFER DATE. — The term "designated transfer date" means the date established under section 1062.

(10) DIRECTOR. — The term "Director" means the Director of the Bureau.

(11) ELECTRONIC CONDUIT SERVICES. — The term "electronic conduit services" —

(A) means the provision, by a person, of electronic data transmission, routing, intermediate or transient storage, or connections to a telecommunications system or network; and

(B) does not include a person that provides electronic conduit services if, when providing such services, the person —

(i) selects or modifies the content of the electronic data;

(ii) transmits, routes, stores, or provides connections for electronic data, including financial data, in a manner that such financial data is differentiated from other types of data of the same form that such person transmits, routes, or stores, or with respect to which, provides connections; or

(iii) is a payee, payor, correspondent, or similar party to a payment transaction with a consumer.

(12) ENUMERATED CONSUMER LAWS. — Except as otherwise specifically provided in section 1029, subtitle G or subtitle H, the term "enumerated consumer laws" means —

(A) the Alternative Mortgage Transaction Parity Act of 1982 (12 U.S.C. 3801 et seq.);

(B)第(A)子款所述主体的任何关联方,前提是该关联方担任该等主体的服务提供者。

(7)**信用**。——"信用"一词系指某一主体向消费者授予的递延偿债权,或者举债并递延偿还的权利,或者购买财产或服务并递延支付购买款项的权利。

(8)**吸收存款活动**。——"吸收存款活动"一词系指——

(A)接受存款、维持存款账户,或为接受存款或维持存款账户提供相关服务;

(B)信贷联盟开展的接受资金、提供与接受资金相关的其他服务,或者维持会员共享账户的活动;或

(C)所涉主体(或所涉主体的代理人)为促进消费者与第三方之间的款项支付或者资金或者资金或价值的转移,而接收或持有资金或接收或持有消费者金融保护局发布的规则或命令所确定的资金等价物的活动。

(9)**指定转移日**。——"指定转移日"一词系指根据第1062条确定的日期。

(10)**消费者金融保护局局长**。——"消费者金融保护局局长"一词系指美国消费者金融保护局的局长。

(11)**电子渠道服务**。——"电子渠道服务"一词——

(A)系指由某一主体提供的电子数据传输、路由、过渡性或临时存储服务,或者电子通讯系统或网络的连接服务;且

(B)不包括在提供电子渠道服务时存在如下情形主体提供的服务——

(i)对电子数据内容进行选择或修改;

(ii)为电子数据(包括金融数据)提供传输、路由、存储或链接服务的方式,不同于该等主体为相同形式的其他类别的数据提供传输、路由、存储或链接服务的方式;或

(iii)在与消费者的支付交易中作为收款人、付款人、代理行或类似当事方行事。

(12)**明文列举的消费者法律**。——除第1029条、第G子编或第H子编另有明确规定的情形外,"明文列举的消费者法律"一词系指——

(A)《1982年另类抵押贷款交易平价法》(《美国法典》第十二编第3801节及其后条文);

(B) the Consumer Leasing Act of 1976 (15 U.S.C. 1667 et seq.);

(C) the Electronic Fund Transfer Act (15 U.S.C. 1693 et seq.), except with respect to section 920 of that Act;

(D) the Equal Credit Opportunity Act (15 U.S.C. 1691 et seq.);

(E) the Fair Credit Billing Act (15 U.S.C. 1666 et seq.);

(F) the Fair Credit Reporting Act (15 U.S.C. 1681 et seq.), except with respect to sections 615(e) and 628 of that Act (15 U.S.C. 1681m(e), 1681w);

(G) the Home Owners Protection Act of 1998 (12 U.S.C. 4901 et seq.);

(H) the Fair Debt Collection Practices Act (15 U.S.C. 1692 et seq.);

(I) subsections (b) through (f) of section 43 of the Federal Deposit Insurance Act (12 U.S.C. 1831t(c) -(f));

(J) sections 502 through 509 of the Gramm-Leach-Bliley Act (15 U.S.C. 6802-6809) except for section 505 as it applies to section 501(b);

(K) the Home Mortgage Disclosure Act of 1975 (12 U.S.C. 2801 et seq.);

(L) the Home Ownership and Equity Protection Act of 1994 (15 U.S.C. 1601 note);

(M) the Real Estate Settlement Procedures Act of 1974 (12 U.S.C. 2601 et seq.);

(N) the S.A.F.E. Mortgage Licensing Act of 2008 (12 U.S.C. 5101 et seq.);

(O) the Truth in Lending Act (15 U.S.C. 1601 et seq.);

(P) the Truth in Savings Act (12 U.S.C. 4301 et seq.);

(Q) section 626 of the Omnibus Appropriations Act, 2009 (Public Law 111-8); and

(R) the Interstate Land Sales Full Disclosure Act (15 U.S.C. 1701).

(13) FAIR LENDING. — The term "fair lending" means fair, equitable, and nondiscriminatory access to credit for consumers.

(14) FEDERAL CONSUMER FINANCIAL LAW. — The term "Federal consumer financial law" means the provisions of this title, the enumerated consumer laws, the laws for which authorities are transferred under subtitles F and H, and any rule or order prescribed by the Bureau under this title, an enumerated consumer law, or pursuant to the authorities transferred under subtitles F and H. The term does not include the Federal Trade Commission Act.

(15) FINANCIAL PRODUCT OR SERVICE. —

(A) IN GENERAL. — The term "financial product or service" means —

(i) extending credit and servicing loans, including acquiring, purchasing, selling, brokering, or other extensions of credit (other than solely extending commercial credit to a person who originates consumer credit transactions);

(ii) extending or brokering leases of personal or real property that are the functional equivalent of purchase finance arrangements, if —

(B)《1976年消费者租赁法》(《美国法典》第十五编第1667节及其后条文);

(C)《电子资金划拨法》(《美国法典》第十五编第1693节及其后条文),但该法第920条除外;

(D)《信贷机会平等法》(《美国法典》第十五编第1691节及其后条文);

(E)《公平信用结账法》(《美国法典》第十五编第1666节及其后条文);

(F)《公平信用报告法》(《美国法典》第十五编第1681节及其后条文),但该法第615(e)条及第628条[《美国法典》第十五编第1681m(e)节及第1681w节]除外;

(G)《1998年业主保护法》(《美国法典》第十二编第4901节及其后条文);

(H)《公平债务催收作业法》(《美国法典》第十五编第1692节及其后条文);

(I)《联邦存款保险法》第43条第(b)子条至第(f)子条(《美国法典》第十二编第1831t(c)~(f)节);

(J)《格雷姆—里奇—比利雷法》第502条至第509条(《美国法典》第十五编第6802~6809节),但适用于第501(b)条时,第505条除外;

(K)《1975年住房抵押贷款披露法》(《美国法典》第十二编第2801节及其后条文);

(L)《1994年住房所有权和房屋权益保护法》(《美国法典》第十五编第1601节注释);

(M)《1974年房地产结算程序法》(《美国法典》第十二编第2601节及其后条文);

(N)《2008年安全和公平执行抵押贷款发起人许可法》(《美国法典》第十二编第5101节及其后条文);

(O)《诚实信贷法》(《美国法典》第十五编第1601节及其后条文);

(P)《诚实储蓄法》(《美国法典》第十二编第4301节及其后条文);

(Q)《2009年综合拨款法》(第111—8号公法)第626条;及

(R)《州际土地销售完全披露法》(《美国法典》第十五编第1701节)。

(13)**公平贷款**。——“公平贷款”一词系指消费者能够公平、公正且不受歧视地获得的信贷。

(14)**联邦消费者金融法律**。——“联邦消费者金融法律”一词系指:本编规定;明文列举的消费者法律;根据第F子编和第H子编将相关职权转移给消费者金融保护局的法律;以及消费者金融保护局根据本编、某一明文列举的消费者法律或根据第F子编和第H子编下转移的权力制定的任何规则或命令。该词不包括《联邦贸易委员会法》。

(15)**金融产品或服务**。——

(A)**一般规定**。——“金融产品或服务”一词系指——

(i)授信和贷款相关服务,包括取得、购买、出售信贷,以及信贷经纪或其他授信活动(仅向消费者信贷交易发起人授予商业信用的行为不在此列);

(ii)提供功能上等同于购买融资安排的动产/不动产租赁,或为该等租赁提供经纪服务,前提是——

(I) the lease is on a non-operating basis;

(II) the initial term of the lease is at least 90 days; and

(III) in the case of a lease involving real property, at the inception of the initial lease, the transaction is intended to result in ownership of the leased property to be transferred to the lessee, subject to standards prescribed by the Bureau;

(iii) providing real estate settlement services, except such services excluded under subparagraph (C), or performing appraisals of real estate or personal property;

(iv) engaging in deposit-taking activities, transmitting or exchanging funds, or otherwise acting as a custodian of funds or any financial instrument for use by or on behalf of a consumer;

(v) selling, providing, or issuing stored value or payment instruments, except that, in the case of a sale of, or transaction to reload, stored value, only if the seller exercises substantial control over the terms or conditions of the stored value provided to the consumer where, for purposes of this clause —

(I) a seller shall not be found to exercise substantial control over the terms or conditions of the stored value if the seller is not a party to the contract with the consumer for the stored value product, and another person is principally responsible for establishing the terms or conditions of the stored value; and

(II) advertising the nonfinancial goods or services of the seller on the stored value card or device is not in itself an exercise of substantial control over the terms or conditions;

(vi) providing check cashing, check collection, or check guaranty services;

(vii) providing payments or other financial data processing products or services to a consumer by any technological means, including processing or storing financial or banking data for any payment instrument, or through any payments systems or network used for processing payments data, including payments made through an online banking system or mobile telecommunications network, except that a person shall not be deemed to be a covered person with respect to financial data processing solely because the person —

(I) is a merchant, retailer, or seller of any nonfinancial good or service who engages in financial data processing by transmitting or storing payments data about a consumer exclusively for purpose of initiating payments instructions by the consumer to pay such person for the purchase of, or to complete a commercial transaction for, such nonfinancial good or service sold directly by such person to the consumer; or

(II) provides access to a host server to a person for purposes of enabling that person to establish and maintain a website;

(viii) providing financial advisory services (other than services relating to securities provided by a person regulated by the Commission or a person regulated by a State securities Commission, but only to the extent that such person acts in a regulated capacity) to

(I)租赁属于非经营性租赁;

(II)租赁的初始期限不短于90天;且

(III)如果租赁涉及不动产,在初始租约签订之时,交易之目的在于在不违反消费者金融保护局所制定标准的前提下,实现租赁财产的所有权向承租人转移;

(iii)提供房地产结算服务[不包括第(C)子款排除的服务],或者开展房地产或动产评估活动;

(iv)从事吸收存款活动、资金转账或汇兑活动,或者以消费者的资金或金融工具的托管人身份开展其他活动;

(v)出售、提供或发行储值或支付工具,但是,对于储值出售交易或储值充存交易而言,必须以销售商对向消费者提供的储值条款或条件拥有实质控制权为前提;在此种情况下,就本项而言——

(I)如果销售商并非与消费者订立储值产品合同的当事方,而由其他主体作为主要负责人设定储值条款或条件,则销售商不得被认定为对储值条款或条件拥有实质控制权;且

(II)仅在储值卡或设备上对销售商的非金融产品或服务进行广告宣传的行为本质上并不意味着对该等条款或条件行使实质控制权;

(vi)提供支票兑现、支票托收或支票担保服务;

(vii)通过任何技术手段向消费者提供支付数据处理产品或服务,或其他金融数据处理产品或服务(包括对任何支付工具的金融或银行数据进行处理或存储),或通过用于处理支付数据的任何支付系统或网络提供前述服务(上文所述支付包括通过网上银行系统或移动电子通信网络进行的支付),但是,不得仅因相关主体存在如下情形,就将其视为金融数据处理的所涉主体——

(I)该主体身为任何非金融产品或服务的商人、零售商或销售商,且其通过传送或存储消费者支付数据从事金融数据处理服务,且其传送或存储消费者支付数据的目的仅在于在该等主体直接向消费者出售非金融产品或服务之时,使消费者能够作出付款指示,向该等主体进行支付,或者完成该等非金融产品或服务的商业交易;或

(II)向他人提供主机服务器接入,以便该人建立和维护网站;

(viii)就具体金融事宜或专有金融产品或服务向消费者提供金融顾问服务(不包括受证券交易委员会或州证券委员会监管的主体以该等受监管身份提供的证券相关服务;也不包括发行任何真正意义上的报纸、新闻杂志或者面向大众并定期发行的商

consumers on individual financial matters or relating to proprietary financial products or services (other than by publishing any bona fide newspaper, news magazine, or business or financial publication of general and regular circulation, including publishing market data, news, or data analytics or investment information or recommendations that are not tailored to the individual needs of a particular consumer), including —

(I) providing credit counseling to any consumer; and

(II) providing services to assist a consumer with debt management or debt settlement, modifying the terms of any extension of credit, or avoiding foreclosure;

(ix) collecting, analyzing, maintaining, or providing consumer report information or other account information, including information relating to the credit history of consumers, used or expected to be used in connection with any decision regarding the offering or provision of a consumer financial product or service, except to the extent that —

(I) a person —

(aa) collects, analyzes, or maintains information that relates solely to the transactions between a consumer and such person;

(bb) provides the information described in item (aa) to an affiliate of such person; or

(cc) provides information that is used or expected to be used solely in any decision regarding the offering or provision of a product or service that is not a consumer financial product or service, including a decision for employment, government licensing, or a residential lease or tenancy involving a consumer; and

(II) the information described in subclause (I)(aa) is not used by such person or affiliate in connection with any decision regarding the offering or provision of a consumer financial product or service to the consumer, other than credit described in section 1027(a)(2)(A);

(x) collecting debt related to any consumer financial product or service; and

(xi) such other financial product or service as may be defined by the Bureau, by regulation, for purposes of this title, if the Bureau finds that such financial product or service is —

(I) entered into or conducted as a subterfuge or with a purpose to evade any Federal consumer financial law; or

(II) permissible for a bank or for a financial holding company to offer or to provide under any provision of a Federal law or regulation applicable to a bank or a financial holding company, and has, or likely will have, a material impact on consumers.

(B) RULE OF CONSTRUCTION. —

(i) IN GENERAL. — For purposes of subparagraph (A)(xi)(II), and subject to clause (ii) of this subparagraph, the following activities provided to a covered person shall not, for purposes of this title, be considered incidental or complementary to a financial activity

业或金融出版物,包括发布非按照具体消费者的个性化需求定制的市场数据、新闻、数据分析或者投资信息或建议),包括——

(I)向任何消费者提供信用咨询服务;及

(II)向消费者提供协助服务,协助其进行债务管理或债务结算、修改授信条款或避免止赎;

(ix)收集、分析、维护或提供消费者报告信息或其他账户信息,包括在就消费者金融产品或服务的要约或提供作出相关决策时,所使用或预计使用的与消费者信用记录相关的信息,但如下情况除外——

(I)该主体——

(aa)收集、分析或维护的信息仅限于消费者与该主体自身之间的交易有关的信息;

(bb)向其关联方提供第(aa)目所述信息;或

(cc)所提供的信息仅用于或预计仅用于与非消费者金融产品或服务的要约或提供相关的任何决策,包括与消费者相关的雇用决策、政府许可决策或者住宅出租或租赁决策;且

(II)该等主体或关联方未将第(I)(aa)子项所述信息用于与消费者金融产品或服务[但第1027(a)(2)(A)条所述信用除外]的要约或提供相关的决策;

(x)催收与任何消费者金融产品或服务相关的债务;及

(xi)消费者金融保护局为本编之宗旨而发布规章界定的任何其他金融产品或服务,前提是消费者金融保护局认定该等金融产品或服务符合如下情形——

(I)该等产品或服务系为掩盖其他目的或为规避任何联邦消费者金融法律而达成或提供;或

(II)银行或金融控股公司可按照适用的联邦法律或规章的任何规定要约或提供该等产品或服务,且该等产品或服务已经或可能对消费者造成重大影响。

(B)**解释规则**。——

(i)**一般规定**。——就第(A)(xi)(II)子款而言,在不违反本子款第(ii)项的前提下,向所涉主体提供的如下活动,就本编而言,不得视为适用于金融控股公司的任何联邦法律或规章规定允许金融控股公司从事的金融活动的附带或补充活动:

permissible for a financial holding company to engage in under any provision of a Federal law or regulation applicable to a financial holding company:

(I) Providing information products or services to a covered person for identity authentication.

(II) Providing information products or services for fraud or identify theft detection, prevention, or investigation.

(III) Providing document retrieval or delivery services.

(IV) Providing public records information retrieval.

(V) Providing information products or services for anti-money laundering activities.

(ii) LIMITATION. — Nothing in clause (i) may be construed as modifying or limiting the authority of the Bureau to exercise any —

(I) examination or enforcement powers authority under this title with respect to a covered person or service provider engaging in an activity described in subparagraph (A)(ix); or

(II) powers authorized by this title to prescribe rules, issue orders, or take other actions under any enumerated consumer law or law for which the authorities are transferred under subtitle F or H.

(C) EXCLUSIONS. — The term "financial product or service" does not include —

(i) the business of insurance; or

(ii) electronic conduit services.

(16) FOREIGN EXCHANGE. — The term "foreign exchange" means the exchange, for compensation, of currency of the United States or of a foreign government for currency of another government.

(17) INSURED CREDIT UNION. — The term "insured credit union" has the same meaning as in section 101 of the Federal Credit Union Act (12 U.S.C. 1752).

(18) PAYMENT INSTRUMENT. — The term "payment instrument" means a check, draft, warrant, money order, traveler's check, electronic instrument[1], or other instrument, payment of funds, or monetary value (other than currency).

(19) PERSON. — The term "person" means an individual, partnership, company, corporation, association (incorporated or unincorporated), trust, estate, cooperative organization, or other entity.

(20) PERSON REGULATED BY THE COMMODITY FUTURES TRADING COMMISSION. — The term "person regulated by the Commodity Futures Trading Commission" means any person that is registered, or required by statute or regulation to be

1 参照美国各州立法中有关"Payment instrument"的定义，本款中"or other instrument, payment of funds, or monetary value (other than currency)"似乎"other instrument"后面缺少介词"for"，否则之后出现的"payment of funds, or monetary value (other than currency)"无法与前文衔接，译文中按有"for"处理。——译者注

(I)为证明身份之目的向所涉主体提供信息产品或服务。

(II)为发现、预防或调查欺诈或身份盗用行为之目的,提供信息产品或服务。

(III)提供文件检索或交付服务。

(IV)提供公共记录信息检索服务。

(V)为反洗钱活动提供信息产品或服务。

(ii)**限制**。——第(i)项的任何内容均不得被解释为修改或限制消费者金融保护局行使如下任何权力的权限——

(I)根据本编规定,针对从事第(A)(ix)子款所述活动的所涉主体或服务提供者进行检查或开展执法的权力;或

(II)按照本编授权,根据任何明文列举的消费者法律,或根据已按照第F子编或第H子将相关职权转移给消费者金融保护局的法律,制定规则、发布命令或采取其他行动的权力。

(C)**除外规定**。——"金融产品或服务"一词不包括——

(i)保险业务;或

(ii)电子渠道服务。

(16)**外汇**。——"外汇"一词系指为获取其他政府的货币,而对美国货币或外国政府货币进行的有偿兑换。

(17)**参保信贷联盟**。——"参保信贷联盟"一词的含义以《联邦信贷联盟法》第101条(《美国法典》第十二编第1752节)的定义为准。

(18)**支付工具**。——"支付工具"一词系指支票、汇票、权证、邮政汇票、旅行支票、电子支付工具以及其他资金或货币价值(不包括货币)的支付工具。

(19)**主体**。——"主体"一词系指个人、合伙、企业、公司、协会(法人制或非法人制)、信托、遗产和破产财团、合作社组织或其他实体。

(20)**受商品期货交易委员会监管的主体**。——"受商品期货交易委员会监管的主体"一词系指在商品期货交易委员会注册的任何主体或者根据制定法或规章应在商品期货交易委员会注册的任何主体,但仅以该等主体从事根据《商品交易法》应受商

registered, with the Commodity Futures Trading Commission, but only to the extent that the activities of such person are subject to the jurisdiction of the Commodity Futures Trading Commission under the Commodity Exchange Act.

(21) PERSON REGULATED BY THE COMMISSION. — The term "person regulated by the Commission" means a person who is —

(A) a broker or dealer that is required to be registered under the Securities Exchange Act of 1934;

(B) an investment adviser that is registered under the Investment Advisers Act of 1940;

(C) an investment company that is required to be registered under the Investment Company Act of 1940, and any company that has elected to be regulated as a business development company under that Act;

(D) a national securities exchange that is required to be registered under the Securities Exchange Act of 1934;

(E) a transfer agent that is required to be registered under the Securities Exchange Act of 1934;

(F) a clearing corporation that is required to be registered under the Securities Exchange Act of 1934;

(G) any self–regulatory organization that is required to be registered with the Commission;

(H) any nationally recognized statistical rating organization that is required to be registered with the Commission;

(I) any securities information processor that is required to be registered with the Commission;

(J) any municipal securities dealer that is required to be registered with the Commission;

(K) any other person that is required to be registered with the Commission under the Securities Exchange Act of 1934; and

(L) any employee, agent, or contractor acting on behalf of, registered with, or providing services to, any person described in any of subparagraphs (A) through (K), but only to the extent that any person described in any of subparagraphs (A) through (K), or the employee, agent, or contractor of such person, acts in a regulated capacity.

(22) PERSON REGULATED BY A STATE INSURANCE REGULATOR. — The term "person regulated by a State insurance regulator" means any person that is engaged in the business of insurance and subject to regulation by any State insurance regulator, but only to the extent that such person acts in such capacity.

(23) PERSON THAT PERFORMS INCOME TAX PREPARATION ACTIVITIES FOR CONSUMERS. — The term "person that performs income tax preparation activities for

品期货交易委员会管辖的活动为限。

(21)**受证券交易委员会监管的主体**。——“受证券交易委员会监管的主体”一词系指如下主体——

(A)应根据《1934年证券交易法》注册的经纪商或自营商;

(B)根据《1940年投资顾问法》注册的投资顾问;

(C)应根据《1940年投资顾问法》注册的投资公司,以及根据该法选择以企业发展支持公司身份接受监管的任何公司;

(D)应根据《1934年证券交易法》注册的全国性证券交易所;

(E)应《1934年证券交易法》注册的过户代理人;

(F)应根据《1934年证券交易法》注册的结算公司;

(G)应在证券交易委员会注册的任何自律监管组织;

(H)应在证券交易委员会注册的任何全国公认统计评级组织;

(I)应在证券交易委员会注册的任何证券信息处理机构;

(J)应在证券交易委员会注册的任何市政证券自营商;

(K)应根据《1934年证券交易法》在证券交易委员会注册的任何其他主体;及

(L)代表第(A)子款至第(K)子款任何子款所述主体行事的、在该等主体处注册或者向该等主体提供服务的任何雇员、代理人或承包商,但仅以该等主体或者该等主体的雇员、代理人或承包商以受监管者身份行事的情形为限。

(22)**受州保险监管者监管的主体**。——“受州保险监管者监管的主体”一词系指从事保险业务并接受任何州保险监管者监管的任何主体,但仅以该等主体以受监管者身份行事的情形为限。

(23)**为消费者提供所得税报税服务的主体**。——“为消费者提供所得税报税服务的主体”一词系指——

consumers" means —

(A) any tax return preparer (as defined in section 7701(a)(36) of the Internal Revenue Code of 1986), regardless of whether compensated, but only to the extent that the person acts in such capacity;

(B) any person regulated by the Secretary under section 330 of title 31, United States Code, but only to the extent that the person acts in such capacity; and

(C) any authorized IRS e-file Providers (as defined for purposes of section 7216 of the Internal Revenue Code of 1986), but only to the extent that the person acts in such capacity.

(24) PRUDENTIAL REGULATOR. — The term "prudential regulator" means —

(A) in the case of an insured depository institution or depository institution holding company (as defined in section 3 of the Federal Deposit Insurance Act), or subsidiary of such institution or company, the appropriate Federal banking agency, as that term is defined in section 3 of the Federal Deposit Insurance Act; and

(B) in the case of an insured credit union, the National Credit Union Administration.

(25) RELATED PERSON. — The term "related person" —

(A) shall apply only with respect to a covered person that is not a bank holding company (as that term is defined in section 2 of the Bank Holding Company Act of 1956), credit union, or depository institution;

(B) shall be deemed to mean a covered person for all purposes of any provision of Federal consumer financial law; and

(C) means —

(i) any director, officer, or employee charged with managerial responsibility for, or controlling shareholder of, or agent for, such covered person;

(ii) any shareholder, consultant, joint venture partner, or other person, as determined by the Bureau (by rule or on a case-by-case basis) who materially participates in the conduct of the affairs of such covered person; and

(iii) any independent contractor (including any attorney, appraiser, or accountant) who knowingly or recklessly participates in any —

(I) violation of any provision of law or regulation; or

(II) breach of a fiduciary duty.

(26) SERVICE PROVIDER. —

(A) IN GENERAL. — The term "service provider" means any person that provides a material service to a covered person in connection with the offering or provision by such covered person of a consumer financial product or service, including a person that —

(i) participates in designing, operating, or maintaining the consumer financial product or service; or

(ii) processes transactions relating to the consumer financial product or service (other

(A)任何报税人[定义见《1986年国内税收法典》第7701(a)(36)条],不论其提供的服务是否有偿,但仅以其以该等身份行事的情形为限;

(B)根据《美国法典》第三十一编第330节受财政部部长监管的任何主体,但仅以其以该等身份行事的情形为限;及

(C)经授权的国税局电子文件提供者(定义见《1986年国内税收法典》第7216条),但仅以其以该等身份行事的情形为限。

(24)**审慎监管者**。——“审慎监管者”一词——

(A)对于参保存款机构或存款机构控股公司(定义见《联邦存款保险法》第3条)或者该等机构或公司的子公司而言,系指相应的联邦银行业监管机关(定义见《联邦存款保险法》第3条);且

(B)对于参保信贷联盟而言,系指国家信贷联盟署。

(25)**关联主体**。——“关联主体”一词——

(A)应仅适用于并非银行控股公司(定义见《1956年银行控股公司法》第2条)、信贷联盟或存款机构的所涉主体;

(B)就任何联邦消费者金融法律规定而言,应视为指所涉主体;且

(C)指——

(i)上述所涉主体的任何董事、管理人员、承担管理责任的职员,或者控股股东或代理人;

(ii)消费者金融保护局发布的规则所确定的或消费者金融保护局基于个案情形判定的实质参与上述所涉主体之业务开展的任何股东、顾问、合营伙伴或其他主体;及

(iii)在知情的情况下或轻率地参与如下任何行为的任何独立缔约人(包括律师、评估师或会计师)——

(I)违反任何法律法规规定的行为;或

(II)违反受信义务的行为。

(26)**服务提供者**。——

(A)**一般规定**。——“服务提供者”一词系指在所涉主体要约或提供消费者金融产品或服务的过程中,向所涉主体提供重要服务的任何主体,包括——

(i)参与消费者金融产品或服务的设计、运作或维护的主体;或

(ii)处理与消费者金融产品或服务相关交易的主体(但无意或意外传送或处理金

than unknowingly or incidentally transmitting or processing financial data in a manner that such data is undifferentiated from other types of data of the same form as the person transmits or processes).

(B) EXCEPTIONS. — The term "service provider" does not include a person solely by virtue of such person offering or providing to a covered person —

(i) a support service of a type provided to businesses generally or a similar ministerial service; or

(ii) time or space for an advertisement for a consumer financial product or service through print, newspaper, or electronic media.

(C) RULE OF CONSTRUCTION. — A person that is a service provider shall be deemed to be a covered person to the extent that such person engages in the offering or provision of its own consumer financial product or service.

(27) STATE. — The term "State" means any State, territory, or possession of the United States, the District of Columbia, the Commonwealth of Puerto Rico, the Commonwealth of the Northern Mariana Islands, Guam, American Samoa, or the United States Virgin Islands or any federally recognized Indian tribe, as defined by the Secretary of the Interior under section 104(a) of the Federally Recognized Indian Tribe List Act of 1994 (25 U.S.C. 479a-1(a)).

(28) STORED VALUE. —

(A) IN GENERAL. — The term "stored value" means funds or monetary value represented in any electronic format, whether or not specially encrypted, and stored or capable of storage on electronic media in such a way as to be retrievable and transferred electronically, and includes a prepaid debit card or product, or any other similar product, regardless of whether the amount of the funds or monetary value may be increased or reloaded.

(B) EXCLUSION. — Notwithstanding subparagraph (A), the term "stored value" does not include a special purpose card or certificate, which shall be defined for purposes of this paragraph as funds or monetary value represented in any electronic format, whether or not specially encrypted, that is —

(i) issued by a merchant, retailer, or other seller of nonfinancial goods or services;

(ii) redeemable only for transactions with the merchant, retailer, or seller of nonfinancial goods or services or with an affiliate of such person, which affiliate itself is a merchant, retailer, or seller of nonfinancial goods or services;

(iii) issued in a specified amount that, except in the case of a card or product used solely for telephone services, may not be increased or reloaded;

(iv) purchased on a prepaid basis in exchange for payment; and

(v) honored upon presentation to such merchant, retailer, or seller of nonfinancial goods or services or an affiliate of such person, which affiliate itself is a merchant, retailer, or seller

融数据，且传送或处理方式与该主体传送或处理相同形式的其他类型的数据并无二致的除外)。

(B)**例外规定**。——任何主体不得仅因其向所涉主体要约或提供如下服务就被视为“服务提供者”——

(i)向企业提供的一般性支持服务或类似的行政服务;或

(ii)通过印刷品、报纸或电子媒体为消费者金融产品或服务提供广告时间或空间。

(C)**解释规则**。——如果服务提供者要约或提供消费者其自有的消费者金融产品或服务,则该等服务提供者应视为所涉主体。

(27)**州**。——“州”一词系指美国的任何州、准州或属地、哥伦比亚特区、波多黎各自由邦、北马里亚纳群岛自由邦、关岛、美属萨摩亚、美属维尔京群岛或内政部部长根据《1994年联邦政府承认的印第安人部落清单法》第104(a)条[《美国法典》第二十五编第479a-1(a)节]所定义的联邦政府承认的任何印第安人部落。

(28)**储值**。——

(A)**一般规定**。——“储值”一词系指任何以电子形式表示并存储或能够存储于电子媒介，且能够进行电子查询和划拨的资金或货币价值（不论是否进行了特殊加密),包括预付费借记卡或产品或者任何其他类似产品,而不论其资金或货币价值的金额是否可以追加或充值。

(B)**除外规定**。——无论第(A)子款如何规定,符合如下条件的特殊用途卡或凭证,不论是否进行了特殊加密,就本款而言,均应定义为以任何电子形式表示的资金或货币价值,而不得被视为“储值”——

(i)由非金融产品或服务的商人、零售商或其他销售商发行;

(ii)仅可通过与非金融产品或服务的商人、零售商或销售商之间的交易赎回,或者与该等主体的关联方(该等关联方本身为非金融产品或服务的商人、零售商或销售商)之间的交易赎回;

(iii)发行金额特定,不可进行追加或充值(但电话服务专用卡或产品除外);

(iv)为了进行付款而在预付基础上进行购买;且

(v)只有在购买非金融产品或服务之时,方可提交该等非金融产品或服务的商人、零售商或销售商或该等主体的关联方(该等关联方本身为非金融产品或服务的商人、

of nonfinancial goods or services, only for any nonfinancial goods or services.

(29) TRANSMITTING OR EXCHANGING FUNDS. — The term "transmitting or exchanging funds" means receiving currency, monetary value, or payment instruments from a consumer for the purpose of exchanging or transmitting the same by any means, including transmission by wire, facsimile, electronic transfer, courier, the Internet, or through bill payment services or through other businesses that facilitate third-party transfers within the United States or to or from the United States.

Subtitle A — Bureau of Consumer Financial Protection

SEC.1011. ESTABLISHMENT OF THE BUREAU OF CONSUMER FINANCIAL PROTECTION.

(a) BUREAU ESTABLISHED. — There is established in the Federal Reserve System, an independent bureau to be known as the "Bureau of Consumer Financial Protection", which shall regulate the offering and provision of consumer financial products or services under the Federal consumer financial laws. The Bureau shall be considered an Executive agency, as defined in section 105 of title 5, United States Code. Except as otherwise provided expressly by law, all Federal laws dealing with public or Federal contracts, property, works, officers, employees, budgets, or funds, including the provisions of chapters 5 and 7 of title 5, shall apply to the exercise of the powers of the Bureau.

(b) DIRECTOR AND DEPUTY DIRECTOR. —

(1) IN GENERAL. — There is established the position of the Director, who shall serve as the head of the Bureau.

(2) APPOINTMENT. — Subject to paragraph (3), the Director shall be appointed by the President, by and with the advice and consent of the Senate.

(3) QUALIFICATION. — The President shall nominate the Director from among individuals who are citizens of the United States.

(4) COMPENSATION. — The Director shall be compensated at the rate prescribed for level Ⅱ of the Executive Schedule under section 5313 of title 5, United States Code.

(5) DEPUTY DIRECTOR. — There is established the position of Deputy Director, who shall —

(A) be appointed by the Director; and

(B) serve as acting Director in the absence or unavailability of the Director.

(c) TERM. —

零售商或销售商)进行承兑。

(29)**资金转账或汇兑**。——“资金转账或汇兑”一词系指从消费者处接收货币、货币价值或支付工具,并通过任何方式(包括电汇、传真、电子划拨、快递、互联网、账单支付服务,或者能够促成第三方在美国境内进行资金过户、从境外汇入资金或将资金汇出境外的其他业务)对该等货币、货币价值或支付工具进行兑换或转账。

第A子编——消费者金融保护局

第1011条 消费者金融保护局的设立

(a)**消费者金融保护局的设立**。——兹于联邦储备系统之下设立独立的“消费者金融保护局”,负责根据联邦消费者金融法律监管消费者金融产品或服务的要约和提供。消费者金融保护局应视为《美国法典》第五编第105节定义的行政机关。除法律另有明确规定的情形外,消费者金融保护局在行使权力时,应适用所有与公共或联邦合同、财产、工程、管理人员、职员、预算或资金相关的联邦法律(包括第五编第五章和第七章的规定)。

(b)**消费者金融保护局局长和副局长**。——

(1)**一般规定**。——兹设立消费者金融保护局局长一职;消费者金融保护局局长应为消费者金融保护局的负责人。

(2)**任命**。——在不违反第(3)款规定的前提下,消费者金融保护局局长应在参议院建议和同意的基础上,由总统任命。

(3)**资格**。——消费者金融保护局局长由总统提名,被提名人应为美国公民。

(4)**薪酬**。——消费者金融保护局局长应按照《美国法典》第五编第5313节规定的“高级公务员序列第二级别”的标准领取薪酬。

(5)**消费者金融保护局副局长**。——兹设立消费者金融保护局副局长一职;消费者金融保护局副局长应——

(A)由消费者金融保护局局长任命;并

(B)在消费者金融保护局局长出现职位空缺或无法履职期间担任代理局长。

(c)**任期**。——

(1) IN GENERAL. — The Director shall serve for a term of 5 years.

(2) EXPIRATION OF TERM. — An individual may serve as Director after the expiration of the term for which appointed, until a successor has been appointed and qualified.

(3) REMOVAL FOR CAUSE. — The President may remove the Director for inefficiency, neglect of duty, or malfeasance in office.

(d) SERVICE RESTRICTION. — No Director or Deputy Director may hold any office, position, or employment in any Federal reserve bank, Federal home loan bank, covered person, or service provider during the period of service of such person as Director or Deputy Director.

(e) OFFICES. — The principal office of the Bureau shall be in the District of Columbia. The Director may establish regional offices of the Bureau, including in cities in which the Federal reserve banks, or branches of such banks, are located, in order to carry out the responsibilities assigned to the Bureau under the Federal consumer financial laws.

SEC. 1012. EXECUTIVE AND ADMINISTRATIVE POWERS.

(a) POWERS OF THE BUREAU. — The Bureau is authorized to establish the general policies of the Bureau with respect to all executive and administrative functions, including —

(1) the establishment of rules for conducting the general business of the Bureau, in a manner not inconsistent with this title;

(2) to bind the Bureau and enter into contracts;

(3) directing the establishment and maintenance of divisions or other offices within the Bureau, in order to carry out the responsibilities under the Federal consumer financial laws, and to satisfy the requirements of other applicable law;

(4) to coordinate and oversee the operation of all administrative, enforcement, and research activities of the Bureau;

(5) to adopt and use a seal;

(6) to determine the character of and the necessity for the obligations and expenditures of the Bureau;

(7) the appointment and supervision of personnel employed by the Bureau;

(8) the distribution of business among personnel appointed and supervised by the Director and among administrative units of the Bureau;

(9) the use and expenditure of funds;

(10) implementing the Federal consumer financial laws through rules, orders, guidance, interpretations, statements of policy, examinations, and enforcement actions; and

(11) performing such other functions as may be authorized or required by law.

(b) DELEGATION OF AUTHORITY. — The Director of the Bureau may delegate to any duly authorized employee, representative, or agent any power vested in the Bureau by law.

(1)**一般规定**。——消费者金融保护局局长的任期应为5年。

(2)**任期届满**。——消费者金融保护局局长任期届满之后,如其继任者尚未获得任命并具备任职资格的,可在其继任者获得任命并具备任职资格之前继续任职。

(3)**有因免职**。——消费者金融保护局局长任职期间出现工作效率低下、失职或渎职行为时,总统可以免除其职务。

(d)**服务限制**。——消费者金融保护局局长或副局长在任职期间,均不得在任何联邦储备银行、联邦住房贷款银行、所涉主体或服务提供者处担任任何职务、职位或与其存在雇佣关系。

(e)**办公场所**。——消费者金融保护局的主要办公场所应位于哥伦比亚特区。消费者金融保护局局长可以设立消费者金融保护局地区办公室(包括在联邦储备银行或其支行所在城市设立地区办公室),以履行联邦消费者金融法律赋予消费者金融保护局的职责。

第1012条　行政和管理权

(a)**消费者金融保护局的权力**。——消费者金融保护局有权针对所有行政和管理职能制定总体政策,包括——

(1)按照符合本编要求的方式,针对消费者金融保护局日常工作的开展制定规则;

(2)作出对消费者金融保护局有约束力的行为,以及订立合同;

(3)指挥消费者金融保护局内部部门或其他办公室的组建和维护,以履行联邦消费者金融法律所赋予的职责,并满足其他适用的法律中的要求;

(4)协调并监督消费者金融保护局所有管理、执法和研究活动的开展;

(5)批准和使用印章;

(6)确定消费者金融保护局负债和支出的性质和必要性;

(7)任命并领导监督消费者金融保护局所聘用的人员;

(8)为消费者金融保护局局长任命和领导管理的人员以及消费者金融保护局的行政单位分配工作;

(9)使用和支出资金;

(10)通过规则、命令、指引、解释、政策声明、检查和执法行动实施联邦消费者金融法律;并

(11)履行法律所赋予或规定的其他职能。

(b)**委托授权**。——消费者金融保护局局长可以将法律授予消费者金融保护局的任何权力委托给任何经正式授权的雇员、代表或代理人行使。

(c) AUTONOMY OF THE BUREAU.—

(1) COORDINATION WITH THE BOARD OF GOVERNORS.— Notwithstanding any other provision of law applicable to the supervision or examination of persons with respect to Federal consumer financial laws, the Board of Governors may delegate to the Bureau the authorities to examine persons subject to the jurisdiction of the Board of Governors for compliance with the Federal consumer financial laws.

(2) AUTONOMY.— Notwithstanding the authorities granted to the Board of Governors under the Federal Reserve Act, the Board of Governors may not—

(A) intervene in any matter or proceeding before the Director, including examinations or enforcement actions, unless otherwise specifically provided by law;

(B) appoint, direct, or remove any officer or employee of the Bureau; or

(C) merge or consolidate the Bureau, or any of the functions or responsibilities of the Bureau, with any division or office of the Board of Governors or the Federal reserve banks.

(3) RULES AND ORDERS.— No rule or order of the Bureau shall be subject to approval or review by the Board of Governors. The Board of Governors may not delay or prevent the issuance of any rule or order of the Bureau.

(4) RECOMMENDATIONS AND TESTIMONY.— No officer or agency of the United States shall have any authority to require the Director or any other officer of the Bureau to submit legislative recommendations, or testimony or comments on legislation, to any officer or agency of the United States for approval, comments, or review prior to the submission of such recommendations, testimony, or comments to the Congress, if such recommendations, testimony, or comments to the Congress include a statement indicating that the views expressed therein are those of the Director or such officer, and do not necessarily reflect the views of the Board of Governors or the President.

(5)CLARIFICATION OF AUTONOMY OF THE BUREAU IN LEGAL PROCE-EDINGS.— The Bureau shall not be liable under any provision of law for any action or inaction of the Board of Governors, and the Board of Governors shall not be liable under any provision of law for any action or inaction of the Bureau.

SEC. 1013. ADMINISTRATION.

(a) PERSONNEL.—

(1) APPOINTMENT.—

(A) IN GENERAL.— The Director may fix the number of, and appoint and direct, all employees of the Bureau, in accordance with the applicable provisions of title 5, United States Code.

(B) EMPLOYEES OF THE BUREAU.— The Director is authorized to employ attorneys, compliance examiners, compliance supervision analysts, economists, statisticians, and other employees as may be deemed necessary to conduct the business of the Bureau.

(c)**消费者金融保护局的自主性**。——

(1)**与联邦储备委员会的协调**。——对于与联邦消费者金融法律相关的对相关主体开展的监管或检查而言,无论适用的法律是否存在任何不同规定,联邦储备委员会均可以将检查受其管辖的主体对联邦消费者金融法律的遵守情况的权力委托给消费者金融保护局。

(2)**自主性**。——不论《联邦储备法》向联邦储备委员会授予何等权限,联邦储备委员会均不得——

(A)干预消费者金融保护局局长处理的任何事项或程序,包括检查或执法行动,但法律另有明确规定的情形除外;

(B)任命、指导或免除消费者金融保护局的任何官员或职员;或

(C)将消费者金融保护局或其任何职能或责任与联邦储备委员会或联邦储备银行的任何部门或办公室进行合并或整合。

(3)**规则和命令**。——消费者金融保护局的任何规则或命令均不必接受联邦储备委员会批准或审查。联邦储备委员会不得拖延或阻止消费者金融保护局发布任何规则或命令。

(4)**建议和证词**。——消费者金融保护局局长或消费者金融保护局的任何其他官员在向国会提交的立法建议、证词或立法意见之中,如包含一份声明,表示该等建议、证词或意见仅代表消费者金融保护局局长或上述官员的意见,并不必然反映联邦储备委员会或总统的意见,则任何联邦官员或任何联邦机关均无权要求消费者金融保护局局长或该等官员在向国会提交立法建议、证词或立法意见之前,将该等建议、证词或意见提交给其批准、发表意见或审查。

(5)**关于消费者金融保护局在法律程序中的自主性的说明**。——消费者金融保护局不应根据任何法律规定对联邦储备委员会的任何作为或不作为承担责任,联邦储备委员会也不应根据任何法律规定对消费者金融保护局的任何作为或不作为承担责任。

第1013条 管理

(a)**人事**。——

(1)**任命**。——

(A)**一般规定**。——消费者金融保护局局长可以按照《美国法典》第五编的适用规定确定消费者金融保护局全体雇员的人数,并对其进行任命和指导。

(B)**消费者金融保护局的雇员**。——消费者金融保护局局长有权聘用律师、合规检查员、合规监管分析师、经济学家、统计学家以及其认为开展消费者金融保护局业务所需的其他必要雇员。除非法律另有明确规定,否则,根据本条任命的任何个人应

Unless otherwise provided expressly by law, any individual appointed under this section shall be an employee as defined in section 2105 of title 5, United States Code, and subject to the provisions of such title and other laws generally applicable to the employees of an Executive agency.

(C) WAIVER AUTHORITY. —

(i) IN GENERAL. — In making any appointment under subparagraph (A), the Director may waive the requirements of chapter 33 of title 5, United States Code, and the regulations implementing such chapter, to the extent necessary to appoint employees on terms and conditions that are consistent with those set forth in section 11(1) of the Federal Reserve Act (12 U.S.C. 248(1)), while providing for —

(I) fair, credible, and transparent methods of establishing qualification requirements for, recruitment for, and appointments to positions;

(II) fair and open competition and equitable treatment in the consideration and selection of individuals to positions;

(III) fair, credible, and transparent methods of assigning, reassigning, detailing, transferring, and promoting employees.

(ii) VETERANS PREFERENCES. — In implementing this subparagraph, the Director shall comply with the provisions of section 2302(b)(11), regarding veterans' preference requirements, in a manner consistent with that in which such provisions are applied under chapter 33 of title 5, United States Code. The authority under this subparagraph to waive the requirements of that chapter 33 shall expire 5 years after the date of enactment of this Act.

(2) COMPENSATION. — Notwithstanding any otherwise applicable provision of title 5, United States Code, concerning compensation, including the provisions of chapter 51 and chapter 53, the following provisions shall apply with respect to employees of the Bureau:

(A) The rates of basic pay for all employees of the Bureau may be set and adjusted by the Director.

(B) The Director shall at all times provide compensation (including benefits) to each class of employees that, at a minimum, are comparable to the compensation and benefits then being provided by the Board of Governors for the corresponding class of employees.

(C) All such employees shall be compensated (including benefits) on terms and conditions that are consistent with the terms and conditions set forth in section 11(1) of the Federal Reserve Act (12 U.S.C. 248(1)).

(3) BUREAU PARTICIPATION IN FEDERAL RESERVE SYSTEM RETIREMENT PLAN AND FEDERAL RESERVE SYSTEM THRIFT PLAN. —

(A) EMPLOYEE ELECTION. — Employees appointed to the Bureau may elect to participate in either —

(i) both the Federal Reserve System Retirement Plan and the Federal Reserve System

属于《美国法典》第五编第2105节所定义的雇员，并应遵守该编规定以及其他适用于行政机关雇员的一般性法律。

(C)**免除权**。——

(i)**一般规定**。——在根据第(A)子款作出任何任命时，消费者金融保护局局长可以在必要范围内免除适用《美国法典》第五编第三十三章及该章实施规章的规定，以按照符合《联邦储备法》第11(1)条[《美国法典》第十二编第248(1)节]的条款和条件任命雇员，同时规定——

(I)设定职位资格要求以及开展招聘和职务任命的公正、可信并透明的方法；

(II)在审查及遴选职位候选人时，实施公正、公开的竞争，并为候选人提供平等待遇；

(III)对雇员进行分配、调整、派遣、调任和晋升的公正、可信并透明的方法。

(ii)**退伍军人优先权**。——对于《美国法典》第2302(b)(11)节关于退伍军人优先权的规定，消费者金融保护局局长在实施本子款规定之时，应按照与该等规定根据《美国法典》第五编第三十三章进行适用的方式相一致的方式，遵守该等规定。本子款规定的免除适用该第三十三章规定的权力应于本法颁布之日后届满五年之日终止。

(2)**薪酬**。——无论《美国法典》第五编与薪酬相关的任何其他适用的条款(包括第五十一章和第五十三章的条款)如何规定，消费者金融保护局的雇员均应适用如下规定：

(A)消费者金融保护局雇员的基本工资等级可以由消费者金融保护局局长设定并调整。

(B)消费者金融保护局局长向每级雇员提供的薪酬(包括福利)至少应始终保持与联邦储备委员会相应级别雇员的薪酬和福利具有可比性。

(C)所有上述雇员据以获得薪酬(包括福利)的条款和条件均应与《联邦储备法》第11(l)条[《美国法典》第十二编第248(l)节]规定的条款和条件相一致。

(3)**消费者金融保护局对联邦储备系统退休计划及联邦储备系统节俭计划的参与。**——

(A)**雇员的选择**。——接受任命在消费者金融保护局任职的雇员——

(i)可选择按照与联邦储备委员会雇员相同的条款以及第1064(i)(1)(C)条规定

Thrift Plan, under the same terms on which such participation is offered to employees of the Board of Governors who participate in such plans and under the terms and conditions specified under section 1064(i)(1)(C); or

(ii) the Civil Service Retirement System under chapter 83 of title 5, United States Code, or the Federal Employees Retirement System under chapter 84 of title 5, United States Code, if previously covered under one of those Federal employee retirement systems.

(B) ELECTION PERIOD. — Bureau employees shall make an election under this paragraph not later than 1 year after the date of appointment by, or transfer under subtitle F to, the Bureau. Participation in, and benefit accruals under, any other retirement plan established or maintained by the Federal Government shall end not later than the date on which participation in, and benefit accruals under, the Federal Reserve System Retirement Plan and Federal Reserve System Thrift Plan begin.

(C) EMPLOYER CONTRIBUTION. — The Bureau shall pay an employer contribution to the Federal Reserve System Retirement Plan, in the amount established as an employer contribution under the Federal Employees Retirement System, as established under chapter 84 of title 5, United States Code, for each Bureau employee who elects to participate in the Federal Reserve System Retirement Plan. The Bureau shall pay an employer contribution to the Federal Reserve System Thrift Plan for each Bureau employee who elects to participate in such plan, as required under the terms of such plan.

(D) CONTROLLED GROUP STATUS. — The Bureau is the same employer as the Federal Reserve System (as comprised of the Board of Governors and each of the 12 Federal reserve banks prior to the date of enactment of this Act) for purposes of subsections (b), (c), (m), and (o) of section 414 of the Internal Revenue Code of 1986, (26 U.S.C. 414).

(4) LABOR–MANAGEMENT RELATIONS. — Chapter 71 of title 5, United States Code, shall apply to the Bureau and the employees of the Bureau.

(5) AGENCY OMBUDSMAN. —

(A) ESTABLISHMENT REQUIRED. — Not later than 180 days after the designated transfer date, the Bureau shall appoint an ombudsman.

(B) DUTIES OF OMBUDSMAN. — The ombudsman appointed in accordance with subparagraph (A) shall —

(i) act as a liaison between the Bureau and any affected person with respect to any problem that such party may have in dealing with the Bureau, resulting from the regulatory activities of the Bureau; and

(ii) assure that safeguards exist to encourage complainants to come forward and preserve confidentiality.

(b) SPECIFIC FUNCTIONAL UNITS. —

(1) RESEARCH. — The Director shall establish a unit whose functions shall include

的条款和条件,同时参加联邦储备系统退休计划和联邦储备系统节俭计划;或

(ii)如果之前曾参加某一联邦雇员退休制度,可选择参加《美国法典》第五编第八十三章规定的公务员退休制度或《美国法典》第五编第八十四章规定的联邦雇员退休制度。

(B)**选择期限**。——消费者金融保护局雇员应在接受消费者金融保护局任命之日后一年内或根据第F子编调任至消费者金融保护局之日后一年内根据本款作出选择。消费者金融保护局雇员对联邦政府设立或维持的任何其他退休计划的参与和以及在该等计划下中应计福利金,至迟应于其参加联邦储备系统退休计划和联邦储备系统节俭计划并产生应计福利金之时终止计算。

(C)**雇主缴费**。——消费者金融保护局应按照《美国法典》第五编第八十四章为联邦雇员退休制度设定的雇主缴费金额,为所有选择参加联邦储备系统退休计划的雇员,向联邦储备系统退休计划支付雇主缴费。消费者金融保护局应按照联邦储备系统节俭计划的条款,为所有选择参加该计划的雇员,向联邦储备系统节俭计划支付雇主缴费。

(D)**受控集团地位**。——就《1986年国内税收法典》第414条第(b)子条、第(c)子条、第(m)子条和第(o)子条(《美国法典》第二十六编第414节)而言,消费者金融保护局与联邦储备系统(由联邦储备委员会以及本法颁布之日前的12家联邦储备银行组成)属于同一雇主。

(4)**劳动管理关系**。——《美国法典》第五编第七十一章应适用于消费者金融保护局及其雇员。

(5)**机关监察专员**。——

(A)**设立要求**。——消费者金融保护局应于指定转移日后180天内任命一名监察专员。

(B)**监察专员的职责**。——按照第(A)子款任命的监察专员应——

(i)在解决消费者金融保护局与任何受其监管活动影响的主体之间可能因消费者金融保护局监管活动而产生的问题时,负责担任消费者金融保护局与该受影响的主体之间的联络人;并

(ii)确保已设有鼓励投诉人进行投诉并对其进行保密的保障措施。

(b)**具体职能部门**。——

(1)**研究**。——消费者金融保护局局长应设立一个职能部门,负责如下事项的研

researching, analyzing, and reporting on —

(A) developments in markets for consumer financial products or services, including market areas of alternative consumer financial products or services with high growth rates and areas of risk to consumers;

(B) access to fair and affordable credit for traditionally underserved communities;

(C) consumer awareness, understanding, and use of disclosures and communications regarding consumer financial products or services;

(D) consumer awareness and understanding of costs, risks, and benefits of consumer financial products or services;

(E) consumer behavior with respect to consumer financial products or services, including performance on mortgage loans; and

(F) experiences of traditionally underserved consumers, including un-banked and under-banked consumers.

(2) COMMUNITY AFFAIRS. — The Director shall establish a unit whose functions shall include providing information, guidance, and technical assistance regarding the offering and provision of consumer financial products or services to traditionally underserved consumers and communities.

(3) COLLECTING AND TRACKING COMPLAINTS. —

(A) IN GENERAL. — The Director shall establish a unit whose functions shall include establishing a single, toll-free telephone number, a website, and a database or utilizing an existing database to facilitate the centralized collection of, monitoring of, and response to consumer complaints regarding consumer financial products or services. The Director shall coordinate with the Federal Trade Commission or other Federal agencies to route complaints to such agencies, where appropriate.

(B) ROUTING CALLS TO STATES. — To the extent practicable, State agencies may receive appropriate complaints from the systems established under subparagraph (A), if —

(i) the State agency system has the functional capacity to receive calls or electronic reports routed by the Bureau systems;

(ii) the State agency has satisfied any conditions of participation in the system that the Bureau may establish, including treatment of personally identifiable information and sharing of information on complaint resolution or related compliance procedures and resources; and

(iii) participation by the State agency includes measures necessary to provide for protection of personally identifiable information that conform to the standards for protection of the confidentiality of personally identifiable information and for data integrity and security that apply to the Federal agencies described in subparagraph (D).

(C) REPORTS TO THE CONGRESS. — The Director shall present an annual report to Congress not later than March 31 of each year on the complaints received by the Bureau in

究、分析和报告——

(A)消费者金融产品或服务市场的发展情况,包括高速增长的替代性消费者金融产品或服务市场领域,以及对消费者造成风险的领域的发展情况;

(B)传统弱势群体获得公平的可负担信贷的机会;

(C)消费者对于消费者金融产品或服务相关披露和宣传的认识、理解和使用;

(D)消费者对于消费者金融产品或服务相关成本、风险及收益的认识和理解;

(E)消费者与消费者金融产品或服务相关的行为,包括其对抵押贷款的履行情况;及

(F)传统弱势消费者(包括未开设银行账户及缺乏足够银行服务的消费者)的经历。

(2)**群体事务**。——消费者金融保护局局长应设立一个职能部门,负责向传统弱势消费者和群体提供与消费者金融产品或服务的要约或提供相关的信息、指导和技术援助。

(3)**投诉意见的收集和跟踪**。——

(A)**一般规定**。——消费者金融保护局局长应设立一个职能部门,负责设立一个统一、免费的电话号码、一个网站及一个数据库,或利用现有数据库,集中收集、监控和回应与消费者金融产品或服务相关的消费者投诉。消费者金融保护局局长应与联邦贸易委员会或其他联邦机关协调,在适当情况下将投诉转交给联邦贸易委员会或其他联邦机关。

(B)**向州机关转交投诉**。——在可行的范围内,州机关可以在如下情况下,通过根据(A)子款设立的系统接收适当的投诉——

(i)州机关系统具有接收消费者金融保护局系统转发的电话或电子报告的功能性能力;

(ii)州机关已满足消费者金融保护局设定的任何系统参与条件,包括对个人身份信息进行处理,以及在投诉处理或相关合规程序和资源方面进行信息共享;且

(iii)州机关参与之时,已制定必要措施,能够按照适用于第(D)子款所述联邦机关的个人身份信息保密标准以及数据完整性和安全性保护标准,保护个人身份信息。

(C)**向国会报告**。——消费者金融保护局局长应于每年3月31日之前就其在上一年收到的与消费者金融产品和服务相关的投诉向国会提交一份年度报告。该报告应

the prior year regarding consumer financial products and services. Such report shall include information and analysis about complaint numbers, complaint types, and, where applicable, information about resolution of complaints.

(D) DATA SHARING REQUIRED. — To facilitate preparation of the reports required under subparagraph (C), supervision and enforcement activities, and monitoring of the market for consumer financial products and services, the Bureau shall share consumer complaint information with prudential regulators, the Federal Trade Commission, other Federal agencies, and State agencies, subject to the standards applicable to Federal agencies for protection of the confidentiality of personally identifiable information and for data security and integrity. The prudential regulators, the Federal Trade Commission, and other Federal agencies shall share data relating to consumer complaints regarding consumer financial products and services with the Bureau, subject to the standards applicable to Federal agencies for protection of confidentiality of personally identifiable information and for data security and integrity.

(c) OFFICE OF FAIR LENDING AND EQUAL OPPORTUNITY. —

(1) ESTABLISHMENT. — The Director shall establish within the Bureau the Office of Fair Lending and Equal Opportunity.

(2) FUNCTIONS. — The Office of Fair Lending and Equal Opportunity shall have such powers and duties as the Director may delegate to the Office, including —

(A) providing oversight and enforcement of Federal laws intended to ensure the fair, equitable, and nondiscriminatory access to credit for both individuals and communities that are enforced by the Bureau, including the Equal Credit Opportunity Act and the Home Mortgage Disclosure Act;

(B) coordinating fair lending efforts of the Bureau with other Federal agencies and State regulators, as appropriate, to promote consistent, efficient, and effective enforcement of Federal fair lending laws;

(C) working with private industry, fair lending, civil rights, consumer and community advocates on the promotion of fair lending compliance and education; and

(D) providing annual reports to Congress on the efforts of the Bureau to fulfill its fair lending mandate.

(3) ADMINISTRATION OF OFFICE. — There is established the position of Assistant Director of the Bureau for Fair Lending and Equal Opportunity, who —

(A) shall be appointed by the Director; and

(B) shall carry out such duties as the Director may delegate to such Assistant Director.

(d) OFFICE OF FINANCIAL EDUCATION. —

(1) ESTABLISHMENT. — The Director shall establish an Office of Financial Education, which shall be responsible for developing and implementing initiatives intended to

包括与投诉数量、投诉类型以及投诉处理(如适用)相关的信息和分析。

(D)**数据共享要求**。——为了协助编制第(C)子款规定的报告,并促进针对消费者金融产品和服务市场的监管与执法活动及监控的开展,消费者金融保护局应在不违反适用于联邦机关的个人身份信息保密标准以及数据完整性和安全性保护标准的前提下,与审慎监管者、联邦贸易委员会、其他联邦机关及州机关共享投诉信息。审慎监管者、联邦贸易委员会及其他联邦机关应在不违反适用于联邦机关的个人身份信息保密标准以及数据完整性和安全性保护标准的前提下,与消费者金融保护局共享与消费者就消费者金融产品和服务提出的投诉相关的数据。

(c)**公平贷款与平等机会办公室**。——

(1)**设立**。——消费者金融保护局局长应于消费者金融保护局之下设立公平贷款与平等机会办公室。

(2)**职能**。——公平贷款与平等机会办公室应行使消费者金融保护局局长委托的权力,并履行消费者金融保护局局长委托的职责,包括——

(A)针对消费者金融保护局负责执行的确保受消费者金融保护局管辖的个人和群体能够公正、公平并不受歧视地获得信贷的联邦法律(包括《信贷机会平等法》和《住房抵押披露法》),提供监督和执行;

(B)与其他联邦监管机关和州监管者就消费者金融保护局的公平贷款工作开展适当的协调,以促进联邦公平贷款法律的一致、高成效和高效率的执行;

(C)在促进公平贷款合规和教育方面,与私营产业倡议者、公平贷款倡议者、民权倡议者、消费者和群体维权人士开展合作;并

(D)就消费者金融保护局履行公平贷款职权的工作向国会提交年度报告。

(3)**公平贷款与平等机会办公室的管理**。——兹设立负责公平贷款与机会平等事务的消费者金融保护局助理局长一职;助理局长应——

(A)由消费者金融保护局局长任命;并

(B)履行消费者金融保护局局长委托的职责。

(d)**金融教育办公室**。——

(1)**设立**。——消费者金融保护局局长应设立金融教育办公室,负责制定和实施相关计划,以教育消费者,并使消费者更明智地作出知情财务决策。

educate and empower consumers to make better informed financial decisions.

(2) OTHER DUTIES. — The Office of Financial Education shall develop and implement a strategy to improve the financial literacy of consumers that includes measurable goals and objectives, in consultation with the Financial Literacy and Education Commission, consistent with the National Strategy for Financial Literacy, through activities including providing opportunities for consumers to access —

(A) financial counseling, including community–based financial counseling, where practicable;

(B) information to assist with the evaluation of credit products and the understanding of credit histories and scores;

(C) savings, borrowing, and other services found at mainstream financial institutions;

(D) activities intended to —

(i) prepare the consumer for educational expenses and the submission of financial aid applications, and other major purchases;

(ii) reduce debt; and

(iii) improve the financial situation of the consumer;

(E) assistance in developing long–term savings strategies; and

(F) wealth building and financial services during the preparation process to claim earned income tax credits and Federal benefits.

(3) COORDINATION. — The Office of Financial Education shall coordinate with other units within the Bureau in carrying out its functions, including —

(A) working with the Community Affairs Office to implement the strategy to improve financial literacy of consumers; and

(B) working with the research unit established by the Director to conduct research related to consumer financial education and counseling.

(4) REPORT. — Not later than 24 months after the designated transfer date, and annually thereafter, the Director shall submit a report on its financial literacy activities and strategy to improve financial literacy of consumers to —

(A) the Committee on Banking, Housing, and Urban Affairs of the Senate; and

(B) the Committee on Financial Services of the House of Representatives.

(5) MEMBERSHIP IN FINANCIAL LITERACY AND EDUCATION COMMISSION. — Section 513 (c)(1) of the Financial Literacy and Education Improvement Act (20 U.S.C. 9702(c)(1)) is amended —

(A) in subparagraph (B), by striking "and" at the end;

(B) by redesignating subparagraph (C) as subparagraph (D); and

(C) by inserting after subparagraph (B) the following new subparagraph:

"(C) the Director of the Bureau of Consumer Financial Protection; and".

(2)**其他职责**。——金融教育办公室应与金融扫盲和教育委员会磋商,按照《全国金融扫盲战略》,向消费者提供获取如下服务、信息或参与如下活动的机会,制定并实施提高消费者金融素养的战略(包括设定可考核的目的和目标)——

(A)金融顾问服务,在可行的情况下,应包括面向群体提供的金融顾问服务;

(B)有助于评估信贷产品以及理解信用记录和评分的信息;

(C)主流金融机构提供的储蓄、借贷和其他服务;

(D)为如下目的开展的活动——

(i)为消费者提供关于教育费用、金融援助申请提交以及其他重大购买行为方面的培训;

(ii)减轻债务;及

(iii)改善消费者的财务状况;

(E)协助消费者制定长期储蓄策略;及

(F)在实施申请所得税抵免和联邦福利的准备工作中提供财富积累计划和金融服务。

(3)**协调**。——金融教育办公室在履行职能时,应与消费者金融保护局内其他部门相协调,包括——

(A)与群体事务办公室合作,实施提高消费者金融素养的战略;并

(B)与消费者金融保护局局长设立的研究部门合作,开展与消费者金融教育和咨询相关的研究。

(4)**报告**。——消费者金融保护局局长应于指定转移日后24个月内,并在此之后的每一年,就其提高消费者金融素养的金融扫盲活动及战略向如下委员会提交报告——

(A)参议院银行、住房与城市事务委员会;及

(B)众议院金融服务委员会。

(5)**金融扫盲和教育委员会的成员资格**。——《金融素养和教育改进法》第513(c)(1)条[《美国法典》第二十编第9702(c)(1)节]修正如下——

(A)在第(B)子款中,删除结尾处的"及";

(B)第(C)子款重新编号为第(D)子款;及

(C)在第(B)子款之后插入如下新子款:

"(C)消费者金融保护局局长;及"。

(6) CONFORMING AMENDMENT. — Section 513(d) of the Financial Literacy and Education Improvement Act (20 U.S.C. 9702(d)) is amended by adding at the end the following: "The Director of the Bureau of Consumer Financial Protection shall serve as the Vice Chairman.".

(7) STUDY AND REPORT ON FINANCIAL LITERACY PROGRAM. —

(A) IN GENERAL. — The Comptroller General of the United States shall conduct a study to identify —

(i) the feasibility of certification of persons providing the programs or performing the activities described in paragraph (2), including recognizing outstanding programs, and developing guidelines and resources for community-based practitioners, including —

(I) a potential certification process and standards for certification;

(II) appropriate certifying entities;

(III) resources required for funding such a process; and

(IV) a cost-benefit analysis of such certification;

(ii) technological resources intended to collect, analyze, evaluate, or promote financial literacy and counseling programs;

(iii) effective methods, tools, and strategies intended to educate and empower consumers about personal finance management; and

(iv) recommendations intended to encourage the development of programs that effectively improve financial education outcomes and empower consumers to make better informed financial decisions based on findings.

(B) REPORT. — Not later than 1 year after the date of enactment of this Act, the Comptroller General of the United States shall submit a report on the results of the study conducted under this paragraph to the Committee on Banking, Housing, and Urban Affairs of the Senate and the Committee on Financial Services of the House of Representatives.

(e) OFFICE OF SERVICE MEMBER AFFAIRS. —

(1) IN GENERAL. — The Director shall establish an Office of Service Member Affairs, which shall be responsible for developing and implementing initiatives for service members and their families intended to —

(A) educate and empower service members and their families to make better informed decisions regarding consumer financial products and services;

(B) coordinate with the unit of the Bureau established under subsection (b)(3), in order to monitor complaints by service members and their families and responses to those complaints by the Bureau or other appropriate Federal or State agency; and

(C) coordinate efforts among Federal and State agencies, as appropriate, regarding consumer protection measures relating to consumer financial products and services offered to, or used by, service members and their families.

(6)**一致性修正**。——在《金融素养和教育改进法》第513(d)条[《美国法典》第二十编第9702(d)节]结尾处增加如下内容,作为对该条的修正:“消费者金融保护局局长应担任副主席。”

(7)**关于金融扫盲计划的研究和报告**。——

(A)**一般规定**。——政府问责办公室主任应开展研究,以确定——

(i)对提供第(2)款所述计划或开展第(2)款所述活动的主体实行认证(包括表彰优秀计划,以及针对为某一群体提供服务的执业人员制定指导方针和为其开发资源)的可行性,包括——

(I)可能采用的认证流程及认证标准;

(II)相应的认证实体;

(III)为认证流程提供资金所需资源;及

(IV)该等认证的成本效益分析;

(ii)用于收集、分析、评估或推广金融扫盲与咨询计划的科技资源;

(iii)用于对消费者进行教育并增强消费者个人金融管理能力的有效方法、工具及战略;及

(iv)为鼓励制定可以有效改善金融教育成果并增强消费者根据研究结果更明智地作出知情财务决策的能力的计划,而提出的相关建议。

(B)**报告**。——政府问责办公室主任应于本法颁布之日后一年内,就根据本款开展的研究之结果向参议院银行、住房与城市事务委员会以及众议院金融服务委员会提交一份报告。

(e)**现役军人事务办公室**。——

(1)**一般规定**。——消费者金融保护局局长应设立现役军人事务办公室,负责制定并实施针对现役军人及其家庭成员的计划,以——

(A)教育现役军人及其家庭成员,使其能够更明智地作出关于消费者金融产品和服务的知情决策;

(B)与消费者金融保护局根据第(b)(3)子条设立的部门协调,监控现役军人及其家庭成员所提出的投诉以及消费者金融保护局或其他相应的联邦机关或州机关对该等投诉作出的回应;并

(C)适当地协调联邦机关和州机关针对向现役军人及其家庭成员要约的或由其使用的消费者金融产品和服务开展的与消费者保护措施相关的工作。

(2) COORDINATION. —

(A) REGIONAL SERVICES. — The Director is authorized to assign employees of the Bureau as may be deemed necessary to conduct the business of the Office of Service Member Affairs, including by establishing and maintaining the functions of the Office in regional offices of the Bureau located near military bases, military treatment facilities, or other similar military facilities.

(B) AGREEMENTS. — The Director is authorized to enter into memoranda of understanding and similar agreements with the Department of Defense, including any branch or agency as authorized by the department, in order to carry out the business of the Office of Service Member Affairs.

(3) DEFINITION. — As used in this subsection, the term "service member" means any member of the United States Armed Forces and any member of the National Guard or Reserves.

(f) TIMING. — The Office of Fair Lending and Equal Opportunity, the Office of Financial Education, and the Office of Service Member Affairs shall each be established not later than 1 year after the designated transfer date.

(g) OFFICE OF FINANCIAL PROTECTION FOR OLDER AMERICANS. —

(1) ESTABLISHMENT. — Before the end of the 180-day period beginning on the designated transfer date, the Director shall establish the Office of Financial Protection for Older Americans, the functions of which shall include activities designed to facilitate the financial literacy of individuals who have attained the age of 62 years or more (in this subsection, referred to as "seniors") on protection from unfair, deceptive, and abusive practices and on current and future financial choices, including through the dissemination of materials to seniors on such topics.

(2) ASSISTANT DIRECTOR. — The Office of Financial Protection for Older Americans (in this subsection referred to as the "Office") shall be headed by an assistant director.

(3) DUTIES. — The Office shall —

(A) develop goals for programs that provide seniors financial literacy and counseling, including programs that —

(i) help seniors recognize warning signs of unfair, deceptive, or abusive practices, protect themselves from such practices;

(ii) provide one-on-one financial counseling on issues including long-term savings and later-life economic security; and

(iii) provide personal consumer credit advocacy to respond to consumer problems caused by unfair, deceptive, or abusive practices;

(B) monitor certifications or designations of financial advisors who advise seniors and

(2)**协调**。——

(A)**地区服务**。——消费者金融保护局局长有权在其认为确属必要的情况下，指派消费者金融保护局的雇员开展现役军人事务办公室的工作，包括安排并保持由邻近军事基地、军事处理设施或其他类似军事设施的消费者金融保护局地区办公室行使现役军人事务办公室的职能。

(B)**协议**。——消费者金融保护局局长有权与国防部(包括经国防部授权的任何分支机构或机关)订立谅解备忘录及类似协议，以开展现役军人事务办公室的工作。

(3)**定义**。——就本子条而言，"现役军人"一词系指美国武装部队成员以及国民警卫队成员或预备役成员。

(f)**时限**。——公平贷款与平等机会办公室、金融教育办公室和现役军人事务办公室均应于指定转移日后一年内设立。

(g)**老年美国人金融保护办公室**。——

(1)**设立**。——消费者金融保护局局长应于指定转移日起180日内设立老年美国人金融保护办公室，其职能包括促进针对年满62周岁的个人（本子条以下简称老年人)开展的金融扫盲活动，使得老年人在当前和将来作出金融选择之时，免受不公平、欺骗性及滥用行为侵害，包括向老年人分发关于前述主题的资料。

(2)**助理局长**。——老年美国人金融保护办公室应由助理局长担任负责人。

(3)**职责**。——老年美国人金融保护办公室应——

(A)针对为老年人提供金融扫盲和咨询服务的计划制定目标，包括以下计划——

(i)帮助老年人识别不公平、欺骗性及滥用行为的警示信号，保护其自身免受该等行为的侵害；

(ii)就长期储蓄和晚年生活经济安全等事宜向老年人提供一对一的金融顾问服务；及

(iii)提供个人消费信用宣传，以应对不公平、欺骗性或滥用行为所造成的消费者问题；

(B)对向老年人提供咨询服务的金融顾问的认证或专业称号进行监控，并将其发

alert the Commission and State regulators of certifications or designations that are identified as unfair, deceptive, or abusive;

(C) not later than 18 months after the date of the establishment of the Office, submit to Congress and the Commission any legislative and regulatory recommendations on the best practices for —

(i) disseminating information regarding the legitimacy of certifications of financial advisers who advise seniors;

(ii) methods in which a senior can identify the financial advisor most appropriate for the senior's needs; and

(iii) methods in which a senior can verify a financial advisor's credentials;

(D) conduct research to identify best practices and effective methods, tools, technology and strategies to educate and counsel seniors about personal finance management with a focus on —

(i) protecting themselves from unfair, deceptive, and abusive practices;

(ii) long–term savings; and

(iii) planning for retirement and long–term care;

(E) coordinate consumer protection efforts of seniors with other Federal agencies and State regulators, as appropriate, to promote consistent, effective, and efficient enforcement; and

(F) work with community organizations, non–profit organizations, and other entities that are involved with educating or assisting seniors (including the National Education and Resource Center on Women and Retirement Planning).

SEC. 1014. CONSUMER ADVISORY BOARD.

(a) ESTABLISHMENT REQUIRED. — The Director shall establish a Consumer Advisory Board to advise and consult with the Bureau in the exercise of its functions under the Federal consumer financial laws, and to provide information on emerging practices in the consumer financial products or services industry, including regional trends, concerns, and other relevant information.

(b) MEMBERSHIP. — In appointing the members of the Consumer Advisory Board, the Director shall seek to assemble experts in consumer protection, financial services, community development, fair lending and civil rights, and consumer financial products or services and representatives of depository institutions that primarily serve underserved communities, and representatives of communities that have been significantly impacted by higher–priced mortgage loans, and seek representation of the interests of covered persons and consumers, without regard to party affiliation. Not fewer than 6 members shall be appointed upon the recommendation of the regional Federal Reserve Bank Presidents, on a rotating basis.

现的不公平、欺骗性或滥用性认证或专业称号提请证券交易委员会和州监管机关注意;

(C)老年美国人金融保护办公室应于设立之日后18个月内,针对如下领域的最佳实践,向国会及证券交易委员会提出立法和监管建议——

(i)针对向老年人提供咨询服务的金融顾问之认证合法性,宣传相关信息;

(ii)老年人能够用以识别最适合其需求的金融顾问的方法;及

(iii)老年人能够用以核实金融顾问证书的方法;

(D)开展研究,以确定在个人金融管理方面为老年人提供教育和咨询服务的最佳实践和有效方法、工具、技术及战略,重点在于——

(i)老年人如何保护自身免受不公平、欺骗性及滥用行为的侵害;

(ii)老年人长期储蓄安排;及

(iii)老年人退休和长期护理规划;

(E)与其他联邦机关和州监管者适当地协调开展老年消费者保护工作,以促进老年消费者保护工作实现高效率和高成效的一致性实施;并

(F)与社区组织、非营利性组织及参与老年人教育或援助的其他实体(包括女性和退休规划国民教育和资源中心)开展合作。

第1014条　消费者顾问委员会

(a)**设立要求**。——消费者金融保护局局长应设立消费者顾问委员会,在消费者金融保护局根据联邦消费者金融法律行使其职能的过程中向消费者金融保护局提供咨询意见并与其磋商,同时为消费者金融保护局提供与消费者金融产品或服务行业新兴实践相关的信息,包括区域发展趋势、关切问题及其他相关信息。

(b)**成员资格**。——在任命消费者顾问委员会成员时,消费者金融保护局局长应尽量选择消费者保护、金融服务、社区发展、公平贷款、公民权利以及消费者金融产品或服务方面的专家,以及主要服务弱势群体的存款机构的代表和遭受高价抵押贷款严重影响的群体的代表,并在不考虑党派属性的情况下,尽力代表所涉主体和消费者的利益。其中至少6名成员应根据地区联邦储备银行主席轮流提出的建议任命。

(c) MEETINGS. — The Consumer Advisory Board shall meet from time to time at the call of the Director, but, at a minimum, shall meet at least twice in each year.

(d) COMPENSATION AND TRAVEL EXPENSES. — Members of the Consumer Advisory Board who are not full-time employees of the United States shall —

(1) be entitled to receive compensation at a rate fixed by the Director while attending meetings of the Consumer Advisory Board, including travel time; and

(2) be allowed travel expenses, including transportation and subsistence, while away from their homes or regular places of business.

SEC. 1015. COORDINATION.

The Bureau shall coordinate with the Commission, the Commodity Futures Trading Commission, the Federal Trade Commission, and other Federal agencies and State regulators, as appropriate, to promote consistent regulatory treatment of consumer financial and investment products and services.

SEC. 1016. APPEARANCES BEFORE AND REPORTS TO CONGRESS.

(a) APPEARANCES BEFORE CONGRESS. — The Director of the Bureau shall appear before the Committee on Banking, Housing, and Urban Affairs of the Senate and the Committee on Financial Services and the Committee on Energy and Commerce of the House of Representatives at semi-annual hearings regarding the reports required under subsection (b).

(b) REPORTS REQUIRED. — The Bureau shall, concurrent with each semi-annual hearing referred to in subsection (a), prepare and submit to the President and to the Committee on Banking, Housing, and Urban Affairs of the Senate and the Committee on Financial Services and the Committee on Energy and Commerce of the House of Representatives, a report, beginning with the session following the designated transfer date. The Bureau may also submit such report to the Committee on Commerce, Science, and Transportation of the Senate.

(c) CONTENTS. — The reports required by subsection (b) shall include —

(1) a discussion of the significant problems faced by consumers in shopping for or obtaining consumer financial products or services;

(2) a justification of the budget request of the previous year;

(3) a list of the significant rules and orders adopted by the Bureau, as well as other significant initiatives conducted by the Bureau, during the preceding year and the plan of the Bureau for rules, orders, or other initiatives to be undertaken during the upcoming period;

(4) an analysis of complaints about consumer financial products or services that the Bureau has received and collected in its central database on complaints during the preceding year;

(5) a list, with a brief statement of the issues, of the public supervisory and enforcement

(c)**会议**。——消费者顾问委员会会议应由消费者金融保护局局长随时召集,但至少应每年举行两次。

(d)**薪酬和差旅费**。——非联邦全职雇员的消费者顾问委员会成员应——

(1)有权在参加消费者顾问委员会会议期间(包括旅途时间)按照消费者金融保护局局长设定的费率领取薪酬;并

(2)有权在远离家庭住所或日常办公场所期间获得差旅费(包括交通和生活补助)。

第1015条　协调

消费者金融保护局应与证券交易委员会、商品期货交易委员会、联邦贸易委员会及其他联邦机关及州监管者进行适当的协调,促进对消费者金融及投资产品和服务实施一致性监管。

第1016条　出席国会听证并向国会报告

(a)**出席国会听证**。——消费者金融保护局局长应出席参议院银行、住房与城市事务委员会、众议院金融服务委员会、众议院能源与商业委员会就第(b)子条规定的报告所举行的半年度听证会。

(b)**报告要求**。——自指定转移日后首次举行第(a)子条所述半年度听证会开始,消费者金融保护局应于每次出席该等会议的同时,编制一份报告,并将其提交给向总统、参议院银行、住房与城市事务委员会、众议院金融服务委员会及众议院能源和商业委员会。消费者金融保护局可同时向参议院商务、科学和运输委员会提交该等报告。

(c)**内容**。——第(b)子条规定的报告应包含如下内容——

(1)对消费者在购买或获取消费者金融产品或服务过程中所遭遇的重大问题的讨论;

(2)关于上一年度预算申请的论证;

(3)消费者金融保护局在上一年度制定的重大规则和命令以及所实施的其他重大计划之清单,以及下一阶段计划制定的规则、命令或计划采取的其他举措;

(4)对消费者金融保护局于上一年度收到的已输入中央投诉数据库的消费者金融产品或服务相关投诉的分析;

(5)消费者金融保护局在上一年度参与的公共监管及执法行动之清单,以及关于

actions to which the Bureau was a party during the preceding year;

(6) the actions taken regarding rules, orders, and supervisory actions with respect to covered persons which are not credit unions or depository institutions;

(7) an assessment of significant actions by State attorneys general or State regulators relating to Federal consumer financial law;

(8) an analysis of the efforts of the Bureau to fulfill the fair lending mission of the Bureau; and

(9) an analysis of the efforts of the Bureau to increase workforce and contracting diversity consistent with the procedures established by the Office of Minority and Women Inclusion.

SEC. 1017. FUNDING; PENALTIES AND FINES.

(a) TRANSFER OF FUNDS FROM BOARD OF GOVERNORS. —

(1) IN GENERAL. — Each year (or quarter of such year), beginning on the designated transfer date, and each quarter thereafter, the Board of Governors shall transfer to the Bureau from the combined earnings of the Federal Reserve System, the amount determined by the Director to be reasonably necessary to carry out the authorities of the Bureau under Federal consumer financial law, taking into account such other sums made available to the Bureau from the preceding year (or quarter of such year).

(2) FUNDING CAP. —

(A) IN GENERAL. — Notwithstanding paragraph (1), and in accordance with this paragraph, the amount that shall be transferred to the Bureau in each fiscal year shall not exceed a fixed percentage of the total operating expenses of the Federal Reserve System, as reported in the Annual Report, 2009, of the Board of Governors, equal to —

(i) 10 percent of such expenses in fiscal year 2011;

(ii) 11 percent of such expenses in fiscal year 2012; and

(iii) 12 percent of such expenses in fiscal year 2013, and in each year thereafter.

(B) ADJUSTMENT OF AMOUNT. — The dollar amount referred to in subparagraph (A)(iii) shall be adjusted annually, using the percent increase, if any, in the employment cost index for total compensation for State and local government workers published by the Federal Government, or the successor index thereto, for the 12-month period ending on September 30 of the year preceding the transfer.

(C) REVIEWABILITY. — Notwithstanding any other provision in this title, the funds derived from the Federal Reserve System pursuant to this subsection shall not be subject to review by the Committees on Appropriations of the House of Representatives and the Senate.

(3) TRANSITION PERIOD. — Beginning on the date of enactment of this Act and until the designated transfer date, the Board of Governors shall transfer to the Bureau the amount estimated by the Secretary needed to carry out the authorities granted to the Bureau under

其中所涉问题的简要说明;

(6)针对不具有信贷联盟和存款机构身份的所涉主体制定的规则、命令及采取的监管行动;

(7)对州总检察长或州监管者所采取的与联邦消费者金融法律相关的重大行动的评估;

(8)对消费者金融保护局为实现其公平贷款宗旨所开展的工作之分析;及

(9)对消费者金融保护局按照少数族裔与女性就业参与办公室制定的程序为提高工作人员和承包商多元化所开展的工作之分析。

第1017条 经费来源;罚款和罚金

(a)**联邦储备委员会划拨经费**。——

(1)**一般规定**。——自指定转移日起,以及在之后的每个季度,联邦储备委员会应按年度(或在该年度内按季度)从联邦储备系统的总收益中向消费者金融保护局划拨一定经费,经费金额以消费者金融保护局局长判定的对于执行联邦消费者金融法律赋予消费者金融保护局的权力确属合理必要的金额为准。在确定该等金额时,消费者金融保护局局长应考虑上一年度(或该年度内的季度)消费者金融保护局通过其他渠道获得的款项。

(2)**经费上限**。——

(A)**一般规定**。——无论第(1)款如何规定,根据本款规定,每一财政年度向消费者金融保护局划拨的经费金额不得超过联邦储备系统总运营费用(以联邦储备委员会2009年年度报告所报告的数额为准)的某一固定比例,即——

(i)2011财政年度,不得超过联邦储备系统总运营费用的10%;

(ii)2012财政年度,不得超过联邦储备系统总运营费用的11%;及

(iii)2013财政年度及之后财政年度,不得超过联邦储备系统总运营费用的12%。

(B)**金额调整**。——第(A)(iii)子款所述金额应按照联邦政府公布的、截至经费划拨前一年度9月30日的12个月期间,州及当地政府职员总薪酬雇用成本指数的增长比例(如有),进行年度调整。

(C)**可审查性**。——无论本编是否存在任何不同规定,根据本子条从联邦储备系统获得的资金不必接受众议院和参议院拨款委员会的审查。

(3)**过渡期**。——自本法颁布之日起直至指定转移日,联邦储备委员会应向消费者金融保护局划拨一定经费,经费金额以财政部部长估算的自本法颁布之日起直至指定转移日执行联邦消费者金融法律赋予消费者金融保护局的权力所需金额为准。

Federal consumer financial law, from the date of enactment of this Act until the designated transfer date.

(4) BUDGET AND FINANCIAL MANAGEMENT.—

(A) FINANCIAL OPERATING PLANS AND FORECASTS. — The Director shall provide to the Director of the Office of Management and Budget copies of the financial operating plans and forecasts of the Director, as prepared by the Director in the ordinary course of the operations of the Bureau, and copies of the quarterly reports of the financial condition and results of operations of the Bureau, as prepared by the Director in the ordinary course of the operations of the Bureau.

(B) FINANCIAL STATEMENTS. — The Bureau shall prepare annually a statement of—

(i) assets and liabilities and surplus or deficit;

(ii) income and expenses; and

(iii) sources and application of funds.

(C) FINANCIAL MANAGEMENT SYSTEMS. — The Bureau shall implement and maintain financial management systems that comply substantially with Federal financial management systems requirements and applicable Federal accounting standards.

(D) ASSERTION OF INTERNAL CONTROLS. — The Director shall provide to the Comptroller General of the United States an assertion as to the effectiveness of the internal controls that apply to financial reporting by the Bureau, using the standards established in section 3512(c) of title 31, United States Code.

(E) RULE OF CONSTRUCTION. — This subsection may not be construed as implying any obligation on the part of the Director to consult with or obtain the consent or approval of the Director of the Office of Management and Budget with respect to any report, plan, forecast, or other information referred to in subparagraph (A) or any jurisdiction or oversight over the affairs or operations of the Bureau.

(F) FINANCIAL STATEMENTS. — The financial statements of the Bureau shall not be consolidated with the financial statements of either the Board of Governors or the Federal Reserve System.

(5) AUDIT OF THE BUREAU.—

(A) IN GENERAL. — The Comptroller General shall annually audit the financial transactions of the Bureau in accordance with the United States generally accepted government auditing standards, as may be prescribed by the Comptroller General of the United States. The audit shall be conducted at the place or places where accounts of the Bureau are normally kept. The representatives of the Government Accountability Office shall have access to the personnel and to all books, accounts, documents, papers, records (including electronic records), reports, files, and all other papers, automated data, things, or

(4)**预算和财务管理**。——

(A)**财务运营计划和预测**。——消费者金融保护局局长应向行政管理和预算局局长提供其在消费者金融保护局日常运营中编制的财务运营计划和预测之复本,以及财务状况和运营成果季度报告之复本。

(B)**财务报表**。——消费者金融保护局应编制关于如下事项的年度报表——

(i)资产和负债以及盈余或赤字;

(ii)收入和支出;及

(iii)资金来源和使用。

(C)**财务管理制度**。——消费者金融保护局所实施并维持的财务管理制度应基本符合联邦财务管理系统要求和适用的联邦会计标准。

(D)**关于内部控制的声明**。——消费者金融保护局局长应向政府问责办公室主任作出声明,说明按照《美国法典》第三十一编第3512(c)节设定的标准,消费者金融保护局财务报告内部控制是否有效。

(E)**解释规则**。——本子条不得被解释为暗示消费者金融保护局局长有义务就第(A)子款所述任何报告、计划、预测或其他信息与行政管理和预算局局长进行磋商或者有义务取得其同意或批准,也不得被解释为暗示消费者金融保护局局长有义务就对于消费者金融保护局事务或运营的任何管辖权或监督权与行政管理和预算局局长进行磋商或者有义务取得其同意或批准。

(F)**财务报表**。——消费者金融保护局的财务报表不得与联邦储备委员会或联邦储备系统的财务报表合并。

(5)**对消费者金融保护局的审计**。——

(A)**一般规定**。——政府问责办公室主任应每年按照政府问责办公室主任制定的联邦公认政府审计标准对消费者金融保护局的金融交易进行审计。审计应在消费者金融保护局通常存放账目的地点进行。政府问责办公室的代表应有权接触消费者金融保护局雇用的与其财务交易有关并有助于审计的必要人员,有权查阅消费者金融保护局拥有、控制或使用与其财务交易有关并有助于审计的所有账簿、账目、文件、文书、记录(包括电子记录)、报告、文档以及其他文书、自动化数据、物品或财产;同时,消费者金融保护局应向该等代表提供充分便利,以便其核实存管机构、财务代理

property belonging to or under the control of or used or employed by the Bureau pertaining to its financial transactions and necessary to facilitate the audit, and such representatives shall be afforded full facilities for verifying transactions with the balances or securities held by depositories, fiscal agents, and custodians. All such books, accounts, documents, records, reports, files, papers, and property of the Bureau shall remain in possession and custody of the Bureau. The Comptroller General may obtain and duplicate any such books, accounts, documents, records, working papers, automated data and files, or other information relevant to such audit without cost to the Comptroller General, and the right of access of the Comptroller General to such information shall be enforceable pursuant to section 716(c) of title 31, United States Code.

(B) REPORT. — The Comptroller General shall submit to the Congress a report of each annual audit conducted under this subsection. The report to the Congress shall set forth the scope of the audit and shall include the statement of assets and liabilities and surplus or deficit, the statement of income and expenses, the statement of sources and application of funds, and such comments and information as may be deemed necessary to inform Congress of the financial operations and condition of the Bureau, together with such recommendations with respect thereto as the Comptroller General may deem advisable. A copy of each report shall be furnished to the President and to the Bureau at the time submitted to the Congress.

(C) ASSISTANCE AND COSTS. — For the purpose of conducting an audit under this subsection, the Comptroller General may, in the discretion of the Comptroller General, employ by contract, without regard to section 3709 of the Revised Statutes of the United States (41 U.S.C. 5), professional services of firms and organizations of certified public accountants for temporary periods or for special purposes. Upon the request of the Comptroller General, the Director of the Bureau shall transfer to the Government Accountability Office from funds available, the amount requested by the Comptroller General to cover the full costs of any audit and report conducted by the Comptroller General. The Comptroller General shall credit funds transferred to the account established for salaries and expenses of the Government Accountability Office, and such amount shall be available upon receipt and without fiscal year limitation to cover the full costs of the audit and report.

(b) CONSUMER FINANCIAL PROTECTION FUND. —

(1) SEPARATE FUND IN FEDERAL RESERVE ESTABLISHED. — There is established in the Federal Reserve a separate fund, to be known as the "Bureau of Consumer Financial Protection Fund" (referred to in this section as the "Bureau Fund"). The Bureau Fund shall be maintained and established at a Federal reserve bank, in accordance with such requirements as the Board of Governors may impose.

(2) FUND RECEIPTS. — All amounts transferred to the Bureau under subsection (a) shall be deposited into the Bureau Fund.

人及托管人持有的结余或证券的交易情况。所有上述账簿、账目、文件、记录、报告、文档、文书及财产均应继续由消费者金融保护局掌握和保管。政府问责办公室主任可以免费获取并复制所有账簿、账目、文件、记录、工作底稿、自动化数据及文档或与该等审计有关的其他信息;政府问责办公室主任查阅该等信息的权利应根据《美国法典》第三十一编第716(c)节的规定强制执行。

(B)**报告**。——政府问责办公室主任应就依本子条规定开展的每项年度审计向国会提交一份报告。向国会提交的报告应说明审计范围,并应包含资产、负债以及盈余或赤字报表、收入和支出报表、资金来源和使用报表以及有助于国会了解消费者金融保护局财务运营和状况的必要意见和信息, 并随附政府问责办公室主任认为可取的相关建议。在向国会提交每份报告时,政府问责办公室主任应同时向总统及消费者金融保护局提供一份该等报告的复本。

(C)**协助与成本**。——在根据本子条开展审计之时,政府问责办公室主任可以在不考虑《美国制定法汇编》(修订版)第3709条(《美国法典》第四十一编第5节)规定的情况下,依其自由裁量权通过合同临时性地或出于特殊目的聘用注册公共会计师事务所和机构,获得其专业性服务。政府问责办公室主任提出要求之时,消费者金融保护局局长应按照其要求的金额,从可用资金中向政府问责办公室划拨相应款项,以支付政府问责办公室主任开展审计和报告产生的全部费用。政府问责办公室主任应将划拨款项计入政府问责办公室开立的薪资和费用账户的贷方,并且该等款项一经到账,即可用于支付审计和报告的全部费用,而不必受财政年度限制。

(b)**消费者金融保护基金**。——

(1)**在联邦储备系统中设立单独基金**。——联邦储备系统下设一项单独基金,即"消费者金融保护局基金"。消费者金融保护基金应按照联邦储备委员会的要求,在联邦储备银行设立并维持。

(2)**经费**。——根据第(a)子条向消费者金融保护局划拨的所有款项均应存入消费者金融保护局基金。

(3) INVESTMENT AUTHORITY. —

(A) AMOUNTS IN BUREAU FUND MAY BE INVESTED. — The Bureau may request the Board of Governors to direct the investment of the portion of the Bureau Fund that is not, in the judgment of the Bureau, required to meet the current needs of the Bureau.

(B) ELIGIBLE INVESTMENTS. — Investments authorized by this paragraph shall be made in obligations of the United States or obligations that are guaranteed as to principal and interest by the United States, with maturities suitable to the needs of the Bureau Fund, as determined by the Bureau.

(C) INTEREST AND PROCEEDS CREDITED. — The interest on, and the proceeds from the sale or redemption of, any obligations held in the Bureau Fund shall be credited to the Bureau Fund.

(c) USE OF FUNDS. —

(1) IN GENERAL. — Funds obtained by, transferred to, or credited to the Bureau Fund shall be immediately available to the Bureau and under the control of the Director, and shall remain available until expended, to pay the expenses of the Bureau in carrying out its duties and responsibilities. The compensation of the Director and other employees of the Bureau and all other expenses thereof may be paid from, obtained by, transferred to, or credited to the Bureau Fund under this section.

(2) FUNDS THAT ARE NOT GOVERNMENT FUNDS. — Funds obtained by or transferred to the Bureau Fund shall not be construed to be Government funds or appropriated monies.

(3) AMOUNTS NOT SUBJECT TO APPORTIONMENT. — Notwithstanding any other provision of law, amounts in the Bureau Fund and in the Civil Penalty Fund established under subsection (d) shall not be subject to apportionment for purposes of chapter 15 of title 31, United States Code, or under any other authority.

(d) PENALTIES AND FINES. —

(1) ESTABLISHMENT OF VICTIMS RELIEF FUND. — There is established in the Federal Reserve a separate fund, to be known as the "Consumer Financial Civil Penalty Fund" (referred to in this section as the "Civil Penalty Fund"). The Civil Penalty Fund shall be maintained and established at a Federal reserve bank, in accordance with such requirements as the Board of Governors may impose. If the Bureau obtains a civil penalty against any person in any judicial or administrative action under Federal consumer financial laws, the Bureau shall deposit into the Civil Penalty Fund, the amount of the penalty collected.

(2) PAYMENT TO VICTIMS. — Amounts in the Civil Penalty Fund shall be available to the Bureau, without fiscal year limitation, for payments to the victims of activities for which

(3)**投资权力**。——

(A)**消费者金融保护局基金内的款项可用于投资**。——对于消费者金融保护局判断不必用于满足消费者金融保护局当期需求的基金款项,消费者金融保护局可以请求联邦储备委员会进行投资。

(B)**适格投资**。——按本款授权开展投资之时,投资对象应为联邦政府债券,或联邦政府担保本金和利息的债券,债券期限由消费者金融保护局判定的符合消费者金融保护局基金需求的期限为准。

(C)**利息和收益的贷记**。——消费者金融保护局基金所持债券产生的利息及其卖出或赎回所得资金均应记入消费者金融保护局基金贷项。

(c)**资金的使用**。——

(1)**一般规定**。——消费者金融保护局基金获得的、向其划拨的或者记入其贷方的资金,应立即可供消费者金融保护局使用,并由消费者金融保护局局长控制,且在被用于支付消费者金融保护局履行其职责和责任所产生的费用之前,应始终保持可支用状态。消费者金融保护局局长及其他雇员的薪酬和所有其他费用均可通过本条规定的消费者金融保护局基金支付、由消费者金融保护局基金提供、向消费者金融保护局基金划拨或记入消费者金融保护局基金贷方。

(2)**并非政府资金的资金**。——消费者金融保护局基金获得的或向其划拨的资金不得视为政府资金或拨款。

(3)**不受制于分配规定的款项**。——无论是否存在任何不同法律规定,消费者金融保护局基金以及根据第(d)子条设立的消费者金融民事罚款基金内的款项不得按照《美国法典》第三十一编第十五章的规定或任何其他法律规定进行分配。

(d)**处罚和罚款**。——

(1)**设立受害人救济基金**。——联邦储备系统下设一项单独基金,即“消费者金融民事罚款基金”。消费者金融民事罚款基金应按照联邦储备委员会提出的要求,在联邦储备银行设立并维持。如果消费者金融保护局根据联邦消费者金融法律规定,在任何司法或行政诉讼中获得针对任何人的民事罚款,则其应将收缴的罚款存入消费者金融民事罚款基金。

(2)**向受害人付款**。——对于已经依联邦消费者金融法律处以民事罚款的违法活动,消费者金融保护局应在不考虑财政年度限制的情况下,利用消费者金融民事罚

civil penalties have been imposed under the Federal consumer financial laws. To the extent that such victims cannot be located or such payments are otherwise not practicable, the Bureau may use such funds for the purpose of consumer education and financial literacy programs.

(e) AUTHORIZATION OF APPROPRIATIONS; ANNUAL REPORT. —

(1) DETERMINATION REGARDING NEED FOR APPROPRIATED FUNDS. —

(A) IN GENERAL. — The Director is authorized to determine that sums available to the Bureau under this section will not be sufficient to carry out the authorities of the Bureau under Federal consumer financial law for the upcoming year.

(B) REPORT REQUIRED. — When making a determination under subparagraph (A), the Director shall prepare a report regarding the funding of the Bureau, including the assets and liabilities of the Bureau, and the extent to which the funding needs of the Bureau are anticipated to exceed the level of the amount set forth in subsection (a)(2). The Director shall submit the report to the President and to the Committee on Appropriations of the Senate and the Committee on Appropriations of the House of Representatives.

(2) AUTHORIZATION OF APPROPRIATIONS. — If the Director makes the determination and submits the report pursuant to paragraph (1), there are hereby authorized to be appropriated to the Bureau, for the purposes of carrying out the authorities granted in Federal consumer financial law, $200,000,000 for each of fiscal years 2010, 2011, 2012, 2013, and 2014.

(3) APPORTIONMENT. — Notwithstanding any other provision of law, the amounts in paragraph (2) shall be subject to apportionment under section 1517 of title 31, United States Code, and restrictions that generally apply to the use of appropriated funds in title 31, United States Code, and other laws.

(4) ANNUAL REPORT. — The Director shall prepare and submit a report, on an annual basis, to the Committee on Appropriations of the Senate and the Committee on Appropriations of the House of Representatives regarding the financial operating plans and forecasts of the Director, the financial condition and results of operations of the Bureau, and the sources and application of funds of the Bureau, including any funds appropriated in accordance with this subsection.

SEC. 1018. EFFECTIVE DATE.

This subtitle shall become effective on the date of enactment of this Act.

款基金内的款项向该等活动的受害人进行支付。如果无法确定受害人,或者因其他原因无法支付该等款项，消费者金融保护局可将该部分资金用于消费者教育和金融扫盲计划。

(e)**拨款授权;年度报告**。——

(1)**拨款需求的判定**。——

(A)**一般规定**。——消费者金融保护局局长有权判定,消费者金融保护局根据本条规定可支用的款项无法满足下一年其执行联邦消费者金融法律赋予的权力的需要。

(B)**报告要求**。——根据第(A)子款作出判定时,消费者金融保护局局长应编制消费者金融保护局经费报告,说明消费者金融保护局的资产和负债,并预计经费需求将在多大程度上超出第(a)(2)子条规定的金额上限。消费者金融保护局局长应向总统以及参议院和众议院的拨款委员会提交上述报告。

(2)**拨款授权**。——兹授权在消费者金融保护局局长根据第(1)款作出判定并提交报告之后,在2010年财政年度、2011年财政年度、2012年财政年度、2013年财政年度和2014年财政年度每一财政年度向消费者金融保护局拨款2亿美元,用于执行联邦消费者金融法律赋予消费者金融保护局的权力。

(3)**分配**。——无论是否存在任何不同法律规定,第(2)款规定的款项应受制于《美国法典》第三十一编第1517节的分配规定以及《美国法典》第三十一编和其他法律中适用于拨款资金使用的一般限制性规定。

(4)**年度报告**。——消费者金融保护局局长应每年就其作出的财务运营计划和预测、消费者金融保护局财务状况和运营成果以及消费者金融保护局的资金来源和使用(包括根据本子条规定获得的拨款)编制一份年度报告,并将其提交给参议院和众议院的拨款委员会。

第1018条　生效日

本子编应于本法颁布之日生效。

Subtitle B — General Powers of the Bureau

SEC. 1021. PURPOSE, OBJECTIVES, AND FUNCTIONS.

(a) PURPOSE. — The Bureau shall seek to implement and, where applicable, enforce Federal consumer financial law consistently for the purpose of ensuring that all consumers have access to markets for consumer financial products and services and that markets for consumer financial products and services are fair, transparent, and competitive.

(b) OBJECTIVES. — The Bureau is authorized to exercise its authorities under Federal consumer financial law for the purposes of ensuring that, with respect to consumer financial products and services —

(1) consumers are provided with timely and understandable information to make responsible decisions about financial transactions;

(2) consumers are protected from unfair, deceptive, or abusive acts and practices and from discrimination;

(3) outdated, unnecessary, or unduly burdensome regulations are regularly identified and addressed in order to reduce unwarranted regulatory burdens;

(4) Federal consumer financial law is enforced consistently, without regard to the status of a person as a depository institution, in order to promote fair competition; and

(5) markets for consumer financial products and services operate transparently and efficiently to facilitate access and innovation.

(c) FUNCTIONS. — The primary functions of the Bureau are —

(1) conducting financial education programs;

(2) collecting, investigating, and responding to consumer complaints;

(3) collecting, researching, monitoring, and publishing information relevant to the functioning of markets for consumer financial products and services to identify risks to consumers and the proper functioning of such markets;

(4) subject to sections 1024 through 1026, supervising covered persons for compliance with Federal consumer financial law, and taking appropriate enforcement action to address violations of Federal consumer financial law;

(5) issuing rules, orders, and guidance implementing Federal consumer financial law; and

(6) performing such support activities as may be necessary or useful to facilitate the other functions of the Bureau.

SEC. 1022. RULEMAKING AUTHORITY.

(a) IN GENERAL. — The Bureau is authorized to exercise its authorities under Federal

第B子编——消费者金融保护局的总体权力

第1021条　宗旨、目的和职能

(a)**宗旨**。——为了确保所有消费者均有机会获得消费者金融产品和服务,并确保消费者金融产品和服务市场的公平、透明和竞争性,消费者金融保护局应努力贯彻实施联邦消费者金融法律,并在适用联邦消费者金融法律之时,对联邦消费者金融法律进行一致性强制执行。

(b)**目的**。——消费者金融保护局有权执行联邦消费者金融法律赋予的权力,以确保对于消费者金融产品和服务而言——

(1)消费者及时获得简明易懂的信息,作出负责任的金融交易决策;

(2)保护消费者免受不公平、欺骗性、滥用行为、做法以及歧视性行为的损害;

(3)过时、不必要或过于繁重的规章得到定期梳理,以减少不必要的监管负担;

(4)联邦消费者金融法律能够得到一致性的强制执行(不论执法对象是否为存款机构),以促进公平竞争;且

(5)消费者金融产品和服务市场实现透明、高效运作,提高市场可及性和创新性。

(c)**职能**。——消费者金融保护局的主要职能如下——

(1)开展金融教育计划;

(2)收集、调查和回应消费者投诉;

(3)收集、研究、监控和发布与消费者金融产品和服务市场运作相关的信息,以发现消费者和该等市场正常运作所面临的风险;

(4)根据第1024条至第1026条规定,监管所涉主体对联邦消费者金融法律的合规情况,并采取适当执法行动,整治违反联邦消费者金融法律的行为;

(5)发布联邦消费者金融法律的实施规则、命令和指引;及

(6)开展对于促进消费者金融保护局其他职能的行使确属必要或有益的支持活动。

第1022条　规则制定权

(a)**一般规定**。——消费者金融保护局有权行使联邦消费者金融法律赋予的权

consumer financial law to administer, enforce, and otherwise implement the provisions of Federal consumer financial law.

(b) RULEMAKING, ORDERS, AND GUIDANCE. —

(1) GENERAL AUTHORITY. — The Director may prescribe rules and issue orders and guidance, as may be necessary or appropriate to enable the Bureau to administer and carry out the purposes and objectives of the Federal consumer financial laws, and to prevent evasions thereof.

(2) STANDARDS FOR RULEMAKING. — In prescribing a rule under the Federal consumer financial laws —

(A) the Bureau shall consider —

(i) the potential benefits and costs to consumers and covered persons, including the potential reduction of access by consumers to consumer financial products or services resulting from such rule; and

(ii) the impact of proposed rules on covered persons, as described in section 1026, and the impact on consumers in rural areas;

(B) the Bureau shall consult with the appropriate prudential regulators or other Federal agencies prior to proposing a rule and during the comment process regarding consistency with prudential, market, or systemic objectives administered by such agencies; and

(C) if, during the consultation process described in subparagraph (B), a prudential regulator provides the Bureau with a written objection to the proposed rule of the Bureau or a portion thereof, the Bureau shall include in the adopting release a description of the objection and the basis for the Bureau decision, if any, regarding such objection, except that nothing in this clause shall be construed as altering or limiting the procedures under section 1023 that may apply to any rule prescribed by the Bureau.

(3) EXEMPTIONS. —

(A) IN GENERAL. — The Bureau, by rule, may conditionally or unconditionally exempt any class of covered persons, service providers, or consumer financial products or services, from any provision of this title, or from any rule issued under this title, as the Bureau determines necessary or appropriate to carry out the purposes and objectives of this title, taking into consideration the factors in subparagraph (B).

(B) FACTORS. — In issuing an exemption, as permitted under subparagraph (A), the Bureau shall, as appropriate, take into consideration —

(i) the total assets of the class of covered persons;

(ii) the volume of transactions involving consumer financial products or services in which the class of covered persons engages; and

(iii) existing provisions of law which are applicable to the consumer financial product or

力,实施、执行和以其他方式落实联邦消费者金融法律规定。

(b)**规则制定、命令和指引**。——

(1)**一般权力**。——消费者金融保护局局长可以制定必要或适当的规则,并发布必要或适当的命令和指引,使消费者金融保护局能够实施、执行联邦消费者金融法律的宗旨和目标,并防范对联邦消费者金融法律的规避行为。

(2)**规则制定标准**。——在根据联邦消费者金融法律制定规则时——

(A)消费者金融保护局应考虑——

(i)该等规则可能给消费者及所涉主体带来收益和成本,包括该等规则导致消费者获得消费者金融产品或服务机会减少的可能性;及

(ii)第1026条所述规则草案对所涉主体的影响,以及对农村地区消费者的影响;

(B)消费者金融保护局在提出规则草案之前,应与相应的审慎监管者或其他联邦机关进行磋商,同时,在就该等规则草案征求意见的过程中,也应就该等规则草案的目标与该等监管者或机关所执行的审慎、市场或系统性目标的一致性,与该等监管者或机关进行磋商;且

(C)如果在第(B)子款所述磋商过程中,审慎监管者针对消费者金融保护局提出的规则草案或其中的任何一部分提出书面反对意见, 消费者金融保护局应在其发布的正式通过规则版本中,说明审慎监管者的反对意见,并且,消费者金融保护局针对该反对意见作出任何决定的,应说明决定理由,但是,本项的任何内容均不得被解释为改变或限制了第1023条所规定的适用于消费者金融保护局所制定任何规则的程序。

(3)**豁免**。——

(A)**一般规定**。——消费者金融保护局可以发布规则,有条件或无条件的向任何类别的所涉主体、服务提供者或者消费者金融产品或服务,授予消费者金融保护局在对第(B)子款所述因素加以考虑后判定对于实现本编宗旨和目的确属必要或适当的豁免,使其不必遵守本编的任何规定或根据本编发布的任何规则。

(B)**因素**。——消费者金融保护局在授予第(A)子款所准许的豁免时,应适当考量如下因素——

(i)该类所涉主体的总资产;

(ii)该类所涉主体从事的涉及消费者金融产品或服务的交易之数量;及

(iii)适用于消费者金融产品或服务的现有法律规定,以及该等规定在多大程度上

service and the extent to which such provisions provide consumers with adequate protections.

(4) EXCLUSIVE RULEMAKING AUTHORITY. —

(A) IN GENERAL. — Notwithstanding any other provisions of Federal law and except as provided in section 1061(b)(5), to the extent that a provision of Federal consumer financial law authorizes the Bureau and another Federal agency to issue regulations under that provision of law for purposes of assuring compliance with Federal consumer financial law and any regulations thereunder, the Bureau shall have the exclusive authority to prescribe rules subject to those provisions of law.

(B) DEFERENCE. — Notwithstanding any power granted to any Federal agency or to the Council under this title, and subject to section 1061(b)(5)(E), the deference that a court affords to the Bureau with respect to a determination by the Bureau regarding the meaning or interpretation of any provision of a Federal consumer financial law shall be applied as if the Bureau were the only agency authorized to apply, enforce, interpret, or administer the provisions of such Federal consumer financial law.

(c) MONITORING. —

(1) IN GENERAL. — In order to support its rulemaking and other functions, the Bureau shall monitor for risks to consumers in the offering or provision of consumer financial products or services, including developments in markets for such products or services.

(2) CONSIDERATIONS. — In allocating its resources to perform the monitoring required by this section, the Bureau may consider, among other factors —

(A) likely risks and costs to consumers associated with buying or using a type of consumer financial product or service;

(B) understanding by consumers of the risks of a type of consumer financial product or service;

(C) the legal protections applicable to the offering or provision of a consumer financial product or service, including the extent to which the law is likely to adequately protect consumers;

(D) rates of growth in the offering or provision of a consumer financial product or service;

(E) the extent, if any, to which the risks of a consumer financial product or service may disproportionately affect traditionally underserved consumers; or

(F) the types, number, and other pertinent characteristics of covered persons that offer or provide the consumer financial product or service.

(3) SIGNIFICANT FINDINGS. —

(A) IN GENERAL. — The Bureau shall publish not fewer than 1 report of significant findings of its monitoring required by this subsection in each calendar year, beginning with the first calendar year that begins at least 1 year after the designated transfer date.

向消费者提供充分保护。

(4)**排他性的规则制定权**。——

(A)**一般规定**。——无论联邦法律是否存在任何不同规定,除第1061(b)(5)条规定的情形外,如果联邦消费者金融法律规定授权消费者金融保护局和另一联邦机关根据该等法律规定发布规章,以确保对联邦消费者金融法律以及依其制定的任何规章的合规,消费者金融保护局应拥有根据该等法律规定制定规则的排他性权力。

(B)**司法尊重**。——不论本编向任何联邦机关或金融稳定监督委员会授予了何种权力,如果法院对于消费者金融保护局就联邦消费者金融法律任何规定的含义或解释作出的判定给予司法尊重,则在不违反第1061(b)(5)(E)条规定的前提下,该等司法尊重应将消费者金融保护局视同唯一有权适用、执行、解释或实施该等联邦消费者金融法律规定的机关。

(c)**监控**。——

(1)**一般规定**。——为了支持消费者金融保护局行使规则制定职能和其他职能,消费者金融保护局应对消费者在消费者金融产品或服务的要约或提供中(包括该等产品或服务市场的发展动态中)所面临的风险进行监控。

(2)**考虑因素**。——为开展本条规定的监控而进行资源分配时,消费者金融保护局可考虑的因素包括但不限于——

(A)购买或使用某一类型的消费者金融产品或服务可能给消费者带来的风险和成本;

(B)消费者对某一类型消费者金融产品或服务风险的认识;

(C)消费者金融产品或服务的要约或提供过程中适用的法律保护,包括法律在多大程度上为消费者提供充分保护;

(D)要约或提供的消费者金融产品或服务的增长率;

(E)消费者金融产品或服务风险可能在多大程度上对传统弱势消费者造成不成比例的影响(如有);或

(F)要约或提供消费者金融产品或服务的所涉主体的类型、数量及其他有关特点。

(3)**重大认定**。——

(A)**一般规定**。——自指定转移日届满至少1年之日起的第一个日历年开始,消费者金融保护局应针对本子条规定的监控,每一日历年发布至少1份重大认定报告。

(B)CONFIDENTIAL INFORMATION. — The Bureau may make public such information obtained by the Bureau under this section as is in the public interest, through aggregated reports or other appropriate formats designed to protect confidential information in accordance with paragraphs (4), (6), (8), and (9).

(4) COLLECTION OF INFORMATION. —

(A) IN GENERAL. — In conducting any monitoring or assessment required by this section, the Bureau shall have the authority to gather information from time to time regarding the organization, business conduct, markets, and activities of covered persons and service providers.

(B) METHODOLOGY. — In order to gather information described in subparagraph (A), the Bureau may —

(i) gather and compile information from a variety of sources, including examination reports concerning covered persons or service providers, consumer complaints, voluntary surveys and voluntary interviews of consumers, surveys and interviews with covered persons and service providers, and review of available databases; and

(ii) require covered persons and service providers participating in consumer financial services markets to file with the Bureau, under oath or otherwise, in such form and within such reasonable period of time as the Bureau may prescribe by rule or order, annual or special reports, or answers in writing to specific questions, furnishing information described in paragraph (4), as necessary for the Bureau to fulfill the monitoring, assessment, and reporting responsibilities imposed by Congress.

(C) LIMITATION. — The Bureau may not use its authorities under this paragraph to obtain records from covered persons and service providers participating in consumer financial services markets for purposes of gathering or analyzing the personally identifiable financial information of consumers.

(5) LIMITED INFORMATION GATHERING. — In order to assess whether a no depository is a covered person, as defined in section 1002, the Bureau may require such no depository to file with the Bureau, under oath or otherwise, in such form and within such reasonable period of time as the Bureau may prescribe by rule or order, annual or special reports, or answers in writing to specific questions.

(6) CONFIDENTIALITY RULES. —

(A) RULEMAKING. — The Bureau shall prescribe rules regarding the confidential treatment of information obtained from persons in connection with the exercise of its authorities under Federal consumer financial law.

(B) ACCESS BY THE BUREAU TO REPORTS OF OTHER REGULATORS. —

(i) EXAMINATION AND FINANCIAL CONDITION REPORTS. — Upon providing reasonable assurances of confidentiality, the Bureau shall have access to any report of

(B)**保密信息**。——消费者金融保护局可以将其根据本条规定获得的有助于维护公共利益的信息,通过汇总报告的方式或旨在根据第(4)款、第(6)款、第(8)款及第(9)款规定保护保密信息的其他适当方式予以公布。

(4)**信息收集**。——

(A)**一般规定**。——消费者金融保护局在开展本条规定的任何监控或评估时,应有权随时收集与所涉主体或服务提供者的组织结构、业务行为、市场和活动相关的信息。

(B)**方法**。——为了收集第(A)子款所述信息,消费者金融保护局可以——

(i)收集和汇编源自各种信息来源的信息,包括关于所涉主体或服务提供者的检查报告、消费者投诉、消费者自愿调查和自愿访谈、所涉主体及服务提供者调查和访谈以及对现有数据库的审查;及

(ii)要求参与消费金融服务市场的所涉主体及服务提供者按照消费者金融保护局发布的规则或命令所规定的形式和合理期限,向消费者金融保护局提交经宣誓或其他程序保证所述内容真实无误的年度报告、特别报告或者对具体问题的书面答复,以便向消费者金融保护局提供第(4)款所述的对协助消费者金融保护局履行国会要求的监控、评估及报告职责确属必要的信息。

(C)**限制**。——消费者金融保护局不得为收集或分析消费者个人身份金融信息之目的,利用本款规定授予的权力,从参与消费金融服务市场的所涉主体及服务提供者处获取相关记录。

(5)**有限信息收集**。——为了评估非存款机构是否构成第1002条定义的所涉主体,消费者金融保护局可以要求该等非存款机构按照消费者金融保护局发布的规则或命令所规定的形式和合理期限,向消费者金融保护局提交经宣誓或其他程序保证所述内容真实无误的年度报告、特别报告或者针对具体问题的书面答复。

(6)**保密规则**。——

(A)**规则制定**。——消费者金融保护局应制定相应规则,对其行使联邦消费者金融法律赋予的权力过程中从他人处获得的信息进行保密处理。

(B)**消费者金融保护局获取其他监管者报告的权利**。——

(i)**检查报告及财务状况报告**。——在提供合理保密保证后,消费者金融保护局应有权获取对所涉主体或服务提供者拥有管辖权的审慎监管者或其他联邦机关所编

examination or financial condition made by a prudential regulator or other Federal agency having jurisdiction over a covered person or service provider, and to all revisions made to any such report.

(ii) PROVISION OF OTHER REPORTS TO THE BUREAU. — In addition to the reports described in clause (i), a prudential regulator or other Federal agency having jurisdiction over a covered person or service provider may, in its discretion, furnish to the Bureau any other report or other confidential supervisory information concerning any insured depository institution, credit union, or other entity examined by such agency under authority of any provision of Federal law.

(C) ACCESS BY OTHER REGULATORS TO REPORTS OF THE BUREAU. —

(i) EXAMINATION REPORTS. — Upon providing reasonable assurances of confidentiality, a prudential regulator, a State regulator, or any other Federal agency having jurisdiction over a covered person or service provider shall have access to any report of examination made by the Bureau with respect to such person, and to all revisions made to any such report.

(ii) PROVISION OF OTHER REPORTS TO OTHER REGULATORS. — In addition to the reports described in clause(i), the Bureau may, in its discretion, furnish to a prudential regulator or other agency having jurisdiction over a covered person or service provider any other report or other confidential supervisory information concerning such person examined by the Bureau under the authority of any other provision of Federal law.

(7) REGISTRATION. —

(A) IN GENERAL. — The Bureau may prescribe rules regarding registration requirements applicable to a covered person, other than an insured depository institution, insured credit union, or related person.

(B) REGISTRATION INFORMATION. — Subject to rules prescribed by the Bureau, the Bureau may publicly disclose registration information to facilitate the ability of consumers to identify covered persons that are registered with the Bureau.

(C) CONSULTATION WITH STATE AGENCIES. — In developing and implementing registration requirements under this paragraph, the Bureau shall consult with State agencies regarding requirements or systems (including coordinated or combined systems for registration), where appropriate.

(8) PRIVACY CONSIDERATIONS. — In collecting information from any person, publicly releasing information held by the Bureau, or requiring covered persons to publicly report information, the Bureau shall take steps to ensure that proprietary, personal, or confidential consumer information that is protected from public disclosure under section 552(b) or 552a of title 5, United States Code, or any other provision of law, is not made public under this title.

制的任何检查报告或财务状况报告,以及对该等报告作出的所有修订。

(ii)**向消费者金融保护局提供其他报告**。——除第(i)项所述报告之外,对所涉主体或服务提供者拥有管辖权的审慎监管者或其他联邦机关可以依其自由裁量权向消费者金融保护局提供关于任何参保存款机构、信贷联盟或该等机关根据联邦法律任何规定赋予的权力而进行检查的其他实体的任何其他报告或其他保密监管信息。

(C)**其他监管者获取消费者金融保护局报告的权利**。——

(i)**检查报告**。——在提供合理保密保证后,对所涉主体或服务提供者拥有管辖权的审慎监管者、州监管者或任何其他联邦机关应有权获取消费者金融保护局针对该等主体编制的任何检查报告,以及对该等报告作出的所有修订。

(ii)**向其他监管者提供其他报告**。——除第(i)项所述报告之外,消费者金融保护局可以依其自由裁量权向对所涉主体或服务提供者拥有管辖权的审慎监管者或其他机关,提供消费者金融保护局根据联邦法律任何其他规定赋予的权力而进行检查的所涉主体的其他报告或其他保密监管信息。

(7)**注册**。——

(A)**一般规定**。——消费者金融保护局可以制定适用于所涉主体(但参保存款机构、参保信贷联盟或关联主体除外)的注册要求规则。

(B)**注册信息**。——消费者金融保护局可以在不违反其制定的规则的前提下,公开披露注册信息,以提升消费者对已在消费者金融保护局注册的所涉主体进行识别的能力。

(C)**与州政府机关进行磋商**。——在制定和实施本款规定的注册要求时,消费者金融保护局应与州机关就注册要求或系统(包括协调或联合注册系统)进行适当的磋商。

(8)**隐私考虑**。——消费者金融保护局在向任何人收集信息、公布消费者金融保护局所持有的信息或要求所涉主体公开报告信息时,应采取相应措施,确保根据《美国法典》第五编第552(b)节或第552a节或任何其他法律规定免予公开披露的专有、个人或保密性质的消费者信息不会根据本编规定被公开。

(9) CONSUMER PRIVACY. —

(A) IN GENERAL. — The Bureau may not obtain from a covered person or service provider any personally identifiable financial information about a consumer from the financial records of the covered person or service provider, except —

(i) if the financial records are reasonably described in a request by the Bureau and the consumer provides written permission for the disclosure of such information by the covered person or service provider to the Bureau; or

(ii) as may be specifically permitted or required under other applicable provisions of law and in accordance with the Right to Financial Privacy Act of 1978(12 U.S.C. 3401 et seq.).

(B) TREATMENT OF COVERED PERSON OR SERVICE PROVIDER. — With respect to the application of any provision of the Right to Financial Privacy Act of 1978, to a disclosure by a covered person or service provider subject to this subsection, the covered person or service provider shall be treated as if it were a "financial institution", as defined in section 1101 of that Act (12 U.S.C. 3401).

(d) ASSESSMENT OF SIGNIFICANT RULES. —

(1) IN GENERAL. — The Bureau shall conduct an assessment of each significant rule or order adopted by the Bureau under Federal consumer financial law. The assessment shall address, among other relevant factors, the effectiveness of the rule or order in meeting the purposes and objectives of this title and the specific goals stated by the Bureau. The assessment shall reflect available evidence and any data that the Bureau reasonably may collect.

(2) REPORTS. — The Bureau shall publish a report of its assessment under this subsection not later than 5 years after the effective date of the subject rule or order.

(3) PUBLIC COMMENT REQUIRED. — Before publishing a report of its assessment, the Bureau shall invite public comment on recommendations for modifying, expanding, or eliminating the newly adopted significant rule or order.

SEC. 1023. REVIEW OF BUREAU REGULATIONS.

(a) REVIEW OF BUREAU REGULATIONS. — On the petition of a member agency of the Council, the Council may set aside a final regulation prescribed by the Bureau, or any provision thereof, if the Council decides, in accordance with subsection (c), that the regulation or provision would put the safety and soundness of the United States banking system or the stability of the financial system of the United States at risk.

(b) PETITION. —

(1) PROCEDURE. — An agency represented by a member of the Council may petition the Council, in writing, and in accordance with rules prescribed pursuant to subsection (f), to stay the effectiveness of, or set aside, a regulation if the member agency filing the petition —

(9)**消费者隐私**。——

(A)**一般规定**。——消费者金融保护局不得通过所涉主体或服务提供者的财务记录获取消费者任何具有个人身份性质的金融信息,但是以下情形除外——

(i)消费者金融保护局在提出要求之时,对该等金融记录进行了合理说明,并且消费者作出书面许可,允许所涉主体或服务提供者向消费者金融保护局披露该等信息;或

(ii)其他适用的法律规定对该等信息的披露给予具体许可或要求,并且该等信息的披露符合《1978年金融隐私权法》(《美国法典》第十二编第3401节及其后条文)的规定。

(B)**所涉主体或服务提供者的待遇**。——如果所涉主体或服务提供者根据本子条规定进行披露之时适用《1978年金融隐私权法》的任何规定,所涉主体或服务提供者应被视同该法第1101条(《美国法典》第十二编第3401节)所定义的"金融机构"。

(d)**对重大规则的评估**。——

(1)**一般规定**。——消费者金融保护局应根据联邦消费者金融法律规定,对其制定的每项重大规则或命令进行评估。该等评估应论述的因素包括但不限于该等规则或命令是否能有效实现本编宗旨、目的以及消费者金融保护局确定的具体目标。该等评估应采用消费者金融保护局合理收集的可用证据和任何数据。

(2)**报告**。——消费者金融保护局应在被评估的规则或命令的生效日后5年内就根据本子条作出的评估发布一份报告。

(3)**征求公众意见要求**。——在发布评估报告之前,消费者金融保护局应就其针对新近制定的重大规则或命令提出的修改、内容增加或废除建议,征求公众意见。

第1023条　对消费者金融保护局规章的审查

(a)**对消费者金融保护局规章的审查**。——经金融稳定监督委员会的成员机关请求,如果金融稳定监督委员会根据第(c)子条认定消费者金融保护局制定的最终规章或其中的任何条款将对美国银行系统的安全稳健或美国金融系统的稳定造成风险,金融稳定监督委员会可以撤销该等规章或条款。

(b)**请求**。——

(1)**程序**。——在下述情形下,金融稳定监督委员会成员所代表的机关可以按照根据第(f)子条制定的规则,以书面形式请求金融稳定监督委员会中止规章的效力或撤销规章——

(A) has in good faith attempted to work with the Bureau to resolve concerns regarding the effect of the rule on the safety and soundness of the United States banking system or the stability of the financial system of the United States; and

(B) files the petition with the Council not later than 10 days after the date on which the regulation has been published in the Federal Register.

(2) PUBLICATION. — Any petition filed with the Council under this section shall be published in the Federal Register and transmitted contemporaneously with filing to the Committee on Banking, Housing, and Urban Affairs of the Senate and the Committee on Financial Services of the House of Representatives.

(c) STAYS AND SET ASIDES. —

(1) STAY. —

(A) IN GENERAL. — Upon the request of any member agency, the Chairperson of the Council may stay the effectiveness of a regulation for the purpose of allowing appropriate consideration of the petition by the Council.

(B) EXPIRATION. — A stay issued under this paragraph shall expire on the earlier of —

(i) 90 days after the date of filing of the petition under subsection (b); or

(ii) the date on which the Council makes a decision under paragraph (3).

(2) NO ADVERSE INFERENCE. — After the expiration of any stay imposed under this section, no inference shall be drawn regarding the validity or enforceability of a regulation which was the subject of the petition.

(3) VOTE. —

(A) IN GENERAL. — The decision to issue a stay of, or set aside, any regulation under this section shall be made only with the affirmative vote in accordance with subparagraph (B) of 2/3 of the members of the Council then serving.

(B) AUTHORIZATION TO VOTE. — A member of the Council may vote to stay the effectiveness of, or set aside, a final regulation prescribed by the Bureau only if the agency or department represented by that member has —

(i) considered any relevant information provided by the agency submitting the petition and by the Bureau; and

(ii) made an official determination, at a public meeting where applicable, that the regulation which is the subject of the petition would put the safety and soundness of the United States banking system or the stability of the financial system of the United States at risk.

(4) DECISIONS TO SET ASIDE. —

(A) EFFECT OF DECISION. — A decision by the Council to set aside a regulation prescribed by the Bureau, or provision thereof, shall render such regulation, or provision

(A)提出申请的成员机关已善意的试图与消费者金融保护局合作解决与该等规章对美国银行系统之安全稳健或美国金融系统之稳定造成的影响相关的问题;且

(B)上述成员机关在该等规章在《联邦公报》上公布之日后10天内向金融稳定监督委员会提出请求。

(2)**公布**。——根据本条向金融稳定监督委员会提出的任何请求均应在《联邦公报》上公布,并同时传送给参议院银行、住房与城市事务委员会以及众议院金融服务委员会。

(c)**中止和撤销**。——

(1)**中止**。——

(A)**一般规定**。——经任何成员机关请求,金融稳定监督委员会主席可以中止被提出请求的规章的效力,以便金融稳定监督委员会对请求进行适当审议。

(B)**到期失效**。——根据本款签发的中止令应于如下日期(以较早者为准)失效——

(i)根据第(b)子条提出请求之日后第90天;或

(ii)金融稳定监督委员会根据第(3)款规定作出决定之日。

(2)禁止作出不利推断。——根据本条签发的任何中止令到期失效之后,不得因该等请求而对被提出请求的规章之效力或可强制执行性作出任何不利推断。

(3)**表决**。——

(A)**一般规定**。——只有在金融稳定监督委员会届时在任成员中的2/3成员按照第(B)子款的规定投赞成票的情况下,方可根据本条规定作出中止或撤销任何规章的决定。

(B)**表决权力**。——只有下述情形下,金融稳定监督委员会的成员方可表决赞成中止消费者金融保护局制定的最终规章的效力或撤销该规章——

(i)该成员所代表的机关或部门已经对提出请求的机关以及消费者金融保护局所提供的相关信息进行了考虑;且

(ii)该成员所代表的机关或部门已经在公开会议上(如适用)正式判定被提出请求的规章将对美国银行系统的安全稳健或美国金融系统的稳定造成风险。

(4)**撤销决定**。——

(A)**决定的效力**。——金融稳定监督委员会对消费者金融保护局制定的规章或其条款作出撤销决定之后,该等规章或条款即丧失强制执行力。

thereof, unenforceable.

(B) TIMELY ACTION REQUIRED. — The Council may not issue a decision to set aside a regulation, or provision thereof, which is the subject of a petition under this section after the expiration of the later of —

(i) 45 days following the date of filing of the petition, unless a stay is issued under paragraph (1); or

(ii) the expiration of a stay issued by the Council under this section.

(C) SEPARATE AUTHORITY. — The issuance of a stay under this section does not affect the authority of the Council to set aside a regulation.

(5) DISMISSAL DUE TO INACTION. — A petition under this section shall be deemed dismissed if the Council has not issued a decision to set aside a regulation, or provision thereof, within the period for timely action under paragraph (4)(B).

(6) PUBLICATION OF DECISION. — Any decision under this subsection to issue a stay of, or set aside, a regulation or provision thereof shall be published by the Council in the Federal Register as soon as practicable after the decision is made, with an explanation of the reasons for the decision.

(7) RULEMAKING PROCEDURES INAPPLICABLE. — The notice and comment procedures under section 553 of title 5, United States Code, shall not apply to any decision under this section of the Council to issue a stay of, or set aside, a regulation.

(8) JUDICIAL REVIEW OF DECISIONS BY THE COUNCIL. — A decision by the Council to set aside a regulation prescribed by the Bureau, or provision thereof, shall be subject to review under chapter 7 of title 5, United States Code.

(d) APPLICATION OF OTHER LAW. — Nothing in this section shall be construed as altering, limiting, or restricting the application of any other provision of law, except as otherwise specifically provided in this section, including chapter 5 and chapter 7 of title 5, United States Code, to a regulation which is the subject of a petition filed under this section.

(e) SAVINGS CLAUSE. — Nothing in this section shall be construed as limiting or restricting the Bureau from engaging in a rulemaking in accordance with applicable law.

(f) IMPLEMENTING RULES. — The Council shall prescribe procedural rules to implement this section.

SEC. 1024. SUPERVISION OF NONDEPOSITORY COVERED PERSONS.

(a) SCOPE OF COVERAGE. —

(1) APPLICABILITY. — Notwithstanding any other provision of this title, and except as provided in paragraph (3), this section shall apply to any covered person who —

(A) offers or provides origination, brokerage, or servicing of loans secured by real estate for use by consumers primarily for personal, family, or household purposes, or loan modification or foreclosure relief services in connection with such loans;

(B)**及时行动要求**。——以下日期届满之后(以较晚者为准),金融稳定监督委员会即不得就依本条规定被提出请求的规章或其条款作出撤销决定——

(i)请求提出之日后第45天,但已根据第(1)款签发中止令的除外;或

(ii)金融稳定监督委员会根据本条签发的中止令到期失效之日。

(C)**独立权力**。——根据本条签发的中止令对金融稳定监督委员会撤销规章的权力不构成影响。

(5)**不作为导致的驳回**。——如果金融稳定监督委员会在第(4)(B)款规定的及时行动期间内未就规章或其条款作出撤销决定,则根据本条提出的请求应视为已被驳回。

(6)**决定的公布**。——金融稳定监督委员会根据本子条规定对规章或其条款作出的任何中止或撤销决定,均应在该等决定作出后尽快在《联邦公报》上公布,并说明作出该等决定的理由。

(7)**不适用的规则制定程序**。——《美国法典》第五编第553节规定的通知和意见征求程序不适用于金融稳定监督委员会根据本条对规章作出的任何中止或撤销决定。

(8)**对金融稳定监督委员会决定的司法审查**。——金融稳定监督委员会对消费者金融保护局制定的规章或其条款作出的撤销决定应按照《美国法典》第五编第七章规定接受司法审查。

(d)**其他法律的适用**。——除本条另有明确规定的情形外,本条的任何内容均不得被解释为改变、限制或禁止任何其他法律规定(包括《美国法典》第五编第五章和第七章)对依本条被提出请求的规章之适用。

(e)**保留条款**。——本条的任何内容均不得被解释为限制或约束消费者金融保护局根据适用法律从事规则制定工作。

(f)**实施规则**。——金融稳定监督委员会应制定实施本条规定的程序规则。

第1024条　对非存款机构所涉主体的监管

(a)**监管范围**。——

(1)**适用范围**。——无论本编是否存在任何不同规定,除第(3)款规定的情形之外,本条应适用于存在如下情形的任何所涉主体——

(A)所涉主体要约或提供主要供消费者个人、家庭或共同居住人使用,以不动产为抵押的贷款的发起、经纪或供给服务,或者与该等贷款有关的贷款修改或止赎救济服务;

(B) is a larger participant of a market for other consumer financial products or services, as defined by rule in accordance with paragraph (2);

(C) the Bureau has reasonable cause to determine, by order, after notice to the covered person and a reasonable opportunity for such covered person to respond, based on complaints collected through the system under section 1013(b)(3) or information from other sources, that such covered person is engaging, or has engaged, in conduct that poses risks to consumers with regard to the offering or provision of consumer financial products or services;

(D) offers or provides to a consumer any private education loan, as defined in section 140 of the Truth in Lending Act (15 U.S.C. 1650), notwithstanding section 1027(a)(2)(A) and subject to section 1027(a)(2)(C); or

(E) offers or provides to a consumer a payday loan.

(2) RULEMAKING TO DEFINE COVERED PERSONS SUBJECT TO THIS SECTION. — The Bureau shall consult with the Federal Trade Commission prior to issuing a rule, in accordance with paragraph (1)(B), to define covered persons subject to this section. The Bureau shall issue its initial rule not later than 1 year after the designated transfer date.

(3) RULES OF CONSTRUCTION. —

(A) CERTAIN PERSONS EXCLUDED. — This section shall not apply to persons described in section 1025(a) or 1026(a).

(B) ACTIVITY LEVELS. — For purposes of computing activity levels under paragraph (1) or rules issued thereunder, activities of affiliated companies (other than insured depository institutions or insured credit unions) shall be aggregated.

(b) SUPERVISION. —

(1) IN GENERAL. — The Bureau shall require reports and conduct examinations on a periodic basis of persons described in subsection (a)(1) for purposes of —

(A) assessing compliance with the requirements of Federal consumer financial law;

(B) obtaining information about the activities and compliance systems or procedures of such person; and

(C) detecting and assessing risks to consumers and to markets for consumer financial products and services.

(2) RISK-BASED SUPERVISION PROGRAM. — The Bureau shall exercise its authority under paragraph(1) in a manner designed to ensure that such exercise, with respect to persons described in subsection (a)(1), is based on the assessment by the Bureau of the risks posed to consumers in the relevant product markets and geographic markets, and taking into consideration, as applicable —

(A) the asset size of the covered person;

(B) the volume of transactions involving consumer financial products or services in which the covered person engages;

(B)所涉主体具有消费者金融保护局根据第(2)款发布的规则所定义的其他消费者金融产品或服务市场大型参与方身份;

(C)消费者金融保护局在向所涉主体发出通知并向其提供合理的答复机会后,根据通过第1013(b)(3)条规定的系统收集的投诉或从其他信息来源获得的信息,基于合理理由,发布命令判定该等所涉主体正在从事或曾经从事与消费者金融产品或服务的要约或提供相关的对消费者造成风险的行为;

(D)无论第1027(a)(2)(A)条如何规定,所涉主体在不违反第1027(a)(2)(C)条规定的情况下,向消费者要约或提供《诚实信贷法》第140条(《美国法典》第十五编第1650节)所定义的任何个人教育贷款;或

(E)所涉主体向消费者要约或提供发薪日贷款。

(2)**制定规则对受制于本条规定的所涉主体进行界定**。——消费者金融保护局应在发布规则之前与联邦贸易委员会磋商,按照第(1)(B)款对受制于本条规定的所涉主体进行界定。消费者金融保护局应于指定转移日后1年内发布初步规则。

(3)解释规则。——

(A)**排除特定主体**。——本条不适用于第1025(a)条或第1026(a)条所述主体。

(B)**活动水平**。——在根据第(1)款或根据依第(1)款规定制定的规则计算所涉主体的活动水平时,关联方(但参保存款机构或参保信贷联盟除外)的活动应合并计算。

(b)**监管**。——

(1)**一般规定**。——消费者金融保护局应要求第(a)(1)子条所述主体定期提交报告并定期对该等主体进行检查,以便——

(A)评估该等主体对联邦消费者金融法律要求的合规情况;

(B)获取与该等主体的活动及合规制度或程序相关的信息;及

(C)检测和评估该等主体对消费者或消费者金融产品和服务市场造成的风险。

(2)**基于风险的监管计划**。——消费者金融保护局应确保对第(a)(1)子条所述主体行使第(1)款规定的权力时,以其对该等主体给相关产品市场及地域市场中消费者造成的风险所做的评估为依据,并考虑如下因素(如适用)——

(A)所涉主体的资产规模;

(B)所涉主体从事的涉及消费者金融产品或服务的交易之数量;

(C) the risks to consumers created by the provision of such consumer financial products or services;

(D) the extent to which such institutions are subject to oversight by State authorities for consumer protection; and

(E) any other factors that the Bureau determines to be relevant to a class of covered persons.

(3) COORDINATION. — To minimize regulatory burden, the Bureau shall coordinate its supervisory activities with the supervisory activities conducted by prudential regulators and the State bank regulatory authorities, including establishing their respective schedules for examining persons described in subsection(a)(1) and requirements regarding reports to be submitted by such persons.

(4) USE OF EXISTING REPORTS. — The Bureau shall, to the fullest extent possible, use —

(A) reports pertaining to persons described in subsection (a)(1) that have been provided or required to have been provided to a Federal or State agency; and

(B) information that has been reported publicly.

(5) PRESERVATION OF AUTHORITY. — Nothing in this title may be construed as limiting the authority of the Director to require reports from persons described in subsection (a)(1), as permitted under paragraph (1), regarding information owned or under the control of such person, regardless of whether such information is maintained, stored, or processed by another person.

(6) REPORTS OF TAX LAW NONCOMPLIANCE. — The Bureau shall provide the Commissioner of Internal Revenue with any report of examination or related information identifying possible tax law noncompliance.

(7) REGISTRATION, RECORDKEEPING AND OTHER REQUIREMENTS FOR CERTAIN PERSONS. —

(A) IN GENERAL. — The Bureau shall prescribe rules to facilitate supervision of persons described in subsection (a)(1) and assessment and detection of risks to consumers.

(B) RECORDKEEPING. — The Bureau may require a person described in subsection (a)(1), to generate, provide, or retain records for the purposes of facilitating supervision of such persons and assessing and detecting risks to consumers.

(C) REQUIREMENTS CONCERNING OBLIGATIONS. — The Bureau may prescribe rules regarding a person described in subsection (a)(1), to ensure that such persons are legitimate entities and are able to perform their obligations to consumers. Such requirements may include background checks for principals, officers, directors, or key personnel and bonding or other appropriate financial requirements.

(D) CONSULTATION WITH STATE AGENCIES. — In developing and implementing

(C)提供该等消费者金融产品或服务对消费者造成的风险;

(D)该等机构在多大程度上受州消费者保护机构监管;及

(E)消费者金融保护局判定与某类所涉主体相关的任何其他因素。

(3)**协调**。——为了将监管负担减到最低限度,消费者金融保护局应与审慎监管者及州银行监管机构就各自开展的监管活动进行协调,包括分别就第(a)(1)子条所述主体制定检查计划及报告提交要求。

(4)**既有报告的利用**。——消费者金融保护局应尽最大可能利用——

(A)已经或应向联邦机关或州机关提供的与第(a)(1)子条所述主体相关的报告;及

(B)已经被公开报告的信息。

(5)**权力保留**。——本编任何内容均不得被解释为对消费者金融保护局局长根据第(1)款规定要求第(a)(1)子条所述主体就其拥有或控制的信息(无论该等信息是否由他人保存、存储或处理)提交报告的权力构成限制。

(6)**关于违反税法行为的报告**。——消费者金融保护局应向国税局局长提供用于发现潜在违反税法行为的任何检查报告或相关信息。

(7)**针对特定主体的注册、记录保存要求和其他要求**。——

(A)**一般规定**。——消费者金融保护局应制定规则,以加强对第(a)(1)子条所述主体的监管以及对该等主体给消费者所造成风险的评估和检测。

(B)**记录保存**。——消费者金融保护局可以要求第(a)(1)子条所述主体编制、提供或保存相关记录,以加强对该等主体的监管以及对该等主体给消费者所造成风险的评估和检测。

(C)**义务相关要求**。——消费者金融保护局可以就第(a)(1)子条所述主体制定规则,以确保该等主体系合法实体并能够履行其对消费者承担的义务。该等要求可包括对负责人、管理人员、董事或主要人员开展背景调查的要求,以及保证金要求或其他适当的财务要求。

(D)**与州机关进行磋商**。——在制定和实施本款所述要求时,消费者金融保护局

requirements under this paragraph, the Bureau shall consult with State agencies regarding requirements or systems (including coordinated or combined systems for registration), where appropriate.

(c) ENFORCEMENT AUTHORITY. —

(1) THE BUREAU TO HAVE ENFORCEMENT AUTHORITY. — Except as provided in paragraph(3) and section 1061, with respect to any person described in subsection (a)(1), to the extent that Federal law authorizes the Bureau and another Federal agency to enforce Federal consumer financial law, the Bureau shall have exclusive authority to enforce that Federal consumer financial law.

(2) REFERRAL. — Any Federal agency authorized to enforce a Federal consumer financial law described in paragraph (1) may recommend in writing to the Bureau that the Bureau initiate an enforcement proceeding, as the Bureau is authorized by that Federal law or by this title.

(3) COORDINATION WITH THE FEDERAL TRADE COMMISSION. —

(A) IN GENERAL. — The Bureau and the Federal Trade Commission shall negotiate an agreement for coordinating with respect to enforcement actions by each agency regarding the offering or provision of consumer financial products or services by any covered person that is described in subsection(a)(1), or service providers thereto. The agreement shall include procedures for notice to the other agency, where feasible, prior to initiating a civil action to enforce any Federal law regarding the offering or provision of consumer financial products or services.

(B) CIVIL ACTIONS. — Whenever a civil action has been filed by, or on behalf of, the Bureau or the Federal Trade Commission for any violation of any provision of Federal law described in subparagraph (A), or any regulation prescribed under such provision of law —

(i) the other agency may not, during the pendency of that action, institute a civil action under such provision of law against any defendant named in the complaint in such pending action for any violation alleged in the complaint; and

(ii) the Bureau or the Federal Trade Commission may intervene as a party in any such action brought by the other agency, and, upon intervening —

(I) be heard on all matters arising in such enforcement action; and

(II) file petitions for appeal in such actions.

(C) AGREEMENT TERMS. — The terms of any agreement negotiated under subparagraph (A) may modify or supersede the provisions of subparagraph (B).

(D) DEADLINE. — The agencies shall reach the agreement required under subparagraph (A) not later than 6 months after the designated transfer date.

(d) EXCLUSIVE RULEMAKING AND EXAMINATION AUTHORITY. — Notwithstanding any other provision of Federal law and except as provided in section 1061, to

应与州机关就上述要求或系统(包括协调或联合注册系统)进行适当的磋商。

(c)**执法权**。——

(1)**消费者金融保护局拥有执法权**。——除第(3)款及第1061条规定的情形外,对于第(a)(1)子条所述任何主体而言,如果联邦法律同时授权消费者金融保护局和另一联邦机关执行联邦消费者金融法律,消费者金融保护局应拥有执行该等联邦消费者金融法律的排他性权力。

(2)**执法建议**。——有权执行第(1)款所述联邦消费者金融法律的任何联邦机关均可采用书面形式建议消费者金融保护局根据上述联邦法律或本编的授权启动执法程序。

(3)**与联邦贸易委员会进行协调**。——

(A)**一般规定**。——消费者金融保护局应与联邦贸易委员会协商达成一份协议,协调各机关针对第(a)(1)子条所述所涉主体或其服务提供者要约或提供消费者金融产品或服务的行为采取的执法行动。该协议的内容应包括双方在针对消费者金融产品或服务的要约或提供启动强制执行任何联邦法律的民事诉讼之前,采用的在可行的范围内向对方机关发送通知的程序。

(B)**民事诉讼**。——如果消费者金融保护局或联邦贸易委员会或其代表针对第(A)子款所述违反任何联邦法律的规定或依其制定的任何规章的行为提起民事诉讼,则——

(i)在上述诉讼未决期间,对方机关不得根据上述法律规定,基于上述诉讼中起诉状所指控的任何违法违规行为对该起诉书中任何被告提起民事诉讼;且

(ii)消费者金融保护局或联邦贸易委员会可以作为当事人参与对方机关所提起的任何上述诉讼,并在参与诉讼之后——

(I)可以就上述执法诉讼中所涉全部事项作出陈述;并

(II)可以就上述诉讼提出上诉请求。

(C)**协议条款**。——双方机关可通过根据第(A)子款磋商达成的任何协议条款,修改或替代第(B)子款的规定。

(D)**最后期限**。——双方机关应在指定转移日后6个月内达成第(A)子款规定的协议。

(d)**排他性的规则制定权和检查权**。——无论联邦法律是否存在任何不同规定,除第1061条规定的情形外,如果联邦法律授权消费者金融保护局及另一联邦机关根

the extent that Federal law authorizes the Bureau and another Federal agency to issue regulations or guidance, conduct examinations, or require reports from a person described in subsection(a)(1) under such law for purposes of assuring compliance with Federal consumer financial law and any regulations thereunder, the Bureau shall have the exclusive authority to prescribe rules, issue guidance, conduct examinations, require reports, or issue exemptions with regard to a person described in subsection (a)(1), subject to those provisions of law.

(e) SERVICE PROVIDERS. — A service provider to a person described in subsection (a)(1) shall be subject to the authority of the Bureau under this section, to the same extent as if such service provider were engaged in a service relationship with a bank, and the Bureau were an appropriate Federal banking agency under section 7(c) of the Bank Service Company Act (12 U.S.C. 1867(c)). In conducting any examination or requiring any report from a service provider subject to this subsection, the Bureau shall coordinate with the appropriate prudential regulator, as applicable.

(f) PRESERVATION OF FARM CREDIT ADMINISTRATION AUTHORITY. — No provision of this title may be construed as modifying, limiting, or otherwise affecting the authority of the Farm Credit Administration.

SEC. 1025. SUPERVISION OF VERY LARGE BANKS, SAVINGS ASSOCIATIONS, AND CREDIT UNIONS.

(a) SCOPE OF COVERAGE. — This section shall apply to any covered person that is —

(1) an insured depository institution with total assets of more than $10,000,000,000 and any affiliate thereof; or

(2) an insured credit union with total assets of more than $10,000,000,000 and any affiliate thereof.

(b) SUPERVISION. —

(1) IN GENERAL. — The Bureau shall have exclusive authority to require reports and conduct examinations on a periodic basis of persons described in subsection (a) for purposes of —

(A) assessing compliance with the requirements of Federal consumer financial laws;

(B) obtaining information about the activities subject to such laws and the associated compliance systems or procedures of such persons; and

(C) detecting and assessing associated risks to consumers and to markets for consumer financial products and services.

(2) COORDINATION. — To minimize regulatory burden, the Bureau shall coordinate its supervisory activities with the supervisory activities conducted by prudential regulators and the State bank regulatory authorities, including consultation regarding their respective

据该等法律就第(a)(1)子条所述主体发布规章或指引、进行检查或要求其提交报告，以确保上述主体对联邦消费者金融法律以及依其制定的任何规章的合规，则消费者金融保护局在不违反该等法律规定的前提下，应拥有排他性的权力，有权就第(a)(1)子条所述主体制定规则、发布指引、进行检查、要求其提交报告或向其授予豁免。

(e)**服务提供者**。——第(a)(1)子条所述主体的服务提供者应受制于本条赋予消费者金融保护局的权力，如同该等服务提供者与银行之间存在服务关系，而消费者金融保护局系《银行服务公司法》第7(c)条[《美国法典》第十二编第1867(c)节]规定的相应的联邦银行业监管机关。在对受制于本子条规定的服务提供者实施任何检查或要求其提交任何报告之时，消费者金融保护局应与相应的审慎监管者进行协调（如适用）。

(f)**农业信贷管理局的权力保持不变**。——本编的任何内容均不得被解释为改变、限制或以其他方式影响农业信贷管理局的权力。

第1025条　对特大型银行、储蓄协会和信贷联盟的监管

(a)**监管范围**。——本条规定适用于符合如下条件的任何所涉主体——

(1)系总资产超过100亿美元的参保存款机构及其任何关联方；或

(2)系总资产超过100亿美元的参保信贷联盟及其任何关联方的所涉主体。

(b)**监管**。——

(1)**一般规定**。——消费者金融保护局应拥有排他性的权力，有权要求第(a)子条所述主体提交定期报告，并对其实施定期检查，以便——

(A)评估该等主体对联邦消费者金融法律要求的合规情况；

(B)获取与受制于该等法律的活动相关的信息，以及与该等主体的相应合规制度或程序相关的信息；及

(C)检测和评估该等主体对消费者以及消费者金融产品和服务市场造成的相关风险。

(2)**协调**。——为了将监管负担减到最低限度，消费者金融保护局应与审慎监管者及州银行监管机构就各自开展的监管活动进行协调，包括分别就第(a)子条所述主体制定检查计划以及报告提交要求。

schedules for examining such persons described in subsection(a) and requirements regarding reports to be submitted by such persons.

(3) USE OF EXISTING REPORTS. — The Bureau shall, to the fullest extent possible, use —

(A) reports pertaining to a person described in subsection(a) that have been provided or required to have been provided to a Federal or State agency; and

(B) information that has been reported publicly.

(4) PRESERVATION OF AUTHORITY. — Nothing in this title may be construed as limiting the authority of the Director to require reports from a person described in subsection (a), as permitted under paragraph (1), regarding information owned or under the control of such person, regardless of whether such information is maintained, stored, or processed by another person.

(5) REPORTS OF TAX LAW NONCOMPLIANCE. — The Bureau shall provide the Commissioner of Internal Revenue with any report of examination or related information identifying possible tax law noncompliance.

(c) PRIMARY ENFORCEMENT AUTHORITY. —

(1) THE BUREAU TO HAVE PRIMARY ENFORCEMENT AUTHORITY. — To the extent that the Bureau and another Federal agency are authorized to enforce a Federal consumer financial law, the Bureau shall have primary authority to enforce that Federal consumer financial law with respect to any person described in subsection (a).

(2) REFERRAL. — Any Federal agency, other than the Federal Trade Commission, that is authorized to enforce a Federal consumer financial law may recommend, in writing, to the Bureau that the Bureau initiate an enforcement proceeding with respect to a person described in subsection (a), as the Bureau is authorized to do by that Federal consumer financial law.

(3) BACKUP ENFORCEMENT AUTHORITY OF OTHER FEDERAL AGENCY. — If the Bureau does not, before the end of the 120–day period beginning on the date on which the Bureau receives a recommendation under paragraph (2), initiate an enforcement proceeding, the other agency referred to in paragraph (2) may initiate an enforcement proceeding, including performing follow up supervisory and support functions incidental thereto, to assure compliance with such proceeding.

(d) SERVICE PROVIDERS. — A service provider to a person described in subsection (a) shall be subject to the authority of the Bureau under this section, to the same extent as if the Bureau were an appropriate Federal banking agency under section 7(c) of the Bank Service Company Act 12 U.S.C. 1867(c). In conducting any examination or requiring any report from a service provider subject to this subsection, the Bureau shall coordinate with the appropriate prudential regulator.

(3)**既有报告的利用**。——消费者金融保护局应尽最大可能利用——

(A)已经或应向联邦机关或州机关提交的与第(a)子条所述主体相关的报告;及

(B)已经被公开报告的信息。

(4)**权力保留**。——本编的任何内容均不得被解释为对消费者金融保护局局长根据第(1)款规定要求第(a)子条所述主体就其拥有或控制的信息(无论该等信息是否由他人保存、存储或处理)提交报告的权力构成限制。

(5)**关于违反税法行为的报告**。——消费者金融保护局应向国税局局长提供用于发现潜在违反税法行为的任何检查报告或相关信息。

(c)**优先执法权**。——

(1)消费者金融保护局拥有优先执法权。——如果消费者金融保护局和另一联邦机关均获得执行联邦消费者金融法律的授权,则对于第(a)子条所述任何主体,消费者金融保护局应拥有执行该等联邦消费者金融法律的优先权力。

(2)**执法建议**。——有权执行联邦消费者金融法律的任何联邦机关(但联邦贸易委员会除外)均可以采用书面形式建议消费者金融保护局根据该等联邦消费者金融法律的授权对第(a)子条所述主体启动执法程序。

(3)**其他联邦机关的后备执法权**。——如果消费者金融保护局在收到第(2)款所述建议之日起120天内未启动执法程序,第(2)款提及的对方机关可以启动执法程序(包括履行伴随该等程序的后续监管和支持职能),以确保该等程序得到遵守。

(d)**服务提供者**。——第(a)子条所述主体的服务提供者应受制于本条赋予消费者金融保护局的权力,如同消费者金融保护局系《银行服务公司法》第7(c)条[《美国法典》第十二编第1867(c)节]规定的相应的联邦银行业监管机关。在对受制于本子条规定的服务提供者进行任何检查或要求其提交任何报告时,消费者金融保护局应与相应的审慎监管者进行协调。

(e) SIMULTANEOUS AND COORDINATED SUPERVISORY ACTION.—

(1) EXAMINATIONS.— A prudential regulator and the Bureau shall, with respect to each insured depository institution, insured credit union, or other covered person described in subsection (a) that is supervised by the prudential regulator and the Bureau, respectively—

(A) coordinate the scheduling of examinations of the insured depository institution, insured credit union, or other covered person described in subsection (a);

(B) conduct simultaneous examinations of each insured depository institution or insured credit union, unless such institution requests examinations to be conducted separately;

(C) share each draft report of examination with the other agency and permit the receiving agency a reasonable opportunity (which shall not be less than a period of 30 days after the date of receipt) to comment on the draft report before such report is made final; and

(D) prior to issuing a final report of examination or taking supervisory action, take into consideration concerns, if any, raised in the comments made by the other agency.

(2) COORDINATION WITH STATE BANK SUPERVISORS.— The Bureau shall pursue arrangements and agreements with State bank supervisors to coordinate examinations, consistent with paragraph (1).

(3) AVOIDANCE OF CONFLICT IN SUPERVISION.—

(A) REQUEST.— If the proposed supervisory determinations of the Bureau and a prudential regulator (in this section referred to collectively as the "agencies") are conflicting, an insured depository institution, insured credit union, or other covered person described in subsection (a) may request the agencies to coordinate and present a joint statement of coordinated supervisory action.

(B) JOINT STATEMENT.— The agencies shall provide a joint statement under subparagraph (A), not later than 30 days after the date of receipt of the request of the insured depository institution, credit union, or covered person described in subsection (a).

(4) APPEALS TO GOVERNING PANEL.—

(A) IN GENERAL.— If the agencies do not resolve the conflict or issue a joint statement required by subparagraph (B), or if either of the agencies takes or attempts to take any supervisory action relating to the request for the joint statement without the consent of the other agency, an insured depository institution, insured credit union, or other covered person described in subsection (a) may institute an appeal to a governing panel, as provided in this subsection, not later than 30 days after the expiration of the period during which a joint statement is required to be filed under paragraph (3)(B).

(B) COMPOSITION OF GOVERNING PANEL.— The governing panel for an appeal under this paragraph shall be composed of—

(i) a representative from the Bureau and a representative of the prudential regulator, both of whom—

(e)**同步和协调监管行动**。——

(1)**检查**。——对于受审慎监管者和消费者金融保护局监管的每一参保存款机构、参保信贷联盟或第(a)子条所述其他所涉主体,审慎监管者和消费者金融保护局应分别——

(A)协调针对上述参保存款机构、参保信贷联盟或第(a)子条所述其他所涉主体的检查时间安排;

(B)对每一参保存款机构或参保信贷联盟开展同步检查,但该等机构请求单独开展检查的除外;

(C)与对方机关共享所有检查报告初稿,并在最终定稿之前给予对方机关就该等报告初稿提出建议的合理机会(提供建议的期限不得少于报告初稿收到之日后30天);并

(D)在发布最终检查报告或采取监管行动之前,考虑对方机关在建议中提出的问题(如有)。

(2)**与州银行监管者的协调**。——消费者金融保护局应根据第(1)款的规定,与州银行监管者达成安排和约定,协调检查行为。

(3)**避免监管冲突**。——

(A)**请求**。——如果消费者金融保护局和审慎监管者(在本条中合称监管机关)拟作出的监管决定相互冲突,则参保存款机构、参保信贷联盟或第(a)子条所述其他所涉主体均可以请求监管机关进行协调,并就协调开展的监管行动作出联合声明。

(B)**联合声明**。——监管机关应在收到参保存款机构、参保信贷联盟或第(a)子条所述其他所涉主体请求之日后30天内,根据第(A)子款作出联合声明。

(4)**提请冲突审查小组进行审查**。——

(A)**一般规定**。——如果监管机关未能解决该等冲突或未能根据第(B)子款的要求发布联合声明,或者任何一方机关在收到联合声明请求之后,未经对方机关同意即采取或试图采取任何监管行动,参保存款机构、参保信贷联盟或第(a)子条所述其他所涉主体可以根据本子条规定,在监管机关根据第(3)(B)款规定应作出联合声明的期限届满后30天内提请冲突审查小组对此进行审查。

(B)**冲突审查小组的组成**。——本款所述冲突审查小组应由下述成员组成——

(i)符合如下条件的消费者金融保护局和审慎监管者代表各一名——

(Ⅰ) have not participated in the material supervisory determinations under appeal; and

(Ⅱ) do not directly or indirectly report to the person who participated materially in the supervisory determinations under appeal; and

(ii) one individual representative, to be determined on a rotating basis, from among the Board of Governors, the Corporation, the National Credit Union Administration, and the Office of the Comptroller of the Currency, other than any agency involved in the subject dispute.

(C) CONDUCT OF APPEAL. — In an appeal under this paragraph —

(i) the insured depository institution, insured credit union, or other covered person described in subsection (a) —

(Ⅰ) shall include in its appeal all the facts and legal arguments pertaining to the matter; and

(Ⅱ) may, through counsel, employees, or representatives, appear before the governing panel in person or by telephone; and

(ii) the governing panel —

(Ⅰ) may request the insured depository institution, insured credit union, or other covered person described in subsection (a), the Bureau , or the prudential regulator to produce additional information relevant to the appeal; and

(Ⅱ) by a majority vote of its members, shall provide a final determination, in writing, not later than 30 days after the date of filing of an information ally complete appeal, or such longer period as the panel and the insured depository institution, insured credit union, or other covered person described in subsection (a) may jointly agree.

(D) PUBLIC AVAILABILITY OF DETERMINATIONS. — A governing panel shall publish all information contained in a determination by the governing panel, with appropriate redactions of information that would be subject to an exemption from disclosure under section 552 of title 5, United States Code.

(E) PROHIBITION AGAINST RETALIATION. — The Bureau and the prudential regulators shall prescribe rules to provide safeguards from retaliation against the insured depository institution, insured credit union, or other covered person described in subsection (a) instituting an appeal under this paragraph, as well as their officers and employees.

(F) LIMITATION. — The process provided in this paragraph shall not apply to a determination by a prudential regulator to appoint a conservator or receiver for an insured depository institution or a liquidating agent for an insured credit union, as the case may be, or a decision to take action pursuant to section 38 of the Federal Deposit Insurance Act (12 U.S.C. 1831o) or section 212 of the Federal Credit Union Act (112 U.S.C. 1790a), as applicable.

(G) EFFECT ON OTHER AUTHORITY. — Nothing in this section shall modify or limit the authority of the Bureau to interpret, or take enforcement action under, any Federal

(I)未曾参与作出被提请审查的重大监管判定;且

(II)不属于作出被提请审查的监管判定的主要参与者的直接或间接下属;及

(ii)从联邦储备委员会、联邦存款保险公司、国家信贷联盟署和货币监理署(但任何涉及相关争议的机关除外)轮流挑选的一名个人代表。

(C)**审查的开展**。——在根据本款规定开展审查的过程中——

(i)参保存款机构、参保信贷联盟或第(a)子条所述其他所涉主体——

(I)应在审查请求中说明与争议事项相关的所有事实和法律论据;并

(II)可以通过法律顾问、雇员或代表亲自或通过电话出席冲突审查小组的审查;且

(ii)冲突审查小组——

(I)可以要求参保存款机构、参保信贷联盟或第(a)子条所述其他所涉主体、消费者金融保护局或审慎监管者提供与审查请求相关的补充信息;且

(II)应在信息完备的审查请求提交之日后30天内,或者冲突审查小组和参保存款机构、参保信贷联盟或第(a)子条所述其他所涉主体共同商定的其他更长期限内,经其成员中多数成员同意,作出最终书面判定。

(D)**判定的公开提供**。——冲突审查小组应公布其判定中包含的全部信息,但对于根据《美国法典》第五编第552节应豁免披露的信息应进行适当编辑。

(E)**禁止报复**。——消费者金融保护局和审慎监管者应制定规则,以保障根据本款提请审查的参保存款机构、参保信贷联盟或第(a)子条所述其他所涉主体及其管理人员和雇员免受报复。

(F)**限制**。——本款规定的程序不适用于审慎监管者为了给参保存款机构指定托管人、代管人或者给参保信贷联盟指定清算代理人(视具体情况而定)而作出的判定,也不适用于审慎监管者为了根据《联邦存款保险法》第38条(《美国法典》第十二编第1831o节)或《联邦信贷联盟法》第212条(《美国法典》第一百一十二编第1790a节)(视具体情况而定)采取行动而作出的决定。

(G)**对其他权力的影响**。——本条任何内容既不改变也不限制消费者金融保护局解释任何联邦消费者金融法律或根据该等法律开展执法行动的权力,同时既不改变

consumer financial law, or the authority of a prudential regulator to interpret or take enforcement action under any other provision of Federal law for safety and soundness purposes.

SEC. 1026. OTHER BANKS, SAVINGS ASSOCIATIONS, AND CREDIT UNIONS.

(a) SCOPE OF COVERAGE. — This section shall apply to any covered person that is —

(1) an insured depository institution with total assets of $10,000,000,000 or less; or

(2) an insured credit union with total assets of $10,000,000,000 or less.

(b) REPORTS. — The Director may require reports from a person described in subsection (a), as necessary to support the role of the Bureau in implementing Federal consumer financial law, to support its examination activities under subsection (c), and to assess and detect risks to consumers and consumer financial markets.

(1) USE OF EXISTING REPORTS. — The Bureau shall, to the fullest extent possible, use —

(A) reports pertaining to a person described in subsection(a) that have been provided or required to have been provided to a Federal or State agency; and

(B) information that has been reported publicly.

(2) PRESERVATION OF AUTHORITY. — Nothing in this subsection may be construed as limiting the authority of the Director from requiring from a person described in subsection (a), as permitted under paragraph (1), information owned or under the control of such person, regardless of whether such information is maintained, stored, or processed by another person.

(3) REPORTS OF TAX LAW NONCOMPLIANCE. — The Bureau shall provide the Commissioner of Internal Revenue with any report of examination or related information identifying possible tax law noncompliance.

(c) EXAMINATIONS. —

(1) IN GENERAL—The Bureau may, at its discretion, include examiners on a sampling basis of the examinations performed by the prudential regulator to assess compliance with the requirements of Federal consumer financial law of persons described in subsection (a).

(2) AGENCY COORDINATION. — The prudential regulator shall —

(A) provide all reports, records, and documentation related to the examination process for any institution included in the sample referred to in paragraph(1) to the Bureau on a timely and continual basis;

(B) involve such Bureau examiner in the entire examination process for such person; and

(C) consider input of the Bureau concerning the scope of an examination, conduct of the

也不限制审慎监管者解释任何其他联邦法律的规定或出于安全和稳健目的根据该等法律规定开展执法行动的权力。

第1026条　其他银行、储蓄协会和信贷联盟

(a)**监管范围**。——本条应适用于符合如下条件的所涉主体——

(1)系总资产低于100亿(含)美元的参保存款机构;或

(2)系总资产低于100亿美元(含)的参保信贷联盟。

(b)**报告**。——消费者金融保护局局长可以要求第(a)子条所述主体提交必要报告,以便支持消费者金融保护局履行实施联邦消费者金融法律的职责,为其根据第(c)子条开展审查活动提供帮助,并促进其对上述主体给消费者和消费者金融市场所带来的风险进行评估和检测。

(1)**既有报告的利用**。——消费者金融保护局应尽最大可能利用——

(A)已经或应向联邦机关或州机关提交的与第(a)子条所述主体相关的报告;及

(B)已经被公开报告的信息。

(2)**权力保留**。——本子条的任何内容均不得被解释为对消费者金融保护局局长根据第(1)款规定要求第(a)子条所述主体就其拥有或控制的信息(无论该等信息是否由他人保存、存储或处理)提交报告的权力构成限制。

(3)**关于违反税法行为的报告**。——消费者金融保护局应向国税局局长提供用于发现潜在违反税法行为的任何检查报告或相关信息。

(c)**检查**。——

(1)**一般规定**。——审慎监管者开展检查活动,评估第(a)子条所述主体对联邦消费者金融法律要求的合规情况之时,消费者金融保护局可依其自由裁量权,选派检查人员参与其随机抽选的检查活动。

(2)**机关之间的协调**。——审慎监管者应——

(A)对于消费者金融保护局按照第(1)款抽选的针对任何机构实施的检查程序,及时并持续向消费者金融保护局提供所有相关报告、记录和文件;

(B)使消费者金融保护局的上述检查人员参与对上述主体开展的整个检查程序;且

(C)在检查范围、检查开展、检查报告内容、需要重点关注之事项的确定以及检查

examination, the contents of the examination report, the designation of matters requiring attention, and examination ratings.

(d) ENFORCEMENT.—

(1) IN GENERAL.—Except for requiring reports under subsection (b), the prudential regulator is authorized to enforce the requirements of Federal consumer financial laws and, with respect to a covered person described in subsection(a), shall have exclusive authority (relative to the Bureau) to enforce such laws.

(2) COORDINATION WITH PRUDENTIAL REGULATOR.—

(A) REFERRAL.—When the Bureau has reason to believe that a person described in subsection(a) has engaged in a material violation of a Federal consumer financial law, the Bureau shall notify the prudential regulator in writing and recommend appropriate action to respond.

(B) RESPONSE.—Upon receiving a recommendation under subparagraph (A), the prudential regulator shall provide a written response to the Bureau not later than 60 days thereafter.

(e) SERVICE PROVIDERS.—A service provider to a substantial number of persons described in subsection (a) shall be subject to the authority of the Bureau under section 1025 to the same extent as if the Bureau were an appropriate Federal banking agency under section 7(c) of the Bank Service Company Act (12 U.S.C. 1867(c)). When conducting any examination or requiring any report from a service provider subject to this subsection, the Bureau shall coordinate with the appropriate prudential regulator.

SEC. 1027. LIMITATIONS ON AUTHORITIES OF THE BUREAU; PRESERVATION OF AUTHORITIES.

(a) EXCLUSION FOR MERCHANTS, RETAILERS, AND OTHER SELLERS OF NONFINANCIAL GOODS OR SERVICES.—

(1) SALE OR BROKERAGE OF NONFINANCIAL GOOD OR SERVICE.—The Bureau may not exercise any rulemaking, supervisory, enforcement or other authority under this title with respect to a person who is a merchant, retailer, or seller of any nonfinancial good or service and is engaged in the sale or brokerage of such nonfinancial good or service, except to the extent that such person is engaged in offering or providing any consumer financial product or service, or is otherwise subject to any enumerated consumer law or any law for which authorities are transferred under subtitle F or H.

(2) OFFERING OR PROVISION OF CERTAIN CONSUMER FINANCIAL PRODUCTS OR SERVICES IN CONNECTION WITH THE SALE OR BROKERAGE OF NONFINANCIAL GOOD OR SERVICE.—

(A) IN GENERAL.—Except as provided in subparagraph (B), and subject to subparagraph (C), the Bureau may not exercise any rulemaking, supervisory, enforcement, or

评级方面考虑消费者金融保护局的意见。

(d)**执法**。——

(1)**一般规定**。——除无权根据第(b)子条要求提交报告外,审慎监管者有权执行联邦消费者金融法律的要求,且相对于消费者金融保护局而言,审慎监管者应拥有对第(a)子条所述所涉主体执行该等法律的排他性权力。

(2)**与审慎监管者进行协调**。——

(A)**执法建议**。——消费者金融保护局有理由认为第(a)子条所述主体实施了严重违反联邦消费者金融法律的行为时,应书面通知审慎监管者,并建议其采取适当的应对行动。

(B)**答复**。——审慎监管者应在收到第(A)子款所述建议后60天内向消费者金融保护局作出书面答复。

(e)**服务提供者**。——向大量第(a)子条所述主体提供服务的服务提供者应受制于第1025条赋予消费者金融保护局的权力,如同消费者金融保护局系《银行服务公司法》第7(c)条[《美国法典》第十二编第1867(c)节]所规定的相应的联邦银行业监管机关。在对受制于本子条规定的服务提供者进行任何检查或要求其提交任何报告时,消费者金融保护局应与相应的审慎监管者进行适当的协调。

第1027条　对消费者金融保护局权力的限制;权力的保留

(a)**适用于提供非金融商品或服务的商人、零售商和其他销售商的除外规定**。——

(1)**非金融产品或服务的销售或经纪**。——消费者金融保护局不得对身为提供非金融商品或服务的商人、零售商或销售商并从事该等非金融商品或服务的销售或经纪业务的任何主体行使任何规则制定权、监管权、执法权或本编规定的其他权力,但该等主体要约或提供任何消费者金融产品或服务,或因其他原因受制于任何明文列举的消费者法律,或受制于已根据第F子编或第H子编转由消费者金融保护局行使执法权的任何法律的除外。

(2)在从事非金融商品或服务的销售或经纪业务过程中要约或提供特定的消费者金融产品或服务。——

(A)**一般规定**。——除第(B)子款规定的情形外,在不违反第(C)子款规定的前提下,消费者金融保护局只有下述情形下,不得对提供非金融商品或服务的商人、零售

other authority under this title with respect to a merchant, retailer, or seller of nonfinancial goods or services, but only to the extent that such person —

(i) extends credit directly to a consumer, in a case in which the good or service being provided is not itself a consumer financial product or service (other than credit described in this subparagraph), exclusively for the purpose of enabling that consumer to purchase such nonfinancial good or service directly from the merchant, retailer, or seller;

(ii) directly, or through an agreement with another person, collects debt arising from credit extended as described in clause (i); or

(iii) sells or conveys debt described in clause (i) that is delinquent or otherwise in default.

(B) APPLICABILITY. — Subparagraph (A) does not apply to any credit transaction or collection of debt, other than as described in subparagraph (C)(i), arising from a transaction described in subparagraph (A) —

(i) in which the merchant, retailer, or seller of nonfinancial goods or services assigns, sells or otherwise conveys to another person such debt owed by the consumer (except for a sale of debt that is delinquent or otherwise in default, as described in subparagraph (A)(iii));

(ii) in which the credit extended significantly exceeds the market value of the nonfinancial good or service provided, or the Bureau otherwise finds that the sale of the nonfinancial good or service is done as a subterfuge, so as to evade or circumvent the provisions of this title; or

(iii) in which the merchant, retailer, or seller of nonfinancial goods or services regularly extends credit and the credit is subject to a finance charge.

(C) LIMITATIONS. —

(i) IN GENERAL. — Notwithstanding subparagraph (B), subparagraph (A) shall apply with respect to a merchant, retailer, or seller of nonfinancial goods or services that is not engaged significantly in offering or providing consumer financial products or services.

(ii) EXCEPTION. — Subparagraph (A) and clause (i) of this subparagraph do not apply to any merchant, retailer, or seller of nonfinancial goods or services —

(I) if such merchant, retailer, or seller of nonfinancial goods or services is engaged in a transaction described in subparagraph (B)(i) or (B)(ii); or

(II) to the extent that such merchant, retailer, or seller is subject to any enumerated consumer law or any law for which authorities are transferred under subtitle F or H, but the Bureau may exercise such authority only with respect to that law.

(D) RULES. —

(i) AUTHORITY OF OTHER AGENCIES. — No provision of this title shall be construed as modifying, limiting, or superseding the supervisory or enforcement authority of the Federal Trade Commission or any other agency (other than the Bureau) with respect to

商或销售商行使任何规则制定权、监管权、执法权或本编规定的其他任何权力：

(i)在上述商人、零售商或销售商提供的商品或服务本身并非消费者金融产品或服务(但本子款所述信用除外)的情况下，其直接向消费者授信，且授信的唯一目的是使消费者能够直接向其购买该等非金融商品或服务；

(ii)上述商人、零售商或销售商直接或通过与其他主体达成协议，催收因第(i)项所述授信产生的债务；或

(iii)上述商人、零售商或销售商出售或转移到期未付的或存在其他拖欠情况的第(i)项所述债务。

(B)**适用范围**。——第(A)子款的规定不适用于第(A)子款中所述交易导致的符合下列条件的任何信贷交易或债务催收活动[但第(C)(i)子款所述信贷交易或债务催收活动除外]：

(i)非金融商品或服务商人、零售商或销售商通过该等信贷交易或债务催收活动，将消费者欠负的债务转让、出售或以其他方式转移给其他主体[但到期未付的或存在其他拖欠情况的第(A)(iii)子款所述债务的出售除外]；

(ii)授信额度大幅超出所提供的非金融产品或服务的市场价值，或消费者金融保护局认定出售非金融产品或服务是为了达到逃避或规避本编规定之目的而实施的诡计；或

(iii)非金融产品或服务商人、零售商或销售商经常开展授信活动，并收取信贷费。

(C)**限制**。——

(i)**一般规定**。——无论第(B)子款如何规定，第(A)子款的规定应适用于并非大规模从事消费者金融产品或服务要约或提供活动的提供非金融商品或服务的商人、零售商或销售商。

(ii)**例外规定**。——在下列情形下，第(A)子款和本子款第(i)项的规定不适用于任何提供非金融商品或服务的商人、零售商或销售商：

(I)该等提供非金融商品或服务的商人、零售商或销售商从事第(B)(i)子款或第(B)(ii)子款所述交易；或

(II)该等提供非金融商品或服务的商人、零售商或销售商受制于任何明文列举的消费者法律，或受制于根据第F子编或第H子编已转由消费者金融保护局行使执法权的任何法律(但是消费者金融保护局仅可以针对该等法律行使上述执法权)。

(D)**规则**。——

(i)**其他机关的权力**。——对于商人或零售商为使消费者能够直接向其购买非金融商品或服务之唯一目的而向消费者进行的授信或者因该等授信而产生的债务催收而言，本编的任何规定均不得被解释为改变、限制或取代联邦贸易委员会或任何其他

credit extended, or the collection of debt arising from such extension, directly by a merchant or retailer to a consumer exclusively for the purpose of enabling that consumer to purchase nonfinancial goods or services directly from the merchant or retailer.

(ii) SMALL BUSINESSES. — A merchant, retailer, or seller of nonfinancial goods or services that would otherwise be subject to the authority of the Bureau solely by virtue of the application of subparagraph (B)(iii) shall be deemed not to be engaged significantly in offering or providing consumer financial products or services under subparagraph (C)(i), if such person —

(I) only extends credit for the sale of nonfinancial goods or services, as described in subparagraph (A)(i);

(II) retains such credit on its own accounts (except to sell or convey such debt that is delinquent or otherwise in default); and

(III) meets the relevant industry size threshold to be a small business concern, based on annual receipts, pursuant to section 3 of the Small Business Act (15 U.S.C. 632) and the implementing rules thereunder.

(iii) INITIAL YEAR. — A merchant, retailer, or seller of nonfinancial goods or services shall be deemed to meet the relevant industry size threshold described in clause (ii)(III) during the first year of operations of that business concern if, during that year, the receipts of that business concern reasonably are expected to meet that size threshold.

(iv) OTHER STANDARDS FOR SMALL BUSINESS. — With respect to a merchant, retailer, or seller of nonfinancial goods or services that is a classified on a basis other than annual receipts for the purposes of section 3 of the Small Business Act (15 U.S.C. 632) and the implementing rules thereunder, such merchant, retailer, or seller shall be deemed to meet the relevant industry size threshold described in clause (ii)(III) if such merchant, retailer, or seller meets the relevant industry size threshold to be a small business concern based on the number of employees, or other such applicable measure, established under that Act.

(E) EXCEPTION FROM STATE ENFORCEMENT. — To the extent that the Bureau may not exercise authority under this subsection with respect to a merchant, retailer, or seller of nonfinancial goods or services, no action by a State attorney general or State regulator with respect to a claim made under this title may be brought under subsection 1042(a), with respect to an activity described in any of clauses (i) through (iii) of subparagraph (A) by such merchant, retailer, or seller of nonfinancial goods or services.

(b) EXCLUSION FOR REAL ESTATE BROKERAGE ACTIVITIES. —

(1) REAL ESTATE BROKERAGE ACTIVITIES EXCLUDED. — Without limiting subsection (a), and except as permitted in paragraph (2), the Bureau may not exercise any rulemaking, supervisory, enforcement, or other authority under this title with respect to a person that is licensed or registered as a real estate broker or real estate agent, in accordance

机关(但消费者金融保护局除外)针对该等授信或债务催收的监管权或执法权。

(ii)**小型企业**。——在下列情形下,仅因第(B)(iii)子款的适用而将受制于消费者金融保护局执法权的提供非金融商品或服务的商人、零售商或销售商,应视为第(C)(i)子款所述并非大规模从事消费者金融产品或服务要约或提供活动的提供非金融商品或服务的商人、零售商或销售商——

(I)如第(A)(i)子款所述,该等主体的授信目的仅在于出售非金融商品或服务;

(II)该等主体为自身利益留存该等信贷(但为出售或转移到期未付的或存在其他拖欠情况的债务而留存的除外);及

(III)根据《小型企业法》第3条(《美国法典》第十五编第632节)及其实施规则,该等主体按年收入计算达到小型企业的相关行业规模门槛。

(iii)**初始年度**。——如果非金融商品或服务商人、零售商或销售商在首个经营年度的收入根据合理预期将达到第(ii)(III)项所述相关行业规模门槛,则该等商人、零售商或销售商应被视为达到该规模门槛。

(iv)**小型企业的其他标准**。——除《小型企业法》第3条(《美国法典》第十五编第632节)及其实施规则规定的年收入标准之外,按照员工人数或者《小型企业法》设定的其他适用指标计算,如果提供非金融商品或服务的商人、零售商或销售商达到小型企业的相关行业规模门槛,则该等商人、零售商或销售商应视为达到第(ii)(III)项所述的相关行业规模门槛。

(E)**州执法的例外规定**。——如果消费者金融保护局无权对提供非金融商品或服务的商人、零售商或销售商行使本子条所述权力,州总检察长或州监管者不得针对提供非金融商品或服务的商人、零售商或销售商从事的第(A)子款第(i)项至第(iii)项所述活动,根据第1042(a)子条的规定提起关于本编所述权利主张的任何诉讼。

(b)**适用于房地产经纪活动的除外规定**。——

(1)**房地产经纪活动除外**。——在不限制第(a)子条规定的前提下,除第(2)款允许的情形外,消费者金融保护局在下列情形下,不得对根据州法律获得房地产经纪人或房地产代理人执照或注册为房地产经纪人或房地产代理人的主体行使任何规则制定权、监管权或本编规定的任何其他权力——

with State law, to the extent that such person —

(A) acts as a real estate agent or broker for a buyer, seller, lessor, or lessee of real property;

(B) brings together parties interested in the sale, purchase, lease, rental, or exchange of real property;

(C) negotiates, on behalf of any party, any portion of a contract relating to the sale, purchase, lease, rental, or exchange of real property (other than in connection with the provision of financing with respect to any such transaction); or

(D) offers to engage in any activity, or act in any capacity, described in subparagraph (A), (B), or (C).

(2) DESCRIPTION OF ACTIVITIES. — The Bureau may exercise rulemaking, supervisory, enforcement, or other authority under this title with respect to a person described in paragraph (1) when such person is —

(A) engaged in an activity of offering or providing any consumer financial product or service, except that the Bureau may exercise such authority only with respect to that activity; or

(B) otherwise subject to any enumerated consumer law or any law for which authorities are transferred under subtitle F or H, but the Bureau may exercise such authority only with respect to that law.

(c) EXCLUSION FOR MANUFACTURED HOME RETAILERS AND MODULAR HOME RETAILERS. —

(1) IN GENERAL. — The Director may not exercise any rulemaking, supervisory, enforcement, or other authority over a person to the extent that —

(A) such person is not described in paragraph (2); and

(B) such person —

(i) acts as an agent or broker for a buyer or seller of a manufactured home or a modular home;

(ii) facilitates the purchase by a consumer of a manufactured home or modular home, by negotiating the purchase price or terms of the sales contract (other than providing financing with respect to such transaction); or

(iii) offers to engage in any activity described in clause (i) or (ii).

(2) DESCRIPTION OF ACTIVITIES. — A person is described in this paragraph to the extent that such person is engaged in the offering or provision of any consumer financial product or service or is otherwise subject to any enumerated consumer law or any law for which authorities are transferred under subtitle F or H.

(3) DEFINITIONS. — For purposes of this subsection, the following definitions shall apply:

(A) MANUFACTURED HOME. — The term "manufactured home" has the same

(A)该等主体担任房地产买方、卖方、出租方或承租方的房地产代理人或经纪人;

(B)该等主体对房地产销售、购买、租赁、出租或交易中的相关方进行撮合;

(C)该等主体代表任何一方参与房地产销售、购买、租赁、出租或交易合同任何部分的谈判(但因向任何前述交易提供融资而参与谈判的除外);或

(D)该等主体要约从事第(A)子款、第(B)子款或第(C)子款所述任何活动,或者以第(A)子款、第(B)子款或第(C)子款所述任何身份行事。

(2)**活动说明**。——在下列情形下,消费者金融保护局可以对第(1)款所述主体行使规则制定权、监管权、执法权或本编规定的其他权力——

(A)该等主体从事要约或提供任何消费者金融产品或服务的活动,但是消费者金融保护局仅可以针对该等活动行使上述权力;或

(B)该等主体受制于任何明文列举的消费者法律,或受制于已根据第F子编或第H子编转由消费者金融保护局行使执法权的任何法律,但消费者金融保护局仅可以针对该等法律行使上述执法权。

(c)**适用于预制房零售商和模块化房屋零售商的除外规定**。——

(1)**一般规定**。——消费者金融保护局局长不得对存在下述情形的主体行使任何规则制定权、监管权、执法权或其他任何权力——

(A)该等主体并非第(2)款所述主体;且

(B)该等主体——

(i)担任预制房或模块化房屋买方或卖方的代理人或经纪人;

(ii)通过参与购买价格或销售合同条款的谈判(但为该等交易提供融资的谈判除外),促成消费者购买预制房或模块化房屋,或

(iii)要约从事第(i)项或第(ii)项所述任何活动。

(2)**活动说明**。——本款所述主体指要约或提供任何消费者金融产品或服务,或者受制于任何明文列举的消费者法律,或受制于已根据第F子编或第H子编转由消费者金融保护局行使执法权的任何法律的主体。

(3)**定义**。——就本子条而言,下列术语应适用如下定义:

(A)**预制房**。——"预制房"一词的含义以《1974年全国工业化住宅建设和安全标

meaning as in section 603 of the National Manufactured Housing Construction and Safety Standards Act of 1974 (42 U.S.C. 5402).

(B) MODULAR HOME. — The term "modular home" means a house built in a factory in 2 or more modules that meet the State or local building codes where the house will be located, and where such modules are transported to the building site, installed on foundations, and completed.

(d) EXCLUSION FOR ACCOUNTANTS AND TAX PREPARERS. —

(1)IN GENERAL. — Except as permitted in paragraph (2), the Bureau may not exercise any rulemaking, supervisory, enforcement, or other authority over —

(A) any person that is a certified public accountant, permitted to practice as a certified public accounting firm, or certified or licensed for such purpose by a State, or any individual who is employed by or holds an ownership interest with respect to a person described in this subparagraph, when such person is performing or offering to perform —

(i) customary and usual accounting activities, including the provision of accounting, tax, advisory, or other services that are subject to the regulatory authority of a State board of accountancy or a Federal authority; or

(ii) other services that are incidental to such customary and usual accounting activities, to the extent that such incidental services are not offered or provided —

(I) by the person separate and apart from such customary and usual accounting activities; or

(II)to consumers who are not receiving such customary and usual accounting activities; or

(B) any person, other than a person described in subparagraph (A) that performs income tax preparation activities for consumers.

(2) DESCRIPTION OF ACTIVITIES. —

(A) IN GENERAL. — Paragraph(1) shall not apply to any person described in paragraph (1)(A) or (1)(B) to the extent that such person is engaged in any activity which is not a customary and usual accounting activity described in paragraph (1)(A) or incidental thereto but which is the offering or provision of any consumer financial product or service, except to the extent that a person described in paragraph(1)(A) is engaged in an activity which is a customary and usual accounting activity described in paragraph (1)(A), or incidental thereto.

(B) NOT A CUSTOMARY AND USUAL ACCOUNTING ACTIVITY. — For purposes of this subsection, extending or brokering credit is not a customary and usual accounting activity, or incidental thereto.

(C) RULE OF CONSTRUCTION. — For purposes of subparagraphs(A) and(B), a person described in paragraph(1)(A) shall not be deemed to be extending credit, if such

准法》第603条(《美国法典》第四十二编第5402节)的定义为准。

(B)**模块化房屋**。——“模块化房屋”一词系指在工厂建造的由符合房屋所在地的州或地方建筑规范的两个(含)以上模块组成的房屋。该等房屋模块应运往建筑场地,并在地基上安装完工。

(d)**适用于会计师和报税员的除外规定**。——

(1)**一般规定**。——除第(2)款允许的情形外,消费者金融保护局不得对下列任何主体行使任何规则制定权、监管权、执法权或其他任何权力——

(A)具有注册公共会计师身份、获许在某州作为注册公共会计师事务所执业,或者已在某州获得注册公共会计师证书或执照的主体,或者被本款所述主体雇用或对该等主体拥有所有权权益的任何个人,前提是该等主体正在从事或要约从事下列活动——

(i)惯常会计活动,包括受州会计委员会或联邦机构监管的会计、税务、咨询或其他服务;或

(ii)伴随上述惯常会计活动而提供的其他服务,前提是——

(I)该等主体并未在上述惯常会计活动之外单独要约或提供该等附带服务;或

(II)该等主体并未向接受上述惯常会计活动的客户之外的客户提供该等附带活动;或

(B)为消费者办理所得税申报的任何主体[但第(A)子款规定的主体除外]。

(2)**活动说明**。——

(A)**一般规定**。——如果第(1)(A)款或第(1)(B)款所述任何主体从事的任何活动不属于第(1)(A)款所述日常普通会计活动或其附带活动,而属于要约或提供任何消费者金融产品或服务的活动,则第(1)款的规定不适用于该等主体,但第(1)(A)款所述主体从事的活动属于第(1)(A)款所述惯常会计活动或其附带活动的除外。

(B)**非惯常会计活动**。——就本子条而言,授信或信贷经纪活动不属于惯常会计活动或其附带活动。

(C)**解释规则**。——就第(A)子款和第(B)子款而言,如果第(1)(A)款所述主体直接向消费者授信的唯一目的在于使该等消费者能够直接向其购买第(1)(A)款第(i)

person is only extending credit directly to a consumer, exclusively for the purpose of enabling such consumer to purchase services described in clause (i) or (ii) of paragraph (1)(A) directly from such person, and such credit is —

(i) not subject to a finance charge; and

(ii) not payable by written agreement in more than 4 installments.

(D) OTHER LIMITATIONS. — Paragraph (1) does not apply to any person described in paragraph (1)(A) or (1)(B) that is otherwise subject to any enumerated consumer law or any law for which authorities are transferred under subtitle F or H.

(e) EXCLUSION FOR PRACTICE OF LAW. —

(1) IN GENERAL. — Except as provided under paragraph (2), the Bureau may not exercise any supervisory or enforcement authority with respect to an activity engaged in by an attorney as part of the practice of law under the laws of a State in which the attorney is licensed to practice law.

(2) RULE OF CONSTRUCTION. — Paragraph (1) shall not be construed so as to limit the exercise by the Bureau of any supervisory, enforcement, or other authority regarding the offering or provision of a consumer financial product or service described in any subparagraph of section 1002(5) —

(A) that is not offered or provided as part of, or incidental to, the practice of law, occurring exclusively within the scope of the attorney-client relationship; or

(B) that is otherwise offered or provided by the attorney in question with respect to any consumer who is not receiving legal advice or services from the attorney in connection with such financial product or service.

(3) EXISTING AUTHORITY. — Paragraph (1) shall not be construed so as to limit the authority of the Bureau with respect to any attorney, to the extent that such attorney is otherwise subject to any of the enumerated consumer laws or the authorities transferred under subtitle F or H.

(f) EXCLUSION FOR PERSONS REGULATED BY A STATE INSURANCE REGULATOR. —

(1) IN GENERAL. — No provision of this title shall be construed as altering, amending, or affecting the authority of any State insurance regulator to adopt rules, initiate enforcement proceedings, or take any other action with respect to a person regulated by a State insurance regulator. Except as provided in paragraph (2), the Bureau shall have no authority to exercise any power to enforce this title with respect to a person regulated by a State insurance regulator.

(2) DESCRIPTION OF ACTIVITIES. — Paragraph (1) does not apply to any person described in such paragraph to the extent that such person is engaged in the offering or provision of any consumer financial product or service or is otherwise subject to any enumerated

项或第(ii)项所述服务,则在下列情形下,该等主体不得被视为从事授信活动——

(i)针对上述授信不收取信贷费;且

(ii)书面偿还协议规定的还款期数不超过4期。

(D)**其他限制**。——第(1)款规定不适用于第(1)(A)款或第(1)(B)款所述受制于任何明文列举的消费者法律,或受制于已根据第F子编或第H子编转由消费者金融保护局行使执法权的任何法律的任何主体。

(e)**适用于法律执业活动的除外规定**。——

(1)**一般规定**。——除第(2)款规定的情形外,对于律师根据其法律执业资格获取地的州法律开展的法律执业活动,消费者金融保护局不得行使任何监管权或执法权。

(2)**解释规则**。——第(1)款不得被解释为限制消费者金融保护局对要约或提供符合下列条件的第1002(5)条任何子款所述消费者金融产品或服务的活动行使任何监管权、执法权或其他权力:

(A)仅在律师—客户关系范围之内并非作为法律执业组成部分,亦非伴随法律执业而要约或提供的消费者金融产品或服务;或

(B)律师向未就该金融产品或服务接受其法律意见或服务的任何消费者要约或提供的消费者金融产品或服务。

(3)**现有权限**。——第(1)款不得被解释为限制消费者金融保护局对下述律师行使权力:受制于任何明文列举的消费者法律,或受制于已根据第F子编或第H子编转由消费者金融保护局行使执法权的任何法律的任何律师。

(f)适用于受州保险监管者监管的主体的除外规定。——

(1)**一般规定**。——本编任何规定均不得被解释为更改、修正或影响任何州保险监管者针对受其监管的主体制定规则、启动执法程序或采取任何其他行动的权力。除第(2)款规定的情形外,消费者金融保护局无权对受州保险监管者监管的主体执行本编的规定。

(2)**活动说明**。——如果第(1)款所述任何主体要约或提供任何消费者金融产品或服务,或受制于任何明文列举的消费者法律,或受制于已根据第F子编或第H子编转由消费者金融保护局行使执法权的任何法律,则第(1)款的规定不适用于该等主体。

consumer law or any law for which authorities are transferred under subtitle F or H.

(3) STATE INSURANCE AUTHORITY UNDER GRAMM–LEACH–BLILEY. — Notwithstanding paragraph (2), the Bureau shall not exercise any authorities that are granted a State insurance authority under section 505(a)(6) of the Gramm–Leach–Bliley Act with respect to a person regulated by a State insurance authority.

(g) EXCLUSION FOR EMPLOYEE BENEFIT AND COMPENSATION PLANS AND CERTAIN OTHER ARRANGEMENTS UNDER THE INTERNAL REVENUE CODE OF 1986. —

(1) PRESERVATION OF AUTHORITY OF OTHER AGENCIES. — No provision of this title shall be construed as altering, amending, or affecting the authority of the Secretary of the Treasury, the Secretary of Labor, or the Commissioner of Internal Revenue to adopt regulations, initiate enforcement proceedings, or take any actions with respect to any specified plan or arrangement.

(2) ACTIVITIES NOT CONSTITUTING THE OFFERING OR PROVISION OF ANY CONSUMER FINANCIAL PRODUCT OR SERVICE. — For purposes of this title, a person shall not be treated as having engaged in the offering or provision of any consumer financial product or service solely because such person is —

(A) a specified plan or arrangement;

(B) engaged in the activity of establishing or maintaining, for the benefit of employees of such person (or for members of an employee organization), any specified plan or arrangement; or

(C) engaged in the activity of establishing or maintaining a qualified tuition program under section 529(b)(1) of the Internal Revenue Code of 1986 offered by a State or other prepaid tuition program offered by a State.

(3) LIMITATION ON BUREAU AUTHORITY. —

(A) IN GENERAL. — Except as provided under subparagraphs (B) and (C), the Bureau may not exercise any rulemaking or enforcement authority with respect to products or services that relate to any specified plan or arrangement.

(B) BUREAU ACTION PURSUANT TO AGENCY REQUEST. —

(i) AGENCY REQUEST. — The Secretary and the Secretary of Labor may jointly issue a written request to the Bureau regarding implementation of appropriate consumer protection standards under this title with respect to the provision of services relating to any specified plan or arrangement.

(ii) AGENCY RESPONSE. — In response to a request by the Bureau, the Secretary and the Secretary of Labor shall jointly issue a written response, not later than 90 days after receipt of such request, to grant or deny the request of the Bureau regarding implementation of appropriate consumer protection standards under this title with respect to the provision of

(3)**《格雷姆—里奇—比利雷法》下的州保险主管机构**。——无论第(2)款如何规定,消费者金融保护局不得对受州保险主管机构监管的主体行使《格雷姆—里奇—比利雷法》第505(a)(6)条授予该等州保险主管机构的任何权力。

(g)**适用于员工福利和薪酬计划以及根据《1986年国内税收法典》制定的其他特定安排的除外规定**。——

(1)**其他机关权力的保留**。——本编任何规定均不得被解释为更改、修正或影响财政部部长、劳动部部长或国税局局长就任何特定计划或安排制定规章、启动执法程序或采取任何行动的权力。

(2)**不构成任何消费者金融产品或服务的要约或提供的活动**。——就本编而言,任何主体均不得仅因下列情形而被视为要约或提供任何消费者金融产品或服务——

(A)该主体系一项特定计划或安排;

(B)该主体为其雇员(或为雇员组织成员)之利益而设立或维持任何特定计划或安排;或

(C)该主体依照《1986年国内税收法典》第529(b)(1)条制订或维持了由州资助的合格学费计划或者其他预付学费计划。

(3)**对消费者金融保护局权力的限制**。——

(A)**一般规定**。——除第(B)子款和第(C)子款规定的情形外,消费者金融保护局不得针对与任何特定计划或安排相关的产品或服务行使任何规则制定权或执法权。

(B)**消费者金融保护局根据机关请求采取的行动**。——

(i)**机关请求**。——财政部部长和劳动部部长可以联合发出书面请求,请求消费者金融保护局针对与任何特定计划或安排相关的服务的提供,实施本编规定的适当的消费者保护标准。

(ii)**机关的答复**。——消费者金融保护局请求财政部部长和劳动部部长针对与任何具体计划或安排相关的服务的提供,实施本编规定的适当的消费者保护标准之时,财政部部长和劳动部部长应在收到该等请求后90天内联合作出书面答复,核准或拒绝该等请求。

services relating to any specified plan or arrangement.

(iii) SCOPE OF BUREAU ACTION. — Subject to a request or response pursuant to clause(i) or clause(ii) by the agencies made under this subparagraph, the Bureau may exercise rulemaking authority, and may act to enforce a rule prescribed pursuant to such request or response, in accordance with the provisions of this title. A request or response made by the Secretary and the Secretary of Labor under this subparagraph shall describe the basis for, and scope of, appropriate consumer protection standards to be implemented under this title with respect to the provision of services relating to any specified plan or arrangement.

(C) DESCRIPTION OF PRODUCTS OR SERVICES. — To the extent that a person engaged in providing products or services relating to any specified plan or arrangement is subject to any enumerated consumer law or any law for which authorities are transferred under subtitle F or H, subparagraph (A) shall not apply with respect to that law.

(4) SPECIFIED PLAN OR ARRANGEMENT. — For purposes of this subsection, the term "specified plan or arrangement" means any plan, account, or arrangement described in section 220, 223, 401(a), 403(a), 403(b), 408, 408A, 529, or 530 of the Internal Revenue Code of 1986, or any employee benefit or compensation plan or arrangement, including a plan that is subject to title I of the Employee Retirement Income Security Act of 1974, or any prepaid tuition program offered by a State.

(h) PERSONS REGULATED BY A STATE SECURITIES COMMISSION. —

(1) IN GENERAL. — No provision of this title shall be construed as altering, amending, or affecting the authority of any securities commission(or any agency or office performing like functions) of any State to adopt rules, initiate enforcement proceedings, or take any other action with respect to a person regulated by any securities commission(or any agency or office performing like functions) of any State. Except as permitted in paragraph (2) and subsection(f), the Bureau shall have no authority to exercise any power to enforce this title with respect to a person regulated by any securities commission(or any agency or office performing like functions) of any State, but only to the extent that the person acts in such regulated capacity.

(2) DESCRIPTION OF ACTIVITIES. — Paragraph (1) shall not apply to any person to the extent such person is engaged in the offering or provision of any consumer financial product or service, or is otherwise subject to any enumerated consumer law or any law for which authorities are transferred under subtitle F or H.

(i) EXCLUSION FOR PERSONS REGULATED BY THE COMMISSION. —

(1) IN GENERAL. — No provision of this title may be construed as altering, amending, or affecting the authority of the Commission to adopt rules, initiate enforcement proceedings, or take any other action with respect to a person regulated by the Commission. The Bureau shall have no authority to exercise any power to enforce this title with respect to a person

(iii)**消费者金融保护局的行动范围**。——在不违反上述机关根据本子款作出的第(i)项或第(ii)项所述请求或答复的前提下,消费者金融保护局可以根据本编的规定行使规则制定权,并采取行动根据本编的规定执行依据该等请求或答复制定的规则。财政部部长和劳动部部长依照本子款作出的请求或答复应说明针对与任何特定计划或安排相关的服务的提供,依据本编所实施的适当消费者保护标准的制定依据和适用范围。

(C)**产品或服务说明**。——如果提供与任何具体计划或安排相关的产品或服务的主体受制于任何明文列举的消费者法律,或受制于已根据第F子编或第H子编转由消费者金融保护局行使执法权的任何法律,则相对于该等法律而言,第(A)子款的规定不适用于该等主体。

(4)**特定计划或安排**。——就本子条而言,“特定计划或安排”一词系指《1986年国内税收法典》第220条、第223条、第401(a)条、第403(a)条、第403(b)条、第408条、第408A条、第529条或第530条所述任何计划、账户或安排,或任何员工福利或薪酬计划或安排,包括受制于《1974年员工退休收入保障法》第一编的计划,或由州资助的任何预付学费计划。

(h)**州证券委员会监管的主体**。——

(1)**一般规定**。——本编任何规定均不得被解释为更改、修正或影响任何州证券委员会(或履行类似职能的任何机关或办公室)针对受其监管的主体制定规则、启动执法程序或采取任何其他措施的权力。除第(2)款和第(f)子条允许的情形外,对于受任何州证券委员会(或履行类似职能的任何机关或办公室)监管的主体而言,消费者金融保护局仅在该等主体以受监管身份行事时,无权对其执行本编的规定。

(2)**活动说明**。——第(1)款不适用于要约或提供任何消费者金融产品或服务,或者受制于任何明文列举的消费者法律,或受制于已根据第F子编或第H子编转由消费者金融保护局行使执法权的任何法律的任何主体。

(i)**适用于受证券交易委员会监管的主体的除外规定**。——

(1)**一般规定**。——本编任何规定均不得被解释为更改、修正或影响证券交易委员会针对受其监管的主体制定规则、启动执法程序或采取任何其他措施的权力。消费者金融保护局无权对受证券交易委员会监管的主体执行本编的规定。

regulated by the Commission.

(2) CONSULTATION AND COORDINATION. — Notwithstanding paragraph (1), the Commission shall consult and coordinate, where feasible, with the Bureau with respect to any rule (including any advance notice of proposed rulemaking) regarding an investment product or service that is the same type of product as, or that competes directly with, a consumer financial product or service that is subject to the jurisdiction of the Bureau under this title or under any other law. In carrying out this paragraph, the agencies shall negotiate an agreement to establish procedures for such coordination, including procedures for providing advance notice to the Bureau when the Commission is initiating a rulemaking.

(j) EXCLUSION FOR PERSONS REGULATED BY THE COMMODITY FUTURES TRADING COMMISSION. —

(1) IN GENERAL. — No provision of this title shall be construed as altering, amending, or affecting the authority of the Commodity Futures Trading Commission to adopt rules, initiate enforcement proceedings, or take any other action with respect to a person regulated by the Commodity Futures Trading Commission. The Bureau shall have no authority to exercise any power to enforce this title with respect to a person regulated by the Commodity Futures Trading Commission.

(2) CONSULTATION AND COORDINATION. — Notwithstanding paragraph (1), the Commodity Futures Trading Commission shall consult and coordinate with the Bureau with respect to any rule (including any advance notice of proposed rulemaking) regarding a product or service that is the same type of product as, or that competes directly with, a consumer financial product or service that is subject to the jurisdiction of the Bureau under this title or under any other law.

(k) EXCLUSION FOR PERSONS REGULATED BY THE FARM CREDIT ADMINISTRATION. —

(1) IN GENERAL. — No provision of this title shall be construed as altering, amending, or affecting the authority of the Farm Credit Administration to adopt rules, initiate enforcement proceedings, or take any other action with respect to a person regulated by the Farm Credit Administration. The Bureau shall have no authority to exercise any power to enforce this title with respect to a person regulated by the Farm Credit Administration.

(2) DEFINITION. — For purposes of this subsection, the term "person regulated by the Farm Credit Administration" means any Farm Credit System institution that is chartered and subject to the provisions of the Farm Credit Act of 1971 (12 U.S.C. 2001 et seq.).

(l)EXCLUSION FOR ACTIVITIES RELATING TO CHARITABLE CONTRIBUTI-ONS.—

(1) IN GENERAL. — The Director and the Bureau may not exercise any rulemaking, supervisory, enforcement, or other authority, including authority to order penalties, over any

(2)**磋商和协调**。——无论第(1)款如何规定,如果投资产品或服务与根据本编或任何其他法律而受消费者金融保护局管辖的消费者金融产品或服务属同类产品,或与之存在直接竞争关系,证券交易委员会应在可行的范围内,与消费者金融保护局就适用于该等投资产品或服务的规则(包括关于拟制定规则的任何事先通知)磋商和协调。在实施本款规定时,上述机关应通过谈判达成协议,确立开展上述协调工作的程序,包括关于证券交易委员会在启动规则制定程序时提前向消费者金融保护局发出通知的程序。

(j)**适用于受商品期货交易委员会监管的主体的除外规定**。——

(1)**一般规定**。——本编任何规定均不得被解释为更改、修正或影响商品期货交易委员会针对受其监管的主体制定规则、启动执法程序或采取任何其他措施的权力。消费者金融保护局无权对受商品期货交易委员会监管的主体执行本编的规定。

(2)**磋商和协调**。——无论第(1)款如何规定,如有产品或服务与根据本编或任何其他法律而受消费者金融保护局管辖的消费者金融产品或服务属同类产品,或与之存在直接竞争关系,商品期货交易委员会应与消费者金融保护局就适用于该等产品或服务的任何规则(包括关于拟制定规则的任何事先通知)磋商和协调。

(k)**适用于受农业信贷管理局监管的主体的除外规定**。——

(1)**一般规定**。——本编任何规定均不得被解释为更改、修正或影响农业信贷管理局针对受其监管的主体制定规则、启动执法程序或采取任何其他措施的权力。消费者金融保护局无权对受农业信贷管理局监管的主体执行本编的规定。

(2)**定义**。——就本子条而言,"受农业信贷管理局监管的主体"一词系指特许注册的并受制于《1971年农业信贷法》(《美国法典》第十二编第2001节及其后条文)的任何农业信贷系统机构。

(l)**适用于慈善捐款相关活动的除外规定**。——

(1)**一般规定**。——对于美国国税局认可的免税组织的任何代理人、志愿者或代表开展的与自愿捐款劝募活动或自愿捐款活动相关的任何活动,消费者金融保护局局

activities related to the solicitation or making of voluntary contributions to a tax-exempt organization as recognized by the Internal Revenue Service, by any agent, volunteer, or representative of such organizations to the extent the organization, agent, volunteer, or representative thereof is soliciting or providing advice, information, education, or instruction to any donor or potential donor relating to a contribution to the organization.

(2) LIMITATION. — The exclusion in paragraph (1) does not apply to other activities not described in paragraph (1) that are the offering or provision of any consumer financial product or service, or are otherwise subject to any enumerated consumer law or any law for which authorities are transferred under subtitle F or H.

(m) INSURANCE. — The Bureau may not define as a financial product or service, by regulation or otherwise, engaging in the business of insurance.

(n) LIMITED AUTHORITY OF THE BUREAU. — Notwithstanding subsections (a) through (h) and (l), a person subject to or described in one or more of such provisions —

(1) may be a service provider; and

(2) may be subject to requests from, or requirements imposed by, the Bureau regarding information in order to carry out the responsibilities and functions of the Bureau and in accordance with section 1022, 1052, or 1053.

(o) NO AUTHORITY TO IMPOSE USURY LIMIT. — No provision of this title shall be construed as conferring authority on the Bureau to establish a usury limit applicable to an extension of credit offered or made by a covered person to a consumer, unless explicitly authorized by law.

(p) ATTORNEY GENERAL. — No provision of this title, including section 1024(c)(1), shall affect the authorities of the Attorney General under otherwise applicable provisions of law.

(q) SECRETARY OF THE TREASURY. — No provision of this title shall affect the authorities of the Secretary, including with respect to prescribing rules, initiating enforcement proceedings, or taking other actions with respect to a person that performs income tax preparation activities for consumers.

(r) DEPOSIT INSURANCE AND SHARE INSURANCE. — Nothing in this title shall affect the authority of the Corporation under the Federal Deposit Insurance Act or the National Credit Union Administration Board under the Federal Credit Union Act as to matters related to deposit insurance and share insurance, respectively.

(s) FAIR HOUSING ACT. — No provision of this title shall be construed as affecting any authority arising under the Fair Housing Act.

SEC. 1028. AUTHORITY TO RESTRICT MANDATORY PRE-DISPUTE ARBITRATION.

(a) STUDY AND REPORT. — The Bureau shall conduct a study of, and shall provide a

长和消费者金融保护局不得行使任何规则制定权、监管权、执法权或其他任何权力（包括下令进行处罚的权力），前提是该等组织或其代理人、志愿者或代表正在向该等组织的任何捐赠者或潜在捐赠者征求或提供与向该等组织进行捐赠相关的意见、信息、教育或指示。

（2）**限制**。——第（1）款中的除外规定不适用于第（1）款所述以外的属于要约或提供任何消费者金融产品或服务的活动，或第（1）款所述以外的受制于任何明文列举的消费者法律，或受制于已根据第F子编或第H子编转由消费者金融保护局行使执法权的任何法律的其他活动。

（m）**保险**。——消费者金融保护局不得发布规章或通过其他形式，将从事保险业务活动界定为金融产品或服务。

（n）**消费者金融保护局的权力限制**。——无论第（a）子条至第（h）子条和第（l）子条如何规定，受制于上述条款的主体，或上述条款所述的主体——

（1）可以是服务提供者；且

（2）消费者金融保护局可以按照第1022条、第1052条或第1053条的规定，为履行其责任和职能，要求该等主体提供信息或向其施加与信息相关的要求。

（o）**无权施加高利限制**。——除非法律有明确授权，否则，本编的任何规定均不得被解释为授权消费者金融保护局就所涉主体向消费者要约发放或发放的信贷设定高利限制。

（p）**联邦总检察长**。——本编任何规定［包括第1024（c）（1）条］均不对联邦总检察长根据其他适用的法律所享有的权力构成影响。

（q）**财政部部长**。——本编任何规定均不对财政部部长的权力（包括针对为消费者提供报税服务的主体制定规则、启动执法程序或采取其他行动的权力）构成影响。

（r）**存款保险和股份保险**。——本编任何规定均不对联邦存款保险公司根据《联邦存款保险法》就存款保险事宜享有的权力和国家信贷联盟署委员会根据《联邦信贷联盟法》就股份保险事宜享有的权力构成影响。

（s）**《公平住房法》**。——本编任何规定不得被解释为对根据《公平住房法》所产生的任何权力构成影响。

第1028条　对强制性纠纷前置仲裁进行限制的权力

（a）**研究和报告**。——对于所涉主体和消费者之间订立的，对要约或提供消费者

report to Congress concerning, the use of agreements providing for arbitration of any future dispute between covered persons and consumers in connection with the offering or providing of consumer financial products or services.

(b) FURTHER AUTHORITY. — The Bureau, by regulation, may prohibit or impose conditions or limitations on the use of an agreement between a covered person and a consumer for a consumer financial product or service providing for arbitration of any future dispute between the parties, if the Bureau finds that such a prohibition or imposition of conditions or limitations is in the public interest and for the protection of consumers. The findings in such rule shall be consistent with the study conducted under subsection (a).

(c) LIMITATION. — The authority described in subsection(b) may not be construed to prohibit or restrict a consumer from entering into a voluntary arbitration agreement with a covered person after a dispute has arisen.

(d) EFFECTIVE DATE. — Notwithstanding any other provision of law, any regulation prescribed by the Bureau under subsection (b) shall apply, consistent with the terms of the regulation, to any agreement between a consumer and a covered person entered into after the end of the 180-day period beginning on the effective date of the regulation, as established by the Bureau.

SEC. 1029. EXCLUSION FOR AUTO DEALERS.

(a) SALE, SERVICING, AND LEASING OF MOTOR VEHICLES EXCLUDED. — Except as permitted in subsection (b), the Bureau may not exercise any rulemaking, supervisory, enforcement or any other authority, including any authority to order assessments, over a motor vehicle dealer that is predominantly engaged in the sale and servicing of motor vehicles, the leasing and servicing of motor vehicles, or both.

(b) CERTAIN FUNCTIONS EXCEPTED. — Subsection (a) shall not apply to any person, to the extent that such person —

(1) provides consumers with any services related to residential or commercial mortgages or self-financing transactions involving real property;

(2) operates a line of business —

(A) that involves the extension of retail credit or retail leases involving motor vehicles; and

(B) in which —

(i) the extension of retail credit or retail leases are provided directly to consumers; and

(ii) the contract governing such extension of retail credit or retail leases is not routinely assigned to an unaffiliated third party finance or leasing source; or

(3) offers or provides a consumer financial product or service not involving or related to the sale, financing, leasing, rental, repair, refurbishment, maintenance, or other servicing of motor vehicles, motor vehicle parts, or any related or ancillary product or service.

金融产品或服务过程中产生的任何未来纠纷之仲裁作出规定的协议的使用情况,消费者金融保护局应开展相关研究并向国会提交报告。

(b)**其他权限**。——对于所涉主体和消费者金融产品或服务的消费者之间订立的对双方任何未来纠纷的仲裁作出规定的协议,消费者金融保护局可以发布规章,禁止该等协议的使用,或对该等协议的使用设定条件或限制,前提是消费者金融保护局认定该等禁止或该等条件或限制的设定符合公共利益并有助于保护消费者。消费者金融保护局在制定上述规则时作出的认定应与其依照第(a)子条开展的研究一致。

(c)**限制**。——第(b)子条所述权力不得被解释为禁止或限制消费者在出现纠纷后与所涉主体自愿达成仲裁协议。

(d)**生效日**。——无论是否存在任何不同法律规定,消费者金融保护局依照第(b)子条制定的任何规章均应按照其条款,适用于消费者和所涉主体在规章生效日(具体日期由消费者金融保护局确定)起届满180天之后达成的任何协议。

第1029条　适用于汽车经销商的除外规定

(a)**汽车销售、维修及租赁除外**。——除第(b)子条允许的情形外,消费者金融保护局不得对以汽车销售与维修和/或汽车租赁与维修为主营业务的汽车经销商行使任何规则制定权、监管权、执法权或其他任何权力(包括发布计征费用命令的任何权力)。

(b)**关于特定职能的例外规定**。——第(a)子条的规定不适用于符合下列条件的任何主体——

(1)该等主体就住房或商业抵押贷款或房地产自融资交易向消费者提供任何相关服务;

(2)该等主体经营的业务范围——

(A)涉及与汽车相关的零售授信或零售租赁业务;且

(B)其中——

(i)零售授信或零售租赁直接面向消费者;且

(ii)零售授信或零售租赁合同通常不转让给作为融资或租赁来源的非关联第三方;或

(3)要约或提供的消费者金融产品或服务既不涉及汽车、汽车零部件或任何相关或配套产品或服务的销售、融资、租赁、出租、修理、翻新、维护或其他保养,也与之无关。

(c) PRESERVATION OF AUTHORITIES OF OTHER AGENCIES. — Except as provided in subsections (b) and(d), nothing in this title, including subtitle F, shall be construed as modifying, limiting, or superseding the operation of any provision of Federal law, or otherwise affecting the authority of the Board of Governors, the Federal Trade Commission, or any other Federal agency, with respect to a person described in subsection (a).

(d) FEDERAL TRADE COMMISSION AUTHORITY. — Notwithstanding section 18 of the Federal Trade Commission Act, the Federal Trade Commission is authorized to prescribe rules under sections 5 and 18(a)(1)(B) of the Federal Trade Commission Act. in accordance with section 553 of title 5, United States Code, with respect to a person described in subsection (a).

(e) COORDINATION WITH OFFICE OF SERVICE MEMBER AFFAIRS. — The Board of Governors and the Federal Trade Commission shall coordinate with the Office of Service Member Affairs, to ensure that —

(1) service members and their families are educated and empowered to make better informed decisions regarding consumer financial products and services offered by motor vehicle dealers, with a focus on motor vehicle dealers in the proximity of military installations; and

(2) complaints by service members and their families concerning such motor vehicle dealers are effectively monitored and responded to, and where appropriate, enforcement action is pursued by the authorized agencies.

(f) DEFINITIONS. — For purposes of this section, the following definitions shall apply:

(1) MOTOR VEHICLE. — The term "motor vehicle" means —

(A) any self–propelled vehicle designed for transporting persons or property on a street, highway, or other road;

(B) recreational boats and marine equipment;

(C) motorcycles;

(D) motor homes, recreational vehicle trailers, and slide–in campers, as those terms are defined in sections 571.3 and 575.103(d) of title 49, Code of Federal Regulations, or any successor thereto; and

(E) other vehicles that are titled and sold through dealers.

(2) MOTOR VEHICLE DEALER. — The term "motor vehicle dealer" means any person or resident in the United States, or any territory of the United States, who —

(A) is licensed by a State, a territory of the United States, or the District of Columbia to engage in the sale of motor vehicles; and

(B) takes title to, holds an ownership in, or takes physical custody of motor vehicles.

SEC. 1029A. EFFECTIVE DATE.

This subtitle shall become effective on the designated transfer date, except that sections

(c)**其他机关权力的保留**。——除第(b)子条和第(d)子条规定的情形外,就第(a)子条所述主体而言,本编的任何规定(包括第F子编)均不得被解释为改变、限制或替代任何联邦法律规定的适用,或对联邦储备委员会、联邦贸易委员会或任何其他联邦机关的权力以其他方式构成影响。

(d)**联邦贸易委员会的权限**。——无论《联邦贸易委员会法》第18条如何规定,联邦贸易委员会均有权按照《美国法典》第五编第553节,针对第(a)子条所述主体依据《联邦贸易委员会法》第5条和第18(a)(1)(B)条制定规则。

(e)**与现役军人事务办公室协调**。——联邦储备委员会和联邦贸易委员会应与现役军人事务办公室相互协调,以确保——

(1)现役军人及其家庭成员拥有消费者金融产品和服务相关知识,并有能力就汽车经销商(尤其是靠近军事设施的汽车经销商)要约的消费者金融产品和服务作出更明智的决定;及

(2)现役军人及其家庭成员对汽车经销商的投诉得到有效监控和答复,并在适当的情形下,确保授权机关采取强制执行行动。

(f)**定义**。——就本条而言,下列术语应适用如下定义:

(1)**汽车**。——"汽车"一词系指——

(A)任何自力推进用于在街道、公路或其他道路上进行客运或货运的交通工具;

(B)游艇及船舶设备;

(C)摩托车;

(D)房车、露营拖车及滑入式露营车[上述词语的定义以《联邦规章汇编》第四十九编第571.3部分和第575.103(d)部分及其任何后续规定为准];及

(E)汽车经销商冠以汽车名称并作为汽车销售的其他交通工具。

(2)**汽车经销商**。——"汽车经销商"一词系指位于美国或美国任何准州内的符合如下条件的任何主体或居民:

(A)经许可在美国某一州、准州或哥伦比亚特区从事汽车销售;且

(B)对汽车拥有产权、所有权或负责对汽车进行实体保管。

第1029A条　生效日

本子编的规定应于指定转移日生效,但第1022条、第1024条及第1025(e)条应于本

1022, 1024, and 1025(e) shall become effective on the date of enactment of this Act.

Subtitle C — Specific Bureau Authorities

SEC. 1031. PROHIBITING UNFAIR, DECEPTIVE, OR ABUSIVE ACTS OR PRACTICES.

(a) IN GENERAL. — The Bureau may take any action authorized under subtitle E to prevent a covered person or service provider from committing or engaging in an unfair, deceptive, or abusive act or practice under Federal law in connection with any transaction with a consumer for a consumer financial product or service, or the offering of a consumer financial product or service.

(b) RULEMAKING. — The Bureau may prescribe rules applicable to a covered person or service provider identifying as unlawful unfair, deceptive, or abusive acts or practices in connection with any transaction with a consumer for a consumer financial product or service, or the offering of a consumer financial product or service. Rules under this section may include requirements for the purpose of preventing such acts or practices.

(c) UNFAIRNESS. —

(1) IN GENERAL. — The Bureau shall have no authority under this section to declare an act or practice in connection with a transaction with a consumer for a consumer financial product or service, or the offering of a consumer financial product or service, to be unlawful on the grounds that such act or practice is unfair, unless the Bureau has a reasonable basis to conclude that —

(A) the act or practice causes or is likely to cause substantial injury to consumers which is not reasonably avoidable by consumers; and

(B) such substantial injury is not outweighed by countervailing benefits to consumers or to competition.

(2) CONSIDERATION OF PUBLIC POLICIES. — In determining whether an act or practice is unfair, the Bureau may consider established public policies as evidence to be considered with all other evidence. Such public policy considerations may not serve as a primary basis for such determination.

(d) ABUSIVE. — The Bureau shall have no authority under this section to declare an act or practice abusive in connection with the provision of a consumer financial product or service, unless the act or practice —

(1) materially interferes with the ability of a consumer to understand a term or condition of a consumer financial product or service; or

法颁布之日生效。

第C子编——消费者金融保护局的具体权限

第1031条　禁止不公平、欺骗性或滥用行为或做法

(a)**一般规定**。——消费者金融保护局可以根据第E子编的授权采取任何行动，防止所涉主体或服务提供者在与消费者开展消费者金融产品或服务交易时，或向消费者要约消费者金融产品或服务时,从事或采取联邦法律规定的不公平、欺骗性或滥用行为或做法。

(b)**规则制定**。——消费者金融保护局可以针对所涉主体或服务提供者制定适用规则,界定所涉主体或服务提供者在与消费者开展消费者金融产品或服务交易时,或要约消费者金融产品或服务时,从事或采取的何种行为或做法构成不公平、欺骗性或滥用行为或做法。消费者金融保护局在根据本条制定规则时,可纳入防范上述行为或做法的相关规定。

(c)**不公平行为或做法**。——

(1)**一般规定**。——对于在与消费者开展消费者金融产品或服务交易或向消费者要约消费者金融产品或服务过程中的行为或做法，除非消费者金融保护局有合理的依据作出如下结论,否则,消费者金融保护局无权基于该等行为或做法不公平的理由,根据本条规定将其宣布为非法行为或做法——

(A)该等行为或做法对或可能对消费者造成其无法合理避免的重大伤害;且

(B)上述重大伤害远远大于该等行为或做法给消费者或竞争带来的抵销性利益。

(2)**对公共政策的考虑**。——在判定某一行为或做法是否不公平时,消费者金融保护局可综合考虑既定公共政策和其他依据,但不得以该等公共政策作为主要依据。

(d)**滥用行为或做法**。——对于提供消费者金融产品或服务过程中的行为或做法,除非存在如下情形,否则,消费者金融保护局无权根据本条规定将该等行为或做法宣布为滥用行为或做法——

(1)该等行为或做法严重干扰了消费者理解消费性金融产品或服务的条款或条件的能力;或

(2) takes unreasonable advantage of —

(A) a lack of understanding on the part of the consumer of the material risks, costs, or conditions of the product or service;

(B) the inability of the consumer to protect the interests of the consumer in selecting or using a consumer financial product or service; or

(C) the reasonable reliance by the consumer on a covered person to act in the interests of the consumer.

(e) CONSULTATION. — In prescribing rules under this section, the Bureau shall consult with the Federal banking agencies, or other Federal agencies, as appropriate, concerning the consistency of the proposed rule with prudential, market, or systemic objectives administered by such agencies.

(f) CONSIDERATION OF SEASONAL INCOME. — The rules of the Bureau under this section shall provide, with respect to an extension of credit secured by residential real estate or a dwelling, if documented income of the borrower, including income from a small business, is a repayment source for an extension of credit secured by residential real estate or a dwelling, the creditor may consider the seasonality and irregularity of such income in the underwriting of and scheduling of payments for such credit.

SEC. 1032. DISCLOSURES.

(a) IN GENERAL. — The Bureau may prescribe rules to ensure that the features of any consumer financial product or service, both initially and over the term of the product or service, are fully, accurately, and effectively disclosed to consumers in a manner that permits consumers to understand the costs, benefits, and risks associated with the product or service, in light of the facts and circumstances.

(b) MODEL DISCLOSURES. —

(1) IN GENERAL. — Any final rule prescribed by the Bureau under this section requiring disclosures may include a model form that may be used at the option of the covered person for provision of the required disclosures.

(2) FORMAT. — A model form issued pursuant to paragraph (1) shall contain a clear and conspicuous disclosure that, at a minimum —

(A) uses plain language comprehensible to consumers;

(B) contains a clear format and design, such as an easily readable type font; and

(C) succinctly explains the information that must be communicated to the consumer.

(3) CONSUMER TESTING. — Any model form issued pursuant to this subsection shall be validated through consumer testing.

(c) BASIS FOR RULEMAKING. — In prescribing rules under this section, the Bureau shall consider available evidence about consumer awareness, understanding of, and responses to disclosures or communications about the risks, costs, and benefits of consumer financial

(2)该等行为或做法不合理地利用了:

(A)消费者对该等产品或服务的重大风险、成本或条件认识不足;

(B)消费者在选择或使用消费者金融产品或服务时保护自身权益能力的缺失;或

(C)消费者对所涉主体代表其权益行事的合理信赖。

(e)**磋商**。——在根据本条制定规则时,消费者金融保护局应与联邦银行业监管机关或其他联邦机关(视具体情而定)进行磋商,确认拟制定的规则与上述机关负责实施的审慎性目标、市场目标或系统性目标是否一致。

(f)**对季节性收入的考虑**。——对于以住房或住宅担保的授信而言,消费者金融保护局根据本条制定的规则应当规定:如果借款人以其有据可查的收入(包括来自小型企业的收入)作为还款来源,则贷款发放人在审核贷款及制定还款时间表时,可将上述收入的季度性和不规律性考虑在内。

第1032条　披露

(a)**一般规定**。——消费者金融保护局可以制定相关规则,确保任何消费者金融产品或服务的特征在最初提供该等产品或服务时以及其整个有效期内,得以完整、准确、有效地向消费者进行披露,使消费者能够根据相关事实和实际情形,了解该等产品或服务的成本、收益及相关风险。

(b)**披露范例**。——

(1)**一般规定**。——消费者金融保护局根据本条制定的任何最终规则包含披露要求的,可以提供相应的披露范例格式,供所涉主体在按要求进行披露时选择使用。

(2)**格式**。——根据第(1)款发布的范例格式应进行清晰、明确的披露,且至少应符合如下标准:

(A)语言平实、易懂;

(B)格式和设计清晰明了,如使用方便阅读的字体;及

(C)简明扼要地说明必须向消费者发布的信息。

(3)**消费者测试**。——根据本子条发布的范例格式应经过消费者测试验证。

(c)**规则制定基础**。——在根据本条制定规则时,对于有关消费性金融产品或服务的风险、成本和收益的披露或发布,消费者金融保护局应当通过可以获得的相关证据,考虑消费者对上述披露或发布的认识、理解和反应。

products or services.

(d) SAFE HARBOR. — Any covered person that uses a model form included with a rule issued under this section shall be deemed to be in compliance with the disclosure requirements of this section with respect to such model form.

(e) TRIAL DISCLOSURE PROGRAMS. —

(1) IN GENERAL. — The Bureau may permit a covered person to conduct a trial program that is limited in time and scope, subject to specified standards and procedures, for the purpose of providing trial disclosures to consumers that are designed to improve upon any model form issued pursuant to subsection (b)(1), or any other model form issued to implement an enumerated statute, as applicable.

(2) SAFE HARBOR. — The standards and procedures issued by the Bureau shall be designed to encourage covered persons to conduct trial disclosure programs. For the purposes of administering this subsection, the Bureau may establish a limited period during which a covered person conducting a trial disclosure program shall be deemed to be in compliance with, or may be exempted from, a requirement of a rule or an enumerated consumer law.

(3) PUBLIC DISCLOSURE. — The rules of the Bureau shall provide for public disclosure of trial disclosure programs, which public disclosure may be limited, to the extent necessary to encourage covered persons to conduct effective trials.

(f) COMBINED MORTGAGE LOAN DISCLOSURE. — Not later than 1 year after the designated transfer date, the Bureau shall propose for public comment rules and model disclosures that combine the disclosures required under the Truth in Lending Act and sections 4 and 5 of the Real Estate Settlement Procedures Act of 1974, into a single, integrated disclosure for mortgage loan transactions covered by those laws, unless the Bureau determines that any proposal issued by the Board of Governors and the Secretary of Housing and Urban Development carries out the same purpose.

SEC. 1033. CONSUMER RIGHTS TO ACCESS INFORMATION.

(a) IN GENERAL. — Subject to rules prescribed by the Bureau, a covered person shall make available to a consumer, upon request, information in the control or possession of the covered person concerning the consumer financial product or service that the consumer obtained from such covered person, including information relating to any transaction, series of transactions, or to the account including costs, charges and usage data. The information shall be made available in an electronic form usable by consumers.

(b) EXCEPTIONS. — A covered person may not be required by this section to make available to the consumer —

(1) any confidential commercial information, including an algorithm used to derive credit scores or other risk scores or predictors;

(2) any information collected by the covered person for the purpose of preventing fraud

(d)**安全港**。——根据本条制定的规则规定了范例格式的,任何所涉主体使用该等范例格式,即应被视为符合本条关于披露范例的要求。

(e)**试披露计划**。——

(1)**一般规定**。——消费者金融保护局可以允许所涉主体根据具体标准和程序,在有限的时间和范围内实施试披露计划,向消费者作出试披露,以改进根据第(b)(1)子条制定的任何范例格式,或改进为实施某项明文列举的制定法而制定的任何其他范例格式(如适用)。

(2)**安全港**。——消费者金融保护局制定的标准和程序应以鼓励所涉主体实施试披露计划为宗旨。为了实施本子条规定,消费者金融保护局可设定一个旨在实现如下目的的有限期限:在该期限内实施试披露计划的所涉主体应被视为符合或者可豁免于遵循某项规则或明文列举的消费者法律的规定。

(3)**公开披露**。——消费者金融保护局制定的规则应规定试披露计划的公开披露,但该等公开披露可以限制在鼓励所涉主体有效开展试披露所必要的范围内。

(f)**综合抵押贷款披露**。——对于如何将《诚实信贷法》规定的披露和《1974年房地产结算程序法》第4条和第5条规定的披露融合成为关于该等法律所规范的住房抵押贷款交易的统一、综合披露,除非消费者金融保护局判定联邦储备委员会和住房与城市发展部部长提出的任何草案对此作出了规定,否则消费者金融保护局应于指定转移日后一年之内,提出规则和披露范例草案,征求公众意见。

第1033条　消费者的信息获取权

(a)**一般规定**。——在不违反消费者金融保护局制定的规则的前提下,消费者从所涉主体处获取消费者金融产品或服务的,该等主体应按照消费者的要求,向消费者提供其控制或掌握的与该等产品或服务相关的信息,包括与任何交易或任何系列交易相关的信息,或账户相关信息(包括成本、收费及用途数据)。该等信息应当以消费者可以使用的电子格式提供。

(b)**例外规定**。——本条规定不得要求所涉主体向消费者提供如下信息——

(1)任何商业保密信息,包括信用评分或其他风险评分或预测指标的算法;

(2)所涉主体为防范欺诈、洗钱、或为发现、举报其他非法行为或潜在非法行为而

or money laundering, or detecting, or making any report regarding other unlawful or potentially unlawful conduct;

(3) any information required to be kept confidential by any other provision of law; or

(4) any information that the covered person cannot retrieve in the ordinary course of its business with respect to that information.

(c) NO DUTY TO MAINTAIN RECORDS. — Nothing in this section shall be construed to impose any duty on a covered person to maintain or keep any information about a consumer.

(d) STANDARDIZED FORMATS FOR DATA. — The Bureau, by rule, shall prescribe standards applicable to covered persons to promote the development and use of standardized formats for information, including through the use of machine readable files, to be made available to consumers under this section.

(e) CONSULTATION. — The Bureau shall, when prescribing any rule under this section, consult with the Federal banking agencies and the Federal Trade Commission to ensure, to the extent appropriate, that the rules —

(1) impose substantively similar requirements on covered persons;

(2) take into account conditions under which covered persons do business both in the United States and in other countries; and

(3) do not require or promote the use of any particular technology in order to develop systems for compliance.

SEC. 1034. RESPONSE TO CONSUMER COMPLAINTS AND INQUIRIES.

(a) TIMELY REGULATOR RESPONSE TO CONSUMERS. — The Bureau shall establish, in consultation with the appropriate Federal regulatory agencies, reasonable procedures to provide a timely response to consumers, in writing where appropriate, to complaints against, or inquiries concerning, a covered person, including —

(1) steps that have been taken by the regulator in response to the complaint or inquiry of the consumer;

(2) any responses received by the regulator from the covered person; and

(3) any follow–up actions or planned follow–up actions by the regulator in response to the complaint or inquiry of the consumer.

(b) TIMELY RESPONSE TO REGULATOR BY COVERED PERSON. — A covered person subject to supervision and primary enforcement by the Bureau pursuant to section 1025 shall provide a timely response, in writing where appropriate, to the Bureau, the prudential regulators, and any other agency having jurisdiction over such covered person concerning a consumer complaint or inquiry, including —

(1) steps that have been taken by the covered person to respond to the complaint or inquiry of the consumer;

收集的任何信息;

(3)任何其他法律规定要求保密的任何信息;或

(4)所涉主体在相关正常业务运作过程中无法重获的任何信息。

(c)**无保存记录职责**。——本条的任何规定均不得被解释为所涉主体有职责保存或保留任何消费者信息。

(d)**标准数据格式**。——消费者金融保护局应制定规则,规定适用于所涉主体的标准,以促进对按照本条规定向消费者提供信息(包括采用机器可读文件等手段)制定和使用标准化格式。

(e)**磋商**。——在根据本条制定任何规则时,消费者金融保护局应与联邦银行业监管机关和联邦贸易委员会进行磋商,确保在适当的范围内,各机关的规则——

(1)对所涉主体施加的要求大致相同;

(2)将所涉主体在美国及其他国家开展业务的条件考虑在内;且

(3)不要求或鼓励在制定合规制度时使用任何特定技术。

第1034条　对消费者投诉和询问的答复

(a)**监管者及时答复消费者**。——消费者金融保护局应在与相应的联邦监管机关磋商之后,制定合理流程,对消费者针对所涉主体的投诉或询问作出及时答复(在适当的情况下作出书面答复)。答复的内容包括——

(1)监管者已经针对消费者的投诉或询问采取的行动;

(2)监管者从所涉主体处收到的任何答复;及

(3)监管者针对消费者的投诉或询问采取的任何后续行动或计划采取的后续行动。

(b)**所涉主体及时答复监管者**。——根据第1025条的规定受消费者金融保护局监管权和优先执法权约束的所涉主体,应及时就消费者的投诉或询问向消费者金融保护局、审慎监管者和其他具有管辖权的机关作出答复(在适当的情况下作出书面答复)。答复的内容包括——

(1)所涉主体已经针对消费者的投诉或询问采取的行动;

(2) responses received by the covered person from the consumer; and

(3) follow–up actions or planned follow–up actions by the covered person to respond to the complaint or inquiry of the consumer.

(c) PROVISION OF INFORMATION TO CONSUMERS. —

(1) IN GENERAL . — A covered person subject to supervision and primary enforcement by the Bureau pursuant to section 1025 shall, in a timely manner, comply with a consumer request for information in the control or possession of such covered person concerning the consumer financial product or service that the consumer obtained from such covered person, including supporting written documentation, concerning the account of the consumer.

(2) EXCEPTIONS. — A covered person subject to supervision and primary enforcement by the Bureau pursuant to section 1025, a prudential regulator, and any other agency having jurisdiction over a covered person subject to supervision and primary enforcement by the Bureau pursuant to section 1025 may not be required by this section to make available to the consumer —

(A) any confidential commercial information, including an algorithm used to derive credit scores or other risk scores or predictors;

(B) any information collected by the covered person for the purpose of preventing fraud or money laundering, or detecting or making any report regarding other unlawful or potentially unlawful conduct;

(C) any information required to be kept confidential by any other provision of law; or

(D) any nonpublic or confidential information, including confidential supervisory information.

(d) AGREEMENTS WITH OTHER AGENCIES. — The Bureau shall enter into a memorandum of understanding with any affected Federal regulatory agency regarding procedures by which any covered person, and the prudential regulators, and any other agency having jurisdiction over a covered person, including the Secretary of the Department of Housing and Urban Development and the Secretary of Education, shall comply with this section.

SEC. 1035. PRIVATE EDUCATION LOAN OMBUDSMAN.

(a) ESTABLISHMENT. — The Secretary, in consultation with the Director, shall designate a Private Education Loan Ombudsman (in this section referred to as the "Ombudsman") within the Bureau, to provide timely assistance to borrowers of private education loans.

(b) PUBLIC INFORMATION. — The Secretary and the Director shall disseminate information about the availability and functions of the Ombudsman to borrowers and potential borrowers, as well as institutions of higher education, lenders, guaranty agencies, loan

(2)所涉主体从消费者处收到的答复;及

(3)所涉主体针对消费者的投诉或询问采取的任何后续行动或计划采取的后续行动。

(c)**向消费者提供信息**。——

(1)**一般规定**。——根据第1025条的规定,所涉主体受消费者金融保护局监管权和优先执法权约束,且消费者从该主体获取消费者金融产品或服务的,该主体应按照消费者的要求,及时向消费者提供该主体所控制或掌握的与该产品或服务相关的信息,包括与消费者账户相关的书面支持文件。

(2)**例外规定**。——本条规定不得要求根据第1025条的规定受消费者金融保护局监管权和优先执法权约束的所涉主体、审慎监管者以及对该等所涉主体具有管辖权的任何其他机关向消费者提供——

(A)任何商业保密信息,包括信用评分或其他风险评分或预测指标的算法;

(B)所涉主体为防范欺诈、洗钱,或为发现、举报其他非法行为或潜在非法行为而收集的任何信息;

(C)其他法律规定要求保密的任何信息;或

(D)任何非公开信息或保密信息,包括保密监管信息。

(d)**与其他机关的协议**。——对于任何所涉主体、审慎监管者,以及对所涉主体具有管辖权的任何其他机关(包括住房与城市发展部部长和教育部部长)遵循本条规定时应采用的流程,消费者金融保护局应与任何受影响的联邦监管机关签订谅解备忘录。

第1035条　个人教育贷款监察官

(a)**设立**。——财政部部长应与消费者金融保护局局长磋商后,在消费者金融保护局内部指定一名个人教育贷款监察官(本条中下称监察官),向个人教育贷款的借款人提供及时协助。

(b)**公开信息**。——财政部部长和消费者金融保护局局长应向借款人、潜在借款人、高等教育机构、贷款人、担保机关、贷款服务机构以及个人教育学生贷款计划的其他参与者传播相关信息,说明其可获得监察官的协助,并提供与监察官职能相关

servicers, and other participants in private education student loan programs.

(c) FUNCTIONS OF OMBUDSMAN. — The Ombudsman designated under this subsection shall —

(1) in accordance with regulations of the Director, receive, review, and attempt to resolve informally complaints from borrowers of loans described in subsection (a), including, as appropriate, attempts to resolve such complaints in collaboration with the Department of Education and with institutions of higher education, lenders, guaranty agencies, loan servicers, and other participants in private education loan programs;

(2) not later than 90 days after the designated transfer date, establish a memorandum of understanding with the student loan ombudsman established under section 141 (f) of the Higher Education Act of 1965 (20 U.S.C. 1018 (f)), to ensure coordination in providing assistance to and serving borrowers seeking to resolve complaints related to their private education or Federal student loans;

(3) compile and analyze data on borrower complaints regarding private education loans; and

(4) make appropriate recommendations to the Director, the Secretary, the Secretary of Education, the Committee on Banking, Housing, and Urban Affairs and the Committee on Health, Education, Labor, and Pensions of the Senate and the Committee on Financial Services and the Committee on Education and Labor of the House of Representatives.

(d) ANNUAL REPORTS. —

(1) IN GENERAL. — The Ombudsman shall prepare an annual report that describes the activities, and evaluates the effectiveness of the Ombudsman during the preceding year.

(2) SUBMISSION. — The report required by paragraph (1) shall be submitted on the same date annually to the Secretary, the Secretary of Education, the Committee on Banking, Housing, and Urban Affairs and the Committee on Health, Education, Labor, and Pensions of the Senate and the Committee on Financial Services and the Committee on Education and Labor of the House of Representatives.

(e) DEFINITIONS. — For purposes of this section, the terms "private education loan" and "institution of higher education" have the same meanings as in section 140 of the Truth in Lending Act (15 U.S.C. 1650).

SEC. 1036. PROHIBITED ACTS.

(a) IN GENERAL. — It shall be unlawful for —

(1) any covered person or service provider —

(A) to offer or provide to a consumer any financial product or service not in conformity with Federal consumer financial law, or otherwise commit any act or omission in violation of a Federal consumer financial law; or

(B) to engage in any unfair, deceptive, or abusive act or practice;

的信息。

(c)**监察官的职能**。——根据本子条指定的监察官应——

(1)根据消费者金融保护局局长的指示,接收、审查并努力以非正式方式解决第(a)子条所述借款人提出的投诉,包括在适当情况下努力与教育部、高等教育机构、贷款人、担保机关、贷款服务机构以及个人教育贷款计划的其他参与者合作解决投诉。

(2)在指定转移日后90天内,与依照《1965年高等教育法》第141(f)条[《美国法典》第二十编第1018(f)节]任命的学生贷款监察官签订谅解备忘录,确保在向寻求解决个人教育或联邦学生贷款投诉的借款人提供协助和服务的过程中,彼此能够实现相互协调。

(3)汇编和分析关于个人教育贷款借款人投诉的数据;并

(4)向消费者金融保护局局长、财政部部长、教育部部长、参议院银行、住房与城市事务委员会、参议院卫生、教育、劳工与养老委员会以及众议院金融服务委员会、众议院教育和劳工委员会提供适当的建议。

(d)**年度报告**。——

(1)**一般规定**。——监察官应当编制一份年度报告,说明上一年度的工作,并对其上一年的工作成效作出评价。

(2)**提交**。——第(1)款规定的报告应在每年同一日期提交给消费者金融保护局局长、财政部部长、教育部部长、参议院银行、住房与城市事务委员会、参议院卫生、教育、劳工与养老委员会以及众议院金融服务委员会、众议院教育和劳工委员会。

(e)**定义**。——就本条而言,"个人教育贷款"和"高等教育机构"的含义以《诚实信贷法》第140条(《美国法典》第十五编第1650节)的定义为准。

第1036条　禁止类行为

(a)**一般规定**。——下列行为属违法行为——

(1)任何所涉主体或服务提供者——

(A)违反联邦消费者金融法律的规定向消费者要约或提供任何金融产品或服务,或者违反联邦消费者金融法律规定实施任何作为或不作为;或

(B)从事任何不公平、欺骗性或滥用行为或做法;

(2) any covered person or service provider to fail or refuse, as required by Federal consumer financial law, or any rule or order issued by the Bureau thereunder —

(A) to permit access to or copying of records;

(B) to establish or maintain records; or

(C) to make reports or provide information to the Bureau; or

(3) any person to knowingly or recklessly provide substantial assistance to a covered person or service provider in violation of the provisions of section 1031, or any rule or order issued thereunder, and notwithstanding any provision of this title, the provider of such substantial assistance shall be deemed to be in violation of that section to the same extent as the person to whom such assistance is provided.

(b) EXCEPTION. — No person shall be held to have violated subsection (a)(1) solely by virtue of providing or selling time or space to a covered person or service provider placing an advertisement.

SEC. 1037. EFFECTIVE DATE.

This subtitle shall take effect on the designated transfer date.

Subtitle D — Preservation of State Law

SEC. 1041. RELATION TO STATE LAW.

(a) IN GENERAL. —

(1) RULE OF CONSTRUCTION. — This title, other than sections 1044 through 1048, may not be construed as annulling, altering, or affecting, or exempting any person subject to the provisions of this title from complying with, the statutes, regulations, orders, or interpretations in effect in any State, except to the extent that any such provision of law is inconsistent with the provisions of this title, and then only to the extent of the inconsistency.

(2) GREATER PROTECTION UNDER STATE LAW. — For purposes of this subsection, a statute, regulation, order, or interpretation in effect in any State is not inconsistent with the provisions of this title if the protection that such statute, regulation, order, or interpretation affords to consumers is greater than the protection provided under this title. A determination regarding whether a statute, regulation, order, or interpretation in effect in any State is inconsistent with the provisions of this title may be made by the Bureau on its own motion or in response to a nonfrivolous petition initiated by any interested person.

(b) RELATION TO OTHER PROVISIONS OF ENUMERATED CONSUMER LAWS THAT RELATE TO STATE LAW. — No provision of this title, except as provided in section 1083, shall be construed as modifying, limiting, or superseding the operation of any provision

(2)任何所涉主体或服务提供者未能或拒绝按照联邦消费者金融法律、消费者金融保护局根据该等法律发布的任何规则或命令的要求——

(A)开放记录的查阅或复制权;

(B)制作或保存记录;或

(C)向消费者金融保护局提交报告或提供信息;或

(3)任何主体在知情的情况下或轻率地违反第1031条或违反根据第1031条制定的任何规则或发布的任何命令,为所涉主体或服务提供者提供实质性协助。不论本编如何规定,上述实质性协助的提供者,应与接受协助的主体一样,同被视为违反了第1031条的规定。

(b)**例外规定**。——任何人均不得仅因向所涉主体或服务提供者提供或出售广告投放时间或空间,而被认定为违反了第(a)(1)子条的规定。

第1037条　生效日

本子编规定应于指定转移日生效。

第D子编——州法律的效力保留

第1041条　与州法律的关系

(a)**一般规定**。——

(1)**解释规则**。——除第1044条至第1048条外,本编任何规定均不得被解释为废除、更改、影响任何州有效适用的制定法、规章、命令或解释,或使受制于本编的任何主体免于遵循该等制定法、规章、命令或解释,但上述法律规定与本编规定不一致的,以本编规定为准,且仅在该不一致情形发生时以本编规定为准。

(2)**州法律提供更大程度保护的情形**。——就本子条而言,如果任何州有效适用的制定法、规章、命令或解释向消费者提供的保护力度强于本编提供的保护,则该等制定法、规章、命令或解释并非与本编的规定不一致。消费者金融保护局可以主动或根据任何利害关系人提出的有正当意义的请求,判定任何州有效适用的制定法、规章、命令或解释是否与本编规定一致。

(b)**与明文列举的消费者法律中与州法律相关的其他规定之间的关系**。——除第1083条规定的情形外,明文列举的消费者法律中对任何州有效适用的法律相对于该等联邦法律的适用效力作出了相关规定的,本编的任何规定均不得被解释为构成

of an enumerated consumer law that relates to the application of a law in effect in any State with respect to such Federal law.

(c) ADDITIONAL CONSUMER PROTECTION REGULATIONS IN RESPONSE TO STATE ACTION.—

(1) NOTICE OF PROPOSED RULE REQUIRED.—The Bureau shall issue a notice of proposed rulemaking whenever a majority of the States has enacted a resolution in support of the establishment or modification of a consumer protection regulation by the Bureau.

(2) BUREAU CONSIDERATIONS REQUIRED FOR ISSUANCE OF FINAL REGULATION.—Before prescribing a final regulation based upon a notice issued pursuant to paragraph (1), the Bureau shall take into account whether—

(A) the proposed regulation would afford greater protection to consumers than any existing regulation;

(B) the intended benefits of the proposed regulation for consumers would outweigh any increased costs or inconveniences for consumers, and would not discriminate unfairly against any category or class of consumers; and

(C) a Federal banking agency has advised that the proposed regulation is likely to present an unacceptable safety and soundness risk to insured depository institutions.

(3) EXPLANATION OF CONSIDERATIONS.—The Bureau—

(A) shall include a discussion of the considerations required in paragraph (2) in the Federal Register notice of a final regulation prescribed pursuant to this subsection; and

(B) whenever the Bureau determines not to prescribe a final regulation, shall publish an explanation of such determination in the Federal Register, and provide a copy of such explanation to each State that enacted a resolution in support of the proposed regulation, the Committee on Banking, Housing, and Urban Affairs of the Senate, and the Committee on Financial Services of the House of Representatives.

(4) RESERVATION OF AUTHORITY.—No provision of this subsection shall be construed as limiting or restricting the authority of the Bureau to enhance consumer protection standards established pursuant to this title in response to its own motion or in response to a request by any other interested person.

(5) RULE OF CONSTRUCTION.—No provision of this subsection shall be construed as exempting the Bureau from complying with subchapter II of chapter 5 of title 5, United States Code.

(6) DEFINITION.—For purposes of this subsection, the term "consumer protection regulation" means a regulation that the Bureau is authorized to prescribe under the Federal consumer financial laws.

SEC. 1042. PRESERVATION OF ENFORCEMENT POWERS OF STATES.

(a) IN GENERAL.—

对该等规定的修改、限制或代替。

(c)**针对州行动向消费者提供保护的其他规章**。——

(1)**规则草案通知要求**。——多数州通过决议,支持消费者金融保护局制定或修改消费者保护规章后,消费者金融保护局应就规章草案发布公告。

(2)**消费者金融保护局发布最终规章时需要考虑的因素**。——在基于根据第(1)款发布的公告制定最终规章之前,消费者金融保护局应考虑——

(A)规章草案向消费者提供的保护力度是否强于任何既存规章;

(B)规章草案为消费者带来的预期利益是否将超过为消费者额外带来的任何成本或不便,以及是否将会对任何类型或类别的消费者形成不平等的歧视;及

(C)联邦银行业监管机关是否认为规章草案可能使参保存款机构面临不可接受的安全及稳定风险。

(3)**考虑因素说明**。——消费者金融保护局——

(A)在《联邦公报》上发布关于根据本子条制定的最终规章的公告时,应论述第(2)款规定的考虑因素;及

(B)如果判定不应制定最终规章,应在《联邦公报》上对该判定作出说明,并向已通过决议,表示支持规章草案制定的各州以及参议院银行、住房和城市事务委员会和众议院金融服务委员会提供该说明。

(4)**权力保留**。——本子条任何规定均不得被解释为限制消费者金融保护局主动或根据任何其他利益关系人的请求提高依据本编制定的消费者保护标准的权力。

(5)**解释规则**。——本子条任何规定均不得被解释为豁免消费者金融保护局遵循《美国法典》第五编第五章第二子章的规定。

(6)**定义**。——就本子条而言,“消费者保护规章”一词系指消费者金融保护局经授权根据联邦消费者金融法律制定的规章。

第1042条　州执法权的保留

(a)**一般规定**。——

(1) ACTION BY STATE. — Except as provided in paragraph (2), the attorney general (or the equivalent thereof) of any State may bring a civil action in the name of such State in any district court of the United States in that State or in State court that is located in that State and that has jurisdiction over the defendant, to enforce provisions of this title or regulations issued under this title, and to secure remedies under provisions of this title or remedies otherwise provided under other law. A State regulator may bring a civil action or other appropriate proceeding to enforce the provisions of this title or regulations issued under this title with respect to any entity that is State–chartered, incorporated, licensed, or otherwise authorized to do business under State law (except as provided in paragraph (2)), and to secure remedies under provisions of this title or remedies otherwise provided under other provisions of law with respect to such an entity.

(2) ACTION BY STATE AGAINST NATIONAL BANK OR FEDERAL SAVINGS ASSOCIATION TO ENFORCE RULES. —

(A) IN GENERAL. — Except as permitted under subparagraph (B), the attorney general (or equivalent thereof) of any State may not bring a civil action in the name of such State against a national bank or Federal savings association to enforce a provision of this title.

(B) ENFORCEMENT OF RULES PERMITTED. — The attorney general (or the equivalent thereof) of any State may bring a civil action in the name of such State against a national bank or Federal savings association in any district court of the United States in the State or in State court that is located in that State and that has jurisdiction over the defendant to enforce a regulation prescribed by the Bureau under a provision of this title and to secure remedies under provisions of this title or remedies otherwise provided under other law.

(3) RULE OF CONSTRUCTION. — No provision of this title shall be construed as modifying, limiting, or superseding the operation of any provision of an enumerated consumer law that relates to the authority of a State attorney general or State regulator to enforce such Federal law.

(b) CONSULTATION REQUIRED. —

(1) NOTICE. —

(A) IN GENERAL. — Before initiating any action in a court or other administrative or regulatory proceeding against any covered person as authorized by subsection (a) to enforce any provision of this title, including any regulation prescribed by the Bureau under this title, a State attorney general or State regulator shall timely provide a copy of the complete complaint to be filed and written notice describing such action or proceeding to the Bureau and the prudential regulator, if any, or the designee thereof.

(B) EMERGENCY ACTION. — If prior notice is not practicable, the State attorney general or State regulator shall provide a copy of the complete complaint and the notice to the Bureau and the prudential regulator, if any, immediately upon instituting the action or

(1)**由州提起的诉讼**。——除第(2)款规定的情形外,任何州的总检察长(或同等职务人员)均可以以本州名义,在本州内的任何联邦地区法院或位于本州并对被告有管辖权的州法院提起民事诉讼,执行本编或依据本编发布的规章,并寻求本编或其他法律规定的救济。除第(2)款规定的情形外,对于在本州获得特许注册、设立、获得执照、被授权依照本州法律开展业务的实体,本州监管者可以提起民事诉讼或其他适当的程序,针对该等实体执行本编或依据本编发布的规章,并寻求本编或其他法律规定的救济。

(2)**各州为执行规则而对国民银行或联邦储蓄协会提起诉讼**。——

(A)**一般规定**。——除第(B)子款许可的情形外,任何州的总检察长(或同等职务人员)均不得以本州名义为执行本编规定之目的而对国民银行或联邦储蓄协会提起民事诉讼。

(B)**可以强制执行规则的情形**。——任何州的总检察长(或同等职务人员)均可以本州名义,针对国民银行或联邦储蓄协会,在本州内的任何联邦地区法院或位于本州并对被告有管辖权的州法院提起民事诉讼,执行消费者金融保护局依照本编规定制定的规章,并寻求本编或其他法律规定的救济。

(3)**解释规则**。——对于明文列举的消费者法律中与州总检察长或州监管者执行该等消费者法律的权力相关的任何规定,本编任何规定均不得被解释为改变、限制或替代该等规定的适用。

(b)**磋商要求**。——

(1)**通知**。——

(A)**一般规定**。——在根据第(a)子条的授权,为执行本编规定(包括消费者金融保护局依照本编制定的任何规章)之目的而针对任何所涉主体向法院提起诉讼或其他行政或监管程序之前,州总检察长或州监管者应及时向消费者金融保护局和审慎监管者(如有)或其指定人员提供将向法院提交的完整的起诉书复本和对上述诉讼或程序进行说明的书面通知。

(B)**紧急行动**。——如果提前发出通知并不可行,州总检察长或州监管者应当在提起诉讼或程序之时,立即向消费者金融保护局和审慎监管者(如有)提供完整的起诉书复本和上述通知。

proceeding.

(C) CONTENTS OF NOTICE. — The notification required under this paragraph shall, at a minimum, describe —

(i) the identity of the parties;

(ii) the alleged facts underlying the proceeding; and

(iii) whether there may be a need to coordinate the prosecution of the proceeding so as not to interfere with any action, including any rulemaking, undertaken by the Bureau, a prudential regulator, or another Federal agency.

(2) BUREAU RESPONSE. — In any action described in paragraph (1), the Bureau may —

(A) intervene in the action as a party;

(B) upon intervening —

(i) remove the action to the appropriate United States district court, if the action was not originally brought there; and

(ii) be heard on all matters arising in the action; and

(C) appeal any order or judgment, to the same extent as any other party in the proceeding may.

(c) REGULATIONS. — The Bureau shall prescribe regulations to implement the requirements of this section and, from time to time, provide guidance in order to further coordinate actions with the State attorneys general and other regulators.

(d) PRESERVATION OF STATE AUTHORITY. —

(1) STATE CLAIMS. — No provision of this section shall be construed as altering, limiting, or affecting the authority of a State attorney general or any other regulatory or enforcement agency or authority to bring an action or other regulatory proceeding arising solely under the law in effect in that State.

(2) STATE SECURITIES REGULATORS. — No provision of this title shall be construed as altering, limiting, or affecting the authority of a State securities commission (or any agency or office performing like functions) under State law to adopt rules, initiate enforcement proceedings, or take any other action with respect to a person regulated by such commission or authority.

(3) STATE INSURANCE REGULATORS. — No provision of this title shall be construed as altering, limiting, or affecting the authority of a State insurance commission or State insurance regulator under State law to adopt rules, initiate enforcement proceedings, or take any other action with respect to a person regulated by such commission or regulator.

SEC. 1043. PRESERVATION OF EXISTING CONTRACTS.

This title, and regulations, orders, guidance, and interpretations prescribed, issued, or established by the Bureau, shall not be construed to alter or affect the applicability of any

(C)**通知内容**。——本款要求提供的通知应至少说明——

(i)当事人的身份;

(ii)州总检察长或州监管者主张引发该等程序的事实;及

(iii)是否有必要协调该等程序的开展,以避免妨碍消费者金融保护局、审慎监管者或其他联邦机关采取的任何行动(包括任何规则制定行为)。

(2)**消费者金融保护局的回应**。——在第(1)款所述的任何诉讼中,消费者金融保护局可以——

(A)作为当事人参与该等诉讼;

(B)参与该等诉讼后——

(i)将该等诉讼移交至相应的联邦地区法院(如果最初受理案件的法院并非联邦地区法院);及

(ii)就该等诉讼中的所有事项作出陈述;及

(C)与该等程序中其他当事人一样,就任何命令或判决提起上诉。

(c)**规章**。——消费者金融保护局应当制定本条的实施规章,并应不时提供指导,以便进一步与州总检察长和其他监管者协调各自的行动。

(d)**州权力的保留**。——

(1)**州的权利主张**。——本条任何规定均不得被解释为改变、限制或影响州总检察长或任何其他监管或执法机关或部门完全依据本州有效适用的法律提起诉讼或其他监管程序的权力。

(2)**州证券监管者**。——本条任何规定均不得被解释为改变、限制或影响州证券委员会(或履行类似职能的任何机关或部门)依据本州法律针对受其监管的主体制定规则、启动执法程序或采取任何其他行动的权力。

(3)**州保险监管者**。——本条任何规定均不得被解释为改变、限制或影响州保险委员会或州保险监管者依据本州法律就受其监管的主体制定规则、启动执法程序或采取任何其他行动的权力。

第1043条　既存合同的保留

货币监理署署长或储蓄机构监理局局长制定、发布或确定的任何规章、命令、指引或解释中,针对依据联邦银行法律制定的州法律对受货币监理署署长监管与规制

regulation, order, guidance, or interpretation prescribed, issued, and established by the Comptroller of the Currency or the Director of the Office of Thrift Supervision regarding the applicability of State law under Federal banking law to any contract entered into on or before the date of enactment of this Act, by national banks, Federal savings associations, or subsidiaries thereof that are regulated and supervised by the Comptroller of the Currency or the Director of the Office of Thrift Supervision, respectively.

SEC. 1044. STATE LAW PREEMPTION STANDARDS FOR NATIONAL BANKS AND SUBSIDIARIES CLARIFIED.

(a) IN GENERAL. — Chapter one of title LXII of the Revised Statutes of the United States(12 U.S.C. 21 et seq.) is amended by inserting after section 5136B the following new section:

"SEC. 5136C. STATE LAW PREEMPTION STANDARDS FOR NATIONAL BANKS AND SUBSIDIARIES CLARIFIED.

"(a) DEFINITIONS. — For purposes of this section, the following definitions shall apply: —

"(1) NATIONAL BANK. — The term 'national bank' includes —

"(A) any bank organized under the laws of the United States; and

"(B) any Federal branch established in accordance with the International Banking Act of 1978.

"(2) STATE CONSUMER FINANCIAL LAWS. — The term 'State consumer financial law' means a State law that does not directly or indirectly discriminate against national banks and that directly and specifically regulates the manner, content, or terms and conditions of any financial transaction (as may be authorized for national banks to engage in), or any account related thereto, with respect to a consumer.

"(3) OTHER DEFINITIONS. — The terms 'affiliate', 'subsidiary', 'includes', and 'including' have the same meanings as in section 3 of the Federal Deposit Insurance Act.

"(b) PREEMPTION STANDARD. —

"(1) IN GENERAL. — State consumer financial laws are preempted, only if —

"(A) application of a State consumer financial law would have a discriminatory effect on national banks, in comparison with the effect of the law on a bank chartered by that State;

"(B) in accordance with the legal standard for preemption in the decision of the Supreme Court of the United States in Barnett Bank of Marion County, N. A. v. Nelson, Florida Insurance Commissioner, et al., 517 U.S. 25 (1996), the State consumer financial law prevents or significantly interferes with the exercise by the national bank of its powers; and any preemption determination under this subparagraph may be made by a court, or by regulation or order of the Comptroller of the Currency on a case-by-case basis, in accordance

的国民银行、受储蓄机构监理局局长监管与规制的联邦储蓄协会或上述二者的子公司在本法颁布日或之前订立的合同的适用性作出了规定的,本编以及消费者金融保护局制定、发布或确定的规章、命令、指引或解释均不得被解释为改变或影响该等规章、命令、指引或解释的适用范围。

第1044条　关于联邦法律对国民银行及其子公司的优先适用标准的说明

(a)**一般规定**。——在《美国制定法汇编》(修订版)第六十二编第一章(《美国法典》第十二编第21节及其后条文)第5136B条之后增加如下条文,作为对该章的修正:

"第5136C条　关于联邦法律对国民银行及其子公司的优先适用标准的说明

(a)**定义**。——就本条而言,下列术语应适用如下定义——

(1)**国民银行**。'国民银行'一词包括——
(A)根据联邦法律组建的任何银行;及
(B)根据《1978年国际银行法》设立的任何联邦分行。

(2)**州消费者金融法律**。——'州消费者金融法律'一词系指不直接或间接对国民银行造成歧视,并对国民银行可以从事的任何金融交易的方式、内容、条款和条件或任何相关账户进行直接、专门监管的州法律。

(3)**其他定义**。——'关联方'、'子公司'、'包括'等词的含义以《联邦存款保险法》第3条的定义为准。
(b)优先适用标准。——
(1)**一般规定**。——只有在下列情形下,方可排除州消费者金融法律的适用——
(A)与在本州特许注册的银行相比,州消费者金融法律的适用对国民银行将造成歧视性影响;
(B)根据美国最高法院在'马里昂郡巴尼特国民银行诉佛罗里达州保险监督官尼尔森等[《美国最高法院判例汇编案例列表》(1996年)第517卷第25页]'一案的判决中确立的优先适用法律标准,州消费者金融法律阻碍或严重干扰国民银行行使其权力;法院可以根据适用的法律,在个案基础上作出本子款规定的任何优先适用判定,货币监理署也可以根据适用的法律,在个案基础上发布规章或命令作出任何优先适用判定;或者

with applicable law; or

"(C) the State consumer financial law is preempted by a provision of Federal law other than this title.

"(2) SAVINGS CLAUSE. — This title and section 24 of the Federal Reserve Act (12 U.S.C. 371) do not preempt, annul, or affect the applicability of any State law to any subsidiary or affiliate of a national bank (other than a subsidiary or affiliate that is chartered as a national bank).

"(3) CASE–BY–CASE BASIS. —

"(A) DEFINITION. — As used in this section the term 'case–by–case basis' refers to a determination pursuant to this section made by the Comptroller concerning the impact of a particular State consumer financial law on any national bank that is subject to that law, or the law of any other State with substantively equivalent terms.

"(B) CONSULTATION. — When making a determination on a case–by–case basis that a State consumer financial law of another State has substantively equivalent terms as one that the Comptroller is preempting, the Comptroller shall first consult with the Bureau of Consumer Financial Protection and shall take the views of the Bureau into account when making the determination.

"(4) RULE OF CONSTRUCTION. — This title does not occupy the field in any area of State law.

"(5) STANDARDS OF REVIEW. —

"(A) PREEMPTION. — A court reviewing any determinations made by the Comptroller regarding preemption of a State law by this title or section 24 of the Federal Reserve Act (12 U.S.C. 371) shall assess the validity of such determinations, depending upon the thoroughness evident in the consideration of the agency, the validity of the reasoning of the agency, the consistency with other valid determinations made by the agency, and other factors which the court finds persuasive and relevant to its decision.

"(B) SAVINGS CLAUSE. — Except as provided in subparagraph(A), nothing in this section shall affect the deference that a court may afford to the Comptroller in making determinations regarding the meaning or interpretation of title LXII of the Revised Statutes of the United States or other Federal laws.

"(6) COMPTROLLER DETERMINATION NOT DELEGABLE. — Any regulation, order, or determination made by the Comptroller of the Currency under paragraph (1)(B) shall be made by the Comptroller, and shall not be delegable to another officer or employee of the Comptroller of the Currency.

"(c) SUBSTANTIAL EVIDENCE. — No regulation or order of the Comptroller of the Currency prescribed under subsection (b)(1)(B), shall be interpreted or applied so as to invalidate, or otherwise declare inapplicable to a national bank, the provision of the State

(C)州消费者金融法律被本编之外的其他联邦法律的规定排除适用。

(2)**保留条款**。——本编的任何规定及《联邦储备法》第24条[《美国法典》第十二编第371节]既不排除也不废止和影响任何州法律对国民银行的任何子公司或关联方的适用范围(但该等子公司或关联方本身特许注册为国民银行的除外)。

(3)**在个案基础上**。——

(A)**定义**。——就本条而言,'在个案基础上'一词系指货币监理署署长根据本条规定,针对特定的州消费者金融法律对受制于该等法律或任何其他州具有基本相同条款之法律的国民银行的影响作出的判定。

(B)**磋商**。——在个案基础上判定其他州的州消费者金融法律与货币监理署署长优先适用的法律是否有基本相同的条款时,货币监理署署长应首先与消费者金融保护局进行磋商,并考虑消费者金融保护局的意见。

(4)**解释规则**。——本编规定不涉入任何州法律领域。

(5)**审查标准**。——

(A)**优先适用**。——对于货币监理署署长作出的本编或《联邦储备法》第24条(《美国法典》第十二编第371节)应优先于州法律适用的任何判定,法院在审查该等判定时,应基于货币监理署署长考虑问题的全面彻底性、理由的有效性、与其作出的其他判定的一致性以及法院认为有说服力并与其判定相关的任何其他因素,评估该等判定的有效性。

(B)**保留条款**。——除第(A)子款规定的情形外,本条任何规定均不影响法院在针对《美国制定法汇编》(修订版)第六十二编的含义或解释作出判定时对货币监理署署长的司法尊重。

(6)**货币监理署署长不得委托他人代为作出决定**。——货币监理署署长依照第(1)(B)款制定的任何规章、命令或作出的任何判定均应由其亲自进行,不得委托货币监理署的其他官员或员工代行。

(c)**实质性证据**。——除非根据美国最高法院在马里昂郡巴尼特美联银行诉佛罗里达州保险监督官尼尔森等(《美国最高法院判例汇编案例列表》(1996年)第517卷第25页)一案的判决中确立的法律标准,被纳入程序记录的实质性证据能够为优先适

consumer financial law, unless substantial evidence, made on the record of the proceeding, supports the specific finding regarding the preemption of such provision in accordance with the legal standard of the decision of the Supreme Court of the United States in Barnett Bank of Marion County, N.A. v. Nelson, Florida Insurance Commissioner, et al., 517 U.S. 25 (1996).

"(d) PERIODIC REVIEW OF PREEMPTION DETERMINATIONS. —

"(1) IN GENERAL. — The Comptroller of the Currency shall periodically conduct a review, through notice and public comment, of each determination that a provision of Federal law preempts a State consumer financial law. The agency shall conduct such review within the 5-year period after prescribing or otherwise issuing such determination, and at least once during each 5-year period thereafter. After conducting the review of, and inspecting the comments made on, the determination, the agency shall publish a notice in the Federal Register announcing the decision to continue or rescind the determination or a proposal to amend the determination. Any such notice of a proposal to amend a determination and the subsequent resolution of such proposal shall comply with the procedures set forth in subsections (a) and (b) of section 5244 of the Revised Statutes of the United States (12 U.S.C. 43 (a), (b)).

"(2) REPORTS TO CONGRESS. — At the time of issuing a review conducted under paragraph (1), the Comptroller of the Currency shall submit a report regarding such review to the Committee on Financial Services of the House of Representatives and the Committee on Banking, Housing, and Urban Affairs of the Senate. The report submitted to the respective committees shall address whether the agency intends to continue, rescind, or propose to amend any determination that a provision of Federal law preempts a State consumer financial law, and the reasons therefor.

"(e) APPLICATION OF STATE CONSUMER FINANCIAL LAW TO SUBSIDIARIES AND AFFILIATES. — Notwithstanding any provision of this title or section 24 of Federal Reserve Act(12 U.S.C. 371), a State consumer financial law shall apply to a subsidiary or affiliate of a national bank(other than a subsidiary or affiliate that is chartered as a national bank) to the same extent that the State consumer financial law applies to any person, corporation, or other entity subject to such State law.

"(f) PRESERVATION OF POWERS RELATED TO CHARGING INTEREST. — No provision of this title shall be construed as altering or otherwise affecting the authority conferred by section 5197 of the Revised Statutes of the United States(12 U.S.C. 85) for the charging of interest by a national bank at the rate allowed by the laws of the State, territory, or district where the bank is located, including with respect to the meaning of 'interest' under such provision.

"(g) TRANSPARENCY OF OCC PREEMPTION DETERMINATIONS .—The Comptroller of the Currency shall publish and update no less frequently than quarterly, a list

用的具体结论提供支持,否则,在对货币监理署署长依照第(b)(1)(B)子条制定的任何规章或命令进行解释或适用时,均不得导致州消费者金融法律的条款无效,或导致该等法律被宣布为不适用于国民银行。

(d)**优先适用判定的定期审查**。——

(1)**一般规定**。——货币监理署署长应通过发布通知和征求公众意见的方式,定期审查联邦法律规定优先于州消费者法律的所有判定。货币监理署应当在该等决定作出或以其他方式发布后5年内进行审查,且此后应每5年至少审查一次。在审查判定并审议相关公众意见之后,货币监理署应在《联邦公报》上发布公告,宣布继续维持或撤销上述判定的决定或者修改上述判定的建议。关于判定修改建议及其后续决议的任何公告均应遵循《美国制定法汇编》(修订版)第5244节第(a)子节和第(b)子节[《美国法典》第十二编第43(a)节和第43(b)节]规定的程序。

(2)**向国会报告**。——在发布根据第(1)款开展的审查之结果时,货币监理署署长应就该审查向众议院金融服务委员会和参议院银行、住房与城市事务委员会提交一份报告。该报告应说明货币监理署是计划继续维持、撤销关于联邦法律规定优先于州消费者金融法律的任何判定,还是计划提出修改该等判定的建议,并说明相关理由。

(e)**州消费者金融法律对国民银行子公司和关联方的适用**。——无论本编或《联邦储备法》第24条(《美国法典》第十二编第371节)如何规定,州消费者金融法律均应适用于国民银行的子公司或关联方(但该等子公司或关联方本身特许注册为国民银行的除外),其适用效力与该等州消费者金融法律适用于受制于该等法律的任何主体、公司或其他实体时并无二致。

(f)**保留与利息计收相关的权力**。——本编任何规定均不得被解释为改变或以其他方式影响《美国制定法汇编》(修订版)第5197节(《美国法典》第十二编第85节)赋予国民银行按其所在州、准州或地区的法律所允许的利率计收利息(包括对于该等规定所述'利息'的含义而言)的权力。

(g)**货币监理署优先适用判定的透明度**。——货币监理署署长应每个季度对其作出的届时有效的优先适用判定清单公布和更新至少一次,说明每项判定涉及的活

of preemption determinations by the Comptroller of the Currency then in effect that identifies the activities and practices covered by each determination and the requirements and constraints determined to be preempted.".

(b) CLERICAL AMENDMENT. — The table of sections for chapter one of title LXII of the Revised Statutes of the United States is amended by inserting after the item relating to section 5136B the following new item:

"SEC. 5136C. State law preemption standards for national banks and subsidiaries clarified.".

SEC. 1045. CLARIFICATION OF LAW APPLICABLE TO NONDEPOSITORY INSTITUTION SUBSIDIARIES.

Section 5136C of the Revised Statutes of the United States (as added by this subtitle) is amended by adding at the end the following:

"(h) CLARIFICATION OF LAW APPLICABLE TO NONDEPOSITORY INSTITUTION SUBSIDIARIES AND AFFILIATES OF NATIONAL BANKS. —

"(1) DEFINITIONS. — For purposes of this subsection, the terms 'depository institution', 'subsidiary', and 'affiliate' have the same meanings as in section 3 of the Federal Deposit Insurance Act.

"(2) RULE OF CONSTRUCTION. — No provision of this title or section 24 of the Federal Reserve Act(12 U.S.C. 371) shall be construed as preempting, annulling, or affecting the applicability of State law to any subsidiary, affiliate, or agent of a national bank (other than a subsidiary, affiliate, or agent that is chartered as a national bank).".

SEC. 1046. STATE LAW PREEMPTION STANDARDS FOR FEDERAL SAVINGS ASSOCIATIONS AND SUBSIDIARIES CLARIFIED.

(a) IN GENERAL. — The Home Owners' Loan Act (12 U.S.C. 1461 et seq.) is amended by inserting after section 5 the following new section:

"SEC. 6. STATE LAW PREEMPTION STANDARDS FOR FEDERAL SAVINGS ASSOCIATIONS CLARIFIED.

"(a) IN GENERAL. — Any determination by a court or by the Director or any successor officer or agency regarding the relation of State law to a provision of this Act or any regulation or order prescribed under this Act shall be made in accordance with the laws and legal standards applicable to national banks regarding the preemption of State law.

"(b) PRINCIPLES OF CONFLICT PREEMPTION APPLICABLE. — Notwithstanding the authorities granted under sections 4 and 5, this Act does not occupy the field in any area of State law.".

(b) CLERICAL AMENDMENT. — The table of sections for the Home Owners' Loan Act (12 U.S.C. 1461 et seq.) is amended by striking the item relating to section 6 and inserting the following new item:

动和行为,以及被该等判定排除适用的要求和限制。”

(b)**目录修正**。——在《美国制定法汇编》(修订版)第六十二编第一章目录中第5136B条的目录项之后增加如下内容,作为对该目录的修正:

“第5136C条 关于联邦法律对国民银行和子公司的优先适用标准的说明。”

第1045条 关于适用于非存款机构子公司的法律的说明

在本子编增加的《美国制定法汇编》(修订版)第5136C条结尾处增加如下内容,作为对该条的修正:

“(h)**关于适用于国民银行非存款机构子公司及关联方的法律的说明**。——

(1)**定义**。——就本子条而言,‘存款机构’、‘子公司’及‘关联方’的含义以《联邦存款保险法》第3条的定义为准。

(2)**解释规则**。——本编的任何规定或《联邦储备法》第24条(《美国法典》第十二编第371节)均不得被解释为排除、废止或影响任何州法律对国民银行的任何子公司、关联方或代理人(但该等子公司、关联方或代理人本身特许注册为国民银行的除外)的适用范围。”

第1046条 关于州法律对联邦储蓄协会及其子公司的优先适用标准的说明

(a)**一般规定**。——在《业主贷款法》(《美国法典》第十二编第1461节及其后条文)第5条之后插入如下新条文,作为对该法的修正:

“第6条 关于州法律对联邦储蓄协会的优先适用标准的说明

(a)**一般规定**。——法院、消费者金融保护局局长或任何继任官员或后继机关针对州法律与本法规定的关系,或针对州法律与依据本法制定的规章或命令的关系作出的任何判定,均应根据适用于国民银行的与州法律的优先适用相关的法律和法定标准作出。

(b)**发生冲突之时的法律适用原则**。——尽管有第4条和第5条授予的权力,本法并不涉入任何州法律领域。”

(b)**目录修正**。——《业主贷款法》(《美国法典》第十二编第1461节及其后条文)条款目录修正如下:删除有关第6条的目录项,替以如下新的目录项:

"Sec. 6. State law preemption standards for Federal savings associations and subsidiaries clarified.".

SEC. 1047. VISITORIAL STANDARDS FOR NATIONAL BANKS AND SAVINGS ASSOCIATIONS.

(a) NATIONAL BANKS. — Section 5136C of the Revised Statutes of the United States (as added by this subtitle) is amended by adding at the end the following:

"(i) VISITORIAL POWERS. —

"(1) IN GENERAL. — In accordance with the decision of the Supreme Court of the United States in Cuomo v. Clearing House Assn., L. L. C.(129 S. Ct. 2710(2009)), no provision of this title which relates to visitorial powers or otherwise limits or restricts the visitorial authority to which any national bank is subject shall be construed as limiting or restricting the authority of any attorney general (or other chief law enforcement officer) of any State to bring an action against a national bank in a court of appropriate jurisdiction to enforce an applicable law and to seek relief as authorized by such law.

"(j) ENFORCEMENT ACTIONS. — The ability of the Comptroller of the Currency to bring an enforcement action under this title or section 5 of the Federal Trade Commission Act does not preclude any private party from enforcing rights granted under Federal or State law in the courts.".

(b) SAVINGS ASSOCIATIONS. — Section 6 of the Home Owners' Loan Act (as added by this title) is amended by adding at the end the following:

"(c) VISITORIAL POWERS. — The provisions of sections 5136C (i) of the Revised Statutes of the United States shall apply to Federal savings associations, and any subsidiary thereof, to the same extent and in the same manner as if such savings associations, or subsidiaries thereof, were national banks or subsidiaries of national banks, respectively."

"(d) ENFORCEMENT ACTIONS. — The ability of the Comptroller of the Currency to bring an enforcement action under this Act or section 5 of the Federal Trade Commission Act does not preclude any private party from enforcing rights granted under Federal or State law in the courts.".

SEC. 1048. EFFECTIVE DATE.

This subtitle shall become effective on the designated transfer date.

Subtitle E — Enforcement Powers

SEC. 1051. DEFINITIONS.

For purposes of this subtitle, the following definitions shall apply:

"第6条　关于州法律对联邦储蓄协会及其子公司的优先适用标准的说明。"

第1047条　适用于国民银行及储蓄协会的巡查标准

(a)**国民银行**。——在本子编增加的《美国制定法汇编》(修订版)第5136C条结尾处增加如下内容,作为对该条的修正:

"(i)**巡查权**。——

(1)**一般规定**。——根据联邦最高法院在科莫诉美国结算协会一案[《美国最高法院判例汇编》第129卷第2710页(2009)]中作出的决定,本编中与针对国民银行行使巡查权相关的任何规定,或限制或约束该等巡查权的任何规定,均不得被解释为限制或约束任何州总检察长(或其他主要执法官员)在具有适当管辖权的法院针对国民银行提起诉讼以便强制执行适用的法律并寻求该等法律授予的救济的权力。

(j)**执法行动**。——货币监理署署长根据本编或《联邦贸易委员会法》第5条提起执法行动的能力并不妨碍任何私人当事方通过法院强制执行联邦法律或州法律向其赋予的权利。"

(b)**储蓄协会**。——在本编增加的《业主贷款法》第6条结尾处增加如下内容,作为对该条的修正:

"(c)**巡查权**。——《美国制定法汇编》(修订版)第5136C(i)条的规定应适用于联邦储蓄协会及其任何子公司,对于适用范围和方式而言,应将该等储蓄协会或其子公司视同国民银行或国民银行的子公司。

(d)**执法诉讼**。——货币监理署署长根据本法或《联邦贸易委员会法》第5条提起执法行动的能力并不妨碍任何私人当事方通过法院强制执行联邦法律或州法律向其赋予的权利。"

第1048条　生效日

本子编规定于指定转移日生效。

第E子编——执　法　权

第1051条　定义

就本子编而言,应适用如下定义:

(1) BUREAU INVESTIGATION. — The term "Bureau investigation" means any inquiry conducted by a Bureau investigator for the purpose of ascertaining whether any person is or has been engaged in any conduct that is a violation, as defined in this section.

(2) BUREAU INVESTIGATOR. — The term "Bureau investigator" means any attorney or investigator employed by the Bureau who is charged with the duty of enforcing or carrying into effect any Federal consumer financial law.

(3) CUSTODIAN. — The term "custodian" means the custodian or any deputy custodian designated by the Bureau.

(4) DOCUMENTARY MATERIAL. — The term "documentary material" includes the original or any copy of any book, document, record, report, memorandum, paper, communication, tabulation, chart, logs, electronic files, or other data or data compilations stored in any medium.

(5) VIOLATION. — The term "violation" means any act or omission that, if proved, would constitute a violation of any provision of Federal consumer financial law.

SEC. 1052. INVESTIGATIONS AND ADMINISTRATIVE DISCOVERY.

(a) JOINT INVESTIGATIONS. —

(1) IN GENERAL. — The Bureau or, where appropriate, a Bureau investigator, may engage in joint investigations and requests for information, as authorized under this title.

(2) FAIR LENDING. — The authority under paragraph (1) includes matters relating to fair lending, and where appropriate, joint investigations with, and requests for information from, the Secretary of Housing and Urban Development, the Attorney General of the United States, or both.

(b) SUBPOENAS. —

(1) IN GENERAL. — The Bureau or a Bureau investigator may issue subpoenas for the attendance and testimony of witnesses and the production of relevant papers, books, documents, or other material in connection with hearings under this title.

(2) FAILURE TO OBEY. — In the case of contumacy or refusal to obey a subpoena issued pursuant to this paragraph and served upon any person, the district court of the United States for any district in which such person is found, resides, or transacts business, upon application by the Bureau or a Bureau investigator and after notice to such person, may issue an order requiring such person to appear and give testimony or to appear and produce documents or other material.

(3) CONTEMPT. — Any failure to obey an order of the court under this subsection may be punished by the court as a contempt thereof.

(c) DEMANDS. —

(1) IN GENERAL. — Whenever the Bureau has reason to believe that any person may be in possession, custody, or control of any documentary material or tangible things, or may

(1)**消费者金融保护局的调查**。——“消费者金融保护局的调查”一词系指消费者金融保护局的调查员为查明某人是否正在或已经从事本条定义的任何违法行为而开展的任何调查。

(2)**消费者金融保护局调查员**。——“消费者金融保护局调查员”一词系指消费者金融保护局聘用的负责执行或实施任何联邦消费者金融法律的任何律师或调查人员。

(3)**保管人**。——“保管人”一词系指消费者金融保护局指定的保管人或任何代理保管人。

(4)**文件材料**。——“文件材料”一词包括存储在任何媒介内的任何账簿、文件、记录、报告、备忘录、文档、通信、表格、图表、日志、电子文档、其他数据或数据集的原件或任何复印件。

(5)**违法行为**。——“违法行为”一词系指一旦被证实,将构成违反任何联邦消费者金融法律规定的任何作为或不作为。

第1052条 调查及行政发现

(a)**联合调查**。——

(1)**一般规定**。——消费者金融保护局或(在适当的情况下)消费者金融保护局调查员可以根据本编的授权实施联合调查,并请求相关方提供信息。

(2)**公平贷款**。——第(1)款规定的权力包括与公平贷款相关的事项,在适当情况下,还包括与住房与城市发展部部长和/或联邦总检察长开展的联合调查,以及从住房与城市发展部部长和/或联邦总检察长处获得信息的请求。

(b)**传票**。——

(1)**一般规定**。——消费者金融保护局或消费者金融保护局调查员可以针对依据本编举行的听证,签发证人出席听证并作证的传票和要求提供相关的文档、账簿、文件或其他材料的传票。

(2)**拒绝服从**。——收到根据本款签发的传票的任何人藐视传票效力或拒不服从传票的,则该人被发现地、居住地或开展交易地所在的任何司法辖区的地区法院,在收到消费者金融保护局或消费者金融保护局调查员的申请并向该人发出通知后,可以签发命令,要求该人出席听证并提供证词,或要求其出席听证并提供相关文件或其他材料。

(3)**藐视法庭**。——对于拒不服从法院按照本子条所签发命令的任何行为,法院可按藐视法庭罪处罚。

(c)**调查令**。——

(1)**一般规定**。——无论何时,如消费者金融保护局有理由相信任何人可能掌握、保管或控制与违法行为相关的任何文件材料或实物,或可能拥有与违法行为相关

have any information, relevant to a violation, the Bureau may, before the institution of any proceedings under the Federal consumer financial law, issue in writing, and cause to be served upon such person, a civil investigative demand requiring such person to —

(A) produce such documentary material for inspection and copying or reproduction in the form or medium requested by the Bureau;

(B) submit such tangible things;

(C) file written reports or answers to questions;

(D) give oral testimony concerning documentary material, tangible things, or other information; or

(E) furnish any combination of such material, answers, or testimony.

(2) REQUIREMENTS. — Each civil investigative demand shall state the nature of the conduct constituting the alleged violation which is under investigation and the provision of law applicable to such violation.

(3) PRODUCTION OF DOCUMENTS. — Each civil investigative demand for the production of documentary material shall —

(A) describe each class of documentary material to be produced under the demand with such definiteness and certainty as to permit such material to be fairly identified;

(B) prescribe a return date or dates which will provide a reasonable period of time within which the material so demanded may be assembled and made available for inspection and copying or reproduction; and

(C) identify the custodian to whom such material shall be made available.

(4) PRODUCTION OF THINGS. — Each civil investigative demand for the submission of tangible things shall —

(A) describe each class of tangible things to be submitted under the demand with such definiteness and certainty as to permit such things to be fairly identified;

(B) prescribe a return date or dates which will provide a reasonable period of time within which the things so demanded may be assembled and submitted; and

(C) identify the custodian to whom such things shall be submitted.

(5) DEMAND FOR WRITTEN REPORTS OR ANSWERS. — Each civil investigative demand for written reports or answers to questions shall —

(A) propound with definiteness and certainty the reports to be produced or the questions to be answered;

(B) prescribe a date or dates at which time written reports or answers to questions shall be submitted; and

(C) identify the custodian to whom such reports or answers shall be submitted.

(6) ORAL TESTIMONY. — Each civil investigative demand for the giving of oral testimony shall —

的任何信息,则消费者金融保护局可以在根据联邦消费者金融法律提起任何程序前,签发一份书面民事调查令,并通过他人将其送达该人,要求该人——

(A)以消费者金融保护局要求的形式或媒介提供上述文件材料以备检查和复印或复制;

(B)提交上述实物;

(C)提交书面报告或问题答复;

(D)提供与文件材料、实物或其他信息相关的口头证词;或

(E)提供上述材料、答复或证词的任何组合。

(2)**要求**。——每一民事调查令均应说明调查所涉被控违法行为之性质,以及适用于该等违法行为的法律规定。

(3)**提供文件**。——要求提供文件材料的每一民事调查令均应——

(A)清晰、明确地说明调查令中要求提供的每类文件材料,以便能够合理地确定该等文件;

(B)规定该等文件材料的交还日期,以便确定整理和准备该等材料供检查、复印或复制所需合理用时;并

(C)指明负责接收该等材料的保管人的身份。

(4)**提供实物**。——要求提供实物的每一民事调查令均应——

(A)清晰、明确地说明调查令中要求提供的每类实物,以便能够合理地确定该等实物;

(B)规定该等实物的交还日期,以便确定整理和准备该等实物所需合理用时;并

(C)指明负责接收该等实物的保管人的身份。

(5)**要求提供书面报告或答复的调查令**。——要求提供书面报告或答复的每一民事调查令均应——

(A)清晰明确地说明需要提供的报告或需要回答的问题;

(B)规定提交书面报告或问题答复的日期;并

(C)指明负责接收该等报告或答复的保管人的身份。

(6)**口头证词**。——要求提供口头证词的每一民事调查令均应——

(A) prescribe a date, time, and place at which oral testimony shall be commenced; and

(B) identify a Bureau investigator who shall conduct the investigation and the custodian to whom the transcript of such investigation shall be submitted.

(7) SERVICE. — Any civil investigative demand issued, and any enforcement petition filed, under this section may be served —

(A) by any Bureau investigator at any place within the territorial jurisdiction of any court of the United States; and

(B) upon any person who is not found within the territorial jurisdiction of any court of the United States —

(i) in such manner as the Federal Rules of Civil Procedure prescribe for service in a foreign nation; and

(ii) to the extent that the courts of the United States have authority to assert jurisdiction over such person, consistent with due process, the United States District Court for the District of Columbia shall have the same jurisdiction to take any action respecting compliance with this section by such person that such district court would have if such person were personally within the jurisdiction of such district court.

(8) METHOD OF SERVICE. — Service of any civil investigative demand or any enforcement petition filed under this section may be made upon a person, including any legal entity, by —

(A) delivering a duly executed copy of such demand or petition to the individual or to any partner, executive officer, managing agent, or general agent of such person, or to any agent of such person authorized by appointment or by law to receive service of process on behalf of such person;

(B) delivering a duly executed copy of such demand or petition to the principal office or place of business of the person to be served; or

(C) depositing a duly executed copy in the United States mails, by registered or certified mail, return receipt requested, duly addressed to such person at the principal office or place of business of such person.

(9) PROOF OF SERVICE. —

(A) IN GENERAL. — A verified return by the individual serving any civil investigative demand or any enforcement petition filed under this section setting forth the manner of such service shall be proof of such service.

(B) RETURN RECEIPTS. — In the case of service by registered or certified mail, such return shall be accompanied by the return post office receipt of delivery of such demand or enforcement petition.

(10) PRODUCTION OF DOCUMENTARY MATERIAL. — The production of documentary material in response to a civil investigative demand shall be made under a sworn

(A)规定该等证词提供的日期、时间及地点;并

(B)指明开展该项调查的消费者金融保护局调查员的身份,以及负责接收调查笔录的保管人的身份。

(7)**送达**。——根据本条签发的任何民事调查令和提交的任何请求执行书——

(A)可由消费者金融保护局调查员在任何联邦法院的地域管辖范围内完成送达;且

(B)对于未能在任何联邦法院的地域管辖范围内发现的任何人,可采用如下方式送达——

(i)《联邦民事诉讼规则》规定的境外送达方式;及

(ii)如果联邦法院有权对该人行使管辖权,则在符合正当程序的前提下,哥伦比亚特区联邦地区法院对该人遵守本条规定的情况有采取任何行动的管辖权,其权限范围以该人位于哥伦比亚特区联邦地区法院的司法辖区内之时,该法院将有权采取的行动为准。

(8)**送达方法**。——根据本条提交的任何民事调查令或任何请求执行书可通过如下方法向相关主体(包括任何法律实体)送达——

(A)将正式签署的调查令或请求执行书的复本直接交付给该主体(如其为自然人),或该主体的任何合伙人、高级管理人员、管理代理人或总代理人,或送交给该主体指定的或法律规定的、可代表其接收法律文书的任何代理人;

(B)将正式签署的调查令或请求执行书复本递送至该主体的主要办公场所或主要营业地;或

(C)通过带回执的美国挂号邮件或带回执邮件,按照该主体主要办公场所或主要营业地的地址,将正式签署的调查令或申请执行书复本寄送给该主体。

(9)**送达证明**。——

(A)**一般规定**。——负责送达根据本条提交的任何民事调查令或任何请求执行书的个人所提供的、载明送达方式的经核证的回执应构成送达证明。

(B)**回执**。——以挂号邮件或带回执邮件送达的,除上述回执外,还应提供送达该调查令或请求执行书的邮局回执。

(10)**文件材料的提供**。——就针对某一主体签发的民事调查令而言,如其为自然人,则该主体应签发一份宣誓证明,并按调查令指定的形式,提供该调查令要求提

certificate, in such form as the demand designates, by the person, if a natural person, to whom the demand is directed or, if not a natural person, by any person having knowledge of the facts and circumstances relating to such production, to the effect that all of the documentary material required by the demand and in the possession, custody, or control of the person to whom the demand is directed has been produced and made available to the custodian.

(11) SUBMISSION OF TANGIBLE THINGS. — The submission of tangible things in response to a civil investigative demand shall be made under a sworn certificate, in such form as the demand designates, by the person to whom the demand is directed or, if not a natural person, by any person having knowledge of the facts and circumstances relating to such production, to the effect that all of the tangible things required by the demand and in the possession, custody, or control of the person to whom the demand is directed have been submitted to the custodian.

(12) SEPARATE ANSWERS. — Each reporting requirement or question in a civil investigative demand shall be answered separately and fully in writing under oath, unless it is objected to, in which event the reasons for the objection shall be stated in lieu of an answer, and it shall be submitted under a sworn certificate, in such form as the demand designates, by the person, if a natural person, to whom the demand is directed or, if not a natural person, by any person responsible for answering each reporting requirement or question, to the effect that all information required by the demand and in the possession, custody, control, or knowledge of the person to whom the demand is directed has been submitted.

(13) TESTIMONY. —

(A) IN GENERAL. —

(i) OATH AND RECORDATION. — The examination of any person pursuant to a demand for oral testimony served under this subsection shall be taken before an officer authorized to administer oaths and affirmations by the laws of the United States or of the place at which the examination is held. The officer before whom oral testimony is to be taken shall put the witness on oath or affirmation and shall personally, or by any individual acting under the direction of and in the presence of the officer, record the testimony of the witness.

(ii) TRANSCRIPTION. — The testimony shall be taken stenographically and transcribed.

(iii) TRANSMISSION TO CUSTODIAN. — After the testimony is fully transcribed, the officer investigator before whom the testimony is taken shall promptly transmit a copy of the transcript of the testimony to the custodian.

(B) PARTIES PRESENT. — Any Bureau investigator before whom oral testimony is to be taken shall exclude from the place where the testimony is to be taken all other persons, except the person giving the testimony, the attorney for that person, the officer before whom the testimony is to be taken, an investigator or representative of an agency with which the

供的文件材料;如其并非自然人,则该等资料应由知晓相关事实及情形的任何主体按调查令指定的形式提供,以确保调查令要求提供的该主体所掌握、保管或控制的全部文件材料均已提供并提交给保管人。

(11)**实物的提供**。——就针对某一主体签发的民事调查令而言,如其为自然人,则该主体应签发一份宣誓证明,并按调查令指定的形式,提供该调查令要求提供的实物;如其并非自然人,则该等实物应由知晓相关事实及情形的任何主体按调查令指定的形式提交,以确保调查令要求提供的该主体所掌握、保管或控制的全部实物均提交给保管人。

(12)**分别答复**。——对于民事调查令中提出的每项报告要求或每一问题,均应分别提供经宣称程序保证所述真实无误的充分书面答复;如答复人对某项报告要求或问题持有反对意见,则答复人应陈述反对理由,而不必提供答复。如该民事调查令的签发对象为自然人,则该主体应签发一份宣誓证明,并按调查令指定的形式提交答复,如其并非自然人,则该等答复应由负责答复的任何主体按调查令指定的形式提交,以确保调查令要求提供的该主体所掌握、保管、控制或所知的全部信息均已提交。

(13)**证词**。——

(A)**一般规定**。——

(i)**宣誓及记录**。——根据本子条送达民事调查令,要求提供口头证词的,应由根据联邦法律或证词提取地的法律有权主持证词宣誓和证词声明程序的官员主持证词提取程序。提取口头证词的官员应要求证人对其证词进行宣誓或作出声明,并亲自记录证人的证词,或指示他人在该官员在场的情况下记录证人的证词。

(ii)**笔录**。——证词应以速记的方式记录,并转录成文。

(iii)**将证词笔录传送给保管人**。——证词完全转录成文之后,主持证词提取程序的调查官员应及时将证词笔录复本传送给保管人。

(B)**出席证词提取程序的当事人**。——主持证词提取程序的消费者金融保护局调查员仅得允许如下人员出席证词提取程序, 除此之外任何他人均不得进入证词提取地点:证词提供人及其律师、主持证词提取程序的官员、与消费者金融保护局联合开展调查的另一机关的调查员或代表,以及证词速记员。

Bureau is engaged in a joint investigation, and any stenographer taking such testimony.

(C) LOCATION. — The oral testimony of any person taken pursuant to a civil investigative demand shall be taken in the judicial district of the United States in which such person resides, is found, or transacts business, or in such other place as may be agreed upon by the Bureau investigator before whom the oral testimony of such person is to be taken and such person.

(D) ATTORNEY REPRESENTATION. —

(i) IN GENERAL. — Any person compelled to appear under a civil investigative demand for oral testimony pursuant to this section may be accompanied, represented, and advised by an attorney.

(ii) AUTHORITY. — The attorney may advise a person described in clause (i), in confidence, either upon the request of such person or upon the initiative of the attorney, with respect to any question asked of such person.

(iii) OBJECTIONS. — A person described in clause (i), or the attorney for that person, may object on the record to any question, in whole or in part, and such person shall briefly state for the record the reason for the objection. An objection may properly be made, received, and entered upon the record when it is claimed that such person is entitled to refuse to answer the question on grounds of any constitutional or other legal right or privilege, including the privilege against self-incrimination, but such person shall not otherwise object to or refuse to answer any question, and such person or attorney shall not otherwise interrupt the oral examination.

(iv) REFUSAL TO ANSWER. — If a person described in clause (i) refuses to answer any question —

(I) the Bureau may petition the district court of the United States pursuant to this section for an order compelling such person to answer such question; and

(II) if the refusal is on grounds of the privilege against self-incrimination, the testimony of such person may be compelled in accordance with the provisions of section 6004 of title 18, United States Code.

(E) TRANSCRIPTS. — For purposes of this subsection —

(i) after the testimony of any witness is fully transcribed, the Bureau investigator shall afford the witness (who may be accompanied by an attorney) a reasonable opportunity to examine the transcript;

(ii) the transcript shall be read to or by the witness, unless such examination and reading are waived by the witness;

(iii) any changes in form or substance which the witness desires to make shall be entered and identified upon the transcript by the Bureau investigator, with a statement of the reasons given by the witness for making such changes;

(C)**地点**。——根据民事调查令对任何人提取口头证词的程序应在该人居住地、被发现地或开展业务地所在的联邦司法辖区内举行,或在主持证词提取程序的消费者金融保护局调查员与该人合意确定的其他地点举行。

(D)**律师的代理**。——

(i)**一般规定**。——按照民事调查令被强制出席本条所述证词提取程序的任何人可由一名律师陪同出席该等程序,并由该律师作为其代理人并为之提供顾问意见。

(ii)**权力**。——该律师可以在保密的基础上,主动或应第(i)项所述之人的请求就该人被询问的问题为该人提供顾问意见。

(iii)**反对意见**。——第(i)项所述之人或该人的律师可以对任何问题提出完全或部分的反对意见,并将其记录在案,该人还应对提出该反对意见的理由进行简要陈述,关于该等理由的陈述也应记录在案。如果该人或其律师主张根据宪法权利或其他法定权利或特权(包括反对强迫自证其罪的特权)其有权拒绝回答上述问题,则其有权针对该问题提出适当的反对意见,且该意见可以按适当程序被接收并记录在案,但该人不得基于其他理由对任何问题提出反对意见或拒绝回答该等问题,且该人或其律师不得基于其他理由中断口头讯问。

(iv)**拒绝回答**。——如果第(i)项所述之人拒绝回答任何问题——

(I)消费者金融保护局可以根据本条规定,请求联邦地区法院签发命令,强制该人回答该问题;且

(II)拒绝回答系基于反对强迫自证其罪的特权的,可根据《美国法典》第十八编第6004节的规定强制该人提供证词。

(E)**笔录**。——就本子条而言——

(i)任何证人的证词完全转录成文之后,消费者金融保护局调查员应向该证人(其可由一名律师陪同)提供审阅笔录的适当机会;

(ii)除非该证人放弃审查并阅读该笔录的权利,否则应向该证人宣读笔录或由其本人阅读;

(iii)该证人希望对证词作出任何形式或内容上的变更的,均应由消费者金融保护局调查员录入笔录并在笔录中注明,同时,该证人应说明作出该等变更的理由;

(iv) the transcript shall be signed by the witness, unless the witness in writing waives the signing, is ill, cannot be found, or refuses to sign; and

(v) if the transcript is not signed by the witness during the 30-day period following the date on which the witness is first afforded a reasonable opportunity to examine the transcript, the Bureau investigator shall sign the transcript and state on the record the fact of the waiver, illness, absence of the witness, or the refusal to sign, together with any reasons given for the failure to sign.

(F) CERTIFICATION BY INVESTIGATOR. — The Bureau investigator shall certify on the transcript that the witness was duly sworn by him or her and that the transcript is a true record of the testimony given by the witness, and the Bureau investigator shall promptly deliver the transcript or send it by registered or certified mail to the custodian.

(G) COPY OF TRANSCRIPT. — The Bureau investigator shall furnish a copy of the transcript (upon payment of reasonable charges for the transcript) to the witness only, except that the Bureau may for good cause limit such witness to inspection of the official transcript of his testimony.

(H) WITNESS FEES. — Any witness appearing for the taking of oral testimony pursuant to a civil investigative demand shall be entitled to the same fees and mileage which are paid to witnesses in the district courts of the United States.

(d) CONFIDENTIAL TREATMENT OF DEMAND MATERIAL. —

(1) IN GENERAL. — Documentary materials and tangible things received as a result of a civil investigative demand shall be subject to requirements and procedures regarding confidentiality, in accordance with rules established by the Bureau.

(2) DISCLOSURE TO CONGRESS. — No rule established by the Bureau regarding the confidentiality of materials submitted to, or otherwise obtained by, the Bureau shall be intended to prevent disclosure to either House of Congress or to an appropriate committee of the Congress, except that the Bureau is permitted to adopt rules allowing prior notice to any party that owns or otherwise provided the material to the Bureau and had designated such material as confidential.

(e) PETITION FOR ENFORCEMENT. —

(1) IN GENERAL. — Whenever any person fails to comply with any civil investigative demand duly served upon him under this section, or whenever satisfactory copying or reproduction of material requested pursuant to the demand cannot be accomplished and such person refuses to surrender such material, the Bureau, through such officers or attorneys as it may designate, may file, in the district court of the United States for any judicial district in which such person resides, is found, or transacts business, and serve upon such person, a petition for an order of such court for the enforcement of this section.

(2) SERVICE OF PROCESS. — All process of any court to which application may be

(iv)笔录应由该证人签署,但该证人以书面形式放弃其签字权,该证人因病无法签字,无法找到该证人,或该证人拒绝签字的除外;且

(v)如果在消费者金融保护局调查员首次向该证人提供审查证词笔录的合理机会之日后30天内,该证人未在证词笔录上签字,则消费者金融保护局调查员应在笔录上签字,并将如下事实记录在案:该证人放弃其签字权,该证人因病无法签字,该证人无法找到,或该证人拒绝签字,以及该证人未能签字的任何原因。

(F)**调查员证明**。——消费者金融保护局调查员应在笔录中证明如下事项:证人在作出证词之前已正式宣誓;该笔录属于证人提供的证词之真实记录。然后,调查员应立即将该笔录交付给保管人,或通过挂号邮件或带回执邮件寄送给保管人。

(G)**笔录复本**。——在证人支付合理费用后,消费者金融保护局调查员应向证人提供一份笔录复本(该等复本仅限于向证人提供),但是,消费者金融保护局可以基于正当理由限制该证人查阅其证词正式笔录的权利。

(H)**证人费用**。——任何根据民事调查令出席证词提取程序提供口头证词的证人均应有权按照在联邦地区法院出庭的证人的标准,获得同等的费用补偿及路费补偿。

(d)**对民事调查令要求提供的资料的保密处理**。——

(1)**一般规定**。——因民事调查令而收到的文件材料和实物应根据消费者金融保护局制定的规则,按照保密要求及程序处理。

(2)**向国会进行披露**。——消费者金融保护局针对向其提交或其另行获取的资料制定的任何保密规则,均无意阻止其向国会或相应的国会委员会披露该等资料,但消费者金融保护局被准许制定符合如下条件的规则的情形除外:允许向拥有该等资料或以其他方式向消费者金融保护局提供该等资料并将该等资料指定为保密信息的任何当事方发出事先通知。

(e)**请求执行书**。——

(1)**一般规定**。——根据本条规定向任何人正式送达民事调查令之后,如果该人未能遵守该调查令,或如果无法按调查令的要求对资料进行符合要求的拷贝或复制,且该人拒绝提交该等资料,则消费者金融保护局可以通过其指定的官员或律师,向该人居住地、被发现地或开展业务地所在司法辖区的联邦法院提交请求书,请求该法院签发强制执行本条规定的命令,并向该人送达该请求书。

(2)**程序文件的送达**。——根据本子条规定可申请获取的任何法院的所有程序

made as provided in this subsection may be served in any judicial district.

(f) PETITION FOR ORDER MODIFYING OR SETTING ASIDE DEMAND. —

(1) IN GENERAL. — Not later than 20 days after the service of any civil investigative demand upon any person under subsection (b), or at any time before the return date specified in the demand, whichever period is shorter, or within such period exceeding 20 days after service or in excess of such return date as may be prescribed in writing, subsequent to service, by any Bureau investigator named in the demand, such person may file with the Bureau a petition for an order by the Bureau modifying or setting aside the demand.

(2) COMPLIANCE DURING PENDENCY. — The time permitted for compliance with the demand in whole or in part, as determined proper and ordered by the Bureau, shall not run during the pendency of a petition under paragraph(1) at the Bureau, except that such person shall comply with any portions of the demand not sought to be modified or set aside.

(3) SPECIFIC GROUNDS. — A petition under paragraph(1) shall specify each ground upon which the petitioner relies in seeking relief, and may be based upon any failure of the demand to comply with the provisions of this section, or upon any constitutional or other legal right or privilege of such person.

(g) CUSTODIAL CONTROL. — At any time during which any custodian is in custody or control of any documentary material, tangible things, reports, answers to questions, or transcripts of oral testimony given by any person in compliance with any civil investigative demand, such person may file, in the district court of the United States for the judicial district within which the office of such custodian is situated, and serve upon such custodian, a petition for an order of such court requiring the performance by such custodian of any duty imposed upon him by this section or rule promulgated by the Bureau.

(h) JURISDICTION OF COURT. —

(1) IN GENERAL. — Whenever any petition is filed in any district court of the United States under this section, such court shall have jurisdiction to hear and determine the matter so presented, and to enter such order or orders as may be required to carry out the provisions of this section.

(2) APPEAL. — Any final order entered as described in paragraph (1) shall be subject to appeal pursuant to section 1291 of title 28, United States Code.

SEC. 1053. HEARINGS AND ADJUDICATION PROCEEDINGS.

(a) IN GENERAL. — The Bureau is authorized to conduct hearings and adjudication proceedings with respect to any person in the manner prescribed by chapter 5 of title 5, United States Code in order to ensure or enforce compliance with —

(1) the provisions of this title, including any rules prescribed by the Bureau under this title; and

(2) any other Federal law that the Bureau is authorized to enforce, including an

文件均可向任何司法辖区送达。

(f)**请求修改或撤销调查令的命令**。——

(1)**一般规定**。——在任何民事调查令根据第(b)子条规定送达任何人后20天内,或在该调查令中具体规定的答复日之前任何时候(以二者中期限较短者为准),或在调查令送达后超过20天的期限内或在晚于该调查令中指定的任何消费者金融保护局调查员在该调查令送达后所书面规定的答复日的期限内,该人可以向消费者金融保护局提交请求书,请求签发修改或撤销该调查令的命令。

(2)**作出决定前的遵守要求**。——在消费者金融保护局对第(1)款所述请求未作出决定之前,消费者金融保护局判定为适当的并已通过命令确定的完全或部分履行该调查令的时限应停止计算,但对于调查令中被调查人未寻求修改或撤销的任何部分,该人仍应承担履行义务。

(3)**具体理由**。——根据第(1)款所述请求书应逐项、具体说明请求人寻求救济所依据的理由。请求人可以调查令不符合本条规定作为依据,或以任何宪法权利或该人的其他法定权利或特权作为依据而提出请求。

(g)**保管控制**。——在任何保管人保管或控制任何人根据民事调查令提供的文件材料、实物、报告、问题答复、口头证词笔录的期间内,该人可以随时向该保管人办公场所所在司法辖区的联邦地区法院提交请求书,请求该法院签发命令,要求该保管人履行本条规定或消费者金融保护局颁发的规则赋予保管人的任何职责,并可以将该请求书送达该保管人。

(h)**法院的管辖权**。——

(1)**一般规定**。——任何请求按照本条规定向任何联邦地区法院提交之后,该法院即应具有对被请求事项进行审理和裁定以及签发实施本条规定所需之命令的管辖权。

(2)**上诉**。——对于第(1)款所述法院作出的任何最终命令,当事人有权根据《美国法典》第二十八编第1291节的规定提起上诉。

第1053条　听证和行政裁决程序

(a)**一般规定**。——消费者金融保护局有权按照《美国法典》第五编第五章规定的方式针对任何人开展听证和行政裁决程序,以确保以下法律、规章及规定得到遵守,或强制执行该等法律、规章及规定——

(1)本编规定,包括消费者金融保护局依据本编制定的任何规则;及

(2)消费者金融保护局有权执行的任何其他联邦法律,包括明文列举的消费者法

enumerated consumer law, and any regulations or order prescribed thereunder, unless such Federal law specifically limits the Bureau from conducting a hearing or adjudication proceeding and only to the extent of such limitation.

(b) SPECIAL RULES FOR CEASE–AND–DESIST PROCEEDINGS. —

(1) ORDERS AUTHORIZED. —

(A) IN GENERAL. — If, in the opinion of the Bureau, any covered person or service provider is engaging or has engaged in an activity that violates a law, rule, or any condition imposed in writing on the person by the Bureau, the Bureau may, subject to sections 1024, 1025, and 1026, issue and serve upon the covered person or service provider a notice of charges in respect thereof.

(B) CONTENT OF NOTICE. — The notice under subparagraph (A) shall contain a statement of the facts constituting the alleged violation or violations, and shall fix a time and place at which a hearing will be held to determine whether an order to cease and desist should issue against the covered person or service provider, such hearing to be held not earlier than 30 days nor later than 60 days after the date of service of such notice, unless an earlier or a later date is set by the Bureau, at the request of any party so served.

(C) CONSENT. — Unless the party or parties served under subparagraph(B) appear at the hearing personally or by a duly authorized representative, such person shall be deemed to have consented to the issuance of the cease–and–desist order.

(D) PROCEDURE. — In the event of consent under subparagraph (C), or if, upon the record, made at any such hearing, the Bureau finds that any violation specified in the notice of charges has been established, the Bureau may issue and serve upon the covered person or service provider an order to cease and desist from the violation or practice. Such order may, by provisions which may be mandatory or otherwise, require the covered person or service provider to cease and desist from the subject activity, and to take affirmative action to correct the conditions resulting from any such violation.

(2) EFFECTIVENESS OF ORDER. — A cease–and–desist order shall become effective at the expiration of 30 days after the date of service of an order under paragraph (1) upon the covered person or service provider concerned (except in the case of a cease–and–desist order issued upon consent, which shall become effective at the time specified therein), and shall remain effective and enforceable as provided therein, except to such extent as the order is stayed, modified, terminated, or set aside by action of the Bureau or a reviewing court.

(3) DECISION AND APPEAL. — Any hearing provided for in this subsection shall be held in the Federal judicial district or in the territory in which the residence or principal office or place of business of the person is located unless the person consents to another place, and shall be conducted in accordance with the provisions of chapter 5 of title 5 of the United

律以及依据该等法律制定的任何规章或命令，但该等联邦法律明确限制消费者金融保护局开展听证或行政裁决程序且仅在该等限制范围内限制消费者金融保护局开展听证或行政裁决程序的除外。

(b)**适用于制止令程序的特别规则**。——

(1)**授权签发制止令**。——

(A)**一般规定**。——如果消费者金融保护局认为,任何所涉主体或服务提供者正在从事或已经从事违反法律、规则或消费者金融保护局以书面形式为其设定的任何条件的活动,则消费者金融保护局可以在不违反第1024条、第1025条和第1026条规定的前提下,针对该主体或服务提供者签发并送达一份指控通知。

(B)**通知内容**。——第(A)子款所述通知应包含一份关于构成被控违法违规行为之事实的声明,并指定听证的举行时间和地点,以便通过该听证判定是否应针对所涉主体或服务提供者签发制止令；听证应在上述通知送达之日后30天至60天的期间内举行，但消费者金融保护局应通知接收方的请求另行指定了更早或更迟的听证时间的除外。

(C)**同意**。——除非收到第(B)子款所述通知的当事人亲自出席或委托其正式授权代表出席听证,否则其应被视为其已同意消费者金融保护局向其签发制止令。

(D)**程序**。——如果出现第(C)子款所述情形,或消费者金融保护局基于听证记认定,指控通知中所述任何违法违规行为已经成立,则消费者金融保护局可以向该所涉主体或服务提供者签发一份命令,责令其停止该违法违规行为或做法。该命令中可载明强制性规定或其他性质的规定,要求所涉主体或服务提供者停止指控通知中指明的活动,并采取积极行动纠正因任何上述违法违规行为导致的状况。

(2)**命令的生效**。——制止令应在根据第(1)款规定送达所涉主体或服务提供者之日后届满30天之日生效(但是,经当事人同意而签发制止令的,应于制止令明确规定的时间生效),并应按其自身规定继续有效并可强制执行,但是消费者金融保护局或审查法院采取行动中止、修改、终止或撤销该制止令的除外。

(3)**决定及上诉**。——本子条规定的任何听证应于所涉主体居住地,或主要办公场所或主要营业地所在的联邦司法辖区或准州内举行，但该人同意在其他地点举行听证的除外;听证应遵照《美国法典》第五编第五章的规定开展。听证结束后,在消费者金融保护局通知各方该案件已提交给消费者金融保护局作出最终决定后,消费者

States Code. After such hearing, and within 90 days after the Bureau has notified the parties that the case has been submitted to the Bureau for final decision, the Bureau shall render its decision (which shall include findings of fact upon which its decision is predicated) and shall issue and serve upon each party to the proceeding an order or orders consistent with the provisions of this section. Judicial review of any such order shall be exclusively as provided in this subsection. Unless a petition for review is timely filed in a court of appeals of the United States, as provided in paragraph (4), and thereafter until the record in the proceeding has been filed as provided in paragraph (4), the Bureau may at any time, upon such notice and in such manner as the Bureau shall determine proper, modify, terminate, or set aside any such order. Upon filing of the record as provided, the Bureau may modify, terminate, or set aside any such order with permission of the court.

(4) APPEAL TO COURT OF APPEALS. — Any party to any proceeding under this subsection may obtain a review of any order served pursuant to this subsection (other than an order issued with the consent of the person concerned) by the filing in the court of appeals of the United States for the circuit in which the principal office of the covered person is located, or in the United States Court of Appeals for the District of Columbia Circuit, within 30 days after the date of service of such order, a written petition praying that the order of the Bureau be modified, terminated, or set aside. A copy of such petition shall be forthwith transmitted by the clerk of the court to the Bureau, and thereupon the Bureau shall file in the court the record in the proceeding, as provided in section 2112 of title 28 of the United States Code. Upon the filing of such petition, such court shall have jurisdiction, which upon the filing of the record shall except as provided in the last sentence of paragraph (3) be exclusive, to affirm, modify, terminate, or set aside, in whole or in part, the order of the Bureau. Review of such proceedings shall be had as provided in chapter 7 of title 5 of the United States Code. The judgment and decree of the court shall be final, except that the same shall be subject to review by the Supreme Court of the United States, upon certiorari, as provided in section 1254 of title 28 of the United States Code.

(5) NO STAY. — The commencement of proceedings for judicial review under paragraph (4) shall not, unless specifically ordered by the court, operate as a stay of any order issued by the Bureau.

(c) SPECIAL RULES FOR TEMPORARY CEASE-AND-DESIST PROCEEDINGS. —

(1) IN GENERAL. — Whenever the Bureau determines that the violation specified in the notice of charges served upon a person, including a service provider, pursuant to subsection (b), or the continuation thereof, is likely to cause the person to be insolvent or otherwise prejudice the interests of consumers before the completion of the proceedings conducted pursuant to subsection (b), the Bureau may issue a temporary order requiring the person to cease and desist from any such violation or practice and to take affirmative action to

金融保护局应在90天内,对该案件作出决定(其中应包含作出该决定所依据的事实认定),并应按照本条规定,向参与该程序每一方签发并送达命令。对任何上述命令的司法审查必须根据本子条的规定进行。除非司法审查请求书已根据第(4)款规定及时提交给联邦上诉法院,否则,消费者金融保护局可以在此后直至上述程序的记录根据第(4)款提交给联邦上诉法院之前的任何时候,在发出其判定确属适当的通知后,按照其判定确属适当的方式修改、终止或撤销任何上述命令。消费者金融保护局在按规定提交上述程序的记录之后,可以在征得上述法院事先允许的前提下,修改、终止或撤销任何上述命令。

(4)**向上诉法院提请上诉**。——对于根据本子条向本子条所述任何听证程序的任何当事人送达的命令(但经其同意而签发的命令除外)而言,该当事人可以在该命令送达之日后30天内,向其主要办公场所所在地的联邦上诉巡回法院或哥伦比亚特区联邦上诉巡回法院提交一份请求书,请求法院修改、终止或撤销消费者金融保护局的命令,从而实现对该命令的审查。收到该请求书之后,上述法院的书记员应随即将该请求书的一份复本传送给消费者金融保护局。收到该复本后,消费者金融保护局应根据《美国法典》第二十八编第2112节的规定将听证程序的记录提交给该法院。除第(3)款最后一句规定的情形外,上述请求书及程序记录提交后,该法院即具有完全或部分地维持、修改、终止或撤销消费者金融保护局命令的排他管辖权。对上述听证程序的审查应根据《美国法典》第五编第七章的规定进行。上述法院作出的判决及判令应具有终局性,但是,联邦最高法院根据《美国法典》第二十八编第1254节的规定签发调案复审令后,该判决及判令应提交给联邦最高法院进行审查。

(5)**不得中止命令的执行**。——除非上述法院作出明确命令,否则第(4)款所述司法审查程序启动之时,消费者金融保护局签发的命令并不因此而中止执行。

(c)**关于临时制止令程序的特别规则**。——

(1)**一般规定**。——如果消费者金融保护局判定,根据第(b)子条向某一主体(包括服务提供者)送达的指控通知中指明的违法违规行为,或该等违法违规行为的持续,可能会导致该主体在根据第(b)子条执行的程序完结前出现资不抵债的状况,或对消费者利益造成其他伤害,则消费者金融保护局可以签发临时命令,要求该主体在上述程序未决期间停止该等违法违规行为或做法,并采取积极行动防范或补救该资不抵债状况或其他状况。该命令中可包含根据本子编授权作出的任何要求。该命令应

prevent or remedy such insolvency or other condition pending completion of such proceedings. Such order may include any requirement authorized under this subtitle. Such order shall become effective upon service upon the person and, unless set aside, limited, or suspended by a court in proceedings authorized by paragraph(2), shall remain effective and enforceable pending the completion of the administrative proceedings pursuant to such notice and until such time as the Bureau shall dismiss the charges specified in such notice, or if a cease–and–desist order is issued against the person, until the effective date of such order.

(2) APPEAL. — Not later than 10 days after the covered person or service provider concerned has been served with a temporary cease–and–desist order, the person may apply to the United States district court for the judicial district in which the residence or principal office or place of business of the person is located, or the United States District Court for the District of Columbia, for an injunction setting aside, limiting, or suspending the enforcement, operation, or effectiveness of such order pending the completion of the administrative proceedings pursuant to the notice of charges served upon the person under subsection (b), and such court shall have jurisdiction to issue such injunction.

(3) INCOMPLETE OR INACCURATE RECORDS. —

(A) TEMPORARY ORDER. — If a notice of charges served under subsection (b) specifies, on the basis of particular facts and circumstances, that the books and records of a covered person or service provider are so incomplete or inaccurate that the Bureau is unable to determine the financial condition of that person or the details or purpose of any transaction or transactions that may have a material effect on the financial condition of that person, the Bureau may issue a temporary order requiring —

(i) the cessation of any activity or practice which gave rise, whether in whole or in part, to the incomplete or inaccurate state of the books or records; or

(ii) affirmative action to restore such books or records to a complete and accurate state, until the completion of the proceedings under subsection (b)(1).

(B) EFFECTIVE PERIOD. — Any temporary order issued under subparagraph (A) —

(i) shall become effective upon service; and

(ii) unless set aside, limited, or suspended by a court in proceedings under paragraph (2), shall remain in effect and enforceable until the earlier of —

(I) the completion of the proceeding initiated under subsection(b) in connection with the notice of charges; or

(II) the date the Bureau determines, by examination or otherwise, that the books and records of the covered person or service provider are accurate and reflect the financial condition thereof.

(d) SPECIAL RULES FOR ENFORCEMENT OF ORDERS. —

(1) IN GENERAL. — The Bureau may in its discretion apply to the United States

在送达该主体后即刻生效。除非根据第(2)款授权所开展程序中的法院撤销、限制或暂停该命令，否则在根据上述通知启动的行政程序结束前，直至消费者金融保护局撤销其在上述通知中所述的指控，或（如果法院针对该主体签发了一份制止令）直至该制止令的生效日，该命令应继续有效并可强制执行。

(2)**上诉**。——在临时制止令送达所涉主体或服务提供者后10天内，该主体可以向其居住地、主要办公场所或主要营业地所在司法辖区的联邦地区法院或哥伦比亚特区联邦地区法院申请一份禁令，以期在基于根据第(b)子条送达至该主体的指控通知所开展的行政程序结束之前，撤销、限制该临时命令或暂停其执行、适用或效力，且该法院应具有签发该禁令的管辖权。

(3)**不完整或不准确的记录**。——

(A)**临时命令**。——如果根据第(b)子条送达的指控通知基于特定的事实和情形，指出所涉主体或服务提供者的账簿和记录不完整或不准确，致使消费者金融保护局无法判断该主体的财务状况或可能对该主体的财务状况造成重大影响的交易之细节或目的，则消费者金融保护局可以签发一份临时命令，要求——

(i)该主体停止任何导致账簿或记录（无论是全部还是部分）不完整或不准确的活动或做法；或

(ii)该主体采取积极行动，恢复该等账簿或记录的完整性及准确性，直至第(b)(1)子条所述程序结束。

(B)**有效期**。——根据第(A)子款签发的临时命令——

(i)应于送达之时立即生效；且

(ii)除非被法院在第(2)款所述程序中撤销、限制或暂停，否则应于以下日期之前（以较早者为准）继续有效并可强制执行——

(I)根据指控通知启动的第(b)子条所述程序结束之日；或

(II)消费者金融保护局通过审查或其他方式作出如下判定之日：该所涉主体或服务提供者的账簿和记录准确无误，能够反映所涉主体的财务状况。

(d)**关于命令执行的特别规则**。——

(1)一般规定。——消费者金融保护局可以依其自由裁量权，申请所涉主体主要

district court within the jurisdiction of which the principal office or place of business of the person is located, for the enforcement of any effective and outstanding notice or order issued under this section, and such court shall have jurisdiction and power to order and require compliance herewith.

(2) EXCEPTION. — Except as otherwise provided in this subsection, no court shall have jurisdiction to affect by injunction or otherwise the issuance or enforcement of any notice or order or to review, modify, suspend, terminate, or set aside any such notice or order.

(e) RULES. — The Bureau shall prescribe rules establishing such procedures as may be necessary to carry out this section.

SEC. 1054. LITIGATION AUTHORITY.

(a) IN GENERAL. — If any person violates a Federal consumer financial law, the Bureau may, subject to sections 1024, 1025, and 1026, commence a civil action against such person to impose a civil penalty or to seek all appropriate legal and equitable relief including a permanent or temporary injunction as permitted by law.

(b) REPRESENTATION. — The Bureau may act in its own name and through its own attorneys in enforcing any provision of this title, rules thereunder, or any other law or regulation, or in any action, suit, or proceeding to which the Bureau is a party.

(c) COMPROMISE OF ACTIONS. — The Bureau may compromise or settle any action if such compromise is approved by the court.

(d) NOTICE TO THE ATTORNEY GENERAL. —

(1) IN GENERAL. — When commencing a civil action under Federal consumer financial law, or any rule thereunder, the Bureau shall notify the Attorney General and, with respect to a civil action against an insured depository institution or insured credit union, the appropriate prudential regulator.

(2) NOTICE AND COORDINATION. —

(A) NOTICE OF OTHER ACTIONS. — In addition to any notice required under paragraph(1), the Bureau shall notify the Attorney General concerning any action, suit, or proceeding to which the Bureau is a party, except an action, suit, or proceeding that involves the offering or provision of consumer financial products or services.

(B) COORDINATION. — In order to avoid conflicts and promote consistency regarding litigation of matters under Federal law, the Attorney General and the Bureau shall consult regarding the coordination of investigations and proceedings, including by negotiating an agreement for coordination by not later than 180 days after the designated transfer date. The agreement under this subparagraph shall include provisions to ensure that parallel investigations and proceedings involving the Federal consumer financial laws are conducted in a manner that avoids conflicts and does not impede the ability of the Attorney General to prosecute violations of Federal criminal laws.

办公场所或主要营业地所在司法辖区的联邦地区法院强制执行根据本条签发的有效但尚未执行的任何通知或命令,且该法院应具有命令并要求所涉主体遵守该通知或命令的管辖权和权力。

(2)**例外规定**。——除本子条另有规定的情形外,任何法院均无权通过禁令或以其他方式影响任何通知或命令的签发及执行,或对该等通知或命令予以审查、修改、暂停、终止或撤销。

(e)**规则**。——消费者金融保护局应制定相关规则,确立实施本条规定所必要的程序。

第1054条 诉讼权

(a)**一般规定**。——任何主体违反了联邦消费者金融法律的,消费者金融保护局可以在不违反第1024条、第1025条和第1026条规定的前提下,针对该主体启动民事诉讼,以便对该主体处以民事罚款或寻求普通法及衡平法上的救济,包括法律所允许的正式或临时禁令。

(b)**代理**。——消费者金融保护局可以其自身的名义和通过其律师,实施本编的任何规定以及根据本编制定的规则或其他法律或规章,或参与任何其作为当事方的行动、诉讼或程序。

(c)**诉讼妥协**。——经法院批准,消费者金融保护局可以针对任何诉讼达成妥协或和解。

(d)**向联邦总检察长发送的通知**。——

(1)**一般规定**。——消费者金融保护局根据联邦消费者金融法律或依据该等法律制定的任何规则启动民事诉讼时,应就此通知联邦总检察长,如该诉讼系针对参保存款机构或参保信贷联盟而提起,则还应通知相应的审慎监管者。

(2)**通知和协调**。——

(A)**关于其他行动的通知**。——除第(1)款规定的通知外,消费者金融保护局还应将其作为当事人参与的任何行动、诉讼或程序通知联邦总检察长,但该等行动、诉讼或程序涉及消费者金融产品或服务的要约或提供的除外。

(B)**协调**。——就针对联邦法律规定的事项开展的行动而言,为避免出现冲突并促进该等行动的一致性,联邦总检察长和消费者金融保护局应就调查和程序的协调问题进行磋商,包括在指定转移日后180天内通过协商,就协调事宜达成一份协议。本子款所述协议应包含相关条款,确保涉及联邦消费者金融法律的各项平行调查和程序的开展方式不会造成冲突,亦不会妨碍联邦总检察长对违反联邦刑法的行为提起公诉的能力。

(C) RULE OF CONSTRUCTION. — Nothing in this paragraph shall be construed to limit the authority of the Bureau under this title, including the authority to interpret Federal consumer financial law.

(e) APPEARANCE BEFORE THE SUPREME COURT. — The Bureau may represent itself in its own name before the Supreme Court of the United States, provided that the Bureau makes a written request to the Attorney General within the 10–day period which begins on the date of entry of the judgment which would permit any party to file a petition for writ of certiorari, and the Attorney General concurs with such request or fails to take action within 60 days of the request of the Bureau.

(f) FORUM. — Any civil action brought under this title may be brought in a United States district court or in any court of competent jurisdiction of a state in a district in which the defendant is located or resides or is doing business, and such court shall have jurisdiction to enjoin such person and to require compliance with any Federal consumer financial law.

(g) TIME FOR BRINGING ACTION. —

(1) IN GENERAL. — Except as otherwise permitted by law or equity, no action may be brought under this title more than 3 years after the date of discovery of the violation to which an action relates.

(2) LIMITATIONS UNDER OTHER FEDERAL LAWS. —

(A) IN GENERAL. — An action arising under this title does not include claims arising solely under enumerated consumer laws.

(B) BUREAU AUTHORITY. — In any action arising solely under an enumerated consumer law, the Bureau may commence, defend, or intervene in the action in accordance with the requirements of that provision of law, as applicable.

(C) TRANSFERRED AUTHORITY. — In any action arising solely under laws for which authorities were transferred under subtitles F and H, the Bureau may commence, defend, or intervene in the action in accordance with the requirements of that provision of law, as applicable.

SEC. 1055. RELIEF AVAILABLE.

(a) ADMINISTRATIVE PROCEEDINGS OR COURT ACTIONS. —

(1) JURISDICTION. — The court (or the Bureau, as the case may be) in an action or adjudication proceeding brought under Federal consumer financial law, shall have jurisdiction to grant any appropriate legal or equitable relief with respect to a violation of Federal consumer financial law, including a violation of a rule or order prescribed under a Federal consumer financial law.

(2) RELIEF. — Relief under this section may include, without limitation —

(A) rescission or reformation of contracts;

(B) refund of moneys or return of real property;

(C)**解释规则**。——本款中的任何规定均不得被解释为对消费者金融保护局根据本编享有的权力(包括对联邦消费者金融法律进行解释的权力)构成限制。

(e)**出席最高法院的审查程序**。——消费者金融保护局可以其自身的名义代表其自身出席联邦最高法院的审查程序，前提是消费者金融保护局在相关判决作出之日后10天内(即允许当事人提交调案复审令签发申请的期限内)向联邦总检察长提交了一份书面请求，且联邦总检察长对该请求表示同意，或联邦总检察长在消费者金融保护局提交该请求后60天内未采取任何行动。

(f)**有管辖权的法院**。——根据本编提起的民事诉讼可在联邦地区法院或被告所在地、居住地或营业地所在地区的任何有管辖权的州法院进行，且该法院应具有对该人签发禁令并要求其遵守联邦消费者金融法律的管辖权。

(g)**诉讼时效**。——

(1)**一般规定**。——除普通法或衡平法另行许可的情形外，违法违规行为自被发现之日后已届满3年的，不得根据本编规定针对该违法违规行为提起诉讼。

(2)**其他联邦法律的限制规定**。——

(A)**一般规定**。——完全基于明文列举的消费者法律提出的权利主张不包括在根据本编提起的诉讼之内。

(B)**消费者金融保护局的权力**。——对于完全基于明文列举的消费者法律提起的任何诉讼，消费者金融保护局可以根据该等法律相关规定的要求，启动该等诉讼、对该等诉讼进行抗辩或参与该等诉讼(视具体情况而定)。

(C)**权力转移**。——对于完全基于已根据第F子编和第H子编转由消费者金融保护局行使执法权的法律提起的任何诉讼，消费者金融保护局可以根据该等法律相关规定的要求，启动完全基于该等法律提起的诉讼，对该等诉讼进行抗辩或参与该等诉讼(视具体情况而定)。

第1055条　可以获得的救济

(a)**行政程序或法院诉讼**。——

(1)**管辖权**。——在根据联邦消费者金融法律提起的诉讼或行政裁决程序中，法院或消费者金融保护局(视具体情况而定)有权针对违反联邦消费者金融法律的行为(包括违反根据联邦消费者金融法律制定的规则或命令的行为)，授予适当的普通法或衡平法救济。

(2)**救济**。——本条所述救济包括但不限于——

(A)解除或修正合同；

(B)退还钱款或归还不动产；

(C) restitution;

(D) disgorgement or compensation for unjust enrichment;

(E) payment of damages or other monetary relief;

(F) public notification regarding the violation, including the costs of notification;

(G) limits on the activities or functions of the person; and

(H) civil money penalties, as set forth more fully in subsection (c).

(3) NO EXEMPLARY OR PUNITIVE DAMAGES. — Nothing in this subsection shall be construed as authorizing the imposition of exemplary or punitive damages.

(b) RECOVERY OF COSTS. — In any action brought by the Bureau, a State attorney general, or any State regulator to enforce any Federal consumer financial law, the Bureau, the State attorney general, or the State regulator may recover its costs in connection with prosecuting such action if the Bureau, the State attorney general, or the State regulator is the prevailing party in the action.

(c) CIVIL MONEY PENALTY IN COURT AND ADMINISTRATIVE ACTIONS. —

(1) IN GENERAL. — Any person that violates, through any act or omission, any provision of Federal consumer financial law shall forfeit and pay a civil penalty pursuant to this subsection.

(2) PENALTY AMOUNTS. —

(A) FIRST TIER. — For any violation of a law, rule, or final order or condition imposed in writing by the Bureau, a civil penalty may not exceed $5,000 for each day during which such violation or failure to pay continues.

(B) SECOND TIER. — Notwithstanding paragraph (A), for any person that recklessly engages in a violation of a Federal consumer financial law, a civil penalty may not exceed $25,000 for each day during which such violation continues.

(C) THIRD TIER. — Notwithstanding subparagraphs (A) and (B), for any person that knowingly violates a Federal consumer financial law, a civil penalty may not exceed $1,000,000 for each day during which such violation continues.

(3) MITIGATING FACTORS. — In determining the amount of any penalty assessed under paragraph (2), the Bureau or the court shall take into account the appropriateness of the penalty with respect to —

(A) the size of financial resources and good faith of the person charged;

(B) the gravity of the violation or failure to pay;

(C) the severity of the risks to or losses of the consumer, which may take into account the number of products or services sold or provided;

(D) the history of previous violations; and

(E) such other matters as justice may require.

(4) AUTHORITY TO MODIFY OR REMIT PENALTY. — The Bureau may compromise,

(C)恢复原状;

(D)没收不当得利或就不当得利作出补偿;

(E)支付损害赔偿金或其他金钱救济;

(F)就违法违规行为发布公开通知,包括通知的费用;

(G)对所涉主体的活动及职能进行限制;及

(H)民事金钱处罚,详见第(c)子条的规定。

(3)**不得判处惩戒性或惩罚性损害赔偿金**。——本子条中的任何规定均不得被解释为授权法院或消费者金融保护局判处惩戒性或惩罚性的损害赔偿金。

(b)**费用的追偿**。——消费者金融保护局、州总检察长或任何州监管者如在为执行联邦消费者金融法律提起的任何诉讼中胜诉,则消费者金融保护局、该州总检察长或州监管者可以追偿因其提起该等诉讼而支付的费用。

(c)**法院及行政诉讼中的民事金钱处罚**。——

(1)**一般规定**。——如果任何主体的作为或不作为违反了联邦消费者金融法律的任何规定,则该主体应根据本子条的规定被处以民事罚款。

(2)**罚款金额**。——

(A)**一级罚款**。——对于违反法律、规则、最终命令或消费者金融保护局以书面形式设定的条件的任何行为,该违法违规行为每持续一天或未支付罚款的情形每持续一天,即可按不高于每天5000美元的标准处以民事罚款。

(B)**二级罚款**。——无论第(A)款如何规定,如果任何主体轻率地从事违反联邦消费者金融法律的行为,则该违法违规行为每持续一天,即可按不高于每天2.5万美元的标准对该主体处以民事罚款。

(C)**三级罚款**。——无论第(A)子款和第(B)子款如何规定,如果任何主体故意违反联邦消费者金融法律,则该违法违规行为每持续一天,即可按不高于每天100万美元的标准对该主体处以民事罚款。

(3)**从轻因素**。——在确定根据第(2)款计征的任何罚款金额时,消费者金融保护局或法院应从以下方面考虑罚款金额的适当性——

(A)被指控人的财务资源的规模及该人的诚信度;

(B)违法违规行为或未能支付罚款行为的严重程度;

(C)对消费者造成的风险或损失的严重程度(可考虑售出或提供的产品或服务的数量);

(D)该人的既往违法违规行为记录;及

(E)为实现公正需要考虑的其他事项。

(4)**变更或免除罚款的权力**。——消费者金融保护局可以降低、变更或免除可能

modify, or remit any penalty which may be assessed or had already been assessed under paragraph (2). The amount of such penalty, when finally determined, shall be exclusive of any sums owed by the person to the United States in connection with the costs of the proceeding, and may be deducted from any sums owing by the United States to the person charged.

(5) NOTICE AND HEARING. — No civil penalty may be assessed under this subsection with respect to a violation of any Federal consumer financial law, unless —

(A) the Bureau gives notice and an opportunity for a hearing to the person accused of the violation; or

(B) the appropriate court has ordered such assessment and entered judgment in favor of the Bureau.

SEC. 1056. REFERRALS FOR CRIMINAL PROCEEDINGS.

If the Bureau obtains evidence that any person, domestic or foreign, has engaged in conduct that may constitute a violation of Federal criminal law, the Bureau shall transmit such evidence to the Attorney General of the United States, who may institute criminal proceedings under appropriate law. Nothing in this section affects any other authority of the Bureau to disclose information.

SEC. 1057. EMPLOYEE PROTECTION.

(a) IN GENERAL. — No covered person or service provider shall terminate or in any other way discriminate against, or cause to be terminated or discriminated against, any covered employee or any authorized representative of covered employees by reason of the fact that such employee or representative, whether at the initiative of the employee or in the ordinary course of the duties of the employee(or any person acting pursuant to a request of the employee), has —

(1) provided, caused to be provided, or is about to provide or cause to be provided, information to the employer, the Bureau, or any other State, local, or Federal, government authority or law enforcement agency relating to any violation of, or any act or omission that the employee reasonably believes to be a violation of, any provision of this title or any other provision of law that is subject to the jurisdiction of the Bureau, or any rule, order, standard, or prohibition prescribed by the Bureau;

(2) testified or will testify in any proceeding resulting from the administration or enforcement of any provision of this title or any other provision of law that is subject to the jurisdiction of the Bureau, or any rule, order, standard, or prohibition prescribed by the Bureau;

(3) filed, instituted, or caused to be filed or instituted any proceeding under any Federal consumer financial law; or

(4) objected to, or refused to participate in, any activity, policy, practice, or assigned

根据第(2)款计征的或已根据该款计征的任何罚款。最终确定的罚款金额不得包括被指控人欠付美国的与诉讼费用相关的任何金额，而美国欠付该人的任何金额可从该罚款中抵扣。

(5)**通知和听证**。——除非满足以下条件,否则不得根据本子条规定,针对违反联邦消费者金融法律的行为计征民事罚款——

(A)消费者金融保护局向被指控实施上述违法行为的主体发出了通知,并向其提供了听证机会;或

(B)相应的法院已下达了计征罚款的命令,且已作出了有利于消费者金融保护局的判决。

第1056条　刑事程序中的证据移交

如果消费者金融保护局获得的证据显示，任何本国或外国主体从事的活动有可能违反联邦刑法,则消费者金融保护局应将该证据移交给联邦总检察长,而联邦总检察长可以根据适当的法律启动刑事程序。本条规定不对消费者金融保护局在信息披露方面的任何其他权力造成影响。

第1057条　员工保护

(a)**一般规定**。——任何所涉员工或其任何授权代表(或根据所涉员工请求行事的任何人)主动或在正常履行职责的过程中采取以下行动的,任何所涉主体或服务提供者均不得以此为由终止与该员工或其授权代表的雇佣关系,或以其他方式对其进行歧视,亦不得致使该雇佣关系被终止,或导致该员工或其授权代表遭受歧视——

(1)已经直接或通过他人,或即将直接或通过他人向雇主、消费者金融保护局或其他州、当地或联邦政府机构或执法机关提供了与违反如下任何法律规定、规则、命令、标准或禁止性规定的行为相关的信息,或提供了与该员工合理相信可构成该等违法违规行为的作为或不作为相关的信息:本编规定、消费者金融保护局拥有管辖权的其他法律规定或消费者金融保护局制定的任何规则、命令、标准或禁止性规定;

(2)已经或将在如下任何程序中作证:因实施或执行本编规定、消费者金融保护局拥有管辖权的任何其他法律规定或消费者金融保护局制定的任何规则、命令、标准或禁止性规定而引发的程序;

(3)已根据任何联邦消费者金融法律亲自或通过他人启动任何程序,或已亲自或通过他人提起该程序;或

(4)反对或拒绝参与如下任何活动、政策、做法或指派任务:该员工(或其他该等

task that the employee (or other such person) reasonably believed to be in violation of any law, rule, order, standard, or prohibition, subject to the jurisdiction of, or enforceable by, the Bureau.

(b) DEFINITION OF COVERED EMPLOYEE. — For the purposes of this section, the term "covered employee" means any individual performing tasks related to the offering or provision of a consumer financial product or service.

(c) PROCEDURES AND TIMETABLES. —

(1) COMPLAINT. —

(A) IN GENERAL. — A person who believes that he or she has been discharged or otherwise discriminated against by any person in violation of subsection (a) may, not later than 180 days after the date on which such alleged violation occurs, file (or have any person file on his or her behalf) a complaint with the Secretary of Labor alleging such discharge or discrimination and identifying the person responsible for such act.

(B) ACTIONS OF SECRETARY OF LABOR. — Upon receipt of such a complaint, the Secretary of Labor shall notify, in writing, the person named in the complaint who is alleged to have committed the violation, of —

(i) the filing of the complaint;

(ii) the allegations contained in the complaint;

(iii) the substance of evidence supporting the complaint; and

(iv) opportunities that will be afforded to such person under paragraph (2).

(2) INVESTIGATION BY SECRETARY OF LABOR. —

(A) IN GENERAL. — Not later than 60 days after the date of receipt of a complaint filed under paragraph (1), and after affording the complainant and the person named in the complaint who is alleged to have committed the violation that is the basis for the complaint an opportunity to submit to the Secretary of Labor a written response to the complaint and an opportunity to meet with a representative of the Secretary of Labor to present statements from witnesses, the Secretary of Labor shall —

(i) initiate an investigation and determine whether there is reasonable cause to believe that the complaint has merit; and

(ii) notify the complainant and the person alleged to have committed the violation of subsection (a), in writing, of such determination.

(B) NOTICE OF RELIEF AVAILABLE. — If the Secretary of Labor concludes that there is reasonable cause to believe that a violation of subsection (a) has occurred, the Secretary of Labor shall, together with the notice under subparagraph (A)(ii), issue a preliminary order providing the relief prescribed by paragraph (4)(B).

(C) REQUEST FOR HEARING. — Not later than 30 days after the date of receipt of notification of a determination of the Secretary of Labor under this paragraph, either the

人员)合理相信将违反消费者金融保护局拥有管辖权或负责执行的任何法律、规则、命令、标准或禁止性规定的任何活动、政策、做法或指派任务。

(b)**所涉员工的定义**。——就本条而言,“所涉员工”一词系指执行与消费者金融产品或服务的要约或提供相关的任务之任何个人。

(c)**程序和时限**。——

(1)申诉书。——

(A)**一般规定**。——如果某人认为任何主体违反第(a)子条规定对其进行了解雇或其他歧视性行为,则该人可以在该被指控的违法违规行为发生后180天内向劳动部部长(或委托任何人代表其向劳动部部长)提交一份申诉书,说明其被解雇或遭受歧视的情形,并指明对等行为负有责任之人的身份。

(B)**劳动部部长的行动**。——劳动部部长应在收到该申诉书后,向该申诉书中指明的被控犯有违法违规行为之主体发出书面通知,通知该主体——

(i)其已被提出申诉;

(ii)申诉中包含的申诉内容;

(iii)支持申诉的证据的具体内容;及

(iv)其根据第(2)款将拥有的机会。

(2)**劳动部部长开展的调查**。——

(A)**一般规定**。——劳动部部长应在收到根据第(1)款提交的申诉书后60天内,向申诉人以及申诉书中指明的被控犯有构成该申诉依据的违法违规行为之主体提供,针对该申诉向劳动部部长提交一份书面答复的机会以及当面向劳动部部长代表提呈证人陈述的机会;在此之后,劳动部部长应——

(i)启动调查,判定是否存在令人信服的合理理由,可证明该申诉具有充分的根据;并

(ii)将该判定书面通知申诉人及被控犯有违反第(a)子条的违法违规行为之主体。

(B)**关于可获得救济的通知**。——如果劳动部部长认定其有合理理由认为违反第(a)子条规定的违法违规行为已发生,则劳动部部长应在签发第(A)(ii)子款所述通知之时,签发一份初步命令,提供第(4)(B)款所述救济。

(C)**听证请求**。——被指控实施上述违法违规行为的主体或申诉人可以在收到劳动部部长根据本款签发的判定通知之日后30天内,提交针对该判定和/或初步命令

person alleged to have committed the violation or the complainant may file objections to the findings or preliminary order, or both, and request a hearing on the record. The filing of such objections shall not operate to stay any reinstatement remedy contained in the preliminary order. Any such hearing shall be conducted expeditiously, and if a hearing is not requested in such 30–day period, the preliminary order shall be deemed a final order that is not subject to judicial review.

(3) GROUNDS FOR DETERMINATION OF COMPLAINTS. —

(A) IN GENERAL. — The Secretary of Labor shall dismiss a complaint filed under this subsection, and shall not conduct an investigation otherwise required under paragraph (2), unless the complainant makes a prima facie showing that any behavior described in paragraphs (1) through (4) of subsection (a) was a contributing factor in the unfavorable personnel action alleged in the complaint.

(B) REBUTTAL EVIDENCE. — Notwithstanding a finding by the Secretary of Labor that the complainant has made the showing required under subparagraph (A), no investigation otherwise required under paragraph (2) shall be conducted, if the employer demonstrates, by clear and convincing evidence, that the employer would have taken the same unfavorable personnel action in the absence of that behavior.

(C) EVIDENTIARY STANDARDS. — The Secretary of Labor may determine that a violation of subsection (a) has occurred only if the complainant demonstrates that any behavior described in paragraphs (1) through (4) of subsection (a) was a contributing factor in the unfavorable personnel action alleged in the complaint. Relief may not be ordered under subparagraph (A) if the employer demonstrates by clear and convincing evidence that the employer would have taken the same unfavorable personnel action in the absence of that behavior.

(4) ISSUANCE OF FINAL ORDERS; REVIEW PROCEDURES. —

(A) TIMING. — Not later than 120 days after the date of conclusion of any hearing under paragraph (2), the Secretary of Labor shall issue a final order providing the relief prescribed by this paragraph or denying the complaint. At any time before issuance of a final order, a proceeding under this subsection may be terminated on the basis of a settlement agreement entered into by the Secretary of Labor, the complainant, and the person alleged to have committed the violation.

(B) PENALTIES. —

(i) ORDER OF SECRETARY OF LABOR. — If, in response to a complaint filed under paragraph (1), the Secretary of Labor determines that a violation of subsection (a) has occurred, the Secretary of Labor shall order the person who committed such violation —

(I) to take affirmative action to abate the violation;

(II) to reinstate the complainant to his or her former position, together with

的反对意见,并请求举行记录在案的听证。提交反对意见的,初步命令中提供的恢复原状救济之效力并不因此而中止。任何上述听证应及时举行。如果被申诉人或申诉人未在该30天期限内提交听证请求,则上述初步命令应视为最终命令,被申诉人或申诉人均不得再提请司法审查。

(3)**对申诉作出判定的依据**。——

(A)**一般规定**。——除非申诉人提供的初步证据证明第(a)子条第(1)款至第(4)款所述的任何行为是导致控告中所述不利人事行动发生的影响因素,否则劳动部部长应驳回申诉人根据本子条提交的申诉书,且不应开展第(2)款另行要求开展的调查。

(B)**反驳证据**。——即使劳动部部长认定申诉人已提供了满足第(A)子款要求的初步证据,如果被控雇主能通过明确且具有说服力的证据,证明即使未发生第(a)子条第(1)款至第(4)款所述行为,其同样会采取相同的不利于该申诉人的人事行动,则劳动部部长不应开展第(2)款另行要求开展的调查。

(C)**证据标准**。——只有在申诉人能够证明第(a)子条第(1)款至第(4)款所述行为系导致申诉书中所述不利人事行动发生的影响因素的情况下,劳动部部长方可判定违反第(a)子条的行为已经发生。如果被控雇主能通过明确且具有说服力的证据,证明即使未发生第(a)子条第(1)款至第(4)款所述行为,其同样会采取相同的不利于该申诉人的人事行动,则劳动部部长不应签发第(A)子款所述救济命令。

(4)**最终命令的签发;审查程序**。——

(A)**时限**。——劳动部部长应于第(2)款所述任何听证结束之日后120天内,签发最终命令,提供本款所述救济或驳回申诉。如果劳动部部长、申诉人及被控犯有违法违规行为之主体在最终命令签发之前的任何时候,达成了和解协议,则本子条所述程序可据此协议终止。

(B)**处罚**。——

(i)劳动部部长的命令。——如果劳动部部长在答复根据第(1)款提交的申诉时判定,违反第(a)子条的行为已经发生,则劳动部部长应命令实施该违法违规行为的主体——

(I)采取积极行动终止该违法违规行为;

(II)恢复申诉人的职位,向申诉人给予补偿(包括补发工资),并恢复与申诉人雇

compensation (including back pay) and restore the terms, conditions, and privileges associated with his or her employment; and

(III) to provide compensatory damages to the complainant.

(ii) PENALTY. — If an order is issued under clause (i), the Secretary of Labor, at the request of the complainant, shall assess against the person against whom the order is issued, a sum equal to the aggregate amount of all costs and expenses (including attorney fees and expert witness fees) reasonably incurred, as determined by the Secretary of Labor, by the complainant for, or in connection with, the bringing of the complaint upon which the order was issued.

(C) PENALTY FOR FRIVOLOUS CLAIMS. — If the Secretary of Labor finds that a complaint under paragraph (1) is frivolous or has been brought in bad faith, the Secretary of Labor may award to the prevailing employer a reasonable attorney fee, not exceeding $1,000, to be paid by the complainant.

(D) DE NOVO REVIEW. —

(i) FAILURE OF THE SECRETARY TO ACT. — If the Secretary of Labor has not issued a final order within 210 days after the date of filing of a complaint under this subsection, or within 90 days after the date of receipt of a written determination, the complainant may bring an action at law or equity for de novo review in the appropriate district court of the United States having jurisdiction, which shall have jurisdiction over such an action without regard to the amount in controversy, and which action shall, at the request of either party to such action, be tried by the court with a jury.

(ii) PROCEDURES. — A proceeding under clause (i) shall be governed by the same legal burdens of proof specified in paragraph (3). The court shall have jurisdiction to grant all relief necessary to make the employee whole, including injunctive relief and compensatory damages, including —

(I) reinstatement with the same seniority status that the employee would have had, but for the discharge or discrimination;

(II) the amount of back pay, with interest; and

(III) compensation for any special damages sustained as a result of the discharge or discrimination, including litigation costs, expert witness fees, and reasonable attorney fees.

(E) OTHER APPEALS. — Unless the complainant brings an action under subparagraph (D), any person adversely affected or aggrieved by a final order issued under subparagraph (A) may file a petition for review of the order in the United States Court of Appeals for the circuit in which the violation with respect to which the order was issued, allegedly occurred or the circuit in which the complainant resided on the date of such violation, not later than 60 days after the date of the issuance of the final order of the Secretary of Labor under subparagraph (A). Review shall conform to chapter 7 of title 5, United States

用相关的条款、条件及特权;并

(III)向申诉人提供补偿性损害赔偿金。

(ii)**罚款**。——劳动部部长签发了第(i)项所述命令的,则在申诉人提出请求之时,劳动部部长应对该命令的签发对象计征罚款,罚款金额应以申诉人因提起该申诉或与该申诉相关的合理承担的全部成本和费用(包括律师费和专家证人费)为准,该等成本和费用金额应由劳动部部长确定。

(C)**对滥用申诉权的处罚**。——如果劳动部部长认定,第(1)款所述申诉属于滥用申诉权的行为或恶意申诉,则劳动部部长可以判令申诉人向胜诉的被指控雇主支付不高于1000美元的合理律师费。

(D)**重新审查**。——

(i)**劳动部部长未采取行动的情形**。——如果劳动部部长未在本子条所述申诉提交之日后210天内签发最终命令,或未在收到书面判定之日后90天内签发最终命令,则申诉人可以依据普通法或衡平法向具有管辖权的相应联邦地区法院提起重新审查诉讼;不论争议金额大小,该法院均应对该诉讼具有管辖权,且该诉讼任何一方提出请求之后,该法院应采取陪审团审理的方式进行审理。

(ii)**程序**。——第(i)项所述诉讼同样应适用第(3)款中关于法定证明责任的具体规定。法院应具有授予使申诉人免受损害的任何必要救济(包括提供禁令救济及补偿性损害赔偿金)的管辖权,该等救济包括——

(I)恢复申诉人若未被解雇或未遭受歧视待遇本应享有的雇用年资;

(II)补发工资及相应利息;及

(III)对申诉人因被解雇或遭受歧视而引发的特殊损害予以赔偿,包括诉讼费、专家证人费及合理的律师费。

(E)**其他相关方提起的上诉**。——如果申诉人未根据第(D)子款提起诉讼,则因根据第(A)子款签发的最终命令而受到不利影响或权益受到侵害的任何人可以在劳动部部长根据第(A)子款签发最终命令之日后60天内,向该命令所针对的被控违法违规行为发生地所在巡回区的联邦上诉法院,或向申诉人在该违法违规行为发生之日的居住地所在巡回区的联邦上诉法院提交一份请求,请求该法院对该命令进行审查。审查应遵守《美国法典》第五编第七章的规定。除非法院另行作出命令,否则,本子款所述程序启动之时,上述命令并不因此而中止适用。对于可根据本子款规定提请审查

Code. The commencement of proceedings under this subparagraph shall not, unless ordered by the court, operate as a stay of the order. An order of the Secretary of Labor with respect to which review could have been obtained under this subparagraph shall not be subject to judicial review in any criminal or other civil proceeding.

(5) FAILURE TO COMPLY WITH ORDER. —

(A) ACTIONS BY THE SECRETARY. — If any person has failed to comply with a final order issued under paragraph (4), the Secretary of Labor may file a civil action in the United States district court for the district in which the violation was found to have occurred, or in the United States district court for the District of Columbia, to enforce such order. In actions brought under this paragraph, the district courts shall have jurisdiction to grant all appropriate relief including injunctive relief and compensatory damages.

(B) CIVIL ACTIONS TO COMPEL COMPLIANCE. — A person on whose behalf an order was issued under paragraph (4) may commence a civil action against the person to whom such order was issued to require compliance with such order. The appropriate United States district court shall have jurisdiction, without regard to the amount in controversy or the citizenship of the parties, to enforce such order.

(C) AWARD OF COSTS AUTHORIZED. — The court, in issuing any final order under this paragraph, may award costs of litigation (including reasonable attorney and expert witness fees) to any party, whenever the court determines such award is appropriate.

(D) MANDAMUS PROCEEDINGS. — Any nondiscretionary duty imposed by this section shall be enforceable in a mandamus proceeding brought under section 1361 of title 28, United States Code.

(d) UNENFORCEABILITY OF CERTAIN AGREEMENTS. —

(1) NO WAIVER OF RIGHTS AND REMEDIES. — Except as provided under paragraph (3), and notwithstanding any other provision of law, the rights and remedies provided for in this section may not be waived by any agreement, policy, form, or condition of employment, including by any predispute arbitration agreement.

(2) NO PREDISPUTE ARBITRATION AGREEMENTS. — Except as provided under paragraph (3), and notwithstanding any other provision of law, no predispute arbitration agreement shall be valid or enforceable to the extent that it requires arbitration of a dispute arising under this section.

(3) EXCEPTION. — Notwithstanding paragraphs (1) and (2), an arbitration provision in a collective bargaining agreement shall be enforceable as to disputes arising under subsection (a)(4), unless the Bureau determines, by rule, that such provision is inconsistent with the purposes of this title.

SEC. 1058. EFFECTIVE DATE.

This subtitle shall become effective on the designated transfer date.

的劳动部部长签发的命令，不得通过任何刑事程序或其他民事程序提请司法审查。

（5）**未遵守命令的情形**。——

（A）**劳动部部长的行动**。——如果任何主体未遵守劳动部部长根据第（4）款签发的最终命令，劳动部部长可以向发现的违法违规行为发生地所在地区的联邦地区法院，或向哥伦比亚特区联邦地区法院提起诉讼，请求强制执行该命令。在根据本款提起的诉讼中，该地区法院有权授予任何适当的救济，包括禁令救济及损害赔偿金。

（B）**为强制执行命令提起的民事诉讼**。——如果申请人申请的命令根据第（4）款规定得以签发，该申请人可以针对该命令的签发对象启动民事诉讼，要求强制执行该命令。无论争议金额大小，亦无论当事人的国籍为何，相应的联邦地区法院均应具有强制执行该命令的管辖权。

（C）**判决费用承担的权限**。——法院在根据本款签发任何最终命令时，可以在其认为适当之时，判令任何一方承担另一方的诉讼成本（包括合理的律师费及专家证人费）。

（D）**执行职务令程序**。——本条规定的任何非自由裁量的职责，均可通过根据《美国法典》第二十八编第1361节规定提起的执行职务令程序强制执行。

（d）**不具强制执行力的特定协议**。——

（1）**权利和救济的不可放弃性**。——无论是否存在任何不同法律规定，除第（3）款规定的情形外，本条规定的权利和救济不得通过任何协议、政策、格式条款或雇用条件（包括纠纷仲裁前置协议）予以放弃。

（2）**纠纷仲裁前置协议无效**。——无论是否存在任何不同法律规定，除第（3）款规定的情形外，任何要求对因本条规定引发的争议进行仲裁的纠纷仲裁前置协议均为无效，且不可强制执行。

（3）**例外规定**。——无论第（1）款和第（2）款如何规定，除非消费者金融保护局发布规则判定集体劳动合同中的仲裁条款不符合本编宗旨，否则对于因第（a）（4）子条引发的争议，该等条款应具有可强制执行力。

第1058条　生效日

本子编规定于指定转移日生效。

Subtitle F — Transfer of Functions and Personnel; Transitional Provisions

SEC.1061. TRANSFER OF CONSUMER FINANCIAL PROTECTION FUNCTIONS.

(a) DEFINED TERMS. — For purposes of this subtitle —

(1) the term "consumer financial protection functions" means —

(A) all authority to prescribe rules or issue orders or guidelines pursuant to any Federal consumer financial law, including performing appropriate functions to promulgate and review such rules, orders, and guidelines; and

(B) the examination authority described in subsection(c)(1), with respect to a person described in subsection 1025(a); and

(2) the terms "transferor agency" and "transferor agencies" mean, respectively —

(A) the Board of Governors (and any Federal reserve bank, as the context requires), the Federal Deposit Insurance Corporation, the Federal Trade Commission, the National Credit Union Administration, the Office of the Comptroller of the Currency, the Office of Thrift Supervision, and the Department of Housing and Urban Development, and the heads of those agencies; and

(B) the agencies listed in subparagraph (A), collectively.

(b) IN GENERAL. — Except as provided in subsection (c), consumer financial protection functions are transferred as follows:

(1) BOARD OF GOVERNORS. —

(A) TRANSFER OF FUNCTIONS. — All consumer financial protection functions of the Board of Governors are transferred to the Bureau.

(B) BOARD OF GOVERNORS AUTHORITY. — The Bureau shall have all powers and duties that were vested in the Board of Governors, relating to consumer financial protection functions, on the day before the designated transfer date.

(2) COMPTROLLER OF THE CURRENCY. —

(A) TRANSFER OF FUNCTIONS. — All consumer financial protection functions of the Comptroller of the Currency are transferred to the Bureau.

(B) COMPTROLLER AUTHORITY. — The Bureau shall have all powers and duties that were vested in the Comptroller of the Currency, relating to consumer financial protection functions, on the day before the designated transfer date.

(3) DIRECTOR OF THE OFFICE OF THRIFT SUPERVISION. —

第F子编——职能转移及人员转移;过渡规定

第1061条 消费者金融保护职能的转移

(a)**术语定义**。——就本子编而言——

(1)“消费者金融保护职能”一词系指——

(A)根据联邦消费者金融法律制定规则、发布命令或指引的所有权力,包括履行适当的职能,以颁发和审查该等规则、命令及指引;及

(B)第(c)(1)子条所述的针对第1025(a)子条所述主体开展检查的权力;

(2)“职能转出机关”一词——

(A)采用单数形式时,系指联邦储备委员会[及任何联邦储备银行(视上下文而定)]、联邦存款保险公司、联邦贸易委员会、国家信贷联盟署、货币监理署、储蓄机构监理局、住房与城市发展部及上述机关的负责人;

(B)采用单数形式时,系指第(A)子款所列全部机关之统称。

(b)**一般规定**。——除第(c)子条规定的情形外,消费者金融保护职能应根据以下规定转移:

(1)**联邦储备委员会**。——

(A)**职能转移**。——联邦储备委员会的所有消费者金融保护职能均应转移至消费者金融保护局。

(B)**联邦储备委员会的权力**。——联邦储备委员会在指定转移日前一天享有和承担的与消费者金融保护职能相关的全部权力及职责,均应转由消费者金融保护局享有和承担。

(2)**货币监理署署长**。——

(A)**职能转移**。——货币监理署署长的所有消费者金融保护职能均应转移至消费者金融保护局。

(B)**货币监理署署长的权力**。——货币监理署署长在指定转移日前一天享有和承担的与消费者金融保护职能相关的全部权力及职责,均应转由消费者金融保护局享有和承担。

(3)**储蓄机构监理局局长**。——

(A) TRANSFER OF FUNCTIONS. — All consumer financial protection functions of the Director of the Office of Thrift Supervision are transferred to the Bureau.

(B) DIRECTOR AUTHORITY. — The Bureau shall have all powers and duties that were vested in the Director of the Office of Thrift Supervision, relating to consumer financial protection functions, on the day before the designated transfer date.

(4) FEDERAL DEPOSIT INSURANCE CORPORATION. —

(A) TRANSFER OF FUNCTIONS. — All consumer financial protection functions of the Federal Deposit Insurance Corporation are transferred to the Bureau.

(B) CORPORATION AUTHORITY. — The Bureau shall have all powers and duties that were vested in the Federal Deposit Insurance Corporation, relating to consumer financial protection functions, on the day before the designated transfer date.

(5) FEDERAL TRADE COMMISSION. —

(A) TRANSFER OF FUNCTIONS. — The authority of the Federal Trade Commission under an enumerated consumer law to prescribe rules, issue guidelines, or conduct a study or issue a report mandated under such law shall be transferred to the Bureau on the designated transfer date. Nothing in this title shall be construed to require a mandatory transfer of any employee of the Federal Trade Commission.

(B) BUREAU AUTHORITY. —

(i) IN GENERAL. — The Bureau shall have all powers and duties under the enumerated consumer laws to prescribe rules, issue guidelines, or to conduct studies or issue reports mandated by such laws, that were vested in the Federal Trade Commission on the day before the designated transfer date.

(ii) FEDERAL TRADE COMMISSION ACT. — Subject to subtitle B, the Bureau may enforce a rule prescribed under the Federal Trade Commission Act by the Federal Trade Commission with respect to an unfair or deceptive act or practice to the extent that such rule applies to a covered person or service provider with respect to the offering or provision of a consumer financial product or service as if it were a rule prescribed under section 1031 of this title.

(C) AUTHORITY OF THE FEDERAL TRADE COMMISSION. —

(i) IN GENERAL. — No provision of this title shall be construed as modifying, limiting, or otherwise affecting the authority of the Federal Trade Commission (including its authority with respect to affiliates described in section 1025(a)(1)) under the Federal Trade Commission Act or any other law, other than the authority under an enumerated consumer law to prescribe rules, issue official guidelines, or conduct a study or issue a report mandated under such law.

(ii) COMMISSION AUTHORITY RELATING TO RULES PRESCRIBED BY THE BUREAU. — Subject to subtitle B, the Federal Trade Commission shall have authority to

(A)**职能转移**。——储蓄机构监理局局长的所有消费者金融保护职能均应转移至消费者金融保护局。

(B)**储蓄机构监理局局长的权力**。——储蓄机构监理局局长在指定转移日前一天享有和承担的与消费者金融保护职能相关的全部权力及职责，均应转由消费者金融保护局享有和承担。

(4)**联邦存款保险公司**。——

(A)**职能转移**。——联邦存款保险公司的所有消费者金融保护职能均应转移至消费者金融保护局。

(B)**联邦存款保险公司的权力**。——联邦存款保险公司在指定转移日前一天享有和承担的与消费者金融保护职能相关的全部权力及职责,均应转由消费者金融保护局享有和承担。

(5)**联邦贸易委员会**。——

(A)**职能转移**。——明文列举的消费者法律向联邦贸易委员会授予的根据该法的强制性要求制定规则、签发指引、开展研究或发布报告的权力,均应在指定转移日转移至消费者金融保护局。本编中的任何规定均不得被解释为要求联邦贸易委员会对任何雇员进行强制转移。

(B)**消费者金融保护局的权力**。——

(i)**一般规定**。——联邦贸易委员会在转移日前一天享有或承担的按照明文列举的消费者法律强制性要求制定规则、签发指引、开展研究或签发报告的全部权力和职责,均应根据该等法律转由消费者金融保护局享有或承担。

(ii)**《联邦贸易委员会法》**。——对于联邦贸易委员会根据《联邦贸易委员会法》针对不公平或欺骗性行为或做法制定的规则而言,只要该等规则适用于要约或提供消费者金融产品或服务的所涉主体或服务提供者,消费者金融保护局在不违反第B子编规定的前提下,即可强制执行该等规则,如同该规则属于根据本编第1031条所制定的规则。

(C)**联邦贸易委员会的权力**。——

(i)**一般规定**。——本编任何规定均不得被解释为修改、限制或以其他方式影响《联邦贸易委员会法》或任何其他法律赋予联邦贸易委员会的权力[包括针对第1025(a)(1)条所述关联方拥有的权力],但明文列举的消费者法律赋予联邦贸易委员会的根据该等法律的强制性要求制定规则、签发官方指引、开展研究或发布报告的权力除外。

(ii)**联邦贸易委员会与消费者金融保护局所制定规则相关的权力**。——涉及依据《联邦贸易委员会法》受联邦贸易委员会管辖的所涉主体,就消费者金融保护局针

enforce under the Federal Trade Commission Act (15 U.S.C. 41 et seq.) a rule prescribed by the Bureau under this title with respect to a covered person subject to the jurisdiction of the Federal Trade Commission under that Act, and a violation of such a rule by such a person shall be treated as a violation of a rule issued under section 18 of that Act (15 U.S.C. 57a) with respect to unfair or deceptive acts or practices.

(D) COORDINATION. — To avoid duplication of or conflict between rules prescribed by the Bureau under section 1031 of this title and the Federal Trade Commission under section 18(a)(1)(B) of the Federal Trade Commission Act that apply to a covered person or service provider with respect to the offering or provision of consumer financial products or services, the agencies shall negotiate an agreement with respect to rulemaking by each agency, including consultation with the other agency prior to proposing a rule and during the comment period.

(E) DEFERENCE. — No provision of this title shall be construed as altering, limiting, expanding, or otherwise affecting the deference that a court affords to the —

(i) Federal Trade Commission in making determinations regarding the meaning or interpretation of any provision of the Federal Trade Commission Act, or of any other Federal law for which the Commission has authority to prescribe rules; or

(ii) Bureau in making determinations regarding the meaning or interpretation of any provision of a Federal consumer financial law (other than any law described in clause (i)).

(6) NATIONAL CREDIT UNION ADMINISTRATION. —

(A) TRANSFER OF FUNCTIONS. — All consumer financial protection functions of the National Credit Union Administration are transferred to the Bureau.

(B) NATIONAL CREDIT UNION ADMINISTRATION AUTHORITY. — The Bureau shall have all powers and duties that were vested in the National Credit Union Administration, relating to consumer financial protection functions, on the day before the designated transfer date.

(7) DEPARTMENT OF HOUSING AND URBAN DEVELOPMENT. —

(A) TRANSFER OF FUNCTIONS. — All consumer protection functions of the Secretary of the Department of Housing and Urban Development relating to the Real Estate Settlement Procedures Act of 1974 (12 U.S.C. 2601 et seq.), the Secure and Fair Enforcement for Mortgage Licensing Act of 2008 (12 U.S.C. 5102 et seq.), and the Interstate Land Sales Full Disclosure Act (15 U.S.C. 1701 et seq.) are transferred to the Bureau.

(B) AUTHORITY OF THE DEPARTMENT OF HOUSING AND URBAN DEVELOPMENT. — The Bureau shall have all powers and duties that were vested in the Secretary of the Department of Housing and Urban Development relating to the Real Estate Settlement Procedures Act of 1974 (12 U.S.C. 2601 et seq.), the Secure and Fair

对该等主体根据本编制定的规则而言,联邦贸易委员会在不违反第B子编规定的前提下有权根据《联邦贸易委员会法》(《美国法典》第十五编第41节及其后条文)强制执行该等规则,且上述主体违反该等规则的行为应视为违反了根据《联邦贸易委员会法》第18条(《美国法典》第十五编第57a节)针对不公平或欺骗性行为或做法发布的规则。

(D)**协调**。——为避免消费者金融保护局根据本编第1031条针对要约或提供消费者金融产品或服务的行为制定的适用于所涉主体的规则，与联邦贸易委员会为此目的根据《联邦贸易委员会法》第18(a)(1)(B)条制定的规则之间发生重复或冲突,上述机关应就各自的规则制定工作进行磋商（包括在提出规则草案前以及在意见征集期内与其他机关进行磋商),以达成一致意见。

(E)**司法尊重**。——法院对以下事项表示司法尊重的,本编任何规定均不得被解释为更改、限制该等司法尊重,或扩大其适用范围,亦不得对该等司法尊重造成其他影响——

(i)联邦贸易委员会针对如下规定的含义或解释作出的判定:《联邦贸易委员会法》的任何规定,或联邦贸易委员会有权对之制定实施规则的任何其他联邦法律的规定;或

(ii)消费者金融保护局针对联邦消费者金融法律[但第(i)项所述法律除外]任何规定的含义或解释作出的判定。

(6)**国家信贷联盟署**。——

(A)**职能转移**。——国家信贷联盟署的所有消费者金融保护职能均应转移至消费者金融保护局。

(B)**国家信贷联盟署的权力**。——国家信贷联盟署在指定转移日当天前一天享有和承担的与消费者金融保护职能相关的全部权力及职责，均应转由消费者金融保护局享有和承担。

(7)**住房与城市发展部**。——

(A)**职能转移**。——住房与城市发展部具有的与如下法律相关的所有消费者保护职能均应转至消费者金融保护局:《1974年房地产结算程序法》(《美国法典》第十二编第2601节及其后条文)、《2008年安全和公平执行抵押贷款发起人许可法》(《美国法典》第十二编第5102节及其后条文)以及《州际土地销售完全披露法》(《美国法典》第十五编第1701节及其后条文)。

(B)**住房与城市发展部的权力**。——住房与城市发展部在指定转移日前一天具有的与如下法律相关的所有权力和职责，均应转由消费者金融保护局享有和承担:《1974年房地产结算程序法》(《美国法典》第十二编第2601节及其后条文)、《2008年安全和公平执行抵押贷款发起人许可法》(《美国法典》 第十二编第5101节及其后条文)

Enforcement for Mortgage Licensing Act of 2008 (12 U.S.C. 5101 et seq.), and the Interstate Land Sales Full Disclosure Act (15 U.S.C. 1701 et seq.), on the day before the designated transfer date.

(c) AUTHORITIES OF THE PRUDENTIAL REGULATORS. —

(1) EXAMINATION. — A transferor agency that is a prudential regulator shall have —

(A) authority to require reports from and conduct examinations for compliance with Federal consumer financial laws with respect to a person described in section 1025(a), that is incidental to the backup and enforcement procedures provided to the regulator under section 1025(c); and

(B) exclusive authority (relative to the Bureau) to require reports from and conduct examinations for compliance with Federal consumer financial laws with respect to a person described in section 1026(a), except as provided to the Bureau under subsections (b) and (c) of section 1026.

(2) ENFORCEMENT. —

(A) LIMITATION. — The authority of a transferor agency that is a prudential regulator to enforce compliance with Federal consumer financial laws with respect to a person described in section 1025(a), shall be limited to the backup and enforcement procedures in described in section 1025(c).

(B) EXCLUSIVE AUTHORITY. — A transferor agency that is a prudential regulator shall have exclusive authority (relative to the Bureau) to enforce compliance with Federal consumer financial laws with respect to a person described in section 1026(a), except as provided to the Bureau under subsections (b) and (c) of section 1026.

(C) STATUTORY ENFORCEMENT. — For purposes of carrying out the authorities under, and subject to the limitations of, subtitle B, each prudential regulator may enforce compliance with the requirements imposed under this title, and any rule or order prescribed by the Bureau under this title, under —

(i) the Federal Credit Union Act (12 U.S.C. 1751 et seq.), by the National Credit Union Administration Board with respect to any covered person or service provider that is an insured credit union, or service provider thereto, or any affiliate of an insured credit union, who is subject to the jurisdiction of the Board under that Act; and

(ii) section 8 of the Federal Deposit Insurance Act(12 U.S.C. 1818), by the appropriate Federal banking agency, as defined in section 3(q) of the Federal Deposit Insurance Act (12 U.S.C. 1813(q)), with respect to a covered person or service provider that is a person described in section 3(q) of that Act and who is subject to the jurisdiction of that agency, as set forth in sections 3(q) and 8 of the Federal Deposit Insurance Act; or

(iii) the Bank Service Company Act (12 U.S.C. 1861 et seq.).

(d) EFFECTIVE DATE. — Subsections (b) and (c) shall become effective on the

以及《州际土地销售完全披露法》(《美国法典》第十五编第1701节及其后条文)。

(c)**审慎监管者的权力**。——

(1)**检查**。——具有审慎监管者身份的职能转出机关应——

(A)有权根据审慎监管者依据第1025(c)条享有的后备执法程序,要求第1025(a)条所述主体提供报告并针对该等主体对联邦消费者金融法律的合规情况进行检查;且

(B)拥有排他性的权力(相对于消费者金融保护局而言),有权要求第1026(a)条所述主体提供报告并针对该等主体对联邦消费者金融法律的合规情况进行检查,但第1026条第(b)子条和第(c)子条将上述权力赋予消费者金融保护局的除外。

(2)**执法**。——

(A)**限制**。——具有审慎监管者身份的职能转出机关针对第1025(a)条所述主体强制执行联邦消费者金融法律的权力,仅限于第1025(c)条所述后备执法程序。

(B)**排他性权力**。——具有审慎监管者身份的职能转出机关拥有排他性的权力(相对于消费者金融保护局而言),有权针对第1026(a)条所述主体强制执行联邦消费者金融法律,但第1026条第(b)子条和第(c)子条将上述权力赋予消费者金融保护局的除外。

(C)**法定执法权**。——就本编施加的要求以及消费者金融保护局依据本编制定的任何规则或命令而言,每一审慎监管者均可以为了履行第B子编授予的权力,在第B子编限制的范围内,按照以下法律强制执行任何该等要求及规则或命令——

(i)由国家信贷联盟署委员会针对具有以下身份的任何所涉主体或服务提供者负责实施的《联邦信贷联盟法》(《美国法典》第十二编第1751节及其后条文):根据该法受国家信贷联盟署委员会管辖的参保信贷联盟,或参保信贷联盟的服务提供者,或参保信贷联盟的任何关联方;及

(ii)由相应的联邦银行业监管机关{定义见《联邦存款保险法》第3(q)条[《美国法典》第十二编第1813(q)节]}针对符合下述情况的所涉主体或服务提供者负责实施的《联邦存款保险法》第8条(《美国法典》第十二编第1818节):属于《联邦存款保险法》第3(q)条所述且根据该法第3(q)条和第8条应接受相应的联邦银行业监管机关管辖的主体;或

(iii)《银行服务公司法》(《美国法典》第十二编第1861节及其后条文)。

(d)**生效日**。——第(b)子条和第(c)子条规定于指定转移日生效。

designated transfer date.

SEC. 1062. DESIGNATED TRANSFER DATE.

(a) IN GENERAL. — Not later than 60 days after the date of enactment of this Act, the Secretary shall —

(1) in consultation with the Chairman of the Board of Governors, the Chairperson of the Corporation, the Chairman of the Federal Trade Commission, the Chairman of the National Credit Union Administration Board, the Comptroller of the Currency, the Director of the Office of Thrift Supervision, the Secretary of the Department of Housing and Urban Development, and the Director of the Office of Management and Budget, designate a single calendar date for the transfer of functions to the Bureau under section 1061; and

(2) publish notice of that designated date in the Federal Register.

(b) CHANGING DESIGNATION. — The Secretary —

(1) may, in consultation with the Chairman of the Board of Governors, the Chairperson of the Federal Deposit Insurance Corporation, the Chairman of the Federal Trade Commission, the Chairman of the National Credit Union Administration Board, the Comptroller of the Currency, the Director of the Office of Thrift Supervision, the Secretary of the Department of Housing and Urban Development, and the Director of the Office of Management and Budget, change the date designated under subsection (a); and

(2) shall publish notice of any changed designated date in the Federal Register.

(c) PERMISSIBLE DATES. —

(1) IN GENERAL. — Except as provided in paragraph (2), any date designated under this section shall be not earlier than 180 days, nor later than 12 months, after the date of enactment of this Act.

(2) EXTENSION OF TIME. — The Secretary may designate a date that is later than 12 months after the date of enactment of this Act if the Secretary transmits to appropriate committees of Congress —

(A) a written determination that orderly implementation of this title is not feasible before the date that is 12 months after the date of enactment of this Act;

(B) an explanation of why an extension is necessary for the orderly implementation of this title; and

(C) a description of the steps that will be taken to effect an orderly and timely implementation of this title within the extended time period.

(3) EXTENSION LIMITED. — In no case may any date designated under this section be later than 18 months after the date of enactment of this Act.

SEC. 1063. SAVINGS PROVISIONS.

(a) BOARD OF GOVERNORS. —

(1) EXISTING RIGHTS, DUTIES, AND OBLIGATIONS NOT AFFECTED. — Section

第1062条　指定转移日

(a)**一般规定**。——财政部部长应于本法颁布之日后60天内——

(1)在与联邦储备委员会主席、联邦存款保险公司主席、联邦贸易委员会主席、国家信贷联盟署委员会主席、货币监理署署长、储蓄机构监理局局长、住房与城市发展部部长及行政管理和预算局局长磋商后,将某一日历日指定为第1061条所述向消费者金融保护局转移职能之日;并

(2)在《联邦公报》上就该指定转移日发布通知。

(b)**指定转移日的变更**。——财政部部长——

(1)可以在与联邦储备委员会主席、联邦存款保险公司主席、联邦贸易委员会主席、国家信贷联盟署委员会主席、货币监理署署长、储蓄机构监理局局长、住房与城市发展部部长及行政管理和预算局局长磋商后,对根据第(a)子条指定的日期进行变更;并

(2)在《联邦公报》上就该指定转移日的任何变更发布通知。

(c)**指定转移日的可选范围**。——

(1)**一般规定**。——除第(2)款规定的情形外,根据本条指定的日期既不得早于本法颁布之日后第180天,亦不得迟于本法颁布之日后12个月。

(2)**期限的延长**。——财政部部长指定的日期可以迟于本法颁布之日后12个月,前提是财政部部长应向相应的国会委员会事先发出——

(A)一份说明在本法颁布之日后届满一年之前有序实施本编规定不具可行性的书面判定;

(B)一份解释必须推迟对本编的有序执行的原因的说明;及

(C)关于为实现本编规定有序、及时的实施将而在延长期内采取的行动的说明。

(3)**期限延长限制**。——在任何情况下,根据本条指定的任何日期均不得迟于本法颁布之日后18个月。

第1063条　保留条款

(a)**联邦储备委员会**。——

(1)**既存权利、职责和义务不受影响**。——联邦政府、联邦储备委员会(或任何联

1061(b)(1) does not affect the validity of any right, duty, or obligation of the United States, the Board of Governors (or any Federal reserve bank), or any other person that —

(A) arises under any provision of law relating to any consumer financial protection function of the Board of Governors transferred to the Bureau by this title; and

(B) existed on the day before the designated transfer date.

(2) CONTINUATION OF SUITS. — No provision of this Act shall abate any proceeding commenced by or against the Board of Governors (or any Federal reserve bank) before the designated transfer date with respect to any consumer financial protection function of the Board of Governors (or any Federal reserve bank) transferred to the Bureau by this title, except that the Bureau, subject to sections 1024, 1025, and 1026, shall be substituted for the Board of Governors (or Federal reserve bank) as a party to any such proceeding as of the designated transfer date.

(b) FEDERAL DEPOSIT INSURANCE CORPORATION. —

(1) EXISTING RIGHTS, DUTIES, AND OBLIGATIONS NOT AFFECTED. — Section 1061(b)(4) does not affect the validity of any right, duty, or obligation of the United States, the Federal Deposit Insurance Corporation, the Board of Directors of that Corporation, or any other person, that —

(A) arises under any provision of law relating to any consumer financial protection function of the Federal Deposit Insurance Corporation transferred to the Bureau by this title; and

(B) existed on the day before the designated transfer date.

(2) CONTINUATION OF SUITS. — No provision of this Act shall abate any proceeding commenced by or against the Federal Deposit Insurance Corporation (or the Board of Directors of that Corporation) before the designated transfer date with respect to any consumer financial protection function of the Federal Deposit Insurance Corporation transferred to the Bureau by this title, except that the Bureau, subject to sections 1024, 1025, and 1026, shall be substituted for the Federal Deposit Insurance Corporation (or Board of Directors) as a party to any such proceeding as of the designated transfer date.

(c) FEDERAL TRADE COMMISSION. — Section 1061(b)(5) does not affect the validity of any right, duty, or obligation of the United States, the Federal Trade Commission, or any other person, that —

(1) arises under any provision of law relating to any consumer financial protection function of the Federal Trade Commission transferred to the Bureau by this title; and

(2) existed on the day before the designated transfer date.

(d) NATIONAL CREDIT UNION ADMINISTRATION. —

(1) EXISTING RIGHTS, DUTIES, AND OBLIGATIONS NOT AFFECTED. — Section 1061(b)(6) does not affect the validity of any right, duty, or obligation of the United States,

邦储备银行）或任何其他主体的下述任何权利、职责或义务的有效性，一概不受第1061(b)(1)条影响——

(A)由于原来由联邦储备委员会行使但按照本编规定转移至消费者金融保护局的与任何消费者金融保护职能相关的任何法律规定,所产生的权利、职责或义务;及

(B)在指定转移日前一天业已存在的权利、职责或义务。

(2)**原有案件继续审理**。——在指定转移日之前,联邦储备委员会(或任何联邦储备银行)提起的或他人针对其提起的,原来由联邦储备委员会行使但按照本编规定转移至消费者金融保护局的与任何消费者金融保护职能相关的任何程序，均不得因本法的任何规定而终止，但是，自指定转移日起，消费者金融保护局应在不违反第1024条、第1025条和第1026条规定的前提下,替代联邦储备委员会(或联邦储备银行)担任该等程序的当事人。

(b)**联邦存款保险公司**。——

(1)**既存权利、职责及义务不受影响**。——联邦政府、联邦存款保险公司及其董事会或任何其他主体的下述任何权利、职责或义务的有效性,一概不受第1061(b)(4)条影响——

(A)由于原来由联邦存款保险公司行使但按照本编规定转移至消费者金融保护局的与任何消费者金融保护职能相关的任何法律规定,所产生的权利、职责及义务;及

(B)在指定转移日前一天业已存在的权利、职责及义务。

(2)**原有案件继续审理**。——在指定转移日之前,联邦存款保险公司(或其董事会)提起的或他人针对其提起的,原来由联邦存款保险公司行使但按照本编规定转移至消费者金融保护局的与任何消费者金融保护职能相关的任何程序，均不得因本法的任何规定而终止,但是,自指定转移日起,消费者金融保护局应在不违反第1024条、第1025条和第1026条规定的前提下,替代联邦存款保险公司(或其董事会)担任该等程序的当事人。

(c)**联邦贸易委员会**。——联邦政府、联邦贸易委员会或任何其他主体的下述任何权利、职责或义务的有效性,一概不受第1061(b)(5)条影响——

(1)由于原来由联邦贸易委员会行使但按照本编规定转移至消费者金融保护局的与任何消费者金融保护职能相关的任何法律规定,所产生的权利、职责及义务;及

(2)在指定转移日前一天业已存在的权利、职责及义务。

(d)**国家信贷联盟署**。——

(1)**既存权利、职责和义务不受影响**。——联邦政府、国家信贷联盟署、国家信贷联盟署委员会或任何其他主体的下述任何权利、职责或义务的有效性,一概不受第

the National Credit Union Administration, the National Credit Union Administration Board, or any other person, that —

(A) arises under any provision of law relating to any consumer financial protection function of the National Credit Union Administration transferred to the Bureau by this title; and

(B) existed on the day before the designated transfer date.

(2) CONTINUATION OF SUITS. — No provision of this Act shall abate any proceeding commenced by or against the National Credit Union Administration (or the National Credit Union Administration Board) before the designated transfer date with respect to any consumer financial protection function of the National Credit Union Administration transferred to the Bureau by this title, except that the Bureau, subject to sections 1024, 1025, and 1026, shall be substituted for the National Credit Union Administration (or National Credit Union Administration Board) as a party to any such proceeding as of the designated transfer date.

(e) OFFICE OF THE COMPTROLLER OF THE CURRENCY. —

(1) EXISTING RIGHTS, DUTIES, AND OBLIGATIONS NOT AFFECTED. — Section 1061(b)(2) does not affect the validity of any right, duty, or obligation of the United States, the Comptroller of the Currency, the Office of the Comptroller of the Currency, or any other person, that —

(A) arises under any provision of law relating to any consumer financial protection function of the Comptroller of the Currency transferred to the Bureau by this title; and

(B) existed on the day before the designated transfer date.

(2) CONTINUATION OF SUITS. — No provision of this Act shall abate any proceeding commenced by or against the Comptroller of the Currency (or the Office of the Comptroller of the Currency) with respect to any consumer financial protection function of the Comptroller of the Currency transferred to the Bureau by this title before the designated transfer date, except that the Bureau, subject to sections 1024, 1025, and 1026, shall be substituted for the Comptroller of the Currency (or the Office of the Comptroller of the Currency) as a party to any such proceeding as of the designated transfer date.

(f) OFFICE OF THRIFT SUPERVISION. —

(1) EXISTING RIGHTS, DUTIES, AND OBLIGATIONS NOT AFFECTED. — Section 1061(b)(3) does not affect the validity of any right, duty, or obligation of the United States, the Director of the Office of Thrift Supervision, the Office of Thrift Supervision, or any other person, that —

(A) arises under any provision of law relating to any consumer financial protection function of the Director of the Office of Thrift Supervision transferred to the Bureau by this title; and

1061(b)(6)条影响——

(A)由于原来由国家信贷联盟署行使但按照本编规定转移至消费者金融保护局的与任何消费者金融保护职能相关的任何法律规定,所产生的权利、职责及义务;及

(B)在指定转移日前一天业已存在的权利、职责及义务。

(2)**原有案件继续审理**。——在指定转移日之前,国家信贷联盟署(或国家信贷联盟署委员会)提起的或他人针对其提起的,原来由国家信贷联盟署行使但按照本编规定转移至消费者金融保护局的与任何消费者金融保护职能相关的任何程序,均不得因本法的任何规定而终止,但是,自指定转移日起,消费者金融保护局应在不违反第1024条、第1025条和第1026条规定的前提下,替代国家信贷联盟署(或其委员会)担任该等程序的当事人。

(e)**货币监理署**。——

(1)**既存权利、职责和义务不受影响**。——联邦政府、货币监理署署长、货币监理署或任何其他主体的下述任何权利、职责或义务的有效性,一概不受第1061(b)(2)条影响——

(A)由于原来由货币监理署署长行使但按照本编规定转移至消费者金融保护局的与任何消费者金融保护职能相关的任何法律规定,所产生的权利、职责及义务;及

(B)在指定转移日前一天业已存在的权利、职责及义务。

(2)**原有案件继续审理**。——在指定转移日之前,货币监理署署长(或货币监理署)提起的或他人针对其提起的,原来由货币监理署署长行使但按照本编规定转移至消费者金融保护局的与消费者金融保护职能相关的任何程序,均不得因本法的任何规定而终止,但是,自指定转移日起,消费者金融保护局应在不违反第1024条、第1025条和第1026条规定的前提下,替代货币监理署署长(或货币监理署)担任该等程序的当事人。

(f)**储蓄机构监理局**。——

(1)**既存权利、职责和义务不受影响**。——联邦政府、储蓄机构监理局局长、储蓄机构监理局或任何其他主体的下述任何权利、职责或义务的有效性,一概不受第1061(b)(3)条影响——

(A)由于原来由储蓄机构监理局局长行使但按照本编规定转移至消费者金融保护局的与任何消费者金融保护职能相关的任何法律规定,所产生的权利、职责及义务;及

(B) that existed on the day before the designated transfer date.

(2) CONTINUATION OF SUITS. — No provision of this Act shall abate any proceeding commenced by or against the Director of the Office of Thrift Supervision (or the Office of Thrift Supervision) with respect to any consumer financial protection function of the Director of the Office of Thrift Supervision transferred to the Bureau by this title before the designated transfer date, except that the Bureau, subject to sections 1024, 1025, and 1026, shall be substituted for the Director (or the Office of Thrift Supervision) as a party to any such proceeding as of the designated transfer date.

(g) DEPARTMENT OF HOUSING AND URBAN DEVELOPMENT. —

(1) EXISTING RIGHTS, DUTIES, AND OBLIGATIONS NOT AFFECTED. — Section 1061(b)(7) shall not affect the validity of any right, duty, or obligation of the United States, the Secretary of the Department of Housing and Urban Development (or the Department of Housing and Urban Development), or any other person, that —

(A) arises under any provision of law relating to any function of the Secretary of the Department of Housing and Urban Development with respect to the Real Estate Settlement Procedures Act of 1974 (12 U.S.C. 2601 et seq.), the Secure and Fair Enforcement for Mortgage Licensing Act of 2008 (12 U.S.C. 5102 et seq.), or the Interstate Land Sales Full Disclosure Act (15 U.S.C. 1701 et seq) transferred to the Bureau by this title; and

(B) existed on the day before the designated transfer date.

(2) CONTINUATION OF SUITS. — This title shall not abate any proceeding commenced by or against the Secretary of the Department of Housing and Urban Development (or the Department of Housing and Urban Development) with respect to any consumer financial protection function of the Secretary of the Department of Housing and Urban Development transferred to the Bureau by this title before the designated transfer date, except that the Bureau, subject to sections 1024, 1025, and 1026, shall be substituted for the Secretary of the Department of Housing and Urban Development (or the Department of Housing and Urban Development) as a party to any such proceeding as of the designated transfer date.

(h) CONTINUATION OF EXISTING ORDERS, RULINGS, DETERMINATIONS, AGREEMENTS, AND RESOLUTIONS. —

(1) IN GENERAL. — Except as provided in paragraph (2) and under subsection (i), all orders, resolutions, determinations, agreements, and rulings that have been issued, made, prescribed, or allowed to become effective by any transferor agency or by a court of competent jurisdiction, in the performance of consumer financial protection functions that are transferred by this title and that are in effect on the day before the designated transfer date, shall continue in effect, and shall continue to be enforceable by the appropriate transferor agency, according to the terms of those orders, resolutions, determinations, agreements, and rulings, and shall

(B)在指定转移日前一天业已存在的权利、职责及义务。

(2)**原有案件继续审理**。——在指定转移日之前,储蓄机构监理局局长(或储蓄机构监理局)提起的或他人针对其提起的,原来由储蓄机构监理局局长行使但按照本编规定转移至消费者金融保护局的与消费者金融保护职能相关的任何程序,均不得因本法的任何规定而终止,但是,自指定转移日起,消费者金融保护局应在不违反第1024条、第1025条和第1026条规定的前提下,替代储蓄机构监理局局长(或储蓄机构监理局)担任该等程序的当事人。

(g)**住房与城市发展部**。——

(1)**既存权利、职责和义务不受影响**。——联邦政府、住房与城市发展部部长(或住房与城市发展部)或任何其他主体的下述任何权利、职责或义务的有效性,一概不受第1061(b)(7)条影响——

(A)由于原来由住房与城市发展部部长根据《1974年房地产结算程序法》(《美国法典》第十二编第2601节及其后条文)、《2008年安全和公平执行抵押贷款发起人许可法》(《美国法典》第十二编第5102节及其后条文)或《州际土地销售完全披露法》(《美国法典》第十五编第1701节及其后条文)行使但按照本编规定转移至消费者金融保护局的与任何消费者金融保护职能相关的任何法律规定,所产生的权利、职责及义务;及

(B)在指定转移日前一天业已存在的权利、职责及义务。

(2)**原有案件继续审理**。——在指定转移日之前,住房与城市发展部部长(或住房与城市发展部)提起的或他人针对其提起的,原来由住房与城市发展部部长行使但按照本编规定转移至消费者金融保护局的与消费者金融保护职能相关的任何程序,均不得因本法的任何规定而终止,但是,自指定转移日起,消费者金融保护局应在不违反第1024条、第1025条和第1026条规定的前提下,替代住房与城市发展部部长(或住房与城市发展部)担任该等程序的当事人。

(h)**既存命令、裁定、判定、协议和决议继续有效**。——

(1)**一般规定**。——除第(2)款和第(i)子条规定的情形外,职能转出机关或有管辖权的法院在履行按照本编规定转移的消费者金融保护职能的过程中签发、作出、规定或允许生效的,且在指定转移日前一天仍然有效适用的所有命令、决议、判定、协议和裁定,均应继续有效,并且应由相关的职能转出机关按照该等命令、决议、判定、协议和裁定的条款继续予以执行, 而不得由消费者金融保护局执行或针对消费者金融保护局执行。

not be enforceable by or against the Bureau.

(2) EXCEPTION FOR ORDERS APPLICABLE TO PERSONS DESCRIBED IN SECTION 1025 (a). — All orders, resolutions, determinations, agreements, and rulings that have been issued, made, prescribed, or allowed to become effective by any transferor agency or by a court of competent jurisdiction, in the performance of consumer financial protection functions that are transferred by this title and that are in effect on the day before the designated transfer date with respect to any person described in section 1025(a), shall continue in effect, according to the terms of those orders, resolutions, determinations, agreements, and rulings, and shall be enforceable by or against the Bureau or transferor agency.

(i) IDENTIFICATION OF RULES AND ORDERS CONTINUED. — Not later than the designated transfer date, the Bureau —

(1) shall, after consultation with the head of each transferor agency, identify the rules and orders that will be enforced by the Bureau; and

(2) shall publish a list of such rules and orders in the Federal Register.

(j) STATUS OF RULES PROPOSED OR NOT YET EFFECTIVE. —

(1) PROPOSED RULES. — Any proposed rule of a transferor agency which that agency, in performing consumer financial protection functions transferred by this title, has proposed before the designated transfer date, but has not been published as a final rule before that date, shall be deemed to be a proposed rule of the Bureau.

(2) RULES NOT YET EFFECTIVE. — Any interim or final rule of a transferor agency which that agency, in performing consumer financial protection functions transferred by this title, has published before the designated transfer date, but which has not become effective before that date, shall become effective as a rule of the Bureau according to its terms.

SEC. 1064. TRANSFER OF CERTAIN PERSONNEL.

(a) IN GENERAL. —

(1) CERTAIN FEDERAL RESERVE SYSTEM EMPLOYEES TRANSFERRED. —

(A) IDENTIFYING EMPLOYEES FOR TRANSFER. — The Bureau and the Board of Governors shall —

(i) jointly determine the number of employees of the Board of Governors necessary to perform or support the consumer financial protection functions of the Board of Governors that are transferred to the Bureau by this title; and

(ii) consistent with the number determined under clause (i), jointly identify employees of the Board of Governors for transfer to the Bureau, in a manner that the Bureau and the Board of Governors, in their sole discretion, determine equitable.

(B) IDENTIFIED EMPLOYEES TRANSFERRED. — All employees of the Board of Governors identified under subparagraph (A)(ii) shall be transferred to the Bureau for

(2)**关于适用于第1025(a)条所述主体的命令的例外规定**。——任何职能转出机关或有管辖权的法院,在履行按照本编规定转移的消费者金融保护职能的过程中,针对第1025(a)条所述主体签发、作出、规定或允许生效的且在指定转移日前一天仍然有效适用的所有命令、决议、判定、协议和裁定,均应按照其条款继续有效,并且应由消费者金融保护局或职能转出机关执行,或者针对消费者金融保护局或职能转出机关执行。

(i)**继续生效的规则与命令的梳理工作**。——消费者金融保护局应在指定转移日之前——

(1)与每一职能转出机关的负责人磋商,确定应由消费者金融保护局执行的规则和命令;及

(2)在《联邦公报》上公布有关该等规则和命令的清单。

(j)**规则草案或尚未生效规则的处理**。——

(1)**规则草案**。——职能转出机关在履行按照本编规定转移的消费者金融保护职能的过程中,于指定转移日之前提出的但在该日期之前尚未作为最终规则发布的任何规则草案,均应视为消费者金融保护局提出的规则草案。

(2)**尚未生效的规则**。——职能转出机关在履行按照本编规定转移的消费者金融保护职能的过程中,于指定转移日之前公布的但在该日期之前尚未生效的任何临时或最终规则,均应按照该规则的条款成为消费者金融保护局生效的规则。

第1064条　特定人员的转移

(a)**一般规定**。——

(1)**联邦储备系统特定雇员的转移**。——

(A)**确定转移雇员**。——消费者金融保护局应与联邦储备委员会——

(i)共同判定消费者金融保护局履行按照本编规定从联邦储备委员会向其转移的消费者金融保护职能或为消费者金融保护局履行该等职能提供支持, 所必需的联邦储备委员会雇员人数;及

(ii)按照根据第(i)项规定判定的人数,以消费者金融保护局和联邦储备委员会完全依其自由裁量权判定为公平的方式,共同确定需转移至消费者金融保护局的联邦储备委员会的具体雇员。

(B)**已确定的转移雇员**。——对于根据第(A)(ii)子款确定的所有联邦储备委员会雇员,其雇佣关系均应转移至消费者金融保护局。

employment.

(C) FEDERAL RESERVE BANK EMPLOYEES. — Employees of any Federal reserve bank who are performing consumer financial protection functions on behalf of the Board of Governors shall be treated as employees of the Board of Governors for purposes of subparagraphs (A) and (B).

(2) CERTAIN FDIC EMPLOYEES TRANSFERRED. —

(A) IDENTIFYING EMPLOYEES FOR TRANSFER. — The Bureau and the Board of Directors of the Federal Deposit Insurance Corporation shall —

(i) jointly determine the number of employees of that Corporation necessary to perform or support the consumer financial protection functions of the Corporation that are transferred to the Bureau by this title; and

(ii) consistent with the number determined under clause (i), jointly identify employees of the Corporation for transfer to the Bureau, in a manner that the Bureau and the Board of Directors of the Corporation, in their sole discretion, determine equitable.

(B) IDENTIFIED EMPLOYEES TRANSFERRED. — All employees of the Corporation identified under subparagraph (A)(ii) shall be transferred to the Bureau for employment.

(3) CERTAIN NCUA EMPLOYEES TRANSFERRED. —

(A) IDENTIFYING EMPLOYEES FOR TRANSFER. — The Bureau and the National Credit Union Administration Board shall —

(i) jointly determine the number of employees of the National Credit Union Administration necessary to perform or support the consumer financial protection functions of the National Credit Union Administration that are transferred to the Bureau by this title; and

(ii) consistent with the number determined under clause (i), jointly identify employees of the National Credit Union Administration for transfer to the Bureau, in a manner that the Bureau and the National Credit Union Administration Board, in their sole discretion, determine equitable.

(B) IDENTIFIED EMPLOYEES TRANSFERRED. — All employees of the National Credit Union Administration identified under subparagraph(A)(ii) shall be transferred to the Bureau for employment.

(4) CERTAIN OFFICE OF THE COMPTROLLER OF THE CURRENCY EMPLOYEES TRANSFERRED. —

(A) IDENTIFYING EMPLOYEES FOR TRANSFER. — The Bureau and the Comptroller of the Currency shall —

(i) jointly determine the number of employees of the Office of the Comptroller of the Currency necessary to perform or support the consumer financial protection functions of the Office of the Comptroller of the Currency that are transferred to the Bureau by this title; and

(ii) consistent with the number determined under clause (i), jointly identify employees

(C)**联邦储备银行雇员**。——就第(A)子款和第(B)子款而言,代表联邦储备委员会履行消费者金融保护职能的任何联邦储备银行的雇员,均应视为联邦储备委员会的雇员。

(2)**联邦存款保险公司特定雇员的转移**。——

(A)**确定转移雇员**。——消费者金融保护局应与联邦存款保险公司董事会——

(i)共同判定消费者金融保护局履行按照本编规定从联邦存款保险公司向其转移的消费者金融保护职能或为消费者金融保护局履行该等职能提供支持,所必需的联邦存款保险公司雇员人数;及

(ii)按照根据第(i)项规定判定的人数,以消费者金融保护局和联邦存款保险公司完全依其自由裁量权判定为公平的方式,共同确定需转移至消费者金融保护局的联邦存款保险公司的具体雇员。

(B)**已确定的转移雇员**。——对于根据第(A)(ii)子款确定的所有联邦存款保险公司雇员,其雇佣关系均应转移至消费者金融保护局。

(3)**国家信贷联盟署特定雇员的转移**。——

(A)**确定转移雇员**。——消费者金融保护局应与国家信贷联盟署委员会应——

(i)共同判定对消费者金融保护局确属必要的原国家信贷联盟署雇员人数,以便履行按照本编规定从国家信贷联盟署向其转移的消费者金融保护职能或为该等职能的履行提供支持;及

(ii)按照根据第(i)项规定判定的人数,以消费者金融保护局和国家信贷联盟署委员会完全依其自由裁量权判定为公平的方式,共同确定需转移至消费者金融保护局的国家信贷联盟署的具体雇员。

(B)**已确定的转移雇员**。——对于根据第(A)(ii)子款确定的所有国家信贷联盟署雇员,其雇佣关系均应转移至消费者金融保护局。

(4)**货币监理署特定雇员的转移**。——

(A)**确定转移雇员**。——消费者金融保护局应与货币监理署署长——

(i)共同判定消费者金融保护局履行按照本编规定从货币监理署向其转移的消费者金融保护职能或为消费者金融保护局履行该等职能提供支持,所必需的货币监理署雇员人数;及

(ii)按照根据第(i)项规定判定的人数,以消费者金融保护局和货币监理署依其自

of the Office of the Comptroller of the Currency for transfer to the Bureau, in a manner that the Bureau and the Office of the Comptroller of the Currency, in their sole discretion, determine equitable.

(B) IDENTIFIED EMPLOYEES TRANSFERRED. — All employees of the Office of the Comptroller of the Currency identified under subparagraph (A)(ii) shall be transferred to the Bureau for employment.

(5) CERTAIN OFFICE OF THRIFT SUPERVISION EMPLOYEES TRANSFERRED.—

(A) IDENTIFYING EMPLOYEES FOR TRANSFER. — The Bureau and the Director of the Office of Thrift Supervision shall —

(i) jointly determine the number of employees of the Office of Thrift Supervision necessary to perform or support the consumer financial protection functions of the Office of Thrift Supervision that are transferred to the Bureau by this title; and

(ii) consistent with the number determined under clause (i), jointly identify employees of the Office of Thrift Supervision for transfer to the Bureau, in a manner that the Bureau and the Office of Thrift Supervision, in their sole discretion, determine equitable.

(B) IDENTIFIED EMPLOYEES TRANSFERRED. — All employees of the Office of Thrift Supervision identified under subparagraph (A)(ii) shall be transferred to the Bureau for employment.

(6) CERTAIN EMPLOYEES OF DEPARTMENT OF HOUSING AND URBAN DEVELOPMENT TRANSFERRED. —

(A) IDENTIFYING EMPLOYEES FOR TRANSFER. — The Bureau and the Secretary of the Department of Housing and Urban Development shall —

(i) jointly determine the number of employees of the Department of Housing and Urban Development necessary to perform or support the consumer protection functions of the Department that are transferred to the Bureau by this title; and

(ii) consistent with the number determined under clause (i), jointly identify employees of the Department of Housing and Urban Development for transfer to the Bureau in a manner that the Bureau and the Secretary of the Department of Housing and Urban Development, in their sole discretion, deem equitable.

(B) IDENTIFIED EMPLOYEES TRANSFERRED. — All employees of the Department of Housing and Urban Development identified under subparagraph (A)(ii) shall be transferred to the Bureau for employment.

(7) CONSUMER EDUCATION, FINANCIAL LITERACY, CONSUMER COMPLAINTS, AND RESEARCH FUNCTIONS. — The Bureau and each of the transferor agencies (except the Federal Trade Commission) shall jointly determine the number of employees and the types and grades of employees necessary to perform the functions of the Bureau under subtitle A, including consumer education, financial literacy, policy analysis,

由裁量权判定为公平的方式,共同确定需转移至消费者金融保护局的货币监理署的具体雇员。

(B)**已确定的转移雇员**。——对于根据第(A)(ii)子款确定的所有货币监理署雇员,其雇佣关系均应转移至消费者金融保护局。

(5)**储蓄机构监理局特定雇员的转移**。——

(A)**确定转移雇员**。——消费者金融保护局应与储蓄机构监理局局长——

(i)共同判定消费者金融保护局履行按照本编规定从储蓄机构监理局向其转移的消费者金融保护职能或为消费者金融保护局履行该等职能提供支持,所必需的储蓄机构监理局雇员人数;及

(ii)按照根据第(i)项规定判定的人数,以消费者金融保护局和储蓄机构监理局依其自由裁量权判定为公平的方式,共同确定需转移至消费者金融保护局的储蓄机构监理局的具体雇员。

(B)**已确定的转移雇员**。——对于根据第(A)(ii)子款规定确定的所有储蓄机构监理局雇员,其雇佣关系均应转移至消费者金融保护局。

(6)**住房与城市发展部特定雇员的转移**。——

(A)**确定转移雇员**。——消费者金融保护局应与住房与城市发展部部长——

(i)共同判定消费者金融保护局履行按照本编规定从住房与城市发展部向其转移的消费者金融保护职能或为消费者金融保护局履行该等职能提供支持,所必需的住房与城市发展部雇员人数;及

(ii)按照根据第(i)项规定判定的人数,以消费者金融保护局和住房与城市发展部依其自由裁量权判定为公平的方式,共同确定需转移至消费者金融保护局的住房与城市发展部的具体雇员。

(B)**已确定的转移雇员**。——对于根据第(A)(ii)子款规定确定的所有住房与城市发展部雇员,其雇佣关系均应转移至消费者金融保护局。

(7)**消费者教育、金融扫盲、消费者投诉以及研究职能**。——消费者金融保护局应与各职能转出机关(但联邦贸易委员会除外)共同判定消费者金融保护局履行第A子编规定的职能(包括消费者教育、金融扫盲、政策分析、消费者投诉回应及咨询、研究以及类似职能)所需的雇员人数、类型和级别。对于消费者金融保护局与职能转出机关根据本款规定共同确定的所有雇员,其雇佣关系均应转移至消费者金融保护局。

responses to consumer complaints and inquiries, research, and similar functions. All employees jointly identified under this paragraph shall be transferred to the Bureau for employment.

(8) AUTHORITY OF THE PRESIDENT TO RESOLVE DISPUTES.—

(A) ACTION AUTHORIZED.— In the event that the Bureau and a transferor agency are unable to reach an agreement under paragraphs (1) through (7) by the designated transfer date, the President, or the designee thereof, may issue an order or directive to the transferor agency to effect the transfer of personnel and property under this subtitle.

(B) TRANSMITTAL TO CONGRESS REQUIRED.— If an order or directive is issued under subparagraph (A), the President shall transmit a copy of the written determination made with respect to such order or directive, including an explanation for the need for the order or directive, to the Committee on Banking, Housing, and Urban Affairs and the Committee on Appropriations of the Senate and the Committee on Financial Services and the Committee on Appropriations of the House of Representatives.

(C) SUNSET.— The authority provided in this paragraph shall terminate 3 years after the designated transfer date.

(9) APPOINTMENT AUTHORITY FOR EXCEPTED SERVICE AND SENIOR EXECUTIVE SERVICE TRANSFERRED.—

(A) IN GENERAL.— In the case of an employee occupying a position in the excepted service or the Senior Executive Service, any appointment authority established pursuant to law or regulations of the Office of Personnel Management for filling such positions shall be transferred, subject to subparagraph (B).

(B) DECLINING TRANSFERS ALLOWED.— An agency or entity may decline to make a transfer of authority under subparagraph (A) (and the employees appointed pursuant thereto) to the extent that such authority relates to positions excepted from the competitive service because of their confidential, policy-making, policy-determining, or policy-advocating character, and non-career positions in the Senior Executive Service (within the meaning of section 3132(a)(7) of title 5, United States Code).

(b) TIMING OF TRANSFERS AND POSITION ASSIGNMENTS.— Each employee to be transferred under this section shall—

(1) be transferred not later than 90 days after the designated transfer date; and

(2) receive notice of a position assignment not later than 120 days after the effective date of his or her transfer.

(c) TRANSFER OF FUNCTION.—

(1) IN GENERAL.— Notwithstanding any other provision of law, the transfer of employees shall be deemed a transfer of functions for the purpose of section 3503 of title 5, United States Code.

(8)**总统解决争议的权限**。——

(A)**授权行动**。——如果消费者金融保护局与职能转出机关无法按照第(1)款至第(7)款的规定在指定转移日之前达成协议,总统或其指定人员可以向职能转出机关下达按照本子编规定转移人员和财产的命令或指令。

(B)**向国会发送文件的要求**。——总统按照第(A)子款的规定下达命令或指令的,应向参议院银行、住房与城市事务委员会、参议院拨款委员会、众议院金融服务委员会以及众议院拨款委员会发送一份关于该命令或指令的书面判定,包括关于有必要下达该命令或指令的说明。

(C)**日落条款**。——本款规定的权力于指定转移日之后届满3年之日终止。

(9)**特招公务员和高级公务员任命权的转移**。——

(A)**一般规定**。——如果雇员属于特招公务员或高级公务员,则在不违反第(B)子款规定的前提下,法律或人事管理局的规章为该职位设立的任命权应予以转移。

(B)**允许拒绝转移**。——如果某一职位因具有保密性政策制定、确定,或倡导职能,而未采用竞聘流程,直接进行特招,且属于高级公务员中的破格任命职位[定义见《美国法典》第五编第3132(a)(7)节],则享有该等职位的任命权的机关或实体可以拒绝按照第(A)子款的规定转移任命权(并可以拒绝转移根据该任命权任命的雇员)。

(b)**转移时间与岗位安排**。——依据本条规定转移的每名雇员均应——

(1)在指定转移日后90天内转移;并

(2)在其转移生效日后120天内收到岗位安排通知。

(c)**职能转移**。——

(1)**一般规定**。——无论是否存在任何不同法律规定,雇员转移均应视为《美国法典》第五编第3503节规定的职能转移。

(2) PRIORITY OF THIS TITLE. — If any provisions of this title conflict with any protection provided to transferred employees under section 3503 of title 5, United States Code, the provisions of this title shall control.

(d) EQUAL STATUS AND TENURE POSITIONS. —

(1) EMPLOYEES TRANSFERRED FROM THE FEDERAL RESERVE SYSTEM, FDIC, HUD, NCUA, OCC, AND OTS. — Each employee transferred to the Bureau from the Board of Governors, a Federal reserve bank, the Federal Deposit Insurance Corporation, the Department of Housing and Urban Development, the National Credit Union Administration, the Office of the Comptroller of the Currency, or the Office of Thrift Supervision shall be placed in a position at the Bureau with the same status and tenure as that employee held on the day before the designated transfer date.

(2) EMPLOYEES TRANSFERRED FROM THE FEDERAL RESERVE SYSTEM. — For purposes of determining the status and position placement of a transferred employee, any period of service with the Board of Governors or a Federal reserve bank shall be credited as a period of service with a Federal agency.

(e) ADDITIONAL CERTIFICATION REQUIREMENTS LIMITED. — Examiners transferred to the Bureau are not subject to any additional certification requirements before being placed in a comparable examiner position at the Bureau examining the same types of institutions as they examined before they were transferred.

(f) PERSONNEL ACTIONS LIMITED. —

(1) 2-YEAR PROTECTION. — Except as provided in paragraph (2), each transferred employee holding a permanent position on the day before the designated transfer date may not, during the 2-year period beginning on the designated transfer date, be involuntarily separated, or involuntarily reassigned outside his or her locality pay area.

(2) EXCEPTIONS. — Paragraph (1) does not limit the right of the Bureau —

(A) to separate an employee for cause or for unacceptable performance;

(B) to terminate an appointment to a position excepted from the competitive service because of its confidential policy-making, policy-determining, or policy-advocating character; or

(C) to reassign a supervisory employee outside of his or her locality pay area when the Bureau determines that the reassignment is necessary for the efficient operation of the Bureau.

(g) PAY. —

(1) 2-YEAR PROTECTION. —

(A) IN GENERAL. — Except as provided in paragraph (2), each transferred employee shall, during the 2-year period beginning on the designated transfer date, receive pay at a rate equal to not less than the basic rate of pay (including any geographic differential) that the

(2)**本编规定的优先性**。——本编的任何规定与《美国法典》第五编第3503节关于转移雇员的任何保护性规定相冲突的,以本编规定为准。

(d)**同等待遇与任职期限**。——

(1)**自联邦储备系统、联邦存款保险公司、住房与城市发展部、国家信贷联盟署、货币监理署和储蓄机构监理局转移的雇员**。——对于从联邦储备委员会、联邦储备银行、联邦存款保险公司、住房与城市发展部、国家信贷联盟署、货币监理署或储蓄机构监理局转移至消费者金融保护局的雇员，其在消费者金融保护局担任的职位应与其在指定转移日之前担任的职位享有同等待遇,并适用同等的任职期限。

(2)**自联邦储备系统转移的雇员**。——在确定转移雇员的待遇和职位安排之时,转移雇员在联邦储备委员会或联邦储备银行工作期间的工龄应计入在联邦机关工作的工龄。

(e)**限制额外认证要求**。——转移雇员如果是检查人员,且该检查人员转移前负责检查的机构类型与转移后在消费者金融保护局工作时负责检查的机构类型并无二致,则消费者金融保护局在安排其从事该等职位之时,不得向其施加任何额外认证要求。

(f)**限制人事行动**。——

(1)**2年保护期**。——除第(2)款规定的情形外,对于在指定转移日前一天担任正式职位的转移雇员,自指定转移日起两年内,不得违背转移雇员的意愿将其解聘或派往其工资分区以外的地区。

(2)**例外规定**。——消费者金融保护局采取如下行动的权利不受第(1)款规定限制——

(A)出于正当理由或由于雇员绩效欠理想而解聘雇员;

(B)终止对具有保密性,或承担政策制定、确定或倡导性质的特招职位的任命;或

(C)消费者金融保护局判定作出重新派遣安排对于保证消费者金融保护局的有效运作确属必要之时,将雇员派往工资分区以外的地区工作。

(g)**工资**。——

(1)**2年保护期**。——

(A)**一般规定**。——除第(2)款规定的情形外,转移雇员的工资自指定转移日起2年内不得低于其在转移日之前最近一个付薪期内获得的基本工资(含任何地区工资级差)。

employee received during the pay period immediately preceding the date of transfer.

(B) LIMITATION. — Notwithstanding subparagraph(A), if the employee was receiving a higher rate of basic pay on a temporary basis(because of a temporary assignment, temporary promotion, or other temporary action) immediately before the date of transfer, the Bureau may reduce the rate of basic pay on the date on which the rate would have been reduced but for the transfer, and the protected rate for the remainder of the 2–year period shall be the reduced rate that would have applied, but for the transfer.

(2) EXCEPTIONS. — Paragraph (1) does not limit the right of the Bureau to reduce the rate of basic pay of a transferred employee —

(A) for cause;

(B) for unacceptable performance; or

(C) with the consent of the employee.

(3) PROTECTION ONLY WHILE EMPLOYED. — Paragraph (1) applies to a transferred employee only while that employee remains employed by the Bureau.

(4) PAY INCREASES PERMITTED. — Paragraph (1) does not limit the authority of the Bureau to increase the pay of a transferred employee.

(h) REORGANIZATION. —

(1) BETWEEN 1ST AND 3RD YEAR. —

(A) IN GENERAL. — If the Bureau determines, during the 2–year period beginning 1 year after the designated transfer date, that a reorganization of the staff of the Bureau is required —

(i) that reorganization shall be deemed a "substantial reorganization" for purposes of affording affected employees retirement under section 8336(d)(2) or 8414 (b)(1)(B) of title 5, United States Code;

(ii) before the reorganization occurs, all employees in the same locality pay area as defined by the Office of Personnel Management shall be placed in a uniform position classification system; and

(iii) any resulting reduction in force shall be governed by the provisions of chapter 35 of title 5, United States Code, except that the Bureau shall —

(I) establish competitive areas (as that term is defined in regulations issued by the Office of Personnel Management) to include at a minimum all employees in the same locality pay area as defined by the Office of Personnel Management;

(II) establish competitive levels (as that term is defined in regulations issued by the Office of Personnel Management) without regard to whether the particular employees have been appointed to positions in the competitive service or the excepted service; and

(III) afford employees appointed to positions in the excepted service (other than to a position excepted from the competitive service because of its confidential policy–making,

(B)**限制**。——无论第(A)子款如何规定,如果转移雇员在转移日前领取的是临时性的较高基本工资(例如,因临时派遣、临时升职或其他临时行动而获得较高基本工资),则自该转移雇员即使不转移也会下调工资之日起,消费者金融保护局可将其基本工资相应下调,而在两年保护期的剩余期限内,该雇员的保护工资标准应为该转移雇员即使不转移也将下调的工资水平。

(2)**例外规定**。——消费者金融保护局基于下列原因下调转移雇员基本工资的权利不受第(1)款规定限制——

(A)存在正当理由;

(B)雇员工作绩效欠理想;或

(C)经雇员同意。

(3)**保护规定仅限于雇佣关系存续期间**。——第(1)款的规定仅适用于转移雇员继续供职于消费者金融保护局的期间。

(4)**允许提高工资**。——第(1)款规定对消费者金融保护局提高转移雇员工资的权力不构成限制。

(h)**重组**。——

(1)**转移日后第1年至第3年进行的重组**。——

(A)**一般规定**。——如果在自指定转移日届满1年之日起2年内,消费者金融保护局判定应对其工作人员进行重组,则——

(i)就根据《美国法典》第五编第8336(d)(2)节或第8414(b)(1)(B)节为受影响雇员提供的退休保障而言,该重组应视为"重大重组";

(ii)重组开始之前,位于人事管理局界定的同一工资分区之内的所有雇员,均应按照统一的职位分类制度确定其职务级别;且

(iii)由此作出的任何裁员均应遵循《美国法典》第五编第三十五章的规定,但是消费者金融保护局应——

(I)确定竞聘区域(定义见人事管理局颁布的规章),且该区域至少应涵盖人事管理局界定的同一工资分区之内的所有雇员;

(II)设定竞聘等级(定义见人事管理局颁布的规章),在设定竞聘等级之时,不考虑特定雇员是否曾被任命担任竞聘性职位或特招公务员职位;并

(III)向接受任命担任特招公务员职位(但因具有保密性,或具有政策制定、确定或倡导性质而特招的岗位除外)的雇员赋予与接受任命担任竞聘性职位的雇员相同

policy–determining, or policy–advocating character) the same assignment rights to positions within the Bureau as employees appointed to positions in the competitive service.

(B) SERVICE CREDIT FOR REDUCTIONS IN FORCE. — For purposes of this paragraph, periods of service with a Federal home loan bank, a joint office of the Federal home loan banks, the Board of Governors, a Federal reserve bank, the Federal Deposit Insurance Corporation, or the National Credit Union Administration shall be credited as periods of service with a Federal agency.

(2) AFTER 3RD YEAR. —

(A) IN GENERAL. — If the Bureau determines, at any time after the 3–year period beginning on the designated transfer date, that a reorganization of the staff of the Bureau is required, any resulting reduction in force shall be governed by the provisions of chapter 35 of title 5, United States Code, except that the Bureau shall establish competitive levels (as that term is defined in regulations issued by the Office of Personnel Management) without regard to types of appointment held by particular employees transferred under this section.

(B) SERVICE CREDIT FOR REDUCTIONS IN FORCE. — For purposes of this paragraph, periods of service with a Federal home loan bank, a joint office of the Federal home loan banks, the Board of Governors, a Federal reserve bank, the Federal Deposit Insurance Corporation, or the National Credit Union Administration shall be credited as periods of service with a Federal agency.

(i) BENEFITS. —

(1) RETIREMENT BENEFITS FOR TRANSFERRED EMPLOYEES. —

(A) IN GENERAL. —

(i) CONTINUATION OF EXISTING RETIREMENT PLAN. — Unless an election is made under clause (iii) or subparagraph (B), each employee transferred pursuant to this subtitle shall remain enrolled in the existing retirement plan of that employee as of the date of transfer, through any period of continuous employment with the Bureau.

(ii) EMPLOYER CONTRIBUTION. — The Bureau shall pay any employer contributions to the existing retirement plan of each transferred employee, as required under that plan.

(iii) OPTION TO ELECT INTO THE FEDERAL RESERVE SYSTEM RETIREMENT PLAN AND FEDERAL RESERVE SYSTEM THRIFT PLAN. — Any employee transferred pursuant to this subtitle may, during the 1–year period beginning 6 months after the designated transfer date, elect to end their participation and benefit accruals under their existing retirement plan or plans and elect to participate in both the Federal Reserve System Retirement Plan and the Federal Reserve System Thrift Plan, through any period of continuous employment with the Bureau, under the same terms as are applicable to Federal Reserve System transferred employees, as provided in subparagraph (C). An election of

的担任消费者金融保护局内部其他职位的权利。

(B)**被裁雇员的工龄**。——就本款而言,在联邦住房贷款银行、联邦住房贷款银行联合办公室、联邦储备委员会、联邦储备银行、联邦存款保险公司或国家信贷联盟署工作期间的工龄应计入在联邦机关工作的工龄。

(2)**转移日第3年之后进行的重组**。——

(A)**一般规定**。——如果在指定转移日起届满三年之后的任何时候,消费者金融保护局判定有必要对其工作人员进行重组,由此进行的任何裁员均应遵循《美国法典》第五编第三十五章的规定,但是,消费者金融保护局应设定竞聘等级(定义见人事管理局颁布的规章),且在设定竞聘等级之时,不考虑根据本条规定转移的特定雇员所担任的职位类型。

(B)**被裁雇员的工龄**。——就本款而言,在联邦住房贷款银行、联邦住房贷款银行联合办公室、联邦储备委员会、联邦储备银行、联邦存款保险公司、国家信贷联盟署工作期间的工龄应计入在联邦机关工作的工龄。

(i)**福利**。——

(1)**转移雇员的退休福利**。——

(A)**一般规定**。——

(i)**既存退休计划继续实施**。——除非按照本子编规定转移的雇员已依据第(iii)项或第(B)子款规定作出选择,否则转移雇员在消费者金融保护局工作期间,应继续参与截至转移日其已经参与的既存退休计划。

(ii)**雇主缴款**。——消费者金融保护局应按照每名转移雇员参与的既存退休计划的要求向该计划缴纳雇主缴款。

(iii)**参与联邦储备系统退休计划和联邦储备系统节俭计划的选择权**。——在自指定转移日届满6个月之日起1年内,根据本子编规定转移的任何雇员均可以选择不再参与既存退休计划并终止其在该等计划中的应计福利,并选择按照第(C)子款规定的适用于联邦储备系统转移雇员的条款,在其持续供职于消费者金融保护局期间,同时参与联邦储备系统退休计划和联邦储备系统节俭计划。转移雇员选择参与联邦储备系统退休计划和联邦储备系统节俭计划的,应自指定转移日起届满18个月之日的次日开始加入这两项计划,其在既存退休计划中的应计福利应自指定转移日届满起18个月之日终止。雇员选择同时参与联邦储备系统退休计划和联邦储备系统节俭计

coverage by the Federal Reserve System Retirement Plan and the Federal Reserve System Thrift Plan shall begin on the day following the end of the 18–month period beginning on the designated transfer date, and benefit accruals under the existing retirement plan of the transferred employee shall end on the last day of the 18–month period beginning on the designated transfer date If an employee elects to participate in the Federal Reserve System Retirement Plan and the Federal Reserve System Thrift Plan, all of the service of the employee that was creditable under their existing retirement plan shall be transferred to the Federal Reserve System Retirement Plan on the day following the end of the 18–month period beginning on the designated transfer date.

(iv) BUREAU CONTRIBUTION. — The Bureau shall pay an employer contribution to the Federal Reserve System Retirement Plan, in the amount established as an employer contribution under the Federal Employees Retirement System, as established under chapter 84 of title 5, United States Code, for each Bureau employee who elects to participate in the Federal Reserve System Retirement Plan under this subparagraph. The Bureau shall pay an employer contribution to the Federal Reserve System Thrift Plan for each Bureau employee who elects to participate in such plan, as required under the terms of the Federal Reserve System Thrift Plan.

(v) ADDITIONAL FUNDING. — The Bureau shall transfer to the Federal Reserve System Retirement Plan an amount determined by the Board of Governors, in consultation with the Bureau, to be necessary to reimburse the Federal Reserve System Retirement Plan for the costs to such plan of providing benefits to employees electing coverage under the Federal Reserve System Retirement Plan under subparagraph (iii), and who were transferred to the Bureau from outside of the Federal Reserve System.

(vi) OPTION TO ELECT INTO THRIFT PLAN CREATED BY THE BUREAU. — If the Bureau chooses to establish a thrift plan, the employees transferred pursuant to this subtitle shall have the option to elect, under such terms and conditions as the Bureau may establish, coverage under such a thrift plan established by the Bureau. Transferred employees may not remain in the thrift plan of the agency from which the employee transferred under this subtitle, if the employee elects to participate in a thrift plan established by the Bureau.

(B) OPTION FOR EMPLOYEES TRANSFERRED FROM FEDERAL RESERVE SYSTEM TO BE SUBJECT TO THE FEDERAL EMPLOYEE RETIREMENT PROGRAM. —

(i) ELECTION. — Any Federal Reserve System transferred employee who was enrolled in the Federal Reserve System Retirement Plan on the day before the date of his or her transfer to the Bureau may, during the 1–year period beginning 6 months after the designated transfer date, elect to be subject to the Federal Employee Retirement Program.

(ii) EFFECTIVE DATE OF COVERAGE. — An election of coverage by the Federal Employee Retirement Program under this subparagraph shall begin on the day following the

划的,自指定转移日起届满18个月之日的次日,该雇员在既存退休计划中可予承认的所有工龄均应转至联邦储备系统退休计划。

(iv)**消费者金融保护局缴款**。——消费者金融保护局应按照《美国法典》第五编第八十四章规定的联邦雇员退休制度中的雇主缴费金额,为根据本子款规定选择参与联邦储备系统退休计划的消费者金融保护局的每一雇员向联邦储备系统退休计划缴纳雇主缴款。消费者金融保护局应按照联邦储备系统节俭计划条款的要求,为选择参与联邦储备系统节俭计划的消费者金融保护局雇员向该计划缴纳雇主缴款。

(v)**补充经费**。——对于从联邦储备系统以外转移至消费者金融保护局,并按照第(iii)项[1]规定选择参与联邦储备系统退休计划的雇员,消费者金融保护局应按照联邦储备委员会与其磋商确定的必要金额,向该计划划拨相应款项,以补偿联邦储备系统退休计划因向该等雇员提供福利而产生的费用。

(vi)**参与消费者金融保护局设立的节俭计划的选择权**。——如果消费者金融保护局选择设立节俭计划,按照本子编规定转移的雇员有权按照消费者金融保护局规定的条款和条件,选择参与该计划。按照本子编规定转移的雇员选择参与消费者金融保护局设立的节俭计划的,不得继续参与职能转出机关的节俭计划。

(B)**原联邦储备系统雇员参与联邦雇员退休计划的选择权**。——

(i)**选择**。——任何原联邦储备系统雇员在其转移至消费者金融保护局之日的前1天具有联邦储备系统退休计划的参与人员身份的,均可以在自指定转移日届满6个月之日起1年内,选择参与联邦雇员退休计划。

(ii)**参与计划的生效日**。——联邦储备系统转移雇员选择按照本子款规定参与

1 第1064(i)(1)(A)(v)条中的subparagraph(iii),按上文,似应为“项”,而非“子款”,译文已按“项”处理。——译者注

end of the 18–month period beginning on the designated transfer date, and benefit accruals under the existing retirement plan of the Federal Reserve System transferred employee shall end on the last day of the 18–month period beginning on the designated transfer date.

(C) BUREAU PARTICIPATION IN FEDERAL RESERVE SYSTEM RETIREMENT PLAN. —

(i) BENEFITS PROVIDED. — Federal Reserve System employees transferred pursuant to this subtitle shall continue to be eligible to participate in the Federal Reserve System Retirement Plan and Federal Reserve System Thrift Plan through any period of continuous employment with the Bureau, unless the employee makes an election under subparagraph (A)(vi) or (B). The retirement benefits, formulas, and features offered to the Federal Reserve System transferred employees shall be the same as those offered to employees of the Board of Governors who participate in the Federal Reserve System Retirement Plan and the Federal Reserve System Thrift Plan, as amended from time to time.

(ii) LIMITATION. — The Bureau shall not have responsibility or authority —

(I) to amend an existing retirement plan (including the Federal Reserve System Retirement Plan or Federal Reserve System Thrift Plan);

(II) for administering an existing retirement plan (including the Federal Reserve System Retirement Plan or Federal Reserve System Thrift Plan); or

(III) for ensuring the plans comply with applicable laws, fiduciary rules, and related responsibilities.

(iii) TAX QUALIFIED STATUS. — Notwithstanding any other provision of law, providing benefits to Federal Reserve System employees transferred to the Bureau pursuant to this subtitle, and to employees who elect coverage pursuant to subparagraph (A)(iii) or under section 1013(a)(2)(B), shall not cause any existing retirement plan (including the Federal Reserve System Retirement Plan and the Federal Reserve System Thrift Plan) to lose its tax–qualified status under sections 401(a) and 501(a) of the Internal Revenue Code of 1986.

(iv) BUREAU CONTRIBUTION. — The Bureau shall pay any employer contributions to the existing retirement plan (including the Federal Reserve System Retirement Plan and the Federal Reserve System Thrift Plan) for each Federal Reserve System transferred employee participating in those plans, as required under the plan, after the designated transfer date.

(v) CONTROLLED GROUP STATUS. — The Bureau is the same employer as the Federal Reserve System (as comprised of the Board of Governors and each of the 12 Federal reserve banks prior to the date of enactment of this Act) for purposes of subsections (b), (c), (m), and (o) of section 414 of the Internal Revenue Code of 1986 (26 U.S.C. 414).

(D) DEFINITIONS. — For purposes of this paragraph —

联邦雇员退休计划的,应自指定转移日起届满18个月之日的次日开始加入该计划,其在既存退休计划中的应计福利应自指定转移日起届满18个月之日终止。

(C)**消费者金融保护局对联邦储备系统退休计划的参与**。——

(i)**提供的福利**。——按照本子编规定转移的联邦储备系统雇员,除非已根据第(A)(vi)子款或第(B)子款规定作出选择,否则,其有资格在持续供职于消费者金融保护局期间,继续参与联邦储备系统退休计划和联邦储备系统节俭计划。向联邦储备系统转移雇员提供的退休福利、计算方案和条件,应与向参与联邦储备系统退休计划和联邦储备系统节俭计划(以不时修正的版本为准)的联邦储备委员会雇员提供的福利、计算方案和条件相同。

(ii)**限制**。——消费者金融保护局没有责任,亦无权——

(I)修正既存退休计划(包括联邦储备系统退休计划或联邦储备系统节俭计划);

(II)管理既存退休计划(包括联邦储备系统退休计划或联邦储备系统节俭计划);或

(III)确保计划符合适用的法律、受信规则并承担相关责任。

(iii)**税惠资格**。——无论是否存在任何不同法律规定,在向按照本子编规定转移至消费者金融保护局的联邦储备系统雇员以及按照第(A)(iii)子款或第1013(a)(2)(B)条规定选择参与相关计划的雇员提供福利时,既存退休计划(包括联邦储备系统退休计划和联邦储备系统节俭计划)不得因此丧失其依据《1986年国内税收法典》第401(a)条和第501(a)条享有的税惠资格。

(iv)**消费者金融保护局的缴款**。——对于参与既存退休计划(包括联邦储备系统退休计划和联邦储备系统节俭计划)的每一联邦储备系统转移雇员,消费者金融保护局应在指定转移日之后,按照该等计划的要求向该计划缴纳雇主缴款。

(v)**受控集团地位**。——就《1986年国内税收法典》第414条(《美国法典》第二十六编第414节)第(b)子条、第(c)子条、第(m)子条和第(o)子条而言,消费者金融保护局与联邦储备系统(由联邦储备委员会以及本法颁布之日前的12家联邦储备银行组成)属于同一雇主。

(D)**定义**。——就本款而言——

(i) the term "existing retirement plan" means, with respect to an employee transferred pursuant to this subtitle, the retirement plan (including the Financial Institutions Retirement Fund) and any associated thrift savings plan, of the agency from which the employee was transferred under this subtitle, in which the employee was enrolled on the day before the date on which the employee was transferred;

(ii) the term "Federal Employee Retirement Program" means either the Civil Service Retirement System established under chapter 83 of title 5, United States Code, or the Federal Employees Retirement System established under chapter 84 of title 5, United States Code, depending upon the service history of the individual;

(iii) the term "Federal Reserve System transferred employee" means a transferred employee who is an employee of the Board of Governors or a Federal reserve bank on the day before the designated transfer date, and who is transferred to the Bureau on the designated transfer date pursuant to this subtitle;

(iv) the term "Federal Reserve System Retirement Plan" means the Retirement Plan for Employees of the Federal Reserve System; and

(v) the term "Federal Reserve System Thrift Plan" means the Thrift Plan for Employees of the Federal Reserve System.

(2) BENEFITS OTHER THAN RETIREMENT BENEFITS FOR TRANSFERRED EMPLOYEES. —

(A) DURING 1ST YEAR. —

(i) EXISTING PLANS CONTINUE. — Each employee transferred pursuant to this subtitle may, for 1 year after the designated transfer date, retain membership in any other employee benefit program of the agency or bank from which the employee transferred, including a medical, dental, vision, long term care, or life insurance program, to which the employee belonged on the day before the designated transfer date.

(ii) EMPLOYER CONTRIBUTION. — The Bureau shall reimburse the agency or bank from which an employee was transferred for any cost incurred by that agency or bank in continuing to extend coverage in the benefit program to the employee, as required under that program or negotiated agreements.

(B) MEDICAL, DENTAL, VISION, OR LIFE INSURANCE AFTER FIRST YEAR. — If, at the end of the 1–year period beginning on the designated transfer date, the Bureau has not established its own, or arranged for participation in another entity's, medical, dental, vision, or life insurance program, an employee transferred pursuant to this subtitle who was a member of such a program at the agency or Federal reserve bank from which the employee transferred may, before the coverage of that employee ends under subparagraph (A)(i), elect to enroll, without regard to any regularly scheduled open season, in —

(i) the enhanced dental benefits program established under chapter 89A of title 5,

(i)"既存退休计划"一词,对于按照本子编规定转移的雇员而言,系指该转移雇员在转移日前一天,已经参与的职能转出机关的退休计划(包括金融机构退休基金)以及任何相关的节俭计划;

(ii)"联邦雇员退休计划"一词系指依据《美国法典》第五编第八十三章设立的公务员退休制度或依据《美国法典》第五编第八十四章设立的联邦雇员退休制度,具体视个人的工作经历而定。

(iii)"联邦储备系统转移雇员" 一词系指在指定转移日前一天在联邦储备委员会或联邦储备银行供职, 并按照本子编规定于指定转移日转移至消费者金融保护局的雇员。

(iv)"联邦储备系统退休计划"一词系指联邦储蓄系统雇员退休计划;及

(v)"联邦储备系统节俭计划"一词系指联邦储蓄系统雇员节俭计划。

(2)**转移雇员退休福利以外的福利**。——

(A)**第1年**。——

(i)**继续参与既存计划**。——在指定转移日后1年之内,按照本子编规定转移的雇员可以继续参与其在指定转移日前一天已经参与的职能转出机关或银行的任何其他雇员福利计划,包括医疗保险计划、牙医保险计划、眼科保险计划、长期医疗保险计划或寿险计划。

(ii)**雇主缴款**。——对于转移雇员的职能转出机关或银行按照相关福利计划的要求或按照磋商达成的协议的要求,继续向转移雇员提供计划保障所发生的费用,消费者金融保护局应向该转移雇员的职能转出机关或银行进行补偿。

(B)**第1年期限届满之后的医疗保险、牙医保险、眼科保险或寿险**。——如果在自指定转移日起届满1年之时,消费者金融保护局尚未设立自身的医疗保险计划、牙医保险计划、眼科保险计划或寿险计划,也未安排雇员参与其他实体的医疗保险计划、牙医保险计划、眼科保险计划或寿险计划,而按照本子编规定转移的雇员在其原供职的机关或联邦储备银行已经参与了该等计划,该雇员可以在第(A)(i)子款提供的保障终止之前,选择参与下列计划,而不受该等计划的常规开放时间表限制——

(i)按照《美国法典》第五编第八十九A章设立的升级版牙医福利计划;

United States Code;

(ii) the enhanced vision benefits established under chapter 89B of title 5, United States Code;

(iii) the Federal Employees Group Life Insurance Program established under chapter 87 of title 5, United States Code, without regard to any requirement of insurability; and

(iv) the Federal Employees Health Benefits Program established under chapter 89 of title 5, United States Code.

(C) LONG TERM CARE INSURANCE AFTER 1ST YEAR. — If, at the end of the 1-year period beginning on the designated transfer date, the Bureau has not established its own, or arranged for participation in another entity's, long term care insurance program, an employee transferred pursuant to this subtitle who was a member of such a program at the agency or Federal reserve bank from which the employee transferred may, before the coverage of that employee ends under subparagraph (A)(i), elect to apply for coverage under the Federal Long Term Care Insurance Program established under chapter 90 of title 5, United States Code, under the underwriting requirements applicable to a new active workforce member (as defined in part 875 of title 5, Code of Federal Regulations).

(D) EMPLOYEE CONTRIBUTION. — An individual enrolled in the Federal Employees Health Benefits program shall pay any employee contribution required by the plan.

(E) ADDITIONAL FUNDING. — The Bureau shall transfer to the Federal Employees Health Benefits Fund established under section 8909 of title 5, United States Code, an amount determined by the Director of the Office of Personnel Management, after consultation with the Bureau and the Office of Management and Budget, to be necessary to reimburse the Fund for the cost to the Fund of providing benefits under this paragraph.

(F) CREDIT FOR TIME ENROLLED IN OTHER PLANS. — For employees transferred under this title, enrollment in a health benefits plan administered by a transferor agency or a Federal reserve bank, as the case may be, immediately before enrollment in a health benefits plan under chapter 89 of title 5, United States Code, shall be considered as enrollment in a health benefits plan under that chapter for purposes of section 8905(b)(1)(A) of title 5, United States Code.

(G) SPECIAL PROVISIONS TO ENSURE CONTINUATION OF LIFE INSURANCE BENEFITS. —

(i) IN GENERAL. — An annuitant (as defined in section 8901(3) of title 5, United States Code) who is enrolled in a life insurance plan administered by a transferor agency on the day before the designated transfer date shall be eligible for coverage by a life insurance plan under sections 8706(b), 8714a, 8714b, and 8714c of title 5, United States Code, or in a life insurance plan established by the Bureau, without regard to any regularly scheduled open

(ii)按照《美国法典》第五编第八十九B章设立的升级版眼科福利计划;

(iii)按照《美国法典》第五编第八十七章设立的联邦雇员集团寿险计划(不受任何参保要求的限制);及

(iv)按照《美国法典》第五编第八十九章设立的联邦雇员健康福利计划;

(C)**第1年期限届满之后的长期医疗保险**。——如果在自指定转移日起届满1年之日,消费者金融保护局尚未设立自身的长期医疗保险计划,也未安排雇员参与其他实体的长期医疗保险计划,而按照本子编规定转移的雇员在其原供职的机关或联邦储备银行已经参与了该等计划,则该雇员可以在第(A)(i)子款提供的保障终止之前,选择申请参与按照《美国法典》第五编第九十章设立的联邦长期医疗保险计划,但应遵守适用于新加入的在职员工(定义见《联邦规章汇编》第5编第875部分)的核保要求。

(D)**雇员缴款**。——参与联邦雇员健康福利计划的个人应按照计划要求缴纳任何雇员缴款。

(E)**补充经费**。——消费者金融保护局应按照人事管理局局长与消费者金融保护局和行政管理和预算局磋商确定的必要金额,向按照《美国法典》第五编第8909节设立的联邦雇员健康福利基金划拨相应款项,以补偿该等基金因按照本子款的规定提供福利而产生的费用。

(F)**对参与其他计划的时间予以认可**。——按照本编规定转移的雇员,如果在按照《美国法典》第五编第八十九章的规定参与健康福利计划前最近的时点,具有职能转出机关或联邦储备银行(视具体情况而定)管理的健康福利计划的参保人身份,则就《美国法典》第五编第8905(b)(1)(A)节而言,该雇员应视为在转移之前即已按照第五编第八十九章参与健康福利计划。

(G)**确保转移雇员继续享受寿险福利的特别规定**。——

(i)**一般规定**。——在指定转移日前一天,已参与职能转出机关管理的寿险计划的年金受益人[定义见《美国法典》第五编第8901(3)节]有资格按照《美国法典》第五编第8706(b)节、第8714a节、第8714b节和第8714c节参与寿险计划或消费者金融保护局设立的寿险计划,而不受该等计划的常规开放时间表和参保要求的限制。

season and requirement of insurability.

(ii) EMPLOYEE CONTRIBUTION. — An individual enrolled in a life insurance plan under this subparagraph shall pay any employee contribution required by the plan.

(iii) ADDITIONAL FUNDING. — The Bureau shall transfer to the Employees' Life Insurance Fund established under section 8714 of title 5, United States Code, an amount determined by the Director of the Office of Personnel Management, after consultation with the Bureau and the Office of Management and Budget, to be necessary to reimburse the Fund for the cost to the Fund of providing benefits under this subparagraph not otherwise paid for by the employee under clause (ii).

(iv) CREDIT FOR TIME ENROLLED IN OTHER PLANS. — For employees transferred under this title, enrollment in a life insurance plan administered by a transferor agency immediately before enrollment in a life insurance plan under chapter 87 of title 5, United States Code, shall be considered as enrollment in a life insurance plan under that chapter for purposes of section 8706(b)(1)(A) of title 5, United States Code.

(3) OPM RULES. — The Office of Personnel Management shall issue such rules as are necessary to carry out this subsection. —

(j) IMPLEMENTATION OF UNIFORM PAY AND CLASSIFICATION SYSTEM. — Not later than 2 years after the designated transfer date, the Bureau shall implement a uniform pay and classification system for all employees transferred under this title.

(k) EQUITABLE TREATMENT. — In administering the provisions of this section, the Bureau —

(1) shall take no action that would unfairly disadvantage transferred employees relative to each other based on their prior employment by the Board of Governors, the Federal Deposit Insurance Corporation, the Department of Housing and Urban Development, the National Credit Union Administration, the Office of the Comptroller of the Currency, the Office of Thrift Supervision, a Federal reserve bank, a Federal home loan bank, or a joint office of the Federal home loan banks; and

(2) may take such action as is appropriate in individual cases so that employees transferred under this section receive equitable treatment, with respect to the status, tenure, pay, benefits (other than benefits under programs administered by the Office of Personnel Management), and accrued leave or vacation time of those employees, for prior periods of service with any Federal agency, including the Board of Governors, the Corporation, the Department of Housing and Urban Development, the National Credit Union Administration, the Office of the Comptroller of the Currency, the Office of Thrift Supervision, a Federal reserve bank, a Federal home loan bank, or a joint office of the Federal home loan banks.

(l) IMPLEMENTATION. — In implementing the provisions of this section, the Bureau shall coordinate with the Office of Personnel Management and other entities having expertise

(ii)**雇员缴款**。——按照本子款规定参与寿险计划的个人应按照计划要求缴纳雇员缴款。

(iii)**补充经费来源**。——消费者金融保护局应按照人事管理局局长与消费者金融保护局和行政管理和预算局磋商确定的必要金额,向按照《美国法典》第五编第8714节设立的联邦雇员寿险基金划拨相应款项，以补偿该等基金因按照本子款的规定提供福利而产生的且雇员未按照第(ii)项规定支付的成本。

(iv)**参与其他计划的时间予以认可**。——在按照《美国法典》第五编第八十七章的规定参与寿险计划前最近的时点，按照本编规定转移的雇员具有职能转出机关管理的寿险计划的参保人身份的,则就《美国法典》第五编第8706(b)(1)(A)节而言,该雇员应视为在转移之前即已按照《美国法典》第五编第八十七章参与寿险计划。

(3)**人事管理局规则**。——人事管理局应发布必要规则,以实施本子条规定——

(j)**实施统一的工资和分类制度**。——消费者金融保护局应在指定转移日后2年期间内,对按照本编规定转移的所有雇员实施统一的工资和分类制度。

(k)**公平待遇**。——在实施本条规定过程中,消费者金融保护局——

(1)不得采取任何将导致如下后果的任何行动:转移雇员彼此之间,由于之前供职于联邦储备委员会、联邦存款保险公司、住房与城市发展部、国家信贷联盟署、货币监理署、储蓄机构监理局、联邦储备银行、联邦住房贷款银行或联邦住房贷款银行联合办公室,而受到次于任何其他转移雇员的不公平待遇;并

(2)可以针对具体个案采取适当措施,确保转移雇员与之前在任何联邦机关(包括联邦储备委员会、联邦存款保险公司、住房与城市发展部、国家信贷联盟署、货币监理署、储蓄机构监理局、联邦储备银行、联邦住房贷款银行或联邦住房贷款银行联合办公室)供职期间相比,在岗位级别、任期、工资、福利(但人事管理局管理的计划所提供的福利除外)以及累积休假时间或假期方面获得公平待遇。

(l)**实施**。——在实施本条规定过程中,消费者金融保护局应与人事管理局和其他在雇佣事项方面具有专长的实体进行协调,确保受影响雇员实现公平有序的过渡。

in matters related to employment to ensure a fair and orderly transition for affected employees.

SEC. 1065. INCIDENTAL TRANSFERS.

(a) INCIDENTAL TRANSFERS AUTHORIZED. — The Director of the Office of Management and Budget, in consultation with the Secretary, shall make such additional incidental transfers and dispositions of assets and liabilities held, used, arising from, available, or to be made available, in connection with the functions transferred by this title, as the Director may determine necessary to accomplish the purposes of this title.

(b) SUNSET. — The authority provided in this section shall terminate 5 years after the date of enactment of this Act.

SEC. 1066. INTERIM AUTHORITY OF THE SECRETARY.

(a) IN GENERAL. — The Secretary is authorized to perform the functions of the Bureau under this subtitle until the Director of the Bureau is confirmed by the Senate in accordance with section 1011.

(b) INTERIM ADMINISTRATIVE SERVICES BY THE DEPARTMENT OF THE TREASURY. — The Department of the Treasury may provide administrative services necessary to support the Bureau before the designated transfer date.

SEC. 1067. TRANSITION OVERSIGHT.

(a) PURPOSE. — The purpose of this section is to ensure that the Bureau —

(1) has an orderly and organized startup;

(2) attracts and retains a qualified workforce; and

(3) establishes comprehensive employee training and benefits programs.

(b) REPORTING REQUIREMENT. —

(1) IN GENERAL. — The Bureau shall submit an annual report to the Committee on Banking, Housing, and Urban Affairs of the Senate and the Committee on Financial Services of the House of Representatives that includes the plans described in paragraph (2).

(2) PLANS. — The plans described in this paragraph are as follows:

(A) TRAINING AND WORKFORCE DEVELOPMENT PLAN. — The Bureau shall submit a training and workforce development plan that includes, to the extent practicable —

(i) identification of skill and technical expertise needs and actions taken to meet those requirements;

(ii) steps taken to foster innovation and creativity;

(iii) leadership development and succession planning; and

(iv) effective use of technology by employees.

(B) WORKPLACE FLEXIBILITIES PLAN. — The Bureau shall submit a workforce flexibility plan that includes, to the extent practicable —

(i) telework;

(ii) flexible work schedules;

第1065条　附带转移

(a)**附带转移授权**。——经与财政部部长磋商,行政管理和预算局局长应对因按照本编规定转移职能而持有、使用、产生以及现在或将来可用的资产和负债,进行其判定对于实现本编宗旨确属必要的额外附带转移和处置。

(b)**日落条款**。——本条规定的权限于本法颁布之日后届满5年之日终止。

第1066条　财政部部长的临时权力

(a)**一般规定**。——在参议院根据第1011条规定确认对消费者金融保护局局长的任命之前,财政部部长有权依据本子编规定行使消费者金融保护局的职能。

(b)**财政部提供的临时性行政管理服务**。——在指定转移日之前,财政部可以提供必要的行政管理服务,为消费者金融保护局的工作提供支持。

第1067条　过渡期间的监督

(a)**目的**。——本条之目的在于确保消费者金融保护局——

(1)有序和有组织地启动;

(2)吸引和留任合格人员;及

(3)建立全面的雇员培训和福利计划。

(b)**报告要求**。——

(1)**一般规定**。——消费者金融保护局应向参议院银行、住房与城市事务委员会和众议院金融服务委员会提交年度报告,其中应包括第(2)款所述计划。

(2)**计划**。——本款所述计划如下:

(A)**培训和人力开发计划**。——消费者金融保护局应提交一份培训和人力开发计划,在可行的范围内,该计划应包括——

(i)关于技能和技术专长需求之说明,以及为满足该等需求采取的行动;

(ii)为鼓励创新和创造而采取的措施;

(iii)领导力开发和继任规划;和

(iv)雇员对技术的有效使用。

(B)**弹性工作计划**。——消费者金融保护局应提交一份人力弹性计划,在可行的范围内,该计划应包括——

(i)远程工作;

(ii)弹性工作时间表;

(iii) phased retirement;

(iv) reemployed annuitants;

(v) part–time work;

(vi) job sharing;

(vii) parental leave benefits and childcare assistance;

(viii) domestic partner benefits;

(ix) other workplace flexibilities; or

(x) any combination of the items described in clauses (i) through (ix).

(C) RECRUITMENT AND RETENTION PLAN. — The Bureau shall submit a recruitment and retention plan that includes, to the extent practicable, provisions relating to —

(i) the steps necessary to target highly qualified applicant pools with diverse backgrounds;

(ii) streamlined employment application processes;

(iii) the provision of timely notification of the status of employment applications to applicants; and

(iv) the collection of information to measure indicators of hiring effectiveness.

(c) EXPIRATION. — The reporting requirement under subsection(b) shall terminate 5 years after the date of enactment of this Act.

(d) RULE OF CONSTRUCTION. — Nothing in this section may be construed to affect —

(1) a collective bargaining agreement, as that term is defined in section 7103(a)(8) of title 5, United States Code, that is in effect on the date of enactment of this Act; or

(2) the rights of employees under chapter 71 of title 5, United States Code.

(e) PARTICIPATION IN EXAMINATIONS. — In order to prepare the Bureau to conduct examinations under section 1025 upon the designated transfer date, the Bureau and the applicable prudential regulator may agree to include, on a sampling basis, examiners on examinations of the compliance with Federal consumer financial law of institutions described in section 1025(a) conducted by the prudential regulators prior to the designated transfer date.

Subtitle G — Regulatory Improvements

SEC. 1071. SMALL BUSINESS DATA COLLECTION.

(a) IN GENERAL. — The Equal Credit Opportunity Act(15 U.S.C. 1691 et seq.) is amended by inserting after section 704A the following:

"SEC. 704B. SMALL BUSINESS LOAN DATA COLLECTION.

"(a) PURPOSE. — The purpose of this section is to facilitate enforcement of fair

(iii)阶段性退休;

(iv)返聘年金受益人;

(v)兼职工作;

(vi)工作分享制度;

(vii)育婴假和儿童保育协助;

(viii)同居伴侣福利;

(ix)其他工作弹性制度;或

(x)第(i)项至第(ix)项规定内容的任何组合。

(C)**招聘和留任计划**。——消费者金融保护局应提交一份招聘和留任计划,在可行的范围内,该计划应包括以下相关规定——

(i)为针对不同背景的高资质人才群体进行招聘而采取的必要措施;

(ii)精简的应聘程序;

(iii)及时通知应聘人应聘申请状态;及

(iv)收集相关信息,以考核招聘成效指标。

(c)**失效**。——第(b)子条规定的报告要求于本法颁布之日后届满5年之日失效。

(d)**解释规则**。——本条中的任何规定均不得被解释为——

(1)对本法颁布之日已生效的集体劳动合同[定义见《美国法典》第五编第7103(a)(8)节]产生任何影响;或

(2)对《美国法典》第五编第七十一章规定的雇员权利产生任何影响。

(e)**参与检查工作**。——为了使消费者金融保护局做好准备,在指定转移日即可按照第1025条规定开展检查工作,消费者金融保护局和相关审慎监管者可以约定,在审慎监管者于指定转移日之前,针对第1025(a)条所述机构开展联邦消费者金融法律合规检查工作之时,选派消费者金融保护局的检查人员参与其随机抽选的该等检查工作。

第G子编——监管完善

第1071条 小型企业数据收集

(a)**一般规定**。——在《信贷机会平等法》(《美国法典》第十五编第1691节及其后条文)第704A条之后插入如下内容,作为对该法的修正:

"第704B条 小型企业贷款数据收集

(a)**目的**。——本条旨在促进公平贷款法律的实施,促使社群、政府实体和贷款发

lending laws and enable communities, governmental entities, and creditors to identify business and community development needs and opportunities of women–owned, minority–owned, and small businesses.

"(b) INFORMATION GATHERING. — Subject to the requirements of this section, in the case of any application to a financial institution for credit for women–owned, minority–owned, or small business, the financial institution shall —

"(1) inquire whether the business is a women–owned, minority–owned, or small business, without regard to whether such application is received in person, by mail, by telephone, by electronic mail or other form of electronic transmission, or by any other means, and whether or not such application is in response to a solicitation by the financial institution; and

"(2) maintain a record of the responses to such inquiry, separate from the application and accompanying information.

"(c) RIGHT TO REFUSE. — Any applicant for credit may refuse to provide any information requested pursuant to subsection (b) in connection with any application for credit.

"(d) NO ACCESS BY UNDERWRITERS. —

"(1) LIMITATION. — Where feasible, no loan underwriter or other officer or employee of a financial institution, or any affiliate of a financial institution, involved in making any determination concerning an application for credit shall have access to any information provided by the applicant pursuant to a request under subsection (b) in connection with such application.

"(2) LIMITED ACCESS. — If a financial institution determines that a loan underwriter or other officer or employee of a financial institution, or any affiliate of a financial institution, involved in making any determination concerning an application for credit should have access to any information provided by the applicant pursuant to a request under subsection (b), the financial institution shall provide notice to the applicant of the access of the underwriter to such information, along with notice that the financial institution may not discriminate on the basis of such information.

"(e) FORM AND MANNER OF INFORMATION. —

"(1) IN GENERAL. — Each financial institution shall compile and maintain, in accordance with regulations of the Bureau, a record of the information provided by any loan applicant pursuant to a request under subsection (b).

"(2) ITEMIZATION. — Information compiled and maintained under paragraph (1) shall be itemized in order to clearly and conspicuously disclose —

"(A) the number of the application and the date on which the application was received;

"(B) the type and purpose of the loan or other credit being applied for;

放人能够发现女性拥有的企业、少数族裔拥有的企业和小型企业的业务和社群发展需求和机会。

(b)**信息收集**。——如果金融机构收到女性拥有的企业、少数族裔拥有的企业或小型企业提出的任何信贷申请,该等金融机构应在不违反本条规定的前提下——

(1)调查该等企业是否为女性拥有的企业、少数族裔拥有的企业或小型企业,而不论该等申请是由专人送达,还是通过邮件、电话、电子邮件、其他电子传输方式或任何其他方式送达,亦不论该等申请是否属于对该等金融机构业务招揽行为的回应;并

(2)在该等申请及其附随信息之外,单独对上述调查的答复情况保存记录。

(c)**拒绝权**。——金融机构依据第(b)子条要求提供与任何信贷申请相关的任何信息时,任何信贷申请人均可予以拒绝。

(d)**禁止贷款审核人查阅相关信息**。——

(1)**限制**。——参与对信贷申请作出任何判定的金融机构的贷款审核人、其他管理人员、职员或任何关联方在可行的范围内,不得查阅申请人按照第(b)子条的要求提供的与该申请相关的任何信息。

(2)**限制性查阅权**。——如果金融机构判定,参与对信贷申请作出任何判定的该等金融机构贷款审核人、其他管理人员、职员或任何关联方应有权查阅申请人按照第(b)子条的要求提供的与该申请相关的任何信息,该等金融机构应将上述贷款审核人对该等信息享有的查阅权通知申请人,并告知申请人该金融机构不得因该等信息而对其进行任何歧视。

(e)**汇编和保存信息记录的格式与方式**。——

(1)**一般规定**。——每一金融机构应按照消费者金融保护局的规章,针对每一名贷款申请人按照第(b)子条要求提供的信息汇编并保存相关记录。

(2)**逐项列明信息**。——按照第(1)款规定汇编和保存记录的信息应逐项列明,以便清晰、显著地披露以下内容——

(A)申请的编号以及收到申请的日期;

(B)申请的贷款或其他信贷的类型和用途;

"(C) the amount of the credit or credit limit applied for, and the amount of the credit transaction or the credit limit approved for such applicant;

"(D) the type of action taken with respect to such application, and the date of such action;

"(E) the census tract in which is located the principal place of business of the women–owned, minority–owned, or small business loan applicant;

"(F) the gross annual revenue of the business in the last fiscal year of the women–owned, minority–owned, or small business loan applicant preceding the date of the application;

"(G) the race, sex, and ethnicity of the principal owners of the business; and

"(H) any additional data that the Bureau determines would aid in fulfilling the purposes of this section.

"(3) NO PERSONALLY IDENTIFIABLE INFORMATION. — In compiling and maintaining any record of information under this section, a financial institution may not include in such record the name, specific address (other than the census tract required under paragraph (1)(E)), telephone number, electronic mail address, or any other personally identifiable information concerning any individual who is, or is connected with, the women–owned, minority–owned, or small business loan applicant.

"(4) DISCRETION TO DELETE OR MODIFY PUBLICLY AVAILABLE DATA. — The Bureau may, at its discretion, delete or modify data collected under this section which is or will be available to the public, if the Bureau determines that the deletion or modification of the data would advance a privacy interest.

"(f) AVAILABILITY OF INFORMATION. —

"(1) SUBMISSION TO BUREAU. — The data required to be compiled and maintained under this section by any financial institution shall be submitted annually to the Bureau.

"(2) AVAILABILITY OF INFORMATION. — Information compiled and maintained under this section shall be —

"(A) retained for not less than 3 years after the date of preparation;

"(B) made available to any member of the public, upon request, in the form required under regulations prescribed by the Bureau;

"(C) annually made available to the public generally by the Bureau, in such form and in such manner as is determined by the Bureau, by regulation.

"(3) COMPILATION OF AGGREGATE DATA. — The Bureau may, at its discretion —

"(A) compile and aggregate data collected under this section for its own use; and

"(B) make public such compilations of aggregate data.

"(g) BUREAU ACTION. —

"(1) IN GENERAL. — The Bureau shall prescribe such rules and issue such guidance

(C)申请人申请的信贷金额或信贷额度,以及申请人获批的信贷交易金额或信贷额度;

(D)针对该申请所采取的行动的类型和日期;

(E)女性拥有的企业、少数族裔拥有的企业或小型企业贷款申请人主要营业地所在的人口普查区;

(F)女性拥有的企业、少数族裔拥有的企业或小型企业贷款申请人在申请日之前最近一个会计年度的年营业收入总额;

(G)企业主要所有人的种族、性别和民族;及

(H)消费者金融保护局判定将有助于实现本条目的之任何其他信息。

(3)**不得记录个人身份信息**。——金融机构在对本条所规定的信息汇编和保存任何记录时,不得将任何女性拥有的企业、少数族裔拥有的企业或小型企业贷款申请人或与其相关的任何个人的姓名、详细地址[但第(1)(E)款规定的普查区除外]、电话号码、电子邮箱地址或其任何个人身份信息纳入该等记录之中。

(4)**删除或修改公开数据的自由裁量权**。——对于按照本条规定收集的目前处于或将来进入公共领域的数据,如果消费者金融保护局判定删除或修改该等数据将有助于保护隐私权,其可以依其自由裁量权删除或修改该等数据。

(f)**信息的提供**。——

(1)**向消费者金融保护局提交信息**。——任何金融机构均应每年向消费者金融保护局提交其按照本条规定应汇编和保存的数据。

(2)**信息的提供**。——按照本条规定汇编和保存相关记录的信息应——

(A)自编制之日起保存不少于3年时间;

(B)在公众提出要求之时,按消费者金融保护局制定的规章所规定的格式向其提供;

(C)通常由消费者金融保护局按照其发布的规章所确定的格式和方式每年向公众公开。

(3)**聚合数据汇编**。——消费者金融保护局可以依其自由裁量权——

(A)出于自身使用之目的,对按照本条规定收集的数据进行汇编和聚合;并

(B)公开聚合数据的汇编情况。

(g)**消费者金融保护局的行动**。——

"(1)**一般规定**。——消费者金融保护局应制定必要的规则,并发布必要的指引,

as may be necessary to carry out, enforce, and compile data pursuant to this section.

"(2) EXCEPTIONS. — The Bureau, by rule or order, may adopt exceptions to any requirement of this section and may, conditionally or unconditionally, exempt any financial institution or class of financial institutions from the requirements of this section, as the Bureau deems necessary or appropriate to carry out the purposes of this section.

"(3) GUIDANCE. — The Bureau shall issue guidance designed to facilitate compliance with the requirements of this section, including assisting financial institutions in working with applicants to determine whether the applicants are women-owned, minority-owned, or small businesses for purposes of this section.

"(h) DEFINITIONS. — For purposes of this section, the following definitions shall apply:

"(1) FINANCIAL INSTITUTION. — The term 'financial institution' means any partnership, company, corporation, association (incorporated or unincorporated), trust, estate, cooperative organization, or other entity that engages in any financial activity.

"(2) SMALL BUSINESS. — The term 'small business' has the same meaning as the term 'small business concern' in section 3 of the Small Business Act (15 U.S.C. 632).

"(3) SMALL BUSINESS LOAN. — The term 'small business loan' means a loan made to a small business.

"(4) MINORITY.—The term 'minority' has the same meaning as in section 1204(c)(3) of the Financial Institutions Reform, Recovery, and Enforcement Act of 1989.

"(5) MINORITY-OWNED BUSINESS. — The term 'minority-owned business' means a business —

"(A) more than 50 percent of the ownership or control of which is held by 1 or more minority individuals; and

"(B) more than 50 percent of the net profit or loss of which accrues to 1 or more minority individuals.

"(6) WOMEN-OWNED BUSINESS. — The term 'women-owned business' means a business —

"(A) more than 50 percent of the ownership or control of which is held by 1 or more women; and

"(B) more than 50 percent of the net profit or loss of which accrues to 1 or more women.".

(b) TECHNICAL AND CONFORMING AMENDMENTS. — Section 701(b) of the Equal Credit Opportunity Act (15 U.S.C. 1691(b)) is amended —

(1) in paragraph (3), by striking "or" at the end;

(2) in paragraph (4), by striking the period at the end and inserting "; or"; and

(3) by inserting after paragraph (4), the following:

以实施、执行本条规定并根据本条规定汇编数据。

(2)**例外规定**。——消费者金融保护局可以发布规则或命令,规定适用本条任何要求的例外情形,有条件或无条件地向任何金融机构或任何类别的金融机构授予其认为对于实现本条目的确属必要或适当的豁免,使其不必遵守本条要求。

(3)**指引**。——消费者金融保护局应发布指引,以促进本条的要求得到遵守,包括协助金融机构与申请人共同判定申请人是否属于本条规定意义上的女性拥有的企业、少数族裔拥有的企业或小型企业。

(h)**定义**。——就本条而言,下列术语应适用如下定义:

(1)**金融机构**。——'金融机构'一词系指从事任何金融活动的任何合伙、企业、公司、协会(法人制或非法人制)、信托、遗产和破产财团、合作社组织或其他实体。

(2)**小型企业**。——'小型企业'一词的含义以《小型企业法》(《美国法典》第十五编第632节)第3条的定义为准。

(3)**小型企业贷款**。——'小型企业贷款'一词系指向小型企业发放的贷款。

(4)**少数族裔**。——'少数族裔'一词的含义以《1989年金融机构改革、复兴与实施法》第1204(c)(3)条的定义为准。

(5)**少数族裔拥有的企业**。——'少数族裔拥有的企业'一词系指符合如下条件的企业——

(A)其超过50%的所有权或控制权由1名或1名以上少数族裔的个人持有;且

(B)其超过50%的净损益归于1名或1名以上少数族裔的个人。

(6)**女性拥有的企业**。——'女性拥有的企业'一词系指符合如下条件的企业——

(A)其超过50%的所有权或控制权由1名或1名以上女性持有;且

(B)其超过50%的净损益归于1名或1名以上女性。"

(b)**技术性和一致性修正**。——《信贷机会平等法》第701(b)条[《美国法典》第十五编第1691(b)节]修正如下——

(1)在第(3)款中,删除结尾处的"或";

(2)在第(4)款中,删除结尾处的句号,替以";或";及

(3)在第(4)款之后插入如下内容:

"(5) to make an inquiry under section 704B, in accordance with the requirements of that section.".

(c) CLERICAL AMENDMENT. — The table of sections for title VII of the Consumer Credit Protection Act is amended by inserting after the item relating to section 704A the following new item:

"704B. Small business loan data collection.".

(d) EFFECTIVE DATE. — This section shall become effective on the designated transfer date.

SEC.1072. ASSISTANCE FOR ECONOMICALLY VULNERABLE INDIVIDUALS AND FAMILIES.

(a) HERA AMENDMENTS. — Section 1132 of the Housing and Economic Recovery Act of 2008 (12 U.S.C. 1701x note) is amended —

(1) in subsection (a), by inserting in each of paragraphs (1), (2), (3), and (4) "or economically vulnerable individuals and families" after "homebuyers" each place that term appears;

(2) in subsection (b)(1), by inserting "or economically vulnerable individuals and families" after "homebuyers";

(3) in subsection (c)(1) —

(A) in subparagraph (A), by striking "or" at the end;

(B) in subparagraph (B), by striking the period at the end and inserting "; or"; and

(C) by adding at the end the following:

"(C) a nonprofit corporation that —

"(i) is exempt from taxation under section 501(c)(3) of the Internal Revenue Code of 1986; and

"(ii) specializes or has expertise in working with economically vulnerable individuals and families, but whose primary purpose is not provision of credit counseling services."; and

(4) in subsection (d)(1), by striking "not more than 5".

(b) APPLICABILITY. — Amendments made by subsection (a) shall not apply to programs authorized by section 1132 of the Housing and Economic Recovery Act of 2008 (12 U.S.C. 1701x note) that are funded with appropriations prior to fiscal year 2011.

SEC. 1073. REMITTANCE TRANSFERS.

(a) TREATMENT OF REMITTANCE TRANSFERS. — The Electronic Fund Transfer Act (15 U.S.C. 1693 et seq.) is amended —

(1) in section 902(b)(15 U.S.C. 1693(b)), by inserting "and remittance" after "electronic fund";

(2) in section 904(c)(15 U.S.C. 1693b(c)), in the first sentence, by inserting "or remittance transfers" after "electronic fund transfers";

“(5)按照第704B条的要求开展该条规定的调查。”

(c)**目录修正**。——《消费者信用保护法》第七编条款目录修正如下:在第704A条的目录项之后插入如下新的目录项:

“**第704B条　小型企业贷款数据收集**。”

(d)**生效日**。——本条规定于指定转移日生效。

第1072条　对经济弱势人士和家庭的援助

(a)**《住房和经济复苏法》的修正**。——《2008年住房和经济复苏法》第1132条(《美国法典》第十二编第1701x节注释)修正如下——

(1)在第(a)子条第(1)款、第(2)款、第(3)款和第(4)款中,在所有“购房人”之后插入“或经济弱势人士和家庭”;

(2)在第(b)(1)子条中,在“购房人”之后插入“或经济弱势人士和家庭”;

(3)在第(c)(1)子条中——

(A)删除第(A)子款结尾处的“或”;

(B)删除第(B)子款结尾处的句号,替以“;或”;及

(C)在结尾处增加如下内容:

“(C)符合以下条件的非营利性公司——

(i)按照《1986年国内税收法典》第501(c)(3)条的规定享有免税待遇;且

(ii)专门从事援助经济弱势人士和家庭的工作,或拥有此领域的专长,但其主要宗旨并非提供信贷咨询服务;及

(4)在第(d)(1)子条中,删除“不超过5项”。

(b)**适用范围**。——根据第(a)子条作出的修正不适用于按照《2008年住房和经济复苏法》第1132条(《美国法典》第十二编第1701x节注释)规定批准的以2011财政年度之前的拨款作为资金来源的计划。

第1073条　资金汇划

(a)**汇划的处理**。——《电子资金划拨法》(《美国法典》第十五编第1693节及其后条文)修正如下——

(1)在第902(b)条[《美国法典》第十五编第1693(b)节]中,在“电子资金”之后插入“以及汇款”;

(2)在第904(c)条[《美国法典》第十五编第1693b(c)节]第1句中,在“电子资金划拨”之后插入“或汇划”;

(3) by redesignating sections 919, 920, 921, and 922 as sections 920, 921, 922, and 923, respectively; and

(4) by inserting after section 918 the following:

"SEC. 919. REMITTANCE TRANSFERS.

"(a) DISCLOSURES REQUIRED FOR REMITTANCE TRANSFERS.—

"(1) IN GENERAL.— Each remittance transfer provider shall make disclosures as required under this section and in accordance with rules prescribed by the Board. Disclosures required under this section shall be in addition to any other disclosures applicable under this title.

"(2) DISCLOSURES.— Subject to rules prescribed by the Board, a remittance transfer provider shall provide, in writing and in a form that the sender may keep, to each sender requesting a remittance transfer, as applicable to the transaction—

"(A) at the time at which the sender requests a remittance transfer to be initiated, and prior to the sender making any payment in connection with the remittance transfer, a disclosure describing—

"(i) the amount of currency that will be received by the designated recipient, using the values of the currency into which the funds will be exchanged;

"(ii) the amount of transfer and any other fees charged by the remittance transfer provider for the remittance transfer; and

"(iii) any exchange rate to be used by the remittance transfer provider for the remittance transfer, to the nearest 1/100th of a point; and

"(B) at the time at which the sender makes payment in connection with the remittance transfer—

"(i) a receipt showing—

"(I) the information described in subparagraph (A);

"(II) the promised date of delivery to the designated recipient; and

"(III) the name and either the telephone number or the address of the designated recipient, if either the telephone number or the address of the designated recipient is provided by the sender; and

"(ii) a statement containing—

"(I) information about the rights of the sender under this section regarding the resolution of errors; and

"(II) appropriate contact information for—

"(aa) the remittance transfer provider; and

"(bb) the State agency that regulates the remittance transfer provider and the Board, including the toll–free telephone number established under section 1013 of the Consumer Financial Protection Act of 2010.

(3)第919条、第920条、第921条和第922条分别重新编号为第920条、第921条、第922条和第923条;及

(4)在第918条之后插入如下内容:

“第919条　汇划

(a)**关于汇划的披露要求**。——

(1)**一般规定**。——汇划服务提供者应按照本条的要求和联邦储备委员会制定的规则进行披露。本条要求的披露不影响本编规定的任何其他相关披露。

(2)**披露**。——在不违反联邦储备委员会制定的规则的前提下,汇划服务提供者应以每一申请汇划的汇款人可以保存的书面和表格形式(根据具体情况而定)——

(A)在汇款人申请进行汇划之时,以及汇款人支付与该汇划相关的任何款项之前,向汇款人进行披露,说明——

(i)指定收款人将收到的外币金额(按作为兑换对象的外币的价值计算);

(ii)划拨资金数额以及汇划服务提供者就该汇划所收取的任何其他费用;及

(iii)汇划服务提供者将在该汇划中使用的任何汇率,精确至小数点后两位;并

(B)在汇款人支付与该汇划相关的款项之时——

(i)向汇款人提供一份显示如下内容的收据——

(I)第(A)子款所述信息;

(II)向指定收款人交付款项的约定付款日;及

(III)指定收款人的姓名以及电话号码或地址(如果汇款人提供了指定收款人的电话号码或地址);并

(ii)向申请汇划的汇款人提供一份含有如下内容的声明——

(I)关于汇款人根据本条规定在错误处理方面所享有权利的信息;及

(II)下述各者的适当联系信息——

(aa)汇划服务提供者;及

(bb)负责对汇划服务提供者进行监管的州机关以及联邦储备委员会,包括根据《2010年消费者金融保护法》第1013条规定开通的免费电话号码。

"(3) RE QUIREMENTS RELATING TO DISCLOSURES. — With respect to each disclosure required to be provided under paragraph (2) a remittance transfer provider shall —

"(A) provide an initial notice and receipt, as required by subparagraphs (A) and (B) of paragraph (2), and an error resolution statement, as required by subsection (d), that clearly and conspicuously describe the information required to be disclosed therein; and

"(B) with respect to any transaction that a sender conducts electronically, comply with the Electronic Signatures in Global and National Commerce Act (15 U.S.C. 7001 et seq.).

"(4) EXCEPTION FOR DISCLOSURES OF AMOUNT RECEIVED. —

"(A) IN GENERAL. — Subject to the rules prescribed by the Board, and except as provided under subparagraph (B), the disclosures required regarding the amount of currency that will be received by the designated recipient shall be deemed to be accurate, so long as the disclosures provide a reasonably accurate estimate of the foreign currency to be received. This paragraph shall apply only to a remittance transfer provider who is an insured depository institution, as defined in section 3 of the Federal Deposit Insurance Act (12 U.S.C. 1813), or an insured credit union, as defined in section 101 of the Federal Credit Union Act (12 U.S.C. 1752), and if —

"(i) a remittance transfer is conducted through a demand deposit, savings deposit, or other asset account that the sender holds with such remittance transfer provider; and

"(ii) at the time at which the sender requests the transaction, the remittance transfer provider is unable to know, for reasons beyond its control, the amount of currency that will be made available to the designated recipient.

"(B) DEADLINE. — The application of subparagraph (A) shall terminate 5 years after the date of enactment of the Consumer Financial Protection Act of 2010, unless the Board determines that termination of such provision would negatively affect the ability of remittance transfer providers described in subparagraph (A) to send remittances to locations in foreign countries, in which case, the Board may, by rule, extend the application of subparagraph (A) to not longer than 10 years after the date of enactment of the Consumer Financial Protection Act of 2010.

"(5) EXEMPTION AUTHORITY. — The Board may, by rule, permit a remittance transfer provider to satisfy the requirements of —

"(A) paragraph (2)(A) orally, if the transaction is conducted entirely by telephone;

"(B) paragraph (2)(B), in the case of a transaction conducted entirely by telephone, by mailing the disclosures required under such subparagraph to the sender, not later than 1 business day after the date on which the transaction is conducted, or by including such documents in the next periodic statement, if the telephone transaction is conducted through a demand deposit, savings deposit, or other asset account that the sender holds with the

(3)**与披露相关的要求**。——对于第(2)款要求提供的每项披露,汇划服务提供者均应——

(A)提供第(2)款第(A)子款和第(B)子款规定的初始通知和收据以及第(d)子条规定的错误处理声明,上述通知、收据以及声明均应清晰、显明地注明应在其中披露的相关信息;并

(B)对于汇款人以电子化方式开展的任何交易,遵守《全球暨全美商业电子签章法》(《美国法典》第十五编第7001节及其后条文)的规定。

(4)**关于收到金额披露的例外规定**。——

(A)**一般规定**。——在不违反联邦储备委员会制定的规则的前提下,除第(B)子款规定的情形外,只要针对指定收款人将收到的外币金额进行的必要披露对外币提供了合理准确的估值,该等披露即应视为准确无误。在下列情形下,本款应仅适用于具有参保存款机构[定义见《联邦存款保险法》第3条(《美国法典》第十二编第1813节)]或参保信贷联盟(定义见《联邦信贷联盟法》第101条(《美国法典》第十二编第1752节)身份的汇划服务提供者——

(i)汇划系通过汇款人在该汇划服务提供者处开立的活期存款账户、储蓄存款账户或其他资产账户进行;且

(ii)汇款人申请汇划交易之时,汇划服务提供者由于自身无法控制的原因而无法获知指定收款人将收到的外币金额。

(B)**最后期限**。——第(A)子款应于《2010年消费者金融保护法》颁布之日后届满五年之日终止适用,但是联邦储备委员会判定终止适用该规定将对第(A)子款所述汇划服务提供者向国外汇款的能力产生不利影响的除外。在该种情况下,联邦储备委员会可以发布规则,延长第(A)子款的适用期限,但是延长之后的期限不得超过《2010年消费者金融保护法》颁布之日后10年。

(5)**豁免权**。——联邦储备委员会可以发布规则——

(A)对于交易完全通过电话进行的情形,准许汇划服务提供者通过口头方式履行第(2)款第(A)子款的要求;

(B)对于交易完全通过电话进行的情形,准许汇划服务提供者通过在交易进行之日后一个营业日内将第(2)款第(B)子款规定的披露文件邮寄给汇款人的方式履行第(2)款第(B)子款的要求,或者,在上述电话交易经由汇款人在汇划服务提供者处开立的活期存款账户、储蓄存款账户或其他资产账户开展的情况下,通过将上述文件纳入下一期定期对账单内的方式履行第(2)款第(B)子款的要求;

remittance transfer provider;

"(C) subparagraphs (A) and (B) of paragraph (2) together in one written disclosure, but only to the extent that the information provided in accordance with paragraph (3)(A) is accurate at the time at which payment is made in connection with the subject remittance transfer; and

"(D) paragraph (2)(A), without compliance with section 101(c) of the Electronic Signatures in Global Commerce Act, if a sender initiates the transaction electronically and the information is displayed electronically in a manner that the sender can keep.

"(6) STOREFRONT AND INTERNET NOTICES. —

"(A) IN GENERAL. —

"(i) PROMINENT POSTING. — Subject to subparagraph (B), the Board may prescribe rules to require a remittance transfer provider to prominently post, and timely update, a notice describing a model remittance transfer for one or more amounts, as the Board may determine, which notice shall show the amount of currency that will be received by the designated recipient, using the values of the currency into which the funds will be exchanged.

"(ii) ONSITE DISPLAYS. — The Board may require the notice prescribed under this subparagraph to be displayed in every physical storefront location owned or controlled by the remittance transfer provider.

"(iii) INTERNET NOTICES. — Subject to paragraph (3), the Board shall prescribe rules to require a remittance transfer provider that provides remittance transfers via the Internet to provide a notice, comparable to a storefront notice described in this subparagraph, located on the home page or landing page (with respect to such remittance transfer services) owned or controlled by the remittance transfer provider.

"(iv) RULEMAKING AUTHORITY. — In prescribing rules under this subparagraph, the Board may impose standards or requirements regarding the provision of the storefront and Internet notices required under this subparagraph and the provision of the disclosures required under paragraphs (2) and (3).

"(B) STUDY AND ANALYSIS. — Prior to proposing rules under subparagraph (A), the Board shall undertake appropriate studies and analyses, which shall be consistent with section 904(a)(2), and may include an advanced notice of proposed rulemaking, to determine whether a storefront notice or Internet notice facilitates the ability of a consumer —

"(i) to compare prices for remittance transfers; and

"(ii) to understand the types and amounts of any fees or costs imposed on remittance transfers.

"(b) FOREIGN LANGUAGE DISCLOSURES. — The disclosures required under this section shall be made in English and in each of the foreign languages principally used by the remittance transfer provider, or any of its agents, to advertise, solicit, or market, either orally

(C)仅对于根据第(3)(A)款提供的信息在与汇划相关的付款进行支付时确属无误的情形,准许汇划服务提供者通过提供一份书面披露文件的方式同时履行第(2)款第(A)子款和第(B)子款的要求。

(D)对于汇款人以电子化方式发起交易且信息以汇款人能够保存的电子化方式列示的情形,准许汇划服务提供者在履行第(2)(A)款的要求时,不必遵守《全球商业电子签章法》第101(c)条的规定。

(6)**店面公告与网上公告**。——

(A)**一般规定**。——

(i)**在显著位置张贴公告**。——在不违反第(B)子款规定的前提下,联邦储备委员会可以制定规则,要求汇划服务提供者在显著位置张贴对联邦储备委员会确定的一笔或多笔款项的汇划示例进行说明的公告,委员会并及时更新该公告。该公告应显示指定收款人将收到的外币金额,即汇款资金按照作为兑换对象的外币的价值计算得出的金额。

(ii)**在营业场所张贴公告**。——联邦储备委员可以要求汇划服务提供者将本子款规定的公告张贴于其拥有或控制的所有实体性营业场所的店面位置。

(iii)**网上通知**。——在不违反第(3)款规定的前提下,联邦储备委员会应制定规则,要求通过因特网进行汇划的汇划服务提供者在其拥有或控制的网站首页或登录页(指与该汇划服务相关的页面),提供与本子款所述店面公告类似的公告。

(iv)**规则制定权**。——在按照本子款规定制定规则时,联邦储备委员会可以针对按照本子款要求提供的店面公告、网上公告以及第(2)款和第(3)款要求提供的披露文件,施加相关标准或要求。

(B)**研究与分析**。——在按照第(A)子款规定提出规则草案之前,联邦储备委员会应遵循第904(a)(2)条的规定,开展适当的研究和分析,并可以就其拟采取的规则制定行为提前发出通知,以判定店面公告或网上公告是否有助于提升消费者的以下能力——

(i)对汇划收费价格进行比较的能力;及

(ii)了解针对汇划收取的任何手续费或成本的类型和金额的能力。

(b)**外语披露**。——本条规定的披露文件的编制应采用英语以及汇划服务提供者或其任何代理人在其营业场所通过口头或书面方式进行业务宣传、招揽或推销时主要使用的每一种外语。

or in writing, at that office.

"(c) REGULATIONS REGARDING TRANSFERS TO CERTAIN NATIONS. — If the Board determines that a recipient nation does not legally allow, or the method by which transactions are made in the recipient country do not allow, a remittance transfer provider to know the amount of currency that will be received by the designated recipient, the Board may prescribe rules (not later than 18 months after the date of enactment of the Consumer Financial Protection Act of 2010) addressing the issue, which rules shall include standards for a remittance transfer provider to provide —

"(1) a receipt that is consistent with subsections (a) and (b); and

"(2) a reasonably accurate estimate of the foreign currency to be received, based on the rate provided to the sender by the remittance transfer provider at the time at which the transaction was initiated by the sender.

"(d) REMITTANCE TRANSFER ERRORS. —

"(1) ERROR RESOLUTION. —

"(A) IN GENERAL. — If a remittance transfer provider receives oral or written notice from the sender within 180 days of the promised date of delivery that an error occurred with respect to a remittance transfer, including the amount of currency designated in subsection (a)(3)(A) that was to be sent to the designated recipient of the remittance transfer, using the values of the currency into which the funds should have been exchanged, but was not made available to the designated recipient in the foreign country, the remittance transfer provider shall resolve the error pursuant to this subsection and investigate the reason for the error.

"(B) REMEDIES. — Not later than 90 days after the date of receipt of a notice from the sender pursuant to subparagraph (A), the remittance transfer provider shall, as applicable to the error and as designated by the sender —

"(i) refund to the sender the total amount of funds tendered by the sender in connection with the remittance transfer which was not properly transmitted;

"(ii) make available to the designated recipient, without additional cost to the designated recipient or to the sender, the amount appropriate to resolve the error;

"(iii) provide such other remedy, as determined appropriate by rule of the Board for the protection of senders; or

"(iv) provide written notice to the sender that there was no error with an explanation responding to the specific complaint of the sender.

"(2) RULES. — The Board shall establish, by rule issued not later than 18 months after the date of enactment of the Consumer Financial Protection Act of 2010, clear and appropriate standards for remittance transfer providers with respect to error resolution relating to remittance transfers, to protect senders from such errors. Standards prescribed under this paragraph shall include appropriate standards regarding record keeping, as required,

(c)**关于向特定国家进行转账的规章**。——如果联邦储备委员会判定,根据收款人国家的法律或在收款人国家开展交易所采用的方法,汇划服务提供者无法获知指定收款人将收到的外币金额,联邦储备委员会可以在《2010年消费者金融保护法》颁布之日后18个月内制定用以解决该问题的规则。该等规则应包括适用于如下各项的标准——

(1)汇划服务提供者如何提供符合第(a)子条和第(b)子条规定的收据;及

(2)汇划服务提供者如何基于其在汇款人发起交易之时向汇款人提供的汇率对指定收款人将收到的外币进行合理准确的估值。

(d)**汇划错误**。——

(1)**错误处理**。——

(A)**一般规定**。——如果汇划服务提供者在约定付款日后180天内收到汇款人的口头或书面通知,说明汇划发生错误,并在通知中包含汇往指定收款人但位于国外的指定收款人并未收到的第(a)(3)(A)子条规定的外币金额(按照作为兑换对象的外币的价值计算),则汇划服务提供者应按照本子条规定处理该错误,并调查错误产生的原因。

(B)**救济**。——在按照第(A)子款规定收到汇款人通知之日后90天内,汇划服务提供者应根据错误情况以及汇款人的指示——

(i)将汇款人因汇划而提供但未正常汇出的资金总额退还给汇款人;

(ii)向指定收款人提供适当金额,使该错误得以解决,但不得另行向指定收款人或汇款人收取任何费用;

(iii)向汇款人提供联邦储备委员会在其发布的规则中判定对于保护汇款人确属适当的其他救济;或

(iv)向汇款人发出书面通知,说明汇款未发生错误,并对汇款人的具体投诉作出解释说明。

(2)**规则**。——联邦储备委员会应于《2010年消费者金融保护法》颁布之日后18个月内发布规则,为汇划服务提供者处理汇划错误确立明确、适当的标准,保护汇款人免受该等错误的影响。按照本款确立的标准按照要求应含有适当的记录保存标准,包括关于以下事项的文件记录标准——

including documentation —

"(A) of the complaint of the sender;

"(B) that the sender provides the remittance transfer provider with respect to the alleged error; and

"(C) of the findings of the remittance transfer provider regarding the investigation of the alleged error that the sender brought to their attention.

"(3) CANCELLATION AND REFUND POLICY RULES. — Not later than 18 months after the date of enactment of the Consumer Financial Protection Act of 2010, the Board shall issue final rules regarding appropriate remittance transfer cancellation and refund policies for consumers.

"(e) APPLICABILITY OF THIS TITLE. —

"(1) IN GENERAL. — A remittance transfer that is not an electronic fund transfer, as defined in section 903, shall not be subject to any of the provisions of sections 905 through 913. A remittance transfer that is an electronic fund transfer, as defined in section 903, shall be subject to all provisions of this title, except for section 908, that are otherwise applicable to electronic fund transfers under this title.

"(2) RULE OF CONSTRUCTION. — Nothing in this section shall be construed —

"(A) to affect the application to any transaction, to any remittance provider, or to any other person of any of the provisions of subchapter II of chapter 53 of title 31, United States Code, section 21 of the Federal Deposit Insurance Act (12 U.S.C. 1829b), or chapter 2 of title I of Public Law 91-508 (12 U.S.C. 1951-1959), or any regulations promulgated thereunder; or

"(B) to cause any fund transfer that would not otherwise be treated as such under paragraph (1) to be treated as an electronic fund transfer, or as otherwise subject to this title, for the purposes of any of the provisions referred to in subparagraph (A) or any regulations promulgated thereunder.

"(f) ACTS OF AGENTS. —

"(1) IN GENERAL. — A remittance transfer provider shall be liable for any violation of this section by any agent, authorized delegate, or person affiliated with such provider, when such agent, authorized delegate, or affiliate acts for that remittance transfer provider.

"(2) OBLIGATIONS OF REMITTANCE TRANSFER PROVIDERS. — The Board shall prescribe rules to implement appropriate standards or conditions of, liability of a remittance transfer provider, including a provider who acts through an agent or authorized delegate. An agency charged with enforcing the requirements of this section, or rules prescribed by the Board under this section, may consider, in any action or other proceeding against a remittance transfer provider, the extent to which the provider had established and maintained policies or procedures for compliance, including policies, procedures, or other

(A)汇款人的投诉;

(B)汇款人向汇划服务提供者提供的与其声称存在的汇划错误相关的文件;及

(C)汇划服务提供者对汇款人声称的汇划错误进行调查后得出的认定结论。

(3)**关于撤销汇划与退款政策的规则**。——联邦储备委员会应在《2010年消费者金融保护法》颁布之日后18个月内发布最终规则,确立关于消费者汇划撤销和退款的适当政策。

(e)**本编规定的适用范围**。——

(1)**一般规定**。——第905条至第913条的任何规定均不适用于并非第903条定义的电子资金划拨的汇划。本编中除第980条以外的因其他原因适用于本编所述电子资金划拨的所有条款均应适用于属于第903条定义的电子资金划拨的汇划。

(2)**解释规则**。——本条的任何内容均不得被解释为——

(A)影响《美国法典》第三十一编第五十三章第二子章、《联邦存款保险法》第21条(《美国法典》第十二编第1829b节)、第91—508号公法第一编第二章(《美国法典》第十二编第1951~1959节)的任何规定或依据该等规定颁发的任何规章对任何交易、任何汇划服务提供者或任何其他人的适用;或

(B)致使本不作为第(1)款所述资金划拨处理的任何资金划拨,就第(A)子款所提及的任何规定或依据该等规定颁发的任何规章而言,被作为电子资金划拨处理或被视为因其他原因受制于本编规定。

(f)**代理人行为**。——

(1)**一般规定**。——如果汇划服务提供者的任何代理人、授权代表或关联方在代其行事时实施任何违反本条规定的行为,汇划服务提供者应对此承担责任。

(2)**汇划服务提供者的义务**。——联邦储备委员会应制定规则,以便针对汇划服务提供者(包括通过代理人或授权代表行事的汇划服务提供者)的责任实施适当的标准或条件。负责实施本条规定或联邦储备委员会依据本条规定所制定的规则的机关在对汇划服务提供者采取的任何行动或其他程序中,可考虑该服务提供者在多大程度上建立和维持了合规政策或程序,包括旨在确保该服务提供者的代理人或授权代表合规的政策、程序或其他适当的监督措施。

appropriate oversight measures designed to assure compliance by an agent or authorized delegate acting for such provider.

"(g) DEFINITIONS. — As used in this section —

"(1) the term 'designated recipient' means any person located in a foreign country and identified by the sender as the authorized recipient of a remittance transfer to be made by a remittance transfer provider, except that a designated recipient shall not be deemed to be a consumer for purposes of this Act;

"(2) the term 'remittance transfer' —

"(A) means the electronic (as defined in section 106(2) of the Electronic Signatures in Global and National Commerce Act (15 U.S.C. 7006(2))) transfer of funds requested by a sender located in any State to a designated recipient that is initiated by a remittance transfer provider, whether or not the sender holds an account with the remittance transfer provider or whether or not the remittance transfer is also an electronic fund transfer, as defined in section 903; and

"(B) does not include a transfer described in subparagraph (A) in an amount that is equal to or lesser than the amount of a small-value transaction determined, by rule, to be excluded from the requirements under section 906(a);

"(3) the term 'remittance transfer provider' means any person or financial institution that provides remittance transfers for a consumer in the normal course of its business, whether or not the consumer holds an account with such person or financial institution; and

"(4) the term 'sender' means a consumer who requests a remittance provider to send a remittance transfer for the consumer to a designated recipient.".

(b) AUTOMATED CLEARINGHOUSE SYSTEM. —

(1) EXPANSION OF SYSTEM. — The Board of Governors shall work with the Federal reserve banks and the Department of the Treasury to expand the use of the automated clearinghouse system and other payment mechanisms for remittance transfers to foreign countries, with a focus on countries that receive significant remittance transfers from the United States, based on —

(A) the number, volume, and size of such transfers;

(B) the significance of the volume of such transfers relative to the external financial flows of the receiving country, including —

(i) the total amount transferred; and

(ii) the total volume of payments made by United States Government agencies to beneficiaries and retirees living abroad;

(C) the feasibility of such an expansion; and

(D) the ability of the Federal Reserve System to establish payment gateways in different geographic regions and currency zones to receive remittance transfers and route them through

(g)**定义**。——就本条而言——

(1)‘指定收款人’一词系指被汇款人确定为汇划服务提供者所提供汇划之授权收款人的位于国外的任何人,但是,指定收款人不得视为本法意义上的消费者。

(2)‘汇划’一词——

(A)系指位于任何州的汇款人申请汇划服务提供者发起的以电子化方式{定义见《全球暨全美商业电子签章法》第106(2)条[《美国法典》第十五编第7006(2)节]}将资金划拨给指定收款人的活动,不论该汇款人是否在该汇划服务提供者处开立了账户,也不论该汇划是否同时属于第903条定义的电子资金划拨;且

(B)不包括第(A)子款所述划拨金额等于或低于如下金额的划拨:相关规则中判定的排除适用第906(a)条规定的小额交易的金额;

(3)‘汇划服务提供者’一词系指正常业务运作过程中向消费者提供汇划服务的任何主体或金融机构,而不论该消费者是否在该主体或金融机构处开立了账户;及

(4)‘汇款人’一词系指申请汇款服务提供者向指定收款人进行汇划的消费者。”

(b)**自动结算所系统**。——

(1)**系统推广**。——联邦储备委员会应与联邦储备银行和财政部协力推广自动结算所系统和其他支付机制在国外汇划中的使用,尤其应针对大规模地接收来自美国的汇划的国家推广上述系统和机制的使用,在确定该等国家时,应基于如下因素——

(A)该等划拨的笔数、规模和金额;

(B)相对于该接收国的对外金融流量,该等划拨规模的重要程度,包括——

(i)划拨的总金额;和

(ii)联邦政府机关向国外生活的受益人和退休人员支付款项的总金额;

(C)该推广的可行性;及

(D)联邦储备系统在不同地理区域和货币区设立用于接收汇划并通过该等支付系统将其转至目的地国的支付网关的能力。

the payments systems in the destination countries.

(2) REPORT TO CONGRESS. — Not later than one calendar year after the date of enactment of this Act, and on April 30 biennially thereafter during the 10–year period beginning on that date of enactment, the Board of Governors shall submit a report to the Committee on Banking, Housing, and Urban Affairs of the Senate and the Committee on Financial Services of the House of Representatives on the status of the automated clearinghouse system and its progress in complying with the requirements of this subsection. The report shall include an analysis of adoption rates of International ACH Transactions rules and formats, the efficacy of increasing adoption rates, and potential recommendations to increase adoption.

(c) EXPANSION OF FINANCIAL INSTITUTION PROVISION OF REMITTANCE TRANSFERS. —

(1) PROVISION OF GUIDELINES TO INSTITUTIONS. — Each of the Federal banking agencies and the National Credit Union Administration shall provide guidelines to financial institutions under the jurisdiction of the agency regarding the offering of low–cost remittance transfers and no–cost or low–cost basic consumer accounts, as well as agency services to remittance transfer providers.

(2) ASSISTANCE TO FINANCIAL LITERACY COMMISSION. — As part of its duties as members of the Financial Literacy and Education Commission, the Bureau, the Federal banking agencies, and the National Credit Union Administration shall assist the Financial Literacy and Education Commission in executing the Strategy for Assuring Financial Empowerment (or the "SAFE Strategy"), as it relates to remittances.

(d) FEDERAL CREDIT UNION ACT CONFORMING AMENDMENT. — Paragraph (12) of section 107 of the Federal Credit Union Act (12 U.S.C. 1757) is amended to read as follows: —

"(12) in accordance with regulations prescribed by the Board —

"(A) to sell, to persons in the field of membership, negotiable checks (including travelers checks), money orders, and other similar money transfer instruments (including international and domestic electronic fund transfers and remittance transfers, as defined in section 919 of the Electronic Fund Transfer Act); and

"(B) to cash checks and money orders for persons in the field of membership for a fee;".

(e) REPORT ON FEASIBILITY OF AND IMPEDIMENTS TO USE OF REMITTANCE HISTORY IN CALCULATION OF CREDIT SCORE. — Before the end of the 365–day period beginning on the date of enactment of this Act, the Director shall submit a report to the President, the Committee on Banking, Housing, and Urban Affairs of the Senate, and the Committee on Financial Services of the House of Representatives regarding —

(1) the manner in which the remittance history of a consumer could be used to enhance

(2)**向国会报告**。——在本法颁布之日后1个日历年内，联邦储备委员会应向参议院银行、住房与城市事务委员会和众议院金融服务委员会提交1份报告，汇报自动结算所系统的状况以及其履行本子条要求的进展状况。在上述日历年之后，联邦储备委员会应于本法颁布之日起10年内每隔1年的4月30日提交1份上述报告。在该报告中，联邦储备委员会应分析国际自动结算所交易规则和格式的采用率、采用率提高所产生的效果以及为提高采用率而可能提出的建议。

(c)**扩大金融机构提供的汇划服务范围**。——

(1)**向金融机构提供指引**。——每一联邦银行业监管机关以及国家信贷联盟署应向其管辖的金融机构提供指引，引导该等金融机构向汇划服务提供者提供低成本的汇划服务、无成本或低成本的消费者基本账户以及代理服务。

(2)**为金融扫盲和教育委员会提供协助**。——由于"确保金融赋权战略"(即SAFE战略)涉及汇款事宜，所以，金融扫盲和教育委员会在执行该战略时，消费者金融保护局、联邦银行业监管机关和国家信贷联盟署作为金融扫盲和教育委员成员应予以协助。

(d)**《联邦信贷联盟法》的一致性修正**。——《联邦信贷联盟法》第107条第(12)款(《美国法典》第十二编第1757节)修正后全文如下——

"(12)根据联邦储备委员会制定的规章——

(A)向具有会员身份的主体出售可转让支票(包括旅行支票)、汇票和其他类似的货币转让工具(包括《电子资金划拨法》第919条定义的国际和国内电子资金划拨以及汇划)；及

(B)为具有会员身份的主体有偿兑现支票和汇票；"。

(e)**关于计算信用评分时使用汇款记录的可行性及所面临阻碍的报告**。——自本法颁布之日起365天内，消费者金融保护局局长应针对以下内容向总统、参议院银行、住房与城市事务委员会和众议院金融服务委员会提交1份报告——

(1)采用何种方式能够将消费者汇款记录用于加强消费者信用评分工作；

the credit score of the consumer;

(2) the current legal and business model barriers and impediments that impede the use of the remittance history of the consumer to enhance the credit score of the consumer; and

(3) recommendations on the manner in which maximum transparency and disclosure to consumers of exchange rates for remittance transfers subject to this title and the amendments made by this title may be accomplished, whether or not such exchange rates are known at the time of origination or payment by the consumer for the remittance transfer, including disclosure to the sender of the actual exchange rate used and the amount of currency that the recipient of the remittance transfer received, using the values of the currency into which the funds were exchanged, as contained in sections 919(a)(2)(D) and 919(a)(3) of the Electronic Fund Transfer Act (as amended by this section).

SEC. 1074. DEPARTMENT OF THE TREASURY STUDY ON ENDING THE CONSERVATORSHIP OF FANNIE MAE, FREDDIE MAC, AND REFORMING THE HOUSING FINANCE SYSTEM.

(a) STUDY REQUIRED. —

(1) IN GENERAL. — The Secretary of the Treasury shall conduct a study of and develop recommendations regarding the options for ending the conservatorship of the Federal National Mortgage Association (in this section referred to as "Fannie Mae") and the Federal Home Loan Mortgage Corporation (in this section referred to as "Freddie Mac"), while minimizing the cost to taxpayers, including such options as —

(A) the gradual wind-down and liquidation of such entities;

(B) the privatization of such entities;

(C) the incorporation of the functions of such entities into a Federal agency;

(D) the dissolution of Fannie Mae and Freddie Mac into smaller companies; or

(E) any other measures the Secretary determines appropriate.

(2) ANALYSES. — The study required under paragraph (1) shall include an analysis of —

(A) the role of the Federal Government in supporting a stable, well-functioning housing finance system, and whether and to what extent the Federal Government should bear risks in meeting Federal housing finance objectives;

(B) how the current structure of the housing finance system can be improved;

(C) how the housing finance system should support the continued availability of mortgage credit to all segments of the market;

(D) how the housing finance system should be structured to ensure that consumers continue to have access to 30-year, fixed rate, pre-payable mortgages and other mortgage products that have simple terms that can be easily understood;

(E) the role of the Federal Housing Administration and the Department of Veterans

(2)将消费者汇款记录用于加强消费者信用评分工作当前存在何种法律和商业模式上的壁垒和障碍;及

(3)对于受制于本编及其修正的汇划之汇率,建议采取能够最大限度地实现透明化并最大限度地向消费者进行披露的方式,而不论消费者在发起汇划或进行支付时是否知晓该等汇率,包括如《电子资金划拨法》第919(a)(2)(D)条和第919(a)(3)条(以本条修正后的版本为准)所规定的,向汇款人披露实际使用的汇率以及汇划收款人收到的外币金额(即汇款资金按照作为兑换对象的外币的价值计算得出金额)。

第1074条　财政部关于结束对房利美和房地美的托管及改革住房金融系统的研究

(a)**研究要求**。——

(1)**一般规定**。——对于选择何种方案在最大限度减少纳税人成本的情况下结束对联邦国民住房贷款协会(本条下称房利美)及联邦住房贷款抵押公司(本条下称房地美)的托管,财政部部长应开展研究,并提出相关建议。该等可供选择的方案包括——

(A)逐步关闭并清算上述实体;

(B)对上述实体实行私有化;

(C)将上述实体之职能纳入联邦机关;

(D)将房利美及房地美分解为规模较小的公司;或

(E)财政部部长判定确属适当的任何其他措施。

(2)**分析**。——第(1)款规定的研究应对如下问题进行分析——

(A)联邦政府在支持稳定和良好运行的住房金融系统方面的作用,以及联邦政府在实现联邦住房金融目标方面是否应当承担风险及承担何种程度的风险;

(B)如何能够完善住房金融系统当前的结构;

(C)住房金融系统应如何支持抵押信贷持续向各细分市场供给;

(D)住房金融系统应采用何种结构安排,以确保消费者能够继续获得30年期固定利率可提前还款的抵押贷款和其他条款简明易懂的抵押贷款产品;

(E)联邦住宅管理局和退伍军人管理局在未来住房体系中的作用;

Affairs in a future housing system;

(F) the impact of reforms of the housing finance system on the financing of rental housing;

(G) the impact of reforms of the housing finance system on secondary market liquidity;

(H) the role of standardization in the housing finance system;

(I) how housing finance systems in other countries offer insights that can help inform options for reform in the United States; and

(J) the options for transition to a reformed housing finance system.

(b) REPORT AND RECOMMENDATIONS. — Not later than January 31, 2011, the Secretary of the Treasury shall submit the report and recommendations required under subsection (a) to the Committee on Banking, Housing, and Urban Affairs of the Senate and the Committee on Financial Services of the House of Representatives.

SEC. 1075. REASONABLE FEES AND RULES FOR PAYMENT CARD TRANSACTIONS.

(a) IN GENERAL. — The Electronic Fund Transfer Act (15 U.S.C. 1693 et seq.) is amended —

(1) by redesignating sections 920 and 921 as sections 921 and 922, respectively; and

(2) by inserting after section 919 the following:

"SEC. 920. REASONABLE FEES AND RULES FOR PAYMENT CARD TRANSACTIONS.

"(a) REASONABLE INTERCHANGE TRANSACTION FEES FOR ELECTRONIC DEBIT TRANSACTIONS. —

"(1)REGULATORY AUTHORITY OVER INTERCHANGE TRANSACTION FEES. — The Board may prescribe regulations, pursuant to section 553 of title 5, United States Code, regarding any interchange transaction fee that an issuer may receive or charge with respect to an electronic debit transaction, to implement this subsection (including related definitions), and to prevent circumvention or evasion of this subsection.

"(2) REASONABLE INTERCHANGE TRANSACTION FEES. — The amount of any interchange transaction fee that an issuer may receive or charge with respect to an electronic debit transaction shall be reasonable and proportional to the cost incurred by the issuer with respect to the transaction.

"(3) RULEMAKING REQUIRED. —

"(A) IN GENERAL. — The Board shall prescribe regulations in final form not later than 9 months after the date of enactment of the Consumer Financial Protection Act of 2010, to establish standards for assessing whether the amount of any interchange transaction fee described in paragraph (2) is reasonable and proportional to the cost incurred by the issuer with respect to the transaction.

(F)住房金融系统改革对租赁房屋融资的影响;

(G)住房金融系统改革对二级市场流动性的影响;

(H)标准化在住房金融系统中的作用;

(I)如何借鉴其他国家在住房金融系统方面的经验帮助美国确定住房金融系统的改革方案;及

(J)采用何种方案实现住房金融系统改革前后的过渡。

(b)**报告与建议**。——财政部部长应于2011年1月31日之前,向参议院银行、住房与城市事务委员会以及众议院金融服务委员会提交第(a)子条规定的报告和建议。

第1075条 支付卡交易的合理费用与规则

(a)**一般规定**。——《电子资金划拨法》(《美国法典》第十五编第1693节及其后条文)修正如下——

(1)第920条和第921条分别重新编号为第921条和第922条;及

(2)在第919条之后插入如下内容:

"第920条 支付卡交易的合理费用与规则

(a)**电子借记交易的合理跨行手续费**。——

(1)**跨行手续费的监管机构**。——联邦储备委员会可以根据《美国法典》第五编第553节就发卡行收取或计收的电子借记交易跨行手续费制定规章,以实施本子条规定(包括相关定义)并防止规避或逃避本子条规定的行为。

(2)**合理跨行手续费**。——发卡行就电子借记交易收取或计收的任何跨行手续费金额均应合理,并与该等发卡行因该等交易发生的成本成比例。

(3)**规则制定要求**。——

(A)**一般规定**。——联邦储备委员会应于《2010年消费者金融保护法》颁布之日后9个月内制定最终规章,以便设定相关标准评估第(2)款所述任何跨行手续费的金额是否合理,以及是否与该等发卡行因该等交易发生的成本成比例。

"(B) INFORMATION COLLECTION. — The Board may require any issuer (or agent of an issuer) or payment card network to provide the Board with such information as may be necessary to carry out the provisions of this subsection and the Board, in issuing rules under subparagraph (A) and on at least a bi-annual basis thereafter, shall disclose such aggregate or summary information concerning the costs incurred, and interchange transaction fees charged or received, by issuers or payment card networks in connection with the authorization, clearance or settlement of electronic debit transactions as the Board considers appropriate and in the public interest.

"(4) CONSIDERATIONS; CONSULTATION. — In prescribing regulations under paragraph (3)(A), the Board shall —

"(A) consider the functional similarity between —

"(i) electronic debit transactions; and

"(ii) checking transactions that are required within the Federal Reserve bank system to clear at par;

"(B) distinguish between —

"(i) the incremental cost incurred by an issuer for the role of the issuer in the authorization, clearance, or settlement of a particular electronic debit transaction, which cost shall be considered under paragraph (2); and

"(ii) other costs incurred by an issuer which are not specific to a particular electronic debit transaction, which costs shall not be considered under paragraph (2); and

"(C) consult, as appropriate, with the Comptroller of the Currency, the Board of Directors of the Federal Deposit Insurance Corporation, the Director of the Office of Thrift Supervision, the National Credit Union Administration Board, the Administrator of the Small Business Administration, and the Director of the Bureau of Consumer Financial Protection.

"(5) ADJUSTMENTS TO INTERCHANGE TRANSACTION FEES FOR FRAUD PREVENTION COSTS. —

"(A) ADJUSTMENTS. — The Board may allow for an adjustment to the fee amount received or charged by an issuer under paragraph (2), if —

"(i) such adjustment is reasonably necessary to make allowance for costs incurred by the issuer in preventing fraud in relation to electronic debit transactions involving that issuer; and

"(ii) the issuer complies with the fraud-related standards established by the Board under subparagraph (B), which standards shall —

"(I) be designed to ensure that any fraud-related adjustment of the issuer is limited to the amount described in clause (i) and takes into account any fraud-related reimbursements (including amounts from charge-backs) received from consumers, merchants, or payment card networks in relation to electronic debit transactions involving the issuer; and

(B)**信息收集**。——联邦储备委员会可以要求任何发卡行(或发卡行的代理行)或支付卡网络向其提供实施本子条规定所需的必要信息。联邦储备委员会应在根据第(A)子款的规定颁布规则时,披露其认为适当且有助于维护公共利益的如下信息,并且以后每年至少将该等信息披露两次:发卡行或支付卡网络因电子借记交易授权、清算或结算而发生的成本及计收或收取的跨行手续费的汇总或摘要信息。

(4)**考虑因素;磋商**。——在根据第(3)(A)款的规定制定规章时,联邦储备委员会应——

(A)考虑以下二者的功能相似性——

(i)电子借记交易;和

(ii)联邦储备银行系统内要求按票面价值进行清算的支票交易;

(B)对以下二者加以区分——

(i)发卡行因在特定电子借记交易的授权、清算或结算中担任发卡行角色而发生的增量成本[该等成本应视为第(2)款规定的成本];和

(ii)发卡行并非因特定电子借记交易而发生的其他成本[该等成本不得视为第(2)款规定的成本];并

(C)与货币监理署署长、联邦存款保险公司董事会、储蓄机构监理局局长、国家信贷联盟署委员会、小企业管理局局长以及消费者金融保护局局长进行适当的磋商。

(5)**基于欺诈防范成本对跨行手续费进行的调整**。——

(A)**调整**。——在下列情形下,联邦储备委员会可以允许发卡行对其按照第(2)款收取或计收的手续费金额进行调整——

(i)为了补贴该发卡行因防范电子借记交易欺诈行为而发生的成本,进行上述调整确属合理必要;且

(ii)发卡行遵守联邦储备委员会根据第(B)子款设定的符合如下条件的反欺诈标准,——

(I)应旨在确保发卡行在进行任何反欺诈调整时,调整范围以第(i)项所述金额为限,并将发卡行因其参与电子借记交易而从消费者、商家或支付卡网络获得的与反欺诈相关的任何补偿金额(包括反向计费金额)考虑进去;并

"(II) require issuers to take effective steps to reduce the occurrence of, and costs from, fraud in relation to electronic debit transactions, including through the development and implementation of cost–effective fraud prevention technology.

"(B) RULEMAKING REQUIRED. —

"(i) IN GENERAL. — The Board shall prescribe regulations in final form not later than 9 months after the date of enactment of the Consumer Financial Protection Act of 2010, to establish standards for making adjustments under this paragraph.

"(ii) FACTORS FOR CONSIDERATION. — In issuing the standards and prescribing regulations under this paragraph, the Board shall consider —

"(I) the nature, type, and occurrence of fraud in electronic debit transactions;

"(II) the extent to which the occurrence of fraud depends on whether authorization in an electronic debit transaction is based on signature, PIN, or other means;

"(III) the available and economical means by which fraud on electronic debit transactions may be reduced;

"(IV) the fraud prevention and data security costs expended by each party involved in electronic debit transactions (including consumers, persons who accept debit cards as a form of payment, financial institutions, retailers and payment card networks);

"(V) the costs of fraudulent transactions absorbed by each party involved in such transactions (including consumers, persons who accept debit cards as a form of payment, financial institutions, retailers and payment card networks);

"(VI) the extent to which interchange transaction fees have in the past reduced or increased incentives for parties involved in electronic debit transactions to reduce fraud on such transactions; and

"(VII) such other factors as the Board considers appropriate.

"(6) EXEMPTION FOR SMALL ISSUERS. —

"(A) IN GENERAL. — This subsection shall not apply to any issuer that, together with its affiliates, has assets of less than $10,000,000,000, and the Board shall exempt such issuers from regulations prescribed under paragraph (3)(A).

"(B) DEFINITION. — For purposes of this paragraph, the term "issuer" shall be limited to the person holding the asset account that is debited through an electronic debit transaction.

"(7) EXEMPTION FOR GOVERNMENT–ADMINISTERED PAYMENT PROGRAMS AND RELOADABLE PREPAID CARDS. —

"(A) IN GENERAL. — This subsection shall not apply to an interchange transaction fee charged or received with respect to an electronic debit transaction in which a person uses —

"(i) a debit card or general–use prepaid card that has been provided to a person pursuant to a Federal, State or local government–administered payment program, in which the

(II)应要求发卡行采取有效措施,包括通过开发并实施具有成本效益的欺诈防范技术的方式,以减少电子借记交易欺诈行为的发生频率,并降低相关成本。

(B)**规则制定要求**。——

(i)**一般规定**。——联邦储备委员会应于《2010年消费者金融保护法》颁布之日后9个月内制定最终规章,以便针对按照本条规定进行的手续费金额调整设定标准。

(ii)**考虑因素**。——在根据本款规定发布标准及制定规章时,联邦储备委员会应考虑如下因素——

(I)电子借记交易中欺诈行为的性质、类型和发生频率;

(II)电子借记交易授权是否基于签名、个人识别码或其他手段作出,在多大程度上决定了欺诈行为的发生频率;

(III)可用并且经济的减少电子借记交易欺诈行为的手段;

(IV)电子借记交易每一参与方(包括消费者、接受借记卡支付方式的主体、金融机构、零售商及支付卡网络)为防范欺诈和保障数据安全支付的成本;

(V)该等交易每一参与方(包括消费者、接受借记卡支付方式的主体、金融机构、零售商及支付卡网络)承担的欺诈交易带来的成本;

(VI)跨行手续费以往曾在多大程度上降低或提高了电子借记交易参与方减少该类交易欺诈行为发生的积极性;及

(VII)联邦储备委员会认为适当的其他因素。

(6)**对小型发卡行的豁免**。——

(A)**一般规定**。——任何发卡行与其关联方合计的资产总额低于100亿美元的,不适用本子条规定。联邦储备委员会应向该等发卡行授予豁免,使其不必适用第(3)(A)款所述规章。

(B)**定义**。——就本款而言,'发卡行'一词仅限于持有以电子借记交易方式进行借记的资产账户的主体。

(7)**针对政府管理的支付计划及可充值预付卡的豁免**。——

(A)**一般规定**。——本子条规定不适用于在符合如下条件的电子借记交易中计收或收取的跨行手续费——

(i)持卡人使用的卡属于依照联邦、州或本地政府管理的支付计划发行的借记卡或通用预付卡,且持卡人只能使用该借记卡或通用预付卡,对依照该计划提供的资

person may only use the debit card or general–use prepaid card to transfer or debit funds, monetary value, or other assets that have been provided pursuant to such program; or

"(ii) a plastic card, payment code, or device that is —

"(I) linked to funds, monetary value, or assets which are purchased or loaded on a prepaid basis;

"(II) not issued or approved for use to access or debit any account held by or for the benefit of the card holder (other than a subaccount or other method of recording or tracking funds purchased or loaded on the card on a prepaid basis);

"(III) redeemable at multiple, unaffiliated merchants or service providers, or automated teller machines;

"(IV) used to transfer or debit funds, monetary value, or other assets; and

"(V) reloadable and not marketed or labeled as a gift card or gift certificate.

"(B) EXCEPTION. — Notwithstanding subparagraph (A), after the end of the 1–year period beginning on the effective date provided in paragraph (9), this subsection shall apply to an interchange transaction fee charged or received with respect to an electronic debit transaction described in subparagraph (A)(i) in which a person uses a general–use prepaid card, or an electronic debit transaction described in subparagraph (A)(ii), if any of the following fees may be charged to a person with respect to the card:

"(i) A fee for an overdraft, including a shortage of funds or a transaction processed for an amount exceeding the account balance.

"(ii) A fee imposed by the issuer for the first withdrawal per month from an automated teller machine that is part of the issuer's designated automated teller machine network.

"(C) DEFINITION. — For purposes of subparagraph (B), the term 'designated automated teller machine network' means either —

"(i) all automated teller machines identified in the name of the issuer; or

"(ii) any network of automated teller machines identified by the issuer that provides reasonable and convenient access to the issuer's customers.

"(D) REPORTING. — Beginning 12 months after the date of enactment of the Consumer Financial Protection Act of 2010, the Board shall annually provide a report to the Congress regarding —

"(i) the prevalence of the use of general–use prepaid cards in Federal, State or local government–administered payment programs; and

"(ii) the interchange transaction fees and cardholder fees charged with respect to the use of such general–use prepaid cards.

"(8) REGULATORY AUTHORITY OVER NETWORK FEES. —

"(A) IN GENERAL. — The Board may prescribe regulations, pursuant to section 553 of title 5, United States Code, regarding any network fee.

金、金钱价值或其他资产进行转账或借记;或

(ii)持卡人使用的是符合如下条件的塑料卡、支付代码或设备——

(I)与在预付基础上购买或充储的资金、金钱价值或资产相关联;

(II)发行或批准用途既不是为了使用或借记持卡人持有的任何账户,也不是为了使用或借记为持卡人之利益持有的任何账户(但子账户,或记录或追踪在预付基础上购买或充储的卡内资金的其他方法除外);

(III)可通过多家非关联商家或服务提供者或者自动取款机进行赎回;

(IV)系用于对资金、金钱价值或其他资产进行转账或借记;且

(V)可充值,但不是作为礼品卡或礼品券进行销售,亦未被标识为礼品卡或礼品券。

(B)**例外规定**。——无论第(A)子款如何规定,在第(9)款规定的生效日起届满1年之后,本子条规定应适用于针对第(A)(i)子款所述持卡人使用通用预付卡的电子借记交易收取或计收的跨行手续费,或针对第(A)(ii)子款所述电子借记交易收取或计收的跨行手续费,前提是持卡人因该卡而被计收了以下任何费用:

(i)透支手续费,包括资金不足或交易金额超过账户余额的情况。

(ii)发卡行针对通过其指定自动取款机网络内的取款机提取的每月首笔款项而收取的手续费。

(C)**定义**。——就第(B)子款而言,'指定自动取款机网络'一词系指——

(i)标有发卡行名称的所有自动取款机;或

(ii)经发卡行确定的向其客户提供合理便捷服务的任何自动取款机网络。

(D)**报告**。——联邦储备委员会应于《2010年消费者金融保护法》颁布之日后12个月内向国会提交1份年度报告,汇报——

(i)联邦、州或本地政府管理的支付计划中通用预付卡使用的普及率;及

(ii)就使用该类通用预付卡所收取的跨行手续费和持卡人费用。

(8)**网络费用的监管机构**。——

(A)**一般规定**。——联邦储备委员会可以针对任何网络费用,根据《美国法典》第五编第553节制定规章。

"(B) LIMITATION. — The authority under subparagraph (A) to prescribe regulations shall be limited to regulations to ensure that —

"(i) a network fee is not used to directly or indirectly compensate an issuer with respect to an electronic debit transaction; and

"(ii) a network fee is not used to circumvent or evade the restrictions of this subsection and regulations prescribed under such subsection.

"(C) RULEMAKING REQUIRED. — The Board shall pre scribe regulations in final form before the end of the 9–month period beginning on the date of the enactment of the Consumer Financial Protection Act of 2010, to carry out the authorities provided under subparagraph (A).

"(9) EFFECTIVE DATE. — This subsection shall take effect at the end of the 12–month period beginning on the date of the enactment of the Consumer Financial Protection Act of 2010.

"(b) LIMITATION ON PAYMENT CARD NETWORK RESTRICTIONS. —

"(1) PROHIBITIONS AGAINST EXCLUSIVITY ARRANGEMENTS. —

"(A) NO EXCLUSIVE NETWORK. — The Board shall, before the end of the 1–year period beginning on the date of the enactment of the Consumer Financial Protection Act of 2010, prescribe regulations providing that an issuer or payment card network shall not directly or through any agent, processor, or licensed member of a payment card network, by contract, requirement, condition, penalty, or otherwise, restrict the number of payment card networks on which an electronic debit transaction may be processed to —

"(i) 1 such network; or

"(ii) 2 or more such networks which are owned, controlled, or otherwise operated by —

"(I) affiliated persons; or

"(II) networks affiliated with such issuer.

"(B) NO ROUTING RESTRICTIONS. — The Board shall, before the end of the 1–year period beginning on the date of the enactment of the Consumer Financial Protection Act of 2010, prescribe regulations providing that an issuer or payment card network shall not, directly or through any agent, processor, or licensed member of the network, by contract, requirement, condition, penalty, or otherwise, inhibit the ability of any person who accepts debit cards for payments to direct the routing of electronic debit transactions for processing over any payment card network that may process such transactions.

"(2) LIMITATION ON RESTRICTIONS ON OFFERING DISCOUNTS FOR USE OF A FORM OF PAYMENT. —

"(A) IN GENERAL. — A payment card network shall not, directly or through any agent, processor, or licensed member of the network, by contract, requirement, condition,

(B)**限制**。——第(A)子款规定的规章制定权应限于制定旨在实现如下目的规章——

(i)确保网络费用不会被直接或间接用于为发卡行提供与电子借记交易相关的补偿;且

(ii)确保网络费用不会被用于规避或逃避本子条以及根据本子条规定制定的规章的限制性规定。

(C)**规则制定要求**。——联邦储备委员会应于《2010年消费者金融保护法》颁布之日起九个月内制定最终规章,以便行使第(A)子款规定的权力。

(9)**生效日**。——本子条规定应于《2010年消费者金融保护法》颁布之日起届满12个月之日生效。

(b)**对限制支付卡网络的限制**。——

(1)**禁止排他性安排**。——

(A)**不得设定排他性网络**。——联邦储备委员会应于《2010年消费者金融保护法》颁布之日起一年内制定规章,规定发卡行或支付卡网络不得直接,亦不得通过任何代理人、处理机构或支付卡网络许可成员,以签订合同、施加要求、设定条件、实施罚款的方式或其他方式,限制能够处理电子借记交易的支付卡网络的数量,即——

(i)不得限制仅有一家支付卡网络可以从事电子借记交易处理;或

(ii)不得限制仅有2家或2家以上由如下主体拥有、控制或以其他方式运营的支付卡网络可以从事电子借记交易处理——

(I)关联主体;或

(II)该发卡行的关联网络。

(B)**不得设定路径限制**。——联邦储备委员会应于《2010年消费者金融保护法》颁布之日起1年内制定规章,规定发卡行或支付卡网络不得直接,亦不得通过任何代理人、处理机构或该网络的许可成员以签订合同、施加要求、设定条件、实施罚款的方式或其他方式,限制任何接受借记卡付款的主体为通过任何可处理该等交易的支付卡网络处理该等交易而指定电子借记交易处理路径的能力。

(2)**对限制为使用某种付款方式提供折扣的限制**。——

(A)**一般规定**。——支付卡网络不得直接,亦不得通过任何代理人、处理机构或该网络的许可成员以签订合同、施加要求、设定条件、实施罚款的方式或其他方式,限

penalty, or otherwise, inhibit the ability of any person to provide a discount or in–kind incentive for payment by the use of cash, checks, debit cards, or credit cards to the extent that —

"(i) in the case of a discount or in–kind incentive for payment by the use of debit cards, the discount or in–kind incentive does not differentiate on the basis of the issuer or the payment card network;

"(ii) in the case of a discount or in–kind incentive for payment by the use of credit cards, the discount or in–kind incentive does not differentiate on the basis of the issuer or the payment card network; and

"(iii) to the extent required by Federal law and applicable State law, such discount or in–kind incentive is offered to all prospective buyers and disclosed clearly and conspicuously.

"(B) LAWFUL DISCOUNTS. — For purposes of this paragraph, the network may not penalize any person for the providing of a discount that is in compliance with Federal law and applicable State law.

"(3) LIMITATION ON RESTRICTIONS ON SETTING TRANSACTION MINIMUMS OR MAXIMUMS. —

"(A) IN GENERAL. — A payment card network shall not, directly or through any agent, processor, or licensed member of the network, by contract, requirement, condition, penalty, or otherwise, inhibit the ability —

"(i) of any person to set a minimum dollar value for the acceptance by that person of credit cards, to the extent that —

"(I) such minimum dollar value does not differentiate between issuers or between payment card networks; and

"(II) such minimum dollar value does not exceed $10.00; or

"(ii) of any Federal agency or institution of higher education to set a maximum dollar value for the acceptance by that Federal agency or institution of higher education of credit cards, to the extent that such maximum dollar value does not differentiate between issuers or between payment card networks.

"(B) INCREASE IN MINIMUM DOLLAR AMOUNT. — The Board may, by regulation prescribed pursuant to section 553 of title 5, United States Code, increase the amount of the dollar value listed in subparagraph (A)(i)(II).

"(4) RULE OF CONSTRUCTION:. — No provision of this sub section shall be construed to authorize any person —

"(A) to discriminate between debit cards within a payment card network on the basis of the issuer that issued the debit card; or

"(B) to discriminate between credit cards within a payment card network on the basis of the issuer that issued the credit card.

"(c) DEFINITIONS. — For purposes of this section, the following definitions shall

制任何主体为使用现金、支票、借记卡或信用卡付款提供折扣或实物激励的能力，前提是——

(i)对于为使用借记卡付款提供折扣或实物激励的情形，该等主体并未基于发卡行或支付卡网络的不同而提供不同的折扣或实物激励；

(ii)对于为使用信用卡付款提供折扣或实物激励的情形，该等主体并未基于发卡行或支付卡网络的不同提供不同的折扣或实物激励；且

(iii)在联邦法律及适用的州法律规定的范围内，该等主体向所有潜在客户提供上述折扣或实物激励，并采用清晰、显明的方式对上述折扣或实物激励进行披露。

(B)**合法折扣**。——就本款而言，支付卡网络不得因任何主体提供符合联邦法律及适用的州法律的折扣而对其进行处罚。

(3)**对限制设定交易最低或最高金额的限制**。——

(A)**一般规定**。——支付卡网络不得直接，亦不得通过任何代理人、处理机构或该网络的许可成员，以签订合同、施加要求、设定条件、实施罚款的方式或其他方式限制——

(i)任何主体对其接受的信用卡付款设定交易最低金额的能力，前提是——

(I)该等主体并未基于发卡行或支付卡网络的不同而设定不同的该等最低金额；且

(II)该等最低金额未超过10.00美元；或

(ii)任何联邦机关或高等教育机构对其接受的信用卡付款设定交易最高金额的能力，前提是该等联邦机构或高等教育机构并未基于发卡行或支付卡网络的不同而设定不同的该等最高金额。

(B)**最低交易金额的提高**。——联邦储备委员会可以根据《美国法典》第五编第553节制定规章，提高第(A)(i)(II)子款所列金额。

(4)**解释规则**。——本子条任何内容均不得被解释为授权任何主体——

(A)基于发行借记卡的发卡行的不同而对支付卡网络内的借记卡进行区别对待；或

(B)基于发行信用卡的发卡行的不同而对支付卡网络内的信用卡进行区别对待。

(c)**定义**。——就本条而言，应适用如下定义：

apply:

"(1) AFFILIATE. — The term 'affiliate' means any company that controls, is controlled by, or is under common control with another company.

"(2) DEBIT CARD. — The term 'debit card' —

"(A) means any card, or other payment code or device, issued or approved for use through a payment card network to debit an asset account (regardless of the purpose for which the account is established), whether authorization is based on signature, PIN, or other means;

"(B) includes a general–use prepaid card, as that term is defined in section 915(a)(2)(A); and

"(C) does not include paper checks.

"(3) CREDIT CARD. — The term 'credit card' has the same meaning as in section 103 of the Truth in Lending Act.

"(4) DISCOUNT. — The term 'discount' —

"(A) means a reduction made from the price that customers are informed is the regular price; and

"(B) does not include any means of increasing the price that customers are informed is the regular price.

"(5) ELECTRONIC DEBIT TRANSACTION. — The term 'electronic debit transaction' means a transaction in which a person uses a debit card.

"(6) FEDERAL AGENCY. — The term 'Federal agency' means —

"(A) an agency (as defined in section 101 of title 31, United States Code); and

"(B) a Government corporation (as defined in section 103 of title 5, United States Code).

"(7) INSTITUTION OF HIGHER EDUCATION. — The term 'institution of higher education' has the same meaning as in 101 and 102 of the Higher Education Act of 1965 (20 U.S.C. 1001, 1002).

"(8) INTERCHANGE TRANSACTION FEE. — The term 'interchange transaction fee' means any fee established, charged or received by a payment card network for the purpose of compensating an issuer for its involvement in an electronic debit transaction.

"(9) ISSUER. — The term 'issuer' means any person who issues a debit card, or credit card, or the agent of such person with respect to such card.

"(10) NETWORK FEE. — The term 'network fee' means any fee charged and received by a payment card network with respect to an electronic debit transaction, other than an interchange transaction fee.

"(11) PAYMENT CARD NETWORK. — The term 'payment card network' means an entity that directly, or through licensed members, processors, or agents, provides the proprietary services, infrastructure, and software that route information and data to conduct

(1)**关联方**。——‘关联方’一词系指控制其他公司、受其他公司控制或与其他公司受同一控制的任何公司。

(2)**借记卡**。——‘借记卡’一词——

(A)系指发行的或被批准的用以通过支付卡网络对资产账户(不论账户的开立目的为何)进行借记的任何卡或者其他付款代码或设备,不论授权是基于签名、个人识别密码还是基于其他方式作出;

(B)包括通用预付卡[定义见第915(a)(2)(A)条];且

(C)不包括纸质支票。

(3)**信用卡**。——‘信用卡’一词的含义以《诚实信贷法》第103条的定义为准。

(4)**折扣**。——‘折扣’一词——

(A)系指客户获知的正常价格的减降;且

(B)不包括客户获知的正常价格的任何形式提高。

(5)**电子借记交易**。——‘电子借记交易’一词系指某一主体使用借记卡进行的交易。

(6)**联邦机关**。——‘联邦机关’一词系指——

(A)机关(定义见《美国法典》第三十一编第101节);及

(B)政府持股公司(定义见《美国法典》第五编第103节)。

(7)**高等教育机构**。——‘高等教育机构’一词的含义以《1965年高等教育法》第101条和第102条(《美国法典》第二十编第1001节和第1002节)的定义为准。

(8)**跨行手续费**。——‘跨行手续费’一词系指支付卡网络出于因发卡行参与电子借贷交易向发卡行支付报酬的目的而设定、计收或收取的任何费用。

(9)**发卡行**。——‘发卡行’一词系指发行借记卡或信用卡的任何主体,或者该等主体的与该卡相关的代理人。

(10)**网络费用**。——‘网络费用’一词系指支付卡网络就电子借记交易所计收和收取的除跨行手续费之外的任何费用。

(11)**支付卡网络**。——‘支付卡网络’一词系指为了进行借记卡或信用卡交易的授权、清算和结算,直接或通过许可成员、处理机构或代理人提供用以按指定路线发送信息和数据的专有服务、基础设施及软件的实体,以及某一主体为了接受通过某个

debit card or credit card transaction authorization, clearance, and settlement, and that a person uses in order to accept as a form of payment a brand of debit card, credit card or other device that may be used to carry out debit or credit transactions.

"(d) ENFORCEMENT.—

"(1) IN GENERAL. — Compliance with the requirements imposed under this section shall be enforced under section 918.

"(2) EXCEPTION. — Sections 916 and 917 shall not apply with respect to this section or the requirements imposed pursuant to this section.".

(b) AMENDMENT TO THE FOOD AND NUTRITION ACT OF 2008. — Section 7(h)(10) of the Food and Nutrition Act of 2008 (7 U.S.C. 2016(h)(10)) is amended to read as follows:

"(10) FEDERAL LAW NOT APPLICABLE. — Section 920 of the Electronic Fund Transfer Act shall not apply to electronic benefit transfer or reimbursement systems under this Act.".

(c) AMENDMENT TO THE FARM SECURITY AND RURAL INVESTMENT ACT OF 2002. — Section 4402 of the Farm Security and Rural Investment Act of 2002 (7 U.S.C. 3007) is amended by adding at the end the following new subsection:

"(f) FEDERAL LAW NOT APPLICABLE. — Section 920 of the Electronic Fund Transfer Act shall not apply to electronic benefit transfer systems established under this section.".

(d) AMENDMENT TO THE CHILD NUTRITION ACT OF 1966. — Section 11 of the Child Nutrition Act of 1966 (42 U.S.C. 1780) is amended by adding at the end the following:

"(c) FEDERAL LAW NOT APPLICABLE. — Section 920 of the Electronic Fund Transfer Act shall not apply to electronic benefit transfer systems established under this Act or the Richard B. Russell National School Lunch Act (42 U.S.C. 1751 et seq.).".

SEC. 1076. REVERSE MORTGAGE STUDY AND REGULATIONS.

(a) STUDY. — Not later than 1 year after the designated transfer date, the Bureau shall conduct a study on reverse mortgage transactions.

(b) REGULATIONS.—

(1) IN GENERAL. — If the Bureau determines through the study required under subsection (a) that conditions or limitations on reverse mortgage transactions are necessary or appropriate for accomplishing the purposes and objectives of this title, including protecting borrowers with respect to the obtaining of reverse mortgage loans for the purpose of funding investments, annuities, and other investment products and the suitability of a borrower in obtaining a reverse mortgage for such purpose.

(2) IDENTIFIED PRACTICES AND INTEGRATED DISCLOSURES. — The

品牌的借记卡、信用卡或其他可以用以执行借记或信用交易的设备进行的付款而利用的实体。

(d)**执行**。——

(1)**一般规定**。——对根据本条施加的要求的合规应根据第918条的规定执行。

(2)**例外规定**。——第916条和第917条不适用于本条或根据本条施加要求。”

(b)**对《2008年食品和营养法》的修正**。——《2008年食品和营养法》第7(h)(10)条(《美国法典》第七编第2016(h)(10)节)修正后全文如下:

“(10)**不适用的联邦法律**。——《电子资金划拨法》第920条不适用于本法规定的电子福利转账或偿付系统。”

(c)**对《2002年农场安全与农村投资法》的修正**。——在《2002年农场安全与农村投资法》第4402条(《美国法典》第七编第3007节)结尾处增加如下新子条,作为对该条的修正:

“(f)**不适用的联邦法律**。——《电子资金划拨法》第920条不适用于本条规定的电子福利转账系统。”

(d)**对《1966年儿童营养法》的修正**。——在《1966年儿童营养法》第11条(《美国法典》第四十二编第1780节)结尾处增加如下内容,作为对该条的修正:

“(c)**不适用的联邦法律**。——《电子资金划拨法》第920条不适用于根据本法或者《理查德B.罗素全国学校午餐法》(《美国法典》第四十二编第1751节及其后条文)的规定设立的电子福利转账系统。”

第1076条　反向抵押贷款研究与相关规章制定

(a)**研究**。——消费者金融保护局应于指定转移日后1年内开展有关反向抵押贷款交易的研究。

(b)**规章**。——

(1)**一般规定**。——如果消费者金融保护局在开展第(a)子条所规定的研究后判定,为实现本编的宗旨和目标,包括在借款人为了开展投资或对年金及其他投资产品进行投资而获取反向抵押贷款时,为了保护借款人,以及为了确定借款人为前述目的获取反向抵押贷款的适当性,对反向抵押贷款交易设定相关条件或限制而言确属必要或适当(,则消费者金融保护局有权制定相关规章,设定该等条件或限制)[1]。

(2)**确定的做法和综合披露**。——经消费者金融保护局判定,依据第(1)款的规定

1　原文只有“If”引导的从句,缺失主句,括号中的内容系译者根据上下文补足。——译者注

regulations prescribed under paragraph (1) may, as the Bureau may so determine —

(A) identify any practice as unfair, deceptive, or abusive in connection with a reverse mortgage transaction; and

(B) provide for an integrated disclosure standard and model disclosures for reverse mortgage transactions, consistent with section 4302 (d), that combines the relevant disclosures required under the Truth in Lending Act (15 U.S.C. 1601 et seq.) and the Real Estate Settlement Procedures Act, with the disclosures required to be provided to consumers for Home Equity Conversion Mortgages under section 255 of the National Housing Act.

(c) RULE OF CONSTRUCTION. — This section shall not be construed as limiting the authority of the Bureau to issue regulations, orders, or guidance that apply to reverse mortgages prior to the completion of the study required under subsection (a).

SEC. 1077. REPORT ON PRIVATE EDUCATION LOANS AND PRIVATE EDUCATIONAL LENDERS.

(a) REPORT. — Not later than 2 years after the date of enactment of this Act, the Director and the Secretary of Education, in consultation with the Commissioners of the Federal Trade Commission, and the Attorney General of the United States, shall submit a report to the Committee on Banking, Housing, and Urban Affairs and the Committee on Health, Education, Labor, and Pensions of the Senate and the Committee on Financial Services and the Committee on Education and Labor of the House of Representatives, on private education loans (as that term is defined in section 140 of the Truth in Lending Act (15 U.S.C. 1650)) and private educational lenders (as that term is defined in such section).

(b) CONTENT. — The report required by this section shall examine, at a minimum —

(1) the growth and changes of the private education loan market in the United States;

(2) factors influencing such growth and changes;

(3) the extent to which students and parents of students rely on private education loans to finance postsecondary education and the private education loan indebtedness of borrowers;

(4) the characteristics of private education loan borrowers, including —

(A) the types of institutions of higher education that they attend;

(B) socioeconomic characteristics (including income and education levels, racial characteristics, geographical background, age, and gender);

(C) what other forms of financing borrowers use to pay for education;

(D) whether they exhaust their Federal loan options before taking out a private loan;

(E) whether such borrowers are dependent or independent students (as determined under part F of title IV of the Higher Education Act of 1965) or parents of such students;

(F) whether such borrowers are students enrolled in a program leading to a certificate, license, or credential other than a degree, an associates degree, a baccalaureate degree, or a graduate or professional degree; and

制定的规章可以——

(A)确定与反向抵押贷款交易相关的任何做法属于不公平、欺骗性或滥用性做法;并

(B)按照第4302(d)条规定为反向抵押贷款交易设定综合披露标准,并提供示范性披露,该等披露标准和示范性披露应综合《诚实信贷法》(《美国法典》第十五编第1601节及其后条文)和《房地产结算程序法》的相关披露要求,以及《国民住房法》第255条关于就住房权益转换抵押贷款向消费者提供披露的要求。

(c)**解释规则**。——本条规定不得被解释为对消费者金融保护局在完成第(a)子条规定的研究之前发布适用于反向抵押贷款的规章、命令或指引的权力构成限制。

第1077条　关于个人教育贷款和个人教育贷款人的报告

(a)**报告**。——消费者金融保护局局长和教育部部长应于本法颁布之日起两年内,与联邦贸易委员会主席及联邦总检察长磋商,针对个人教育贷款[定义见《诚实信贷法》第140条(《美国法典》第十五编第1650节)]和个人教育贷款人(定义见《诚实信贷法》第140条)向参议院银行、住房与城市事务委员会、参议院健康、教育、劳动与养老委员会、众议院金融服务委员会以及众议院教育与劳动委员会提交一份报告。

(b)**内容**。——本条规定的报告至少应对如下各项进行调查——

(1)美国个人教育贷款市场的发展与变化;

(2)影响该等发展与变化的因素;

(3)学生及其家长在高等教育费支付方面对个人教育贷款的依赖程度,以及借款人的个人教育贷款负债情况;

(4)个人教育贷款借款人的特点,包括——

(A)就读的高等教育机构的类型;

(B)社会经济特征(包括收入和教育水平、种族特征、地理背景、年龄及性别);

(C)借款人用以支付教育费用的其他融资手段;

(D)借款人在获得私人贷款之前是否用尽其获取联邦贷款的选择权;

(E)借款人是经济独立或非独立的学生(具体情况根据《1965年高等教育法》第四编第F部分进行确定)还是该等学生的家长;

(F)借款人被录取就读的课程是颁发证书、执照或证明,还是颁发学位、专科学位、学士学位或者研究生或专业学位;及

(G) if practicable, employment and repayment behaviors;

(5) the characteristics of private educational lenders, including whether such creditors are for-profit, non-profit, or institutions of higher education;

(6) the underwriting criteria used by private educational lenders, including the use of cohort default rate (as such term is defined in section 435(m) of the Higher Education Act of 1965);

(7) the terms, conditions, and pricing of private education loans;

(8) the consumer protections available to private education loan borrowers, including the effectiveness of existing disclosures and requirements and borrowers' awareness and understanding about terms and conditions of various financial products;

(9) whether Federal regulators and the public have access to information sufficient to provide them with assurances that private education loans are provided in accord with the Nation's fair lending laws and that allows public officials to determine lender compliance with fair lending laws; and

(10) any statutory or legislative recommendations necessary to improve consumer protections for private education loan borrowers and to better enable Federal regulators and the public to ascertain private educational lender compliance with fair lending laws.

SEC. 1078. STUDY AND REPORT ON CREDIT SCORES.

(a) STUDY. — The Bureau shall conduct a study on the nature, range, and size of variations between the credit scores sold to creditors and those sold to consumers by consumer reporting agencies that compile and maintain files on consumers on a nationwide basis (as defined in section 603(p) of the Fair Credit Reporting Act; 15 U.S.C. 1681a(p)), and whether such variations disadvantage consumers.

(b) REPORT TO CONGRESS. — The Bureau shall submit a report to Congress on the results of the study conducted under subsection (a) not later than 1 year after the date of enactment of this Act.

SEC. 1079. REVIEW, REPORT, AND PROGRAM WITH RESPECT TO EXCHANGE FACILITATORS.

(a) REVIEW. — The Director shall review all Federal laws and regulations relating to the protection of consumers who use exchange facilitators for transactions primarily for personal, family, or household purposes.

(b) REPORT. — Not later than 1 year after the designated transfer date, the Director shall submit to Congress a report describing —

(1) recommendations for legislation to ensure the appropriate protection of consumers who use exchange facilitators for transactions primarily for personal, family, or household purposes;

(2) recommendations for updating the regulations of Federal departments and agencies

(G)就业和还款情况(如可行);

(5)个人教育贷款人的特点,包括该等贷款人是营利性机构、非营利性机构还是高等教育机构;

(6)个人教育贷款人使用的贷款审核标准,包括对群体违约比率的使用["群体违约比率"一词的定义见《1965年高等教育法》第435(m)条];

(7)个人教育贷款的条款、条件和定价;

(8)个人教育贷款借款人可以获得的消费者保护,包括现有披露和要求的有效性,以及借款人对各类金融产品条款和条件的认识和了解;

(9)联邦监管者和公众是否有权获得充分信息,足以使其确信个人教育贷款符合国家公平贷款法律,并且使政府官员能够判定贷款人对公平贷款法律的合规情况;及

(10)为增强向个人教育贷款借款人提供的消费者保护,以及更大程度上使联邦监管者及公众能够确定个人教育贷款人对公平贷款法律的合规情况,而有必要提出的任何制定法或立法建议。

第1078条　信用评分研究与报告

(a)**研究**。——对于在全国范围内编制并维持消费者信用文件的消费者征信机构[定义见《公平信用报告法》第603(p)条(《美国法典》第十五编第1681a(p)节)]向贷款发放人和消费者出售的信用评分之间的差异的性质、范围和规模以及该等差异是否对消费者不利,消费者金融保护局应开展研究。

(b)**向国会报告**。——消费者金融保护局应于本法颁布之日起一年内就根据第(a)子条所开展研究的结果向国会提交一份报告。

第1079条　关于交易中介的审查、报告和计划

(a)**审查**。——对于主要出于个人、家庭或共同居住人目的而使用交易中介进行交易的消费者,消费者金融保护局局长应审查与该等消费者之保护相关的所有联邦法律和规章。

(b)**报告**。——消费者金融保护局局长应于指定转移日后一年内向国会提交一份报告,说明如下内容——

(1)对于主要出于个人、家庭或共同居住人目的而使用交易中介进行交易的消费者,为确保向该等消费者提供适当保护而提出的立法建议;

(2)为确保向上述消费者提供适当保护而提出的更新联邦部门和机关规章的建

to ensure the appropriate protection of such consumers; and

(3) recommendations for regulations to ensure the appropriate protection of such consumers.

(c) PROGRAM. — Not later than 2 years after the date of the submission of the report under subsection (b), the Bureau shall, consistent with subtitle B, propose regulations or otherwise establish a program to protect consumers who use exchange facilitators.

(d) EXCHANGE FACILITATOR DEFINED. — In this section, the term "exchange facilitator" means a person that —

(1) facilitates, for a fee, an exchange of like kind property by entering into an agreement with a taxpayer by which the exchange facilitator acquires from the taxpayer the contractual rights to sell the taxpayer's relinquished property and transfers a replacement property to the taxpayer as a qualified intermediary (within the meaning of Treasury Regulations section 1.1031(k)-1(g)(4)) or enters into an agreement with the taxpayer to take title to a property as an exchange accommodation titleholder (within the meaning of Revenue Procedure 2000-37) or enters into an agreement with a taxpayer to act as a qualified trustee or qualified escrow holder (within the meaning of Treasury Regulations section 1.1031(k)-1(g)(3));

(2) maintains an office for the purpose of soliciting business to perform the services described in paragraph (1); or

(3) advertises any of the services described in paragraph (1) or solicits clients in printed publications, direct mail, television or radio advertisements, telephone calls, facsimile transmissions, or other electronic communications directed to the general public for purposes of providing any such services.

SEC. 1079A. FINANCIAL FRAUD PROVISIONS.

(a) SENTENCING GUIDELINES. —

(1) SECURITIES FRAUD. —

(A) DIRECTIVE. — Pursuant to its authority under section 994 of title 28, United States Code, and in accordance with this paragraph, the United States Sentencing Commission shall review and, if appropriate, amend the Federal Sentencing Guidelines and policy statements applicable to persons convicted of offenses relating to securities fraud or any other similar provision of law, in order to reflect the intent of Congress that penalties for the offenses under the guidelines and policy statements appropriately account for the potential and actual harm to the public and the financial markets from the offenses.

(B) REQUIREMENTS. — In making any amendments to the Federal Sentencing Guidelines and policy statements under subparagraph (A), the United States Sentencing Commission shall —

(i) ensure that the guidelines and policy statements, particularly section 2B1.1(b)(14)

议;及

(3)为确保向上述消费者提供适当保护而提出的规章建议。

(c)**计划**。——消费者金融保护局应于提交第(b)子条所述报告之日后2年内,按照第B子编的规定提出规章草案或以其他方式制定计划,以保护使用交易中介的消费者。

(d)**交易中介的定义**。——就本条而言,"交易中介"一词系指符合如下条件的主体——

(1)通过与纳税人签署交易中介作为合格中介[定义见《联邦税务管理办法》第1.1031(k)-1(g)(4)条]获取出售纳税人所出让财产的合同权利并向纳税人转让替代财产的协议,有偿促成同类财产交换;或者与纳税人签署协议,作为交换寄存产权持有人(定义见《税务规程2000-37》)获得财产产权;或者与纳税人签署协议,以合格受托人或合格托管人[定义见《联邦税务管理办法》第1.1031(k)-1(g)(3)条]身份行事;

(2)出于招揽业务以开展第(1)款所述服务的目的而拥有办公场所;或

(3)为提供第(1)款所述任何服务,通过印刷出版物、直邮、电视或电台广告、电话、传真或其他面向一般公众的电子通讯手段,对第(1)款所述服务进行广告宣传或招揽客户。

第1079A条　关于金融欺诈的法律规定

(a)**量刑指引**。——

(1)**证券欺诈**。——

(A)**方针**。——美国量刑委员会应基于其根据《美国法典》第二十八编第994节规定获得的权力,按照本款规定审查适用于被判犯有证券欺诈罪行或违反任何其他类似法律规定之人的《联邦量刑指引》和政策陈述,并对其进行适当的修正,以反映国会力求量刑指引和政策陈述规定的处罚与该等罪行对公众和金融市场造成的潜在和实际损害相适应的意图。

(B)**要求**。——在根据第(A)子款对《联邦量刑指引》和政策陈述进行修正时,美国量刑委员会应——

(i)确保量刑指引和政策陈述,特别是第2B1.1(b)(14)条与第2B1.1(b)(17)条(及

and section 2B1.1(b)(17)(and any successors thereto), reflect —

(I) the serious nature of the offenses described in subparagraph (A);

(II) the need for an effective deterrent and appropriate punishment to prevent the offenses; and

(III) the effectiveness of incarceration in furthering the objectives described in subclauses (I) and (II);

(ii) consider the extent to which the guidelines appropriately account for the potential and actual harm to the public and the financial markets resulting from the offenses;

(iii) ensure reasonable consistency with other relevant directives and guidelines and Federal statutes;

(iv) make any necessary conforming changes to guidelines; and

(v) ensure that the guidelines adequately meet the purposes of sentencing, as set forth in section 3553(a)(2) of title 18, United States Code.

(2) FINANCIAL INSTITUTION FRAUD. —

(A) DIRECTIVE. — Pursuant to its authority under section 994 of title 28, United States Code, and in accordance with this paragraph, the United States Sentencing Commission shall review and, if appropriate, amend the Federal Sentencing Guidelines and policy statements applicable to persons convicted of fraud offenses relating to financial institutions or federally related mortgage loans and any other similar provisions of law, to reflect the intent of Congress that the penalties for the offenses under the guidelines and policy statements ensure appropriate terms of imprisonment for offenders involved in substantial bank frauds or other frauds relating to financial institutions.

(B) REQUIREMENTS. — In making any amendments to the Federal Sentencing Guidelines and policy statements under subparagraph (A), the United States Sentencing Commission shall —

(i) ensure that the guidelines and policy statements reflect —

(I) the serious nature of the offenses described in subparagraph (A);

(II) the need for an effective deterrent and appropriate punishment to prevent the offenses; and

(III) the effectiveness of incarceration in furthering the objectives described in subclauses (I) and (II);

(ii) consider the extent to which the guidelines appropriately account for the potential and actual harm to the public and the financial markets resulting from the offenses;

(iii) ensure reasonable consistency with other relevant directives and guidelines and Federal statutes;

(iv) make any necessary conforming changes to guidelines; and

(v) ensure that the guidelines adequately meet the purposes of sentencing, as set forth in

前述条款的任何后续规定)的规定,反映——

(I)第(A)子款所述罪行的严重性质;

(II)为防范上述罪行采取具有有效威慑力的适当处罚措施的必要性;及

(III)采用监禁的处罚方式对于促进实现第(I)子项和第(II)子项所述目标的有效性;

(ii)考虑量刑指引与上述罪行对公众和金融市场造成的潜在和实际损害相适应的程度;

(iii)确保与其他相关方针、指引以及联邦制定法规定保持合理一致;

(iv)对量刑指引进行任何必要的一致性修正;并

(v)确保量刑指引充分达到《美国法典》第十八编第3553(a)(2)节规定的量刑目的。

(2)**金融机构欺诈**。——

(A)**方针**。——美国量刑委员会应基于其根据《美国法典》第二十八编第994节规定获得的权力,按照本款规定审查适用于被判犯有金融机构或联邦抵押贷款欺诈罪行或违反任何其他类似法律规定之人的《联邦量刑指引》和政策陈述,并对其进行适当的修正,以反映国会确保按照量刑指引和政策陈述对上述罪行实施的处罚保证使实施重大银行欺诈行为或与金融机构相关的其他欺诈行为的犯罪人获判适当刑期的意图。

(B)**要求**。——在根据第(A)子款对《联邦量刑指引》和政策陈述进行修正时,美国量刑委员会应——

(i)确保量刑指引和政策陈述反映——

(I)第(A)子款所述罪行的严重性质;

(II)为防范上述罪行采取具有有效威慑力的适当处罚措施的必要性;及

(III)采用监禁的处罚方式对于促进实现第(I)子项和第(II)子项所述目标的有效性;

(ii)考虑量刑指引与上述罪行对公众和金融市场造成的潜在和实际损害相适应的程度;

(iii)确保与其他相关方针、指引以及联邦制定法规定保持合理一致;

(iv)对量刑指引进行任何必要的一致性修正;并

(v)确保量刑指引充分达到《美国法典》第十八编第3553(a)(2)节规定的量刑目的。

section 3553(a)(2) of title 18, United States Code.

(b) EXTENSION OF STATUTE OF LIMITATIONS FOR SECURITIES FRAUD VIOLATIONS. —

(1) IN GENERAL. — Chapter 213 of title 18, United States Code, is amended by adding at the end the following:

"§ 3301. Securities fraud offenses

"(a) DEFINITION. — In this section, the term 'securities fraud offense' means a violation of, or a conspiracy or an attempt to violate —

"(1) section 1348;

"(2) section 32(a) of the Securities Exchange Act of 1934 (15 U.S.C. 78ff(a));

"(3) section 24 of the Securities Act of 1933 (15 U.S.C. 77x);

"(4) section 217 of the Investment Advisers Act of 1940 (15 U.S.C. 80b–17);

"(5) section 49 of the Investment Company Act of 1940 (15 U.S.C. 80a–48); or

"(6) section 325 of the Trust Indenture Act of 1939 (15 U.S.C. 77yyy).

"(b) LIMITATION. — No person shall be prosecuted, tried, or punished for a securities fraud offense, unless the indictment is found or the information is instituted within 6 years after the commission of the offense.".

(2) TECHNICAL AND CONFORMING AMENDMENT. — The table of sections for chapter 213 of title 18, United States Code, is amended by adding at the end the following:

"3301. Securities fraud offenses.".

(c) AMENDMENTS TO THE FALSE CLAIMS ACT RELATING TO LIMITATIONS ON ACTIONS. — Section 3730(h) of title 31, United States Code, is amended —

(1) in paragraph (1), by striking "or agent on behalf of the employee, contractor, or agent or associated others in furtherance of other efforts to stop 1 or more violations of this subchapter" and inserting "agent or associated others in furtherance of an action under this section or other efforts to stop 1 or more violations of this subchapter"; and

(2) by adding at the end the following:

"(3) LIMITATION ON BRINGING CIVIL ACTION. — A civil action under this subsection may not be brought more than 3 years after the date when the retaliation occurred.".

Subtitle H — Conforming Amendments

SEC. 1081. AMENDMENTS TO THE INSPECTOR GENERAL ACT.

Effective on the date of enactment of this Act, the Inspector General Act of 1978 (5 U.S.

(b)**延长对证券欺诈违法违规行为提起诉讼的诉讼时效**。——

(1)**一般规定**。——在《美国法典》第十八编第二百一十三章结尾处增加如下内容,作为对该章的修正:

“第3301节　证券欺诈犯罪

(a)**定义**。——就本节而言,‘证券欺诈犯罪’一词系指违反、共谋或试图违反如下法律的行为——

(1)第1348节;

(2)《1934年证券交易法》第32(a)条[《美国法典》第十五编第78ff(a)节];

(3)《1933年证券法》第24条(《美国法典》第十五编第77x节);

(4)《1940年投资顾问法》第217条(《美国法典》第十五编第80b-17节);

(5)《1940年投资公司法》第49条(《美国法典》第十五编第80a-48节);或

(6)《1939年信托契约法》第325条(《美国法典》第十五编第77yyy节)。

(b)**限制**。——除非在犯罪行为实施后六年内提交检察官起诉书和大陪审团起诉书,否则不得基于证券欺诈犯罪行为对任何人进行起诉、审判或处罚。”

(2)**技术和一致性修正**。——在《美国法典》第十八编第二百一十三章条款目录结尾处增加如下内容,作为对该目录的修正:

“第3301节　证券欺诈犯罪。”

(c)**对《反欺骗政府法》中与诉讼限制相关规定的修正**。——《美国法典》第三十一编第3730(h)节修正如下——

(1)在第(1)款中,删除“或作为雇员、承包商的代理人,或者作为他人的代理人或与他人共同积极制止一项或一项以上违反本子章规定的行为”,替以“作为他人的代理人,或与他人共同促进根据本节规定提起的诉讼,或者采取其他措施积极制止一项或一项以上违反本子章规定的行为”;及

(2)在结尾处增加如下内容:

“(3)**对提起民事诉讼的限制**。——本子条规定的民事诉讼必须在报复行为发生之日后三年内提起。”

第H子编——一致性修正

第1081条　对《监察长法》的修正

《1978年监察长法》(《美国法典》第五编附件3)修正如下(该等修正自本法颁布之

C. App. 3) is amended —

(1) in section 8G (a)(2), by inserting "and the Bureau of Consumer Financial Protection" after "Board of Governors of the Federal Reserve System";

(2) in section 8G(c), by adding at the end the following:

"For purposes of implementing this section, the Chairman of the Board of Governors of the Federal Reserve System shall appoint the Inspector General of the Board of Governors of the Federal Reserve System and the Bureau of Consumer Financial Protection. The Inspector General of the Board of Governors of the Federal Reserve System and the Bureau of Consumer Financial Protection shall have all of the authorities and responsibilities provided by this Act with respect to the Bureau of Consumer Financial Protection, as if the Bureau were part of the Board of Governors of the Federal Reserve System."; and

(3) in section 8G(g)(3), by inserting "and the Bureau of Consumer Financial Protection" after "Board of Governors of the Federal Reserve System" the first place that term appears.

SEC. 1082. AMENDMENTS TO THE PRIVACY ACT OF 1974.

Effective on the date of enactment of this Act, section 552a of title 5, United States Code, is amended by adding at the end the following:

"(w) APPLICABILITY TO BUREAU OF CONSUMER FINANCIALPROTECTION. — Except as provided in the Consumer Financial Protection Act of 2010, this section shall apply with respect to the Bureau of Consumer Financial Protection.".

SEC.1083. AMENDMENTS TO THE ALTERNATIVE MORTGAGE TRANSACTION PARITY ACT OF 1982.

(a) IN GENERAL. — The Alternative Mortgage Transaction Parity Act of 1982 (12 U.S.C. 3801 et seq.) is amended —

(1) in section 803(12 U.S.C. 3802(1)), by striking "1974" and all that follows through "described and defined" and inserting the following: "1974), in which the interest rate or finance charge may be adjusted or renegotiated, described and defined"; and

(2) in section 804 (12 U.S.C. 3803) —

(A) in subsection (a) —

(i) in each of paragraphs (1), (2), and (3), by inserting after "transactions made" each place that term appears "on or before the designated transfer date, as determined under section 1062 of the Consumer Financial Protection Act of 2010,";

(ii) in paragraph (2), by striking "and" at the end;

(iii) in paragraph (3), by striking the period at the end and inserting "; and"; and

(iv) by adding at the end the following new paragraph:

"(4) with respect to transactions made after the designated transfer date, only in accordance with regulations governing alternative mortgage transactions, as issued by the

日起生效)——

(1)在第8G(a)(2)条中,在"联邦储备委员会"之后插入"和消费者金融保护局";

(2)在第8G(c)条中,在结尾处增加如下内容:

"为了实施本条规定,联邦储备委员会主席应任命联邦储备委员会和消费者金融保护局的监察长。联邦储备委员会和消费者金融保护局的监察长在针对消费者金融保护局开展工作时,应拥有本法规定的所有权力,并承担本法规定的所有职责,如同消费者金融保护局属于联邦储备委员会的一部分。";及

(3)在第8G(g)(3)条中,在首次出现的"联邦储备委员会"之后插入"和消费者金融保护局"。

第1082条　对《1974年隐私权法》的修正

在《美国法典》第五编第552a节结尾处增加如下内容,作为对该节的修正(该等修正自本法颁布之日起生效):

"(w)**对消费者金融保护局的适用性**。——除《2010年消费者金融保护法》规定的情形外,本条规定应适用于消费者金融保护局。"

第1083条　对《1982年另类抵押贷款交易平价法》的修正

(a)**一般规定**。——《1982年另类抵押贷款交易平价法》(《美国法典》第十二编第3801节及其后条文)修正如下——

(1)在第803条(《美国法典》第十二编第3802(1)节)中,删除"1974年"及其后直至"如相关规章所说明和定义。"的全部内容,替以"1974年),且贷款或信贷销售中的利率或财务费用可以调整或重新商定以及说明并定义。";及

(2)在第804条(《美国法典》第十二编第3803节)中——

(A)第(a)子条——

(i)分别在第(1)款、第(2)款和第(3)款中,在所有"开展的交易"前插入"在《2010年消费者金融保护法》第1062条规定的指定转移日(含)之前,";

(ii)第(2)款删除结尾处的"及";

(iii)第(3)款删除结尾处的句号,替以";及";并

(iv)在结尾处增加如下新款:

"(4)对于在指定转移日之后开展的交易而言,必须符合消费者金融保护局根据本条之外的其他法律规定赋予的规则制定权力,针对联邦特许注册的住房贷款发放

Bureau of Consumer Financial Protection for federally chartered housing creditors, in accordance with the rulemaking authority granted to the Bureau of Consumer Financial Protection with regard to federally chartered housing creditors under provisions of law other than this section.";

(B) by striking subsection (c) and inserting the following:

"(c) PREEMPTION OF STATE LAW. — An alternative mortgage transaction may be made by a housing creditor in accordance with this section, notwithstanding any State constitution, law, or regulation that prohibits an alternative mortgage transaction. For purposes of this subsection, a State constitution, law, or regulation that prohibits an alternative mortgage transaction does not include any State constitution, law, or regulation that regulates mortgage transactions generally, including any restriction on prepayment penalties or late charges."; and

(C) by adding at the end the following:

"(d) BUREAU ACTIONS. — The Bureau of Consumer Financial Protection shall —

"(1) review the regulations identified by the Comptroller of the Currency and the National Credit Union Administration, (as those rules exist on the designated transfer date), as applicable under paragraphs (1) through (3) of subsection (a);

"(2) determine whether such regulations are fair and not deceptive and otherwise meet the objectives of the Consumer Financial Protection Act of 2010; and

"(3) promulgate regulations under subsection (a)(4) after the designated transfer date.

"(e) DESIGNATED TRANSFER DATE. — As used in this section, the term 'designated transfer date' means the date determined under section 1062 of the Consumer Financial Protection Act of 2010.".

(b) EFFECTIVE DATE. — This section and the amendments made by this section shall become effective on the designated transfer date.

(c) RULE OF CONSTRUCTION. — The amendments made by subsection (a) shall not affect any transaction covered by the Alternative Mortgage Transaction Parity Act of 1982 (12 U.S.C. 3801 et seq.) and entered into on or before the designated transfer date.

SEC. 1084. AMENDMENTS TO THE ELECTRONIC FUND TRANSFER ACT.

The Electronic Fund Transfer Act (15 U.S.C. 1693 et seq.) is amended —

(1) by striking "Board" each place that term appears and inserting "Bureau", except in subsections (a) and (e) of section 904 (as amended in paragraph (3) of this section) and in 918 (15 U.S.C. 1693o)(as so designated by the Credit Card Act of 2009) and section 920 (as added by section 1076);

(2) in section 903 (15 U.S.C. 1693a) —

(A) by redesignating paragraphs (3) through (11) as paragraphs (4) through (12), respectively; and

人发布的规制另类抵押贷款交易的规章。”;

(B)删除第(c)子条,替以如下内容:

“(c)**对州法律的排除适用**。——即使任何州的宪法、法律或规章禁止开展另类抵押贷款交易,住房贷款发放人仍可以根据本条规定从事另类抵押贷款交易。就本子条而言,对抵押贷款交易进行一般性监管的任何州宪法、法律或规章(包括对提前还款违约金或滞纳金进行限制的规定),均不属于禁止开展另类抵押贷款交易的州宪法、法律或规章。”;及

(C)在结尾处增加如下内容:

“(d)**消费者金融保护局的行动**。——消费者金融保护局应——

(1)审查货币监理署署长和国家信贷联盟署确定的,在指定转移日已有效适用,且根据第(a)子条第(1)款至第(3)款具有适用性的规章;

(2)判定上述规章是否公平、不具有欺骗性,并符合《2010年消费者金融保护法》的宗旨;并

(3)在指定转移日之后根据第(a)(4)子条颁发规章。

(e)**指定转移日**。——就本条而言,‘指定转移日’一词系指根据《2010年消费者金融保护法》第1062条确定的日期。”

(b)**生效日**。——本条以及本条作出的修正均于指定转移日生效。

(c)**解释规则**。——(a)子条作出的修正不得影响适用《1982年另类抵押贷款交易平价法》(《美国法典》第十二编第3801节及其后条文)并在指定转移日(含)之前达成的任何交易。

第1084条　对《电子资金划拨法》的修正

《电子资金划拨法》(《美国法典》第十五编第1693节及其后条文)修正如下——

(1)删除所有的“联邦储备委员会”,全部替以“消费者金融保护局”,但第904条第(a)子条和第(e)子条[以本条第(3)款修正后的版本为准]、第918条(《美国法典》第十五编第1693o节)(以《2009年信用卡法》序号为准)以及第1076条增加的第920条中的“联邦储备委员会”仍应保留;

(2)在第903条(《美国法典》第十五编第1693a节)中——

(A)第(3)款至第(11)款分别重新编号为第(4)款至第(12)款;及

(B) by inserting after paragraph (3) the following:

"(4) the term 'Bureau' means the Bureau of Consumer Financial Protection;";

(3) in section 904 (15 U.S.C. 1693b)—

(A) in subsection (a), by striking "(a) PRESCRIPTION BY BOARD.—The Board shall prescribe regulations to carry out the purposes of this title." and inserting the following:

"(a) PRESCRIPTION BY THE BUREAU AND THE BOARD.—

"(1) IN GENERAL.—Except as provided in paragraph (2), the Bureau shall prescribe rules tocarry out the purposes of this title.

"(2) AUTHORITY OF THE BOARD.—The Board shall have sole authority to prescribe rules—

"(A) to carry out the purposes of this title with respect to a person described in section 1029(a) of the Consumer Financial Protection Act of 2010; and

"(B) to carry out the purposes of section 920."; and (B) by adding at the end the following new subsection:

"(e) DEFERENCE.—No provision of this title may be construed as altering, limiting, or otherwise affecting the deference that a court affords to—

"(1) the Bureau in making determinations regarding the meaning or interpretation of any provision of this title for which the Bureau has authority to prescribe regulations; or

"(2) the Board in making determinations regarding the meaning or interpretation of section 920.".

(4) in section 916(d)(15 U.S.C. 1693m)(as so designated by the Credit CARD Act of 2009)—

(A) in the subsection heading, by striking "OF BOARD OR APPROVAL OF DULY AUTHORIZED OFFICIAL OR EMPLOYEE OF FEDERAL RESERVE SYSTEM";

(B) by inserting "Bureau or the" before "Board" each place that term appears; and

(C) by inserting "Bureau of Consumer Financial Protection or the" before "Federal Reserve System"; and

(5) in section 918 (15 U.S.C. 1693o)(as so designated by the Credit CARD Act of 2009)—

(A) in subsection (a)—

(i) by striking "Compliance" and inserting "Subject to subtitle B of the Consumer Financial Protection Act of 2010, compliance";

(ii) by striking paragraphs (1) and (2), and inserting the following:

"(1) section 8 of the Federal Deposit Insurance Act, by the appropriate Federal banking agency, as defined in section 3 (q) of the Federal Deposit Insurance Act (12 U.S.C. 1813 (q)), with respect to—

"(A) national banks, Federal savings associations, and Federal branches and Federal

(B)在第(3)款之后插入如下内容:

"(4)'消费者金融保护局'一词系指联邦储备系统下的消费者金融保护局;";

(3)在第904条(《美国法典》第十五编第1693b节)中——

(A)**第(a)子条删除"(a)联邦储备委员会的规章制定行为**。——联邦储备委员会应制定相关规章,执行本编宗旨。",替以如下内容:

"(a)消费者金融保护局和联邦储备委员会的规章制定行为。——

(1)**一般规定**。——除第(2)款规定的情形外,消费者金融保护局应制定相关规则,执行本编宗旨。

(2) **联邦储备委员会的权力**。——联邦储备委员会拥有为如下目的制定规则的排他性权力——

(A)针对《2010年消费者金融保护法》第1029(a)条所述主体执行本编宗旨;并

(B)执行第920条的目的。";及

(B)在结尾处增加如下新子条:

"(e)**司法尊重**。——本编任何内容均不得被解释为改变、限制或以其他方式影响法院对如下决定表示的司法尊重——

(1)消费者金融保护局针对其有权制定实施规章的本编规定之含义或解释作出的判定;或

(2)联邦储备委员会针对第920条之含义或解释作出的判定。"

(4)在第916(d)条(《美国法典》第十五编第1693m节)(以《2009年信用卡法》序号为准)中——

(A)删除子条标题中的"联邦储备委员会"以及"或联邦储备系统正式授权官员或职员的批准";

(B)在所有出现的"联邦储备委员会"一词前插入"消费者金融保护局或";且

(C)在"联邦储备系统"前插入"消费者金融保护局或";及

(5)在第918条(《美国法典》第十五编第1693o节)(以《2009年信用卡法》序号为准)中——

(A)第(a)子条——

(i)起始处插入"在不违反《2010年消费者金融保护法》第B子编规定的前提下合规";

(ii)删除第(1)款和第(2)款,替以如下内容:

"(1)对于以下实体而言,应按照《联邦存款保险法》第8条的规定由相应的联邦银行业监管机关[定义见《联邦存款保险法》第3(q)条(《美国法典》第12编第1813(q)节)]强制执行——

(A)国民银行、联邦储蓄协会以及外国银行的联邦分行和联邦代理行;

agencies of foreign banks;

"(B) member banks of the Federal Reserve System (other than national banks), branches and agencies of foreign banks (other than Federal branches, Federal agencies, and insured State branches of foreign banks), commercial lending companies owned or controlled by foreign banks, and organizations operating under section 25 or 25A of the Federal Reserve Act; and

"(C) banks and State savings associations insured by the Federal Deposit Insurance Corporation (other than members of the Federal Reserve System), and insured State branches of foreign banks;";

(iii) by redesignating paragraphs (3) through (5) as paragraphs (2) through (4), respectively;

(iv) in paragraph (2)(as so redesignated), by striking the period at the end and inserting a semicolon;

(v) in paragraph (3)(as so redesignated), by striking "and" at the end;

(vi) in paragraph (4)(as so redesignated), by striking the period at the end and inserting "and"; and

(vii) by adding at the end the following:

"(5) subtitle E of the Consumer Financial Protection Act of 2010, by the Bureau, with respect to any person subject to this title, except that the Bureau shall not have authority to enforce the requirements of section 920 or any regulations prescribed by the Board under section 920.";

(B) in subsection (b), by inserting "any of paragraphs (1) through (4) of" before "subsection (a)" each place that term appears; and

(C) by striking subsection (c) and inserting the following:

"(c) OVERALL ENFORCEMENT AUTHORITY OF THE FEDERAL TRADE COMMISSION. — Except to the extent that enforcement of the requirements imposed under this title is specifically committed to some other Government agency under any of paragraphs (1) through (4) of subsection (a), and subject to subtitle B of the Consumer Financial Protection Act of 2010, the Federal Trade Commission shall be authorized to enforce such requirements. For the purpose of the exercise by the Federal Trade Commission of its functions and powers under the Federal Trade Commission Act, a violation of any requirement imposed under this title shall be deemed a violation of a requirement imposed under that Act. All of the functions and powers of the Federal Trade Commission under the Federal Trade Commission Act are available to the Federal Trade Commission to enforce compliance by any person subject to the jurisdiction of the Federal Trade Commission with the requirements imposed under this title, irrespective of whether that person is engaged in commerce or meets any other jurisdictional tests under the Federal Trade Commission Act.".

（B）联邦储备系统的成员银行（但国民银行除外）、外国银行的分行和代理行（外国银行的联邦分行、联邦代理行及州参保分行除外）、外国银行拥有或控制的商业贷款公司以及依照《联邦储备法》第25条或第25A条开展运营的组织；及

（C）由联邦存款保险公司承保的银行和州储蓄协会（联邦储备系统的成员除外）以及外国银行的州参保分行；”；

（iii）第（3）款至第（5）款分别重新编号为第（2）款至第（4）款；

（iv）在第（2）款（以重新编号后的序号为准）中，删除结尾处的句号，替以分号；

（v）在第（3）款（以重新编号后的序号为准）中，删除结尾处的“及”；

（vi）在第（4）款（以重新编号后的序号为准）中，删除结尾处的句号，替以“及”；并

（vii）在结尾处增加如下内容：

“（5）对于受本编规定管辖的任何主体，应按照《2010年消费者金融保护法》第E子编的规定由消费者金融保护局强制执行，但是消费者金融保护局无权强制执行第920条或由联邦储备委员会根据第920条制定的任何规章的要求。”；

（B）在第（b）子条中，在所有“第（a）子条”一词之后插入“第（1）款至第（4）款中的任何一款”；及

（C）删除第（c）子条，替以如下内容：

“（c）**联邦贸易委员会的总体执法权**。——除非第（a）子条第（1）款至第（4）款已将对本编要求的执法权明确授予其他政府机关，否则，在不违反《2010年消费者金融保护法》第B子编规定的前提下，联邦贸易委员会应有权执行本编施加的要求。联邦贸易委员会在行使《联邦贸易委员会法》规定的职能和权力之时，对本编施加的任何要求的违反均应被视为对《联邦贸易委员会法》施加的要求的违反。联邦贸易委员会在对受其管辖的任何主体强制执行本编施加的要求之时，有权行使其根据《联邦贸易委员会法》享有的所有职能和权力，不论该等主体是否从事商业，亦不论其是否符合《联邦贸易委员会法》规定的任何其他管辖权标准。”

SEC. 1085. AMENDMENTS TO THE EQUAL CREDIT OPPORTUNITY ACT

The Equal Credit Opportunity Act (15 U.S.C. 1691 et seq.) is amended —

(1) by striking "Board" each place that term appears, other than in section 703(f)(as added by this section) and section 704(a)(4)(15 U.S.C. 1691c(a)(4)), and inserting "Bureau";

(2) in section 702 (15 U.S.C. 1691a), by striking subsection (c) and inserting the following:

"(c) The term 'Bureau' means the Bureau of Consumer Financial Protection.";

(3) in section 703 (15 U.S.C. 1691b) —

(A) by striking the section heading and inserting the following:

"SEC. 703. PROMULGATION OF REGULATIONS BY THE BUREAU.";

(B) by striking "(a) REGULATIONS. — ";

(C) by striking subsection (b);

(D) by redesignating paragraphs (1) through (5) as subsections (a) through (e), respectively;

(E) in subsection (c), as so redesignated, by striking "paragraph (2) " and inserting "subsection (b) "; and

(F) by adding at the end the following:

"(f) BOARD AUTHORITY. — Notwithstanding subsection (a), the Board shall prescribe regulations to carry out the purposes of this title with respect to a person described in section 1029(a) of the Consumer Financial Protection Act of 2010. These regulations may contain but are not limited to such classifications, differentiation, or other provision, and may provide for such adjustments and exceptions for any class of transactions, as in the judgment of the Board are necessary or proper to effectuate the purposes of this title, to prevent circumvention or evasion thereof, or to facilitate or substantiate compliance therewith.

"(g) DEFERENCE. — Notwithstanding any power granted to any Federal agency under this title, the deference that a court affords to a Federal agency with respect to a determination made by such agency relating to the meaning or interpretation of any provision of this title that is subject to the jurisdiction of such agency shall be applied as if that agency were the only agency authorized to apply, enforce, interpret, or administer the provisions of this title";

(4) in section 704 (15 U.S.C. 1691c) —

(A) in subsection (a) —

(i) by striking "Compliance" and inserting "Subject to subtitle B of the Consumer Protection Financial Protection Act of 2010";

(ii) by striking paragraphs (1) and (2) and inserting the following:

"(1) section 8 of the Federal Deposit Insurance Act, by the appropriate Federal banking agency, as defined in section 3(q) of the Federal Deposit Insurance Act (12 U.S.C. 1813

第1085条　对《信贷机会平等法》的修正

《信贷机会平等法》(《美国法典》第十五编第1691节及其后条文)修正如下——

(1)删除所有的"联邦储备委员会",全部替以"消费者金融保护局",但第704(a)(4)条[《美国法典》第十五编第1691c(a)(4)节]以及本条增加的第703(f)条中的"联邦储备委员会"除外;

(2)在第702条(《美国法典》第十五编第1691a节)中,删除第(c)子条,替以如下内容:

"(c)'消费者金融保护局'一词系指联邦储备系统下的消费者金融保护局。";

(3)在第703条(《美国法典》第十五编第1691b节)中——

(A)删除该条标题,替以如下内容:

"第703条　消费者金融保护局颁发规章的行为";

(B)删除"(a)**规章**。——";

(C)删除第(b)子条;

(D)第(1)款至第(5)款分别重新编号为第(a)子条至第(e)子条;

(E)在第(c)子条(以重新编号后的序号为准)中,删除"第(2)款",替以"第(b)子条";且

(F)在结尾处增加如下内容:

"(f)**联邦储备委员会的权力**。——无论第(a)子条如何规定,但是,联邦储备委员会仍应制定相关规章,针对《2010年消费者金融保护法》第1029(a)条所述主体执行本编的宗旨。联邦储备委员会在制定该等规章时,可以为执行本编宗旨、防范对本编宗旨的规避或逃避或促进或加强对本编宗旨的合规之目的,而制定联邦储备委员会判断确属必要或宜应制定的分类规定、区分规定或其他规定,并且还可规定适用于任何类别交易的调整及例外情形。

(g)**司法尊重**。——不论本编向任何联邦机关赋予了任何权力,对于联邦机关对其有管辖权的本编任何规定之含义或解释作出的判定,如法院对该等决定表示司法尊重,则在适用该等司法尊重时,应将该联邦机关视同为唯一有权适用、执行、解释或实施本编规定的机关";

(4)在第704条(《美国法典》第十五编第1691c节)中——

(A)第(a)子条——

(i)在起始处插入"在不违反《2010年消费者金融保护法》第B子编规定的前提下";

(ii)删除第(1)款和第(2)款,替以如下内容:

"(1)对于以下实体而言,应按照《联邦存款保险法》第8条的规定由相应的联邦银行业监管机关(定义见《联邦存款保险法》第3(q)条[《美国法典》第十二编第1813(q)

(q)), with respect to—

"(A) national banks, Federal savings associations, and Federal branches and Federal agencies of foreign banks;

"(B) member banks of the Federal Reserve System (other than national banks), branches and agencies of foreign banks (other than Federal branches, Federal agencies, and insured State branches of foreign banks), commercial lending companies owned or controlled by foreign banks, and organizations operating under section 25 or 25A of the Federal Reserve Act; and

"(C) banks and State savings associations insured by the Federal Deposit Insurance Corporation (other than members of the Federal Reserve System), and insured State branches of foreign banks;";

(iii) by redesignating paragraphs (3) through (9) as paragraphs (2) through (8), respectively;

(iv) in paragraph (7)(as so redesignated), by striking "and" at the end;

(v) in paragraph (8)(as so redesignated), by striking the period at the end, and inserting "; and"; and

(vi) by adding at the end the following:

"(9) Subtitle E of the Consumer Financial Protection Act of 2010, by the Bureau, with respect to any person subject to this title.";

(B) by striking subsection (c) and inserting the following:

"(c) OVERALL ENFORCEMENT AUTHORITY OF FEDERAL TRADE COMMISSION.—Except to the extent that enforcement of the requirements imposed under this title is specifically committed to some other Government agency under any of paragraphs (1) through (8) of subsection (a), and subject to subtitle B of the Consumer Financial Protection Act of 2010, the Federal Trade Commission shall be authorized to enforce such requirements. For the purpose of the exercise by the Federal Trade Commission of its functions and powers under the Federal Trade Commission Act (15 U.S.C. 41 et seq.), a violation of any requirement imposed under this subchapter shall be deemed a violation of a requirement imposed under that Act. All of the functions and powers of the Federal Trade Commission under the Federal Trade Commission Act are available to the Federal Trade Commission to enforce compliance by any person with the requirements imposed under this title, irrespective of whether that person is engaged in commerce or meets any other jurisdictional tests under the Federal Trade Commission Act, including the power to enforce any rule prescribed by the Bureau under this title in the same manner as if the violation had been a violation of a Federal Trade Commission trade regulation rule."; and

(C) in subsection (d), by striking "Board" and inserting "Bureau";

(5) in section 706(e)(15 U.S.C. 1691e(e))—

节)]强制执行——

(A)国民银行、联邦储蓄协会以及外国银行的联邦分行和联邦代理行;

(B)联邦储备系统的成员银行(但国民银行除外)、外国银行的分行和代理行(但外国银行的联邦分行、联邦代理行及州参保分行除外)、外国银行拥有或控制的商业贷款公司以及依照《联邦储备法》第25条或第25A条开展运营的组织;及

(C)由联邦存款保险公司承保的银行和州储蓄协会(但联邦储备系统的成员除外)以及外国银行的州参保分行;";

(iii)第(3)款至第(9)款分别重新编号为第(2)款至第(8)款;

(iv)在第(7)款(以重新编号后的序号为准)中,删除结尾处的"及";

(v)在第(8)款(以重新编号后的序号为准)中,删除结尾处的句号,替以";及";并

(vi)在结尾处增加如下内容:

"(9)对于受本编规定管辖的任何主体,应按照《2010年消费者金融保护法》第E子编的规定由消费者金融保护局强制执行。";

(B)删除第(c)子条,替以如下内容:

"(c)**联邦贸易委员会的总体执法权**。——除非第(a)子条第(1)款至第(8)款已将本编要求的执法权明确授予其他政府机关,否则,在不违反《2010年消费者金融保护法》第B子编规定的前提下,联邦贸易委员会应有权执行本编施加的要求。联邦贸易委员会在行使《联邦贸易委员会法》(《美国法典》第十五编第41节及其后条文)规定的职能和权力之时,对本编施加的任何要求的违反均应被视为对《联邦贸易委员会法》施加的要求的违反。联邦贸易委员会在对任何主体强制执行本编施加的要求之时,有权行使其根据《联邦贸易委员会法》享有的所有职能和权力,不论该等主体是否从事商业,亦不论其是否符合《联邦贸易委员会法》规定的任何其他管辖权标准,包括有权强制执行消费者金融保护局依据本编制定的任何规则,如同违反该等规则的行为属于违反联邦贸易委员会贸易制定的规章的行为。";且

(C)在第(d)子条中,删除"联邦储备委员会",替以"消费者金融保护局";

(5)在第706(e)条[《美国法典》第十五编第1691e(e)节]中——

(A) in the subsection heading—

(i) by striking "BOARD" each place that term appears and inserting "BUREAU"; and

(ii) by striking "FEDERAL RESERVE SYSTEM" and inserting "BUREAU OF CONSUMER FINANCIAL PROTECTION"; and

(B) by striking "Federal Reserve System" and inserting "Bureau of Consumer Financial Protection";

(6) in section 706(g)(15 U.S.C. 1691e(g)), by striking "(3)" and inserting "(9)"; and

(7) in section 706(f)(15 U.S.C. 1691e(f)), by striking "two years from" each place that term appears and inserting "5 years after".

SEC. 1086. AMENDMENTS TO THE EXPEDITED FUNDS AVAILABILITY ACT.

(a) AMENDMENT TO SECTION 603.—Section 603 (d)(1) of the Expedited Funds Availability Act (12 U.S.C. 4002) is amended by inserting after "Board" the following ", jointly with the Director of the Bureau of Consumer Financial Protection,".

(b) AMENDMENTS TO SECTION 604.—Section 604 of the Expedited Funds Availability Act (12 U.S.C. 4003) is amended—

(1) by inserting after "Board" each place that term appears, other than in subsection (f), the following: ", jointly with the Director of the Bureau of Consumer Financial Protection,"; and

(2) in subsection (f), by striking "Board." each place that term appears and inserting the following: "Board, jointly with the Director of the Bureau of Consumer Financial Protection.".

(c) AMENDMENTS TO SECTION 605.—Section 605 of the Expedited Funds Availability Act (12 U.S.C. 4004) is amended—

(1) by inserting after "Board" each place that term appears, other than in the heading for section 605 (f)(1), the following: ", jointly with the Director of the Bureau of Consumer Financial Protection,"; and

(2) in subsection (f)(1), in the paragraph heading, by inserting "AND BUREAU" after "BOARD".

(d) AMENDMENTS TO SECTION 609.—Section 609 of the Expedited Funds Availability Act (12 U.S.C. 4008) is amended:

(1) in subsection (a), by inserting after "Board" the following ", jointly with the Director of the Bureau of Consumer Financial Protection,"; and

(2) by striking subsection (e) and inserting the following:

"(e) CONSULTATIONS.—In prescribing regulations under subsections (a) and (b), the Board and the Director of the Bureau of Consumer Financial Protection, in the case of subsection (a), and the Board, in the case of subsection (b), shall consult with the

(A)子条标题——

(i)删除所有的“**联邦储备委员会**”,全部替以“**消费者金融保护局**”;及

(ii)删除所有的“**联邦储备委员会**”,全部替以“**消费者金融保护局**”;及

(B)删除“联邦储备系统”,替以“消费者金融保护局”;

(6)在第706(g)条[《美国法典》第十五编第1691e(g)节]中,删除“(3)”,替以“(9)”;及

(7)在第706(f)条[《美国法典》第十五编第1691e(f)节]中,删除所有的“2年”,全部替以“5年”。

第1086条　对《加速资金到位法》的修正

(a)**对第603条的修正**。——《加速资金到位法》第603(d)(1)条(《美国法典》第十二编第4002节)修正如下:在“联邦储备委员会”之后插入“与消费者金融保护局局长共同,”。

(b)**对第604条的修正**。——《加速资金到位法》第604条(《美国法典》第十二编第4003节)修正如下——

(1)在所有的“联邦储备委员会”一词之后插入“与消费者金融保护局局长共同,”,但第(f)子条除外;及

(2)在第(f)子条中,删除所有的“联邦储备委员会”,全部替以“联邦储备委员会与消费者金融保护局局长共同”。

(c)**对第605条的修正**。——《加速资金到位法》第605条(《美国法典》第十二编第4004节)修正如下——

(1)除第605(f)(1)条标题外,在所有的“联邦储备委员会”一词之后插入如下内容:“与消费者金融保护局局长共同,”;及

(2)在第(f)(1)子条中,该款标题在“联邦储备委员会”之后插入“及消费者金融保护局”。

(d)**对第609条的修正**。——《加速资金到位法》第609条(《美国法典》第十二编第4008节)修正如下:

(1)在第(a)子条中,在“联邦储备委员会”之后插入如下内容:“与消费者金融保护局局长共同,”;及

(2)删除第(e)子条,替以如下内容:

“(e)**磋商**。——在根据第(a)子条制定规章时,联邦储备委员会和消费者金融保护局局长应与货币监理署署长、联邦存款保险公司董事会以及国家信贷联盟署委员会进行磋商;在根据第(b)子条制定规章时,联邦储备委员会应与货币监理署署长、联

Comptroller of the Currency, the Board of Directors of the Federal Deposit Insurance Corporation, and the National Credit Union Administration Board.".

(e) EXPEDITED FUNDS AVAILABILITY IMPROVEMENTS. — Section 603 of the Expedited Funds Availability Act (12 U.S.C. 4002) is amended —

(1) in subsection (a)(2)(D), by striking "$100" and inserting "$200"; and

(2) in subsection (b)(3)(C), in the subparagraph heading, by striking "$100" and inserting "$200"; and

(3) in subsection (c)(1)(B)(iii), in the clause heading, by striking "$100" and inserting "$200".

(f) REGULAR ADJUSTMENTS FOR INFLATION. — Section 607 of the Expedited Funds Availability Act (12 U.S.C. 4006) is amended by adding at the end the following:

"(f) ADJUSTMENTS TO DOLLAR AMOUNTS FOR INFLATION. — The dollar amounts under this title shall be adjusted every 5 years after December 31, 2011, by the annual percentage increase in the Consumer Price Index for Urban Wage Earners and Clerical Workers, as published by the Bureau of Labor Statistics, rounded to the nearest multiple of $25.".

SEC. 1087. AMENDMENTS TO THE FAIR CREDIT BILLING ACT.

The Fair Credit Billing Act (15 U.S.C. 1666–1666j) is amended by striking "Board" each place that term appears, other than in section 105 (i)(as added by this subtitle) and inserting "Bureau".

SEC. 1088. AMENDMENTS TO THE FAIR CREDIT REPORTING ACT AND THE FAIR AND ACCURATE CREDIT TRANSACTIONS ACT OF 2003.

(a) FAIR CREDIT REPORTING ACT. — The Fair Credit Reporting Act (15 U.S.C. 1681 et seq.) is amended —

(1) in section 603 (15 U.S.C. 1681a) —

(A) by redesignating subsections (w) and (x) as subsections (x) and (y), respectively; and

(B) by inserting after subsection (v) the following:

"(w) The term 'Bureau' means the Bureau of Consumer Financial Protection."; and

(2) except as otherwise specifically provided in this subsection —

(A) by striking "Federal Trade Commission" each place that term appears and inserting "Bureau";

(B) by striking "FTC" each place that term appears and inserting "Bureau";

(C) by striking "the Commission" each place that term appears, other than sections 615 (e)(15 U.S.C. 1681m(e)) and 628(a)(1)(15 U.S.C. 1681w(a)(1)), and inserting "the Bureau"; and

邦存款保险公司董事会以及国家信贷联盟署委员会进行磋商。”

(e)**加速资金到位的完善规定**。——《加速资金到位法》第603条(《美国法典》第12编第4002节)修正如下——

(1)在第(a)(2)(D)子条中,删除“100美元”,替以“200美元”;及

(2)在第(b)(3)(C)子条中,子款标题删除“100美元”,替以“200美元”;及

(3)在第(c)(1)(B)(iii)子条中,该项标题删除“100美元”,替以“200美元”。

(f)**定期通胀调整**。——在《加速资金到位法》第607条(《美国法典》第十二编第4006节)结尾处增加如下内容,作为对该条的修正:

“(f)**金额通胀调整**。——2011年12月31日之后,本编规定的美元金额应每5年调整一次,调整幅度为劳动统计局公布的城市工薪阶层和文职人员的消费物价指数的年度增幅,并按最接近25美元的倍数取整。”

第1087条　对《公平信用结账法》的修正

《公平信用结账法》(《美国法典》第十五编第1666-1666j节)修正如下:删除所有的“联邦储备委员会”,全部替以“消费者金融保护局”,但本子编增加的第105(i)条中的“联邦储备委员会”仍应保留。

第1088条　对《公平信用报告法》和《2003年公平准确信用交易法》的修正

(a)**《公平信用报告法》**。——《公平信用报告法》(《美国法典》第十五编第1681节及其后条文)修正如下——

(1)在第603条(《美国法典》第十五编第1681a节)中——

(A)第(w)子条和第(x)子条分别重新编号为第(x)子条和第(y)子条;及

(B)在第(v)子条之后插入如下内容:

“(w)‘消费者金融保护局’一词系指联邦储备系统下的消费者金融保护局。”;及

(2)除本子条另有明确规定的情形外——

(A)删除所有的“联邦贸易委员会”,全部替以“消费者金融保护局”;

(B)删除所有的联邦贸易委员会的英文简称“FTC”,全部替以“消费者金融保护局”;

(C)删除所有的“联邦贸易委员会”,全部替以“消费者金融保护局”,但第615(e)条[《美国法典》第十五编第1681m(e)节]以及第628(a)(1)条[《美国法典》第十五编第1681w(a)(1)节]中的“联邦贸易委员会”仍应保留;及

(D) by striking "The Federal banking agencies, the National Credit Union Administration, and the Commission shall jointly" each place that term appears, other than section 615(e)(1)(15 U.S.C. 1681m(e)) and section 628(a)(1)(15 U.S.C. 1681w(a)(1)), and inserting "The Bureau shall";

(3) in section 603(k)(2)(15 U.S.C. 1681a(k)(2)), by striking "Board of Governors of the Federal Reserve System" and inserting "Bureau";

(4) in section 604(g)(15 U.S.C. 1681b(g))—

(A) in paragraph (3), by striking subparagraph (C) and inserting the following:

"(C) as otherwise determined to be necessary and appropriate, by regulation or order, by the Bureau or the applicable State insurance authority (with respect to any person engaged in providing insurance or annuities)."; and

(B) by striking paragraph (5) and inserting the following:

"(5) REGULATIONS AND EFFECTIVE DATE FOR PARAGRAPH (2).—

"(A) REGULATIONS REQUIRED. — The Bureau may, after notice and opportunity for comment, prescribe regulations that permit transactions under paragraph (2) that are determined to be necessary and appropriate to protect legitimate operational, transactional, risk, consumer, and other needs (and which shall include permitting actions necessary for administrative verification purposes), consistent with the intent of paragraph (2) to restrict the use of medical information for inappropriate purposes.";

(5) in section 605(h)(2)(A)(15 U.S.C. 1681c(h)(2)(A)), by striking "with respect to the entities that are subject to their respective enforcement authority under section 621" and inserting ", in consultation with the Federal banking agencies, the National Credit Union Administration, and the Federal Trade Commission,".

(6) in section 611 (e)(2)(15 U.S.C. 1681i (e)), by striking paragraph (2) and inserting the following:

"(2) EXCLUSION. — Complaints received or obtained by the Bureau pursuant to its investigative authority under the Consumer Financial Protection Act of 2010 shall not be subject to paragraph (1).";

(7) in section 615(d)(2)(B)(15 U.S.C. 1681m(d)(2)(B)), by striking "the Federal banking agencies" and inserting "the Federal Trade Commission, the Federal banking agencies,";

(8) in section 615 (e)(1)(15 U.S.C. 1681m (e)(1)), by striking "and the Commission" and inserting "the Federal Trade Commission, the Commodity Futures Trading Commission, and the Securities and Exchange Commission";

(9) in section 615(h)(6)(15 U.S.C. 1681m(h)(6)), by striking subparagraph (A) and inserting the following:

"(A) RULES REQUIRED. — The Bureau shall prescribe rules to carry out this

(D)删除所有的“联邦银行业监管机关、国家信贷联盟署以及联邦贸易委员会应联合”,全部替以“消费者金融保护局应”,但第615(e)(1)条[《美国法典》第十五编第1681m(e)节]以及第628(a)(1)条[《美国法典》第十五编第1681w(a)(1)节]中的“联邦银行业监管机关、国家信贷联盟署以及联邦贸易委员会应联合”仍应保留;

(3)在第603(k)(2)条[《美国法典》第十五编第1681a(k)(2)节]中,删除“联邦储备委员会”,替以“消费者金融保护局”;

(4)在第604(g)条[《美国法典》第十五编第1681b(g)节]中——

(A)第(3)款删除第(C)子款,替以如下内容:

“(C)消费者金融保护局或相应的州保险监管机构判定确属必要且适当之时,针对从事提供保险或年金服务的任何主体发布的规章或命令。”;及

(B)删除第(5)款,替以如下内容:

“(5)**规章以及第(2)款的生效日**。——

(A)**规章要求**。——消费者金融保护局可以在发出通知并征求意见之后,制定相关规章,在符合第(2)款之意图,即限制出于不当目的使用医疗信息的行为的前提下,允许按照第(2)款开展被判定对保护合法经营需求、交易需求、风险、消费者和其他需求而必要且适当的交易(且该等规章应包括允许为行政审核之目的采取必要行动)。”;

(5)在第605(h)(2)(A)条[《美国法典》第十五编第1681c(h)(2)(A)节]中,删除“对于根据第621条受各自的执法机构管辖的实体而言”,替以“,与联邦银行业监管机关、国家信贷联盟署以及联邦贸易委员会进行磋商,”。

(6)在第611(e)(2)条[《美国法典》第十五编第1681i(e)节]中,删除第(2)款,替以如下内容:

“(2)**除外规定**。——消费者金融保护局根据《2010年消费者金融保护法》规定的调查权收到或获得的投诉不必受制于第(1)款的规定。”;

(7)在第615(d)(2)(B)条[《美国法典》第十五编第1681m(d)(2)(B)节]中,删除“联邦银行业监管机关”,替以“联邦贸易委员会、联邦银行业监管机关、”;

(8)在第615(e)(1)条[《美国法典》第十五编第1681m(e)(1)节]中,删除“且联邦贸易委员会”,替以“联邦贸易委员会、商品期货交易委员会以及证券交易委员会”;

(9)在第615(h)(6)条[《美国法典》第十五编第1681m(h)(6)节]中,删除第(A)子款,替以如下内容:

“(A)**规则制定要求**。——消费者金融保护局应制定相关规则,以执行本子条规定。”;

subsection.";

(10) in section 621 (15 U.S.C. 1681s) —

(A) by striking subsection (a) and inserting the following:

"(a) ENFORCEMENT BY FEDERAL TRADE COMMISSION. —

"(1) IN GENERAL. — The Federal Trade Commission shall be authorized to enforce compliance with the requirements imposed by this title under the Federal Trade Commission Act (15 U.S.C. 41 et seq.), with respect to consumer reporting agencies and all other persons subject thereto, except to the extent that enforcement of the requirements imposed under this title is specifically committed to some other Government agency under any of subparagraphs (A) through (G) of subsection (b)(1), and subject to subtitle B of the Consumer Financial Protection Act of 2010, subsection(b). For the purpose of the exercise by the Federal Trade Commission of its functions and powers under the Federal Trade Commission Act, a violation of any requirement or prohibition imposed under this title shall constitute an unfair or deceptive act or practice in commerce, in violation of section 5(a) of the Federal Trade Commission Act (15 U.S.C. 45 (a)), and shall be subject to enforcement by the Federal Trade Commission under section 5 (b) of that Act with respect to any consumer reporting agency or person that is subject to enforcement by the Federal Trade Commission pursuant to this subsection, irrespective of whether that person is engaged in commerce or meets any other jurisdictional tests under the Federal Trade Commission Act. The Federal Trade Commission shall have such procedural, investigative, and enforcement powers, including the power to issue procedural rules in enforcing compliance with the requirements imposed under this title and to require the filing of reports, the production of documents, and the appearance of witnesses, as though the applicable terms and conditions of the Federal Trade Commission Act were part of this title. Any person violating any of the provisions of this title shall be subject to the penalties and entitled to the privileges and immunities provided in the Federal Trade Commission Act as though the applicable terms and provisions of such Act are part of this title.

"(2) PENALTIES. —

"(A) KNOWING VIOLATIONS. — Except as otherwise provided by subtitle B of the Consumer Financial Protection Act of 2010, in the event of a knowing violation, which constitutes a pattern or practice of violations of this title, the Federal Trade Commission may commence a civil action to recover a civil penalty in a district court of the United States against any person that violates this title. In such action, such person shall be liable for a civil penalty of not more than $2,500 per violation.

"(B) DETERMINING PENALTY AMOUNT. — In determining the amount of a civil penalty under subparagraph (A), the court shall take into account the degree of culpability, any history of such prior conduct, ability to pay, effect on ability to continue to do business,

(10)在第621条(《美国法典》第十五编第1681s节)中——

(A)删除第(a)子条,替以如下内容:

"(a)**联邦贸易委员会的执法权**。——

(1)**一般规定**。——除非第(b)(1)子条第(A)款至第(G)款已将本编要求的执法权明确授予其他政府机关,否则,在不违反《2010年消费者金融保护法》第B子编规定的前提下,联邦贸易委员会应有权根据《联邦贸易委员会法》(《美国法典》第十五编第41节及其后条文)针对消费者征信机构以及受其监管的所有其他主体执行本编施加的要求。联邦贸易委员会在行使其在《联邦贸易委员会法》中的职能和权力之时,违反本编施加的任何要求或禁止性规定的行为均应视为构成违反该法》第5(a)条[《美国法典》第十五编第45(a)节]的不公平或欺骗性商业行为或做法,并且如从事该等违法违规行为的主体是一家消费者征信机构或根据本子条应受联邦贸易委员会执法权管辖的任何主体,则联邦贸易委员会均有权根据该法第5(b)条行使执法权,不论该等主体是否从事商业,亦不论其是否符合《联邦贸易委员会法》规定的任何其他管辖权标准。联邦贸易委员会应拥有相应的程序权、调查权及执法权,包括为执行本编施加的要求而发布程序性规则的权力,以及要求提交报告、提供文件和要求证人出席作证的权力,如同《联邦贸易委员会法》的相关条款和条件属于本编的一部分。违反本编规定的任何人,均应按照《联邦贸易委员会法》规定接受处罚,并享有该法规定的特权和豁免权,如同该法的相关条款和规定属于本编的一部分。

(2)**罚款**。——

(A)**故意违法违规行为**。——除《2010年消费者金融保护法》第B子编另有规定的情形外,任何故意违法违规行为,形成违反本编规定之范例或实践的,联邦贸易委员会可以在联邦地区法院,针对该等违法违规行为人提起民事诉讼,要求对其处以民事罚款。在该等诉讼中,违法主体对于每项违法违规行为承担的民事罚款均不得超过2500美元。

(B)**确定罚款金额**。——在确定第(A)子款所述民事罚款的金额时,法院应考虑当事人罪责程度、违法违规行为记录、支付能力、对其继续开展业务的影响以及为实现公正需要考虑的其他事项。

and such other matters as justice may require.

"(C) LIMITATION. — Notwithstanding paragraph (2), a court may not impose any civil penalty on a person for a violation of section 623(a)(1), unless the person has been enjoined from committing the violation, or ordered not to commit the violation, in an action or proceeding brought by or on behalf of the Federal Trade Commission, and has violated the injunction or order, and the court may not impose any civil penalty for any violation occurring before the date of the violation of the injunction or order.";

(B) by striking subsection (b) and inserting the following:

"(b) ENFORCEMENT BY OTHER AGENCIES. —

"(1) IN GENERAL. — Subject to subtitle B of the Consumer Financial Protection Act of 2010, compliance with the require ments imposed under this title with respect to consumer reporting agencies, persons who use consumer reports from such agencies, persons who furnish information to such agen cies, and users of information that are subject to section 615 (d) shall be enforced under —

"(A) section 8 of the Federal Deposit Insurance Act (12 U.S.C. 1818), by the appropriate Federal banking agency, as defined in section 3(q) of the Federal Deposit Insurance Act (12 U.S.C. 1813(q)), with respect to —

"(i) any national bank or State savings association, and any Federal branch or Federal agency of a foreign bank;

"(ii) any member bank of the Federal Reserve System (other than a national bank), a branch or agency of a foreign bank (other than a Federal branch, Federal agency, or insured State branch of a foreign bank), a commercial lending company owned or controlled by a foreign bank, and any organization operating under section 25 or 25A of the Federal Reserve Act; and

"(iii) any bank or Federal savings association insured by the Federal Deposit Insurance Corporation (other than a member of the Federal Reserve System) and any insured State branch of a foreign bank;

"(B) the Federal Credit Union Act (12 U.S.C. 1751 et seq.), by the Administrator of the National Credit Union Administration with respect to any Federal credit union;

"(C) subtitle IV of title 49, United States Code, by the Secretary of Transportation, with respect to all carriers subject to the jurisdiction of the Surface Transportation Board;

"(D) the Federal Aviation Act of 1958 (49 U.S.C. App. 1301 et seq.), by the Secretary of Transportation, with respect to any air carrier or foreign air carrier subject to that Act;

"(E) the Packers and Stockyards Act, 1921 (7 U.S.C. 181 et seq.)(except as provided in section 406 of that Act), by the Secretary of Agriculture, with respect to any activities subject to that Act;

（C）**限制**。——无论第（2）款如何规定，对于违反第623（a）（1）条的主体，除非该主体在联邦贸易委员会或其代表提起的诉讼或法律程序中已被责成或命令不得从事上述违法违规行为但事后仍违反了该等禁令或命令，否则法院不得对其处以任何民事罚款，且法院不得对其在该主体违反该等禁令或命令之前进行的任何违法违规行为处以民事罚款。”；

（B）删除第（b）子条，替以如下内容：

“（b）**其他机关的执法权**。——

（1）**一般规定**。——在不违反《2010年消费者金融保护法》第B子编规定的前提下，对于消费者征信机构、使用消费者征信机构提供的消费者报告的主体、向消费者征信机构提供信息的主体以及受制于第615（d）条规定的信息使用者而言，本编施加的要求应按如下规定执行——

（A）对于以下实体而言，应按照《联邦存款保险法》第8条[《美国法典》第十二编第1818节）]的规定由相应的联邦银行业监管机关（定义见《联邦存款保险法》第3（q）条[《美国法典》第十二编第1813（q）节）]强制执行——

（i）任何国民银行或州储蓄协会，以及外国银行的联邦分行或联邦代理行；

（ii）联邦储备系统的任何成员银行（但国民银行除外）、外国银行的分行和代理行（但外国银行的联邦分行、联邦代理行或州参保分行除外）、外国银行拥有或控制的商业贷款公司以及依照《联邦储备法》第25条或第25A条开展运营的组织；及

（iii）由联邦存款保险公司承保的任何银行或联邦储蓄协会（联邦储备系统的成员除外）以及外国银行的州参保分行；

（B）对于任何联邦信贷联盟而言，应由国家信贷联盟署委员会委员根据《联邦信贷联盟法》（《美国法典》第十二编第1751节及其后条文）的规定强制执行；

（C）对于受地面交通委员会管辖的所有运输机构而言，应由交通部部长根据《美国法典》第四十九编第IV子编的规定强制执行；

（D）对于受《1958年联邦航空法》（《美国法典》第四十九编附件1301及其后条文）管辖的所有航空运输机构或外国航空运输机构而言，应由交通部部长根据该法的规定强制执行；

（E）对于受《1921年包装食品生产厂及牲畜围栏法》（《美国法典》第七编第181节及其后条文）管辖的所有相关活动而言，应由农业部部长根据该法规定（但该法第406条规定的情形外除外）强制执行；

"(F) the Commodity Exchange Act, with respect to a person subject to the jurisdiction of the Commodity Futures Trading Commission;

"(G) the Federal securities laws, and any other laws that are subject to the jurisdiction of the Securities and Exchange Commission, with respect to a person that is subject to the jurisdiction of the Securities and Exchange Commission; and

"(H) subtitle E of the Consumer Financial Protection Act of 2010, by the Bureau, with respect to any person subject to this title.

"(2) INCORPORATED DEFINITIONS. — The terms used in paragraph (1) that are not defined in this title or otherwise defined in section 3(s) of the Federal Deposit Insurance Act (12 U.S.C. 1813(s)) have the same meanings as in section 1(b) of the International Banking Act of 1978 (12 U.S.C. 3101).";

(C) in subsection (c)(2) —

(i) by inserting "and the Federal Trade Commission" before "or the appropriate"; and

(ii) by inserting "and the Federal Trade Commission" before "or appropriate" each place that term appears;

(D) in subsection (c)(4), by inserting before "or the appropriate" each place that term appears the following: ", the Federal Trade Commission,";

(E) by striking subsection (e) and inserting the following:

"(e) REGULATORY AUTHORITY. —

"(1) IN GENERAL. — The Bureau shall prescribe such regulations as are necessary to carry out the purposes of this title, except with respect to sections 615(e) and 628. The Bureau may prescribe regulations as may be necessary or appropriate to administer and carry out the purposes and objectives of this title, and to prevent evasions thereof or to facilitate compliance therewith. Except as provided in section 1029(a) of the Consumer Financial Protection Act of 2010, the regulations prescribed by the Bureau under this title shall apply to any person that is subject to this title, notwithstanding the enforcement authorities granted to other agencies under this section.

"(2) DEFERENCE. — Notwithstanding any power granted to any Federal agency under this title, the deference that a court affords to a Federal agency with respect to a determination made by such agency relating to the meaning or interpretation of any provision of this title that is subject to the jurisdiction of such agency shall be applied as if that agency were the only agency authorized to apply, enforce, interpret, or administer the provisions of this title The regulations prescribed by the Bureau under this title shall apply to any person that is subject to this title, notwithstanding the enforcement authorities granted to other agencies under this section."; and

(F) in subsection (f)(2), by striking "the Federal banking agencies" and insert "the Federal Trade Commission, the Federal banking agencies,";

(F)对于商品期货交易委员会管辖的主体而言,应根据《商品交易法》强制执行;

(G)对于受证券交易委员会管辖的主体而言,应根据联邦证券法律以及证券交易委员会有管辖权的任何其他法律强制执行;及

(H)对于受本编管辖的主体而言,应由消费者金融保护局根据《2010年消费者金融保护法》第E子编的规定强制执行。

(2)**援引纳入的定义**。——在第(1)款中出现,但本编或《联邦存款保险法》第3(s)条[《美国法典》第十二编第1813(s)节]未予定义的术语,其含义应以《1978年国际银行法》第1(b)条(《美国法典》第十二编第3101节)的定义为准。”;

(C)在第(c)(2)子条中——

(i)在“或相应的”前插入“及联邦贸易委员会”;及

(ii)在所有的“或相应的”前插入“及联邦贸易委员会”;

(D)第(c)(4)子条在所有的“或相应的”前插入如下内容:“、联邦贸易委员会”;

(E)删除第(e)子条,替以如下内容:

“(e)**监管权**。——

(1)**一般规定**。——消费者金融保护局应制定必要规章,执行本编[但第615(e)条和第628条除外]的宗旨。消费者金融保护局可以制定必要且适当的规章,以实施和执行本编的宗旨和目标,防范规避本编规定的行为,并促进对本编规定的合规。除《2010年消费者金融保护法》第1029(a)条规定的情形外,即使本条向其他机关赋予了执法权,消费者金融保护局根据本编制定的规章仍应适用于受本编管辖的所有主体。

(2)**司法尊重**。——不论本编向任何其他联邦机关赋予了任何权力,某联邦机关对其管辖的本编任何规定之含义或解释作出了判定且法院对该等判定表示司法尊重的,则在适用该等司法尊重时,应将该联邦机关视同为唯一有权适用、执行、解释或实施本编规定的机关。即使本条向其他机关赋予了执法权,消费者金融保护局根据本编制定的规章仍应适用于受本编管辖的所有主体。”;及

(F)在第(f)(2)子条中,删除“联邦银行业监管机关”,替以“联邦贸易委员会、联邦银行业监管机关、”;

(11) in section 623 (15 U.S.C. 1681s-2) —

(A) in subsection (a)(7), by striking subparagraph (D) and inserting the following:

"(D) MODEL DISCLOSURE. —

"(i) DUTY OF BUREAU. — The Bureau shall prescribe a brief model disclosure that a financial institution may use to comply with subparagraph (A), which shall not exceed 30 words.

"(ii) USE OF MODEL NOT REQUIRED. — No provision of this paragraph may be construed to require a financial institution to use any such model form prescribed by the Bureau.

"(iii) COMPLIANCE USING MODEL. — A financial institution shall be deemed to be in compliance with subparagraph (A) if the financial institution uses any model form prescribed by the Bureau under this subparagraph, or the financial institution uses any such model form and rearranges its format."; (B) in subsection (a)(8), by inserting ", in consultation with the Federal Trade Commission, the Federal banking agencies, and the National Credit Union Administration," before "shall jointly"; and

(C) by striking subsection (e) and inserting the following:

"(e) ACCURACY GUIDELINES AND REGULATIONS REQUIRED. —

"(1) GUIDELINES. — The Bureau shall, with respect to persons or entities that are subject to the enforcement authority of the Bureau under section 621 —

"(A) establish and maintain guidelines for use by each person that furnishes information to a consumer reporting agency regarding the accuracy and integrity of the information relating to consumers that such entities furnish to consumer reporting agencies, and update such guidelines as often as necessary; and

"(B) prescribe regulations requiring each person that furnishes information to a consumer reporting agency to establish reasonable policies and procedures for implementing the guidelines established pursuant to subparagraph (A).

"(2) CRITERIA. — In developing the guidelines required by paragraph (1)(A), the Bureau shall —

"(A) identify patterns, practices, and specific forms of activity that can compromise the accuracy and integrity of information furnished to consumer reporting agencies;

"(B) review the methods (including technological means) used to furnish information relating to consumers to consumer reporting agencies;

"(C) determine whether persons that furnish information to consumer reporting agencies maintain and enforce policies to ensure the accuracy and integrity of information furnished to consumer reporting agencies; and

"(D) examine the policies and processes that persons that furnish information to consumer reporting agencies employ to conduct reinvestigations and correct inaccurate

(11)在第623条(《美国法典》第十五编第1681s–2节)中——

(A)第(a)(7)子条删除第(D)子款,替以如下内容:

"(D)**披露范例**。——

(i)**消费者金融保护局的职责**。——消费者金融保护局应制定篇幅不超过30个单词的简要披露范例,供金融机构在遵守第(A)子款规定之时使用。

(ii)**不要求使用范例格式**。——本款任何内容均不得被解释为要求金融机构必须使用消费者金融保护局制定的任何范例格式。

(iii)**使用范例格式即视为合规**。——如果金融机构使用消费者金融保护局根据本子款制定的任何范例格式,或者使用前述范例格式对其格式进行重新安排,其应被视为符合第(A)子款规定。";(B)在第(a)(8)子条中,在"应联合"前插入",在与联邦贸易委员会、联邦银行业监管机关以及国家信贷联盟署磋商后";及

(C)删除第(e)子条,替以如下内容:

"(e)**准确性指引和规章要求**。——

(1)**指引**。——对于根据第621条受制于消费者金融保护局的执法权力的个人或实体而言,消费者金融保护局应——

(A)就该等实体向消费者征信机构提供的消费者相关信息的准确性和完整性制定并维持一份指引,以供相关主体在向消费者征信机构提供信息时使用,并随时对该等指引进行必要的更新;并

(B)制定规章,要求向消费者征信机构提供信息的所有主体均制定合理的政策和程序,以实施根据第(A)子款制定的上述指引。

(2)**标准**。——在按照第(1)(A)款的要求制定指引之时,消费者金融保护局应——

(A)对能够损害向消费者征信机构提供的信息之准确性和完整性的范例、实践和具体活动形式进行确认;

(B)对用以向消费者征信机构提供与消费者相关的信息的方法(包括技术手段)进行审查;

(C)判定向消费者征信机构提供信息的主体是否维持并执行了相关政策,确保向消费者征信机构提供的信息之准确性和完整性;并

(D)审查向消费者征信机构提供信息的主体对已经向消费者征信机构提供的不准确的消费者相关信息进行重新调查和纠正的政策和程序。";

information relating to consumers that has been furnished to consumer reporting agencies.";

(12) in section 628(a)(1)(15 U.S.C. 1681w(a)(1)), by striking "Not later than" and all that follows through "Exchange Commission," and inserting "The Federal Trade Commission, the Securities and Exchange Commission, the Commodity Futures Trading Commission, the Federal banking agencies, and the National Credit Union Administration, with respect to the entities that are subject to their respective enforcement authority under section 621,"; and

(13) in section 628(a)(3)(15 U.S.C. 1681w(a)(3)), by striking "the Federal banking agencies, the National Credit Union Administration, the Commission, and the Securities and Exchange Commission" and inserting "the agencies identified in paragraph (1)".

(b) FAIR AND ACCURATE CREDIT TRANSACTIONS ACT OF 2003. — The Fair and Accurate Credit Transactions Act of 2003 (Public Law 108–159) is amended —

(1) in section 112(b)(15 U.S.C. 1681c–1 note), by striking "Commission" and inserting "Bureau";

(2) in section 211(d)(15 U.S.C. 1681j note), by striking "Commission" each place that term appears and inserting "Bureau";

(3) in section 214(b)(15 U.S.C. 1681s–3 note), by striking paragraph (1) and inserting the following:

"(1) IN GENERAL. — Regulations to carry out section 624 of the Fair Credit Reporting Act (15 U.S.C. 1681s–3), shall be prescribed, as described in paragraph (2), by —

"(A) the Commodity Futures Trading Commission, with respect to entities subject to its enforcement authorities;

"(B) the Securities and Exchange Commission, with respect to entities subject to its enforcement authorities; and

"(C) the Bureau, with respect to other entities subject to this Act."; and

(4) in section 214(e)(1)(15 U.S.C. 1681s–3 note), by striking "Commission" and inserting "Bureau".

SEC. 1089. AMENDMENTS TO THE FAIR DEBT COLLECTION PRACTICES ACT.

The Fair Debt Collection Practices Act (15 U.S.C. 1692 et seq.) is amended —

(1) by striking "Commission" each place that term appears and inserting "Bureau";

(2) in section 803 (15 U.S.C. 1692a) —

(A) by striking paragraph (1) and inserting the following:

"(1) The term 'Bureau' means the Bureau of Consumer Financial Protection.";

(3) in section 814 (15 U.S.C. 1692l) —

(A) by striking subsection (a) and inserting the following:

(12)在第628(a)(1)条[《美国法典》第十五编第1681w(a)(1)节]中,删除"不迟于"直至"交易委员会"的全部内容,替以"联邦贸易委员会、证券交易委员会、商品期货交易委员会、联邦银行业监管机关以及国家信贷联盟署,对于根据第621条其分别拥有执法权的实体而言";并

(13)在第628(a)(3)条[《美国法典》第十五编第1681w(a)(3)节]中,删除"联邦银行业监管机关、国家信贷联盟署、联邦贸易委员会以及证券交易委员会",替以"第(1)款所列机关"。

(b)**《2003年公平准确信用交易法》**。——《2003年公平准确信用交易法》(第108—159号公法)修正如下——

(1)在第112(b)条(《美国法典》第十五编第1681c-1节注释)中,删除"联邦贸易委员会",替以"消费者金融保护局";

(2)在第211(d)条(《美国法典》第十五编第1681j节注释)中,删除所有的"联邦贸易委员会",全部替以"消费者金融保护局";

(3)在第214(b)条(《美国法典》第十五编第1681s-3节注释)中,删除第(1)款,替以如下内容:

"(1)**一般规定**。——第(2)款所述《公平信用报告法》第624条(《美国法典》第十五编第1681s-3节)的实施规章应按如下规定制定——

(A)对于受制于商品期货交易委员会的执法权的实体而言,由商品期货交易委员会制定;

(B)对于受制于证券交易委员会的执法权的实体而言,由证券交易委员会制定;

(C)对于受本法管辖的其他实体而言,由消费者金融保护局制定。";及

(4)在第214(e)(1)条(《美国法典》第十五编第1681s-3节注释)中,删除"联邦贸易委员会",替以"消费者金融保护局"。

第1089条　对《公平债务催收作业法》的修正

《公平债务催收作业法》(《美国法典》第十五编第1692节及其后条文)修正如下——

(1)删除所有的"联邦贸易委员会",全部替以"消费者金融保护局";

(2)在第803条(《美国法典》第十五编第1692a节)中——

(A)删除第(1)款,替以如下内容:

"(1)'消费者金融保护局'一词系指联邦储备系统下的消费者金融保护局。";

(3)在第814条(《美国法典》第十五编第1692l节)中——

(A)删除第(a)子条,替以如下内容:

"(a) FEDERAL TRADE COMMISSION. — The Federal Trade Commission shall be authorized to enforce compliance with this title, except to the extent that enforcement of the requirements imposed under this title is specifically committed to another Government agency under any of paragraphs (1) through (5) of subsection (b), subject to subtitle B of the Consumer Financial Protection Act of 2010. For purpose of the exercise by the Federal Trade Commission of its functions and powers under the Federal Trade Commission Act (15 U.S.C. 41 et seq.), a violation of this title shall be deemed an unfair or deceptive act or practice in violation of that Act. All of the functions and powers of the Federal Trade Commission under the Federal Trade Commission Act are available to the Federal Trade Commission to enforce compliance by any person with this title, irrespective of whether that person is engaged in commerce or meets any other jurisdictional tests under the Federal Trade Commission Act, including the power to enforce the provisions of this title, in the same manner as if the violation had been a violation of a Federal Trade Commission trade regulation rule."; and

(B) in subsection (b) —

(i) by striking "Compliance" and inserting "Subject to subtitle B of the Consumer Financial Protection Act of 2010, compliance";

(ii) by striking paragraphs (1) and (2) and inserting the following:

"(1) section 8 of the Federal Deposit Insurance Act, by the appropriate Federal banking agency, as defined in section 3(q) of the Federal Deposit Insurance Act (12 U.S.C. 1813 (q)), with respect to —

"(A) national banks, Federal savings associations, and Federal branches and Federal agencies of foreign banks;

"(B) member banks of the Federal Reserve System (other than national banks), branches and agencies of foreign banks (other than Federal branches, Federal agencies, and insured State branches of foreign banks), commercial lending companies owned or controlled by foreign banks, and organizations operating under section 25 or 25A of the Federal Reserve Act; and

"(C) banks and State savings associations insured by the Federal Deposit Insurance Corporation (other than members of the Federal Reserve System), and insured State branches of foreign banks;";

(iii) by redesignating paragraphs (3) through (6), as paragraphs (2) through (5), respectively;

(iv) in paragraph (4)(as so redesignated), by striking "and" at the end;

(v) in paragraph (5)(as so redesignated), by striking the period at the end and inserting "; and"; and

(vi) by inserting before the undesignated matter at the end the following:

"(6) subtitle E of the Consumer Financial Protection Act of 2010, by the Bureau, with

“(a)**联邦贸易委员会**。——在不违反《2010年消费者金融保护法》第B子编规定的前提下,联邦贸易委员会有权强制执行本编规定,但是,第(b)子条第(1)款至第(5)款明确指明由其他政府机关强制执行的本编规定除外。联邦贸易委员会在根据《联邦贸易委员会法》(《美国法典》第十五编第41节及其后条文)行使职能和权力之时,违反本编规定的行为应被视为违反该法的不公平或欺骗性行为或做法。联邦贸易委员会对任何人强制执行本编规定时,不论该人是否从事商业,亦不论其是否符合《联邦贸易委员会法》规定的任何其他管辖权标准,联邦贸易委员会均有权行使《联邦贸易委员会法》赋予的所有职能和权力,包括强制执行本编的规定的权力,如同该项违法违规行为属于违反联邦贸易委员会某一贸易监管规则的行为。”;及

(B)第(b)子条——

(i)删除“遵从”,替以“在不违反《2010年消费者金融保护法》第B子编规定的前提下,”;

(ii)删除第(1)款和第(2)款,替以如下内容:

“(1)对于以下实体,《联邦存款保险法》第8条的规定应由相应的联邦银行业监管机关(定义见《联邦存款保险法》第3(q)条[《美国法典》第十二编第1813(q)节)]强制执行——

(A)国民银行、联邦储蓄协会以及外国银行的联邦分行和联邦代理行;

(B)联邦储备系统的成员银行(但国民银行除外)、外国银行的分行和代理行(但外国银行的联邦分行、联邦代理行以及州参保分行除外)、外国银行拥有或控制的商业贷款公司以及根据《联邦储备法》第25条或第25A条运营的组织;及

(C)在联邦存款保险公司参保的银行和州储蓄协会(但联邦储备系统成员除外)以及外国银行的州参保分行;”;

(iii)第(3)款至第(6)款分别重新编号为第(2)款至第(5)款;

(iv)在第(4)款(以重新编号后的序号为准)中,删除结尾处的“及”;

(v)在第(5)款(以重新编号后的序号为准)中,删除结尾处的句号,替以“;及”;并

(vi)在结尾处的无编号内容前插入如下内容:

“(6)对于受本编管辖的任何人,《2010年消费者金融保护法》第E子编的规定均应

respect to any person subject to this title.".

(4) in subsection (d), by striking "Neither the Commission" and all that follows through the end of the subsection and inserting the following: "Except as provided in section 1029 (a) of the Consumer Financial Protection Act of 2010, the Bureau may prescribe rules with respect to the collection of debts by debt collectors, as defined in this title.".

SEC. 1090. AMENDMENTS TO THE FEDERAL DEPOSIT INSURANCE ACT.

The Federal Deposit Insurance Act (12 U.S.C. 1811 et seq.) is amended —

(1) in section 8(t)(12 U.S.C. 1818(t)), by adding at the end the following:

"(6) REFERRAL TO BUREAU OF CONSUMER FINANCIAL PROTECTION. — Subject to subtitle B of the Consumer Financial Protection Act of 2010, each appropriate Federal banking agency shall make a referral to the Bureau of Consumer Financial Protection when the Federal banking agency has a reasonable belief that a violation of an enumerated consumer law, as defined in the Consumer Financial Protection Act of 2010, has been committed by any insured depository institution or institution–affiliated party within the jurisdiction of that appropriate Federal banking agency."; and

(2) in section 43 (12 U.S.C. 1831t) —

(A) in subsection (c), by striking "Federal Trade Commission" and inserting "Bureau";

(B) in subsection (d), by striking "Federal Trade Commission" and inserting "Bureau";

(C) in subsection (e) —

(i) in paragraph (2), by striking "Federal Trade Commission" and inserting "Bureau"; and

(ii) by adding at the end the following new paragraph:

"(5) BUREAU. — The term 'Bureau' means the Bureau of Consumer Financial Protection."; and

(D) in subsection (f) —

(i) by striking paragraph (1) and inserting the following:

"(1) LIMITED ENFORCEMENT AUTHORITY. — Compliance with the requirements of subsections (b), (c), and (e), and any regulation prescribed or order issued under such subsection, shall be enforced under the Consumer Financial Protection Act of 2010, by the Bureau, subject to subtitle B of the Consumer Financial Protection Act of 2010, and under the Federal Trade Commission Act(15 U.S.C. 41 et seq.) by the Federal Trade Commission."; and

(ii) in paragraph (2), by striking subparagraph (C) and inserting the following:

"(C) LIMITATION ON STATE ACTION WHILE FEDERAL ACTION PENDING. — If the Bureau or Federal Trade Commission has instituted an enforcement action for a

由消费者金融保护局强制执行。”

（4）在第（d）子条中，删除“联邦贸易委员会”直至该子条结尾的全部内容，替以如下内容：“除《2010年消费者金融保护法》第1029（a）条规定的情形外，消费者金融保护局可以就本编定义的收债人催收债务行为制定规则。”

第1090条　对《联邦存款保险法》的修正

《联邦存款保险法》（《美国法典》第十二编第1811节及其后条文）修正如下——

（1）在第8（t）条［《美国法典》第十二编第1818（t）节］结尾处增加如下内容：

“（6）移交消费者金融保护局。——在不违反《2010年消费者金融保护法》第B子编规定的前提下，任何相应的联邦银行业监管机关一旦合理相信受其管辖的任何参保存款机构或机构关联方从事了《2010年消费者金融保护法》定义的违反明文列举的消费者法律之行为，均应将其移交消费者金融保护局。”；及

（2）在第43条（《美国法典》第十二编第1831t节）中——

（A）第（c）子条删除“联邦贸易委员会”，替以“消费者金融保护局”；

（B）第（d）子条删除“联邦贸易委员会”，替以“消费者金融保护局”；

（C）第（e）子条——

（i）第（2）款删除“联邦贸易委员会”，替以“消费者金融保护局”；及

（ii）在结尾处增加如下新款：

“（5）**消费者金融保护局**。——‘消费者金融保护局’一词系指联邦储备系统下的消费者金融保护局。”；及

（D）第（f）子条——

（i）删除第（1）款，替以如下内容：

“（1）**有限的强制执行权**。——第（b）子条、第（c）子条和第（e）子条的规定以及根据该等子条制定的任何规章或发布的任何命令，均应由消费者金融保护局在不违反《2010年消费者金融保护法》第B子编规定的前提下，根据《2010年消费者金融保护法》强制执行，以及由联邦贸易委员会根据《联保贸易委员会法》（《美国法典》第十五编第41节及其后条文）强制执行。”及

（ii）在第（2）款中，删除第（C）子款，替以如下内容：

“（C）**联邦诉讼未决期间对州诉讼的限制**。——消费者金融保护局或联邦贸易委员会就违反本条的行为启动了执法诉讼之后，在诉讼未决期间，任何相应的州监管机

violation of this section, no appropriate State supervisory agency may, during the pendency of such action, bring an action under this section against any defendant named in the complaint of the Bureau or Federal Trade Commission for any violation of this section that is alleged in that complaint.".

SEC. 1091. AMENDMENT TO FEDERAL FINANCIAL INSTITUTIONS EXAMINATION COUNCIL ACT OF 1978.

Section 1004(a)(4) of the Federal Financial Institutions Examination Council Act of 1978(12 U.S.C. 3303(a)(4)) is amended by striking "Director, Office of Thrift Supervision" and inserting "Director of the Consumer Financial Protection Bureau".

SEC. 1092. AMENDMENTS TO THE FEDERAL TRADE COMMISSION ACT.

Section 18(f) of the Federal Trade Commission Act (15 U.S.C. 57a(f)) is amended —

(1) by striking the subsection heading and inserting the following:

"(f) DEFINITIONS OF BANKS, SAVINGS AND LOAN INSTITUTIONS, AND FEDERAL CREDIT UNIONS. — ".

(2) by striking paragraph (1) and inserting the following:

"(1) [Repealed.]";

(3) by striking paragraphs (5) through (7);

(4) in paragraph (2) —

(A) by striking "(2) ENFORCEMENT" and all that follows through "in the case of" and inserting the following:

"(2) DEFINITION. — For purposes of this Act, the term 'bank' means";

(B) in subparagraph (A), by striking ", by the division" and all that follows through "Currency";

(C) in subparagraph (B) —

(i) by striking ", by the division" and all that follows through "System"; and

(ii) by striking "25(a)" and inserting "25A"; and

(D) in subparagraph (C) —

(i) by striking "(other" and inserting "(other than"; and

(ii) by striking ", by the division" and all that follows through "Corporation";

(5) in paragraph (3), by striking "Compliance" and all that follows through "as defined in" and inserting the following: "For purposes of this Act, the term "savings and loan institution" has the same meaning as in"; and

(6) in paragraph (4), by striking "Compliance" and all that follows through "credit unions under" and inserting the following: "For purposes of this Act, the term "Federal credit union" has the same meaning as in".

SEC. 1093. AMENDMENTS TO THE GRAMM-LEACH-BLILEY ACT.

Title V of the Gramm-Leach-Bliley Act (15 U.S.C. 6801 et seq.) is amended —

关均不得针对消费者金融保护局或联邦贸易委员会申诉书中的被告，基于该申诉书中所指称的任何违反本条的行为按照本条提起诉讼。”

第1091条　对《1978年联邦金融机构检查委员会法》的修正

在《1978年联邦金融机构检查委员会法》第1004(a)(4)条[《美国法典》第十二编第3303(a)(4)节]中,删除“储蓄机构监理局局长”,替以“消费者金融保护局局长”。

第1092条　对《联邦贸易委员会法》的修正

《联邦贸易委员会法》第18(f)条[《美国法典》第十五编第57a(f)节]修正如下——

(1)删除该子条标题,替以如下内容:

“(f)**银行、储蓄和贷款机构以及联邦信贷联盟的定义**。——”

(2)删除第(1)款,替以如下内容:

“(1)[已废止。]”;

(3)删除第(5)款至第(7)款;

(4)在第(2)款中——

(A)删除“(2)强制执行”直至“应遵照第12编第1818节的规定,并按照以下规定强制执行”的全部内容,替以如下内容:

“(2)**定义**。——就本法而言,‘银行’一词系指”;

(B)第(A)子款删除“由货币监理署设立的消费者事务部强制执行”;

(C)第(B)子款——

(i)删除“由联邦储备委员会设立的消费者事务部强制执行”;及

(ii)删除“25(a)”,替以“25A”;及

(D)第(C)子款——

(i)删除“(其他”,替以“(不包括”;及

(ii)删除“由联邦存款保险公司董事会设立的消费者事务部强制执行”;

(5)在第(3)款中,删除“对于第十二编第1813节定义的储蓄协会而言,根据本子条制定的规章应按照第十二编第1818节的规定强制执行”,替以如下内容:

“就本法而言,‘储蓄和贷款机构’一词的含义以第十二编第1813节的定义为准。”;及

(6)在第(4)款中,删除“根据本子条制定的规章应针对第十二编第1766节和第1786节定义的联邦信贷联盟强制执行”,替以如下内容:“就本法而言,‘联邦信贷联盟’一词的含义以第十二编第1766节和第1786节的定义为准。”

第1093条　对《格雷姆—里奇—比利雷法》的修正

《格雷姆—里奇—比利雷法》第五编(《美国法典》第十五编第6801节及其后条文)

(1) in section 501(b)(15 U.S.C. 6801(b)), by inserting ", other than the Bureau of Consumer Financial Protection," after "505(a)";

(2) in section 502(e)(5)(15 U.S.C. 6802(e)(5)), by inserting "the Bureau of Consumer Financial Protection" after "(including";

(3) in section 504(a)(15 U.S.C. 6804(a))—

(A) by striking paragraphs (1) and (2) and inserting the following:

"(1) RULEMAKING.—

"(A) IN GENERAL.—Except as provided in subparagraph (C), the Bureau of Consumer Financial Protection and the Securities and Exchange Commission shall have authority to prescribe such regulations as may be necessary to carry out the purposes of this subtitle with respect to financial institutions and other persons subject to their respective jurisdiction under section 505 (and notwithstanding subtitle B of the Consumer Financial Protection Act of 2010), except that the Bureau of Consumer Financial Protection shall not have authority to prescribe regulations with respect to the standards under section 501.

"(B) CFTC.—The Commodity Futures Trading Commission shall have authority to prescribe such regulations as may be necessary to carry out the purposes of this subtitle with respect to financial institutions and other persons subject to the jurisdiction of the Commodity Futures Trading Commission under section 5g of the Commodity Exchange Act.

"(C) FEDERAL TRADE COMMISSION AUTHORITY.—Notwithstanding the authority of the Bureau of Consumer Financial Protection under subparagraph (A), the Federal Trade Commission shall have authority to prescribe such regulations as may be necessary to carry out the purposes of this subtitle with respect to any financial institution that is a person described in section 1029(a) of the Consumer Financial Protection Act of 2010.

"(D) RULE OF CONSTRUCTION.—Nothing in this paragraph shall be construed to alter, affect, or otherwise limit the authority of a State insurance authority to adopt regulations to carry out this subtitle.

"(2) COORDINATION, CONSISTENCY, AND COMPARABILITY.—Each of the agencies authorized under paragraph (1) to prescribe regulations shall consult and coordinate with the other such agencies and, as appropriate, and with representatives of State insurance authorities designated by the National Association of Insurance Commissioners, for the purpose of assuring, to the extent possible, that the regulations prescribed by each such agency are consistent and comparable with the regulations prescribed by the other such agencies."; and

(B) in paragraph (3), by striking ", and shall be issued in final form not later than 6 months after the date of enactment of this Act";

(4) in section 505(a)(15 U.S.C. 6805(a))—

修正如下——

(1)在第501(b)条[《美国法典》第十五编第6801(b)节]中,在"第505(a)条所述每一机关或主管机构"之后插入"(但消费者金融保护局除外)";

(2)在第502(e)(5)条[《美国法典》第十五编第6802(e)(5)节]中,在"(包括"之后插入"消费者金融保护局";

(3)在第504(a)条[《美国法典》第15编第6804(a)节]中——

(A)删除第(1)款和第(2)款,替以如下内容:

"(1)**规则制定**。——

(A)**一般规定**。——除第(C)子款规定的情形外,消费者金融保护局和证券交易委员会有权制定必要规章,以针对金融机构及根据第505条受其各自管辖的其他主体执行本子编之宗旨(不论《2010年消费者金融保护法》第B子编是否存在任何相反规定),但是,消费者金融保护局无权就第501条规定的标准制定规章。

(B)**商品期货交易委员会**。——商品期货交易委员会有权制定必要规章,以针对金融机构及根据《商品交易法》第5g条受商品期货交易委员会管辖的其他主体执行本子编之宗旨。

(C)**联邦贸易委员会的权力**。——尽管第(A)子款向消费者金融保护局赋予了相关权力,但是,对于身为《2010年消费者金融保护法》第1029(a)条所述主体的金融机构,联邦贸易委员会有权为针对该等金融机构执行本子编之宗旨而制定必要规章。

(D)**解释规则**。——本款的任何规定均不得被解释为更改、影响或以其他方式限制州保险监管机构为实施本子编规定而制定相关规章的权力。

(2)**协调、一致性及可比性**。——根据第(1)款授权制定规章的各个机关,应相互磋商和协调,并在适当情况下,与美国保险监督官协会指定的州保险监管机构代表进行磋商和协调,以尽可能确保各机关制定的规章之间实现相互协调并具有可比性。"及

(B)在第(3)款中,删除",并应在本法颁布之日起6个月内颁布最终版本";

(4)在第505(a)条[《美国法典》第十五编第6805(a)节]中——

(A) by striking "This subtitle" and all that follows through "as follows:" and inserting "Subject to subtitle B of the Consumer Financial Protection Act of 2010, this subtitle and the regulations prescribed thereunder shall be enforced by the Bureau of Consumer Financial Protection, the Federal functional regulators, the State insurance authorities, and the Federal Trade Commission with respect to financial institutions and other persons subject to their jurisdiction under applicable law, as follows:";

(B) in paragraph (1)—

(i) in the matter preceding subparagraph (A), by inserting "by the appropriate Federal banking agency, as defined in section 3 (q) of the Federal Deposit Insurance Act," after "Act,";

(ii) in subparagraph (A), by striking ", by the Office of the Comptroller of the Currency";

(iii) in subparagraph (B), by striking ", by the Board of Governors of the Federal Reserve System";

(iv) in subparagraph (C), by striking ", by the Board of Directors of the Federal Deposit Insurance Corporation"; and

(v) in subparagraph (D), by striking ", by the Director of the Office of Thrift Supervision"; and

(C) by adding at the end the following:

"(8) Under subtitle E of the Consumer Financial Protection Act of 2010, by the Bureau of Consumer Financial Protection, in the case of any financial institution and other covered person or service provider that is subject to the jurisdiction of the Bureau and any person subject to this subtitle, but not with respect to the standards under section 501.";

(5) in section 505(b)(1)(15 U.S.C. 6805(b)(1)), by inserting ", other than the Bureau of Consumer Financial Protection," after "subsection (a)"; and

(6) in section 507(b)(15 U.S.C. 6807), by striking "Federal Trade Commission" and inserting "Bureau of Consumer Financial Protection".

SEC. 1094. AMENDMENTS TO THE HOME MORTGAGE DISCLOSURE ACT OF 1975.

The Home Mortgage Disclosure Act of 1975 (12 U.S.C. 2801 et seq.) is amended—

(1) by striking "Board" each place that term appears, other than in sections 303, 304 (h), 305 (b)(as amended by this section), and 307(a)(as amended by this section) and inserting "Bureau".

(2) in section 303 (12 U.S.C. 2802)—

(A) by redesignating paragraphs (1) through (6) as paragraphs (2) through (7), respectively; and

(A)删除“本子编”直至“具体如下：”的所有内容，替以“在不违反《2010年消费者金融保护法》第B子编规定的前提下，本子编以及根据本子编制定的规章应由消费者金融保护局、联邦功能监管者、州保险监管机构以及联邦贸易委员会针对金融机构以及根据适用法律受其管辖的其他主体强制执行，具体如下：”；

(B)第(1)款——

(i)第(A)子款之前的内容在“按照《联邦存款保险法》第8条的规定强制执行”前插入“由《联邦存款保险法》第3(q)条定义的相应的联邦银行业监管机关”；

(ii)第(A)子款删除“，由货币监理署强制执行”；

(iii)第(B)子款删除“，由联邦储备委员会强制执行”；

(iv)第(C)子款删除“，由联邦存款保险公司董事会强制执行”；及

(v)第(D)子款删除“，由储蓄机构监理局局长强制执行”；及

(C)在结尾处增加如下内容：

“(8)对于任何金融机构以及其他受消费者金融保护局管辖的所涉主体或服务提供者以及受本子编管辖的任何主体而言，由消费者金融保护局根据《2010年消费者金融保护法》第E子编的规定强制执行，但第501条规定的标准除外。”

(5)在第505(b)(1)条[《美国法典》第十五编第6805(b)(1)节]中，在“第(a)子条所述每一机关或主管机构”之后插入“(但消费者金融保护局除外)”；及

(6)在第507(b)条(《美国法典》第十五编第6807节)中，删除“联邦贸易委员会”，替以“消费者金融保护局”。

第1094条 对《1975年住房抵押贷款披露法》的修正

《1975年住房抵押贷款披露法》(《美国法典》第十二编第2801节及其后条文)修正如下——

(1)删除在第303条、第304(h)条、第305(b)条(以本条修正后的版本为准)以及第307(a)条(以本条修正后的版本为准)以外出现的所有“联邦储备委员会”，全部替以“消费者金融保护局”。

(2)在第303条(《美国法典》第十二编第2802节)中——

(A)第(1)款至第(6)款分别重新编号为第(2)款至第(7)款；及

(B) by inserting before paragraph (2) the following:

"(1) the term 'Bureau' means the Bureau of Consumer Financial Protection;";

(3) in section 304 (12 U.S.C. 2803)—

(A) in subsection (b)—

(i) in paragraph (4), by inserting "age," before "and gender";

(ii) in paragraph (3), by striking "and" at the end;

(iii) in paragraph (4), by striking the period at the end and inserting a semicolon; and

(iv) by adding at the end the following:

"(5) the number and dollar amount of mortgage loans grouped according to measurements of—

"(A) the total points and fees payable at origination in connection with the mortgage as determined by the Bureau, taking into account 15 U.S.C. 1602(aa)(4);

"(B) the difference between the annual percentage rate associated with the loan and a benchmark rate or rates for all loans;

"(C) the term in months of any prepayment penalty or other fee or charge payable on repayment of some portion of principal or the entire principal in advance of scheduled payments; and

"(D) such other information as the Bureau may require; and

"(6) the number and dollar amount of mortgage loans and completed applications grouped according to measurements of—

"(A) the value of the real property pledged or proposed to be pledged as collateral;

"(B) the actual or proposed term in months of any introductory period after which the rate of interest may change;

"(C) the presence of contractual terms or proposed contractual terms that would allow the mortgagor or applicant to make payments other than fully amortizing payments during any portion of the loan term;

"(D) the actual or proposed term in months of the mortgage loan;

"(E) the channel through which application was made, including retail, broker, and other relevant categories;

"(F) as the Bureau may determine to be appropriate, a unique identifier that identifies the loan originator as set forth in section 1503 of the S.A.F.E. Mortgage Licensing Act of 2008;

"(G) as the Bureau may determine to be appropriate, a universal loan identifier;

"(H) as the Bureau may determine to be appropriate, the parcel number that corresponds to the real property pledged or proposed to be pledged as collateral;

"(I) the credit score of mortgage applicants and mortgagors, in such form as the Bureau may prescribe; and

(B)在第(2)款前插入如下内容:

"(1)'消费者金融保护局'一词系指联邦储备系统下的消费者金融保护局;";

(3)在第304条(《美国法典》第十二编第2803节)中——

(A)第(b)子条——

(i)第(4)款在"及性别"前插入"年龄";

(ii)删除第(3)款结尾处的"及";

(iii)第(4)款删除结尾处的句号,替以分号;及

(iv)在结尾处增加如下内容:

"(5)依据如下指标分类的抵押贷款数量和金额——

(A)由消费者金融保护局参照《美国法典》第十五编第1602(aa)(4)节规定确定的抵押贷款发起时的总点数和应付费用;

(B)该贷款年利率和所有贷款基准利率之间的差异;

(C)早于预定还款日期提前偿还部分或全部本金时,所应付的提前还款违约金或其他费用或收费的期限(按月计算);及

(D)消费者金融保护局要求提供的其他信息;及

(6)依据如下指标分类的抵押贷款数量和金额,以及已填妥的申请——

(A)作为担保品已质押或拟作为担保品质押的不动产之价值;

(B)导入期(导入期届满之后利率可能发生变化)的实际期限或拟设定的期限(按月计算);

(C)是否存在合同条款或拟定的合同条款,允许抵押人或申请人除了在贷款期内的任何时段分期完全摊还贷款之外,选择其他还款方式;

(D)实际或拟定的抵押贷款期限(按月计算);

(E)申请贷款的渠道,包括零售、经纪以及其他相关类别的渠道;

(F)识别《2008年安全和公平执行抵押贷款发起人许可法》第1503条所述贷款发起人的唯一识别码(如消费者金融保护局判定确属适当);

(G)通用贷款识别码(如消费者金融保护局判定确属适当);

(H)作为担保品已质押或拟作为担保品质押的不动产所对应的宗地号(如消费者金融保护局判定确属适当);

(I)抵押贷款申请人和抵押人的信用评分(其格式以消费者金融保护局的规定为准);及

"(J) such other information as the Bureau may require.";

(B) by striking subsection (h) and inserting the following:

"(h) SUBMISSION TO AGENCIES.—

"(1) IN GENERAL.—The data required to be disclosed under subsection (b) shall be submitted to the Bureau or to the appropriate agency for the institution reporting under this title, in accordance with rules prescribed by the Bureau. Notwithstanding the requirement of subsection (a)(2)(A) for disclosure by census tract, the Bureau, in consultation with other appropriate agencies described in paragraph (2) and, after notice and comment, shall develop regulations that—

"(A) prescribe the format for such disclosures, the method for submission of the data to the appropriate agency, and the procedures for disclosing the information to the public;

"(B) require the collection of data required to be disclosed under subsection (b) with respect to loans sold by each institution reporting under this title;

"(C) require disclosure of the class of the purchaser of such loans;

"(D) permit any reporting institution to submit in writing to the Bureau or to the appropriate agency such additional data or explanations as it deems relevant to the decision to originate or purchase mortgage loans; and

"(E) modify or require modification of itemized information, for the purpose of protecting the privacy interests of the mortgage applicants or mortgagors, that is or will be available to the public.

"(2) OTHER APPROPRIATE AGENCIES.—The appropriate agen cies described in this paragraph are—

"(A) the appropriate Federal banking agencies, as defined in section 3 (q) of the Federal Deposit Insurance Act (12 U.S.C. 1813 (q)), with respect to the entities that are subject to the jurisdiction of each such agency, respectively;

"(B) the Federal Deposit Insurance Corporation for banks insured by the Federal Deposit Insurance Corporation (other than members of the Federal Reserve System), mutual savings banks, insured State branches of foreign banks, and any other depository institution described in section 303(2)(A) which is not otherwise referred to in this paragraph;

"(C) the National Credit Union Administration Board with respect to credit unions; and

"(D) the Secretary of Housing and Urban Development with respect to other lending institutions not regulated by the agencies referred to in subparagraph (A) or (B).

"(3) RULES FOR MODIFICATIONS UNDER PARAGRAPH (1).—

"(A) APPLICATION.—A modification under paragraph (1)(E) shall apply to information concerning—

"(i) credit score data described in subsection (b)(6)(I), in a manner that is consistent with the purpose described in paragraph (1)(E); and

(J)消费者金融保护局要求提供的其他信息。”

(B)删除第(h)子条,替以如下内容:

“(h)**向各机关提交数据**。——

(1)**一般规定**。——第(b)子条要求披露的数据应按照消费者金融保护局制定的规则,提交给消费者金融保护局,或提交给相应的机关,以便完成本编规定的机构报告。尽管有第(a)(2)(A)子条要求按人口普查区进行披露的规定,但是,消费者金融保护局仍应在与第(2)款所述相关机关磋商,并发出通知和征求意见后,制定规章——

(A)规定该等披露的格式、向相关机关提交数据的方法以及向公众披露信息的程序;

(B)要求在按照本编作出的每次机构报告中,均应收集根据第(b)子条必须披露的关于出售贷款的数据;

(C)要求披露该等贷款购买者的类别;

(D)允许任何报告机构向消费者金融保护局或相应的机关以书面形式提交其认为与发起或购买抵押贷款的决定有关的补充数据或解释;及

(E)修改或要求修改已向公众提供或将向公众提供的逐项列出的信息,以保护抵押贷款申请人和抵押人的隐私利益。

(2)**其他相关机关**。——本款所述相关机关——

(A)对于受《联邦存款保险法》第3(q)条[《美国法典》第十二编第1813(q)节]定义的相应的联邦银行业监管机关管辖的实体而言,指其各自的主管联邦银行业监管机关;

(B)对于在联邦存款保险公司参保的银行(但联邦储备系统成员除外)、互助储蓄银行、外国银行的州参保分行以及第303(2)(A)条所述但本款未提及的任何其他存款机构而言,指联邦存款保险公司;

(C)对于信贷联盟而言,指国家信贷联盟署委员会;及

(D)对于不受第(A)子款或第(B)子款所提及的机关监管的其他贷款机构而言,指住房与城市发展部部长。

(3)关于按照第(1)款作出的修改的规则。——

(A)**适用范围**。——按照第(1)(E)款作出的修改应适用于以下信息——

(i)第(b)(6)(I)子条所述信用评分数据[其适用方式不得违背第(1)(E)款所述宗旨];及

"(ii) age or any other category of data described in paragraph (5) or (6) of subsection (b), as the Bureau determines to be necessary to satisfy the purpose described in paragraph (1)(E), and in a manner consistent with that purpose.

"(B) STANDARDS. — The Bureau shall prescribe standards for any modification under paragraph (1)(E) to effectuate the purposes of this title, in light of the privacy interests of mortgage applicants or mortgagors. Where necessary to protect the privacy interests of mortgage applicants or mortgagors, the Bureau shall provide for the disclosure of information described in subparagraph (A) in aggregate or other reasonably modified form, in order to effectuate the purposes of this title.";

(C) in subsection (i), by striking "subsection (b)(4) " and inserting "subsections (b)(4), (b)(5), and (b)(6) ";

(D) in subsection (j) —

(i) by striking paragraph (3) and inserting the following:

"(3) CHANGE OF FORM NOT REQUIRED. — A depository institution meets the disclosure requirement of paragraph (1) if the institution provides the information required under such paragraph in such formats as the Bureau may require"; and

(ii) in paragraph (2)(A), by striking "in the format in which such information is maintained by the institution" and inserting "in such formats as the Bureau may require";

(E) in subsection (m), by striking paragraph (2) and inserting the following:

"(2) FORM OF INFORMATION. — In complying with paragraph (1), a depository institution shall provide the person requesting the information with a copy of the information requested in such formats as the Bureau may require."; and

(F) by adding at the end the following:

"(n) TIMING OF CERTAIN DISCLOSURES. — The data required to be disclosed under subsection (b) shall be submitted to the Bureau or to the appropriate agency for any institution reporting under this title, in accordance with regulations prescribed by the Bureau. Institutions shall not be required to report new data under paragraph (5) or (6) of subsection (b) before the first January 1 that occurs after the end of the 9-month period beginning on the date on which regulations are issued by the Bureau in final form with respect to such disclosures.";

(4) in section 305 (12 U.S.C. 2804) —

(A) by striking subsection (b) and inserting the following:

"(b) POWERS OF CERTAIN OTHER AGENCIES. —

"(1) IN GENERAL. — Subject to subtitle B of the Consumer Financial Protection Act of 2010, compliance with the require ments of this title shall be enforced —

"(A) under section 8 of the Federal Deposit Insurance Act, the appropriate Federal banking agency, as defined in section 3(q) of the Federal Deposit Insurance Act (12 U.S.C.

(ii)第(b)子条第(5)款或第(6)款所述年龄或任何其他类型的数据(以消费者金融保护局判定为实现第(1)(E)款所述宗旨所必需的数据为准,且其适用方式不得违背该等宗旨);

(B)**标准**。——消费者金融保护局应在考虑抵押贷款申请人或抵押人的隐私利益的基础上,就按照第(1)(E)款作出的修改制定标准,以实现本编的宗旨。如为保护抵押贷款申请人或抵押人的隐私利益所必要，消费者金融保护局还应规定以汇总形式或其他经合理修改的格式披露第(A)子款所述信息,以实现本编的宗旨。"

(C)在第(i)子条中,删除"第(b)(4)子条",替以"第(b)(4)子条、第(b)(5)子条及第(b)(6)子条";

(D)第(j)子条——

(i)删除第(3)款,替以如下内容:

"(3)**不必修改格式**。——存款机构按照消费者金融保护局所要求的格式提供了第(1)款规定的信息的,即视为符合该款的披露要求";及

(ii)第(2)(A)款删除"按照该机构维持该项信息的格式",替以"按照消费者金融保护局要求的格式";

(E)第(m)子条删除第(2)款,替以如下内容:

"(2)**信息格式**。——在履行第(1)款的规定之时,存款机构应按照消费者金融保护局要求的格式向提出信息请求的人提供所请求信息的复本。";及

(F)在结尾处增加如下内容:

"(n)**特定披露的时间安排**。——第(b)子条要求披露的数据应按照消费者金融保护局制定的规章,提交给消费者金融保护局或相应的机关,以便完成本编规定的机构报告。在消费者金融保护局就上述披露发布最终规章之日起届满9个月之后的首个1月1日之前,不得要求各机构根据第(b)子条第(5)款或第(6)款的规定报告新数据。"

(4)在第305条(《美国法典》第十二编第2804节)中——

(A)删除第(b)子条,替以如下内容:

"(b)**其他特定机关的权力**。——

(1)**一般规定**。——在不违反《2010年消费者金融保护法》第B子编规定的前提下,本编的要求——

(A)对于以下实体而言,应由《联邦存款保险法》第3(q)条[《美国法典》第十二编第1813(q)节]定义的相应的联邦银行业监管机关根据该法第8条强制执行——

1813(q)), with respect to —

"(i) any national bank or Federal savings association, and any Federal branch or Federal agency of a foreign bank;

"(ii) any member bank of the Federal Reserve System (other than a national bank), branch or agency of a foreign bank (other than a Federal branch, Federal agency, and insured State branch of a foreign bank), commercial lending company owned or controlled by a foreign bank, and any organization operating under section 25 or 25A of the Federal Reserve Act; and

"(iii) any bank or State savings association insured by the Federal Deposit Insurance Corporation (other than a member of the Federal Reserve System), any mutual savings bank as, defined in section 3(f) of the Federal Deposit Insurance Act (12 U.S.C. 1813(f)), any insured State branch of a foreign bank, and any other depository institution not referred to in this paragraph or subparagraph (B) or (C);

"(B) under subtitle E of the Consumer Financial Protection Act of 2010, by the Bureau, with respect to any person subject to this subtitle;

"(C) under the Federal Credit Union Act, by the Administrator of the National Credit Union Administration with respect to any insured credit union; and

"(D) with respect to other lending institutions, by the Secretary of Housing and Urban Development.

"(2) INCORPORATED DEFINITIONS. — The terms used in paragraph (1) that are not defined in this title or otherwise defined in section 3(s) of the Federal Deposit Insurance Act(12 U.S.C. 1813(s)) shall have the same meanings as in section 1(b) of the International Banking Act of 1978 (12 U.S.C. 3101)."; and

(B) by adding at the end the following:

"(d) OVERALL ENFORCEMENT AUTHORITY OF THE BUREAU OF CONSUMER FINANCIAL PROTECTION. — Subject to subtitle B of the Consumer Financial Protection Act of 2010, enforcement of the requirements imposed under this title is committed to each of the agencies under subsection (b). To facilitate research, examinations, and enforcement, all data collected pursuant to section 304 shall be available to the entities listed under subsection (b). The Bureau may exercise its authorities under the Consumer Financial Protection Act of 2010 to exercise principal authority to examine and enforce compliance by any person with the requirements of this title.";

(5) in section 306 (12 U.S.C. 2805(b)), by striking subsection (b) and inserting the following:

"(b) EXEMPTION AUTHORITY. — The Bureau may, by regulation, exempt from the requirements of this title any State–chartered depository institution within any State or subdivision thereof, if the agency determines that, under the law of such State or subdivision,

(i)任何国民银行或联邦储蓄协会,以及外国银行的联邦分行和联邦代理行;

(ii)联邦储备系统的任何成员银行(但国民银行除外)、外国银行的分行或代理行(但外国银行的联邦分行、联邦代理行以及外国银行的州参保分行除外)、外国银行拥有或控制的商业贷款公司以及根据《联邦储备法》第25条或第25A条运营的任何组织;及

(iii)在联邦存款保险公司参保的任何银行或州储蓄协会(但联邦储备系统的成员除外)、《联邦存款保险法》第3(f)条[《美国法典》第十二编第1813(f)节]定义的互助储蓄银行、外国银行的州参保分行以及本款中或第(B)子款或第(C)子款中未提及的任何其他存款机构;

(B)对于受本子编管辖的任何主体而言,应由消费者金融保护局根据《2010年消费者金融保护法》第E子编的规定针对其强制执行;

(C)对于参保信贷联盟而言,应由国家信贷联盟署委员会委员根据《联邦信贷联盟法》的规定强制执行;及

(D)对于其他贷款机构而言,应由住房与城市发展部部长强制执行。

(2)**援引纳入的定义**。——第(1)款中使用的术语,如本编或《联邦存款保险法》第3(s)条[《美国法典》第十二编第1813(s)节]未作定义,其含义应以《1978年国际银行法》第1(b)条(《美国法典》第十二编第3101节)的定义为准。"及

(B)在结尾处增加如下内容:

"(d)**消费者金融保护局的总体执法权**。——在不违反《2010年消费者金融保护法》第B子编规定的前提下,本编施加的要求应由第(b)子条规定的各个机关执行。为便利研究、检查和执法工作的开展,根据第304条收集的所有数据均应向第(b)子条所列实体提供。消费者金融保护局可以按照《2010年消费者金融保护法》行使权力,以检查任何人对本编要求的合规情况,以及强制执行本编的要求。"

(5)在第306条[《美国法典》第十二编第2805(b)节]中,删除第(b)子条,替以如下内容:

"(b)**豁免权**。——消费者金融保护局可以发布规章,向任何州或州下属行政区域之内的州特许注册的存款机构授予豁免,获得豁免的存款机构不必受本编要求限制,前提是消费者金融保护局判定,根据该州或该行政区域的法律,该机构所受制的

that institution is subject to requirements that are substantially similar to those imposed under this title, and that such law contains adequate provisions for enforcement. Notwithstanding any other provision of this subsection, compliance with the requirements imposed under this subsection shall be enforced by the Office of the Comptroller of the Currency under section 8 of the Federal Deposit Insurance Act, in the case of national banks and Federal savings associations, the deposits of which are insured by the Federal Deposit Insurance Corporation."; and

(6) by striking section 307 (12 U.S.C. 2806) and inserting the following:

"SEC. 307. COMPLIANCE IMPROVEMENT METHODS.

"(a) IN GENERAL.—

"(1) CONSULTATION REQUIRED. — The Director of the Bureau of Consumer Financial Protection, with the assistance of the Secretary, the Director of the Bureau of the Census, the Board of Governors of the Federal Reserve System, the Federal Deposit Insurance Corporation, and such other persons as the Bureau deems appropriate, shall develop or assist in the improvement of, methods of matching addresses and census tracts to facilitate compliance by depository institutions in as economical a manner as possible with the requirements of this title.

"(2) AUTHORIZATION OF APPROPRIATIONS. — There are authorized to be appropriated, such sums as may be necessary to carry out this subsection.

"(3) CONTRACTING AUTHORITY. — The Director of the Bureau of Consumer Financial Protection is authorized to utilize, contract with, act through, or compensate any person or agency in order to carry out this subsection.

"(b) RECOMMENDATIONS TO CONGRESS. — The Director of the Bureau of Consumer Financial Protection shall recommend to the Committee on Banking, Housing, and Urban Affairs of the Senate and the Committee on Financial Services of the House of Representatives, such additional legislation as the Director of the Bureau of Consumer Financial Protection deems appropriate to carry out the purpose of this title.".

SEC. 1095. AMENDMENTS TO THE HOMEOWNERS PROTECTION ACT OF 1998.

Section 10 of the Homeowners Protection Act of 1998 (12 U.S.C. 4909) is amended—

(1) in subsection (a)—

(A) by striking "Compliance" and all that follows through the end of paragraph (1) and inserting the following:

"Subject to subtitle B of the Consumer Financial Protection Act of 2010, compliance with the requirements imposed under this Act shall be enforced under—

"(1) section 8 of the Federal Deposit Insurance Act, by the appropriate Federal banking agency (as defined in section 3(q) of that Act), with respect to—

要求与本编施加的要求基本类似，并且该州或该行政区域的法律包括充分的强制执行规定。无论本子条其他条款是否存在任何不同规定，对于其存款由联邦存款保险公司承保的国民银行和联邦储蓄协会而言，本子条的要求均应由货币监理署根据《联邦存款保险法》第8条的规定强制执行。”及

(6)删除第307条(《美国法典》第十二编第2806节)，替以如下内容：

“第307条　合规改善方法

(a)**一般规定**。——

(1)**磋商要求**。——消费者金融保护局局长应在财政部部长、人口普查局局长、联邦储备委员会、联邦存款保险公司以及消费者金融保护局认为相应的其他主体的协助下，制定对地址和人口普查区予进行匹配的方法，或协助改良该等方法，以促使存款机构以尽可能经济的方式遵守本编要求。

(2)**拨款授权**。——兹授权拨付履行本子条所必要的款项。

(3)**缔约权**。——兹授权消费者金融保护局局长为履行本子条规定而使用任何人或机关，与任何人或机关订立合同、通过其行事或向其提供薪酬。

(b)**向国会提出建议**。——消费者金融保护局局长应向参议院银行、住房与城市事务委员会和众议院金融服务委员会提出其认为对履行本编之宗旨而言属于适当的其他立法建议。”

第1095条　对《1998年业主保护法》的修正

《1998年业主保护法》第10条(《美国法典》第十二编第4909节)修正如下——

(1)在第(a)子条中——

(A)删除“对本法合规要求的强制执行”直至第(1)款结尾的全部内容，替以如下内容：

“在不违反《2010年消费者金融保护法》第B子编规定的前提下，本法施加的要求——

(1)对于以下实体而言，应由《联邦存款保险法》第3(q)条定义的相应的联邦银行业监管机关根据该法第8条强制执行——

"(A) insured depository institutions (as defined in section 3(c)(2) of that Act);

"(B) depository institutions described in clause (i), (ii), or (iii) of section 19(b)(1)(A) of the Federal Reserve Act which are not insured depository institutions (as defined in section 3(c)(2) of the Federal Deposit Insurance Act); and

"(C) depository institutions described in clause (v) or (vi) of section 19(b)(1)(A) of the Federal Reserve Act which are not insured depository institutions (as defined in section 3(c)(2) of the Federal Deposit Insurance Act);";

(B) in paragraph (2), by striking "and" at the end;

(C) in paragraph (3), by striking the period at the end and inserting "; and"; and

(D) by adding at the end the following:

"(4) subtitle E of the Consumer Financial Protection Act of 2010, by the Bureau of Consumer Financial Protection, with respect to any person subject to this Act."; and

(2) in subsection (b)(2), by inserting before the period at the end the following: ", subject to subtitle B of the Consumer Financial Protection Act of 2010".

SEC. 1096. AMENDMENTS TO THE HOME OWNERSHIP AND EQUITY PROTECTION ACT OF 1994.

The Home Ownership and Equity Protection Act of 1994 (15 U.S.C. 1601 note) is amended —

(1) in section 158(a), by striking "Board of Governors of the Federal Reserve System, in consultation with the Consumer Advisory Council of the Board" and inserting "Bureau, in consultation with the Advisory Board to the Bureau"; and

(2) in section 158(b), by striking "Board of Governors of the Federal Reserve System" and inserting "Bureau".

SEC. 1097. AMENDMENTS TO THE OMNIBUS APPROPRIATIONS ACT, 2009.

Section 626 of the Omnibus Appropriations Act, 2009 (15 U.S.C. 1638 note) is amended —

(1) by striking subsection (a) and inserting the following:

"(a)(1) The Bureau of Consumer Financial Protection shall have authority to prescribe rules with respect to mortgage loans in accordance with section 553 of title 5, United States Code. Such rulemaking shall relate to unfair or deceptive acts or practices regarding mortgage loans, which may include unfair or deceptive acts or practices involving loan modification and foreclosure rescue services. Any violation of a rule prescribed under this paragraph shall be treated as a violation of a rule prohibiting unfair, deceptive, or abusive acts or practices under the Consumer Financial Protection Act of 2010 and a violation of a rule under section 18 of the Federal Trade Commission Act (15 U.S.C. 57a) regarding unfair or deceptive acts or practices.

(A)参保存款机构[定义见该法第3(c)(2)条];

(B)《联邦储备法》第19(b)(1)(A)条第(i)项、第(ii)项或第(iii)项所述并非参保存款机构[定义见《联邦存款保险法》第3(c)(2)条]的存款机构;及

(C)《联邦储备法》第19(b)(1)(A)条第(v)项或第(vi)项所述并非参保存款机构[定义见《联邦存款保险法》第3(c)(2)条]的存款机构;";

(B)第(2)款删除结尾处的"及";

(C)第(3)款删除结尾处的句号,替以";及";并

(D)在结尾处增加如下内容:

"(4)对于受本法管辖的任何主体而言,由消费者金融保护局根据《2010年消费者金融保护法》第E子编强制执行。"及

(2)在第(b)(2)子条结尾处的句号前插入如下内容:",在不违反《2010年消费者金融保护法》第B子编规定的前提下"。

第1096条　对《1994年住房所有权和房屋权益保护法》的修正

《1994年住房所有权和房屋权益保护法》(《美国法典》第十五编第1601节注释)修正如下——

(1)在第158(a)条中,删除"联邦储备委员会在与其消费者顾问委员会磋商后",替以"消费者金融保护局在与其顾问委员会磋商后";及

(2)在第158(b)条中,删除"联邦储备委员会",替以"消费者金融保护局"。

第1097条　对《2009年综合拨款法》的修正

《2009年综合拨款法》第626条(《美国法典》第十五编第1638节注释)修正如下——

(1)删除第(a)子条,替以如下内容:

"(a)(1)消费者金融保护局有权根据《美国法典》第五编第553节的规定,就抵押贷款制定规则。按照上述规定制定的规则,应对抵押贷款的不公平或欺骗性行为或做法进行规制,包括涉及贷款修改和止赎救助的不公平或欺骗性行为或做法。任何违反根据本款制定的规则的行为,均应作为违反以下规则的行为处理:《2010年消费者金融保护法》中止不公平、欺骗性或滥用行为或做法的规则,以及《联邦贸易委员会法》第18条(《美国法典》第十五编第57a节)中关于不公平或欺骗性行为或做法的规则。

"(2) The Bureau of Consumer Financial Protection shall enforce the rules issued under paragraph (1) in the same manner, by the same means, and with the same jurisdiction, powers, and duties, as though all applicable terms and provisions of the Consumer Financial Protection Act of 2010 were incorporated into and made part of this subsection.

"(3) Subject to subtitle B of the Consumer Financial Protection Act of 2010, the Federal Trade Commission shall enforce the rules issued under paragraph (1), in the same manner, by the same means, and with the same jurisdiction, as though all applicable terms and provisions of the Federal Trade Commission Act were incorporated into and made part of this section."; and

(2) in subsection (b)—

(A) by striking paragraph (1) and inserting the following:

"(1) Except as provided in paragraph (6), in any case in which the attorney general of a State has reason to believe that an interest of the residents of the State has been or is threatened or adversely affected by the engagement of any person subject to a rule prescribed under subsection (a) in practices that violate such rule, the State, as parens patriae, may bring a civil action on behalf of its residents in an appropriate district court of the United States or other court of competent jurisdiction—

"(A) to enjoin that practice;

"(B) to enforce compliance with the rule;

"(C) to obtain damages, restitution, or other compensation on behalf of the residents of the State; or

"(D) to obtain penalties and relief provided under the Consumer Financial Protection Act of 2010, the Federal Trade Commission Act, and such other relief as the court deems appropriate.";

(B) in paragraphs (2) and (3), by striking "the primary Federal regulator" each time the term appears and inserting "the Bureau of Consumer Financial Protection or the Commission, as appropriate";

(C) in paragraph (3), by inserting "and subject to subtitle B of the Consumer Financial Protection Act of 2010," after "paragraph (2),"; and

(D) in paragraph (6), by striking "the primary Federal regulator" each place that term appears and inserting "the Bureau of Consumer Financial Protection or the Commission".

SEC. 1098. AMENDMENTS TO THE REAL ESTATE SETTLEMENT PROCEDURES ACT OF 1974.

The Real Estate Settlement Procedures Act of 1974 (12 U.S.C. 2601 et seq.) is amended—

(1) in section 3 (12 U.S.C. 2602)—

(A) in paragraph (7), by striking "and" at the end;

(2)消费者金融保护局在执行根据第(1)款颁发的规则之时,在确定其可以采用的执法方式、手段,及其享有的管辖权、权力和承担的职责时,应视同《2010年消费者金融保护法》的所有适用条款和规定均已纳入本子条并构成本子条一部分。

(3)在不违反《2010年消费者金融保护法》第B子编规定的前提下,联邦贸易委员会在执行根据第(1)款发布的规则之时,在确定其可以采用的执法方式、手段,及其享有的管辖权时,应视同《联邦贸易委员会法》的所有适用条款和规定均已纳入本条并构成本条的一部分。";及

(2)在第(b)子条中——

(A)删除第(1)款,替以如下内容:

"(1)除第(6)款规定的情形外,如某一州的州检察长有理由相信,受依据第(a)子条制定的规则管辖的任何主体从事了违反上述规则的做法,从而已经或有可能危及本州居民的利益,或对其造成不利影响,该州应以国家监护人的身份,代表其居民向相应的联邦地区法院或其他有管辖权的法院提起民事诉讼,以便——

(A)禁止该做法;

(B)强制执行该项规则;

(C)代表本州居民获得损害赔偿金、不当得利的归还或其他赔偿;或

(D)获取《2010年消费者金融保护法》和《联邦贸易委员会法》所规定的罚款、救济以及法院认为适当的其他救济。"

(B)第(2)款和第(3)款删除所有的"优先联邦监管者",全部替以"消费者金融保护局或联邦贸易委员会(视具体情况而定)";

(C)第(3)款在"在收到第(2)款规定的通知之后,"之后插入"且在不违反《2010年消费者金融保护法》第B子编规定的前提下,";及

(D)第(6)款删除所有的"优先联邦监管者",全部替以"消费者金融保护局或联邦贸易委员会"。

第1098条　对《1974年房地产结算程序法》的修正

《1974年房地产结算程序法》(《美国法典》第十二编第2601节及其后条文)修正如下——

(1)在第3条(《美国法典》第十二编第2602节)中——

(A)第(7)款删除结尾处的"及";

(B) in paragraph (8), by striking the period at the end and inserting "; and"; and

(C) by adding at the end the following:

"(9) the term 'Bureau' means the Bureau of Consumer Financial Protection.";

(2) in section 4 (12 U.S.C. 2603)—

(A) in subsection (a), by striking the first sentence and inserting the following: "The Bureau shall publish a single, integrated disclosure for mortgage loan transactions (including real estate settlement cost statements) which includes the disclosure requirements of this section and section 5, in conjunction with the disclosure requirements of the Truth in Lending Act that, taken together, may apply to a transaction that is subject to both or either provisions of law. The purpose of such model disclosure shall be to facilitate compliance with the disclosure requirements of this title and the Truth in Lending Act, and to aid the borrower or lessee in understanding the transaction by utilizing readily understandable language to simplify the technical nature of the disclosures.";

(B) by striking "Secretary" each place that term appears and inserting "Bureau"; and

(C) by striking "form" each place that term appears and inserting "forms";

(3) in section 5 (12 U.S.C. 2604)—

(A) by striking "Secretary" each place that term appears and inserting "Bureau"; and

(B) in subsection (a), by striking the first sentence and inserting the following: "The Bureau shall prepare and distribute booklets jointly addressing compliance with the requirements of the Truth in Lending Act and the provisions of this title, in order to help persons borrowing money to finance the purchase of residential real estate better to understand the nature and costs of real estate settlement services.";

(4) in section 6(j)(3)(12 U.S.C. 2605(j)(3))—

(A) by striking "Secretary" and inserting "Bureau"; and

(B) by striking ", by regulations that shall take effect not later than April 20, 1991,";

(5) in section 7(b)(12 U.S.C. 2606(b)) by striking "Secretary" and inserting "Bureau";

(6) in section 8(c)(5)(12 U.S.C. 2607(c)(5)), by striking "Secretary" and inserting "Bureau";

(7) in section 8(d)(12 U.S.C. 2607(d))—

(A) in the subsection heading, by inserting "BUREAU AND" before "SECRETARY"; and

(B) by striking paragraph (4), and inserting the following:

"(4) The Bureau, the Secretary, or the attorney general or the insurance commissioner of any State may bring an action to enjoin violations of this section. Except, to the extent that a person is subject to the jurisdiction of the Bureau, the Secretary, or the attorney general or the insurance commissioner of any State, the Bureau shall have primary authority to enforce or

(B)第(8)款删除结尾处的句号,替以";及";并

(C)在结尾处增加如下内容;

"(9)'消费者金融保护局'一词系指联邦储备系统下的消费者金融保护局。";

(2)在第4条(《美国法典》第十二编第2603节)中——

(A)第(a)子条删除第一句,替以如下内容:"消费者金融保护局应公布一份关于抵押贷款交易的统一、综合的披露(包括房地产结算成本报表),其中应包括本条和第5条的规定的披露以及《诚实信贷法》规定的披露,并对受此两项法律或其中任一法律的规定管辖的交易,同时适用上述披露要求。作出上述披露范例的目的为促进对本编和《诚实信贷法》披露要求的合规,以及通过简明易懂的语言简化披露的技术性质,帮助借款人或承租人理解交易。"

(B)删除所有的"财政部部长",全部替以"消费者金融保护局";及

(C)删除"格式"一词的所有单数形式"form",全部替以复数形式"forms";

(3)在第5条(《美国法典》第十二编第2604节)中——

(A)删除所有的"财政部部长",全部替以"消费者金融保护局";及

(B)第(a)子条删除第一句,替以如下内容:"消费者金融保护局应制作和传发相关手册,说明对《诚实信贷法》和本编规定的合规问题,帮助为购买住宅房地产而融资借款的人更好地理解房地产结算服务的性质和成本。"

(4)在第6(j)(3)条[《美国法典》第十二编第2605(j)(3)节]中——

(A)删除"财政部部长",替以"消费者金融保护局";及

(B)删除",制定生效日不迟于1991年4月20日的规章";

(5)在第7(b)条[《美国法典》第十二编第2606(b)节]中,删除"财政部部长",替以"消费者金融保护局";

(6)在第8(c)(5)条[《美国法典》第十二编第2607(c)(5)节]中,删除"财政部部长",替以"消费者金融保护局";

(7)在第8(d)条[《美国法典》第十二编第2607(d)节]中——

(A)子条标题在"财政部部长"前插入"消费者金融保护局和";及

(B)删除第(4)款,替以如下内容:

"(4)消费者金融保护局、财政部部长或任何州检察长或州保险监督官,均可以提起诉讼,以禁止违反本条规定的行为。然而,对于受消费者金融保护局、财政部部长或任何州检察长或州保险监督官管辖的主体,消费者金融保护局应在不违反《2010年消费者金融保护法》第B子编规定的情形下,拥有执行或实施本条的优先权。"

administer this section, subject to subtitle B of the Consumer Financial Protection Act of 2010.";

(8) in section 10(c)(12 U.S.C. 2609(c) and (d)), by striking "Secretary" and inserting "Bureau";

(9) in section 16 (12 U.S.C. 2614), by inserting "the Bureau," before "the Secretary";

(10) in section 18 (12 U.S.C. 2616), by striking "Secretary" each place that term appears and inserting "Bureau"; and

(11) in section 19 (12 U.S.C. 2617) —

(A) in the section heading by striking "SECRETARY" and inserting "BUREAU";

(B) in subsection (a), by striking "Secretary" each place that term appears and inserting "Bureau"; and

(C) in subsections (b) and (c), by striking "the Secretary" each place that term appears and inserting "the Bureau".

SEC. 1098A. AMENDMENTS TO THE INTERSTATE LAND SALES FULL DISCLOSURE ACT.

The Interstate Land Sales Full Disclosure Act (15 U.S.C. 1701 et seq.) is amended —

(1) by striking "Secretary" each place that term appears and inserting "Director";

(2) by striking "Department of Housing and Urban Development" each place that term appears and inserting "Bureau of Consumer Financial Protection";

(3) by striking "Department" each place that term appears and inserting "Bureau";

(4) in section 1402 (15 U.S.C. 1701) —

(A) by striking paragraph (1) and inserting the following:

"(1) 'Director' means the Director of the Bureau of Consumer Financial Protection;";

(B) in paragraph (10), by striking "and" at the end;

(C) in paragraph (11), by striking the period at the end and inserting "; and"; and

(D) by adding at the end the following:

"(12) 'Bureau' means the Bureau of Consumer Financial Protection."; and

(5) in section 1416(a)(15 U.S.C. 1715(a)), by striking "Secretary of Housing and Urban Development" and inserting "Director of the Bureau of Consumer Financial Protection".

SEC. 1099. AMENDMENTS TO THE RIGHT TO FINANCIAL PRIVACY ACT OF 1978.

The Right to Financial Privacy Act of 1978 (12 U.S.C. 3401 et seq.) is amended —

(1) in section 1101 —

(A) in paragraph (6) —

(8)在第10(c)条[《美国法典》第十二编第2609(c)节和第2609(d)节]中,删除"财政部部长",替以"消费者金融保护局";

(9)在第16条(《美国法典》第十二编第2614节)中,在"财政部部长"前插入"消费者金融保护局";

(10)在第18条(《美国法典》第十二编第2616节)中,删除所有的"财政部部长",全部替以"消费者金融保护局";及

(11)在第19条(《美国法典》第十二编第2617节)中——

(A)该条标题删除"财政部部长",替以"消费者金融保护局";

(B)第(a)子条删除所有的"财政部部长",全部替以"消费者金融保护局";及

(C)第(b)子条和第(c)子条删除所有的"财政部部长",全部替以"消费者金融保护局"。

第1098A条　对《州际土地销售完全披露法》的修正

《州际土地销售完全披露法》(《美国法典》第十五编第1701节及其后条文)修正如下——

(1)删除所有的"财政部部长",全部替以"消费者金融保护局局长";

(2)删除所有的"住房与城市发展部",全部替以"消费者金融保护局";

(3)删除所有的"住房与城市发展部",全部替以"消费者金融保护局";

(4)在第1402条(《美国法典》第十五编第1701节)中——

(A)删除第(1)款,替以如下内容:

"(1)'局长'一词系指消费者金融保护局局长;";

(B)第(10)款删除结尾处的"及";

(C)第(11)款删除结尾处的句号,替以";及";并

(D)在结尾处增加如下内容:

"(12)'消费者金融保护局'一词系指联邦储备系统下的消费者金融保护局。"及

(5)在第1416(a)条[《美国法典》第十五编第1715(a)节]中,删除"住房与城市发展部部长",替以"消费者金融保护局局长"。

第1099条　对《1978年金融隐私权法》的修正

《1978年金融隐私权法》(《美国法典》第十二编第3401节及其后条文)修正如下——

(1)在第1101条中——

(A)第(6)款——

(i) in subparagraph (A), by inserting "and" after the semicolon;

(ii) in subparagraph (B), by striking "and" at the end; and

(iii) by striking subparagraph (C); and

(B) in paragraph (7), by striking subparagraph (B), and inserting the following:

"(B) the Bureau of Consumer Financial Protection;";

(2) in section 1112(e)(12 U.S.C. 3412(e)), by striking "and the Commodity Futures Trading Commission is permitted" and inserting "the Commodity Futures Trading Commission, and the Bureau of Consumer Financial Protection is permitted"; and

(3)in section 1113(12 U.S.C. 3413), by adding at the end the following new subsection:

"(r) DISCLOSURE TO THE BUREAU OF CONSUMER FINANCIAL PROTECTION. — Nothing in this title shall apply to the examination by or disclosure to the Bureau of Consumer Financial Protection of financial records or information in the exercise of its authority with respect to a financial institution.".

SEC. 1100. AMENDMENTS TO THE SECURE AND FAIR ENFORCEMENT FOR MORTGAGE LICENSING ACT OF 2008.

The S.A.F.E. Mortgage Licensing Act of 2008 (12 U.S.C. 5101 et seq.) is amended —

(1) by striking "a Federal banking agency" each place that term appears, other than in paragraphs (7) and (11) of section 1503 and section 1507 (a)(1), and inserting "the Bureau";

(2) by striking "Federal banking agencies" each place that term appears and inserting "Bureau"; and

(3) by striking "Secretary" each place that term appears and inserting "Director";

(4) in section 1503 (12 U.S.C. 5102) —

(A) by redesignating paragraphs (2) through (12) as (3) through (13), respectively;

(B) by striking paragraph (1) and inserting the following:

"(1) BUREAU. — The term 'Bureau' means the Bureau of Consumer Financial Protection.

"(2) FEDERAL BANKING AGENCY. — The term 'Federal banking agency' means the Board of Governors of the Federal Reserve System, the Office of the Comptroller of the Currency, the National Credit Union Administration, and the Federal Deposit Insurance Corporation."; and

(C) by striking paragraph (10), as so designated by this section, and inserting the following:

"(10) DIRECTOR. — The term 'Director' means the Director of the Bureau of Consumer Financial Protection."; and

(i)在第(A)子款的分号之后插入“及”;

(ii)第(B)子款删除结尾处的“及”;并

(iii)删除第(C)子款;及

(B)第(7)款删除第(B)子款,替以如下内容:

“(B)消费者金融保护局;”;

(2)在第1112(e)条[《美国法典》第十二编第3412(e)节]中,删除“以及商品期货交易委员会”,替以“商品期货交易委员会和消费者金融保护局”;及

(3)在第1113条(《美国法典》第十二编第3413节)结尾处增加如下新子条:

“(r)**向消费者金融保护局进行的披露**。——本编的任何规定均不适用于消费者金融保护局在针对金融机构行使其权力的过程中,对财务记录或信息进行的检查,亦不适用于在此过程中向消费者金融保护局作出的财务记录或信息披露。”

第1100条　对《2008年安全和公平执行抵押贷款发起人许可法》的修正

《2008年安全和公平执行抵押贷款发起人许可法》(《美国法典》第十二编第5101节及其后条文)修正如下——

(1)删除所有在第1503条第(7)款和第(11)款以及第1507(a)(1)条以外出现的单数形式的“某一联邦银行业监管机关”,全部替以“消费者金融保护局”;

(2)删除所有复数形式的“联邦银行业监管机关”,全部替以“消费者金融保护局”;及

(3)删除所有的“财政部部长”,全部替以“消费者金融保护局局长”;

(4)在第1503条(《美国法典》第十二编第5102节)中——

(A)第(2)款至第(12)款分别重新编号为第(3)款至第(13)款;

(B)删除第(1)款,替以如下内容:

“(1)**消费者金融保护局**。——‘消费者金融保护局’一词系指联邦储备系统下的消费者金融保护局。

(2)**联邦银行业监管机关**。——‘联邦银行业监管机关’一词系指联邦储备委员会、货币监理署、国家信贷联盟署以及联邦存款保险公司。”及

(C)删除第(10)款(以本条序号为准),替以如下内容:

“(10)**局长**。——‘局长’一词系指消费者金融保护局局长。”及

(5) in section 1507 (12 U.S.C. 5106) —

(A) in subsection (a) —

(i) by striking paragraph (1) and inserting the following:

"(1) IN GENERAL. — The Bureau shall develop and maintain a system for registering employees of a depository institution, employees of a subsidiary that is owned and controlled by a depository institution and regulated by a Federal banking agency, or employees of an institution regulated by the Farm Credit Administration, as registered loan originators with the Nationwide Mortgage Licensing System and Registry. The system shall be implemented before the end of the 1–year period beginning on the date of enactment of the Consumer Financial Protection Act of 2010."; and

(ii) in paragraph (2) —

(I) by striking "appropriate Federal banking agency and the Farm Credit Administration" and inserting "Bureau"; and

(II) by striking "employees's identity" and inserting "identity of the employee"; and

(B) in subsection (b), by striking "through the Financial Institutions Examination Council, and the Farm Credit Administration", and inserting "and the Bureau of Consumer Financial Protection";

(6) in section 1508 (12 U.S.C. 5107) —

(A) by striking the section heading and inserting the following:

"SEC. 1508. BUREAU OF CONSUMER FINANCIAL PROTECTION BACKUP AUTHORITY TO ESTABLISH LOAN ORIGINATOR LICENSING SYSTEM."; and

(B) by adding at the end the following:

"(f) REGULATION AUTHORITY. —

"(1) IN GENERAL. — The Bureau is authorized to promulgate regulations setting minimum net worth or surety bond requirements for residential mortgage loan originators and minimum requirements for recovery funds paid into by loan originators.

"(2) CONSIDERATIONS. — In issuing regulations under paragraph (1), the Bureau shall take into account the need to provide originators adequate incentives to originate affordable and sustainable mortgage loans, as well as the need to ensure a competitive origination market that maximizes consumer access to affordable and sustainable mortgage loans.";

(7) by striking section 1510 (12 U.S.C. 5109) and inserting the following:

"SEC. 1510. FEES.

"The Bureau, the Farm Credit Administration, and the Nationwide Mortgage Licensing System and Registry may charge reasonable fees to cover the costs of maintaining and providing access to information from the Nationwide Mortgage Licensing System and Registry, to the extent that such fees are not charged to consumers for access to such system and

(5)在第1507条(《美国法典》第十二编第5106节)中——

(A)第(a)子条——

(i)删除第(1)款,替以如下内容:

"(1)**一般规定**。——消费者金融保护局应制定和维持一项制度,在全国性抵押贷款发起人许可系统和注册名册中将存款机构的员工、存款机构拥有和控制并受联邦银行业监管机关监管的子公司之员工,或受农业信贷管理局监管的机构之员工登记为注册贷款发起人。该制度应在自《2010年消费者金融保护法》颁布之日起一年内予以实施。"及

(ii)在第(2)款中——

(I)删除"相应的联邦银行业监管机关和农业信贷管理局",替以"消费者金融保护局";及

(II)删除"各员工的身份",替以"该员工的身份";及

(B)第(b)子条删除"通过金融机构检查委员会,和农业信贷管理局",替以"和消费者金融保护局";

(6)在第1508条(《美国法典》第十二编第5107节)中——

(A)删除该条标题,替以如下内容:

"第1508条　消费者金融保护局建立贷款发起人许可制度的后备权力";及

(B)在结尾处增加如下内容:

"(f)**监管权**。——

(1)**一般规定**。——消费者金融保护局有权颁发规章,设定住房抵押贷款发起人的最低净资产值或履约保证要求以及贷款发起人的最低赔偿基金缴存要求。

(2)**考虑因素**。——在根据第(1)款发布规章时,消费者金融保护局应考虑到,需要向发起人提供充分激励,使发起人发起可负担和可持续的抵押贷款,同时应考虑确保建立充分竞争的发起市场的需要,以期使可获得可负担和可持续抵押贷款的消费者人数尽可能提高。"

(7)删除第1510条(《美国法典》第十二编第5109节),替以如下内容:

"第1510条　费用

消费者金融保护局、农业信贷管理局以及全国性抵押贷款发起人许可系统和注册名册可以收取合理的费用,以收回维持全国性抵押贷款发起人许可系统和注册名册的成本,以及提供信息查询权的成本,但是,上述费用不得向访问该系统和名册的消费者收取。"

registry.";

(8) by striking section 1513 (12 U.S.C. 5112) and inserting the following:

"SEC. 1513. LIABILITY PROVISIONS.

"The Bureau, any State official or agency, or any organization serving as the administrator of the Nationwide Mortgage Licensing System and Registry or a system established by the Director under section 1509, or any officer or employee of any such entity, shall not be subject to any civil action or proceeding for monetary damages by reason of the good faith action or omission of any officer or employee of any such entity, while acting within the scope of office or employment, relating to the collection, furnishing, or dissemination of information concerning persons who are loan originators or are applying for licensing or registration as loan originators."; and

(9) in section 1514 (12 U.S.C. 5113) in the section heading, by striking "**UNDER HUD BACKUP LICENSING SYSTEM" and inserting "BY THE BUREAU**".

SEC. 1100A. AMENDMENTS TO THE TRUTH IN LENDING ACT.

The Truth in Lending Act (15 U.S.C. 1601 et seq.) is amended —

(1) in section 103 (15 U.S.C. 1602) —

(A) by redesignating subsections (b) through (bb) as subsections (c) through (cc), respectively; and

(B) by inserting after subsection (a) the following:

"(b) BUREAU. — The term 'Bureau' means the Bureau of Consumer Financial Protection.";

(2) by striking "Board" each place that term appears, other than in section 140(d) and sections 105(i) and 108(a), as amended by this section, and inserting "Bureau";

(3) by striking "Federal Trade Commission" each place that term appears, other than in section 108(c) and section 129(m), as amended by this Act, and other than in the context of a reference to the Federal Trade Commission Act, and inserting "Bureau";

(4) in section 105(a)(15 U.S.C. 1604(a)), in the second sentence —

(A) by striking "Except in the case of a mortgage referred to in section 103(aa), these regulations may contain such" and inserting "Except with respect to the provisions of section 129 that apply to a mortgage referred to in section 103(aa), such regulations may contain such additional requirements,"; and

(B) by inserting "all or" after "exceptions for";

(5) in section 105(b)(15 U.S.C. 1604(b)), by striking the first sentence and inserting the following: "The Bureau shall publish a single, integrated disclosure for mortgage loan transactions (including real estate settlement cost statements) which includes the disclosure requirements of this title in conjunction with the disclosure requirements of the Real Estate Settlement Procedures Act of 1974 that, taken together, may apply to a transaction that is

(8)删除第1513条(《美国法典》第十二编第5112节),替以如下内容:

"第1513条　责任条款

消费者金融保护局、任何州官员或机关,或任何担任全国性抵押贷款发起人许可系统和注册名册的管理人的组织,或担任消费者金融保护局局长根据第1509条设立的系统的管理人的组织,或上述任何实体的任何官员或员工,均不得因以下作为或不作为而成为损害赔偿金民事诉讼或程序的当事人:上述实体的官员或员工,在其职务权限范围内,收集、提供或传播关于贷款发起人或以贷款发起人身份申请贷款许可或注册的人的信息的善意作为或不作为。"及

(9)在第1514条(《美国法典》第十二编第5113节)的标题中,删除"**住房与城市发展部的后备许可系统下的**",替以"**消费者金融保护局的**"。

第1100A条　对《诚实信贷法》的修正

《诚实信贷法》(《美国法典》第十五编第1601节及其后条文)修正如下——

(1)在第103条(《美国法典》第十五编第1602节)中——

(A)第(b)子条至第(bb)子条分别重新编号为第(c)子条至第(cc)子条;及

(B)在第(a)子条之后插入如下内容:

"(b)**消费者金融保护局**。——'消费者金融保护局'一词系指联邦储备系统下的消费者金融保护局。"

(2)删除所有在经本条修正后的第140(d)条、第105(i)条和第108(a)条以外出现的"联邦储备委员会",全部替以"消费者金融保护局";

(3)除在经本法修正后的第108(c)条和第129(m)条以及提及《联邦贸易委员会法》的上下文中出现的"联邦贸易委员会"之外,删除所有其他的"联邦贸易委员会",全部替以"消费者金融保护局";

(4)在第105(a)条[《美国法典》第十五编第1604(a)节]第二句中——

(A)删除"除涉及第103(aa)条所述抵押贷款的情形外,此等规章可包含",替以"除了第129条中适用于第103(aa)条所述抵押贷款的规定外,该等规章可包含相关额外要求,";及

(B)在"任何类型的交易"前插入"所有或";

(5)在第105(b)条[《美国法典》第十五编第1604(b)节]中,删除第一句,替以如下内容:"消费者金融保护局应发布一份关于抵押贷款交易的统一、综合的披露(包括房地产结算成本报表),其中应包括本编规定的披露,以及《1974年房地产结算程序法》规定的披露,并对受此两项法律或其中任一法律的规定管辖的交易,同时适用上述披露要求。上述披露范例的目的为促进对本编和《1974年房地产结算程序法》披露要求

subject to both or either provisions of law. The purpose of such model disclosure shall be to facilitate compliance with the disclosure requirements of this title and the Real Estate Settlement Procedures Act of 1974, and to aid the borrower or lessee in understanding the transaction by utilizing readily understandable language to simplify the technical nature of the disclosures.";

(6) in section 105(f)(1)(15 U.S.C. 1604(f)(1)), by inserting "all or" after "from all or part of this title";

(7) in section 105 (15 U.S.C. 1604), by adding at the end the following:

"(i) AUTHORITY OF THE BOARD TO PRESCRIBE RULES. — Notwithstanding subsection (a), the Board shall have authority to prescribe rules under this title with respect to a person described in section 1029 (a) of the Consumer Financial Protection Act of 2010. Regulations prescribed under this subsection may contain such classifications, differentiations, or other provisions, as in the judgment of the Board are necessary or proper to effectuate the purposes of this title, to prevent circumvention or evasion thereof, or to facilitate compliance therewith.";

(8) in section 108 (15 U.S.C. 1604), by adding at the end the following:

(A) by striking subsection (a) and inserting the following:

"(a) ENFORCING AGENCIES. — Subject to subtitle B of the Consumer Financial Protection Act of 2010, compliance with the requirements imposed under this title shall be enforced under —

"(1) section 8 of the Federal Deposit Insurance Act, by the appropriate Federal banking agency, as defined in section 3(q) of the Federal Deposit Insurance Act (12 U.S.C. 1813(q)), with respect to —

"(A) national banks, Federal savings associations, and Federal branches and Federal agencies of foreign banks;

"(B) member banks of the Federal Reserve System (other than national banks), branches and agencies of foreign banks (other than Federal branches, Federal agencies, and insured State branches of foreign banks), commercial lending companies owned or controlled by foreign banks, and organizations operating under section 25 or 25A of the Federal Reserve Act; and

"(C) banks and State savings associations insured by the Federal Deposit Insurance Corporation (other than members of the Federal Reserve System), and insured State branches of foreign banks;

"(2) the Federal Credit Union Act, by the Director of the National Credit Union Administration, with respect to any Federal credit union;

"(3) the Federal Aviation Act of 1958, by the Secretary of Transportation, with respect to any air carrier or foreign air carrier subject to that Act;

的合规,以及通过简明易懂的语言简化披露的技术性质,帮助借款人或承租人理解交易。”

(6)在第105(f)(1)条[《美国法典》第十五编第1604(f)(1)节]中,删除“豁免任何类型的交易”,替以“豁免所有或任何类型的交易”;

(7)在第105条(《美国法典》第十五编第1604节)的结尾处增加如下内容:

“(i)**联邦储备委员会的规则制定权**。——无论第(a)子条如何规定,但是,联邦储备委员会仍有权根据本编针对《2010年消费者金融保护法》第1029(a)条所述主体制定规则。根据本子条制定的规章可包括联邦储备委员会判断为实现本编宗旨、防范规避或逃避本编规定或促使本编规定得到遵守所必要或恰当的分类、区分或其他规定。”

(8)在第108条(《美国法典》第十五编第1604节)结尾处增加如下内容:

(A)删除第(a)子条,替以如下内容:

“(a)**执法机构**。——在不违反《2010年消费者金融保护法》第B子编规定的前提下,本编施加的要求——

(1)对于以下实体而言,应由《联邦存款保险法》第3(q)条[《美国法典》第十二编第1813(q)节]定义的相应的联邦银行业监管机关根据该法第8条强制执行——

(A)国民银行、联邦储蓄协会以及外国银行的联邦分行和联邦代理行;

(B)联邦储备系统的成员银行(但国民银行除外)、外国银行的分行和代理行(但外国银行的联邦分行、联邦代理行以及州参保分行除外)、外国银行拥有或控制的商业贷款公司以及根据《联邦储备法》第25条或第25A条运营的组织;及

(C)在联邦存款保险公司参保的银行和州储蓄协会(但联邦储备系统成员除外)以及外国银行的州参保分行;

(2)对于联邦信贷联盟而言,应由国家信贷联盟署主任根据《联邦信贷联盟法》强制执行;

(3)对于航空公司或受《1958年联邦民航法》管辖的外资航空公司而言,应由交通部部长根据《1958年联邦民航法》强制执行;

"(4) the Packers and Stockyards Act, 1921 (except as provided in section 406 of that Act), by the Secretary of Agriculture, with respect to any activities subject to that Act;

"(5) the Farm Credit Act of 1971, by the Farm Credit Administration with respect to any Federal land bank, Federal land bank association, Federal intermediate credit bank, or production credit association; and

"(6) subtitle E of the Consumer Financial Protection Act of 2010, by the Bureau, with respect to any person subject to this title."; and

(B) by striking subsection (c) and inserting the following:

"(c) OVERALL ENFORCEMENT AUTHORITY OF THE FEDERAL TRADE COMMISSION. — Except to the extent that enforcement of the requirements imposed under this title is specifically committed to some other Government agency under any of paragraphs (1) through (5) of subsection (a), and subject to subtitle B of the Consumer Financial Protection Act of 2010, the Federal Trade Commission shall be authorized to enforce such requirements. For the purpose of the exercise by the Federal Trade Commission of its functions and powers under the Federal Trade Commission Act, a violation of any requirement imposed under this title shall be deemed a violation of a requirement imposed under that Act. All of the functions and powers of the Federal Trade Commission under the Federal Trade Commission Act are available to the Federal Trade Commission to enforce compliance by any person with the requirements under this title, irrespective of whether that person is engaged in commerce or meets any other jurisdictional tests under the Federal Trade Commission Act."; and

(9) in section 129 (15 U.S.C. 1639), by striking subsection (m) and inserting the following:

"(m) CIVIL PENALTIES IN FEDERAL TRADE COMMISSION ENFORCEMENT ACTIONS. — For purposes of enforcement by the Federal Trade Commission, any violation of a regulation issued by the Bureau pursuant to subsection (l)(2) shall be treated as a violation of a rule promulgated under section 18 of the Federal Trade Commission Act (15 U.S.C. 57a) regarding unfair or deceptive acts or practices."; and

(10) in chapter 5 (15 U.S.C. 1667 et seq.) —

(A) by striking "the Board" each place that term appears and inserting "the Bureau"; and

(B) by striking "The Board" each place that term appears and inserting "The Bureau".

SEC. 1100B. AMENDMENTS TO THE TRUTH IN SAVINGS ACT.

The Truth in Savings Act (12 U.S.C. 4301 et seq.) is amended —

(1) by striking "Board" each place that term appears, other than in section 272(b)(12 U.S.C. 4311), and inserting "Bureau";

(4)对于受《1921年包装食品生产厂及牲畜围栏法》管辖的活动而言,应由农业部部长根据《1921年包装食品生产厂及牲畜围栏法》(但该法第406条规定的情形除外)强制执行;

(5)对于任何联邦土地银行、联邦土地银行协会、联邦中间信贷银行或生产信贷协会而言,应由农业信贷管理局根据《1971年农业信贷法》强制执行;及

(6)对于受本编管辖的主体而言,应由消费者金融保护局根据《2010年消费者金融保护法》第E子编的规定强制执行。”及

(B)删除第(c)子条,替以如下内容:

“(c)**联邦贸易委员会的总体执法权**。——除非第(a)子条第(1)款至第(5)款已经指定其他政府机关强制执行本编施加的要求,在不违反《2010年消费者金融保护法》第B子编规定的前提下,联邦贸易委员会有权强制执行本编规定。联邦贸易委员会在按照《联邦贸易委员会法》(《美国法典》第十五编第41节及其后条文)行使职能和权力之时,违反本编施加的任何要求的行为均应视为构成违反该法施加的要求的行为。联邦贸易委员会在针对任何人强制执行本编规定之时,有权按照《联邦贸易委员会法》行使所有职能和权力,不论该人是否从事商业,亦不论其是否符合《联邦贸易委员会法》规定的任何其他管辖权标准。”及

(9)在第129条(《美国法典》第十五编第1639节)中,删除第(m)子条,替以如下内容:

“(m)**联邦贸易委员会执法行动中的民事罚款**。——联邦贸易委员会在执法之时,任何违反消费者金融保护局根据第(l)(2)子条发布的规章的行为,均应作为违反根据《联邦贸易委员会法》第18条(《美国法典》第十五编第57a节)颁布的关于不公平或欺骗性行为或做法的规则的行为处理。”及

(10)在第五章(《美国法典》第十五编第1667节及其后条文)中——

(A)删除所有的“联邦储备委员会”,全部替以“消费者金融保护局”;及

(B)删除所有的“联邦储备委员会”,全部替以“消费者金融保护局”。

第1100B条　对《诚实储蓄法》的修正

《诚实储蓄法》(《美国法典》第十二编第4301节及其后条文)修正如下——

(1)删除所有在第272(b)条(《美国法典》第十二编第4311节)以外出现的“联邦储备委员会”,全部替以“消费者金融保护局”;

(2) in section 270(a)(12 U.S.C. 4309)—

(A) by striking "Compliance" and all that follows through the end of paragraph (1) and inserting: "Subject to subtitle B of the Consumer Financial Protection Act of 2010, compliance with the requirements imposed under this subtitle shall be enforced under—

"(1) section 8 of the Federal Deposit Insurance Act by the appropriate Federal banking agency (as defined in section 3(q) of that Act), with respect to—

"(A) insured depository institutions (as defined in section 3(c)(2) of that Act);

"(B) depository institutions described in clause (i), (ii), or (iii) of section 19(b)(1)(A) of the Federal Reserve Act which are not insured depository institutions (as defined in section 3(c)(2) of the Federal Deposit Insurance Act); and

"(C) depository institutions described in clause (v) or (vi) of section 19(b)(1)(A) of the Federal Reserve Act which are not insured depository institutions (as defined in section 3(c)(2) of the Federal Deposit Insurance Act);";

(B) in paragraph (2), by striking the period at the end and inserting "; and"; and

(C) by adding at the end the following:

"(3) subtitle E of the Consumer Financial Protection Act of 2010, by the Bureau, with respect to any person subject to this subtitle.";

(3) in section 272(b)(12 U.S.C. 4311(b)), by striking "regulation prescribed by the Board" each place that term appears and inserting "regulation prescribed by the Bureau"; and

(4) in section 274(12 U.S.C. 4313), by striking paragraph (4) and inserting the following:

"(4) BUREAU. — The term 'Bureau' means the Bureau of Consumer Financial Protection.".

SEC. 1100C. AMENDMENTS TO THE TELEMARKETING AND CONSUMER FRAUD AND ABUSE PREVENTION ACT.

(a) AMENDMENTS TO SECTION 3. — Section 3 of the Telemarketing and Consumer Fraud and Abuse Prevention Act (15 U.S.C. 6102) is amended by striking subsections (b) and (c) and inserting the following:

"(b) RULEMAKING AUTHORITY. — The Commission shall have authority to prescribe rules under subsection (a), in accordance with section 553 of title 5, United States Code. In prescribing a rule under this section that relates to the provision of a consumer financial product or service that is subject to the Consumer Financial Protection Act of 2010, including any enumerated consumer law thereunder, the Commission shall consult with the Bureau of Consumer Financial Protection regarding the consistency of a proposed rule with standards, purposes, or objectives administered by the Bureau of Consumer Financial Protection.

(2)在第270(a)条(《美国法典》第十二编第4309节)中——

(A)删除"对本编施加的要求的合规"直至第(1)款结尾的全部内容,替以:"在不违反《2010年消费者金融保护法》第B子编规定的前提下,对本子编施加的要求——

"(1)对于以下实体而言,应由《联邦存款保险法》第3(q)条定义的相应的联邦银行业监管机关根据该法第8条强制执行——

(A)参保存款机构[定义见该法第3(c)(2)条];

(B)《联邦储备法》第19(b)(1)(A)条第(i)项、第(ii)项或第(iii)项所述并非参保存款机构[定义见《联邦存款保险法》第3(c)(2)条]的存款机构;及

(C)《联邦储备法》第19(b)(1)(A)条第(v)项或第(vi)项所述并非参保存款机构[定义见《联邦存款保险法》第3(c)(2)条]的存款机构;";

(B)第(2)款删除结尾处的句号,替以";及";并

(C)在结尾处增加如下内容:

"(3)对于受本编管辖的主体而言,应由消费者金融保护局根据《2010年消费者金融保护法》第E子编的规定强制执行。"

(3)在第272(b)条[《美国法典》第十二编第4311(b)节]中,删除所有的"联邦储备委员会制定的规章",全部替以"消费者金融保护局制定的规章";及

(4)在第274条(《美国法典》第十二编第4313节)中,删除第(4)款,替以如下内容:

"(4)**消费者金融保护局**。——'消费者金融保护局'一词系指联邦储备系统下的消费者金融保护局。"

第1100C条　对《电话营销与消费者欺诈及滥用防范法》的修正

(a)**对第3条的修正**。——删除《电话营销与消费者欺诈及滥用防范法》第3条(《美国法典》第十五编第6102节)第(b)子条和第(c)子条,替以如下内容:

"(b)**规则制定权**。——联邦贸易委员会有权根据《美国法典》第五编第553节,制定第(a)子条的细则。在针对提供受《2010年消费者金融保护法》(包括该法明文列举的消费者法律)管辖的消费者金融产品或服务的行为,制定本条的规则时,联邦贸易委员会应与消费者金融保护局磋商,确定规则草案是否与消费者金融保护局执行的标准、宗旨或目标相符。

"(c) VIOLATIONS. — Any violation of any rule prescribed under subsection (a) —

"(1) shall be treated as a violation of a rule under section 18 of the Federal Trade Commission Act regarding unfair or deceptive acts or practices; and

"(2) that is committed by a person subject to the Consumer Financial Protection Act of 2010 shall be treated as a violation of a rule under section 1031 of that Act regarding unfair, deceptive, or abusive acts or practices.".

(b) AMENDMENTS TO SECTION 4. — Section 4(d) of the Telemarketing and Consumer Fraud and Abuse Prevention Act (15 U.S.C. 6103 (d)) is amended by inserting after "Commission" each place that term appears the following: "or the Bureau of Consumer Financial Protection".

(c) AMENDMENTS TO SECTION 5. — Section 5(c) of the Telemarketing and Consumer Fraud and Abuse Prevention Act (15 U.S.C. 6104(c)) is amended by inserting after "Commission" each place that term appears the following: "or the Bureau of Consumer Financial Protection".

(d) AMENDMENT TO SECTION 6. — Section 6 of the Telemarketing and Consumer Fraud and Abuse Prevention Act (15 U.S.C. 6105) is amended by adding at the end the following:

"(d) ENFORCEMENT BY BUREAU OF CONSUMER FINANCIAL PROTECTION. — Except as otherwise provided in sections 3(d), 3(e), 4, and 5, and subject to subtitle B of the Consumer Financial Protection Act of 2010, this Act shall be enforced by the Bureau of Consumer Financial Protection under subtitle E of the Consumer Financial Protection Act of 2010, with respect to the offering or provision of a consumer financial product or service subject to that Act.".

SEC. 1100D. AMENDMENTS TO THE PAPERWORK REDUCTION ACT.

(a) DESIGNATION AS AN INDEPENDENT AGENCY. — Section 2(5) of the Paperwork Reduction Act (44 U.S.C. 3502(5)) is amended by inserting "the Bureau of Consumer Financial Protection, the Office of Financial Research," after "the Securities and Exchange Commission,".

(b) COMPARABLE TREATMENT. — Section 3513 of title 44, United States Code, is amended by adding at the end the following:

"(c) COMPARABLE TREATMENT. — Notwithstanding any other provision of law, the Director shall treat or review a rule or order prescribed or proposed by the Director of the Bureau of Consumer Financial Protection on the same terms and conditions as apply to any rule or order prescribed or proposed by the Board of Governors of the Federal Reserve System.".

SEC. 1100E. ADJUSTMENTS FOR INFLATION IN THE TRUTH IN LENDING ACT.

(a) CAPS. —

(c)**违反**。——任何违反根据第(a)子条制定的规则的行为——

(1)均应作为违反《联邦贸易委员会法》第18条中关于不公平或欺骗性行为或做法的规则的行为处理;及

(2)如果从事该行为的人受《2010年消费者金融保护法》所管辖,则应作为违反该法第1031条中关于不公平、欺骗性或滥用行为或做法的规则的行为处理。”

(b)**对第4条的修正**。——在《电话营销与消费者欺诈及滥用防范法》第4(d)条[《美国法典》第十五编第6103(d)节]中的所有“联邦贸易委员会”之后插入“或消费者金融保护局”。

(c)**对第5条的修正**。——在《电话营销与消费者欺诈及滥用防范法》第5(c)条[《美国法典》第十五编第6104(c)节]中的所有“联邦储备委员会”之后插入“或消费者金融保护局”,作为对该条的修正。

(d)**对第6条的修正**。——在《电话营销与消费者欺诈及滥用防范法》第6条(《美国法典》第十五编第6105节)结尾处增加如下内容:

“(d)**消费者金融保护局的强制执行**。——除第3(d)条、第3(e)条、第4条和第5条规定的情形外,在不违反《2010年消费者金融保护法》第B子编规定的前提下,对于要约或提供受该法管辖的消费者金融产品或服务的行为,本法应由消费者金融保护局根据《2010年消费者金融保护法》第E子编的规定强制执行。”

第1100D条　对《文书削减法》的修正

(a)**独立机关的指定**。——在《文书削减法》第2(5)条[《美国法典》第四十四编第3502(5)节]的“证券交易委员会、”之后插入“消费者金融保护局、金融研究办公室、”,作为对该条的修正。

(b)**可比处理**。——在《美国法典》第四十四编第3513节结尾处增加如下内容:

“(c)**可比处理**。——无论是否存在任何不同法律规定,消费者金融保护局局长在处理或审查其制定或提议的规则或命令时,其条款和条件应等同于处理或审查联邦储备委员会制定或提议的规则或命令时适用的条款和条件。”

第1100E　对《诚实信贷法》规定的金额的通胀调整

(a)**上限**。——

(1) CREDIT TRANSACTIONS. — Section 104(3) of the Truth in Lending Act (15 U.S.C. 1603(3)) is amended by striking "$25,000" and inserting "$50,000".

(2) CONSUMER LEASES. — Section 181(1) of the Truth in Lending Act (15 U.S.C. 1667(1)) is amended by striking "$25,000" and inserting "$50,000".

(b) ADJUSTMENTS FOR INFLATION. — On and after December 31, 2011, the Bureau shall adjust annually the dollar amounts described in sections 104(3) and 181(1) of the Truth in Lending Act (as amended by this section), by the annual percentage increase in the Consumer Price Index for Urban Wage Earners and Clerical Workers, as published by the Bureau of Labor Statistics, rounded to the nearest multiple of $100, or $1,000, as applicable.

SEC. 1100F. USE OF CONSUMER REPORTS.

Section 615 of the Fair Credit Reporting Act (15 U.S.C. 1681m) is amended —

(1) in subsection (a) —

(A) by redesignating paragraphs (2) and (3) as paragraphs (3) and (4), respectively;

(B) by inserting after paragraph (1) the following:

"(2) provide to the consumer written or electronic disclosure —

"(A) of a numerical credit score as defined in section 609(f)(2)(A) used by such person in taking any adverse action based in whole or in part on any information in a consumer report; and

"(B) of the information set forth in subparagraphs (B) through (E) of section 609(f)(1);"; and

(C) in paragraph (4)(as so redesignated), by striking "paragraph (2)" and inserting "paragraph (3)"; and (2) in subsection (h)(5) —

(A) in subparagraph (C), by striking "; and" and inserting a semicolon;

(B) in subparagraph (D), by striking the period and inserting "; and"; and

(C) by inserting at the end the following:

"(E) include a statement informing the consumer of —

"(i) a numerical credit score as defined in section 609(f)(2)(A), used by such person in making the credit decision described in paragraph (1) based in whole or in part on any information in a consumer report; and

"(ii) the information set forth in subparagraphs(B) through(E) of section 609(f)(1).".

SEC. 1100G. SMALL BUSINESS FAIRNESS AND REGULATORY TRANSPARENCY.

(a) PANEL REQUIREMENT. — Section 609(d) of title 5, United States Code, is amended by striking "means the" and all that follows and inserting the following: "means —

"(1) the Environmental Protection Agency;

"(2) the Consumer Financial Protection Bureau of the Federal Reserve System; and

"(3) the Occupational Safety and Health Administration of the Department of Labor.".

(1)**信用交易**。——删除《诚实信贷法》第104(3)条[《美国法典》第十五编第1603(3)节]中的"2.5万美元",替以"5万美元"。

(2)**消费租赁**。——删除《诚实信贷法》第181(1)条[《美国法典》第十五编第1667(1)节]中的"2.5万美元",替以"5万美元"。

(b)**通胀调整**。——消费者金融保护局应于2011年12月31日及其后,按照劳工统计局发布的城市工薪族和文员的消费者物价指数的年增长率,对《诚实信贷法》第104(3)条和第181(1)条(以经本条修正后的版本为准)所述金额进行年度调整(根据实际情况按最接近的100美元或1000美元的倍数取整)。

第1100F条 对消费者报告的利用

《公平信用报告法》第615条(《美国法典》第十五编第1681m节)修正如下——

(1)在第(a)子条中——

(A)第(2)款和第(3)款分别重新编号为第(3)款和第(4)款;

(B)在第(1)款之后插入如下内容:

"(2)以书面形式或电子方式向消费者披露——

(A)该等主体完全或部分地基于消费者报告中的任何信息而采取不利行动时所使用的、第609(f)(2)(A)条所定义的信用评分数值;及

(B)第609(f)(1)条第(B)子款至第(E)子款所列信息;";及

(C)在第(4)款(以重新编号后的序号为准)中,删除"第(2)款",替以"第(3)款";及(2)在第(h)(5)子条中——

(A)第(C)子款删除";及",替以分号;

(B)第(D)子款删除句号,替以";及";并

(C)在结尾处插入如下内容:

"(E)纳入一份声明,向消费者提供如下信息——

(i)上述主体完全或部分地基于消费者报告中的任何信息作出第(1)款所述信用决定时所使用的、第609(f)(2)(A)条所定义的信用评分数值;及

(ii)第609(f)(1)条第(B)子款至第(E)子款所列信息。"

第1100G条 小型企业公平和监管透明度

(a)**审查小组要求**。——在《美国法典》第五编第609(d)节中,删除"系指"及其后的所有内容,替以如下内容作为对该节的修正:"系指——

(1)环保局;

(2)联邦储备系统下的消费者金融保护局;及

(3)劳动部的职业安全与卫生管理局。"

(b) INITIAL REGULATORY FLEXIBILITY ANALYSIS. — Section 603 of title 5, United States Code, is amended by adding at the end the following:

"(d)(1) For a covered agency, as defined in section 609(d)(2), each initial regulatory flexibility analysis shall include a description of —

"(A) any projected increase in the cost of credit for small entities;

"(B) any significant alternatives to the proposed rule which accomplish the stated objectives of applicable statutes and which minimize any increase in the cost of credit for small entities; and

"(C) advice and recommendations of representatives of small entities relating to issues described in subparagraphs (A) and (B) and subsection (b).

"(2) A covered agency, as defined in section 609 (d)(2), shall, for purposes of complying with paragraph (1)(C) —

"(A) identify representatives of small entities in consultation with the Chief Counsel for Advocacy of the Small Business Administration; and

"(B) collect advice and recommendations from the representatives identified under subparagraph (A) relating to issues described in subparagraphs (A) and (B) of paragraph (1) and subsection (b).".

(c) FINAL REGULATORY FLEXIBILITY ANALYSIS. — Section 604 (a) of title 5, United States Code, is amended —

(1) in paragraph (4), by striking "and" at the end;

(2) in paragraph (5), by striking the period at the end and inserting "; and"; and

(3) by adding at the end the following:

"(6) for a covered agency, as defined in section 609(d)(2), a description of the steps the agency has taken to minimize any additional cost of credit for small entities.".

SEC. 1100H. EFFECTIVE DATE.

Except as otherwise provided in this subtitle and the amendments made by this subtitle, this subtitle and the amendments made by this subtitle, other than sections 1081 and 1082, shall become effective on the designated transfer date.

(b)**初步监管弹性分析**。——在《美国法典》第五编第603节结尾处增加如下内容,作为对该节的修正:

"(d)(1)对于第609(d)(2)条定义的所涉机关,每份初步监管灵活性分析均应包括以下内容——

(A)小型实体信贷成本的任何预计增长;

(B)同样能够实现适用制定法明文规定的立法宗旨,并将小型实体信贷成本增长减到最低限度的,规则草案的任何重要的替代性规则;及

(C)小型实体代表就第(A)子款、第(B)子款以及第(b)子条所述问题提出的意见和建议。

(2)为遵守第(1)(C)款的规定,第609(d)(2)条定义的所涉机关应——

(A)与小型企业管理局的首席维权律师磋商,确定小型实体的代表;及

(B)针对第(1)款第(A)子款和第(B)子款以及第(b)子条所述的问题,收集根据第(A)子款确定的代表提出的相关意见和建议。"

(c)**最终监管弹性分析**。——《美国法典》第五编第604(a)节修正如下——

(1)删除第(4)款结尾处的"及";

(2)在第(5)款中,删除结尾处的句号,替以";及";及

(3)在结尾处增加如下内容:

"(6)对于第609(d)(2)条定义的所涉机关,应说明该机关将采取何种措施,将小型实体的新增信贷成本(如有)减到最低限度。"

第1100H条 生效日

除本子编以及本子编作出的修正另有规定的情形外,本子编以及本子编作出的修正,除第1081条和第1082条外,均于指定转移日生效。

TITLE XI — FEDERAL RESERVE SYSTEM PROVISIONS

SEC. 1101. FEDERAL RESERVE ACT AMENDMENTS ON EMERGENCY LENDING AUTHORITY.

(a) FEDERAL RESERVE ACT. — The third undesignated paragraph of section 13 of the Federal Reserve Act (12 U.S.C. 343) (relating to emergency lending authority) is amended —

(1) by inserting "(3)(A)" before "In unusual";

(2) by striking "individual, partnership, or corporation" the first place that term appears and inserting the following: "participant in any program or facility with broad-based eligibility";

(3) by striking "exchange for an individual or a partnership or corporation" and inserting "exchange,";

(4) by striking "such individual, partnership, or corporation" and inserting the following: "such participant in any program or facility with broad-based eligibility";

(5) by striking "for individuals, partnerships, corporations" and inserting "for any participant in any program or facility with broad-based eligibility"; and

(6) by striking "may prescribe." and inserting the following: "may prescribe.

"(B)(i) As soon as is practicable after the date of enactment of this subparagraph, the Board shall establish, by regulation, in consultation with the Secretary of the Treasury, the policies and procedures governing emergency lending under this paragraph. Such policies and procedures shall be designed to ensure that any emergency lending program or facility is for the purpose of providing liquidity to the financial system, and not to aid a failing financial company, and that the security for emergency loans is sufficient to protect taxpayers from losses and that any such program is terminated in a timely and orderly fashion. The policies and procedures established by the Board shall require that a Federal reserve bank assign, consistent with sound risk management practices and to ensure protection for the taxpayer, a lendable value to all collateral for a loan executed by a Federal reserve bank under this

第十一编——联邦储备系统的相关规定

第1101条　对《联邦储备法》中与紧急贷款权相关规定的修正

(a)**《联邦储备法》**。——《联邦储备法》第13条(《美国法典》第十二编第343节)第三个无编号段落(关于紧急贷款权的规定)修正如下——

(1)在“在非常和紧急情况下”前插入编号“(3)(A)”;

(2)删除首次出现的“个人、合伙或公司”,替以“任何适格主体广泛的计划或安排的参与者”;

(3)删除“个人、合伙或公司的汇票”,替以“汇票、”;

(4)删除“该等个人、合伙或公司”,替以“该等适格主体广泛的计划或安排的参与者”;

(5)删除“为个人、合伙或公司”,替以“为适格主体广泛的计划或安排的任何参与者”;及

(6)删除“可能规定的限制和规则。”,替以:“可能规定的限制和规则。

(B)(i)自本子款规定颁布之日起,联邦储备委员会应尽快与财政部部长磋商,发布规章,为本款规定的紧急贷款制定相关政策和程序。在设计该等政策和程序时,应确保任何紧急贷款计划或安排的目的均为向金融系统提供流动性,而非为经营失败的金融公司提供救助;而且为紧急贷款提供的担保应足以保护纳税人免受损失,且任何该等计划均应及时有序地终止。联邦储备委员会制定的政策和程序应当规定,联邦储备银行在判定就本款而言,贷款是否已获得本款意义上令人满意的担保之时,应在符合健全的风险管理实践并确保纳税人受到保护的前提下,为其根据本款规定执行的每一笔贷款的所有担保品确定一个可借贷价值。

paragraph in determining whether the loan is secured satisfactorily for purposes of this paragraph.

"(ii) The Board shall establish procedures to prohibit borrowing from programs and facilities by borrowers that are insolvent. Such procedures may include a certification from the chief executive officer (or other authorized officer) of the borrower, at the time the borrower initially borrows under the program or facility (with a duty by the borrower to update the certification if the information in the certification materially changes), that the borrower is not insolvent. A borrower shall be considered insolvent for purposes of this subparagraph, if the borrower is in bankruptcy, resolution under title II of the Dodd–Frank Wall Street Reform and Consumer Protection Act, or any other Federal or State insolvency proceeding.

"(iii) A program or facility that is structured to remove assets from the balance sheet of a single and specific company, or that is established for the purpose of assisting a single and specific company avoid bankruptcy, resolution under title II of the Dodd–Frank Wall Street Reform and Consumer Protection Act, or any other Federal or State insolvency proceeding, shall not be considered a program or facility with broad–based eligibility.

"(iv) The Board may not establish any program or facility under this paragraph without the prior approval of the Secretary of the Treasury.

"(C) The Board shall provide to the Committee on Banking, Housing, and Urban Affairs of the Senate and the Committee on Financial Services of the House of Representatives —

"(i) not later than 7 days after the Board authorizes any loan or other financial assistance under this paragraph, a report that includes —

"(I) the justification for the exercise of authority to provide such assistance;

"(II) the identity of the recipients of such assistance;

"(III) the date and amount of the assistance, and form in which the assistance was provided; and

"(IV) the material terms of the assistance, including —

"(aa) duration;

"(bb) collateral pledged and the value thereof;

"(cc) all interest, fees, and other revenue or items of value to be received in exchange for the assistance;

"(dd) any requirements imposed on the recipient with respect to employee compensation, distribution of dividends, or any other corporate decision in exchange for the assistance; and

"(ee) the expected costs to the taxpayers of such assistance; and

"(ii) once every 30 days, with respect to any outstanding loan or other financial assistance under this paragraph, written updates on —

"(I) the value of collateral;

(ii)联邦储备委员会应制定相关程序,禁止计划或安排向资不抵债的借款人提供贷款。该等程序可包括要求借款人的首席执行官(或其他授权管理人员)在借款人最初通过该计划或安排借款时,出具一份借款人并非资不抵债的自查证明(证明中所含信息发生重大变化的,借款人有义务更新该证明)。如果借款人处于破产程序、《多德—弗兰克华尔街改革与消费者保护法》第二编规定的清盘程序,或任何其他联邦或州的资不抵债程序之中,则就本子款而言,该借款人应被视为处于资不抵债的状态。

(iii)为了将资产从某一特定公司的资产负债表上移除而设立的贷款计划或安排,或为了援助某一特定公司,使其避免进入破产程序,《多德—弗兰克华尔街改革与消费者保护法》第二编规定的清盘程序或任何其他联邦或州的资不抵债程序而设立的贷款计划或安排,均不得被视为适格主体广泛的计划或安排。

(iv)未经财政部部长事先批准,联邦储备委员会不得设立本款规定的任何计划或安排。

(C)联邦储备委员会应按如下规定向参议院银行、住房与城市事务委员会和众议院金融服务委员会提交相关材料——

(i)在联邦储备委员会根据本款核准任何贷款或其他财务援助后7天内,提交一份包含以下内容的报告——

(I)行使援助权的正当性;

(II)援助对象的身份信息;

(III)援助的日期、金额及形式;及

(IV)援助的重大条款,包括——

(aa)期限;

(bb)质押的担保品及其价值;

(cc)作为援助对价,所获得的所有利息、费用、其他收入或有价物品;

(dd)作为援助的条件,向援助对象施加的有关雇员薪酬、股息分配或任何其他公司决策事项的要求;及

(ee)纳税人预计将为该等援助支付的成本;并

(ii)每30天,就本款规定的任何未清偿贷款或其他财务援助提供一份书面的更新材料,说明以下信息——

(I)担保品价值;

"(II) the amount of interest, fees, and other revenue or items of value received in exchange for the assistance; and

"(III) the expected or final cost to the taxpayers of such assistance.

"(D) The information required to be submitted to Congress under subparagraph (C) related to —

"(i) the identity of the participants in an emergency lending program or facility commenced under this paragraph;

"(ii) the amounts borrowed by each participant in any such program or facility;

"(iii) identifying details concerning the assets or collateral held by, under, or in connection with such a program or facility,

shall be kept confidential, upon the written request of the Chairman of the Board, in which case such information shall be made available only to the Chairpersons or Ranking Members of the Committees described in subparagraph (C).

"(E) If an entity to which a Federal reserve bank has provided a loan under this paragraph becomes a covered financial company, as defined in section 201 of the Dodd–Frank Wall Street Reform and Consumer Protection Act, at any time while such loan is outstanding, and the Federal reserve bank incurs a realized net loss on the loan, then the Federal reserve bank shall have a claim equal to the amount of the net realized loss against the covered entity, with the same priority as an obligation to the Secretary of the Treasury under section 210(b) of the Dodd–Frank Wall Street Reform and Consumer Protection Act.".

(b) CONFORMING AMENDMENT. — Section 507(a)(2) of title 11, United States Code, is amended by inserting "unsecured claims of any Federal reserve bank related to loans made through programs or facilities authorized under section 13(3) of the Federal Reserve Act (12 U.S.C. 343)," after "this title,".

(c) REFERENCES. — On and after the date of enactment of this Act, any reference in any provision of Federal law to the third undesignated paragraph of section 13 of the Federal Reserve Act(12 U.S.C. 343) shall be deemed to be a reference to section 13(3) of the Federal Reserve Act, as so designated by this section.

SEC. 1102. AUDITS OF SPECIAL FEDERAL RESERVE CREDIT FACILITIES.

(a) AUDITS. — Section 714 of title 31, United States Code, is amended by adding at the end the following:

"(f) AUDITS OF CREDIT FACILITIES OF THE FEDERAL RESERVE SYSTEM. —

"(1) DEFINITIONS. — In this subsection, the following definitions shall apply:

"(A) CREDIT FACILITY. — The term 'credit facility' means a program or facility, including any special purpose vehicle or other entity established by or on behalf of the Board of Governors of the Federal Reserve System or a Federal reserve bank, authorized by the Board of Governors under section 13(3) of the Federal Reserve Act (12 U.S.C. 343), that is

(II)作为援助对价,所获得的利息、费用、其他收入或有价物品之金额;且

(III)纳税人预计将为或最终为该等援助支付的成本。

(D)在联邦储备委员会主席提出书面请求之时,根据第(C)子款向国会提交的与如下各项相关的信息均应予以保密——

(i)根据本款启动的紧急贷款计划或安排的参与者身份信息;

(ii)该贷款计划或安排的每一参与者的借款金额;

(iii)该计划或安排持有的、在该计划或安排项下持有的或因该计划或安排而持有的资产或担保品的识别性详细信息,在该等保密情况下,该等信息仅能提供给第(C)子款规定的参议院银行、住房与城市事务委员会和众议院金融服务委员会的主席或副主席。

(E)如果接受联邦储备银行根据本款提供的贷款的实体成为《多德—弗兰克华尔街改革与消费者保护法》第201条定义的所涉金融公司,则只要该贷款尚未清偿,且联邦储备银行已就该贷款发生了已实现的净损失,则联邦储备银行对该所涉实体拥有的债权金额应与已实现净损失相等,该债权的优先顺序应与《多德—弗兰克华尔街改革与消费者保护法》第210(b)条规定的向财政部部长承担的义务相同。"

(b)**一致性修正**。——《美国法典》第十一编第507(a)(2)节修正如下:在"本编第503(b)节允许的行政费用、"之后插入"联邦储备银行对根据《联邦储备法》第13(3)条(《美国法典》第十二编第343节)核准的计划或安排发放的贷款拥有的无担保债权,"。

(c)**指称**。——自本法颁布之日起,任何联邦法律的规定中指称的《联邦储备法》第13条(《美国法典》第十二编第343节)的第三个无编号段落时,应被视为对《联邦储备法》第13(3)条(以本条序号为准)的指称。

第1102条 对特殊联邦储备信贷安排的审计

(a)**审计**。——在《美国法典》第三十一编第714节结尾处增加如下内容,作为对该节的修正:

"(f)**对联邦储备系统信贷安排的审计**。——

(1)**定义**。——就本子节而言,应适用如下定义:

(A)**信贷安排**。——'信贷安排'一词系指联邦储备委员会根据《联邦储备法》第13(3)条(《美国法典》第十二编第343节)授权的不在第(e)子条规定的审计范围之内的计划或安排,包括由联邦储备委员会或联邦储备银行设立的或者代表其利益的任何特殊目的载体或其他实体。

not subject to audit under subsection (e).

"(B) COVERED TRANSACTION. — The term 'covered transaction' means any open market transaction or discount window advance that meets the definition of 'covered transaction' in section 11(s) of the Federal Reserve Act.

"(2) AUTHORITY FOR AUDITS AND EXAMINATIONS. — Subject to paragraph (3), and notwithstanding any limitation in subsection (b) on the auditing and oversight of certain functions of the Board of Governors of the Federal Reserve System or any Federal reserve bank, the Comptroller General of the United States may conduct audits, including onsite examinations, of the Board of Governors, a Federal reserve bank, or a credit facility, if the Comptroller General determines that such audits are appropriate, solely for the purposes of assessing, with respect to a credit facility or a covered transaction —

"(A) the operational integrity, accounting, financial reporting, and internal controls governing the credit facility or covered transaction;

"(B) the effectiveness of the security and collateral policies established for the facility or covered transaction in mitigating risk to the relevant Federal reserve bank and taxpayers;

"(C) whether the credit facility or the conduct of a covered transaction inappropriately favors one or more specific participants over other institutions eligible to utilize the facility; and

"(D) the policies governing the use, selection, or payment of third-party contractors by or for any credit facility or to conduct any covered transaction.

"(3) REPORTS AND DELAYED DISCLOSURE. —

"(A) REPORTS REQUIRED. — A report on each audit conducted under paragraph (2) shall be submitted by the Comptroller General to the Congress before the end of the 90-day period beginning on the date on which such audit is completed.

"(B) CONTENTS. — The report under subparagraph (A) shall include a detailed description of the findings and conclusions of the Comptroller General with respect to the matters described in paragraph (2) that were audited and are the subject of the report, together with such recommendations for legislative or administrative action relating to such matters as the Comptroller General may determine to be appropriate.

"(C) DELAYED RELEASE OF CERTAIN INFORMATION. —

"(i) IN GENERAL. — The Comptroller General shall not disclose to any person or entity, including to Congress, the names or identifying details of specific participants in any credit facility or covered transaction, the amounts borrowed by or transferred by or to specific participants in any credit facility or covered transaction, or identifying details regarding assets or collateral held or transferred by, under, or in connection with any credit facility or covered transaction, and any report provided under subparagraph (A) shall be redacted to ensure that such names and details are not disclosed.

(B)**所涉交易**。——‘所涉交易’一词系指满足《联邦储备法》第11(s)条‘所涉交易’定义的任何公开市场操作或贴现窗口贷款。

(2)**审计和检查权**。——尽管第(b)子条限制了对联邦储备委员会或任何联邦储备银行特定职能进行的审计和监督,但是,在不违反第(3)款规定的前提下,如果政府问责办公室主任判定,为实现对信贷安排或所涉交易的以下事项进行评估之唯一目的,对联邦储备委员会、联邦储备银行或信贷安排开展审计确属适当,则政府问责办公室主任可以针对联邦储备委员会、联邦储备银行或任何信贷安排进行审计,包括进行现场检查——

(A)信贷安排或所涉交易运作的诚信度、会计、财务报告和内部控制;

(B)针对信贷安排或所涉交易设立的担保和抵押政策在缓释相关联邦储备银行和纳税人风险方面的有效性;

(C)相对于有资格利用该信贷安排的其他机构,该信贷安排或所涉交易的开展是否不恰当地偏向某一或某些特定参与者;及

(D)任何信贷安排或开展任何所涉交易时,使用、选择第三方承包商或向其付款的相关政策。

(3)**报告和延迟披露**。——

(A)**报告要求**。——政府问责办公室主任应在根据第(2)款开展的每次审计结束之日后90天内,针对该等审计向国会提交一份报告。

(B)**内容**。——根据第(A)子款提交的报告应详细描述政府问责办公室主任对其审计的第(2)款所述事项(即报告的主题)进行审计之后得出的认定和结论,并就该等事项提出政府问责办公室主任判定确属适当的立法或行政行动建议。

(C)**特定信息的延迟发布**。——

(i)**一般规定**。——政府问责办公室不得向任何人或实体(包括国会)披露下述信息:任何信贷安排或所涉交易的具体参与者名称/姓名或识别性详细信息;该等参与者在该等信贷安排或所涉交易中举借、受让或转让的金额;任何信贷安排或所述交易持有或转让的、在该等信贷安排或交易项下所持有或转让的或因该等信贷安排或交易所持有或转让的财产或担保品的识别性详细信息。根据第(A)子款提供的报告亦应予以相应的编辑处理,以避免披露上述信息。

"(ii) DELAYED RELEASE. — The nondisclosure obligation under clause (i) shall expire with respect to any participant on the date on which the Board of Governors, directly or through a Federal reserve bank, publicly discloses the identity of the subject participant or the identifying details of the subject assets, collateral, or transaction.

"(iii) GENERAL RELEASE. — The Comptroller General shall release a nonredacted version of any report on a credit facility 1 year after the effective date of the termination by the Board of Governors of the authorization for the credit facility. For purposes of this clause, a credit facility shall be deemed to have terminated 24 months after the date on which the credit facility ceases to make extensions of credit and loans, unless the credit facility is otherwise terminated by the Board of Governors.

"(iv) EXCEPTIONS. — The nondisclosure obligation under clause (i) shall not apply to the credit facilities Maiden Lane, Maiden Lane II, and Maiden Lane III.

"(v) RELEASE OF COVERED TRANSACTION INFORMATION. — The Comptroller General shall release a nonredacted version of any report regarding covered transactions upon the release of the information regarding such covered transactions by the Board of Governors of the Federal Reserve System, as provided in section 11(s) of the Federal Reserve Act.".

(b) ACCESS TO RECORDS. — Section 714(d) of title 31, United States Code, is amended —

(1) in paragraph (2), by inserting "or any person or entity described in paragraph (3)(A)" after "used by an agency";

(2) in paragraph (3), by inserting "or (f)" after "subsection (e)" each place that term appears;

(3) in clauses (i) and (ii) of paragraph (3)(A), by inserting "or the Federal Reserve banks" after "by the Board" each place that term appears;

(4) in paragraph (3)(A)(ii), by inserting "participating in or" after "any entity"; and

(5) in paragraph (3)(B), by adding at the end the following:

"The Comptroller General may make and retain copies of books, accounts, and other records provided under subparagraph (A) as the Comptroller General deems appropriate. The Comptroller General shall provide to any person or entity described in subparagraph (A) a current list of officers and employees to whom, with proper identification, records and property may be made available, and who may make notes or copies necessary to carry out a audit or examination under this subsection.".

SEC. 1103. PUBLIC ACCESS TO INFORMATION.

(a) IN GENERAL. — Section 2B of the Federal Reserve Act (12 U.S.C. 225b) is amended by adding at the end the following:

"(c) PUBLIC ACCESS TO INFORMATION. — The Board shall place on its home Internet website, a link entitled 'Audit', which shall link to a webpage that shall serve as a

(ii)**延迟发布**。——对于任何参与者而言,第(i)项规定的不披露义务的失效日期,应为联邦储备委员会直接或通过联邦储备银行公开披露具体参与者的身份,或相关资产、担保品或交易的识别性详细信息之日。

(iii)**一般发布**。——联邦储备委员会终止对信贷安排的授权的,政府问责办公室主任应在该等终止生效日后一年之内,发布关于该信贷安排的未经编辑的报告。就本项而言,信贷安排停止授信或发放借款之日后届满24个月之日,应被视为信贷安排终止之日,但联邦储备委员会另行终止该信贷安排的情形除外。

(iv)**例外规定**。——第(i)项规定的不披露义务不适用于如下信贷安排:Maiden Lane I、Maiden Lane II和Maiden Lane III。

(v)**所涉交易信息的发布**。——联邦储备委员会根据《联邦储备法》第11(s)条发布所涉交易的信息之时,政府问责办公室应发布一份关于该所涉交易的未经编辑的报告。"

(b)**记录查阅权**。——《美国法典》第三十一编第714(d)节修正如下——

(1)在第(2)款中,在"机关"之后插入"或第(3)(A)款所述任何主体或实体";

(2)在第(3)款中,在所有的"第(e)子节"之后插入"或第(f)子节";

(3)在第(3)(A)款的第(i)项和第(ii)项中,在所有的"联邦储备委员会"之后插入"或联邦储备银行";

(4)在第(3)(A)(ii)款中,在"接受援助的任何实体"前插入"参加或";且

(5)在第(3)(B)款结尾处增加如下内容:

"如政府问责办公室认为恰当,其可以复制根据第(A)子款提供的账簿、账册和其他记录,并保留复印件。政府问责办公室应向第(A)子款所述任何主体或实体提供一份最新名单,并注明适当的身份信息,说明可以接触该等记录和财产,以及可以为开展本子节规定的审计或检查而摘抄或复制记录和财产的官员和职员。"

第1103条　公众知情权

(a)**一般规定**。——在《联邦储备法》第2B条(《美国法典》第十二编第225b节)结尾处增加如下内容,作为对该条的修正:

"(c)**公众知情权**。——联邦储备委员会应在其官网主页上设置名为'审计'的链接,该链接应指向公众开放的信息库网页,信息的提供期间应合理,不得短于信息发

repository of information made available to the public for a reasonable period of time, not less than 6 months following the date of release of the relevant information, including —

"(1) the reports prepared by the Comptroller General under section 714 of title 31, United States Code;

"(2) the annual financial statements prepared by an independent auditor for the Board in accordance with section 11B;

"(3) the reports to the Committee on Banking, Housing, and Urban Affairs of the Senate required under section 13(3)(relating to emergency lending authority); and

"(4) such other information as the Board reasonably believes is necessary or helpful to the public in understanding the accounting, financial reporting, and internal controls of the Board and the Federal reserve banks.".

(b) FEDERAL RESERVE TRANSPARENCY AND RELEASE OF INFORMATION. — Section 11 of the Federal Reserve Act (12 U.S.C. 248) is amended by adding at the end the following new subsection:

"(s) FEDERAL RESERVE TRANSPARENCY AND RELEASE OF INFORMATION.—

"(1) IN GENERAL. — In order to ensure the disclosure in a timely manner consistent with the purposes of this Act of information concerning the borrowers and counterparties participating in emergency credit facilities, discount window lending programs, and open market operations authorized or conducted by the Board or a Federal reserve bank, the Board of Governors shall disclose, as provided in paragraph (2) —

"(A) the names and identifying details of each borrower, participant, or counterparty in any credit facility or covered transaction;

"(B) the amount borrowed by or transferred by or to a specific borrower, participant, or counterparty in any credit facility or covered transaction;

"(C) the interest rate or discount paid by each borrower, participant, or counterparty in any credit facility or covered transaction; and

"(D) information identifying the types and amounts of collateral pledged or assets transferred in connection with participation in any credit facility or covered transaction.

"(2) MANDATORY RELEASE DATE. In the case of —

"(A) a credit facility, the Board shall disclose the information described in paragraph (1) on the date that is 1 year after the effective date of the termination by the Board of the authorization of the credit facility; and

"(B) a covered transaction, the Board shall disclose the information described in paragraph (1) on the last day of the eighth calendar quarter following the calendar quarter in which the covered transaction was conducted.

"(3) EARLIER RELEASE DATE AUTHORIZED. — The Chairman of the Board may publicly release the information described in paragraph (1) before the relevant date specified

布后6个月。该等信息包括——

(1)按《美国法典》第三十一编第714节规定由政府问责办公室编制的报告;

(2)按第11B节规定由联邦储备委员会的独立审计师编制的年度财务报表;

(3)按第13(3)节(与紧急贷款权相关的规定)的要求向参议院银行、住房与城市事务委员会提交的报告;及

(4)联邦储备委员会合理认为对公众理解联邦储备委员会和联邦储备银行的会计、财务报告和内部控制确属必要或有帮助的其他信息。”

(b)**联邦储备信息的透明度和发布**。——在《联邦储备法》第11条(《美国法典》第十二编第248节)结尾处增加如下新子条,作为对该条的修正:

“(s)**联邦储备信息的透明度和发布**。——

(1)**一般规定**。——对于参与联邦储备委员会或联邦储备银行核准或开展的紧急信贷安排、贴现窗口贷款计划和公开市场操作的借款人和对手方的相关信息,为确保该信息按照符合本法宗旨的方式及时得以披露,联邦储备委员会应按照第(2)款的规定披露以下信息——

(A)任何信贷安排或所涉交易的每一借款人、参与者或对手方的名称/姓名和识别性详细信息;

(B)在任何信贷安排或所涉交易中,某一具体借款人、参与者或对手方举借、转让或受让的金额;

(C)任何信贷安排或所涉交易的每一借款人、参与者或对手方支付的利息或贴息;及

(D)参加任何信贷安排或所涉交易之时,质押的担保品或转移的资产之类型和金额的识别性信息。

(2)**强制发布日**。——

(A)对于信贷安排而言,联邦储备委员会终止对信贷安排的授权的,联邦储备委员会应在终止生效日后届满1年时披露第(1)款规定的信息;及

(B)对于所涉交易而言,联邦储备委员会应当在该所涉交易开展之日所在的日历季度之后的第8个日历季度的最后一天披露第(1)款规定的信息。

(3)**获准提前发布之日**。——如联邦储备委员会主席判定提前发布信息符合公共利益且不会损害相关信贷安排的有效性或所涉交易之目的或开展,联邦储备委员

in paragraph (2), if the Chairman determines that such disclosure would be in the public interest and would not harm the effectiveness of the relevant credit facility or the purpose or conduct of covered transactions.

"(4) DEFINITIONS. — For purposes of this subsection, the following definitions shall apply:

"(A) CREDIT FACILITY. — The term 'credit facility' has the same meaning as in section 714(f)(1)(A) of title 31, United States Code.

"(B) COVERED TRANSACTION. — The term 'covered transaction' means —

"(i) any open market transaction with a nongovernmental third party conducted under the first undesignated paragraph of section 14 or subparagraph (a), (b), or (c) of the 2nd undesignated paragraph of such section, after the date of enactment of the Dodd–Frank Wall Street Reform and Consumer Protection Act; and

"(ii) any advance made under section 10B after the date of enactment of that Act.

"(5) TERMINATION OF CREDIT FACILITY BY OPERATION OF LAW. — A credit facility shall be deemed to have terminated as of the end of the 24–month period beginning on the date on which the credit facility ceases to make extensions of credit and loans, unless the credit facility is otherwise terminated by the Board before such date.

"(6) CONSISTENT TREATMENT OF INFORMATION. — Except as provided in this subsection or section 13(3)(D), or in section 714(f)(3)(C) of title 31, United States Code, the information described in paragraph (1) and information concerning the transactions described in section 714 (f) of such title, shall be confidential, including for purposes of section 552(b)(3) of title 5 of such Code, until the relevant mandatory release date described in paragraph (2), unless the Chairman of the Board determines that earlier disclosure of such information would be in the public interest and would not harm the effectiveness of the relevant credit facility or the purpose of conduct of the relevant transactions.

"(7) PROTECTION OF PERSONAL PRIVACY. — This subsection and section 13(3)(C), section 714 (f)(3)(C) of title 31, United States Code, and subsection (a) or (c) of section 1109 of the Dodd–Frank Wall Street Reform and Consumer Protection Act shall not be construed as requiring any disclosure of nonpublic personal information (as defined for purposes of section 502 of the Gramm–Leach–Bliley Act (12 U.S.C. 6802)) concerning any individual who is referenced in collateral pledged or assets transferred in connection with a credit facility or covered transaction, unless the person is a borrower, participant, or counterparty under the credit facility or covered transaction.

"(8) STUDY OF FOIA EXEMPTION IMPACT. —

"(A) STUDY. — The Inspector General of the Board of Governors of the Federal Reserve System shall —

"(i) conduct a study on the impact that the exemption from section 552(b)(3) of title 5

会主席可以在第(2)款规定的发布日之前公开发布第(1)款规定的信息。

(4)**定义**。——就本子条而言,应适用如下定义:

(A)**信贷安排**。——'信贷安排'一词的含义以《美国法典》第三十一编第714(f)(1)(A)节的定义为准。

(B)**所涉交易**。——'所涉交易'一词系指——

(i)自《多德—弗兰克华尔街改革与消费者保护法》颁布之日起,根据第14条第一个无编号段落或该条第二个无编号段落第(a)子款、第(b)子款或第(c)子款同非政府第三方开展的任何公开市场操作;及

(ii)本法颁布之日起根据第10B条提供的任何预支款。

(5)**信贷安排的法定终止**。——信贷安排停止授信和发放贷款之日起届满24个月之日,应被视为其终止日,但联邦储备委员会在该等日期之前提前终止信贷安排的情形除外。

(6)**对信息的一致性处理**。——除本子条、第13(3)(D)条或《美国法典》第三十一编第714(f)(3)(C)节规定的情形外,在第(2)款规定的相关强制发布日之前,第(1)款所述信息以及与该编第714(f)节所述交易相关的信息应予保密(包括在适用《美国法典》第五编第552(b)(3)节的规定之时,亦应保密),但联邦储备委员会主席判定提前披露信息符合公共利益,且不会损害相关信贷安排的有效性或开展所涉交易之目的的除外。

(7)**保护个人隐私**。——对于与信贷安排或所涉交易相关的担保品质押或财产转移文书中所提及的任何个人而言,本子条、第13(3)(C)条、《美国法典》第三十一编第714(f)(3)(C)节和《多德—弗兰克华尔街改革与消费者保护法》第1109条第(a)子条或第(c)子条,均不得被解释为要求对该等个人的非公开私人信息[定义见《格雷姆—里奇—比利雷法》(《美国法典》第十二编第6802节)]进行任何披露,但该个人身为该信贷安排或所涉交易的借款人、参与者或对手方的除外。

(8)**关于《信息自由法》豁免影响的研究**。——

(A)**研究**。——联邦储备委员会的监察长应——

(i)针对第(6)款中关于豁免适用《美国法典》第五编第552(b)(3)节(即《信息自由

(known as the Freedom of Information Act) established under paragraph (6) has had on the ability of the public to access information about the administration by the Board of Governors of emergency credit facilities, discount window lending programs, and open market operations; and

"(ii) make any recommendations on whether the exemption described in clause (i) should remain in effect.

"(B) REPORT. — Not later than 30 months after the date of enactment of this section, the Inspector General of the Board of Governors of the Federal Reserve System shall submit a report on the findings of the study required under subparagraph (A) to the Committee on Banking, Housing, and Urban Affairs of the Senate and the Committee on Financial Services of the House of Representatives, and publish the report on the website of the Board.

"(9) RULE OF CONSTRUCTION. — Nothing in this section is meant to affect any pending litigation or lawsuit filed under section 552 of title 5, United States Code (popularly known as the Freedom of Information Act), on or before the date of enactment of the Dodd–Frank Wall Street Reform and Consumer Protection Act.".

SEC. 1104. LIQUIDITY EVENT DETERMINATION.

(a) DETERMINATION AND WRITTEN RECOMMENDATION. —

(1) DETERMINATION REQUEST. — The Secretary may request the Corporation and the Board of Governors to determine whether a liquidity event exists that warrants use of the guarantee program authorized under section 1105.

(2) REQUIREMENTS OF DETERMINATION. — Any determination pursuant to paragraph (1) shall —

(A) be written; and

(B) contain an evaluation of the evidence that —

(i) a liquidity event exists;

(ii) failure to take action would have serious adverse effects on financial stability or economic conditions in the United States; and

(iii) actions authorized under section 1105 are needed to avoid or mitigate potential adverse effects on the United States financial system or economic conditions.

(b) PROCEDURES. — Notwithstanding any other provision of Federal or State law, upon the determination of both the Corporation (upon a vote of not fewer than 2/3 of the members of the Corporation then serving) and the Board of Governors (upon a vote of not fewer than 2/3 of the members of the Board of Governors then serving) under subsection (a) that a liquidity event exists that warrants use of the guarantee program authorized under section 1105, and with the written consent of the Secretary —

(1) the Corporation shall take action in accordance with section 1105(a); and

(2) the Secretary (in consultation with the President) shall take action in accordance

法》)的规定对公众获取如下信息的能力之影响开展研究:与联邦储备委员会管理紧急信贷安排、贴现窗口贷款计划和公开市场操作的方式相关之信息;及

(ii)对第(i)项所述豁免是否应继续有效提出任何建议。

(B)**报告**。——联邦储备委员会的监察长应于本条规定颁布之日后30个月内,针对第(A)子款要求开展的研究之结果,向参议院银行、住房与城市事务委员会和众议院金融服务委员会提交一份报告,并在联邦储备委员会的网站上发布该报告。

(9)**解释规则**。——本条的任何规定均不影响在《多德—弗兰克华尔街改革与消费者保护法》颁布之日或之前,已根据《美国法典》第五编第552节(即《信息自由法》)提起的任何未决诉讼或案件。”

第1104条　流动性事件的判定

(a)**判定和书面建议**。——

(1)**判定请求**。——财政部部长可以请求联邦存款保险公司和联邦储备委员会判定是否存在有必要启动第1105条准许提供的担保计划的流动性事件。

(2)**判定要求**。——根据第(1)款作出的判定应当——

(A)采用书面形式;并

(B)包含对证明以下事项的证据的评价——

(i)存在流动性事件;

(ii)不采取行动将对美国的金融稳定或经济状况造成严重不利影响;及

(iii)为避免或减轻对美国金融系统或经济状况可能造成的不利影响,需要采取第1105条准许采取的行动。

(b)**程序**。——无论联邦法律或州法律是否存在任何不同规定,联邦存款保险公司(经至少2/3届时在任的委员表决通过)和联邦储备委员会(经至少2/3届时在任的委员表决通过)根据第(a)子条共同作出存在需要启动第1105条批准的担保项目应对的流动性事件之判定的,则经财政部部长书面同意——

(1)联邦存款保险公司应根据第1105(a)条采取行动;且

(2)财政部部长应在与总统磋商之后,根据第1105(c)条采取行动。

with section 1105(c).

(c) DOCUMENTATION AND REVIEW.—

(1) DOCUMENTATION.—The Secretary shall—

(A) maintain the written documentation of each determination of the Corporation and the Board of Governors under this section; and

(B) provide the documentation for review under paragraph (2).

(2) GAO REVIEW.—The Comptroller General of the United States shall review and report to Congress on any determination of the Corporation and the Board of Governors under subsection (a), including—

(A) the basis for the determination; and

(B) the likely effect of the actions taken.

(d) REPORT TO CONGRESS.—On the earlier of the date of a submission made to Congress under section 1105(c), or within 30 days of the date of a determination under subsection (a), the Secretary shall provide written notice of the determination of the Corporation and the Board of Governors to the Committee on Banking, Housing, and Urban Affairs of the Senate and the Committee on Financial Services of the House of Representatives, including a description of the basis for the determination.

SEC. 1105. EMERGENCY FINANCIAL STABILIZATION.

(a) IN GENERAL.—Upon the written determination of the Corporation and the Board of Governors under section 1104, the Corporation shall create a widely available program to guarantee obligations of solvent insured depository institutions or solvent depository institution holding companies (including any affiliates thereof) during times of severe economic distress, except that a guarantee of obligations under this section may not include the provision of equity in any form.

(b) RULEMAKING AND TERMS AND CONDITIONS.—

(1) POLICIES AND PROCEDURES.—As soon as is practicable after the date of enactment of this Act, the Corporation shall establish, by regulation, and in consultation with the Secretary, policies and procedures governing the issuance of guarantees authorized by this section. Such policies and procedures may include a requirement of collateral as a condition of any such guarantee.

(2) TERMS AND CONDITIONS.—The terms and conditions of any guarantee program shall be established by the Corporation, with the concurrence of the Secretary.

(c) DETERMINATION OF GUARANTEED AMOUNT.—

(1) IN GENERAL.—In connection with any program established pursuant to subsection (a) and subject to paragraph (2) of this subsection, the Secretary (in consultation with the President) shall determine the maximum amount of debt outstanding that the Corporation may guarantee under this section, and the President may transmit to Congress a

(c)**文件编制和审查**。——

(1)**文件编制**。——财政部部长应——

(A)对于联邦存款保险公司和联邦储备委员会根据本条作出的每一判定,保存书面文件;并

(B)提供该等文件,以便开展第(2)款规定的审查。

(2)**政府问责办公室的审查**。——政府问责办公室主任应对联邦存款保险公司和联邦储备委员会根据第(a)子条作出的任何判定进行审查,并向国会提交报告,包括——

(A)判定的依据;及

(B)采取行动之后可能产生的效果。

(d)**向国会报告**。——在根据第1105(c)条向国会提交报告之日或根据第(a)子条作出判定之日后30天内(以较早者为准),财政部部长应将联邦存款保险公司和联邦储备委员会作出的判定书面通知参议院银行、住房与城市事务委员会和众议院金融服务委员会,并在通知中说明作出该判定的依据。

第1105条　紧急金融稳定

(a)**一般规定**。——一旦联邦存款保险公司和联邦储备委员会按照第1104条作出书面判定,联邦存款保险公司即应立即成立一个计划,广泛地为处于严重经济困境中有偿债能力的参保存款机构或有偿债能力的存款机构控股公司(包括其任何关联方)的债务提供担保,但是本条规定的债务担保不得包括提供任何形式的股权。

(b)**规则制定以及条款和条件**。——

(1)**政策和程序**。——本法颁布之日起,联邦存款保险公司应与财政部部长磋商,尽快发布规章制定对本条准许提供的担保的提供进行规范的政策和程序。在该等政策和程序中,可以要求提供担保品,作为提供该等担保的条件。

(2)**条款和条件**。——任何担保计划的条款和条件应由联邦存款保险公司制定,并征得财政部部长同意。

(c)**担保金额的判定**。——

(1)**一般规定**。——在不违反本子条第(2)款规定的前提下,对于按照第(a)子条制定的任何计划,财政部部长应在与总统磋商之后,判定联邦存款保险公司可以按照本条规定担保的未清偿债务的最高金额。对于联邦存款保险公司按照本条规定,在上述最高金额限度之内行使提供担保权的计划,总统可以向国会发送一份书面报告,并

written report on the plan of the Corporation to exercise the authority under this section to issue guarantees up to that maximum amount and a request for approval of such plan. The Corporation shall exercise the authority under this section to issue guarantees up to that specified maximum amount upon passage of the joint resolution of approval, as provided in subsection (d). Absent such approval, the Corporation shall issue no such guarantees.

(2) ADDITIONAL DEBT GUARANTEE AUTHORITY. — If the Secretary (in consultation with the President) determines, after a submission to Congress under paragraph (1), that the maximum guarantee amount should be raised, and the Council concurs with that determination, the President may transmit to Congress a written report on the plan of the Corporation to exercise the authority under this section to issue guarantees up to the increased maximum debt guarantee amount. The Corporation shall exercise the authority under this section to issue guarantees up to that specified maximum amount upon passage of the joint resolution of approval, as provided in subsection (d). Absent such approval, the Corporation shall issue no such guarantees.

(d) RESOLUTION OF APPROVAL. —

(1) ADDITIONAL DEBT GUARANTEE AUTHORITY. — A request by the President under this section shall be considered granted by Congress upon adoption of a joint resolution approving such request. Such joint resolution shall be considered in the Senate under expedited procedures.

(2) FAST TRACK CONSIDERATION IN SENATE. —

(A) RECONVENING. — Upon receipt of a request under subsection (c), if the Senate has adjourned or recessed for more than 2 days, the majority leader of the Senate, after consultation with the minority leader of the Senate, shall notify the Members of the Senate that, pursuant to this section, the Senate shall convene not later than the second calendar day after receipt of such message.

(B) PLACEMENT ON CALENDAR. — Upon introduction in the Senate, the joint resolution shall be placed immediately on the calendar.

(C) FLOOR CONSIDERATION. —

(i) IN GENERAL. — Notwithstanding Rule XXII of the Standing Rules of the Senate, it is in order at any time during the period beginning on the 4th day after the date on which Congress receives a request under subsection (c), and ending on the 7th day after that date (even though a previous motion to the same effect has been disagreed to) to move to proceed to the consideration of the joint resolution, and all points of order against the joint resolution (and against consideration of the joint resolution) are waived. The motion to proceed is not debatable. The motion is not subject to a motion to postpone. A motion to reconsider the vote by which the motion is agreed to or disagreed to shall not be in order. If a motion to proceed to the consideration of the resolution is agreed to, the joint resolution shall remain the unfinished

请求国会批准该计划。在该计划按照第(d)子条的规定获得联合决议批准通过之后,联邦存款保险公司应依据本条规定,在上述规定的最高金额限度内行使提供担保权。在未取得上文所述批准的情况下,联邦存款保险公司不得提供担保。

(2)**额外债务担保权**。——如果财政部部长在按照第(1)款规定向国会提交报告并与总统磋商之后,判定应上调最高担保金额,且金融稳定监督委员会同意该判定,则,对于联邦存款保险公司按照本条规定,在上调最高金额限度之内行使提供担保权的计划,总统可以向国会发送一份书面报告。在该计划按照第(d)子条的规定获得联合决议批准通过之后,联邦存款保险公司应依据本条规定,在上述规定的最高金额限度内行使提供担保权。在未取得上文所述批准的情况下,联邦存款保险公司不得提供担保。

(d)**批准决议**。——

(1)**额外债务担保权**。——总统按照本条规定提出的请求获得联合决议通过的,即应被视为已获国会批准。该联合决议应由参议院按照快速程序进行审议。

(2)**参议院的快速审议**。——

(A)**重新召集会议**。——如果在收到第(c)子条所述请求后,参议院已经休会2天以上,则参议院多数党领袖应在与参议院少数党领袖磋商后,向参议院全体议员发出通知,说明根据本条规定,参议院最迟应在收到该消息后第2个日历日召开会议。

(B)**日程安排**。——联合决议一经提交至参议院,即应立即提上议事日程。

(C)**全体议员审议**。——

(i)**一般规定**。——无论《参议院议事规则》第22条规则如何规定,在国会收到第(c)子条规定的请求之日起第4天至第7天之间的任何时候,提出对联合决议进行审议的动议并不违反程序(即使此前提出的相同动议曾被否决),并且针对联合决议(以及对联合决议的审议)提出的所有程序异议均搁置不议。启动审议的动议不容辩论。不得针对该动议提出任何推迟审议的动议。对动议作出同意或不同意的表决之后,不得再提出对表决票数进行重新审议的动议。如果启动对决议进行审议的动议获得同意,则联合决议在获得最终处理之前,仍应处于效力未定状态。

business until disposed of.

(ii) DEBATE. — Debate on the joint resolution, and on all debatable motions and appeals in connection therewith, shall be limited to not more than 10 hours, which shall be divided equally between the majority and minority leaders or their designees. A motion further to limit debate is in order and not debatable. An amendment to, or a motion to postpone, or a motion to proceed to the consideration of other business, or a motion to recommit the joint resolution is not in order.

(iii) VOTE ON PASSAGE. — The vote on passage shall occur immediately following the conclusion of the debate on the joint resolution, and a single quorum call at the conclusion of the debate if requested in accordance with the rules of the Senate.

(iv) RULINGS OF THE CHAIR ON PROCEDURE. — Appeals from the decisions of the Chair relating to the application of the rules of the Senate, as the case may be, to the procedure relating to a joint resolution shall be decided without debate.

(3) RULES. —

(A) COORDINATION WITH ACTION BY HOUSE OF REPRESENTATIVES. — If, before the passage by the Senate of a joint resolution of the Senate, the Senate receives a joint resolution, from the House of Representatives, then the following procedures shall apply:

(i) The joint resolution of the House of Representatives shall not be referred to a committee.

(ii) With respect to a joint resolution of the Senate —

(I) the procedure in the Senate shall be the same as if no joint resolution had been received from the other House; but

(II) the vote on passage shall be on the joint resolution of the House of Representatives.

(B) TREATMENT OF JOINT RESOLUTION OF HOUSE OF REPRESENTATIVES. — If the Senate fails to introduce or consider a joint resolution under this section, the joint resolution of the House of Representatives shall be entitled to expedited floor procedures under this subsection.

(C) TREATMENT OF COMPANION MEASURES. — If, following passage of the joint resolution in the Senate, the Senate then receives the companion measure from the House of Representatives, the companion measure shall not be debatable.

(D) RULES OF THE SENATE. — This subsection is enacted by Congress —

(i) as an exercise of the rulemaking power of the Senate, and as such it is deemed a part of the rules of the Senate, but applicable only with respect to the procedure to be followed in the Senate in the case of a joint resolution, and it supersedes other rules, only to the extent that it is inconsistent with such rules; and

(ii) with full recognition of the constitutional right of the Senate to change the rules (so far as relating to the procedure of the Senate) at any time, in the same manner, and to the

(ii)**辩论**。——针对联合决议以及与此相关的所有可辩论的动议和请求开展的辩论,时间不得超过10个小时。该时间应在多数党领袖或其指定人员,以及少数党领袖或其指定人员之间平均分配。提出进一步限制辩论时间的动议不违反程序,且该动议不容辩论。修正对其他事项的审议、提出推迟对其他事项的审议的动议、提出启动对其他事项的审议的动议,或者提出重新提交联合决议的动议均违反程序。

(iii)**投票表决**。——针对联合决议的辩论结束之后,应立即开始投票表决;并且,按照参议院规则提出查点确认法定人数的请求的,应在辩论结束时进行一次查点确认。

(iv)**参议院议长对程序事项的裁定**。——针对参议院议长视具体情况作出的将参议院规则适用于联合决议程序的决定,所提出的异议可直接裁决,不必进行辩论。

(3)**规则**。——

(A)**与众议院行动的协调**。——如果参议院在通过其联合决议之前,先收到了众议院的联合决议,则应适用如下程序:

(i)众议院的联合决议不得转给任何委员会。

(ii)对于参议院的联合决议——

(I)参议院的程序仍应保持不变,如同其从未收到来自众议院的任何联合决议;但是

(II)对于众议院的联合决议,应进行投票表决。

(B)**对于众议院联合决议的处理**。——如果参议院未能按照本条规定提出或审议联合决议,众议院的联合决议应按照本子条规定适用快速全体审议程序。

(C)**众议院同步议案的处理**。——如果参议院通过联合决议之后,收到来自众议院的同步议案,则该同步议案不容辩论。

(D)**参议院的规则**。——本子条规定由国会制定颁布——

(i)该等制定颁布行为属于参议院对规则制定权的行使,因此,本子条规定应被视为参议院规则的组成部分,但是本子条规定仅适用于参议院审议联合决议时遵守的程序,并且,仅在与其他规则不一致时,才能取代其他规则;且

(ii)参议院拥有充分的宪法权利,有权在任何时候以与修改参议院任何其他规则相同的方式和程度,修改本子条的规则(只要与参议院的程序相关)。

same extent as in the case of any other rule of the Senate.

(4) DEFINITION. — As used in this subsection, the term "joint resolution" means only a joint resolution —

(A) that is introduced not later than 3 calendar days after the date on which the request referred to in subsection (c) is received by Congress;

(B) that does not have a preamble;

(C) the title of which is as follows: "Joint resolution relating to the approval of a plan to guarantee obligations under section 1105 of the Dodd–Frank Wall Street Reform and Consumer Protection Act"; and

(D) the matter after the resolving clause of which is as follows: "That Congress approves the obligation of any amount described in section 1105(c) of the Dodd–Frank Wall Street Reform and Consumer Protection Act.".

(e) FUNDING. —

(1) FEES AND OTHER CHARGES. — The Corporation shall charge fees and other assessments to all participants in the program established pursuant to this section, in such amounts as are necessary to offset projected losses and administrative expenses, including amounts borrowed pursuant to paragraph (3), and such amounts shall be available to the Corporation.

(2) EXCESS FUNDS. — If, at the conclusion of the program established under this section, there are any excess funds collected from the fees associated with such program, the funds shall be deposited in the General Fund of the Treasury.

(3) AUTHORITY OF CORPORATION. — The Corporation —

(A) may borrow funds from the Secretary of the Treasury and issue obligations of the Corporation to the Secretary for amounts borrowed, and the amounts borrowed shall be available to the Corporation for purposes of carrying out a program established pursuant to this section, including the payment of reasonable costs of administering the program, and the obligations issued shall be repaid in full with interest through fees and charges paid by participants in accordance with paragraphs (1) and (4), as applicable; and

(B) may not borrow funds from the Deposit Insurance Fund established pursuant to section 11(a)(4) of the Federal Deposit Insurance Act.

(4) BACKUP SPECIAL ASSESSMENTS. — To the extent that the funds collected pursuant to paragraph (1) are insufficient to cover any losses or expenses, including amounts borrowed pursuant to paragraph (3), arising from a program established pursuant to this section, the Corporation shall impose a special assessment solely on participants in the program, in amounts necessary to address such insufficiency, and which shall be available to the Corporation to cover such losses or expenses.

(5) AUTHORITY OF THE SECRETARY. — The Secretary may purchase any

(4)**定义**。——就本子条而言,“联合决议”一词系仅指符合如下条件的联合决议——

(A)作出时间在国会收到第(c)子条所述请求后3个日历日之内;

(B)不存在序文;

(C)其名称如下:“关于批准根据《多德—弗兰克华尔街改革与消费者保护法》第1105条规定为债务提供担保的计划的联合决议”;且

(D)其决议条款之后的内容如下:“国会批准《多德—弗兰克华尔街改革与消费者保护法》第1105(c)条所述任何金额的债务。”

(e)**经费来源**。——

(1)**费用和其他收费**。——联邦存款保险公司应向参与按照本条规定制定的计划的所有参与者征收必要金额的费用和其他计征费,以抵销预期损失和行政费用[包括根据第(3)款借入的金额],并且该等金额应可供联邦存款保险公司使用。

(2)**过剩资金**。——如果按照本条规定制定的计划结束之时,由于收取的与该计划相关的费用而存在过剩资金,则该等过剩资金应存入财政部普通基金。

(3)**联邦存款保险公司的权力**。——联邦存款保险公司——

(A)可以通过向财政部部长发行债务的方式,向其举借资金。联邦存款保险公司可利用借款金额实施按照本条规定制定的计划,包括支付该计划行政管理的合理成本。联邦存款保险公司发行的债务,应通过参与者按照第(1)款和第(4)款规定(视具体情况而定)支付的费用,予以全额偿还,并支付利息;且

(B)不得向按照《联邦存款保险法》第11(a)(4)条设立的存款保险基金借款。

(4)**后备特殊计征费**。——如果按照第(1)款收取的资金不足以偿付因依据本条制定的计划而产生的所有损失或费用[包括按照第(3)款借入的金额],则联邦存款保险公司应仅向该计划的参与者征收必要金额的特殊计征费,以解决资金不足问题。联邦存款保险公司可利用该特殊计征费偿付上述损失或费用。

(5)**财政部部长的权力**。——财政部部长可以购买按照第(3)(A)款发行的债务。

obligations issued under paragraph (3)(A). For such purpose, the Secretary may use the proceeds of the sale of any securities issued under chapter 31 of title 31, United States Code, and the purposes for which securities may be issued under that chapter 31 are extended to include such purchases, and the amount of any securities issued under that chapter 31 for such purpose shall be treated in the same manner as securities issued under section 208(n)(5)(E).

(f) RULE OF CONSTRUCTION. — For purposes of this section, a guarantee of deposits held by insured depository institutions shall not be treated as a debt guarantee program.

(g) DEFINITIONS. — For purposes of this section, the following definitions shall apply:

(1) COMPANY. — The term "company" means any entity other than a natural person that is incorporated or organized under Federal law or the laws of any State.

(2) DEPOSITORY INSTITUTION HOLDING COMPANY. — The term "depository institution holding company" has the same meaning as in section 3 of the Federal Deposit Insurance Act (12 U.S.C. 1813).

(3) LIQUIDITY EVENT. — The term "liquidity event" means —

(A) an exceptional and broad reduction in the general ability of financial market participants —

(i) to sell financial assets without an unusual and significant discount; or

(ii) to borrow using financial assets as collateral without an unusual and significant increase in margin; or

(B) an unusual and significant reduction in the ability of financial market participants to obtain unsecured credit.

(4) SOLVENT. — The term "solvent" means that the value of the assets of an entity exceed its obligations to creditors.

SEC. 1106. ADDITIONAL RELATED AMENDMENTS.

(a) SUSPENSION OF PARALLEL FEDERAL DEPOSIT INSURANCE ACT AUTHORITY. — Effective upon the date of enactment of this section, the Corporation may not exercise its authority under section 13(c)(4)(G)(i) of the Federal Deposit Insurance Act(12 U.S.C. 1823(c)(4)(G)(i)) to establish any widely available debt guarantee program for which section 1105 would provide authority.

(b) FEDERAL DEPOSIT INSURANCE ACT. — Section 13(c)(4)(G) of the Federal Deposit Insurance Act (12 U.S.C. 1823(c)(4)(G)) is amended —

(1) in clause (i) —

(A) in subclause (I), by inserting "for which the Corporation has been appointed receiver" before "would have serious"; and

(B) in the undesignated matter following subclause (II), by inserting "for the purpose

为实现该目的,财政部部长可以使用按照《美国法典》第三十一编第三十一章规定发行的证券出售所获资金。兹扩大按照《美国法典》第三十一编第三十一章规定发行证券的目的范围,使之涵盖上述债务购买。为上述目的而按照《美国法典》第三十一编第三十一章规定发行的证券金额,与按照第208(n)(5)(E)条发行的证券金额,应以同等方式处理。

(f)**解释规则**。——就本条而言,参保存款机构持有的存款担保不得视为债务担保计划。

(g)**定义**。——就本条而言,下列术语应适用如下定义:

(1)**公司**。——“公司”一词系指按照联邦法律或任何州法律设立或组建的,除自然人之外的任何实体。

(2)**存款机构控股公司**。——“存款机构控股公司”一词的含义以《联邦存款保险法》第3条[《美国法典》第十二编第1813节]的定义为准。

(3)**流动性事件**。——“流动性事件”一词系指—

(A)金融市场参与者的以下整体能力出现异常、大幅下降——

(i)在无特别大幅折扣的情况下,销售金融资产的能力;或

(ii)在保证金无特别大幅增加的情况下,以金融资产作为担保品进行借款的能力;或

(B)金融市场参与者获取无担保信贷能力出现异常、大幅下降。

(4)**有偿债能力**。——“有偿债能力”一词系指某一实体的资产价值超过其对债权人负担的债务。

第1106条　其他相关修正

(a)**暂停《联邦存款保险法》平行授予的权力**。——自本条规定颁布之日起,对于第1105条将提供授权的任何广泛提供的债务担保计划,联邦存款保险公司不得行使《联邦存款保险法》第13(c)(4)(G)(i)条[《美国法典》第十二编第1823(c)(4)(G)(i)节]授予的权力,制定该等广泛提供的债务担保计划。

(b)**《联邦存款保险法》**。——《联邦存款保险法》第13(c)(4)(G)条[《美国法典》第十二编第1823(c)(4)(G)节]修正如下——

(1)在第(i)项中——

(A)第(I)子项在“参保存款机构”前插入“联邦存款保险公司被指定担任接管人的”;及

(B)第(II)子项之后的无编号内容在“按照本条规定提供援助”之后插入“,以便对

of winding up the insured depository institution for which the Corporation has been appointed receiver" after "provide assistance under this section"; and

(2) in clause (v)(I), by striking "The" and inserting "Not later than 3 days after making a determination under clause (i), the".

(c) EFFECT OF DEFAULT ON AN FDIC GUARANTEE. — If an insured depository institution or depository institution holding company (as those terms are defined in section 3 of the Federal Deposit Insurance Act) participating in a program under section 1105, or any participant in a debt guarantee program established pursuant to section 13(c)(4)(G)(i) of the Federal Deposit Insurance Act defaults on any obligation guaranteed by the Corporation after the date of enactment of this Act, the Corporation shall —

(1) appoint itself as receiver for the insured depository institution that defaults; and

(2) with respect to any other participating company that is not an insured depository institution that defaults —

(A) require —

(i) consideration of whether a determination shall be made, as provided in section 203 to resolve the company under section 202; and

(ii) the company to file a petition for bankruptcy under section 301 of title 11, United States Code, if the Corporation is not appointed receiver pursuant to section 202 within 30 days of the date of default; or

(B) file a petition for involuntary bankruptcy on behalf of the company under section 303 of title 11, United States Code.

SEC. 1107. FEDERAL RESERVE ACT AMENDMENTS ON FEDERAL RESERVE BANK GOVERNANCE.

The 5th subparagraph of the 4th undesignated paragraph of section 4 of the Federal Reserve Act (12 U.S.C. 341) is amended by striking the 2nd sentence and inserting the following: "The president shall be the chief executive officer of the bank and shall be appointed by the Class B and Class C directors of the bank, with the approval of the Board of Governors of the Federal Reserve System, for a term of 5 years; and all other executive officers and all employees of the bank shall be directly responsible to the president.".

SEC. 1108. FEDERAL RESERVE ACT AMENDMENTS ON SUPERVISION AND REGULATION POLICY.

(a) ESTABLISHMENT OF THE POSITION OF VICE CHAIRMAN FOR SUPERVISION. —

(1) POSITION ESTABLISHED. — The second undesignated paragraph of section 10 of the Federal Reserve Act (12 U.S.C. 242)(relating to the Chairman and Vice Chairman of the Board) is amended by striking the third sentence and inserting the following: "Of the persons thus appointed, 1 shall be designated by the President, by and with the advice and consent of

联邦存款保险公司担任指定接管人的参保存款机构进行清盘”;及

(2)第(v)(I)项在句首前插入“在按照(i)项规定作出判定后三天内,”。

(c)**联邦存款保险公司担保的债务发生违约的后果**。——如果在本法颁布之日后,根据第1105条参与某项计划的参保存款机构或存款机构控股公司(定义见《联邦存款保险法》第3条),或任何参与根据《联邦存款保险法》第13(c)(4)(G)(i)条制定的债务担保计划的参与者,对联邦存款保险公司担保的债务构成违约,则,联邦存款保险公司应——

(1)主动担任违约参保存款机构的接管人;并

(2)对于参与计划的并非参保存款机构的任何其他违约公司而言——

(A)要求——

(i)考虑是否应按照第203条规定作出判定,依据第202条解散该公司;及

(ii)该公司按照《美国法典》第十一编第301节的规定提出破产请求(如果联邦存款保险公司未在违约之日后30天内按照第202条的规定被指定为接管人);或

(B)按照《美国法典》第十一编第303节的规定,代表该公司提出强制性破产请求。

第1107条　对《联邦储备法》中与联邦储备银行治理相关规定的修正

《联邦储备法》第4条(《美国法典》第十二编第341节)第4个无编号段落的第五个子段落修正如下:删除第2句,替以如下内容:“行长应担任银行的首席执行官,并在获得联邦储备委员会批准的情况下,由该行的B类和C类董事任命,任期为五年;该行的所有其他高级管理人员和所有雇员均应直接对行长负责。”

第1108条　对《联邦储备法》中与监管与规制政策相关规定的修正

(a)**设置监督副主席一职**。——

(1)**职位设置**。——《联邦储备法》第10条(《美国法典》第十二编第242节)第2个无编号段落(与联邦储备委员会主席和副主席相关的规定)修正如下:删除第3句,替以如下内容:“经参议院建议和同意,总统应从以上述方式任命的人员中指定一人担任联邦储备委员会主席,任期为4年;并且,经参议院建议和同意,总统还应指定其中2

the Senate, to serve as Chairman of the Board for a term of 4 years, and 2 shall be designated by the President, by and with the advice and consent of the Senate, to serve as Vice Chairmen of the Board, each for a term of 4 years, 1 of whom shall serve in the absence of the Chairman, as provided in the fourth undesignated paragraph of this section, and 1 of whom shall be designated Vice Chairman for Supervision. The Vice Chairman for Supervision shall develop policy recommendations for the Board regarding supervision and regulation of depository institution holding companies and other financial firms supervised by the Board, and shall oversee the supervision and regulation of such firms.".

(2) EFFECTIVE DATE. — The amendment made by subsection (a) takes effect on the date of enactment of this title and applies to individuals who are designated by the President on or after that date to serve as Vice Chairman of Supervision.(b) APPEARANCES BEFORE CONGRESS. — Section 10 of the Federal Reserve Act (12 U.S.C. 241 et seq.) is amended by adding at the end the following:

"(12) APPEARANCES BEFORE CONGRESS. — The Vice Chairman for Supervision shall appear before the Committee on Banking, Housing, and Urban Affairs of the Senate and the Committee on Financial Services of the House of Representatives and at semi–annual hearings regarding the efforts, activities, objectives, and plans of the Board with respect to the conduct of supervision and regulation of depository institution holding companies and other financial firms supervised by the Board.".

(c) BOARD RESPONSIBILITY TO SET SUPERVISION AND REGULATORY POLICY. — Section 11 of the Federal Reserve Act (12 U.S.C. 248)(relating to enumerated powers of the Board) is amended by adding at the end of subsection (k)(relating to delegation) the following: "The Board of Governors may not delegate to a Federal reserve bank its functions for the establishment of policies for the supervision and regulation of depository institution holding companies and other financial firms supervised by the Board of Governors.".

(d) EXERCISE OF FEDERAL RESERVE AUTHORITY. —

(1) NO DECISIONS BY FEDERAL RESERVE BANK PRESIDENTS. — No provision of title I relating to the authority of the Board of Governors shall be construed as conferring any decision–making authority on presidents of Federal reserve banks.

(2) VOTING DECISIONS BY BOARD. — The Board of Governors shall not delegate the authority to make any voting decision that the Board of Governors is authorized or required to make under title I of this Act in contravention of section 11(k) of the Federal Reserve Act.

SEC. 1109. GAO AUDIT OF THE FEDERAL RESERVE FACILITIES; PUBLICATION OF BOARD ACTIONS.

(a) GAO AUDIT. —

人担任联邦储备委员会副主席,任期各为4年,其中一名副主席应按照本条第4个无编号段落的规定,在主席职位出现空缺时担任主席,另一名副主席应被指定为监督副主席。对于受联邦储备委员会监管的存款机构控股公司和其他金融公司,监督副主席应向联邦储备委员会提出监管与规制政策建议,并应负责对该等公司的监管与规制工作。”

(2)**生效日**。——根据第(a)子条作出的修正应自本编颁布之日起生效,并适用于总统在该日期(含)之后指定的担任监督副主席的人。(b)**出席国会听证**——在《联邦储备法》第10条(《美国法典》第十二编第241节及其后条文)结尾处增加如下内容,作为对该条的修正:

“(12)**出席国会听证**。——监督副主席应出席参议院银行、住房与城市事务委员会和众议院金融服务委员会的听证,并且,对于针对联邦储备委员会对受其监管的存款机构控股公司和其他金融公司开展的监管与规制工作、活动、目标和计划而举行的半年度听证会,其也应出席。”

(c)**联邦储备委员会制定监管与规制政策的责任**。——《联邦储备法》第11条(《美国法典》第十二编第248节)(明文列举联邦储备委员会权力的相关规定)修正如下:在第(k)子条(与职能委托相关的规定)结尾处增加如下内容:“对于受联邦储备委员会监管的存款机构控股公司和其他金融公司,联邦储备委员会不得将其针对该等公司制定监管与规制政策的职能委托给联邦储备银行行使。”

(d)**联邦储备权力的行使**。——

(1)**联邦储备银行行长不享有决策权**。——第一编与联邦储备委员会权力相关的任何规定均不得被解释为授予联邦储备银行行长任何决策权。

(2)**联邦储备委员会通过投票作出的决定**。——对于本法第一编批准或要求联邦储备委员会通过投票作出的任何决定,联邦储备委员会均不得违反《联邦储备法》第11(k)条的规定,将其作出该等决定的权力委托给任何其他机构。

第1109条　政府问责办公室对联邦储备系统信贷安排的审计;联邦储备委员会行动的公布

(a)**政府问责办公室的审计**。——

(1) IN GENERAL. — Notwithstanding section 714(b) of title 31, United States Code, or any other provision of law, the Comptroller General of the United States (in this subsection referred to as the "Comptroller General") shall conduct a one-time audit of all loans and other financial assistance provided during the period beginning on December 1, 2007 and ending on the date of enactment of this Act by the Board of Governors or a Federal reserve bank under the Asset-Backed Commercial Paper Money Market Mutual Fund Liquidity Facility, the Term Asset-Backed Securities Loan Facility, the Primary Dealer Credit Facility, the Commercial Paper Funding Facility, the Term Securities Lending Facility, the Term Auction Facility, Maiden Lane, Maiden Lane II, Maiden Lane III, the agency Mortgage-Backed Securities program, foreign currency liquidity swap lines, and any other program created as a result of section 13(3) of the Federal Reserve Act (as so designated by this title).

(2) ASSESSMENTS. — In conducting the audit under paragraph (1), the Comptroller General shall assess —

(A) the operational integrity, accounting, financial reporting, and internal controls of the credit facility;

(B) the effectiveness of the security and collateral policies established for the facility in mitigating risk to the relevant Federal reserve bank and taxpayers;

(C) whether the credit facility inappropriately favors one or more specific participants over other institutions eligible to utilize the facility;

(D) the policies governing the use, selection, or payment of third-party contractors by or for any credit facility; and

(E) whether there were conflicts of interest with respect to the manner in which such facility was established or operated.

(3) TIMING. — The audit required by this subsection shall be commenced not later than 30 days after the date of enactment of this Act, and shall be completed not later than 12 months after that date of enactment.

(4) REPORT REQUIRED. — The Comptroller General shall submit a report on the audit conducted under paragraph (1) to the Congress not later than 12 months after the date of enactment of this Act, and such report shall be made available to —

(A) the Speaker of the House of Representatives;

(B) the majority and minority leaders of the House of Representatives;

(C) the majority and minority leaders of the Senate;

(D) the Chairman and Ranking Member of the Committee on Banking, Housing, and Urban Affairs of the Senate and of the Committee on Financial Services of the House of Representatives; and

(E) any member of Congress who requests it.

(1)**一般规定**。——无论《美国法典》第三十一编第714(b)节如何规定,也无论是否存在任何其他法律规定,对于联邦储备委员会或联邦储备银行在2007年12月1日起至本法颁布之日止的期间内,按照资产支持商业票据货币市场共同基金流动性安排、定期资产支持证券贷款安排、一级交易商信贷安排、商业票据融资安排、定期融券安排、定期拍卖安排、Maiden Lane计划、Maiden Lane II计划和Maiden Lane III计划、联邦机关住房抵押贷款支持证券计划、外币流动性互换机制,以及因《联邦储备法》第13(3)条(以本编序号为准)之适用而制定的任何其他计划,提供的所有贷款和其他金融援助,美国政府问责办公室主任(在本条中,简称为政府问责办公室主任)应开展一次性地审计。

(2)**评估**。——按照第(1)款规定开展审计时,政府问责办公室主任应评估——

(A)信贷安排的运作诚信度、会计、财务报告和内部控制机制;

(B)针对信贷安排制定的担保和抵押政策在缓释相关联邦储备银行和纳税人风险方面的有效性;

(C)相对于有资格利用信贷安排的其他机构而言,信贷安排是否不恰当地偏向某一或某些特定参与者;

(D)信贷安排或其代表使用、选择第三方承包商或向其付款的政策;及

(E)该信贷安排的设立方式或运作方式是否存在利益冲突。

(3)**时间**。——本子条规定的审计应于本法颁布之日后30天内启动,并在本法颁布之日后12月内结束。

(4)**报告要求**。——对于按照第(1)款规定开展的审计,政府问责办公室主任应于本法颁布之日后12个月内,向国会提交一份报告。该报告应向下述人员提供——

(A)众议院议长;

(B)众议院的多数党领袖和少数党领袖;

(C)参议院的多数党领袖和少数党领袖;

(D)参议院银行、住房与城市事务委员会和众议院金融服务委员会的主席和副主席;及

(E)索要该报告的任何国会议员。

(b) AUDIT OF FEDERAL RESERVE BANK GOVERNANCE. —

(1) AUDIT. —

(A) IN GENERAL. — Not later than 1 year after the date of enactment of this Act, the Comptroller General shall complete an audit of the governance of the Federal reserve bank system.

(B) REQUIRED EXAMINATIONS. — The audit required under subparagraph (A) shall —

(i) examine the extent to which the current system of appointing Federal reserve bank directors effectively represents "the public, without discrimination on the basis of race, creed, color, sex or national origin, and with due but not exclusive consideration to the interests of agriculture, commerce, industry, services, labor, and consumers" in the selection of bank directors, as such requirement is set forth under section 4 of the Federal Reserve Act;

(ii) examine whether there are actual or potential conflicts of interest created when the directors of Federal reserve banks, which execute the supervisory functions of the Board of Governors of the Federal Reserve System, are elected by member banks;

(iii) examine the establishment and operations of each facility described in subsection (a)(1) and each Federal reserve bank involved in the establishment and operations thereof; and

(iv) identify changes to selection procedures for Federal reserve bank directors, or to other aspects of Federal reserve bank governance, that would —

(I) improve how the public is represented;

(II) eliminate actual or potential conflicts of interest in bank supervision;

(III) increase the availability of information useful for the formation and execution of monetary policy; or

(IV) in other ways increase the effectiveness or efficiency of reserve banks.

(2) REPORT REQUIRED. — A report on the audit conducted under paragraph (1) shall be submitted by the Comptroller General to the Congress before the end of the 90–day period beginning on the date on which such audit is completed, and such report shall be made available to —

(A) the Speaker of the House of Representatives;

(B) the majority and minority leaders of the House of Representatives;

(C) the majority and minority leaders of the Senate;

(D) the Chairman and Ranking Member of the Committee on Banking, Housing, and Urban Affairs of the Senate and of the Committee on Financial Services of the House of Representatives; and

(E) any member of Congress who requests it.

(c) PUBLICATION OF BOARD ACTIONS. — Notwithstanding any other provision of

(b)**对联邦储备银行治理的审计**。——

(1)**审计**。——

(A)**一般规定**。——政府问责办公室主任应于本法颁布之日后一年内,完成对联邦储备银行系统治理的审计。

(B)**检查要求**。——第(A)子款规定的审计应——

(i)检查当前的联邦储备银行董事任命制度在选任银行董事时,按照《联邦储备法》第4条的规定,"不分种族、信仰、肤色、性别或民族,并适当但非排他性地考虑农业、商业、工业、服务业、劳工和消费者利益的情况下,有效代表公众"的程度;

(ii)检查行使联邦储备委员会监管职能的联邦储备银行的董事被成员银行选为董事时,是否存在实际或潜在的利益冲突;

(iii)检查第(a)(1)子条所述每项信贷安排的设立和运作以及其设立和运作中所涉及的每家联邦银行;及

(iv)识别对将产生如下效果的联邦储备银行董事选任程序的变动,或联邦储备银行治理的其他方面发生的变动——

(I)提高代表公众的程度;

(II)消除银行监管中存在的实际或潜在利益冲突;

(III)加强有助于制定和执行货币政策的信息之提供;或

(IV)以其他方式提高联邦储备银行的工作成效或效率。

(2)**报告要求**。——对于按照第(1)款开展的审计,政府问责办公室主任应在审计结束之日后90天内,向国会提交一份报告。该报告应向下述人员提供——

(A)众议院议长;

(B)众议院的多数党领袖和少数党领袖;

(C)参议院的多数党领袖和少数党领袖;

(D)参议院银行、住房与城市事务委员会和众议院金融服务委员会的主席和副主席;及

(E)索要该报告的任何国会议员。

(c)**联邦储备委员会行动的公布**。——无论是否存在任何不同法律规定,联邦储

law, the Board of Governors shall publish on its website, not later than December 1, 2010, with respect to all loans and other financial assistance provided during the period beginning on December 1, 2007 and ending on the date of enactment of this Act under the Asset-Backed Commercial Paper Money Market Mutual Fund Liquidity Facility, the Term Asset-Backed Securities Loan Facility, the Primary Dealer Credit Facility, the Commercial Paper Funding Facility, the Term Securities Lending Facility, the Term Auction Facility, Maiden Lane, Maiden Lane II, Maiden Lane III, the agency Mortgage-Backed Securities program, foreign currency liquidity swap lines, and any other program created as a result of section 13(3) of the Federal Reserve Act (as so designated by this title) —

(1) the identity of each business, individual, entity, or foreign central bank to which the Board of Governors or a Federal reserve bank has provided such assistance;

(2) the type of financial assistance provided to that business, individual, entity, or foreign central bank;

(3) the value or amount of that financial assistance;

(4) the date on which the financial assistance was provided;

(5) the specific terms of any repayment expected, including the repayment time period, interest charges, collateral, limitations on executive compensation or dividends, and other material terms; and

(6) the specific rationale for each such facility or program.

备委员会均应于2010年12月1日之前,针对联邦储备委员会或联邦储备银行在2007年12月1日起至本法颁布之日止的期间内,按照资产支持商业票据货币市场共同基金流动性安排、定期资产支持证券贷款安排、一级交易商信贷安排、商业票据融资安排、定期融券安排、定期拍卖安排、Maiden Lane计划、Maiden Lane II计划和Maiden Lane III计划、联邦机关住房抵押贷款支持证券计划、外币流动性互换机制,以及因《联邦储备法》第13(3)条(以本编序号为准)之适用而制定的任何其他计划,提供的所有贷款和其他金融援助,在其网站上公布如下信息——

(1)接受联邦储备委员会或联邦储备银行援助的每一企业、个人、实体或外国中央银行的身份;

(2)向该企业、个人、实体或外国中央银行提供的金融援助的类型;

(3)该金融援助的价值或金额;

(4)提供该金融援助的日期;

(5)任何预期还款的具体条款,包括还款期间、利息费用、担保品、高管薪酬或股息水平的限制以及其他重大条款;及

(6)每一该等安排或计划的具体理念。

TITLE XII — IMPROVING ACCESS TO MAINSTREAM FINANCIAL INSTITUTIONS

SEC. 1201. SHORT TITLE.

This title may be cited as the "Improving Access to Mainstream Financial Institutions Act of 2010".

SEC. 1202. PURPOSE.

The purpose of this title is to encourage initiatives for financial products and services that are appropriate and accessible for millions of Americans who are not fully incorporated into the financial mainstream.

SEC. 1203. DEFINITIONS.

In this title, the following definitions shall apply:

(1) ACCOUNT. — The term "account" means an agreement between an individual and an eligible entity under which the individual obtains from or through the entity 1 or more banking products and services, and includes a deposit account, a savings account (including a money market savings account), an account for a closed-end loan, and other products or services, as the Secretary deems appropriate.

(2) COMMUNITY DEVELOPMENT FINANCIAL INSTITUTION. — The term "community development financial institution" has the same meaning as in section 103(5) of the Community Development Banking and Financial Institutions Act of 1994 (12 U.S.C. 4702(5)).

(3) ELIGIBLE ENTITY. — The term "eligible entity" means —

(A) an organization described in section 501(c)(3) of the Internal Revenue Code of 1986, and exempt from tax under section 501(a) of such Code;

(B) a federally insured depository institution;

(C) a community development financial institution;

(D) a State, local, or tribal government entity; or

(E) a partnership or other joint venture comprised of 1 or more of the entities described

第十二编——改进主流金融机构可及性

第1201条 简称

引述本编时,可简称为《2010年主流金融机构可及性改进法》。

第1202条 目的

本编旨在鼓励主流金融机构积极开发适宜于尚未完全融入主流金融市场的数以百万计的美国民众,且对于该等民众而言具有可及性的金融产品和服务。

第1203条 定义

就本编而言,下列术语应适用如下定义:

(1)**账户**。——"账户"一词系指个人为了从适格实体处获得或通过其获得一种或一种以上银行产品和服务而与该实体签订的协议,包括存款账户、储蓄账户(包括货币市场储蓄账户)、封闭式贷款账户以及财政部部长认为适当的任何其他产品或服务。

(2)**社区发展金融机构**。——"社区发展金融机构"一词的含义以《1994年社区发展银行与金融机构法》第103(5)条[《美国法典》第十二编第4702(5)节]的定义为准。

(3)**适格实体**。——"适格实体"一词系指——

(A)《1986年国内税收法典》第501(c)(3)条所述,并按照《1986年国内税收法典》第501(a)条获得免税资格的组织;

(B)联邦参保存款机构;

(C)社区发展金融机构;

(D)州、地方或部落政府实体;或

(E)第(A)子款至第(D)子款所述一个或一个以上实体按照财政部部长依据本编

in subparagraphs (A) through (D), in accordance with regulations prescribed by the Secretary under this title.

(4) FEDERALLY INSURED DEPOSITORY INSTITUTION. — The term "federally insured depository institution" means any insured depository institution (as that term is defined in section 3 of the Federal Deposit Insurance Act (12 U.S.C. 1813)) and any insured credit union (as that term is defined in section 101 of the Federal Credit Union Act (12 U.S.C. 1752)).

SEC. 1204. EXPANDED ACCESS TO MAINSTREAM FINANCIAL INSTITUTIONS.

(a) IN GENERAL. — The Secretary is authorized to establish a multiyear program of grants, cooperative agreements, financial agency agreements, and similar contracts or undertakings to promote initiatives designed —

(1) to enable low– and moderate–income individuals to establish one or more accounts in a federally insured depository institution that are appropriate to meet the financial needs of such individuals; and

(2) to improve access to the provision of accounts, on reasonable terms, for low– and moderate–income individuals.

(b) PROGRAM ELIGIBILITY AND ACTIVITIES. —

(1) IN GENERAL. — The Secretary shall restrict participation in any program established under subsection (a) to an eligible entity. Subject to regulations prescribed by the Secretary under this title, 1 or more eligible entities may participate in 1 or several programs established under subsection (a).

(2) ACCOUNT ACTIVITIES. — Subject to regulations prescribed by the Secretary, an eligible entity may, in participating in a program established under subsection (a), offer or provide to low– and moderate–income individuals products and services relating to accounts, including —

(A) small–dollar value loans; and

(B) financial education and counseling relating to conducting transactions in and managing accounts.

SEC. 1205. LOW–COST ALTERNATIVES TO SMALL DOLLAR LOANS.

(a) GRANTS AUTHORIZED. — The Secretary is authorized to establish multiyear demonstration programs by means of grants, cooperative agreements, financial agency agreements, and similar contracts or undertakings, with eligible entities to provide low–cost, small loans to consumers that will provide alternatives to more costly small dollar loans.

(b) TERMS AND CONDITIONS. —

(1) IN GENERAL. — Loans under this section shall be made on terms and conditions, and pursuant to lending practices, that are reasonable for consumers.

规定制定的规章组建的合伙或其他合营企业。

(4)**联邦参保存款机构**。——“联邦参保存款机构”一词系指任何参保存款机构(定义见《联邦存款保险法》第3条(《美国法典》第十二编第1813节)和任何参保信贷联盟[定义见《联邦信贷联盟法》第101条(《美国法典》第十二编第1752节)]。

第1204条　提高主流金融机构的可及性

(a)**一般规定**。——财政部部长有权制定有关补助金、合作协议、金融代理协议和类似合同或承诺的多年期计划,以推动旨在实现如下目的之行动——

(1)使得中低收入个人能够在联邦参保存款机构处开立一个或一个以上的适当账户,以满足其金融需求;及

(2)使中低收入个人能够更容易地以合理的条件获得账户。

(b)**计划参与资格和账户活动**。——

(1)**一般规定**。——财政部部长应将根据第(a)子条制定的计划的参与者限制在适格实体范围之内。在不违反财政部部长按照本编制定的规章的前提下,一个或一个以上适格实体有权参与按照第(a)子条制定的一个或多个计划。

(2)**账户活动**。——在不违反财政部部长制定的规章的前提下,适格实体可以在参与按照第(a)子条设立的计划之时,向中低收入个人要约或提供与账户相关的产品和服务,包括——

(A)小额贷款;及

(B)与在账户中开展交易相关的金融教育和咨询,以及与账户管理相关的金融教育和咨询。

第1205条　小额贷款的低成本替代品

(a)**补助金的核准**。——财政部部长有权通过给予适格主体补助金或与适格实体签订合作协议、金融代理协议和类似合同或承诺的方式,设立多年期示范性计划,向消费者提供低成本小额贷款,使得消费者在高成本小额贷款之外拥有其他选择。

(b)**条款和条件**。——

(1)**一般规定**。——本条规定的贷款应按照对消费者而言合理的条款和条件,并依据对其而言合理的借贷做法,向消费者发放。

(2) FINANCIAL LITERACY AND EDUCATION OPPORTUNITIES. —

(A) IN GENERAL. — Each eligible entity awarded a grant under this section shall promote and take appropriate steps to ensure the provision of financial literacy and education opportunities, such as relevant counseling services, educational courses, or wealth building programs, to each consumer provided with a loan pursuant to this section.

(B) AUTHORITY TO EXPAND ACCESS. — As part of the grants, agreements, and undertakings established under this section, the Secretary may implement reasonable measures or programs designed to expand access to financial literacy and education opportunities, including relevant counseling services, educational courses, or wealth building programs to be provided to individuals who obtain loans from eligible entities under this section.

SEC. 1206. GRANTS TO ESTABLISH LOAN–LOSS RESERVE FUNDS.

The Community Development Banking and Financial Institutions Act of 1994(12 U.S.C. 4701 et seq.) is amended by adding at the end the following:

"SEC. 122. GRANTS TO ESTABLISH LOAN–LOSS RESERVE FUNDS.

"(a) PURPOSES. — The purposes of this section are —

"(1) to make financial assistance available from the Fund in order to help community development financial institutions defray the costs of operating small dollar loan programs, by providing the amounts necessary for such institutions to establish their own loan loss reserve funds to mitigate some of the losses on such small dollar loan programs; and

"(2) to encourage community development financial institutions to establish and maintain small dollar loan programs that would help give consumers access to mainstream financial institutions and combat high cost small dollar lending.

"(b) GRANTS. —

"(1) LOAN–LOSS RESERVE FUND GRANTS. — The Fund shall make grants to community development financial institutions or to any partnership between such community development financial institutions and any other federally insured depository institution with a primary mission to serve targeted investment areas, as such areas are defined under section 103 (16), to enable such institutions or any partnership of such institutions to establish a loan–loss reserve fund in order to defray the costs of a small dollar loan program established or maintained by such institution.

"(2) MATCHING REQUIREMENT. — A community development financial institution or any partnership of institutions established pursuant to paragraph (1) shall provide non–Federal matching funds in an amount equal to 50 percent of the amount of any grant received under this section.

"(3) USE OF FUNDS. — Any grant amounts received by a community development financial institution or any partnership between or among such institutions under paragraph

(2)**金融扫盲和教育机会**。——

(A)**一般规定**。——依据本条规定获得补助金的每一适格实体,均应推广针对按照本条规定获得贷款的消费者提供的金融扫盲和教育机会(例如,相关的咨询服务、教育课程或财富积累计划),并采取适当措施确保该等消费者获得金融扫盲和教育机会。

(B)**拓展消费者获得金融扫盲和教育机会的渠道的权力**。——作为本条规定的补助金、协议和承诺的组成部分,财政部部长可以实施合理的措施或计划,拓展消费者获得金融扫盲和教育机会的渠道,包括向按照本条规定从适格实体处获得贷款的个人提供相关咨询服务、教育课程或财富积累计划。

第1206条　为设立贷款损失准备基金而发放的补助金

在《1994年社区发展银行与金融机构法》(《美国法典》第十二编第4701节及其后条文)结尾处增加如下内容,作为对该法的修正:

"第122条　为设立贷款损失准备基金而发放的补助金

(a)**目的**。——本条旨在——

(1)由贷款损失准备基金提供金融援助,以便通过向社区发展金融机构提供设立自身的贷款损失准备基金的必要资金,帮助该等机构支付小额贷款计划的运作成本,进而减轻该等小额贷款计划的某些损失;及

(2)鼓励社区发展金融机构设立并维持小额贷款计划,帮助消费者获得主流金融机构的服务并抵制高成本小额贷款。

(b)**补助金**。——

(1)**贷款损失准备基金补助金**。——对于社区发展金融机构,或者社区发展金融机构与任何其他联邦参保存款机构设立的主要目的在于向目标投资领域[定义见第103(16)条]提供服务的合伙,贷款损失准备基金应向该等机构或合伙提供补助金,以便其设立贷款损失准备基金,以便支付该等机构制定或维持的小额贷款计划的成本。

(2)**对等资金要求**。——社区发展金融机构或按照第(1)款设立的任何机构的合伙在按照本条规定获得任何补助金之时,均应按该补助金金额的50%提供非联邦对等资金。

(3)**资金的使用**。——一家社区发展金融机构或多个该等机构按照第(1)款规定共同设立的一家合伙所获得的补助金——

(1)—

"(A) may not be used by such institution to provide direct loans to consumers;

"(B) may be used by such institution to help recapture a portion or all of a defaulted loan made under the small dollar loan program of such institution; and

"(C) may be used to designate and utilize a fiscal agent for services normally provided by such an agent.

"(4) TECHNICAL ASSISTANCE GRANTS. — The Fund shall make technical assistance grants to community development financial institutions or any partnership between or among such institutions to support and maintain a small dollar loan program. Any grant amounts received under this paragraph may be used for technology, staff support, and other costs associated with establishing a small dollar loan program.

"(c) DEFINITIONS. — For purposes of this section —

"(1) the term 'consumer reporting agency that compiles and maintains files on consumers on a nationwide basis' has the same meaning given such term in section 603(p) of the Fair Credit Reporting Act (15 U.S.C. 1681a(p)); and

"(2) the term 'small dollar loan program' means a loan program wherein a community development financial institution or any partnership between or among such institutions offers loans to consumers that —

"(A) are made in amounts not exceeding $2,500;

"(B) must be repaid in installments;

"(C) have no pre–payment penalty;

"(D) the institution has to report payments regarding the loan to at least 1 of the consumer reporting agencies that compiles and maintains files on consumers on a nationwide basis; and

"(E) meet any other affordability requirements as may be established by the Administrator.".

SEC. 1207. PROCEDURAL PROVISIONS.

An eligible entity desiring to participate in a program or obtain a grant under this title shall submit an application to the Secretary, in such form and containing such information as the Secretary may require.

SEC. 1208. AUTHORIZATION OF APPROPRIATIONS.

(a) AUTHORIZATION TO THE SECRETARY. — There are authorized to be appropriated to the Secretary, such sums as are necessary to both administer and fund the programs and projects authorized by this title, to remain available until expended.

(b) AUTHORIZATION TO THE FUND. — There is authorized to be appropriated to the Fund for each fiscal year beginning in fiscal year 2010, an amount equal to the amount of the administrative costs of the Fund for the operation of the grant program established under

(A)不得被该等机构用于直接向消费者提供贷款;

(B)可以被该等机构用于帮助收回该机构按照小额贷款计划发放的全部或部分违约贷款;且

(C)可以用于指定财务代理人以及使用通常由财务代理人提供的服务。

(4)**技术援助补助金**。——贷款损失准备基金应向社区发展金融机构或多个该等机构共同设立的任何合伙提供技术援助补助金,以支持和维持小额贷款计划。按照本款规定获得的任何补助金,均可用于与制定小额贷款计划相关的技术和人员支持,以及用于支付其他相关费用。

(c)**定义**。——就本条而言——

(1)'编制和保存全国消费者档案的消费者征信机构'一词的含义以《公平信用报告法》第603(p)条[《美国法典》第十五编第1681a(p)节]的定义为准;且

(2)'小额贷款计划'一词系指社区发展金融机构或多个该等机构共同设立的任何合伙向消费者提供的具有如下特征的贷款计划——

(A)贷款金额不超过2500美元;

(B)贷款必须分期偿付;

(C)不含提前还款违约金规定;

(D)对于贷款的还款情况,金融机构至少应向一家编制和保存全国消费者档案的消费者征信机构报告;且

(E)贷款满足基金管理人可能制定的其他可负担性要求。"

第1207条　程序性规定

希望参加本编规定的计划或获得本编规定的补助金的适格实体,应按照财政部部长规定的格式和内容要求,向财政部部长提交申请。

第1208条　拨款授权

(a)**授权向财政部部长拨款**。——兹授权向财政部部长拨付必要款项,用于管理和资助本编授权的计划和项目,且该等款项应随时处于可支用状态,不得另作他用。

(b)**授权向贷款损失准备基金拨款**。——兹授权自2010财政年度起,在每一财政年度,按照贷款损失准备基金因运作依本编规定设立的补助金计划而产生的行政费用金额,向该基金拨付该笔金额。

this title.

SEC. 1209. REGULATIONS.

(a) IN GENERAL. — The Secretary is authorized to promulgate regulations to implement and administer the grant programs and undertakings authorized by this title.

(b) REGULATORY AUTHORITY. — Regulations prescribed under this section may contain such classifications, differentiations, or other provisions, and may provide for such adjustments and exceptions for any class of grant programs, undertakings, or eligible entities, as, in the judgment of the Secretary, are necessary or proper to effectuate the purposes of this title, to prevent circumvention or evasion of this title, or to facilitate compliance with this title.

SEC. 1210. EVALUATION AND REPORTS TO CONGRESS.

For each fiscal year in which a program or project is carried out under this title, the Secretary shall submit a report to the Committee on Banking, Housing, and Urban Affairs of the Senate and the Committee on Financial Services of the House of Representatives containing a description of the activities funded, amounts distributed, and measurable results, as appropriate and available.

第1209条　规章

(a)**一般规定**。——财政部部长有权颁发旨在实施和管理本编授权的补助金计划和承诺的规章。

(b)**监管权**。——财政部部长在按照本条制定规章时,可以为了实现本编之宗旨、防范规避或逃避本编规定的行为或者为促进对本编规定的合规,而订立其认为必要或适当的分类、区分性规定或其他规定,并可以针对任何类别的补助金计划、承诺或适格实体作出财政部部长认为必要或宜应作出的调整和例外规定。

第1210条　评价和向国会报告

在按照本编规定实施相关计划或项目的每一个财政年度,财政部部长均应向参议院银行、住房与城市事务委员会和众议院金融服务委员会提交一份报告,在其可以获得的相关信息范围内,针对受资助活动、已分发的金额和相关量化结果提供适当说明。

TITLE XIII — PAY IT BACK ACT

SEC. 1301. SHORT TITLE.

This title may be cited as the "Pay It Back Act".

SEC. 1302. AMENDMENT TO REDUCE TARP AUTHORIZATION.

Section 115(a) of the Emergency Economic Stabilization Act of 2008 (12 U.S.C. 5225(a)) is amended —

(1) in paragraph (3) —

(A) by striking ", $700,000,000,000, as such amount is reduced by $1,259,000,000, as such amount is reduced by $1,244,000,000" and inserting "$475,000,000,000"; and

(B) by striking "outstanding at any one time"; and

(2) by adding at the end the following:

"(4) For purposes of this subsection, the amount of authority considered to be exercised by the Secretary shall not be reduced by —

"(A) any amounts received by the Secretary before, on, or after the date of enactment of the Pay It Back Act from repayment of the principal of financial assistance by an entity that has received financial assistance under the TARP or any other program enacted by the Secretary under the authorities granted to the Secretary under this Act;

"(B) any amounts committed for any guarantees pursuant to the TARP that became or become uncommitted; or

"(C) any losses realized by the Secretary.

"(5) No authority under this Act may be used to incur any obligation for a program or initiative that was not initiated prior to June 25, 2010.".

SEC. 1303. REPORT.

Section 106 of the Emergency Economic Stabilization Act of 2008 (12 U.S.C. 5216) is amended by inserting at the end the following:

"(f) REPORT. — The Secretary of the Treasury shall report to Congress every 6 months on amounts received and transferred to the general fund under subsection (d).".

第十三编——《还款法》

第1301条　简称

引述本编时,可简称为《还款法》。

第1302条　降低不良资产救助计划授权金额的修正

《2008年紧急经济稳定法》第115(a)条[《美国法典》第十二编第5225(a)节]修正如下——

(1)在第(3)款中——

(A)删除",7000亿美元,减去12.59亿美元,再减去12.44亿美元",替以"4750亿美元";及

(B)删除"每次购买问题资产的权力应限于未清偿的";及

(2)在结尾处增加如下内容:

"(4)就本子条而言,被视为应由财政部部长行使权力购买问题资产的金额不得扣减如下金额——

(A)财政部部长在《还款法》颁布日之前以及颁布日(含)之后收到的任何如下还款,即由于按照财政部部长根据《2008年紧急经济稳定法》的授权设立的不良资产救助计划或任何其他计划而获得资金援助的任何实体,所偿还的援助资金本金;

(B)最初按照不良资产救助计划被指定用于提供担保,但随后被取消指定用途限制的资金金额;或

(C)财政部部长遭受的任何已实现损失。

(5)不得为了2010年6月25日之前尚未启动的计划或行动,而动用本法授予的任何权力产生任何债务。"

第1303条　报告

在《2008年紧急经济稳定法》第106条(《美国法典》第十二编第5216节)结尾处插入如下内容,作为对该条的修正:

"(f)**报告**。——财政部部长应每6个月向国会提交一份报告,说明其按照第(d)子条规定收到并转入普通基金的资金数额。"

SEC. 1304. AMENDMENTS TO HOUSING AND ECONOMIC RECOVERY ACT OF 2008.

(a) SALE OF FANNIE MAE OBLIGATIONS AND SECURITIES BY THE TREASURY; DEFICIT REDUCTION. — Section 304(g)(2) of the Federal National Mortgage Association Charter Act (12 U.S.C. 1719(g)(2)) is amended —

(1) by redesignating subparagraph (C) as subparagraph (D); and

(2) by inserting after subparagraph (B) the following:

"(C) DEFICIT REDUCTION. — The Secretary of the Treasury shall deposit in the General Fund of the Treasury any amounts received by the Secretary from the sale of any obligation acquired by the Secretary under this subsection, where such amounts shall be —

"(i) dedicated for the sole purpose of deficit reduction; and

"(ii) prohibited from use as an offset for other spending increases or revenue reductions.".

(b) SALE OF FREDDIE MAC OBLIGATIONS AND SECURITIES BY THE TREASURY; DEFICIT REDUCTION. — Section 306(l)(2) of the Federal Home Loan Mortgage Corporation Act (12 U.S.C. 1455(l)(2)) is amended —

(1) by redesignating subparagraph (C) as subparagraph (D); and

(2) by inserting after subparagraph (B) the following:

"(C) DEFICIT REDUCTION. — The Secretary of the Treasury shall deposit in the General Fund of the Treasury any amounts received by the Secretary from the sale of any obligation acquired by the Secretary under this subsection, where such amounts shall be —

"(i) dedicated for the sole purpose of deficit reduction; and

"(ii) prohibited from use as an offset for other spending increases or revenue reductions.".

(c) SALE OF FEDERAL HOME LOAN BANKS OBLIGATIONS BY THE TREASURY; DEFICIT REDUCTION. — Section 11(l)(2) of the Federal Home Loan Bank Act (12 U.S.C. 1431(l)(2)) is amended —

(1) by redesignating subparagraph (C) as subparagraph (D); and

(2) by inserting after subparagraph (B) the following:

"(C) DEFICIT REDUCTION. — The Secretary of the Treasury shall deposit in the General Fund of the Treasury any amounts received by the Secretary from the sale of any obligation acquired by the Secretary under this subsection, where such amounts shall be —

"(i) dedicated for the sole purpose of deficit reduction; and

"(ii) prohibited from use as an offset for other spending increases or revenue reductions.".

(d) REPAYMENT OF FEES. — Any periodic commitment fee or any other fee or assessment paid by the Federal National Mortgage Association or Federal Home Loan

第1304条　对《2008年住房和经济复苏法》的修正

(a)**财政部对房利美债务和证券的出售;赤字削减**。——《联邦国民抵押贷款协会章程法》第304(g)(2)条[《美国法典》第十二编第1719(g)(2)节]修正如下——

(1)第(C)子款重新编号为第(D)子款;及
(2)在第(B)子款之后插入如下内容:
"(C)**赤字削减**。——财政部部长因按照本子条规定出售其获得的任何债务而收到的任何款项,均应存入财政部普通基金,此时,该等款项应——

(i)专门用于削减赤字之唯一目的;且
(ii)禁止用于抵销其他支出增加或收入减少。"

(b)**财政部对房地美债务和证券的出售;赤字削减**。——《联邦住房贷款抵押公司法》第306(l)(2)条[《美国法典》第十二编第1455(l)(2)节]修正如下——

(1)第(C)子款重新编号为第(D)子款;及
(2)在第(B)子款之后插入如下内容:
"(C)**赤字削减**。——财政部部长因按照本子条规定出售其获得的任何债务而收到的任何款项,均应存入财政部普通基金,且该等款项应——

(i)专门用于削减赤字之唯一目的;且
(ii)禁止用于抵销其他支出增加或收入减少。"

(c)**财政部对联邦住房贷款银行债务的出售;赤字削减**。——《联邦住房贷款银行法》第11(l)(2)条[《美国法典》第十二编第1431(l)(2)节]修正如下——

(1)第(C)子款重新编号为第(D)子款;及
(2)在第(B)子款之后插入如下内容:
"(C)**赤字削减**。——财政部部长因按照本子条规定出售其获得的任何债务而收到的任何款项,均应存入财政部普通基金,且该等款项应——

(i)专门用于削减赤字之唯一目的;且
(ii)禁止用于抵销其他支出增加或收入减少。"

(d)**费用偿还**。——联邦国民抵押贷款协会或联邦住房贷款抵押公司,因优先股购买协议、住房抵押贷款支持证券购买计划或根据《2008年住房和经济复苏法》第

Mortgage Corporation to the Secretary of the Treasury as a result of any preferred stock purchase agreement, mortgage–backed security purchase program, or any other program or activity authorized or carried out pursuant to the authorities granted to the Secretary of the Treasury under section 1117 of the Housing and Economic Recovery Act of 2008 (Public Law 110–289; 122 Stat. 2683), including any fee agreed to by contract between the Secretary and the Association or Corporation, shall be deposited in the General Fund of the Treasury where such amounts shall be —

(1) dedicated for the sole purpose of deficit reduction; and

(2) prohibited from use as an offset for other spending increases or revenue reductions.

SEC. 1305. FEDERAL HOUSING FINANCE AGENCY REPORT.

The Director of the Federal Housing Finance Agency shall submit to Congress a report on the plans of the Agency to continue to support and maintain the Nation's vital housing industry, while at the same time guaranteeing that the American taxpayer will not suffer unnecessary losses.

SEC. 1306. REPAYMENT OF UNOBLIGATED ARRA FUNDS.

(a) REJECTION OF ARRA FUNDS BY STATE. — Section 1607 of the American Recovery and Reinvestment Act of 2009 (Public Law 111–5; 123 Stat. 305) is amended by adding at the end the following:

"(d) STATEWIDE REJECTION OF FUNDS. — If funds provided to any State in any division of this Act are not accepted for use by the Governor of the State pursuant to subsection (a) or by the State legislature pursuant to subsection (b), then all such funds shall be —

"(1) rescinded; and

"(2) deposited in the General Fund of the Treasury where such amounts shall be —

"(A) dedicated for the sole purpose of deficit reduction; and

"(B) prohibited from use as an offset for other spending increases or revenue reductions.".

(b) WITHDRAWAL OR RECAPTURE OF UNOBLIGATED FUNDS. — Title XVI of the American Recovery and Reinvestment Act of 2009 (Public Law 111–5; 123 Stat. 302) is amended by adding at the end the following:

"SEC. 1613. WITHDRAWAL OR RECAPTURE OF UNOBLIGATED FUNDS.

"Notwithstanding any other provision of this Act, if the head of any executive agency withdraws or recaptures for any reason funds appropriated or otherwise made available under this division, and such funds have not been obligated by a State to a local government or for a specific project, such recaptured funds shall be —

"(1) rescinded; and

"(2) deposited in the General Fund of the Treasury where such amounts shall be —

1117条(第110—289号公法;《美国制定法汇编》第122卷第2683页)向财政部部长授予的权力而授权或实施的其他计划或活动,而向财政部部长支付的任何定期承诺费、任何其他费用或计征费(包括财政部部长与该协会或该公司在合同中约定的任何费用在内)均应存入财政部普通基金,并且该等款项应——

(1)专门用于削减赤字之唯一目的;且

(2)禁止用于抵销其他支出增加或收入减少。

第1305条 联邦住房金融局的报告

联邦住房金融局局长应向国会提交一份关于联邦住房金融局继续支持和维持美国关键性住宅产业的各项计划,与此同时还应保证美国纳税人免遭不必要损失。

第1306条 《美国复苏与再投资法》中未指定用途资金的偿还

(a)**州拒绝接受《美国复苏与再投资法》资金的情形**。——在《2009年美国复苏与再投资法》第1607条(第111—5号公法;《美国制定法汇编》第123卷第305页)结尾处增加如下内容,作为对该条的修正:

"(d)**在全州范围内拒绝接受资金**。——针对按照《2009年美国复苏与再投资法》任何一卷的规定向任何州提供的资金,如果该州州长按照第(a)子条规定或该州立法机关按照(b)子条规定拒绝使用,则该等资金应全部——

(1)予以撤销;并

(2)存入财政部的普通基金,并且该等款项应——

(A)专门用于削减赤字之唯一目的;且

(B)禁止用于抵销其他支出增加或收入减少。"

(b)**未指定用途资金的撤回或收回**。——在《2009年美国复苏与再投资法》第十六编(第111—5号公法;《美国制定法汇编》第123卷第302页)结尾处增加如下内容,作为对该编的修正:

"第1613条 未指定用途资金的撤回或收回

无论《2009年美国复苏与再投资法》是否存在任何不同规定,如果任何行政机关的负责人出于任何原因,撤回或收回按照本卷规定拨付的或以其他方式提供的资金,且相关州尚未指定该等资金的用途,即未将其用于地方政府或具体项目,则该等收回的资金应——

(1)予以撤销;并

(2)存入财政部的普通基金,并且该等款项应——

"(A) dedicated for the sole purpose of deficit reduction; and

"(B) prohibited from use as an offset for other spending increases or revenue reductions.".

(c) RETURN OF UNOBLIGATED FUNDS BY END OF 2012. — Section 1603 of the American Recovery and Reinvestment Act of 2009 (Public Law 111–5; 123 Stat. 302) is amended by —

(1) striking "All funds" and inserting "(a) IN GENERAL. — All funds"; and

(2) adding at the end the following:

"(b) REPAYMENT OF UNOBLIGATED FUNDS. — Any discretionary appropriations made available in this division that have not been obligated as of December 31, 2012, are hereby rescinded, and such amounts shall be deposited in the General Fund of the Treasury where such amounts shall be —

"(1) dedicated for the sole purpose of deficit reduction; and

"(2) prohibited from use as an offset for other spending increases or revenue reductions.

"(c) PRESIDENTIAL WAIVER AUTHORITY. —

"(1) IN GENERAL. — The President may waive the requirements under subsection (b), if the President determines that it is not in the best interest of the Nation to rescind a specific unobligated amount after December 31, 2012.

"(2) REQUESTS. — The head of an executive agency may also apply to the President for a waiver from the requirements under subsection (b).".

(A)专门用于削减赤字之唯一目的;且

(B)禁止用于抵销其他支出增加或收入减少。”

(c)**截至2012年年底尚未指定用途的资金之退还**。——《2009年美国复苏与再投资法》第1603条(第111—5号公法;《美国制定法汇编》第123卷第302页)修正如下——

(1)删除“所有资金”,替以“(a)**一般规定**。——所有资金”;及

(2)在结尾处增加如下内容:

(b)**未指定用途资金的偿还**。——按照本卷规定提供但截至2012年12月31日尚未指定用途的任何自主拨款均应予以撤销，并存入财政部普通基金，并且该等款项应——

(1)专门用于削减赤字之唯一目的;且

(2)禁止用于抵销其他支出增加或收入减少。

(c)**总统的免除权**。——

(1)**一般规定**。——如果总统判定,在2012年12月31日以后撤销某一特定的未指定用途资金并不符合美国的最佳利益,则总统可以免除第(b)子条规定之适用。

(2)**请求**。——行政机关负责人亦可以请求总统免除第(b)子条规定之适用。”

TITLE XIV—MORTGAGE REFORM AND ANTI–PREDATORY LENDING ACT

SEC. 1400. SHORT TITLE; DESIGNATION AS ENUMERATED CONSUMER LAW.

(a) SHORT TITLE. —This title may be cited as the "Mortgage Reform and Anti–Predatory Lending Act".

(b) DESIGNATION AS ENUMERATED CONSUMER LAW UNDER THE PURVIEW OF THE BUREAU OF CONSUMER FINANCIAL PROTECTION. — Subtitles A, B, C, and E and sections 1471, 1472, 1475, and 1476, and the amendments made by such subtitles and sections, shall be enumerated consumer laws, as defined in section 1002, and come under the purview of the Bureau of Consumer Financial Protection for purposes of title X, including the transfer of functions and personnel under subtitle F of title X and the savings provisions of such subtitle.

(c) REGULATIONS; EFFECTIVE DATE. —

(1) REGULATIONS. —The regulations required to be prescribed under this title or the amendments made by this title shall—

(A) be prescribed in final form before the end of the 18–month period beginning on the designated transfer date; and

(B) take effect not later than 12 months after the date of issuance of the regulations in final form.

(2) EFFECTIVE DATE ESTABLISHED BY RULE. —Except as provided in paragraph (3), a section, or provision thereof, of this title shall take effect on the date on which the final regulations implementing such section, or provision, take effect.

(3) EFFECTIVE DATE. —A section of this title for which regulations have not been issued on the date that is 18 months after the designated transfer date shall take effect on such date.

第十四编——《抵押贷款改革和反掠夺性借贷法》

第1400条　简称;明文列举的消费者权益保护法律之指定

(a)**简称**。——引述本编时,可简称为《抵押贷款改革和反掠夺性借贷法》。

(b)**纳入消费者金融保护局的执法权之内的明文列举的消费者权益保护法律之指定**。——第A子编、第B子编、第C子编、第E子编、第1471条、第1472条、第1475条和第1476条,以及依据该等子编和条款作出的修正,均应属于第1002条定义的明文列举的消费者权益保护法律,并且就第十编而言,应纳入消费者金融保护局的执法权之内,包括按照第十编第F子编和该子编的保留条款应予开展的职能和人员转移。

(c)**规章;生效日**。——
(1)**规章**。——本编或本编所做修正要求制定的规章应——

(A)在指定转移日起18个月内,制定最终版本;及

(B)在规章最终版本颁布之日后12个月内生效。

(2)**通过规则确立生效日**。——除第(3)款规定的情形外,本编的条款或规定应于该等条款或规定的最终实施规章生效之日生效。

(3) **生效日**。——在指定转移日后届满18个月之日尚未颁布实施规章的本编条款,应于指定转移日届满18个月之日生效。

Subtitle A—Residential Mortgage Loan Origination Standards

SEC. 1401. DEFINITIONS.

Section 103 of the Truth in Lending Act (15 U. S. C. 1602) is amended by adding at the end the following new subsection:

"(cc) DEFINITIONS RELATING TO MORTGAGE ORIGINATION AND RESIDENTIAL MORTGAGE LOANS.—

"(1) COMMISSION.—Unless otherwise specified, the term 'Commission' means the Federal Trade Commission.

"(2) MORTGAGE ORIGINATOR.—The term 'mortgage originator'—

"(A) means any person who, for direct or indirect compensation or gain, or in the expectation of direct or indirect compensation or gain—

"(i) takes a residential mortgage loan application;

"(ii) assists a consumer in obtaining or applying to obtain a residential mortgage loan; or

"(iii) offers or negotiates terms of a residential mortgage loan;

"(B) includes any person who represents to the public, through advertising or other means of communicating or providing information (including the use of business cards, stationery, brochures, signs, rate lists, or other promotional items), that such person can or will provide any of the services or perform any of the activities described in subparagraph (A);

"(C) does not include any person who is (i) not otherwise described in subparagraph (A) or (B) and who performs purely administrative or clerical tasks on behalf of a person who is described in any such subparagraph, or (ii) an employee of a retailer of manufactured homes who is not described in clause (i) or (iii) of subparagraph (A) and who does not advise a consumer on loan terms (including rates, fees, and other costs);

"(D) does not include a person or entity that only performs real estate brokerage activities and is licensed or registered in accordance with applicable State law, unless such person or entity is compensated by a lender, a mortgage broker, or other mortgage originator or by any agent of such lender, mortgage broker, or other mortgage originator;

"(E) does not include, with respect to a residential mortgage loan, a person, estate, or trust that provides mortgage financing for the sale of 3 properties in any 12-month period to purchasers of such properties, each of which is owned by such person, estate, or trust and

第A子编——住房抵押贷款发起标准

第1401条　定义

在《诚实信贷法》第103条(《美国法典》第十五编第1602节)结尾处增加如下新子条,作为对该条的修正:

"(cc)**抵押贷款发起和住房抵押贷款相关术语的定义**。——

(1)**联邦贸易委员会**。——除非另有明确规定,否则'联邦贸易委员会'一词系指美国的联邦贸易委员会。

(2)**抵押贷款发起人**。——'抵押贷款发起人'一词——

(A)系指为了直接或间接获得报酬或收益,或者期望直接或间接获得报酬或收益,而从事如下任一事项的主体——

(i)接受住房抵押贷款申请;

(ii)协助消费者获取或申请住房抵押贷款;或

(iii)对住房抵押贷款进行要约或对住房抵押贷款的条款进行谈判;

(B)包括任何如下所述之人,即通过广告或其他信息传播或提供手段(包括使用商务名片、文具、宣传册、标牌、价目表或其他宣传品)向公众表示其能够或将会提供第(A)子款所述任何服务或开展该子款所述任何活动的人;

(C)不包括任何如下所述之人:(i)未在第(A)子款或第(B)子款中列出,而仅代表该等子款规定之人开展纯粹的行政或文员工作的人,或(ii)未在第(A)子款第(i)项或第(iii)项中列出,且不针对贷款条款(包括费率、手续费和其他费用)向消费者提供咨询的预制房屋零售商的雇员;

(D)不包括已按照适用的州法律注册或持有执照的,仅开展房地产经纪业务的人或实体,但该人或实体接受贷款人、住房抵押贷款经纪商、其他住房抵押贷款发起人或者上述各者的任何代理人提供的报酬的除外;

(E)不包括下列人、遗产和破产财团或信托:该人、遗产和破产财团或信托在任何12个月的期间内为了3幢房地产的出售而向该等房地产的购买人提供住房抵押贷款融资,并且每处该等房地产均为该人、遗产和破产财团或信托所有,作为贷款的担保,

serves as security for the loan, provided that such loan —

"(i) is not made by a person, estate, or trust that has constructed, or acted as a contractor for the construction of, a residence on the property in the ordinary course of business of such person, estate, or trust;

"(ii) is fully amortizing;

"(iii) is with respect to a sale for which the seller determines in good faith and documents that the buyer has a reasonable ability to repay the loan;

"(iv) has a fixed rate or an adjustable rate that is adjustable after 5 or more years, subject to reasonable annual and lifetime limitations on interest rate increases; and

"(v) meets any other criteria the Board may prescribe;

"(F) does not include the creditor (except the creditor in a table-funded transaction) under paragraph (1), (2), or (4) of section 129B(c); and

"(G) does not include a servicer or servicer employees, agents and contractors, including but not limited to those who offer or negotiate terms of a residential mortgage loan for purposes of renegotiating, modifying, replacing and subordinating principal of existing mortgages where borrowers are behind in their payments, in default or have a reasonable likelihood of being in default or falling behind.

"(3) NATIONWIDE MORTGAGE LICENSING SYSTEM AND REGISTRY. — The term 'Nationwide Mortgage Licensing System and Registry' has the same meaning as in the Secure and Fair Enforcement for Mortgage Licensing Act of 2008.

"(4) OTHER DEFINITIONS RELATING TO MORTGAGE ORIGINATOR. — For purposes of this subsection, a person 'assists a consumer in obtaining or applying to obtain a residential mortgage loan' by, among other things, advising on residential mortgage loan terms (including rates, fees, and other costs), preparing residential mortgage loan packages, or collecting information on behalf of the consumer with regard to a residential mortgage loan.

"(5) RESIDENTIAL MORTGAGE LOAN. — The term 'residential mortgage loan' means any consumer credit transaction that is secured by a mortgage, deed of trust, or other equivalent consensual security interest on a dwelling or on residential real property that includes a dwelling, other than a consumer credit transaction under an open end credit plan or, for purposes of sections 129B and 129C and section 128(a)(16), (17), (18), and (19), and sections 128(f) and 130(k), and any regulations promulgated thereunder, an extension of credit relating to a plan described in section 101(53D) of title 11, United States Code.

"(6) SECRETARY. — The term 'Secretary', when used in connection with any transaction or person involved with a residential mortgage loan, means the Secretary of Housing and Urban Development.

"(7) SERVICER. — The term 'servicer' has the same meaning as in section 6(i)(2) of the Real Estate Settlement Procedures Act of 1974 (12 U. S. C. 2605(i)(2)).".

前提是该住房抵押贷款满足下列条件——

(i)该贷款的发放人并非在正常业务运作中在该等房地产上建造了住房或以该等住房的建造承包身份行事的人、遗产和破产财团或信托;

(ii)该贷款属于全额摊还贷款;

"(iii)在与该贷款相关的房地产销售中,出售人善意判定并通过文件证明购买人拥有合理的贷款偿还能力;

(iv)该贷款适用固定利率,或适用仅能在五年或更多年以后调整的可调利率,且该可调利率不得违反合理的年度利率上调限制和贷款期间内的利率上调限制;及

(v)该贷款满足联邦储备委员会规定的任何其他标准;

(F)不包括第129B(c)条第(1)款、第(2)款或第(4)款规定的贷款发放人(但在发起贷款并转让贷款权益的交易中的贷款发放人除外);且

(G)不包括服务机构或服务机构的雇员、代理人和承包商(包括但不限于:在既存的抵押贷款的借款人逾期还款、拖欠还款或存在拖欠还款或逾期还款的合理可能性的情况下,为了就该等既存贷款的本金重新谈判或修改、重定和降低本金,而就住房抵押贷款进行要约或对住房抵押贷款的条款进行谈判的服务机构或其雇员、代理人和承包商)。

(3)**全国性抵押贷款发起人许可系统和注册名册**。——'全国性抵押贷款发起人许可系统和注册名册'一词的含义以《2008年安全和公平执行抵押贷款发起人许可法》的定义为准。

(4)**与住房抵押贷款发起人相关的其他术语之定义**。——就本子条而言,抵押贷款发起人'协助消费者获取或申请住房抵押贷款'的方式,包括针对住房抵押贷款条款(包括费率、手续费和其他费用)提供咨询、制定住房抵押贷款方案、代表消费者收集住房抵押贷款相关信息等。

(5)**住房抵押贷款**。——'住房抵押贷款'一词系指以抵押物、信托契约为担保的消费者信用交易,或以住所或包括住所在内的住宅房地产的其他同等合意担保权益为担保的消费者信用交易,但不包括依开放式信用计划开展的消费者信用交易以及129B条、第129C条、第128(a)(16)条、第128(a)(17)条、第128(a)(18)条、第128(a)(19)条、第128(f)条和第130(k)条以及依据上述条款颁发的任何规章意义上的消费者信用交易,也不包括与《美国法典》第十一编第101(53D)节所述计划相关的授信。

(6)**部长**。——'部长'一词,在针对住房抵押贷款所涉交易或主体使用时,系指住房与城市发展部部长。

(7)**服务机构**。——'服务机构'一词的含义以《1974年房地产结算程序法》第6(i)(2)条(《美国法典》第十二编第2605(i)(2)节)的定义为准。"

SEC. 1402. RESIDENTIAL MORTGAGE LOAN ORIGINATION.

(a) IN GENERAL. —Chapter 2 of the Truth in Lending Act (15 U. S. C. 1631 et seq.) is amended —

(1) by redesignating the 2nd of the 2 sections designated as section 129 (15 U. S. C. 1639a)(relating to duty of servicers of residential mortgages) as section 129A; and

(2) by inserting after section 129A (as so redesignated) the following new section:

" § 129B. Residential mortgage loan origination

"(a) FINDING AND PURPOSE. —

"(1) FINDING. — The Congress finds that economic stabilization would be enhanced by the protection, limitation, and regulation of the terms of residential mortgage credit and the practices related to such credit, while ensuring that responsible, affordable mortgage credit remains available to consumers.

"(2) PURPOSE. — It is the purpose of this section and section 129C to assure that consumers are offered and receive residential mortgage loans on terms that reasonably reflect their ability to repay the loans and that are understandable and not unfair, deceptive or abusive.

"(b) DUTY OF CARE. —

"(1) STANDARD. — Subject to regulations prescribed under this subsection, each mortgage originator shall, in addition to the duties imposed by otherwise applicable provisions of State or Federal law —

"(A) be qualified and, when required, registered and licensed as a mortgage originator in accordance with applicable State or Federal law, including the Secure and Fair Enforcement for Mortgage Licensing Act of 2008; and

"(B) include on all loan documents any unique identifier of the mortgage originator provided by the Nationwide Mortgage Licensing System and Registry.

"(2) COMPLIANCE PROCEDURES REQUIRED. — The Board shall prescribe regulations requiring depository institutions to establish and maintain procedures reasonably designed to assure and monitor the compliance of such depository institutions, the subsidiaries of such institutions, and the employees of such institutions or subsidiaries with the requirements of this section and the registration procedures established under section 1507 of the Secure and Fair Enforcement for Mortgage Licensing Act of 2008. ".

(b) CLERICAL AMENDMENT. — The table of sections for chapter 2 of the Truth in Lending Act is amended by inserting after the item relating to section 129 the following new items:

"129A. Fiduciary duty of servicers of pooled residential mortgages.

"129B. Residential mortgage loan origination. ".

第1402条　住房抵押贷款的发起

(a)**一般规定**。——《诚实信贷法》第二章(《美国法典》第十五编第1631节及其后条文)修正如下——

(1)编号为第129条的两项条款中的第2项条款(《美国法典》第十五编第1639a节)(关于住房抵押贷款服务机构义务的规定)重新编号为第129A条;及

(2)在第129A条(以重新编号后的序号为准)之后插入如下新条文:

"第129B条　住房抵押贷款的发起

(a)**认定与目的**。——

(1)**认定**。——国会认定:在确保消费者仍然能够获得负责任的且可负担的住房抵押贷款的同时,对住房抵押贷款的条款以及与该等贷款相关的实践进行保护、限制和监管,将有助于促进经济稳定。

(2)**目的**。——本条和第129C条旨在确保向消费者要约的以及消费者得到的住房抵押贷款条款,能够合理反映消费者的还款能力、易于理解、具有公平性,且不存在欺骗或滥用情形。

(b)**注意义务**。——

(1)**标准**。——在不违反依据本子条制定的规章的前提下,每一抵押贷款发起人,除承担适用的州法律或联邦法律另行施加的义务之外,还应——

(A)按照适用的州法律或联邦法律(包括《2008年安全和公平执行抵押贷款发起人许可法》)的规定具有抵押贷款发起人的资格,且如有规定,还有义务办理抵押贷款发起人注册和获取相应执照;及

(B)在所有贷款文件上注明全国性抵押贷款发起人许可系统和注册名册针对该抵押贷款发起人指定的唯一识别码。

(2)**合规程序要求**。——联邦储备委员会应制定规章,据以要求存款机构制定并维持合理的程序,以期确保该等存款机构及其子公司或该等存款机构或子公司的雇员遵守本条规定和依据《2008年安全和公平执行抵押贷款发起人许可法》第1507条制定的注册程序,并监控其对该等规定和注册程序的合规情况。"

(b)目录修正。——《诚实信贷法》第二章条款目录修正如下:在第129条的目录项之后插入如下新的目录项:

"第129A条　集合住房抵押贷款服务机构的受信义务。

第129B条　住房抵押贷款的发起。"

SEC. 1403. PROHIBITION ON STEERING INCENTIVES.

Section 129B of the Truth in Lending Act (as added by section 1402(a)) is amended by inserting after subsection (b) the following new subsection:

"(c) PROHIBITION ON STEERING INCENTIVES. —

"(1) IN GENERAL. — For any residential mortgage loan, no mortgage originator shall receive from any person and no person shall pay to a mortgage originator, directly or indirectly, compensation that varies based on the terms of the loan (other than the amount of the principal).

"(2) RESTRUCTURING OF FINANCING ORIGINATION FEE. —

"(A) IN GENERAL. — For any mortgage loan, a mortgage originator may not receive from any person other than the consumer and no person, other than the consumer, who knows or has reason to know that a consumer has directly compensated or will directly compensate a mortgage originator may pay a mortgage originator any origination fee or charge except bona fide third party charges not retained by the creditor, mortgage originator, or an affiliate of the creditor or mortgage originator.

"(B) EXCEPTION. — Notwithstanding subparagraph (A), a mortgage originator may receive from a person other than the consumer an origination fee or charge, and a person other than the consumer may pay a mortgage originator an origination fee or charge, if —

"(i) the mortgage originator does not receive any compensation directly from the consumer; and

"(ii) the consumer does not make an upfront payment of discount points, origination points, or fees, however denominated (other than bona fide third party charges not retained by the mortgage originator, creditor, or an affiliate of the creditor or originator), except that the Board may, by rule, waive or provide exemptions to this clause if the Board determines that such waiver or exemption is in the interest of consumers and in the public interest.

"(3) REGULATIONS. — The Board shall prescribe regulations to prohibit —

"(A) mortgage originators from steering any consumer to a residential mortgage loan that —

"(i) the consumer lacks a reasonable ability to repay (in accordance with regulations prescribed under section 129C(a)); or

"(ii) has predatory characteristics or effects (such as equity stripping, excessive fees, or abusive terms);

"(B) mortgage originators from steering any consumer from a residential mortgage loan for which the consumer is qualified that is a qualified mortgage (as defined in section 129C (b)(2)) to a residential mortgage loan that is not a qualified mortgage;

"(C) abusive or unfair lending practices that promote disparities among consumers of equal credit worthiness but of different race, ethnicity, gender, or age; and

"(D) mortgage originators from —

第1403条　关于引导性激励的禁止性规定

第1402(a)条增加的《诚实信贷法》第129B条修正如下:在第(b)子条之后插入如下新子条:

“(c)**关于引导性激励的禁止性规定**。——

(1)**一般规定**。——对于任何住房抵押贷款,任何抵押贷款发起人均不得直接或间接向任何人收取基于贷款条款而变动的报酬(基于本金数额而变动的报酬不在此例),同时,任何人均不得直接或间接向抵押贷款发起人支付该等报酬。

(2)**贷款发起手续费的调整**。——

(A)**一般规定**。——抵押贷款发起人不得就任何抵押贷款向消费者之外的任何人收取任何贷款发起手续费,并且,除消费者之外,任何人在知晓或有理由知晓消费者已经或将直接向抵押贷款发起人支付报酬的情况下,均不得向抵押贷款发起人支付任何贷款发起手续费,但是贷款发放人、抵押贷款发起人或者该贷款发放人或抵押贷款发起人的关联方未予留存的善意第三方收费除外。

(B)**例外规定**。——无论第(A)子款如何规定,在下列情形下,抵押贷款发起人可以向消费者之外的人收取贷款发起手续费,消费者之外的人也可以向抵押贷款发起人支付贷款发起手续费——

(i)抵押贷款发起人未收到消费者直接支付的任何报酬;且

(ii)消费者未提前支付任何形式的折扣点数、贷款发起点数或手续费(但抵押贷款发起人、贷款发放人或者该等贷款发放人或抵押贷款发起人的关联方未予留存的善意第三方收费除外),但是,如果联邦储备委员会判定,免除或豁免本项规定对消费者的适用符合消费者利益和公共利益,则联邦储备委员会可以发布规则,免除或豁免本项规定的适用。

(3)**规章**。——联邦储备委员会应制定规章,以——

(A)禁止抵押贷款发起人引导消费者举借如下住房抵押贷款——

(i)按照依据第129C(a)条制定的规章,消费者没有合理能力偿还的贷款;或

(ii)具有掠夺性特征或效果的贷款(例如权益剥离、收费过高或滥用性条款);

(B)禁止抵押贷款发起人引导消费者不举借其有资格获取,且属于合格抵押贷款[定义见第129C(b)(2)条]的住房抵押贷款,而引导其举借不属于合格抵押贷款的住房抵押贷款;

(C)禁止使种族、民族、性别或年龄不同但具有同等资信的消费者遭受不平等待遇的滥用性或不公平借贷做法;及

(D)禁止抵押贷款发起人——

"(i) mischaracterizing the credit history of a consumer or the residential mortgage loans available to a consumer;

"(ii) mischaracterizing or suborning the mischaracterization of the appraised value of the property securing the extension of credit; or

"(iii) if unable to suggest, offer, or recommend to a consumer a loan that is not more expensive than a loan for which the consumer qualifies, discouraging a consumer from seeking a residential mortgage loan secured by a consumer's principal dwelling from another mortgage originator.

"(4) RULES OF CONSTRUCTION. — No provision of this sub section shall be construed as —

"(A) permitting any yield spread premium or other similar compensation that would, for any residential mortgage loan, permit the total amount of direct and indirect compensation from all sources permitted to a mortgage originator to vary based on the terms of the loan (other than the amount of the principal);

"(B) limiting or affecting the amount of compensation received by a creditor upon the sale of a consummated loan to a subsequent purchaser;

"(C) restricting a consumer's ability to finance, at the option of the consumer, including through principal or rate, any origination fees or costs permitted under this subsection, or the mortgage originator's right to receive such fees or costs (including compensation) from any person, subject to paragraph (2)(B), so long as such fees or costs do not vary based on the terms of the loan (other than the amount of the principal) or the consumer's decision about whether to finance such fees or costs; or

"(D) prohibiting incentive payments to a mortgage originator based on the number of residential mortgage loans originated within a specified period of time.".

SEC. 1404. LIABILITY.

Section 129B of the Truth in Lending Act is amended by inserting after subsection (c) (as added by section 1403) the following new subsection:

"(d) LIABILITY FOR VIOLATIONS. —

"(1) IN GENERAL. — For purposes of providing a cause of action for any failure by a mortgage originator, other than a creditor, to comply with any requirement imposed under this section and any regulation prescribed under this section, section 130 shall be applied with respect to any such failure by substituting 'mortgage originator' for 'creditor' each place such term appears in each such subsection.

"(2) MAXIMUM. — The maximum amount of any liability of a mortgage originator under paragraph (1) to a consumer for any violation of this section shall not exceed the greater of actual damages or an amount equal to 3 times the total amount of direct and indirect compensation or gain accruing to the mortgage originator in connection with the residential

(i)错误描述消费者的信用记录或消费者可获得的住房抵押贷款;

(ii)错误描述或唆使错误描述为授信提供担保的房地产的评估价值;或

(iii)在其无法向消费者建议、要约或推荐成本不高于该消费者有资格获取的贷款的贷款之时,阻挠该消费者向其他抵押贷款发起人申请以消费者主要住所担保的住房抵押贷款。

(4)**解释规则**。——本子条的任何规定均不得被解释为——

(A)允许支付任何可以产生如下效果的利差溢价或其他类似报酬:贷款发起人从各个来源获得的直接和间接报酬总额将基于贷款条款而变动(基于本金数额而变动的不在此例);

(B)限制或影响贷款发放人向后手购买人出售已订立合同的贷款之时获得的报酬数额;

(C)限制消费者按其选择的方式,为支付本子条准许收取的任何贷款发起手续费或费用而进行融资的能力(包括通过本金或利率的方式进行融资的能力),或者限制抵押贷款发起人在不违反第(2)(B)款规定的情况下,向任何人收取该等手续费或费用(包括报酬)的权利,但前提条件是该等手续费或费用并不基于贷款条款而变动(基于本金数额而变动的不在此例),亦不因消费者是否为该等手续费或费用进行融资的决定而变动;或

(D)禁止基于在规定期间内发起的住房抵押贷款笔数向抵押贷款发起人支付激励性报酬。"

第1404条 责任

《诚实信贷法》第129B条修正如下:在第1403条增加的第(c)子条之后插入如下新子条:

"(d)**违法责任**。——

(1)**一般规定**。——在贷款发放人之外的抵押贷款发起人未遵守本条和依据本条施加的任何要求的情况下而确立相关诉因时,应适用第130条的规定,并将该子条中所有的'贷款发放人'全部替以'抵押贷款发起人'。

(2)**最高责任金额**。——抵押贷款发起人违反本条规定的,其按照第(1)款规定应向消费者支付的最高责任金额不得超过按如下方式计算的金额:与该违法违规行为所涉住房抵押贷款相关的实际损害赔偿金,或该违法违规行为所涉抵押贷款发起人因该贷款获得的直接和间接报酬或收益总额三倍的金额(以二者中数额较高者为

mortgage loan involved in the violation, plus the costs to the consumer of the action, including a reasonable attorney's fee. ".

SEC. 1405. REGULATIONS.

(a) DISCRETIONARY REGULATORY AUTHORITY. —Section 129B of the Truth in Lending Act is amended by inserting after subsection (d)(as added by section 1404) the following new subsection:

"(e) DISCRETIONARY REGULATORY AUTHORITY. —

"(1) IN GENERAL. — The Board shall, by regulations, prohibit or condition terms, acts or practices relating to residential mortgage loans that the Board finds to be abusive, unfair, deceptive, predatory, necessary or proper to ensure that responsible, affordable mortgage credit remains available to consumers in a manner consistent with the purposes of this section and section 129C, necessary or proper to effectuate the purposes of this section and section 129C, to prevent circumvention or evasion thereof, or to facilitate compliance with such sections, or are not in the interest of the borrower.

"(2) APPLICATION. — The regulations prescribed under paragraph (1) shall be applicable to all residential mortgage loans and shall be applied in the same manner as regulations prescribed under section 105.

"(f) Section 129B and any regulations promulgated thereunder do not apply to an extension of credit relating to a plan described in section 101 (53D) of title 11, United States Code. ".

(b) DISCLOSURES. — Notwithstanding any other provision of this title, in order to improve consumer awareness and understanding of transactions involving residential mortgage loans through the use of disclosures, the Board may, by rule, exempt from or modify disclosure requirements, in whole or in part, for any class of residential mortgage loans if the Board determines that such exemption or modification is in the interest of consumers and in the public interest.

SEC. 1406. STUDY OF SHARED APPRECIATION MORTGAGES.

(a) STUDY. — The Secretary of Housing and Urban Development, in consultation with the Secretary of the Treasury and other relevant agencies, shall conduct a comprehensive study to determine prudent statutory and regulatory requirements sufficient to provide for the widespread use of shared appreciation mortgages to strengthen local housing markets, provide new opportunities for affordable homeownership, and enable homeowners at risk of foreclosure to refinance or modify their mortgages.

(b) REPORT. — Not later than the expiration of the 6–month period beginning on the date of the enactment of this Act, the Secretary of Housing and Urban Development shall submit a report to the Congress on the results of the study, which shall include recommendations for the regulatory and legislative requirements referred to in subsection (a).

准),加上消费者诉讼费用(含一笔合理的律师费)之和。”

第1405条　规章

(a)**监管自由裁量权**。——《诚实信贷法》第129B条修正如下:在第1404条增加的第(d)子条之后插入如下新子条:

“(e)**监管自由裁量权**。——

(1)**一般规定**。——为了确保消费者能够继续以与本条和第129C条目的相符的方式获得负责任且可负担的抵押贷款、实现本条和第129C条的目的、防范规避或逃避该等条款的行为或促进对该等条款的合规,联邦储备委员会应制定必要的或宜应制定的规章,对其认定的与住房抵押贷款相关的滥用性、不公平、欺骗性、掠夺性条件、条款、行为或做法或不符合借款人利益的条件、条款、行为或做法予以禁止或施加条件。

(2)**适用**。——根据第(1)款制定的规章应适用于所有住房抵押贷款,且其适用方式应与根据第105条制定的规章一致。

(f)第129B条和根据第129B条颁发的任何规章不适用于与《美国法典》第十一编第101(53D)节所述计划相关的授信。”

(b)**披露**。——无论本编是否存在任何不同规定,为了通过披露制度来提高消费者对涉及住房抵押贷款的交易的认识和理解,联邦储备委员会可以制定规则,对任何类别的住房抵押贷款适用的披露要求授予完全或部分的豁免,或进行完全或部分修改,前提是联邦储备委员会判定该等豁免或修改符合消费者利益和公共利益。

第1406条　关于共享增值抵押贷款的研究

(a)**研究**。——为了使共享增值抵押贷款能够获得广泛使用,从而完善地方住宅市场,以及为了提供获得可负担的住房的新机会,和使存在止赎风险的业主能够为其抵押贷款进行再融资或修改其抵押贷款,住房与城市发展部部长应在与财政部部长和其他相关机关磋商之后,开展一项全面的研究,确定充分审慎的立法和监管要求。

(b)**报告**。——住房与城市发展部部长应于本法颁布之日起6个月内,向国会提交研究结果报告,说明针对第(a)子条所述监管和立法要求提出的建议。

Subtitle B—Minimum Standards For Mortgages

SEC. 1411. ABILITY TO REPAY.

(a) IN GENERAL. —

(1) RULE OF CONSTRUCTION. — No regulation, order, or guidance issued by the Bureau under this title shall be construed as requiring a depository institution to apply mortgage underwriting standards that do not meet the minimum underwriting standards required by the appropriate prudential regulator of the depository institution.

(2) AMENDMENT TO TRUTH IN LENDING ACT. — Chapter 2 of the Truth in Lending Act (15 U. S. C. 1631 et seq.) is amended by inserting after section 129B (as added by section 1402(a)) the following new section:

“ § 129C. Minimum standards for residential mortgage loans

“(a) ABILITY TO REPAY. —

“(1) IN GENERAL. — In accordance with regulations prescribed by the Board, no creditor may make a residential mortgage loan unless the creditor makes a reasonable and good faith determination based on verified and documented information that, at the time the loan is consummated, the consumer has a reasonable ability to repay the loan, according to its terms, and all applicable taxes, insurance (including mortgage guarantee insurance), and assessments.

“(2) MULTIPLE LOANS. — If the creditor knows, or has reason to know, that 1 or more residential mortgage loans secured by the same dwelling will be made to the same consumer, the creditor shall make a reasonable and good faith determination, based on verified and documented information, that the consumer has a reasonable ability to repay the combined payments of all loans on the same dwelling according to the terms of those loans and all applicable taxes, insurance (including mortgage guarantee insurance), and assessments.

“(3) BASIS FOR DETERMINATION. — A determination under this subsection of a consumer’s ability to repay a residential mortgage loan shall include consideration of the consumer’s credit history, current income, expected income the consumer is reasonably assured of receiving, current obligations, debt–to–income ratio or the residual income the consumer will have after paying non–mortgage debt and mortgage–related obligations, employment status, and other financial resources other than the consumer’s equity in the dwelling or real property that secures repayment of the loan. A creditor shall determine the ability of the consumer to repay using a payment schedule that fully amortizes the loan over the term of the loan.

第B子编——抵押贷款最低标准

第1411条　还款能力

(a)**一般规定**。——

(1)**解释规则**。——消费者金融保护局依据本编发布的任何规章、命令或指引均不得被解释为要求存款机构适用未达到存款机构之相应的审慎监管者所规定的最低贷款标准的抵押贷款审核标准。

(2)**对《诚实信贷法》的修正**。——在《诚实信贷法》第二章(《美国法典》第十五编第1631节及其后条文)中,在第1402(a)条增加的第129B条之后插入如下新条文,作为对该章的修正:

"第129C条　住房抵押贷款最低标准

(a)**还款能力**。——

(1)**一般规定**。——根据联邦储备委员会制定的规章,除非贷款发放人基于经核实的文件合理和善意地判定,在贷款合同订立时消费者拥有根据贷款条款偿还贷款以及所有适用税费、保费(包括抵押担保保险)和计征费的合理能力,否则贷款发放人不得提供住房抵押贷款。

(2)**多笔贷款**。——如果贷款发放人知晓或有理由知晓同一住宅担保的一笔或多笔住房抵押贷款将向同一消费者提供,则贷款发放人应基于经核实的文件合理和善意地判定,消费者拥有根据贷款条款偿还该同一住宅担保的所有该等贷款以及所有适用税费、保费(包括抵押担保保险)和计征费的合理能力。

(3) **判定的依据**。——在根据本子条判定某一消费者清偿住房抵押贷款的能力时,应考虑消费者的信用记录、当前收入、消费者可合理确定地获得的预期收入、现有债务、负债收入比或消费者在支付无抵押债务和抵押债务后的收入余额、就业状况,以及除了对用于担保贷款之清偿的房屋或不动产所享有的权益之外,消费者其他的经济来源。贷款发放人应基于在贷款期限内全额摊还贷款的还款计划表判定消费者的还款能力。

"(4) INCOME VERIFICATION. —A creditor making a residential mortgage loan shall verify amounts of income or assets that such creditor relies on to determine repayment ability, including expected income or assets, by reviewing the consumer's Internal Revenue Service Form W–2, tax returns, payroll receipts, financial institution records, or other third–party documents that provide reasonably reliable evidence of the consumer's income or assets. In order to safeguard against fraudulent reporting, any consideration of a consumer's income history in making a determination under this subsection shall include the verification of such income by the use of —

"(A) Internal Revenue Service transcripts of tax returns; or

"(B) a method that quickly and effectively verifies income documentation by a third party subject to rules prescribed by the Board.

"(5) EXEMPTION. — With respect to loans made, guaranteed, or insured by Federal departments or agencies identified in subsection (b)(3)(B)(ii), such departments or agencies may exempt refinancings under a streamlined refinancing from this income verification requirement as long as the following conditions are met:

"(A) The consumer is not 30 days or more past due on the prior existing residential mortgage loan.

"(B) The refinancing does not increase the principal balance outstanding on the prior existing residential mortgage loan, except to the extent of fees and charges allowed by the department or agency making, guaranteeing, or insuring the refinancing.

"(C) Total points and fees (as defined in section 103(aa)(4), other than bona fide third party charges not retained by the mortgage originator, creditor, or an affiliate of the creditor or mortgage originator) payable in connection with the refinancing do not exceed 3 percent of the total new loan amount.

"(D) The interest rate on the refinanced loan is lower than the interest rate of the original loan, unless the borrower is refinancing from an adjustable rate to a fixed–rate loan, under guidelines that the department or agency shall establish for loans they make, guarantee, or issue.

"(E) The refinancing is subject to a payment schedule that will fully amortize the refinancing in accordance with the regulations prescribed by the department or agency making, guaranteeing, or insuring the refinancing.

"(F) The terms of the refinancing do not result in a balloon payment, as defined in subsection (b)(2)(A)(ii).

"(G) Both the residential mortgage loan being refinanced and the refinancing satisfy all requirements of the department or agency making, guaranteeing, or insuring the refinancing.

"(6) NONSTANDARD LOANS. —

"(A) VARIABLE RATE LOANS THAT DEFER REPAYMENT OF ANY PRINCIPAL

(4)**收入核实**。——提供住房抵押贷款的贷款发放人应审查消费者的《国家税务局W-2表格》、报税单、工资条、金融机构记录,或可为消费者的收入或资产提供合理可信的证明的其他第三方文件，核实其判定消费者的还款能力时采信的消费者收入或资产金额(包括预期收入或资产金额)。为了杜绝欺骗性报告,在根据本子条开展判定的过程中，审查某一消费者的收入记录时应利用以下文件和方法对该等收入进行核实——

(A)国家税务局的报税单记录;或

(B)第三方在遵守联邦储备委员会制定的规则的前提下,所使用的及时有效地核实收入凭证的方法。

(5)**豁免**。——对于第(b)(3)(B)(ii)子条所确定的联邦政府部门或机关授予、担保或承保的贷款而言,在满足下列条件的情况下,该等部门或机关可以向采用简易再融资程序的再融资授予豁免,使其不必遵守上述收入核实要求:

(A)对于之前已经存在的住房抵押贷款,消费者未曾逾期付款达30天(含)以上。

(B)除授予、担保或承保再融资的部门或机关允许的费用和收费外,再融资并未造成之前已经存在的住房抵押贷款的未清偿本金余额增加。

(C)再融资的所有应付点数和费用[定义见第103(aa)(4)条,但抵押贷款发起人、贷款发放人或抵押贷款发起人或贷款发放人的某一关联方未留存的善意第三方收费除外]不超过新贷款总额的3%。

(D)再融资贷款的利率低于初始贷款的利率,但是按照相关联邦部门或机关确立的该等部门或机关授予、担保或承保的贷款指导原则,借款人在再融资时将可调利率转变为固定利率的除外。

(E)根据再融资的还款计划,再融资将遵循授予、担保或承保再融资的部门或机关所制定的规章,按照全额摊还的还款时间表偿还。

(F)再融资条款不得导致出现第(b)(2)(A)(ii)子条定义的大额尾付。

(G)进行再融资的住房抵押贷款和再融资均完全符合授予、担保或承保再融资的部门或机关的要求。

(6)**非标准贷款**。——

(A)**延期偿还任何本金或利息的浮动利率贷款**。——住房抵押贷款允许或要求

OR INTEREST. —For purposes of determining, under this subsection, a consumer's ability to repay a variable rate residential mortgage loan that allows or requires the consumer to defer the repayment of any principal or interest, the creditor shall use a fully amortizing repayment schedule.

"(B) INTEREST-ONLY LOANS. — For purposes of determining, under this subsection, a consumer's ability to repay a residential mortgage loan that permits or requires the payment of interest only, the creditor shall use the payment amount required to amortize the loan by its final maturity.

"(C) CALCULATION FOR NEGATIVE AMORTIZATION. —In making any determination under this subsection, a creditor shall also take into consideration any balance increase that may accrue from any negative amortization provision.

"(D) CALCULATION PROCESS. — For purposes of making any determination under this subsection, a creditor shall calculate the monthly payment amount for principal and interest on any residential mortgage loan by assuming —

"(i) the loan proceeds are fully disbursed on the date of the consummation of the loan;

"(ii) the loan is to be repaid in substantially equal monthly amortizing payments for principal and interest over the entire term of the loan with no balloon payment, unless the loan contract requires more rapid repayment (including balloon payment), in which case the calculation shall be made (I) in accordance with regulations prescribed by the Board, with respect to any loan which has an annual percentage rate that does not exceed the average prime offer rate for a comparable transaction, as of the date the interest rate is set, by 1. 5 or more percentage points for a first lien residential mortgage loan; and by 3.5 or more percentage points for a subordinate lien residential mortgage loan; or (II) using the contract's repayment schedule, with respect to a loan which has an annual percentage rate, as of the date the interest rate is set, that is at least 1. 5 percentage points above the average prime offer rate for a first lien residential mortgage loan; and 3. 5 percentage points above the average prime offer rate for a subordinate lien residential mortgage loan; and

"(iii) the interest rate over the entire term of the loan is a fixed rate equal to the fully indexed rate at the time of the loan closing, without considering the introductory rate.

"(E) REFINANCE OF HYBRID LOANS WITH CURRENT LENDER. — In considering any application for refinancing an existing hybrid loan by the creditor into a standard loan to be made by the same creditor in any case in which there would be a reduction in monthly payment and the mortgagor has not been delinquent on any payment on the existing hybrid loan, the creditor may —

"(i) consider the mortgagor's good standing on the existing mortgage;

"(ii) consider if the extension of new credit would prevent a likely default should the original mortgage reset and give such concerns a higher priority as an acceptable underwriting

消费者延期偿付贷款本金或利息的,在依据本子条判定消费者偿还该等贷款的能力之时,贷款发放人应采用全额摊还还款计划。

(B)**仅付利息贷款**。——住房抵押贷款允许或要求消费者仅偿付利息的,在依据本子条判定消费者偿还该等贷款的能力之时,贷款发放人应采用在贷款最终到期日前摊还贷款所需的还款金额进行判定。

(C)**负值摊还本金的计算**。——在根据本子条的规定判定消费者的还款能力之时,贷款发放人还应考虑因任何负值摊还本金规定可能导致的任何余额增加。

(D)**计算过程**。——在根据本子条的规定判定消费者的还款能力之时,贷款发放人应计算在以下假定条件下任何住房抵押贷款每月应付的本金和利息金额——

(i)贷款资金在贷款合同订立之日已全额到位;

(ii)除非贷款合同要求加速还款(包括大额尾付),否则在整个贷款期限内,贷款本金和利息应每月按大体相等的摊还金额偿还,不得留有大额尾付,在该等情况下,(I)如贷款为第一顺位留置权住房抵押贷款,且截至利率设定之日,贷款年利率不超过可比交易的平均最优惠利率1.5(含)个百分点,或者,如贷款为次级留置权住房抵押贷款,且截至利率设定之日,贷款年利率不超过可比交易的平均最优惠利率3.5(含)个百分点,则应按照联邦储备委员会制定的规章计算每月还款金额;或(II)如贷款为第一顺位留置权住房抵押贷款,且截至利率设定之日,贷款年利率超过可比交易的平均最优惠利率至少1.5(含)个百分点,或者,如贷款为次级留置权住房抵押贷款,且截至利率设定之日,贷款年利率超过可比交易的平均最优惠利率至少3.5(含)个百分点,则应采用合同规定的偿还计划计算每月还款金额;及

(iii)在整个贷款期限内,利率为固定利率,且与贷款成交时的完全指数利率相等(不考虑先期利率)。

(E)**当前贷款人授予的混合贷款的再融资**。——如果抵押人申请对贷款发放人向其授予的既存混合贷款进行再融资,使其成为同一贷款发放人发放的标准贷款,且由此导致抵押人的每月还款金额减少,并且抵押人从未有过拖欠偿还既存混合贷款的记录,则贷款发放人在审查该等申请时——

(i)可以考虑抵押人在既存抵押贷款上的还款信誉;

(ii)可以考虑如果重新设定原有抵押贷款的利率,新的授信是否可以防范可能发生的违约,并且有权按照可接受的贷款审核做法,优先考虑该等违约的防范因素;

practice; and

"(iii) offer rate discounts and other favorable terms to such mortgagor that would be available to new customers with high credit ratings based on such underwriting practice.

"(7) FULLY–INDEXED RATE DEFINED. — For purposes of this subsection, the term 'fully indexed rate' means the index rate prevailing on a residential mortgage loan at the time the loan is made plus the margin that will apply after the expiration of any introductory interest rates.

"(8) REVERSE MORTGAGES AND BRIDGE LOANS. — This subsection shall not apply with respect to any reverse mortgage or temporary or bridge loan with a term of 12 months or less, including to any loan to purchase a new dwelling where the consumer plans to sell a different dwelling within 12 months.

"(9) SEASONAL INCOME. — If documented income, including income from a small business, is a repayment source for a residential mortgage loan, a creditor may consider the seasonality and irregularity of such income in the underwriting of and scheduling of payments for such credit.".

(b) CLERICAL AMENDMENT. — The table of sections for chapter 2 of the Truth in Lending Act is amended by inserting after the item relating to section 129B (as added by section 1402(b)) the following new item:

"129C. Minimum standards for residential mortgage loans.".

SEC. 1412. SAFE HARBOR AND REBUTTABLE PRESUMPTION.

Section 129C of the Truth in Lending Act is amended by inserting after subsection (a) (as added by section 1411) the following new subsection:

"(b) PRESUMPTION OF ABILITY TO REPAY. —

"(1) IN GENERAL. — Any creditor with respect to any residential mortgage loan, and any assignee of such loan subject to liability under this title, may presume that the loan has met the requirements of subsection (a), if the loan is a qualified mortgage.

"(2) DEFINITIONS. — For purposes of this subsection, the following definitions shall apply:

"(A) QUALIFIED MORTGAGE.— The term 'qualified mortgage' means any residential mortgage loan —

"(i) for which the regular periodic payments for the loan may not —

"(I) result in an increase of the principal balance; or

"(II) except as provided in subparagraph (E), allow the consumer to defer repayment of principal;

"(ii) except as provided in subparagraph (E), the terms of which do not result in a balloon payment, where a 'balloon payment' is a scheduled payment that is more than twice as large as the average of earlier scheduled payments;

(iii)可以向抵押人提供利率优惠,以及按照上述贷款审核做法向高信用评级的新客户提供的其他优惠条款。

(7)**完全指数利率的定义**。——就本子条而言,'完全指数利率'一词系指住房抵押贷款成交之时住房抵押贷款的现行指数利率加上任何先期利率到期后将适用的利差之和。

(8)**反向抵押贷款和过桥贷款**。——本子条不适用于任何反向抵押贷款,亦不适用于贷款期限短于12个月(含)的任何临时性贷款或过桥贷款,包括为使消费者能够在出售住所后12个月内购买另一处住所,而向消费者发放的任何贷款。

(9)**季节性收入**。——如果有据可查的收入(包括来自小型企业的收入)是住房抵押贷款的还款来源之一,贷款发放人在对该贷款的发放进行审批和安排其还款时间时,可以考虑该收入的季节性和不定期性。"

(b)**目录修正**。——《诚实信贷法》第二章条款目录修正如下:在第1402(b)条增加的第129B条的目录项之后插入如下新的目录项:

"第129C条　住房抵押贷款最低标准。"

第1412条　安全港和可予推翻的推定

《诚实信贷法》第129C条修正如下:在第1411条增加的第(a)子条之后插入如下新子条:

"(b)**关于还款能力的推定**。——

(1)**一般规定**。——如果任何住房抵押贷款属于合格抵押贷款,则该贷款的贷款发放人以及受本编规定的责任约束的任何贷款受让人均可推定该贷款符合第(a)子条的要求。

(2)**定义**。——就本子条而言,下列词语应适用如下定义:

(A)**合格抵押贷款**。——'合格抵押贷款'一词系指符合如下条件的任何住房抵押贷款——

(i)该贷款的定期还款不得——

(I)导致本金余额增加;或

(II)除第(E)子款规定的情形外,允许消费者延期偿还本金;

(ii)除第(E)子款规定的情形外,该贷款的条款不会导致出现大额尾付,就本款规定而言,'大额尾付'一词系指金额超过之前各期还款平均金额两倍的计划还款;

"(iii) for which the income and financial resources relied upon to qualify the obligors on the loan are verified and documented;

"(iv) in the case of a fixed rate loan, for which the underwriting process is based on a payment schedule that fully amortizes the loan over the loan term and takes into account all applicable taxes, insurance, and assessments;

"(v) in the case of an adjustable rate loan, for which the underwriting is based on the maximum rate permitted under the loan during the first 5 years, and a payment schedule that fully amortizes the loan over the loan term and takes into account all applicable taxes, insurance, and assessments;

"(vi) that complies with any guidelines or regulations established by the Board relating to ratios of total monthly debt to monthly income or alternative measures of ability to pay regular expenses after payment of total monthly debt, taking into account the income levels of the borrower and such other factors as the Board may determine relevant and consistent with the purposes described in paragraph (3)(B)(i);

"(vii) for which the total points and fees (as defined in subparagraph (C)) payable in connection with the loan do not exceed 3 percent of the total loan amount;

"(viii) for which the term of the loan does not exceed 30 years, except as such term may be extended under paragraph (3), such as in high–cost areas; and

"(ix) in the case of a reverse mortgage (except for the purposes of subsection (a) of section 129C, to the extent that such mortgages are exempt altogether from those requirements), a reverse mortgage which meets the standards for a qualified mortgage, as set by the Board in rules that are consistent with the purposes of this subsection.

"(B) AVERAGE PRIME OFFER RATE. — The term 'average prime offer rate' means the average prime offer rate for a comparable transaction as of the date on which the interest rate for the transaction is set, as published by the Board. .

"(C) POINTS AND FEES. —

"(i) IN GENERAL. —For purposes of subparagraph (A), the term 'points and fees' means points and fees as defined by section 103(aa)(4)(other than bona fide third party charges not retained by the mortgage originator, creditor, or an affiliate of the creditor or mortgage originator).

"(ii) COMPUTATION. — For purposes of computing the total points and fees under this subparagraph, the total points and fees shall exclude either of the amounts described in the following subclauses, but not both:

"(I) Up to and including 2 bona fide discount points payable by the consumer in connection with the mortgage, but only if the interest rate from which the mortgage's interest rate will be discounted does not exceed by more than 1 percentage point the average prime offer rate.

(iii)在认定借款人的资格时所采信的借款人收入和经济来源数据均已核实,并有据可查;

(iv)如果该贷款属于固定利率贷款,则进行贷款审核时,应以在整个贷款期限对贷款进行全额摊还的还款计划为根据,并考虑了所有适用税费、保费和计征费;

(v)如果该贷款属于可调利率贷款,则进行贷款审核时,应以该贷款在第一个5年内允许适用的最高利率以及在整个贷款期限对贷款进行全额摊还的还款计划为根据,并考虑了所有适用税费、保费和计征费;

(vi)该贷款符合联邦储备委员会考虑了借款人收入水平和其判定符合第(3)(B)(i)款目的之其他相关因素后制定的任何如下指引或规章,即关于月度总债务收入比的指引或规章,或者关于用于借款人支付月度总债务后支付定期费用能力的其他计量指标的指引或规章;

(vii)该贷款的应付总点数和手续费[定义见第(C)子款]不超过贷款总金额的3%;

(viii)该贷款期限不超过30年,但是该期限可以按照第(3)款的规定延长,例如在高成本地区可以延长;及

(ix)如果该贷款属于反向抵押贷款[但是,就第129C条第(a)子条而言,该等抵押贷款全部豁免于遵守该等要求],该贷款应满足联邦储备委员会制定的与本子条目的一致的规则所规定的合格抵押贷款标准。

(B)**平均最优惠利率**。——'平均最优惠利率'一词系指截至交易利率设定之日,联邦储备委员会公布的可比交易的平均最优惠利率。

(C)**点数与手续费**。——

(i)**一般规定**。——就第(A)子款而言,'点数和手续费'一词系指第103(aa)(4)条定义的点数和费用(但抵押贷款发起人、贷款发放人或贷款发放人或抵押贷款发起人的关联方未予留存的善意第三方收费除外)。

(ii)**计算**。——在按照本子款的规定计算总点数和手续费之时,应排除下述子项中任一子项规定的金额,但不得同时排除二者规定的金额:

(I)应排除消费者应就抵押贷款支付的善意折扣点数[最高可排除2(含)个点数],但仅在折扣前的抵押贷款利率超出平均最优惠利率的幅度不高于1个百分点的情况下,方可排除该等折扣点数。

"(II) Unless 2 bona fide discount points have been excluded under subclause (I), up to and including 1 bona fide discount point payable by the consumer in connection with the mortgage, but only if the interest rate from which the mortgage's interest rate will be discounted does not exceed by more than 2 percentage points the average prime offer rate.

"(iii) BONA FIDE DISCOUNT POINTS DEFINED. — For purposes of clause (ii), the term 'bona fide discount points' means loan discount points which are knowingly paid by the consumer for the purpose of reducing, and which in fact result in a bona fide reduction of, the interest rate or time–price differential applicable to the mortgage.

"(iv) INTEREST RATE REDUCTION. — Subclauses (I) and (II) of clause (ii) shall not apply to discount points used to purchase an interest rate reduction unless the amount of the interest rate reduction purchased is reasonably consistent with established industry norms and practices for secondary mortgage market transactions.

"(D) SMALLER LOANS. — The Board shall prescribe rules adjusting the criteria under subparagraph (A)(vii) in order to permit lenders that extend smaller loans to meet the requirements of the presumption of compliance under paragraph (1). In prescribing such rules, the Board shall consider the potential impact of such rules on rural areas and other areas where home values are lower.

"(E) BALLOON LOANS. — The Board may, by regulation, provide that the term 'qualified mortgage' includes a balloon loan —

"(i) that meets all of the criteria for a qualified mortgage under subparagraph (A) (except clauses (i)(II), (ii), (iv), and (v) of such subparagraph);

"(ii) for which the creditor makes a determination that the consumer is able to make all scheduled payments, except the balloon payment, out of income or assets other than the collateral;

"(iii) for which the underwriting is based on a payment schedule that fully amortizes the loan over a period of not more than 30 years and takes into account all applicable taxes, insurance, and assessments; and

"(iv) that is extended by a creditor that —

"(I) operates predominantly in rural or underserved areas;

"(II) together with all affiliates, has total annual residential mortgage loan originations that do not exceed a limit set by the Board;

"(III) retains the balloon loans in portfolio; and

"(IV) meets any asset size threshold and any other criteria as the Board may establish, consistent with the purposes of this subtitle.

"(3) REGULATIONS. —

"(A) IN GENERAL. — The Board shall prescribe regulations to carry out the purposes of this subsection.

(II)除非已按照第(I)子项的规定将2个善意折扣点数排除在外,否则,应排除消费者应就抵押贷款支付的善意折扣点数[最高可排除1(含)个点数],但仅在折扣前的抵押贷款利率超出平均最优惠利率的幅度不高于2个百分点的情况下,方可排除该等折扣点数。

(iii)**善意折扣点数的定义**。——就第(ii)项而言,'善意折扣点数'一词系指消费者在知情的情况下,为了降低抵押贷款的适用利率,或者为了降低分期还款与一次性还款的还款差额而支付的贷款折扣点数,并且该等折扣点数事实上导致了该利率善意降低,或导致了分期还款与一次性还款的还款差额的善意降低。

(iv)**利率优惠**。——第(ii)项的第(I)子项和第(II)子项不适用于被用于购买利率优惠的折扣点数,但是购买的利率优惠数额合理符合二级抵押贷款市场交易适用的既定行业标准和惯例的情形除外。

(D)**小额贷款**。——联邦储备委员会应制定规则,对第(A)(vii)子款规定的标准进行调整,以便小额贷款的贷款人满足第(1)款规定的推定合规要求。在制定该等规则时,联邦储备委员会应考虑该等规则对农村地区和房屋价值较低的其他地区的潜在影响。

(E)**大额尾付贷款**。——联邦储备委员会可以发布规章,将符合以下条件的大额尾付贷款纳入'合格抵押贷款'定义之内——

(i)该贷款满足第(A)子款[但该子款的第(i)(II)项、第(ii)项、第(iv)项和第(v)项除外]规定的合格抵押贷款标准;

(ii)该贷款的贷款发放人判定消费者有能力凭抵押物之外的收入或资产支付所有计划还款(但大额尾付款除外)。

(iii)进行贷款审核时,以在不超过30年期限内对贷款进行全额摊还的还款计划为根据,并考虑了所有适用的税费、保费和计征费;及

(iv)该贷款由符合以下条件的贷款发放人发放——

(I)主要在农村或贫困地区运营;

(II)该贷款发放人及其所有关联方每年发起的住房抵押贷款总额不超过联邦储备委员会设定的限额;

(III)其产品组合中包括大额尾付贷款;及

(IV)满足联邦储备委员会按照本子编宗旨制定的最低资产规模门槛和任何其他标准。

(3)**规章**。——

(A)**一般规定**。——联邦储备委员会应制定相关规章,实施本子条的目的。

"(B) REVISION OF SAFE HARBOR CRITERIA. —

"(i) IN GENERAL. — The Board may prescribe regulations that revise, add to, or subtract from the criteria that define a qualified mortgage upon a finding that such regulations are necessary or proper to ensure that responsible, affordable mortgage credit remains available to consumers in a manner consistent with the purposes of this section, necessary and appropriate to effectuate the purposes of this section and section 129B, to prevent circumvention or evasion thereof, or to facilitate compliance with such sections.

"(ii) LOAN DEFINITION. — The following agencies shall, in consultation with the Board, prescribe rules defining the types of loans they insure, guarantee, or administer, as the case may be, that are qualified mortgages for purposes of paragraph (2)(A), and such rules may revise, add to, or subtract from the criteria used to define a qualified mortgage under paragraph (2)(A), upon a finding that such rules are consistent with the purposes of this section and section 129B, to prevent circumvention or evasion thereof, or to facilitate compliance with such sections:

"(I) The Department of Housing and Urban Development, with regard to mortgages insured under the National Housing Act (12 U. S. C. 1707 et seq.).

"(II) The Department of Veterans Affairs, with regard to a loan made or guaranteed by the Secretary of Veterans Affairs.

"(III) The Department of Agriculture, with regard loans guaranteed by the Secretary of Agriculture pursuant to 42 U. S. C. 1472(h).

"(IV) The Rural Housing Service, with regard to loans insured by the Rural Housing Service. ".

SEC. 1413. DEFENSE TO FORECLOSURE.

Section 130 of the Truth in Lending Act (15 U. S. C. 1640) is amended by adding at the end the following new subsection:

"(k) DEFENSE TO FORECLOSURE. —

"(1) IN GENERAL. — Notwithstanding any other provision of law, when a creditor, assignee, or other holder of a residential mortgage loan or anyone acting on behalf of such creditor, assignee, or holder, initiates a judicial or nonjudicial foreclosure of the residential mortgage loan, or any other action to collect the debt in connection with such loan, a consumer may assert a violation by a creditor of paragraph (1) or (2) of section 129B(c), or of section 129C(a), as a matter of defense by recoupment or set off without regard for the time limit on a private action for damages under subsection (e).

"(2) AMOUNT OF RECOUPMENT OR SETOFF. —

"(A) IN GENERAL. — The amount of recoupment or set–off under paragraph (1) shall equal the amount to which the consumer would be entitled under subsection (a) for damages for a valid claim brought in an original action against the creditor, plus the costs to the

(B)**安全港标准的修订**。——

(i)**一般规定**。——如联邦储备委员会认定,为了确保能够继续以与本条目的相符的方式向消费者提供负责任且可负担的抵押贷款、实现本条和第129B条的目的、防范规避或逃避本条和第129B条规定的行为或为促进对该等条款的合规,联邦储备委员会应制定必要的或宜应制定的规章,以对合格抵押贷款的界定标准进行修订、补充或删减,则联邦储备委员会可以制定该等规章。

(ii)**贷款的定义**。——下述机关应在与联邦储备委员会磋商之后,制定规则以明确界定其承保、担保或管理的(视具体情况而定)且属于第(2)(A)款规定的合格抵押贷款之贷款类型;并且,如其认定,制定该等规则对第(2)(A)款项下用以界定合格抵押贷款的标准进行修订、补充或删减有助于实现本条和第129B条的目的,或者有助于防范规避或逃避本条和第129B条规定的行为或促进对该等条款的合规,则其可以制定该等规则:

(I)住房与城市发展部,应当针对按照《国民住房法》(《美国法典》第十二编第1707节及其后条文)承保的抵押贷款制定相关规则。

(II)退伍军人事务部,应当针对退伍军人事务部部长所发放或担保的贷款制定规则。

(III)农业部,应当针对农业部部长按照《美国法典》第四十二编第1472(h)节所担保的贷款制定规则。

(IV)农村住房服务局,应当针对农村住房服务局承保的贷款制定规则。”

第1413条 止赎抗辩

在《诚实信贷法》第130条(《美国法典》第十五编第1640节)结尾处增加如下新子条,作为对该条的修正:

“(k)**止赎抗辩**。——

(1)**一般规定**。——无论是否存在任何不同法律规定,住房抵押贷款的贷款发放人、受让人或其他持有人亲自或通过其代表针对住房抵押贷款启动司法或非司法止赎行动,或者为追收与该贷款相关的债务而提起任何其他行动之时,消费者可以主张贷款发放人违反了第129(B)(c)条第(1)款或第(2)款或第129C(a)条的规定,以此作为扣减抗辩或抵销抗辩,而不受第(e)子条规定的私人赔偿金诉讼的时限限制。

(2)**扣减或抵销金额**。——

(A)**一般规定**。——第(1)款规定的扣减或抵销的金额应等于消费者在原始诉讼中针对贷款发放人提出有效主张时,其按照第(a)子条规定将有权获得的赔偿金金额,再加上消费者支出的诉讼费用(包括一笔合理的律师费)之和。

consumer of the action, including a reasonable attorney's fee.

"(B) SPECIAL RULE. — Where such judgment is rendered after the expiration of the applicable time limit on a private action for damages under subsection (e), the amount of recoupment or set–off under paragraph (1) derived from damages under subsection (a)(4) shall not exceed the amount to which the consumer would have been entitled under subsection (a)(4) for damages computed up to the day preceding the expiration of the applicable time limit.".

SEC. 1414. ADDITIONAL STANDARDS AND REQUIREMENTS.

(a) IN GENERAL. — Section 129C of the Truth in Lending Act is amended by inserting after subsection (b)(as added by this title) the following new subsections:

"(c) PROHIBITION ON CERTAIN PREPAYMENT PENALTIES. —

"(1) PROHIBITED ON CERTAIN LOANS. —

"(A) IN GENERAL. — A residential mortgage loan that is not a 'qualified mortgage', as defined under subsection (b)(2), may not contain terms under which a consumer must pay a prepayment penalty for paying all or part of the principal after the loan is consummated.

"(B) EXCLUSIONS. — For purposes of this subsection, a 'qualified mortgage' may not include a residential mortgage loan that —

"(i) has an adjustable rate; or

"(ii) has an annual percentage rate that exceeds the average prime offer rate for a comparable transaction, as of the date the interest rate is set —

"(I) by 1. 5 or more percentage points, in the case of a first lien residential mortgage loan having an original principal obligation amount that is equal to or less than the amount of the maximum limitation on the original principal obligation of mortgage in effect for a residence of the applicable size, as of the date of such interest rate set, pursuant to the 6th sentence of section 305(a)(2) the Federal Home Loan Mortgage Corporation Act (12 U. S. C. 1454(a)(2));

"(II) by 2. 5 or more percentage points, in the case of a first lien residential mortgage loan having a original principal obligation amount that is more than the amount of the maximum limitation on the original principal obligation of mortgage in effect for a residence of the applicable size, as of the date of such interest rate set, pursuant to the 6th sentence of section 305(a)(2) the Federal Home Loan Mortgage Corporation Act (12 U. S. C. 1454(a)(2)); and

"(III) by 3. 5 or more percentage points, in the case of a subordinate lien residential mortgage loan.

"(2) PUBLICATION OF AVERAGE PRIME OFFER RATE AND APR THRESHOLDS. — The Board —

"(A) shall publish, and update at least weekly, average prime offer rates;

(B)**特别规则**。——如果上述判决的作出时间在第(e)子条规定的私人赔偿金诉讼的适用时限届满之后,则按照第(1)款规定,通过第(a)(4)子条规定的赔偿金进行扣减或抵销的金额,不得超过截至适用时限届满之日前一天,消费者按照第(a)(4)子条规定将有权获得的赔偿金的累计金额。”

第1414条　补充标准和要求

(a)**一般规定**。——《诚实信贷法》第129C条修正如下:在本编增加的第(b)子条之后插入如下新子条:

“(c)**对特定提前还款违约金的禁止性规定**。——

(1)**对特定贷款的禁止性规定**。——

(A)**一般规定**。——任何住房抵押贷款,如不属于第(b)(2)子条定义的‘合格抵押贷款’,均不得包含要求消费者在贷款合同订立之后偿还全部或部分本金时必须缴纳提前还款违约金的条款。

(B)**除外规定**。——就本子条而言,‘合格抵押贷款’不得包括符合如下条件的住房抵押贷款——

(i)利率可以调整;或

(ii)截至利率设定之日,其年利率超过可比交易的平均最优惠利率——

(I)在下述情形下,其年利率超过可比交易的平均最优惠利率1.5(含)个百分点以上:截至利率设定之日,按照《联邦住房贷款抵押公司法》第305(a)(2)条[《美国法典》第十二编第1454(a)(2)节]第6句的规定,享有第一顺位留置权的住房抵押贷款的初始本金金额,不超过届时有效适用的以同等面积住宅担保的抵押贷款的初始本金上限;

(II)在下述情形下,其年利率超过可比交易的平均最优惠利率2.5(含)个百分点以上:截至利率设定之日,按照《联邦住房贷款抵押公司法》第305(a)(2)条(《美国法典》第十二编第1454(a)(2)节)第6句的规定,享有第一顺位留置权的住房抵押贷款的初始本金金额,超过了届时有效适用的以同等面积住宅担保的抵押贷款的初始本金的上限;及

(III)对于享有次级留置权的住房抵押贷款,其年利率超过可比交易的平均最优惠利率3.5(含)个百分点以上。

(2)**平均最优惠利率及年利率门槛的发布**。——联邦储备委员会——

(A)应发布平均最优惠利率,并至少应每周进行一次更新;

"(B) may publish multiple rates based on varying types of mortgage transactions; and

"(C) shall adjust the thresholds established under subclause (I), (II), and (III) of paragraph (1)(B)(ii) as necessary to reflect significant changes in market conditions and to effectuate the purposes of the Mortgage Reform and Anti–Predatory Lending Act.

"(3) PHASED–OUT PENALTIES ON QUALIFIED MORTGAGES. — A qualified mortgage (as defined in subsection (b)(2)) may not contain terms under which a consumer must pay a prepayment penalty for paying all or part of the principal after the loan is consummated in excess of the following limitations:

"(A) During the 1–year period beginning on the date the loan is consummated, the prepayment penalty shall not exceed an amount equal to 3 percent of the outstanding balance on the loan.

"(B) During the 1–year period beginning after the period described in subparagraph (A), the prepayment penalty shall not exceed an amount equal to 2 percent of the outstanding balance on the loan.

"(C) During the 1–year period beginning after the 1–year period described in subparagraph (B), the prepayment penalty shall not exceed an amount equal to 1 percent of the outstanding balance on the loan.

"(D) After the end of the 3–year period beginning on the date the loan is consummated, no prepayment penalty may be imposed on a qualified mortgage.

"(4) OPTION FOR NO PREPAYMENT PENALTY REQUIRED. — A creditor may not offer a consumer a residential mortgage loan product that has a prepayment penalty for paying all or part of the principal after the loan is consummated as a term of the loan without offering the consumer a residential mortgage loan product that does not have a prepayment penalty as a term of the loan.

"(d) SINGLE PREMIUM CREDIT INSURANCE PROHIBITED. — No creditor may finance, directly or indirectly, in connection with any residential mortgage loan or with any extension of credit under an open end consumer credit plan secured by the principal dwelling of the consumer, any credit life, credit disability, credit unemployment, or credit property insurance, or any other accident, loss–of–income, life, or health insurance, or any payments directly or indirectly for any debt cancellation or suspension agreement or contract, except that —

"(1) insurance premiums or debt cancellation or suspension fees calculated and paid in full on a monthly basis shall not be considered financed by the creditor; and

"(2) this subsection shall not apply to credit unemployment insurance for which the unemployment insurance premiums are reasonable, the creditor receives no direct or indirect compensation in connection with the unemployment insurance premiums, and the unemployment insurance premiums are paid pursuant to another insurance contract and not

(B)可以根据抵押贷款交易的不同类型发布多个平均最优惠利率;及

(C)应对按照第(1)(B)(ii)款第(I)子项、第(II)子项和第(III)子项制定的年利率门槛进行必要调整,以反映市场状况发生的重大变化并实现《抵押贷款改革和反掠夺性借贷法》的立法宗旨。

(3)**逐步取消合格抵押贷款的提前还款违约金**。——合格抵押贷款[定义见第(b)(2)子条]不得包含要求消费者在贷款合同订立之后偿还全部或部分本金之时必须缴纳超过以下限额的提前还款违约金的条款:

(A)在自贷款合同订立之日起一年内提前还款的,提前还款违约金不得超过未清偿贷款余额的3%。

(B)在第(A)子款规定期限届满后1年内提前还款的,提前还款违约金不得超过未清偿贷款余额的2%。

(C)在第(B)子款规定的1年期限届满后1年内提前还款的,提前还款违约金不得超过未清偿贷款余额的1%。

(D)在贷款合同订立之日起届满3年之后提前还款的,不得对合格抵押贷款收取提前还款违约金。

(4)**消费者应有享受无提前还款违约金条款的选择权**。——对于含有提前还款违约金条款(规定消费者在贷款合同订立之后偿还全部或部分本金之时必须缴纳提前还款违约金)的住房抵押贷款产品,贷款发放人在未向消费者要约一份不含提前还款违约金条款的住房抵押贷款产品的情况下,不得向消费者要约该等含有提前还款违约金条款的住房抵押贷款产品。

(d)**禁止趸缴信用保险**。——对于与任何住房抵押贷款相关的或与开放式消费者信用计划中以消费者主要住所担保的任何授信相关的信用人寿保险、信用残疾保险、信用失业保险或信用财产保险,或者任何其他意外险、收入损失险、人寿保险或健康保险,或者对于为债务撤销或暂停协议或合同所直接或间接支付的任何款项,任何贷款发放人均不得直接或间接提供融资,但是——

(1)按月计算并全额缴付的保费或债务撤销或暂停手续费不得视为系由贷款发放人提供融资;且

(2)本子条不适用于符合如下条件的信用失业保险:失业保险费金额合理;贷款发放人未因失业保险费获得直接或间接报酬;且失业保险费系根据另一保险合同的规定交纳且并非向贷款发放人的关联方交纳。

paid to an affiliate of the creditor.

"(e) ARBITRATION.—

"(1) IN GENERAL.— No residential mortgage loan and no extension of credit under an open end consumer credit plan secured by the principal dwelling of the consumer may include terms which require arbitration or any other nonjudicial procedure as the method for resolving any controversy or settling any claims arising out of the transaction.

"(2) POST–CONTROVERSY AGREEMENTS.— Subject to paragraph (3), paragraph (1) shall not be construed as limiting the right of the consumer and the creditor or any assignee to agree to arbitration or any other nonjudicial procedure as the method for resolving any controversy at any time after a dispute or claim under the transaction arises.

"(3) NO WAIVER OF STATUTORY CAUSE OF ACTION.— No provision of any residential mortgage loan or of any extension of credit under an open end consumer credit plan secured by the principal dwelling of the consumer, and no other agreement between the consumer and the creditor relating to the residential mortgage loan or extension of credit referred to in paragraph (1), shall be applied or interpreted so as to bar a consumer from bringing an action in an appropriate district court of the United States, or any other court of competent jurisdiction, pursuant to section 130 or any other provision of law, for damages or other relief in connection with any alleged violation of this section, any other provision of this title, or any other Federal law.

"(f) MORTGAGES WITH NEGATIVE AMORTIZATION.— No creditor may extend credit to a borrower in connection with a consumer credit transaction under an open or closed end consumer credit plan secured by a dwelling or residential real property that includes a dwelling, other than a reverse mortgage, that provides or permits a payment plan that may, at any time over the term of the extension of credit, result in negative amortization unless, before such transaction is consummated—

"(1) the creditor provides the consumer with a statement that—

"(A) the pending transaction will or may, as the case may be, result in negative amortization;

"(B) describes negative amortization in such manner as the Board shall prescribe;

"(C) negative amortization increases the outstanding principal balance of the account; and

"(D) negative amortization reduces the consumer's equity in the dwelling or real property; and

"(2) in the case of a first–time borrower with respect to a residential mortgage loan that is not a qualified mortgage, the first–time borrower provides the creditor with sufficient documentation to demonstrate that the consumer received homeownership counseling from organizations or counselors certified by the Secretary of Housing and Urban Development as

“(e)**仲裁**。——

(1)**一般规定**。——任何住房抵押贷款以及开放式消费者信用计划中以消费者主要住所担保的任何授信,均不得包含要求在因交易引发任何争议或任何索赔时采用仲裁或任何其他非司法程序作为解决方法的条款。

(2)**争议发生后订立的协议**。——在不违反第(3)款规定的前提下,第(1)款的规定不得被解释为限制消费者、贷款发放人或任何受让人在因交易引发纠纷或索赔之后的任何时候,达成协议,将仲裁或任何其他非司法程序选定为争议解决方法的权利。

(3)**不放弃法定诉因**。——在适用或解释住房抵押贷款的任何规定或开放式消费者信用计划中以消费者主要住所为担保的授信的任何规定之时,以及适用或解释消费者与贷款发放人之间就第(1)款所述住房抵押贷款或授信签署的其他协议之时,均不得禁止消费者按照第130条规定或任何其他法律规定向相应的联邦地区法院或任何其他有管辖权的法院提起诉讼,以对违反本条规定、本编任何其他规定或任何其他联邦法律的行为提出指控并请求赔偿金或其他救济的权利。

(f)**引发负值摊还本金的抵押贷款**。——对于开放式或封闭式消费者信用计划中以住所或包括住所在内的住宅房地产作为担保的消费者信用交易,任何贷款发放人就该等交易向借款人授予的信用(但反向抵押贷款除外)均不得规定或允许订立可能导致在授信期限内任何时候引发负值摊还本金的还款计划,除非,在该交易合同订立之前——

(1)贷款发放人已向消费者提供一份声明——

(A)说明该交易将会或可能(视具体情况而定)引发负值摊还本金;

(B)按照联邦储备委员会规定的方式,对负值摊还本金进行了说明;

(C)说明负值摊还本金将增加账户中的未清偿本金余额;且

(D)说明负值摊还本金将减少消费者对住所或房地产享有的权益;且

(2)如果借款人是第一次申请不属于合格抵押贷款的住房抵押贷款,则借款人应向贷款发放人提供充分的证明文件,证明消费者接受了经住房与城市发展部部长认证的组织或咨询顾问提供的房屋所有权咨询。”

competent to provide such counseling. ".

(b) CONFORMING AMENDMENT RELATING TO ENFORCEMENT.—Section 108(a) of the Truth in Lending Act (15 U. S. C. 1607(a)) is amended by inserting after paragraph (6) the following new paragraph:

"(7) sections 21B and 21C of the Securities Exchange Act of 1934, in the case of a broker or dealer, other than a depository institution, by the Securities and Exchange Commission. ".

(c) PROTECTION AGAINST LOSS OF ANTI-DEFICIENCY PROTECTION. — Section 129C of the Truth in Lending Act is amended by inserting after subsection (f)(as added by subsection (a)) the following new subsection:

"(g) PROTECTION AGAINST LOSS OF ANTI-DEFICIENCY PROTECTION. —

"(1) DEFINITION. — For purposes of this subsection, the term 'anti-deficiency law' means the law of any State which provides that, in the event of foreclosure on the residential property of a consumer securing a mortgage, the consumer is not liable, in accordance with the terms and limitations of such State law, for any deficiency between the sale price obtained on such property through foreclosure and the outstanding balance of the mortgage.

"(2) NOTICE AT TIME OF CONSUMMATION. — In the case of any residential mortgage loan that is, or upon consummation will be, subject to protection under an anti-deficiency law, the creditor or mortgage originator shall provide a written notice to the consumer describing the protection provided by the anti-deficiency law and the significance for the consumer of the loss of such protection before such loan is consummated.

"(3) NOTICE BEFORE REFINANCING THAT WOULD CAUSE LOSS OF PROTECTION. — In the case of any residential mortgage loan that is subject to protection under an anti-deficiency law, if a creditor or mortgage originator provides an application to a consumer, or receives an application from a consumer, for any type of refinancing for such loan that would cause the loan to lose the protection of such anti-deficiency law, the creditor or mortgage originator shall provide a written notice to the consumer describing the protection provided by the anti-deficiency law and the significance for the consumer of the loss of such protection before any agreement for any such refinancing is consummated. ".

(d) POLICY REGARDING ACCEPTANCE OF PARTIAL PAYMENT. — Section 129C of the Truth in Lending Act is amended by inserting after subsection (g)(as added by subsection (c)) the following new subsection:

"(h) POLICY REGARDING ACCEPTANCE OF PARTIAL PAYMENT. — In the case of any residential mortgage loan, a creditor shall disclose prior to settlement or, in the case of a person becoming a creditor with respect to an existing residential mortgage loan, at the time such person becomes a creditor —

"(1) the creditor's policy regarding the acceptance of partial payments; and

(b)**与执法相关的一致性修正**。——《诚实信贷法》第108(a)条[《美国法典》第十五编第1607(a)节]修正如下:在第(6)款之后插入如下新款:

“(7)对于经纪商或自营商(但存款机构除外)而言,由证券交易委员会根据《1934年证券交易法》第21B条和第21C条的规定强制执行。”

(c)**防止消费者丧失禁止追索差额保护**。——《诚实信贷法》第129C条修正如下:在第(a)子条增加的第(f)子条之后插入如下新子条:

“(g)**防止消费者丧失禁止追索差额保护**。——

(1)**定义**。——就本子条而言,‘禁止追索差额法律’一词系指作出如下规定的任何州法律:消费者的为抵押贷款提供担保的居住性房地产被止赎之时,在遵守该州法律规定和限制的情况下,消费者对该止赎房地产售价与未清偿抵押贷款余额之间的差额不承担任何责任。

(2)**贷款合同订立之时的通知**。——如果任何住房抵押贷款当前受到或合同订立之后将受到禁止追索差额法律的保护,则贷款发放人或抵押贷款发起人应向消费者提供一份书面通知,说明禁止追索差额法律提供的保护,以及如在该贷款合同订立之前丧失该保护将对消费者造成的重大影响。

(3)**在提供将导致保护丧失的再融资之前向消费者发出的通知**。——对于受禁止追索差额法律保护的任何住房抵押贷款, 如果贷款发放人或抵押贷款发起人向消费者提供,或收到消费者提交的任何类型的再融资申请表,且该等类型的再融资将会导致该贷款丧失禁止追索差额法律提供的保护,则该贷款发放人或抵押贷款发起人应向消费者提供一份书面通知,说明该禁止追索贷款差额损法律提供的保护,以及在就该等再融资订立协议之前丧失该保护将对消费者造成的重大影响。”

(d)**关于接受部分还款的政策**。——《诚实信贷法》第129C条修正如下:在第(c)子条增加的第(g)子条之后插入如下新子条:

“(h)**关于接受部分还款的政策**。——对于住房抵押贷款而言,贷款发放人应在对该贷款进行结算之前披露如下信息,或者,如果某一主体即将成为某一笔既存住房抵押贷款的贷款发放人,则在该主体应于成为贷款发放人之时,披露如下信息——

(1)贷款发放人关于接受部分还款的政策;及

"(2) if partial payments are accepted, how such payments will be applied to such mortgage and if such payments will be placed in escrow.

"(i) TIMESHARE PLANS. — This section and any regulations promulgated under this section do not apply to an extension of credit relating to a plan described in section 101(53D) of title 11, United States Code. ".

SEC. 1415. RULE OF CONSTRUCTION.

Except as otherwise expressly provided in section 129B or 129C of the Truth in Lending Act (as added by this title), no provision of such section 129B or 129C shall be construed as superseding, repealing, or affecting any duty, right, obligation, privilege, or remedy of any person under any other provision of the Truth in Lending Act or any other provision of Federal or State law.

SEC. 1416. AMENDMENTS TO CIVIL LIABILITY PROVISIONS.

(a) INCREASE IN AMOUNT OF CIVIL MONEY PENALTIES FOR CERTAIN VIOLATIONS. — Section 130(a) of the Truth in Lending Act (15 U. S. C. 1640(a)) is amended —

(1) in paragraph (2)(A)(ii) —

(A) by striking "$100" and inserting "$200"; and

(B) by striking "$1, 000" and inserting "$2, 000";

(2) in paragraph (2)(B), by striking "$500, 000" and inserting "$1, 000, 000"; and

(3) in paragraph (4), by inserting ", paragraph (1) or (2) of section 129B(c), or section 129C(a)" after "section 129".

(b) STATUTE OF LIMITATIONS EXTENDED FOR SECTION 129 VIOLATIONS. — Section 130(e) of the Truth in Lending Act (15 U. S. C. 1640(e)) is amended —

(1) in the first sentence, by striking "Any action" and inserting "Except as provided in the subsequent sentence, any action"; and

(2) by inserting after the first sentence the following new sentence: "Any action under this section with respect to any violation of section 129, 129B, or 129C may be brought in any United States district court, or in any other court of competent jurisdiction, before the end of the 3–year period beginning on the date of the occurrence of the violation. ".

SEC.1417. LENDER RIGHTS IN THE CONTEXT OF BORROWER DECEPTION.

Section 130 of the Truth in Lending Act (15 U. S. C. 1640) is amended by adding after subsection (k)(as added by this title) the following new subsection:

"(l) EXEMPTION FROM LIABILITY AND RESCISSION IN CASE OF BORROWER FRAUD OR DECEPTION. — In addition to any other remedy available by law or contract, no creditor or assignee shall be liable to an obligor under this section, if such obligor, or co–obligor has been convicted of obtaining by actual fraud such residential mortgage loan. ".

(2)如果接受部分还款,该还款将如何用于偿还抵押贷款,以及该还款是否需要由第三方代管。

(i)**分时使用权计划**。——本条和依据本条颁发的任何规章均不适用于与《美国法典》第十一编第101(53D)节所述计划相关的授信。”

第1415条　解释规则

除本编增加的《诚实信贷法》第129B条或第129C条另有明确规定的情形外,该第129B或第129C条的任何规定不得被解释为取代、废止或影响任何主体根据《诚实信贷法》的任何其他规定或联邦法律或州法律的任何其他规定承担的职责、义务,以及享有的权利、特权或救济。

第1416条　民事责任条款的修正

(a)**提高特定违法违规行为的民事罚款金额。**——《诚实信贷法》第130(a)条[《美国法典》第十五编第1640(a)节]修正如下——

(1)在第(2)(A)(ii)款中——

(A)删除“100美元”,替以“200美元”;及

(B)删除“1000美元”,替以“2000美元”;

(2)在第(2)(B)款中,删除“50万美元”,替以“100万美元”;及

(3)在第(4)款中,在“第129条”之后插入“、第129B(c)条第(1)款或第(2)款,或者第129C(a)条”。

(b)**延长针对违反第129条规定的行为提起诉讼的诉讼时效。**——《诚实信贷法》第130(e)条[《美国法典》第十五编第1640(e)节]修正如下——

(1)在第一句中,删除“任何诉讼”,替以“除下一句规定的情形外,任何诉讼”;及

(2)在第一句之后插入如下新句:“对于违反第129条、第129B条或第129C条的行为,可以在该违法违规行为发生之日起3年之内,按照本条的规定在任何联邦地区法院或任何其他有管辖权的法院提起诉讼。”

第1417条　借款人出现欺骗行为时贷款人享有的权利

《诚实信贷法》第130条(《美国法典》第十五编第1640节)修正如下:在本编增加的第(k)子条之后插入如下新子条:

“(l)**借款人出现欺诈或欺骗行为时的免责和合同撤销**。——如果借款人或共同借款人被法院判决认定系通过实际的欺诈手段获取住房抵押贷款,则贷款发放人和受让人,除了享有法律或合同规定的其他救济之外,还可以依据本条规定不对借款人承担任何责任。”

SEC. 1418. SIX–MONTH NOTICE REQUIRED BEFORE RESET OF HYBRID ADJUSTABLE RATE MORTGAGES.

(a) IN GENERAL. — Chapter 2 of the Truth in Lending Act (15 U. S. C. 1631 et seq.) is amended by inserting after section 128 the following new section:

" § 128A. Reset of hybrid adjustable rate mortgages

"(a) HYBRID ADJUSTABLE RATE MORTGAGES DEFINED. — For purposes of this section, the term 'hybrid adjustable rate mortgage' means a consumer credit transaction secured by the consumer's principal residence with a fixed interest rate for an introductory period that adjusts or resets to a variable interest rate after such period.

"(b) NOTICE OF RESET AND ALTERNATIVES. — During the 1–month period that ends 6 months before the date on which the interest rate in effect during the introductory period of a hybrid adjustable rate mortgage adjusts or resets to a variable interest rate or, in the case of such an adjustment or resetting that occurs within the first 6 months after consummation of such loan, at consummation, the creditor or servicer of such loan shall provide a written notice, separate and distinct from all other correspondence to the consumer, that includes the following:

"(1) Any index or formula used in making adjustments to or resetting the interest rate and a source of information about the index or formula.

"(2) An explanation of how the new interest rate and payment would be determined, including an explanation of how the index was adjusted, such as by the addition of a margin.

"(3) A good faith estimate, based on accepted industry standards, of the creditor or servicer of the amount of the monthly payment that will apply after the date of the adjustment or reset, and the assumptions on which this estimate is based.

"(4) A list of alternatives consumers may pursue before the date of adjustment or reset, and descriptions of the actions consumers must take to pursue these alternatives, including—

"(A) refinancing;

"(B) renegotiation of loan terms;

"(C) payment forbearances; and

"(D) pre–foreclosure sales.

"(5) The names, addresses, telephone numbers, and Internet addresses of counseling agencies or programs reasonably available to the consumer that have been certified or approved and made publicly available by the Secretary of Housing and Urban Development or a State housing finance authority (as defined in section 1301 of the Financial Institutions Reform, Recovery, and Enforcement Act of 1989).

"(6) The address, telephone number, and Internet address for the State housing finance authority (as so defined) for the State in which the consumer resides.

"(c) SAVINGS CLAUSE. — The Board may require the notice in paragraph (b) or

第1418条　须在重新设定混合型可调利率抵押贷款的利率之前6个月发出通知

(a)一般规定。——《诚实信贷法》第二章(《美国法典》第十五编第1631节及其后条文)修正如下:在第128条之后插入如下新条文:

"第128A条　混合型可调利率抵押贷款的利率重新设定

(a)**混合型可调利率抵押贷款的定义**。——就本条而言,"混合型可调利率抵押贷款"一词系指以消费者主要住所担保的,在导入期内采用固定利率,而在导入期届满之后调整或重新设定为浮动利率的消费者信用交易。

(b)**利率重新设定的通知与替代性方法**。——在混合型可调利率抵押贷款导入期有效适用的利率调整或重新设定为浮动利率之日之前的第7个月中,或如果该利率调整或重置在该贷款合同订立后6个月内发生,则在该贷款合同订立之时,该贷款的贷款发放人或服务机构应向消费者提供一份包含如下内容的书面通知,且该通知应独立并区别于贷款发放人或服务机构与消费者之间的所有其他通信往来:

(1)调整或重新设定利率时采用的任何指数或公式,以及该指数或公式的信息来源。

(2)关于确定新利率和还款金额的方式之说明,包括对指数调整方式的说明,例如,通过加上利差的方式对指数进行调整。

(3)贷款发放人或服务机构根据公认行业标准,对利率调整或利率重新设定日之后适用的月度还款金额进行的善意估算,以及开展该等估算所依据的假设。

(4)消费者在利率调整或利率重新设定日之前可以采用的替代性方法之清单,并说明消费者如希望采用该等替代性方法,必须采取的措施,包括——

(A)再融资;

(B)重新商定贷款条款;

(C)还款宽限;及

(D)在止赎之前进行出售。

(5)住房与城市发展部部长或州住房金融局(定义见《1989年金融机构改革、复兴与实施法》第1301条)认证或批准并公布的,消费者可以合理获得其服务的咨询机构或咨询计划的名称、地址、电话号码和互联网网址。

(6)消费者居住地所在州的州住房金融局(定义见《1989年金融机构改革、复兴与实施法》第1301条)的地址、电话号码和互联网网址。

(c)**保留条款**。——抵押贷款不属于混合型可调利率抵押贷款的,联邦储备委员

other notice consistent with this Act for adjustable rate mortgage loans that are not hybrid adjustable rate mortgage loans. ".

(b) CLERICAL AMENDMENT. — The table of sections for chapter 2 of the Truth in Lending Act is amended by inserting after the item relating to section 128 the following new item:

"128A. Reset of hybrid adjustable rate mortgages. ".

SEC. 1419. REQUIRED DISCLOSURES.

Section 128(a) of Truth in Lending Act (15 U. S. C. 1638(a)) is amended by adding at the end the following new paragraphs:

"(16) In the case of a variable rate residential mortgage loan for which an escrow or impound account will be established for the payment of all applicable taxes, insurance, and assessments —

"(A) the amount of initial monthly payment due under the loan for the payment of principal and interest, and the amount of such initial monthly payment including the monthly payment deposited in the account for the payment of all applicable taxes, insurance, and assessments; and

"(B) the amount of the fully indexed monthly payment due under the loan for the payment of principal and interest, and the amount of such fully indexed monthly payment including the monthly payment deposited in the account for the payment of all applicable taxes, insurance, and assessments.

"(17) In the case of a residential mortgage loan, the aggregate amount of settlement charges for all settlement services provided in connection with the loan, the amount of charges that are included in the loan and the amount of such charges the borrower must pay at closing, the approximate amount of the wholesale rate of funds in connection with the loan, and the aggregate amount of other fees or required payments in connection with the loan.

"(18) In the case of a residential mortgage loan, the aggregate amount of fees paid to the mortgage originator in connection with the loan, the amount of such fees paid directly by the consumer, and any additional amount received by the originator from the creditor.

"(19) In the case of a residential mortgage loan, the total amount of interest that the consumer will pay over the life of the loan as a percentage of the principal of the loan. Such amount shall be computed assuming the consumer makes each monthly payment in full and on-time, and does not make anyover-payments. ".

SEC. 1420. DISCLOSURES REQUIRED IN MONTHLY STATEMENTS FOR RESIDENTIAL MORTGAGE LOANS.

Section 128 of the Truth in Lending Act (15 U. S. C. 1638) is amended by adding at the end the following new subsection:

"(f) PERIODIC STATEMENTS FOR RESIDENTIAL MORTGAGE LOANS. —

会可以要求贷款发放人发出第(b)款规定的通知或符合本法规定的其他通知。”

(b)**目录修正**。——《诚实信贷法》第二章条款目录修正如下:在第128条的目录项之后插入如下新的目录项:

“第128A条　混合型可调利率抵押贷款的利率重新设定。”

第1419条　披露要求

在《诚实信贷法》第128(a)条[《美国法典》第十五编第1638(a)节]结尾处增加如下新款,作为对该条的修正:

“(16)对于将开立代管账户或扣押账户,用以支付所有适用税费、保费和计征费的浮动利率住房抵押贷款而言——

(A)该贷款项下到期应付之本金和利息的初始月供金额,以及含有下列款项的初始月供金额:用于支付所有适用税费、保费和计征费的账户中所存入的每月款项;及

(B)该贷款项下到期应付之本金和利息的完全指数月供金额,以及含有下列款项的完全指数月供金额:用于支付适用税费、保费和计征费的账户中所存入的每月款项。

(17)对于住房抵押贷款而言,就为该贷款提供的所有结算服务而收取的结算费用总金额、包含在该贷款中的费用金额、借款人在贷款成交之时必须支付的费用金额、该贷款资金大致的批发性利率以及与该贷款相关的其他收费或必须支付的款项的合计金额。

(18)对于住房抵押贷款而言,向抵押贷款发起人支付的与该贷款相关的费用的合计金额、消费者直接支付的该等费用的金额以及抵押贷款发起人从贷款发放人处收到的任何其他款项。

(19)对于住房抵押贷款而言,消费者在该贷款有效期内将按照贷款本金百分比支付的利息总金额。计算该利息金额时,应假设消费者按时、一次性全额支付月度还款,且不进行任何超额还款。”

第1420条　住房抵押贷款月度对账单的披露要求

在《诚实信贷法》第128条(《美国法典》第十五编第1638节)结尾处增加如下新子条,作为对该条的修正:

“(f)**住房抵押贷款的定期对账单**。——

"(1) IN GENERAL. — The creditor, assignee, or servicer with respect to any residential mortgage loan shall transmit to the obligor, for each billing cycle, a statement setting forth each of the following items, to the extent applicable, in a conspicuous and prominent manner:

"(A) The amount of the principal obligation under the mortgage.

"(B) The current interest rate in effect for the loan.

"(C) The date on which the interest rate may next reset or adjust.

"(D) The amount of any prepayment fee to be charged, if any.

"(E) A description of any late payment fees.

"(F) A telephone number and electronic mail address that may be used by the obligor to obtain information regarding the mortgage.

"(G) The names, addresses, telephone numbers, and Internet addresses of counseling agencies or programs reasonably available to the consumer that have been certified or approved and made publicly available by the Secretary of Housing and Urban Development or a State housing finance authority (as defined in section 1301 of the Financial Institutions Reform, Recovery, and Enforcement Act of 1989).

"(H) Such other information as the Board may prescribe in regulations.

"(2) DEVELOPMENT AND USE OF STANDARD FORM. — The Board shall develop and prescribe a standard form for the disclosure required under this subsection, taking into account that the statements required may be transmitted in writing or electronically.

"(3) EXCEPTION. — Paragraph (1) shall not apply to any fixed rate residential mortgage loan where the creditor, assignee, or servicer provides the obligor with a coupon book that provides the obligor with substantially the same information as required in paragraph (1).".

SEC. 1421. REPORT BY THE GAO.

(a) REPORT REQUIRED. — The Comptroller General of the United States shall conduct a study to determine the effects the enactment of this Act will have on the availability and affordability of credit for consumers, small businesses, homebuyers, and mortgage lending, including the effect —

(1) on the mortgage market for mortgages that are not within the safe harbor provided in the amendments made by this subtitle;

(2) on the ability of prospective homebuyers to obtain financing;

(3) on the ability of homeowners facing resets or adjustments to refinance — for example, do they have fewer refinancing options due to the unavailability of certain loan products that were available before the enactment of this Act;

(4) on minorities' ability to access affordable credit compared with other prospective borrowers;

(5) on home sales and construction;

(1)**一般规定**。——住房抵押贷款的贷款发放人、受让人或服务机构应就每个账单周期,向借款人发送一份对账单。该对账单应在适用范围内,以明确、显著的方式列明如下项目:

(A)该抵押贷款项下的本金金额。

(B)该贷款当前有效适用的利率。

(C)下次利率可能重新设定或调整的日期。

(D)将收取的提前还款手续费(如有)之金额。

(E)有关任何逾期还款手续费的说明。

(F)借款人可能为获取抵押贷款信息而使用的电话号码和电子邮箱地址。

(G)住房与城市发展部部长或州住房金融局(定义见《1989年金融机构改革、复兴与实施法》第1301条)认证或批准且公布的、消费者可以合理获得其服务的咨询机构或咨询计划之名称、地址、电话和互联网网址。

(H)联邦储备委员会可能在规章中规定的其他信息。

(2)**标准格式的制定和使用**。——在就本子条要求披露的文件制定和规定标准格式之时,联邦储备委员会应考虑到规定的对账单可能通过书面或电子化方式发送。

(3)**例外规定**。——对于贷款发放人、受让人或服务机构已向借款人提供一份宣传册,且其中包含的信息与第(1)款规定的信息基本一致的任何固定利率住房抵押贷款,不适用第(1)款的规定。

第1421条　政府问责办公室的报告

(a)**报告要求**。——美国政府问责办公室主任应开展研究,以期判定本法的颁布对消费者、小型企业和购房人获得和负担信用的能力产生之影响,以及对抵押贷款的影响,包括——

(1)对本子编作出的修正中所规定的安全港范围之外的抵押贷款之市场的影响;

(2)对潜在购买人筹资能力的影响;

(3)对面临利率重新设定或调整的业主再融资能力的影响——例如,本法之颁布是否会导致其无法获得之前可以获得的特定贷款产品,从而使其可选的再融资受限;

(4)与其他潜在借款人相比,对少数族裔获得可负担信用的能力之影响;

(5)对房屋销售和建设的影响;

(6) of extending the rescission right, if any, on adjustable rate loans and its impact on litigation;

(7) of State foreclosure laws and, if any, an investor's ability to transfer a property after foreclosure;

(8) of expanding the existing provisions of the Home Ownership and Equity Protection Act of 1994;

(9) of prohibiting prepayment penalties on high–cost mortgages; and

(10) of establishing counseling services under the Department of Housing and Urban Development and offered through the Office of Housing Counseling.

(b) REPORT. — Before the end of the 1–year period beginning on the date of the enactment of this Act, the Comptroller General shall submit a report to the Congress containing the findings and conclusions of the Comptroller General with respect to the study conducted pursuant to subsection (a).

(c) EXAMINATION RELATED TO CERTAIN CREDIT RISK RETENTION PROVISIONS. — The report required by subsection (b) shall also include an analysis by the Comptroller General of the effect on the capital reserves and funding of lenders of credit risk retention provisions for non–qualified mortgages, including an analysis of the exceptions and adjustments authorized in section 129C(b)(3) of the Truth in Lending Act and a recommendation on whether a uniform standard is needed.

(d) ANALYSIS OF CREDIT RISK RETENTION PROVISIONS. — The report required by subsection (b) shall also include —

(1) an analysis by the Comptroller General of whether the credit risk retention provisions have significantly reduced risks to the larger credit market of the repackaging and selling of securitized loans on a secondary market; and

(2) recommendations to the Congress on adjustments that should be made, or additional measures that should be undertaken.

SEC. 1422. STATE ATTORNEY GENERAL ENFORCEMENT AUTHORITY.

Section 130(e) of the Truth in Lending Act (15 U. S. C. 1640(e)) is amended by striking "section 129 may also" and inserting "section 129, 129B, 129C, 129D, 129E, 129F, 129G, or 129H of this Act may also".

(6)授予合同撤销权(如有)对可调利率贷款的影响及对诉讼的影响;

(7)州止赎法律(如有)对投资者在止赎之后转让房地产能力的影响;

(8)增加《1994年住房所有权和房屋权益保护法》现有规定所产生的影响;

(9)禁止收取提前还款违约金对高成本抵押贷款的影响;及

(10)住房与城市发展部设立住房咨询办公室提供咨询服务所产生的影响。

(b)报告。——政府问责办公室主任应于本法颁布之日起一年内,向国会提交一份报告,说明政府问责办公室主任按照第(a)子条规定开展研究得出的认定和结论。

(c)**关于特定信用风险自留条款的审查**。——在按照第(b)子条要求提供的报告中,政府问责办公室主任还应分析不合格抵押贷款的信用风险自留条款对贷款人资本公积金和经费来源的影响,包括分析《诚实信贷法》第129C(b)(3)条授权的例外待遇和调整,以及关于是否需要统一标准的建议。

(d)**关于信用风险自留条款的分析**。——第(b)子条规定的报告还应包括——

(1)针对信用风险自留条款是否大幅降低了二级市场上证券化贷款的重新打包和出售对整体信贷市场的风险,政府问责办公室主任进行的分析;及

(2)政府问责办公室主任针对需要作出的调整或采取的其他措施向国会提出的建议。

第1422条　州总检察长的执法权

《诚实信贷法》第130(e)条[《美国法典》第十五编第1640(e)节]修正如下:删除"第129条亦可",替以"本法第129条、第129B条、第129C条、第129D条、第129E条、第129F条、第129G条或第129H条亦可"。

Subtitle C—High–Cost Mortgages

SEC. 1431. DEFINITIONS RELATING TO HIGH–COST MORTGAGES.

(a) HIGH–COST MORTGAGE DEFINED. — Section 103(aa) of the Truth in Lending Act (15 U. S. C. 1602 (aa)) is amended by striking all that precedes paragraph (2) and inserting the following:

"(aa) HIGH–COST MORTGAGE. —

"(1) DEFINITION. —

"(A) IN GENERAL. — The term 'high–cost mortgage', and a mortgage referred to in this subsection, means a consumer credit transaction that is secured by the consumer's principal dwelling, other than a reverse mortgage transaction, if —

"(i) in the case of a credit transaction secured —

"(I) by a first mortgage on the consumer's principal dwelling, the annual percentage rate at consummation of the transaction will exceed by more than 6. 5 percentage points (8. 5 percentage points, if the dwelling is personal property and the transaction is for less than $50, 000) the average prime offer rate, as defined in section 129C(b)(2)(B), for a comparable transaction; or

"(II) by a subordinate or junior mortgage on the consumer's principal dwelling, the annual percentage rate at consummation of the transaction will exceed by more than 8. 5 percentage points the average prime offer rate, as defined in section 129C(b)(2)(B), for a comparable transaction;

"(ii) the total points and fees payable in connection with the transaction, other than bona fide third party charges not retained by the mortgage originator, creditor, or an affiliate of the creditor or mortgage originator, exceed —

"(I) in the case of a transaction for $20, 000 or more, 5 percent of the total transaction amount; or

"(II) in the case of a transaction for less than $20, 000, the lesser of 8 percent of the total transaction amount or $1, 000 (or such other dollar amount as the Board shall prescribe by regulation); or

"(iii) the credit transaction documents permit the creditor to charge or collect prepayment fees or penalties more than 36 months after the transaction closing or such fees or penalties exceed, in the aggregate, more than 2 percent of the amount prepaid.

"(B) INTRODUCTORY RATES TAKEN INTO ACCOUNT. — For purposes of subparagraph (A)(i), the annual percentage rate of interest shall be determined based on the

第C子编——高成本抵押贷款

第1431条　高成本抵押贷款相关术语的定义

(a)**高成本抵押贷款的定义**。——《诚实信贷法》第103(aa)条[《美国法典》第十五编第1602(aa)节]修正如下:删除第(2)款之前的所有内容,替以如下内容:

“(aa)**高成本抵押贷款**。——

(1)**定义**。——

(A)**一般规定**。——‘高成本抵押贷款’一词及本条提及的抵押贷款均指反向抵押贷款交易之外的以消费者主要住所担保的消费者信用交易,前提是——

(i)该等信用交易的年利率满足如下标准——

(I)对于以消费者主要住所第一顺位抵押权担保的信用交易而言,交易合同订立之时的年利率将超出可比交易的平均最优惠利率[定义见第129C(b)(2)(B)条]6.5个百分点以上(如果该住所属于私人财产,且交易金额少于5万美元,则超出8.5个百分点以上);或

(II)对于以消费者主要住所的次级或次位抵押权担保的信用交易而言,交易合同订立之时的年利率将超出可比交易的平均最优惠利率(定义见第129C(b)(2)(B)条)8.5个百分点以上;

(ii)除抵押贷款发起人、贷款发放人或贷款发放人或抵押贷款发起人的关联方未留存的善意第三方收费之外,与交易相关的应付总点数和手续费——

(I)在交易金额超过2万美元(含)之时,超过交易总金额的5%;或

(II)在交易金额少于2万美元之时,超过总交易金额的8%或1000美元(以金额较低者为准),或超过联邦储备委员会发布的规章所规定的其他金额;或

(iii)信用交易文件允许贷款发放人在交易成交届满36个月之后收取提前还款手续费或违约金,或允许该等费用或罚款合计金额超过提前还款金额的2%。

(B)**考虑先期利率**。——就第(A)(i)子款而言,年利率应基于如下利率确定:

following interest rate:

"(i) In the case of a fixed–rate transaction in which the annual percentage rate will not vary during the term of the loan, the interest rate in effect on the date of consummation of the transaction.

"(ii) In the case of a transaction in which the rate of interest varies solely in accordance with an index, the interest rate determined by adding the index rate in effect on the date of consummation of the transaction to the maximum margin permitted at any time during the loan agreement.

"(iii) In the case of any other transaction in which the rate may vary at any time during the term of the loan for any reason, the interest charged on the transaction at the maximum rate that may be charged during the term of the loan.

"(C) MORTGAGE INSURANCE. — For the purposes of computing the total points and fees under paragraph (4), the total points and fees shall exclude —

"(i) any premium provided by an agency of the Federal Government or an agency of a State;

"(ii) any amount that is not in excess of the amount payable under policies in effect at the time of origination under section 203(c)(2)(A) of the National Housing Act (12 U. S. C. 1709(c)(2)(A)), provided that the premium, charge, or fee is required to be refundable on a pro–rated basis and the refund is automatically issued upon notification of the satisfaction of the underlying mortgage loan; and

"(iii) any premium paid by the consumer after closing. ".

(b) ADJUSTMENT OF PERCENTAGE POINTS. — Section 103(aa)(2) of the Truth in Lending Act (15 U. S. C. 1602(aa)(2)) is amended by striking subparagraph (B) and inserting the following new subparagraph:

"(B) An increase or decrease under subparagraph (A) —

"(i) may not result in the number of percentage points referred to in paragraph (1)(A)(i)(I) being less than 6 percentage points or greater than 10 percentage points; and

"(ii) may not result in the number of percentage points referred to in paragraph (1)(A)(i)(II) being less than 8 percentage points or greater than 12 percentage points. ".

(c) POINTS AND FEES DEFINED. —

(1) IN GENERAL. — Section 103(aa)(4) of the Truth in Lending Act (15 U. S. C. 1602(aa)(4)) is amended —

(A) by striking subparagraph (B) and inserting the following:

"(B) all compensation paid directly or indirectly by a consumer or creditor to a mortgage originator from any source, including a mortgage originator that is also the creditor in a table–funded transaction; ";

(B) by redesignating subparagraph (D) as subparagraph (G); and

(i)对于年利率在贷款期限内保持不变的固定利率交易,交易合同订立之日有效适用的利率。

(ii)对于利率仅根据指数变化的交易,交易合同订立之日有效适用的指数利率加上贷款协议期限内任何时候准许采用的最大利差得出的利率。

(iii)对于利率可能因任何原因在贷款期限内任何时候发生变化的任何其他交易,按照贷款期限内可以收取的最高利率对该交易收取的利息。

(C)**抵押贷款保险**。——在按照第(4)款规定计算总点数和手续费之时,总点数和手续费不得包括——

(i)联邦政府机关或州机关支付的任何保费;

(ii)不超过根据《国民住房法》第203(c)(2)(A)条[《美国法典》第十二编第1709(c)(2)(A)节]发起贷款时有效保单项下应付保费的金额,前提是保费、收费或手续费应可以按比例退还,并且退还金额应在相应抵押贷款偿清通知发出之后立即自动退还;及

(iii)消费者在贷款成交之后支付的任何保费。”

(b)**百分点的调整**。——《诚实信贷法》第103(aa)(2)条[《美国法典》第十五编第1602(aa)(2)节]修正如下:删除第(B)子款,替以如下新子款:

“(B)第(A)子款规定的数额的增减——

(i)不得导致第(1)(A)(i)(I)款规定的百分点低于6个百分点或高于10个百分点;且

(ii)不得导致第(1)(A)(i)(II)款规定的百分点低于8个百分点或高于12个百分点。”

(c)**点数与手续费的定义**。——

(1)**一般规定**。——《诚实信贷法》第103(aa)(4)条[《美国法典》第十五编第1602(aa)(4)节]修正如下——

(A)删除第(B)子款,替以如下内容:

“(B)消费者或贷款发放人依靠任何资金来源直接或间接向抵押贷款发起人支付的所有报酬,包括在发起贷款并转让贷款权益的交易中同时担任贷款发放人的抵押贷款发起人;”;

(B)第(D)子款重新编号为第(G)子款;及

(C) by inserting after subparagraph (C) the following new subparagraphs:

"(D) premiums or other charges payable at or before closing for any credit life, credit disability, credit unemployment, or credit property insurance, or any other accident, loss-of-income, life or health insurance, or any payments directly or indirectly for any debt cancellation or suspension agreement or contract, except that insurance premiums or debt cancellation or suspension fees calculated and paid in full on a monthly basis shall not be considered financed by the creditor;

"(E) the maximum prepayment fees and penalties which may be charged or collected under the terms of the credit transaction;

"(F) all prepayment fees or penalties that are incurred by the consumer if the loan refinances a previous loan made or currently held by the same creditor or an affiliate of the creditor; and".

(2) CALCULATION OF POINTS AND FEES FOR OPEN-END CONSUMER CREDIT PLANS. — Section 103(aa) of the Truth in Lending Act (15 U. S. C. 1602(aa)) is amended —

(A) by redesignating paragraph (5) as paragraph (6); and

(B) by inserting after paragraph (4) the following new paragraph:

"(5) CALCULATION OF POINTS AND FEES FOR OPEN-END CONSUMER CREDIT PLANS. — In the case of open-end consumer credit plans, points and fees shall be calculated, for purposes of this section and section 129, by adding the total points and fees known at or before closing, including the maximum prepayment penalties which may be charged or collected under the terms of the credit transaction, plus the minimum additional fees the consumer would be required to pay to draw down an amount equal to the total credit line.".

(d) BONA FIDE DISCOUNT LOAN DISCOUNT POINTS. — Section 103 of the Truth in Lending Act (15 U. S. C. 1602) is amended by inserting after subsection (cc)(as added by section 1401) the following new subsection:

"(dd) BONA FIDE DISCOUNT POINTS AND PREPAYMENT PENALTIES. — For the purposes of determining the amount of points and fees for purposes of subsection (aa), either the amounts described in paragraph (1) or (2) of the following paragraphs, but not both, shall be excluded:

"(1) Up to and including 2 bona fide discount points payable by the consumer in connection with the mortgage, but only if the interest rate from which the mortgage's interest rate will be discounted does not exceed by more than 1 percentage point —

"(A) the average prime offer rate, as defined in section 129C; or

"(B) if secured by a personal property loan, the average rate on a loan in connection with which insurance is provided under title I of the National Housing Act (12 U. S. C. 1702

(C)在第(C)子款之后插入如下内容:

"(D)在交易成交之时或之前,对于任何信用人寿保险、信用残疾保险、信用失业保险或信用财产保险,或者任何其他意外保险、收入损失保险、人寿保险或健康保险,应支付的保费或其他收费,或者为债务撤销或债务暂停协议或合同所直接或间接支付的任何款项,但是,按月计算并全额支付的保费或债务撤销或暂停手续费不得视为系由贷款发放人提供的融资;

(E)根据信用交易条款的规定可以收取的最高提前还款手续费和违约金;

(F)消费者承担的所有提前还款手续费或违约金(如果该贷款的性质系为同一贷款发放人或其关联方之前发放或目前持有的贷款提供再融资);及"。

(2)**开放式消费者信用计划点数和手续费的计算**。——《诚实信贷法》第103(aa)条[《美国法典》第十五编第1602(aa)节]修正如下——

(A)第(5)款重新编号为第(6)款;及

(B)在第(4)款之后插入如下新款:

"(5)**开放式消费者信用计划点数和手续费的计算**。——对于开放式消费者信用计划而言,在为本条和第129条之目的计算点数和手续费之时,应采用如下方法:交易成交之时或之前已知的总点数和手续费(包括根据信用交易条款可以收取的最高提前还款违约金)加上消费者提取与总信贷额度相等的金额之时,将需支付的最低数额的加收费用。"

(d)**贴现贷款的善意折扣点数**。——《诚实信贷法》第103条[《美国法典》第十五编第1602节]修正如下:在第1401条增加的第(cc)子条之后插入如下新子条:

"(dd)**善意折扣点数与提前还款违约金**。——在确定第(aa)子条规定的点数和手续费的金额之时,应排除下文第(1)款或第(2)款中任一款规定的金额,但不得同时排除两款规定的金额:

"(1)应排除消费者应就抵押贷款支付的善意折扣点数[最高可排除2个(含)点数],但仅在折扣前的抵押贷款利率超出如下利率的幅度不高于1个百分点的情况下,方可排除该等折扣点数——

(A)第129C条定义的平均最优惠利率;或

(B)对于以动产抵押贷款担保的,按照《国民住房法》第一编[《美国法典》第十二编第1702节及其后条文]规定提供保险的贷款的平均利率。

et seq.) .

"(2) Unless 2 bona fide discount points have been excluded under paragraph (1), up to and including 1 bona fide discount point payable by the consumer in connection with the mortgage, but only if the interest rate from which the mortgage's interest rate will be discounted does not exceed by more than 2 percentage points —

"(A) the average prime offer rate, as defined in section 129C; or

"(B) if secured by a personal property loan, the average rate on a loan in connection with which insurance is provided under title I of the National Housing Act (12 U. S. C. 1702 et seq.) .

"(3) For purposes of paragraph (1), the term 'bona fide discount points' means loan discount points which are knowingly paid by the consumer for the purpose of reducing, and which in fact result in a bona fide reduction of, the interest rate or time–price differential applicable to the mortgage.

"(4) Paragraphs (1) and (2) shall not apply to discount points used to purchase an interest rate reduction unless the amount of the interest rate reduction purchased is reasonably consistent with established industry norms and practices for secondary mortgage market transactions. ".

SEC. 1432. AMENDMENTS TO EXISTING REQUIREMENTS FOR CERTAIN MORTGAGES.

(a) PREPAYMENT PENALTY PROVISIONS. — Section 129(c)(2) of the Truth in Lending Act (15 U. S. C. 1639(c)(2)) is hereby repealed.

(b) NO BALLOON PAYMENTS. — Section 129(e) of the Truth in Lending Act (15 U. S. C. 1639(e)) is amended to read as follows:

"(e) NO BALLOON PAYMENTS. — No high–cost mortgage may contain a scheduled payment that is more than twice as large as the average of earlier scheduled payments. This subsection shall not apply when the payment schedule is adjusted to the seasonal or irregular income of the consumer. ".

SEC. 1433. ADDITIONAL REQUIREMENTS FOR CERTAIN MORTGAGES.

(a) ADDITIONAL REQUIREMENTS FOR CERTAIN MORTGAGES. —Section 129 of the Truth in Lending Act (15 U. S. C. 1639) is amended —

(1) by redesignating subsections (j), (k), (l) and (m) as subsections (n), (o), (p), and (q) respectively; and

(2) by inserting after subsection (i) the following new subsections:

"(j) RECOMMENDED DEFAULT. — No creditor shall recommend or encourage default on an existing loan or other debt prior to and in connection with the closing or planned closing of a high–cost mortgage that refinances all or any portion of such existing loan or debt.

(2)除非已按照第(1)款的规定将2个善意折扣点数排除在外,否则,应排除消费者应就抵押贷款支付的善意折扣点数[最高可排除1个(含)点数],但仅在折扣前的抵押贷款利率超出如下利率的幅度不高于2个百分点的情况下,方可排除该等折扣点数——

(A)第129C条定义的平均最优惠利率;或

(B)对于有动产抵押贷款担保的抵押贷款,按照《国民住房法》第一编(《美国法典》第十二编第1702节及其后条文)规定承保的贷款的平均利率。

(3)就第(1)款而言,'善意折扣点数'一词系指消费者在知情的情况下,为了降低抵押贷款的适用利率,或者为了降低分期还款与一次性还款的还款差额而支付的贷款折扣点数,并且该等折扣点数事实上导致了该利率善意降低,或导致了分期还款与一次性还款的还款差额的善意降低。

(4)第(1)款和第(2)款不适用于被用于购买利率优惠的折扣点数,但是购买的利率优惠数额合理符合二级抵押贷款市场交易适用的既定行业标准和惯例的情形除外。"

第1432条　针对特定抵押贷款的现有要求作出的修正

(a)**提前还款违约金规定**。——《诚实信贷法》第129(c)(2)条[《美国法典》第十五编第1639(c)(2)节]兹予废止。

(b)**禁止大额尾付**。——《诚实信贷法》第129(e)条[《美国法典》第十五编第1639(e)节]修正后全文如下:

"(e)**禁止大额尾付**。——在高成本抵押贷款中,任何一笔计划还款均不得超过以往计划还款平均值的两倍以上。由于消费者收入的季节性或不规律性对还款计划进行调整时,不适用本子条的规定。"

第1433条　针对特定抵押贷款的额外要求

(a)针对特定抵押贷款的额外要求。——《诚实信贷法》第129条(《美国法典》第十五编第1639节)修正如下——

(1)第(j)子条、第(k)子条、第(l)子条和第(m)子条分别重新编号为第(n)子条、第(o)子条、第(p)子条和第(q)子条;及

(2)在第(i)子条之后插入如下新子条:

"(j)**建议拖欠还款**。——对于为全部或部分既存贷款或其他债务提供再融资的高成本抵押贷款,任何贷款发放人不得在该高成本抵押贷款的成交或计划成交之前以及由于该高成本抵押贷款的成交或计划成交而建议或鼓励债务人拖欠对既存贷款

"(k) LATE FEES. —

"(1) IN GENERAL. — No creditor may impose a late payment charge or fee in connection with a high–cost mortgage —

"(A) in an amount in excess of 4 percent of the amount of the payment past due;

"(B) unless the loan documents specifically authorize the charge or fee;

"(C) before the end of the 15–day period beginning on the date the payment is due, or in the case of a loan on which interest on each installment is paid in advance, before the end of the 30–day period beginning on the date the payment is due; or

"(D) more than once with respect to a single late payment.

"(2) COORDINATION WITH SUBSEQUENT LATE FEES. — If a payment is otherwise a full payment for the applicable period and is paid on its due date or within an applicable grace period, and the only delinquency or insufficiency of payment is attributable to any late fee or delinquency charge assessed on any earlier payment, no late fee or delinquency charge may be imposed on such payment.

"(3) FAILURE TO MAKE INSTALLMENT PAYMENT. — If, in the case of a loan agreement the terms of which provide that any payment shall first be applied to any past due principal balance, the consumer fails to make an installment payment and the consumer subsequently resumes making installment payments but has not paid all past due installments, the creditor may impose a separate late payment charge or fee for any principal due (without deduction due to late fees or related fees) until the default is cured.

"(l) ACCELERATION OF DEBT. — No high–cost mortgage may contain a provision which permits the creditor to accelerate the indebtedness, except when repayment of the loan has been accelerated by default in payment, or pursuant to a due–on–sale provision, or pursuant to a material violation of some other provision of the loan document unrelated to payment schedule.

"(m) RESTRICTION ON FINANCING POINTS AND FEES. — No creditor may directly or indirectly finance, in connection with any high–cost mortgage, any of the following:

"(1) Any prepayment fee or penalty payable by the consumer in a refinancing transaction if the creditor or an affiliate of the creditor is the noteholder of the note being refinanced.

"(2) Any points or fees. ".

(b) PROHIBITIONS ON EVASIONS. — Section 129 of the Truth in Lending Act (15 U. S. C. 1639) is amended by inserting after subsection (q)(as so redesignated by subsection (a)(1)) the following new subsection:

"(r) PROHIBITIONS ON EVASIONS, STRUCTURING OF TRANSACTIONS, AND RECIPROCAL ARRANGEMENTS. — A creditor may not take any action in connection with

或债务的还款。

(k)**滞纳金**。——

(1)**一般规定**。——任何贷款发放人在针对高成本抵押贷款收取逾期还款滞纳金或手续费之时——

(A)逾期还款滞纳金均不得超过逾期未付还款金额的4%;

(B)贷款文件明确允许的方得收取;

(C)收取逾期还款滞纳金或手续费的时间不得早于还款到期应付之日起15天内,或者,对于每笔分期还款的利息均已提前支付的贷款而言,不得早于还款到期应付之日起30天内;或

(D)不得对一笔逾期还款多次收取逾期还款滞纳金或手续费。

(2)**与后续滞纳金的协调**。——如果某笔还款本应构成相应还款期的足额还款,且已在还款到期日或相应宽限期内支付,并且所拖欠或未足额支付的金额完全属于针对以往还款计征的滞纳金或拖欠还贷罚款,则不得对该笔还款收取任何滞纳金或拖欠还贷罚款。

(3)**未进行分期还款的情形**。——如果贷款协议中规定还款应首先用于支付逾期未付的本金余额,而消费者出现未支付分期还款的情形,但随后恢复按期分期还款,但并未全额偿还所有逾期未付的分期还款,则贷款发放人可以对到期应付的本金单独计收逾期还款滞纳金或手续费(不可以其他滞纳金或相关费用抵扣),直至拖欠还款全部付清为止。

(l)**债务加速到期**。——任何高成本抵押贷款均不得含有允许贷款发放人加速债务到期的条款,但是由于以下情形导致提前还款的除外:债务人拖欠还款;适用出售即到期条款;或出现关于贷款文件中与还款计划无关的某些其他条款的重大违约行为。

(m)**点数和手续费的融资限制**。——任何贷款发放人均不得直接或间接为任何高成本抵押贷款的下述款项或费用提供融资:

(1)消费者在再融资交易中应支付的任何提前还款手续费或违约金,但前提是贷款发放人或其关联方是进行再融资的票据的持有人。

(2)任何点数或手续费。”

(b)**禁止规避**。——《诚实信贷法》第129条(《美国法典》第十五编第1639节)修正如下:在第(q)子条[以第(a)(1)子条重新编号后的序号为准]之后插入如下新子条:

“(r)**禁止规避、交易构建以及互惠安排**。——对于高成本抵押贷款,任何贷款发放人均不得——

a high–cost mortgage —

"(1) to structure a loan transaction as an open–end credit plan or another form of loan for the purpose and with the intent of evading the provisions of this title; or

"(2) to divide any loan transaction into separate parts for the purpose and with the intent of evading provisions of this title. ".

(c) MODIFICATION OR DEFERRAL FEES. — Section 129 of the Truth in Lending Act (15 U. S. C. 1639) is amended by inserting after subsection (r)(as added by subsection (b) of this section) the following new subsection:

"(s) MODIFICATION AND DEFERRAL FEES PROHIBITED. — A creditor, successor in interest, assignee, or any agent of any of the above, may not charge a consumer any fee to modify, renew, extend, or amend a high–cost mortgage, or to defer any payment due under the terms of such mortgage. ".

(d) PAYOFF STATEMENT. — Section 129 of the Truth in Lending Act (15 U. S. C. 1639) is amended by inserting after subsection (s)(as added by subsection (c) of this section) the following new subsection:

"(t) PAYOFF STATEMENT. —

"(1) FEES. —

"(A) IN GENERAL. — Except as provided in subparagraph (B), no creditor or servicer may charge a fee for informing or transmitting to any person the balance due to pay off the outstanding balance on a high–cost mortgage.

"(B) TRANSACTION FEE. — When payoff information referred to in subparagraph (A) is provided by facsimile transmission or by a courier service, a creditor or servicer may charge a processing fee to cover the cost of such transmission or service in an amount not to exceed an amount that is comparable to fees imposed for similar services provided in connection with consumer credit transactions that are secured by the consumer's principal dwelling and are not high–cost mortgages.

"(C) FEE DISCLOSURE. — Prior to charging a transaction fee as provided in subparagraph (B), a creditor or servicer shall disclose that payoff balances are available for free pursuant to subparagraph (A).

"(D) MULTIPLE REQUESTS. — If a creditor or servicer has provided payoff information referred to in subparagraph (A) without charge, other than the transaction fee allowed by subparagraph (B), on 4 occasions during a calendar year, the creditor or servicer may thereafter charge a reasonable fee for providing such information during the remainder of the calendar year.

"(2) PROMPT DELIVERY. — Payoff balances shall be provided within 5 business days after receiving a request by a consumer or a person authorized by the consumer to obtain such information. ".

(1)为了规避本编规定,将贷款交易构建为开放式信用计划或其他形式的贷款;或

(2)为了规避本编规定,将任何贷款交易拆分成不同的部分。”

(c)**贷款修改或延期还款费**。——《诚实信贷法》第129条[《美国法典》第十五编第1639节]修正如下:在本条第(b)子条增加的第(r)子条之后插入如下新子条:

“(s)**禁止收取贷款修改费和延期还款费**。——任何贷款发放人及其权益继受人、受让人或上述各者的任何代理人,均不得针对高成本抵押贷款的修改、展期、延期或修正,或者针对该抵押贷款条款规定的到期款项的延期支付,向消费者收取任何费用。”

(d)**贷款清偿声明**。——《诚实信贷法》第129条(《美国法典》第十五编第1639节)修正如下:在本条第(c)子条增加的第(s)子条之后插入如下新子条:

“(t)**贷款清偿声明**。——

(1)**费用**。——

(A)**一般规定**。——除第(B)子款规定的情形外,任何贷款发放人或服务机构均不得因向任何人通知或传达清偿高成本抵押贷款应支付的到期余额,而收取任何费用。

(B)**手续费**。——如果第(A)子款所述贷款清偿信息系通过传真提供或通过快递送达,贷款发放人或服务机构可以按照传真或快递成本收取手续费,但该手续费的金额不得超过就下述交易提供类似服务时收取的可比金额:以消费者主要住所为担保,且不属于高成本抵押贷款的消费者信用交易。

(C)**费用披露**。——在收取第(B)子款规定的手续费之前,贷款发放人或服务机构应进行披露,说明未偿余额信息系按照第(A)子款的规定免费提供。

(D)**多次信息申请**。——如果贷款发放人或服务机构在某一日历年内已经4次免费[但第(B)子款允许收取的手续费除外]提供第(A)子款所述贷款清偿信息,则该贷款发放人或服务机构在该日历年剩余时间内再提供该等信息时,可以收取合理的费用。

(2)**及时送达**。——消费者或经其授权获取贷款清偿信息的人提出获取贷款清偿信息请求的,贷款发放人或服务机构应在收到请求后的5个营业日内予以提供。

(e) PRE–LOAN COUNSELING REQUIRED. — Section 129 of the Truth in Lending Act (15 U. S. C. 1639) is amended by inserting after subsection (t)(as added by subsection (d) of this section) the following new subsection:

"(u) PRE–LOAN COUNSELING. —

"(1) IN GENERAL. —A creditor may not extend credit to a consumer under a high–cost mortgage without first receiving certification from a counselor that is approved by the Secretary of Housing and Urban Development, or at the discretion of the Secretary, a State housing finance authority, that the consumer has received counseling on the advisability of the mortgage. Such counselor shall not be employed by the creditor or an affiliate of the creditor or be affiliated with the creditor.

"(2) DISCLOSURES REQUIRED PRIOR TO COUNSELING. —No counselor may certify that a consumer has received counseling on the advisability of the high–cost mortgage unless the counselor can verify that the consumer has received each statement required (in connection with such loan) by this section or the Real Estate Settlement Procedures Act of 1974 with respect to the transaction.

"(3) REGULATIONS. — The Board may prescribe such regulations as the Board determines to be appropriate to carry out the requirements of paragraph (1) . ".

(f) CORRECTIONS AND UNINTENTIONAL VIOLATIONS. — Section 129 of the Truth in Lending Act (15 U. S. C. 1639) is amended by inserting after subsection (u)(as added by subsection (e)) the following new subsection:

"(v) CORRECTIONS AND UNINTENTIONAL VIOLATIONS. — A creditor or assignee in a high–cost mortgage who, when acting in good faith, fails to comply with any requirement under this section will not be deemed to have violated such requirement if the creditor or assignee establishes that either —

"(1) within 30 days of the loan closing and prior to the institution of any action, the consumer is notified of or discovers the violation, appropriate restitution is made, and whatever adjustments are necessary are made to the loan to either, at the choice of the consumer —

"(A) make the loan satisfy the requirements of this chapter; or

"(B) in the case of a high–cost mortgage, change the terms of the loan in a manner beneficial to the consumer so that the loan will no longer be a high–cost mortgage; or

"(2) within 60 days of the creditor's discovery or receipt of notification of an unintentional violation or bona fide error and prior to the institution of any action, the consumer is notified of the compliance failure, appropriate restitution is made, and whatever adjustments are necessary are made to the loan to either, at the choice of the consumer —

"(A) make the loan satisfy the requirements of this chapter; or

"(B) in the case of a high–cost mortgage, change the terms of the loan in a manner

(e)**贷款之前的咨询要求**。——《诚实信贷法》第129条(《美国法典》第十五编第1639节)修正如下:在本条第(d)子条增加的第(t)子条之后插入如下新子条:

"(u)**贷款之前的咨询**。——

(1)**一般规定**。——如果贷款发放人未先收到住房与城市发展部部长批准的咨询顾问出具的证明或住房与城市发展部部长依其自由裁量权指定的州住房金融局批准的咨询顾问出具的证明,即关于高成本抵押贷款消费者已就该高成本抵押贷款的可取性获得咨询的证明,则不得向该消费者发放贷款。该咨询顾问不得与贷款发放人或其关联方存在雇佣关系,或与贷款发放人存在关联关系。

(2)**咨询之前的披露要求**。——除非咨询顾问能够核实消费者已经收到本条或《1974年房地产结算程序法》规定的与高成本抵押贷款相关的每一说明书,否则,其不得证明消费者已经就该高成本抵押贷款的可取性接受了咨询。

(3)**规章**。——联邦储备委员会可以制定其判定对于实施第(1)款规定确属适当的规章。"

(f)**违法违规行为的整改和非故意违法违规行为**。——《诚实信贷法》第129条(《美国法典》第十五编第1639节)修正如下:在第(e)子条增加的第(u)子条之后插入如下新子条:

"(v)**违法违规行为的整改和非故意违法违规行为**。——高成本抵押贷款中的贷款发放人或受让人善意行事时,未能遵守本条任何规定的,不得被视为构成对该等规定的违反,前提是该贷款发放人或受让人能够证明——

(1)在贷款成交之日后30天内,且在任何诉讼提起之前,消费者已被通知或已发现该违法违规行为,且贷款发放人或受让人已对消费者作出适当的不当得利返还,并对贷款做出了必要的调整,以便按照消费者的选择——

(A)使贷款满足本章的要求;或

(B)对于高成本抵押贷款,以对消费者有利的方式修改贷款条款,使该贷款不再构成高成本抵押贷款;或

(2)在贷款发放人发现非故意违法违规行为或善意过错或收到有关该违法违规行为或过错通知之日后60天内,且在任何诉讼提起之前,消费者已被通知该违法违规行为,且贷款发放人或受让人已向消费者作出适当的不当得利返还,并对贷款作出了必要的调整,以便按照消费者的选择——

(A)使贷款满足本章的要求;或

(B)对于高成本抵押贷款,以对消费者有利的方式修改贷款条款,使该贷款不再

beneficial so that the loan will no longer be a high–cost mortgage. ".

Subtitle D—Office of Housing Counseling

SEC. 1441. SHORT TITLE.

This subtitle may be cited as the "Expand and Preserve Home Ownership through Counseling Act".

SEC. 1442. ESTABLISHMENT OF OFFICE OF HOUSING COUNSELING.

Section 4 of the Department of Housing and Urban Development Act (42 U. S. C. 3533) is amended by adding at the end the following new subsection:

"(g) OFFICE OF HOUSING COUNSELING. —

"(1) ESTABLISHMENT. — There is established, in the Department, the Office of Housing Counseling.

"(2) DIRECTOR. — There is established the position of Director of Housing Counseling. The Director shall be the head of the Office of Housing Counseling and shall be appointed by, and shall report to, the Secretary. Such position shall be a career–reserved position in the Senior Executive Service.

"(3) FUNCTIONS. —

"(A) IN GENERAL. — The Director shall have primary responsibility within the Department for all activities and matters relating to homeownership counseling and rental housing counseling, including —

"(i) research, grant administration, public outreach, and policy development relating to such counseling; and

"(ii) establishment, coordination, and administration of all regulations, requirements, standards, and performance measures under programs and laws administered by the Department that relate to housing counseling, homeownership counseling (including maintenance of homes), mortgage–related counseling (including home equity conversion mortgages and credit protection options to avoid foreclosure), and rental housing counseling, including the requirements, standards, and performance measures relating to housing counseling.

"(B) SPECIFIC FUNCTIONS. — The Director shall carry out the functions assigned to the Director and the Office under this section and any other provisions of law. Such functions shall include establishing rules necessary for —

"(i) the counseling procedures under section 106(g)(1) of the Housing and Urban Development Act of 1968 (12 U. S. C. 1701x(h)(1));

构成高成本抵押贷款。”

第D子编——住房咨询办公室

第1441条　简称

引述本子编时,可简称为《促进与保护置业咨询法》。

第1442条　设立住房咨询办公室

在《住房与城市发展部法》第4条(《美国法典》第四十二编第3533节)结尾处增加如下新子条,作为对该条的修正:

“(g)**住房咨询办公室**。——

(1)**设立**。——兹于住房与城市发展部之下设立住房咨询办公室。

(2)**主任**。——兹设住房咨询办公室主任一职。住房咨询办公室主任作为住房咨询办公室的负责人,由住房与城市发展部部长任命,并向住房与城市发展部部长汇报工作。该职位属于“高级公务员序列”中通过指定方式任命的职位。

(3)**职能**。——

(A)**一般规定**。——在住房与城市发展部内部,住房咨询办公室主任应对与房屋所有权咨询和租赁住房咨询相关的活动和事宜承担主要责任,包括——

(i)与上述咨询有关的研究、补助金管理、宣传和政策制定工作;及

(ii)对于住房与城市发展部负责实施的计划和法律,但凡关乎住房咨询、房屋所有权咨询(包括房屋维护)、抵押贷款咨询(包括房屋权益转换抵押贷款和防止银行止赎的可选信用保护方法)和租赁住房咨询的,住房咨询办公室主任均应制定、协调和实施该等计划中和依据该等法律制定的所有规章、要求、标准和绩效指标,包括与住房咨询相关的要求、标准和绩效指标。

(B)**具体职能**。——住房咨询办公室主任应履行本条以及任何其他法律规定赋予住房咨询办公室主任及住房咨询办公室的职能,包括针对以下工作的开展制定必要的规则——

(i)落实《1968年住房与城市发展法》第106(g)(1)条[《美国法典》第十二编第1701x(h)(1)节]规定的咨询程序;

"(ii) carrying out all other functions of the Secretary under section 106(g) of the Housing and Urban Development Act of 1968, including the establishment, operation, and publication of the availability of the toll-free telephone number under paragraph (2) of such section;

"(iii) contributing to the distribution of home buying information booklets pursuant to section 5 of the Real Estate Settlement Procedures Act of 1974 (12 U. S. C. 2604);

"(iv) carrying out the certification program under section 106 (e) of the Housing and Urban Development Act of 1968 (12 U. S. C. 1701x(e));

"(v) carrying out the assistance program under section 106(a)(4) of the Housing and Urban Development Act of 1968, including criteria for selection of applications to receive assistance;

"(vi) carrying out any functions regarding abusive, deceptive, or unscrupulous lending practices relating to residential mortgage loans that the Secretary considers appropriate, which shall include conducting the study under section 6 of the Expand and Preserve Home Ownership Through Counseling Act;

"(vii) providing for operation of the advisory committee established under paragraph (4) of this subsection;

"(viii) collaborating with community-based organizations with expertise in the field of housing counseling; and

"(ix) providing for the building of capacity to provide housing counseling services in areas that lack sufficient services, including underdeveloped areas that lack basic water and sewer systems, electricity services, and safe, sanitary housing.

"(4) ADVISORY COMMITTEE. —

"(A) IN GENERAL. — The Secretary shall appoint an advisory committee to provide advice regarding the carrying out of the functions of the Director.

"(B) MEMBERS. — Such advisory committee shall consist of not more than 12 individuals, and the membership of the committee shall equally represent the mortgage and real estate industry, including consumers and housing counseling agencies certified by the Secretary.

"(C) TERMS. — Except as provided in subparagraph (D), each member of the advisory committee shall be appointed for a term of 3 years. Members may be reappointed at the discretion of the Secretary.

"(D) TERMS OF INITIAL APPOINTEES. — As designated by the Secretary at the time of appointment, of the members first appointed to the advisory committee, 4 shall be appointed for a term of 1 year and 4 shall be appointed for a term of 2 years.

"(E) PROHIBITION OF PAY; TRAVEL EXPENSES. — Members of the advisory committee shall serve without pay, but shall receive travel expenses, including per diem in

(ii)落实住房与城市发展部部长在《1968年住房与城市发展法》第106(g)条下承担的所有其他职能，包括开通、运作并公布该条第(2)款规定的免费电话号码；

(iii)协助传播《1974年房地产结算程序法》第5条(《美国法典》第十二编第2604节)制作的房屋购买信息宣传册；

(iv)实施《1968年住房与城市发展法》第106(e)条[《美国法典》第十二编第1701x(e)节]规定的认证计划；

(v)实施《1968年住房与城市发展法》第106(a)(4)条规定的援助计划，包括落实援助申请的筛选标准；

(vi)针对住房抵押贷款中的滥用性、欺骗性或不道德的借贷做法，行使任何住房与城市发展部部长认为适当的职能，包括按照《促进与保护置业咨询法》第6条的要求开展研究；

(vii)支持按照本子条第(4)款要求设立的顾问委员会的运作；

(viii)与专业提供住房咨询服务的社区组织开展协作；及

(ix)支持相关能力建设，在服务不充分的区域提供住房咨询服务，包括在缺乏基本供排水系统、电力服务和安全清洁住房条件的经济欠发达地区提供该等咨询服务。

(4)**顾问委员会**。——

(A)**一般规定**。——住房与城市发展部部长应任命组建顾问委员会，就住房咨询办公室主任职能的履行提供建议。

(B)**成员**。——顾问委员会的组成成员不得超过12名个人，委员会的成员组成结构应能够平等地代表抵押贷款和房地产行业，包括消费者和经住房与城市发展部部长认证的住房咨询机构。

(C)**任期**。——除第(D)子款规定的情形外，顾问委员会所有成员的任期均为3年。住房与城市发展部部长可以依其自由裁量权任命会员连任。

(D)**首届成员的任期**。——住房与城市发展部部长在任命顾问委员会首届成员之时，其中4名成员的任期为1年，另外4名成员的任期为2年。

(E)**禁止支付报酬；差旅费**。——顾问委员会成员不得领取报酬，但可领取差旅费，包括按照《美国法典》第五编第五十七章第一子章适用的规定领取每日津贴，作为

lieu of subsistence, in accordance with applicable provisions under subchapter I of chapter 57 of title 5, United States Code.

"(F) ADVISORY ROLE ONLY. — The advisory committee shall have no role in reviewing or awarding housing counseling grants.

"(5) SCOPE OF HOMEOWNERSHIP COUNSELING. — In carrying out the responsibilities of the Director, the Director shall ensure that homeownership counseling provided by, in connection with, or pursuant to any function, activity, or program of the Department addresses the entire process of homeownership, including the decision to purchase a home, the selection and purchase of a home, issues arising during or affecting the period of ownership of a home (including refinancing, default and foreclosure, and other financial decisions), and the sale or other disposition of a home.".

SEC. 1443. COUNSELING PROCEDURES.

(a) IN GENERAL. — Section 106 of the Housing and Urban Development Act of 1968 (12 U. S. C. 1701x) is amended by adding at the end the following new subsection:

"(g) PROCEDURES AND ACTIVITIES. —

"(1) COUNSELING PROCEDURES. —

"(A) IN GENERAL. — The Secretary shall establish, coordinate, and monitor the administration by the Department of Housing and Urban Development of the counseling procedures for homeownership counseling and rental housing counseling provided in connection with any program of the Department, including all requirements, standards, and performance measures that relate to homeownership and rental housing counseling.

"(B) HOMEOWNERSHIP COUNSELING. — For purposes of this subsection and as used in the provisions referred to in this subparagraph, the term 'homeownership counseling' means counseling related to homeownership and residential mortgage loans. Such term includes counseling related to homeownership and residential mortgage loans that is provided pursuant to —

"(i) section 105(a)(20) of the Housing and Community Development Act of 1974 (42 U. S. C. 5305(a)(20));

"(ii) in the United States Housing Act of 1937 —

"(I) section 9(e)(42 U. S. C. 1437g(e));

"(II) section 8(y)(1)(D)(42 U. S. C. 1437f(y)(1)(D));

"(III) section 18(a)(4)(D)(42 U. S. C. 1437p(a)(4)(D));

"(IV) section 23(c)(4)(42 U. S. C. 1437u(c)(4));

"(V) section 32(e)(4)(42 U. S. C. 1437z–4(e)(4));

"(VI) section 33(d)(2)(B)(42 U. S. C. 1437z– 5(d)(2)(B));

"(VII) sections 302(b)(6) and 303(b)(7)(42 U. S. C. 1437aaa–1(b)(6), 1437aaa–2(b)(7)); and

生活补助的替代。

(F)**仅得行使顾问职能**。——顾问委员会不得参与审查或发放住房咨询补助金。

(5)**房屋所有权咨询范围**。——住房咨询办公室主任在履行其职责之时,应确保与住房与城市发展部的职能、活动或计划有关的,或根据该部职能、活动或计划提供的房屋所有权咨询服务应覆盖房屋所有权的整个流程,包括购房决定、房屋选购、房屋所有权期内产生的事宜或影响房屋所有权期的事宜(包括再融资、违约和止赎以及其他财务决定),以及房屋的出售或其他处置。”

第1443条　咨询流程

(a)**一般规定**。——在《1968年住房与城市发展法》第106条(《美国法典》第十二编第1701x节)结尾处增加如下新子条,作为对该条的修正:

“(g)**程序与活动**。——

(1)**咨询程序**。——

(A)**一般规定**。——住房与城市发展部部长应建立、协调和监控与该部计划有关的房屋所有权咨询程序和租赁住房所有权咨询程序,包括有关房屋所有权咨询和租赁住房咨询的所有要求、标准和绩效指标。

(B)**房屋所有权咨询**。——就本子条以及本子款所述条款而言,‘房屋所有权咨询’一词系指有关房屋所有权和住房抵押贷款的咨询服务。该词包括根据以下条款提供的房屋所有权咨询和住房抵押贷款咨询——

(i)《1974年住房与社区发展法》第105(a)(20)条(《美国法典》第四十二编第5305(a)(20)节);

(ii)《1937年联邦住房法》的如下条款——

(I)第9(e)条[《美国法典》第四十二编第1437g(e)节];

(II)第8(y)(1)(D)条[《美国法典》第四十二编第1437f(y)(1)(D)节];

(III)第18(a)(4)(D)条[《美国法典》第四十二编第1437p(a)(4)(D)节];

(IV)第23(c)(4)条[《美国法典》第四十二编第1437u(c)(4)节];

(V)第32(e)(4)条[《美国法典》第四十二编第1437z-4(e)(4)节];

(VI)第33(d)(2)(B)条[《美国法典》第四十二编第1437z-5(d)(2)(B)节];

(VII)第302(b)(6)条和第303(b)(7)条[《美国法典》第四十二编第1437aaa-1(b)(6)节和第1437aaa-2(b)(7)节];及

"(VIII) section 304(c)(4)(42 U. S. C. 1437aaa– 3(c)(4));

"(iii) section 302(a)(4) of the American Homeownership and Economic Opportunity Act of 2000 (42 U. S. C. 1437f note);

"(iv) sections 233 (b)(2) and 258 (b) of the Cranston–Gonzalez National Affordable Housing Act (42 U. S. C. 12773(b)(2), 12808(b));

"(v) this section and section 101(e) of the Housing and Urban Development Act of 1968 (12 U. S. C. 1701x, 1701w(e));

"(vi) section 220(d)(2)(G) of the Low–Income Housing Preservation and Resident Homeownership Act of 1990 (12 U. S. C. 4110(d)(2)(G));

"(vii) sections 422(b)(6), 423(b)(7), 424(c)(4), 442(b)(6), and 443(b)(6) of the Cranston–Gonzalez National Affordable Housing Act (42 U. S. C. 12872(b)(6), 12873 (b)(7), 12874(c)(4), 12892(b)(6), and 12893(b)(6));

"(viii) section 491(b)(1)(F)(iii) of the McKinney–Vento Homeless Assistance Act (42 U. S. C. 11408(b)(1)(F)(iii));

"(ix) sections 202(3) and 810(b)(2)(A) of the Native American Housing and Self–Determination Act of 1996 (25 U. S. C. 4132(3), 4229(b)(2)(A));

"(x) in the National Housing Act —

"(I) in section 203 (12 U. S. C. 1709), the penultimate undesignated paragraph of paragraph (2) of subsection (b), subsection (c)(2)(A), and subsection (r)(4);

"(II) subsections (a) and (c)(3) of section 237 (12 U. S. C. 1715z–2); and

"(III) subsections (d)(2)(B) and (m)(1) of section 255 (12 U. S. C. 1715z–20);

"(xi) section 502 (h)(4)(B) of the Housing Act of 1949 (42 U. S. C. 1472 (h)(4) (B));

"(xii) section 508 of the Housing and Urban Development Act of 1970 (12 U. S. C. 1701z–7); and

"(xiii) section 106 of the Energy Policy Act of 1992 (42 U. S. C. 12712 note).

"(C) RENTAL HOUSING COUNSELING. — For purposes of this subsection, the term 'rental housing counseling' means counseling related to rental of residential property, which may include counseling regarding future homeownership opportunities and providing referrals for renters and prospective renters to entities providing counseling and shall include counseling related to such topics that is provided pursuant to —

"(i) section 105(a)(20) of the Housing and Community Development Act of 1974 (42 U. S. C. 5305(a)(20));

"(ii) in the United States Housing Act of 1937 —

"(I) section 9(e)(42 U. S. C. 1437g(e));

"(II) section 18(a)(4)(D)(42 U. S. C. 1437p(a)(4)(D));

（VIII）第304（c）（4）条［《美国法典》第四十二编第1437aaa-3（c）（4）节］；

（iii）《2000年美国房屋所有权与经济机会法》第302（a）（4）条［《美国法典》第四十二编第1437f节注释］；

（iv）《克兰斯顿—冈塞雷斯国家住房保障法》第233（b）（2）条和第258（b）条［《美国法典》第四十二编第12773（b）（2）节和第12808（b）节］；

（v）本条以及《1968年住房与城市发展法》第101（e）条［《美国法典》第十二编第1701x节和第1701w（e）节］；

（vi）《1990年低收入住房保护和居民房屋所有权法》第220（d）（2）（G）条［《美国法典》第十二编第4110（d）（2）（G）节］；

（vii）《克兰斯顿—冈塞雷斯国家住房保障法》第422（b）（6）条、第423（b）（7）条、第424（c）（4）条、第442（b）（6）条及第443（b）（6）条［《美国法典》第四十二编第12872（b）（6）节、第12873（b）（7）节、第12874（c）（4）节、第12892（b）（6）节和第12893（b）（6）节］；

（viii）《麦金尼—文托无房者援助法》第491（b）（1）（F）（iii）条［《美国法典》第四十二编第11408（b）（1）（F）（iii）节］；

（ix）《1996年美国原住民住房援助与自决法》第202（3）条和第810（b）（2）（A）条［《美国法典》第二十五编第4132（3）节和第4229（b）（2）（A）节］；

（x）《国民住房法》的如下条款——

（I）第203条（《美国法典》第十二编第1709节），第（b）子条第（2）款的倒数第二个无编号段落、第（c）（2）（A）子条和第（r）（4）子条；

（II）第237条的第（a）子条和第（c）（3）子条（《美国法典》第十二编第1715z-2节）；及

（III）第255条的第（d）（2）（B）子条和第（m）（1）子条［《美国法典》第十二编第1715z-20节］；

（xi）《1949年住房法》第502（h）（4）（B）条［《美国法典》第四十二编第1472（h）（4）（B）节］；

（xii）《1970年住房与城市发展法》第508条（《美国法典》第十二编第1701z-7节）；及

（xiii）《1992年能源政策法》第106条（《美国法典》第四十二编第12712节注释）。

（C）**租赁住房咨询**。——就本子条而言，‘租赁住房咨询’一词系指有关住宅房地产租赁的咨询，可包括关于未来房屋所有权机会的咨询，以及将租赁者或潜在租赁者转介绍给咨询服务实体的行为，且应包括按照以下规定就上述主题提供的咨询内容——

（i）《1974年住房与社区发展法》第105（a）（20）条［（《美国法典》第四十二编第5305（a）（20）节］；

（ii）《1937年联邦住房法》的如下条款——

（I）第9（e）条［《美国法典》第四十二编第1437（g）（e）节］；

（II）第18（a）（4）（D）条［《美国法典》第四十二编第1437p（a）（4）（D）节］；

"(III) section 23(c)(4)(42 U. S. C. 1437u(c)(4));

"(IV) section 32(e)(4)(42 U. S. C. 1437z–4(e)(4));

"(V) section 33(d)(2)(B)(42 U. S. C. 1437z– 5(d)(2)(B)); and

"(VI) section 302(b)(6)(42 U. S. C. 1437aaa– 1(b)(6));

"(iii) section 233 (b)(2) of the Cranston–Gonzalez National Affordable Housing Act (42 U. S. C. 12773(b)(2));

"(iv) section 106 of the Housing and Urban Development Act of 1968 (12 U. S. C. 1701x);

"(v) section 422(b)(6) of theCranston–Gonzalez National Affordable Housing Act (42 U. S. C. 12872(b)(6));

"(vi) section 491(b)(1)(F)(iii) of the McKinney–Vento Homeless Assistance Act (42 U. S. C. 11408(b)(1)(F)(iii));

"(vii) sections 202(3) and 810(b)(2)(A) of theNative American Housing and Self–Determination Act of 1996 (25 U. S. C. 4132(3), 4229(b)(2)(A)); and

"(viii) the rental assistance program under section 8 of the United States Housing Act of 1937 (42 U. S. C. 1437f).

"(2) STANDARDS FOR MATERIALS. — The Secretary, in consultation with the advisory committee established under subsection (g)(4) of the Department of Housing and Urban Development Act, shall establish standards for materials and forms to be used, as appropriate, by organizations providing homeownership counseling services, including any recipients of assistance pursuant to subsection (a)(4).

"(3) MORTGAGE SOFTWARE SYSTEMS. —

"(A) CERTIFICATION. — The Secretary shall provide for the certification of various computer software programs for consumers to use in evaluating different residential mortgage loan proposals. The Secretary shall require, for such certification, that the mortgage software systems take into account —

"(i) the consumer's financial situation and the cost of maintaining a home, including insurance, taxes, and utilities;

"(ii) the amount of time the consumer expects to remain in the home or expected time to maturity of the loan; and

"(iii) such other factors as the Secretary considers appropriate to assist the consumer in evaluating whether to pay points, to lock in an interest rate, to select an adjustable or fixed rate loan, to select a conventional or government–insured or guaranteed loan and to make other choices during the loan application process.

If the Secretary determines that available existing software is inadequate to assist consumers during the residential mortgage loan application process, the Secretary shall

(Ⅲ)第23(c)(4)条[《美国法典》第四十二编第1437u(c)(4)节];

(Ⅳ)第32(e)(4)条[《美国法典》第四十二编第1437z-4(e)(4)节];

(Ⅴ)第33(d)(2)(B)条[《美国法典》第四十二编第1437z-5(d)(2)(B)节];及

(Ⅵ)第302(b)(6)条[《美国法典》第四十二编第1437aaa-1(b)(6)节];

(iii)《克兰斯顿—冈塞雷斯国家住房保障法》第233(b)(2)条[《美国法典》第四十二编第12773(b)(2)节];

(iv)《1968年住房与城市发展法》第106条[《美国法典》第十二编第1701x节];

(v)《克兰斯顿—冈塞雷斯国家住房保障法》第422(b)(6)条[《美国法典》第四十二编第12872(b)(6)节];

(vi)《麦金尼—文托无房者援助法》第491(b)(1)(F)(iii)条[《美国法典》第四十二编第11408(b)(1)(F)(iii)节];

(vii)《1996年美国原住民住房援助与自决法》[1] 第202(3)条和第810(b)(2)(A)条[《美国法典》第二十五编第4132(3)节和第4229(b)(2)(A)节];及

(viii)《1937年联邦住房法》第8条(《美国法典》第四十二编第1437f节)规定的租赁援助计划。

(2)**材料标准**。——住房与城市发展部部长应在与根据《住房与城市发展部法》第(g)(4)子条设立的顾问委员会磋商之后,制定适当的材料和表格标准,并将之适用于提供房屋所有权咨询服务的组织,包括按照第(a)(4)子条接受援助的组织。

(3)**抵押贷款软件系统**。——

(A)**认证**。——住房与城市发展部部长应为各类计算机软件提供认证,供消费者用于对不同的住房抵押贷款建议方案的评估。在进行认证之时,住房与城市发展部部长应要求抵押贷款软件系统中应将以下因素纳入考虑——

(i)消费者的财务状况和维持一套房屋的成本,包括保费、税费以及公用设施费用;

(ii)消费者对房屋使用期的估计,或者该贷款的预期偿还期;及

(iii)住房与城市发展部部长认为能协助消费者对以下事项进行评估的其他适当因素:是否应该支付贷款点数或锁定某一利率;选择可调利率贷款或固定利率贷款;选择传统贷款或政府承保或担保的贷款;以及在贷款申请过程中作出其他决定。

如果住房与城市发展部部长判定,现有软件无法在住房抵押贷款申请过程中为消费者提供充分的帮助,则住房与城市发展部部长应作出相应安排,由私营软件公司

1 本法的全称为“Native American Housing Assistance and Self-Determination Act of 1996”,原文中似乎遗漏了“Assistance”一词,译文中对该词进行了补译。——译者注

arrange for the development by private sector software companies of new mortgage software systems that meet the Secretary's specifications.

"(B) USE AND INITIAL AVAILABILITY. — Such certified computer software programs shall be used to supplement, not replace, housing counseling. The Secretary shall provide that such programs are initially used only in connection with the assistance of housing counselors certified pursuant to subsection (e).

"(C) AVAILABILITY. — After a period of initial availability under subparagraph (B) as the Secretary considers appropriate, the Secretary shall take reasonable steps to make mortgage software systems certified pursuant to this paragraph widely available through the Internet and at public locations, including public libraries, senior–citizen centers, public housing sites, offices of public housing agencies that administer rental housing assistance vouchers, and housing counseling centers.

"(D) BUDGET COMPLIANCE. — This paragraph shall be effective only to the extent that amounts to carry out this paragraph are made available in advance in appropriations Acts.

"(4) NATIONAL PUBLIC SERVICE MULTIMEDIA CAMPAIGNS TO PROMOTE HOUSING COUNSELING. —

"(A) IN GENERAL. — The Director of Housing Counseling shall develop, implement, and conduct national public service multimedia campaigns designed to make persons facing mortgage foreclosure, persons considering a subprime mortgage loan to purchase a home, elderly persons, persons who face language barriers, low–income persons, minorities, and other potentially vulnerable consumers aware that it is advisable, before seeking or maintaining a residential mortgage loan, to obtain homeownership counseling from an unbiased and reliable sources and that such homeownership counseling is available, including through programs sponsored by the Secretary of Housing and Urban Development.

"(B) CONTACT INFORMATION. — Each segment of the multimedia campaign under subparagraph (A) shall publicize the toll–free telephone number and website of the Department of Housing and Urban Development through which persons seeking housing counseling can locate a housing counseling agency in their State that is certified by the Secretary of Housing and Urban Development and can provide advice on buying a home, renting, defaults, foreclosures, credit issues, and reverse mortgages.

"(C) AUTHORIZATION OF APPROPRIATIONS. — There are authorized to be appropriated to the Secretary, not to exceed $3, 000, 000 for fiscal years 2009, 2010, and 2011, for the development, implementation, and conduct of national public service multimedia campaigns under this paragraph.

"(D) FORECLOSURE RESCUE EDUCATION PROGRAMS. —

"(i) IN GENERAL. — Ten percent of any funds appropriated pursuant to the authorization under subparagraph (C) shall be used by the Director of Housing Counseling to

开发新的抵押贷款软件系统,以满足住房与城市发展部部长提出的具体要求。

(B)**使用和初期启用认证软件**。——上述经认证的计算机软件应用于辅助住房咨询服务,而不得用以取代住房咨询服务。住房与城市发展部部长应规定,此类软件初期启用时,仅得用于辅助根据第(e)子条认证的住房咨询顾问的工作。

(C)**推广使用**。——在经过第(B)子款规定并由住房与城市发展部部长确定的适当的初期使用期之后,住房与城市发展部部长应采取合理措施,通过互联网和公共场所(包括公共图书馆、老年中心、政府资助的公共房屋、管理租赁住房援助券的公共住房机构的办公室以及住房咨询中心等),使得经本款认证的抵押贷款软件系统得到广泛的使用。

(D)**预算合规**。——执行本款规定产生的费用不得超过拨款法律针对本款规定之落实而事先提供的资金。

(4)**旨在推广住房咨询的全国公共服务多媒体宣传活动**。——

(A)**一般规定**。——住房咨询办公室主任应制定、落实并开展全国公共服务多媒体宣传活动,包括通过住房与城市发展部部长支持的计划,针对面临止赎的人士、考虑申请次级房贷购房的人士、老年人、具有语言障碍的人士、低收入人士、少数族裔以及其他弱势群体开展宣传,提高其意识,强调在申请或维持住房抵押贷款之前,宜先向中立可靠的机构获取住房所有权咨询,并强调公众确实可以获得此类住房所有权咨询意见。

(B)**联系信息**。——按照第(A)子款开展多媒体宣传活动时,在宣传活动的每一环节均应公布住房与城市发展部的免费电话号码和网站;需要获取住房咨询的人士可通过该电话或网站,在其所在的州联系到经住房与城市发展部部长认证的住房咨询机构,通过该机构获得关于购房、租房、房贷违约、止赎、信用问题和反向抵押贷款等问题的咨询意见。

(C)**拨款授权**。——兹授权向住房与城市发展部部长拨付不超过300万美元的金额,用于在2009财政年度、2010财政年度和2011财政年度按照本款制定、落实和开展全国公共服务多媒体宣传活动。

(D)**止赎救助教育项目**。——

(i)**一般规定**。——住房咨询办公室主任应将第(C)子款授权拨款的10%用于在高止赎率地区开展教育项目。该教育项目包括通过直邮方式向在上述地区居住的人

conduct an education program in areas that have a high density of foreclosure. Such program shall involve direct mailings to persons living in such areas describing —

"(I) tips on avoiding foreclosure rescue scams;

"(II) tips on avoiding predatory lending mortgage agreements;

"(III) tips on avoiding for-profit foreclosure counseling services; and

"(IV) local counseling resources that are approved by the Department of Housing and Urban Development.

"(ii) PROGRAM EMPHASIS. — In conducting the education program described under clause (i), the Director of Housing Counseling shall also place an emphasis on serving communities that have a high percentage of retirement communities or a high percentage of low-income minority communities.

"(iii) TERMS DEFINED. — For purposes of this subparagraph:

"(I) HIGH DENSITY OF FORECLOSURES. — An area has a 'high density of foreclosures' if such area is one of the metropolitan statistical areas (as that term is defined by the Director of the Office of Management and Budget) with the highest home foreclosure rates.

"(II) HIGH PERCENTAGE OF RETIREMENT COMMUNITIES. — An area has a 'high percentage of retirement communities' if such area is one of the metropolitan statistical areas (as that term is defined by the Director of the Office of Management and Budget) with the highest percentage of residents aged 65 or older.

"(III) HIGH PERCENTAGE OF LOW-INCOME MINORITY COMMUNITIES. — An area has a 'high percentage of low-income minority communities' if such area contains a higher-than-normal percentage of residents who are both minorities and low-income, as defined by the Director of Housing Counseling.

"(5) EDUCATION PROGRAMS. — The Secretary shall provide advice and technical assistance to States, units of general local government, and nonprofit organizations regarding the establishment and operation of, including assistance with the development of content and materials for, educational programs to inform and educate consumers, particularly those most vulnerable with respect to residential mortgage loans (such as elderly persons, persons facing language barriers, low-income persons, minorities, and other potentially vulnerable consumers), regarding home mortgages, mortgage refinancing, home equity loans, home repair loans, and where appropriate by region, any requirements and costs associated with obtaining flood or other disaster-specific insurance coverage.".

(b) CONFORMING AMENDMENTS TO GRANT PROGRAM FOR HOME-OWNERSHIP COUNSELING ORGANIZATIONS. — Section 106(c)(5)(A)(ii) of the Housing and Urban Development Act of 1968 (12 U.S.C. 1701x(c)(5)(A)(ii)) is amended —

士寄送以下信息——

(I)如何避免止赎救助欺诈;
(II)如何避免掠夺性抵押贷款协议;
(III)如何避免以营利为目的之止赎咨询服务;及
(IV)住房与城市发展部批准的本地咨询资源。

(ii)**计划重点**。——在开展第(i)项所述教育计划之时,住房咨询办公室主任应特别重视为退休人口占比较高的社区或低收入少数族裔人口占比较高的社区提供服务。

(iii)**术语定义**。——就本子款而言:

(I)**'高止赎率'**。——如果某一地区属于银行止赎率最高的大都市统计区之一(该词的含义以管理和预算办公室主任的定义为准),则该地区属于'高止赎率地区'。

(II)**'退休人口占比较高的社区'**。——如果某一地区属于65岁及以上居民占比最高的大都市统计区之一(该词的含义以管理和预算办公室主任的定义为准),则该地区属于'退休人口占比较高的社区'。

(III)**低收入少数族裔人口占比较高的社区**。——如果某一地区既属于少数族裔又属于低收入的居民(以住房咨询办公室主任的定义为准)占全部人口的比例超过正常水平,则该地区属于'低收入少数族裔人口占比较高的社区'。

(5)**教育计划**。——住房与城市发展部部长应向各州、一般地方政府行政分区和非盈利组织提供建议和技术援助,协助其设立和运作相关教育计划(包括协助编制计划的内容和材料),向消费者(特别是在住房抵押贷款方面最弱势的人士,如老年人、存在语言障碍的人士、低收入人士、少数族裔及其他可能需要帮助的消费者)提供信息和教育,帮助消费者了解房屋抵押贷款、抵押贷款再融资、房屋权益贷款、房屋修葺贷款,以及(根据各地区具体情况而定)与获得洪灾险或其它专门的灾难保险相关的要求和费用问题。"

(b)**有关住房所有权咨询组织补助金计划的一致性修正**。——《1968年住房与城市发展法》第106(c)(5)(A)(ii)条[《美国法典》第十二编第1701x(c)(5)(A)(ii)节]修正如下——

(1) in subclause (III), by striking "and" at the end;

(2) in subclause (IV) by striking the period at the end and inserting "; and"; and

(3) by inserting after subclause (IV) the following new subclause:

"(V) notify the housing or mortgage applicant of the availability of mortgage software systems provided pursuant to subsection (g)(3).".

SEC. 1444. GRANTS FOR HOUSING COUNSELING ASSISTANCE.

Section 106(a) of the Housing and Urban Development Act of 1968 (12 U. S. C. 1701x (a)) is amended by adding at the end the following new paragraph:

"(4) HOMEOWNERSHIP AND RENTAL COUNSELING ASSISTANCE. —

"(A) IN GENERAL. — The Secretary shall make financial assistance available under this paragraph to HUD-approved housing counseling agencies and State housing finance agencies.

"(B) QUALIFIED ENTITIES. — The Secretary shall establish standards and guidelines for eligibility of organizations (including governmental and nonprofit organizations) to receive assistance under this paragraph, in accordance with subparagraph (D).

"(C) DISTRIBUTION. — Assistance made available under this paragraph shall be distributed in a manner that encourages efficient and successful counseling programs and that ensures adequate distribution of amounts for rural areas having traditionally low levels of access to such counseling services, including areas with insufficient access to the Internet. In distributing such assistance, the Secretary may give priority consideration to entities serving areas with the highest home foreclosure rates.

"(D) LIMITATION ON DISTRIBUTION OF ASSISTANCE. —

"(i) IN GENERAL. — None of the amounts made available under this paragraph shall be distributed to —

"(I) any organization which has been convicted for a violation under Federal law relating to an election for Federal office; or

"(II) any organization which employs applicable individuals.

"(ii) DEFINITION OF APPLICABLE INDIVIDUALS. — In this subparagraph, the term 'applicable individual' means an individual who —

"(I) is —

"(aa) employed by the organization in a permanent or temporary capacity;

"(bb) contracted or retained by the organization; or

"(cc) acting on behalf of, or with the express or apparent authority of, the organization; and

"(II) has been convicted for a violation under Federal law relating to an election for Federal office.

"(E) GRANTMAKING PROCESS. — In making assistance available under this

(1)删除第(III)子项结尾处的“及”;

(2)删除第(IV)子项结尾处的句号,替以“;及”;及

(3)在第(IV)子项之后插入如下新子项:

“(V)通知住房或抵押贷款申请者,说明其可以使用按照第(g)(3)子条提供的抵押贷款软件系统。”

第1444条 住房咨询补助金

在《1968年住房与城市发展法》第106(a)条[《美国法典》第十二编第1701x(a)节]结尾处增加如下新款,作为对该条的修正:

“(4)**住房所有权与租赁咨询援助**。——

(A)**一般规定**。——住房与城市发展部部长应按照本款规定向住房与城市发展部批准的住房咨询机构和州住房融资机构提供财务援助。

(B)**合格实体**。——住房与城市发展部部长应制定标准和指引,用以判断有资格按照第(D)子款规定获得本款提供的补助金的组织(包括政府组织和非营利组织)。

(C)**补助金的发放**。——按照本款发放补助金之时,应采取能够为高效和成功的咨询计划提供激励的方式,并确保长期以来较难获得此类咨询服务的农村地区,包括互联网覆盖不足的地区能够获得充分的补助金。在发放补助金之时,住房与城市发展部部长应优先考虑为止赎率最高的地区提供服务的实体。

(D)**补助金发放的限制**。——

(i)**一般规定**。——按照本款规定提供的款项不得向以下组织发放——

(I)曾被判定违反关于联邦职务选举的联邦法律的任何组织;或

(II)雇用相关个人的任何组织。

(ii)**相关个人的定义**。——就本子款而言,‘相关个人’一词系指具有以下特征的个人——

(I)具有如下身份——

(aa)该组织的正式或临时员工;

(bb)承接该组织外包工作或受其聘用的个人;或

(cc)代表该组织行事的个人,或获得该组织明示授权或表见授权的个人;且

(II)曾被判定违反关于联邦职务选举的联邦法律的任何组织。

(E)**补助金发放流程**。——按照本款规定提供补助金之时,住房与城市发展部部

paragraph, the Secretary shall consider appropriate ways of streamlining and improving the processes for grant application, review, approval, and award.

"(F) AUTHORIZATION OF APPROPRIATIONS. — There are authorized to be appropriated $45, 000, 000 for each of fiscal years 2009 through 2012 for —

"(i) the operations of the Office of Housing Counseling of the Department of Housing and Urban Development;

"(ii) the responsibilities of the Director of Housing Counseling under paragraphs (2) through (5) of subsection (g); and

"(iii) assistance pursuant to this paragraph for entities providing homeownership and rental counseling. ".

SEC. 1445. REQUIREMENTS TO USE HUD-CERTIFIED COUNSELORS UNDER HUD PROGRAMS.

Section 106(e) of the Housing and Urban Development Act of 1968 (12 U. S. C. 1701x (e)) is amended —

(1) by striking paragraph (1) and inserting the following new paragraph:

"(1) REQUIREMENT FOR ASSISTANCE. — An organization may not receive assistance for counseling activities under subsection (a)(1)(iii), (a)(2), (a)(4), (c), or (d) of this section, or under section 101(e), unless the organization, or the individuals through which the organization provides such counseling, has been certified by the Secretary under this subsection as competent to provide such counseling. ";

(2) in paragraph (2) —

(A) by inserting "and for certifying organizations" before the period at the end of the first sentence; and

(B) in the second sentence by striking "for certification" and inserting ", for certification of an organization, that each individual through which the organization provides counseling shall demonstrate, and, for certification of an individual, ";

(3) in paragraph (3), by inserting "organizations and" before "individuals";

(4) by redesignating paragraph (3) as paragraph (5); and

(5) by inserting after paragraph (2) the following new paragraphs:

"(3) REQUIREMENT UNDER HUD PROGRAMS. — Any homeownership counseling or rental housing counseling (as such terms are defined in subsection (g)(1)) required under, or provided in connection with, any program administered by the Department of Housing and Urban Development shall be provided only by organizations or counselors certified by the Secretary under this subsection as competent to provide such counseling.

"(4) OUTREACH. — The Secretary shall take such actions as the Secretary considers appropriate to ensure that individuals and organizations providing homeownership or rental housing counseling are aware of the certification requirements and standards of this

长应考虑采取优化并改进补助金申请、审查、批准和发放流程的适当措施。

(F)**拨款授权**。——兹授权对于2009年至2012年的每一个财政年度,拨付4500万美元的款项用于以下开支——

(i)住房与城市发展部下属住房咨询办公室的运作;

(ii)住房咨询办公室主任履行第(g)子条第(2)款至第(5)款规定的职责;及

(iii)按照本款规定向提供住房所有权咨询和租赁咨询的实体提供援助。”

第1445条　关于在住房与城市发展部计划中使用住房与城市发展部认证的咨询顾问的要求

《1968年住房与城市发展法》第106(e)条[《美国法典》第十二编第1701x(e)节]修正如下——

(1)删除第(1)款,替以如下新款:

“(1)**援助要求**。——任何组织如需按照本条第(a)(1)(iii)子条、第(a)(2)子条、第(a)(4)子条、第(c)子条或第(d)子条或按照第101(e)条申请咨询活动援助,该组织或通过该组织提供咨询服务的个人均须事先获得住房与城市发展部部长按照本子条做出的认证,确认该组织或个人有能力提供该咨询服务。”

(2)在第(2)款中——

(A)在第一句结尾处的句号前插入“以及提供认证的组织”;及

(B)第二句删去“在认证之时,”,替以“,在对组织进行认证之时,该组织提供咨询服务的每一个人均应证明,且,对个人进行认证之时,”;

(3)在第(3)款中,在“个人”前插入“组织和”;

(4)第(3)款重新编号为第(5)款;及

(5)在第(2)款之后插入如下新款:

“(3)**住房与城市发展部计划的要求**。——住房与城市发展部负责实施的计划要求提供的,或与此类计划相关的住房所有权咨询服务或租赁住房咨询服务[上述术语之定义见第(g)(1)子条],应由住房与城市发展部部长按照本子条认证为有能力提供该等咨询服务的组织或咨询顾问提供。

(4)宣传。——住房与城市发展部部长有权采取其认为适当的行动,确保提供住房所有权咨询或租赁住房咨询的个人和组织均了解本子条的认证要求和标准,并了解第(f)子条规定的培训和认证计划。”

subsection and of the training and certification programs under subsection (f).".

SEC. 1446. STUDY OF DEFAULTS AND FORECLOSURES.

The Secretary of Housing and Urban Development shall conduct an extensive study of the root causes of default and foreclosure of home loans, using as much empirical data as are available. The study shall also examine the role of escrow accounts in helping prime and nonprime borrowers to avoid defaults and foreclosures, and the role of computer registries of mortgages, including those used for trading mortgage loans. Not later than 12 months after the date of the enactment of this Act, the Secretary shall submit to the Congress a preliminary report regarding the study. Not later than 24 months after such date of enactment, the Secretary shall submit a final report regarding the results of the study, which shall include any recommended legislation relating to the study, and recommendations for best practices and for a process to identify populations that need counseling the most.

SEC. 1447. DEFAULT AND FORECLOSURE DATABASE.

(a) ESTABLISHMENT. — The Secretary of Housing and Urban Development and the Director of the Bureau, in consultation with the Federal agencies responsible for regulation of banking and financial institutions involved in residential mortgage lending and servicing, shall establish and maintain a database of information on foreclosures and defaults on mortgage loans for one– to four–unit residential properties and shall make such information publicly available, subject to subsection (e).

(b) CENSUS TRACT DATA. — Information in the database may be collected, aggregated, and made available on a census tract basis.

(c) REQUIREMENTS. — Information collected and made available through the database shall include —

(1) the number and percentage of such mortgage loans that are delinquent by more than 30 days;

(2) the number and percentage of such mortgage loans that are delinquent by more than 90 days;

(3) the number and percentage of such properties that are real estate–owned;

(4) number and percentage of such mortgage loans that are in the foreclosure process;

(5) the number and percentage of such mortgage loans that have an outstanding principal obligation amount that is greater than the value of the property for which the loan was made; and

(6) such other information as the Secretary of Housing and Urban Development and the Director of the Bureau consider appropriate.

(d) RULE OF CONSTRUCTION. — Nothing in this section shall be construed to encourage discriminatory or unsound allocation of credit or lending policies or practices.

(e) PRIVACY AND CONFIDENTIALITY. — In establishing and maintaining the

第1446条　关于违约和止赎的研究

住房与城市发展部部长应尽可能多地利用现有实证数据,开展一项关于住房贷款违约和止赎的根本原因的广泛研究。在开展研究的过程中,应审查在帮助高信用借款人和低信用借款人防止违约和止赎过程中,代管账户所起到的作用,以及抵押贷款计算机登记册(包括用于对抵押贷款进行交易的登记册)的作用。住房与城市发展部部长应于本法颁布后12个月内,就该研究向国会提交一份初步报告,并于本法颁布后24个月内就研究结果向国会提交最终报告。最终报告应基于上述研究,向国会提出立法建议,以及关于最佳实践和用以确定最需要咨询服务的人群的流程的相关建议。

第1447条　违约和止赎数据库

(a)**数据库的建立**。——住房与城市发展部部长和消费者金融保护局局长应在与负责对从事住房抵押贷款和服务的银行和金融机构进行监管的联邦机关磋商后,针对购买一至四个单元的住宅房地产的抵押贷款建立并维护止赎和违约信息数据库,并应在不违反第(e)子条的前提下公布该等信息。

(b)**人口普查区数据**。——数据库中的信息可按照人口普查区收集、汇总和提供。

(c)**要求**。——通过该数据库收集并提供的信息应包括——

(1)违约超过30天的抵押贷款的数量和比例;

(2)违约超过90天的抵押贷款的数量和比例;

(3)由贷款人拥有的止赎房地产的数量和比例;

(4)处于止赎过程中的抵押贷款的数量和比例;

(5)未清偿本金金额超过通过该贷款购买的房地产价值的抵押贷款的数量和比例;及

(6)住房与城市发展部部长和消费者金融保护局局长认为应予收集的其他信息。

(d)**解释规则**。——本条的任何内容均不得被解释为鼓励歧视性的或欠稳健的信用分配或借贷政策或做法。

(e)**隐私权和保密权**。——在按照第(a)子条建立并维护数据库之时,住房与城市

database described in subsection (a), the Secretary of Housing and Urban Development and the Director of the Bureau shall —

(1) be subject to the standards applicable to Federal agencies for the protection of the confidentiality of personally identifiable information and for data security and integrity;

(2) implement the necessary measures to conform to the standards for data integrity and security described in paragraph (1); and

(3) collect and make available information under this section, in accordance with paragraphs (5) and (6) of section 1022(c) and the rules prescribed under such paragraphs, in order to protect privacy and confidentiality.

SEC. 1448. DEFINITIONS FOR COUNSELING–RELATED PROGRAMS.

Section 106 of the Housing and Urban Development Act of 1968 (12 U. S. C. 1701x), as amended by the preceding provisions of this subtitle, is amended by adding at the end the following new subsection:

"(h) DEFINITIONS. — For purposes of this section:

"(1) NONPROFIT ORGANIZATION. — The term 'nonprofit organization' has the meaning given such term in section 104(5) of the Cranston–Gonzalez National Affordable Housing Act (42 U. S. C. 12704(5)), except that subparagraph (D) of such section shall not apply for purposes of this section.

"(2) STATE. — The term 'State' means each of the several States, the Commonwealth of Puerto Rico, the District of Columbia, the Commonwealth of the Northern Mariana Islands, Guam, the Virgin Islands, American Samoa, the Trust Territories of the Pacific, or any other possession of the United States.

"(3) UNIT OF GENERAL LOCAL GOVERNMENT. — The term 'unit of general local government' means any city, county, parish, town, township, borough, village, or other general purpose political subdivision of a State.

"(4) HUD–APPROVED COUNSELING AGENCY. — The term 'HUD–approved counseling agency' means a private or public nonprofit organization that is —

"(A) exempt from taxation under section 501(c) of the Internal Revenue Code of 1986; and

"(B) certified by the Secretary to provide housing counseling services.

"(5) STATE HOUSING FINANCE AGENCY. — The term 'State housing finance agency' means any public body, agency, or instrumentality specifically created under State statute that is authorised to finance activities designed to provide housing and related facilities throughout an entire State through land acquisition, construction, or rehabilitation. ".

SEC. 1449. ACCOUNTABILITY AND TRANSPARENCY FOR GRANT RECIPIENTS.

Section 106 of the Housing and Urban Development Act of 1968 (12 U. S. C. 1701x),

发展部部长和消费者金融保护局局长应——

(1)遵守适用于联邦机关的用以保护个人身份信息保密性和数据安全及完整性的各项标准;

(2)实施遵守第(1)款所述保护数据安全及完整性的各项标准的必要措施;及

(3)在按照本条收集并公布信息时,遵守第1022(c)条第(5)款和第(6)款的规定以及依据上述条款制定的规则,以保护隐私权和保密性。

第1448条　适用于与咨询相关的计划的定义

在经本子编前文规定修正后的《1968年住房与城市发展法》第106条(《美国法典》第十二编第1701x节)结尾处增加如下新子条,作为对该条的进一步修正:

"(h)**定义**。——就本条而言:

(1)**非营利组织**。——'非营利组织'一词的含义以《克兰斯顿—冈塞雷斯国家住房保障法》第104(5)条[《美国法典》第四十二编第12704(5)节]的定义为准,但该条第(D)子款不适用于本条。

(2)**州**。——'州'一词系指美国各州、波多黎各自由邦、哥伦比亚特区、北马里亚纳群岛、关岛、维尔京群岛、美属萨摩亚群岛、太平洋群岛托管地或美国的任何其他属地。

(3)**一般地方政府行政分区**。——'一般地方政府行政分区'一词系指任何市、郡、教区、镇、市镇、乡、村或各州其他一般行政区域。

(4)**住房与城市发展部批准的咨询机构**。——'住房与城市发展部批准的咨询机构'一词系指具有以下特征的私人或公众非营利组织——

(A)按照《1986年国内税收法典》第501(c)条获得免税待遇;及

(B)获得住房与城市发展部部长认证提供住房咨询服务。

(5)**州住房融资机构**。——'州住房融资机构'一词系指根据州制定法特别创设,有权为如下活动提供融资的任何公共机构、机关或职能部门:通过购买土地、建设房屋或翻修房屋,在全州范围提供住房和相关设施的活动。"

第1449条　补助金获得者的问责制和透明度要求

在经本子编前文规定修正后的《1968年住房与城市发展法》第106条(《美国法典》

as amended by the preceding provisions of this subtitle, is amended by adding at the end the following:

"(i) ACCOUNTABILITY FOR RECIPIENTS OF COVERED ASSISTANCE. —

"(1) TRACKING OF FUNDS. — The Secretary shall —

"(A) develop and maintain a system to ensure that any organization or entity that receives any covered assistance uses all amounts of covered assistance in accordance with this section, the regulations issued under this section, and any requirements or conditions under which such amounts were provided; and

"(B) require any organization or entity, as a condition of receipt of any covered assistance, to agree to comply with such requirements regarding covered assistance as the Secretary shall establish, which shall include —

"(i) appropriate periodic financial and grant activity reporting, record retention, and audit requirements for the duration of the covered assistance to the organization or entity to ensure compliance with the limitations and requirements of this section, the regulations under this section, and any requirements or conditions under which such amounts were provided; and

"(ii) any other requirements that the Secretary determines are necessary to ensure appropriate administration and compliance.

"(2) MISUSE OF FUNDS. — If any organization or entity that receives any covered assistance is determined by the Secretary to have used any covered assistance in a manner that is materially in violation of this section, the regulations issued under this section, or any requirements or conditions under which such assistance was provided —

"(A) the Secretary shall require that, within 12 months after the determination of such misuse, the organization or entity shall reimburse the Secretary for such misused amounts and return to the Secretary any such amounts that remain unused or uncommitted for use; and

"(B) such organization or entity shall be ineligible, at any time after such determination, to apply for or receive any further covered assistance. The remedies under this paragraph are in addition to any other remedies that may be available under law.

"(3) COVERED ASSISTANCE. — For purposes of this subsection, the term 'covered assistance' means any grant or other financial assistance provided under this section.".

SEC. 1450. UPDATING AND SIMPLIFICATION OF MORTGAGE INFORMATION BOOKLET.

Section 5 of the Real Estate Settlement Procedures Act of 1974 (12 U. S. C. 2604) is amended —

(1) in the section heading, by striking "SPECIAL" and inserting "HOME BUYING";

(2) by striking subsections (a) and (b) and inserting the following new subsections:

"(a) PREPARATION AND DISTRIBUTION. — The Director of the Bureau of

第十二编第1701x节)结尾处增加如下内容,作为对该条的修正:

"(i)**所涉补助金获得者的问责制**。——

(1)**资金追踪**。——住房与城市发展部部长应——

(A)制定并维护资金追踪系统,确保获得所涉补助金的任何组织或实体在使用所涉补助金时,符合本条规定、依据本条发布的规章以及发放该补助金时所设定的任何要求或条件;及

(B)作为发放所涉补助金的条件,要求申请所涉补助金的任何组织或实体同意遵守住房与城市发展部部长制定的相关要求,包括——

(i)在向该等组织或实体提供所涉补助金期间,该等组织或实体应定期、适当地报告财务和补助金使用情况,保存相关记录并遵守审计要求,从而确保该等补助金的使用符合本条的限制和要求、依据本条发布的规章以及发放该补助金时设定的任何条件或要求;及

(ii)住房与城市发展部部长为确保适当的管理和合规,认为有必要设定的任何其他要求。

(2)**资金滥用**。——如果住房与城市发展部部长判定,接受任何所涉补助金的组织或实体对任何所涉补助金的使用严重违反本条规定,或严重违反依据本条发布的规章或任何发放条件或要求,则——

(A)住房与城市发展部部长应要求该组织或实体在判定做出后12个月内,将该等滥用款项赔偿给住房与城市发展部部长,并将未使用或未指定用途的剩余资金返还给住房与城市发展部部长;且

(B)在住房与城市发展部部长作出存在资金滥用情形的判定后,该组织或实体将丧失申请或获得任何其他所涉补助金的资格。本款规定的救济与法律规定的任何其他救济具有并存性,前者不限制后者。

(3)**所涉补助金**。——就本子条而言,"所涉补助金"一词系指按照本条提供的任何补助金或其他财务援助。"

第1450条　更新并简化抵押贷款信息宣传册

《1974年房地产结算程序法》第5条(《美国法典》第十二编第2604节)修正如下——

(1)在本条标题中,删除"特别",替以"购房";

(2)删除第(a)子条和第(b)子条,替以如下新子条:

"(a)**宣传册的制作和派放**。——消费者金融保护局局长应至少每5年制定一份宣

Consumer Financial Protection (hereafter in this section referred to as the 'Director') shall prepare, at least once every 5 years, a booklet to help consumers applying for federally related mortgage loans to understand the nature and costs of real estate settlement services. The Director shall prepare the booklet in various languages and cultural styles, as the Director determines to be appropriate, so that the booklet is understandable and accessible to homebuyers of different ethnic and cultural backgrounds. The Director shall distribute such booklets to all lenders that make federally related mortgage loans. The Director shall also distribute to such lenders lists, organized by location, of homeownership counselors certified under section 106(e) of the Housing and Urban Development Act of 1968 (12 U. S. C. 1701x(e)) for use in complying with the requirement under subsection (c) of this section.

"(b) CONTENTS. — Each booklet shall be in such form and detail as the Director shall prescribe and, in addition to such other information as the Director may provide, shall include in plain and understandable language the following information:

"(1) A description and explanation of the nature and purpose of the costs incident to a real estate settlement or a federally related mortgage loan. The description and explanation shall provide general information about the mortgage process as well as specific information concerning, at a minimum —

"(A) balloon payments;

"(B) prepayment penalties;

"(C) the advantages of prepayment; and

"(D) the trade–off between closing costs and the interest rate over the life of the loan.

"(2) An explanation and sample of the uniform settlement statement required by section 4.

"(3) A list and explanation of lending practices, including those prohibited by the Truth in Lending Act or other applicable Federal law, and of other unfair practices and unreasonable or unnecessary charges to be avoided by the prospective buyer with respect to a real estate settlement.

"(4) A list and explanation of questions a consumer obtaining a federally related mortgage loan should ask regarding the loan, including whether the consumer will have the ability to repay the loan, whether the consumer sufficiently shopped for the loan, whether the loan terms include prepayment penalties or balloon payments, and whether the loan will benefit the borrower.

"(5) An explanation of the right of rescission as to certain transactions provided by sections 125 and 129 of the Truth in Lending Act.

"(6) A brief explanation of the nature of a variable rate mortgage and a reference to the booklet entitled 'Consumer Handbook on Adjustable Rate Mortgages', published by the Director, or to any suitable substitute of such booklet that the Director may subsequently

传册,帮助申请联邦抵押贷款的消费者了解房地产结算服务的性质和费用。宣传册应备有各种语言版本,并符合不同文化的阅读理解习惯(具体以消费者金融保护局局长判定确属适当的为准),从而使得不同种族和文化背景的购房者均可理解并使用该宣传册。消费者金融保护局局长应将宣传册派放给所有发放联邦抵押贷款的贷款人,并向该等贷款人派放按照《1968年住房与城市发展法》第106(e)条[《美国法典》第十二编第1701x(e)节]获得认证的住房所有权咨询顾问的名单(按地理区域进行编排),以便各银行遵守本条第(c)子条的要求。

(b)**内容**。——每份宣传册的格式和详细内容均应以消费者金融保护局局长规定的为准。除了消费者金融保护局局长可能另行要求提供的信息之外,该宣传册还应以简明易懂的语言提供如下信息:

(1)关于房地产结算或联邦抵押贷款相关费用的性质和目的之说明和解释。该等说明和解释文字应提供关于抵押贷款申请流程的一般性信息,同时,至少应提供与以下各项相关的具体信息——

(A)大额尾付式还款;

(B)提前还款违约金;

(C)提前还款的好处;及

(D)贷款成交费用与贷款期内的利息之间的权衡比较。

(2)解释第4条规定的统一结算说明,并提供样本。

(3)列明并解释各种借贷做法(包括《诚实信贷法》或其他适用的联邦法律禁止的借贷做法)、其他不公平做法和潜在购房者应予避免的不合理或不必要的房地产结算费用。

(4)列明并解释申请联邦抵押贷款的消费者应了解的贷款问题,包括该消费者是否有能力还款,该消费者在贷款前是否已充分了解所有可选的贷款,该联邦抵押贷款条款是否包含提前还款违约金或大额尾付,以及该联邦抵押贷款是否对该借款人有利。

(5)解释《诚实信贷法》第125条和第129条规定的特定交易的解约权。

(6)简要解释浮动利率抵押贷款的性质,并提及消费者金融保护局局长编发的名为《可调利率抵押贷款消费者手册》的宣传册,或者消费者金融保护局局长按照本条规定编发的后继宣传册。

adopt pursuant to such section.

"(7) A brief explanation of the nature of a home equity line of credit and a reference to the pamphlet required to be provided under section 127A of the Truth in Lending Act.

"(8) Information about homeownership counseling services made available pursuant to section 106(a)(4) of the Housing and Urban Development Act of 1968 (12 U. S. C. 1701x (a)(4)), a recommendation that the consumer use such services, and notification that a list of certified providers of homeownership counseling in the area, and their contact information, is available.

"(9) An explanation of the nature and purpose of escrow accounts when used in connection with loans secured by residential real estate and the requirements under section 10 of this Act regarding such accounts.

"(10) An explanation of the choices available to buyers of residential real estate in selecting persons to provide necessary services incidental to a real estate settlement.

"(11) An explanation of a consumer's responsibilities, liabilities, and obligations in a mortgage transaction.

"(12) An explanation of the nature and purpose of real estate appraisals, including the difference between an appraisal and a home inspection.

"(13) Notice that the Office of Housing of the Department of Housing and Urban Development has made publicly available a brochure regarding loan fraud and a World Wide Web address and toll-free telephone number for obtaining the brochure. The booklet prepared pursuant to this section shall take into consideration differences in real estate settlement procedures that may exist among the several States and territories of the United States and among separate political subdivisions within the same State and territory. ";

(3) in subsection (c), by inserting at the end the following new sentence: "Each lender shall also include with the booklet a reasonably complete or updated list of homeownership counselors who are certified pursuant to section 106(e) of the Housing and Urban Development Act of 1968 (12 U. S. C. 1701x(e)) and located in the area of the lender. "; and

(4) in subsection (d), by inserting after the period at the end of the first sentence the following: "The lender shall provide the booklet in the version that is most appropriate for the person receiving it. ".

SEC. 1451. HOME INSPECTION COUNSELING.

(a) PUBLIC OUTREACH. —

(1) IN GENERAL. — The Secretary of Housing and Urban Development (in this section referred to as the "Secretary") shall take such actions as may be necessary to inform potential homebuyers of the availability and importance of obtaining an independent home inspection. Such actions shall include —

(7)简要解释房屋权益贷款信用额度的性质,并提及按《诚实信贷法》第127A条规定制作的宣传资料。

(8)按照《1968年住房与城市发展法》第106(a)(4)条[《美国法典》第十二编第1701x(a)(4)节]提供的住房所有权咨询服务的相关信息,并建议消费者使用该等服务,向消费者告知其可以获得当地经认证的房屋所有权咨询服务提供商名单及其联系方式。

(9)解释在以住宅房地产为担保的贷款中使用的代管账户之性质和目的,并解释本法第10条关于该等账户的要求。

(10)解释住宅房地产购买者在为房地产结算选择附带的必要服务的提供者时拥有的选择。

(11)解释抵押贷款交易中消费者的职责、责任和义务。

(12)解释不同的房地产评估项目的性质和目的,包括说明估价和验房的差异。

(13)相关通知,说明住房与城市发展部下属的住房办公室已经向公众发布一份有关贷款欺诈的手册,并提供获取该手册的万维网地址和免费电话号码。按照本条规定编制该手册之时,应考虑美国不同的州和准州之间以及同一个州或准州内不同行政区域关于房地产结算程序的不同规定。”

(3)在第(c)子条结尾处插入下句规定:“每一贷款人均应在该宣传册中纳入合理完整或合理更新的房屋所有权咨询顾问名单,名单上的顾问均应已按照《1968年住房与城市发展法》第106(e)条[《美国法典》第十二编第1701x(e)节]获得认证,且身处该贷款人所在区域。”及

(4)在第(d)子条第一句结尾处的句号之后插入如下内容:“贷款人提供的宣传册版本应为对于收到宣传册的人士最为适当的版本。”

第1451条　验房咨询

(a)**社会宣传**。——

(1)**一般规定**。——住房与城市发展部部长应采取必要行动,告知潜在购房者其可以获得独立的验房服务,并告知该等服务的重要性。此类必要行动应包括——

(A) publication of the HUD/FHA form HUD 92564–CN entitled "For Your Protection: Get a Home Inspection", in both English and Spanish languages;

(B) publication of the HUD/FHA booklet entitled "For Your Protection: Get a Home Inspection", in both English and Spanish languages;

(C) development and publication of a HUD booklet entitled "For Your Protection — Get a Home Inspection" that does not reference FHA–insured homes, in both English and Spanish languages; and

(D) publication of the HUD document entitled "Ten Important Questions To Ask Your Home Inspector", in both English and Spanish languages.

(2) AVAILABILITY. — The Secretary shall make the materials specified in paragraph (1) available for electronic access and, where appropriate, inform potential homebuyers of such availability through home purchase counseling public service announcements and toll–free telephone hotlines of the Department of Housing and Urban Development. The Secretary shall give special emphasis to reaching first–time and low–income homebuyers with these materials and efforts.

(3) UPDATING. — The Secretary may periodically update and revise such materials, as the Secretary determines to be appropriate.

(b) REQUIREMENT FOR FHA–APPROVED LENDERS. — Each mortgagee approved for participation in the mortgage insurance programs under title II of the National Housing Act shall provide prospective homebuyers, at first contact, whether upon pre–qualification, pre–approval, or initial application, the materials specified in subparagraphs (A), (B), and (D) of subsection (a)(1).

(c) REQUIREMENTS FOR HUD–APPROVED COUNSELING AGENCIES. — Each counseling agency certified pursuant by the Secretary to provide housing counseling services shall provide each of their clients, as part of the home purchase counseling process, the materials specified in subparagraphs (C) and (D) of subsection (a)(1).

(d) TRAINING. — Training provided the Department of Housing and Urban Development for housing counseling agencies, whether such training is provided directly by the Department or otherwise, shall include —

(1) providing information on counseling potential homebuyers of the availability and importance of getting an independent home inspection;

(2) providing information about the home inspection process, including the reasons for specific inspections such as radon and lead–based paint testing;

(3) providing information about advising potential homebuyers on how to locate and select a qualified home inspector; and

(4) review of home inspection public outreach materials of the Department.

(A)印发题为“使用验房服务,更好地保护自己”的《住房与城市发展部/联邦住房管理局HUD 92564-CN表格》,表格应包括英文版本和西班牙语版本;

(B)印发题为“使用验房服务,更好地保护自己”的住房与城市发展部/联邦住房管理局宣传册,宣传册应包括英文版本和西班牙语版本;

(C)编写并印发题为“使用验房服务,更好地保护自己”的住房与城市发展部宣传册,该等宣传册不应涉及联邦住房管理局承保的房屋,应提供英文版本和西班牙语版本;及

(D)印发题为“应向验房师询问的十大重要问题”的住房与城市发展部文件,应提供英文版本和西班牙语版本。

(2)**宣传资料的提供**。——住房与城市发展部部长确保第(1)款所述宣传资料能够通过电子方式访问,并应在适当的时候,通过购房咨询公共服务公告和住房与城市发展部的免费热线电话,通知潜在购房者其可获得上述宣传资料。住房与城市发展部部长应特别重视使用上述宣传资料和宣传手段向首次购房者和低收入购房者传达相关信息。

(3)**更新**。——住房与城市发展部部长可以在其判定确属适当的时候,定期更新和修订上述宣传资料。

(b)**适用于经联邦住房管理局批准的贷款人的要求**。——获批参与《国民住房法》第二编规定的抵押贷款保险计划的抵押权人在与潜在购房者首次接触时(不论是在资格预审、预批准或首次申请之时),一律应向潜在购房者提供第(a)(1)子条第(A)子款、第(B)子款和第(D)子款规定的资料。

(c)**适用于经住房与城市发展部批准的咨询机构的要求**。——获得住房与城市发展部部长认证可以提供住房咨询服务的咨询机构,应向所有客户提供第(a)(1)子条第(C)子款和第(D)子款规定的资料,将该等资料的提供作为提供购房咨询服务流程中的一个环节。

(d)**培训**。——住房与城市发展部直接或间接向住房咨询机构提供的培训,均应包含以下内容——

(1)提供相关信息,说明如何向潜在购房者提供咨询,包括应告知潜在购房者其可以获得独立验房服务以及该等服务的重要性;

(2)提供有关验房流程的信息,包括开展特定具体检查项目(如含氡涂料测试和含铅涂料测试)的原因;

(3)提供相关信息,就如何寻找并选择合格的验房师向潜在购房者提供建议;及

(4)审查该部制定的验房宣传材料。

SEC. 1452. WARNINGS TO HOMEOWNERS OF FORECLOSURE RESCUE SCAMS.

(a) ASSISTANCE TO NRC. — Notwithstanding any other provision of law, of any amounts made available for any fiscal year pursuant to section 106(a)(4)(F) of the Housing and Urban Development Act of 1968 (12 U. S. C. 1701x (a)(4)(F))(as added by section 1444), 10 percent shall be used only for assistance to the Neighborhood Reinvestment Corporation for activities, in consultation with servicers of residential mortgage loans, to provide notice to borrowers under such loans who are delinquent with respect to payments due under such loans that makes such borrowers aware of the dangers of fraudulent activities associated with foreclosure.

(b) NOTICE. — The Neighborhood Reinvestment Corporation, in consultation with servicers of residential mortgage loans, shall use the amounts provided pursuant to subsection (a) to carry out activities to inform borrowers under residential mortgage loans —

(1) that the foreclosure process is complex and can be confusing;

(2) that the borrower may be approached during the foreclosure process by persons regarding saving their home and they should use caution in any such dealings;

(3) that there are Federal Government and nonprofit agencies that may provide information about the foreclosure process, including the Department of Housing and Urban Development;

(4) that they should contact their lender immediately, contact the Department of Housing and Urban Development to find a housing counseling agency certified by the Department to assist in avoiding foreclosure, or visit the Department's website regarding tips for avoiding foreclosure; and

(5) of the telephone number of the loan servicer or successor, the telephone number of the Department of Housing and Urban Development housing counseling line, and the Uniform Resource Locators (URLs) for the Department of Housing and Urban Development Web sites for housing counseling and for tips for avoiding foreclosure.

Subtitle E—Mortgage Servicing

SEC. 1461. ESCROW AND IMPOUND ACCOUNTS RELATING TO CERTAIN CONSUMER CREDIT TRANSACTIONS.

(a) IN GENERAL. — Chapter 2 of the Truth in Lending Act (15 U. S. C. 1631 et seq.) is amended by inserting after section 129C (as added by section 1411) the following new section:

第1452条　提醒业主警惕止赎救助欺诈

(a)**向社区再投资公司提供援助**。——无论是否存在任何不同法律规定,对于在任一财政年度,根据第1444条增加的《1968年住房与城市发展法》第106(a)(4)(F)条[《美国法典》第十二编第1701x(a)(4)(F)节]规定提供的资金,其中的10%必须作为专款,用于为社区再投资公司的活动提供援助,社区再投资公司应在与住房抵押贷款服务机构磋商之后,向拖欠抵押贷款的借款人发出通知,提醒其警惕与止赎相关的欺诈性行为。

(b)**通知**。——社区再投资公司应在与住房抵押贷款服务机构磋商之后,利用按照第(a)子条提供的资金,开展向住房抵押贷款的借款人说明如下信息的活动——

(1)止赎程序相当复杂且可能会很难理解;

(2)在止赎程序中,可能会有人与借款人接洽,声称能帮助借款人避免止赎的发生,借款人应提高警惕,谨慎对待;

(3)联邦政府(包括住房与城市发展部)和非盈利机构可以提供有关止赎程序的信息;

(4)借款人应立即联系贷款人,或联系住房与城市发展部,以寻找获得经住房与城市发展部认证的住房咨询机构来协助该借款人避免止赎,或登录住房与城市发展部的网站查询有关避免银行止赎的建议;及

(5)贷款服务机构或其继任单位的电话号码、住房与城市发展部住房咨询热线的电话号码、住房与城市发展部官方网站关于住房咨询和避免止赎建议的链接。

第E子编——抵押贷款服务

第1461条　与特定消费者信用交易有关的代管和扣押账户

(a)**一般规定。**——《诚实信贷法》(《美国法典》第十五编第1631节及其后条文)第二章修正如下:在第1411条增加的第129C条之后插入如下新条文:

" § 129D. Escrow or impound accounts relating to certain consumer credit transactions

"(a) IN GENERAL. —Except as provided in subsection (b), (c), (d), or (e), a creditor, in connection with the consummation of a consumer credit transaction secured by a first lien on the principal dwelling of the consumer, other than a consumer credit transaction under an open end credit plan or a reverse mortgage, shall establish, before the consummation of such transaction, an escrow or impound account for the payment of taxes and hazard insurance, and, if applicable, flood insurance, mortgage insurance, ground rents, and any other required periodic payments or premiums with respect to the property or the loan terms, as provided in, and in accordance with, this section.

"(b) WHEN REQUIRED. — No impound, trust, or other type of account for the payment of property taxes, insurance premiums, or other purposes relating to the property may be required as a condition of a real property sale contract or a loan secured by a first deed of trust or mortgage on the principal dwelling of the consumer, other than a consumer credit transaction under an open end credit plan or a reverse mortgage, except when —

"(1) any such impound, trust, or other type of escrow or impound account for such purposes is required by Federal or State law;

"(2) a loan is made, guaranteed, or insured by a State or Federal governmental lending or insuring agency;

"(3) the transaction is secured by a first mortgage or lien on the consumer's principal dwelling having an original principal obligation amount that —

"(A) does not exceed the amount of the maximum limitation on the original principal obligation of mortgage in effect for a residence of the applicable size, as of the date such interest rate set, pursuant to the sixth sentence of section 305(a)(2) the Federal Home Loan Mortgage Corporation Act (12 U. S. C. 1454(a)(2)), and the annual percentage rate will exceed the average prime offer rate as defined in section 129C by 1. 5 or more percentage points; or

"(B) exceeds the amount of the maximum limitation on the original principal obligation of mortgage in effect for a residence of the applicable size, as of the date such interest rate set, pursuant to the sixth sentence of section 305(a)(2) the Federal Home Loan Mortgage Corporation Act (12 U. S. C. 1454(a)(2)), and the annual percentage rate will exceed the average prime offer rate as defined in section 129C by 2. 5 or more percentage points; or

"(4) so required pursuant to regulation.

"(c) EXEMPTIONS. — The Board may, by regulation, exempt from the requirements of subsection (a) a creditor that —

"(1) operates predominantly in rural or underserved areas;

"(2) together with all affiliates, has total annual mortgage loan originations that do not exceed a limit set by the Board;

“第129D条　与特定消费者信用交易有关的代管或扣押账户

“(a)**一般规定**。——除第(b)子条、第(c)子条、第(d)子条或第(e)子条规定的情形外,对于以消费者主要住所第一顺位留置权作为抵押订立的消费者信用交易合同(但根据开放式信用计划或者反向抵押贷款开展的消费者信用交易除外)而言,贷款发放人应在交易合同订立前,设立代管或扣押账户,用以支付税费和灾害险,并且,还应用于支付洪灾险、抵押贷款保险、地租(如适用),以及按照本条规定,支付本条规定的与该房地产或贷款条款相关的任何其他定期付款或保费。

(b)**需要设立代管或扣押账户的情形**。——如果在消费者主要住所上设立第一顺位信托契约或抵押权作为房地产销售合同或贷款的担保(但根据开放式信用计划或者反向抵押贷款开展的消费者信用交易除外),则不得要求必须先设立扣押账户、信托账户或其他类型的账户用以支付财产税、保费或与房地产有关的其他费用,即不得以此类账户的设立作为上述合同或贷款的前提条件,但存在以下情形的除外——

(1)联邦法律或州法律要求为上述目的设立任何该等扣押账户、信托账户或其他类型的账户;

(2)该等贷款由州政府或联邦政府的贷款或保险机关所提供、担保或承保;

(3)该等交易由该消费者主要住所的第一顺位抵押权或第一顺位留置权为担保,且截至利率设定之日,其初始本金数额——

(A)按照《联邦住房贷款抵押公司法》第305(a)(2)条第六句[《美国法典》第十二编第1454(a)(2)节]的规定,不超过届时有效适用的同等面积住宅的初始抵押贷款本金上限,且年利率将超过第129C条定义的平均最优惠利率1.5(含)个百分点以上;或

(B)按照《联邦住房贷款抵押贷款公司法》第305(a)(2)条第六句[《美国法典》第十二编第1454(a)(2)节]的规定,超过届时有效适用的同等面积住宅的初始抵押贷款本金上限,且年利率将超过第129C条定义的平均最优惠利率2.5(含)个百分点以上;或

(4)相关规章要求设立该等账户。

(c)**豁免**。——联邦储备委员会可以发布规章,向符合以下条件的贷款发放人授予豁免,获得豁免的贷款发放人不必遵守第(a)子条的规定——

(1)主要在农村地区或欠发达地区开展经营;

(2)贷款发放人及其所有关联方每年发起的抵押贷款总额不超过联邦储备委员会设定的限额;

"(3) retains its mortgage loan originations in portfolio; and

"(4) meets any asset size threshold and any other criteria the Board may establish, consistent with the purposes of this subtitle.

"(d) DURATION OF MANDATORY ESCROW OR IMPOUND ACCOUNT. — An escrow or impound account established pursuant to subsection (b) shall remain in existence for a minimum period of 5 years, beginning with the date of the consummation of the loan, unless and until —

"(1) such borrower has sufficient equity in the dwelling securing the consumer credit transaction so as to no longer be required to maintain private mortgage insurance;

"(2) such borrower is delinquent;

"(3) such borrower otherwise has not complied with the legal obligation, as established by rule; or

"(4) the underlying mortgage establishing the account is terminated.

"(e) LIMITED EXEMPTIONS FOR LOANS SECURED BY SHARES IN A COOPERATIVE OR IN WHICH AN ASSOCIATION MUST MAINTAIN A MASTER INSURANCE POLICY. — Escrow accounts need not be established for loans secured by shares in a cooperative. Insurance premiums need not be included in escrow accounts for loans secured by dwellings or units, where the borrower must join an association as a condition of ownership, and that association has an obligation to the dwelling or unit owners to maintain a master policy insuring the dwellings or units.

"(f) CLARIFICATION ON ESCROW ACCOUNTS FOR LOANS NOT MEETING STATUTORY TEST. — For mortgages not covered by the requirements of subsection (b), no provision of this section shall be construed as precluding the establishment of an impound, trust, or other type of account for the payment of property taxes, insurance premiums, or other purposes relating to the property —

"(1) on terms mutually agreeable to the parties to the loan;

"(2) at the discretion of the lender or servicer, as provided by the contract between the lender or servicer and the borrower; or

"(3) pursuant to the requirements for the escrowing of flood insurance payments for regulated lending institutions in section 102(d) of the Flood Disaster Protection Act of 1973.

"(g) ADMINISTRATION OF MANDATORY ESCROW OR IMPOUND ACCO-UNTS. —

"(1) IN GENERAL. — Except as may otherwise be provided for in this title or in regulations prescribed by the Board, escrow or impound accounts established pursuant to subsection (b) shall be established in a federally insured depository institution or credit union.

"(2) ADMINISTRATION. — Except as provided in this section or regulations

(3)在贷款组合中持有其发起的抵押贷款;且

(4)符合联邦储备委员会可能根据本子编宗旨设定的任何资产规模最低门槛和任何其他标准。

(d)**强制性代管或扣押账户的期限**。——按照第(b)子条设立的代管或扣押账户至少应存续5年(自贷款交易合同订立日起算),除非且直至——

(1)该借款人用以为消费者信用交易提供担保的房屋权益已达一定水平,以致其可以不用再维持私人抵押贷款保险;

(2)该借款人拖欠还款;

(3)该借款人违反相关规则设定的法律义务;或

(4)与该账户相关的抵押贷款已终止。

(e)**适用于以合作社股份抵押的贷款的有限豁免,以及协会必须为其维持主保险单的贷款的有限豁免**。——对于以合作社股份抵押的贷款,不必设立代管账户。如果借款人必须加入协会方可获得房屋或公寓单元的所有权,且该协会有义务为该房屋或公寓单元所有人维持主保险单从而为该房屋或公寓单元投保,则以该房屋或公寓单元抵押的贷款的代管账户不必包含保费。

(f)**关于不符合法定标准的贷款代管账户的说明**。——对于不符合第(b)子条规定的抵押贷款,本条的任何规定均不得被解释为禁止设立扣押账户、信托账户或其他类型的用以支付财产税、保费或与该房地产相关的其他费用的账户,只要该等账户满足下列条件——

(1)账户条款由贷款双方共同协商达成;

(2)账户之设立系由贷款人或贷款服务机构根据其与借款人签订的合同依其自由裁量权决定的;或

(3)账户系按照《1973年洪水灾害防御法》第102(d)条针对受监管贷款机构的洪灾险赔款的代管要求设立。

(g)**强制性代管或扣押账户的管理**。——

(1)**一般规定**。——除本编或联邦储备委员会制定的规章另有规定的情形外,按照第(b)子条设立的代管或扣押账户应在联邦政府承保的存款机构或信贷联盟处开立。

(2)**管理**。——除本条或按本条制定的规章另有规定的情形外,按本条设立的代

prescribed under this section, an escrow or impound account subject to this section shall be administered in accordance with —

"(A) the Real Estate Settlement Procedures Act of 1974 and regulations prescribed under such Act;

"(B) the Flood Disaster Protection Act of 1973 and regulations prescribed under such Act; and

"(C) the law of the State, if applicable, where the real property securing the consumer credit transaction is located.

"(3) APPLICABILITY OF PAYMENT OF INTEREST. — If prescribed by applicable State or Federal law, each creditor shall pay interest to the consumer on the amount held in any impound, trust, or escrow account that is subject to this section in the manner as prescribed by that applicable State or Federal law.

"(4) PENALTY COORDINATION WITH RESPA. — Any action or omission on the part of any person which constitutes a violation of the Real Estate Settlement Procedures Act of 1974 or any regulation prescribed under such Act for which the person has paid any fine, civil money penalty, or other damages shall not give rise to any additional fine, civil money penalty, or other damages under this section, unless the action or omission also constitutes a direct violation of this section.

"(h) DISCLOSURES RELATING TO MANDATORY ESCROW OR IMPOUND ACCOUNT. — In the case of any impound, trust, or escrow account that is required under subsection (b), the creditor shall disclose by written notice to the consumer at least 3 business days before the consummation of the consumer credit transaction giving rise to such account or in accordance with timeframes established in prescribed regulations the following information:

"(1) The fact that an escrow or impound account will be established at consummation of the transaction.

"(2) The amount required at closing to initially fund the escrow or impound account.

"(3) The amount, in the initial year after the consummation of the transaction, of the estimated taxes and hazard insurance, including flood insurance, if applicable, and any other required periodic payments or premiums that reflects, as appropriate, either the taxable assessed value of the real property securing the transaction, including the value of any improvements on the property or to be constructed on the property (whether or not such construction will be financed from the proceeds of the transaction) or the replacement costs of the property.

"(4) The estimated monthly amount payable to be escrowed for taxes, hazard insurance (including flood insurance, if applicable) and any other required periodic payments or premiums.

管或扣押账户应遵照如下规定进行管理——

(A)《1974年房地产结算程序法》以及依据该法制定的规章;

(B)《1973年洪水灾害防御法》以及依据该法制定的规章;及

(C)为消费者信用交易提供担保的房地产所在州的法律(如适用)。

(3)**利息支付规定**。——如果相关州法律或联邦法律有规定,则每一贷款发放人均应按相关州法律或联邦法律规定的方式,就在按照本条设立的任何扣押账户、信托账户或代管账户中持有的金额向消费者支付利息。

(4)**避免与《1974年房地产结算程序法》下的罚款构成双重罚款**。——任何人的任何作为或不作为如果构成对《1974年房地产结算程序法》或依据该法制定的任何规章的违反,且已就此缴纳罚金、民事罚款或其他赔偿金,则不应依照本条另行针对该等作为或不作为征收额外的罚金、民事罚款或其他赔偿金,但该等作为或不作为同时构成对本条规定的直接违反的除外。

(h)**关于强制性代管或扣押账户的披露**。——对于第(b)子条要求设立的任何扣押账户、信托账户或代管账户,贷款发放人至少应在与该账户相关的消费者信用交易合同订立前3个营业日,或按照相关规章设定的时间表,以书面形式向该消费者披露如下信息:

(1)交易合同订立之时将设立代管或扣押账户此一事实。

(2)交易成交时必须存入该代管或扣押账户的首笔资金金额。

(3)交易合同订立后首年相关税费和灾害险(如适用,还应包括洪灾险)的预估金额,以及任何其他须定期支付的金额或保费,该等金额或保费应适当地反映用以为该交易提供担保的房地产的应税估值(包括房地产已作出的改良工程之价值或将要在该房地产上作出的改良工程之价值,不论该改良工程的融资是否来自于该交易所获资金)或者该房地产的重置成本。

(4)每月应予代管,用于支付税费、灾害险(如适用,还应包括洪灾险)的预估金额以及任何其他须定期支付的金额或保费。

"(5) The fact that, if the consumer chooses to terminate the account in the future, the consumer will become responsible for the payment of all taxes, hazard insurance, and flood insurance, if applicable, as well as any other required periodic payments or premiums on the property unless a new escrow or impound account is established.

"(6) Such other information as the Board determines necessary for the protection of the consumer.

"(i) DEFINITIONS. — For purposes of this section, the following definitions shall apply:

"(1) FLOOD INSURANCE. — The term 'flood insurance' means flood insurance coverage provided under the national flood insurance program pursuant to the National Flood Insurance Act of 1968.

"(2) HAZARD INSURANCE. — The term 'hazard insurance' shall have the same meaning as provided for 'hazard insurance', 'casualty insurance', 'homeowner's insurance', or other similar term under the law of the State where the real property securing the consumer credit transaction is located.".

(b) EXEMPTIONS AND MODIFICATIONS. — The Board may prescribe rules that revise, add to, or subtract from the criteria of section 129D(b) of the Truth in Lending Act if the Board determines that such rules are in the interest of consumers and in the public interest.

(c) CLERICAL AMENDMENT. — The table of sections for chapter 2 of the Truth in Lending Act is amended by inserting after the item relating to section 129C (as added by section 1411) the following new item:

"129D. Escrow or impound accounts relating to certain consumer credit transactions.".

SEC. 1462. DISCLOSURE NOTICE REQUIRED FOR CONSUMERS WHO WAIVE ESCROW SERVICES.

Section 129D of the Truth in Lending Act (as added by section 1461) is amended by adding at the end the following new subsection:

"(j) DISCLOSURE NOTICE REQUIRED FOR CONSUMERS WHO WAIVE ESCROW SERVICES. —

"(1) IN GENERAL. — If —

"(A) an impound, trust, or other type of account for the payment of property taxes, insurance premiums, or other purposes relating to real property securing a consumer credit transaction is not established in connection with the transaction; or

"(B) a consumer chooses, and provides written notice to the creditor or servicer of such choice, at any time after such an account is established in connection with any such transaction and in accordance with any statute, regulation, or contractual agreement, to close such account, the creditor or servicer shall provide a timely and clearly written disclosure to

(5)如果消费者在未来选择终止该账户，则该消费者将负责支付与该房地产相关的所有税费、灾害险、洪灾险(如适用)以及任何其他须定期支付的金额或保费(但消费者另行开立新的存管或扣押账户的除外)此一事实。

(6)联邦储备委员会判定对于消费者保护而言必要的其他信息。

(i)**定义**。——就本条而言，应适用如下定义：

(1)**洪灾险**。——‘洪灾险’一词系指按照《1968年全国洪灾保险法》设立的全国洪灾保险计划所提供的洪灾险。

(2)**灾害险**。——‘灾害险’一词的含义以为消费者信用交易提供担保的房地产所在州的法律对于‘灾害险’、‘伤害险’、‘业主险’或其他类似术语的定义为准。”

(b)**豁免和修改**。——如果联邦储备委员会判定为保护消费者利益和公共利益有必要制定规则，以修订、补充或删减《诚实信贷法》第129D(b)条规定的标准，则联邦储备委员会可以制定该等规则。

(c)**目录修正**。——《诚实信贷法》第二章条款目录修正如下：在第1411条增加的第129C条的目录项之后插入如下新的目录项：

“第129D条　与特定消费者信用交易相关的代管或扣押账户。”

第1462条　在消费者放弃代管服务之时向其发出披露通知的要求

在第1461条增加的《诚实信贷法》第129D条结尾处新插入如下子条，作为对该条的修正：

“(j)**在消费者放弃代管服务之时向其发出披露通知的要求**。——

(1)**一般规定**。——如果——

(A)并未针对该交易设立扣押账户、信托账户或其他类型的账户，用于支付财产税、保费或与作为消费者信用交易担保的房地产相关的其他费用；或

(B)在针对该交易设立该等账户之后的任何时候，消费者按照任何制定法、规章的规定或合同约定，选择取消该等账户，并将其决定书面通知贷款发放人或贷款服务机构，则该贷款发放人或贷款服务机构应及时、明确地向该消费者作出信息披露，告知消费者在没有任何该等账户的情况下，消费者自己将担负的责任以及对消费者产

the consumer that advises the consumer of the responsibilities of the consumer and implications for the consumer in the absence of any such account.

"(2) DISCLOSURE REQUIREMENTS. — Any disclosure provided to a consumer under paragraph (1) shall include the following:

"(A) Information concerning any applicable fees or costs associated with either the non–establishment of any such account at the time of the transaction, or any subsequent closure of any such account.

"(B) A clear and prominent statement that the consumer is responsible for personally and directly paying the non–escrowed items, in addition to paying the mortgage loan payment, in the absence of any such account, and the fact that the costs for taxes, insurance, and related fees can be substantial.

"(C) A clear explanation of the consequences of any failure to pay non–escrowed items, including the possible requirement for the forced placement of insurance by the creditor or servicer and the potentially higher cost (including any potential commission payments to the servicer) or reduced coverage for the consumer in the event of any such creditor–placed insurance.

"(D) Such other information as the Board determines necessary for the protection of the consumer. ".

SEC. 1463. REAL ESTATE SETTLEMENT PROCEDURES ACT OF 1974 AMENDMENTS.

(a) SERVICER PROHIBITIONS. — Section 6 of the Real Estate Settlement Procedures Act of 1974 (12 U. S. C. 2605) is amended by adding at the end the following new subsections:

"(k) SERVICER PROHIBITIONS. —

"(1) IN GENERAL. — A servicer of a federally related mortgage shall not—

"(A) obtain force–placed hazard insurance unless there is a reasonable basis to believe the borrower has failed to comply with the loan contract's requirements to maintain property insurance;

"(B) charge fees for responding to valid qualified written requests (as defined in regulations which the Bureau of Consumer Financial Protection shall prescribe) under this section;

"(C) fail to take timely action to respond to a borrower's requests to correct errors relating to allocation of payments, final balances for purposes of paying off the loan, or avoiding foreclosure, or other standard servicer's duties;

"(D) fail to respond within 10 business days to a request from a borrower to provide the identity, address, and other relevant contact information about the owner or assignee of the loan; or

生的影响。

(2)**披露要求**。——根据第(1)款向消费者作出的披露应包含如下信息:

(A)在交易之时不设立该等账户将产生的任何相关手续费或费用之信息,或在交易之后取消已设立的账户将产生的相关手续费或费用之信息。

(B)在显著位置清楚地说明,在没有任何该等账户的情况下,消费者除要支付抵押贷款还款外,还应负责亲自直接支付非代管款项,并应清楚说明各项税费、保费和相关费用可能金额庞大。

(C)清楚解释未支付非代管款项的后果,包括贷款发放人或贷款服务机构可能会强制消费者购买保险,且可能会因此产生更高的费用(包括任何可能需向该贷款服务机构支付佣金),或者,在任何该等贷款发放人强制购买保险的情况下,消费者的获保金额将会降低。

(D)联邦储备委员会判定为保护消费者而必须披露的其他信息。"

第1463条 对《1974年房地产结算程序法》的修正

(a)**关于贷款服务机构的禁止性规定**。——在《1974年房地产结算程序法》第6条(《美国法典》第十二编第2605节)结尾处增加如下新子条,作为对该条的修正:

"(k)**关于贷款服务机构的禁止性规定**。——

(1)**一般规定**。——联邦抵押贷款的贷款服务机构不得——

(A)强制借款人购买灾害险,除非该贷款服务机构有合理理由相信该借款人未按照贷款合同的要求维持财产保险;

(B)为处理借款人按照本条规定作出的有效合格书面请求(以消费者金融保护局制定的规章所做定义为准)而收取费用;

(C)不及时采取行动对借款人提出的错误改正请求作出回应,包括关于如下事项的错误:付款分配、还清贷款时的最终余额、避免止赎或贷款服务机构的其他标准职责;

(D)不在10个营业日之内对借款人提出的信息请求作出回应,包括关于如下信息的请求:贷款所有人或受让人的身份信息、地址及其他相关的联系信息;或

"(E) fail to comply with any other obligation found by the Bureau of Consumer Financial Protection, by regulation, to be appropriate to carry out the consumer protection purposes of this Act.

"(2) FORCE–PLACED INSURANCE DEFINED. — For purposes of this subsection and subsections (l) and (m), the term 'force–placed insurance' means hazard insurance coverage obtained by a servicer of a federally related mortgage when the borrower has failed to maintain or renew hazard insurance on such property as required of the borrower under the terms of the mortgage.

"(l) REQUIREMENTS FOR FORCE–PLACED INSURANCE. — A servicer of a federally related mortgage shall not be construed as having a reasonable basis for obtaining force–placed insurance unless the requirements of this subsection have been met.

"(1) WRITTEN NOTICES TO BORROWER. — A servicer may not impose any charge on any borrower for force–placed insurance with respect to any property securing a federally related mortgage unless —

"(A) the servicer has sent, by first–class mail, a written notice to the borrower containing —

"(i) a reminder of the borrower's obligation to maintain hazard insurance on the property securing the federally related mortgage;

"(ii) a statement that the servicer does not have evidence of insurance coverage of such property;

"(iii) a clear and conspicuous statement of the procedures by which the borrower may demonstrate that the borrower already has insurance coverage; and

"(iv) a statement that the servicer may obtain such coverage at the borrower's expense if the borrower does not provide such demonstration of the borrower's existing coverage in a timely manner;

"(B) the servicer has sent, by first–class mail, a second written notice, at least 30 days after the mailing of the notice under subparagraph (A) that contains all the information described in each clause of such subparagraph; and

"(C) the servicer has not received from the borrower any demonstration of hazard insurance coverage for the property securing the mortgage by the end of the 15–day period beginning on the date the notice under subparagraph (B) was sent by the servicer.

"(2) SUFFICIENCY OF DEMONSTRATION. — A servicer of a federally related mortgage shall accept any reasonable form of written confirmation from a borrower of existing insurance coverage, which shall include the existing insurance policy number along with the identity of, and contact information for, the insurance company or agent, or as otherwise required by the Bureau of Consumer Financial Protection.

"(3) TERMINATION OF FORCE–PLACED INSURANCE. — Within 15 days of the

(E)不遵守消费者金融保护局发布规章认定的,为实现本法的消费者保护宗旨而宜应遵守的其他义务。

(2)**强制购买的保险的定义**。——对于本子条、第(l)子条和第(m)子条而言,'强制购买的保险'一词系指借款人未能按照抵押贷款条款的要求为相关房地产维持或续展灾害险的情况下,联邦抵押贷款的贷款服务机构为该房地产获取的灾害险。

(l)**与强制购买的保险相关的要求**。——除非满足本子条规定的所有要求,否则,联邦抵押贷款的贷款服务机构不得被视为有合理理由获得强制购买的保险。

(1)**向借款人发出书面通知**。——在强制借款人购买保险时,贷款服务机构不得针对任何为联邦抵押贷款提供担保的财产收取任何费用,除非——

(A)贷款服务机构已通过普通邮件向借款人发出一份书面通知,说明如下信息——

(i)提醒借款人有义务为联邦抵押贷款的担保财产维持灾害险;

(ii)说明该贷款服务机构并未获得任何证明该财产已购买灾害险的证据;

(iii)以明确、显著的方式说明借款人欲证明其已经为该财产购买灾害险其可采用的证明程序;及

(iv)说明如果借款人未能及时提供关于已为该财产获取灾害险的证明,则贷款服务机构可代为获取灾害险,且相关费用将由借款人承担;

(B)贷款服务机构至少已在按照第(A)子款寄出通知30天之后,通过普通邮件寄出第二份书面通知,说明第(A)子款每一项规定的所有信息;及

(C)贷款服务机构在按照第(B)子款发出通知之日起15天内,仍未收到借款人证明该借款人已为该抵押贷款的担保财产获取灾害险的材料。

(2)**证明的充分性**。——联邦抵押贷款的贷款服务机构应接受任何形式合理的关于借款人已获取的保险的书面确认材料,包括已获取的保险保单号以及保险公司或保险代理人的身份信息和联系方式,或者消费者金融保护局另行要求的其他信息。

(3)**强制购买的保险的终止**。——贷款服务机构应在收到关于借款人已获取的

receipt by a servicer of confirmation of a borrower's existing insurance coverage, the servicer shall—

"(A) terminate the force-placed insurance; and

"(B) refund to the consumer all force-placed insurance premiums paid by the borrower during any period during which the borrower's insurance coverage and the force-placed insurance coverage were each in effect, and any related fees charged to the consumer's account with respect to the force-placed insurance during such period.

"(4) CLARIFICATION WITH RESPECT TO FLOOD DISASTER PROTECTION ACT. —No provision of this section shall be construed as prohibiting a servicer from providing simultaneous or concurrent notice of a lack of flood insurance pursuant to section 102(e) of the Flood Disaster Protection Act of 1973.

"(m) LIMITATIONS ON FORCE-PLACED INSURANCE CHARGES. — All charges, apart from charges subject to State regulation as the business of insurance, related to force-placed insurance imposed on the borrower by or through the servicer shall be bona fide and reasonable. ".

(b) INCREASE IN PENALTY AMOUNTS. — Section 6(f) of the Real Estate Settlement Procedures Act of 1974 (12 U. S. C. 2605(f)) is amended —

(1) in paragraphs (1)(B) and (2)(B), by striking "$1, 000" each place such term appears and inserting "$2, 000"; and

(2) in paragraph (2)(B)(i), by striking "$500, 000" and inserting "$1, 000, 000".

(c) DECREASE IN RESPONSE TIMES. — Section 6(e) of the Real Estate Settlement Procedures Act of 1974 (12 U. S. C. 2605(e)) is amended —

(1) in paragraph (1)(A), by striking "20 days" and inserting "5 days";

(2) in paragraph (2), by striking "60 days" and inserting "30 days"; and

(3) by adding at the end the following new paragraph: "(4) LIMITED EXTENSION OF RESPONSE TIME. — The 30-day period described in paragraph (2) may be extended for not more than 15 days if, before the end of such 30-day period, the servicer notifies the borrower of the extension and the reasons for the delay in responding. ".

(d) PROMPT REFUND OF ESCROW ACCOUNTS UPON PAYOFF. — Section 6(g) of the Real Estate Settlement Procedures Act of 1974 (12 U. S. C. 2605(g)) is amended by adding at the end the following new sentence: "Any balance in any such account that is within the servicer's control at the time the loan is paid off shall be promptly returned to the borrower within 20 business days or credited to a similar account for a new mortgage loan to the borrower with the same lender. ".

SEC. 1464. TRUTH IN LENDING ACT AMENDMENTS.

(a) REQUIREMENTS FOR PROMPT CREDITING OF HOME LOAN PAYMENTS. — Chapter 2 of the Truth in Lending Act (15 U. S. C. 1631 et seq.) is amended by inserting

保险的确认材料之后15天内——

(A)终止强制购买的保险;及

(B)借款人的自购灾害险和贷款服务机构强制购买的灾害险的有效期出现重叠的，贷款服务机构应向该消费者返还借款人在该期间内为所有强制购买的保险所支付的保费，以及在该期间内向该消费者的账户就该强制购买的保险收取之任何相关费用。

(4)**关于《洪水灾害防御法》的说明**。——本条的任何规定均不得被解释为禁止贷款服务机构按照《1973年洪水灾害防御法》第102(e)条同时发出关于缺乏洪灾险的通知。

(m) **强制购买的保险的收费限制**。——除了作为保险业务而按照各州规章收取的费用之外,与强制购买的保险有关的、由贷款服务机构或通过贷款服务机构向借款人收取的所有收费均须善意且合理。”

(b)**提高罚款金额**。——《1974年房地产结算程序法》第6(f)条[《美国法典》第十二编第2605(f)节]修正如下——

(1)在第(1)(B)款和第(2)(B)款中,删除所有的“1000美元”,全部替以“2000美元”;及

(2)在第(2)(B)(i)款中,删除“50万美元”,替以“100万美元”。

(c)缩短回应时间。——《1974年房地产结算程序法》第6(e)条[《美国法典》第十二编第2605(e)节]修正如下——

(1)在第(1)(A)款中,删除“20天”,替以“五天”;

(2)在第(2)款中,删除“60天”,替以“30天”;及

(3)在结尾处增加如下新款:“(4)**延长回应时间的限制**。——在第(2)款所述30天的回应时间届满之前,贷款服务机构通知借款人需要延期,并说明延期理由的,该30天的回应时间可以延长,但延长的时间不得超过15天。”

(d)**还清贷款时须及时返还代管账户资金**。——在《1974年房地产结算程序法》第6(g)条[《美国法典》第十二编第2605(g)节]结尾处增加如下内容,作为对该条的修正:“贷款还清之时任何该等账户内处于贷款服务机构控制范围之内的任何余额,均应在20个营业日内及时返还给借款人,或者贷记入该借款人为同一贷款人向其新发放的抵押贷款而开立的类似账户。”

第1464条　对《诚实信贷法》的修正

(a)**关于及时贷记住房贷款还款的要求**。——《诚实信贷法》第二章(《美国法典》第十五编第1631节及其后条文)在第1472条增加的第129E条之后插入如下内容,作为

after section 129E (as added by section 1472) the following new section:

"§ 129F. Requirements for prompt crediting of home loan payments

"(a) IN GENERAL. — In connection with a consumer credit transaction secured by a consumer's principal dwelling, no servicer shall fail to credit a payment to the consumer's loan account as of the date of receipt, except when a delay in crediting does not result in any charge to the consumer or in the reporting of negative information to a consumer reporting agency, except as required in subsection (b).

"(b) EXCEPTION. — If a servicer specifies in writing requirements for the consumer to follow in making payments, but accepts a payment that does not conform to the requirements, the servicer shall credit the payment as of 5 days after receipt.".

(b) REQUESTS FOR PAYOFF AMOUNTS. — Chapter 2 of the Truth in Lending Act (15 U. S. C. 1631 et seq.), as amended by this title, is amended by inserting after section 129F (as added by subsection (a)) the following new section:

"§ 129G. Requests for payoff amounts of home loan

"A creditor or servicer of a home loan shall send an accurate payoff balance within a reasonable time, but in no case more than 7 business days, after the receipt of a written request for such balance from or on behalf of the borrower.".

SEC. 1465. ESCROWS INCLUDED IN REPAYMENT ANALYSIS.

Section 128(b) of the Truth in Lending Act (15 U. S. C. 1638(b)) is amended by adding at the end the following new paragraph:

"(4) REPAYMENT ANALYSIS REQUIRED TO INCLUDE ESCROW PAYMENTS. —

"(A) IN GENERAL. — In the case of any consumer credit transaction secured by a first mortgage or lien on the principal dwelling of the consumer, other than a consumer credit transaction under an open end credit plan or a reverse mortgage, for which an impound, trust, or other type of account has been or will be established in connection with the transaction for the payment of property taxes, hazard and flood (if any) insurance premiums, or other periodic payments or premiums with respect to the property, the information required to be provided under subsection(a) with respect to the number, amount, and due dates or period of payments scheduled to repay the total of payments shall take into account the amount of any monthly payment to such account for each such repayment in accordance with section 10(a)(2) of the Real Estate Settlement Procedures Act of 1974.

"(B) ASSESSMENT VALUE. — The amount taken into account under subparagraph (A) for the payment of property taxes, hazard and flood (if any) insurance premiums, or other periodic payments or premiums with respect to the property shall reflect the taxable assessed value of the real property securing the transaction after the consummation of the transaction, including the value of any improvements on the property or to be constructed on the property (whether or not such construction will be financed from the proceeds of the

对该章的修正：

“第129F条　关于及时贷记房贷还款的要求。

(a)**一般规定**。——除第(b)子条规定的情形外，对于以消费者主要住所为担保的消费者信用交易，贷款服务机构必须在收到还款当天将该还款贷记入该消费者的贷款账户，但是贷款服务机构未及时进行贷记既不导致消费者因此支付额外费用，也不导致因此向消费者征信机构报告负面信息的情形除外。

(b)**例外规定**。——如果贷款服务机构以书面形式具体列明了消费者在还款时应遵守的相关要求，但也接受了未按照该要求做出的还款，则贷款服务机构应在收到未按要求做出的还款后五天内将该还款贷记入消费者的贷款账户。”

(b)**查询未偿余额的请求**。——在经本编修正后的《诚实信贷法》第二章(《美国法典》第十五编第1631节及其后条文)第(a)子条增加的第129F条之后插入如下内容，作为对该章的修正：

“第129G条　查询房贷未偿余额的请求

住房贷款的贷款发放人或贷款服务机构在收到借款人或其代表发出的查询未偿余额的书面请求之后，应在合理期间内(但无论如何不得超过7个营业日)寄出准确的未偿余额声明。”

第1465条　将代管款项纳入还款分析

在《诚实信贷法》第128(b)条[《美国法典》第十五编第1638(b)节]结尾处增加如下新款，作为对该条的修正：

“(4)**将代管款项纳入还款分析的要求**。——

(A)**一般规定**。——对于以消费者主要住所第一顺位抵押权或第一顺位留置权作为担保开展的消费者信用交易而言（但根据开放式信用计划或者反向抵押贷款开展的消费者信用交易除外），如已经或将为该等交易设立扣押账户、信托账户或其他类型的账户，用以支付房地产税、灾害险和洪灾险(如有)的保费或与该财产有关的其他须定期支付的费用或保费，则在按照第(a)子条要求提供关于分期支付全部还款金额的期数、每期金额、每期还款到期日或还款期的信息之时，应将按照《1974年房地产结算程序法》第10(a)(2)条就每笔该等还款而向该账户支付的任何月付款项纳入考虑。

(B)**估值**。——按照第(A)子款纳入还款分析的与该房地产有关的房地产税、灾害险和洪灾险(如有)的保费或其他须定期支付的费用或保费，应反映用于为该交易提供担保的房地产在交易合同订立之后的应税估值(包括房地产已作出的改良工程之价值或将要在该房地产上作出的改良工程之价值，不论该改良工程的融资是否来自该交易所获资金)，以及交易合同订立后首年该房地产的灾害险的重置成本(如已知)。”

transaction), if known, and the replacement costs of the property for hazard insurance, in the initial year after the transaction.".

Subtitle F—Appraisal Activities

SEC. 1471. PROPERTY APPRAISAL REQUIREMENTS.

Chapter 2 of the Truth in Lending Act (15 U. S. C. 1631 et seq.) is amended by inserting after 129G (as added by section 1464(b)) the following new section:

"§ 129H. Property appraisal requirements

"(a) IN GENERAL. — A creditor may not extend credit in the form of a higher-risk mortgage to any consumer without first obtaining a written appraisal of the property to be mortgaged prepared in accordance with the requirements of this section.

"(b) APPRAISAL REQUIREMENTS. —

"(1) PHYSICAL PROPERTY VISIT. — Subject to the rules prescribed under paragraph (4), an appraisal of property to be secured by a higher-risk mortgage does not meet the requirement of this section unless it is performed by a certified or licensed appraiser who conducts a physical property visit of the interior ofthe mortgaged property.

"(2) SECOND APPRAISAL UNDER CERTAIN CIRCUMSTANCES. —

"(A) IN GENERAL. — If the purpose of a higher-risk mortgage is to finance the purchase or acquisition of the mortgaged property from a person within 180 days of the purchase or acquisition of such property by that person at a price that was lower than the current sale price of the property, the creditor shall obtain a second appraisal from a different certified or licensed appraiser. The second appraisal shall include an analysis of the difference in sale prices, changes in market conditions, and any improvements made to the property between the date of the previous sale and the current sale.

"(B) NO COST TO APPLICANT. — The cost of any second appraisal required under subparagraph (A) may not be charged to the applicant.

"(3) CERTIFIED OR LICENSED APPRAISER DEFINED. — For purposes of this section, the term 'certified or licensed appraiser' means a person who —

"(A) is, at a minimum, certified or licensed by the State in which the property to be appraised is located; and

"(B) performs each appraisal in conformity with the Uniform Standards of Professional Appraisal Practice and title XI of the Financial Institutions Reform, Recovery, and Enforcement Act of 1989, and the regulations prescribed under such title, as in effect on the date of the appraisal.

第F子编——评估活动

第1471条　房地产评估要求

《诚实信贷法》第二章(《美国法典》第十五编第1631节及其后条文)在第1464(b)条增加的第129G条之后插入如下新条文,作为对该章的修正:

“第129H条　房地产评估要求

“(a)**一般规定**。——贷款发放人在取得按照本条规定编制的抵押房地产评估书之前,不得以高风险抵押贷款的形式向任何消费者授信。

(b)**评估要求**。——

(1)**对房地产的现场检验**。——在不违反根据第(4)款制定的规则的前提下,除非获认证或执照的评估师在对用于担保高风险抵押贷款的房地产进行评估时,对房地产的内部情况进行了现场检验,否则,对该房地产的评估应视为不符合本条的要求。

(2)**特定情形下的二次评估**。——

(A)一般规定。——如果高风险抵押贷款的目的是获取融资,以便在某人购买或获得抵押房地产之日后180天内向该人购买或获得该房地产,且该等当初购买或获得该房地产之价格低于该房地产当前售价,则贷款发放人应安排一名不同的获认证或执照的评估师对该房地产进行二次评估。在二次评估中,应分析售价差异、市场状况变化以及上一出售日至当前销售日期间对该房地产作出的任何改良。

(B)**申请人不必承担费用**。——第(A)子款规定的任何二次评估之费用,不得由申请人承担。

(3)**获认证或执照的评估师的定义**。——就本条而言,‘获认证或执照的评估师’一词系指满足以下条件的人——

(A)至少已在被评估房地产所在州进行注册,获得该州的认证或执照;且

(B)遵循在评估日有效适用的《专业评估执业统一标准》、《1989年金融机构改革、复兴与实施法》第十一编和依据该编制定的规章开展每次评估。

"(4) REGULATIONS.—

"(A) IN GENERAL. — The Board, the Comptroller of the Currency, the Federal Deposit Insurance Corporation, the National Credit Union Administration Board, the Federal Housing Finance Agency, and the Bureau shall jointly prescribe regulations to implement this section.

"(B) EXEMPTION. — The agencies listed in subparagraph (A) may jointly exempt, by rule, a class of loans from the requirements of this subsection or subsection (a) if the agencies determine that the exemption is in the public interest and promotes the safety and soundness of creditors.

"(c) FREE COPY OF APPRAISAL. — A creditor shall provide 1 copy of each appraisal conducted in accordance with this section in connection with a higher–risk mortgage to the applicant without charge, and at least 3 days prior to the transaction closing date.

"(d) CONSUMER NOTIFICATION. — At the time of the initial mortgage application, the applicant shall be provided with a statement by the creditor that any appraisal prepared for the mortgage is for the sole use of the creditor, and that the applicant may choose to have a separate appraisal conducted at the expense of the applicant.

"(e) VIOLATIONS. — In addition to any other liability to any person under this title, a creditor found to have willfully failed to obtain an appraisal as required in this section shall be liable to the applicant or borrower for the sum of $2, 000.

"(f) HIGHER–RISK MORTGAGE DEFINED. — For purposes of this section, the term 'higher–risk mortgage' means a residential mortgage loan, other than a reverse mortgage loan that is a qualified mortgage, as defined in section 129C, secured by a principal dwelling —

"(1) that is not a qualified mortgage, as defined in section 129C; and

"(2) with an annual percentage rate that exceeds the average prime offer rate for a comparable transaction, as defined in section 129C, as of the date the interest rate is set —

"(A) by 1. 5 or more percentage points, in the case of a first lien residential mortgage loan having an original principal obligation amount that does not exceed the amount of the maximum limitation on the original principal obligation of mortgage in effect for a residence of the applicable size, as of the date of such interest rate set, pursuant to the sixth sentence of section 305(a)(2) the Federal Home Loan Mortgage Corporation Act (12 U. S. C. 1454(a)(2));

"(B) by 2. 5 or more percentage points, in the case of a first lien residential mortgage loan having an original principal obligation amount that exceeds the amount of the maximum limitation on the original principal obligation of mortgage in effect for a residence of the applicable size, as of the date of such interest rate set, pursuant to the sixth sentence of section 305(a)(2) the Federal Home Loan Mortgage Corporation Act (12 U. S. C. 1454(a)(2)); and

(4)**规章**。——

(A)**一般规定**。——联邦储备委员会应与货币监理署署长、联邦存款保险公司、国家信贷联盟署委员会、联邦住房金融局和消费者金融保护局共同制定旨在执行本条规定的规章。

(B)**豁免**。——第(A)子款所列机关可以联合发布规则,就某一类别的贷款授予豁免,获得豁免的贷款不必遵守本子条或第(a)子条的要求,前提是该等机关判定该项豁免符合公共利益,且可以提升贷款发放人的安全性和稳健性。

(c)免费提供评估报告。——按本条规定就高风险抵押贷款开展评估的,贷款发放人应在交易成交之前至少提前3天免费向申请人提供一份所做每次评估之报告复本。

(d)**向消费者发出的通知**。——申请人首次提交抵押贷款申请的,贷款发放人应向其提供一份声明,说明为抵押贷款编制的所有评估报告均仅供贷款发放人专用且申请人可以选择自费另行开展评估。

(e)**违法行为**。——如果发现贷款发放人故意不按本条规定安排评估,除了根据本编规定向任何人承担任何其他责任之外,该贷款发放人还应承担向申请人或借款人支付2000美元的责任。

(f)**高风险抵押贷款的定义**。——就本条而言,‘高风险抵押贷款’一词系指由主要住所担保,且具有以下特征的住房抵押贷款,但不包括属于第129C条定义的合格抵押贷款的反向抵押贷款——

(1)不属于第129C条定义的合格抵押贷款;且

(2)截至利率设定之日,其年利率超出第129C条定义的可比交易的平均最优惠利率幅度达到——

(A)在下述情形下,1.5(含)个百分点以上:截至上述利率设定之日,按照《联邦住房贷款抵押公司法》第305(a)(2)条[《美国法典》第十二编第1454(a)(2)节]第6句的规定,享有第一顺位留置权的住房抵押贷款的初始本金金额,不超过届时有效适用的,以同等面积住宅担保的抵押贷款的初始本金上限;

(B)在下述情形下,2.5(含)个百分点以上:截至上述利率设定之日,按照《联邦住房贷款抵押公司法》第305(a)(2)条[《美国法典》第十二编第1454(a)(2)节]第6句的规定,享有第一顺位留置权的住房抵押贷款的初始本金金额,超过届时有效适用的,以同等面积住宅担保的抵押贷款的初始本金上限;及

"(C) by 3. 5 or more percentage points for a subordinate lien residential mortgage loan.".

SEC. 1472. APPRAISAL INDEPENDENCE REQUIREMENTS.

(a) IN GENERAL. — Chapter 2 of the Truth in Lending Act (15 U. S. C. 1631 et seq.) is amended by inserting after section 129D (as added by section 1461(a)) the following new section:

§ 129E. Appraisal independence requirements

"(a) IN GENERAL. — It shall be unlawful, in extending credit or in providing any services for a consumer credit transaction secured by the principal dwelling of the consumer, to engage in any act or practice that violates appraisal independence as described in or pursuant to regulations prescribed under this section.

"(b) APPRAISAL INDEPENDENCE. — For purposes of subsection (a), acts or practices that violate appraisal independence shall include —

"(1) any appraisal of a property offered as security for repayment of the consumer credit transaction that is conducted in connection with such transaction in which a person with an interest in the underlying transaction compensates, coerces, extorts, colludes, instructs, induces, bribes, or intimidates a person, appraisal management company, firm, or other entity conducting or involved in an appraisal, or attempts, to compensate, coerce, extort, collude, instruct, induce, bribe, or intimidate such a person, for the purpose of causing the appraised value assigned, under the appraisal, to the property to be based on any factor other than the independent judgment of the appraiser;

"(2) mischaracterizing, or suborning any mischaracterization of, the appraised value of the property securing the extension of the credit;

"(3) seeking to influence an appraiser or otherwise to encourage a targeted value in order to facilitate the making or pricing of the transaction; and

"(4) withholding or threatening to withhold timely payment for an appraisal report or for appraisal services rendered when the appraisal report or services are provided for in accordance with the contract between the parties.

"(c) EXCEPTIONS. — The requirements of subsection (b) shall not be construed as prohibiting a mortgage lender, mortgage broker, mortgage banker, real estate broker, appraisal management company, employee of an appraisal management company, consumer, or any other person with an interest in a real estate transaction from asking an appraiser to undertake 1 or more of the following:

"(1) Consider additional, appropriate property information, including the consideration of additional comparable properties to make or support an appraisal.

"(2) Provide further detail, substantiation, or explanation for the appraiser's value conclusion.

(C)在享有次级留置权的住房抵押贷款的情形下,3.5(含)个百分点以上。”

第1472条　评估独立性要求

(a)**一般规定**。——《诚实信贷法》第二章(《美国法典》第十五编第1631节及其后条文)在第1461(a)条增加的第129D条之后插入如下新条文,作为对该章的修正:

“第129E条　评估独立性要求

(a)**一般规定**。——贷款发放人在针对以消费者主要住所担保的消费者信用交易授信或提供服务之时,不得从事违反本条所述的或依据本条制定的规章所述的评估独立性要求的任何行为或做法,否则当属违法。

(b)**评估独立性**。——就第(a)子条而言,违反评估独立性要求的行为或做法包括——

(1)在针对为消费者信用交易还款提供担保的房地产开展与该交易相关的任何评估之时,与该交易存在利害关系的人强迫、威逼、勾结、指令、引诱、贿赂或恐吓开展或涉及评估工作的人、评估管理公司、机构或其他实体或向其提供报酬,或试图实施上述行为,以使评估师基于其独立判断之外的任何因素确定该房地产的评估价值;

(2)错误描述为授信提供担保的房地产的评估价值,或唆使评估师错误描述该房地产的评估价值;

(3)试图对评估师施加影响,或以其他方式怂恿评估师按事先设定的价值对房地产进行评估,以便促成交易的成交或定价;及

(4)对于评估师按照双方合同约定提供的评估报告或评估服务,拒绝及时付费或威胁拒绝及时付费。

(c)**例外规定**。——第(b)子条的要求不得被解释为禁止抵押贷款人、抵押贷款经纪人、抵押贷款银行家、房地产经纪人、评估管理公司、评估管理公司雇员、消费者或与房地产交易存在利害关系的任何其他人要求评估师从事下列一种或一种以上行为:

(1)考虑更多的适当的房地产信息,包括考虑更多的可比房地产,以便开展评估或为评估提供支持;

(2)就评估师得出的评估价值结论,提供进一步的详细信息、论证或解释;或

"(3) Correct errors in the appraisal report.

"(d) PROHIBITIONS ON CONFLICTS OF INTEREST. — No certified or licensed appraiser conducting, and no appraisal management company procuring or facilitating, an appraisal in connection with a consumer credit transaction secured by the principal dwelling of a consumer may have a direct or indirect interest, financial or otherwise, in the property or transaction involving the appraisal.

"(e) MANDATORY REPORTING. — Any mortgage lender, mortgage broker, mortgage banker, real estate broker, appraisal management company, employee of an appraisal management company, or any other person involved in a real estate transaction involving an appraisal in connection with a consumer credit transaction secured by the principal dwelling of a consumer who has a reasonable basis to believe an appraiser is failing to comply with the Uniform Standards of Professional Appraisal Practice, is violating applicable laws, or is otherwise engaging in unethical or unprofessional conduct, shall refer the matter to the applicable State appraiser certifying and licensing agency.

"(f) NO EXTENSION OF CREDIT. — In connection with a consumer credit transaction secured by a consumer's principal dwelling, a creditor who knows, at or before loan consummation, of a violation of the appraisal independence standards established in subsections (b) or (d) shall not extend credit based on such appraisal unless the creditor documents that the creditor has acted with reasonable diligence to determine that the appraisal does not materially misstate or misrepresent the value of such dwelling.

"(g) RULES AND INTERPRETIVE GUIDELINES. —

"(1) IN GENERAL. — Except as provided under paragraph (2), the Board, the Comptroller of the Currency, the Federal Deposit Insurance Corporation, the National Credit Union Administration Board, the Federal Housing Finance Agency, and the Bureau may jointly issue rules, interpretive guidelines, and general statements of policy with respect to acts or practices that violate appraisal independence in the provision of mortgage lending services for a consumer credit transaction secured by the principal dwelling of the consumer and mortgage brokerage services for such a transaction, within the meaning of subsections (a), (b), (c), (d), (e), (f), (h), and (i).

"(2) INTERIM FINAL REGULATIONS. — The Board shall, for purposes of this section, prescribe interim final regulations no later than 90 days after the date of enactment of this section defining with specificity acts or practices that violate appraisal independence in the provision of mortgage lending services for a consumer credit transaction secured by the principal dwelling of the consumer or mortgage brokerage services for such a transaction and defining any terms in this section or such regulations. Rules prescribed by the Board under this paragraph shall be deemed to be rules prescribed by the agencies jointly under paragraph (1).

(3)改正评估报告中的错误。

(d)**禁止利益冲突**。——就以消费者主要住所担保的消费者信用交易开展评估的任何获认证或执照的评估师,以及取得或促成该项评估业务的任何评估管理公司,均不得对该评估所涉房地产或交易拥有直接或间接的经济利益或其他利害关系。

(e)**强制报告**。——如果抵押贷款人、抵押贷款经纪人、抵押贷款银行家、房地产经纪人、评估管理公司、评估管理公司雇员或任何其他人所涉及的房地产交易牵涉到房地产评估,而该房地产交易与以消费者主要住所担保的消费者信用交易相关,且该消费者有合理理由认为评估师未遵守《专业评估执业统一标准》,违反了适用的法律的规定,或存在其他违反职业道德或缺乏专业性的行为,则上述主体应将该事宜提交负责对评估师进行认证和颁发执照的州机关处理。

(f)**不得授信的情形**。——对于以消费者主要住所担保的消费者信用交易,如果贷款发放人在贷款合同订立之时或之前,获知存在违反第(b)子条或第(d)子条设定的评估独立性标准的行为,则贷款发放人不得基于该评估授信,但贷款发放人提供书面文件,证明其已开展合理尽职调查判定该评估并未严重误报或误述该住所价值的除外。

(g)**规则和解释性指引**。——

(1)**一般规定**。——除第(2)款规定的情形外,联邦储备委员会、货币监理署署长、联邦存款保险公司、国家信贷联盟署委员会、联邦住房金融局和消费者金融保护局可以在第(a)子条、第(b)子条、第(c)子条、第(d)子条、第(e)子条、第(f)子条、第(h)子条和第(i)子条规定的范围内,针对在为以消费者主要住所为担保的消费者信用交易提供抵押贷款服务以及抵押贷款经纪服务的过程中违反评估独立性要求的行为或做法,联合发布规则、解释性指引和一般性政策声明。

(2)**暂行最终规章**。——为实现本条之目的,联邦储备委员会应于本条规定颁布之日起90天内制定暂行最终规章,明确界定在为以消费者主要住所担保的消费者信用交易提供抵押贷款服务或抵押贷款经纪服务的过程中违反评估独立性要求的行为或做法,并对本条或该等规章中的术语予以定义。联邦储备委员会根据本款制定的规则应视为第(1)款所述各机关联合制定的规则。

"(h) APPRAISAL REPORT PORTABILITY. — Consistent with the requirements of this section, the Board, the Comptroller of the Currency, the Federal Deposit Insurance Corporation, the National Credit Union Administration Board, the Federal Housing Finance Agency, and the Bureau may jointly issue regulations that address the issue of appraisal report portability, including regulations that ensure the portability of the appraisal report between lenders for a consumer credit transaction secured by a 1–4 unit single family residence that is the principal dwelling of the consumer, or mortgage brokerage services for such a transaction.

"(i) CUSTOMARY AND REASONABLE FEE. —

"(1) IN GENERAL. — Lenders and their agents shall compensate fee appraisers at a rate that is customary and reasonable for appraisal services performed in the market area of the property being appraised. Evidence for such fees may be established by objective third–party information, such as government agency fee schedules, academic studies, and independent private sector surveys. Fee studies shall exclude assignments ordered by known appraisal management companies.

"(2) FEE APPRAISER DEFINITION. — For purposes of this section, the term 'fee appraiser' means a person who is not an employee of the mortgage loan originator or appraisal management company engaging the appraiser and is —

"(A) a State licensed or certified appraiser who receives a fee for performing an appraisal and certifies that the appraisal has been prepared in accordance with the Uniform Standards of Professional Appraisal Practice; or

"(B) a company not subject to the requirements of section 1124 of the Financial Institutions Reform, Recovery, and Enforcement Act of 1989 (12 U. S. C. 3331 et seq.) that utilizes the services of State licensed or certified appraisers and receives a fee for performing appraisals in accordance with the Uniform Standards of Professional Appraisal Practice.

"(3) EXCEPTION FOR COMPLEX ASSIGNMENTS. — In the case of an appraisal involving a complex assignment, the customary and reasonable fee may reflect the increased time, difficulty, and scope of the work required for such an appraisal and include an amount over and above the customary and reasonable fee for non–complex assignments.

"(j) SUNSET. — Effective on the date the interim final regulations are promulgated pursuant to subsection (g), the Home Valuation Code of Conduct announced by the Federal Housing Finance Agency on December 23, 2008, shall have no force or effect.

"(k) PENALTIES. —

"(1) FIRST VIOLATION. — In addition to the enforcement provisions referred to in section 130, each person who violates this section shall forfeit and pay a civil penalty of not more than $10, 000 for each day any such violation continues.

"(2) SUBSEQUENT VIOLATIONS. — In the case of any person on whom a civil

(h)**评估报告的可转移性**。——联邦储备委员会、货币监理署署长、联邦存款保险公司、国家信贷联盟署委员会、联邦住房金融局和消费者金融保护局可以按照本条的要求,联合发布解决评估报告可转移性问题的规章,包括旨在针对作为消费者主要住所的1~4个单元的独户住宅担保的消费者信用交易,确保评估报告在不同贷款人之间或不同抵押贷款经纪服务提供人之间具有可转移性的规章。

(i)**惯常合理费用**。——

(1)**一般规定**。——对于收费的评估师就被评估房地产提供的评估服务,贷款人及其代理人应向其支付惯常合理费用,按被评估房地产所在区域市场的水平确定。在确定该等惯常合理费用时,可借助客观的第三方信息,例如,政府机关费率表、学术研究和独立私营部门的调查等。开展该等费用研究之时,不得纳入具体评估管理公司聘用第三方所做研究的结果。

(2)**收费的评估师的定义**。——就本条而言,'收费的评估师'一词系指并非抵押贷款发起人或聘用该评估师的评估管理公司的雇员,且满足以下任一条件的主体——

(A)是获得州执照或认证的评估师,开展收费的评估工作并作出评估报告的编制符合《专业评估执业统一标准》的认证;或

(B)是一家不受《1989年金融机构改革、复兴与实施法》第1124条(《美国法典》第十二编第3331节及其后条文)规定约束的公司,并聘用获得州执照或认证的评估师按照《专业评估执业统一标准》开展收费的评估工作。

(3)**适用于复杂评估工作的例外规定**。——如果评估涉及复杂工作任务,则可以在惯常合理费用中体现评估工作所需的额外工作时间、难度和范围,且其金额可超过非复杂工作任务的惯常合理费用。

(j)**日落条款**。——自暂行最终规章依照第(g)子条规定颁发之日起,联邦住房金融局于2008年12月23日发布的《住房估值行为守则》应予废止。

(k)**处罚**。——

(1)**初次违法**。——违反本条规定行为的人,除须受制于第130条提及的执法条款之外,还应在违法行为存续期间按照每天不高于1万美元的标准承担并支付民事罚款。

(2)**后续违法**。——如果依照第(1)款规定对任何人处以民事罚款之后,该人再

penalty has been imposed under paragraph (1), paragraph (1) shall be applied by substituting '$20, 000' for '$10, 000' with respect to all subsequent violations.

"(3) ASSESSMENT. — The agency referred to in subsection (a) or (c) of section 108 with respect to any person described in paragraph (1) shall assess any penalty under this subsection to which such person is subject.".

(b) CLERICAL AMENDMENT. — The table of sections for chapter 2 of the Truth in Lending Act is amended by inserting after the item relating to section 129D (as added by section 1461(c)) the following new items:

"129E. Appraisal independence requirements.

"129F. Requirements for prompt crediting of home loan payments.

"129G. Requests for payoff amounts of home loan.

"129H. Property appraisal requirements.".

(c) DEFERENCE. — Section 105 of the Truth in Lending Act (15 U. S. C. 1604) is amended by adding at the end the following:

"(h) DEFERENCE. — Notwithstanding any power granted to any Federal agency under this title, the deference that a court affords to the Bureau with respect to a determination made by the Bureau relating to the meaning or interpretation of any provision of this title, other than section 129E or 129H, shall be applied as if the Bureau were the only agency authorized to apply, enforce, interpret, or administer the provisions of this title.".

(d) CONFORMING AMENDMENTS IN TITLE X NOT APPLICABLE TO SECTIONS 129E AND 129H. —Notwithstanding section 1099A, the term "Board" in sections 129E and 129H, as added by this subtitle, shall not be substituted by the term "Bureau".

SEC. 1473. AMENDMENTS RELATING TO APPRAISAL SUBCOMMITTEE OF FFIEC, APPRAISER INDEPENDENCE MONITORING, APPROVED APPRAISER EDUCATION, APPRAISAL MANAGEMENT COMPANIES, APPRAISER COMPLAINT HOTLINE, AUTOMATED VALUATION MODELS, AND BROKER PRICE OPINIONS.

(a) THRESHOLD LEVELS. — Section 1112(b) of the Financial Institutions Reform, Recovery, and Enforcement Act of 1989 (12 U. S. C. 3341(b)) is amended by inserting before the period the following: ", and receives concurrence from the Bureau of Consumer Financial Protection that such threshold level provides reasonable protection for consumers who purchase 1–4 unit single–family residences".

(b) ANNUAL REPORT OF APPRAISAL SUBCOMMITTEE. — Section 1103 (a) of the Financial Institutions Reform, Recovery, and Enforcement Act of 1989 (12 U. S. C. 3332(a)) is amended at the end by inserting the following new paragraph:

"(5) transmit an annual report to the Congress not later than June 15 of each year that describes the manner in which each function assigned to the Appraisal Subcommittee has

出现后续违法行为的，则其应在该等后续违法行为存续期间按每天不高于2万美元[而非第(1)款规定的1万美元]的标准承担并支付民事罚款。

(3)**计征罚款**。——对于第(1)款所述之人,应由第108条第(a)子条或第(c)子条所述机关按照本子条规定计征对其适用的任何罚款金额。”

(b)**目录修正**。——在《诚实信贷法》第二章条款目录中,在第1461(c)条增加的第129D条的目录项之后插入如下新的目录项,作为对该目录的修正:

“第129E条　评估独立性要求

第129F条　关于及时贷记房贷还款的要求

第129G条　查询房贷未偿余额的请求

第129H条　房地产评估要求。”

(c)**司法尊重**。——在《诚实信贷法》第105条(《美国法典》第十五编第1604节)结尾处增加如下内容,作为对该条的修正:

“(h)**司法尊重**。——不论本编赋予了任何联邦机关任何权力,如消费者金融保护局就本编除第129E条或第129H条之外任何其他规定的含义或解释作出判定,且法院对该等判定表示司法尊重,则在适用该等司法尊重时,应将消费者金融保护局视同为唯一有权适用、执行、解释或实施本编规定的机关。”

(d)**第十编的一致性修正不适用于第129E条和第129H条**。——无论第1099A条如何规定,本子编增加的第129E条和第129H条中的“联邦储备委员会”一词不得替以“消费者金融保护局”。

第1473条　关于联邦金融机构检查委员会评估小组委员会、评估师独立性监控、已获批准的评估师教育课程、评估管理公司、评估师投诉热线、自动估值模型和经纪人价格意见的修正

(a)**最低门槛**。——在《1989年金融机构改革、复兴与实施法》第1112(b)条[《美国法典》第十二编第3341(b)节]的句号前插入如下内容,作为对该条的修正:“,并收到消费者金融保护局发出的同意意见,该同意意见认可了该等最低门槛为购买1~4个单元的独户住宅的消费者提供了合理保护之事实”。

(b)**评估小组委员会的年度报告**。——在《1989年金融机构改革、复兴与实施法》第1103(a)条[《美国法典》第十二编第3332(a)节]结尾处插入如下新款,作为对该条的修正:

“(5)在每年6月15日之前向国会发送一份年度报告,说明评估小组委员会在上一年度履行其各项职能的方式。报告还应详细列明评估小组委员会的活动,包括州评估

been carried out during the preceding year. The report shall also detail the activities of the Appraisal Subcommittee, including the results of all audits of State appraiser regulatory agencies, and provide an accounting of disapproved actions and warnings taken in the previous year, including a description of the conditions causing the disapproval and actions taken to achieve compliance. ".

(c) OPEN MEETINGS. — Section 1104(b) of the Financial Institutions Reform, Recovery, and Enforcement Act of 1989 (12 U. S. C. 3333(b)) is amended —

(1) by inserting "in public session after notice in the Federal Register, but may close certain portions of these meetings related to personnel and review of preliminary State audit reports, " after "shall meet"; and

(2) by adding after the final period the following: "The subject matter discussed in any closed or executive session shall be described in the Federal Register notice of the meeting. ".

(d) REGULATIONS. — Section 1106 of the Financial Institutions Reform, Recovery, and Enforcement Act of 1989 (12 U. S. C. 3335) is amended —

(1) by inserting "prescribe regulations in accordance with chapter 5 of title 5, United States Code (commonly referred to as the Administrative Procedures Act) after notice and opportunity for comment, " after "hold hearings"; and

(2) at the end by inserting "Any regulations prescribed by the Appraisal Subcommittee shall (unless otherwise provided in this title) be limited to the following functions: temporary practice, national registry, information sharing, and enforcement. For purposes of prescribing regulations, the Appraisal Subcommittee shall establish an advisory committee of industry participants, including appraisers, lenders, consumer advocates, real estate agents, and government agencies, and hold meetings as necessary to support the development of regulations. ".

(e) APPRAISAL REVIEWS AND COMPLEX APPRAISALS. —

(1) SECTION 1110. — Section 1110 of the Financial Institutions Reform, Recovery, and Enforcement Act of 1989 (12 U. S. C. 3339) is amended —

(A) in paragraph (1), by striking "and";

(B) in paragraph (2), by striking the period at the end and inserting "; and"; and

(C) by inserting after paragraph (2) the following:

"(3) that such appraisals shall be subject to appropriate review for compliance with the Uniform Standards of Professional Appraisal Practice. ".

(2) SECTION 1113. — Section 1113 of the Financial Institutions and Reform, Recovery, and Enforcement Act of 1989 (12 U. S. C. 3342) is amended by inserting before the period the following: ", where a complex 1-to-4 unit single family residential appraisal means an appraisal for which the property to be appraised, the form of ownership, the property

师监管机关开展的所有审计之结果，并列明上一年度采取的不批准行动和给予的警告(包括说明导致其采取不批准行动的情形)以及为实现合规而采取的行动。”

(c)**公开会议**。——《1989年金融机构改革、复兴与实施法》第1104(b)条[《美国法典》第十二编第3333(b)节]修正如下——

(1)在“应举行”之后插入“公开会议,在会议举行之前,应在《联邦公报》上发布通知,但是,该等会议中有关人事和州初步审计报告之审查的部分可以不公开举行,”;及

(2)在该条结尾处的句号之后增加如下内容:“任何非公开会议或行政会议讨论的主题均应在《联邦公报》发布的会议通知中予以说明。”

(d)**规章**。——《1989年金融机构改革、复兴与实施法》第1106条(《美国法典》第十二编第3335节)修正如下——

(1)在“举行听证”之后插入“,并在发布公告和征求公众意见后,按照《美国法典》第五编第五章(通常简称为《行政程序法》)的规定制定规章”;及

(2)在结尾处插入:“除非本编另有规定,否则评估小组委员会制定的任何规章均应限于如下职能范围:临时执业、全国性注册名册、信息共享和执法。在制定规章之时,评估小组委员会应设立由行业参与者组成的顾问委员会,包括评估师、贷款人、消费者维权人士、房地产代理人和政府机关,并且顾问委员会应举行必要会议,以为制定规章提供支持。”

(e)**评估审查和复杂评估**。——

(1)**第1110条。**——《1989年金融机构改革、复兴与实施法》第1110条(《美国法典》第十二编第3339节)修正如下——

(A)在第(1)款中,删除“且”;

(B)在第(2)款中,删除结尾处的句号,替以“;且”;及

(C)在第(2)款之后插入如下内容:

“(3)该等评估应接受适当审查,以确定其是否符合《专业评估执业统一标准》。”

(2)**第1113条**。——在《1989年金融机构改革、复兴与实施法》第1113条(《美国法典》第十二编第3342节)的句号前插入如下内容,作为对该条的修正:“,在此情形下,‘1~4个单元的独户住宅的复杂评估’一词系指被评估的房地产、所有权形式、房地产特点或市场状况具有非典型特质的评估”。

characteristics, or the market conditions are atypical".

(f) APPRAISAL MANAGEMENT SERVICES. —

(1) SUPERVISION OF THIRD PARTY PROVIDERS OF APPRAISAL MANAGEMENT SERVICES. — Section 1103(a) of the Financial Institutions Reform, Recovery, and Enforcement Act of 1989 (12 U. S. C. 3332 (a))(as previously amended by this section) is amended —

(A) by amending paragraph (1) to read as follows:

"(1) monitor the requirements established by States —

"(A) for the certification and licensing of individuals who are qualified to perform appraisals in connection with federally related transactions, including a code of professional responsibility; and

"(B) for the registration and supervision of the operations and activities of an appraisal management company; "; and

(B) by adding at the end the following new paragraph:

"(6) maintain a national registry of appraisal management companies that either are registered with and subject to supervision of a State appraiser certifying and licensing agency or are operating subsidiaries of a Federally regulated financial institution. ".

(2) APPRAISAL MANAGEMENT COMPANY MINIMUM REQUIREMENTS. — Title XI of the Financial Institutions Reform, Recovery, and Enforcement Act of 1989 (12 U. S. C. 3331 et seq.) is amended by adding at the end the following new section (and amending the table of contents accordingly):

"SEC. 1124. APPRAISAL MANAGEMENT COMPANY MINIMUM REQUIREMENTS.

"(a) IN GENERAL. — The Board of Governors of the Federal Reserve System, the Comptroller of the Currency, the Federal Deposit Insurance Corporation, the National Credit Union Administration Board, the Federal Housing Finance Agency, and the Bureau of Consumer Financial Protection shall jointly, by rule, establish minimum requirements to be applied by a State in the registration of appraisal management companies. Such requirements shall include a requirement that such companies —

"(1) register with and be subject to supervision by a State appraiser certifying and licensing agency in each State in which such company operates;

"(2) verify that only licensed or certified appraisers are used for federally related transactions;

"(3) require that appraisals coordinated by an appraisal management company comply with the Uniform Standards of Professional Appraisal Practice; and

"(4) require that appraisals are conducted independently and free from inappropriate influence and coercion pursuant to the appraisal independence standards established under section 129E of the Truth in Lending Act.

(f)**评估管理服务**。——

(1)**第三方评估管理服务提供者的监管**。——《1989年金融机构改革、复兴与实施法》第1103(a)条[《美国法典》第十二编第3332(a)节](以先前经本条修正后的版本为准)进一步修正如下——

(A)第(1)款修正后全文如下:

"(1)监控各州制定的——

(A)具有就联邦相关交易开展评估的资格的个人,为获认证和执照所应达到的要求,包括职业责任守则;及

"(B)关于评估管理公司的注册要求,以及关于其运营和活动监管的要求;";及

(B)在该条结尾处增加如下新款:

"(6) 针对在州评估师的认证和执照颁发机关注册并接受其监管的评估管理公司,或是身为受联邦监管的金融机构的运营子公司的评估管理公司,维持一份全国性注册名册。"

(2)**关于评估管理公司的最低限度要求**。——在《1989年金融机构改革、复兴与实施法》第十一编(《美国法典》第十二编第3331节及其后条文)结尾处增加如下新条文(并修正相应的目录),作为对该编的修正:

"第1124条　关于评估管理公司的最低要求

(a)**一般规定**。——联邦储备委员会、货币监理署署长、联邦存款保险公司、国家信贷联盟署委员会、联邦住房金融局和消费者金融保护局应联合发布规则,确立各州在对评估管理公司进行注册时应适用的最低要求。该等要求应包括——

(1)该等公司应在其运营的每个州的州评估师认证和执照颁发机关办理注册,并接受其监管;

(2)该等公司应进行核实,确保其所聘用的对联邦相关交易开展评估的评估师仅限于获认证或执照的评估师;

(3)该等公司应要求经评估管理公司协调开展的各项评估应符合《专业评估执业统一标准》;及

(4)该等公司应要求按照《诚实信贷法》第129E条确立的评估独立性标准独立开展评估,不得受到任何不当影响或强迫。

"(b) RELATION TO STATE LAW. — Nothing in this section shall be construed to prevent States from establishing requirements in addition to any rules promulgated under subsection (a).

"(c) FEDERALLY REGULATED FINANCIAL INSTITUTIONS. — The requirements of subsection (a) shall apply to an appraisal management company that is a subsidiary owned and controlled by a financial institution and regulated by a Federal financial institution regulatory agency. An appraisal management company that is a subsidiary owned and controlled by a financial institution regulated by a Federal financial institution regulatory agency shall not be required to register with a State.

"(d) REGISTRATION LIMITATIONS. —An appraisal management company shall not be registered by a State or included on the national registry if such company, in whole or in part, directly or indirectly, is owned by any person who has had an appraiser license or certificate refused, denied, cancelled, surrendered in lieu of revocation, or revoked in any State. Additionally, each person that owns more than 10 percent of an appraisal management company shall be of good moral character, as determined by the State appraiser certifying and licensing agency, and shall submit to a background investigation carried out by the State appraiser certifying and licensing agency.

"(e) REPORTING. — The Board of Governors of the Federal Reserve System, the Comptroller of the Currency, the Federal Deposit Insurance Corporation, the National Credit Union Administration Board, the Federal Housing Finance Agency, and the Bureau of Consumer Financial Protection shall jointly promulgate regulations for the reporting of the activities of appraisal management companies to the Appraisal Subcommittee in determining the payment of the annual registry fee.

"(f) EFFECTIVE DATE. —

"(1) IN GENERAL. — No appraisal management company may perform services related to a federally related transaction in a State after the date that is 36 months after the date on which the regulations required to be prescribed under subsection (a) are prescribed in final form unless such company is registered with such State or subject to oversight by a Federal financial institutions regulatory agency.

"(2) EXTENSION OF EFFECTIVE DATE. — Subject to the approval of the Council, the Appraisal Subcommittee may extend by an additional 12 months the requirements for the registration and supervision of appraisal management companies if it makes a written finding that a State has made substantial progress in establishing a State appraisal management company registration and supervision system that appears to conform with the provisions of this title.".

(3) STATE APPRAISER CERTIFYING AND LICENSING AGENCY AUTHORITY. — Section 1117 of the Financial Institutions Reform, Recovery, and Enforcement Act of 1989

(b)**与州法律的关系**。——本条的任何规定均不得被解释为妨碍各州在按照第(a)子条颁发的任何规则之外制定其他要求。

(c)**受联邦监管的金融机构**。——第(a)子条的要求适用于身为金融机构所有并控制的子公司并受联邦金融机构监管机关监管的评估管理公司。不得要求如上所述的评估管理公司在任何州办理注册。

(d)**注册限制**。——如果任何人曾被任何州拒发评估师执照或认证证明，或其执照或认证证明曾被任何州拒不承认、取消、吊销或撤销，则该人直接或间接、完全或部分拥有的评估管理公司不得在该州办理注册，亦不得在全国性注册名册中登记。此外，持有评估管理公司10%以上所有权的人应具有州评估师认证和执照颁发机关所判定的良好道德品格，并应接受州评估师认证和执照颁发机关开展的背景调查。

(e)**报告**。——联邦储备委员会、货币监理署署长、联邦存款保险公司、国家信贷署委员会、联邦住房金融局和消费者金融保护局应联合颁发规章，规范评估管理公司向评估小组委员会作出的活动报告，以便据以判定其年度注册费缴纳金额。

(f)**生效日**。——

(1)**一般规定**。——在按照第(a)子条的规定制定最终规章之日届满36个月之后，任何评估管理公司均不得在该州就联邦相关交易开展服务，但该公司已在该州注册或接受联邦金融监管机关监督的除外。

(2)**生效日的延长**。——如果评估小组委员会书面认定某一州在建设州评估管理公司注册和监管制度方面已取得重大进展，且该等制度从表面判断符合本编规定，则，经联邦金融机构检查委员会批准，评估小组委员会可以将评估管理公司办理注册和接受监管的要求另行延长12个月。”

(3)**州评估师认证和执照颁发机关的权力**。——在《1989年金融机构改革、复兴与实施法》第1117条（《美国法典》第十二编第3346节）结尾处增加如下内容，作为对该

(12 U. S. C. 3346) is amended by adding at the end the following: "The duties of such agency may additionally include the registration and supervision of appraisal management companies and the addition of information about the appraisal management company to the national registry.".

(4) APPRAISAL MANAGEMENT COMPANY DEFINITION. — Section 1121 of the Financial Institutions Reform, Recovery, and Enforcement Act of 1989 (12 U. S. C. 3350) is amended by adding at the end the following:

"(11) APPRAISAL MANAGEMENT COMPANY. — The term 'appraisal management company' means, in connection with valuing properties collateralizing mortgage loans or mortgages incorporated into a securitization, any external third party authorized either by a creditor of a consumer credit transaction secured by a consumer's principal dwelling or by an underwriter of or other principal in the secondary mortgage markets, that oversees a network or panel of more than 15 certified or licensed appraisers in a State or 25 or more nationally within a given year —

"(A) to recruit, select, and retain appraisers;

"(B) to contract with licensed and certified appraisers to perform appraisal assignments;

"(C) to manage the process of having an appraisal performed, including providing administrative duties such as receiving appraisal orders and appraisal reports, submitting completed appraisal reports to creditors and underwriters, collecting fees from creditors and underwriters for services provided, and reimbursing appraisers for services performed; or

"(D) to review and verify the work of appraisers.".

(g) STATE AGENCY REPORTING REQUIREMENT. — Section 1109(a) of the Financial Institutions Reform, Recovery, and Enforcement Act of 1989 (12 U. S. C. 3338(a)) is amended —

(1) by striking "and" after the semicolon in paragraph (1);

(2) by redesignating paragraph (2) as paragraph (4); and

(3) by inserting after paragraph (1) the following new paragraphs:

"(2) transmit reports on the issuance and renewal of licenses and certifications, sanctions, disciplinary actions, license and certification revocations, and license and certification suspensions on a timely basis to the national registry of the Appraisal Subcommittee;

"(3) transmit reports on a timely basis of supervisory activities involving appraisal management companies or other third-party providers of appraisals and appraisal management services, including investigations initiated and disciplinary actions taken; and".

(h) REGISTRY FEES MODIFIED. —

(1) IN GENERAL. — Section 1109(a) of the Financial Institutions Reform, Recovery, and Enforcement Act of 1989 (12 U. S. C. 3338(a)) is amended —

条的修正:“该机关的职能还可包括对评估管理公司进行注册和监管，以及将有关评估管理公司的信息登记录入全国性注册名册。”

(4)**评估管理公司的定义**。——在《1989年金融机构改革、复兴与实施法》第1121条(《美国法典》第十二编第3350节)结尾处增加如下内容,作为对该条的修正:

“(11)**评估管理公司**。——‘评估管理公司’一词系指在以消费者主要住所担保的消费者信用交易中，贷款发放人或二级抵押贷款市场上的贷款审核人或其他委托人为对抵押贷款的担保房地产进行估值或对被证券化的抵押贷款进行估值而委托的任何外部第三方,且该外部第三方在相关年度内,在某一州管理的获认证或执照的评估师网络或团队成员达15名以上,或者在全国范围内管理的获认证或执照的评估师网络或团队成员达25名以上,并有权——

(A)招聘、遴选和聘用评估师;

(B)与获执照或认证的评估师订立合同,委托其开展评估工作;

(C)管理他人开展评估的流程,包括履行管理职能,例如,接收评估订单和评估报告、向贷款发放人和贷款审核人提供完整的评估报告、就已提供的服务向贷款发放人和贷款审核人收取服务费以及就已履行的服务向评估师支付服务费;或

(D)审核和核实评估师的工作。”

(g)**州机关的报告要求**。——《1989年金融机构改革、复兴与实施法》第1109(a)条[《美国法典》第十二编第3338(a)节]修正如下——

(1)删除第(1)款分号之后的“及”;

(2)第(2)款重新编号为第(4)款;及

(3)在第(1)款之后插入如下新款:

“(2)及时向评估小组委员会提交有关执照和认证证明的颁发和续展、处罚、纪律处分以及执照和认证证明的撤销和暂停的报告,以便登记录入全国性注册名册;

(3)及时向评估小组委员会提交关于评估管理公司或其他第三方评估服务提供者和评估管理服务提供者的监管活动的报告(包括对其开展的调查和采取的纪律处分);及”。

(h)**注册费调整**。——

(1)**一般规定**。——《1989年金融机构改革、复兴与实施法》第1109(a)条[《美国法典》第十二编第3338(a)节]修正如下——

(A) by amending paragraph (4)(as modified by section 1473(g)) to read as follows:

"(4) collect —

"(A) from such individuals who perform or seek to perform appraisals in federally related transactions, an annual registry fee of not more than $40, such fees to be transmitted by the State agencies to the Council on an annual basis; and

"(B) from an appraisal management company that either has registered with a State appraiser certifying and licensing agency in accordance with this title or operates as a subsidiary of a federally regulated financial institution, an annual registry fee of —

"(i) in the case of such a company that has been in existence for more than a year, $25 multiplied by the number of appraisers working for or contracting with such company in such State during the previous year, but where such $25 amount may be adjusted, up to a maximum of $50, at the discretion of the Appraisal Subcommittee, if necessary to carry out the Subcommittee's functions under this title; and

"(ii) in the case of such a company that has not been in existence for more than a year, $25 multiplied by an appropriate number to be determined by the Appraisal Subcommittee, and where such number will be used for determining the fee of all such companies that were not in existence for more than a year, but where such $25 amount may be adjusted, up to a maximum of $50, at the discretion of the Appraisal Subcommittee, if necessary to carry out the Subcommittee's functions under this title. "; and

(B) by amending the matter following paragraph (4), as redesignated, to read as follows:

"Subject to the approval of the Council, the Appraisal Subcommittee may adjust the dollar amount of registry fees under paragraph (4)(A), up to a maximum of $80 per annum, as necessary to carry out its functions under this title. The Appraisal Subcommittee shall consider at least once every 5 years whether to adjust the dollar amount of the registry fees to account for inflation. In implementing any change in registry fees, the Appraisal Subcommittee shall provide flexibility to the States for multi-year certifications and licenses already in place, as well as a transition period to implement the changes in registry fees. In establishing the amount of the annual registry fee for an appraisal management company, the Appraisal Subcommittee shall have the discretion to impose a minimum annual registry fee for an appraisal management company to protect against the under reporting of the number of appraisers working for or contracted by the appraisal management company. ".

(2) INCREMENTAL REVENUES. — Incremental revenues collected pursuant to the increases required by this subsection shall be placed in a separate account at the United States Treasury, entitled the "— Appraisal Subcommittee Account".

(i) GRANTS AND REPORTS. — Section 1109(b) of the Financial Institutions Reform, Recovery, and Enforcement Act of 1989 (12 U. S. C. 3338(b)) is amended —

(1) by striking "and" after the semicolon in paragraph (3);

(A)第(4)款[以经第1473(g)条修改后的版本为准]修正后全文如下:

“(4)按如下规定收取费用——

(A)对于就或试图就联邦相关交易开展评估活动的个人,收取不高于40美元的年度注册费,该费用应每年由州机关上缴至联邦金融机构检查委员会;及

(B)对于已经按照本编规定在州评估师认证与执照颁发机关办理注册的评估管理公司,或作为受联邦监管的金融机构的子公司运营的评估管理公司,年度注册费应按如下规定计算——

(i)如果该公司已经存续一年以上,年度注册费应为25美元乘以上一年度在该州为该公司工作的或与其签约的评估师的人数,但是,评估小组委员会可以为履行本编规定的职能之目的,依其自由裁量权对该25美元的标准予以必要调整,调整后的金额最高不得超过50美元;且

(ii)如果该公司存续时间不足一年,则年度注册费应为25美元乘以评估小组委员会判定的适当数目,此时,该数目应用于判定所有存续时间不足一年的公司的年度注册费,但是,评估小组委员会可以为履行本编规定的职能之目的,依其自由裁量权对该25美元的标准予以必要调整,调整后的金额最高不得超过50美元。”及

(B)第(4)款(以重新编号后的序号为准)之后的内容修正如下:

“经联邦金融机构检查委员会批准,评估小组委员会可以为履行本编规定的职能之目的,对第(4)(A)款规定的注册费金额予以必要调整,调整后的金额最高不得超过每年80美元。评估小组委员会至少应每隔五年,考虑是否调整注册费金额,以便计入通货膨胀因素。在对注册费实施任何变更之时,对于已经颁发的多年期的认证证明和执照,评估小组委员会应为各州提供灵活调整空间,并为注册费变更的执行设定相应的过渡期。在确定评估管理公司年度注册费的金额时,为了防止评估管理公司少报为其工作的或与其签约的评估师的人数,评估小组委员会有权依其自由裁量权决定评估管理公司的最低年度注册费。”

(2)**增量收入**。——因按照本子条要求提高注册费而获得的增量收入应存入在美国财政部开设的名为“——评估小组委员会账户”的独立账户。

(i)**拨款与报告**。——《1989年金融机构改革、复兴与实施法》第1109(b)条[《美国法典》第十二编第3338(b)节]修正如下——

(1)删除第(3)款分号之后的“及”;

(2) by striking the period at the end of paragraph (4) and inserting a semicolon;

(3) by adding at the end the following new paragraphs:

"(5) to make grants to State appraiser certifying and licensing agencies, in accordance with policies to be developed by the Appraisal Subcommittee, to support the efforts of such agencies to comply with this title, including —

"(A) the complaint process, complaint investigations, and appraiser enforcement activities of such agencies; and

"(B) the submission of data on State licensed and certified appraisers and appraisal management companies to the National appraisal registry, including information affirming that the appraiser or appraisal management company meets the required qualification criteria and formal and informal disciplinary actions; and

"(6) to report to all State appraiser certifying and licensing agencies when a license or certification is surrendered, revoked, or suspended. ". Obligations authorized under this subsection may not exceed 75 percent of the fiscal year total of incremental increase in fees collected and deposited in the "Appraisal Subcommittee Account" pursuant to subsection (h).

(j) CRITERIA. — Section 1116 of the Financial Institutions Reform, Recovery, and Enforcement Act of 1989 (12 U. S. C. 3345) is amended —

(1) in subsection (c), by inserting "whose criteria for the licensing of a real estate appraiser currently meet or exceed the minimum criteria issued by the Appraisal Qualifications Board of The Appraisal Foundation for the licensing of real estate appraisers" before the period at the end; and

(2) by striking subsection (e) and inserting the following new subsection:

"(e) MINIMUM QUALIFICATION REQUIREMENTS. — Any requirements established for individuals in the position of 'Trainee Appraiser' and 'Supervisory Appraiser' shall meet or exceed the minimum qualification requirements of the Appraiser Qualifications Board of The Appraisal Foundation. The Appraisal Subcommittee shall have the authority to enforce these requirements. ".

(k) MONITORING OF STATE APPRAISER CERTIFYING AND LICENSING AGENCIES. — Section 1118 of the Financial Institutions Reform, Recovery, and Enforcement Act of 1989 (12 U. S. C. 3347) is amended —

(1) by amending subsection (a) to read as follows:

"(a) IN GENERAL. — The Appraisal Subcommittee shall monitor each State appraiser certifying and licensing agency for the purposes of determining whether such agency —

(2)删除第(4)款结尾处的句号,替以分号;

(3)在结尾处增加如下新款:

"(5)按照评估小组委员会制定的政策,向州评估师认证和执照颁发机关拨款,以支持该机关开展实施本编规定工作,包括——

(A)该等机关的投诉制度、投诉调查和针对评估师的执法活动;及

(B)提交关于获得州执照和认证的评估师的数据,以及评估管理公司的数据,包括确认评估师或评估管理公司符合规定的资格标准的信息,以及正式和非正式的纪律处分,以便登记录入全国性评估师注册名册;及

(6)在评估师执照和认证证明被收回、撤销或暂停之时,向所有州评估师认证和执照颁发机关报告。"按照本子条批准拨付的款项不得超过该财政年度按照第(h)子条收取并存入"评估小组委员会账户"的费用的增量总额的75%。

(j)**标准**。——《1989年金融机构改革、复兴与实施法》第1116条(《美国法典》第十二编第3345节)修正如下——

(1)在第(c)子条中,在结尾处句号前插入"且当前,其房地产评估师执照颁发标准的严格程度不低于评估基金会的评估师资格委员会发布的关于房地产评估师执照颁发的最低标准";及

(2)删除第(e)子条,替以如下内容:

"(e)**最低资格要求**。——针对担任'实习评估师'和'主管评估师'的个人制定的要求之严格程度不得低于评估基金会的评估师资格委员会[1]发布的最低资格要求。评估小组委员会有权强制执行该等要求。"

(k)**对州评估师认证和执照颁发机关的监控**。——《1989年金融机构改革、复兴与实施法》第1118条(《美国法典》第十二编第3347节)修正如下——

(1)第(a)子条修正后全文如下:

"(a)**一般规定**。——评估小组委员会应对各州评估师认证和执照颁发机关进行监控,以判定该等机关——

---

1 原文Appraisal Qualifications Board疑误,经查,似应为"Appraiser Qualifications Board",译文按后者处理。——译者注

"(1) has policies, practices, funding, staffing, and procedures that are consistent with this title;

"(2) processes complaints and completes investigations in a reasonable time period;

"(3) appropriately disciplines sanctioned appraisers and appraisal management companies;

"(4) maintains an effective regulatory program; and

"(5) reports complaints and disciplinary actions on a timely basis to the national registries on appraisers and appraisal management companies maintained by the Appraisal Subcommittee.

The Appraisal Subcommittee shall have the authority to remove a State licensed or certified appraiser or a registered appraisal management company from a national registry on an interim basis, not to exceed 90 days, pending State agency action on licensing, certification, registration, and disciplinary proceedings. The Appraisal Subcommittee and all agencies, instrumentalities, and Federally recognized entities under this title shall not recognize appraiser certifications and licenses from States whose appraisal policies, practices, funding, staffing, or procedures are found to be inconsistent with this title. The Appraisal Subcommittee shall have the authority to impose sanctions, as described in this section, against a State agency that fails to have an effective appraiser regulatory program. In determining whether such a program is effective, the Appraisal Subcommittee shall include an analysis of the licensing and certification of appraisers, the registration of appraisal management companies, the issuance of temporary licenses and certifications for appraisers, the receiving and tracking of submitted complaints against appraisers and appraisal management companies, the investigation of complaints, and enforcement actions against appraisers and appraisal management companies. The Appraisal Subcommittee shall have the authority to impose interim actions and suspensions against a State agency as an alternative to, or in advance of, the derecognition of a State agency. ".

(2) in subsection (b)(2), by inserting after "authority" the following: "or sufficient funding".

(1) RECIPROCITY. — Subsection (b) of section 1122 of the Financial Institutions Reform, Recovery, and Enforcement Act of 1989 (12 U. S. C. 3351(b)) is amended to read as follows:

"(b) RECIPROCITY. — Notwithstanding any other provisions of this title, a federally related transaction shall not be appraised by a certified or licensed appraiser unless the State appraiser certifying or licensing agency of the State certifying or licensing such appraiser has in place a policy of issuing a reciprocal certification or license for an individual from another State when —

"(1) the appraiser licensing and certification program of such other State is in

(1)其政策、实践、经费、人员配置和程序是否符合本编规定;

(2)是否在合理的时间内处理投诉并完成调查;

(3)是否对受到处罚的评估师和评估管理公司进行了适当的处分;

(4)是否维持了有效的监管计划;及

(5)是否及时向评估小组委员会报告其所收到的投诉和所采取的纪律处分,以便登记录入评估小组委员会所维持的评估师和评估管理公司全国性注册名册。

在州机关就执照颁发、认证、注册和纪律处分程序采取行动的期间,评估小组委员会有权临时将获得州执照或认证的评估师或注册评估管理公司从全国性注册名册中予以移除,但时间不得超过90天。对于评估政策、实践、经费、人员配置或程序被认定为不符合本编规定的州颁发的评估师认证证明和执照,评估小组委员会及本编规定的任何机关、职能机构和联邦认可的实体均不得予以承认。对尚未制定有效的评估师监管计划的州机关,评估小组委员会有权按本条规定处以相应的处罚。在判定该等计划是否有效时,评估小组委员会应对下述事项进行分析:评估师执照的颁发与认证、评估管理公司的注册、评估师临时执照和认证证明的颁发、投诉人针对评估师和评估管理公司提起的投诉之受理与追踪、投诉调查以及针对评估师和评估管理公司的执法行动。评估小组委员会有权对州机关采取临时措施和暂停其工作,作为撤销承认州机关的替代性措施或前置措施。”

(2)在第(b)(2)子条中,在“权力”之后插入如下内容:“或充足的经费”。

(l)**互相承认**。——《1989年金融机构改革、复兴与实施法》第1122条第(b)子条[《美国法典》第十二编第3351(b)节]修正后全文如下:

“(b)**互相承认**。——无论本编是否存在任何不同规定,对联邦相关交易进行评估的获认证或执照的评估师必须满足下列条件:对该评估师进行认证或向其颁发执照的州评估师认证或执照颁发机关已经制定了相应政策,规定在下述情况下,将向其他州的个人颁发认证证明或执照,承认其评估师资格——

(1)该等其他州的评估师执照颁发和认证制度符合本编规定;且

compliance with the provisions of this title; and

"(2) the appraiser holds a valid certification from a State whose requirements for certification or licensing meet or exceed the licensure standards established by the State where an individual seeks appraisal licensure.".

(m) CONSIDERATION OF PROFESSIONAL APPRAISAL DESIGNATIONS. — Section 1122(d) of the Financial Institutions Reform, Recovery, and Enforcement Act of 1989 (12 U. S. C. 3351(d)) is amended by striking "shall not exclude" and all that follows through the end of the subsection and inserting the following: "may include education achieved, experience, sample appraisals, and references from prior clients. Membership in a nationally recognized professional appraisal organization may be a criteria considered, though lack of membership therein shall not be the sole bar against consideration for an assignment under these criteria.".

(n) APPRAISER INDEPENDENCE. — Section 1122 of the Financial Institutions Reform, Recovery, and Enforcement Act of 1989 (12 U. S. C. 3351) is amended by adding at the end the following new subsection:

"(g) APPRAISER INDEPENDENCE MONITORING. — The Appraisal Subcommittee shall monitor each State appraiser certifying and licensing agency for the purpose of determining whether such agency's policies, practices, and procedures are consistent with the purposes of maintaining appraiser independence and whether such State has adopted and maintains effective laws, regulations, and policies aimed at maintaining appraiser independence.".

(o) APPRAISER EDUCATION. — Section 1122 of the Financial Institutions Reform, Recovery, and Enforcement Act of 1989 (12 U. S. C. 3351) is amended by inserting after subsection (g)(as added by subsection (l) of this section) the following new subsection:

"(h) APPROVED EDUCATION. — The Appraisal Subcommittee shall encourage the States to accept courses approved by the Appraiser Qualification Board's Course Approval Program.".

(p) APPRAISAL COMPLAINT HOTLINE. — Section 1122 of the Financial Institutions Reform, Recovery, and Enforcement Act of 1989 (12 U. S. C. 3351), as amended by this section, is amended by adding at the end the following new subsection:

"(i) APPRAISAL COMPLAINT NATIONAL HOTLINE. — If, 6 months after the date of the enactment of this subsection, the Appraisal Subcommittee determines that no national hotline exists to receive complaints of non-compliance with appraisal independence standards and Uniform Standards of Professional Appraisal Practice, including complaints from appraisers, individuals, or other entities concerning the improper influencing or attempted improper influencing of appraisers or the appraisal process, the Appraisal Subcommittee shall establish and operate such a national hotline, which shall include a toll-free telephone

(2)该评估师持有其他州的有效认证证明,且该州的认证证明或执照颁发要求之严格程度不低于该评估师申请评估执照的州的执照颁发标准。”

(m)**对专业评估师称号的考虑**。——《1989年金融机构改革、复兴与实施法》第1122(d)条[《美国法典》第十二编第3351(d)节]修正如下:删除“不得包括”直至该子条结尾的全部内容,替以如下内容:“可以包括教育程度、工作经历、评估案例及以往客户的推荐信。全国认可的专业评估组织的会员资格可以作为考虑的标准之一,但是不得仅因申请人不具有该等会员资格而拒绝根据本标准向其授予称号。”

(n)**评估师的独立性**。——在《1989年金融机构改革、复兴与实施法》第1122条(《美国法典》第十二编第3351节)结尾处增加如下内容,作为对该条的修正:

“(g)**对评估师独立性的监控**。——评估小组委员会应对各州评估师认证和执照颁发机关进行监控,以判定其政策、实践和程序是否符合维持评估师独立性之目的,以及该州是否已经制定并维持旨在维持评估师独立性的有效法律、规章和政策。”

(o)**评估师的教育**。——《1989年金融机构改革、复兴与实施法》第1122条(《美国法典》第十二编第3351节)在依本条的第(l)子条增加的第(g)子条之后插入以下内容,作为对该条的修正:

“(h)**已获批准的教育课程**。——评估小组委员会应鼓励各州接受经“评估师资格委员会课程批准计划”批准的课程。”

(p)**评估师投诉热线**。——在经本条修正后的《1989年金融机构改革、复兴与实施法》第1122条(《美国法典》第十二编第3351节)结尾处增加如下新子条,作为对该条的修正:

“(i)**评估投诉全国热线**。——如果在本子条规定颁布之日届满6个月之后,评估小组委员会判定不存在任何相关的全国热线,无法接收针对违反评估独立性标准和《专业评估执业统一标准》行为提出的投诉,包括评估师、个人或其他实体针对不当影响或试图不当影响评估师或评估过程的行为提出的投诉,则,评估小组委员会应开通并运行全国热线(包括免费电话号码和电子邮箱地址)。评估小组委员会运行该全国热线时,应将投诉移交相应的政府机构,包括州评估师认证和执照颁发机关、金融机构监管者或其他相应的合法监管机构,以便上述各者采取进一步行动。对于移交给州

number and an email address. If the Appraisal Subcommittee operates such a national hotline, the Appraisal Subcommittee shall refer complaints for further action to appropriate governmental bodies, including a State appraiser certifying and licensing agency, a financial institution regulator, or other appropriate legal authorities. For complaints referred to State appraiser certifying and licensing agencies or to Federal regulators, the Appraisal Subcommittee shall have the authority to follow up such complaint referrals in order to determine the status of the resolution of the complaint. ".

(q) AUTOMATED VALUATION MODELS. — Title XI of the Financial Institutions Reform, Recovery, and Enforcement Act of 1989 (12 U. S. C. 3331 et seq.), as amended by this section, is amended by adding at the end the following new section (and amending the table of contents accordingly):

"SEC. 1125. AUTOMATED VALUATION MODELS USED TO ESTIMATE COLLATERAL VALUE FOR MORTGAGE LENDING PURPOSES.

"(a) IN GENERAL. — Automated valuation models shall adhere to quality control standards designed to —

"(1) ensure a high level of confidence in the estimates produced by automated valuation models;

"(2) protect against the manipulation of data;

"(3) seek to avoid conflicts of interest;

"(4) require random sample testing and reviews; and

"(5) account for any other such factor that the agencies listed in subsection (b) determine to be appropriate.

"(b) ADOPTION OF REGULATIONS. — The Board, the Comptroller of the Currency, the Federal Deposit Insurance Corporation, the National Credit Union Administration Board, the Federal Housing Finance Agency, and the Bureau of Consumer Financial Protection, in consultation with the staff of the Appraisal Subcommittee and the Appraisal Standards Board of the Appraisal Foundation, shall promulgate regulations to implement the quality control standards required under this section.

"(c) ENFORCEMENT. — Compliance with regulations issued under this subsection shall be enforced by —

"(1) with respect to a financial institution, or subsidiary owned and controlled by a financial institution and regulated by a Federal financial institution regulatory agency, the Federal financial institution regulatory agency that acts as the primary Federal supervisor of such financial institution or subsidiary; and

"(2) with respect to other participants in the market for appraisals of 1-to-4 unit single family residential real estate, the Federal Trade Commission, the Bureau of Consumer Financial Protection, and a State attorney general.

评估师认证和执照颁发机关或联邦监管者的投诉，评估小组委员会有权对该等投诉进行追踪,以确定投诉的处理情况。”

(q)**自动估值模型**。——在经本条修正后的《1989年金融机构改革、复兴与实施法》第十一编(《美国法典》第十二编第3331节及其后条文)结尾处增加如下新条文(并修正相应的目录),作为对该编的修正:

“第1125条　抵押贷款人对抵押物进行估值时使用的自动估值模型

(a)**一般规定**。——自动估值模型应符合针对如下目的设计的质量控制标准——

(1)确保通过自动估值模型作出的估值达到较高的置信度;

(2)防范数据操纵行为;
(3)力图避免利益冲突;
(4)要求进行随机抽样测试和审查;及
(5)反映第(b)子条所列机关判定确属适当的任何其他因素。

(b)**规章的制定**。——联邦储备委员会、货币监理署署长、联邦存款保险公司、国家信贷署委员会、联邦住房金融局和消费者金融保护局,应在与评估小组委员会和评估基金会的评估标准委员会的工作人员磋商后颁发据以执行本条规定的质量控制标准的规章。

(c)**执行**。——根据本子条发布的规章应按如下规定执行——

(1)对金融机构而言,或对金融机构拥有和控制的且受联邦金融机构监管机关监管的子公司而言,由作为该金融机构或该子公司的优先联邦监管者的联邦金融机构监管机关执行;及

(2)对于1至4个单元的独户住宅房地产评估市场的其他参与者而言,由联邦贸易委员会、消费者金融保护局和州总检察长执行。

"(d) AUTOMATED VALUATION MODEL DEFINED. — For purposes of this section, the term 'automated valuation model' means any computerized model used by mortgage originators and secondary market issuers to determine the collateral worth of a mortgage secured by a consumer's principal dwelling. ".

(r) BROKER PRICE OPINIONS. — Title XI of the Financial Institutions Reform, Recovery, and Enforcement Act of 1989 (12 U. S. C. 3331 et seq.), as amended by this section, is amended by adding at the end the following new section (and amending the table of contents accordingly):

"SEC. 1126. BROKER PRICE OPINIONS.

"(a) GENERAL PROHIBITION. — In conjunction with the purchase of a consumer's principal dwelling, broker price opinions may not be used as the primary basis to determine the value of a piece of property for the purpose of a loan origination of a residential mortgage loan secured by such piece of property.

"(b) BROKER PRICE OPINION DEFINED. — For purposes of this section, the term 'broker price opinion' means an estimate prepared by a real estate broker, agent, or sales person that details the probable selling price of a particular piece of real estate property and provides a varying level of detail about the property's condition, market, and neighborhood, and information on comparable sales, but does not include an automated valuation model, as defined in section 1125(c). ".

(s) AMENDMENTS TO APPRAISAL SUBCOMMITTEE. — Section 1011 of the Federal Financial Institutions Examination Council Act of 1978 (12 U. S. C. 3310) is amended —

(1) in the first sentence, by adding before the period the following: ", the Bureau of Consumer Financial Protection, and the Federal Housing Finance Agency"; and

(2) by inserting at the end the following: "At all times at least one member of the Appraisal Subcommittee shall have demonstrated knowledge and competence through licensure, certification, or professional designation within the appraisal profession. ".

(t) TECHNICAL CORRECTIONS. —

(1) Section 1119(a)(2) of theFinancial Institutions Reform, Recovery, and Enforcement Act of 1989 (12 U. S. C. 3348(a)(2)) is amended by striking "council, " and inserting "Council, ".

(2) Section 1121(6) of the Financial Institutions Reform, Recovery, and Enforcement Act of 1989 (12 U. S. C. 3350(6)) is amended by striking "Corporations, " and inserting "Corporation, ".

(3) Section 1121(8) of the Financial Institutions Reform, Recovery, and Enforcement Act of 1989 (12 U. S. C. 3350(8)) is amended by striking "council" and inserting "Council".

(d)**自动估值模型的定义**。——就本条而言,‘自动估值模型’一词系指在以消费者主要住所为担保的抵押贷款中,抵押贷款发起人和二级市场发行人为确定抵押物价值所使用的计算模型。”

(r)**经纪人价格意见**。——在经本条修正后的《1989年金融机构改革、复兴与实施法》第十一编(《美国法典》第十二编第3331节及其后条文)结尾处增加如下新条文(并修正相应的目录),作为对该编的修正:

“第1126条　经纪人价格意见

(a)**一般禁止性规定**。——在发放由房地产担保的住房抵押贷款之时,与消费者主要住所之购买相关的经纪人价格意见不得作为确定该房地产价值的主要依据。

(b)**经纪人价格意见的定义**。——就本条而言,‘经纪人价格意见’一词系指房地产经纪人、代理人或销售人员作出的估计,其中详细列明某一具体房地产可能的销售价格,提供的关于该房地产状况、市场状况、所在社区和可比销售信息的信息详细程度不尽相同,但不包括第1125(c)条定义的自动估值模型。”

(s)**对与评估小组委员会相关的规定的修正**。——《1978年联邦金融机构检查委员会法》第1011条(《美国法典》第十二编第3310节)修正如下——

(1)在第一句的句号前增加如下内容:“、消费者金融保护局及联邦住房金融局”;及

(2)在该条结尾处增加如下内容:“无论何时,评估小组委员会均应至少有1名成员拥有评估行业的相关执照、认证证明或专业称号,证明其具有确凿娴熟的知识和技能。”

(t)**技术性改正**。——

(1)在《1989年金融机构改革、复兴与实施法》第1119(a)(2)条[《美国法典》第十二编第3348(a)(2)节]中,删除首字母小写的“金融机构检查委员会(council)”,替以首字母大写的“金融机构检查委员会(Council)”,作为对该条的修正。

(2)在《1989年金融机构改革、复兴与实施法》第1121(6)条[《美国法典》第十二编第3350(6)节]中,删除复数形式的“联邦存款保险公司(Corporations)”,替以单数形式的“联邦存款保险公司(Corporation)”,作为对该条的修正。

(3)在《1989年金融机构改革、复兴与实施法》第1121(8)条[《美国法典》第十二编第3350(8)节]中,删除首字母小写的“金融机构检查委员会(council)”,替以首字母大写的“金融机构检查委员会(Council)”,作为对该条的修正。

(4) Section 1122 of the Financial Institutions Reform, Recovery, and Enforcement Act of 1989 (12 U. S. C. 3351) is amended —

(A) in subsection (a)(1) by moving the left margin of subparagraphs (A), (B), and (C) 2 ems to the right; and

(B) in subsection (c) —

(i) by striking "Federal Financial Institutions Examination Council" and inserting "Financial Institutions Examination Council"; and

(ii) by striking "the council's functions" and inserting "the Council's functions".

SEC. 1474. EQUAL CREDIT OPPORTUNITY ACT AMENDMENT.

Subsection (e) of section 701 of the Equal Credit Opportunity Act (15 U. S. C. 1691) is amended to read as follows:

"(e) COPIES FURNISHED TO APPLICANTS. —

"(1) IN GENERAL. — Each creditor shall furnish to an applicant a copy of any and all written appraisals and valuations developed in connection with the applicant's application for a loan that is secured or would have been secured by a first lien on a dwelling promptly upon completion, but in no case later than 3 days prior to the closing of the loan, whether the creditor grants or denies the applicant's request for credit or the application is incomplete or withdrawn.

"(2) WAIVER. — The applicant may waive the 3 day requirement provided for in paragraph (1), except where otherwise required in law.

"(3) REIMBURSEMENT. — The applicant may be required to pay a reasonable fee to reimburse the creditor for the cost of the appraisal, except where otherwise required in law.

"(4) FREE COPY. — Notwithstanding paragraph (3), the creditor shall provide a copy of each written appraisal or valuation at no additional cost to the applicant.

"(5) NOTIFICATION TO APPLICANTS. — At the time of application, the creditor shall notify an applicant in writing of the right to receive a copy of each written appraisal andvaluation under this subsection.

"(6) VALUATION DEFINED. — For purposes of this subsection, the term 'valuation' shall include any estimate of the value of a dwelling developed in connection with a creditor's decision to provide credit, including those values developed pursuant to a policy of a government sponsored enterprise or by an automated valuation model, a broker price opinion, or other methodology or mechanism. ".

SEC. 1475. REAL ESTATE SETTLEMENT PROCEDURES ACT OF 1974 AMENDMENT RELATING TO CERTAIN APPRAISAL FEES.

Section 4 of the Real Estate Settlement Procedures Act of 1974 is amended by adding at

(4)《1989年金融机构改革、复兴与实施法》第1122条(《美国法典》第十二编第3351节)修正如下——

(A)在第(a)(1)子条中,第(A)子款、第(B)子款和第(C)子款左侧的段前空白向右缩进2个空格;及

(B)在第(c)子条中——

(i)删除"联邦金融机构检查委员会",替以"金融机构检查委员会";及

(ii)删除"委员会"一词首字母小写的"金融机构检查委员会的职能(the council's functions)",替以"委员会"一词首字母大写的"金融机构检查委员会的职能(the Council's functions)"。

第1474条　对《信贷机会平等法》的修正

《信贷机会平等法》第701条第(e)子条(《美国法典》第十五编第1691节)修正后全文如下:

"(e)**向申请人提供的文件**。——

(1)**一般规定**。——申请人申请以或本应以住宅第一顺位留置权担保的贷款时,贷款发放人应在就该等贷款申请编制的所有书面评估报告和估值报告完成之后,及时(但无论如何不得迟于贷款成交之日前3天)将该等报告的一份复本提供给申请人,不论贷款发放人最后决定批准或拒绝该贷款申请,也不论申请人提交的申请是否不完备或最终被申请人被撤回。

(2)**弃权**。——除非法律另有规定,否则,申请人可以放弃第(1)款规定的3天期限的要求。

(3)**偿付**。——除非法律另有规定,否则,贷款发放人可以要求申请人支付合理费用,以偿付评估费用。

(4)**免费提供文件**。——无论第(3)款如何规定,贷款发放人向申请人提供书面评估报告或估值报告之时,不得收取额外费用。

(5)**通知申请人**。——申请人提出申请时,贷款发放人应向申请人发出书面通知,告知其有权按照本子条规定获得书面评估报告和估值报告的一份复本。

(6)**估值的定义**。——就本子条而言,'估值'一词应包括贷款发放人在作出提供贷款的决定时对住宅价值做出的任何估算,包括根据政府创办的企业之政策或者依据自动估值模型、经纪人价格意见或通过其他方法或机制对该等价值作出的估算。"

第1475条　对《1974年房地产结算程序法》中关于某些评估费的修正

在《1974年房地产结算程序法》第4条结尾处增加如下新子条,作为对该条的

the end the following new subsection:

"(c) The standard form described in subsection (a) may include, in the case of an appraisal coordinated by an appraisal management company (as such term is defined in section 1121(11) of the Financial Institutions Reform, Recovery, and Enforcement Act of 1989 (12 U. S. C. 3350(11))), a clear disclosure of—

"(1) the fee paid directly to the appraiser by such company; and

"(2) the administration fee charged by such company.".

SEC. 1476. GAO STUDY ON THE EFFECTIVENESS AND IMPACT OF VARIOUS APPRAISAL METHODS, VALUATION MODELS AND DISTRIBUTIONS CHANNELS, AND ON THE HOME VALUATION CODE OF CONDUCT AND THE APPRAISAL SUBCOMMITTEE.

(a) IN GENERAL.—The Government Accountability Office shall conduct a study on—

(1) the effectiveness and impact of—

(A) appraisal methods, including the cost approach, the comparative sales approach, the income approach, and others that may be available;

(B) appraisal valuation models, including licensed and certified appraisals, broker-priced opinions, and automated valuation models; and

(C) appraisal distribution channels, including appraisal management companies, independent appraisal operations within mortgage originators, and fee-for-service appraisers;

(2) the Home Valuation Code of Conduct; and

(3) the Appraisal Subcommittee's functions pursuant to title XI of the Financial Institutions Reform, Recovery, and Enforcement Act of 1989.

(b) STUDY.—Not later than—

(1) 12 months after the date of enactment of this Act, the Government Accountability Office shall submit a study to the Committee on Banking, Housing, and Urban Affairs of the Senate and the Committee on Financial Services of the House of Representatives; and

(2) 90 days after the date of enactment of this Act, the Government Accountability Office shall provide a report on the status of the study and any preliminary findings to the Committee on Banking, Housing, and Urban Affairs of the Senate and the Committee on Financial Services of the House of Representatives.

(c) CONTENT OF STUDY.—The study required by this section shall include an examination of the following:

(1) APPRAISAL APPROACHES, VALUATION MODELS, AND DISTRIBUTION CHANNELS.—

(A) The prevalence, alone or in combination, of certain appraisal approaches, models, and channels in purchase-money and refinance mortgage transactions.

(B) The accuracy of these approaches, models, and channels in assessing the property

修正：

“(c)对于由评估管理公司(定义见《1989年金融机构改革、复兴与实施法》第1121(11)条[《美国法典》第十二编第3350(11)节)]协调开展的评估，第(a)子条规定的标准格式可以包括对如下各项的明确披露——

(1)该公司直接向评估师支付的费用；及

(2)该公司收取的管理费。”

第1476条　政府问责办公室关于各类评估方法、估值模型和发布渠道的有效性和影响的研究以及关于《住房估值行为守则》和评估小组委员会的研究

(a)**一般规定**。——政府问责办公室应针对如下事项开展研究——

(1)下列各项的有效性和影响——

(A)评估方法，包括成本法、可比销售法、收入法及其他可利用的方法；

(B)评估估值模型，包括获得执照和认证的评估师开展的评估、经纪人价格意见和自动估值模型；及

(C)评估发布渠道，包括评估管理公司、抵押贷款发起人内部的独立评估部门及按服务收费的评估师；

(2)《住房估值行为守则》；及

(3)评估小组委员会根据《1989年金融机构改革、复兴与实施法》第十一编承担的职能。

(b)**研究**。——

(1)政府问责办公室应于本法颁布之日后12个月内，向参议院银行、住房与城市事务委员会及众议院金融服务委员会提交一份研究报告；及

(2)政府问责办公室应于本法颁布之日起90天内，向参议院银行、住房与城市事务委员会及众议院金融服务委员会报告研究进度及初步研究结果。

(c)**研究内容**。——按照本条规定开展研究之时，应对如下事项进行审查：

(1)**评估方法、估值模型和发布渠道**。——

(A)特定评估方法、模型和渠道或该等方法、模型和渠道的组合，在购买款项抵押贷款交易和再融资抵押贷款交易中的采用率。

(B)该等方法、模型和渠道在对作为抵押物的房地产进行估值时的准确度。

as collateral.

(C) Whether and how these approaches, models, and channels contributed to price speculation during the previous cycle.

(D) The costs to consumers of these approaches, models, and channels.

(E) The disclosure of fees to consumers in the appraisal process.

(F) To what extent the usage of these approaches, models, and channels may be influenced by a conflict of interest between the mortgage lender and the appraiser and the mechanism by which the lender selects and compensates the appraiser.

(G) The suitability of these approaches, models, and channels in rural versus urban areas.

(2) HOME VALUATION CODE OF CONDUCT (HVCC). —

(A) How the HVCC affects mortgage lenders' selection of appraisers.

(B) How the HVCC affects State regulation of appraisers and appraisal distribution channels.

(C) How the HVCC affects the quality and cost of appraisals and the length of time to obtain an appraisal.

(D) How the HVCC affects mortgage brokers, small businesses, and consumers.

(d) ADDITIONAL STUDY REQUIRED. —

(1) IN GENERAL. — Not later than 18 months after the date of enactment of this Act, the Government Accountability Office shall submit a study to the Committee on Banking, Housing, and Urban Affairs of the Senate and the Committee on Financial Services of the House of Representatives.

(2) CONTENT OF ADDITIONAL STUDY. —The study required under paragraph (1) shall include —

(A) an examination of —

(i) the Appraisal Subcommittee's ability to monitor and enforce State and Federal certification requirements and standards, including by providing a summary with a statistical breakdown of enforcement actions taken during the last 10 years;

(ii) whether existing Federal financial institutions regulatory agency exemptions on appraisals for federally related transactions needs to be revised; and

(iii) whether new means of data collection, such as the establishment of a national repository, would benefit the Appraisal Subcommittee's ability to perform its functions; and

(B) recommendations from this examination for administrative and legislative action at the Federal and State level.

(C)该等方法、模型和渠道在上一周期是否助长了价格投机现象,如助长了该等现象,说明原因。

(D)该等方法、模型和渠道给消费者带来的费用。

(E)在评估流程中向消费者作出的费用披露。

(F) 抵押贷款人与评估师之间的利益冲突以及贷款人挑选评估师并向其支付报酬的机制对该等方法、模型和渠道使用的影响程度。

(G)该等方法、模型和渠道在农村和城市地区的适当性之比较。

(2)**《住房估值行为守则》(HVCC)**。——

(A)在评估师的挑选过程中,《住房估值行为守则》对抵押贷款人的影响。

(B)《住房估值行为守则》对各州对评估师和评估发布渠道之监管的影响。

(C)《住房估值行为守则》对评估质量和费用及获取评估的时间长度的影响。

(D)《住房估值行为守则》对抵押贷款经纪人、小型企业和消费者的影响。

(d)**补充研究要求**。——

(1)**一般规定**。——政府问责办公室应于本法颁布之日后18个月内,向参议院银行、住房与城市事务委员会以及众议院金融服务委员会提交一份研究报告。

(2)**补充研究的内容**。——根据第(1)款规定开展的研究应包括——

(A)对如下事项的审查——

(i)评估小组委员会监控和执行州和联邦认证要求和标准的能力,包括提供关于过去10年的执法行动统计明细表的摘要总结;

(ii)联邦金融机构监管机关当前对联邦相关交易之评估授予的豁免是否需要修改;及

(iii)新型数据收集手段(例如,建设全国性的数据存管机构)是否将有助于提高评估小组委员会履行职能的能力;及

(B)基于该等审查而提出的关于联邦和州行政及立法行动的建议。

Subtitle G—Mortgage Resolution and Modification

SEC. 1481. MULTIFAMILY MORTGAGE RESOLUTION PROGRAM.

(a) ESTABLISHMENT. — The Secretary of Housing and Urban Development shall develop a program under this subsection to ensure the protection of current and future tenants and at–risk multifamily properties, where feasible, based on criteria that may include —

(1) creating sustainable financing of such properties, that may take into consideration such factors as —

(A) the rental income generated by such properties; and

(B) the preservation of adequate operating reserves;

(2) maintaining the level of Federal, State, and city subsidies in effect as of the date of the enactment of this Act;

(3) providing funds for rehabilitation; and

(4) facilitating the transfer of such properties, when appropriate and with the agreement of owners, to responsible new owners and ensuring affordability of such properties.

(b) COORDINATION. — The Secretary of Housing and Urban Development may, in carrying out the program developed under this section, coordinate with the Secretary of the Treasury, the Federal Deposit Insurance Corporation, the Board of Governors of the Federal Reserve System, the Federal Housing Finance Agency, and any other Federal Government agency that the Secretary considers appropriate.

(c) DEFINITION. — For purposes of this section, the term "multifamily properties" means a residential structure that consists of 5 or more dwelling units.

(d) PREVENTION OF QUALIFICATION FOR CRIMINAL APPLICANTS. —

(1) IN GENERAL. — No person shall be eligible to begin receiving assistance from the Making Home Affordable Program authorized under the Emergency Economic Stabilization Act of 2008 (12 U. S. C. 5201 et seq.), or any other mortgage assistance program authorized or funded by that Act, on or after 60 days after the date of the enactment of this Act, if such person, in connection with a mortgage or real estate transaction, has been convicted, within the last 10 years, of any one of the following:

(A) Felony larceny, theft, fraud, or forgery.

(B) Money laundering.

(C) Tax evasion.

(2) PROCEDURES. — The Secretary shall establish procedures to ensure compliance

第G子编——抵押贷款的处置和修改

第1481条　多户抵押贷款处置计划

(a)**计划制定**。——住房与城市发展部部长应根据本子条规定,在可行的情况下基于包括如下内容的标准,制定旨在保护当前和未来承租人及存在风险的多户房地产的计划。制定该等计划时,所基于的标准可包括——

(1)为该等房地产创造可持续的资金来源,此时,可考虑如下等因素——

(A)该等房地产产生的租金收入;及

(B)保持充足的运营准备金;

(2)将联邦、州和市补贴金维持在本法颁布之日有效适用的水平;

(3)提供翻修资金;及

(4)在适当之时并经原有业主同意,促成该等房地产转让给有责任感的新业主,并确保该等房地产的价格保持在消费者负担能力之内。

(b)**协调**。——在实施根据本条制定的计划时,住房与城市发展部部长可以与财政部部长、联邦存款保险公司、联邦储备委员会、联邦住房金融局及住房与城市发展部部长认为相应的其他联邦政府机关进行协调。

(c)**定义**。——就本条而言,"多户房地产"一词系指由5(含)个以上居住单元组成的一幢住宅建筑。

(d)**防止有犯罪记录的申请人获得资格**。——

(1)**一般规定**。——如果任何人在过去10年内由于抵押贷款或房地产交易而被判犯有以下罪行,则,自本法颁布届满60(含)天之日后,其无资格获得根据《2008年紧急经济稳定法》(《美国法典》第十二编第5201节及其后条文)核准的《房贷可负担计划》或该法授权或资助的任何其他抵押贷款援助计划提供的援助:

(A)偷盗重罪、盗窃重罪、诈骗重罪或伪造重罪。

(B)洗钱罪。

(C)偷税罪。

(2)**程序**。——住房与城市发展部部长应制定相关程序,确保本子条规定得以

with this subsection.

(3) REPORT. — The Secretary shall report to the Committee on Financial Services of the House of Representatives and the Committee on Banking, Housing, and Urban Affairs of the Senate regarding the implementation of this provision. The report shall also describe the steps taken to implement this subsection.

SEC. 1482. HOME AFFORDABLE MODIFICATION PROGRAM GUIDE–LINES.

(a) NET PRESENT VALUE INPUT DATA. — The Secretary of the Treasury (in this section referred to as the "Secretary") shall revise the supplemental directives and other guidelines for the Home Affordable Modification Program of the Making Home Affordable initiative of the Secretary of the Treasury, authorized under the Emergency Economic Stabilization Act of 2008 (Public Law 110–343), to require each mortgage servicer participating in such program to provide each borrower under a mortgage whose request for a mortgage modification under the Program is denied with all borrower–related and mortgage–related input data used in any net present value (NPV) analyses performed in connection with the subject mortgage. Such input data shall be provided to the borrower at the time of such denial.

(b) WEB–BASED SITE FOR NPV CALCULATOR AND APPLICATION. —

(1) NPV CALCULATOR. — In carrying out the Home Affordable Modification Program, the Secretary shall establish and maintain a site on the World Wide Web that provides a calculator for net present value analyses of a mortgage, based on the Secretary's methodology for calculating such value, that mortgagors can use to enter information regarding their own mortgages and that provides a determination after entering such information regarding a mortgage of whether such mortgage would be accepted or rejected for modification under the Program, using such methodology.

(2) DISCLOSURE. — Such Web site shall also prominently disclose that each mortgage servicer participating in such Program may use a method for calculating net present value of a mortgage that is different than the method used by such calculator.

(3) APPLICATION. — The Secretary shall make a reasonable effort to include on such World Wide Web site a method for homeowners to apply for a mortgage modification under the Home Affordable Modification Program.

(c) PUBLIC AVAILABILITY OF NPV METHODOLOGY, COMPUTER MODEL, AND VARIABLES. — The Secretary shall make publicly available, including by posting on a World Wide Web site of the Secretary —

(1) the Secretary's methodology and computer model, including all formulae used in such computer model, used for calculating net present value of a mortgage that is used by the calculator established pursuant to subsection (b); and

遵守。

(3)**报告**。——住房与城市发展部部长应向众议院金融服务委员会和参议院银行、住房与城市事务委员会报告本规定的实施情况,并在报告中说明为实施本子条规定采取的措施。

第1482条 《可负担房贷修改计划》指引

(a)**净现值输入数据**。——对于财政部部长根据《2008年紧急经济稳定法》(第110—343号公法)授权制定的“可负担房贷”行动之《可负担房贷修改计划》,财政部部长应修订与之相关的补充指令和其他指引,要求参与该计划的每一抵押贷款服务机构向按该计划提出抵押贷款修改申请但被驳回的借款人提供在该抵押的贷款净现值(NPV)分析中使用的与借款人和抵押贷款相关的所有输入数据。该等输入数据应于申请被驳回之时提供给借款人。

(b)**网络净现值计算器和抵押贷款修改申请**。——

(1)**净现值计算器**。——实施《可负担房贷修改计划》时,财政部部长应在互联网上开设并维护一个网站,并在网站上提供一个净现值计算器,该计算器应能按财政部部长使用的净现值计算方法对抵押贷款的净现值进行分析计算。抵押人将其自身抵押贷款的相关信息输入该计算器,计算器即可以输出结论,说明按照该等计算方法,该抵押贷款修改申请将被接受或被驳回。

(2)**披露**。——该网站还应在显著位置披露,参与该计划的每一抵押贷款服务机构在计算抵押贷款净现值之时均可使用与该计算器不同的方法。

(3)**申请**。——财政部部长应尽合理努力,在该网站上说明业主可以利用何种方法来按照《可负担房贷修改计划》申请对抵押贷款进行修改。

(c)**净现值计算方法、计算模型和变量的公开提供**。——财政部部长应公开提供,包括在财政部部长网站上发布以下内容——

(1)按照第(b)子条设置的计算器在计算抵押贷款净现值时使用的财政部部长的计算方法和计算模型,包括该计算模型使用的所有公式;及

(2) all non–proprietary variables used in such net present value analysis.

SEC. 1483. PUBLIC AVAILABILITY OF INFORMATION OF MAKING HOME AFFORDABLE PROGRAM.

(a) REVISIONS TO PROGRAM GUIDELINES. — The Secretary of the Treasury (in this section referred to as the "Secretary") shall revise the guidelines for the Home Affordable Modification Program of the Making Home Affordable initiative of the Secretary of the Treasury, authorized under the Emergency Economic Stabilization Act of 2008 (Public Law 110–343), to provide that the data being collected by the Secretary from each mortgage servicer and lender participating in the Program is made public in accordance with subsection (b).

(b) PUBLIC AVAILABILITY. — Data shall be made available according to the following guidelines:

(1) Not more than 14 days after each monthly deadline for submission of data by mortgage servicers and lenders participating in the Program, reports shall be made publicly available by means of a World Wide Web site of the Secretary, and by submitting a report to the Congress, that shall includes the following information:

(A) The number of requests for mortgage modifications under the Program that the servicer or lender has received.

(B) The number of requests for mortgage modifications under the Program that the servicer or lender has processed.

(C) The number of requests for mortgage modifications under the Program that the servicer or lender has approved.

(D) The number of requests for mortgage modifications under the Program that the servicer or lender has denied.

(2) Not more than 60 days after each monthly deadline for submission of data by mortgage servicers and lenders participating in the Program, the Secretary shall make data tables available to the public at the individual record level. The Secretary shall issue regulations prescribing —

(A) the procedures for disclosing such data to the public; and

(B) such deletions as the Secretary may determine to be appropriate to protect any privacy interest of any mortgage modification applicant, including the deletion or alteration of the applicant's name and identification number.

SEC. 1484. PROTECTING TENANTS AT FORECLOSURE EXTENSION AND CLARIFICATION.

The Protecting Tenants at Foreclosure Act is amended —

(1) in section 702 (12 U. S. C. 5220 note) —

(A) in subsection (a)(2), by striking ", as of the date of such notice of foreclosure";

(2)在该净现值分析中使用的所有非专有变量。

第1483条 《房贷可负担计划》信息的公开提供

(a)**计划指引的修订**。——对于财政部部长根据《2008年紧急经济稳定法》(第110—343号公法)授权制定的"可负担房贷"行动之《可负担房贷修改计划》,财政部部长应修订与之相关的指引,规定财政部部长从参与该计划的每一抵押贷款服务机构和贷款人处收集的数据均应按照第(b)子条的规定公开。

(b)**公开提供**。——提供数据时应遵守以下指引:

(1)参与计划的抵押贷款服务机构和贷款人每月提交数据的最后期限届满后14天之内,财政部部长应通过财政部的网站公开报告,并向国会提交一份报告,该报告应包含以下信息:

(A)服务机构或贷款人收到的按照该计划提出的抵押贷款修改申请的份数。

(B)服务机构或贷款人处理的按照该计划提出的抵押贷款修改申请的份数。

(C)服务机构或贷款人批准的按照该计划提出的抵押贷款修改申请的份数。

(D)服务机构或贷款人驳回的按照该计划提出的抵押贷款修改申请的份数。

(2)参与计划的抵押贷款服务机构和贷款人每月提交数据的最后期限届满后60天之内,财政部部长应向公众提供数据表(数据表应细化至单笔贷款记录水平)。财政部部长应发布规章,对以下事项作出规定——

(A)向公众披露该等数据的程序;及

(B)财政部部长判定的为保护任何抵押贷款修改申请人的隐私利益而宜应进行的删除,包括删除或修改申请人的姓名和身份识别号码。

第1484条 《止赎时承租人权益保护法》的期限延长与相关问题的说明

《止赎时承租人权益保护法》修正如下——

(1)在第702条(《美国法典》第十二编第5220节注释)中——

(A)第(a)(2)子条删除"截至该止赎通知之日";及

and

(B) in subsection (c), by inserting after the period the following: "For purposes of this section, the date of a notice of foreclosure shall be deemed to be the date on which complete title to a property is transferred to a successor entity or person as a result of an order of a court or pursuant to provisions in a mortgage, deed of trust, or security deed. "; and

(2) in section 704 (12 U. S. C. 5201 note), by striking "2012" and inserting "2014".

Subtitle H—Miscellaneous Provisions

SEC. 1491. SENSE OF CONGRESS REGARDING THE IMPORTANCE OF GOVERNMENT-SPONSORED ENTERP RISES REFORM TO ENHANCE THE PROTECTION, LIMITATION, AND REGULATION OF THE TERMS OF RESIDENTIAL MORTGAGE CREDIT.

(a) FINDINGS. — The Congress finds as follows:

(1) The Government-sponsored enterprises, Federal National Mortgage Association (Fannie Mae) and the Federal Home Loan Mortgage Corporation (Freddie Mac), were chartered by Congress to ensure a reliable and affordable supply of mortgage funding, but enjoy a dual legal status as privately owned corporations with Government mandated affordable housing goals.

(2) In 1996, the Department of Housing and Urban Development required that 42 percent of Fannie Mae's and Freddie Mac's mortgage financing should go to borrowers with income levels below the median for a given area.

(3) In 2004, the Department of Housing and Urban Development revised those goals, increasing them to 56 percent of their overall mortgage purchases by 2008, and additionally mandated that 12 percent of all mortgage purchases by Fannie Mae and Freddie Mac be "special affordable" loans made to borrowers with incomes less than 60 percent of an area's median income, a target that ultimately increased to 28 percent for 2008.

(4) To help fulfill those mandated affordable housing goals, in 1995 the Department of Housing and Urban Development authorized Fannie Mae and Freddie Mac to purchase subprime securities that included loans made to low-income borrowers.

(5) After this authorization to purchase subprime securities, subprime and near-prime loans increased from 9 percent of securitized mortgages in 2001 to 40 percent in 2006, while the market share of conventional mortgages dropped from 78. 8 percent in 2003 to 50. 1 percent by 2007 with a corresponding increase in subprime and Alt-A loans from 10. 1

(B)第(c)子条在句号之后插入如下内容:“就本条而言,止赎通知日期应视为房地产的完整所有权按照法院命令或抵押契约、信托契约或担保契约规定转让给继受实体或继受人的日期。”;及

(2)在第704条(《美国法典》第十二编第5201节注释)中,删除“2012年”,替以“2014年”。

第H子编——其他规定

第1491条　为加强住房抵押贷款条款的保护、限制和监管,国会对政府创办的企业的改革重要性所持态度

(a)**认定**。——国会兹作出如下认定:

(1)为了确保可靠且可负担的抵押贷款资金供应,国会特许注册了两家政府创办的企业——联邦国民住房贷款协会(房利美)和联邦住房贷款抵押公司(房地美);但是,这两家公司一方面是私人所有的公司,另一方面具有政府强制规定的提供可负担住房的目标,因而具有双重法律身份。

(2)1996年,住房与城市发展部要求,房利美和房地美的抵押贷款资金中42%应投向收入低于所涉地区平均水平的借款人。

(3)2004年,住房与城市发展部对该目标进行了修订,要求房利美和房地美在2008年之前将上述标准提升至其总体抵押贷款购买数额的56%,此外,还强制房利美和房地美应将其全部抵押贷款购买数额的12%用于为收入水平低于地区平均收入60%的借款人发放“特殊可负担”住房贷款,并且在2008年,该标准应最终提升至28%。

(4)为了帮助实现上述强制性的可负担住房供给目标,1995年,住房与城市发展部授权房利美和房地美购买含有向低收入借款人发放的住房贷款的次级证券。

(5)房利美和房地美获得购买次级证券的授权后,次级贷款和准优级贷款在证券化抵押贷款中所占比例从2001年的9%猛增至2006年的40%,而传统抵押贷款的市场份额则从2003年的78.8%骤降至2007年的50.1%,同期次级贷款和准优级贷款的市场份额则从10.1%上升至32.7%。

percent to 32. 7 percent over the same period.

(6) In 2004 alone, Fannie Mae and Freddie Mac purchased $175, 000, 000, 000 in subprime mortgage securities, which accounted for 44 percent of the market that year, and from 2005 through 2007, Fannie Mae and Freddie Mac purchased approximately $1, 000, 000, 000, 000 in subprime and Alt-A loans, while Fannie Mae's acquisitions of mortgages with less than 10 percent down payments almost tripled.

(7) According to data from the Federal Housing Finance Agency (FHFA) for the fourth quarter of 2008, Fannie Mae and Freddie Mac own or guarantee 75 percent of all newly originated mortgages, and Fannie Mae and Freddie Mac currently own 13. 3 percent of outstanding mortgage debt in the United States and have issued mortgage-backed securities for 31. 0 percent of the residential debt market, a combined total of 44. 3 percent of outstanding mortgage debt in the United States.

(8) On September 7, 2008, the FHFA placed Fannie Mae and Freddie Mac into conservatorship, with the Treasury Department subsequently agreeing to purchase at least $200, 000, 000, 000 of preferred stock from each enterprise in exchange for warrants for the purchase of 79. 9 percent of each enterprise's common stock.

(9) The conservatorship for Fannie Mae and Freddie Mac has potentially exposed taxpayers to upwards of $5, 300, 000, 000, 000 worth of risk.

(10) The hybrid public-private status of Fannie Mae and Freddie Mac is untenable and must be resolved to assure that consumers are offered and receive residential mortgage loans on terms that reasonably reflect their ability to repay the loans and that are understandable and not unfair, deceptive, or abusive.

(b) SENSE OF THE CONGRESS. — It is the sense of the Congress that efforts to enhance by the protection, limitation, and regulation of the terms of residential mortgage credit and the practices related to such credit would be incomplete without enactment of meaningful structural reforms of Fannie Mae and Freddie Mac.

SEC. 1492. GAO STUDY REPORT ON GOVERNMENT EFFORTS TO COMBAT MORTGAGE FORECLOSURE RESCUE SCAMS AND LOAN MODIFICATION FRAUD.

(a) STUDY. — The Comptroller General of the United States shall conduct a study of the current inter-agency efforts of the Secretary of the Treasury, the Secretary of Housing and Urban Development, the Attorney General, and the Federal Trade Commission to crackdown on mortgage foreclosure rescue scams and loan modification fraud in order to advise the Congress to the risks and vulnerabilities of emerging schemes in the loan modification arena.

(b) REPORT. —

(1) IN GENERAL. — The Comptroller General shall submit a report to the Congress on the study conducted under subsection (a) containing such recommendations for legislative

(6)仅2004年一年,房利美和房地美即购买了1750亿美元的次级抵押贷款证券,占当年市场总量的44%。2005年至2007年,房利美和房地美购买了约1万亿美元的次级贷款和准优级贷款,而房利美购买的首付款比例低于10%的抵押贷款几乎增长了3倍。

(7)根据联邦住房金融局(FHFA)提供的2008年第四季度的数据,新发起的抵押贷款的75%由房利美和房地美拥有或担保,房利美和房地美目前持有全美境内未清偿购房抵押债务的13.3%,并且全美住房债务市场中有31.0%已由房利美和房地美发行抵押贷款支持证券,合计占全美境内未清偿购房抵押债务的44.3%。

(8)2008年9月7日,联邦住房金融局接管了房利美和房地美,随后,财政部同意分别向房利美和房地美至少购买2000亿美元的优先股,以换取可以购买其各自79.9%的普通股认股权证。

(9)由于联邦住房金融局对房利美和房地美的接管,纳税人可能要面临价值5.3万亿美元以上的风险敞口。

(10)房利美和房地美公私混营的身份无以为继,必须予以解决,以确保向消费者提供住房抵押贷款的条款以及消费者获得住房抵押贷款的条款能合理体现消费者的偿贷能力,且易于理解、公平和不存在欺骗或滥用情况。

(b)**国会的态度**。——国会认为,如果不对房利美和房地美进行真正意义上的结构性变革,仅仅加强对住房抵押贷款条款的保护、限制和监管以及完善与该等贷款相关的做法将不足以实现改革目的。

第1492条　政府问责办公室关于政府打击抵押止赎救助诈骗活动和抵押贷款修改欺诈活动的研究报告

(a)**研究**。——政府问责办公室主任应针对财政部部长、住房与城市发展部部长、联邦总检察长和联邦贸易委员会当前在打击抵押止赎救助诈骗活动和抵押贷款修改欺诈活动领域中采取的跨机关行动开展研究,并基于该等研究向国会报告抵押贷款修改领域新出现的计划所面临的风险和存在的弱点。

(b)**报告**。——

(1)**一般规定**。——对于按照第(a)子条开展的研究,政府问责办公室主任应向国会提交一份报告,并在报告中提出第(2)款规定的建议和政府问责办公室主任判定确

and administrative actions as the Comptroller General may determine to be appropriate in addition to the recommendations required under paragraph (2).

(2) SPECIFIC TOPICS. — The report made under paragraph (1) shall include —

(A) an evaluation of the effectiveness of the inter–agency task force current efforts to combat mortgage foreclosure rescue scams and loan modification fraud scams;

(B) specific recommendations on agency or legislative action that are essential to properly protect homeowners from mortgage foreclosure rescue scams and loan modification fraud scams; and

(C) the adequacy of financial resources that the Federal Government is allocating to —

(i) crackdown on loan modification and foreclosure rescue scams; and

(ii) the education of homeownersabout fraudulent scams relating to loan modification and foreclosure rescues.

SEC. 1493. REPORTING OF MORTGAGE DATA BY STATE.

(a) IN GENERAL. — Section 104(a) of the Helping Families Save Their Homes Act of 2009 (division A of Public Law 111–22) is amended —

(1) in paragraph (2), by striking "resulting" and inserting "in each State that result";

(2) in paragraph (3), by inserting "each State for" after "modifications in"; and

(3) in paragraph (4), by inserting "in each State" after "total number of loans".

(b) CONFORMING AMENDMENT. — Section 104 (b)(1)(A) of such Act is amended by adding at the end the following sentence: "Not later than 60 days after the date of the enactment of the Dodd–Frank Wall Street Reform and Consumer Protection Act, the Comptroller of the Currency and the Director of the Office of Thrift Supervision shall update such requirements to reflect amendments made to this section by such Act.".

SEC. 1494. STUDY OF EFFECT OF DRYWALL PRESENCE ON FORECLOSURES.

(a) STUDY. — The Secretary of Housing and Urban Development, in consultation with the Secretary of the Treasury, shall conduct a study of the effect on residential mortgage loan foreclosures of —

(1) the presence in residential structures subject to such mortgage loans of drywall that was imported from China during the period beginning with 2004 and ending at the end of 2007; and

(2) the availability of property insurance for residential structures in which such drywall is present.

(b) REPORT. — Not later than the expiration of the 120–day period beginning on the date of the enactment of this Act, the Secretary of Housing and Urban Development shall submit to the Congress a report on the study conducted under subsection (a) containing its findings, conclusions, and recommendations.

属适当的立法和行政行动建议。

(2)**具体议题**。——按照第(1)款规定提交的报告应包含如下信息——

(A)针对跨机关特别工作组当前在打击抵押止赎救助诈骗活动和抵押贷款修改欺诈活动领域开展的工作的有效性评价;

(B)为妥善保护业主不受抵押止赎救助诈骗活动和抵押贷款修改欺诈活动危害提出的具体机关行动或立法行动建议;及

(C)联邦政府为以下事项投入的财务资源的充分性——

(i)打击抵押贷款修改和止赎救助诈骗活动;及

(ii)针对抵押贷款修改和止赎救助诈骗活动向业主提供的教育。

第1493条　以州为单位报告抵押贷款数据

(a)**一般规定**。——《2009年协助家庭保全房屋法》第104(a)条(第111—22号公法第A卷)修正如下——

(1)在第(2)款中,删除"导致如下后果的",替以"在每一州内导致如下后果的";

(2)在第(3)款中,在"抵押贷款修改总数"前插入"每一州的";及

(3)在第(4)款中,在"修改之后出现违约的贷款总笔数"前插入"每一州的"。

(b)**一致性修正**。——在《2009年协助家庭保全房屋法》第104(b)(1)(A)条结尾处增加下句规定,作为对该条的修正:"在《多德—弗兰克华尔街改革与消费者保护法》颁布后60天内,货币监理署署长和储蓄机构监理局局长应对该等要求进行更新,以体现该法对本条作出的修正。"

第1494条　关于石膏板对止赎影响的研究

(a)**研究**。——住房与城市发展部部长应在与财政部部长磋商之后,就下述事项对住房抵押贷款止赎的影响开展研究——

(1)有住宅抵押贷款的住宅建筑上是否使用了2004年年初至2007年年末这一期间,从中国进口的石膏板;及

(2)使用该等石膏板的住宅建筑是否可以获得财产保险。

(b)**报告**。——住房与城市发展部部长应于本法颁布之日后120天内,针对按照第(a)子条规定开展的研究向国会提交一份报告,说明其研究得出的认定、结论和提出的建议。

SEC. 1495. DEFINITION.

For purposes of this title, the term "designated transfer date" means the date established under section 1062 of this Act.

SEC. 1496. EMERGENCY MORTGAGE RELIEF.

(a) EMERGENCY HOMEOWNERS' RELIEF FUND. — Effective October 1, 2010, and notwithstanding any other provision of law, there is hereby made available to the Secretary of Housing and Urban Development such sums as are necessary to provide $1, 000, 000, 000 in assistance through the Emergency Homeowners' Relief Fund, which such Secretary shall establish pursuant to section 107 of the Emergency Housing Act of 1975 (12 U. S. C. 2706), as such Act is amended by this section, for use for emergency mortgage assistance in accordance with title I of such Act.

(b) REAUTHORIZATION OF EMERGENCY MORTGAGE RELIEF PROGRAM. — Title I of the Emergency Housing Act of 1975 is amended —

(1) in section 103 (12 U. S. C. 2702) —

(A) in paragraph (2) —

(i) by striking "have indicated" and all that follows through "regulation of the holder" and insert "have certified";

(ii) by striking "(such as the volume of delinquent loans in its portfolio)"; and

(iii) by striking ", except that such statement" and all that follows through "purposes of this title"; and

(B) in paragraph (4), by inserting "or medical conditions" after "adverse economic conditions";

(2) in section 104 (12 U. S. C. 2703) —

(A) in subsection (b), by striking ", but such assistance" and all that follows through the period at the end and inserting the following: ". The amount of assistance provided to a homeowner under this title shall be an amount that the Secretary determines is reasonably necessary to supplement such amount as the homeowner is capable of contributing toward such mortgage payment, except that the aggregate amount of such assistance provided for any homeowner shall not exceed $50, 000. ";

(B) in subsection (d), by striking "interest on a loan or advance" and all that follows through the end of the subsection and inserting the following: "(1) the rate of interest on any loan or advance of credit insured under this title shall be fixed for the life of the loan or advance of credit and shall not exceed the rate of interest that is generally charged for mortgages on single–family housing insured by the Secretary of Housing and Urban Development under title II of the National Housing Act at the time such loan or advance of credit is made, and (2) no interest shall be charged on interest which is deferred on a loan or advance of credit made under this title. In establishing rates, terms and conditions for loans or

第1495条　定义

就本编而言,"指定转移日"一词系指本法第1062条规定的日期。

第1496条　紧急抵押贷款救助

(a)**业主紧急救助基金**。——无论是否存在任何不同法律规定,兹向住房与城市发展部部长提供必要资金,以通过业主紧急救助基金提供10亿美元的援助,上述规定于2010年10月1日生效。该项基金应由住房与城市发展部部长依照《1975年紧急住房法》(以经本条修正后的版本为准)第107条(《美国法典》第十二编第2706节)设立,用于按照该法第一编提供紧急抵押贷款援助。

(b)**紧急抵押贷款援助计划的重新批准**。——《1975年紧急住房法》第一编修正如下——

(1)在第103条(《美国法典》第十二编第2702节)中——

(A)第(2)款——

(i)删除"已经以书面形式,向住房与城市发展部部长及负责对持有人进行监管的任何联邦机关或部门说明",替以"已经证明";

(ii)删除"(例如其贷款组合中拖欠贷款的数量)";及

(iii)删除"但是,住房与城市发展部部长认为有助于实现本编宗旨的,有权放弃要求抵押贷款持有人提供该等声明";及

(B)第(4)款在"不利经济条件"之后插入"或者医疗状况";

(2)在第104条(《美国法典》第十二编第2703节)中——

(A)第(b)子条删除",但是该等援助"直至结尾处句号前的全部内容,替以如下内容:"。依据本编向某一业主提供的援助数额应当为住房与城市发展部部长判定的合理必要数额,作为业主有能力支付的抵押贷款还款的补充;但是,对任何业主的援助总额均不得超过5万美元。"

(B)第(d)子条删除"贷款或预支款利息"直至该子条结尾处的全部内容,替以如下内容:"(1)依据本编获保的任何贷款或信用预支款的利率在其整个期限内均应固定不变,并且不得超过提供该等贷款或信用预支款之时住房与城市发展部部长依照《国家住房法》第二编承保的独户住房抵押贷款一般适用的利率,且(2)不得对按照本编提供的贷款或信用预支款的递延利息计收利息。在确定按照本编提供的贷款或信用预支款的利率时,住房与城市发展部部长还应考虑业主偿还贷款或信用预支款的能力。"及

advances of credit made under this title, the Secretary shall take into account a homeowner's ability to repay such loan or advance of credit. "; and

(C) in subsection (e), by inserting after the period at the end of the first sentence the following: "Any eligible homeowner who receives a grant or an advance of credit under this title may repay the loan in full, without penalty, by lump sum or by installment payments at any time before the loan becomes due and payable. ";

(3) in section 105 (12 U. S. C. 2704) —

(A) by striking subsection (b);

(B) in subsection (e) —

(i) by inserting "and emergency mortgage relief payments made under section 106" after "insured under this section"; and

(ii) by striking "$1, 500, 000, 000 at any one time" and inserting "$3, 000, 000, 000";

(C) by redesignating subsections (c), (d), and (e) as subsections (b), (c), and (d), respectively; and

(D) by adding at the end the following new subsection:

"(e) The Secretary shall establish underwriting guidelines or procedures to allocate amounts made available for loans and advances insured under this section and for emergency relief payments made under section 106 based on the likelihood that a mortgagor will be able to resume mortgage payments, pursuant to the requirement under section 103(5) . ";

(4) in section 107 —

(A) by striking "(a)"; and

(B) by striking subsection (b);

(5) in section 108 (12 U. S. C. 2707), by adding at the end the following new subsection:

"(d) COVERAGE OF EXISTING PROGRAMS. — The Secretary shall allow funds to be administered by a State that has an existing program that is determined by the Secretary to provide substantially similar assistance to homeowners. After such determination is made such State shall not be required to modify such program to comply with the provisions of this title. ";

(6) in section 109 (12 U. S. C. 2708) —

(A) in the section heading, by striking "AUTHORIZATION AND";

(B) by striking subsection (a);

(C) by striking "(b)"; and

(D) by striking "1977" and inserting "2011";

(7) by striking sections 110, 111, and 113 (12 U. S. C. 2709, 2710, 2712); and

(8) by redesignating section 112 (12 U. S. C. 2711) as section 110.

(C)在第(e)子条中,在第一句结尾处的句号之后插入如下内容:“依据本编获授补助金或者信用预支款的任何适格业主,均可在贷款到期应付之前的任何时候一次性或分期还清贷款;任何适格业主在贷款到期之前提前偿清贷款的,不必缴纳任何罚款。”

(3)在第105条(《美国法典》第十二编第2704节)中——

(A)删除第(b)子条;

(B)第(e)子条——

(i)在“每次按照本条获保的贷款和预支款”之后插入“以及按照第106条进行的任何紧急抵押救助付款”;及

(ii)删除“每次”;删除“15亿美元”,替以“30亿美元”;

(C)第(c)子条、第(d)子条和第(e)子条分别重新编号为第(b)子条、第(c)子条和第(d)子条;及

(D)在结尾处增加如下新子条:

“(e)住房与城市发展部部长应当依据第103(5)条规定的要求,编制审核指引或程序,以根据抵押人恢复抵押还款的可能性,为按照本条获保的贷款和预支款以及按照第106条进行的紧急救助付款分配资金。”

(4)在第107条中——

(A)删除“(a)”;及

(B)删除第(b)子条;

(5)在第108条(《美国法典》第十二编第2707节)中,在结尾处增加如下新子条:

“(d)**既存计划覆盖的范围**。——任何州如有既存的计划被住房与城市发展部部长判定属于为业主提供基本类似的援助,则住房与城市发展部部长应允许其管理相关资金。在住房与城市发展部部长作出上述判定后,不得要求该州为满足本编要求而修改该等计划。”

(6)在第109条(《美国法典》第十二编第2708节)中——

(A)该条标题删除**“授权和”**;

(B)删除第(a)子条;

(C)删除“(b)”;及

(D)删除“1977年”,替以“2011年”;

(7)删除第110条、第111条和第113条(《美国法典》第十二编第2709节、第2710节和第2712节);及

(8)第112条(《美国法典》第十二编第2711节)重新编号为第110条。

SEC. 1497. ADDITIONAL ASSISTANCE FOR NEIGHBORHOOD STABILIZATION PROGRAM.

(a) IN GENERAL. — Effective October 1, 2010, out of funds in the Treasury not otherwise appropriated, there is hereby made available to the Secretary of Housing and Urban Development $1, 000, 000, 000, and the Secretary of Housing and Urban Development shall use such amounts for assistance to States and units of general local government for the redevelopment of abandoned and foreclosed homes, in accordance with the same provisions applicable under the second undesignated paragraph under the heading "Community Planning and Development — Community Development Fund" in title XII of division A of the American Recovery and Reinvestment Act of 2009 (Public Law 111–5; 123 Stat. 217) to amounts made available under such second undesignated paragraph, except as follows:

(1) Notwithstanding the matter of such second undesignated paragraph that precedes the first proviso, amounts made available by this section shall remain available until expended.

(2) The 3rd, 4th, 5th, 6th, 7th, and 15th provisos of such second undesignated paragraph shall not apply to amounts made available by this section.

(3) Amounts made available by this section shall be allocated based on a funding formula for such amounts established by the Secretary in accordance with section 2301(b) of the Housing and Economic Recovery Act of 2008 (42 U. S. C. 5301 note), except that —

(A) notwithstanding paragraph (2) of such section 2301(b), the formula shall be established not later than 30 days after the date of the enactment of this Act;

(B) notwithstanding such section 2301 (b), each State shall receive, at a minimum, not less than 0. 5 percent of funds made available under this section;

(C) the Secretary may establish a minimum grant amount for direct allocations to units of general local government located within a State, which shall not exceed $1, 000, 000;

(D) each State and local government receiving grant amounts shall establish procedures to create preferences for the development of affordable rental housing for properties assisted with amounts made available by this section; and

(E) the Secretary may use not more than 2 percent of the funds made available under this section for technical assistance to grantees.

(4) Paragraph (1) of section 2301(c) of the Housing and Economic Recovery Act of 2008 shall not apply to amounts made available by this section.

(5) The fourth proviso from the end of such second undesignated paragraph shall be applied to amounts made available by this section by substituting "2013" for "2012".

(6) Notwithstanding section 2301(a) of the Housing and Economic Recovery Act of 2008, the term "State" means any State, as defined in section 102 of the Housing and Community Development Act of 1974 (42 U. S. C. 5302), and the District of Columbia,

第1497条　为社区稳定计划提供的额外援助

(a)**一般规定**。——自2010年10月1日起,兹从国库中未拨作他用的资金中,向住房与城市发展部部长提供10亿美元,由住房与城市发展部部长将该等资金用于为各州和一般地方政府行政分区提供援助,对被放弃和被止赎的住房进行重新开发;住房与城市发展部部长在使用该等资金时,应遵守《2009年美国复苏与再投资法》(第111—5号公法;《美国制定法汇编》第123卷第217页)第A卷第十二编"社区规划和发展——社区发展基金"标题下第二个无编号段落中适用于按照该第二个无编号段落提供的资金的相同规定,但是:

(1)无论该第二个无编号段落的首项限制性条款之前的内容如何规定,依照本条提供的款项在支出前不得转作他用。

(2)该第二个无编号段落的第3项、第4项、第5项、第6项、第7项和第15项限制性条款不适用于依照本条提供的款项。

(3)依照本条提供的款项应当按照住房与城市发展部部长依据《2008年住房和经济复苏法》第2301(b)条(《美国法典》第四十二编第5301节注释)确立的资金分配公式进行分配,但是——

(A)无论上述第2301(b)条第(2)款如何规定,该资金分配公式至迟应于本法颁布之日后30天内确立;

(B)无论上述第2301(b)条如何规定,在按照本条提供的资金中,每个州均应至少获得0.5%;

(C)住房与城市发展部部长可以设定向位于某一州的一般地方政府行政分区进行直接分配的最低补助金数额,该数额不得超过100万美元;

(D)每一接受补助金的州和地方政府均应制定一套程序,针对获得本条规定的资金支持的房地产,设定优先开发可负担的租赁住房的要求;且

(E)住房与城市发展部部长可以将不高于本条提供之资金的2%用于向获得补助金的人提供技术援助。

(4)《2008年住房和经济复苏法》第2301(c)条第(1)款不适用于依据本条提供的款项。

(5)该第二个无编号段落的倒数第四项限制性条款适用于本条提供的款项,但是其中的"2012年"应替为"2013年"。

(6)无论《2008年住房和经济复苏法》第2301(a)条如何规定,就本条和本编中适用于根据本条提供的款项的规定而言,"州"一词系指《1974年住房与社区发展法》第102条(《美国法典》第四十二编第5302节)所定义的任何州以及哥伦比亚特区。

for purposes of this section and this title, as applied to amounts made available by this section.

(7)(A) None of the amounts made available by this section shall be distributed to —

(i) any organization which has been convicted for a violation under Federal law relating to an election for Federal office; or

(ii) any organization which employs applicable individuals.

(B) In this paragraph, the term "applicable individual" means an individual who—

(i) is —

(I) employed by the organization in a permanent or temporary capacity;

(II) contracted or retained by the organization; or

(III) acting on behalf of, or with the express or apparent authority of, the organization; and

(ii) has been convicted for a violation under Federal law relating to an election for Federal office.

(8) An eligible entity receiving a grant under this section shall, to the maximum extent feasible, provide for the hiring of employees who reside in the vicinity, as such term is defined by the Secretary, of projects funded under this section or contract with small businesses that are owned and operated by persons residing in the vicinity of such projects.

(b) ADDITIONAL AMENDMENTS. —

(1) SECTION 2301. — Section 2301(f)(3)(A)(ii) of the Housing and Economic Recovery Act of 2008 (42 U. S. C. 5301(f)(3)(A)(ii)) —

(A) is amended by striking "for the purchase and redevelopment of abandoned and foreclosed upon homes or residential properties that will be used"; and

(B) shall apply with respect to any unexpended or unobligated balances, including recaptured and reallocated funds made available under this Act, section 2301 of the Housing and Economic Recovery Act of 2008 (42 U. S. C. 5301), and the heading "Community Planning and Development — Community Development Fund" in title XII of division A of the American Recovery and Reinvestment Act of 2009 (Public Law 111–5; 123 Stat. 217).

(2) NOTICE OF FORECLOSURE. — For any amounts made available under this section, under division B, title III of the Housing and Economic Recovery Act of 2008 (42 U. S. C. 5301), or under the heading "Community Planning and Development — Community Development Fund" in title XII of division A of the American Recovery and Reinvestment Act of 2009 (Public Law 111–5; 123 Stat. 217), the date of a notice of foreclosure shall be deemed to be the date on which complete title to a property is transferred to a successor entity or person as a result of an order of a court or pursuant to provisions in a mortgage, deed of trust, or security deed.

(7)(A)本条提供的任何款项均不得向下列组织分配——

(i)曾被判违反有关联邦职务选举的联邦法律的任何组织;或

(ii)雇用相关个人的任何组织。

(B)就本款而言,"相关个人"一词系指具有以下特征的个人——

(i)具有如下身份——

(I)该组织的正式或临时员工;

(II)承接该组织外包工作或受其聘用的个人;或

(III)代表该组织行事的个人,或获得该组织明示授权或表见授权的个人;且

(ii)曾被判定违反关于联邦职务选举的联邦法律。

(8)有资格按照本条获得补助金的实体,应当在最大可行范围内规定聘用在按照本条获得资助的项目周边地区("周边地区"一词以住房与城市发展部部长的定义为准)居住的雇员,或者应当与居住在该等计划周边地区的人拥有和运营的小型企业缔约。

(b)**补充修正**。——

(1)**第2301条**。——《2008年住房和经济复苏法》第2301(f)(3)(A)(ii)条[《美国法典》第四十二编第5301(f)(3)(A)(ii)节]——

(A)修正如下:删除"购买和重新开发被放弃或被止赎的房屋或住宅,将其用于";且

(B)应适用于任何尚未支出或者未被指定用途的余额,包括根据本法、《2008年住房和经济复苏法》第2301条(《美国法典》第四十二编第5301节)以及《2009年美国复苏与再投资法》(第111—5号公法;《美国制定法汇编》第123卷第217页)第A卷第十二编"社区规划和发展——社区发展基金"提供的收回和重新分配的资金。

(2)**止赎通知**。——对于根据本条、《2008年住房和经济复苏法》第B卷第三编(《美国法典》第四十二编第5301节)或者《2009年美国复苏与再投资法》(第111—5号公法;《美国制定法汇编》第123卷第217页)第A卷第十二编"社区规划和发展——社区发展基金"提供的任何款项,止赎通知日期应视为房地产的完整所有权按照法院命令或抵押契约、信托契约或担保契约规定转让给继受实体或继受人之日。

SEC. 1498. LEGAL ASSISTANCE FOR FORECLOSURE-RELATED ISSUES.

(a) ESTABLISHMENT. — The Secretary of Housing and Urban Development (hereafter in this section referred to as the "Secretary") shall establish a program for making grants for providing a full range of foreclosure legal assistance to low–and moderate–income homeowners and tenants related to home ownership preservation, home foreclosure prevention, and tenancy associated with home foreclosure.

(b) COMPETITIVE ALLOCATION. — The Secretary shall allocate amounts made available for grants under this section to State and local legal organizations on the basis of a competitive process. For purposes of this subsection "State and local legal organizations" are those State and local organizations whose primary business or mission is to provide legal assistance.

(c) PRIORITY TO CERTAIN AREAS. — In allocating amounts in accordance with subsection (b), the Secretary shall give priority consideration to State and local legal organizations that are operating in the 125 metropolitan statistical areas (as that term is defined by the Director of the Office of Management and Budget) with the highest home foreclosure rates.

(d) LEGAL ASSISTANCE. —

(1) IN GENERAL. — Any State or local legal organization that receives financial assistance pursuant to this section may use such amounts only to assist —

(A) homeowners of owner–occupied homes with mortgages in default, in danger of default, or subject to or at risk of foreclosure; and

(B) tenants at risk of or subject to eviction as a result of foreclosure of the property in which such tenant resides.

(2) COMMENCE USE WITHIN 90 DAYS. — Any State or local legal organization that receives financial assistance pursuant to this section shall begin using any financial assistance received under this section within 90 days after receipt of the assistance.

(3) PROHIBITION ON CLASS ACTIONS. — No funds provided to a State or local legal organization under this section may be used to support any class action litigation.

(4) LIMITATION ON LEGAL ASSISTANCE. — Legal assistance funded with amounts provided under this section shall be limited to mortgage–related default, eviction, or foreclosure proceedings, without regard to whether such foreclosure is judicial or nonjudicial.

(5) EFFECTIVE DATE. — Notwithstanding any other provision of this Act, this subsection shall take effect on the date of the enactment of this Act.

(e) LIMITATION ON DISTRIBUTION OF ASSISTANCE. —

(1) IN GENERAL. — None of the amounts made available under this section shall be distributed to—

第1498条 为止赎相关事项提供的法律援助

(a)**计划设立**。——住房与城市发展部部长应当设立一项补助金计划,针对房屋所有权保护、预防房屋止赎以及与房屋止赎相关的租赁,为中低收入业主和租户提供全套止赎法律援助。

(b)**竞争性分配**。——住房与城市发展部部长应当通过竞争性程序,将按照本条提供的补助金款项分配给州和地方法律组织。就本子条而言,"州和地方法律组织"一词系指以提供法律援助为主营业务或宗旨的州和地方组织。

(c)**优先向特定地区提供的补助金**。——按照第(b)子条分配款项时,住房与城市发展部部长应当优先考虑在房屋止赎率最高的125个大都市统计区(该词的含义以行政管理和预算办公室主任的定义为准)之内运营的州和地方法律组织。

(d)**法律援助**。——

(1)**一般规定**。——依据本条获得财政援助的任何州或地方法律组织均仅得将该等款项用于协助——

(A)存在如下情形的自住房屋的业主:拖欠房贷或者存在拖欠房贷的危险,或者其房屋已被止赎或存在止赎危险;及

(B)由于房地产止赎而被要求或可能被要求退租的租户。

(2)**在90天内开始使用**。——依据本条获得任何财政援助的任何州或地方法律组织均应在收到援助后90天内开始使用该等援助。

(3)**集体诉讼禁止性规定**。——按照本条向州或地方法律组织提供的资金不得用于支持任何集体诉讼。

(4)**对法律援助的限制**。——按照本条提供的法律援助资金应当仅限于与抵押贷款有关的违约、退租或者止赎程序(无论是司法或是非司法性质的止赎)。

(5)**生效日**。——无论本法是否存在任何不同规定,本子条规定均应于本法颁布之日生效。

(e)**对援助分配的限制**。——

(1)**一般规定**。——按照本条提供的任何资金均不得向下列组织分配——

(A) any organization which has been convicted for a violation under Federal law relating to an election for Federal office; or

(B) any organization which employs applicable individuals.

(2) DEFINITION OF APPLICABLE INDIVIDUALS. — In this subsection, the term "applicable individual" means an individual who —

(A) is —

(i) employed by the organization in a permanent or temporary capacity;

(ii) contracted or retained by the organization; or

(iii) acting on behalf of, or with the express or apparent authority of, the organization; and

(B) has been convicted for a violation under Federal law relating to an election for Federal office.

(f) AUTHORIZATION OF APPROPRIATIONS. — There are authorized to be appropriated to the Secretary $35, 000, 000 for each of fiscal years 2011 through 2012 for grants under this section.

(A)曾被判违反有关联邦职务选举的联邦法律的任何组织;或

(B)雇用相关个人的任何组织。

(2)**相关个人的定义**。——就本子条中,“相关个人”一词系指具有以下特征的个人——

(A)具有如下身份——

(i)该组织的正式或临时员工;

(ii)承接该组织外包工作或受其聘用的个人;或

(iii)代表该组织行事的个人,或获得该组织明示授权或表见授权的个人;且

(B)曾被判违反有关联邦职务选举的联邦法律。

(f)**拨款授权**。——兹授权在2011财政年度和2012财政年度分别向住房与城市发展部部长拨款3500万美元,以提供本条规定的补助金。

TITLE XV—MISCELLANEOUS PROVISIONS

SEC. 1501. RESTRICTIONS ON USE OF UNITED STATES FUNDS FOR FOREIGN GOVERNMENTS; PROTECTION OF AMERICAN TAXPAYERS.

The Bretton Woods Agreements Act (22 U. S. C. 286 et seq.) is amended by adding at the end the following:

"SEC. 68. RESTRICTIONS ON USE OF UNITED STATES FUNDS FOR FOREIGN GOVERNMENTS; PROTECTION OF AMERICAN TAX–PAYERS.

"(a) IN GENERAL. — The Secretary of the Treasury shall instruct the United States Executive Director at the International Monetary Fund —

"(1) to evaluate, prior to consideration by the Board of Executive Directors of the Fund, any proposal submitted to the Board for the Fund to make a loan to a country if —

"(A) the amountof the public debt of the country exceeds the gross domestic product of the country as of the most recent year for which such information is available; and

"(B) the country is not eligible for assistance from the International Development Association.

"(2) OPPOSITION TO LOANS UNLIKELY TO BE REPAID IN FULL. — If any such evaluation indicates that the proposed loan is not likely to be repaid in full, the Secretary of the Treasury shall instruct the United States Executive Director at the Fund to use the voice and vote of the United States to oppose the proposal.

"(b) REPORTS TO CONGRESS. — Within 30 days after the Board of Executive Directors of the Fund approves a proposal described in subsection (a), and annually thereafter by June 30, for the duration of any program approved under such proposals, the Secretary of the Treasury shall report in writing to the Committee on Financial Services of the House of Representatives and the Committee on Foreign Relations and the Committee on Banking, Housing, and Urban Affairs of the Senate assessing the likelihood that loans made pursuant to such proposals will be repaid in full, including —

"(1) the borrowing country's current debt status, including, to the extent possible, its maturity structure, whether it has fixed or floating rates, whether it is indexed, and by whom it is held;

第十五编 其他规定

第1501条 向外国政府提供美国资金的限制;对美国纳税人的保护

在《布雷顿森林协定法》(《美国法典》第二十二编第286节及其后条文)结尾处增加如下内容,作为对该法的修正:

"第68条 向外国政府提供美国资金的限制;对美国纳税人的保护

(a)**一般规定**。——财政部部长应当指示国际货币基金组织的美国执行董事——

(1)在国际货币基金组织的执行董事会审议向某国提供贷款的提案之前,评估——

(A)截至可获得相关信息的最近一个年度,该国的公共债务数额是否超过国内生产总值;及

(B)该国是否并无资格获得国际开发协会的援助。

(2)**对全额清偿可能性很低的贷款提出反对**。——如果任何该等评估表明该提议贷款获得全额清偿的可能性很低,财政部部长应当指示国际货币基金组织的美国执行董事利用美国的发言权和表决权对该提案提出反对意见。

(b)**向国会报告**。——在国际货币基金组织执行董事会批准第(a)子条所述提案之后30天内,以及此后在根据该等提案批准的任何计划存续期内每一年的6月30日之前,财政部部长均应向众议院金融服务委员会、参议院对外关系委员会和参议院银行、住房与城市事务委员会提交一份书面报告,评估根据该等提案提供的贷款获得清偿的可能性,包括——

(1)借款国的当前债务状况,包括在可能的范围内,说明债务的到期结构、实行固定或浮动利率、是否已经指数化以及由谁持有;

"(2) the borrowing country's external and internal vulnerabilities that could potentially affect its ability to repay; and

"(3) the borrowing country's debt management strategy.".

SEC. 1502. CONFLICT MINERALS.

(a) SENSE OF CONGRESS ON EXPLOITATION AND TRADE OF CONFLICT MINERALS ORIGINATING IN THE DEMOCRATIC REPUBLIC OF THE CONGO. — It is the sense of Congress that the exploitation and trade of conflict minerals originating in the Democratic Republic of the Congo is helping to finance conflict characterized by extreme levels of violence in the eastern Democratic Republic of the Congo, particularly sexual- and gender-based violence, and contributing to an emergency humanitarian situation therein, warranting the provisions of section 13(p) of the Securities Exchange Act of 1934, as added by subsection (b).

(b) DISCLOSURE RELATING TO CONFLICT MINERALS ORIGINATING IN THE DEMOCRATIC REPUBLIC OF THE CONGO. — Section 13 of the Securities Exchange Act of 1934 (15 U. S. C. 78m), as amended by this Act, is amended by adding at the end the following new subsection:

"(p) DISCLOSURES RELATING TO CONFLICT MINERALS ORIGINATING IN THE DEMOCRATIC REPUBLIC OF THE CONGO. —

"(1) REGULATIONS. —

"(A) IN GENERAL. — Not later than 270 days after the date of the enactment of this subsection, the Commission shall promulgate regulations requiring any person described in paragraph (2) to disclose annually, beginning with the person's first full fiscal year that begins after the date of promulgation of such regulations, whether conflict minerals that are necessary as described in paragraph (2)(B), in the year for which such reporting is required, did originate in the Democratic Republic of the Congo or an adjoining country and, in cases in which such conflict minerals did originate in any such country, submit to the Commission a report that includes, with respect to the period covered by the report —

"(i) a description of the measures taken by the person to exercise due diligence on the source and chain of custody of such minerals, which measures shall include an independent private sector audit of such report submitted through the Commission that is conducted in accordance with standards established by the Comptroller General of the United States, in accordance with rules promulgated by the Commission, in consultation with the Secretary of State; and

"(ii) a description of the products manufactured or contracted to be manufactured that are not DRC conflict free ('DRC conflict free' is defined to mean the products that do not contain minerals that directly or indirectly finance or benefit armed groups in the Democratic Republic of the Congo or an adjoining country), the entity that conducted the independent

(2)借款国存在的,可能影响其偿债能力的内外部弱点;及

(3)借款国的债务管理战略。"

第1502条　冲突矿物

(a)**国会对产自刚果民主共和国的冲突矿物的开采和贸易所持态度**。——国会认为刚果民主共和国冲突矿物的开采和贸易正在为该国东部地区具有极端暴力(特别是性暴力和性别暴力)特征的冲突提供资金援助,并促使该地区人道主义状况的紧急恶化,这是制定第(b)子条增加的《1934年证券交易法》第13(p)条的理由。

(b)**与产自刚果民主共和国的冲突矿物相关的披露**。——在经本法修正后的《1934年证券交易法》第13条(《美国法典》第十五编第78m节)结尾处增加如下新子条,作为对该条的进一步修正:

(p)**与产自刚果民主共和国的冲突矿物相关的披露**。——

(1)**规章**。——

(A)**一般规定**。——证券交易委员会应于本子条规定颁布之日后270天内,颁发规章要求第(2)款所述的任何主体自该等规章颁发之日后开始的第一个完整会计年度起,在应作出报告的年度内,对第(2)(B)款所述的必要冲突矿物是否来自刚果民主共和国或其邻国进行年度披露,并且,如果冲突矿物确实来自任何该等国家,应向证券交易委员会提交一份报告,针对报告所覆盖的期间说明如下内容——

(i)该主体针对该等矿产的来源和产销监管链进行尽职调查时采取的措施,该等措施应包括聘用私营部门对通过证券交易委员会提交的该等报告进行独立审计。审计标准应由政府问责办公室主任与国务卿磋商后,按照证券交易委员会颁发的规则确立;及

(ii)说明以下各项:制造或者委托他人制造的涉及刚果冲突的产品('不涉及刚果冲突'一词系指不含有如下矿物的产品:为刚果民主共和国或其邻国的武装团体提供直接或间接资助的矿物,或者该等武装团体能够直接或间接受益的矿物)、依照第(i)项开展独立私营部门审计的实体、用于加工冲突矿物的设施、冲突矿物的原产国,以

private sector audit in accordance with clause (i), the facilities used to process the conflict minerals, the country of origin of the conflict minerals, and the efforts to determine the mine or location of origin with the greatest possible specificity.

"(B) CERTIFICATION. — The person submitting a report under subparagraph (A) shall certify the audit described in clause (i) of such subparagraph that is included in such report. Such a certified audit shall constitute a critical component of due diligence in establishing the source and chain of custody of such minerals.

"(C) UNRELIABLE DETERMINATION. — If a report required to be submitted by a person under subparagraph (A) relies on a determination of an independent private sector audit, as described under subparagraph (A)(i), or other due diligence processes previously determined by the Commission to be unreliable, the report shall not satisfy the requirements of the regulations promulgated under subparagraph (A)(i).

"(D) DRC CONFLICT FREE. — For purposes of this paragraph, a product may be labeled as 'DRC conflict free' if the product does not contain conflict minerals that directly or indirectly finance or benefit armed groups in the Democratic Republic of the Congo or an adjoining country.

"(E) INFORMATION AVAILABLE TO THE PUBLIC. — Each person described under paragraph (2) shall make available to the public on the Internet website of such person the information disclosed by such person under subparagraph (A).

"(2) PERSON DESCRIBED. — A person is described in this paragraph if —

"(A) the person is required to file reports with the Commission pursuant to paragraph (1)(A); and

"(B) conflict minerals are necessary to the functionality or production of a product manufactured by such person.

"(3) REVISIONS AND WAIVERS. — The Commission shall revise or temporarily waive the requirements described in paragraph (1) if the President transmits to the Commission a determination that —

"(A) such revision or waiver is in the national security interest of the United States and the President includes the reasons therefor; and

"(B) establishes a date, not later than 2 years after the initial publication of such exemption, on which such exemption shall expire.

"(4) TERMINATION OF DISCLOSURE REQUIREMENTS. — The requirements of paragraph (1) shall terminate on the date on which the President determines and certifies to the appropriate congressional committees, but in no case earlier than the date that is one day after the end of the 5–year period beginning on the date of the enactment of this subsection, that no armed groups continue to be directly involved and benefitting from commercial activity involving conflict minerals.

及为了尽可能精确地确定矿山或原产国位置所开展的工作。

(B)**核证**。——根据第(A)子款提交报告的主体应对该子款第(i)项所述、该报告中所包含的审计工作进行核证。在为确定上述矿物的来源和产销监管链而开展尽职调查工作时,该等经核证的审计应构成尽职调查工作的关键组成部分。

(C)**不可靠的判定**。——如果某一主体根据第(A)子款提交的报告采信了第(A)(i)子款所述私营部门独立作出的审计作出的判定,或者采信了之前已被证券交易委员会判定为不可靠的其他尽职调查程序,则该报告应视为不满足第(A)(i)子款下颁发的规章的要求。

(D)**不涉及刚果冲突**。——就本款而言,如果某项产品不含有为刚果民主共和国或其邻国的武装团体提供直接或间接资助或使其直接或间接受益的矿物, 则其可标注为'不涉及刚果冲突'。

(E)**公开信息**。——第(2)款所述每一主体均应通过其因特网网站,公开发布其根据第(A)子款披露的信息。

(2)**本款所述主体**。——具有如下特征的主体为本款所述主体——

(A)有义务按照第(1)(A)款的规定向证券交易委员会提交报告;且

(B)冲突矿物为实现其制造的产品的功能所必需,或为其产品生产所必需。

(3)**修订和免除**。——美国总统向证券交易委员会传达了下列判定的,证券交易委员会应当修订或者暂时免除第(1)款所述要求——

(A)该等修订或免除有利于美国的国家安全,并且总统说明了相关理由;且

(B)总统设定了该等豁免的到期日(该日期应不迟于豁免首次公布后2年)。

(4)**披露要求的终止**。——在总统判定并向相应的国会委员会证明涉及冲突矿物的商业活动不再涉及任何武装团体,亦不再有任何武装团体从中获益之日起,第(1)款的要求应当终止,但是该日期不得早于自本子条规定颁布之日起届满5年之后第一天。

"(5) DEFINITIONS. —For purposes of this subsection, the terms 'adjoining country', 'appropriate congressional committees', 'armed group', and 'conflict mineral' have the meaning given those terms under section 1502 of the Dodd–Frank Wall Street Reform and Consumer Protection Act. ".

(c) STRATEGY AND MAP TO ADDRESS LINKAGES BETWEEN CONFLICT MINERALS AND ARMED GROUPS. —

(1) STRATEGY. —

(A) IN GENERAL. — Not later than 180 days after the date of the enactment of this Act, the Secretary of State, in consultation with the Administrator of the United States Agency for International Development, shall submit to the appropriate congressional committees a strategy to address the linkages between human rights abuses, armed groups, mining of conflict minerals, and commercial products.

(B) CONTENTS. — The strategy required by subparagraph (A) shall include the following:

(i) A plan to promote peace and security in the Democratic Republic of the Congo by supporting efforts of the Government of the Democratic Republic of the Congo, including the Ministry of Mines and other relevant agencies, adjoining countries, and the international community, in particular the United Nations Group of Experts on the Democratic Republic of Congo, to —

(I) monitor and stop commercial activities involving the natural resources of the Democratic Republic of the Congo that contribute to the activities of armed groups and human rights violations in the Democratic Republic of the Congo; and

(II) develop stronger governance and economic institutions that can facilitate and improve transparency in the cross–border trade involving the natural resources of the Democratic Republic of the Congo to reduce exploitation by armed groups and promote local and regional development.

(ii) A plan to provide guidance to commercial entities seeking to exercise due diligence on and formalize the origin and chain of custody of conflict minerals used in their products and on their suppliers to ensure that conflict minerals used in the products of such suppliers do not directly or indirectly finance armed conflict or result in labor or human rights violations.

(iii) A description of punitive measures that could be taken against individuals or entities whose commercial activities are supporting armed groups and human rights violations in the Democratic Republic of the Congo.

(2) MAP. —

(A) IN GENERAL. — Not later than 180 days after the date of the enactment of this Act, the Secretary of State shall, in accordance with the recommendation of the United

(5)**定义**。——就本子条而言,‘邻国’、‘相应的国会委员会’、‘武装团体’和‘冲突矿物’的定义以《多德—弗兰克华尔街改革与消费者保护法》第1502条的定义为准。”

(c)**处理冲突矿物和武装团体之间的联系的战略和地图**。——

(1)**战略**。——

(A)**一般规定**。——国务卿应于本法颁布后180天内,在与美国国际开发署署长磋商之后,向相应的国会委员会提交一项关于处理侵犯人权的行为、武装团体、冲突矿物开采与商用产品之间的联系的战略。

(B)**内容**。——第(A)子款规定的战略应当包含如下内容:

(i)为刚果民主共和国政府(包括矿产部)及其他相关机关、邻国以及国际社会(特别是联合国刚果民主共和国专家组)的工作提供支持,从而促进刚果民主共和国实现和平与安全的计划,以便——

(I)监控商业活动是否涉及有助于刚果民主共和国武装团体行动和侵犯人权行为的刚果自然资源,并制止涉及该等自然资源的商业活动;及

(II)发展更强大的治理和经济机构,促进和改善涉及刚果民主共和国自然资源的跨境交易的透明度,减少武装团体对自然资源的利用,并促进地方和地区发展。

(ii)提供一份指导计划,指导商业实体对其产品中使用的冲突矿物的来源和产销监管链及其供应商进行尽职调查和作出正式认定,确保该等供应商的产品中所使用的冲突矿物不为武装冲突提供任何直接或间接资助,亦不会导致对劳工权利或人权的侵犯。

(iii)说明对于通过商业活动为刚果民主共和国境内的武装团体和人权侵权行为提供支持的个人或实体可能采取的惩罚措施。

(2)**地图**。——

(A)**一般规定**。——国务卿应于本法颁布后180天内,按照联合国刚果民主共和国专家组在2008年12月的报告中提出的建议——

Nations Group of Experts on the Democratic Republic of the Congo in their December 2008 report —

(i) produce a map of mineral-rich zones, trade routes, and areas under the control of armed groups in the Democratic Republic of the Congo and adjoining countries based on data from multiple sources, including —

(I) the United Nations Group of Experts on the Democratic Republic of the Congo;

(II) the Government of the Democratic Republic of the Congo, the governments of adjoining countries, and the governments of other Member States of the United Nations; and

(III) local and international nongovernmental organizations;

(ii) make such map available to the public; and

(iii) provide to the appropriate congressional committees an explanatory note describing the sources of information from which such map is based and the identification, where possible, of the armed groups or other forces in control of the mines depicted.

(B) DESIGNATION. — The map required under subparagraph (A) shall be known as the "Conflict Minerals Map", and mines located in areas under the control of armed groups in the Democratic Republic of the Congo and adjoining countries, as depicted on such Conflict Minerals Map, shall be known as "Conflict Zone Mines".

(C) UPDATES. — The Secretary of State shall update the map required under subparagraph (A) not less frequently than once every 180 days until the date on which the disclosure requirements under paragraph (1) of section 13(p) of the Securities Exchange Act of 1934, as added by subsection (b), terminate in accordance with the provisions of paragraph (4) of such section 13(p).

(D) PUBLICATION IN FEDERAL REGISTER. — The Secretary of State shall add minerals to the list of minerals in the definition of conflict minerals under section 1502, as appropriate. The Secretary shall publish in the Federal Register notice of intent to declare a mineral as a conflict mineral included in such definition not later than one year before such declaration.

(d) REPORTS. —

(1) BASELINE REPORT. — Not later than 1 year after the date of the enactment of this Act and annually thereafter until the termination of the disclosure requirements under section 13 (p) of the Securities Exchange Act of 1934, the Comptroller General of the United States shall submit to appropriate congressional committees a report that includes an assessment of the rate of sexual- and gender-based violence in wartorn areas of the Democratic Republic of the Congo and adjoining countries.

(2) REGULAR REPORT ON EFFECTIVENESS. — Not later than 2 years after the date of the enactment of this Act and annually thereafter, the Comptroller General of the United States shall submit to the appropriate congressional committees a report that includes

(i)基于多种不同来源的数据编制一份地图,注明刚果民主共和国和邻国境内蕴含丰富矿藏的地区、贸易路线以及武装团体控制的地区。上述数据来源包括——

(I)联合国刚果民主共和国专家组;

(II)刚果民主共和国政府、邻国政府以及其他联合国成员国的政府;及

(III)地方和国际非政府组织;

(ii)将该等地图向公众公开;及

(iii)向相应的国会委员会提供关于该等地图所依据的信息来源的说明，如有可能,还应对控制相关矿物的武装团体或其他武装力量进行描述。

(B)**名称**。——第(A)子款所述地图应称为“冲突矿物地图”,而冲突矿物地图上描述的刚果民主共和国和邻国武装团体控制的地区内的矿物应称为“冲突地区矿物”。

(C)**更新**。——国务卿至少应每180天对第(A)子款规定的地图进行一次更新,直至第(b)子条增加的《1934年证券交易法》第13(p)条第(1)款的披露要求按照该第13(p)条第(4)款的规定终止之日为止。

(D)**在《联邦公报》上发布**。——国务卿应视适当情形,将符合条件的相关矿物加入第1502条中被定义为冲突矿物的矿物清单之中。国务卿至少应在宣布之前,提前1年在《联邦公报》上发布通告,说明其宣布将某种矿物纳入冲突矿物定义的意图。

(d)**报告**。——

(1)**基础报告**。——在本法颁布日后1年之内,以及此后在《1934年证券交易法》第13(p)条规定的披露要求终止之前的每一年,政府问责办公室主任均应向相应的国会委员会提交一份报告，对刚果民主共和国及其邻国受战争蹂躏地区的性暴力和性别暴力的犯罪率进行评估。

(2)**对成效进行评估的定期报告**。——在本法颁布日之后2年期间内,以及此后的每一年,政府问责办公室主任均应向相应的国会委员会提交一份报告,说明如下内容:

the following:

(A) An assessment of the effectiveness of section 13(p) of the Securities Exchange Act of 1934, as added by subsection (b), in promoting peace and security in the Democratic Republic of the Congo and adjoining countries.

(B) A description of issues encountered by the Securities and Exchange Commission in carrying out the provisions of such section 13(p).

(C)(i) A general review of persons described in clause (ii) and whether information is publicly available about —

(I) the use of conflict minerals by such persons; and

(II) whether such conflict minerals originate from the Democratic Republic of the Congo or an adjoining country.

(ii) A person is described in this clause if —

(I) the person is not required to file reports with the Securities and Exchange Commission pursuant to section 13(p)(1)(A) of the Securities Exchange Act of 1934, as added by subsection (b); and

(II) conflict minerals are necessary to the functionality or production of a product manufactured by such person.

(3) REPORT ON PRIVATE SECTOR AUDITING. — Not later than 30 months after the date of the enactment of this Act, and annually thereafter, the Secretary of Commerce shall submit to the appropriate congressional committees a report that includes the following:

(A) An assessment of the accuracy of the independent private sector audits and other due diligence processes described under section 13(p) of the Securities Exchange Act of 1934.

(B) Recommendations for the processes used to carry out such audits, including ways to —

(i) improve the accuracy of such audits; and

(ii) establish standards of best practices.

(C) A listing of all known conflict mineral processing facilities worldwide.

(e) DEFINITIONS. — For purposes of this section:

(1) ADJOINING COUNTRY. — The term "adjoining country", with respect to the Democratic Republic of the Congo, means a country that shares an internationally recognized border with the Democratic Republic of the Congo.

(2) APPROPRIATE CONGRESSIONAL COMMITTEES. — The term "appropriate congressional committees" means —

(A) the Committee on Appropriations, the Committee on Foreign Affairs, the Committee on Ways and Means, and the Committee on Financial Services of the House of Representatives; and

(B) the Committee on Appropriations, the Committee on Foreign Relations, the

(A)评估第(b)子条增加的《1934年证券交易法》第13(p)条在促进刚果民主共和国及其邻国的和平与安全方面的成效;

(B)说明证券交易委员会在实施上述第13(p)条的规定时遇到的问题;

(C)(i)对第(ii)项所述主体进行综合审查,并审查下述信息是否已经公开——

(I)关于上述主体使用冲突矿物的信息;及
(II)关于该等冲突矿物是否源自刚果民主共和国或其邻国的信息。

(ii)具有如下特征的主体为本项所述主体——
(I)不必按照第(b)子条增加的《1934年证券交易法》第13(p)(1)(A)条向证券交易委员会提交报告;且

(II)冲突矿物为实现其制造的产品的功能所必需,或为其产品生产所必需。

(3)**私营部门审计报告**。——在本法颁布日后30个月内,以及此后的每一年,商务部部长均应向相应的国会委员会提交一份报告,内容包括:

(A)评估《1934年证券交易法》第13(p)条所述私营部门独立做出的审计以及其他尽职调查程序的准确性;

(B)针对实施该等审计时采用的程序提出建议,包括——

(i)提高该等审计准确性的方法;及
(ii)制定最佳实践标准。
(C)世界范围内所有已知冲突矿物加工设施的清单。
(e)**定义**。——就本条而言:
(1)**邻国**。——“邻国”一词系指与刚果民主共和国拥有任何共同的国际公认的国界线的国家。

(2)**相应的国会委员会**。——“相应的国会委员会”一词系指——

(A)众议院拨款委员会、外事委员会、筹款委员会和金融服务委员会;及

(B)参议院拨款委员会、对外关系委员会、财政委员会以及银行、住房与城市事务

Committee on Finance, and the Committee on Banking, Housing, and Urban Affairs of the Senate.

(3) ARMED GROUP. — The term "armed group" means an armed group that is identified as perpetrators of serious human rights abuses in the annual Country Reports on Human Rights Practices under sections 116(d) and 502B(b) of the Foreign Assistance Act of 1961 (22 U. S. C. 2151n(d) and 2304(b)) relating to the Democratic Republic of the Congo or an adjoining country.

(4) CONFLICT MINERAL. — The term "conflict mineral" means —

(A) columbite–tantalite (coltan), cassiterite, gold, wolframite, or their derivatives; or

(B) any other mineral or its derivatives determined by the Secretary of State to be financing conflict in the Democratic Republic of the Congo or an adjoining country.

(5) UNDER THE CONTROL OF ARMED GROUPS. — The term "under the control of armed groups" means areas within the Democratic Republic of the Congo or adjoining countries in which armed groups —

(A) physically control mines or force labor of civilians to mine, transport, or sell conflict minerals;

(B) tax, extort, or control any part of trade routes for conflict minerals, including the entire trade route from a Conflict Zone Mine to the point of export from the Democratic Republic of the Congo or an adjoining country; or

(C) tax, extort, or control trading facilities, in whole or in part, including the point of export from the Democratic Republic of the Congo or an adjoining country.

SEC. 1503. REPORTING REQUIREMENTS REGARDING COAL OR OTHER MINE SAFETY.

(a) REPORTING MINE SAFETY INFORMATION. — Each issuer that is required to file reports pursuant to section 13(a) or 15(d) of the Securities Exchange Act of 1934 (15 U. S. C. 78m, 78o) and that is an operator, or that has a subsidiary that is an operator, of a coal or other mine shall include, in each periodic report filed with the Commission under the securities laws on or after the date of enactment of this Act, the following information for the time period covered by such report:

(1) For each coal or other mine of which the issuer or a subsidiary of the issuer is an operator —

(A) the total number of violations of mandatory health or safety standards that could significantly and substantially contribute to the cause and effect of a coal or other mine safety or health hazard under section 104 of the Federal Mine Safety and Health Act of 1977 (30 U. S. C. 814) for which the operator received a citation from the Mine Safety and Health Administration;

(B) the total number of orders issued under section 104(b) of such Act (30 U. S. C.

委员会。

(3)**武装团体**。——“武装团体”一词系指在根据《1961年对外援助法》第116(d)条和第502B(b)条[《美国法典》第二十二编第2151n(d)节和第2304(b)节]发布的年度《国家人权工作报告》中,被认定犯有与刚果民主共和国或其邻国有关的严重侵犯人权罪行的武装团体。

(4)**冲突矿物**。——“冲突矿物”一词系指——

(A)铌—钽(钶钽铁矿)、锡、金、钨或其衍生物;或

(B)国务卿判定的,为刚果民主共和国或其邻国冲突提供资助的任何其他矿物或其衍生物。

(5)**武装团体控制的地区**。——“武装团体控制的地区”一词系指刚果民主共和国或其邻国符合下列情况的地区——

(A)武装团体以实体方式控制矿山,或者强迫平民劳动力开采、运输或出售冲突矿物;

(B)武装团体对冲突矿物贸易路线(包括从冲突地区矿山至刚果民主共和国或其邻国出口地点之间的完整贸易路线)的任何部分实施征税、勒索或控制;或

(C)武装团体对全部或部分贸易设施(包括刚果民主共和国或其邻国的出口地点)实施征税、勒索或控制。

第1503条　关于煤矿或其他种类矿山安全的报告要求

(a)**关于矿山安全信息的报告。**——任何发行人,如其有义务根据《1934年证券交易法》第13(a)条或第15(d)条[《美国法典》第十五编第78m节或第78o节]提交报告,并且其本身或其子公司身为煤矿或其他种类矿山的经营者,均应在自本法颁布之日(含)起根据证券法律向证券交易委员会提交的每份定期报告中,针对报告所覆盖期间提供下列信息:

(1)发行人或其子公司作为经营者经营的每座煤矿或其他种类矿山——

(A)在违反强制性健康或安全标准的情况下,对《1977年联邦矿山安全和健康法》第104条(《美国法典》第三十编第814节)规定的煤矿或其他种类矿山的安全或健康危害的成因和影响有重大和实质的促成作用,并因此收到矿山安全和健康管理局签发的传票的总次数;

(B)收到根据该法第104(b)条[《美国法典》第三十编第814(b)节]签发的命令的

814(b));

(C) the total number of citations and orders for unwarrantable failure of the mine operator to comply with mandatory health or safety standards under section 104(d) of such Act (30 U. S. C. 814(d));

(D) the total number of flagrant violations under section 110(b)(2) of such Act (30 U. S. C. 820(b)(2));

(E) the total number of imminent danger orders issued under section 107(a) of such Act (30 U. S. C. 817(a));

(F) the total dollar value of proposed assessments from the Mine Safety and Health Administration under such Act (30 U. S. C. 801 et seq.); and

(G) the total number of mining–related fatalities.

(2) A list of such coal or other mines, of which the issuer or a subsidiary of the issuer is an operator, that receive written notice from the Mine Safety and Health Administration of—

(A) a pattern of violations of mandatory health or safety standards that are of such nature as could have significantly and substantially contributed to the cause and effect of coal or other mine health or safety hazards under section 104(e) of such Act (30 U. S. C. 814 (e)); or

(B) the potential to have such a pattern.

(3) Any pending legal action before the Federal Mine Safety and Health Review Commission involving such coal or other mine.

(b) REPORTING SHUTDOWNS AND PATTERNS OF VIOLATIONS. — Beginning on and after the date of enactment of this Act, each issuer that is an operator, or that has a subsidiary that is an operator, of a coal or other mine shall file a current report with the Commission on Form 8–K (or any successor form) disclosing the following regarding each coal or other mine of which the issuer or subsidiary is an operator:

(1) The receipt of an imminent danger order issued under section 107(a) of the Federal Mine Safety and Health Act of 1977 (30 U. S. C. 817(a)) .

(2) The receipt of written notice from the Mine Safety and Health Administration that the coal or other mine has —

(A) a pattern of violations of mandatory health or safety standards that are of such nature as could have significantly and substantially contributed to the cause and effect of coal or other mine health or safety hazards under section 104(e) of such Act (30 U. S. C. 814 (e)); or

(B) the potential to have such a pattern.

(c) RULE OF CONSTRUCTION. — Nothing in this section shall be construed to affect any obligation of a person to make a disclosure under any other applicable law in effect

总次数;

(C)矿山经营者无正当理由不遵守该法第104(d)条[《美国法典》第三十编第814(d)节]规定的强制性健康或安全标准而收到传票和命令的总次数;

(D)公然违反该法第110(b)(2)条[《美国法典》第三十编第820(b)(2)节]规定的总次数;

(E)收到根据该法第107(a)条[《美国法典》第三十编第817(a)节]签发的迫切危险令的总次数;

(F)矿山安全和健康管理局拟根据该法(《美国法典》第三十编第801节及其后条文)计征费用的总金额;及

(G)矿难死亡事故的总次数。

(2)发行人本身或其子公司作为经营者经营,并符合下述情况的煤矿或其他种类矿山之清单——

(A)矿山安全和健康管理局发出书面通知,说明该等煤矿或其他种类矿山存在违反强制性健康或安全标准的运营模式,且其性质可能对该法第104(e)条[《美国法典》第三十编第814(e)节]规定的煤矿或其他种类矿山的健康或安全危害的成因和影响有重大和实质的促成作用;或

(B)矿山安全和健康管理局发出书面通知,说明该等煤矿或其他种类矿山存在上述违规的运营模式。

(3)联邦矿山安全和健康审查委员会主持开展的涉及该等煤矿或其他种类矿山的任何未决法律诉讼。

(b)**关于停工和违规行为的报告**。——自本法颁布之日(含)起,任何发行人,如其本身或其子公司作为经营者经营煤矿或其他种类矿山,均应使用《8—K表格》(或者任何后继表格)向证券交易委员会提交最新报告,披露关于每一该等煤矿或其他种类矿山的下列信息:

(1)该等煤矿或其他种类矿山收到了根据《1977年联邦矿山安全和健康法》第107(a)条[《美国法典》第三十编第817(a)节]发布的迫切危险令;

(2)该等煤矿或其他种类矿山收到矿山安全和健康管理局发出的书面通知,说明该等煤矿或其他种类矿山——

(A)存在违反强制性健康或安全标准的运营模式,且其性质可能对该法第104(e)条[《美国法典》第三十编第814(e)节]规定的煤矿或其他种类矿山的健康或安全危害的成因和影响有重大和实质的促成作用;或

(B)可能存在发生上述违规的运营模式。

(c)**解释规则**。——本条任何规定均不得被解释为影响任何主体根据在本法颁布日之前或颁布日(含)之后有效适用的任何其他法律作出披露的义务。

before, on, or after the date of enactment of this Act.

(d) COMMISSION AUTHORITY.—

(1) ENFORCEMENT. — A violation by any person of this section, or any rule or regulation of the Commission issued under this section, shall be treated for all purposes in the same manner as a violation of the Securities Exchange Act of 1934 (15 U. S. C. 78a et seq.) or the rules and regulations issued thereunder, consistent with the provisions of this section, and any such person shall be subject to the same penalties, and to the same extent, as for a violation of such Act or the rules or regulations issued thereunder.

(2) RULES AND REGULATIONS. —The Commission is authorized to issue such rules or regulations as are necessary or appropriate for the protection of investors and to carry out the purposes of this section.

(e) DEFINITIONS. — In this section —

(1) the terms "issuer" and "securities laws" have the meaning given the terms in section 3 of the Securities Exchange Act of 1934 (15 U. S. C. 78c);

(2) the term "coal or other mine" means a coal or other mine, as defined in section 3 of the Federal Mine Safety and Health Act of 1977 (30 U. S. C. 802), that is subject to the provisions of such Act (30 U. S. C. 801 et seq.); and

(3) the term "operator" has the meaning given the term in section 3 of the Federal Mine Safety and Health Act of 1977 (30 U. S. C. 802).

(f) EFFECTIVE DATE. — This section shall take effect on the day that is 30 days after the date of enactment of this Act.

SEC. 1504. DISCLOSURE OF PAYMENTS BY RESOURCE EXTRACTION ISSUERS.

Section 13 of the Securities Exchange Act of 1934 (15 U. S. C. 78m), as amended by this Act, is amended by adding at the end the following:

"(q) DISCLOSURE OF PAYMENTS BY RESOURCE EXTRACTION ISSUERS.—

"(1) DEFINITIONS. — In this subsection —

"(A) the term 'commercial development of oil, natural gas, or minerals' includes exploration, extraction, processing, export, and other significant actions relating to oil, natural gas, or minerals, or the acquisition of a license for any such activity, as determined by the Commission;

"(B) the term 'foreign government' means a foreign government, a department, agency, or instrumentality of a foreign government, or a company owned by a foreign government, as determined by the Commission;

"(C) the term 'payment' —

"(i) means a payment that is —

"(I) made to further the commercial development of oil, natural gas, or minerals; and

(d)**证券交易委员会的权力**。——

(1)**执法**。——在任何情况下,任何人违反本条规定或者违反证券交易委员会按照本条规定发布的任何规则或规章的,在任何方面均应依照本条规定视同为违反《1934年证券交易法》(《美国法典》第十五编第78a节及其后条文)或依据该法发布的规则和规章的行为,应按相同方式予以相应处理,并应受到相同程度的处罚。

(2)**规则和规章**。——证券交易委员会有权为保护投资者及执行本条目的,发布必要或适当的规则或规章。

(e)**定义**。——就本条而言——

(1)"发行人"和"证券法律"的含义以《1934年证券交易法》第3条(《美国法典》第十五编第78c节)的定义为准;

(2)"煤矿或其他种类矿山"一词系指《1977年联邦矿山安全和健康法》第3条(《美国法典》第三十编第802节)所定义的,并且受到该法(《美国法典》第三十编第801节及其后条文)管辖的煤矿或其他种类矿山;及

(3)"经营者"一词的含义以《1977年联邦矿山安全和健康法》第3条(《美国法典》第三十编第802节)的定义为准。

(f)**生效日**。——本条规定应于本法颁布之日起届满30天之日生效。

第1504条　资源采掘发行人的付款披露

在经本法修正后的《1934年证券交易法》第13条(《美国法典》第十五编第78m节)结尾处增加如下内容,作为对该条的进一步修正:

"(q)**资源采掘发行人的付款披露**。——

(1)**定义**。——就本子条而言——

(A)'石油、天然气或矿物的商业开发'一词涵盖证券交易委员会所判定的,与石油、天然气或矿物有关的勘探、采掘、加工、出口以及其他重大行动,或者为开展该等活动获得执照的行为;

(B)'外国政府'一词系指证券交易委员会所判定的外国政府、外国政府的部门、机关、职能机构或者外国政府拥有的公司;

(C)'付款'一词系指——

(i)符合下列情况的付款——

(I)为推动石油、天然气或矿物的商业开发而支付的款项;且

"(II) not de minimis; and

"(ii) includes taxes, royalties, fees (including license fees), production entitlements, bonuses, and other material benefits, that the Commission, consistent with the guidelines of the Extractive Industries Transparency Initiative (to the extent practicable), determines are part of the commonly recognized revenue stream for the commercial development of oil, natural gas, or minerals;

"(D) the term 'resource extraction issuer' means an issuer that —

"(i) is required to file an annual report with the Commission; and

"(ii) engages in the commercial development of oil, natural gas, or minerals;

"(E) the term 'interactive data format' means an electronic data format in which pieces of information are identified using an interactive data standard; and

"(F) the term 'interactive data standard' means standardized list of electronic tags that mark information included in the annual report of a resource extraction issuer.

"(2) DISCLOSURE. —

"(A) INFORMATION REQUIRED. — Not later than 270 days after the date of enactment of the Dodd–Frank Wall Street Reform and Consumer Protection Act, the Commission shall issue final rules that require each resource extraction issuer to include in an annual report of the resource extraction issuer information relating to any payment made by the resource extraction issuer, a subsidiary of the resource extraction issuer, or an entity under the control of the resource extraction issuer to a foreign government or the Federal Government for the purpose of the commercial development of oil, natural gas, or minerals, including —

"(i) the type and total amount of such payments made for each project of the resource extraction issuer relating to the commercial development of oil, natural gas, or minerals; and

"(ii) the type and total amount of such payments made to each government.

"(B) CONSULTATION IN RULEMAKING. —In issuing rules under subparagraph (A), the Commission may consult with any agency or entity that the Commission determines is relevant.

"(C) INTERACTIVE DATA FORMAT. — The rules issued under subparagraph (A) shall require that the information included in the annual report of a resource extraction issuer be submitted in an interactive data format.

"(D) INTERACTIVE DATA STANDARD. —

"(i) IN GENERAL. — The rules issued under subparagraph (A) shall establish an interactive data standard for the information included in the annual report of a resource extraction issuer.

"(ii) ELECTRONIC TAGS. — The interactive data standard shall include electronic tags that identify, for any payments made by a resource extraction issuer to a foreign

(Ⅱ)不属于金额可忽略不计的付款;及

(ii)包括被证券交易委员会在可行范围内,按照《采掘业透明度倡议》的指导方针判定为属于石油、天然气或矿物商业开发的公认收入流的税费、采矿权使用费、收费(包括执照费)、产量分成、奖金以及其他物质利益;

(D)'资源采掘发行人'一词系指符合下列情况的发行人——

(i)有义务向证券交易委员会提交年度报告;及

(ii)从事石油、天然气或矿物的商业开发;

(E)'交互式数据格式'一词系指使用交互式数据标准识别每条信息的电子数据格式;及

(F)'交互式数据标准'一词系指对资源采掘发行人的年度报告中包含的信息进行标注的标准化电子标签清单。

(2)**披露**。——

(A)**有义务披露的信息**。——证券交易委员会应于《多德—弗兰克华尔街改革与消费者保护法》颁布之日后270天之内,发布最终规则,要求每名资源采掘发行人在其年报中提供相关信息,说明该资源采掘发行人、其子公司或其所控制的实体就石油、天然气或矿物的商业开发向外国政府或联邦政府支付的任何款项,包括——

(i)为资源采掘发行人每一关于石油、天然气或矿物商业开发的项目支付的款项的类型和总额;及

(ii)向每一政府支付的上述款项的类型和总额。

(B)**规则制定过程中的磋商**。——在根据第(A)子款发布规则之时,证券交易委员会可以与其判定具有相关性的任何机关或实体进行磋商。

(C)**交互式数据格式**。——根据第(A)子款发布的规则应当要求资源采掘发行人以交互式数据格式提交年度报告中包含的信息。

(D)**交互式数据标准**。——

(i)**一般规定**。——根据第(A)子款发布的规则应当为资源采掘发行人的年度报告中包含的信息设定交互式数据标准。

(ii)**电子标签**。——交互式数据标准应当包含电子标签,用以识别资源采掘发行人向外国政府或联邦政府支付的任何款项的下述信息——

government or the Federal Government —

"(I) the total amounts of the payments, by category;

"(II) the currency used to make the payments;

"(III) the financial period in which the payments were made;

"(IV) the business segment of the resource extraction issuer that made the payments;

"(V) the government that received the payments, and the country in which the government is located;

"(VI) the project of the resource extraction issuer to which the payments relate; and

"(VII) such other information as the Commission may determine is necessary or appropriate in the public interest or for the protection of investors.

"(E) INTERNATIONAL TRANSPARENCY EFFORTS. — To the extent practicable, the rules issued under subparagraph (A) shall support the commitment of the Federal Government to international transparency promotion efforts relating to the commercial development of oil, natural gas, or minerals.

"(F) EFFECTIVE DATE. — With respect to each resource extraction issuer, the final rules issued under subparagraph (A) shall take effect on the date on which the resource extraction issuer is required to submit an annual report relating to the fiscal year of the resource extraction issuer that ends not earlier than 1 year after the date on which the Commission issues final rules under subparagraph (A).

"(3) PUBLIC AVAILABILITY OF INFORMATION. —

"(A) IN GENERAL. — To the extent practicable, the Commission shall make available online, to the public, a compilation of the information required to be submitted under the rules issued under paragraph (2)(A).

"(B) OTHER INFORMATION. — Nothing in this paragraph shall require the Commission to make available online information other than the information required to be submitted under the rules issued under paragraph (2)(A).

"(4) AUTHORIZATION OF APPROPRIATIONS. — There are authorized to be appropriated to the Commission such sums as may be necessary to carry out this subsection.".

SEC. 1505. STUDY BY THE COMPTROLLER GENERAL.

(a) IN GENERAL. — Not later than 1 year after the date of enactment of this Act, the Comptroller General of the United States shall issue a report assessing the relative independence, effectiveness, and expertise of presidentially appointed inspectors general and inspectors general of designated Federal entities, as such term is defined under section 8G of the Inspector General Act of 1978, and the effects on independence of the amendments to the Inspector General Act of 1978 made by this Act.

(b) REPORT. — The report required by subsection (a) shall be issued to the Committees

(I)款项总额(按类分列);

(II)付款货币;

(III)付款所在的财务期间;

(IV)作为付款方的资源采掘发行人的业务分部;

(V)作为收款方的政府以及政府所在国家;

(VI)与付款有关的资源采掘发行人的项目;及

(VII)证券交易委员会可能判定的,对保护投资者或公共利益所必要或适当的其他信息。

(E)**国际透明度促进工作**。——在可行范围内,依据第(A)子款发布的规则应当支持联邦政府针对石油、天然气或矿物商业开发作出的,促进国际透明度的承诺。

(F)**生效日**。——对于每名资源采掘发行人而言,依据第(A)子款发布的最终规则均应于该发行人有义务就其在证券交易委员会发布该等规则1年(含)后结束的会计年度提交年度报告之日生效。

(3)**信息的公开提供**。——

(A)**一般规定**。——在可行范围内,证券交易委员会应通过网络向公众在线公开依据第(2)(A)款发布的规则要求提交的信息之汇编。

(B)**其他信息**。——除依据第(2)(A)款发布的规则要求提交的信息之外,本款不要求证券交易委员会在线公开任何信息。

(4)**拨款授权**。——兹授权向证券交易委员会拨付执行本子条规定所需的必要金额。”

第1505条　政府问责办公室主任的研究

(a)**一般规定**。——政府问责办公室主任应于本法颁布之日后1年内发布1份报告,评估总统任命的监察长以及指定联邦实体(定义见《1978年监察长法》第8G条)的监察长的相对独立性、工作成效和专长,以及本法对《1978年监察长法》所做修正对其独立性的影响。

(b)**报告**。——第(a)子条规定的报告应向众议院金融服务委员会、众议院监督和

on Financial Services and Oversight and Government Reform of the House of Representatives and the Committees on Banking, Housing, and Urban Affairs and Homeland Security and Governmental Affairs of the Senate.

SEC. 1506. STUDY ON CORE DEPOSITS AND BROKERED DEPOSITS.

(a) STUDY.—The Corporation shall conduct a study to evaluate—

(1) the definition of core deposits for the purpose of calculating the insurance premiums of banks;

(2) the potential impact on the Deposit Insurance Fund of revising the definitions of brokered deposits and core deposits to better distinguish between them;

(3) an assessment of the differences between core deposits and brokered deposits and their role in the economy and banking sector of the United States;

(4) the potential stimulative effect on local economies of redefining core deposits; and

(5) the competitive parity between large institutions and community banks that could result from redefining core deposits.

(b) REPORT TO CONGRESS.— Not later than 1 year after the date of enactment of this Act, the Corporation shall submit to the Committee on Banking, Housing, and Urban Affairs of the Senate and the Committee on Financial Services of the House of Representatives a report on the results of the study under subsection (a) that includes legislative recommendations, if any, to address concerns arising in connection with the definitions of core deposits and brokered deposits.

政府改革委员会、参议院银行、住房与城市事务委员会以及参议院国土安全和政府事务委员会提交。

第1506条 关于核心存款和经纪存款的研究

(a)**研究**。——联邦存款保险公司应开展研究,以评价——

(1)计算银行保费之时使用的核心存款之定义;

(2)为了更明确地区分经纪存款和核心存款而修订二者的定义对存款保险基金的潜在影响;

(3)核心存款和经纪存款之间的差额的评估,及其在美国经济和银行业中起到的作用;

(4)重新定义核心存款对地方经济的潜在刺激作用;及

(5)重新定义核心存款之后,大型机构和社区银行之间可能形成的竞争对等地位。

(b)**向国会提交报告**。——联邦存款保险公司应于本法颁布之日后1年内,针对依据第(a)子款开展的研究之结果,向参议院银行、住房与城市事务委员会以及众议院金融服务委员会提交1份报告;如联邦存款保险公司针对核心存款和经纪存款的定义引发的问题提出了立法建议,该等立法建议亦应纳入报告之中。

TITLE XVI—SECTION 1256 CONTRACTS

SEC. 1601. CERTAIN SWAPS, ETC. , NOT TREATED AS SECTION 1256 CONTRACTS.

(a) IN GENERAL. — Subsection (b) of section 1256 of the Internal Revenue Code of 1986 is amended —

(1) by redesignating paragraphs (1) through (5) as subparagraphs (A) through (E), respectively, and by indenting such subparagraphs (as so redesignated) accordingly,

(2) by striking "For purposes of " and inserting the following:

"(1) IN GENERAL. — For purposes of ", and

(3) by striking the last sentence and inserting the following new paragraph:

"(2) EXCEPTIONS. — The term 'section 1256 contract' shall not include —

"(A) any securities futures contract or option on such a contract unless such contract or option is a dealer securities futures contract, or

"(B) any interest rate swap, currency swap, basis swap, interest rate cap, interest rate floor, commodity swap, equity swap, equity index swap, credit default swap, or similar agreement. ".

(b) EFFECTIVE DATE. — The amendments made by this section shall apply to taxable years beginning after the date of the enactment of this Act.

Speaker of the House of Representatives.

Vice President of the United States and
President of the Senate.

第十六编——第1256条规定的合约

第1601条　不视同第1256条规定的合约的特定互换等

(a)**一般规定**。——《1986年国内税收法典》第1256条第(b)子条修正如下——

(1)第(1)款至第(5)款分别重新编号为第(A)子款到第(E)子款,并且相应调整该等重新编号后的子款的缩进距离;

(2)删除“就本子编而言”,替以如下内容:

“(1)**一般规定**。——就本子编而言”,及

(3)删除最后一句,替以如下新款:

“(2)**例外规定**。——‘第1256条规定的合约’一词不包括——

(A)任何证券期货合约或者该等合约的期权,但该等合约或期权属于交易商证券期货合约的除外;或

(B)任何利率互换、货币互换、基差互换、利率上限期权、利率下限期权、商品互换、股权互换、股权指数互换、信用违约互换或类似协议。”

(b)**生效日**。——本条作出的修正应适用于起始日在本法颁布之日后的各纳税年度。

众议院议长

美国副总统兼参议院议长

Glossary 词汇表

Abusive swap	滥用性互换
Accelerated filer	加速报告人
Acceptance of securities	证券承兑
Acceptances	承兑汇票
Accredited investor	获许投资者
Accreted original issue discount	原始发行折价增值
Actual direct compensatory damages	实际直接损害赔偿/实际直接损害赔偿金
Administrative hearing	行政听证
Affiliate	关联方
Affiliate transactions	关联交易
Affiliated group	关联集团
Affiliations	关联关系
Agency consultation	机关磋商
Agency ombudsman	机关监察专员
Agricultural swap	农产品互换
Alaska Native Claims Settlement Act	《阿拉斯加原住民土地权处理法》
Allocated transaction	分配交易
Alternating examinations	替代性检查
Alternative Mortgage Transaction Parity Act of 1982	《1982 年另类抵押贷款交易平价法》
Anti-deficiency law	禁止追索差额法律
Antievasion	反规避
Antitrust laws	反垄断法律
Appropriate congressional committees	相应的国会委员会
Appropriate Federal banking agency	相应的联邦银行业监管机关
Appropriate financial regulator	相应的金融监管者
Arbitrage	套利
Armed group	武装团体
Assessment	计征费/计征款项/评估
Assessment base	计征基数

续表

Asset-threshold	资产门槛
Associated person of a securities holding company	证券控股公司关联人
Associated person of a swap dealer or major swap participant	互换交易商或主要互换参与者的业务相关人
Assuming insurer	再保险分入公司
Attachment	扣押令/扣押
Attestation	鉴证/证明
Attorney General	总检察长
Authority to enforce contracts	合约的强制执行权
Automated clearinghouse system	自动结算所系统
Average prime offer rate	平均最优惠利率
Avoidable transfers	可撤销的转让
Backup authority	后备权力
Back-up examination	后备检查权
Balance sheet	资产负债表
Balanced Budget and Emergency Deficit Control Act of 1985	《1985 年平衡预算和紧急赤字控制法》
Balloon payments	大额尾付
Bank Enterprise Act of 1991	《1991 年银行企业法》
Bank holding company	银行控股公司
Bank Holding Company Act Amendments of 1970	《1970 年银行控股公司法修正案》
Bank Holding Company Act of 1956	《1956 年银行控股公司法》
Bank Merger Act	《银行兼并法》
Bank Service Company Act	《银行服务公司法》
Banking entity	银行实体
Banking supervisors	银行监督官
Bankruptcy Code	《破产法》
Baseline	基本情形/基准/基础
Basis swap	基差互换
Block trades	大宗交易
Board of Governors	联邦储备委员会

续表

Board of trade	交易场所
Bona fide hedge positions	真正的套期保值持仓
Bretton Woods Agreements Act	《布雷顿森林协定法》
Bridge financial company	过渡金融公司
Bridge loan	过桥贷款
Broker	经纪商/经纪人
Broker licensing	经纪人执照
Brokerage	经纪费/经纪/经纪业务
Bureau of Consumer Financial Protection	消费者金融保护局
Bureau of Economic Analysis	经济分析局
Call	看涨期权/召集/需求
Capital adequacy	资本充足性
Capital stock and surplus	股本和资本公积金
Casualty insurance	意外险
Catalog of finacial entities and instruments	金融实体和工具目录
Cause of action	诉因
Cease and desist order	制止令
Cease-and-desist proceeding	制止令程序
Ceding insurer	再保险分出公司
Census tract	人口普查区
Central Registration Depository	集中注册信息存管系统
Certificate of deposit	存单
Certified Risk Manager/CRM	注册风险管理经理
Chapter	章
Chartered Property and Casualty Underwriter/CPCU	特许财产及意外险核保人
Chief compliance officer	首席合规官
Child Nutrition Act Of 1966	《1966 年儿童营养法》
Claims for damages for repudiation	拒绝履约赔偿请求权
Clayton Act	《克莱顿法》
Clearing agency	结算机构
Cohort default rate	群体违约比率

续表

Commercial paper	商业票据
Commercial risk	商业风险
Committee on Banking, Housing, and Urban Affairs of the Senate	参议院银行、住房与城市事务委员会
Committee on Financial Services of the House of Representatives	众议院金融服务委员会
Committee on the Judiciary of the House of Representatives	众议院司法委员会
Committee on the Judiciary of the Senate	参议院司法委员会
Commodity broker	商品经纪商
Commodity Futures Trading Commission	商品期货交易委员会
Commodity pool	商品基金
Commodity pool operator	商品基金管理人
Commodity swap	商品互换
Commodity trading advisor	商品交易顾问
Common stock	普通股
Commonwealth	准州
Community Development Banking and Financial Institutions Act of 1994	《1994 年社区发展银行与金融机构法》
Community development financial institution	社区发展金融机构
Community Reinvestment Act of 1977	《1977 年社区再投资法》
Compensation Committee	薪酬委员会
Compliance examiners	合规检查员
Compliance office	合规办公室
Component of Tier 1 capital	一级资本构成要素
Components of capital	资本构成要素
Compromise of action	诉讼妥协
Comptroller General of the United States	政府问责办公室主任
Comptroller of the Currency	货币监理署署长
Concentration limit	集中度限制
Concentrations in assets	资产集中
Conflict minerals	冲突矿物

续表

Consolidated supervision	并表监管
Consumer Financial Protection Fund	消费者金融保护基金
Consumer Handbook on Adjustable Rate Mortgages	《可调利率抵押贷款消费者手册》
Consumer Leasing Act of 1976	《1976 年消费者租赁法》
Contingent capital	或有资本
Contract proposals	合同建议书
Contractor	承包商/缔约人
Contracts to extend credit	授信合同
Cost and availability of credit in the United States	美国信贷成本和可获得性
Coupon book	宣传册
Covered agreement	所涉协定
Covered assistance	所涉补助金
Covered employee	所涉员工
Covered financial company	所涉金融公司
Cranston-Gonzalez National Affordable Housing Act	《克兰斯顿—冈塞雷斯国家住房国家住房保障法》
Credit card	信用卡
Credit card bank	信用卡银行
Credit default swap	信用违约互换
Credit exposure	信用风险敞口
Credit facility	信贷安排
Credit for reinsurance	再保险信用
Credit market	信贷市场
Credit risk	信用风险
Credit risk retention	信用风险自留
Credit spread	信贷息差
Credit swap	信贷互换
Credit union	信贷联盟
Crime Control Act of 1990	《1990 年犯罪控制法》
Cross-currency rate swap	跨货币利率互换
Cross-guarantees	交叉担保

续表

Currency swap	货币互换
CUSIP number	库斯普编号
Customer name securities	客户名下证券
Damages for pain and suffering	疼痛和精神痛苦赔偿
Data Center	数据中心
De minimis investment	微量投资
Debit card	借记卡
Debt index swap	债务指数互换
Debt swap	债务互换
Default	违约
Defense to foreclosure	止赎抗辩
Defenses	抗辩
Deferred compensation	递延薪酬
Department of Housing and Urban Development	住房与城市发展部
Department of Justice	司法部
Deposit insurance	存款保险
Depository institution	存款机构
Depository institution holding company	存款机构控股公司
Depository Institutions Management Interlocks Act	《禁止存款机构管理层交叉任职法》
Deposit-taking activity	吸收存款活动
Derivative transaction	衍生品交易
Derivative transactions in lending	衍生品交易借贷
Derivatives clearing organization	衍生品结算组织
Designated automated teller machine network	指定自动取款机网络
Designated clearing entity	指定结算实体
Designated financial market utility	指定金融市场服务平台
Designated transfer date	指定转移日
Director of the Federal Insurance Office	联邦保险办公室主任
Director of the Office of Thrift Supervision	储蓄机构监理局局长
Disclosure exemption	披露豁免
Discount window	贴现窗口

续表

Disruptive practices	扰乱性做法
District of Columbia savings and loan association	哥伦比亚特区储贷协会
Divestiture order	资产剥离令
Dual registration	双重注册
Dual service	双重任职
Electronic conduit services	电子渠道服务
Electronic debit transaction	电子借记交易
Electronic Fund Transfer Act	《电子资金划拨法》
Electronic Signatures in Global and National Commerce Act	《全球暨全美商业电子签章法》
Eligible bankers' acceptances	适格银行承兑汇票
Eligible contract participant	适格合约参与者
Emergency Economic Stabilization Act of 2008	《2008 年紧急经济稳定法》
Emergency Exception	紧急例外规定
Emergency Homeowners' Relief Act	《紧急业主救济法》
Emissions swap	排放互换
Employer's contribution	雇主缴款
Endorsement	背书
Energy Information Administration	能源信息署
Energy swap	能源互换
Enhancing Financial Institution Safety and Soundness Act of 2010	《2010 年金融机构安全性与稳健性改良法》
Equal Credit Opportunity Act	《信贷机会平等法》
Equitable remedies	衡平救济
Equity index swap	股指互换
Equity swap	股权互换
Event contract	事件合约
Excess funds	过剩资金
Exchange facilitator	交易中介
Executive Schedule	高级公务员序列
Exempt commercial purchaser	豁免商业购买人

续表

Exempt tax status	税收豁免地位
Existing retirement plan	既存退休计划
Expedited Funds Availability Act	《加速资金到位法》
Expedition	加急处理
Externally audited financial statement	经外部审计的财务报表
Failure to deliver shares sold short	卖空股份交割失信
Fair And Accurate Credit Transactions Act of 2003	《2003 年公平准确信用交易法》
Fair Credit Billing Act	《公平信用结账法》
Fair Credit Reporting Act	《公平信用报告法》
Fair Debt Collection Practices Act	《公平债务催收作业法》
Fair Housing Act	《公平住房法》
False Claims Act	《反欺骗政府法》
Family office	家族理财室
Fannie Mae	房利美
Farm Credit Act of 1971	《1971 年农业信贷法》
Farm Credit Administration	农业信贷管理局
Farm Credit System institution	农业信贷系统机构
Federal Advisory Committee Act/FACA	《联邦顾问委员会法》
Federal Agricultural Mortgage Corporation	联邦农业抵押贷款公司
Federal Aviation Act of 1958	《1958 年联邦民航法》
Federal Banking Agency	联邦银行业监管机关
Federal Deposit Insurance Act	《联邦存款保险法》
Federal Deposit Insurance Corporation	联邦存款保险公司
Federal Deposit Insurance Corporation Improvement Act of 1991	《1991 年联邦存款保险公司改良法》
Federal depository institution	联邦存款机构
Federal Employee Retirement Program	联邦雇员退休计划
Federal Energy Regulatory Commission	联邦能源监管委员会
Federal financial regulatory agency	联邦金融监管机关
Federal Home Loan Bank	联邦住房贷款银行
Federal Home Loan Bank Act	《联邦住房贷款银行法》

续表

Federal Home Loan Mortgage Corporation	联邦住房贷款抵押公司
Federal Housing Enterprises Financial Safety and Soundness Act of 1992	《1992 年联邦住房企业财务安全和稳健法》
Federal Housing Finance Agency	联邦住房金融局
Federal Insurance Office	联邦保险办公室
Federal Insurance Office Act of 2010	《2010 年联邦保险办公室法》
Federal National Mortgage Association	联邦国民抵押贷款协会
Federal Power Act	《联邦电力法》
Federal Property and Administrative Services Act of 1949	《1949 年联邦财产和行政服务法》
Federal Register	《联邦公报》
Federal Reserve Act	《联邦储备法》
Federal Reserve System Retirement Plan	联邦储备系统退休计划
Federal Reserve System Thrift Plan	联邦储备系统节俭计划
Federal Rules of Civil Procedure	《联邦民事诉讼规则》
Federal savings association	联邦储蓄协会
Federal Sentencing Guidelines	《联邦量刑指引》
Federal Trade Commission Act	《联邦贸易委员会法》
Federally Recognized Indian Tribe List Act of 1994	《1994 年联邦政府承认的印第安人部落清单法》
Fellowship program	英才计划
Fiduciary duty	受信义务
Filing date	破产申请日/报批日期/申报日期
Finance Board	金融委员会
Financial Accounting Statements	《财务会计准则公告》
Financial company	金融公司
Financial company reference database	金融公司参考数据库
Financial contract	金融合约
Financial decline	财务困境
Financial guarantee	金融担保
Financial holding company	金融控股公司
Financial Industry Regulatory Authority, FINRA	金融业监管局

续表

Financial Institutions Reform, Recovery, and Enforcement Act of 1989	《1989 年金融机构改革、复兴与实施法》
Financial Institutions Retirement Fund	金融机构退休基金
Financial Institutions Supervisory Act of 1966	《1966 年金融机构监管法》
Financial instrument	金融工具
Financial integrity	财务完整性
Financial literacy	金融扫盲/金融素养
Financial Literacy and Education Commission	金融扫盲和教育委员会
Financial Literacy and Education Improvement Act	《金融素养和教育改进法》
Financial market utilities	金融市场服务平台
Financial planners	金融理财师
Financial Privacy Act of 1978	《1978 年金融隐私权法》
Financial Research Fund	金融研究基金
Financial Stability Act of 2010	《2010 年金融稳定法》
Financial Stability Oversight Council	金融稳定监督委员会
Financial statement	财务报表
Financial transaction data	金融交易数据
Financing Corporation, and the Resolution Funding Corporation	融资公司以及清盘融资公司
Financing priority	融资优先性
Flood Disaster Protection Act of 1973	《1973 年洪水灾害防御法》
Floor broker	场内经纪商
Floor trader	场内交易商
Food and Nutrition Act Of 2008	《2008 年食品和营养法》
Foreign bank	外国银行
Foreign exchange forward	外汇远期
Foreign exchange swap	外汇互换
Foreign nonbank financial company	外国非银行金融公司
Foreign private adviser	外国私人顾问
Forward contract	远期合约
Forward-looking indicator	前瞻性指标

续表

Fraudulent transfers	欺诈性转让
Freddie Mac	房地美
Freedom of Information Act	《信息自由法》
Fully indexed rate	完全指数利率
Functionally regulated subsidiary	受制于功能监管的子公司
Futures	期货
Futures and options contracts	期货和期权合约
Futures commission merchant	期货经纪商
General Accounting Office; / GAO	政府问责办公室
Global Analyst Research Settlements	《全球分析师研究协议》
Global and National Commerce Act	《全球暨全美商业电子签章法》
Global Risk Management Institute	全球风险管理学会
Golden parachute benefits	金色降落伞福利
Government bond	政府债券
Government National Mortgage Association	美国政府国民抵押贷款协会
Graduated assessment rate	计征费分级费率
Gramm-Leach-Bliley Act	《格雷姆—里奇—比利雷法》
Grandfather Provision	不溯及既往条款
Guarantee	保函/担保/保证
Guaranteed investment contract	担保投资合约
Hart-Scott-Rodino Filing Requirement	《哈特—斯科—罗迪诺反垄断改进法》
Hazard insurance	灾害险
Hedge fund	对冲基金
Hedge transaction	套期保值交易
Helping Families Save Their Homes Act of 2009	《2009 年协助家庭保全房屋法》
Higher Education Act of 1965	《1965 年高等教育法》
High-frequency trading	高频交易
Home Affordable Modification Program Guidlines	《可负担房贷修改计划》
Home Mortgage Disclosure Act of 1975	《1975 年住房抵押贷款披露法》
Home Owners Protection Act of 1998	《1998 年业主保护法》
Home Owners' Loan Act	《业主贷款法》

续表

Home Ownership and Equity Protection Act of 1994	《1994 年住房所有权和房屋权益保护法》
Home Valuation Code of Conduct	《住房估值行为守则》
Homeowner's insurance	业主险
Housing Act of 1948	《1948 年住房法》
Housing and Community Development Act of 1992	《1992 年住房与社区发展法》
Housing and Urban-Rural Recovery Act of 1983	《1983 年住房与城乡复苏法》
HUD-approved counseling agency	住房与城市发展部批准的咨询机构
Hybrid capital instrument	混合资本工具
Illiquid fund	非流动性基金
Implementation expenses	实施费用
Independent director	独立董事
Independently procured insurance	独立购买的保险
Industrial bank	产业银行
Inflation swap	通货膨胀互换
Insider	内幕人士
Insolvency	资不抵债
Inspector General Act of 1978	《1978 年监察长法》
Institution of higher education	高等教育机构
Insurance commissioner	保险监督官
Insurance for Noninterest-Bearing Transaction Accounts	无息交易账户保险
Insurance Institute of America	美国保险学会
Insurance of transaction accounts	交易账户保险
Insured bank	参保银行
Insured branch	参保分支机构/参保分行
Insured depository institution	参保存款机构
Interactive data format	交互式数据格式
Interactive data standard	交互式数据标准
Interchange transaction fee	跨行手续费
Interest rate swap	利率互换
Interested parties	利害关系人

续表

Intermediate Holding Company	中间控股公司
Internal Revenue Code of 1986	《1986 年国内税收法典》
International Banking Act of 1978	《1978 年国际银行法》
International Lending Supervision Act of 1983	《1983 年国际贷款监管法》
International Swap Regulation	国际互换监管
Interstate Land Sales Full Disclosure Act	《州际土地销售完全披露法》
Introducing broker	介绍经纪商
Invalid dividends	无效股息
Investment adviser	投资顾问
Investment Adviser Registration Depository system	投资顾问注册信息存管系统
Investment Advisers Act of 1940	《1940 年投资顾问法》
Investment company	投资公司
Investment Company Act of 1940	《1940 年投资公司法》
Ipso Facto Clauses	破产约定条款
Irrevocable	不可撤销
Judicial discretion	司法自由裁量权
Judicial review	司法审查
Judicial stay	司法中止
Junior lien	次位留置权
Jury	陪审团
Large financial institution	大型金融机构
Large swap trader reporting	互换大户报告
Late fee	滞纳金
Leasehold interest	承租权益
Legal Certainty for Bank Products Act of 2000	《2000 年银行产品法律确定性法》
Letters of credit	信用证
Leverage	杠杆/杠杆率
Leverage capital	杠杆资本
Leverage transaction merchant	杠杆交易商
Lien	留置权
Life insurance program	寿险计划

续表

Line of credit	信用额度
Liquidation or rehabilitation	清算或整顿
Liquidity	流动性
Liquidity event	流动性事件
Liquidity measures	流动性指标
Loan-transaction coupled with a securities collar transaction	证券封顶保底交易附随的贷款交易
Long term care	长期医疗保险
Major swap participant	主要互换参与者
Mandatory regulations	强制性规章
Manufactured home	预制房
Margin loan	保证金贷款
Market discipline	市场约束
Material financial distress	重大财务困境
Maximum amount of liability	最高责任金额
McKinney-Vento Homeless Assistance Act	《麦金尼—文托无房者援助法》
Measures of the financial condition	财务状况计量指标
Member agency	成员机关
Memorandum	备忘录
Metal swap	金属互换
Minimum capital requirements	最低资本要求
Minimum leverage capital requirement	最低杠杆资本要求
Minimum reserve ratio	最低准备金率
Minimum risk-based capital requirement	最低风险基础资本要求
Minority	少数族裔/少数党
Minority-owned business	少数族裔拥有的企业
Misleading designation	误导性称号
Misleading or fraudulent marketing	误导性或欺诈性营销
Missing security holder	失去联络的证券持有人
Mitigation of risk	风险的缓释
Mixed swap	混合互换

续表

Model Regulations on the Use of Senior-Specific Certifications and Professional Designations in the Sale of Life Insurance and Annuities, Model Regulation on the Use of Senior-Specific Certifications and Professional Designations in the Sale of Life Insurance and Annuities	《美国保险监督官协会关于在人寿保险和年金销售中面向老年人的认证和专业称号的使用示范管理办法》
Model Rule on the Use of Senior-Specific Certifications and Professional Designations	《北美证券管理者协会关于面向老年人的认证和专业称号的使用示范规则》
Modular home	模块化房屋
Money damages	金钱损害赔偿
Mortgage loan	抵押贷款
Municipal advisor	市政顾问
Municipal securities dealer	市政证券自营商
Mutual Fund	共同基金
Narrow-based security index	窄基证券指数
NASAA Model Rule on the Use of Senior-Specific Certifications and Professional Designations	《北美证券管理者协会关于面向老年人的认证和专业称号的使用示范规则》
National Alliance for Insurance Education & Research	全国保险教育和研究联盟
national banking association	国民银行协会
National Credit Union Administration Board	国家信贷联盟署委员会
National Credit Union Share Insurance Fund	国家信贷联盟股份保险基金
National Endowment for the Humanities	全国人文基金会
National Endowment of the Arts	全国艺术基金会
National Housing Act	《国民住房法》
National member bank	国民成员银行
National nonmember bank	国民非成员银行
National securities exchange	全国性证券交易所
National Strategy for Financial Literacy	《全国金融扫盲战略》
National treatment	国民待遇
Nationally recognized statistical rating organization	全国公认统计评级组织
Natural Gas Act	《天然气法》
Negative amortization	负值摊还本金

续表

Neighborhood Reinvestment Corporation Act	《社区再投资公司法》
Net amount of insurance payable	应付保险净额
Net equity	权益净额
Net present value	净现值
Network fee	网络费用
Nonadmitted and Reinsurance Reform Act of 2010	《2010年非本州监管保险和再保险改革法》
Non-Admitted Insurance Model Act	《非本州监管保险示范法》
Nonadmitted premium taxes	非本州监管保险的保费税金
Nonbank financial company	非银行金融公司
Nonbank financial company supervised by the Board of Governors	受联邦储备委员会监管的非银行金融公司
Non-cleared option	非集中结算的期权
Non-cleared security-based swap	非集中结算的基于证券的互换
Noninterest-bearing transaction account	无息交易账户
Nonprofit organization	非营利组织
Non-United States insurer	非美国保险公司
North American Securities Administrators Association/NASAA	北美证券管理者协会
Notice of deficiencies	缺陷通知
Off-balance-sheet activities	表外活动
Off-balance-sheet exposures	表外风险敞口/表外风险
Off-balance-sheet item	表外项目
Office of Credit Ratings	信用评级办公室
Office of Financial Protection for Older Americans	老年美国人金融保护办公室
Office of Financial Research	金融研究办公室
Office of Personnel Management	人事管理局
Office of Service Member Affairs	现役军人事务办公室
Office of the Comptroller of the Currency	货币监理署
Office of the Investor Advocate	投资者维权办公室
Office of Thrift Supervision	储蓄机构监理局
Officer of the United States	联邦官员

续表

Ombudsman	监察专员
Omnibus Appropriations Act, 2009	《2009 年综合拨款法》
Open repurchase agreement	开放式回购协议
Open reverse repurchase agreement	开放式逆回购协议
Option	期权
Options contract	期权合约
Orderly liquidation	有序清算
Orderly Liquidation Fund	有序清算基金
Overall risk management	整体风险管理
Packers and Stockyards Act, 1921	《1921 年包装食品生产厂及牲畜围栏法》
Paperwork Reduction Act	《文书削减法》
Paragraph	款
Pay It Back Act	《还款法》
Paying agent	付款代理人
Payment card network	支付卡网络
Payment, Clearing, and Settlement Supervision Act of 2010	《2010 年支付、清算和结算监管法》
Permissive Regulation	选择性规章
Person regulated by the Farm Credit Administration	受农业信贷管理局监管的主体
Phased retirement	阶段性退休
Points and fees	点数和费用
Portfolio margining account of a customer	客户投资组合保证金
Position accountability	持仓说明制度
Position data	持仓数据
Position limitations	持仓限额/限仓制度
Preferential transfers	偏颇性转让
Premium tax	保费税金
Prepaid securities forward transaction	预付证券远期交易
Prepaid variable forward contract	预付可变远期合约
Prepayment penalties	提前还款违约金
Primary financial regulatory agency	优先金融监管机关

续表

Primary Financial Regulatory Agency Inspector General	优先金融监管机关监察长
Prime brokerage transaction	大宗经纪交易
Principal office	主要办公场所
Principal place of business	主要营业地
Prior review	事先审查
Privacy Act of 1974	《1974 年隐私权法》
Private Education Loan Ombudsman	个人教育贷款监察官
Private Equity Fund	私募股权基金
Private Fund Investment Advisers Registration Act of 2010	《2010 年私募基金投资顾问注册法》
Private right of action	私人诉讼权利
Private Securities Litigation Act of 1995	《1995 年私人证券诉讼法》
Privilege	优先权/特权/会员权/保密特权
Procedure for expedited relief	加速救济程序
Procyclical assessments	顺周期计征费
Property interest	房产权益
Proprietary trading	自营交易
Proprietary trading in derivatives	衍生品自营交易
Protecting Tenants at Foreclosure Act	《止赎时承租人权益保护法》
Prudential standards	审慎性标准
Public Company Accounting Over sight Board	公众公司会计监督委员会
Public debt transactions	公共债务交易
Public disclosure	公开披露
Public Utility Holding Company Act of 1935	《1935 年公用事业控股公司法》
Punitive or exemplary damages	惩罚性赔偿金
Put	看跌期权
Qualified risk manager	合格风险经理
Rate cap	利率上限期权
Rate collar	保护性封顶保底利率期权
Rate floor	利率下限期权

续表

Real Estate Settlement Procedures	《1974年房地产结算程序法》
Real Estate Settlement Procedures Act of 1974	《1974年房地产结算程序法》
ReaL-time public reporting	实时公开报告
Recording tax	登记税
Reemployed annuitants	返聘年金受益人
Regulation	管理办法/规章/监管/法规
Regulatory capital	监管资本
Reinsurance	再保险
Related action	关联诉讼
Related person	关联主体
Reporting systems for risks to the financial stability of the United States	美国金融稳定的风险指标和报告系统
Repudiate contracts	拒绝履约
Repurchase agreement	回购协议
Rescission	撤销
Research and Analysis Center	研究分析中心
Reserve ratio	准备金率
Resolution mechanisms	清盘机制
Resolution plan	清盘计划
Resolution Trust Corporation	清盘信托公司
Resource extraction issuer	资源采掘发行人
Restitution remedies	恢复原状救济
Retail foreign exchange transactions	零售外汇交易
Retail transactions	零售交易
Retention of records	记录留存
Reverse mortgage	反向抵押贷款
Reverse repurchase agreement	逆回购协议
Revesting of assets	资产的重新占有
Revised Statutes of the United States	《美国制定法汇编》(修订版)
Richard B. Russell National School Lunch Act	《理查·B.罗素全国学校午餐法》
Right to Financial Privacy Act of 1978	《1978年金融隐私权法》

续表

Risk Committee	风险委员会
Risk management expert	风险管理专家
Risk participations in bankers' acceptance	银行承兑汇票的风险参与
Risk profile	风险特征
Risk-based capital	风险基础资本
Safe harbor	安全港
Sale and repurchase agreement	出售和回购协议
Sale or securitization of loan	贷款的出售或证券化
Sarbanes-Oxley Act of 2002	《2002 年萨班斯—奥克斯法》
Savings and loan holding company	储贷控股公司
Savings association	储蓄协会
Savings clause	保留条款
Savings provisions	保留条款
Secretary of Health and Human Services	卫生及公共服务部部长
Secretary of the Treasury	财政部部长
Section	条
Secure and Fair Enforcement/S. A. F. E. for Mortgage Licensing Act of 2008	《2008 年安全和公平执行抵押贷款发起人许可法》
Secured creditor haircuts	有担保债权人本金折价
Securities and Exchange Commission	证券交易委员会
Securities borrowing and lending transaction	融券交易
Securities contract	证券合约
Securities Exchange Act of 1934	《1934 年证券交易法》
Securities fraud offense	证券欺诈犯罪
Securities holding company	证券控股公司
Securities Investor Protection Act of 1970	《1970 年证券投资者保护法》
Securities Investor Protection Corporation/SIPC	证券投资者保护公司
Securities laws	证券法/证券法律
Securitized product	证券化产品
Security-based swap	证券类互换
Security-based swap data repository	证券类互换数据存管机构

续表

Security-based swap dealer	证券类互换交易商
Security-based swap execution facility	证券类互换执行设施
Self-regulatory organizations	自律组织
Self-reported error	自报失误
Senior executives	高级公务员/高级管理人员/高管
Senior liability	优先债务
Separate resolution	单独清盘/单独决议
Separately accounted	单独核算
Service periods	工龄
Setoff	抵销
Share insurance	股份保险
Short-swing profit reporting	短线收益报告
Short-term debt	短期债务
Significant bank holding company	重要非银行金融公司
Significant nonbank financial company	重要银行控股公司
Significant price discovery	重要价格发现
Single security	单一证券
Small Bank Holding Company Policy Statement of the Board of Governors	《联邦储备委员会关于小型银行控股公司的政策声明》
Small Business Act	《小型企业法》
Small Business Investment Act of 1958	《1958 年小型企业投资法》
Small business loan	小型企业贷款
Source of strength	财务后盾
Special Committee on Aging of the Senate	参议院老龄问题特别委员会
Special financial resolution court	特殊金融清盘法庭
Spoofing	电子欺诈
Stable value contract	稳定价值合约
Standard maximum cash advance amount	最高预付标准现金额
Standby letters of credit	备用信用证
State bank	州银行
State depository institution	州存款机构

续表

State housing finance agency	州住房融资机构
State insurance regulator	州保险监管者
State member bank	州成员银行
State nonmember bank	州非成员银行
State savings association	州储蓄协会
State -chartered corporation	特许注册公司
Statutory disqualification	法定失格
Statute of limitations	诉讼时效
Statutory Pay-As-You-Go-Act of 2010	《法定 2010 年财政收支平衡法》
Stock borrowed agreement	股票借入协议
Stockbroker	股票经纪商
Straddle	跨式期权组合
Stress test	压力测试
Subcontractor	分包商
Subparagraph	子款
Subpoena	传票
Subsection	子条
Subsidiary	子公司
Substantial position	大额持仓
Subtilte	子编
Suitability in Annuity Transactions Model Regulation of the National Association of Insurance Commissioners	《美国保险监督官协会关于在人寿保险和年金销售中面向老年人的认证和专业称号的使用示范管理办法》
Sunset	日落条款
Supervised securities holding company	受监管证券控股公司
Surplus lines broker	非本州监管保险的经纪人
Swap	互换
Swap agreement	互换协议
Swap data repository	互换数据存管机构
Swap dealer	互换交易商
Swap execution facility	互换执行设施
Swaps entity	互换实体

续表

Systemic risk	系统性风险
Systemic risk regulators	系统性风险监管者
Systemically important	系统重要性
Systemwide risk levels and patterns	系统性风险水平和模式
Tax qualified status	税惠资格
Tax-exempt securities	免税证券
Technical and Professional Advisory Committee	技术与专业顾问委员会
Telemarketing and Consumer Fraud and Abuse Prevention Act	《电话营销与消费者欺诈及滥用防范法》
Territory	属地
Terrorism Risk Insurance Act of 2002	《2002 年恐怖主义风险保险法》
Testimony by the chairperson	主席证词
The Bank Service Company Act	《银行服务公司法》
The Office of Financial Education	金融教育办公室
Title	编
Total consolidated assets	并表资产总额
Total return swap	总回报互换
Trading account	交易账户
Transactions in municipal securities	市政证券交易
Transfer agent	过户代理人
Transfer date	转移日
Transferor agency	职能转出机关
Transferred employee	转移雇员
Transition period	过渡期
Transition reserve ratio	过渡准备金率
Transitional provisions	过渡条款
Trust bank	信托银行
Trust Indenture Act of 1939	《1939 年信托契约法》
Trust preferred share	信托优先股份
Truth in Lending Act	《诚实信贷法》
Truth in Savings Act	《诚实储蓄法》

续表

Underwriters	承销商/贷款审核人
Uniform Standards of Professional Appraisal Practice	《专业评估执业统一标准》
Unit of general local government	一般地方政府行政分区
Unitary savings and loan holding company	单一储贷控股公司
United States Code	《美国法典》
United States District Court for the District of Columbia	哥伦比亚特区联邦地区法院
Valuation	估值
Valuation models	估值模型
Walkaway clause	走避条款
Wall Street Transparency and Accountability Act of 2010	《2010 年华尔街透明度与问责法》
Ways and Means of the House of Representatives	众议院筹款委员会
Weather swap	气候互换
Wells notification	韦尔斯通知
Whistleblower	举报人
Work papers	工作底稿
Workforce flexibility plan	弹性工作计划
Writ of Certiorari	调案复审令
Yield spread premium	利差溢价

Postscript

The Dodd-Frank Wall Street Reform and Consumer Protection Act was enacted in order to bolster the financial market system, to enhance the transparency of the financial markets and to protect the interests of financial consumers in the post-financial crisis context of the USA in 2008. This reform is the largest shakeup to happen to the American financial supervisory system since the 1930s. With the USA holding a decisive role in the global economic and financial system, the ups and downs of its domestic economy and financial industry have substantial influence on the global economy and financial industry. Consequently, to a certain extent, the reform of financial laws and regulations in the USA can influence and even guide the direction of similar reforms in other countries throughout the world. As China dedicates itself to steadily driving forward financial market reform, innovation and opening up, it is imperative to be proactive, to keep ourselves updated with the reform of the legal system in the USA financial markets and to draw experience from their sophisticated and properly designed systems and arrangements for our own development. For the aforementioned purposes, the China Securities Regulatory Commission (CSRC) has initiated the project and entrusted the Shanghai Futures Exchange to translate the Dodd-Frank Wall Street Reform and Consumer Protection Act and publish it as part of "the Digest of Legislation Related to Foreign Capital Markets" (hereinafter referred to as the "Digest").

To facilitate the implementation of the project, the Shanghai Futures Exchange has strictly observed the requirements set by the CSRC in entrusting the translation to a translation team through a bidding process and the translation review to relevant experts to ensure the quality of translation, using appropriate compensation and academic prominence as incentives throughout the project. During the bidding process, the translation team was selected based on its competence in legal translation and quality of its trial translation. In addition, the translation draft was reviewed and validated by individuals from appropriate units and divisions of and affiliated with the CSRC as well as prestigious universities. The team of reviewers, whose field of study and work experience are the most relevant to the

后　记

《多德—弗兰克华尔街改革与消费者保护法》是2008年金融危机后美国为巩固金融市场体系、提高金融市场透明度、保护金融消费者的利益而制定的，是美国"20世纪30年代以来最大规模的"金融监管制度改革法案。美国在全球经济和金融体系中具有举足轻重的地位，其国内经济和金融业的兴衰成败对全球经济和金融业具有实质性的重要影响，美国金融法律制度改革也随之在相当程度上影响甚至引导着世界各国金融法律制度改革的走向。在我国积极稳妥地推进金融市场改革创新和对外开放的背景下，我们有必要充分发挥后发优势，及时了解和关注美国金融市场法律制度改革的内容，学习和借鉴其先进、合理的制度安排，为我所用。为此，中国证监会启动并委托上海期货交易所组织翻译《多德—弗兰克华尔街改革与消费者保护法》，并将翻译成果编辑成《境外资本市场重要法律文献译丛》(以下简称《译丛》)公开出版发行。

为做好此项工作，上海期货交易所严格依照中国证监会提出的"竞标择优确定翻译人员、专家评审保证翻译质量、适当报酬和学术声誉结合激励"的要求，严把选人关、严把审校关。一方面，以法律文献翻译实力和试译稿质量为标准，采用竞标择优方式选定翻译单位；另一方面，从证监会系统相关单位、部门和知名高校推荐的"三通"专家(精通中外语言、精通中外法律、精通中外资本市场)中，抽选工作研究经历与本项目最相关的专家负责审校翻译初稿，翻译稿由两位专家负责审校，再集体讨论定稿，并由一位权威专家负责统稿审校工作。

subject matters dealt with in the project, are deemed to be linguistic experts in the concerned languages, well versed in Chinese and relevant foreign laws and having an in–depth knowledge of both Chinese and foreign capital markets. Each section of the translation was examined respectively by two experts in an independent manner and finalized after collective discussions. Their revised version was eventually submitted to an authoritative expert for final review and overall proofreading for consistency.

The Dodd–Frank Wall Street Reform and Consumer Protection Act covers an extensive range of contents and totals approximately 387,780 words. Despite the various challenges in this demanding translation project, the Shanghai Futures Exchange has been able to deliver with excellence. With the Dodd–Frank Wall Street Reform and Consumer Protection Act about to be published, as the organizer of the project, we would like to express our most sincere and profound gratitude to the following organizations and individuals. First of all, we would like to thank the Shanghai Futures Exchange for its dedication in the project, especially Chairman of the Board Mr. Yang Maijun, the Presidont and CEO Mr. Liu Nengyuan, who headed the project, Executive Vice President Mr. Xi Zhiyong, who provided constructive suggestions and insights during discussions on terminology and internal seminars, and Department of Legal Affairs and Department of International Cooperation for their invaluable professional input and technical support. Secondly, we would like to give our thanks to the translation team from Ubica Translation Center Beijing led by Ms. Chu Naiming and the panel of review including Prof. Luo Peixin. They have timely completed the translation and review with utmost diligence and professionalism. In particular, we owe our gratitude to Prof. Wu Zhipan from Peking University, who took up the overall and final review of the book despite his tight schedule. Finally, we thank the staff at Law Press·China, especially Ms. Shen Xiaoying, Ms. Chen Ni, Ms. Hu Yifang, who contributed enormously to the editing and publication of the book.

Due to the time constraints pertaining to the translation and editing work, errors and inaccuracies in the book will be inevitable. Any comments, criticism or corrections would be gratefully received.

Shanghai Futures Exchange

September, 2013

《多德—弗兰克华尔街改革与消费者保护法》涉及内容多,约387,780个英文单词,翻译难度大,但上海期货交易所克服种种困难,圆满完成了任务。在本法案翻译稿即将付梓之际,作为《译丛》的组织者,首先,我们要真诚地感谢上海期货交易所为翻译本项目付出的努力,感谢上海期货交易所理事长杨迈军先生和总经理刘能元先生亲自组织和指导本次翻译工作,感谢上海期货交易所副总经理席志勇先生多次参加本项目统稿会和内部讨论会,提出了许多非常具有建设性的建议和意见,感谢上海期货交易所法律事务部、国际合作部同人从专业角度为本项目翻译提出的中肯建议和重要技术支持;其次,感谢瞿乃明女士带领的北京优笔客翻译中心的翻译团队,以及罗培新教授等审校专家,他们以认真负责的态度、严谨务实的作风、按时保质完成了翻译和审校工作,特别要感谢北京大学吴志攀教授在百忙之中拨冗亲自承担总审校;最后,感谢法律出版社及其相关工作人员,尤其是沈小英女士、陈妮女士和胡艺芳女士为本书的编辑、出版做了大量工作。我们在此一并致以诚挚的谢意!

由于编译时间有限,书中难免有疏漏、不足之处,欢迎读者批评指正。

上海期货交易所

2013年9月

图书在版编目(CIP)数据

美国多德—弗兰克华尔街改革与消费者保护法:全2册 / 中国证券监督管理委员会组织编译. —北京:法律出版社,2014.1

(境外资本市场重要法律文献译丛)

ISBN 978-7-5118-5312-7

Ⅰ.①美… Ⅱ.①中… Ⅲ.①金融法—法案—研究—美国 Ⅳ.①D971.222.8

中国版本图书馆CIP数据核字(2013)第201781号

责任编辑/胡艺芳　　**装帧设计**/贾丹丹

出版/法律出版社　　**编辑统筹**/财税出版分社
总发行/中国法律图书有限公司　　**经销**/新华书店
印刷/北京中科印刷有限公司　　**责任印制**/吕亚莉

开本/787毫米×1092毫米 1/16　　**印张**/60　**字数**/1341千
版本/2014年1月第1版　　**印次**/2014年1月第1次印刷

法律出版社/北京市丰台区莲花池西里7号(100073)
电子邮件/info@lawpress.com.cn　　**销售热线**/010-63939792/9779
网址/www.lawpress.com.cn　　**咨询电话**/010-63939796

中国法律图书有限公司/北京市丰台区莲花池西里7号(100073)
全国各地中法图分、子公司电话:
第一法律书店/010-63939781/9782　**西安分公司**/029-85388843　**重庆公司**/023-65382816/2908
上海公司/021-62071010/1636　**北京分公司**/010-62534456　**深圳公司**/0755-83072995

书号:ISBN 978-7-5118-5312-7　　**定价(上、下册):**780.00元

(如有缺页或倒装,中国法律图书有限公司负责退换)

译者说明

《多德—弗兰克华尔街改革与消费者保护法》(Dodd-Frank Wall Street Reform and Consumer Protection Act)(以下简称《多德—弗兰克法》)是美国联邦政府为了应对2008年肇始于美国并迅速席卷全球的金融风暴而制定的一部大规模的金融改革法案。综观该法案的制定过程不难看出,美国政府在推行金融监管体制改革、弥补金融体系缺陷方面,可谓步履维艰。

2009年6月17日,奥巴马政府正式发布实施一系列全面彻底的金融监管改革措施,之后各大利益集团之间开始了长达一年多的激烈博弈,国会众议院和参议院分别于2009年12月11日和2010年5月20日通过了各自版本的金融监管法案。为协调立法分歧,两院任命了联席委员会,修改并形成了两院统一版本的《多德—弗兰克法》。2010年7月15日,参议院通过了该法案的最终版本。2010年7月21日,美国总统奥巴马在法案上签字,《多德—弗兰克法》正式生效。

这份鸿篇巨制的金融改革法案,标志着美国完成了历时近两年的金融改革立法,体现了美国对于金融危机爆发的原因的深刻反思,并由此开启了与新自由主义分道扬镳的金融监管路径。该法案不仅是美国在全球范围内率先针对危机中饱受诟病的金融监管体制建立的新规则,更是今后各国进行金融监管改革的新标尺,对美国境内以及全球范围的金融生态产生了深远影响。

一、《多德—弗兰克法》的立法背景

金融监管体制改革向来具有"危机指向"的特征,《多德—弗兰克法》的出台亦是一种事后立法改革的具体举措。

华尔街,这一曾经创造无数荣耀、辉煌与梦想的金融"麦加"圣地,几十年来一直引领着全球金融市场的发展方向,但却在2008年以其贪婪无度与极端不负责为全球金融体系带来了一次沉重打击。单就美国而言,在这场继大萧条以来最糟糕的金融危机中,800万个就业机会付诸东流,企业破产,房价下跌,个人储蓄蒸发……经济衰退的背后是实体经济与虚拟经济比例的严重失衡,是房地产资本泡沫的彻底破灭,是金融衍生工具的过度创新,是金融机构道德风险的肆意泛滥,是信用评级机构剧烈的利益冲突,而这一切的一切,将美国金融监管体制的内生性缺陷暴露无遗。

在金融危机爆发之时,美国"双线多头"的金融监管体制呈现出多种弊端,在这样一种"伞形"的金融监管体系下,监管机构之间的职能既有分工,又有交叉,多个监管机构并存。此种模式在飞速发展的金融市场中,引发了监管重叠、监管真空和监管套利等情况,暴露出了诸多难以胜任市场发展现状的缺陷,如各监管机构之间协调性差,容易出现监管真空地带;各监管机构之间难以统一号令,不可避免地产生摩擦;针对混业经营体制而实行分业监管,容易导致重复监管;多重监管之下易催生监管套利行为;从整体上看,金融监管机构庞大,导致监管成本较高等。

在这种情况下,只有通过一场根本性的重大革新,才能消弭美国金融监管体系的结构性缺陷。而在此过程中,如何在不减损美国金融市场的全球竞争力的同时,重塑行之有效的金融监管机制,同时维持金融市场的稳定并保护金融消费者的合法权益,无疑是一场艰难的平衡。

回顾美国金融监管法律法规的历史变迁,可以发现其经历了一条在“管制与自由之间”、在“金融监管与市场发展之间”不断寻求平衡点的曲折道路,美国的整个金融法制史就是一个“放松管制—加强管制—再放松管制—再次重构管制”的循环过程。

具体来说,在20世纪30年代的大萧条背景之下,罗斯福总统颁布了具有里程碑意义的《格拉斯—斯蒂格尔法》,将投资银行和商业银行分离,逐步形成分业经营、分业监管的格局,美国金融发展逐渐法制化和机构化;此后,面对20世纪70年代开始的产业空心化和滞胀局面,美国国会于1999年通过了《金融服务现代化法》,打破了分业经营的界限,以“效率与竞争”的理念整合了美国的金融法律体系,放松管制成为这一时期的主要趋势;在金融实践的新自由主义舞台上,美国金融机构的经营规模越来越大,金融创新越来越多,在市场份额迅速扩张的乐观局面下,酝酿着不断累积的系统性金融风险,终于在2008年全面爆发。

这场监管放松与金融自由化的“滑铁卢”所带来了巨大灾难,直接催生了《多德—弗兰克法》,其方向直指“重构管制”。

二、《多德—弗兰克法》的主要内容及特点

《多德—弗兰克法》充分体现了后危机时代美国金融监管理念和监管模式的变革方向,篇幅宏大、规定细致,共设16编,1600多条规定,文本多达2300多页。该法案对包括银行、证券、保险、对冲基金、信用评级机构、交易商、投资咨询机构、会计制度、上市公司等在内的金融体系运行规则和监管架构进行了全面改革与修订。

《多德—弗兰克法》的核心宗旨主要体现在以下两方面:其一,改变目前超级金融机构“太大而不能倒”的局面,有效防范系统性风险;其二,保护金融市场中的弱势群体,避免金融消费者受到欺诈。

围绕系统性风险和消费者金融保护两大核心问题,法案从系统性风险、消费者金融保护、重构原有监管机构和监管职能、提高对“具有系统重要性”金融机构的监管标准、填补关于对冲基金等金融行业的监管空白、对证券化及场外衍生品金融市场进行规范和约束、严格银行资本金监管和业务监管、华尔街高管薪酬监管等几个方面对现有监管规则进行了调整和改革。

在金融监管机构方面的改革,主要体现为以下三方面:

其一,设立了金融稳定监督委员会(Financial Stability Oversight Council)。该法案规

定，由财政部部长担任主席，领导10名成员设立金融稳定监督委员会，负责监测和处理危及全美金融稳定的系统风险金融。金融稳定监督委员会有权认定哪些金融机构可能对市场产生系统性冲击，从而在资本金和流动性方面对这些机构提出更加严格的监管要求，并识别、审查具有系统重要性的金融市场服务平台及各类金融活动，促进市场秩序、消除美国金融体系稳定所面临的潜在威胁。

其二，成立了金融研究办公室（Office of Financial Research）。法案规定，在财政部管辖下再成立金融研究办公室，此办公室旨在为金融稳定监督委员会及其附属机构提供行政、技术、预算分析等服务。办公室由数据中心和调查分析中心构成，有权利制定管制措施以及收集报告、数据和信息，无须国会批准。

其三，新建消费者金融保护局（Bureau of Consumer Financial Protection）。在美国联邦储备委员会下新设消费者金融保护局，并赋予其在规划和执行消费者金融产品和服务标准时的广泛的实质性权力。消费者金融保护局负责对提供信用卡、抵押贷款和其他贷款等消费者金融产品及服务的金融机构实施监管，还被授权根据金融产品和服务的特征来制定披露相关信息规则。该局接受美国总审计局的审计，并且每半年得向参议院银行委员会和众议院金融服务委员会汇报。

除了这三个机构的新设之外，《多德—弗兰克法》还对现有的监管机构进行了一系列改革及职能的重新定位，明晰界定各自的职责，以防止出现监管竞次的局面。

在具体内容方面，该法案的修订主要涉及以下几方面：

其一，终结金融机构"太大而不能倒"（too-big-to-fail）现象，停止政府救市。具体措施包括：当金融机构经营失败时，对其采取安全的清算程序；规定新的严格的资本金充足率及流动性要求使金融机构自觉不宜过大；更新美联储的权力，允许其提供系统范围内的支持，但不再扶持个别金融机构；建立更加严格的标准和监督体系以保护美国经济、消费者、投资者和企业的利益。

其二，杜绝不公平、欺诈性的金融产品或金融活动，打击隐蔽费用、条款滥用等欺骗行为，确保消费者获取信用卡公司、房地产抵押贷款经纪人、银行等金融机构提供的有关贷款或其他金融产品的详尽信息，以保护消费者权益。

其三，改进金融监管法规，采纳"沃克尔规则"，限制大金融机构的投机性交易，禁止银行或拥有银行的机构从事违背客户要求的自营交易或投资套利基金，限制银行持有的最大负债额，以保证银行机构资产结构合理和管理制度完善。

其四，强化金融衍生产品交易管理，剥离掉期业务与场外市场场内化。法案对于美国银行设立私募基金、对冲基金，信用卡消费等方面作出了诸多限制以及规定，禁止联邦政府救济任何掉期交易企业或从事任何掉期、证券支持掉期交易或其他交易活动，要求场外金融衍生产品交易通过集中清算系统完成，防止金融体系出现不当风险行为。

其五，改革保险监管，迈向全国集中统一监管模式。法案规定由美国联邦政府对保险业进行集中统一监管，而不再由各州分散监管。法案试图在保险监管的两个领域，即保险市场和再保险市场设立全国统一标准。

其六,规制公司高层薪酬水平,在公司高层薪酬待遇方面,为股东提供发言权,使其对高层薪酬水平和高管解职补偿费等方面取得不具约束力的投票权,进一步完善公司治理。

三、《多德—弗兰克法》的现实意义与启示

《多德—弗兰克法》是美国金融体制立法上的一项历史性革新,通过对该法案具体内容的梳理,可以看出其在重构美国金融监管体系的努力中所遵循的思路,即注重宏观审慎监管、严格金融监管标准、扩大监管覆盖范围以及强调跨机构协调监管。

就宏观层面而言,法案基于对金融市场本质的思考,对金融市场的功能重新进行了定位,推动了金融机构向传统业务的回归。就微观层面而言,法案对金融机构的非审慎行为进行了纠正,强调了将所有具有系统重要性的金融机构纳入宏观审慎的监管框架之下,对有系统性风险的金融机构,提出了更高的资本充足率、杠杆限制和风险集中度要求,还对银行自营交易及高风险的衍生品交易进行了更为严格的限制,并将此前缺乏监管的场外衍生品市场、对冲基金、私募基金等金融市场参与者纳入了监管视野。

事实上,该法案并没有全盘否定20世纪以来的金融自由化思想和放松监管模式,而是透过危机认识到金融监管结构中的弊端和不足,有针对性地调整监管架构和创设监管规则,从而使美国现行的金融监管制度能够适应金融体系的新变化,以防范金融体系中新变化可能带来的风险。的确,绝对依靠监管或绝对信赖市场这两种极端的模式均不能创造出良好的金融体系,只有在金融监管与市场力量中寻找到一个平衡,才能更好地实现金融稳定、风险控制及高效率的金融发展。

《多德—弗兰克法》正是在保留过去30多年金融自由化的基本成果、确认市场化仍是美国金融业未来发展基本方向的前提下,致力于改善和提高金融监管的技术和艺术,并将其尽可能覆盖所有的金融产品和服务、所有的金融市场和所有的金融机构。

当然,我们也应当认识到,《多德—弗兰克法》的立法意图在于维持金融稳定,但这仅仅是进一步实现金融发展的保障与条件,而非最终目的。没有任何一种监管模式可以称得上完美,这次金融体制改革也不例外。具体来说,该法案依然存在种种不足,如没有对真正引起危机的房利美和房地美进行约束,出于对美国房市稳定的考虑,两房问题成为此次改革中的空白区域;而且此法案仅仅确定了改革的框架,其具体实施还有待相关监管当局制定进一步的细则。但是,金融监管具有天生的滞后性,在具体问题暴露出来以后,监管者要对此进行逐步调整和完善,构建出一个比此前的金融监管制度更为适合的整体框架,达到促进金融市场健康、有序发展的基本要求。公允地说,只要在一次改革中能够为上一阶段金融体系新发展所带来的负面效应提供些许有益的解决方案,那么这次改革的价值就不容低估。

华东政法大学国际金融法律学院　罗培新

总译校：

吴志攀，北京大学教授、博士研究生导师，中国法学会副会长，北京大学党委常委、常务副校长、法律总顾问，兼任北京大学亚太研究院院长、北京大学金融法研究中心主任，最高人民法院专家咨询员。北京大学法学博士，美国哈佛大学法学院访问学者，美国艾森豪威尔基金会学者。出版《金融法概论》、《国际金融法》等十余部专著。

审校人员：

罗培新，华东政法大学国际金融法律学院院长、科研处处长，教授、博士研究生导师。北京大学国际金融法专业博士，中国社会科学院法学所博士后，美国耶鲁大学、英国牛津大学访问学者。国家教育部新世纪优秀人才、上海市第三届十大"优秀中青年法学家"。在《中国社会科学》、《中国法学》、《法学研究》发表论文若干篇，出版专著、译著10多部。

宋金莹，北京思必锐翻译公司译审。通过全国翻译专业资格英语一级笔译考试。北京外国语大学高级翻译学院翻译硕士、中国人民大学法学学士、南开大学英语语言文学学士。曾就职于司法部司法协助交流中心、司法协助与外事司，担任高级翻译。负责审校《美国多德—弗兰克华尔街改革与消费者保护法》第一章到第八章、第十章到第十六章以及最后的统稿工作。

翻译人员：

瞿乃明，法国巴黎高等翻译学院翻译学硕士、法国巴黎第九大学国际企业管理硕士、台湾大学经济学学士，北京优笔客翻译中心总经理。主要翻译作品有《欧盟金融工具市场指令》、《中国证监会2011年年报》、《美国商品交易法》、《美国证券交易委员会自身组织与通用规章》、《欧盟金融监管体制改革法规汇编》、《欧盟证券监管法规汇编》和《欧盟另类投资基金管理人指令》等。

艾飞，北京大学法学院法学学士。2007年通过中国司法考试，北京优笔客翻译中心质量经理。主要翻译作品有《美国商品交易法》、《美国证券交易委员会自身组织与通用规章》和《欧盟证券监管法规汇编》。

董雷召，天津外国语大学英美文学学士、南开大学法学院法律硕士。2005年通过中国司法考试，北京优笔客翻译中心专职译者。主要翻译作品有《美国商品交易法》和《欧盟另类投资基金管理人指令》等。

福宇，北京外国语大学英语学士。曾任北京优笔客翻译中心专职译者，现任中国铁建国际集团有限公司专职译者。主要翻译作品有《美国证券交易委员会自身组织与通用规章》。

范一，中国政法大学中美法学院比较法硕士、中国政法大学法学学士。2007年通过中国司法考试，北京优笔客翻译中心专职译者。主要翻译作品有《美国证券交易委员会自身组织与通用规章》。

冯永杰，烟台师范学院外语系英语学士，华东政法大学法律硕士。2009年通过中国司法考试，曾任某知名律师事务所翻译部负责人，现任优笔客翻译中心兼职译者。

梁霏，美国纽约大学法学院法学硕士、中国人民大学经济学学士及法学硕士。曾长期执业于国际律师事务所北京及香港分所,并任职诺基亚西门子通信和惠普中国区法律顾问。现任北京市君泰律师事务所合伙人律师。

周舒诞,美国波士顿大学法学院法律博士(J.D.)、上海外国语大学高级翻译学院翻译学硕士、中山大学中文系中国语言文学学士。现任国际律师事务所伦敦总部美国税法律师。主要翻译作品有《欧盟金融工具市场指令》和《美国商品交易法》等。

程宇凡,首都经贸大学法律学士。现任某美国律师事务所专职法律翻译。主要翻译作品有《美国证券交易委员会自身组织与通用规章》、《欧盟金融监管体制改革法规汇编》和《欧盟另类投资基金管理人指令》等。

钱淳,北京语言大学文学学士。北京优笔客翻译中心专职译者。主要翻译作品有《美国证券交易委员会自身组织与通用规章》等。

区欣,波兰什切青大学伊拉斯谟世界(Erasmus Mundus)硕士课程班学习欧盟法和欧盟指令,中山大学西方哲学硕士。北京优笔客翻译中心专职译者。主要翻译作品有《欧盟金融监管体制改革法规汇编》和《欧盟证券监管法规汇编》等。

总　　序

中国资本市场是适应我国经济体制改革和对外开放的形势要求逐步建立发展起来的。为了有效借鉴境外成熟市场的制度经验，中国资本市场从成立伊始，就特别注重按照“立足国情，为我所用”的原则，不断学习、消化和吸收境外成熟市场的运行规则和监管制度。目前，中国资本市场现行有效的法律、法规、规章、规范性文件共521件，加上大量的交易所和协会的自律规则，基本形成了我国资本市场的法律制度规范体系。这些制度规范构建起一整套与国际通行原则基本相符的法律框架、交易规则和监管体系，有效维护了市场秩序，保证了市场功能和作用的发挥，保护了投资者的合法权益。

经过20余年的改革发展，我国资本市场进入了创新发展的新阶段。立足于服务实体经济发展的大局需要，重点解决资本市场自身结构不平衡、服务实体经济能力不足、为居民提供投资理财产品相对匮乏等突出现实问题，资本市场现有的以股票公开发行并在交易所上市交易为主的境内市场体系，将逐步发展成为一个公募与私募并重、股票与债券平衡、场内与场外协调发展的资本市场体系。与此相适应，需要进一步发展壮大财富管理行业，立足于功能监管的制度定位，统一资产管理行为规则，放松行政管制，增强创新活力。实现这样的改革目标，需要我们更加重视学习境外成熟市场的制度经验，充分借鉴境外市场有关私募发行、债权融资、资产管理、期货及衍生品等方面的法律制度，在尊重市场规律的前提下，大胆进行制度和机制创新，确保我们的各项制度适应和满足市场改革的实际需要。

坚持对外开放是中国资本市场改革和发展的一贯方针。在经济全球化深入发展的时代背景下，适应我国经济结构调整和经济方式转变和“逐步实现人民币资本项目可兑换”的金融对外开放的总体要求，中国资本市场必须以更加积极的态度参与全球经济竞争，提高在全球范围内配置资源，服务实体经济发展的能力。不论是支持境内企业到境外发行融资，鼓励境内机构和个人到境外进行证券投资，还是畅通境外企业到境内发行融资渠道，平等保护境外机构和个人到境内进行证券投资，都需要在立足国情的前提下，实现制度衔接互通，消除制度壁垒。特别重要的是，市场竞争首先是制度规则的竞争，增强我国资本市场的国际竞争力，一方面要确保我国市场通过制度规则体现法治环境吸引力，另一方面还要增强我国在涉及资本市场对外开放的国际规则的制定中的话语权,增强我国在国际监管合作和跨境执法合作中的主动权。

同时,我们也注意到,2008年国际金融危机发生后,境外资本市场对监管体制、机制做了较为重大的调整,提出了不少新的监管要求,出台了不少新的法律文件。例如,美国制定了具有金融综合监管性质的《多德—弗兰克华尔街改革与消费者保护法》,英国则将原来集证券、银行、保险于一身的《2000年金融服务与市场法》修改成《2010年金融服务法》。对于境外相关法律制度的动态发展,需要及时掌握情况,借鉴有益经验,为进一步完善我国资本市场的基础性制度建设提供参考。

经过长期的努力,中国资本市场的制度借鉴和引进已经越过了概念化、碎片状的发展阶段,进入全面、系统、精细化的更高阶段。由于种种原因,对境外资本市场法律制度的介绍,无论是在法学界、法律界,还是在证券期货行业内,一直以来都存在及时性不够、系统性不足、权威性不强的情况。特别是翻译介绍的质量不高、精品不多,这在客观上影响了对境外经验的学习和借鉴。

为了适应资本市场学习借鉴境外制度经验的形势要求,中国证监会精选了境外资本市场国家和地区的重要法律文献,包括境外主要资本市场的重要法律、监管部门的监管规则、经典的司法判例、最新的资本市场立法成果以及相关法学理论权威著作等,组织翻译出版了这套《境外资本市场重要法律文献译丛》。译丛的翻译出版工作,在系统单位、部门和关心市场发展的专家学者的共同努力下,紧紧抓住保质量、出精品的关键环节,建立了"竞标择优确定翻译人员、知名专家评审保证翻译质量、适当报酬和学术声誉结合激励"的工作机制,落实"精选译题、精细翻译、精心审校、精致出版"的工作要求,是中国证监会打造国人了解国际资本市场法律制度权威平台的有益尝试。为此,愿以本文向参与丛书翻译、审校的国际金融、法律方面的专家和学者表示感谢,并与大家共勉,共同为建设起一个权利公平、机会公平、规则公平的资本市场而努力。

中国证监会

2013年2月

序

党的十八大明确指出，树立社会主义法治理念，增强全社会学法尊法守法用法意识，提高领导干部运用法治思维和法治方式深化改革、推动发展、化解矛盾、维护稳定的能力。对期货与衍生品市场而言，法规就是市场的生命线，因此，加强我国期货与衍生品市场的法制建设，首先就是要学习、研究国际期货与衍生品市场的法规规则。2010年出台的《多德—弗兰克华尔街改革与消费者保护法》（以下简称《多德—弗兰克法》）作为美国20世纪30年代后颁布的最大规模的金融监管改革法案，对全球期货与衍生品市场发展产生了深远影响。因此，对该法案进行翻译与学习对我国期货与衍生品市场发展具有重要意义。

近年来，世界经济正在发生深刻变化，全球经济的一体化进程加快，促使生产要素和金融资本在全球范围内快速流动，商品和各类金融资产价格剧烈波动，经济、金融体系中的不确定因素明显增多，与经济发展密切相关的汇率、能源、金属和农产品等价格大幅波动。在交易电子化与网络化的背景下，期货与衍生品市场交易量快速增长，已成为国际资本市场的重要组成部分。相较境外成熟资本市场，我国期货及衍生品发展不足的问题还很突出。“十二五”时期，中国资本市场应更好地承担起服务经济社会发展大局的历史责任，金融衍生品的发展可以大大拓展资本市场的深度，起到价格发现和风险管理的作用。但是，复杂的衍生品本身隐含风险。2008年肇始于美国华尔街并席卷全球的金融危机，已经让各国政府及监管机构充分认识到金融衍生品的高杠杆、高风险性和迅速的风险传递性。因此，完善金融衍生品市场法规，加强金融衍生品市场的监管是非常必要的。从美国2000年《商品期货交易现代化法》全面放松金融监管，到《多德—弗兰克法》对金融监管的再次重构历程中可以看出，金融衍生品市场的稳步发展需要完善的法律制度支撑和保障。

推动我国期货与衍生品市场由数量扩张向质量提升转变，对于保障我国经济战略安全具有重要意义。我国期货与衍生品市场发展较晚，是在学习、借鉴境外主要期货与衍生品市场经验的基础上建立并发展起来的，期货与衍生品市场法规规则也是在学习、借鉴境外主要期货与衍生品市场经验的基础上建立并发展起来的。因此，学习借鉴《多德—弗兰克法》等国际法规，促进我国期货与衍生品市场的法制建设与业务发展非常必要。

为防范系统性风险同时加大对投资者的保护，《多德—弗兰克法》从总体上加强了对场外衍生品市场的监管力度,抑制过度性投机,立体化拓宽了风险控制制度和措施,同时注重不同风险类型市场间的风险隔离,通过适当放宽市场操纵等市场欺诈行为的认定标准,进一步加大了对欺诈行为的打击力度,多维度加强了对市场安全的维护。这些新的监管思路和措施,对我国进一步发展期货与衍生品市场,完善监管制度有很大的启示意义。

此外,衍生品市场的国际化和电子化也进一步加剧了全球衍生品市场间的竞争,交易电子化越来越普及,几乎在世界任何一个角落都可以交易全球的产品。在交易标的、投资者与影响力等因素全球化的背景下,我国期货与衍生品市场与境外市场已存在被动的竞争关系,亟待通过“走出去”和“引进来”逐步完成期货市场的对外开放。在这个过程中,一方面需要完善相关制度与规则,为境内机构创造条件,使其逐步接近国际市场的运作标准;另一方面需要降低外资进入门槛,分阶段允许境外投资者进入我国期货与衍生品市场交易,积极构建一个稳定、有竞争力的衍生品市场。

为此,我们都要继续加大国内外期货与衍生品法规规则的研究力度,在深刻把握我国期货与衍生品市场发展规律的基础上,不断对我国现有规则、制度、机制进行调整,建立一套适合我国国情又与国际接轨的高效法规规则体系,通过法规规则和制度创新,带动业务发展,夯实我国期货与衍生品市场发展的制度基础。

杨迈军

2013 年 9 月

CONTENTS

目　录

Dodd–Frank Wall Street Reform and Consumer Protection Act

美国多德—弗兰克华尔街改革与消费者保护法

One Hundred Eleventh Congress of the United States of America

AT THE SECOND SESSION

Begun and held at the City of Washington on Tuesday, the fifth day of January, two thousand and ten

An Act

To promote the financial stability of the United States by improving accountability and transparency in the financial system, to end "too big to fail", to protect the American taxpayer by ending bailouts, to protect consumers from abusive financial services practices, and for other purposes.

Be it enacted by the Senate and House of Representatives of the United States of America in Congress assembled,

SECTION 1. SHORT TITLE; TABLE OF CONTENTS.

(a) SHORT TITLE. — This Act may be cited as the "Dodd–Frank Wall Street Reform and Consumer Protection Act".

(b) TABLE OF CONTENTS. — The table of contents for this Act is as follows:

SEC. 2. DEFINITIONS.

As used in this Act, the following definitions shall apply, except as the context otherwise requires or as otherwise specifically provided in this Act:

(1) AFFILIATE. — The term "affiliate" has the same meaning as in section 3 of the Federal Deposit Insurance Act (12 U.S.C. 1813).

(2) APPROPRIATE FEDERAL BANKING AGENCY. — On and after the transfer date, the term "appropriate Federal banking agency" has the same meaning as in section 3(q) of the Federal Deposit Insurance Act (12 U.S.C. 1813(q)), as amended by title III.

第111届
美国国会

第二次会期

2010 年 1 月 5 日(周二),于华盛顿

法　　案

旨在完善金融体系的问责制、提高金融体系的透明度,借以提高美国的金融稳定性,结束“大到不能倒”和政府埋单现象,保护美国纳税人,使消费者免受金融服务滥用所导致的负面影响及实现其他相关宗旨。

由美国参议院和众议院于国会会议通过

第1条　简称;目录

(a)简称。——引述本法时,可简称为《多德—弗兰克华尔街改革与消费者保护法》。

(b)目录。——本法目录如次:(参见目录)

第2条　定义

除非上下文另有所指或本法另有明确规定,否则,就本法而言,下列术语应适用如下定义:

(1)**关联方**。——“关联方”一词的含义以《联邦存款保险法》第3条(《美国法典》第十二编第1813节)的定义为准。

(2)**相应的联邦银行业监管机关**。——在转移日(含)之后,“相应的联邦银行业监管机关”一词的含义以《联邦存款保险法》第3(q)条[《美国法典》第十二编第1813(q)节](以经第三编修正后的版本为准)的定义为准。

(3) BOARD OF GOVERNORS. — The term "Board of Governors" means the Board of Governors of the Federal Reserve System.

(4) BUREAU. — The term "Bureau" means the Bureau of Consumer Financial Protection established under title X.

(5) COMMISSION. — The term "Commission" means the Securities and Exchange Commission, except in the context of the Commodity Futures Trading Commission.

(6) COMMODITY FUTURES TERMS. — The terms "futures commission merchant", "swap", "swap dealer", "swap execution facility", "derivatives clearing organization", "board of trade", "commodity trading advisor", "commodity pool", and "commodity pool operator" have the same meanings as given the terms in section 1a of the Commodity Exchange Act (7 U.S.C. 1 et seq.).

(7) CORPORATION. — The term "Corporation" means the Federal Deposit Insurance Corporation.

(8) COUNCIL. — The term "Council" means the Financial Stability Oversight Council established under title I.

(9) CREDIT UNION. — The term "credit union" means a Federal credit union, State credit union, or State–chartered credit union, as those terms are defined in section 101 of the Federal Credit Union Act (12 U.S.C. 1752).

(10) FEDERAL BANKING AGENCY. — The term —

(A) "Federal banking agency" means, individually, the Board of Governors, the Office of the Comptroller of the Currency, and the Corporation; and

(B) "Federal banking agencies" means all of the agencies referred to in subparagraph (A), collectively.

(11) FUNCTIONALLY REGULATED SUBSIDIARY. — The term "functionally regulated subsidiary" has the same meaning as in section 5(c)(5) of the Bank Holding Company Act of 1956 (12 U.S.C. 1844(c)(5)).

(12) PRIMARY FINANCIAL REGULATORY AGENCY. — The term "primary financial regulatory agency" means —

(A) the appropriate Federal banking agency, with respect to institutions described in section 3(q) of the Federal Deposit Insurance Act, except to the extent that an institution is or the activities of an institution are otherwise described in subparagraph (B), (C), (D), or (E);

(B) the Securities and Exchange Commission, with respect to —

(i) any broker or dealer that is registered with the Commission under the Securities

(3)**联邦储备委员会**。——“联邦储备委员会”一词系指美国联邦储备系统管理委员会。

(4)**消费者金融保护局**。——“消费者金融保护局”一词系指根据第十编设立的消费者金融保护局。

(5)**证券交易委员会**。——除非按上下文应指美国商品期货交易委员会,否则“委员会”特指证券交易委员会。[1]

(6)**商品期货术语**。——“期货经纪商”、“互换”、“互换交易商”、“互换执行设施”、“衍生品结算组织”、“交易场所”、“商品交易顾问”、“商品基金”以及“商品基金管理人”的含义以《商品交易法》第1a条(《美国法典》第七编第1节及其后条文)的定义为准。

(7)**联邦存款保险公司**。——“联邦存款保险公司”一词系指美国联邦存款保险公司。

(8)**金融稳定监督委员会**。——“金融稳定监督委员会”一词系指根据第一编设立的金融稳定监督委员会。

(9)**信贷联盟**。——“信贷联盟”一词系指《联邦信贷联盟法》第101条(《美国法典》第十二编第1752节)定义的联邦信贷联盟、州信贷联盟或州特许注册信贷联盟。

(10)**联邦银行业监管机关**。——“联邦银行业监管机关”一词——

(A)采用单数形式时,系指联邦储备委员会、货币监理署和联邦存款保险公司中的任一者;及

(B)采用复数形式时,系指第(A)子款所述全部机关之统称。

(11)**受制于功能监管的子公司**。——“受制于功能监管的子公司”一词的含义以《1956年银行控股公司法》第5(c)(5)条[《美国法典》第十二编第1844(c)(5)节]的定义为准。

(12)**优先金融监管机关**。——“优先金融监管机关”一词——

(A)对于《联邦存款保险法》第3(q)条所述机构而言,系指相应的联邦银行业监管机关,但第(B)子款、第(C)子款、第(D)子款或第(E)子款对该等机构或机构活动另行规定了优先金融监管机关的除外;

(B)对于以下实体而言,系指证券交易委员会——

(i)根据《1934年证券交易法》在证券交易委员会注册的任何经纪商或自营商[2],但

1 鉴于全文出现各种不同的委员会,译文中都采用全称。因此,此处的“Commission”在中文文本中采用全称“证券交易委员会”,而未采用简称“委员会”。——译者注

2 《1934 年证券交易法》对“dealer”一词明确定义为“自营商”。因此,本书涉及证券语境(即“broker”和“dealer”并列的语境)时,将“dealer”译为“自营商”,同时从事自营和经纪业务的业者“broker-dealer”译为“经纪自营商”。在期货语境中,“dealer”则指“交易商”,例如,“swap dealer”一词译为“互换交易商”。——译者注

Exchange Act of 1934, with respect to the activities of the broker or dealer that require the broker or dealer to be registered under that Act;

(ii) any investment company that is registered with the Commission under the Investment Company Act of 1940, with respect to the activities of the investment company that require the investment company to be registered under that Act;

(iii) any investment adviser that is registered with the Commission under the Investment Advisers Act of 1940, with respect to the investment advisory activities of such company and activities that are incidental to such advisory activities;

(iv) any clearing agency registered with the Commission under the Securities Exchange Act of 1934, with respect to the activities of the clearing agency that require the agency to be registered under such Act;

(v) any nationally recognized statistical rating organization registered with the Commission under the Securities Exchange Act of 1934;

(vi) any transfer agent registered with the Commission under the Securities Exchange Act of 1934;

(vii) any exchange registered as a national securities exchange with the Commission under the Securities Exchange Act of 1934;

(viii) any national securities association registered with the Commission under the Securities Exchange Act of 1934;

(ix) any securities information processor registered with the Commission under the Securities Exchange Act of 1934;

(x) the Municipal Securities Rulemaking Board established under the Securities Exchange Act of 1934;

(xi) the Public Company Accounting Oversight Board established under the Sarbanes-Oxley Act of 2002 (15 U.S.C. 7211 et seq.);

(xii) the Securities Investor Protection Corporation established under the Securities Investor Protection Act of 1970 (15 U.S.C. 78aaa et seq.); and

(xiii) any security-based swap execution facility, security-based swap data repository, security-based swap dealer or major security-based swap participant registered with the Commission under the Securities Exchange Act of 1934, with respect to the security-based swap activities of the person that require such person to be registered under such Act;

(C) the Commodity Futures Trading Commission, with respect to —

(i) any futures commission merchant registered with the Commodity Futures Trading Commission under the Commodity Exchange Act (7 U.S.C. 1 et seq.), with respect to the activities of the futures commission merchant that require the futures commission merchant to be registered under that Act;

监管针对的是该等经纪商或自营商必须根据该法注册才能从事的活动；

(ii)根据《1940年投资公司法》在证券交易委员会注册的任何投资公司,但监管针对的是该等投资公司必须根据该法注册才能从事的活动；

(iii)根据《1940年投资顾问法》在证券交易委员会注册的任何投资顾问,但监管针对的是该等公司的投资顾问活动以及该等顾问活动的附属活动；

(iv)根据《1934年证券交易法》在证券交易委员会注册的任何结算机构,但监管针对的是该等结算机构必须根据该法注册才能从事的活动；

(v)根据《1934年证券交易法》在证券交易委员会注册的任何全国公认统计评级组织；

(vi)根据《1934年证券交易法》在证券交易委员会注册的任何过户代理人；

(vii)根据《1934年证券交易法》在证券交易委员会注册的任何全国性证券交易所；

(viii)根据《1934年证券交易法》在证券交易委员会注册的任何全国性证券协会；

(ix)根据《1934年证券交易法》在证券交易委员会注册的任何证券信息处理商；

(x)根据《1934年证券交易法》设立的市政证券规则制定委员会；

(xi)根据《2002年萨班斯—奥克斯利法》(《美国法典》第十五编第7211节及其后条文)设立的公众公司会计监督委员会；

(xii)根据《1970年证券投资者保护法》(《美国法典》第十五编第78aaa节及其后条文)设立的证券投资者保护公司;及

(xiii)根据《1934年证券交易法》在证券交易委员会注册的任何证券类互换执行设施、证券类互换数据存管机构、证券类互换交易商或主要的证券类互换参与者,但监管针对的是该等主体必须根据该法注册才能从事的证券类互换活动；

(C)对于以下实体而言,系指商品期货交易委员会——

(i)根据《商品交易法》(《美国法典》第七编第1节及其后条文)在商品期货交易委员会注册的任何期货经纪商,但监管针对的是该等期货经纪商必须根据该法注册才能从事的活动；

(ii) any commodity pool operator registered with the Commodity Futures Trading Commission under the Commodity Exchange Act (7 U.S.C. 1 et seq.), with respect to the activities of the commodity pool operator that require the commodity pool operator to be registered under that Act, or a commodity pool, as defined in that Act;

(iii) any commodity trading advisor or introducing broker registered with the Commodity Futures Trading Commission under the Commodity Exchange Act (7 U.S.C. 1 et seq.), with respect to the activities of the commodity trading advisor or introducing broker that require the commodity trading adviser or introducing broker to be registered under that Act;

(iv) any derivatives clearing organization registered with the Commodity Futures Trading Commission under the Commodity Exchange Act (7 U.S.C. 1 et seq.), with respect to the activities of the derivatives clearing organization that require the derivatives clearing organization to be registered under that Act;

(v) any board of trade designated as a contract market by the Commodity Futures Trading Commission under the Commodity Exchange Act (7 U.S.C. 1 et seq.);

(vi) any futures association registered with the Commodity Futures Trading Commission under the Commodity Exchange Act (7 U.S.C. 1 et seq.);

(vii) any retail foreign exchange dealer registered with the Commodity Futures Trading Commission under the Commodity Exchange Act (7 U.S.C. 1 et seq.), with respect to the activities of the retail foreign exchange dealer that require the retail foreign exchange dealer to be registered under that Act;

(viii) any swap execution facility, swap data repository, swap dealer, or major swap participant registered with the Commodity Futures Trading Commission under the Commodity Exchange Act (7 U.S.C. 1 et seq.) with respect to the swap activities of the person that require such person to be registered under that Act; and

(ix) any registered entity under the Commodity Exchange Act (7 U.S.C. 1 et seq.), with respect to the activities of the registered entity that require the registered entity to be registered under that Act;

(D) the State insurance authority of the State in which an insurance company is domiciled, with respect to the insurance activities and activities that are incidental to such insurance activities of an insurance company that is subject to supervision by the State insurance authority under State insurance law; and

(E) the Federal Housing Finance Agency, with respect to Federal Home Loan Banks or the Federal Home Loan Bank System, and with respect to the Federal National Mortgage Association or the Federal Home Loan Mortgage Corporation.

(13) PRUDENTIAL STANDARDS. — The term "prudential standards" means enhanced supervision and regulatory standards developed by the Board of Governors

（ii）根据《商品交易法》在商品期货交易委员会注册的任何商品基金管理人，但监管针对的是该等商品基金管理人必须根据该法注册才能从事的活动，或者《商品交易法》（《美国法典》第七编第1节及其后条文）定义的商品基金；

（iii）根据《商品交易法》（《美国法典》第七编第1节及其后条文）在商品期货交易委员会注册的任何商品交易顾问或介绍经纪商，但监管针对的是该等商品交易顾问或介绍经纪商必须根据该法注册才能从事的活动；

（iv）根据《商品交易法》（《美国法典》第七编第1节及其后条文）在商品期货交易委员会注册的任何衍生品结算组织，但监管针对的是该等衍生品结算组织必须根据该法注册才能从事的活动；

（v）商品期货交易委员会根据《商品交易法》（《美国法典》第七编第1节及其后条文）指定为合约市场的任何交易场所；

（vi）根据《商品交易法》（《美国法典》第七编第1节及其后条文）在商品期货交易委员会注册的任何期货协会；

（vii）根据《商品交易法》（《美国法典》第七编第1节及其后条文）在商品期货交易委员会注册的任何零售外汇交易商，但监管针对的是该等零售外汇交易商必须根据该法注册才能从事的活动；

（viii）根据《商品交易法》（《美国法典》第七编第1节及其后条文）在商品期货交易委员会注册的任何互换执行设施、互换数据存管机构、互换交易商或主要互换参与者，但监管针对的是该等主体必须根据该法注册才能从事的互换活动；且

（ix）根据《商品交易法》（《美国法典》第七编第1节及其后条文）注册的任何注册实体，但监管针对的是该等注册实体必须根据该法注册才能从事的活动；

（D）对于从事保险活动，且根据州保险法受制于州保险监管机关的保险公司的保险活动以及该等保险活动的附属活动而言，系指保险公司住所地所在州的州保险监管机构；及

（E）对于联邦住房贷款银行或联邦住房贷款银行系统而言，以及对于联邦国民抵押贷款协会或联邦住宅贷款抵押公司而言，系指联邦住房金融局。

（13）**审慎性标准**。——“审慎性标准”一词系指联邦储备委员会根据第165条制定的强化的监管与规制标准。

under section 165.

(14) SECRETARY. — The term "Secretary" means the Secretary of the Treasury.

(15) SECURITIES TERMS. — The —

(A) terms "broker", "dealer", "issuer", "nationally recognized statistical rating organization", "security", and "securities laws" have the same meanings as in section 3 of the Securities Exchange Act of 1934 (15 U.S.C. 78c);

(B) term "investment adviser" has the same meaning as in section 202 of the Investment Advisers Act of 1940 (15 U.S.C. 80b–2); and

(C) term "investment company" has the same meaning as in section 3 of the Investment Company Act of 1940 (15 U.S.C. 80a–3).

(16) STATE. — The term "State" means any State, commonwealth, territory, or possession of the United States, the District of Columbia, the Commonwealth of Puerto Rico, the Commonwealth of the Northern Mariana Islands, American Samoa, Guam, or the United States Virgin Islands.

(17) TRANSFER DATE. — The term "transfer date" means the date established under section 311.

(18) OTHER INCORPORATED DEFINITIONS. —

(A) FEDERAL DEPOSIT INSURANCE ACT. — The terms "bank", "bank holding company", "control", "deposit", "depository institution", "Federal depository institution", "Federal savings association", "foreign bank", "including", "insured branch", "insured depository institution", "national member bank", "national nonmember bank", "savings association", "State bank", "State depository institution", "State member bank", "State nonmember bank", "State savings association", and "subsidiary" have the same meanings as in section 3 of the Federal Deposit Insurance Act (12 U.S.C. 1813).

(B) HOLDING COMPANIES. — The term —

(i) "bank holding company" has the same meaning as in section 2 of the Bank Holding Company Act of 1956 (12 U.S.C. 1841);

(ii) "financial holding company" has the same meaning as in section 2(p) of the Bank Holding Company Act of 1956 (12 U.S.C. 1841(p)); and

(iii) "savings and loan holding company" has the same meaning as in section 10 of the Home Owners' Loan Act (12 U.S.C. 1467a(a)).

SEC. 3. SEVERABILITY.

If any provision of this Act, an amendment made by this Act, or the application of such provision or amendment to any person or circumstance is held to be unconstitutional, the remainder of this Act, the amendments made by this Act, and the application of the provisions of such to any person or circumstance shall not be affected thereby.

(14)**财政部部长**。——“财政部部长”一词系指美国财政部部长。

(15)**证券术语**。——

(A)“经纪商”、“自营商”、“发行人”、“全国公认统计评级组织”、“证券”以及“证券法律”等词语的含义以《1934年证券交易法》第3条(《美国法典》第十五编第78c节)的定义为准。

(B)“投资顾问”一词的含义以《1940年投资顾问法》第202条(《美国法典》第十五编第80b—2节)的定义为准;及

(C)“投资公司”一词的含义以《1940年投资公司法》第3条(《美国法典》第十五编第80a—3节)的定义为准。

(16)**州**。——“州”一词系指美国的任何州、准州或属地、哥伦比亚特区、波多黎各自由邦、北马里亚纳群岛、美属萨摩亚、关岛或美属维京尔群岛。

(17)**转移日**。——“转移日”一词系指第311条确定的日期。

(18)**其他援引纳入的定义**。——

(A)**《联邦存款保险法》**。——“银行”、“银行控股公司”、“控制”、“存款”、“存款机构”、“联邦存款机构”、“联邦储蓄协会”、“外国银行”、“包括”、“参保分支机构”、“参保存款机构”、“国民成员银行”、“国民非成员银行”、“储蓄协会”、“州银行”、“州存款机构”、“州成员银行”、“州非成员银行”、“州储蓄协会”及“子公司”的含义以《联邦存款保险法》第3条(《美国法典》第十二编第1813节)的定义为准。

(B)**控股公司**。——

(i)“银行控股公司”一词的含义以《1956年银行控股公司法》第2条(《美国法典》第十二编第1841节)的定义为准;

(ii)“金融控股公司”一词的含义以《1956年银行控股公司法》第2(p)条[《美国法典》第十二编第1841(p)节]的定义为准;及

(iii)“储贷控股公司”一词的含义以《业主贷款法》第10条[《美国法典》第十二编第1467a(a)节]的定义为准。

第3条　可分割性

本法的任何规定、本法所做的任何修正,或者任何该等规定或修正对任何人或任何情形的适用被认定为违宪的,本法其余规定、本法所做的其余修正或者任何该等规定或修正对任何人或情形的适用一概不受影响。

SEC. 4. EFFECTIVE DATE.

Except as otherwise specifically provided in this Act or the amendments made by this Act, this Act and such amendments shall take effect 1 day after the date of enactment of this Act.

SEC. 5. BUDGETARY EFFECTS.

The budgetary effects of this Act, for the purpose of complying with the Statutory Pay–As–You–Go–Act of 2010, shall be determined by reference to the latest statement titled "Budgetary Effects of PAYGO Legislation" for this Act, jointly submitted for printing in the Congressional Record by the Chairmen of the House and Senate Budget Committees, provided that such statement has been submitted prior to the vote on passage in the House acting first on this conference report or amendment between the Houses.

SEC. 6. ANTITRUST SAVINGS CLAUSE.

Nothing in this Act, or any amendment made by this Act, shall be construed to modify, impair, or supersede the operation of any of the antitrust laws, unless otherwise specified. For purposes of this section, the term "antitrust laws" has the same meaning as in subsection (a) of the first section of the Clayton Act, except that such term includes section 5 of the Federal Trade Commission Act, to the extent that such section 5 applies to unfair methods of competition.

第4条 生效日

除非本法或本法所做修正另有明确规定,否则本法以及本法所做修正应于本法颁布次日生效。

第5条 预算影响

为遵守《法定2010年财政收支平衡法》的规定,本法对预算的影响应参照众议院预算委员会主席和参议院预算委员会主席共同提交并纳入国会记录的最近一版关于本法的《〈财政收支平衡法〉的预算影响》报告确定。前提是在参众两院当中对于协商会议报告或两院之间的修正先予表决的议院进行投票表决之前,该报告已经提交。

第6条 反垄断法律保留条款

除非另有明确规定,否则本法的任何规定或对本法所做的任何修正均不得被解释为对任何反垄断法律适用的修改、损害或替代。就本条而言,“反垄断法律”一词的含义应以《克莱顿法》第1条第(a)子条的定义为准。但是,在《联邦贸易委员会法》第5条的规定适用于不正当竞争方式的前提下,该条规定亦应包括在“反垄断法律”之内。

TITLE I — FINANCIAL STABILITY

SEC. 101. SHORT TITLE.

This title may be cited as the "Financial Stability Act of 2010".

SEC. 102. DEFINITIONS.

(a) IN GENERAL. — For purposes of this title, unless the context otherwise requires, the following definitions shall apply:

(1) BANK HOLDING COMPANY. — The term "bank holding company" has the same meaning as in section 2 of the Bank Holding Company Act of 1956 (12 U.S.C. 1841). A foreign bank or company that is treated as a bank holding company for purposes of the Bank Holding Company Act of 1956, pursuant to section 8(a) of the International Banking Act of 1978 (12 U.S.C. 3106(a)), shall be treated as a bank holding company for purposes of this title.

(2) CHAIRPERSON. — The term "Chairperson" means the Chairperson of the Council.

(3) MEMBER AGENCY. — The term "member agency" means an agency represented by a voting member of the Council.

(4) NONBANK FINANCIAL COMPANY DEFINITIONS. —

(A) FOREIGN NONBANK FINANCIAL COMPANY. — The term "foreign nonbank financial company" means a company (other than a company that is, or is treated in the United States as, a bank holding company) that is —

(i) incorporated or organized in a country other than the United States; and

(ii) predominantly engaged in, including through a branch in the United States, financial activities, as defined in paragraph (6).

(B) U.S. NONBANK FINANCIAL COMPANY. — The term "U.S. nonbank financial company" means a company (other than a bank holding company, a Farm Credit System institution chartered and subject to the provisions of the Farm Credit Act of 1971 (12 U.S.C. 2001 et seq.), or a national securities exchange (or parent thereof), clearing agency (or parent thereof, unless the parent is a bank holding company), security–based swap execution facility, or security–based swap data repository registered with the Commission,

第一编——金融稳定

第101条　简称

引述本编时,可简称为《2010年金融稳定法》。

第102条　定义

(a)**一般规定**。——就本编而言,除非上下文另有所指,否则下列术语应适用如下定义:

(1)**银行控股公司**。——“银行控股公司”一词的含义以《1956年银行控股公司法》第2条(《美国法典》第十二编第1841节)的定义为准。如果外国银行或公司按照《1978年国际银行法》第8(a)条[《美国法典》第十二编第3106(a)节]的规定被视为《1956年银行控股公司法》意义上的银行控股公司,则就本编而言,该等外国银行或公司亦应视为银行控股公司。

(2)**主席**。——“主席”一词系指金融稳定监督委员会主席。

(3)**成员机关**。——“成员机关”一词系指金融稳定监督委员会的有表决权成员所代表的机关。

(4)**非银行金融公司的定义**。——

(A)**外国非银行金融公司**。——“外国非银行金融公司”一词系指符合以下条件的公司(但银行控股公司或在美国被视为银行控股公司的公司除外)——

(i)在美国之外的国家设立或组建;且

(ii)主营(包括通过位于美国境内的分支机构主营)第(6)款所定义的金融活动。

(B)**美国非银行金融公司**。——“美国非银行金融公司”一词系指符合以下条件的:公司(但银行控股公司和根据《1971年农业信贷法》(《美国法典》第十二编第2001节及其后条文)的规定特许注册并受制于该法规定的农业信贷系统机构除外);或者,在证券交易委员会注册的全国性证券交易所(或其母公司)、结算机构(或其母公司,除非该母公司为银行控股公司)、证券类互换执行设施或证券类互换数据存管机构;或者,在商品期货交易委员会注册的被指定为合约市场的交易场所(或其母公司)、衍

or a board of trade designated as a contract market (or parent thereof), or a derivatives clearing organization (or parent thereof, unless the parent is a bank holding company), swap execution facility or a swap data repository registered with the Commodity Futures Trading Commission), that is —

(i) incorporated or organized under the laws of the United States or any State; and

(ii) predominantly engaged in financial activities, as defined in paragraph (6).

(C) NONBANK FINANCIAL COMPANY. — The term "nonbank financial company" means a U.S. nonbank financial company and a foreign nonbank financial company.

(D) NONBANK FINANCIAL COMPANY SUPERVISED BY THE BOARD OF GOVERNORS. — The term "nonbank financial company supervised by the Board of Governors" means a nonbank financial company that the Council has determined under section 113 shall be supervised by the Board of Governors.

(5) OFFICE OF FINANCIAL RESEARCH. — The term "Office of Financial Research" means the office established under section 152.

(6) PREDOMINANTLY ENGAGED. — A company is "predominantly engaged in financial activities" if —

(A) the annual gross revenues derived by the company and all of its subsidiaries from activities that are financial in nature (as defined in section 4(k) of the Bank Holding Company Act of 1956) and, if applicable, from the ownership or control of one or more insured depository institutions, represents 85 percent or more of the consolidated annual gross revenues of the company; or

(B) the consolidated assets of the company and all of its subsidiaries related to activities that are financial in nature (as defined in section 4(k) of the Bank Holding Company Act of 1956) and, if applicable, related to the ownership or control of one or more insured depository institutions, represents 85 percent or more of the consolidated assets of the company.

(7) SIGNIFICANT INSTITUTIONS. — The terms "significant nonbank financial company" and "significant bank holding company" have the meanings given those terms by rule of the Board of Governors, but in no instance shall the term "significant nonbank financial company" include those entities that are excluded under paragraph (4)(B).

(b) DEFINITIONAL CRITERIA. — The Board of Governors shall establish, by regulation, the requirements for determining if a company is predominantly engaged in financial activities, as defined in subsection (a)(6).

(c) FOREIGN NONBANK FINANCIAL COMPANIES. — For purposes of the application of subtitles A and C (other than section 113(b)) with respect to a foreign nonbank financial company, references in this title to "company" or "subsidiary" include

生品结算组织(或其母公司,除非该母公司为银行控股公司)、互换执行设施或互换数据存管机构——

(i)按照美国联邦法律或任何州法律设立或组建;且

(ii)主营第(6)款所定义的金融活动。

(C)**非银行金融公司**。——“非银行金融公司”一词系指美国非银行金融公司及外国非银行金融公司。

(D)**受联邦储备委员会监管的非银行金融公司**。——“受联邦储备委员会监管的非银行金融公司”一词系指金融稳定监督委员会根据第113条判定应由联邦储备委员会监管的非银行金融公司。

(5)**金融研究办公室**。——“金融研究办公室”一词系指按照第152条规定设立的办公室。

(6)**主营金融业务**。——以下情形下,公司将被认定为“主营金融业务”——

(A)公司及其全部子公司通过金融性质活动[定义见《1956年银行控股公司法》第4(k)条]获得的以及(如适用)通过拥有或者控制一家或一家以上参保存款机构获得的年度总收入,在该公司并表年度总收入中占比达85%(含)以上;或

(B)公司及其全部子公司与金融性质活动[定义见《1956年银行控股公司法》第4(k)条]相关的,以及(如适用)与拥有或者控制一家或一家以上参保存款机构相关的并表资产,在该公司并表资产中占比达85%(含)以上。

(7)**重要机构**。——“重要非银行金融公司”及“重要银行控股公司”的含义以联邦储备委员会发布的规则中的定义为准,但在任何情况下“重要非银行金融公司”一词均不包括第(4)(B)款所排除的实体。

(b) **定义标准**。——联邦储备委员会应发布规章制定相关标准,以判定以第(a)(6)子条的定义而言,公司是否主营金融活动。

(c)**外国非银行金融公司**。——除非另有规定,否则,在针对外国非银行金融公司适用第A子编和第C子编[但第113(b)条除外]的规定时,外国非银行金融公司仅在美国从事活动之时方得被视为本编所提及的“公司”,而该等公司的美国子公司方得被

only the United States activities and subsidiaries of such foreign company, except as otherwise provided.

Subtitle A — Financial Stability Oversight Council

SEC. 111. FINANCIAL STABILITY OVERSIGHT COUNCIL ESTABLISHED.

(a) ESTABLISHMENT. — Effective on the date of enactment of this Act, there is established the Financial Stability Oversight Council.

(b) MEMBERSHIP. — The Council shall consist of the following members:

(1) VOTING MEMBERS. — The voting members, who shall each have 1 vote on the Council shall be —

(A) the Secretary of the Treasury, who shall serve as Chairperson of the Council;

(B) the Chairman of the Board of Governors;

(C) the Comptroller of the Currency;

(D) the Director of the Bureau;

(E) the Chairman of the Commission;

(F) the Chairperson of the Corporation;

(G) the Chairperson of the Commodity Futures Trading Commission;

(H) the Director of the Federal Housing Finance Agency;

(I) the Chairman of the National Credit Union Administration Board; and

(J) an independent member appointed by the President, by and with the advice and consent of the Senate, having insurance expertise.

(2) NONVOTING MEMBERS. — The nonvoting members, who shall serve in an advisory capacity as a nonvoting member of the Council, shall be —

(A) the Director of the Office of Financial Research;

(B) the Director of the Federal Insurance Office;

(C) a State insurance commissioner, to be designated by a selection process determined by the State insurance commissioners;

(D) a State banking supervisor, to be designated by a selection process determined by the State banking supervisors; and

(E) a State securities commissioner (or an officer performing like functions), to be designated by a selection process determined by such State securities commissioners.

(3) NONVOTING MEMBER PARTICIPATION. — The nonvoting members of the Council shall not be excluded from any of the proceedings, meetings, discussions, or deliberations of the Council, except that the Chairperson may, upon an affirmative vote of

视为本编所提及的“子公司”。

第A子编——金融稳定监督委员会

第111条　设立金融稳定监督委员会

(a)**设立**。——金融稳定监督委员会自本法颁布之日起设立。

(b)**成员**。——金融稳定监督委员会由以下成员组成:

(1)**有表决权成员**。——金融稳定监督委员会的每名有表决权成员拥有一票表决权,包括——

(A)财政部部长,任金融稳定监督委员会主席;

(B)联邦储备委员会主席;

(C)货币监理署署长;

(D)消费者金融保护局局长;

(E)证券交易委员会主席;

(F)联邦存款保险公司主席;

(G)商品期货交易委员会主席;

(H)联邦住房金融局局长;

(I)国家信贷联盟署委员会主席;及

(J)经参议院建议和同意,由总统任命的一名具有保险专长的独立成员。

(2)**无表决权成员**。——无表决权成员以顾问身份参与金融稳定监督委员会,不享有表决权,其中包括——

(A)金融研究办公室主任;

(B)联邦保险办公室主任;

(C)按照各州保险监督官确定的遴选程序指定的一名州保险监督官;

(D)按照各州银行监管者确定的遴选程序指定的一名州银行监督官;及

(E)按照各州证券监督官确定的遴选程序指定的一名州证券监督官(或履行类似职能的一名官员)。

(3)**无表决权成员的参与**。——金融稳定监督委员会举行或开展任何程序、会议、讨论或审议时,均不得将无表决权成员排除在外,但是经成员机关表决赞成,在必要时,金融稳定监督委员会主席可以出于保护并促进保密性监管信息自由交流之目

the member agencies, exclude the nonvoting members from any of the proceedings, meetings, discussions, or deliberations of the Council when necessary to safeguard and promote the free exchange of confidential supervisory information.

(c) TERMS; VACANCY. —

(1) TERMS. — The independent member of the Council shall serve for a term of 6 years, and each nonvoting member described in subparagraphs (C), (D), and (E) of subsection (b)(2) shall serve for a term of 2 years.

(2) VACANCY. — Any vacancy on the Council shall be filled in the manner in which the original appointment was made.

(3) ACTING OFFICIALS MAY SERVE. — In the event of a vacancy in the office of the head of a member agency or department, and pending the appointment of a successor, or during the absence or disability of the head of a member agency or department, the acting head of the member agency or department shall serve as a member of the Council in the place of that agency or department head.

(d) TECHNICAL AND PROFESSIONAL ADVISORY COMMITTEES. — The Council may appoint such special advisory, technical, or professional committees as may be useful in carrying out the functions of the Council, including an advisory committee consisting of State regulators, and the members of such committees may be members of the Council, or other persons, or both.

(e) MEETINGS. —

(1) TIMING. — The Council shall meet at the call of the Chairperson or a majority of the members then serving, but not less frequently than quarterly.

(2) RULES FOR CONDUCTING BUSINESS. — The Council shall adopt such rules as may be necessary for the conduct of the business of the Council. Such rules shall be rules of agency organization, procedure, or practice for purposes of section 553 of title 5, United States Code.

(f) VOTING. — Unless otherwise specified, the Council shall make all decisions that it is authorized or required to make by a majority vote of the voting members then serving.

(g) NONAPPLICABILITY OF FACA. — The Federal Advisory Committee Act (5 U.S.C. App.) shall not apply to the Council, or to any special advisory, technical, or professional committee appointed by the Council, except that, if an advisory, technical, or professional committee has one or more members who are not employees of or affiliated with the United States Government, the Council shall publish a list of the names of the members of such committee.

(h) ASSISTANCE FROM FEDERAL AGENCIES. — Any department or agency of the United States may provide to the Council and any special advisory, technical, or

的,将无表决权成员排除在金融稳定监督委员会的任何程序、会议、讨论或审议之外。

(c)**任期;席位空缺。**——

(1)**任期**。——金融稳定监督委员会独立成员的任期为6年;第(b)(2)子条第(C)子款、第(D)子款及第(E)子款所述每一无表决权成员的任期均为2年。

(2)**席位空缺**。——金融稳定监督委员会出现任何席位空缺的,均应按照原任命方式进行填补。

(3)**代理官员可履行成员职责**。——成员机关或部门的负责人职位出现空缺且尚未任命继任负责人,或者成员机关或部门的负责人缺席或丧失行为能力的,在上述期间内,该成员机关或部门的代理负责人应代为履行金融稳定监督委员会成员的职责。

(d)**技术与专业顾问委员会**。——金融稳定监督委员会可以成立特别顾问、技术或专业委员会,协助金融稳定监督委员会履行职能,包括可以成立由州监管者组成的顾问委员会。该等委员会的成员可以为金融稳定监督委员会成员、其他人士或兼涉二者。

(e)**会议**。——

(1)**时间**。——金融稳定监督委员会会议应由主席或过半数届时在任成员召集,但会议召开频率不得低于每季度一次。

(2)**业务开展规则**。——金融稳定监督委员会应根据业务开展需要制定必要规则。该等规则应属于《美国法典》第五编第553节规定的机关组织、程序或工作规则。

(f)**表决**。——除非另有规定,否则,金融稳定监督委员会有权或有义务作出的所有决定均应由过半数届时在任有表决权的成员表决通过。

(g)**不适用《联邦顾问委员会法》**。——《联邦顾问委员会法》(《美国法典》第五编附件)不得适用于金融稳定监督委员会或其成立的任何特别顾问、技术或专业委员会;但是,如果顾问、技术或专业委员会包括一名或一名以上不具有美国政府雇员或美国政府关联人员身份的成员,金融稳定监督委员会应公布该等委员会的成员名单。

(h)**联邦机关提供的协助**。——任何美国联邦部门或机关均可向金融稳定监督委员会及其成立的任何特别顾问、技术或专业委员会提供金融稳定监督委员会判定

professional committee appointed by the Council, such services, funds, facilities, staff, and other support services as the Council may determine advisable.

(i) COMPENSATION OF MEMBERS. —

(1) FEDERAL EMPLOYEE MEMBERS. — All members of the Council who are officers or employees of the United States shall serve without compensation in addition to that received for their services as officers or employees of the United States.

(2) COMPENSATION FOR NON–FEDERAL MEMBER. — Section 5314 of title 5, United States Code, is amended by adding at the end the following:

"Independent Member of the Financial Stability Oversight Council (1). ".

(j) DETAIL OF GOVERNMENT EMPLOYEES. — Any employee of the Federal Government may be detailed to the Council without reimbursement, and such detail shall be without interruption or loss of civil service status or privilege. An employee of the Federal Government detailed to the Council shall report to and be subject to oversight by the Council during the assignment to the Council, and shall be compensated by the department or agency from which the employee was detailed.

SEC. 112. COUNCIL AUTHORITY.

(a) PURPOSES AND DUTIES OF THE COUNCIL. —

(1) IN GENERAL. — The purposes of the Council are —

(A) to identify risks to the financial stability of the United States that could arise from the material financial distress or failure, or ongoing activities, of large, interconnected bank holding companies or nonbank financial companies, or that could arise outside the financial services marketplace;

(B) to promote market discipline, by eliminating expectations on the part of shareholders, creditors, and counterparties of such companies that the Government will shield them from losses in the event of failure; and

(C) to respond to emerging threats to the stability of the United States financial system.

(2) DUTIES. — The Council shall, in accordance with this title —

(A) collect information from member agencies, other Federal and State financial regulatory agencies, the Federal Insurance Office and, if necessary to assess risks to the United States financial system, direct the Office of Financial Research to collect information from bank holding companies and nonbank financial companies;

(B) provide direction to, and request data and analyses from, the Office of Financial Research to support the work of the Council;

(C) monitor the financial services marketplace in order to identify potential threats to the financial stability of the United States;

(D) to monitor domestic and international financial regulatory proposals and

为有益的服务、资金、设施、人员及其他支持服务。

(i)**成员薪酬**。——

(1)**身为联邦政府雇员的成员**。——身为美国联邦政府官员或职员的金融稳定监督委员会成员,除因担任美国联邦政府官员或职员而获得薪酬之外,不得因在金融稳定监督委员会任职而获得额外报酬。

(2)**非联邦政府成员的薪酬**。——在《美国法典》第五编第5314节结尾处增加如下内容,作为对该节的修正:

"金融稳定监督委员会的独立成员(1)。"

(j)**政府雇员的选派**。——联邦政府的任何雇员均可无偿选派至金融稳定监督委员会任职,且其公务员身份或特权不因该等选派而中断或丧失。选派至金融稳定监督委员会的联邦政府雇员在派遣期间应向金融稳定监督委员会汇报工作并接受其监督,且应由该雇员的派遣部门或机关支付薪酬。

第112条　金融稳定监督委员会的权力

(a)**金融稳定监督委员会的宗旨和职责**。——

(1)**一般规定**。——金融稳定监督委员会的宗旨为——

(A)识别相互关联的大型银行控股公司或非银行金融公司的重大财务困境、经营失败或者正在开展的活动可能导致的金融稳定风险,或者金融服务市场之外可能产生的金融稳定风险;

(B)矫正该等公司股东、债权人及对手方的观念,使之不再预期政府在该等公司经营失败时为其损失埋单,从而加强市场约束;及

(C)应对美国金融体系稳定面临的新威胁。

(2)**职责**。——金融稳定监督委员会应按照本编规定——

(A)向成员机关、其他联邦金融监管机关和州金融监管机关以及联邦保险办公室收集信息,对美国金融体系面临的风险进行必要评估,并指令金融研究办公室向银行控股公司和非银行金融公司收集信息;

(B)为金融研究办公室提供指导,要求其提供相关数据和分析,为金融稳定监督委员会的工作提供支持;

(C)监控金融服务市场,识别美国金融稳定面临的潜在威胁;

(D)监控国内和国际金融监管新理念和发展动态,包括保险及会计事宜,并就相

developments, including insurance and accounting issues, and to advise Congress and make recommendations in such areas that will enhance the integrity, efficiency, competitiveness, and stability of the U.S. financial markets;

(E) facilitate information sharing and coordination among the member agencies and other Federal and State agencies regarding domestic financial services policy development, rulemaking, examinations, reporting requirements, and enforcement actions;

(F) recommend to the member agencies general supervisory priorities and principles reflecting the outcome of discussions among the member agencies;

(G) identify gaps in regulation that could pose risks to the financial stability of the United States;

(H) require supervision by the Board of Governors for nonbank financial companies that may pose risks to the financial stability of the United States in the event of their material financial distress or failure, or because of their activities pursuant to section 113;

(I) make recommendations to the Board of Governors concerning the establishment of heightened prudential standards for risk-based capital, leverage, liquidity, contingent capital, resolution plans and credit exposure reports, concentration limits, enhanced public disclosures, and overall risk management for nonbank financial companies and large, interconnected bank holding companies supervised by the Board of Governors;

(J) identify systemically important financial market utilities and payment, clearing, and settlement activities (as that term is defined in title VIII);

(K) make recommendations to primary financial regulatory agencies to apply new or heightened standards and safeguards for financial activities or practices that could create or increase risks of significant liquidity, credit, or other problems spreading among bank holding companies, nonbank financial companies, and United States financial markets;

(L) review and, as appropriate, may submit comments to the Commission and any standard—setting body with respect to an existing or proposed accounting principle, standard, or procedure;

(M) provide a forum for —

(i) discussion and analysis of emerging market developments and financial regulatory issues; and

(ii) resolution of jurisdictional disputes among the members of the Council; and

(N) annually report to and testify before Congress on —

(i) the activities of the Council;

(ii) significant financial market and regulatory developments, including insurance and accounting regulations and standards, along with an assessment of those developments on the stability of the financial system;

(iii) potential emerging threats to the financial stability of the United States;

关领域向国会提供意见和建议,促进美国金融市场的诚信度、效率、竞争力和稳定性;

(E)促进成员机关以及其他联邦机关和州机关之间在国内金融服务政策制定、规则制定、检查、报告要求及执法行动方面实现信息共享和协调;

(F)基于成员机关之间的讨论结果,就总体监管重点和原则向成员机关提出建议;

(G)识别可能对美国金融稳定造成风险的监管漏洞;

(H)在非银行金融公司出现重大财务困境、经营失败或者依第113条从事的活动,可能对美国金融稳定造成风险之时,要求联邦储备委员会对非银行金融公司进行监管;

(I)就受联邦储备委员会监管的非银行金融公司和相互关联的大型银行控股公司而言,针对其风险基础资本、杠杆、流动性、或有资本、清盘计划及信用风险敞口报告、集中度限制、更严格的公开披露及整体风险管理,建议联邦储备委员会制定更严格的审慎性标准;

(J)识别具有系统重要性的金融市场服务平台及支付、清算和结算活动(定义见第八编);

(K)针对可能引发或加深重大流动性、信用或其他问题的风险在银行控股公司、非银行金融公司及美国金融市场之间相互传播的活动或做法,建议优先金融监管机关适用新的或更严格的标准和保障措施;

(L)审查现行或作为草案提出的会计原则、标准或程序,并在适当情况下,向证券交易委员会及任何标准制定机构提交审查意见;

(M)为以下活动提供平台——

(i)讨论并分析新兴市场发展和金融监管事宜;及

(ii)解决金融稳定监督委员会成员之间的管辖权争议;及

(N)就以下事项向国会提交年度报告并向国会作证——

(i)金融稳定监督委员会的活动;

(ii)重大金融市场及监管发展动态(包括保险及会计规章和标准),以及该等发展动态对金融体系稳定性的影响的评估;

(iii)美国金融稳定面临的新的潜在威胁;

(iv) all determinations made under section 113 or title VIII, and the basis for such determinations;

(v) all recommendations made under section 119 and the result of such recommendations; and

(vi) recommendations —

(I) to enhance the integrity, efficiency, competitiveness, and stability of United States financial markets;

(II) to promote market discipline; and

(III) to maintain investor confidence.

(b) STATEMENTS BY VOTING MEMBERS OF THE COUNCIL. — At the time at which each report is submitted under subsection (a), each voting member of the Council shall —

(1) if such member believes that the Council, the Government, and the private sector are taking all reasonable steps to ensure financial stability and to mitigate systemic risk that would negatively affect the economy, submit a signed statement to Congress stating such belief; or

(2) if such member does not believe that all reasonable steps described under paragraph (1) are being taken, submit a signed statement to Congress stating what actions such member believes need to be taken in order to ensure that all reasonable steps described under paragraph (1) are taken.

(c) TESTIMONY BY THE CHAIRPERSON. — The Chairperson shall appear before the Committee on Financial Services of the House of Representatives and the Committee on Banking, Housing, and Urban Affairs of the Senate at an annual hearing, after the report is submitted under subsection (a) —

(1) to discuss the efforts, activities, objectives, and plans of the Council; and

(2) to discuss and answer questions concerning such report.

(d) AUTHORITY TO OBTAIN INFORMATION. —

(1) IN GENERAL. — The Council may receive, and may request the submission of, any data or information from the Office of Financial Research, member agencies, and the Federal Insurance Office, as necessary —

(A) to monitor the financial services marketplace to identify potential risks to the financial stability of the United States; or

(B) to otherwise carry out any of the provisions of this title.

(2) SUBMISSIONS BY THE OFFICE AND MEMBER AGENCIES. — Notwithstanding any other provision of law, the Office of Financial Research, any member agency, and the Federal Insurance Office, are authorized to submit information to the Council.

(iv)根据第113条或第八编作出的所有判定,以及作出该等判定的依据;

(v)根据第119条提出的所有建议,以及该等建议的结果;及

(vi)为如下目的提出的建议——

(I)促进美国金融市场的诚信度、效率、竞争力和稳定性;

(II)加强市场约束;及

(III)保持投资者信心。

(b)**金融稳定监督委员会有表决权成员的声明**。——根据第(a)子条规定提交每一份报告时,金融稳定监督委员会的每一有表决权成员——

(1)如果认为金融稳定监督委员会、政府及私人部门正在采取所有的合理措施,确保金融稳定并缓释可能对经济产生负面影响的系统性风险,则应向国会提交一份经签署的声明说明上述观点;或

(2)如果认为金融稳定监督委员会、政府及私人部门没有采取第(1)款所述所有的合理措施,则应向国会提交一份经签署的声明,说明其认为需要采取何等行动以确保第(1)款所述所有的合理措施得以落实。

(c)**主席证词**。——在根据第(a)子条规定提交报告后,主席应出席众议院金融服务委员会以及参议院银行、住房与城市事务委员会召集的年度听证会——

(1)讨论金融稳定监督委员会的工作、活动、目标和计划;及

(2)讨论和答复与上述报告相关的问题。

(d)**信息获取权**。——

(1)**一般规定**。——金融稳定监督委员会可以接收金融研究办公室、成员机关及联邦保险办公室呈报的任何必要数据和信息,并可以要求该等机关呈报必要数据和信息,以——

(A)监控金融服务市场,识别美国金融稳定面临的潜在风险;或

(B)实施本编任何规定。

(2)**办公室及成员机关的信息呈报**。——无论是否存在任何不同法律规定,金融研究办公室、任何成员机关及联邦保险办公室均可以向金融稳定监督委员会呈报信息。

(3) FINANCIAL DATA COLLECTION. —

(A) IN GENERAL. — The Council, acting through the Office of Financial Research, may require the submission of periodic and other reports from any nonbank financial company or bank holding company for the purpose of assessing the extent to which a financial activity or financial market in which the nonbank financial company or bank holding company participates, or the nonbank financial company or bank holding company itself, poses a threat to the financial stability of the United States.

(B) MITIGATION OF REPORT BURDEN. — Before requiring the submission of reports from any nonbank financial company or bank holding company that is regulated by a member agency or any primary financial regulatory agency, the Council, acting through the Office of Financial Research, shall coordinate with such agencies and shall, whenever possible, rely on information available from the Office of Financial Research or such agencies.

(C) MITIGATION IN CASE OF FOREIGN FINANCIAL COMPANIES. — Before requiring the submission of reports from a company that is a foreign nonbank financial company or foreign-based bank holding company, the Council shall, acting through the Office of Financial Research, to the extent appropriate, consult with the appropriate foreign regulator of such company and, whenever possible, rely on information already being collected by such foreign regulator, with English translation.

(4) BACK-UP EXAMINATION BY THE BOARD OF GOVERNORS. — If the Council is unable to determine whether the financial activities of a U.S. nonbank financial company pose a threat to the financial stability of the United States, based on information or reports obtained under paragraphs (1) and (3), discussions with management, and publicly available information, the Council may request the Board of Governors, and the Board of Governors is authorized, to conduct an examination of the U.S. nonbank financial company for the sole purpose of determining whether the nonbank financial company should be supervised by the Board of Governors for purposes of this title.

(5) CONFIDENTIALITY. —

(A) IN GENERAL. — The Council, the Office of Financial Research, and the other member agencies shall maintain the confidentiality of any data, information, and reports submitted under this title.

(B) RETENTION OF PRIVILEGE. — The submission of any nonpublicly available data or information under this subsection and subtitle B shall not constitute a waiver of, or otherwise affect, any privilege arising under Federal or State law (including the rules of any Federal or State court) to which the data or information is otherwise subject.

(C) FREEDOM OF INFORMATION ACT. — Section 552 of title 5, United States Code, including the exceptions thereunder, shall apply to any data or information

(3)**金融数据收集**。——

(A)**一般规定**。——金融稳定监督委员会可以通过金融研究办公室要求任何非银行金融公司或银行控股公司提交定期报告及其他报告,以评估非银行金融公司或银行控股公司参与的金融活动或金融市场对美国金融稳定造成的威胁程度,或者非银行金融公司或银行控股公司本身对美国金融稳定造成的威胁程度。

(B)**减轻报告负担**。——在要求受成员机关或任何优先金融监管机关监管的任何非银行金融公司或银行控股公司提交报告之前,金融稳定监督委员会应通过金融研究办公室与该等成员机关或监管机关协调,并尽可能采信金融研究办公室或该等机关提供的信息。

(C)**减轻外国金融公司的报告负担**。——在要求外国非银行金融公司或外国银行控股公司提交报告之前,金融稳定监督委员会应通过金融研究办公室,在适当范围内与该等公司的适当外国监管者磋商,并尽可能采信该等外国监管者已经收集的具有英文译本的信息。

(4)**联邦储备委员会的后备检查权**。——如果金融稳定监督委员会基于根据第(1)款和第(3)款规定获取的相关信息或报告、与管理层开展的讨论以及公开信息,仍无法判定美国非银行金融公司的金融活动是否对美国金融稳定构成威胁,金融稳定监督委员会可以请求联邦储备委员会对该美国非银行金融公司开展检查,且联邦储备委员会有权开展该等检查,但检查目的必须仅限于判定该非银行金融公司就本编而言是否应受联邦储备委员会监管。

(5)**保密**。——

(A)**一般规定**。——金融稳定监督委员会、金融研究办公室及其他成员机关应对依本编规定提交的任何数据、信息和报告进行保密。

(B)**保留保密特权**。——根据本子条及第B子编规定提交任何非公开数据或信息,并不表示提交人放弃依据适用于该等数据或信息的联邦法律或州法律(包括任何联邦法院或州法院的规则)享有的任何保密特权,也不对该等保密特权产生其他影响。

(C)**《信息自由法》**。——依据本子条及第B子编规定提交的任何数据或信息,均应适用《美国法典》第五编第552节的规定(包括其中的例外规定)。

submitted under this subsection and subtitle B.

SEC. 113. AUTHORITY TO REQUIRE SUPERVISION AND REGULATION OF CERTAIN NONBANK FINANCIAL COMPANIES.

(a) U.S. NONBANK FINANCIAL COMPANIES SUPERVISED BY THE BOARD OF GOVERNORS. —

(1) DETERMINATION. — The Council, on a nondelegable basis and by a vote of not fewer than 2/3 of the voting members then serving, including an affirmative vote by the Chairperson, may determine that a U.S. nonbank financial company shall be supervised by the Board of Governors and shall be subject to prudential standards, in accordance with this title, if the Council determines that material financial distress at the U.S. nonbank financial company, or the nature, scope, size, scale, concentration, interconnectedness, or mix of the activities of the U.S. nonbank financial company, could pose a threat to the financial stability of the United States.

(2) CONSIDERATIONS. — In making a determination under paragraph (1), the Council shall consider —

(A) the extent of the leverage of the company;

(B) the extent and nature of the off–balance–sheet exposures of the company;

(C) the extent and nature of the transactions and relationships of the company with other significant nonbank financial companies and significant bank holding companies;

(D) the importance of the company as a source of credit for households, businesses, and State and local governments and as a source of liquidity for the United States financial system;

(E) the importance of the company as a source of credit for low–income, minority, or underserved communities, and the impact that the failure of such company would have on the availability of credit in such communities;

(F) the extent to which assets are managed rather than owned by the company, and the extent to which ownership of assets under management is diffuse;

(G) the nature, scope, size, scale, concentration, inter–connectedness, and mix of the activities of the company;

(H) the degree to which the company is already regulated by 1 or more primary financial regulatory agencies;

(I) the amount and nature of the financial assets of the company;

(J) the amount and types of the liabilities of the company, including the degree of reliance on short–term funding; and

(K) any other risk–related factors that the Council deems appropriate.

(b) FOREIGN NONBANK FINANCIAL COMPANIES SUPERVISED BY THE BOARD OF GOVERNORS. —

第113条　要求对特定非银行金融公司进行监管与规制的权力

(a)**受联邦储备委员会监管的美国非银行金融公司**。——

(1)**判定**。——如果金融稳定监督委员会判定,某美国非银行金融公司发生的重大财务困境或其活动性质、范围、数额、规模、集中度、相互关联程度或组合可能对美国金融稳定造成威胁,则经至少2/3届时在任的有表决权成员表决通过(且其中必须包括主席的赞成票),金融稳定监督委员会可以按照本编规定判定,该美国非银行金融公司应受联邦储备委员会监管并遵守审慎性标准(金融稳定监督委员会不得将此权力委托给任何其他机构)。

(2)**考虑因素**。——根据第(1)款作出判定时,金融稳定监督委员会应考虑如下因素——

(A)公司的杠杆率;

(B)公司表外风险的范围和性质;

(C)公司与其他重要非银行金融公司及重要银行控股公司之间的交易和关系之范围和性质;

(D)公司作为家庭、企业以及州政府和地方政府信贷来源所具有的重要性,或作为美国金融体系流动性来源所具有的重要性;

(E)公司作为低收入群体、少数族裔或弱势群体信贷来源所具有的重要性,以及公司经营失败会对该等群体获取信贷的能力的影响;

(F)公司管理的非自有资产的占比,以及其管理的资产的所有权分散程度;

(G)公司活动的性质、范围、数额、规模、集中度、相互关联程度或组合;

(H)公司已受一家或一家以上优先金融监管机关监管的程度;

(I)公司金融资产的金额及性质;

(J)公司债务的金额及类型,包括对短期融资的依赖程度;及

(K)金融稳定监督委员会认为适当的任何其他风险因素。

(b)**受联邦储备委员会监管的外国非银行金融公司**。——

(1) DETERMINATION. — The Council, on a nondelegable basis and by a vote of not fewer than 2/3 of the voting members then serving, including an affirmative vote by the Chairperson, may determine that a foreign nonbank financial company shall be supervised by the Board of Governors and shall be subject to prudential standards, in accordance with this title, if the Council determines that material financial distress at the foreign nonbank financial company, or the nature, scope, size, scale, concentration, interconnectedness, or mix of the activities of the foreign nonbank financial company, could pose a threat to the financial stability of the United States.

(2) CONSIDERATIONS. — In making a determination under paragraph (1), the Council shall consider —

(A) the extent of the leverage of the company;

(B) the extent and nature of the United States related off–balance–sheet exposures of the company;

(C) the extent and nature of the transactions and relationships of the company with other significant nonbank financial companies and significant bank holding companies;

(D) the importance of the company as a source of credit for United States households, businesses, and State and local governments and as a source of liquidity for the United States financial system;

(E) the importance of the company as a source of credit for low–income, minority, or underserved communities in the United States, and the impact that the failure of such company would have on the availability of credit in such communities;

(F) the extent to which assets are managed rather than owned by the company and the extent to which ownership of assets under management is diffuse;

(G) the nature, scope, size, scale, concentration, inter–connectedness, and mix of the activities of the company;

(H) the extent to which the company is subject to prudential standards on a consolidated basis in its home country that are administered and enforced by a comparable foreign supervisory authority;

(I) the amount and nature of the United States financial assets of the company;

(J) the amount and nature of the liabilities of the company used to fund activities and operations in the United States, including the degree of reliance on short –term funding; and

(K) any other risk–related factors that the Council deems appropriate.

(c) ANTIEVASION. —

(1) DETERMINATIONS. — In order to avoid evasion of this title, the Council, on its own initiative or at the request of the Board of Governors, may determine, on a nondelegable basis and by a vote of not fewer than 2/3 of the voting members then

(1)**判定**。——如果金融稳定监督委员会判定，某外国非银行金融公司发生的重大财务困境或其活动的性质、范围、数额、规模、集中度、相互关联程度或组合可能对美国金融稳定造成威胁，则经至少2/3届时在任的有表决权成员表决通过(且其中必须包括主席的赞成票)，金融稳定监督委员会可以按照本编规定判定，该外国非银行金融公司应受联邦储备委员会监管并遵守审慎性标准(金融稳定监督委员会不得将此权力委托给任何其他机构)。

(2)**考虑因素**。——根据第(1)款作出判定时，金融稳定监督委员会应考虑如下因素——

(A)该公司的杠杆率；

(B)该公司表外风险敞口的范围和性质；

(C)该公司与其他重要非银行金融公司及重要银行控股公司之间的交易和关系之范围和性质；

(D)该公司作为家庭、企业以及州政府和地方政府信贷来源所具有的重要性，或作为美国金融体系流动性来源所具有的重要性；

(E)该公司作为美国低收入群体、少数族裔或弱势群体信贷来源所具有的重要性，以及公司经营失败会对该等群体获取信贷的能力产生的影响；

(F)该公司管理的非自有资产的占比，以及其管理的资产的所有权分散程度；

(G)该公司活动的性质、范围、数额、规模、集中度、相互关联程度或组合；

(H)在多大程度上，该公司在母国受制于外国监管机构实施并执行的具有可比性的并表审慎性标准；

(I)该公司美国境内金融资产的金额及性质；

(J)该公司用于为美国境内活动及运营提供资金的债务金额及类型，包括对短期融资的依赖程度；及

(K)金融稳定监督委员会认为适当的任何其他风险因素。

(c)**反规避**。——

(1)**判定**。——为了防范规避本编规定的行为，经至少2/3届时在任的有表决权成员表决通过(且其中必须包括主席的赞成票)，金融稳定监督委员会可以主动或按照联邦储备委员会的请求作出如下判定(金融稳定监督委员会不得将此权力委托给任

serving, including an affirmative vote by the Chairperson, that —

(A) material financial distress related to, or the nature, scope, size, scale, concentration, interconnectedness, or mix of, the financial activities conducted directly or indirectly by a company incorporated or organized under the laws of the United States or any State or the financial activities in the United States of a company incorporated or organized in a country other than the United States would pose a threat to the financial stability of the United States, based on consideration of the factors in subsection (a)(2) or (b)(2), as applicable;

(B) the company is organized or operates in such a manner as to evade the application of this title; and

(C) such financial activities of the company shall be supervised by the Board of Governors and subject to prudential standards in accordance with this title, consistent with paragraph (3).

(2) REPORT. — Upon making a determination under paragraph (1), the Council shall submit a report to the appropriate committees of Congress detailing the reasons for making such determination.

(3) CONSOLIDATED SUPERVISION OF ONLY FINANCIAL ACTIVITIES; ESTABLISHMENT OF AN INTERMEDIATE HOLDING COMPANY. —

(A) ESTABLISHMENT OF AN INTERMEDIATE HOLDING COMPANY. — Upon a determination under paragraph (1), the company that is the subject of the determination may establish an intermediate holding company in which the financial activities of such company and its subsidiaries shall be conducted (other than the activities described in section 167(b)(2)) in compliance with any regulations or guidance provided by the Board of Governors. Such intermediate holding company shall be subject to the supervision of the Board of Governors and to prudential standards under this title as if the intermediate holding company were a nonbank financial company supervised by the Board of Governors.

(B) ACTION OF THE BOARD OF GOVERNORS. — To facilitate the supervision of the financial activities subject to the determination in paragraph (1), the Board of Governors may require a company to establish an intermediate holding company, as provided for in section 167, which would be subject to the supervision of the Board of Governors and to prudential standards under this title, as if the intermediate holding company were a nonbank financial company supervised by the Board of Governors.

(4) NOTICE AND OPPORTUNITY FOR HEARING AND FINAL DETERMINATION; JUDICIAL REVIEW. — Subsections (d) through (h) shall apply to determinations made by the Council pursuant to paragraph (1) in the same manner as such subsections apply to nonbank financial companies.

何其他机构)——

(A)金融稳定监督委员会在考虑第(a)(2)子条或第(b)(2)子条规定的适用因素之后判定,按照美国联邦法律或任何州法律设立或组建的公司所直接或间接开展的金融活动,或者在美国之外的其他国家设立或组建的公司在美国境内开展的金融活动,所发生的重大财务困境或性质、范围、数额、规模、集中度、相互关联程度或组合将对美国金融稳定造成威胁;

(B)公司组建或运营的方式以规避本编规定之适用为目的;且

(C)按照第(3)款的规定,公司的该等金融活动应按照本编规定受联邦储备委员会监管并遵守审慎性标准。

(2)**报告**。——根据第(1)款作出判定后,金融稳定监督委员会应向相应的国会委员会提交一份报告,具体说明作出该等判定的理由。

(3)**仅针对金融活动的并表监管;设立中间控股公司**。——

(A)**设立中间控股公司**。——在金融稳定监督委员会根据第(1)款规定作出判定后,被作出判定的公司可设立中间控股公司,按照联邦储备委员会规定的任何规章或指引,通过该中间控股公司开展该公司及其子公司的金融活动[但第167(b)(2)条所述活动除外]。该中间控股公司应受联邦储备委员会监管并遵守本编规定的审慎性标准,如同其为受联邦储备委员会监管的非银行金融公司。

(B)**联邦储备委员会的行动**。——为了促进对第(1)款判定所涉金融活动的监管,联邦储备委员会可以要求相关公司按照第167条规定设立中间控股公司,该中间控股公司应受联邦储备委员会监管并遵守本编规定的审慎性标准,如同其为受联邦储备委员会监管的非银行金融公司。

(4)**听证通知和机会及最终判定;司法审查**。——第(d)子条至第(h)子条规定应适用于金融稳定监督委员会根据第(1)款作出的判定,适用方式与适用于非银行金融公司之时完全一致。

(5) COVERED FINANCIAL ACTIVITIES. — For purposes of this subsection, the term "financial activities" —

(A) means activities that are financial in nature (as defined in section 4(k) of the Bank Holding Company Act of 1956);

(B) includes the ownership or control of one or more insured depository institutions; and

(C) does not include internal financial activities conducted for the company or any affiliate thereof, including internal treasury, investment, and employee benefit functions.

(6) ONLY FINANCIAL ACTIVITIES SUBJECT TO PRUDENTIAL SUPERVISION. — Nonfinancial activities of the company shall not be subject to supervision by the Board of Governors and prudential standards of the Board. For purposes of this Act, the financial activities that are the subject of the determination in paragraph (1) shall be subject to the same requirements as a nonbank financial company supervised by the Board of Governors. Nothing in this paragraph shall prohibit or limit the authority of the Board of Governors to apply prudential standards under this title to the financial activities that are subject to the determination in paragraph (1).

(d) REEVALUATION AND RESCISSION. — The Council shall —

(1) not less frequently than annually, reevaluate each determination made under subsections (a) and (b) with respect to such nonbank financial company supervised by the Board of Governors; and

(2) rescind any such determination, if the Council, by a vote of not fewer than 2/3 of the voting members then serving, including an affirmative vote by the Chairperson, determines that the nonbank financial company no longer meets the standards under subsection (a) or (b), as applicable.

(e) NOTICE AND OPPORTUNITY FOR HEARING AND FINAL DETERMINATION. —

(1) IN GENERAL. — The Council shall provide to a nonbank financial company written notice of a proposed determination of the Council, including an explanation of the basis of the proposed determination of the Council, that a nonbank financial company shall be supervised by the Board of Governors and shall be subject to prudential standards in accordance with this title.

(2) HEARING. — Not later than 30 days after the date of receipt of any notice of a proposed determination under paragraph (1), the nonbank financial company may request, in writing, an opportunity for a written or oral hearing before the Council to contest the proposed determination. Upon receipt of a timely request, the Council shall fix a time (not later than 30 days after the date of receipt of the request) and place at which such company may appear, personally or through counsel, to submit written materials (or,

(5)**本子条所涉金融活动**。——就本子条而言,“金融活动”一词——

(A)系指金融性质的活动[定义见《1956年银行控股公司法》第4(k)条];

(B)包括对一家或一家以上参保存款机构的所有或控制;且

(C)不包括为公司或其任何关联方开展的内部金融活动(内部金融活动涵盖内部财务、投资及雇员福利职能活动)。

(6)**审慎监管的对象以金融活动为限**。——公司的非金融活动不必受联邦储备委员会监管,也不必遵守其审慎性标准。就本法而言,按第(1)款作出的判定所涉金融活动适用的监管要求,应与联邦储备委员会对非银行金融公司的监管要求一致。本款任何规定均不禁止或限制联邦储备委员会根据本编规定对按第(1)款作出的判定所涉金融活动适用审慎性标准的权限。

(d)**重新评价和撤销**。——金融稳定监督委员会应——

(1)对根据第(a)子条及第(b)子条就受联邦储备委员会监管的该等非银行金融公司作出的所有判定,至少每年进行一次重新评价;及

(2)在金融稳定监督委员会经至少2/3届时在任的有表决权成员表决通过(且其中必须包括主席的赞成票),判定非银行金融公司不再符合第(a)子条或第(b)子条规定的标准(视具体情况而定)之时,撤销任何上述判定。

(e)**听证通知、机会及最终判定**。——

(1)**一般规定**。——金融稳定监督委员会拟判定某一非银行金融公司应受联邦储备委员会监管并按本编规定遵守审慎性标准的,应向该非银行金融公司发出一份书面通知,通知中应说明金融稳定监督委员会拟作出该等判定的理由。

(2)**听证**。——收到第(1)款所述任何拟议判定的通知后30天内,非银行金融公司可以书面请求金融稳定监督委员会提供书面或口头听证机会,在金融稳定监督委员会对拟作出的判定进行质疑。金融稳定监督委员会收到非银行金融公司及时提出的听证请求后,应指定时间(不迟于请求收到之日后的第30天)和地点,以便该公司亲自或通过律师提交书面材料(或者提供口头证词和进行口头辩护,具体情况完全由金融稳定监督委员会依其自由裁量权决定)。

at the sole discretion of the Council, oral testimony and oral argument).

(3) FINAL DETERMINATION. — Not later than 60 days after the date of a hearing under paragraph (2), the Council shall notify the nonbank financial company of the final determination of the Council, which shall contain a statement of the basis for the decision of the Council.

(4) NO HEARING REQUESTED. — If a nonbank financial company does not make a timely request for a hearing, the Council shall notify the nonbank financial company, in writing, of the final determination of the Council under subsection (a) or (b), as applicable, not later than 10 days after the date by which the company may request a hearing under paragraph (2).

(f) EMERGENCY EXCEPTION. —

(1) IN GENERAL. — The Council may waive or modify the requirements of subsection (e) with respect to a nonbank financial company, if the Council determines, by a vote of not fewer than 2/3 of the voting members then serving, including an affirmative vote by the Chairperson, that such waiver or modification is necessary or appropriate to prevent or mitigate threats posed by the nonbank financial company to the financial stability of the United States.

(2) NOTICE. — The Council shall provide notice of a waiver or modification under this subsection to the nonbank financial company concerned as soon as practicable, but not later than 24 hours after the waiver or modification is granted.

(3) INTERNATIONAL COORDINATION. — In making a determination under paragraph (1), the Council shall consult with the appropriate home country supervisor, if any, of the foreign nonbank financial company that is being considered for such a determination.

(4) OPPORTUNITY FOR HEARING. — The Council shall allow a nonbank financial company to request, in writing, an opportunity for a written or oral hearing before the Council to contest a waiver or modification under this subsection, not later than 10 days after the date of receipt of notice of the waiver or modification by the company. Upon receipt of a timely request, the Council shall fix a time (not later than 15 days after the date of receipt of the request) and place at which the nonbank financial company may appear, personally or through counsel, to submit written materials (or, at the sole discretion of the Council, oral testimony and oral argument).

(5) NOTICE OF FINAL DETERMINATION. — Not later than 30 days after the date of any hearing under paragraph (4), the Council shall notify the subject nonbank financial company of the final determination of the Council under this subsection, which shall contain a statement of the basis for the decision of the Council.

(g) CONSULTATION. — The Council shall consult with the primary financial

(3)**最终判定**。——金融稳定监督委员会应在根据第(2)款举行听证后60天内将其最终判定通知非银行金融公司,通知中应说明其作出该等判定的理由。

(4)**未收到听证请求的情形**。——如果非银行金融公司未及时提出听证请求,金融稳定监督委员会应在按第(2)款规定的公司可以要求举行听证的时限届满后10天内将其根据第(a)子条或第(b)子条(视具体情况而定)作出的最终判定书面通知该非银行金融公司。

(f)**紧急例外规定**。——

(1)**一般规定**。——金融稳定监督委员会可以豁免或修改第(e)子条所述关于非银行金融公司的要求,前提是金融稳定监督委员会判定为防范或缓解该非银行金融公司对美国金融稳定造成的威胁,该等豁免或修改确属必要或适当,且经至少2/3届时在任的有表决权成员表决通过(其中必须包括主席的赞成票)。

(2)**通知**。——金融稳定监督委员会应尽快(但不得迟于豁免或修改作出后24小时)向该当事非银行金融公司发出关于本子条所述豁免或修改的通知。

(3)**国际协作**。——根据第(1)款规定作出判定时,金融稳定监督委员会应与判定所涉外国非银行金融公司的相应母国监管者(如有)进行磋商。

(4)**听证机会**。——金融稳定监督委员会应允许非银行金融公司能够在收到本子条所述豁免或修改通知后10天内以书面形式请求金融稳定监督委员会提供书面或口头听证机会,对根据本子条作出的豁免或修改进行质疑。金融稳定监督委员会收到非银行金融公司及时提出的听证请求后,应指定时间(不迟于请求收到之日后的第15天)和地点,以便该公司亲自或通过律师提交书面材料(或者提供口头证词和进行口头辩护,具体情况完全由金融稳定监督委员会依其自由裁量权决定)。

(5)**最终判定通知**。——金融稳定监督委员会应在根据第(4)款举行任何听证之后30天内将其根据本子条作出的最终判定通知当事非银行金融公司,通知中应说明其作出该等判定的理由。

(g)**磋商**。——对于正在依本条规定考虑是否应受联邦储备委员会监管的每一非

regulatory agency, if any, for each nonbank financial company or subsidiary of a nonbank financial company that is being considered for supervision by the Board of Governors under this section before the Council makes any final determination with respect to such nonbank financial company under subsection (a), (b), or (c).

(h) JUDICIAL REVIEW. — If the Council makes a final determination under this section with respect to a nonbank financial company, such nonbank financial company may, not later than 30 days after the date of receipt of the notice of final determination under subsection (d)(2), (e)(3), or (f)(5), bring an action in the United States district court for the judicial district in which the home office of such nonbank financial company is located, or in the United States District Court for the District of Columbia, for an order requiring that the final determination be rescinded, and the court shall, upon review, dismiss such action or direct the final determination to be rescinded. Review of such an action shall be limited to whether the final determination made under this section was arbitrary and capricious.

(i) INTERNATIONAL COORDINATION. — In exercising its duties under this title with respect to foreign nonbank financial companies, foreign –based bank holding companies, and cross –border activities and markets, the Council shall consult with appropriate foreign regulatory authorities, to the extent appropriate.

SEC. 114. REGISTRATION OF NONBANK FINANCIAL COMPANIES SUPERVISED BY THE BOARD OF GOVERNORS.

Not later than 180 days after the date of a final Council determination under section 113 that a nonbank financial company is to be supervised by the Board of Governors, such company shall register with the Board of Governors, on forms prescribed by the Board of Governors, which shall include such information as the Board of Governors, in consultation with the Council, may deem necessary or appropriate to carry out this title.

SEC. 115. ENHANCED SUPERVISION AND PRUDENTIAL STANDARDS FOR NONBANK FINANCIAL COMPANIES SUPERVISED BY THE BOARD OF GOVERNORS AND CERTAIN BANK HOLDING COMPANIES.

(a) IN GENERAL. —

(1) PURPOSE. — In order to prevent or mitigate risks to the financial stability of the United States that could arise from the material financial distress, failure, or ongoing activities of large, interconnected financial institutions, the Council may make recommendations to the Board of Governors concerning the establishment and refinement of prudential standards and reporting and disclosure requirements applicable to nonbank financial companies supervised by the Board of Governors and large, interconnected bank holding companies, that —

(A) are more stringent than those applicable to other nonbank financial companies

银行金融公司或其子公司,金融稳定监督委员会应在根据第(a)子条、第(b)子条或第(c)子条就该等非银行金融公司作出任何最终判定之前,与该等公司的优先监管机关(如有)进行磋商。

(h)**司法审查**。——如果金融稳定监督委员会根据本条规定针对非银行金融公司作出任何最终判定,则该等非银行金融公司可以在收到依据第(d)(2)子条、第(e)(3)子条或第(f)(5)子条作出的最终判定通知后30天内,向其总部所在司法辖区的联邦地区法院或哥伦比亚特区联邦地区法院提起诉讼,请求法院发布命令撤销金融稳定监督委员会作出的最终判定;法院在完成审查后应驳回该等诉讼,或命令撤销最终判定。诉讼的审查范围应仅限于依本条规定作出的最终判定是否恣意、专断。

(i)**国际协作**。——在根据本编规定针对外国非银行金融公司、外国银行控股公司、跨境活动及市场履行职责时,金融稳定监督委员会应在适当范围内与相应的外国监管机关进行磋商。

第114条　受联邦储备委员会监管的非银行金融公司的注册

金融稳定监督委员会根据第113条作出非银行金融公司应受联邦储备委员会监管的最终判定的,非银行金融公司应在该等判定作出后180天内,提交联邦储备委员会规定应提交的表格,以便在联邦储备委员会注册,表格中应包括联邦储备委员会与金融稳定监督委员会磋商后认为对于实施本编规定所必要或合理的信息。

第115条　强化对受联邦储备委员会监管的非银行金融公司和特定银行控股公司的监管并提高审慎性标准

(a)**一般规定**。——

(1)**目的**。——为了防范或缓释因相互关联的大型金融机构的财务困境、经营失败或者正在开展的活动而对美国金融稳定产生的风险,金融稳定监督委员会可建议联邦储备委员会,制定并完善适用于受联邦储备委员会监管的非银行金融公司以及相互关联的大型银行控股公司的审慎性标准及报告和披露要求,且该等标准和要求应——

(A)比适用于对美国金融稳定不具有类似风险的其他非银行金融公司和银行控

and bank holding companies that do not present similar risks to the financial stability of the United States; and

(B) increase in stringency, based on the considerations identified in subsection (b)(3).

(2) RECOMMENDED APPLICATION OF REQUIRED STANDARDS. — In making recommendations under this section, the Council may —

(A) differentiate among companies that are subject to heightened standards on an individual basis or by category, taking into consideration their capital structure, riskiness, complexity, financial activities (including the financial activities of their subsidiaries), size, and any other risk-related factors that the Council deems appropriate; or

(B) recommend an asset threshold that is higher than $50, 000, 000, 000 for the application of any standard described in subsections (c) through (g).

(b) DEVELOPMENT OF PRUDENTIAL STANDARDS. —

(1) IN GENERAL. — The recommendations of the Council under subsection (a) may include —

(A) risk-based capital requirements;

(B) leverage limits;

(C) liquidity requirements;

(D) resolution plan and credit exposure report requirements;

(E) concentration limits;

(F) a contingent capital requirement;

(G) enhanced public disclosures;

(H) short-term debt limits; and

(I) overall risk management requirements.

(2) PRUDENTIAL STANDARDS FOR FOREIGN FINANCIAL COMPANIES. — In making recommendations concerning the standards set forth in paragraph (1) that would apply to foreign nonbank financial companies supervised by the Board of Governors or foreign-based bank holding companies, the Council shall —

(A) give due regard to the principle of national treatment and equality of competitive opportunity; and

(B) take into account the extent to which the foreign nonbank financial company or foreign-based bank holding company is subject on a consolidated basis to home country standards that are comparable to those applied to financial companies in the United States.

(3) CONSIDERATIONS. — In making recommendations concerning prudential standards under paragraph (1), the Council shall —

(A) take into account differences among nonbank financial companies supervised by

股公司的要求更为严格;及

(B)基于第(b)(3)子条确定的考虑因素,进一步提高严格程度。

(2)**建议适用的必要标准**。——根据本条规定提出建议时,金融稳定监督委员会可以——

(A)考虑公司的资本结构、风险程度、复杂程度、金融活动(包括其子公司的金融活动)、规模及金融稳定监督委员会认为适当的任何其他风险因素,区别对待适用更严格的标准的每一公司或按类别区别对待该等公司;或

(B)对于第(c)子条至第(g)子条所述任何标准之适用,建议采用高于500亿美元的资产门槛。

(b)**审慎性标准的制定**。——

(1)**一般规定**。——第(a)子条所述金融稳定监督委员会的建议可包括——

(A)风险基础资本要求;

(B)杠杆率限制;

(C)流动性要求;

(D)清盘计划和信用风险敞口报告要求;

(E)集中度限制;

(F)或有资本要求;

(G)加强公开披露;

(H)短期债务限制;及

(I)整体风险管理要求。

(2)**适用于外国金融公司的审慎性标准**。——就第(1)款所述适用于受联邦储备委员会监管的外国非银行金融公司或外国银行控股公司的标准提出建议时,金融稳定监督委员会应——

(A)适当考虑国民待遇和竞争机会均等原则;及

(B)考虑在多大程度上,外国非银行金融公司或外国银行控股公司在母国受制于与美国境内金融公司适用的标准具有可比性的并表标准。

(3)**考虑因素**。——在根据第(1)款就审慎性标准提出建议时,金融稳定监督委员会应——

(A)考虑受联邦储备委员会监管的非银行金融公司及第(a)子条所述的银行控股

the Board of Governors and bank holding companies described in subsection (a), based on —

(i) the factors described in subsections (a) and (b) of section 113;

(ii) whether the company owns an insured depository institution;

(iii) nonfinancial activities and affiliations of the company; and

(iv) any other factors that the Council determines appropriate;

(B) to the extent possible, ensure that small changes in the factors listed in subsections (a) and (b) of section 113 would not result in sharp, discontinuous changes in the prudential standards established under section 165; and

(C) adapt its recommendations as appropriate in light of any predominant line of business of such company, including assets under management or other activities for which particular standards may not be appropriate.

(c) CONTINGENT CAPITAL. —

(1) STUDY REQUIRED. — The Council shall conduct a study of the feasibility, benefits, costs, and structure of a contingent capital requirement for nonbank financial companies supervised by the Board of Governors and bank holding companies described in subsection (a), which study shall include —

(A) an evaluation of the degree to which such requirement would enhance the safety and soundness of companies subject to the requirement, promote the financial stability of the United States, and reduce risks to United States taxpayers;

(B) an evaluation of the characteristics and amounts of contingent capital that should be required;

(C) an analysis of potential prudential standards that should be used to determine whether the contingent capital of a company would be converted to equity in times of financial stress;

(D) an evaluation of the costs to companies, the effects on the structure and operation of credit and other financial markets, and other economic effects of requiring contingent capital;

(E) an evaluation of the effects of such requirement on the international competitiveness of companies subject to the requirement and the prospects for international coordination in establishing such requirement; and

(F) recommendations for implementing regulations.

(2) REPORT. — The Council shall submit a report to Congress regarding the study required by paragraph (1) not later than 2 years after the date of enactment of this Act.

(3) RECOMMENDATIONS. —

(A) IN GENERAL. — Subsequent to submitting a report to Congress under paragraph (2), the Council may make recommendations to the Board of Governors to

公司之间的差别,考虑因素包括——

(i)第113条第(a)子条及第(b)子条所述因素;

(ii)公司是否拥有参保存款机构;

(iii)公司的非金融活动和关联关系;及

(iv)金融稳定监督委员会判定确属适当的任何其他因素;

(B)尽可能确保第113条第(a)子条及第(b)子条所列因素发生的轻微变化不会导致依第165条设立的审慎性标准发生急剧、不连续的变化;及

(C)根据该等公司的任何主营业务(包括可能不宜适用特定标准的该等公司所管理的资产或其他活动)对其建议进行适当调整。

(c)**或有资本**。——

(1)**研究要求**。——金融稳定监督委员会应就对受联邦储备委员会监管的非银行金融公司及第(a)子条所述的银行控股公司设定或有资本要求的可行性、收益、成本及结构开展研究,研究应包括——

(A)评估该等要求在多大程度上会提高受制于该等要求的公司的安全性和稳健性、促进美国金融稳定并降低美国纳税人承担的风险;

(B)评估要求的或有资本特征及应达到的金额;

(C)对潜在审慎性标准进行分析(该标准用于判定出现财务困境时,是否进行公司或有资本转增股本);

(D)评估设定或有资本要求将对公司造成的成本、对信贷市场及其他金融市场结构和运作的影响以及任何其他经济影响;

(E)评估该等要求对受制于该等要求的公司国际竞争力的影响,以及在该等要求的设立上实现国际协作的可能性;及

(F)关于实施规章的建议。

(2)**报告**。——金融稳定监督委员会应在本法颁布之日后2年内就第(1)款要求开展的研究向国会提交报告。

(3)**建议**。——

(A)**一般规定**。——在根据第(2)款规定向国会提交报告后,金融稳定监督委员会可建议联邦储备委员会要求受联邦储备委员会监管的任何非银行金融公司及第(a)

require any nonbank financial company supervised by the Board of Governors and any bank holding company described in subsection (a) to maintain a minimum amount of contingent capital that is convertible to equity in times of financial stress.

(B) FACTORS TO CONSIDER. — In making recommendations under this subsection, the Council shall consider —

(i) an appropriate transition period for implementation of a conversion under this subsection;

(ii) the factors described in subsection (b)(3);

(iii) capital requirements applicable to a nonbank financial company supervised by the Board of Governors or a bank holding company described in subsection (a), and subsidiaries thereof;

(iv) results of the study required by paragraph (1); and

(v) any other factor that the Council deems appropriate.

(d) RESOLUTION PLAN AND CREDIT EXPOSURE REPORTS. —

(1) RESOLUTION PLAN. — The Council may make recommendations to the Board of Governors concerning the requirement that each nonbank financial company supervised by the Board of Governors and each bank holding company described in subsection (a) report periodically to the Council, the Board of Governors, and the Corporation, the plan of such company for rapid and orderly resolution in the event of material financial distress or failure.

(2) CREDIT EXPOSURE REPORT. — The Council may make recommendations to the Board of Governors concerning the advisability of requiring each nonbank financial company supervised by the Board of Governors and bank holding company described in subsection (a) to report periodically to the Council, the Board of Governors, and the Corporation on —

(A) the nature and extent to which the company has credit exposure to other significant nonbank financial companies and significant bank holding companies; and

(B) the nature and extent to which other such significant nonbank financial companies and significant bank holding companies have credit exposure to that company.

(e) CONCENTRATION LIMITS. — In order to limit the risks that the failure of any individual company could pose to nonbank financial companies supervised by the Board of Governors or bank holding companies described in subsection (a), the Council may make recommendations to the Board of Governors to prescribe standards to limit such risks, as set forth in section 165.

(f) ENHANCED PUBLIC DISCLOSURES. — The Council may make recommendations to the Board of Governors to require periodic public disclosures by bank holding companies described in subsection (a) and by nonbank financial companies

子条所述的任何银行控股公司维持最低金额的或有资本,以便在出现财务困境时转增股本。

(B)**考虑因素**。——在根据本子条提出建议时,金融稳定监督委员会应考虑——

(i)实施本子条的或有资本转增股本规定所需的适当过渡期;

(ii)第(b)(3)子条所述因素;

(iii)适用于受联邦储备委员会监管的非银行金融公司或第(a)子条所述的银行控股公司及上述各者的子公司的资本要求;

(iv)按第(1)款要求开展的研究之结果;及

(v)金融稳定监督委员会认为适当的任何其他因素。

(d)**清盘计划与信用风险敞口报告**。——

(1)**清盘计划**。——金融稳定监督委员会可建议联邦储备委员会要求受联邦储备委员会监管的每一非银行金融公司及第(a)子条所述的每一银行控股公司定期向金融稳定监督委员会、联邦储备委员会及联邦存款保险公司报告该等公司在重大财务困境或经营失败情况下将采取的快速有序清盘计划。

(2)**信用风险敞口报告**。——金融稳定监督委员会可以向联邦储备委员会提出建议,说明要求受联邦储备委员会监管的每一非银行金融公司及第(a)子条所述的每一银行控股公司就下列事项向金融稳定监督委员会、联邦储备委员会及联邦存款保险公司提供定期报告的做法是否可取——

(A)公司对其他重要非银行金融公司及重要银行控股公司的信用风险敞口的性质及范围;及

(B)其他该等重要非银行金融公司及重要银行控股公司对该公司的信用风险敞口的性质及范围。

(e)**集中度限制**。——为了限制因任何一家公司经营失败而可能对受联邦储备委员会监管的非银行金融公司或第(a)子条所述的银行控股公司造成的风险,金融稳定监督委员会可建议联邦储备委员会根据第165条规定制定相关标准,对该等风险进行限制。

(f)**加强公开披露**。——金融稳定监督委员会可建议联邦储备委员会要求第(a)子条所述的银行控股公司及受联邦储备委员会监管的非银行金融公司定期进行公开披露,以支持对该等公司的风险特征、资本充足性及风险管理能力进行市场评估。

supervised by the Board of Governors, in order to support market evaluation of the risk profile, capital adequacy, and risk management capabilities thereof.

(g) SHORT–TERM DEBT LIMITS. — The Council may make recommendations to the Board of Governors to require short–term debt limits to mitigate the risks that an over–accumulation of such debt could pose to bank holding companies described in subsection (a), nonbank financial companies supervised by the Board of Governors, or the financial system.

SEC. 116. REPORTS.

(a) IN GENERAL. — Subject to subsection (b), the Council, acting through the Office of Financial Research, may require a bank holding company with total consolidated assets of $50, 000, 000, 000 or greater or a nonbank financial company supervised by the Board of Governors, and any subsidiary thereof, to submit certified reports to keep the Council informed as to —

(1) the financial condition of the company;

(2) systems for monitoring and controlling financial, operating, and other risks;

(3) transactions with any subsidiary that is a depository institution; and

(4) the extent to which the activities and operations of the company and any subsidiary thereof, could, under adverse circumstances, have the potential to disrupt financial markets or affect the overall financial stability of the United States.

(b) USE OF EXISTING REPORTS. —

(1) IN GENERAL. — For purposes of compliance with subsection (a), the Council, acting through the Office of Financial Research, shall, to the fullest extent possible, use —

(A) reports that a bank holding company, nonbank financial company supervised by the Board of Governors, or any functionally regulated subsidiary of such company has been required to provide to other Federal or State regulatory agencies or to a relevant foreign supervisory authority;

(B) information that is otherwise required to be reported publicly; and

(C) externally audited financial statements.

(2) AVAILABILITY. — Each bank holding company described in subsection (a) and nonbank financial company supervised by the Board of Governors, and any subsidiary thereof, shall provide to the Council, at the request of the Council, copies of all reports referred to in paragraph (1).

(3) CONFIDENTIALITY. — The Council shall maintain the confidentiality of the reports obtained under subsection (a) and paragraph (1)(A) of this subsection.

SEC. 117. TREATMENT OF CERTAIN COMPANIES THAT CEASE TO BE BANK HOLDING COMPANIES.

(a) APPLICABILITY. — This section shall apply to —

(g)**短期债务限制**。——金融稳定监督委员会可建议联邦储备委员会制定短期债务限制要求,以缓释该等债务的过度积累可能对第(a)子条所述的银行控股公司、受联邦储备委员会监管的非银行金融公司或金融体系造成的风险。

第116条　报告

(a)**一般规定**。——在不违反第(b)子条规定的前提下,金融稳定监督委员会可通过金融研究办公室,要求并表资产总额500亿美元(含)以上的银行控股公司或受联邦储备委员会监管的非银行金融公司及上述各者的任何子公司提交经认证的报告,随时通知金融稳定监督委员会以下情况——

(1)公司的财务状况;

(2)财务、运营和其他风险的监控和控制系统;

(3)与具有存款机构身份的任何子公司开展的交易;及

(4)在不利情况下,公司及其任何子公司的活动及运营可能对金融市场造成扰乱或影响美国总体金融稳定的程度。

(b)**既有报告的利用**。——

(1)**一般规定**。——金融稳定监督委员会在通过金融研究办公室实施第(a)子条的规定时,应尽最大可能利用——

(A)银行控股公司、受联邦储备委员会监管的非银行金融公司或该等公司的受制于功能监管的任何子公司已经按要求向其他联邦监管机关、州监管机关或相关外国监管机关提供的报告;

(B)应另行公开报告的信息;及

(C)经外部审计的财务报表。

(2)**报告的提供**。——第(a)子条所述的每一银行控股公司和受联邦储备委员会监管的非银行金融公司及上述各者的任何子公司,均应按照金融稳定监督委员会要求向其提供第(1)款所述所有报告的复本。

(3)**保密**。——金融稳定监督委员会应对依第(a)子条及本子条第(1)(A)款获得的报告保密。

第117条　对于不再构成银行控股公司之特定公司的处理

(a)**适用范围**。——本条规定适用于——

(1) any entity that —

(A) was a bank holding company having total consolidated assets equal to or greater than $50, 000, 000, 000 as of January 1, 2010; and

(B) received financial assistance under or participated in the Capital Purchase Program established under the Troubled Asset Relief Program authorized by the Emergency Economic Stabilization Act of 2008; and

(2) any successor entity (as defined by the Board of Governors, in consultation with the Council) to an entity described in paragraph (1).

(b) TREATMENT. — If an entity described in subsection (a) ceases to be a bank holding company at any time after January 1, 2010, then such entity shall be treated as a nonbank financial company supervised by the Board of Governors, as if the Council had made a determination under section 113 with respect to that entity.

(c) APPEAL. —

(1) REQUEST FOR HEARING. — An entity may request, in writing, an opportunity for a written or oral hearing before the Council to appeal its treatment as a nonbank financial company supervised by the Board of Governors in accordance with this section. Upon receipt of the request, the Council shall fix a time (not later than 30 days after the date of receipt of the request) and place at which such entity may appear, personally or through counsel, to submit written materials (or, at the sole discretion of the Council, oral testimony and oral argument).

(2) DECISION. —

(A) PROPOSED DECISION. — A Council decision to grant an appeal under this subsection shall be made by a vote of not fewer than 2/3 of the voting members then serving, including an affirmative vote by the Chairperson. Not later than 60 days after the date of a hearing under paragraph (1), the Council shall submit a report to, and may testify before, the Committee on Banking, Housing, and Urban Affairs of the Senate and the Committee on Financial Services of the House of Representatives on the proposed decision of the Council regarding an appeal under paragraph (1), which report shall include a statement of the basis for the proposed decision of the Council.

(B) NOTICE OF FINAL DECISION. — The Council shall notify the subject entity of the final decision of the Council regarding an appeal under paragraph (1), which notice shall contain a statement of the basis for the final decision of the Council, not later than 60 days after the later of —

(i) the date of the submission of the report under subparagraph (A); or

(ii) if, not later than 1 year after the date of submission of the report under subparagraph (A), the Committee on Banking, Housing, and Urban Affairs of the Senate or the Committee on Financial Services of the House of Representatives holds one or more

(1)符合以下条件的任何实体——

(A)于2010年1月1日,具有银行控股公司身份且并表资产总额达500亿美元(含)以上;且

(B)曾参与依《2008年紧急经济稳定法》核准的问题资产救助计划而设立的资本收购计划,或曾获得该等资本收购计划提供的财政援助;及

(2)第(1)款所述实体的任何继任实体(以联邦储备委员会与金融稳定监督委员会磋商后作出的定义为准)。

(b)**处理**。——如果第(a)子条所述实体在2010年1月1日之后的任何时候不再构成银行控股公司,则该等实体应视为受联邦储备委员会监管的非银行金融公司,如同金融稳定监督委员会已按第113条规定对该实体作出判定。

(c)**复议申请**。——

(1)**听证请求**。——某一实体按照本条规定被视为受联邦储备委员会监管的非银行金融公司的,可以以书面形式请求金融稳定监督委员会提供书面或口头听证机会,对此进行复议。金融稳定监督委员会收到上述实体提出的请求后,应指定时间(不迟于请求收到之日后的第30天)和地点,以便该实体亲自或通过律师提交书面材料(或者提供口头证词和进行口头辩护,具体情况完全由金融稳定监督委员会依其自由裁量权决定)。

(2)**决定**。——

(A)**拟议决定**。——金融稳定监督委员会根据本子条作出准予复议的决定的,须经至少2/3届时在任的有表决权成员表决通过(且其中必须包括主席的赞成票)。金融稳定监督委员会应在按照第(1)款举行听证后60天内就其拟针对第(1)款所述复议作出的决定向参议院银行、住房与城市事务委员会以及众议院金融服务委员会提交报告,且可以向上述委员会作证;报告中应说明金融稳定监督委员会拟作出的决定的理由。

(B)**最终决定通知**。——金融稳定监督委员会应在以下日期(以较晚者为准)后60天内将其针对第(1)款所述复议作出的最终决定通知当事实体,通知中应说明金融稳定监督委员会作出的最终决定的理由——

(i)根据第(A)子款提交报告之日;或

(ii)如果在根据第(A)子款提交报告后一年内参议院银行、住房与城市事务委员会或众议院金融服务委员会就该等报告举行了一次或一次以上听证,则为最后一次举行听证之日。

hearings regarding such report, the date of the last such hearing.

(C) CONSIDERATIONS. — In making a decision regarding an appeal under paragraph (1), the Council shall consider whether the company meets the standards under section 113(a) or 113(b), as applicable, and the definition of the term "nonbank financial company" under section 102. The decision of the Council shall be final, subject to the review under paragraph (3).

(3) REVIEW. — If the Council denies an appeal under this subsection, the Council shall, not less frequently than annually, review and reevaluate the decision.

SEC. 118. COUNCIL FUNDING.

Any expenses of the Council shall be treated as expenses of, and paid by, the Office of Financial Research.

SEC. 119. RESOLUTION OF SUPERVISORY JURISDICTIONAL DISPUTES AMONG MEMBER AGENCIES.

(a) REQUEST FOR COUNCIL RECOMMENDATION. — The Council shall seek to resolve a dispute among 2 or more member agencies, if —

(1) a member agency has a dispute with another member agency about the respective jurisdiction over a particular bank holding company, nonbank financial company, or financial activity or product (excluding matters for which another dispute mechanism specifically has been provided under title X);

(2) the Council determines that the disputing agencies cannot, after a demonstrated good faith effort, resolve the dispute without the intervention of the Council; and

(3) any of the member agencies involved in the dispute —

(A) provides all other disputants prior notice of the intent to request dispute resolution by the Council; and

(B) requests in writing, not earlier than 14 days after providing the notice described in subparagraph (A), that the Council seek to resolve the dispute.

(b) COUNCIL RECOMMENDATION. — The Council shall seek to resolve each dispute described in subsection (a) —

(1) within a reasonable time after receiving the dispute resolution request;

(2) after consideration of relevant information provided by each agency party to the dispute; and

(3) by agreeing with 1 of the disputants regarding the entirety of the matter, or by determining a compromise position.

(c) FORM OF RECOMMENDATION. — Any Council recommendation under this section shall —

(1) be in writing;

(2) include an explanation of the reasons therefor; and

(C)**考虑因素**。——在根据第(1)款就复议作出决定时,金融稳定监督委员会应考虑该公司是否符合第113(a)条或第113(b)条(视具体情况而定)规定的标准,以及是否符合第102条中对"非银行金融公司"的定义。金融稳定监督委员会的决定应当是终局的,但可根据第(3)款规定进行审查。

(3)**审查**。——如果金融稳定监督委员会驳回依据本子条提出的复议申请,则金融稳定监督委员会至少应每年对上述决定进行一次审查和重新评价。

第118条　金融稳定监督委员会的经费来源

金融稳定监督委员会的任何费用均应视为金融研究办公室的费用,并由金融研究办公室支付。

第119条　成员机关间监管管辖权争议的解决

(a)**请求金融稳定监督委员会提供建议**。——在下述情形下,金融稳定监督委员会应尽力解决两名或多名成员机关之间的争议——

(1)一个成员机关与另一个成员机关对其各自针对某特定银行控股公司、非银行金融公司或者金融活动或产品拥有的管辖权产生争议(但第十编已明确规定采用其他争议解决机制的事项除外);

(2)金融稳定监督委员会判定争议当事机关已经作出确凿的善意努力,但仍然无法在没有金融稳定监督委员会干预的情况下解决争议;且

(3)争议涉及的任何成员机关——

(A)已向全体其他争议当事人发出事先通知,表明其希望请求金融稳定监督委员会解决争议;及

(B)在发出第(A)子款所述通知后的第14天或其他更晚的日期,书面请求金融稳定监督委员会解决争议。

(b)**金融稳定监督委员会的建议**。——对于第(a)子条所述每一争议,金融稳定监督委员会均应——

(1)尽力在收到争议解决请求后的合理时间内解决争议;

(2)考虑各争议当事机关提供的相关信息;及

(3)通过完全支持一方当事人的主张或确定一个折中立场的方式解决每一争议。

(c)**建议的形式**。——金融稳定监督委员会根据本条规定作出的任何建议均应——

(1)采用书面形式;

(2)说明作出该建议的理由;及

(3) be approved by the affirmative vote of 2/3 of the voting members of the Council then serving.

(d) NONBINDING EFFECT. — Any recommendation made by the Council under subsection (c) shall not be binding on the Federal agencies that are parties to the dispute.

SEC. 120. ADDITIONAL STANDARDS APPLICABLE TO ACTIVITIES OR PRACTICES FOR FINANCIAL STABILITY PURPOSES.

(a) IN GENERAL. — The Council may provide for more stringent regulation of a financial activity by issuing recommendations to the primary financial regulatory agencies to apply new or heightened standards and safeguards, including standards enumerated in section 115, for a financial activity or practice conducted by bank holding companies or nonbank financial companies under their respective jurisdictions, if the Council determines that the conduct, scope, nature, size, scale, concentration, or interconnectedness of such activity or practice could create or increase the risk of significant liquidity, credit, or other problems spreading among bank holding companies and nonbank financial companies, financial markets of the United States, or low–income, minority, or under–served communities.

(b) PROCEDURE FOR RECOMMENDATIONS TO REGULATORS. —

(1) NOTICE AND OPPORTUNITY FOR COMMENT. — The Council shall consult with the primary financial regulatory agencies and provide notice to the public and opportunity for comment for any proposed recommendation that the primary financial regulatory agencies apply new or heightened standards and safeguards for a financial activity or practice.

(2) CRITERIA. — The new or heightened standards and safeguards for a financial activity or practice recommended under paragraph (1) —

(A) shall take costs to long–term economic growth into account; and

(B) may include prescribing the conduct of the activity or practice in specific ways (such as by limiting its scope, or applying particular capital or risk management requirements to the conduct of the activity) or prohibiting the activity or practice.

(c) IMPLEMENTATION OF RECOMMENDED STANDARDS. —

(1) ROLE OF PRIMARY FINANCIAL REGULATORY AGENCY. —

(A) IN GENERAL. — Each primary financial regulatory agency may impose, require reports regarding, examine for compliance with, and enforce standards in accordance with this section with respect to those entities for which it is the primary financial regulatory agency.

(B) RULE OF CONSTRUCTION. — The authority under this paragraph is in addition to, and does not limit, any other authority of a primary financial regulatory

(3)经至少2/3届时在任的有表决权成员表决通过。

(d)**不具约束力**。——金融稳定监督委员会根据第(c)子条规定作出的任何建议对作为争议方的联邦机关均不具约束力。

第120条　为实现金融稳定之目的而对活动或做法适用的补充标准

(a)**一般规定**。——如果金融稳定监督委员会判定,在各优先金融监管机关各自管辖范围内的银行控股公司或非银行金融公司开展的金融活动或做法及其范围、性质、数额、规模、集中度或相互关联程度,可能造成或加深重大流动性、信用或其他问题的风险在银行控股公司、非银行金融公司、美国金融市场或者低收入群体、少数族裔或弱势群体之间的相互传播,则金融稳定监督委员会可建议优先金融监管机关对该等活动或做法适用新的或更严格的标准和保障措施(包括第115条所列标准),以期实现对金融活动更加严格的监管。

(b)**向监管者提出建议的程序**。——

(1)**公告和征求公众意见**。——金融稳定监督委员会拟作出任何建议优先金融监管机关对金融活动或做法适用新的或更严格的标准和保障措施的,应与优先金融监管机关进行磋商,予以公告,并征求公众意见。

(2)**标准**。——根据第(1)款建议针对金融活动或做法适用的新的或更严格的标准和保障措施——

(A)应考虑对长期经济增长造成的负面效应;及

(B)可规定开展活动或做法的具体方式(如限制活动开展范围或者对活动开展适用具体的资本或风险管理要求),或禁止开展该等活动或做法。

(c)**建议标准之实施**。——

(1)**优先金融监管机关的作用**。——

(A)**一般规定**。——每一优先金融监管机关均可以按照本条规定向受其优先金融监管的实体施加标准,要求该等实体提交与该等标准相关的报告、检查该等标准合规的情况并强制执行该等标准。

(B)**解释规则**。——本款规定的权力与优先金融监管机关的任何其他权力具有并存性,前者不限制后者。任一优先金融监管机关根据本条规定针对某一实体采取的

agency. Compliance by an entity with actions taken by a primary financial regulatory agency under this section shall be enforceable in accordance with the statutes governing the respective jurisdiction of the primary financial regulatory agency over the entity, as if the agency action were taken under those statutes.

(2) IMPOSITION OF STANDARDS. — The primary financial regulatory agency shall impose the standards recommended by the Council in accordance with subsection (a), or similar standards that the Council deems acceptable, or shall explain in writing to the Council, not later than 90 days after the date on which the Council issues the recommendation, why the agency has determined not to follow the recommendation of the Council.

(d) REPORT TO CONGRESS. — The Council shall report to Congress on —

(1) any recommendations issued by the Council under this section;

(2) the implementation of, or failure to implement, such recommendation on the part of a primary financial regulatory agency; and

(3) in any case in which no primary financial regulatory agency exists for the nonbank financial company conducting financial activities or practices referred to in subsection (a), recommendations for legislation that would prevent such activities or practices from threatening the stability of the financial system of the United States.

(e) EFFECT OF RESCISSION OF IDENTIFICATION. —

(1) NOTICE. — The Council may recommend to the relevant primary financial regulatory agency that a financial activity or practice no longer requires any standards or safeguards implemented under this section.

(2) DETERMINATION OF PRIMARY FINANCIAL REGULATORY AGENCY TO CONTINUE. —

(A) IN GENERAL. — Upon receipt of a recommendation under paragraph (1), a primary financial regulatory agency that has imposed standards under this section shall determine whether such standards should remain in effect.

(B) APPEAL PROCESS. — Each primary financial regulatory agency that has imposed standards under this section shall promulgate regulations to establish a procedure under which entities under its jurisdiction may appeal a determination by such agency under this paragraph that standards imposed under this section should remain in effect.

SEC. 121. MITIGATION OF RISKS TO FINANCIAL STABILITY.

(a) MITIGATORY ACTIONS. — If the Board of Governors determines that a bank holding company with total consolidated assets of $50, 000, 000, 000 or more, or a nonbank financial company supervised by the Board of Governors, poses a grave threat to the financial stability of the United States, the Board of Governors, upon an affirmative vote of not fewer than 2/3 of the voting members of the Council then serving, shall —

行动,均可依据规范该优先管辖机关对该实体管辖权的制定法予以强制执行,如同该机关行动系按照该制定法作出。

(2)**标准的施行**。——优先金融监管机关应施行金融稳定监督委员会按照第(a)子条建议的标准或金融稳定监督委员会认可的类似标准,或者应在金融稳定监督委员会提出建议后90天内向金融稳定监督委员会书面解释其决定不遵循该等建议的原因。

(d)**向国会报告**。——金融稳定监督委员会应就以下内容向国会提交报告——

(1)金融稳定监督委员会根据本条规定提出的任何建议;

(2)优先金融监管机关对该等建议的实施情况,或者其未实施该等建议的事实;及

(3)在开展第(a)子条所述金融活动或做法的非银行金融公司不存在相应的优先金融监管机关的情况下,提出立法建议,以防范该等活动或做法对美国的金融体系稳定造成威胁。

(e)**撤销风险判定的效力**。——

(1)**通知**。——金融稳定监督委员会可向相关优先金融监管机关提出建议,说明不必再依据本条规定针对某一金融活动或做法实施任何标准或保障措施。

(2)**优先金融监管机关关于继续实施标准的判定**。——

(A)**一般规定**。——收到金融稳定监督委员会根据第(1)款规定提出的建议后,已按本条规定施加标准的优先金融监管机关应判定该等标准是否应继续有效。

(B)**复议程序**。——已按本条规定施加标准的每一优先金融监管机关均应颁发规章,制定复议程序,如果优先金融监管机关根据本款判定依本条规定施加的标准应继续有效,则受其管辖的实体可以通过该程序对该决定申请复议。

第121条　金融稳定风险的缓释

(a)**风险缓释行动**。——如果联邦储备委员会判定并表资产总额达500亿美元(含)以上的银行控股公司或受联邦储备委员会监管的非银行金融公司对美国金融稳定构成严重威胁,则经金融稳定监督委员会至少2/3届时在任的有表决权成员表决赞成,联邦储备委员会应——

(1) limit the ability of the company to merge with, acquire, consolidate with, or otherwise become affiliated with another company;

(2) restrict the ability of the company to offer a financial product or products;

(3) require the company to terminate one or more activities;

(4) impose conditions on the manner in which the company conducts 1 or more activities; or

(5) if the Board of Governors determines that the actions described in paragraphs (1) through (4) are inadequate to mitigate a threat to the financial stability of the United States in its recommendation, require the company to sell or otherwise transfer assets or off-balance-sheet items to unaffiliated entities.

(b) NOTICE AND HEARING. —

(1) IN GENERAL. — The Board of Governors, in consultation with the Council, shall provide to a company described in subsection (a) written notice that such company is being considered for mitigatory action pursuant to this section, including an explanation of the basis for, and description of, the proposed mitigatory action.

(2) HEARING. — Not later than 30 days after the date of receipt of notice under paragraph (1), the company may request, in writing, an opportunity for a written or oral hearing before the Board of Governors to contest the proposed mitigatory action. Upon receipt of a timely request, the Board of Governors shall fix a time (not later than 30 days after the date of receipt of the request) and place at which such company may appear, personally or through counsel, to submit written materials (or, at the discretion of the Board of Governors, in consultation with the Council, oral testimony and oral argument).

(3) DECISION. — Not later than 60 days after the date of a hearing under paragraph (2), or not later than 60 days after the provision of a notice under paragraph (1) if no hearing was held, the Board of Governors shall notify the company of the final decision of the Board of Governors, including the results of the vote of the Council, as described in subsection (a).

(c) FACTORS FOR CONSIDERATION. — The Board of Governors and the Council shall take into consideration the factors set forth in subsection (a) or (b) of section 113, as applicable, in making any determination under subsection (a).

(d) APPLICATION TO FOREIGN FINANCIAL COMPANIES. — The Board of Governors may prescribe regulations regarding the application of this section to foreign nonbank financial companies supervised by the Board of Governors and foreign-based bank holding companies —

(1) giving due regard to the principle of national treatment and equality of competitive opportunity; and

(2) taking into account the extent to which the foreign nonbank financial company

(1)限制该公司与其他公司兼并、收购其他公司、与其他公司合并或与其他公司形成其他关联关系的能力;

(2)限制公司要约金融产品或其他产品的能力;

(3)要求公司终止一项或一项以上活动;

(4)对公司开展一项或一项以上活动的方式施加条件;或

(5)要求公司向非关联实体出售或转让资产或表外项目,前提是联邦储备委员会判定第(1)款至第(4)款所述行动不足以缓解其建议中认定的对美国金融稳定的威胁。

(b)**通知和听证**。——

(1)**一般规定**。——联邦储备委员会应在与金融稳定监督委员会磋商后,向第(a)子条所述公司发出书面通知,说明其正在考虑依据本条规定对该公司实施风险缓释行动,同时应介绍其拟采取的风险缓释行动及采取该等行动的理由。

(2)**听证**。——上述公司可在收到第(1)款所述通知后30天内书面请求联邦储备委员会提供书面或口头听证机会,对联邦储备委员会拟采取的风险缓释行动进行质疑。联邦储备委员会收到该等公司及时提出的听证请求后,应指定时间(不迟于请求收到之日后的第30天)和地点,以便该公司亲自或通过律师提交书面材料(或者提供口头证词和进行口头辩护,具体情况由联邦储备委员会在与金融稳定监督委员会磋商后依其自由裁量权决定)。

(3)**决定**。——联邦储备委员会应在根据第(2)款举行听证后60天内,或者在根据第(1)款发出通知后60天内(如果未举行任何听证)将其最终决定通知该公司,包括第(a)子条所述金融稳定监督委员会的表决结果。

(c)**考虑因素**。——联邦储备委员会和金融稳定监督委员会在根据第(a)子条作出任何判定时,均应考虑第113条第(a)子条或第(b)子条(视具体情况而定)规定的因素。

(d)**对外国金融公司的适用**。——联邦储备委员会可以针对本条规定对受联邦储备委员会监管的外国非银行金融公司及外国银行控股公司之适用制定规章,在制定规章时,应——

(1)适当考虑国民待遇及竞争机会均等原则;及

(2)考虑在多大程度上,外国非银行金融公司或外国银行控股公司在母国受制于

or foreign –based bank holding company is subject on a consolidated basis to home country standards that are comparable to those applied to financial companies in the United States.

SEC. 122. GAO AUDIT OF COUNCIL.

(a) AUTHORITY TO AUDIT. — The Comptroller General of the United States may audit the activities of —

(1) the Council; and

(2) any person or entity acting on behalf of or under the authority of the Council, to the extent that such activities relate to work for the Council by such person or entity.

(b) ACCESS TO INFORMATION. —

(1) IN GENERAL. — Notwithstanding any other provision of law, the Comptroller General shall, upon request and at such reasonable time and in such reasonable form as the Comptroller General may request, have access to —

(A) any records or other information under the control of or used by the Council;

(B) any records or other information under the control of a person or entity acting on behalf of or under the authority of the Council, to the extent that such records or other information is relevant to an audit under subsection (a); and

(C) the officers, directors, employees, financial advisors, staff, working groups, and agents and representatives of the Council (as related to the activities on behalf of the Council of such agent or representative), at such reasonable times as the Comptroller General may request.

(2) COPIES. — The Comptroller General may make and retain copies of such books, accounts, and other records, access to which is granted under this section, as the Comptroller General considers appropriate.

SEC. 123. STUDY OF THE EFFECTS OF SIZE AND COMPLEXITY OF FINANCIAL INSTITUTIONS ON CAPITAL MARKET EFFICIENCY AND ECONOMIC GROWTH.

(a) STUDY REQUIRED. —

(1) IN GENERAL. — The Chairperson of the Council shall carry out a study of the economic impact of possible financial services regulatory limitations intended to reduce systemic risk. Such study shall estimate the benefits and costs on the efficiency of capital markets, on the financial sector, and on national economic growth, of —

(A) explicit or implicit limits on the maximum size of banks, bank holding companies, and other large financial institutions;

(B) limits on the organizational complexity and diversification of large financial institutions;

(C) requirements for operational separation between business units of large financial

与美国境内金融公司适用的标准具有可比性的并表标准。

第122条　政府问责办公室对金融稳定监督委员会的审计

(a)**审计权**。——政府问责办公室主任可以审计以下主体的活动——

(1)金融稳定监督委员会;及

(2)代表金融稳定监督委员会或根据其授权行事的任何人或实体,但审计范围以与该人或实体为金融稳定监督委员会开展的工作相关的活动为限。

(b)**信息获取权**。——

(1)**一般规定**。——无论是否存在任何不同法律规定,政府问责办公室主任在提出要求后,可以按照其要求的合理时间和合理方式查阅或接触——

(A)金融稳定监督委员会控制或者使用的任何记录或其他信息;

(B)代表金融稳定监督委员会或者根据其授权行事的任何人或实体控制的任何记录或其他信息,但以该等记录或其他信息与第(a)子条所述审计相关为限;及

(C)金融稳定监督委员会的官员、主任、雇员、金融顾问、工作人员、工作组、代理人及代表(接触该等代理人或代表时应限于该等代表或代理人代表金融稳定监督委员会开展的活动),接触时间以政府问责办公室主任要求的合理时间为限。

(2)**复本**。——政府问责办公室主任认为适当时,可以制作并保留依本条规定其可以查阅的账册、账簿及其他记录的复本。

第123条　金融机构的规模和复杂程度对资本市场效率和经济增长的影响之研究

(a)**研究要求**。——

(1)**一般规定**。——对于为减少系统性风险而可能采取的金融服务监管限制,金融稳定监督委员会主席应就该等限制的经济影响开展研究。研究中应对下列各项限制或要求的收益和成本进行估测(指在资本市场效率、金融行业及国家经济增长方面的收益和成本)——

(A)对银行、银行控股公司及其他大型金融机构规模的显性或隐性限制;

(B)对大型金融机构组织复杂程度和多元化的限制;

(C)为加快经营失败时的清盘进程,对大型金融机构各业务单位施加运营

institutions in order to expedite resolution in case of failure;

(D) limits on risk transfer between business units of large financial institutions;

(E) requirements to carry contingent capital or similar mechanisms;

(F) limits on commingling of commercial and financial activities by large financial institutions;

(G) segregation requirements between traditional financial activities and trading or other high–risk operations in large financial institutions; and

(H) other limitations on the activities or structure of large financial institutions that may be useful to limit systemic risk.

(2) RECOMMENDATIONS. — The study required by this section shall include recommendations for the optimal structure of any limits considered in subparagraphs (A) through (E), in order to maximize their effectiveness and minimize their economic impact.

(b) REPORT. — Not later than the end of the 180–day period beginning on the date of enactment of this title, and not later than every 5 years thereafter, the Chairperson shall issue a report to the Congress containing any findings and determinations made in carrying out the study required under subsection (a).

Subtitle B — Office of Financial Research

SEC. 151. DEFINITIONS.

For purposes of this subtitle —

(1) the terms "Office" and "Director" mean the Office of Financial Research established under this subtitle and the Director thereof, respectively;

(2) the term "financial company" has the same meaning as in title II, and includes an insured depository institution and an insurance company;

(3) the term "Data Center" means the data center established under section 154;

(4) the term "Research and Analysis Center" means the research and analysis center established under section 154;

(5) the term "financial transaction data" means the structure and legal description of a financial contract, with sufficient detail to describe the rights and obligations between counterparties and make possible an independent valuation;

(6) the term "position data" —

(A) means data on financial assets or liabilities held on the balance sheet of a financial company, where positions are created or changed by the execution of a financial transaction; and

分离要求;

(D)对大型金融机构各业务单位之间风险转移的限制;

(E)对或有资产或类似机制的实施要求;

(F)对大型金融机构的商业活动和财务活动混合运作的限制;

(G)对大型金融机构施加对传统金融活动与交易或其他高风险业务进行分离的要求;及

(H)可能有利于限制系统性风险的对大型金融机构的活动或结构的其他限制。

(2)**建议**。——对于第(A)子款至第(E)子款所述限制,按本条要求开展的研究应提出优化的结构建议,从而最大限度地提高其有效性并将其对经济的影响减到最低限度。

(b)**报告**。——金融稳定监督委员会主席应于本编颁布之日起180天内,向国会提交一份报告,说明其在按照第(a)子条要求开展研究期间作出的任何认定和判定;且此后应至少每5年提交一份报告。

第B子编——金融研究办公室

第151条　定义

在本子编中——

(1)“金融研究办公室”一词系指依据本子编设立的金融研究办公室,“金融研究办公室主任”一词系指该金融研究办公室的主任;

(2)“金融公司”一词的含义以第二编的定义为准,且包括参保存款机构和保险公司;

(3)“数据中心”一词系指依据第154条设立的数据中心;

(4)“研究分析中心”一词系指依据第154条设立的研究分析中心;

(5)“金融交易数据”一词系指对金融合约的结构和法律描述,该等描述应充分详细地说明对手方之间的权利和义务,且足以据此作出独立估值;

(6)“持仓数据”一词——

(A)系指某一金融公司资产负债表显示的持有的金融资产或负债数据,其中建仓和持仓量的变动均通过金融交易的执行来实现;且

(B) includes information that identifies counterparties, the valuation by the financial company of the position, and information that makes possible an independent valuation of the position;

(7) the term "financial contract" means a legally binding agreement between 2 or more counterparties, describing rights and obligations relating to the future delivery of items of intrinsic or extrinsic value among the counterparties; and

(8) the term "financial instrument" means a financial contract in which the terms and conditions are publicly available, and the roles of one or more of the counterparties are assignable without the consent of any of the other counterparties (including common stock of a publicly traded company, government bonds, or exchange traded futures and options contracts).

SEC. 152. OFFICE OF FINANCIAL RESEARCH ESTABLISHED.

(a) ESTABLISHMENT. — There is established within the Department of the Treasury the Office of Financial Research.

(b) DIRECTOR. —

(1) IN GENERAL. — The Office shall be headed by a Director, who shall be appointed by the President, by and with the advice and consent of the Senate.

(2) TERM OF SERVICE. — The Director shall serve for a term of 6 years, except that, in the event that a successor is not nominated and confirmed by the end of the term of service of a Director, the Director may continue to serve until such time as the next Director is appointed and confirmed.

(3) EXECUTIVE LEVEL. — The Director shall be compensated at Level III of the Executive Schedule.

(4) PROHIBITION ON DUAL SERVICE. — The individual serving in the position of Director may not, during such service, also serve as the head of any financial regulatory agency.

(5) RESPONSIBILITIES, DUTIES, AND AUTHORITY. — The Director shall have sole discretion in the manner in which the Director fulfills the responsibilities and duties and exercises the authorities described in this subtitle.

(c) BUDGET. — The Director, in consultation with the Chairperson, shall establish the annual budget of the Office.

(d) OFFICE PERSONNEL. —

(1) IN GENERAL. — The Director, in consultation with the Chairperson, may fix the number of, and appoint and direct, all employees of the Office.

(2) COMPENSATION. — The Director, in consultation with the Chairperson, shall fix, adjust, and administer the pay for all employees of the Office, without regard to chapter 51 or sub–chapter III of chapter 53 of title 5, United States Code, relating to

(B)包括对手方的识别性详细信息、金融公司对持仓的估值以及对持仓进行独立估值所必要的信息;

(7)“金融合约”一词系指两个或两个以上的对手方针对具有内在价值或外在价值的对象之远期交割订立的具有法律约束力,且规定了对手方之间的相关权利和义务的协议;及

(8)“金融工具”一词系指其条款和条件可公开获得,且不必经过任何其他对手方同意,其中一个或数个对手方即可进行转让的金融合约(包括公开交易的公司的普通股、政府债券或交易所交易的期货和期权合约)。

第152条 设立金融研究办公室

(a)**设立**。——财政部下设金融研究办公室。

(b)金融研究办公室主任。——

(1)**一般规定**。——金融研究办公室由金融研究办公室主任领导;金融研究办公室主任由参议院推荐、同意,并由总统任命。

(2)**任期**。——金融研究办公室主任任期为6年;但是,如果其任期届满时尚未提名并确认继任人选,则该办公室主任可以继续任职,直至下一任主任被提名并确认人选之时为止。

(3)**行政级别**。——金融研究办公室主任享受“高级公务员序列第三级别”的薪酬待遇。

(4)**双重任职的禁止性规定**。——金融研究办公室主任在任职期间内不得兼任任何金融监管机关的负责人。

(5)**责任、职责和权力**。——金融研究办公室主任应完全依其自由裁量权决定履行本子编规定的责任和职责以及行使本子编规定的权力的方式。

(c)**预算**。——金融研究办公室主任应与金融稳定监督委员会主席磋商,确定金融研究办公室的年度预算。

(d)**金融研究办公室的组成人员**。——

(1)**一般规定**。——金融研究办公室主任应与金融稳定监督委员会主席磋商,确定金融研究办公室的雇员总数,并任命、领导全体雇员。

(2)**薪酬**。——金融研究办公室主任应与金融稳定监督委员会主席磋商以确定、调整和管理金融研究办公室全体雇员的薪资,而不必考虑《美国法典》第五编第五十一章或第五十三章第三子章关于职位分类和一般职位序列薪资的规定。

classification of positions and General Schedule pay rates.

(3) COMPARABILITY. — Section 1206(a) of the Financial Institutions Reform, Recovery, and Enforcement Act of 1989 (12 U.S.C. 1833b(a)) is amended —

(A) by striking "Finance Board, " and inserting "Finance Board, the Office of Financial Research, and the Bureau of Consumer Financial Protection"; and

(B) by striking "and the Office of Thrift Supervision, ".

(4) SENIOR EXECUTIVES. — Section 3132(a)(1)(D) of title 5, United States Code, is amended by striking "and the National Credit Union Administration; " and inserting "the National Credit Union Administration, the Bureau of Consumer Financial Protection, and the Office of Financial Research; ".

(e) ASSISTANCE FROM FEDERAL AGENCIES. — Any department or agency of the United States may provide to the Office and any special advisory, technical, or professional committees appointed by the Office, such services, funds, facilities, staff, and other support services as the Office may determine advisable. Any Federal Government employee may be detailed to the Office without reimbursement, and such detail shall be without interruption or loss of civil service status or privilege.

(f) PROCUREMENT OF TEMPORARY AND INTERMITTENT SERVICES. — The Director may procure temporary and intermittent services under section 3109(b) of title 5, United States Code, at rates for individuals which do not exceed the daily equivalent of the annual rate of basic pay prescribed for Level V of the Executive Schedule under section 5316 of such title.

(g) POST–EMPLOYMENT PROHIBITIONS. — The Secretary, with the concurrence of the Director of the Office of Government Ethics, shall issue regulations prohibiting the Director and any employee of the Office who has had access to the transaction or position data maintained by the Data Center or other business confidential information about financial entities required to report to the Office from being employed by or providing advice or consulting services to a financial company, for a period of 1 year after last having had access in the course of official duties to such transaction or position data or business confidential information, regardless of whether that entity is required to report to the Office. For employees whose access to business confidential information was limited, the regulations may provide, on a case–by–case basis, for a shorter period of post–employment prohibition, provided that the shorter period does not compromise business confidential information.

(h) TECHNICAL AND PROFESSIONAL ADVISORY COMMITTEES. — The Office, in consultation with the Chairperson, may appoint such special advisory, technical, or professional committees as may be useful in carrying out the functions of the Office, and the members of such committees may be staff of the Office, or other persons, or both.

(3)**可比性**。——《1989年金融机构改革、复兴与实施法》第1206(a)条[《美国法典》第十二编第1833b(a)节]修正如下:

(A)删除“金融委员会、”,替以“金融委员会、金融研究办公室和消费者金融保护局”;及

(B)删除“和储蓄机构监理局,”。

(4)**“高级公务员”**。——《美国法典》第五编第3132(a)(1)(D)节修正如下:删除“和国家信贷联盟署;”替以“国家信贷联盟署、消费者金融保护局和金融研究办公室”。

(e)**联邦机关提供的协助**。——任何美国联邦部门或机关均可向金融研究办公室及其成立的任何特别顾问、技术或专业委员会提供金融研究办公室认为有益的服务、资金、设施、人员及其他支持服务。联邦政府的任何雇员均可无偿选派至金融研究办公室任职,且其公务员身份或特权不会因该等选派而中断或丧失。

(f)**获取临时性和非常年服务**。——金融研究办公室主任可获得《美国法典》第五编第3109(b)节规定的临时性和非常年服务,服务人员的费率不得超过按该编第5316节规定的“高级公务员序列第五级别”基本薪资年度费率计算的日均金额。

(g)**脱密规定**。——对于金融研究办公室主任和任何金融研究办公室雇员(只要该等雇员曾经接触过数据中心保存的交易或持仓数据或按照要求应向金融研究办公室报告的与金融实体相关的其他业务保密信息),经政府道德署署长同意,财政部部长即应颁布规章,规定该等人员在其正式任职期间最后一次接触上述交易或持仓数据或业务保密信息后1年之内,不得受聘于任何金融公司或为任何金融公司提供建议或咨询服务,而无论该等金融公司是否有向金融研究办公室报告的义务。对于被限制接触业务保密信息的雇员,在不危害业务保密信息的条件下,规章中可在个案基础上规定较短的脱密禁止期。

(h)**技术与专业顾问委员会**。——金融研究办公室可以在与金融稳定监督委员会主席磋商后成立特别顾问、技术或专业委员会,协助金融研究办公室履行职能。该等委员会的成员可以为金融研究办公室工作人员、其他人士或兼涉二者。

(i) FELLOWSHIP PROGRAM. — The Office, in consultation with the Chairperson, may establish and maintain an academic and professional fellowship program, under which qualified academics and professionals shall be invited to spend not longer than 2 years at the Office, to perform research and to provide advanced training for Office personnel.

(j) EXECUTIVE SCHEDULE COMPENSATION. — Section 5314 of title 5, United States Code, is amended by adding at the end the following new item:

"Director of the Office of Financial Research. ".

SEC. 153. PURPOSE AND DUTIES OF THE OFFICE.

(a) PURPOSE AND DUTIES. — The purpose of the Office is to support the Council in fulfilling the purposes and duties of the Council, as set forth in subtitle A, and to support member agencies, by —

(1) collecting data on behalf of the Council, and providing such data to the Council and member agencies;

(2) standardizing the types and formats of data reported and collected;

(3) performing applied research and essential long-term research;

(4) developing tools for risk measurement and monitoring;

(5) performing other related services;

(6) making the results of the activities of the Office available to financial regulatory agencies; and

(7) assisting such member agencies in determining the types and formats of data authorized by this Act to be collected by such member agencies.

(b) ADMINISTRATIVE AUTHORITY. — The Office may —

(1) share data and information, including software developed by the Office, with the Council, member agencies, and the Bureau of Economic Analysis, which shared data, information, and software —

(A) shall be maintained with at least the same level of security as is used by the Office; and

(B) may not be shared with any individual or entity without the permission of the Council;

(2) sponsor and conduct research projects; and

(3) assist, on a reimbursable basis, with financial analyses undertaken at the request of other Federal agencies that are not member agencies.

(c) RULEMAKING AUTHORITY. —

(1) SCOPE. — The Office, in consultation with the Chairperson, shall issue rules, regulations, and orders only to the extent necessary to carry out the purposes and duties described in paragraphs (1), (2), and (7) of subsection (a).

(2) STANDARDIZATION. — Member agencies, in consultation with the Office,

(i)**英才计划**。——金融研究办公室可以在与金融稳定监督委员会主席磋商后，设立和维持一个学术和专业英才计划，邀请具有相应资质的学术和专业人员，在不超过2年的期间内在金融研究办公室开展研究工作，并向金融研究办公室的工作人员提供高水平的培训。

(j)**"高级公务员序列薪酬"**。——在《美国法典》第五编第5314节结尾处增列一目，作为对该节的修正：

"金融研究办公室主任。"

第153条 金融研究办公室的设立宗旨和职责

(a)**设立宗旨和职责**。——金融研究办公室的宗旨为辅助金融稳定监督委员会实现第A子编规定的目的和职责，并为其成员机关提供支持，具体方式包括——

(1)代表金融稳定监督委员会收集数据，并将该等数据提供给金融稳定监督委员会及其成员机关；

(2)对报告和收集的数据的类型和格式制定标准；

(3)开展应用研究和重要长期研究；

(4)开发风险计量和监控工具；

(5)实施其他相关服务；

(6)向金融监管机关提供金融研究办公室的工作成果；及

(7)协助成员机关确定该等成员机关根据本法授权收集的数据的类型和格式。

(b)**行政管理权**。——金融研究办公室可以——

(1)与金融稳定监督委员会、成员机关和经济分析局共享数据和信息(包括金融研究办公室开发的软件)，条件是金融稳定监督委员会、成员机关和经济分析局——

(A)至少应按照金融研究办公室使用的同等安全保护级别，保管该等共享数据、信息和软件；且

(B)未经金融稳定监督委员会同意，不得与任何个人或实体共享该等数据、信息和软件；

(2)资助和开展研究项目；及

(3)经成员机关之外的其他联邦机关请求，协助开展金融分析，相关费用应由请求协助的联邦机关偿付。

(c)**规则制定权**。——

(1)**范围**。——金融研究办公室应在与金融稳定监督委员会主席磋商后发布规则、规章和命令，但必须以实施第(a)子条第(1)款、第(2)款和第(7)款规定的宗旨和职责所必要者为限。

(2)**标准化**。——成员机关应在与金融研究办公室磋商后，实施金融研究办公室

shall implement regulations promulgated by the Office under paragraph (1) to standardize the types and formats of data reported and collected on behalf of the Council, as described in subsection (a)(2). If a member agency fails to implement such regulations prior to the expiration of the 3-year period following the date of publication of final regulations, the Office, in consultation with the Chairperson, may implement such regulations with respect to the financial entities under the jurisdiction of the member agency. This paragraph shall not supersede or interfere with the independent authority of a member agency under other law to collect data, in such format and manner as the member agency requires.

(d) TESTIMONY. —

(1) IN GENERAL. — The Director of the Office shall report to and testify before the Committee on Banking, Housing, and Urban Affairs of the Senate and the Committee on Financial Services of the House of Representatives annually on the activities of the Office, including the work of the Data Center and the Research and Analysis Center, and the assessment of the Office of significant financial market developments and potential emerging threats to the financial stability of the United States.

(2) NO PRIOR REVIEW. — No officer or agency of the United States shall have any authority to require the Director to submit the testimony required under paragraph (1) or other congressional testimony to any officer or agency of the United States for approval, comment, or review prior to the submission of such testimony. Any such testimony to Congress shall include a statement that the views expressed therein are those of the Director and do not necessarily represent the views of the President.

(e) ADDITIONAL REPORTS. — The Director may provide additional reports to Congress concerning the financial stability of the United States. The Director shall notify the Council of any such additional reports provided to Congress.

(f) SUBPOENA. —

(1) IN GENERAL. — The Director may require from a financial company, by subpoena, the production of the data requested under subsection (a)(1) and section 154(b)(1), but only upon a written finding by the Director that —

(A) such data is required to carry out the functions described under this subtitle; and

(B) the Office has coordinated with the relevant primary financial regulatory agency, as required under section 154(b)(1)(B)(ii).

(2) FORMAT. — Subpoenas under paragraph (1) shall bear the signature of the Director, and shall be served by any person or class of persons designated by the Director for that purpose.

(3) ENFORCEMENT. — In the case of contumacy or failure to obey a subpoena,

根据第(1)款颁发的规章,以按照第(a)(2)子条的规定对代表金融稳定监督委员会报告和收集的数据之类型和格式制定统一标准。如果某一成员机关未在最终规章颁布后3年期限届满前实施该等规章,则金融研究办公室可以在与金融稳定监督委员会主席磋商后,直接针对受该等成员机关管辖的金融实体实施有关规章。本款规定并不替代或影响任一成员机关根据其他法律享有的按照其要求的格式和方法独立收集数据的权力。

(d)**作证**。——

(1)**一般规定**。——金融研究办公室主任应每年就金融研究办公室开展的活动(包括数据中心和研究分析中心的工作、金融研究办公室对重大金融市场发展动态以及美国金融稳定面临的新的潜在威胁作出的评估)向参议院银行、住房与城市事务委员会和众议院金融服务委员会提交报告,并向上述委员会作证。

(2)**无事先审查**。——在金融研究办公室主任按照第(1)款规定提交证词之前,任何美国联邦官员或机关均无权要求金融研究办公室主任向任何美国联邦官员或机关提供该等证词或其他国会听证会证词,供事先批准、评议或审查。向国会提供的任何证词中应包括一份声明,说明证词中的观点属于金融研究办公室主任的观点,并不必然代表总统的观点。

(e)**补充报告**。——金融研究办公室主任可以向国会提供关于美国金融稳定的补充报告;金融研究办公室主任向国会提交上述任何补充报告的,应通知金融稳定监督委员会。

(f)**传票**。——

(1)**一般规定**。——金融办公室主任可以通过传票的方式要求金融公司出示第(a)(1)子条和第154(b)(1)条规定的数据,前提是金融研究办公室主任已作出如下书面认定——

(A)该等数据为履行本子编规定的职能所必需;且

(B)金融研究办公室已按照第154(b)(1)(B)(ii)条的规定与相关优先金融监管机关进行了协调。

(2)**格式**。——根据第(1)款发送的传票应由金融研究办公室主任签字,并由其专门指定的任何一名或任一类别的人员送达。

(3)**强制执行**。——如果发生拒不执行或拒不服从传票的情形,应由任何相应的

the subpoena shall be enforceable by order of any appropriate district court of the United States. Any failure to obey the order of the court may be punished by the court as a contempt of court.

SEC. 154. ORGANIZATIONAL STRUCTURE; RESPONSIBILITIES OF PRIMARY PROGRAMMATIC UNITS.

(a) IN GENERAL. — There are established within the Office, to carry out the programmatic responsibilities of the Office —

(1) the Data Center; and

(2) the Research and Analysis Center.

(b) DATA CENTER. —

(1) GENERAL DUTIES. —

(A) DATA COLLECTION. — The Data Center, on behalf of the Council, shall collect, validate, and maintain all data necessary to carry out the duties of the Data Center, as described in this subtitle. The data assembled shall be obtained from member agencies, commercial data providers, publicly available data sources, and financial entities under subparagraph (B).

(B) AUTHORITY. —

(i) IN GENERAL. — The Office may, as determined by the Council or by the Director in consultation with the Council, require the submission of periodic and other reports from any financial company for the purpose of assessing the extent to which a financial activity or financial market in which the financial company participates, or the financial company itself, poses a threat to the financial stability of the United States.

(ii) MITIGATION OF REPORT BURDEN. — Before requiring the submission of a report from any financial company that is regulated by a member agency, any primary financial regulatory agency, a foreign supervisory authority, or the Office shall coordinate with such agencies or authority, and shall, whenever possible, rely on information available from such agencies or authority.

(iii) COLLECTION OF FINANCIAL TRANSACTION AND POSITION DATA. — The Office shall collect, on a schedule determined by the Director, in consultation with the Council, financial transaction data and position data from financial companies.

(C) RULEMAKING. — The Office shall promulgate regulations pursuant to subsections (a)(1), (a)(2), (a)(7), and (c)(1) of section 153 regarding the type and scope of the data to be collected by the Data Center under this paragraph.

(2) RESPONSIBILITIES. —

(A) PUBLICATION. — The Data Center shall prepare and publish, in a manner that is easily accessible to the public —

联邦地区法院下达强制执行传票的命令。对于拒不服从法院命令的任何行为,法院可按藐视法庭罪处罚。

第154条　组织结构;主要职能单位的责任

(a)**一般规定**。——金融研究办公室下设以下单位,负责履行金融研究办公室的职能责任——

(1)数据中心;及

(2)研究分析中心。

(b)**数据中心**。——

(1)**一般职责**。——

(A)**数据收集**。——数据中心应代表金融稳定监督委员会,负责收集、确认和保存全部必要数据,以履行本子编规定的数据中心职责。数据中心所收集的数据应按照第(B)子款的规定,从成员机关、商业数据提供商、公开的数据来源以及金融实体处获取。

(B)**权力**。——

(i)**一般规定**。——根据金融稳定监督委员会作出的判定或金融研究办公室主任与金融稳定监督委员会磋商后作出的判定,金融研究办公室可以要求任何金融公司提交定期报告和其他报告,以评估金融公司参与的金融活动或金融市场或金融公司对美国金融稳定造成的威胁程度。

(ii)**减轻报告负担**。——在要求任何金融公司呈交报告之前,如果该等金融公司由某一成员机关、任何优先金融监管机关或外国监管机关负责监管,[1]金融研究办公室应与该等机关或机构进行协调,并尽可能采信从该等机构或机关获取的信息。

(iii)**金融交易和持仓数据的收集**。——金融研究办公室应按照金融研究办公室主任与金融稳定监督委员会磋商后确定的时间安排,向金融公司收集金融交易数据和持仓数据。

(C)**规则制定**。——金融研究办公室应按照第153条第(a)(1)子条、第(a)(2)子条、第(a)(7)子条和第(c)(1)子条的规定颁发相关规章,对数据中心将依据本款规定收集的数据之类型和范围作出规定。

(2)**责任**。——

(A)**发布**。——数据中心应以便于公众查阅的方式编制和发布——

1　原文“or the Office”中的“or”似为衍词,译文中未翻译。——译者注

(i) a financial company reference database;

(ii) a financial instrument reference database; and

(iii) formats and standards for Office data, including standards for reporting financial transaction and position data to the Office.

(B) CONFIDENTIALITY. — The Data Center shall not publish any confidential data under subparagraph (A).

(3) INFORMATION SECURITY. — The Director shall ensure that data collected and maintained by the Data Center are kept secure and protected against unauthorized disclosure.

(4) CATALOG OF FINANCIAL ENTITIES AND INSTRUMENTS. — The Data Center shall maintain a catalog of the financial entities and instruments reported to the Office.

(5) AVAILABILITY TO THE COUNCIL AND MEMBER AGENCIES. — The Data Center shall make data collected and maintained by the Data Center available to the Council and member agencies, as necessary to support their regulatory responsibilities.

(6) OTHER AUTHORITY. — The Office shall, after consultation with the member agencies, provide certain data to financial industry participants and to the general public to increase market transparency and facilitate research on the financial system, to the extent that intellectual property rights are not violated, business confidential information is properly protected, and the sharing of such information poses no significant threats to the financial system of the United States.

(c) RESEARCH AND ANALYSIS CENTER. —

(1) GENERAL DUTIES. — The Research and Analysis Center, on behalf of the Council, shall develop and maintain independent analytical capabilities and computing resources —

(A) to develop and maintain metrics and reporting systems for risks to the financial stability of the United States;

(B) to monitor, investigate, and report on changes in systemwide risk levels and patterns to the Council and Congress;

(C) to conduct, coordinate, and sponsor research to support and improve regulation of financial entities and markets;

(D) to evaluate and report on stress tests or other stability-related evaluations of financial entities overseen by the member agencies;

(E) to maintain expertise in such areas as may be necessary to support specific requests for advice and assistance from financial regulators;

(F) to investigate disruptions and failures in the financial markets, report findings, and make recommendations to the Council based on those findings;

(i)金融公司参考数据库;

(ii)金融工具参考数据库;及

(iii)金融研究办公室的数据格式和标准,包括向金融研究办公室提交金融交易和持仓数据报告的标准。

(B)**保密**。——数据中心不得根据第(A)子款公开任何保密数据。

(3)**信息安全**。——金融研究办公室主任应确保数据中心收集和维持的数据得到安全保管和保护,防止未经授权擅自披露。

(4)**金融实体和工具目录**。——对于向金融研究办公室报告的金融实体和工具,数据中心应维持一份目录。

(5)**金融稳定监督委员会和成员机关的数据获取权**。——数据中心应将其收集和保存的数据提供给金融稳定监督委员会和成员机关,为金融稳定监督委员会和成员机关履行监管责任提供必要支持。

(6)**其他权力**。——金融研究办公室应在与成员机关磋商后,在不侵犯知识产权,商业保密信息得到妥善保护,且信息共享不会对美国金融体系造成严重威胁的前提下,向金融业参与者和一般公众提供特定数据,以提高市场透明度,并为与金融体系有关的研究提供便利。

(c)**研究分析中心**。——

(1)**一般职责**。——研究分析中心应代表金融稳定监督委员会开发和维持独立的分析能力和计算资源,以便——

(A)开发和维持美国金融稳定的风险指标和报告系统;

(B)监控、调查和向金融稳定监督委员会和国会报告系统性风险水平和模式的变化情况;

(C)为支持和改进金融实体和市场的监管工作开展、协调和资助各项研究;

(D)对成员机关所监管的金融实体的压力测试或其他稳定性评估作出评价和报告;

(E)在相关领域维持必要的专业技能水平,以满足金融监管者可能提出的具体建议或协助要求;

(F)调查金融市场中出现的运转失灵和受到扰乱的情况,报告调查结论,并基于调查结论向金融稳定监督委员会提出建议;

(G) to conduct studies and provide advice on the impact of policies related to systemic risk; and

(H) to promote best practices for financial risk management.

(d) REPORTING RESPONSIBILITIES. —

(1) REQUIRED REPORTS. — Not later than 2 years after the date of enactment of this Act, and not later than 120 days after the end of each fiscal year thereafter, the Office shall prepare and submit a report to Congress.

(2) CONTENT. — Each report required by this subsection shall assess the state of the United States financial system, including —

(A) an analysis of any threats to the financial stability of the United States;

(B) the status of the efforts of the Office in meeting the mission of the Office; and

(C) key findings from the research and analysis of the financial system by the Office.

SEC. 155. FUNDING.

(a) FINANCIAL RESEARCH FUND. —

(1) FUND ESTABLISHED. — There is established in the Treasury of the United States a separate fund to be known as the "Financial Research Fund".

(2) FUND RECEIPTS. — All amounts provided to the Office under subsection (c), and all assessments that the Office receives under subsection (d) shall be deposited into the Financial Research Fund.

(3) INVESTMENTS AUTHORIZED. —

(A) AMOUNTS IN FUND MAY BE INVESTED. — The Director may request the Secretary to invest the portion of the Financial Research Fund that is not, in the judgment of the Director, required to meet the needs of the Office.

(B) ELIGIBLE INVESTMENTS. — Investments shall be made by the Secretary in obligations of the United States or obligations that are guaranteed as to principal and interest by the United States, with maturities suitable to the needs of the Financial Research Fund, as determined by the Director.

(4) INTEREST AND PROCEEDS CREDITED. — The interest on, and the proceeds from the sale or redemption of, any obligations held in the Financial Research Fund shall be credited to and form a part of the Financial Research Fund.

(b) USE OF FUNDS. —

(1) IN GENERAL. — Funds obtained by, transferred to, or credited to the Financial Research Fund shall be immediately available to the Office, and shall remain available until expended, to pay the expenses of the Office in carrying out the duties and responsibilities of the Office.

(2) FEES, ASSESSMENTS, AND OTHER FUNDS NOT GOVERNMENT FUNDS. —

(G)对系统性风险相关政策所产生的影响开展研究和提供建议;及

(H)推广金融风险管理的最佳实践。

(d)**报告责任**。——

(1)**报告要求**。——金融研究办公室应在本法颁布之日后2年内,编制并向国会提交一份报告。且此后每一财政年度,金融研究办公室均应在财政年度结束后120天内编制并向国会提交一份报告。

(2)**内容**。——按照本子条规定提交的每份报告均应对美国金融体系的状况作出评估,包括——

(A)关于任何威胁美国金融稳定的因素之分析;

(B)金融研究办公室为完成自身任务所做的工作现状;及

(C)金融研究办公室通过对金融体系的研究和分析得出的重要结论。

第155条　经费来源

(a)**金融研究基金**。——

(1)**基金的设立**。——美国财政部兹设立一项单独基金,即"金融研究基金"。

(2)**经费**。——按照第(c)子条的规定向金融研究办公室提供的所有款项,以及金融研究办公室按照第(d)子条的规定收取的所有计征费均应存入金融研究基金。

(3)**经授权作出投资**。——

(A)**基金款项可用于投资**。——对于金融研究办公室主任判断不必用于满足金融研究办公室需求的金融研究基金之部分资金,金融研究办公室主任可要求财政部部长对该部分基金进行投资。

(B)**适格投资**。——投资应由财政部部长作出,投资标的应为美国国债,或者美国政府担保本金和利息的债券,债券期限应为金融研究办公室主任基于金融研究基金需求确定为适当的期限。

(4)**计入贷方的利息和收益**。——金融研究基金所持任何债券产生的利息以及卖出或赎回所获资金均应计入基金贷方,构成基金的一部分。

(b)**资金的使用**。——

(1)**一般规定**。——金融研究基金取得、收到的资金或计入金融研究基金贷方的资金均可立即用于支付金融研究办公室在履行职责和责任过程中发生的费用,且在支用完毕之前,可始终用于前述目的。

(2)**费用、计征费和政府资金之外的任何资金**。——金融研究基金取得、收到的

Funds obtained by, transferred to, or credited to the Financial Research Fund shall not be construed to be Government funds or appropriated moneys.

(3) AMOUNTS NOT SUBJECT TO APPORTIONMENT. — Notwithstanding any other provision of law, amounts in the Financial Research Fund shall not be subject to apportionment for purposes of chapter 15 of title 31, United States Code, or under any other authority, or for any other purpose.

(c) INTERIM FUNDING. — During the 2-year period following the date of enactment of this Act, the Board of Governors shall provide to the Office an amount sufficient to cover the expenses of the Office.

(d) PERMANENT SELF-FUNDING. — Beginning 2 years after the date of enactment of this Act, the Secretary shall establish, by regulation, and with the approval of the Council, an assessment schedule, including the assessment base and rates, applicable to bank holding companies with total consolidated assets of $50, 000, 000, 000 or greater and nonbank financial companies supervised by the Board of Governors, that takes into account differences among such companies, based on the considerations for establishing the prudential standards under section 115, to collect assessments equal to the total expenses of the Office.

SEC. 156. TRANSITION OVERSIGHT.

(a) PURPOSE. — The purpose of this section is to ensure that the Office —

(1) has an orderly and organized startup;

(2) attracts and retains a qualified workforce; and

(3) establishes comprehensive employee training and benefits programs.

(b) REPORTING REQUIREMENT. —

(1) IN GENERAL. — The Office shall submit an annual report to the Committee on Banking, Housing, and Urban Affairs of the Senate and the Committee on Financial Services of the House of Representatives that includes the plans described in paragraph (2).

(2) PLANS. — The plans described in this paragraph are as follows:

(A) TRAINING AND WORKFORCE DEVELOPMENT PLAN. — The Office shall submit a training and workforce development plan that includes, to the extent practicable —

(i) identification of skill and technical expertise needs and actions taken to meet those requirements;

(ii) steps taken to foster innovation and creativity;

(iii) leadership development and succession planning; and

(iv) effective use of technology by employees.

(B) WORKPLACE FLEXIBILITY PLAN. — The Office shall submit a workforce flexibility plan that includes, to the extent practicable —

资金或计入金融研究基金贷方的资金不得被视为政府资金或拨付款项。

(3)**基金款项不得进行分配**。——无论是否存在任何不同法律规定,严禁为《美国法典》第三十一编第十五章规定的目的、按照任何其他法律依据或出于任何其他目的对金融研究基金中的款项作出分配。

(c)**短期经费来源**。——本法颁布后2年内,联邦储备委员会应向金融研究办公室提供一笔足以支付其费用的款项。

(d)**长期自行筹措资金**。——本法颁布之日起届满2年之后,经金融稳定监督委员会批准,财政部部长应发布规章,制定一份费用计征表,适用于并表资产总额达500亿美元(含)以上的银行控股公司和受联邦储备委员会监管的非银行金融公司。计征表应说明计征基数和比率,应对该等公司之间的差异予以考量,并基于根据第115条确立审慎性标准时应考虑的因素,其目的在于按照金融研究办公室的费用总额计征同等金额的款项。

第156条 过渡期间的监督

(a)**目的**。——本条的目的在于确保金融研究办公室——

(1)有序和有组织地启动;

(2)吸引和留任合格人力;及

(3)建立全面的雇员培训和福利计划。

(b)**报告要求**。——

(1)**一般规定**。——金融研究办公室应向参议院银行、住房与城市事务委员会和众议院金融服务委员会提交年度报告,其中应包括第(2)款所述计划。

(2)**计划**。——本款所述计划如下:

(A)**培训和人力开发计划**。——金融研究办公室应提交一份培训和人力开发计划,在可行的范围内,该计划应包括:

(i)关于技能和技术专长需求之说明,以及为满足该等需求采取的行动;

(ii)为鼓励创新和创造采取的措施;

(iii)领导力开发和继任规划;及

(iv)雇员对技术的有效使用。

(B)**弹性工作计划**。——金融研究办公室应提交一份人力弹性工作计划,在可行的范围内,该计划应包括——

(i) telework;

(ii) flexible work schedules;

(iii) phased retirement;

(iv) reemployed annuitants;

(v) part-time work;

(vi) job sharing;

(vii) parental leave benefits and childcare assistance;

(viii) domestic partner benefits;

(ix) other workplace flexibilities; or

(x) any combination of the items described in clauses (i) through (ix).

(C) RECRUITMENT AND RETENTION PLAN. — The Office shall submit a recruitment and retention plan that includes, to the extent practicable, provisions relating to —

(i) the steps necessary to target highly qualified applicant pools with diverse backgrounds;

(ii) streamlined employment application processes;

(iii) the provision of timely notification of the status of employment applications to applicants; and

(iv) the collection of information to measure indicators of hiring effectiveness.

(c) EXPIRATION. — The reporting requirement under subsection (b) shall terminate 5 years after the date of enactment of this Act.

(d) RULE OF CONSTRUCTION. — Nothing in this section may be construed to affect —

(1) a collective bargaining agreement, as that term is defined in section 7103(a)(8) of title 5, United States Code, that is in effect on the date of enactment of this Act; or

(2) the rights of employees under chapter 71 of title 5, United States Code.

Subtitle C — Additional Board of Governors Authority for Certain Nonbank Financial Companies and Bank Holding Companies

SEC. 161. REPORTS BY AND EXAMINATIONS OF NONBANK FINANCIAL COMPANIES BY THE BOARD OF GOVERNORS.

(a) REPORTS. —

(1) IN GENERAL. — The Board of Governors may require each nonbank financial company supervised by the Board of Governors, and any subsidiary thereof, to submit

(i)远程工作;
(ii)弹性工作时间表;
(iii)阶段性退休;
(iv)返聘年金受益人;
(v)兼职工作;
(vi)工作分享制度;
(vii)育婴假和儿童保育协助;
(viii)同居伴侣福利;
(ix)其他工作弹性制度;或
(x)第(i)项至第(ix)项规定内容的任何组合。

(C)**招聘和留才计划**。——金融研究办公室应提交一份招聘和留才计划,在可行的范围内,该计划应包括以下相关规定——

(i)为针对不同背景的高资质人才群体进行招聘而采取的必要措施;

(ii)精简的应聘程序;
(iii)及时通知应聘人应聘申请状态;及

(iv)收集相关信息,以考核招聘成效指标。

(c)**失效**。——第(b)子条规定的报告要求于本法颁布之日起届满5年失效。

(d)**解释规则**。——本条中的任何规定均不得被解释为——

(1)对本法颁布之日已生效的集体劳动合同[定义见《美国法典》第五编第7103(a)(8)节]产生任何影响;或

(2)对《美国法典》第五编第七十一章规定的雇员权利产生任何影响。

第C子编——联邦储备委员会就特定非银行金融公司和银行控股公司享有的其他权力

第161条 要求非银行金融公司提交报告和联邦储备委员会对非银行金融公司的检查

(a)**报告**。——

(1)**一般规定**。——联邦储备委员会可以要求受其监管的每一家非银行金融公司及其任何子公司提交一份经宣誓程序保证所述内容真实无误的报告,以便联邦储

reports under oath, to keep the Board of Governors informed as to —

(A) the financial condition of the company or subsidiary, systems of the company or subsidiary for monitoring and controlling financial, operating, and other risks, and the extent to which the activities and operations of the company or subsidiary pose a threat to the financial stability of the United States; and

(B) compliance by the company or subsidiary with the requirements of this title.

(2) USE OF EXISTING REPORTS AND INFORMATION. — In carrying out subsection (a), the Board of Governors shall, to the fullest extent possible, use —

(A) reports and supervisory information that a nonbank financial company or subsidiary thereof has been required to provide to other Federal or State regulatory agencies;

(B) information otherwise obtainable from Federal or State regulatory agencies;

(C) information that is otherwise required to be reported publicly; and

(D) externally audited financial statements of such company or subsidiary.

(3) AVAILABILITY. — Upon the request of the Board of Governors, a nonbank financial company supervised by the Board of Governors, or a subsidiary thereof, shall promptly provide to the Board of Governors any information described in paragraph (2).

(b) EXAMINATIONS. —

(1) IN GENERAL. — Subject to paragraph (2), the Board of Governors may examine any nonbank financial company supervised by the Board of Governors and any subsidiary of such company, to inform the Board of Governors of —

(A) the nature of the operations and financial condition of the company and such subsidiary;

(B) the financial, operational, and other risks of the company or such subsidiary that may pose a threat to the safety and soundness of such company or subsidiary or to the financial stability of the United States;

(C) the systems for monitoring and controlling such risks; and

(D) compliance by the company or such subsidiary with the requirements of this title.

(2) USE OF EXAMINATION REPORTS AND INFORMATION. — For purposes of this subsection, the Board of Governors shall, to the fullest extent possible, rely on reports of examination of any subsidiary depository institution or functionally regulated subsidiary made by the primary financial regulatory agency for that subsidiary, and on information described in subsection (a)(2).

(c) COORDINATION WITH PRIMARY FINANCIAL REGULATORY AGENCY. — The Board of Governors shall —

(1) provide reasonable notice to, and consult with, the primary financial regulatory

备委员会了解——

(A)该公司或子公司的财务状况及财务、运营和其他风险的监控和控制系统,以及该公司或子公司的活动和运营对美国金融稳定的威胁程度;及

(B)该公司或子公司对本编规定的合规情况。

(2)**既有报告和信息的利用**。——在实施第(a)子条的规定时,联邦储备委员会应尽最大可能利用——

(A) 其他联邦监管机关或州监管机关已经要求非银行金融公司或其子公司提供的报告和监管信息;

(B)联邦监管机关或州监管机关可另行获得的其他信息;

(C)另行公开报告的其他信息;及

(D)非银行金融公司或其子公司经外部审计的财务报表。

(3)**信息提供**。——联邦储备委员会提出要求时,受联邦储备委员会监管的非银行金融公司或其子公司应及时向联邦储备委员会提供第(2)款所述的任何信息。

(b)**检查**。——

(1)**一般规定**。——在不违反第(2)款规定的前提下,联邦储备委员会可以对受其监管的任何非银行金融公司或其任何子公司开展检查工作,以便获得以下信息——

(A)该公司及其子公司的运营性质和财务状况;

(B)该公司或其子公司面临的,可能对其自身安全性、稳健性或对美国的金融稳定构成威胁的财务、运营和其他风险;

(C)该等风险的监控和控制系统;及

(D)该公司或其子公司对本编规定的合规情况。

(2)**检查报告和信息的利用**。——就本子条而言,联邦储备委员会应尽最大可能采信优先金融监管机关针对任何子公司存款机构或受制于功能监管的子公司制作的检查报告,并采信第(a)(2)子条规定的信息。

(c)**与优先金融监管机关的协调**。——联邦储备委员会应——

(1)在按照本条规定要求任何子公司提交报告或启动对某一子公司的检查之前,

agency for any subsidiary before requiring a report or commencing an examination of such subsidiary under this section; and

(2) avoid duplication of examination activities, reporting requirements, and requests for information, to the fullest extent possible.

SEC. 162. ENFORCEMENT.

(a) IN GENERAL. — Except as provided in subsection (b), a nonbank financial company supervised by the Board of Governors and any subsidiaries of such company (other than any depository institution subsidiary) shall be subject to the provisions of subsections (b) through (n) of section 8 of the Federal Deposit Insurance Act (12 U.S.C. 1818), in the same manner and to the same extent as if the company were a bank holding company, as provided in section 8(b)(3) of the Federal Deposit Insurance Act (12 U.S.C. 1818(b)(3)).

(b) ENFORCEMENT AUTHORITY FOR FUNCTIONALLY REGULATED SUBSIDIARIES. —

(1) REFERRAL. — If the Board of Governors determines that a condition, practice, or activity of a depository institution subsidiary or functionally regulated subsidiary of a nonbank financial company supervised by the Board of Governors does not comply with the regulations or orders prescribed by the Board of Governors under this Act, or otherwise poses a threat to the financial stability of the United States, the Board of Governors may recommend, in writing, to the primary financial regulatory agency for the subsidiary that such agency initiate a supervisory action or enforcement proceeding. The recommendation shall be accompanied by a written explanation of the concerns giving rise to the recommendation.

(2) BACK–UP AUTHORITY OF THE BOARD OF GOVERNORS. — If, during the 60–day period beginning on the date on which the primary financial regulatory agency receives a recommendation under paragraph (1), the primary financial regulatory agency does not take supervisory or enforcement action against a subsidiary that is acceptable to the Board of Governors, the Board of Governors (upon a vote of its members) may take the recommended supervisory or enforcement action, as if the subsidiary were a bank holding company subject to supervision by the Board of Governors.

SEC. 163. ACQUISITIONS.

(a) ACQUISITIONS OF BANKS; TREATMENT AS A BANK HOLDING COMPANY. — For purposes of section 3 of the Bank Holding Company Act of 1956 (12 U.S.C. 1842), a nonbank financial company supervised by the Board of Governors shall be deemed to be, and shall be treated as, a bank holding company.

(b) ACQUISITION OF NONBANK COMPANIES. —

(1) PRIOR NOTICE FOR LARGE ACQUISITIONS. — Notwithstanding section 4

向该子公司的优先金融监管机关提供合理通知,并与之进行磋商;及

(2)尽最大可能避免重复的检查活动,并避免提出重复的报告要求和信息提供要求。

第162条 执法

(a)**一般规定**。——除第(b)子条规定的情形外,受联邦储备委员会监管的非银行金融公司和该等公司的任何子公司(不包括任何存款机构子公司)均应受制于《联邦存款保险法》第8条[《美国法典》第十二编第1818节]第(b)子条至第(n)子条的规定,其方式和范围均与《联邦存款保险法》第8(b)(3)条[《美国法典》第十二编第1818(b)(3)节]规定的银行控股公司完全一致。

(b)**受制于功能监管的子公司的执法机构**。——

(1)**移交**。——如果对于受联邦储备委员会监管的非银行金融公司的存款机构子公司或受制于功能监管的子公司,联邦储备委员会判定该等子公司的某项状态、做法或活动不符合联邦储备委员会根据本法制定的规章或命令,或者对美国的金融稳定构成威胁,则联邦储备委员会可以书面形式建议该等子公司的优先金融监管机关采取监管行动或启动执法程序。联邦储备委员会提出上述建议的,应随附一份书面说明,解释导致其提出该等建议的关切问题。

(2)**联邦储备委员会的后备权力**。——在收到根据第(1)款发送的建议之日起60天内,优先金融监管机关未对子公司采取联邦储备委员会认可的监管行动或执法行动的,则联邦储备委员会(经其成员表决通过)可以采取其建议的监管行动或执法行动,如同该等子公司是一家受联邦储备委员会监管的银行控股公司。

第163条 收购

(a)**对银行的收购;作为银行控股公司处理**。——就《1956年银行控股公司法》第3条(《美国法典》第十二编第1842节)而言,受联邦储备委员会监管的非银行金融公司应视为银行控股公司,并作为银行控股公司处理。

(b)**对非银行公司的收购**。——

(1)**大规模收购的预先通知**。——无论《1956年银行控股公司法》第4(k)(6)(B)

(k)(6)(B) of the Bank Holding Company Act of 1956 (12 U.S.C. 1843 (k)(6)(B)), a bank holding company with total consolidated assets equal to or greater than $50, 000, 000, 000 or a nonbank financial company supervised by the Board of Governors shall not acquire direct or indirect ownership or control of any voting shares of any company (other than an insured depository institution) that is engaged in activities described in section 4 (k) of the Bank Holding Company Act of 1956 having total consolidated assets of $10, 000, 000, 000 or more, without providing written notice to the Board of Governors in advance of the transaction.

(2) EXEMPTIONS. — The prior notice requirement in paragraph (1) shall not apply with regard to the acquisition of shares that would qualify for the exemptions in section 4(c) or section 4(k)(4)(E) of the Bank Holding Company Act of 1956 (12 U.S.C. 1843(c) and (k)(4)(E)).

(3) NOTICE PROCEDURES. — The notice procedures set forth in section 4(j)(1) of the Bank Holding Company Act of 1956 (12 U.S.C. 1843 (j)(1)), without regard to section 4(j)(3) of that Act, shall apply to an acquisition of any company (other than an insured depository institution) by a bank holding company with total consolidated assets equal to or greater than $50, 000, 000, 000 or a nonbank financial company supervised by the Board of Governors, as described in paragraph (1), including any such company engaged in activities described in section 4(k) of that Act.

(4) STANDARDS FOR REVIEW. — In addition to the standards provided in section 4(j)(2) of the Bank Holding Company Act of 1956 (12 U.S.C. 1843(j)(2)), the Board of Governors shall consider the extent to which the proposed acquisition would result in greater or more concentrated risks to global or United States financial stability or the United States economy.

(5) HART-SCOTT-RODINO FILING REQUIREMENT. — Solely for purposes of section 7A(c)(8) of the Clayton Act (15 U.S.C. 18a(c)(8)), the transactions subject to the requirements of paragraph (1) shall be treated as if Board of Governors approval is not required.

SEC. 164. PROHIBITION AGAINST MANAGEMENT INTERLOCKSBETWEEN CERTAIN FINANCIAL COMPANIES.

A nonbank financial company supervised by the Board of Governors shall be treated as a bank holding company for purposes of the Depository Institutions Management Interlocks Act (12 U.S.C. 3201 et seq.), except that the Board of Governors shall not exercise the authority provided in section 7 of that Act (12 U.S.C. 3207) to permit service by a management official of a nonbank financial company supervised by the Board of Governors as a management official of any bank holding company with total consolidated assets equal to or greater than $50, 000, 000, 000, or other nonaffiliated

条[《美国法典》第十二编第1843(k)(6)(B)节]如何规定,并表资产总额达500亿美元(含)以上的银行控股公司或受联邦储备委员会监管的非银行金融公司,如果未在交易前向联邦储备委员会提交事先书面通知,则不得收购从事《1956年银行控股公司法》第4(k)条所述活动且并表资产总额达100亿美元(含)以上的任何公司(但参保存款机构除外)之任何表决股的直接或间接所有权或控制权。

(2)**豁免**。——第(1)款规定的预先通知要求不适用于根据《1956年银行控股公司法》第4(c)条或第4(k)(4)(E)条[《美国法典》第十二编第1843(c)节和第1843(k)(4)(E)节]规定可以享有豁免资格的股份收购。

(3)**通知程序**。——《1956年银行控股公司法》第4(j)(1)条[《美国法典》第十二编第1843(j)(1)节]规定的通知程序,应适用于第(1)款所述并表资产总额达500亿美元(含)以上的银行控股公司或受联邦储备委员会监管的非银行金融公司[包括从事该法第4(k)条所述活动的任何上述公司]对任何公司(但参保存款机构除外)的收购,而不必考虑该法第4(j)(3)条的规定。

(4)**审查标准**。——除《1956年银行控股公司法》第4(j)(2)条[《美国法典》第十二编第1843(j)(2)节]规定的标准外,联邦储备委员会还应考虑拟进行的收购对全球或美国的金融稳定或美国经济造成更大或更为集中的风险的可能性。

(5)**哈特—斯科特—罗迪诺反垄断改进法**。——仅就《克莱顿法》第7A(c)(8)条[《美国法典》第十五编第18a(c)(8)节]而言,受制于第(1)款要求的交易应视同不必取得联邦储备委员会批准的交易处理。

第164条 特定金融公司管理层之间交叉任职之禁止性规定

就《禁止存款机构管理层交叉任职法》(《美国法典》第十二编第3201节及其后条文)而言,受联邦储备委员会监管的非银行金融公司应视同银行控股公司处理,但是,联邦储备委员会不得行使该法第7条(《美国法典》第十二编第3207节)规定的权力,即不得允许受联邦储备委员会监管的非银行金融公司的管理人员担任并表资产总额达500亿美元(含)以上的任何银行控股公司或受联邦储备委员会监管的其他非关联非银行金融公司的管理人员职务(但是联邦储备委员会有权对因兼并、收购或合并引起的交叉任职授予临时豁免)。

nonbank financial company supervised by the Board of Governors (other than to provide a temporary exemption for interlocks resulting from a merger, acquisition, or consolidation).

SEC. 165. ENHANCED SUPERVISION AND PRUDENTIAL STANDARDS FOR NONBANK FINANCIAL COMPANIES SUPERVISED BY THE BOARD OF GOVERNORS AND CERTAIN BANK HOLDING COMPANIES.

(a) IN GENERAL. —

(1) PURPOSE. — In order to prevent or mitigate risks to the financial stability of the United States that could arise from the material financial distress or failure, or ongoing activities, of large, interconnected financial institutions, the Board of Governors shall, on its own or pursuant to recommendations by the Council under section 115, establish prudential standards for nonbank financial companies supervised by the Board of Governors and bank holding companies with total consolidated assets equal to or greater than $50, 000, 000, 000 that —

(A) are more stringent than the standards and requirements applicable to nonbank financial companies and bank holding companies that do not present similar risks to the financial stability of the United States; and

(B) increase in stringency, based on the considerations identified in subsection (b)(3).

(2) TAILORED APPLICATION. —

(A) IN GENERAL. — In prescribing more stringent prudential standards under this section, the Board of Governors may, on its own or pursuant to a recommendation by the Council in accordance with section 115, differentiate among companies on an individual basis or by category, taking into consideration their capital structure, riskiness, complexity, financial activities (including the financial activities of their subsidiaries), size, and any other risk-related factors that the Board of Governors deems appropriate.

(B) ADJUSTMENT OF THRESHOLD FOR APPLICATION OF CERTAIN STANDARDS. — The Board of Governors may, pursuant to a recommendation by the Council in accordance with section 115, establish an asset threshold above $50, 000, 000, 000 for the application of any standard established under subsections (c) through (g).

(b) DEVELOPMENT OF PRUDENTIAL STANDARDS. —

(1) IN GENERAL. —

(A) REQUIRED STANDARDS. — The Board of Governors shall establish prudential standards for nonbank financial companies supervised by the Board of Governors and bank holding companies described in subsection (a), that shall include —

(i) risk-based capital requirements and leverage limits, unless the Board of Governors, in consultation with the Council, determines that such requirements are not appropriate for a company subject to more stringent prudential standards because of the

第165条　强化对受联邦储备委员会监管的非银行金融公司和特定银行控股公司的监管并提高审慎性标准

(a)**一般规定**。——

(1)**目的**。——为了防范或缓释相互关联的大型金融机构的重大财务困境、经营失败或正在开展的活动可能对美国金融稳定造成的风险,联邦储备委员会应自行或根据金融稳定监督委员会按照第115条规定提出的建议,设定适用于受联邦储备委员会监管的非银行金融公司和并表资产总额达500亿美元(含)以上的银行控股公司的审慎性标准,且该等标准应——

(A)比适用于对美国金融稳定不具有类似风险的非金融公司和银行控股公司的标准和要求更为严格;及

(B)基于第(b)(3)子条确定的考虑因素,进一步提高严格程度。

(2)**差异化适用**。——

(A)**一般规定**。——在根据本条制定更为严格的审慎性标准过程中,联邦储备委员会可自行决定或根据金融稳定监督委员会按照第115条规定提出的建议,考虑公司的资本结构、风险程度、复杂程度、金融活动(包括其子公司的金融活动)、规模及联邦储备委员会认为适当的任何其他风险因素,区别对待每一公司或按类别区别对待。

(B)**调整特定标准的适用门槛**。——联邦储备委员会可根据金融稳定监督委员会按照第115条规定提出的建议,就按照第(c)子条至第(g)子条设定的任何标准之适用设立一个高于500亿美元的资产门槛。

(b)**审慎性标准的制定**。——

(1)**一般规定**。——

(A)**标准要求**。——联邦储备委员会应就受其监管的非银行金融公司和第(a)子条所述的银行控股公司设定审慎性标准,其中应包括——

(i)风险基础资本要求和杠杆率限制,除非联邦储备委员会在与金融稳定监督委员会磋商后判定,鉴于该公司的活动(例如,投资公司活动或所管理的资产)或结构,该公司不宜适用该等要求(前提是其已受制于更为严格的审慎性标准),在前述情况

activities of such company (such as investment company activities or assets under management) or structure, in which case, the Board of Governors shall apply other standards that result in similarly stringent risk controls;

(ii) liquidity requirements;

(iii) overall risk management requirements;

(iv) resolution plan and credit exposure report requirements; and

(v) concentration limits.

(B) ADDITIONAL STANDARDS AUTHORIZED. — The Board of Governors may establish additional prudential standards for nonbank financial companies supervised by the Board of Governors and bank holding companies described in subsection (a), that include —

(i) a contingent capital requirement;

(ii) enhanced public disclosures;

(iii) short–term debt limits; and

(iv) such other prudential standards as the Board or Governors, on its own or pursuant to a recommendation made by the Council in accordance with section 115, determines are appropriate.

(2) STANDARDS FOR FOREIGN FINANCIAL COMPANIES. — In applying the standards set forth in paragraph (1) to any foreign nonbank financial company supervised by the Board of Governors or foreign –based bank holding company, the Board of Governors shall —

(A) give due regard to the principle of national treatment and equality of competitive opportunity; and

(B) take into account the extent to which the foreign financial company is subject on a consolidated basis to home country standards that are comparable to those applied to financial companies in the United States.

(3) CONSIDERATIONS. — In prescribing prudential standards under paragraph (1), the Board of Governors shall —

(A) take into account differences among nonbank financial companies supervised by the Board of Governors and bank holding companies described in subsection (a), based on —

(i) the factors described in subsections (a) and (b) of section 113;

(ii) whether the company owns an insured depository institution;

(iii) nonfinancial activities and affiliations of the company; and

(iv) any other risk–related factors that the Board of Governors determines appropriate;

(B) to the extent possible, ensure that small changes in the factors listed in

下,联邦储备委员会应采用其他标准,但该等标准的风险控制应达到类似的严格程度;

(ii)流动性要求;
(iii)整体风险管理要求;
(iv)清盘计划和信用风险敞口报告要求;及
(v)集中度限制。

(B)**授权设定其他标准**。——联邦储备委员会可以就受联邦储备委员会监管的非银行金融公司和第(a)子条所述的银行控股公司设立其他审慎性标准,包括——

(i)或有资本要求;
(ii)加强公开披露;
(iii)短期债务限制;及
(iv)联邦储备委员会自行或根据金融稳定监督委员会按照第115条规定提出的建议,判定确属适当的任何其他审慎性标准。

(2)**适用于外国金融公司的标准**。——在对受联邦储备委员会监管的任何外国非银行金融公司或外国银行控股公司适用第(1)款规定的标准时,联邦储备委员会应——

(A)适当考虑国民待遇和竞争机会均等原则;及

(B)考虑在多大程度上,外国金融公司在母国受制于与美国境内金融公司适用的标准具有可比性的并表标准。

(3)**考虑因素**。——在根据第(1)款制定审慎性标准时,联邦储备委员会应:

(A)考虑受联邦储备委员会监管的非银行金融公司与第(a)子条所述的银行控股公司之间的差别,考虑因素包括——

(i)第113条第(a)子条和第(b)子条所述因素;
(ii)公司是否拥有参保存款机构;
(iii)公司的非金融活动和关联关系;及
(iv)联邦储备委员会判定确属适当的任何其他风险因素;

(B)尽可能确保第113条第(a)子条和第(b)子条所列因素的轻微变化不会导致依

subsections (a) and (b) of section 113 would not result in sharp, discontinuous changes in the prudential standards established under paragraph (1) of this subsection;

(C) take into account any recommendations of the Council under section 115; and

(D) adapt the required standards as appropriate in light of any predominant line of business of such company, including assets under management or other activities for which particular standards may not be appropriate.

(4) CONSULTATION. — Before imposing prudential standards or any other requirements pursuant to this section, including notices of deficiencies in resolution plans and more stringent requirements or divestiture orders resulting from such notices, that are likely to have a significant impact on a functionally regulated subsidiary or depository institution subsidiary of a nonbank financial company supervised by the Board of Governors or a bank holding company described in subsection (a), the Board of Governors shall consult with each Council member that primarily supervises any such subsidiary with respect to any such standard or requirement.

(5) REPORT. — The Board of Governors shall submit an annual report to Congress regarding the implementation of the prudential standards required pursuant to paragraph (1), including the use of such standards to mitigate risks to the financial stability of the United States.

(c) CONTINGENT CAPITAL. —

(1) IN GENERAL. — Subsequent to submission by the Council of a report to Congress under section 115(c), the Board of Governors may issue regulations that require each nonbank financial company supervised by the Board of Governors and bank holding companies described in subsection (a) to maintain a minimum amount of contingent capital that is convertible to equity in times of financial stress.

(2) FACTORS TO CONSIDER. — In issuing regulations under this subsection, the Board of Governors shall consider —

(A) the results of the study undertaken by the Council, and any recommendations of the Council, under section 115(c);

(B) an appropriate transition period for implementation of contingent capital under this subsection;

(C) the factors described in subsection (b)(3)(A);

(D) capital requirements applicable to the nonbank financial company supervised by the Board of Governors or a bank holding company described in subsection (a), and subsidiaries thereof; and

(E) any other factor that the Board of Governors deems appropriate.

(d) RESOLUTION PLAN AND CREDIT EXPOSURE REPORTS. —

(1) RESOLUTION PLAN. — The Board of Governors shall require each nonbank

本子条第(1)款设立的审慎性标准之适用发生急剧、不连续的变化;

(C)考虑金融稳定监督委员会按照第115条规定提出的任何建议;及

(D)根据该等公司的任何主营业务范围(包括不宜适用特定标准的该等公司所管理的资产或其他活动)对设定的标准进行适当调整。

(4)**磋商**。——在根据本条对受联邦储备委员会监管的非银行金融公司、第(a)子条所述的银行控股公司下属的某一受制于功能监管的子公司或存款机构子公司,实施可能对其产生重大影响的审慎性标准或任何其他要求之前(包括就清盘计划发出缺陷通知,以及因该等通知引发的更为严格的要求或资产剥离令),联邦储备委员会应就该等标准或要求征求对任何该等子公司负有优先监管责任的金融稳定监督委员会成员的意见。

(5)**报告**。——联邦储备委员会应每年向国会提交一份报告,说明第(1)款规定的审慎性标准的实施情况,包括利用该等标准缓释美国金融稳定风险的情况。

(c)**或有资本**。——

(1)**一般规定**。——在联邦储备委员会按照第115(c)条规定向国会提交报告后,联邦储备委员会可以发布规章,要求受其监管的每一非银行金融公司以及第(a)子条所述的银行控股公司维持一定的最低金额的或有资本,以便在发生财务困境时转增股本。

(2)**考虑因素**。——在按照本子条发布规章时,联邦储备委员会应考虑以下因素——

(A)金融稳定监督委员会按照第115(c)条开展的研究之结果和提出的任何建议;

(B)实施本子条的或有资本所需的适当过渡期;

(C)第(b)(3)(A)子条所述因素;

(D)对受联邦储备委员会监管的非银行金融公司或第(a)子条所述的银行控股公司及上述各者的子公司适用的资本要求;及

(E)联邦储备委员会判定确属适当的任何其他因素。

(d)**清盘计划和信用风险敞口报告**。——

(1)**清盘计划**。——联邦储备委员会应要求其监管的每一非银行金融公司以及

financial company supervised by the Board of Governors and bank holding companies described in subsection (a) to report periodically to the Board of Governors, the Council, and the Corporation the plan of such company for rapid and orderly resolution in the event of material financial distress or failure, which shall include —

(A) information regarding the manner and extent to which any insured depository institution affiliated with the company is adequately protected from risks arising from the activities of any nonbank subsidiaries of the company;

(B) full descriptions of the ownership structure, assets, liabilities, and contractual obligations of the company;

(C) identification of the cross–guarantees tied to different securities, identification of major counterparties, and a process for determining to whom the collateral of the company is pledged; and

(D) any other information that the Board of Governors and the Corporation jointly require by rule or order.

(2) CREDIT EXPOSURE REPORT. — The Board of Governors shall require each nonbank financial company supervised by the Board of Governors and bank holding companies described in subsection (a) to report periodically to the Board of Governors, the Council, and the Corporation on —

(A) the nature and extent to which the company has credit exposure to other significant nonbank financial companies and significant bank holding companies; and

(B) the nature and extent to which other significant nonbank financial companies and significant bank holding companies have credit exposure to that company.

(3) REVIEW. — The Board of Governors and the Corporation shall review the information provided in accordance with this subsection by each nonbank financial company supervised by the Board of Governors and bank holding company described in subsection (a).

(4) NOTICE OF DEFICIENCIES. — If the Board of Governors and the Corporation jointly determine, based on their review under paragraph (3), that the resolution plan of a nonbank financial company supervised by the Board of Governors or a bank holding company described in subsection (a) is not credible or would not facilitate an orderly resolution of the company under title 11, United States Code —

(A) the Board of Governors and the Corporation shall notify the company of the deficiencies in the resolution plan; and

(B) the company shall resubmit the resolution plan within a timeframe determined by the Board of Governors and the Corporation, with revisions demonstrating that the plan is credible and would result in an orderly resolution under title 11, United States Code, including any proposed changes in business operations and corporate structure to facilitate

第(a)子条所述的银行控股公司,定期向联邦储备委员会、金融稳定监督委员会和联邦存款保险公司报告该等公司在重大财务困境或经营失败情况下将采取的快速有序清盘计划,其中应包括以下信息——

(A)对于因公司的任何非银行子公司活动造成的风险,充分保护公司的任何关联参保存款机构免受该等风险影响的保护方式和程度;

(B)关于公司所有权结构、资产、负债和合同义务的全面说明;

(C)识别与不同证券绑定的交叉担保,识别主要的对手方,以及确定公司担保品之担保权人;及

(D)联邦储备委员会和联邦存款保险公司联合发布规则或命令要求提供的任何其他信息。

(2)**信用风险敞口报告**。——联邦储备委员会应要求其监管的每一非银行金融公司以及第(a)子条所述的银行控股公司,定期向联邦储备委员会、金融稳定监督委员会和联邦存款保险公司报告——

(A)该公司对其他重要非银行金融公司和重要银行控股公司的信用风险敞口的性质和范围;及

(B)其他重要非银行金融公司和重要银行控股公司对该公司的信用风险敞口的性质和范围。

(3)**审查**。——联邦储备委员会和联邦存款保险公司应审查受联邦储备委员会监管的每一非银行金融公司以及第(a)子条所述的银行控股公司根据本子条规定提供的信息。

(4)**缺陷通知**。——联邦储备委员会和联邦存款保险公司按照第(3)款规定进行审查之后,基于审查结果共同判定受联邦储备委员会监管的非银行金融公司或第(a)子条所述的银行控股公司的清盘计划缺乏可信性,或者将不利于按照《美国法典》第十一编规定对公司进行有序清盘的,则——

(A)联邦储备委员会和联邦存款保险公司应通知该公司清盘计划存在的缺陷;且

(B)该公司应在联邦储备委员会和联邦存款保险公司确定的期限内重新提交清盘计划,修订后的清盘计划应证明计划的可信性,并证明该计划将实现《美国法典》第十一编规定的有序清盘,同时应提出业务运营和公司结构的任何变更提案,以促进清盘计划的实施。

implementation of the plan.

(5) FAILURE TO RESUBMIT CREDIBLE PLAN. —

(A) IN GENERAL. — If a nonbank financial company supervised by the Board of Governors or a bank holding company described in subsection (a) fails to timely resubmit the resolution plan as required under paragraph (4), with such revisions as are required under subparagraph (B), the Board of Governors and the Corporation may jointly impose more stringent capital, leverage, or liquidity requirements, or restrictions on the growth, activities, or operations of the company, or any subsidiary thereof, until such time as the company resubmits a plan that remedies the deficiencies.

(B) DIVESTITURE. — The Board of Governors and the Corporation, in consultation with the Council, may jointly direct a nonbank financial company supervised by the Board of Governors or a bank holding company described in subsection (a), by order, to divest certain assets or operations identified by the Board of Governors and the Corporation, to facilitate an orderly resolution of such company under title 11, United States Code, in the event of the failure of such company, in any case in which —

(i) the Board of Governors and the Corporation have jointly imposed more stringent requirements on the company pursuant to subparagraph (A); and

(ii) the company has failed, within the 2-year period beginning on the date of the imposition of such requirements under subparagraph (A), to resubmit the resolution plan with such revisions as were required under paragraph (4)(B).

(6) NO LIMITING EFFECT. — A resolution plan submitted in accordance with this subsection shall not be binding on a bankruptcy court, a receiver appointed under title II, or any other authority that is authorized or required to resolve the nonbank financial company supervised by the Board, any bank holding company, or any subsidiary or affiliate of the foregoing.

(7) NO PRIVATE RIGHT OF ACTION. — No private right of action may be based on any resolution plan submitted in accordance with this subsection.

(8) RULES. — Not later than 18 months after the date of enactment of this Act, the Board of Governors and the Corporation shall jointly issue final rules implementing this subsection.

(e) CONCENTRATION LIMITS. —

(1) STANDARDS. — In order to limit the risks that the failure of any individual company could pose to a nonbank financial company supervised by the Board of Governors or a bank holding company described in subsection (a), the Board of Governors, by regulation, shall prescribe standards that limit such risks.

(2) LIMITATION ON CREDIT EXPOSURE. — The regulations prescribed by the Board of Governors under paragraph (1) shall prohibit each nonbank financial company

(5)**未能重新提交可信的清盘计划的情形**。——

(A)**一般规定**。——如果受联邦储备委员会监管的非银行金融公司或第(a)子条所述的银行控股公司未能按照第(4)款规定及时重新提交清盘计划以及第(B)子款规定的修订,则联邦储备委员会和联邦存款保险公司可以联合对该公司或其任何子公司施加更为严格的资本、杠杆率或流动性要求,或者对公司的发展、业务或运营施加限制,直至公司重新提交清盘计划纠正上述缺陷为止。

(B)**剥离**。——如果受联邦储备委员会监管的非银行金融公司或第(a)子条所述的银行控股公司经营失败且符合以下条件的,则联邦储备委员会和联邦存款保险公司可以在与金融稳定监督委员会磋商后联合发布命令,责令该公司剥离联邦储备委员会和联邦存款保险公司确定的特定资产或经营,以利于该公司按照《美国法典》第十一编的规定进行有序清盘——

(i)联邦储备委员会和联邦存款保险公司已按照第(A)子款联合对该公司施加更为严格的要求;且

(ii)在联邦储备委员会和联邦存款保险公司按照第(A)子款施加要求之日起2年内,该公司未能按照第(4)(B)款的规定重新提交清盘计划及相关修订。

(6)**无限制效力**。——根据本子条提交的清盘计划对以下机构或主体不具有约束力:破产法院、根据第二编指定的破产接管人、有权或有义务对受联邦储备委员会监管的非银行金融公司、任何银行控股公司或者其以上各者的任何子公司或关联方执行清盘的任何其他机构。

(7)**无私人诉讼权利**。——不得基于根据本子条提交的任何清盘计划主张任何私人诉讼权利。

(8)**规则**。——联邦储备委员会和联邦存款保险公司应在本法颁布之日后18个月内,联合发布本子条的最终规则。

(e)**集中度限制**。——

(1)**标准**。——为了限制任何一家公司经营失败可能对受联邦储备委员会监管的某一非银行金融公司或对第(a)子条所述某一银行控股公司造成的风险,联邦储备委员会应发布规章,制定标准限制该等风险。

(2)**信用风险敞口限制**。——联邦储备委员会应在根据第(1)款制定的规章中规定,任何受联邦储备委员会监管的非银行金融公司以及第(a)子条所述的银行控股公

supervised by the Board of Governors and bank holding company described in subsection (a) from having credit exposure to any unaffiliated company that exceeds 25 percent of the capital stock and surplus (or such lower amount as the Board of Governors may determine by regulation to be necessary to mitigate risks to the financial stability of the United States) of the company.

(3) CREDIT EXPOSURE. — For purposes of paragraph (2), "credit exposure" to a company means —

(A) all extensions of credit to the company, including loans, deposits, and lines of credit;

(B) all repurchase agreements and reverse repurchase agreements with the company, and all securities borrowing and lending transactions with the company, to the extent that such transactions create credit exposure for the nonbank financial company supervised by the Board of Governors or a bank holding company described in subsection (a);

(C) all guarantees, acceptances, or letters of credit (including endorsement or standby letters of credit) issued on behalf of the company;

(D) all purchases of or investment in securities issued by the company;

(E) counterparty credit exposure to the company in connection with a derivative transaction between the nonbank financial company supervised by the Board of Governors or a bank holding company described in subsection (a) and the company; and

(F) any other similar transactions that the Board of Governors, by regulation, determines to be a credit exposure for purposes of this section.

(4) ATTRIBUTION RULE. — For purposes of this subsection, any transaction by a nonbank financial company supervised by the Board of Governors or a bank holding company described in subsection (a) with any person is a transaction with a company, to the extent that the proceeds of the transaction are used for the benefit of, or transferred to, that company.

(5) RULEMAKING. — The Board of Governors may issue such regulations and orders, including definitions consistent with this section, as may be necessary to administer and carry out this subsection.

(6) EXEMPTIONS. — This subsection shall not apply to any Federal home loan bank. The Board of Governors may, by regulation or order, exempt transactions, in whole or in part, from the definition of the term "credit exposure" for purposes of this subsection, if the Board of Governors finds that the exemption is in the public interest and is consistent with the purpose of this subsection.

(7) TRANSITION PERIOD. —

(A) IN GENERAL. — This subsection and any regulations and orders of the Board of Governors under this subsection shall not be effective until 3 years after the date of

司对任何非关联企业的信用风险敞口不得超过该公司股本和资本公积金的25%(联邦储备委员会亦可以发布规章确定对缓释美国金融稳定风险确属必要的其他较低比例)。

(3)**信用风险敞口**。——在第(2)款中,一家公司的“信用风险敞口”系指——

(A)该公司获授的所有信贷,包括贷款、存款和信用额度;

(B)与该公司订立的所有回购协议和逆回购协议、与该公司达成的所有融券交易(以该等交易对受联邦储备委员会监管的非银行金融公司或第(a)子条所述的银行控股公司造成信用风险敞口的为限);

(C)以该公司名义出具的所有担保、承兑汇票或信用证(包括背书或备用信用证);

(D)对该公司发行证券的所有购买或投资;

(E)该公司所面临的,与受联邦储备委员会监管的非银行金融公司或者第(a)子条所述的银行控股公司作为一方、该公司作为另一方达成的衍生品交易相关的对手方信用风险敞口;及

(F)联邦储备委员会发布规章判定的确属本条意义上的信用风险敞口的任何其他类似交易。

(4)**归属规则**。——就本子条而言,受联邦储备委员会监管的非银行金融公司或第(a)子条所述的银行控股公司与任何主体之间的交易,只要交易所获资金为某一公司之利益而使用或被转移给该公司,即应被视为与该公司之间开展的交易。

(5)**规则制定**。——联邦储备委员会可以为执行和实施本子条的规定发布必要的规章和命令,包括作出符合本条规定的定义。

(6)**豁免**。——本子条的规定不适用于任何联邦住房贷款银行。如果联邦储备委员会认定豁免符合公共利益且符合本子条的目的,则联邦储备委员会可以发布规章或命令,将交易全部或部分豁免于本子条“信用风险敞口”定义的适用。

(7)**过渡期**。——

(A)**一般规定**。——本子条的规定以及联邦储备委员会根据本子条发布的任何规章和命令在本法颁布之日起届满3年之后方可生效。

enactment of this Act.

(B) EXTENSION AUTHORIZED. — The Board of Governors may extend the period specified in subparagraph (A) for not longer than an additional 2 years.

(f) ENHANCED PUBLIC DISCLOSURES. — The Board of Governors may prescribe, by regulation, periodic public disclosures by nonbank financial companies supervised by the Board of Governors and bank holding companies described in subsection (a) in order to support market evaluation of the risk profile, capital adequacy, and risk management capabilities thereof.

(g) SHORT-TERM DEBT LIMITS. —

(1) IN GENERAL. — In order to mitigate the risks that an over-accumulation of short-term debt could pose to financial companies and to the stability of the United States financial system, the Board of Governors may, by regulation, prescribe a limit on the amount of short-term debt, including off-balance sheet exposures, that may be accumulated by any bank holding company described in subsection (a) and any nonbank financial company supervised by the Board of Governors.

(2) BASIS OF LIMIT. — Any limit prescribed under paragraph (1) shall be based on the short-term debt of the company described in paragraph (1) as a percentage of capital stock and surplus of the company or on such other measure as the Board of Governors considers appropriate.

(3) SHORT-TERM DEBT DEFINED. — For purposes of this subsection, the term "short-term debt" means such liabilities with short-dated maturity that the Board of Governors identifies, by regulation, except that such term does not include insured deposits.

(4) RULEMAKING AUTHORITY. — In addition to prescribing regulations under paragraphs (1) and (3), the Board of Governors may prescribe such regulations, including definitions consistent with this subsection, and issue such orders, as may be necessary to carry out this subsection.

(5) AUTHORITY TO ISSUE EXEMPTIONS AND ADJUSTMENTS. — Notwithstanding the Bank Holding Company Act of 1956 (12 U.S.C. 1841 et seq.), the Board of Governors may, if it determines such action is necessary to ensure appropriate heightened prudential supervision, with respect to a company described in paragraph (1) that does not control an insured depository institution, issue to such company an exemption from or adjustment to the limit prescribed under paragraph (1).

(h) RISK COMMITTEE. —

(1) NONBANK FINANCIAL COMPANIES SUPERVISED BY THE BOARD OF GOVERNORS. — The Board of Governors shall require each nonbank financial company supervised by the Board of Governors that is a publicly traded company to establish a risk

(B)**延期授权**。——联邦储备委员会可以延长第(A)子款规定的期限,但延长期不得超过2年。

(f)**加强公开披露**。——联邦储备委员会可以发布规章,要求受联邦储备委员会监管的非银行金融公司以及第(a)子条所述的银行控股公司定期作出公开披露,以有助于市场对公司的风险特征、资本充足性和风险管理能力的评估。

(g)**短期债务限制**。——

(1)**一般规定**。——为了缓释短期债务过度积累可能对金融公司和美国的金融体系稳定造成的风险,联邦储备委员会可以发布规章,对受联邦储备委员会监管的任何非银行金融公司以及第(a)子条所述任何银行控股公司所累积的短期债务金额(包括表外风险敞口)作出限制性规定。

(2)**限制依据**。——根据第(1)款作出的限制性规定应以该款所述公司短期债务在该公司股本和资本公积金中的占比或联邦储备委员会认为适当的其他指标作为依据。

(3)**短期债务的定义**。——在本子条中,"短期债务"一词系指联邦储备委员会发布规章确定的在短期内到期的负债,但不包括参保存款。

(4)**规则制定权**。——除第(1)款和第(3)款所述规章外,联邦储备委员会还可以为实施本子条的规定制定必要的规章(包括作出符合本条规定的定义)和发布必要的命令。

(5)**豁免和调整权**。——无论《1956年银行控股公司法》(《美国法典》第十二编第1841节及其后条文)如何规定,只要联邦储备委员会判定,为了确保适当、严格的审慎性监管,有必要将第(1)款所述且未持有任何参保存款机构控制权的某一公司豁免于第(1)款的限制性规定,或对该等限制性规定作出调整,则联邦储备委员会可以对该公司采取上述必要的豁免或调整行动。

(h)**风险委员会**。——

(1)**受联邦储备委员会监管的非银行金融公司**。——联邦储备委员会应要求受其监管的身为公开交易公司的每一均非银行金融公司按照第(3)款的规定设立一个风险委员会,设立时间不得迟于该等非银行金融公司收到联邦储备委员会依照第113

committee, as set forth in paragraph (3), not later than 1 year after the date of receipt of a notice of final determination under section 113(e)(3) with respect to such nonbank financial company supervised by the Board of Governors.

(2) CERTAIN BANK HOLDING COMPANIES. —

(A) MANDATORY REGULATIONS. — The Board of Governors shall issue regulations requiring each bank holding company that is a publicly traded company and that has total consolidated assets of not less than $10, 000, 000, 000 to establish a risk committee, as set forth in paragraph (3).

(B) PERMISSIVE REGULATIONS. — The Board of Governors may require each bank holding company that is a publicly traded company and that has total consolidated assets of less than $10, 000, 000, 000 to establish a risk committee, as set forth in paragraph (3), as determined necessary or appropriate by the Board of Governors to promote sound risk management practices.

(3) RISK COMMITTEE. — A risk committee required by this subsection shall —

(A) be responsible for the oversight of the enterprise -wide risk management practices of the nonbank financial company supervised by the Board of Governors or bank holding company described in subsection (a), as applicable;

(B) include such number of independent directors as the Board of Governors may determine appropriate, based on the nature of operations, size of assets, and other appropriate criteria related to the nonbank financial company supervised by the Board of Governors or a bank holding company described in subsection (a), as applicable; and

(C) include at least 1 risk management expert having experience in identifying, assessing, and managing risk exposures of large, complex firms.

(4) RULEMAKING. — The Board of Governors shall issue final rules to carry out this subsection, not later than 1 year after the transfer date, to take effect not later than 15 months after the transfer date.

(i) STRESS TESTS. —

(1) BY THE BOARD OF GOVERNORS. —

(A) ANNUAL TESTS REQUIRED. — The Board of Governors, in coordination with the appropriate primary financial regulatory agencies and the Federal Insurance Office, shall conduct annual analyses in which nonbank financial companies supervised by the Board of Governors and bank holding companies described in subsection (a) are subject to evaluation of whether such companies have the capital, on a total consolidated basis, necessary to absorb losses as a result of adverse economic conditions.

(B) TEST PARAMETERS AND CONSEQUENCES. — The Board of Governors —

(i) shall provide for at least 3 different sets of conditions under which the evaluation required by this subsection shall be conducted, including baseline, adverse, and severely

(e)(3)条针对其作出的最终判定通知后1年。

(2)**特定银行控股公司**。——

(A)**强制性规章**。——对于并表资产总额不低于100亿美元且身为公开交易公司的任何银行控股公司,联邦储备委员会应发布规章要求其按照第(3)款的规定设立风险委员会。

(B)**选择性规章**——对于并表资产总额低于100亿美元且身为公开交易公司的任何银行控股公司,在联邦储备委员会为促进健全的风险管理实践而判定确属必要或适当的情况下,联邦储备委员会可要求其按照第(3)款的规定设立风险委员会。

(3)**风险委员会**。——本子条规定的风险委员会应——

(A)负责对受联邦储备委员会监管的非银行金融公司或第(a)子条所述的银行控股公司(视具体情况而定)的企业风险管理实践进行监督;

(B)包含适当人数的独立董事,独立董事的人数应由联邦储备委员会基于受联邦储备委员会监管的非银行金融公司或第(a)子条所述的银行控股公司(视具体情况而定)的运营性质、资产规模和其他适当的相关标准确定;且

(C)至少包含1名风险管理专家,且该专家应拥有识别、评估和管理大型综合企业风险敞口的经验。

(4)**规则制定**。——联邦储备委员会应在转移日后1年内颁布本子条的最终实施规则,该规则应在转移日后15个月之内生效。

(i)**压力测试**。——

(1)**联邦储备委员会组织开展的测试**。——

(A)**年度测试要求**。——联邦储备委员会应在与相应的优先金融监管机关和联邦保险办公室协调后,开展对受联邦储备委员会监管的非银行金融公司和第(a)子条所述的银行控股公司的年度分析,评估该公司是否拥有必要的并表资本总额,使其足以吸收不利经济状况所致损失。

(B)**测试参数和结果**。——联邦储备委员会——

(i)至少应提供三种不同情景(包括基本情形、不利情形和严重不利情形),并在该等情景下开展本子条规定的评估;

adverse;

(ii) may require the tests described in subparagraph (A) at bank holding companies and nonbank financial companies, in addition to those for which annual tests are required under subparagraph (A);

(iii) may develop and apply such other analytic techniques as are necessary to identify, measure, and monitor risks to the financial stability of the United States;

(iv) shall require the companies described in subparagraph (A) to update their resolution plans required under subsection (d)(1), as the Board of Governors determines appropriate, based on the results of the analyses; and

(v) shall publish a summary of the results of the tests required under subparagraph (A) or clause (ii) of this subparagraph.

(2) BY THE COMPANY. —

(A) REQUIREMENT. — A nonbank financial company supervised by the Board of Governors and a bank holding company described in subsection (a) shall conduct semiannual stress tests. All other financial companies that have total consolidated assets of more than $10, 000, 000, 000 and are regulated by a primary Federal financial regulatory agency shall conduct annual stress tests. The tests required under this subparagraph shall be conducted in accordance with the regulations prescribed under subparagraph (C).

(B) REPORT. — A company required to conduct stress tests under subparagraph (A) shall submit a report to the Board of Governors and to its primary financial regulatory agency at such time, in such form, and containing such information as the primary financial regulatory agency shall require.

(C) REGULATIONS. — Each Federal primary financial regulatory agency, in coordination with the Board of Governors and the Federal Insurance Office, shall issue consistent and comparable regulations to implement this paragraph that shall —

(i) define the term "stress test" for purposes of this paragraph;

(ii) establish methodologies for the conduct of stress tests required by this paragraph that shall provide for at least 3 different sets of conditions, including baseline, adverse, and severely adverse;

(iii) establish the form and content of the report required by subparagraph (B); and

(iv) require companies subject to this paragraph to publish a summary of the results of the required stress tests.

(j) LEVERAGE LIMITATION. —

(1) REQUIREMENT. — The Board of Governors shall require a bank holding company with total consolidated assets equal to or greater than $50, 000, 000, 000 or a nonbank financial company supervised by the Board of Governors to maintain a debt to equity ratio of no more than 15 to 1, upon a determination by the Council that such

(ii)除第(A)子款规定的应接受年度测试的公司外,还可以要求对其他银行控股公司和非银行金融公司进行第(A)子款规定的测试;

(iii)可以为识别、计量和监控美国的金融稳定风险,开发和使用其他必要的分析技术;

(iv)基于分析结果,若联邦储备委员会判定确属适当,应要求第(A)子款所述公司对第(d)(1)子条规定的清盘计划作出更新;及

(v)应发布根据第(A)子款或本子款第(ii)项开展的测试结果之摘要。

(2)**公司组织开展的测试**。——

(A)**要求**。——受联邦储备委员会监管的非银行金融公司和第(a)子条所述的银行控股公司须每半年进行一次压力测试。并表资产总额超过100亿美元且受优先联邦金融监管机关监管的所有其他金融公司须每年进行一次压力测试。实施本子款规定的测试时应遵循按照第(C)子款制定的规章。

(B)**报告**。——根据第(A)子款规定须进行压力测试的公司,应按照优先金融监管机关规定的时间、格式和信息要求向联邦储备委员会和其优先金融监管机关提交报告。

(C)**规章**。——各联邦优先金融监管机关均应在与联邦储备委员会和联邦保险办公室协调后,针对本款规定颁布具有一致性和可比性的实施规章,其中应——

(i)界定"压力测试"一词在本款中的含义;

(ii)确定实施本款所述压力测试的方法,该方法至少应规定三种不同情景(包括基本情形、不利情形和严重不利情形);

(iii)规定第(B)子款所述报告的格式和内容;及

(iv)要求须按照本款进行压力测试的公司发布测试结果摘要。

(j)**杠杆率限制**。——

(1)**要求**。——对于并表资产总额达500亿美元(含)以上的银行控股公司或受联邦储备委员会监管的非银行金融公司,如果金融稳定监督委员会判定该公司对美国金融稳定构成严重威胁,且为了缓释该等风险有必要要求该公司维持不高于15:1的债务股本比,则联邦储备委员会应要求该等公司遵守该比率。本款规定不适用于联邦

company poses a grave threat to the financial stability of the United States and that the imposition of such requirement is necessary to mitigate the risk that such company poses to the financial stability of the United States. Nothing in this paragraph shall apply to a Federal home loan bank.

(2) CONSIDERATIONS. — In making a determination under this subsection, the Council shall consider the factors described in subsections (a) and (b) of section 113 and any other risk-related factors that the Council deems appropriate.

(3) REGULATIONS. — The Board of Governors shall promulgate regulations to establish procedures and timelines for complying with the requirements of this subsection.

(k) INCLUSION OF OFF-BALANCE-SHEET ACTIVITIES IN COMPUTING CAPITAL REQUIREMENTS. —

(1) IN GENERAL. — In the case of any bank holding company described in subsection (a) or nonbank financial company supervised by the Board of Governors, the computation of capital for purposes of meeting capital requirements shall take into account any off-balance-sheet activities of the company.

(2) EXEMPTIONS. — If the Board of Governors determines that an exemption from the requirement under paragraph (1) is appropriate, the Board of Governors may exempt a company, or any transaction or transactions engaged in by such company, from the requirements of paragraph (1).

(3) OFF-BALANCE-SHEET ACTIVITIES DEFINED. — For purposes of this subsection, the term "off-balance-sheet activities" means an existing liability of a company that is not currently a balance sheet liability, but may become one upon the happening of some future event, including the following transactions, to the extent that they may create a liability:

(A) Direct credit substitutes in which a bank substitutes its own credit for a third party, including standby letters of credit.

(B) Irrevocable letters of credit that guarantee repayment of commercial paper or tax-exempt securities.

(C) Risk participations in bankers' acceptances.

(D) Sale and repurchase agreements.

(E) Asset sales with recourse against the seller.

(F) Interest rate swaps.

(G) Credit swaps.

(H) Commodities contracts.

(I) Forward contracts.

(J) Securities contracts.

(K) Such other activities or transactions as the Board of Governors may, by rule, define.

住房贷款银行。

(2)**考虑因素**。——金融稳定监督委员会根据本子条规定作出判定时,应考虑第113条第(a)子条和第(b)子条所述因素以及金融稳定监督委员会判定确属适当的任何其他风险因素。

(3)**规章**。——联邦储备委员会应颁发相关规章,确定本子条规定的履行程序和时间期限。

(k)**在计算资本要求时应涵括表外活动**。——

(1)**一般规定**。——在对第(a)子条所述任何银行控股公司或受联邦储备委员会监管的非银行金融公司进行资本计算,以确定其是否符合资本要求时,应当考虑公司的任何表外活动。

(2)**豁免**。——在联邦储备委员会判定确属适当的情况下,其可以向某一公司或该公司开展的任何一项或数项交易授予豁免,获得豁免的公司或交易不必遵守第(1)款的要求。

(3)**表外活动的定义**。——就本子条而言,“表外活动”一词系指某一公司当前未列入资产负债表,但在发生某未来事件的情况下可以转化为表内负债的现有负债,包括以下交易(以可能创设负债者为限):

(A)某一银行以其自身信用替代某一第三方信用的直接信用替代,包括备用信用证;

(B)为商业票据或免税证券的偿付提供有担保且不可撤销的信用证;

(C)银行承兑汇票的风险参与;

(D)出售和回购协议;

(E)附带对卖方的追索权的资产出售;

(F)利率互换;

(G)信贷互换;

(H)商品合约;

(I)远期合约;

(J)证券合约;

(K)联邦储备委员会发布规则确定的任何其他活动或交易。

SEC. 166. EARLY REMEDIATION REQUIREMENTS.

(a) IN GENERAL. — The Board of Governors, in consultation with the Council and the Corporation, shall prescribe regulations establishing requirements to provide for the early remediation of financial distress of a nonbank financial company supervised by the Board of Governors or a bank holding company described in section 165(a), except that nothing in this subsection authorizes the provision of financial assistance from the Federal Government.

(b) PURPOSE OF THE EARLY REMEDIATION REQUIREMENTS. — The purpose of the early remediation requirements under subsection (a) shall be to establish a series of specific remedial actions to be taken by a nonbank financial company supervised by the Board of Governors or a bank holding company described in section 165(a) that is experiencing increasing financial distress, in order to minimize the probability that the company will become insolvent and the potential harm of such insolvency to the financial stability of the United States.

(c) REMEDIATION REQUIREMENTS. — The regulations prescribed by the Board of Governors under subsection (a) shall —

(1) define measures of the financial condition of the company, including regulatory capital, liquidity measures, and other forward–looking indicators; and

(2) establish requirements that increase in stringency as the financial condition of the company declines, including —

(A) requirements in the initial stages of financial decline, including limits on capital distributions, acquisitions, and asset growth; and

(B) requirements at later stages of financial decline, including a capital restoration plan and capital–raising requirements, limits on transactions with affiliates, management changes, and asset sales.

SEC. 167. AFFILIATIONS.

(a) AFFILIATIONS. — Nothing in this subtitle shall be construed to require a nonbank financial company supervised by the Board of Governors, or a company that controls a nonbank financial company supervised by the Board of Governors, to conform the activities thereof to the requirements of section 4 of the Bank Holding Company Act of 1956 (12 U.S.C. 1843).

(b) REQUIREMENT. —

(1) IN GENERAL. —

(A) BOARD AUTHORITY. — If a nonbank financial company supervised by the Board of Governors conducts activities other than those that are determined to be financial in nature or incidental thereto under section 4(k) of the Bank Holding Company Act of 1956, the Board of Governors may require such company to establish and conduct all or a

第166条 及早补救要求

(a)**一般规定**。——联邦储备委员会应在与金融稳定监督委员会和联邦存款保险公司磋商后制定规章,确立对受联邦储备委员会监管的非银行金融公司或第165(a)条所述的银行控股公司的财务困境及早作出补救的要求,但本子条任何内容均不授权联邦政府提供任何财务援助。

(b)**及早补救要求的目的**。——第(a)子条所述及早补救要求旨在针对面临日益加剧的重大财务困境的受联邦储备委员会监管的非银行金融公司或第165(a)条所述的银行控股公司,确定其应采取的系列具体补救行动,以便将该等公司发生资不抵债的可能性以及该等资不抵债可能对美国金融稳定造成的损害减到最低限度。

(c)**补救要求**。——联邦储备委员会应在按照第(a)子条制定的规章中——

(1)确定公司的财务状况计量指标,包括监管资本、流动性指标和其他前瞻性指标;及

(2)设立严格程度随公司财务状况的恶化而提高的要求,包括:

(A)财务困境初期阶段的要求,包括资本分配、收购和资产增长方面的限制;及

(B)财务困境后期阶段的要求,包括资本恢复计划和资本筹措要求以及关联交易、管理层变更和资产出售方面的限制。

第167条 关联关系

(a)**关联关系**。——本子编中的任何规定均不得被解释为要求受联邦储备委员会监管的非银行金融公司或拥有该等非银行金融公司控制权的公司从事的活动必须符合《1956年银行控股公司法》第4条(《美国法典》第十二编第1843节)的规定。

(b)**要求**。——

(1)**一般规定**。——

(A)**联邦储备委员会的权力**。——如果除根据《1956年银行控股公司法》第4(k)条判定的金融性质活动或附属金融活动之外,受联邦储备委员会监管的非银行金融公司还从事其他业务活动,那么,联邦储备委员会可以要求该等非银行金融公司在收到联邦储备委员会根据本条作出的判定之日后90天内(或联邦储备委员会认为适当

portion of such activities that are determined to be financial in nature or incidental thereto in or through an intermediate holding company established pursuant to regulation of the Board of Governors, not later than 90 days (or such longer period as the Board of Governors may deem appropriate) after the date on which the nonbank financial company supervised by the Board of Governors is notified of the determination of the Board of Governors under this section.

(B) NECESSARY ACTIONS. — Notwithstanding subparagraph (A), the Board of Governors shall require a nonbank financial company supervised by the Board of Governors to establish an intermediate holding company if the Board of Governors makes a determination that the establishment of such intermediate holding company is necessary to —

(i) appropriately supervise activities that are determined to be financial in nature or incidental thereto; or

(ii) to ensure that supervision by the Board of Governors does not extend to the commercial activities of such nonbank financial company.

(2) INTERNAL FINANCIAL ACTIVITIES. — For purposes of this subsection, activities that are determined to be financial in nature or incidental thereto under section 4(k) of the Bank Holding Company Act of 1956, as described in paragraph (1), shall not include internal financial activities, including internal treasury, investment, and employee benefit functions. With respect to any internal financial activity engaged in for the company or an affiliate and a non–affiliate of such company during the year prior to the date of enactment of this Act, such company (or an affiliate that is not an intermediate holding company or subsidiary of an intermediate holding company) may continue to engage in such activity, as long as not less than 2/3 of the assets or 2/3 of the revenues generated from the activity are from or attributable to such company or an affiliate, subject to review by the Board of Governors, to determine whether engaging in such activity presents undue risk to such company or to the financial stability of the United States.

(3) SOURCE OF STRENGTH. — A company that directly or indirectly controls an intermediate holding company established under this section shall serve as a source of strength to its subsidiary intermediate holding company.

(4) PARENT COMPANY REPORTS. — The Board of Governors may, from time to time, require reports under oath from a company that controls an intermediate holding company, and from the appropriate officers or directors of such company, solely for purposes of ensuring compliance with the provisions of this section, including assessing the ability of the company to serve as a source of strength to its subsidiary intermediate holding company pursuant to paragraph (3) and enforcing such compliance.

的其他更长的期间内),在根据联邦储备委员会规章组建的中间控股公司内部,或者通过该等中间控股公司设立并开展所有或部分前述金融性质活动或附属金融活动。

(B)**必要行动**。——无论第(A)子款如何规定,如果联邦储备委员会出于以下因素判定有必要组建中间控股公司,则联邦储备委员会应要求受其监管的非银行金融公司组建中间控股公司——

(i)任何活动被判定为金融性质活动或附属金融活动的,应对其进行适当监管;或

(ii)确保联邦储备委员会的监管工作不扩展至该等非银行金融公司从事的商业活动。

(2)**内部金融活动**。——就本子条而言,第(1)款所述根据《1956年银行控股公司法》第4(k)条被判定的金融性质活动或附属金融活动不包括内部金融活动(该等内部金融活动包括内部财务、投资及雇员福利职能活动)。对于在本法颁布之日以前1年内为该等公司或其关联方或非关联方从事的任何内部金融活动,在至少2/3的资产或2/3的活动收入来自或可归属于该公司或其关联方的情况下,该公司(或并非一家中间控股公司的关联方或并非一家中间控股公司子公司的关联方)可以继续从事前述内部金融活动,但是联邦储备委员会须审查并判定从事该等活动是否会对该公司或对美国的金融稳定构成不当风险。

(3)**财务后盾**。——对于根据本条规定设立的中间控股公司而言,直接或间接持有其控制权的公司应起到该中间控股子公司的财务后盾的作用。

(4)**母公司报告**。——联邦储备委员会可以不时要求对中间控股公司持有控制权的公司以及该等公司的相应管理人员或董事提交一份经宣誓程序保证所述内容真实无误的报告,但其目的应以确保对本条规定的合规为限,包括根据第(3)款评估该等公司作为财务后盾为其中间控股子公司提供支持的能力以及强制执行本条规定。

(5) LIMITED PARENT COMPANY ENFORCEMENT. —

(A) IN GENERAL. — In addition to any other authority of the Board of Governors, the Board of Governors may enforce compliance with the provisions of this subsection that are applicable to any company described in paragraph (1) that controls an intermediate holding company under section 8 of the Federal Deposit Insurance Act, and such company shall be subject to such section (solely for such purposes) in the same manner and to the same extent as if such company were a bank holding company.

(B) APPLICATION OF OTHER ACT. — Any violation of this subsection by any company that controls an intermediate holding company may also be treated as a violation of the Federal Deposit Insurance Act for purposes of subparagraph (A).

(C) NO EFFECT ON OTHER AUTHORITY. — No provision of this paragraph shall be construed as limiting any authority of the Board of Governors or any other Federal agency under any other provision of law.

(c) REGULATIONS. — The Board of Governors —

(1) shall promulgate regulations to establish the criteria for determining whether to require a nonbank financial company supervised by the Board of Governors to establish an intermediate holding company under subsection (b); and

(2) may promulgate regulations to establish any restrictions or limitations on transactions between an intermediate holding company or a nonbank financial company supervised by the Board of Governors and its affiliates, as necessary to prevent unsafe and unsound practices in connection with transactions between such company, or any subsidiary thereof, and its parent company or affiliates that are not subsidiaries of such company, except that such regulations shall not restrict or limit any transaction in connection with the bona fide acquisition or lease by an unaffiliated person of assets, goods, or services.

SEC. 168. REGULATIONS.

The Board of Governors shall have authority to issue regulations to implement subtitles A and C and the amendments made thereunder. Except as otherwise specified in subtitle A or C, not later than 18 months after the effective date of this Act, the Board of Governors shall issue final regulations to implement subtitles A and C, and the amendments made thereunder.

SEC. 169. AVOIDING DUPLICATION.

The Board of Governors shall take any action that the Board of Governors deems appropriate to avoid imposing requirements under this subtitle that are duplicative of requirements applicable to bank holding companies and nonbank financial companies under other provisions of law.

(5)**对母公司强制执行的限制规定**。——

(A)**一般规定**。——除任何其他权力外,联邦储备委员会也可以针对第(1)款所述对《联邦存款保险法》第8条规定的中间控股公司持有控制权的任何公司,强制执行本子条的适用规定。在且仅在上述情形下,该等公司有义务遵守本子条的规定,其方式及范围均与银行控股公司完全一致。

(B)**其他法律的适用**。——就第(A)子款而言,对中间控股公司持有控制权的任何公司违反本子条规定的任何行为,均可作为违反《联邦存款保险法》的行为处理。

(C)**不影响其他权力**。——本款中的任何规定均不得被解释为构成对联邦储备委员会或任何其他联邦机关根据任何其他法律规定享有的任何权力之限制。

(c)**规章**。——联邦储备委员会——

(1)应颁发规章,设定相关标准,用于判定是否应要求受联邦储备委员会监管的某一非银行金融公司根据第(b)子条设立中间控股公司;且

(2)可以颁发规章,对中间控股公司或受联邦储备委员会监管的非银行金融公司与其关联方之间的交易设定任何必要的约束或限制条件,以便对在该等公司或其任何子公司作为一方与其母公司或其子公司之外的关联方作为另一方开展任何交易的过程中,防范欠安全和欠稳健的做法,但该等规章不得对非关联主体善意收购或租赁资产、货物或服务的交易施加约束或限制。

第168条　规章

联邦储备委员会有权为实施第A子编和第C子编的规定及其修正内容发布规章。除第A子编和第C子编另有规定的情形外,联邦储备委员会应在本法生效日后18个月内就第A子编和第C子编的规定及其修正内容发布最终实施规章。

第169条　避免重复规定

联邦储备委员会应采取其认为适当的任何行动,避免在其他法律规定已对银行控股公司和非金融公司作出适用要求的情况下,再根据本子编作出重复性规定。

SEC. 170. SAFE HARBOR.

(a) REGULATIONS. — The Board of Governors shall promulgate regulations on behalf of, and in consultation with, the Council setting forth the criteria for exempting certain types or classes of U.S. nonbank financial companies or foreign nonbank financial companies from supervision by the Board of Governors.

(b) CONSIDERATIONS. — In developing the criteria under subsection (a), the Board of Governors shall take into account the factors for consideration described in subsections (a) and (b) of section 113 in determining whether a U.S. nonbank financial company or foreign nonbank financial company shall be supervised by the Board of Governors.

(c) RULE OF CONSTRUCTION. — Nothing in this section shall be construed to require supervision by the Board of Governors of a U.S. nonbank financial company or foreign nonbank financial company, if such company does not meet the criteria for exemption established under subsection (a).

(d) REVISIONS. —

(1) IN GENERAL. — The Board of Governors shall, in consultation with the Council, review the regulations promulgated under subsection (a), not less frequently than every 5 years, and based upon the review, the Board of Governors may revise such regulations on behalf of, and in consultation with, the Council to update as necessary the criteria set forth in such regulations.

(2) TRANSITION PERIOD. — No revisions under paragraph (1) shall take effect before the end of the 2-year period after the date of publication of such revisions in final form.

(e) REPORT. — The Chairman of the Board of Governors and the Chairperson of the Council shall submit a joint report to the Committee on Banking, Housing, and Urban Affairs of the Senate and the Committee on Financial Services of the House of Representatives not later than 30 days after the date of the issuance in final form of regulations under subsection (a), or any subsequent revision to such regulations under subsection (d), as applicable. Such report shall include, at a minimum, the rationale for exemption and empirical evidence to support the criteria for exemption.

SEC. 171. LEVERAGE AND RISK-BASED CAPITAL REQUIREMENTS.

(a) DEFINITIONS. — For purposes of this section, the following definitions shall apply:

(1) GENERALLY APPLICABLE LEVERAGE CAPITAL REQUIREMENTS. — The term "generally applicable leverage capital requirements" means —

(A) the minimum ratios of tier 1 capital to average total assets, as established by the appropriate Federal banking agencies to apply to insured depository institutions under the

第170条　安全港

(a)**规章**。——联邦储备委员会应在与金融稳定监督委员会磋商后代表金融稳定监督委员会颁发规章,制定相关标准,用以判断是否应将特定类型或类别的美国非银行金融公司或外国非银行金融公司豁免于联邦储备委员会的监管。

(b)**考虑因素**。——在按照第(a)子条制定标准时,联邦储备委员会应考虑第113条第(a)子条和第(b)子条规定的因素以判定某一美国非银行金融公司或外国非银行金融公司是否应受联邦储备委员会监管。

(c)**解释规则**。——本条中的任何规定均不得被解释为要求联邦储备委员会在某一美国非银行金融公司或外国非银行金融公司不符合根据第(a)子条制定的豁免标准的情况下对该非银行金融公司实施监管。

(d)**修订**。——

(1)**一般规定**。——联邦储备委员会应在与金融稳定监督委员会磋商后,对按照第(a)子条颁发的规章进行审查(审查频率不得低于5年一次),并在审查结果的基础上,与金融稳定监督委员会磋商后代表金融稳定监督委员会对该等规章作出修订,以便对其中规定的标准作出必要的更新。

(2)**过渡期**。——根据第(1)款作出的修订生效日不得早于最终修订文本公布后届满2周年之日。

(e)**报告**。——按照第(a)子条规定发布最终规章文本或按照第(d)子条规定发布该等规章的任何后续修订的(视具体情况而定),联邦储备委员会主席和金融稳定监督委员会主席应在上述发布日后30天内向参议院银行、住房与城市事务委员会和众议院金融服务委员会提交一份联合报告,其中至少应说明豁免的理论依据和支持豁免标准的实证证据。

第171条　杠杆率和风险基础资本要求

(a)**定义**。——就本条而言,应适用如下定义:

(1)**普遍适用的杠杆资本要求**。——“普遍适用的杠杆资本要求”一词——

(A)系指相应的联邦银行业监管机关根据及时纠正措施规章(指《联邦存款保险法》第38条的实施规章)所设定的,对参保存款机构适用的一级资本与平均资产总额

prompt corrective action regulations implementing section 38 of the Federal Deposit Insurance Act, regardless of total consolidated asset size or foreign financial exposure; and

(B) includes the regulatory capital components in the numerator of that capital requirement, average total assets in the denominator of that capital requirement, and the required ratio of the numerator to the denominator.

(2) GENERALLY APPLICABLE RISK-BASED CAPITAL REQUIREMENTS. — The term "generally applicable risk-based capital requirements" means —

(A) the risk-based capital requirements, as established by the appropriate Federal banking agencies to apply to insured depository institutions under the prompt corrective action regulations implementing section 38 of the Federal Deposit Insurance Act, regardless of total consolidated asset size or foreign financial exposure; and

(B) includes the regulatory capital components in the numerator of those capital requirements, the risk-weighted assets in the denominator of those capital requirements, and the required ratio of the numerator to the denominator.

(3) DEFINITION OF DEPOSITORY INSTITUTION HOLDING COMPANY. — The term "depository institution holding company" means a bank holding company or a savings and loan holding company (as those terms are defined in section 3 of the Federal Deposit Insurance Act) that is organized in the United States, including any bank or savings and loan holding company that is owned or controlled by a foreign organization, but does not include the foreign organization.

(b) MINIMUM CAPITAL REQUIREMENTS. —

(1) MINIMUM LEVERAGE CAPITAL REQUIREMENTS. — The appropriate Federal banking agencies shall establish minimum leverage capital requirements on a consolidated basis for insured depository institutions, depository institution holding companies, and nonbank financial companies supervised by the Board of Governors. The minimum leverage capital requirements established under this paragraph shall not be less than the generally applicable leverage capital requirements, which shall serve as a floor for any capital requirements that the agency may require, nor quantitatively lower than the generally applicable leverage capital requirements that were in effect for insured depository institutions as of the date of enactment of this Act.

(2) MINIMUM RISK-BASED CAPITAL REQUIREMENTS. — The appropriate Federal banking agencies shall establish minimum risk-based capital requirements on a consolidated basis for insured depository institutions, depository institution holding companies, and nonbank financial companies supervised by the Board of Governors. The minimum risk-based capital requirements established under this paragraph shall not be less than the generally applicable risk-based capital requirements, which shall serve as a floor for any capital requirements that the agency may require, nor quantitatively lower

的最低比率,而不必考虑参保存款机构的并表资产总额或外国金融风险敞口;且

(B)在该资本要求计算公式中,应以监管资本为分子,以平均总资产为分母,分子和分母之间应符合规定比率。

(2)**普遍适用的风险基础资本要求**。——“普遍适用的风险基础资本要求”一词——

(A)系指相应的联邦银行业监管机关根据及时纠正措施规章(指《联邦存款保险法》第38条的实施规章)所设定的,对参保存款机构适用的风险基础资本要求,而不考虑参保存款机构的并表资产总额或外国金融风险敞口;且

(B)在该资本要求计算公式中,应以监管资本为分子,以风险加权资产为分母,分子和分母之间应符合规定比率。

(3)**存款机构控股公司的定义**。——“存款机构控股公司”一词系指在美国组建的银行控股公司或储贷控股公司(该等术语之定义见《联邦存款保险法》第3条),包括外国组织拥有或控制的任何银行或储贷控股公司,但不包括外国组织本身。

(b)**最低资本要求**。——

(1)**最低杠杆资本要求**。——相应的联邦银行业监管机关应就参保存款机构、存款机构控股公司和受联邦储备委员会监管的非银行金融公司设定最低并表杠杆资本要求。根据本款设定的最低杠杆资本要求不得低于普遍适用的杠杆资本要求,该等适用的杠杆资本要求应作为联邦银行业监管机关规定的任何资本要求下限;数量上亦不得低于本法颁布之日有效适用的对参保存款机构普遍适用的杠杆资本要求。

(2)**最低风险基础资本要求**。——相应的联邦银行业监管机关应为参保存款机构、存款机构控股公司和受联邦储备委员会监管的非银行金融公司设定最低并表风险基础资本要求。根据本款设定的最低风险基础资本要求不得低于普遍适用的风险基础资本要求,该等适用的杠杆资本要求应作为联邦银行业监管机关规定的任何资本要求下限;数量上亦不得低于本法颁布之日有效适用的对参保存款机构普遍适用的风险基础资本要求。

than the generally applicable risk–based capital requirements that were in effect for insured depository institutions as of the date of enactment of this Act.

(3) INVESTMENTS IN FINANCIAL SUBSIDIARIES. — For purposes of this section, investments in financial subsidiaries that insured depository institutions are required to deduct from regulatory capital under section 5136A of the Revised Statutes of the United States or section 46(a)(2) of the Federal Deposit Insurance Act need not be deducted from regulatory capital by depository institution holding companies or nonbank financial companies supervised by the Board of Governors, unless such capital deduction is required by the Board of Governors or the primary financial regulatory agency in the case of nonbank financial companies supervised by the Board of Governors.

(4) EFFECTIVE DATES AND PHASE–IN PERIODS. —

(A) DEBT OR EQUITY INSTRUMENTS ON OR AFTER MAY 19, 2010. — For debt or equity instruments issued on or after May 19, 2010, by depository institution holding companies or by nonbank financial companies supervised by the Board of Governors, this section shall be deemed to have become effective as of May 19, 2010.

(B) DEBT OR EQUITY INSTRUMENTS ISSUED BEFORE MAY 19, 2010. — For debt or equity instruments issued before May 19, 2010, by depository institution holding companies or by nonbank financial companies supervised by the Board of Governors, any regulatory capital deductions required under this section shall be phased in incrementally over a period of 3 years, with the phase–in period to begin on January 1, 2013, except as set forth in subparagraph (C).

(C) DEBT OR EQUITY INSTRUMENTS OF SMALLER INSTITUTIONS. — For debt or equity instruments issued before May 19, 2010, by depository institution holding companies with total consolidated assets of less than $15, 000, 000, 000 as of December 31, 2009, and by organizations that were mutual holding companies on May 19, 2010, the capital deductions that would be required for other institutions under this section are not required as a result of this section.

(D) DEPOSITORY INSTITUTION HOLDING COMPANIES NOT PREVIOUSLY SUPERVISED BY THE BOARD OF GOVERNORS. — For any depository institution holding company that was not supervised by the Board of Governors as of May 19, 2010, the requirements of this section, except as set forth in subparagraphs (A) and (B), shall be effective 5 years after the date of enactment of this Act.

(E) CERTAIN BANK HOLDING COMPANY SUBSIDIARIES OF FOREIGN BANKING ORGANIZATIONS. — For bank holding company subsidiaries of foreign banking organizations that have relied on Supervision and Regulation Letter SR–01–1 issued by the Board of Governors (as in effect on May 19, 2010), the requirements of this section, except as set forth in subparagraph (A), shall be effective 5 years after the date

(3)**对金融子公司的投资**。——根据《美国制定法汇编(修订版)》第5136A条或《联邦存款保险法》第46(a)(2)条的规定,参保存款机构应从监管资本中扣除对金融子公司的投资,但就本条而言,存款机构控股公司或受联邦储备委员会监管的非银行金融公司不必从监管资本中扣除对金融子公司的该等投资,除非联邦储备委员会或优先金融监管机关(对受联邦储备委员会监管的非银行金融公司而言)要求作出该等资本扣除。

(4)**生效日和逐步实施期间**。——

(A)**2010年5月19日及其后发行的债务或股权工具**。——对于存款机构控股公司或受联邦储备委员会监管的非银行金融公司在2010年5月19日或之后发行的债务或股权工具,本条的规定应视为于2010年5月19日生效。

(B)**2010年5月19日之前发行的债务或股权工具**。——对于存款机构控股公司或受联邦储备委员会监管的非银行金融公司在2010年5月19日之前发行的债务或股权工具,本条规定的任何监管资本扣除应从2013年1月1日开始在3年期间内逐步实施,但第(C)子款规定的情形除外。

(C)**规模较小的机构的债务或股权工具**。——对于截至2009年12月31日并表资产总额低于150亿美元的任何存款机构控股公司和截至2010年5月19日性质为互助控股公司的组织在2010年5月19日之前发行的债务或股权工具,不必作出本条中对其他机构规定的资本扣除。

(D)**之前不受联邦储备委员会监管的存款机构控股公司**。——对于截至2010年5月19日不受联邦储备委员会监管的任何存款机构控股公司,除第(A)子款和第(B)子款规定的情形外,本条的规定应于本法颁布之日起届满5年之后生效。

(E)**外国银行组织的某些银行控股公司子公司**。——对于援引联邦储备委员会发布的于2010年5月19日有效适用的《第SR—01—1号监管与规制函》的外国银行组织的银行控股公司子公司,本条的规定[但第(A)子款的规定除外]应在本法颁布之日届满5年之后生效。

of enactment of this Act.

(5) EXCEPTIONS. — This section shall not apply to —

(A) debt or equity instruments issued to the United States or any agency or instrumentality thereof pursuant to the Emergency Economic Stabilization Act of 2008, and prior to October 4, 2010;

(B) any Federal home loan bank; or

(C) any small bank holding company that is subject to the Small Bank Holding Company Policy Statement of the Board of Governors, as in effect on May 19, 2010.

(6) STUDY AND REPORT ON SMALL INSTITUTION ACCESS TO CAPITAL. —

(A) STUDY REQUIRED. — The Comptroller General of the United States, after consultation with the Federal banking agencies, shall conduct a study of access to capital by smaller insured depository institutions.

(B) SCOPE. — For purposes of this study required by subparagraph (A), the term "smaller insured depository institution" means an insured depository institution with total consolidated assets of $5, 000, 000, 000 or less.

(C) REPORT TO CONGRESS. — Not later than 18 months after the date of enactment of this Act, the Comptroller General of the United States shall submit to the Committee on Banking, Housing, and Urban Affairs of the Senate and the Committee on Financial Services of the House of Representatives a report summarizing the results of the study conducted under subparagraph (A), together with any recommendations for legislative or regulatory action that would enhance the access to capital of smaller insured depository institutions, in a manner that is consistent with safe and sound banking operations.

(7) CAPITAL REQUIREMENTS TO ADDRESS ACTIVITIES THAT POSE RISKS TO THE FINANCIAL SYSTEM. —

(A) IN GENERAL. — Subject to the recommendations of the Council, in accordance with section 120, the Federal banking agencies shall develop capital requirements applicable to insured depository institutions, depository institution holding companies, and nonbank financial companies supervised by the Board of Governors that address the risks that the activities of such institutions pose, not only to the institution engaging in the activity, but to other public and private stakeholders in the event of adverse performance, disruption, or failure of the institution or the activity.

(B) CONTENT. — Such rules shall address, at a minimum, the risks arising from —

(i) significant volumes of activity in derivatives, securitized products purchased and sold, financial guarantees purchased and sold, securities borrowing and lending, and repurchase agreements and reverse repurchase agreements;

(ii) concentrations in assets for which the values presented in financial reports are

(5)**例外规定**。——本条的规定不适用于——

(A)在2010年10月4日之前根据《2008年紧急经济稳定法》向美国或任何美国联邦机关或职能部门发行的债务或股权工具;

(B)任何联邦住房贷款银行;或

(C)受制于2010年5月19日有效适用的《联邦储备委员会关于小型银行控股公司的政策声明》的任何小型银行控股公司。

(6)**关于小型机构资本获取渠道的研究和报告**。——

(A)**研究要求**。——政府问责办公室主任应在与联邦银行业监管机关磋商后,对小型参保存款机构的资本获取渠道开展研究。

(B)**范围**。——就第(A)子款规定的研究而言,"小型参保存款机构"一词系指并表资产总额不高于50亿美元的参保存款机构。

(C)**向国会报告**。——政府问责办公室主任应在本法颁布之日后18个月内,向参议院银行、住房与城市事务委员会和众议院金融服务委员会提交一份报告,概要说明根据第(A)子款规定开展的研究之结果,并提出任何立法或监管行动建议,以通过符合安全稳健的银行运营方式增强小型参保存款机构获取资本的能力。

(7)**就对金融体系构成风险的活动设定的资本要求**。——

(A)**一般规定**。——联邦银行业监管机关应按照金融稳定监督委员会根据第120条提出的建议,制定适用于参保存款机构、存款机构控股公司和受联邦储备委员会监管的非银行金融公司的资本要求,以应对该等机构的活动导致的风险。此处的风险不仅包括对开展该等活动的机构造成的风险,也包括在该等机构或该等活动在绩效不良、遭受扰乱或经营失败的情况下给公共和私人利益相关者造成的风险。

(B)**内容**。——该等规则至少应对以下原因引起的风险作出规定——

(i)大规模的衍生品活动、证券化产品买卖、金融担保买卖、融券、回购协议和逆回购协议活动;

(ii)资产集中(此处的资产指财务报告列报的价值系基于模型,而非基于深层和

based on models rather than historical cost or prices deriving from deep and liquid 2–way markets; and

(iii) concentrations in market share for any activity that would substantially disrupt financial markets if the institution is forced to unexpectedly cease the activity.

SEC. 172. EXAMINATION AND ENFORCEMENT ACTIONS FOR INSURANCE AND ORDERLY LIQUIDATION PURPOSES.

(a) EXAMINATIONS FOR INSURANCE AND RESOLUTION PURPOSES. — Section 10(b)(3) of the Federal Deposit Insurance Act (12 U.S.C. 1820(b)(3)) is amended —

(1) by striking "In addition" and inserting the following: "(A) IN GENERAL. — In addition"; and

(2) by striking "whenever the board of directors determines" and all that follows through the period and inserting the following: "or nonbank financial company supervised by the Board of Governors or a bank holding company described in section 165(a) of the Financial Stability Act of 2010, whenever the Board of Directors determines that a special examination of any such depository institution is necessary to determine the condition of such depository institution for insurance purposes, or of such nonbank financial company supervised by the Board of Governors or bank holding company described in section 165 (a) of the Financial Stability Act of 2010, for the purpose of implementing its authority to provide for orderly liquidation of any such company under title II of that Act, provided that such authority may not be used with respect to any such company that is in a generally sound condition.

"(B) LIMITATION. — Before conducting a special examination of a nonbank financial company supervised by the Board of Governors or a bank holding company described in section 165(a) of the Financial Stability Act of 2010, the Corporation shall review any available and acceptable resolution plan that the company has submitted in accordance with section 165(d) of that Act, consistent with the nonbinding effect of such plan, and available reports of examination, and shall coordinate to the maximum extent practicable with the Board of Governors, in order to minimize duplicative or conflicting examinations.".

(b) ENFORCEMENT AUTHORITY. — Section 8 (t) of the Federal Deposit Insurance Act (12 U.S.C. 1818(t)) is amended —

(1) in paragraph (1), by inserting ", any depository institution holding company," before "or any institution–affiliated party";

(2) in paragraph (2) —

(A) by striking "or" at the end of subparagraph (B);

(B) at the end of subparagraph (C), by striking the period and inserting "or"; and

流动的双向市场所形成的历史成本或价格而确定的资产);及

(iii)符合以下情况的任何活动的市场份额集中度:上述机构被迫意外停止开展该等活动,将导致金融市场遭受严重扰乱。

第172条　为保险和有序清算之目的实施的检查和执法行动

(a)**为保险和清盘之目的实施的检查**。——《联邦存款保险法》第10(b)(3)条[《美国法典》第十二编第1820(b)(3)节]修正如下——

(1)删除“另外”,替以“(A)**一般规定**。——另外”;及

(2)删除“只要联邦储备委员会判定”直至句号之前的所有内容,替以“或受联邦储备委员会监管的非银行金融公司或《2010年金融稳定法》第165(a)条所述的银行控股公司,只要联邦储备委员会判定,出于保险的目的,为了判断该等存款机构现况、受联邦储备委员会监管的该等非银行金融公司或《2010年金融稳定法》第165(a)条所述该等银行控股公司的现况,而有必要对任何该等存款机构实施专项检查,以便联邦储备委员会根据本法第二编的规定行使指令任何该等公司进行有序清算的权力。但是,不得对整体状况良好的任何该等公司行使该等权力。”

“(B)**限制**。——在对受联邦储备委员会监管的非银行金融公司或《2010年金融稳定法》第165(a)条所述的银行控股公司实施专项检查之前,联邦存款保险公司应审查公司根据该法第165(d)条提交的任何可获取和可接受的清盘计划(审查时应考虑该等计划不具拘束力)和可获得的检查报告,同时应尽最大可能与联邦储备委员会进行协调,将重复的或相互冲突的检查减到最低限度。”

(b)**执法权**。——《联邦存款保险法》第8(t)条[《美国法典》第十二编第1818(t)节]修正如下——

(1)在第(1)款中,在“或任何机构关联方”前插入“,任何存款机构控股公司”;

(2)在第(2)款中——

(A)删除第(B)子款结尾处的“或者”;

(B)删除第(C)子款结尾处的句号并替以“或者”;及

(C) by inserting at the end the following new subparagraph:

"(D) the conduct or threatened conduct (including any acts or omissions) of the depository institution holding company poses a risk to the Deposit Insurance Fund, provided that such authority may not be used with respect to a depository institution holding company that is in generally sound condition and whose conduct does not pose a foreseeable and material risk of loss to the Deposit Insurance Fund; "; and

(3) by adding at the end the following:

"(6) POWERS AND DUTIES WITH RESPECT TO DEPOSITORY INSTITUTION HOLDING COMPANIES. — For purposes of exercising the backup authority provided in this subsection —

"(A) the Corporation shall have the same powers with respect to a depository institution holding company and its affiliates as the appropriate Federal banking agency has with respect to the holding company and its affiliates; and

"(B) the holding company and its affiliates shall have the same duties and obligations with respect to the Corporation as the holding company and its affiliates have with respect to the appropriate Federal banking agency. ".

(c) RULE OF CONSTRUCTION. — Nothing in this Act shall be construed to limit or curtail the Corporation's current authority to examine or bring enforcement actions with respect to any insured depository institution or institution-affiliated party.

SEC. 173. ACCESS TO UNITED STATES FINANCIAL MARKET BY FOREIGN INSTITUTIONS.

(a) ESTABLISHMENT OF FOREIGN BANK OFFICES IN THE UNITED STATES. — Section 7(d)(3) of the International Banking Act of 1978 (12 U.S.C. 3105(d)(3)) is amended —

(1) in subparagraph (C), by striking "and" at the end;

(2) in subparagraph (D), by striking the period at the end of and inserting "; and"; and

(3) by adding at the end the following new subparagraph:

"(E) for a foreign bank that presents a risk to the stability of United States financial system, whether the home country of the foreign bank has adopted, or is making demonstrable progress toward adopting, an appropriate system of financial regulation for the financial system of such home country to mitigate such risk. ".

(b) TERMINATION OF FOREIGN BANK OFFICES IN THE UNITED STATES. — Section 7(e)(1) of the International Banking Act of 1978 (12 U.S.C. 3105(e)(1)) is amended —

(1) in subparagraph (A), by striking "or" at the end;

(2) in subparagraph (B), by striking the period at the end of and inserting "; or"; and

(C)在结尾处增如下新子款:

"(D)存款机构控股公司采取或可能采取的行为(包括任何作为或不作为)构成对存款保险基金的风险,但是,不得对整体状况良好且其行为未对存款保险基金构成可预见和重大损失风险的存款机构控股公司行使该等权力;"及

(3)在结尾处增加如下内容:

"(6)**存款机构控股公司的权力和职责**。——考虑在行使本子条规定的后备权力之目的——

(A)联邦存款保险公司对存款机构控股公司及其关联方拥有的权力,应当与相应的联邦银行业监管机关对存款机构控股公司及其关联方拥有的权力相同;且

(B)控股公司及其关联方对联邦存款保险公司负有的职责和义务,应当与其对相应的联邦银行业监管机关负有的职责和义务相同。"

(c)**解释规则**。——本法中的任何规定均不得被解释为对联邦存款保险公司当前拥有的对任何参保存款机构或机构关联方开展检查或启动强制执法行动的权力作出任何限制或限缩。

第173条　外国机构在美国金融市场的市场准入

(a)**在美国境内设立外国银行办事处**。——《1978年国际银行法》第7(d)(3)条[《美国法典》第十二编第3105(d)(3)节]修正如下——

(1)删除第(C)子款结尾处的"和";

(2)删除第(D)子款结尾处的句号,替以";及";及

(3)在结尾处增加如下新子款:

"(E)对美国金融体系稳定构成风险的外国银行,无论其母国是否已经为缓释该等风险实行对该国金融体系确属适当的金融监管体制,或是否正在为实行该等金融监管体制作出确凿的努力。"

(b)**外国银行办事处在美国的终止**。——《1978年国际银行法》第7(e)(1)条[《美国法典》第十二编第3105(e)(1)节]修正如下——

(1)在第(A)子款中,删除结尾处的"或者"一词;

(2)在第(B)子款中,删除结尾处的句号,替以";或";及

(3) by inserting after subparagraph (B), the following new subparagraph:

"(C) for a foreign bank that presents a risk to the stability of the United States financial system, the home country of the foreign bank has not adopted, or made demonstrable progress toward adopting, an appropriate system of financial regulation to mitigate such risk. ".

(c) REGISTRATION OR SUCCESSION TO A UNITED STATES BROKER OR DEALER AND TERMINATION OF SUCH REGISTRATION. — Section 15 of the Securities Exchange Act of 1934 (15 U.S.C. 78o) is amended by adding at the end the following new subsections:

"(k) REGISTRATION OR SUCCESSION TO A UNITED STATES BROKER OR DEALER. — In determining whether to permit a foreign person or an affiliate of a foreign person to register as a United States broker or dealer, or succeed to the registration of a United States broker or dealer, the Commission may consider whether, for a foreign person, or an affiliate of a foreign person that presents a risk to the stability of the United States financial system, the home country of the foreign person has adopted, or made demonstrable progress toward adopting, an appropriate system of financial regulation to mitigate such risk.

"(l) TERMINATION OF A UNITED STATES BROKER OR DEALER. — For a foreign person or an affiliate of a foreign person that presents such a risk to the stability of the United States financial system, the Commission may determine to terminate the registration of such foreign person or an affiliate of such foreign person as a broker or dealer in the United States, if the Commission determines that the home country of the foreign person has not adopted, or made demonstrable progress toward adopting, an appropriate system of financial regulation to mitigate such risk. ".

SEC. 174. STUDIES AND REPORTS ON HOLDING COMPANY CAPITAL REQUIREMENTS.

(a) STUDY OF HYBRID CAPITAL INSTRUMENTS. — The Comptroller General of the United States, in consultation with the Board of Governors, the Comptroller of the Currency, and the Corporation, shall conduct a study of the use of hybrid capital instruments as a component of Tier 1 capital for banking institutions and bank holding companies. The study shall consider —

(1) the current use of hybrid capital instruments, such as trust preferred shares, as a component of Tier 1 capital;

(2) the differences between the components of capital permitted for insured depository institutions and those permitted for companies that control insured depository institutions;

(3) the benefits and risks of allowing such instruments to be used to comply with

(3)在第(B)子款之后增加如下新子款：

"(C)对美国金融体系稳定构成风险的外国银行，其母国没有为缓释该等风险实行适当的金融监管体制，也没有为实行该等金融监管体制作出任何确凿的努力。"

(c)**美国经纪商或自营商的注册或继任以及该等注册的终止**。——在《1934年证券交易法》第15条(《美国法典》第十五编第78o节)结尾处增加如下新子条：

"(k)**美国经纪商或自营商的注册或继任**。——在判定是否应允许某一外国主体或外国主体的某一关联方注册为美国经纪商或自营商，或继任某一美国经纪商或自营商的注册时，如果该外国主体或外国主体的关联方对美国的金融体系稳定构成风险，证券交易委员会可考虑该外国主体的母国是否已为缓释该等风险实行了适当的金融监管体制，或是否正在为实行该等金融监管体制作出确凿的努力。

(l)**美国经纪商或自营商的注册终止**。——如果某一外国主体或外国主体的某一关联方对美国的金融体系稳定构成风险，且证券交易委员会判定该等外国主体的母国没有为缓释该等风险实行适当的金融监管体制，也没有为实行该等金融监管体制作出任何确凿的努力，则证券交易委员会可以判定终止该等外国主体或该等外国主体的关联方在美国境内的经纪商或自营商注册资格。"

第174条 关于控股公司资本要求的研究和报告

(a)**混合资本工具研究**。——政府问责办公室主任应在与联邦储备委员会、货币监理署和联邦存款保险公司磋商后，就银行机构和银行控股公司将混合资本工具作为一级资本构成要素的情况开展研究。此项研究应考虑以下因素——

(1)目前将混合资本工具(如信托优先股份)作为一级资本构成要素使用的情况；

(2)参保存款机构获许采用的资本构成要素与控制该等机构的公司获许采用的资本构成要素之间的差异；

(3)允许使用该等工具满足一级资本要求的益处和风险；

Tier 1 capital requirements;

(4) the economic impact of prohibiting the use of such capital instruments for Tier 1;

(5) a review of the consequences of disqualifying trust preferred instruments, and whether it could lead to the failure or undercapitalization of existing banking organizations;

(6) the international competitive implications prohibiting hybrid capital instruments for Tier 1;

(7) the impact on the cost and availability of credit in the United States from such a prohibition;

(8) the availability of capital for financial institutions with less than $10, 000, 000, 000 in total assets; and

(9) any other relevant factors relating to the safety and soundness of our financial system and potential economic impact of such a prohibition.

(b) STUDY OF FOREIGN BANK INTERMEDIATE HOLDING COMPANY CAPITAL REQUIREMENTS. — The Comptroller General of the United States, in consultation with the Secretary, the Board of Governors, the Comptroller of the Currency, and the Corporation, shall conduct a study of capital requirements applicable to United States intermediate holding companies of foreign banks that are bank holding companies or savings and loan holding companies. The study shall consider —

(1) current Board of Governors policy regarding the treatment of intermediate holding companies;

(2) the principle of national treatment and equality of competitive opportunity for foreign banks operating in the United States;

(3) the extent to which foreign banks are subject on a consolidated basis to home country capital standards comparable to United States capital standards;

(4) potential effects on United States banking organizations operating abroad of changes to United States policy regarding intermediate holding companies;

(5) the impact on the cost and availability of credit in the United States from a change in United States policy regarding intermediate holding companies; and

(6) any other relevant factors relating to the safety and soundness of our financial system and potential economic impact of such a prohibition.

(c) REPORT. — Not later than 18 months after the date of enactment of this Act, the Comptroller General of the United States shall submit reports to the Committee on Banking, Housing, and Urban Affairs of the Senate and the Committee on Financial Services of the House of Representatives summarizing the results of the studies required under subsection (a). The reports shall include specific recommendations for legislative or regulatory action regarding the treatment of hybrid capital instruments, including trust

(4)禁止将该等资本工具作为一级资本使用的经济影响;

(5)评估不允许使用信托优先工具的后果,以及不允许使用信托优先工具是否会导致现有银行组织机构经营失败或资本不足;

(6)禁止将混合资本工具作为一级资本使用可能对国际竞争力造成的影响;

(7)将混合资本工具作为一级资本使用的禁止性规定可能对美国信贷成本和可获得性造成的影响;

(8)资产总额低于100亿美元的金融机构的资本可获得性;及

(9)与美国金融体系的安全性和稳健性相关的任何其他因素以及该等禁止性规定可能造成的经济影响。

(b)**关于外国银行中间控股公司资本要求的研究**。——政府问责办公室主任应在与财政部部长、联邦储备委员会、货币监理署和联邦存款保险公司磋商后,就具有银行控股公司或储贷控股公司身份的外国银行的美国中间控股公司所适用的资本要求开展研究。此项研究应考虑以下因素——

(1)联邦储备委员会关于处理中间控股公司的现行政策;

(2)在美国开展运营活动的外国银行享有的国民待遇和竞争机会均等原则;

(3)在多大程度上,外国银行在其母国受制于与美国资本标准具有可比性的并表资本标准;

(4)变更美国关于中间控股公司政策的做法可能对在美国境外开展运营活动的美国银行组织造成的影响;

(5)变更美国关于中间控股公司政策的做法可能对美国信贷成本和可获得性造成的影响;及

(6)与美国金融体系的安全性和稳健性相关的任何其他因素,以及该等禁止性规定可能造成的经济影响。

(c)报告。——政府问责办公室主任应在本法颁布之日后的18个月内,向参议院银行、住房与城市事务委员会和众议院金融服务委员会提交一份关于按照第(a)子条规定开展的研究结果的摘要报告。报告中应就处理混合资本工具(包括信托优先股份)所应采取的立法或监管行动提出具体建议,并说明该等建议的依据。

preferred shares, and shall explain the basis for such recommendations.

SEC. 175. INTERNATIONAL POLICY COORDINATION.

(a) BY THE PRESIDENT. — The President, or a designee of the President, may coordinate through all available international policy channels, similar policies as those found in United States law relating to limiting the scope, nature, size, scale, concentration, and interconnectedness of financial companies, in order to protect financial stability and the global economy.

(b) BY THE COUNCIL. — The Chairperson of the Council, in consultation with the other members of the Council, shall regularly consult with the financial regulatory entities and other appropriate organizations of foreign governments or international organizations on matters relating to systemic risk to the international financial system.

(c) BY THE BOARD OF GOVERNORS AND THE SECRETARY. — The Board of Governors and the Secretary shall consult with their foreign counterparts and through appropriate multilateral organizations to encourage comprehensive and robust prudential supervision and regulation for all highly leveraged and interconnected financial companies.

SEC. 176. RULE OF CONSTRUCTION.

No regulation or standard imposed under this title may be construed in a manner that would lessen the stringency of the requirements of any applicable primary financial regulatory agency or any other Federal or State agency that are otherwise applicable. This title, and the rules and regulations or orders prescribed pursuant to this title, do not divest any such agency of any authority derived from any other applicable law.

第175条　国际政策协调

(a)**总统进行的协调**。——总统或总统指定的人员可以通过所有可用的国际政策渠道,协调与美国法律中限制金融公司经营范围、性质、数额、规模、集中度和相互关联程度政策类似的政策,以保护金融稳定和全球经济。

(b)**金融稳定监督委员会进行的协调**。——金融稳定监督委员会主席应在与金融稳定监督委员会其他成员磋商后，就与国际金融体系的系统性风险相关的事宜与外国政府的金融监管实体以及其他相应的组织或与国际组织定期磋商。

(c)**联邦储备委员会和财政部部长进行的协调**。——联邦储备委员会和财政部部长应与其他国家的对等机关或官员磋商,并通过相应的多边组织促进对具有高杠杆率和高关联度的所有金融公司实施全面并且健全的审慎性监管与规制。

第176条　解释规则

依据本编施行的任何规章或标准均不得被解释为导致削弱任何相应的优先金融监管机关或任何其他相关联邦机关或州机关的要求的严格程度。本编以及根据本编制定的任何规则、规章或命令,并不解除任何上述机关根据任何其他适用的法律所享有的任何权力。

TITLE II—ORDERLY LIQUIDATION AUTHORITY

SEC. 201. DEFINITIONS.

(a) IN GENERAL. — In this title, the following definitions shall apply:

(1) ADMINISTRATIVE EXPENSES OF THE RECEIVER. — The term "administrative expenses of the receiver" includes —

(A) the actual, necessary costs and expenses incurred by the Corporation as receiver for a covered financial company in liquidating a covered financial company; and

(B) any obligations that the Corporation as receiver for a covered financial company determines are necessary and appropriate to facilitate the smooth and orderly liquidation of the covered financial company.

(2) BANKRUPTCY CODE. — The term "Bankruptcy Code" means title 11, United States Code.

(3) BRIDGE FINANCIAL COMPANY. — The term "bridge financial company" means a new financial company organized by the Corporation in accordance with section 210(h) for the purpose of resolving a covered financial company.

(4) CLAIM. — The term "claim" means any right to payment, whether or not such right is reduced to judgment, liquidated, unliquidated, fixed, contingent, matured, unmatured, disputed, undisputed, legal, equitable, secured, or unsecured.

(5) COMPANY. — The term "company" has the same meaning as in section 2(b) of the Bank Holding Company Act of 1956 (12 U.S.C. 1841(b)), except that such term includes any company described in paragraph (11), the majority of the securities of which are owned by the United States or any State.

(6) COURT. — The term "Court" means the United States District Court for the District of Columbia, unless the context otherwise requires.

(7) COVERED BROKER OR DEALER. — The term "covered broker or dealer" means a covered financial company that is a broker or dealer that —

(A) is registered with the Commission under section 15(b) of the Securities Exchange Act of 1934 (15 U.S.C. 78o(b)); and

第二编——有序清算权

第201条　定义

(a)**一般规定**。——就本编而言,下列术语应适用如下定义:

(1)**接管人的行政费用**。——"接管人的行政费用"一词包括——

(A)联邦存款保险公司作为所涉金融公司接管人对所涉金融公司进行清算时,发生的实际、必要费用和支出;及

(B)联邦存款保险公司作为所涉金融公司的接管人判定的对于促进对该所涉金融公司进行顺利有序清算确属必要且适当的任何义务。

(2)**《破产法》**。——《破产法》一词系指《美国法典》第十一编。

(3)**过渡金融公司**。——"过渡金融公司"一词系指联邦存款保险公司为对所涉金融公司进行清盘之目的,而根据第210(h)条新组建的一家金融公司。

(4)**权利主张**。——"权利主张"一词系指要求获得支付的任何权利,无论其是否已形成判决,亦不论其属于已清算或未清算、确定或或有、到期或未到期、有争议或无争议、普通法律或衡平法、有担保或无担保的权利。

(5)**公司**。——"公司"一词的含义以《1956年银行控股公司法》第2(b)条[《美国法典》第十二编第1841(b)节]的定义为准,但是该词包括第(11)款所述其多数证券之所有权由联邦政府或任何州所有的任何公司。

(6)**法院**。——除非上下文另有所指,否则"法院"一词系指哥伦比亚特区联邦地区法院。

(7)**所涉经纪商或自营商**。——"所涉经纪商或自营商"一词系指性质为经纪商或自营商,且符合下述条件的所涉金融公司——

(A)已根据《1934年证券交易法》第15(b)条[《美国法典》第十五编第78o(b)节]在证券交易委员会进行注册;且

(B) is a member of SIPC.

(8) COVERED FINANCIAL COMPANY. — The term "covered financial company" —

(A) means a financial company for which a determination has been made under section 203(b); and

(B) does not include an insured depository institution.

(9) COVERED SUBSIDIARY. — The term "covered subsidiary" means a subsidiary of a covered financial company, other than —

(A) an insured depository institution;

(B) an insurance company; or

(C) a covered broker or dealer.

(10) DEFINITIONS RELATING TO COVERED BROKERS AND DEALERS. — The terms "customer", "customer name securities", "customer property", and "net equity" in the context of a covered broker or dealer, have the same meanings as in section 16 of the Securities Investor Protection Act of 1970 (15 U.S.C. 78lll).

(11) FINANCIAL COMPANY. — The term "financial company" means any company that —

(A) is incorporated or organized under any provision of Federal law or the laws of any State;

(B) is —

(i) a bank holding company, as defined in section 2(a) of the Bank Holding Company Act of 1956 (12 U.S.C. 1841(a));

(ii) a nonbank financial company supervised by the Board of Governors;

(iii) any company that is predominantly engaged in activities that the Board of Governors has determined are financial in nature or incidental thereto for purposes of section 4(k) of the Bank Holding Company Act of 1956 (12 U.S.C. 1843(k)) other than a company described in clause (i) or (ii); or

(iv) any subsidiary of any company described in any of clauses (i) through (iii) that is predominantly engaged in activities that the Board of Governors has determined are financial in nature or incidental thereto for purposes of section 4(k) of the Bank Holding Company Act of 1956 (12 U.S.C. 1843(k)) (other than a subsidiary that is an insured depository institution or an insurance company); and

(C) is not a Farm Credit System institution chartered under and subject to the provisions of the Farm Credit Act of 1971, as amended (12 U.S.C. 2001 et seq.), a governmental entity, or a regulated entity, as defined under section 1303(20) of the Federal Housing Enterprises Financial Safety and Soundness Act of 1992 (12 U.S.C. 4502(20)).

(12) FUND. — The term "Fund" means the Orderly Liquidation Fund established

(B)身为证券投资者保护公司的会员。

(8)**所涉金融公司**。——“所涉金融公司”一词——

(A)系指已根据第203(b)条被作出判定的金融公司;且

(B)不包括参保存款机构。

(9)**所涉子公司**。——“所涉子公司”一词系指所涉金融公司的子公司,但以下主体除外——

(A)参保存款机构;

(B)保险公司;或

(C)所涉经纪商或自营商。

(10)**与所涉经纪商和自营商相关的定义**。——在上下文涉及所涉经纪商或自营商时,“客户”、“客户名下证券”、“客户财产”以及“权益净额”之含义以《1970年证券投资者保护法》第16条(《美国法典》第十五编第78lll节)的定义为准。

(11)**金融公司**。——“金融公司”一词系指具有以下特征的任何公司——

(A)根据联邦法律或任何州法律成立或组建;

(B)性质为——

(i)银行控股公司[定义见《1956年银行控股公司法》第2(a)条(《美国法典》第十二编第1841(a)节)];

(ii)受联邦储备委员会监管的非银行金融公司;

(iii)主营业务为联邦储备委员会所判定的属于《1956年银行控股公司法》第4(k)条[《美国法典》第十二编第1843(k)节]意义上的金融性质活动或其附属活动的任何公司[但第(i)项或第(ii)项所述公司除外];或

(iv)第(i)项至第(iii)项所述任何公司的主营业务为联邦储备委员会所判定的属于《1956年银行控股公司法》第4(k)条[《美国法典》第十二编第1843(k)节]意义上的金融性质活动或其附属活动的任何子公司(但性质为参保存款机构或保险公司的子公司的除外);且

(C)并非根据《1971年农业信贷法》(修正版)(《美国法典》第十二编第2001节及其后条文)特许注册并受制于该法规定的农业信贷系统机构,同时并非政府实体或受监管实体,定义见《1992年联邦住房企业财务安全和稳健法》第1303(20)条[《美国法典》第十二编第4502(20)节]。

(12)**有序清算基金**。——“有序清算基金”一词系指根据第210(n)条设立的有序

under section 210(n).

(13) INSURANCE COMPANY. — The term "insurance company" means any entity that is —

(A) engaged in the business of insurance;

(B) subject to regulation by a State insurance regulator; and

(C) covered by a State law that is designed to specifically deal with the rehabilitation, liquidation, or insolvency of an insurance company.

(14) NONBANK FINANCIAL COMPANY. — The term "nonbank financial company" has the same meaning as in section 102(a)(4)(C).

(15) NONBANK FINANCIAL COMPANY SUPERVISED BY THE BOARD OF GOVERNORS. — The term "nonbank financial company supervised by the Board of Governors" has the same meaning as in section 102(a)(4)(D).

(16) SIPC. — The term "SIPC" means the Securities Investor Protection Corporation.

(b) DEFINITIONAL CRITERIA. — For purpose of the definition of the term "financial company" under subsection (a)(11), no company shall be deemed to be predominantly engaged in activities that the Board of Governors has determined are financial in nature or incidental thereto for purposes of section 4(k) of the Bank Holding Company Act of 1956 (12 U.S.C. 1843(k)), if the consolidated revenues of such company from such activities constitute less than 85 percent of the total consolidated revenues of such company, as the Corporation, in consultation with the Secretary, shall establish by regulation. In determining whether a company is a financial company under this title, the consolidated revenues derived from the ownership or control of a depository institution shall be included.

SEC. 202. JUDICIAL REVIEW.

(a) COMMENCEMENT OF ORDERLY LIQUIDATION. —

(1) PETITION TO DISTRICT COURT. —

(A) DISTRICT COURT REVIEW. —

(i) PETITION TO DISTRICT COURT. — Subsequent to a determination by the Secretary under section 203 that a financial company satisfies the criteria in section 203(b), the Secretary shall notify the Corporation and the covered financial company. If the board of directors (or body performing similar functions) of the covered financial company acquiesces or consents to the appointment of the Corporation as receiver, the Secretary shall appoint the Corporation as receiver. If the board of directors (or body performing similar functions) of the covered financial company does not acquiesce or consent to the appointment of the Corporation as receiver, the Secretary shall petition the United States District Court for the District of Columbia for an order authorizing the

清算基金。

(13)**保险公司**。——“保险公司”一词系指具有以下特征的任何实体——

(A)从事保险业务;

(B)接受州保险监管者监管;且

(C)属于为处理保险公司整顿、清算或资不抵债而专门制定的州法律的适用对象。

(14)**非银行金融公司**。——“非银行金融公司”一词的含义以第102(a)(4)(C)条的定义为准。

(15)**受联邦储备委员会监管的非银行金融公司**。——“受联邦储备委员会监管的非银行金融公司”一词的含义以第102(a)(4)(D)条的定义为准。

(16)**SIPC**。——“SIPC”一词系指证券投资者保护公司。

(b)**定义标准**。——就第(a)(11)子条对“金融公司”的定义而言,任何公司如因从事联邦储备委员会判定的属于《1956年银行控股公司法》第4(k)条[《美国法典》第十二编第1843(k)节]意义上的金融性质活动或其附属活动而获得的并表收入低于该公司并表收入总额的85%,则不得被认定为主营该等活动。联邦存款保险公司应在与财政部部长磋商后,发布规章明确确立上述标准。根据本编判定某公司是否是一家金融公司时,应将该公司因拥有或控制存款机构而产生的并表收入纳入考虑范围。

第202条　司法审查

(a)**有序清算的启动**。——

(1)**向地区法院提交请求书**。——

(A)**地区法院审查**。——

(i)**向地区法院提交请求书**。——财政部部长根据第203条判定某金融公司符合第203(b)条规定的标准后,应通知联邦存款保险公司和该所涉金融公司。该所涉金融公司的董事会(或履行类似职能的机构)默许或同意将联邦存款保险公司指定为接管人的,则财政部部长应将联邦存款保险公司指定为接管人。该所涉金融公司董事会(或履行类似职能的机构)未默许或同意将联邦存款保险公司指定为接管人的,则财政部部长应请求哥伦比亚特区联邦地区法院签发命令,准许财政部部长将联邦存款保险公司指定为接管人。

Secretary to appoint the Corporation as receiver.

(ii) FORM AND CONTENT OF ORDER. — The Secretary shall present all relevant findings and the recommendation made pursuant to section 203 (a) to the Court. The petition shall be filed under seal.

(iii) DETERMINATION. — On a strictly confidential basis, and without any prior public disclosure, the Court, after notice to the covered financial company and a hearing in which the covered financial company may oppose the petition, shall determine whether the determination of the Secretary that the covered financial company is in default or in danger of default and satisfies the definition of a financial company under section 201(a)(11) is arbitrary and capricious.

(iv) ISSUANCE OF ORDER. — If the Court determines that the determination of the Secretary that the covered financial company is in default or in danger of default and satisfies the definition of a financial company under section 201(a)(11) —

(I) is not arbitrary and capricious, the Court shall issue an order immediately authorizing the Secretary to appoint the Corporation as receiver of the covered financial company; or

(II) is arbitrary and capricious, the Court shall immediately provide to the Secretary a written statement of each reason supporting its determination, and afford the Secretary an immediate opportunity to amend and refile the petition under clause (i).

(v) PETITION GRANTED BY OPERATION OF LAW. — If the Court does not make a determination within 24 hours of receipt of the petition —

(I) the petition shall be granted by operation of law;

(II) the Secretary shall appoint the Corporation as receiver; and

(III) liquidation under this title shall automatically and without further notice or action be commenced and the Corporation may immediately take all actions authorized under this title.

(B) EFFECT OF DETERMINATION. — The determination of the Court under subparagraph (A) shall be final, and shall be subject to appeal only in accordance with paragraph (2). The decision shall not be subject to any stay or injunction pending appeal. Upon conclusion of its proceedings under subparagraph (A), the Court shall provide immediately for the record a written statement of each reason supporting the decision of the Court, and shall provide copies thereof to the Secretary and the covered financial company.

(C) CRIMINAL PENALTIES. — A person who recklessly discloses a determination of the Secretary under section 203(b) or a petition of the Secretary under subparagraph (A), or the pendency of court proceedings as provided for under subparagraph (A), shall be fined not more than $250, 000, or imprisoned for not more than 5 years, or both.

(ii)**请求书**[1]**的格式和内容**。——财政部部长应向法院提交其根据第203(a)条作出的全部相关认定和建议。该请求书须加盖公章提交。

(iii)**判定**。——法院应向所涉金融公司发出通知并举行听证,所涉金融公司可以在听证中提出反对意见。听证结束之后,法院应判定财政部部长作出的关于所涉金融公司已处于违约状态或有违约之虞且符合第201(a)(11)条金融公司定义的判定是否恣意、专断。该判定应在严格保密的基础上作出,不得进行任何事先公开披露。

(iv)**签发命令**。——对于财政部部长作出的,关于所涉金融公司已处于违约状态或有违约之虞且符合第201(a)(11)条中金融公司定义的判定——

(I)法院判定上述财政部部长所做判定不具有恣意性和专断性的,则法院应立即签发命令,准许财政部部长将联邦存款保险公司指定为该所涉金融公司的接管人;或

(II)法院判定上述财政部部长所做判定具有恣意性和专断性的,则法院应立即向财政部部长提供一份关于支持其判定的各项原因的书面说明,并向财政部部长提供根据第(i)项立即进行修正并重新提交请求书的机会。

(v)**依法自动批准请求**。——法院在收到请求书后24小时内未作出判定的,则——

(I)该请求将被自动依法批准;

(II)财政部部长应将联邦存款保险公司指定为接管人;且

(III)本编规定的清算程序应自动启动,而不必发出进一步通知或采取进一步行动,且联邦存款保险公司可立即采取其依据本编有权采取的全部行动。

(B)**判定的效力**。——法院根据第(A)子款作出的判定应为最终判定,且对该判定的上诉仅得根据第(2)款规定进行。该判定在上诉未决期间,不得被签发任何中止令或禁令。法院在第(A)子款规定的程序完结后,应立即制作一份关于支持其判定的各项理由的书面说明,并应向财政部部长和所涉金融公司提供该说明的复本。

(C)**刑事处罚**。——任何人如出于轻率的主观态度泄露财政部部长根据第203(b)条作出的某项判定,或者泄露财政部部长根据第(A)子款提交的请求或尚未完结的第(A)子款所述法院程序,应单处或并处不高于25万美元的罚款或5年以下监禁。

---

1 按上下文,此处的“命令”(order)似应为“请求书”(petition),译文中按“请求”(petition)处理。——译者注

(2) APPEAL OF DECISIONS OF THE DISTRICT COURT. —

(A) APPEAL TO COURT OF APPEALS. —

(i) IN GENERAL. — Subject to clause (ii), the United States Court of Appeals for the District of Columbia Circuit shall have jurisdiction of an appeal of a final decision of the Court filed by the Secretary or a covered financial company, through its board of directors, notwithstanding section 210(a)(1)(A)(i), not later than 30 days after the date on which the decision of the Court is rendered or deemed rendered under this subsection.

(ii) CONDITION OF JURISDICTION. — The Court of Appeals shall have jurisdiction of an appeal by a covered financial company only if the covered financial company did not acquiesce or consent to the appointment of a receiver by the Secretary under paragraph (1)(A).

(iii) EXPEDITION. — The Court of Appeals shall consider any appeal under this subparagraph on an expedited basis.

(iv) SCOPE OF REVIEW. — For an appeal taken under this subparagraph, review shall be limited to whether the determination of the Secretary that a covered financial company is in default or in danger of default and satisfies the definition of a financial company under section 201(a)(11) is arbitrary and capricious.

(B) APPEAL TO THE SUPREME COURT. —

(i) IN GENERAL. — A petition for a writ of certiorari to review a decision of the Court of Appeals under subparagraph (A) may be filed by the Secretary or the covered financial company, through its board of directors, notwithstanding section 210 (a)(1)(A)(i), with the Supreme Court of the United States, not later than 30 days after the date of the final decision of the Court of Appeals, and the Supreme Court shall have discretionary jurisdiction to review such decision.

(ii) WRITTEN STATEMENT. — In the event of a petition under clause (i), the Court of Appeals shall immediately provide for the record a written statement of each reason for its decision.

(iii) EXPEDITION. — The Supreme Court shall consider any petition under this subparagraph on an expedited basis.

(iv) SCOPE OF REVIEW. — Review by the Supreme Court under this subparagraph shall be limited to whether the determination of the Secretary that the covered financial company is in default or in danger of default and satisfies the definition of a financial company under section 201(a)(11) is arbitrary and capricious.

(b) ESTABLISHMENT AND TRANSMITTAL OF RULES AND PROCEDURES. —

(1) IN GENERAL. — Not later than 6 months after the date of enactment of this Act, the Court shall establish such rules and procedures as may be necessary to ensure the orderly conduct of proceedings, including rules and procedures to ensure that the 24–

(2)**对地区法院裁决的上诉**。——

(A)**向上诉法院的上诉**。——

(i)**一般规定**。——无论第210(a)(1)(A)(i)条如何规定,如果在法院根据本子条作出或被视为作出最终裁决之日后30天内,财政部部长或所涉金融公司(通过其董事会)仍对该最终裁决提起了上诉,则在不违反第(ii)项规定的前提下,该上诉应由美国哥伦比亚特区巡回上诉法院管辖。

(ii)**管辖权条件**。——对于所涉金融公司提起的上诉,哥伦比亚特区巡回上诉法院仅在以下前提下方具有管辖权:该所涉金融公司未默许或同意财政部部长根据第(1)(A)款作出的接管人指定。

(iii)**加急处理**。——哥伦比亚特区巡回上诉法院应加急处理根据本子款提起的任何上诉。

(iv)**审查范围**。——就根据本子款提起的上诉而言,审查范围应仅限于:审查财政部部长作出的关于所涉金融公司已处于违约状态或有违约之虞且符合第201(a)(11)条金融公司定义的判定是否恣意、专断。

(B)**向最高法院提起的上诉**。——

(i)**一般规定**。——无论第210(a)(1)(A)(i)条如何规定,哥伦比亚特区巡回上诉法院作出最终判定之日后30天内,财政部部长或所涉金融公司(通过其董事会)仍可以提请美国最高法院签发调案复审令,对哥伦比亚特区巡回上诉法院根据第(A)子款作出的最终判定进行审查。最高法院应依其自由裁量权自行决定是否对该最终判定进行审查。

(ii)**书面说明**。——财政部部长或所涉金融公司根据第(i)项提交了请求的,则哥伦比亚特区巡回上诉法院应立即制作一份关于支持其决定的各项理由的书面说明。

(iii)**加急处理**。——最高法院应加急处理根据本子款提交的任何请求。

(iv)**审查范围**。——最高法院根据本子款进行审查时,审查范围应仅限于:审查财政部部长作出的关于所涉金融公司已处于违约状态或有违约之虞且符合第201(a)(11)条金融公司定义的判定是否恣意、专断。

(b)**规则和程序的制定与传发**。——

(1)**一般规定**。——哥伦比亚特区巡回法院应于本法颁布之日后6个月内制定必要的规则和程序,以确保审查程序的有序开展,包括确保24小时的时限规定得到遵守,且财政部部长有根据第(a)(1)子条修正并重新提交请求书的持续的机会。

hour deadline is met and that the Secretary shall have an ongoing opportunity to amend and refile petitions under subsection (a)(1).

(2) PUBLICATION OF RULES. — The rules and procedures established under paragraph (1), and any modifications of such rules and procedures, shall be recorded and shall be transmitted to —

(A) the Committee on the Judiciary of the Senate;

(B) the Committee on Banking, Housing, and Urban Affairs of the Senate;

(C) the Committee on the Judiciary of the House of Representatives; and

(D) the Committee on Financial Services of the House of Representatives.

(c) PROVISIONS APPLICABLE TO FINANCIAL COMPANIES. —

(1) BANKRUPTCY CODE. — Except as provided in this subsection, the provisions of the Bankruptcy Code and rules issued thereunder or otherwise applicable insolvency law, and not the provisions of this title, shall apply to financial companies that are not covered financial companies for which the Corporation has been appointed as receiver.

(2) THIS TITLE. — The provisions of this title shall exclusively apply to and govern all matters relating to covered financial companies for which the Corporation is appointed as receiver, and no provisions of the Bankruptcy Code or the rules issued thereunder shall apply in such cases, except as expressly provided in this title.

(d) TIME LIMIT ON RECEIVERSHIP AUTHORITY. —

(1) BASELINE PERIOD. — Any appointment of the Corporation as receiver under this section shall terminate at the end of the 3-year period beginning on the date on which such appointment is made.

(2) EXTENSION OF TIME LIMIT. — The time limit established in paragraph (1) may be extended by the Corporation for up to 1 additional year, if the Chairperson of the Corporation determines and certifies in writing to the Committee on Banking, Housing, and Urban Affairs of the Senate and the Committee on Financial Services of the House of Representatives that continuation of the receivership is necessary —

(A) to —

(i) maximize the net present value return from the sale or other disposition of the assets of the covered financial company; or

(ii) minimize the amount of loss realized upon the sale or other disposition of the assets of the covered financial company; and

(B) to protect the stability of the financial system of the United States.

(3) SECOND EXTENSION OF TIME LIMIT. —

(A) IN GENERAL. — The time limit under this subsection, as extended under paragraph (2), may be extended for up to 1 additional year, if the Chairperson of the Corporation, with the concurrence of the Secretary, submits the certifications described in

(2)**规则公布**。——根据第(1)款制定的规则和程序及其任何修正均应记录在案,并传发给下述委员会——

(A)参议院司法委员会;

(B)参议院银行、住房与城市事务委员会;

(C)众议院司法委员会;及

(D)众议院金融服务委员会。

(c)**适用于金融公司的规定**。——

(1)**《破产法》**。——除非本子条规定的情形外,《破产法》、根据《破产法》发布的规则或其他适用的资不抵债法的规定(但本编规定除外)应适用于联邦存款保险公司作为接管人接管的所涉金融公司之外的金融公司。

(2)**本编**。——本编规定仅适用于且仅管辖以联邦存款保险公司作为接管人的所涉金融公司相关的全部事项,且除非本编另有明确规定,否则《破产法》或根据《破产法》发布的规则对该等事项均不具有适用性。

(d)**接管期限**。——

(1)**基础期限**。——联邦存款保险公司根据本条规定被指定为接管人的,该项指定的效力应于自该项指定作出之日起届满3年时终止。

(2)**延期**。——联邦存款保险公司可以将第(1)款规定的时限延长不超过1年的期间,只要联邦存款保险公司主席作出了如下判定,并就此向参议院银行、住房与城市事务委员会和众议院金融服务委员会提交了书面证明:延长接管期限——

(A)系为实现以下目的所必需——

(i)将出售或以其他方式处置所涉金融公司资产产生的净现值回报最大化;或

(ii)将出售或以其他方式处置所涉金融公司资产所造成的任何损失金额减到最低限度;及

(B)系为保护美国金融体系的稳定所必需。

(3)**二次延期**。——

(A)**一般规定**。——本子条规定的期限根据第(2)款规定延长后,可再次延长不超过1年的期间,只要联邦存款保险公司主席在征得财政部部长同意的情况下提交了第(2)款所述证明。

paragraph (2).

(B) ADDITIONAL REPORT REQUIRED. — Not later than 30 days after the date of commencement of the extension under subparagraph (A), the Corporation shall submit a report to the Committee on Banking, Housing, and Urban Affairs of the Senate and the Committee on Financial Services of the House of Representatives describing the need for the extension and the specific plan of the Corporation to conclude the receivership before the end of the second extension.

(4) ONGOING LITIGATION. — The time limit under this subsection, as extended under paragraph (3), may be further extended solely for the purpose of completing ongoing litigation in which the Corporation as receiver is a party, provided that the appointment of the Corporation as receiver shall terminate not later than 90 days after the date of completion of such litigation, if —

(A) the Council determines that the Corporation used its best efforts to conclude the receivership in accordance with its plan before the end of the time limit described in paragraph (3);

(B) the Council determines that the completion of longer–term responsibilities in the form of ongoing litigation justifies the need for an extension; and

(C) the Corporation submits a report approved by the Council not later than 30 days after the date of the determinations by the Council under subparagraphs (A) and (B) to the Committee on Banking, Housing, and Urban Affairs of the Senate and the Committee on Financial Services of the House of Representatives, describing —

(i) the ongoing litigation justifying the need for an extension; and

(ii) the specific plan of the Corporation to complete the litigation and conclude the receivership.

(5) REGULATIONS. — The Corporation may issue regulations governing the termination of receiverships under this title.

(6) NO LIABILITY. — The Corporation and the Deposit Insurance Fund shall not be liable for unresolved claims arising from the receivership after the termination of the receivership.

(e) STUDY OF BANKRUPTCY AND ORDERLY LIQUIDATION PROCESS FOR FINANCIAL COMPANIES. —

(1) STUDY. —

(A) IN GENERAL. — The Administrative Office of the United States Courts and the Comptroller General of the United States shall each monitor the activities of the Court, and each such Office shall conduct separate studies regarding the bankruptcy and orderly liquidation process for financial companies under the Bankruptcy Code.

(B) ISSUES TO BE STUDIED. — In conducting the study under subparagraph (A),

(B)**需要补充提交的报告**。——在第(A)子款所述延期起始日后30天内,联邦存款保险公司应向参议院银行、住房与城市事务委员会和众议院金融服务委员会提交一份报告,说明延期的需要以及联邦存款保险公司在该二次延期的期限内完成其接管人职责的具体计划。

(4)**进行中的诉讼**。——在下述情形下,如果联邦存款保险公司作为接管人而以当事人身份参与的诉讼尚未完结,则本子条规定的期限在根据第(3)款延长后,可以再次延长,但延长的目的应仅限于完成该诉讼,其前提是,联邦存款保险公司被指定的接管人身份应于该诉讼完结后90天内终止——

(A)金融稳定监督委员会判定,联邦存款保险公司已尽最大努力在第(3)款所述的延期期限结束前根据其计划完成接管人职责;

(B)金融稳定监督委员会判定,利用进行中的诉讼完成具有长远意义的责任可以成为延期的合理理由;且

(C)联邦存款保险公司在金融稳定监督委员会根据第(A)子款和第(B)子款作出判定后30天内向参议院银行、住房与城市事务委员会和众议院金融服务委员会提交了一份经金融稳定监督委员会批准的报告,对下列各项进行说明——

(i)作为其需要延期之理由的进行中的诉讼;及

(ii)联邦存款保险公司完成该诉讼及其接管人职责的具体计划。

(5)**规章**。——联邦存款保险公司可以发布规章,对其根据本编获得的接管人身份之终止作出规定。

(6)**不承担责任**。——接管终止之后,联邦存款保险公司以及存款保险基金对因接管产生的尚未解决的权利主张均不承担任何责任。

(e)**关于金融公司破产和有序清算程序的研究**。——

(1)**研究**。——

(A)**一般规定**。——联邦法院行政管理局和政府问责办公室主任应分别监控法院的行为,并应分别针对《破产法》规定的金融公司破产和有序清算程序开展独立研究。

(B)**研究事项**。——联邦法院行政管理局和政府问责办公室主任在根据第(A)子

the Administrative Office of the United States Courts and the Comptroller General of the United States each shall evaluate —

(i) the effectiveness of chapter 7 or chapter 11 of the Bankruptcy Code in facilitating the orderly liquidation or reorganization of financial companies;

(ii) ways to maximize the efficiency and effectiveness of the Court; and

(iii) ways to make the orderly liquidation process under the Bankruptcy Code for financial companies more effective.

(2) REPORTS. — Not later than 1 year after the date of enactment of this Act, in each successive year until the third year, and every fifth year after that date of enactment, the Administrative Office of the United States Courts and the Comptroller General of the United States shall submit to the Committee on Banking, Housing, and Urban Affairs and the Committee on the Judiciary of the Senate and the Committee on Financial Services and the Committee on the Judiciary of the House of Representatives separate reports summarizing the results of the studies conducted under paragraph (1).

(f) STUDY OF INTERNATIONAL COORDINATION RELATING TO BANKRUPTCY PROCESS FOR FINANCIAL COMPANIES. —

(1) STUDY. —

(A) IN GENERAL. — The Comptroller General of the United States shall conduct a study regarding international coordination relating to the orderly liquidation of financial companies under the Bankruptcy Code.

(B) ISSUES TO BE STUDIED. — In conducting the study under subparagraph (A), the Comptroller General of the United States shall evaluate, with respect to the bankruptcy process for financial companies —

(i) the extent to which international coordination currently exists;

(ii) current mechanisms and structures for facilitating international cooperation;

(iii) barriers to effective international coordination; and

(iv) ways to increase and make more effective international coordination.

(2) REPORT. — Not later than 1 year after the date of enactment of this Act, the Comptroller General of the United States shall submit to the Committee on Banking, Housing, and Urban Affairs and the Committee on the Judiciary of the Senate and the Committee on Financial Services and the Committee on the Judiciary of the House of Representatives and the Secretary a report summarizing the results of the study conducted under paragraph (1).

(g) STUDY OF PROMPT CORRECTIVE ACTION IMPLEMENTATION BY THE APPROPRIATE FEDERAL AGENCIES. —

(1) STUDY. — The Comptroller General of the United States shall conduct a study regarding the implementation of prompt corrective action by the appropriate Federal

款开展研究时,应对下列各项进行评价——

(i)《破产法》第七章或第十一章在促进金融公司有序清算或重组方面的成效;

(ii)将法院效率和成效最大化的方式;及
(iii)提高金融公司按照《破产法》有序清算的成效的方式。

(2)**报告**。——联邦法院行政管理局和政府问责办公室主任应在本法颁布之日后1年内,就其根据第(1)款开展的研究,分别向参议院银行、住房与城市事务委员会、参议院司法委员会、众议院金融服务委员会和众议院司法委员会提交一份研究结果摘要报告,并分别在随后的2年中每年提交该报告;本法颁布届满3年以后,应在本法颁布日后的每个第5年提交该报告。

(f)**关于金融公司破产程序中国际协作的研究**。——

(1)**研究**。——
(A)**一般规定**。——政府问责办公室主任应针对金融公司按照《破产法》进行的有序清算程序中的国际协作开展研究。

(B)**研究事项**。——在根据第(A)子款开展研究时,政府问责办公室主任应针对金融公司破产程序对以下各项进行评价——

(i)当前国际协作的范围和程度;
(ii)促进国际合作的现有机制和架构;
(iii)有效实施国际协作的障碍;及
(iv)加强国际协作、提高国际协作成效的方式。
(2)**报告**。——政府问责办公室主任应在本法颁布之日后1年内,就其根据第(1)款开展的研究向参议院银行、住房与城市事务委员会、参议院司法委员会、众议院金融服务委员会、众议院司法委员会和财政部部长提交一份研究结果摘要报告。

(g)**关于相应的联邦机关及时实施纠正行动的研究**。——

(1)**研究**。——政府问责办公室主任应针对相应的联邦银行业监管机关对纠正行动的及时实施开展研究。

banking agencies.

(2) ISSUES TO BE STUDIED. — In conducting the study under paragraph (1), the Comptroller General shall evaluate —

(A) the effectiveness of implementation of prompt corrective action by the appropriate Federal banking agencies and the resolution of insured depository institutions by the Corporation; and

(B) ways to make prompt corrective action a more effective tool to resolve the insured depository institutions at the least possible long-term cost to the Deposit Insurance Fund.

(3) REPORT TO COUNCIL. — Not later than 1 year after the date of enactment of this Act, the Comptroller General shall submit a report to the Council on the results of the study conducted under this subsection.

(4) COUNCIL REPORT OF ACTION. — Not later than 6 months after the date of receipt of the report from the Comptroller General under paragraph (3), the Council shall submit a report to the Committee on Banking, Housing, and Urban Affairs of the Senate and the Committee on Financial Services of the House of Representatives on actions taken in response to the report, including any recommendations made to the Federal primary financial regulatory agencies under section 120.

SEC. 203. SYSTEMIC RISK DETERMINATION.

(a) WRITTEN RECOMMENDATION AND DETERMINATION. —

(1) VOTE REQUIRED. —

(A) IN GENERAL. — On their own initiative, or at the request of the Secretary, the Corporation and the Board of Governors shall consider whether to make a written recommendation described in paragraph (2) with respect to whether the Secretary should appoint the Corporation as receiver for a financial company. Such recommendation shall be made upon a vote of not fewer than 2/3 of the members of the Board of Governors then serving and 2/3 of the members of the board of directors of the Corporation then serving.

(B) CASES INVOLVING BROKERS OR DEALERS. — In the case of a broker or dealer, or in which the largest United States subsidiary (as measured by total assets as of the end of the previous calendar quarter) of a financial company is a broker or dealer, the Commission and the Board of Governors, at the request of the Secretary, or on their own initiative, shall consider whether to make the written recommendation described in paragraph (2) with respect to the financial company. Subject to the requirements in paragraph (2), such recommendation shall be made upon a vote of not fewer than 2/3 of the members of the Board of Governors then serving and 2/3 of the members of the Commission then serving, and in consultation with the Corporation.

(C) CASES INVOLVING INSURANCE COMPANIES. — In the case of an

(2)**研究事项**。——政府问责办公室主任在根据第(1)款开展研究时,应评估——

(A)相应的联邦银行业监管机关及时实施纠正行动的效率,以及联邦存款保险公司对参保存款机构实施清盘的效率;及

(B)如何在将存款保险基金承担的长期成本最小化的情况下,使及时纠正行动成为更加有效地对参保存款机构进行清算的工具。

(3)**向金融稳定监督委员会提交的报告**。——政府问责办公室主任应于本法颁布之日后1年内,就其根据本子条开展的研究结果向金融稳定监督委员会提交一份报告。

(4)**金融稳定监督委员会的行动报告**。——金融稳定监督委员会应在收到政府问责办公室主任根据第(3)款提交的报告后6个月内,就其针对该报告采取的相应行动(包括根据第120条向联邦优先金融监管机关提供的任何建议)向参议院银行、住房与城市事务委员会和众议院金融服务委员会提交一份报告。

第203条　系统性风险的判定

(a)**书面建议和判定**。——

(1)**表决要求**。——

(A)**一般规定**。——就财政部部长是否应将联邦存款保险公司指定为某一金融公司的接管人这一问题而言,联邦存款保险公司和联邦储备委员会应主动或应财政部部长的请求,考虑是否作出第(2)款所述书面建议。联邦储备委员会和联邦存款保险公司董事会作出该建议的,应获得其各自至少2/3届时在任的成员表决同意。

(B)**涉及经纪商或自营商的情形**。——对于涉及经纪商或自营商的情形,或对于金融公司下属最大的美国子公司(按截至上一日历季度季末的资产总额计量)是一家经纪商或自营商的情形,证券交易委员会和联邦储备委员会应主动或应财政部部长的请求,对是否应就该金融公司作出第(2)款所述书面建议进行考虑。在不违反第(2)款规定的前提下,联邦储备委员会和证券交易委员会在作出该建议时,至少应获得其各自2/3届时在任的成员表决同意,且应与联邦存款保险公司进行磋商。

(C)**涉及保险公司的情形**。——对于涉及保险公司的情形,或金融公司下属最大

insurance company, or in which the largest United States subsidiary (as measured by total assets as of the end of the previous calendar quarter) of a financial company is an insurance company, the Director of the Federal Insurance Office and the Board of Governors, at the request of the Secretary or on their own initiative, shall consider whether to make the written recommendation described in paragraph (2) with respect to the financial company. Subject to the requirements in paragraph (2), such recommendation shall be made upon a vote of not fewer than 2/3 of the Board of Governors then serving and the affirmative approval of the Director of the Federal Insurance Office, and in consultation with the Corporation.

(2) RECOMMENDATION REQUIRED. — Any written recommendation pursuant to paragraph (1) shall contain —

(A) an evaluation of whether the financial company is in default or in danger of default;

(B) a description of the effect that the default of the financial company would have on financial stability in the United States;

(C) a description of the effect that the default of the financial company would have on economic conditions or financial stability for low income, minority, or underserved communities;

(D) a recommendation regarding the nature and the extent of actions to be taken under this title regarding the financial company;

(E) an evaluation of the likelihood of a private sector alternative to prevent the default of the financial company;

(F) an evaluation of why a case under the Bankruptcy Code is not appropriate for the financial company;

(G) an evaluation of the effects on creditors, counterparties, and shareholders of the financial company and other market participants; and

(H) an evaluation of whether the company satisfies the definition of a financial company under section 201.

(b) DETERMINATION BY THE SECRETARY. — Notwithstanding any other provision of Federal or State law, the Secretary shall take action in accordance with section 202(a)(1)(A), if, upon the written recommendation under subsection (a), the Secretary (in consultation with the President) determines that —

(1) the financial company is in default or in danger of default;

(2) the failure of the financial company and its resolution under otherwise applicable Federal or State law would have serious adverse effects on financial stability in the United States;

(3) no viable private sector alternative is available to prevent the default of the

的美国子公司(按截至上一日历季度季末的资产总额计量)是一家保险公司的情形,联邦保险办公室主任和联邦储备委员会应主动或应财政部部长的请求,就是否应就该金融公司作出第(2)款所述书面建议进行考虑。在不违反第(2)款规定的前提下,联邦储备委员会和联邦保险办公室主任作出该建议时应获得联邦储备委员会至少2/3届时在任的成员表决同意,并获得联邦保险办公室主任的批准,且应与联邦存款保险公司进行磋商。

(2)**需要提交的建议**。——根据第(1)款提交的任何书面建议均应包括如下信息——

(A)对该金融公司是否处于违约状态或有违约之虞的评估;

(B)关于该金融公司违约将给美国金融稳定造成的影响的说明;

(C)关于该金融公司违约将给低收入群体、少数族裔或者弱势群体经济状况或财务稳定造成的影响的说明;

(D)关于应根据本编采取的与该金融公司有关的行动之性质和范围的建议;

(E)关于借助私人部门防止该金融公司违约的可能性的评估;

(F)为何不应根据《破产法》对该金融公司启动案件的评估;

(G)对该金融公司的债权人、对手方和股东以及其他市场参与者将受到的影响的评估;及

(H)对该公司是否符合第201条对金融公司的定义的评估。

(b)**财政部部长作出的判定**。——无论联邦法律或州法律是否存在任何不同规定,只要财政部部长在收到根据第(a)子条提交的书面建议并与总统磋商后作出以下判定,财政部部长即应根据第202(a)(1)(A)条采取相应行动——

(1)该金融公司处于违约状态或有违约之虞;

(2)该金融公司的经营失败和该金融公司根据其他适用的联邦法律或州法律进行清算将对美国金融稳定造成严重不利影响;

(3)没有找到借助私人部门防止该金融公司违约的方案;

financial company;

(4) any effect on the claims or interests of creditors, counterparties, and shareholders of the financial company and other market participants as a result of actions to be taken under this title is appropriate, given the impact that any action taken under this title would have on financial stability in the United States;

(5) any action under section 204 would avoid or mitigate such adverse effects, taking into consideration the effectiveness of the action in mitigating potential adverse effects on the financial system, the cost to the general fund of the Treasury, and the potential to increase excessive risk taking on the part of creditors, counterparties, and shareholders in the financial company;

(6) a Federal regulatory agency has ordered the financial company to convert all of its convertible debt instruments that are subject to the regulatory order; and

(7) the company satisfies the definition of a financial company under section 201.

(c) DOCUMENTATION AND REVIEW. —

(1) IN GENERAL. — The Secretary shall —

(A) document any determination under subsection (b);

(B) retain the documentation for review under paragraph (2); and

(C) notify the covered financial company and the Corporation of such determination.

(2) REPORT TO CONGRESS. — Not later than 24 hours after the date of appointment of the Corporation as receiver for a covered financial company, the Secretary shall provide written notice of the recommendations and determinations reached in accordance with subsections (a) and (b) to the Majority Leader and the Minority Leader of the Senate and the Speaker and the Minority Leader of the House of Representatives, the Committee on Banking, Housing, and Urban Affairs of the Senate, and the Committee on Financial Services of the House of Representatives, which shall consist of a summary of the basis for the determination, including, to the extent available at the time of the determination —

(A) the size and financial condition of the covered financial company;

(B) the sources of capital and credit support that were available to the covered financial company;

(C) the operations of the covered financial company that could have had a significant impact on financial stability, markets, or both;

(D) identification of the banks and financial companies which may be able to provide the services offered by the covered financial company;

(E) any potential international ramifications of resolution of the covered financial company under other applicable insolvency law;

(F) an estimate of the potential effect of the resolution of the covered financial

(4)根据本编采取行动对该金融公司的债权人、对手方、股东以及其他市场参与者的权利主张或权益产生的任何影响确属适当(在作出该判定时,应考虑该等行动将对美国金融体系的稳定产生的影响);

(5)根据第204条采取的任何行动将避免或减轻前述不利影响(作出该判定时,应考虑如下因素:该行动对减轻该金融公司将遭受的潜在不利影响的成效、财政部普通基金将负担的成本以及该金融公司的债权人、对手方和股东过度的涉险情况恶化的可能性);

(6)联邦监管机关已命令该金融公司将其受制于监管命令的全部可转换债务工具进行转化;且

(7)该公司符合第201条对金融公司的定义。

(c)**文件编制和审查**。——

(1)**一般规定**。——财政部部长应——

(A)将第(b)子条所述任何判定形成书面文件;

(B)根据第(2)款规定保留该等文件以备接受审查;及

(C)通知所涉金融公司和联邦存款保险公司上述判定。

(2)**向国会提交报告**。——财政部部长在将联邦存款保险公司指定为所涉金融公司的接管人后24小时内,应书面通知参议院多数党领袖、参议院少数党领袖、众议院议长、众议院少数党领袖、参议院银行、住房与城市事务委员会以及众议院金融服务委员会其根据第(a)子条和第(b)子条作出的建议和判定,该通知应概要说明作出上述判定的依据,包括在作出判定时可以获得的如下信息——

(A)该所涉金融公司的规模和财务状况;

(B)该所涉金融公司可获得的资本和信贷支持的来源;

(C)可能已对金融稳定和/或市场造成重大影响的该所涉金融公司的运营情况;

(D)识别可能有能力提供该所涉金融公司要约的服务的具体银行或金融公司;

(E)因根据其他适用的资不抵债法对该所涉金融公司进行清盘而可能产生的任何国际影响;

(F)该所涉金融公司根据其他适用的资不抵债法接受清盘将对美国金融稳定造

company under other applicable insolvency law on the financial stability of the United States;

(G) the potential effect of the appointment of a receiver by the Secretary on consumers;

(H) the potential effect of the appointment of a receiver by the Secretary on the financial system, financial markets, and banks and other financial companies; and

(I) whether resolution of the covered financial company under other applicable insolvency law would cause banks or other financial companies to experience severe liquidity distress.

(3) REPORTS TO CONGRESS AND THE PUBLIC. —

(A) IN GENERAL. — Not later than 60 days after the date of appointment of the Corporation as receiver for a covered financial company, the Corporation shall file a report with the Committee on Banking, Housing, and Urban Affairs of the Senate and the Committee on Financial Services of the House of Representatives —

(i) setting forth information on the financial condition of the covered financial company as of the date of the appointment, including a description of its assets and liabilities;

(ii) describing the plan of, and actions taken by, the Corporation to wind down the covered financial company;

(iii) explaining each instance in which the Corporation waived any applicable requirements of part 366 of title 12, Code of Federal Regulations (or any successor thereto) with respect to conflicts of interest by any person in the private sector who was retained to provide services to the Corporation in connection with such receivership;

(iv) describing the reasons for the provision of any funding to the receivership out of the Fund;

(v) setting forth the expected costs of the orderly liquidation of the covered financial company;

(vi) setting forth the identity of any claimant that is treated in a manner different from other similarly situated claimants under subsection (b)(4), (d)(4), or (h)(5)(E), the amount of any additional payment to such claimant under subsection (d)(4), and the reason for any such action; and

(vii) which report the Corporation shall publish on an online website maintained by the Corporation, subject to maintaining appropriate confidentiality.

(B) AMENDMENTS. — The Corporation shall, on a timely basis, not less frequently than quarterly, amend or revise and resubmit the reports prepared under this paragraph, as necessary.

(C) CONGRESSIONAL TESTIMONY. — The Corporation and the primary financial

成的潜在影响之预估;

(G)财政部部长指定接管人之事实对消费者的潜在影响;

(H)财政部部长指定接管人之事实对金融体系、金融市场、银行和其他金融公司的潜在影响;及

(I)该所涉金融公司根据其他适用的资不抵债法接受清盘是否将导致银行或其他金融公司遭遇严重的流动性危机。

(3)**向国会和公众提供报告**。——

(A)**一般规定**。——联邦存款保险公司应在其被指定为所涉金融公司接管人后60天内,向参议院银行、住房与城市事务委员会和众议院金融服务委员会提交一份报告,该报告应——

(i)列明该所涉金融公司在上述指定日的财务状况信息,包括对其资产和负债的说明;

(ii)说明联邦存款保险公司对该所涉金融公司进行停业清理的计划,以及联邦存款保险公司就此采取的行动;

(iii)如果任何私人部门任何主体在受聘向联邦存款保险公司提供接管相关服务时,联邦存款保险公司放弃了《联邦规章汇编》第十二编第366部分(或其任何后续规定)任何关于利益冲突的规定之适用,则应对每一该等情况进行解释说明;

(iv)详细说明向接管人提供有序清算基金以外的任何资金的原因;

(v)列明对所涉金融公司进行有序清算的预期成本;

(vi)如果对任何权利主张人的处理方式不同于第(b)(4)子条、第(d)(4)子条或第(h)(5)(E)子条规定的情形类似的其他权利主张人的处理方式,则应列明该等权利主张人的身份信息,并说明根据第(d)(4)子条向该等权利主张人所作出的任何额外支付以及作出任何额外支付的原因;及

(vii)联邦存款保险公司在保持适当机密性的前提下,应在其网站上公布该报告。

(B)**修正**。——联邦存款保险公司应及时(至少应每季度)对根据本款制作的报告进行必要的修正或修订,并重新提交该报告。

(C)**向国会作证**。——如果国会提出要求,联邦存款保险公司以及联邦存款保险

regulatory agency, if any, of the financial company for which the Corporation was appointed receiver under this title shall appear before Congress, if requested, not later than 30 days after the date on which the Corporation first files the reports required under subparagraph (A).

(4) DEFAULT OR IN DANGER OF DEFAULT. — For purposes of this title, a financial company shall be considered to be in default or in danger of default if, as determined in accordance with subsection (b) —

(A) a case has been, or likely will promptly be, commenced with respect to the financial company under the Bankruptcy Code;

(B) the financial company has incurred, or is likely to incur, losses that will deplete all or substantially all of its capital, and there is no reasonable prospect for the company to avoid such depletion;

(C) the assets of the financial company are, or are likely to be, less than its obligations to creditors and others; or

(D) the financial company is, or is likely to be, unable to pay its obligations (other than those subject to a bona fide dispute) in the normal course of business.

(5) GAO REVIEW. — The Comptroller General of the United States shall review and report to Congress on any determination under subsection (b), that results in the appointment of the Corporation as receiver, including —

(A) the basis for the determination;

(B) the purpose for which any action was taken pursuant thereto;

(C) the likely effect of the determination and such action on the incentives and conduct of financial companies and their creditors, counterparties, and shareholders; and

(D) the likely disruptive effect of the determination and such action on the reasonable expectations of creditors, counterparties, and shareholders, taking into account the impact any action under this title would have on financial stability in the United States, including whether the rights of such parties will be disrupted.

(d) CORPORATION POLICIES AND PROCEDURES. — As soon as is practicable after the date of enactment of this Act, the Corporation shall establish policies and procedures that are acceptable to the Secretary governing the use of funds available to the Corporation to carry out this title, including the terms and conditions for the provision and use of funds under sections 204(d), 210(h)(2)(G)(iv), and 210(h)(9).

(e) TREATMENT OF INSURANCE COMPANIES AND INSURANCE COMPANY SUBSIDIARIES. —

(1) IN GENERAL. — Notwithstanding subsection (b), if an insurance company is a covered financial company or a subsidiary or affiliate of a covered financial company, the liquidation or rehabilitation of such insurance company, and any subsidiary or affiliate of

公司根据本编规定作为接管人接管的金融公司的优先金融监管机关(如有),应在联邦存款保险公司根据第(A)子款规定首次提交报告后30天内出席国会听证会。

(4)**违约或有违约之虞**。——就本编而言,金融公司根据第(b)子条被判定存在以下情形的,即应视为处于违约状态或有违约之虞——

(A)已经根据《破产法》针对该金融公司启动案件或有可能很快启动该案件;

(B)该金融公司已经遭受或可能遭受将耗尽或基本耗尽其资本的损失,且据合理预期,无法避免上述情况发生;

(C)该金融公司的资产不足以或很可能不足以履行其应向债权人或其他人承担的义务;或

(D)该金融公司不具有或很可能丧失在其正常业务运作过程中偿付其债务(但存在善意争议的债务除外)的能力。

(5)**政府问责办公室的审查**。——政府问责办公室主任应对根据第(b)子条作出的并导致联邦存款保险公司被指定为接管人的任何判定进行审查,并向国会提交报告。该报告内容应包括——

(A)判定的依据;

(B)根据该子条采取的任何行动之目的;

(C)该判定和行动可能对金融公司及其债权人、对手方和股东的积极性和行为造成的潜在影响;及

(D)该判定和行动将会对债权人、对手方和股东的合理预期造成的潜在扰乱性影响(此时应考虑根据本编规定采取的任何行动可能对美国金融稳定产生的影响,包括债权人、对手方和股东的权利是否会因此遭到扰乱)。

(d)**联邦存款保险公司的政策和程序**。——联邦存款保险公司应在本法颁布之日后,尽快制定获得财政部部长认可的政策和程序,对其可用以实施本编规定的资金之使用作出规定,包括对根据第204(d)条、第210(h)(2)(G)(iv)条和第210(h)(9)条提供并使用资金的条款和条件作出规定。

(e)**对保险公司和保险公司子公司的处理**。——

(1)**一般规定**。——无论第(b)子条如何规定,如果保险公司是一家所涉金融公司,或一家所涉金融公司的子公司或关联方,则针对该保险公司及其未被第(2)款排除的任何子公司或关联方的清算或整顿程序应根据适用的州法律执行。

such company that is not excepted under paragraph (2), shall be conducted as provided under applicable State law.

(2) EXCEPTION FOR SUBSIDIARIES AND AFFILIATES. — The requirement of paragraph (1) shall not apply with respect to any subsidiary or affiliate of an insurance company that is not itself an insurance company.

(3) BACKUP AUTHORITY. — Notwithstanding paragraph (1), with respect to a covered financial company described in paragraph (1), if, after the end of the 60–day period beginning on the date on which a determination is made under section 202(a) with respect to such company, the appropriate regulatory agency has not filed the appropriate judicial action in the appropriate State court to place such company into orderly liquidation under the laws and requirements of the State, the Corporation shall have the authority to stand in the place of the appropriate regulatory agency and file the appropriate judicial action in the appropriate State court to place such company into orderly liquidation under the laws and requirements of the State.

SEC. 204. ORDERLY LIQUIDATION OF COVERED FINANCIAL COMPANIES.

(a) PURPOSE OF ORDERLY LIQUIDATION AUTHORITY. — It is the purpose of this title to provide the necessary authority to liquidate failing financial companies that pose a significant risk to the financial stability of the United States in a manner that mitigates such risk and minimizes moral hazard. The authority provided in this title shall be exercised in the manner that best fulfills such purpose, so that —

(1) creditors and shareholders will bear the losses of the financial company;

(2) management responsible for the condition of the financial company will not be retained; and

(3) the Corporation and other appropriate agencies will take all steps necessary and appropriate to assure that all parties, including management, directors, and third parties, having responsibility for the condition of the financial company bear losses consistent with their responsibility, including actions for damages, restitution, and recoupment of compensation and other gains not compatible with such responsibility.

(b) CORPORATION AS RECEIVER. — Upon the appointment of the Corporation under section 202, the Corporation shall act as the receiver for the covered financial company, with all of the rights and obligations set forth in this title.

(c) CONSULTATION. — The Corporation, as receiver —

(1) shall consult with the primary financial regulatory agency or agencies of the covered financial company and its covered subsidiaries for purposes of ensuring an orderly liquidation of the covered financial company;

(2) may consult with, or under subsection (a)(1)(B)(v) or (a)(1)(L) of section

(2)**被排除的子公司和关联方**。——保险公司的任何子公司或关联方本身并非保险公司的,则就该子公司或关联方而言,第(1)款的规定不具有适用性。

(3)**后备权力**。——无论第(1)款如何规定,就该款所述所涉金融公司而言,如果按照第202(a)条规定针对该公司作出判定届满60天之后,相应的监管机关仍未向相应的州法院提起旨在按照该州法律及要求对该公司进行有序清算的适当司法行动,则联邦存款保险公司有权代替该相应的监管机关向相应的州法院提起适当的司法行动,按照该州法律及要求对该公司进行有序清算。

第204条　所涉金融公司的有序清算

(a)**有序清算权的目的**。——本编的目的在于提供必要的权力,就对美国金融稳定构成重大风险的经营失败的金融公司进行清算,并确保清算能够以缓释该等风险并将道德风险减到最低限度的方式进行。本编规定的权力应以能够最大限度地实现上述目的之方式行使,以确保——

(1)债权人和股东承担该金融公司的损失;

(2)对该金融公司状况负有责任的管理层被免职;及

(3)联邦存款保险公司和其他相应的监管机关采取全部必要且适当的行动,以确保对该金融公司状况负有责任的各方(包括管理层、董事和第三方)按照其各自的责任承担相应损失,包括提起损害赔偿诉讼、不当得利返还诉讼以及索回其在承担上述责任的情况下无权获得的薪酬和其他收益的诉讼。

(b)**联邦存款保险公司的接管人身份**。——联邦存款保险公司根据第202条接受指定后,即应以所涉金融公司接管人的身份行事,并具有本编规定的全部权利和义务。

(c)**磋商**。——联邦存款保险公司作为接管人——

(1)应与所涉金融公司及其所涉子公司的1个或1个以上优先金融监管机关进行磋商,以确保完成对该所涉金融公司的有序清算;

(2)可以在有序清算过程中与任何相应的外部专家磋商,根据第210条第(a)(1)

210, acquire the services of, any outside experts, as appropriate to inform and aid the Corporation in the orderly liquidation process;

(3) shall consult with the primary financial regulatory agency or agencies of any subsidiaries of the covered financial company that are not covered subsidiaries, and coordinate with such regulators regarding the treatment of such solvent subsidiaries and the separate resolution of any such insolvent subsidiaries under other governmental authority, as appropriate; and

(4) shall consult with the Commission and the Securities Investor Protection Corporation in the case of any covered financial company for which the Corporation has been appointed as receiver that is a broker or dealer registered with the Commission under section 15(b) of the Securities Exchange Act of 1934 (15 U.S.C. 78o(b)) and is a member of the Securities Investor Protection Corporation, for the purpose of determining whether to transfer to a bridge financial company organized by the Corporation as receiver, without consent of any customer, customer accounts of the covered financial company.

(d) FUNDING FOR ORDERLY LIQUIDATION. — Upon its appointment as receiver for a covered financial company, and thereafter as the Corporation may, in its discretion, determine to be necessary or appropriate, the Corporation may make available to the receivership, subject to the conditions set forth in section 206 and subject to the plan described in section 210(n)(9), funds for the orderly liquidation of the covered financial company. All funds provided by the Corporation under this subsection shall have a priority of claims under subparagraph (A) or (B) of section 210(b)(1), as applicable, including funds used for —

(1) making loans to, or purchasing any debt obligation of, the covered financial company or any covered subsidiary;

(2) purchasing or guaranteeing against loss the assets of the covered financial company or any covered subsidiary, directly or through an entity established by the Corporation for such purpose;

(3) assuming or guaranteeing the obligations of the covered financial company or any covered subsidiary to 1 or more third parties;

(4) taking a lien on any or all assets of the covered financial company or any covered subsidiary, including a first priority lien on all unencumbered assets of the covered financial company or any covered subsidiary to secure repayment of any transactions conducted under this subsection;

(5) selling or transferring all, or any part, of such acquired assets, liabilities, or obligations of the covered financial company or any covered subsidiary; and

(6) making payments pursuant to subsections (b)(4), (d)(4), and (h)(5)(E) of

(B)(v)子条或第(a)(1)(L)子条获取相应的任何外部专家提供的服务,以便获得相关信息和协助;

(3)应与所涉金融公司的所涉子公司之外的任何子公司的1个或1个以上优先金融监管机关进行磋商,并与该等监管者就未丧失偿债能力的子公司的处理进行适当协调,并对受其他政府部门管辖的无偿债能力的任何子公司进行单独清盘;且

(4)如果联邦存款保险公司作为接管人接管的任何所涉金融公司是一家根据《1934年证券交易法》第15(b)条[《美国法典》第十五编第78o(b)节]在证券交易委员会注册的经纪商或自营商,并且身为证券投资者保护公司的会员,则联邦存款保险公司应与证券交易委员会和证券投资者保护公司进行磋商,以判定是否将该所涉金融公司的客户账户转让给联邦存款保险公司作为接管人组建的过渡金融公司,而不必征得任何客户同意。

(d)**有序清算经费来源**。——联邦存款保险公司在其被指定为所涉金融公司接管人之时以及依其自由裁量权判定确属必要或适当的其他较晚时间,可以在不违反第206条所述条件的前提下并根据第201(n)(9)条所述计划,为所涉金融公司的有序清算提供接管资金。联邦存款保险公司根据本子条提供的全部资金均应按照第210(b)(1)条第(A)子款或第(B)子款(视具体情况而定)规定的权利主张的优先顺序使用,包括将其用于——

(1)向所涉金融公司或任何所涉子公司提供贷款,或者购买其任何债务;

(2)直接购买所涉金融公司或任何所涉子公司的资产或为该等资产提供损失担保,或者通过联邦存款保险公司为上述目的成立的实体购买该等资产或提供该等担保;

(3)承担或担保所涉金融公司或任何所涉子公司对1个或1个以上第三方负担的义务;

(4)在所涉金融公司或任何所涉子公司的任何或全部资产上设置留置权,包括在所涉金融公司或任何所涉子公司全部的无权利负担的资产上设置第一优先留置权,以确保根据本子条执行的任何交易可获偿付;

(5)出售或转让通过以上方式取得的所涉金融公司或任何所涉子公司的全部或部分资产、负债或义务;及

(6)根据第210条第(b)(4)子条、第(d)(4)子条和第(h)(5)(E)子条作出支付。

section 210.

SEC. 205. ORDERLY LIQUIDATION OF COVERED BROKERS AND DEALERS.

(a) APPOINTMENT OF SIPC AS TRUSTEE. —

(1) APPOINTMENT. — Upon the appointment of the Corporation as receiver for any covered broker or dealer, the Corporation shall appoint, without any need for court approval, the Securities Investor Protection Corporation to act as trustee for the liquidation under the Securities Investor Protection Act of 1970 (15 U.S.C. 78aaa et seq.) of the covered broker or dealer.

(2) ACTIONS BY SIPC. —

(A) FILING. — Upon appointment of SIPC under paragraph (1), SIPC shall promptly file with any Federal district court of competent jurisdiction specified in section 21 or 27 of the Securities Exchange Act of 1934 (15 U.S.C. 78u, 78aa), an application for a protective decree under the Securities Investor Protection Act of 1970 (15 U.S.C. 78aaa et seq.) as to the covered broker or dealer. The Federal district court shall accept and approve the filing, including outside of normal business hours, and shall immediately issue the protective decree as to the covered broker or dealer.

(B) ADMINISTRATION BY SIPC. — Following entry of the protective decree, and except as otherwise provided in this section, the determination of claims and the liquidation of assets retained in the receivership of the covered broker or dealer and not transferred to the bridge financial company shall be administered under the Securities Investor Protection Act of 1970 (15 U.S.C. 78aaa et seq.) by SIPC, as trustee for the covered broker or dealer.

(C) DEFINITION OF FILING DATE. — For purposes of the liquidation proceeding, the term "filing date" means the date on which the Corporation is appointed as receiver of the covered broker or dealer.

(D) DETERMINATION OF CLAIMS. — As trustee for the covered broker or dealer, SIPC shall determine and satisfy, consistent with this title and with the Securities Investor Protection Act of 1970 (15 U.S.C. 78aaa et seq.), all claims against the covered broker or dealer arising on or before the filing date.

(b) POWERS AND DUTIES OF SIPC. —

(1) IN GENERAL. — Except as provided in this section, upon its appointment as trustee for the liquidation of a covered broker or dealer, SIPC shall have all of the powers and duties provided by the Securities Investor Protection Act of 1970 (15 U.S.C. 78aaa et seq.), including, without limitation, all rights of action against third parties, and shall conduct such liquidation in accordance with the terms of the Securities Investor Protection Act of 1970 (15 U.S.C. 78aaa et seq.), except that SIPC shall have no powers or duties

第205条　所涉经纪商和自营商的有序清算

(a)**将证券投资者保护公司指定为清算受托人**。——

(1)**指定**。——联邦存款保险公司在被指定为任何所涉经纪商或自营商的接管人后,即应根据《1970年证券投资者保护法》(《美国法典》第十五编第78aaa节及其后条文)将证券投资者保护公司指定为所涉经纪商或自营商的清算受托人,而不必取得法院批准。

(2)**证券投资者保护公司采取的行动**。——

(A)**提交申请**。——证券投资者保护公司根据第(1)款接受指定后,应及时根据《1970年证券投资者保护法》(《美国法典》第十五编第78aaa节及其后条文),向《1934年证券交易法》第21条或第27条(《美国法典》第十五编第78u节或第78aa节)规定的具有管辖权的任何联邦地区法院,针对该所涉经纪商或自营商提交保护令申请。该联邦地区法院应受理并批准该申请(包括在正常工作时间以外的时间进行受理和批准),并立即就该所涉经纪商或自营商签发保护令。

(B)**证券投资者保护公司实施的管理**。——除本条另有规定的情形外,证券投资者保护公司在法院发出该保护令之后,应根据《1970年证券投资者保护法》(《美国法典》第十五编第78aaa节及其后条文)对权利主张的判定进行管理,并对其以清算受托人身份保留且未转让给过渡金融公司的所涉经纪商和自营商的资产清算进行管理。

(C)**破产申请日的定义**。——就清算程序而言,"破产申请日"一词系指联邦存款保险公司被指定为所涉经纪商或自营商接管人之日。

(D)**权利主张的判定**。——证券投资者保护公司作为所涉经纪商或自营商的清算受托人,应根据本编以及《1970年证券投资者保护法》(《美国法典》第十五编第78aaa节及其后条文),对破产申请日或之前产生的针对该所涉经纪商或自营商的全部权利主张进行判定和清偿。

(b)**证券投资者保护公司的权力和职责**。——

(1)**一般规定**。——除本条规定的情形外,证券投资者保护公司在被指定为所涉经纪商或自营商清算受托人之后,应具有《1970年证券投资者保护法》(《美国法典》第十五编第78aaa节及其后条文)规定的全部权力和职责,包括但不限于针对第三方采取行动的全部权利,并应根据该法的规定实施清算,但是,就联邦存款保险公司从所涉经纪商或自营商转让至根据本编成立的任何过渡金融公司之资产和负债而言,证券投资者保护公司不具有任何权力和职责。

with respect to assets and liabilities transferred by the Corporation from the covered broker or dealer to any bridge financial company established in accordance with this title.

(2) LIMITATION OF POWERS. — The exercise by SIPC of powers and functions as trustee under subsection (a) shall not impair or impede the exercise of the powers and duties of the Corporation with regard to —

(A) any action, except as otherwise provided in this title —

(i) to make funds available under section 204(d);

(ii) to organize, establish, operate, or terminate any bridge financial company;

(iii) to transfer assets and liabilities;

(iv) to enforce or repudiate contracts; or

(v) to take any other action relating to such bridge financial company under section 210; or

(B) determining claims under subsection (e).

(3) PROTECTIVE DECREE. — SIPC and the Corporation, in consultation with the Commission, shall jointly determine the terms of the protective decree to be filed by SIPC with any court of competent jurisdiction under section 21 or 27 of the Securities Exchange Act of 1934 (15 U.S.C. 78u, 78aa), as required by subsection (a).

(4) QUALIFIED FINANCIAL CONTRACTS. — Notwithstanding any provision of the Securities Investor Protection Act of 1970 (15 U.S.C. 78aaa et seq.) to the contrary (including section 5(b)(2)(C) of that Act (15 U.S.C. 78eee(b)(2)(C))), the rights and obligations of any party to a qualified financial contract (as that term is defined in section 210 (c)(8)) to which a covered broker or dealer for which the Corporation has been appointed receiver is a party shall be governed exclusively by section 210, including the limitations and restrictions contained in section 210(c)(10)(B).

(c) LIMITATION ON COURT ACTION. — Except as otherwise provided in this title, no court may take any action, including any action pursuant to the Securities Investor Protection Act of 1970 (15 U.S.C. 78aaa et seq.) or the Bankruptcy Code, to restrain or affect the exercise of powers or functions of the Corporation as receiver for a covered broker or dealer and any claims against the Corporation as such receiver shall be determined in accordance with subsection (e) and such claims shall be limited to money damages.

(d) ACTIONS BY CORPORATION AS RECEIVER. —

(1) IN GENERAL. — Notwithstanding any other provision of this title, no action taken by the Corporation as receiver with respect to a covered broker or dealer shall —

(A) adversely affect the rights of a customer to customer property or customer name securities;

(B) diminish the amount or timely payment of net equity claims of customers; or

(2)**权力限制**。——证券投资者保护公司在根据第(a)子条作为清算受托人行使相关权力和履行相关职责时，既不得损害也不得阻碍联邦存款保险公司针对以下事项行使权力和履行职责——

(A)为如下目的采取的任何行动(除本编另有规定的情形外)——

(i)根据第204(d)条提供资金；

(ii)组建、成立、运营或终止任何过渡金融公司；

(iii)转让资产和负债；

(iv)强制执行或拒绝履行合同;或

(v)根据第210条采取与该等过渡金融公司相关的任何其他行动;或者

(B)根据第(e)子条对权利主张进行判定。

(3)**保护令**。——证券投资者保护公司和联邦存款保险公司应在与证券交易委员会磋商后,共同按照第(a)子条的要求确定保护令条款,该保护令系由证券投资者保护公司向《1934年证券交易法》第21条或第27条(《美国法典》第十五编第78u节或第78aa节)规定的有管辖权的任何法院提交的保护令。

(4)**合格金融合约**。——无论《1970年证券投资者保护法》(《美国法典》第十五编第78aaa节及其后条文)是否存在任何相反规定{包括该法第5(b)(2)(C)条[《美国法典》第十五编第78eee(b)(2)(C)节]},对于联邦存款保险公司作为接管人接管的所涉经纪商或自营商签订的合格金融合约[定义见第210(c)(8)条]而言,任何合约方的权利和义务应仅受第210条[包括第210(c)(10)(B)条所述限制和约束条件]规制。

(c)**法院行动限制**。——除本编另有规定的情形外,任何法院均无权采取任何行动约束或影响联邦存款保险公司作为所涉经纪商或自营商的接管人行使其权力或履行其职能[包括无权为该等目的根据《1970年证券投资者保护法》(《美国法典》第十五编第78aaa节及其后条文)或《破产法》采取行动];且向作为所涉经纪商或自营商的接管人的联邦存款保险公司提起的任何权利主张均应根据第(e)子条进行判定,并且该等权利主张应仅限于金钱损害赔偿。

(d)**联邦存款保险公司作为接管人采取的行动**。——

(1)**一般规定**。——无论本编是否存在任何其他规定,联邦存款保险公司作为接管人针对所涉经纪商或自营商采取的任何行动,均不得——

(A)客户对客户财产的权利或对客户名下证券的权利造成不利影响;

(B)减损客户的所有者权利主张净额,或影响该等所有者权利主张的及时支付;或

(C) otherwise impair the recoveries provided to a customer under the Securities Investor Protection Act of 1970 (15 U.S.C. 78aaa et seq.).

(2) NET PROCEEDS. — The net proceeds from any transfer, sale, or disposition of assets of the covered broker or dealer, or proceeds thereof by the Corporation as receiver for the covered broker or dealer shall be for the benefit of the estate of the covered broker or dealer, as provided in this title.

(e) CLAIMS AGAINST THE CORPORATION AS RECEIVER. — Any claim against the Corporation as receiver for a covered broker or dealer for assets transferred to a bridge financial company established with respect to such covered broker or dealer —

(1) shall be determined in accordance with section 210(a)(2); and

(2) may be reviewed by the appropriate district or territorial court of the United States in accordance with section 210(a)(5).

(f) SATISFACTION OF CUSTOMER CLAIMS. —

(1) OBLIGATIONS TO CUSTOMERS. — Notwithstanding any other provision of this title, all obligations of a covered broker or dealer or of any bridge financial company established with respect to such covered broker or dealer to a customer relating to, or net equity claims based upon, customer property or customer name securities shall be promptly discharged by SIPC, the Corporation, or the bridge financial company, as applicable, by the delivery of securities or the making of payments to or for the account of such customer, in a manner and in an amount at least as beneficial to the customer as would have been the case had the actual proceeds realized from the liquidation of the covered broker or dealer under this title been distributed in a proceeding under the Securities Investor Protection Act of 1970 (15 U.S.C. 78aaa et seq.) without the appointment of the Corporation as receiver and without any transfer of assets or liabilities to a bridge financial company, and with a filing date as of the date on which the Corporation is appointed as receiver.

(2) SATISFACTION OF CLAIMS BY SIPC. — SIPC, as trustee for a covered broker or dealer, shall satisfy customer claims in the manner and amount provided under the Securities Investor Protection Act of 1970 (15 U.S.C. 78aaa et seq.), as if the appointment of the Corporation as receiver had not occurred, and with a filing date as of the date on which the Corporation is appointed as receiver. The Corporation shall satisfy customer claims, to the extent that a customer would have received more securities or cash with respect to the allocation of customer property had the covered financial company been subject to a proceeding under the Securities Investor Protection Act (15 U.S.C. 78aaa et seq.) without the appointment of the Corporation as receiver, and with a filing date as of the date on which the Corporation is appointed as receiver.

(g) PRIORITIES. —

(C)以其他方式损害客户根据《1970年证券投资者保护法》(《美国法典》第十五编第78aaa节及其后条文)有权获得的补偿款项。

(2)**所获资金净额**。——所涉经纪商或自营商资产的任何转让、出售或处置的所获资金净额,或者联邦存款保险公司作为所涉经纪商或自营商接管人进行该等转让、出售或处置所获资金净额,应当根据本编规定记入该所涉经纪商或自营商的破产财团。

(e)**向作为接管人的联邦存款保险公司提起的权利主张**。——因转让给就所涉经纪商或自营商设立的过渡金融公司的资产,而向作为该所涉经纪商或自营商接管人的联邦存款保险公司提出的任何权利主张——

(1)应根据第210(a)(2)条的规定进行判定;且

(2)可由相应的联邦地区法院或准州法院根据第210(a)(5)条的规定进行审查。

(f)**客户权利主张的清偿**。——

(1)**向客户承担的义务**。——无论本编是否存在任何不同规定,所涉经纪商或自营商或就该所涉经纪商或自营商设立的任何过渡金融公司应向某一客户承担的与客户财产或客户名下证券相关的义务,或者基于客户财产或客户名下证券而享有的所有者权利主张净额,均应由证券投资者保护公司、联邦存款保险公司或该过渡金融公司(视具体情况而定)通过向该客户账户交付证券或作出支付的方式及时清偿,清偿的方式和金额至少应确保客户获得的利益不低于在如下条件下本可获得的利益:联邦存款保险公司未被指定为接管人,且任何资产或负债均未转让给过渡金融公司,且对所涉经纪商或自营商按照本编进行清算实现的实际所得已按照《1970年证券投资者保护法》(《美国法典》第十五编第78aaa节及其后条文)规定的程序完成了分配,并且破产申请日为联邦存款保险公司被指定为接管人之日。

(2)**证券投资者保护公司对权利主张的清偿**。——证券投资者保护公司作为所涉经纪商或自营商的清算受托人,应以《1970年证券投资者保护法》(《美国法典》第十五编第78aaa节及其后条文)规定的方式和金额清偿客户权利主张,如同联邦存款保险公司未被指定为接管人,且破产申请日为联邦存款保险公司被指定为接管人之日。如果联邦存款保险公司未被指定为接管人且破产申请日为联邦存款保险公司被指定为接管人之日,并且在所涉金融公司按照《证券投资者保护法》(《美国法典》第十五编第78aaa节及其后条文)规定的程序被处理的情况下某一客户在分配客户财产时将获得更多的证券或现金,则联邦存款保险公司应对客户在上述情况下本可享有的权利主张进行清偿。

(g)**财产**。——

(1) CUSTOMER PROPERTY. — As trustee for a covered broker or dealer, SIPC shall allocate customer property and deliver customer name securities in accordance with section 8(c) of the Securities Investor Protection Act of 1970 (15 U.S.C. 78fff-2(c)).

(2) OTHER CLAIMS. — All claims other than those described in paragraph (1) (including any unpaid claim by a customer for the allowed net equity claim of such customer from customer property) shall be paid in accordance with the priorities in section 210(b).

(h) RULEMAKING. — The Commission and the Corporation, after consultation with SIPC, shall jointly issue rules to implement this section.

SEC. 206. MANDATORY TERMS AND CONDITIONS FOR ALL ORDERLY LIQUIDATION ACTIONS.

In taking action under this title, the Corporation shall —

(1) determine that such action is necessary for purposes of the financial stability of the United States, and not for the purpose of preserving the covered financial company;

(2) ensure that the shareholders of a covered financial company do not receive payment until after all other claims and the Fund are fully paid;

(3) ensure that unsecured creditors bear losses in accordance with the priority of claim provisions in section 210;

(4) ensure that management responsible for the failed condition of the covered financial company is removed (if such management has not already been removed at the time at which the Corporation is appointed receiver);

(5) ensure that the members of the board of directors (or body performing similar functions) responsible for the failed condition of the covered financial company are removed, if such members have not already been removed at the time the Corporation is appointed as receiver; and

(6) not take an equity interest in or become a shareholder of any covered financial company or any covered subsidiary.

SEC. 207. DIRECTORS NOT LIABLE FOR ACQUIESCING IN APPOINTMENT OF RECEIVER.

The members of the board of directors (or body performing similar functions) of a covered financial company shall not be liable to the shareholders or creditors thereof for acquiescing in or consenting in good faith to the appointment of the Corporation as receiver for the covered financial company under section 203.

SEC. 208. DISMISSAL AND EXCLUSION OF OTHER ACTIONS.

(a) IN GENERAL. — Effective as of the date of the appointment of the Corporation as receiver for the covered financial company under section 202 or the appointment of SIPC as trustee for a covered broker or dealer under section 205, as applicable, any case

(1)**客户财产**。——证券投资者保护公司作为所涉经纪商或自营商的清算受托人,应根据《1970年证券投资者保护法》第8(c)条[《美国法典》第十五编第78fff—2(c)节]的规定分配客户财产并交付客户名下证券。

(2)**其他权利主张**。——除第(1)款所述权利主张之外的所有其他权利主张(包括任何客户已获认可但尚未清偿的,要求通过客户财产清偿的所有者权利主张净额),均应根据第210(b)条规定的优先顺序清偿。

(h)**规则制定**。——证券交易委员会和联邦存款保险公司应在与证券投资者保护公司磋商后,联合发布本条的细则。

第206条　统一适用于所有有序清算行动的强制性条款和条件

联邦存款保险公司根据本编采取行动时,应——

(1) 判定该行动对维护美国金融体系稳定性确属必要且其并非以维持所涉金融公司为目的;

(2)确保在所有其他权利主张和有序清算基金均获全额清偿之前,所涉金融公司的股东不会收到任何支付;

(3)确保无担保债权人根据第210条规定的权利主张的先后顺序承担损失;

(4)对所涉金融公司经营失败状况负有责任的管理人员,在联邦存款保险公司被指定为接管人之时尚未被免职的,确保其被免职;

(5)对所涉金融公司经营失败状况负有责任的董事会(或履行类似职能的其他机构)成员,在联邦存款保险公司被指定为接管人之时尚未被免职的,确保其被免职;且

(6)不得获取任何所涉金融公司或任何所涉子公司的股权权益,或者成为任何所涉金融公司或任何所涉子公司的股东。

第207条　董事不就默许接管人的指定承担任何责任

所涉金融公司的董事会(或履行类似职能的其他机构)成员根据第203条规定善意默许或同意将联邦存款保险公司指定为该所涉金融公司接管人的,该等成员不必就此向该所涉金融公司的股东或债权人承担任何责任。

第208条　其他诉讼的驳回与排除

(a)**一般规定**。——通知破产法院(对于根据《破产法》启动的案件而言)联邦存款保险公司根据第202条规定被指定为所涉金融公司接管人后,或通知证券投资者保护公司(对于所涉经纪商或自营商而言)证券投资者保护公司根据第205条规定被指定

or proceeding commenced with respect to the covered financial company under the Bankruptcy Code or the Securities Investor Protection Act of 1970 (15 U.S.C. 78aaa et seq.) shall be dismissed, upon notice to the bankruptcy court (with respect to a case commenced under the Bankruptcy Code), and upon notice to SIPC (with respect to a covered broker or dealer) and no such case or proceeding may be commenced with respect to a covered financial company at any time while the orderly liquidation is pending.

(b) REVESTING OF ASSETS. — Effective as of the date of appointment of the Corporation as receiver, the assets of a covered financial company shall, to the extent they have vested in any entity other than the covered financial company as a result of any case or proceeding commenced with respect to the covered financial company under the Bankruptcy Code, the Securities Investor Protection Act of 1970 (15 U.S.C. 78aaa et seq.), or any similar provision of State liquidation or insolvency law applicable to the covered financial company, revest in the covered financial company.

(c) LIMITATION. — Notwithstanding subsections (a) and (b), any order entered or other relief granted by a bankruptcy court prior to the date of appointment of the Corporation as receiver shall continue with the same validity as if an orderly liquidation had not been commenced.

SEC. 209. RULEMAKING; NON-CONFLICTING LAW.

The Corporation shall, in consultation with the Council, prescribe such rules or regulations as the Corporation considers necessary or appropriate to implement this title, including rules and regulations with respect to the rights, interests, and priorities of creditors, counterparties, security entitlement holders, or other persons with respect to any covered financial company or any assets or other property of or held by such covered financial company, and address the potential for conflicts of interest between or among individual receiverships established under this title or under the Federal Deposit Insurance Act. To the extent possible, the Corporation shall seek to harmonize applicable rules and regulations promulgated under this section with the insolvency laws that would otherwise apply to a covered financial company.

SEC. 210. POWERS AND DUTIES OF THE CORPORATION.

(a) POWERS AND AUTHORITIES. —

(1) GENERAL POWERS. —

(A) SUCCESSOR TO COVERED FINANCIAL COMPANY. — The Corporation shall, upon appointment as receiver for a covered financial company under this title, succeed to —

(i) all rights, titles, powers, and privileges of the covered financial company and its assets, and of any stockholder, member, officer, or director of such company; and

为所涉经纪商或自营商的清算受托人后,根据《破产法》或《1970年证券投资者保护法》(《美国法典》第十五编第78aaa节及其后条文)针对所涉金融公司启动的案件或程序即应驳回,并且,在有序清算结束之前不得针对所涉金融公司启动任何该等案件或程序;上述规定自联邦存款保险公司根据第202条规定被指定为所涉金融公司接管人之日起,或者自证券投资者保护公司根据第205条规定被指定为所涉经纪商或自营商清算受托人之日起(视具体情况而定)生效。

(b)**资产的重新占有**。——如果根据《破产法》、《1970年证券投资者保护法》(《美国法典》第十五编第78aaa节及其后条文),或者根据适用于该所涉金融公司的州清算法或资不抵债法的任何类似规定针对该所涉金融公司启动的任何案件或程序,导致该所涉金融公司的资产的占有权已归属于该所涉金融公司之外的任何其他实体,则自联邦存款保险公司被指定为接管人之日起,该等资产应由该所涉金融公司重新占有。

(c)**限制**。——无论第(a)子条和第(b)子条如何规定,在联邦存款保险公司被指定为接管人之日前破产法院已作出的任何命令或已授予的救济应继续保持原有效力,如同有序清算程序未曾启动。

第209条　规则制定;避免法律冲突

联邦存款保险公司应在与金融稳定监督委员会磋商后,制定其认为必要或者适当的规则或规章,以实施本编规定(包括针对债权人、对手方、法定担保权益持有人或其他人就任何所涉金融公司或者该所涉金融公司拥有或持有的任何资产或其他财产享有的权利、权益和优先权制定规则和规章),并解决根据本编或《联邦存款保险法》确立的各项接管之间的潜在利益冲突。联邦存款保险公司应尽可能使根据本条颁发的适用规则和规章与其他适用于所涉金融公司的资不抵债法相协调。

第210条　联邦存款保险公司的权力和职责

(a)**权力和权限**。——

(1)**一般权力**。——

(A)**所涉金融公司的继受人**。——联邦存款保险公司被指定为所涉金融公司的接管人后,应继受——

(i)所涉金融公司及其资产以及其任何股东、成员、管理人员或董事的全部权利、所有权、权力和特权;及

(ii) title to the books, records, and assets of any previous receiver or other legal custodian of such covered financial company.

(B) OPERATION OF THE COVERED FINANCIAL COMPANY DURING THE PERIOD OF ORDERLY LIQUIDATION. — The Corporation, as receiver for a covered financial company, may —

(i) take over the assets of and operate the covered financial company with all of the powers of the members or shareholders, the directors, and the officers of the covered financial company, and conduct all business of the covered financial company;

(ii) collect all obligations and money owed to the covered financial company;

(iii) perform all functions of the covered financial company, in the name of the covered financial company;

(iv) manage the assets and property of the covered financial company, consistent with maximization of the value of the assets in the context of the orderly liquidation; and

(v) provide by contract for assistance in fulfilling any function, activity, action, or duty of the Corporation as receiver.

(C) FUNCTIONS OF COVERED FINANCIAL COMPANY OFFICERS, DIRECTORS, AND SHAREHOLDERS. — The Corporation may provide for the exercise of any function by any member or stockholder, director, or officer of any covered financial company for which the Corporation has been appointed as receiver under this title.

(D) ADDITIONAL POWERS AS RECEIVER. — The Corporation shall, as receiver for a covered financial company, and subject to all legally enforceable and perfected security interests and all legally enforceable security entitlements in respect of assets held by the covered financial company, liquidate, and wind-up the affairs of a covered financial company, including taking steps to realize upon the assets of the covered financial company, in such manner as the Corporation deems appropriate, including through the sale of assets, the transfer of assets to a bridge financial company established under subsection (h), or the exercise of any other rights or privileges granted to the receiver under this section.

(E) ADDITIONAL POWERS WITH RESPECT TO FAILING SUBSIDIARIES OF A COVERED FINANCIAL COMPANY. —

(i) IN GENERAL. — In any case in which a receiver is appointed for a covered financial company under section 202, the Corporation may appoint itself as receiver of any covered subsidiary of the covered financial company that is organized under Federal law or the laws of any State, if the Corporation and the Secretary jointly determine that —

(I) the covered subsidiary is in default or in danger of default;

(II) such action would avoid or mitigate serious adverse effects on the financial stability or economic conditions of the United States; and

(ii)该所涉金融公司任何前任接管人或其他法定托管人对账簿、记录和资产的所有权。

(B)**所涉金融公司在有序清算期内的运营**。——联邦存款保险公司作为所涉金融公司的接管人,可以——

(i)接管该所涉金融公司的资产,运用其成员或股东、董事以及管理人员的全部权力运营该所涉金融公司,并开展该所涉金融公司的全部活动;

(ii)追收第三方欠付该所涉金融公司的全部债务和现金;

(iii)以该所涉金融公司的名义履行该所涉金融公司的所有职能;

(iv)在有序清算过程中以资产价值最大化原则管理该所涉金融公司的资产和财产;并

(v)订立合同,协助联邦存款保险公司作为接管人履行或开展任何职能、活动、行动或职责。

(C)**所涉金融公司的管理人员、董事和股东的职能**。——联邦存款保险公司根据本编规定被指定为任何所涉金融公司的接管人的,可以对该所涉金融公司任何成员或股东、董事或管理人员的任何职能的行使作出规定。

(D)**接管人的其他权力**。——所涉金融公司持有的资产上存在可依法强制执行且无瑕疵的担保权益以及可依法强制执行的法定担保权利的,联邦存款保险公司作为该所涉金融公司接管人应在上述全部权益和权利的制约下清算并了结所涉金融公司的事务,包括采取其认为适当的方式对所涉金融公司资产进行变现[变现方式包括通过出售资产、将资产转让给根据第(h)子条成立的过渡金融公司或通过行使本条规定授予接管人的任何其他权利或特权]。

(E)**对于所涉金融公司面临经营失败的子公司的其他权力**。——

(i)**一般规定**。——如果所涉金融公司根据第202条规定被指定了接管人,则联邦存款保险公司可将其自身指定为该所涉金融公司的依据联邦法律或任何州法律组建的任何所涉子公司之接管人,只要联邦存款保险公司和财政部部长共同作出如下判定——

(I)该所涉子公司处于违约状态或有违约之虞;

(II)该等指定将避免或减轻对美国金融稳定或经济状况的不利影响;及

(III) such action would facilitate the orderly liquidation of the covered financial company.

(ii) TREATMENT AS COVERED FINANCIAL COMPANY. — If the Corporation is appointed as receiver of a covered subsidiary of a covered financial company under clause (i), the covered subsidiary shall thereafter be considered a covered financial company under this title, and the Corporation shall thereafter have all the powers and rights with respect to that covered subsidiary as it has with respect to a covered financial company under this title.

(F) ORGANIZATION OF BRIDGE COMPANIES. — The Corporation, as receiver for a covered financial company, may organize a bridge financial company under subsection (h).

(G) MERGER; TRANSFER OF ASSETS AND LIABILITIES. —

(i) IN GENERAL. — Subject to clauses (ii) and (iii), the Corporation, as receiver for a covered financial company, may —

(I) merge the covered financial company with another company; or

(II) transfer any asset or liability of the covered financial company (including any assets and liabilities held by the covered financial company for security entitlement holders, any customer property, or any assets and liabilities associated with any trust or custody business) without obtaining any approval, assignment, or consent with respect to such transfer.

(ii) FEDERAL AGENCY APPROVAL; ANTITRUST REVIEW. — With respect to a transaction described in clause (i)(I) that requires approval by a Federal agency —

(I) the transaction may not be consummated before the 5th calendar day after the date of approval by the Federal agency responsible for such approval;

(II) if, in connection with any such approval, a report on competitive factors is required, the Federal agency responsible for such approval shall promptly notify the Attorney General of the United States of the proposed transaction, and the Attorney General shall provide the required report not later than 10 days after the date of the request; and

(III) if notification under section 7A of the Clayton Act is required with respect to such transaction, then the required waiting period shall end on the 15th day after the date on which the Attorney General and the Federal Trade Commission receive such notification, unless the waiting period is terminated earlier under subsection (b)(2) of such section 7A, or is extended pursuant to subsection (e)(2) of such section 7A.

(iii) SETOFF. — Subject to the other provisions of this title, any transferee of assets from a receiver, including a bridge financial company, shall be subject to such claims or rights as would prevail over the rights of such transferee in such assets under applicable

(Ⅲ)该等指定将促进上述所涉金融公司的有序清算。

(ii)**作为所涉金融公司处理**。——联邦存款保险公司根据第(i)项规定被指定为所涉金融公司的所涉子公司接管人后,该所涉子公司应视为本编规定的所涉金融公司,在上述指定作出后,联邦存款保险公司对该所涉子公司享有的全部权力和权利与其对本编规定的所涉金融公司享有的全部权力和权利相同。

(F)**过渡公司的组建**。——联邦存款保险公司作为所涉金融公司的接管人,可以按照第(h)子条的规定组建过渡金融公司。

(G)**兼并;资产和负债转让**。——

(i)**一般规定**。——在不违反第(ii)项和第(iii)项规定的前提下,联邦存款保险公司作为所涉金融公司的接管人,可以——

(Ⅰ)将所涉金融公司并入另一家公司;或

(Ⅱ)转让所涉金融公司的任何资产或负债(包括所涉金融公司为法定担保权利人持有的任何资产和负债、任何客户财产或者任何信托或托管业务的任何资产和负债),而不必取得任何转让批准、指定或同意。

(ii)**联邦机关批准;反垄断审查**。——就第(i)(Ⅰ)项所述应由某联邦机关批准的交易而言——

(Ⅰ)该交易合同订立的时间不得早于负责批准的联邦机关批准交易之日后第5个日历日;

(Ⅱ)如果按规定作出任何上述批准时应提供一份竞争要素报告,则负责批准的联邦机关应及时通知联邦总检察长该拟议交易,并且联邦总检察长应在收到申请后10天内提供上述报告;且

(Ⅲ)根据《克莱顿法》第7A条应提供交易通知的,则规定的等待期应于联邦总检察长和联邦贸易委员会收到该通知之日后第15天终止,除非该等待期根据《克莱顿法》第7A条第(b)(2)子条提前终止,或者根据该第7A条第(e)(2)子条被延长。

(iii)**抵销**。——在不违反本编其他规定的前提下,接管人转让资产的,任何资产受让人(包括过渡金融公司)对受让资产享有的权利之优先性将次于根据资不抵债法以外的适用的法律主张的其他债权或权利,即前述资产受让人应服从该等其他债权

noninsolvency law.

(H) PAYMENT OF VALID OBLIGATIONS. — The Corporation, as receiver for a covered financial company, shall, to the extent that funds are available, pay all valid obligations of the covered financial company that are due and payable at the time of the appointment of the Corporation as receiver, in accordance with the prescriptions and limitations of this title.

(I) APPLICABLE NONINSOLVENCY LAW. — Except as may otherwise be provided in this title, the applicable noninsolvency law shall be determined by the noninsolvency choice of law rules otherwise applicable to the claims, rights, titles, persons, or entities at issue.

(J) SUBPOENA AUTHORITY. —

(i) IN GENERAL. — The Corporation, as receiver for a covered financial company, may, for purposes of carrying out any power, authority, or duty with respect to the covered financial company (including determining any claim against the covered financial company and determining and realizing upon any asset of any person in the course of collecting money due the covered financial company), exercise any power established under section 8 (n) of the Federal Deposit Insurance Act, as if the Corporation were the appropriate Federal banking agency for the covered financial company, and the covered financial company were an insured depository institution.

(ii) RULE OF CONSTRUCTION. — This subparagraph may not be construed as limiting any rights that the Corporation, in any capacity, might otherwise have to exercise any powers described in clause (i) or under any other provision of law.

(K) INCIDENTAL POWERS. — The Corporation, as receiver for a covered financial company, may exercise all powers and authorities specifically granted to receivers under this title, and such incidental powers as shall be necessary to carry out such powers under this title.

(L) UTILIZATION OF PRIVATE SECTOR. — In carrying out its responsibilities in the management and disposition of assets from the covered financial company, the Corporation, as receiver for a covered financial company, may utilize the services of private persons, including real estate and loan portfolio asset management, property management, auction marketing, legal, and brokerage services, if such services are available in the private sector, and the Corporation determines that utilization of such services is practicable, efficient, and cost effective.

(M) SHAREHOLDERS AND CREDITORS OF COVERED FINANCIAL COMPANY. — Notwithstanding any other provision of law, the Corporation, as receiver for a covered financial company, shall succeed by operation of law to the rights, titles, powers, and privileges described in subparagraph (A), and shall terminate all rights and claims that

或权利。

(H)**偿付有效债务**。——联邦存款保险公司作为所涉金融公司的接管人,只要存在可支配的资金,即应根据本编的规定和限制偿付所涉金融公司于联邦存款保险公司被指定为接管人之日到期应付的全部有效债务。

(I)**资不抵债法以外的适用的法律**——除本编另有规定的情形外,资不抵债法以外的适用的法律应通过另行适用于相关债权、权利、所有权、人或实体的冲突法规则确定。

(J)**签发传票的权力**。——

(i)**一般规定**。——联邦存款保险公司作为所涉金融公司的接管人,有权出于就所涉金融公司行使任何权力、权限或职责之目的(包括判定债权人对所涉金融公司提起的任何权利主张,以及在追缴他人欠负所涉金融公司的款项过程中对任何人的任何资产作出判定并进行变现),行使《联邦存款保险法》第8(n)条确定的任何权力,如同联邦存款保险公司系所涉金融公司的相应的联邦银行业监管机关,而所涉金融公司具有参保存款机构的身份。

(ii)**解释规则**。——联邦存款保险公司可以以任何身份行使第(i)项所述任何权力或根据任何其他法律规定行使任何权力的,本子款不得被解释为构成对上述权力的限制。

(K)**附属权力**。——联邦存款保险公司作为所涉金融公司的接管人,可以行使本编明确授予接管人的全部权力和权限,并可以为按照本编行使该等权力而行使必要的附属权力。

(L)**私人部门的使用**。——联邦存款保险公司在作为所涉金融公司的接管人履行其对所涉金融公司资产的管理和处置责任时,可以使用私人部门的服务,包括不动产与贷款组合资产管理服务、财产管理服务、拍卖市场服务、法律服务和经纪服务,只要私人部门可提供该等服务且联邦存款保险公司判定使用该等服务可行、高效且符合成本效益。

(M)**所涉金融公司的股东和债权人**。——无论是否存在任何不同法律规定,联邦存款保险公司作为所涉金融公司的接管人,应依法继受第(A)子款所述权利、所有权、权力和特权,并终止所涉金融公司股东及债权人因其股东或债权人身份针对所涉金融公司或联邦存款保险公司的资产行使的所有权利及债权,但上述股东及债权人根

the stockholders and creditors of the covered financial company may have against the assets of the covered financial company or the Corporation arising out of their status as stockholders or creditors, except for their right to payment, resolution, or other satisfaction of their claims, as permitted under this section. The Corporation shall ensure that shareholders and unsecured creditors bear losses, consistent with the priority of claims provisions under this section.

(N) COORDINATION WITH FOREIGN FINANCIAL AUTHORITIES. — The Corporation, as receiver for a covered financial company, shall coordinate, to the maximum extent possible, with the appropriate foreign financial authorities regarding the orderly liquidation of any covered financial company that has assets or operations in a country other than the United States.

(O) RESTRICTION ON TRANSFERS. —

(i) SELECTION OF ACCOUNTS FOR TRANSFER. — If the Corporation establishes one or more bridge financial companies with respect to a covered broker or dealer, the Corporation shall transfer to one of such bridge financial companies, all customer accounts of the covered broker or dealer, and all associated customer name securities and customer property, unless the Corporation, after consulting with the Commission and SIPC, determines that —

(I) the customer accounts, customer name securities, and customer property are likely to be promptly transferred to another broker or dealer that is registered with the Commission under section 15(b) of the Securities Exchange Act of 1934 (15 U.S.C. 73o(b)) and is a member of SIPC; or

(II) the transfer of the accounts to a bridge financial company would materially interfere with the ability of the Corporation to avoid or mitigate serious adverse effects on financial stability or economic conditions in the United States.

(ii) TRANSFER OF PROPERTY. — SIPC, as trustee for the liquidation of the covered broker or dealer, and the Commission shall provide any and all reasonable assistance necessary to complete such transfers by the Corporation.

(iii) CUSTOMER CONSENT AND COURT APPROVAL NOT REQUIRED. — Neither customer consent nor court approval shall be required to transfer any customer accounts or associated customer name securities or customer property to a bridge financial company in accordance with this section.

(iv) NOTIFICATION OF SIPC AND SHARING OF INFORMATION. — The Corporation shall identify to SIPC the customer accounts and associated customer name securities and customer property transferred to the bridge financial company. The Corporation and SIPC shall cooperate in the sharing of any information necessary for each entity to discharge its obligations under this title and under the Securities Investor

据本条规定享有的就其债权获得支付、清盘或其他清偿的权利除外。联邦存款保险公司应确保股东和无担保债权人根据本条关于权利主张优先性的规定承担相关损失。

(N)**与外国金融监管机构的协作**。——所涉金融公司在美国之外的其他国家拥有资产或从事运营的,联邦存款保险公司作为所涉金融公司的接管人,应尽最大可能就任何所涉金融公司的有序清算与相应的外国金融监管机构进行协作。

(O)**转让限制**。——

(i)**转让账户的选择**。——联邦存款保险公司就所涉经纪商或自营商成立了一家或一家以上过渡金融公司的,联邦存款保险公司应将所涉经纪商或自营商的全部客户账户以及所有相关的客户名下证券和客户资产转让给其中一家过渡金融公司,除非联邦存款保险公司在与证券投资者保护公司磋商后判定——

(I)上述客户账户、客户名下证券和客户财产可能可以迅速地转让给另一家根据《1934年证券交易法》第15(b)条[《美国法典》第十五编第73o(b)节]注册且具有证券投资者保护公司会员身份的经纪商或自营商;或

(II)将账户转让给过渡金融公司将严重干扰联邦存款保险公司避免或减轻使美国金融稳定或经济状况遭受重大不利影响的能力。

(ii)**财产转让**。——证券投资者保护公司作为所涉经纪商或自营商的清算受托人,应与证券交易委员会共同向联邦存款保险公司提供任何和所有合理且必要的协助,帮助联邦存款保险公司完成该等转让。

(iii)**不必取得客户同意和法院批准**。——根据本条规定向过渡金融公司转让任何客户账户或相关客户名下证券或客户财产不必征得客户同意,也不必获得法院批准。

(iv)**向证券投资者保护公司提供的通知和信息共享**。——联邦存款保险公司应向证券投资者保护公司明确指出已转让给过渡金融公司的客户账户、相关客户名下证券和客户财产。联邦存款保险公司和证券投资者保护公司应相互协作,共享任何必要信息,以便按照本编及《1970年证券投资者保护法》(《美国法典》第十五编第78aaa节及其后条文)的规定履行各自的义务,包括向彼此提供所涉金融公司和根据本编规定

Protection Act of 1970 (15 U.S.C. 78aaa et seq.) including by providing access to the books and records of the covered financial company and any bridge financial company established in accordance with this title.

(2) DETERMINATION OF CLAIMS. —

(A) IN GENERAL. — The Corporation, as receiver for a covered financial company, shall report on claims, as set forth in section 203(c)(3). Subject to paragraph (4) of this subsection, the Corporation, as receiver for a covered financial company, shall determine claims in accordance with the requirements of this subsection and regulations prescribed under section 209.

(B) NOTICE REQUIREMENTS. — The Corporation, as receiver for a covered financial company, in any case involving the liquidation or winding up of the affairs of a covered financial company, shall —

(i) promptly publish a notice to the creditors of the covered financial company to present their claims, together with proof, to the receiver by a date specified in the notice, which shall be not earlier than 90 days after the date of publication of such notice; and

(ii) republish such notice 1 month and 2 months, respectively, after the date of publication under clause (i).

(C) MAILING REQUIRED. — The Corporation as receiver shall mail a notice similar to the notice published under clause (i) or (ii) of subparagraph (B), at the time of such publication, to any creditor shown on the books and records of the covered financial company —

(i) at the last address of the creditor appearing in such books;

(ii) in any claim filed by the claimant; or

(iii) upon discovery of the name and address of a claimant not appearing on the books and records of the covered financial company, not later than 30 days after the date of the discovery of such name and address.

(3) PROCEDURES FOR RESOLUTION OF CLAIMS. —

(A) DECISION PERIOD. —

(i) IN GENERAL. — Prior to the 180th day after the date on which a claim against a covered financial company is filed with the Corporation as receiver, or such later date as may be agreed as provided in clause (ii), the Corporation shall notify the claimant whether it allows or disallows the claim, in accordance with subparagraphs (B), (C), and (D).

(ii) EXTENSION OF TIME. — By written agreement executed not later than 180 days after the date on which a claim against a covered financial company is filed with the Corporation, the period described in clause (i) may be extended by written agreement between the claimant and the Corporation. Failure to notify the claimant of any

成立的任何过渡金融公司的账簿和记录的查阅权。

(2)**权利主张的判定**。——

(A) **一般规定**。——联邦存款保险公司作为所涉金融公司的接管人，应按照第203(c)(3)条的规定提供关于权利主张的报告。在不违反本子条第(4)款规定的前提下,联邦存款保险公司作为所涉金融公司的接管人,应根据本子条的要求和根据第209条制定的规章对权利主张进行判定。

(B)**通知要求**。——只要相关事务涉及所涉金融公司事务的清算或了结,联邦存款保险公司作为所涉金融公司的接管人应——

(i)及时向所涉金融公司的债权人发布通知,说明债权人应在通知指定的日期前向联邦存款保险公司申报权利主张及相关证明,但是该指定日期不得早于该通知发布日之后第90天;并

(ii)分别在第(i)项所述发布日后第一个月和第二个月届满时重新发布上述通知。

(C)**寄送要求**。——联邦存款保险公司作为接管人,应根据下述规定在上述发布日向所涉金融公司的账簿及记录所示任何债权人寄送与第(B)子款第(i)项或第(ii)项所述通知相类似的通知——

(i)按照上述账簿所示的债权人最新的地址寄送;

(ii)按照任何权利主张申报文件所示的地址寄送;或

(iii)权利主张人的名称及地址未在所涉金融公司的账簿和记录上显示的,在上述名称及地址发现日后30天之内寄送。

(3)**权利主张了结程序**。——

(A)**判定期**。——

(i)**一般规定**。——联邦存款保险公司应在权利主张人针对所涉金融公司向联邦存款保险公司申报权利主张后第180天之前或按照第(ii)项的规定约定的其他较晚日期之前,根据第(B)子款、第(C)子款和第(D)子款的规定通知权利主张人,说明联邦存款保险公司是否认可其权利主张。

(ii)**时限延长**。——权利主张人和联邦存款保险公司可以通过一份书面协议延长第(i)项所述时限,但该协议需在权利主张人向联邦存款保险公司申报对所涉金融公司的权利主张后180天内签署。联邦存款保险公司未在第(i)项规定的时限内或根据本项可能通过书面协议延长的时限内向权利主张人发出通知的,应视为联邦存款保

disallowance within the time period set forth in clause (i), as it may be extended by agreement under this clause, shall be deemed to be a disallowance of such claim, and the claimant may file or continue an action in court, as provided in paragraph (4).

(iii) MAILING OF NOTICE SUFFICIENT. — The requirements of clause (i) shall be deemed to be satisfied if the notice of any decision with respect to any claim is mailed to the last address of the claimant which appears —

(I) on the books, records, or both of the covered financial company;

(II) in the claim filed by the claimant; or

(III) in documents submitted in proof of the claim.

(iv) CONTENTS OF NOTICE OF DISALLOWANCE. — If the Corporation as receiver disallows any claim filed under clause (i), the notice to the claimant shall contain —

(I) a statement of each reason for the disallowance; and

(II) the procedures required to file or continue an action in court, as provided in paragraph (4).

(B) ALLOWANCE OF PROVEN CLAIM. — The receiver shall allow any claim received by the receiver on or before the date specified in the notice under paragraph (2)(B)(i), which is proved to the satisfaction of the receiver.

(C) DISALLOWANCE OF CLAIMS FILED AFTER END OF FILING PERIOD. —

(i) IN GENERAL. — Except as provided in clause (ii), claims filed after the date specified in the notice published under paragraph (2)(B)(i) shall be disallowed, and such disallowance shall be final.

(ii) CERTAIN EXCEPTIONS. — Clause (i) shall not apply with respect to any claim filed by a claimant after the date specified in the notice published under paragraph (2)(B)(i), and such claim may be considered by the receiver under subparagraph (B), if —

(I) the claimant did not receive notice of the appointment of the receiver in time to file such claim before such date; and

(II) such claim is filed in time to permit payment of such claim.

(D) AUTHORITY TO DISALLOW CLAIMS. —

(i) IN GENERAL. — The Corporation may disallow any portion of any claim by a creditor or claim of a security, preference, setoff, or priority which is not proved to the satisfaction of the Corporation.

(ii) PAYMENTS TO UNDERSECURED CREDITORS. — In the case of a claim against a covered financial company that is secured by any property or other asset of such covered financial company, the receiver —

(I) may treat the portion of such claim which exceeds an amount equal to the fair

险公司不认可该等权利主张,权利主张人可以根据第(4)款的规定向法院提起诉讼或继续已开展的诉讼。

(iii)**通知邮寄的充分性**。——联邦存款保险公司已按照下列文件所示权利主张人的最新地址寄送任何权利主张判定通知的,应视为已满足第(i)项的要求——

(I)所涉金融公司的账簿和/或记录;

(II)权利主张申报文件;或

(III)已提交的权利主张的证明文件。

(iv)**不认可决定通知的内容**。——联邦存款保险公司作为接管人不认可依据第(i)项规定提交的任何权利主张的,其向权利主张人发送的通知应包含以下内容——

(I)关于每项不认可原因的说明;及

(II)按照第(4)款规定向法院提起诉讼或继续已开展的诉讼的必要程序。

(B)**对已证实权利主张的认可**。——接管人在第(2)(B)(i)款所述通知指定的日期或该日期之前收到任何权利主张,且该权利主张已获得令接管人满意的证实的,接管人应认可该权利主张。

(C)**申报期终止后申报的权利主张不予认可**。——

(i)**一般规定**。——除第(ii)项规定的情形外,在根据第(2)(B)(i)款发布的通知所指定的日期之后才申报的权利主张将不予认可,并且该等不认可决定具有终局性。

(ii)**特定例外规定**。——在下列情形下,在根据第(2)(B)(i)款发布的通知指定的日期之后才申报的任何权利主张不应适用第(i)项的规定,且在下列情形下接管人可根据第(B)子款的规定考虑是否认可该等权利主张——

(I)权利主张人未及时收到指定接管人的通知,故未能在上述日期前申报权利主张;且

(II)该权利主张仍然及时作了申报,因而可对该权利主张进行支付。

(D)**不认可权利主张的权力**。——

(i)**一般规定**。——债权人的债权主张的任何部分,或者任何权利主张人主张的担保权、优先偿还权、抵销权或优先权的任何部分,如未能获得令联邦存款保险公司满意的证实,联邦存款保险公司可以不予认可。

(ii)**对无充分担保的债权人的支付规定**。——如针对所涉金融公司的权利主张存在该所涉金融公司的任何财产或其他资产所提供的担保,则接管人——

(I)可以将该权利主张超出上述财产或资产公允市值之部分作为无担保权利主张

market value of such property or other asset as an unsecured claim; and

(II) may not make any payment with respect to such unsecured portion of the claim, other than in connection with the disposition of all claims of unsecured creditors of the covered financial company.

(iii) EXCEPTIONS. — No provision of this paragraph shall apply with respect to —

(I) any extension of credit from any Federal reserve bank, or the Corporation, to any covered financial company; or

(II) subject to clause (ii), any legally enforceable and perfected security interest in the assets of the covered financial company securing any such extension of credit.

(E) LEGAL EFFECT OF FILING. —

(i) STATUTE OF LIMITATIONS TOLLED. — For purposes of any applicable statute of limitations, the filing of a claim with the receiver shall constitute a commencement of an action.

(ii) NO PREJUDICE TO OTHER ACTIONS. — Subject to paragraph (8), the filing of a claim with the receiver shall not prejudice any right of the claimant to continue any action which was filed before the date of appointment of the receiver for the covered financial company.

(4) JUDICIAL DETERMINATION OF CLAIMS. —

(A) IN GENERAL. — Subject to subparagraph (B), a claimant may file suit on a claim(or continue an action commenced before the date of appointment of the Corporation as receiver) in the district or territorial court of the United States for the district within which the principal place of business of the covered financial company is located (and such court shall have jurisdiction to hear such claim).

(B) TIMING. — A claim under subparagraph (A) may be filed before the end of the 60-day period beginning on the earlier of —

(i) the end of the period described in paragraph (3)(A)(i) (or, if extended by agreement of the Corporation and the claimant, the period described in paragraph (3)(A)(ii)) with respect to any claim against a covered financial company for which the Corporation is receiver; or

(ii) the date of any notice of disallowance of such claim pursuant to paragraph (3)(A)(i).

(C) STATUTE OF LIMITATIONS. — If any claimant fails to file suit on such claim (or to continue an action on such claim commenced before the date of appointment of the Corporation as receiver) prior to the end of the 60-day period described in subparagraph (B), the claim shall be deemed to be disallowed (other than any portion of such claim which was allowed by the receiver) as of the end of such period, such disallowance shall be final, and the claimant shall have no further rights or remedies with respect to such claim.

处理;并

(II)不得对上述权利主张的该等无担保部分进行任何支付,但在处置所涉金融公司无担保债权人的全部权利主张时除外。

(iii)**例外规定**。——本款任何规定均不适用于——

(I)任何联邦储备银行或联邦存款保险公司对任何所涉金融公司的任何授信;或

(II)在不违反第(ii)项规定的前提下,所涉金融公司资产上存在的为任何上述授信提供担保的所有可依法强制执行且无瑕疵的任何担保权益。

(E)**申报的法律效力**。——

(i)**诉讼时效中断**。——就任何适用诉讼时效而言,向接管人申报权利主张之时即视为启动了诉讼。

(ii)**不影响其他诉讼**。——在不违反第(8)款规定的前提下,向接管人申报权利主张的行为不影响权利主张人继续开展在联邦存款保险公司被指定为所涉金融公司接管人之日前已提起的任何诉讼的权利。

(4)**权利主张的司法判定**。——

(A)**一般规定**。——在不违反第(B)子款规定的前提下,权利主张人可以基于其权利主张,在所涉金融公司主要营业地所在联邦地区或准州法院(该法院应拥有审理该权利主张的司法管辖权)提起诉讼(或继续开展在联邦存款保险公司被指定为接管人之日前已启动的诉讼)。

(B)**时限**。——第(A)子款所述权利主张可在以下日期(以较早者为准)起60天内提起——

(i)如该权利主张为针对联邦存款保险公司作为接管人接管的所涉金融公司提出的任何权利主张,则第(3)(A)(i)款所述期限终止之日[或该期限由联邦存款保险公司和权利主张人协议延长的,第(3)(A)(ii)款所述期限终止之日];或

(ii)根据第(3)(A)(i)款规定,就该权利主张发出任何不予认可通知之日。

(C)**诉讼时效**。——任何权利主张人未基于上述权利主张在第(B)子款所述60天期限内提起诉讼的(或未继续开展在联邦存款保险公司被指定为接管人之日前已启动的诉讼的),则自上述期限结束之日起,应视为接管人已作出不认可该权利主张的决定(但接管人已认可的任何部分除外),且该等不认可决定具有终局性,权利主张人不得就该权利主张享有任何进一步的权利或救济。

(5) EXPEDITED DETERMINATION OF CLAIMS. —

(A) PROCEDURE REQUIRED. — The Corporation shall establish a procedure for expedited relief outside of the claims process established under paragraph (3), for any claimant that alleges —

(i) having a legally valid and enforceable or perfected security interest in property of a covered financial company or control of any legally valid and enforceable security entitlement in respect of any asset held by the covered financial company for which the Corporation has been appointed receiver; and

(ii) that irreparable injury will occur if the claims procedure established under paragraph (3) is followed.

(B) DETERMINATION PERIOD. — Prior to the end of the 90 –day period beginning on the date on which a claim is filed in accordance with the procedures established pursuant to subparagraph (A), the Corporation shall —

(i) determine —

(I) whether to allow or disallow such claim, or any portion thereof; or

(II) whether such claim should be determined pursuant to the procedures established pursuant to paragraph (3);

(ii) notify the claimant of the determination; and

(iii) if the claim is disallowed, provide a statement of each reason for the disallowance and the procedure for obtaining a judicial determination.

(C) PERIOD FOR FILING OR RENEWING SUIT. — Any claimant who files a request for expedited relief shall be permitted to file suit (or continue a suit filed before the date of appointment of the Corporation as receiver) seeking a determination of the rights of the claimant with respect to such security interest (or such security entitlement) after the earlier of —

(i) the end of the 90–day period beginning on the date of the filing of a request for expedited relief; or

(ii) the date on which the Corporation denies the claim or a portion thereof.

(D) STATUTE OF LIMITATIONS. — If an action described in subparagraph (C) is not filed, or the motion to renew a previously filed suit is not made, before the end of the 30–day period beginning on the date on which such action or motion may be filed in accordance with subparagraph (C), the claim shall be deemed to be disallowed as of the end of such period (other than any portion of such claim which was allowed by the receiver), such disallowance shall be final, and the claimant shall have no further rights or remedies with respect to such claim.

(E) LEGAL EFFECT OF FILING. —

(i) STATUTE OF LIMITATIONS TOLLED. — For purposes of any applicable

(5)**权利主张的加速判定**。——

(A)**程序要求**。——除根据第(3)款制定的权利主张处理程序外,在下述情形下,联邦存款保险公司还应就任何权利主张人制定加速救济程序——

(i)权利主张人对联邦存款保险公司作为接管人接管的所涉金融公司的财产拥有合法有效的可强制执行或无瑕疵的担保权益,或者对该等所涉金融公司持有的任何资产拥有任何合法有效且可强制执行的法定担保权利的控制权;且

(ii)适用根据第(3)款制定的权利主张处理程序将导致不可弥补的损害。

(B)**判定期**。——在根据第(A)子款设定的程序申报权利主张之日起90天内,联邦存款保险公司应——

(i)判定——

(I)是否认可该权利主张或该权利主张的任何部分;或

(II)该权利主张是否应按照根据第(3)款制定的程序进行判定;

(ii)将上述判定通知权利主张人;且

(iii)对权利主张作出不予认可决定的,应逐项说明不予认可的原因及获得司法判定的程序。

(C)**提起诉讼或继续已开展的诉讼的期限**。——任何提交加速救济申请的权利主张人有权在以下日期(以较早者为准)之后提起诉讼(或继续开展在联邦存款保险公司被指定为接管人之日前已启动的诉讼),请求法院就其对上述担保权益(或法定担保权利)享有的权利作出判定——

(i)加速救济申请提交之日起第90天;或

(ii)联邦存款保险公司对该权利主张或其中任何部分予以否决之日。

(D)**诉讼时效**。——如自权利主张人根据第(C)子款可以提起诉讼之日起或可以提出继续开展此前已提起诉讼的动议之日起30天内,权利主张人未提起该等诉讼或动议,则自上述期限届满之日起,应视为接管人已作出不认可该权利主张的决定(但任何接管人已认可的部分除外),且该等不认可决定具有终局性,权利主张人不得就该权利主张享有任何进一步的权利或救济。

(E)**申报的法律效力**。——

(i)**诉讼时效中断**。——就任何适用诉讼时效而言,向接管人申报权利主张之时

statute of limitations, the filing of a claim with the receiver shall constitute a commencement of an action.

(ii) NO PREJUDICE TO OTHER ACTIONS. — Subject to paragraph (8), the filing of a claim with the receiver shall not prejudice any right of the claimant to continue any action which was filed before the appointment of the Corporation as receiver for the covered financial company.

(6) AGREEMENTS AGAINST INTEREST OF THE RECEIVER. — No agreement that tends to diminish or defeat the interest of the Corporation as receiver in any asset acquired by the receiver under this section shall be valid against the receiver, unless such agreement —

(A) is in writing;

(B) was executed by an authorized officer or representative of the covered financial company, or confirmed in the ordinary course of business by the covered financial company; and

(C) has been, since the time of its execution, an official record of the company or the party claiming under the agreement provides documentation, acceptable to the receiver, of such agreement and its authorized execution or confirmation by the covered financial company.

(7) PAYMENT OF CLAIMS. —

(A) IN GENERAL. — Subject to subparagraph (B), the Corporation as receiver may, in its discretion and to the extent that funds are available, pay creditor claims, in such manner and amounts as are authorized under this section, which are —

(i) allowed by the receiver;

(ii) approved by the receiver pursuant to a final determination pursuant to paragraph (3) or (5), as applicable; or

(iii) determined by the final judgment of a court of competent jurisdiction.

(B) LIMITATION. — A creditor shall, in no event, receive less than the amount that the creditor is entitled to receive under paragraphs (2) and (3) of subsection (d), as applicable.

(C) PAYMENT OF DIVIDENDS ON CLAIMS. — The Corporation as receiver may, in its sole discretion, and to the extent otherwise permitted by this section, pay dividends on proven claims at any time, and no liability shall attach to the Corporation as receiver, by reason of any such payment or for failure to pay dividends to a claimant whose claim is not proved at the time of any such payment.

(D) RULEMAKING BY THE CORPORATION. — The Corporation may prescribe such rules, including definitions of terms, as the Corporation deems appropriate to establish an interest rate for or to make payments of post–insolvency interest to creditors

即视为启动了诉讼。

(ii)**不影响其他诉讼**。——在不违反第(8)款规定的前提下,向接管人申报权利主张的行为不影响权利主张人继续开展在联邦存款保险公司被指定为所涉金融公司接管人之日前已提起的任何诉讼的任何权利。

(6)**不利于接管人权益的协议**。——任何协议如试图缩小联邦存款保险公司作为接管人对其根据本条规定所获任何资产享有的权益,或试图使该等权益归于无效,均对接管人无效,除非该等协议——

(A)属于书面协议;

(B)由所涉金融公司的授权管理人员或授权代表签署,或已在所涉金融公司的正常业务运作中获得确认;且

(C)自签署之后,已成为公司的一项正式记录,或者根据该协议提出权利主张的一方可提供证明文件,证明该协议的存在以及该协议已获得所涉金融公司授权签署或确认,且该等证明文件获得接管人认可。

(7)**对权利主张的支付**。——

(A)**一般规定**。——在不违反第(B)子款规定的前提下,联邦存款保险公司作为接管人,可以依其自由裁量权在其可支取资金的范围内,按照本条准许采用的方式和准许支付的金额对债权人的权利主张进行支付,前提是该权利主张——

(i)已获接管人认可;

(ii)已由接管人根据第(3)款或第(5)款(视具体情况而定)作出的最终判定予以批准;或

(iii)已由有管辖权的法院作出最终判定予以认定。

(B)**限制**。——在任何情况下,债权人获得的金额均不得低于其根据第(d)子条第(2)款或第(3)款(视具体情况而定)有权获得的金额。

(C)**基于权利主张支付破产偿金**。——在本条另行许可的范围内,联邦存款保险公司作为接管人,可完全依其自由裁量权,在任何时候针对已证实权利主张支付破产偿金,且联邦存款保险公司向权利主张已获证实的权利主张人支付任何该等破产偿金,或不向在支付之时权利主张尚未获证实的权利主张人支付任何破产偿金,均不会导致联邦存款保险公司由于其接管人身份而承担任何责任。

(D)**联邦存款保险公司的规则制定权**。——联邦存款保险公司可以制定其认为适当的规则(包括对相关术语作出定义),在债权人就该所涉金融公司的被接管破产财团拥有已证实权利主张的情况下,就应付给该债权人的资不抵债后所发生的利息,

holding proven claims against the receivership estate of a covered financial company, except that no such interest shall be paid until the Corporation as receiver has satisfied the principal amount of all creditor claims.

(8) SUSPENSION OF LEGAL ACTIONS. —

(A) IN GENERAL. — After the appointment of the Corporation as receiver for a covered financial company, the Corporation may request a stay in any judicial action or proceeding in which such covered financial company is or becomes a party, for a period of not to exceed 90 days.

(B) GRANT OF STAY BY ALL COURTS REQUIRED. — Upon receipt of a request by the Corporation pursuant to subparagraph (A), the court shall grant such stay as to all parties.

(9) ADDITIONAL RIGHTS AND DUTIES. —

(A) PRIOR FINAL ADJUDICATION. — The Corporation shall abide by any final, non–appealable judgment of any court of competent jurisdiction that was rendered before the appointment of the Corporation as receiver.

(B) RIGHTS AND REMEDIES OF RECEIVER. — In the event of any appealable judgment, the Corporation as receiver shall —

(i) have all the rights and remedies available to the covered financial company (before the date of appointment of the Corporation as receiver under section 202) and the Corporation, including removal to Federal court and all appellate rights; and

(ii) not be required to post any bond in order to pursue such remedies.

(C) NO ATTACHMENT OR EXECUTION. — No attachment or execution may be issued by any court upon assets in the possession of the Corporation as receiver for a covered financial company.

(D) LIMITATION ON JUDICIAL REVIEW. — Except as otherwise provided in this title, no court shall have jurisdiction over —

(i) any claim or action for payment from, or any action seeking a determination of rights with respect to, the assets of any covered financial company for which the Corporation has been appointed receiver, including any assets which the Corporation may acquire from itself as such receiver; or

(ii) any claim relating to any act or omission of such covered financial company or the Corporation as receiver.

(E) DISPOSITION OF ASSETS. — In exercising any right, power, privilege, or authority as receiver in connection with any covered financial company for which the Corporation is acting as receiver under this section, the Corporation shall, to the greatest extent practicable, conduct its operations in a manner that —

(i) maximizes the net present value return from the sale or disposition of such assets;

设定所适用的利率或支付该等利息,但是,在作为接管人付清债权人全部权利主张的本金之前,联邦存款保险公司不得支付任何上述利息。

(8)**法律诉讼的暂停**。——

(A)**一般规定**。——某一所涉金融公司身为或将成为任何司法诉讼或司法程序的当事人的,联邦存款保险公司在被指定为该所涉金融公司的接管人之后,可以申请暂停上述诉讼或程序,但中止期不得超过90天。

(B)**所有法院均应核准暂停司法诉讼或程序的申请**。——法院在收到联邦存款保险公司根据第(A)子款提交的申请后,应向所有当事人核准上述暂停申请。

(9)**其他权利和职责**。——

(A)**已作出的最终判决**。——如果在联邦存款保险公司被指定为接管人之前,任何有管辖权的法院已作出不可上诉的任何最终判决,则联邦存款保险公司应履行该等判决。

(B)**接管人的权利与救济**。——在判决仍可上诉的情况下,联邦存款保险公司作为接管人,应——

(i)享有所涉金融公司(在联邦存款保险公司根据第202条规定被指定为接管人之前)可获得的全部权利和救济,以及联邦存款保险公司可获得的全部权利和救济,包括将诉讼移交联邦法院的权利以及所有的上诉权;且

(ii)不必为寻求上述救济提供任何保证金。

(C)**不得签发扣押令或执行令**。——对于联邦存款保险公司作为所涉金融公司接管人持有的资产,任何法院均不得就该等资产签发扣押令或执行令。

(D)**司法审查限制**。——除本编另有规定的情形外,任何法院均不得对以下主张或诉讼享有管辖权——

(i)联邦存款保险公司被指定为所涉金融公司的接管人后,任何针对该所涉金融公司资产(包括联邦存款保险公司可能以接管人身份从其自身处获得的任何资产)要求予以支付的权利主张或诉讼,或者任何寻求法院就其对该等资产享有的权利作出判定的诉讼;或

(ii)与上述所涉金融公司或联邦存款保险公司以接管人身份作出的任何作为或不作为相关的任何权利主张。

(E)**资产处置**。——联邦存款保险公司在根据本条规定以任何所涉金融公司接管人身份行使与该所涉金融公司相关的任何权利、权力、特权或权限时,应在最大可行范围内,以如下方式开展工作——

(i)将出售或处置上述资产所得的净现值最大化;

(ii) minimizes the amount of any loss realized in the resolution of cases;

(iii) mitigates the potential for serious adverse effects to the financial system;

(iv) ensures timely and adequate competition and fair and consistent treatment of offerors; and

(v) prohibits discrimination on the basis of race, sex, or ethnic group in the solicitation and consideration of offers.

(10) STATUTE OF LIMITATIONS FOR ACTIONS BROUGHT BY RECEIVER. —

(A) IN GENERAL. — Notwithstanding any provision of any contract, the applicable statute of limitations with regard to any action brought by the Corporation as receiver for a covered financial company shall be —

(i) in the case of any contract claim, the longer of —

(I) the 6–year period beginning on the date on which the claim accrues; or

(II) the period applicable under State law; and

(ii) in the case of any tort claim, the longer of —

(I) the 3–year period beginning on the date on which the claim accrues; or

(II) the period applicable under State law.

(B) DATE ON WHICH A CLAIM ACCRUES. — For purposes of subparagraph (A), the date on which the statute of limitations begins to run on any claim described in subparagraph (A) shall be the later of —

(i) the date of the appointment of the Corporation as receiver under this title; or

(ii) the date on which the cause of action accrues.

(C) REVIVAL OF EXPIRED STATE CAUSES OF ACTION. —

(i) IN GENERAL. — In the case of any tort claim described in clause (ii) for which the applicable statute of limitations under State law has expired not more than 5 years before the date of appointment of the Corporation as receiver for a covered financial company, the Corporation may bring an action as receiver on such claim without regard to the expiration of the statute of limitations.

(ii) CLAIMS DESCRIBED. — A tort claim referred to in clause (i) is a claim arising from fraud, intentional misconduct resulting in unjust enrichment, or intentional misconduct resulting in substantial loss to the covered financial company.

(11) AVOIDABLE TRANSFERS. —

(A) FRAUDULENT TRANSFERS. — The Corporation, as receiver for any covered financial company, may avoid a transfer of any interest of the covered financial company in property, or any obligation incurred by the covered financial company, that was made or incurred at or within 2 years before the date on which the Corporation was appointed receiver, if —

(i) the covered financial company voluntarily or involuntarily —

(ii)将了结相关案件实现的任何损失金额减到最低限度;

(iii)尽量减轻对金融体系产生重大不利影响的可能性;

(iv)确保及时充分的竞争和公允、一致地对待各要约方;及

(v)在招揽和评估要约时杜绝种族、性别或民族歧视。

(10)**接管人提起诉讼的诉讼时效**。——

(A)**一般规定**。——无论任何合同如何规定,联邦存款保险公司作为所涉金融公司接管人提起的任何诉讼所适用的诉讼时效应按如下规定确定——

(i)对于依据任何合同提起的权利主张,以如下二者中较长者为准——

(I)6年,自权利主张发生之日起算;或

(II)相关州法律规定的适用期限;及

(ii)对于任何侵权主张,以如下二者中较长者为准——

(I)3年,自权利主张发生之日起算;或

(II)相关州法律规定的适用期限。

(B)**权利主张发生日**。——就第(A)子款而言,第(A)子款所述任何权利主张诉讼时效的起算日应为以下日期中较晚者——

(i)联邦存款保险公司根据本编规定被指定为接管人之日;或

(ii)诉因发生之日。

(C)**过期诉因的重新生效**。——

(i)**一般规定**。——在联邦存款保险公司被指定为所涉金融公司接管人之前,根据相关州法律,第(ii)项所述任何侵权主张的诉讼时效届满尚不超过5年的,联邦存款保险公司可不受该诉讼时效届满的限制,可以接管人身份就上述主张提起诉讼。

(ii)**第(i)项所述权利主张**。——第(i)项所述侵权主张系指因导致不当得利的欺诈、故意不当行为而引发的主张,或因造成所涉金融公司重大损失的故意不当行为而引发的主张。

(11)**可撤销的转让**。——

(A)**欺诈性转让**。——在下述情形下,联邦存款保险公司作为任何所涉金融公司的接管人,可以撤销所涉金融公司在联邦存款保险公司被指定为接管人之前2年内进行的任何财产权益转让或产生的任何义务——

(i)该所涉金融公司主动或被动地——

(I) made such transfer or incurred such obligation with actual intent to hinder, delay, or defraud any entity to which the covered financial company was or became, on or after the date on which such transfer was made or such obligation was incurred, indebted; or

(II) received less than a reasonably equivalent value in exchange for such transferor obligation; and

(ii) the covered financial company voluntarily or involuntarily —

(I) was insolvent on the date that such transfer was made or such obligation was incurred, or became insolvent as a result of such transfer or obligation;

(II) was engaged in business or a transaction, or was about to engage in business or a transaction, for which any property remaining with the covered financial company was an unreasonably small capital;

(III) intended to incur, or believed that the covered financial company would incur, debts that would be beyond the ability of the covered financial company to pay as such debts matured; or

(IV) made such transfer to or for the benefit of an insider, or incurred such obligation to or for the benefit of an insider, under an employment contract and not in the ordinary course of business.

(B) PREFERENTIAL TRANSFERS. — The Corporation as receiver for any covered financial company may avoid a transfer of an interest of the covered financial company in property —

(i) to or for the benefit of a creditor;

(ii) for or on account of an antecedent debt that was owed by the covered financial company before the transfer was made;

(iii) that was made while the covered financial company was insolvent;

(iv) that was made —

(I) 90 days or less before the date on which the Corporation was appointed receiver; or

(II) more than 90 days, but less than 1 year before the date on which the Corporation was appointed receiver, if such creditor at the time of the transfer was an insider; and

(v) that enables the creditor to receive more than the creditor would receive if —

(I) the covered financial company had been liquidated under chapter 7 of the Bankruptcy Code;

(II) the transfer had not been made; and

(III) the creditor received payment of such debt to the extent provided by the provisions of chapter 7 of the Bankruptcy Code.

(I)作出上述转让或产生上述义务的真实意图为:对在上述转让作出或者义务产生之日或之后身为或成为该所涉金融公司之债权人的任何实体造成妨碍、延误或进行欺诈;或

(II)收到的价值低于转让人义务被交换时所应获得的合理对等价值;且

(ii)所涉金融公司主动或被动地——

(I)在上述转让或义务产生之日丧失偿债能力,或者由于上述转让或义务而丧失偿债能力;

(II)从事或即将从事某业务或交易,而相对于该等业务或交易而言,所涉金融公司的任何剩余财产资本显然属于规模过小的资本;

(III)试图产生或认为所涉金融公司将产生在到期时将超出其偿付能力的债务;或

(IV)根据雇佣合同且并非在正常业务运作中向内幕人士或为内幕人士的利益作出上述转让,或代内幕人士或为内幕人士利益产生上述债务。

(B)**偏颇性转让**。——对任何所涉金融公司财产权益作出的转让,如符合下述条件,联邦存款保险公司作为所涉金融公司的接管人,可以予以撤销——

(i)该转让系向债权人作出,或为债权人利益而作出;

(ii)该转让系因转让前所涉金融公司所欠先前之债而作出;

(iii)该转让系在所涉金融公司处于资不抵债状态时作出;

(iv)该转让系在——

(I)联邦存款保险公司被指定为接管人之前90天内作出;或

(II)联邦存款保险公司被指定为接管人之前90天以上但1年以内作出,且债权人在转让发生时系内幕人士;且

(v)债权人通过该转让获得的权益高于其在以下情况下将获得的权益——

(I)所涉金融公司按照《破产法》第七章规定被清算;

(II)该转让并未作出;且

(III)债权人在《破产法》第七章的规定范围内收到了相应的债务偿付。

(C) POST-RECEIVERSHIP TRANSACTIONS. — The Corporation as receiver for any covered financial company may avoid a transfer of property of the receivership that occurred after the Corporation was appointed receiver that was not authorized under this title by the Corporation as receiver.

(D) RIGHT OF RECOVERY. — To the extent that a transfer is avoided under subparagraph (A), (B), or (C), the Corporation may recover, for the benefit of the covered financial company, the property transferred or, if a court so orders, the value of such property (at the time of such transfer) from —

(i) the initial transferee of such transfer or the person for whose benefit such transfer was made; or

(ii) any immediate or mediate transferee of any such initial transferee.

(E) RIGHTS OF TRANSFEREE OR OBLIGEE. — The Corporation may not recover under subparagraph (D)(ii) from —

(i) any transferee that takes for value, including in satisfaction of or to secure a present or antecedent debt, in good faith, and without knowledge of the voidability of the transfer avoided; or

(ii) any immediate or mediate good faith transferee of such transferee.

(F) DEFENSES. — Subject to the other provisions of this title —

(i) a transferee or obligee from which the Corporation seeks to recover a transfer or to avoid an obligation under subparagraph (A), (B), (C), or (D) shall have the same defenses available to a transferee or obligee from which a trustee seeks to recover a transfer or avoid an obligation under sections 547, 548, and 549 of the Bankruptcy Code; and

(ii) the authority of the Corporation to recover a transfer or avoid an obligation shall be subject to subsections (b) and (c) of section 546, section 547(c), and section 548(c) of the Bankruptcy Code.

(G) RIGHTS UNDER THIS SECTION. — The rights of the Corporation as receiver under this section shall be superior to any rights of a trustee or any other party (other than a Federal agency) under the Bankruptcy Code.

(H) RULES OF CONSTRUCTION; DEFINITIONS. — For purposes of —

(i) subparagraphs (A) and (B) —

(I) the term "insider" has the same meaning as in section 101(31) of the Bankruptcy Code;

(II) a transfer is made when such transfer is so perfected that a bona fide purchaser from the covered financial company against whom applicable law permits such transfer to be perfected cannot acquire an interest in the property transferred that is superior to the interest in such property of the transferee, but if such transfer is not so perfected before

(C)**接管之后的交易**。——如果联邦存款保险公司被指定为接管人之后发生接管财产转让,而该等转让并未获得联邦存款保险公司以接管人身份根据本编规定作出的批准,则联邦存款保险公司作为任何所涉金融公司接管人,可以撤销该等转让。

(D)**追回权**。——某项转让根据第(A)子款、第(B)子款或第(C)子款规定被撤销的,联邦存款保险公司可以为所涉金融公司的利益向以下受让人追回被转让财产,或按照法院命令追回上述财产的价值(指转让时的价值)——

(i)该转让的最初受让人或该转让的受益人;或

(ii)该最初受让人的任何直接或间接受让人。

(E)**受让人或权利人的权利**。——联邦存款保险公司无权向以下受让人执行第(D)(ii)子款所述追回权——

(i)善意、有偿取得被转让财产("有偿"包括清偿某项当前或先前之债,或为之提供担保),且不知晓该等转让具有可撤销性的任何受让人;或

(ii)上述受让人的任何直接或间接善意受让人。

(F)**抗辩**。——在不违反本编其他规定的前提下——

(i)如联邦存款保险公司根据第(A)子款、第(B)子款、第(C)子款或第(D)子款规定向受让人追回被转让财产或撤销对权利人承担的某项义务,该受让人或权利人享有的抗辩权应与破产管理人根据《破产法》第547条、第548条及第549条向受让人追回被转让财产或撤销对权利人承担的某项义务时,受让人或权利人所享有的抗辩权相同;且

(ii)联邦存款保险公司追回某项被转让财产或撤销某项义务的权力应受制于《破产法》第546条第(b)子条及第(c)子条、第547(c)条和第548(c)条的规定。

(G)**本条规定的权利**。——联邦存款保险公司根据本条规定作为接管人享有的权利应优先于破产管理人或任何其他当事方(但联邦机关除外)根据《破产法》享有的任何权利。

(H)**解释规则;定义**。——就

(i)第(A)子款和第(B)子款而言——

(I)"内幕人士"一词的含义以《破产法》第101(31)条的定义为准;

(II)如果转让已经取得合法效力,以致根据适用的法律有权获得合法转让的所涉金融公司的善意购买人无法取得优先于受让人对被转让财产享有的权益,转让即应视为已经作出;但是,如果转让在联邦存款保险公司被指定为所涉金融公司接管人之前尚未取得上述合法效力,则该等转让应视为在上述指定日前最近的时点作出;且

the date on which the Corporation is appointed as receiver for the covered financial company, such transfer is made immediately before the date of such appointment; and

(III) the term "value" means property, or satisfaction or securing of a present or antecedent debt of the covered financial company, but does not include an unperformed promise to furnish support to the covered financial company; and

(ii) subparagraph (B) —

(I) the covered financial company is presumed to have been insolvent on and during the 90-day period immediately preceding the date of appointment of the Corporation as receiver; and

(II) the term "insolvent" has the same meaning as in section 101(32) of the Bankruptcy Code.

(12) SETOFF. —

(A) GENERALLY. — Except as otherwise provided in this title, any right of a creditor to offset a mutual debt owed by the creditor to any covered financial company that arose before the Corporation was appointed as receiver for the covered financial company against a claim of such creditor may be asserted if enforceable under applicable noninsolvency law, except to the extent that —

(i) the claim of the creditor against the covered financial company is disallowed;

(ii) the claim was transferred, by an entity other than the covered financial company, to the creditor —

(I) after the Corporation was appointed as receiver of the covered financial company; or

(II)(aa) after the 90-day period preceding the date on which the Corporation was appointed as receiver for the covered financial company; and

(bb) while the covered financial company was insolvent (except for a setoff in connection with a qualified financial contract); or

(iii) the debt owed to the covered financial company was incurred by the covered financial company —

(I) after the 90-day period preceding the date on which the Corporation was appointed as receiver for the covered financial company;

(II) while the covered financial company was insolvent; and

(III) for the purpose of obtaining a right of setoff against the covered financial company (except for a setoff in connection with a qualified financial contract).

(III)“有偿”一词系指提供财产,或者对所涉金融公司当前或先前之债提供偿付或担保,但不包括尚未履行的向所涉金融公司提供支持的承诺;且

(ii)就第(B)子款而言——

(I)所涉金融公司被推定为在联邦存款保险公司被指定为接管人之日及之前90天内已处于资不抵债状态;且

(II)“破产”一词的含义以《破产法》第101(32)条的定义为准。

(12)**抵销**。——

(A)**一般规定**。——除本编另有规定的情形外,如果债权人在联邦存款保险公司被指定为任何所涉金融公司接管人之前与所涉金融公司存在互欠债务,且根据资不抵债法以外的法律,债权人以该债务抵销其某项权利主张的做法具有可执行性,则该债权人可以主张该抵销权,除非——

(i)债权人针对所涉金融公司提出的权利主张未被认可;

(ii)该权利主张已在下述时间或状况下由所涉金融公司之外的实体转让给债权人——

(I)在联邦存款保险公司被指定为所涉金融公司接管人之后;或

(II)(aa)在联邦存款保险公司被指定为所涉金融公司接管人之日前90天的期限之内;[1]且

(bb)所涉金融公司处于资不抵债状态(但与合格金融合约相关的抵销不在此限);或

(iii)欠付所涉金融公司的债务系由所涉金融公司在以下时间和情形下为以下目的所产生——

(I)在联邦存款保险公司被指定为所涉金融公司接管人之日前90天的期限之内;

(II)所涉金融公司处于资不抵债状态;且

(III)目的是取得针对所涉金融公司的抵销权(但与合格金融合约相关的抵销除外)。

1　本处的上下文为对债权人行使其抵销权的限制,债权人在特定时间内获得的债权,不得进行抵销。该句子按字面意思应译为“被指定为所涉金融公司接管人之日前90天的期限届满之后”,与第(I)子项所述重复。本规定之立法意图应为防止在所涉金融公司出现财务困境时出现恶意的债权转让,其实际意思应为在联邦存款保险公司被指定为所涉金融公司接管人之前第90天以后至其被指定为接管人之日这段时间内发生的债权转让,此处的“after”似应指“within”,即译为“90天的期限之内”似乎更妥,译文中按此处理。——译者注

(B) INSUFFICIENCY. —

(i) IN GENERAL. — Except with respect to a setoff in connection with a qualified financial contract, if a creditor offsets a mutual debt owed to the covered financial company against a claim of the covered financial company on or within the 90-day period preceding the date on which the Corporation is appointed as receiver for the covered financial company, the Corporation may recover from the creditor the amount so offset, to the extent that any insufficiency on the date of such setoff is less than the insufficiency on the later of —

(I) the date that is 90 days before the date on which the Corporation is appointed as receiver for the covered financial company; or

(II) the first day on which there is an insufficiency during the 90-day period preceding the date on which the Corporation is appointed as receiver for the covered financial company.

(ii) DEFINITION OF INSUFFICIENCY. — In this subparagraph, the term "insufficiency" means the amount, if any, by which a claim against the covered financial company exceeds a mutual debt owed to the covered financial company by the holder of such claim.

(C) INSOLVENCY. — The term "insolvent" has the same meaning as in section 101(32) of the Bankruptcy Code.

(D) PRESUMPTION OF INSOLVENCY. — For purposes of this paragraph, the covered financial company is presumed to have been insolvent on and during the 90-day period preceding the date of appointment of the Corporation as receiver.

(E) LIMITATION. — Nothing in this paragraph (12) shall be the basis for any right of setoff where no such right exists under applicable noninsolvency law.

(F) PRIORITY CLAIM. — Except as otherwise provided in this title, the Corporation as receiver for the covered financial company may sell or transfer any assets free and clear of the setoff rights of any party, except that such party shall be entitled to a claim, subordinate to the claims payable under subparagraphs (A), (B), (C), and (D) of subsection (b)(1), but senior to all other unsecured liabilities defined in subsection (b)(1)(E), in an amount equal to the value of such setoff rights.

(13) ATTACHMENT OF ASSETS AND OTHER INJUNCTIVE RELIEF. — Subject to paragraph (14), any court of competent jurisdiction may, at the request of the Corporation as receiver for a covered financial company, issue an order in accordance with Rule 65 of the Federal Rules of Civil Procedure, including an order placing the assets of any person designated by the Corporation under the control of the court and appointing a trustee to hold such assets.

(14) STANDARDS. —

(B)**不足金额**。——

(i)**一般规定**。——除了与合格金融合约相关的抵销外,债权人在联邦存款保险公司被指定为所涉金融公司接管人之日或该指定日之前90天的期限之内以欠付所涉金融公司的相互债务抵销其对所涉金融公司拥有的权利主张的,只要在该抵销日存在的不足金额少于在以下日期(以较晚者为准)存在的任何不足金额,联邦存款保险公司即可以向债权人追收该等抵销金额——

(I)联邦存款保险公司被指定为所涉金融公司接管人之日前第90天;或

(II)联邦存款保险公司被指定为所涉金融公司接管人之日前90天内出现不足金额的首日。

(ii)**不足金额的定义**。——就本子款而言,"不足金额"一词系指针对所涉金融公司拥有的权利主张金额超过该权利主张人欠负所涉金融公司的相互债务的金额(如有)。

(C)**资不抵债**。——"资不抵债"一词的含义以《破产法》第101(32)条的定义为准。

(D)**资不抵债推定**。——就本款而言,所涉金融公司应被推定为在联邦存款保险公司被指定为接管人之日及该日前90天内已处于资不抵债状态。

(E)**限制**。——如根据资不抵债法以外的适用的法律不享有抵销权,则不得援引本第(12)款的任何规定作为获得抵销权的依据。

(F)**权利主张的优先性**。——除本编另有规定的情形外,联邦存款保险公司作为所涉金融公司的接管人,可以出售或转让任何资产,被出售或转让的任何资产不受制于任何一方的抵销权,但是,享有抵销权的一方应拥有金额与该等抵销权价值相等的权利主张,其权利主张的优先性低于根据第(b)(1)子条第(A)子款、第(B)子款、第(C)子款和第(D)子款中的应付权利主张,但高于第(b)(1)(E)子条定义的任何其他无担保债务。

(13)**资产扣押和其他禁令救济**。——在不违反第(14)款规定的前提下,在联邦存款保险公司作为所涉金融公司的接管人提出请求时,任何有管辖权的法院均可以根据《联邦民事诉讼规则》的《65规则》签发命令,包括将联邦存款保险公司指定的任何人的资产置于法院控制之下,并指定持有该等资产的破产管理人。

(14)**标准**。——

(A) SHOWING. — Rule 65 of the Federal Rules of Civil Procedure shall apply with respect to any proceeding under paragraph (13), without regard to the requirement that the applicant show that the injury, loss, or damage is irreparable and immediate.

(B) STATE PROCEEDING. — If, in the case of any proceeding in a State court, the court determines that rules of civil procedure available under the laws of the State provide substantially similar protections of the right of the parties to due process as provided under Rule 65 (as modified with respect to such proceeding by subparagraph (A)), the relief sought by the Corporation pursuant to paragraph (14) may be requested under the laws of such State.

(15) TREATMENT OF CLAIMS ARISING FROM BREACH OF CONTRACTS EXECUTED BY THE CORPORATION AS RECEIVER. — Notwithstanding any other provision of this title, any final and non–appealable judgment for monetary damages entered against the Corporation as receiver for a covered financial company for the breach of an agreement executed or approved by the Corporation after the date of its appointment shall be paid as an administrative expense of the receiver. Nothing in this paragraph shall be construed to limit the power of a receiver to exercise any rights under contract or law, including to terminate, breach, cancel, or otherwise discontinue such agreement.

(16) ACCOUNTING AND RECORDKEEPING REQUIREMENTS. —

(A) IN GENERAL. — The Corporation as receiver for a covered financial company shall, consistent with the accounting and reporting practices and procedures established by the Corporation, maintain a full accounting of each receivership or other disposition of any covered financial company.

(B) ANNUAL ACCOUNTING OR REPORT. — With respect to each receivership to which the Corporation is appointed, the Corporation shall make an annual accounting or report, as appropriate, available to the Secretary and the Comptroller General of the United States.

(C) AVAILABILITY OF REPORTS. — Any report prepared pursuant to subparagraph (B) and section 203(c)(3) shall be made available to the public by the Corporation.

(D) RECORDKEEPING REQUIREMENT. —

(i) IN GENERAL. — The Corporation shall prescribe such regulations and establish such retention schedules as are necessary to maintain the documents and records of the Corporation generated in exercising the authorities of this title and the records of a covered financial company for which the Corporation is appointed receiver, with due regard for —

(I) the avoidance of duplicative record retention; and

(II) the expected evidentiary needs of the Corporation as receiver for a covered

(A)**证明**。——《联邦民事诉讼规则》的《65规则》适用于根据第(13)款开展的任何程序,申请人不必证明伤害、损失或损害的不可补救性和直接性。

(B)**在州法院开展的程序**。——对于在某一州法院开展的任何程序,如该法院判定该州法律规定的民事诉讼规则为当事人提供的正当程序保护与《65规则》[以经第(A)子款对该等程序作出修改后的版本为准]规定的保护实质类似,联邦存款保险公司依据第(14)款规定所寻求的救济可以通过依照该州法律提出请求而实现。

(15)**因联邦存款保险公司违反其以接管人身份签署的合同而引起的权利主张之处理**。——无论本编是否存在任何不同规定,联邦存款保险公司违反其被指定为所涉金融公司接管人之后签署或批准的某项协议,因而被作出任何具有终局性且不可上诉的金钱赔偿判决的,该等判决之履行应作为接管人的一项行政费用支出处理。本款中的任何规定均不得被解释为限制接管人有权根据合同或法律行使任何权利(包括终止、不履行、取消或以其他方式中止上述协议的权利)。

(16)**会计与记录保存要求**。——

(A)**一般规定**。——联邦存款保险公司作为所涉金融公司的接管人,应根据其制定的会计与报告实践和程序,针对其每次接管任何所涉金融公司或对所涉金融公司进行其他处置的行为维持一份完整的会计记录。

(B)**年度财务报表或报告**。——联邦存款保险公司被指定为接管人的,应针对其每次接管行为向联邦财政部部长和政府问责办公室主任提供年度财务报表或报告(视具体情况而定)。

(C)**报告的提供**。——联邦存款保险公司根据第(B)子款和第203(c)(3)条编制的任何报告均应向公众公开。

(D)**记录保存要求**。——

(i)**一般规定**。——联邦存款保险公司应制定必要的规章和记录留存计划,以保存其在行使本编规定的权力的过程中产生的文件和记录,并保存其作为指定接管人接管的所涉金融公司的记录,在制定该等规章和计划时,应适当考虑如下因素——

(I)避免重复性的记录留存;及

(II)联邦存款保险公司作为所涉金融公司接管人以及公众将所涉金融公司记录

financial company and the public regarding the records of covered financial companies.

(ii) RETENTION OF RECORDS. — Unless otherwise required by applicable Federal law or court order, the Corporation may not, at any time, destroy any records that are subject to clause (i).

(iii) RECORDS DEFINED. — As used in this subparagraph, the terms "records" and "records of a covered financial company" mean any document, book, paper, map, photograph, microfiche, microfilm, computer or electronically-created record generated or maintained by the covered financial company in the course of and necessary to its transaction of business.

(b) PRIORITY OF EXPENSES AND UNSECURED CLAIMS. —

(1) IN GENERAL. — Unsecured claims against a covered financial company, or the Corporation as receiver for such covered financial company under this section, that are proven to the satisfaction of the receiver shall have priority in the following order:

(A) Administrative expenses of the receiver.

(B) Any amounts owed to the United States, unless the United States agrees or consents otherwise.

(C) Wages, salaries, or commissions, including vacation, severance, and sick leave pay earned by an individual (other than an individual described in subparagraph (G)), but only to the extent of $11, 725 for each individual (as indexed for inflation, by regulation of the Corporation) earned not later than 180 days before the date of appointment of the Corporation as receiver.

(D) Contributions owed to employee benefit plans arising from services rendered not later than 180 days before the date of appointment of the Corporation as receiver, to the extent of the number of employees covered by each such plan, multiplied by $11, 725 (as indexed for inflation, by regulation of the Corporation), less the aggregate amount paid to such employees under subparagraph (C), plus the aggregate amount paid by the receivership on behalf of such employees to any other employee benefit plan.

(E) Any other general or senior liability of the covered financial company (which is not a liability described under subparagraph (F), (G), or (H)).

(F) Any obligation subordinated to general creditors (which is not an obligation described under subparagraph (G) or (H)).

(G) Any wages, salaries, or commissions, including vacation, severance, and sick leave pay earned, owed to senior executives and directors of the covered financial company.

(H) Any obligation to shareholders, members, general partners, limited partners, or other persons with interests in the equity of the covered financial company arising as a result of their status as shareholders, members, general partners, limited partners, or other

用作证据的潜在需要。

(ii)**记录留存**。——除非适用的联邦法律或法庭命令另有要求,否则联邦存款保险公司无论何时均不得销毁受制于第(i)项规定的任何记录。

(iii)**记录的定义**。——在本子款中,“记录”和“所涉金融公司的记录”系指所涉金融公司在其日常业务中产生或保存的开展业务所必要的任何文件、账簿、文档、示意图、照片、缩微平片、微缩胶卷和以电脑或电子手段制作的记录。

(b)**费用和无担保权利主张的先后顺序**。——

(1)**一般规定**。——针对所涉金融公司提出的或根据本条规定针对作为所涉金融公司接管人的联邦存款保险公司提出的无担保但已获得令接管人满意的证明的权利主张,应按如下先后顺序清偿:

(A)接管人的行政费用。

(B)欠付联邦政府的任何金额,但联邦政府另行同意或允许降低其优先顺序的除外。

(C)在联邦存款保险公司被指定为接管人之日前180天内任何个人[但第(G)子款所述个人除外]赚取的工资、薪金或佣金,包括假期工资、离职金和病假工资,但每名人员应以11725美元为上限(该数字应根据联邦存款保险公司的规章进行通胀调整)。

(D)因在联邦存款保险公司被指定为接管人之日前180天内提供的服务而产生的应向雇员福利计划支付的缴款,应以按如下公式计算出的金额为限:上述每一计划覆盖的雇员人数乘以11725美元(该数字应根据联邦存款保险公司的规章进行通胀调整),减去根据第(C)子款规定向该等雇员支付的总计金额,加上接管人代表该等雇员向任何其他雇员福利计划缴纳的总金额。

(E)所涉金融公司的任何其他普通债务或优先债务[指第(F)子款、第(G)子款或第(H)子款所述债务之外的债务]。

(F)优先顺序次于普通债权人的任何义务[指第(G)子款或第(H)子款所述义务之外的义务]。

(G)应向所涉金融公司高级管理人员和董事支付的任何工资、薪金或佣金,包括假期工资、离职金和病假工资。

(H)对于所涉金融公司的股东、成员、普通合伙人、有限合伙人或拥有所涉金融公司股权权益的其他人的任何义务,该等义务系因该等人员的上述身份而产生的;

persons with interests in the equity of the covered financial company.

(2) POST-RECEIVERSHIP FINANCING PRIORITY. — In the event that the Corporation, as receiver for a covered financial company, is unable to obtain unsecured credit for the covered financial company from commercial sources, the Corporation as receiver may obtain credit or incur debt on the part of the covered financial company, which shall have priority over any or all administrative expenses of the receiver under paragraph (1)(A).

(3) CLAIMS OF THE UNITED STATES. — Unsecured claims of the United States shall, at a minimum, have a higher priority than liabilities of the covered financial company that count as regulatory capital.

(4) CREDITORS SIMILARLY SITUATED. — All claimants of a covered financial company that are similarly situated under paragraph (1) shall be treated in a similar manner, except that the Corporation may take any action (including making payments, subject to subsection (o)(1)(D)(i)) that does not comply with this subsection, if —

(A) the Corporation determines that such action is necessary —

(i) to maximize the value of the assets of the covered financial company;

(ii) to initiate and continue operations essential to implementation of the receivership or any bridge financial company;

(iii) to maximize the present value return from the sale or other disposition of the assets of the covered financial company; or

(iv) to minimize the amount of any loss realized upon the sale or other disposition of the assets of the covered financial company; and

(B) all claimants that are similarly situated under paragraph (1) receive not less than the amount provided in paragraphs (2) and (3) of subsection (d).

(5) SECURED CLAIMS UNAFFECTED. — This section shall not affect secured claims or security entitlements in respect of assets or property held by the covered financial company, except to the extent that the security is insufficient to satisfy the claim, and then only with regard to the difference between the claim and the amount realized from the security.

(6) PRIORITY OF EXPENSES AND UNSECURED CLAIMS IN THE ORDERLY LIQUIDATION OF SIPC MEMBER. — Where the Corporation is appointed as receiver for a covered broker or dealer, unsecured claims against such covered broker or dealer, or the Corporation as receiver for such covered broker or dealer under this section, that are proven to the satisfaction of the receiver under section 205(e), shall have the priority prescribed in paragraph (1), except that —

(A) SIPC shall be entitled to recover administrative expenses incurred in performing its responsibilities under section 205 on an equal basis with the Corporation, in

（2）**接管后的融资优先性**。——联邦存款保险公司作为所涉金融公司的接管人，无法通过商业渠道为所涉金融公司获得无担保信贷的，联邦存款保险公司作为接管人，可以代表所涉金融公司获取信贷或产生债务，且该等信贷或债务的优先性应高于第（1）（A）款所述接管人的任何或全部行政费用。

（3）**联邦政府的权利主张**。——联邦政府享有的无担保权利主张之优先性至少应在所涉金融公司记入监管资本的负债之前。

（4）**情形类似的债权人**。——所涉金融公司与第（1）款规定的情形类似的全部权利主张人均应按类似方式处理，但在以下情形下，联邦存款保险公司可以采取与本子条规定不一致的任何行动[包括在不违反第（o）（1）（D）（i）子条规定的前提下，作出支付]——

（A）联邦存款保险公司判定该行动系对实现以下目的确属必要——

（i）将所涉金融公司资产价值最大化；

（ii）启动和继续开展对履行接管人职责或对任何过渡金融公司而言必不可少的运营；

（iii）将出售或以其他方式处置所涉金融公司资产所获得的现值最大化；或

（iv）将出售或以其他方式处置所涉金融公司资产造成的任何损失的金额减到最低限度；且

（B）所有与第（1）款规定的情形类似的权利主张人收到的金额均不低于第（d）子条第（2）款和第（3）款规定的金额。

（5）**有担保权利主张不受影响**。——本条规定不影响对所涉金融公司持有的资产或财产享有的有担保权利主张或法定担保权利，但担保不足以偿付权利主张的除外，此时，本条规定将仅适用于权利主张与担保实现金额之间的差额。

（6）**证券投资者保护公司会员有序清算过程中发生的费用和无担保权利主张的优先性**。——联邦存款保险公司被指定为所涉经纪商或自营商的接管人的，针对该所涉经纪商或自营商提出的，或者根据本条规定针对作为该所涉经纪商或自营商的接管人的联邦存款保险公司提出的无担保但已根据第205（e）条规定获得令接管人满意的证实的权利主张，应按第（1）款规定的先后顺序清偿，但是——

（A）证券投资者保护公司有权根据第（1）（A）款的规定，在平等的基础上向联邦存款保险公司追收其在根据第205条履行职责过程中发生的行政费用；

accordance with paragraph (1)(A);

(B) the Corporation shall be entitled to recover any amounts paid to customers or to SIPC pursuant to section 205(f), in accordance with paragraph (1)(B);

(C) SIPC shall be entitled to recover any amounts paid out of the SIPC Fund to meet its obligations under section 205 and under the Securities Investor Protection Act of 1970 (15 U.S.C. 78aaa et seq.), which claim shall be subordinate to the claims payable under subparagraphs (A) and (B) of paragraph (1), but senior to all other claims; and

(D) the Corporation may, after paying any proven claims to customers under section 205 and the Securities Investor Protection Act of 1970 (15 U.S.C. 78aaa et seq.), and as provided above, pay dividends on other proven claims, in its discretion, and to the extent that funds are available, in accordance with the priorities set forth in paragraph (1).

(c) PROVISIONS RELATING TO CONTRACTS ENTERED INTO BEFORE APPOINTMENT OF RECEIVER. —

(1) AUTHORITY TO REPUDIATE CONTRACTS. — In addition to any other rights that a receiver may have, the Corporation as receiver for any covered financial company may disaffirm or repudiate any contract or lease —

(A) to which the covered financial company is a party;

(B) the performance of which the Corporation as receiver, in the discretion of the Corporation, determines to be burdensome; and

(C) the disaffirmance or repudiation of which the Corporation as receiver determines, in the discretion of the Corporation, will promote the orderly administration of the affairs of the covered financial company.

(2) TIMING OF REPUDIATION. — The Corporation, as receiver for any covered financial company, shall determine whether or not to exercise the rights of repudiation under this section within a reasonable period of time.

(3) CLAIMS FOR DAMAGES FOR REPUDIATION. —

(A) IN GENERAL. — Except as provided in paragraphs (4), (5), and (6) and in subparagraphs (C), (D), and (E) of this paragraph, the liability of the Corporation as receiver for a covered financial company for the disaffirmance or repudiation of any contract pursuant to paragraph (1) shall be —

(i) limited to actual direct compensatory damages; and

(ii) determined as of —

(I) the date of the appointment of the Corporation as receiver; or

(II) in the case of any contract or agreement referred to in paragraph (8), the date of the disaffirmance or repudiation of such contract or agreement.

(B) NO LIABILITY FOR OTHER DAMAGES. — For purposes of subparagraph (A), the term "actual direct compensatory damages" does not include —

（B）联邦存款保险公司有权根据第（1）（B）款的规定，追收根据第205（f）条向客户或证券投资者保护公司支付的任何金额；

（C）证券投资者保护公司有权追收其为履行第205条和《1970年证券投资者保护法》（《美国法典》第十五编第78aaa节及其后条文）规定的义务而从证券投资者保护公司基金中支出的任何金额，该项权利主张在优先性上应低于第（1）款第（A）子款和第（B）子款规定的应付权利主张，但高于所有其他权利主张；且

（D）联邦存款保险公司可以在根据第205条和《1970年证券投资者保护法》（《美国法典》第十五编第78aaa节及其后条文）以及上文规定完成对任何已证实权利主张的支付后，依其自由裁量权，在其可支配资金的范围内根据第（1）款规定的先后顺序就其他已证实权利主张支付破产偿金。

（c）**关于指定接管人之前订立的合同的规定**。——

（1）**拒绝履约权**。——联邦存款保险公司作为任何所涉金融公司的接管人，除享有接管人的任何其他权利之外，还可以拒绝履行具有以下特征的任何合同或租约，或宣告其无效——

（A）所涉金融公司是该合同或租约的一方；

（B）联邦存款保险公司作为接管人依其自由裁量权判定履行该合同或租约将造成沉重负担；且

（C）联邦存款保险公司作为接管人依其自由裁量权判定拒绝履行该合同或租约或宣告其无效将促进所涉金融公司事务的有序管理。

（2）**拒绝履行的时限**。——联邦存款保险公司作为任何所涉金融公司的接管人，应在合理的期限内决定是否行使本条规定的拒绝履约权。

（3）**拒绝履约赔偿请求权**。——

（A）**一般规定**。——除第（4）款、第（5）款和第（6）款以及本款第（C）子款、第（D）子款和第（E）子款规定的情形外，联邦存款保险公司作为所涉金融公司的接管人根据第（1）款规定拒绝履行任何合同或宣告任何合同无效的，其因此承担的责任——

（i）应限于实际直接损害赔偿；且

（ii）基于截至以下日期的状况来确定该等责任——

（I）联邦存款保险公司被指定为接管人之日；或

（II）对于第（8）款所述任何合同或协议而言，联邦存款保险公司拒不履行该合同或协议，或宣布该合同或协议无效之日。

（B）**不对其他损害赔偿承担责任**。——就第（A）子款而言，"实际直接损害赔偿"不包括——

(i) punitive or exemplary damages;

(ii) damages for lost profits or opportunity; or

(iii) damages for pain and suffering.

(C) MEASURE OF DAMAGES FOR REPUDIATION OF QUALIFIED FINANCIAL CONTRACTS. — In the case of any qualified financial contract or agreement to which paragraph (8) applies, compensatory damages shall be —

(i) deemed to include normal and reasonable costs of cover or other reasonable measures of damages utilized in the industries for such contract and agreement claims; and

(ii) paid in accordance with this paragraph and subsection (d), except as otherwise specifically provided in this subsection.

(D) MEASURE OF DAMAGES FOR REPUDIATION OR DISAFFIRMANCE OF DEBT OBLIGATION. — In the case of any debt for borrowed money or evidenced by a security, actual direct compensatory damages shall be no less than the amount lent plus accrued interest plus any accreted original issue discount as of the date the Corporation was appointed receiver of the covered financial company and, to the extent that an allowed secured claim is secured by property the value of which is greater than the amount of such claim and any accrued interest through the date of repudiation or disaffirmance, such accrued interest pursuant to paragraph (1).

(E) MEASURE OF DAMAGES FOR REPUDIATION OR DISAFFIRMANCE OF CONTINGENT OBLIGATION. — In the case of any contingent obligation of a covered financial company consisting of any obligation under a guarantee, letter of credit, loan commitment, or similar credit obligation, the Corporation may, by rule or regulation, prescribe that actual direct compensatory damages shall be no less than the estimated value of the claim as of the date the Corporation was appointed receiver of the covered financial company, as such value is measured based on the likelihood that such contingent claim would become fixed and the probable magnitude thereof.

(4) LEASES UNDER WHICH THE COVERED FINANCIAL COMPANY IS THE LESSEE. —

(A) IN GENERAL. — If the Corporation as receiver disaffirms or repudiates a lease under which the covered financial company is the lessee, the receiver shall not be liable for any damages (other than damages determined pursuant to subparagraph (B)) for the disaffirmance or repudiation of such lease.

(B) PAYMENTS OF RENT. — Notwithstanding subparagraph (A), the lessor under a lease to which subparagraph (A) would otherwise apply shall —

(i) be entitled to the contractual rent accruing before the later of the date on which —

(I) the notice of disaffirmance or repudiation is mailed; or

(i)惩罚性赔偿金;

(ii)利润损失或机会损失赔偿;或

(iii)疼痛和精神痛苦赔偿。

(C)**拒绝履行合格金融合约的损害赔偿之计量**。——就适用第(8)款规定的任何合格金融合约或协议而言,损害赔偿应——

(i)视为包括正常且合理的成本项目,或采用业内就该类合约和协议主张所使用的其他计量损害赔偿的合理方法;并

(ii)根据本款和第(d)子条支付,但本子条另有明确规定的除外。

(D)**拒绝履行或宣布债务无效的损害赔偿之确定**。——就任何现金借款债务,或以证券作为凭证的债务而言,实际直接损害赔偿金不得低于按如下规定计算出的金额:所借任何本金加上截至联邦存款保险公司被指定为所涉金融公司接管人之日的应计利息、原始发行折价增值,同时,如果某项权利主张已被认可,且作为其担保的财产的价值高于截至拒绝履行或宣布无效之日该权利主张加上任何应计利息的金额,则还应加上第(1)款规定的该等应计利息。

(E)**拒绝履行或有义务,或宣布或有义务无效的损害赔偿之计量**。——如果所涉金融公司的任何或有义务中包括保证、信用证、贷款承诺项下的义务或类似的信贷义务,则联邦存款保险公司应发布规则或规章,规定与该等义务相关的实际直接损害赔偿金额不得低于截至联邦存款保险公司被指定为所涉金融公司接管人之日该权利主张的估算价值,该价值应基于该或有权利主张成为确定权利主张的可能性和潜在的金额估算。

(4)**所涉金融公司作为承租人签订的租约**。——

(A)**一般规定**。——联邦存款保险公司作为接管人拒绝履行所涉金融公司作为承租人签订的租约或宣布该等租约无效的,接管人不就此承担任何损害赔偿责任[但根据第(B)子款确定的损害赔偿除外]。

(B)**租金支付**。——无论第(A)子款如何规定,因其他原因而应适用第(A)子款规定的租约的出租人将——

(i)有权获得在以下日期(以较晚者为准)之前累计的约定租金——

(I)宣布无效或拒绝履行通知的寄送日;或

(II) the disaffirmance or repudiation becomes effective, unless the lessor is in default or breach of the terms of the lease;

(ii) have no claim for damages under any acceleration clause or other penalty provision in the lease; and

(iii) have a claim for any unpaid rent, subject to all appropriate offsets and defenses, due as of the date of the appointment which shall be paid in accordance with this paragraph and subsection (d).

(5) LEASES UNDER WHICH THE COVERED FINANCIAL COMPANY IS THE LESSOR. —

(A) IN GENERAL. — If the Corporation as receiver for a covered financial company repudiates an unexpired written lease of real property of the covered financial company under which the covered financial company is the lessor and the lessee is not, as of the date of such repudiation, in default, the lessee under such lease may either —

(i) treat the lease as terminated by such repudiation; or

(ii) remain in possession of the leasehold interest for the balance of the term of the lease, unless the lessee defaults under the terms of the lease after the date of such repudiation.

(B) PROVISIONS APPLICABLE TO LESSEE REMAINING IN POSSESSION. — If any lessee under a lease described in subparagraph (A) remains in possession of a leasehold interest pursuant to clause (ii) of subparagraph (A) —

(i) the lessee —

(I) shall continue to pay the contractual rent pursuant to the terms of the lease after the date of the repudiation of such lease; and

(II) may offset against any rent payment which accrues after the date of the repudiation of the lease, any damages which accrue after such date due to the nonperformance of any obligation of the covered financial company under the lease after such date; and

(ii) the Corporation as receiver shall not be liable to the lessee for any damages arising after such date as a result of the repudiation, other than the amount of any offset allowed under clause (i)(II).

(6) CONTRACTS FOR THE SALE OF REAL PROPERTY. —

(A) IN GENERAL. — If the receiver repudiates any contract (which meets the requirements of subsection (a)(6)) for the sale of real property, and the purchaser of such real property under such contract is in possession and is not, as of the date of such repudiation, in default, such purchaser may either —

(i) treat the contract as terminated by such repudiation; or

(ii) remain in possession of such real property.

(II)宣布无效或拒绝履行的生效日,但出租人不履行或违反租约条款在先的除外;

(ii)不得根据租约中的任何提前偿付条款或其他罚款规定主张损害赔偿;且

(iii)在受制于全部适当的抵销和抗辩的前提下,有权主张截至上述指定日根据本款和第(d)子条应付但未付的任何租金。

(5)**所涉金融公司作为出租人签订的租约**。——

(A)**一般规定**。——联邦存款保险公司作为所涉金融公司的接管人拒绝履行所涉金融公司作为出租人就其不动产签订的尚未到期的书面租约,且截至该拒绝履约决定作出之时承租人并未违约的,该租约的承租人可以——

(i)将租约视为已在联邦存款保险公司作出拒绝履约决定之时终止;或

(ii)继续保有剩余租期的承租权益,但承租人在上述拒绝履约日之后违反租约条款的除外。

(B)**适用于继续保有承租权益的承租人的规定**。——第(A)子款所述租约的任何承租人根据第(A)子款第(ii)项规定继续保有承租权益的——

(i)该承租人——

(I)应在联邦存款保险公司拒绝履约之日后根据租约条款继续支付约定租金;且

(II)拒绝履约日后所涉金融公司的任何租约义务未得到履行,从而产生任何损害赔偿的,承租人可以以该等损害赔偿抵销拒绝履约之日起累计的任何应付租金;且

(ii)除第(i)(II)项允许抵销的金额外,联邦存款保险公司作为接管人,不必在拒绝履约日后就拒绝履约行为向承租人承担任何损害赔偿责任。

(6)**不动产出售合同**。——

(A)**一般规定**。——如果接管人拒绝履行符合第(a)(6)子条要求的任何不动产出售合同,并且,该等合同中的不动产购买人在拒绝履约日已占有该不动产且并未违约,则该购买人可以——

(i)将合同视为已在联邦存款保险公司作出拒绝履约决定之时终止;或

(ii)继续占有该不动产。

(B) PROVISIONS APPLICABLE TO PURCHASER REMAINING IN POSSESSION. — If any purchaser of real property under any contract described in subparagraph (A) remains in possession of such property pursuant to clause (ii) of subparagraph (A) —

(i) the purchaser —

(I) shall continue to make all payments due under the contract after the date of the repudiation of the contract; and

(II) may offset against any such payments any damages which accrue after such date due to the nonperformance (after such date) of any obligation of the covered financial company under the contract; and

(ii) the Corporation as receiver shall —

(I) not be liable to the purchaser for any damages arising after such date as a result of the repudiation, other than the amount of any offset allowed under clause (i)(II);

(II) deliver title to the purchaser in accordance with the provisions of the contract; and

(III) have no obligation under the contract other than the performance required under subclause (II).

(C) ASSIGNMENT AND SALE ALLOWED. —

(i) IN GENERAL. — No provision of this paragraph shall be construed as limiting the right of the Corporation as receiver to assign the contract described in subparagraph (A) and sell the property, subject to the contract and the provisions of this paragraph.

(ii) NO LIABILITY AFTER ASSIGNMENT AND SALE. — If an assignment and sale described in clause (i) is consummated, the Corporation as receiver shall have no further liability under the contract described in subparagraph (A) or with respect to the real property which was the subject of such contract.

(7) PROVISIONS APPLICABLE TO SERVICE CONTRACTS. —

(A) SERVICES PERFORMED BEFORE APPOINTMENT. — In the case of any contract for services between any person and any covered financial company for which the Corporation has been appointed receiver, any claim of such person for services performed before the date of appointment shall be —

(i) a claim to be paid in accordance with subsections (a), (b), and (d); and

(ii) deemed to have arisen as of the date on which the receiver was appointed.

(B) SERVICES PERFORMED AFTER APPOINTMENT AND PRIOR TO REPUDIATION. — If, in the case of any contract for services described in subparagraph (A), the Corporation as receiver accepts performance by the other person before making any determination to exercise the right of repudiation of such contract under this section —

(i) the other party shall be paid under the terms of the contract for the services performed; and

(B)**适用于继续占有不动产的购买人的规定**。——第(A)子款所述的任何合同的任何不动产购买人根据第(A)子款第(ii)项规定继续占有不动产的——

(i)该购买人——

(I)应在联邦存款保险公司拒绝履约之日后继续支付合同规定的全部应付款项;且

(II)拒绝履约日后所涉金融公司的任何合同义务未得到履行,从而产生任何损害赔偿的,购买人有权以该等损害赔偿抵销任何上述付款;且

(ii)联邦存款保险公司作为接管人——

(I)除第(i)(II)项允许任何抵销的金额外,不必在拒绝履约日后就拒绝履约行为向购买人承担任何损害赔偿责任;

(II)应根据合同约定向购买人交付所有权;且

(III)除履行第(II)子项规定的义务外,不必承担该合同规定的任何义务。

(C)**允许的转让和出售**。——

(i)**一般规定**。——在不违反合同约定及本款规定的前提下,本款任何规定均不得被解释为限制联邦存款保险公司作为接管人转让第(A)子款所述合同和出售该不动产的权利。

(ii)**转让和出售后不承担任何责任**。——第(i)项所述转让和出售已经订立合同的,联邦存款保险公司作为接管人,不必根据第(A)子款所述合同承担任何责任,也不必就作为上述合同标的之不动产承担任何责任。

(7)**适用于服务合同的规定**。——

(A)**指定日之前履行的服务**。——任何人与联邦存款保险公司作为指定接管人接管的任何所涉金融公司之间存在服务合同关系的,该人就指定日之前已履行的服务提出的任何权利主张应——

(i)属于应根据第(a)子条、第(b)子条和第(d)子条支付的权利主张;且

(ii)视为在接管人被指定之日产生的权利主张。

(B)**指定日之后、拒绝履约日之前履行的服务**。——就第(A)子款所述任何服务合同而言,如联邦存款保险公司作为接管人,在根据本条规定作出行使拒绝履约权的任何决定之前接受了另一方履行的服务,则——

(i)另一方有权根据该合同条款就已履行的服务获得支付;且

(ii) the amount of such payment shall be treated as an administrative expense of the receivership.

(C) ACCEPTANCE OF PERFORMANCE NO BAR TO SUBSEQUENT REPUDIATION. — The acceptance by the Corporation as receiver for services referred to in subparagraph (B) in connection with a contract described in subparagraph (B) shall not affect the right of the Corporation as receiver to repudiate such contract under this section at any time after such performance.

(8) CERTAIN QUALIFIED FINANCIAL CONTRACTS. —

(A) RIGHTS OF PARTIES TO CONTRACTS. — Subject to subsection (a)(8) and paragraphs (9) and (10) of this subsection, and notwithstanding any other provision of this section, any other provision of Federal law, or the law of any State, no person shall be stayed or prohibited from exercising —

(i) any right that such person has to cause the termination, liquidation, or acceleration of any qualified financial contract with a covered financial company which arises upon the date of appointment of the Corporation as receiver for such covered financial company or at any time after such appointment;

(ii) any right under any security agreement or arrangement or other credit enhancement related to one or more qualified financial contracts described in clause (i); or

(iii) any right to offset or net out any termination value, payment amount, or other transfer obligation arising under or in connection with 1 or more contracts or agreements described in clause (i), including any master agreement for such contracts or agreements.

(B) APPLICABILITY OF OTHER PROVISIONS. — Subsection (a)(8) shall apply in the case of any judicial action or proceeding brought against the Corporation as receiver referred to in subparagraph (A), or the subject covered financial company, by any party to a contract or agreement described in subparagraph (A)(i) with such covered financial company.

(C) CERTAIN TRANSFERS NOT AVOIDABLE. —

(i) IN GENERAL. — Notwithstanding subsection (a)(11), (a)(12), or (c)(12), section 5242 of the Revised Statutes of the United States, or any other provision of Federal or State law relating to the avoidance of preferential or fraudulent transfers, the Corporation, whether acting as the Corporation or as receiver for a covered financial company, may not avoid any transfer of money or other property in connection with any qualified financial contract with a covered financial company.

(ii) EXCEPTION FOR CERTAIN TRANSFERS. — Clause (i) shall not apply to any transfer of money or other property in connection with any qualified financial contract with a covered financial company if the transferee had actual intent to hinder, delay, or

(ii)该支付金额应作为履行接管职责的一项行政费用处理。

(C)**接受服务履行不妨碍随后行使拒绝履约权**。——联邦存款保险公司作为接管人接受与第(B)子款所述合同相关的第(B)子款提及的服务,不妨碍联邦存款保险公司作为接管人根据本条规定在该服务履行后的任何时候拒绝履约的权利。

(8)**特定合格金融合约**。——

(A)**合约当事方的权利**。——在不违反第(a)(8)子条和本子条第(9)款、第(10)款规定的前提下,无论本条任何其他条款、联邦法律或任何州法律是否存在任何不同规定,任何人均不得被中止或禁止行使以下权利——

(i)在联邦存款保险公司被指定为所涉金融公司接管人之日或之后任何时候产生的,该人拥有的责成终止、清算或提前履行与所涉金融公司之间的任何合格金融合约的权利;

(ii)与第(i)项所述某一或某些合格金融合约相关的任何担保协议、安排或其他信用增级措施中的任何权利;或

(iii)针对由于第(i)项所述某一或某些合约或协议产生的或者与该等合约或协议(包括该等合约或协议的任何主协议)相关的任何终止价值、支付金额或其他转让义务的抵销权或净额冲抵权。

(B)**其他规定的适用性**。——第(A)(i)子款所述与所涉金融公司签订的合约或协议的任何一方,对第(A)子款所述作为接管人的联邦存款保险公司或其接管的所涉金融公司提起任何司法诉讼或程序的,应适用第(a)(8)子条的规定。

(C)**不可撤销的特定转让**。——

(i)**一般规定**。——无论第(a)(11)子条、第(a)(12)子条、第(c)(12)子条、《美国制定法汇编》(修订版)第5242条或者联邦法律或任何州法律关于撤销偏颇性或欺诈性转让的任何其他条款如何规定,联邦存款保险公司以其自身身份或作为所涉金融公司接管人,均无权撤销根据与所涉金融公司达成的任何合格金融合约作出的任何现金转让或其他财产转让。

(ii)**关于特定转让的例外规定**。——在根据与所涉金融公司达成的任何合格金融合约实施任何现金转让或其他财产转让时,如受让人的实际意图为对该公司、该公司债权人或被指定为该公司接管人的联邦存款保险公司造成妨碍、延误或欺诈的,则

defraud such company, the creditors of such company, or the Corporation as receiver appointed for such company.

(D) CERTAIN CONTRACTS AND AGREEMENTS DEFINED. — For purposes of this subsection, the following definitions shall apply:

(i) QUALIFIED FINANCIAL CONTRACT. — The term "qualified financial contract" means any securities contract, commodity contract, forward contract, repurchase agreement, swap agreement, and any similar agreement that the Corporation determines by regulation, resolution, or order to be a qualified financial contract for purposes of this paragraph.

(ii) SECURITIES CONTRACT. — The term "securities contract" —

(I) means a contract for the purchase, sale, or loan of a security, a certificate of deposit, a mortgage loan, any interest in a mortgage loan, a group or index of securities, certificates of deposit, or mortgage loans or interests therein (including any interest therein or based on the value thereof), or any option on any of the foregoing, including any option to purchase or sell any such security, certificate of deposit, mortgage loan, interest, group or index, or option, and including any repurchase or reverse repurchase transaction on any such security, certificate of deposit, mortgage loan, interest, group or index, or option (whether or not such repurchase or reverse repurchase transaction is a "repurchase agreement", as defined in clause (v));

(II) does not include any purchase, sale, or repurchase obligation under a participation in a commercial mortgage loan unless the Corporation determines by regulation, resolution, or order to include any such agreement within the meaning of such term;

(III) means any option entered into on a national securities exchange relating to foreign currencies;

(IV) means the guarantee (including by novation) by or to any securities clearing agency of any settlement of cash, securities, certificates of deposit, mortgage loans or interests therein, group or index of securities, certificates of deposit or mortgage loans or interests therein (including any interest therein or based on the value thereof) or an option on any of the foregoing, including any option to purchase or sell any such security, certificate of deposit, mortgage loan, interest, group or index, or option (whether or not such settlement is in connection with any agreement or transaction referred to in subclauses (I) through (XII) (other than subclause (II)));

(V) means any margin loan;

(VI) means any extension of credit for the clearance or settlement of securities transactions;

(VII) means any loan transaction coupled with a securities collar transaction, any

该转让不得适用第(i)项的规定。

(D)**特定合约和协议的定义**。——就本子条而言,应适用如下定义:

(i)**合格金融合约**。——“合格金融合约”一词系指任何证券合约、商品合约、远期合约、回购协议、互换协议以及通过联邦存款保险公司发布规章、决议或命令判定的属于本款意义上合格金融合约的任何类似协议。

(ii)**证券合约**。——“证券合约”一词——

(I)系指对如下所列各项进行购买、出售或贷款的合约:证券、存单、抵押贷款、任何抵押贷款权益;证券、存单、抵押贷款或抵押贷款权益的集合或指数(包括对该等集合或指数的任何权益或者基于该等集合或指数价值的任何权益);或上述任何各者的任何期权,包括购买或出售任何该等证券、存单、抵押贷款、权益、集合或指数或期权的期权,也包括针对任何该等证券、存单、抵押贷款、权益、集合或指数或期权开展的任何回购交易或逆回购交易[无论该回购交易或逆回购交易是否属于第(v)项定义的“回购协议”];

(II)不包括参与商业抵押贷款时承担的任何购买、出售或回购义务,但联邦存款保险公司发布规章、决议或命令,将任何上述协议纳入“证券合约”定义的除外;

(III)系指在全国性证券交易所达成的与外币相关的任何期权;

(IV)系指向证券结算机构或由任何证券结算机构作出的关于下列各项之任何结算的保证(包括通过更替形式承担的保证):现金、证券、存单、抵押贷款或抵押贷款权益;证券、存单、抵押贷款或抵押贷款权益的集合或指数(包括对该等集合或指数的任何权益或者基于该等集合或指数价值的任何权益);或上述任何各者的任何期权,包括购买或出售任何该等证券、存单、抵押贷款、权益、集合或指数或期权的期权,而无论上述各项的结算是否与第(I)子项至第(XII)子项[但第(II)子项除外]所述任何协议或交易相关;

(V)系指任何保证金贷款;

(VI)系指为清算或结算证券交易之目的作出的任何授信;

(VII)系指证券封顶保底交易附随的任何贷款交易、任何预付证券远期交易或证

prepaid securities forward transaction, or any total return swap transaction coupled with a securities sale transaction;

(VIII) means any other agreement or transaction that is similar to any agreement or transaction referred to in this clause;

(IX) means any combination of the agreements or transactions referred to in this clause;

(X) means any option to enter into any agreement or transaction referred to in this clause;

(XI) means a master agreement that provides for an agreement or transaction referred to in any of subclauses (I) through (X), other than subclause (II), together with all supplements to any such master agreement, without regard to whether the master agreement provides for an agreement or transaction that is not a securities contract under this clause, except that the master agreement shall be considered to be a securities contract under this clause only with respect to each agreement or transaction under the master agreement that is referred to in any of subclauses (I) through (X), other than subclause (II); and

(XII) means any security agreement or arrangement or other credit enhancement related to any agreement or transaction referred to in this clause, including any guarantee or reimbursement obligation in connection with any agreement or transaction referred to in this clause.

(iii) COMMODITY CONTRACT. — The term "commodity contract" means —

(I) with respect to a futures commission merchant, a contract for the purchase or sale of a commodity for future delivery on, or subject to the rules of, a contract market or board of trade;

(II) with respect to a foreign futures commission merchant, a foreign future;

(III) with respect to a leverage transaction merchant, a leverage transaction;

(IV) with respect to a clearing organization, a contract for the purchase or sale of a commodity for future delivery on, or subject to the rules of, a contract market or board of trade that is cleared by such clearing organization, or commodity option traded on, or subject to the rules of, a contract market or board of trade that is cleared by such clearing organization;

(V) with respect to a commodity options dealer, a commodity option;

(VI) any other agreement or transaction that is similar to any agreement or transaction referred to in this clause;

(VII) any combination of the agreements or transactions referred to in this clause;

(VIII) any option to enter into any agreement or transaction referred to in this clause;

券出售交易附随的任何总回报互换交易;

(VIII)系指与本项所述协议或交易类似的任何其他协议或交易;

(IX)系指本项所述协议或交易的任何组合;

(X)系指达成本项所述任何协议或交易的任何期权;

(XI)系指规定了第(I)子项至第(X)子项中任一子项[但第(II)子项除外]所述某项协议或交易的某一主协议以及任何该等主协议的全部补充协议,而不论该主协议是否规定了并非本项定义的证券合约的协议或交易,但是,只有对于第(I)子项至第(X)子项中任一子项[但第(II)子项除外]所述的各项协议或交易而言,该主协议始得视为本项定义的证券合约;且

(XII)系指与本项所述任何协议或交易相关的任何担保协议、安排或其他信用增级措施,包括与本项所述任何协议或交易相关的任何保证或补偿义务。

(iii)**商品合约**。——"商品合约"一词——

(I)就期货经纪商而言,系指在合约市场、交易场所或按其规则进行远期交割的商品的买卖合约;

(II)就外国期货经纪商而言,系指外国期货;

(III)就杠杆交易商而言,系指杠杆交易;

(IV)就结算组织而言,系指由该结算组织集中结算的在合约市场、交易场所或按其规则进行远期交割的商品的买卖合约,或者由该结算组织集中结算的在合约市场、交易场所或按其规则交易的商品期权;

(V)就商品期权交易商而言,系指商品期权;

(VI)系指与本项所述任何协议或交易类似的任何其他协议或交易;

(VII)系指本项所述协议或交易的任何组合;

(VIII)系指达成本项所述任何协议或交易的任何期权;

(IX) a master agreement that provides for an agreement or transaction referred to in any of subclauses (I) through (VIII), together with all supplements to any such master agreement, without regard to whether the master agreement provides for an agreement or transaction that is not a commodity contract under this clause, except that the master agreement shall be considered to be a commodity contract under this clause only with respect to each agreement or transaction under the master agreement that is referred to in any of subclauses (I) through (VIII); or

(X) any security agreement or arrangement or other credit enhancement related to any agreement or transaction referred to in this clause, including any guarantee or reimbursement obligation in connection with any agreement or transaction referred to in this clause.

(iv) FORWARD CONTRACT. — The term "forward contract" means —

(I) a contract (other than a commodity contract) for the purchase, sale, or transfer of a commodity or any similar good, article, service, right, or interest which is presently or in the future becomes the subject of dealing in the forward contract trade, or product or byproduct thereof, with a maturity date that is more than 2 days after the date on which the contract is entered into, including a repurchase or reverse repurchase transaction (whether or not such repurchase or reverse repurchase transaction is a "repurchase agreement", as defined in clause (v)), consignment, lease, swap, hedge transaction, deposit, loan, option, allocated transaction, unallocated transaction, or any other similar agreement;

(II) any combination of agreements or transactions referred to in subclauses (I) and (III);

(III) any option to enter into any agreement or transaction referred to in subclause (I) or (II);

(IV) a master agreement that provides for an agreement or transaction referred to in subclause (I), (II), or (III), together with all supplements to any such master agreement, without regard to whether the master agreement provides for an agreement or transaction that is not a forward contract under this clause, except that the master agreement shall be considered to be a forward contract under this clause only with respect to each agreement or transaction under the master agreement that is referred to in subclause (I), (II), or (III); or

(V) any security agreement or arrangement or other credit enhancement related to any agreement or transaction referred to in subclause (I), (II), (III), or (IV), including any guarantee or reimbursement obligation in connection with any agreement or transaction referred to in any such subclause.

(v) REPURCHASE AGREEMENT. — The term "repurchase agreement" (which

(IX)系指规定了第(I)子项至第(VIII)子项中任一子项所述某项协议或交易的某一主协议以及任何该等主协议的全部补充协议,而不论该主协议是否规定了并非本项定义的商品合约的协议或交易,但是,只有对于第(I)子项至第(VIII)子项中任一子项所述的各项协议或交易而言,该主协议始得视为本项定义的商品合约;或

(X)系指与本项所述任何协议或交易相关的任何担保协议、安排或其他信用增级措施,包括与本项所述任何协议或交易相关的任何保证或补偿义务。

(iv)**远期合约**。——“远期合约”一词——

(I)系指当前属于或未来将成为远期合约交易标的之商品或任何类似货物、物品、服务、权利或权益或上述各者的产品、副产品的购买、出售或转让合约(但商品合约除外),且合约到期日应为合约达成之日起超过两天以后,包括回购或逆回购交易[无论该回购交易或逆回购交易是否属于第(v)项定义的“回购协议”]、寄售、租约、互换、套期保值交易、存款、贷款、期权、分配交易、非分配交易或任何其他类似协议;

(II)系指第(I)子项和第(III)子项所述协议或交易的任何组合;

(III)系指达成第(I)子项或第(II)子项所述任何协议或交易的任何期权;

(IV)系指规定了第(I)子项、第(II)子项或第(III)子项所述某项协议或交易的某一主协议以及任何该等主协议的全部补充协议,而不论该主协议是否规定了并非本项定义的远期合约的协议或交易,但是,只有对第(I)子项、第(II)子项或第(III)子项中任一子项所述的各项协议或交易而言,该主协议始得视为本项定义的远期合约;或

(V)系指与第(I)子项、第(II)子项、第(III)子项或第(IV)子项所述任何协议或交易相关的任何担保协议、安排或其他信用增级措施,包括与任何该等子项所述任何协议或交易相关的任何保证或补偿义务。

(v)**回购协议**。——“回购协议”一词(该词定义也适用于逆回购协议)——

definition also applies to a reverse repurchase agreement) —

(I) means an agreement, including related terms, which provides for the transfer of one or more certificates of deposit, mortgage related securities (as such term is defined in section 3 of the Securities Exchange Act of 1934), mortgage loans, interests in mortgage–related securities or mortgage loans, eligible bankers' acceptances, qualified foreign government securities (which, for purposes of this clause, means a security that is a direct obligation of, or that is fully guaranteed by, the central government of a member of the Organization for Economic Cooperation and Development, as determined by regulation or order adopted by the Board of Governors), or securities that are direct obligations of, or that are fully guaranteed by, the United States or any agency of the United States against the transfer of funds by the transferee of such certificates of deposit, eligible bankers' acceptances, securities, mortgage loans, or interests with a simultaneous agreement by such transferee to transfer to the transferor thereof certificates of deposit, eligible bankers' acceptances, securities, mortgage loans, or interests as described above, at a date certain not later than 1 year after such transfers or on demand, against the transfer of funds, or any other similar agreement;

(II) does not include any repurchase obligation under a participation in a commercial mortgage loan, unless the Corporation determines, by regulation, resolution, or order to include any such participation within the meaning of such term;

(III) means any combination of agreements or transactions referred to in subclauses (I) and (IV);

(IV) means any option to enter into any agreement or transaction referred to in subclause (I) or (III);

(V) means a master agreement that provides for an agreement or transaction referred to in subclause (I), (III), or (IV), together with all supplements to any such master agreement, without regard to whether the master agreement provides for an agreement or transaction that is not a repurchase agreement under this clause, except that the master agreement shall be considered to be a repurchase agreement under this subclause only with respect to each agreement or transaction under the master agreement that is referred to in subclause (I), (III), or (IV); and

(VI) means any security agreement or arrangement or other credit enhancement related to any agreement or transaction referred to in subclause (I), (III), (IV), or (V), including any guarantee or reimbursement obligation in connection with any agreement or transaction referred to in any such subclause.

(vi) SWAP AGREEMENT. — The term "swap agreement" means —

(I) any agreement, including the terms and conditions incorporated by reference in any such agreement, which is an interest rate swap, option, future, or forward agreement,

(I)系指规定了对转让标的(具体说明如下)进行转让(包括相关条款)且与此同时受让方同意在转让之后的一定时间将转让标的转回给转让方(转让与转回方式具体说明如下)的协议,或者任何其他类似的协议:转让标的指一项或一项以上存单、抵押相关证券(定义见《1934年证券交易法》第3条)、抵押贷款、抵押相关证券权益或抵押贷款权益、适格银行承兑汇票、适格外国政府证券(就本项而言,指联邦储备委员会制定的规章或命令所判定的属于经济合作与发展组织成员国中央政府的直接债务或由该中央政府全额担保的证券)或属于美国联邦政府或任何联邦政府机关的直接债务或者由美国联邦政府或任何联邦政府机关全额担保的证券;实施转让时,上述存单、适格银行承兑汇票、证券、抵押贷款或权益之受让方向转让方转移资金,与此同时受让方同意,在上述转让实施后1年内的某一特定日期,或经上述存单、合格银行承兑汇票、证券、抵押贷款或权益之转让方要求,即向该转让方转回上述存单、适格银行承兑汇票、证券、抵押贷款或权益并且转让方向受让方转回资金;

(II)不包括参与某项商业抵押贷款时承担的任何回购义务,但联邦存款保险公司依据其发布规章、决议或命令判定将该等参与纳入"回购协议"定义的情形除外;

(III)系指第(I)子项和第(IV)子项所述协议或交易的任何组合;

(IV)系指达成第(I)子项或第(III)子项所述任何协议或交易的任何期权;

(V)系指规定了第(I)子项、第(III)子项或第(IV)子项所述某项协议或交易的某一主协议以及任何该等主协议的全部补充协议,而不论该主协议是否规定了并非本项定义的回购协议的协议或交易,但是,只有对于第(I)子项、第(III)子项或第(IV)子项所述的每项协议或交易而言,该主协议始得视为本子项定义的回购协议;且

(VI)系指与第(I)子项、第(III)子项、第(IV)子项或第(V)子项所述任何协议或交易相关的任何担保协议、安排或其他信用增级措施,包括与任一该等子项所述任何协议或交易相关的任何保证或补偿义务。

(vi)**互换协议**。——"互换协议"一词——

(I)系指任何以下协议,包括任何该等协议引用纳入的条款和条件:利率互换、期权、期货或远期协议,包括利率下限期权、利率上限期权、保护性封顶保底利率期权、

including a rate floor, rate cap, rate collar, cross–currency rate swap, and basis swap; a spot, same day–tomorrow, tomorrow–next, forward, or other foreign exchange, precious metals, or other commodity agreement; a currency swap, option, future, or forward agreement; an equity index or equity swap, option, future, or forward agreement; a debt index or debt swap, option, future, or forward agreement; a total return, credit spread or credit swap, option, future, or forward agreement; a commodity index or commodity swap, option, future, or forward agreement; weather swap, option, future, or forward agreement; an emissions swap, option, future, or forward agreement; or an inflation swap, option, future, or forward agreement;

(II) any agreement or transaction that is similar to any other agreement or transaction referred to in this clause and that is of a type that has been, is presently, or in the future becomes, the subject of recurrent dealings in the swap or other derivatives markets (including terms and conditions incorporated by reference in such agreement) and that is a forward, swap, future, option, or spot transaction on one or more rates, currencies, commodities, equity securities or other equity instruments, debt securities or other debt instruments, quantitative measures associated with an occurrence, extent of an occurrence, or contingency associated with a financial, commercial, or economic consequence, or economic or financial indices or measures of economic or financial risk or value;

(III) any combination of agreements or transactions referred to in this clause;

(IV) any option to enter into any agreement or transaction referred to in this clause;

(V) a master agreement that provides for an agreement or transaction referred to in subclause (I), (II), (III), or (IV), together with all supplements to any such master agreement, without regard to whether the master agreement contains an agreement or transaction that is not a swap agreement under this clause, except that the master agreement shall be considered to be a swap agreement under this clause only with respect to each agreement or transaction under the master agreement that is referred to in subclause (I), (II), (III), or (IV); and

(VI) any security agreement or arrangement or other credit enhancement related to any agreement or transaction referred to in any of subclauses (I) through (V), including any guarantee or reimbursement obligation in connection with any agreement or transaction referred to in any such clause.

(vii) DEFINITIONS RELATING TO DEFAULT. — When used in this paragraph and paragraphs (9) and (10) —

(I) the term "default" means, with respect to a covered financial company, any

跨货币利率互换以及基差互换;外汇、贵金属或其他商品的即期互换、当日换明日、明日换后日、远期互换或其他协议;货币互换、期权、期货或远期协议;股权指数或股权互换、期权、期货或远期协议;债务指数或债务互换、期权、期货或远期协议;总回报、信贷息差或信贷互换、期权、期货或远期协议;商品指数或商品互换、期权、期货或远期协议;气候互换、期权、期货或远期协议;排放互换、期权、期货或远期协议;或者通货膨胀互换、期权、期货或远期协议;

(II)系指与本项所述任何其他协议或交易类似且具有如下特征的任何协议或交易:已成为、当前属于或在未来成为互换或其他衍生品市场经常性交易标的之协议或交易(包括该等协议引用纳入的条款和条件)并且该协议或交易属于如下各者的远期、互换、期货、期权或即期交易:一项或一项以上比率;货币;商品;股权证券或其他股权工具;债务证券或其他债务工具;与伴随有金融、商业或经济后果的某一事件的发生、某一事件发生的范围或程度或者或有事件发生的可能性相关的量化指标;或者经济或金融风险或价值的经济或金融指数或指标;

(III)系指本项所述协议或交易的任何组合;

(IV)系指达成本项所述任何协议或交易的任何期权;

(V)系指规定了第(I)子项、第(II)子项、第(III)子项或第(IV)子项所述某项协议或交易的某一主协议以及任何该等主协议的全部补充协议,而不论该主协议是否同时包含了并非本项定义的互换协议的协议或交易,但是,只有对于第(I)子项、第(II)子项、第(III)子项或第(IV)子项所述每项协议或交易而言,该主协议始得视为本项定义的互换协议;且

(VI)系指与第(I)子项至第(V)子项中任一子项所述任何协议或交易相关的任何担保协议、安排或其他信用增级措施,包括与上述任一子项[1]所述任何协议或交易相关的任何保证或补偿义务。

(vii)**与违约相关的定义**。——在本款以及第(9)款和第(10)款中——

(I)就所涉金融公司而言,"违约"一词系指任何有管辖权的法院或其他公共权力

1 根据本子项所述的"第(I)子项至第(V)子项中任一子项"并参考本项下其他子项中的索引,此处索引似乎不指向"项"("clause"),而指向"子项"("subclause"),译文中按后者处理。——译者注

adjudication or other official decision by any court of competent jurisdiction, or other public authority pursuant to which the Corporation has been appointed receiver; and

(II) the term "in danger of default" means a covered financial company with respect to which the Corporation or appropriate State authority has determined that —

(aa) in the opinion of the Corporation or such authority —

(AA) the covered financial company is not likely to be able to pay its obligations in the normal course of business; and

(BB) there is no reasonable prospect that the covered financial company will be able to pay such obligations without Federal assistance; or

(bb) in the opinion of the Corporation or such authority —

(AA) the covered financial company has incurred or is likely to incur losses that will deplete all or substantially all of its capital; and

(BB) there is no reasonable prospect that the capital will be replenished without Federal assistance.

(viii) TREATMENT OF MASTER AGREEMENT AS ONE AGREEMENT. — Any master agreement for any contract or agreement described in any of clauses (i) through (vi) (or any master agreement for such master agreement or agreements), together with all supplements to such master agreement, shall be treated as a single agreement and a single qualified financial contact. If a master agreement contains provisions relating to agreements or transactions that are not themselves qualified financial contracts, the master agreement shall be deemed to be a qualified financial contract only with respect to those transactions that are themselves qualified financial contracts.

(ix) TRANSFER. — The term "transfer" means every mode, direct or indirect, absolute or conditional, voluntary or involuntary, of disposing of or parting with property or with an interest in property, including retention of title as a security interest and foreclosure of the equity of redemption of the covered financial company.

(x) PERSON. — The term "person" includes any governmental entity in addition to any entity included in the definition of such term in section 1, title 1, United States Code.

(E) CLARIFICATION. — No provision of law shall be construed as limiting the right or power of the Corporation, or authorizing any court or agency to limit or delay, in any manner, the right or power of the Corporation to transfer any qualified financial contract or to disaffirm or repudiate any such contract in accordance with this subsection.

(F) WALKAWAY CLAUSES NOT EFFECTIVE. —

(i) IN GENERAL. — Notwithstanding the provisions of subparagraph (A) of this paragraph and sections 403 and 404 of the Federal Deposit Insurance Corporation Improvement Act of 1991, no walkaway clause shall be enforceable in a qualified financial contract of a covered financial company in default.

机构作出的将联邦存款保险公司指定为所涉金融公司接管人的任何裁决或其他正式决定;且

(II)"有违约之虞"一词系指联邦存款保险公司或相应的州监管机构已就所涉金融公司作出了如下判定——

(aa)联邦存款保险公司或相应的州监管机构认为——

(AA)该所涉金融公司在正常业务运作过程中完成债务偿付的可能性微乎其微;且

(BB)无法合理预期,该所涉金融公司在未获得联邦援助的情况下能够偿付上述债务;或

(bb)联邦存款保险公司或上述监管机构认为——

(AA)该所涉金融公司已遭受或可能遭受将耗尽或基本耗尽其资本的损失;且

(BB)无法合理预期,该所涉金融公司在未获得联邦援助的情况下能够实现资本补充。

(viii)**将主协议视为单一协议**。——第(i)项至第(vi)项所述任何合约或协议的任何主协议(或一项或一项以上该等主协议的任何主协议)以及该等主协议的全部补充协议,均应视为单一的协议和单一的合格金融合约。主协议的规定涉及本身并非合格金融合约的协议或交易的,则该主协议仅针对本身构成合格金融合约的交易被视为合格金融合约。

(ix)**转让**。——"转让"一词系指直接或间接、无条件或有条件、主动或被动地处置或分离的财产或财产权益(包括保留所有权作为担保权益的转让,以及因为所设金融公司丧失作为担保品股权的赎回权实现的权益转让)。

(x)**人或主体**。——除《美国法典》第一编第1节关于"人"或"主体"的定义中包括的任何实体外,"人"或"主体"一词还包括任何政府实体。

(E)**说明**。——联邦存款保险公司拥有根据本子条规定转让任何合格金融合约,拒绝履行该等合约或宣告该等合约无效的权利或权力,任何法律规定均不得被解释为构成对上述权利或权力的限制,亦不得被解释为授权任何法院或机关以任何方式限制或推迟上述权利或权力。

(F)**走避条款无效**。——

(i)**一般规定**。——无论本款第(A)子款和《1991年联邦存款保险公司改良法》第403条和第404条如何规定,处于违约状态的所涉金融公司达成的合格金融合约中的任何走避条款均不得强制执行。

(ii) LIMITED SUSPENSION OF CERTAIN OBLIGATIONS. — In the case of a qualified financial contract referred to in clause (i), any payment or delivery obligations otherwise due from a party pursuant to the qualified financial contract shall be suspended from the time at which the Corporation is appointed as receiver until the earlier of —

(I) the time at which such party receives notice that such contract has been transferred pursuant to paragraph (10)(A); or

(II) 5: 00 p. m. (eastern time) on the business day following the date of the appointment of the Corporation as receiver.

(iii) WALKAWAY CLAUSE DEFINED. — For purposes of this subparagraph, the term "walkaway clause" means any provision in a qualified financial contract that suspends, conditions, or extinguishes a payment obligation of a party, in whole or in part, or does not create a payment obligation of a party that would otherwise exist, solely because of the status of such party as a nondefaulting party in connection with the insolvency of a covered financial company that is a party to the contract or the appointment of or the exercise of rights or powers by the Corporation as receiver for such covered financial company, and not as a result of the exercise by a party of any right to offset, setoff, or net obligations that exist under the contract, any other contract between those parties, or applicable law.

(G) CERTAIN OBLIGATIONS TO CLEARING ORGANIZATIONS. — In the event that the Corporation has been appointed as receiver for a covered financial company which is a party to any qualified financial contract cleared by or subject to the rules of a clearing organization (as defined in paragraph (9)(D)), the receiver shall use its best efforts to meet all margin, collateral, and settlement obligations of the covered financial company that arise under qualified financial contracts (other than any margin, collateral, or settlement obligation that is not enforceable against the receiver under paragraph (8)(F)(i) or paragraph (10)(B)), as required by the rules of the clearing organization when due. Notwithstanding any other provision of this title, if the receiver fails to satisfy any such margin, collateral, or settlement obligations under the rules of the clearing organization, the clearing organization shall have the immediate right to exercise, and shall not be stayed from exercising, all of its rights and remedies under its rules and applicable law with respect to any qualified financial contract of the covered financial company, including, without limitation, the right to liquidate all positions and collateral of such covered financial company under the company's qualified financial contracts, and suspend or cease to act for such covered financial company, all in accordance with the rules of the clearing organization.

(H) RECORDKEEPING. —

(i) JOINT RULEMAKING. — The Federal primary financial regulatory agencies

(ii)**特定义务的有限暂停履行**。——就第(i)项所述合格金融合约而言,自联邦存款保险公司被指定为接管人起直至以下时间(以较早者为准),合约方应暂停履行其根据该合约本应履行的任何支付或交付义务——

(I)该方收到该合约已根据第(10)(A)款完成转让的通知;或

(II)联邦存款保险公司被指定为接管人的下一个营业日下午5点(美国东部时间)。

(iii)**走避条款的定义**。——就本子款而言,"走避条款"一词系指合格金融合约中任何规定只要出现以下原因,合约一方即不必承担本应承担的某项支付义务,或其本应履行的某项支付义务即应完全或部分暂停、受相关条件限制或消灭的条款:作为合约一方的所涉金融公司在出现资不抵债情况时,或者联邦存款保险公司被指定为该所涉金融公司的接管人或行使接管人的权利或权力时,该方未处于违约状态;且上述合约方不必承担上述支付义务,或其支付义务被暂停、受相关条件限制或消灭,并非由于该方针对该合约、上述各方之间的任何其他合约或适用的法律规定的义务行使任何对冲权、抵销权或净额结算权所导致。

(G)**应向结算组织承担的特定义务**。——联邦存款保险公司被指定为所涉金融公司接管人,且该所涉金融公司系由结算组织[定义见第(9)(D)款]或应按其规则集中结算的任何合格金融合约之当事方的,接管人应尽最大努力按该结算组织的规则要求履行该所涉金融公司依据合格金融合约到期应履行的全部保证金、担保品以及结算义务[根据第(8)(F)(i)款或第(10)(B)款对接管人不具强制执行力的任何保证金、担保品以及结算义务除外]。无论本编是否存在任何不同规定,接管人未根据该结算组织的规则要求履行任何上述保证金、担保品或结算义务的,该结算组织有权直接根据其规则以及适用的法律的规定,就该所涉金融公司的任何合格金融合约行使其享有的全部权利和救济措施,包括但不限于根据该结算组织规则,对该所涉金融公司在该公司的合格金融合约项下的全部持仓和担保品进行平仓,以及暂停或停止代表该所涉金融公司行事的权利;结算组织行使上述权利和救济措施的,不得被中止。

(H)**记录保存**。——

(i)**联合制定规则**。——各联邦优先金融监管机关应联合制定规章,要求金融公

shall jointly prescribe regulations requiring that financial companies maintain such records with respect to qualified financial contracts (including market valuations) that the Federal primary financial regulatory agencies determine to be necessary or appropriate in order to assist the Corporation as receiver for a covered financial company in being able to exercise its rights and fulfill its obligations under this paragraph or paragraph (9) or (10).

(ii) TIME FRAME. — The Federal primary financial regulatory agencies shall prescribe joint final or interim final regulations not later than 24 months after the date of enactment of this Act.

(iii) BACK-UP RULEMAKING AUTHORITY. — If the Federal primary financial regulatory agencies do not prescribe joint final or interim final regulations within the time frame in clause (ii), the Chairperson of the Council shall prescribe, in consultation with the Corporation, the regulations required by clause (i).

(iv) CATEGORIZATION AND TIERING. — The joint regulations prescribed under clause (i) shall, as appropriate, differentiate among financial companies by taking into consideration their size, risk, complexity, leverage, frequency and dollar amount of qualified financial contracts, interconnectedness to the financial system, and any other factors deemed appropriate.

(9) TRANSFER OF QUALIFIED FINANCIAL CONTRACTS. —

(A) IN GENERAL. — In making any transfer of assets or liabilities of a covered financial company in default, which includes any qualified financial contract, the Corporation as receiver for such covered financial company shall either —

(i) transfer to one financial institution, other than a financial institution for which a conservator, receiver, trustee in bankruptcy, or other legal custodian has been appointed or which is otherwise the subject of a bankruptcy or insolvency proceeding —

(I) all qualified financial contracts between any person or any affiliate of such person and the covered financial company in default;

(II) all claims of such person or any affiliate of such person against such covered financial company under any such contract (other than any claim which, under the terms of any such contract, is subordinated to the claims of general unsecured creditors of such company);

(III) all claims of such covered financial company against such person or any affiliate of such person under any such contract; and

(IV) all property securing or any other credit enhancement for any contract described in subclause (I) or any claim described in subclause (II) or (III) under any such contract; or

(ii) transfer none of the qualified financial contracts, claims, property or other credit

司就合格金融合约(包括市场估值)维持其判定确属必要或适当的记录,以便为联邦存款保险公司提供协助,使其能够作为所涉金融公司接管人行使并履行本款、第(9)款或第(10)款规定的权利和义务。

(ii)**时限**。——各联邦优先金融监管机关应于本法颁布之日起24个月内,联合制定最终规章或暂行最终规章。

(iii)**后备规则制定权**。——各联邦优先金融监管机关未在第(ii)项规定的时限内联合制定最终规章或暂行最终规章的,金融稳定监督委员会主席应在与联邦存款保险公司磋商后,按照第(i)项的要求制定该等规章。

(iv)**按类别和层级区别对待**。——根据第(i)项要求联合制定的规章应考虑各金融公司合格金融合约的规模、风险程度、复杂程度、杠杆率、频率、金额和与金融体系的相互关联性以及所涉监管机关认为适当的任何其他因素,并在此基础上对该等金融公司进行适当区别对待。

(9)**合格金融合约的转让**。——

(A)**一般规定**。——联邦存款保险公司作为违约的所涉金融公司接管人,对该所涉金融公司的资产或负债(包括任何合格金融合约)进行任何转让时——

(i)应将以下各项转让给某一金融机构(但已被指定破产托管人、接管人、破产管理人或其他法定托管人,或者已另行进入破产或资不抵债程序的金融机构除外)——

(I)任何人或其任何关联方与该违约的所涉金融公司之间达成的全部合格金融合约;

(II)该人或其任何关联方依据任何该等合格金融合约对该所涉金融公司享有的全部权利主张(但根据任何该等合约条款,其受偿顺序次于该公司普通无担保债权人的任何权利主张的除外);

(III)该所涉金融公司依据任何该等合格金融合约对该人或其任何关联方享有的全部权利主张;及

(IV)为第(I)子项所述任何合约或第(II)子项或第(III)子项所述任何该等合约中的任何权利主张提供担保的全部财产或任何其他信用增级措施;或

(ii)不转让第(i)项所述的与该人及其任何关联方相关的任何合格金融合约、权利

enhancement referred to in clause (i) (with respect to such person and any affiliate of such person).

(B) TRANSFER TO FOREIGN BANK, FINANCIAL INSTITUTION, OR BRANCH OR AGENCY THEREOF. — In transferring any qualified financial contracts and related claims and property under subparagraph (A)(i), the Corporation as receiver for the covered financial company shall not make such transfer to a foreign bank, financial institution organized under the laws of a foreign country, or a branch or agency of a foreign bank or financial institution unless, under the law applicable to such bank, financial institution, branch or agency, to the qualified financial contracts, and to any netting contract, any security agreement or arrangement or other credit enhancement related to one or more qualified financial contracts, the contractual rights of the parties to such qualified financial contracts, netting contracts, security agreements or arrangements, or other credit enhancements are enforceable substantially to the same extent as permitted under this section.

(C) TRANSFER OF CONTRACTS SUBJECT TO THE RULES OF A CLEARING ORGANIZATION. — In the event that the Corporation as receiver for a financial institution transfers any qualified financial contract and related claims, property, or credit enhancement pursuant to subparagraph (A)(i) and such contract is cleared by or subject to the rules of a clearing organization, the clearing organization shall not be required to accept the transferee as a member by virtue of the transfer.

(D) DEFINITIONS. — For purposes of this paragraph —

(i) the term "financial institution" means a broker or dealer, a depository institution, a futures commission merchant, a bridge financial company, or any other institution determined by the Corporation, by regulation, to be a financial institution; and

(ii) the term "clearing organization" has the same meaning as in section 402 of the Federal Deposit Insurance Corporation Improvement Act of 1991.

(10) NOTIFICATION OF TRANSFER. —

(A) IN GENERAL. —

(i) NOTICE. — The Corporation shall provide notice in accordance with clause (ii), if —

(I) the Corporation as receiver for a covered financial company in default or in danger of default transfers any assets or liabilities of the covered financial company; and

(II) the transfer includes any qualified financial contract.

(ii) TIMING. — The Corporation as receiver for a covered financial company shall notify any person who is a party to any contract described in clause (i) of such transfer not later than 5: 00 p. m. (eastern time) on the business day following the date of the appointment of the Corporation as receiver.

主张、财产或其他信用增级措施。

(B)**向外国银行、金融机构或者其分行或代理行进行的转让**。——联邦存款保险公司作为所涉金融公司接管人,对第(A)(i)子款所述任何合格金融合约、相关权利主张和财产进行转让时,不得将该等金融合约、权利主张和财产转让给根据外国法律组建的外国银行、外国金融机构或外国银行、外国金融机构的分行或代理行,除非,根据适用于该等银行、金融机构、分行或代理行的法律,以及适用于该等合格金融合约以及与一份或一份以上合格金融合约相关的任何净额结算合约、任何担保协议或安排或者其他信用增级措施的法律,该等合格金融合约、净额结算合约、担保协议或安排或者其他信用增级措施的各当事方的合约权利可以在与本条规定基本相当的范围内强制执行。

(C)**根据结算组织规则进行的合约转让**。——联邦存款保险公司作为所涉金融公司接管人,根据第(A)(i)子款对任何合格金融合约、相关权利主张、财产或信用增级措施进行转让,而该等合约系由结算组织或根据其规则进行集中结算的,则该结算组织没有义务因该转让而接受受让人作为其会员。

(D)**定义**。——就本款而言——

(i)"金融机构"一词系指经纪商或自营商、存款机构、期货经纪商、过渡金融公司或联邦存款保险公司发布规章判定的属于金融机构的任何其他机构;且

(ii)"结算组织"一词的含义以《1991年联邦存款保险公司改良法》第402条的定义为准。

(10)**转让通知**。——

(A)**一般规定**。——

(i)**通知**。——在以下情形下,联邦存款保险公司应根据第(ii)项的规定提供相关通知——

(I)联邦存款保险公司作为违约或有违约之虞的所涉金融公司的接管人,转让该所涉金融公司的任何资产或负债;且

(II)该转让包括任何合格金融合约。

(ii)**时限**。——联邦存款保险公司作为所涉金融公司的接管人,最迟应于其被指定为接管人的下一个营业日下午5点(美国东部时间),向第(i)项所述任何合约的任何当事方发出关于上述转让的通知。

(B) CERTAIN RIGHTS NOT ENFORCEABLE. —

(i) RECEIVERSHIP. — A person who is a party to a qualified financial contract with a covered financial company may not exercise any right that such person has to terminate, liquidate, or net such contract under paragraph (8)(A) solely by reason of or incidental to the appointment under this section of the Corporation as receiver for the covered financial company (or the insolvency or financial condition of the covered financial company for which the Corporation has been appointed as receiver) —

(I) until 5: 00 p. m. (eastern time) on the business day following the date of the appointment; or

(II) after the person has received notice that the contract has been transferred pursuant to paragraph (9)(A).

(ii) NOTICE. — For purposes of this paragraph, the Corporation as receiver for a covered financial company shall be deemed to have notified a person who is a party to a qualified financial contract with such covered financial company, if the Corporation has taken steps reasonably calculated to provide notice to such person by the time specified in subparagraph (A).

(C) TREATMENT OF BRIDGE FINANCIAL COMPANY. — For purposes of paragraph (9), a bridge financial company shall not be considered to be a financial institution for which a conservator, receiver, trustee in bankruptcy, or other legal custodian has been appointed, or which is otherwise the subject of a bankruptcy or insolvency proceeding.

(D) BUSINESS DAY DEFINED. — For purposes of this paragraph, the term "business day" means any day other than any Saturday, Sunday, or any day on which either the New York Stock Exchange or the Federal Reserve Bank of New York is closed.

(11) DISAFFIRMANCE OR REPUDIATION OF QUALIFIED FINANCIAL CONTRACTS. — In exercising the rights of disaffirmance or repudiation of the Corporation as receiver with respect to any qualified financial contract to which a covered financial company is a party, the Corporation shall either —

(A) disaffirm or repudiate all qualified financial contracts between —

(i) any person or any affiliate of such person; and

(ii) the covered financial company in default; or

(B) disaffirm or repudiate none of the qualified financial contracts referred to in subparagraph (A) (with respect to such person or any affiliate of such person).

(12) CERTAIN SECURITY AND CUSTOMER INTERESTS NOT AVOIDABLE. — No provision of this subsection shall be construed as permitting the avoidance of any —

(A) legally enforceable or perfected security interest in any of the assets of any covered financial company, except in accordance with subsection (a)(11); or

(B)**不可强制执行的特定权利**。——

(i)**接管**。——某人与所涉金融公司达成合格金融合约的,该人作为合约当事方,不得仅因为或基于联邦存款保险公司根据本条规定被指定为所涉金融公司的接管人(或者仅因被指定由联邦存款保险公司担任接管人的该所涉金融公司的资不抵债状态或财务状况),而在下述期间根据第(8)(A)款行使其对该合约进行终止、平仓或净额结算的任何权利——

(I)该项指定日的下一个营业日下午5点(美国东部时间)之前;或

(II)该人收到关于该合约已根据第(9)(A)款转让的通知之后。

(ii)**通知**。——就本款而言,在某人与所涉金融公司达成合格金融合约的情形下,如果联邦存款保险公司作为该所涉金融公司的接管人且已采取了经过合理计算的措施向该人在第(A)子款规定的时限之前发出通知,则联邦存款保险公司应视为已履行其通知义务。

(C)**对过渡金融公司的处理**。——就第(9)款而言,过渡金融公司不得视为已被指定破产托管人、接管人、破产管理人或其他法定托管人,或者已另行进入破产或资不抵债程序的金融机构。

(D)**营业日的定义**。——就本款而言,"营业日"一词系指除任何周六、周日或纽约证券交易所或纽约联邦储备银行闭门不营业之日以外的任何一日。

(11)**拒绝履行合格金融合约或宣告其无效**。——联邦存款保险公司作为接管人,对所涉金融公司签订的任何合格金融合约行使拒绝履约权或宣告合约无效权的,应——

(A)宣告以下双方达成的一切合格金融合约无效或拒绝履行该等合约——

(i)任何人或其任何关联方;及

(ii)违约的所涉金融公司;或

(B)不针对该人或其任何关联方宣告第(A)子款所述任何合格金融合约无效,亦不针对该人或其任何关联方拒绝履行任何该等合约。

(12)**不可撤销的特定担保权益和客户权益**。——本子条的任何规定均不得被解释为允许撤销——

(A)任何所涉金融公司资产上存在的任何可依法强制执行或无瑕疵的担保权益,但根据第(a)(11)子条规定允许撤销的除外;或

(B) legally enforceable interest in customer property, security entitlements in respect of assets or property held by the covered financial company for any security entitlement holder.

(13) AUTHORITY TO ENFORCE CONTRACTS. —

(A) IN GENERAL. — The Corporation, as receiver for a covered financial company, may enforce any contract, other than a liability insurance contract of a director or officer, a financial institution bond entered into by the covered financial company, notwithstanding any provision of the contract providing for termination, default, acceleration, or exercise of rights upon, or solely by reason of, insolvency, the appointment of or the exercise of rights or powers by the Corporation as receiver, the filing of the petition pursuant to section 202 (a) (1), or the issuance of the recommendations or determination, or any actions or events occurring in connection therewith or as a result thereof, pursuant to section 203.

(B) CERTAIN RIGHTS NOT AFFECTED. — No provision of this paragraph may be construed as impairing or affecting any right of the Corporation as receiver to enforce or recover under a liability insurance contract of a director or officer or financial institution bond under other applicable law.

(C) CONSENT REQUIREMENT AND IPSO FACTO CLAUSES. —

(i) IN GENERAL. — Except as otherwise provided by this section, no person may exercise any right or power to terminate, accelerate, or declare a default under any contract to which the covered financial company is a party (and no provision in any such contract providing for such default, termination, or acceleration shall be enforceable), or to obtain possession of or exercise control over any property of the covered financial company or affect any contractual rights of the covered financial company, without the consent of the Corporation as receiver for the covered financial company during the 90 day period beginning from the appointment of the Corporation as receiver.

(ii) EXCEPTIONS. — No provision of this subparagraph shall apply to a director or officer liability insurance contract or a financial institution bond, to the rights of parties to certain qualified financial contracts pursuant to paragraph (8), or to the rights of parties to netting contracts pursuant to subtitle A of title IV of the Federal Deposit Insurance Corporation Improvement Act of 1991 (12 U.S.C. 4401 et seq.), or shall be construed as permitting the Corporation as receiver to fail to comply with otherwise enforceable provisions of such contract.

(D) CONTRACTS TO EXTEND CREDIT. — Notwithstanding any other provision in this title, if the Corporation as receiver enforces any contract to extend credit to the covered financial company or bridge financial company, any valid and enforceable obligation to repay such debt shall be paid by the Corporation as receiver, as an

(B)客户财产上存在的可依法强制执行的权益,以及所涉金融公司为任何法定担保权益持有人持有的资产或财产上的法定担保权益。

(13)**合约的强制执行权**。——

(A)**一般规定**。——除所涉金融公司订立的董事或管理人员责任险合同和金融机构保函外,联邦存款保险公司作为该所涉金融公司的接管人可以强制执行该所涉金融公司订立的任何其他合同,即使该等合同规定在发生以下情况时合同一方有权终止、不履行、提前履行该合同或行使权利:所涉金融公司出现资不抵债的情况;联邦存款保险公司被指定为接管人,或者行使接管人的权利或权力;财政部部长根据第202(a)(1)条规定提交请求;或者联邦存款保险公司或联邦储备委员会根据第203条签发建议或判定,或采取与之相关的任何行动或因此导致了相关事件发生,又或,只要发生上述任何情况,联邦存款保险公司作为该所涉金融公司的接管人也可以强制执行该所涉金融公司订立的任何其他合同。

(B)**特定权利不受影响**。——联邦存款保险公司作为接管人,根据其他适用的法律有权强制执行董事或管理人员责任险合同或金融机构保函或根据该等合同或保函获得补救的,本款的任何规定均不得被解释为构成对上述任何权利的削弱或影响。

(C)**征求同意要求和破产约定条款**。——

(i)**一般规定**。——除本条另有规定的情形外,任何人如果未在自联邦存款保险公司被指定为所涉金融公司接管人之日起90天内征得联邦存款保险公司的同意,则不得根据该所涉金融公司作为一方签订的任何合同行使任何终止、提前履行合同或宣告不履约的权利或权力(且任何该等合同中规定上述不履约、终止合同或提前履约的任何条款均不得强制执行),亦不得取得所涉金融公司财产的占有权或对该等财产行使控制权,或影响该所涉金融公司的任何合同权利。

(ii)**例外规定**。——本子款的任何规定均不适用于董事或管理人员责任险合同或金融机构保函,亦不得适用于某些合格金融合约的当事方根据第(8)款有权行使的权利,或净额结算合约当事方根据《1991年联邦存款保险公司改良法》第四编第A子编(《美国法典》第十二编第4401节及其后条文)有权行使的权利,也不得被解释为联邦存款保险公司作为接管人,有权不遵守该等合同中本可强制执行的条款。

(D)**授信合同**。——无论本编是否存在任何不同规定,如果联邦存款保险公司作为接管人强制执行向所涉金融公司或过渡金融公司授信的任何合同,则任何有效且可强制执行的偿还该等债务之义务均应由联邦存款保险公司作为接管人清偿,该等款项作为接管工作的行政费用处理。

administrative expense of the receivership.

(14) EXCEPTION FOR FEDERAL RESERVE BANKS AND CORPORATION SECURITY INTEREST. — No provision of this subsection shall apply with respect to —

(A) any extension of credit from any Federal reserve bank or the Corporation to any covered financial company; or

(B) any security interest in the assets of the covered financial company securing any such extension of credit.

(15) SAVINGS CLAUSE. — The meanings of terms used in this subsection are applicable for purposes of this subsection only, and shall not be construed or applied so as to challenge or affect the characterization, definition, or treatment of any similar terms under any other statute, regulation, or rule, including the Gramm–Leach–Bliley Act, the Legal Certainty for Bank Products Act of 2000, the securities laws (as that term is defined in section 3(a)(47) of the Securities Exchange Act of 1934), and the Commodity Exchange Act.

(16) ENFORCEMENT OF CONTRACTS GUARANTEED BY THE COVERED FINANCIAL COMPANY. —

(A) IN GENERAL. — The Corporation, as receiver for a covered financial company or as receiver for a subsidiary of a covered financial company (including an insured depository institution) shall have the power to enforce contracts of subsidiaries or affiliates of the covered financial company, the obligations under which are guaranteed or otherwise supported by or linked to the covered financial company, notwithstanding any contractual right to cause the termination, liquidation, or acceleration of such contracts based solely on the insolvency, financial condition, or receivership of the covered financial company, if —

(i) such guaranty or other support and all related assets and liabilities are transferred to and assumed by a bridge financial company or a third party (other than a third party for which a conservator, receiver, trustee in bankruptcy, or other legal custodian has been appointed, or which is otherwise the subject of a bankruptcy or insolvency proceeding) within the same period of time as the Corporation is entitled to transfer the qualified financial contracts of such covered financial company; or

(ii) the Corporation, as receiver, otherwise provides adequate protection with respect to such obligations.

(B) RULE OF CONSTRUCTION. — For purposes of this paragraph, a bridge financial company shall not be considered to be a third party for which a conservator, receiver, trustee in bankruptcy, or other legal custodian has been appointed, or which is otherwise the subject of a bankruptcy or insolvency proceeding.

(d) VALUATION OF CLAIMS IN DEFAULT. —

(14)**联邦储备银行和联邦存款保险公司担保权益的例外规定**。——本子条的任何规定均不适用于——

(A)任何联邦储备银行或联邦存款保险公司对任何所涉金融公司的任何授信;或

(B)所涉金融公司资产上存在的为上述任何授信提供担保的任何担保权益。

(15)**保留条款**。——本子条中各术语的含义仅适用于本子条之规定,解释或适用时不得用于质疑或影响任何其他制定法、规章或规则{包括《格雷姆—里奇—比利雷法》、《2000年银行产品法律确定性法》、证券法律[定义见《1934年证券交易法》第3(a)(47)条]和《商品交易法》}中对任何类似术语的特征描述、定义或处理。

(16)**强制执行所涉金融公司担保的合约**。——

(A)**一般规定**。——如果所涉金融公司子公司或关联方的合约项下的义务由该所涉金融公司担保、提供支持或与其存在关联,则在以下情形下,作为该所涉金融公司或该所涉金融公司子公司(包括参保存款机构)的接管人,联邦存款保险公司有权强制执行该等合约,即使该等合约规定,只要该所涉金融公司发生资不抵债、出现特定财务状况或被接管的情形,合约另一方即有权责成终止、提前履行合约或对合约进行平仓——

(i)在联邦存款保险公司有权转让该所涉金融公司的合格金融合约的期间内,该等担保、支持以及所有相关资产和负债均已转让给过渡金融公司、第三方或者由该等过渡金融公司或第三方承担(但已被指定破产托管人、接管人、破产管理人或其他法定托管人,或者已另行进入破产或资不抵债程序的第三方除外);或

(ii)联邦存款保险公司作为接管人,已通过其他方式为该等义务提供了充分保护。

(B)**解释规则**。——就本款而言,过渡金融公司不得视为已被指定破产托管人、接管人、破产管理人或其他法定托管人,或者已另行进入破产或资不抵债程序的第三方。

(d)**公司处于违约状态时权利主张的估值**。——

(1) IN GENERAL. — Notwithstanding any other provision of Federal law or the law of any State, and regardless of the method utilized by the Corporation for a covered financial company, including transactions authorized under subsection (h), this subsection shall govern the rights of the creditors of any such covered financial company.

(2) MAXIMUM LIABILITY. — The maximum liability of the Corporation, acting as receiver for a covered financial company or in any other capacity, to any person having a claim against the Corporation as receiver or the covered financial company for which the Corporation is appointed shall equal the amount that such claimant would have received if —

(A) the Corporation had not been appointed receiver with respect to the covered financial company; and

(B) the covered financial company had been liquidated under chapter 7 of the Bankruptcy Code, or any similar provision of State insolvency law applicable to the covered financial company.

(3) SPECIAL PROVISION FOR ORDERLY LIQUIDATION BY SIPC. — The maximum liability of the Corporation, acting as receiver or in its corporate capacity for any covered broker or dealer to any customer of such covered broker or dealer, with respect to customer property of such customer, shall be —

(A) equal to the amount that such customer would have received with respect to such customer property in a case initiated by SIPC under the Securities Investor Protection Act of 1970 (15 U.S.C. 78aaa et seq.); and

(B) determined as of the close of business on the date on which the Corporation is appointed as receiver.

(4) ADDITIONAL PAYMENTS AUTHORIZED. —

(A) IN GENERAL. — Subject to subsection (o)(1)(D)(i), the Corporation, with the approval of the Secretary, may make additional payments or credit additional amounts to or with respect to or for the account of any claimant or category of claimants of the covered financial company, if the Corporation determines that such payments or credits are necessary or appropriate to minimize losses to the Corporation as receiver from the orderly liquidation of the covered financial company under this section.

(B) LIMITATIONS. —

(i) PROHIBITION. — The Corporation shall not make any payments or credit amounts to any claimant or category of claimants that would result in any claimant receiving more than the face value amount of any claim that is proven to the satisfaction of the Corporation.

(ii) NO OBLIGATION. — Notwithstanding any other provision of Federal or State law, or the Constitution of any State, the Corporation shall not be obligated, as a result of having made any payment under subparagraph (A) or credited any amount described in

(1)**一般规定**。——无论联邦法律或任何州法律其他条款是否存在任何不同规定,且无论联邦存款保险公司就所涉金融公司采用了何种方法[包括执行第(h)子条授权开展的交易],该所涉金融公司债权人的权利均应受本子条规定规制。

(2)**最高责任金额**。——任何人针对履行接管人职责的联邦存款保险公司,或针对联邦存款保险公司接管的所涉金融公司提出某项权利主张的,联邦存款保险公司作为该所涉金融公司接管人或以任何其他身份向该人承担的最高责任金额应与该人在以下情形下将会收到的金额相等——

(A)若联邦存款保险公司未被指定为该所涉金融公司的接管人;且

(B)若该所涉金融公司已根据《破产法》第七章或适用于该所涉金融公司的州资不抵债法的任何类似规定进行清算。

(3)**证券投资者保护公司有序清算的特别规定**。——联邦存款保险公司以接管人身份或以其自身公司身份为任何所涉经纪商或自营商向该等所涉经纪商或自营商的任何客户就该客户之客户财产所承担的最高责任金额——

(A)应等于该客户在证券投资者保护公司根据《1970年证券投资者保护法》(《美国法典》第十五编第78aaa节及其后条文)提起的案件中,基于其财产将有权获得的金额;且

(B)应基于联邦存款保险公司被指定为接管人之日的营业时间结束之时的数值来确定该等金额。

(4)**授权进行的额外支付**。——

(A)**一般规定**。——在不违反第(o)(1)(D)(i)子条规定的前提下,如果联邦存款保险公司判定,向所涉金融公司的任何权利主张人或某类别的权利主张人的账户进行额外支付或贷记额外金额,对将联邦存款保险公司在根据本条规定对所涉金融公司进行有序清算中作为接管人面临的损失减到最低限度而言确属必要或适当,那么,经财政部部长批准,联邦存款保险公司可以作出上述支付或贷记。

(B)**限制**。——

(i)**禁止性规定**。——如联邦存款保险公司向任何权利主张人或某类别的权利主张人进行任何支付或贷记后,将导致任何权利主张人收到的金额高于获得令联邦存款保险公司满意的证明的权利主张的面值金额,则联邦存款保险公司不得进行上述任何支付或贷记。

(ii)**无义务**。——无论联邦法律、州法律或任何州的宪法是否存在任何不同规定,联邦存款保险公司按第(A)子款的规定向任何权利主张人或任何类别的权利主张人的账户作出了任何支付或贷记的,并不因此而有义务向任何其他权利主张人或其

subparagraph (A) to or with respect to, or for the account, of any claimant or category of claimants, to make payments to any other claimant or category of claimants.

(C) MANNER OF PAYMENT. — The Corporation may make payments or credit amounts under subparagraph (A) directly to the claimants or may make such payments or credit such amounts to a company other than a covered financial company or a bridge financial company established with respect thereto in order to induce such other company to accept liability for such claims.

(e) LIMITATION ON COURT ACTION. — Except as provided in this title, no court may take any action to restrain or affect the exercise of powers or functions of the receiver hereunder, and any remedy against the Corporation or receiver shall be limited to money damages determined in accordance with this title.

(f) LIABILITY OF DIRECTORS AND OFFICERS. —

(1) IN GENERAL. — A director or officer of a covered financial company may be held personally liable for monetary damages in any civil action described in paragraph (2) by, on behalf of, or at the request or direction of the Corporation, which action is prosecuted wholly or partially for the benefit of the Corporation —

(A) acting as receiver for such covered financial company;

(B) acting based upon a suit, claim, or cause of action purchased from, assigned by, or otherwise conveyed by the Corporation as receiver; or

(C) acting based upon a suit, claim, or cause of action purchased from, assigned by, or otherwise conveyed in whole or in part by a covered financial company or its affiliate in connection with assistance provided under this title.

(2) ACTIONS COVERED. — Paragraph (1) shall apply with respect to actions for gross negligence, including any similar conduct or conduct that demonstrates a greater disregard of a duty of care (than gross negligence) including intentional tortious conduct, — as such terms are defined and determined under applicable State law.

(3) SAVINGS CLAUSE. — Nothing in this subsection shall impair or affect any right of the Corporation under other applicable law.

(g) DAMAGES. — In any proceeding related to any claim against a director, officer, employee, agent, attorney, accountant, or appraiser of a covered financial company, or any other party employed by or providing services to a covered financial company, recoverable damages determined to result from the improvident or otherwise improper use or investment of any assets of the covered financial company shall include principal losses and appropriate interest.

(h) BRIDGE FINANCIAL COMPANIES. —

(1) ORGANIZATION. —

(A) PURPOSE. — The Corporation, as receiver for one or more covered financial

他类别的权利主张人进行支付。

(C)**支付方式**。——联邦存款保险公司可以向权利主张人直接作出第(A)子款所述支付或贷记，亦可以向除所涉金融公司或就所涉金融公司设立的过渡金融公司之外的公司作出该等支付或贷记,以作为该公司就该等权利主张承担相关责任的诱因。

(e)**法院行动限制**。——除本编另有规定的情形外,任何法院均不得采取任何行动限制或影响接管人行使本编所述权力或职能,并且,针对联邦存款保险公司或接管人享有的任何救济应仅限于根据本编确定的金钱损害赔偿。

(f)**董事和管理人员的责任**。——

(1)**一般规定**。——按照下述规定,完全或部分为联邦存款保险公司之利益而提起第(2)款所述任何民事诉讼(无论是由联邦存款保险公司自行提起、由他人代表其提起或者应其请求或指示而提起的诉讼)时,可追究所涉金融公司的董事或管理人员的个人金钱损害赔偿责任,并且在该等诉讼中——

(A)联邦存款保险公司以所涉金融公司的接管人的身份行事;

(B)联邦存款保险公司基于向其购买的、由其转让的或以其他方式转移的相关案件、权利主张或诉因,以接管人的身份行事;或

(C)联邦存款保险公司基于如下案件、权利主张或诉因行事:所涉金融公司或其关联方就根据本编规定提供的援助而购买的、由其转让的或以其他方式转移的相关案件、权利主张或诉因。

(2)**所涉诉讼**。——第(1)款规定应适用于就以下原因提起的诉讼:重大过失,包括任何类似行为或比重大过失更为严重的漠视注意义务的行为(包括故意侵权行为)——上述各术语的定义以及上述行为的判定均应以适用州法律为依据。

(3)**保留条款**。——本子条的任何规定均不得削弱或影响联邦存款保险公司根据其他适用的法律享有的任何权利。

(g)**损害赔偿**。——针对所涉金融公司的董事、管理人员、职员、代理人、律师、会计师或评估师或所涉金融公司聘用的或为之提供服务的任何其他人提起的任何权利主张而言,如任何相关程序判定,上述人员存在草率或不当使用所涉金融公司任何资产的行为,或者以该等资产进行了草率或不当投资的行为,并被判定应为此支付损害赔偿的,该等损害赔偿应包括损失本金,并加计适当的利息。

(h)**过渡金融公司**。——

(1)**组建**。——

(A)**目的**。——联邦存款保险公司在担任一家或一家以上所涉金融公司接管人

companies or in anticipation of being appointed receiver for one or more covered financial companies, may organize one or more bridge financial companies in accordance with this subsection.

(B) AUTHORITIES. — Upon the creation of a bridge financial company under subparagraph (A) with respect to a covered financial company, such bridge financial company may —

(i) assume such liabilities (including liabilities associated with any trust or custody business, but excluding any liabilities that count as regulatory capital) of such covered financial company as the Corporation may, in its discretion, determine to be appropriate;

(ii) purchase such assets (including assets associated with any trust or custody business) of such covered financial company as the Corporation may, in its discretion, determine to be appropriate; and

(iii) perform any other temporary function which the Corporation may, in its discretion, prescribe in accordance with this section.

(2) CHARTER AND ESTABLISHMENT. —

(A) ESTABLISHMENT. — Except as provided in subparagraph (H), where the covered financial company is a covered broker or dealer, the Corporation, as receiver for a covered financial company, may grant a Federal charter to and approve articles of association for one or more bridge financial company or companies, with respect to such covered financial company which shall, by operation of law and immediately upon issuance of its charter and approval of its articles of association, be established and operate in accordance with, and subject to, such charter, articles, and this section.

(B) MANAGEMENT. — Upon its establishment, a bridge financial company shall be under the management of a board of directors appointed by the Corporation.

(C) ARTICLES OF ASSOCIATION. — The articles of association and organization certificate of a bridge financial company shall have such terms as the Corporation may provide, and shall be executed y such representatives as the Corporation may designate.

(D) TERMS OF CHARTER; RIGHTS AND PRIVILEGES. — Subject to and in accordance with the provisions of this subsection, the Corporation shall —

(i) establish the terms of the charter of a bridge financial company and the rights, powers, authorities, and privileges of a bridge financial company granted by the charter or as an incident thereto; and

(ii) provide for, and establish the terms and conditions governing, the management (including the bylaws and the number of directors of the board of directors) and operations of the bridge financial company.

(E) TRANSFER OF RIGHTS AND PRIVILEGES OF COVERED FINANCIAL COMPANY. —

期间,或在预期即将被指定为一家或一家以上所涉金融公司接管人之时,可以根据本子条规定组建一家或一家以上过渡金融公司。

(B)**权力**。——根据第(A)子款规定针对所涉金融公司成立过渡金融公司后,该过渡金融公司可以——

(i)承担联邦存款保险公司依其自由裁量权判定确属适当的该所涉金融公司的负债(包括与任何信托或托管业务相关的负债,但不包括记入监管资本的负债);

(ii)购买联邦存款保险公司依其自由裁量权判定确属适当的该所涉金融公司的资产(包括与信托或托管业务相关的资产);并

(iii)履行联邦存款保险公司依其自由裁量权根据本条规定确定的任何其他临时职能。

(2)**执照与成立**。——

(A)**成立**。——除第(H)子款另有规定的情形外,在所涉金融公司是一家所涉经纪商或自营商的情形下,联邦存款保险公司作为所涉金融公司的接管人,可以向与该所涉金融公司相关的一家或一家以上过渡金融公司授予联邦执照并批准其章程。该等过渡金融公司在联邦存款保险公司签发上述执照并批准其章程后,即应依法成立,并应根据该执照、章程以及本条规定开展运营。

(B)**管理**。——过渡金融公司成立后,应由联邦存款保险公司任命的董事会进行管理。

(C)**章程**。——过渡金融公司的章程及组建证书中应包含联邦存款保险公司规定的条款,并由联邦存款保险公司指定的代表签署。

(D)**执照条款;权利及特权**。——在不违反本子条规定的前提下,联邦存款保险公司应根据本子条规定——

(i)确定过渡金融公司执照的条款,并确定该执照授予或附带的过渡金融公司的权利、权力、权限和特权;并

(ii)规定并确定规范过渡金融公司管理和运营的条款和条件(包括章程细则和董事会的董事人数)。

(E)**所涉金融公司权利和特权的转让**。——

(i) IN GENERAL. — Notwithstanding any other provision of Federal or State law, the Corporation may provide for a bridge financial company to succeed to and assume any rights, powers, authorities, or privileges of the covered financial company with respect to which the bridge financial company was established and, upon such determination by the Corporation, the bridge financial company shall immediately and by operation of law succeed to and assume such rights, powers, authorities, and privileges.

(ii) EFFECTIVE WITHOUT APPROVAL. — Any succession to or assumption by a bridge financial company of rights, powers, authorities, or privileges of a covered financial company under clause (i) or otherwise shall be effective without any further approval under Federal or State law, assignment, or consent with respect thereto.

(F) CORPORATE GOVERNANCE AND ELECTION AND DESIGNATION OF BODY OF LAW. — To the extent permitted by the Corporation and consistent with this section and any rules, regulations, or directives issued by the Corporation under this section, a bridge financial company may elect to follow the corporate governance practices and procedures that are applicable to a corporation incorporated under the general corporation law of the State of Delaware, or the State of incorporation or organization of the covered financial company with respect to which the bridge financial company was established, as such law may be amended from time to time.

(G) CAPITAL. —

(i) CAPITAL NOT REQUIRED. — Notwithstanding any other provision of Federal or State law, a bridge financial company may, if permitted by the Corporation, operate without any capital or surplus, or with such capital or surplus as the Corporation may in its discretion determine to be appropriate.

(ii) NO CONTRIBUTION BY THE CORPORATION REQUIRED. — The Corporation is not required to pay capital into a bridge financial company or to issue any capital stock on behalf of a bridge financial company established under this subsection.

(iii) AUTHORITY. — If the Corporation determines that such action is advisable, the Corporation may cause capital stock or other securities of a bridge financial company established with respect to a covered financial company to be issued and offered for sale in such amounts and on such terms and conditions as the Corporation may, in its discretion, determine.

(iv) OPERATING FUNDS IN LIEU OF CAPITAL AND IMPLEMENTATION PLAN. — Upon the organization of a bridge financial company, and thereafter as the Corporation may, in its discretion, determine to be necessary or advisable, the Corporation may make available to the bridge financial company, subject to the plan described in subsection (n)(9), funds for the operation of the bridge financial company in lieu of capital.

(H) BRIDGE BROKERS OR DEALERS. —

(i)**一般规定**。——无论联邦法律或州法律是否存在任何不同规定,联邦存款保险公司均可以规定过渡金融公司应继受并承担该所涉金融公司的权利、权力、权限或特权,联邦存款保险公司作出上述规定后,该过渡金融公司应立即依法继受并承担该等权利、权力、权限或特权。

(ii)**不必批准即可生效**。——过渡金融公司根据第(i)项或其他规定继受并承担所涉金融公司的权利、权力、权限或特权的,不必根据联邦法律或州法律取得任何进一步批准、指定或同意便可生效。

(F)**公司治理及适用的法律的选择和指定**。——在联邦存款保险公司允许的范围内,并在符合本条规定和联邦存款保险公司根据本条规定发布的任何规则、规章或指令的前提下,过渡金融公司可以选择遵守根据特拉华州普通公司法(以不时修正的版本为准)成立的公司所适用的公司治理惯例和程序,或选择遵守根据所涉金融公司成立或组建地所在州的普通公司法(以不时修正的版本为准)成立的公司所适用的公司治理惯例和程序。

(G)**资本**。——

(i)**无资本要求**。——无论联邦法律或州法律是否存在任何不同规定,如果联邦存款保险公司允许,过渡金融公司可以在无资本或资本公积金的状态下运营,或者以联邦存款保险公司依其自由裁量权判定确属适当的资本或资本公积金开展运营。

(ii)**联邦存款保险公司不承担出资义务**。——联邦存款保险公司不必承担向过渡金融公司出资的义务,也不必代表根据本子条成立的过渡金融公司发行任何股本。

(iii)**权力**。——如果联邦存款保险公司判定确属发行并要约出售过渡金融公司的股本或其他证券可取,其可以责令进行该等发行和要约,联邦存款保险公司可以依其自由裁量权判定该等被发行和要约出售的股本或证券的数量以及其发行和要约出售的条款和条件。

(iv)**代替资本的运营资金和实施计划**。——联邦存款保险公司可以在过渡金融公司组建伊始,以及在依其自由裁量权判定确属必要或可取的其他较晚时间,根据第(n)(9)子条所述计划向过渡金融公司提供运营资金,作为过渡金融公司资本的替代。

(H)**过渡经纪商或自营商**。——

(i) IN GENERAL. — The Corporation, as receiver for a covered broker or dealer, may approve articles of association for one or more bridge financial companies with respect to such covered broker or dealer, which bridge financial company or companies shall, by operation of law and immediately upon approval of its articles of association —

(I) be established and deemed registered with the Commission under the Securities Exchange Act of 1934 and a member of SIPC;

(II) operate in accordance with such articles and this section; and

(III) succeed to any and all registrations and memberships of the covered financial company with or in any self–regulatory organizations.

(ii) OTHER REQUIREMENTS. — Except as provided in clause (i), and notwithstanding any other provision of this section, the bridge financial company shall be subject to the Federal securities laws and all requirements with respect to being a member of a self–regulatory organization, unless exempted from any such requirements by the Commission, as is necessary or appropriate in the public interest or for the protection of investors.

(iii) TREATMENT OF CUSTOMERS. — Except as otherwise provided by this title, any customer of the covered broker or dealer whose account is transferred to a bridge financial company shall have all the rights, privileges, and protections under section 205 (f) and under the Securities Investor Protection Act of 1970 (15 U.S.C. 78aaa et seq.), that such customer would have had if the account were not transferred from the covered financial company under this subparagraph.

(iv) OPERATION OF BRIDGE BROKERS OR DEALERS. — Notwithstanding any other provision of this title, the Corporation shall not operate any bridge financial company created by the Corporation under this title with respect to a covered broker or dealer in such a manner as to adversely affect the ability of customers to promptly access their customer property in accordance with applicable law.

(3) INTERESTS IN AND ASSETS AND OBLIGATIONS OF COVERED FINANCIAL COMPANY. — Notwithstanding paragraph (1) or (2) or any other provision of law —

(A) a bridge financial company shall assume, acquire, or succeed to the assets or liabilities of a covered financial company (including the assets or liabilities associated with any trust or custody business) only to the extent that such assets or liabilities are transferred by the Corporation to the bridge financial company in accordance with, and subject to the restrictions set forth in, paragraph (1)(B); and

(B) a bridge financial company shall not assume, acquire, or succeed to any obligation that a covered financial company for which the Corporation has been appointed receiver may have to any shareholder, member, general partner, limited partner, or other

(i)**一般规定**。——联邦存款保险公司作为所涉经纪商或自营商的接管人,可以批准为该所涉经纪商或自营商成立的一家或一家以上过渡金融公司的章程,该等过渡金融公司在联邦存款保险公司批准其章程后,即应依法——

(I)成立,并视为已根据《1934年证券交易法》在证券交易委员会完成注册,并已成为证券投资者保护公司的会员;

(II)根据该章程和本条规定开展运营;并

(III)继任该所涉金融公司在任何自律组织的所有注册身份和成员资格。

(ii)**其他要求**。——除第(i)项另有规定的情形外,且无论本条是否存在任何不同规定,过渡金融公司均应受制于联邦证券法律以及与自律组织会员身份相关的全部要求;但是,证券交易委员会为维护公共利益和保护投资者,向该过渡金融公司授予了必要或适当豁免的情形例外。

(iii)**对客户的处理**。——除本编另有规定的情形外,对于所涉经纪商或自营商的任何客户而言,即便其账户已转让给过渡金融公司,该等客户仍将享有第205(f)条和《1970年证券投资者保护法》(《美国法典》第十五编第78aaa节及其后条文)规定并提供的全部权利、特权及保护,如同其账户未根据本子款从所涉金融公司转出一般。

(iv)**过渡经纪商或自营商的运营**。——无论本编是否存在任何不同规定,联邦存款保险公司根据本编规定就所涉经纪商或自营商成立过渡金融公司的,联邦存款保险公司运营该过渡金融公司的方式不得对客户按适用的法律及时支取其财产的能力造成不利影响。

(3)**对所涉金融公司拥有的权益、资产和义务**。——无论第(1)款、第(2)款或法律其他条款是否存在任何不同规定——

(A)过渡金融公司应承担、收购或继受所涉金融公司的资产或负债(包括与任何信托或托管业务相关的资产或负债),但前提是,联邦存款保险公司已根据第(1)(B)款并在不违反该款限制条件的前提下将该等资产或负债转让给该过渡金融公司;且

(B)联邦存款保险公司被指定为其接管人的所涉金融公司之股东、成员、普通合伙人、有限合伙人或其他对所涉金融公司拥有股权权益的人,因其对所涉金融公司拥有股权权利主张,导致所涉金融公司向其负有义务的,过渡金融公司不得承担、收购

person with an interest in the equity of the covered financial company that arises as a result of the status of that person having an equity claim in the covered financial company.

(4) BRIDGE FINANCIAL COMPANY TREATED AS BEING IN DEFAULT FOR CERTAIN PURPOSES. — A bridge financial company shall be treated as a covered financial company in default at such times and for such purposes as the Corporation may, in its discretion, determine.

(5) TRANSFER OF ASSETS AND LIABILITIES. —

(A) AUTHORITY OF CORPORATION. — The Corporation, as receiver for a covered financial company, may transfer any assets and liabilities of a covered financial company (including any assets or liabilities associated with any trust or custody business) to one or more bridge financial companies, in accordance with and subject to the restrictions of paragraph (1).

(B) SUBSEQUENT TRANSFERS. — At any time after the establishment of a bridge financial company with respect to a covered financial company, the Corporation, as receiver, may transfer any assets and liabilities of such covered financial company as the Corporation may, in its discretion, determine to be appropriate in accordance with and subject to the restrictions of paragraph (1).

(C) TREATMENT OF TRUST OR CUSTODY BUSINESS. — For purposes of this paragraph, the trust or custody business, including fiduciary appointments, held by any covered financial company is included among its assets and liabilities.

(D) EFFECTIVE WITHOUT APPROVAL. — The transfer of any assets or liabilities, including those associated with any trust or custody business of a covered financial company, to a bridge financial company shall be effective without any further approval under Federal or State law, assignment, or consent with respect thereto.

(E) EQUITABLE TREATMENT OF SIMILARLY SITUATED CREDITORS. — The Corporation shall treat all creditors of a covered financial company that are similarly situated under subsection (b)(1), in a similar manner in exercising the authority of the Corporation under this subsection to transfer any assets or liabilities of the covered financial company to one or more bridge financial companies established with respect to such covered financial company, except that the Corporation may take any action (including making payments, subject to subsection (o)(1)(D)(i)) that does not comply with this subparagraph, if —

(i) the Corporation determines that such action is necessary —

(I) to maximize the value of the assets of the covered financial company;

(II) to maximize the present value return from the sale or other disposition of the assets of the covered financial company; or

或继受该等义务。

(4)**为了特定目的而将过渡金融公司视为违约**。——过渡金融公司应在联邦存款保险公司依其自由裁量权所判定的时间、为了联邦存款保险公司依其自由裁量权所判定的目的而被视为违约的所涉金融公司。

(5)**资产和负债转让**。——

(A)**联邦存款保险公司的权力**。——联邦存款保险公司作为所涉金融公司的接管人,可以根据第(1)款规定并在不违反该款限制条件的前提下,将所涉金融公司的任何资产和负债(包括与任何信托或托管业务相关的任何资产或负债)转让给一家或一家以上过渡金融公司。

(B)**后续转让**。——联邦存款保险公司作为接管人,在为所涉金融公司成立过渡金融公司后,可以随时根据第(1)款规定并在不违反该款限制条件的前提下,依其自由裁量权,对该所涉金融公司的任何资产和负债进行联邦存款保险公司判定确属适当的转让。

(C)**信托或托管业务的处理**。——就本款而言,任何所涉金融公司持有的信托或托管业务(包括因被指定为受信义务人而持有的业务),应纳入该所涉金融公司的资产和负债之中。

(D)**不必批准即可生效**。——所涉金融公司向过渡金融公司转让任何资产或负债的(包括与任何信托或托管业务相关的任何资产或负债),不必根据联邦法律或州法律取得任何进一步的批准、指定或同意便可生效。

(E)**公平处理情形类似的债权人**。——联邦存款保险公司在行使本子条规定的权力,将所涉金融公司任何资产或负债转让给为该所涉金融公司成立的一家或一家以上过渡金融公司时,应以类似方式处理该所涉金融公司所有在第(b)(1)子条规定项下情形类似的债权人,但是,在以下情形下,联邦存款保险公司可以采取与本子款规定不一致的任何行动[包括在不违反第(o)(1)(D)(i)子条的前提下进行支付]——

(i)联邦存款保险公司判定该等行动对于实现以下目的而言确属必要——

(I)将所涉金融公司资产的价值最大化;

(II)将出售或以其他方式处置所涉金融公司资产产生的现值回报最大化;或

(III) to minimize the amount of any loss realized upon the sale or other disposition of the assets of the covered financial company; and

(ii) all creditors that are similarly situated under subsection (b)(1) receive not less than the amount provided under paragraphs (2) and (3) of subsection (d).

(F) LIMITATION ON TRANSFER OF LIABILITIES. — Notwithstanding any other provision of law, the aggregate amount of liabilities of a covered financial company that are transferred to, or assumed by, a bridge financial company from a covered financial company may not exceed the aggregate amount of the assets of the covered financial company that are transferred to, or purchased by, the bridge financial company from the covered financial company.

(6) STAY OF JUDICIAL ACTION. — Any judicial action to which a bridge financial company becomes a party by virtue of its acquisition of any assets or assumption of any liabilities of a covered financial company shall be stayed from further proceedings for a period of not longer than 45 days (or such longer period as may be agreed to upon the consent of all parties) at the request of the bridge financial company.

(7) AGREEMENTS AGAINST INTEREST OF THE BRIDGE FINANCIAL COMPANY. — No agreement that tends to diminish or defeat the interest of the bridge financial company in any asset of a covered financial company acquired by the bridge financial company shall be valid against the bridge financial company, unless such agreement —

(A) is in writing;

(B) was executed by an authorized officer or representative of the covered financial company or confirmed in the ordinary course of business by the covered financial company; and

(C) has been on the official record of the company, since the time of its execution, or with which, the party claiming under the agreement provides documentation of such agreement and its authorized execution or confirmation by the covered financial company that is acceptable to the receiver.

(8) NO FEDERAL STATUS. —

(A) AGENCY STATUS. — A bridge financial company is not an agency, establishment, or instrumentality of the United States.

(B) EMPLOYEE STATUS. — Representatives for purposes of paragraph (1)(B), directors, officers, employees, or agents of a bridge financial company are not, solely by virtue of service in any such capacity, officers or employees of the United States. Any employee of the Corporation or of any Federal instrumentality who serves at the request of the Corporation as a representative for purposes of paragraph (1)(B), director, officer, employee, or agent of a bridge financial company shall not —

(III)将出售或以其他方式处置所涉金融公司资产造成的任何损失金额减到最低限度;且

(ii)所有在第(b)(1)子条项下情形类似的债权人收到的金额均不低于第(d)子条第(2)款和第(3)款规定的金额。

(F)**负债转让限制**。——无论是否存在任何不同法律规定,过渡金融公司受让或承担的所涉金融公司的负债总额,不得超过过渡金融公司受让或购买的所涉金融公司的资产总额。

(6)**司法诉讼中止**。——过渡金融公司因其收购所涉金融公司任何资产或承担所涉金融公司任何负债而成为司法诉讼当事人的,如该过渡金融公司提出请求,则该诉讼应中止,中止期不得超过45天(或诉讼各当事人同意的更长的期间)。

(7)**不利于过渡金融公司权益的协议**。——任何协议如果易于减损或消灭过渡金融公司对其收购的所涉金融公司资产享有之权益,则对该过渡金融公司一概无效,除非该协议——

(A)属于书面协议;

(B)已由所涉金融公司的授权管理人员或授权代表签署,或已在所涉金融公司的正常业务运作中获得确认;且

(C)自签署之后,已成为公司的一项正式记录,或者根据该协议提出权利主张的一方已提供获得证明文件,证明该协议的存在以及该协议已获得所涉金融公司授权签署或确认,且该等证明文件获得接管人认可。

(8)**无联邦机关身份**。——

(A)**机关身份**。——过渡金融公司不具有美国联邦机关、组织或职能机构的身份。

(B)**雇员身份**。——为实现第(1)(B)款目的之任何代表,以及过渡金融公司的董事、管理人员、职员或代理人并不仅因其上述职务而具有美国联邦官员或职员的身份。应联邦存款保险公司的请求,为实现第(1)(B)款目的而担任代表,或者担任过渡金融公司董事、管理人员、职员或代理人的联邦存款保险公司或联邦职能机构的任何雇员均不得——

(i) solely by virtue of service in any such capacity lose any existing status as an officer or employee of the United States for purposes of title 5, United States Code, or any other provision of law; or

(ii) receive any salary or benefits for service in any such capacity with respect to a bridge financial company in addition to such salary or benefits as are obtained through employment with the Corporation or such Federal instrumentality.

(9) FUNDING AUTHORIZED. — The Corporation may, subject to the plan described in subsection (n)(9), provide funding to facilitate any transaction described in subparagraph (A), (B), (C), or (D) of paragraph (13) with respect to any bridge financial company, or facilitate the acquisition by a bridge financial company of any assets, or the assumption of any liabilities, of a covered financial company for which the Corporation has been appointed receiver.

(10) EXEMPT TAX STATUS. — Notwithstanding any other provision of Federal or State law, a bridge financial company, its franchise, property, and income shall be exempt from all taxation now or hereafter imposed by the United States, by any territory, dependency, or possession thereof, or by any State, county, municipality, or local taxing authority.

(11) FEDERAL AGENCY APPROVAL; ANTITRUST REVIEW. — If a transaction involving the merger or sale of a bridge financial company requires approval by a Federal agency, the transaction may not be consummated before the 5th calendar day after the date of approval by the Federal agency responsible for such approval with respect thereto. If, in connection with any such approval a report on competitive factors from the Attorney General is required, the Federal agency responsible for such approval shall promptly notify the Attorney General of the proposed transaction and the Attorney General shall provide the required report within 10 days of the request. If a notification is required under section 7A of the Clayton Act with respect to such transaction, the required waiting period shall end on the 15th day after the date on which the Attorney General and the Federal Trade Commission receive such notification, unless the waiting period is terminated earlier under section 7A(b)(2) of the Clayton Act, or extended under section 7A(e)(2) of that Act.

(12) DURATION OF BRIDGE FINANCIAL COMPANY. — Subject to paragraphs (13) and (14), the status of a bridge financial company as such shall terminate at the end of the 2-year period following the date on which it was granted a charter. The Corporation may, in its discretion, extend the status of the bridge financial company as such for no more than 3 additional 1-year periods.

(13) TERMINATION OF BRIDGE FINANCIAL COMPANY STATUS. — The status of any bridge financial company as such shall terminate upon the earliest of —

(i)仅因其担任上述职务而丧失其当前具有的《美国法典》第五编或任何其他法律规定意义上的美国联邦官员或职员的身份;或

(ii)在因其受雇于联邦存款保险公司或该联邦职能机构而获得的工资或福利之外,就其在过渡金融公司担任的职位获取任何额外工资或福利。

(9)**授权提供融资**。——联邦存款保险公司可以根据第(n)(9)子条所述计划,提供资金为第(13)款第(A)子款、第(B)子款、第(C)子款或第(D)子款所述与任何过渡金融公司相关的交易提供融通便利,或为过渡金融公司收购联邦存款保险公司作为接管人接管的所涉金融公司的任何资产或承担该所涉金融公司的任何债务提供融通便利。

(10)**税收豁免地位**。——无论联邦法律或州法律是否存在任何不同规定,过渡金融公司及其特许业务、财产和收入均应豁免于美国、美国任何准州或属地或任何州、郡、郡级市或地方税务机关当前或此后施加的纳税义务。

(11)**联邦机关的批准;反垄断审查**。——如涉及兼并或出售一家过渡金融公司的交易须获得联邦机关批准,则该交易合同订立的时间不得早于相应的联邦负责机关批准该交易之日后的第5个日历日。如作出任何该等批准需要联邦总检察长提供一份关于竞争要素的报告,则负责该等批准的联邦机关应及时将该拟议交易通知联邦总检察长,联邦总检察长应在收到申请后10天内提供上述报告。如《克莱顿法》第7A条要求就该交易提供通知,则规定的等待期应于联邦总检察长和联邦贸易委员会收到该通知之日后第15天终止,除非该等待期根据《克莱顿法》第7A(b)(2)条提前终止,或者根据该法第7A(e)(2)条延长。

(12)**过渡金融公司的存续期**。——在不违反第(13)款和第(14)款规定的前提下,过渡金融公司的身份应在其获授执照之日起届满2年之日终止。联邦存款保险公司可以依其自由裁量权延长上述期限,每次延期为1年,但延期次数最多不得超过3次。

(13)**过渡金融公司身份的终止**。——过渡金融公司的身份应于以下日期或以下事件发生之日(以最早者为准)终止——

(A) the date of the merger or consolidation of the bridge financial company with a company that is not a bridge financial company;

(B) at the election of the Corporation, the sale of a majority of the capital stock of the bridge financial company to a company other than the Corporation and other than another bridge financial company;

(C) the sale of 80 percent, or more, of the capital stock of the bridge financial company to a person other than the Corporation and other than another bridge financial company;

(D) at the election of the Corporation, either the assumption of all or substantially all of the liabilities of the bridge financial company by a company that is not a bridge financial company, or the acquisition of all or substantially all of the assets of the bridge financial company by a company that is not a bridge financial company, or other entity as permitted under applicable law; and

(E) the expiration of the period provided in paragraph (12), or the earlier dissolution of the bridge financial company, as provided in paragraph (15).

(14) EFFECT OF TERMINATION EVENTS. —

(A) MERGER OR CONSOLIDATION. — A merger or consolidation, described in paragraph (13)(A) shall be conducted in accordance with, and shall have the effect provided in, the provisions of applicable law. For the purpose of effecting such a merger or consolidation, the bridge financial company shall be treated as a corporation organized under the laws of the State of Delaware (unless the law of another State has been selected by the bridge financial company in accordance with paragraph (2)(F)), and the Corporation shall be treated as the sole shareholder thereof, notwithstanding any other provision of State or Federal law.

(B) CHARTER CONVERSION. — Following the sale of a majority of the capital stock of the bridge financial company, as provided in paragraph (13)(B), the Corporation may amend the charter of the bridge financial company to reflect the termination of the status of the bridge financial company as such, whereupon the company shall have all of the rights, powers, and privileges under its constituent documents and applicable Federal or State law. In connection therewith, the Corporation may take such steps as may be necessary or convenient to reincorporate the bridge financial company under the laws of a State and, notwithstanding any provisions of Federal or State law, such State-chartered corporation shall be deemed to succeed by operation of law to such rights, titles, powers, and interests of the bridge financial company as the Corporation may provide, with the same effect as if the bridge financial company had merged with the State-chartered corporation under provisions of the corporate laws of such State.

(C) SALE OF STOCK. — Following the sale of 80 percent or more of the capital

(A)该过渡金融公司与并非过渡金融公司的公司兼并或合并之日;

(B)联邦存款保险公司选择将该过渡金融公司的多数股本出售给并非联邦存款保险公司、亦非另一家过渡金融公司的公司;

(C)该过渡金融公司80%或80%以上的股本被出售给并非联邦存款保险公司、亦非另一家过渡金融公司的人;

(D)联邦存款保险公司选择一家并非过渡金融公司的公司或适用的法律允许的其他实体承担该过渡金融公司全部或绝大部分负债,或者收购该过渡金融公司全部或基本全部资产;及

(E)第(12)款规定的期限届满,或该过渡金融公司根据第(15)款的规定提前解散。

(14)**终止事件的效力**。——

(A)**兼并或合并**。——第(13)(A)款所述兼并或合并应根据适用的法律规定执行,并具有适用的法律规定所规定的效力。为使该兼并或合并生效,过渡金融公司应视为根据特拉华州法律组建的公司[除非该过渡金融公司根据第(2)(F)款选择适用另一州的州法律],且联邦存款保险公司应视为该过渡金融公司的唯一股东,而无论州法律或联邦法律是否存在任何不同规定。

(B)**执照的变更**。——过渡金融公司的多数股本根据第(13)(B)款的规定完成出售后,联邦存款保险公司可以修正该过渡金融公司的执照,以反映其过渡金融公司身份的终止,此后,该公司将享有其章程和适用的联邦法律或州法律规定的全部权利、权力和特权。联邦存款保险公司可以就上述目的采取必要或便利的行动,根据某一州的州法律重新成立该过渡金融公司,且无论联邦法律或州法律是否存在任何不同规定。该重新成立的州特许注册公司均应视为已按照联邦存款保险公司的规定,依法继受该过渡金融公司的权利、所有权、权力和权益,其效力应如同该过渡金融公司已根据该州的公司法规定与该州特许注册公司兼并。

(C)**股本出售**。——过渡金融公司的80%或80%以上的股本根据第(13)(C)款的

stock of a bridge financial company, as provided in paragraph (13)(C), the company shall have all of the rights, powers, and privileges under its constituent documents and applicable Federal or State law. In connection therewith, the Corporation may take such steps as may be necessary or convenient to reincorporate the bridge financial company under the laws of a State and, notwithstanding any provisions of Federal or State law, the State–chartered corporation shall be deemed to succeed by operation of law to such rights, titles, powers and interests of the bridge financial company as the Corporation may provide, with the same effect as if the bridge financial company had merged with the State–chartered corporation under provisions of the corporate laws of such State.

(D) ASSUMPTION OF LIABILITIES AND SALE OF ASSETS. — Following the assumption of all or substantially all of the liabilities of the bridge financial company, or the sale of all or substantially all of the assets of the bridge financial company, as provided in paragraph (13)(D), at the election of the Corporation, the bridge financial company may retain its status as such for the period provided in paragraph (12) or may be dissolved at the election of the Corporation.

(E) AMENDMENTS TO CHARTER. — Following the consummation of a transaction described in subparagraph (A), (B), (C), or (D) of paragraph (13), the charter of the resulting company shall be amended to reflect the termination of bridge financial company status, if appropriate.

(15) DISSOLUTION OF BRIDGE FINANCIAL COMPANY. —

(A) IN GENERAL. — Notwithstanding any other provision of Federal or State law, if the status of a bridge financial company as such has not previously been terminated by the occurrence of an event specified in subparagraph (A), (B), (C), or (D) of paragraph (13) —

(i) the Corporation may, in its discretion, dissolve the bridge financial company in accordance with this paragraph at any time; and

(ii) the Corporation shall promptly commence dissolution proceedings in accordance with this paragraph upon the expiration of the 2–year period following the date on which the bridge financial company was chartered, or any extension thereof, as provided in paragraph (12).

(B) PROCEDURES. — The Corporation shall remain the receiver for a bridge financial company for the purpose of dissolving the bridge financial company. The Corporation as receiver for a bridge financial company shall wind up the affairs of the bridge financial company in conformity with the provisions of law relating to the liquidation of covered financial companies under this title. With respect to any such bridge financial company, the Corporation as receiver shall have all the rights, powers, and privileges and shall perform the duties related to the exercise of such rights, powers,

规定完成出售后,该公司将据此享有其章程和适用的联邦法律或州法律规定的全部权利、权力和特权。联邦存款保险公司可以就上述目的采取必要或便利的行动,根据某一州的州法律重新成立该过渡金融公司,且无论联邦法律或州法律是否存在任何不同规定,该重新成立的州特许注册公司均应视为已按照联邦存款保险公司的规定,依法继受该过渡金融公司的权利、所有权、权力和权益,其效力应如同该过渡金融公司已根据该州的公司法规定与该州特许注册公司兼并。

(D)**负债承担和资产出售**。——过渡金融公司的全部或绝大部分负债根据第(13)(D)款已转由他方承担,或该过渡金融公司的全部或基本全部资产已根据该款完成出售的,该过渡金融公司可以在第(12)款规定的期间内保留其过渡金融公司的身份,联邦存款保险公司亦可以选择将其解散。

(E)**执照修正**。——第(13)款第(A)子款、第(B)子款、第(C)子款或第(D)子款所述交易合同订立后,应对存续的公司的执照进行修正,以反映过渡金融公司身份的终止(如适用)。

(15)**过渡金融公司的解散**。——

(A)**一般规定**。——无论联邦法律或州法律是否存在任何不同规定,如过渡金融公司的身份未在第(13)款第(A)子款、第(B)子款、第(C)子款或第(D)子款所述事件发生之前终止,则——

(i)联邦存款保险公司可以依其自由裁量权,根据本款规定随时解散该过渡金融公司;且

(ii)联邦存款保险公司应根据本款规定,在该过渡金融公司特许注册之日起的2年期限届满之日或第(12)款规定的延长期限届满之日及时启动该过渡金融公司的解散程序。

(B)**程序**。——为实现解散过渡金融公司的目的,联邦存款保险公司应保留其作为该过渡金融公司接管人的身份。联邦存款保险公司作为过渡金融公司的接管人,应遵守与本编规定的所涉金融公司清算相关的法律规定,了结该过渡金融公司的事务。就任何该等过渡金融公司而言,联邦存款保险公司作为接管人,应具有法律赋予本编规定的所涉金融公司接管人的全部权利、权力和特权,并应履行与行使该等权利、权力或特权相关的职责,且无论是否存在任何不同法律规定,联邦存款保险公司在行使该等权利、权力和特权时,均不得受制于任何州机关或联邦机关的指示或监管。

or privileges granted by law to the Corporation as receiver for a covered financial company under this title and, notwithstanding any other provision of law, in the exercise of such rights, powers, and privileges, the Corporation shall not be subject to the direction or supervision of any State agency or other Federal agency.

(16) AUTHORITY TO OBTAIN CREDIT. —

(A) IN GENERAL. — A bridge financial company may obtain unsecured credit and issue unsecured debt.

(B) INABILITY TO OBTAIN CREDIT. — If a bridge financial company is unable to obtain unsecured credit or issue unsecured debt, the Corporation may authorize the obtaining of credit or the issuance of debt by the bridge financial company —

(i) with priority over any or all of the obligations of the bridge financial company;

(ii) secured by a lien on property of the bridge financial company that is not otherwise subject to a lien; or

(iii) secured by a junior lien on property of the bridge financial company that is subject to a lien.

(C) LIMITATIONS. —

(i) IN GENERAL. — The Corporation, after notice and a hearing, may authorize the obtaining of credit or the issuance of debt by a bridge financial company that is secured by a senior or equal lien on property of the bridge financial company that is subject to a lien, only if —

(I) the bridge financial company is unable to otherwise obtain such credit or issue such debt; and

(II) there is adequate protection of the interest of the holder of the lien on the property with respect to which such senior or equal lien is proposed to be granted.

(ii) HEARING. — The hearing required pursuant to this subparagraph shall be before a court of the United States, which shall have jurisdiction to conduct such hearing and to authorize a bridge financial company to obtain secured credit under clause (i).

(D) BURDEN OF PROOF. — In any hearing under this paragraph, the Corporation has the burden of proof on the issue of adequate protection.

(E) QUALIFIED FINANCIAL CONTRACTS. — No credit or debt obtained or issued by a bridge financial company may contain terms that impair the rights of a counterparty to a qualified financial contract upon a default by the bridge financial company, other than the priority of such counterparty's unsecured claim (after the exercise of rights) relative to the priority of the bridge financial company's obligations in respect of such credit or debt, unless such counterparty consents in writing to any such impairment.

(17) EFFECT ON DEBTS AND LIENS. — The reversal or modification on appeal of

(16)**获取信贷权**。——

(A)**一般规定**。——过渡金融公司可以获取无担保信贷并发行无担保债务。

(B)**无法获得信用的情形**。——过渡金融公司无法获得无担保信贷或发行无担保债务的,联邦存款保险公司可以核准该过渡金融公司——

(i)获取或发行优先顺序高于该过渡金融公司部分或全部义务的信贷或债务;

(ii)在该过渡金融公司的不存在其他留置权的财产上设定留置权,作为获取信贷或发行债务的担保;或

(iii)在该过渡金融公司已存在留置权的财产上设定次位留置权,作为获取信贷或发行债务的担保。

(C)**限制**。——

(i)**一般规定**。——联邦存款保险公司有权在发出通知并进行听证后,核准过渡金融公司在其财产上设定优先顺序高于或等同于现有的过渡金融公司财产留置权的留置权,作为获取信贷或发行债务的担保,其前提是——

(I)该过渡金融公司无法以其他方式获取该信贷或发行该债务;且

(II)拟在已存在留置权的财产上设定优先顺序更高或同等的留置权时,该等既有留置权持有人的权益已获充分保护。

(ii)**听证**。——本子款规定的听证应在美国法院举行,该法院应具有举行该听证并批准过渡金融公司根据第(i)项规定获取担保信贷的权力。

(D)**证明责任**。——在根据本款举行的听证中,联邦存款保险公司应就保护充分性问题承担证明责任。

(E)**合格金融合约**。——除非经对手方书面同意,否则过渡金融公司获取的信贷或发行的债务的任何条款均不得损害合格金融合约对手方在该过渡金融公司出现违约时享有的权利,但过渡金融公司就该信贷或债务承担之义务的优先顺序,可以高于该对手方行权后享有的无担保权利主张的优先顺序。

(17)**债务和留置权的效力**。——如信贷的获取或债务的发行已根据本子条规定

an authorization under this subsection to obtain credit or issue debt, or of a grant under this section of a priority or a lien, does not affect the validity of any debt so issued, or any priority or lien so granted, to an entity that extended such credit in good faith, whether or not such entity knew of the pendency of the appeal, unless such authorization and the issuance of such debt, or the granting of such priority or lien, were stayed pending appeal.

(i) SHARING RECORDS. — If the Corporation has been appointed as receiver for a covered financial company, other Federal regulators shall make all records relating to the covered financial company available to the Corporation, which may be used by the Corporation in any manner that the Corporation determines to be appropriate.

(j) EXPEDITED PROCEDURES FOR CERTAIN CLAIMS. —

(1) TIME FOR FILING NOTICE OF APPEAL. — The notice of appeal of any order, whether interlocutory or final, entered in any case brought by the Corporation against a director, officer, employee, agent, attorney, accountant, or appraiser of the covered financial company, or any other person employed by or providing services to a covered financial company, shall be filed not later than 30 days after the date of entry of the order. The hearing of the appeal shall be held not later than 120 days after the date of the notice of appeal. The appeal shall be decided not later than 180 days after the date of the notice of appeal.

(2) SCHEDULING. — The court shall expedite the consideration of any case brought by the Corporation against a director, officer, employee, agent, attorney, accountant, or appraiser of a covered financial company or any other person employed by or providing services to a covered financial company. As far as practicable, the court shall give such case priority on its docket.

(3) JUDICIAL DISCRETION. — The court may modify the schedule and limitations stated in paragraphs (1) and (2) in a particular case, based on a specific finding that the ends of justice that would be served by making such a modification would outweigh the best interest of the public in having the case resolved expeditiously.

(k) FOREIGN INVESTIGATIONS. — The Corporation, as receiver for any covered financial company, and for purposes of carrying out any power, authority, or duty with respect to a covered financial company —

(1) may request the assistance of any foreign financial authority and provide assistance to any foreign financial authority in accordance with section 8(v) of the Federal Deposit Insurance Act, as if the covered financial company were an insured depository institution, the Corporation were the appropriate Federal banking agency for the company, and any foreign financial authority were the foreign banking authority; and

(2) may maintain an office to coordinate foreign investigations or investigations on behalf of foreign financial authorities.

获批准，或某项优先权或留置权已根据本条规定授予，则即使该等批准或授予被提起上诉并被撤销或变更，对于善意提供该信贷的实体而言，已经发行的债务或已经授予的优先权或留置权的效力均不得因此受到影响，无论该实体是否知晓上诉已被提起并处于待决状态，除非在上诉期间，该等批准、债务发行或该等优先权或留置权的授予已被中止。

(i)**记录共享**。——联邦存款保险公司被指定为所涉金融公司接管人的，其他联邦监管者应向联邦存款保险公司提供与该所涉金融公司相关的全部记录，联邦存款保险公司可以其认为适当的任何方式使用该等记录。

(j)**适用于特定权利主张的加急程序**。——

(1)**提交上诉通知的时限**。——在联邦存款保险公司针对所涉金融公司的董事、管理人员、职员、代理人、律师、会计师或评估师或所涉金融公司雇用的或为之提供服务的任何人提起的案件中作出某一中间或最终命令的，针对该命令的上诉通知应在该命令正式作出之日后30天内提交。对该上诉的听证应在上诉通知提交之日后120天内举行，并应在上诉通知提交之日后180天内作出裁决。

(2)**时间安排**。——法院应加急审理联邦存款保险公司针对所涉金融公司的董事、管理人员、职员、代理人、律师、会计师或评估师或所涉金融公司雇用的或为之提供服务的任何人提起的案件。法院应尽可能将该案件安排在其备审案件目录表的优先位置。

(3)**司法自由裁量权**——如法院明确认定，变更第(1)款和第(2)款规定的时间安排和限制以实现司法公正，比及时解决案件实现公众的最佳利益更为重要，则法院可以在特定的案件中变更第(1)款和第(2)款所述的时间安排和限制。

(k)**外国调查**。——联邦存款保险公司作为所涉金融公司的接管人，在就所涉金融公司履行其权力、权限或职责之时——

(1)可以根据《联邦存款保险法》第8(v)条请求任何外国金融监管机构提供援助，并向外国金融监管机构提供援助，如同所涉金融公司是一家参保存款机构，而联邦存款保险公司系该公司的相应的联邦银行业监管机关，且外国金融监管机构具有外国银行业监管机构身份；及

(2)可以维持一个办公室，以协调在外国进行的调查或代表外国金融监管机构开展的调查。

(l) PROHIBITION ON ENTERING SECRECY AGREEMENTS AND PROTECTIVE ORDERS. — The Corporation may not enter into any agreement or approve any protective order which prohibits the Corporation from disclosing the terms of any settlement of an administrative or other action for damages or restitution brought by the Corporation in its capacity as receiver for a covered financial company.

(m) LIQUIDATION OF CERTAIN COVERED FINANCIAL COMPANIES OR BRIDGE FINANCIAL COMPANIES. —

(1) IN GENERAL. — Except as specifically provided in this section, and notwithstanding any other provision of law, the Corporation, in connection with the liquidation of any covered financial company or bridge financial company with respect to which the Corporation has been appointed as receiver, shall —

(A) in the case of any covered financial company or bridge financial company that is a stockbroker, but is not a member of the Securities Investor Protection Corporation, apply the provisions of subchapter III of chapter 7 of the Bankruptcy Code, in respect of the distribution to any customer of all customer name security and customer property and member property, as if such covered financial company or bridge financial company were a debtor for purposes of such subchapter; or

(B) in the case of any covered financial company or bridge financial company that is a commodity broker, apply the provisions of subchapter IV of chapter 7 the Bankruptcy Code, in respect of the distribution to any customer of all customer property and member property, as if such covered financial company or bridge financial company were a debtor for purposes of such subchapter.

(2) DEFINITIONS. — For purposes of this subsection —

(A) the terms "customer", "customer name security", and "customer property and member property" have the same meanings as in sections 741 and 761 of title 11, United States Code; and

(B) the terms "commodity broker" and "stockbroker" have the same meanings as in section 101 of the Bankruptcy Code.

(n) ORDERLY LIQUIDATION FUND. —

(1) ESTABLISHMENT. — There is established in the Treasury of the United States a separate fund to be known as the "Orderly Liquidation Fund", which shall be available to the Corporation to carry out the authorities contained in this title, for the cost of actions authorized by this title, including the orderly liquidation of covered financial companies, payment of administrative expenses, the payment of principal and interest by the Corporation on obligations issued under paragraph (5), and the exercise of the authorities of the Corporation under this title.

(2) PROCEEDS. — Amounts received by the Corporation, including assessments

(l)**订立保密协议和保护令的禁止性规定**。——联邦存款保险公司作为所涉金融公司的接管人,就损害赔偿或不当得利返还提起的行政诉讼或其他诉讼已达成和解的,联邦存款保险公司不得为禁止披露该等和解条款而订立任何协议或批准任何保护令。

(m)**特定所涉金融公司或特定过渡金融公司的清算**。——

(1)**一般规定**。——除本条另有明确规定的情形外,无论是否存在任何不同法律规定,在任何所涉金融公司或过渡金融公司接受清算时,联邦存款保险公司作为该所涉金融公司或过渡金融公司的接管人的,应在以下情形下分别适用以下法律规定——

(A)如所涉金融公司或过渡金融公司是一家股票经纪商,但并非证券投资者保护公司会员,则联邦存款保险公司在向任何客户分配任何客户名下证券、客户财产和会员财产时,应适用《破产法》第七章第三子章的规定,如同该所涉金融公司或过渡金融公司身为该子编规定的债务人;或

(B)如所涉金融公司或过渡金融公司是一家商品经纪商,则联邦存款保险公司在向任何客户分配任何客户财产和会员财产时,应适用《破产法》第七章第四子章的规定,如同该所涉金融公司或过渡金融公司身为该子编规定的债务人。

(2)**定义**。——就本子条而言——

(A)"客户"、"客户名下证券"和"客户财产和会员财产"的含义以《美国法典》第十一编第741节和第761节的定义为准;且

(B)"商品经纪商"和"股票经纪商"的含义以《破产法》第101条的定义为准。

(n)**有序清算基金**。——

(1)**设立**。——美国财政部下设名为"有序清算基金"的独立基金,以便联邦存款保险公司在行使其在本编中的权力时,利用该基金支付本编授权其采取的行动的费用,该等行动包括:对所涉金融公司的有序清算、支付行政费用、联邦存款保险公司偿付根据第(5)款发行的债务之本金和利息以及行使本编规定的联邦存款保险公司的权力。

(2)**所得资金**。——联邦存款保险公司收到的款项,包括根据第(o)子条收取的计

received under subsection (o), proceeds of obligations issued under paragraph (5), interest and other earnings from investments, and repayments to the Corporation by covered financial companies, shall be deposited into the Fund.

(3) MANAGEMENT. — The Corporation shall manage the Fund in accordance with this subsection and the policies and procedures established under section 203(d).

(4) INVESTMENTS. — At the request of the Corporation, the Secretary may invest such portion of amounts held in the Fund that are not, in the judgment of the Corporation, required to meet the current needs of the Corporation, in obligations of the United States having suitable maturities, as determined by the Corporation. The interest on and the proceeds from the sale or redemption of such obligations shall be credited to the Fund.

(5) AUTHORITY TO ISSUE OBLIGATIONS. —

(A) CORPORATION AUTHORIZED TO ISSUE OBLIGATIONS. — Upon appointment by the Secretary of the Corporation as receiver for a covered financial company, the Corporation is authorized to issue obligations to the Secretary.

(B) SECRETARY AUTHORIZED TO PURCHASE OBLIGATIONS. — The Secretary may, under such terms and conditions as the Secretary may require, purchase or agree to purchase any obligations issued under subparagraph (A), and for such purpose, the Secretary is authorized to use as a public debt transaction the proceeds of the sale of any securities issued under chapter 31 of title 31, United States Code, and the purposes for which securities may be issued under chapter 31 of title 31, United States Code, are extended to include such purchases.

(C) INTEREST RATE. — Each purchase of obligations by the Secretary under this paragraph shall be upon such terms and conditions as to yield a return at a rate determined by the Secretary, taking into consideration the current average yield on outstanding marketable obligations of the United States of comparable maturity, plus an interest rate surcharge to be determined by the Secretary, which shall be greater than the difference between —

(i) the current average rate on an index of corporate obligations of comparable maturity; and

(ii) the current average rate on outstanding marketable obligations of the United States of comparable maturity.

(D) SECRETARY AUTHORIZED TO SELL OBLIGATIONS. — The Secretary may sell, upon such terms and conditions as the Secretary shall determine, any of the obligations acquired under this paragraph.

(E) PUBLIC DEBT TRANSACTIONS. — All purchases and sales by the Secretary of such obligations under this paragraph shall be treated as public debt transactions of the United States, and the proceeds from the sale of any obligations acquired by the Secretary

征费、根据第(5)款发行债务募集的资金、投资产生的利息和其他收益以及所涉金融公司向联邦存款保险公司的偿还款项,均应存入有序清算基金。

(3)**管理**。——联邦存款保险公司应根据本子条以及根据203(d)条制定的政策和程序管理有序清算基金。

(4)**投资**。——如联邦存款保险公司判断不需要动用有序清算基金持有的任何部分金额来满足联邦存款保险公司当前的需求,则经联邦存款保险公司请求,财政部部长可以利用该部分金额对美国债券进行投资,投资债券的期限应为联邦存款保险公司判定确属适当的期限。上述债券的利息以及出售或赎回所得均应贷记入有序清算基金。

(5)**债务发行权**。——

(A)**联邦存款保险公司的债务发行权**。——财政部部长指定联邦存款保险公司担任所涉金融公司接管人后,联邦存款保险公司即有权向财政部部长发行债务。

(B)**财政部部长的债务购买权**。——财政部部长可以按其规定的条款和条件购买或同意购买根据第(A)子款发行的任何债务,且财政部部长有权为此目的,使用根据《美国法典》第三十一编第三十一章发行的任何证券出售所获资金;该等购买应视同公共债务交易,且应纳入根据《美国法典》第三十一编第三十一章发行的证券的发行目的范围之内。

(C)**利率**。——根据本款购买的每笔债务的条款和条件应使其能达到财政部部长确定的收益率,财政部部长确定该等收益率时应考虑未清偿的且期限相当的美国联邦流通债券的平均收益率,加上财政部部长按高于以下二者之差的利率确定的附加利息——

(i)期限相当的公司债务指数的当前平均利率;及

(ii)未清偿的且期限相当的联邦流通债券的当前平均利率。

(D)**财政部部长的债务出售权**。——财政部部长可以按照其确定的条款和条件出售根据本款规定购买的任何债务。

(E)**公共债务交易**。——财政部部长根据本款实施的全部购买和出售均应视为美国公共债务交易,且财政部部长出售根据本款购买的任何债务所获全部资金均应作为杂项收入存入美国财政部。

under this paragraph shall be deposited into the Treasury of the United States as miscellaneous receipts.

(6) MAXIMUM OBLIGATION LIMITATION. — The Corporation may not, in connection with the orderly liquidation of a covered financial company, issue or incur any obligation, if, after issuing or incurring the obligation, the aggregate amount of such obligations outstanding under this subsection for each covered financial company would exceed —

(A) an amount that is equal to 10 percent of the total consolidated assets of the covered financial company, based on the most recent financial statement available, during the 30-day period immediately following the date of appointment of the Corporation as receiver (or a shorter time period if the Corporation has calculated the amount described under subparagraph (B)); and

(B) the amount that is equal to 90 percent of the fair value of the total consolidated assets of each covered financial company that are available for repayment, after the time period described in subparagraph (A).

(7) RULEMAKING. — The Corporation and the Secretary shall jointly, in consultation with the Council, prescribe regulations governing the calculation of the maximum obligation limitation defined in this paragraph.

(8) RULE OF CONSTRUCTION. —

(A) IN GENERAL. — Nothing in this section shall be construed to affect the authority of the Corporation under subsection (a) or (b) of section 14 or section 15(c)(5) of the Federal Deposit Insurance Act (12 U.S.C. 1824, 1825(c)(5)), the management of the Deposit Insurance Fund by the Corporation, or the resolution of insured depository institutions, provided that —

(i) the authorities of the Corporation contained in this title shall not be used to assist the Deposit Insurance Fund or to assist any financial company under applicable law other than this Act;

(ii) the authorities of the Corporation relating to the Deposit Insurance Fund, or any other responsibilities of the Corporation under applicable law other than this title, shall not be used to assist a covered financial company pursuant to this title; and

(iii) the Deposit Insurance Fund may not be used in any manner to otherwise circumvent the purposes of this title.

(B) VALUATION. — For purposes of determining the amount of obligations under this subsection —

(i) the Corporation shall include as an obligation any contingent liability of the Corporation pursuant to this title; and

(ii) the Corporation shall value any contingent liability at its expected cost to the

(6)**最高债务额度限制**。——在对所涉金融公司进行有序清算时,如果发行或产生任何债务后,每家所涉金融公司在本子条下未清偿的债务总额均会超过如下金额,则联邦存款保险公司不得发行或发生任何该等债务——

(A)该所涉金融公司的并表资产总额的10%,该并表资产总额指联邦存款保险公司被指定为接管人之日后紧接的30天期间[如联邦存款保险公司已完成了第(B)子款所述金额的计算,则上述期间可以更短]的并表资产总额,应基于可获得的最近一期财务报表进行计算;且

(B)在第(A)子款所述的期间届满之后,每家所涉金融公司可用于偿还债务的并表资产公允价值的90%。

(7)**规则制定**。——联邦存款保险公司和财政部部长应在与金融稳定监督委员会磋商后,共同就本款界定的最高债务额度之计算制定规章。

(8)**解释规则**。——

(A)**一般规定**。——本条任何规定均不得被解释为对以下各项造成任何影响:联邦存款保险公司根据《联邦存款保险法》第14条第(a)子条或第(b)子条或第15(c)(5)条[《美国法典》第十二编第1824节或第1825(c)(5)节]享有的权力、联邦存款保险公司对存款保险基金的管理或对参保存款机构的清盘,但是——

(i)联邦存款保险公司不得利用其在本编中的权力,向存款保险基金提供援助,或向本法以外的适用的法律规定的任何金融公司提供援助;

(ii)联邦存款保险公司不得利用其与存款保险基金相关的权力,或本编以外其他的法律规定的任何其他职责,对本编规定的所涉金融公司提供援助;且

(iii)不得以任何旨在规避本编规定的方式使用存款保险基金。

(B)**估值**。——在确定本子条规定的债务的金额之时——

(i)联邦存款保险公司应根据本编规定将其或有负债记入债务金额;且

(ii)联邦存款保险公司应基于或有负债将对联邦存款保险公司造成的预期成本

Corporation.

(9) ORDERLY LIQUIDATION AND REPAYMENT PLANS. —

(A) ORDERLY LIQUIDATION PLAN. — Amounts in the Fund shall be available to the Corporation with regard to a covered financial company for which the Corporation is appointed receiver after the Corporation has developed an orderly liquidation plan that is acceptable to the Secretary with regard to such covered financial company, including the provision and use of funds, including taking any actions specified under section 204(d) and subsection (h)(2)(G)(iv) and (h)(9) of this section, and payments to third parties. The orderly liquidation plan shall take into account actions to avoid or mitigate potential adverse effects on low income, minority, or underserved communities affected by the failure of the covered financial company, and shall provide for coordination with the primary financial regulatory agencies, as appropriate, to ensure that such actions are taken. The Corporation may, at any time, amend any orderly liquidation plan approved by the Secretary with the concurrence of the Secretary.

(B) MANDATORY REPAYMENT PLAN. —

(i) IN GENERAL. — No amount authorized under paragraph (6)(B) may be provided by the Secretary to the Corporation under paragraph (5), unless an agreement is in effect between the Secretary and the Corporation that —

(I) provides a specific plan and schedule to achieve the repayment of the outstanding amount of any borrowing under paragraph (5); and

(II) demonstrates that income to the Corporation from the liquidated assets of the covered financial company and assessments under subsection (o) will be sufficient to amortize the outstanding balance within the period established in the repayment schedule and pay the interest accruing on such balance within the time provided in subsection (o)(1)(B).

(ii) CONSULTATION WITH AND REPORT TO CONGRESS. — The Secretary and the Corporation shall —

(I) consult with the Committee on Banking, Housing, and Urban Affairs of the Senate and the Committee on Financial Services of the House of Representatives on the terms of any repayment schedule agreement; and

(II) submit a copy of the repayment schedule agreement to the Committees described in subclause (I) before the end of the 30–day period beginning on the date on which any amount is provided by the Secretary to the Corporation under paragraph (5).

(10) IMPLEMENTATION EXPENSES. —

(A) IN GENERAL. — Reasonable implementation expenses of the Corporation incurred after the date of enactment of this Act shall be treated as expenses of the Council.

对该或有负债进行估值。

（9）**有序清算和偿还计划**。——

（A）**有序清算计划**。——联邦存款保险公司针对其被指定接管的所涉金融公司制定的有序清算计划（包括资金的提供和使用）获得财政部部长认可后，联邦存款保险公司即可为所涉金融公司使用有序清算基金中的资金，包括采取第204（d）条、本条第（h）（2）（G）（iv）子条和第（h）（9）子条规定的任何行动，以及向第三方进行支付。就遭受所涉金融公司经营失败影响的低收入群体、少数族裔或弱势群体而言，有序清算计划中应考虑采取必要行动，以避免或减轻对该等群体造成的不利影响，并规定应与优先金融监管机关进行适当协作，确保该等行动得以落实。经财政部部长同意，联邦存款保险公司可随时对财政部部长批准的有序清算计划进行修正。

（B）**强制性偿还计划**。——

（i）**一般规定**。——财政部部长不得根据第（5）款规定向联邦存款保险公司提供第（6）（B）款授权提供的任何金额，除非财政部部长与联邦存款保险公司已经签订有效协议，且该协议——

（I）就根据第（5）款发生的任何借款的未清偿余额规定了具体偿付计划和时间安排；且

（II）证明联邦存款保险公司从所涉金融公司清算资产获得的收入和根据第（o）子条收取的计征费足以在该偿还计划规定的期间内摊还未清偿余额，并在第（o）（1）（B）子条规定的时间内该等支付未偿余额的应计利息。

（ii）**与国会进行协商并向国会报告**。——财政部部长和联邦存款保险公司应——

（I）就任何偿还计划协议的条款与参议院银行、住房与城市事务委员会和众议院金融服务委员会磋商；及

（II）在财政部部长根据第（5）款向联邦存款保险公司提供任何金额之日起30天内，向第（I）子项所述各委员会各提交一份该偿还计划协议的复本。

（10）**实施费用**。——

（A）**一般规定**。——联邦存款保险公司在本法颁布之日后产生的合理实施费用应作为金融稳定监督委员会的费用处理。

(B) REQUESTS FOR REIMBURSEMENT. — The Corporation shall periodically submit a request for reimbursement for implementation expenses to the Chairperson of the Council, who shall arrange for prompt reimbursement to the Corporation of reasonable implementation expenses.

(C) DEFINITION. — As used in this paragraph, the term "implementation expenses" —

(i) means costs incurred by the Corporation beginning on the date of enactment of this Act, as part of its efforts to implement this title that do not relate to a particular covered financial company; and

(ii) includes the costs incurred in connection with the development of policies, procedures, rules, and regulations and other planning activities of the Corporation consistent with carrying out this title.

(o) ASSESSMENTS. —

(1) RISK–BASED ASSESSMENTS. —

(A) ELIGIBLE FINANCIAL COMPANIES DEFINED. — For purposes of this subsection, the term "eligible financial company" means any bank holding company with total consolidated assets equal to or greater than $50, 000, 000, 000 and any nonbank financial company supervised by the Board of Governors.

(B) ASSESSMENTS. — The Corporation shall charge one or more risk –based assessments in accordance with the provisions of subparagraph (D), if such assessments are necessary to pay in full the obligations issued by the Corporation to the Secretary under this title within 60 months of the date of issuance of such obligations.

(C) EXTENSIONS AUTHORIZED. — The Corporation may, with the approval of the Secretary, extend the time period under subparagraph (B), if the Corporation determines that an extension is necessary to avoid a serious adverse effect on the financial system of the United States.

(D) APPLICATION OF ASSESSMENTS. — To meet the requirements of subparagraph (B), the Corporation shall —

(i) impose assessments, as soon as practicable, on any claimant that received additional payments or amounts from the Corporation pursuant to subsection (b)(4), (d)(4), or (h)(5)(E), except for payments or amounts necessary to initiate and continue operations essential to implementation of the receivership or any bridge financial company, to recover on a cumulative basis, the entire difference between —

(I) the aggregate value the claimant received from the Corporation on a claim pursuant to this title (including pursuant to subsection (b)(4), (d)(4), and (h)(5)(E)), as of the date on which such value was received; and

(II) the value the claimant was entitled to receive from the Corporation on such

(B)**偿付请求**。——联邦存款保险公司应向金融稳定监督委员会主席定期提交偿付实施费用的请求，金融稳定监督委员会主席应作出安排，及时向联邦存款保险公司偿付该等费用。

(C)**定义**。——就本款而言，"实施费用"一词——

(i)系指联邦存款保险公司自本法颁布之日起在实施本编规定的过程中产生的，且并非仅与某一特定的所涉金融公司相关的费用；且

(ii)包括联邦存款保险公司为实施本编规定而制定政策、程序、规则、规章和开展其他规划活动所产生的费用。

(o)**计征费**。——

(1)**风险计征费**。——

(A)**适格金融公司的定义**。——就本子条而言，"适格金融公司"一词系指并表资产总额等于或高于500亿美元的任何银行控股公司和受联邦储备委员会监管的任何非银行金融公司。

(B)**计征费**。——为了根据本编规定在联邦存款保险公司向财政部部长发行债务后60个月内向财政部部长全额偿清该等债务，在确有必要的情况下，联邦存款保险公司应根据第(D)子款征收必要的一项或一项以上风险计征费。

(C)**授权延期**。——经财政部部长批准，联邦存款保险公司可以出于避免美国金融体系遭受严重不利影响之目的，对第(B)子款规定的时限进行其判定确属必要的延长。

(D)**计征费的适用**。——为满足第(B)子款的要求，联邦存款保险公司——

(i)应尽快向根据第(b)(4)子条、第(d)(4)子条或第(h)(5)(E)子条收到了联邦存款保险公司的额外支付或金额的权利主张人征收计征费(但为启动并继续开展对履行接管人职责或者对任何过渡金融公司必不可少的运营活动所必需的支付或金额除外)，以全额累积弥补以下二者的差额——

(I)权利主张人申报权利主张后，根据本编规定[包括根据第(b)(4)子条、第(d)(4)子条和第(h)(5)(E)子条的规定]从联邦存款保险公司收到的价值总额(该等金额按收到该等价值之日的数值确定)；且

(II)权利主张人申报权利主张后，根据本编规定有权从联邦存款保险公司处收到

claim solely from the proceeds of the liquidation of the covered financial company under this title; and

(ii) if the amounts to be recovered on a cumulative basis under clause (i) are insufficient to meet the requirements of subparagraph (B), after taking into account the considerations set forth in paragraph (4), impose assessments on —

(I) eligible financial companies; and

(II) financial companies with total consolidated assets equal to or greater than $50, 000, 000, 000 that are not eligible financial companies.

(E) PROVISION OF FINANCING. — Payments or amounts necessary to initiate and continue operations essential to implementation of the receivership or any bridge financial company described in subparagraph (D)(i) shall not include the provision of financing, as defined by rule of the Corporation, to third parties.

(2) GRADUATED ASSESSMENT RATE. — The Corporation shall impose assessments on a graduated basis, with financial companies having greater assets and risk being assessed at a higher rate.

(3) NOTIFICATION AND PAYMENT. — The Corporation shall notify each financial company of that company's assessment under this subsection. Any financial company subject to assessment under this subsection shall pay such assessment in accordance with the regulations prescribed pursuant to paragraph (6).

(4) RISK-BASED ASSESSMENT CONSIDERATIONS. — In imposing assessments under paragraph (1)(D)(ii), the Corporation shall use a risk matrix. The Council shall make a recommendation to the Corporation on the risk matrix to be used in imposing such assessments, and the Corporation shall take into account any such recommendation in the establishment of the risk matrix to be used to impose such assessments. In recommending or establishing such risk matrix, the Council and the Corporation, respectively, shall take into account —

(A) economic conditions generally affecting financial companies so as to allow assessments to increase during more favorable economic conditions and to decrease during less favorable economic conditions;

(B) any assessments imposed on a financial company or an affiliate of a financial company that —

(i) is an insured depository institution, assessed pursuant to section 7 or 13(c)(4)(G) of the Federal Deposit Insurance Act;

(ii) is a member of the Securities Investor Protection Corporation, assessed pursuant to section 4 of the Securities Investor Protection Act of 1970 (15 U.S.C. 78ddd);

(iii) is an insured credit union, assessed pursuant to section 202(c)(1)(A)(i) of the Federal Credit Union Act (12 U.S.C. 1782(c)(1)(A)(i)); or

的,仅从所涉金融公司根据本编清算所获资金中获得分配的价值;且

(ii)如根据第(i)项规定累积弥补的金额不足以满足第(B)子款的要求,则应在考虑第(4)款规定的考虑因素后,向以下主体征收计征费——

(I)适格金融公司;及

(II)并表资产总额等于或高于500亿美元但不具有适格金融公司身份的金融公司。

(E)**提供融资**。——第(D)(i)子款所述为启动并继续开展对履行接管人职责或者对任何过渡金融公司必不可少的运营活动所必需的支付或金额,不应包括联邦存款保险公司发布的规则所定义的向第三方提供的融资。

(2)**计征费分级费率**。——联邦存款保险公司应分级征收计征费,资产金额和风险等级均较高的金融公司应适用较高的费率。

(3)**通知和支付**。——联邦存款保险公司应将通知每一金融公司各自根据本子条应缴纳的计征费。根据本子条应缴纳计征费的金融公司应根据依第(6)款制定的规章缴纳该等计征费。

(4)**与风险计征费相关的考虑因素**。——联邦存款保险公司在根据第(1)(D)(ii)款规定征收计征费时,应使用风险矩阵。金融稳定监督委员会应就拟用于征收计征费的风险矩阵向联邦存款保险公司提出建议,且联邦存款保险公司在设定该风险矩阵时应考虑该等建议。金融稳定监督委员会在就该风险矩阵提供建议,以及联邦存款保险公司在设定该矩阵时,均应考虑如下因素——

(A)对各金融公司具有普遍影响的总体经济状况,以便在经济状况较为有利的时期提高计征费,在经济状况较为不利的时期降低计征费;

(B)对具有以下身份的金融公司或金融公司关联方征收的计征费——

(i)根据《联邦存款保险法》第7条或第13(c)(4)(G)条征收计征费的参保存款机构;

(ii)根据《1970年证券投资者保护法》第4条(《美国法典》第十五编第78ddd节)征收计征费的证券投资者保护公司的会员;

(iii)根据《联邦信贷联盟法》第202(c)(1)(A)(i)条[《美国法典》第十二编第1782(c)(1)(A)(i)节]征收计征费的参保信贷联盟;或

(iv) is an insurance company, assessed pursuant to applicable State law to cover (or reimburse payments made to cover) the costs of the rehabilitation, liquidation, or other State insolvency proceeding with respect to 1 or more insurance companies;

(C) the risks presented by the financial company to the financial system and the extent to which the financial company has benefitted, or likely would benefit, from the orderly liquidation of a financial company under this title, including —

(i) the amount, different categories, and concentrations of assets of the financial company and its affiliates, including both on–balance sheet and off–balance sheet assets;

(ii) the activities of the financial company and its affiliates;

(iii) the relevant market share of the financial company and its affiliates;

(iv) the extent to which the financial company is leveraged;

(v) the potential exposure to sudden calls on liquidity precipitated by economic distress;

(vi) the amount, maturity, volatility, and stability of the company's financial obligations to, and relationship with, other financial companies;

(vii) the amount, maturity, volatility, and stability of the liabilities of the company, including the degree of reliance on short–term funding, taking into consideration existing systems for measuring a company's risk–based capital;

(viii) the stability and variety of the company's sources of funding;

(ix) the company's importance as a source of credit for households, businesses, and State and local governments and as a source of liquidity for the financial system;

(x) the extent to which assets are simply managed and not owned by the financial company and the extent to which ownership of assets under management is diffuse; and

(xi) the amount, different categories, and concentrations of liabilities, both insured and uninsured, contingent and noncontingent, including both on–balance sheet and off–balance sheet liabilities, of the financial company and its affiliates;

(D) any risks presented by the financial company during the 10–year period immediately prior to the appointment of the Corporation as receiver for the covered financial company that contributed to the failure of the covered financial company; and

(E) such other risk–related factors as the Corporation, or the Council, as applicable, may determine to be appropriate.

(5) COLLECTION OF INFORMATION. — The Corporation may impose on covered financial companies such collection of information requirements as the Corporation deems necessary to carry out this subsection after the appointment of the Corporation as receiver under this title.

(6) RULEMAKING. —

(A) IN GENERAL. — The Corporation shall prescribe regulations to carry out this

(iv)根据适用的州法律征收计征费以支付如下费用(或为偿付为如下费用所支付的款项)的保险公司:一家或一家以上保险公司的整顿程序、清算程序或其他州资不抵债程序的费用;

(C)金融公司对金融体系造成的风险,以及该金融公司在多大程度上已经或将会因根据本编规定接受有序清算而受益,包括——

(i)该金融公司及其关联方表内和表外资产的金额、类别和集中程度;

(ii)该金融公司及其关联方的活动;

(iii)该金融公司及其关联方的相关市场份额;

(iv)该金融公司的杠杆率;

(v)因经济衰退而出现突然性的流动性需求时,将导致的潜在风险敞口;

(vi)该金融公司向其他金融公司承担的金融义务的金额、期限、波动性和稳定性,以及与其他金融公司的关系;

(vii)该金融公司负债的金额、期限、波动性和稳定性,包括对短期资金的依赖程度(此时应考虑用于计量金融公司风险基础资本的现有体系);

(viii)该金融公司资金来源的稳定程度和多元性;

(ix)该金融公司作为家庭、企业以及州政府和地方政府信贷来源所具有的重要性,或作为美国金融体系流动性来源所具有的重要性;

(x)该金融公司管理的非自有资产的占比,以及其管理的资产的所有权分散程度;及

(xi)该金融公司及其关联方表内和表外的有保险负债和无保险负债,以及或有负债和非或有负债的金额、类别和集中程度;

(D)在联邦存款保险公司在被指定为所涉金融公司接管人之前的最近10年中,金融公司产生的,且促成所涉金融公司经营失败的风险;及

(E)联邦存款保险公司或金融稳定监督委员会(视具体情况而定)判定确属适当的其他风险因素。

(5)**信息收集**。——联邦存款保险公司根据本编被指定为接管人之后,可以向所涉金融公司施加其认为对实施本子条确属必要的信息收集要求。

(6)**规则制定**。——

(A)**一般规定**。——联邦存款保险公司应制定本子条的实施规章。联邦存款保险

subsection. The Corporation shall consult with the Secretary in the development and finalization of such regulations.

(B) EQUITABLE TREATMENT. — The regulations prescribed under subparagraph (A) shall take into account the differences in risks posed to the financial stability of the United States by financial companies, the differences in the liability structures of financial companies, and the different bases for other assessments that such financial companies may be required to pay, to ensure that assessed financial companies are treated equitably and that assessments under this subsection reflect such differences.

(p) UNENFORCEABILITY OF CERTAIN AGREEMENTS. —

(1) IN GENERAL. — No provision described in paragraph (2) shall be enforceable against or impose any liability on any person, as such enforcement or liability shall be contrary to public policy.

(2) PROHIBITED PROVISIONS. — A provision described in this paragraph is any term contained in any existing or future standstill, confidentiality, or other agreement that, directly or indirectly —

(A) affects, restricts, or limits the ability of any person to offer to acquire or acquire;

(B) prohibits any person from offering to acquire or acquiring; or

(C) prohibits any person from using any previously disclosed information in connection with any such offer to acquire or acquisition of, all or part of any covered financial company, including any liabilities, assets, or interest therein, in connection with any transaction in which the Corporation exercises its authority under this title.

(q) OTHER EXEMPTIONS. —

(1) IN GENERAL. — When acting as a receiver under this title —

(A) the Corporation, including its franchise, its capital, reserves and surplus, and its income, shall be exempt from all taxation imposed by any State, county, municipality, or local taxing authority, except that any real property of the Corporation shall be subject to State, territorial, county, municipal, or local taxation to the same extent according to its value as other real property is taxed, except that, notwithstanding the failure of any person to challenge an assessment under State law of the value of such property, such value, and the tax thereon, shall be determined as of the period for which such tax is imposed;

(B) no property of the Corporation shall be subject to levy, attachment, garnishment, foreclosure, or sale without the consent of the Corporation, nor shall any involuntary lien attach to the property of the Corporation; and

(C) the Corporation shall not be liable for any amounts in the nature of penalties or fines, including those arising from the failure of any person to pay any real property,

公司在制定该等规章以及最终定稿时,应与财政部部长磋商。

(B)**公平处理**。——根据第(A)子款制定的规章应考虑不同金融公司对美国金融稳定构成的风险之差异,该等金融公司负债结构的差异,以及该等金融公司所应缴纳的其他计征费的不尽相同的计征依据,以确保被征收计征费的各家金融公司均获得公平处理,并确保根据本子条规定征收的计征费能够反映上述差异。

(p)**不具强制执行力的特定协议**。——

(1)**一般规定**。——第(2)款所述任何禁止作出的规定由于违反公共政策,不得对任何人强制执行,或向任何人施加任何责任。

(2)**禁止作出的规定**。——本款所述禁止作出的规定指任何既存的或未来的中止协议、保密协议或其他协议中包含的任何具有如下直接或间接效力的条款——

(A)影响、约束或限制任何人在联邦存款保险公司根据本编规定的权力开展交易时的能力;

(B)禁止任何人在联邦存款保险公司根据本编规定的权力开展交易时,要约收购或收购所涉金融公司之整体或部分(包括其任何负债、资产或权益);或

(C)禁止任何人在联邦存款保险公司根据本编规定的权力开展交易时,使用此前已披露的与上述对所涉金融公司之整体或部分(包括其任何负债、资产或权益)所做之要约收购或收购相关的任何信息。

(q)**其他豁免**。——

(1)**一般规定**。——联邦存款保险公司根据本编以接管人身份行事时——

(A)联邦存款保险公司(包括其特许业务、资本、准备金和资本公积金以及收入)应豁免于任何州、郡、郡级市或地方税务机关施加的所有纳税义务,但是,联邦存款保险公司的不动产应如同其他应税不动产一样,基于自身的价值按照相同的税率缴纳州、准州、郡、郡级市或地方税务机关施加的所有纳税义务,然而,即使任何人均未对根据州法律基于该不动产价值计征的税金提出质疑,在确定该价值和基于该价值计征的税金时应基于该项税收的纳税期间的数值计算;

(B)未经联邦存款保险公司同意,联邦存款保险公司的任何财产均不得受制于任何保全、扣押、债权冻结、止赎程序,亦不得予以出售,联邦存款保险公司的财产上亦不得设立任何非自愿的留置权;且

(C)联邦存款保险公司对任何处罚或罚款性质的金额均不承担责任,包括因任何人未缴纳到期应缴的任何不动产税、动产税、遗嘱认证税、登记税或者任何登记或申

personal property, probate, or recording tax or any recording or filing fees when due; and

(D) the Corporation shall be exempt from all prosecution by the United States or any State, county, municipality, or local authority for any criminal offense arising under Federal, State, county, municipal, or local law, which was allegedly committed by the covered financial company, or persons acting on behalf of the covered financial company, prior to the appointment of the Corporation as receiver.

(2) LIMITATION. — Paragraph (1) shall not apply with respect to any tax imposed (or other amount arising) under the Internal Revenue Code of 1986.

(r) CERTAIN SALES OF ASSETS PROHIBITED. —

(1) PERSONS WHO ENGAGED IN IMPROPER CONDUCT WITH, OR CAUSED LOSSES TO, COVERED FINANCIAL COMPANIES. — The Corporation shall prescribe regulations which, at a minimum, shall prohibit the sale of assets of a covered financial company by the Corporation to —

(A) any person who —

(i) has defaulted, or was a member of a partnership or an officer or director of a corporation that has defaulted, on 1 or more obligations, the aggregate amount of which exceeds $1, 000, 000, to such covered financial company;

(ii) has been found to have engaged in fraudulent activity in connection with any obligation referred to in clause (i); and

(iii) proposes to purchase any such asset in whole or in part through the use of the proceeds of a loan or advance of credit from the Corporation or from any covered financial company;

(B) any person who participated, as an officer or director of such covered financial company or of any affiliate of such company, in a material way in any transaction that resulted in a substantial loss to such covered financial company; or

(C) any person who has demonstrated a pattern or practice of defalcation regarding obligations to such covered financial company.

(2) CONVICTED DEBTORS. — Except as provided in paragraph (3), a person may not purchase any asset of such institution from the receiver, if that person —

(A) has been convicted of an offense under section 215, 656, 657, 1005, 1006, 1007, 1008, 1014, 1032, 1341, 1343, or 1344 of title 18, United States Code, or of conspiring to commit such an offense, affecting any covered financial company; and

(B) is in default on any loan or other extension of credit from such covered financial company which, if not paid, will cause substantial loss to the Fund or the Corporation.

(3) SETTLEMENT OF CLAIMS. — Paragraphs (1) and (2) shall not apply to the sale or transfer by the Corporation of any asset of any covered financial company to any person, if the sale or transfer of the asset resolves or settles, or is part of the resolution or

报费产生的处罚或罚款金额;且

(D)对于联邦存款保险公司被指定为接管人之前,所涉金融公司或其代表所作出的涉嫌刑事犯罪的行为,联邦存款保险公司应豁免于联邦或任何州、郡、郡级市或地方政府根据联邦法律、州法律、郡法、郡级市法或地方法为追究该刑事犯罪而提起的所有诉讼。

(2)**限制**。——第(1)款规定不得适用于根据《1986年国内税收法典》征收的任何税金(或根据该法典应予支付的其他金额)。

(r)**禁止出售特定财产**。——

(1)**与所涉金融公司共同从事不当行为或对所涉金融公司造成损失的人**。——联邦存款保险公司应制定至少应禁止向下列主体出售所涉金融公司资产的规章——

(A)具有以下特征的任何主体——

(i)未履行向所涉金融公司负有的总额超过100万美元的一项或一项以上义务,或身为未履行上述义务的一家合伙的成员或一家公司的管理人员或董事;

(ii)经认定从事了与第(i)项所述义务相关的欺诈活动;且

(iii)建议使用联邦存款保险公司或任何所涉金融公司授予的贷款或预支款资金,整体或部分购买该等资产;

(B)作为该所涉金融公司或其任何关联方的管理人员或董事,实质参与了导致该所涉金融公司蒙受重大损失的任何交易的主体;或

(C)已通过迹象或行为表示其将不履行向该所涉金融公司承担的义务的主体。

(2)**被判定有罪或违约的债务人**。——除第(3)款规定的情形外,任何存在下述情形的主体均不得向接管人购买所涉金融公司的任何资产——

(A)被判定犯有影响任何所涉金融公司的《美国法典》第十八编第215节、第656节、第657节、第1005节、第1006节、第1007节、第1008节、第1014节、第1032节、第1341节、第1343节或第1344节规定的罪行,或被判定密谋实施该等罪行;及

(B)对所涉金融公司授予的任何贷款或其他信贷违约,且如果该贷款或信贷无法获得偿付,将对有序清算基金或联邦存款保险公司造成重大损失。

(3)**权利主张的和解**。——如果联邦存款保险公司向任何人出售或转让所涉金融公司的任何资产,将构成对联邦存款保险公司已向或本可向该人提出的一项或一项以上权利主张的完全或部分解决或和解,则该等出售或转让不适用第(1)款和第

settlement, of 1 or more claims that have been, or could have been, asserted by the Corporation against the person.

(4) DEFINITION OF DEFAULT. — For purposes of this subsection, the term "default" means a failure to comply with the terms of a loan or other obligation to such an extent that the property securing the obligation is foreclosed upon.

(s) RECOUPMENT OF COMPENSATION FROM SENIOR EXECUTIVES AND DIRECTORS. —

(1) IN GENERAL. — The Corporation, as receiver of a covered financial company, may recover from any current or former senior executive or director substantially responsible for the failed condition of the covered financial company any compensation received during the 2-year period preceding the date on which the Corporation was appointed as the receiver of the covered financial company, except that, in the case of fraud, no time limit shall apply.

(2) COST CONSIDERATIONS. — In seeking to recover any such compensation, the Corporation shall weigh the financial and deterrent benefits of such recovery against the cost of executing the recovery.

(3) RULEMAKING. — The Corporation shall promulgate regulations to implement the requirements of this subsection, including defining the term "compensation" to mean any financial remuneration, including salary, bonuses, incentives, benefits, severance, deferred compensation, or golden parachute benefits, and any profits realized from the sale of the securities of the covered financial company.

SEC. 211. MISCELLANEOUS PROVISIONS.

(a) CLARIFICATION OF PROHIBITION REGARDING CONCEALMENT OF ASSETS FROM RECEIVER OR LIQUIDATING AGENT. — Section 1032(1) of title 18, United States Code, is amended by inserting "the Federal Deposit Insurance Corporation acting as receiver for a covered financial company, in accordance with title II of the Dodd–Frank Wall Street Reform and Consumer Protection Act, " before "or the National Credit".

(b) CONFORMING AMENDMENT. — Section 1032 of title 18, United States Code, is amended in the section heading, by striking "**of financial institution**".

(c) FEDERAL DEPOSIT INSURANCE CORPORATION IMPROVEMENT ACT OF 1991. — Section 403(a) of the Federal Deposit Insurance Corporation Improvement Act of 1991 (12 U.S.C. 4403(a)) is amended by inserting "section 210(c) of the Dodd–Frank Wall Street Reform and Consumer Protection Act, section 1367 of the Federal Housing Enterprises Financial Safety and Soundness Act of 1992 (12 U.S.C. 4617(d)), " after "section 11(e) of the Federal Deposit Insurance Act, ".

(d) FDIC INSPECTOR GENERAL REVIEWS. —

(2)款的规定。

(4)**违约的定义**。——就本子条而言,“违约”一词系指未履行某项贷款或其他义务的条款,致使担保该等义务的财产被止赎。

(s)**向高管和董事索回薪酬**。——

(1)**一般规定**。——对于对所涉金融公司经营失败负有实质责任的任何当前或前任高管或董事,联邦存款保险公司作为所涉金融公司的接管人,可以索回其在被指定为该所涉金融公司接管人之日前2年内,该等高管或董事收到的任何薪酬;如该等高管或董事存在欺诈行为,则该索回不受任何时间限制。

(2)**成本考虑**。——联邦存款保险公司在寻求索回上述薪酬时,应对该索回所带来的财务利益和威慑作用,以及实施该等索回的成本进行权衡。

(3)**规则制定**。——联邦存款保险公司应颁发本子条的实施规章,包括将“薪酬”一词定义为任何财务报酬,包括工资、奖金、激励、福利、离职金、递延薪酬或金色降落伞福利,以及因出售所涉金融公司证券而实现的利润。

第211条　其他规定

(a)**关于向接管人或清算代理人隐瞒资产的禁止性规定之说明**。——《美国法典》第十八编第1032(1)节在“或全国信贷”前插入“根据《多德—弗兰克华尔街改革与消费者保护法》第二编的规定,作为所涉金融公司的接管人的联邦存款保险公司,”作为对该节的修正。

(b)**一致性修正**。——删除《美国法典》第十八编第1032节标题中的“**金融机构的**”。

(c)**《1991年联邦存款保险公司改良法》**。——《1991年联邦存款保险公司改良法》第403(a)条[《美国法典》第十二编第4403(a)节]在“《联邦存款保险法》第11(e)条、”之后插入“《多德—弗兰克华尔街改革与消费者保护法》第210(c)条、《1992年联邦住房企业财务安全和稳健法》第1367条[《美国法典》第12编第4617(d)节]、”作为对该条的修正。

(d)**联邦存款保险公司监察长的审查**。——

(1) SCOPE. — The Inspector General of the Corporation shall conduct, supervise, and coordinate audits and investigations of the liquidation of any covered financial company by the Corporation as receiver under this title, including collecting and summarizing —

(A) a description of actions taken by the Corporation as receiver;

(B) a description of any material sales, transfers, mergers, obligations, purchases, and other material transactions entered into by the Corporation;

(C) an evaluation of the adequacy of the policies and procedures of the Corporation under section 203(d) and orderly liquidation plan under section 210(n)(14);

(D) an evaluation of the utilization by the Corporation of the private sector in carrying out its functions, including the adequacy of any conflict–of–interest reviews; and

(E) an evaluation of the overall performance of the Corporation in liquidating the covered financial company, including administrative costs, timeliness of liquidation process, and impact on the financial system.

(2) FREQUENCY. — Not later than 6 months after the date of appointment of the Corporation as receiver under this title and every 6 months thereafter, the Inspector General of the Corporation shall conduct the audit and investigation described in paragraph (1).

(3) REPORTS AND TESTIMONY. — The Inspector General of the Corporation shall include in the semiannual reports required by section 5(a) of the Inspector General Act of 1978 (5 U.S.C. App.), a summary of the findings and evaluations under paragraph (1), and shall appear before the appropriate committees of Congress, if requested, to present each such report.

(4) FUNDING. —

(A) INITIAL FUNDING. — The expenses of the Inspector General of the Corporation in carrying out this subsection shall be considered administrative expenses of the receivership.

(B) ADDITIONAL FUNDING. — If the maximum amount available to the Corporation as receiver under this title is insufficient to enable the Inspector General of the Corporation to carry out the duties under this subsection, the Corporation shall pay such additional amounts from assessments imposed under section 210.

(5) TERMINATION OF RESPONSIBILITIES. — The duties and responsibilities of the Inspector General of the Corporation under this subsection shall terminate 1 year after the date of termination of the receivership under this title.

(e) TREASURY INSPECTOR GENERAL REVIEWS. —

(1) SCOPE. — The Inspector General of the Department of the Treasury shall conduct, supervise, and coordinate audits and investigations of actions taken by the

(1)**范围**。——对于联邦存款保险公司根据本编规定作为接管人对所涉金融公司进行的清算,联邦存款保险公司监察长应执行、监督并协调针对该清算的审计和调查,包括收集并总结如下信息——

(A)关于联邦存款保险公司作为接管人所采取的行动之说明;

(B)关于联邦存款保险公司达成的任何重大出售、转让、兼并、义务、购买以及其他重要交易之说明;

(C)对联邦存款保险公司根据第203(d)条制定的政策和程序的充分性和根据第210(n)(14)条制定的有序清算计划的充分性进行的评价;

(D)对联邦存款保险公司在履行其职能时使用私人部门的情况进行的评价,包括对利益冲突审查的充分性进行的评估;及

(E)对联邦存款保险公司在清算所涉金融公司过程中的总体表现进行的评价,评估内容包括行政费用、清算程序的及时性以及对金融体系的影响。

(2)**频率**。——联邦存款保险公司监察长应在联邦存款保险公司根据本编被指定为接管人之日后6个月内,执行第(1)款所述审计和调查,并在此后每隔6个月执行该等审计和调查。

(3)**报告和作证**。——联邦存款保险公司监察长应根据《1978年监察长法》第5(a)条(《美国法典》第五编附录)的要求提交半年报告,并将其根据第(1)款作出的认定结论和评价之摘要纳入该报告,且如国会相应的委员会提出要求,还应出席该等委员会的听证会并对每份该等报告进行汇报。

(4)**经费来源**。——

(A)**初始经费来源**。——联邦存款保险公司监察长实施本子条规定的费用应视为接管人的行政费用。

(B)**补充经费来源**。——如根据本编规定联邦存款保险公司作为接管人可支配的最高金额不足以使联邦存款保险公司监察长履行本子条规定的职责,则联邦存款保险公司应使用根据第210条征收的计征费支付额外所需的金额。

(5)**职责终止**。——联邦存款保险公司承担的接管人职责和责任根据本编终止后届满1年之日,本子条规定的联邦存款保险公司监察长的职责和责任应予终止。

(e)**财政部监察长的审查**。——

(1)**范围**。——对于财政部部长在所涉金融公司根据本编接受清算时所采取的行动,财政部监察长应执行、监督并协调针对该等行动的审计和调查,包括收集并总

Secretary related to the liquidation of any covered financial company under this title, including collecting and summarizing —

(A) a description of actions taken by the Secretary under this title;

(B) an analysis of the approval by the Secretary of the policies and procedures of the Corporation under section 203 and acceptance of the orderly liquidation plan of the Corporation under section 210; and

(C) an assessment of the terms and conditions underlying the purchase by the Secretary of obligations of the Corporation under section 210.

(2) FREQUENCY. — Not later than 6 months after the date of appointment of the Corporation as receiver under this title and every 6 months thereafter, the Inspector General of the Department of the Treasury shall conduct the audit and investigation described in paragraph (1).

(3) REPORTS AND TESTIMONY. — The Inspector General of the Department of the Treasury shall include in the semiannual reports required by section 5 (a) of the Inspector General Act of 1978 (5 U.S.C. App.), a summary of the findings and assessments under paragraph (1), and shall appear before the appropriate committees of Congress, if requested, to present each such report.

(4) TERMINATION OF RESPONSIBILITIES. — The duties and responsibilities of the Inspector General of the Department of the Treasury under this subsection shall terminate 1 year after the date on which the obligations purchased by the Secretary from the Corporation under section 210 are fully redeemed.

(f) PRIMARY FINANCIAL REGULATORY AGENCY INSPECTOR GENERAL REVIEWS. —

(1) SCOPE. — Upon the appointment of the Corporation as receiver for a covered financial company supervised by a Federal primary financial regulatory agency or the Board of Governors under section 165, the Inspector General of the agency or the Board of Governors shall make a written report reviewing the supervision by the agency or the Board of Governors of the covered financial company, which shall —

(A) evaluate the effectiveness of the agency or the Board of Governors in carrying out its supervisory responsibilities with respect to the covered financial company;

(B) identify any acts or omissions on the part of agency or Board of Governors officials that contributed to the covered financial company being in default or in danger of default;

(C) identify any actions that could have been taken by the agency or the Board of Governors that would have prevented the company from being in default or in danger of default; and

(D) recommend appropriate administrative or legislative action.

结如下信息——

(A)关于财政部部长所采取的行动之说明;

(B)对财政部部长就联邦存款保险公司根据第203条制定的政策和程序作出的批准以及就联邦存款保险公司根据第210条制定的有序清算计划的认可进行分析;及

(C)对财政部部长根据第210条购买联邦存款保险公司发行的债务的条款和条件的评估。

(2)**频率**。——财政部监察长应在联邦存款保险公司根据本编规定被指定为接管人之日后6个月内,执行第(1)款所述审计和调查,并在此后每隔6个月执行该等审计和调查。

(3)**报告和作证**。——财政部监察长应根据《1978年监察长法》第5(a)条(《美国法典》第五编附录)的要求提交半年报告,并将其根据第(1)款作出的认定结论和评价之摘要纳入该报告,且如国会相应的委员会提出要求,还应出席该等委员会的听证会并对每份该等报告进行汇报。

(4)**职责终止**。——本子条规定的财政部监察长的职责和责任应于财政部部长根据第210条向联邦存款保险公司购买的全部债务已悉数赎回之日起届满1年之日终止。

(f)**优先金融监管机关监察长的审查**。——

(1)**范围**。——联邦存款保险公司被指定为根据第165条接受联邦优先金融监管机关或联邦储备委员会监管的所涉金融公司的接管人后,该机关或联邦储备委员会的监察长应针对该机关或联邦储备委员会就该所涉金融公司开展的监管工作制作一份书面审查报告,该报告应——

(A)对该机关或联邦储备委员会就该所涉金融公司执行的监管职责的成效进行评价;

(B)指出该机关或联邦储备委员会的官员导致该所涉金融公司进入违约或违约之虞状态的任何作为或不作为;

(C)指出该机关或联邦储备委员会本可采取的防范该所涉金融公司进入违约或违约之虞状态的任何行动;及

(D)建议采取适当的行政或立法行动。

(2) REPORTS AND TESTIMONY. — Not later than 1 year after the date of appointment of the Corporation as receiver under this title, the Inspector General of the Federal primary financial regulatory agency or the Board of Governors shall provide the report required by paragraph (1) to such agency or the Board of Governors, and along with such agency or the Board of Governors, as applicable, shall appear before the appropriate committees of Congress, if requested, to present the report required by paragraph (1). Not later than 90 days after the date of receipt of the report required by paragraph (1), such agency or the Board of Governors, as applicable, shall provide a written report to Congress describing any actions taken in response to the recommendations in the report, and if no such actions were taken, describing the reasons why no actions were taken.

SEC. 212. PROHIBITION OF CIRCUMVENTION AND PREVENTION OF CONFLICTS OF INTEREST.

(a) NO OTHER FUNDING. — Funds for the orderly liquidation of any covered financial company under this title shall only be provided as specified under this title.

(b) LIMIT ON GOVERNMENTAL ACTIONS. — No governmental entity may take any action to circumvent the purposes of this title.

(c) CONFLICT OF INTEREST. — In the event that the Corporation is appointed receiver for more than 1 covered financial company or is appointed receiver for a covered financial company and receiver for any insured depository institution that is an affiliate of such covered financial company, the Corporation shall take appropriate action, as necessary to avoid any conflicts of interest that may arise in connection with multiple receiverships.

SEC. 213. BAN ON CERTAIN ACTIVITIES BY SENIOR EXECUTIVES AND DIRECTORS.

(a) PROHIBITION AUTHORITY. — The Board of Governors or, if the covered financial company was not supervised by the Board of Governors, the Corporation, may exercise the authority provided by this section.

(b) AUTHORITY TO ISSUE ORDER. — The appropriate agency described in subsection (a) may take any action authorized by subsection (c), if the agency determines that —

(1) a senior executive or a director of the covered financial company, prior to the appointment of the Corporation as receiver, has, directly or indirectly —

(A) violated —

(i) any law or regulation;

(ii) any cease–and–desist order which has become final;

(iii) any condition imposed in writing by a Federal agency in connection with any action on any application, notice, or request by such company or senior executive; or

(2)**报告和作证**。——联邦优先金融监管机关或联邦储备委员会的监察长应在联邦存款保险公司根据本编规定被指定为接管人后1年之内,向该机关或联邦储备委员会提供第(1)款规定的报告,且如国会相应的委员会提出要求,还应与该机关或联邦储备委员会(视具体情况而定)共同出席该等委员会的听证会并就第(1)款规定的每一报告进行汇报。该机关或联邦储备委员会(视具体情况而定)应在收到第(1)款规定的报告后90天内,向国会提供一份书面报告,详细说明针对报告中所述建议采取的任何相应行动,且如未采取相应行动,应详细说明原因。

第212条　对于规避行为的禁止性规定和避免利益冲突

(a)**禁止使用其他资金**。——对适用本编规定的任何所涉金融公司进行有序清算时,仅得按照本编规定的方式获取资金。

(b)**政府行动限制**。——任何政府实体均不得采取任何行动规避本编宗旨。

(c)**利益冲突**。——如果联邦存款保险公司同时被指定为2个或2个以上所涉金融公司的接管人,或者在被指定为一家所涉金融公司的接管人时,同时被指定为与该所涉金融公司存在关联关系的任何参保存款机构的接管人,则联邦存款保险公司应采取适当的必要行动,避免多重接管身份造成的任何利益冲突。

第213条　禁止高级管理人员和董事从事特定活动

(a)**作出禁止性规定的权力**。——联邦储备委员会或联邦存款保险公司(如果所涉金融公司不受联邦储备委员会监管)可以行使本条规定的权力。

(b)**签发命令的权力**。——第(a)子条所述相应的机关作出以下判定之时,可以根据第(c)子条授权采取任何相应行动——

(1)在联邦存款保险公司被指定为接管人之前,所涉金融公司的高级管理人员或董事曾直接或间接——

(A)违反——

(i)任何法律法规;

(ii)任何已产生终局效力的制止令;

(iii)联邦机关针对该公司或高级管理人员提出或发出的任何申请、通知或请求而采取任何行动时施加的书面条件;或

(iv) any written agreement between such company and such agency;

(B) engaged or participated in any unsafe or unsound practice in connection with any financial company; or

(C) committed or engaged in any act, omission, or practice which constitutes a breach of the fiduciary duty of such senior executive or director;

(2) by reason of the violation, practice, or breach described in any subparagraph of paragraph (1), such senior executive or director has received financial gain or other benefit by reason of such violation, practice, or breach and such violation, practice, or breach contributed to the failure of the company; and

(3) such violation, practice, or breach —

(A) involves personal dishonesty on the part of such senior executive or director; or

(B) demonstrates willful or continuing disregard by such senior executive or director for the safety or soundness of such company.

(c) AUTHORIZED ACTIONS. —

(1) IN GENERAL. — The appropriate agency for a financial company, as described in subsection (a), may serve upon a senior executive or director described in subsection (b) a written notice of the intention of the agency to prohibit any further participation by such person, in any manner, in the conduct of the affairs of any financial company for a period of time determined by the appropriate agency to be commensurate with such violation, practice, or breach, provided such period shall be not less than 2 years.

(2) PROCEDURES. — The due process requirements and other procedures under section 8(e) of the Federal Deposit Insurance Act (12 U.S.C. 1818(e)) shall apply to actions under this section as if the covered financial company were an insured depository institution and the senior executive or director were an institution–affiliated party, as those terms are defined in that Act.

(d) REGULATIONS. — The Corporation and the Board of Governors, in consultation with the Council, shall jointly prescribe rules or regulations to administer and carry out this section, including rules, regulations, or guidelines to further define the term senior executive for the purposes of this section.

SEC. 214. PROHIBITION ON TAXPAYER FUNDING.

(a) LIQUIDATION REQUIRED. — All financial companies put into receivership under this title shall be liquidated. No taxpayer funds shall be used to prevent the liquidation of any financial company under this title.

(b) RECOVERY OF FUNDS. — All funds expended in the liquidation of a financial company under this title shall be recovered from the disposition of assets of such financial company, or shall be the responsibility of the financial sector, through assessments.

(iv)上述公司和该机关之间的任何书面协议;

(B)从事或参与了与任何金融公司相关的任何欠安全或欠稳健做法;或

(C)作出或从事了违反该高级管理人员或董事的受信义务的任何作为、不作为或做法;

(2)该高级管理人员或董事由于第(1)款中任一子款的违反行为、欠安全或欠稳健做法或者违反受信义务的行为或做法获取了经济收益或其他形式的利益,且该等违反行为、欠安全或欠稳健做法或者违反受信义务的行为或做法是导致该公司经营失败的原因之一;且

(3)上述违反行为、欠安全或欠稳健做法或者违反受信义务的行为或做法——

(A)事关该高级管理人员或董事的个人诚信;或

(B)表明该高级管理人员或董事故意或持续性地漠视公司的安全性或稳健性。

(c)**授权行动**。——

(1)**一般规定**。——第(a)子条所述对金融公司进行监管的相应的机关可以向第(b)子条所述高级管理人员或董事发出书面通知,告知其有意禁止该高级管理人员或董事以任何形式继续参与任何金融公司活动的开展,禁止期限由该相应的机关决定,视违反行为、欠安全或欠稳健做法或者违反受信义务的行为或做法的情节而定,但不得短于2年。

(2)**程序**。——按照本条采取的行动均应遵循《联邦存款保险法》第8(e)条[《美国法典》第十二编第1818(e)节]规定的正当程序要求以及其他流程,如同所涉金融公司是一家参保存款机构,而高级管理人员或董事身为参保存款机构的关联方(“参保存款机构”和“关联方”的定义见《联邦存款保险法》)。

(d)**规章**。——联邦存款保险公司和联邦储备委员会应在与金融稳定监督委员会磋商后,联合制定规则或规章,以实施并执行本条规定,包括发布规则、规章或指引,进一步界定本条使用的“高级管理人员”一词。

第214条　不得使用纳税人资金的禁止性规定

(a)**流动性要求**。——按照本编规定被接管的所有金融公司均应进行清算。不得使用纳税人资金阻止任何金融公司按照本编规定进行清算。

(b)**资金收回**。——金融公司按照本编规定进行清算产生的所有支出均应通过处置该金融公司的资产予以收回,或通过计征费由金融行业承担。

(c) NO LOSSES TO TAXPAYERS. — Taxpayers shall bear no losses from the exercise of any authority under this title.

SEC. 215. STUDY ON SECURED CREDITOR HAIRCUTS.

(a) STUDY REQUIRED. — The Council shall conduct a study evaluating the importance of maximizing United States taxpayer protections and promoting market discipline with respect to the treatment of fully secured creditors in the utilization of the orderly liquidation authority authorized by this Act. In carrying out such study, the Council shall —

(1) not be prejudicial to current or past laws or regulations with respect to secured creditor treatment in a resolution process;

(2) study the similarities and differences between the resolution mechanisms authorized by the Bankruptcy Code, the Federal Deposit Insurance Corporation Improvement Act of 1991, and the orderly liquidation authority authorized by this Act;

(3) determine how various secured creditors are treated in such resolution mechanisms and examine how a haircut (of various degrees) on secured creditors could improve market discipline and protect taxpayers;

(4) compare the benefits and dynamics of prudent lending practices by depository institutions in secured loans for consumers and small businesses to the lending practices of secured creditors to large, interconnected financial firms;

(5) consider whether credit differs according to different types of collateral and different terms and timing of the extension of credit; and

(6) include an examination of stakeholders who were unsecured or under – collateralized and seek collateral when a firm is failing, and the impact that such behavior has on financial stability and an orderly resolution that protects taxpayers if the firm fails.

(b) REPORT. — Not later than the end of the 1–year period beginning on the date of enactment of this Act, the Council shall issue a report to the Congress containing all findings and conclusions made by the Council in carrying out the study required under subsection (a).

SEC. 216. STUDY ON BANKRUPTCY PROCESS FOR FINANCIAL AND NONBANK FINANCIAL INSTITUTIONS.

(a) STUDY. —

(1) IN GENERAL. — Upon enactment of this Act, the Board of Governors, in consultation with the Administrative Office of the United States Courts, shall conduct a study regarding the resolution of financial companies under the Bankruptcy Code, under chapter 7 or 11 thereof .

(2) ISSUES TO BE STUDIED. — Issues to be studied under this section include —

(A) the effectiveness of chapter 7 and chapter 11 of the Bankruptcy Code in facilitating the orderly resolution or reorganization of systemic financial companies;

(B) whether a special financial resolution court or panel of special masters or judges

(c)**不得由纳税人承担损失**。——因行使本编规定授予的任何权力而产生的损失不得转嫁于纳税人。

第215条　关于有担保债权人本金折价的研究

(a)**研究要求**。——金融稳定监督委员会应开展研究,评估在行使本法规定的有序清算权对拥有全额担保的债权人进行处理的同时,兼顾充分保护美国纳税人和促进市场约束的重要性。开展该等研究时,金融稳定监督委员会——

(1)对于有担保债权人在清盘过程中所得到的处理相关的现行或过往法律或规章,不应造成负面影响;

(2)应研究《破产法》和《1991年联邦存款保险公司改良法》授权实施的清盘机制与本法案授予的有序清算权之间的异同;

(3)应研究该等清盘机制对各类有担保债权人的处理方式,并研究对有担保债权人进行(不同程度的)本金折价可能对改善市场约束和保护纳税人产生的作用;

(4)针对存款机构向消费者和小型企业发放有担保贷款的审慎借贷做法,以及有担保债权人向相互关联的大型金融公司发放贷款的借贷做法,比较上述二者各自的优点和发展动态;

(5)考虑信用是否由于抵押品类型的不同、授信条款和时间的不同而有所差异;及

(6)对无担保或担保不足,在公司经营失败时才寻求抵押的利益相关者进行审视,研究该等做法对金融稳定的影响,以及对公司经营失败时旨在保护纳税人的有序清盘所产生的影响。

(b)**报告**。——在本法颁布之日起1年内,金融稳定监督委员会应向国会提交报告,阐述金融稳定监督委员会按第(a)子条规定开展研究后作出的所有事实认定和研究结论。

第216条　关于金融机构及非银行金融机构破产程序的研究

(a)**研究**。——

(1)**一般规定**。——本法颁布后,联邦储备委员会应立即与美国联邦法院行政管理局磋商,对金融公司按照《破产法》第七章或第十一章进行的清盘开展研究。

(2)**研究事项**。——本条要求研究的事项包括——

(A)《破产法》第七章和第十一章在促进系统性金融公司的有序清盘或重组中取得的成效;

(B)是否应设立特殊金融清盘法庭、特别专家小组或法官小组来监督涉及金融公

should be established to oversee cases involving financial companies to provide for the resolution of such companies under the Bankruptcy Code, in a manner that minimizes adverse impacts on financial markets without creating moral hazard;

(C) whether amendments to the Bankruptcy Code should be adopted to enhance the ability of the Code to resolve financial companies in a manner that minimizes adverse impacts on financial markets without creating moral hazard;

(D) whether amendments should be made to the Bankruptcy Code, the Federal Deposit Insurance Act, and other insolvency laws to address the manner in which qualified financial contracts of financial companies are treated; and

(E) the implications, challenges, and benefits to creating a new chapter or subchapter of the Bankruptcy Code to deal with financial companies.

(b) REPORTS TO CONGRESS. — Not later than 1 year after the date of enactment of this Act, and in each successive year until the fifth year after the date of enactment of this Act, the Administrative Office of the United States courts shall submit to the Committees on Banking, Housing, and Urban Affairs and the Judiciary of the Senate and the Committees on Financial Services and the Judiciary of the House of Representatives a report summarizing the results of the study conducted under subsection (a).

SEC. 217. STUDY ON INTERNATIONAL COORDINATION RELATING TO BANKRUPTCY PROCESS FOR NONBANK FINANCIAL INSTITUTIONS.

(a) STUDY. —

(1) IN GENERAL. — The Board of Governors, in consultation with the Administrative Office of the United States Courts, shall conduct a study regarding international coordination relating to the resolution of systemic financial companies under the United States Bankruptcy Code and applicable foreign law.

(2) ISSUES TO BE STUDIED. — With respect to the bankruptcy process for financial companies, issues to be studied under this section include —

(A) the extent to which international coordination currently exists;

(B) current mechanisms and structures for facilitating international cooperation;

(C) barriers to effective international coordination; and

(D) ways to increase and make more effective international coordination of the resolution of financial companies, so as to minimize the impact on the financial system without creating moral hazard.

(b) REPORT TO CONGRESS. — Not later than 1 year after the date of enactment of this Act, the Administrative office of the United States Courts shall submit to the Committees on Banking, Housing, and Urban Affairs and the Judiciary of the Senate and the Committees on Financial Services and the Judiciary of the House of Representatives a report summarizing the results of the study conducted under subsection (a).

司的案件,将对金融市场造成的负面影响减到最低限度,并在不形成道德风险的情况下,协助此类公司按照《破产法》进行清盘;

(C)是否应修正《破产法》,使得能够将对金融市场造成的负面影响减到最低限度,并在不形成道德风险的情况下,依据《破产法》对金融公司进行清盘;

(D)是否应修正《破产法》、《联邦存款保险法》以及其他关于资不抵债的法律,对处理金融公司的合格金融合约的方式作出规定;及

(E)如果在《破产法》增补新的一章或新的子章专门对金融公司作出规定,将产生何种影响、带来何种挑战和益处。

(b)**向国会报告**。——本法颁布之日后1年内,且在本法颁布之日起5年内的每1年,美国联邦法院行政管理局均应基于按照第(a)子条开展的研究结果编制一份摘要报告,提交给参议院银行、住房与城市事务委员会和司法委员会,以及众议院金融服务委员会和司法委员会。

第217条　关于非银行金融机构破产程序中的国际协作之研究

(a)**研究**。——

(1)**一般规定**。——联邦储备委员会应与美国联邦法院行政管理局磋商,对系统性金融公司按照《美国破产法》和适用的外国法律进行清盘时的国际协作开展研究。

(2)**研究事项**。——就金融公司的破产流程而言,本条要求研究的事项包括——

(A)当前开展的国际协作的程度;

(B)促进国际合作的现行机制和结构;

(C)妨碍国际协作有效开展的壁垒;及

(D)如何增加金融机构清盘过程中的国际合作,并提高国际合作的成效,以在不产生道德风险的情况下,将对金融体系造成的影响减到最低限度。

(b)**向国会报告**。——本法颁布之日后1年内,美国联邦法院行政管理局应基于按照第(a)子条开展的研究结果编制一份摘要报告,提交给参议院银行、住房与城市事务委员会和司法委员会,以及众议院金融服务委员会和司法委员会。

TITLE III — TRANSFER OF POWERS TO THE COMPTROLLER OF THE CURRENCY, THE CORPORATION, AND THE BOARD OF GOVERNORS

SEC. 300. SHORT TITLE.

This title may be cited as the "Enhancing Financial Institution Safety and Soundness Act of 2010".

SEC. 301. PURPOSES.

The purposes of this title are —

(1) to provide for the safe and sound operation of the banking system of the United States;

(2) to preserve and protect the dual system of Federal and State -chartered depository institutions;

(3) to ensure the fair and appropriate supervision of each depository institution, regardless of the size or type of charter of the depository institution; and

(4) to streamline and rationalize the supervision of depository institutions and the holding companies of depository institutions.

SEC. 302. DEFINITION.

In this title, the term "transferred employee" means, as the context requires, an employee transferred to the Office of the Comptroller of the Currency or the Corporation under section 322.

Subtitle A — Transfer of Powers and Duties

SEC. 311. TRANSFER DATE.

(a) TRANSFER DATE. — Except as provided in subsection (b), the term "transfer

第三编——向货币监理署、联邦存款保险公司和联邦储备委员会转移权力

第300条 简称

引述本编时,可简称为《2010年金融机构安全性与稳健性改良法》。

第301条 目的

本编旨在——

(1)就美国银行体系的安全稳健运行作出规定;

(2)保留并保护联邦注册存款机构和州特许注册存款机构并存的双轨制;

(3)确保各存款机构得到公平适当的监管,不因其规模或执照类型的不同而有所差别;及

(4)精简和优化对存款机构和存款机构控股公司的监管。

第302条 定义

在本编中,"转移雇员"一词系指按照第322条规定转移至货币监理署或联邦存款保险公司(具体视上下文而定)的雇员。

第A子编——权力和职责的转移

第311条 转移日

(a)**转移日**。——除第(b)子条规定的情形外,"转移日"一词系指本法颁布届满1

date" means the date that is 1 year after the date of enactment of this Act.

(b) EXTENSION PERMITTED. —

(1) NOTICE REQUIRED. — The Secretary, in consultation with the Comptroller of the Currency, the Director of the Office of Thrift Supervision, the Chairman of the Board of Governors, and the Chairperson of the Corporation, may extend the period under subsection (a) and designate a transfer date that is not later than 18 months after the date of enactment of this Act, if the Secretary transmits to the Committee on Banking, Housing, and Urban Affairs of the Senate and the Committee on Financial Services of the House of Representatives —

(A) a written determination that commencement of the orderly process to implement this title is not feasible by the date that is 1 year after the date of enactment of this Act;

(B) an explanation of why an extension is necessary to commence the process of orderly implementation of this title;

(C) the transfer date designated under this subsection; and

(D) a description of the steps that will be taken to initiate the process of an orderly and timely implementation of this title within the extended time period.

(2) PUBLICATION OF NOTICE. — Not later than 270 days after the date of enactment of this Act, the Secretary shall publish in the Federal Register notice of any transfer date designated under paragraph (1).

SEC. 312. POWERS AND DUTIES TRANSFERRED.

(a) EFFECTIVE DATE. — This section, and the amendments made by this section, shall take effect on the transfer date.

(b) FUNCTIONS OF THE OFFICE OF THRIFT SUPERVISION. —

(1) SAVINGS AND LOAN HOLDING COMPANY FUNCTIONS TRANSFERRED. —

(A) TRANSFER OF FUNCTIONS. — There are transferred to the Board of Governors all functions of the Office of Thrift Supervision and the Director of the Office of Thrift Supervision (including the authority to issue orders) relating to —

(i) the supervision of —

(I) any savings and loan holding company; and

(II) any subsidiary (other than a depository institution) of a savings and loan holding company; and

(ii) all rulemaking authority of the Office of Thrift Supervision and the Director of the Office of Thrift Supervision relating to savings and loan holding companies.

(B) POWERS, AUTHORITIES, RIGHTS, AND DUTIES. — The Board of Governors shall succeed to all powers, authorities, rights, and duties that were vested in the Office of Thrift Supervision and the Director of the Office of Thrift Supervision on the day before the transfer date relating to the functions and authority transferred under subparagraph (A).

年之日。

（b）**允许的延期**。——

（1）**通知要求**。——财政部部长可以在与货币监理署署长、储蓄机构监理局局长、联邦储备委员会主席以及联邦存款保险公司主席磋商后，延长第（a）子条规定的期限，另行指定转移日，但该另行指定的日期不得迟于本法颁布之日起18个月期限届满之日。在作出上述延期决定之前，财政部部长应向参议院银行、住房与城市事务委员会和众议院金融服务委员会提交以下材料——

（A）财政部部长的书面判定，说明在本法颁布后届满1年之日开始有序执行本编规定是不可行的；

（B）解释必须推迟本编规定的有序执行的原因；

（C）说明根据本子条另行指定的转移日；及

（D）说明将采取何种措施，在延期的期间内开始有序及时地执行本编规定。

（2）**通知发布**。——本法颁布后270天内，财政部部长应在《联邦公报》上公布按照第（1）款另行指定的任何转移日期。

第312条　转移的权力和职责

（a）**生效日**。——本条以及本条所做修正应于转移日当日生效。

（b）**储蓄机构监理局的职能**。——

（1）**转移储贷控股公司职能**。——

（A）**职能转移**。——储蓄机构监理局和储蓄机构监理局局长与以下各项相关的职能（包括发布命令的权力）全部转由联邦储备委员会行使——

（i）对以下机构的监管——

（I）任何储贷控股公司；及

（II）储贷控股公司的任何子公司（但存款机构除外）；及

（ii）储蓄机构监理局和储蓄机构监理局局长享有的与储贷控股公司相关的所有规则制定权。

（B）**权力、授权、权利和职责**。——储蓄机构监理局和储蓄机构监理局局长在转移日前一天享有的，与第（A）子款所述职能和权力转移相关的所有权力、授权、权利和职责，均应转由联邦储备委员会享有和承担。

(2) ALL OTHER FUNCTIONS TRANSFERRED. —

(A) BOARD OF GOVERNORS. — All rulemaking authority of the Office of Thrift Supervision and the Director of the Office of Thrift Supervision under section 11 of the Home Owners' Loan Act (12 U.S.C. 1468) relating to transactions with affiliates and extensions of credit to executive officers, directors, and principal shareholders and under section 5(q) of such Act relating to tying arrangements is transferred to the Board of Governors.

(B) COMPTROLLER OF THE CURRENCY. — Except as provided in paragraph (1) and subparagraph (A) —

(i) there are transferred to the Office of the Comptroller of the Currency and the Comptroller of the Currency —

(I) all functions of the Office of Thrift Supervision and the Director of the Office of Thrift Supervision, respectively, relating to Federal savings associations; and

(II) all rulemaking authority of the Office of Thrift Supervision and the Director of the Office of Thrift Supervision, respectively, relating to savings associations; and

(ii) the Office of the Comptroller of the Currency and the Comptroller of the Currency shall succeed to all powers, authorities, rights, and duties that were vested in the Office of Thrift Supervision and the Director of the Office of Thrift Supervision, respectively, on the day before the transfer date relating to the functions and authority transferred under clause (i).

(C) CORPORATION. — Except as provided in paragraph (1) and subparagraphs (A) and (B) —

(i) all functions of the Office of Thrift Supervision and the Director of the Office of Thrift Supervision relating to State savings associations are transferred to the Corporation; and

(ii) the Corporation shall succeed to all powers, authorities, rights, and duties that were vested in the Office of Thrift Supervision and the Director of the Office of Thrift Supervision on the day before the transfer date relating to the functions transferred under clause (i).

(c) CONFORMING AMENDMENTS. — Section 3 of the Federal Deposit Insurance Act (12 U.S.C. 1813) is amended —

(1) in subsection (q), by striking paragraphs (1) through (4) and inserting the following:

"(1) the Office of the Comptroller of the Currency, in the case of —

"(A) any national banking association;

"(B) any Federal branch or agency of a foreign bank; and

"(C) any Federal savings association;

(2)**所有转移的其他职能**。——

(A)**联邦储备委员会**。——储蓄机构监理局和储蓄机构监理局局长根据《业主贷款法》第11条(《美国法典》第十二编第1468节)享有的与关联方交易以及高级管理人员、董事及主要股东获得授信相关的所有规则制定权,以及根据《业主贷款法》第5(q)条享有的与搭售安排相关的所有规则制定权,均转由联邦储备委员会享有。

(B)**货币监理署署长**。——除第(1)款和第(A)子款规定的情形外——

(i)以下职能和权力应转由货币监理署和货币监理署署长行使——

(I)储蓄机构监理局以及储蓄机构监理局局长与联邦储蓄协会相关的所有职能;及

(II)储蓄机构监理局以及储蓄机构监理局局长与储蓄协会相关的所有规则制定权;且

(ii)储蓄机构监理局和储蓄机构监理局局长在转移日前一天享有的,与第(i)项所述职能和权力转移相关的所有权力、授权、权利和职责,均应转由货币监理署和货币监理署署长享有和承担。

(C)**联邦存款保险公司**。——除第(1)款和第(A)子款和第(B)子款规定的情形外——

(i) 原属储蓄机构监理局和储蓄机构监理局局长的与州储蓄协会相关的所有职能,均应转由联邦存款保险公司行使;且

(ii)储蓄机构监理局和储蓄机构监理局局长在转移日前一天享有的,与第(i)项所述职能转移相关的所有权力、授权、权利和职责,均应转由联邦存款保险公司享有和承担。

(c)**一致性修正**。——《联邦存款保险法》第3条(《美国法典》第十二编第1813节)修正如下——

(1)在第(q)子条中,删除第(1)款至第(4)款,替以以下内容:

“(1)对于以下主体而言,指货币监理署——

(A)任何国民银行协会;

(B)任何外国银行的联邦分行或代理行;及

(C)任何联邦储蓄协会;

"(2) the Federal Deposit Insurance Corporation, in the case of —

"(A) any State nonmember insured bank;

"(B) any foreign bank having an insured branch; and

"(C) any State savings association;

"(3) the Board of Governors of the Federal Reserve System, in the case of —

"(A) any State member bank;

"(B) any branch or agency of a foreign bank with respect to any provision of the Federal Reserve Act which is made applicable under the International Banking Act of 1978;

"(C) any foreign bank which does not operate an insured branch;

"(D) any agency or commercial lending company other than a Federal agency;

"(E) supervisory or regulatory proceedings arising from the authority given to the Board of Governors under section 7(c)(1) of the International Banking Act of 1978, including such proceedings under the Financial Institutions Supervisory Act of 1966;

"(F) any bank holding company and any subsidiary (other than a depository institution) of a bank holding company; and

"(G) any savings and loan holding company and any subsidiary (other than a depository institution) of a savings and loan holding company."; and

(2) in paragraphs (1) and (3) of subsection (u), by striking "(other than a bank holding company" and inserting "(other than a bank holding company or savings and loan holding company".

(d) CONSUMER PROTECTION. — Nothing in this section may be construed to limit or otherwise affect the transfer of powers under title X.

SEC. 313. ABOLISHMENT.

Effective 90 days after the transfer date, the Office of Thrift Supervision and the position of Director of the Office of Thrift Supervision are abolished.

SEC. 314. AMENDMENTS TO THE REVISED STATUTES.

(a) AMENDMENT TO SECTION 324. — Section 324 of the Revised Statutes of the United States (12 U.S.C. 1) is amended to read as follows:

"SEC. 324.COMPTROLLER OF THE CURRENCY.

"(a) OFFICE OF THE COMPTROLLER OF THE CURRENCY ESTABLISHED. — There is established in the Department of the Treasury a bureau to be known as the 'Office of the Comptroller of the Currency' which is charged with assuring the safety and soundness of, and compliance with laws and regulations, fair access to financial services, and fair treatment of customers by, the institutions and other persons subject to its jurisdiction.

"(b) COMPTROLLER OF THE CURRENCY. —

(2)对于以下主体而言,指联邦存款保险公司——

(A)任何州非成员参保银行;

(B)任何拥有参保分行的外国银行;及

(C)任何州储蓄协会;

(3)对于以下主体而言,指联邦储备系统的联邦储备委员会——

(A)任何州成员银行;

(B)根据《1978年国际银行法》而适用《联邦储备法》任何规定的外国银行的任何分行或代理行;

(C)不运营参保分行的任何外国银行;

(D)联邦机关以外的任何机关或商业贷款公司;

(E)联邦储备委员会因行使《1978年国际银行法》第7(c)(1)条赋予的权力而开展的监管或规制程序,包括根据《1966年金融机构监管法》开展的程序;

(F)任何银行控股公司及银行控股公司的任何子公司(但具有存款机构身份的子公司除外);及

(G)任何储贷控股公司及储贷控股公司的任何子公司(但具有存款机构身份的子公司除外)";及

(2)在第(u)子条的第(1)款和第(3)款中,删除"(银行控股公司除外",替以"(银行控股公司或储贷控股公司除外"。

(d)消费者保护。——本条任何规定均不得被解释为限制或影响第十编规定的权力转移。

第313条　撤销

转移日后第90天起,储蓄机构监理局即予撤销,储蓄机构监理局局长一职亦相应撤销。

第314条　对《美国制定法汇编》(修订版)的修正

(a) 对第324条的修正。——《美国制定法汇编》(修订版)第324条(《美国法典》第十二编第1节)修正后全文如下:

"第324条　货币监理署署长。——

(a)**设立货币监理署**。——财政部下设'货币监理署',负责确保管辖范围内的机构和其他主体的安全性和稳健性,确保此类机构和主体遵守法律法规,能够公平使用金融服务,并公平对待客户。

(b)**货币监理署署长**。——

"(1) IN GENERAL. — The chief officer of the Office of the Comptroller of the Currency shall be known as the Comptroller of the Currency. The Comptroller of the Currency shall perform the duties of the Comptroller of the Currency under the general direction of the Secretary of the Treasury. The Secretary of the Treasury may not delay or prevent the issuance of any rule or the promulgation of any regulation by the Comptroller of the Currency, and may not intervene in any matter or proceeding before the Comptroller of the Currency (including agency enforcement actions), unless otherwise specifically provided by law.

"(2) ADDITIONAL AUTHORITY. — The Comptroller of the Currency shall have the same authority with respect to functions transferred to the Comptroller of the Currency under the Enhancing Financial Institution Safety and Soundness Act of 2010 as was vested in the Director of the Office of Thrift Supervision on the transfer date, as defined in section 311 of that Act.".

(b) SUPERVISION OF FEDERAL SAVINGS ASSOCIATIONS. — Chapter 9 of title VII of the Revised Statutes of the United States (12 U.S.C. 1 et seq.) is amended by inserting after section 327A (12 U.S.C. 4a) the following:

"SEC. 327B. DEPUTY COMPTROLLER FOR THE SUPERVISION AND EXAMINATION OF FEDERAL SAVINGS ASSOCIATIONS.

"The Comptroller of the Currency shall designate a Deputy Comptroller, who shall be responsible for the supervision and examination of Federal savings associations.".

(c) AMENDMENT TO SECTION 329. — Section 329 of the Revised Statutes of the United States (12 U.S.C. 11) is amended by inserting before the period at the end the following: "or any Federal savings association".

(d) EFFECTIVE DATE. — This section, and the amendments made by this section, shall take effect on the transfer date.

SEC. 315. FEDERAL INFORMATION POLICY.

Section 3502(5) of title 44, United States Code, is amended by inserting "Office of the Comptroller of the Currency," after "the Securities and Exchange Commission,".

SEC. 316. SAVINGS PROVISIONS.

(a) OFFICE OF THRIFT SUPERVISION. —

(1) EXISTING RIGHTS, DUTIES, AND OBLIGATIONS NOT AFFECTED. — Sections 312 (b) and 313 shall not affect the validity of any right, duty, or obligation of the United States, the Director of the Office of Thrift Supervision, the Office of Thrift Supervision, or any other person, that existed on the day before the transfer date.

(2) CONTINUATION OF SUITS. — This title shall not abate any action or proceeding commenced by or against the Director of the Office of Thrift Supervision or the Office of Thrift Supervision before the transfer date, except that —

(1)**一般规定**。——货币监理署的最高领导人为货币监理署署长。货币监理署署长应在财政部部长的总体领导下履行货币监理署署长的职责。除非法律另有明确规定,否则,财政部部长不得延误或阻止货币监理署署长发布任何规则或颁发任何规章,亦不得介入货币监理署署长处理的任何事务或程序(包括机关执法行动)。

(2)**其他权力**。——转移日(转移日的定义见本法第311条)当天,原属储蓄机构监理局局长的职能应按照《2010年金融机构安全性与稳健性改良法》转移给货币监理署署长,转移之后,对于此类职能,货币监理署署长应拥有与储蓄机构监理局局长相同的权力。”

(b)**对联邦储蓄协会的监管**。——在《美国制定法汇编》(修订版)第七编第9章(《美国法典》第十二编第1节及其后条文)第327A条(《美国法典》第十二编第4a节)之后插入如下内容,作为对该章的修正:

“第327B条　货币监理署副署长负责对联邦储蓄协会进行监管和检查

货币监理署署长应指定一名副署长,负责对联邦储蓄协会进行监管和检查。”

(c)**对第329条的修正**。——在《美国制定法汇编》(修订版)第329条(《美国法典》第十二编第11节)结尾处的句号前插入如下内容,作为对该条的修正,“或任何联邦储蓄协会”。

(d)**生效日**。——本条以及本条所做修正应于转移日生效。

第315条　联邦信息政策

《美国法典》第四十四编第3502(5)节在“证券交易委员会”之后插入“货币监理署”,作为对该节的修正。

第316条　保留条款

(a)**储蓄机构监理局**。——

(1)**既存权利、职责和义务不受影响**。——第312(b)条和第313条规定不影响美国联邦政府、储蓄机构监理局局长、储蓄机构监理局或任何其他主体于转移日当天或之前即已拥有或承担的任何权力、职责或义务的有效性。

(2)**继续开展原有诉讼**。——储蓄机构监理局局长或储蓄机构监理局于转移日之前启动的,或者针对储蓄机构监理局局长或储蓄机构监理局而启动的任何诉讼或程序不得因为本编规定而终止,但是——

(A) for any action or proceeding arising out of a function of the Office of Thrift Supervision or the Director of the Office of Thrift Supervision transferred to the Board of Governors by this title, the Board of Governors shall be substituted for the Office of Thrift Supervision or the Director of the Office of Thrift Supervision as a party to the action or proceeding on and after the transfer date;

(B) for any action or proceeding arising out of a function of the Office of Thrift Supervision or the Director of the Office of Thrift Supervision transferred to the Office of the Comptroller of the Currency or the Comptroller of the Currency by this title, the Office of the Comptroller of the Currency or the Comptroller of the Currency shall be substituted for the Office of Thrift Supervision or the Director of the Office of Thrift Supervision, as the case may be, as a party to the action or proceeding on and after the transfer date; and

(C) for any action or proceeding arising out of a function of the Office of Thrift Supervision or the Director of the Office of Thrift Supervision transferred to the Corporation by this title, the Corporation shall be substituted for the Office of Thrift Supervision or the Director of the Office of Thrift Supervision as a party to the action or proceeding on and after the transfer date.

(b) CONTINUATION OF EXISTING OTS ORDERS, RESOLUTIONS, DETERMINATIONS, AGREEMENTS, REGULATIONS, ETC. — All orders, resolutions, determinations, agreements, and regulations, interpretative rules, other interpretations, guidelines, procedures, and other advisory materials, that have been issued, made, prescribed, or allowed to become effective by the Office of Thrift Supervision or the Director of the Office of Thrift Supervision, or by a court of competent jurisdiction, in the performance of functions that are transferred by this title and that are in effect on the day before the transfer date, shall continue in effect according to the terms of such orders, resolutions, determinations, agreements, and regulations, interpretative rules, other interpretations, guidelines, procedures, and other advisory materials, and shall be enforceable by or against —

(1) the Board of Governors, — in the case of a function of the Office of Thrift Supervision or the Director of the Office of Thrift Supervision transferred to the Board of Governors, until modified, terminated, set aside, or superseded in accordance with applicable law by the Board of Governors, by any court of competent jurisdiction, or by operation of law;

(2) the Office of the Comptroller of the Currency or the Comptroller of the Currency, in the case of a function of the Office of Thrift Supervision or the Director of the Office of Thrift Supervision transferred to the Office of the Comptroller of the Currency or the Comptroller of the Currency, respectively, until modified, terminated, set aside, or superseded in accordance with applicable law by the Office of the Comptroller of the

(A)如果任何相关诉讼或程序系因原属储蓄机构监理局或储蓄机构监理局局长但已按本编规定转由联邦储备委员会行使的职能所引起,则联邦储备委员会应于转移日当天及之后取代该局或该局长成为该诉讼或程序的一方;

(B)如果任何诉讼或程序系因原属储蓄机构监理局或储蓄机构监理局局长但已按本编规定转由货币监理署或货币监理署署长行使的职能所引起,则货币监理署或货币监理署署长应于转移日当天及之后取代储蓄机构监理局或储蓄机构监理局局长(视具体情况而定)成为该诉讼或程序的一方;且

(C)如果任何诉讼或程序系因原属储蓄机构监理局或储蓄机构监理局局长但已按本编规定转由联邦存款保险公司行使的职能所引起,则联邦存款保险公司应于转移日当天及之后取代储蓄机构监理局或储蓄机构监理局局长成为该诉讼或程序的一方。

(b)**现行命令、决议、判定、协议和规章等继续有效**。——储蓄机构监理局或储蓄机构监理局局长在履行按本编规定进行转移的职能时,储蓄机构监理局、储蓄机构监理局局长或有管辖权的法院签发、作出、制定或允许生效的所有相关命令、决议、判定、协议、规章、解释规则、其他解释性文件、指引、程序和其他建议性材料,在转移日前一天尚属有效的,应继续按该等命令、决议、判定、协议、规章、解释规则、其他解释性文件、指引、程序和其他建议性材料的内容有效,并由以下主体执行或针对以下主体执行——

(1)联邦储备委员会——在原属储蓄机构监理局或储蓄机构监理局局长的某项职能已转由联邦储备委员会行使的情形下,该项职能由联邦储备委员会执行或针对联邦储备委员会执行,直至上述命令、决议、判定、协议、规章、解释规则、其他解释性文件、指引、程序和其他建议性材料被联邦储备委员会、任何有管辖权的法院或法律规定修改、终止、撤销或取代;

(2)货币监理署或货币监理署署长——在原属储蓄机构监理局或储蓄机构监理局局长的某项职能已分别转由货币监理署或货币监理署署长行使的情形下,该项职能由货币监理署或货币监理署署长执行或针对货币监理署或货币监理署署长执行,直至上述命令、决议、判定、协议、规章、解释规则、其他解释性文件、指引、程序和其他建议性材料被货币监理署、货币监理署署长、任何有管辖权的法院或法律规定修改、

Currency or the Comptroller of the Currency, by any court of competent jurisdiction, or by operation of law; and

(3) the Corporation, in the case of a function of the Office of Thrift Supervision or the Director of the Office of Thrift Supervision transferred to the Corporation, until modified, terminated, set aside, or superseded in accordance with applicable law by the Corporation, by any court of competent jurisdiction, or by operation of law.

(c) IDENTIFICATION OF REGULATIONS CONTINUED. —

(1) BY THE BOARD OF GOVERNORS. — Not later than the transfer date, the Board of Governors shall —

(A) identify the regulations continued under subsection (b) that will be enforced by the Board of Governors; and

(B) publish a list of the regulations identified under subparagraph (A) in the Federal Register.

(2) BY OFFICE OF THE COMPTROLLER OF THE CURRENCY. — Not later than the transfer date, the Office of the Comptroller of the Currency shall —

(A) after consultation with the Corporation, identify the regulations continued under subsection (b) that will be enforced by the Office of the Comptroller of the Currency; and

(B) publish a list of the regulations identified under subparagraph (A) in the Federal Register.

(3) BY THE CORPORATION. — Not later than the transfer date, the Corporation shall —

(A) after consultation with the Office of the Comptroller of the Currency, identify the regulations continued under subsection (b) that will be enforced by the Corporation; and

(B) publish a list of the regulations identified under subparagraph (A) in the Federal Register.

(d) STATUS OF REGULATIONS PROPOSED OR NOT YET EFFECTIVE. —

(1) PROPOSED REGULATIONS. — Any proposed regulation of the Office of Thrift Supervision, which the Office of Thrift Supervision in performing functions transferred by this title, has proposed before the transfer date but has not published as a final regulation before such date, shall be deemed to be a proposed regulation of the Office of the Comptroller of the Currency or the Board of Governors, as appropriate, according to the terms of the proposed regulation.

(2) REGULATIONS NOT YET EFFECTIVE. — Any interim or final regulation of the Office of Thrift Supervision, which the Office of Thrift Supervision, in performing functions transferred by this title, has published before the transfer date but which has not become effective before that date, shall become effective as a regulation of the Office of

终止、撤销或取代;及

(3)联邦存款保险公司——在原属储蓄机构监理局或储蓄机构监理局局长的某项职能已转由联邦存款保险公司行使的情形下,该项职能由联邦存款保险公司执行或针对联邦存款保险公司执行,直至上述命令、决议、判定、协议、规章、解释规则、其他解释性文件、指引、程序和其他建议性材料被联邦存款保险公司、任何有管辖权的法院或法律规定修改、终止、撤销或取代。

(c)**确认继续有效的规章**。——

(1)**联邦储备委员会进行的确认**。——联邦储备委员会最迟应于转移日——

(A)确认根据第(b)子条规定应继续有效,且将由联邦储备委员会执行的规章;及

(B)在《联邦公报》发布按照第(A)子款确认的规章清单。

(2)**货币监理署进行的确认**。——货币监理署最迟应于转移日——

(A)与联邦存款保险公司进行磋商,确认根据第(b)子条规定应继续有效且将由货币监理署执行的规章;及

(B)在《联邦公报》发布按照第(A)子款确认的规章清单。

(3)**联邦存款保险公司进行的确认**。——联邦存款保险公司最迟应于转移日——

(A)与货币监理署进行磋商,确认根据第(b)子条规定应继续有效且将由联邦存款保险公司执行的规章;及

(B)在《联邦公报》发布按照第(A)子款确认的规章清单。

(d)**规章草案或尚未生效的规章的性质**。——

(1)**规章草案**。——储蓄机构监理局于转移日之前在履行本编转移的职能过程中提出的,但在转移日前尚未公布为最终规章的任何规章草案,均应保留其原有条款,视为货币监理署或联邦储备委员会(视具体情况而定)的规章草案。

(2)**尚未生效的规章**。——储蓄机构监理局于转移日之前,在履行本编转移的职能过程中公布的,但在转移日前尚未生效的任何暂行规章或最终规章,均应保留其原有条款,作为货币监理署或联邦储备委员会(视具体情况而定)的规章生效,直至该等规章被货币监理署或联邦储备委员会(视具体情况而定)、任何有管辖权的法院或法

the Comptroller of the Currency or the Board of Governors, as appropriate, according to the terms of the interim or final regulation, unless modified, terminated, set aside, or superseded in accordance with applicable law by the Office of the Comptroller of the Currency or the Board of Governors, as appropriate, by any court of competent jurisdiction, or by operation of law.

SEC. 317. REFERENCES IN FEDERAL LAW TO FEDERAL BANKING AGENCIES.

On and after the transfer date, any reference in Federal law to the Director of the Office of Thrift Supervision or the Office of Thrift Supervision, in connection with any function of the Director of the Office of Thrift Supervision or the Office of Thrift Supervision transferred under section 312(b) or any other provision of this subtitle, shall be deemed to be a reference to the Comptroller of the Currency, the Office of the Comptroller of the Currency, the Chairperson of the Corporation, the Corporation, the Chairman of the Board of Governors, or the Board of Governors, as appropriate and consistent with the amendments made in subtitle E.

SEC. 318. FUNDING.

(a) COMPENSATION OF EXAMINERS. — Section 5240 of the Revised Statutes of the United States (12 U.S.C. 481 et seq.) is amended —

(1) in the second undesignated paragraph (12 U.S.C. 481), in the fourth sentence, by striking "without regard to the provisions of other laws applicable to officers or employees of the United States" and inserting the following: "set and adjusted subject to chapter 71 of title 5, United States Code, and without regard to the provisions of other laws applicable to officers or employees of the United States"; and

(2) in the third undesignated paragraph (12 U.S.C. 482), in the first sentence, by striking "shall fix" and inserting "shall, subject to chapter 71 of title 5, United States Code, fix".

(b) FUNDING OF OFFICE OF THE COMPTROLLER OF THE CURRENCY. — Chapter 4 of title LXII of the Revised Statutes is amended by inserting after section 5240 (12 U.S.C. 481, 482) the following:

"SEC. 5240A. The Comptroller of the Currency may collect an assessment, fee, or other charge from any entity described in section 3(q)(1) of the Federal Deposit Insurance Act (12 U.S.C. 1813(q)(1)), as the Comptroller determines is necessary or appropriate to carry out the responsibilities of the Office of the Comptroller of the Currency. In establishing the amount of an assessment, fee, or charge collected from an entity under this section, the Comptroller of the Currency may take into account the nature and scope of the activities of the entity, the amount and type of assets that the entity holds, the financial and managerial condition of the entity, and any other factor, as the Comptroller

律规定修改、终止、撤销或取代。

第317条 联邦法律中提及联邦银行业监管机关的内容

在转移日当天及其后，联邦法律中指称的任何储蓄机构监理局局长或储蓄机构监理局,与根据第312(b)条或本子编任何其他规定转移的原属储蓄机构监理局局长或储蓄机构监理局的任何职能相关时,应被视为指称货币监理署署长、货币监理署、联邦存款保险公司主席、联邦存款保险公司、联邦储备委员会主席或联邦储备委员会(视具体情况而定且应与第E子编所做的修正一致)。

第318条 经费来源

(a)**检查人员的薪酬**。——《美国制定法汇编》(修订版)第5240条(《美国法典》第十二编第481节及其后条文)修正如下——

(1)在第二个无编号段落(《美国法典》第十二编第481节)第四个句子中,删除“不论适用于联邦官员或职员的其他法律如何规定”,替以“按照《美国法典》第五编第71章进行设定和调整,而不论适用于联邦官员或职员的其他法律如何规定”;且

(2)在第三个无编号段落(《美国法典》第十二编第482节)第一个句子中,删除“应确定”,替以“应按照《美国法典》第五编第71章确定”。

(b)**货币监理署的经费来源**。——在《美国制定法汇编》(修订版)第六十二编第四章第5240节(《美国法典》第十二编第481节或第482节)之后插入如下内容,作为对该章的修正:

“第5240A条 货币监理署署长可以向《联邦存款保险法》第3(q)(1)条[《美国法典》第十二编第1813(q)(1)节]所述任何实体收取其判定对履行货币监理署职责确属必要或适当的计征费、费用或其他收费。在按照本条规定确定计征费、费用或收费的金额时,货币监理署署长可考虑该等实体活动的性质和范围、持有资产的数量和类型、财务和管理状况以及货币监理署署长认为适当的任何其他因素。对于因按照本条规定收取计征费、费用、收费或付款而获得的资金,货币监理署署长可按照第5234条的规定进行存储。上述资金不得视作政府资金或拨款,也不得按照《美国法典》第三十一编第十五章或任何其他法律规定进行分配。本条向货币监理署署长赋予的权力与

of the Currency determines is appropriate. Funds derived from any assessment, fee, or charge collected or payment made pursuant to this section may be deposited by the Comptroller of the Currency in accordance with the provisions of section 5234. Such funds shall not be construed to be Government funds or appropriated monies, and shall not be subject to apportionment for purposes of chapter 15 of title 31, United States Code, or any other provision of law. The authority of the Comptroller of the Currency under this section shall be in addition to the authority under section 5240.

"The Comptroller of the Currency shall have sole authority to determine the manner in which the obligations of the Office of the Comptroller of the Currency shall be incurred and its disbursements and expenses allowed and paid, in accordance with this section, except asprovided in chapter 71 of title 5, United States Code (with respect to compensation).".

(c) FUNDING OF BOARD OF GOVERNORS. — Section 11 of the Federal Reserve Act (12 U.S.C. 248) is amended by adding at the end the following:

"(s) ASSESSMENTS, FEES, AND OTHER CHARGES FOR CERTAIN COMPANIES. —

"(1) IN GENERAL. — The Board shall collect a total amount of assessments, fees, or other charges from the companies described in paragraph (2) that is equal to the total expenses the Board estimates are necessary or appropriate to carry out the supervisory and regulatory responsibilities of the Board with respect to such companies.

"(2) COMPANIES. — The companies described in this paragraph are —

"(A) all bank holding companies having total consolidated assets of $50,000,000,000 or more;

"(B) all savings and loan holding companies having total consolidated assets of $50,000,000,000 or more; and

" (C) all nonbank financial companies supervised by the Board under section 113 of the Dodd–Frank Wall Street Reform and Consumer Protection Act.".

(d) CORPORATION EXAMINATION FEES. — Section 10 (e) of the Federal Deposit Insurance Act (12 U.S.C. 1820(e)) is amended by striking paragraph (1) and inserting the following:

"(1) REGULAR AND SPECIAL EXAMINATIONS OF DEPOSITORY INSTITUTIONS. — The cost of conducting any regular examination or special examination of any depository institution under subsection (b)(2), (b)(3), or (d) or of any entity described in section 3(q)(2) may be assessed by the Corporation against the institution or entity to meet the expenses of the Corporation in carrying out such examinations.".

(e) EFFECTIVE DATE. — This section, and the amendments made by this section,

第5240条赋予货币监理署署长的权力具有并存性,前者不限制后者。

货币监理署产生债务的方式以及允许支付和实际支付的开支和费用,由货币监理署署长按照本条规定全权决定,但《美国法典》第五编第七十一章(关于薪酬的规定)另有规定的除外。"

(c)**联邦储备委员会的经费来源**。——在《联邦储备法》第11条(《美国法典》第十二编第248节)结尾处增加如下内容,作为对该条的修正:

"(s)**特定公司的计征费、费用和其他收费**——

(1)**一般规定**。——联邦储备委员会向第(2)款所述公司收取的计征费、费用或其他收费的总额应等于联邦储备委员会预估对该等公司开展监管与规制工作所必要或适当的费用总额。

(2)**公司**。——本款所述公司指——

(A)并表总资产达500亿美元(含)以上的银行控股公司;

(B)并表总资产达500亿美元(含)以上的储贷控股公司;及

(C)联邦储备委员会按照《多德—弗兰克华尔街改革与消费者保护法》第113条进行监管的非银行金融公司。"

(d)**联邦存款保险公司的检查费用**。——删除《联邦存款保险法》第10(e)条[《美国法典》第十二编第1820(e)节]第(1)款,并替以如下内容,作为对该条的修正:

"(1)**对存款机构开展的常规和特殊检查**。——按照第(b)(2)子条、第(b)(3)子条或第(d)子条对任何存款机构进行任何常规或特殊检查,或对第3(q)(2)条所述任何实体开展任何常规或特殊检查之时,联邦存款保险公司均可对被检查机构或实体计征相关费用,以抵销联邦存款保险公司开展上述检查的费用。"

(e)**生效日**。——本条以及本条所做修正于转移日生效。

shall take effect on the transfer date.

SEC. 319. CONTRACTING AND LEASING AUTHORITY.

Notwithstanding the Federal Property and Administrative Services Act of 1949 (41 U.S.C. 251 et seq.) or any other provision of law (except the full and open competition requirements of the Competition in Contracting Act), the Office of the Comptroller of the Currency may —

(1) enter into and perform contracts, execute instruments, and acquire real property (or property interest) as the Comptroller deems necessary to carry out the duties and responsibilities of the Office of the Comptroller of the Currency; and

(2) hold, maintain, sell, lease, or otherwise dispose of the property (or property interest) acquired under paragraph (1).

Subtitle B — Transitional Provisions

SEC. 321. INTERIM USE OF FUNDS, PERSONNEL, AND PROPERTY OF THE OFFICE OF THRIFT SUPERVISION.

(a) IN GENERAL. — Before the transfer date, the Office of the Comptroller of the Currency, the Corporation, and the Board of Governors shall —

(1) consult and cooperate with the Office of Thrift Supervision to facilitate the orderly transfer of functions to the Office of the Comptroller of the Currency, the Corporation, and the Board of Governors in accordance with this title;

(2) determine jointly, from time to time —

(A) the amount of funds necessary to pay any expenses associated with the transfer of functions (including expenses for personnel, property, and administrative services) during the period beginning on the date of enactment of this Act and ending on the transfer date;

(B) which personnel are appropriate to facilitate the orderly transfer of functions by this title; and

(C) what property and administrative services are necessary to support the Office of the Comptroller of the Currency, the Corporation, and the Board of Governors during the period beginning on the date of enactment of this Act and ending on the transfer date; and

(3) take such actions as may be necessary to provide for the orderly implementation of this title.

(b) AGENCY CONSULTATION. — When requested jointly by the Office of the Comptroller of the Currency, the Corporation, and the Board of Governors to do so before

第319条　合同外包和租赁权

不论《1949年联邦财产和行政服务法》(《美国法典》第四十一编第251节及其后条文)或任何其他法律规定是否存在任何不同规定(但《合同外包竞争法》关于充分、公开竞争的要求除外),货币监理署可以——

(1)签署并履行合同、签署法律文书并购买房地产(或房产权益),前提是货币监理署署长认为该等行为对履行货币监理署的职责和责任而言确属必要;及

(2)持有、维护、出售、出租或以其他方式处置按照第(1)款购得的房产(或房产权益)。

第B子编——过渡条款

第321条　暂时使用储蓄机构监理局的资金、人员和财产

(a)**一般规定**。——货币监理署、联邦存款保险公司和联邦储备委员会应于转移日之前——

(1)与储蓄机构监理局磋商并合作,使相关职能顺利地按本编规定有序转移给货币监理署、联邦存款保险公司和联邦储备委员会;

(2)不时共同判定下列事项——

(A)为支付本法颁布日到转移日期间与转移职能相关的费用(包括人员、财产或行政服务方面的费用)所需的资金金额;

(B)何等人员能使相关职能顺利地按本编规定有序转移;及

(C)从本法颁布日到转移日期间,货币监理署、联邦存款保险公司和联邦储备委员会开展工作必不可少的财产和行政服务;及

(3)采取必要措施,促进本编规定的有序实施。

(b)**机关磋商**。——如果在转移日之前,货币监理署、联邦存款保险公司和联邦储备委员会共同提出相关请求,则储蓄机构监理局应——

the transfer date, the Office of Thrift Supervision shall —

(1) pay to the Office of the Comptroller of the Currency, the Corporation, or the Board of Governors, as applicable, from funds obtained by the Office of Thrift Supervision through assessments, fees, or other charges that the Office of Thrift Supervision is authorized by law to impose, such amounts as the Office of the Comptroller of the Currency, the Corporation, and the Board of Governors jointly determine to be necessary under subsection (a);

(2) detail to the Office of the Comptroller of the Currency, the Corporation, or the Board of Governors, as applicable, such personnel as the Office of the Comptroller of the Currency, the Corporation, and the Board of Governors jointly determine to be appropriate under subsection (a); and

(3) make available to the Office of the Comptroller of the Currency, the Corporation, or the Board of Governors, as applicable, such property and provide to the Office of the Comptroller of the Currency, the Corporation, or the Board of Governors, as applicable, such administrative services as the Office of the Comptroller of the Currency, the Corporation, and the Board of Governors jointly determine to be necessary under subsection (a).

(c) NOTICE REQUIRED. — The Office of the Comptroller of the Currency, the Corporation, and the Board of Governors shall jointly give the Office of Thrift Supervision reasonable prior notice of any request that the Office of the Comptroller of the Currency, the Corporation, and the Board of Governors jointly intend to make under subsection (b).

SEC. 322. TRANSFER OF EMPLOYEES.

(a) IN GENERAL. —

(1) OFFICE OF THRIFT SUPERVISION EMPLOYEES. —

(A) IN GENERAL. — Except as provided in section 1064, all employees of the Office of Thrift Supervision shall be transferred to the Office of the Comptroller of the Currency or the Corporation for employment in accordance with this section.

(B) ALLOCATING EMPLOYEES FOR TRANSFER TO RECEIVING AGENCIES. — The Director of the Office of Thrift Supervision, the Comptroller of the Currency, and the Chairperson of the Corporation shall —

(i) jointly determine the number of employees of the Office of Thrift Supervision necessary to perform or support the functions that are transferred to the Office of the Comptroller of the Currency or the Corporation by this title; and

(ii) consistent with the determination under clause (i), jointly identify employees of the Office of Thrift Supervision for transfer to the Office of the Comptroller of the Currency or the Corporation.

(2) EMPLOYEES TRANSFERRED; SERVICE PERIODS CREDITED. — For

(1)使用储蓄机构监理局依法收取的计征费、费用或其他收费获得的资金,向货币监理署、联邦存款保险公司或联邦储备委员会(视具体情况而定)支付相应金额,具体数额以货币监理署、联邦存款保险公司和联邦储备委员会联合判定对第(a)子条而言确属必要的为准;

(2)向货币监理署、联邦存款保险公司或联邦储备委员会(视具体情况而定)派遣相关人员,具体派遣人员以货币监理署、联邦存款保险公司和联邦储备委员会联合判定对第(a)子条而言确属适当的为准;及

(3)向货币监理署、联邦存款保险公司或联邦储备委员会(视具体情况而定)提供财产或行政服务,具体财产和服务以货币监理署、联邦存款保险公司和联邦储备委员会联合判定对第(a)子条而言确属必要的为准。

(c)**通知要求**。——货币监理署、联邦存款保险公司和联邦储备委员会拟根据第(b)子条提出任何联合请求的,应向储蓄机构监理局联合发出合理期限的事先通知。

第322条　雇员转移

(a)**一般规定**。——

(1)**储蓄机构监理局雇员**。——

(A)**一般规定**。——除第1064条规定的情形外,储蓄机构监理局的全体雇员均应按照本条规定转移至货币监理署或联邦存款保险公司。

(B)**转移到不同接收机关之雇员分配**。——储蓄机构监理局局长、货币监理署署长和联邦存款保险公司主席应——

(i)共同判定货币监理署或者联邦存款保险公司履行按照本编规定从储蓄机构监理局向其转移的职能或者为货币监理署或联邦存款保险公司履行该等职能提供支持,所必需的储蓄机构监理局雇员人数;及

(ii)按照根据第(i)项规定判定的人数,共同确定应转移至货币监理署或联邦存款保险公司的原储蓄机构监理局具体雇员。

(2)**转移雇员;承认工龄**。——就本条而言,在联邦住房贷款银行、联邦住房贷款

purposes of this section, periods of service with a Federal home loan bank, a joint office of Federal home loan banks, or a Federal reserve bank shall be credited as periods of service with a Federal agency.

(3) APPOINTMENT AUTHORITY FOR EXCEPTED SERVICE TRANSFERRED. —

(A) IN GENERAL. — Except as provided in subparagraph (B), any appointment authority of the Office of Thrift Supervision under Federal law that relates to the functions transferred under section 312, including the regulations of the Office of Personnel Management, for filling the positions of employees in the excepted service shall be transferred to the Comptroller of the Currency or the Chairperson of the Corporation, as appropriate.

(B) DECLINING TRANSFERS ALLOWED. — The Comptroller of the Currency or the Chairperson of the Corporation may decline to accept a transfer of authority under subparagraph (A) (and the employees appointed under that authority) to the extent that such authority relates to positions excepted from the competitive service because of their confidential, policy–making, policy–determining, or policy–advocating character.

(4) ADDITIONAL APPOINTMENT AUTHORITY. — Notwithstanding any other provision of law, the Office of the Comptroller of the Currency and the Corporation may appoint transferred employees to positions in the Office of the Comptroller of the Currency or the Corporation, respectively.

(b) TIMING OF TRANSFERS AND POSITION ASSIGNMENTS. — Each employee to be transferred under subsection (a)(1) shall —

(1) be transferred not later than 90 days after the transfer date; and

(2) receive notice of the position assignment of the employee not later than 120 days after the effective date of the transfer of the employee.

(c) TRANSFER OF FUNCTIONS. —

(1) IN GENERAL. — Notwithstanding any other provision of law, the transfer of employees under this subtitle shall be deemed a transfer of functions for the purpose of section 3503 of title 5, United States Code.

(2) PRIORITY. — If any provision of this subtitle conflicts with any protection provided to a transferred employee under section 3503 of title 5, United States Code, the provisions of this subtitle shall control.

(d) EMPLOYEE STATUS AND ELIGIBILITY. — The transfer of functions and employees under this subtitle, and the abolishment of the Office of Thrift Supervision under section 313, shall not affect the status of the transferred employees as employees of an agency of the United States under any provision of law.

(e) EQUAL STATUS AND TENURE POSITIONS. —

(1) STATUS AND TENURE. — Each transferred employee from the Office of Thrift

银行的联合办公室或联邦储备银行工作期间的工龄应获承认，计入在联邦机关工作的工龄。

(3)**特招雇员任命权的转移**。——

(A)**一般规定**。——除第(B)子款规定的情形外，联邦法律（包括人事管理局的规章）赋予储蓄机构监理局的并与第312条规定的职能转移相关的特招雇员任命权，应转由货币监理署署长或联邦存款保险公司主席（视具体情况而定）享有。

(B)**允许拒绝转移**。——如果某一职位因具有保密性或承担政策制定、确定或倡导性质，而未采用竞聘流程，直接进行特招，则货币监理署署长或联邦存款保险公司主席可以拒绝接受按第(A)子款转移的任命权（并可以拒绝接受根据该等任命权任命的雇员）。

(4)**其他任命权**。——无论是否存在任何不同法律规定，货币监理署和联邦存款保险公司均可以将转移雇员分别任命到货币监理署或联邦存款保险公司处任职。

(b)**转移时间与岗位安排**。——依据第(a)(1)子条规定转移的每名雇员均应——

(1)在转移日后90天内转移；并

(2)在该雇员的转移生效日后120天内收到岗位安排通知。

(c)**职能转移**。——

(1)**一般规定**。——无论是否存在任何不同法律规定，按照本子编进行的雇员转移均应视为《美国法典》第五编第3503节规定的职能转移。

(2)**优先适用**。——本子编的任何规定与《美国法典》第五编第3503节关于转移雇员的任何保护性规定相冲突的，以本子编的规定为准。

(d)**雇员身份和适格性**。——按本子编规定进行职能转移和雇员转移以及按第313条规定撤销储蓄机构监理局，不影响转移雇员在任何法律规定下的联邦机关雇员身份。

(e)**职位级别和工龄不变**。——

(1)**职位级别和工龄**。——从储蓄机构监理局转移至货币监理署或联邦存款保

Supervision shall be placed in a position at the Office of the Comptroller of the Currency or the Corporation with the same status and tenure as the transferred employee held on the day before the date on which the employee was transferred.

(2) FUNCTIONS. — To the extent practicable, each transferred employee shall be placed in a position at the Office of the Comptroller of the Currency or the Corporation, as applicable, responsible for the same functions and duties as the transferred employee had on the day before the date on which the employee was transferred, in accordance with the expertise and preferences of the transferred employee.

(f) NO ADDITIONAL CERTIFICATION REQUIREMENTS. — An examiner who is a transferred employee shall not be subject to any additional certification requirements before being placed in a comparable position at the Office of the Comptroller of the Currency or the Corporation, if the examiner carries out examinations of the same type of institutions as an employee of the Office of the Comptroller of the Currency or the Corporation as the employee was responsible for carrying out before the date on which the employee was transferred.

(g) PERSONNEL ACTIONS LIMITED. —

(1) PROTECTION. —

(A) IN GENERAL. — Except as provided in paragraph (2), each affected employee shall not, during the 30-month period beginning on the transfer date, be involuntarily separated, or involuntarily reassigned outside his or her locality pay area.

(B) AFFECTED EMPLOYEES. — For purposes of this paragraph, the term "affected employee" means —

(i) an employee transferred from the Office of Thrift Supervision holding a permanent position on the day before the transfer date; and

(ii) an employee of the Office of the Comptroller of the Currency or the Corporation holding a permanent position on the day before the transfer date.

(2) EXCEPTIONS. — Paragraph (1) does not limit the right of the Office of the Comptroller of the Currency or the Corporation to —

(A) separate an employee for cause or for unacceptable performance;

(B) terminate an appointment to a position excepted from the competitive service because of its confidential policy-making, policy-determining, or policy-advocating character; or

(C) reassign an employee outside such employee's locality pay area when the Office of the Comptroller of the Currency or the Corporation determines that the reassignment is necessary for the efficient operation of the agency.

(h) PAY. —

(1) 30-MONTH PROTECTION. — Except as provided in paragraph (2), during the

险公司的每名雇员的岗位级别和工龄均应与转移日前一天的级别和工龄保持一致。

(2)**职能**。——货币监理署或联邦存款保险公司(视具体情况而定)给每名转移雇员安排岗位时,在可行范围内应尽量根据转移雇员的专长和个人选择,确保雇员在转移后承担的工作职能和职责与该雇员在转移日前一天承担的职能和职责保持一致。

(f)**不要求额外认证**。——转移雇员如果是检查人员,且该检查人员转移前负责检查的机构类型与转移后在货币监理署或联邦存款保险公司工作时负责检查的机构类型并无二致,则货币监理署或联邦存款保险公司在安排其从事该等职位之时,不得向其施加任何额外认证要求。

(g)**限制人事行动**。——

(1)**保护**。——

(A)**一般规定**。——除第(2)款规定的情形外,自转移日起30个月内,不得违背受影响雇员意愿将其解聘或派往其工资分区以外的地区。

(B)**受影响雇员**。——就本款而言,"受影响雇员"一词系指——

(i)在转移日前一天拥有正式工作岗位的、从储蓄机构监理局转出的雇员;及

(ii)在转移日前一天拥有正式工作岗位的、供职于货币监理署或联邦存款保险公司的雇员。

(2)**例外规定**。——第(1)款规定并不限制货币监理署或联邦存款保险公司进行以下安排的权力——

(A)出于正当理由或由于雇员绩效欠理想而解聘雇员;

(B)终止对具有保密性,或者承担政策制定、确定或倡导性质的特招职位的任命;或

(C)货币监理署或联邦存款保险公司判定作出重新派遣安排对于保证该机关的有效运作确属必要之时,将雇员派往工资分区以外的地区工作。

(h)**工资**。——

(1)**30个月的保护期**。——除第(2)款规定的情形外,从雇员按照本子编转移之

30-month period beginning on the date on which the employee was transferred under this subtitle, a transferred employee shall be paid at a rate that is not less than the basic rate of pay, including any geographic differential, that the transferred employee received during the pay period immediately preceding the date on which the employee was transferred. Notwithstanding the preceding sentence, if the employee was receiving a higher rate of basic pay on a temporary basis (because of a temporary assignment, temporary promotion, or other temporary action) immediately before the transfer, the Agency may reduce the rate of basic pay on the date the rate would have been reduced but for the transfer, and the protected rate for the remainder of the 30-month period will be the reduced rate that would have applied but for the transfer.

(2) EXCEPTIONS. — The Comptroller of the Currency or the Corporation may reduce the rate of basic pay of a transferred employee —

(A) for cause, including for unacceptable performance; or

(B) with the consent of the transferred employee.

(3) PROTECTION ONLY WHILE EMPLOYED. — This subsection shall apply to a transferred employee only during the period that the transferred employee remains employed by Office of the Comptroller of the Currency or the Corporation.

(4) PAY INCREASES PERMITTED. — Nothing in this subsection shall limit the authority of the Comptroller of the Currency or the Chairperson of the Corporation to increase the pay of a transferred employee.

(i) BENEFITS. —

(1) RETIREMENT BENEFITS FOR TRANSFERRED EMPLOYEES. —

(A) IN GENERAL. —

(i) CONTINUATION OF EXISTING RETIREMENT PLAN. — Each transferred employee shall remain enrolled in the retirement plan of the transferred employee, for as long as the transferred employee is employed by the Office of the Comptroller of the Currency or the Corporation.

(ii) EMPLOYER'S CONTRIBUTION. — The Comptroller of the Currency or the Chairperson of the Corporation, as appropriate, shall pay any employer contributions to the existing retirement plan of each transferred employee, as required under each such existing retirement plan.

(B) DEFINITION. — In this paragraph, the term "existing retirement plan" means, with respect to a transferred employee, the retirement plan (including the Financial Institutions Retirement Fund), and any associated thrift savings plan, of the agency from which the employee was transferred in which the employee was enrolled on the day before the date on which the employee was transferred.

(2) BENEFITS OTHER THAN RETIREMENT BENEFITS. —

日起30个月内，该转移雇员的工资不得低于其在转移日之前最近一个付薪期获得的基本工资(在确定上述标准时应考虑含任何地区工资级差)。无论上一句如何规定,如果转移雇员在转移日前领取的是临时性的较高基本工资(例如,因临时派遣、临时升职或其他临时行动而获得较高基本工资),则自该转移雇员即使不转移也会下调工资之日起,新的接收机关可将其基本工资相应下调,而在30个月保护期的剩余期限内，该雇员的保护工资标准应为该转移雇员即使不转移也将下调的工资水平。

(2)**例外规定**。——货币监理署署长或联邦存款保险公司可以基于下列原因下调转移雇员的基本工资——

(A)存在正当理由,包括雇员绩效欠理想;或

(B)经转移雇员同意。

(3)**保护规定仅限于雇佣关系存续期间**。——本子条仅适用于转移雇员继续供职于货币监理署或联邦存款保险公司的期间。

(4)**允许提高工资**。——本子条的任何规定对货币监理署署长或联邦存款保险公司主席提高转移雇员工资的权力均不构成限制。

(i)**福利**。——

(1)**转移雇员的退休福利**。——

(A)**一般规定**。——

(i)**既存退休计划继续实施**。——只要转移雇员供职于货币监理署或联邦存款保险公司,即应继续参与该转移雇员的退休计划。

(ii)**雇主缴款**。——货币监理署署长或联邦存款保险公司主席(视具体情况而定)应按照每名转移雇员参与的既存退休计划的要求向每一该等退休计划缴纳任何雇主缴款。

(B)**定义**。——就本款而言,“既存退休计划”一词系指转移雇员在转移日前一天,在职能转出机关已经参与的退休计划(包括金融机构退休基金)以及任何相关的储蓄计划。

(2)**退休福利以外的福利**。——

(A) DURING FIRST YEAR. —

(i) EXISTING PLANS CONTINUE. — During the 1-year period following the transfer date, each transferred employee may retain membership in any employee benefit program (other than a retirement benefit program) of the agency from which the employee was transferred under this title, including any dental, vision, long term care, or life insurance program to which the employee belonged on the day before the transfer date.

(ii) EMPLOYER'S CONTRIBUTION. — The Office of the Comptroller of the Currency or the Corporation, as appropriate, shall pay any employer cost required to extend coverage in the benefit program to the transferred employee as required under that program or negotiated agreements.

(B) DENTAL, VISION, OR LIFE INSURANCE AFTER FIRST YEAR. — If, after the 1-year period beginning on the transfer date, the Office of the Comptroller of the Currency or the Corporation determines that the Office of the Comptroller of the Currency or the Corporation, as the case may be, will not continue to participate in any dental, vision, or life insurance program of an agency from which an employee was transferred, a transferred employee who is a member of the program may, before the decision takes effect and without regard to any regularly scheduled open season, elect to enroll in —

(i) the enhanced dental benefits program established under chapter 89A of title 5, United States Code;

(ii) the enhanced vision benefits established under chapter 89B of title 5, United States Code; and

(iii) the Federal Employees' Group Life Insurance Program established under chapter 87 of title 5, United States Code, without regard to any requirement of insurability.

(C) LONG TERM CARE INSURANCE AFTER 1ST YEAR. — If, after the 1-year period beginning on the transfer date, the Office of the Comptroller of the Currency or the Corporation determines that the Office of the Comptroller of the Currency or the Corporation, as appropriate, will not continue to participate in any long term care insurance program of an agency from which anemployee transferred, a transferred employee who is a member of such a program may, before the decision takes effect, elect to apply for coverage under the Federal Long Term Care Insurance Program established under chapter 90 of title 5, United States Code, under the underwriting requirements applicable to a new active workforce member, as described in part 875 of title 5, Code of Federal Regulations (or any successor thereto).

(D) CONTRIBUTION OF TRANSFERRED EMPLOYEE. —

(i) IN GENERAL. — Subject to clause (ii), a transferred employee who is enrolled in a plan under the Federal Employees Health Benefits Program shall pay any employee

(A)**第一年**。——

(i)**既存计划将继续实施**。——在转移日后1年之内,每一转移雇员均可继续参与本编中的职能转出机关的任何雇员福利计划(但退休福利计划除外),包括该雇员在转移日前一天已经参与的任何牙医保险、眼科保险、长期医疗保险或寿险计划。

(ii)**雇主缴款**。——货币监理署或联邦存款保险公司(视具体情况而定)应按照计划要求或按照磋商达成的协议的要求,缴纳福利计划中的任何雇主缴款,使转移雇员可继续享受该福利计划。

(B)**第一年期限届满之后的牙医保险、眼科保险或寿险**。——自转移日起届满1年之后,如果货币监理署或联邦存款保险公司(视具体情况而定)决定不再参与转移雇员的职能转出机关的任何牙医保险、眼科保险或寿险计划,则已经参与该计划的转移雇员可在上述决定生效前选择参与以下计划, 而不受该等计划的任何常规开放时间表限制——

(i)按照《美国法典》第五编第89A章设立的升级版牙医福利计划;

(ii)按照《美国法典》第五编第89B章设立的升级版眼科福利计划;

(iii)按照《美国法典》第五编第87章设立的联邦雇员团体寿险计划(不受任何参保要求的限制)。

(C)**第一年期限届满之后的长期医疗保险**。——自转移日起届满1年之后,如果货币监理署或联邦存款保险公司(视具体情况而定)决定不再参与转移雇员的职能转出机关的任何长期医疗保险计划,则原已参与该计划的转移雇员可在上述决定生效前,按照《联邦规章汇编》第五编第875部分(或其后续规定)适用于新雇员的参保要求,选择申请参与按照《美国法典》第五编第90章设立的联邦长期医疗保险计划。

(D)**转移雇员缴款**。——

(i)**一般规定**。——在不违反第(ii)项要求的前提下,在联邦雇员卫生福利计划下参与任何计划的转移雇员应按照该计划要求缴纳任何雇员缴款。

contribution required under the plan.

(ii) COST DIFFERENTIAL. — The Office of the Comptroller of the Currency or the Corporation, as applicable, shall pay any difference in cost between the employee contribution required under the plan provided to transferred employees by the agency from which the employee transferred on the date of enactment of this Act and the plan provided by the Office of the Comptroller of the Currency or the Corporation, as the case may be, under this section.

(iii) FUNDS TRANSFER. — The Office of the Comptroller of the Currency or the Corporation, as the case may be, shall transfer to the Employees Health Benefits Fund established under section 8909 of title 5, United States Code, an amount determined by the Director of the Office of Personnel Management, after consultation with the Comptroller of the Currency or the Chairperson of the Corporation, as the case may be, and the Office of Management and Budget, to be necessary to reimburse the Fund for the cost to the Fund of providing any benefits under this subparagraph that are not otherwise paid for by a transferred employee under clause (i).

(E) SPECIAL PROVISIONS TO ENSURE CONTINUATION OF LIFE INSURANCE BENEFITS. —

(i) IN GENERAL. — An annuitant, as defined in section 8901 of title 5, United States Code, who is enrolled in a life insurance plan administered by an agency from which employees are transferred under this title on the day before the transfer date shall be eligible for coverage by a life insurance plan under sections 8706(b), 8714a, 8714b, or 8714c of title 5, United States Code, or by a life insurance plan established by the Office of the Comptroller of the Currency or the Corporation, as applicable, without regard to any regularly scheduled open season or any requirement of insurability.

(ii) CONTRIBUTION OF TRANSFERRED EMPLOYEE. —

(I) IN GENERAL. — Subject to subclause (II), a transferred employee enrolled in a life insurance plan under this subparagraph shall pay any employee contribution required by the plan.

(II) COST DIFFERENTIAL. — The Office of the Comptroller of the Currency or the Corporation, as the case may be, shall pay any difference in cost between the benefits provided by the agency from which the employee transferred on the date of enactment of this Act and the benefits provided under this section.

(III) FUNDS TRANSFER. — The Office of the Comptroller of the Currency or the Corporation, as the case may be, shall transfer to the Federal Employees' Group Life Insurance Fund established under section 8714 of title 5, United States Code, an amount determined by the Director of the Office of Personnel Management, after consultation with

(ii)**费用差异**。——于本法颁布之日,转移雇员在职能转出机关提供的福利计划下所承担的费用,与在货币监理署或联邦存款保险公司(视具体情况而定)根据本条提供的计划下承担的费用相比,存在任何差额的,货币监理署或联邦存款保险公司(视具体情况而定)应按照本条规定代为缴纳。

(iii)**资金转移**。——货币监理署或联邦存款保险公司(视具体情况而定)应向按照《美国法典》第五编第8909节设立的雇员卫生福利基金转移必要资金,以补偿该基金根据本子款提供的任何福利而产生的且并非转移雇员应在第(i)项下支付的费用,具体金额由人事管理局局长与货币监理署署长或联邦存款保险公司主席(视具体情况而定)以及行政管理和预算局磋商后确定。

(E)**保证转移雇员继续享受寿险福利的特别规定**。——

(i)**一般规定**。——在转移日前一天已参与本编下职能转出机关管理的寿险计划的年金受益人(定义见《美国法典》第五编第8901节)有资格按照《美国法典》第五编第8706(b)节、第8714a节、第8714b节或第8714c节参与寿险计划,或者有资格参加货币监理署或联邦存款保险公司(视具体情况而定)设立的寿险计划,而不受该等计划的任何常规开放时间表或任何参保要求的限制。

(ii)**转移雇员缴款**。——

(I)**一般规定**。——在不违反第(II)子项要求的前提下,按照本子款参与寿险计划的转移雇员应按照计划要求缴纳雇员缴款。

(II)**费用差异**。——于本法颁布之日,转移雇员在职能转出机关提供的福利计划下承担的费用,与在货币监理署或联邦存款保险公司(视具体情况而定)根据本条提供的计划下承担的费用相比,存在任何差额的,货币监理署或联邦存款保险公司(视具体情况而定)应按照本条规定代为缴纳。

(III)**资金转移**。——货币监理署或联邦存款保险公司(视具体情况而定)应向按照《美国法典》第五编第8714节设立的联邦雇员团体人寿保险基金转移必要资金,以补偿该基金根据本子款提供的任何福利而产生的且并非转移雇员应在第(I)子项下支付的费用,具体金额由人事管理局局长与货币监理署署长或联邦存款保险公司主席

the Comptroller of the Currency or the Chairperson of the Corporation, as the case may be, and the Office of Management and Budget, to be necessary to reimburse the Federal Employees' Group Life Insurance Fund for the cost to the Federal Employees' Group Life Insurance Fund of providing benefits under this subparagraph not otherwise paid for by a transferred employee under subclause (I).

(IV) CREDIT FOR TIME ENROLLED IN OTHER PLANS. — For any transferred employee, enrollment in a life insurance plan administered by the agency from which the employee transferred, immediately before enrollment in a life insurance plan under chapter 87 of title 5, United States Code, shall be considered as enrollment in a life insurance plan under that chapter for purposes of section 8706(b)(1)(A) of title 5, United States Code.

(j) INCORPORATION INTO AGENCY PAY SYSTEM. — Not later than 30 months after the transfer date, the Comptroller of the Currency and the Chairperson of the Corporation shall place each transferred employee into the established pay system and structure of the appropriate employing agency.

(k) EQUITABLE TREATMENT. — In administering the provisions of this section, the Comptroller of the Currency and the Chairperson of the Corporation —

(1) may not take any action that would unfairly disadvantage a transferred employee relative to any other employee of the Office of the Comptroller of the Currency or the Corporation on the basis of prior employment by the Office of Thrift Supervision;

(2) may take such action as is appropriate in an individual case to ensure that a transferred employee receives equitable treatment, with respect to the status, tenure, pay, benefits (other than benefits under programs administered by the Office of Personnel Management), and accrued leave or vacation time for prior periods of service with any Federal agency of the transferred employee;

(3) shall, jointly with the Director of the Office of Thrift Supervision, develop and adopt procedures and safeguards designed to ensure that the requirements of this subsection are met; and

(4) shall conduct a study detailing the position assignments of all employees transferred pursuant to subsection (a), describing the procedures and safeguards adopted pursuant to paragraph (3), and demonstrating that the requirements of this subsection have been met; and shall, not later than 365 days after the transfer date, submit a copy of such study to Congress.

(l) REORGANIZATION. —

(1) IN GENERAL. — If the Comptroller of the Currency or the Chairperson of the Corporation determines, during the 2-year period beginning 1 year after the transfer date, that a reorganization of the staff of the Office of the Comptroller of the Currency or the

(视具体情况而定)以及行政管理和预算局磋商后确定。

(Ⅳ)**其他计划参与时间的认可**。——在按照《美国法典》第五编第八十七章的规定参与寿险计划前最近的时点，任何转移雇员具有职能转出机关管理的寿险计划的参保人身份的,则就《美国法典》第五编第8706(b)(1)(A)节而言,该转移雇员应视为在转移之前即已按照《美国法典》第五编第八十七章参与寿险计划。

(j)**纳入机关薪酬体系**。——转移日后30个月内,货币监理署署长和联邦存款保险公司主席应将所有转移雇员纳入相关雇佣机关的既有薪酬体系和结构之内。

(k)**公平待遇**。——在实施本条规定过程中,货币监理署署长和联邦存款保险公司主席——

(1)不得采取任何将导致转移雇员遭受如下后果的任何行动:由于之前供职于储蓄机构监理局，而受到次于货币监理署或联邦存款保险公司任何其他雇员的不公平待遇;

(2)可以针对具体个案采取适当措施,确保转移雇员与之前在职能转出机关供职期间相比,在岗位级别、任期、工资、福利(但人事管理局管理的计划所提供的福利除外)以及累积休假时间或假期方面获得公平待遇;

(3)应与储蓄机构监理局局长联合制定并通过旨在确保本子条的要求得到遵守的程序和保障措施;且

(4)应开展研究,对按照第(a)子条转移的所有雇员的岗位安排作出详细说明,描述按照第(3)款采取的程序和保障措施,并证明本子条的要求已得到遵守;同时,应在转移日后365天内将该研究报告提交国会。

(l)**重组**。——

(1)**一般规定**。——如果在转移日届满1年之日起2年内,货币监理署署长或联邦存款保险公司主席判定应对货币监理署或联邦存款保险公司人员进行重组，则在按照《美国法典》第五编第8336(d)(2)节或第8414(b)(1)(B)节的规定确定受影响雇员

Corporation, respectively, is required, the reorganization shall be deemed a "major reorganization" for purposes of affording affected employees retirement under section 8336(d)(2) or 8414(b)(1)(B) of title 5, United States Code.

(2) SERVICE CREDIT. — For purposes of this subsection, periods of service with a Federal home loan bank or a joint office of Federal home loan banks shall be credited as periods of service with a Federal agency.

SEC. 323. PROPERTY TRANSFERRED.

(a) PROPERTY DEFINED. — For purposes of this section, the term "property" includes all real property (including leaseholds) and all personal property, including computers, furniture, fixtures, equipment, books, accounts, records, reports, files, memoranda, paper, reports of examination, work papers, and correspondence related to such reports, and any other information or materials.

(b) PROPERTY OF THE OFFICE OF THRIFT SUPERVISION. —

(1) IN GENERAL. — No later than 90 days after the transfer date, all property of the Office of Thrift Supervision (other than property described under paragraph (b)(2)) that the Comptroller of the Currency and the Chairperson of the Corporation jointly determine is used, on the day before the transfer date, to perform or support the functions of the Office of Thrift Supervision transferred to the Office of the Comptroller of the Currency or the Corporation under this title, shall be transferred to the Office of the Comptroller of the Currency or the Corporation in a manner consistent with the transfer of employees under this subtitle.

(2) PERSONAL PROPERTY. — All books, accounts, records, reports, files, memoranda, papers, documents, reports of examination, work papers, and correspondence of the Office of Thrift Supervision that the Comptroller of the Currency, the Chairperson of the Corporation, and the Chairman of the Board of Governors jointly determine is used, on the day before the transfer date, to perform or support the functions of the Office of Thrift Supervision transferred to the Board of Governors under this title shall be transferred to the Board of Governors in a manner consistent with the purposes of this title.

(c) CONTRACTS RELATED TO PROPERTY TRANSFERRED. — Each contract, agreement, lease, license, permit, and similar arrangement relating to property transferred to the Office of the Comptroller of the Currency or the Corporation by this section shall be transferred to the Office of the Comptroller of the Currency or the Corporation, as appropriate, together with the property to which it relates.

(d) PRESERVATION OF PROPERTY. — Property identified for transfer under this section shall not be altered, destroyed, or deleted before transfer under this section.

的退休待遇时,该重组应视为“重大重组”。

(2)**工龄**。——就本子条而言,在联邦住房贷款银行或联邦住房贷款银行联合办公室工作期间的工龄应计入在联邦机关工作的工龄。

第323条　财产转移

(a)**财产定义**。——就本条而言,“财产”一词包括所有不动产(包括租赁不动产)和所有动产,包括电脑、家具、固定装置、设备、书籍、账目、记录、报告、档案、备忘录、文件、检查报告、工作底稿、与上述报告有关的往来信件以及任何其他信息或材料。

(b)**储蓄机构监理局的财产**。——

(1)**一般规定**。——货币监理署署长和联邦存款保险公司主席应共同判定,在转移日前一天储蓄机构监理局哪些财产用于开展或支持储蓄机构监理局按照本编规定转移给货币监理署或联邦存款保险公司的职能,并且所有该等财产[但第(b)(2)款所述财产除外]均应于转移日后90天内转移至货币监理署或联邦存款保险公司,转移方式应与按照本子编进行的雇员转移方式一致。

(2)**动产**。——货币监理署署长、联邦存款保险公司主席和联邦储备委员会主席应共同判定,在转移日前一天储蓄机构监理局哪些书籍、账目、记录、报告、档案、备忘录、文件、检查报告、工作底稿以及与上述报告相关的往来信件用于开展或支持储蓄机构监理局按照本编规定转移给联邦储备委员会的职能,并且所有该等财产均应转移至联邦储备委员会,转移方式应与本编宗旨一致。

(c)**与转移财产相关的合同**。——与按照本条规定转移至货币监理署或联邦存款保险公司的财产相关的所有合同、协议、租约、执照、许可和类似安排,均应与相关财产一并转移至货币监理署或联邦存款保险公司(视具体情况而定)。

(d)**财产保护**。——按照本条确定的待转移的财产,在按照本条完成转移之前不得改动、毁坏或移除。

SEC. 324. FUNDS TRANSFERRED.

The funds that, on the day before the transfer date, the Director of the Office of Thrift Supervision (in consultation with the Comptroller of the Currency, the Chairperson of the Corporation, and the Chairman of the Board of Governors) determines are not necessary to dispose of the affairs of the Office of Thrift Supervision under section 325 and are available to the Office of Thrift Supervision to pay the expenses of the Office of Thrift Supervision —

(1) relating to the functions of the Office of Thrift Supervision transferred under section 312(b)(2)(B), shall be transferred to the Office of the Comptroller of the Currency on the transfer date;

(2) relating to the functions of the Office of Thrift Supervision transferred under section 312(b)(2)(C), shall be transferred to the Corporation on the transfer date; and

(3) relating to the functions of the Office of Thrift Supervision transferred under section 312(b)(1)(A), shall be transferred to the Board of Governors on the transfer date.

SEC. 325. DISPOSITION OF AFFAIRS.

(a) AUTHORITY OF DIRECTOR. — During the 90–day period beginning on the transfer date, the Director of the Office of Thrift Supervision —

(1) shall, solely for the purpose of winding up the affairs of the Office of Thrift Supervision relating to any function transferred to the Office of the Comptroller of the Currency, the Corporation, or the Board of Governors under this title —

(A) manage the employees of the Office of Thrift Supervision who have not yet been transferred and provide for the payment of the compensation and benefits of the employees that accrue before the date on which the employees are transferred under this title; and

(B) manage any property of the Office of Thrift Supervision, until the date on which the property is transferred under section 323; and

(2) may take any other action necessary to wind up the affairs of the Office of Thrift Supervision.

(b) STATUS OF DIRECTOR. —

(1) IN GENERAL. — Notwithstanding the transfer of functions under this subtitle, during the 90–day period beginning on the transfer date, the Director of the Office of Thrift Supervision shall retain and may exercise any authority vested in the Director of the Office of Thrift Supervision on the day before the transfer date, only to the extent necessary —

(A) to wind up the Office of Thrift Supervision; and

第324条　资金转移

如果储蓄机构监理局局长(在与货币监理署署长、联邦存款保险公司主席和联邦储备委员会主席磋商后)判定,在转移日前一天,某些资金对处理第325条规定的储蓄机构监理局事务而言非属必要,但是——

(1)若该资金属于可用于支付与储蓄机构监理局按照第312(b)(2)(B)条转移的职能相关的费用,则应于转移日转移至货币监理署;

(2)若该资金属于可用于支付与储蓄机构监理局按照第312(b)(2)(C)条转移的职能相关的费用,则应于转移日转移至联邦存款保险公司;且

(3)若该资金属于可用于支付与储蓄机构监理局按照第312(b)(1)(A)条转移的职能相关的费用,则应于转移日转移至联邦储备委员会。

第325条　事务处理

(a)**储蓄机构监理局局长的权力**。——自转移日起90天内,储蓄机构监理局局长应——

(1)仅出于了结储蓄机构监理局与按照本编规定转移至货币监理署、联邦存款保险公司或联邦储备委员会的任何职能相关的事务之目的——

(A)管理储蓄机构监理局尚未转移的雇员,并向该等雇员支付其在按照本编规定被转移之前的累积薪酬和福利;及

(B)管理储蓄机构监理局的任何财产,直至该财产按照第323条完成转移;及

(2)为了了结储蓄机构监理局的事务而采取任何其他必要措施。

(b)**储蓄机构监理局局长的身份**。——

(1)**一般规定**。——尽管本子编规定了对职能的转移,但在转移日后90天内,储蓄机构监理局局长仍应保有并且可以行使储蓄机构监理局局长在转移日前一天拥有的任何权力,但须以对实现下列目的确属必要为限——

(A)了结储蓄机构监理局的事务;及

(B) to carry out the transfer under this subtitle during such 90-day period.

(2) OTHER PROVISIONS. — For purposes of paragraph (1), the Director of the Office of Thrift Supervision shall, during the 90-day period beginning on the transfer date, continue to be —

(A) treated as an officer of the United States; and

(B) entitled to receive compensation at the same annual rate of basic pay that the Director of the Office of Thrift Supervision received on the day before the transfer date.

SEC. 326. CONTINUATION OF SERVICES

Any agency, department, or other instrumentality of the United States, and any successor to any such agency, department, or instrumentality, that was, before the transfer date, providing support services to the Office of Thrift Supervision in connection with functions transferred to the Office of the Comptroller of the Currency, the Corporation or the Board of Governors under this title, shall —

(1) continue to provide such services, subject to reimbursement by the Office of the Comptroller of the Currency, the Corporation, or the Board of Governors, until the transfer of functions under this title is complete; and

(2) consult with the Comptroller of the Currency, the Chairperson of the Corporation, or the Chairman of the Board of Governors, as appropriate, to coordinate and facilitate a prompt and orderly transition.

SEC. 327. IMPLEMENTATION PLAN AND REPORTS.

(a) PLAN SUBMISSION. — Within 180 days of the enactment of the Dodd-Frank Wall Street Reform and Consumer Protection Act, the Board of Governors, the Corporation, the Office of the Comptroller of the Currency, and the Office of Thrift Supervision, shall jointly submit a plan to the Committee on Banking, Housing, and Urban Affairs of the Senate, the Committee on Financial Services of the House of Representatives, and the Inspectors General of the Department of the Treasury, the Corporation, and the Board of Governors detailing the steps the Board of Governors, the Corporation, the Office of the Comptroller of the Currency, and the Office of Thrift Supervision will take to implement the provisions of sections 301 through 326, and the provisions of the amendments made by such sections.

(b) INSPECTORS GENERAL REVIEW OF THE PLAN. — Within 60 days of receiving the plan required under subsection (a), the Inspectors General of the Department of the Treasury, the Corporation, and the Board of Governors shall jointly provide a written report to the Board of Governors, the Corporation, the Office of the Comptroller of the Currency, and the Office of Thrift Supervision and shall submit a copy to the Committee on Banking, Housing, and Urban Affairs of the Senate and the

(B)在转移日后90天内按照本子编规定进行相关转移。

(2)**其他规定**。——就第(1)款而言，在转移日后90天内，储蓄机构监理局局长应继续——

(A)保持联邦官员身份；并

(B)按照与其在转移日前一天所享受的基本年薪相同的水平继续领取薪酬。

第326条　继续提供服务

任何联邦机关、部门或其他职能部门(及任何该等机关的任何继任单位)如果在转移日之前针对按照本编转移给货币监理署、联邦存款保险公司或联邦储备委员会的职能向储蓄机构监理局提供支持服务的，则该等机关、部门或职能部门应——

(1)继续提供该等服务，但应由货币监理署、联邦存款保险公司或联邦储备委员会偿付费用，直至按照本编进行的职能转移全部完成为止；及

(2)与货币监理署署长、联邦存款保险公司主席或联邦储备委员会主席(视具体情况而定)磋商，以便为过渡阶段及时有序地完成进行协调并提供便利。

第327条　实施计划和报告

(a)**提交报告**。——《多德—弗兰克华尔街改革与消费者保护法》颁布后180天内，联邦储备委员会、联邦存款保险公司、货币监理署和储蓄机构监理局应联合向参议院银行、住房与城市事务委员会、众议院金融服务委员会，以及财政部、联邦存款保险公司和联邦储备委员会各自的监察长提交一份计划，详细说明联邦储备委员会、联邦存款保险公司、货币监理署和储蓄机构监理局为实施第301条至第326条的规定以及由该等条款作出的修正规定所将采取的措施。

(b)**监察长对计划的审查**。——在收到按照第(a)子条要求提交的计划后60天内，财政部、联邦存款保险公司和联邦储备委员会各自的监察长应向联邦储备委员会、联邦存款保险公司、货币监理署以及储蓄机构监理局联合提交一份书面报告，并向参议院银行、住房与城市事务委员会以及众议院金融服务委员会提交一份报告复本，详细说明上述计划是否符合第301条至第326条的规定以及由该等条款作出的修正规定，包括——

Committee on Financial Services of the House of Representatives detailing whether the plan conforms with the provisions of sections 301 through 326, and the provisions of the amendments made by such sections, including —

(1) whether the plan sufficiently takes into consideration the orderly transfer of personnel;

(2) whether the plan describes procedures and safeguards to ensure that the Office of Thrift Supervision employees are not unfairly disadvantaged relative to employees of the Office of the Comptroller of the Currency and the Corporation;

(3) whether the plan sufficiently takes into consideration the orderly transfer of authority and responsibilities;

(4) whether the plan sufficiently takes into consideration the effective transfer of funds;

(5) whether the plan sufficiently takes in consideration the orderly transfer of property; and

(6) any additional recommendations for an orderly and effective process.

(c) IMPLEMENTATION REPORTS. — Not later than 6 months after the date on which the Committee on Banking, Housing, and Urban Affairs of the Senate and the Committee on Financial Services of the House of Representatives receives the report required under subsection (b), and every 6 months thereafter until all aspects of the plan have been implemented, the Inspectors General of the Department of the Treasury, the Corporation, and the Board of Governors shall jointly provide a written report on the status of the implementation of the plan to the Board of Governors, the Corporation, the Office of the Comptroller of the Currency, and the Office of Thrift Supervision and shall submit a copy to the Committee on Banking, Housing, and Urban Affairs of the Senate and the Committee on Financial Services of the House of Representatives.

Subtitle C — Federal Deposit Insurance Corporation

SEC. 331. DEPOSIT INSURANCE REFORMS.

(a) SIZE DISTINCTIONS. — Section 7(b)(2) of the Federal Deposit Insurance Act (12 U.S.C. 1817(b)(2)) is amended —

(1) by striking subparagraph (D); and

(2) by redesignating subparagraph (C) as subparagraph (D).

(b) ASSESSMENT BASE. — The Corporation shall amend the regulations issued by the Corporation under section 7(b)(2) of the Federal Deposit Insurance Act (12 U.S.C.

(1)该计划是否充分考虑了人员的有序转移;

(2)该计划是否阐述了旨在确保储蓄机构监理局的雇员不会受到低于货币监理署和联邦存款保险公司雇员的不公平待遇的程序和保障措施;

(3)该计划是否充分考虑了权力和责任的有序转移;

(4)该计划是否充分考虑了资金的有效转移;

(5)该计划是否充分考虑了财产的有序转移;及

(6)为保证有序高效地进行转移所做的任何其他建议。

(c)**实施报告**。——参议院银行、住房与城市事务委员会以及众议院金融服务委员会在收到按照第(b)子条要求提交的报告后6个月内,以及其后的每6个月(直至该计划在所有方面均已得到完全落实),财政部、联邦存款保险公司以及联邦储备委员会各自的监察长应就计划的实施状态向联邦储备委员会、联邦存款保险公司、货币监理署以及储蓄机构监理局联合提供一份书面报告,并应向参议院银行、住房与城市事务委员会以及众议院金融服务委员会提供一份报告复本。

第C子编——联邦存款保险公司

第331条 存款保险改革

(a)**规模区分**。——《联邦存款保险法》第7(b)(2)条[《美国法典》第十二编第1817(b)(2)节]修正如下——

(1)删除第(D)子款;及

(2)第(C)子款重新编号为第(D)子款。

(b)**计征基数**。——联邦存款保险公司应修正其根据《联邦存款保险法》第7(b)(2)条[《美国法典》第十二编第1817(b)(2)节]发布的规章,从而将第7(b)(2)条规定

1817(b)(2)) to define the term "assessment base" with respect to an insured depository institution for purposes of that section 7(b)(2), as an amount equal to —

(1) the average consolidated total assets of the insured depository institution during the assessment period; minus

(2) the sum of —

(A) the average tangible equity of the insured depository institution during the assessment period; and

(B) in the case of an insured depository institution that is a custodial bank (as defined by the Corporation, based on factors including the percentage of total revenues generated by custodial businesses and the level of assets under custody) or a banker's bank (as that term is used in section 5136 of the Revised Statutes (12 U.S.C. 24)), to establish assessments consistent with the definition under section 7(b)(1) of the Federal Deposit Insurance Act (12 U.S.C. 1817(b)(1)) for a custodial bank or a banker's bank.

SEC. 332. ELIMINATION OF PROCYCLICAL ASSESSMENTS.

Section 7(e) of the Federal Deposit Insurance Act is amended —

(1) in paragraph (2) —

(A) by amending subparagraph (B) to read as follows:

"(B) LIMITATION. — The Board of Directors may, in its sole discretion, suspend or limit the declaration of payment of dividends under subparagraph (A).";

(B) by amending subparagraph (C) to read as follows:

"(C) NOTICE AND OPPORTUNITY FOR COMMENT. — The Corporation shall prescribe, by regulation, after notice and opportunity for comment, the method for the declaration, calculation, distribution, and payment of dividends under this paragraph"; and

(C) by striking subparagraphs (D) through (G); and

(2) in paragraph (4)(A) by striking "paragraphs (2)(D) and" and inserting "paragraphs (2) and".

SEC. 333. ENHANCED ACCESS TO INFORMATION FOR DEPOSIT INSURANCE PURPOSES.

(a) Section 7 (a)(2)(B) of the Federal Deposit Insurance Act is amended by striking "agreement" and inserting "consultation".

的参保存款机构“计征基数”确定为如下金额——

(1)参保存款机构在费用计征期间的平均并表资产总额;减去

(2)下列金额的总和——
(A)参保存款机构在费用计征期间的平均有形权益;及

(B)如果参保存款机构为托管银行(托管银行的定义由联邦存款保险公司根据托管业务总收入在总体业务收入中的占比以及托管资产水平等因素界定)或银行家的银行(定义见《美国制定法汇编》(修订版)第5136条(《美国法典》第十二编第24节),则为了能根据《联邦存款保险法》第7(b)(1)条[《美国法典》第十二编第1817(b)(1)节]规定的托管银行的定义或银行家的银行的定义确定计征费,经联邦存款保险有限公司判定确属必要的金额。[1]

第332条　取消顺周期计征费
《联邦存款保险法》第7(e)条修正如下——
(1)在第(2)款中——
(A)第(B)子款修正为:
“(B)**限制**——董事会可完全依其自由裁量权决定暂停根据第(A)子款宣布的股息支付或对其施加限制”;
(B)第(C)子款修正为:
“(C)**通知与征求意见的机会**——联邦存款保险公司在提供通知和征求意见的机会后,应发布规章,对本款中股息宣布、计算、分配和支付的方法作出规定”;及

(C)删除第(D)子款至第(G)子款;及
(2)在第(4)(A)款中,删除“第(2)(D)款和”,替以“第(2)款和”。

第333条　加强关于储蓄保险的信息获取渠道

(a)《联邦存款保险法》第7(a)(2)(B)条修正如下:删除“协议”,替以“磋商”。

1　(B)项中有遗漏,经检索office of the law revision counsel的网站,此处(B)项完整的表述应为“(B) in the case of an insured depository institution that is a custodial bank　(as defined by the Corporation, based on factors including the percentage of total revenues generated by custodial businesses and the level of assets under custody) or a banker's bank (as that term is used in section 5136 of the Revised Statutes　(12 U.S.C. 24)), an amount that the Corporation determines is necessary to establish assessments consistent with the definition under section 7(b)(1) of the Federal Deposit Insurance Act (12 U.S.C. 1817(b)(1)) for a custodial bank or a banker's bank.”,遗漏了“an amount that the Corporation determines is necessary”。在译文中已按完整的表达并进行翻译。——译者注

(b) Section 7(b)(1)(E) of the Federal Deposit Insurance Act is amended —

(1) in clause (i), by striking "such as" and inserting "including"; and

(2) in clause (iii), by striking "Corporation" and inserting "Corporation, except as provided in section 7(a)(2)(B)".

SEC. 334. TRANSITION RESERVE RATIO REQUIREMENTS TO REFLECT NEW ASSESSMENT BASE.

(a) Section 7(b)(3)(B) of the Federal Deposit Insurance Act is amended to read as follows:

"(B) MINIMUM RESERVE RATIO. — The reserve ratio designated by the Board of Directors for any year may not be less than 1.35 percent of estimated insured deposits, or the comparable percentage of the assessment base set forth in paragraph (2)(C).".

(b) Section 3(y)(3) of the Federal Deposit Insurance Act is amended by inserting ", or such comparable percentage of the assessment base set forth in section 7(b)(2)(C)" before the period.

(c) For a period of not less than 5 years after the date of the enactment of this title, the Federal Deposit Insurance Corporation shall make available to the public the reserve ratio and the designated reserve ratio using both estimated insured deposits and the assessment base under section 7(b)(2)(C) of the Federal Deposit Insurance Act.

(d) RESERVE RATIO. — Notwithstanding the timing requirements of section 7(b)(3)(E)(ii) of the Federal Deposit Insurance Act, the Corporation shall take such steps as may be necessary for the reserve ratio of the Deposit Insurance Fund to reach 1.35 percent of estimated insured deposits by September 30, 2020.

(e) OFFSET. — In setting the assessments necessary to meet the requirements of subsection (d), the Corporation shall offset the effect of subsection (d) on insured depository institutions with total consolidated assets of less than $10,000,000,000.

SEC. 335. PERMANENT INCREASE IN DEPOSIT AND SHARE INSURANCE.

(a) PERMANENT INCREASE IN DEPOSIT INSURANCE. — Section 11(a)(1)(E) of the Federal Deposit Insurance Act (12 U.S.C. 1821(a)(1)(E)) is amended —

(1) by striking "$100,000" and inserting "$250,000"; and

(2) by adding at the end the following new sentences:

"Notwithstanding any other provision of law, the increase in the standard maximum deposit insurance amount to $250,000 shall apply to depositors in any institution for which the Corporation was appointed as receiver or conservator on or after January 1, 2008, and before October 3, 2008. The Corporation shall take such actions as are necessary to carry out the requirements of this section with respect to such depositors, without regard to any time limitations under this Act. In implementing this and the preceding 2 sentences, any payment on a deposit claim made by the Corporation as

(b)《联邦存款保险法》第7(b)(1)(E)条修正如下——

(1)在第(i)项中,删除“例如”,替以“包括”;及

(2)在第(iii)项中,删除“公司”,替以“公司,但第7(a)(2)(B)条规定的情形除外”。

第334条 反映新计征基数的过渡准备金率要求

(a)《联邦存款保险法》第7(b)(3)(B)条修正后全文如下:

“(B)**最低准备金率**。——董事会就任何年度指定的准备金率均不得低于预估参保存款的1.35%,或第(2)(C)款规定的计征基数具有可比性的百分比。”

(b)在《联邦存款保险法》第3(y)(3)条的句号前插入“,或第7(b)(2)(C)条规定的计征基数具有可比性的百分比”,作为对该条的修正。

(c)联邦存款保险公司应在本编颁布至少5年以后,向公众公布准备金率以及同时基于参保存款预估数额和《联邦存款保险法》第7(b)(2)(C)条规定的计征基数二者计算出的指定准备金率。

(d)**准备金率**。——无论《联邦存款保险法》第7(b)(3)(E)(ii)条有任何不同的时间要求,联邦存款保险公司都应采取必要措施使存款保险基金的准备金率在2020年9月30日之前达到预估参保存款的1.35%。

(e)**抵销**。——在确定满足第(d)子条要求所需的计征费时,联邦存款保险公司应抵销第(d)子条对并表总资产低于100亿美元的参保存款机构的影响数。

第335条 正式提高储蓄和股份保险金额

(a)**正式提高储蓄保险金额**。——《联邦存款保险法》第11(a)(1)(E)条[《美国法典》第十二编第1821(a)(1)(E)节]修正如下——

(1)删除“10万美元”,替以“25万美元”;及

(2)在该条结尾处增加如下新的内容:

“无论是否存在任何不同法律规定,在2008年1月1日(含)至2008年10月3日之前的期间,任何机构被指定由联邦存款保险公司担任接管人或财产管理人的,该等机构的存款人均得适用提高后的最高标准储蓄保险金额,即25万美元。联邦存款保险公司应采取为达到本条中与该等存款人相关之要求所必要的行动,而不必考虑本法规定的任何时间限制。在实施本句规定及之前两句的规定时,联邦存款保险公司作为接管人或财产管理人依存款人的权利主张向存款人支付的金额超出其被指定为接管人或财产管理人之日有效适用的标准最高储蓄保险数额的部分,应被视为第(B)子款规定

receiver or conservator to a depositor above the standard maximum deposit insurance amount in effect at the time of the appointment of the Corporation as receiver or conservator shall be deemed to be part of the net amount due to the depositor under subparagraph (B)."

(b) PERMANENT INCREASE IN SHARE INSURANCE. — Section 207(k)(5) of the Federal Credit Union Act (12 U.S.C. 1787 (k)(5)) is amended by striking "$100,000" and inserting "$250,000".

SEC. 336. MANAGEMENT OF THE FEDERAL DEPOSIT INSURANCE CORPORATION.

(a) IN GENERAL. — Section 2 of the Federal Deposit Insurance Act (12 U.S.C. 1812) is amended —

(1) in subsection (a)(1)(B), by striking "Director of the Office of Thrift Supervision" and inserting "Director of the Consumer Financial Protection Bureau";

(2) by amending subsection (d)(2) to read as follows:

"(2) ACTING OFFICIALS MAY SERVE. — In the event of a vacancy in the office of the Comptroller of the Currency or the office of Director of the Consumer Financial Protection Bureau and pending the appointment of a successor, or during the absence or disability of the Comptroller of the Currency or the Director of the Consumer Financial Protection Bureau, the acting Comptroller of the Currency or the acting Director of the Consumer Financial Protection Bureau, as the case may be, shall be a member of the Board of Directors in the place of the Comptroller or Director."; and

(3) in subsection (f)(2), by striking "Office of Thrift Supervision" and inserting "Consumer Financial Protection Bureau".

(b) EFFECTIVE DATE. — This section, and the amendments made by this section, shall take effect on the transfer date.

Subtitle D — Other Matters

SEC. 341. BRANCHING.

Notwithstanding the Federal Deposit Insurance Act (12 U.S.C. 1811 et seq.), the Bank Holding Company Act of 1956 (12 U.S.C. 1841 et seq.), or any other provision of Federal or State law, a savings association that becomes a bank may —

(1) continue to operate any branch or agency that the savings association operated immediately before the savings association became a bank; and

(2) establish, acquire, and operate additional branches and agencies at any location

的应向存款人支付的净额。”

(b)**正式提高股份保险金额**。——删除《联邦信贷联盟法》第207(k)(5)条[《美国法典》第十二编第1787(k)(5)节]中的“10万美元”,替以“25万美元”。

第336条 联邦存款保险公司的管理

(a)**一般规定**。——《联邦存款保险法》第2条(《美国法典》第十二编第1812节)修正如下——

(1)在第(a)(1)(B)子条中,删除“储蓄机构监理局局长”,替以“消费者金融保护局局长”;

(2)第(d)(2)子条修正后全文如下:

“(2)**代理官员可代为履职**。——货币监理署署长或消费者金融保护局局长的职位出现空缺且尚未任命继任者,或者货币监理署署长或消费者金融保护局局长无法履职或丧失行为能力的,应由代理货币监理署署长或代理消费者金融保护局局长(视具体情况而定)代其担任理事会成员。”及

(3)删除第(f)(2)子条中的“储蓄机构监理局”,替以“消费者金融保护局”。

(b)**生效日**。——本条及本条作出的修正应于转移日生效。

第D子编——其他事项

第341条 分行设立

不论《联邦存款保险法》(《美国法典》第十二编第1811节及其后条文)、《1956年银行控股公司法》(《美国法典》第十二编第1841节及其后条文)或者任何其他联邦法律或州法律其他条款是否存在任何不同规定,获得银行身份的储蓄协会可以——

(1)继续运营其在获得银行身份前最近的时点所运营的任何分行或代理行;及

(2)在该储蓄协会获得银行身份前最近的时点所运营的分行所在州,设立、收购

within any State in which the savings association operated a branch immediately before the savings association became a bank, if the law of the State in which the branch is located, or is to be located, would permit establishment of the branch if the bank were a State bank chartered by such State.

SEC. 342. OFFICE OF MINORITY AND WOMEN INCLUSION.

(a) OFFICE OF MINORITY AND WOMEN INCLUSION. —

(1) ESTABLISHMENT. —

(A) IN GENERAL. — Except as provided in subparagraph (B), not later than 6 months after the date of enactment of this Act, each agency shall establish an Office of Minority and Women Inclusion that shall be responsible for all matters of the agency relating to diversity in management, employment, and business activities.

(B) BUREAU. — The Bureau shall establish an Office of Minority and Women Inclusion not later than 6 months after the designated transfer date established under section 1062.

(2) TRANSFER OF RESPONSIBILITIES. — Each agency that, on the day before the date of enactment of this Act, assigned the responsibilities described in paragraph (1) (or comparable responsibilities) to another office of the agency shall ensure that such responsibilities are transferred to the Office.

(3) DUTIES WITH RESPECT TO CIVIL RIGHTS LAWS. — The responsibilities described in paragraph (1) do not include enforcement of statutes, regulations, or executive orders pertaining to civil rights, except each Director shall coordinate with the agency administrator, or the designee of the agency administrator, regarding the design and implementation of any remedies resulting from violations of such statutes, regulations, or executive orders.

(b) DIRECTOR. —

(1) IN GENERAL. — The Director of each Office shall be appointed by, and shall report to, the agency administrator. The position of Director shall be a career reserved position in the Senior Executive Service, as that position is defined in section 3132 of title 5, United States Code, or an equivalent designation.

(2) DUTIES. — Each Director shall develop standards for —

(A) equal employment opportunity and the racial, ethnic, and gender diversity of the workforce and senior management of the agency;

(B) increased participation of minority–owned and women–owned businesses in the programs and contracts of the agency, including standards for coordinating technical assistance to such businesses; and

(C) assessing the diversity policies and practices of entities regulated by the agency.

和运营其他分行或代理行,前提是根据该州法律,该银行若为该州特许注册银行将会获许成立该等分行。

第342条　少数族裔与女性融入事务办公室

(a)**少数族裔与女性融入事务办公室**。——

(1)**设立**。——

(A)**一般规定**。——除第(B)子款规定的情形外,每一机关均应在本法颁布之日起6个月内设立少数族裔与女性融入事务办公室,负责该机关在管理、雇佣和业务活动中与多元性相关的全部事宜。

(B)**消费者金融保护局**——消费者金融保护局应在根据第1062条指定的转移日后6个月内设立少数族裔与女性融入事务办公室。

(2)**责任转移**。——各机关在本法颁布日前一天向本机关其他办公室转移了第(1)款规定的责任(或具有可比性的责任)的,应确保将该等责任转移给少数族裔与女性融入事务办公室。

(3)**与民权法相关的职责**——第(1)款所述责任不包括执行与民权相关的制定法、规章或行政命令,但是,在针对违反上述法律、规章或行政命令的行为制定和实施任何救济措施之时,各少数族裔与女性融入事务办公室主任应配合机关负责人或其指定人员的工作。

(b)**少数族裔与女性融入事务办公室主任**——

(1)**一般规定**。——各少数族裔与女性融入事务办公室主任应由机关负责人任命并向机关负责人汇报工作。少数族裔与女性融入事务办公室主任之职应为"高级公务员序列"中的保留职位(定义见《美国法典》第五编第3132节)或同等职位。

(2)**职责**。——少数族裔与女性融入事务办公室主任应制定关于下列各项标准——

(A)机关工作人员和高级管理人员职位的就业机会均等以及种族、民族和性别多元性;

(B)增加少数族裔和女性拥有的企业参与机关的项目和合同的机会,包括用于协调为该等企业提供技术援助的标准;及

(C)评估受机关监管的实体的多元性政策和实践。

(3) OTHER DUTIES. — Each Director shall advise the agency administrator on the impact of the policies and regulations of the agency on minority–owned and women–owned businesses.

(4) RULE OF CONSTRUCTION. — Nothing in paragraph (2)(C) may be construed to mandate any requirement on or otherwise affect the lending policies and practices of any regulated entity, or to require any specific action based on the findings of the assessment.

(c) INCLUSION IN ALL LEVELS OF BUSINESS ACTIVITIES. —

(1) IN GENERAL. — The Director of each Office shall develop and implement standards and procedures to ensure, to the maximum extent possible, the fair inclusion and utilization of minorities, women, and minority–owned and women–owned businesses in all business and activities of the agency at all levels, including in procurement, insurance, and all types of contracts.

(2) CONTRACTS. — The procedures established by each agency for review and evaluation of contract proposals and for hiring service providers shall include, to the extent consistent with applicable law, a component that gives consideration to the diversity of the applicant. Such procedure shall include a written statement, in a form and with such content as the Director shall prescribe, that a contractor shall ensure, to the maximum extent possible, the fair inclusion of women and minorities in the workforce of the contractor and, as applicable, subcontractors.

(3) TERMINATION. —

(A) DETERMINATION. — The standards and procedures developed and implemented under this subsection shall include a procedure for the Director to make a determination whether an agency contractor, and, as applicable, a subcontractor has failed to make a good faith effort to include minorities and women in their workforce.

(B) EFFECT OF DETERMINATION. —

(i) RECOMMENDATION TO AGENCY ADMINISTRATOR. — Upon a determination described in subparagraph (A), the Director shall make a recommendation to the agency administrator that the contract be terminated.

(ii) ACTION BY AGENCY ADMINISTRATOR. — Upon receipt of a recommendation under clause (i), the agency administrator may —

(I) terminate the contract;

(II) make a referral to the Office of Federal Contract Compliance Programs of the Department of Labor; or

(III) take other appropriate action.

(d) APPLICABILITY. — This section shall apply to all contracts of an agency for

(3)**其他职责**——各少数族裔与女性融入事务办公室主任应就各自机关的政策和规章对少数族裔和女性拥有的企业造成之影响,向机关负责人提供建议。

(4)**解释规则**。——第(2)(C)款的任何内容均不得被解释为对任何受监管实体的借贷政策和做法强制施加任何要求或影响,也不要求基于评估结果采取任何具体行动。

(c)**融入各层级的业务活动中**。——

(1)**一般规定**。——各少数族裔与女性融入事务办公室主任应制定并执行相关标准和流程,以确保少数族裔、女性和由少数族裔和女性拥有的企业能够尽可能公平地参与和利用机关各层级的业务和活动(包括采购、保险)以及各种类型的合同。

(2)**合同**。——各机关制定的关于合同建议书和服务提供商聘用的审查和评估流程中,在符合适用的法律的前提下,应有考虑申请者多元性问题的环节。按照该流程,承包商应提供一份按少数族裔与女性融入事务办公室主任规定的格式和内容作出的书面声明,声明其应尽最大可能确保女性和少数族裔公平参与到承包商和分包商(如适用)的工作团队中。

(3)**终止**。——

(A)**判定**。——根据本子条制定和实施的标准和流程应包括一项由少数族裔与女性融入事务办公室主任判定某一机关承包商以及分包商(如适用)是否未尽善意努力将少数族裔和女性纳入其工作团队之中的流程。

(B)**判定的效力**。——

(i)**向机关负责人提出建议**。——合同如被少数族裔与女性融入事务办公室主任作出第(A)子款所述判定,则应建议机关负责人终止该合同。

(ii)**机关负责人采取的行动**。——机关负责人在收到第(i)项规定的建议后,可以——

(I)终止合同;

(II)将其转交劳动部联邦合同合规项目办公室处理;或

(III)采取其他适当行动。

(d)**适用范围**。——本条规定适用于各机关任何类型的服务合同,包括金融机

services of any kind, including the services of financial institutions, investment banking firms, mortgage banking firms, asset management firms, brokers, dealers, financial services entities, underwriters, accountants, investment consultants, and providers of legal services. The contracts referred to in this subsection include all contracts for all business and activities of an agency, at all levels, including contracts for the issuance or guarantee of any debt, equity, or security, the sale of assets, the management of the assets of the agency, the making of equity investments by the agency, and the implementation by the agency of programs to address economic recovery.

(e) REPORTS. — Each Office shall submit to Congress an annual report regarding the actions taken by the agency and the Office pursuant to this section, which shall include —

(1) a statement of the total amounts paid by the agency to contractors since the previous report;

(2) the percentage of the amounts described in paragraph (1) that were paid to contractors described in subsection (c)(1);

(3) the successes achieved and challenges faced by the agency in operating minority and women outreach programs;

(4) the challenges the agency may face in hiring qualified minority and women employees and contracting with qualified minority–owned and women–owned businesses; and

(5) any other information, findings, conclusions, and recommendations for legislative or agency action, as the Director determines appropriate.

(f) DIVERSITY IN AGENCY WORKFORCE. — Each agency shall take affirmative steps to seek diversity in the workforce of the agency at all levels of the agency in a manner consistent with applicable law. Such steps shall include —

(1) recruiting at historically black colleges and universities, Hispanic–serving institutions, women's colleges, and colleges that typically serve majority minority populations;

(2) sponsoring and recruiting at job fairs in urban communities;

(3) placing employment advertisements in newspapers and magazines oriented toward minorities and women;

(4) partnering with organizations that are focused on developing opportunities for minorities and women to place talented young minorities and women in industry internships, summer employment, and full–time positions;

(5) where feasible, partnering with inner–city high schools, girls' high schools, and

构、投资银行公司、抵押贷款银行公司、资产管理公司、经纪商、自营商/交易商、[1]金融服务实体、承销商、会计师、投资顾问以及法律服务提供商所提供的各类服务。本子条所述合同包括机关各个层级所有业务和活动所适用的全部合同,包括任何债务、股权或担保的发行合同或保证合同、资产出售合同、机关资产管理合同、机关股权投资合同的订立以及机关实施的各项经济复苏计划。

(e)**报告**。——各少数族裔与女性融入事务办公室应就其所属机关及少数族裔与女性融入事务办公室本身根据本条采取的行动,向国会提交包括下列内容的年度报告——

(1)自提交上一篇报告以来,该机关向各承包商支付的总金额的说明;

(2)第(1)款所述金额当中支付给第(c)(1)子条所述承包商的金额所占百分比;

(3)该机关执行少数族裔和女性融入计划取得的成就和面临的挑战;

(4)该机关在雇用合格少数族裔和女性雇员以及向少数族裔和女性拥有的企业发包过程中可能面临的挑战;及

(5)少数族裔与女性融入事务办公室主任认为适当的任何其他信息、结果、结论以及对立法或机关行动的建议。

(f)**机关工作人员的多元性**。——各机关应采取平权措施,以便以符合适用的法律的方式,实现机关内各级工作人员的多元性,该等措施应包括——

(1)在传统的黑人院校、西语裔院校、女子学院以及少数族裔占多数的院校进行招聘;

(2)赞助城市社区招聘会,并在该等招聘会上进行招聘;

(3)在以少数族裔和女性为目标读者的报纸杂志上刊登招聘广告;

(4)与专门为少数族裔和女性开拓机会的组织开展合作,以便向有才华的青年少数族裔和青年女性提供实习、暑期工作和全职岗位;

(5)如条件可行,与老城区的高中、女子高中以及少数族裔占多数的高中开展合

1 如前所述,“dealer”一词在证券语境中译为“自营商”,在期货语境中译为“交易商”,但此处语境无法判断是否仅涉及证券,有可能也包括期货在内,所以“dealer”一词译为“自营商/交易商”。——译者注

high schools with majority minority populations to establish or enhance financial literacy programs and provide mentoring; and

(6) any other mass media communications that the Office determines necessary.

(g) DEFINITIONS. — For purposes of this section, the following definitions shall apply:

(1) AGENCY. — The term "agency" means —

(A) the Departmental Offices of the Department of the Treasury;

(B) the Corporation;

(C) the Federal Housing Finance Agency;

(D) each of the Federal reserve banks;

(E) the Board;

(F) the National Credit Union Administration;

(G) the Office of the Comptroller of the Currency;

(H) the Commission; and

(I) the Bureau.

(2) AGENCY ADMINISTRATOR. — The term "agency administrator" means the head of an agency.

(3) MINORITY. — The term "minority" has the same meaning as in section 1204(c) of the Financial Institutions Reform, Recovery, and Enforcement Act of 1989 (12 U.S.C. 1811 note).

(4) MINORITY–OWNED BUSINESS. — The term "minority–owned business" has the same meaning as in section 21A(r)(4)(A) of the Federal Home Loan Bank Act (12 U.S.C. 1441a(r)(4)(A)), as in effect on the day before the transfer date.

(5) OFFICE. — The term "Office" means the Office of Minority and Women Inclusion established by an agency under subsection (a).

(6) WOMEN–OWNED BUSINESS. — The term "women–owned business" has the meaning given the term "women's business" in section 21A(r)(4)(B) of the Federal Home Loan Bank Act (12 U.S.C. 1441a(r)(4)(B)), as in effect on the day before the transfer date.

SEC. 343. INSURANCE OF TRANSACTION ACCOUNTS.

(a) BANKS AND SAVINGS ASSOCIATIONS. —

(1) AMENDMENTS. — Section 11(a)(1) of the Federal Deposit Insurance Act (12 U.S.C. 1821(a)(1)) is amended —

(A) in subparagraph (B) —

(i) by striking "The net amount" and inserting the following:

"(i) IN GENERAL. — Subject to clause (ii), the net amount"; and

作,以建立或加强金融扫盲计划并提供指导;及

(6)少数族裔与女性融入事务办公室判定确属必要的任何其他大众媒体宣传。

(g)**定义**。——就本条而言,下列术语应适用如下定义:

(1)**机关**。——“机关”一词系指——

(A)财政部各部门;
(B)联邦存款保险公司;
(C)联邦住房金融局;
(D)各联邦储备银行;
(E)联邦储备委员会;
(F)国家信贷联盟署;
(G)货币监理署;
(H)证券交易委员会;及
(I)消费者金融保护局。

(2)机关负责人。——“机关负责人”一词系指各机关的负责人。

(3)少数族裔。——“少数族裔”一词的含义以《1989年金融机构改革、复兴与实施法》第1204(c)条(《美国法典》第十二编第1811节注释)的定义为准。

(4)少数族裔拥有的企业——“少数族裔拥有的企业”一词的含义以在转移日前一天有效适用的《联邦住房贷款银行法》第21A(r)(4)(A)条[《美国法典》第十二编第1441a(r)(4)(A)节]的定义为准。

(5)少数族裔与女性融入事务办公室——“少数族裔与女性融入事务办公室”一词系指各机关根据第(a)子条设立的少数族裔与女性融入事务办公室。

(6)女性拥有的企业——“女性拥有的企业”一词的含义以在转移日前一天有效适用的《联邦住房贷款银行法》第21A(r)(4)(B)条[《美国法典》第十二编第1441a(r)(4)(B)节]的定义为准。

第343条　交易账户保险

(a)银行和存款机构。——

(1)修正。——《联邦存款保险法》第11(a)(1)条[《美国法典》第十二编第1821(a)(1)节]修正如下——

(A)在第(B)子款中——

(i)删除“净额”,替以如下内容:

“(i)一般规定。——在不违反第(ii)项规定的前提下,净额”;及

(ii) by adding at the end the following new clauses:

"(ii) INSURANCE FOR NONINTEREST-BEARING TRANSACTION ACCOUNTS. — Notwithstanding clause (i), the Corporation shall fully insure the net amount that any depositor at an insured depository institution maintains in a noninterest-bearing transaction account. Such amount shall not be taken into account when computing the net amount due to such depositor under clause (i).

"(iii) NONINTEREST-BEARING TRANSACTION ACCOUNT DEFINED. — For purposes of this subparagraph, the term 'noninterest-bearing transaction account' means a deposit or account maintained at an insured depository institution —

"(I) with respect to which interest is neither accrued nor paid;

"(II) on which the depositor or account holder is permitted to make withdrawals by negotiable or transferable instrument, payment orders of withdrawal, telephone or other electronic media transfers, or other similar items for the purpose of making payments or transfers to third parties or others; and

"(III) on which the insured depository institution does not reserve the right to require advance notice of an intended withdrawal."; and

(B) in subparagraph (C), by striking "subparagraph (B)" and inserting "subparagraph (B)(i)".

(2) EFFECTIVE DATE. — The amendments made by paragraph (1) shall take effect on December 31, 2010.

(3) PROSPECTIVE REPEAL. — Effective January 1, 2013, section 11(a)(1) of the Federal Deposit Insurance Act (12 U.S.C. 1821(a)(1)), as amended by paragraph (1), is amended —

(A) in subparagraph (B) —

(i) by striking "DEPOSIT. — " and all that follows through "clause (ii), the net amount" and insert "DEPOSIT. — The net amount"; and

(ii) by striking clauses (ii) and (iii); and

(B) in subparagraph (C), by striking "subparagraph (B)(i)" and inserting "subparagraph (B)".

(b) CREDIT UNIONS. —

(1) AMENDMENTS. — Section 207(k)(1) of the Federal Credit Union Act (12 U.S.C. 1787(k)(1)) is amended —

(A) in subparagraph (A) —

(i) by striking "Subject to the provisions of paragraph (2), the net amount" and inserting the following:

"(i) NET AMOUNT OF INSURANCE PAYABLE. — Subject to clause (ii) and the provisions of paragraph (2), the net amount"; and

(ii)在结尾处增加如下新条文:

“(ii)**无息交易账户保险**。——无论第(i)项如何规定,联邦存款保险公司仍应全额承保任何参保存款机构储户在无息交易账户中持有的存款净额。该等金额不应计入根据第(i)项计算的应向该储户支付的净额。

(iii)**无息交易账户的定义**。——就本子款而言,‘无息交易账户’一词系指在参保存款机构持有且符合下列条件的存款或账户——

(I)不产生也不支付利息;

(II)允许储户或账户持有人通过可流通或可转让票据、提款支付指令、电话转账或其他电子媒介转账或者其他类似方式提款,从而实现对第三方或其他方的付款或转账;及

(III)参保存款机构未保留要求储户或账户持有人在提款前先发通知的权利。”及

(B)第(C)子款删除“第(B)子款”,替以“第(B)(i)子款”。

(2)**生效日**。——第(1)款作出的修正应于2010年12月31日生效。

(3)**预期失效**。——经第(1)款修正后的《联邦存款保险法》第11(a)(1)条[《美国法典》第十二编第1821(a)(1)节]加入如下修正,并于2013年1月1日生效——

(A)在第(B)子款中——

(i)删除从“存款。——”直至“第(ii)项,净额”的全部内容,替以“**存款**。——净额”;及

(ii)删除第(ii)项和第(iii)项;及

(B)第(C)子款删除“第(B)(i)子款”,替以“第(B)子款”。

(b)**信贷联盟**。——

(1)**修正**。——《联邦信贷联盟法》第207(k)(1)条[《美国法典》第十二编第1787(k)(1)节]修正如下——

(A)在第(A)子款中——

(i)删除“在不违反第(2)款规定的前提下,净额”,替以如下内容:

“(i)**应付保险净额**。——在不违反第(ii)项及第(2)款规定的前提下,净额”;及

(ii) by adding at the end the following new clauses:

"(ii) INSURANCE FOR NONINTEREST–BEARING TRANSACTION ACCOUNTS. — Notwithstanding clause (i), the Board shall fully insure the net amount that any member or depositor at an insured credit union maintains in a noninterest–bearing transaction account. Such amount shall not be taken into account when computing the net amount due to such member or depositor under clause (i).

"(iii) NONINTEREST–BEARING TRANSACTION ACCOUNT DEFINED. — For purposes of this subparagraph, the term 'noninterest–bearing transaction account' means an account or deposit maintained at an insured credit union —

"(I) with respect to which interest is neither accrued nor paid;

"(II) on which the account holder or depositor is permitted to make withdrawals by negotiable or transferable instrument, payment orders of withdrawal, telephone or other electronic media transfers, or other similar items for the purpose of making payments or transfers to third parties or others; and

"(III) on which the insured credit union does not reserve the right to require advance notice of an intended withdrawal."; and

(B) in subparagraph (B), by striking "subparagraph (A)" and inserting "subparagraph (A)(i)".

(2) EFFECTIVE DATE. — The amendments made by paragraph (1) shall take effect upon the date of the enactment of this Act

(3) PROSPECTIVE REPEAL. — Effective January 1, 2013, section 207(k)(1) of the Federal Credit Union Act (12 U.S.C. 1787(k)(1)), as amended by paragraph (1), is amended —

(A) in subparagraph (A) —

(i) by striking "(i) NET AMOUNT OF INSURANCE PAYABLE. —" and all that follows through "paragraph (2), the net amount" and inserting "Subject to the provisions of paragraph (2), the net amount"; and

(ii) by striking clauses (ii) and (iii); and

(B) in subparagraph (B), by striking "subparagraph (A)(i)" and inserting "subparagraph (A)".

(ii)在结尾处增加如下新条文:

“(ii)**无息交易账户保险**。——无论第(i)项如何规定,联邦储备委员会仍应全额承保任何参保信贷联盟成员或储户在无息交易账户中持有的存款净额。计算根据第(i)项应向该成员或储户支付的净额时,不应计入该等金额。

(iii)**无息交易账户的定义**。——就本子款而言,‘无息交易账户’一词系指在参保信贷联盟持有且符合下列条件的账户或存款——

(I)不产生也不支付利息;

(II)账户持有人或储户可以通过可流通或可转让票据、提款支付指示、电话或者其他电子媒介转账手段或其他类似方式进行提款,从而向第三方或其他方付款或转账;及

(III)参保信贷联盟未保留要求储户或账户持有人在提款前事先发出通知的权利”;及

(B)第(B)子款删除“第(A)子款”,替以“第(A)(i)子款”。

(2)**生效日**。——第(1)款作出的修正应于本法颁布之日生效。

(3)**预期失效**。——经第(1)款修正后的《联邦信贷联盟法》第207(k)(1)条[《美国法典》第十二编第1787(k)(1)节]修正如下,并于2013年1月1日生效——

(A)在第(A)子款中——

(i)删除“(i)**应付保险净额**。——”直至“第(2)款,净额”的全部内容,替以“在不违反第(2)款规定的前提下,净额”;及

(ii)删除第(ii)项和第(iii)项;及

(B)第(B)子款删除“第(A)(i)子款”,替以“第(A)子款”。

Subtitle E — Technical and Conforming Amendments

SEC. 351. EFFECTIVE DATE.

Except as provided in section 364 (a),the amendments made by this subtitle shall take effect on the transfer date.

SEC. 352. BALANCED BUDGET AND EMERGENCY DEFICIT CONTROL ACT OF 1985.

Section 256 (h) of the Balanced Budget and Emergency Deficit Control Act of 1985 (2 U.S.C. 906 (h)) is amended —

(1) in paragraph (4),by striking subparagraphs (C) and (G); and

(2) by redesignating subparagraphs (D), (E), (F),and (H) as subparagraphs (C), (D), (E),and (F),respectively.

SEC. 353. BANK ENTERPRISE ACT OF 1991.

Section 232 (a) of the Bank Enterprise Act of 1991 (12 U.S.C. 1834 (a)) is amended —

(1) in the subsection heading,by striking "BY FEDERAL RESERVE BOARD";

(2) in paragraph (1) —

(A) by striking "The Board of Governors of the Federal Reserve System," and inserting "The Comptroller of the Currency"; and

(B) by striking "section 7 (b) (2) (H)" and inserting "section 7 (b) (2) (E)";

(3) in paragraph (2) (A),by striking "Board" and inserting "Comptroller"; and

(4) in paragraph (3) —

(A) by redesignating subparagraphs (A) through (C) as subparagraphs (B) through (D),respectively; and

(B) by inserting before subparagraph (B) the following:

" (A) COMPTROLLER. — The term 'Comptroller' means the Comptroller of the Currency.".

SEC. 354. BANK HOLDING COMPANY ACT OF 1956.

The Bank Holding Company Act of 1956 (12 U.S.C. 1841 et seq.) is amended —

(1) in section 2 (j) (3) (12 U.S.C. 1841 (j) (3)),strike "Director of the Office of Thrift Supervision" and inserting "appropriate Federal banking agency";

(2) in section 4 (12 U.S.C. 1843) —

(A) in subsection (i) —

第E子编——技术性和一致性修正

第351条　生效日

除第364(a)条规定的情形外,本子编作出的修正应于转移日生效。

第352条　《1985年平衡预算和紧急赤字控制法》

《1985年平衡预算和紧急赤字控制法》第256(h)条[《美国法典》第二编第906(h)节]修正如下——

(1)在第(4)款中,删除第(C)子款和第(G)子款;及

(2)第(D)子款、第(E)子款、第(F)子款和第(H)子款分别重新编号为第(C)子款、第(D)子款、第(E)子款和第(F)子款。

第353条　《1991年银行企业法》

《1991年银行企业法》第232(a)条[《美国法典》第十二编第1834(a)节]修正如下——

(1)删除该子条标题中的“**由联邦储备委员会**”;

(2)在第(1)款中——

(A)删除“联邦储备委员会,”替以“货币监理署署长”;及

(B)删除“第7(b)(2)(H)条”,替以“第7(b)(2)(E)条”;

(3)在第(2)(A)款中,删除“联邦储备委员会”,替以“货币监理署署长”;及

(4)在第(3)款中——

(A)第(A)子款至第(C)子款分别重新编号为第(B)子款至第(D)子款;及

(B)在第(B)子款前插入如下内容:

“(A)**货币监理署署长**——‘货币监理署署长’一词系指美国货币监理署署长。”

第354条　《1956年银行控股公司法》

《1956年银行控股公司法》(《美国法典》第十二编第1841节及其后条文)修正如下——

(1)在第2(j)(3)条[《美国法典》第十二编第1841(j)(3)节]中,删除“储蓄机构监理局局长”,替以“相应的联邦银行业监管机关”;

(2)在第4条(《美国法典》第十二编第1843节)中——

(A)第(i)子条——

(i) in paragraph (4)—

(I) in subparagraph (A)—

(aa) in the subparagraph heading,by striking "TO DIRECTOR"; and

(bb) by striking "Board" and all that follows through the end of the subparagraph and inserting "Board shall solicit comments and recommendations from—

"(i) the Comptroller of the Currency,with respect to the acquisition of a Federal savings association; and

"(ii) the Federal Deposit Insurance Corporation,with respect to the acquisition of a State savings association.".

(II) in subparagraph (B), by striking "Director" each place that term appears and inserting "Comptroller of the Currency or the Federal Deposit Insurance Corporation,as applicable,";

(ii) in paragraph (5)—

(I) in subparagraph (B),by striking "Director with" and inserting "Comptroller of the Currency or the Federal Deposit Insurance Corporation,as applicable,with"; and

(II) by striking "Director" each place that term appears and inserting "Comptroller of the Currency or the Federal Deposit Insurance Corporation";

(iii) in paragraph (6),by striking "Director" and inserting "Comptroller of the Currency or the Federal Deposit Insurance Corporation,as applicable,"; and

(iv) by striking paragraph (7); and

(3) in section 5 (f) (12 U.S.C. 1844 (f))—

(A) by striking "subpena" each place that term appears and inserting "subpoena";

(B) by striking "subpenas" each place that term appears and inserting "subpoenas"; and

(C) by striking "subpenaed" and inserting "subpoenaed".

SEC. 355. BANK HOLDING COMPANY ACT AMENDMENTS OF 1970.

Section 106 (b) (1) of the Bank Holding Company Act Amendments of 1970 (12 U.S.C. 1972 (1)) is amended in the undesignated matter following subparagraph (E) by inserting "issue such regulations as are necessary to carry out this section,and,in consultation with the Comptroller of the Currency and the Federal Deposit Insurance Company,may" after "The Board may".

SEC. 356. BANK PROTECTION ACT OF 1968.

The Bank Protection Act of 1968 (12 U.S.C. 1881 et seq.) is amended—

(1) in section 2 (12 U.S.C. 1881),by striking "the term" and all that follows through the end of the section and inserting "the term 'Federal supervisory agency' means the appropriate Federal banking agency,as defined in section 3 (q) of the Federal Deposit

(i)第(4)款——

(I)第(A)子款——

(aa)删除该子款标题中的“**向储蓄机构监理局局长**”;及

(bb)删除从“联邦储备委员会”直至该子款结尾处的全部内容,替以“联邦储备委员会应向下列各方征求意见和建议——

(i)涉及联邦储蓄协会收购的,向货币监理署署长征求意见和建议;及

(ii)涉及州储蓄协会收购的,向联邦存款保险公司征求意见和建议。”

(II)第(B)子款删除本子款出现的所有“储蓄机构监理局局长”,全部替以“货币监理署署长或联邦存款保险公司(视具体情况而定),”;

(ii)第(5)款——

(I)第(B)子款删除“储蓄机构监理局局长”,替以“货币监理署署长或联邦存款保险公司(视具体情况而定),”;及

(II)删除本款出现的所有“储蓄机构监理局局长”,全部替以“货币监理署署长或联邦存款保险公司”;

(iii)第(6)款删除“储蓄机构监理局局长”,替以“货币监理署署长或联邦存款保险公司(视具体情况而定),”;及

(iv)删除第(7)款;及

(3)在第5(f)条[《美国法典》第十二编第1844(f)节]中——

(A)删除本条出现的所有“传票”的错误拼写“subpena”,全部替以正确拼写“subpoena”;

(B)删除本条出现的所有“传票”的错误拼写“subpenas”,全部替以正确拼写“subpoenas”;及

(C)删除“被签发传票”的错误拼写“subpenaed”,替以正确拼写“subpoenaed”。

第355条 《1970年银行控股公司法修正案》

《1970年银行控股公司法修正案》第106(b)(1)条[《美国法典》第十二编第1972(1)节]第(E)子款后的无编号内容修正如下:在“联邦储备委员会可以”之后插入“发布对实施本条规定确属必要的规章,且在与货币监理署署长和联邦存款保险公司磋商后,可以”。

第356条 《1968年银行保护法》

《1968年银行保护法》(《美国法典》第十二编第1881节及其后条文)修正如下——

(1)在第2条(《美国法典》第十二编第1881节)中,删除从“期限”直至该条结尾处的全部内容,替以“‘联邦监管机关’一词系指《联邦存款保险法》第3(q)条[《美国法典》第十二编第1813(q)节]定义的相应的联邦银行业监管机关。”;

Insurance Act (12 U.S.C. 1813 (q)) . ";

(2) in section 3 (12 U.S.C. 1882) ,by striking "and loan" each place that term appears; and

(3) in section 5 (12 U.S.C. 1884) ,by striking "and loan".

SEC. 357. BANK SERVICE COMPANY ACT.

The Bank Service Company Act (12 U.S.C. 1861 et seq.) is amended —

(1) in section 1 (b) (4) (12 U.S.C. 1861 (b) (4)) —

(A) by inserting after "an insured bank," the following: "a savings association,";

(B) by striking "Director of the Office of Thrift Supervision" and inserting "appropriate Federal banking agency"; and

(C) by striking ",the Federal Savings and Loan Insurance Corporation,";

(2) in section 1 (b) (5) ,by striking "term 'insured depository institution' has the same meaning as in section 3 (c) " and inserting "terms 'depository institution' and 'savings association' have the same meanings as in section 3"; and

(3) in section 7 (c) (2) (12 U.S.C. 1867 (c) (2)) ,by inserting "each" after "notify"

.

SEC. 358. COMMUNITY REINVESTMENT ACT OF 1977.

The Community Reinvestment Act of 1977 (12 U.S.C. 2901 et seq.) is amended —

(1) in section 803 (12 U.S.C. 2902) —

(A) in paragraph (1) —

(i) in subparagraph (A) , by inserting "and Federal savings associations (the deposits of which are insured by the Federal Deposit Insurance Corporation) " after "banks";

(ii) in subparagraph (B) , by striking "and bank holding companies" and inserting ",ank holding companies,and savings and loan holding companies"; and

(iii) in subparagraph (C) , by striking "; and" and inserting ",and State savings associations (the deposits of which are insured by the Federal Deposit Insurance Corporation) . "; and

(B) by striking paragraph (2) (relating to the Office of Thrift Supervision) ,as added by section 744 (q) of the Financial Institutions Reform, Recovery, and Enforcement Act of 1989 (Public Law 101-73; 103 Stat. 440) ; and

(2) in section 806 (12 U.S.C. 2905) ,by inserting ",except that the Comptroller of the Currency shall prescribe regulations applicable to savings associations and the Board of Governors shall prescribe regulations applicable to insured State member banks,bank holding companies and savings and loan holding companies," after "supervisory agency".

SEC. 359. CRIME CONTROL ACT OF 1990.

The Crime Control Act of 1990 is amended —

(2)在第3条(《美国法典》第十二编第1882节)中,删除本条出现的所有“及贷款”;及

(3)在第5条(《美国法典》第十二编第1884节)中,删除“及贷款”。

第357条 《银行服务公司法》

《银行服务公司法》(《美国法典》第十二编第1861节及其后条文)修正如下——

(1)在第1(b)(4)条[《美国法典》第十二编第1861(b)(4)节]中——

(A)在“参保银行”之后插入如下内容:“储蓄协会,”;

(B)删除“储蓄机构监理局局长”,替以“相应的联邦银行业监管机关”;及

(C)删除“,联邦储贷保险公司,”;

(2)在第1(b)(5)条中,删除“‘参保存款机构’一词的含义以第3(c)条的规定为准”,替以“‘存款机构’和‘储蓄协会’的含义以第3条的定义为准”;及

(3)在第7(c)(2)条[《美国法典》第十二编第1867(c)(2)节]中,在“通知”后加入“每一”。

第358条 《1977年社区再投资法》

《1977年社区再投资法》(《美国法典》第十二编第2901节及其后条文)修正如下——

(1)在第803条(《美国法典》第十二编第2902节)中——

(A)第(1)款——

(i)第(A)子款在“银行”之后插入“及联邦储蓄协会(其存款已由联邦存款保险公司承保)”;

(ii)第(B)子款删除“以及银行控股公司”,替以“,银行控股公司以及储贷控股公司”;及

(iii)第(C)子款删除“;及”,替以“,及州储蓄协会(其存款已由联邦存款保险公司承保)。”;及

(B)删除《1989年金融机构改革、复兴与实施法》第744(q)条(第101—73号公法;《美国制定法汇编》第103卷第440页)增加的第(2)款(关于储蓄机构监理局的规定);及

(2)在第806条(《美国法典》第十二编第2905节)中,在“监管机关”之后插入“,但是,货币监理署署长应制定适用于储蓄协会的规章,且联邦储备委员会应制定适用于参保州成员银行、银行控股公司以及储贷控股公司的规章,”。

第359条 《1990年犯罪控制法》

《1990年犯罪控制法》修正如下——

(1) in section 2539 (c) (2) (28 U.S.C. 509 note) —

(A) by striking subparagraphs (C) and (D) ; and

(B) by redesignating subparagraphs (E) through (H) as subparagraphs (C) through (G) , respectively; and

(2) in section 2554 (b) (2) (Public Law 101-647; 104 Stat. 4890) —

(A) in subparagraph (A) , by striking ",the Director of the Office of Thrift Supervision," and inserting "the Comptroller of the Currency"; and

(B) in subparagraph (B) , by striking ",the Director" and all that follows through "Trust Corporation" and inserting "or the Federal Deposit Insurance Corporation".

SEC. 360. DEPOSITORY INSTITUTION MANAGEMENT INTERLOCKS ACT.

The Depository Institution Management Interlocks Act (12 U.S.C. 3201 et seq.) is amended —

(1) in section 207 (12 U.S.C. 3206) —

(A) in paragraph (1) ,by inserting before the comma at the end the following: "and Federal savings associations (the deposits of which are insured by the Federal Deposit Insurance Corporation) ";

(B) in paragraph (2) ,by striking ",and bank holding companies" and inserting ",bank holding companies,and savings and loan holding companies";

(C) in paragraph (3) ,by striking "Corporation," and inserting "Corporation and State savings associations (the deposits of which are insured by the Federal Deposit Insurance Corporation) ,";

(D) by striking paragraph (4) ;

(E) by redesignating paragraphs (5) and (6) as paragraphs (4) and (5) , respectively; and

(F) in paragraph (5) , as so redesignated,by striking "through (5) " and inserting "through (4) ";

(2) in section 209 (12 U.S.C. 3207) —

(A) in paragraph (1) , by inserting before the comma at the end the following: "and Federal savings associations (the deposits of which are insured by the Federal Deposit Insurance Corporation) ";

(B) in paragraph (2) , by striking ",and bank holding companies" and inserting ",bank holding companies,and savings and loan holding companies";

(C) in paragraph (3) , by striking "Corporation," and inserting "Corporation and State savings associations (the deposits of which are insured by the Federal Deposit Insurance Corporation) ,";

(1)在第2539(c)(2)条(《美国法典》第二十八编第509节注释)中——

(A)删除第(C)子款和第(D)子款;及

(B)第(E)子款至第(H)子款分别重新编号为第(C)子款至第(G)子款;及

(2)在第2554(b)(2)条(第101—647号公法;《美国制定法汇编》第104卷第4890页)中——

(A)第(A)子款删除",储蓄机构监理局局长,"替以"货币监理署署长";及

(B)第(B)子款删除从",储蓄机构监理局局长,"直至"信托公司"的全部内容,替以"或联邦存款保险公司"。

第360条 《禁止存款机构管理层交叉任职法》

《禁止存款机构管理层交叉任职法》(《美国法典》第十二编第3201节及其后条文)修正如下——

(1)在第207条(《美国法典》第十二编第3206节)中——

(A)第(1)款结尾处的逗号前插入如下内容:"及联邦储蓄协会(其存款已由联邦存款保险公司承保)";

(B)第(2)款删除",及银行控股公司",替以",银行控股公司及储贷控股公司";

(C)第(3)款删除"联邦存款保险公司",替以"联邦存款公司及州储蓄协会(其存款已由联邦存款保险公司承保),";

(D)删除第(4)款;

(E)第(5)款和第(6)款分别重新编号为第(4)款和第(5)款;及

(F)第(5)款(以重新编号后的序号为准)删除"至第(5)款",替以"至第(4)款";

(2)在第209条(《美国法典》第十二编第3207节)中——

(A)第(1)款结尾处的逗号前插入如下内容:"及联邦储蓄协会(其存款已由联邦存款保险公司承保)";

(B)第(2)款删除",及银行控股公司",替以",银行控股公司及储贷控股公司";

(C)第(3)款删除"联邦存款保险公司",替以"联邦存款保险公司及州储蓄协会(其存款已由联邦存款保险公司承保)";

(D) by striking paragraph (4); and

(E) by redesignating paragraph (5) as paragraph (4); and

(3) in section 210 (a) (12 U.S.C. 3208 (a))—

(A) by striking "his" and inserting "the"; and

(B) by inserting "of the Attorney General" after "enforcement functions".

SEC. 361. EMERGENCY HOMEOWNERS' RELIEF ACT

Section 110 of the Emergency Homeowners' Relief Act (12 U.S.C. 2709) is amended in the second sentence,by striking "Home Loan Bank Board,the Federal Savings and Loan Insurance Corporation" and inserting "Housing Finance Agency".

SEC. 362. FEDERAL CREDIT UNION ACT.

The Federal Credit Union Act (12 U.S.C. 1751 et seq.) is amended—

(1) in section 107 (8) (12 U.S.C. 1757 (8)), by striking "or the Federal Savings and Loan Insurance Corporation";

(2) in section 205 (12 U.S.C. 1785)—

(A) in subsection (b) (2) (G) (i),by striking "the Office of Thrift Supervision and"; and

(B) in subsection (i) (1),by striking "or the Federal Savings and Loan Insurance Corporation"; and

(3) in section 206 (g) (7) (12 U.S.C. 1786 (g) (7))—

(A) in subparagraph (A)—

(i) in clause (ii), by striking "(b) (8)" and inserting "(b) (9)";

(ii) in clause (v)—

(I) by striking "depository" and inserting "financial"; and

(II) by adding "and" at the end;

(iii) in clause (vi)—

(I) by striking "Board" and inserting "Agency"; and

(II) by striking "; and" and inserting a period; and

(iv) by striking clause (vii); and

(B) in subparagraph (D)—

(i) in clause (iii), by adding "and" at the end;

(ii) in clause (iv)—

(I) by striking "Board" and inserting "Agency"; and

(II) by striking "and" at the end; and

(iii) by striking clause (v).

SEC. 363. FEDERAL DEPOSIT INSURANCE ACT.

The Federal Deposit Insurance Act (12 U.S.C. 1811 et seq.) is amended—

(1) in section 3 (12 U.S.C. 1813)—

(D)删除第(4)款;及

(E)第(5)款重新编号为第(4)款;及

(3)在第210(a)条[《美国法典》第十二编第3208(a)节]中——

(A)删除“其”,替以“该”;及

(B)在“执法职能”前插入“总检察长的”。

第361条 《紧急业主救济法》

《紧急业主救济法》第110条(《美国法典》第十二编第2709节)第二句修正如下:删除“住房贷款银行委员会、联邦储贷保险公司”,替以“联邦住房金融局”。

第362条 《联邦信贷联盟法》

《联邦信贷联盟法》(《美国法典》第十二编第1751节及其后条文)修正如下——

(1)在第107(8)条[《美国法典》第十二编第1757(8)节]中,删除“或联邦储贷保险公司”;

(2)在第205条(《美国法典》第十二编第1785节)中——

(A)第(b)(2)(G)(i)子条删除“储蓄机构监理局及”;及

(B)第(i)(1)子条删除“或联邦储贷保险公司”;及

(3)在第206(g)(7)条[《美国法典》第十二编第1786(g)(7)节]中——

(A)第(A)子款——

(i)第(ii)项删除“(b)(8)”,替以“(b)(9)”;

(ii)第(v)项——

(I)删除“存款”,替以“金融”;及

(II)结尾处增加“及”;

(iii)在第(vi)项中——

(I)删除“联邦储备委员会”,替以“联邦住房金融局”;及

(II)删除“;及”,替以句号;及

(iv)删除第(vii)项;及

(B)第(D)子款——

(i)第(iii)项结尾处增加“及”;

(ii)第(iv)项——

(I)删除“联邦储备委员会”,替以“联邦住房金融局”;及

(II)删除结尾处的“及”;及

(iii)删除第(v)项。

第363条 《联邦存款保险法》

《联邦存款保险法》(《美国法典》第十二编第1811节及其后条文)修正如下——

(1)在第3条(《美国法典》第十二编第1813节)中——

(A) in subsection (b) (1) (C), by striking "Director of the Office of Thrift Supervision" and inserting "Comptroller of the Currency";

(B) in subsection (l) (5), in the matter preceding subparagraph (A), by striking "Director of the Office of Thrift Supervision,"; and

(C) in subsection (z), by striking "the Director of the Office of Thrift Supervision,";

(2) in section 7 (12 U.S.C. 1817) —

(A) in subsection (a) —

(i) in paragraph (2) —

(I) in subparagraph (A) —

(aa) in the first sentence, by striking "the Director of the Office of Thrift Supervision,";

(bb) in the second sentence —

(AA) by striking "the Director of the Office of Thrift Supervision," and inserting "to"; and

(BB) by inserting "to" before "any Federal home"; and

(cc) by striking "Finance Board" each place that term appears and inserting "Finance Agency"; and

(II) in subparagraph (B), by striking "the Comptroller of the Currency, the Board of Governors of the Federal Reserve System, and the Director of the Office of Thrift Supervision," and inserting "the Comptroller of the Currency and the Board of Governors of the Federal Reserve System,";

(ii) in paragraph (3), in the first sentence, by striking "Comptroller of the Currency, the Chairman of the Board of Governors of the Federal Reserve System, and the Director of the Office of Thrift Supervision." and inserting "Comptroller of the Currency, and the Chairman of the Board of Governors of the Federal Reserve System.";

(iii) in paragraph (6), by striking "section 232 (a) (3) (C)" and inserting "section 232 (a) (3) (D)"; and

(iv) in paragraph (7), by striking ", the Director of the Office of Thrift Supervision,"; and

(B) in subsection (n) —

(i) in the heading, by striking "DIRECTOR OF THE OFFICE OF THRIFT SUPERVISION" and inserting "COMPTROLLER OF THE CURRENCY";

(ii) in the first sentence —

(I) by striking "the Director of the Office of Thrift Supervision" and inserting "the Comptroller of the Currency"; and

(II) by inserting "Federal" before "savings associations";

(iii) in the third sentence, by striking ", the Financing Corporation, and the Resolution Funding Corporation"; and

(A)第(b)(1)(C)子条删除“储蓄机构监理局局长”,替以“货币监理署署长”;

(B)第(l)(5)子条在第(A)子款之前的内容删除“储蓄机构监理局局长,”;及

(C)第(z)子条删除“储蓄机构监理局局长,”;
(2)在第7条(《美国法典》第十二编第1817节)中——
(A)第(a)子条——
(i)第(2)款——
(I)第(A)子款——
(aa)第一句删除“储蓄机构监理局局长,”;
(bb)第二句——
(AA)删除“储蓄机构监理局局长,”,替以“向”;及

(BB)在“任何联邦住房”前插入“向”;及
(cc)删除本子款出现的所有“金融委员会”,全部替以“金融局”;及

(II)第(B)子款删除“货币监理署署长、联邦储备委员会以及储蓄机构监理局局长,”替以“货币监理署署长和联邦储备委员会,”;

(ii)第(3)款第一句删除“货币监理署署长、联邦储备委员会主席以及储蓄机构监理局局长。”替以“货币监理署署长和联邦储备委员会主席。”;

(iii)第(6)款删除“第232(a)(3)(C)条”,替以“第232(a)(3)(D)条”;及

(iv)第(7)款删除“,储蓄机构监理局局长,”;及

(B)第(n)子条——
(i)删除标题中的“**储蓄机构监理局局长**,”,替以“**货币监理署署长**”;

(ii)第一句——
(I)删除“储蓄机构监理局局长”,替以“货币监理署署长”;及

(II)在“储蓄协会”前插入“联邦”;
(iii)第三句删除“、融资公司以及清盘融资公司”;及

(iv) by striking "the Director" each place that term appears and inserting "the Comptroller";

(3) in section 8 (12 U.S.C. 1818)—

(A) in subsection (a) (8) (B) (ii) ,in the last sentence, by striking "Director of the Office of Thrift Supervision" each place that term appears and inserting "Comptroller of the Currency";

(B) in subsection (b) (3)—

(i) by inserting "any savings and loan holding company and any subsidiary (other than a depository institution) of a savings and loan holding company (as such terms are defined in section 10 of Home Owners' Loan Act)), any noninsured State member bank" after "Bank Holding Company Act of 1956,"; and

(ii) by inserting "or against a savings and loan holding company or any subsidiary thereof (other than a depository institution or a subsidiary of such depository institution) " before the period at the end;

(C) by striking paragraph (9) of subsection (b) and inserting the following new paragraph:

" (9) [Repealed]".

(D) in subsection (e) (7)—

(i) in subparagraph (A)—

(I) in clause (v) ,by inserting "and" after the semicolon;

(II) in clause (vi)—

(aa) by striking "Board" and inserting "Agency"; and

(bb) by striking "; and" and inserting a period; and

(III) by striking clause (vii) ; and

(ii) in subparagraph (D)—

(I) in clause (iii), by inserting "and" after the semicolon;

(II) in clause (iv)—

(aa) by striking "Board" and inserting "Agency"; and

(bb) by striking "; and" and inserting a period; and

(III) by striking clause (v);

(E) in subsection (j)—

(i) in paragraph (2), by striking ", or as a savings association under subsection (b) (9) of this section";

(ii) in paragraph (3), by inserting "or" after the semicolon;

(iii) in paragraph (4), by striking "; or" and inserting a comma; and

(iv) by striking paragraph (5);

(F) in subsection (o), by striking "Director of the Office of Thrift Supervision" and

(iv)删除本子条出现的所有“储蓄机构监理局局长”,全部替以“货币监理署署长”;

(3)在第8条(《美国法典》第十二编第1818节)中——

(A)第(a)(8)(B)(ii)子条最后一句删除本句出现的所有“储蓄机构监理局局长”,全部替以“货币监理署署长”;

(B)第(b)(3)子条——

(i)“《1956年银行控股公司法》,”之后插入“任何储贷控股公司及其任何子公司(但存款机构除外)(上述词语定义见《业主贷款法》第10条)、任何未参保州成员银行”;及

(ii)结尾处的句号前插入“或针对储贷控股公司或其任何子公司(但存款机构或该等存款机构的子公司除外)”;

(C)删除第(b)子条第(9)款,替以如下新款:

“(9)[已废止]”。

(D)第(e)(7)子条——

(i)第(A)子款——

(I)第(v)项在分号之后插入“及”;

(II)第(vi)项——

(aa)删除“联邦储备委员会”,替以“联邦住房金融局”;及

(bb)删除“;及”,替以句号;及

(III)删除第(vii)项;及

(ii)第(D)子款——

(I)第(iii)项在分号之后插入“及”;

(II)第(iv)项——

(aa)删除“联邦储备委员会”,替以“联邦住房金融局”;及

(bb)删除“;及”,替以句号;及

(III)删除第(v)项;

(E)第(j)子条——

(i)第(2)款删除“,或本条第(b)(9)子条规定的储蓄协会”;

(ii)第(3)款在分号之后插入“或”;

(iii)第(4)款删除“;或”,替以逗号;及

(iv)删除第(5)款;

(F)第(o)子条删除“储蓄机构监理局局长”,替以“货币监理署署长”;及

inserting "Comptroller of the Currency"; and

(G) in subsection (w)(3)(A), by striking "and the Office of Thrift Supervision";

(4) in section 10 (12 U.S.C. 1820)—

(A) in subsection (d)(5), by striking "or the Resolution Trust Corporation" each place that term appears; and

(B) in subsection (k)(5)(B)—

(i) in clause (ii), by inserting "and" after the semicolon;

(ii) in clause (iii), by striking "; and" and inserting a period; and

(iii) by striking clause (iv);

(5) in section 11 (12 U.S.C. 1821)—

(A) in subsection (c)—

(i) in paragraph (2)(A)(ii), by striking "(other than section 21A of the Federal Home Loan Bank Act)";

(ii) in paragraph (4), by striking "Except as otherwise provided in section 21A of the Federal Home Loan Bank Act and notwithstanding" and inserting "Notwithstanding";

(iii) in paragraph (6)—

(I) in the heading, by striking "DIRECTOR OF THE OFFICE OF THRIFT SUPERVISION" and inserting "COMPTROLLER OF THE CURRENCY";

(II) in subparagraph (A)—

(aa) by striking "or the Resolution Trust Corporation"; and

(bb) by striking "Director of the Office of Thrift Supervision" and inserting "Comptroller of the Currency"; and

(III) by amending subparagraph (B) to read as follows:

"(B) RECEIVER.—The Corporation may, at the discretion of the Comptroller of the Currency, be appointed receiver and the Corporation may accept any such appointment.";

(iv) in paragraph (12)(A), by striking "or the Resolution Trust Corporation";

(B) in subsection (d)—

(i) in paragraph (17)(A), by striking "or the Director of the Office of Thrift Supervision"; and

(ii) in paragraph (18)(B), by striking "or the Director of the Office of Thrift Supervision";

(C) in subsection (m)—

(i) in paragraph (9), by striking "or the Director of the Office of Thrift Supervision, as appropriate";

(ii) in paragraph (16), by striking "or the Director of the Office of Thrift Supervision, as appropriate" each place that term appears; and

(iii) in paragraph (18), by striking "or the Director of the Office of Thrift Supervision,

(G)第(w)(3)(A)子条删除“及储蓄机构监理局”;

(4)在第10条(《美国法典》第十二编第1820节)中——

(A)第(d)(5)子条删除本条出现的所有的“或清盘信托公司”;及

(B)第(k)(5)(B)子条——

(i)第(ii)项在分号之后插入“及”;

(ii)第(iii)项删除“;及”,替以句号;及

(iii)删除第(iv)项;

(5)在第11条(《美国法典》第十二编第1821节)中——

(A)第(c)子条——

(i)第(2)(A)(ii)款删除“(但《联邦住房贷款银行法》第21A条除外)”;

(ii)第(4)款删除“除《联邦住房贷款银行法》第21A条另有规定的情形外,且尽管”,替以“尽管”;

(iii)第(6)款——

(I)删除标题中的“**储蓄机构监理局局长**”,替以“**货币监理署署长**”;

(II)第(A)子款——

(aa)删除“或清盘信托公司”;及

(bb)删除“储蓄机构监理局局长”,替以“货币监理署署长”;及

(III)第(B)子款修正后全文如下:

“(B)接管人。——货币监理署署长依其自由裁量权指定联邦存款保险公司担任接管人,且联邦存款保险公司可接受任何该等指定。”

(iv)第(12)(A)款删除“或清盘信托公司”;

(B)第(d)子条——

(i)第(17)(A)款删除“或储蓄机构监理局局长”;及

(ii)第(18)(B)款删除“或储蓄机构监理局局长”;

(C)第(m)子条——

(i)第(9)款删除“或储蓄机构监理局局长(视具体情况而定)”;

(ii)第(16)款删除所有的“或储蓄机构监理局局长(视具体情况而定)”;及

(iii)第(18)款删除所有的“或储蓄机构监理局局长(视具体情况而定)”;

as appropriate" each place that term appears;

(D) in subsection (n)—

(i) in paragraph (1) (A)—

(I) by striking ", or the Director of the Office of Thrift Supervision,with respect to" and inserting "or"; and

(II) by striking "applicable,," and inserting "applicable,";

(ii) in paragraph (2)(A), by striking "or the Director of the Office of Thrift Supervision";

(iii) in paragraph (4)(D), by striking "and the Director of the Office of Thrift Supervision,as appropriate,";

(iv) in paragraph (4)(G), by striking "and the Director of the Office of Thrift Supervision,as appropriate,"; and

(v) in paragraph (12) (B)—

(I) by inserting "as" after "shall appoint the Corporation";

(II) by striking "or the Director of the Office of Thrift Supervision,as appropriate," each place such term appears;

(E) in subsection (p)—

(i) in paragraph (2) (B), by striking "the Corporation,the FSLIC Resolution Fund,or the Resolution Trust Corporation," and inserting "or the Corporation,"; and

(ii) in paragraph (3)(B), by striking ",the FSLIC Resolution Fund,the Resolution Trust Corporation,"; and

(F) in subsection (r), by striking "and the Resolution Trust Corporation";

(6) in section 13 (k) (1) (A) (iv) (12 U.S.C. 1823 (k) (1) (A) (iv)) ,by striking "Director of the Office of Thrift Supervision" and inserting "Comptroller of the Currency";

(7) in section 18 (12 U.S.C. 1828)—

(A) in subsection (c) (2)—

(i) in subparagraph (A) ,by inserting "or a Federal savings association" before the semicolon;

(ii) in subparagraph (B), by adding "and" at the end;

(iii) in subparagraph (C), by striking " (except" and all that follows through "; and" and inserting "or a State savings association. "; and

(iv) by striking subparagraph (D);

(B) in subsection (g) (1), by striking "the Director of the Office of Thrift Supervision" and inserting "the Comptroller of the Currency";

(C) in subsection (i) (2) (C), by striking "Director of the Office of Thrift Supervision" and inserting "Corporation"; and

(D) in subsection (m)—

(D)第(n)子条——

(i)第(1)(A)款——

(I)删除“或者就一个或一个以上参保储蓄协会而言,储蓄机构监理局局长”,替以“或者一个或一个以上参保储蓄协会”;及

(II)删除“适用,,”,替以“适用,”;

(ii)第(2)(A)款删除“或储蓄机构监理局局长”;

(iii)第(4)(D)款删除“和储蓄机构监理局局长(视具体情况而定),”;

(iv)第(4)(G)款删除“和储蓄机构监理局局长(视具体情况而定),”;及

(v)第(12)(B)款——

(I)在“应指定联邦存款保险公司”之后插入“担任”;

(II)删除本款出现的所有的“或储蓄机构监理局局长(视具体情况而定)”;

(E)第(p)子条——

(i)第(2)(B)款删除“联邦存款保险公司、联邦储贷保险公司清盘基金或清盘信托公司,”替以“或联邦存款保险公司,”;及

(ii)第(3)(B)款删除“,联邦储贷保险公司清盘基金、清盘信托公司,”;及

(F)第(r)子条删除“和清盘信托公司”;

(6)第13(k)(1)(A)(iv)条[《美国法典》第十二编第1823(k)(1)(A)(iv)节]删除“储蓄机构监理局局长”,替以“货币监理署署长”;

(7)在第18条(《美国法典》第十二编第1828节)中——

(A)第(c)(2)子条——

(i)第(A)子款在分号前插入“或联邦储蓄协会”;

(ii)第(B)子款结尾处增加“及”;

(iii)第(C)子款删除从“(除”直至“;及”的全部内容,替以“或州储蓄协会。”;及

(iv)删除第(D)子款;

(B)第(g)(1)子条删除“储蓄机构监理局局长”,替以“货币监理署署长”;

(C)第(i)(2)(C)子条删除“储蓄机构监理局局长”,替以“联邦存款保险公司”;及

(D)第(m)子条——

(i) in paragraph (1)—

(I) in subparagraph (A),by striking "and the Director of the Office of Thrift Supervision" and inserting "or the Comptroller of the Currency,as appropriate,"; and

(II) in subparagraph (B), by striking "and orders of the Director of the Office of Thrift Supervision" and inserting "of the Comptroller of the Currency and orders of the Corporation and the Comptroller of the Currency";

(ii) in paragraph (2)—

(I) in subparagraph (A), by striking "Director of the Office of Thrift Supervision" and inserting "Comptroller of the Currency,as appropriate,"; and

(II) in subparagraph (B)—

(aa) in the matter before clause (i), by striking "Director of the Office of Thrift Supervision" and inserting "Corporation or the Comptroller of the Currency,as appropriate,"; and

(bb) in the matter following clause (ii)—

(AA) in the first sentence,by striking "Director of the Office of Thrift Supervision" and inserting "Office of the Comptroller of the Currency,as appropriate,"; and

(BB) by striking the second sentence and inserting the following: "The Corporation or the Comptroller of the Currency, as appropriate,may take any other corrective measures with respect to the subsidiary, including the authority to require the subsidiary to terminate the activities or operations posing such risks,as the Corporation or the Comptroller of the Currency,respectively,may deem appropriate. "; and

(iii) in paragraph (3)—

(I) in subparagraph (A),in the second sentence—

(aa) by inserting ",in the case of a Federal savings association," before "consult with"; and

(bb) by striking "Director of the Office of Thrift Supervision" and inserting "Comptroller of the Currency"; and

(II) in subparagraph (B)—

(aa) in the subparagraph heading,by striking "DIRECTOR" and inserting "COMPTROLLER OF THE CURRENCY";

(bb) by striking "Office of Thrift Supervision" and inserting "Comptroller of the Currency";

(cc) by inserting a comma after "soundness"; and

(dd) by inserting "as to Federal savings associations" after "compliance";

(8) in section 19 (e) (12 U.S.C. 1829 (e))—

(A) in paragraph (1),by striking "Director of the Office of Thrift Supervision" and inserting "Board of Governors of the Federal Reserve System"; and

(i)第(1)款——

(I)第(A)子款删除“及储蓄机构监理局局长”,替以“或货币监理署署长(视具体情况而定),”;及

(II)第(B)子款删除“和储蓄机构监理局局长的命令”,替以“货币监理署署长制定的规章以及联邦存款保险公司和货币监理署署长的命令”;

(ii)第(2)款——

(I)第(A)子款删除“储蓄机构监理局局长”,替以“货币监理署署长(视具体情况而定),”;及

(II)第(B)子款——

(aa)第(i)项之前的内容删除“储蓄机构监理局局长”,替以“联邦存款保险公司或货币监理署署长(视具体情况而定),”;及

(bb)第(ii)项之后的内容——

(AA)第一句删除“储蓄机构监理局局长”,替以“货币监理署署长(视具体情况而定),”;及

(BB)删除第二句,替以如下内容:“联邦存款保险公司或货币监理署署长(视具体情况而定)可以对子公司采取其各自认为适当的任何其他整改措施,包括有权要求子公司终止产生该等风险的活动或运营。”及

(iii)在第(3)款中——

(I)第(A)子款第二句——

(aa)在“磋商”前插入“涉及联邦储蓄协会时”;及

(bb)删除“储蓄机构监理局局长”,替以“货币监理署署长”;及

(II)第(B)子款——

(aa)删除子款标题中的“**储蓄机构监理局局长**”,替以“**货币监理署署长**”;

(bb)删除“储蓄机构监理局”,替以“货币监理署署长”;

(cc)在“稳健”之后插入逗号;及

(dd)在“合规”之后插入“关于联邦储蓄协会”;

(8)在第19(e)条[《美国法典》第十二编第1829(e)节]中——

(A)第(1)款删除“储蓄机构监理局局长”,替以“联邦储备委员会”;及

(B) in paragraph (2), by striking "Director of the Office of Thrift Supervision" and inserting "Board of Governors of the Federal Reserve System";

(9) in section 28 (12 U.S.C. 1831e) —

(A) in subsection (e) —

(i) in paragraph (2) —

(I) in subparagraph (A) (ii), by striking "Director of the Office of Thrift Supervision" and inserting "Comptroller of the Currency or the Corporation,as appropriate";

(II) in subparagraph (C), by striking "Director of the Office of Thrift Supervision" and inserting "Comptroller of the Currency or the Corporation,as appropriate,"; and

(III) in subparagraph (F), by striking "Director of the Office of Thrift Supervision" and inserting "Comptroller of the Currency or the Corporation,as appropriate"; and

(ii) in paragraph (3) —

(I) in subparagraph (A), by striking "Director of the Office of Thrift Supervision" and inserting "Comptroller of the Currency or the Corporation,as appropriate"; and

(II) in subparagraph (B), by striking "Director of the Office of Thrift Supervision" and inserting "Comptroller of the Currency or the Corporation,as appropriate,"; and

(B) in subsection (h) (2), by striking "Director of the Office of Thrift Supervision" and inserting "Comptroller of the Currency,of the Corporation,"; and

(10) in section 33 (e) (12 U.S.C. 1831j (e)), by striking "Federal Housing Finance Board,the Comptroller of the Currency,and the Director of the Office of Thrift Supervision" and inserting "Federal Housing Finance Agency and the Comptroller of the Currency".

SEC. 364. FEDERAL HOME LOAN BANK ACT.

(a) REPEAL OF SECTION 18 (c). — Effective 90 days after the transfer date,section 18 (c) of the Federal Home Loan Bank Act (12 U.S.C. 1438 (c)) is repealed.

(b) REPEAL OF SECTION 21A. — Section 21A of the Federal Home Loan Bank Act (12 U.S.C. 1441a) is repealed.

SEC. 365. FEDERAL HOUSING ENTERPRISES FINANCIAL SAFETY AND SOUNDNESS ACT OF 1992.

The Federal Housing Enterprises Financial Safety and Soundness Act of 1992 (12 U.S.C. 4501 et seq.) is amended —

(1) in section 1315 (b) (12 U.S.C. 4515 (b)), by striking "the Federal Deposit Insurance Corporation,and the Office of Thrift Supervision. " and inserting "and the Federal Deposit Insurance Corporation. "; and

(2) in section 1317 (c) (12 U.S.C. 4517 (c)), by striking "the Federal Deposit Insurance Corporation, or the Director of the Office of Thrift Supervision" and inserting "or the Federal Deposit Insurance Corporation".

(B)第(2)款删除“储蓄机构监理局局长”,替以“联邦储备委员会”;

(9)在第28条(《美国法典》第十二编第1831e节)中——

(A)第(e)子条——

(i)第(2)款——

(I)第(A)(ii)子款删除“储蓄机构监理局局长”,替以“货币监理署署长或联邦存款保险公司(视具体情况而定),”;

(II)第(C)子款删除“储蓄机构监理局局长”,替以“货币监理署署长或联邦存款保险公司(视具体情况而定),”;及

(III)第(F)子款删除“储蓄机构监理局局长”,替以“货币监理署署长或联邦存款保险公司(视具体情况而定),”;及

(ii)第(3)款——

(I)第(A)子款删除“储蓄机构监理局局长”,替以“货币监理署署长或联邦存款保险公司(视具体情况而定)”;及

(II)第(B)子款删除“储蓄机构监理局局长”,替以“货币监理署署长或联邦存款保险公司(视具体情况而定),”;及

(B)第(h)(2)子条删除“储蓄机构监理局局长”,替以“货币监理署署长或联邦存款保险公司,”;及

(10)第33(e)条[《美国法典》第十二编第1831j(e)节]删除“联邦住房金融委员会、货币监理署署长和储蓄机构监理局局长”, 替以 “联邦住房金融局和货币监理署署长”。

第364条 《联邦住房贷款银行法》

(a)废止第18(c)条。——《联邦住房贷款银行法》第18(c)条[《美国法典》第十二编第1438(c)节]自转移日后第90天失效。

(b)废止第21A条。——《联邦住房贷款银行法》(《美国法典》第十二编第1441a节)第21A条兹予废止。

第365条 《1992年联邦住房企业财务安全和稳健法》

《1992年联邦住房企业财务安全和稳健法》(《美国法典》 第十二编第4501节及其后条文)修正如下——

(1)在第1315(b)条[《美国法典》第十二编第4515(b)节]中,删除“联邦存款保险公司及储蓄机构监理局。”,替以“及联邦存款保险公司。”;及

(2)在第1317(c)条[《美国法典》第十二编第4517(c)节]中,删除“联邦存款保险公司或储蓄机构监理局局长”,替以“或联邦存款保险公司”。

SEC. 366. FEDERAL RESERVE ACT.

The Federal Reserve Act (12 U.S.C. 221 et seq.) is amended —

(1) in section 11 (a) (2) (12 U.S.C. 248 (a) (2)) —

(A) by inserting "State savings associations that are insured depository institutions (as defined in section 3 of the Federal Deposit Insurance Act) ," after "case of insured";

(B) by striking "Director of the Office of Thrift Supervision" and inserting "Comptroller of the Currency";

(C) by inserting "Federal" before "savings association which"; and

(D) by striking "savings and loan association" and inserting "savings association"; and

(2) in section 19 (b) (12 U.S.C. 461 (b)) —

(A) in paragraph (1) (F) , by striking "Director of the Office of Thrift Supervision" and inserting "Comptroller of the Currency"; and

(B) in paragraph (4) (B) , by striking "Director of the Office of Thrift Supervision" and inserting "Comptroller of the Currency".

SEC. 367. FINANCIAL INSTITUTIONS REFORM, RECOVERY, AND ENFORCEMENT ACT OF 1989.

The Financial Institutions Reform, Recovery, and Enforcement Act of 1989 is amended —

(1) in section 203 (12 U.S.C. 1812 note) , by striking subsection (b) ;

(2) in section 302 (1) (12 U.S.C. 1467a note) , by striking "Director of the Office of Thrift Supervision" and inserting "Comptroller of the Currency";

(3) in section 305 (12 U.S.C. 1464 note) ,by striking subsection (b) ;

(4) in section 308 (12 U.S.C. 1463 note) —

(A) in subsection (a) ,by striking "Director of the Office of Thrift Supervision" and inserting "Chairman of the Board of Governors of the Federal Reserve System,the Comptroller of the Currency,the Chairman of the National Credit Union Administration,"; and

(B) by adding at the end the following new subsection:

"(c) REPORTS. — The Secretary of the Treasury,the Chairman of the Board of Governors of the Federal Reserve System,the Comptroller of the Currency,the Chairman of the National Credit Union Administration,and the Chairperson of Board of Directors of the Federal Deposit Insurance Corporation shall each submit an annual report to the Congress containing a description of actions taken to carry out this section. ";

(5) in section 402 (12 U.S.C. 1437 note) —

(A) in subsection (a) , by striking "Director of the Office of Thrift Supervision" and inserting "Comptroller of the Currency";

(B) by striking subsection (b) ;

(C) in subsection (e) —

第366条 《联邦储备法》

《联邦储备法》(《美国法典》第十二编第221节及其后条文)修正如下——

(1)在第11(a)(2)条[《美国法典》第十二编第248(a)(2)节]中——

(A)在“对于”之后插入“性质为参保存款机构(定义见《联邦存款保险法》第3条)的参保州储蓄协会而言,”;

(B)删除“储蓄机构监理局局长”,替以“货币监理署署长”;

(C)在“储蓄协会”前插入“联邦”;及

(D)删除“储贷协会”,替以“储蓄协会”;及

(2)在第19(b)条[《美国法典》第十二编第461(b)节]中——

(A)第(1)(F)款删除“储蓄机构监理局局长”,替以“货币监理署署长”;及

(B)第(4)(B)款删除“储蓄机构监理局局长”,替以“货币监理署署长”。

第367条 《1989年金融机构改革、复兴与实施法》

《1989年金融机构改革、复兴与实施法》修正如下——

(1)在第203条(《美国法典》第十二编第1812节注释)中,删除第(b)子条;

(2)在第302(1)条(《美国法典》第十二编第1467a节注释)中,删除“储蓄机构监理局局长”,替以“货币监理署署长”;

(3)在第305条(《美国法典》第十二编第1464节注释)中,删除第(b)子条;

(4)在第308条(《美国法典》第十二编第1463节注释)中——

(A)第(a)子条删除“储蓄机构监理局局长”,替以“联邦储备委员会主席、货币监理署署长、国家信贷联盟署署长、”;及

(B)该条结尾处增加如下新子条:

“(c)**报告**。——财政部部长、联邦储备委员会主席、货币监理署署长、国家信贷联盟署署长、联邦存款保险公司董事会主席应分别向国会提交一份年度报告,说明为实施本条规定所采取的行动。”

(5)在第402条(《美国法典》第十二编第1437节注释)中——

(A)第(a)子条删除“储蓄机构监理局局长”,替以“货币监理署署长”;

(B)删除第(b)子条;

(C)第(e)子条——

(i) in paragraph (1), by striking "Office of Thrift Supervision" and inserting "Comptroller of the Currency"; and

(ii) in each of paragraphs (2), (3), and (4), by striking "Director of the Office of Thrift Supervision" each place that term appears and inserting "Comptroller of the Currency"; and

(D) by striking "Federal Housing Finance Board" each place that term appears and inserting "Federal Housing Finance Agency";

(6) in section 1103 (a) (12 U.S.C. 3332 (a)), by striking "and the Resolution Trust Corporation";

(7) in section 1205 (b) (12 U.S.C. 1818 note)—

(A) in paragraph (1)—

(i) by striking subparagraph (B); and

(ii) by redesignating subparagraphs (C) through (F) as subparagraphs (B) through (E), respectively; and

(B) in paragraph (2), by striking "paragraph (1) (F)" and inserting "paragraph (1) (E)";

(8) in section 1206 (12 U.S.C. 1833b)—

(A) by striking "Board, the Oversight Board of the Resolution Trust Corporation" and inserting "Agency, and"; and

(B) by striking ", and the Office of Thrift Supervision";

(9) in section 1216 (12 U.S.C. 1833e)—

(A) in subsection (a)—

(i) in paragraph (3), by adding "and" at the end;

(ii) in paragraph (4), by striking the semicolon at the end and inserting a period;

(iii) by striking paragraphs (2), (5), and (6); and

(iv) by redesignating paragraphs (3) and (4), as paragraphs (2) and (3), respectively;

(B) in subsection (c)—

(i) by striking "the Director of the Office of Thrift Supervision," and inserting "and"; and

(ii) by striking "the Thrift Depositor Protection Oversight Board of the Resolution Trust Corporation, and the Resolution Trust Corporation"; and

(C) in subsection (d)—

(i) by striking paragraphs (3), (5), and (6); and

(ii) by redesignating paragraphs (4), (7), and (8) as paragraphs (3), (4), and (5), respectively.

SEC. 368. FLOOD DISASTER PROTECTION ACT OF 1973.

Section 3 (a) (5) of the Flood Disaster Protection Act of 1973 (42 U.S.C. 4003 (a) (5))

(i)第(1)款删除“储蓄机构监理局”,替以“货币监理署署长”;及

(ii)第(2)款、第(3)款和第(4)款删除该款出现的所有的“储蓄机构监理局局长”,全部替以“货币监理署署长”;及

(D)删除本条出现的所有的“联邦住房金融委员会”,全部替以“联邦住房金融局”;

(6)在第1103(a)条[《美国法典》第十二编第3332(a)节]中,删除“以及清盘信托公司”;

(7)在第1205(b)条(《美国法典》第十二编第1818节注释)中——

(A)第(1)款——

(i)删除第(B)子款;及

(ii)第(C)子款至第(F)子款分别重新编号为第(B)子款至第(E)子款;及

(B)第(2)款删除“第(1)(F)款”,替以“第(1)(E)款”;

(8)在第1206条(《美国法典》第十二编第1833b节)中——

(A)删除“联邦储备委员会、清盘信托公司监督委员会”,替以“联邦住房金融局,及”;及

(B)删除“,及储蓄机构监理局”;

(9)在第1216条(《美国法典》第十二编第1833e节)中——

(A)第(a)子条——

(i)第(3)款结尾处插入“及”;

(ii)第(4)款删除结尾处的分号,替以句号;

(iii)删除第(2)款、第(5)款和第(6)款;及

(iv)第(3)款和第(4)款分别重新编号为第(2)款和第(3)款;

(B)第(c)子条——

(i)删除“储蓄机构监理局局长,”替以“及”;及

(ii)删除“清盘信托公司的储蓄机构存款人保护监督委员会和清盘信托公司”;及

(C)第(d)子条——

(i)删除第(3)款、第(5)款和第(6)款;及

(ii)第(4)款、第(7)款和第(8)款分别重新编号为第(3)款、第(4)款和第(5)款。

第368条 《1973年洪水灾害防御法》

删除《1973年洪水灾害防御法》第3(a)(5)条[《美国法典》第四十二编第4003(a)

is amended by striking ",the Office of Thrift Supervision".

SEC. 369. HOME OWNERS' LOAN ACT.

The Home Owners' Loan Act (12 U.S.C. 1461 et seq.) is amended —

(1) in section 1 (12 U.S.C. 1461), by striking the table of contents;

(2) in section 2 (12 U.S.C. 1462), as amended by this Act —

(A) by striking paragraphs (1) and (3);

(B) by redesignating paragraph (2) as paragraph (1);

(C) by redesignating paragraphs (4) through (9) as paragraphs (2) through (7), respectively; and

(D) by adding at the end the following:

" (8) BOARD. — The term 'Board',other than in the context of the Board of Directors of the Corporation,means the Board of Governors of the Federal Reserve System.

" (9) COMPTROLLER. — The term 'Comptroller' means the Comptroller of the Currency. ";

(3) in section 3 (12 U.S.C. 1462a) —

(A) by striking the section heading and inserting the following:

"SEC. 3. ADMINISTRATIVE PROVISIONS. ";

(B) by striking subsections (a), (b), (c), (d), (g), (h), (i),and (j);

(C) by redesignating subsections (e) and (f) as subsections (a) and (b), respectively;

(D) in subsection (a),as so redesignated —

(i) in the heading by striking "OF THE DIRECTOR"; and

(ii) in the matter preceding paragraph (1),by striking "The Director" and inserting "In accordance with subtitle A of title III of the Dodd–Frank Wall Street Reform and Consumer Protection Act,the appropriate Federal banking agency"; and

(E) in subsection (b), as so redesignated,by striking "Director" and inserting "appropriate Federal banking agency";

(4) in section 4 (12 U.S.C. 1463) —

(A) in subsection (a) —

(i) in the subsection heading,by striking "FEDERAL";

(ii) by striking paragraphs (1) and (2) and inserting the following:

" (1) EXAMINATION AND SAFE AND SOUND OPERATION. —

" (A) FEDERAL SAVINGS ASSOCIATIONS. — The Comptroller shall provide for the examination and safe and sound operation of Federal savings associations.

" (B) STATE SAVINGS ASSOCIATIONS. — The Corporation shall provide for the examination and safe and sound operation of State savings associations.

" (2) REGULATIONS FOR SAVINGS ASSOCIATIONS. — The Comptroller may

(5)节]中的“,储蓄机构监理局”。

第369条 《业主贷款法》

《业主贷款法》(《美国法典》第十二编第1461节及其后条文)修正如下——

(1)在第1条(《美国法典》第十二编第1461节)中,删除目录;

(2)第2条(《美国法典》第十二编第1462节)修正如下——

(A)删除第(1)款和第(3)款;

(B)第(2)款重新编号为第(1)款;

(C)第(4)款至第(9)款分别重新编号为第(2)款至第(7)款;及

(D)在该条结尾处增加如下内容:

“(8)**委员会**。——除非根据上下文另指联邦存款保险公司董事会,否则‘委员会’一词应指联邦储备委员会。

(9)**监理署署长**。——‘监理署署长’一词系指货币监理署署长。”

(3)在第3条(《美国法典》第十二编第1462a节)中——

(A)删除该条标题,替以:

“第3条 管理规定”;

(B)删除第(a)子条、第(b)子条、第(c)子条、第(d)子条、第(g)子条、第(h)子条、第(i)子条和第(j)子条;

(C)第(e)子条和第(f)子条分别重新编号为第(a)子条和第(b)子条;

(D)第(a)子条(以重新编号后的序号为准)——

(i)删除本子条标题中的“**储蓄机构监理局局长的**”;及

(ii)第(1)款之前的内容删除“储蓄机构监理局局长”,替以“根据《多德—弗兰克华尔街改革与消费者保护法》第三编第A子编,相应的联邦银行业监管机关”;及

(E)第(b)子条(以重新编号后的序号为准)删除“储蓄机构监理局局长”,替以“相应的联邦银行业监管机关”;

(4)在第4条(《美国法典》第十二编第1463节)中——

(A)第(a)子条——

(i)删除标题中的“**联邦**”;

(ii)删除第(1)款和第(2)款,替以如下内容:

“(1)**检查及安全稳健运营**。——

(A)**联邦储蓄协会**。——货币监理署署长应对联邦储蓄协会进行检查,并对其安全稳健运营负责。

(B)**州储蓄协会**。——联邦存款保险公司应对州储蓄协会进行检查,并对其安全稳健运营负责。

(2)**适用于储蓄协会的规章**。——货币监理署署长可以为实现本法宗旨,针对储

prescribe regulations with respect to savings associations,as the Comptroller determines to be appropriate to carry out the purposes of this Act. "; and

(iii) in paragraph (3), by striking "Director" each place that term appears and inserting "Comptroller and the Corporation";

(B) in subsection (b)—

(i) in paragraph (2)—

(I) in subparagraph (A), by adding "and" at the end;

(II) in subparagraph (B), by striking "; and" and inserting a period; and

(III) by striking subparagraph (C); and

(ii) by striking "Director" each place that term appears and inserting "Comptroller";

(C) in subsection (c)—

(i) by striking "All regulations and policies of the Director" and inserting "The regulations of the Comptroller and the policies of the Comptroller and the Corporation"; and

(ii) by striking "of the Currency";

(D) in subsection (e)(5), by striking "Director" and inserting "Comptroller";

(E) in subsection (f), by striking "Director" each place that term appears and inserting "appropriate Federal banking agency"; and

(F) in subsection (h), by striking "Director" each place that term appears and inserting "appropriate Federal banking agency";

(5) in section 5 (12 U.S.C. 1464)—

(A) in subsection (a), by striking "Director",each place such term appears and inserting "Comptroller of the Currency";

(B) in subsection (b), by striking "Director",each place such term appears and inserting "Comptroller of the Currency";

(C) in subsection (c)—

(i) in paragraph (5)—

(I) in subparagraph (A),by striking "Director" and inserting "appropriate Federal banking agency"; and

(II) in subparagraph (B)—

(aa) by striking "The Director" and inserting "The appropriate Federal banking agency"; and

(bb) by striking "the Director" and inserting "the appropriate Federal banking agency";

(D) in subsection (d)—

(i) in paragraph (1)—

(I) in subparagraph (A)—

(aa) in the first sentence, by striking "Director" and inserting "appropriate Federal banking agency";

蓄协会制定其判定确属适当的规章。”及

(iii)第(3)款删除本款出现的所有的“储蓄机构监理局局长”,全部替以“货币监理署署长和联邦存款保险公司”;

(B)第(b)子条——

(i)第(2)款——

(I)第(A)子款在结尾处增加“及”;

(II)第(B)子款删除“;及”,替以句号;及

(III)删除第(C)子款;及

(ii)删除所有的“储蓄机构监理局局长”,全部替以“货币监理署署长”;

(C)第(c)子条——

(i)删除“储蓄机构监理局局长制定的所有规章和政策”,替以“货币监理署署长制定的规章,以及货币监理署署长和联邦存款保险公司制定的政策”;及

(ii)删除“货币”;

(D)第(e)(5)子条删除“储蓄机构监理局局长”,替以“货币监理署署长”;

(E)第(f)子条删除本子条出现的所有的“储蓄机构监理局局长”,全部替以“相应的联邦银行业监管机关”;及

(F)第(h)子条删除本子条出现的所有的“储蓄机构监理局局长”,全部替以“相应的联邦银行业监管机关”;

(5)在第5条(《美国法典》第十二编第1464节)中——

(A)第(a)子条删除本子条出现的所有的“储蓄机构监理局局长”,全部替以“货币监理署署长”;

(B)第(b)子条删除所有的“储蓄机构监理局局长”,全部替以“货币监理署署长”;

(C)第(c)子条——

(i)第(5)款——

(I)第(A)子款删除“储蓄机构监理局局长”,替以“相应的联邦银行业监管机关”;及

(II)第(B)子款——

(aa)删除“储蓄机构监理局局长”,替以“相应的联邦银行业监管机关”;及

(bb)删除“储蓄机构监理局局长”,替以“相应的联邦银行业监管机关”;

(D)第(d)子条——

(i)第(1)款——

(I)第(A)子款——

(aa)第一句删除“储蓄机构监理局局长”,替以“相应的联邦银行业监管机关”;

(bb) in the second sentence —

(AA) by striking "Director's own name and through the Director's own attorneys" and inserting "name of the appropriate Federal banking agency and through the attorneys of the appropriate Federal banking agency"; and

(BB) by striking "Director" each place that term appears and inserting "appropriate Federal banking agency"; and

(cc) in the third sentence, by striking "Director" each place that term appears and inserting "Comptroller";

(II) in subparagraph (B) —

(aa) in clauses (i) through (iv), by striking "Director" each place that term appears and inserting "appropriate Federal banking agency";

(III) in clause (v) —

(aa) in the matter preceding subclause (I), by striking "Director" and inserting "appropriate Federal banking agency";

(bb) in subclause (II), by striking "subpenas" and inserting "subpoenas"; and

(cc) in the matter following subclause (II), by striking "subpena" and inserting "subpoena";

(IV) in clause (vi) —

(aa) in the first sentence, by striking "Director" and inserting "appropriate Federal banking agency"; and

(bb) in the second sentence, by striking "Director" and inserting "Comptroller";

(V) in clause (vii) —

(aa) in the first sentence, by striking "subpena" and inserting "subpoena";

(bb) in the second sentence, by striking "subpenaed" and inserting "subpoenaed"; and

(cc) in the third sentence, by striking "Director" and inserting "appropriate Federal banking agency";

(ii) in paragraph (2) —

(I) in subparagraph (A) —

(aa) by striking "Director of the Office of Thrift Supervision" and inserting "appropriate Federal banking agency";

(bb) by striking "any insured savings association" and inserting "an insured savings association"; and

(cc) by striking "Director determines,in the Director's discretion" and inserting "appropriate Federal banking agency determines, in the discretion of the appropriate Federal banking agency";

(II) in subparagraph (B), by striking "Director" each place that term appears and

(bb)第二句——

(AA)删除“储蓄机构监理局局长自身的名义并通过储蓄机构监理局局长自身的法律代理人”,替以“相应的联邦银行业监管机关的名义并通过相应的联邦银行业监管机关的法律代理人”;及

(BB)删除所有的“储蓄机构监理局局长”,全部替以“相应的联邦银行业监管机关”;及

(cc)第三句删除所有的“储蓄机构监理局局长”,全部替以“货币监理署署长”;

(II)第(B)子款——

(aa)第(i)项至第(iv)项删除所有的“储蓄机构监理局局长”,全部替以“相应的联邦银行业监管机关”;

(III)第(v)项——

(aa)第(I)子项之前的内容删除“储蓄机构监理局局长”,替以“相应的联邦银行业监管机关”;

(bb)第(II)子项删除“传票”的错误拼写“subpenas”,替以正确拼写“subpoenas”;及

(cc)第(II)子项之后的内容删除“传票”的错误拼写“subpena”,替以正确拼写“subpoena”;

(IV)第(vi)项——

(aa)第一句删除“储蓄机构监理局局长”,替以“相应的联邦银行业监管机关”;及

(bb)第二句删除“储蓄机构监理局局长”,替以“货币监理署署长”;

(V)第(vii)项——

(aa)第一句删除“传票”的错误拼写“subpena”,替以正确拼写“subpoena”;

(bb)第二句删除“被签发传票的”的错误拼写“subpenaed”,替以正确拼写“subpoenaed”;及

(cc)第三句删除“储蓄机构监理局局长”,替以“相应的联邦银行业监管机关”;

(ii)第(2)款——

(I)第(A)子款——

(aa)删除“储蓄机构监理局局长”,替以“相应的联邦银行业监管机关”;

(bb)删除“任何参保储蓄协会”,替以“某一参保储蓄协会”;及

(cc)删除“储蓄机构监理局局长依其自由裁量权判定”,替以“相应的联邦银行业监管机关依其自由裁量权判定”;

(II)第(B)子款删除所有的“储蓄机构监理局局长”,全部替以“相应的联邦银行业

inserting "appropriate Federal banking agency";

(III) in subparagraphs (C) and (D), by striking "Director" and inserting "appropriate Federal banking agency";

(IV) in subparagraph (E)—

(aa) in clause (ii)—

(AA) in the clause heading,by striking "OR RTC"; and

(BB) by striking "or the Resolution Trust Corporation,as appropriate," each place that term appears; and

(bb) by striking "Director" each place that term appears and inserting "appropriate Federal banking agency"; and

(iii) in paragraph (3)—

(I) in subparagraph (A), by striking "Director" each place that term appears and inserting "Comptroller"; and

(II) in subparagraph (B)—

(aa) in the subparagraph heading,by striking "OR RTC";

(bb) by striking "Corporation or the Resolution Trust"; and

(cc) by striking "Director" and inserting "Comptroller";

(iv) in paragraph (4), by striking "Director" and inserting "appropriate Federal banking agency";

(v) in paragraph (6)—

(I) in subparagraph (A),by striking "Director" and inserting "Comptroller"; and

(II) in subparagraphs (B) and (C), by striking "Director" each place that term appears and inserting "appropriate Federal banking agency";

(vi) in paragraph (7)—

(I) in subparagraphs (A), (B),and (D), by striking "Director" each place that term appears and inserting "appropriate Federal banking agency";

(II) in subparagraph (C), by striking "Director" and inserting "Federal Deposit Insurance Corporation or the Comptroller,as appropriate,"; and

(III) by striking subparagraph (E) and inserting the following:

"(E) ADMINISTRATION BY THE COMPTROLLER AND THE CORPORATION. —The Comptroller may issue such regulations, and the appropriate Federal banking agency may issue such orders,including those issued pursuant to section 8 of the Federal Deposit Insurance Act,as may be necessary to administer and carry out this paragraph and to prevent evasion of this paragraph. ";

(E) in subsection (e)(2), strike "Director" and insert "Comptroller";

(F) in subsection (i)—

(i) by striking "Director", each place such term appears,and inserting "Comptroller";

监管机关”;

(III)第(C)子款和第(D)子款删除“储蓄机构监理局局长”,替以“相应的联邦银行业监管机关”;

(IV)第(E)子款——

(aa)第(ii)项——

(AA)删除标题中的“**或清盘信托公司**”;及

(BB)删除所有的“或清盘信托公司(视具体情况而定),”;及

(bb)删除所有的“储蓄机构监理局局长”,全部替以“相应的联邦银行业监管机关”;及

(iii)第(3)款——

(I)第(A)子款删除所有的“储蓄机构监理局局长”,全部替以“货币监理署署长”;及

(II)第(B)子款——

(aa)删除标题中的“**或清盘信托公司**”;

(bb)删除“联邦存款保险公司或清盘信托公司”;及

(cc)删除“储蓄机构监理局局长”,替以“货币监理署署长”;

(iv)第(4)款删除“储蓄机构监理局局长”,替以“相应的联邦银行业监管机关”;

(v)第(6)款——

(I)第(A)子款删除“储蓄机构监理局局长”,替以“货币监理署署长”;及

(II)第(B)子款和第(C)子款删除所有的“储蓄机构监理局局长”,全部替以“相应的联邦银行业监管机关”;

(vi)第(7)款——

(I)第(A)子款、第(B)子款和第(D)子款删除所有的“储蓄机构监理局局长”,全部替以“相应的联邦银行业监管机关”;

(II)第(C)子款删除“储蓄机构监理局局长”,替以“联邦存款保险公司或货币监理署署长(视具体情况而定),”;及

(III)删除第(E)子款,替以如下内容:

“(E)**货币监理署署长和联邦存款保险公司负责实施本款规定**。——为实施并执行本款规定并防范对本款的规避行为,货币监理署署长可以发布必要的规章,且相应的联邦银行业监管机关亦可以为相同目的签发必要的命令,包括根据《联邦存款保险法》第8条发布规章和签发命令。”;

(E)第(e)(2)子条删除“储蓄机构监理局局长”,替以“货币监理署署长”;

(F)第(i)子条——

(i)删除所有的“储蓄机构监理局局长”,全部替以“货币监理署署长”;

(ii) in paragraph (2) ,in the heading, by striking "DIRECTOR" and inserting "COMPTROLLER";

(iii) in paragraph (5) (A), by striking "of the Currency"; and

(iv) except as provided in clauses (i) through (iii), by striking "Director" each place such term appears and inserting "Comptroller";

(G) in subsection (o)—

(i) in paragraph (1), by striking "Director" and inserting "Comptroller"; and

(ii) in paragraph (2)(B), by striking "Director's determination" and inserting "determination of the Comptroller";

(H) in subsections (m), (n), (o), and (p), by striking "Director", each place such term appears,and inserting "Comptroller";

(I) in subsection (q)—

(i) in paragraph (6) ,by striking "of Governors of the Federal Reserve System";

(ii) by striking "Director" each place that term appears and inserting "Board"; and

(iii) by inserting "in consultation with the Comptroller and the Corporation," before "considers";

(J) in subsection (r)(3), by striking "Director" and inserting "Comptroller of the Currency";

(K) in subsection (s)—

(i) in paragraph (1), strike "Director" and insert "Comptroller of the Currency";

(ii) in paragraph (2), strike "Director" and insert "Comptroller of the Currency";

(iii) in paragraph (3), by striking "Director's discretion,the Director" and inserting "discretion of the appropriate Federal banking agency,the appropriate Federal banking agency,";

(iv) in paragraph (4), by striking "Director" each place that term appears and inserting "appropriate Federal banking agency"; and

(v) in paragraph (5)—

(I) by striking "Director", each place such term appears,and inserting "appropriate Federal banking agency"; and

(II) by striking "Director's approval" and inserting "approval of the appropriate Federal banking agency";

(L) in subsection (t)—

(i) in paragraph (1), by striking subparagraph (D);

(ii) by striking paragraph (3) and inserting the following:

"(3) [Repealed]. ";

(iii) in paragraph (5)—

(I) in subparagraph (B), by striking "Corporation,in its sole discretion" and inserting

(ii)删除第(2)款标题中的“**储蓄机构监理局局长**”,替以“**货币监理署署长**”;

(iii)第(5)(A)款删除“货币”;及

(iv)除第(i)至第(iii)项规定的情形外,删除所有的“储蓄机构监理局局长”,全部替以“货币监理署署长”;

(G)第(o)子条——

(i)第(1)款删除“储蓄机构监理局局长”,替以“货币监理署署长”;及

(ii)第(2)(B)款删除“储蓄机构监理局局长的判定”,替以“货币监理署署长的判定”;

(H)第(m)子条、第(n)子条、第(o)子条和第(p)子条删除所有的“储蓄机构监理局局长”,全部替以“货币监理署署长”;

(I)第(q)子条——

(i)第(6)款删除“联邦储备委员会的”;

(ii)删除所有的“储蓄机构监理局局长”,全部替以“联邦储备委员会”;及

(iii)在“考虑”前插入“与货币监理署署长和联邦存款保险公司磋商后”;

(J)第(r)(3)子条删除“储蓄机构监理局局长”,替以“货币监理署署长”;

(K)第(s)子条——

(i)第(1)款删除“储蓄机构监理局局长”,替以“货币监理署署长”;

(ii)第(2)款删除“储蓄机构监理局局长”,替以“货币监理署署长”;

(iii)第(3)款删除“储蓄机构监理局局长依其自由裁量权,”,替以“相应的联邦银行业监管机关依其自由裁量权,”;

(iv)第(4)款删除所有的“储蓄机构监理局局长”,全部替以“相应的联邦银行业监管机关”;及

(v)第(5)款——

(I)删除所有的“储蓄机构监理局局长”,全部替以“相应的联邦银行业监管机关”;及

(II)删除“储蓄机构监理局局长的批准”,替以“相应的联邦银行业监管机关的批准”;

(L)第(t)子条——

(i)第(1)款删除第(D)子款;

(ii)删除第(3)款,替以

“(3)[已废止]。”

(iii)第(5)款——

(I)第(B)子款删除“联邦存款保险公司可完全依其自由裁量权,”替以“相应的联

"appropriate Federal banking agency,in the sole discretion of the appropriate Federal banking agency"; and

(II) by striking subparagraph (D);

(iv) in paragraph (6)—

(I) by striking subparagraph (A) and inserting the following: " (A) [Reserved]. ";

(II) in subparagraph (B), by striking "Director" each place that term appears and inserting "appropriate Federal banking agency";

(III) in subparagraph (C)—

(aa) in clause (i), by striking "Director's prior approval" and inserting "prior approval of the appropriate Federal banking agency";

(bb) in clause (ii), by striking "Director's discretion" and inserting "discretion of the appropriate Federal banking agency"; and

(cc) by striking "Director" each place that term appears and inserting "appropriate Federal banking agency";

(IV) in subparagraph (E), by striking "Director shall" and inserting "appropriate Federal banking agency may"; and

(V) in subparagraph (F), by striking "Director" and all that follows through the end of the subparagraph and inserting "appropriate Federal banking agency under this Act or any other provision of law. ";

(v) in paragraph (7),by striking "Director" each place that term appears and inserting "appropriate Federal banking agency";

(vi) by striking paragraph (8) and inserting the following: " (8) [Repealed]. ";

(vii) in paragraph (9)—

(I) in subparagraph (A), by striking "Director" and inserting "Comptroller";

(II) in subparagraph (C), by striking "of the Currency"; and

(III) by striking subparagraph (B) and redesignating subparagraphs (C) and (D) as subparagraphs (B) and (C), respectively; and

(viii) except as provided in clauses (i) through (vii), by striking "Director" each place that term appears and inserting "appropriate Federal banking agency";

(M) in subsection (u), by striking "Director" each place that term appears and inserting "appropriate Federal banking agency";

(N) in subsection (v)—

(i) in paragraph (2), by striking "Director's determinations" and inserting "determinations of the appropriate Federal banking agency"; and

(ii) by striking "Director" each place that term appears and inserting "appropriate Federal banking agency";

(O) in subsection (w)(1)—

邦银行业监管机关可完全依其自由裁量权,";及

(Ⅱ)删除第(D)子款;

(iv)在第(6)款中——

(Ⅰ)删除第(A)子款,替以"(A)[本子款内容删除,序号予以保留]。";

(Ⅱ)第(B)子款删除所有的"储蓄机构监理局局长",全部替以"相应的联邦银行业监管机关";

(Ⅲ)第(C)子款——

(aa)第(i)项删除"储蓄机构监理局局长的事先批准",替以"相应的联邦银行业监管机关的事先批准";

(bb)第(ii)项删除"储蓄机构监理局局长的自由裁量权",替以"相应的联邦银行业监管机关的自由裁量权";及

(cc)删除所有的"储蓄机构监理局局长",全部替以"相应的联邦银行业监管机关";

(Ⅳ)第(E)子款删除"储蓄机构监理局局长应",替以"相应的联邦银行业监管机关可以";及

(Ⅴ)第(F)子款删除"储蓄机构监理局局长"直至结尾的全部内容,替以"相应的联邦银行业监管机关根据本法或其他法律规定。"

(v)第(7)款删除所有的"储蓄机构监理局局长",全部替以"相应的联邦银行业监管机关";

(vi)删除第(8)款,替以"(8)[已废止]。";

(vii)第(9)款——

(Ⅰ)第(A)子款删除"储蓄机构监理局局长",替以"货币监理署署长";

(Ⅱ)第(C)子款删除"货币";及

(Ⅲ)删除第(B)子款,并且第(C)子款和第(D)子款分别重新编号为第(B)子款和第(C)子款;及

(viii)除第(1)项至第(vii)项规定的情形外,删除所有的"储蓄机构监理局局长",全部替以"相应的联邦银行业监管机关";

(M)第(u)子条删除所有的"储蓄机构监理局局长",全部替以"相应的联邦银行业监管机关";

(N)第(v)子条——

(i)第(2)款删除"储蓄机构监理局局长的判定",替以"相应的联邦银行业监管机关的判定";及

(ii)删除所有的"储蓄机构监理局局长",全部替以"相应的联邦银行业监管机关";

(O)第(w)(1)子条——

(i) in subparagraph (A)(II), by striking "Director's intention" and inserting "intention of the Comptroller"; and

(ii) in subparagraph (B), by striking "Director's intention" and inserting "intention of the Comptroller"; and

(P) except as provided in subparagraphs (A) through (J), by striking "Director" each place that term appears and inserting "Comptroller";

(6) in section 8 (12 U.S.C. 1466a), by striking "Director" each place that term appears and inserting "Comptroller";

(7) in section 9 (12 U.S.C. 1467)—

(A) in subsection (a), by striking "assessed by the Director" and all that follows through the end of the subsection and inserting the following: "assessed by—

"(1) the Comptroller, against each such Federal savings association, as the Comptroller deems necessary or appropriate; and

"(2) the Corporation, against each such State savings association, as the Corporation deems necessary or appropriate.";

(B) in subsection (b), by striking "Director", each place such term appears, and inserting "Comptroller or Corporation, as appropriate";

(C) in subsection (e)—

(i) by striking "Only the Director" and inserting "The Comptroller"; and

(ii) by striking "Director's designee" and inserting "designee of the Comptroller";

(D) by striking subsection (f) and inserting the following: "(f) [Reserved].";

(E) in subsection (g)—

(i) in paragraph (1), by striking "Director" and inserting "appropriate Federal banking agency"; and

(ii) in paragraph (2), by striking "Director, or the Corporation, as the case may be," and inserting "appropriate Federal banking agency for the savings association";

(F) in subsection (i), by striking "Director" each place that term appears and inserting "appropriate Federal banking agency";

(G) in subsection (j), by striking "Director's sole discretion" and inserting "sole discretion of the appropriate Federal banking agency";

(H) in subsection (k), by striking "Director may assess against institutions for which the Director is the appropriate Federal banking agency, as defined in section 3 of the Federal Deposit Insurance Act," and inserting "appropriate Federal banking agency may assess against an institution"; and

(I) except as provided in subparagraphs (A) through (G), by striking "Director" each place that term appears and inserting "appropriate Federal banking agency";

(i)第(A)(II)子款删除“储蓄机构监理局局长的意图”,替以“货币监理署署长的意图”;及

(ii)第(B)子款删除“储蓄机构监理局局长的意图”,替以“货币监理署署长的意图”;及

(P)除第(A)子款至第(J)子款规定的情形外,删除所有的“储蓄机构监理局局长”,全部替以“货币监理署署长”;

(6)第8条(《美国法典》第十二编第1466a节)删除所有的“储蓄机构监理局局长”,全部替以“货币监理署署长”;

(7)在第9条(《美国法典》第十二编第1467节)中——

(A)第(a)子条删除“应由储蓄机构监理局局长计征”直至该子条结尾的全部内容,替以:“应由——

(1)货币监理署署长对其判定确属必要或适当的每一该等联邦储蓄协会进行计征;及

(2)联邦存款保险公司对其判定确属必要或适当的每一该等州储蓄协会进行计征。”

(B)第(b)子条删除所有的“储蓄机构监理局局长”,全部替以“货币监理署署长或联邦存款保险公司(视具体情况而定),”;

(C)第(e)子条——

(i)删除“仅储蓄机构监理局局长”,替以“货币监理署署长”;及

(ii)删除“储蓄机构监理局局长的指定人员”,替以“货币监理署署长的指定人员”;

(D)删除第(f)子条,替以:“(f)[本子条内容删除,但序号予以保留]。”

(E)第(g)子条——

(i)第(1)款删除“储蓄机构监理局局长”,替以“相应的联邦银行业监管机关”;及

(ii)第(2)款删除“储蓄机构监理局局长或联邦存款保险公司(视具体情况而定)”,替以“储蓄协会的相应的联邦银行业监管机关”;

(F)第(i)子条删除所有的“储蓄机构监理局局长”,全部替以“相应的联邦银行业监管机关”;

(G)第(j)子条删除“储蓄机构监理局局长可完全依其自由裁量权”,替以“相应的联邦银行业监管机关可完全依其自由裁量权”;

(H)第(k)子条删除“就储蓄机构监理局作为相应的联邦银行业监管机关(定义见《联邦存款保险法》第3条)监管的机构而言,储蓄机构监理局局长可以针对该等机构计征费用”,替以“相应的联邦银行业监管机关可以对一家机构计征费用”;及

(I)除第(A)子款至第(G)子款规定的情形外,删除所有的“储蓄机构监理局局长”,全部替以“相应的联邦银行业监管机关”;

(8) in section 10 (12 U.S.C. 1467a) —

(A) in subsection (a) (1) ,by striking "Director" each place that term appears and inserting "appropriate Federal banking agency";

(B) in subsection (b) —

(i) in paragraph (2) , by striking "and the regional office of the Director of the district in which its principal office is located,"; and

(ii) in paragraph (6) , by striking "Director's own motion or application" and inserting "motion or application of the Board";

(C) in subsection (c) —

(i) in paragraph (2) (F) , by striking "of Governors of the Federal Reserve System";

(ii) in paragraph (4) (B) , in the subparagraph heading,by striking "BY DIRECTOR";

(iii) in paragraph (6) (D) , in the subparagraph heading,by striking "BY DIRECTOR"; and

(iv) in paragraph (9) (E) , by inserting " (in consultation with the appropriate Federal banking agency) " after "including a determination";

(D) in subsection (g) (5) (B) , by striking "the Director's discretion" and inserting "the discretion of the Board";

(E) in subsection (l) , by striking "Director" each place that term appears and inserting "appropriate Federal banking agency";

(F) in subsection (m) , by striking "Director" and inserting "appropriate Federal banking agency";

(G) in subsection (p) —

(i) in paragraph (1) —

(I) by striking "Director determines" the 1st place such term appears and inserting "Board or the appropriate Federal banking agency for the savings association determines";

(II) by striking "Director may" and inserting "Board may"; and

(III) by striking "Director determines" the 2nd place such term appears and inserting "Board,in consultation with the appropriate Federal banking agency for the savings association determines"; and

(ii) in paragraph (2) , by striking "Director", each place such term appears,and inserting "Board";

(H) in subsection (q) , by striking "Director", each place such term appears,and inserting "Board";

(I) in subsection (r) , by striking "Director", each place such term appears, and inserting "Board or appropriate Federal banking agency";

(J) in subsection (s) —

(i) in paragraph (2) —

（8）第10条（《美国法典》第十二编第1467a节）——

（A）第（a）（1）子条删除所有的“储蓄机构监理局局长”，全部替以“相应的联邦银行业监管机关”；

（B）第（b）子条——

（i）第（2）款删除“其主要办公场所所在地区的储蓄机构监理局局长地区办公室，”；及

（ii）第（6）款删除“储蓄机构监理局局长自身的动议或申请”，替以“联邦储备委员会的动议或申请”；

（C）第（c）子条——

（i）第（2）（F）款删除“联邦储备委员会的”；

（ii）第（4）（B）款删除子款标题中的“**由储蓄机构监理局局长**”；

（iii）第（6）（D）款删除子款标题中的“**由储蓄机构监理局局长**”；及

（iv）第（9）（E）款在“包括一项判定”之后插入“（在与相应的联邦银行业监管机关磋商后）”；

（D）第（g）（5）（B）子条删除“储蓄机构监理局局长的自由裁量权”，替以“联邦储备委员会的自由裁量权”；

（E）第（l）子条删除所有的“储蓄机构监理局局长”，全部替以“相应的联邦银行业监管机关”；

（F）第（m）子条删除“储蓄机构监理局局长”，替以“相应的联邦银行业监管机关”；

（G）第（p）子条——

（i）第（1）款——

（I）删除首次出现的“储蓄机构监理局局长判定”，替以“联邦储备委员会或储蓄协会的相应的联邦银行业监管机关判定”；

（II）删除“储蓄机构监理局局长可以”，替以“联邦储备委员会可以”；及

（III）删除第二次出现的“储蓄机构监理局局长判定”，替以“联邦储备委员会在与储蓄协会的相应的联邦银行业监管机关磋商后判定”；及

（ii）第（2）款删除所有的“储蓄机构监理局局长”，全部替以“联邦储备委员会”；

（H）第（q）子条删除所有的“储蓄机构监理局局长”，全部替以“联邦储备委员会”；

（I）第（r）子条删除所有的“储蓄机构监理局局长”，全部替以“联邦储备委员会或相应的联邦银行业监管机关”；

（J）第（s）子条——

（i）第（2）款——

(I) in subparagraph (B) (ii) ,by striking "Director's judgment" and inserting "judgment of the appropriate Federal banking agency for the savings association"; and

(II) by striking "Director" each place that term appears and inserting "appropriate Federal banking agency for the savings association"; and

(ii) in paragraph (4) , by striking "Director" and inserting "Comptroller"; and

(K) except as provided in subparagraphs (A) through (J) , by striking "Director" each place that term appears and inserting "Board";

(9) in section 11 (12 U.S.C. 1468) , by striking "Director" each place that term appears and inserting "appropriate Federal banking agency";

(10) in section 12 (12 U.S.C. 1468a) , by striking "the Director" and inserting "a Federal banking agency"; and

(11) in section 13 (12 U.S.C. 1468a) is amended by striking "Director" and inserting "a Federal banking agency".

SEC. 370. HOUSING ACT OF 1948.

Section 502 (c) of the Housing Act of 1948 (12 U.S.C. 1701c (c)) is amended —

(1) in the matter preceding paragraph (1) , by striking "and the Director of the Office of Thrift Supervision" and inserting ", the Comptroller of the Currency,and the Federal Deposit Insurance Corporation"; and

(2) in paragraph (3) , by striking "Board" and inserting "Agency".

SEC. 371. HOUSING AND COMMUNITY DEVELOPMENT ACT OF 1992.

Section 543 of the Housing and Community Development Act of 1992 (Public Law 102–550; 106 Stat. 3798) is amended —

(1) in subsection (c) (1) —

(A) by striking subparagraphs (D) through (F) ; and

(B) by redesignating subparagraphs (G) and (H) as subparagraphs (D) and (E) , respectively; and

(2) in subsection (f) —

(A) in paragraph (2) , by striking "the Office of Thrift Supervision," each place that term appears; and

(B) in paragraph (3) —

(i) in the matter preceding subparagraph (A) ,by striking "the Office of Thrift Supervision,"; and

(ii) in subparagraph (D) , by striking "Office of Thrift Supervision,".

SEC. 372. HOUSING AND URBAN–RURAL RECOVERY ACT OF 1983.

Section 469 of the Housing and Urban–Rural Recovery Act of 1983 (12 U.S.C. 1701p–1) is amended in the first sentence,by striking "Federal Home Loan Bank Board" and

(I)第(B)(ii)子款删除“储蓄机构监理局局长的判断”,替以“储蓄协会的相应的联邦银行业监管机关的判断”;及

(II)删除所有的“储蓄机构监理局局长”,全部替以“储蓄协会的相应的联邦银行业监管机关”;及

(ii)第(4)款删除“储蓄机构监理局局长”,替以“货币监理署署长”;及

(K)除第(A)子款至第(J)子款规定的情形外,删除所有的“储蓄机构监理局局长”,全部替以“联邦储备委员会”;

(9)第11条(《美国法典》第十二编第1468节)删除所有的“储蓄机构监理局局长”,全部替以“相应的联邦银行业监管机关”;

(10)第12条(《美国法典》第十二编第1468a节)删除“储蓄机构监理局局长”,替以“某一联邦银行业监管机关”;及

(11)第13条(《美国法典》第十二编第1468a节)删除“储蓄机构监理局局长”,替以“某一联邦银行业监管机关”。

第370条 《1948年住房法》

《1948年住房法》第502(c)条[《美国法典》第十二编第1701c(c)节]修正如下——

(1)第(1)款之前的内容删除“以及储蓄机构监理局局长”,替以“,货币监理署署长和联邦存款保险公司”;及

(2)第(3)款删除“联邦储备委员会”,替以“联邦住房金融局”。

第371条 《1992年住房与社区发展法》

《1992年住房与社区发展法》第543条(第102—550号公法;《美国制定法汇编》第106卷第3798页)修正如下——

(1)在第(c)(1)子条中——

(A)删除第(D)子款至第(F)子款;及

(B)第(G)子款和第(H)子款分别重新编号为第(D)子款和第(E)子款;及

(2)在第(f)子条中——

(A)第(2)款删除所有的“储蓄机构监理局,”;及

(B)第(3)款——

(i)第(A)子款之前的内容删除“储蓄机构监理局,”;及

(ii)第(D)子款删除“储蓄机构监理局,”。

第372条 《1983年住房与城乡复苏法》

《1983年住房与城乡复苏法》第469条(《美国法典》第十二编第1701p—1节)第一句修正如下:删除“联邦住房贷款银行委员会”,替以“联邦住房金融局”。

inserting "Federal Housing Finance Agency".

SEC. 373. NATIONAL HOUSING ACT.

Section 202 (f) of the National Housing Act (12 U.S.C. 1708 (f)) is amended —

(1) by striking paragraph (5) and inserting the following: " (5) if the mortgagee is a national bank, a subsidiary or affiliate of such bank,a Federal savings association or a subsidiary or affiliate of a savings association,the Comptroller of the Currency; ";

(2) in paragraph (6) , by adding "and" at the end;

(3) in paragraph (7) —

(A) by inserting "or State savings association" after "State bank"; and

(B) by striking "; and" and inserting a period; and

(4) by striking paragraph (8) .

SEC. 374. NEIGHBORHOOD REINVESTMENT CORPORATION ACT.

Section 606 (c) (3) of the Neighborhood Reinvestment Corporation Act (42 U.S.C. 8105 (c) (3)) is amended by striking "Federal Home Loan Bank Board" and inserting "Federal Housing Finance Agency".

SEC. 375. PUBLIC LAW 93–100.

Section 5 (d) of Public Law 93–100 (12 U.S.C. 1470 (a)) is amended —

(1) in paragraph (1) , by striking "Federal Savings and Loan Insurance Corporation with respect to insured institutions, the Board of Governors of the Federal Reserve System with respect to State member insured banks, and the Federal Deposit Insurance Corporation with respect to State nonmember insured banks" and inserting "appropriate Federal banking agency, with respect to the institutions subject to the jurisdiction of each such agency,"; and

(2) in paragraph (2) , by striking "supervisory" and inserting "banking".

SEC. 376. SECURITIES EXCHANGE ACT OF 1934.

The Securities Exchange Act of 1934 (15 U.S.C. 78a et seq.) is amended —

(1) in section 3 (a) (34) (15 U.S.C. 78c (a) (34)) —

(A) in subparagraph (A) —

(i) in clause (i) ,by striking "or a subsidiary or a department or division of any such bank" and inserting "a subsidiary or a department or division of any such bank,a Federal savings association (as defined in section 3 (b) (2) of the Federal Deposit Insurance Act (12 U.S.C. 1813 (b) (2))) , the deposits of which are insured by the Federal Deposit Insurance Corporation,or a subsidiary or department or division of any such Federal savings association";

(ii) in clause (ii) , by striking "or a subsidiary or a department or division of such subsidiary" and inserting "a subsidiary or a department or division of such subsidiary,or a savings and loan holding company";

(iii) in clause (iii) , by striking "or a subsidiary or department or division thereof; " and

第373条　《国民住房法》

《国民住房法》第202(f)条(《美国法典》第十二编第1708(f)节)修正如下——

(1)删除第(5)款,替以如下内容:"(5)如果抵押权人是国民银行、国民银行的子公司或关联方、联邦储蓄协会或某一储蓄协会的子公司或关联方,则为货币监理署署长;";

(2)在第(6)款结尾处增加"及";

(3)在第(7)款中——

(A)在"州银行"之后插入"或州储蓄协会";及

(B)删除";及",替以句号;及

(4)删除第(8)款。

第374条　《社区再投资公司法》

《社区再投资公司法》第606(c)(3)条[《美国法典》第四十二编第8105(c)(3)节]修正如下:删除"联邦住房贷款银行委员会",替以"联邦住房金融局"。

第375条　第93—100号公法

第93—100号公法第5(d)条[《美国法典》第十二编第1470(a)节]修正如下——

(1)在第(1)款中,删除"就参保机构而言,指联邦储贷保险公司,就州成员参保银行而言,指联邦储备委员会,以及就州非成员参保银行而言,指联邦存款保险公司",替以"就每一该等监管机关管辖范围内的机构而言,指相应的联邦银行业监管机关,";及

(2)在第(2)款中,删除"监管",替以"银行"。

第376条　《1934年证券交易法》

《1934年证券交易法》(《美国法典》第十五编第78a节及其后条文)修正如下——

(1)在第3(a)(34)条[《美国法典》第十五编第78c(a)(34)节]中——

(A)第(A)子款——

(i)第(i)项删除"或任何该等银行的子公司、部门或单位",替以"任何该等银行的子公司、部门或单位,其存款由联邦存款保险公司承保的联邦储蓄协会{定义见《联邦存款保险法》第3(b)(2)条[《美国法典》第十二编第1813(b)(2)节)]},或者任何该等联邦储蓄协会的子公司或部门或单位";

(ii)第(ii)项删除"或某一子公司或该子公司的部门或单位",替以"某一子公司,或该子公司的部门或单位,或者储贷控股公司";

(iii)第(iii)项删除"或其子公司、部门或单位;",替以"任何该等银行的子公司、部

inserting "a subsidiary or department or division of any such bank,a State savings association (as defined in section 3 (b) (3) of the Federal Deposit Insurance Act (12 U.S.C. 1813 (b) (3))) ,the deposits of which are insured by the Federal Deposit Insurance Corporation,or a subsidiary or a department or division of any such State savings association; and";

(iv) by striking clause (iv) ; and

(v) by redesignating clause (v) as clause (iv) ;

(B) in subparagraph (B) —

(i) in clause (i) ,by striking "or a subsidiary of any such bank" and inserting "a subsidiary of any such bank,a Federal savings association (as defined in section 3 (b) (2) of the Federal Deposit Insurance Act (12 U.S.C. 1813 (b) (2))) , the deposits of which are insured by the Federal Deposit Insurance Corporation,or a subsidiary of any such Federal savings association";

(ii) in clause (ii) ,by striking "or a subsidiary of a bank holding company which is a bank other than a bank specified in clause (i) , (iii) , or (iv) of this subparagraph" and inserting "a subsidiary of a bank holding company that is a bank other than a bank specified in clause (i) or (iii) of this subparagraph,or a savings and loan holding company";

(iii) in clause (iii) , by striking "or a subsidiary thereof; " and inserting "a subsidiary of any such bank,a State savings association (as defined in section 3 (b) (3) of the Federal Deposit Insurance Act (12 U.S.C. 1813 (b) (3))) , the deposits of which are insured by the Federal Deposit Insurance Corporation,or a subsidiary of any such State savings association; and";

(iv) by striking clause (iv) ; and

(v) by redesignating clause (v) as clause (iv) ;

(C) in subparagraph (C) —

(i) in clause (i) ,by striking "bank" and inserting "bank or a Federal savings association (as defined in section 3 (b) (2) of the Federal Deposit Insurance Act (12 U.S.C. 1813 (b) (2))) , the deposits of which are insured by the Federal Deposit Insurance Corporation";

(ii) in clause (ii) ,by striking "or a subsidiary of a bank holding company which is a bank other than a bank specified in clause (i) , (iii) , or (iv) of this subparagraph" and inserting "a subsidiary of a bank holding company that is a bank other than a bank specified in clause (i) or (iii) of this subparagraph,or a savings and loan holding company";

(iii) in clause (iii) , by striking "System) " and inserting, "System) or a State savings association (as defined in section 3 (b) (3) of the Federal Deposit Insurance Act (12 U.S.C. 1813 (b) (3))), the deposits of which are insured by the Federal Deposit Insurance Corporation; and";

(iv) by striking clause (iv) ; and

门或单位,其存款由联邦存款保险公司承保的州储蓄协会{定义见《联邦存款保险法》第3(b)(3)条[《美国法典》第十二编第1813(b)(3)节]},或者任何该等州储蓄协会的子公司、部门或单位;及”;

(iv)删除第(iv)项;及

(v)第(v)项重新编号为第(iv)项;

(B)第(B)子款——

(i)第(i)项删除“或任何该等银行的子公司”,替以“任何该等银行的子公司,其存款由联邦存款保险公司承保的联邦储蓄协会{定义见《联邦存款保险法》第3(b)(2)条[《美国法典》第十二编第1813(b)(2)节]},或者任何该等联邦储蓄协会的子公司”;

(ii)第(ii)项删除“或银行控股公司的具有银行身份的子公司[但本子款第(i)项、第(iii)项或第(iv)项所述银行的子公司除外]”,替以“银行控股公司具有银行身份的子公司[但本子款第(i)项或第(iii)项所述银行的子公司除外],或者储贷控股公司”;

(iii)第(iii)项删除“或其子公司;”,替以“任何该等银行的子公司、其存款由联邦存款保险公司承保的州储蓄协会{定义见《联邦存款保险法》第3(b)(3)条[《美国法典》第十二编第1813(b)(3)节]},或者任何该等州储蓄协会的子公司;及”;

(iv)删除第(iv)项;及

(v)第(v)项重新编号为第(iv)项;

(C)第(C)子款——

(i)第(i)项删除“银行”,替以“银行或其存款由联邦存款保险公司承保的联邦储蓄协会{定义见《联邦存款保险法》第3(b)(2)条[《美国法典》第十二编第1813(b)(2)节]}”;

(ii)第(ii)项删除“或银行控股公司具有银行身份的子公司[但性质为本子款第(i)项、第(iii)项或第(iv)项所述银行的子公司除外]”,替以“银行控股公司具有银行身份的子公司[但本子款第(i)项或第(iii)项所述银行的子公司除外],或者储贷控股公司”;

(iii)第(iii)项删除“联邦储备委员会)”,替以“联邦储备委员会)或其存款由联邦存款保险公司承保的州储蓄协会{定义见《联邦存款保险法》第3(b)(3)条[《美国法典》第12编第1813(b)(3)节]};及”;

(iv)删除第(iv)项;及

(v) by redesignating clause (v) as clause (iv);

(D) in subparagraph (D)—

(i) in clause (i), by inserting after "bank" the following: "or a Federal savings association (as defined in section 3 (b) (2) of the Federal Deposit Insurance Act (12 U.S.C. 1813 (b) (2))), the deposits of which are insured by the Federal Deposit Insurance Corporation";

(ii) in clause (ii), by adding "and" at the end;

(iii) by striking clause (iii);

(iv) by redesignating clause (iv) as clause (iii); and

(v) in clause (iii), as so redesignated, by inserting after "bank" the following: "or a State savings association (as defined in section 3 (b) (3) of the Federal Deposit Insurance Act (12 U.S.C. 1813 (b) (3))), the deposits of which are insured by the Federal Deposit Insurance Corporation";

(E) in subparagraph (F)—

(i) in clause (i), by inserting after "bank" the following: "or a Federal savings association (as defined in section 3 (b) (2) of the Federal Deposit Insurance Act (12 U.S.C. 1813 (b) (2), the deposits of which are insured by the Federal Deposit Insurance Corporation";

(ii) by striking clause (ii);

(iii) by redesignating clauses (iii), (iv), and (v) as clauses (ii), (iii), and (iv), respectively; and

(iv) in clause (iii), as so redesignated, by inserting before the semicolon the following: "or a State savings association (as defined in section 3 (b) (3) of the Federal Deposit Insurance Act (12 U.S.C. 1813 (b) (3))), the deposits of which are insured by the Federal Deposit Insurance Corporation";

(F) in subparagraph (G)—

(i) in clause (i), by inserting after "national bank" the following: ", a Federal savings association (as defined in section 3 (b) (2) of the Federal Deposit Insurance Act), the deposits of which are insured by the Federal Deposit Insurance Corporation,";

(ii) in clause (iii)—

(I) by inserting after "bank)" the following: ", a State savings association (as defined in section 3 (b) (3) of the Federal Deposit Insurance Act), the deposits of which are insured by the Federal Deposit Insurance Corporation,"; and

(II) by adding "and" at the end;

(iii) by striking clause (iv); and

(iv) by redesignating clause (v) as clause (iv); and

(G) in the undesignated matter following subparagraph (H), by striking ", and the term

（v）第（v）项重新编号为第（iv）项；

（D）第（D）子款——

（i）第（i）项在“银行”之后插入“或其存款由联邦存款保险公司承保的联邦储蓄协会｛定义见《联邦存款保险法》第3（b）（2）条［《美国法典》第十二编第1813（b）（2）节］｝”；

（ii）第（ii）项结尾处增加“及”；

（iii）删除第（iii）项；

（iv）第（iv）项重新编号为第（iii）项；及

（v）第（iii）项（以重新编号后的序号为准）在“银行”之后插入“或其存款由联邦存款保险公司承保的州储蓄协会｛定义见《联邦存款保险法》第3（b）（3）条［《美国法典》第十二编第1813（b）（3）节］｝”；

（E）第（F）子款——

（i）第（i）项在“银行”之后插入“或其存款由联邦存款保险公司承保的联邦储蓄协会｛定义见《联邦存款保险法》第3（b）（2）条［《美国法典》第十二编第1813（b）（2）节］｝”；

（ii）删除第（ii）项；

（iii）第（iii）项、第（iv）项和第（v）项分别重新编号为第（ii）项、第（iii）项和第（iv）项；及

（iv）在第（iii）项（以重新编号后的序号为准）的分号前插入“或其存款由联邦存款保险公司承保的州储蓄协会｛定义见《联邦存款保险法》第3（b）（3）条［《美国法典》第十二编第1813（b）（3）节］｝”；

（F）第（G）子款——

（i）第（i）项在“国民银行”之后插入“，其存款由联邦存款保险公司承保的联邦储蓄协会［定义见《联邦存款保险法》第3（b）（2）条］，”；

（ii）第（iii）项——

（I）在“银行）”之后插入“，其存款由联邦存款保险公司承保的州储蓄协会［定义见《联邦存款保险法》第3（b）（3）条］，”；及

（II）在该项结尾处增加“及”；

（iii）删除第（iv）项；及

（iv）第（v）项重新编号为第（iv）项；及

（G）在第（H）子款后的无编号内容中，删除“，‘哥伦比亚特区储贷协会’一词系指

'District of Columbia savings and loan association' means any association subject to examination and supervision by the Office of Thrift Supervision under section 8 of the Home Owners' Loan Act of 1933";

(2) in section 12 (i) (15 U.S.C. 78l (i))—

(A) in paragraph (1) ,by inserting after "national banks" the following: "and Federal savings associations,the accounts of which are insured by the Federal Deposit Insurance Corporation";

(B) by striking "(3)" and all that follows through "vested in the Office of Thrift Supervision" and inserting "and (3) with respect to all other insured banks and State savings associations,the accounts of which are insured by the Federal Deposit Insurance Corporation,are vested in the Federal Deposit Insurance Corporation"; and

(C) in the second sentence,by striking "the Federal Deposit Insurance Corporation,and the Office of Thrift Supervision" and inserting "and the Federal Deposit Insurance Corporation";

(3) in section 15C (g) (1) (15 U.S.C. 78o–5 (g) (1)) ,by striking "the Director of the Office of Thrift Supervision,the Federal Savings and Loan Insurance Corporation,"; and

(4) in section 23 (b) (1) (15 U.S.C. 78w (b) (1)) ,by striking ",other than the Office of Thrift Supervision,".

SEC. 377. TITLE 18,UNITED STATES CODE.

Title 18,United States Code,is amended—

(1) in section 212 (c) (2)—

(A) by striking subparagraph (C) ; and

(B) by redesignating subparagraphs (D) through (H) as subparagraphs (C) through (G) ,respectively;

(2) in section 657,by striking "Office of Thrift Supervision,the Resolution Trust Corporation,";

(3) in section 981 (a) (1) (D)—

(A) by striking "Resolution Trust Corporation,"; and

(B) by striking "or the Office of Thrift Supervision";

(4) in section 982 (a) (3)—

(A) by striking "Resolution Trust Corporation,"; and

(B) by striking "or the Office of Thrift Supervision";

(5) in section 1006—

(A) by striking "Office of Thrift Supervision,"; and

(B) by striking "the Resolution Trust Corporation,";

(6) in section 1014—

(A) by striking "the Office of Thrift Supervision"; and

根据《1933年业主贷款法》第8条须接受储蓄机构监理局检查和监管的任何协会”;

(2)在第12(i)条[《美国法典》第十五编第78l(i)节]中——

(A)第(1)款在“国民银行”之后插入“以及其账户由联邦存款保险公司承保的联邦储蓄协会”;

(B)删除“(3)”直至“属于储蓄机构监理局”的全部内容,替以“且(3)就其账户由联邦存款保险公司承保的全部其他参保银行和州储蓄协会而言,属于联邦存款保险公司”;及

(C)第二句删除“联邦存款保险公司和储蓄机构监理局”,替以“以及联邦存款保险公司”;

(3)第15C(g)(1)条[《美国法典》第十五编第78o—5(g)(1)节]删除“储蓄机构监理局局长、联邦储贷保险公司,”;及

(4)第23(b)(1)条[《美国法典》第十五编第78w(b)(1)节]删除“,储蓄机构监理局除外,”。

第377条 《美国法典》第十八编

《美国法典》第十八编修正如下——

(1)在第212(c)(2)节中——

(A)删除第(C)子款;及

(B)第(D)子款至第(H)子款重新编号为第(C)子款至第(G)子款;

(2)在第657节中,删除“储蓄机构监理局、清盘信托公司、”;

(3)在第981(a)(1)(D)节中——

(A)删除“清盘信托公司,”;及

(B)删除“或储蓄机构监理局”;

(4)在第982(a)(3)节中——

(A)删除“清盘信托公司,”;及

(B)删除“或储蓄机构监理局”;

(5)在第1006节中——

(A)删除“储蓄机构监理局,”;及

(B)删除“清盘信托公司,”;及

(6)在第1014节中——

(A)删除“储蓄机构监理局”;及

(B) by striking "the Resolution Trust Corporation,"; and

(7) in section 1032 (1) —

(A) by striking "the Resolution Trust Corporation,"; and

(B) by striking "or the Director of the Office of Thrift Supervision".

SEC. 378. TITLE 31,UNITED STATES CODE.

Title 31,United States Code,is amended —

(1) in section 321 —

(A) in subsection (c) —

(i) in paragraph (1), by adding "and" at the end;

(ii) in paragraph (2), by striking "; and" and inserting a period; and

(iii) by striking paragraph (3); and

(B) by striking subsection (e); and

(2) in section 714 (a), by striking "the Office of the Comptroller of the Currency, and the Office of Thrift Supervision." and inserting "and the Office of the Comptroller of the Currency.".

(B)删除“清盘信托公司,”;及

(7)在第1032(1)节中——

(A)删除“清盘信托公司,”;及

(B)删除“或储蓄机构监理局局长”。

第378条 《美国法典》第三十一编

《美国法典》第三十一编修正如下——

(1)在第321节中——

(A)第(c)子节——

(i)在第(1)款结尾处增加“及”;

(ii)第(2)款删除“;及”,替以句号;及

(iii)删除第(3)款;及

(B)删除第(e)子节;及

(2)在第714(a)节中,删除“货币监理署以及储蓄机构监理局。”替以“货币监理署。”

TITLE Ⅳ — REGULATION OF ADVISERS TO HEDGE FUNDS AND OTHERS

SEC. 401. SHORT TITLE.

This title may be cited as the "Private Fund Investment Advisers Registration Act of 2010".

SEC. 402. DEFINITIONS.

(a) INVESTMENT ADVISERS ACT OF 1940 DEFINITIONS. — Section 202 (a) of the Investment Advisers Act of 1940 (15 U.S.C. 80b–2 (a)) is amended by adding at the end the following:

" (29) The term 'private fund' means an issuer that would be an investment company, as defined in section 3 of the Investment Company Act of 1940 (15 U.S.C. 80a–3) ,but for section 3 (c)(1) or 3 (c)(7) of that Act.

" (30) The term 'foreign private adviser' means any investment adviser who —

" (A) has no place of business in the United States;

" (B) has,in total,fewer than 15 clients and investors in the United States in private funds advised by the investment adviser;

" (C) has aggregate assets under management attributable to clients in the United States and investors in the United States in private funds advised by the investment adviser of less than $25,000,000,or such higher amount as the Commission may,by rule,deem appropriate in accordance with the purposes of this title; and

" (D) neither —

" (i) holds itself out generally to the public in the United States as an investment adviser; nor

" (ii) acts as —

" (I) an investment adviser to any investment company registered under the Investment Company Act of 1940; or

" (II) a company that has elected to be a business development company pursuant to section 54 of the Investment Company Act of 1940 (15 U.S.C. 80a–53) , and has not

第四编——对于对冲基金顾问和其他基金顾问的监管

第401条 简称

引述本编时,可简称为《2010年私募基金投资顾问注册法》。

第402条 定义

(a)**《1940年投资顾问法》中的定义**。——在《1940年投资顾问法》第202(a)条[《美国法典》第十五编第80b—2(a)节]结尾处增加如下内容,作为对该条的修正:

"(29)'私募基金'一词系指若非适用了《1940年投资公司法》第3(c)(1)条或第3(c)(7)条的规定,将会构成该法第3条(《美国法典》第十五编80a—3节)定义的投资公司的发行人。

(30)'外国私人顾问'一词系指具有如下特征的任何投资顾问——

(A)在美国无营业场所;

(B)接受其顾问服务的客户和私募基金的美国境内投资者总数不超过15名;

(C)接受其顾问服务的美国境内客户和接受其顾问服务的私募基金美国境内投资者,委托该投资顾问管理的资产总额低于2500万美元,或低于证券交易委员会根据本编宗旨认为适当的并发布规则确定的其他较高标准;且

(D)既未——

(i)对美国公众以投资顾问身份自居;也未

(ii)以如下身份行事——

(I)根据《1940年投资公司法》注册的任何投资公司的投资顾问;或

(II)根据《1940年投资公司法》第54条(《美国法典》第十五编第80a—53节)已选择企业开发公司身份,且未撤销该等选择的公司。"

withdrawn its election. ".

(b) OTHER DEFINITIONS. — As used in this title,the terms "investment adviser" and "private fund" have the same meanings as in section 202 of the Investment Advisers Act of 1940,as amended by this title.

SEC. 403. ELIMINATION OF PRIVATE ADVISER EXEMPTION; LIMITED EXEMPTION FOR FOREIGN PRIVATE ADVISERS; LIMITED INTRASTATE EXEMPTION.

Section 203 (b) of the Investment Advisers Act of 1940 (15 U.S.C. 80b-3 (b)) is amended —

(1) in paragraph (1) , by inserting ",other than an investment adviser who acts as an investment adviser to any private fund," before "all of whose";

(2) by striking paragraph (3) and inserting the following:

" (3) any investment adviser that is a foreign private adviser;"; and

(3) in paragraph (5) ,by striking "or" at the end;

(4) in paragraph (6) —

(A) by striking "any investment adviser" and inserting " (A) any investment adviser";

(B) by redesignating subparagraphs (A) and (B) as clauses (i) and (ii) , respectively; and

(C) in clause (ii)(as so redesignated) ,by striking the period at the end and inserting "; or"; and

(D) by adding at the end the following:

" (B) any investment adviser that is registered with the Commodity Futures Trading Commission as a commodity trading advisor and advises a private fund,provided that,if after the date of enactment of the Private Fund Investment Advisers Registration Act of 2010,the business of the advisor should become predominately the provision of securities-related advice,then such adviser shall register with the Commission. ".

(5) by adding at the end the following:

" (7) any investment adviser,other than any entity that has elected to be regulated or is regulated as a business development company pursuant to section 54 of the Investment Company Act of 1940 (15 U.S.C. 80a-54) ,who solely advises —

" (A) small business investment companies that are licensees under the Small Business Investment Act of 1958;

" (B) entities that have received from the Small Business Administration notice to proceed to qualify for a license as a small business investment company under the Small Business Investment Act of 1958, which notice or license has not been revoked; or

" (C) applicants that are affiliated with 1 or more licensed small business investment companies described in subparagraph (A) and that have applied for another license under

(b)**其他定义**。——就本编而言,“投资顾问”和“私募基金”的含义以《1940年投资顾问法》第202条(以经本编修正后的版本为准)的定义为准。

第403条　取消私人顾问豁免;对外国私人顾问的有限豁免;州际有限豁免

《1940年投资顾问法》第203(b)条[《美国法典》第十五编第80b—3(b)节]修正如下——

(1)在第(1)款“其全部客户为”前插入“,以任何私募基金的投资顾问身份行事的投资顾问除外,”;

(2)删除第(3)款,替以:

“(3)任何具有外国私人顾问身份的投资顾问;”;及

(3)删除第(5)款结尾处的“或”;

(4)在第(6)款中——

(A)删除“任何投资顾问”,替以“(A)任何投资顾问”;

(B)第(A)子款和第(B)子款分别重新编号为第(i)项和第(ii)项;及

(C)在重新编号后的第(ii)项中删除结尾处的句号,替以“;或”;及

(D)在第(6)款结尾处增加如下内容:

“(B)在商品期货交易委员会注册为商品交易顾问并为私募基金提供顾问服务的任何投资顾问,但是,在《2010年私募基金投资顾问注册法》颁布之日后,该顾问以提供证券顾问服务为主营业务的,应在证券交易委员会注册。”

(5)在结尾处增加如下内容:

“(7)并非根据《1940年投资公司法》第54条(《美国法典》第十五编第80a—54节)选择以企业开发公司身份受监管或事实上被作为企业开发公司监管的任何实体,且仅为以下对象提供顾问服务的任何投资顾问——

(A)根据《1958年小型企业投资法》获得执照的小型企业投资公司;

(B)已收到小型企业管理局通知,可根据《1958年小型企业投资法》完成相关手续获得小型企业投资公司执照的实体,且上述通知或执照未被撤销;或

(C)与第(A)子款所述一家或一家以上已获得执照的小型企业投资公司相关联,并已根据《1958年小型企业投资法》单独申请执照,但尚未获批的申请人。”

the Small Business Investment Act of 1958,which application remains pending. ".

SEC. 404. COLLECTION OF SYSTEMIC RISK DATA; REPORTS; EXAMINATIONS; DISCLOSURES.

Section 204 of the Investment Advisers Act of 1940 (15 U.S.C. 80b–4) is amended —

(1) by redesignating subsections (b) and (c) as subsections (c) and (d), respectively; and

(2) by inserting after subsection (a) the following:

" (b) RECORDS AND REPORTS OF PRIVATE FUNDS. —

" (1) IN GENERAL. — The Commission may require any investment adviser registered under this title —

" (A) to maintain such records of,and file with the Commission such reports regarding, private funds advised by the investment adviser,as necessary and appropriate in the public interest and for the protection of investors,or for the assessment of systemic risk by the Financial Stability Oversight Council (in this subsection referred to as the 'Council'); and

" (B) to provide or make available to the Council those reports or records or the information contained therein.

" (2) TREATMENT OF RECORDS. — The records and reports of any private fund to which an investment adviser registered under this title provides investment advice shall be deemed to be the records and reports of the investment adviser.

" (3) REQUIRED INFORMATION. — The records and reports required to be maintained by an investment adviser and subject to inspection by the Commission under this subsection shall include, for each private fund advised by the investment adviser, a description of —

" (A) the amount of assets under management and use of leverage,including off–balance–sheet leverage;

" (B) counterparty credit risk exposure;

" (C) trading and investment positions;

" (D) valuation policies and practices of the fund;

" (E) types of assets held;

" (F) side arrangements or side letters,whereby certain investors in a fund obtain more favorable rights or entitlements than other investors;

" (G) trading practices; and

" (H) such other information as the Commission,in consultation with the Council, determines is necessary and appropriate in the public interest and for the protection of investors or for the assessment of systemic risk, which may include the establishment of different reporting requirements for different classes of fund advisers, based on the type or size of private fund being advised.

第404条　系统性风险数据的收集;报告;检查;披露

《1940年投资顾问法》第204条(《美国法典》第十五编第80b—4节)修正如下——

(1)第(b)子条和第(c)子条分别重新编号为第(c)子条和第(d)子条;及

(2)在第(a)子条之后插入如下内容:

"(b)**私募基金的记录和报告**。——

(1)**一般规定**。——证券交易委员会可以要求根据本编规定注册的任何投资顾问——

(A)为维护公共利益和保护投资者或为金融稳定监督委员会评估系统性风险之目的,就接受其顾问服务的私募基金保存必要且适当的记录,并就该等基金向证券交易委员会提交必要且适当的报告;及

(B)向金融稳定监督委员会提供或开放上述报告或记录或其中包含的信息。

(2)**记录的处理**。——根据本编规定注册的投资顾问为任何私募基金提供投资顾问服务的,该私募基金的记录和报告即应视为该投资顾问的记录和报告。

(3)**信息要求**。——投资顾问应根据本子条规定保存接受其顾问服务的每一私募基金的记录和报告,并接受证券交易委员会检查。记录和报告应包含以下内容——

(A)管理资产的金额和杠杆的使用,包括资产负债表外杠杆的使用;

(B)对手方信用风险敞口;

(C)交易和投资持仓;

(D)基金估值政策和惯例;

(E)所持资产的类型;

(F)特定基金投资者可据以获取更特惠的权利或资格的补充安排或补充合意函;

(G)交易方式;及

(H)经证券交易委员会与金融稳定监督委员会磋商后判定的,对维护公共利益和保护投资者或评估系统性风险必要且适当的其他信息,其中可能包括:按照接受顾问服务的私募基金类型或规模针对不同类别基金顾问设定的差异化报告制度。

“(4) MAINTENANCE OF RECORDS. — An investment adviser registered under this title shall maintain such records of private funds advised by the investment adviser for such period or periods as the Commission,by rule,may prescribe as necessary and appropriate in the public interest and for the protection of investors,or for the assessment of systemic risk.

“(5) FILING OF RECORDS. — The Commission shall issue rules requiring each investment adviser to a private fund to file reports containing such information as the Commission deems necessary and appropriate in the public interest and for the protection of investors or for the assessment of systemic risk.

“(6) EXAMINATION OF RECORDS. —

“(A) PERIODIC AND SPECIAL EXAMINATIONS. — The Commission —

“(i) shall conduct periodic inspections of the records of private funds maintained by an investment adviser registered under this title in accordance with a schedule established by the Commission; and

“(ii) may conduct at any time and from time to time such additional,special,and other examinations as the Commission may prescribe as necessary and appropriate in the public interest and for the protection of investors,or for the assessment of systemic risk.

“(B) AVAILABILITY OF RECORDS. — An investment adviser registered under this title shall make available to the Commission any copies or extracts from such records as may be prepared without undue effort,expense,or delay,as the Commission or its representatives may reasonably request.

“(7) INFORMATION SHARING. —

“(A) IN GENERAL. — The Commission shall make available to the Council copies of all reports,documents,records,and information filed with or provided to the Commission by an investment adviser under this subsection as the Council may consider necessary for the purpose of assessing the systemic risk posed by a private fund.

“(B) CONFIDENTIALITY. — The Council shall maintain the confidentiality of information received under this paragraph in all such reports,documents,records,and information,in a manner consistent with the level of confidentiality established for the Commission pursuant to paragraph (8). The Council shall be exempt from section 552 of title 5,United States Code,with respect to any information in any report,document,record,or information made available,to the Council under this subsection.”.

“(8) COMMISSION CONFIDENTIALITY OF REPORTS. — Notwithstanding any other provision of law,the Commission may not be compelled to disclose any report or information contained therein required to be filed with the Commission under this subsection, except that nothing in this subsection authorizes the Commission —

“(A) to withhold information from Congress,upon an agreement of confidentiality; or

“(B) prevent the Commission from complying with —

(4)**记录保存**。——出于维护公共利益和保护投资者或评估系统性风险之目的，根据本编注册的投资顾问应按证券交易委员会发布的规则明确规定的一个或一个以上的记录期，就接受其顾问服务的私募基金保存必要且适当的记录。

(5)**记录的提交**。——证券交易委员会应发布规则，要求私募基金的每一投资顾问均提交报告，说明证券交易委员会认为对维护公共利益和保护投资者或评估系统性风险必要且适当的信息。

(6)**记录检查**。——

(A)**定期及特别检查**。——证券交易委员会——

(i)应根据其制定的时间表，对依据本编规定注册的投资顾问所保存的私募基金记录进行定期检查;及

(ii)可以随时和不时对上述记录进行其认为对维护公共利益和保护投资者或评估系统性风险必要且适当的补充检查、特别检查或其他形式的检查。

(B)**记录的提供**。——根据本编规定注册的投资顾问应在证券交易委员会或其代表提出合理请求时，向证券交易委员会提供上述记录的任何复本或摘要，但以文件准备工作不必付出不合理的努力、成本和时间为限。

(7)**信息共享**。——

(A)**一般规定**。——为评估某一个私募基金的系统性风险，当金融稳定监督委员会认为必要时，证券交易委员会应向金融稳定监督委员会提供，投资顾问根据本子条规定向证券交易委员会提交或提供的所有报告、文件、记录和信息的复本。

(B)**保密**。——金融稳定监督委员会应按证券交易委员会根据第(8)款规定设定的保密级别，维持其根据本款收到的上述所有报告、文件、记录和信息的保密性。就根据本子条规定向金融稳定监督委员会提供的任何报告、文件、记录或信息而言，金融稳定监督委员会应豁免于《美国法典》第五编第552节的规定。

(8)**证券交易委员会对报告承担的保密责任**。——无论是否存在任何不同法律规定，证券交易委员会均不得被强制披露根据本子条规定应向其提交的任何报告或报告所含任何信息，但本子条的任何规定均不授权证券交易委员会——

(A)在达成保密协议后，仍拒不向国会透露上述信息;或

(B)拒不遵守或履行——

"(i) a request for information from any other Federal department or agency or any self–regulatory organization requesting the report or information for purposes within the scope of its jurisdiction; or

"(ii) an order of a court of the United States in an action brought by the United States or the Commission.

"(9) OTHER RECIPIENTS CONFIDENTIALITY. — Any department,agency,or self–regulatory organization that receives reports or information from the Commission under this subsection shall maintain the confidentiality of such reports,documents,records,and information in a manner consistent with the level of confidentiality established for the Commission under paragraph (8).

"(10) PUBLIC INFORMATION EXCEPTION. —

"(A) IN GENERAL. — The Commission,the Council,and any other department, agency,or self–regulatory organization that receives information,reports,documents,records,or information from the Commission under this subsection,shall be exempt from the provisions of section 552 of title 5,United States Code,with respect to any such report,document,record,or information. Any proprietary information of an investment adviser ascertained by the Commission from any report required to be filed with the Commission pursuant to this subsection shall be subject to the same limitations on public disclosure as any facts ascertained during an examination,as provided by section 210 (b) of this title.

"(B) PROPRIETARY INFORMATION. — For purposes of this paragraph,proprietary information includes sensitive,non–public information regarding —

"(i) the investment or trading strategies of the investment adviser;

"(ii) analytical or research methodologies;

"(iii) trading data;

"(iv) computer hardware or software containing intellectual property; and

"(v) any additional information that the Commission determines to be proprietary.

"(11) ANNUAL REPORT TO CONGRESS. — The Commission shall report annually to Congress on how the Commission has used the data collected pursuant to this subsection to monitor the markets for the protection of investors and the integrity of the markets.".

SEC. 405. DISCLOSURE PROVISION AMENDMENT.

Section 210 (c) of the Investment Advisers Act of 1940 (15 U.S.C. 80b–10 (c)) is amended by inserting before the period at the end the following: "or for purposes of assessment of potential systemic risk".

SEC. 406. CLARIFICATION OF RULEMAKING AUTHORITY.

Section 211 of the Investment Advisers Act of 1940 (15 U.S.C. 80b–11) is amended —

(1) in subsection (a), by inserting before the period at the end of the first sentence the following: ",including rules and regulations defining technical,trade,and other terms used in

(i)任何其他联邦部门或机关或任何自律组织因其管辖范围内之事项提出的获取上述报告或信息的请求;或

(ii)在美国或证券交易委员会提起的诉讼过程中,联邦法院签发的命令。

(9)**其他接收者的保密义务**。——任何根据本子条规定收到证券交易委员会提供的报告或信息的部门、机关或自律组织均应根据第(8)款为证券交易委员会确定的保密级别,维持该等报告、文件、记录及信息的保密性。

(10)**公开披露信息的例外规定**。——

(A)**一般规定**。——证券交易委员会、金融稳定监督委员会以及根据本子条规定从证券交易委员会处收到报告、文件、记录或信息的任何其他部门、机关或自律组织,就任何上述报告、文件、记录或信息而言,应豁免于《美国法典》第五编第552节的规定。证券交易委员会根据报告提交人依本子条规定应向其提交的任何报告所查明的任何投资顾问的专有信息,应与其在检查工作中所查明的任何事实一样受制于本编第210(b)条的公开披露限制规定。

(B)**专有信息**。——就本款而言,专有信息包括与下列各项相关的敏感、非公开信息——

(i)投资顾问的投资或交易策略;

(ii)分析或研究方法;

(iii)交易数据;

(iv)含有知识产权的电脑硬件或软件;及

(v)证券交易委员会判定为专有信息的任何其他信息。

(11)**向国会提交年度报告**。——证券交易委员会应向国会提交年度报告,说明为实施市场监控,实现投资者保护和确保市场完整性之目标,其对根据本子条规定收集的数据的使用情况。"

第405条 对披露规定的修正

在《1940年投资顾问法》第210(c)条[《美国法典》第十五编第80b—10(c)节]结尾处的句号前插入如下内容:"或为评估系统性风险之目的",作为对该条的修正。

第406条 对规则制定权的说明

《1940年投资顾问法》第211条(《美国法典》第十二编第80b—11节)修正如下——

(1)在第(a)子条中,在第一句结尾处的句号前插入如下内容:",包括界定本编中使用的技术术语、交易术语和其他术语的规则与规章,但就第206条第(1)款和第(2)

this title,except that the Commission may not define the term 'client' for purposes of paragraphs (1) and (2) of section 206 to include an investor in a private fund managed by an investment adviser,if such private fund has entered into an advisory contract with such adviser"; and

(2) by adding at the end the following:

" (e) DISCLOSURE RULES ON PRIVATE FUNDS. — The Commission and the Commodity Futures Trading Commission shall,after consultation with the Council but not later than 12 months after the date of enactment of the Private Fund Investment Advisers Registration Act of 2010,jointly promulgate rules to establish the form and content of the reports required to be filed with the Commission under subsection 204 (b) and with the Commodity Futures Trading Commission by investment advisers that are registered both under this title and the Commodity Exchange Act (7 U.S.C. 1a et seq.) . ".

SEC. 407. EXEMPTION OF AND REPORTING BY VENTURE CAPITAL FUND ADVISERS.

Section 203 of the Investment Advisers Act of 1940 (15 U.S.C. 80b-3) is amended by adding at the end the following:

" (l) EXEMPTION OF VENTURE CAPITAL FUND ADVISERS. — No investment adviser that acts as an investment adviser solely to 1 or more venture capital funds shall be subject to the registration requirements of this title with respect to the provision of investment advice relating to a venture capital fund. Not later than 1 year after the date of enactment of this subsection,the Commission shall issue final rules to define the term 'venture capital fund' for purposes of this subsection. The Commission shall require such advisers to maintain such records and provide to the Commission such annual or other reports as the Commission determines necessary or appropriate in the public interest or for the protection of investors. ".

SEC. 408. EXEMPTION OF AND REPORTING BY CERTAIN PRIVATE FUND ADVISERS.

Section 203 of the Investment Advisers Act of 1940 (15 U.S.C. 80b-3) is amended by adding at the end the following:

" (m) EXEMPTION OF AND REPORTING BY CERTAIN PRIVATE FUND ADVISERS. —

" (1) IN GENERAL. — The Commission shall provide an exemption from the registration requirements under this section to any investment adviser of private funds,if each of such investment adviser acts solely as an adviser to private funds and has assets under management in the United States of less than $150,000,000.

" (2) REPORTING. — The Commission shall require investment advisers exempted by reason of this subsection to maintain such records and provide to the Commission such annual or other reports as the Commission determines necessary or appropriate in the public interest

款而言,如某私募基金已与某投资顾问签订顾问合同,则证券交易委员会无权在'客户'一词的定义中纳入该投资顾问所管理的私募基金的投资者;"及

(2)在本条结尾处增加如下内容:

"(e)**关于私募基金的披露规则**。——证券交易委员会和商品期货交易委员会应在与金融稳定监督委员会磋商后,在《2010年私募基金投资顾问注册法》颁布之日起12个月内,联合颁发规则,明确规定同时根据本编及《商品交易法》(《美国法典》第七编第1a节及其后条文)注册的投资顾问按照第204(b)子条应向证券交易委员会提交的报告以及应向商品期货交易委员会提交的报告之格式和内容。"

第407条　风险投资基金顾问的豁免和报告

在《1940年投资顾问法》第203条(《美国法典》第十五编第80b—3节)结尾处增加如下内容,作为对该条的修正:

"(l)**对风险投资基金顾问的豁免**。——任何投资顾问的顾问服务对象如仅限于一只或一只以上风险投资基金,则就该等投资顾问提供的与风险投资基金相关的投资顾问服务而言,该等投资顾问不必受制于本编规定的注册要求。证券交易委员会应在本子条规定颁布之日后1年内,发布最终规则,对本子条中的'风险投资基金'一词作出定义。证券交易委员会应要求该等投资顾问保存证券交易委员会判定的对维护公共利益或保护投资者所必要或适当的记录,并向证券交易委员会提供证券交易委员会判定对维护公共利益或保护投资者所必要或适当的年度报告或其他报告。"

第408条　特定私募基金顾问的豁免和报告

在《1940年投资顾问法》第203条(《美国法典》第十五编第80b—3节)结尾处增加如下内容,作为对该条的修正:

"(m)**特定私募基金顾问的豁免和报告**。——

(1)**一般规定**。——任何投资顾问的顾问服务对象如仅限于私募基金,且其在美国境内的管理资产金额低于1.5亿美元,证券交易委员会应向该等投资顾问授予豁免,获得豁免的投资顾问不必遵守本条规定的注册要求。

(2)**报告**。——证券交易委员会应要求依据本子条规定获得豁免的投资顾问保存证券交易委员会判定对维护公共利益或保护投资者所必要或适当的记录,并向证券交易委员会提供证券交易委员会判定对维护公共利益或保护投资者所必要或适当

or for the protection of investors.

“(n) REGISTRATION AND EXAMINATION OF MID–SIZED PRIVATE FUND ADVISERS. — In prescribing regulations to carry out the requirements of this section with respect to investment advisers acting as investment advisers to mid–sized private funds,the Commission shall take into account the size,governance,and investment strategy of such funds to determine whether they pose systemic risk,and shall provide for registration and examination procedures with respect to the investment advisers of such funds which reflect the level of systemic risk posed by such funds.”.

SEC. 409. FAMILY OFFICES.

(a) IN GENERAL. — Section 202 (a)(11) of the Investment Advisers Act of 1940 (15 U.S.C. 80b–2 (a)(11)) is amended by striking “or (G)” and inserting the following: “; (G) any family office,as defined by rule,regulation,or order of the Commission,in accordance with the purposes of this title; or (H)”.

(b) RULEMAKING. — The rules,regulations,or orders issued by the Commission pursuant to section 202 (a)(11)(G) of the Investment Advisers Act of 1940,as added by this section,regarding the definition of the term “family office” shall provide for an exemption that —

(1) is consistent with the previous exemptive policy of the Commission,as reflected in exemptive orders for family offices in effect on the date of enactment of this Act,and the grandfathering provisions in paragraph (3);

(2) recognizes the range of organizational,management,and employment structures and arrangements employed by family offices; and

(3) does not exclude any person who was not registered or required to be registered under the Investment Advisers Act of 1940 on January 1,2010 from the definition of the term “family office”,solely because such person provides investment advice to,and was engaged before January 1,2010 in providing investment advice to —

(A) natural persons who,at the time of their applicable investment,are officers,directors, or employees of the family office who —

(i) have invested with the family office before January 1,2010; and

(ii) are accredited investors,as defined in Regulation D of the Commission (or any successor thereto) under the Securities Act of 1933,or,as the Commission may prescribe by rule,the successors–in–interest thereto;

(B) any company owned exclusively and controlled by members of the family of the family office,or as the Commission may prescribe by rule;

(C) any investment adviser registered under the Investment Adviser Act of 1940 that provides investment advice to the family office and who identifies investment opportunities to the family office,and invests in such transactions on substantially the same terms as the family

的年度报告或其他报告。

(n)**中等规模私募基金顾问的注册及审查**。——证券交易委员会在针对中等规模私募基金的投资顾问制定规章以实施本条规定之时,应考虑该等基金的规模、治理结构及投资战略,以判定其是否具有系统性风险,并应基于该等基金的系统性风险级别,就该等基金的投资顾问规定相应的注册及检查程序。”

第409条 家族理财室

(a)**一般规定**。——《1940年投资顾问法》第202(a)(11)条[《美国法典》第十五编第80b-2(a)(11)节]修正如下:删除“或(G)”,替以“;(G)证券交易委员会根据本编宗旨发布规则、规章或命令定义的任何家族理财室;或(H)”。

(b)**规则制定**。——证券交易委员会在根据本条增加的《1940年投资顾问法》第202(a)(11)(G)条就“家族理财室”一词定义发布规则、规章或命令时,应作出豁免规定,且该项豁免规定——

(1)应与本法颁布之日已生效的家族理财室豁免命令所反映的证券交易委员会此前的豁免政策以及第(3)款中的不溯及既往条款相一致;

(2)应考虑家族理财室采用的组织结构、管理结构和雇佣结构及安排的范围;且

(3)对于在2010年1月1日未根据或不必根据《1940年投资顾问法》注册的任何人,不得仅因该人向以下对象提供投资顾问服务或在2010年1月1日之前受以下对象委托为其提供投资顾问服务而将该人排除在“家族理财室”一词的定义之外——

(A)在进行相关投资时身为家族理财室的管理人员、董事或职员,并具有以下特征的自然人——

(i)在2010年1月1日前即已对该家族理财室进行投资;且

(ii)身为证券交易委员会根据《1933年证券法》制定的《D管理办法》(或其任何后续规定)所定义的获许投资者,或证券交易委员会发布规则明确规定的获许投资者的权益继受人;

(B)家族理财室的家族成员独自所有并控制的任何公司,或者证券交易委员会发布规则明确规定的其他公司;

(C)根据《1940年投资顾问法》注册的向家族理财室提供投资顾问服务并为家族理财室识别投资机会,同时具有如下特征的任何投资顾问:按照实质相同的条款投资于家族理财室投资的交易,但不对接受家族理财室顾问服务的其他基金进行投资,且

office invests,but does not invest in other funds advised by the family office,and whose assets as to which the family office directly or indirectly provides investment advice represent,in the aggregate,not more than 5 percent of the value of the total assets as to which the family office provides investment advice.

(c) ANTIFRAUD AUTHORITY. — A family office that would not be a family office,but for subsection (b)(3) ,shall be deemed to be an investment adviser for the purposes of paragraphs (1) , (2) and (4) of section 206 of the Investment Advisers Act of 1940.

SEC. 410. STATE AND FEDERAL RESPONSIBILITIES; ASSET THRESHOLD FOR FEDERAL REGISTRATION OF INVESTMENT ADVISERS.

Section 203A (a) of the of the Investment Advisers Act of 1940 (15 U.S.C. 80b–3a (a)) is amended —

(1) by redesignating paragraph (2) as paragraph (3) ; and

(2) by inserting after paragraph (1) the following:

" (2) TREATMENT OF MID–SIZED INVESTMENT ADVISERS. —

" (A) IN GENERAL. — No investment adviser described in subparagraph (B) sha ll register under section 203,unless the investment adviser is an adviser to an investment company registered under the Investment Company Act of 1940,or a company which has elected to be a business development company pursuant to section 54 of the Investment Company Act of 1940,and has not withdrawn the election,except that,if by effect of this paragraph an investment adviser would be required to register with 15 or more States,then the adviser may register under section 203.

" (B) COVERED PERSONS. — An investment adviser described in this subparagraph is an investment adviser that —

" (i) is required to be registered as an investment adviser with the securities commissioner (or any agency or office performing like functions) of the State in which it maintains its principal office and place of business and,if registered,would be subject to examination as an investment adviser by any such commissioner,agency,or office; and

" (ii) has assets under management between —

" (I) the amount specified under subparagraph (A) of paragraph (1) ,as such amount may have been adjusted by the Commission pursuant to that subparagraph; and

" (II) $100,000,000,or such higher amount as the Commission may,by rule,deem appropriate in accordance with the purposes of this title. ".

SEC. 411. CUSTODY OF CLIENT ASSETS.

The Investment Advisers Act of 1940 (15 U.S.C. 80b–1 et seq.) is amended by adding at the end the following new section:

"SEC. 223. CUSTODY OF CLIENT ACCOUNTS.

"An investment adviser registered under this title shall take such steps to safeguard

其接受家族理财室直接或间接顾问服务的资产总额在接受该家族理财室投资顾问服务的全部资产价值中占比不超过5%。

(c)**反欺诈权**。——对于若非适用了第(b)(3)子条的规定,将不构成家族理财室的家族理财室,应视为《1940年投资顾问法》第206条第(1)款、第(2)款和第(4)款所述的投资顾问。

第410条　州及联邦的责任;投资顾问进行联邦注册的资产门槛

《1940年投资顾问法》第203A(a)条[《美国法典》第十五编第80b—3a(a)节]修正如下——

(1)第(2)款重新编号为第(3)款;及

(2)在第(1)款之后插入如下内容:

"(2)**对中等规模投资顾问的处理**。——

(A)**一般规定**。——除非具有根据《1940年投资公司法》注册的投资公司的投资顾问身份,或已根据《1940年投资公司法》第54条规定选择企业开发公司身份,并且未撤销该等选择,否则第(B)子款所述任何投资顾问均不得根据第203条办理注册。但是,如因本款之适用将导致投资顾问需要在15个或15个以上的州办理注册,则该等顾问可以根据第203条规定办理注册。

(B)**适用本子款规定的主体**。——本子款所述投资顾问指具有以下特征的投资顾问——

(i)有义务在其主要办公场所或主要营业地所在州的州证券监督官(或行使类似职能的任何机关或办公室)处注册为投资顾问,且一经注册,便将作为投资顾问接受任何该等监督官、机关或办公室的检查;且

(ii)其管理的资产金额在以下两个额度之间——

(I)第(1)款第(A)子款明确规定的金额,但证券交易委员会根据该子款对该金额进行了调整的,以调整后的金额为准;及

(II)1亿美元或证券交易委员会根据本编宗旨认为适当并发布规则设定的更高标准。"

第411条　客户资产的托管

在《1940年投资顾问法》(《美国法典》第十五编第80b—1节及其后条文)结尾处增加如下新条文,作为对该法的修正:

"第223条　客户账户的托管

根据本编规定注册的投资顾问应采取证券交易委员会在其发布的规则中明确规

client assets over which such adviser has custody,including,without limitation,verification of such assets by an independent public accountant,as the Commission may,by rule,prescribe. ".

SEC. 412. COMPTROLLER GENERAL STUDY ON CUSTODY RULE COSTS.

The Comptroller General of the United States shall —

(1) conduct a study of —

(A) the compliance costs associated with the current Securities and Exchange Commission rules 204–2 (17 C. F. R. Parts 275. 204–2) and rule 206 (4)–2 (17 C. F. R. 275. 206 (4)–2) under the Investment Advisers Act of 1940 regarding custody of funds or securities of clients by investment advisers; and

(B) the additional costs if subsection (b)(6) of rule 206 (4)–2 (17 C. F. R. 275. 206 (4)–2 (b)(6)) relating to operational independence were eliminated; and

(2) submit a report to the Committee on Banking,Housing,and Urban Affairs of the Senate and the Committee on Financial Services of the House of Representatives on the results of such study,not later than 3 years after the date of enactment of this Act.

SEC. 413. ADJUSTING THE ACCREDITED INVESTOR STANDARD.

(a) IN GENERAL. — The Commission shall adjust any net worth standard for an accredited investor,as set forth in the rules of the Commission under the Securities Act of 1933,so that the individual net worth of any natural person,or joint net worth with the spouse of that person,at the time of purchase,is more than $1,000,000 (as such amount is adjusted periodically by rule of the Commission) ,excluding the value of the primary residence of such natural person,except that during the 4–year period that begins on the date of enactment of this Act,any net worth standard shall be $1,000,000,excluding the value of the primary residence of such natural person.

(b) REVIEW AND ADJUSTMENT. —

(1) INITIAL REVIEW AND ADJUSTMENT. —

(A) INITIAL REVIEW. — The Commission may undertake a review of the definition of the term "accredited investor",as such term applies to natural persons,to determine whether the requirements of the definition,excluding the requirement relating to the net worth standard described in subsection (a) ,should be adjusted or modified for the protection of investors,in the public interest,and in light of the economy.

(B) ADJUSTMENT OR MODIFICATION. — Upon completion of a review under subparagraph (A) ,the Commission may,by notice and comment rulemaking,make such adjustments to the definition of the term "accredited investor",excluding adjusting or modifying the requirement relating to the net worth standard described in subsection (a) ,as such term applies to natural persons,as the Commission may deem appropriate for the protection of investors,in the public interest,and in light of the economy.

定的措施,对其负责托管的客户资产进行保护,包括但不限于使用独立公共会计师对上述资产进行核验。”

第412条 政府问责办公室主任对托管规则成本的总体研究

政府问责办公室主任应——

(1)就以下成本开展研究——

(A)如下规则相关的合规成本:证券交易委员会依据《1940年投资顾问法》制定的关于投资顾问托管客户基金或证券的现行有效的《204—2规则》(《联邦规章汇编》第十七编第275.204—2部分)和《206(4)—2规则》[《联邦规章汇编》第十七编第275.206(4)—2部分];及

(B)如果关于运营独立性的《206(4)—2规则》第(b)(6)子条[《联邦规章汇编》第十七编第275.206(4)—2(b)(6)部分]被取消将导致的额外成本;及

(2)在本法颁布之日起3年内就上述研究结果向参议院银行、住房与城市事务委员会和众议院金融服务委员会提交一份报告。

第413条 获许投资者标准的调整

(a)**一般规定**。——证券交易委员会应对其依据《1933年证券法》制定的规则中规定的获许投资者的任何净值标准进行调整,要求任何自然人在进行购买时其个人净值或与其配偶的联合净值(不包括该自然人主要住所的价值)高于100万美元(证券交易委员会可发布规则对该金额定期调整),但是,在本法颁布之日后4年内,任何净值标准(不包括该自然人主要住所的价值)应维持在100万美元。

(b)**审查和调整**。——

(1)**初始审查和调整**。——

(A)**初始审查**。——证券交易委员会可以出于保护投资者和公共利益之目,并在考虑经济状况的前提下,对适用于自然人的“获许投资者”一词之定义进行审查,以判定是否应对该定义提出的各项要求[但第(a)子条中所述关于净值标准的要求除外]进行调整或修改。

(B)**调整或修改**。——证券交易委员会可以在完成第(A)子款所述审查并发布公告和征求公众意见后制定规则,对适用于自然人的“获准投资者”一词之定义[但不得调整或修改第(a)子条所述关于净值标准的要求]作出其认为对保护投资者和公共利益而言适当并符合经济状况的调整。

(2) SUBSEQUENT REVIEWS AND ADJUSTMENT. —

(A) SUBSEQUENT REVIEWS. — Not earlier than 4 years after the date of enactment of this Act,and not less frequently than once every 4 years thereafter,the Commission shall undertake a review of the definition,in its entirety,of the term "accredited investor",as defined in section 230. 215 of title 17,Code of Federal Regulations,or any successor thereto,as such term applies to natural persons,to determine whether the requirements of the definition should be adjusted or modified for the protection of investors,in the public interest,and in light of the economy.

(B) ADJUSTMENT OR MODIFICATION. — Upon completion of a review under subparagraph (A) ,the Commission may,by notice and comment rulemaking,make such adjustments to the definition of the term "accredited investor",as defined in section 230. 215 of title 17,Code of Federal Regulations,or any successor thereto,as such term applies to natural persons,as the Commission may deem appropriate for the protection of investors,in the public interest,and in light of the economy.

SEC. 414. RULE OF CONSTRUCTION RELATING TO THE COMMODITIES EXCHANGE ACT.

The Investment Advisers Act of 1940 (15 U.S.C. 80b-1 et seq.) is further amended by adding at the end the following new section:

"SEC. 224. RULE OF CONSTRUCTION RELATING TO THE COMMODITIES EXCHANGE ACT.

"Nothing in this title shall relieve any person of any obligation or duty,or affect the availability of any right or remedy available to the Commodity Futures Trading Commission or any private party,arising under the Commodity Exchange Act (7 U.S.C. 1 et seq.) governing commodity pools,commodity pool operators,or commodity trading advisors. ".

SEC. 415. GAO STUDY AND REPORT ON ACCREDITED INVESTORS.

The Comptroller General of the United States shall conduct a study on the appropriate criteria for determining the financial thresholds or other criteria needed to qualify for accredited investor status and eligibility to invest in private funds,and shall submit a report to the Committee on Banking,Housing,and Urban Affairs of the Senate and the Committee on Financial Services of the House of Representatives on the results of such study not later than 3 years after the date of enactment of this Act.

SEC. 416. GAO STUDY ON SELF-REGULATORY ORGANIZATION FOR PRIVATE FUNDS.

The Comptroller General of the United States shall —

(1) conduct a study of the feasibility of forming a self-regulatory organization to oversee private funds; and

(2) submit a report to the Committee on Banking,Housing,and Urban Affairs of the

(2)**后续审查和调整**。——

(A)**后续审查**。——在本法颁布之日起届满4年之后,证券交易委员会至少应每隔4年对《联邦规章汇编》第十七编第230.215部分(或其任何后续规定)定义的适用于自然人的"获许投资者"一词进行全面审查,以判定是否有必要出于保护投资者和公共利益之目的并在考虑经济状况的前提下,对该定义要素进行调整或修改。

(B)**调整或修改**。——证券交易委员会可以在完成第(A)子款所述审查并发布公告和征求公众意见后制定规则,对《联邦规章汇编》第十七编第230.215部分(或其任何后续规定)定义的适用于自然人的"获准投资者"一词之定义作出其认为对保护投资者和公共利益而言适当并符合经济状况的调整。

第414条　关于《商品交易法》的解释规则

在《1940年投资顾问法》(《美国法典》第十五编第80b—1节及其后条文)结尾处增加如下新条文,作为对该法的进一步修正:

"第224条　关于《商品交易法》的解释规则

对于规制商品基金、商品基金管理人或商品交易顾问的《商品交易法》(《美国法典》第七编第1节及其后条文)而言,本编的任何规定均不免除任何人因该法而承担的任何义务或职责,亦不影响商品期货交易委员会或任何私人当事方因该法而享有的任何权利或救济。"

第415条　政府问责办公室关于获许投资者的研究和报告

政府问责办公室主任应开展旨在确定如下适当标准的研究,即任何主体欲获得获许投资者身份及私募基金适格投资者身份所须满足的适当的财务门槛标或其他标准。政府问责办公室主任应在本法颁布之日起3年内就上述研究结果向参议院银行、住房与城市事务委员会和众议院金融服务委员会提交一份报告。

第416条　政府问责办公室关于私募基金自律组织的研究

政府问责办公室主任应——

(1)就成立自律组织对私募基金进行监督开展可行性研究;及

(2)在本法颁布之日后1年内就上述研究结果向参议院银行、住房与城市事务委

Senate and the Committee on Financial Services of the House of Representatives on the results of such study,not later than 1 year after the date of enactment of this Act.

SEC. 417. COMMISSION STUDY AND REPORT ON SHORT SELLING.

(a) STUDIES. — The Division of Risk,Strategy,and Financial Innovation of the Commission shall conduct —

(1) a study,taking into account current scholarship,on the state of short selling on national securities exchanges and in the over–the–counter markets,with particular attention to the impact of recent rule changes and the incidence of —

(A) the failure to deliver shares sold short; or

(B) delivery of shares on the fourth day following the short sale transaction; and

(2) a study of —

(A) the feasibility,benefits,and costs of requiring reporting publicly,in real time short sale positions of publicly listed securities,or,in the alternative,reporting such short positions in real time only to the Commission and the Financial Industry Regulatory Authority; and

(B) the feasibility,benefits,and costs of conducting a voluntary pilot program in which public companies will agree to have all trades of their shares marked "short","market maker short","buy","buy–to–cover",or "long",and reported in real time through the Consolidated Tape.

(b) REPORTS. — The Commission shall submit a report to the Committee on Banking, Housing,and Urban Affairs of the Senate and the Committee on Financial Services of the House of Representatives —

(1) on the results of the study required under subsection (a)(1),including recommendations for market improvements,not later than 2 years after the date of enactment of this Act; and

(2) on the results of the study required under subsection (a)(2),not later than 1 year after the date of enactment of this Act.

SEC. 418. QUALIFIED CLIENT STANDARD.

Section 205 (e) of the Investment Advisers Act of 1940 (15 U.S.C. 80b–5(e)) is amended by adding at the end the following: "With respect to any factor used in any rule or regulation by the Commission in making a determination under this subsection,if the Commission uses a dollar amount test in connection with such factor,such as a net asset threshold,the Commission shall,by order,not later than 1 year after the date of enactment of the Private Fund Investment Advisers Registration Act of 2010,and every 5 years thereafter, adjust for the effects of inflation on such test. Any such adjustment that is not a multiple of $100,000 shall be rounded to the nearest multiple of $100,000. ".

SEC. 419. TRANSITION PERIOD.

Except as otherwise provided in this title,this title and the amendments made by this title

员会和众议院金融服务委员会提交一份报告。

第417条 证券交易委员会关于卖空情况的研究和报告

(a)**研究**。——证券交易委员会的风险、战略和金融创新部应——

(1)在现有学术成果的基础上,对全国性证券和场外交易市场的卖空情况开展研究,尤其应注重近期规则变更的影响和以下情况的发生率——

(A)卖空股份交割失信;或

(B)在卖空交易之后第四天交割股份;及

(2)对以下问题开展研究——

(A)要求对公开上市证券的卖空持仓进行公开实时报告,或者(作为替代方案)仅要求向证券交易委员会及金融业监管局实时报告上述持仓的可行性、收益和成本;及

(B)开展自愿性试点计划,要求参与试点的公众公司同意将其所有股票交易标识为"卖空"、"做市商卖空"、"买入"、"卖空补回"或"买空",并通过证券交易汇总记录带进行实时报告之可行性、收益和成本。

(b)**报告**。——证券交易委员会应按如下规定向参议院银行、住房与城市事务委员会和众议院金融服务委员会提交报告——

(1)在本法颁布之日起2年内就按照第(a)(1)子条开展的研究之结果提交一份报告,报告内容应包括市场改进建议;及

(2)在本法颁布之日起1年内就按照第(a)(2)子条开展的研究之结果提交一份报告。

第418条 合格客户标准

在《1940年投资顾问法》第205(e)条[《美国法典》第80b—5(e)节]结尾处增加如下内容,作为对该法的修正:"如果证券交易委员会在其发布的任何规则或规章中,针对本子条任何证券交易委员会判定要素采用了一项测试金额(例如,资产门槛净额),则证券交易委员会应在《2010年私募基金投资顾问注册法》颁布之日起1年内以及其后每隔5年发布命令,就通货膨胀对上述测试标准造成的影响进行调整。调整额度如非10万美元的整数倍,应取与该数额最为接近的10万美元的整数倍。"

第419条 过渡期

除本编另有规定的情形外,本编以及本编作出的修正应于本法颁布届满1年之日

shall become effective 1 year after the date of enactment of this Act,except that any investment adviser may,at the discretion of the investment adviser,register with the Commission under the Investment Advisers Act of 1940 during that 1–year period,subject to the rules of the Commission.

生效,但是,在不违反证券交易委员会规则的前提下,投资顾问可以在本法颁布后1年内依其自由裁量权自行选择根据《1940年投资顾问法》在证券交易委员会办理注册。

TITLE V — INSURANCE

Subtitle A — Federal Insurance Office

SEC. 501. SHORT TITLE.

This subtitle may be cited as the "Federal Insurance Office Act of 2010".

SEC. 502. FEDERAL INSURANCE OFFICE.

(a) ESTABLISHMENT OF OFFICE. — Subchapter I of chapter 3 of subtitle I of title 31, United States Code, is amended —

(1) by redesignating section 312 as section 315;

(2) by redesignating section 313 as section 312; and

(3) by inserting after section 312 (as so redesignated) the following new sections:

"SEC. 313. FEDERAL INSURANCE OFFICE.

"(a) ESTABLISHMENT. — There is established within the Department of the Treasury the Federal Insurance Office.

"(b) LEADERSHIP. — The Office shall be headed by a Director, who shall be appointed by the Secretary of the Treasury. The position of Director shall be a career reserved position in the Senior Executive Service, as that position is defined under section 3132 of title 5, United States Code.

"(c) FUNCTIONS. —

"(1) AUTHORITY PURSUANT TO DIRECTION OF SECRETARY. — The Office, pursuant to the direction of the Secretary, shall have the authority —

"(A) to monitor all aspects of the insurance industry, including identifying issues or gaps in the regulation of insurers that could contribute to a systemic crisis in the insurance industry or the United States financial system;

"(B) to monitor the extent to which traditionally underserved communities and

第五编——保　　险

第A子编——联邦保险办公室

第501条　简称

引述本子编时,可简称为《2010年联邦保险办公室法》。

第502条　联邦保险办公室

(a)**联邦保险办公室的设立**。——《美国法典》第三十一编第一子编第三章第一子章修正如下——

(1)第312条重新编号为第315条;

(2)第313条重新编号为第312条;及

(3)在第312条(以重新编号后的序号为准)之后增加如下新条文:

"第313条　联邦保险办公室

(a)**设立**。——财政部下设联邦保险办公室。

(b)**领导**。——联邦保险办公室在联邦保险办公室主任的领导下开展工作,联邦保险办公室主任由财政部部长任命。联邦保险办公室主任属于'高级公务员'中的保留职位(定义见《美国法典》第五编第3132节)。

(c)**职能**。——

(1)**在财政部部长领导下享有的权力**。——在财政部部长的领导下,联邦保险办公室拥有以下权力——

(A)对保险业各方面进行监控,包括识别可能导致保险业或美国金融体系系统性危机的保险公司监管问题或漏洞;

(B)对以下群体在多大程度上能够获得能力负担范围之内的各类保险产品(但健

consumers, minorities (as such term is defined in section 1204 (c) of the Financial Institutions Reform, Recovery, and Enforcement Act of 1989 (12 U.S.C. 1811 note)), and low–and moderate–income persons have access to affordable insurance products regarding all lines of insurance, except health insurance;

" (C) to recommend to the Financial Stability Oversight Council that it designate an insurer, including the affiliates of such insurer, as an entity subject to regulation as a nonbank financial company supervised by the Board of Governors pursuant to title I of the Dodd–Frank Wall Street Reform and Consumer Protection Act;

" (D) to assist the Secretary in administering the Terrorism Insurance Program established in the Department of the Treasury under the Terrorism Risk Insurance Act of 2002 (15 U.S.C. 6701 note);

" (E) to coordinate Federal efforts and develop Federal policy on prudential aspects of international insurance matters, including representing the United States, as appropriate, in the International Association of Insurance Supervisors (or a successor entity) and assisting the Secretary in negotiating covered agreements (as such term is defined in subsection (r));

" (F) to determine, in accordance with subsection (f), whether State insurance measures are preempted by covered agreements;

" (G) to consult with the States (including State insurance regulators) regarding insurance matters of national importance and prudential insurance matters of international importance; and

" (H) to perform such other related duties and authorities as may be assigned to the Office by the Secretary.

" (2) ADVISORY FUNCTIONS.— The Office shall advise the Secretary on major domestic and prudential international insurance policy issues.

" (3) ADVISORY CAPACITY ON COUNCIL.— The Director shall serve in an advisory capacity on the Financial Stability Oversight Council established under the Financial Stability Act of 2010.

" (d) SCOPE.— The authority of the Office shall extend to all lines of insurance except —

" (1) health insurance, as determined by the Secretary in coordination with the Secretary of Health and Human Services based on section 2791 of the Public Health Service Act (42 U.S.C. 300gg–91);

" (2) long–term care insurance, except long–term care insurance that is included with life or annuity insurance components, as determined by the Secretary in coordination with the Secretary of Health and Human Services, and in the case of long–term care insurance that is included with such components, the Secretary shall coordinate with the Secretary of Health and Human Services in performing the functions of the Office; and

康险除外)进行监督:传统弱势群体和消费者、少数族裔[定义见《1989年金融机构改革、复兴与实施法》第1204(c)条(《美国法典》第十二编第1811节注释)]和中低收入人群;

(C)建议金融稳定监督委员会将某一保险公司(包括该保险公司的关联方)指定为须受联邦储备委员会根据《多德—弗兰克华尔街改革与消费者保护法》第一编规定进行监管的非银行金融公司;

(D)协助财政部部长实施财政部根据《2002年恐怖主义风险保险法》(《美国法典》第十五编第6701节注释)制订的恐怖主义保险计划;

(E)就国际保险事务的审慎问题协调联邦工作并制定联邦政策,包括在适当情况下在国际保险监管者协会(或其继任实体)中担任美国的代表,并协助财政部部长就所涉协定[定义见第(r)子条]进行谈判;

(F)根据第(f)子条的规定判定州保险措施是否已经被所涉协定排除适用;

(G)就具有全国重要性的保险事宜和具有国际重要性的审慎保险事宜与各州(包括各州保险监管者)进行磋商;及

(H)履行和行使财政部部长指定的其他相关职责和权力。

(2)**顾问职能**。——联邦保险办公室应就重大的国内保险政策问题和重大的审慎国际保险政策问题向财政部部长提供意见。

(3)**在金融稳定监督委员会的顾问职务**。——联邦保险办公室主任应在根据《2010年金融稳定法》设立的金融稳定监督委员会担任顾问职务。

(d)**权力范围**。——联邦保险办公室的权力范围应覆盖除以下险种外的全部险种——

(1)财政部部长协同卫生及公共服务部部长根据《公共健康服务法》第2791条(《美国法典》第四十二编第300gg—91节)界定的健康险;

(2)财政部部长协同卫生及公共服务部部长判定的长期医疗保险(但不包括含有人寿或年金保险要素的长期医疗保险),长期医疗保险包括上述要素的,则财政部部长应协同卫生及公共服务部部长履行联邦保险办公室的职能;及

" (3) crop insurance, as established by the Federal Crop Insurance Act (7 U.S.C. 1501 et seq.).

" (e) GATHERING OF INFORMATION. —

" (1) IN GENERAL. — In carrying out the functions required under subsection (c) , the Office may —

" (A) receive and collect data and information on and from the insurance industry and insurers;

" (B) enter into information-sharing agreements;

" (C) analyze and disseminate data and information; and

" (D) issue reports regarding all lines of insurance except health insurance.

" (2) COLLECTION OF INFORMATION FROM INSURERS AND AFFILIATES. —

" (A) IN GENERAL. — Except as provided in paragraph (3) , the Office may require an insurer, or any affiliate of an insurer, to submit such data or information as the Office may reasonably require in carrying out the functions described under subsection (c) .

" (B) RULE OF CONSTRUCTION. — Notwithstanding any other provision of this section, for purposes of subparagraph (A) , the term 'insurer' means any entity that writes insurance or reinsures risks and issues contracts or policies in 1 or more States.

" (3) EXCEPTION FOR SMALL INSURERS. — Paragraph (2) shall not apply with respect to any insurer or affiliate thereof that meets a minimum size threshold that the Office may establish, whether by order or rule.

" (4) ADVANCE COORDINATION. — Before collecting any data or information under paragraph (2) from an insurer, or affiliate of an insurer, the Office shall coordinate with each relevant Federal agency and State insurance regulator (or other relevant Federal or State regulatory agency, if any, in the case of an affiliate of an insurer) and any publicly available sources to determine if the information to be collected is available from, and may be obtained in a timely manner by, such Federal agency or State insurance regulator, individually or collectively, other regulatory agency, or publicly available sources. If the Director determines that such data or information is available, and may be obtained in a timely manner, from such an agency, regulator, regulatory agency, or source, the Director shall obtain the data or information from such agency, regulator, regulatory agency, or source. If the Director determines that such data or information is not so available, the Director may collect such data or information from an insurer (or affiliate) only if the Director complies with the requirements of subchapter I of chapter 35 of title 44, United States Code (relating to Federal information policy; commonly known as the Paperwork Reduction Act) , in collecting such data or information. Notwithstanding any other provision of law, each such relevant Federal agency and State insurance regulator or other Federal or State regulatory agency is authorized to provide to the Office such data or information.

(3)农作物保险，定义见《联邦农作物保险法》(《美国法典》第七编第1501节及其后条文)。

(e)**信息收集**。——

(1)**一般规定**。——在履行第(c)子条规定的职能时，联邦保险办公室可以——

(A)接收并收集关于保险业和保险公司的数据和信息，以及由保险业及保险公司提供的数据和信息；

(B)订立信息共享协议；

(C)分析并发布数据和信息；及

(D)发布关于除健康险外所有险种的报告。

(2)**从保险公司及其关联方收集信息**。——

(A)**一般规定**。——除第(3)款另有规定的情形外，联邦保险办公室可以要求某一保险公司或该保险公司的任何关联方提交联邦保险办公室履行第(c)子条所述职能过程中合理所需的数据或信息。

(B)**解释规则**。——无论本条是否存在任何不同规定，就第(A)子款而言，'保险公司'一词系指在一个或一个以上的州对风险进行承保或再保险，并签发保险合同或保单的任何实体。

(3)**关于小型保险公司的例外规定**。——联邦保险办公室可以发布命令或规则设定保险公司的最小规模门槛，符合该等门槛规定的任何保险公司或其关联方不得适用第(2)款的规定。

(4)**事先协调**。——联邦保险办公室在根据第(2)款向保险公司或保险公司的关联方收集任何相关数据或信息之前，应与每一相关联邦机关及州保险监管者[向保险公司关联方收集数据或信息的，还应与其他相关联邦监管机关或州监管机关(如有)]以及任何可公开获得的信息来源进行协调，以期判定上述联邦机关或州保险监管者是否可单独或共同及时提供和获取联邦保险办公室需要收集的信息，以及判定其他监管机关或可公开获得的信息来源是否可及时提供和获取联邦保险办公室需要收集的信息。如果联邦保险办公室主任判定上述机关、监管者、监管机关或信息来源可以及时提供和获取联邦保险办公室需要收集的数据或信息，联邦保险办公室主任应从上述机关、监管者、监管机关或信息来源处获取该等数据或信息。如果联邦保险办公室主任判定无法以上述方式获取该等数据或信息，联邦保险办公室主任可以向保险公司(或保险公司的关联方)收集该等数据或信息，但是，联邦保险办公室主任仅得在遵守《美国法典》第四十四编第三十五章第一子章(关于联邦信息政策的规定，通常被称为'《文书削减法》')的要求的条件下收集该等数据或信息。无论是否存在任何不同法律规定，每一上述相关联邦机关、州保险监管者或者其他联邦监管机关或州监管机关均有权向联邦保险办公室提供上述数据或信息。

“(5) CONFIDENTIALITY. —

“(A) RETENTION OF PRIVILEGE. — The submission of any nonpublicly available data and information to the Office under this subsection shall not constitute a waiver of, or otherwise affect, any privilege arising under Federal or State law (including the rules of any Federal or State court) to which the data or information is otherwise subject.

“(B) CONTINUED APPLICATION OF PRIOR CONFIDENTIALITY AGREEMENTS — Any requirement under Federal or State law to the extent otherwise applicable, or any requirement pursuant to a written agreement in effect between the original source of any nonpublicly available data or information and the source of such data or information to the Office, regarding the privacy or confidentiality of any data or information in the possession of the source to the Office, shall continue to apply to such data or information after the data or information has been provided pursuant to this subsection to the Office.

“(C) INFORMATION–SHARING AGREEMENT. — Any data or information obtained by the Office may be made available to State insurance regulators, individually or collectively, through an information–sharing agreement that —

“(i) shall comply with applicable Federal law; and

“(ii) shall not constitute a waiver of, or otherwise affect, any privilege under Federal or State law (including the rules of any Federal or State court) to which the data or information is otherwise subject.

“(D) AGENCY DISCLOSURE REQUIREMENTS. — Section 552 of title 5, United States Code, shall apply to any data or information submitted to the Office by an insurer or an affiliate of an insurer.

“(6) SUBPOENAS AND ENFORCEMENT. — The Director shall have the power to require by subpoena the production of the data or information requested under paragraph (2), but only upon a written finding by the Director that such data or information is required to carry out the functions described under subsection (c) and that the Office has coordinated with such regulator or agency as required under paragraph (4). Subpoenas shall bear the signature of the Director and shall be served by any person or class of persons designated by the Director for that purpose. In the case of contumacy or failure to obey a subpoena, the subpoena shall be enforceable by order of any appropriate district court of the United States. Any failure to obey the order of thecourt may be punished by the court as a contempt of court.

“(f) PREEMPTION OF STATE INSURANCE MEASURES. —

“(1) STANDARD. — A State insurance measure shall be preempted pursuant to this section or section 314 if, and only to the extent that the Director determines, in accordance with this subsection, that the measure —

“(A) results in less favorable treatment of a non–United States insurer domiciled in a foreign jurisdiction that is subject to a covered agreement than a United States insurer

(5)**保密**。——

(A)**保留保密特权**。——根据本子条规定向联邦保险办公室提交的任何非公开数据及信息,如依据其他适用的联邦法律或州法律(包括任何联邦法院或州法院的规则)应受任何保密特权保护,则提交上述非公开数据及信息不得影响该等保密特权,或构成对该等权利的放弃。

(B)**先前保密协议继续适用**。——根据本子条规定向联邦保险办公室提供的非公开数据或信息应继续适用以下要求:联邦法律或州法律中另行适用的,或者任何非公开数据或信息的原始来源与向联邦保险办公室提供该等数据或信息的信息来源之间签订的有效书面协议中的,关于联邦保险办公室的信息来源所掌握的任何数据或信息之隐私性或保密性的任何要求。

(C)**信息共享协议**。——联邦保险办公室获取的任何数据或信息均可通过信息共享协议单独或共同提供给各州保险监管者,但是——

(i)该等信息共享协议应符合适用的联邦法律;且

(ii)上述数据或信息如根据另行适用的联邦法律或州法律(包括任何联邦法院或州法院的规则)应受任何保密特权保护的,该等信息共享协议不得影响上述保密特权或构成对该等权利的放弃。

(D)**机关披露要求**。——保险公司或保险公司关联方向联邦保险办公室提交的任何数据或信息应适用《美国法典》第五编第552节的规定。

(6)**传票和执行**。——联邦保险办公室主任有权签发传票,要求被签发人提供第(2)款规定的数据或信息,但仅得在以下情况下签发该等传票,即联邦保险办公室主任已作出一份书面认定,判定该等数据或信息为履行第(c)子条所述职能所必需,且联邦保险办公室已根据第(4)款规定与相关监管者或机关进行了协调。联邦保险办公室主任应在该传票上签字,并由其专门指定的任何人或任何类别人员进行送达。被签发人拒不履行或未能履行传票要求的,该传票应由任何相应的联邦地区法院签发命令强制执行。被签发人拒绝服从法院命令的,法院可以以蔑视法庭罪对其进行处罚。

(f)**排除州保险措施的适用**。——

(1)**标准**。——当且仅当联邦保险办公室主任根据本子条规定就某一州的保险措施作出如下判定后,始得根据本条或第314条的规定排除该保险措施的适用性——

(A)该措施将导致适用所涉协定的住所位于外国司法辖区的非美国保险公司所获待遇的优惠性次于住所位于该州、在该州取得执照或以其他形式被该州认可的美

domiciled, licensed, or otherwise admitted in that State; and

" (B) is inconsistent with a covered agreement.

" (2) DETERMINATION. —

" (A) NOTICE OF POTENTIAL INCONSISTENCY — Before making any determination under paragraph (1), the Director shall —

" (i) notify and consult with the appropriate State regarding any potential inconsistency or preemption;

" (ii) notify and consult with the United States Trade Representative regarding any potential inconsistency or preemption;

" (iii) cause to be published in the Federal Register notice of the issue regarding the potential inconsistency or preemption, including a description of each State insurance measure at issue and any applicable covered agreement;

" (iv) provide interested parties a reasonable opportunity to submit written comments to the Office; and

" (v) consider any comments received.

" (B) SCOPE OF REVIEW. — For purposes of this subsection, any determination of the Director regarding State insurance measures, and any preemption under paragraph (1) as a result of such determination, shall be limited to the subject matter contained within the covered agreement involved and shall achieve a level of protection for insurance or reinsurance consumers that is substantially equivalent to the level of protection achieved under State insurance or reinsurance regulation.

" (C) NOTICE OF DETERMINATION OF INCONSISTENCY. — Upon making any determination under paragraph (1), the Director shall —

" (i) notify the appropriate State of the determination and the extent of the inconsistency;

" (ii) establish a reasonable period of time, which shall not be less than 30 days, before the determination shall become effective; and

" (iii) notify the Committees on Financial Services and Ways and Means of the House of Representatives and the Committees on Banking, Housing, and Urban Affairs and Finance of the Senate.

" (3) NOTICE OF EFFECTIVENESS. — Upon the conclusion of the period referred to in paragraph (2)(C)(ii), if the basis for such determination still exists, the determination shall become effective and the Director shall —

" (A) cause to be published a notice in the Federal Register that the preemption has become effective, as well as the effective date; and

" (B) notify the appropriate State.

" (4) LIMITATION. — No State may enforce a State insurance measure to the extent that such measure has been preempted under this subsection.

国保险公司;且

(B)该措施与所涉协定不一致。

(2)**判定**。——

(A)**潜在不一致通知**。——联邦保险办公室主任在作出第(1)款所述任何判定前,应——

(i)就上述任何潜在不一致性或排除适用的判定向相关的州发出通知并与之进行磋商;

(ii)就上述任何潜在不一致性或排除适用的判定向美国贸易代表发出通知并与之磋商;

(iii)责成在《联邦公报》上发布关于潜在不一致性或适用排除问题的通知,通知中应说明涉及的每一项州保险措施和任何适用的所涉协定;

(iv)为利害关系人提供向联邦保险办公室提交书面意见的合理机会;及

(v)审议所收到的任何意见。

(B)**审查范围**。——就本子条而言,联邦保险办公室主任根据第(1)款的规定就州保险措施作出的任何判定及由于该判定导致的州保险措施适用性的任何排除,其范围均应仅限于所涉协定之标的,且对保险或再保险消费者进行的保护水平应与在州保险或再保险法规下实现的保护水平基本相当。

(C)**关于不一致判定的通知**。——联邦保险办公室在根据第(1)款规定作出任何判定后,应——

(i)就该判定以及不一致的程度向相应的州发出通知;

(ii)规定该判定生效前必须经过的合理期间(不得短于30天);并

(iii)就该判定向众议院金融服务委员会、众议院筹款委员会、参议院银行、住房与城市事务委员会和参议院财政委员会发出通知。

(3)**生效通知**。——第(2)(c)(ii)款所述期间终止时,作出该判定的依据仍然存在的,该判定应立即生效,且联邦保险办公室主任应——

(A)责成在《联邦公报》上发布相关通知,说明该适用排除已生效以及生效日;及

(B)通知相应的州。

(4)**限制**。——任何州保险措施的适用性已根据本子条被排除的,该州不得执行该措施。

"(g) APPLICABILITY OF ADMINISTRATIVE PROCEDURES ACT. —Determinations of inconsistency made pursuant to subsection (f)(2) shall be subject to the applicable provisions of subchapter II of chapter 5 of title 5, United States Code (relating to administrative procedure), and chapter 7 of such title (relating to judicial review), except that in any action for judicial review of a determination of inconsistency, the court shall determine the matter de novo.

"(h) REGULATIONS, POLICIES, AND PROCEDURES. — The Secretary may issue orders, regulations, policies, and procedures to implement this section.

"(i) CONSULTATION. — The Director shall consult with State insurance regulators, individually or collectively, to the extent the Director determines appropriate, in carrying out the functions of the Office.

"(j) SAVINGS PROVISIONS. — Nothing in this section shall —

"(1) preempt —

"(A) any State insurance measure that governs any insurer's rates, premiums, underwriting, or sales practices;

"(B) any State coverage requirements for insurance;

"(C) the application of the antitrust laws of any State to the business of insurance; or

"(D) any State insurance measure governing the capital or solvency of an insurer, except to the extent that such State insurance measure results in less favorable treatment of a non-United State insurer than a United States insurer;

"(2) be construed to alter, amend, or limit any provision of the Consumer Financial Protection Agency Act of 2010; or

"(3) affect the preemption of any State insurance measure otherwise inconsistent with and preempted by Federal law.

"(k) RETENTION OF EXISTING STATE REGULATORY AUTHORITY. — Nothing in this section or section 314 shall be construed to establish or provide the Office or the Department of the Treasury with general supervisory or regulatory authority over the business of insurance.

"(l) RETENTION OF AUTHORITY OF FEDERAL FINANCIAL REGULATORY AGENCIES. — Nothing in this section or section 314 shall be construed to limit the authority of any Federal financial regulatory agency, including the authority to develop and coordinate policy, negotiate, and enter into agreements with foreign governments, authorities, regulators, and multinational regulatory committees and to preempt State measures to affect uniformity with international regulatory agreements.

"(m) RETENTION OF AUTHORITY OF UNITED STATES TRADE REPRESENTATIVE. — Nothing in this section or section 314 shall be construed to affect the authority of the Office of the United States Trade Representative pursuant to section 141 of

(g)**《行政程序法》的适用性**。——根据第(f)(2)子条规定作出的关于不一致性的判定应受制于《美国法典》第五编第五章第二子章(关于行政程序的规定)的适用规定和该编第七章(关于司法审查的规定)的适用规定,但是,在关于不一致性判定的任何司法审查诉讼中,法院应对该事项作出重新判定。

(h)**规章、政策和程序**。——财政部部长可以为实施本条规定而发布相关命令、规章、政策及程序。

(i)**磋商**。——联邦保险办公室主任在行使联邦保险办公室职能的过程中,应与其判定的相应的州保险监管者进行单独或共同磋商。

(j)**保留条款**。——本条中的任何规定均不得——

(1)排除以下任一项的适用性——

(A)规范任何保险公司费率、保费、承保或销售做法的任何州保险措施;

(B)任何州关于保险范围的要求;

(C)任何州的反垄断法律对保险业务的适用;或

(D)规范保险公司资本或偿付能力的任何州保险措施,除非该措施将导致非美国保险公司所获待遇的优惠性次于美国保险公司;

(2)被解释为构成对《2010年消费者金融保护局法》任何规定的修改、修正或限制;或

(3)影响对如下任何州保险措施适用性的排除:因与联邦法律存在其他不一致而被联邦法律排除适用的州保险措施。

(k)**保留现有的州监管权**。——本条或第314条的任何规定均不得被解释为确立了联邦保险办公室或财政部对保险业务的总体监管权或规制权,或者被解释为向联邦保险办公室或财政部提供了该等权力。

(l)**保留联邦金融监管机关的权力**。——本条或第314条的任何规定均不得被解释为构成对任何联邦金融监管机关的权力的限制,包括制定并协调相关政策的权力,与外国政府、监管机构、监管者和跨国监管委员会谈判并达成协定的权力,以及排除影响全球监管协定统一性的州措施之适用的权力。

(m)**保留美国贸易代表的权力**。——本条或第314条的任何规定均不得被解释为影响《1974年贸易法》第141条(《美国法典》第十九编第2171节)或任何其他法律规定赋予联邦贸易代表办公室的权力,包括制定并协调联邦国际贸易政策的权力和实施

the Trade Act of 1974 (19 U.S.C. 2171) or any other provision of law, including authority over the development and coordination of United States international trade policy and the administration of the United States trade agreements program.

"(n) ANNUAL REPORTS TO CONGRESS. —

"(1) SECTION 313 (f) REPORTS. — Beginning September 30, 2011, the Director shall submit a report on or before September 30 of each calendar year to the President and to the Committees on Financial Services and Ways and Means of the House of Representatives and the Committees on Banking, Housing, and Urban Affairs and Finance of the Senate on any actions taken by the Office pursuant to subsection (f) (regarding preemption of inconsistent State insurance measures).

"(2) INSURANCE INDUSTRY. — Beginning September 30, 2011, the Director shall submit a report on or before September 30 of each calendar year to the President and to the Committee on Financial Services of the House of Representatives and the Committee on Banking, Housing, and Urban Affairs of the Senate on the insurance industry and any other information as deemed relevant by the Director or requested by such Committees.

"(o) REPORTS ON U.S. AND GLOBAL REINSURANCE MARKET. —The Director shall submit to the Committee on Financial Services of the House of Representatives and the Committee on Banking, Housing, and Urban Affairs of the Senate —

"(1) a report received not later than September 30, 2012, describing the breadth and scope of the global reinsurance market and the critical role such market plays in supporting insurance in the United States; and

"(2) a report received not later than January 1, 2013, and updated not later than January 1, 2015, describing the impact of part II of the Nonadmitted and Reinsurance Reform Act of 2010 on the ability of State regulators to access reinsurance information for regulated companies in their jurisdictions.

"(p) STUDY AND REPORT ON REGULATION OF INSURANCE. —

"(1) IN GENERAL. — Not later than 18 months after the date of enactment of this section, the Director shall conduct a study and submit a report to Congress on how to modernize and improve the system of insurance regulation in the United States.

"(2) CONSIDERATIONS. — The study and report required under paragraph (1) shall be based on and guided by the following considerations:

"(A) Systemic risk regulation with respect to insurance.

"(B) Capital standards and the relationship between capital allocation and liabilities, including standards relating to liquidity and duration risk.

"(C) Consumer protection for insurance products and practices, including gaps in State regulation.

"(D) The degree of national uniformity of State insurance regulation.

联邦贸易协定计划的权力。

(n)**向国会提交年度报告**。——

(1)**关于第313(f)条的报告**。——自2011年9月30日起,联邦保险办公室主任应在每一日历年的9月30日或9月30日之前,就联邦保险办公室根据第(f)子条(关于排除不一致州保险措施适用性的规定)采取的任何行动向总统、众议院金融服务委员会、众议院筹款委员会以及参议院银行、住房与城市事务委员会和参议院财政委员会提交一份报告。

(2)**关于保险业的报告**。——自2011年9月30日起,联邦保险办公室主任应在每一日历年的9月30日或9月30日之前,就保险业以及联邦保险办公室主任认为相关的任何其他信息或众议院金融服务委员会和参议院银行、住房与城市事务委员会要求提供的任何其他信息,向总统和上述委员会提交一份报告。

(o)**关于美国和全球再保险市场的报告**。——联邦保险办公室主任应向众议院金融服务委员会和参议院银行、住房与城市事务委员会提交以下报告——

(1)关于全球再保险市场的市场广度和范围以及该市场对美国保险业的关键支持作用之报告,报告的收到时间不得迟于2012年9月30日;及

(2)关于《2010年非本州监管保险和再保险改革法》第2部分对州监管者获取其管辖范围内的受监管公司的再保险信息能力的影响之报告,报告的收到时间不得迟于2013年1月1日,且最迟应于2015年1月1日完成更新。

(p)**关于保险监管的研究和报告**。——

(1)**一般规定**。——联邦保险办公室主任应在本条规定颁布之日后18个月内针对如何实现美国保险监管体系的现代化和改良开展研究,并就此向国会提交一份报告。

(2)**考虑因素**。——第(1)款所述研究和报告应基于以下考虑因素,并以之为指导:

(A)保险的系统性风险监管。

(B)资本标准以及资本配置与债务的关系,包括与流动性风险和期限风险相关的标准。

(C)在保险产品和保险惯例方面(包括州监管漏洞)的消费者保护。

(D)州保险监管的全国一致性程度。

"(E) The regulation of insurance companies and affiliates on a consolidated basis.

"(F) International coordination of insurance regulation.

"(3) ADDITIONAL FACTORS. — The study and report required under paragraph (1) shall also examine the following factors:

"(A) The costs and benefits of potential Federal regulation of insurance across various lines of insurance (except health insurance).

"(B) The feasibility of regulating only certain lines of insurance at the Federal level, while leaving other lines of insurance to be regulated at the State level.

"(C) The ability of any potential Federal regulation or Federal regulators to eliminate or minimize regulatory arbitrage.

"(D) The impact that developments in the regulation of insurance in foreign jurisdictions might have on the potential Federal regulation of insurance.

"(E) The ability of any potential Federal regulation or Federal regulator to provide robust consumer protection for policyholders.

"(F) The potential consequences of subjecting insurance companies to a Federal resolution authority, including the effects of any Federal resolution authority —

"(i) on the operation of State insurance guaranty fund systems, including the loss of guaranty fund coverage if an insurance company is subject to a Federal resolution authority;

"(ii) on policyholder protection, including the loss of the priority status of policyholder claims over other unsecured general creditor claims;

"(iii) in the case of life insurance companies, on the loss of the special status of separate account assets and separate account liabilities; and

"(iv) on the international competitiveness of insurance companies.

"(G) Such other factors as the Director determines necessary or appropriate, consistent with the principles set forth in paragraph (2).

"(4) REQUIRED RECOMMENDATIONS. — The study and report required under paragraph (1) shall also contain any legislative, administrative, or regulatory recommendations, as the Director determines appropriate, to carry out or effectuate the findings set forth in such report.

"(5) CONSULTATION. — With respect to the study and report required under paragraph (1), the Director shall consult with the State insurance regulators, consumer organizations, representatives of the insurance industry and policyholders, and other organizations and experts, as appropriate.

"(q) USE OF EXISTING RESOURCES. — To carry out this section, the Office may employ personnel, facilities, and any other resource of the Department of the Treasury available to the Secretary and the Secretary shall dedicate specific personnel to the Office.

"(r) DEFINITIONS. — In this section and section 314, the following definitions shall

(E)对保险公司和保险公司关联方的并表监管。

(F)保险监管的国际协作。

(3)**其他因素**。——第(1)款规定的研究及报告还应审查以下因素：

(A)如果在联邦层面对保险进行跨险种(但健康险除外)监管,该等监管之成本和收益。

(B)仅对某些险种在联邦层面进行监管,而其他险种仍在州层面进行监管的可行性。

(C)如选择联邦监管,任何联邦监管或联邦监管者是否有能力消除监管套利或将监管套利减到最低限度。

(D)外国司法辖区保险监管的发展可能对保险体系联邦监管这一选择造成的影响。

(E)如选择联邦监管,任何联邦监管或联邦监管者是否有能力为投保人提供稳健的消费者保护。

(F)使保险公司受制于联邦清盘权的潜在后果,包括任何联邦清盘权对以下各项的影响——

(i)对州保险保障基金体系运行的影响,包括保险公司如受制于联邦清盘权所将丧失的保障基金提供的担保;

(ii)对投保人保护的影响,包括投保人主张丧失相对于其他无担保的普通债权人主张的优先性;

(iii)对人寿保险公司独立账户资产和独立账户债务的特殊地位之丧失的影响;及

(iv)对保险公司国际竞争力的影响。

(G)联邦保险办公室主任判定确属必要或适当的与第(2)款规定的原则相符的其他因素。

(4)**应包含的建议**。——第(1)款规定的研究和报告还应包括联邦保险办公室主任判定对于实施或完成该等报告结论确属适当的任何立法、行政或监管建议。

(5)**磋商**。——联邦保险办公室主任应就第(1)款规定的研究和报告与州保险监管者、消费者组织、保险业和投保人代表以及其他相应的组织或专家磋商。

(q)**现有资源的使用**。——为了实施本条规定,联邦保险办公室可以使用可供财政部部长支配的财政部的人员、设施以及任何其他资源,财政部部长应指定专人供联邦保险办公室使用。

(r)**定义**。——就本条和第314条而言,应适用如下定义：

apply:

“(1) AFFILIATE. — The term ‘affiliate’ means, with respect to an insurer, any person who controls, is controlled by, or is under common control with the insurer.

“(2) COVERED AGREEMENT. — The term ‘covered agreement’ means a written bilateral or multilateral agreement regarding prudential measures with respect to the business of insurance or reinsurance that —

“(A) is entered into between the United States and one or more foreign governments, authorities, or regulatory entities; and

“(B) relates to the recognition of prudential measures with respect to the business of insurance or reinsurance that achieves a level of protection for insurance or reinsurance consumers that is substantially equivalent to the level of protection achieved under State insurance or reinsurance regulation.

“(3) INSURER. — The term ‘insurer’ means any person engaged in the business of insurance, including reinsurance.

“(4) FEDERAL FINANCIAL REGULATORY AGENCY. — The term ‘Federal financial regulatory agency’ means the Department of the Treasury, the Board of Governors of the Federal Reserve System, the Office of the Comptroller of the Currency, the Office of Thrift Supervision, the Securities and Exchange Commission, the Commodity Futures Trading Commission, the Federal Deposit Insurance Corporation, the Federal Housing Finance Agency, or the National Credit Union Administration.

“(5) NON–UNITED STATES INSURER. — The term ‘non–United States insurer’ means an insurer that is organized under the laws of a jurisdiction other than a State, but does not include any United States branch of such an insurer.

“(6) OFFICE. — The term ‘Office’ means the Federal Insurance Office established by this section.

“(7) STATE INSURANCE MEASURE. —The term ‘State insurance measure’ means any State law, regulation, administrative ruling, bulletin, guideline, or practice relating to or affecting prudential measures applicable to insurance or reinsurance.

“(8) STATE INSURANCE REGULATOR. — The term ‘State insurance regulator’ means any State regulatory authority responsible for the supervision of insurers.

“(9) SUBSTANTIALLY EQUIVALENT TO THE LEVEL OF PROTECTION ACHIEVED. — The term ‘substantially equivalent to the level of protection achieved’ means the prudential measures of a foreign government, authority, or regulatory entity achieve a similar outcome in consumer protection as the outcome achieved under State insurance or reinsurance regulation.

“(10) UNITED STATES INSURER. — The term ‘United States insurer’ means —

“(A) an insurer that is organized under the laws of a State; or

(1)**关联方**。——‘关联方’一词就保险公司而言,系指控制该保险公司的、受该保险公司控制的或与该保险公司受同一控制的任何人。

(2)**所涉协定**。——‘所涉协定’一词系指与保险或再保险业务审慎措施相关的具有以下特征的双边或多边书面协定——

(A)系由美国与一个或一个以上外国政府、监管机构或监管实体订立;及

(B)作出了相关规定,以承认保险或再保险业务的审慎措施所实现的对保险或再保险客户的保护水平与州保险或再保险监管下所实现的对保险或再保险客户的保护水平基本相当。

(3)**保险公司**。——‘保险公司’一词系指任何从事保险业务(包括再保险业务)的人。

(4)**联邦金融监管机关**。——‘联邦金融监管机关’一词系指财政部、联邦储备委员会、货币监理署、储蓄机构监理局、证券交易委员会、商品期货交易委员会、联邦存款保险公司、联邦住房金融局或国家信贷联盟署。

(5)**非美国保险公司**。——‘非美国保险公司’一词系指按照美国任何州以外的司法辖区法律组建的保险公司,但不包括该保险公司的任何美国分公司。

(6)**联邦保险办公室**。——‘联邦保险办公室’一词系指根据本条规定设立的联邦保险办公室。

(7)**州保险措施**。——‘州保险措施’一词系指与适用于保险或再保险的州审慎性措施相关或影响该等措施的任何州法律、规章、行政裁定、公报、指引或惯例。

(8)**州保险监管者**。——‘州保险监管者’一词系指负责监管保险公司的任何州监管机构。

(9)**基本相当的保护水平**。——‘基本相当的保护水平’一词系指外国政府、监管机构或监管实体的保险措施实现的消费者保护效果与州保险或再保险监管所实现的消费者保护效果类似。

(10)**美国保险公司**。——‘美国保险公司’一词系指——

(A)根据美国某一州法律组建的保险公司;或

"(B) a United States branch of a non–United States insurer.

"(s) AUTHORIZATION OF APPROPRIATIONS. — There are authorized to be appropriated for the Office for each fiscal year such sums as may be necessary.

"SEC. 314. COVERED AGREEMENTS.

"(a) AUTHORITY. — The Secretary and the United States Trade Representative are authorized, jointly, to negotiate and enter into covered agreements on behalf of the United States.

"(b) REQUIREMENTS FOR CONSULTATION WITH CONGRESS. —

"(1) IN GENERAL. — Before initiating negotiations to enter into a covered agreement under subsection (a), during such negotiations, and before entering into any such agreement, the Secretary and the United States Trade Representative shall jointly consult with the Committee on Financial Services and the Committee on Ways and Means of the House of Representatives and the Committee on Banking, Housing, and Urban Affairs and the Committee on Finance of the Senate.

"(2) SCOPE. — The consultation described in paragraph (1) shall include consultation with respect to —

"(A) the nature of the agreement;

"(B) how and to what extent the agreement will achieve the applicable purposes, policies, priorities, and objectives of section 313 and this section; and

"(C) the implementation of the agreement, including the general effect of the agreement on existing State laws.

"(c) SUBMISSION AND LAYOVER PROVISIONS. — A covered agreement under subsection (a) may enter into force with respect to the United States only if —

"(1) the Secretary and the United States Trade Representative jointly submit to the congressional committees specified in subsection (b)(1), on a day on which both Houses of Congress are in session, a copy of the final legal text of the agreement; and

"(2) a period of 90 calendar days beginning on the date on which the copy of the final legal text of the agreement is submitted to the congressional committees under paragraph (1) has expired.".

(b) DUTIES OF SECRETARY. — Section 321 (a) of title 31, United States Code, is amended —

(1) in paragraph (7), by striking "; and" and inserting a semicolon;

(2) in paragraph (8)(C), by striking the period at the end and inserting "; and"; and

(3) by adding at the end the following new paragraph:

"(9) advise the President on major domestic and international prudential policy issues in connection with all lines of insurance except health insurance.".

(c) CLERICAL AMENDMENT. — The table of sections for subchapter I of chapter 3

(B)非美国保险公司的美国分支机构。

(s)**拨款授权**。——兹授权在每一财政年度向联邦保险办公室拨付必要数额的款项。

第314条　所涉协定

(a)**权力**。——财政部部长和联邦贸易代表有权代表美国共同参与所涉协定的谈判和订立。

(b)**与国会磋商的要求**。——

(1)**一般规定**。——根据第(a)子条的规定启动所涉协定的谈判订立工作前,以及在谈判过程中、订立所涉协定前,财政部部长和美国贸易代表均应共同与众议院金融服务委员会、众议院筹款委员会、参议院银行、住房与城市事务委员会和参议院财政委员会磋商。

(2)**磋商范围**。——第(1)款所述磋商应包括就以下问题开展的磋商——

(A)上述协定的性质;

(B)该协定将如何并在多大程度上实现第313条和本条的相关目的、政策、重点任务和目标;及

(C)协定的实施,包括协定对现有各州法律的一般影响。

(c)**提交和暂缓生效期规定**。——第(a)子条下所涉协定仅可在满足以下条件的前提下始得对美国生效——

(1)财政部部长和美国贸易代表在国会两院均处于会期之日共同向第(b)(1)子条所述国会各委员会提交一份该协定的最终法律文本;及

(2)自该协定最终法律文本提交给第(1)款所述国会委员会之日起已届满90天。”

(b)**财政部部长的职责**。——《美国法典》第三十一编第321(a)节修正如下——

(1)在第(7)款中删除“;及”,替以分号;

(2)在第(8)(C)款中删除结尾处的句号,替以“;及”;及

(3)在该节结尾处增加如下新款:

“(9)就与所有险种(但健康险除外)相关的国内和国际重大审慎政策问题向总统提供意见。”

(c)**目录修正**。——《美国法典》第三十一编第三章第一子章各节目录修正如下:

of title 31, United States Code, is amended by striking the item relating to section 312 and inserting the following new items:

"Sec. 312. Terrorism and financial intelligence.

"Sec. 313. Federal Insurance Office.

"Sec. 314. Covered agreements.

"Sec. 315. Continuing in office. ".

Subtitle B — State–Based Insurance Reform

SEC. 511. SHORT TITLE.

This subtitle may be cited as the "Nonadmitted and Reinsurance Reform Act of 2010".

SEC. 512. EFFECTIVE DATE.

Except as otherwise specifically provided in this subtitle, this subtitle shall take effect upon the expiration of the 12–month period beginning on the date of the enactment of this subtitle.

PART I — NONADMITTED INSURANCE

SEC. 521. REPORTING, PAYMENT, AND ALLOCATION OF PREMIUM TAXES.

(a) HOME STATE'S EXCLUSIVE AUTHORITY. — No State other than the home State of an insured may require any premium tax payment for nonadmitted insurance.

(b) ALLOCATION OF NONADMITTED PREMIUM TAXES. —

(1) IN GENERAL. — The States may enter into a compact or otherwise establish procedures to allocate among the States the premium taxes paid to an insured's home State described in subsection (a).

(2) EFFECTIVE DATE. — Except as expressly otherwise provided in such compact or other procedures, any such compact or other procedures —

(A) if adopted on or before the expiration of the 330–day period that begins on the date of the enactment of this subtitle, shall apply to any premium taxes that, on or after such date of enactment, are required to be paid to any State that is subject to such compact or procedures; and

(B) if adopted after the expiration of such 330–day period, shall apply to any premium taxes that, on or after January 1 of the first calendar year that begins after the expiration of such 330–day period, are required to be paid to any State that is subject to such compact or procedures.

删除与第312节相关的目录项,替以如下新目录项:

“第312节　恐怖主义情报和金融情报。
第313节　联邦保险办公室。
第314节　所涉协定。
第315条　连任。”

第B子编——州保险改革

第511条　简称

引述本子编时,可简称为《2010年非本州监管保险和再保险改革法》。

第512条　生效日

除本子编另有特别规定的情形外,否则本子编应自本子编颁布之日起届满12个月之日生效。

第1部分——非本州监管保险

第521条　保费税金的申报、支付和分配

(a)**参保人所在州的排他性权力**。——除参保人所在州外,任何州均不得要求参保人就非本州监管保险支付任何保费税金。

(b)**非本州监管保险的保费税金的分配**。——

(1)**一般规定**。——各州可订立协约或以其他方式制定相关程序,在各州间分配向第(a)子条所述参保人所在州支付的保费税金。

(2)**生效日**。——除任何上述协约或其他程序中另有明确规定的情形外——

(A)该协约或程序系在本子编颁布之日后330天期限届满之前通过的,则应适用于在本子编颁布之日或之后,按规定应向受制于该协约或程序的任何州支付的任何保费税金;且

(B)该协约或程序系在本子编颁布之日后330天期限届满之后通过的,则应适用于上述330天期限届满后第一个日历年的1月1日或之后,按规定应向受制于该协约或程序的任何州支付的任何保费税金。

(3) REPORT. — Upon the expiration of the 330–day period referred to in paragraph (2) , the NAIC may submit a report to the Committee on Financial Services and the Committee on the Judiciary of the House of Representatives and the Committee on Banking, Housing, and Urban Affairs of the Senate identifying and describing any compact or other procedures for allocation among the States of premium taxes that have been adopted during such period by any States.

(4) NATIONWIDE SYSTEM. — The Congress intends that each State adopt nationwide uniform requirements, forms, and procedures, such as an interstate compact, that provide for the reporting, payment, collection, and allocation of premium taxes for nonadmitted insurance consistent with this section.

(c) ALLOCATION BASED ON TAX ALLOCATION REPORT. — To facilitate the payment of premium taxes among the States, an insured's home State may require surplus lines brokers and insureds who have independently procured insurance to annually file tax allocation reports with the insured's home State detailing the portion of the nonadmitted insurance policy premium or premiums attributable to properties, risks, or exposures located in each State. The filing of a nonadmitted insurance tax allocation report and the payment of tax may be made by a person authorized by the insured to act as its agent.

SEC. 522. REGULATION OF NONADMITTED INSURANCE BY INSURED'S HOME STATE.

(a) HOME STATE AUTHORITY. — Except as otherwise provided in this section, the placement of nonadmitted insurance shall be subject to the statutory and regulatory requirements solely of the insured's home State.

(b) BROKER LICENSING. — No State other than an insured's home State may require a surplus lines broker to be licensed in order to sell, solicit, or negotiate nonadmitted insurance with respect to such insured.

(c) ENFORCEMENT PROVISION. — With respect to section 521 and subsections (a) and (b) of this section, any law, regulation, provision, or action of any State that applies or purports to apply to nonadmitted insurance sold to, solicited by, or negotiated with an insured whose home State is another State shall be preempted with respect to such application.

(d) WORKERS' COMPENSATION EXCEPTION. — This section may not be construed to preempt any State law, rule, or regulation that restricts the placement of workers' compensation insurance or excess insurance for self–funded workers' compensation plans with a nonadmitted insurer.

SEC. 523. PARTICIPATION IN NATIONAL PRODUCER DATABASE.

After the expiration of the 2–year period beginning on the date of the enactment of this subtitle, a State may not collect any fees relating to licensing of an individual or entity as a

(3)**报告**。——第(2)款所述330天的期限届满之后,美国保险监督官协会可向众议院金融服务委员会、众议院司法委员会以及参议院银行、住房与城市事务委员会提交一份报告,指明并描述在上述期限内任何州已经通过的关于在各州之间分配保费税金的任何协约或其他程序。

(4)**全国性体系**。——国会的意图是,每个州均就非本州监管保险的保费税金的申报、支付、征收和分配制定与本条规定相符的且全国统一的要求、形式及制度(如州际协约)。

(c)**基于税收分配报告的分配**。——为促进州际间保费税金的支付,参保人所在州可以要求非本州监管保险的经纪人和已独立购买保险的参保人向参保人所在州提交年度报告,详细说明属于非本州监管保单保费的部分,或详细说明归于位于每一州的财产、风险或风险敞口的保费。参保人可授权他人作为其代理人,提交非本州监管保险税金分配报告并支付该税金。

第522条　参保人所在州对非本州监管保险的监管

(a)**参保人所在州的权力**。——除本条另有规定的情形外,对非本州监管保险的投保仅得受制于参保人所在州的法定要求及监管要求。

(b)**经纪人执照**。——除参保人所在州外,任何州均不得要求非本州监管保险的经纪人必须获得执照才能向该参保人销售、招揽或与之洽商非本州监管的保险。

(c)**执行规定**。——就第521条和本条第(a)子条和第(b)子条而言,任何州的任何法律、规章、规定或行动,如适用于或意图适用于向其他州的参保人出售的、该参保人申购的或与该参保人洽商的非本州监管的保险,其适用性均应予以排除。

(d)**工伤补偿的例外规定**。——对于限制自筹资金的工伤补偿计划向非本州监管保险公司投保工伤补偿险或超额险的任何州的法律、规则或规章,本条规定不得被解释为排除任何该等州法律、规则或规章的适用性。

第523条　加入全国保险中介数据库

自本子编颁布之日起届满2年之后,任何州均不得在向个人或实体颁发非本州监管保险的经纪人执照时收取任何相关费用,除非该州在其时已经制定并实施相关法

surplus lines broker in the State unless the State has in effect at such time laws or regulations that provide for participation by the State in the national insurance producer database of the NAIC, or any other equivalent uniform national database, for the licensure of surplus lines brokers and the renewal of such licenses.

SEC. 524. UNIFORM STANDARDS FOR SURPLUS LINES ELIGIBILITY.

A State may not —

(1) impose eligibility requirements on, or otherwise establish eligibility criteria for, nonadmitted insurers domiciled in a United States jurisdiction, except in conformance with such requirements and criteria in sections 5A (2) and 5C (2)(a) of the Non-Admitted Insurance Model Act, unless the State has adopted nationwide uniform requirements, forms, and procedures developed in accordance with section 521 (b) of this subtitle that include alternative nationwide uniform eligibility requirements; or

(2) prohibit a surplus lines broker from placing nonadmitted insurance with, or procuring nonadmitted insurance from, a nonadmitted insurer domiciled outside the United States that is listed on the Quarterly Listing of Alien Insurers maintained by the International Insurers Department of the NAIC.

SEC. 525. STREAMLINED APPLICATION FOR COMMERCIAL PURCHA - SERS.

A surplus lines broker seeking to procure or place nonadmitted insurance in a State for an exempt commercial purchaser shall not be required to satisfy any State requirement to make a due diligence search to determine whether the full amount or type of insurance sought by such exempt commercial purchaser can be obtained from admitted insurers if —

(1) the broker procuring or placing the surplus lines insurance has disclosed to the exempt commercial purchaser that such insurance may or may not be available from the admitted market that may provide greater protection with more regulatory oversight; and

(2) the exempt commercial purchaser has subsequently requested in writing the broker to procure or place such insurance from a nonadmitted insurer.

SEC. 526. GAO STUDY OF NONADMITTED INSURANCE MARKET.

(a) IN GENERAL. — The Comptroller General of the United States shall conduct a study of the nonadmitted insurance market to determine the effect of the enactment of this part on the size and market share of the nonadmitted insurance market for providing coverage typically provided by the admitted insurance market.

(b) CONTENTS. — The study shall determine and analyze —

(1) the change in the size and market share of the nonadmitted insurance market and in the number of insurance companies and insurance holding companies providing such business in the 18-month period that begins upon the effective date of this subtitle;

(2) the extent to which insurance coverage typically provided by the admitted insurance

律或规章，规定为颁发及延展非本州监管保险的经纪人执照之目的，该州应加入美国保险监督官协会的全国保险中介数据库或与该数据库相当的任何其他统一的全国性数据库。

第524条　非本州监管保险的经纪人的统一适格性标准

任何州均不得——

(1)向住所位于美国司法辖区的非本州监管保险公司施加适格性要求或另行设定适格性标准，但与《非本州监管保险示范法》第5A(2)条和第5C(2)(a)条所述要求及标准相符的要求或标准除外，除非该州已采用了根据本子编第521(b)条制定的全国统一要求、形式及制度，且该等要求、形式及制度中含有备选适用的全国统一适格性要求；或

(2)禁止非本州监管保险的经纪人向住所位于美国境外的、在美国保险监督官协会的外国保险公司部所维持的外国保险公司季度名单上的非本州监管保险公司投保非本州监管保险或向该等公司获取非本州监管保险。

第525条　商业购买人的精简申请程序

非本州监管保险的经纪人计划在某一州为豁免商业购买人获取或投保非本州监管保险的，不必按照任何州的要求开展尽职调查即可判断是否可从本州监管保险公司全额获得该豁免商业购买人需要的保险或获得该险种，其前提是——

(1)该意图获取或投保非本州监管保险的经纪商已向豁免商业购买人披露，该保险可以或无法从保护和监管程度更强的本州监管保险市场获得；且

(2)该豁免商业购买人在获得上述披露后，已书面要求该经纪商向非本州监管保险公司获取或投保上述保险。

第526条　政府问责办公室关于非本州监管保险市场的研究

(a)**一般规定**。——政府问责办公室主任应对非本州监管保险市场开展研究，从而判定本部分规定颁布后，对于通常由本州监管保险市场提供的保险而言，非本州监管保险市场在其中所占规模和市场份额将产生的变化。

(b)**研究内容**。——该项研究应对以下问题进行判定和分析——

(1)自本子编生效之日后18个月内，非本州监管保险市场规模和市场份额的变化，以及提供非本州监管保险业务的保险公司和保险控股公司的数量变化；

(2)通常由本州监管保险市场提供的保险向非本州监管保险市场的转移程度；

market has shifted to the nonadmitted insurance market;

(3) the consequences of any change in the size and market share of the nonadmitted insurance market, including differences in the price and availability of coverage available in both the admitted and nonadmitted insurance markets;

(4) the extent to which insurance companies and insurance holding companies that provide both admitted and nonadmitted insurance have experienced shifts in the volume of business between admitted and nonadmitted insurance; and

(5) the extent to which there has been a change in the number of individuals who have nonadmitted insurance policies, the type of coverage provided under such policies, and whether such coverage is available in the admitted insurance market.

(c) CONSULTATION WITH NAIC. — In conducting the study under this section, the Comptroller General shall consult with the NAIC.

(d) REPORT. — The Comptroller General shall complete the study under this section and submit a report to the Committee on Banking, Housing, and Urban Affairs of the Senate and the Committee on Financial Services of the House of Representatives regarding the findings of the study not later than 30 months after the effective date of this subtitle.

SEC. 527. DEFINITIONS.

For purposes of this part, the following definitions shall apply:

(1) ADMITTED INSURER. — The term "admitted insurer" means, with respect to a State, an insurer licensed to engage in the business of insurance in such State.

(2) AFFILIATE. — The term "affiliate" means, with respect to an insured, any entity that controls, is controlled by, or is under common control with the insured.

(3) AFFILIATED GROUP. — The term "affiliated group" means any group of entities that are all affiliated.

(4) CONTROL. — An entity has "control" over another entity if—

(A) the entity directly or indirectly or acting through 1 or more other persons owns, controls, or has the power to vote 25 percent or more of any class of voting securities of the other entity; or

(B) the entity controls in any manner the election of a majority of the directors or trustees of the other entity.

(5) EXEMPT COMMERCIAL PURCHASER. — The term "exempt commercial purchaser" means any person purchasing commercial insurance that, at the time of placement, meets the following requirements:

(A) The person employs or retains a qualified risk manager to negotiate insurance coverage.

(B) The person has paid aggregate nationwide commercial property and casualty insurance premiums in excess of $100, 000 in the immediately preceding 12 months.

(3)非本州监管保险市场规模和市场份额任何变化的后果,包括本州监管保险市场和非本州监管保险市场均可提供的保险的价格差异和可获得性的差异;

(4)同时提供本州监管保险和非本州监管保险的保险公司和保险控股公司的本州监管保险业务量和非本州监管保险的业务量比重的变动程度;及

(5)已持有非本州监管保险保单的个人的数量和该等保单提供的保险范围类型的变动程度,以及是否可从本州监管保险市场获得该等保险。

(c)**与美国保险监督官协会的磋商**。——政府问责办公室主任在开展本条所述研究时,应与美国保险监督官协会磋商。

(d)**报告**。——政府问责办公室主任应完成本条所述研究,并在本子编生效之日后30个月内就研究结果向参议院银行、住房与城市事务委员会和众议院金融服务委员会提交一份报告。

第527条　定义

就本部分而言,应适用如下定义:

(1)**本州监管保险公司**。——“本州监管保险公司”一词就某一州而言,系指获得在该州从事保险业务的执照的保险公司。

(2)**关联方**。——“关联方”一词就被保险人而言,系指控制该被保险人、受该被保险人控制或与之受同一控制的任何人。

(3)**关联集团**。——“关联集团”一词系指相互关联的任何一组实体。

(4)**控制**。——符合以下条件的实体应认定为“控制”另一实体——

(A)直接或间接地或通过一名或一名以上其他人拥有、控制另一实体任何类别的25%(含)以上的表决股,或者拥有另一实体任何类别的25%(含)以上的表决股的表决权;或

(B)以任何方式拥有控制选举另一实体过半数董事或信托受托人的权力。

(5)**豁免商业购买人**。——“豁免商业购买人”一词系指购买商业保险,且在投保时符合以下条件的任何主体:

(A)该主体雇用或聘用了一名合格风险经理,负责就保险范围开展谈判。

(B)该主体在投保前12个月内缴纳的全国商业财产和意外险的保费总额超过10万美元。

(C)(i) The person meets at least 1 of the following criteria:

(I) The person possesses a net worth in excess of $20, 000, 000, as such amount is adjusted pursuant to clause (ii).

(II) The person generates annual revenues in excess of $50, 000, 000, as such amount is adjusted pursuant to clause (ii).

(III) The person employs more than 500 full-time or full-time equivalent employees per individual insured or is a member of an affiliated group employing more than 1, 000 employees in the aggregate.

(IV) The person is a not-for-profit organization or public entity generating annual budgeted expenditures of at least $30, 000, 000, as such amount is adjusted pursuant to clause (ii).

(V) The person is a municipality with a population in excess of 50, 000 persons.

(ii) Effective on the fifth January 1 occurring after the date of the enactment of this subtitle and each fifth January 1 occurring thereafter, the amounts in subclauses (I), (II), and (IV) of clause (i) shall be adjusted to reflect the percentage change for such 5-year period in the Consumer Price Index for All Urban Consumers published by the Bureau of Labor Statistics of the Department of Labor.

(6) HOME STATE. —

(A) IN GENERAL. — Except as provided in subparagraph (B), the term "home State" means, with respect to an insured —

(i) the State in which an insured maintains its principal place of business or, in the case of an individual, the individual's principal residence; or

(ii) if 100 percent of the insured risk is located out of the State referred to in clause (i), the State to which the greatest percentage of the insured's taxable premium for that insurance contract is allocated.

(B) AFFILIATED GROUPS. — If more than 1 insured from an affiliated group are named insureds on a single nonadmitted insurance contract, the term "home State" means the home State, as determined pursuant to subparagraph (A), of the member of the affiliated group that has the largest percentage of premium attributed to it under such insurance contract.

(7) INDEPENDENTLY PROCURED INSURANCE. — The term "independently procured insurance" means insurance procured directly by an insured from a nonadmitted insurer.

(8) NAIC. — The term "NAIC" means the National Association of Insurance Commissioners or any successor entity.

(9) NONADMITTED INSURANCE. — The term "nonadmitted insurance" means any property and casualty insurance permitted to be placed directly or through a surplus lines

(C)(i)该主体至少符合以下一项标准:

(I)该主体的资产净值超过2000万美元[该金额标准可根据第(ii)项规定调整]。

(II)该主体的年度收入超过5000万美元[该金额标准可根据第(ii)项规定调整]。

(III)该单个参保主体雇用了500名以上全职雇员或可视同为全职雇员的雇员,或者具有某一关联集团的成员身份,而该关联集团雇用的雇员达1000名以上。

(IV)该主体是一家非营利组织或公共实体,且其年度预算支出不低于3000万美元[该金额标准可根据第(ii)项规定调整]。

(V)该主体是一个人口超过5万人的郡级市。

(ii)在本子编颁布之日后的第五年的1月1日,以及此后每隔5年的1月1日,应对第(i)项的第(I)子项、第(II)子项和第(IV)子项所述金额标准进行调整,以反映劳动部劳动统计局公布的所有城市消费者的消费者物价指数在上述5年期间内的百分比变化。

(6)**参保人所在州**。——

(A)一般规定。——除第(B)子款规定的情形外,"参保人所在州"一词——

(i)指参保人主要营业地所在州,或者(参保人为个人的)主要居住地所在州;或

(ii)如果参保风险100%位于第(i)项所述州之外,则指参保人的保险合同的应税保费分配百分比最高的州。

(B)**关联集团**。——某一关联集团中一个以上的成员被指定为同一份非本州监管保险合同的参保人的,"参保人所在州"一词系指根据该合同的应付保费占比最高的关联集团成员所在州[该成员所在州按第(A)子款判定]。

(7)**独立购买的保险**。——"独立购买的保险"一词系指参保人向非本州监管保险公司直接购买的保险。

(8)**美国保险监督官协会**。——"美国保险监督官协会"一词系指美国的保险监督官协会或该协会的任何继任实体。

(9)**非本州监管保险**。——"非本州监管保险"一词系指可直接向非本州监管保险公司投保的或通过非本州监管保险的经纪人向非本州监管保险公司投保的任何财

broker with a nonadmitted insurer eligible to accept such insurance.

(10) NON-ADMITTED INSURANCE MODEL ACT. — The term "Non-Admitted Insurance Model Act" means the provisions of the Non-Admitted Insurance Model Act, as adopted by the NAIC on August 3, 1994, and amended on September 30, 1996, December 6, 1997, October 2, 1999, and June 8, 2002.

(11) NONADMITTED INSURER. — The term "nonadmitted insurer" —

(A) means, with respect to a State, an insurer not licensed to engage in the business of insurancein such State; but

(B) does not include a risk retention group, as that term is defined in section 2 (a)(4) of the Liability Risk Retention Act of 1986 (15 U.S.C. 3901 (a)(4)).

(12) PREMIUM TAX. — The term "premium tax" means, with respect to surplus lines or independently procured insurance coverage, any tax, fee, assessment, or other charge imposed by a government entity directly or indirectly based on any payment made as consideration for an insurance contract for such insurance, including premium deposits, assessments, registration fees, and any other compensation given in consideration for a contract of insurance.

(13) QUALIFIED RISK MANAGER. — The term "qualified risk manager" means, with respect to a policyholder of commercial insurance, a person who meets all of the following requirements:

(A) The person is an employee of, or third-party consultant retained by, the commercial policyholder.

(B) The person provides skilled services in loss prevention, loss reduction, or risk and insurance coverage analysis, and purchase of insurance.

(C) The person —

(i)(I) has a bachelor's degree or higher from an accredited college or university in risk management, business administration, finance, economics, or any other field determined by a State insurance commissioner or other State regulatory official or entity to demonstrate minimum competence in risk management; and

(II) (aa) has 3 years of experience in risk financing, claims administration, loss prevention, risk and insurance analysis, or purchasing commercial lines of insurance; or

(bb) has —

(AA) a designation as a Chartered Property and Casualty Underwriter (in this subparagraph referred to as "CPCU") issued by the American Institute for CPCU/Insurance Institute of America;

(BB) a designation as an Associate in Risk Management (ARM) issued by the American Institute for CPCU/Insurance Institute of America;

(CC) a designation as Certified Risk Manager (CRM) issued by the National Alliance

产及意外险,但该非本州监管保险公司应具有接受上述投保的适格性。

(10)**《非本州监管保险示范法》**。——"《非本州监管保险示范法》"一词系指美国保险监督官协会于1994年8月3日通过并分别于1996年9月30日、1997年12月6日、1999年10月2日和2002年6月8日修正的《非本州监管保险示范法》的条款。

(11)**非本州监管保险公司**。——"非本州监管保险公司"一词——

(A)就某一州而言,系指未获得在该州从事保险业务的执照的保险公司;但

(B)不包括风险自留集团{定义见《1986年责任风险自留法》第2(a)(4)条[《美国法典》第十五编第3901(a)(4)节]}。

(12)**保费税金**。——就通过非本州监管保险的经纪人购买的或独立购买的保险而言,"保费税金"一词系指由政府实体基于上述保险合同的对价所做任何付款(包括预付保费、计征费、注册费以及保险合同任何其他对价报酬)直接或间接征收的任何税金、费用、计征费或任何其他收费。

(13)**合格风险经理**。——"合格风险经理"一词就商业保险投保人而言,系指符合以下全部要求的人:

(A)该人是商业保险投保人的雇员或该商业保险投保人聘用的第三方顾问。

(B)该人在损失防范、损失降低或风险及保险范围分析以及保险购买方面为商业保险投保人提供具有专业性的服务。

(C)该人——

(i)(I)持有经认证的学院或大学颁发的风险管理专业、商业管理专业、金融专业、经济学专业的学士或以上学位,或者州保险监督官、其他州监管官员或实体判定的任何其他专业的学士或以上学位,证明其具备基本风险管理能力;且

(II)(aa)在风险融资、索赔管理、损失防范、风险及保险分析或商业险种购买方面具有3年经验;或

(bb)持有——

(AA)美国特许财产及意外险核保人学会/美国保险学会颁发的特许注册的财产及意外险核保人(本子款中简称特许财产及意外险核保人)认证指定;

(BB)美国特许财产及意外险核保人学会/美国保险学会颁发的风险管理师(ARM)认证指定;

(CC)全国保险教育和研究联盟颁发的注册风险管理经理(CRM)认证指定;

for Insurance Education & Research;

(DD) a designation as a RIMS Fellow (RF) issued by the Global Risk Management Institute; or

(EE) any other designation, certification, or license determined by a State insurance commissioner or other State insurance regulatory official or entity to demonstrate minimum competency in risk management;

(ii)(I) has at least 7 years of experience in risk financing, claims administration, loss prevention, risk and insurance coverage analysis, or purchasing commercial lines of insurance; and

(II) has any 1 of the designations specified in subitems (AA) through (EE) of clause (i)(II)(bb);

(iii) has at least 10 years of experience in risk financing, claims administration, loss prevention, risk and insurance coverage analysis, or purchasing commercial lines of insurance; or

(iv) has a graduate degree from an accredited college or university in risk management, business administration, finance, economics, or any other field determined by a State insurance commissioner or other State regulatory official or entity to demonstrate minimum competence in risk management.

(14) REINSURANCE. — The term "reinsurance" means the assumption by an insurer of all or part of a risk undertaken originally by another insurer.

(15) SURPLUS LINES BROKER. — The term "surplus lines broker" means an individual, firm, or corporation which is licensed in a State to sell, solicit, or negotiate insurance on properties, risks, or exposures located or to be performed in a State with nonadmitted insurers.

(16) STATE. — The term "State" includes any State of the United States, the District of Columbia, the Commonwealth of Puerto Rico, Guam, the Northern Mariana Islands, the Virgin Islands, and American Samoa.

PART II — REINSURANCE

SEC. 531. REGULATION OF CREDIT FOR REINSURANCE AND REINSURANCE AGREEMENTS.

(a) CREDIT FOR REINSURANCE. — If the State of domicile of a ceding insurer is an NAIC-accredited State, or has financial solvency requirements substantially similar to the requirements necessary for NAIC accreditation, and recognizes credit for reinsurance for the insurer's ceded risk, then no other State may deny such credit for reinsurance.

(b) ADDITIONAL PREEMPTION OF EXTRATERRITORIAL APPLICATION OF STATE LAW. — In addition to the application of subsection (a), all laws, regulations,

(DD)全球风险管理学会颁发的风险与保险管理学会会员(RF)认证指定;或

(EE)州保险监督官或者其他州保险监管者或实体判定的任何其他可证明其具备基本风险管理能力的认证指定、证书或执照;

(ii)(I)在风险融资、索赔管理、损失防范、风险及保险范围分析或商业险种购买方面具有至少7年经验;及

(II)持有第(i)(II)(bb)项第(AA)子目至第(EE)子目所述任何一项认证指定;

(iii)在风险融资、索赔管理、损失防范、风险及保险范围分析或商业险种购买方面具有至少10年经验;或

(iv)持有经认证的学院或大学颁发的风险管理专业、商业管理专业、金融专业、经济学专业的硕士学位,或者州保险监督官或其他州监管官员或实体判定的任何其他专业的硕士学位,证明其具备基本风险管理能力。

(14)**再保险**。——"再保险"一词系指某一保险公司承担原本由另一保险公司承担的全部或部分风险。

(15)**非本州监管保险的经纪人**。——"非本州监管保险的经纪人"一词系指在某一州获得执照,可以与非本州监管保险公司共同就位于该州的或将在该州履行的财产、风险或风险敞口保险开展销售、招揽或业务洽谈的个人、机构或公司。

(16)州。——"州"一词包括美国的任何州、哥伦比亚特区、波多黎各自由邦、关岛、北马里亚纳群岛、维尔京群岛和美属萨摩亚。

第2部分——再　保　险

第531条　再保险和再保险协议的信用的规制

(a)**再保险信用**。——如再保险分出公司住所所在州已获美国保险监督官协会认证,或者该州的财务偿付能力要求与获得美国保险监督官协会认证所应满足的要求基本类似,且该州承认保险公司分出风险的再保险信用,则其他任何州均不得不承认该等再保险信用的效力。

(b)**补充排除州法律的域外适用**。——作为第(a)子条的适用的补充,再保险分出公司住所所在州之外的州,其所有法律、规章、规定或其他行动(但与对保险公司或保

provisions, or other actions of a State that is not the domiciliary State of the ceding insurer, except those with respect to taxes and assessments on insurance companies or insurance income, are preempted to the extent that they —

(1) restrict or eliminate the rights of the ceding insurer or the assuming insurer to resolve disputes pursuant to contractual arbitration to the extent such contractual provision is not inconsistent with the provisions of title 9, United States Code;

(2) require that a certain State's law shall govern the reinsurance contract, disputes arising from the reinsurance contract, or requirements of the reinsurance contract;

(3) attempt to enforce a reinsurance contract on terms different than those set forth in the reinsurance contract, to the extent that the terms are not inconsistent with this part; or

(4) otherwise apply the laws of the State to reinsurance agreements of ceding insurers not domiciled in that State.

SEC. 532. REGULATION OF REINSURER SOLVENCY.

(a) DOMICILIARY STATE REGULATION. — If the State of domicile of a reinsurer is an NAIC–accredited State or has financial solvency requirements substantially similar to the requirements necessary for NAIC accreditation, such State shall be solely responsible for regulating the financial solvency of the reinsurer.

(b) NONDOMICILIARY STATES. —

(1) LIMITATION ON FINANCIAL INFORMATION REQUIREMENTS. — If the State of domicile of a reinsurer is an NAIC–accredited State or has financial solvency requirements substantially similar to the requirements necessary for NAIC accreditation, no other State may require the reinsurer to provide any additional financial information other than the information the reinsurer is required to file with its domiciliary State.

(2) RECEIPT OF INFORMATION. — No provision of this section shall be construed as preventing or prohibiting a State that is not the State of domicile of a reinsurer from receiving a copy of any financial statement filed with its domiciliary State.

SEC. 533. DEFINITIONS.

For purposes of this part, the following definitions shall apply:

(1) CEDING INSURER. — The term "ceding insurer" means an insurer that purchases reinsurance.

(2) DOMICILIARY STATE. — The terms "State of domicile" and "domiciliary State" mean, with respect to an insurer or reinsurer, the State in which the insurer or reinsurer is incorporated or entered through, and licensed.

(3) NAIC. — The term "NAIC" means the National Association of Insurance Commissioners or any successor entity.

(4) REINSURANCE. — The term "reinsurance" means the assumption by an insurer of all or part of a risk undertaken originally by another insurer.

险所得征收税收和计征费相关的除外)只要具有以下特征,其适用性即应被排除——

(1)限制或取消再保险分出公司或再保险分入公司根据仲裁合同解决纠纷的权利,但前提是该合同规定不得违反《美国法典》第九编的规定;

(2)要求再保险合同、因再保险合同产生的纠纷或再保险合同的规定必须受某一州的法律规制;

(3)在再保险合同所载条款并不违反本部分规定的情况下,试图按与之相异的条款强制执行该再保险合同;或

(4)以其他方式将该州法律适用于住所并非位于该州的再保险分出公司。

第532条 对再保险公司偿付能力的监管

(a)**再保险公司住所所在州的监管**。——如再保险公司住所所在州已获美国保险监督官协会认证,或该州的财务偿付能力要求与获得美国保险监督官协会认证所应满足的要求基本类似,则对该再保险公司偿付能力的监管应完全由该州负责。

(b)**再保险公司住所所在州之外的州**。——

(1)**财务信息要求的限制**。——如果再保险公司住所所在州已获美国保险监督官协会认证,或该州的财务偿付能力要求与获得美国保险监督官协会认证所应满足的要求基本类似,则除再保险公司按要求须向其住所所在州提交的信息外,任何其他州均不得要求该再保险公司提供任何额外财务信息。

(2)**信息接收**。——再保险公司住所所在州之外的州有权接收再保险公司向其住所所在州提交的任何财务报表的复本,本条中的任何规定均不得被解释为构成对上述权利的妨碍或禁止。

第533条 定义

就本部分而言,应适用如下定义:

(1)**再保险分出公司**。——"再保险分出公司"一词系指购买再保险的保险公司。

(2)**住所所在州**。——就保险公司或再保险公司而言,该保险公司在哪一州组建或通过哪一州进入美国市场并在哪一州获得执照,该州即为该保险公司的"住所所在州"。

(3)**美国保险监督官协会**。——"美国保险监督官协会"一词系指美国保险监督官协会或其任何继任实体。

(4)**再保险**。——"再保险"一词系指某一保险公司承担原本由另一保险公司承担的全部或部分风险。

(5) REINSURER. —

(A) IN GENERAL. — The term "reinsurer" means an insurer to the extent that the insurer —

(i) is principally engaged in the business of reinsurance;

(ii) does not conduct significant amounts of direct insurance as a percentage of its net premiums; and

(iii) is not engaged in an ongoing basis in the business of soliciting direct insurance.

(B) DETERMINATION. — A determination of whether an insurer is a reinsurer shall be made under the laws of the State of domicile in accordance with this paragraph.

(6) STATE. — The term "State" includes any State of the United States, the District of Columbia, the Commonwealth of Puerto Rico, Guam, the Northern Mariana Islands, the Virgin Islands, and American Samoa.

PART III — RULE OF CONSTRUCTION

SEC. 541. RULE OF CONSTRUCTION.

Nothing in this subtitle or the amendments made by this subtitle shall be construed to modify, impair, or supersede the application of the antitrust laws. Any implied or actual conflict between this subtitle and any amendments to this subtitle and the antitrust laws shall be resolved in favor of the operation of the antitrust laws.

SEC. 542. SEVERABILITY.

If any section or subsection of this subtitle, or any application of such provision to any person or circumstance, is held to be unconstitutional, the remainder of this subtitle, and the application of the provision to any other person or circumstance, shall not be affected.

(5)**再保险公司**。——

(A)**一般规定**。——“再保险公司”一词系指具有以下特征的保险公司——

(i)主营业务为再保险业务;

(ii)从事直接保险获得的保费在其保费净额中所占百分比不大;且

(iii)并不持续从事招揽直接保险的业务。

(B)**判定**。——某一保险公司是否是一家再保险公司,应根据本款按照该保险公司住所所在州的州法律判定。

(6)**州**。——“州”一词包括美国的任何州、哥伦比亚特区、波多黎各自由邦、关岛、北马里亚纳群岛、维尔京群岛和美属萨摩亚。

第3部分——解 释 规 则

第541条　解释规则

本子编的任何规定或本子编作出的任何修正均不得被解释为对反垄断法律适用的修改、削弱或替代。本子编和对本子编的任何修正与反垄断法律存在任何隐含冲突或实际冲突的,应以有利于反垄断法律实施的原则解决。

第542条　可分割性

本子编的任何条款或该等条款对任何人或情形的任何适用被判定违宪的,本子编其余部分及该等条款对任何其他人或其他情形的适用不受影响。

TITLE Ⅵ — IMPROVEMENTS TO REGULATION OF BANK AND SAVINGS ASSOCIATION HOLDING COMPANIES AND DEPOSITORY INSTITUTIONS

SEC. 601. SHORT TITLE.

This title may be cited as the "Bank and Savings Association Holding Company and Depository Institution Regulatory Improvements Act of 2010".

SEC. 602. DEFINITION.

For purposes of this title, a company is a "commercial firm" if the annual gross revenues derived by the company and all of its affiliates from activities that are financial in nature (as defined in section 4 (k) of the Bank Holding Company Act of 1956 (12 U.S.C. 1843 (k))) and, if applicable, from the ownership or control of one or more insured depository institutions, represent less than 15 percent of the consolidated annual gross revenues of the company.

SEC. 603. MORATORIUM AND STUDY ON TREATMENT OF CREDIT CARD BANKS, INDUSTRIAL LOAN COMPANIES, AND CERTAIN OTHER COMPANIES UNDER THE BANK HOLDING COMPANY ACT OF 1956.

(a) MORATORIUM. —

(1) DEFINITIONS. — In this subsection —

(A) the term "credit card bank" means an institution described in section 2 (c)(2)(F) of the Bank Holding Company Act of 1956 (12 U.S.C. 1841 (c)(2)(F));

(B) the term "industrial bank" means an institution described in section 2 (c)(2)(H) of the Bank Holding Company Act of 1956 (12 U.S.C. 1841 (c)(2)(H)); and

(C) the term "trust bank" means an institution described in section 2 (c)(2)(D) of the Bank Holding Company Act of 1956 (12 U.S.C. 1841 (c)(2)(D)).

(2) MORATORIUM ON PROVISION OF DEPOSIT INSURANCE. — The Corporation may not approve an application for deposit insurance under section 5 of the Federal Deposit Insurance Act (12 U.S.C. 1815) that is received after November 23, 2009,

第六编——改进对银行、储蓄协会控股公司和存款机构的监管

第601条　简称

引述本编时,可简称为《2010年银行、储蓄协会控股公司和存款机构监管改进法》。

第602条　定义

就本编而言,如某一公司自身及其全体关联方从金融性质活动{定义见《1956年银行控股公司法》第4(k)条[《美国法典》第十二编第1843(k)节]}获得的,和(如适用)从其对一家或一家以上参保存款机构的所有权或控制权而获得的年度总收入低于该公司并表年度总收入的15%,则该公司是一家“商业公司”。

第603条　延期履行权和关于对《1956年银行控股公司法》中的信用卡银行、产业贷款公司及特定其他公司的处理之研究

(a)**延期履行权**。——

(1)**定义**。——在本子条中——

(A)“信用卡银行”一词系指《1956年银行控股公司法》第2(c)(2)(F)条[《美国法典》第十二编第1841(c)(2)(F)节]所述机构;

(B)“产业银行”一词系指《1956年银行控股公司法》第2(c)(2)(H)条[《美国法典》第十二编第1841(c)(2)(H)节]所述机构;及

(C)“信托银行”一词系指《1956年银行控股公司法》第2(c)(2)(D)条[《美国法典》第十二编第1841(c)(2)(D)节]所述机构。

(2)**存款保险条款的延期履行**。——对于为商业公司直接或间接拥有或控制的产业银行、信用卡银行或信托银行申请的《联邦存款保险法》第5条[《美国法典》第十二编第1815节]所述存款保险,如联邦存款保险公司收到该等申请的日期晚于2009年

for an industrial bank, a credit card bank, or a trust bank that is directly or indirectly owned or controlled by a commercial firm.

(3) CHANGE IN CONTROL. —

(A) IN GENERAL. — Except as provided in subparagraph (B), the appropriate Federal banking agency shall disapprove a change in control, as provided in section 7 (j) of the Federal Deposit Insurance Act (12 U.S.C. 1817 (j)), of an industrial bank, a credit card bank, or a trust bank if the change in control would result in direct or indirect control of the industrial bank, credit card bank, or trust bank by a commercial firm.

(B) EXCEPTIONS. — Subparagraph (A) shall not apply to a change in control of an industrial bank, credit card bank, or trust bank —

(i) that —

(I) is in danger of default, as determined by the appropriate Federal banking agency;

(II) results from the merger or whole acquisition of a commercial firm that directly or indirectly controls the industrial bank, credit card bank, or trust bank in a bona fide merger with or acquisition by another commercial firm, as determined by the appropriate Federal banking agency; or

(III) results from an acquisition of voting shares of a publicly traded company that controls an industrial bank, credit card bank, or trust bank, if, after the acquisition, the acquiring shareholder (or group of shareholders acting in concert) holds less than 25 percent of any class of the voting shares of the company; and

(ii) that has obtained all regulatory approvals otherwise required for such change of control under any applicable Federal or State law, including section 7 (j) of the Federal Deposit Insurance Act (12 U.S.C. 1817 (j)).

(4) SUNSET. — This subsection shall cease to have effect 3 years after the date of enactment of this Act.

(b) GOVERNMENT ACCOUNTABILITY OFFICE STUDY OF EXCEPTIONS UNDER THE BANK HOLDING COMPANY ACT OF 1956. —

(1) STUDY REQUIRED. — The Comptroller General of the United States shall carry out a study to determine whether it is necessary, in order to strengthen the safety and soundness of institutions or the stability of the financial system, to eliminate the exceptions under section 2 of the Bank Holding Company Act of 1956 (12 U.S.C. 1841) for institutions described in —

(A) section 2 (a)(5)(E) of the Bank Holding Company Act of 1956 (12 U.S.C. 1841 (a)(5)(E));

(B) section 2 (a)(5)(F) of the Bank Holding Company Act of 1956 (12 U.S.C. 1841 (a)(5)(F));

(C) section 2 (c)(2)(D) of the Bank Holding Company Act of 1956 (12 U.S.C. 1841

11月23日,则联邦存款保险公司可以不予批准。

(3)**控制权变更**。——

(A)**一般规定**。——除第(B)子款规定的情形外,产业银行、信用卡银行或信托银行发生控制权变更{相关规定见《联邦存款保险法》第7(j)条[《美国法典》第十二编第1817(j)节]}且该等变更可能导致该产业银行、信用卡银行或信托银行被商业公司直接或间接控制的,则相应的联邦银行业监管机关不得批准该等变更。

(B)**例外规定**。——在以下情形下,不适用第(A)子款的规定——

(i)产业银行、信用卡银行或信托银行——

(I)据相应的联邦银行业监管机关判定,存在违约风险;

(II)其控制权变更系由以下原因产生:直接或间接控制该产业银行、信用卡银行或信托银行的商业公司,在一项善意的并购中被另一商业公司兼并或完全收购,并购是否属于善意并购由相应的联邦银行业监管机关判定;或

(III)其控制权变更系由以下原因产生:控制该产业银行、信用卡银行或信托银行的公开交易公司的表决股被收购,且收购完成后,收购表决股的股东(或一致行动的若干股东)在该公司任何类别的表决股中持有的份额均低于25%;且

(ii)已根据任何适用的联邦法律或州法律{包括《联邦存款保险法》第7(j)条[《美国法典》第十二编第1817(j)节]}就控制权变更取得所有其他必要的监管批准。

(4)**日落条款**。——本法颁布之日起届满3年之后,本子条应停止生效。

(b)**政府问责办公室对《1956年银行控股公司法》的例外规定的研究**。——

(1)**研究要求**。——政府问责办公室主任应开展一项研究,以判定为加强相关机构的安全和稳健水平或金融体系的稳定性,是否应取消下述机构根据《1956年银行控股公司法》第2条(《美国法典》第十二编第1841节)享有的例外待遇——

(A)《1956年银行控股公司法》第2(a)(5)(E)条[《美国法典》第十二编第1841(a)(5)(E)节]所述机构;

(B)《1956年银行控股公司法》第2(a)(5)(F)条[《美国法典》第十二编第1841(a)(5)(F)节]所述机构;

(C)《1956年银行控股公司法》第2(c)(2)(D)条[《美国法典》第十二编第1841(c)

(c)(2)(D));

(D) section 2 (c)(2)(F) of the Bank Holding Company Act of 1956 (12 U.S.C. 1841 (c)(2)(F));

(E) section 2 (c)(2)(H) of the Bank Holding Company Act of 1956 (12 U.S.C. 1841 (c)(2)(H)); and

(F) section 2 (c)(2)(B) of the Bank Holding Company Act of 1956 (12 U.S.C. 1841 (c)(2)(B)).

(2) CONTENT OF STUDY. —

(A) IN GENERAL. — The study required under paragraph (1), with respect to the institutions referenced in each of subparagraphs (A) through (E) of paragraph (1), shall, to the extent feasible be based on information provided to the Comptroller General by the appropriate Federal or State regulator, and shall —

(i) identify the types and number of institutions excepted from section 2 of the Bank Holding Company Act of 1956 (12 U.S.C. 1841) under each of the subparagraphs described in subparagraphs (A) through (E) of paragraph (1);

(ii) generally describe the size and geographic locations of the institutions described in clause (i);

(iii) determine the extent to which the institutions described in clause (i) are held by holding companies that are commercial firms;

(iv) determine whether the institutions described in clause (i) have any affiliates that are commercial firms;

(v) identify the Federal banking agency responsible for the supervision of the institutions described in clause (i) on and after the transfer date;

(vi) determine the adequacy of the Federal bank regulatory framework applicable to each category of institution described in clause (i), including any restrictions (including limitations on affiliate transactions or cross–marketing) that apply to transactions between an institution, the holding company of the institution, and any other affiliate of the institution; and

(vii) evaluate the potential consequences of subjecting the institutions described in clause (i) to the requirements of the Bank Holding Company Act of 1956, including with respect to the availability and allocation of credit, the stability of the financial system and the economy, the safe and sound operation of each category of institution, and the impact on the types of activities in which such institutions, and the holding companies of such institutions, may engage.

(B) SAVINGS ASSOCIATIONS. — With respect to institutions described in paragraph (1)(F), the study required under paragraph (1) shall —

(i) determine the adequacy of the Federal bank regulatory framework applicable to such

(2)(D)节]所述机构;

(D)《1956年银行控股公司法》第2(c)(2)(F)条[《美国法典》第十二编第1841(c)(2)(F)节]所述机构;

(E)《1956年银行控股公司法》第2(c)(2)(H)条[《美国法典》第十二编第1841(c)(2)(H)节]所述机构;及

(F)《1956年银行控股公司法》第2(c)(2)(B)条[《美国法典》第十二编第1841(c)(2)(B)节]所述机构;

(2)**研究内容**。——

(A)**一般规定**。——在可行范围内,第(1)款要求针对第(1)款第(A)子款至第(E)子款其中每一子款所述机构开展的研究,应以相应的联邦监管者或州监管者向政府问责办公室主任提供的信息为基础,并应——

(i)指明上文第(1)款第(A)子款至第(E)子款提及的每一子款所述的且可以享受例外待遇的,不必适用《1956年银行控股公司法》第2条(《美国法典》第十二编第1841节)的机构的类型和数量;

(ii)对第(i)项所述机构的规模和地理位置提供一般性描述;

(iii)判定具有商业公司身份的控股公司对第(i)项所述机构的控制程度;

(iv)判定第(i)项所述机构是否拥有具有商业公司身份的任何关联方;

(v)指明在转移日和转移日之后负责监管第(i)项所述机构的联邦银行业监管机关;

(vi)判定第(i)项所述机构适用的联邦银行监管框架是否完备,包括适用于某一机构、该机构的控股公司及任何其他关联方之间交易的任何限制(包括对关联交易或交叉营销的限制)的完备程度;及

(vii)评估可能对第(i)项所述机构适用《1956年银行控股公司法》的规定将产生的潜在影响,包括对信用的可获得性和分配、金融体系及经济稳定以及上述每一类机构安全稳健运营的影响,以及对该等机构及其控股公司可以从事的活动类型的影响。

(B)**储蓄协会**。——就第(1)(F)款所述机构而言,按第(1)款要求开展的研究应——

(i)判定适用于该等机构的联邦银行监管框架是否完备,包括适用于该等机构、该

institutions, including any restrictions (including limitations on affiliate transactions or cross-marketing) that apply to transactions between an institution, the holding company of the institution, and any other affiliate of the institution; and

(ii) evaluate the potential consequences of subjecting the institutions described in paragraph (1)(F) to the requirements of the Bank Holding Company Act of 1956, including with respect to the availability and allocation of credit, the stability of the financial system and the economy, the safe and sound operation of such institutions, and the impact on the types of activities in which such institutions, and the holding companies of such institutions, may engage.

(3) REPORT. — Not later than 18 months after the date of enactment of this Act, the Comptroller General shall submit to the Committee on Banking, Housing, and Urban Affairs of the Senate and the Committee on Financial Services of the House of Representatives a report on the study required under paragraph (1).

SEC. 604. REPORTS AND EXAMINATIONS OF HOLDING COMPANIES; REGULATION OF FUNCTIONALLY REGULATED SUBSIDIARIES.

(a) REPORTS BY BANK HOLDING COMPANIES. — Sections 5 (c)(1) of the Bank Holding Company Act of 1956 (12 U.S.C. 1844 (c)(1)) is amended —

(1) by striking subclause (A)(ii) and inserting the following:

"(ii) compliance by the bank holding company or subsidiary with —

"(I) this Act;

"(II) Federal laws that the Board has specific jurisdiction to enforce against the company or subsidiary; and

"(III) other than in the case of an insured depository institution or functionally regulated subsidiary, any other applicable provision of Federal law.";

(2) by striking subparagraph (B) and inserting the following:

"(B) USE OF EXISTING REPORTS AND OTHER SUPERVISORY INFORMATION. — The Board shall, to the fullest extent possible, use —

"(i) reports and other supervisory information that the bank holding company or any subsidiary thereof has been required to provide to other Federal or State regulatory agencies;

"(ii) externally audited financial statements of the bank holding company or subsidiary;

"(iii) information otherwise available from Federal or State regulatory agencies; and

"(iv) information that is otherwise required to be reported publicly."; and

(3) by adding at the end the following:

"(C) AVAILABILITY. — Upon the request of the Board, the bank holding company or a subsidiary of the bank holding company shall promptly provide to the Board any information described in clauses (i) through (iii) of subparagraph (B).".

(b) EXAMINATIONS OF BANK HOLDING COMPANIES. — Section 5 (c)(2) of the

等机构的控股公司及任何其他关联方之间交易的任何限制(包括对关联方交易或交叉营销的限制)的完备程度;及

(ii)评估可能对第(1)(F)款所述机构适用《1956年银行控股公司法》的规定将产生的潜在影响,包括对信用的可获得性和分配、金融体系及经济稳定、该等机构安全稳健运营的影响,以及对该等机构及其控股公司可以从事的活动类型的影响。

(3)**报告**。——政府问责办公室主任应在本法颁布之日后18个月内向参议院银行、住房与城市事务委员会和众议院金融服务委员会就按第(1)款要求开展的研究提交一份研究报告。

第604条　银行控股公司报告及检查;对受制于功能监管的子公司的监管

(a)**银行控股公司的报告**。——《1956年银行控股公司法》第5(c)(1)条[《美国法典》第十二编第1844(c)(1)节]修正如下——

(1)删除第(A)(ii)子项,替以如下内容:

"(ii)银行控股公司或其子公司对以下法律的合规情况——

(I)本法;

(II)联邦储备委员会有明确的管辖权,可针对银行控股公司或其子公司执行的联邦法律;及

(III)联邦法律任何其他适用的规定(对于参保存款机构或受制于功能监管的子公司之外的实体而言)。"

(2)删除第(B)子款,替以如下内容:

"(B)**既有报告和其他监管信息的利用**。——联邦储备委员会应尽最大可能利用——

(i)银行控股公司或其任何子公司已按要求向其他联邦监管机关或州监管机关提供的报告和其他监管信息;

(ii)银行控股公司或其子公司经外部审计的财务报表;

(iii)联邦监管机关或州监管机关可另行提供的其他信息;及

(iv)要求公开报告的其他信息。"及

(3)在该条结尾处增加如下内容:

"(C)**信息提供**。——联邦储备委员会提出要求时,银行控股公司或其子公司应及时向联邦储备委员会提供第(B)子款第(i)项至第(iii)项所述的任何信息。"

(b)**对银行控股公司的检查**。——《1956年银行控股公司法》第5(c)(2)条[《美国

Bank Holding Company Act of 1956 (12 U.S.C. 1844 (c)(2)) is amended to read as follows:

"(2) EXAMINATIONS. —

"(A) IN GENERAL. — Subject to subtitle B of the Consumer Financial Protection Act of 2010, the Board may make examinations of a bank holding company and each subsidiary of a bank holding company in order to —

"(i) inform the Board of —

"(I) the nature of the operations and financial condition of the bank holding company and the subsidiary;

"(II) the financial, operational, and other risks within the bank holding company system that may pose a threat to —

"(aa) the safety and soundness of the bank holding company or of any depository institution subsidiary of the bank holding company; or

"(bb) the stability of the financial system of the United States; and

"(III) the systems of the bank holding company for monitoring and controlling the risks described in subclause (II); and

"(ii) monitor the compliance of the bank holding company and the subsidiary with —

"(I) this Act;

"(II) Federal laws that the Board has specific jurisdiction to enforce against the company or subsidiary; and

"(III) other than in the case of an insured depository institution or functionally regulated subsidiary, any other applicable provisions of Federal law.

"(B) USE OF REPORTS TO REDUCE EXAMINATIONS. — For purposes of this paragraph, the Board shall, to the fullest extent possible, rely on —

"(i) examination reports made by other Federal or State regulatory agencies relating to a bank holding company and any subsidiary of a bank holding company; and

"(ii) the reports and other information required under paragraph (1).

"(C) COORDINATION WITH OTHER REGULATORS. — The Board shall —

"(i) provide reasonable notice to, and consult with, the appropriate Federal banking agency, the Securities and Exchange Commission, the Commodity Futures Trading Commission, or State regulatory agency, as appropriate, for a subsidiary that is a depository institution or a functionally regulated subsidiary of a bank holding company before commencing an examination of the subsidiary under this section; and

"(ii) to the fullest extent possible, avoid duplication of examination activities, reporting requirements, and requests for information.".

(c) AUTHORITY TO REGULATE FUNCTIONALLY REGULATED SUBSIDIARIES OF BANK HOLDING COMPANIES. — The Bank Holding Company Act of 1956 (12 U.S.C. 1841 et seq.) is amended —

法典》第十二编第1844(c)(2)节]修正后全文如下:

“(2)**检查**。——

(A)**一般规定**。——在不违反《2010年消费者金融保护法》第B子编规定的前提下,联邦储备委员会可以对银行控股公司及其每一子公司进行检查,以便——

(i)获取如下信息——

(I)银行控股公司及其子公司的经营性质和财务状况;

(II)银行控股公司体系之内可能对以下各项构成威胁的财务、运营和其他风险——

(aa)银行控股公司或具有存款机构身份的任何银行控股公司子公司的安全性和稳健性;或

(bb)美国金融体系的稳定;及

(III)银行控股公司对第(II)子项所述风险的监控和控制系统;及

(ii)监控银行控股公司及其子公司对以下法律的合规情况——

(I)本法;

(II)联邦储备委员会有明确的管辖权,可对银行控股公司或其子公司执行的联邦法律;及

(III)联邦法律任何其他适用的规定(对于参保存款机构或受制于功能监管的子公司之外的实体而言)。

(B)**利用报告减少检查工作**。——就本款而言,联邦储备委员会应尽最大可能采信——

(i)其他联邦监管机关或州监管机关就银行控股公司及其任何子公司作出的检查报告;及

(ii)第(1)款规定的报告和其他信息。

(C)**与其他监管者的协调**。——联邦储备委员会应——

(i)在根据本条规定对具有存款机构身份的银行控股公司子公司或受制于功能监管的银行控股公司子公司开始检查前,向相应的联邦银行业监管机关、证券交易委员会、商品期货交易委员会或州监管机关(视具体情况而定)提供合理的通知并与之磋商;及

(ii)尽最大可能避免重复检查,并避免提出重复的报告要求和信息提供要求。”

(c)**对受制于功能监管的银行控股公司子公司的监管权**。——《1956年银行控股公司法》(《美国法典》第十二编第1841节及其后条文)修正如下——

(1) in section 5 (c)(5)(B)(12 U.S.C. 1844 (c)(5)(B)), by striking clause (v) and inserting the following: " (v) an entity that is subject to regulation by, or registration with, the Commodity Futures Trading Commission, with respect to activities conducted as a futures commission merchant, commodity trading adviser, commodity pool, commodity pool operator, swap execution facility, swap data repository, swap dealer, major swap participant, and activities that are incidental to such commodities and swaps activities. "; and

(2) by striking section 10A (12 U.S.C. 1848a).

(d) ACQUISITIONS OF BANKS. — Section 3 (c) of the Bank Holding Company Act of 1956 (12 U.S.C. 1842 (c)) is amended by adding at the end the following:

" (7) FINANCIAL STABILITY. — In every case, the Board shall take into consideration the extent to which a proposed acquisition, merger, or consolidation would result in greater or more concentrated risks to the stability of the United States banking or financial system. ".

(e) ACQUISITIONS OF NONBANKS. —

(1) NOTICE PROCEDURES. — Section 4 (j)(2)(A) of the Bank Holding Company Act of 1956 (12 U.S.C. 1843 (j)(2)(A)) is amended by striking "or unsound banking practices" and inserting "unsound banking practices, or risk to the stability of the United States banking or financial system".

(2) ACTIVITIES THAT ARE FINANCIAL IN NATURE. — Section 4 (k)(6)(B) of the Bank Holding Company Act of 1956 (12 U.S.C. 1843 (k)(6)(B)) is amended to read as follows:

" (B) APPROVAL NOT REQUIRED FOR CERTAIN FINANCIAL ACTIVITIES. —

" (i) IN GENERAL. — Except as provided in subsection (j) with regard to the acquisition of a savings association and clause (ii), a financial holding company may commence any activity, or acquire any company, pursuant to paragraph (4) or any regulation prescribed or order issued under paragraph (5), without prior approval of the Board.

" (ii) EXCEPTION. — A financial holding company may not acquire a company, without the prior approval of the Board, in a transaction in which the total consolidated assets to be acquired by the financial holding company exceed $10, 000, 000, 000.

" (iii) HART–SCOTT–RODINO FILING REQUIREMENT. — Solely for purposes of section 7A (c)(8) of the Clayton Act (15 U.S.C. 18a (c)(8)), the transactions subject to the requirements of this paragraph shall be treated as if the approval of the Board is not required. ".

(f) BANK MERGER ACT TRANSACTIONS. — Section 18 (c)(5) of the Federal Deposit Insurance Act (12 U.S.C. 1828 (c)(5)) is amended, in the matter immediately following subparagraph (B), by striking "and the convenience and needs of the community to be served" and inserting "the convenience and needs of the community to be served, and the risk to the stability of the United States banking or financial system".

(1)在第5(c)(5)(B)条[《美国法典》第十二编第1844(c)(5)(B)节]中删除第(v)项,并替以如下内容:“(v)对于以期货经纪商、商品交易顾问、商品基金、商品基金管理人、互换执行设施、互换数据存管机构、互换交易商、主要互换参与者身份从事的活动,以及上述商品活动和互换活动的附带活动而言,受商品期货交易委员会监管或在商品期货交易委员会注册的实体。”及

(2)删除第10A条(《美国法典》第十二编第1848a节)。

(d)**对银行的收购**。——在《1956年银行控股公司法》第3(c)条[《美国法典》第十二编第1842(c)节]之后增加如下内容,作为对该条的修正:

“(7)**金融稳定**。——对于任何拟开展的收购、兼并或合并,联邦储备委员会均应考虑其在多大程度上会对美国银行体系或金融体系造成更大或更集中的风险。”

(e)**对非银行机构的收购**。——

(1)**通知程序**。——《1956年银行控股公司法》第4(j)(2)(A)条[《美国法典》第十二编第1843(j)(2)(A)节]修正如下:删除“或欠稳健的银行做法”,替以“欠稳健的银行做法,或对美国银行体系或金融体系稳定构成威胁的风险”。

(2)**金融性质活动**。——《1956年银行控股公司法》第4(k)(6)(B)条[《美国法典》第十二编第1843(k)(6)(B)节]修正后全文如下:

“(B)**特定金融活动不必获取批准**。——

(i)**一般规定**。——除第(j)子条针对储蓄协会的收购和第(ii)项规定的情形外,金融控股公司可根据第(4)款的规定或根据第(5)款颁布的任何规章或命令开始任何活动,或收购任何公司,而不必征得联邦储备委员会的事先批准。

(ii)**例外规定**。——如金融控股公司在交易中拟收购的并表资产总额超过100亿美元,则未经联邦储备委员会事先批准,金融控股公司不得通过该等交易收购任何公司。

(iii)**《哈特—斯科特—罗迪诺反垄断改进法》**的申请批准要求。——仅就《克莱顿法》第7A(c)(8)条[《美国法典》第十五编第18a(c)(8)节]而言,受制于本款要求的交易应视同不必取得联邦储备委员会批准的交易。”

(f)**《银行兼并法》交易**。——《联邦存款保险法》第18(c)(5)条[《美国法典》第十二编第1828(c)(5)节]修正如下:在紧接第(B)子款之后的内容中删除“目标社区的便利和需求”,替以“目标社区的便利和需求以及对美国银行体系或金融体系稳定造成威胁的风险”。

(g) REPORTS BY SAVINGS AND LOAN HOLDING COMPANIES. — Section 10 (b)(2) of the Home Owners' Loan Act (12 U.S.C. 1467a (b)(2) is amended —

(1) by striking "Each savings" and inserting the following: " (A) IN GENERAL. — Each savings"; and

(2) by adding at the end the following:

" (B) USE OF EXISTING REPORTS AND OTHER SUPERVISORY INFORMATION. — The Board shall, to the fullest extent possible, use —

" (i) reports and other supervisory information that the savings and loan holding company or any subsidiary thereof has been required to provide to other Federal or State regulatory agencies;

" (ii) externally audited financial statements of the savings and loan holding company or subsidiary;

" (iii) information that is otherwise available from Federal or State regulatory agencies; and

" (iv) information that is otherwise required to be reported publicly.

" (C) AVAILABILITY. — Upon the request of the Board, a savings and loan holding company or a subsidiary of a savings and loan holding company shall promptly provide to the Board any information described in clauses (i) through (iii) of subparagraph (B) . ".

(h) EXAMINATION OF SAVINGS AND LOAN HOLDING COMPANIES. —

(1) DEFINITIONS. — Section 2 of the Home Owners' Loan Act (12 U.S.C. 1462) is amended by adding at the end the following:

" (10) APPROPRIATE FEDERAL BANKING AGENCY. — The term 'appropriate Federal banking agency' has the same meaning as in section 3 (q) of the Federal Deposit Insurance Act (12 U.S.C. 1813 (q)) .

" (11) FUNCTIONALLY REGULATED SUBSIDIARY. — The term 'functionally regulated subsidiary' has the same meaning as in section 5 (c)(5) of the Bank Holding Company Act of 1956 (12 U.S.C. 1844 (c)(5)) . ".

(2) EXAMINATION. — Section 10 (b) of the Home Owners' Loan Act (12 U.S.C. 1467a (b)) is amended by striking paragraph (4) and inserting the following:

" (4) EXAMINATIONS. —

" (A) IN GENERAL. — Subject to subtitle B of the Consumer Financial Protection Act of 2010, the Board may make examinations of a savings and loan holding company and each subsidiary of a savings and loan holding company system, in order to —

" (i) inform the Board of —

" (I) the nature of the operations and financial condition of the savings and loan holding company and the subsidiary;

" (II) the financial, operational, and other risks within the savings and loan holding

(g)**储贷控股公司报告**。——《业主贷款法》第10(b)(2)条[《美国法典》第十二编第1467a(b)(2)节]修正如下——

(1)删除"每笔存款",替以"(A)**一般规定**。——每笔存款";及

(2)在该条结尾处增加如下内容:

"(B)**既有报告和其他监管信息的利用**。——联邦储备委员会应尽最大可能利用——

(i)储贷控股公司或其任何子公司已按要求向其他联邦监管机关或州监管机关提供的报告和其他监管信息;

(ii)储贷控股公司或其子公司经外部审计的财务报表;

(iii)联邦监管机关或州监管机关可另行提供的其他信息;及

(iv)要求公开报告的其他信息。

(C)**信息提供**。——联邦储备委员会提出要求时,储贷控股公司或其子公司应及时向联邦储备委员会提供第(B)子款第(i)项至第(iii)项所述的任何信息。"

(h)**对储贷控股公司的检查**。——

(1)**定义**。——在《业主贷款法》第2条(《美国法典》第十二编第1462节)结尾处增加如下内容,作为对该条的修正:

"(10)**相应的联邦银行业监管机关**。——'相应的联邦银行业监管机关'一词的含义以《联邦存款保险法》第3(q)条[《美国法典》第十二编第1813(q)节]的定义为准。

(11)**受制于功能监管的子公司**。——'受制于功能监管的子公司'一词的含义以《1956年银行控股公司法》第5(c)(5)条[《美国法典》第十二编第1844(c)(5)节]的定义为准。"

(2)**检查**。——《业主贷款法》第10(b)条[《美国法典》第十二编第1467a(b)节]修正如下:删除第(4)款,替以如下内容:

"(4)**检查**。——

(A)**一般规定**。——在不违反《2010年消费者金融保护法》第B子编的前提下,联邦储备委员会可以对储贷控股公司及其体系内的每一子公司进行检查,以便——

(i)获取如下信息——

(I)储贷控股公司及其子公司的经营性质和财务状况;

(II)储贷控股公司体系之内可能对以下各项构成威胁的财务、运营和其他风

company system that may pose a threat to —

" (aa) the safety and soundness of the savings and loan holding company or of any depository institution subsidiary of the savings and loan holding company; or

" (bb) the stability of the financial system of the United States; and

" (III) the systems of the savings and loan holding company for monitoring and controlling the risks described in subclause (II) ; and

" (ii) monitor the compliance of the savings and loan holding company and the subsidiary with —

" (I) this Act;

" (II) Federal laws that the Board has specific jurisdiction to enforce against the company or subsidiary; and

" (III) other than in the case of an insured depository institution or functionally regulated subsidiary, any other applicable provisions of Federal law.

" (B) USE OF REPORTS TO REDUCE EXAMINATIONS. — For purposes of this subsection, the Board shall, to the fullest extent possible, rely on —

" (i) the examination reports made by other Federal or State regulatory agencies relating to a savings and loan holding company and any subsidiary; and

" (ii) the reports and other information required under paragraph (2) .

" (C) COORDINATION WITH OTHER REGULATORS. — The Board shall —

" (i) provide reasonable notice to, and consult with, the appropriate Federal banking agency, the Securities and Exchange Commission, the Commodity Futures Trading Commission, or State regulatory agency, as appropriate, for a subsidiary that is a depository institution or a functionally regulated subsidiary of a savings and loan holding company before commencing an examination of the subsidiary under this section; and

" (ii) to the fullest extent possible, avoid duplication of examination activities, reporting requirements, and requests for information. ".

(i) DEFINITION OF THE TERM "SAVINGS AND LOAN HOLDING COMPANY". — Section 10 (a)(1)(D)(ii) of the Home Owners' Loan Act (12 U.S.C. 1467a (a)(1)(D)(ii)) is amended to read as follows:

" (ii) EXCLUSION. — The term 'savings and loan holding company' does not include —

" (I) a bank holding company that is registered under, and subject to, the Bank Holding Company Act of 1956 (12 U.S.C. 1841 et seq.) , or to any company directly or indirectly controlled by such company (other than a savings association) ;

" (II) a company that controls a savings association that functions solely in a trust or

险——

(aa) 储贷控股公司或具有存款机构身份的任何储贷控股公司子公司的安全性和稳健性;或

(bb)美国金融体系的稳定;及

(III)储贷控股公司对第(II)子项所述风险的监控和控制系统;及

(ii)监控储贷控股公司及其子公司对以下法律的合规情况——

(I)本法;

(II)联邦储备委员会有明确的管辖权,可对储贷控股公司或其子公司执行的联邦法律;及

(III)联邦法律任何其他适用的规定(对于参保存款机构或受制于功能监管的子公司之外的实体而言)。

(B)**利用报告减少检查工作**。——就本子条而言,联邦储备委员会应尽最大可能采信——

(i)其他联邦监管机关或州监管机关就储贷控股公司及其任何子公司作出的检查报告;及

(ii)第(2)款规定的报告和其他信息。

(C)**与其他监管者的协调**。——联邦储备委员会应——

(i)在根据本条规定对具有存款机构身份的储贷控股公司子公司或受制于功能监管的储贷控股公司子公司开始检查前,向相应的联邦银行业监管机关、证券交易委员会、商品期货交易委员会或州监管机关(视具体情况而定)提供合理的通知并与之进行磋商;及

(ii)尽最大可能避免重复检查,并避免提出重复的报告要求和信息提供要求。"

(i)**"储贷控股公司"的定义**。——《业主贷款法》第10(a)(1)(D)(ii)条[《美国法典》第十二编第1467a(a)(1)(D)(ii)节]修正后全文如下:

"(ii)**除外规定**。——'储贷控股公司'一词不包括——

(I)根据《1956年银行控股公司法》(《美国法典》第十二编第1841节及其后条文)注册并受制于该法规定的银行控股公司,或者[1]受该公司直接或间接控制的任何公司(但存款协会除外);

(II)控制《1956年银行控股公司法》2(c)(2)(D)条[《美国法典》第十二编第1841

1 原文"or to"中的"to"疑为衍词,单用"or"即可,对译文无影响。——译者注

fiduciary capacity as described in section 2 (c)(2)(D) of the Bank Holding Company Act of 1956 (12 U.S.C. 1841 (c)(2)(D)); or

"(III) a company described in subsection (c)(9)(C) solely by virtue of such company's control of an intermediate holding company established pursuant to section 10A.".

(j) EFFECTIVE DATE. — The amendments made by this section shall take effect on the transfer date.

SEC. 605. ASSURING CONSISTENT OVERSIGHT OF PERMISSIBLE ACTIVITIES OF DEPOSITORY INSTITUTION SUBSIDIARIES OF HOLDING COMPANIES.

(a) IN GENERAL. — The Federal Deposit Insurance Act (12 U.S.C. 1811 et seq.) is amended by inserting after section 25 the following new section:

"SEC. 26. ASSURING CONSISTENT OVERSIGHT OF SUBSIDIARIES OF HOLDING COMPANIES.

"(a) DEFINITIONS. — For purposes of this section:

"(1) BOARD. — The term 'Board' means the Board of Governors of the Federal Reserve System.

"(2) FUNCTIONALLY REGULATED SUBSIDIARY. — The term 'functionally regulated subsidiary' has the same meaning as in section 5 (c)(5) of the Bank Holding Company Act.

"(3) LEAD INSURED DEPOSITORY INSTITUTION. — The term 'lead insured depository institution' has the same meaning as in section 2 (o)(8) of the Bank Holding Company Act.

"(b) EXAMINATION REQUIREMENTS. — Subject to subtitle B of the Consumer Financial Protection Act of 2010, the Board shall examine the activities of a nondepository institution subsidiary (other than a functionally regulated subsidiary or a subsidiary of a depository institution) of a depository institution holding company that are permissible for the insured depository institution subsidiaries of the depository institution holding company in the same manner, subject to the same standards, and with the same frequency as would be required if such activities were conducted in the lead insured depository institution of the depository institution holding company.

"(c) STATE COORDINATION. —

"(1) CONSULTATION AND COORDINATION. — If a nondepository institution subsidiary is supervised by a State bank supervisor or other State regulatory authority, the Board, in conducting the examinations required in subsection (b), shall consult and coordinate with such State regulator.

"(2) ALTERNATING EXAMINATIONS PERMITTED. — The examinations required under subsection (b) may be conducted in joint or alternating manner with a State regulator,

(c)(2)(D)节]所述仅履行信托或受信职能的存款协会的公司;或

(III)第(c)(9)(C)子条所述公司,只要其控制有根据第10A条成立的一家中介控股公司。”

(j)**生效日**。——本条作出的各项修正应于转移日生效。

第605条 确保对控股公司的存款机构子公司被允许开展的活动进行一致的监督

(a)**一般规定**。——在《联邦存款保险法》(《美国法典》第十二编第1811节及其后条文)第25条结尾处增加如下新条文,作为对该条的修正:

“第26条 确保针对控股公司的子公司进行一致的监督

(a)**定义**。——就本条而言:

(1)**联邦储备委员会**。——‘联邦储备委员会’一词系指美国联邦储备系统管理委员会。

(2)**受制于功能监管的子公司**。——‘受制于功能监管的子公司’一词的含义以《银行控股公司法》第5(c)(5)条的定义为准。

(3)**主参保存款机构**。——‘主参保存款机构’一词的含义以《银行控股公司法》第2(o)(8)条的定义为准。

(b)**检查要求**。——在不违反《2010年消费者金融保护法》第B子编规定的前提下,如存款机构控股公司的非存款机构子公司(但受制于功能监管的子公司或存款机构的子公司除外)从事了该存款机构控股公司的参保存款机构子公司被允许从事的活动,则联邦储备委员会应对该等活动进行检查,确定检查方式、标准和频率时,应以该等活动由该存款机构控股公司的主参保存款机构所从事时将采取的方式、标准和频率为准。

(c)**与州监管者的协调**。——

(1)**磋商与协调**。——对于受州银行监管者或其他州监管机构监管的非存款机构子公司,联邦储备委员会在按第(b)子条规定对其进行检查时,应与上述州监管者磋商和协调。

(2)**允许替代性检查**。——如联邦储备委员会判定州监管者对某一非存款机构子公司的检查可实现本条之目的,则可与州监管者共同执行或由州监管者独立执行

if the Board determines that an examination of a nondepository institution subsidiary conducted by the State carries out the purposes of this section.

"(d) APPROPRIATE FEDERAL BANKING AGENCY BACKUP EXAMINATION AUTHORITY. —

"(1) IN GENERAL. — In the event that the Board does not conduct examinations required under subsection (b) in the same manner, subject to the same standards, and with the same frequency as would be required if such activities were conducted by the lead insured depository institution subsidiary of the depository institution holding company, the appropriate Federal banking agency for the lead insured depository institution may recommend in writing (which shall include a written explanation of the concerns giving rise to the recommendation) that the Board perform the examination required under subsection (b).

"(2) EXAMINATION BY AN APPROPRIATE FEDERAL BANKING AGENCY. — If the Board does not, before the end of the 60-day period beginning on the date on which the Board receives a recommendation under paragraph (1), begin an examination as required under subsection (b) or provide a written explanation or plan to the appropriate Federal banking agency making such recommendation responding to the concerns raised by the appropriate Federal banking agency for the lead insured depository institution, the appropriate Federal banking agency for the lead insured depository institution may, subject to the Consumer Financial Protection Act of 2010, examine the activities that are permissible for a depository institution subsidiary conducted by such nondepository institution subsidiary (other than a functionally regulated subsidiary or a subsidiary of a depository institution) of the depository institution holding company as if the nondepository institution subsidiary were an insured depository institution for which the appropriate Federal banking agency of the lead insured depository institution was the appropriate Federal banking agency, to determine whether the activities —

"(A) pose a material threat to the safety and soundness of any insured depository institution subsidiary of the depository institution holding company;

"(B) are conducted in accordance with applicable Federal law; and

"(C) are subject to appropriate systems for monitoring and controlling the financial, operating, and other material risks of the activities that may pose a material threat to the safety and soundness of the insured depository institution subsidiaries of the holding company.

"(3) AGENCY COORDINATION WITH THE BOARD. — An appropriate Federal banking agency that conducts an examination pursuant to paragraph (2) shall coordinate examination of the activities of nondepository institution subsidiaries described in subsection (b) with the Board in a manner that —

"(A) avoids duplication;

第(b)子条规定的检查。

(d)**相应的联邦银行业监管机关的后备检查权**。——

(1)**一般规定**。——如果联邦储备委员会进行第(b)子条规定的检查时所采用的方式、标准和频率,与如果上述活动系为存款机构控股公司的主参保存款机构子公司所从事时将采取的方式、标准和频率不一致,则主参保存款机构的相应的联邦银行业监管机关可以书面建议联邦储备委员会(建议中应对提出该建议的原因提供书面说明)执行第(b)子条规定的检查。

(2)**相应的联邦银行业监管机关的检查**。——如果联邦储备委员会未在收到第(1)款所述建议之日起60天内启动第(b)子条规定的检查,也未向提出上述建议的主参保存款机构的相应的联邦银行业监管机关提供一份对该联邦银行业监管机关的关切问题作出答复的书面说明或计划,则该联邦银行业监管机关在不违反《2010年消费者金融保护法》的前提下,可以对该存款机构控股公司的非存款机构子公司(但受制于功能监管的子公司或存款机构的子公司除外)所从事的存款机构子公司允许从事的活动进行检查,如同该非存款机构身为受其相应的联邦银行业监管的参保存款机构,以判定该等活动——

(A)是否对存款机构控股公司的任何参保存款机构子公司的安全性和稳健性构成重大威胁;

(B)是否根据适用的联邦法律开展;及

(C)是否受制于适当的风险监控和控制系统(该等系统旨在对于可能对控股公司的参保存款机构子公司的安全性和稳健性造成重大威胁的财务、运营和其他风险进行监控和控制)。

(3)**监管机关与联邦储备委员会的协调**。——相应的联邦银行业监管机关在根据第(2)款规定开展检查时,应就针对第(b)子条所述非存款机构子公司开展的检查活动与联邦储备委员会开展协调,以便——

(A)避免重复的检查;

"(B) shares information relevant to the supervision of the depository institution holding company;

"(C) achieves the objectives of subsection (b); and

"(D) ensures that the depository institution holding company and the subsidiaries of the depository institution holding company are not subject to conflicting supervisory demands by such agency and the Board.

"(4) FEE PERMITTED FOR EXAMINATION COSTS. — An appropriate Federal banking agency that conducts an examination or enforcement action pursuant to this section may collect an assessment, fee, or such other charge from the subsidiary as the appropriate Federal banking agency determines necessary or appropriate to carry out the responsibilities of the appropriate Federal banking agency in connection with such examination.

"(e) REFERRALS FOR ENFORCEMENT BY APPROPRIATE FEDERAL BANKING AGENCY. —

"(1) RECOMMENDATION OF ENFORCEMENT ACTION. — The appropriate Federal banking agency for the lead insured depository institution, based upon its examination of a nondepository institution subsidiary conducted pursuant to subsection (d), or other relevant information, may submit to the Board, in writing, a recommendation that the Board take enforcement action against such nondepository institution subsidiary, together with an explanation of the concerns giving rise to the recommendation, if the appropriate Federal banking agency determines (by a vote of its members, if applicable) that the activities of the nondepository institution subsidiary pose a material threat to the safety and soundness of any insured depository institution subsidiary of the depository institution holding company.

"(2) BACK-UP AUTHORITY OF THE APPROPRIATE FEDERAL BANKING AGENCY. — If, within the 60-day period beginning on the date on which the Board receives a recommendation under paragraph (1), the Board does not take enforcement action against the nondepository institution subsidiary or provide a plan for supervisory or enforcement action that is acceptable to the appropriate Federal banking agency that made the recommendation pursuant to paragraph (1), such agency may take the recommended enforcement action against the nondepository institution subsidiary, in the same manner as if the nondepository institution subsidiary were an insured depository institution for which the agency was the appropriate Federal banking agency.

"(f) COORDINATION AMONG APPROPRIATE FEDERAL BANKING AGENCIES. — Each Federal banking agency, prior to or when exercising authority under subsection (d) or (e) shall —

"(1) provide reasonable notice to, and consult with, the appropriate Federal banking agency or State bank supervisor (or other State regulatory agency) of the nondepository institution subsidiary of a depository institution holding company that is described in

(B)共享与存款机构控股公司的监管相关的信息;

(C)实现第(b)子条的目标;及

(D)确保该联邦银行业监管机关和联邦储备委员会不会对存款机构控股公司及存款机构控股公司的子公司施加冲突性的监管要求。

(4)**允许基于检查成本收取检查费用**。——相应的联邦银行业监管机关根据本条规定开展检查或执法行动时,可以向相关子公司收取据该相应的联邦银行业监管机关判定对履行该相应的联邦银行业监管机关检查职责确属必要或适当的计征费、收费或其他费用。

(e)**交由相应的联邦银行业监管机关采取执法行动**。——

(1)**执法行动建议**。——如主参保存款机构的相应的联邦银行业监管机关判定(如适用,应通过其成员进行表决)该非存款机构子公司的活动对存款机构控股公司的任何参保存款机构子公司的安全性和稳健性构成重大威胁,该联邦银行业监管机关可以基于其根据第(d)子条对非存款机构子公司进行的检查或其他相关信息书面建议联邦储备委员会针对该非存款机构子公司实施执法行动,建议中应说明其作出上述建议时所考虑的关切问题。

(2)**相应的联邦银行业监管机关的后备权力**。——联邦储备委员会在收到第(1)款所述建议之日起60天内未针对该非存款机构子公司采取执法行动,也未提供一份获得根据第(1)款提出建议的相应的联邦银行业监管机关认可的监管或执法行动计划,则该联邦银行业监管机关可以针对该非存款机构子公司采取其所建议的执法行动,如同该非存款机构身为受其相应的联邦银行业监管的参保存款机构。

(f)**相应的联邦银行业监管机关之间的协调**。——每一相应的联邦银行业监管机关在根据第(d)子条或第(e)子条行使其权力前或行使其权力之时,均应——

(1)在针对第(d)子条所述存款机构控股公司的非存款机构子公司启动任何检查之前,向该子公司的相应的联邦银行业监管机关或州银行监管者(或其他州监管机关)提供合理通知,并与之进行磋商;

subsection (d) before commencing any examination of the subsidiary;

" (2) to the fullest extent possible —

" (A) rely on the examinations, inspections, and reports of the appropriate Federal banking agency or the State bank supervisor (or other State regulatory agency) of the subsidiary;

" (B) avoid duplication of examination activities, reporting requirements, and requests for information; and

" (C) ensure that the depository institution holding company and the subsidiaries of the depository institution holding company are not subject to conflicting supervisory demands by the appropriate Federal banking agencies.

" (g) RULE OF CONSTRUCTION. — No provision of this section shall be construed as limiting any authority of the Board, the Corporation, or the Comptroller of the Currency under any other provision of law. ".

(b) EFFECTIVE DATE. — The amendment made by subsection (a) shall take effect on the transfer date.

SEC. 606. REQUIREMENTS FOR FINANCIAL HOLDING COMPANIES TO REMAIN WELL CAPITALIZED AND WELL MANAGED.

(a) AMENDMENT. — Section 4 (l)(1) of the Bank Holding Company Act of 1956 (12 U.S.C. 1843 (l)(1)) is amended —

(1) in subparagraph (B), by striking "and" at the end;

(2) by redesignating subparagraph (C) as subparagraph (D);

(3) by inserting after subparagraph (B) the following: " (C) the bank holding company is well capitalized and well managed; and"; and

(4) in subparagraph (D)(ii), as so redesignated, by striking "subparagraphs (A) and (B) " and inserting "subparagraphs (A), (B), and (C) ".

(b) HOME OWNERS' LOAN ACT AMENDMENT. — Section 10 (c)(2) of the Home Owners' Loan Act (12 U.S.C. 1467a (c)(2)) is amended by adding at the end the following new subparagraph:

" (H) Any activity that is permissible for a financial holding company (as such term is defined under section 2 (p) of the Bank Holding Company Act of 1956 (12 U.S.C. 1841 (p)) to conduct under section 4 (k) of the Bank Holding Company Act of 1956 if —

" (i) the savings and loan holding company meets all of the criteria to qualify as a financial holding company, and complies with all of the requirements applicable to a financial holding company, under sections 4 (l) and 4 (m) of the Bank Holding Company Act and section 804 (c) of the Community Reinvestment Act of 1977 (12 U.S.C. 2903 (c)) as if the savings and loan holding company was a bank holding company; and

" (ii) the savings and loan holding company conducts the activity in accordance with the

(2)尽最大可能——

(A)采信该子公司的相应的联邦银行业监管机关或州银行监管者(或其他州监管机关)作出的审查、检查和报告;

(B)避免重复的检查活动,并避免提出重复的报告要求和信息提供要求;及

(C)确保相应的联邦银行业监管机关不会对存款机构控股公司及存款机构控股公司的子公司施加冲突性的监管要求。

(g)**解释规则**。——本条中的任何规定均不得被解释为构成对联邦储备委员会、联邦存款保险公司、货币监理署依据任何其他法律规定享有的权力之限制。”

(b)**生效日**。——第(a)子条作出的修正应于转移日生效。

第606条　金融控股公司维持良好资本状况和良好管理的要求

(a)**修正**。——《1956年银行控股公司法》第4(l)(1)条[《美国法典》第十二编第1843(l)(1)节]修正如下——

(1)删除第(B)子款结尾处的“且”;

(2)第(C)子款重新编号为第(D)子款;

(3)在第(B)子款之后插入:“(C)银行控股公司资本状况良好且管理良好;且”;及

(4)在第(D)(ii)子款(以重新编号后的序号为准)中删除“第(A)子款和第(B)子款”,替以“第(A)子款、第(B)子款和第(C)子款”。

(b)**对《业主贷款法》的修正**。——在《业主贷款法》第10(c)(2)条[《美国法典》第十二编第1467a(c)(2)节]结尾处增加如下新子款,作为对该条的修正:

“(H)根据《1956年银行控股公司法》第4(k)条,金融控股公司{定义见《1956年银行控股公司法》第2(p)条[《美国法典》第十二编第1841(p)节]}允许开展的任何活动,但前提是——

(i)储贷控股公司应满足金融控股公司的所有资格标准,并符合《银行控股公司法》第4(l)条、第4(m)条以及《1977年社区再投资法》第804(c)条[《美国法典》第十二编第2903(c)节]规定的适用于金融控股公司的全部要求,如同该储贷控股公司身为银行控股公司;且

(ii)储贷控股公司开展活动时适用的条款、条件及要求,与银行控股公司根据

same terms, conditions, and requirements that apply to the conduct of such activity by a bank holding company under the Bank Holding Company Act of 1956 and the Board's regulations and interpretations under such Act.".

(c) EFFECTIVE DATE. — The amendments made by this section shall take effect on the transfer date.

SEC. 607. STANDARDS FOR INTERSTATE ACQUISITIONS.

(a) ACQUISITION OF BANKS. — Section 3 (d)(1)(A) of the Bank Holding Company Act of 1956 (12 U.S.C. 1842 (d)(1)(A)) is amended by striking "adequately capitalized and adequately managed" and inserting "well capitalized and well managed".

(b) INTERSTATE BANK MERGERS. — Section 44 (b)(4)(B) of the Federal Deposit Insurance Act (12 U.S.C. 1831u (b)(4)(B)) is amended by striking "will continue to be adequately capitalized and adequately managed" and inserting "will be well capitalized and well managed".

(c) EFFECTIVE DATE. — The amendments made by this section shall take effect on the transfer date.

SEC. 608. ENHANCING EXISTING RESTRICTIONS ON BANK TRANS-ACTIONS WITH AFFILIATES.

(a) AFFILIATE TRANSACTIONS. — Section 23A of the Federal Reserve Act (12 U.S.C. 371c) is amended —

(1) in subsection (b) —

(A) in paragraph (1), by striking subparagraph (D) and inserting the following:

"(D) any investment fund with respect to which a member bank or affiliate thereof is an investment adviser; and"; and

(B) in paragraph (7) —

(i) in subparagraph (A), by inserting before the semicolon at the end the following: ", including a purchase of assets subject to an agreement to repurchase";

(ii) in subparagraph (C), by striking ", including assets subject to an agreement to repurchase,";

(iii) in subparagraph (D) —

(I) by inserting "or other debt obligations" after "acceptance of securities"; and

(II) by striking "or" at the end; and

(iv) by adding at the end the following:

"(F) a transaction with an affiliate that involves the borrowing or lending of securities, to the extent that the transaction causes a member bank or a subsidiary to have credit exposure to the affiliate; or

"(G) a derivative transaction, as defined in paragraph (3) of section 5200 (b) of the Revised Statutes of the United States (12 U.S.C. 84 (b)), with an affiliate, to the extent that

《1956年银行控股公司法》及联邦储备委员会依据该法颁布的规章及解释开展该等活动时所适用的条款、条件及要求相同。”

(c)**生效日**。——本条作出的各项修正应于转移日生效。

第607条 州际收购标准

(a)**对银行的收购**。——《1956年银行控股公司法》第3(d)(1)(A)条[《美国法典》第十二编第1842(d)(1)(A)节]修正如下:删除“资本充足且管理完备”,替以“资本状况良好且管理良好”。

(b)**州际银行兼并**。——《联邦存款保险法》第44(b)(4)(B)条[《美国法典》第十二编第1831u(b)(4)(B)节]修正如下:删除“将继续保持资本充足且管理完备状态”,替以“将具有资本状况良好且管理良好状态”。

(c)**生效日**。——本条作出的各项修正应于转移日生效。

第608条 加强对银行关联交易的既有限制

(a)**关联交易**。——《联邦储备法》第23A条(《美国法典》第十二编第371c节)修正如下——

(1)在第(b)子条中——

(A)第(1)款删除第(D)子款,替以如下内容:

“(D)成员银行或其关联方担任投资顾问的任何投资基金;及”;及

(B)第(7)款——

(i)在第(A)子款结尾处的分号前插入:“,包括受制于回购协议的资产收购”;

(ii)第(C)子款删除“,包括受制于回购协议的资产,”;

(iii)第(D)子款——

(I)在“证券承兑”之后插入“或其他债务凭证”;及

(II)删除结尾处的“或”;及

(iv)在结尾处增加如下内容:

“(F)与关联方开展的涉及融券的交易,前提是该等交易导致成员银行或子公司对该关联方的信用风险敞口;或

(G)与关联方开展的衍生品交易{定义见《美国制定法汇编》(修订版)第5200(b)条第(3)款[《美国法典》第十二编第84(b)节]},前提是该等交易导致成员银行或子公

the transaction causes a member bank or a subsidiary to have credit exposure to the affiliate; ";

(2) in subsection (c) —

(A) in paragraph (1) —

(i) in the matter preceding subparagraph (A), by striking "subsidiary" and all that follows through "time of the transaction" and inserting "subsidiary, and any credit exposure of a member bank or a subsidiary to an affiliate resulting from a securities borrowing or lending transaction, or a derivative transaction, shall be secured at all times"; and

(ii) in each of subparagraphs (A) through (D), by striking "or letter of credit" and inserting "letter of credit, or credit exposure";

(B) by striking paragraph (2);

(C) by redesignating paragraphs (3) through (5) as paragraphs (2) through (4), respectively;

(D) in paragraph (2), as so redesignated, by inserting before the period at the end ", or credit exposure to an affiliate resulting from a securities borrowing or lending transaction, or derivative transaction"; and

(E) in paragraph (3), as so redesignated —

(i) by inserting "or other debt obligations" after "securities"; and

(ii) by striking "or guarantee" and all that follows through "behalf of, " and inserting "guarantee, acceptance, or letter of credit issued on behalf of, or credit exposure from a securities borrowing or lending transaction, or derivative transaction to, ";

(3) in subsection (d)(4), in the matter preceding subparagraph (A), by striking "or issuing" and all that follows through "behalf of, " and inserting "issuing a guarantee, acceptance, or letter of credit on behalf of, or having credit exposure resulting from a securities borrowing or lending transaction, or derivative transaction to, "; and

(4) in subsection (f) —

(A) in paragraph (2) —

(i) by striking "or order";

(ii) by striking "if it finds" and all that follows through the end of the paragraph and inserting the following: "if —

" (i) the Board finds the exemption to be in the public interest and consistent with the purposes of this section, and notifies the Federal Deposit Insurance Corporation of such finding; and

" (ii) before the end of the 60-day period beginning on the date on which the Federal Deposit Insurance Corporation receives notice of the finding under clause (i), the Federal Deposit Insurance Corporation does not object, in writing, to the finding, based on a determination that the exemption presents an unacceptable risk to the Deposit Insurance Fund. ";

司对该关联方的信用风险敞口;"

(2)在第(c)子条中——

(A)第(1)款——

(i)第(A)子款之前的内容删除"子公司"直至"交易时间"的全部内容,替以"子公司,以及因融券交易或衍生品交易导致成员银行或子公司对关联方的任何信用风险敞口无论何时均应有担保";及

(ii)在第(A)子款至第(D)子款的每一子款中均删除"或信用证",替以"信用证或信用风险敞口";

(B)删除第(2)款;

(C)第(3)款至第(5)款分别重新编号为第(2)款至第(4)款;

(D)在第(2)款(以重新编号后的序号为准)结尾处的句号前插入",或因融券交易或衍生品交易导致的对关联方的信用风险敞口";及

(E)第(3)款(以重新编号后的序号为准)——

(i)在"证券"之后插入"或其他债务凭证";及

(ii)删除"或担保"直至"代表"的全部内容,替以"代表关联方签发的担保函、承兑汇票或信用证,或者因融券交易或衍生品交易导致的信用风险敞口,";

(3)在第(d)(4)子条第(A)子款之前的内容中,删除"或签发"直至"代表"的全部内容,替以"代其签发担保函、承兑汇票或信用证,或者因融券交易或衍生品交易而存在关联方信用风险敞口,";及

(4)在第(f)子条中——

(A)第(2)款——

(i)删除"或命令";

(ii)删除"如果其认定"直至该款结尾处的全部内容,替以如下内容:"前提是——

(i)联邦储备委员会认定该项豁免符合公共利益并与本条目的相一致,且将该认定结论通知了联邦存款保险公司;且

(ii)联邦存款保险公司在收到第(i)项所述认定结论通知之日起60天内,并未判定该项豁免对存款保险基金造成不可接受的风险,且并未基于此项判定对该认定结论提出书面反对意见。"

(iii) by striking the Board and inserting the following:

" (A) IN GENERAL. — The Board"; and

(iv) by adding at the end the following:

" (B) ADDITIONAL EXEMPTIONS. —

" (i) NATIONAL BANKS. — The Comptroller of the Currency may, by order, exempt a transaction of a national bank from the requirements of this section if —

" (I) the Board and the Office of the Comptroller of the Currency jointly find the exemption to be in the public interest and consistent with the purposes of this section and notify the Federal Deposit Insurance Corporation of such finding; and

" (II) before the end of the 60-day period beginning on the date on which the Federal Deposit Insurance Corporation receives notice of the finding under subclause (I), the Federal Deposit Insurance Corporation does not object, in writing, to the finding, based on a determination that the exemption presents an unacceptable risk to the Deposit Insurance Fund.

" (ii) STATE BANKS. — The Federal Deposit Insurance Corporation may, by order, exempt a transaction of a State nonmember bank, and the Board may, by order, exempt a transaction of a State member bank, from the requirements of this section if —

" (I) the Board and the Federal Deposit Insurance Corporation jointly find that the exemption is in the public interest and consistent with the purposes of this section; and

" (II) the Federal Deposit Insurance Corporation finds that the exemption does not present an unacceptable risk to the Deposit Insurance Fund. "; and

(B) by adding at the end the following:

" (4) AMOUNTS OF COVERED TRANSACTIONS. — The Board may issue such regulations or interpretations as the Board determines are necessary or appropriate with respect to the manner in which a netting agreement may be taken into account in determining the amount of a covered transaction between a member bank or a subsidiary and an affiliate, including the extent to which netting agreements between a member bank or a subsidiary and an affiliate may be taken into account in determining whether a covered transaction is fully secured for purposes of subsection (d)(4). An interpretation under this paragraph with respect to a specific member bank, subsidiary, or affiliate shall be issued jointly with the appropriate Federal banking agency for such member bank, subsidiary, or affiliate. ".

(b) TRANSACTIONS WITH AFFILIATES. — Section 23B (e) of the Federal Reserve Act (12 U.S.C. 371c-1 (e)) is amended —

(1) by striking the undesignated matter following subparagraph (B);

(2) by redesignating subparagraphs (A) and (B) as clauses (i) and (ii), respectively, and adjusting the clause margins accordingly;

(3) by redesignating paragraphs (1) and (2) as subparagraphs (A) and (B),

(iii)删除“联邦储备委员会”,替以“(A)**一般规定**。——联邦储备委员会”;及

(iv)在该款结尾处增加如下内容:

“(B)**补充豁免**。——

(i)**国民银行**。——货币监理署可以签发命令向某一国民银行开展的某项交易授予豁免,获得豁免的交易不必受本条规定约束,其前提是——

(I)联邦储备委员会和货币监理署共同认定该项豁免符合公共利益并与本条目的相一致,且将该认定结论通知了联邦存款保险公司;且

(II)联邦存款保险公司在收到第(I)子项所述通知之日起60天内,并未判定该项豁免将对存款保险基金造成不可接受的风险,且并未基于此项判定对该认定结论提出书面反对意见。

(ii)**州银行**。——联邦存款保险公司可以签发命令向某一州非成员银行授予豁免,并且联邦储备委员会可以签发命令向某一州成员银行开展的某项交易授予豁免,获得豁免的非成员州银行和交易不必受本条规定约束,其前提是——

(I)联邦储备委员会和联邦存款保险公司共同认定该项豁免符合公共利益并与本条目的相一致;且

(II)联邦存款保险公司认定该项豁免不会对存款保险基金造成不可接受的风险。”及

(B)在结尾处增加如下内容:

“(4)**所涉交易的金额**。——联邦储备委员会可以发布其判定确属必要或适当的规章或解释,明确规定在判定成员银行或其子公司与某一关联方之间开展的所涉交易之金额时,按照何种方式将净额结算协议纳入考虑,包括就第(d)(4)子条而言,在判定所涉交易是否获得了全额担保时,可在多大程度上将成员银行或其子公司与某一关联方之间的净额结算协议纳入考虑。联邦储备委员会根据本款针对某一具体成员银行或其子公司或关联方的解释,应与该等成员银行、子公司或关联方的相应的联邦银行业监管机关联合发布。”

(b)**与关联方开展的交易**。——《联邦储备法》第23B(e)条[《美国法典》第十二编第371c—1(e)节]修正如下——

(1)删除第(B)子款之后的无编号内容;

(2)第(A)子款和第(B)子款分别重新编号为第(i)项和第(ii)项,并相应调整其缩进距离;

(3)第(1)款和第(2)款分别重新编号为第(A)子款和第(B)子款,并相应调整其缩

respectively, and adjusting the subparagraph margins accordingly;

(4) by striking "The Board" and inserting the following:

"(1) IN GENERAL. —The Board";

(5) in paragraph (1)(B), as so redesignated—

(A) in the matter preceding clause (i), by inserting before "regulations" the following: "subject to paragraph (2), if the Board finds that an exemption or exclusion is in the public interest and is consistent with the purposes of this section, and notifies the Federal Deposit Insurance Corporation of such finding, "; and

(B) in clause (ii), by striking the comma at the end and inserting a period; and

(6) by adding at the end the following:

"(2) EXCEPTION. — The Board may grant an exemption or exclusion under this subsection only if, during the 60–day period beginning on the date of receipt of notice of the finding from the Board under paragraph (1)(B), the Federal Deposit Insurance Corporation does not object, in writing, to such exemption or exclusion, based on a determination that the exemption presents an unacceptable risk to the Deposit Insurance Fund. ".

(c) HOME OWNERS' LOAN ACT. —Section 11 of the Home Owners' Loan Act (12 U.S.C. 1468) is amended by adding at the end the following:

"(d) EXEMPTIONS. —

"(1) FEDERAL SAVINGS ASSOCIATIONS. — The Comptroller of the Currency may, by order, exempt a transaction of a Federal savings association from the requirements of this section if—

"(A) the Board and the Office of the Comptroller of the Currency jointly find the exemption to be in the public interest and consistent with the purposes of this section and notify the Federal Deposit Insurance Corporation of such finding; and

"(B) before the end of the 60–day period beginning on the date on which the Federal Deposit Insurance Corporation receives notice of the finding under subparagraph (A), the Federal Deposit Insurance Corporation does not object, in writing, to the finding, based on a determination that the exemption presents an unacceptable risk to the Deposit Insurance Fund.

"(2) STATE SAVINGS ASSOCIATION. — The Federal Deposit Insurance Corporation may, by order, exempt a transaction of a State savings association from the requirements of this section if the Board and the Federal Deposit Insurance Corporation jointly find that—

"(A) the exemption is in the public interest and consistent with the purposes of this section; and

"(B) the exemption does not present an unacceptable risk to the Deposit Insurance Fund. ".

进距离;

(4)删除“联邦储备委员会”,替以:

“(1)**一般规定**。——联邦储备委员会”;

(5)在第(1)(B)款中(以重新编号后的序号为准)——

(A)第(i)项之前的内容在“规章”前插入如下内容:“在不违反第(2)款的规定的前提下,如果联邦储备委员会认定某项豁免或排除符合公共利益并与本条目的相一致,并将该认定结论通知了联邦存款保险公司,”;及

(B)第(ii)项删除项末的逗号,替以句号;及

(6)在结尾处增加如下内容:

“(2)**例外规定**。——联邦储备委员会根据本子条授予某项豁免或排除的,必须以下述条件为前提:联邦存款保险公司在收到联邦储备委员会根据第(1)(B)款规定发出的认定结论通知之日起60天内,未判定该项豁免或排除将对存款保险基金造成不可接受的风险,且并未基于此项判定对该认定结论提出书面反对意见。”

(c)**《业主贷款法》**。——在《业主贷款法》第11条(《美国法典》第十二编第1468节)结尾处增加如下内容,作为对该条的修正:

“(d)**豁免**。——

(1)**联邦储蓄协会**。——货币监理署可以签发命令,向某一联邦储蓄协会开展的某项交易授予豁免,获得豁免的交易不必受本条规定约束,前提是——

(A)联邦储备委员会和货币监理署共同认定该项豁免符合公共利益并与本条目的相一致,且将该认定结论通知了联邦存款保险公司;且

(B)联邦存款保险公司在收到第(A)子款所述通知之日起60天内,并未判定该项豁免或排除将对存款保险基金造成不可接受的风险,且并未基于此项判定对该认定结论提出书面反对意见。

(2)**州储蓄协会**。——联邦存款保险公司可以签发命令,向某一州储蓄协会开展的某项交易授予豁免,获得豁免的交易不必受本条规定约束,前提是联邦储备委员会和联邦存款保险公司共同认定——

(A)该项豁免符合公共利益并与本条目的相一致;且

(B)该项豁免不会对存款保险基金造成不可接受的风险。”

(d) EFFECTIVE DATE. — The amendments made by this section shall take effect 1 year after the transfer date.

SEC. 609. ELIMINATING EXCEPTIONS FOR TRANSACTIONS WITH FINANCIAL SUBSIDIARIES.

(a) AMENDMENT. — Section 23A (e) of the Federal Reserve Act (12 U.S.C. 371c (e)) is amended —

(1) by striking paragraph (3); and

(2) by redesignating paragraph (4) as paragraph (3).

(b) PROSPECTIVE APPLICATION OF AMENDMENT. — The amendments made by this section shall apply with respect to any covered transaction between a bank and a subsidiary of the bank, as those terms are defined in section 23A of the Federal Reserve Act (12 U.S.C. 371c), that is entered into on or after the date of enactment of this Act.

(c) EFFECTIVE DATE. — The amendments made by this section shall take effect 1 year after the transfer date.

SEC. 610. LENDING LIMITS APPLICABLE TO CREDIT EXPOSURE ON DERIVATIVE TRANSACTIONS, REPURCHASE AGREEMENTS, REVERSE REPURCHASE AGREEMENTS, AND SECURITIES LENDING AND BORROWING TRANSACTIONS.

(a) NATIONAL BANKS. — Section 5200 (b) of the Revised Statutes of the United States (12 U.S.C. 84 (b)) is amended —

(1) in paragraph (1), by striking "shall include" and all that follows through the end of the paragraph and inserting the following: "shall include —

" (A) all direct or indirect advances of funds to a person made on the basis of any obligation of that person to repay the funds or repayable from specific property pledged by or on behalf of the person;

" (B) to the extent specified by the Comptroller of the Currency, any liability of a national banking association to advance funds to or on behalf of a person pursuant to a contractual commitment; and

" (C) any credit exposure to a person arising from a derivative transaction, repurchase agreement, reverse repurchase agreement, securities lending transaction, or securities borrowing transaction between the national banking association and the person; ";

(2) in paragraph (2), by striking the period at the end and inserting "; and"; and

(3) by adding at the end the following:

" (3) the term 'derivative transaction' includes any transaction that is a contract, agreement, swap, warrant, note, or option that is based, in whole or in part, on the value of, any interest in, or any quantitative measure or the occurrence of any event relating to, one or more commodities, securities, currencies, interest or other rates, indices, or other assets. ".

(d)**生效日**。——本条作出的各项修正应于转移日届满1年之日生效。

第609条 取消与金融子公司开展的交易适用的例外规定

(a)**修正**。——《联邦储备法》第23A(e)条[《美国法典》第十二编第371c(e)节]修正如下——

(1)删除第(3)款;及

(2)第(4)款重新编号为第(3)款。

(b)**修正的未来适用**。——银行与银行子公司之间在本法颁布之日或之后达成的任何所涉交易[银行、银行子公司和所涉交易的定义见《联邦储备法》第23A条(《美国法典》第十二编第371c节)]应适用本条作出的各项修正。

(c)**生效日**。——本条作出的各项修正应于转移日届满1年之日生效。

第610条 适用于衍生品交易、回购协议、逆回购协议和融券交易的信用风险敞口的借贷限制

(a)**国民银行**。——《美国制定法汇编》(修订版)第5200(b)条[《美国法典》第十二编第84(b)节]修正如下——

(1)在第(1)款中,删除“应包括”直至本款结尾的全部内容,替以如下内容:“应包括——

“(A)向某人直接或间接提供的所有预支款,且根据贷款条件,该人负有返还资金的任何义务,或者负有通过该人或该人代表质押的特定财产返还资金的义务;

(B)在货币监理署规定的范围内,某一国民银行协会根据合同承诺向某人或代表某人提供预支款的任何责任;及

(C)因国民银行协会与某人之间签订的衍生品交易、回购协议、逆回购协议或融券交易对该人产生的任何信用风险敞口;”

(2)在第(2)款中,删除结尾处的句号,替以“;且”;及

(3)在该款结尾处增加如下内容:

“(3)‘衍生品交易’一词包括属于合约、协议、互换、权证、票据或期权,且完全或部分基于如下各项的任何交易:一项或一项以上商品、证券、货币、任何利息或其他比率、指数或其他资产的价值,上述各者的权益或任何量化指标,或者与该等商品、证券、货币、利息或其他比率、指数或其他资产相关的任何事件的发生。”

(b) SAVINGS ASSOCIATIONS. — Section 5 (u)(3) of the Home Owners' Loan Act (12 U.S.C. 1464 (u)(3)) is amended by striking "Director" each place that term appears and inserting "Comptroller of the Currency".

(c) EFFECTIVE DATE. — The amendments made by this section shall take effect 1 year after the transfer date.

SEC. 611. CONSISTENT TREATMENT OF DERIVATIVE TRANSACTIONS IN LENDING LIMITS.

(a) AMENDMENT. — Section 18 of the Federal Deposit Insurance Act (12 U.S.C. 1828) is amended by adding at the end the following:

" (y) STATE LENDING LIMIT TREATMENT OF DERIVATIVES TRANSACTIONS. — An insured State bank may engage in a derivative transaction, as defined in section 5200 (b)(3) of the Revised Statutes of the United States (12 U.S.C. 84 (b)(3)), only if the law with respect to lending limits of the State in which the insured State bank is chartered takes into consideration credit exposure to derivative transactions. ".

(b) EFFECTIVE DATE. — The amendment made by this section shall take effect 18 months after the transfer date.

SEC. 612. RESTRICTION ON CONVERSIONS OF TROUBLED BANKS.

(a) CONVERSION OF A NATIONAL BANKING ASSOCIATION. — The Act entitled "An Act to provide for the conversion of national banking associations into and their merger or consolidation with State banks, and for other purposes. " (12 U.S.C. 214 et seq.) is amended by adding at the end the following:

"SEC. 10. PROHIBITION ON CONVERSION.

"A national banking association may not convert to a State bank or State savings association during any period in which the national banking association is subject to a cease and desist order (or other formal enforcement order) issued by, or a memorandum of understanding entered into with, the Comptroller of the Currency with respect to a significant supervisory matter. ".

(b) CONVERSION OF A STATE BANK OR SAVINGS ASSOCIATION. — Section 5154 of the Revised Statutes of the United States (12 U.S.C. 35) is amended by adding at the end the following: "The Comptroller of the Currency may not approve the conversion of a State bank or State savings association to a national banking association or Federal savings association during any period in which the State bank or State savings association is subject to a cease and desist order (or other formal enforcement order) issued by, or a memorandum of understanding entered into with, a State bank supervisor or the appropriate Federal banking agency with respect to a significant supervisory matter or a final enforcement action by a State Attorney General. ".

(c) CONVERSION OF A FEDERAL SAVINGS ASSOCIATION. — Section 5 (i) of

(b)**储蓄协会**。——《业主贷款法》第5(u)(3)条[《美国法典》第十二编第1464(u)(3)节]修正如下:删除在该条中出现的所有“储蓄机构监理局局长”,全部替以“货币监理署署长”。

(c)**生效日**。——本条作出的各项修正应于转移日届满一年之日生效。

第611条　对衍生品交易借贷限制的一致性处理

(a)**修正**。——在《联邦存款保险法》第18条(《美国法典》第十二编第1828节)结尾处增加如下内容,作为对该条的修正:

“(y)**针对衍生品交易的州借贷限制处理**。——仅在满足下述条件的情况下,参保州银行方得从事衍生品交易{定义见《美国制定法汇编》(修订版)第5200(b)(3)条[《联邦法典》第十二编第84(b)(3)节]}:该参保州银行特许注册地所在州关于借贷限制的法律已将衍生品交易的信用风险敞口纳入考虑。”

(b)**生效日**。——本条作出的修正应于转移日届满18个月之日生效。

第612条　问题银行的形式变更限制

(a)**国民银行协会的形式变更**。——在《关于国民银行协会变更为州银行及与州银行兼并或合并等事项的法律》(《美国法典》第十二编第214节及其后条文)结尾处增加如下内容,作为对该法的修正:

“第10条　形式变更之禁止性规定

货币监理署署长就重大监管事宜向国民银行协会签发制止令（或其他正式的执法令)或国民银行协会与货币监理署署长就重大监管事宜达成谅解备忘录的,国民银行协会在受制于该等命令或备忘录的任何期间内不得变更为州银行或州储蓄协会。”

(b)**州银行或储蓄协会的形式变更**。——在《美国制定法汇编》(修订版)第5154条(《美国法典》第十二编第35节)结尾处增加如下内容,作为对该条的修正:“州银行监管者或相应的联邦银行业监管机关就重大监管事宜向某一州银行或州储蓄协会签发制止令(或其他正式的执法令),该州银行或州储蓄协会与该州银行业监管机关或相应的联邦银行业监管机关达成谅解备忘录，或者州总检察长针对该州银行或州储蓄协会采取最终执法行动的,则在该州银行或州储蓄协会受制于上述命令、备忘录或执法行动的任何期间内，货币监理署署长不得批准该州银行或州储蓄协会变更为国民银行协会或联邦储蓄协会。”

(c)**联邦储蓄协会的形式变更**。——在《业主贷款法》第5(i)条[《美国法典》第十

the Home Owners' Loan Act (12 U.S.C. 1464 (i)) is amended by adding at the end the following:

"(6) LIMITATION ON CERTAIN CONVERSIONS BY FEDERAL SAVINGS ASSOCIATIONS. — A Federal savings association may not convert to a State bank or State savings association during any period in which the Federal savings association is subject to a cease and desist order (or other formal enforcement order) issued by, or a memorandum of understanding entered into with, the Office of Thrift Supervision or the Comptroller of the Currency with respect to a significant supervisory matter.".

(d) EXCEPTION. — The prohibition on the approval of conversions under the amendments made by subsections (a), (b), and (c) shall not apply, if —

(1) the Federal banking agency that would be the appropriate Federal banking agency after the proposed conversion gives the appropriate Federal banking agency or State bank supervisor that issued the cease and desist order (or other formal enforcement order) or memorandum of understanding, as appropriate, written notice of the proposed conversion including a plan to address the significant supervisory matter in a manner that is consistent with the safe and sound operation of the institution;

(2) within 30 days of receipt of the written notice required under paragraph (1), the appropriate Federal banking agency or State bank supervisor that issued the cease and desist order (or other formal enforcement order) or memorandum of understanding, as appropriate, does not object to the conversion or the plan to address the significant supervisory matter;

(3) after conversion of the insured depository institution, the appropriate Federal banking agency after the conversion implements such plan; and

(4) in the case of a final enforcement action by a State Attorney General, approval of the conversion is conditioned on compliance by the insured depository institution with the terms of such final enforcement action.

(e) NOTIFICATION OF PENDING ENFORCEMENT ACTIONS. —

(1) COPY OF CONVERSION APPLICATION. — At the time an insured depository institution files a conversion application, the insured depository institution shall transmit a copy of the conversion application to —

(A) the appropriate Federal banking agency for the insured depository institution; and

(B) the Federal banking agency that would be the appropriate Federal banking agency of the insured depository institution after the proposed conversion.

(2) NOTIFICATION AND ACCESS TO INFORMATION. — Upon receipt of a copy of the application described in paragraph (1), the appropriate Federal banking agency for the insured depository institution proposing the conversion shall —

(A) notify the Federal banking agency that would be the appropriate Federal banking agency for the institution after the proposed conversion in writing of any ongoing supervisory

二编第1464(i)节]结尾处增加如下内容,作为对该条的修正:

“(6)**联邦储蓄协会的特定形式变更限制**。——储蓄机构监理局或货币监理署署长就重大监管事宜向联邦储蓄协会签发制止令(或其他正式的执法令),或联邦储蓄协会与储蓄机构监理局或货币监理署署长达成谅解备忘录的,联邦储蓄协会在受制于该等命令或备忘录的任何期间内不得变更为州银行或州储蓄协会。”

(d)**例外规定**。——在以下情形,第(a)子条、第(b)子条和第(c)子条作出的修正中禁止批准形式变更之规定不得适用——

(1)在提议的形式变更完成后将成为相应的联邦银行业监管机关的联邦银行业监管机关,向签发制止令(或其他正式的执法令)或谅解备忘录(视具体情况而定)的相应的联邦银行业监管机关或州银行监管者发出了一份关于该拟进行的形式变更的通知,其中包含有一份处理重大监管事宜的方案,处理方式与实现该机构安全、稳健运营之目标相符;

(2)签发制止令(或其他正式的执法令)或谅解备忘录(视具体情况而定)的相应的联邦银行业监管机关或州银行监管者在收到第(1)款规定的书面通知后30天内,未对该项形式变更或处理重大监管事宜的方案提出反对意见;

(3)参保存款机构完成形式变更后,相应的联邦银行业监管机关实施了上述方案;且

(4)州总检察长实施最终执法行动的,形式变更的批准以参保存款机构遵守州总检察长在该最终执法行动中设定的条款为前提。

(e)**关于尚未实施的执法行动的通知**。——

(1)**形式变更申请书复本**。——参保存款机构提交形式变更申请时,应向下述机关发送该形式变更申请书的复本——

(A)与该参保存款机构的相应的联邦银行业监管机关;及

(B)在提议的形式变更完成后,将成为与参保存款机构相应的联邦银行业监管机关的联邦银行业监管机关。

(2)**通知及信息查阅**。——提出形式变更请求的参保存款机构的相应的联邦银行业监管机关在收到第(1)款所述申请书复本后,应——

(A)向在提议的形式变更完成后将成为参保存款机构的相应的联邦银行业监管机关的联邦银行业监管机关发送一份书面通知,说明正在针对该参保存款机构进行

or investigative proceedings that the appropriate Federal banking agency for the institution proposing to convert believes is likely to result, in the near term and absent the proposed conversion, in a cease and desist order (or other formal enforcement order) or memorandum of understanding with respect to a significant supervisory matter; and

(B) provide the Federal banking agency that would be the appropriate Federal banking agency for the institution after the proposed conversion access to all investigative and supervisory information relating to the proceedings described in subparagraph (A).

SEC. 613. DE NOVO BRANCHING INTO STATES.

(a) NATIONAL BANKS. — Section 5155 (g)(1)(A) of the Revised Statutes of the United States (12 U.S.C. 36 (g)(1)(A)) is amended to read as follows:

"(A) the law of the State in which the branch is located, or is to be located, would permit establishment of the branch, if the national bank were a State bank chartered by such State; and".

(b) STATE INSURED BANKS. — Section 18 (d)(4)(A)(i) of the Federal Deposit Insurance Act (12 U.S.C. 1828 (d)(4)(A)(i)) is amended to read as follows:

"(i) the law of the State in which the branch is located, or is to be located, would permit establishment of the branch, if the bank were a State bank chartered by such State; and".

SEC. 614. LENDING LIMITS TO INSIDERS.

(a) EXTENSIONS OF CREDIT. — Section 22 (h)(9)(D)(i) of the Federal Reserve Act (12 U.S.C. 375b (9)(D)(i)) is amended —

(1) by striking the period at the end and inserting "; or";

(2) by striking "a person" and inserting "the person";

(3) by striking "extends credit by making" and inserting the following: "extends credit to a person by —

"(I) making"; and

(4) by adding at the end the following:

"(II) having credit exposure to the person arising from a derivative transaction (as defined in section 5200 (b) of the Revised Statutes of the United States (12 U.S.C. 84 (b))), repurchase agreement, reverse repurchase agreement, securities lending transaction, or securities borrowing transaction between the member bank and the person.".

(b) EFFECTIVE DATE. — The amendments made by this section shall take effect 1 year after the transfer date.

SEC. 615. LIMITATIONS ON PURCHASES OF ASSETS FROM INSIDE-RS.

(a) AMENDMENT TO THE FEDERAL DEPOSIT INSURANCE ACT. — Section 18 of the Federal Deposit Insurance Act (12 U.S.C. 1828) is amended by adding at the end the following:

的任何监管或调查程序,前提是其认为如不进行该形式变更,该等程序有可能会导致该参保存款机构被签发关于重大监管事宜的制止令(或其他正式的执法令)或谅解备忘录;及

(B)向在提议的形式变更完成后将成为参保存款机构的相应的联邦银行业监管机关的联邦银行业监管机关提供查阅与第(A)子款所述程序相关的全部调查信息和监管信息的权力。

第613条 重新设立州分行

(a)**国民银行**。——《美国制定法汇编》(修订版)第5155(g)(1)(A)条[《美国法典》第十二编第36(g)(1)(A)节]修正后全文如下:

"(A)该国民银行若为在其分行设立地或拟设立地所在州特许注册的州银行,则该州法律将会允许其设立分行;且。"

(b)**州参保银行**。——《联邦存款保险法》第18(d)(4)(A)(i)条[《美国法典》第十二编第1828(d)(4)(A)(i)节]修正后全文如下:

"(i)该银行若为在其分行设立地或拟设立地所在州特许注册的州银行,则该州法律将会允许其设立分行;且"。

第614条 对内幕人士的借贷限制

(a)**授信**。——《联邦储备法》第22(h)(9)(D)(i)条[《美国法典》第十二编第375b(9)(D)(i)节]修正如下——

(1)删除结尾处的句号,替以";或";

(2)删除"某人",替以"该人";

(3)删除"通过如下方式授信",替以"以如下方式向某人授信——

(I)通过";及

(4)在该条结尾处增加如下内容:

"(II)因该成员银行与该人之间的衍生品交易{定义见《美国制定法汇编》(修订版)第5200(b)条[《美国法典》第十二编第84(b)节]}、回购协议、逆回购协议、融券交易产生的对该人的信用风险敞口。"

(b)**生效日**。——本条作出的各项修正应于转移日届满1年之日生效。

第615条 向内幕人士购买资产的限制

(a)**对《联邦存款保险法》的修正**。——在《联邦存款保险法》第18条(《美国法典》第十二编第1828节)结尾处增加如下内容,作为对该条的修正:

"(z) GENERAL PROHIBITION ON SALE OF ASSETS. —

"(1) IN GENERAL. — An insured depository institution may not purchase an asset from, or sell an asset to, an executive officer, director, or principal shareholder of the insured depository institution, or any related interest of such person (as such terms are defined in section 22 (h) of Federal Reserve Act), unless —

"(A) the transaction is on market terms; and

"(B) if the transaction represents more than 10 percent of the capital stock and surplus of the insured depository institution, the transaction has been approved in advance by a majority of the members of the board of directors of the insured depository institution who do not have an interest in the transaction.

"(2) RULEMAKING. — The Board of Governors of the Federal Reserve System may issue such rules as may be necessary to define terms and to carry out the purposes this subsection. Before proposing or adopting a rule under this paragraph, the Board of Governors of the Federal Reserve System shall consult with the Comptroller of the Currency and the Corporation as to the terms of the rule.".

(b) AMENDMENTS TO THE FEDERAL RESERVE ACT. — Section 22 (d) of the Federal Reserve Act (12 U.S.C. 375) is amended to read as follows:

"(d) [Reserved]".

(c) EFFECTIVE DATE. — The amendments made by this section shall take effect on the transfer date.

SEC. 616. REGULATIONS REGARDING CAPITAL LEVELS.

(a) CAPITAL LEVELS OF BANK HOLDING COMPANIES. — Section 5 (b) of the Bank Holding Company Act of 1956 (12 U.S.C. 1844 (b)) is amended —

(1) by inserting after "orders" the following: ", including regulations and orders relating to the capital requirements for bank holding companies,"; and

(2) by adding at the end the following: "In establishing capital regulations pursuant to this subsection, the Board shall seek to make such requirements countercyclical, so that the amount of capital required to be maintained by a company increases in times of economic expansion and decreases in times of economic contraction, consistent with the safety and soundness of the company.".

(b) CAPITAL LEVELS OF SAVINGS AND LOAN HOLDING COMPANIES. — Section 10 (g)(1) of the Home Owners' Loan Act (12U.S.C. 1467a(g)(1)) is amended—

(1) by inserting after "orders" the following: ", including regulations and orders relating to capital requirements for savings and loan holding companies,"; and

(2) by inserting at the end the following: "In establishing capital regulations pursuant to this subsection, the appropriate Federal banking agency shall seek to make such requirements countercyclical so that the amount of capital required to be maintained by a company

"(z)**资产出售的一般禁止性规定**。——

(1)**一般规定**。——参保存款机构不得向该参保存款机构的高级管理人员、董事或主要股东购买或出售资产或该人的任何相关权益[上述词语的定义见《联邦储备法》第22(h)条],除非——

(A)该交易系按照市场条款进行;且

(B)如该交易占该参保存款机构股本和资本公积金10%以上,该交易已获得参保存款机构过半数对该交易不具有任何利益关联的董事会成员事先批准。

(2)**规则制定**。——联邦储备委员会可以为界定术语和实施本子条之目的发布必要规则。联邦储备委员会在根据本款提出某项规则草案或通过某项规则之前,应就该规则的条款与货币监理署和联邦存款保险公司磋商。"

(b)**对《联邦储备法》的修正**。——《联邦储备法》第22(d)条(《美国法典》第十二编第375节)修正后全文如下:

"(d)[本条内容删除,但序号予以保留]"。

(c)**生效日**。——本条作出的各项修正应于转移日生效。

第616条　与资本水平相关的规章

(a)**银行控股公司的资本水平**。——《1956年银行控股公司法》第5(b)条[《美国法典》第十二编第1844(b)节]修正如下——

(1)在"命令"之后插入",包括与针对银行控股公司资本要求相关的规章及命令,";及

(2)在该条结尾处增加如下内容:"联邦储备委员会在根据本子条制定资本规章时,应按照实现公司安全性和稳健性的目标,使资本要求具有逆周期特性,即在经济扩张时期,提高公司必须维持的资本金额,而在经济萎缩时期,降低公司必须维持的资本金额。"

(b)**储贷控股公司的资本水平**。——《业主贷款法》第10(g)(1)条[《美国法典》第十二编第1467a(g)(1)节]修正如下——

(1)在"命令"之后插入",包括与储贷控股公司资本要求相关的规章及命令,";及

(2)在该条结尾处增加如下内容:"相应的联邦银行业监管机关在根据本子条制定资本规章时,应按照实现公司安全性和稳健性的目标,使资本要求具有逆周期特性,即在经济扩张时期,提高公司必须维持的资本金额;而在经济萎缩时期,降低公司

increases in times of economic expansion and decreases in times of economic contraction, consistent with the safety and soundness of the company. ".

(c) CAPITAL LEVELS OF INSURED DEPOSITORY INSTITUTIONS. — Section 908 (a)(1) of the International Lending Supervision Act of 1983 (12 U.S.C. 3907 (a)(1)) is amended by adding at the end the following: "Each appropriate Federal banking agency shall seek to make the capital standards required under this section or other provisions of Federal law for insured depository institutions countercyclical so that the amount of capital required to be maintained by an insured depository institution increases in times of economic expansion and decreases in times of economic contraction, consistent with the safety and soundness of the insured depository institution. "

(d) SOURCE OF STRENGTH. — The Federal Deposit Insurance Act (12 U.S.C. 1811 et seq.) is amended by inserting after section 38 (12 U.S.C. 1831o) the following:

"SEC. 38A. SOURCE OF STRENGTH.

" (a) HOLDING COMPANIES. — The appropriate Federal banking agency for a bank holding company or savings and loan holding company shall require the bank holding company or savings and loan holding company to serve as a source of financial strength for any subsidiary of the bank holding company or savings and loan holding company that is a depository institution.

" (b) OTHER COMPANIES. — If an insured depository institution is not the subsidiary of a bank holding company or savings and loan holding company, the appropriate Federal banking agency for the insured depository institution shall require any company that directly or indirectly controls the insured depository institution to serve as a source of financial strength for such institution.

" (c) REPORTS. — The appropriate Federal banking agency for an insured depository institution described in subsection (b) may, from time to time, require the company, or a company that directly or indirectly controls the insured depository institution, to submit a report, under oath, for the purposes of —

" (1) assessing the ability of such company to comply with the requirement under subsection (b) ; and

" (2) enforcing the compliance of such company with the requirement under subsection (b) .

" (d) RULES. — Not later than 1 year after the transfer date, as defined in section 311 of the Enhancing Financial Institution Safety and Soundness Act of 2010, the appropriate Federal banking agencies shall jointly issue final rules to carry out this section.

" (e) DEFINITION. — In this section, the term 'source of financial strength' means the ability of a company that directly or indirectly owns or controls an insured depository

必须维持的资本金额。”

(c)**参保存款机构的资本水平**。——在《1983年国际贷款监管法》第908(a)(1)条[《美国法典》第十二编第3907(a)(1)节]结尾处增加如下内容,作为对该条的修正:“每一相应的联邦银行业监管机关在根据本条或其他联邦法律的规定制定参保存款机构的资本标准时,均应按照实现参保存款机构安全性和稳健性的目标,使资本要求具有逆周期特性,即在经济扩张时期,提高参保存款机构必须维持的资本金额;而在经济萎缩时期,降低参保存款机构必须维持的资本金额。”

(d)**财务后盾**。——在《联邦存款保险法》第38条(《美国法典》第十二编第1831o节)之后插入如下内容,作为对《联邦存款保险法》(《美国法典》第十二编第1811节及其后条文)的修正:

“第38A条　财务后盾

(a)**控股公司**。——银行控股公司或储贷控股公司的相应的联邦银行业监管机关应要求该等银行控股公司或储贷控股公司成为其具有存款机构身份的任何子公司的财务后盾。

(b)**其他公司**。——对于不具有银行控股公司或储贷控股公司子公司身份的参保存款机构,该参保存款机构的相应的联邦银行业监管机关应要求直接或间接控制该参保存款机构的任何公司成为该等机构的财务后盾。

(c)**报告**。——对于第(b)子条所述参保存款机构,其相应的联邦银行业监管机关可以不时要求该公司或者直接或间接控制参保存款机构的公司提交一份经宣誓程序保证所述内容真实无误的报告,以便——

(1)对该公司遵守第(b)子条之要求的能力进行评估;及

(2)对该公司强制执行第(b)子条的要求。

(d)**规则**。——各相应的联邦银行业监管机关应于转移日(定义见《2010年金融机构安全性与稳健性改良法》第311条)后1年内联合发布本条的最终实施规则。

(e)**定义**。——就本条而言,‘财务后盾’一词系指直接或间接拥有或控制某一参保存款机构的公司在该参保存款机构处于财务困境时向其提供财务援助的能力。”

institution to provide financial assistance to such insured depository institution in the event of the financial distress of the insured depository institution. ".

(e) EFFECTIVE DATE. — The amendments made by this section shall take effect on the transfer date.

SEC. 617. ELIMINATION OF ELECTIVE INVESTMENT BANK HOLDING COMPANY FRAMEWORK.

(a) AMENDMENT. — Section 17 of the Securities Exchange Act of 1934 (15 U.S.C. 78q) is amended —

(1) by striking subsection (i); and

(2) by redesignating subsections (j) and (k) as subsections (i) and (j), respectively.

(b) EFFECTIVE DATE. — The amendments made by this section shall take effect on the transfer date.

SEC. 618. SECURITIES HOLDING COMPANIES.

(a) DEFINITIONS. — In this section —

(1) the term "associated person of a securities holding company" means a person directly or indirectly controlling, controlled by, or under common control with, a securities holding company;

(2) the term "foreign bank" has the same meaning as in section 1 (b)(7) of the International Banking Act of 1978 (12 U.S.C. 3101 (7));

(3) the term "insured bank" has the same meaning as in section 3 of the Federal Deposit Insurance Act (12 U.S.C. 1813);

(4) the term "securities holding company" —

(A) means —

(i) a person (other than a natural person) that owns or controls 1 or more brokers or dealers registered with the Commission; and

(ii) the associated persons of a person described in clause (i); and

(B) does not include a person that is —

(i) a nonbank financial company supervised by the Board under title I;

(ii) an insured bank (other than an institution described in subparagraphs (D), (F), or (H) of section 2 (c)(2) of the Bank Holding Company Act of 1956 (12 U.S.C. 1841 (c)(2)) or a savings association;

(iii) an affiliate of an insured bank (other than an institution described in subparagraphs (D), (F), or (H) of section 2 (c)(2) of the Bank Holding Company Act of 1956 (12 U.S.C. 1841 (c)(2)) or an affiliate of a savings association;

(iv) a foreign bank, foreign company, or company that is described in section 8 (a) of the International Banking Act of 1978 (12 U.S.C. 3106 (a));

(v) a foreign bank that controls, directly or indirectly, a corporation chartered under

(e)**生效日**。——本条作出的各项修正应于转移日生效。

第617条　取消投资银行控股公司的选择性制度

(a)**修正**。——《1934年证券交易法》第17条(《美国法典》第十五编第78q节)修正如下——

(1)删除第(i)子条;及

(2)第(j)子条和第(k)子条分别重新编号为第(i)子条和第(j)子条。

(b)**生效日**。——本条作出的各项修正应于转移日生效。

第618条　证券控股公司

(a)**定义**。——就本条而言——

(1)"证券控股公司关联人"一词系指,直接或间接控制该证券控股公司、被该证券控股公司控制或与之受同一控制的任何人;

(2)"外国银行"一词的含义以《1978年国际银行法》第1(b)(7)条[《美国法典》第十二编第3101(7)节]的定义为准;

(3)"参保银行"一词的含义以《联邦存款保险法》第3条(《美国法典》第十二编第1813节)的定义为准;

(4)"证券控股公司"一词——

(A)系指——

(i)拥有或控制一家或一家以上已在证券交易委员会注册的经纪商或自营商的人(但自然人除外);及

(ii)第(i)项所述之人的关联人;且

(B)不包括——

(i)根据第一编接受联邦储备委员会监管的非银行金融公司;

(ii)参保银行{但《1956年银行控股公司法》第2(c)(2)条[《美国法典》第十二编第1841(c)(2)节]第(D)子款、第(F)子款或第(H)子款所述机构除外}或储蓄协会;

(iii)参保银行的关联方{但《1956年银行控股公司法》第2(c)(2)条[《美国法典》第十二编第1841(c)(2)节]第(D)子款、第(F)子款或第(H)子款所述机构除外}或储蓄协会的关联方;

(iv)《1978年国际银行法》第8(a)条[《美国法典》第十二编第3106(a)节]所述外国银行、外国公司或公司;

(v)直接或间接控制根据《联邦储备法》第25A条(《美国法典》第十二编第611节及

section 25A of the Federal Reserve Act (12 U.S.C. 611 et seq.); or

(vi) subject to comprehensive consolidated supervision by a foreign regulator;

(5) the term "supervised securities holding company" means a securities holding company that is supervised by the Board of Governors under this section; and

(6) the terms "affiliate", "bank", "bank holding company", "company", "control", "savings association", and "subsidiary" have the same meanings as in section 2 of the Bank Holding Company Act of 1956.

(b) SUPERVISION OF A SECURITIES HOLDING COMPANY NOT HAVING A BANK OR SAVINGS ASSOCIATION AFFILIATE. —

(1) IN GENERAL. — A securities holding company that is required by a foreign regulator or provision of foreign law to be subject to comprehensive consolidated supervision may register with the Board of Governors under paragraph (2) to become a supervised securities holding company. Any securities holding company filing such a registration shall be supervised in accordance with this section, and shall comply with the rules and orders prescribed by the Board of Governors applicable to supervised securities holding companies.

(2) REGISTRATION AS A SUPERVISED SECURITIES HOLDING COMPANY. —

(A) REGISTRATION. — A securities holding company that elects to be subject to comprehensive consolidated supervision shall register by filing with the Board of Governors such information and documents as the Board of Governors, by regulation, may prescribe as necessary or appropriate in furtherance of the purposes of this section.

(B) EFFECTIVE DATE. — A securities holding company that registers under subparagraph (A) shall be deemed to be a supervised securities holding company, effective on the date that is 45 days after the date of receipt of the registration information and documents under subparagraph (A) by the Board of Governors, or within such shorter period as the Board of Governors, by rule or order, may determine.

(c) SUPERVISION OF SECURITIES HOLDING COMPANIES. —

(1) RECORDKEEPING AND REPORTING. —

(A) RECORDKEEPING AND REPORTING REQUIRED. — Each supervised securities holding company and each affiliate of a supervised securities holding company shall make and keep for periods determined by the Board of Governors such records, furnish copies of such records, and make such reports, as the Board of Governors determines to be necessary or appropriate to carry out this section, to prevent evasions thereof, and to monitor compliance by the supervised securities holding company or affiliate with applicable provisions of law.

(B) FORM AND CONTENTS. —

(i) IN GENERAL. — Any record or report required to be made, furnished, or kept under this paragraph shall —

(I) be prepared in such form and according to such specifications (including

其后条文)特许注册公司的外国银行;或

(vi)受外国监管者全面并表监管的人;

(5)“受监管证券控股公司” 一词系指根据本条规定受联邦储备委员会监管的证券控股公司;且

(6)“关联方”、“银行”、“银行控股公司”、“公司”、“控制”、“储蓄协会”以及“子公司”的含义以《1956年银行控股公司法》第2条的定义为准。

(b)**针对不拥有银行或储蓄协会关联方的证券控股公司的监管**。——

(1)**一般规定**。——按照外国监管者或外国法律规定的要求受制于全面并表监管的证券控股公司,可以根据第(2)款的规定在联邦储备委员会注册为受全面监管的证券控股公司。提交上述注册申请的任何证券控股公司应根据本条规定接受监管,且应遵守联邦储备委员会制定的适用于受监管证券控股公司的规则和命令。

(2)**注册为受监管证券控股公司**。——

(A)**注册**。——选择接受全面并表监管的证券控股公司应向联邦储备委员会提交联邦储备委员会在其发布的规章中所规定的对实现本条目的确属必要或适当的信息及文件,以便在联邦储备委员会注册。

(B)**生效日**。——根据第(A)子款注册的证券控股公司,在联邦储备委员会收到第(A)子款所述注册信息和文件之日起届满45天之日,或者在联邦储备委员会在其发布的规则或命令中所判定的更短时限之内,应视为受监管证券控股公司。

(c)**对证券控股公司的监管**。——

(1)**记录保存和报告**。——

(A)**记录保存和报告要求**。——每一受监管证券控股公司及其每一关联方,均应在联邦储备委员会规定的期间内,留存联邦储备委员会判定对实施本条规定、防范上述控股公司及其关联方的规避行为并监控其对适用的法律规定之合规情况确属必要或适当的记录,向联邦储备委员会提供其判定确属必要或适当的记录复本,并作出联邦储备委员会判定确属必要或适当的报告。

(B)**格式和内容**。——

(i)**一般规定**。——按照本款要求制作、提交或保存的任何记录或报告均应——

(I)按照联邦储备委员会要求的格式和具体要求(包括注册公共会计师事务所的

certification by a registered public accounting firm), as the Board of Governors may require; and

(II) be provided promptly to the Board of Governors at any time, upon request by the Board of Governors.

(ii) CONTENTS. — Records and reports required to be made, furnished, or kept under this paragraph may include —

(I) a balance sheet or income statement of the supervised securities holding company or an affiliate of a supervised securities holding company;

(II) an assessment of the consolidated capital and liquidity of the supervised securities holding company;

(III) a report by an independent auditor attesting to the compliance of the supervised securities holding company with the internal risk management and internal control objectives of the supervised securities holding company; and

(IV) a report concerning the extent to which the supervised securities holding company or affiliate has complied with the provisions of this section and any regulations prescribed and orders issued under this section.

(2) USE OF EXISTING REPORTS. —

(A) IN GENERAL. — The Board of Governors shall, to the fullest extent possible, accept reports in fulfillment of the requirements of this paragraph that a supervised securities holding company or an affiliate of a supervised securities holding company has been required to provide to another regulatory agency or a self–regulatory organization.

(B) AVAILABILITY. — A supervised securities holding company or an affiliate of a supervised securities holding company shall promptly provide to the Board of Governors, at the request of the Board of Governors, any report described in subparagraph (A), as permitted by law.

(3) EXAMINATION AUTHORITY. —

(A) FOCUS OF EXAMINATION AUTHORITY. — The Board of Governors may make examinations of any supervised securities holding company and any affiliate of a supervised securities holding company to carry out this subsection, to prevent evasions thereof, and to monitor compliance by the supervised securities holding company or affiliate with applicable provisions of law.

(B) DEFERENCE TO OTHER EXAMINATIONS. — For purposes of this subparagraph, the Board of Governors shall, to the fullest extent possible, use the reports of examination made by other appropriate Federal or State regulatory authorities with respect to any functionally regulated subsidiary or any institution described in subparagraph (D), (F), or (H) of section 2 (c)(2) of the Bank Holding Company Act of 1956 (12 U.S.C. 1841 (c)(2)).

认证)制作;及

(Ⅱ)在任何时候,如联邦储备委员会在任何时候提出要求,及时向其提供。

(ⅱ)**内容**。——按照本款要求制作、提交或保存的任何记录或报告可包含——

(Ⅰ)受监管证券控股公司或其关联方的资产负债表或损益表;

(Ⅱ)受监管证券控股公司的并表资本和流动性评估;及

(Ⅲ)独立审计师出具的鉴证受监管证券控股公司符合其内部风险管理和内部控制目标的报告;及

(Ⅳ)关于受监管证券控股公司或其关联方对本条规定及根据本条制定的任何规章和发布的任何命令的遵守情况的报告。

(2)**既有报告的利用**。——

(A)**一般规定**。——联邦储备委员会在履行本款要求时,应尽最大可能承认受监管证券控股公司或其关联方已按要求向其他监管机关或自律组织提供报告。

(B)**信息提供**。——联邦储备委员会提出要求时,受监管证券控股公司或其关联方应在法律允许的范围内,及时向联邦储备委员会提供第(A)子款所述的任何报告。

(3)**检查权**。——

(A)**检查权的重点**。——为了实施本子条规定、防范任何受监管证券控股公司或其任何关联方的规避行为,并监控其对适用的法律规定的合规情况,联邦储备委员会可以对该受监管证券控股公司及其任何关联方进行检查。

(B)**遵从其他检查的结果**。——就本子款而言,联邦储备委员会应尽最大可能利用其他相应的联邦监管机关或州监管机构针对受制于任何功能监管的子公司或《1956年银行控股公司法》第2(c)(2)条[《美国法典》第十二编第1841(c)(2)节]第(D)子款、第(F)子款或第(H)子款所述的任何机构作出的检查报告。

(d) CAPITAL AND RISK MANAGEMENT. —

(1) IN GENERAL. — The Board of Governors shall, by regulation or order, prescribe capital adequacy and other risk management standards for supervised securities holding companies that are appropriate to protect the safety and soundness of the supervised securities holding companies and address the risks posed to financial stability by supervised securities holding companies.

(2) DIFFERENTIATION. — In imposing standards under this subsection, the Board of Governors may differentiate among supervised securities holding companies on an individual basis, or by category, taking into consideration the requirements under paragraph (3).

(3) CONTENT. — Any standards imposed on a supervised securities holding company under this subsection shall take into account —

(A) the differences among types of business activities carried out by the supervised securities holding company;

(B) the amount and nature of the financial assets of the supervised securities holding company;

(C) the amount and nature of the liabilities of the supervised securities holding company, including the degree of reliance on short–term funding;

(D) the extent and nature of the off–balance sheet exposures of the supervised securities holding company;

(E) the extent and nature of the transactions and relationships of the supervised securities holding company with other financial companies;

(F) the importance of the supervised securities holding company as a source of credit for households, businesses, and State and local governments, and as a source of liquidity for the financial system; and

(G) the nature, scope, and mix of the activities of the supervised securities holding company.

(4) NOTICE. — A capital requirement imposed under this subsection may not take effect earlier than 180 days after the date on which a supervised securities holding company is provided notice of the capital requirement.

(e) OTHER PROVISIONS OF LAW APPLICABLE TO SUPERVISED SECURITIES HOLDING COMPANIES. —

(1) FEDERAL DEPOSIT INSURANCE ACT. — Subsections (b), (c) through (s), and (u) of section 8 of the Federal Deposit Insurance Act (12 U.S.C. 1818) shall apply to any supervised securities holding company, and to any subsidiary (other than a bank or an institution described in subparagraph (D), (F), or (H) of section 2 (c)(2) of the Bank Holding Company Act of 1956 (12 U.S.C. 1841 (c)(2))) of a supervised securities holding company, in the same manner as such subsections apply to a bank holding company for which

(d)**资本及风险管理**。——

(1)**一般规定**。——联邦储备委员会应发布规章或命令,针对受监管证券控股公司规定适当的资本充足性标准及其他风险管理标准,以保护该等公司的安全性和稳健性,并处理该等公司对金融稳定造成的风险。

(2)**区别处理**。——联邦储备委员会在根据本子条规定向受监管证券控股公司施加标准时,可考虑第(3)款的要求,区别对待每一受监管证券控股公司或按类别区别对待该等公司。

(3)**内容**。——根据本子条对受监管证券控股公司施加的任何标准均应考虑如下因素——

(A)受监管证券控股公司业务活动类型的差别;

(B)受监管证券控股公司金融资产的金额和性质;

(C)受监管证券控股公司债务的金额和性质,包括其对短期融资的依赖程度;

(D)受监管证券控股公司资产负债表之外的风险敞口的程度和性质;

(E)受监管证券控股公司与其他金融公司之间的交易和关系之范围和性质;

(F)受监管证券控股公司作为家庭、企业、州政府和地方政府信贷来源的重要性,及其作为金融体系流动性来源的重要性;及

(G)受监管证券控股公司活动的性质、范围和组合。

(4)**通知**。——根据本子条施加的资本要求的生效时间不得早于向受监管证券控股公司发出资本要求通知后第180天。

(e)**适用于受监管证券控股公司的其他法律规定**。——

(1)《**联邦存款保险法**》。——《联邦存款保险法》第8条(《美国法典》第十二编第1818节)第(b)子条、第(c)子条至第(s)子条和第(u)子条,应适用于任何受监管证券控股公司及其任何子公司{但《1956年银行控股公司法》第2(c)(2)条[《美国法典》第十二编第1841(c)(2)节]第(D)子款、第(F)子款或第(H)子款所述银行或机构除外},并且适用方式应与该等子条适用于联邦储备委员会作为相应的联邦银行业监管机关监管的银行控股公司的方式相一致。在将上述子条适用于受监管证券控股公司或其子公

the Board of Governors is the appropriate Federal banking agency. For purposes of applying such subsections to a supervised securities holding company or a subsidiary (other than a bank or an institution described in subparagraph (D), (F), or (H) of section 2 (c)(2) of the Bank Holding Company Act of 1956 (12 U.S.C. 1841 (c)(2))) of a supervised securities holding company, the Board of Governors shall be deemed the appropriate Federal banking agency for the supervised securities holding company or subsidiary.

(2) BANK HOLDING COMPANY ACT OF 1956. — Except as the Board of Governors may otherwise provide by regulation or order, a supervised securities holding company shall be subject to the provisions of the Bank Holding Company Act of 1956 (12 U.S.C. 1841 et seq.) in the same manner and to the same extent a bank holding company is subject to such provisions, except that a supervised securities holding company may not, by reason of this paragraph, be deemed to be a bank holding company for purposes of section 4 of the Bank Holding Company Act of 1956 (12 U.S.C. 1843).

SEC. 619. PROHIBITIONS ON PROPRIETARY TRADING AND CERTAIN RELATIONSHIPS WITH HEDGE FUNDS AND PRIVATE EQUITY FUNDS.

The Bank Holding Company Act of 1956 (12 U.S.C. 1841 et seq.) is amended by adding at the end the following:

"SEC. 13. PROHIBITIONS ON PROPRIETARY TRADING AND CERTAIN RELATIONSHIPS WITH HEDGE FUNDS AND PRIVATE EQUITY FUNDS.

"(a) IN GENERAL. —

"(1) PROHIBITION. — Unless otherwise provided in this section, a banking entity shall not —

"(A) engage in proprietary trading; or

"(B) acquire or retain any equity, partnership, or other ownership interest in or sponsor a hedge fund or a private equity fund.

"(2) NONBANK FINANCIAL COMPANIES SUPERVISED BY THE BOARD. — Any nonbank financial company supervised by the Board that engages in proprietary trading or takes or retains any equity, partnership, or other ownership interest in or sponsors a hedge fund or a private equity fund shall be subject, by rule, as provided in subsection (b)(2), to additional capital requirements for and additional quantitative limits with regards to such proprietary trading and taking or retaining any equity, partnership, or other ownership interest in or sponsorship of a hedge fund or a private equity fund, except that permitted activities as described in subsection (d) shall not be subject to the additional capital and additional quantitative limits except as provided in subsection (d)(3), as if the nonbank financial company supervised by the Board were a banking entity.

"(b) STUDY AND RULEMAKING. —

"(1) STUDY. — Not later than 6 months after the date of enactment of this section, the

司时{但《1956年银行控股公司法》第2(c)(2)条[《美国法典》第十二编第1841(c)(2)节]第(D)子款、第(F)子款或第(H)子款所述银行或机构除外}时,联邦储备委员会应视为受监管证券控股公司或其子公司的相应的联邦银行业监管机关。

(2)**《1956年银行控股公司法》**。——除联邦储备委员会发布的规章或命令另有规定的情形外,受监管证券控股公司应以与银行控股公司同样的方式和范围遵守《1956年银行控股公司法》(《美国法典》第十二编第1841节及其后条文),但是受监管证券控股公司不得因为本款而被视为《1956年银行控股公司法》第4条(《美国法典》第十二编第1843节)意义上的银行控股公司。

第619条　自营交易之禁止性规定及与对冲基金和私募股权基金发生特定关系之禁止性规定

在《1956年银行控股公司法》(《美国法典》第十二编第1841节及其后条文)结尾处增加如下内容,作为对该法的修正:

"第13条　自营交易之禁止性规定及与对冲基金和私募股权基金发生特定关系之禁止性规定

(a)**一般规定**。——

(1)**禁止性规定**。——除非本条另有规定,否则银行实体不得——

(A)从事自营交易;或

(B)取得或持有对冲基金或私募股权基金中的股权、合伙权益或其他所有权权益,或者发起对冲基金或私募股权基金。

(2)**受联邦储备委员会监管的非银行金融公司**。——受联邦储备委员会监管,且从事自营交易,或取得或持有对冲基金或私募股权基金中的任何股权、合伙权益或其他所有权权益,或者发起对冲基金或私募股权基金的任何非银行金融公司,应受制于按照第(b)(2)子条制定的规则就上述自营交易、取得或持有股权、合伙权益或其他所有权权益或者发起基金的行为所施加的附加资本要求和附加量化限制,但是,除第(d)(3)子条规定的情形外,第(d)子条允许开展的活动不应受制于上述附加资本要求和附加量化限制,此时,受联邦储备委员会监管的非银行金融公司应视同银行实体。

(b)**研究和规则制定**。——

(1)**研究**。——金融稳定监督委员会应在本条规定颁布起6个月内就本条规定的

Financial Stability Oversight Council shall study and make recommendations on implementing the provisions of this section so as to —

“(A) promote and enhance the safety and soundness of banking entities;

“(B) protect taxpayers and consumers and enhance financial stability by minimizing the risk that insured depository institutions and the affiliates of insured depository institutions will engage in unsafe and unsound activities;

“(C) limit the inappropriate transfer of Federal subsidies from institutions that benefit from deposit insurance and liquidity facilities of the Federal Government to unregulated entities;

“(D) reduce conflicts of interest between the self–interest of banking entities and nonbank financial companies supervised by the Board, and the interests of the customers of such entities and companies;

“(E) limit activities that have caused undue risk or loss in banking entities and nonbank financial companies supervised by the Board, or that might reasonably be expected to create undue risk or loss in such banking entities and nonbank financial companies supervised by the Board;

“(F) appropriately accommodate the business of insurance within an insurance company, subject to regulation in accordance with the relevant insurance company investment laws, while protecting the safety and soundness of any banking entity with which such insurance company is affiliated and of the United States financial system; and

“(G) appropriately time the divestiture of illiquid assets that are affected by the implementation of the prohibitions under subsection (a).

“(2) RULEMAKING. —

“(A) IN GENERAL. — Unless otherwise provided in this section, not later than 9 months after the completion of the study under paragraph (1), the appropriate Federal banking agencies, the Securities and Exchange Commission, and the Commodity Futures Trading Commission, shall consider the findings of the study under paragraph (1) and adopt rules to carry out this section, as provided in subparagraph (B).

“(B) COORDINATED RULEMAKING. —

“(i) REGULATORY AUTHORITY. — The regulations issued under this paragraph shall be issued by —

“(I) the appropriate Federal banking agencies, jointly, with respect to insured depository institutions;

“(II) the Board, with respect to any company that controls an insured depository institution, or that is treated as a bank holding company for purposes of section 8 of the International Banking Act, any nonbank financial company supervised by the Board, and any subsidiary of any of the foregoing (other than a subsidiary for which an agency described in

实施情况开展研究并提出建议,以便——

(A)提高并加强银行实体的安全性及稳健性;

(B)尽量降低参保存款机构及其关联方从事欠安全、欠稳健活动的风险,从而保护纳税人和消费者并加强金融稳定性;

(C)限制受益于联邦政府存款保险和流动性安排的机构向不受监管的实体不适当地转让联邦补贴;

(D)减少受联邦储备委员会监管的银行实体和非银行金融公司的自身利益与该等实体和公司的客户利益之间的冲突;

(E)限制已导致或根据合理预期将导致受联邦储备委员会监管的银行实体和非银行金融公司遭受不当风险或损失的活动;

(F)在不违反按照相关的保险公司投资法律进行的监管的前提下,适当地调整保险公司的保险业务,同时保护与该等保险公司存在关联关系的任何银行实体的安全性和稳健性,以及美国金融体系的安全性和稳健性;及

(G)对于受第(a)子条禁止性规定之实施影响的非流动性资产,适当地制定剥离该等资产的时间计划。

(2)**规则制定**。——

(A)**一般规定**。——除本条规定的情形外,在第(1)款要求开展的研究完成后9个月内,相应的联邦银行业监管机关、证券交易委员会和商品期货交易委员会应审议该项研究的结果,并根据第(B)子款的规定制定实施本条的规则。

(B)**协调完成规则制定**。——

(i)**监管权**。——本款所述规章应由以下机关发布——

(I)对于参保存款机构而言,应由各相应的联邦银行业监管机关联合发布;

(II)对于控制某一参保存款机构的任何公司、根据《国际银行法》第8条被视同银行控股公司的公司、受联邦储备委员会监管的任何非银行金融公司和前述任何各者的任何子公司[但第(I)子项、第(III)子项或第(IV)子项所述机关作为优先金融监管机关监管的子公司除外]而言,应由联邦储备委员会发布;

subclause (I), (III), or (IV) is the primary financial regulatory agency);

"(III) the Commodity Futures Trading Commission, with respect to any entity for which the Commodity Futures Trading Commission is the primary financial regulatory agency, as defined in section 2 of the Dodd–Frank Wall Street Reform and Consumer Protection Act; and

"(IV) the Securities and Exchange Commission, with respect to any entity for which the Securities and Exchange Commission is the primary financial regulatory agency, as defined in section 2 of the Dodd–Frank Wall Street Reform and Consumer Protection Act.

"(ii) COORDINATION, CONSISTENCY, AND COMPARABILITY. — In developing and issuing regulations pursuant to this section, the appropriate Federal banking agencies, the Securities and Exchange Commission, and the Commodity Futures Trading Commission shall consult and coordinate with each other, as appropriate, for the purposes of assuring, to the extent possible, that such regulations are comparable and provide for consistent application and implementation of the applicable provisions of this section to avoid providing advantages or imposing disadvantages to the companies affected by this subsection and to protect the safety and soundness of banking entities and nonbank financial companies supervised by the Board.

"(iii) COUNCIL ROLE. — The Chairperson of the Financial Stability Oversight Council shall be responsible for coordination of the regulations issued under this section.

"(c) EFFECTIVE DATE. —

"(1) IN GENERAL. — Except as provided in paragraphs (2) and (3), this section shall take effect on the earlier of —

"(A) 12 months after the date of the issuance of final rules under subsection (b); or

"(B) 2 years after the date of enactment of this section.

"(2) CONFORMANCE PERIOD FOR DIVESTITURE. — A banking entity or nonbank financial company supervised by the Board shall bring its activities and investments into compliance with the requirements of this section not later than 2 years after the date on which the requirements become effective pursuant to this section or 2 years after the date on which the entity or company becomes a nonbank financial company supervised by the Board. The Board may, by rule or order, extend this two–year period for not more than one year at a time, if, in the judgment of the Board, such an extension is consistent with the purposes of this section and would not be detrimental to the public interest. The extensions made by the Board under the preceding sentence may not exceed an aggregate of 3 years.

"(3) EXTENDED TRANSITION FOR ILLIQUID FUNDS. —

"(A) APPLICATION. — The Board may, upon the application of a banking entity, extend the period during which the banking entity, to the extent necessary to fulfill a contractual obligation that was in effect on May 1, 2010, may take or retain its equity, partnership, or

(III)对于商品期货交易委员会作为优先金融监管机关(定义见《多德—弗兰克华尔街改革与消费者保护法》第2条)监管的任何实体而言,应由商品期货交易委员会发布;及

(IV)对于证券交易委员会作为优先金融监管机关(定义见《多德—弗兰克华尔街改革与消费者保护法》第2条)监管的任何实体而言,应由证券交易委员会发布。

(ii)**协调、一致性及可比性**。——各相应的联邦银行业监管机关、证券交易委员会和商品期货交易委员会在根据本条规定制定并发布规章时,应相互进行适当的磋商和协调,以期尽可能确保该等规章具有可比性,并对本条相关条款的一致适用及实施作出规定,避免给受本子条规定影响的公司带来有利或不利条件,并保护受联邦储备委员会监管的银行实体和非银行金融公司的安全性和稳健性。

(iii)**金融稳定监督委员会的作用**。——金融稳定监督委员会主席应负责协调根据本条规定发布的各项规章。

(c)**生效日**。——

(1)**一般规定**。——除非第(2)款和第(3)款另有规定,否则,本条应在以下日期(以较早者为准)生效——

(A)第(b)子条所述最终规则发布后届满12个月之日;或

(B)本条规定颁布之日起届满2年之日。

(2)**剥离的合规期限**。——受联邦储备委员会监管的银行实体或非银行金融公司应在本条的各项要求根据本条规定生效后2年内,或者该实体或公司成为受联邦储备委员会监管的非银行金融公司之日后2年内,使其各项活动和投资均符合本条的各项要求。如联邦储备委员会认为延期与本条目的相一致且无损于公共利益,则联邦储备委员会有权发布规则或命令,延长上文规定的2年期限,但每次延长期不得超过1年。联邦储备委员会根据前一句规定所做各次延期总计时长不得超过3年。

(3)**非流动性基金过渡期的延长**。——

(A)**申请**。——银行实体为完成某项在2010年5月1日已生效的合同义务而有必要延期,向联邦储备委员会提出申请后,联邦储备委员会可延长上述期限,使该实体可为完成上述义务而在延长期内取得或继续持有其在某一非流动性基金中的股权、

other ownership interest in, or otherwise provide additional capital to, an illiquid fund.

"(B) TIME LIMIT ON APPROVAL. — The Board may grant 1 extension under subparagraph (A), which may not exceed 5 years.

"(4) DIVESTITURE REQUIRED. — Except as otherwise provided in subsection (d)(1)(G), a banking entity may not engage in any activity prohibited under subsection (a)(1)(B) after the earlier of —

"(A) the date on which the contractual obligation to invest in the illiquid fund terminates; and

"(B) the date on which any extensions granted by the Board under paragraph (3) expire.

"(5) ADDITIONAL CAPITAL DURING TRANSITION PERIOD. — Notwithstanding paragraph (2), on the date on which the rules are issued under subsection (b)(2), the appropriate Federal banking agencies, the Securities and Exchange Commission, and the Commodity Futures Trading Commission shall issue rules, as provided in subsection (b)(2), to impose additional capital requirements, and any other restrictions, as appropriate, on any equity, partnership, or ownership interest in or sponsorship of a hedge fund or private equity fund by a banking entity.

"(6) SPECIAL RULEMAKING. — Not later than 6 months after the date of enactment of this section, the Board shall issues rules to implement paragraphs (2) and (3).

"(d) PERMITTED ACTIVITIES. —

"(1) IN GENERAL. — Notwithstanding the restrictions under subsection (a), to the extent permitted by any other provision of Federal or State law, and subject to the limitations under paragraph (2) and any restrictions or limitations that the appropriate Federal banking agencies, the Securities and Exchange Commission, and the Commodity Futures Trading Commission, may determine, the following activities (in this section referred to as 'permitted activities') are permitted:

"(A) The purchase, sale, acquisition, or disposition of obligations of the United States or any agency thereof, obligations, participations, or other instruments of or issued by the Government National Mortgage Association, the Federal National Mortgage Association, the Federal Home Loan Mortgage Corporation, a Federal Home Loan Bank, the Federal Agricultural Mortgage Corporation, or a Farm Credit System institution chartered under and subject to the provisions of the Farm Credit Act of 1971 (12 U.S.C. 2001 et seq.), and obligations of any State or of any political subdivision thereof.

"(B) The purchase, sale, acquisition, or disposition of securities and other instruments described in subsection (h)(4) in connection with underwriting or market-making-related activities, to the extent that any such activities permitted by this subparagraph are designed not to exceed the reasonably expected near term demands of clients, customers, or

合伙权益或其他所有权权益,或者另行向该非流动性基金提供附加资本。

(B)**批准时限**。——联邦储备委员会可以根据第(A)子款准许一次延期,但该延期时长不得超过5年。

(4)**剥离要求**。——除第(d)(1)(G)子条另有规定的情形外,银行实体在以下日期(以较早者为准)之后不得从事第(a)(1)(B)子条禁止的任何活动——

(A)对非流动性基金投资的合同义务的终止日;及

(B)联邦储备委员会根据第(3)款规定批准的任何延期之到期日。

(5)**过渡期内的附加资本要求**。——无论第(2)款如何规定,相应的联邦银行业监管机关、证券交易委员会和商品期货交易委员会应在第(b)(2)子条规定的规则发布之日,发布第(b)(2)子条所述规则,针对银行实体在对冲基金或私募股权基金中持有的任何股权、合伙权益或所有权权益或其对该等基金的发起施加附加资本要求和任何其他适当限制。

(6)**特别规则制定**。——联邦储备委员会应于本条规定颁布之日后6个月内,发布实施第(2)款和第(3)款的规则。

(d)**获许活动**。——

(1)**一般规定**。——尽管有第(a)子条的限制规定,在任何其他联邦法律或州法律许可的范围内,并在受制于第(2)款的限制条件和相应的联邦银行业监管机关、证券交易委员会和商品期货交易委员会判定的任何限制或约束条件的前提下,允许开展以下活动(本条中简称获许活动):

(A)购买、出售、获得或处置联邦政府或任何联邦机关的债务,美国政府国民抵押贷款协会、联邦国民抵押贷款协会、联邦住房贷款抵押公司、联邦住房贷款银行、联邦农业抵押贷款公司或根据《1971年农业信贷法》(《美国法典》第十二编第2001节及其后条文)特许注册并受制于该法规定的农业信贷系统机构拥有或发行的债务、参与份额或其他工具,以及任何州或州下属行政区域的债务。

(B)购买、出售、获得或处置第(h)(4)子条所述与承销或做市行为相关的证券和其他工具,只要根据本子款获许开展的任何该等行为并未超出委托方、客户或对手方的合理预期的近期需求量。

counterparties.

"(C) Risk–mitigating hedging activities in connection with and related to individual or aggregated positions, contracts, or other holdings of a banking entity that are designed to reduce the specific risks to the banking entity in connection with and related to such positions, contracts, or other holdings.

"(D) The purchase, sale, acquisition, or disposition of securities and other instruments described in subsection (h)(4) on behalf of customers.

"(E) Investments in one or more small business investment companies, as defined in section 102 of the Small Business Investment Act of 1958 (15 U.S.C. 662), investments designed primarily to promote the public welfare, of the type permitted under paragraph (11) of section 5136 of the Revised Statutes of the United States (12 U.S.C. 24), or investments that are qualified rehabilitation expenditures with respect to a qualified rehabilitated building or certified historic structure, as such terms are defined in section 47 of the Internal Revenue Code of 1986 or a similar State historic tax credit program.

"(F) The purchase, sale, acquisition, or disposition of securities and other instruments described in subsection (h)(4) by a regulated insurance company directly engaged in the business of insurance for the general account of the company and by any affiliate of such regulated insurance company, provided that such activities by any affiliate are solely for the general account of the regulated insurance company, if—

"(i) the purchase, sale, acquisition, or disposition is conducted in compliance with, and subject to, the insurance company investment laws, regulations, and written guidance of the State or jurisdiction in which each such insurance company is domiciled; and

"(ii) the appropriate Federal banking agencies, after consultation with the Financial Stability Oversight Council and the relevant insurance commissioners of the States and territories of the United States, have not jointly determined, after notice and comment, that a particular law, regulation, or written guidance described in clause (i) is insufficient to protect the safety and soundness of the banking entity, or of the financial stability of the United States.

"(G) Organizing and offering a private equity or hedge fund, including serving as a general partner, managing member, or trustee of the fund and in any manner selecting or controlling (or having employees, officers, directors, or agents who constitute) a majority of the directors, trustees, or management of the fund, including any necessary expenses for the foregoing, only if—

"(i) the banking entity provides bona fide trust, fiduciary, or investment advisory services;

"(ii) the fund is organized and offered only in connection with the provision of bona fide trust, fiduciary, or investment advisory services and only to persons that are customers of

(C)与银行实体的个别或合并持仓、合约或其他持仓状况相关的,旨在降低与该等持仓、合约或其他持仓状况相关的特定风险的风险缓释套期保值行为。

(D)代表客户购买、出售、获得或处置第(h)(4)子条所述证券和其他工具。

(E)对一家或一家以上小型商业投资公司[定义见《1958年小型企业投资法》第102条(《美国法典》第十五编第662节)]的投资;主要目的是提高公共福利,且属于《美国制定法汇编》(修订版)第5136条第(11)款(《美国法典》第十二编第24节)所允许之类型的投资;或者与合格的复建建筑物或经认证的历史性建筑相关的,符合复建支出标准的投资(合格的复建建筑物、经认证的历史性建筑之定义见《1986年国内税收法典》第47条或类似的州历史遗迹税收抵免计划)。

(F)直接从事保险业务的受监管保险公司为其一般账户,或该等受监管保险公司的任何关联方(仅为该等受监管保险公司的一般账户)购买、出售、获得或处置第(h)(4)子条证券和其他工具,只要——

(i)该等购买、出售、获得或处置符合并受制于该保险公司住所所在州或司法辖区的保险公司投资法律、规章和书面指引;及

(ii)相应的联邦银行业监管机关在与金融稳定监督委员会和美国州及准州相关的保险监督官磋商后,并在通知和意见征求期届满之后,并未共同判定,第(i)项所述具体法律、规章或书面指引对于保护银行实体的安全性和稳健性或美国的金融稳定并不充分。

(G)组建和要约私募股权基金或对冲基金,包括担任该基金的普通合伙人、管理团队成员或受托人,并以任何方式(包括控制相关的任何必要费用)选任或控制该基金的过半数董事、受托人或管理团队成员(或该基金的过半数董事、受托人或管理团队成员均属于该银行实体的职员、管理人员、董事或代理人),但前提是——

(i)该银行实体提供善意的信托、受信或投资顾问服务;

(ii)该基金的组建与发行仅与善意提供信托、受信或投资顾问服务有关,且其发行对象仅为接受该金融实体的该等信托、受信或投资顾问服务的客户;

such services of the banking entity;

"(iii) the banking entity does not acquire or retain an equity interest, partnership interest, or other ownership interest in the funds except for a de minimis investment subject to and in compliance with paragraph (4);

"(iv) the banking entity complies with the restrictions under paragraphs (1) and (2) of subparagraph (f);

"(v) the banking entity does not, directly or indirectly, guarantee, assume, or otherwise insure the obligations or performance of the hedge fund or private equity fund or of any hedge fund or private equity fund in which such hedge fund or private equity fund invests;

"(vi) the banking entity does not share with the hedge fund or private equity fund, for corporate, marketing, promotional, or other purposes, the same name or a variation of the same name;

"(vii) no director or employee of the banking entity takes or retains an equity interest, partnership interest, or other ownership interest in the hedge fund or private equity fund, except for any director or employee of the banking entity who is directly engaged in providing investment advisory or other services to the hedge fund or private equity fund; and

"(viii) the banking entity discloses to prospective and actual investors in the fund, in writing, that any losses in such hedge fund or private equity fund are borne solely by investors in the fund and not by the banking entity, and otherwise complies with any additional rules of the appropriate Federal banking agencies, the Securities and Exchange Commission, or the Commodity Futures Trading Commission, as provided in subsection (b)(2), designed to ensure that losses in such hedge fund or private equity fund are borne solely by investors in the fund and not by the banking entity.

"(H) Proprietary trading conducted by a banking entity pursuant to paragraph (9) or (13) of section 4 (c), provided that the trading occurs solely outside of the United States and that the banking entity is not directly or indirectly controlled by a banking entity that is organized under the laws of the United States or of one or more States.

"(I) The acquisition or retention of any equity, partnership, or other ownership interest in, or the sponsorship of, a hedge fund or a private equity fund by a banking entity pursuant to paragraph (9) or (13) of section 4 (c) solely outside of the United States, provided that no ownership interest in such hedge fund or private equity fund is offered for sale or sold to a resident of the United States and that the banking entity is not directly or indirectly controlled by a banking entity that is organized under the laws of the United States or of one or more States.

"(J) Such other activity as the appropriate Federal banking agencies, the Securities and Exchange Commission, and the Commodity Futures Trading Commission determine, by rule,

(iii)该银行实体并未取得或保留该基金中的某项股权、合伙权益或其他所有权权益,但受制于并满足第(4)款规定的微量投资除外;

(iv)该银行实体符合第(f)子条[1]第(1)款和第(2)款规定的限制条件;

(v)该银行实体并未直接或间接地担保、承担该对冲基金或者私募股权基金或者该对冲基金或私募股权基金投资的任何对冲基金或者私募股权基金之义务或履约责任,或对该等义务或履约责任提供保险。

(vi)该银行实体并未出于公司目的、营销目的、促销目的或其他目的与该对冲基金或私募股权基金共用同一名称或同一名称的变体;

(vii)该银行实体的任何董事或雇员均未购买或持有该对冲基金或私募股权基金的股权、合伙权益或其他所有权权益,但该银行实体直接为该对冲基金或私募股权基金提供投资顾问服务的董事或雇员除外;及

(viii)该银行实体须向该基金的潜在投资者和实际投资者作出如下书面披露:该对冲基金或私募股权基金的任何亏损均将仅由投资者而非银行实体承担;同时,该银行实体应遵守相应的联邦银行业监管机关、证券交易委员会或商品期货交易委员会根据第(b)(2)子条规定发布的,旨在确保该对冲基金或私募股权基金的所有亏损均将仅由投资者而非该银行实体承担的任何补充规则。

(H)银行实体根据第4(c)条第(9)款或第(13)款的规定开展的自营交易,前提是该交易仅在美国境外开展,且该银行实体并非由根据美国联邦法律或美国的一个或一个以上的州之法律所组建的另一银行实体所直接或间接控制。

(I)银行实体根据第4(c)条第(9)款或第(13)款的规定仅在美国境外开展的取得或继续持有对冲基金或私募股权基金中的任何股权、合伙权益或其他所有权权益的行为,或者发起某一对冲基金或私募股权基金的行为,前提是,该对冲基金或私募股权基金中的任何所有权权益均不得向美国居民要约出售或出售,且该银行实体并非由根据美国联邦法律或美国一个或一个以上的州之法律组建的另一银行实体所直接或间接控制。

(J)相应的联邦银行业监管机关、证券交易委员会和商品期货交易委员会根据第(b)(2)子条发布的规则判定的有助于促进并保护银行实体的安全性和稳健性以及美

1　按照全文的条款编辑体例,此处的“subparagraph”似乎应为“subsection”,译文中按后者处理。——译者注

as provided in subsection (b)(2), would promote and protect the safety and soundness of the banking entity and the financial stability of the United States.

"(2) LIMITATION ON PERMITTED ACTIVITIES. —

"(A) IN GENERAL. — No transaction, class of transactions, or activity may be deemed a permitted activity under paragraph (1) if the transaction, class of transactions, or activity —

"(i) would involve or result in a material conflict of interest (as such term shall be defined by rule as provided in subsection (b)(2)) between the banking entity and its clients, customers, or counterparties;

"(ii) would result, directly or indirectly, in a material exposure by the banking entity to high-risk assets or high-risk trading strategies (as such terms shall be defined by rule as provided in subsection (b)(2));

"(iii) would pose a threat to the safety and soundness of such banking entity; or

"(iv) would pose a threat to the financial stability of the United States.

"(B) RULEMAKING. — The appropriate Federal banking agencies, the Securities and Exchange Commission, and the Commodity Futures Trading Commission shall issue regulations to implement subparagraph (A), as part of the regulations issued under subsection (b)(2).

"(3) CAPITAL AND QUANTITATIVE LIMITATIONS. — The appropriate Federal banking agencies, the Securities and Exchange Commission, and the Commodity Futures Trading Commission shall, as provided in subsection (b)(2), adopt rules imposing additional capital requirements and quantitative limitations, including diversification requirements, regarding the activities permitted under this section if the appropriate Federal banking agencies, the Securities and Exchange Commission, and the Commodity Futures Trading Commission determine that additional capital and quantitative limitations are appropriate to protect the safety and soundness of banking entities engaged in such activities.

"(4) DE MINIMIS INVESTMENT. —

"(A) IN GENERAL. — A banking entity may make and retain an investment in a hedge fund or private equity fund that the banking entity organizes and offers, subject to the limitations and restrictions in subparagraph (B) for the purposes of —

"(i) establishing the fund and providing the fund with sufficient initial equity for investment to permit the fund to attract unaffiliated investors; or

"(ii) making a de minimis investment.

"(B) LIMITATIONS AND RESTRICTIONS ON INVESTMENTS. —

"(i) REQUIREMENT TO SEEK OTHER INVESTORS. — A banking entity shall actively seek unaffiliated investors to reduce or dilute the investment of the banking entity to the amount permitted under clause (ii).

国金融稳定的其他活动。

(2)**针对获许活动的限制**。——

(A)**一般规定**。——任何交易、交易类型或活动如存在以下情形,均不得被视为第(1)款规定的获许活动——

(i)将涉及或导致银行实体与其委托方、客户或对手方之间的重大利益冲突[该等术语应由按照第(b)(2)子条规定发布的规则进行定义];

(ii)将直接或间接导致银行实体对高风险资产或高风险交易策略的重大风险敞口[该等术语应由按照第(b)(2)子条规定发布的规则进行定义];

(iii)将对银行实体的安全性和稳健性构成威胁;或

(iv)将对美国的金融稳定构成威胁。

(B)**规则制定**。——相应的联邦银行业监管机关、证券交易委员会和商品期货交易委员会应发布规章,实施第(A)子款的规定,该等实施规章应作为根据第(b)(2)子条发布的规章的组成部分。

(3)**资本及量化限制**。——如果相应的联邦银行业监管机关、证券交易委员会和商品期货交易委员会判定附加资本和量化限制对保护从事本条允许的活动的银行实体之安全性和稳健性确属适当,则上述机关应根据第(b)(2)子条的规定,针对该等活动制定施加附加资本要求及量化限制(包括分散限制)的规则。

(4)**微量投资**。——

(A)**一般规定**。——在受制于第(B)子款所述限制及约束条件的前提下,银行实体可以出于以下目的,向其组建和要约的对冲基金或私募股权基金进行投资或保留该等投资——

(i)成立该基金并向该基金提供充足的初始投资股权,以便该基金能够吸引非关联投资者;或

(ii)进行微量投资。

(B)**投资的限制和约束条件**。——

(i)**吸纳其他投资者的要求**。——银行实体应积极吸纳非关联投资者,以将其投资降低或稀释至第(ii)项规定的许可金额。

“(ii) LIMITATIONS ON SIZE OF INVESTMENTS. — Notwithstanding any other provision of law, investments by a banking entity in a hedge fund or private equity fund shall —

“(Ⅰ) not later than 1 year after the date of establishment of the fund, be reduced through redemption, sale, or dilution to an amount that is not more than 3 percent of the total ownership interests of the fund;

“(Ⅱ) be immaterial to the banking entity, as defined, by rule, pursuant to subsection (b)(2), but in no case may the aggregate of all of the interests of the banking entity in all such funds exceed 3 percent of the Tier 1 capital of the banking entity.

“(iii) CAPITAL. — For purposes of determining compliance with applicable capital standards under paragraph (3), the aggregate amount of the outstanding investments by a banking entity under this paragraph, including retained earnings, shall be deducted from the assets and tangible equity of the banking entity, and the amount of the deduction shall increase commensurate with the leverage of the hedge fund or private equity fund.

“(C) EXTENSION. — Upon an application by a banking entity, the Board may extend the period of time to meet the requirements under subparagraph (B)(ii)(I) for 2 additional years, if the Board finds that an extension would be consistent with safety and soundness and in the public interest.

“(e) ANTI-EVASION. —

“(1) RULEMAKING. — The appropriate Federal banking agencies, the Securities and Exchange Commission, and the Commodity Futures Trading Commission shall issue regulations, as part of the rulemaking provided for in subsection (b)(2), regarding internal controls and recordkeeping, in order to insure compliance with this section.

“(2) TERMINATION OF ACTIVITIES OR INVESTMENT. — Notwithstanding any other provision of law, whenever an appropriate Federal banking agency, the Securities and Exchange Commission, or the Commodity Futures Trading Commission, as appropriate, has reasonable cause to believe that a banking entity or nonbank financial company supervised by the Board under the respective agency's jurisdiction has made an investment or engaged in an activity in a manner that functions as an evasion of the requirements of this section (including through an abuse of any permitted activity) or otherwise violates the restrictions under this section, the appropriate Federal banking agency, the Securities and Exchange Commission, or the Commodity Futures Trading Commission, as appropriate, shall order, after due notice and opportunity for hearing, the banking entity or nonbank financial company supervised by the Board to terminate the activity and, as relevant, dispose of the investment. Nothing in this paragraph shall be construed to limit the inherent authority of any Federal agency or State regulatory authority to further restrict any investments or activities under otherwise applicable provisions of law.

“(f) LIMITATIONS ON RELATIONSHIPS WITH HEDGE FUNDS AND PRIVATE

(ii)**投资规模限制**。——无论是否存在任何不同法律规定,银行实体向对冲基金或私募股权基金的投资均——

(Ⅰ)应在该基金成立之日后1年内,通过赎回、出售或稀释降低至不超过该基金全部所有权权益的3%;

(Ⅱ)不得对该银行实体具有重大意义[‘重大意义’应由按照第(b)(2)子条规定发布的规则进行定义],但无论如何,该银行实体在上述基金中的全部权益之总额不得超过该银行实体一级资本的3%。

(iii)**资本**。——在判定银行实体是否符合第(3)款规定的适用资本标准之时,本款所述银行实体的未实现投资总额(包括留存收益)应从该银行实体的资产和有形权益中扣除,且对冲基金或私募股权基金的杠杆率越高,扣除金额也应越高。

(C)**延期**。——如银行实体提出延期申请,且联邦储备委员会认定该项延期将有助于实现安全性和稳健性并符合公共利益,联邦储备委员会可以将第(B)(ii)(I)子款规定的合规期限延长2年。

(e)**反规避**。——

(1)**规则制定**。——作为第(b)(2)子条要求制定的规则的一部分,相应的联邦银行业监管机关、证券交易委员会和商品期货交易委员会应发布规章,就内部控制和记录保存作出规定,以确保本条的规定得以遵守。

(2)**活动或投资的终止**。——无论是否存在任何不同法律规定,只要相应的联邦银行业监管机关、证券交易委员会或商品期货交易委员会(视具体情况而定)有合理理由相信在其各自管辖范围内的受联邦储备委员会监管的银行实体或非银行金融公司开展的投资或从事的活动构成对本条规定之规避(包括对任何获许活动的滥用),或以其他方式违反了本条规定的限制条件,相应的联邦银行业监管机关、证券交易委员会或商品期货交易委员会(视具体情况而定)在发出适当的通知并提供听证机会后,应命令上述受联邦储备委员会监管的银行实体或非银行金融公司终止其活动或(如适用)处置上述投资。任何联邦机关或州监管机关根据其他适用的法律规定具有对任何投资或活动进行进一步限制的权力的,本款的任何规定均不得被解释为构成对上述固有权力的限制。

(f)**对于与对冲基金和私募股权基金的关系的限制**。——

EQUITY FUNDS. —

"(1) IN GENERAL. — No banking entity that serves, directly or indirectly, as the investment manager, investment adviser, or sponsor to a hedge fund or private equity fund, or that organizes and offers a hedge fund or private equity fund pursuant to paragraph (d)(1)(G), and no affiliate of such entity, may enter into a transaction with the fund, or with any other hedge fund or private equity fund that is controlled by such fund, that would be a covered transaction, as defined in section 23A of the Federal Reserve Act (12 U.S.C. 371c), with the hedge fund or private equity fund, as if such banking entity and the affiliate thereof were a member bank and the hedge fund or private equity fund were an affiliate thereof.

"(2) TREATMENT AS MEMBER BANK. — A banking entity that serves, directly or indirectly, as the investment manager, investment adviser, or sponsor to a hedge fund or private equity fund, or that organizes and offers a hedge fund or private equity fund pursuant to paragraph (d)(1)(G), shall be subject to section 23B of the Federal Reserve Act (12 U.S.C. 371c-1), as if such banking entity were a member bank and such hedge fund or private equity fund were an affiliate thereof.

"(3) PERMITTED SERVICES. —

"(A) IN GENERAL. — Notwithstanding paragraph (1), the Board may permit a banking entity to enter into any prime brokerage transaction with any hedge fund or private equity fund in which a hedge fund or private equity fund managed, sponsored, or advised by such banking entity has taken an equity, partnership, or other ownership interest, if—

"(i) the banking entity is in compliance with each of the limitations set forth in subsection (d)(1)(G) with regard to a hedge fund or private equity fund organized and offered by such banking entity;

"(ii) the chief executive officer (or equivalent officer) of the banking entity certifies in writing annually (with a duty to update the certification if the information in the certification materially changes) that the conditions specified in subsection (d)(1)(g)(v) are satisfied; and

"(iii) the Board has determined that such transaction is consistent with the safe and sound operation and condition of the banking entity.

"(B) TREATMENT OF PRIME BROKERAGE TRANSACTIONS. — For purposes of subparagraph (A), a prime brokerage transaction described in subparagraph (A) shall be subject to section 23B of the Federal Reserve Act (12 U.S.C. 371c-1) as if the counterparty were an affiliate of the banking entity.

"(4) APPLICATION TO NONBANK FINANCIAL COMPANIES SUPERVISED BY THE BOARD. — The appropriate Federal banking agencies, the Securities and Exchange Commission, and the Commodity Futures Trading Commission shall adopt rules, as provided in subsection (b)(2), imposing additional capital charges or other restrictions for nonbank

(1)**一般规定**。——任何直接或间接担任对冲基金或私募股权基金的投资管理人、投资顾问或发起人,或者根据第(d)(1)(G)款的规定组建并要约对冲基金或私募股权基金的银行实体及其关联方,均不得与该基金或由该基金控制的任何其他对冲基金或私募股权基金达成将构成与该对冲基金或私募股权基金的所涉交易[‘所涉交易’一词的定义见《联邦储备法》第23A条(《美国法典》第十二编第371c节)]之交易,如同该银行实体及其关联方是一家成员银行,而该对冲基金或私募股权基金是成员银行的关联方。

(2)**作为成员银行处理**。——直接或间接担任对冲基金或私募股权基金的投资管理人、投资顾问或发起人,或根据第(d)(1)(G)款的规定组建并要约对冲基金或私募股权基金的银行实体,应受制于《联邦储备法》第23B条(《美国法典》第十二编第371c—1节)的规定,如同该银行实体是一家成员银行,而该对冲基金或私募股权基金是成员银行的关联方。

(3)**获许服务**。——

(A)**一般规定**。——无论第(1)款如何规定,对于由银行实体管理、发起或提供顾问服务的对冲基金或私募股权基金持有股权、合伙权益或其他所有权权益的任何对冲基金或私募基金,联邦储备委员会均可允许银行实体与其达成任何大宗经纪交易,前提是——

(i)对于该银行实体组建和要约的对冲基金或私募股权基金而言,该银行实体遵守了第(d)(1)(G)子条所述每项限制;

(ii)该银行实体的首席执行官(或与之相当的管理人员)每年提供一份关于第(d)(1)(g)(v)子条规定的各项条件均已得到满足的书面自查证明(证明中的信息出现重大变更的,该首席执行官或与之相当的管理人员有责任予以更新);且

(iii)联邦储备委员会已判定该交易有助于实现该银行实体安全稳健的运营和状况。

(B)**对大宗经纪交易的处理**。——就第(A)子款而言,该子款所述大宗经纪交易应受制于《联邦储备法》第23B条(《美国法典》第十二编第371c—1节)的规定,如同交易的对手方是该银行实体的关联方。

(4)**对受联邦储备委员会监管的非银行金融公司的适用**。——相应的联邦银行业监管机关、证券交易委员会和商品期货交易委员会应根据第(b)(2)子条的规定制定规则,对受联邦储备委员会监管的非银行金融公司施加附加资本成本要求或其他限制,以应对本子条第(1)款、第(2)款和第(3)款所述银行实体的风险和利益冲突。

financial companies supervised by the Board to address the risks to and conflicts of interest of banking entities described in paragraphs (1), (2), and (3) of this subsection.

"(g) RULES OF CONSTRUCTION. —

"(1) LIMITATION ON CONTRARY AUTHORITY. — Except as provided in this section, notwithstanding any other provision of law, the prohibitions and restrictions under this section shall apply to activities of a banking entity or nonbank financial company supervised by the Board, even if such activities are authorized for a banking entity or nonbank financial company supervised by the Board.

"(2) SALE OR SECURITIZATION OF LOANS. — Nothing in this section shall be construed to limit or restrict the ability of a banking entity or nonbank financial company supervised by the Board to sell or securitize loans in a manner otherwise permitted by law.

"(3) AUTHORITY OF FEDERAL AGENCIES AND STATE REGULATORY AUTHORITIES. — Nothing in this section shall be construed to limit the inherent authority of any Federal agency or State regulatory authority under otherwise applicable provisions of law.

"(h) DEFINITIONS. — In this section, the following definitions shall apply:

"(1) BANKING ENTITY. — The term 'banking entity' means any insured depository institution (as defined in section 3 of the Federal Deposit Insurance Act (12 U.S.C. 1813)), any company that controls an insured depository institution, or that is treated as a bank holding company for purposes of section 8 of the International Banking Act of 1978, and any affiliate or subsidiary of any such entity. For purposes of this paragraph, the term 'insured depository institution' does not include an institution that functions solely in a trust or fiduciary capacity, if —

"(A) all or substantially all of the deposits of such institution are in trust funds and are received in a bona fide fiduciary capacity;

"(B) no deposits of such institution which are insured by the Federal Deposit Insurance Corporation are offered or marketed by or through an affiliate of such institution;

"(C) such institution does not accept demand deposits or deposits that the depositor may withdraw by check or similar means for payment to third parties or others or make commercial loans; and

"(D) such institution does not —

"(i) obtain payment or payment related services from any Federal Reserve bank, including any service referred to in section 11A of the Federal Reserve Act (12 U.S.C. 248a); or

"(ii) exercise discount or borrowing privileges pursuant to section 19 (b)(7) of the Federal Reserve Act (12 U.S.C. 461 (b)(7)).

"(2) HEDGE FUND; PRIVATE EQUITY FUND. — The terms 'hedge fund' and 'private equity fund' mean an issuer that would be an investment company, as defined in the

(g)**解释规则**。——

(1)**针对相反权力的限制**。——除本条规定的情形外,无论是否存在任何不同法律规定,受联邦储备委员会监管的银行实体或非银行金融公司的活动即使已获核准,亦应适用本条各项禁止性规定和限制。

(2)**贷款的出售或证券化**。——受联邦储备委员会监管的银行实体或非银行金融公司可以按法律允许的其他方式出售贷款或将贷款证券化,本条中的任何规定均不得被解释为构成对该等能力的限制或约束。

(3)**联邦机关和州监管部门的权力**。——本条中的任何规定均不得被解释为对任何联邦机关或州监管机构根据其他适用的法律规定享有的固有权力构成限制。

(h)**定义**。——就本条而言,应适用如下定义:

(1)**银行实体**。——'银行实体'一词系指:任何参保存款机构[定义见《联邦存款保险法》第3条(《美国法典》第十二编第1813节)]、控制参保存款机构或被作为《1978年国际银行法》第8条意义上的银行控股公司处理的任何公司,以及任何上述实体的任何关联方或子公司。就本款而言,在下列情形下,'参保存款机构'一词不包括仅履行信托或受信职能的机构——

(A)该机构的全部存款或基本全部存款均处于信托基金之中,且信托基金系以善意受信义务人的身份接收该等存款;

(B)联邦存款保险公司为之提供保险的该机构的任何存款均未由其关联方或通过其关联方要约或推介;

(C)该机构不接受具有以下特征的活期存款或存款:存款人可通过支票或类似手段提取,用于向第三方或其他人支付或作为商业贷款使用的存款;且

(D)该机构——

(i)未获取任何联邦储备银行的支付或与支付相关的服务,包括《联邦储备法》第11A条(《美国法典》第十二编第248a节)所述的任何服务;或

(ii)未根据《联邦储备法》第19(b)(7)条[《美国法典》第十二编第461(b)(7)节]行使贴现或借款权。

(2)**对冲基金;私募股权基金**。——'对冲基金'和'私募股权基金'系指,若非适用了《1940投资公司法》第3(c)(1)条或第3(c)(7)条之规定,将会构成投资公司(定义

Investment Company Act of 1940 (15 U.S.C. 80a-1 et seq.), but for section 3 (c)(1) or 3 (c)(7) of that Act, or such similar funds as the appropriate Federal banking agencies, the Securities and Exchange Commission, and the Commodity Futures Trading Commission may, by rule, as provided in subsection (b)(2), determine.

"(3) NONBANK FINANCIAL COMPANY SUPERVISED BY THE BOARD. — The term 'nonbank financial company supervised by the Board' means a nonbank financial company supervised by the Board of Governors, as defined in section 102 of the Financial Stability Act of 2010.

"(4) PROPRIETARY TRADING. — The term 'proprietary trading', when used with respect to a banking entity or nonbank financial company supervised by the Board, means engaging as a principal for the trading account of the banking entity or nonbank financial company supervised by the Board in any transaction to purchase or sell, or otherwise acquire or dispose of, any security, any derivative, any contract of sale of a commodity for future delivery, any option on any such security, derivative, or contract, or any other security or financial instrument that the appropriate Federal banking agencies, the Securities and Exchange Commission, and the Commodity Futures Trading Commission may, by rule as provided in subsection (b)(2), determine.

"(5) SPONSOR. — The term to 'sponsor' a fund means —

"(A) to serve as a general partner, managing member, or trustee of a fund;

"(B) in any manner to select or to control (or to have employees, officers, or directors, or agents who constitute) a majority of the directors, trustees, or management of a fund; or

"(C) to share with a fund, for corporate, marketing, promotional, or other purposes, the same name or a variation of the same name.

"(6) TRADING ACCOUNT. — The term 'trading account' means any account used for acquiring or taking positions in the securities and instruments described in paragraph (4) principally for the purpose of selling in the near term (or otherwise with the intent to resell in order to profit from short-term price movements), and any such other accounts as the appropriate Federal banking agencies, the Securities and Exchange Commission, and the Commodity Futures Trading Commission may, by rule as provided in subsection (b)(2), determine.

"(7) ILLIQUID FUND. —

"(A) IN GENERAL. — The term 'illiquid fund' means a hedge fund or private equity fund that —

"(i) as of May 1, 2010, was principally invested in, or was invested and contractually committed to principally invest in, illiquid assets, such as portfolio companies, real estate investments, and venture capital investments; and

见《1940年投资公司法》(《美国法典》第十五编第80a—1节及其后条文))的发行人，或者相应的联邦银行业监管机关、证券交易委员会和商品期货交易委员会根据第(b)(2)子条之规定发布的规则确定的类似基金。

(3)**受联邦储备委员会监管的非银行金融公司**。——‘受联邦储备委员会监管的非银行金融公司’一词系指受美国联邦储备委员会监管的非银行金融公司(定义见《2010年金融稳定法》第102条)。

(4)**自营交易**。——就受联邦储备委员会监管的银行实体或非银行金融公司而言，‘自营交易’一词系指，该等受联邦储备委员会监管的银行实体或非银行金融公司为自身的交易账户从事以下交易：买入、卖出或以其他方式取得或处置任何证券、任何衍生品或任何远期交割商品出售合约、任何该等证券、衍生品或合约的任何期权或相应的联邦银行业监管机关、证券交易委员会和商品期货交易委员会在其根据第(b)(2)子条之规定发布的规则中所判定的任何其他证券或金融工具。

(5)**发起**。——为某一基金提供‘发起’系指——

(A)担任某一基金的普通合伙人、管理团队成员或受托人；

(B)以任何方式选任或控制某一基金的过半数董事、受托人或管理团队成员(或该基金的过半数股东、受托人或管理团队成员均身为其职员、管理人员、董事或代理人)；或

(C)出于公司目的、营销目的、促销目的或其他目的与某一基金共用同一名称或同一名称的变体。

(6)**交易账户**。——‘交易账户’一词系指，以近期出售(或意图从短期价格波动中获利的转售)为主要目的，为了获得或持有第(4)款所述证券和工具的持仓所使用的任何账户，以及相应的联邦银行业监管机关、证券交易委员会和商品期货交易委员会根据第(b)(2)子条之规定发布的规则所判定的任何其他账户。

(7)**非流动性基金**。——

(A)**一般规定**。——‘非流动性基金’一词系指，具有以下特征的对冲基金或私募股权基金——

(i)截至2010年5月1日，主要投资于，或已投资于且根据合同承诺将主要投资于非流动性资产，例如投资组合公司、不动产投资和风险资本投资；且

"(ii) makes all investments pursuant to, and consistent with, an investment strategy to principally invest in illiquid assets. In issuing rules regarding this subparagraph, the Board shall take into consideration the terms of investment for the hedge fund or private equity fund, including contractual obligations, the ability of the fund to divest of assets held by the fund, and any other factors that the Board determines are appropriate.

"(B) HEDGE FUND. — For the purposes of this paragraph, the term 'hedge fund' means any fund identified under subsection (h)(2), and does not include a private equity fund, as such term is used in section 203 (m) of the Investment Advisers Act of 1940 (15 U.S.C. 80b–3 (m))."

SEC. 620. STUDY OF BANK INVESTMENT ACTIVITIES.

(a) STUDY. —

(1) IN GENERAL. — Not later than 18 months after the date of enactment of this Act, the appropriate Federal banking agencies shall jointly review and prepare a report on the activities that a banking entity, as such term is defined in the Bank Holding Company Act of 1956 (12 U.S.C. 1841 et. seq.), may engage in under Federal and State law, including activities authorized by statute and by order, interpretation and guidance.

(2) CONTENT. — In carrying out the study under paragraph (1), the appropriate Federal banking agencies shall review and consider —

(A) the type of activities or investments;

(B) any financial, operational, managerial, or reputation risks associated with or presented as a result of the banking entity engaged in the activity or making the investment; and

(C) risk mitigation activities undertaken by the banking entity with regard to the risks.

(b) REPORT AND RECOMMENDATIONS TO THE COUNCIL AND TO CONGRESS. — The appropriate Federal banking agencies shall submit to the Council, the Committee on Financial Services of the House of Representatives, and the Committee on Banking, Housing, and Urban Affairs of the Senate the study conducted pursuant to subsection (a) no later than 2 months after its completion. In addition to the information described in subsection (a), the report shall include recommendations regarding —

(1) whether each activity or investment has or could have a negative effect on the safety and soundness of the banking entity or the United States financial system;

(2) the appropriateness of the conduct of each activity or type of investment by banking entities; and

(3) additional restrictions as may be necessary to address risks to safety and soundness arising from the activities or types of investments described in subsection (a).

SEC. 621. CONFLICTS OF INTEREST.

(a) IN GENERAL. — The Securities Act of 1933 (15 U.S.C. 77a et seq.) is amended

(ii)其所有投资均系根据一项以非流动性资产投资为主的投资策略作出,且与该策略相符。联邦储备委员会在发布关于本子款的规则时,应考虑对冲基金或私募股权基金的投资条款,包括合同义务、该基金剥离其持有资产的能力以及联邦储备委员会判定确属适当的任何其他因素。

(B)**对冲基金**。——就本款而言,'对冲基金'一词系指第(h)(2)子条指明的任何基金,但不包括《1940年投资顾问法》第203(m)条[《美国法典》第十五编第80b—3(m)节]所述私募股权基金。"

第620条 关于银行投资活动的研究

(a)**研究**。——

(1)**一般规定**。——各相应的联邦银行业监管机关应于本法颁布后18个月内,共同审查银行实体{定义见《1956年银行控股公司法》[《美国法典》第十二编第1841节及其后条文]}根据联邦法律和州法律可以从事的活动(包括相关制定法、命令、解释及指引核准从事的活动),并编制审查报告。

(2)**内容**。——在按照第(1)款规定的开展研究时,相应的联邦银行业监管机关应审查并考虑——

(A)活动或投资的类型;

(B)与从事上述活动或进行上述投资的银行实体相关的或者由其导致的任何财务风险、运营风险、管理风险或声誉风险;及

(C)银行实体针对该等风险采取的风险缓释行为。

(b)**向金融稳定监督委员会和国会提交报告和建议**。——在完成第(a)子条所述研究之后2个月内,相应的联邦银行业监管机关应将研究结果提交给金融稳定监督委员会、众议院金融服务委员会和参议院银行、住房与城市事务委员会。除第(a)子条所述信息外,该报告还应包括关于以下方面的建议——

(1)各项活动或投资是否已经或可能对银行实体或美国金融体系的安全性和稳健性造成不良影响;

(2)银行实体各项活动或投资类型的适当性;及

(3)为应对第(a)子条所述活动或投资类型产生的安全性和稳健性风险而有必要施加的附加约束条件。

第621条 利益冲突

(a)**一般规定**。——在《1933年证券法》(《美国法典》第十五编第77a节及其后条

by inserting after section 27A the following:

"SEC. 27B. CONFLICTS OF INTEREST RELATING TO CERTAIN SECURITIZATIONS.

"(a) IN GENERAL. — An underwriter, placement agent, initial purchaser, or sponsor, or any affiliate or subsidiary of any such entity, of an asset-backed security (as such term is defined in section 3 of the Securities and Exchange Act of 1934 (15 U.S.C. 78c), which for the purposes of this section shall include a synthetic asset-backed security), shall not, at any time for a period ending on the date that is one year after the date of the first closing of the sale of the asset-backed security, engage in any transaction that would involve or result in any material conflict of interest with respect to any investor in a transaction arising out of such activity.

"(b) RULEMAKING. — Not later than 270 days after the date of enactment of this section, the Commission shall issue rules for the purpose of implementing subsection (a).

"(c) EXCEPTION. — The prohibitions of subsection (a) shall not apply to —

"(1) risk-mitigating hedging activities in connection with positions or holdings arising out of the underwriting, placement, initial purchase, or sponsorship of an asset-backed security, provided that such activities are designed to reduce the specific risks to the underwriter, placement agent, initial purchaser, or sponsor associated with positions or holdings arising out of such underwriting, placement, initial purchase, or sponsorship; or

"(2) purchases or sales of asset-backed securities made pursuant to and consistent with —

"(A) commitments of the underwriter, placement agent, initial purchaser, or sponsor, or any affiliate or subsidiary of any such entity, to provide liquidity for the asset-backed security, or

"(B) bona fide market-making in the asset backed security.

"(d) RULE OF CONSTRUCTION. — This subsection shall not otherwise limit the application of section 15G of the Securities Exchange Act of 1934.".

(b) EFFECTIVE DATE. — Section 27B of the Securities Act of 1933, as added by this section, shall take effect on the effective date of final rules issued by the Commission under subsection (b) of such section 27B, except that subsections (b) and (d) of such section 27B shall take effect on the date of enactment of this Act.

SEC. 622. CONCENTRATION LIMITS ON LARGE FINANCIAL FIRMS.

The Bank Holding Company Act of 1956 (12 U.S.C. 1841 et seq.) is amended by adding at the end the following:

"SEC. 14. CONCENTRATION LIMITS ON LARGE FINANCIAL FIRMS.

"(a) DEFINITIONS. — In this section —

"(1) the term 'Council' means the Financial Stability Oversight Council;

文)第27A条之后插入如下内容,作为对该法的修正:

"第27B条　与特定证券化相关的利益冲突

(a)**一般规定**。——资产支持证券(定义见《1934年证券交易法》第3条(《美国法典》第十五编第78c节);就本条而言,应包括合成资产支持证券)的承销商、配售代理人、初始购买人或保荐人或上述任何实体的任何关联方或子公司,均不得在出售资产支持证券的首次交割日后1年内的任何时候,从事将涉及或导致与其上述活动产生的交易中的任何投资者产生任何重大利益冲突的任何交易。

(b)**规则制定**。——证券交易委员会应在本条规定颁布之日后270天内,为第(a)子条的实施发布规则。

(c)**例外规定**。——第(a)子条的禁止性规定不得适用于——

(1)与因承销、配售、初始购买或保荐资产支持证券产生的头寸或持仓量相关的风险缓释套期保值行为,前提是该等行为之目的为降低承销商、配售代理人、初始购买人或保荐人与上述承销、配售、初始购买或保荐产生的头寸和持仓量相关的具体风险;或

(2)根据以下承诺或行为作出并与之相符的资产支持证券的买入或卖出——

(A)承销商、配售代理人、初始购买人或者保荐人或者上述任何实体的任何关联方或子公司为资产支持证券提供流动性的承诺,或

(B)资产支持证券的善意做市行为。

(d)**解释规则**。——本子条的规定不得另行限制《1934年证券交易法》第15G条的适用。"

(b)**生效日**。——本条增加的《1933年证券法》第27B条应于证券交易委员会根据该第27B条第(b)子条发布的最终规则之生效日生效,但是该第27B条的第(b)子条和第(d)子条应于本法颁布之日生效。

第622条　大型金融公司的集中度限制

在《1956年银行控股公司法》(《美国法典》第十二编第1841节及其后条文)结尾处增加如下内容,作为对该法的修订:

"第14条　大型金融公司的集中度限制

(a)**定义**。——就本条而言——

(1)'金融稳定监督委员会'一词系指美国金融稳定监督委员会;

“(2) the term ‘financial company’ means —

“(A) an insured depository institution;

“(B) a bank holding company;

“(C) a savings and loan holding company;

“(D) a company that controls an insured depository institution;

“(E) a nonbank financial company supervised by the Board under title I of the Dodd–Frank Wall Street Reform and Consumer Protection Act; and

“(F) a foreign bank or company that is treated as a bank holding company for purposes of this Act; and

“(3) the term ‘liabilities’ means —

“(A) with respect to a United States financial company —

“(i) the total risk–weighted assets of the financial company, as determined under the risk–based capital rules applicable to bank holding companies, as adjusted to reflect exposures that are deducted from regulatory capital; less

“(ii) the total regulatory capital of the financial company under the risk–based capital rules applicable to bank holding companies;

“(B) with respect to a foreign–based financial company —

“(i) the total risk–weighted assets of the United States operations of the financial company, as determined under the applicable risk–based capital rules, as adjusted to reflect exposures that are deducted from regulatory capital; less

“(ii) the total regulatory capital of the United States operations of the financial company, as determined under the applicable risk–based capital rules; and

“(C) with respect to an insurance company or other nonbank financial company supervised by the Board, such assets of the company as the Board shall specify by rule, in order to provide for consistent and equitable treatment of such companies.

“(b) CONCENTRATION LIMIT. — Subject to the recommendations by the Council under subsection (e), a financial company may not merge or consolidate with, acquire all or substantially all of the assets of, or otherwise acquire control of, another company, if the total consolidated liabilities of the acquiring financial company upon consummation of the transaction would exceed 10 percent of the aggregate consolidated liabilities of all financial companies at the end of the calendar year preceding the transaction.

“(c) EXCEPTION TO CONCENTRATION LIMIT. — With the prior written consent of the Board, the concentration limit under subsection (b) shall not apply to an acquisition —

“(1) of a bank in default or in danger of default;

“(2) with respect to which assistance is provided by the Federal Deposit Insurance Corporation under section 13 (c) of the Federal Deposit Insurance Act (12 U.S.C. 1823(c)); or

(2)‘金融公司’一词系指——

(A)参保存款机构;

(B)银行控股公司;

(C)储贷控股公司;

(D)控制参保存款机构的公司;

(E)根据《多德—弗兰克华尔街改革与消费者保护法》第一编规定接受联邦储备委员会监管的非银行金融公司;及

(F)在本法中被作为银行控股公司处理的外国银行或公司;且

(3)‘负债’一词——

(A)就美国金融公司而言,系指——

(i)根据适用于银行控股公司的风险基础资本规则确定的,为反映从监管资本中扣除的风险敞口而经过调整的该金融公司的风险加权资产总额;减去

(ii)根据适用于银行控股公司的风险基础资本规则确定的该金融公司的监管资本总额;

(B)就外国金融公司而言,系指——

(i)根据适用的风险基础资本规则确定的,为反映从监管资本中扣除的风险敞口而经过调整的该金融公司的美国运营的风险加权资产总额;减去

(ii)根据适用的风险基础资本规则确定的该金融公司的美国运营的监管资本总额;及

(C)就受联邦储备委员会监管的保险公司或其他非银行金融公司而言,指联邦储备委员会为公平、一致地对待该等公司而发布的规则所指明的资产。

(b)**集中度限制**。——在不违反金融稳定监督委员会根据第(e)子条提出的建议的前提下,如金融公司与另一公司兼并或合并,或者收购另一公司的全部资产或基本全部资产或者通过其他方式取得另一公司的控制权,将导致在上述交易合同订立之时,作为收购方的金融公司的并表负债总额将超过截至上述交易的前一日历年年末所有金融公司并表负债总额的10%,则该公司不得进行该等兼并、合并、收购或取得控制权。

(c)**集中度限制的例外规定**。——经联邦储备委员会事先书面同意,第(b)子条所述集中度限制不得适用于——

(1)对违约或有违约之虞银行的收购;

(2)联邦存款保险公司根据《联邦存款保险法》第13(c)条[《美国法典》第十二编第1823(c)节]的规定为之提供援助的收购;或

"(3) that would result only in a de minimis increase in the liabilities of the financial company.

"(d) RULEMAKING AND GUIDANCE. — The Board shall issue regulations implementing this section in accordance with the recommendations of the Council under subsection (e), including the definition of terms, as necessary. The Board may issue interpretations or guidance regarding the application of this section to an individual financial company or to financial companies in general.

"(e) COUNCIL STUDY AND RULEMAKING. —

"(1) STUDY AND RECOMMENDATIONS. — Not later than 6 months after the date of enactment of this section, the Council shall —

"(A) complete a study of the extent to which the concentration limit under this section would affect financial stability, moral hazard in the financial system, the efficiency and competitiveness of United States financial firms and financial markets, and the cost and availability of credit and other financial services to households and businesses in the United States; and

"(B) make recommendations regarding any modifications to the concentration limit that the Council determines would more effectively implement this section.

"(2) RULEMAKING. — Not later than 9 months after the date of completion of the study under paragraph (1), and notwithstanding subsections (b) and (d), the Board shall issue final regulations implementing this section, which shall reflect any recommendations by the Council under paragraph (1)(B).".

SEC. 623. INTERSTATE MERGER TRANSACTIONS.

(a) INTERSTATE MERGER TRANSACTIONS. — Section 18 (c) of the Federal Deposit Insurance Act (12 U.S.C. 1828 (c)) is amended by adding at the end the following:

"(13)(A) Except as provided in subparagraph (B), the responsible agency may not approve an application for an interstate merger transaction if the resulting insured depository institution (including all insured depository institutions which are affiliates of the resulting insured depository institution), upon consummation of the transaction, would control more than 10 percent of the total amount of deposits of insured depository institutions in the United States.

"(B) Subparagraph (A) shall not apply to an interstate merger transaction that involves 1 or more insured depository institutions in default or in danger of default, or with respect to which the Corporation provides assistance under section 13.

"(C) In this paragraph —

"(i) the term 'interstate merger transaction' means a merger transaction involving 2 or more insured depository institutions that have different home States and that are not affiliates; and

(3)将仅导致金融公司负债微量提高的收购。

(d)**规则制定和指引**。——联邦储备委员会应根据第(e)子条所述金融稳定监督委员会建议,发布本条的实施规章,包括对术语进行必要的定义。联邦储备委员会可以针对某一具体金融公司或一般性地针对各金融公司发布与本条的适用相关的解释或指引。

(e)**金融稳定监督委员会的研究和规则制定**。——

(1)**研究和建议**。——金融稳定监督委员会应于本条规定颁布之日后6个月内——

(A)完成如下研究:本条规定的集中度限制将在多大程度上影响金融稳定、金融体系道德风险、美国金融公司和金融市场的效率和竞争力以及美国家庭和企业获得信用和其他金融服务的成本及能力;及

(B)提供其判定为将有助于更有效地实施本条规定的关于任何修改集中度限制的建议。

(2)**规则制定**。——无论第(b)子条和第(d)子条如何规定,自第(1)款要求开展的研究完成后9个月内,联邦储备委员会应发布本条的最终实施规章,规章中应反映第(1)(B)款所述金融稳定监督委员会的任何建议。”

第623条　州际兼并交易

(a)**州际兼并交易**。——在《联邦存款保险法》第18(c)条[《美国法典》第十二编第1828(c)节]结尾处增加如下内容,作为对该条的修正:

“(13)(A)除第(B)子款规定的情形外,存续参保存款机构(包括身为该存续参保存款机构关联方的全部参保存款机构)在某项州际兼并交易合同订立之后将会控制美国境内所有参保存款机构10%以上存款总额的,负责机关不得批准该兼并交易申请。

(B)对于涉及一个或一个以上违约或有违约之虞的参保存款机构的州际兼并交易,或者联邦存款保险公司根据第13条的规定为之提供援助的州际兼并交易,不得适用第(A)子款的规定。

(C)就本款而言——

(i)‘州际兼并交易’一词系指兼并交易所涉之两个或两个以上参保存款机构的所在州彼此不同且参保存款机构互不关联的兼并交易;及

"(ii) the term 'home State' means—

"(I) with respect to a national bank, the State in which the main office of the bank is located;

"(II) with respect to a State bank or State savings association, the State by which the State bank or State savings association is chartered; and

"(III) with respect to a Federal savings association, the State in which the home office (as defined by the regulations of the Director of the Office of Thrift Supervision, or, on and after the transfer date, the Comptroller of the Currency) of the Federal savings association is located.".

(b) ACQUISITIONS BY BANK HOLDING COMPANIES.—

(1) IN GENERAL.—Section 4 of the Bank Holding Company Act of 1956 (12 U.S.C. 1843) is amended—

(A) in subsection (i), by adding at the end the following:

"(8) INTERSTATE ACQUISITIONS.—

"(A) IN GENERAL.—The Board may not approve an application by a bank holding company to acquire an insured depository institution under subsection (c)(8) or any other provision of this Act if—

"(i) the home State of such insured depository institution is a State other than the home State of the bank holding company; and

"(ii) the applicant (including all insured depository institutions which are affiliates of the applicant) controls, or upon consummation of the transaction would control, more than 10 percent of the total amount of deposits of insured depository institutions in the United States.

"(B) EXCEPTION.—Subparagraph (A) shall not apply to an acquisition that involves an insured depository institution in default or in danger of default, or with respect to which the Federal Deposit Insurance Corporation provides assistance under section 13 of the Federal Deposit Insurance Act (12 U.S.C. 1823)."; and

(B) in subsection (k)(6)(B), by striking "savings association" and inserting "insured depository institution".

(2) DEFINITIONS.—Section 2 (o)(4) of the Bank Holding Company Act of 1956 (12 U.S.C. 1841 (o)(4)) is amended—

(A) in subparagraph (B), by striking "and" at the end;

(B) in subparagraph (C)(ii), by striking the period at the end and inserting a semicolon; and

(C) by adding at the end the following:

"(D) with respect to a State savings association, the State by which the savings association is chartered; and

"(E) with respect to a Federal savings association, the State in which the home office

(ii)‘所在州’一词——

(I)就国民银行而言,系指该银行总部所在州;

(II)就州银行或州储蓄协会而言,系指州银行或州储蓄协会获得特许注册的州;及

(III)就联邦储蓄协会而言系指,该联邦储蓄协会总部所在州(‘总部’一词由储蓄机构监理局局长发布规章定义,或者由货币监理署署长在转移日或转移日之后发布规章定义)。”

(b)**银行控股公司进行的收购**。——

(1)**一般规定**。——《1956年银行控股公司法》第4条(《美国法典》第十二编第1843节)修正如下——

(A)在第(i)子条结尾处增加如下内容:

“(8)**州际收购**。——

(A)**一般规定**。——在以下情形下,联邦储备委员会不得批准银行控股公司根据第(c)(8)子条或本法任何其他条款提出的收购参保存款机构的申请——

(i)该参保存款机构所在州并非该银行控股公司所在州;且

(ii)申请人(包括身为该申请人关联方的全部参保存款机构)控制或在该收购交易合同订立之后将会控制美国境内所有参保存款机构10%以上的存款总额。

(B)**例外规定**。——对于涉及违约或有违约之虞的参保存款机构的收购,或者联邦存款保险公司根据《联邦存款保险法》第13条(《美国法典》第十二编第1823节)的规定为之提供援助的收购,不得适用第(A)子款的规定。”及

(B)在第(k)(6)(B)子条中,删除“储蓄协会”,替以“参保存款机构”。

(2)**定义**。——《1956年银行控股公司法》第2(o)(4)条[《美国法典》第十二编第1841(o)(4)节]修正如下——

(A)在第(B)子款中,删除结尾处的“且”;

(B)在第(C)(ii)子款中,删除结尾处的句号,替以分号;及

(C)在该条结尾处增加如下内容:

“(D)就州储蓄协会而言,指该储蓄协会获得特许注册的州;且

(E)就联邦储蓄协会而言,指该联邦储蓄协会总部所在州(‘总部’一词应由储蓄

(as defined by the regulations of the Director of the Office of Thrift Supervision, or, on and after the transfer date, the Comptroller of the Currency) of the Federal savings association is located.".

(c) ACQUISITIONS BY SAVINGS AND LOAN HOLDING COMPANIES. — Section 10 (e)(2) of the Home Owners' Loan Act (12 U.S.C. 1467a (e)(2)) is amended —

(1) in paragraph (2) —

(A) in subparagraph (C), by striking "or" at the end;

(B) in subparagraph (D), by striking the period at the end and inserting ", or"; and

(C) by adding at the end the following:

"(E) in the case of an application by a savings and loan holding company to acquire an insured depository institution, if —

"(i) the home State of the insured depository institution is a State other than the home State of the savings and loan holding company;

"(ii) the applicant (including all insured depository institutions which are affiliates of the applicant) controls, or upon consummation of the transaction would control, more than 10 percent of the total amount of deposits of insured depository institutions in the United States; and

"(iii) the acquisition does not involve an insured depository institution in default or in danger of default, or with respect to which the Federal Deposit Insurance Corporation provides assistance under section 13 of the Federal Deposit Insurance Act (12 U.S.C. 1823).", and

(2) by adding at the end the following:

"(7) DEFINITIONS. — For purposes of paragraph (2)(E) —

"(A) the terms 'default', 'in danger of default', and 'insured depository institution' have the same meanings as in section 3 of the Federal Deposit Insurance Act (12 U.S.C. 1813); and

"(B) the term 'home State' means —

"(i) with respect to a national bank, the State in which the main office of the bank is located;

"(ii) with respect to a State bank or State savings association, the State by which the savings association is chartered;

"(iii) with respect to a Federal savings association, the State in which the home office (as defined by the regulations of the Director of the Office of Thrift Supervision, or, on and after the transfer date, the Comptroller of the Currency) of the Federal savings association is located; and

"(iv) with respect to a savings and loan holding company, the State in which the amount of total deposits of all insured depository institution subsidiaries of such company was

机构监理局局长发布规章定义，或者由货币监理署署长在转移日或转移日之后发布规章定义)。”

(c)**储贷控股公司进行的收购**。——《业主贷款法》第10(e)(2)条[《美国法典》第十二编第1467a(e)(2)节]修正如下——

(1)在第(2)款中——

(A)删除第(C)子款结尾处的“或”;

(B)删除第(D)子款结尾处的句号,替以“,或”;及

(C)在该款结尾处增加如下内容:

“(E)储贷控股公司申请收购参保存款机构,只要——

(i)该参保存款机构所在州并非该储贷控股公司所在州;

(ii)申请人(包括身为该申请人关联方的全部参保存款机构)控制或在该收购交易合同订立之后将会控制美国境内所有参保存款机构10%以上的存款总额;且

(iii)该收购未涉及违约或有违约之虞的参保存款机构,或联邦存款保险公司根据《联邦存款保险法》第13条(《美国法典》第十二编第1823节)的规定为之提供援助的参保存款机构。”及

(2)在该条结尾处增加如下内容:

“(7)定义。——就第(2)(E)款而言——

(A)‘违约’、‘有违约之虞’和‘参保存款机构’的含义以《联邦存款保险法》第3条(《美国法典》第十二编第1813节)的定义为准;且

(B)‘所在州’一词——

(i)就国民银行而言,系指该银行总部所在州;

(ii)就州银行或州储蓄协会而言,系指州银行或州储蓄协会获得特许注册的州;且

(iii)就联邦储蓄协会而言,系指该联邦储蓄协会总部所在州(‘总部’一词应由储蓄机构监理局局长发布规章定义,或者由货币监理署署长在转移日或转移日之后发布规章定义);且

(iv)就储贷控股公司而言,系指在该公司成为储贷控股公司之日,该公司全部参保存款机构子公司存款总额中的最大份额所在州。”

the greatest on the date on which the company became a savings and loan holding company. ".

SEC. 624. QUALIFIED THRIFT LENDERS.

Section 10 (m)(3) of the Home Owners' Loan Act (12 U.S.C. 1467a (m)(3)) is amended —

(1) by striking subparagraph (A) and inserting the following:

" (A) IN GENERAL. — A savings association that fails to become or remain a qualified thrift lender shall immediately be subject to the restrictions under subparagraph (B). "; and

(2) in subparagraph (B)(i), by striking subclause (III) and inserting the following:

" (III) DIVIDENDS. — The savings association may not pay dividends, except for dividends that —

" (aa) would be permissible for a national bank;

" (bb) are necessary to meet obligations of a company that controls such savings association; and

" (cc) are specifically approved by the Comptroller of the Currency and the Board after a written request submitted to the Comptroller of the Currency and the Board by the savings association not later than 30 days before the date of the proposed payment.

" (IV) REGULATORY AUTHORITY. — A savings association that fails to become or remain a qualified thrift lender shall be deemed to have violated section 5 of the Home Owners' Loan Act (12 U.S.C. 1464) and subject to actions authorized by section 5 (d) of the Home Owners' Loan Act (12 U.S.C. 1464 (d)). ".

SEC. 625. TREATMENT OF DIVIDENDS BY CERTAIN MUTUAL HOLDING COMPANIES.

(a) IN GENERAL. — Section 10 (o) of the Home Owners' Loan Act (12 U.S.C. 1467a (o) is amended by adding at the end the following:

" (11) DIVIDENDS. —

" (A) DECLARATION OF DIVIDENDS. —

" (i) ADVANCE NOTICE REQUIRED. —Each subsidiary of a mutual holding company that is a savings association shall give the appropriate Federal banking agency and the Board notice not later than 30 days before the date of a proposed declaration by the board of directors of the savings association of any dividend on the guaranty, permanent, or other nonwithdrawable stock of the savings association.

" (ii) INVALID DIVIDENDS. — Any dividend described in clause (i) that is declared without giving notice to the appropriate Federal banking agency and the Board under clause (i), or that is declared during the 30-day period preceding the date of a proposed declaration for which notice is given to the appropriate Federal banking agency and the Board under clause (i), shall be invalid and shall confer no rights or benefits upon the holder of any such stock.

第624条　合格储蓄机构贷款人

《业主贷款法》第10(m)(3)条[《美国法典》第十二编第1467a(m)(3)节]修正如下——

(1)删除第(A)子款,替以如下内容:

"(A)**一般规定**。——未能获得或保留合格储蓄机构贷款人资格的储蓄协会应立即受制于第(B)子款的约束条件。"及

(2)删除第(B)(i)子款的第(III)子项,替以如下内容:

"(III)**股息**。——储蓄协会不得支付任何股息,除非——

(aa)股息属于国民银行可以支付的股息;

(bb)股息的支付系为履行控制该等储蓄协会的公司的义务所必需;且

(cc)储蓄协会在拟议的支付日前,至少已提前30天向货币监理署和联邦储备委员会提交书面请求,且已获得货币监理署和联邦储备委员会的特别批准。

(IV)**监管权**。——未能获得或保留合格储蓄机构贷款人资格的储蓄协会应视为违反了《业主贷款法》第5条(《美国法典》第十二编第1464节)的规定,并应受制于该法第5(d)条[《美国法典》第十二编第1464(d)节]授权的执法行动。"

第625条　特定互助控股公司对股息的处理

(a)**一般规定**。——在《业主贷款法》第10(o)条[《美国法典》第十二编第1467a(o)节]结尾处增加如下内容,作为对该条的修正:

"(11)**股息**。——

(A)**股息宣布**。——

(i) **事先通知要求**。——对于互助控股公司的每一性质为储蓄协会的子公司,如其董事会拟就该储蓄协会的担保股票、永久性股票或其他不可撤销的股票宣布任何股息,该子公司应在拟定宣布日前,至少已提前30天将该意图通知相应的联邦银行业监管机关和联邦储备委员会。

(ii)**无效股息**。——未根据第(i)项向相应的联邦银行业监管机关和联邦储备委员会发出通知便宣布第(i)项所述的任何股息的,或者根据第(i)项规定向相应的联邦银行业监管机关和联邦储备委员会发出了事先通知,但在通知的拟定宣布日之前30天期间内便宣布第(i)项所述股息的,该股息无效,且相关持股人不得因此获得任何权利或利益。

"(B) WAIVER OF DIVIDENDS. —A mutual holding company may waive the right to receive any dividend declared by a subsidiary of the mutual holding company, if—

"(i) no insider of the mutual holding company, associate of an insider, or tax-qualified or non-tax-qualified employee stock benefit plan of the mutual holding company holds any share of the stock in the class of stock to which the waiver would apply; or

"(ii) the mutual holding company gives written notice to the Board of the intent of the mutual holding company to waive the right to receive dividends, not later than 30 days before the date of the proposed date of payment of the dividend, and the Board does not object to the waiver.

"(C) RESOLUTION INCLUDED IN WAIVER NOTICE. — A notice of a waiver under subparagraph (B) shall include a copy of the resolution of the board of directors of the mutual holding company, in such form and substance as the Board may determine, together with any supporting materials relied upon by the board of directors of the mutual holding company, concluding that the proposed dividend waiver is consistent with the fiduciary duties of the board of directors to the mutual members of the mutual holding company.

"(D) STANDARDS FOR WAIVER OF DIVIDEND. —The Board may not object to a waiver of dividends under subparagraph (B) if—

"(i) the waiver would not be detrimental to the safe and sound operation of the savings association;

"(ii) the board of directors of the mutual holding company expressly determines that a waiver of the dividend by the mutual holding company is consistent with the fiduciary duties of the board of directors to the mutual members of the mutual holding company; and

"(iii) the mutual holding company has, prior to December 1, 2009 —

"(I) reorganized into a mutual holding company under subsection (o);

"(II) issued minority stock either from its mid-tier stock holding company or its subsidiary stock savings association; and

"(III) waived dividends it had a right to receive from the subsidiary stock savings association.

"(E) VALUATION. —

"(i) IN GENERAL. —The appropriate Federal banking agency shall consider waived dividends in determining an appropriate exchange ratio in the event of a full conversion to stock form.

"(ii) EXCEPTION. —In the case of a savings association that has reorganized into a mutual holding company, has issued minority stock from a mid-tier stock holding company or a subsidiary stock savings association of the mutual holding company, and has waived dividends it had a right to receive from a subsidiary savings association before December 1, 2009, the appropriate Federal banking agency shall not consider waived dividends in

(B)**放弃股息**。——就互助控股公司的子公司宣布的任何股息而言,在以下情形下,互助控股公司可以放弃接收任何股息的权利——

(i)该互助控股公司的任何内幕人士、内幕人士的业务相关人或该互助控股公司的任何具有免税资格或不具有免税资格的雇员股票福利计划,对该项弃权适用的股票类别不持有任何股份;或

(ii)该互助控股公司已在该股息的拟定支付日前,至少提前30天向联邦储备委员会发出了书面通知,说明其放弃接收该股息的意图,且联邦储备委员会并未对此提出反对意见。

(C)**弃权通知中包含的决议**。——第(B)子款所述弃权通知中应包含一份互助控股公司董事会决议的复本,以及董事会采信的任何支持性文件,表明以下结论:该项股息弃权符合董事会对互助控股公司的互助成员承担的受信义务;上述决议的格式和内容以联邦储备委员会确定的格式和内容为准。

(D)**放弃股息的认可标准**。——在以下情形下,联邦储备委员会不得反对第(B)子款所述对股息权利的放弃——

(i)该项弃权无损于相关储蓄协会的安全稳健运营;

(ii)该互助控股公司的董事会已明确判定互助控股公司对股息权利的放弃符合董事会对该互助控股公司的互助成员承担的受信义务;且

(iii)该互助控股公司在2009年12月1日之前——

(I)已重组为第(o)子条所述互助控股公司;

(II)已通过其中间控股公司或其股份储蓄协会子公司发行了少数权益股票。且

(III)已放弃了其有权接收的其股份储蓄协会子公司的股息。

(E)**估值**。——

(i)**一般规定**。——相应的联邦银行业监管机关在确定股息全部转换为股票时需采用的适当转换比率时,应考虑该等被放弃的股息。

(ii)**例外规定**。——如果在2009年12月1日前,某一储蓄协会重组为互助控股公司,已通过该互助控股公司的中间控股公司或股份储蓄协会子公司发行少数权益股票,且该重组为互助控股公司的储蓄协会已放弃其有权接收的其储蓄协会子公司的股息,则相应的联邦银行业监管机关在判定股息全部转换为股票时需采用的适当转换比率时,不应考虑该等被放弃的股息。”

determining an appropriate exchange ratio in the event of a full conversion to stock form. ".

(b) EFFECTIVE DATE. — The amendment made by subsection (a) shall take effect on the transfer date.

SEC. 626. INTERMEDIATE HOLDING COMPANIES.

The Home Owners' Loan Act (12 U.S.C. 1461 et seq.) is amended by inserting after section 10 (12 U.S.C. 1467a) the following new section:

"SEC. 10A. INTERMEDIATE HOLDING COMPANIES.

" (a) DEFINITION. — For purposes of this section:

" (1) FINANCIAL ACTIVITIES. — The term 'financial activities' means activities described in clauses (i) and (ii) of section 10 (c)(9)(A).

" (2) GRANDFATHERED UNITARY SAVINGS AND LOAN HOLDING COMPANY. — The term 'grandfathered unitary savings and loan holding company' means a company described in section 10 (c)(9)(C).

" (3) INTERNAL FINANCIAL ACTIVITIES. — The term 'internal financial activities' includes —

" (A) internal financial activities conducted by a grandfathered savings and loan holding company or any affiliate; and

" (B) internal treasury, investment, and employee benefit functions.

" (b) REQUIREMENT. —

" (1) IN GENERAL. —

" (A) ACTIVITIES OTHER THAN FINANCIAL ACTIVITIES. — If a grandfathered unitary savings and loan holding company conducts activities other than financial activities, the Board may require such company to establish and conduct all or a portion of such financial activities in or through an intermediate holding company, which shall be a savings and loan holding company, established pursuant to regulations of the Board, not later than 90 days (or such longer period as the Board may deem appropriate) after the transfer date.

" (B) OTHER ACTIVITIES. — Notwithstanding subparagraph (A), the Board shall require a grandfathered unitary savings and loan holding company to establish an intermediate holding company if the Board makes a determination that the establishment of such intermediate holding company is necessary —

" (i) to appropriately supervise activities that are determined to be financial activities; or

" (ii) to ensure that supervision by the Board does not extend to the activities of such company that are not financial activities.

" (2) INTERNAL FINANCIAL ACTIVITIES. —

" (A) TREATMENT OF INTERNAL FINANCIAL ACTIVITIES. — For purposes of this subsection, the internal financial activities of a grandfathered unitary savings and loan holding

(b)生效日。——第(a)子条作出的修正应于转移日生效。

第626条　中间控股公司

在《业主贷款法》(《美国法典》第十二编第1461节及其后条文)第10条(《美国法典》第十二编第1467a节)之后插入如下新条文,作为对该法的修正:

"第10A条　中间控股公司

(a)**定义**。——就本条而言:

(1)**金融活动**。——'金融活动'一词系指第10(c)(9)(A)条第(i)项和第(ii)项所述活动。

(2)**适用既往规定的单一储贷控股公司**。——'适用既往规定的单一储贷控股公司'一词系指第10(c)(9)(C)条所述公司。

(3)**内部金融活动**。——'内部金融活动'一词包括——

(A)适用既往规定的单一储贷控股公司或其任何关联方从事的内部金融活动;及

(B)内部财务、投资和雇员福利职能。

(b)**要求**。——

(1)**一般规定**。——

(A)**金融活动以外的活动**。——适用既往规定的单一储贷控股公司从事金融活动以外的活动的,联邦储备委员会可以要求该公司在转移日后90天内(或联邦储备委员会认为适当的更长期限内)根据联邦储备委员会的规章建立一家具有储贷控股公司身份的中间控股公司,并将其全部或部分金融活动转移至该中间控股公司开展,或者通过该公司开展其全部或部分金融活动。

(B)**其他活动**。——无论第(A)子款如何规定,如联邦储备委员会判定为实现以下目的建立中间控股公司确属必要,则联邦储备委员会应要求适用既往规定的单一储贷控股公司建立一家中间控股公司——

(i)适当地对被判定为金融活动的活动进行监管;或

(ii)确保联邦储备委员会的监管范围未延伸至该公司金融活动以外的活动。

(2)**内部金融活动**。——

(A)**对内部金融活动的处理**。——就本子条而言,不得要求适用既往规定的单一储贷控股公司将内部金融活动转移给中间控股公司。

company shall not be required to be placed in an intermediate holding company.

“(B) GRANDFATHERED ACTIVITIES. —A grandfathered unitary savings and loan holding company may continue to engage in an internal financial activity, subject to review by the Board to determine whether engaging in such activity presents undue risk to the grandfathered unitary savings and loan holding company or to the financial stability of the United States, if—

“(i) the grandfathered unitary savings and loan holding company engaged in the activity during the year before the date of enactment of this section; and

“(ii) at least 2/3 of the assets or 2/3 of the revenues generated from the activity are from or attributable to the grandfathered unitary savings and loan holding company.

“(3) SOURCE OF STRENGTH. —A grandfathered unitary savings and loan holding company that directly or indirectly controls an intermediate holding company established under this section shall serve as a source of strength to its subsidiary intermediate holding company.

“(4) PARENT COMPANY REPORTS. —The Board, may from time to time, examine and require reports under oath from a grandfathered unitary savings and loan holding company that controls an intermediate holding company, and from the appropriate officers or directors of such company, solely for purposes of ensuring compliance with the provisions of this section, including assessing the ability of the company to serve as a source of strength to its subsidiary intermediate holding company as required under paragraph (3) and enforcing compliance with such requirement.

“(5) LIMITED PARENT COMPANY ENFORCEMENT. —

“(A) IN GENERAL. —In addition to any other authority of the Board, the Board may enforce compliance with the provisions of this subsection that are applicable to any company described in paragraph (1)(A) that controls an intermediate holding company under section 8 of the Federal Deposit Insurance Act, and a company described in paragraph (1)(A) shall be subject to such section (solely for purposes of this subparagraph) in the same manner and to the same extent as if the company described in paragraph (1)(A) were a savings and loan holding company.

“(B) APPLICATION OF OTHER ACT. —Any violation of this subsection by a grandfathered unitary savings and loan holding company that controls an intermediate holding company may also be treated as a violation of the Federal Deposit Insurance Act for purposes of subparagraph (A).

“(C) NO EFFECT ON OTHER AUTHORITY. —No provision of this paragraph shall be construed as limiting any authority of the Board or any other Federal agency under any other provision of law.

“(c) REGULATIONS. —The Board—

(B)**适用既往规定的活动**。——在以下情形下,适用既往规定的单一储贷控股公司可以继续从事内部金融活动,但须接受联邦储备委员会的审查,以便联邦储备委员会判定该等适用既往规定的单一储贷控股公司从事内部金融活动是否会对其自身或美国金融稳定造成不当风险——

(i)该适用既往规定的单一储贷控股公司在本条规定颁布之日前的1年期间内即已从事上述活动;且

(ii)该活动至少2/3的资产或2/3的收入系源于或归于该适用既往规定的单一储贷控股公司。

(3)**财务后盾**。——适用既往规定的单一储贷控股公司直接或间接控制根据本条规定成立的中间控股公司的,该适用既往规定的单一储贷控股公司应作为其子公司(即该中间控股公司)的财务后盾。

(4)**母公司报告**。——联邦储备委员会可以不时要求控制一家中间控股公司的适用既往规定的单一储贷控股公司和该公司的适当管理人员或董事提交一份经宣誓程序保证所述内容真实无误的报告,并对该等报告进行审查,但其目的仅限于确保本条规定的合规,包括评估该适用既往规定的单一储贷控股公司是否符合第(3)款的要求,具有担任其子公司(即其中间控股公司)财务后盾之能力,以及强制执行该合规要求。

(5)**针对母公司实施合规要求的限制规定**。——

(A)**一般规定**。——除任何其他权力外,联邦储备委员会还可以针对第(1)(A)款所述,且控制《联邦存款保险法》第8条规定的中间控股公司的任何公司强制执行本条的适用规定,并且仅就本子款而言,第(1)(A)款所述公司应受制于《联邦存款保险法》第8条的规定,且其受制于该等规定的方式和范围如同其系一家储贷控股公司。

(B)**其他法律的适用**。——就第(A)子款而言,任何控制中间控股公司,且适用既往规定的单一储贷控股公司违反本子条任何规定的行为,均可作为违反《联邦存款保险法》的行为处理。

(C)**不影响其他权力**。——本款的任何规定均不得被解释为构成对联邦储备委员会或任何其他联邦机关根据任何其他法律规定享有的任何权力之限制。

(c)**规章**。——联邦储备委员会——

"(1) shall promulgate regulations to establish the criteria for determining whether to require a grandfathered unitary savings and loan holding company to establish an intermediate holding company under subsection (b); and

"(2) may promulgate regulations to establish any restrictions or limitations on transactions between an intermediate holding company or a parent of such company and its affiliates, as necessary to prevent unsafe and unsound practices in connection with transactions between the intermediate holding company, or any subsidiary thereof, and its parent company or affiliates that are not subsidiaries of the intermediate holding company, except that such regulations shall not restrict or limit any transaction in connection with the bona fide acquisition or lease by an unaffiliated person of assets, goods, or services.

"(d) RULES OF CONSTRUCTION. —

"(1) ACTIVITIES. — Nothing in this section shall be construed to require a grandfathered unitary savings and loan holding company to conform its activities to permissible activities.

"(2) PERMISSIBLE CORPORATE REORGANIZATION. — The formation of an intermediate holding company as required in subsection (b) shall be presumed to be a permissible corporate reorganization as described in section 10 (c)(9)(D).".

SEC. 627. INTEREST-BEARING TRANSACTION ACCOUNTS AUTHORIZED.

(a) REPEAL OF PROHIBITION ON PAYMENT OF INTEREST ON DEMAND DEPOSITS. —

(1) FEDERAL RESERVE ACT. — Section 19 (i) of the Federal Reserve Act (12 U.S.C. 371a) is amended to read as follows:

"(i) [Repealed]".

(2) HOME OWNERS' LOAN ACT. — The first sentence of section 5 (b)(1)(B) of the Home Owners' Loan Act (12 U.S.C. 1464 (b)(1)(B)) is amended by striking "savings association may not — " and all that follows through "(ii) permit any" and inserting "savings association may not permit any".

(3) FEDERAL DEPOSIT INSURANCE ACT. — Section 18 (g) of the Federal Deposit Insurance Act (12 U.S.C. 1828 (g)) is amended to read as follows:

"(g) [Repealed]".

(b) EFFECTIVE DATE. — The amendments made by subsection (a) shall take effect 1 year after the date of the enactment of this Act.

SEC. 628. CREDIT CARD BANK SMALL BUSINESS LENDING.

Section 2 (c)(2)(F)(v) of the Bank Holding Company Act of 1956 (12 U.S.C. 1841

(1)应颁发规章,以便制定相关标准,据以判定是否应要求某一适用既往规定的单一储贷控股公司按第(b)子条的规定设立中间控股公司;及

(2)可以颁发规章,对中间控股公司或其母公司与其关联方之间的交易制定任何必要的约束或限制条件,以防范在中间控股公司或其任何子公司与其母公司或其子公司之外的关联方开展交易过程中出现欠安全和欠稳健的做法;但该等规章不得对非关联主体善意收购或租赁资产、货物或服务的任何交易施加约束或限制。

(d)**解释规则**。——

(1)**活动**。——本条中的任何规定均不得被解释为要求适用既往规定的单一储贷控股公司将其活动限于获许的活动。

(2)**允许进行的公司重组**。——按照第(b)子条的要求成立中间控股公司的行为应被推定为第10(c)(9)(D)条所述的允许进行的公司重组。”

第627条　批准开立计息交易账户

(a)**支付活期存款利息的禁止性规定之废止**。——

(1)**《联邦储备法》**。——《联邦储备法》第19(i)条(《美国法典》第十二编第371a节)修正后全文如下:

“(i)[已废止]”。

(2)**《业主贷款法》**。——《业主贷款法》第5(b)(1)(B)条[《美国法典》第十二编第1464(b)(1)(B)节]第一句修正如下:删除“储蓄协会不得”直至“(ii)允许任何”的全部内容,替以“储蓄协会不得允许任何”。

(3)**《联邦存款保险法》**。——《联邦存款保险法》第18(g)条[《美国法典》第十二编第1828(g)节]修正后全文如下:

“(g)[已废止]”。

(b)**生效日**。——第(a)子条中作出的各项修正应于本法颁布日届满1年之日生效。

第628条　信用卡银行小企业贷款

在《1956年银行控股公司法》第2(c)(2)(F)(v)条[《美国法典》第十二编第1841(c)

(c)(2)(F)(v)) is amended by inserting before the period the following: ", other than credit card loans that are made to businesses that meet the criteria for a small business concern to be eligible for business loans under regulations established by the Small Business Administration under part 121 of title 13, Code of Federal Regulations".

(2)(F)(v)节]的句号前插入如下内容,作为对该条的修正:",向以下企业提供的信用卡贷款除外:符合小企业标准,且按照小企业管理局根据《联邦规章汇编》第十三编第121部分制定的规章,有资格获得企业贷款的企业"。

TITLE VII — WALL STREET TRANSPARENCY AND ACCOUNTABILITY

SEC.701. SHORT TITLE.

This title may be cited as the "Wall Street Transparency and Accountability Act of 2010".

Subtitle A — Regulation of Over–the–Counter Swaps Markets

PART I — REGULATORY AUTHORITY

SEC.711. DEFINITIONS.

In this subtitle, the terms "prudential regulator", "swap", "swap dealer", "major swap participant", "swap data repository", "associated person of a swap dealer or major swap participant", "eligible contract participant", "swap execution facility", "security–based swap", "security–based swap dealer", "major security–based swap participant", and "associated person of a security–based swap dealer or major security–based swap participant" have the meanings given the terms in section 1a of the Commodity Exchange Act (7 U.S.C. 1a), including any modification of the meanings under section 721(b) of this Act.

SEC.712. REVIEW OF REGULATORY AUTHORITY.

(a) CONSULTATION. —

(1) COMMODITY FUTURES TRADING COMMISSION. — Before commencing any rulemaking or issuing an order regarding swaps, swap dealers, major swap participants, swap data repositories, derivative clearing organizations with regard to swaps, persons associated with a swap dealer or major swap participant, eligible contract participants, or swap execution facilities pursuant to this subtitle, the Commodity Futures Trading Commission shall consult and coordinate to the extent possible with the Securities and Exchange Commission and the

第七编——华尔街透明度与问责法

第701条　简称

引述本编时,可简称为《2010年华尔街透明度与问责法》。

第 A 子编——场外互换市场监管

第 1 部分——监管权

第711条　定义

在本子编中,“审慎监管者”、“互换”、“互换交易商”、“主要互换参与者”、“互换数据存管机构”、“互换交易商或主要互换参与者的业务相关人”、“适格合约参与者”、“互换执行设施”、“证券类互换”、“证券类互换交易商”、“主要的证券类互换参与者”和“证券类互换交易商或主要的证券类互换参与者的业务相关人”等术语的含义以《商品交易法》第1a条(《美国法典》第七编第1a节)[包括本法第721(b)条作出的任何修改]的定义为准。

第712条　监管权审查

(a)**磋商**。——

(1)**商品期货交易委员会**。——针对互换、互换交易商、主要互换参与者、互换数据存管机构、互换的衍生品结算组织、互换交易商或主要互换参与者的业务相关人、适格合约参与者或互换执行设施,商品期货交易委员会在根据本子编开始任何规则制定工作或签发任何命令之前,应尽可能与证券交易委员会和审慎监管者磋商和协作,以便尽可能保证彼此监管的一致性和可比性。

prudential regulators for the purposes of assuring regulatory consistency and comparability, to the extent possible.

(2) SECURITIES AND EXCHANGE COMMISSION. — Before commencing any rulemaking or issuing an order regarding security-based swaps, security-based swap dealers, major security-based swap participants, security-based swap data repositories, clearing agencies with regard to security-based swaps, persons associated with a security-based swap dealer or major security-based swap participant, eligible contract participants with regard to security-based swaps, or security-based swap execution facilities pursuant to subtitle B, the Securities and Exchange Commission shall consult and coordinate to the extent possible with the Commodity Futures Trading Commission and the prudential regulators for the purposes of assuring regulatory consistency and comparability, to the extent possible.

(3) PROCEDURES AND DEADLINE. — Such regulations shall be prescribed in accordance with applicable requirements of title 5, United States Code, and shall be issued in final form not later than 360 days after the date of enactment of this Act.

(4) APPLICABILITY. — The requirements of paragraphs (1) and (2) shall not apply to an order issued —

(A) in connection with or arising from a violation or potential violation of any provision of the Commodity Exchange Act (7 U.S.C. 1 et seq.);

(B) in connection with or arising from a violation or potential violation of any provision of the securities laws; or

(C) in any proceeding that is conducted on the record in accordance with sections 556 and 557 of title 5, United States Code.

(5) EFFECT. — Nothing in this subsection authorizes any consultation or procedure for consultation that is not consistent with the requirements of subchapter II of chapter 5, and chapter 7, of title 5, United States Code (commonly known as the "Administrative Procedure Act").

(6) RULES; ORDERS. — In developing and promulgating rules or orders pursuant to this subsection, each Commission shall consider the views of the prudential regulators.

(7) TREATMENT OF SIMILAR PRODUCTS AND ENTITIES. —

(A) IN GENERAL. — In adopting rules and orders under this subsection, the Commodity Futures Trading Commission and the Securities and Exchange Commission shall treat functionally or economically similar products or entities described in paragraphs (1) and (2) in a similar manner.

(B) EFFECT. — Nothing in this subtitle requires the Commodity Futures Trading Commission or the Securities and Exchange Commission to adopt joint rules or orders that treat functionally or economically similar products or entities described in paragraphs (1) and (2) in an identical manner.

(2)**证券交易委员会**。——针对证券类互换、证券类互换交易商、主要的证券类互换参与者、证券类互换数据存管机构、证券类互换的结算机构、证券类互换交易商或主要的证券类互换参与者的业务相关人、证券类互换的适格合约参与者或证券类互换执行设施,证券交易委员会在根据第B子编开始任何规则制定工作或签发任何命令之前,应尽可能与商品期货交易委员会和审慎监管者磋商和协作,以便尽可能保证彼此监管的一致性和可比性。

(3)**程序及期限**。——该等规章应依照《美国法典》第五编的相关要求制定,并在本法颁布之日起360天内颁布最终版本。

(4)**适用范围**。——第(1)款及第(2)款的要求不适用于——

(A)签发的与违反或可能违反《商品交易法》(《美国法典》第七编第1节及其后条文)任何规定的行为相关的命令,或因该等行为签发的命令;

(B)签发的与违反或可能违反证券法任何规定的行为相关的命令,或因该等行为签发的命令;或

(C)在根据《美国法典》第五编第556节和第557节开展的记录在案的任何程序中签发的命令。

(5)**影响**。——本子条任何内容均不授权开展与《美国法典》第五编第五章第二子章和第七章(一般称为《行政程序法》)的要求相悖的任何磋商,亦不授权启动与该等要求相悖的任何磋商程序。

(6)**规则;命令**。——在根据本子条制定和颁发规则或命令时,证券交易委员会和商品期货交易委员会均应考虑审慎监管者的意见。

(7)**类似产品和实体的处理**。——

(A)**一般规定**。——在按本子条制定规则和命令时,商品期货交易委员会和证券交易委员会对于第(1)款和第(2)款所述的在功能上或经济上类似的产品或实体,应采取类似的处理方式。

(B)**影响**。——本子编任何内容均不要求商品期货交易委员会和证券交易委员会联合制定规则或命令,以相同方式处理第(1)款和第(2)款所述的功能上或经济上类似的产品或实体。

(8) MIXED SWAPS. — The Commodity Futures Trading Commission and the Securities and Exchange Commission, after consultation with the Board of Governors, shall jointly prescribe such regulations regarding mixed swaps, as described in section 1a(47)(D) of the Commodity Exchange Act (7 U.S.C. 1a(47)(D)) and in section 3(a)(68)(D) of the Securities Exchange Act of 1934 (15 U.S.C. 78c(a)(68)(D)), as may be necessary to carry out the purposes of this title.

(b) LIMITATION. —

(1) COMMODITY FUTURES TRADING COMMISSION. — Nothing in this title, unless specifically provided, confers jurisdiction on the Commodity Futures Trading Commission to issue a rule, regulation, or order providing for oversight or regulation of —

(A) security–based swaps; or

(B) with regard to its activities or functions concerning security–based swaps —

(i) security–based swap dealers;

(ii) major security–based swap participants;

(iii) security–based swap data repositories;

(iv) associated persons of a security–based swap dealer or major security–based swap participant;

(v) eligible contract participants with respect to security–based swaps; or

(vi) swap execution facilities with respect to security–based swaps.

(2) SECURITIES AND EXCHANGE COMMISSION. — Nothing in this title, unless specifically provided, confers jurisdiction on the Securities and Exchange Commission or State securities regulators to issue a rule, regulation, or order providing for oversight or regulation of —

(A) swaps; or

(B) with regard to its activities or functions concerning swaps —

(i) swap dealers;

(ii) major swap participants;

(iii) swap data repositories;

(iv) persons associated with a swap dealer or major swap participant;

(v) eligible contract participants with respect to swaps; or

(vi) swap execution facilities with respect to swaps.

(3) PROHIBITION ON CERTAIN FUTURES ASSOCIATIONS AND NATIONAL SECURITIES ASSOCIATIONS. —

(A) FUTURES ASSOCIATIONS. — Notwithstanding any other provision of law (including regulations), unless otherwise authorized by this title, no futures association registered under section 17 of the Commodity Exchange Act (7 U.S.C. 21) may issue a rule, regulation, or order for the oversight or regulation of, or otherwise assert jurisdiction over, for

(8)**混合互换**。——为实现本子编的宗旨,商品期货交易委员会和证券交易委员会应在与联邦储备委员会磋商后,就《商品交易法》第1a(47)(D)条[《美国法典》第七编第1a(47)(D)节]和《1934年证券交易法》第3(a)(68)(D)条[《美国法典》第十五编第78c(a)(68)(D)节]所述的混合互换联合制定规章。

(b)**限制**。——

(1)**商品期货交易委员会**。——除非另有明确规定,否则本编任何内容均不赋予商品期货交易委员会就以下各者的监管或规制发布规则、规章或命令的管辖权——

(A)证券类互换;或

(B)下述各者与证券类互换相关的活动或职能——

(i)证券类互换交易商;

(ii)主要的证券类互换参与者;

(iii)证券类互换数据存管机构;

(iv)证券类互换交易商或主要的证券类互换参与者的业务相关人;

(v)证券类互换的适格合约参与者;或

(vi)证券类互换的互换执行设施。

(2)**证券交易委员会**。——除非另有明确规定,否则本编任何内容均不赋予证券交易委员会或州证券监管者就以下各者的监管或规制发布规则、规章或命令的管辖权——

(A)互换;或

(B)下述各者与互换相关的活动或职能:

(i)互换交易商;

(ii)主要互换参与者;

(iii)互换数据存管机构;

(iv)互换交易商或主要互换参与者的业务相关人;

(v)互换的适格合约参与者;或

(vi)互换的互换执行设施。

(3)**关于特定期货协会和全国性证券协会的禁止性规定**。——

(A)**期货协会**。——除非本编另行授权,否则,无论法律(包括规章)是否存在任何不同规定,依照《商品交易法》第17条(《美国法典》第七编第21节)注册的任何期货协会均不得就任何证券类互换之监管或规制发布规则、规章或命令,也不得出于任何目的以其他方式主张对任何证券类互换的管辖权,但是,本子款对注册的期货协会检

any purpose, any security–based swap, except that this subparagraph shall not limit the authority of a registered futures association to examine for compliance with, and enforce, its rules on capital adequacy.

(B) NATIONAL SECURITIES ASSOCIATIONS. — Notwithstanding any other provision of law (including regulations), unless otherwise authorized by this title, no national securities association registered under section 15A of the Securities Exchange Act of 1934 (15 U.S.C. 78o–3) may issue a rule, regulation, or order for the oversight or regulation of, or otherwise assert jurisdiction over, for any purpose, any swap, except that this subparagraph shall not limit the authority of a national securities association to examine for compliance with, and enforce, its rules on capital adequacy.

(c) OBJECTION TO COMMISSION REGULATION. —

(1) FILING OF PETITION FOR REVIEW. —

(A) IN GENERAL. — If either Commission referred to in this section determines that a final rule, regulation, or order of the other Commission conflicts with subsection (a)(7) or (b), then the complaining Commission may obtain review of the final rule, regulation, or order in the United States Court of Appeals for the District of Columbia Circuit by filing in the court, not later than 60 days after the date of publication of the final rule, regulation, or order, a written petition requesting that the rule, regulation, or order be set aside.

(B) EXPEDITED PROCEEDING. — A proceeding described in subparagraph (A) shall be expedited by the United States Court of Appeals for the District of Columbia Circuit.

(2) TRANSMITTAL OF PETITION AND RECORD. —

(A) IN GENERAL. — A copy of a petition described in paragraph (1) shall be transmitted not later than 1 business day after the date of filing by the complaining Commission to the Secretary of the responding Commission.

(B) DUTY OF RESPONDING COMMISSION. — On receipt of the copy of a petition described in paragraph (1), the responding Commission shall file with the United States Court of Appeals for the District of Columbia Circuit —

(i) a copy of the rule, regulation, or order under review (including any documents referred to therein); and

(ii) any other materials prescribed by the United States Court of Appeals for the District of Columbia Circuit.

(3) STANDARD OF REVIEW. — The United States Court of Appeals for the District of Columbia Circuit shall —

(A) give deference to the views of neither Commission; and

(B) determine to affirm or set aside a rule, regulation, or order of the responding Commission under this subsection, based on the determination of the court as to whether the rule, regulation, or order is in conflict with subsection (a)(7) or (b), as applicable.

查其资本充足性规则是否得以遵守和执行的权力不构成限制。

(B)**全国性证券协会**。——除非本编另行授权,否则,无论法律(包括规章)是否存在任何不同规定,依据《1934年证券交易法》第15A条(《美国法典》第十五编第78o—3节)注册的任何全国性证券协会均不得就任何互换之监管或规制发布规则、规章或命令,也不得出于任何目的以其他方式主张对任何互换的管辖权,但是,本子款对全国性证券协会检查其资本充足性规则是否得以遵守和执行的权力不构成限制。

(c)**对证券交易委员会或商品期货交易委员会规章提出的异议**。——

(1)**提交司法审查请求书**。——

(A)**一般规定**。——本条所述证券交易委员会或商品期货交易委员会判定对方的最终规则、规章或命令与第(a)(7)子条或第(b)子条相冲突的,异议方可以在该等最终规则、规章或命令公布之日起60天内向哥伦比亚特区联邦巡回上诉法院提出司法审查请求书,请求法院审查并撤销该等最终规则、规章或命令。

(B)**加急处理**。——对于第(A)子款所述程序,哥伦比亚特区联邦巡回上诉法院应当进行加急处理。

(2)**请求书和记录的传送**。——

(A)**一般规定**。——作为请求方的委员会最迟应于提交第(1)款所述请求书之日起1个营业日内向作为被请求方的委员会的秘书传送一份请求书的复本。

(B)**作为被请求方的委员会的责任**。——在收到第(1)款所述请求书后,作为被请求方的委员会应向哥伦比亚特区联邦巡回上诉法院提交:

(i)被提请司法审查的规则、规章或命令(包括其中引用的任何文件)的一份复本;及

(ii)哥伦比亚特区联邦巡回上诉法院规定的任何其他材料。

(3)**审查标准**。——哥伦比亚特区联邦巡回上诉法院——

(A)不得采纳证券交易委员会或商品期货交易委员会中任何一方的意见;并

(B)应就作为被请求方的委员会的规则、规章或命令是否与第(a)(7)子条或第(b)子条(视具体情况而定)相冲突作出判定,并基于该等判定作出维持或撤销该规则、规章或命令的判定。

(4) JUDICIAL STAY. — The filing of a petition by the complaining Commission pursuant to paragraph (1) shall operate as a stay of the rule, regulation, or order until the date on which the determination of the United States Court of Appeals for the District of Columbia Circuit is final (including any appeal of the determination).

(d) JOINT RULEMAKING. —

(1) IN GENERAL. — Notwithstanding any other provision of this title and subsections (b) and (c), the Commodity Futures Trading Commission and the Securities and Exchange Commission, in consultation with the Board of Governors, shall further define the terms "swap", "security-based swap", "swap dealer", "security-based swap dealer", "major swap participant", "major security-based swap participant", "eligible contract participant", and "security-based swap agreement" in section 1a(47)(A)(v) of the Commodity Exchange Act (7 U.S.C. 1a(47)(A)(v)) and section 3(a)(78) of the Securities Exchange Act of 1934 (15 U.S.C. 78c(a)(78)).

(2) AUTHORITY OF THE COMMISSIONS. —

(A) IN GENERAL. — Notwithstanding any other provision of this title, the Commodity Futures Trading Commission and the Securities and Exchange Commission, in consultation with the Board of Governors, shall jointly adopt such other rules regarding such definitions as the Commodity Futures Trading Commission and the Securities and Exchange Commission determine are necessary and appropriate, in the public interest, and for the protection of investors.

(B) TRADE REPOSITORY RECORDKEEPING. — Notwithstanding any other provision of this title, the Commodity Futures Trading Commission and the Securities and Exchange Commission, in consultation with the Board of Governors, shall engage in joint rulemaking to jointly adopt a rule or rules governing the books and records that are required to be kept and maintained regarding security-based swap agreements by persons that are registered as swap data repositories under the Commodity Exchange Act, including uniform rules that specify the data elements that shall be collected and maintained by each repository.

(C) BOOKS AND RECORDS. — Notwithstanding any other provision of this title, the Commodity Futures Trading Commission and the Securities and Exchange Commission, in consultation with the Board of Governors, shall engage in joint rulemaking to jointly adopt a rule or rules governing books and records regarding security-based swap agreements, including daily trading records, for swap dealers, major swap participants, security-based swap dealers, and security-based swap participants.

(D) COMPARABLE RULES. — Rules and regulations prescribed jointly under this title by the Commodity Futures Trading Commission and the Securities and Exchange Commission shall be comparable to the maximum extent possible, taking into consideration differences in instruments and in the applicable statutory requirements.

(4)**司法中止**。——作为请求方的委员会根据第(1)款提交请求书的,被提请司法审查的规则、规章或命令即应中止适用,直至哥伦比亚特区联邦巡回上诉法院作出的判定产生终局效力之日(法院的判定被提起上诉的,则直至该等上诉获得最终解决之日)。

(d)**联合制定规则**。——

(1)**一般规定**。——无论本编和第(b)子条和第(c)子条是否存在任何不同规定,商品期货交易委员会和证券交易委员会应在与联邦储备委员会磋商后,对《商品交易法》第1a(47)(A)(v)条[《美国法典》第七编第1a(47)(A)(v)节]和《1934年证券交易法》第3(a)(78)条[《美国法典》第十五编第78c(a)(78)节]中的"互换"、"证券类互换"、"互换交易商"、"证券类互换交易商"、"主要互换参与者"、"主要的证券类互换参与者"、"适格合约参与者"及"证券类互换协议"等术语作出进一步界定。

(2)**证券交易委员会和商品期货交易委员会的权力**。——

(A)**一般规定**。——无论本编是否存在任何不同规定,商品期货交易委员会和证券交易委员会应在与联邦储备委员会磋商后,针对上述定义联合制定双方均判定符合公共利益并且对于保护投资者确属必要且适当的其他规则。

(B)**交易信息存管机构的记录保存**。——无论本编是否存在任何不同规定,商品期货交易委员会和证券交易委员会应在与联邦储备委员会磋商后,联合制定规则,对根据《商品交易法》注册为互换数据存管机构的主体需要就证券类互换协议保存和维护的账簿和记录进行规制,包括就各存管机构均应收集并保存的数据元素制定统一规则。

(C)**账簿及记录**。——无论本编是否存在任何不同规定,商品期货交易委员会和证券交易委员会应在与联邦储备委员会磋商后,联合制定规则,对证券类互换协议的账簿和记录进行规制,包括就互换交易商、主要互换参与者、证券类互换交易商以及证券类互换参与者的每日交易记录制定规则。

(D)**规则的可比性**。——商品期货交易委员会和证券交易委员会根据本编联合制定的规则及规章,应在考虑不同工具之间差异的基础上以及在该等工具适用的法定要求差异的基础上,具有尽可能高的可比性。

(E) TRACKING UNCLEARED TRANSACTIONS. — Any rules prescribed under subparagraph (A) shall require the maintenance of records of all activities relating to security–based swap agreement transactions defined under subparagraph (A) that are not cleared.

(F) SHARING OF INFORMATION. — The Commodity Futures Trading Commission shall make available to the Securities and Exchange Commission information relating to security–based swap agreement transactions defined in subparagraph (A) that are not cleared.

(3) FINANCIAL STABILITY OVERSIGHT COUNCIL. — In the event that the Commodity Futures Trading Commission and the Securities and Exchange Commission fail to jointly prescribe rules pursuant to paragraph (1) or (2) in a timely manner, at the request of either Commission, the Financial Stability Oversight Council shall resolve the dispute —

(A) within a reasonable time after receiving the request;

(B) after consideration of relevant information provided by each Commission; and

(C) by agreeing with 1 of the Commissions regarding the entirety of the matter or by determining a compromise position.

(4) JOINT INTERPRETATION. — Any interpretation of, or guidance by either Commission regarding, a provision of this title, shall be effective only if issued jointly by the Commodity Futures Trading Commission and the Securities and Exchange Commission, after consultation with the Board of Governors, if this title requires the Commodity Futures Trading Commission and the Securities and Exchange Commission to issue joint regulations to implement the provision.

(e) GLOBAL RULEMAKING TIMEFRAME. — Unless otherwise provided in this title, or an amendment made by this title, the Commodity Futures Trading Commission or the Securities and Exchange Commission, or both, shall individually, and not jointly, promulgate rules and regulations required of each Commission under this title or an amendment made by this title not later than 360 days after the date of enactment of this Act.

(f) RULES AND REGISTRATION BEFORE FINAL EFFECTIVE DATES. — Beginning on the date of enactment of this Act and notwithstanding the effective date of any provision of this Act, the Commodity Futures Trading Commission and the Securities and Exchange Commission may, in order to prepare for the effective dates of the provisions of this Act —

(1) promulgate rules, regulations, or orders permitted or required by this Act;

(2) conduct studies and prepare reports and recommendations required by this Act;

(3) register persons under the provisions of this Act; and

(4) exempt persons, agreements, contracts, or transactions from provisions of this Act,

(E)**跟踪非集中结算的交易**。——对于第(A)子款定义的非集中结算的基于证券的互换协议交易,根据第(A)子款制定的任何规则均应要求保存与该等交易相关的活动之记录。

(F)**信息共享**。——对于第(A)子款定义的非集中结算的证券类互换协议交易,商品期货交易委员会应向证券交易委员会提供与该等交易相关的信息。

(3)**金融稳定监督委员会**。——商品期货交易委员会和证券交易委员会未及时根据第(1)款或第(2)款联合制定规则的,则二者中任何一方提出请求之后,金融稳定监督委员会应按如下规定解决争议——

(A)在收到请求后的合理时间内解决争议;

(B)先审议商品期货交易委员会和证券交易委员会提供的相关信息,再解决争议;及

(C)通过完全支持证券交易委员会和商品期货交易委员会中任何一方对争议事项的看法的方式,或通过确定一个折中立场的方式,解决争议。

(4)**联合解释**。——如果本编要求商品期货交易委员会和证券交易委员会联合发布规章,以便实施本编的任何规定,则商品期货交易委员会或证券交易委员会对该规定的任何解释或指引必须由双方在与联邦储备委员会磋商后联合颁布后方可生效。

(e)**规则制定的统一时间表**。——除非本编或本编作出的修正另有规定,否则,商品期货交易委员会或证券交易委员会或二者应在本法颁布之日起360天内,按照本编或本编所做修正的要求单独(而非联合)颁发相关规则及规章。

(f)**在最终生效日之前制定规则及进行注册**。——自本法颁布之日起(不考虑本法任何规定何时生效),商品期货交易委员会和证券交易委员会可以出于为使本法规定按时生效而做好准备之目的——

(1)颁发本法许可或要求的规则、规章或命令;

(2)开展研究并编制本法要求的报告和建议;

(3)按照本法规定对相关主体进行注册;及

(4)根据本法的条款豁免相关主体、协议、合约或交易适用本法规定,但第(1)款

under the terms contained in this Act, provided, however, that no action by the Commodity Futures Trading Commission or the Securities and Exchange Commission described in paragraphs (1) through (4) shall become effective prior to the effective date applicable to such action under the provisions of this Act.

SEC.713. PORTFOLIO MARGINING CONFORMING CHANGES.

(a) SECURITIES EXCHANGE ACT OF 1934. — Section 15(c)(3) of the Securities Exchange Act of 1934 (15 U.S.C. 78o (c) (3)) is amended by adding at the end the following:

"(C) Notwithstanding any provision of sections 2(a)(1)(C)(i) or 4d(a)(2) of the Commodity Exchange Act and the rules and regulations thereunder, and pursuant to an exemption granted by the Commission under section 36 of this title or pursuant to a rule or regulation, cash and securities may be held by a broker or dealer registered pursuant to subsection (b)(1) and also registered as a futures commission merchant pursuant to section 4f(a)(1) of the Commodity Exchange Act, in a portfolio margining account carried as a futures account subject to section 4d of the Commodity Exchange Act and the rules and regulations thereunder, pursuant to a portfolio margining program approved by the Commodity Futures Trading Commission, and subject to subchapter IV of chapter 7 of title 11 of the United States Code and the rules and regulations thereunder. The Commission shall consult with the Commodity Futures Trading Commission to adopt rules to ensure that such transactions and accounts are subject to comparable requirements to the extent practicable for similar products.".

(b) COMMODITY EXCHANGE ACT. — Section 4d of the Commodity Exchange Act (7 U.S.C. 6d) is amended by adding at the end the following:

"(h) Notwithstanding subsection (a)(2) or the rules and regulations thereunder, and pursuant to an exemption granted by the Commission under section 4(c) of this Act or pursuant to a rule or regulation, a futures commission merchant that is registered pursuant to section 4f(a)(1) of this Act and also registered as a broker or dealer pursuant to section 15 (b)(1) of the Securities Exchange Act of 1934 may, pursuant to a portfolio margining program approved by the Securitiesand Exchange Commission pursuant to section 19(b) of the Securities Exchange Act of 1934, hold in a portfolio margining account carried as a securities account subject to section 15(c)(3) of the Securities Exchange Act of 1934 and the rules and regulations thereunder, a contract for the purchase or sale of a commodity for future delivery or an option on such a contract, and any money, securities or other property received from a customer to margin, guarantee or secure such a contract, or accruing to a customer as the result of such a contract. The Commission shall consult with the Securities and Exchange Commission to adopt rules to ensure that such transactions and accounts are subject to comparable requirements to the extent practical for similar products.".

至第(4)款所述商品期货交易委员会或证券交易委员会采取的任何行动均不得在本法规定的该等行动的生效日之前生效。

第713条　投资组合保证金制度规定的一致性变更

(a)**《1934年证券交易法》**。——在《1934年证券交易法》第15(c)(3)条[《美国法典》第十五编第78o(c)(3)节]结尾处增加如下内容,作为对该条的修正:

"(C)无论《商品交易法》第2(a)(1)(C)(i)条或第4d(a)(2)条及依上述条文制定的规则和规章如何规定,根据证券交易委员会依照本编第36条或某项规则或规章授予的豁免,依第(b)(1)子条注册的经纪商或自营商同时也根据《商品交易法》第4f(a)(1)条注册为期货经纪商的,可根据商品期货交易委员会批准的且受制于《美国法典》第十一编第七章第四子章及依其制定的规则和规章的投资组合保证金计划,在投资组合保证金账户中持有现金和证券,但该等保证金账户应为受制于《商品交易法》第4d条及依其制定的规则和规章的期货账户。经与商品期货交易委员会磋商,证券交易委员会应制定相关规则,确保该等交易和账户在可行范围内受制于类似产品的可比要求。"

(b)**《商品交易法》**。——在《商品交易法》第4d条(《美国法典》第七编第6d节)结尾处增加如下内容,作为对该条的修正:

"(h)无论第(a)(2)子条或依其制定的规则或规章如何规定,根据本法第4f(a)(1)条注册的期货经纪商同时也根据《1934年证券交易法》第15(b)(1)条注册为经纪商或自营商的,该期货经纪商可以基于商品期货交易委员会依据本法第4(c)条或某项规则或规章授予的豁免资格,按照证券交易委员会依《1934年证券交易法》第19(b)条批准的投资组合保证金计划,在投资组合保证金账户中持有远期交割商品买卖合约或该等合约的期权,以及从客户处收到的用于为该等合约提供保证金、保证或担保的任何现金、证券或其他财产,或因该等合约而产生并归属于该客户的任何现金、证券或其他财产,但该等保证金账户应为受制于《1934年证券交易法》第15(c)(3)条或依该条规定制定的规则和规章的证券账户。经与证券交易委员会磋商,商品期货交易委员会应制定相关规则,确保该等交易和账户在可行范围内符合适用于类似产品的具有可比性的要求。"

(c) DUTY OF COMMODITY FUTURES TRADING COMMISSION. — Section 20 of the Commodity Exchange Act (7 U.S.C. 24) is amended by adding at the end the following:

"(c) The Commission shall exercise its authority to ensure that securities held in a portfolio margining account carried as a futures account are customer property and the owners of those accounts are customers for the purposes of subchapter IV of chapter 7 of title 11 of the United States Code.".

SEC.714. ABUSIVE SWAPS.

The Commodity Futures Trading Commission or the Securities and Exchange Commission, or both, individually may, by rule or order —

(1) collect information as may be necessary concerning the markets for any types of —

(A) swap (as defined in section 1a of the Commodity Exchange Act (7 U.S.C. 1a)); or

(B) security–based swap (as defined in section 1a of the Commodity Exchange Act (7 U.S.C. 1a)); and

(2) issue a report with respect to any types of swaps or security–based swaps that the Commodity Futures Trading Commission or the Securities and Exchange Commission determines to be detrimental to —

(A) the stability of a financial market; or

(B) participants in a financial market.

SEC.715. AUTHORITY TO PROHIBIT PARTICIPATION IN SWAP ACTIVITIES.

Except as provided in section 4 of the Commodity Exchange Act (7 U.S.C. 6), if the Commodity Futures Trading Commission or the Securities and Exchange Commission determines that the regulation of swaps or security–based swaps markets in a foreign country undermines the stability of the United States financial system, either Commission, in consultation with the Secretary of the Treasury, may prohibit an entity domiciled in the foreign country from participating in the United States in any swap or security–based swap activities.

SEC.716. PROHIBITION AGAINST FEDERAL GOVERNMENT BAILOUTS OF SWAPS ENTITIES.

(a) PROHIBITION ON FEDERAL ASSISTANCE. — Notwithstanding any other provision of law (including regulations), no Federal assistance may be provided to any swaps entity with respect to any swap, security–based swap, or other activity of the swaps entity.

(b) DEFINITIONS. — In this section:

(1) FEDERAL ASSISTANCE. — The term "Federal assistance" means the use of any advances from any Federal Reserve credit facility or discount window that is not part of a program or facility with broad–based eligibility under section 13 (3) (A) of the Federal Reserve Act, Federal Deposit Insurance Corporation insurance or guarantees for the purpose of —

(A) making any loan to, or purchasing any stock, equity interest, or debt obligation of,

(c)**商品期货交易委员会的职责**。——在《商品交易法》第20条(《美国法典》第七编第24节)结尾处增加如下内容,作为对该条的修正:

“(c)商品期货交易委员会应行使其职权,确保在作为期货账户的投资组合保证金账户中持有的证券属于客户财产,且该等账户的所有人是《美国法典》第十一编第七章第四子章中规定的客户。”

第714条 滥用性互换

商品期货交易委员会或证券交易委员会一方或双方可以单独发布规则或命令——

(1)收集关于下述各者的市场必要信息——

(A)任何类型的互换[定义见《商品交易法》第1a条(《美国法典》第七编第1a节)];或

(B)任何类型的证券类互换(定义见《商品交易法》第1a条(《美国法典》第七编第1a节);及

(2)就商品期货交易委员会或证券交易委员会判定的对下列各项不利的任何类型的互换或证券类互换发布报告——

(A)某一金融市场的稳定;或

(B)某一金融市场的参与者。

第715条 禁止参与互换活动的权力

除《商品交易法》第4条《美国法典》第七编第6节)规定的情形外,如果商品期货交易委员会或证券交易委员会判定外国对互换市场或证券类互换市场的监管有损美国金融体系的稳定性,则经与财政部部长磋商,商品期货交易委员会或证券交易委员会可以禁止在该外国注册的实体在美国参与任何互换活动或证券类互换活动。

第716条 禁止联邦政府为了挽救互换实体而为其埋单

(a)**禁止提供联邦援助**。——无论法律(包括规章)是否存在任何不同规定,联邦政府不得就任何互换实体的任何互换、证券类互换或其他活动向该等互换实体提供联邦援助。

(b)**定义**。——在本条中:

(1)**联邦援助**。——“联邦援助”一词系指为了实现以下目的而使用来自联邦储备系统的任何信贷安排或贴现窗口[且该等信贷安排或贴现窗口并不属于《联邦储备法》第13(3)(A)条规定的适格主体广泛的计划或安排的一部分]的任何预支款,或使用联邦存款保险公司的保险或担保——

(A)向任何互换实体提供任何贷款或购买该实体的任何股票、股权权益或债务

any swaps entity;

(B) purchasing the assets of any swaps entity;

(C) guaranteeing any loan or debt issuance of any swaps entity; or

(D) entering into any assistance arrangement (including tax breaks), loss sharing, or profit sharing with any swaps entity.

(2) SWAPS ENTITY. —

(A) IN GENERAL. — The term "swaps entity" means any swap dealer, security-based swap dealer, major swap participant, major security-based swap participant, that is registered under —

(i) the Commodity Exchange Act (7 U.S.C. 1 et seq.); or

(ii) the Securities Exchange Act of 1934 (15 U.S.C. 78a et seq.).

(B) EXCLUSION. — The term "swaps entity" does not include any major swap participant or major security-based swap participant that is an insured depository institution.

(c) AFFILIATES OF INSURED DEPOSITORY INSTITUTIONS. — The prohibition on Federal assistance contained in subsection (a) does not apply to and shall not prevent an insured depository institution from having or establishing an affiliate which is a swaps entity, as long as such insured depository institution is part of a bank holding company, or savings and loan holding company, that is supervised by the Federal Reserve and such swaps entity affiliate complies with sections 23A and 23B of the Federal Reserve Act and such other requirements as the Commodity Futures Trading Commission or the Securities Exchange Commission, as appropriate, and the Board of Governors of the Federal Reserve System, may determine to be necessary and appropriate.

(d) ONLY BONA FIDE HEDGING AND TRADITIONAL BANK ACTIVITIES PERMITTED. — The prohibition in subsection (a) shall apply to any insured depository institution unless the insured depository institution limits its swap or security-based swap activities to:

(1) Hedging and other similar risk mitigating activities directly related to the insured depository institution's activities.

(2) Acting as a swaps entity for swaps or security-based swaps involving rates or reference assets that are permissible for investment by a national bank under the paragraph designated as "Seventh." of section 5136 of the Revised Statutes of the United States (12 U.S.C. 24), other than as described in paragraph (3).

(3) LIMITATION ON CREDIT DEFAULT SWAPS. — Acting as a swaps entity for credit default swaps, including swaps or security-based swaps referencing the credit risk of asset-backed securities as defined in section 3(a)(77) of the Securities Exchange Act of 1934 (15 U.S.C. 78c(a)(77)) (as amended by this Act) shall not be considered a bank permissible activity for purposes of subsection (d)(2) unless such swaps or security-based

凭证;

(B)购买任何互换实体的资产;

(C)为任何互换实体的任何贷款或债务发行提供担保;或

(D)与任何互换实体达成任何援助安排(包括减税)、损失分摊或利润共享约定。

(2)**互换实体**。——

(A)**一般规定**。——"互换实体"一词系指根据下列法律注册的任何互换交易商、证券类互换交易商、主要互换参与者以及主要的证券类互换参与者——

(i)《商品交易法》(《美国法典》第七编第1节及其后条文);或

(ii)《1934年证券交易法》(《美国法典》第十五编第78a节及其后条文)。

(B)**除外规定**。——"互换实体"一词不包括具有参保存款机构身份的任何主要互换参与者或主要的证券类互换参与者。

(c)**参保存款机构的关联方**。——第(a)子条中关于禁止提供联邦援助的规定不适用于拥有或设立了具有互换实体身份的关联方的参保存款机构,亦不妨碍参保存款机构拥有或设立具有互换实体身份的关联方,其前提是该等参保存款机构属于受联邦储备系统监管的银行控股公司或储贷控股公司的一部分,且具有互换实体身份的该等关联方符合《联邦储备法》第23A条和第23B条的规定以及商品期货交易委员会或证券交易委员会(视具体情况而定)及联邦储备委员会判定确属必要且适当的其他要求。

(d)**仅允许开展真正的套期保值业务和传统银行活动**。——第(a)子条中的禁止规定性适用于任何参保存款机构,除非该等参保存款机构将其互换活动或证券类互换活动限制在下列范围内:

(1)与该等参保存款机构的活动直接相关的套期保值活动及其他类似的风险缓释活动。

(2)以互换实体身份从事涉及比率或参考资产的互换活动或证券类互换活动,且该等活动属于《美国制定法》(修订版)第5136条第"7"款(《美国法典》第十二编第24节)允许的国民银行投资行为,但第(3)款所述行为除外。

(3)**对信用违约互换的限制**。——以互换实体身份从事的信用违约互换活动,包括涉及资产担保证券[定义见《1934年证券交易法》第3(a)(77)条(《美国法典》第十五编第78c(a)(77)节](以经本法修正后的版本为准)的信用风险的互换活动或证券类互换活动,不应被视为第(d)(2)子条所述的允许开展的银行活动,除非该等证券或证券类互换由以下机构进行集中结算:依据《商品交易法》注册或豁免注册为衍生品结算

swaps are cleared by a derivatives clearing organization (as such term is defined in section la of the Commodity Exchange Act (7 U.S.C. la)) or a clearing agency (as such term is defined in section 3 of the Securities Exchange Act (15 U.S.C. 78c)) that is registered, or exempt from registration, as a derivatives clearing organization under the Commodity Exchange Act or as a clearing agency under the Securities Exchange Act, respectively.

(e) EXISTING SWAPS AND SECURITY–BASED SWAPS. — The prohibition in subsection (a) shall only apply to swaps or security–based swaps entered into by an insured depository institution after the end of the transition period described in subsection (f).

(f) TRANSITION PERIOD. — To the extent an insured depository institution qualifies as a "swaps entity" and would be subject to the Federal assistance prohibition in subsection (a), the appropriate Federal banking agency, after consulting with and considering the views of the Commodity Futures Trading Commission or the Securities Exchange Commission, as appropriate, shall permit the insured depository institution up to 24 months to divest the swaps entity or cease the activities that require registration as a swaps entity. In establishing the appropriate transition period to effect such divestiture or cessation of activities, which may include making the swaps entity an affiliate of the insured depository institution, the appropriate Federal banking agency shall take into account and make written findings regarding the potential impact of such divestiture or cessation of activities on the insured depository institution's (1) mortgage lending, (2) small business lending, (3) job creation, and (4) capital formation versus the potential negative impact on insured depositors and the Deposit Insurance Fund of the Federal Deposit Insurance Corporation. The appropriate Federal banking agency may consider such other factors as may be appropriate. The appropriate Federal banking agency may place such conditions on the insured depository institution's divestiture or ceasing of activities of the swaps entity as it deems necessary and appropriate. The transition period under this subsection may be extended by the appropriate Federal banking agency, after consultation with the Commodity Futures Trading Commission and the Securities and Exchange Commission, for a period of up to 1 additional year.

(g) EXCLUDED ENTITIES. — For purposes of this section, the term "swaps entity" shall not include any insured depository institution under the Federal Deposit Insurance Act or a covered financial company under title II which is in a conservatorship, receivership, or a bridge bank operated by the Federal Deposit Insurance Corporation.

(h) EFFECTIVE DATE. — The prohibition in subsection (a) shall be effective 2 years following the date on which this Act is effective.

(i) LIQUIDATION REQUIRED. —

(1) IN GENERAL. —

(A) FDIC INSURED INSTITUTIONS. — All swaps entities that are FDIC insured institutions that are put into receivership or declared insolvent as a result of swap or

组织的衍生品结算组织[定义见《商品交易法》第1a条(《美国法典》第七编第1a节)],或依据《证券交易法》注册或豁免注册为结算机构的结算机构[定义见《证券交易法》第3条(《美国法典》第十五编第78c节)]。

(e)**既存的互换和证券类互换**。——第(a)子条的禁止规定仅适用于参保存款机构在第(f)子条所述过渡期结束后达成的互换或证券类互换。

(f)**过渡期**。——如果参保存款机构具有“互换实体”资格,并将受制于第(a)子条关于禁止联邦援助的规定,则经与商品期货交易委员会或证券交易委员会(视具体情况而定)磋商并考虑其意见后,相应的联邦银行业监管机关应允许,该等参保存款机构在长达24个月的期限内剥离互换实体或停止其必须注册为互换实体才能从事的活动。在为实施该等剥离或停止该等活动(其方式可能包括使互换实体成为该参保存款机构的关联方)而确定适当的过渡期时,相应的联邦银行业监管机关应考虑该等剥离或停止该等活动可能在以下各方面对该等参保存款机构产生的影响:(1)抵押贷款;(2)小企业贷款;(3)提供就业机会;及(4)资本形成,以及该等剥离或停止该等活动可能对参保存款人和联邦存款保险公司的存款保险基金产生的消极影响,并在对两种影响进行对比后作出书面认定。相应的联邦银行业监管机关还可考虑其他适当的因素,并可以对该等参保存款机构剥离该等互换实体或停止该等互换实体活动的行为施加其认为必要且适当的条件。经与商品期货交易委员会和证券交易委员会磋商,相应的联邦银行业监管机关可以将本子条规定的过渡期另行延长1年。

(g)**除外实体**。——在本条中,“互换实体”一词不包括《联邦存款保险法》中规定的任何参保存款机构或第二编中规定的处于托管或接管状态的所涉金融公司,或由联邦存款保险公司经营的过渡银行。

(h)**生效日**。——第(a)子条中的禁止性规定应自本法生效日届满2年之日生效。

(i)**清算要求**。——

(1)**一般规定**。——

(A)**在联邦存款保险公司参保的机构**。——在联邦存款保险公司参保的所有互换实体,因其互换活动或证券类互换活动而被接管或被宣布丧失偿债能力的,应根据

security–based swap activity of the swaps entities shall be subject to the termination or transfer of that swap or security–based swap activity in accordance with applicable law prescribing the treatment of those contracts. No taxpayer funds shall be used to prevent the receivership of any swap entity resulting from swap or security–based swap activity of the swaps entity.

(B) INSTITUTIONS THAT POSE A SYSTEMIC RISK AND ARE SUBJECT TO HEIGHTENED PRUDENTIAL SUPERVISION AS REGULATED UNDER SECTION 113. — All swaps entities that are institutions that pose a systemic risk and are subject to heightened prudential supervision as regulated under section 113, that are put into receivership or declared insolvent as a result of swap or security–based swap activity of the swaps entities shall be subject to the termination or transfer of that swap or security–based swap activity in accordance with applicable law prescribing the treatment of those contracts. No taxpayer funds shall be used to prevent the receivership of any swap entity resulting from swap or security–based swap activity of the swaps entity.

(C) NON–FDIC INSURED, NON–SYSTEMICALLY SIGNIFICANT INSTITUTIONS NOT SUBJECT TO HEIGHTENED PRUDENTIAL SUPERVISION AS REGULATED UNDER SECTION 113. — No taxpayer resources shall be used for the orderly liquidation of any swaps entities that are non–FDIC insured, non–systemically significant institutions not subject to heightened prudential supervision as regulated under section 113.

(2) RECOVERY OF FUNDS. — All funds expended on the termination or transfer of the swap or security–based swap activity of the swaps entity shall be recovered in accordance with applicable law from the disposition of assets of such swap entity or through assessments, including on the financial sector as provided under applicable law.

(3) NO LOSSES TO TAXPAYERS. — Taxpayers shall bear no losses from the exercise of any authority under this title.

(j) PROHIBITION ON UNREGULATED COMBINATION OF SWAPS ENTITIES AND BANKING. — At no time following adoption of the rules in subsection (k) may a bank or bank holding company be permitted to be or become a swap entity unless it conducts its swap or security–based swap activity in compliance with such minimum standards set by its prudential regulator as are reasonably calculated to permit the swaps entity to conduct its swap or security–based swap activities in a safe and sound manner and mitigate systemic risk.

(k) RULES. — In prescribing rules, the prudential regulator for a swaps entity shall consider the following factors:

(1) The expertise and managerial strength of the swaps entity, including systems for effective oversight.

(2) The financial strength of the swaps entity.

(3) Systems for identifying, measuring and controlling risks arising from the swaps

适用的法律中关于该等合约处理的规定终止或转让该等互换活动或证券类互换活动。纳税人资金不得被用于阻止任何互换实体因互换活动或证券类互换活动进入被接管状态。

(B)**产生系统性风险并应根据第113条接受更严格的审慎监管的机构**。——产生系统性风险并应根据第113条接受更严格的审慎监管的所有互换实体,因其互换活动或证券类互换活动而被接管或宣布丧失偿债能力的,应根据适用的法律中关于该等合约的处理的规定终止或转让该等互换活动或证券类互换活动。纳税人资金不得被用于阻止任何互换实体因互换活动或证券类互换活动进入被接管状态。

(C)**未在联邦存款保险公司参保、不具有系统重要性且不必根据第113条的规定接受更严格的审慎监管的机构**。——对于任何未在联邦存款保险公司参保、不具有系统重要性且不必根据第113条的规定接受更严格的审慎监管的互换实体而言,不得利用任何纳税人资源对其进行有序清算。

(2)**资金的收回**。——互换实体为终止或转让其互换活动或证券类互换活动所花费的所有资金,均应根据适用的法律通过处置该等互换实体的资产或通过计征费(包括根据适用的法律对金融行业计征费用)的方式收回。

(3)**纳税人不承担损失**。——本编中规定的任何权力的行使不得给纳税人造成任何损失。

(j)**禁止互换实体与银行业之间开展不受监管的合并**。——第(k)子条中的规则正式通过之后,银行或银行控股公司在任何时候均不得作为或成为互换实体,除非其在开展互换活动或证券类互换活动时,遵循其审慎监管者通过合理计划设定的旨在确保互换实体以安全稳健的方式开展互换活动或证券类互换活动并缓释系统性风险的最低标准。

(k)**规则**。——互换实体的审慎监管者在制定规则时应考虑以下因素:

(1)互换实体的专业技能及管理能力,包括有效的监管制度。

(2)互换实体的财力。

(3)识别、计量和控制互换实体运营所产生的风险的系统。

entity's operations.

(4) Systems for identifying, measuring and controlling the swaps entity's participation in existing markets.

(5) Systems for controlling the swaps entity's participation or entry into in new markets and products.

(l) AUTHORITY OF THE FINANCIAL STABILITY OVERSIGHT COUNCIL. — The Financial Stability Oversight Council may determine that, when other provisions established by this Act are insufficient to effectively mitigate systemic risk and protect taxpayers, that swaps entities may no longer access Federal assistance with respect to any swap, security–based swap, or other activity of the swaps entity. Any such determination by the Financial Stability Oversight Council of a prohibition of federal assistance shall be made on an institution–by–institution basis, and shall require the vote of not fewer than two–thirds of the members of the Financial Stability Oversight Council, which must include the vote by the Chairman of the Council, the Chairman of the Board of Governors of the Federal Reserve System, and the Chairperson of the Federal Deposit Insurance Corporation. Notice and hearing requirements for such determinations shall be consistent with the standards provided in title I.

(m) BAN ON PROPRIETARY TRADING IN DERIVATIVES. — An insured depository institution shall comply with the prohibition on proprietary trading in derivatives as required by section 619 of the Dodd–Frank Wall Street Reform and Consumer Protection Act.

SEC.717. NEW PRODUCT APPROVAL CFTC — SEC PROCESS.

(a) AMENDMENTS TO THE COMMODITY EXCHANGE ACT. — Section 2(a)(1)(C) of the Commodity Exchange Act (7 U.S.C. 2(a)(1)(C)) is amended —

(1) in clause (i) by striking "This" and inserting "(I) Except as provided in subclause (II), this"; and

(2) by adding at the end of clause (i) the following:

"(II) This Act shall apply to and the Commission shall have jurisdiction with respect to accounts, agreements, and transactions involving, and may permit the listing for trading pursuant to section 5c(c) of, a put, call, or other option on 1 or more securities (as defined in section 2(a)(1) of the Securities Act of 1933 or section 3(a)(10) of the Securities Exchange Act of 1934 on the date of enactment of the Futures Trading Act of 1982), including any group or index of such securities, or any interest therein or based on the value thereof, that is exempted by the Securities and Exchange Commission pursuant to section 36(a)(1) of the Securities Exchange Act of 1934 with the condition that the Commission exercise concurrent jurisdiction over such put, call, or other option; provided, however, that nothing in this paragraph shall be construed to affect the jurisdiction and authority of the Securities and Exchange Commission over such put, call, or other option.".

(4)识别、计量和控制互换实体对现有市场参与的情况的系统。

(5)控制互换实体参与或进入新市场和新产品的情况的系统。

(l)**金融稳定监督委员会的权力**。——金融稳定监督委员会可以判定,当本法中的其他规定不足以有效地缓释系统性风险并保护纳税人时,互换实体在其任何互换、证券类互换或其他活动中不得再获得联邦援助。金融稳定监督委员会的任何禁止联邦援助的判定均应在各机构的个案基础上逐一作出,并获得金融稳定监督委员会至少2/3的届时在任的成员表决通过,其中必须包括金融稳定监督委员会主席、联邦储备委员会主席及联邦存款保险公司主席的赞成票。该等判定的通知及听证要求应与第一编中规定的标准保持一致。

(m)**禁止衍生品自营交易**。——参保存款机构应当遵循《多德—弗兰克华尔街改革与消费者保护法》第619条中关于禁止衍生品自营交易的规定。

第717条　商品期货交易委员会——证券交易委员会批准新产品的程序

(a)**对《商品交易法》的修正**。——《商品交易法》第2(a)(1)(C)条[《美国法典》第七编第2(a)(1)(C)节]修正如下——

(1)删除第(i)项中的"本",增加"(I)除第(II)子项规定的情形外,本";及

(2)在第(i)项结尾处增加如下内容:

"(II)本法适用于证券交易委员会根据《1934年证券交易法》第36(a)(1)条授予豁免的涉及一只或一只以上证券[定义见《1982年期货交易法》颁布之日有效适用的《1933年证券法》第2(a)(1)条或《1934年证券交易法》第3(a)(10)条,包括该等证券的任何集合或指数,或者该等证券的任何权益或者该等集合或指数的任何权益,或者基于该等证券价值的任何权益或者基于该等集合或指数价值的任何权益]的看跌期权、看涨期权或其他期权之账户、协议和交易,商品期货交易委员会应对该等账户、协议和交易享有管辖权,并且可以允许该等看跌期权、看涨期权或其他期权按照第5c(c)条上市交易,其前提是商品期货交易委员会对该等看跌期权、看涨期权或其他期权行使的管辖权是共同管辖权。但是,本款的任何内容均不得被解释为影响证券交易委员会对该等看跌期权、看涨期权或其他期权所享有的管辖权和职权。"

(b) AMENDMENTS TO THE SECURITIES EXCHANGE ACT OF 1934. — The Securities Exchange Act of 1934 is amended by adding the following section after section 3A (15 U.S.C. 78c–1):

"SEC.3B. SECURITIES–RELATED DERIVATIVES.

"(a) Any agreement, contract, or transaction (or class thereof) that is exempted by the Commodity Futures Trading Commission pursuant to section 4 (c) (1) of the Commodity Exchange Act (7 U.S.C. 6 (c) (1)) with the condition that the Commission exercise concurrent jurisdiction over such agreement, contract, or transaction (or class thereof) shall be deemed a security for purposes of the securities laws.

"(b) With respect to any agreement, contract, or transaction (or class thereof) that is exempted by the Commodity Futures Trading Commission pursuant to section 4(c)(1) of the Commodity Exchange Act (7 U.S.C. 6 (c) (1)) with the condition that the Commission exercise concurrent jurisdiction over such agreement, contract, or transaction (or class thereof), references in the securities laws to the 'purchase' or 'sale' of a security shall be deemed to include the execution, termination (prior to its scheduled maturity date), assignment, exchange, or similar transfer or conveyance of, or extinguishing of rights or obligations under such agreement, contract, or transaction, as the context may require.".

(c) AMENDMENT TO SECURITIES EXCHANGE ACT OF 1934. — Section 19(b) of the Securities Exchange Act of 1934 (15 U.S.C. 78s(b)) is amended by adding at the end the following:

"(10) Notwithstanding paragraph (2), the time period within which the Commission is required by order to approve a proposed rule change or institute proceedings to determine whether the proposed rule change should be disapproved is stayed pending a determination by the Commission upon the request of the Commodity Futures Trading Commission or its Chairman that the Commission issue a determination as to whether a product that is the subject of such proposed rule change is a security pursuant to section 718 of the Wall Street Transparency and Accountability Act of 2010.".

(d) AMENDMENT TO COMMODITY EXCHANGE ACT. — Section 5c(c)(1) of the Commodity Exchange Act (7 U.S.C. 7a–2(c)(1)) is amended —

(1) by striking "Subject to paragraph (2)" and inserting the following:

"(A) ELECTION. — Subject to paragraph (2)"; and

(2) by adding at the end the following:

"(B) CERTIFICATION. — The certification of a product pursuant to this paragraph shall be stayed pending a determination by the Commission upon the request of the Securities and Exchange Commission or its Chairman that the Commission issue a determination as to whether the product that is the subject of such certification is a contract of sale of a commodity for future delivery, an option on such a contract, or an option on a commodity pursuant to

(b)**对《1934年证券交易法》的修正**。——在《1934年证券交易法》第3A条(《美国法典》第十五编第78c—1节)结尾处增加如下内容,作为对该法的修正:

"第3B条 与证券相关的衍生品

(a)商品期货交易委员会根据《商品交易法》第4(c)(1)条[《美国法典》第七编第6(c)(1)节]授予豁免的但证券交易委员会享有共同管辖权的任何(或任何类型的)协议、合约或交易均应视为证券法意义上的证券。

(b)对于商品期货交易委员会根据《商品交易法》第4(c)(1)条[《美国法典》第七编第6(c)(1)节]授予豁免的但证券交易委员会享有共同管辖权的任何(或任何类型的)协议、合约或交易,证券法律中提及的证券'买入'或'卖出',应根据上下文的要求,视为包括该等协议、合约或交易的执行、终止(指在预定的到期日之前终止)、转让、交换或该等协议、合约或交易规定的权利或义务的类似转移、让与或消灭。"

(c)**对《1934年证券交易法》的修正**。——在《1934年证券交易法》第19(b)条[《美国法典》第十五编第78s(b)节]结尾处增加如下内容,作为对该条的修正:

"(10)无论第(2)款如何规定,如果商品期货交易委员会或其主席请求证券交易委员会判定规则变更提案所规范的产品是否属于《2010年华尔街透明度与问责法》第718条规定的证券,则在证券交易委员会作出该等判定之前,下述期限应中止计算:证券交易委员会应通过发布命令来批准该等规则变更提案的期限,或证券交易委员会应通过发布命令来启动判定该等规则变更提案是否应予否决的程序的期限。"

(d)**对《商品交易法》的修正**。——《商品交易法》第5c(c)(1)条[《美国法典》第七编第7a—2(c)(1)节]修正如下——

(1)删除"在不违反第(2)款的前提下"并替以如下内容:

"(A)**选择**。——在不违反第(2)款的前提下";及

(2)在结尾处增加如下内容:

"(B)**自查证明**。——根据本款规定为产品提供自查证明时,如证券交易委员会或其主席请求商品期货交易委员会判定应提供自查证明的产品是否属于《2010年华尔街透明度与问责法》第718条规定的远期交割商品出售合约、该等合约的期权或商品期权,则在商品期货交易委员会作出该等判定之前,应中止提供前述自查证明。"

section 718 of the Wall Street Transparency and Accountability Act of 2010.".

SEC.718. DETERMINING STATUS OF NOVEL DERIVATIVE PRODUCTS.

(a) PROCESS FOR DETERMINING THE STATUS OF A NOVEL DERIVATIVE PRODUCT.—

(1) NOTICE.—

(A) IN GENERAL.— Any person filing a proposal to list or trade a novel derivative product that may have elements of both securities and contracts of sale of a commodity for future delivery (or options on such contracts or options on commodities) may concurrently provide notice and furnish a copy of such filing with the Securities and Exchange Commission and the Commodity Futures Trading Commission. Any such notice shall state that notice has been made with both Commissions.

(B) NOTIFICATION.— If no concurrent notice is made pursuant to subparagraph (A), within 5 business days after determining that a proposal that seeks to list or trade a novel derivative product may have elements of both securities and contracts of sale of a commodity for future delivery (or options on such contracts or options on commodities), the Securities and Exchange Commission or the Commodity Futures Trading Commission, as applicable, shall notify the other Commission and provide a copy of such filing to the other Commission.

(2) REQUEST FOR DETERMINATION.—

(A) IN GENERAL.— No later than 21 days after receipt of a notice under paragraph (1), or upon its own initiative if no such notice is received, the Commodity Futures Trading Commission may request that the Securities and Exchange Commission issue a determination as to whether a product is a security, as defined in section 3(a)(10) of the Securities Exchange Act of 1934 (15 U.S.C. 78c(a)(10)).

(B) REQUEST.— No later than 21 days after receipt of a notice under paragraph (1), or upon its own initiative if no such notice is received, the Securities and Exchange Commission may request that the Commodity Futures Trading Commission issue a determination as to whether a product is a contract of sale of a commodity for future delivery, an option on such a contract, or an option on a commodity subject to the Commodity Futures Trading Commission's exclusive jurisdiction under section 2(a)(1)(A) of the Commodity Exchange Act (7 U.S.C. 2(a)(1)(A)).

(C) REQUIREMENT RELATING TO REQUEST.— A request under subparagraph (A) or (B) shall be made by submitting such request, in writing, to the Securities and Exchange Commission or the Commodity Futures Trading Commission, as applicable.

(D) EFFECT.— Nothing in this paragraph shall be construed to prevent—

(i) the Commodity Futures Trading Commission from requesting that the Securities and Exchange Commission grant an exemption pursuant to section 36(a)(1) of the Securities Exchange Act of 1934 (15 U.S.C. 78mm(a)(1)) with respect to a product that is the subject

第718条 新型衍生产品性质的判定

(a)**新型衍生产品性质的判定程序**。——

(1)**通知**。——

(A)**一般规定**。——任何主体申请上市或交易同时包含证券和远期交割商品出售合约(或者该等合约的期权或商品期权)要素的新型衍生产品的,可同时向证券交易委员会和商品期货交易委员会发出通知并提供该等申请的复本。任何上述通知中均应说明通知已同时发送给证券交易委员会和商品期货交易委员会。

(B)**通知**。——在判定拟上市或交易的新型衍生产品可能同时包含证券和远期交割商品出售合约(或者该等合约的期权或商品期权)要素之后,如申请人未在5个营业日内按照第(A)子款的规定同时向证券交易委员会和商品期货交易委员会发出通知,则证券交易委员会或商品期货交易委员会(视具体情况而定)应通知对方委员会并提供一份该等申请的复本。

(2)**判定请求**。——

(A)**一般规定**。——商品期货交易委员会可以在收到第(1)款所述通知后21天内请求,或者在未收到该等通知的情况下主动请求证券交易委员会判定产品是否属于《1934年证券交易法》第3(a)(10)条[《美国法典》第十五编第78c(a)(10)节]所定义的证券。

(B)**请求**。——证券交易委员会可以在收到第(1)款规定的通知后21天内请求,或者在未收到该等通知的情况下主动请求商品期货交易委员会判定产品是否属于根据《商品交易法》第2(a)(1)(A)条[《美国法典》第七编第2(a)(1)(A)节]的规定受商品期货交易委员会排他管辖的远期交割商品出售合约、该等合约的期权或商品期权。

(C)**与请求相关的规定**。——第(A)子款或第(B)子款所述请求应以书面形式向证券交易委员会或商品期货交易委员会(视具体情况而定)提出。

(D)**影响**。——本款的任何内容均不得被解释为——

(i)阻止商品期货交易委员会请求证券交易委员会根据《1934年证券交易法》第36(a)(1)条[《美国法典》第十五编第78mm(a)(1)节]向第(1)款所述申请针对的产品授予豁免;或

of a filing under paragraph (1); or

(ii) the Securities and Exchange Commission from requesting that the Commodity Futures Trading Commission grant an exemption pursuant to section 4 (c) (1) of the Commodity Exchange Act (7 U.S.C. 6(c)(1)) with respect to a product that is the subject of a filing under paragraph (1), Provided, however, that nothing in this subparagraph shall be construed to require the Commodity Futures Trading Commission or the Securities and Exchange Commission to issue an exemption requested pursuant to this subparagraph; provided further, That an order granting or denying an exemption described in this subparagraph and issued under paragraph (3)(B) shall not be subject to judicial review pursuant to subsection (b).

(E) WITHDRAWAL OF REQUEST. — A request under subparagraph (A) or (B) may be withdrawn by the Commission making the request at any time prior to a determination being made pursuant to paragraph (3) for any reason by providing written notice to the head of the other Commission.

(3) DETERMINATION. — Notwithstanding any other provision of law, no later than 120 days after the date of receipt of a request —

(A) under subparagraph (A) or (B) of paragraph (2), unless such request has been withdrawn pursuant to paragraph (2)(E), the Securities and Exchange Commission or the Commodity Futures Trading Commission, as applicable, shall, by order, issue the determination requested in subparagraph (A) or (B) of paragraph (2), as applicable, and the reasons therefor; or

(B) under paragraph (2)(D), unless such request has been withdrawn, the Securities and Exchange Commission or the Commodity Futures Trading Commission, as applicable, shall grant an exemption or provide reasons for not granting such exemption, provided that any decision by the Securities and Exchange Commission not to grant such exemption shall not be reviewable under section 25 of the Securities Exchange Act of 1934 (15 U.S.C. 78y).

(b) JUDICIAL RESOLUTION. —

(1) IN GENERAL. — The Commodity Futures Trading Commission or the Securities and Exchange Commission may petition the United States Court of Appeals for the District of Columbia Circuit for review of a final order of the other Commission issued pursuant to subsection (a)(3)(A), with respect to a novel derivative product that may have elements of both securities and contracts of sale of a commodity for future delivery (or options on such contracts or options on commodities) that it believes affects its statutory jurisdiction within 60 days after the date of entry of such order, a written petition requesting a review of the order. Any such proceeding shall be expedited by the Court of Appeals.

(2) TRANSMITTAL OF PETITION AND RECORD. — A copy of a petition described in paragraph (1) shall be transmitted not later than 1 business day after filing by the

(ii)阻止证券交易委员会要求商品期货交易委员会根据《商品交易法》第4(c)(1)条[《美国法典》第七编第6(c)(1)节]向第(1)款所述申请针对的产品授予豁免,但是,本子款的任何内容均不得被解释为要求商品期货交易委员会或证券交易委员会对依本子款规定提出的请求授予豁免;此外,对于根据第(3)(B)款签发的授予或拒绝本子款所述豁免的命令,不得根据第(b)子条提请司法审查。

(E)**撤回请求**。——在对方委员会根据第(3)款作出判定之前的任何时候,提出请求的委员会可出于任何理由向对方委员会负责人发出书面通知撤回依据第(A)子款或第(B)子款提出的请求。

(3)**判定**。——无论是否存在任何不同法律规定,在收到请求后120天内——

(A)根据第(2)款第(A)子款或第(B)子款规定,除非该等请求已经按照第(2)(E)款撤回,否则证券交易委员会或商品期货交易委员会(视具体情况而定)应发布命令,对依第(2)款第(A)子款或第(B)子款(视具体情况而定)提出之请求作出判定,并说明判定作出的理由;或

(B)根据第(2)(D)款规定,除非该等请求已经撤回,否则证券交易委员会或商品期货交易委员会(视具体情况而定)应授予豁免或说明不予豁免的理由,但是对于证券交易委员会作出的不予豁免的任何决定,均不得根据《1934年证券交易法》第25条(《美国法典》第十五编第78y节)提请司法审查。

(b)**司法裁决**。——

(1)**一般规定**。——商品期货交易委员会或证券交易委员会可以向哥伦比亚特区联邦巡回上诉法院提出请求,要求审查对方委员会根据第(a)(3)(A)子条就可能同时包含证券及远期交割商品出售合约(或者该等合约的期权或商品期权)要素的新型衍生产品作出的、其认为影响其法定管辖权的最终命令,司法审查请求应在该等命令作出之日起60天内以书面形式提出。任何该等程序均应由上诉法院加急处理。

(2)**请求书和记录的传送**。——作为请求方的委员会应在提交请求书后1个营业日内向作为被请求方的委员会传送一份第(1)款所述请求书的复本。在收到请求书

complaining Commission to the responding Commission. On receipt of the petition, the responding Commission shall file with the court a copy of the order under review and any documents referred to therein, and any other materials prescribed by the court.

(3) STANDARD OF REVIEW. — The court, in considering a petition filed pursuant to paragraph (1), shall give no deference to, or presumption in favor of, the views of either Commission.

(4) JUDICIAL STAY. — The filing of a petition by the complaining Commission pursuant to paragraph (1) shall operate as a stay of the order, until the date on which the determination of the court is final (including any appeal of the determination).

SEC.719. STUDIES.

(a) STUDY ON EFFECTS OF POSITION LIMITS ON TRADING ON EXCHANGES IN THE UNITED STATES. —

(1) STUDY. — The Commodity Futures Trading Commission, in consultation with each entity that is a designated contract market under the Commodity Exchange Act, shall conduct a study of the effects (if any) of the position limits imposed pursuant to the other provisions of this title on excessive speculation and on the movement of transactions from exchanges in the United States to trading venues outside the United States.

(2) REPORT TO THE CONGRESS. — Within 12 months after the imposition of position limits pursuant to the other provisions of this title, the Commodity Futures Trading Commission, in consultation with each entity that is a designated contract market under the Commodity Exchange Act, shall submit to the Congress a report on the matters described in paragraph (1).

(3) REQUIRED HEARING. — Within 30 legislative days after the submission to the Congress of the report described in paragraph (2), the Committee on Agriculture of the House of Representatives shall hold a hearing examining the findings of the report.

(4) BIENNIAL REPORTING. — In addition to the study required in paragraph (1), the Chairman of the Commodity Futures Trading Commission shall prepare and submit to the Congress biennial reports on the growth or decline of the derivatives markets in the United States and abroad, which shall include assessments of the causes of any such growth or decline, the effectiveness of regulatory regimes in managing systemic risk, a comparison of the costs of compliance at the time of the report for market participants subject to regulation by the United States with the costs of compliance in December 2008 for the market participants, and the quality of the available data. In preparing the report, the Chairman shall solicit the views of, consult with, and address the concerns raised by, market participants, regulators, legislators, and other interested parties.

(b) STUDY ON FEASIBILITY OF REQUIRING USE OF STANDARDIZED ALGORITHMIC DESCRIPTIONS FOR FINANCIAL DERIVATIVES. —

后,作为被请求方的委员会应向法院提交被提请司法审查的命令的一份复本,并提交命令中所提及的所有文件以及法院规定的任何其他资料。

(3)**审查标准**。——法院在审议根据第(1)款提出的请求时,不得基于任何一方委员会的意见做判定,亦不得作出有利于任何一方委员会意见的推定。

(4)**司法中止**。——申诉的委员会根据第(1)款提出请求的,被提请司法审查的命令即应中止适用,直至法院作出的判定产生终局效力之日(法院的判定被提起上诉的,则直至该等上诉获得最终解决之日)。

第719条 研究

(a)**研究持仓限额对美国境内交易所交易的影响**。——

(1)**研究**。——商品期货交易委员会应与身为《商品交易法》规定的指定合约市场的每一实体磋商,研究根据本编其他规定设定的持仓限额对过度投机以及交易从美国境内交易所流向境外交易场所的影响(如有)。

(2)**向国会报告**。——商品期货交易委员会应与身为《商品交易法》中的指定合约市场的每一实体磋商,在根据本编其他规定设定持仓限额后12个月内就第(1)款所述事宜向国会提交报告。

(3)**听证要求**。——众议院农业委员会应在向国会提交第(2)款所述报告后30个立法日内举行听证,对该等报告作出的认定进行审查。

(4)**2年期报告**。——除第(1)款要求开展的研究外,商品期货交易委员会主席还应就美国境内及海外衍生品市场的增长或萎缩情况编制2年期报告并向国会提交,报告中应包括市场增长或萎缩的原因评估、管理系统性风险的监管制度的成效、报告编制之时受美国监管的市场参与者的合规成本与2008年12月时该等市场参与者的合规成本的比较,以及可获得数据的质量。商品期货交易委员会主席在编制报告期间,应征求市场参与者、监管者、立法者及其他利害关系人的意见,与其进行磋商并对其关切问题予以论述。

(b)**研究要求金融衍生品适用标准化算法说明的可行性**。——

(1) IN GENERAL. — The Securities and Exchange Commission and the Commodity Futures Trading Commission shall conduct a joint study of the feasibility of requiring the derivatives industry to adopt standardized computer-readable algorithmic descriptions which may be used to describe complex and standardized financial derivatives.

(2) GOALS. — The algorithmic descriptions defined in the study shall be designed to facilitate computerized analysis of individual derivative contracts and to calculate net exposures to complex derivatives. The algorithmic descriptions shall be optimized for simultaneous use by —

(A) commercial users and traders of derivatives;

(B) derivative clearing houses, exchanges and electronic trading platforms;

(C) trade repositories and regulator investigations of market activities; and

(D) systemic risk regulators. The study will also examine the extent to which the algorithmic description, together with standardized and extensible legal definitions, may serve as the binding legal definition of derivative contracts. The study will examine the logistics of possible implementations of standardized algorithmic descriptions for derivatives contracts. The study shall be limited to electronic formats for exchange of derivative contract descriptions and will not contemplate disclosure of proprietary valuation models.

(3) INTERNATIONAL COORDINATION. — In conducting the study, the Securities and Exchange Commission and the Commodity Futures Trading Commission shall coordinate the study with international financial institutions and regulators as appropriate and practical.

(4) REPORT. — Within 8 months after the date of the enactment of this Act, the Securities and Exchange Commission and the Commodity Futures Trading Commission shall jointly submit to the Committees on Agriculture and on Financial Services of the House of Representatives and the Committees on Agriculture, Nutrition, and Forestry and on Banking, Housing, and Urban Affairs of the Senate a written report which contains the results of the study required by paragraphs (1) through (3).

(c) INTERNATIONAL SWAP REGULATION. —

(1) IN GENERAL. — The Commodity Futures Trading Commission and the Securities and Exchange Commission shall jointly conduct a study —

(A) relating to —

(i) swap regulation in the United States, Asia, and Europe; and

(ii) clearing house and clearing agency regulation in the United States, Asia, and Europe; and

(B) that identifies areas of regulation that are similar in the United States, Asia and Europe and other areas of regulation that could be harmonized

(2) REPORT. — Not later than 18 months after the date of enactment of this Act, the Commodity Futures Trading Commission and the Securities and Exchange Commission shall

(1)**一般规定**。——对于是否应要求衍生品行业采用标准化且计算机可读的算法说明(该算法可用于提供对复杂的及标准化金融衍生品的说明),证券交易委员会和商品期货交易委员会应联合开展可行性研究。

(2)**目的**。——研究中界定的算法说明应旨在促进对单个衍生品合约品种进行计算机分析,并计算对复杂衍生品的净风险敞口。算法说明应进行优化,便于以下主体能够同时使用——

(A)商业用户和衍生品交易商;

(B)衍生品结算所、交易所及电子交易平台;

(C)交易数据存管机构以及监管者对市场活动的调查;及

(D)系统性风险监管者。进行该等研究时还应考察该等算法说明以及标准化和可扩展的法律定义在多大程度上能够作为衍生品合约的具有约束力的法律定义,同时需要考察若对衍生品合约实施标准化算法说明所需作出后勤安排。研究应限于对衍生品合约说明进行交流的电子格式,不涉及专有估值模型的披露。

(3)**国际协作**。——证券交易委员会和商品期货交易委员会应在开展研究过程中与国际金融机构和监管者进行适当、可行的协作。

(4)**报告**。——证券交易委员会和商品期货交易委员会应在本法颁布之日后8个月内联合向众议院农业委员会、众议院金融服务委员会、参议院农业、营养与林业委员会、参议院银行及住房与城市事务委员会提交书面报告,说明第(1)款至第(3)款所述研究的结果。

(c)**国际互换监管**。——

(1)**一般规定**。——商品期货交易委员会和证券交易委员会应——

(A)联合开展与以下事项相关的研究——

(i)美国、亚洲和欧洲的互换监管;及

(ii)美国、亚洲和欧洲的结算所及结算机构监管;及

(B)联合开展研究,识别美国、亚洲和欧洲之间类似的监管领域以及可以进行协调的其他监管领域。

(2)**报告**。——商品期货交易委员会和证券交易委员会应于本法颁布之日起18个月内向参议院农业、营养与林业委员会、参议院银行、住房与城市事务委员会、众议

submit to the Committee on Agriculture, Nutrition, and Forestry and the Committee on Banking, Housing, and Urban Affairs of the Senate and the Committee on Agriculture and the Committee on Financial Services of the House of Representatives a report that includes a description of the results of the study under subsection (a), including —

(A) identification of the major exchanges and their regulator in each geographic area for the trading of swaps and security–based swaps including a listing of the major contracts and their trading volumes and notional values as well as identification of the major swap dealers participating in such markets;

(B) identification of the major clearing houses and clearing agencies and their regulator in each geographic area for the clearing of swaps and security–based swaps, including a listing of the major contracts and the clearing volumes and notional values as well as identification of the major clearing members of such clearing houses and clearing agencies in such markets;

(C) a description of the comparative methods of clearing swaps in the United States, Asia, and Europe; and

(D) a description of the various systems used for establishing margin on individual swaps, security–based swaps, and swap portfolios.

(d) STABLE VALUE CONTRACTS. —

(1) DETERMINATION. —

(A) STATUS. — Not later than 15 months after the date of the enactment of this Act, the Securities and Exchange Commission and the Commodity Futures Trading Commission shall, jointly, conduct a study to determine whether stable value contracts fall within the definition of a swap. In making the determination required under this subparagraph, the Commissions jointly shall consult with the Department of Labor, the Department of the Treasury, and the State entities that regulate the issuers of stable value contracts.

(B) REGULATIONS. — If the Commissions determine that stable value contracts fall within the definition of a swap, the Commissions jointly shall determine if an exemption for stable value contracts from the definition of swap is appropriate and in the public interest. The Commissions shall issue regulations implementing the determinations required under this paragraph. Until the effective date of such regulations, and notwithstanding any other provision of this title, the requirements of this title shall not apply to stable value contracts.

(C) LEGAL CERTAINTY. — Stable value contracts in effect prior to the effective date of the regulations described in subparagraph (B) shall not be considered swaps.

(2) DEFINITION. — For purposes of this subsection, the term "stable value contract" means any contract, agreement, or transaction that provides a crediting interest rate and guaranty or financial assurance of liquidity at contract or book value prior to maturity offered by a bank, insurance company, or other State or federally regulated financial institution for the

院农业委员会以及众议院金融服务委员会提交书面报告,说明第(a)子条所述研究的结果,包括——

(A)识别每一地理区域内的互换和证券类互换的主要交易所及其监管者,包括一份关于主要合约及其成交量和名义价值的清单,并识别该等市场中的主要互换交易商;

(B)识别每一地理区域内对互换和证券类互换进行集中结算的主要结算所和结算机构及其监管者,包括一份关于主要合约及其结算量和名义价值的清单,并识别该等市场中的该等结算所和结算机构的主要结算会员;

(C)说明美国、亚洲和欧洲之间互换集中结算方法的比较;及

(D)说明确定单个互换品种、单个证券类互换品种以及互换组合的保证金所使用的各类系统。

(d)**稳定价值合约**。——

(1)**判定**。——

(A)**性质**。——证券交易委员会和商品期货交易委员会应于本法颁布之日后15个月内联合开展研究,以期判定稳定价值合约是否符合互换定义。在作出本子款规定之判定时,证券交易委员会和商品期货交易委员会应共同与劳动部、财政部以及对稳定价值合约发行人进行监管的州实体进行磋商。

(B)**规章**。——如果证券交易委员会和商品期货交易委员会判定稳定价值合约符合互换定义,其应共同判定将稳定价值合约豁免于互换定义的适用是否确属适当并符合公共利益。证券交易委员会和商品期货交易委员会应发布规章,据以实施根据本款作出的判定。无论本编是否存在任何不同规定,在该等规章的生效日之前,本编规定不得适用于稳定价值合约。

(C)**法律确定性**。——第(B)子款所述规章生效日之前已生效的稳定价值合约不得视为互换。

(2)**定义**。——就本子条而言,"稳定价值合约"一词系指为了对下列任一计划进行投资而提供的任何单独或混合基金的利益,而由银行、保险公司或者其他州或联邦监管的金融机构要约的任何如下合约、协议或交易,即在下列任一计划未到期前按照合约或账面价值提供结算利率和担保或者流动性之金融保证的合约、协议或交易:按

benefit of any individual or commingled fund available as an investment in an employee benefit plan (as defined in section 3(3) of the Employee Retirement Income Security Act of 1974, including plans described in section 3 (32) of such Act) subject to participant direction, an eligible deferred compensation plan (as defined in section 457 (b) of the Internal Revenue Code of 1986) that is maintained by an eligible employer described in section 457(e)(1)(A) of such Code, an arrangement described in section 403(b) of such Code, or a qualified tuition program (as defined in section 529 of such Code).

SEC.720. MEMORANDUM.

(a) (1) The Commodity Futures Trading Commission and the Federal Energy Regulatory Commission shall, not later than 180 days after the date of the enactment of this Act, negotiate a memorandum of understanding to establish procedures for —

(A) applying their respective authorities in a manner so as to ensure effective and efficient regulation in the public interest;

(B) resolving conflicts concerning overlapping jurisdiction between the 2 agencies; and

(C) avoiding, to the extent possible, conflicting or duplicative regulation.

(2) Such memorandum and any subsequent amendments to the memorandum shall be promptly submitted to the appropriate committees of Congress.

(b) The Commodity Futures Trading Commission and the Federal Energy Regulatory Commission shall, not later than 180 days after the date of the enactment of this section, negotiate a memorandum of understanding to share information that may be requested where either Commission is conducting an investigation into potential manipulation, fraud, or market power abuse in markets subject to such Commission's regulation or oversight. Shared information shall remain subject to the same restrictions on disclosure applicable to the Commission initially holding the information.

PART II — REGULATION OF SWAP MARKETS

SEC.721. DEFINITIONS.

(a) IN GENERAL. — Section 1a of the Commodity Exchange Act (7 U.S.C. 1a) is amended —

(1) by redesignating paragraphs (2), (3) and (4), (5) through (17), (18) through (23), (24) through (28), (29), (30), (31) through (33), and (34) as paragraphs (6), (8) and (9), (11) through (23), (26) through (31), (34) through (38), (40), (41), (44) through (46), and (51), respectively;

(2) by inserting after paragraph (1) the following:

"(2) APPROPRIATE FEDERAL BANKING AGENCY. — The term 'appropriate Federal banking agency' —

参与者指令执行的员工福利计划[定义见《1974年员工退休收入保障法》第3(3)条,包括该法第3(32)条所述计划]、《1986年国内税收法典》第457(e)(1)(A)条所述适格雇主维持的适格递延薪酬计划[定义见该法典第457(b)条]、《1986年国内税收法典》第403(b)条所述安排或者合格学费计划(定义见《1986年国内税收法典》第529条)。

第720条　备忘录

(a)(1)商品期货交易委员会和联邦能源监管委员会应于本法颁布之日起180天内就一份制定如下程序的谅解备忘录进行谈判——

(A)行使其各自权力的程序,以确保监管的成效和效率,并确保监管符合公共利益;

(B)解决商品期货交易委员会和联邦能源监管委员会之间管辖权重叠引起的冲突;及

(C)尽量避免冲突或重复的监管。

(2)上述备忘录及其任何后续修正均应及时向相应的国会委员会提交。

(b)商品期货交易委员会和联邦能源监管委员会应于本条规定颁布之日起180天内就一份关于信息共享的谅解备忘录进行谈判,以便在对其所规制或监督的市场的潜在操纵、欺诈或市场支配力滥用进行调查时,共享被请求提供的信息。最初持有共享信息的委员会对该等信息施以披露限制的,获得共享信息的委员会应继续施加相同的披露限制。

第2部分——互换市场的监管

第721条　定义

(a)**一般规定**。——《商品交易法》第1a条(《美国法典》第七编第1a节)修正如下——

(1)第(2)款、第(3)款和第(4)款、第(5)款至第(17)款、第(18)款至第(23)款、第(24)款至第(28)款、第(29)款、第(30)款、第(31)款至第(33)款和第(34)款分别重新编号为第(6)款、第(8)款和第(9)款、第(11)款至第(23)款、第(26)款至第(31)款、第(34)款至第(38)款、第(40)款、第(41)款、第(44)款至第(46)款和第(51)款;

(2)在第(1)款之后插入如下内容:

"(2)**相应的联邦银行业监管机关**。——'相应的联邦银行业监管机关'一词——

"(A) has the meaning given the term in section 3 of the Federal Deposit Insurance Act (12 U.S.C. 1813);

"(B) means the Board in the case of a noninsured State bank; and

"(C) is the Farm Credit Administration for farm credit system institutions.

"(3) ASSOCIATED PERSON OF A SECURITY-BASED SWAP DEALER OR MAJOR SECURITY-BASED SWAP PARTICIPANT. — The term 'associated person of a security-based swap dealer or major security-based swap participant' has the meaning given the term in section 3(a) of the Securities Exchange Act of 1934 (15 U.S.C. 78c(a)).

"(4) ASSOCIATED PERSON OF A SWAP DEALER OR MAJOR SWAP PARTICIPANT. —

"(A) IN GENERAL. — The term 'associated person of a swap dealer or major swap participant' means a person who is associated with a swap dealer or major swap participant as a partner, officer, employee, or agent (or any person occupying a similar status or performing similar functions), in any capacity that involves —

"(i) the solicitation or acceptance of swaps; or

"(ii) the supervision of any person or persons so engaged.

"(B) EXCLUSION. — Other than for purposes of section 4s (b) (6), the term 'associated person of a swap dealer or major swap participant' does not include any person associated with a swap dealer or major swap participant the functions of which are solely clerical or ministerial.

"(5) BOARD. — The term 'Board' means the Board of Governors of the Federal Reserve System.";

(3) by inserting after paragraph (6) (as redesignated by paragraph (1)) the following:

"(7) CLEARED SWAP. — The term 'cleared swap' means any swap that is, directly or indirectly, submitted to and cleared by a derivatives clearing organization registered with the Commission.";

(4) in paragraph (9) (as redesignated by paragraph (1)), by striking "except onions" and all that follows through the period at the end and inserting the following: "except onions (as provided by the first section of Public Law 85-839 (7 U.S.C. 13-1)) and motion picture box office receipts (or any index, measure, value, or data related to such receipts), and all services, rights, and interests (except motion picture box office receipts, or any index, measure, value or data related to such receipts) in which contracts for future delivery are presently or in the future dealt in.";

(5) by inserting after paragraph (9) (as redesignated by paragraph (1)) the following:

"(10) COMMODITY POOL. —

"(A) IN GENERAL. — The term 'commodity pool' means any investment trust, syndicate, or similar form of enterprise operated for the purpose of trading in commodity

(A)含义应以《联邦存款保险法》第3条[《美国法典》第十二编第1813节]的定义为准;

(B)对未参保的州银行而言,系指联邦储备委员会;且

(C)对农业信贷系统机构而言,系指农业信贷管理局。

(3) **证券类互换交易商或主要的证券类互换参与者的业务相关人**。——'证券类互换交易商或主要的证券类互换参与者的业务相关人'一词的含义以《1934年证券交易法》第3(a)条[《美国法典》第十五编第78c(a)节]的定义为准。

(4)**互换交易商或主要互换参与者的业务相关人**。——

(A)**一般规定**。——'互换交易商或主要互换参与者的业务相关人'一词系指作为互换交易商或主要互换参与者的合伙人、管理人员、职员或代理人(或任何担任类似职位或履行类似职能的人),与互换交易商或主要互换参与者产生业务关联,并以任何身份从事下列活动的人——

(i)互换的招揽或接受;或

(ii)对任何招揽或接受互换之人的领导监督。

(B)**除外规定**。——除用于第4s(b)(6)条之外,'互换交易商或主要互换参与者的业务相关人'一词不包括任何仅因履行文员或行政职能而与互换交易商或主要互换参与者产生业务关联的人。

(5)**联邦储备委员会**。——'联邦储备委员会'一词系指美国联邦储备系统管理委员会。"

(3)在第(6)款[以第(1)款重新编号后的序号为准]之后插入如下内容:

"(7)**集中结算的互换**。——'集中结算的互换'一词系指直接或间接提交给已在商品期货交易委员会注册的衍生品结算组织进行集中结算的任何互换。"

(4)在第(9)款[以第(1)款重新编号后的序号为准]中,删除"但洋葱"直至结尾处句号前的全部内容,替以:"但洋葱[见第85-839号公法第1条(《美国法典》第七编第13-1节)的规定]和电影票房收入(或与电影票房收入相关的任何指数、指标、价值或数据)除外,以及作为现在交易或未来交易的远期交割合约标的之一切服务、权利以及权益(但电影票房收入或与电影票房收入相关的任何指数、指标、价值或数据除外。"

(5)在第(9)款[以第(1)款重新编号后的序号为准]之后插入如下内容:

"(10)**商品基金**。——

(A) **一般规定**。——'商品基金'一词系指为交易商品权益之目的而经营的任何投资信托、辛迪加或类似形式的企业。商品权益包括任何——

interests, including any —

"(i) commodity for future delivery, security futures product, or swap;

"(ii) agreement, contract, or transaction described in section 2(c)(2)(C)(i) or section 2(c)(2)(D)(i);

"(iii) commodity option authorized under section 4c; or

"(iv) leverage transaction authorized under section 19.

"(B) FURTHER DEFINITION. — The Commission, by rule or regulation, may include within, or exclude from, the term 'commodity pool' any investment trust, syndicate, or similar form of enterprise if the Commission determines that the rule or regulation will effectuate the purposes of this Act.";

(6) by striking paragraph (11) (as redesignated by paragraph (1)) and inserting the following:

"(11) COMMODITY POOL OPERATOR. —

"(A) IN GENERAL. — The term 'commodity pool operator' means any person —

"(i) engaged in a business that is of the nature of a commodity pool, investment trust, syndicate, or similar form of enterprise, and who, in connection therewith, solicits, accepts, or receives from others, funds, securities, or property, either directly or through capital contributions, the sale of stock or other forms of securities, or otherwise, for the purpose of trading in commodity interests, including any —

"(I) commodity for future delivery, security futures product, or swap;

"(II) agreement, contract, or transaction described in section 2(c)(2)(C)(i) or section 2(c)(2)(D)(i);

"(III) commodity option authorized under section 4c; or

"(IV) leverage transaction authorized under section 19; or

"(ii) who is registered with the Commission as a commodity pool operator.

"(B) FURTHER DEFINITION. — The Commission, by rule or regulation, may include within, or exclude from, the term 'commodity pool operator' any person engaged in a business that is of the nature of a commodity pool, investment trust, syndicate, or similar form of enterprise if the Commission determines that the rule or regulation will effectuate the purposes of this Act.";

(7) in paragraph (12) (as redesignated by paragraph (1)), in subparagraph (A) —

(A) in clause (i) —

(i) in subclause (I), by striking "made or to be made on or subject to the rules of a contract market or derivatives transaction execution facility" and inserting ", security futures product, or swap";

(ii) by redesignating subclauses (II) and (III) as subclauses (III) and (IV);

(iii) by inserting after subclause (I) the following:

(i)远期交割的商品、证券期货产品或互换;

(ii)第2(c)(2)(C)(i)条或第2(c)(2)(D)(i)条所述协议、合约或交易;

(iii)根据第4c条获得核准的商品期权;或

(iv)根据第19条获得核准的杠杆交易。

(B)**进一步界定**。——商品期货交易委员会可以发布规则或规章,将任何投资信托、辛迪加或类似形式的企业纳入'商品基金'一词的定义之内或排除在该词的定义之外,其前提是商品期货交易委员会判定该等规则或规章有助于实现本法宗旨。"

(6)删除第(11)款[以第(1)款重新编号后的序号为准],并替以:

"(11)**商品基金管理人**。——

(A)**一般规定**。——'商品基金管理人'一词系指以下任何主体——

(i)为交易商品权益之目的,从事性质属于商品基金、投资信托、辛迪加或类似形式企业的业务,且在该等业务中直接从他人处招揽、接受或者收取资金、证券或财产,或通过资本缴纳、出售股票或其他形式证券的方式或者通过其他方式从他人处招揽、接受或收取资金、证券或财产的主体。商品权益包括任何——

(I)远期交割的商品、证券期货产品或互换;

(II)第2(c)(2)(C)(i)条或第2(c)(2)(D)(i)条所述协议、合约或交易;

(III)根据第4c条获得核准的商品期权;或

(IV)根据第19条获得核准的杠杆交易;或

(ii)在商品期货交易委员会注册为商品基金管理人的主体。

(B)**进一步界定**。——商品期货交易委员会可以发布规则或规章,将从事性质属于商品基金、投资信托、辛迪加或类似形式企业的业务的任何主体,纳入'商品基金管理人'一词的定义之内或排除在该词的定义之外,其前提是商品期货交易委员会判定该等规则或规章有助于实现本法宗旨。"

(7)在第(12)款[以第(1)款重新编号后的序号为准]第(A)子款中——

(A)第(i)项——

(i)第(I)子项删除"远期交割商品出售合约,且该合约已经或将在某一合约市场或某一衍生品交易执行设施上达成或按其规则达成",替以"、证券期货产品或互换";

(ii)第(II)子项和第(III)子项重新编号为第(III)子项和第(IV)子项;

(iii)在第(I)子项之后插入如下内容:

"(II) any agreement, contract, or transaction described in section 2(c)(2)(C)(i) or section 2(c)(2)(D)(i)"; and

(iv) in subclause (IV) (as so redesignated), by striking "or";

(B) in clause (ii), by striking the period at the end and inserting a semicolon; and

(C) by adding at the end the following:

"(iii) is registered with the Commission as a commodity trading advisor; or

"(iv) the Commission, by rule or regulation, may include if the Commission determines that the rule or regulation will effectuate the purposes of this Act.";

(8) in paragraph (17) (as redesignated by paragraph (1)), in subparagraph (A), in the matter preceding clause (i), by striking "paragraph (12)(A)" and inserting "paragraph (18)(A)";

(9) in paragraph (18) (as redesignated by paragraph (1)) —

(A) in subparagraph (A) —

(i) in the matter following clause (vii)(III) —

(I) by striking "section 1a (11)(A)" and inserting "paragraph (17)(A)"; and

(II) by striking "$25,000,000" and inserting "$50,000,000"; and

(ii) in clause (xi), in the matter preceding subclause (I), by striking "total assets in an amount" and inserting "amounts invested on a discretionary basis, the aggregate of which is";

(10) by striking paragraph (22) (as redesignated by paragraph (1)) and inserting the following:

"(22) FLOOR BROKER. —

"(A) IN GENERAL. — The term 'floor broker' means any person —

"(i) who, in or surrounding any pit, ring, post, or other place provided by a contract market for the meeting of persons similarly engaged, shall purchase or sell for any other person —

"(I) any commodity for future delivery, security futures product, or swap; or

"(II) any commodity option authorized under section 4c; or

"(ii) who is registered with the Commission as a floor broker.

"(B) FURTHER DEFINITION. — The Commission, by rule or regulation, may include within, or exclude from, the term 'floor broker' any person in or surrounding any pit, ring, post, or other place provided by a contract market for the meeting of persons similarly engaged who trades for any other person if the Commission determines that the rule or regulation will effectuate the purposes of this Act.";

(11) by striking paragraph (23) (as redesignated by paragraph (1)) and inserting the following:

"(23) FLOOR TRADER. —

"(A) IN GENERAL. — The term 'floor trader' means any person —

“(II)任何第2(c)(2)(C)(i)条或第2(c)(2)(D)(i)条所述协议、合约或交易”;及

(iv)第(IV)子项(以重新编号后的序号为准)删除“或”;

(B)第(ii)项删除结尾处的句号并替以分号;及

(C)在结尾处增加如下内容:

“(iii)在商品期货交易委员会注册为商品交易顾问的主体;或

(iv)商品期货交易委员会发布规则或规章将其纳入‘商品交易顾问’定义之内的任何主体,其前提是商品期货交易委员会判定该等规则或规章有助于实现本法宗旨。”

(8)在第(17)款[以第(1)款重新编号后的序号为准]第(A)子款第(i)项之前的内容中,删除“第(12)(A)款”,替以“第(18)(A)款”;

(9)在第(18)款[以第(1)款重新编号后的序号为准]中——

(A)第(A)子款——

(i)第(vii)(III)项之后的内容——

(I)删除“第1a(11)(A)条”,替以“第(17)(A)款”;及

(II)删除“2500万美元”,替以“5000万美元”;及

(ii)在第(xi)项第(I)子项之前的内容中,删除“总资产”,替以“自主投资总额”;

(10)删除第(22)款[以第(1)款重新编号后的序号为准],并替以如下内容:

“(22)**场内经纪商**。——

(A)**一般规定**。——‘场内经纪商’一词系指下述任何主体——

(i)在合约市场为类似从业人员聚集所提供的任何交易池、交易圈、交易站或其他场所之内或其周围为任何其他人买卖以下各项的主体——

(I)任何远期交割商品、证券期货产品或互换;或

(II)根据第4c条获得核准的任何商品期权;或

(ii)在商品期货交易委员会注册为场内经纪商的主体。

(B)**进一步界定**。——商品期货交易委员会可以发布规则或规章,将在合约市场为类似从业人员聚集所提供的任何交易池、交易圈、交易站或其他场所之内或其周围为任何其他人从事交易的任何主体,纳入‘场内经纪商’一词的定义之内或排除在该词的定义之外, 前提是商品期货交易委员会判定该等规则或规章有助于实现本法宗旨。”

(11)删除第(23)款[以第(1)款重新编号后的序号为准],并替以:

“(23)**场内交易商**。——

(A)**一般规定**。——‘场内交易商’一词系指下述任何主体——

"(i) who, in or surrounding any pit, ring, post, or other place provided by a contract market for the meeting of persons similarly engaged, purchases, or sells solely for such person's own account —

"(I) any commodity for future delivery, security futures product, or swap; or

"(II) any commodity option authorized under section 4c; or

"(ii) who is registered with the Commission as a floor trader.

"(B) FURTHER DEFINITION. — The Commission, by rule or regulation, may include within, or exclude from, the term 'floor trader' any person in or surrounding any pit, ring, post, or other place provided by a contract market for the meeting of persons similarly engaged who trades solely for such person's own account if the Commission determines that the rule or regulation will effectuate the purposes of this Act.";

(12) by inserting after paragraph (23) (as redesignated by paragraph (1)) the following:

"(24) FOREIGN EXCHANGE FORWARD. — The term 'foreign exchange forward' means a transaction that solely involves the exchange of 2 different currencies on a specific future date at a fixed rate agreed upon on the inception of the contract covering the exchange.

"(25) FOREIGN EXCHANGE SWAP. — The term 'foreign exchange swap' means a transaction that solely involves —

"(A) an exchange of 2 different currencies on a specific date at a fixed rate that is agreed upon on the inception of the contract covering the exchange; and

"(B) a reverse exchange of the 2 currencies described in subparagraph (A) at a later date and at a fixed rate that is agreed upon on the inception of the contract covering the exchange.";

(13) by striking paragraph (28) (as redesignated by paragraph (1)) and inserting the following:

"(28) FUTURES COMMISSION MERCHANT. —

"(A) IN GENERAL. — The term 'futures commission merchant' means an individual, association, partnership, corporation, or trust —

"(i) that —

"(I) is —

"(aa) engaged in soliciting or in accepting orders for —

"(AA) the purchase or sale of a commodity for future delivery;

"(BB) a security futures product;

"(CC) a swap;

"(DD) any agreement, contract, or transaction described in section 2(c)(2)(C)(i) or section 2(c)(2)(D)(i);

"(EE) any commodity option authorized under section 4c; or

(i)在合约市场为类似从业人员聚集所提供的任何交易池、交易圈、交易站或其他场所之内或其周围仅为自身账户买卖以下各项的主体——

(I)任何远期交割商品、证券期货产品或互换;或

(II)根据第4c条获得核准的任何商品期权;或

(ii)在商品期货交易委员会注册为场内交易商的主体。

(B)**进一步界定**。——商品期货交易委员会可以发布规则或规章,将在合约市场为类似从业人员聚集所提供的任何交易池、交易圈、交易站或其他场所之内或其周围仅为自身账户交易的任何主体,纳入'场内交易商'一词的定义之内或排除在该词的定义之外,前提是商品期货交易委员会判定该等规则或规章有助于实现本法宗旨。"

(12)在第(23)款[以第(1)款重新编号后的序号为准]之后插入如下内容:

"(24)**外汇远期**。——'外汇远期'一词系指仅涉及两种不同货币在未来某一特定日期按照交换合约订立时所约定的固定比率进行交换的交易。

(25)**外汇互换**。——'外汇互换'一词系指仅涉及如下交换的交易——

(A)两种不同货币在某一特定日期按照交换合约订立时所约定的固定比率进行的交换;及

(B)第(A)子款所述的两种货币在某一较晚的日期按照交换合约订立时所约定的固定比率进行的反向交换。"

(13)删除第(28)款[以第(1)款重新编号后的序号为准],并替以:

"(28)**期货经纪商**。——

(A)**一般规定**。——'期货经纪商'一词系指具有以下特征的个人、协会、合伙、公司或信托——

(i)其——

(I)具有以下特征——

(aa)从事关于以下各项的交易指令的招揽或接受——

(AA)远期交割商品买卖;

(BB)证券期货产品;

(CC)互换;

(DD)第2(c)(2)(C)(i)条或第2(c)(2)(D)(i)条所述任何协议、合约或交易";

(EE)根据第4c条获得核准的任何商品期权;或

"(FF) any leverage transaction authorized under section 19; or

"(bb) acting as a counterparty in any agreement, contract, or transaction described in section 2(c)(2)(C)(i) or section 2(c)(2)(D)(i); and

"(II) in or in connection with the activities described in items (aa) or (bb) of subclause (I), accepts any money, securities, or property (or extends credit in lieu thereof) to margin, guarantee, or secure any trades or contracts that result or may result therefrom; or

"(ii) that is registered with the Commission as a futures commission merchant.

"(B) FURTHER DEFINITION. — The Commission, by rule or regulation, may include within, or exclude from, the term 'futures commission merchant' any person who engages in soliciting or accepting orders for, or acting as a counterparty in, any agreement, contract, or transaction subject to this Act, and who accepts any money, securities, or property (or extends credit in lieu thereof) to margin, guarantee, or secure any trades or contracts that result or may result therefrom, if the Commission determines that the rule or regulation will effectuate the purposes of this Act.";

(14) in paragraph (30) (as redesignated by paragraph (1)), in subparagraph (B), by striking "state" and inserting "State";

(15) by striking paragraph (31) (as redesignated by paragraph (1) and inserting the following:

"(31) INTRODUCING BROKER. —

"(A) IN GENERAL. — The term 'introducing broker' means any person (except an individual who elects to be and is registered as an associated person of a futures commission merchant) —

"(i) who —

"(I) is engaged in soliciting or in accepting orders for —

"(aa) the purchase or sale of any commodity for future delivery, security futures product, or swap;

"(bb) any agreement, contract, or transaction described in section 2(c)(2)(C)(i) or section 2(c)(2)(D)(i);

"(cc) any commodity option authorized under section 4c; or

"(dd) any leverage transaction authorized under section 19; and

"(II) does not accept any money, securities, or property (or extend credit in lieu thereof) to margin, guarantee, or secure any trades or contracts that result or may result therefrom; or

"(ii) who is registered with the Commission as an introducing broker.

"(B) FURTHER DEFINITION. — The Commission, by rule or regulation, may include within, or exclude from, the term 'introducing broker' any person who engages in soliciting or accepting orders for any agreement, contract, or transaction subject to this Act, and who does

(FF)根据第19条获得核准的任何杠杆交易;或

(bb)以第2(c)(2)(C)(i)条或第2(c)(2)(D)(i)条所述任何协议、合约或交易中的对手方身份行事;且

(II)在从事第(I)子项第(aa)目或第(bb)目所述活动时或在该等活动相关事宜中,接受用于为该等活动产生的或可能产生的任何交易或合约提供保证金、保证或担保的任何现金、证券或财产(或进行用于该等目的之替代性授信);或

(ii)已在商品期货交易委员会注册为期货经纪商。

(B)**进一步界定**。——商品期货交易委员会可以发布规则或规章,将从事关于受制于本法规定的任何协议、合约或交易的指令的招揽或接受或在该等协议、合约或交易中担任对手方的活动,并且接受用于为该等活动产生的或可能产生的任何交易或合约提供保证金、保证或担保的任何现金、证券或财产(或进行用于该等目的之替代性授信)的任何主体,纳入'期货经纪商'一词的定义之内或排除在该词的定义之外,前提是商品期货交易委员会判定该等规则或规章有助于实现本法宗旨。"

(14)在第(30)款[以第(1)款重新编号后的序号为准]第(B)子款中删除首字母小写的"州"("state")并替以首字母大写的"州"("State");

(15)删除第(31)款[以第(1)款重新编号后的序号为准],并替以:

"(31)**介绍经纪商**。——

(A)**一般规定**。——'介绍经纪商'一词系指具有以下特征的任何主体(但选择成为并且已注册成为期货经纪商业务相关人的个人除外)——

(i)其——

(I)从事关于以下各项的交易指令的招揽或接受——

(aa)任何远期交割商品、证券期货产品或互换的买卖;

(bb)第2(c)(2)(C)(i)条或第2(c)(2)(D)(i)条所述任何协议、合约或交易;

(cc)根据第4c条获得核准的任何商品期权;或

(dd)根据第19条获得核准的任何杠杆交易;且

(II)并不接受用于为该等活动产生的或可能产生的任何交易或合约提供保证金、保证或担保的任何现金、证券或财产(也不进行用于该等目的之替代性授信);或

(ii)已在商品期货交易委员会注册为介绍经纪商。

(B)**进一步界定**。——商品期货交易委员会可以发布规则或规章,将从事关于受制于本法规定的任何协议、合约或交易的指令的招揽或接受,但不接受用于为该等活动产生的或可能产生的任何交易或合约提供保证金、保证或担保的任何现金、证券或

not accept any money, securities, or property (or extend credit in lieu thereof) to margin, guarantee, or secure any trades or contracts that result or may result therefrom, if the Commission determines that the rule or regulation will effectuate the purposes of this Act.";

(16) by inserting after paragraph (31) (as redesignated by paragraph (1)) the following:

"(32) MAJOR SECURITY-BASED SWAP PARTICIPANT. — The term 'major security-based swap participant' has the meaning given the term in section 3(a) of the Securities Exchange Act of 1934 (15 U.S.C. 78c(a)).

"(33) MAJOR SWAP PARTICIPANT. —

"(A) IN GENERAL. — The term 'major swap participant' means any person who is not a swap dealer, and —

"(i) maintains a substantial position in swaps for any of the major swap categories as determined by the Commission, excluding —

"(I) positions held for hedging or mitigating commercial risk; and

"(II) positions maintained by any employee benefit plan (or any contract held by such a plan) as defined in paragraphs (3) and (32) of section 3 of the Employee Retirement Income Security Act of 1974 (29 U.S.C. 1002) for the primary purpose of hedging or mitigating any risk directly associated with the operation of the plan;

"(ii) whose outstanding swaps create substantial counterparty exposure that could have serious adverse effects on the financial stability of the United States banking system or financial markets; or

"(iii)(I) is a financial entity that is highly leveraged relative to the amount of capital it holds and that is not subject to capital requirements established by an appropriate Federal banking agency; and

"(II) maintains a substantial position in outstanding swaps in any major swap category as determined by the Commission.

"(B) DEFINITION OF SUBSTANTIAL POSITION. — For purposes of subparagraph (A), the Commission shall define by rule or regulation the term 'substantial position' at the threshold that the Commission determines to be prudent for the effective monitoring, management, and oversight of entities that are systemically important or can significantly impact the financial system of the United States. In setting the definition under this subparagraph, the Commission shall consider the person's relative position in uncleared as opposed to cleared swaps and may take into consideration the value and quality of collateral held against counterparty exposures.

"(C) SCOPE OF DESIGNATION. — For purposes of subparagraph (A), a person may be designated as a major swap participant for 1 or more categories of swaps without being classified as a major swap participant for all classes of swaps.

财产(也不进行用于该等目的之替代性授信)的任何主体,纳入'介绍经纪商'一词的定义之内或排除在该词的定义之外,前提是商品期货交易委员会判定该等规则或规章有助于实现本法宗旨。"

(16)在第(31)款[以第(1)款重新编号后的序号为准]之后插入如下内容:

"(32)**主要的证券类互换参与者**。——'主要的证券类互换参与者'一词的含义以《1934年证券交易法》第3(a)条[《美国法典》第十五编第78c(a)节]的定义为准。

(33)**主要互换参与者**。——

(A)**一般规定**。——'主要互换参与者'一词系指互换交易商以外的具有以下特征的任何主体——

(i)对商品期货交易委员会认定的任何类别的主要互换持有大额互换持仓,但该等持仓不包括——

(I)为了对商业风险进行套期保值或缓释而持有的持仓;及

(II)任何员工福利计划[定义见《1974年员工退休收入保障法》(《美国法典》第二十九编第1002节)第3条第(3)款和第(32)款]维持的主要旨在对与该等计划运作直接相关的任何风险进行套期保值或缓释的持仓(或该等计划为此目的持有的任何合约);

(ii)其尚未了结的互换形成重大对手方风险敞口,而该等敞口可能给美国银行体系或金融市场的金融稳定带来重大不利影响;或

(iii)(I)系一家杠杆率相对于其持有的资本额而言过高且不受制于相应的联邦银行业监管机关设定的资本要求的金融实体;且

(II)对商品期货交易委员会认定的任何类别的主要互换持有大额未了结的持仓。

(B)**大额持仓的定义**。——就第(A)子款而言,商品期货交易委员会应当按照其判定确属审慎的门槛标准,发布规则或规章对'大额持仓'一词作出定义,以便有效监控、管理和监督具有系统重要性的或可能对美国金融体系产生重大影响的实体。在按照本子款确定上述定义时,商品期货交易委员会应考虑该等主体非集中结算的互换的持仓和集中结算的互换的持仓二者间的比例,并可将该等主体为了担保对手方风险敞口所持有的担保品价值和质量纳入考虑。

(C)**指定范围**。——就第(A)子款而言,任何主体均可被指定为一类或一类以上互换的主要互换参与者,而不必同时被指定为所有类别的互换的主要互换参与者。

"(D) EXCLUSIONS. — The definition under this paragraph shall not include an entity whose primary business is providing financing, and uses derivatives for the purpose of hedging underlying commercial risks related to interest rate and foreign currency exposures, 90 percent or more of which arise from financing that facilitates the purchase or lease of products, 90 percent or more of which are manufactured by the parent company or another subsidiary of the parent company.";

(17) by inserting after paragraph (38) (as redesignated by paragraph (1)) the following:

"(39) PRUDENTIAL REGULATOR. — The term 'prudential regulator' means —

"(A) the Board in the case of a swap dealer, major swap participant, security-based swap dealer, or major security-based swap participant that is —

"(i) a State-chartered bank that is a member of the Federal Reserve System;

"(ii) a State-chartered branch or agency of a foreign bank;

"(iii) any foreign bank which does not operate an insured branch;

"(iv) any organization operating under section 25A of the Federal Reserve Act or having an agreement with the Board under section 225 of the Federal Reserve Act;

"(v) any bank holding company (as defined in section 2 of the Bank Holding Company Act of 1965 (12 U.S.C. 1841)), any foreign bank (as defined in section 1(b)(7) of the International Banking Act of 1978 (12 U.S.C. 3101(b)(7)) that is treated as a bank holding company under section 8(a) of the International Banking Act of 1978 (12 U.S.C. 3106(a)), and any subsidiary of such a company or foreign bank (other than a subsidiary that is described in subparagraph (A) or (B) or that is required to be registered with the Commission as a swap dealer or major swap participant under this Act or with the Securities and Exchange Commission as a security-based swap dealer or major security-based swap participant);

"(vi) after the transfer date (as defined in section 311 of the Dodd-Frank Wall Street Reform and Consumer Protection Act), any savings and loan holding company (as defined in section 10 of the Home Owners' Loan Act (12 U.S.C. 1467a)) and any subsidiary of such company (other than a subsidiary that is described in subparagraph (A) or (B) or that is required to be registered as a swap dealer or major swap participant with the Commission under this Act or with the Securities and Exchange Commission as a security-based swap dealer or major security-based swap participant); or

"(vii) any organization operating under section 25A of the Federal Reserve Act (12U.S.C. 611 et seq.) or having an agreement with the Board under section 25 of the Federal Reserve Act (12 U.S.C. 601 et seq.);

"(B) the Office of the Comptroller of the Currency in the case of a swap dealer, major swap participant, security-based swap dealer, or major security-based swap

(D)**除外规定**。——本款定义不包括具有如下特征的实体:以提供融资为主营业务并利用衍生品对与利率和外币风险敞口相关的基础商业风险进行套期保值,而该等风险90%(含)以上来自为产品购买或承租提供便利的融资并且该等产品90%(含)以上由其母公司或母公司的另一子公司制造。”

(17)在第(38)款[以第(1)款重新编号后的序号为准]之后插入如下内容:

“(39)**审慎监管者**。——‘审慎监管者’一词——

(A)就具有以下身份的互换交易商、主要互换参与者、证券类互换交易商或主要的证券类互换参与者而言,系指联邦储备委员会——

(i)身为联邦储备系统成员的州特许注册银行;

(ii)外国银行的州特许注册分行或代理行;

(iii)不运营参保分行的任何外国银行;

(iv)根据《联邦储备法》第25A条规定运营的任何组织,或根据《联邦储备法》第225条与联邦储备委员会存在协议关系的任何组织;

(v)任何银行控股公司[定义见《1965年银行控股公司法》第2条(《美国法典》第12编第1841节)]、根据《1978年国际银行法》第8(a)条[《美国法典》第十二编第3106(a)节]被作为银行控股公司处理的任何外国银行[定义见《1978年国际银行法》第1(b)(7)条(《美国法典》第十二编第3101(b)(7)节)]及该等公司或外国银行的任何子公司[但第(A)子款或第(B)子款所述的子公司、按本法规定应在商品期货交易委员会注册为互换交易商或主要互换参与者的子公司或者应在证券交易委员会注册为证券类互换交易商或主要的证券类互换参与者的子公司除外];

(vi)转移日(定义见《多德—弗兰克华尔街改革与消费者保护法》第311条)之后,任何储贷控股公司[定义见《业主贷款法》第10条(《美国法典》第十二编第1467a节)]以及该等公司的任何子公司[但第(A)子款或第(B)子款所述的子公司、按本法规定应在商品期货交易委员会注册为互换交易商或主要互换参与者的子公司或者应在证券交易委员会注册为证券类互换交易商或主要的证券类互换参与者的子公司除外];或

(vii)根据《联邦储备法》第25A条(《美国法典》第十二编第611节及其后条文)运营的任何组织或根据《联邦储备法》第25条(《美国法典》第十二编第601节及其后条文)与联邦储备委员会存在协议关系的任何组织;

(B)就具有以下身份的互换交易商、主要互换参与者、证券类互换交易商或主要的证券类互换参与者而言,系指货币监理署——

participant that is —

"(i) a national bank;

"(ii) a federally chartered branch or agency of a foreign bank; or

"(iii) any Federal savings association;

"(C) the Federal Deposit Insurance Corporation in the case of a swap dealer, major swap participant, security–based swap dealer, or major security–based swap participant that is —

"(i) a State–chartered bank that is not a member of the Federal Reserve System; or

"(ii) any State savings association;

"(D) the Farm Credit Administration, in the case of a swap dealer, major swap participant, security–based swap dealer, or major security–based swap participant that is an institution chartered under the Farm Credit Act of 1971 (12 U.S.C. 2001 et seq.); and

"(E) the Federal Housing Finance Agency in the case of a swap dealer, major swap participant, security–based swap dealer, or major security–based swap participant that is a regulated entity (as such term is defined in section 1303 of the Federal Housing Enterprises Financial Safety and Soundness Act of 1992).";

(18) in paragraph (40) (as redesignated by paragraph (1)) —

(A) by striking subparagraph (B);

(B) by redesignating subparagraphs (C), (D), and (E) as subparagraphs (B), (C), and (F), respectively;

(C) in subparagraph (C) (as so redesignated), by striking "and"; and

(D) by inserting after subparagraph (C) (as so redesignated) the following:

"(D) a swap execution facility registered under section 5h;

"(E) a swap data repository registered under section 21; and";

(19) by inserting after paragraph (41) (as redesignated by paragraph (1)) the following:

"(42) SECURITY–BASED SWAP. — The term 'security–based swap' has the meaning given the term in section 3(a) of the Securities Exchange Act of 1934 (15 U.S.C. 78c(a)).

"(43) SECURITY–BASED SWAP DEALER. — The term 'security–based swap dealer' has the meaning given the term in section 3(a) of the Securities Exchange Act of 1934 (15 U.S.C. 78c(a)).";

(20) in paragraph (46) (as redesignated by paragraph (1)), by striking "subject to section 2(h)(7)" and inserting "subject to section 2(h)(5)";

(21) by inserting after paragraph (46) (as redesignated by paragraph (1)) the following:

"(47) SWAP. —

（i）国民银行；

（ii）外国银行的联邦特许注册分行或代理行；或

（iii）任何联邦储蓄协会；

（C）就具有以下身份的互换交易商、主要互换参与者、证券类互换交易商或主要的证券类互换参与者而言，系指联邦存款保险公司——

（i）并非联邦储备系统成员的州特许注册银行；或

（ii）任何州储蓄协会；

（D）就具有根据《1971年农业信贷法》（《美国法典》第十二编第2001节及其后条文）特许注册的机构身份的互换交易商、主要互换参与者、证券类互换交易商或主要的证券类互换参与者而言，系指农业信贷管理局；及

（E）就具有受监管实体（定义见《1992年联邦住房企业财务安全和稳健法》第1303条）身份的互换交易商、主要互换参与者、证券类互换交易商或主要的证券类互换参与者而言，系指联邦住房金融局。”

（18）在第（40）款[以第（1）款重新编号后的序号为准]中——

（A）删除第（B）子款；

（B）第（C）子款、第（D）子款和第（E）子款分别重新编号为第（B）子款、第（C）子款和第（F）子款；

（C）第（C）子款（以重新编号后的序号为准）删除“及”；及

（D）在第（C）子款（以重新编号后的序号为准）之后插入：

“（D）根据第5h条注册的互换执行设施；

（E）根据第21条注册的互换数据存管机构；及”；

（19）在第（41）款[以第（1）款重新编号后的序号为准]之后插入如下内容：

“（42）**证券类互换**。——‘证券类互换’一词的含义以《1934年证券交易法》第3（a）条[《美国法典》第十五编第78c（a）节]的定义为准。

（43）**证券类互换交易商**。——‘证券类互换交易商’一词的含义以《1934年证券交易法》第3（a）条[《美国法典》第十五编第78c（a）节]的定义为准。”

（20）在第（46）款[以第（1）款重新编号后的序号为准]中删除“受制于第2（h）（7）条规定的”，替以“受制于第2（h）（5）条规定的”；

（21）在第（46）款[以第（1）款重新编号后的序号为准]之后插入：

“（47）**互换**。——

"(A) IN GENERAL. — Except as provided in subparagraph (B), the term 'swap' means any agreement, contract, or transaction —

"(i) that is a put, call, cap, floor, collar, or similar option of any kind that is for the purchase or sale, or based on the value, of 1 or more interest or other rates, currencies, commodities, securities, instruments of indebtedness, indices, quantitative measures, or other financial or economic interests or property of any kind;

"(ii) that provides for any purchase, sale, payment, or delivery (other than a dividend on an equity security) that is dependent on the occurrence, nonoccurrence, or the extent of the occurrence of an event or contingency associated with a potential financial, economic, or commercial consequence;

"(iii) that provides on an executory basis for the exchange, on a fixed or contingent basis, of 1 or more payments based on the value or level of 1 or more interest or other rates, currencies, commodities, securities, instruments of indebtedness, indices, quantitative measures, or other financial or economic interests or property of any kind, or any interest therein or based on the value thereof, and that transfers, as between the parties to the transaction, in whole or in part, the financial risk associated with a future change in any such value or level without also conveying a current or future direct or indirect ownership interest in an asset (including any enterprise or investment pool) or liability that incorporates the financial risk so transferred, including any agreement, contract, or transaction commonly known as —

"(I) an interest rate swap;

"(II) a rate floor;

"(III) a rate cap;

"(IV) a rate collar;

"(V) a cross-currency rate swap;

"(VI) a basis swap;

"(VII) a currency swap;

"(VIII) a foreign exchange swap;

"(IX) a total return swap;

"(X) an equity index swap;

"(XI) an equity swap;

"(XII) a debt index swap;

"(XIII) a debt swap;

"(XIV) a credit spread;

"(XV) a credit default swap;

"(XVI) a credit swap;

"(XVII) a weather swap;

(A)**一般规定**。——除第(B)子款规定的情形外,'互换'一词系指具有以下特征的任何协议、合约或交易——

(i)系以买卖下列各项(或基于下列各项的价值)为目的之看跌期权、看涨期权、上限期权、下限期权、保护性封顶保底期权或任何种类的类似期权:一项或一项以上利率或其他比率、货币、商品、证券、债务工具、指数、量化指标或其他任何种类的金融或经济权益或财产;

(ii)其所规定的任何买卖、支付或交割(但股权证券的股息除外)取决于:伴随有潜在金融、经济或商业后果的某一事件的发生、某一事件的不发生或某一事件发生的范围或程度,或者伴随有潜在金融、经济或商业后果的或有事件发生的可能性;

(iii)其所规定的于未来执行的一项或一项以上支付的交换(不论是在确定的基础上,或在或有的基础上进行的交换)系基于下列各项的价值或水平:一项或一项以上利率或其他比率、货币、商品、证券、债务工具、指数、量化指标或其他任何种类的金融或经济权益或财产,或上述各者的任何权益或基于上述各者价值的任何权益。此外,该等协议、合约或交易将任何上述价值或水平未来发生变动时伴随的全部或部分金融风险,从交易的一方转移到另一方,但是与此同时,并不转移含有该等被转移的金融风险的资产(包括任何企业或投资基金)或负债之当前或未来的直接或间接所有权权益。该等协议、合约或交易包括通常被冠以如下名称的任何协议、合约或交易——

(Ⅰ)利率互换;
(Ⅱ)利率下限期权;
(Ⅲ)利率上限期权;
(Ⅳ)保护性封顶保底利率期权;
(Ⅴ)跨货币利率互换;
(Ⅵ)基差互换;
(Ⅶ)货币互换;
(Ⅷ)外汇互换;
(Ⅸ)总回报互换;
(Ⅹ)股指互换;
(Ⅺ)股权互换;
(Ⅻ)债务指数互换;
(XIII)债务互换;
(XIV)信贷息差;
(XV)信用违约互换;
(XVI)信贷互换;
(XVII)气候互换;

"(XVIII) an energy swap;

"(XIX) a metal swap;

"(XX) an agricultural swap;

"(XXI) an emissions swap; and

"(XXII) a commodity swap;

"(iv) that is an agreement, contract, or transaction that is, or in the future becomes, commonly known to the trade as a swap;

"(v) including any security-based swap agreement which meets the definition of 'swap agreement' as defined in section 206A of the Gramm-Leach-Bliley Act (15 U.S.C. 78c note) of which a material term is based on the price, yield, value, or volatility of any security or any group or index of securities, or any interest therein; or

"(vi) that is any combination or permutation of, or option on, any agreement, contract, or transaction described in any of clauses (i) through (v).

"(B) EXCLUSIONS. — The term 'swap' does not include —

"(i) any contract of sale of a commodity for future delivery (or option on such a contract), leverage contract authorized under section 19, security futures product, or agreement, contract, or transaction described in section 2(c)(2)(C)(i) or section 2(c)(2)(D)(i);

"(ii) any sale of a nonfinancial commodity or security for deferred shipment or delivery, so long as the transaction is intended to be physically settled;

"(iii) any put, call, straddle, option, or privilege on any security, certificate of deposit, or group or index of securities, including any interest therein or based on the value thereof, that is subject to —

"(I) the Securities Act of 1933 (15 U.S.C. 77a et seq.); and

"(II) the Securities Exchange Act of 1934 (15 U.S.C. 78a et seq.);

"(iv) any put, call, straddle, option, or privilege relating to a foreign currency entered into on a national securities exchange registered pursuant to section 6 (a) of the Securities Exchange Act of 1934 (15 U.S.C. 78f(a));

"(v) any agreement, contract, or transaction providing for the purchase or sale of 1 or more securities on a fixed basis that is subject to —

"(I) the Securities Act of 1933 (15 U.S.C. 77a et seq.); and

"(II) the Securities Exchange Act of 1934 (15 U.S.C. 78a et seq.);

"(vi) any agreement, contract, or transaction providing for the purchase or sale of 1 or more securities on a contingent basis that is subject to the Securities Act of 1933 (15 U.S.C. 77a et seq.) and the Securities Exchange Act of 1934 (15 U.S.C. 78a et seq.), unless the agreement, contract, or transaction predicates the purchase or sale on the occurrence of a bona fide contingency that might reasonably be expected to affect or be affected by the

(XVIII)能源互换;
(XIX)金属互换;
(XX)农产品互换;
(XXI)排放互换;及
(XXII)商品互换;
(iv)当前或将来通常被业界称为互换的协议、合约或交易;

(v)包括符合'互换协议'定义的任何证券类互换协议['互换协议'定义见《格雷姆—里奇—比利雷法》第206A条(《美国法典》第十五编第78c节注释)],且该等证券类互换协议的某项重要条款系基于任何证券、任何证券集合、证券指数或上述各者的任何权益之价格、收益率、价值或波动性;或

(vi)属于第(i)至第(v)项所述任何协议、合约或交易的任何组合或排列,或该等协议、合约或交易的任何期权。

(B)**除外规定**。——'互换'一词不包括——

(i)任何远期交割的商品的出售合约(或该等合约的期权)、根据第19条获得核准的杠杆合约、证券期货产品,或者第2(c)(2)(C)(i)条或第2(c)(2)(D)(i)条所述协议、合约或交易;

(ii)旨在进行实物交割的任何延期装运或延期交割的非金融商品或证券的任何出售;

(iii)受制于以下法律规定的任何证券、存单或证券集合或证券指数(包括上述各者的任何权益或基于上述各者价值的任何权益)的任何看跌期权、看涨期权、跨式期权组合、其他期权或优先权——

(I)《1933年证券法》(《美国法典》第十五编第77a节及其后条文);及

(II)《1934年证券交易法》(《美国法典》第十五编第78a节及其后条文);

(iv)在根据《1934年证券交易法》第6(a)条[《美国法典》第十五编第78f(a)节]注册的全国性证券交易所达成的与外币相关的任何看跌期权、看涨期权、跨式期权组合、其他期权或优先权;

(v)规定了一只或一只以上受制于以下法律规定之证券的确定性买卖的任何协议、合约或交易——

(I)《1933年证券法》(《美国法典》第十五编第77a节及其后条文);及

(II)《1934年证券交易法》(《美国法典》第十五编第78a节及其后条文);

(vi)规定了一只或一只以上受制于《1933年证券法》(《美国法典》第十五编第77a节及其后条文)和《1934年证券交易法》(《美国法典》第十五编第78a节及其后条文)规定之证券的或有买卖的任何协议、合约或交易,除非该等协议、合约或交易要求以如下状况的发生作为买卖的前提条件:根据合理预期,可能会影响该等协议、合约或交易的非当事方信誉度的善意或有事件,或者可能受该非当事方信誉度影响的善意或

creditworthiness of a party other than a party to the agreement, contract, or transaction;

"(vii) any note, bond, or evidence of indebtedness that is a security, as defined in section 2(a)(1) of the Securities Act of 1933 (15 U.S.C. 77b(a)(1));

"(viii) any agreement, contract, or transaction that is —

"(I) based on a security; and

"(II) entered into directly or through an underwriter (as defined in section 2(a)(11) of the Securities Act of 1933 (15 U.S.C. 77b(a)(11)) by the issuer of such security for the purposes of raising capital, unless the agreement, contract, or transaction is entered into to manage a risk associated with capital raising;

"(ix) any agreement, contract, or transaction a counterparty of which is a Federal Reserve bank, the Federal Government, or a Federal agency that is expressly backed by the full faith and credit of the United States; and

"(x) any security–based swap, other than a security–based swap as described in subparagraph (D).

"(C) RULE OF CONSTRUCTION REGARDING MASTER AGREEMENTS. —

"(i) IN GENERAL. — Except as provided in clause (ii), the term 'swap' includes a master agreement that provides for an agreement, contract, or transaction that is a swap under subparagraph (A), together with each supplement to any master agreement, without regard to whether the master agreement contains an agreement, contract, or transaction that is not a swap pursuant to subparagraph (A).

"(ii) EXCEPTION. — For purposes of clause (i), the master agreement shall be considered to be a swap only with respect to each agreement, contract, or transaction covered by the master agreement that is a swap pursuant to subparagraph (A).

"(D) MIXED SWAP. — The term 'security–based swap' includes any agreement, contract, or transaction that is as described in section 3(a)(68)(A) of the Securities Exchange Act of 1934 (15 U.S.C. 78c(a)(68)(A)) and also is based on the value of 1 or more interest or other rates, currencies, commodities, instruments of indebtedness, indices, quantitative measures, other financial or economic interest or property of any kind (other than a single security or a narrow–based security index), or the occurrence, non–occurrence, or the extent of the occurrence of an event or contingency associated with a potential financial, economic, or commercial consequence (other than an event described in subparagraph (A)(iii)).

"(E) TREATMENT OF FOREIGN EXCHANGE SWAPS AND FORWARDS. —

"(i) IN GENERAL. — Foreign exchange swaps and foreign exchange forwards shall be considered swaps under this paragraph unless the Secretary makes a written determination under section 1b that either foreign exchange swaps or foreign exchange forwards or both —

"(I) should be not be regulated as swaps under this Act; and

有事件;

(vii)属于证券{定义见《1933年证券法》第2(a)(1)条[《美国法典》第十五编第77b(a)(1)节]}的任何票据、债券或债务证明;

(viii)任何具有以下特征的协议、合约或交易——

(I)系基于某一证券;且

(II)该等协议、合约或交易系由该证券的发行人以资金募集之目的直接达成或通过承销商{定义见《1933年证券法》第2(a)(11)条[《美国法典》第十五编第77b(a)(11)节]}达成,但达成该等协议、合约或交易是为了管理与资金募集相关的风险的情况除外;

(ix)任何协议、合约或交易的对手方是联邦储备银行、联邦政府或明确具有联邦十足诚信和信用担保的联邦机构;及

(x)第(D)子款所述证券类互换之外的任何证券类互换。

(C)**关于主协议的解释规则**。——

(i)**一般规定**。——除第(ii)项规定的情形外,'互换'一词包括:对属于第(A)子款项下互换的协议、合约或交易作出规定的主协议及任何主协议的所有补充协议,不论该主协议是否含有不属于第(A)子款规定之互换的协议、合约或交易。

(ii)**例外规定**。——就第(i)项而言,主协议应当仅得针对该主协议所涉及的属于第(A)子款规定之互换的每一协议、合同或交易时始得被视为互换。

(D)**混合互换**。——'证券类互换'一词包括《1934年证券交易法》第3(a)(68)(A)条[《美国法典》第十五编第78c(a)(68)(A)节]所述的并且同时基于一项或一项以上利率或其他比率、货币、商品、债务工具、指数、量化指标、任何其他种类的金融或经济权益或财产(但单一证券或窄基证券指数除外)的价值的任何协议、合约或交易,或者,《1934年证券交易法》第3(a)(68)(A)条[《美国法典》第十五编第78c(a)(68)(A)节]所述的并且同时基于伴随有潜在金融、经济或商业后果的某一事件的发生、某一事件的不发生或某一事件发生的范围或程度的任何协议、合约或交易,或者伴随有潜在金融、经济或商业后果的或有事件发生的可能性[但第(A)(iii)子款所述事件除外]的任何协议、合约或交易。

(E)**外汇互换和外汇远期的处理**。——

(i)**一般规定**。——外汇互换和外汇远期应视为本款规定的互换,除非财政部部长按照第1b条规定作出如下书面判定,即外汇互换和/或外汇远期——

(I)不应根据本法作为互换进行规制;且

"(II) are not structured to evade the Dodd–Frank Wall Street Reform and Consumer Protection Act in violation of any rule promulgated by the Commission pursuant to section 721 (c) of that Act.

"(ii) CONGRESSIONAL NOTICE; EFFECTIVENESS. — The Secretary shall submit any written determination under clause (i) to the appropriate committees of Congress, including the Committee on Agriculture, Nutrition, and Forestry of the Senate and the Committee on Agriculture of the House of Representatives. Any such written determination by the Secretary shall not be effective until it is submitted to the appropriate committees of Congress.

"(iii) REPORTING. — Notwithstanding a written determination by the Secretary under clause (i), all foreign exchange swaps and foreign exchange forwards shall be reported to either a swap data repository, or, if there is no swap data repository that would accept such swaps or forwards, to the Commission pursuant to section 4r within such time period as the Commission may by rule or regulation prescribe.

"(iv) BUSINESS STANDARDS. — Notwithstanding a written determination by the Secretary pursuant to clause (i), any party to a foreign exchange swap or forward that is a swap dealer or major swap participant shall conform to the business conduct standards contained in section 4s(h).

"(v) SECRETARY. — For purposes of this subparagraph, the term 'Secretary' means the Secretary of the Treasury.

"(F) EXCEPTION FOR CERTAIN FOREIGN EXCHANGE SWAPS AND FORWARDS. —

"(i) REGISTERED ENTITIES. — Any foreign exchange swap and any foreign exchange forward that is listed and traded on or subject to the rules of a designated contract market or a swap execution facility, or that is cleared by a derivatives clearing organization, shall not be exempt from any provision of this Act or amendments made by the Wall Street Transparency and Accountability Act of 2010 prohibiting fraud or manipulation.

"(ii) RETAIL TRANSACTIONS. — Nothing in subparagraph (E) shall affect, or be construed to affect, the applicability of this Act or the jurisdiction of the Commission with respect to agreements, contracts, or transactions in foreign currency pursuant to section 2(c)(2).

"(48) SWAP DATA REPOSITORY. — The term 'swap data repository' means any person that collects and maintains information or records with respect to transactions or positions in, or the terms and conditions of, swaps entered into by third parties for the purpose of providing a centralized recordkeeping facility for swaps.

"(49) SWAP DEALER. —

"(A) IN GENERAL. — The term 'swap dealer' means any person who —

(II)就其构建方式而言,无意通过违反商品期货交易委员会根据《多德—弗兰克华尔街改革与消费者保护法》第721(c)条颁发的任何规则而达到规避该法的目的。

(ii)**国会通知;生效**。——财政部部长应向相应的国会委员会(包括参议院农业、营养与林业委员会以及众议院的农业委员会)提交第(i)项所述的任何书面判定。财政部部长作出的任何上述判定在提交给相应的国会委员会之前不得生效。

(iii)**报告**。——即使财政部部长根据第(i)项的规定作出了书面判定,所有外汇互换和外汇远期仍应在商品期货交易委员会发布的规则或规章所规定的时限内根据第4r条的规定向一家互换数据存管机构报告。如果没有互换数据存管机构愿意受理该等外汇互换或外汇远期的报告,则应向商品期货交易委员会报告。

(iv)**业务标准**。——即使财政部部长根据第(i)项的规定作出了书面判定,任何外汇互换或外汇远期的一方身份为互换交易商或主要互换参与者的,仍应遵守第4s(h)条所述的业务行为准则。

(v)**财政部部长**。——就本子款而言,'财政部部长'一词系指美国财政部部长。

(F)**关于某些外汇互换和外汇远期的例外规定**。——

(i)**注册实体**。——在指定合约市场或互换执行设施或按其规则上市交易的任何外汇互换和任何外汇远期,或由衍生品结算组织集中结算的任何外汇互换和任何外汇远期,均不得豁免于本法关于禁止欺诈或操纵的任何规定,亦不得豁免于《2010年华尔街透明度与问责法》就禁止欺诈或操纵作出的任何相关修正。

(ii)**零售交易**。——第(E)子款的任何内容均不影响,亦不得被解释为影响本法对第2(c)(2)条所述的外汇协议、合约或交易的适用性或商品期货交易委员会对该等外汇协议、合约或交易的管辖权。

(48)**互换数据存管机构**。——'互换数据存管机构'一词系指为了给互换提供集中的记录保存设施,就第三方达成的互换交易或持仓的相关信息或记录以及与该等互换的条款和条件相关的信息或记录,进行收集和保存的任何主体。

(49)**互换交易商**。——

(A)**一般规定**。——'互换交易商'一词系指具有以下特征的任何主体——

"(i) holds itself out as a dealer in swaps;

"(ii) makes a market in swaps;

"(iii) regularly enters into swaps with counterparties as an ordinary course of business for its own account; or

"(iv) engages in any activity causing the person to be commonly known in the trade as a dealer or market maker in swaps, provided however, in no event shall an insured depository institution be considered to be a swap dealer to the extent it offers to enter into a swap with a customer in connection with originating a loan with that customer.

"(B) INCLUSION. — A person may be designated as a swap dealer for a single type or single class or category of swap or activities and considered not to be a swap dealer for other types, classes, or categories of swaps or activities.

"(C) EXCEPTION. — The term 'swap dealer' does not include a person that enters into swaps for such person's own account, either individually or in a fiduciary capacity, but not as a part of a regular business.

"(D) DE MINIMIS EXCEPTION. — The Commission shall exempt from designation as a swap dealer an entity that engages in a de minimis quantity of swap dealing in connection with transactions with or on behalf of its customers. The Commission shall promulgate regulations to establish factors with respect to the making of this determination to exempt.

"(50) SWAP EXECUTION FACILITY. — The term 'swap execution facility' means a trading system or platform in which multiple participants have the ability to execute or trade swaps by accepting bids and offers made by multiple participants in the facility or system, through any means of interstate commerce, including any trading facility, that —

"(A) facilitates the execution of swaps between persons; and

"(B) is not a designated contract market.".

(22) in paragraph (51) (as redesignated by paragraph (1), in subparagraph (A)(i), by striking "partipants" and inserting "participants".

(b) AUTHORITY TO DEFINE TERMS. — The Commodity Futures Trading Commission may adopt a rule to define —

(1) the term "commercial risk"; and

(2) any other term included in an amendment to the Commodity Exchange Act (7 U.S.C. 1 et seq.) made by this subtitle.

(c) MODIFICATION OF DEFINITIONS. — To include transactions and entities that have been structured to evade this subtitle (or an amendment made by this subtitle), the Commodity Futures Trading Commission shall adopt a rule to further define the terms "swap", "swap dealer", "major swap participant", and "eligible contract participant".

(d) EXEMPTIONS. — Section 4(c)(1) of the Commodity Exchange Act (7 U.S.C. 6(c)(1)) is amended by striking "except that" and all that follows through the period at the

(i)以互换交易商身份自居;

(ii)为互换做市;

(iii)为其自身账户在正常业务运作中经常地与对手方达成互换;或

(iv)因其从事的任何活动导致其通常被业界称为互换交易商或做市商,但是,参保存款机构因对客户发起某项贷款而向该客户要约达成某一互换的,不得将该等参保存款机构视为互换交易商。

(B)**包含的主体**。——任何主体均可在被指定为某单一类型、类别或种类的互换或活动的互换交易商的同时,而不被视为其他类型、类别或种类的互换或活动的互换交易商。

(C)**例外规定**。——‘互换交易商’一词不包括:虽以自身身份或受信义务人身份为自身账户达成互换,但并不以此为常规业务的主体。

(D)**微量豁免**。——对于因为与其客户进行的交易或代表其客户进行的交易而从事微量互换交易的实体,商品期货交易委员会应授予其豁免,使其不必被指定为互换交易商。商品期货交易委员会应颁发规章,明确规定作出上述豁免判定时应予考虑的因素。

(50)**互换执行设施**。——‘互换执行设施’一词系指具有如下特征的交易系统或平台:众多参与者可以通过任何州际商业手段接受设施内或系统内众多参与者的买卖报价以执行或交易互换。该等系统或平台包括符合下述条件的任何交易设施——

(A)为不同主体之间的互换执行提供便利;且

(B)并非指定的合约市场。”

(22)在第(51)款[以第(1)款重新编号后的序号为准]第(A)(i)子款中删除“参与者”的错误拼写“partipants”,替以正确拼写“participants”。

(b)**术语定义权**。——商品期货交易委员会有权发布规则,对如下术语作出定义——

(1)“商业风险”;及

(2)本子编对《商品交易法》(《美国法典》第七编第1节及其后条文)作出的修正中包含的任何其他术语。

(c)**定义修改**。——对于就其构建方式而言有意规避本子编规定(或本子编所做修正)的交易和实体,商品期货交易委员会应制定规则,对下列术语进行进一步界定,将该等交易或实体纳入本子编的管辖范围:“互换”、“互换交易商”、“主要互换参与者”和“适格合约参与者”。

(d)**豁免**。——《商品交易法》第4(c)(1)条[《美国法典》第七编第6(c)(1)节]修正如下:删除“但”直至结尾处句号前的全部内容,并替以:“但是下列情形除外——

end and inserting the following: "except that —

"(A) unless the Commission is expressly authorized by any provision described in this subparagraph to grant exemptions, with respect to amendments made by subtitle A of the Wall Street Transparency and Accountability Act of 2010 —

"(i) with respect to —

"(I) paragraphs (2), (3), (4), (5), and (7), paragraph (18)(A)(vii)(III), paragraphs (23), (24), (31), (32), (38), (39), (41), (42), (46), (47), (48), and (49) of section 1a, and sections 2(a)(13), 2(c)(1)(D), 4a(a), 4a(b), 4d(c), 4d(d), 4r, 4s, 5b(a), 5b(b), 5(d), 5(g), 5(h), 5b(c), 5b(i), 8e, and 21; and

"(II) section 206(e) of the Gramm–Leach–Bliley Act (Public Law 106 – 102; 15 U.S.C. 78c note); and

"(ii) in sections 721(c) and 742 of the Dodd–Frank Wall Street Reform and Consumer Protection Act; and

"(B) the Commission and the Securities and Exchange Commission may by rule, regulation, or order jointly exclude any agreement, contract, or transaction from section 2(a)(1)(D)) if the Commissions determine that the exemption would be consistent with the public interest.".

(e) CONFORMING AMENDMENTS. —

(1) Section 2(c)(2)(B)(i)(II) of the Commodity Exchange Act (7 U.S.C. 2(c)(2)(B)(i)(II)) is amended —

(A) in item (cc) —

(i) in subitem (AA), by striking "section 1a(20)" and inserting "section 1a"; and

(ii) in subitem (BB), by striking "section 1a(20)" and inserting "section 1a"; and

(B) in item (dd), by striking "section 1a(12)(A)(ii)" and inserting "section 1a(18)(A)(ii)".

(2) Section 4m(3) of the Commodity Exchange Act (7 U.S.C. 6m(3)) is amended by striking "section 1a(6)" and inserting "section 1a".

(3) Section 4q(a)(1) of the Commodity Exchange Act (7 U.S.C. 6o – 1(a)(1)) is amended by striking "section 1a(4)" and inserting "section 1a(9)".

(4) Section 5(e)(1) of the Commodity Exchange Act (7 U.S.C. 7(e)(1)) is amended by striking "section 1a(4)" and inserting "section 1a(9)".

(5) Section 5a(b)(2)(F) of the Commodity Exchange Act (7 U.S.C. 7a(b)(2)(F)) is amended by striking "section 1a(4)" and inserting "section 1a(9)".

(6) Section 5b(a) of the Commodity Exchange Act (7 U.S.C. 7a – 1(a)) is amended, in the matter preceding paragraph (1), by striking "section 1a (9)" and inserting "section 1a".

(A)除非商品期货交易委员会有权根据本子款任何规定的明确授权就《2010年华尔街透明度与问责法》第A子编作出的以下修正授予豁免——

(i)就以下条款作出的修正——

(I)第1a条第(2)款、第(3)款、第(4)款、第(5)款和第(7)款、第(18)(A)(vii)(III)款、第(23)款、第(24)款、第(31)款、第(32)款、第(38)款、第(39)款、第(41)款、第(42)款、第(46)款、第(47)款、第(48)款和第(49)款,以及第2(a)(13)条、第2(c)(1)(D)条、第4a(a)条、第4a(b)条、第4d(c)条、第4d(d)条、第4r条、第4s条、第5b(a)条、第5b(b)条、第5(d)条、第5(g)条、第5(h)条、第5b(c)条、第5b(i)条、第8e条和第21条;及

(II)《格雷姆—里奇—比利雷法》第206(e)条(第106—102号公法;《美国法典》第十五编第78c节注释);及

(ii)在《多德—弗兰克华尔街改革与消费者保护法》第721(c)条和第742条中作出的修正;且

(B)商品期货交易委员会和证券交易委员会可以联合发布规则、规章或命令,将任何协议、合约或交易排除在第2(a)(1)(D)条的适用范围之外,其前提是商品期货交易委员会判定该等豁免将符合公共利益。"

(e)**一致性修正**。——

(1)《商品交易法》第2(c)(2)(B)(i)(II)条[《美国法典》第7编第2(c)(2)(B)(i)(II)节]修正如下——

(A)在第(cc)目中——

(i)第(AA)子目删除"第1a(20)条",替以"第1a条";及

(ii)第(BB)子目删除"第1a(20)条",替以"第1a条";及

(B)第(dd)目删除"第1a(12)(A)(ii)条",替以"第1a(18)(A)(ii)条"

(2)《商品交易法》第4m(3)条[《美国法典》第七编第6m(3)节]修正如下:删除"第1a(6)条",替以"第1a条"。

(3)《商品交易法》第4q(a)(1)条[《美国法典》第七编第6o-1(a)(1)节]修正如下:删除"第1a(4)条",替以"第1a(9)条"。

(4)《商品交易法》第5(e)(1)条[《美国法典》第七编第7(e)(1)节]修正如下:删除"第1a(4)条",替以"第1a(9)条"。

(5)《商品交易法》第5a(b)(2)(F)条[《美国法典》第七编第7a(b)(2)(F)节]修正如下:删除"第1a(4)条",替以"第1a(9)条"。

(6)《商品交易法》第5b(a)条(《美国法典》第7编第7a-1(a)节]修正如下:在第(1)款之前的内容中,删除"第1a(9)条",替以"第1a条"。

(7) Section 5c(c)(2)(B) of the Commodity Exchange Act (7 U.S.C. 7a–2(c)(2)(B)) is amended by striking "section 1a(4)" and inserting "section 1a(9)".

(8) Section 6(g)(5)(B)(i) of the Securities Exchange Act of 1934 (15 U.S.C. 78f(g)(5)(B)(i)) is amended —

(A) in subclause (I), by striking "section 1a(12)(B)(ii)" and inserting "section 1a(18)(B)(ii)"; and

(B) in subclause (II), by striking "section 1a(12)" and inserting "section 1a(18)".

(9) Section 402 of the Legal Certainty for Bank Products Act of 2000 (7 U.S.C. 27 et seq.) is amended —

(A) in subsection (a)(7), by striking "section 1a(20)" and inserting "section 1a";

(B) in subsection (b)(2), by striking "section 1a(12)" and inserting "section 1a"; and

(C) in subsection (c), by striking "section 1a(4)" and inserting "section 1a".

(10) The first section of Public Law 85–839 (7 U.S.C. 13–1) is amended in subsection (a), in the first sentence, by inserting "motion picture box office receipts (or any index, measure, value, or data related to such receipts) or" after "sale of".

(f) EFFECTIVE DATE. — Notwithstanding any other provision of this Act, the amendments made by subsection (a)(4) shall take effect on June 1, 2010.

SEC.722. JURISDICTION.

(a) EXCLUSIVE JURISDICTION. — Section 2(a)(1) of the Commodity Exchange Act (7 U.S.C. 2(a)(1)) is amended —

(1) in subparagraph (A), in the first sentence —

(A) by inserting "the Wall Street Transparency and Accountability Act of 2010 (including an amendment made by that Act) and" after "otherwise provided in";

(B) by striking "(C) and (D)" and inserting "(C), (D), and (I)";

(C) by striking "(c) through (i) of this section" and inserting "(c) and (f)";

(D) by striking "contracts of sale" and inserting "swaps or contracts of sale"; and

(E) by striking "or derivatives transaction execution facility registered pursuant to section 5 or 5a" and inserting "pursuant to section 5 or a swap execution facility pursuant to section 5h"; and

(2) by adding at the end the following:

"(G)(i) Nothing in this paragraph shall limit the jurisdiction conferred on the Securities and Exchange Commission by the Wall Street Transparency and Accountability Act of 2010 with regard to security–based swap agreements as defined pursuant to section 3(a)(78) of the Securities Exchange Act of 1934, and security–based swaps.

"(ii) In addition to the authority of the Securities and Exchange Commission described in clause (i), nothing in this subparagraph shall limit or affect any statutory authority of the Commission with respect to an agreement, contract, or transaction described in clause (i).

(7)《商品交易法》第5c(c)(2)(B)条[《美国法典》第7编第7a—2(c)(2)(B)节]修正如下:删除“第1a(4)条”,替以“第1a(9)条”。

(8)《1934年证券交易法》第6(g)(5)(B)(i)条[《美国法典》第十五编第78f(g)(5)(B)(i)节]修正如下——

(A)在第(I)子项中,删除“第1a(12)(B)(ii)条”,替以“第1a(18)(B)(ii)条”;及

(B)在第(II)子项中,删除“第1a(12)条”,替以“第1a(18)条”。

(9)《2000年银行产品法律确定性法》第402条(《美国法典》第七编第27节及其后条文)修正如下——

(A)在第(a)(7)子条中,删除“第1a(20)条”,替以“第1a条”;

(B)在第(b)(2)子条中,删除“第1a(12)条”,替以“第1a条”;及

(C)在第(c)子条中,删除“第1a(4)条”,替以“第1a条”。

(10)第85-839号公法第1条(《美国法典》第七编第13-1节)第(a)子条修正如下:在第一句中,在“销售”前插入“电影票房收入(或与电影票房收入相关的任何指数、指标、价值或数据)或”。

(f)**生效日**。——无论本法是否存在任何不同规定,第(a)(4)子条作出的全部修正均应于2010年6月1日生效。

第722条　管辖权

(a)**排他管辖权**。——《商品交易法》第2(a)(1)条[《美国法典》第七编第2(a)(1)节]修正如下——

(1)在第(A)子款第一句中——

(A)在“本款第(c)子款”前插入“《2010年华尔街透明度与问责法》(包括该法作出的修正)及”;

(B)删除“第(C)子款和第(D)子款”,替以“第(C)子款、第(D)子款和第(I)子款”;

(C)删除“本条第(c)子条至第(i)子条”,替以“第(c)子条和第(f)子条”;

(D)删除“出售合约”,替以“互换或远期交割商品出售合约”;及

(E)删除“依本法第5条或第5a条指定的合约市场或注册的衍生品交易执行设施”,替以“依本法第5条指定的合约市场或依本法第5h条指定的互换执行设施”;同时

(2)在结尾处增加如下内容:

“(G)(i)本款任何内容均不限制《2010年华尔街透明度与问责法》赋予证券交易委员会的对《1934年证券交易法》第3(a)(78)条所定义的证券类互换协议的管辖权,以及对证券类互换的管辖权。

(ii)除了既不限制也不影响第(i)项所述证券交易委员会的权力之外,本子款任何内容同样既不限制也不影响商品期货交易委员会对第(i)项所述协议、合约或交易享有的任何法定权力。

"(H) Notwithstanding any other provision of law, the Wall Street Transparency and Accountability Act of 2010 shall not apply to, and the Commodity Futures Trading Commission shall have no jurisdiction under such Act (or any amendments to the Commodity Exchange Act made by such Act) with respect to, any security other than a security–based swap.".

(b) REGULATION OF SWAPS UNDER FEDERAL AND STATE LAW. — Section 12 of the Commodity Exchange Act (7 U.S.C. 16) is amended by adding at the end the following:

"(h) REGULATION OF SWAPS AS INSURANCE UNDER STATE LAW. — A swap —

"(1) shall not be considered to be insurance; and

"(2) may not be regulated as an insurance contract under the law of any State.".

(c) AGREEMENTS, CONTRACTS, AND TRANSACTIONS TRADED ON AN ORGANIZED EXCHANGE. — Section 2(c)(2)(A) of the Commodity Exchange Act (7 U.S.C. 2(c)(2)(A)) is amended —

(1) in clause (i), by striking "or" at the end;

(2) by redesignating clause (ii) as clause (iii); and

(3) by inserting after clause (i) the following:

"(ii) a swap; or".

(d) APPLICABILITY. — Section 2 of the Commodity Exchange Act (7 U.S.C. 2) (as amended by section 723(a)(3)) is amended by adding at the end the following:

"(i) APPLICABILITY. — The provisions of this Act relating to swaps that were enacted by the Wall Street Transparency and Accountability Act of 2010 (including any rule prescribed or regulation promulgated under that Act), shall not apply to activities outside the United States unless those activities —

"(1) have a direct and significant connection with activities in, or effect on, commerce of the United States; or

"(2) contravene such rules or regulations as the Commission may prescribe or promulgate as are necessary or appropriate to prevent the evasion of any provision of this Act that was enacted by the Wall Street Transparency and Accountability Act of 2010.".

(e) FEDERAL ENERGY REGULATORY COMMISSION. — Section 2(a)(1) of the Commodity Exchange Act (7 U.S.C. 2(a)(1)) is amended by adding at the end the following:

"(I)(i) Nothing in this Act shall limit or affect any statutory authority of the Federal Energy Regulatory Commission or a State regulatory authority (as defined in section 3(21) of the Federal Power Act (16 U.S.C. 796(21)) with respect to an agreement, contract, or transaction that is entered into pursuant to a tariff or rate schedule approved by the Federal Energy Regulatory Commission or a State regulatory authority and is —

"(I) not executed, traded, or cleared on a registered entity or trading facility; or

"(II) executed, traded, or cleared on a registered entity or trading facility owned or

（H）无论是否存在任何不同法律规定，《2010年华尔街透明度与问责法》不适用于证券类互换之外的任何证券，且商品期货交易委员会亦不得根据该法（或该法对《商品交易法》作出的任何修正）对证券类互换之外的任何证券享有管辖权。”

（b）**联邦法律及州法律规定的互换监管**。——在《商品交易法》（《美国法典》第七编第16节）第12条结尾处增加如下内容，作为对该法的修正：

“（h）**根据州法律将互换视为保险进行监管**。——任何互换均——

（1）不得被视为保险；并

（2）不得作为任何州法律规定的保险合同予以监管。”

（c）**在有组织的交易所交易的协议、合约和交易**——《商品交易法》第2（c）（2）（A）条［《美国法典》第七编第2（c）（2）（A）节］修正如下——

（1）删除第（i）项中最后的“或”；

（2）第（ii）项重新编号为第（iii）项；及

（3）在第（i）项之后插入如下内容：

“（ii）属于互换；或”。

（d）**适用范围**。——在《商品交易法》第2条（《美国法典》第七编第2节）［以经第723（a）（3）条修正后的版本为准］结尾处增加如下内容，作为对该条的修正：

“（i）**适用范围**。——《2010年华尔街透明度与问责法》（包括根据该法制定的任何规则或颁发的任何规章）中制定的本法关于互换的规定不适用于美国境外的活动，除非该等活动——

（1）与美国境内商业活动具有直接重大关联，或对其具有直接重大影响；或

（2）违反商品期货交易委员会为防范对《2010年华尔街透明度与问责法》制定的本法任何规定的规避行为而制定或颁发的必要或适当的规则或规章。”

（e）**联邦能源监管委员会**。——在《商品交易法》第2（a）（1）条［《美国法典》第七编第2（a）（1）节］结尾处增加如下内容，作为对该条的修正：

“（I）（i）本法任何规定既不限制也不影响联邦能源监管委员会或州监管机构{定义见《联邦电力法》第3（21）条［《美国法典》第十六编第796（21）节］}对以下协议、合约或交易享有的任何法定权力：依据联邦能源监管委员会或州监管机构批准的电价表或价目表达成的，并且符合以下条件的协议、合约或交易——

（I）既不是在注册实体或交易设施进行执行、交易或结算；也

（II）不是在区域输电组织或独立系统运营商所拥有或运营的注册实体或交易设

operated by a regional transmission organization or independent system operator.

"(ii) In addition to the authority of the Federal Energy Regulatory Commission or a State regulatory authority described in clause (i), nothing in this subparagraph shall limit or affect —

"(I) any statutory authority of the Commission with respect to an agreement, contract, or transaction described in clause (i); or

"(II) the jurisdiction of the Commission under subparagraph (A) with respect to an agreement, contract, or transaction that is executed, traded, or cleared on a registered entity or trading facility that is not owned or operated by a regional transmission organization or independent system operator (as defined by sections 3(27) and (28) of the Federal Power Act (16 U.S.C. 796(27), 796(28))).".

(f) PUBLIC INTEREST WAIVER. — Section 4(c) of the Commodity Exchange Act (7 U.S.C. 6 (c)) (as amended by section 721 (d)) is amended by adding at the end the following:

"(6) If the Commission determines that the exemption would be consistent with the public interest and the purposes of this Act, the Commission shall, in accordance with paragraphs (1) and (2), exempt from the requirements of this Act an agreement, contract, or transaction that is entered into —

"(A) pursuant to a tariff or rate schedule approved or permitted to take effect by the Federal Energy Regulatory Commission;

"(B) pursuant to a tariff or rate schedule establishing rates or charges for, or protocols governing, the sale of electric energy approved or permitted to take effect by the regulatory authority of the State or municipality having jurisdiction to regulate rates and charges for the sale of electric energy within the State or municipality; or

"(C) between entities described in section 201(f) of the Federal Power Act (16 U.S.C. 824(f)).".

(g) AUTHORITY OF FERC. — Nothing in the Wall Street Transparency and Accountability Act of 2010 or the amendments to the Commodity Exchange Act made by such Act shall limit or affect any statutory enforcement authority of the Federal Energy Regulatory Commission pursuant to section 222 of the Federal Power Act and section 4A of the Natural Gas Act that existed prior to the date of enactment of the Wall Street Transparency and Accountability Act of 2010.

(h) DETERMINATION. — The Commodity Exchange Act is amended by inserting after section 1a (7 U.S.C. 1a) the following:

"SEC.1b. REQUIREMENTS OF SECRETARY OF THE TREASURY REGARDING EXEMPTION OF FOREIGN EXCHANGE SWAPS AND FOREIGN EXCHANGE FORWARDS FROM DEFINITION OF THE TERM 'SWAP'.

施进行执行、交易或结算。

(ii)除了既不限制也不影响第(i)项所述联邦能源监管委员会或州监管机构的权力之外,本子款任何内容同样既不限制也不影响——

(I)商品期货交易委员会对于第(i)项所述协议、合约或交易享有的任何法定权力;或

(II)商品期货交易委员会依据第(A)子款对如下协议、合约或交易享有的管辖权,即其不在由区域输电组织或独立系统运营商{定义见《联邦电力法》第3(27)条和第3(28)条[《美国法典》第十六编第796(27)节及第796(28)节]}所拥有或运营的注册实体或交易设施执行、交易或结算的协议、合约或交易。"

(f)**公共利益豁免**。——在《商品交易法》第4(c)条[《美国法典》第七编第6(c)节][以经第721(d)条修正后的版本为准]结尾处增加如下内容,作为对该条的修正:

"(6)商品期货交易委员会判定豁免将符合公共利益以及本法宗旨的,应按照第(1)款和第(2)款规定将下列协议、合约或交易豁免于本法规定的适用——

(A)根据联邦能源监管委员会批准或许可生效的电价表或价目表而达成的协议、合约或交易;

(B)根据设定电力出售费率或收费的电价表或价目表或者电力出售协议而达成的协议、合约或交易,且该等电价表、价目表或电力出售协议已获得对在该州或该市出售电力之费率及收费享有监管管辖权的该州或该市监管机构批准或许可生效;或

(C)《联邦电力法》第201(f)条[《美国法典》第十六编第824(f)节]所述实体之间达成的协议、合约或交易。"

(g)**联邦能源监管委员会的权力**。——《2010年华尔街透明度与问责法》的任何规定或该法对《商品交易法》作出的任何修正均不限制或影响联邦能源监管委员会根据在《2010年华尔街透明度与问责法》颁布之日前已经生效的《联邦电力法》第222条及《天然气法》第4A条享有的法定执行权。

(h)**判定**。——在《商品交易法》第1a条(《美国法典》第七编第1a节)之后插入如下内容,作为对该法的修正:

"第1b条　财政部部长授予外汇互换和外汇远期豁免于'互换'定义时的要求

"(a) REQUIRED CONSIDERATIONS. — In determining whether to exempt foreign exchange swaps and foreign exchange forwards from the definition of the term 'swap', the Secretary of the Treasury (referred to in this section as the 'Secretary') shall consider —

"(1) whether the required trading and clearing of foreign exchange swaps and foreign exchange forwards would create systemic risk, lower transparency, or threaten the financial stability of the United States;

"(2) whether foreign exchange swaps and foreign exchange forwards are already subject to a regulatory scheme that is materially comparable to that established by this Act for other classes of swaps;

"(3) the extent to which bank regulators of participants in the foreign exchange market provide adequate supervision, including capital and margin requirements;

"(4) the extent of adequate payment and settlement systems; and

"(5) the use of a potential exemption of foreign exchange swaps and foreign exchange forwards to evade otherwise applicable regulatory requirements.

"(b) DETERMINATION. — If the Secretary makes a determination to exempt foreign exchange swaps and foreign exchange forwards from the definition of the term 'swap', the Secretary shall submit to the appropriate committees of Congress a determination that contains —

"(1) an explanation regarding why foreign exchange swaps and foreign exchange forwards are qualitatively different from other classes of swaps in a way that would make the foreign exchange swaps and foreign exchange forwards ill-suited for regulation as swaps; and

"(2) an identification of the objective differences of foreign exchange swaps and foreign exchange forwards with respect to standard swaps that warrant an exempted status.

"(c) EFFECT OF DETERMINATION. — A determination by the Secretary under subsection (b) shall not exempt any foreign exchange swaps and foreign exchange forwards traded on a designated contract market or swap execution facility from any applicable antifraud and antimanipulation provision under this title.".

SEC.723. CLEARING.

(a) CLEARING REQUIREMENT. —

(1) IN GENERAL. — Section 2 of the Commodity Exchange Act (7 U.S.C. 2) is amended —

(A) by striking subsections (d), (e), (g), and (h); and

(B) by redesignating subsection (i) as subsection (g).

(2) SWAPS; LIMITATION ON PARTICIPATION. — Section 2 of the Commodity Exchange Act (7 U.S.C. 2) (as amended by paragraph (1)) is amended by inserting after subsection (c) the following:

"(d) SWAPS. — Nothing in this Act (other than subparagraphs (A), (B), (C), (D),

(a)**应考虑的因素**。——判定外汇互换和外汇远期是否应豁免适用‘互换’的定义时，财政部部长(本条以下简称部长)应考虑下列因素——

(1)按相关要求交易和结算外汇互换和外汇远期是否会引发系统性风险、导致透明度降低或威胁美国的金融稳定；

(2)外汇互换和外汇远期已受到的监管是否与本法对其他类别互换所建立的监管制度具有实质可比性；

(3)监管外汇市场参与者的银行业监管者在多大范围内作出了充分的监管(包括在资本和保证金要求方面的监管)；

(4)在多大范围内使用了充分的支付和结算系统；及

(5)申请豁免外汇互换和外汇远期的目的是否是规避其他本应适用的监管要求。

(b)**判定**。——如果部长判定应使外汇互换和外汇远期豁免适用‘互换’的定义，则部长应向相应的国会委员会提交其判定书——

(1)解释为何外汇互换和外汇远期与其他类别互换存在本质上的差异，因此不适合作为互换监管；及

(2)指出外汇互换和外汇远期与标准互换存在何等客观差异，因此有必要获得豁免资格。

(c)**判定的影响**。——部长依据第(b)子条作出豁免判定的，在指定合约市场或互换执行设施交易的任何外汇互换和外汇远期就本编关于反欺诈和反操纵的任何适用的规定而言应不受该项豁免影响，其应继续遵守该等规定。”

第723条　集中结算

(a)**集中结算要求**。——

(1)**一般规定**。——《商品交易法》(《美国法典》第七编第2节)第2条修正如下——

(A)删除第(d)子条、第(e)子条、第(g)子条及第(h)子条；及

(B)第(i)子条重新编号为第(g)子条。

(2)**互换；参与限制**。——在《商品交易法》第2条(《美国法典》第七编第2节)[以经第(1)款修正后的版本为准]第(c)子条之后插入如下内容，作为对该条的修正：

“(d)**互换**。——本法任何规定既不规制也不适用于互换[以下规定除外：第(a)

(G), and (H) of subsection (a)(1), subsections (f) and (g), sections 1a, 2(a)(13), 2(c)(2)(A)(ii), 2(e), 2(h), 4(c), 4a, 4b, and 4b–1, subsections (a), (b), and (g) of section 4c, sections 4d, 4e, 4f, 4g, 4h, 4i, 4j, 4k, 4l, 4m, 4n, 4o, 4p, 4r, 4s, 4t, 5, 5b, 5c, 5e, and 5h, subsections (c) and (d) of section 6, sections 6c, 6d, 8, 8a, and 9, subsections (e)(2), (f), and (h) of section 12, subsections (a) and (b) of section 13, sections 17, 20, 21, and 22(a)(4), and any other provision of this Act that is applicable to registered entities or Commission registrants) governs or applies to a swap.

"(e) LIMITATION ON PARTICIPATION. — It shall be unlawful for any person, other than an eligible contract participant, to enter into a swap unless the swap is entered into on, or subject to the rules of, a board of trade designated as a contract market under section 5.".

(3) MANDATORY CLEARING OF SWAPS. — Section 2 of the Commodity Exchange Act (7 U.S.C. 2) is amended by inserting after subsection (g) (as redesignated by paragraph (1)(B)) the following:

"(h) CLEARING REQUIREMENT. —

"(1) IN GENERAL. —

"(A) STANDARD FOR CLEARING. — It shall be unlawful for any person to engage in a swap unless that person submits such swap for clearing to a derivatives clearing organization that is registered under this Act or a derivatives clearing organization that is exempt from registration under this Act if the swap is required to be cleared.

"(B) OPEN ACCESS. — The rules of a derivatives clearing organization described in subparagraph (A) shall —

"(i) prescribe that all swaps (but not contracts of sale of a commodity for future delivery or options on such contracts) submitted to the derivatives clearing organization with the same terms and conditions are economically equivalent within the derivatives clearing organization and may be offset with each other within the derivatives clearing organization; and

"(ii) provide for non–discriminatory clearing of a swap (but not a contract of sale of a commodity for future delivery or option on such contract) executed bilaterally or on or through the rules of an unaffiliated designated contract market or swap execution facility.

"(2) COMMISSION REVIEW. —

"(A) COMMISSION–INITIATED REVIEW. —

"(i) The Commission on an ongoing basis shall review each swap, or any group, category, type, or class of swaps to make a determination as to whether the swap or group, category, type, or class of swaps should be required to be cleared.

"(ii) The Commission shall provide at least a 30–day public comment period regarding any determination made under clause (i).

"(B) SWAP SUBMISSIONS. —

(1)子条第(A)子款、第(B)子款、第(C)子款、第(D)子款、第(G)子款及第(H)子款;第(f)子条和第(g)子条;第1a条、第2(a)(13)条、第2(c)(2)(A)(ii)条、第2(e)条、第2(h)条、第4(c)条、第4a条、第4b条和第4b-1条;第4c条第(a)子条、第(b)子条和第(g)子条;第4d条、第4e条、第4f条、第4g条、第4h条、第4i条、第4j条、第4k条、第4l条、第4m条、第4n条、第4o条、第4p条、第4r条、第4s条、第4t条、第5条、第5b条、第5c条、第5e条和第5h条;第6条第(c)子条和第(d)子条;第6c条、第6d条、第8条、第8a条和第9条;第12条第(e)(2)子条、第(f)子条和第(h)子条;第13条第(a)子条和第(b)子条;第17条、第20条、第21条和第22(a)(4)条,以及本法中适用于注册实体或在商品期货交易委员会注册之实体的任何其他规定]。

(e)**参与限制**。——适格合约参与者之外的任何人,除在根据第5条被指定为合约市场的交易场所或按其规则达成互换以外,不得达成互换,否则当属违法。”

(3)**互换的强制集中结算**。——在《商品交易法》第2条(《美国法典》第七编第2节)第(g)子条[以第(1)(B)款重新编号后的序号为准]之后插入如下内容,作为对该条的修正:

“(h)**集中结算要求**。——

(1)**一般规定**。——

(A)**集中结算标准**。——对于必须进行集中结算的互换,若非将该等互换提交根据本法注册的或者根据本法豁免注册的衍生品结算组织进行集中结算,任何人不得从事该等互换,否则当属违法。

(B)**准入开放性**。——第(A)子款所述衍生品结算组织的规则应——

(i)规定提交给该衍生品结算组织的具有相同条款及条件的所有互换(但不包括远期交割商品出售合约或该等合约的期权)在该衍生品结算组织内应具有同等经济意义,并可在该衍生品结算组织内相互对冲;且

(ii)为双边执行的互换,或在非关联指定合约市场或互换执行设施执行的或通过其规则执行的互换(但不包括远期交割商品出售合约或该等合约的期权)提供无差别对待的集中结算。

(2)**商品期货交易委员会审查**。——

(A)**商品期货交易委员会发起的审查**。——

(i)商品期货交易委员会应对每一互换或任何互换集合、种类、类型或类别进行持续性审查,判定该等互换或互换集合、种类、类型或类别是否应进行集中结算。

(ii)商品期货交易委员会按照第(i)项作出任何判定的,至少应提供30天的公众意见征求期。

(B)**拟受理结算的互换的呈报**。——

"(i) A derivatives clearing organization shall submit to the Commission each swap, or any group, category, type, or class of swaps that it plans to accept for clearing, and provide notice to its members (in a manner to be determined by the Commission) of the submission.

"(ii) Any swap or group, category, type, or class of swaps listed for clearing by a derivative clearing organization as of the date of enactment of this subsection shall be considered submitted to the Commission.

"(iii) The Commission shall —

"(I) make available to the public submissions received under clauses (i) and (ii);

"(II) review each submission made under clauses (i) and (ii), and determine whether the swap, or group, category, type, or class of swaps described in the submission is required to be cleared; and

"(III) provide at least a 30-day public comment period regarding its determination as to whether the clearing requirement under paragraph (1)(A) shall apply to the submission.

"(C) DEADLINE. — The Commission shall make its determination under subparagraph (B)(iii) not later than 90 days after receiving a submission made under subparagraphs (B)(i) and (B)(ii), unless the submitting derivatives clearing organization agrees to an extension for the time limitation established under this subparagraph.

"(D) DETERMINATION. —

"(i) In reviewing a submission made under subparagraph (B), the Commission shall review whether the submission is consistent with section 5b(c)(2).

"(ii) In reviewing a swap, group of swaps, or class of swaps pursuant to subparagraph (A) or a submission made under subparagraph (B), the Commission shall take into account the following factors:

"(I) The existence of significant outstanding notional exposures, trading liquidity, and adequate pricing data.

"(II) The availability of rule framework, capacity, operational expertise and resources, and credit support infrastructure to clear the contract on terms that are consistent with the material terms and trading conventions on which the contract is then traded.

"(III) The effect on the mitigation of systemic risk, taking into account the size of the market for such contract and the resources of the derivatives clearing organization available to clear the contract.

"(IV) The effect on competition, including appropriate fees and charges applied to clearing.

"(V) The existence of reasonable legal certainty in the event of the insolvency of the relevant derivatives clearing organization or 1 or more of its clearing members with regard to the treatment of customer and swap counterparty positions, funds, and property.

"(iii) In making a determination under subparagraph (A) or (B)(iii) that the clearing

(i)衍生品结算组织应将拟受理结算的每一互换或任何互换集合、种类、类型或类别呈报给商品期货交易委员会,并按商品期货交易委员会确定的方式向衍生品结算组织会员提供相应通知。

(ii) 截至在本子条规定颁布之日衍生品结算组织已挂牌结算的任何互换或互换集合、种类、类型或类别均应视为已呈报商品期货交易委员会。

(iii)商品期货交易委员会应——

(I)向公众公开其根据第(i)项和第(ii)项收到的呈报信息;

(II)对按照第(i)项和第(ii)项进行的每项呈报进行审查,判定呈报材料中所述的互换或互换集合、种类、类型或类别是否应进行集中结算;及

(III)在对呈报的互换或互换集合、种类、类型或类别是否应按照第(1)(A)款的规定进行集中结算作出判定前,提供至少30天的公众意见征求期。

(C)**最后期限**。——除非进行呈报的衍生品结算组织同意延长本子款规定的期限,否则商品期货交易委员会应在收到依据第(B)(i)子款和第(B)(ii)子款进行的呈报后90天内按照第(B)(iii)子款作出判定。

(D)**判定**。——

(i)商品期货交易委员会应审查根据第(B)子款进行的呈报是否符合第5b(c)(2)条的规定。

(ii)商品期货交易委员会根据第(A)子款规定审查某一互换、互换集合或互换类别时或者审查根据第(B)子款进行的呈报时,应考虑下列因素:

(I)是否存在重大未平仓名义风险敞口、交易流动性及充分的定价数据。

(II)是否具有充分的规则框架、能力、运营专长和资源以及信用支持基础设施,能够按照与合约届时交易所依据的重要条款及与交易惯例一致的条款对合约进行结算。

(III)对缓释系统性风险的作用(此时应考虑该合约的市场规模及衍生品结算组织可用的结算该合约的资源)。

(IV)对竞争(包括针对结算收取的适当的费用和收费)的影响。

(V)若相关衍生品结算组织或其一个或一个以上结算会员出现资不抵债的情况,对客户及互换对手方的持仓、资金及财产的处理是否存在合理的法律确定性。

(iii)商品期货交易委员会根据第(A)子款或第(B)(iii)子款判定应进行集中结算

requirement shall apply, the Commission may require such terms and conditions to the requirement as the Commission determines to be appropriate.

"(E) RULES. — Not later than 1 year after the date of the enactment of this subsection, the Commission shall adopt rules for a derivatives clearing organization's submission for review, pursuant to this paragraph, of a swap, or a group, category, type, or class of swaps, that it seeks to accept for clearing. Nothing in this subparagraph limits the Commission from making a determination under subparagraph (B)(iii) for swaps described in subparagraph (B)(ii).

"(3) STAY OF CLEARING REQUIREMENT. —

"(A) IN GENERAL. — After making a determination pursuant to paragraph (2)(B), the Commission, on application of a counterparty to a swap or on its own initiative, may stay the clearing requirement of paragraph (1) until the Commission completes a review of the terms of the swap (or the group, category, type, or class of swaps) and the clearing arrangement.

"(B) DEADLINE. — The Commission shall complete a review undertaken pursuant to subparagraph (A) not later than 90 days after issuance of the stay, unless the derivatives clearing organization that clears the swap, or group, category, type, or class of swaps agrees to an extension of the time limitation established under this subparagraph.

"(C) DETERMINATION. — Upon completion of the review undertaken pursuant to subparagraph (A), the Commission may —

"(i) determine, unconditionally or subject to such terms and conditions as the Commission determines to be appropriate, that the swap, or group, category, type, or class of swaps must be cleared pursuant to this subsection if it finds that such clearing is consistent with paragraph (2)(D); or

"(ii) determine that the clearing requirement of paragraph (1) shall not apply to the swap, or group, category, type, or class of swaps.

"(D) RULES. — Not later than 1 year after the date of the enactment of the Wall Street Transparency and Accountability Act of 2010, the Commission shall adopt rules for reviewing, pursuant to this paragraph, a derivatives clearing organization's clearing of a swap, or a group, category, type, or class of swaps, that it has accepted for clearing.

"(4) PREVENTION OF EVASION. —

"(A) IN GENERAL. — The Commission shall prescribe rules under this subsection (and issue interpretations of rules prescribed under this subsection) as determined by the Commission to be necessary to prevent evasions of the mandatory clearing requirements under this Act.

"(B) DUTY OF COMMISSION TO INVESTIGATE AND TAKE CERTAIN ACTIONS. — To the extent the Commission finds that a particular swap, group, category,

时,可就该等要求的条款和条件作出其判定确属适当的规定。

(E)**规则**。——商品期货交易委员会应在本子条规定颁布之日后1年内,针对衍生品结算组织呈报的就其拟受理结算的互换或互换集合、种类、类型或类别的集中结算根据本款规定进行审查的事宜,制定相关规则。本子款任何规定均不限制商品期货交易委员会依据第(B)(iii)子款规定就第(B)(ii)子款所述互换作出判定。

(3)**集中结算要求的中止**。——

(A)**一般规定**。——商品期货交易委员会在按照第(2)(B)款作出判定后,可根据互换对手方提出的申请或主动中止第(1)款所述集中结算要求,直至其完成对互换(或互换集合、种类、类型或类别)的条款及结算安排的审查。

(B)**最后期限**。——除非对互换或互换集合、种类、类型或类别进行集中结算的衍生品结算组织同意延长本子款规定的期限,否则商品期货交易委员会应在发出中止令后90天内完成根据第(A)子款规定执行的审查。

(C)**判定**。——商品期货交易委员会在完成根据第(A)子款执行的审查后,可以——

(i)判定互换或互换集合、种类、类型或类别必须无条件地按照本子条的规定进行集中结算,或在不违反商品期货交易委员会判定确属适当的条款及条件的情况下按照本子条的规定进行集中结算,前提是其认定该等结算符合第(2)(D)款的规定;或

(ii)判定互换或互换集合、种类、类型或类别不适用第(1)款的集中结算要求。

(D)**规则**。——商品期货交易委员会应在《2010年华尔街透明度与问责法》颁布之日起1年内,就衍生品结算组织已受理进行集中结算的互换或任何互换集合、种类、类型或类别的结算情况根据本款规定进行审查的事宜,制定相关规则。

(4)**防范规避**。——

(A)**一般规定**。——商品期货交易委员会应依据本子条规定制定其判定确属必要的规则(并就该等规则发布必要的解释),以防范规避本法的强制集中结算要求的行为。

(B)**商品期货交易委员会开展调查及采取特定行动的职责**。——若商品期货交易委员会认定某一特定互换或互换集合、种类、类型或类别本应受制于强制集中结算

type, or class of swaps would otherwise be subject to mandatory clearing but no derivatives clearing organization has listed the swap, group, category, type, or class of swaps for clearing, the Commission shall —

"(i) investigate the relevant facts and circumstances;

"(ii) within 30 days issue a public report containing the results of the investigation; and

"(iii) take such actions as the Commission determines to be necessary and in the public interest, which may include requiring the retaining of adequate margin or capital by parties to the swap, group, category, type, or class of swaps.

"(C) EFFECT ON AUTHORITY. — Nothing in this paragraph —

"(i) authorizes the Commission to adopt rules requiring a derivatives clearing organization to list for clearing a swap, group, category, type, or class of swaps if the clearing of the swap, group, category, type, or class of swaps would threaten the financial integrity of the derivatives clearing organization; and

"(ii) affects the authority of the Commission to enforce the open access provisions of paragraph (1)(B) with respect to a swap, group, category, type, or class of swaps that is listed for clearing by a derivatives clearing organization.

"(5) REPORTING TRANSITION RULES. — Rules adopted by the Commission under this section shall provide for the reporting of data, as follows:

"(A) Swaps entered into before the date of the enactment of this subsection shall be reported to a registered swap data repository or the Commission no later than 180 days after the effective date of this subsection.

"(B) Swaps entered into on or after such date of enactment shall be reported to a registered swap data repository or the Commission no later than the later of —

"(i) 90 days after such effective date; or

"(ii) such other time after entering into the swap as the Commission may prescribe by rule or regulation.

"(6) CLEARING TRANSITION RULES. —

"(A) Swaps entered into before the date of the enactment of this subsection are exempt from the clearing requirements of this subsection if reported pursuant to paragraph (5)(A).

"(B) Swaps entered into before application of the clearing requirement pursuant to this subsection are exempt from the clearing requirements of this subsection if reported pursuant to paragraph (5)(B).

"(7) EXCEPTIONS. —

"(A) IN GENERAL. — The requirements of paragraph (1)(A) shall not apply to a swap if 1 of the counterparties to the swap —

"(i) is not a financial entity;

"(ii) is using swaps to hedge or mitigate commercial risk; and

要求,但无任何衍生品结算组织对该互换或互换集合、种类、类型或类别进行挂牌结算,则商品期货交易委员会应——

(i)对相关事实及情况进行调查;

(ii)在30天内就调查结果发布公开报告;及

(iii)采取其判定确属必要且符合公共利益的行动,该等行动可包括:要求该互换或互换集合、种类、类型或类别的交易方留存充足的保证金或资本。

(C)**对商品期货交易委员会权力的影响**。——本款的任何规定——

(i)不授权商品期货交易委员会制定规则,要求衍生品结算组织在互换或互换集合、种类、类型或类别的集中结算将会威胁该衍生品结算组织财务完整性的情况下仍须对该互换或互换集合、种类、类型或类别进行挂牌结算;且

(ii)不影响商品期货交易委员会就衍生品结算组织挂牌结算的互换、互换集合、种类、类型或类别执行第(1)(B)款的准入开放性规定的权力。

(5)**过渡性报告规则**。——商品期货交易委员会依据本条制定的规则应对数据报告作出如下规定:

(A)本子条规定颁布之日以前达成的互换应在本子条生效之日后180天内向注册的互换数据存管机构或商品期货交易委员会报告。

(B)本子条规定颁布之日或之后达成的互换应向注册的互换数据存管机构或商品期货交易委员会报告,报告日不得迟于下述日期(以较晚者为准)——

(i)本子条生效之日后第90天;或

(ii)商品期货交易委员会发布的规则或规章所另行规定的互换达成后的其他时间。

(6)**过渡性集中结算规则**。——

(A)本子条规定颁布之日以前达成的互换已按照第(5)(A)款的规定报告的,可豁免本子条的集中结算要求。

(B)在集中结算要求按本子条开始适用之前达成的互换,已按照第(5)(B)款的规定报告的,可豁免本子条的集中结算要求。

(7)**例外规定**。——

(A)**一般规定**。——在下述情形下,互换不适用第(1)(A)款规定的要求:互换对手方之一——

(i)并非金融实体;

(ii)正在利用互换对商业风险进行套期保值或缓释;且

"(iii) notifies the Commission, in a manner set forth by the Commission, how it generally meets its financial obligations associated with entering into non–cleared swaps.

"(B) OPTION TO CLEAR. — The application of the clearing exception in subparagraph (A) is solely at the discretion of the counterparty to the swap that meets the conditions of clauses (i) through (iii) of subparagraph (A).

"(C) FINANCIAL ENTITY DEFINITION.—

"(i) IN GENERAL. — For the purposes of this paragraph, the term 'financial entity' means —

"(I) a swap dealer;

"(II) a security–based swap dealer;

"(III) a major swap participant;

"(IV) a major security–based swap participant;

"(V) a commodity pool;

"(VI) a private fund as defined in section 202(a) of the Investment Advisers Act of 1940 (15 U.S.C. 80–b–2(a));

"(VII) an employee benefit plan as defined in paragraphs (3) and (32) of section 3 of the Employee Retirement Income Security Act of 1974 (29 U.S.C. 1002);

"(VIII) a person predominantly engaged in activities that are in the business of banking, or in activities that are financial in nature, as defined in section 4(k) of the Bank Holding Company Act of 1956.

"(ii) EXCLUSION. — The Commission shall consider whether to exempt small banks, savings associations, farm credit system institutions, and credit unions, including —

"(I) depository institutions with total assets of $10,000,000,000 or less;

"(II) farm credit system institutions with total assets of $10,000,000,000 or less; or

"(III) credit unions with total assets of $10,000,000,000 or less.

"(iii) LIMITATION. — Such definition shall not include an entity whose primary business is providing financing, and uses derivatives for the purpose of hedging underlying commercial risks related to interest rate and foreign currency exposures, 90 percent or more of which arise from financing that facilitates the purchase or lease of products, 90 percent or more of which are manufactured by the parent company or another subsidiary of the parent company.

"(D) TREATMENT OF AFFILIATES.—

"(i) IN GENERAL. — An affiliate of a person that qualifies for an exception under subparagraph (A) (including affiliate entities predominantly engaged in providing financing for the purchase of the merchandise or manufactured goods of the person) may qualify for the exception only if the affiliate, acting on behalf of the person and as an agent, uses the swap to hedge or mitigate the commercial risk of the person or other affiliate of the person that is not a

(iii)已按照商品期货交易委员会规定的方式告知商品期货交易委员会通常情况下其履行与达成非集中结算的互换相关的财务义务的方式。

(B)**选择进行集中结算的权利**。——符合第(A)子款第(i)项至第(iii)项各项条件的互换对手方可完全依其自由裁量权决定是否适用第(A)子款中关于集中结算的例外规定。

(C)**金融实体的定义**。——

(i)**一般规定**。——就本款而言,'金融实体'一词系指——

(I)互换交易商;

(II)证券类互换交易商;

(III)主要互换参与者;

(IV)主要的证券类互换参与者;

(V)商品基金;

(VI)《1940年投资顾问法》第202(a)条[《美国法典》第十五编第80-b-2(a)节]定义的私募基金;

(VII)《1974年员工退休收入保障法》第3条第(3)款和第(32)款(《美国法典》第二十九编第1002节)定义的员工福利计划;

(VIII)主营业务为银行业务或金融性质活动[金融性质活动定义见《1956年银行控股公司法》第4(k)条]的人。

(ii)**除外规定**。——商品期货交易委员会应考虑是否将下列实体豁免于上述定义:小型银行、储蓄协会、农业信贷系统机构和信贷联盟,包括——

(I)总资产100亿美元(含)以下的存款机构;

(II)总资产100亿美元(含)以下的农业信贷系统机构;或

(III)总资产100亿美元(含)以下的信贷联盟。

(iii)**限制**。——上述定义不包括具有如下特征的实体:以提供融资为主营业务并利用衍生品对与利率和外币风险敞口相关的基础商业风险进行套期保值,而该等敞口90%(含)以上来自为产品购买或承租提供便利的融资并且该等产品90%(含)以上由其母公司或母公司的另一子公司制造。

(D)**关联方的处理**。——

(i)**一般规定**。——对于符合第(A)子款例外资格之主体,只有以代理人身份代表该主体利用互换对该主体或该主体另一非金融实体关联方之商业风险进行套期保值或缓释的关联方(包括以为该主体之商品或产成品的购买提供融资作为主营业务的关联实体),方可被认定为符合该例外规定。

financial entity.

"(ii) PROHIBITION RELATING TO CERTAIN AFFILIATES. — The exception in clause (i) shall not apply if the affiliate is —

"(I) a swap dealer;

"(II) a security–based swap dealer;

"(III) a major swap participant;

"(IV) a major security–based swap participant;

"(V) an issuer that would be an investment company, as defined in section 3 of the Investment Company Act of 1940 (15 U.S.C. 80a–3), but for paragraph (1) or (7) of subsection (c) of that Act (15 U.S.C. 80a–3(c));

"(VI) a commodity pool; or

"(VII) a bank holding company with over $50,000,000,000 in consolidated assets.

"(iii) TRANSITION RULE FOR AFFILIATES. — An affiliate, subsidiary, or a wholly owned entity of a person that qualifies for an exception under subparagraph (A) and is predominantly engaged in providing financing for the purchase or lease of merchandise or manufactured goods of the person shall be exempt from the margin requirement described in section 4s(e) and the clearing requirement described in paragraph (1) with regard to swaps entered into to mitigate the risk of the financing activities for not less than a 2–year period beginning on the date of enactment of this clause.

"(E) ELECTION OF COUNTERPARTY. —

"(i) SWAPS REQUIRED TO BE CLEARED. — With respect to any swap that is subject to the mandatory clearing requirement under this subsection and entered into by a swap dealer or a major swap participant with a counterparty that is not a swap dealer, major swap participant, security–based swap dealer, or major security–based swap participant, the counterparty shall have the sole right to select the derivatives clearing organization at which the swap will be cleared.

"(ii) SWAPS NOT REQUIRED TO BE CLEARED. — With respect to any swap that is not subject to the mandatory clearing requirement under this subsection and entered into by a swap dealer or a major swap participant with a counterparty that is not a swap dealer, major swap participant, security–based swap dealer, or major security–based swap participant, the counterparty —

"(I) may elect to require clearing of the swap; and

"(II) shall have the sole right to select the derivatives clearing organization at which the swap will be cleared.

"(F) ABUSE OF EXCEPTION. — The Commission may pre scribe such rules or issue interpretations of the rules as the Commission determines to be necessary to prevent abuse of the exceptions described in this paragraph. The Commission may also request information

(ii)**关于特定关联方的禁止规定**。——关联方具有下列身份的，不得适用第(i)项所述的例外规定——

(I)互换交易商；

(II)证券类互换交易商；

(III)主要互换参与者；

(IV)主要的证券类互换参与者；

(V)若非适用了《1940年投资公司法》第(c)子条[《美国法典》第十五编第80a-3(c)节]第(1)款或第(7)款的规定，将会构成该法第3条[《美国法典》第十五编第80a-3节]定义之投资公司的发行人；

(VI)商品基金；或

(VII)并表资产超过500亿美元的银行控股公司。

(iii)**过渡性关联方规则**。——某主体的关联方、子公司或全资拥有的实体符合第(A)子款所述例外规定资格，且主营业务是为该主体之商品或产成品的购买或承租提供融资的，则就为缓释融资活动风险而达成的互换而言，该等关联方、子公司或全资拥有的实体应豁免于第4s(e)条的保证金要求和第(1)款的集中结算要求，豁免期限至少2年，自本项规定颁布之日起算。

(E)**对手方选择衍生品结算组织的权利**。——

(i)**要求进行集中结算的互换**。——互换交易商或主要互换参与者与对手方达成的任何互换如受制于本子条规定的强制集中结算要求，且该对手方并不具有互换交易商、主要互换参与者、证券类互换交易商或主要的证券类互换参与者身份，则该对手方应可以全权自行挑选在哪一衍生品结算组织进行该互换的集中结算。

(ii) **不要求进行集中结算的互换**。——互换交易商或主要互换参与者与对手方达成的任何互换如不受制于本子条规定的强制集中结算要求，且该对手方并不具有互换交易商、主要互换参与者、证券类互换交易商或主要的证券类互换参与者身份，则该对手方——

(I)可以自行选择要求对该互换进行集中结算；并

(II)应可以全权自行挑选在哪一衍生品结算组织进行该互换的集中结算。

(F)**例外规定的滥用**。——商品期货交易委员会可以制定其判定确属必要的规则或针对该等规则发布必要的解释，防止本子条的例外规定被滥用。商品期货交易委员会亦可要求申请适用集中结算例外规定的主体提供相关信息，以防止本子条的例

from those persons claiming the clearing exception as necessary to prevent abuse of the exceptions described in this paragraph.

"(8) TRADE EXECUTION. —

"(A) IN GENERAL. — With respect to transactions involving swaps subject to the clearing requirement of paragraph (1), counterparties shall —

"(i) execute the transaction on a board of trade designated as a contract market under section 5; or

"(ii) execute the transaction on a swap execution facility registered under 5h or a swap execution facility that is exempt from registration under section 5h(f) of this Act.

"(B) EXCEPTION. — The requirements of clauses (i) and (ii) of subparagraph (A) shall not apply if no board of trade or swap execution facility makes the swap available to trade or for swap transactions subject to the clearing exception under paragraph (7).".

(b) COMMODITY EXCHANGE ACT. — Section 2 of the Commodity Exchange Act (7 U.S.C. 2) is amended by adding at the end the following:

"(j) COMMITTEE APPROVAL BY BOARD. — Exemptions from the requirements of subsection (h)(1) to clear a swap and subsection (h)(8) to execute a swap through a board of trade or swap execution facility shall be available to a counterparty that is an issuer of securities that are registered under section 12 of the Securities Exchange Act of 1934 (15 U.S.C. 78l) or that is required to file reports pursuant to section 15 (d) of the Securities Exchange Act of 1934 (15 U.S.C. 78o) only if an appropriate committee of the issuer's board or governing body has reviewed and approved its decision to enter into swaps that are subject to such exemptions.".

(c) GRANDFATHER PROVISIONS. —

(1) LEGAL CERTAINTY FOR CERTAIN TRANSACTIONS IN EXEMPT COMMODITIES. — Not later than 60 days after the date of enactment of this Act, a person may submit to the Commodity Futures Trading Commission a petition to remain subject to section 2(h) of the Commodity Exchange Act (7 U.S.C. 2(h)) (as in effect on the day before the date of enactment of this Act).

(2) CONSIDERATION; AUTHORITY OF COMMODITY FUTURES TRADING COMMISSION. — The Commodity Futures Trading Commission —

(A) shall consider any petition submitted under subparagraph (A) in a prompt manner; and

(B) may allow a person to continue operating subject to section 2(h) of the Commodity Exchange Act (7 U.S.C. 2(h)) (as in effect on the day before the date of enactment of this Act) for not longer than a 1-year period.

(3) AGRICULTURAL SWAPS. —

(A) IN GENERAL. — Except as provided in subparagraph (B), no person shall offer to

外规定被滥用。

(8)**交易执行**。——

(A)**一般规定**。——涉及互换的交易受制于第(1)款的集中结算要求的，对手方应——

(i)在根据第5条被指定为合约市场的交易场所执行该等交易；或

(ii)在根据本法第5h条注册的互换执行设施或根据本法第5h(f)条豁免注册的互换执行设施执行该等交易。

(B)**例外规定**。——如果没有任何交易场所或互换执行设施提供互换以供交易，则在不违反第(7)款的集中结算例外规定的前提下，不应适用第(A)子款第(i)项和第(ii)项的要求。”

(b)**商品交易法**。——在《商品交易法》第2条(《美国法典》第七编第2节)结尾处增加如下内容，作为对该条的修正：

“(j)**董事会批准**。——如对手方具有根据《1934年证券交易法》第12条(《美国法典》第十五编第78l节)注册的证券的发行人身份，或有义务根据《1934年证券交易法》第15(d)条(《美国法典》第十五编第78o节)提交报告，则该对手方可以豁免于第(h)(1)子条规定的互换集中结算要求和第(h)(8)子条要求通过交易场所或互换执行设施执行互换的规定，前提是该发行人的董事会或管理机构下属相应的委员会已审议并批准了该发行人作出的达成适用上述豁免的互换之决定。”

(c)**不溯及既往条款**。——

(1)**特定豁免商品交易的法律确定性**。——任何人均可以于本法颁布之日起60天内向商品期货交易委员会提交一份请求，申请继续适用《商品交易法》第2(h)条[《美国法典》第七编第2(h)节]的规定(以本法颁布前1天有效适用的版本为准)。

(2)**审议；商品期货交易委员会的权力**。——商品期货交易委员会——

(A)应及时审议依据第(A)子款提交的任何请求；及

(B)可以允许请求人在不超过1年的期间内，按照《商品交易法》第2(h)条[《美国法典》第七编第2(h)节](以本法颁布前1天有效适用的版本为准)继续开展运营。

(3)**农产品互换**。——

(A)**一般规定**。——除第(B)子款规定的情形外，任何人均不得要约达成、达成或

enter into, enter into, or confirm the execution of, any swap in an agricultural commodity (as defined by the Commodity Futures Trading Commission).

(B) EXCEPTION. — Notwithstanding subparagraph (A), a person may offer to enter into, enter into, or confirm the execution of, any swap in an agricultural commodity pursuant to section 4(c) of the Commodity Exchange Act (7 U.S.C. 6(c)) or any rule, regulation, or order issued thereunder (including any rule, regulation, or order in effect as of the date of enactment of this Act) by the Commodity Futures Trading Commission to allow swaps under such terms and conditions as the Commission shall prescribe.

(4) REQUIRED REPORTING. — If the exception described in section 2(h)(8)(B) of the Commodity Exchange Act applies, the counterparties shall comply with any recordkeeping and transaction reporting requirements that may be prescribed by the Commission with respect to swaps subject to section 2(h)(8)(B) of the Commodity Exchange Act.

SEC.724. SWAPS; SEGREGATION AND BANKRUPTCY TREATMENT.

(a) SEGREGATION REQUIREMENTS FOR CLEARED SWAPS. — Section 4d of the Commodity Exchange Act (7 U.S.C. 6d) (as amended by section 732) is amended by adding at the end the following:

"(f) SWAPS. —

"(1) REGISTRATION REQUIREMENT. — It shall be unlawful for any person to accept any money, securities, or property (or to extend any credit in lieu of money, securities, or property) from, for, or on behalf of a swaps customer to margin, guarantee, or secure a swap cleared by or through a derivatives clearing organization (including money, securities, or property accruing to the customer as the result of such a swap), unless the person shall have registered under this Act with the Commission as a futures commission merchant, and the registration shall not have expired nor been suspended nor revoked.

"(2) CLEARED SWAPS. —

"(A) SEGREGATION REQUIRED. — A futures commission merchant shall treat and deal with all money, securities, and property of any swaps customer received to margin, guarantee, or secure a swap cleared by or though a derivatives clearing organization (including money, securities, or property accruing to the swaps customer as the result of such a swap) as belonging to the swaps customer.

"(B) COMMINGLING PROHIBITED. — Money, securities, and property of a swaps customer described in subparagraph (A) shall be separately accounted for and shall not be commingled with the funds of the futures commission merchant or be used to margin, secure, or guarantee any trades or contracts of any swaps customer or person other than the person for whom the same are held.

"(3) EXCEPTIONS. —

"(A) USE OF FUNDS. —

确认执行任何农产品互换(以商品期货交易委员会的定义为准)。

(B)**例外规定**。——无论第(A)子款是否存在任何相反规定,任何人均可以根据《商品交易法》第4(c)条[《美国法典》第七编第6(c)节]或者商品期货交易委员会根据上述条款制定的允许按其规定的条款和条件进行互换相关活动的任何规则、规章或命令(包括本法颁布日之前有效适用的任何规则、规章或命令),要约达成、达成或确认执行任何农产品互换(以商品期货交易委员会的定义为准)。

(4)**报告要求**。——适用《商品交易法》第2(h)(8)(B)条所述例外规定之时,对手方应遵守商品期货交易委员会就受制于《商品交易法》第2(h)(8)(B)条的互换规定的任何记录保存和交易报告要求。

第724条　互换;分离和破产处理

(a)**集中结算的互换的分离要求**。——在《商品交易法》第4d条(《美国法典》第七编第6d节)(以经第732条修正后的版本为准)结尾处增加如下内容,作为对该条的修正:

"(f)**互换**。——

(1)**注册要求**。——对于由衍生品结算组织集中结算的或通过其集中结算的互换而言,任何人不得出于为该等互换提供保证金、保证或担保之目的,而接受互换客户的任何现金、证券或财产(包括因该等互换而产生并归属于该客户的现金、证券或财产)或为该互换客户接受或者代表该互换客户接受该等现金、证券或财产,亦不得进行替代性授信,否则当属违法,除非该人已经根据本法在商品期货交易委员会注册为期货经纪商,且该注册尚未过期,也未被暂停或撤销。

(2)**集中结算的互换**。——

(A)**分离要求**。——对于由衍生品结算组织集中结算的或通过其集中结算的互换而言,期货经纪商应将其收到的用于为该等互换提供保证金、保证或担保的任何互换客户的所有现金、证券和财产(包括因该等互换而产生并归属于该客户的现金、证券或财产)作为属于该互换客户的现金、证券和财产来对待和处理。

(B)**禁止混合**。——第(A)子款所述互换客户的现金、证券和财产应单独核算,不得与该期货经纪商的自有资金混合,亦不得用于为该等现金、证券和财产所属客户以外的任何互换客户或任何人的任何交易或合约提供保证金、担保或保证。

(3)**例外规定**。——

(A)**资金使用**。——

"(i) IN GENERAL. — Notwithstanding paragraph (2), money, securities, and property of swap customers of a futures commission merchant described in paragraph (2) may, for convenience, be commingled and deposited in the same account or accounts with any bank or trust company or with a derivatives clearing organization.

"(ii) WITHDRAWAL. — Notwithstanding paragraph (2), such share of the money, securities, and property described in clause (i) as in the normal course of business shall be necessary to margin, guarantee, secure, transfer, adjust, or settle a cleared swap with a derivatives clearing organization, or with any member of the derivatives clearing organization, may be withdrawn and applied to such purposes, including the payment of commissions, brokerage, interest, taxes, storage, and other charges, lawfully accruing in connection with the cleared swap.

"(B) COMMISSION ACTION. — Notwithstanding paragraph (2), in accordance with such terms and conditions as the Commission may prescribe by rule, regulation, or order, any money, securities, or property of the swaps customers of a futures commission merchant described in paragraph (2) may be commingled and deposited in customer accounts with any other money, securities, or property received by the futures commission merchant and required by the Commission to be separately accounted for and treated and dealt with as belonging to the swaps customer of the futures commission merchant.

"(4) PERMITTED INVESTMENTS. — Money described in paragraph (2) may be invested in obligations of the United States, in general obligations of any State or of any political subdivision of a State, and in obligations fully guaranteed as to principal and interest by the United States, or in any other investment that the Commission may by rule or regulation prescribe, and such investments shall be made in accordance with such rules and regulations and subject to such conditions as the Commission may prescribe.

"(5) COMMODITY CONTRACT. — A swap cleared by or through a derivatives clearing organization shall be considered to be a commodity contract as such term is defined in section 761 of title 11, United States Code, with regard to all money, securities, and property of any swaps customer received by a futures commission merchant or a derivatives clearing organization to margin, guarantee, or secure the swap (including money, securities, or property accruing to the customer as the result of the swap).

"(6) PROHIBITION. — It shall be unlawful for any person, including any derivatives clearing organization and any depository institution, that has received any money, securities, or property for deposit in a separate account or accounts as provided in paragraph (2) to hold, dispose of, or use any such money, securities, or property as belonging to the depositing futures commission merchant or any person other than the swaps customer of the futures commission merchant.".

(b) BANKRUPTCY TREATMENT OF CLEARED SWAPS. — Section 761 of title 11,

(i)**一般规定**。——无论第(2)款如何规定,第(2)款所述期货经纪商可以出于便利目的,将其互换客户的现金、证券和财产混合存入任何银行或信托公司或者衍生品结算组织的一个或一个以上相同账户之中。

(ii)**提取**。——无论第(2)款如何规定,上述期货经纪商可以在正常业务运作中提取必要份额的第(i)项所述现金、证券和财产,用于为衍生品结算组织或其任何会员结算的互换提供保证金、保证、担保,或者进行移仓、调整或结算操作,包括支付因集中的结算互换而合法产生的佣金、经纪费、利息、税费、存储费及其他收费。

(B)**商品期货交易委员会的行动**。——无论第(2)款如何规定,根据商品期货交易委员会发布的规则、规章或命令所规定的条款和条件,以下二者可混合存储于客户账户,即第(2)款所述期货经纪商的互换客户的任何现金、证券或财产,以及该期货经纪商收到的按照商品期货交易委员会要求应单独核算并当作属于该期货经纪商的互换客户所有的现金、证券或财产处理和对待的任何其他现金、证券或财产。

(4)**允许的投资**。——第(2)款所述现金可投资于美国国债、任何州或州下属任何行政区域的一般债券、联邦政府全额担保本金和利息的债券或者商品期货交易委员会在其发布的规则或规章中所规定的任何其他投资,但是该等投资应按照商品期货交易委员会制定的规则和规章作出,并受制于其规定的条件。

(5)**商品合约**。——对于期货经纪商或衍生品结算组织收到的用于为互换提供保证金、保证或担保的任何互换客户的所有现金、证券和财产(包括因该等互换而产生并归属于该客户的现金、证券或财产)而言,由衍生品结算组织集中结算的或通过其进行集中结算的互换应视为《美国法典》第十一编第761节定义的商品合约。

(6)**禁止性规定**。——已收到依据第(2)款规定应存入独立账户的任何现金、证券或财产的任何人(包括任何衍生品结算组织及任何存款机构),不得将该等现金、证券或财产当作属于实施存储操作的期货经纪商的现金、证券或财产或属于该期货经纪商的互换客户以外的任何人的现金、证券或财产进行持有、处置或使用,否则当属违法。"

(b)**集中结算的互换的破产处理**。——《美国法典》第十一编第761节修正

United States Code, is amended —

(1) in paragraph (4), by striking subparagraph (F) and inserting the following:

"(F)(i) any other contract, option, agreement, or transaction that is similar to a contract, option, agreement, or transaction referred to in this paragraph; and

"(ii) with respect to a futures commission merchant or a clearing organization, any other contract, option, agreement, or transaction, in each case, that is cleared by a clearing organization;"; and

(2) in paragraph (9)(A)(i), by striking "the commodity futures account" and inserting "a commodity contract account".

(c) SEGREGATION REQUIREMENTS FOR UNCLEARED SWAPS. — Section 4s of the Commodity Exchange Act (as added by section 731) is amended by adding at the end the following:

"(1) SEGREGATION REQUIREMENTS. —

"(1) SEGREGATION OF ASSETS HELD AS COLLATERAL IN UNCLEARED SWAP TRANSACTIONS. —

"(A) NOTIFICATION. — A swap dealer or major swap participant shall be required to notify the counterparty of the swap dealer or major swap participant at the beginning of a swap transaction that the counterparty has the right to require segregation of the funds or other property supplied to margin, guarantee, or secure the obligations of the counterparty.

"(B) SEGREGATION AND MAINTENANCE OF FUNDS. — At the request of a counterparty to a swap that provides funds or other property to a swap dealer or major swap participant to margin, guarantee, or secure the obligations of the counterparty, the swap dealer or major swap participant shall —

"(i) segregate the funds or other property for the benefit of the counterparty; and

"(ii) in accordance with such rules and regulations as the Commission may promulgate, maintain the funds or other property in a segregated account separate from the assets and other interests of the swap dealer or major swap participant.

"(2) APPLICABILITY. — The requirements described in paragraph (1) shall —

"(A) apply only to a swap between a counterparty and a swap dealer or major swap participant that is not submitted for clearing to a derivatives clearing organization; and

"(B)(i) not apply to variation margin payments; or

"(ii) not preclude any commercial arrangement regarding —

"(I) the investment of segregated funds or other property that may only be invested in such investments as the Commission may permit by rule or regulation; and

"(II) the related allocation of gains and losses resulting from any investment of the segregated funds or other property.

"(3) USE OF INDEPENDENT THIRD–PARTY CUSTODIANS. — The segregated

如下——

(1)第(4)款中,删除第(F)子款,并替以如下内容:

“(F)(i)与本款所述合约、期权、协议或交易类似的任何其他合约、期权、协议或交易;及

(ii)对于期货经纪商或结算组织而言,由结算组织进行集中结算的任何其他合约、期权、协议或交易;”及

(2)在第(9)(A)(i)款中,删除“该商品期货账户”,替以“商品合约账户”。

(c)**非集中结算的互换的分离要求**。——在第731条增加的《商品交易法》第4s条结尾处增加如下内容,作为对该条的修正:

“(1)**担保品分离要求**。——

(1)**用作非集中结算的互换交易担保品的资产应分离管理**。——

(A)**通知**。——互换交易开始之时,互换交易商或主要互换参与者即应通知互换交易商或主要互换参与者的对手方,告知该对手方有权要求对用于为对手方债务提供保证金、保证或担保的资金或其他财产进行分离管理。

(B)**资金的分离和存储**。——互换对手方向互换交易商或主要互换参与者提供资金或其他财产用于为该对手方债务提供保证金、保证或担保的,经该互换对手方提出请求,互换交易商或主要互换参与者应——

(i)为了对手方的利益对该等资金或其他财产进行分离管理;及

(ii)根据商品期货交易委员会颁发的规则与规章,将该等资金或其他财产存储在分离的账户中,与互换交易商或主要互换参与者的自有资产和其他权益独立开来。

(2)**适用范围**。——第(1)款所述的要求应——

(A)仅适用于在对手方和互换交易商或主要互换参与者之间达成的不提交给衍生品结算组织进行集中结算的互换;且

(B)(i)不适用于追加保证金款项;亦

(ii)也不排除以下任何商业安排——

(I)分离资金或其他财产的投资(仅能投资于商品期货交易委员会发布的规则或规章所允许的投资);及

(II)该分离的资金或其他财产进行任何投资产生的收益和损失的相关分配。

(3)**使用独立的第三方存管人**。——第(1)款所述分离账户应——

account described in paragraph (1) shall be —

"(A) carried by an independent third–party custodian; and

"(B) designated as a segregated account for and on behalf of the counterparty.

"(4) REPORTING REQUIREMENT. — If the counterparty does not choose to require segregation of the funds or other property supplied to margin, guarantee, or secure the obligations of the counterparty, the swap dealer or major swap participant shall report to the counterparty of the swap dealer or major swap participant on a quarterly basis that the back office procedures of the swap dealer or major swap participant relating to margin and collateral requirements are in compliance with the agreement of the counterparties.".

SEC.725. DERIVATIVES CLEARING ORGANIZATIONS.

(a) REGISTRATION REQUIREMENT. — Section 5b of the Commodity Exchange Act (7 U.S.C. 7a – 1) is amended by striking subsections (a) and (b) and inserting the following:

"(a) REGISTRATION REQUIREMENT. —

"(1) IN GENERAL. — Except as provided in paragraph (2), it shall be unlawful for a derivatives clearing organization, directly or indirectly, to make use of the mails or any means or instrumentality of interstate commerce to perform the functions of a derivatives clearing organization with respect to —

"(A) a contract of sale of a commodity for future delivery (or an option on the contract of sale) or option on a commodity, in each case, unless the contract or option is —

"(i) excluded from this Act by subsection (a)(1)(C)(i), (c), or (f) of section 2; or

"(ii) a security futures product cleared by a clearing agency registered with the Securities and Exchange Commission under the Securities Exchange Act of 1934 (15 U.S.C. 78a et seq.); or

"(B) a swap.

"(2) EXCEPTION. — Paragraph (1) shall not apply to a derivatives clearing organization that is registered with the Commission.

"(b) VOLUNTARY REGISTRATION. — A person that clears 1 or more agreements, contracts, or transactions that are not required to be cleared under this Act may register with the Commission as a derivatives clearing organization.".

(b) REGISTRATION FOR DEPOSITORY INSTITUTIONS AND CLEARING AGENCIES; EXEMPTIONS; COMPLIANCE OFFICER; ANNUAL REPORTS. — Section 5b of the Commodity Exchange Act (7 U.S.C. 7a–1) is amended by adding at the end the following:

"(g) EXISTING DEPOSITORY INSTITUTIONS AND CLEARING AGENCIES. —

"(1) IN GENERAL. — A depository institution or clearing agency registered with the

(A)由独立的第三方存管人持有;且

(B)被指明系为了并代表该对手方持有的分离账户。

(4)**报告要求**。——针对用于为对手方债务提供保证金、保证或担保的资金或其他财产,如果该对手方选择不要求进行分离管理,则互换交易商或主要互换参与者应每季度向该对手方作出报告,表明该互换交易商或主要互换参与者关于保证金和担保品要求的后台管理流程符合对手方协议。”

第725条　衍生品结算组织

(a)**注册要求**。——删除《商品交易法》(《美国法典》第七编第7a-1节)第5b条第(a)子条和第(b)子条,并替以如下内容,作为对该条的修正:

“(a)**注册要求**。——

(1)**一般规定**。——除第(2)款规定的情形外,衍生品结算组织不得直接或间接使用邮件或任何州际商业手段或工具就下列任何一项内容履行衍生品结算组织的职能,否则当属违法——

(A)远期交割商品出售合约(或该等出售合约的期权)或商品期权,除非该等合约或期权符合以下条件——

(i)被第2条第(a)(1)(C)(i)子条、第(c)子条或第(f)子条排除在本法适用范围之外;或

(ii)属于由依《1934年证券交易法》(《美国法典》第十五编第78a节及其后条文)在证券交易委员会注册的结算机构集中结算的证券期货产品;或

(B)互换。

(2)**例外规定**。——第(1)款不适用于在商品期货交易委员会注册的衍生品结算组织。

(b)**自愿注册**。——对不必根据本法进行集中结算的协议、合约或交易进行集中结算的主体,可在商品期货交易委员会注册为衍生品结算组织。”

(b)**存款机构和结算机构的注册;豁免;合规官;年度报告**。——在《商品交易法》(《美国法典》第七编第7a-1节)第5b条结尾处增加如下内容,作为对该条的修正:

“(g)**已注册的存款机构和结算机构**。——

(1)**一般规定**。——本条要求注册为衍生品结算组织的机构,已根据《1934年证

Securities and Exchange Commission under the Securities Exchange Act of 1934 (15 U.S.C. 78a et seq.) that is required to be registered as a derivatives clearing organization under this section is deemed to be registered under this section to the extent that, before the date of enactment of this subsection —

"(A) the depository institution cleared swaps as a multilateral clearing organization; or

"(B) the clearing agency cleared swaps.

"(2) CONVERSION OF DEPOSITORY INSTITUTIONS. — A depository institution to which this subsection applies may, by the vote of the shareholders owning not less than 51 percent of the voting interests of the depository institution, be converted into a State corporation, partnership, limited liability company, or similar legal form pursuant to a plan of conversion, if the conversion is not in contravention of applicable State law.

"(3) SHARING OF INFORMATION. — The Securities and Exchange Commission shall make available to the Commission, upon request, all information determined to be relevant by the Securities and Exchange Commission regarding a clearing agency deemed to be registered with the Commission under paragraph (1).

"(h) EXEMPTIONS. — The Commission may exempt, conditionally or unconditionally, a derivatives clearing organization from registration under this section for the clearing of swaps if the Commission determines that the derivatives clearing organization is subject to comparable, comprehensive supervision and regulation by the Securities and Exchange Commission or the appropriate government authorities in the home country of the organization. Such conditions may include, but are not limited to, requiring that the derivatives clearing organization be available for inspection by the Commission and make available all information requested by the Commission.

"(i) DESIGNATION OF CHIEF COMPLIANCE OFFICER. —

"(1) IN GENERAL. — Each derivatives clearing organization shall designate an individual to serve as a chief compliance officer.

"(2) DUTIES. — The chief compliance officer shall —

"(A) report directly to the board or to the senior officer of the derivatives clearing organization;

"(B) review the compliance of the derivatives clearing organization with respect to the core principles described in subsection (c)(2);

"(C) in consultation with the board of the derivatives clearing organization, a body performing a function similar to the board of the derivatives clearing organization, or the senior officer of the derivatives clearing organization, resolve any conflicts of interest that may arise;

"(D) be responsible for administering each policy and procedure that is required to be established pursuant to this section;

券交易法》(《美国法典》第十五编第78a节及其后条文)在证券交易委员会注册为存款机构或结算机构的,视为已按照本条规定注册,其前提是在本子条规定颁布日期之前——

(A)该存款机构曾作为多边结算组织提供互换集中结算服务;或

(B)该结算机构曾提供互换集中结算服务。

(2)**存款机构的形式变更**。——经拥有存款机构51%以上表决权益的股东表决同意,适用本子条规定的存款机构可根据形式变更计划变更为州公司、合伙、有限责任公司或与之类似的法律形式,但该等形式变更不得违反适用的州法律。

(3)**信息共享**。——对于根据第(1)款被视为已在商品期货交易委员会注册的结算机构而言,证券交易委员会应按照商品期货交易委员会要求,向其提供证券交易委员会判定与该等结算机构相关的全部信息。

(h)**豁免**。——如果商品期货交易委员会判定,某衍生品结算组织受到的来自证券交易委员会或该衍生品结算组织母国相应的政府机构的监管和规制足够全面,且与商品期货交易委员会的监管和规制具有可比性,则商品期货交易委员会可有条件或无条件地豁免该衍生品结算组织,使其不必依照本条对互换结算活动办理注册。上述条件包括但不限于要求衍生品结算组织接受商品期货交易委员会检查并按商品期货交易委员会的要求提供一切信息。

(i)**首席合规官的指定**。——

(1)**一般规定**。——每一衍生品结算组织均应指定一名个人担任首席合规官。

(2)**职责**。——首席合规官应——

(A)向衍生品结算组织的董事会或高级管理人员直接汇报工作;

(B)审查衍生品结算组织对第(c)(2)子条所述核心原则的遵守情况;

(C)与衍生品结算组织的董事会、履行与董事会类似职能的机构或高级管理人员磋商,解决任何可能发生的利益冲突问题;

(D)负责实施应当依据本条要求制定的每一项政策和程序;

"(E) ensure compliance with this Act (including regulations) relating to agreements, contracts, or transactions, including each rule prescribed by the Commission under this section;

"(F) establish procedures for the remediation of non compliance issues identified by the compliance officer through any —

"(i) compliance office review;

"(ii) look-back;

"(iii) internal or external audit finding;

"(iv) self-reported error; or

"(v) validated complaint; and

"(G) establish and follow appropriate procedures for the handling, management response, remediation, re testing, and closing of noncompliance issues.

"(3) ANNUAL REPORTS. —

"(A) IN GENERAL. — In accordance with rules prescribed by the Commission, the chief compliance officer shall annually prepare and sign a report that contains a description of—

"(i) the compliance of the derivatives clearing organization of the compliance officer with respect to this Act (including regulations); and

"(ii) each policy and procedure of the derivatives clearing organization of the compliance officer (including the code of ethics and conflict of interest policies of the derivatives clearing organization).

"(B) REQUIREMENTS. — A compliance report under subparagraph (A) shall —

"(i) accompany each appropriate financial report of the derivatives clearing organization that is required to be furnished to the Commission pursuant to this section; and

"(ii) include a certification that, under penalty of law, the compliance report is accurate and complete.".

(c) CORE PRINCIPLES FOR DERIVATIVES CLEARING ORGANIZATIONS. — Section 5b(c) of the Commodity Exchange Act (7 U.S.C. 7a - 1(c)) is amended by striking paragraph (2) and inserting the following:

"(2) CORE PRINCIPLES FOR DERIVATIVES CLEARING ORGANIZATIONS. —

"(A) COMPLIANCE. —

"(i) IN GENERAL. — To be registered and to maintain registration as a derivatives clearing organization, a derivatives clearing organization shall comply with each core principle described in this paragraph and any requirement that the Commission may impose by rule or regulation pursuant to section 8a(5).

"(ii) DISCRETION OF DERIVATIVES CLEARING ORGANIZATION. — Subject to any rule or regulation prescribed by the Commission, a derivatives clearing organization shall have reasonable discretion in establishing the manner by which the derivatives clearing

(E)确保本法(包括规章)中与协议、合约或交易相关的规定(包括商品期货交易委员会依据本条制定的每项规则)均得到遵守;

(F)制定相关程序,据以对首席合规官通过以下任何方式识别的不合规问题采取补救措施——

(i)合规办公室的审查工作;

(ii)回顾工作;

(iii)内部或外部的审计认定结论;

(iv)自报失误;或

(v)有效的投诉;及

(G)制定并遵守用以对不合规问题进行处理、管理回应、补救、重新测试和终结的适当程序。

(3)**年度报告**。——

(A)**一般规定**。——首席合规官应根据商品期货交易委员会制定的规则每年编制并签署一份报告,其中应包含以下内容——

(i)首席合规官所属的衍生品结算组织对本法(包括规章)的合规情况;及

(ii)首席合规官所属的衍生品结算组织的每项政策和程序(包括该衍生品结算组织的职业道德准则和利益冲突处理政策)。

(B)**要求**。——按照第(A)子款编制的合规报告应——

(i)与按本条规定应向商品期货交易委员会提交的衍生品结算组织每份相应的财务报告一并提交;及

(ii)包含一份自查证明,证明该合规报告的准确性和完整性,并明确表示其知晓作伪证将招致法律惩罚。"

(c)**适用于衍生品结算组织的核心原则**。——删除《商品交易法》第5b(c)条[《美国法典》第七编第7a-1(c)节]第(2)款,并替以如下内容,作为对该条的修正:

"(2)**适用于衍生品结算组织的核心原则**。——

(A)**合规**。——

(i)**一般规定**。——要获得并维持衍生品结算组织的注册资格,衍生品结算组织应当遵守本款所述每项核心原则以及商品期货交易委员会依据第8a(5)条发布的规则或规章所施加的任何要求。

(ii)**衍生品结算组织的自由裁量权**。——在不违反商品期货交易委员会制定的任何规则或规章的前提下,衍生品结算组织应依其合理的自由裁量权决定其遵守本款所述每项核心原则的方式。

organization complies with described in this paragraph.

"(B) FINANCIAL RESOURCES.—

"(i) IN GENERAL.— Each derivatives principle clearing organization shall have adequate financial, operational, and managerial resources, as determined by the Commission, to discharge each responsibility of the derivatives clearing organization.

"(ii) MINIMUM AMOUNT OF FINANCIAL RESOURCES.— Each derivatives clearing organization shall possess financial resources that, at a minimum, exceed the total amount that would—

"(I) enable the organization to meet its financial obligations to its members and participants notwithstanding a default by the member or participant creating the largest financial exposure for that organization in extreme but plausible market conditions; and

"(II) enable the derivatives clearing organization to cover the operating costs of the derivatives clearing organization for a period of 1 year (as calculated on a rolling basis).

"(C) PARTICIPANT AND PRODUCT ELIGIBILITY.—

"(i) IN GENERAL.— Each derivatives clearing organization shall establish—

"(I) appropriate admission and continuing eligibility standards (including sufficient financial resources and operational capacity to meet obligations arising from participation in the derivatives clearing organization) for members of, and participants in, the derivatives clearing organization; and

"(II) appropriate standards for determining the eligibility of agreements, contracts, or transactions submitted to the derivatives clearing organization for clearing.

"(ii) REQUIRED PROCEDURES.— Each derivatives clearing organization shall establish and implement procedures to verify, on an ongoing basis, the compliance of each participation and membership requirement of the derivatives clearing organization.

"(iii) REQUIREMENTS.— The participation and membership requirements of each derivatives clearing organization shall—

"(I) be objective;

"(II) be publicly disclosed; and

"(III) permit fair and open access.

"(D) RISK MANAGEMENT.—

"(i) IN GENERAL.— Each derivatives clearing organization shall ensure that the derivatives clearing organization possesses the ability to manage the risks associated with discharging the responsibilities of the derivatives clearing organization through the use of appropriate tools and procedures.

"(ii) MEASUREMENT OF CREDIT EXPOSURE.— Each derivatives clearing organization shall—

"(I) not less than once during each business day of the derivatives clearing organization,

(B)**财务资源**。——

(i)**一般规定**。——每一衍生品结算组织均应具备充足的财务、运营和管理资源,以履行衍生品结算组织的各项责任,财务、运营和管理资源的充足性以商品期货交易委员会的判定为准。

(ii)**财务资源的最低金额**。——每一衍生品结算组织拥有的财务资源最低均应超过满足下列条件所需的总金额——

(I)足以使该衍生品结算组织履行对其会员和参与者承担的财务责任(即使在极端但可能发生的市场状况中,形成最大财务风险敞口的该组织会员或参与者发生违约的情况下,也不例外);及

(II)足以使衍生品结算组织支付1年的运营成本(以滚动方式计算)。

(C)**参与者和产品的适格性**。——

(i)**一般规定**。——每一衍生品结算组织均应——

(I)为衍生品结算组织会员和参与者制定适当的准入标准和持续的适格性标准(包括就财务资源和运营能力制定充足性标准,以确保会员和参与者能够履行因参与衍生品结算组织而产生的义务);及

(II)制定用以判定提交给衍生品结算组织进行集中结算的协议、合约或交易的适当的适格性标准。

(ii)**程序要求**。——每一衍生品结算组织均应制定并实施相关程序,持续审核对每项参与要求和会员要求的合规情况。

(iii)**要求**。——每一衍生品结算组织的参与要求和会员要求均应——

(I)客观;

(II)公开披露;且

(III)提供公平、公开的准入。

(D)**风险管理**。——

(i)**一般规定**。——每一衍生品结算组织均应确保其有能力使用适当的工具和流程管理履行责任过程中产生的风险。

(ii)**信用风险敞口的计量**。——每一衍生品结算组织均应——

(I)计量对其每一会员和参与者的信用风险敞口,计量频率不得低于每个营业日

measure the credit exposures of the derivatives clearing organization to each member and participant of the derivatives clearing organization; and

"(II) monitor each exposure described in subclause (I) periodically during the business day of the derivatives clearing organization.

"(iii) LIMITATION OF EXPOSURE TO POTENTIAL LOSSES FROM DEFAULTS. — Each derivatives clearing organization, through margin requirements and other risk control mechanisms, shall limit the exposure of the derivatives clearing organization to potential losses from defaults by members and participants of the derivatives clearing organization to ensure that —

"(I) the operations of the derivatives clearing organization would not be disrupted; and

"(II) nondefaulting members or participants would not be exposed to losses that nondefaulting members or participants cannot anticipate or control.

"(iv) MARGIN REQUIREMENTS. — The margin required from each member and participant of a derivatives clearing organization shall be sufficient to cover potential exposures in normal market conditions.

"(v) REQUIREMENTS REGARDING MODELS AND PARAMETERS. — Each model and parameter used in setting margin requirements under clause (iv) shall be —

"(I) risk-based; and

"(II) reviewed on a regular basis.

"(E) SETTLEMENT PROCEDURES. — Each derivatives clearing organization shall —

"(i) complete money settlements on a timely basis (but not less frequently than once each business day);

"(ii) employ money settlement arrangements to eliminate or strictly limit the exposure of the derivatives clearing organization to settlement bank risks (including credit and liquidity risks from the use of banks to effect money settlements);

"(iii) ensure that money settlements are final when effected;

"(iv) maintain an accurate record of the flow of funds associated with each money settlement;

"(v) possess the ability to comply with each term and condition of any permitted netting or offset arrangement with any other clearing organization;

"(vi) regarding physical settlements, establish rules that clearly state each obligation of the derivatives clearing organization with respect to physical deliveries; and

"(vii) ensure that each risk arising from an obligation described in clause (vi) is identified and managed.

"(F) TREATMENT OF FUNDS. —

"(i) REQUIRED STANDARDS AND PROCEDURES. — Each derivatives clearing

一次(指衍生品结算组织的营业日);并

(II)在衍生品结算组织的每个营业日内定期监控第(I)子项所述每一风险敞口。

(iii)**限制对违约可能产生的损失的风险敞口**。——每一衍生品结算组织应通过保证金要求以及其他风险控制机制限制对其会员和参与者违约可能产生之损失的风险敞口,以确保——

(I)衍生品结算组织的运营不会受到扰乱;且

(II)非违约会员或参与者不会受到其无法预料或控制的风险影响。

(iv)**保证金要求**。——要求衍生品结算组织每一会员和参与者提供的保证金应足以弥补正常市场状况下的潜在风险敞口。

(v)**模型和参数要求**。——根据第(iv)项设定保证金要求时使用的每一模型和参数均应——

(I)基于风险;并

(II)定期进行审查。

(E)**结算程序**。——每一衍生品结算组织均应——

(i)及时完成现金结算(频率不得低于每个营业日一次);

(ii)采用现金结算安排来消除或严格限制衍生品结算组织对结算银行风险(包括通过银行实施现金结算产生的信用和流动性风险)的风险敞口;

(iii)确保当货币结算完成时该等结算具有终局性;

(iv)就每笔现金结算保存相关资金流动的准确记录;

(v)有能力遵守与任何其他结算组织达成的任何获许净额结算或对冲安排的每项条款和条件;

(vi)对于实物结算而言,制定相关规则,明确规定其在实物交割方面的所有义务;并

(vii)确保第(vi)项所述义务产生的每一风险均得以识别和管理。

(F)**资金处理**。——

(i)**标准和流程要求**。——每一衍生品结算组织均应制定相关标准和流程,以保

organization shall establish standards and procedures that are designed to protect and ensure the safety of member and participant funds and assets.

"(ii) HOLDING OF FUNDS AND ASSETS. — Each derivatives clearing organization shall hold member and participant funds and assets in a manner by which to minimize the risk of loss or of delay in the access by the derivatives clearing organization to the assets and funds.

"(iii) PERMISSIBLE INVESTMENTS. — Funds and assets invested by a derivatives clearing organization shall be held in instruments with minimal credit, market, and liquidity risks.

"(G) DEFAULT RULES AND PROCEDURES. —

"(i) IN GENERAL. — Each derivatives clearing organization shall have rules and procedures designed to allow for the efficient, fair, and safe management of events during which members or participants —

"(I) become insolvent; or

"(II) otherwise default on the obligations of the members or participants to the derivatives clearing organization.

"(ii) DEFAULT PROCEDURES. — Each derivatives clearing organization shall —

"(I) clearly state the default procedures of the derivatives clearing organization;

"(II) make publicly available the default rules of the derivatives clearing organization; and

"(III) ensure that the derivatives clearing organization may take timely action —

"(aa) to contain losses and liquidity pressures; and

"(bb) to continue meeting each obligation of the derivatives clearing organization.

"(H) RULE ENFORCEMENT. — Each derivatives clearing organization shall —

"(i) maintain adequate arrangements and resources for —

"(I) the effective monitoring and enforcement of compliance with the rules of the derivatives clearing organization; and

"(II) the resolution of disputes;

"(ii) have the authority and ability to discipline, limit, suspend, or terminate the activities of a member or participant due to a violation by the member or participant of any rule of the derivatives clearing organization; and

"(iii) report to the Commission regarding rule enforcement activities and sanctions imposed against members and participants as provided in clause (ii).

"(I) SYSTEM SAFEGUARDS. — Each derivatives clearing organization shall —

"(i) establish and maintain a program of risk analysis and oversight to identify and minimize sources of operational risk through the development of appropriate controls and procedures, and automated systems, that are reliable, secure, and have adequate scalable

护和确保会员和参与者的资金及资产安全。

(ii)**资金和资产的持有**。——每一衍生品结算组织在持有会员和参与者的资金和资产时，所采取的方式应能将其丧失或延迟对该等资产和资金的支取能力的风险减到最低限度。

(iii)**允许的投资**。——衍生品结算组织投资的资金和资产应通过信用、市场和流动性风险最小的工具持有。

(G)**违约处理规则和程序**。——

(i)**一般规定**。——每一衍生品结算组织均应设有旨在对会员或参与者的以下情形实施高效、公平、安全管理的规则和程序——

(I)资不抵债;或

(II)由于其他原因无法履行其对衍生品结算组织的会员或参与者的义务。

(ii)**违约处理程序**。——每一衍生品结算组织均应——

(I)明确规定其违约处理程序;

(II)公布其违约处理规则;并

(III)确保其可及时采取行动——

(aa)控制损失和流动性压力;及

(bb)继续履行其承担的各项义务。

(H)**规则的执行**。——每一衍生品结算组织均应——

(i)为以下各项工作维持充足的安排和资源——

(I)对其规则的合规情况进行有效监控和执行;及

(II)争议解决;

(ii)拥有相关权力和能力,对违反其任何规则的会员或参与者进行纪律处分并限制、暂停或终止该会员或参与者的活动;并

(iii)向商品期货交易委员会报告规则执行活动以及按第(ii)项规定对会员和参与者实施的处分;

(I)**系统保障**。——每一衍生品结算组织均应——

(i)建立并维持风险分析和监控计划,以便通过设置可靠、安全并具备充分的升级能力的适当控制措施和程序以及自动化系统,识别运营风险源并将其减到最低限度;

capacity;

"(ii) establish and maintain emergency procedures, backup facilities, and a plan for disaster recovery that allows for —

"(I) the timely recovery and resumption of operations of the derivatives clearing organization; and

"(II) the fulfillment of each obligation and responsibility of the derivatives clearing organization; and

"(iii) periodically conduct tests to verify that the backup resources of the derivatives clearing organization are sufficient to ensure daily processing, clearing, and settlement.

"(J) REPORTING. — Each derivatives clearing organization shall provide to the Commission all information that the Commission determines to be necessary to conduct oversight of the derivatives clearing organization.

"(K) RECORDKEEPING. — Each derivatives clearing organization shall maintain records of all activities related to the business of the derivatives clearing organization as a derivatives clearing organization —

"(i) in a form and manner that is acceptable to the Commission; and

"(ii) for a period of not less than 5 years.

"(L) PUBLIC INFORMATION. —

"(i) IN GENERAL. — Each derivatives clearing organization shall provide to market participants sufficient information to enable the market participants to identify and evaluate accurately the risks and costs associated with using the services of the derivatives clearing organization.

"(ii) AVAILABILITY OF INFORMATION. — Each derivatives clearing organization shall make information concerning the rules and operating and default procedures governing the clearing and settlement systems of the derivatives clearing organization available to market participants.

"(iii) PUBLIC DISCLOSURE. — Each derivatives clearing organization shall disclose publicly and to the Commission information concerning —

"(I) the terms and conditions of each contract, agreement, and transaction cleared and settled by the derivatives clearing organization;

"(II) each clearing and other fee that the derivatives clearing organization charges the members and participants of the derivatives clearing organization;

"(III) the margin–setting methodology, and the size and composition, of the financial resource package of the derivatives clearing organization;

"(IV) daily settlement prices, volume, and open interest for each contract settled or cleared by the derivatives clearing organization; and

"(V) any other matter relevant to participation in the settlement and clearing activities

(ii)建立并维持应急程序、备用设施和灾难恢复计划,以便——

(I)及时恢复和重启该衍生品结算组织的运营;并

(II)履行该衍生品结算组织承担的各项责任和义务;并

(iii)定期开展测试,以核实该衍生品结算组织的备用资源是否足以确保交易的每日处理、清算和结算。

(J)**报告**。——每一衍生品结算组织均应向商品期货交易委员会提供商品期货交易委员会判定对于该衍生品结算组织的监控确属必要的所有信息。

(K)**记录保存**。——每一衍生品结算组织均应就其作为衍生品结算组织开展的业务相关的所有活动保存记录,并且——

(i)按照商品期货交易委员会认可的格式和方式保存记录;且

(ii)记录保存期至少应为5年。

(L)**公开信息**。——

(i)**一般规定**。——每一衍生品结算组织均应向市场参与者提供充分信息,使其能够识别并准确评估与使用该衍生品结算组织服务相关的风险和成本。

(ii)**信息的提供**。——每一衍生品结算组织均应向市场参与者提供与其清算和结算系统的规则、运作程序和违约处理程序相关的信息。

(iii)**公开披露**。——每一衍生品结算组织均应向公众和商品期货交易委员会披露以下信息——

(I)其所清算和结算的每一合约、协议和交易品种的条款和条件;

(II)向会员和参与者收取的每项结算费用和其他费用;

(III)保证金设定方法以及财务资源组合的规模和构成;

(IV)其所结算或清算的每一合约品种的每日结算价格、成交量及未平仓量;及

(V)与参与结算和清算活动相关的任何其他事项。

of the derivatives clearing organization.

"(M) INFORMATION-SHARING. — Each derivatives clearing organization shall —

"(i) enter into, and abide by the terms of, each appropriate and applicable domestic and international information-sharing agreement; and

"(ii) use relevant information obtained from each agreement described in clause (i) in carrying out the risk management program of the derivatives clearing organization.

"(N) ANTITRUST CONSIDERATIONS. — Unless necessary or appropriate to achieve the purposes of this Act, a derivatives clearing organization shall not —

"(i) adopt any rule or take any action that results in any unreasonable restraint of trade; or

"(ii) impose any material anticompetitive burden.

"(O) GOVERNANCE FITNESS STANDARDS. —

"(i) GOVERNANCE ARRANGEMENTS. — Each derivatives clearing organization shall establish governance arrangements that are transparent —

"(I) to fulfill public interest requirements; and

"(II) to permit the consideration of the views of owners and participants.

"(ii) FITNESS STANDARDS. — Each derivatives clearing organization shall establish and enforce appropriate fitness standards for —

"(I) directors;

"(II) members of any disciplinary committee;

"(III) members of the derivatives clearing organization;

"(IV) any other individual or entity with direct access to the settlement or clearing activities of the derivatives clearing organization; and

"(V) any party affiliated with any individual or entity described in this clause.

"(P) CONFLICTS OF INTEREST. — Each derivatives clearing organization shall —

"(i) establish and enforce rules to minimize conflicts of interest in the decision-making process of the derivatives clearing organization; and

"(ii) establish a process for resolving conflicts of interest described in clause (i).

"(Q) COMPOSITION OF GOVERNING BOARDS. — Each derivatives clearing organization shall ensure that the composition of the governing board or committee of the derivatives clearing organization includes market participants.

"(R) LEGAL RISK. — Each derivatives clearing organization shall have a well-founded, transparent, and enforceable legal framework for each aspect of the activities of the derivatives clearing organization.".

(d) CONFLICTS OF INTEREST. — The Commodity Futures Trading Commission shall adopt rules mitigating conflicts of interest in connection with the conduct of business by a swap dealer or a major swap participant with a derivatives clearing organization, board of

(M)**信息共享**。——每一衍生品结算组织均应——

(i)订立并遵守适当和适用的国内和国际信息共享协议;且

(ii)在实施其风险管理计划时使用通过第(i)项所述每一协议获取的相关信息。

(N)**反垄断考量**。——除非对实现本法宗旨确属必要或适当,否则衍生品结算组织不得——

(i)制定对交易造成任何不合理限制的任何规则或采取对交易造成任何不合理限制的任何行动;或

(ii)施加任何阻碍竞争的实质性负担。

(O)**治理的适合性标准**。——

(i)**治理安排**。——每一衍生品结算组织均应建立透明的治理安排,以便——

(I)满足公共利益的要求;并

(II)使管理机构能够考虑到所有者和参与者的意见。

(ii) **适合性标准**。——每一衍生品结算组织均应针对以下各者制定和执行适当的适合性标准——

(I)董事;

(II)任何纪律委员会的成员;

(III)其会员;

(IV)能直接接触其结算或清算活动的任何其他个人或实体;及

(V)本项所述任何个人的或实体的关联方。

(P)**利益冲突**。——每一衍生品结算组织均应——

(i)制定并执行相关规则,将其决策过程中的利益冲突减到最低限度;并

(ii)制定解决第(i)项所述利益冲突的程序。

(Q)**管理机构的组成**。——每一衍生品结算组织均应确保其管理机构或委员会组成人员中包括市场参与者。

(R)**法律风险**。——每一衍生品结算组织均应针对其活动的各个方面设置具有充分依据、透明并且可强制执行的法律框架。”

(d)**利益冲突**。——商品期货交易委员会应制定规则,在互换交易商或主要互换参与者对于对互换进行结算或交易的衍生品结算组织、交易场所或互换执行设施拥有重大债务或重大股权投资的情况下,将互换交易商或主要互换参与者与该等衍生

trade, or a swap execution facility that clears or trades swaps in which the swap dealer or major swap participant has a material debt or material equity investment.

(e) REPORTING REQUIREMENTS. — Section 5b of the Commodity Exchange Act (7 U.S.C. 7a – 1) (as amended by subsection (b)) is amended by adding at the end the following:

"(k) REPORTING REQUIREMENTS. —

"(1) DUTY OF DERIVATIVES CLEARING ORGANIZATIONS. — Each derivatives clearing organization that clears swaps shall provide to the Commission all information that is determined by the Commission to be necessary to perform each responsibility of the Commission under this Act.

"(2) DATA COLLECTION AND MAINTENANCE REQUIREMENTS. — The Commission shall adopt data collection and maintenance requirements for swaps cleared by derivatives clearing organizations that are comparable to the corresponding requirements for —

"(A) swaps data reported to swap data repositories; and

"(B) swaps traded on swap execution facilities.

"(3) REPORTS ON SECURITY–BASED SWAP AGREEMENTS TO BE SHARED WITH THE SECURITIES AND EXCHANGE COMMISSION. —

"(A) IN GENERAL. — A derivatives clearing organization that clears security–based swap agreements (as defined in section 1a (47) (A) (v)) shall, upon request, open to inspection and examination to the Securities and Exchange Commission all books and records relating to such security–based swap agreements, consistent with the confidentiality and disclosure requirements of section 8.

"(B) JURISDICTION. — Nothing in this paragraph shall affect the exclusive jurisdiction of the Commission to prescribe recordkeeping and reporting requirements for a derivatives clearing organization that is registered with the Commission.

"(4) INFORMATION SHARING. — Subject to section 8, and upon request, the Commission shall share information collected under paragraph (2) with —

"(A) the Board;

"(B) the Securities and Exchange Commission;

"(C) each appropriate prudential regulator;

"(D) the Financial Stability Oversight Council;

"(E) the Department of Justice; and

"(F) any other person that the Commission determines to be appropriate, including —

"(i) foreign financial supervisors (including foreign futures authorities);

"(ii) foreign central banks; and

"(iii) foreign ministries.

"(5) CONFIDENTIALITY AND INDEMNIFICATION AGREEMENT. — Before the

品结算组织、交易场所或互换执行设施之间开展业务而产生的利益冲突限制在最低范围之内。

(e)**报告要求**。——在《商品交易法》第5b条(《美国法典》第七编第7a-1节)[以经第(b)子条修正后的版本为准]结尾处增加如下内容,作为对该条的修正:

"(k)**报告要求**。——

(1)**衍生品结算组织的职责**。——提供互换集中结算服务的每一衍生品结算组织均应向商品期货交易委员会提供商品期货交易委员会判定确属必要的所有信息,以便商品期货交易委员会履行本法规定的各项责任。

(2)**数据收集和保存要求**。——对于衍生品结算组织集中结算的互换,商品期货交易委员会应制定与适用于以下各项的要求具有可比性的数据收集和保存要求——

(A)向互换数据存管机构报告的互换数据;及

(B)在互换执行设施交易的互换。

(3)**与证券交易委员会共享的证券类互换协议报告**。——

(A)**一般规定**。——对证券类互换协议[定义见第1a(47)(A)(v)条]进行集中结算的衍生品结算组织应在不违背第8条的保密和披露要求的前提下,按照证券交易委员会要求,将与该等证券类互换协议有关的所有账簿和记录提供给证券交易委员会检查和核查。

(B)**管辖权**。——对于在商品期货交易委员会注册的衍生品结算组织,商品期货交易委员会享有制定记录保存和报告要求的排他管辖权,本款任何内容均不影响商品期货交易委员会的该管辖权。

(4)**信息共享**。——在不违反第8条规定的前提下,经下述机构提出请求,商品期货交易委员会应与其共享依据第(2)款收集的信息——

(A)联邦储备委员会;

(B)证券交易委员会;

(C)每一相应的审慎监管者;

(D)金融稳定监督委员会;

(E)司法部;及

(F)商品期货交易委员会判定确属适当的任何其他主体,包括——

(i)外国金融监管者(包括外国期货监管机构);

(ii)外国中央银行;及

(iii)外国部委。

(5)**保密和补偿协议**。——在商品期货交易委员会与第(4)款所述任何实体共享

Commission may share information with any entity described in paragraph (4) —

"(A) the Commission shall receive a written agreement from each entity stating that the entity shall abide by the confidentiality requirements described in section 8 relating to the information on swap transactions that is provided; and

"(B) each entity shall agree to indemnify the Commission for any expenses arising from litigation relating to the information provided under section 8.

"(6) PUBLIC INFORMATION. — Each derivatives clearing organization that clears swaps shall provide to the Commission (including any designee of the Commission) information under paragraph (2) in such form and at such frequency as is required by the Commission to comply with the public reporting requirements contained in section 2(a)(13).".

(f) PUBLIC DISCLOSURE. — Section 8(e) of the Commodity Exchange Act (7 U.S.C. 12(e)) is amended in the last sentence —

(1) by inserting ", central bank and ministries," after "department" each place it appears; and

(2) by striking ". is a party." and inserting ", is a party.".

(g) LEGAL CERTAINTY FOR IDENTIFIED BANKING PRODUCTS. —

(1) REPEALS. — The Legal Certainty for Bank Products Act of 2000 (7 U.S.C. 27 et seq.) is amended —

(A) by striking sections 404 and 407 (7 U.S.C. 27b, 27e);

(B) in section 402 (7 U.S.C. 27), by striking subsection (d); and

(C) in section 408 (7 U.S.C. 27f) —

(i) in subsection (c) —

(I) by striking "in the case" and all that follows through "a hybrid" and inserting "in the case of a hybrid";

(II) by striking "; or" and inserting a period; and

(III) by striking paragraph (2);

(ii) by striking subsection (b); and

(iii) by redesignating subsection (c) as subsection (b).

(2) LEGAL CERTAINTY FOR BANK PRODUCTS ACT OF 2000. — Section 403 of the Legal Certainty for Bank Products Act of 2000 (7 U.S.C. 27a) is amended to read as follows:

"SEC.403. EXCLUSION OF IDENTIFIED BANKING PRODUCT.

"(a) EXCLUSION. — Except as provided in subsection (b) or (c) —

"(1) the Commodity Exchange Act (7 U.S.C. 1 et seq.) shall not apply to, and the Commodity Futures Trading Commission shall not exercise regulatory authority under the Commodity Exchange Act (7 U.S.C. 1 et seq.) with respect to, an identified banking product;

信息之前——

(A)商品期货交易委员会应已收到一份来自每一实体的书面协议,说明该实体将遵守第8条关于所提供的互换交易信息的保密要求;且

(B)每一实体均应同意,如果依照第8条提供的信息引发相关诉讼,其将补偿商品期货交易委员会由此发生的任何费用。

(6)**公开信息**。——提供互换集中结算服务的每一衍生品结算组织均应按照商品期货交易委员会要求的格式和频率向商品期货交易委员会(包括商品期货交易委员会指定的任何人员)提供第(2)款规定的信息,以履行第2(a)(13)条的公开报告要求。"

(f)**公开披露**。——《商品交易法》[《美国法典》第七编第12(e)节]第8(e)条最后一句修正如下——

(1)在所有"部门"之后插入"、中央银行和部委,";及

(2)将"作为当事方"之前的句号改为逗号。

(g)**确定的银行产品的法律确定性**。——

(1)**废止**。——《2000年银行产品法律确定性法》(《美国法典》第七编第27节及其后条文)修正如下——

(A)删除第404条和第407条(《美国法典》第七编第27b节和第27e节);

(B)在第402条(《美国法典》第七编第27节)中,删除第(d)子条;及

(C)在第408条(《美国法典》第七编第27f节)中——

(i)第(c)子条——

(I)删除"如果"及之后内容直至"混合",替以"如果为混合";

(II)删除";或",替以句号;及

(III)删除第(2)款;

(ii)删除第(b)子条;及

(iii)第(c)子条重新编号为第(b)子条。

(2)**《2000年银行产品法律确定性法》**。——《2000年银行产品法律确定性法》(《美国法典》第七编第27a节)第403条修正后全文如下:

"第403条 关于确定的银行产品的除外规定

(a)**除外规定**。——除第(b)子条或第(c)子条规定的情形外——

(1)《商品交易法》(《美国法典》第七编第1节及其后条文)不适用于确定的银行产品,且商品期货交易委员会不得依据《商品交易法》(《美国法典》第七编第1节及其后条文)对确定的银行产品行使监管权;且

and

"(2) the definitions of 'security-based swap' in section 3(a)(68) of the Securities Exchange Act of 1934 and 'security-based swap agreement' in section 1a(47)(A)(v) of the Commodity Exchange Act and section 3(a)(78) of the Securities Exchange Act of 1934 do not include any identified bank product.

"(b) EXCEPTION. — An appropriate Federal banking agency may except an identified banking product of a bank under its regulatory jurisdiction from the exclusion in subsection (a) if the agency determines, in consultation with the Commodity Futures Trading Commission and the Securities and Exchange Commission, that the product —

"(1) would meet the definition of a 'swap' under section 1a(47) of the Commodity Exchange Act (7 U.S.C. 1a) or a 'security-based swap' under that section 3(a)(68) of the Securities Exchange Act of 1934; and

"(2) has become known to the trade as a swap or security-based swap, or otherwise has been structured as an identified banking product for the purpose of evading the provisions of the Commodity Exchange Act (7 U.S.C. 1 et seq.), the Securities Act of 1933 (15 U.S.C. 77a et seq.), or the Securities Exchange Act of 1934 (15 U.S.C. 78a et seq.).

"(c) EXCEPTION. — The exclusions in subsection (a) shall not apply to an identified bankproduct that —

"(1) is a product of a bank that is not under the regulatory jurisdiction of an appropriate Federal banking agency;

"(2) meets the definition of swap in section 1a(47) of the Commodity Exchange Act or security-based swap in section 3(a)(68) of the Securities Exchange Act of 1934; and

"(3) has become known to the trade as a swap or security-based swap, or otherwise has been structured as an identified banking product for the purpose of evading the provisions of the Commodity Exchange Act (7 U.S.C. 1 et seq.), the Securities Act of 1933 (15 U.S.C. 77a et seq.), or the Securities Exchange Act of 1934 (15 U.S.C. 78a et seq.).".

(h) REDUCING CLEARING SYSTEMIC RISK. — Section 5b(f)(1) of the Commodity Exchange Act (7 U.S.C. 7a-1(F)(i)) is amended by adding at the end the following: "In order to minimize systemic risk, under no circumstances shall a derivatives clearing organization be compelled to accept the counterparty credit risk of another clearing organization.".

SEC.726. RULEMAKING ON CONFLICT OF INTEREST.

(a) IN GENERAL. — In order to mitigate conflicts of interest, not later than 180 days after the date of enactment of the Wall Street Transparency and Accountability Act of 2010, the Commodity Futures Trading Commission shall adopt rules which may include numerical limits on the control of, or the voting rights with respect to, any derivatives clearing organization that clears swaps, or swap execution facility or board of trade designated as a

(2)《1934年证券交易法》第3(a)(68)条对‘证券类互换’定义,以及《商品交易法》第1a(47)(A)(v)条和《1934年证券交易法》第3(a)(78)条对‘证券类互换协议’的定义,均不包括任何确定的银行产品。

(b)**例外规定**——相应的联邦银行业监管机关可规定受其监管的银行的确定的银行产品不适用第(a)子条的除外规定,其前提是该机关在与商品期货交易委员会和证券交易委员会磋商后判定该产品——

(1)符合《商品交易法》(《美国法典》第七编第1a节)第1a(47)条对‘互换’的定义或者符合《1934年证券交易法》第3(a)(68)条对‘证券类互换’的定义;且

(2)已经被业界通称为互换或证券类互换,或者被构建为确定的银行产品,但其目的是规避《商品交易法》(《美国法典》第七编第1节及其后条文)、《1933年证券法》(《美国法典》第十五编第77a节及其后条文)或《1934年证券交易法》(《美国法典》第十五编第78a节及其后条文)的规定。

(c)**例外规定**。——第(a)子条的除外规定不得适用于以下确定的银行产品——

(1)不受相应的联邦银行业监管机关监管的银行的产品;

(2)符合《商品交易法》第1a(47)条对互换的定义或者符合《1934年证券交易法》第3(a)(68)条对证券类互换的定义;及

(3)已经被业界通称为互换或证券类互换,或者被构建为确定的银行产品,但其目的是规避《商品交易法》(《美国法典》第七编第1节及其后条文)、《1933年证券法》(《美国法典》第十五编第77a节及其后条文)或《1934年证券交易法》(《美国法典》第十五编第78a节及其后条文)的规定。”

(h)**降低结算系统性风险**。——在《商品交易法》第5b(f)(1)条[《美国法典》第七编第7a-1(F)(i)节]结尾处增加如下内容,作为对该条的修正:“为了将系统性风险减到最低限度,在任何情况下均不得强制衍生品结算组织接受另一结算组织的对手方信用风险。”

第726条　利益冲突规则的制定

(a)**一般规定**。——在《2010年华尔街透明度与问责法》颁布之日起180天内,商品期货交易委员会应为化解利益冲突之目的制定相关规则,包括控制权或表决权的数量限制规则,以限制以下实体对提供互换集中结算服务的任何衍生品结算组织,或者对发布互换或提供互换以供交易的互换执行设施或被指定为合约市场的交易场所拥有的控制权或表决权:并表资产总额达500亿美元(含)以上的银行控股公司[定义见

contract market that posts swaps or makes swaps available for trading, by a bank holding company (as defined in section 2 of the Bank Holding Company Act of 1956 (12 U.S.C. 1841)) with total consolidated assets of $50,000,000,000 or more, a nonbank financial company (as defined in section 102) supervised by the Board, an affiliate of such a bank holding company or nonbank financial company, a swap dealer, major swap participant, or associated person of a swap dealer or major swap participant.

(b) PURPOSES. — The Commission shall adopt rules if it determines, after the review described in subsection (a), that such rules are necessary or appropriate to improve the governance of, or to mitigate systemic risk, promote competition, or mitigate conflicts of interest in connection with a swap dealer or major swap participant's conduct of business with, a derivatives clearing organization, contract market, or swap execution facility that clears or posts swaps or makes swaps available for trading and in which such swap dealer or major swap participant has a material debt or equity investment.

(c) CONSIDERATIONS. — In adopting rules pursuant to this section, the Commodity Futures Trading Commission shall consider any conflicts of interest arising from the amount of equity owned by a single investor, the ability to vote, cause the vote of, or withhold votes entitled to be cast on any matters by the holders of the ownership interest, and the governance arrangements of any derivatives clearing organization that clears swaps, or swap execution facility or board of trade designated as a contract market that posts swaps or makes swaps available for trading.

SEC.727. PUBLIC REPORTING OF SWAP TRANSACTION DATA.

Section 2(a) of the Commodity Exchange Act (7 U.S.C. 2(a)) is amended by adding at the end the following:

"(13) PUBLIC AVAILABILITY OF SWAP TRANSACTION DATA. —

"(A) DEFINITION OF REAL-TIME PUBLIC REPORTING. — In this paragraph, the term 'real-time public reporting' means to report data relating to a swap transaction, including price and volume, as soon as technologically practicable after the time at which the swap transaction has been executed.

"(B) PURPOSE. — The purpose of this section is to authorize the Commission to make swap transaction and pricing data available to the public in such form and at such times as the Commission determines appropriate to enhance price discovery.

"(C) GENERAL RULE. — The Commission is authorized and required to provide by rule for the public availability of swap transaction and pricing data as follows:

"(i) With respect to those swaps that are subject to the mandatory clearing requirement described in subsection (h)(1) (including those swaps that are excepted from the requirement pursuant to subsection (h)(7)), the Commission shall require real-time public reporting for such transactions.

《1956年银行控股公司法》第2条(《美国法典》第十二编第1841节)]、受联邦储备委员会监管的非银行金融公司(定义见第102条)、上述银行控股公司或非银行金融公司的关联方、互换交易商、主要互换参与者或该等交易商或参与者的业务相关人。

(b)**目的**。——商品期货交易委员会应在开展第(a)子条所述审查后,制定必要或适当的规则,以改善互换交易商或主要互换参与者的治理,缓释其系统性风险,促进竞争或减少其开展业务时与下述主体之间的利益冲突:由互换交易商或主要互换参与者拥有重大债务或股权投资的,结算、发布互换或提供互换以供交易的衍生品结算组织、合约市场或互换执行设施。

(c)**考虑因素**。——根据本条制定规则时,商品期货交易委员会应考虑以下因素:因单个投资者拥有的股权金额产生的利益冲突;直接表决能力、促使所有权权益持有人就其有权表决的任何事项进行表决或放弃表决的能力;以及提供互换结算服务的任何衍生品结算组织,或被指定为合约市场的发布互换或提供互换以供交易的互换执行设施或交易场所的治理安排。

第727条　互换交易数据的公开报告

在《商品交易法》第2(a)条[《美国法典》第七编第2(a)节]结尾处增加如下内容,作为对该条的修正:

"(13)**互换交易数据的公开提供**。——

(A)**实时公开报告的定义**。——就本款而言,'实时公开报告'一词系指在互换交易执行之后技术可行的第一时间报告与互换交易相关的数据,包括成交价格和成交量。

(B)**目的**。——本条规定旨在授权商品期货交易委员会以其判定确属适当的格式和时间,向公众公开提供互换交易和定价数据,以加强价格发现。

(C)**一般规定**。——商品期货交易委员会有权并有义务发布规则,对互换交易和定价数据的公开提供作出如下规定:

(i)对于受制于第(h)(1)子条所述强制集中结算要求的互换[包括根据第(h)(7)子条作为例外不适用该等要求的互换],商品期货交易委员会应要求对该等交易进行实时公开报告。

"(ii) With respect to those swaps that are not subject to the mandatory clearing requirement described in subsection (h)(1), but are cleared at a registered derivatives clearing organization, the Commission shall require real–time public reporting for such transactions.

"(iii) With respect to swaps that are not cleared at a registered derivatives clearing organization and which are reported to a swap data repository or the Commission under subsection (h)(6), the Commission shall require real–time public reporting for such transactions, in a manner that does not disclose the business transactions and market positions of any person.

"(iv) With respect to swaps that are determined to be required to be cleared under subsection (h)(2) but are not cleared, the Commission shall require real–time public reporting for such transactions.

"(D) REGISTERED ENTITIES AND PUBLIC REPORTING. — The Commission may require registered entities to publicly disseminate the swap transaction and pricing data required to be reported under this paragraph.

"(E) RULEMAKING REQUIRED. — With respect to the rule providing for the public availability of transaction and pricing data for swaps described in clauses (i) and (ii) of subparagraph (C), the rule promulgated by the Commission shall contain provisions —

"(i) to ensure such information does not identify the participants;

"(ii) to specify the criteria for determining what constitutes a large notional swap transaction (block trade) for particular markets and contracts;

"(iii) to specify the appropriate time delay for reporting large notional swap transactions (block trades) to the public; and

"(iv) that take into account whether the public disclosure will materially reduce market liquidity.

"(F) TIMELINESS OF REPORTING. — Parties to a swap (including agents of the parties to a swap) shall be responsible for reporting swap transaction information to the appropriate registered entity in a timely manner as may be prescribed by the Commission.

"(G) REPORTING OF SWAPS TO REGISTERED SWAP DATA REPOSITORIES. — Each swap (whether cleared or uncleared) shall be reported to a registered swap data repository.

"(14) SEMIANNUAL AND ANNUAL PUBLIC REPORTING OF AGGREGATE SWAP DATA. —

"(A) IN GENERAL. — In accordance with subparagraph (B), the Commission shall issue a written report on a semiannual and annual basis to make available to the public information relating to —

"(i) the trading and clearing in the major swap categories; and

(ii)对于不受制于第(h)(1)子条所述强制集中结算要求,但仍在注册衍生品结算组织进行集中结算的互换,商品期货交易委员会应要求对该等交易进行实时公开报告。

(iii)对于不在注册衍生品结算组织进行集中结算,但根据第(h)(6)子条的规定向互换数据存管机构或商品期货交易委员会报告的互换,商品期货交易委员会应要求以不披露任何人的业务交易和市场持仓量的方式,对该等交易进行实时公开报告。

(iv)对于被判定应根据第(h)(2)子条的规定进行集中结算但结果并未集中结算的互换,商品期货交易委员会应要求对该等交易进行实时公开报告。

(D)**注册实体和公开报告**。——商品期货交易委员会可以要求注册实体公开发布本款要求报告的互换交易和定价数据。

(E)**规则制定要求**。——商品期货交易委员会颁发关于第(C)子款第(i)项和第(ii)项所述互换的交易和定价数据的公开提供规则时,应纳入相关规定,以——

(i)确保该等信息不会透露参与者的身份;

(ii)具体规定对于特定市场和合约而言,构成大额名义互换交易(大宗交易)的判定标准;

(iii)具体规定对于大额名义互换交易(大宗交易)而言,向公众报告时可以适度延迟的时间;并

(iv)考虑公开披露是否会严重降低市场流动性。

(F)**及时报告**。——互换的交易方(包括互换的交易方的代理人)有责任按照商品期货交易委员会规定的方式,及时向相应的注册实体报告互换交易信息。

(G)**向注册的互换数据存管机构进行互换报告**。——每一互换(不论是否集中结算)均应向注册的互换数据存管机构进行报告。

(14)**汇总互换数据的半年公开报告和年度公开报告**。——

(A)**一般规定**。——商品期货交易委员会应根据第(B)子款的规定,发布书面的半年度报告和年度报告,向公众提供与如下各项相关的信息——

(i)主要互换类别的交易和集中结算情况;及

"(ii) the market participants and developments in new products.

"(B) USE; CONSULTATION. — In preparing a report under subparagraph (A), the Commission shall —

"(i) use information from swap data repositories and derivatives clearing organizations; and

"(ii) consult with the Office of the Comptroller of the Currency, the Bank for International Settlements, and such other regulatory bodies as may be necessary.

"(C) AUTHORITY OF THE COMMISSION. — The Commission may, by rule, regulation, or order, delegate the public reporting responsibilities of the Commission under this paragraph in accordance with such terms and conditions as the Commission determines to be appropriate and in the public interest.".

SEC.728. SWAP DATA REPOSITORIES.

The Commodity Exchange Act is amended by inserting after section 20 (7 U.S.C. 24) the following:

"SEC.21. SWAP DATA REPOSITORIES.

"(a) REGISTRATION REQUIREMENT. —

"(1) REQUIREMENT; AUTHORITY OF DERIVATIVES CLEARING ORGANIZATION. —

"(A) IN GENERAL. — It shall be unlawful for any person, unless registered with the Commission, directly or indirectly to make use of the mails or any means or instrumentality of interstate commerce to perform the functions of a swap data repository.

"(B) REGISTRATION OF DERIVATIVES CLEARING ORGANIZATIONS. — A derivatives clearing organization may register as a swap data repository.

"(2) INSPECTION AND EXAMINATION. — Each registered swap data repository shall be subject to inspection and examination by any representative of the Commission.

"(3) COMPLIANCE WITH CORE PRINCIPLES. —

"(A) IN GENERAL. — To be registered, and maintain registration, as a swap data repository, the swap data repository shall comply with —

"(i) the requirements and core principles described in this section; and

"(ii) any requirement that the Commission may impose by rule or regulation pursuant to section 8a(5).

"(B) REASONABLE DISCRETION OF SWAP DATA REPOSITORY. — Unless otherwise determined by the Commission by rule or regulation, a swap data repository described in subparagraph (A) shall have reasonable discretion in establishing the manner in which the swap data repository complies with the core principles described in this section.

"(b) STANDARD SETTING. —

"(1) DATA IDENTIFICATION. —

(ii)新产品的市场参与者和开发情况。

(B)**信息使用;磋商**。——在编制第(A)子款规定的报告时,商品期货交易委员会应——

(i)使用互换数据存管机构和衍生品结算组织提供的信息;并

(ii)与货币监理署、国际清算银行及其他必要的监管机构磋商。

(C)**商品期货交易委员会的权力**。——商品期货交易委员会可以发布规则、规章或命令,按其判定确属适当且符合公共利益的条款及条件,将其根据本款承担的公开报告责任委托给其他主体履行。”

第728条　互换数据存管机构

在《商品交易法》第20条(《美国法典》第七编第24节)之后插入如下内容,作为对该法的修正:

“第21条　互换数据存管机构

(a)**注册要求**。——

(1)**要求;衍生品结算组织的权力**。——

(A)**一般规定**。——除非已在商品期货交易委员会注册,否则任何人直接或间接使用邮件或任何州际商业手段或工具履行互换数据存管机构职能的行为,当属违法。

(B)**衍生品结算组织的注册**。——衍生品结算组织可以注册为互换数据存管机构。

(2)**检查和核查**。——每一注册的互换数据存管机构均应接受商品期货交易委员会任何代表的检查和核查。

(3)**核心原则合规**。——

(A)**一般规定**。——要注册为互换数据存管机构并维持该注册,互换数据存管机构应当遵守:

(i)本条所述的要求和核心原则;及

(ii)商品期货交易委员会依据第8a(5)条发布的规则或规章所施加的任何要求。

(B)**互换数据存管机构合理的自由裁量权**。——除非商品期货交易委员会发布的规则或规章作出不同判定,否则第(A)子款所述互换数据存管机构应依其合理的自由裁量权决定其遵守本条所述核心原则的方式。

(b)**标准设定**。——

(1)**数据识别**。——

"(A) IN GENERAL. — In accordance with subparagraph (B), the Commission shall prescribe standards that specify the data elements for each swap that shall be collected and maintained by each registered swap data repository.

"(B) REQUIREMENT. — In carrying out subparagraph (A), the Commission shall prescribe consistent data element standards applicable to registered entities and reporting counterparties.

"(2) DATA COLLECTION AND MAINTENANCE. — The Commission shall prescribe data collection and data maintenance standards for swap data repositories.

"(3) COMPARABILITY. — The standards prescribed by the Commission under this subsection shall be comparable to the data standards imposed by the Commission on derivatives clearing organizations in connection with their clearing of swaps.

"(c) DUTIES. — A swap data repository shall —

"(1) accept data prescribed by the Commission for each swap under subsection (b);

"(2) confirm with both counterparties to the swap the accuracy of the data that was submitted;

"(3) maintain the data described in paragraph (1) in such form, in such manner, and for such period as may be required by the Commission;

"(4)(A) provide direct electronic access to the Commission (or any designee of the Commission, including another registered entity); and

"(B) provide the information described in paragraph (1) in such form and at such frequency as the Commission may require to comply with the public reporting requirements contained in section 2(a)(13);

"(5) at the direction of the Commission, establish automated systems for monitoring, screening, and analyzing swap data, including compliance and frequency of end user clearing exemption claims by individual and affiliated entities;

"(6) maintain the privacy of any and all swap transaction information that the swap data repository receives from a swap dealer, counterparty, or any other registered entity; and

"(7) on a confidential basis pursuant to section 8, upon request, and after notifying the Commission of the request, make available all data obtained by the swap data repository, including individual counterparty trade and position data, to —

"(A) each appropriate prudential regulator;

"(B) the Financial Stability Oversight Council;

"(C) the Securities and Exchange Commission;

"(D) the Department of Justice; and

"(E) any other person that the Commission determines to be appropriate, including —

"(i) foreign financial supervisors (including foreign futures authorities);

"(ii) foreign central banks; and

(A)**一般规定**。——根据第(B)子款,商品期货交易委员会应制定标准,具体规定各个注册的互换数据存管机构针对每一互换品种应收集和保存的数据元素。

(B)**要求**。——执行第(A)子款的规定时,商品期货交易委员会应制定适用于注册实体和报告对手方的统一数据元素标准。

(2)**数据的收集和保存**。——商品期货交易委员会应针对互换数据存管机构制定数据收集和保存标准。

(3)**可比性**。——商品期货交易委员会依据本子条制定的标准应与其对衍生品结算组织的互换结算设定的数据标准具有可比性。

(c)**职责**。——互换数据存管机构应——

(1)受理商品期货交易委员会针对第(b)子条的每一互换品种所规定的数据;

(2)与互换对手双方确认提交的数据的准确性;

(3)按照商品期货交易委员会要求的格式、方式和期限保存第(1)款所述数据;

(4)(A)向商品期货交易委员会(或商品期货交易委员会的任何指定人,包括其他注册实体)提供直接的电子接入;且

(B)按照商品期货交易委员会要求的格式和频率提供第(1)款规定的信息,以遵守第2(a)(13)条的公开报告要求;

(5)在商品期货交易委员会的指导下,建立自动系统用以监控、筛选和分析互换数据,包括单个实体和关联实体申请获得最终用户豁免集中结算的合规性和频率;

(6)维持互换数据存管机构从互换交易商、对手方或任何其他注册实体处获取的所有互换交易数据的隐私性;并

(7)在遵守第8条保密规定的基础上,在以下机构提出请求时并在向商品期货交易委员会通知该等请求后,向以下机构提供该互换数据存管机构获取的所有数据,包括具体单个对手方的交易和持仓数据——

(A)每一相应的审慎监管者;

(B)金融稳定监督委员会;

(C)证券交易委员会;

(D)司法部;及

(E)商品期货交易委员会判定确属适当的任何其他主体,包括——

(i)外国金融监管者(包括外国期货监管机构);

(ii)外国中央银行;及

"(iii) foreign ministries; and

"(8) establish and maintain emergency procedures, backup facilities, and a plan for disaster recovery that allows for the timely recovery and resumption of operations and the fulfillment of the responsibilities and obligations of the organization.

"(d) CONFIDENTIALITY AND INDEMNIFICATION AGREEMENT. — Before the swap data repository may share information with any entity described in subsection (c)(7) —

"(1) the swap data repository shall receive a written agreement from each entity stating that the entity shall abide by the confidentiality requirements described in section 8 relating to the information on swap transactions that is provided; and

"(2) each entity shall agree to indemnify the swap data repository and the Commission for any expenses arising from litigation relating to the information provided under section 8.

"(e) DESIGNATION OF CHIEF COMPLIANCE OFFICER. —

"(1) IN GENERAL. — Each swap data repository shall designate an individual to serve as a chief compliance officer.

"(2) DUTIES. — The chief compliance officer shall —

"(A) report directly to the board or to the senior officer of the swap data repository;

"(B) review the compliance of the swap data repository with respect to the requirements and core principles described in this section;

"(C) in consultation with the board of the swap data repository, a body performing a function similar to the board of the swap data repository, or the senior officer of the swap data repository, resolve any conflicts of interest that may arise;

"(D) be responsible for administering each policy and procedure that is required to be established pursuant to this section;

"(E) ensure compliance with this Act (including regulations) relating to agreements, contracts, or transactions, including each rule prescribed by the Commission under this section;

"(F) establish procedures for the remediation of noncompliance issues identified by the chief compliance officer through any —

"(i) compliance office review;

"(ii) look-back;

"(iii) internal or external audit finding;

"(iv) self-reported error; or

"(v) validated complaint; and

"(G) establish and follow appropriate procedures for the handling, management response, remediation, retesting, and closing of noncompliance issues.

"(3) ANNUAL REPORTS. —

"(A) IN GENERAL. — In accordance with rules prescribed by the Commission, the

(iii)外国部委;并

(8)建立并维持应急程序、备用设施以及灾难恢复计划,以便能及时恢复和重启该互换数据存管机构的运营,并履行其承担的责任和义务。

(d)**保密和补偿协议**。——在互换数据存管机构与第(c)(7)子条所述任何实体共享信息之前——

(1)互换数据存管机构应从每一实体处收到一份书面协议,说明该实体将遵守第8条关于所提供的互换交易信息的保密要求;且

(2)每一实体均应同意,如果依照第8条提供的信息引发诉讼,其将补偿互换数据存管机构和商品期货交易委员会由此发生的任何费用。

(e)**首席合规官的指定**。——

(1)**一般规定**。——每一互换数据存管机构均应指定一名个人担任首席合规官。

(2)**职责**。——首席合规官应——

(A)向互换数据存管机构的董事会或高级管理人员直接汇报工作;

(B)审查互换数据存管机构对本条所述要求和核心原则的遵守情况;

(C)与互换数据存管机构的董事会、履行与董事会类似职能的机构或高级管理人员磋商,解决任何可能发生的利益冲突问题;

(D)负责实施依据本条要求制定的每一项政策和程序;

(E)确保本法(包括规章)中与协议、合约或交易相关的规定(包括商品期货交易委员会依据本条制定的每项规则)均得到遵守;

(F)制定相关程序,据以对首席合规官通过以下任何方式识别的不合规问题采取补救措施——

(i)合规办公室的审查工作;

(ii)回顾工作;

(iii)内部或外部的审计认定结论;

(iv)自报失误;或

(v)有效的投诉;及

(G)制定并遵守用以对不合规问题进行处理、管理回应、补救、重新测试和终结的适当程序。

(3)**年度报告**。——

(A) **一般规定**。——首席合规官应根据商品期货交易委员会的规则每年编制并

chief compliance officer shall annually prepare and sign a report that contains a description of —

"(i) the compliance of the swap data repository of the chief compliance officer with respect to this Act (including regulations); and

"(ii) each policy and procedure of the swap data repository of the chief compliance officer (including the code of ethics and conflict of interest policies of the swap data repository).

"(B) REQUIREMENTS. — A compliance report under subparagraph (A) shall —

"(i) accompany each appropriate financial report of the swap data repository that is required to be furnished to the Commission pursuant to this section; and

"(ii) include a certification that, under penalty of law, the compliance report is accurate and complete.

"(f) CORE PRINCIPLES APPLICABLE TO SWAP DATA REPOSITORIES. —

"(1) ANTITRUST CONSIDERATIONS. — Unless necessary or appropriate to achieve the purposes of this Act, a swap data repository shall not —

"(A) adopt any rule or take any action that results in any unreasonable restraint of trade; or

"(B) impose any material anticompetitive burden on the trading, clearing, or reporting of transactions.

"(2) GOVERNANCE ARRANGEMENTS. — Each swap data repository shall establish governance arrangements that are transparent —

"(A) to fulfill public interest requirements; and

"(B) to support the objectives of the Federal Government, owners, and participants.

"(3) CONFLICTS OF INTEREST. — Each swap data repository shall —

"(A) establish and enforce rules to minimize conflicts of interest in the decision–making process of the swap data repository; and

"(B) establish a process for resolving conflicts of interest described in subparagraph (A).

"(4) ADDITIONAL DUTIES DEVELOPED BY COMMISSION. —

"(A) IN GENERAL. — The Commission may develop 1 or more additional duties applicable to swap data repositories.

"(B) CONSIDERATION OF EVOLVING STANDARDS. — In developing additional duties under subparagraph (A), the Commission may take into consideration any evolving standard of the United States or the international community.

"(C) ADDITIONAL DUTIES FOR COMMISSION DESIGNEES. — The Commission shall establish additional duties for any registrant described in section 1a(48) in order to minimize conflicts of interest, protect data, ensure compliance, and guarantee the safety and

签署一份报告,其中应包含以下内容——

(i)首席合规官所属的互换数据存管机构对本法(包括规章)的合规情况;及

(ii)首席合规官所属的互换数据存管机构的每项政策和程序(包括该互换数据存管机构的职业道德准则和利益冲突处理政策)。

(B)**要求**。——按照第(A)子款编制的合规报告应——

(i)与按本条规定应向商品期货交易委员会提交的互换数据存管机构每份相应的财务报告一并提交;并

(ii)包含一份自查证明,证明该合规报告的准确性和完整性,并明确表示其知晓作伪证将招致法律惩罚。

(f)**适用于互换数据存管机构的核心原则**。——

(1)**反垄断考量**。——除非对本法宗旨的实现确属必要或适当,否则互换数据存管机构不得——

(A)制定对交易造成任何不合理限制的任何规则或采取对交易造成任何不合理限制的任何行动;或

(B)对交易、结算或交易报告施加任何阻碍竞争的实质性负担。

(2)**治理安排**。——每一互换数据存管机构均应建立透明的治理安排,以——

(A)满足公共利益的要求;并

(B)支持联邦政府、所有者和参与者实现其目标。

(3)**利益冲突**。——每一互换数据存管机构均应——

(A)制定并执行相关规则,将其决策过程中的利益冲突减到最低限度;并

(B)制定解决第(A)子款所述利益冲突的程序。

(4)**商品期货交易委员会设定的新增职责**。——

(A)**一般规定**。——商品期货交易委员会可以针对互换数据存管机构规定一项或一项以上新增职责。

(B)**对标准产生的变化的考虑**。——在根据第(A)子款设定新增职责时,商品期货交易委员会可以考虑美国或者国际标准的任何变化。

(C)**商品期货交易委员会指定人的新增职责**。——商品期货交易委员会应设定第1a(48)条所述任何注册人的新增职责,以期将利益冲突减到最低限度、保护数据、确保互换数据存管机构合规并保证其安全和安保。

security of the swap data repository.

"(g) REQUIRED REGISTRATION FOR SWAP DATA REPOSITORIES. — Any person that is required to be registered as a swap data repository under this section shall register with the Commission regardless of whether that person is also licensed as a bank or registered with the Securities and Exchange Commission as a swap data repository.

"(h) RULES. — The Commission shall adopt rules governing persons that are registered under this section.".

SEC.729. REPORTING AND RECORDKEEPING.

The Commodity Exchange Act is amended by inserting after section 4q (7 U.S.C. 6o–1) the following:

"SEC.4r. REPORTING AND RECORDKEEPING FOR UNCLEARED SWAPS.

"(a) REQUIRED REPORTING OF SWAPS NOT ACCEPTED BY ANY DERIVATIVES CLEARING ORGANIZATION. —

"(1) IN GENERAL. — Each swap that is not accepted for clearing by any derivatives clearing organization shall be reported to —

"(A) a swap data repository described in section 21; or

"(B) in the case in which there is no swap data repository that would accept the swap, to the Commission pursuant to this section within such time period as the Commission may by rule or regulation prescribe.

"(2) TRANSITION RULE FOR PREENACTMENT SWAPS. —

"(A) SWAPS ENTERED INTO BEFORE THE DATE OF ENACTMENT OF THE WALL STREET TRANSPARENCY AND ACCOUNTABILITY ACT OF 2010. — Each swap entered into before the date of enactment of the Wall Street Transparency and Accountability Act of 2010, the terms of which have not expired as of the date of enactment of that Act, shall be reported to a registered swap data repository or the Commission by a date that is not later than —

"(i) 30 days after issuance of the interim final rule; or

"(ii) such other period as the Commission determines to be appropriate.

"(B) COMMISSION RULEMAKING. — The Commission shall promulgate an interim final rule within 90 days of the date of enactment of this section providing for the reporting of each swap entered into before the date of enactment as referenced in subparagraph (A).

"(C) EFFECTIVE DATE. — The reporting provisions described in this section shall be effective upon the enactment of this section.

"(3) REPORTING OBLIGATIONS. —

"(A) SWAPS IN WHICH ONLY 1 COUNTERPARTY IS A SWAP DEALER OR MAJOR SWAP PARTICIPANT. — With respect to a swap in which only 1 counterparty is a swap dealer or major swap participant, the swap dealer or major swap participant shall report

(g)**互换数据存管机构的注册要求**。——按照本条规定应注册为互换数据存管机构的任何主体，无论其是否同时拥有银行执照或已同时在证券交易委员会注册为互换数据存管机构，均应在商品期货交易委员会注册。

(h)**规则**。——商品期货交易委员会应针对依据本条规定注册的人制定相关规则。”

第729条　报告和记录保存

在《商品交易法》第4q条(《美国法典》第七编第6o-1节)结尾处增加如下内容，作为对该法的修正：

“第4r条　非集中结算的互换的报告和记录保存

(a)**未被任何衍生品结算组织受理进行集中结算的互换的报告要求**。——

(1)**一般规定**。——未被任何衍生品结算组织受理进行集中结算的每一互换均——

(A)应向第21条所述互换数据存管机构报告；或

(B)无任何互换数据存管机构受理该互换报告的，应在商品期货交易委员会发布的规则或规章所规定的期限内依照本条规定向商品期货交易委员会报告。

(2)**《2010年华尔街透明度与问责法》颁布之日以前达成的互换的过渡规则**。——

(A)**《2010年华尔街透明度与问责法》颁布之日前达成的互换**。——《2010年华尔街透明度与问责法》颁布之日以前达成的每一互换，其条款截至该法颁布之日尚未到期的，应不迟于以下期限向注册的互换数据存管机构或商品期货交易委员会报告——

(i)最终规则(暂行版)颁发后第30天；或

(ii)商品期货交易委员会判定确属适当的任何其他期限。

(B)**商品期货交易委员会的规则制定**。——商品期货交易委员会应于本条规定颁布之日起90天内颁发最终规则(暂行版)，规定对第(A)子款提及的颁布前达成的每一互换进行报告。

(C)**生效日**。——本条规定颁布后，其关于报告的规定当即生效。

(3)**报告义务**。——

(A)**互换中只有一个对手方是互换交易商或主要互换参与者的情形**。——如果互换中只有一个对手方是互换交易商或主要互换参与者，则该互换交易商或主要互换参与者应按第(1)款和第(2)款的规定进行互换报告。

the swap as required under paragraphs (1) and (2).

"(B) SWAPS IN WHICH COUNTERPARTY IS A SWAP DEALER AND THE OTHER A MAJOR SWAP PARTICIPANT. — With respect to a swap in which 1 counterparty is a swap dealer and the other a major swap participant, the swap dealer shall report the swap as required under paragraphs (1) and (2).

"(C) OTHER SWAPS. — With respect to any other swap not described in subparagraph (A) or (B), the counterparties to the swap shall select a counterparty to report the swap as required under paragraphs (1) and (2).

"(b) DUTIES OF CERTAIN INDIVIDUALS. — Any individual or entity that enters into a swap shall meet each requirement described in subsection (c) if the individual or entity did not —

"(1) clear the swap in accordance with section 2(h)(1); or

"(2) have the data regarding the swap accepted by a swap data repository in accordance with rules (including timeframes) adopted by the Commission under section 21.

"(c) REQUIREMENTS. — An individual or entity described in sub section (b) shall —

"(1) upon written request from the Commission, provide reports regarding the swaps held by the individual or entity to the Commission in such form and in such manner as the Commission may request; and

"(2) maintain books and records pertaining to the swaps held by the individual or entity in such form, in such manner, and for such period as the Commission may require, which shall be open to inspection by —

"(A) any representative of the Commission;

"(B) an appropriate prudential regulator;

"(C) the Securities and Exchange Commission;

"(D) the Financial Stability Oversight Council; and

"(E) the Department of Justice.

"(d) IDENTICAL DATA. — In prescribing rules under this section, the Commission shall require individuals and entities described in subsection (b) to submit to the Commission a report that contains data that is not less comprehensive than the data required to be collected by swap data repositories under section 21.".

SEC.730. LARGE SWAP TRADER REPORTING.

The Commodity Exchange Act (7 U.S.C. 1 et seq.) is amended by adding after section 4s (as added by section 731) the following:

"SEC.4t. LARGE SWAP TRADER REPORTING.

"(a) PROHIBITION. —

"(1) IN GENERAL. — Except as provided in paragraph (2), it shall be unlawful for any person to enter into any swap that the Commission determines to perform a significant

(B)**互换中有一个对手方是互换交易商而另一个对手方是主要互换参与者的情形**。——如果互换中有一个对手方是互换交易商而另一个对手方是主要互换参与者,则该互换交易商应按第(1)和第(2)款的规定进行互换报告。

(C)**其他互换**。——就不属于第(A)子款或第(B)子款所述的任何其他互换而言,互换对手方应从双方之中选定一方,由其按第(1)款和第(2)款的规定进行互换报告。

(b)**特定个人的职责**。——达成互换的任何个人或实体在下列情形下应遵守第(c)子条的每项要求——

(1)该个人或实体并未按第2(h)(1)条的规定对该互换进行集中结算;或

(2)该个人或实体不掌握与如下互换相关的数据,即互换数据存管机构按照商品期货交易委员会根据第21条制定的规则(包括期限方面的规则)受理的互换。

(c)**要求**。——第(b)子条所述个人或实体——

(1)经商品期货交易委员会提出书面要求,应按照商品期货交易委员会要求的格式和方式,对其持有的互换向商品期货交易委员会提交报告;且

(2)应对其持有的互换保存账簿和记录,保存格式、方式和期限应符合商品期货交易委员会的相关要求,并可供以下机构检查——

(A)商品期货交易委员会的任何代表;

(B)相应的审慎监管者;

(C)证券交易委员会;

(D)金融稳定监督委员会;及

(E)司法部。

(d)**相同的数据**。——依据本条制定规则时,商品期货交易委员会应要求第(b)子条所述的个人和实体向商品期货交易委员会提交全面的数据报告,且其所含数据的全面程度应不亚于第21条要求互换数据存管机构收集的数据。”

第730条　互换大户报告

在第731条增加的《商品交易法》(《美国法典》第七编第1节及其后条文)第4s条之后插入如下内容,作为对该法的修正:

“第4t条　互换大户报告

(a)**禁止性规定**。——

(1)**一般规定**。——除第(2)款规定的情形外,如果商品期货交易委员会判定某一品种互换对注册实体具有重要价格发现功能,则在下列情形下,任何人不得达成该

price discovery function with respect to registered entities if—

"(A) the person directly or indirectly enters into the swap during any 1 day in an amount equal to or in excess of such amount as shall be established periodically by the Commission; and

"(B) the person directly or indirectly has or obtains a position in the swap equal to or in excess of such amount as shall be established periodically by the Commission.

"(2) EXCEPTION.— Paragraph (1) shall not apply if—

"(A) the person files or causes to be filed with the properly designated officer of the Commission such reports regarding any transactions or positions described in subparagraphs (A) and (B) of paragraph (1) as the Commission may require by rule or regulation; and

"(B) in accordance with the rules and regulations of the Commission, the person keeps books and records of all such swaps and any transactions and positions in any related commodity traded on or subject to the rules of any designated contract market or swap execution facility, and of cash or spot transactions in, inventories of, and purchase and sale commitments of, such a commodity.

"(b) REQUIREMENTS.—

"(1) IN GENERAL.— Books and records described in subsection (a)(2)(B) shall—

"(A) show such complete details concerning all transactions and positions as the Commission may prescribe by rule or regulation;

"(B) be open at all times to inspection and examination by any representative of the Commission; and

"(C) be open at all times to inspection and examination by the Securities and Exchange Commission, to the extent such books and records relate to transactions in swaps (as that term is defined in section 1a(47)(A)(v)), and consistent with the confidentiality and disclosure requirements of section 8.

"(2) JURISDICTION. — Nothing in paragraph (1) shall affect the exclusive jurisdiction of the Commission to prescribe recordkeeping and reporting requirements for large swap traders under this section.

"(c) APPLICABILITY.— For purposes of this section, the swaps, futures, and cash or spot transactions and positions of any person shall include the swaps, futures, and cash or spot transactions and positions of any persons directly or indirectly controlled by the person.

"(d) SIGNIFICANT PRICE DISCOVERY FUNCTION.— In making a determination as to whether a swap performs or affects a significant price discovery function with respect to registered entities, the Commission shall consider the factors described in section 4a(a)(3).".

等互换,否则当属违法——

(A)任何一天内该人直接或间接达成的该品种互换金额达到或超过商品期货交易委员会定期设定的数额;及

(B)该人直接或间接持有或获得的该品种互换持仓达到或超过商品期货交易委员会定期设定的数额。

(2)**例外规定**。——在下列情形下,不适用第(1)款的规定——

(A)针对第(1)款第(A)子款和第(B)子款所述的任何交易或持仓,该人向商品期货交易委员会恰当地指定的官员提交商品期货交易委员会发布的规则或规章所要求的报告或促使他人向该等官员提交该报告;及

(B)该人按商品期货交易委员会的规则与规章,就所有该等互换以及在任何指定合约市场或互换执行设施或按其规则交易的任何相关商品的任何交易和持仓保存账簿和记录,并且应就任何该商品现货或即期交易、库存、买入和卖出承诺保存账簿和记录。

(b)**要求**。——

(1)**一般规定**。——第(a)(2)(B)子条所述账簿和记录——

(A)应载明商品期货交易委员会发布的规则或规章所规定的关于所有交易和持仓的完备详情;

(B)应随时可供商品期货交易委员会任何代表检查和核查;且

(C)账簿和记录涉及互换交易[定义见第1a(47)(A)(v)条]的,应在符合第8条的保密和信息披露要求的情形下,随时可供证券交易委员会检查和核查。

(2)**管辖权**。——对于互换大户,商品期货交易委员会依据本条享有制定记录保存和报告要求的排他管辖权,而第(1)款的任何内容均不影响商品期货交易委员会的该排他管辖权。

(c)**适用范围**。——就本条而言,任何人的互换、期货以及现货或即期交易和持仓均应包括由该人直接或间接控制的任何其他人的互换、期货以及现货或即期交易和持仓。

(d)**重要价格发现功能**。——判定某互换品种是否对注册实体具有重要价格发现功能或影响该等功能时,商品期货交易委员会应考虑第4a(a)(3)条规定的因素。”

SEC.731. REGISTRATION AND REGULATION OF SWAP DEALERS AND MAJOR SWAP PARTICIPANTS.

The Commodity Exchange Act (7 U.S.C. 1 et seq.) is amended by inserting after section 4r (as added by section 729) the following:

"SEC.4s. REGISTRATION AND REGULATION OF SWAP DEALERS AND MAJOR SWAP PARTICIPANTS.

"(a) REGISTRATION. —

"(1) SWAP DEALERS. — It shall be unlawful for any person to act as a swap dealer unless the person is registered as a swap dealer with the Commission.

"(2) MAJOR SWAP PARTICIPANTS. — It shall be unlawful for any person to act as a major swap participant unless the person is registered as a major swap participant with the Commission.

"(b) REQUIREMENTS. —

"(1) IN GENERAL. — A person shall register as a swap dealer or major swap participant by filing a registration application with the Commission.

"(2) CONTENTS. —

"(A) IN GENERAL. — The application shall be made in such form and manner as prescribed by the Commission, and shall contain such information, as the Commission considers necessary concerning the business in which the applicant is or will be engaged.

"(B) CONTINUAL REPORTING. — A person that is registered as a swap dealer or major swap participant shall continue to submit to the Commission reports that contain such information pertaining to the business of the person as the Commission may require.

"(3) EXPIRATION. — Each registration under this section shall expire at such time as the Commission may prescribe by rule or regulation.

"(4) RULES. — Except as provided in subsections (d) and (e), the Commission may prescribe rules applicable to swap dealers and major swap participants, including rules that limit the activities of swap dealers and major swap participants.

"(5) TRANSITION. — Rules under this section shall provide for the registration of swap dealers and major swap participants not later than 1 year after the date of enactment of the Wall Street Transparency and Accountability Act of 2010.

"(6) STATUTORY DISQUALIFICATION. — Except to the extent otherwise specifically provided by rule, regulation, or order, it shall be unlawful for a swap dealer or a major swap participant to permit any person associated with a swap dealer or a major swap participant who is subject to a statutory disqualification to effect or be involved in effecting swaps on behalf of the swap dealer or major swap participant, if the swap dealer or major swap participant knew, or in the exercise of reasonable care should have known, of the statutory disqualification.

第731条　互换交易商和主要互换参与者的注册和监管

在第729条增加的《商品交易法》(《美国法典》第七编第1节及其后条文)第4r条之后插入如下内容,作为对该法的修正:

"第4s条　互换交易商和主要互换参与者的注册和监管

(a)**注册**。——

(1)**互换交易商**。——任何人除非已在商品期货交易委员会注册为互换交易商,否则该人以互换交易商的身份行事当属违法。

(2)**主要互换参与者**。——任何人除非已在商品期货交易委员会注册为主要互换参与者,否则该人以主要互换参与者的身份行事当属违法。

(b)**要求**。——

(1)**一般规定**。——任何人如欲注册为互换交易商或主要互换参与者,应向商品期货交易委员会提交注册申请。

(2)**内容**。——

(A)**一般规定**。——注册申请应当按照商品期货交易委员会规定的格式和方式提交,并应包含商品期货交易委员会认为对于申请人目前从事或将要从事的业务确属必要的信息。

(B)**持续报告**。——注册为互换交易商或主要互换参与者的任何人应持续地向商品期货交易委员会提交商品期货交易委员会要求的与该人业务有关的信息报告。

(3)**注册到期**。——依据本条完成的注册于商品期货交易委员会发布的规则或规章所规定的时间到期。

(4)**规则**。——除第(d)子条和第(e)子条规定的情形外,商品期货交易委员会可以制定适用于互换交易商和主要互换参与者的规则,包括限制互换交易商和主要互换参与者活动的规则。

(5)**过渡**。——根据本条制定的规则应规定互换交易商和主要互换参与者在《2010年华尔街透明度与问责法》颁布之日后1年内注册。

(6)**法定失格**。——除非有相关规则、规章或命令另做具体规定,否则,如果互换交易商或主要互换参与者明知或尽合理注意后应知其任何业务相关人处于法定失格状态,则该互换交易商或主要互换参与者不得允许任何该等业务相关人代表其实施互换交易或参与互换交易的实施工作,否则当属违法。

"(c) DUAL REGISTRATION.—

"(1) SWAP DEALER.—Any person that is required to be registered as a swap dealer under this section shall register with the Commission regardless of whether the person also is a depository institution or is registered with the Securities and Exchange Commission as a security-based swap dealer.

"(2) MAJOR SWAP PARTICIPANT.—Any person that is required to be registered as a major swap participant under this section shall register with the Commission regardless of whether the person also is a depository institution or is registered with the Securities and Exchange Commission as a major security-based swap participant.

"(d) RULEMAKINGS.—

"(1) IN GENERAL.—The Commission shall adopt rules for persons that are registered as swap dealers or major swap participants under this section.

"(2) EXCEPTION FOR PRUDENTIAL REQUIREMENTS.—

"(A) IN GENERAL.—The Commission may not prescribe rules imposing prudential requirements on swap dealers or major swap participants for which there is a prudential regulator.

"(B) APPLICABILITY.—Subparagraph (A) does not limit the authority of the Commission to prescribe rules as directed under this section.

"(e) CAPITAL AND MARGIN REQUIREMENTS.—

"(1) IN GENERAL.—

"(A) SWAP DEALERS AND MAJOR SWAP PARTICIPANTS THAT ARE BANKS.—Each registered swap dealer and major swap participant for which there is a prudential regulator shall meet such minimum capital requirements and minimum initial and variation margin requirements as the prudential regulator shall by rule or regulation prescribe under paragraph (2)(A).

"(B) SWAP DEALERS AND MAJOR SWAP PARTICIPANTS THAT ARE NOT BANKS.—Each registered swap dealer and major swap participant for which there is not a prudential regulator shall meet such minimum capital requirements and minimum initial and variation margin requirements as the Commission shall by rule or regulation prescribe under paragraph (2)(B).

"(2) RULES.—

"(A) SWAP DEALERS AND MAJOR SWAP PARTICIPANTS THAT ARE BANKS.—The prudential regulators, in consultation with the Commission and the Securities and Exchange Commission, shall jointly adopt rules for swap dealers and major swap participants, with respect to their activities as a swap dealer or major swap participant, for which there is a prudential regulator imposing—

"(i) capital requirements; and

(c)**双重注册**。——

(1)**互换交易商**。——根据本条规定应注册为互换交易商的任何主体,无论其是否同时也是存款机构或已在证券交易委员会注册为证券类互换交易商,均应在商品期货交易委员会办理注册。

(2)**主要互换参与者**。——根据本条规定应注册为主要互换参与者的任何人,无论其是否同时也是存款机构或已在证券交易委员会注册为主要的证券类互换参与者,均应在商品期货交易委员会办理注册。

(d)**规则制定**。——

(1)**一般规定**。——商品期货交易委员会应就依本条注册为互换交易商或主要互换参与者的人制定规则。

(2)**关于审慎要求的例外规定**。——

(A)**一般规定**。——商品期货交易委员会不得针对受审慎监管者监管的互换交易商或主要互换参与者制定施加审慎要求的规则。

(B)**适用范围**。——第(A)子款并不限制商品期货交易委员会制定本条要求的规则的权力。

(e)**资本和保证金要求**。——

(1)**一般规定**。——

(A)**互换交易商和主要互换参与者为银行的情形**。——受审慎监管者监管的每一注册互换交易商和主要互换参与者均应达到该审慎监管者依据第(2)(A)款发布的规则或规章所规定的最低资本要求、最低初始保证金要求和追加保证金要求。

(B)**互换交易商和主要互换参与者并非银行的情形**。——不受审慎监管者监管的每一注册互换交易商和主要互换参与者均应达到商品期货交易委员会依据第(2)(B)款发布的规则或规章所规定的最低资本要求、最低初始保证金要求和追加保证金要求。

(2)**规则**。——

(A)**互换交易商和主要互换参与者为银行的情形**。——审慎监管者应与商品期货交易委员会和证券交易委员会进行磋商,针对受审慎监管者监管的互换交易商和主要互换参与者以互换交易商或主要互换参与者身份开展的活动,联合制定施加如下要求的规则——

(i)资本要求;及

"(ii) both initial and variation margin requirements on all swaps that are not cleared by a registered derivatives clearing organization.

"(B) SWAP DEALERS AND MAJOR SWAP PARTICIPANTS THAT ARE NOT BANKS. — The Commission shall adopt rules for swap dealers and major swap participants, with respect to their activities as a swap dealer or major swap participant, for which there is not a prudential regulator imposing —

"(i) capital requirements; and

"(ii) both initial and variation margin requirements on all swaps that are not cleared by a registered derivatives clearing organization.

"(C) CAPITAL. — In setting capital requirements for a person that is designated as a swap dealer or a major swap participant for a single type or single class or category of swap or activities, the prudential regulator and the Commission shall take into account the risks associated with other types of swaps or classes of swaps or categories of swaps engaged in and the other activities conducted by that person that are not otherwise subject to regulation applicable to that person by virtue of the status of the person as a swap dealer or a major swap participant.

"(3) STANDARDS FOR CAPITAL AND MARGIN. —

"(A) IN GENERAL. — To offset the greater risk to the swap dealer or major swap participant and the financial system arising from the use of swaps that are not cleared, the requirements imposed under paragraph (2) shall —

"(i) help ensure the safety and soundness of the swap dealer or major swap participant; and

"(ii) be appropriate for the risk associated with the non-cleared swaps held as a swap dealer or major swap participant.

"(B) RULE OF CONSTRUCTION. —

"(i) IN GENERAL. — Nothing in this section shall limit, or be construed to limit, the authority —

"(I) of the Commission to set financial responsibility rules for a futures commission merchant or introducing broker registered pursuant to section 4f(a) (except for section 4f(a)(3)) in accordance with section 4f(b); or

"(II) of the Securities and Exchange Commission to set financial responsibility rules for a broker or dealer registered pursuant to section 15(b) of the Securities Exchange Act of 1934 (15 U.S.C. 78o(b)) (except for section 15(b)(11) of that Act (15 U.S.C. 78o(b)(11)) in accordance with section 15(c)(3) of the Securities Exchange Act of 1934 (15 U.S.C. 78o(c)(3)).

"(ii) FUTURES COMMISSION MERCHANTS AND OTHER DEALERS. — A futures commission merchant, introducing broker, broker, or dealer shall maintain sufficient capital to

(ii)不在注册衍生品结算组织进行集中结算的所有互换施加初始保证金要求和追加保证金要求。

(B)**互换交易商和主要互换参与者并非银行的情形**——商品期货交易委员会应针对不受任何审慎监管者监管的互换交易商和主要互换参与者以互换交易商或主要互换参与者身份开展的活动,制定施加如下要求的规则——

(i)资本要求;及

(ii)不在注册衍生品结算组织进行集中结算的所有互换的初始保证金要求和追加保证金要求。

(C)**资本**。——如果某人因某单一类型或者某单一类别或某单一种类的互换或活动被指定为互换交易商或主要互换参与者,审慎监管者和商品期货交易委员会在对其设定资本要求时,应考虑其从事的其他类型或者其他类别或其他种类的互换和开展的其他活动(该等互换或活动并不受该人以互换交易商或主要互换参与者身份所受到的监管约束)所产生的风险。

(3)**资本和保证金标准**。——

(A)**一般规定**。——为了吸收由于使用非集中结算的互换给互换交易商或主要互换参与者及金融体系带来的额外风险,依据第(2)款施加的要求应——

(i)有助于确保互换交易商或主要互换参与者的安全性和稳健性;且

(ii)对于以互换交易商或主要互换参与者身份持有的非集中结算的互换产生的风险而言,确属适当。

(B)**解释规则**。——

(i)**一般规定**。——本条任何内容均不限制以下权力,亦不得被解释为限制以下权力——

(I)商品期货交易委员会根据第4f(b)条针对依第4f(a)条[但第4f(a)(3)条除外]注册的期货经纪商或介绍经纪商制定财务责任规则的权力;或

(II)证券交易委员会根据《1934年证券交易法》第15(c)(3)条[《美国法典》第十五编第78o(c)(3)节]针对依《1934年证券交易法》第15(b)条[《美国法典》第十五编第78o(b)节]{该法第15(b)(11)条[但《美国法典》第十五编第78o(b)(11)节]除外}注册的经纪商或自营商制定财务责任规则的权力。

(ii)**期货经纪商和其他交易商**。——期货经纪商、介绍经纪商、经纪商或自营商应根据本法或《1934年证券交易法》(《美国法典》第十五编第78a节及其后条文)要求其

comply with the stricter of any applicable capital requirements to which such futures commission merchant, introducing broker, broker, or dealer is subject to under this Act or the Securities Exchange Act of 1934 (15 U.S.C. 78a et seq.).

"(C) MARGIN REQUIREMENTS. — In prescribing margin requirements under this subsection, the prudential regulator with respect to swap dealers and major swap participants for which it is the prudential regulator and the Commission with respect to swap dealers and major swap participants for which there is no prudential regulator shall permit the use of noncash collateral, as the regulator or the Commission determines to be consistent with —

"(i) preserving the financial integrity of markets trading swaps; and

"(ii) preserving the stability of the United States financial system.

"(D) COMPARABILITY OF CAPITAL AND MARGIN REQUIREMENTS. —

"(i) IN GENERAL. — The prudential regulators, the Commission, and the Securities and Exchange Commission shall periodically (but not less frequently than annually) consult on minimum capital requirements and minimum initial and variation margin requirements.

"(ii) COMPARABILITY. — The entities described in clause (i) shall, to the maximum extent practicable, establish and maintain comparable minimum capital requirements and minimum initial and variation margin requirements, including the use of non cash collateral, for —

"(I) swap dealers; and

"(II) major swap participants.

"(f) REPORTING AND RECORDKEEPING. —

"(1) IN GENERAL. — Each registered swap dealer and major swap participant —

"(A) shall make such reports as are required by the Commission by rule or regulation regarding the transactions and positions and financial condition of the registered swap dealer or major swap participant;

"(B)(i) for which there is a prudential regulator, shall keep books and records of all activities related to the business as a swap dealer or major swap participant in such form and manner and for such period as may be prescribed by the Commission by rule or regulation; and

"(ii) for which there is no prudential regulator, shall keep books and records in such form and manner and for such period as may be prescribed by the Commission by rule or regulation;

"(C) shall keep books and records described in subparagraph (B) open to inspection and examination by any representative of the Commission; and

"(D) shall keep any such books and records relating to swaps defined in section 1a(47)(A)(v) open to inspection and examination by the Securities and Exchange Commission.

"(2) RULES. — The Commission shall adopt rules governing reporting and

遵守的任何资本要求中最严格的一项维持充足的资本。

(C)**保证金要求**。——依据本子条对保证金要求水平作出规定时,审慎监管者应允许受其审慎监管的互换交易商和主要互换参与者使用非现金担保品,商品期货交易委员会则应允许不受审慎监管者监管的互换交易商和主要互换参与者使用非现金担保品,前提是该监管者或商品期货交易委员会判定非现金担保品有利于——

(i)维护互换交易市场的财务完整性;及

(ii)维护美国金融体系的稳定性。

(D)**具有可比性的资本和保证金要求**。——

(i)**一般规定**。——审慎监管者、商品期货交易委员会和证券交易委员会应定期(频率不得低于每年一次)就最低资本要求和最低初始保证金及追加保证金要求进行磋商。

(ii)**可比性**。——第(i)项所述实体对以下各者分别设定最低资本要求、最低初始保证金及追加保证金要求时(包括就非现金担保品的使用设定要求时),应尽最大可能维持其水平具有可比性——

(I)互换交易商;及

(II)主要互换参与者。

(f)**报告和记录保存**。——

(1)**一般规定**。——每一注册互换交易商和主要互换参与者——

(A)均应按照商品期货交易委员会发布的规则或规章的要求,制作关于其交易及持仓和财务状况的报告;

(B)(i)如受审慎监管者监管,则均应按照商品期货交易委员会在其发布的规则或规章中所规定的格式、方式和期限,就其以互换交易商或主要互换参与者身份从事的所有业务活动保存相关账簿和记录;且

(ii)如不受审慎监管者监管,则均应按照商品期货交易委员会在其发布的规则或规章中所规定的格式、方式和期限保存账簿和记录;并

(C)均应将按照第(B)子款保存的账簿和记录提供给商品期货交易委员会任何代表检查和核查;且

(D)均应将就第1a(47)(A)(v)条所定义的互换保存的任何账簿和记录提供给证券交易委员会检查和核查。

(2)**规则**。——商品期货交易委员会应针对互换交易商和主要互换参与者制定

recordkeeping for swap dealers and major swap participants.

"(g) DAILY TRADING RECORDS. —

"(1) IN GENERAL. — Each registered swap dealer and major swap participant shall maintain daily trading records of the swaps of the registered swap dealer and major swap participant and all related records (including related cash or forward transactions) and recorded communications, including electronic mail, instant messages, and recordings of telephone calls, for such period as may be required by the Commission by rule or regulation.

"(2) INFORMATION REQUIREMENTS. — The daily trading records shall include such information as the Commission shall require by rule or regulation.

"(3) COUNTERPARTY RECORDS. — Each registered swap dealer and major swap participant shall maintain daily trading records for each counterparty in a manner and form that is identifiable with each swap transaction.

"(4) AUDIT TRAIL. — Each registered swap dealer and major swap participant shall maintain a complete audit trail for conducting comprehensive and accurate trade reconstructions.

"(5) RULES. — The Commission shall adopt rules governing daily trading records for swap dealers and major swap participants.

"(h) BUSINESS CONDUCT STANDARDS. —

"(1) IN GENERAL. — Each registered swap dealer and major swap participant shall conform with such business conduct standards as prescribed in paragraph (3) and as may be prescribed by the Commission by rule or regulation that relate to —

"(A) fraud, manipulation, and other abusive practices involving swaps (including swaps that are offered but not entered into);

"(B) diligent supervision of the business of the registered swap dealer and major swap participant;

"(C) adherence to all applicable position limits; and

"(D) such other matters as the Commission determines to be appropriate.

"(2) RESPONSIBILITIES WITH RESPECT TO SPECIAL ENTITIES. —

"(A) ADVISING SPECIAL ENTITIES. — A swap dealer or major swap participant that acts as an advisor to a special entity regarding a swap shall comply with the requirements of subparagraph (4) with respect to such Special Entity.

"(B) ENTERING OF SWAPS WITH RESPECT TO SPECIAL ENTITIES. — A swap dealer that enters into or offers to enter into swap with a Special Entity shall comply with the requirements of subparagraph (5) with respect to such Special Entity.

"(C) SPECIAL ENTITY DEFINED. — For purposes of this subsection, the term 'special entity' means —

"(i) a Federal agency;

报告规则和记录保存规则。

(g)**每日交易记录**。——

(1)**一般规定**。——每一注册互换交易商和主要互换参与者均应按照商品期货交易委员会发布的规则或规章所规定的期限，就其互换保存每日交易记录以及所有相关的记录(包括相关的现货交易或远期交易)和通信记录(包括电子邮件、即时信息、电话录音等)。

(2)**信息要求**。——每日交易记录应包含商品期货交易委员会发布的规则或规章所规定的信息。

(3)**对手方记录**。——每一注册互换交易商和主要互换参与者均应为每一对手方保存每日交易记录，方式和格式应能够使人识别与每笔互换交易相对应的交易记录。

(4)**审计留痕**。——每一注册互换交易商和主要互换参与者均应保持完整的审计留痕记录,以便进行全面而准确的交易回溯。

(5)**规则**。——商品期货交易委员会应制定规范互换交易商和主要互换参与者的每日交易记录的规则。

(h)**业务行为准则**。——

(1)**一般规定**。——每一注册互换交易商和主要互换参与者均应遵守第(3)款规定的业务行为准则,并应遵守商品期货交易委员会发布的规则或规章对以下行为所规定的业务行为准则——

(A)涉及互换(包括已要约但未达成的互换)的欺诈、操纵和其他滥用行为;

(B)对该注册互换交易商和主要互换参与者业务的尽职监管;

(C)对所有适用的持仓限额规定的遵守;及

(D)商品期货交易委员会判定确属适当的任何其他事项。

(2)**与特殊实体相关的责任**。——

(A)**充当特殊实体的顾问**。——互换交易商或主要互换参与者如果就某一互换品种充当特殊实体的顾问,则应遵守第(4)子款就该等特殊实体规定的相关要求。

(B)**与特殊实体达成互换**。——与特殊实体达成或要约达成互换的互换交易商应遵守第(5)子款规定的关于该等特殊实体的要求。

(C)**特殊实体的定义**。——就本子条而言,‘特殊实体’一词系指——

(i)联邦机关;

"(ii) a State, State agency, city, county, municipality, or other political subdivision of a State;

"(iii) any employee benefit plan, as defined in section 3 of the Employee Retirement Income Security Act of 1974 (29 U.S.C. 1002);

"(iv) any governmental plan, as defined in section 3 of the Employee Retirement Income Security Act of 1974 (29 U.S.C. 1002); or

"(v) any endowment, including an endowment that is an organization described in section 501(c)(3) of the Internal Revenue Code of 1986.

"(3) BUSINESS CONDUCT REQUIREMENTS. — Business conduct requirements adopted by the Commission shall —

"(A) establish a duty for a swap dealer or major swap participant to verify that any counterparty meets the eligibility standards for an eligible contract participant;

"(B) require disclosure by the swap dealer or major swap participant to any counterparty to the transaction (other than a swap dealer, major swap participant, security–based swap dealer, or major security–based swap participant) of —

"(i) information about the material risks and characteristics of the swap;

"(ii) any material incentives or conflicts of interest that the swap dealer or major swap participant may have in connection with the swap; and

"(iii)(I) for cleared swaps, upon the request of the counterparty, receipt of the daily mark of the transaction from the appropriate derivatives clearing organization; and

"(II) for uncleared swaps, receipt of the daily mark of the transaction from the swap dealer or the major swap participant;

"(C) establish a duty for a swap dealer or major swap participant to communicate in a fair and balanced manner based on principles of fair dealing and good faith; and

"(D) establish such other standards and requirements as the Commission may determine are appropriate in the public interest, for the protection of investors, or otherwise in furtherance of the purposes of this Act.

"(4) SPECIAL REQUIREMENTS FOR SWAP DEALERS ACTING AS ADVISORS. —

"(A) IN GENERAL. — It shall be unlawful for a swap dealer or major swap participant —

"(i) to employ any device, scheme, or artifice to defraud any Special Entity or prospective customer who is a Special Entity;

"(ii) to engage in any transaction, practice, or course of business that operates as a fraud or deceit on any Special Entity or prospective customer who is a Special Entity; or

"(iii) to engage in any act, practice, or course of business that is fraudulent, deceptive or manipulative.

"(B) DUTY. — Any swap dealer that acts as an advisor to a Special Entity shall have a

(ii)州、州机关、州级市、郡、郡级市或州下属的其他行政区域;

(iii)任何员工福利计划[定义见《1974年员工退休收入保障法》第3条(《美国法典》第二十九编第1002节)];

(iv)任何政府计划[定义见《1974年员工退休收入保障法》第3条(《美国法典》第二十九编第1002节)];或

(v)任何捐赠基金,包括性质属于《1986年国内税收法典》第501(c)(3)条所述组织的捐赠基金。

(3)**业务行为要求**。——商品期货交易委员会制定的业务行为要求应——

(A)规定互换交易商或主要互换参与者有义务就每一对手方核实其是否符合适格合约参与者的适格性标准;

(B)要求该等互换交易商或主要互换参与者向任何交易对手方(指并非互换交易商、主要互换参与者、证券类互换交易商或主要的证券类互换参与者的对手方)披露以下信息——

(i)关于该等互换的重大风险和特征的信息;

(ii)互换交易商或主要互换参与者可能有的与该等互换相关的任何重大激励因素或利益冲突;及

(iii)(I)对集中结算的互换而言,经对手方提出请求,应披露从相应的衍生品结算组织处收到的交易逐日盯市信息;及

(II)对非集中结算的互换而言,应披露从互换交易商或主要互换参与者处收到的交易逐日盯市信息。

(C)规定互换交易商或主要互换参与者有责任基于公平交易原则和善意原则开展公平、公正的沟通;并

(D)设定商品期货交易委员会判定确属适当的其他标准和要求,以维护公共利益、保护投资者或促进本法其他宗旨的实现。

(4)**充当顾问的互换交易商应遵守的特殊要求**。——

(A)**一般规定**。——互换交易商或主要互换参与者不得从事以下活动,否则当属违法——

(i)使用任何手段、计谋或诡计欺诈任何特殊实体或具有特殊实体身份的潜在客户;

(ii)从事对任何特殊实体或具有特殊实体身份的潜在客户构成欺诈或欺骗的交易、做法或业务运作;或

(iii)从事具有欺诈性、欺骗性或操纵性的任何行为、做法或业务运作。

(B)**职责**。——充当特殊实体顾问的任何互换交易商有责任以符合特殊实体最

duty to act in the best interests of the Special Entity.

"(C) REASONABLE EFFORTS. — Any swap dealer that acts as an advisor to a Special Entity shall make reasonable efforts to obtain such information as is necessary to make a reasonable determination that any swap recommended by the swap dealer is in the best interests of the Special Entity, including information relating to —

"(i) the financial status of the Special Entity;

"(ii) the tax status of the Special Entity;

"(iii) the investment or financing objectives of the Special Entity; and

"(iv) any other information that the Commission may prescribe by rule or regulation.

"(5) SPECIAL REQUIREMENTS FOR SWAP DEALERS AS COUNTERPARTIES TO SPECIAL ENTITIES. —

"(A) Any swap dealer or major swap participant that offers to enter or enters into a swap with a Special Entity shall —

"(i) comply with any duty established by the Commission for a swap dealer or major swap participant, with respect to a counterparty that is an eligible contract participant within the meaning of subclause (I) or (II) of clause (vii) of section 1a(18) of this Act, that requires the swap dealer or major swap participant to have a reasonable basis to believe that the counterparty that is a Special Entity has an independent representative that —

"(I) has sufficient knowledge to evaluate the transaction and risks;

"(II) is not subject to a statutory disqualification;

"(III) is independent of the swap dealer or major swap participant;

"(IV) undertakes a duty to act in the best interests of the counterparty it represents;

"(V) makes appropriate disclosures;

"(VI) will provide written representations to the Special Entity regarding fair pricing and the appropriateness of the transaction; and

"(VII) in the case of employee benefit plans subject to the Employee Retirement Income Security act of 1974, is a fiduciary as defined in section 3 of that Act (29 U.S.C. 1002); and

"(ii) before the initiation of the transaction, disclose to the Special Entity in writing the capacity in which the swap dealer is acting; and

"(B) the Commission may establish such other standards and requirements as the Commission may determine are appropriate in the public interest, for the protection of investors, or otherwise in furtherance of the purposes of this Act.

"(6) RULES. — The Commission shall prescribe rules under this subsection governing business conduct standards for swap dealers and major swap participants.

"(7) APPLICABILITY. — This section shall not apply with respect to a transaction that is —

佳利益的方式行事。

(C)**合理努力**。——充当特殊实体顾问的任何互换交易商应尽合理努力获取必要信息,以合理判定其推荐的任何互换是否符合特殊实体的最佳利益,该等必要信息包括——

(i)特殊实体的财务状况信息;

(ii)特殊实体的税务状况信息;

(iii)特殊实体的投融资目标信息;及

(iv)商品期货交易委员会发布的规则或规章所规定的任何其他信息。

(5)**充当特殊实体对手方的互换交易商所应遵守的特殊要求**。——

(A)任何互换交易商或主要互换参与者如要约与特殊实体达成互换或与特殊实体达成互换,均应——

(i)遵守商品期货交易委员会设定的作为适格合约参与者对手方的互换交易商或主要互换参与者的职责[适格合约参与者的定义见本法第1a(18)条第(vii)项第(I)子项或第(II)子项],该等职责指,在交易对手方具有特殊实体身份的情况下,互换交易商或主要互换参与者应有合理的依据确信该对手方有一名符合下述条件的独立代表——

(I)拥有评估交易和风险的充分知识;

(II)不存在法定失格情形;

(III)独立于互换交易商或主要互换参与者;

(IV)负有为其所代表的对手方最佳利益行事的职责;

(V)进行适当披露;

(VI)将就交易的公平定价和交易的适当性向特殊实体提供书面声明;且

(VII)就受制于《1974年员工退休收入保障法》规定的员工福利计划而言,身为该法第3条(《美国法典》第二十九编第1002节)所定义的受信义务人;且

(ii)在发起交易之前,向特殊实体书面披露互换交易商行事的身份;及

(B)为了维护公共利益、保护投资者或促进本法其他宗旨的实现,商品期货交易委员会可以设定其判定确属适当的其他标准和要求。

(6)**规则**。——商品期货交易委员会应根据本子条制定规则,规范互换交易商和主要互换参与者的业务行为准则。

(7)**适用范围**。——本条不适用于如下交易——

"(A) initiated by a Special Entity on an exchange or swap execution facility; and

"(B) one in which the swap dealer or major swap participant does not know the identity of the counterparty to the transaction.

"(i) DOCUMENTATION STANDARDS. —

"(1) IN GENERAL. — Each registered swap dealer and major swap participant shall conform with such standards as may be prescribed by the Commission by rule or regulation that relate to timely and accurate confirmation, processing, netting, documentation, and valuation of all swaps.

"(2) RULES. — The Commission shall adopt rules governing documentation standards for swap dealers and major swap participants.

"(j) DUTIES. — Each registered swap dealer and major swap participant at all times shall comply with the following requirements:

"(1) MONITORING OF TRADING. — The swap dealer or major swap participant shall monitor its trading in swaps to prevent violations of applicable position limits.

"(2) RISK MANAGEMENT PROCEDURES. — The swap dealer or major swap participant shall establish robust and professional risk management systems adequate for managing the day-to-day business of the swap dealer or major swap participant.

"(3) DISCLOSURE OF GENERAL INFORMATION. — The swap dealer or major swap participant shall disclose to the Commission and to the prudential regulator for the swap dealer or major swap participant, as applicable, information concerning —

"(A) terms and conditions of its swaps;

"(B) swap trading operations, mechanisms, and practices;

"(C) financial integrity protections relating to swaps; and

"(D) other information relevant to its trading in swaps.

"(4) ABILITY TO OBTAIN INFORMATION. — The swap dealer or major swap participant shall —

"(A) establish and enforce internal systems and procedures to obtain any necessary information to perform any of the functions described in this section; and

"(B) provide the information to the Commission and to the prudential regulator for the swap dealer or major swap participant, as applicable, on request.

"(5) CONFLICTS OF INTEREST. — The swap dealer and major swap participant shall implement conflict-of-interest systems and procedures that —

"(A) establish structural and institutional safeguards to ensure that the activities of any person within the firm relating to research or analysis of the price or market for any commodity or swap or acting in a role of providing clearing activities or making determinations as to accepting clearing customers are separated by appropriate informational partitions within the firm from the review, pressure, or oversight of persons whose involvement in pricing,

(A)由特殊实体在交易所或互换执行设施发起的交易;及

(B)互换交易商或主要互换参与者不知道交易对手方身份的交易。

(i)**文档记录标准**。——

(1)**一般规定**。——每一注册互换交易商和主要互换参与者均应遵照执行商品期货交易委员会发布的规则或规章所规定的关于对所有互换进行及时准确的确认、处理、净额结算、文档记录和估值的标准。

(2)**规则**。——商品期货交易委员会应制定规则,规范互换交易商和主要互换参与者的文档记录标准。

(j)**职责**。——每一注册互换交易商和主要互换参与者均应始终遵守如下要求:

(1)**交易监控**。——互换交易商或主要互换参与者应监控其互换交易,从而防范违反适用的持仓限额的行为。

(2)**风险管理程序**。——互换交易商或主要互换参与者应建立健全的、专业的风险管理制度,充分管理互换交易商或主要互换参与者的日常业务。

(3)**一般信息披露**。——互换交易商或主要互换参与者应向商品期货交易委员会和其审慎监管者(视具体情况而定)披露如下信息——

(A)其互换的条款和条件;

(B)互换交易的运作、机制和惯例;

(C)与互换相关的财务完整性保护措施;及

(D)与互换交易相关的其他信息。

(4)**获取信息的能力**。——互换交易商或主要互换参与者应——

(A)建立并执行内部制度和流程,以获取履行本条所述职能所需的任何必要信息;并

(B)按照商品期货交易委员会及其审慎监管者要求,向其提供互换交易商或主要互换参与者(视具体情况而定)的信息。

(5)**利益冲突**。——互换交易商和主要互换参与者应实施利益冲突处理制度和程序,该等制度和程序应——

(A)设立结构性和制度性保障,以确保通过该等机构内部适当的信息隔离墙,将下列两类活动分开,即该等机构内部与任何商品或互换之价格或市场研究或者分析相关的任何人的活动,或者负责提供结算活动或负责判断是否受理结算客户的人的活动,以及具有以下特征的人员开展的审查、施压或监督工作,即该等人员若参与定价、交易或结算活动,该等人员的判断或领导监管工作即可能产生偏差并违反准入开

trading, or clearing activities might potentially bias their judgment or supervision and contravene the core principles of open access and the business conduct standards described in this Act; and

"(B) address such other issues as the Commission determines to be appropriate.

"(6) ANTITRUST CONSIDERATIONS. — Unless necessary or appropriate to achieve the purposes of this Act, a swap dealer or major swap participant shall not —

"(A) adopt any process or take any action that results in any unreasonable restraint of trade; or

"(B) impose any material anticompetitive burden on trading or clearing.

"(7) RULES. — The Commission shall prescribe rules under this subsection governing duties of swap dealers and major swap participants.

"(k) DESIGNATION OF CHIEF COMPLIANCE OFFICER. —

"(1) IN GENERAL. — Each swap dealer and major swap participant shall designate an individual to serve as a chief compliance officer.

"(2) DUTIES. — The chief compliance officer shall —

"(A) report directly to the board or to the senior officer of the swap dealer or major swap participant;

"(B) review the compliance of the swap dealer or major swap participant with respect to the swap dealer and major swap participant requirements described in this section;

"(C) in consultation with the board of directors, a body performing a function similar to the board, or the senior officer of the organization, resolve any conflicts of interest that may arise;

"(D) be responsible for administering each policy and procedure that is required to be established pursuant to this section;

"(E) ensure compliance with this Act (including regulations) relating to swaps, including each rule prescribed by the Commission under this section;

"(F) establish procedures for the remediation of noncompliance issues identified by the chief compliance officer through any —

"(i) compliance office review;

"(ii) look-back;

"(iii) internal or external audit finding;

"(iv) self-reported error; or

"(v) validated complaint; and

"(G) establish and follow appropriate procedures for the handling, management response, remediation, retesting, and closing of noncompliance issues.

"(3) ANNUAL REPORTS. —

"(A) IN GENERAL. — In accordance with rules prescribed by the Commission, the chief

放性的核心原则及本编所述业务行为准则;及

(B)处理商品期货交易委员会判定确属适当的其他事项。

(6)**反垄断考量**。——除非对实现本法宗旨确属必要或适当,否则互换交易商或主要互换参与者不得——

(A)制定对交易造成任何不合理限制的任何程序或采取对交易造成任何不合理限制的任何行动;或

(B)对交易或结算施加任何阻碍竞争的实质性负担。

(7)**规则**。——商品期货交易委员会应根据本子条对互换交易商和主要互换参与者的职责制定规则。

(k)**首席合规官的指定**。——

(1)**一般规定**。——每一互换交易商和主要互换参与者均应指定一名个人担任首席合规官。

(2)**职责**。——首席合规官应——

(A)向互换交易商或主要互换参与者的董事会或高级管理人员直接汇报工作;

(B)审查互换交易商或主要互换参与者对本条针对互换交易商和主要互换参与者规定的要求的遵守情况;

(C)与其所属组织的董事会、履行与董事会类似职能的机构或高级管理人员磋商,解决任何可能发生的利益冲突问题;

(D)负责实施应当依据本条要求制定的每一项政策和程序;

(E)确保本法(包括规章)中与互换相关的规定(包括商品期货交易委员会依据本条制定的每项规则)均得到遵守;

(F)制定相关程序,据以对首席合规官通过以下任何方式识别的不合规问题采取补救措施——

(i)合规办公室的审查工作;

(ii)回顾工作;

(iii)内部或外部审计认定结论;

(iv)自报失误;或

(v)有效的投诉;及

(G)制定并遵守用以对不合规问题进行处理、管理回应、补救、重新测试和终结的适当程序。

(3)**年度报告**。——

(A)**一般规定**。——首席合规官应根据商品期货交易委员会制定的规则每年编

compliance officer shall annually prepare and sign a report that contains a description of—

"(i) the compliance of the swap dealer or major swap participant with respect to this Act (including regulations); and

"(ii) each policy and procedure of the swap dealer or major swap participant of the chief compliance officer (including the code of ethics and conflict of interest policies).

"(B) REQUIREMENTS. — A compliance report under subparagraph (A) shall —

"(i) accompany each appropriate financial report of the swap dealer or major swap participant that is required to be furnished to the Commission pursuant to this section; and

"(ii) include a certification that, under penalty of law, the compliance report is accurate and complete.".

SEC.732. CONFLICTS OF INTEREST.

Section 4d of the Commodity Exchange Act (7 U.S.C. 6d) is amended —

(1) by redesignating subsection (c) as subsection (e); and

(2) by inserting after subsection (b) the following:

"(c) CONFLICTS OF INTEREST. — The Commission shall require that futures commission merchants and introducing brokers imple ment conflict–of–interest systems and procedures that —

"(1) establish structural and institutional safeguards to ensure that the activities of any person within the firm relating to research or analysis of the price or market for any commodity are separated by appropriate informational partitions within the firm from the review, pressure, or oversight of persons whose involvement in trading or clearing activities might potentially bias the judgment or supervision of the persons; and

"(2) address such other issues as the Commission determines to be appropriate.

"(d) DESIGNATION OF CHIEF COMPLIANCE OFFICER. — Each futures commission merchant shall designate an individual to serve as its Chief Compliance Officer and perform such duties and responsibilities as shall be set forth in regulations to be adopted by the Commission or rules to be adopted by a futures association registered under section 17.".

SEC.733. SWAP EXECUTION FACILITIES.

The Commodity Exchange Act is amended by inserting after section 5g (7 U.S.C. 7b–2) the following:

"SEC.5h. SWAP EXECUTION FACILITIES.

"(a) REGISTRATION. —

"(1) IN GENERAL. — No person may operate a facility for the trading or processing of swaps unless the facility is registered as a swap execution facility or as a designated contract market under this section.

"(2) DUAL REGISTRATION. — Any person that is registered as a swap execution

制并签署一份报告,其中应包含以下内容——

(i)互换交易商或主要互换参与者对本法(包括规章)的合规情况;及

(ii)首席合规官所属的互换交易商或主要互换参与者的每项政策和程序(包括职业道德准则和利益冲突处理政策)。

(B)**要求**。——按照第(A)子款编制的合规报告应——

(i)与按本条规定应向商品期货交易委员会提交的互换交易商或主要互换参与者每份相应的财务报告一并提交;并

(ii)包含一份自查证明,证明该合规报告的准确性和完整性,并明确表示其知晓作伪证将招致法律惩罚。"

第732条　利益冲突

《商品交易法》第4d条(《美国法典》第七编第6d节)修正如下——

(1)第(c)子条重新编号为第(e)子条;及

(2)在第(b)子条之后插入如下内容:

"(c)**利益冲突**。——商品期货交易委员会应要求期货经纪商和介绍经纪商实施符合下列条件的利益冲突处理制度和程序——

(1)设立结构性和制度性保障措施,以确保通过该等机构内部适当的信息隔离墙,将下列两类活动分开,即该等机构内部与任何商品之价格或市场研究或分析相关的任何人的活动,以及具有以下特征的人员开展的审查、施压或监督工作,即该等人员若参与参与交易或结算活动,该等人员的判断或领导监督工作即可能产生偏差;及

(2)处理商品期货交易委员会判定确属适当的其他事项。

(d)**首席合规官的指定**。——每一期货经纪商均应指定一名个人担任首席合规官,履行商品期货交易委员会制定的规章或根据第17条注册的期货协会制定的规则所规定的义务和责任。"

第733条　互换执行设施

在《商品交易法》第5g条(《美国法典》第七编第7b-2节)之后插入如下内容,作为对该法的修正:

"第5h条　互换执行设施

(a)**注册**。——

(1)**一般规定**。——任何人不得出于交易或处理互换之目的运营未依据本条注册为互换执行设施或指定合约市场的设施,否则当属违法。

(2)**双重注册**。——根据本条规定注册为互换执行设施的任何主体,无论其是否

facility under this section shall register with the Commission regardless of whether the person also is registered with the Securities and Exchange Commission as a swap execution facility.

"(b) TRADING AND TRADE PROCESSING. —

"(1) IN GENERAL. — Except as specified in paragraph (2), a swap execution facility that is registered under subsection (a) may —

"(A) make available for trading any swap; and

"(B) facilitate trade processing of any swap.

"(2) AGRICULTURAL SWAPS. — A swap execution facility may not list for trading or confirm the execution of any swap in an agricultural commodity (as defined by the Commission) except pursuant to a rule or regulation of the Commission allowing the swap under such terms and conditions as the Commission shall prescribe.

"(c) IDENTIFICATION OF FACILITY USED TO TRADE SWAPS BY CONTRACT MARKETS. — A board of trade that operates a contract market shall, to the extent that the board of trade also operates a swap execution facility and uses the same electronic trade execution system for listing and executing trades of swaps on or through the contract market and the swap execution facility, identify whether the electronic trading of such swaps is taking place on or through the contract market or the swap execution facility.

"(d) RULE–WRITING. —

"(1)The Securities and Exchange Commission and Commodity Futures Trading Commission may promulgate rules defining the universe of swaps that can be executed on a swap execution facility. These rules shall take into account the price and nonprice requirements of the counterparties to a swap and the goal of this section as set forth in subsection (e).

"(2) For all swaps that are not required to be executed through a swap execution facility as defined in paragraph (1), such trades may be executed through any other available means of interstate commerce.

"(3)The Securities and Exchange Commission and Commodity Futures Trading Commission shall update these rules as necessary to account for technological and other innovation.

"(e)RULE OF CONSTRUCTION. — The goal of this section is to promote the trading of swaps on swap execution facilities and to promote pre–trade price transparency in the swaps market.

"(f)CORE PRINCIPLES FOR SWAP EXECUTION FACILITIES. —

"(1)COMPLIANCE WITH CORE PRINCIPLES. —

"(A)IN GENERAL. — To be registered, and maintain registration, as a swap execution facility, the swap execution facility shall comply with —

"(i)the core principles described in this subsection; and

同时也在证券交易委员会注册为互换执行设施,均应在商品期货交易委员会办理注册。

(b)**交易和交易处理**。——

(1)**一般规定**。——除第(2)款具体规定的情形外,依第(a)子条注册的互换执行设施可以——

(A)提供任何互换以供交易;并

(B)为任何互换的交易处理提供便利。

(2)**农产品互换**。——对于某一农产品(以商品期货交易委员会的定义为准)的任何互换,除非遵循商品期货交易委员会颁发的允许按商品期货交易委员会规定的条款和条件进行该等农产品互换的规则或规章,否则互换执行设施不得上市交易或确认执行任何该等农产品互换。

(c)**指明合约市场用于交易互换的设施**。——如果运营某合约市场的交易场所同时也运营互换执行设施,并使用同一套电子交易执行系统在该合约市场和该互换执行设施(或通过该市场和该设施)进行互换的上市和互换的交易执行,则该交易场所应指明该等互换的电子交易是在(或通过)该合约市场还是在(或通过)该互换执行设施进行的。

(d)**规则拟定**。——

(1)证券交易委员会和商品期货交易委员会可以颁发规则,界定可以在互换执行设施执行的互换的范围。该等规则应考虑互换各对手方的价格和非价格要求,并考虑第(e)子条阐述的本条目标。

(2)任何互换如果并未被要求必须通过第(1)款所定义的互换执行设施才能执行,则可通过任何其他可用的州际商业手段交易。

(3)证券交易委员会和商品期货交易委员会应对上述规则进行必要更新,以反映科技和其他方面的创新。

(e)**解释规则**。——本条旨在促进在互换执行设施上进行互换交易,并提高互换市场的交易前价格透明度。

(f)**互换执行设施的核心原则**。——

(1)**核心原则合规**。——

(A)**一般规定**。——要注册为互换执行设施并维持该注册,互换执行设施应遵守——

(i)本子条所述核心原则;及

"(ii) any requirement that the Commission may impose by rule or regulation pursuant to section 8a(5).

"(B) REASONABLE DISCRETION OF SWAP EXECUTION FACILITY. — Unless otherwise determined by the Commission by rule or regulation, a swap execution facility described in subparagraph (A) shall have reasonable discretion in establishing the manner in which the swap execution facility complies with the core principles described in this subsection.

"(2) COMPLIANCE WITH RULES. — A swap execution facility shall —

"(A) establish and enforce compliance with any rule of the swap execution facility, including —

"(i) the terms and conditions of the swaps traded or processed on or through the swap execution facility; and

"(ii) any limitation on access to the swap execution facility;

"(B) establish and enforce trading, trade processing, and participation rules that will deter abuses and have the capacity to detect, investigate, and enforce those rules, including means —

"(i) to provide market participants with impartial access to the market; and

"(ii) to capture information that may be used in establishing whether rule violations have occurred;

"(C) establish rules governing the operation of the facility, including rules specifying trading procedures to be used in entering and executing orders traded or posted on the facility, including block trades; and

"(D) provide by its rules that when a swap dealer or major swap participant enters into or facilitates a swap that is subject to the mandatory clearing requirement of section 2(h), the swap dealer or major swap participant shall be responsible for compliance with the mandatory trading requirement under section 2(h)(8).

"(3) SWAPS NOT READILY SUSCEPTIBLE TO MANIPULATION. — The swap execution facility shall permit trading only in swaps that are not readily susceptible to manipulation.

"(4) MONITORING OF TRADING AND TRADE PROCESSING. — The swap execution facility shall —

"(A) establish and enforce rules or terms and conditions defining, or specifications detailing —

"(i) trading procedures to be used in entering and executing orders traded on or through the facilities of the swap execution facility; and

"(ii) procedures for trade processing of swaps on or through the facilities of the swap execution facility; and

(ii)商品期货交易委员会依据第8a(5)条发布的规则或规章所施加的任何要求。

(B)**互换执行设施合理的自由裁量权**。——除非商品期货交易委员会发布的规则或规章作出不同判定,否则第(A)子款所述互换执行设施应依其合理的自由裁量权决定其遵守本子条所述核心原则的方式。

(2)**规则合规**。——互换执行设施应——

(A)制定并执行包括如下各项在内的该互换执行设施的任何规则——

(i)在该互换执行设施或通过该互换执行设施交易或处理的互换的条款及条件;及

(ii)该互换执行设施的任何接入限制;

(B)制定并执行对滥用行为具有威慑作用的交易规则、交易处理规则和参与规则,并有能力发现、调查和执行上述规则,包括拥有——

(i)向市场参与者提供公平的市场准入的手段;及

(ii)捕捉用以判定是否存在违规行为的信息的手段;

(C)制定规范该设施运行的规则,包括对如下交易程序作出具体规定的规则,即对于在该设施交易的或发布的指令(包括大宗交易)之录入和执行所采用的交易程序;并

(D)通过颁发规则作出如下规定,即互换交易商或主要互换参与者达成受制于第2(h)条规定的强制集中结算要求的互换或为该等互换提供便利的,应有责任遵守第2(h)(8)条规定的强制性交易要求。

(3)**不易受操纵的互换**。——互换执行设施应仅允许对不易受操纵的互换进行交易。

(4)**交易和交易处理的监控**。——互换执行设施应——

(A)制定并执行界定下列程序的规则或条款和条件,或制定并执行对以下程序作出具体规定的细则——

(i)对于在该互换执行设施的设施或通过该等设施交易的指令之录入和执行所采用的交易程序;及

(ii)对在该互换执行设施的设施或通过该等设施实施的互换进行交易处理的程序;并

"(B) monitor trading in swaps to prevent manipulation, price distortion, and disruptions of the delivery or cash settlement process through surveillance, compliance, and disciplinary practices and procedures, including methods for conducting real–time monitoring of trading and comprehensive and accurate trade reconstructions.

"(5) ABILITY TO OBTAIN INFORMATION. — The swap execution facility shall —

"(A) establish and enforce rules that will allow the facility to obtain any necessary information to perform any of the functions described in this section;

"(B) provide the information to the Commission on request; and

"(C) have the capacity to carry out such international information–sharing agreements as the Commission may require.

"(6) POSITION LIMITS OR ACCOUNTABILITY. —

"(A) IN GENERAL. — To reduce the potential threat of market manipulation or congestion, especially during trading in the delivery month, a swap execution facility that is a trading facility shall adopt for each of the contracts of the facility, as is necessary and appropriate, position limitations or position accountability for speculators.

"(B) POSITION LIMITS. — For any contract that is subject to a position limitation established by the Commission pursuant to section 4a(a), the swap execution facility shall —

"(i) set its position limitation at a level no higher than the Commission limitation; and

"(ii) monitor positions established on or through the swap execution facility for compliance with the limit set by the Commission and the limit, if any, set by the swap execution facility.

"(7) FINANCIAL INTEGRITY OF TRANSACTIONS. — The swap execution facility shall establish and enforce rules and procedures for ensuring the financial integrity of swaps entered on or through the facilities of the swap execution facility, including the clearance and settlement of the swaps pursuant to section 2(h)(1).

"(8) EMERGENCY AUTHORITY. — The swap execution facility shall adopt rules to provide for the exercise of emergency authority, in consultation or cooperation with the Commission, as is necessary and appropriate, including the authority to liquidate or transfer open positions in any swap or to suspend or curtail trading in a swap.

"(9) TIMELY PUBLICATION OF TRADING INFORMATION. —

"(A) IN GENERAL. — The swap execution facility shall make public timely information on price, trading volume, and other trading data on swaps to the extent prescribed by the Commission.

"(B) CAPACITY OF SWAP EXECUTION FACILITY. — The swap execution facility shall be required to have the capacity to electronically capture and transmit trade information with respect to transactions executed on the facility.

"(10) RECORDKEEPING AND REPORTING. —

(B)通过监测、合规、纪律处分实践和程序(包括进行交易实时监控和全面而准确的交易回溯的方法)来监控互换交易,从而防范操纵和价格扭曲,并防范交割或现金结算过程受到扰乱。

(5)**获取信息的能力**。——互换执行设施应——

(A)制定并执行相关规则,使该设施能够获取对履行本条所述任何职能确属必要的任何信息;

(B)经商品期货交易委员会提出要求即向其提供上述信息;且

(C)有能力按商品期货交易委员会的要求执行国际信息共享协议。

(6)**限仓制度或持仓说明制度**。——

(A)**一般规定**。——为了降低市场操纵或阻塞的潜在威胁(特别是在交割月的交易中),互换执行设施如果同时也是交易设施,则应就该设施的每一合约品种对投资者采取必要且适当的限仓制度或持仓说明制度。

(B)**限仓制度**。——如果商品期货交易委员会已依据第4a(a)条对任何品种的合约设定了持仓限额,则互换执行设施应针对该品种合约——

(i)设定不高于商品期货交易委员会所设限额水平的持仓限额;并

(ii)监控在该互换执行设施或通过该互换执行设施建立的持仓,以期符合商品期货交易委员会设定的限额和该设施设定的限额(如有)。

(7)**交易的财务完整性**。——互换执行设施应制定并执行相关规则和程序,以确保在该互换执行设施的设施或通过该等设施达成的互换[包括根据第2(h)(1)条对互换进行的清算和结算]的财务完整性。

(8)**紧急权力**。——互换执行设施应在与商品期货交易委员会磋商后制定相关规则,或与商品期货交易委员会合作制定相关规则,以对必要且适当的紧急权力(包括对未平仓的任何互换进行平仓或移仓的权力,或者暂停或停止互换交易的权力)的行使作出规定。

(9)**及时公布交易信息**。——

(A)**一般规定**。——互换执行设施应在商品期货交易委员会的规定范围内及时公布互换的成交价格、成交量和其他交易数据信息。

(B)**互换执行设施的能力**。——该设施应当有能力通过电子方式捕获和传送在互换执行设施执行的交易的信息。

(10)**记录保存和报告**。——

"(A) IN GENERAL. — A swap execution facility shall —

"(i) maintain records of all activities relating to the business of the facility, including a complete audit trail, in a form and manner acceptable to the Commission for a period of 5 years;

"(ii) report to the Commission, in a form and manner acceptable to the Commission, such information as the Commission determines to be necessary or appropriate for the Commission to perform the duties of the Commission under this Act; and

"(iii) shall keep any such records relating to swaps defined in section 1a(47)(A)(v) open to inspection and examination by the Securities and Exchange Commission."

"(B) REQUIREMENTS. — The Commission shall adopt data collection and reporting requirements for swap execution facilities that are comparable to corresponding requirements for derivatives clearing organizations and swap data repositories.

"(11) ANTITRUST CONSIDERATIONS. — Unless necessary or appropriate to achieve the purposes of this Act, the swap execution facility shall not —

"(A) adopt any rules or taking any actions that result in any unreasonable restraint of trade; or

"(B) impose any material anticompetitive burden on trading or clearing.

"(12) CONFLICTS OF INTEREST. — The swap execution facility shall —

"(A) establish and enforce rules to minimize conflicts of interest in its decision–making process; and

"(B) establish a process for resolving the conflicts of interest.

"(13) FINANCIAL RESOURCES. —

"(A) IN GENERAL. — The swap execution facility shall have adequate financial, operational, and managerial resources to discharge each responsibility of the swap execution facility.

"(B) DETERMINATION OF RESOURCE ADEQUACY. — The financial resources of a swap execution facility shall be considered to be adequate if the value of the financial resources exceeds the total amount that would enable the swap execution facility to cover the operating costs of the swap execution facility for a 1–year period, as calculated on a rolling basis.

"(14) SYSTEM SAFEGUARDS. — The swap execution facility shall —

"(A) establish and maintain a program of risk analysis and oversight to identify and minimize sources of operational risk, through the development of appropriate controls and procedures, and automated systems, that —

"(i) are reliable and secure; and

"(ii) have adequate scalable capacity;

"(B) establish and maintain emergency procedures, backup facilities, and a plan for

(A)**一般规定**。——互换执行设施应——

(i)按照商品期货交易委员会认可的格式和方式保存与该设施业务相关的所有活动记录,包括完整的审计留痕记录,记录保存期限为5年;

(ii)按照商品期货交易委员会认可的格式和方式向其报告商品期货交易委员会判定对其履行本法规定的职责确属必要或适当的相关信息;且

(iii)应保存与第1a(47)(A)(v)条定义的互换相关的任何上述记录,供证券交易委员会检查和核查。

(B)**要求**。——商品期货交易委员会对互换执行设施制定的数据收集和报告要求,应与其就衍生品结算组织和互换数据存管机构制定的相应要求具有可比性。

(11)**反垄断考量**。——除非对实现本法宗旨确属必要或适当,否则互换执行设施不得——

(A)制定对交易造成任何不合理限制的任何规则或采取对交易造成任何不合理限制的任何行动;或

(B)对交易或结算施加任何阻碍竞争的实质性负担。

(12)**利益冲突**。——互换执行设施应——

(A)制定并执行相关规则,将其决策过程中的利益冲突减到最低限度;并

(B)制定解决利益冲突的程序。

(13)**财务资源**。——

(A)**一般规定**。——互换执行设施应具备充足的财务、运营和管理资源,以履行互换执行设施的每项责任。

(B)**对资源充足性的判定**。——如果互换执行设施的财务资源价值超过其开展1年运营所需成本总额(以滚动方式计算),则该互换执行设施应视为拥有充足的财务资源。

(14)**系统保障**。——互换执行设施应当——

(A)建立并维持风险分析和监控计划,以便通过设置具有以下特征的适当的控制措施和程序以及自动化系统,识别运营风险源并将其减到最低限度——

(i)可靠、安全;并

(ii)具备充分的升级能力;

(B)建立并维持应急程序、备用设施和灾难恢复计划,以便——

disaster recovery that allow for —

"(i) the timely recovery and resumption of operations; and

"(ii) the fulfillment of the responsibilities and obligations of the swap execution facility; and

"(C) periodically conduct tests to verify that the backup resources of the swap execution facility are sufficient to ensure continued —

"(i) order processing and trade matching;

"(ii) price reporting;

"(iii) market surveillance and

"(iv) maintenance of a comprehensive and accurate audit trail.

"(15) DESIGNATION OF CHIEF COMPLIANCE OFFICER. —

"(A) IN GENERAL. — Each swap execution facility shall designate an individual to serve as a chief compliance officer.

"(B) DUTIES. — The chief compliance officer shall —

"(i) report directly to the board or to the senior officer of the facility;

"(ii) review compliance with the core principles in this subsection;

"(iii) in consultation with the board of the facility, a body performing a function similar to that of a board, or the senior officer of the facility, resolve any conflicts of interest that may arise;

"(iv) be responsible for establishing and administering the policies and procedures required to be established pursuant to this section;

"(v) ensure compliance with this Act and the rules and regulations issued under this Act, including rules prescribed by the Commission pursuant to this section; and

"(vi) establish procedures for the remediation of noncompliance issues found during compliance office reviews, look backs, internal or external audit findings, self–reported errors, or through validated complaints.

"(C) REQUIREMENTS FOR PROCEDURES. — In establishing procedures under subparagraph (B)(vi), the chief compliance officer shall design the procedures to establish the handling, management response, remediation, retesting, and closing of noncompliance issues.

"(D) ANNUAL REPORTS. —

"(i) IN GENERAL. — In accordance with rules prescribed by the Commission, the chief compliance officer shall annually prepare and sign a report that contains a description of —

"(I) the compliance of the swap execution facility with this Act; and

"(II) the policies and procedures, including the code of ethics and conflict of interest policies, of the swap execution facility.

"(ii) REQUIREMENTS. — The chief compliance officer shall —

(i)及时恢复和重启运营;及

(ii)履行该互换执行设施承担的各项责任和义务;及

(C)定期开展测试,以核实该互换执行设施的备用资源是否足以确保下列活动的持续进行——

(i)指令处理和交易匹配;

(ii)价格报告;

(iii)市场监测;及

(iv)保持全面且准确的审计留痕记录。

(15)**指定首席合规官**。——

(A)**一般规定**。——每一互换执行设施均应指定一名个人担任首席合规官。

(B)**职责**。——首席合规官应——

(i)向互换执行设施的董事会或高级管理人员直接汇报工作;

(ii)审查对本子条核心原则的遵守情况;

(iii)与互换执行设施的董事会、履行与董事会类似职能的机构或高级管理人员磋商,解决任何可能发生的利益冲突问题;

(iv)负责制定并实施应当依据本条制定的每一项政策和程序;

(v)确保本法以及依据本法发布的规则与规章(包括商品期货交易委员会依据本条制定的规则)均得到遵守;及

(vi)制定相关程序,据以对合规办公室的审查工作、回顾工作、内部或外部的审计认定结论、自报失误或有效的投诉中发现的不合规问题,采取补救措施。

(C)**程序要求**。——根据第(B)(vi)子款制定相关程序时,首席合规官应设计用以对不合规问题进行处理、管理回应、补救、重新测试和终结的适当程序。

(D)**年度报告**。——

(i)**一般规定**。——首席合规官应根据商品期货交易委员会的规则每年编制并签署一份报告,其中应包含以下内容——

(I)互换执行设施对本法的合规情况;及

(II)互换执行设施的政策和程序(包括职业道德准则和利益冲突处理政策)。

(ii)**要求**。——首席合规官应——

"(I) submit each report described in clause (i) with the appropriate financial report of the swap execution facility that is required to be submitted to the Commission pursuant to this section; and

"(II) include in the report a certification that, under penalty of law, the report is accurate and complete.

"(g) EXEMPTIONS. — The Commission may exempt, conditionally or unconditionally, a swap execution facility from registration under this section if the Commission finds that the facility is subject to comparable, comprehensive supervision and regulation on a consolidated basis by the Securities and Exchange Commission, a prudential regulator, or the appropriate governmental authorities in the home country of the facility.

"(h) RULES. — The Commission shall prescribe rules governing the regulation of alternative swap execution facilities under this section.".

SEC.734. DERIVATIVES TRANSACTION EXECUTION FACILITIES AND EXEMPT BOARDS OF TRADE.

(a) IN GENERAL. — Sections 5a and 5d of the Commodity Exchange Act (7 U.S.C. 7a, 7a–3) are repealed.

(b) CONFORMING AMENDMENTS. —

(1) Section 2 of the Commodity Exchange Act (7 U.S.C. 2) is amended —

(A) in subsection (a)(1)(A), in the first sentence, by striking "or 5a"; and

(B) in paragraph (2) of subsection (g) (as redesignated by section 723(a)(1)(B)), by striking "section 5a of this Act" and all that follows through "5d of this Act" and inserting "section 5b of this Act".

(2) Section 6(g)(1)(A) of the Securities Exchange Act of 1934 (15 U.S.C. 78f(g)(1)(A)) is amended —

(A) by striking "that — " and all that follows through "(i) has been designated" and inserting "that has been designated";

(B) by striking "; or" and inserting "; and" and

(C) by striking clause (ii).

(c) ABILITY TO PETITION COMMISSION. —

(1) IN GENERAL. — Prior to the final effective dates in this title, a person may petition the Commodity Futures Trading Commission to remain subject to the provisions of section 5d of the Commodity Exchange Act, as such provisions existed prior to the effective date of this subtitle.

(2) CONSIDERATION OF PETITION. — The Commodity Futures Trading Commission shall consider any petition submitted under paragraph (1) in a prompt manner and may allow a person to continue operating subject to the provisions of section 5d of the Commodity Exchange Act for up to 1 year after the effective date of this subtitle.

(I)将第(i)项所述的每份报告与按本条规定应向商品期货交易委员会提交的相应的互换执行设施财务报告一并提交;及

(II)在报告中纳入一份自查证明,证明该合规报告的准确性和完整性,并明确表示其知晓作伪证将招致法律惩罚。

(g)**豁免**。——如果商品期货交易委员会认定,某互换执行设施所受到的来自证券交易委员会、审慎监管者或该互换执行设施的母国相应的政府机关的监管和规制整体而言足够全面,与商品期货交易委员会的监管和规制具有可比性,则商品期货交易委员会可有条件或无条件地豁免该互换执行设施, 使其不必依照本条规定进行注册。

(h)**规则**。——商品期货交易委员会应制定相关规则,规范根据本条规定对另类互换执行设施的监管。”

第734条 衍生产品交易执行设施以及豁免交易场所

(a)**一般规定**。——《商品交易法》第5a条和第5d条(《美国法典》第七编第7a节和第7a-3节)现予废除。

(b)**一致性修正**。——

(1)《商品交易法》第2条(《美国法典》第七编第2节)修正如下——

(A)在第(a)(1)(A)子条第一句中,删除“或第5a条”;及

(B)第(g)子条第(2)款[以第723(a)(1)(B)条重新编号后的序号为准]中,删除“本法第5a条”直至“本法第5d条”,并插入“本法第5b条”。

(2)《1934年证券交易法》第6(g)(1)(A)条[《美国法典》第十五编第78f(g)(1)(A)节]修正如下——

(A)删除“该交易所——”直至“(i)已被商品期货交易委员会指定为合约市场”,并插入“该交易所已被商品期货交易委员会指定为合约市场”;

(B)删除“;或”,并插入“;且”及

(C)删除第(ii)项。

(c)**向商品期货交易委员会提出请求的资格**。——

(1)**一般规定**。——在本编规定最终生效日之前,任何主体可以向商品期货交易委员会请求继续适用《商品交易法》第5d条规定,且该规定以本子编生效日之前已存在的版本为准。

(2)**对请求的审议**。——对于根据第(1)款提交的任何请求,商品期货交易委员会应及时审议,并允许在不超过本子编规定生效日后 1 年的期间内继续按照《商品交易法》第5d条规定运营。

SEC.735. DESIGNATED CONTRACT MARKETS.

(a) CRITERIA FOR DESIGNATION. — Section 5 of the Commodity Exchange Act (7 U.S.C. 7) is amended by striking subsection (b).

(b) CORE PRINCIPLES FOR CONTRACT MARKETS. — Section 5 of the Commodity Exchange Act (7 U.S.C. 7) is amended by striking subsection (d) and inserting the following:

"(d) CORE PRINCIPLES FOR CONTRACT MARKETS. —

"(1) DESIGNATION AS CONTRACT MARKET. —

"(A) IN GENERAL. — To be designated, and maintain a designation, as a contract market, a board of trade shall comply with —

"(i) any core principle described in this subsection; and

"(ii) any requirement that the Commission may impose by rule or regulation pursuant to section 8a(5).

"(B) REASONABLE DISCRETION OF CONTRACT MARKET. — Unless otherwise determined by the Commission by rule or regulation, a board of trade described in subparagraph (A) shall have reasonable discretion in establishing the manner in which the board of trade complies with the core principles described in this subsection.

"(2) COMPLIANCE WITH RULES. —

"(A)IN GENERAL. — The board of trade shall establish, monitor, and enforce compliance with the rules of the contract market, including —

"(i) access requirements;

"(ii) the terms and conditions of any contracts to be traded on the contract market; and

"(iii) rules prohibiting abusive trade practices on the contract market.

"(B) CAPACITY OF CONTRACT MARKET. — The board of trade shall have the capacity to detect, investigate, and apply appropriate sanctions to any person that violates any rule of the contract market.

"(C) REQUIREMENT OF RULES. — The rules of the contract market shall provide the board of trade with the ability and authority to obtain any necessary information to perform any function described in this subsection, including the capacity to carry out such international information–sharing agreements as the Commission may require.

"(3) CONTRACTS NOT READILY SUBJECT TO MANIPULATION. — The board of trade shall list on the contract market only contracts that are not readily susceptible to manipulation.

"(4) PREVENTION OF MARKET DISRUPTION. — The board of trade shall have the capacity and responsibility to prevent manipulation, price distortion, and disruptions of the delivery or cash–settlement process through market surveillance, compliance, and enforcement practices and procedures, including —

第735条　指定合约市场

(a)**指定的标准**。——删除《商品交易法》(《美国法典》第七编第7节)第5条第(b)子条,作为对该条的修正。

(b)**合约市场的核心原则**。——《商品交易法》(《美国法典》第七编第7节)第5条修正如下:删除第(d)子条,并替以如下内容:

"(d)**合约市场的核心原则**。——

(1)**指定合约市场**。——

(A)**一般规定**。——要获得并维持指定合约市场资格,交易场所应遵守以下规定——

(i)本子条所述任何核心原则;及

(ii)商品期货交易委员会根据第8a(5)条发布的规则或规章所提出的任何要求。

(B) **合约市场合理的自由裁量权**。——除非商品期货交易委员会发布的规则或规章作出不同判定,否则,第(A)子款所述交易场所应依其合理的自由裁量权决定其遵守本子条核心原则的方式。

(2)**规则合规**。——

(A)**一般规定**。——交易场所应制定、监控并执行合约市场规则,包括——

(i)准入要求;

(ii)任何合约在合约市场上交易的条款和条件;及

(iii)禁止合约市场滥用性交易行为的规则。

(B)**合约市场的能力**。——交易场所应有能力发现、调查违反任何合约市场规则的任何人并对其处以适当处罚。

(C)**规则的要求**。——合约市场规则应赋予交易场所相关能力和权力,使之能够获取履行本子条所述各项职能所必要的任何信息,包括按照商品期货交易委员会的要求执行国际信息共享协议的能力。

(3)**不易受操纵的合约**。——交易场所仅得在合约市场上市不易受操纵的合约。

(4)**防范市场扰乱**。——交易场所应有能力和责任通过市场监测、合规和规则执行措施及程序来防范操纵行为、价格扭曲以及扰乱交割或现金结算过程的行为,包括——

"(A) methods for conducting real–time monitoring of trading; and

"(B) comprehensive and accurate trade reconstructions.

"(5) POSITION LIMITATIONS OR ACCOUNTABILITY.—

"(A) IN GENERAL. — To reduce the potential threat of market manipulation or congestion (especially during trading in the delivery month), the board of trade shall adopt for each contract of the board of trade, as is necessary and appropriate, position limitations or position accountability for speculators.

"(B) MAXIMUM ALLOWABLE POSITION LIMITATION. — For any contract that is subject to a position limitation established by the Commission pursuant to section 4a(a), the board of trade shall set the position limitation of the board of trade at a level not higher than the position limitation established by the Commission.

"(6) EMERGENCY AUTHORITY. — The board of trade, in consultation or cooperation with the Commission, shall adopt rules to provide for the exercise of emergency authority, as is necessary and appropriate, including the authority —

"(A) to liquidate or transfer open positions in any contract;

"(B) to suspend or curtail trading in any contract; and

"(C) to require market participants in any contract to meet special margin requirements.

"(7) AVAILABILITY OF GENERAL INFORMATION. — The board of trade shall make available to market authorities, market participants, and the public accurate information concerning —

"(A) the terms and conditions of the contracts of the contract market; and

"(B)(i) the rules, regulations, and mechanisms for executing transactions on or through the facilities of the contract market; and

"(ii) the rules and specifications describing the operation of the contract market's —

"(I) electronic matching platform; or

"(II) trade execution facility.

"(8) DAILY PUBLICATION OF TRADING INFORMATION. — The board of trade shall make public daily information on settlement prices, volume, open interest, and opening and closing ranges for actively traded contracts on the contract market.

"(9) EXECUTION OF TRANSACTIONS.—

"(A) IN GENERAL. — The board of trade shall provide a competitive, open, and efficient market and mechanism for executing transactions that protects the price discovery process of trading in the centralized market of the board of trade.

"(B) RULES. — The rules of the board of trade may authorize, for bona fide business purposes —

"(i) transfer trades or office trades;

"(ii) an exchange of —

(A)对交易开展实时监控的方法;及

(B)全面、准确的交易回溯。

(5)**限仓制度或持仓说明制度**——

(A)**一般规定**。——为了降低市场操纵或阻塞的潜在威胁(特别是在交割月的交易中),交易场所应就该交易场所的每一合约品种对投机者采取必要且适当的限仓制度或持仓说明制度。

(B)**允许的最高持仓限额**。——对于受制于商品期货交易委员会根据第4a(a)条规定的持仓限额的任何合约而言,交易场所设定的该交易场所之持仓限额不得高于商品期货交易委员会规定的水平。

(6)**紧急权力**。——交易场所应在与商品期货交易委员会磋商后制定相关规则,或与商品期货交易委员会合作制定相关规则,以对必要且适当的紧急权力的行使作出规定,包括以下权力——

(A)对任何未平仓合约进行平仓或移仓的权力;

(B)暂停或限制任何合约交易的权力;及

(C)要求任何合约的市场参与者满足特殊保证金要求的权力。

(7)**一般信息的提供**。——交易场所应向市场主管部门、市场参与者及公众提供关于以下各项的准确信息——

(A)合约市场中合约的条款和条件;及

(B)(i)在合约市场设施或通过合约市场设施执行交易的规则、规章和机制;及

(ii)合约市场以下各者的运行规则和规范——

(I)电子匹配平台;或

(II)交易执行设施。

(8)**每日公布交易信息**。——对于合约市场上交易活跃的合约,交易场所应每日公布其结算价格、成交量、未平仓量以及开盘和收盘价格区间方面的信息。

(9)**交易执行**。——

(A)**一般规定**。——交易场所应为交易的执行提供有竞争力、公开且高效的市场和机制,以保护交易场所的集中市场的交易价格发现过程。

(B)**规则**。——交易场所规则可出于善意商业目的,准许进行——

(i)内部移仓或外部移仓;

(ii)以下交易——

"(I) futures in connection with a cash commodity transaction;

"(II) futures for cash commodities; or

"(III) futures for swaps; or

"(iii) a futures commission merchant, acting as principal or agent, to enter into or confirm the execution of a contract for the purchase or sale of a commodity for future delivery if the contract is reported, recorded, or cleared in accordance with the rules of the contract market or a derivatives clearing organization.

"(10) TRADE INFORMATION. — The board of trade shall maintain rules and procedures to provide for the recording and safe storage of all identifying trade information in a manner that enables the contract market to use the information —

"(A) to assist in the prevention of customer and market abuses; and

"(B) to provide evidence of any violations of the rules of the contract market.

"(11) FINANCIAL INTEGRITY OF TRANSACTIONS. — The board of trade shall establish and enforce —

"(A) rules and procedures for ensuring the financial integrity of transactions entered into on or through the facilities of the contract market (including the clearance and settlement of the transactions with a derivatives clearing organization); and

"(B) rules to ensure —

"(i) the financial integrity of any —

"(I) futures commission merchant; and

"(II) introducing broker; and

"(ii) the protection of customer funds.

"(12) PROTECTION OF MARKETS AND MARKET PARTICIPANTS. — The board of trade shall establish and enforce rules —

"(A) to protect markets and market participants from abusive practices committed by any party, including abusive practices committed by a party acting as an agent for a participant; and

"(B) to promote fair and equitable trading on the contract market.

"(13) DISCIPLINARY PROCEDURES. — The board of trade shall establish and enforce disciplinary procedures that authorize the board of trade to discipline, suspend, or expel members or market participants that violate the rules of the board of trade, or similar methods for performing the same functions, including delegation of the functions to third parties.

"(14) DISPUTE RESOLUTION. — The board of trade shall establish and enforce rules regarding, and provide facilities for alternative dispute resolution as appropriate for, market participants and any market intermediaries.

"(15) GOVERNANCE FITNESS STANDARDS. — The board of trade shall establish

(I)套期保值;

(II)期货转现货;或

(III)期货转互换;或

(iii)期货经纪商以委托人或代理人身份,为买卖远期交割的商品而达成或确认执行合约,其前提是该等合约的报告、记录或结算符合该合约市场或衍生品结算组织的规则。

(10)**交易信息**。——交易场所应维持相关规则和程序,对所有识别性交易信息的记录和安全保存作出规定,以便使合约市场能够利用该等信息——

(A)为防范对客户和市场的滥用行为提供协助;并

(B)就任何违反合约市场规则的行为提供证据。

(11)**交易的财务完整性**。——交易场所应制定并执行——

(A)相关规则和程序,以确保在合约市场设施或通过该等合约市场设施达成的交易(包括衍生品结算组织进行的交易清算和结算)的财务完整性;及

(B)相关规则,确保——

(i)以下任何机构的财务完整性——

(I)期货经纪商;及

(II)介绍经纪商;及

(ii)客户资金的保护。

(12)**市场和市场参与者的保护**。——交易场所应制定并执行相关规则——

(A)保护市场和市场参与者免受任何一方的滥用行为(包括参与者代理人的滥用行为)的损害;并

(B)促进合约市场的公平、公正交易。

(13)**纪律处分程序**。——交易场所应制定并执行纪律处分程序,该等程序赋予交易场所如下权力:处分违反交易场所规则的会员或市场参与者,或暂停或取消该等会员或参与者的资格,或者制定并执行履行相同职能的类似方法,包括委托第三方行使该等处分权。

(14)**争议解决**。——交易场所应就市场参与者及任何市场中介机构制定并执行相关规则,并为其提供适当的替代性争议解决方式。

(15)**治理适合性标准**。——交易场所应对以下人员制定并执行适当的适合性标

and enforce appropriate fitness standards for directors, members of any disciplinary committee, members of the contract market, and any other person with direct access to the facility (including any party affiliated with any person described in this paragraph).

"(16) CONFLICTS OF INTEREST. — The board of trade shall establish and enforce rules —

"(A) to minimize conflicts of interest in the decision-making process of the contract market; and

"(B) to establish a process for resolving conflicts of interest described in subparagraph (A).

"(17) COMPOSITION OF GOVERNING BOARDS OF CONTRACT MARKETS. — The governance arrangements of the board of trade shall be designed to permit consideration of the views of market participants.

"(18) RECORDKEEPING. — The board of trade shall maintain records of all activities relating to the business of the contract market —

"(A) in a form and manner that is acceptable to the Commission; and

"(B) for a period of at least 5 years.

"(19) ANTITRUST CONSIDERATIONS. — Unless necessary or appropriate to achieve the purposes of this Act, the board of trade shall not —

"(A) adopt any rule or taking any action that results in any unreasonable restraint of trade; or

"(B) impose any material anticompetitive burden on trading on the contract market.

"(20) SYSTEM SAFEGUARDS. — The board of trade shall —

"(A) establish and maintain a program of risk analysis and oversight to identify and minimize sources of operational risk, through the development of appropriate controls and procedures, and the development of automated systems, that are reliable, secure, and have adequate scalable capacity;

"(B) establish and maintain emergency procedures, backup facilities, and a plan for disaster recovery that allow for the timely recovery and resumption of operations and the fulfillment of the responsibilities and obligations of the board of trade; and

"(C) periodically conduct tests to verify that backup resources are sufficient to ensure continued order processing and trade matching, price reporting, market surveillance, and maintenance of a comprehensive and accurate audit trail.

"(21) FINANCIAL RESOURCES. —

"(A) IN GENERAL. — The board of trade shall have adequate financial, operational, and managerial resources to discharge each responsibility of the board of trade.

"(B) DETERMINATION OF ADEQUACY. — The financial resources of the board of trade shall be considered to be adequate if the value of the financial resources exceeds the

准:董事、任何纪律处分委员会的成员、合约市场会员以及有权直接接入设施的任何其他人(包括本款所述人士的任何关联方)。

(16)**利益冲突**。——交易场所应制定并执行相关规则,以便——

(A)将合约市场决策过程中的利益冲突减到最低限度;及

(B)制定解决第(A)子款所述利益冲突的程序。

(17)**合约市场管理机构的组成**。——设计交易场所的治理安排时,应使管理机构能够考虑到市场参与者的意见。

(18)**记录保存**。——交易场所应就与合约市场业务相关的所有活动保存记录,并且——

(A)按照商品期货交易委员会认可的格式和方式保持记录;且

(B)记录保存期至少应为5年。

(19)**反垄断考量**。——除非对实现本法宗旨确属必要或适当,否则交易场所不得——

(A)制定对交易造成任何不合理限制的任何规则或采取对交易造成任何不合理限制的任何行动;或

(B)对合约市场上的交易施加任何阻碍竞争的实质性负担。

(20)**系统保障**。——交易场所应当——

(A)建立并维持风险分析和监控计划,以便通过设置可靠、安全并具备充分的升级能力的适当控制措施和程序以及自动化系统,识别运营风险源并将其减到最低限度;

(B)建立并维持应急程序、备用设施和灾难恢复计划,以便及时恢复和重启该交易场所的运营,并履行其承担的各项责任和义务;并

(C)定期开展测试,以核实其备用资源是否足以确保下列活动的持续进行:指令处理和交易匹配、价格报告、市场监测以及保持全面且准确的审计留痕记录。

(21)**财务资源**。——

(A)**一般规定**。——交易场所应拥有履行其各项责任所需的充足财务、运营和管理资源。

(B)**对资源充足性的判定**。——如果交易场所的财务资源价值超过其开展1年运营所需成本总额(以滚动方式计算),则该交易场所应视为拥有充足的财务资源。

total amount that would enable the contract market to cover the operating costs of the contract market for a 1–year period, as calculated on a rolling basis.

"(22) DIVERSITY OF BOARD OF DIRECTORS. — The board of trade, if a publicly traded company, shall endeavor to recruit individuals to serve on the board of directors and the other decision–making bodies (as determined by the Commission) of the board of trade from among, and to have the composition of the bodies reflect, a broad and culturally diverse pool of qualified candidates.

"(23) SECURITIES AND EXCHANGE COMMISSION. — The board of trade shall keep any such records relating to swaps defined in section 1a(47)(A)(v) open to inspection and examination by the Securities and Exchange Commission.".

SEC.736. MARGIN.

Section 8a(7) of the Commodity Exchange Act (7 U.S.C. 12a(7)) is amended —

(1) in subparagraph (C), by striking ", excepting the setting of levels of margin";

(2) by redesignating subparagraphs (D) through (F) as subparagraphs (E) through (G), respectively; and

(3) by inserting after subparagraph (C) the following:

"(D) margin requirements, provided that the rules, regulations, or orders shall —

"(i) be limited to protecting the financial integrity of the derivatives clearing organization;

"(ii) be designed for risk management purposes to protect the financial integrity of transactions; and

"(iii) not set specific margin amounts;".

SEC.737. POSITION LIMITS.

(a) AGGREGATE POSITION LIMITS. — Section 4a(a) of the Commodity Exchange Act (7 U.S.C. 6a(a)) is amended —

(1) by inserting after "(a)" the following:

"(1) IN GENERAL. — ";

(2) in the first sentence, by striking "on electronic trading facilities with respect to a significant price discovery contract" and inserting "swaps that perform or affect a significant price discovery function with respect to registered entities";

(3) in the second sentence —

(A) by inserting ", including any group or class of traders," after "held by any person"; and

(B) by striking "on an electronic trading facility with respect to a significant price discovery contract," and inserting "swaps traded on or subject to the rules of a designated contract market or a swap execution facility, or swaps not traded on or subject to the rules of a designated contract market or a swap execution facility that performs a significant price

(22)**董事会的多元性**。——如果交易场所为一家公开交易公司,其应尽力从具有广泛性和文化多元性的合格候选人群体中聘用相关人员在交易场所董事会或商品期货交易委员会确定的其他决策机构中任职,并在机构人员组成中体现会员的广泛性和文化多元性。

(23)**证券交易委员会**。——交易场所应向证券交易委员会公开与第1a(47)(A)(v)条定义的互换相关的任何该等记录,供其检查和核查。”

第736条 保证金

《商品交易法》第8a(7)条[《美国法典》第七编第12a(7)节]修正如下——

(1)在第(C)子款中,删除“,但不包括设定保证金水平的规定”;

(2)第(D)子款至第(F)子款分别重新编号为第(E)子款至第(G)子款;及

(3)在第(C)子款之后插入如下内容:

“(D)保证金要求,前提是该等规则、规章或命令——

(i)应仅限于保护衍生品结算组织财务完整性的规则、规章或命令;

(ii)出于风险管理之目的,应设计成能保护交易财务完整性;且

(iii)不得设定具体的保证金金额;”。

第737条 持仓限额

(a)**合并持仓限额**。——《商品交易法》第4a(a)条[《美国法典》第七编第6a(a)节]修正如下——

(1)在“(a)”之后插入如下内容:

“(1)**一般规定**。——”

(2)第一句删除“针对重要价格发现合约而言,在电子交易设施上”,替以“对注册实体具有重要价格发现功能的或影响该等功能的互换”;

(3)第二句——

(A)在“由任何人所持有的”之后插入“(包括任何群体或类别的交易商)”;及

(B)删除“针对重要价格发现合约而言,在电子交易设施上,”替以“在指定合约市场或互换执行设施交易的或按其规则交易的互换;既不在指定合约市场或互换执行设施交易,也不按其规则交易,但对某注册实体具有重要价格发现功能的互换。”及

discovery function with respect to a registered entity,"; and

(4) by adding at the end the following:

"(2) ESTABLISHMENT OF LIMITATIONS. —

"(A) IN GENERAL. — In accordance with the standards set forth in paragraph (1) of this subsection and consistent with the good faith exception cited in subsection (b)(2), with respect to physical commodities other than excluded commodities as defined by the Commission, the Commission shall by rule, regulation, or order establish limits on the amount of positions, as appropriate, other than bona fide hedge positions, that may be held by any person with respect to contracts of sale for future delivery or with respect to options on the contracts or commodities traded on or subject to the rules of a designated contract market.

"(B) TIMING. —

"(i) EXEMPT COMMODITIES. — For exempt commodities, the limits required under subparagraph (A) shall be established within 180 days after the date of the enactment of this paragraph.

"(ii) AGRICULTURAL COMMODITIES. — For agricultural commodities, the limits required under subparagraph(A) shall be established within 270 days after the date of the enactment of this paragraph.

"(C) GOAL. — In establishing the limits required under subparagraph (A), the Commission shall strive to ensure that trading on foreign boards of trade in the same commodity will be subject to comparable limits and that any limits to be imposed by the Commission will not cause price discovery in the commodity to shift to trading on the foreign boards of trade.

"(3) SPECIFIC LIMITATIONS. — In establishing the limits required in paragraph (2), the Commission, as appropriate, shall set limits —

"(A) on the number of positions that may be held by any person for the spot month, each other month, and the aggregate number of positions that may be held by any person for all months; and

"(B) to the maximum extent practicable, in its discretion —

"(i) to diminish, eliminate, or prevent excessive speculation as described under this section;

"(ii) to deter and prevent market manipulation, squeezes, and corners;

"(iii) to ensure sufficient market liquidity for bona fide hedgers; and

"(iv) to ensure that the price discovery function of the underlying market is not disrupted.

"(4) SIGNIFICANT PRICE DISCOVERY FUNCTION. — In making a determination whether a swap performs or affects a significant price discovery function with respect to regulated markets, the Commission shall consider, as appropriate:

(4)在结尾处增加如下内容:

(2)**设定限额**——

(A)**一般规定**。——根据本子条第(1)款规定的标准并在符合第(b)(2)子条所述善意例外规定的情况下，针对并非商品期货交易委员会所定义的除外商品的实物商品,商品期货交易委员会应发布规则、规章或命令,就下列持仓(不包括真正的套期保值持仓)设定适当的限额,即任何人对远期交割出售合约的持仓,或者任何人对在指定合约市场交易的或按其规则交易的合约或商品的期权的持仓。

"(B)**时间**。——

(i)**豁免商品**。——对于豁免商品,第(A)子款规定的限额应在本款规定颁布之日后180天内设定。

(ii)**农产品**。——对于农产品,第(A)子款规定的限额应在本款规定颁布之日后270天内设定。

(C)**目标**。——设定第(A)子款规定的限额时,商品期货交易委员会应努力确保在外国交易场所交易的同一品种商品的限额与商品期货交易委员会设定的任何限额具有可比性，并确保其设定的限额不会致使该商品的价格发现活动转移到外国交易场所。

(3)**特殊限制**。——设定第(2)款规定的限额时,商品期货交易委员会应适当地——

(A)对任何人在现货月份和其他每个月份的可持仓量设定限额,并对任何人在所有月份的合并可持仓量设定限额;并

(B)尽最大可能依其自由裁量权——

(i)减少、消除或防范本条所述的过度投机;

(ii)威慑和防范市场操纵、挤压和囤积行为;

(iii)确保真正的套期保值者有充足的市场流动性;并

(iv)确保基础市场的价格发现功能不受到扰乱。

(4)**重要价格发现功能**。——判定某互换对受监管市场是否具有重要价格发现功能或影响该等功能时,商品期货交易委员会应适当考虑下列因素:

"(A) PRICE LINKAGE. — The extent to which the swap uses or otherwise relies on a daily or final settlement price, or other major price parameter, of another contract traded on a regulated market based upon the same underlying commodity, to value a position, transfer or convert a position, financially settle a position, or close out a position.

"(B) ARBITRAGE. — The extent to which the price for the swap is sufficiently related to the price of another contract traded on a regulated market based upon the same underlying commodity so as to permit market participants to effectively arbitrage between the markets by simultaneously maintaining positions or executing trades in the swaps on a frequent and recurring basis.

"(C) MATERIAL PRICE REFERENCE. — The extent to which, on a frequent and recurring basis, bids, offers, or transactions in a contract traded on a regulated market are directly based on, or are determined by referencing, the price generated by the swap.

"(D) MATERIAL LIQUIDITY. — The extent to which the volume of swaps being traded in the commodity is sufficient to have a material effect on another contract traded on a regulated market.

"(E) OTHER MATERIAL FACTORS. — Such other material factors as the Commission specifies by rule or regulation as relevant to determine whether a swap serves a significant price discovery function with respect to a regulated market.

"(5) ECONOMICALLY EQUIVALENT CONTRACTS. —

"(A) Notwithstanding any other provision of this section, the Commission shall establish limits on the amount of positions, including aggregate position limits, as appropriate, other than bona fide hedge positions, that may be held by any person with respect to swaps that are economically equivalent to contracts of sale for future delivery or to options on the contracts or commodities traded on or subject to the rules of a designated contract market subject to paragraph (2).

"(B) In establishing limits pursuant to subparagraph (A), the Commission shall —

"(i) develop the limits concurrently with limits established under paragraph (2), and the limits shall have similar requirements as under paragraph (3)(B); and

"(ii) establish the limits simultaneously with limits established under paragraph (2).

"(6) AGGREGATE POSITION LIMITS. — The Commission shall, by rule or regulation, establish limits (including related hedge exemption provisions) on the aggregate number or amount of positions in contracts based upon the same underlying commodity (as defined by the Commission) that may be held by any person, including any group or class of traders, for each month across —

"(A) contracts listed by designated contract markets;

"(B) with respect to an agreement, contract, or transaction that settles against any price (including the daily or final settlement price) of 1 or more contracts listed for trading on a

(A)**价格联系**。——该互换在多大程度上采用或依赖在受监管市场交易的另一品种合约(该合约与该互换基于同一基础商品)的每日或最终结算价格或其他重要价格参数进行持仓估值、转移或换算、财务结算或了结。

(B)**套利**。——该互换的价格在多大程度上与在受监管市场交易的另一品种合约(该合约与该互换基于同一品种基础商品)的价格具有充分的相关性,从而使市场参与者能通过频繁反复地同时维持互换持仓或执行互换交易而在不同市场之间有效套利。

(C)**重大价格参考**。——在受监管市场交易的合约的买卖报价或交易,在多大程度上频繁反复地直接建基于该互换产生的价格,或在多大程度上频繁反复地参照该价格予以确定。

(D)**重大流动性**。——商品互换的成交量在多大程度上足以对在受监管市场交易的另一品种合约产生重大影响。

(E)**其他重要因素**。——商品期货交易委员会发布的规则或规章具体规定的据以判定互换对受监管市场是否具有重要价格发现功能的其他重要因素。

(5)**具有同等经济意义的合约**。——

(A)无论本条是否存在任何不同规定,商品期货交易委员会应对任何人持有的具有以下特征的互换持仓(不包括真正的套期保值持仓)设定适当限额(包括合并持仓限额):从经济意义角度而言,等同于受制于第(2)款规定的远期交割出售合约或者在指定合约市场交易的或者按其规则交易的合约或商品的期权。

(B)依第(A)子款设定限额的,商品期货交易委员会——

(i)在设定第(2)款规定的限额时,应配套制定第(A)子款规定的限额,且第(A)子款规定的限额要求应与第(3)(B)款的要求相似;且

(ii)在设定第(2)款规定的限额时,应同时设定第(A)子款规定的限额。

(6)**合并持仓限额**。——商品期货交易委员会应发布规则或规章,就任何人(包括任何群体或类别的交易商)持有的基于同一品种基础商品(以商品期货交易委员会的定义为准)的合约之合并持仓数量或金额设定限额(包括相关的套值保期豁免条款),以下列各项每一月份的持仓为口径——

(A)各指定合约市场所上市的合约品种;

(B)对于依据在某一注册实体上市交易的一个或一个以上合约品种的任何价格(包括每日或最终结算价格)进行结算的协议、合约或交易而言:还应包括在相关外国

registered entity, contracts traded on a foreign board of trade that provides members or other participants located in the United States with direct access to its electronic trading and order matching system; and

"(C) swap contracts that perform or affect a significant price discovery function with respect to regulated entities.

"(7) EXEMPTIONS. — The Commission, by rule, regulation, or order, may exempt, conditionally or unconditionally, any person or class of persons, any swap or class of swaps, any contract of sale of a commodity for future delivery or class of such contracts, any option or class of options, or any transaction or class of transactions from any requirement it may establish under this section with respect to position limits.".

(b) CONFORMING AMENDMENTS. — Section 4a(b) of the Commodity Exchange Act (7 U.S.C. 6a(b)) is amended —

(1) in paragraph (1), by striking "or derivatives transaction execution facility or facilities or electronic trading facility" and inserting "or swap execution facility or facilities"; and

(2) in paragraph (2), by striking "or derivatives transaction execution facility or facilities or electronic trading facility" and inserting "or swap execution facility".

(c) BONA FIDE HEDGING TRANSACTION. — Section 4a(c) of the Commodity Exchange Act is amended —

(1) by inserting "(1)" after "(c)"; and

(2) by adding at the end the following:

"(2) For the purposes of implementation of subsection (a)(2) for contracts of sale for future delivery or options on the contracts or commodities, the Commission shall define what constitutes a bona fide hedging transaction or position as a transaction or position that —

"(A)(i) represents a substitute for transactions made or to be made or positions taken or to be taken at a later time in a physical marketing channel;

"(ii) is economically appropriate to the reduction of risks in the conduct and management of a commercial enterprise; and

"(iii) arises from the potential change in the value of —

"(I) assets that a person owns, produces, manufactures, processes, or merchandises or anticipates owning, producing, manufacturing, processing, or merchandising;

"(II) liabilities that a person owns or anticipates incurring; or

"(III) services that a person provides, purchases, or anticipates providing or purchasing; or

"(B) reduces risks attendant to a position resulting from a swap that —

"(i) was executed opposite a counterparty for which the transaction would qualify as a bona fide hedging transaction pursuant to subparagraph (A); or

交易场所（指向美国境内会员或其他参与者提供电子交易直接接入和指令匹配系统直接接入的外国交易场所)交易的合约;及

(C)对受监管实体具有重要价格发现功能的或影响该等功能的互换合约。

(7)**豁免**。——商品期货交易委员会可以发布规则、规章或命令,有条件或无条件地豁免任何主体或任何类别的主体、任何互换或任何类别的互换、任何远期交割商品出售合约或任何类别的远期交割商品出售合约、任何期权或任何类别的期权、任何交易或任何类别的交易，使其不必遵守商品期货交易委员会按本条规定设定的持仓限额。”

(b)**一致性修正**。——《商品交易法》[《美国法典》第七编第6a(b)节]第4a(b)条修正如下—

(1)在第(1)款中,删除“或衍生品交易执行设施或电子交易设施”,替以“或一个或一个以上互换执行设施”;及

(2)在第(2)款中,删除“或衍生品交易执行设施或电子交易设施”,替以“或(针对重要价格发现合约而言)互换执行设施”。

(c)**真正的套期保值交易**。——《商品交易法》第4a(c)条修正如下——

(1)在“(c)”之后插入“(1)”;及

(2)在结尾处增加如下内容:

“(2)为实施第(a)(2)子条针对远期交割出售合约或合约期权或商品期权的规定,商品期货交易委员会应将真正的套期保值交易或持仓定义为具有以下特征的交易或持仓——

(A)(i)可以替代通过现货市场渠道已订立或将订立的交易或者已持有或将持有的头寸;

(ii)对于降低商业企业的运营和管理风险具有经济益处;且

(iii)由以下价值可能发生的变化而产生——

(I)某人所拥有、生产、制造、加工或售卖的资产,或某人预期将拥有、生产、制造、加工或售卖的资产;

(II)某人负有的债务或预期将产生的债务;或

(III)某人提供或购买的或者预期将提供或购买的服务;或

(B)可以降低由于持有下列互换的持仓而产生的风险——

(i)对于对手方而言,根据第(A)子款规定构成真正的套期保值交易的互换;或

"(ii) meets the requirements of subparagraph (A).".

(d) EFFECTIVE DATE. — This section and the amendments made by this section shall become effective on the date of the enactment of this section.

SEC.738. FOREIGN BOARDS OF TRADE.

(a) IN GENERAL. — Section 4(b) of the Commodity Exchange Act (7 U.S.C. 6(b)) is amended —

(1) in the first sentence, by striking "The Commission" and inserting the following:

"(2) PERSONS LOCATED IN THE UNITED STATES. —

"(A) IN GENERAL. — The Commission";

(2) in the second sentence, by striking "Such rules and regulations" and inserting the following:

"(B)DIFFERENT REQUIREMENTS. — Rules and regulations described in subparagraph (A)";

(3) in the third sentence —

(A) by striking "No rule or regulation" and inserting the following:

"(C) PROHIBITION. — Except as provided in paragraphs (1) and (2), no rule or regulation";

(B) by striking "that (1) requires" and inserting the following: "that —

"(i) requires"; and

(C) by striking "market, or (2) governs" and inserting the following: "market; or

"(ii) governs"; and

(4) by inserting before paragraph (2) (as designated by paragraph (1)) the following:

"(1) FOREIGN BOARDS OF TRADE. —

"(A) REGISTRATION. — The Commission may adopt rules and regulations requiring registration with the Commission for a foreign board of trade that provides the members of the foreign board of trade or other participants located in the United States with direct access to the electronic trading and order matching system of the foreign board of trade, including rules and regulations prescribing procedures and requirements applicable to the registration of such foreign boards of trade. For purposes of this paragraph, 'direct access' refers to an explicit grant of authority by a foreign board of trade to an identified member or other participant located in the United States to enter trades directly into the trade matching system of the foreign board of trade. In adopting such rules and regulations, the commission shall consider —

"(i) whether any such foreign board of trade is subject to comparable, comprehensive supervision and regulation by the appropriate governmental authorities in the foreign board of

(ii)符合第(A)子款规定的互换。”

(d)**生效日**。——本条及本条所做修正应于本条规定颁布之日起生效。

第738条 外国交易场所

(a)**一般规定**。——《商品交易法》第4(b)条[《美国法典》第七编第6(b)节]修正如下——

(1)在第一句中,删除“商品期货交易委员会”并替以:

“(2)**位于美国境内的人**。——

(A)**一般规定**。——商品期货交易委员会”;

(2)在第二句中,删除“该等规则和规章”并替以:

“(B)**差异化要求**。——第(A)子款所述规则与规章”;

(3)在第三句中——

(A)删除“任何规则或规章均不得”并替以:

“(C)**禁止性规定**。——除第(1)款和第(2)款规定的情形外,商品期货交易委员会不得根据本子条制定下列规则和规章”;

(B)删除“其(1)要求”并替以:“其——

(i)要求”;及

(C)删除“要求任何外国交易场所、交易所或市场或上述各者的结算所的任何合约、规则、规章或行动必须获得商品期货交易委员会批准,或(2)规范”并替以:“要求任何外国交易场所、交易所或市场或上述各者的结算所的任何合约、规则、规章或行动必须获得商品期货交易委员会批准;或

(ii)以任何方式规范”;及

(4)在第(2)款[以第(1)款进行的编号为准]前插入如下内容:

“(1)**外国交易场所**。——

(A)**注册**。——商品期货交易委员会可以制定规则和规章,在外国交易场所向其位于美国境内的会员或其他参与者提供其电子交易和指令匹配系统的直接接入的情形下,要求其在商品期货交易委员会进行注册,包括制定相关规则和规章对外国交易场所注册应适用的程序和要求作出规定。就本款而言,‘直接接入’一词系指外国交易场所明确授权其位于美国境内的具体会员或其他参与者直接进入该外国交易场所的交易匹配系统进行交易。制定该等规则和规章时,商品期货交易委员会应考虑——

(i)任何上述外国交易场所是否受到来自母国相应的政府机构的具有可比性且全面的监管与规制;及

trade's home country; and

"(ii) any previous commission findings that the foreign board of trade is subject to comparable comprehensive supervision and regulation by the appropriate government authorities in the foreign board of trade's home country.

"(B)LINKED CONTRACTS. — The Commission may not permit a foreign board of trade to provide to the members of the foreign board of trade or other participants located in the United States direct access to the electronic trading and order–matching system of the foreign board of trade with respect to an agreement, contract, or transaction that settles against any price (including the daily or final settlement price) of 1 or more contracts listed for trading on a registered entity, unless the Commission determines that —

"(i) the foreign board of trade makes public daily trading information regarding the agreement, contract, or transaction that is comparable to the daily trading information published by the registered entity for the 1 or more contracts against which the agreement, contract, or transaction traded on the foreign board of trade settles; and

"(ii) the foreign board of trade (or the foreign futures authority that oversees the foreign board of trade) —

"(I) adopts position limits (including related hedge exemption provisions) for the agreement, contract, or transaction that are comparable to the position limits (including related hedge exemption provisions) adopted by the registered entity for the 1 or more contracts against which the agreement, contract, or transaction traded on the foreign board of trade settles;

"(II) has the authority to require or direct market participants to limit, reduce, or liquidate any position the foreign board of trade (or the foreign futures authority that oversees the foreign board of trade) determines to be necessary to prevent or reduce the threat of price manipulation, excessive speculation as described in section 4a, price distortion, or disruption of delivery or the cash settlement process;

"(III) agrees to promptly notify the Commission, with regard to the agreement, contract, or transaction that settles against any price (including the daily or final settlement price) of 1 or more contracts listed for trading on a registered entity, of any change regarding —

"(aa) the information that the foreign board of trade will make publicly available;

"(bb) the position limits that the foreign board of trade or foreign futures authority will adopt and enforce;

"(cc) the position reductions required to prevent manipulation, excessive speculation as described in section 4a, price distortion, or disruption of delivery or the cash settlement process; and

"(dd) any other area of interest expressed by the Commission to the foreign board of trade or foreign futures authority;

(ii)商品期货交易委员会之前作出的确认该等外国交易场所受到来自其母国相应的政府机构的具有可比性且全面的监管与规制的任何认定。

(B)**有价格联系的合约**。——任何协议、合约或交易如依据在某一注册实体上市交易的一个或一个以上品种合约的任何价格(包括每日或最终结算价格)结算,则商品期货交易委员会不得允许外国交易场所就该等协议、合约或交易向其位于美国境内的会员或其他参与者提供其电子交易和指令匹配系统的直接接入,除非商品期货交易委员会判定——

(i)该外国交易场所就该等协议、合约或交易公布的每日交易信息,与该注册实体公布的、作为外国交易场所交易的该等协议、合约或交易结算依据的一个或一个以上品种合约的每日交易信息具有可比性;且

(ii)该外国交易场所(或负责监督该外国交易场所的外国期货监管机构)——

(I)对该等协议、合约或交易采用的持仓限额(包括相关套期保值豁免规定),与该注册实体对作为外国交易场所交易之协议、合约或交易结算依据的一个或一个以上品种合约所采用的持仓限额(包括相关套期保值豁免规定),二者具有可比性;

(II)有权力要求或引导市场参与者进行其判定确属必要的限仓、减仓或平仓,以防范或减低价格操纵威胁、第4a条所述过度投机威胁、价格扭曲威胁或者交割或现金结算过程受到扰乱的威胁;

(III)对于依据在某一注册实体上市交易的一个或一个以上品种合约的任何价格(包括每日或最终结算价格)进行结算的任何协议、合约或交易,同意将以下各项的任何变化及时通知商品期货交易委员会——

(aa)该外国交易场所将予公布的信息;

(bb)该外国交易场所或者外国期货监管机构将设定并执行的持仓限额;

(cc)为了防范价格操纵、第4a条所述过度投机、价格扭曲或者交割或现金结算过程受到扰乱而要求进行的减仓;及

(dd)商品期货交易委员会要求该外国交易场所或外国期货监管机构提供的任何其他领域的信息;

"(IV) provides information to the Commission regarding large trader positions in the agreement, contract, or transaction that is comparable to the large trader position information collected by the Commission for the 1 or more contracts against which the agreement, contract, or transaction traded on the foreign board of trade settles; and

"(V) provides the Commission such information as is necessary to publish reports on aggregate trader positions for the agreement, contract, or transaction traded on the foreign board of trade that are comparable to such reports on aggregate trader positions for the 1 or more contracts against which the agreement, contract, or transaction traded on the foreign board of trade settles.

"(C) EXISTING FOREIGN BOARDS OF TRADE. — Subparagraphs (A) and (B) shall not be effective with respect to any foreign board of trade to which, prior to the date of enactment of this paragraph, the Commission granted direct access permission until the date that is 180 days after that date of enactment.".

(b) LIABILITY OF REGISTERED PERSONS TRADING ON A FOREIGN BOARD OF TRADE. — Section 4 of the Commodity Exchange Act (7 U.S.C. 6) is amended —

(1) in subsection (a), in the matter preceding paragraph (1), by inserting "or by subsection (e)" after "Unless exempted by the Commission pursuant to subsection (c)"; and

(2) by adding at the end the following:

"(e) LIABILITY OF REGISTERED PERSONS TRADING ON A FOREIGN BOARD OF TRADE. —

"(1) IN GENERAL. — A person registered with the Commission, or exempt from registration by the Commission, under this Act may not be found to have violated subsection (a) with respect to a transaction in, or in connection with, a contract of sale of a commodity for future delivery if the person —

"(A) has reason to believe that the transaction and the contract is made on or subject to the rules of a foreign board of trade that is —

"(i) legally organized under the laws of a foreign country;

"(ii) authorized to act as a board of trade by a foreign futures authority; and

"(iii) subject to regulation by the foreign futures authority; and

"(B) has not been determined by the Commission to be operating in violation of subsection (a).

"(2) RULE OF CONSTRUCTION. — Nothing in this subsection shall be construed as implying or creating any presumption that a board of trade, exchange, or market is located outside the United States, or its territories or possessions, for purposes of subsection (a).".

(c) CONTRACT ENFORCEMENT FOR FOREIGN FUTURES CONTRACTS. — Section 22(a) of the Commodity Exchange Act (7 U.S.C. 25(a)) (as amended by section

(Ⅳ)向商品期货交易委员会提供协议、合约或交易的大户持仓信息,且该等信息应与商品期货交易委员会就该外国交易场所交易的协议、合约或交易结算所依据的一个或一个以上品种合约所收集的大户持仓信息具有可比性;及

(Ⅴ)向商品期货交易委员会提供必要信息,以便商品期货交易委员会能够就该外国交易场所交易之协议、合约或交易发布合并持仓报告,且该等报告应与该外国交易场所交易之协议、合约或交易的结算所依据的一个或一个以上品种合约的合并持仓报告具有可比性。

(C)**现有外国交易场所**。——在本款规定颁布日期之前商品期货交易委员会已授予直接接入许可的任何外国交易场所,不适用第(A)子款和第(B)子款的规定,直至本款规定颁布180天后才适用。"

(b)**在外国交易场所交易注册的主体的法律责任**。——《商品交易法》(《美国法典》第七编第6节)第4条修正如下——

(1)在第(a)子条中,在第(1)款之前的内容中,删除"除商品期货交易委员会依第(c)子条准予豁免的情况外",替以"除商品期货交易委员会依第(c)子条或第(e)子条予以豁免的情况外";及

(2)在结尾处增加如下内容:

"(e)**在外国交易场所交易注册的主体的法律责任**。——

(1)**一般规定**。——下列情形下,根据本法在商品期货交易委员会注册的或者被商品期货交易委员会豁免注册的主体不得被认定为违反了第(a)子条关于远期交割商品出售合约交易或相关交易的规定,即该主体——

(A)有理由认为交易及合约是在符合下述条件的外国交易场所或按其规则进行的——

(i)根据外国法律依法设立;

(ii)经外国期货监管机构核准作为交易场所开展运营;并

(iii)受外国期货监管机构监管;且

(B)未曾被商品期货交易委员会判定为违反第(a)子条的规定开展运营。

(2)**解释规则**。——就第(a)子条而言,本子条任何内容不得被解释为暗示或作出了以下任何推定:交易场所、交易所或市场位于美国、其准州或属地之外。"

(c)**外国期货合约的合约执行**。——在《商品交易法》第22(a)条[《美国法典》第七编第25(a)节](以经第739条修正后的版本为准)结尾处增加如下内容,作为对该条的

739) is amended by adding at the end the following:

"(6) CONTRACT ENFORCEMENT FOR FOREIGN FUTURES CONTRACTS. — A contract of sale of a commodity for future delivery traded or executed on or through the facilities of a board of trade, exchange, or market located outside the United States for purposes of section 4(a) shall not be void, voidable, or unenforceable, and a party to such a contract shall not be entitled to rescind or recover any payment made with respect to the contract, based on the failure of the foreign board of trade to comply with any provision of this Act.".

SEC.739. LEGAL CERTAINTY FOR SWAPS.

Section 22(a) of the Commodity Exchange Act (7 U.S.C. 25(a)) is amended by striking paragraph (4) and inserting the following:

"(4) CONTRACT ENFORCEMENT BETWEEN ELIGIBLE COUNTERPARTIES. —

"(A) IN GENERAL. — No hybrid instrument sold to any investor shall be void, voidable, or unenforceable, and no party to a hybrid instrument shall be entitled to rescind, or recover any payment made with respect to, the hybrid instrument under this section or any other provision of Federal or State law, based solely on the failure of the hybrid instrument to comply with the terms or conditions of section 2(f) or regulations of the Commission.

"(B) SWAPS. — No agreement, contract, or transaction between eligible contract participants or persons reasonably believed to be eligible contract participants shall be void, voidable, or unenforceable, and no party to such agreement, contract, or transaction shall be entitled to rescind, or recover any payment made with respect to, the agreement, contract, or transaction under this section or any other provision of Federal or State law, based solely on the failure of the agreement, contract, or transaction —

"(i) to meet the definition of a swap under section 1a; or

"(ii) to be cleared in accordance with section 2(h)(1).

"(5) LEGAL CERTAINTY FOR LONG-TERM SWAPS ENTERED INTO BEFORE THE DATE OF ENACTMENT OF THE WALL STREET TRANSPARENCY AND ACCOUNTABILITY ACT OF 2010. —

"(A) EFFECT ON SWAPS. — Unless specifically reserved in the applicable swap, neither the enactment of the Wall Street Transparency and Accountability Act of 2010, nor any requirement under that Act or an amendment made by that Act, shall constitute a termination event, force majeure, illegality, increased costs, regulatory change, or similar event under a swap (including any related credit support arrangement) that would permit a party to terminate, renegotiate, modify, amend, or supplement 1 or more transactions under the swap.

"(B) POSITION LIMITS. — Any position limit established under the Wall Street Transparency and Accountability Act of 2010 shall not apply to a position acquired in good

修正:

“(6)**外国期货合约的合约执行**。——就第4(a)条而言,在美国境外交易场所、交易所或市场的设施上或通过该等设施交易或执行的远期交割商品销售合约,不得因该外国交易场所不符合本法任何规定而归于无效、可撤销或不可执行,且合约方无权以此为由撤销或收回已就合约支付的任何款项。”

第739条 互换的法律确定性

《商品交易法》第22(a)条[《美国法典》第七编第25(a)节]修正如下:删除第(4)款,并替以如下内容:

“(4)**适格对手方之间的合约执行**。——

(A)**一般规定**。——卖给任何投资者的任何混合工具均不得仅因混合工具不符合第2(f)条或商品期货交易委员会规章的条款或条件而归于无效、可撤销或不可执行,且混合工具的当事方无权仅以此为由撤销或收回已根据本条或者联邦法律或州法律的任何其他规定就混合工具支付的款项。

(B)**互换**。——适格合约参与者或被合理认为具有适格合约参与者身份的人员之间的任何协议、合约或交易均不得仅因下述理由而归于无效、可撤销或不可执行,且该协议、合约或交易的当事方无权仅基于下述理由撤销或收回已根据本条或者联邦法律或州法律的任何其他规定就所述协议、合约或交易支付的款项——

(i)该协议、合约或交易不符合第1a条所述互换定义;或

(ii)该协议、合约或交易未按照第2(h)(1)条的规定进行集中结算。

(5)**《2010年华尔街透明度与问责法》颁布之日前达成的长期互换的法律确定性**。——

(A)**对互换的影响**。——除非适用的互换作出明确保留,否则《2010年华尔街透明度与问责法》及该法的任何要求或该法作出的任何修正之颁布均不构成互换(包括任何相关信用支持安排)的终止事件、不可抗力、非法情形、成本增加、监管变更或类似事件,且任何一方均无权据此终止互换项下的一项或多项交易或对之进行重新磋商、修改、修正或作出补充规定。

(B)**持仓限额**。——根据《2010年华尔街透明度与问责法》设定的任何持仓限额,均不得适用于依据设定该持仓的该法所制定的任何规则、规章或命令生效日之前善

faith prior to the effective date of any rule, regulation, or order under the Act that establishes the position limit; provided, however, that such positions shall be attributed to the trader if the trader's position is increased after the effective date of such position limit rule, regulation, or order.".

SEC.740. MULTILATERAL CLEARING ORGANIZATIONS.

Sections 408 and 409 of the Federal Deposit Insurance Corporation Improvement Act of 1991 (12 U.S.C. 4421, 4422) are repealed.

SEC.741. ENFORCEMENT.

(a) ENFORCEMENT AUTHORITY. — The Commodity Exchange Act is amended by inserting after section 4b (7 U.S.C. 6b) the following:

"SEC.4b-1. ENFORCEMENT AUTHORITY.

"(a) COMMODITY FUTURES TRADING COMMISSION. — Except as provided in subsections (b), (c), and (d), the Commission shall have exclusive authority to enforce the provisions of subtitle A of the Wall Street Transparency and Accountability Act of 2010 with respect to any person.

"(b) PRUDENTIAL REGULATORS. — The prudential regulators shall have exclusive authority to enforce the provisions of section 4s(e) with respect to swap dealers or major swap participants for which they are the prudential regulator.

"(c) REFERRALS. —

"(1) PRUDENTIAL REGULATORS. — If the prudential regulator for a swap dealer or major swap participant has cause to believe that the swap dealer or major swap participant, or any affiliate or division of the swap dealer or major swap participant, may have engaged in conduct that constitutes a violation of the nonprudential requirements of this Act (including section 4s or rules adopted by the Commission under that section), the prudential regulator may promptly notify the Commission in a written report that includes —

"(A) a request that the Commission initiate an enforcement proceeding under this Act; and

"(B) an explanation of the facts and circumstances that led to the preparation of the written report.

"(2) COMMISSION. — If the Commission has cause to believe that a swap dealer or major swap participant that has a prudential regulator may have engaged in conduct that constitutes a violation of any prudential requirement of section 4s or rules adopted by the Commission under that section, the Commission may notify the prudential regulator of the conduct in a written report that includes —

"(A) a request that the prudential regulator initiate an enforcement proceeding under this Act or any other Federal law (including regulations); and

"(B) an explanation of the concerns of the Commission, and a description of the facts

意获得的持仓;但是,如果交易商持仓在该持仓限额任何规则、规章或命令生效日之后增加,则该持仓应计入交易商的持仓。”

第740条 多边结算组织

《1991年联邦存款保险公司改良法》第408条和第409条(《美国法典》第十二编第4421节和第4422节)现予废止。

第741条 执法

(a)**执法权**。——在《商品交易法》第4b条(《美国法典》第七编第6b节)之后插入如下内容,作为对该法的修正:

“第4b-1条 执法权

(a)**商品期货交易委员会**。——除第(b)子条、第(c)子条和第(d)子条规定的情形外,商品期货交易委员会应对《2010年华尔街透明度与问责法》第A子编的规定享有排他执法权,有权对任何主体执行该等规定。

(b)**审慎监管者**。——审慎监管者应对第4s(e)条的规定享有排他执法权,有权对受其审慎监管的互换交易商或主要互换参与者执行该等规定。

(c)**移交**。——

(1)**审慎监管者**。——如果互换交易商或主要互换参与者的审慎监管者有理由相信,互换交易商或主要互换参与者(或者该互换交易商或主要互换参与者的任何关联方或其任何下属单位)可能作出了违反本法非审慎性要求(包括第4s条或商品期货交易委员会根据该条制定的规则)的行为,则该审慎监管者可以及时向商品期货交易委员会提交书面报告,通知以下内容——

(A)请求商品期货交易委员会根据本法规定启动执法程序;并

(B)对促使其编制该书面报告的事实和情况作出解释。

(2)**商品期货交易委员会**。——如果商品期货交易委员会有理由相信,受审慎监管者监管的互换交易商或主要互换参与者可能作出了违反第4s条任何审慎要求或商品期货交易委员会根据该条制定的规则的行为,则商品期货交易委员会可以向该审慎监管者提交书面报告,通知该等违法行为及以下内容——

(A)请求该审慎监管者根据本法或任何其他联邦法律(包括规章)启动执法程序;并

(B)解释其所关切的问题,对促使其编制该书面报告的事实和情况作出说明。

and circumstances, that led to the preparation of the written report.

"(d) BACKSTOP ENFORCEMENT AUTHORITY.—

"(1)INITIATION OF ENFORCEMENT PROCEEDING BY PRUDENTIAL REGULATOR. — If the Commission does not initiate an enforcement proceeding before the end of the 90–day period beginning on the date on which the Commission receives a written report under subsection (c)(1), the prudential regulator may initiate an enforcement proceeding.

"(2) INITIATION OF ENFORCEMENT PROCEEDING BY COMMISSION. — If the prudential regulator does not initiate an enforcement proceeding before the end of the 90–day period beginning on the date on which the prudential regulator receives a written report under subsection (c)(2), the Commission may initiate an enforcement proceeding.".

(b) CONFORMING AMENDMENTS.—

(1) Section 4b of the Commodity Exchange Act (7 U.S.C. 6b) is amended—

(A) in subsection (a)(2), by striking "or other agreement, contract, or transaction subject to paragraphs (1) and (2) of section 5a(g)," and inserting "or swap,";

(B) in subsection (b), by striking "or other agreement, contract or transaction subject to paragraphs (1) and (2) of section 5a(g)," and inserting "or swap,"; and

(C) by adding at the end the following:

"(e) It shall be unlawful for any person, directly or indirectly, by the use of any means or instrumentality of interstate commerce, or of the mails, or of any facility of any registered entity, in or in connection with any order to make, or the making of, any contract of sale of any commodity for future delivery (or option on such a contract), or any swap, on a group or index of securities (or any interest therein or based on the value thereof)—

"(1) to employ any device, scheme, or artifice to defraud;

"(2) to make any untrue statement of a material fact or to omit to state a material fact necessary in order to make the statements made, in the light of the circumstances under which they were made, not misleading; or

"(3) to engage in any act, practice, or course of business which operates or would operate as a fraud or deceit upon any person.".

(2) Section 4c (a) (1) of the Commodity Exchange Act (7 U.S.C. 6c (a) (1)) is amended by inserting "or swap" before "if the transaction is used or may be used".

(3) Section 6(c) of the Commodity Exchange Act (7 U.S.C. 9) is amended in the first

(d)**后备执法权**。——

(1)**由审慎监管者启动执法程序**。——如果商品期货交易委员会未在收到根据第(c)(1)子条提交的书面报告后90天期限届满前启动执法程序,则审慎监管者可以自行启动执法程序。

(2)**由商品期货交易委员会启动执法程序**。——如果审慎监管者未在收到根据第(c)(2)子条提交的书面报告后90天期限届满前启动执法程序,则商品期货交易委员会可以自行启动执法程序。"

(b)**一致性修正**。——

(1)《商品交易法》(《美国法典》第七编第6b节)第4b条修正如下——

(A)在第(a)(2)子条中,删除"受第5a(g)条第(1)款和第(2)款管辖的其他协议、合约或交易,"替以"或互换,";

(B)在第(b)子条中,删除"受第5a(g)条第(1)款和第(2)款管辖的任何其他协议、合约或交易,"替以"或互换,";及

(C)在结尾处增加如下内容:

"(e)任何人直接或间接利用任何州际商业手段或工具或者邮件或者任何注册实体的任何设施,针对订立某一证券集合或证券指数(或者该等证券的任何权益或该等集合或者指数的任何权益,或者基于该等证券价值的任何权益或者基于该等集合或指数价值的任何权益)之任何远期交割商品的任何出售合约(或该等合约的期权)的指令或订立某一证券集合或证券指数(或者该等证券的任何权益或该等集合或指数的任何权益,或者基于该等证券价值的任何权益或基于该等集合或指数价值的任何权益)之互换的指令,或针对该等合约或互换的订立,而作出以下行为或者就相关事宜作出以下行为的,当属违法——

(1)使用任何手段、计谋或诡计进行欺诈;

(2)为了使已作出的声明在原有情形下不致具有误导性,作出任何重大事实的不实陈述,或者遗漏必要的重大事实;或

(3)从事对任何其他人构成或将会构成欺诈或欺骗的任何行为、做法或业务运作。"

(2)《商品交易法》第4c(a)(1)条[《美国法典》第七编第6c(a)(1)节]修正如下:在"任何人出于下列目的或者可能出于下列目的而要约达成、达成或者确认执行涉及远期交割商品买卖的第(2)款所述交易(或者该等交易的任何期权或某商品的任何期权)"之后插入"或互换"

(3)《商品交易法》第6(c)条(《美国法典》第七编第9节)修正如下:在第一句"或按

sentence by inserting "or of any swap," before "or has willfully made".

(4) Section 6(d) of the Commodity Exchange Act (7 U.S.C. 13b) is amended in the first sentence, in the matter preceding the proviso, by inserting "or of any swap," before "or otherwise is violating".

(5) Section 6c(a) of the Commodity Exchange Act (7 U.S.C. 13a–1(a)) is amended in the matter preceding the proviso by inserting "or any swap" after "commodity for future delivery".

(6) Section 9 of the Commodity Exchange Act (7 U.S.C. 13) is amended—

(A) in subsection (a)—

(i) in paragraph (2), by inserting "or of any swap," before "or to corner"; and

(ii) in paragraph (4), by inserting "swap data repository," before "or futures association" and

(B) in subsection (e)(1)—

(i) by inserting "swap data repository," before "or registered futures association"; and

(ii) by inserting ", or swaps," before "on the basis".

(7) Section 9 (a) of the Commodity Exchange Act (7 U.S.C. 13 (a)) is amended by adding at the end the following:

"(6) Any person to abuse the end user clearing exemption under section 2(h)(4), as determined by the Commission.".

(8) Section 2(c)(2)(B) of the Commodity Exchange Act (7 U.S.C. 2(c)(2)(B)) is amended—

(A) by striking "(dd)," each place it appears;

(B) in clause (iii), by inserting ", and accounts or pooled investment vehicles described in clause (vi)," before "shall be subject to"; and

(C) by adding at the end the following:

"(vi) This Act applies to, and the Commission shall have jurisdiction over, an account or pooled investment vehicle that is offered for the purpose of trading, or that trades, any agreement, contract, or transaction in foreign currency described in clause (i).".

(9) Section 2(c)(2)(C) of the Commodity Exchange Act (7 U.S.C. 2(c)(2)(C)) is amended—

(A) by striking "(dd)," each place it appears;

(B) in clause (ii)(I), by inserting ", and accounts or pooled investment vehicles described in clause (vii)," before "shall be subject to"; and

(C) by adding at the end the following:

"(vii) This Act applies to, and the Commission shall have jurisdiction over, an account or pooled investment vehicle that is offered for the purpose of trading, or that trades, any agreement, contract, or transaction in foreign currency described in clause (i).".

其规则进行远期交割任何商品的价格”之后插入“,或任何互换”。

(4)《商品交易法》第6(d)条(《美国法典》第七编第13b节)修正如下:第一句但书之前的内容中,在“或以其他方式违反”之后插入“或任何互换”。

(5)《商品交易法》第6c(a)条[《美国法典》第七编第13a-1(a)节]修正如下:在但书之前的内容中,在“任何远期交割商品”之后插入“或互换”。

(6)《商品交易法》(《美国法典》第七编第13节)第9条修正如下——

(A)在第(a)子条中——

(i)第(2)款在“对任何该等商品囤积或试图囤积”前插入“或任何互换的价格;”;及

(ii)第(4)款在“或期货协会”前插入“、互换数据存管机构”;及

(B)在第(e)(1)子条中——

(i)在“或注册期货协会”前插入“、互换数据存管机构”;及

(ii)在“远期交割的合约的交易或该等合约的期权交易”之后插入“或者互换交易”。

(7)在《商品交易法》第9(a)条[《美国法典》第7编第13(a)节]结尾处增加如下内容,作为对该条的修正:

“(6)根据商品期货交易委员会的判定,任何人滥用第2(h)(4)条的终端用户集中结算豁免规定。”

(8)《商品交易法》第2(c)(2)(B)条[《美国法典》第七编第2(c)(2)(B)节]修正如下——

(A)删除所有“(dd)”字样;

(B)第(iii)项在“系由注册为期货经纪商或零售外汇交易商的主体所要约或达成”前插入“以及第(vi)项所述账户或集合投资载体,”;及

(C)在结尾处增加如下内容:

“(vi)为交易第(i)项所述任何外汇协议、合约或交易而要约的账户或集合投资载体,或者实际交易该等外汇协议、合约或交易的账户或集合投资载体,适用本法并应接受商品期货交易委员会的管辖。”

(9)《商品交易法》第2(c)(2)(C)条[《美国法典》第七编第2(c)(2)(C)节]修正如下——

(A)删除所有“(dd)”字样;

(B)第(ii)(I)项在“,应当受制于”之前插入“,以及第(vii)项所述账户或集合投资载体”;及

(C)在结尾处增加如下内容:

“(vii)为交易第(i)项所述任何外汇协议、合约或交易而要约的账户或集合投资载体,或者实际交易该等外汇协议、合约或交易的账户或集合投资载体,适用本法并接受商品期货交易委员会的管辖。”

(10) Section 1a(19)(A)(iv)(II) of the Commodity Exchange Act (7 U.S.C. 1a(19)(A)(iv)(II)) (as redesignated by section 721(a)(1)) is amended by inserting before the semicolon at the end the following: "provided, however, that for purposes of section 2(c)(2)(B)(vi) and section 2(c)(2)(C)(vii), the term 'eligible contract participant' shall not include a commodity pool in which any participant is not otherwise an eligible contract participant".

(11) Section 6(e) of the Commodity Exchange Act (7 U.S.C. 9a) is amended by adding at the end the following:

"(4) Any designated clearing organization that knowingly or recklessly evades or participates in or facilitates an evasion of the requirements of section 2(h) shall be liable for a civil money penalty in twice the amount otherwise available for a violation of section 2(h).

"(5) Any swap dealer or major swap participant that knowingly or recklessly evades or participates in or facilitates an evasion of the requirements of section 2(h) shall be liable for a civil money penalty in twice the amount otherwise available for a violation of section 2(h).".

(c) SAVINGS CLAUSE. — Notwithstanding any other provision of this title, nothing in this subtitle shall be construed as divesting any appropriate Federal banking agency of any authority it may have to establish or enforce, with respect to a person for which such agency is the appropriate Federal banking agency, prudential or other standards pursuant to authority granted by Federal law other than this title.

SEC.742. RETAIL COMMODITY TRANSACTIONS.

(a) IN GENERAL. — Section 2(c) of the Commodity Exchange Act (7 U.S.C. 2(c)) is amended —

(1) in paragraph (1), by striking "5a (to the extent provided in section 5a(g)), 5b, 5d, or 12(e)(2)(B))" and inserting ", 5b, or 12(e)(2)(B))"; and

(2) in paragraph (2), by adding at the end the following:

"(D) RETAIL COMMODITY TRANSACTIONS. —

"(i) APPLICABILITY. — Except as provided in clause (ii), this subparagraph shall apply to any agreement, contract, or transaction in any commodity that is —

"(I) entered into with, or offered to (even if not entered into with), a person that is not an eligible contract participant or eligible commercial entity; and

"(II) entered into, or offered (even if not entered into), on a leveraged or margined basis, or financed by the offeror, the counterparty, or a person acting in concert with the offeror or counterparty on a similar basis.

"(ii) EXCEPTIONS. — This subparagraph shall not apply to —

"(I)an agreement, contract, or transaction described in paragraph (1) or subparagraphs (A), (B), or (C), including any agreement, contract, or transaction specifically excluded from subparagraph (A), (B), or (C);

(10)在《商品交易法》第1a(19)(A)(iv)(II)条[《美国法典》第七编第1a(19)(A)(iv)(II)节][以第721(a)(1)条重新编号后的序号为准]在最后的分号前插入如下内容,作为对该条的修正:“但是,就第2(c)(2)(B)(vi)条和第2(c)(2)(C)(vii)条而言,如果商品基金的任何参与者由于其他原因而并非适格合约参与者,则‘适格合约参与者’一词的定义不得包括该等商品基金。”

(11)在《商品交易法》第6(e)条(《美国法典》第七编第9a节)结尾处增加如下内容,作为对该条的修正:

“(4)任何指定结算组织如因故意或漠视而造成规避第2(h)条的要求、参与他人规避该等要求的行为或为他人规避该等要求提供便利,均应按违反第2(h)条时应付之罚款的两倍金额缴纳民事罚款。

(5)任何互换交易商或主要互换参与者如因故意或漠视而造成规避第2(h)条的要求、参与他人规避该等要求的行为或为他人规避该等要求提供便利,均应按违反第2(h)条时应纳之罚款的两倍金额缴纳民事罚款。”

(c)**保留条款**。——无论本编是否存在任何不同规定,如任何相应的联邦银行业监管机关根据本编之外的联邦法律规定的授权,可以对受其相应的联邦银行业监管的主体制定或执行审慎性标准或其他标准,则本子编的任何规定均不得被解释为解除该等监管机关所享有的上述权力。

第742条　零售商品交易

(a)**一般规定**。——《商品交易法》第2(c)条[《美国法典》第7编第2(c)节]修正如下——

(1)在第(1)款中,删除“但第5a条[涉及第5a(g)条规定内容的]、第5b条、第5d条或第12(e)(2)(B)条例外]”,替以“但第5b条或第12(e)(2)(B)条例外”;及

(2)在第(2)款结尾处增加如下内容:

“(D)**零售商品交易**。——

(i)**适用范围**。——除第(ii)项规定的情形外,本子款应适用于具有以下特征的任何商品协议、合约或交易——

(I)相对立约人或受要约人(即使结果并未达成协议、合约或交易)并非适格合约参与者,也非适格商业实体;且

(II)由要约人、对手方或与要约人或对手方以类似方式一致行动的人,通过杠杆或保证金方式达成或要约(即使结果并未达成协议、合约或交易),或者由上述各者提供融资。

(ii)**例外规定**。——本子款不适用于——

(I)第(1)款或第(A)子款、第(B)子款或第(C)子款所述协议、合约或交易,包括第(A)子款、第(B)子款或第(C)子款明确排除的任何协议、合约或交易;

"(II) any security;

"(III) a contract of sale that —

"(aa) results in actual delivery within 28 days or such other longer period as the Commission may determine by rule or regulation based upon the typical commercial practice in cash or spot markets for the commodity involved; or

"(bb) creates an enforceable obligation to deliver between a seller and a buyer that have the ability to deliver and accept delivery, respectively, in connection with the line of business of the seller and buyer; or

"(IV) an agreement, contract, or transaction that is listed on a national securities exchange registered under section 6(a) of the Securities Exchange Act of 1934 (15 U.S.C. 78f(a)); or

"(V) an identified banking product, as defined in section 402(b) of the Legal Certainty for Bank Products Act of 2000 (7 U.S.C.27(b)).

"(iii) ENFORCEMENT. — Sections 4(a), 4(b), and 4b apply to any agreement, contract, or transaction described in clause (i), as if the agreement, contract, or transaction was a contract of sale of a commodity for future delivery.

"(iv) ELIGIBLE COMMERCIAL ENTITY. — For purposes of this subparagraph, an agricultural producer, packer, or handler shall be considered to be an eligible commercial entity for any agreement, contract, or transaction for a commodity in connection with the line of business of the agricultural producer, packer, or handler.".

(b) GRAMM-LEACH-BLILEY ACT. — Section 206 (a) of the Gramm-Leach-Bliley Act (Public Law 106-102; 15 U.S.C. 78c note) is amended, in the matter preceding paragraph (1), by striking "For purposes of" and inserting "Except as provided in subsection (e), for purposes of".

(c) CONFORMING AMENDMENTS RELATING TO RETAIL FOREIGN EXCHANGE TRANSACTIONS. —

(1) Section 2(c)(2)(B)(i)(II) of the Commodity Exchange Act (7 U.S.C. 2(c)(2)(B)(i)(II)) is amended —

(A) in item (aa), by inserting "United States" before "financial institution";

(B) by striking items (dd) and (ff);

(C) by redesignating items (ee) and (gg) as items (dd) and (ff), respectively; and

(D) in item (dd) (as so redesignated), by striking the semicolon and inserting "; or".

(2) Section 2(c)(2) of the Commodity Exchange Act (7 U.S.C. 2(c)(2)) (as amended by subsection (a)(2)) is amended by adding at the end the following:

"(E) PROHIBITION. —

"(i) DEFINITION OF FEDERAL REGULATORY AGENCY. — In this subparagraph, the term 'Federal regulatory agency' means —

(II)任何证券;

(III)符合以下条件的出售合约——

(aa)在28天内进行实际交割,或者在商品期货交易委员会基于所涉商品的现货或即期市场的典型商业实践而通过规则或规章确定的其他更长时限内进行实际交割;或

(bb)在有能力在其业务范围内进行交割的卖方与有能力在其业务范围内接受交割的买方之间,创设了可强制执行的交割义务;或

(IV)在根据《1934年证券交易法》第6(a)条[《美国法典》第十五编第78f(a)节]注册的全国性证券交易所上市的协议、合约或交易;或

(V)《2000年银行产品法律确定性法》[《美国法典》第七编第27(b)节]第402(b)条所定义的确定的银行产品。

(iii)**执行**。——第4(a)条、第4(b)条及第4b条适用于第(i)项所述任何协议、合约或交易,如同该等协议、合约或交易属于远期交割商品出售合约。

(iv)**适格商业实体**。——就本子款而言,农产品生产商、包装商或装卸商应被视为其业务范围内商品的任何协议、合约或交易的适格商业实体。"

(b)**《格雷姆—里奇—比利雷法》**。——在《格雷姆—里奇—比利雷法》(第106—102号公法;《美国法典》第十五编第78c节注释)第206(a)条修正如下:第(1)款之前的内容中,在"就……而言"前插入"除第(e)子条规定的情形外,"。

(c)**关于零售外汇交易的一致性修正**。——

(1)《商品交易法》第2(c)(2)(B)(i)(II)条[《美国法典》第七编第2(c)(2)(B)(i)(II)节]修正如下——

(A)在第(aa)目中,在"金融机构"前插入"美国";

(B)删除第(dd)目和第(ff)目;

(C)第(ee)目和第(gg)目分别重新编号为第(dd)目和第(ff)目;及

(D)在第(dd)目中(以重新编号后的序号为准),删除分号,替以";或"。

(2)在《商品交易法》第2(c)(2)条[《美国法典》第七编第2(c)(2)节][以经第(a)(2)子条修正后的版本为准]结尾处增加如下内容,作为对该条的修正:

"(E)**禁止性规定**。——

(i)**联邦监管机关的定义**。——在本子款中,联'邦监管机关'一词系指——

"(Ⅰ) the Commission;

"(Ⅱ) the Securities and Exchange Commission;

"(Ⅲ) an appropriate Federal banking agency;

"(Ⅳ) the National Credit Union Association; and

"(Ⅴ) the Farm Credit Administration.

"(ii) PROHIBITION. —

"(Ⅰ) IN GENERAL. — Except as provided in subclause (Ⅱ), a person described in subparagraph (B)(i)(Ⅱ) for which there is a Federal regulatory agency shall not offer to, or enter into with, a person that is not an eligible contract participant, any agreement, contract, or transaction in foreign currency described in subparagraph (B)(i)(Ⅰ) except pursuant to a rule or regulation of a Federal regulatory agency allowing the agreement, contract, or transaction under such terms and conditions as the Federal regulatory agency shall prescribe.

"(Ⅱ) EFFECTIVE DATE. — With regard to persons described in subparagraph (B)(i)(Ⅱ) for which a Federal regulatory agency has issued a proposed rule concerning agreements, contracts, or transactions in foreign currency described in subparagraph (B)(i)(Ⅰ) prior to the date of enactment of this subclause, subclause (Ⅰ) shall take effect 90 days after the date of enactment of this subclause.

"(iii) REQUIREMENTS OF RULES AND REGULATIONS. —

"(Ⅰ) IN GENERAL. — The rules and regulations described in clause (ii) shall prescribe appropriate requirements with respect to —

"(aa) disclosure;

"(bb) recordkeeping;

"(cc) capital and margin;

"(dd) reporting;

"(ee) business conduct;

"(ff) documentation; and

"(gg) such other standards or require ments as the Federal regulatory agency shall determine to be necessary.

"(Ⅱ) TREATMENT. — The rules or regulations described in clause (ii) shall treat all agreements, contracts, and transactions in foreign currency described in subparagraph (B)(i)(Ⅰ), and all agreements, contracts, and transactions in foreign currency that are functionally or economically similar to agreements, contracts, or transactions described in subparagraph (B)(i)(Ⅰ), similarly.".

SEC.743. OTHER AUTHORITY.

Unless otherwise provided by the amendments made by this subtitle, the amendments made by this subtitle do not divest any appropriate Federal banking agency, the Commodity Futures Trading Commission, the Securities and Exchange Commission, or other Federal or

(I)商品期货交易委员会;

(II)证券交易委员会;

(III)相应的联邦银行业监管机关;

(IV)全美信贷联盟协会;及

(V)农业信贷管理局。

(ii)**禁止性规定**。——

(I)**一般规定**。——除第(II)子项规定的情形外,第(B)(i)(II)子款所述受联邦监管机关监管之主体不得向非适格合约参与者要约或与其达成第(B)(i)(I)子款所述任何外汇协议、合约或交易,除非为联邦监管机关的规则或规章所允许,并且符合联邦监管机关规定的条款和条件。

(II)**生效日**。——如果在本子项颁布之前,联邦监管机关已就第(B)(i)(I)子款所述任何外汇协议、合约或交易针对第(B)(i)(II)子款所述之主体发布规则草案,则第(I)子项的规定应于本子项颁布之日后第90天生效。

(iii)**规则及规章要求**。——

(I)**一般规定**。——第(ii)项所述规则与规章应对以下各项作出适当的要求——

(aa)披露;

(bb)记录保存;

(cc)资本和保证金;

(dd)报告;

(ee)业务行为;

(ff)文件记录;及

(gg)联邦监管机关确定的其他必要标准或要求。

(II)**处理**。——对于第(B)(i)(I)子款所述的所有外汇协议、合约及交易,以及与第(B)(i)(I)子款所述协议、合约或交易在功能上或经济上类似的所有外汇协议、合约及交易,第(ii)项所述规则或规章应予以类似处理。”

第743条　其他权力

除非本子编所做修正另有规定,否则,本子编所做修正不解除任何相应的联邦银行业监管机关、商品期货交易委员会、证券交易委员会或其他联邦机关或州机关根据任何其他适用的法律所享有的任何权力。

State agency of any authority derived from any other applicable law.

SEC.744. RESTITUTION REMEDIES.

Section 6c (d) of the Commodity Exchange Act (7 U.S.C. 13a–1 (d)) is amended by adding at the end the following:

"(3) EQUITABLE REMEDIES. — In any action brought under this section, the Commission may seek, and the court may impose, on a proper showing, on any person found in the action to have committed any violation, equitable remedies including —

"(A) restitution to persons who have sustained losses proximately caused by such violation (in the amount of such losses); and

"(B) disgorgement of gains received in connection with such violation.".

SEC.745. ENHANCED COMPLIANCE BY REGISTERED ENTITIES.

(a) EFFECT OF INTERPRETATION. — Section 5c(a) of the Commodity Exchange Act (7 U.S.C. 7a–2(a)) is amended by striking paragraph (2) and inserting the following:

"(2) EFFECT OF INTERPRETATION. — An interpretation issued under paragraph (1) may provide the exclusive means for complying with each section described in paragraph (1).".

(b) NEW CONTRACTS, NEW RULES, AND RULE AMENDMENTS. —

Section 5c of the Commodity Exchange Act (7 U.S.C. 7a–2) is amended by striking subsection (c) and inserting the following:

"(c) NEW CONTRACTS, NEW RULES, AND RULE AMENDMENTS. —

"(1) IN GENERAL. — A registered entity may elect to list for trading or accept for clearing any new contract, or other instrument, or may elect to approve and implement any new rule or rule amendment, by providing to the Commission (and the Secretary of the Treasury, in the case of a contract of sale of a government security for future delivery (or option on such a contract) or a rule or rule amendment specifically related to such a contract) a written certification that the new contract or instrument or clearing of the new contract or instrument, new rule, or rule amendment complies with this Act (including regulations under this Act).

"(2) RULE REVIEW. — The new rule or rule amendment described in paragraph (1) shall become effective, pursuant to the certification of the registered entity and notice of such certification to its members (in a manner to be determined by the Commission), on the date that is 10 business days after the date on which the Commission receives the certification (or such shorter period as determined by the Commission by rule or regulation) unless the Commission notifies the registered entity within such time that it is staying the certification because there exist novel or complex issues that require additional time to analyze, an inadequate explanation by the submitting registered entity, or a potential inconsistency with this Act (including regulations under this Act).

第744条　恢复原状救济

在《商品交易法》第6c(d)条[《美国法典》第七编第13a-1(d)节]结尾处增加如下内容,作为对该条的修正:

"(3)**衡平救济**。——针对在根据本条提起的任何诉讼中被认定从事了违法违规行为的任何人,商品期货交易委员会可以寻求如下衡平救济,并且,在有适当证明的情况下,法院可给予如下衡平救济——

(A)对于因该违法违规行为直接遭受损失之人返还不当得利款项(以该等损失金额为准);及

(B)没收因该违法违规行为而获得的非法所得。"

第745条　加强注册实体合规

(a)**解释的效力**。——删除《商品交易法》第5c(a)条[《美国法典》第七编第7a-2(a)节]第(2)款,并替以如下内容,作为对该条的修正:

"(2)**解释的效力**。——根据第(1)款发布的解释可以规定遵守第(1)款所述每一条款的唯一方式。"

(b)**新合约、新规则及规则修正**。——

删除《商品交易法》第5c条(《美国法典》第七编第7a-2节)第(c)子条,并替以如下内容,作为对该条的修正:

"(c)**新合约、新规则及规则修正**。——

(1)**一般规定**。——注册实体可选择上市交易任何新合约品种或其他工具,或受理其结算,也可选择批准和执行任何新规则或规则修正。在作出该等选择时,应向商品期货交易委员会提供一份关于新合约品种或工具、新合约品种或工具的结算或者新规则或规则修正符合本法(包括依据本法发布的规章)的规定的书面自查证明,涉及远期交割的政府证券出售合约(或该等合约的期权)的,或者涉及该等合约专门的规则或规则修正的,该等书面自查证明还应提供给财政部部长。

(2)**规则审查**。——第(1)款所述新规则或规则修正应根据注册实体的自查证明以及注册实体就该等证明向其会员发出的通知中的规定生效(通知应以商品期货交易委员会确定的方式发出),生效时间为商品期货交易委员会收到该等证明之日后第10个营业日(或商品期货交易委员会发布的规则或规章所确定的较早时间),除非商品期货交易委员会在前述期间内通知注册实体,说明由于以下原因商品期货交易委员会决定中止该自查证明:存在无先例可循的或复杂的事项,其需要更长的分析时间;注册实体提交的解释欠充分;或者可能存在不符合本法(包括依据本法发布的规章)的情形。

"(3) STAY OF CERTIFICATION FOR RULES.—

"(A) A notification by the Commission pursuant to paragraph (2) shall stay the certification of the new rule or rule amendment for up to an additional 90 days from the date of the notification.

"(B) A rule or rule amendment subject to a stay pursuant to subparagraph (A) shall become effective, pursuant to the certification of the registered entity, at the expiration of the period described in subparagraph (A) unless the Commission—

"(i) withdraws the stay prior to that time; or

"(ii) notifies the registered entity during such period that it objects to the proposed certification on the grounds that it is inconsistent with this Act (including regulations under this Act).

"(C) The Commission shall provide a not less than 30–day public comment period, within the 90–day period in which the stay is in effect as described in subparagraph (A), whenever the Commission reviews a rule or rule amendment pursuant to a notification by the Commission under this paragraph.

"(4) PRIOR APPROVAL.—

"(A) IN GENERAL.—A registered entity may request that the Commission grant prior approval to any new contract or other instrument, new rule, or rule amendment.

"(B) PRIOR APPROVAL REQUIRED.—Notwithstanding any other provision of this section, a designated contract market shall submit to the Commission for prior approval each rule amendment that materially changes the terms and conditions, as determined by the Commission, in any contract of sale for future delivery of a commodity specifically enumerated in section 1a(10) (or any option thereon) traded through its facilities if the rule amendment applies to contracts and delivery months which have already been listed for trading and have open interest.

"(C) DEADLINE.—If prior approval is requested under subparagraph (A), the Commission shall take final action on the request not later than 90 days after submission of the request, unless the person submitting the request agrees to an extension of the time limitation established under this subparagraph.

"(5) APPROVAL.—

"(A) RULES.—The Commission shall approve a new rule, or rule amendment, of a registered entity unless the Commission finds that the new rule, or rule amendment, is inconsistent with this subtitle (including regulations).

"(B) CONTRACTS AND INSTRUMENTS.—The Commission shall approve a new contract or other instrument unless the Commission finds that the new contract or other instrument would violate this Act (including regulations).

"(C) SPECIAL RULE FOR REVIEW AND APPROVAL OF EVENT CONTRACTS

(3)**规则自查证明的中止**。——

(A)商品期货交易委员会根据第(2)款发出通知中止该等新规则或规则修正的自查证明的,中止期间最长不超过90天(自通知日起算)。

(B)按照第(A)子款被中止的规则或规则修正,应根据注册实体的自查证明于第(A)子款所述期间届满之时生效,除非商品期货交易委员会——

(i)在届满日期之前撤销该中止;或

(ii)在该等期间内通知注册实体其提出的自查证明不符合本法(包括依据本法发布的规章)规定,因此予以拒绝。

(C)商品期货交易委员会根据其依本款发出的通知对规则或规则修正进行审查时,应在第(A)子款所述90天的中止有效期内提供至少30天的公众意见征求期。

(4)**事先批准**。——

(A)**一般规定**。——注册实体可以请求商品期货交易委员会对任何新合约或其他工具、新规则或规则修正授予事先批准。

(B)**事先批准要求**。——无论本条是否存在任何不同规定,如果商品期货交易委员会判定,规则修正实质性地变更了通过指定合约市场设施交易的第1a(10)条具体列明的某一商品的远期交割出售合约(或该商品的期权)的条款和条件,并且,如果规则修正内容适用于已经上市交易且尚有未平仓量的合约和交割月,则该指定合约市场应将该等每项修正的内容提交给商品期货交易委员会,以征得其事先批准。

(C)**最后期限**。——按照第(A)子款提出事先批准请求的,商品期货交易委员会应在请求提交后90天内采取最终行动,除非提交请求的人同意延长本子款规定的期限。

(5)**批准**。——

(A)**规则**。——除非商品期货交易委员会认定注册实体的新规则或规则修正违反本子编(包括规章)的规定,否则商品期货交易委员会应批准该等新规则或规则修正。

(B)**合约及工具**。——除非商品期货交易委员会认定新合约或其他工具将会违反本法(包括规章),否则商品期货交易委员会应批准该等新合约或工具。

(C)**事件合约及互换合约的特别审批规则**。——

AND SWAPS CONTRACTS. —

"(i) EVENT CONTRACTS. — In connection with the listing of agreements, contracts, transactions, or swaps in excluded commodities that are based upon the occurrence, extent of an occurrence, or contingency (other than a change in the price, rate, value, or levels of a commodity described in section 1a (2) (i)), by a designated contract market or swap execution facility, the Commission may determine that such agreements, contracts, or transactions are contrary to the public interest if the agreements, contracts, or transactions involve —

"(I) activity that is unlawful under any Federal or State law;

"(II) terrorism;

"(III) assassination;

"(IV) war;

"(V) gaming; or

"(VI) other similar activity determined by the Commission, by rule or regulation, to be contrary to the public interest.

"(ii) PROHIBITION. — No agreement, contract, or transaction determined by the Commission to be contrary to the public interest under clause (i) may be listed or made available for clearing or trading on or through a registered entity.

"(iii) SWAPS CONTRACTS. —

"(I) IN GENERAL. — In connection with the listing of a swap for clearing by a derivatives clearing organization, the Commission shall determine, upon request or on its own motion, the initial eligibility, or the continuing qualification, of a derivatives clearing organization to clear such a swap under those criteria, conditions, or rules that the Commission, in its discretion, determines.

"(II) REQUIREMENTS. — Any such criteria, conditions, or rules shall consider —

"(aa) the financial integrity of the derivatives clearing organization; and

"(bb) any other factors which the Commission determines may be appropriate.

"(iv) DEADLINE. — The Commission shall take final action under clauses (i) and (ii) in not later than 90 days from the commencement of its review unless the party seeking to offer the contract or swap agrees to an extension of this time limitation.".

(c) VIOLATION OF CORE PRINCIPLES. — Section 5c of the Commodity Exchange Act (7 U.S.C. 7a–2) is amended by striking subsection (d).

SEC.746. INSIDER TRADING.

Section 4c(a) of the Commodity Exchange Act (7 U.S.C. 6c(a)) is amended by adding at the end the following:

"(3) CONTRACT OF SALE. — It shall be unlawful for any employee or agent of any department or agency of the Federal Government who, by virtue of the employment or position

(i)**事件合约**。——对于由指定合约市场或互换执行设施上市的关于除外商品的协议、合约、交易或互换而言,如该等协议、合约、交易或互换系基于某一事件的发生、某一事件发生的范围或程度或者或有事件发生的可能性[基于第1a(2)(i)条所述商品价格、费率、价值或水平变化的除外],且涉及以下内容,则商品期货交易委员会可以判定该等协议、合约或交易有悖公共利益——

(I)任何联邦法律或州法律规定的非法活动;

(II)恐怖活动;

(III)暗杀;

(IV)战争;

(V)博彩;或

(VI)商品期货交易委员会发布的规则或规章所确定的有悖公共利益的其他类似活动。

(ii)**禁止性规定**。——商品期货交易委员会根据第(i)项规定判定的有悖公共利益的协议、合约或交易,不得在注册实体或通过注册实体挂牌结算或上市交易。

(iii)**互换合约**。——

(I)**一般规定**。——对于衍生品结算组织挂牌结算的互换而言,商品期货交易委员会应根据其依自由裁量权确定的标准、条件或规则,就提供互换结算服务的衍生品结算组织的初始适格性或持续合格性,应衍生品结算组织提出的要求作出判定或依其自由裁量权作出判定。

(II)**要求**。——任何该等标准、条件或规则均应考虑——

(aa)衍生品结算组织的财务完整性;及

(bb)商品期货交易委员会判定确属适当的任何其他因素。

(iv)**最后期限**。——除非有意对相关合约或互换进行要约的当事人同意延长期限,否则商品期货交易委员会应在审查开始后90天内,根据第(i)项和第(ii)项规定采取最终行动。”

(c)**核心原则之违反**。——删除《商品交易法》第5c条(《美国法典》第七编第7a-2节)第(d)子条,作为对该条的修正。

第746条　内幕交易

在《商品交易法》第4c(a)条[《美国法典》第七编第6c(a)节]结尾处增加如下内容,作为对该条的修正:

“(3)**出售合约**。——如果联邦政府任何部门或机关的任何雇员或代理人利用其雇佣关系或雇员或代理人职务获取可能影响或易于影响州际商业中的任何商品价

of the employee or agent, acquires information that may affect or tend to affect the price of any commodity in interstate commerce, or for future delivery, or any swap, and which information has not been disseminated by the department or agency of the Federal Government holding or creating the information in a manner which makes it generally available to the trading public, or disclosed in a criminal, civil, or administrative hearing, or in a congressional, administrative, or Government Accountability Office report, hearing, audit, or investigation, to use the information in his personal capacity and for personal gain to enter into, or offer to enter into —

"(A) a contract of sale of a commodity for future delivery (or option on such a contract);

"(B) an option (other than an option executed or traded on a national securities exchange registered pursuant to section 6(a) of the Securities Exchange Act of 1934 (15 U.S.C. 78f(a)); or

"(C) a swap.

"(4) NONPUBLIC INFORMATION. —

"(A) IMPARTING OF NONPUBLIC INFORMATION. — It shall be unlawful for any employee or agent of any department or agency of the Federal Government who, by virtue of the employment or position of the employee or agent, acquires information that may affect or tend to affect the price of any commodity in interstate commerce, or for future delivery, or any swap, and which information has not been disseminated by the department or agency of the Federal Government holding or creating the information in a manner which makes it generally available to the trading public, or disclosed in a criminal, civil, or administrative hearing, or in a congressional, administrative, or Government Accountability Office report, hearing, audit, or investigation, to impart the information in his personal capacity and for personal gain with intent to assist another person, directly or indirectly, to use the information to enter into, or offer to enter into —

"(i) a contract of sale of a commodity for future delivery (or option on such a contract);

"(ii) an option (other than an option executed or traded on a national securities exchange registered pursuant to section 6(a) of the Securities Exchange Act of 1934 (15 U.S.C. 78f(a)); or

"(iii) a swap.

"(B) KNOWING USE. — It shall be unlawful for any person who receives information imparted by any employee or agent of any department or agency of the Federal Government as described in subparagraph (A) to knowingly use such information to enter into, or offer to enter into —

"(i) a contract of sale of a commodity for future delivery (or option on such a contract);

"(ii) an option (other than an option executed or traded on a national securities exchange registered pursuant to section 6(a) of the Securities Exchange Act of 1934 (15 U.S.

格、远期交割的任何商品价格或任何互换价格的信息,而掌握或生成该等信息的联邦政府部门或机关尚未以可以使交易公众普遍知晓的方式发布该等信息,且该等信息未在刑事、民事听审或行政听证中披露,亦未在国会、行政部门或政府问责办公室主持开展的报告、听证、审计或调查程序中披露,则上述人员以其个人身份并以个人牟利为目的利用上述信息达成或要约达成下列合约的行为,当属违法——

(A)远期交割商品出售合约(或该等合约的期权);

(B)期权{但在根据《1934年证券交易法》第6(a)条[《美国法典》第十五编第78f(a)节]注册的全国性证券交易所执行或交易的期权除外};或

(C)互换。

(4)**非公开信息**。——

(A)**非公开信息的泄露**。——如果联邦政府任何部门或机关的任何雇员或代理人利用其雇佣关系或雇员或代理人职务获取可能影响或易于影响州际商业中的任何商品价格、远期交割的任何商品价格或任何互换价格的信息,而掌握或生成该等信息的联邦政府部门或机关尚未以可以使交易公众普遍知晓的方式发布该等信息,且该等信息未在刑事、民事听审或行政听证中披露,亦未在国会、行政部门或政府问责办公室主持开展的报告、听证、审计或调查程序中披露,则上述人员为了直接或间接协助他人利用上述信息以达成或要约达成下列合约的意图而以其个人身份并以个人牟利为目的泄露上述信息的行为,当属违法——

(i)远期交割商品出售合约(或该等合约的期权);

(ii)期权(但在根据《1934年证券交易法》第6(a)条[《美国法典》第十五编第78f(a)节]注册的全国性证券交易所执行或交易的期权除外);或

(iii)互换。

(B)**知情利用**。——如果任何人收到第(A)子款所述的联邦政府任何部门或机关的任何雇员或代理人泄露的信息,则上述人员在知情情况下利用上述信息以达成或要约达成下列合约的行为,当属违法——

(i)远期交割商品出售合约(或该等合约的期权);

(ii)期权{但在根据《1934年证券交易法》第6(a)条[《美国法典》第十五编第78f(a)节]注册的全国性证券交易所执行或交易的期权除外};或

C. 78f(a)); or

"(iii) a swap.

"(C) THEFT OF NONPUBLIC INFORMATION. — It shall be unlawful for any person to steal, convert, or misappropriate, by any means whatsoever, information held or created by any department or agency of the Federal Government that may affect or tend to affect the price of any commodity in interstate commerce, or for future delivery, or any swap, where such person knows, or acts in reckless disregard of the fact, that such information has not been disseminated by the department or agency of the Federal Government holding or creating the information in a manner which makes it generally available to the trading public, or disclosed in a criminal, civil, or administrative hearing, or in a congressional, administrative, or Government Accountability Office report, hearing, audit, or investigation, and to use such information, or to impart such information with the intent to assist another person, directly or indirectly, to use such information to enter into, or offer to enter into —

"(i) a contract of sale of a commodity for future delivery (or option on such a contract);

"(ii)an option (other than an option executed or traded on a national securities exchange registered pursuant to section 6(a) of the Securities Exchange Act of 1934 (15 U.S. C. 78f(a)); or

"(iii) a swap, provided, however, that nothing in this subparagraph shall preclude a person that has provided information concerning, or generated by, the person, its operations or activities, to any employee or agent of any department or agency of the Federal Government, voluntarily or as required by law, from using such information to enter into, or offer to enter into, a contract of sale, option, or swap described in clauses (i), (ii), or (iii).".

SEC.747. ANTIDISRUPTIVE PRACTICES AUTHORITY.

Section 4c (a) of the Commodity Exchange Act (7 U.S.C. 6c (a)) (as amended by section 746) is amended by adding at the end the following:

"(5) DISRUPTIVE PRACTICES. — It shall be unlawful for any person to engage in any trading, practice, or conduct on or subject to the rules of a registered entity that —

"(A) violates bids or offers;

"(B)demonstrates intentional or reckless disregard for the orderly execution of transactions during the closing period; or

"(C) is, is of the character of, or is commonly known to the trade as, 'spoofing' (bidding or offering with the intent to cancel the bid or offer before execution).

"(6) RULEMAKING AUTHORITY. — The Commission may make and promulgate such rules and regulations as, in the judgment of the Commission, are reasonably necessary to prohibit the trading practices described in paragraph (5) and any other trading practice that is disruptive of fair and equitable trading.

(iii)互换。

(C)**盗用非公开信息**。——对于联邦政府任何部门或机关掌握或生成的可能影响或易于影响州际商业中的任何商品价格、远期交割的任何商品价格或任何互换价格的信息,如果任何人明知或漠视上述联邦政府部门或机关尚未以可以使交易公众普遍知晓的方式发布该等信息,且该等信息未在刑事、民事听审或行政听证中披露,亦未在国会、行政部门或政府问责办公室主持开展的报告、听证、审计或调查程序中披露,则上述人员以任何方式盗用、侵占或滥用上述信息,并利用该等信息达成或要约达成下列合约的行为,或向他人泄露该等信息,意图直接或间接协助他人利用该等信息达成或要约达成下列合约的行为,当属违法——

(i)远期交割商品出售合约(或该等合约的期权);

(ii)期权{但在根据《1934年证券交易法》第6(a)条[《美国法典》第十五编第78f(a)节]注册的全国性证券交易所执行或交易的期权除外};或

(iii)互换,但是,某人已经自愿或者按照法律规定,向联邦政府任何部门或机关的任何雇员或代理人提供关于其自身或其经营、活动的信息或者其自身或其经营、活动所生成的信息的,本子款任何规定均不禁止该人利用上述信息达成或要约达成第(i)项、第(ii)项或第(iii)项所述的出售合约、期权或互换。”

第747条 打击扰乱性做法的权力

《商品交易法》第4c(a)条[《美国法典》第七编第6c(a)节](以经第746条修正后的版本为准)结尾处增加如下内容,作为对该条的修正:

“(5)**扰乱性做法**。——任何人在注册实体或按其规则从事下列任何交易、做法或行为的,当属违法——

(A)违反买入报价或卖出报价的交易、做法或行为;

(B)在收盘期间故意无视或者漠视交易的有序执行交易、做法或行为;或

(C)构成‘电子欺诈’、具有‘电子欺诈’的特质,或通常被业界冠以该名称(‘电子欺诈’指作出买入报价或卖出报价时,意图在交易执行之前撤销该买入报价或卖出报价)的交易、做法或行为。

(6)**规则制定权**。——商品期货交易委员会可以制定并颁发依其判断确属合理必要的规则与规章,禁止第(5)款所述交易做法以及任何其他扰乱公平公正交易的交易做法。

"(7) USE OF SWAPS TO DEFRAUD. — It shall be unlawful for any person to enter into a swap knowing, or acting in reckless disregard of the fact, that its counterparty will use the swap as part of a device, scheme, or artifice to defraud any third party.".

SEC.748. COMMODITY WHISTLEBLOWER INCENTIVES AND PROTE-CTION.

The Commodity Exchange Act (7 U.S.C. 1 et seq.) is amended by adding at the end the following:

"SEC.23. COMMODITY WHISTLEBLOWER INCENTIVES AND PROTECTION.

(a) DEFINITIONS. — In this section:

"(1) COVERED JUDICIAL OR ADMINISTRATIVE ACTION. — The term 'covered judicial or administrative action' means any judicial or administrative action brought by the Commission under this Act that results in monetary sanctions exceeding $1,000,000.

"(2) FUND. — The term 'Fund' means the Commodity Futures Trading Commission Customer Protection Fund established under subsection (g).

"(3) MONETARY SANCTIONS. — The term 'monetary sanctions', when used with respect to any judicial or administrative action means —

"(A) any monies, including penalties, disgorgement, restitution, and interest ordered to be paid; and

"(B) any monies deposited into a disgorgement fund or other fund pursuant to section 308(b) of the Sarbanes-Oxley Act of 2002 (15 U.S.C. 7246(b)), as a result of such action or any settlement of such action.

"(4) ORIGINAL INFORMATION. — The term 'original information' means information that —

"(A) is derived from the independent knowledge or analysis of a whistleblower;

"(B) is not known to the Commission from any other source, unless the whistleblower is the original source of the information; and

"(C) is not exclusively derived from an allegation made in a judicial or administrative hearing, in a governmental report, hearing, audit, or investigation, or from the news media, unless the whistleblower is a source of the information.

"(5) RELATED ACTION. — The term 'related action', when used with respect to any judicial or administrative action brought by the Commission under this Act, means any judicial or administrative action brought by an entity described in subclauses (I) through (VI) of subsection (h)(2)(C) that is based upon the original information provided by a whistleblower pursuant to subsection (a) that led to the successful enforcement of the Commission action.

"(6) SUCCESSFUL RESOLUTION. — The term 'successful resolution', when used with respect to any judicial or administrative action brought by the Commission under this

(7)**利用互换进行欺诈**。——任何人在明知或漠视其对手方将在欺诈任何第三方的手段、计谋或诡计中使用互换这一事实的情况下,仍与其对手方达成该互换的行为,当属违法。”

第748条　对商品违法违规行为举报人的激励和保护

在《商品交易法》(《美国法典》第七编第1节及其后条文)结尾处增加如下内容,作为对该法的修正:

“第23条　对商品违法行为举报人的激励和保护

(a)**定义**。——在本条中:

(1)**所涉司法或行政诉讼**。——‘所涉司法或行政诉讼’一词系指商品期货交易委员会根据本法提起的导致100万美元以上金钱制裁的任何司法或行政诉讼。

(2)**基金**。——‘基金’一词系指根据第(g)子条设立的商品期货交易委员会客户保护基金。

(3)**金钱制裁**。——就任何司法或行政诉讼而言,‘金钱制裁’一词系指——

(A)被勒令支付的任何钱款,包括罚款、没收款项、不当得利返还款项和利息;且

(B)因上述诉讼或诉讼和解而依据《2002年萨班斯—奥克斯法》第308(b)条[《美国法典》第十五编第7246(b)节]存入没收基金或其他基金的任何钱款。

(4)**原始信息**。——‘原始信息’一词系指符合下述条件的信息——

(A)完全因举报人自身掌握的情况或分析而获取的信息;

(B)商品期货交易委员会并非从任何其他来源获知的信息,但是原始来源为举报人的信息除外;且

(C)并非完全源自司法听审或行政听证、政府报告、听证、审计、调查或新闻媒体的信息,但是源自举报人的信息除外。

(5)**关联诉讼**。——就商品期货交易委员会依据本法提起的任何司法或行政诉讼而言,‘关联诉讼’一词系指第(h)(2)(c)子条第(1)子项至第(6)子项所述任何实体基于举报人依据第(a)子条提供的原始信息提起的任何司法或行政诉讼,且该原始信息导致了商品期货交易委员会胜诉。

(6)**成功解决**。——就商品期货交易委员会依据本法提起的任何司法或行政诉讼而言,‘成功解决’一词包括诉讼的任何和解。

Act, includes any settlement of such action.

"(7) WHISTLEBLOWER. — The term 'whistleblower' means any individual, or 2 or more individuals acting jointly, who provides information relating to a violation of this Act to the Commission, in a manner established by rule or regulation by the Commission.

"(b) AWARDS. —

"(1) IN GENERAL. — In any covered judicial or administrative action, or related action, the Commission, under regulations prescribed by the Commission and subject to subsection (c), shall pay an award or awards to 1 or more whistleblowers who voluntarily provided original information to the Commission that led to the successful enforcement of the covered judicial or administrative action, or related action, in an aggregate amount equal to —

"(A) not less than 10 percent, in total, of what has been collected of the monetary sanctions imposed in the action or related actions; and

"(B) not more than 30 percent, in total, of what has been collected of the monetary sanctions imposed in the action or related actions.

"(2) PAYMENT OF AWARDS. — Any amount paid under paragraph (1) shall be paid from the Fund.

"(c) DETERMINATION OF AMOUNT OF AWARD; DENIAL OF AWARD. —

"(1) DETERMINATION OF AMOUNT OF AWARD. —

"(A) DISCRETION. — The determination of the amount of an award made under subsection (b) shall be in the discretion of the Commission.

"(B) CRITERIA. — In determining the amount of an award made under subsection (b), the Commission —

"(i) shall take into consideration —

"(I) the significance of the information provided by the whistleblower to the success of the covered judicial or administrative action;

"(II) the degree of assistance provided by the whistleblower and any legal representative of the whistleblower in a covered judicial or administrative action;

"(III) the programmatic interest of the Commission in deterring violations of the Act (including regulations under the Act) by making awards to whistleblowers who provide information that leads to the successful enforcement of such laws; and

"(IV) such additional relevant factors as the Commission may establish by rule or regulation; and

"(ii) shall not take into consideration the balance of the Fund.

"(2) DENIAL OF AWARD. — No award under subsection (b) shall be made —

"(A) to any whistleblower who is, or was at the time the whistleblower acquired the original information submitted to the Commission, a member, officer, or employee of —

(7)**举报人**。——‘举报人’一词系指按商品期货交易委员会发布的规则或规章所规定的方式向商品期货交易委员会提供与违反本法规定的行为相关的信息的任何个人,或共同提供上述信息的2名(含)以上的个人。

(b)**奖励**。——

(1)**一般规定**。——在任何所涉司法或行政诉讼或关联诉讼中,对于自愿向商品期货交易委员会提供原始信息并导致所涉司法或行政诉讼或关联诉讼胜诉的1名或1名以上举报人,商品期货交易委员会应根据其所制定的规章并在不违反第(c)子条的前提下向其提供奖励,奖励总额应——

(A)不低于诉讼或关联诉讼中收取的金钱制裁的10%;且

(B)不高于诉讼或关联诉讼中收取的金钱制裁的30%。

(2)**奖励支付**。——第(1)款规定的所有金额均应通过基金支付。

(c)**奖励金额的确定;不授予奖励的情形**。——

(1)**奖励金额的确定**。——

(A)**自由裁量权**。——第(b)子条规定的奖励金额应由商品期货交易委员会依其自由裁量权确定。

(B)**标准**。——在确定第(b)子条规定的奖励金额时,商品期货交易委员会——

(i)应考虑如下因素——

(I)举报人提供的信息对于所涉司法或行政诉讼胜诉的重要性;

(II)举报人及其任何法律代理人在所涉司法或行政诉讼中提供协助的程度;

(III)举报人提供信息帮助商品期货交易委员会成功执行本法规定(包括依据本法发布的规章)的,商品期货交易委员会向举报人授予奖励以期威慑违反本法(包括依据本法发布的规章)的行为而获得的战略性效益;及

(IV)商品期货交易委员会发布的规则或规章所确定的其他相关因素;且

(ii)不得将基金余额作为确定奖励金额的考虑因素。

(2)**不授予奖励的情形**。——在以下情形下,不得向举报人授予第(b)子条规定的奖励——

(A)任何举报人身为下述组织或机关的成员、官员或雇员的举报人,或者任何举报人在获取提交给商品期货交易委员会的原始信息时身为下列组织或机构的成员、

"(i) a appropriate regulatory agency;

"(ii) the Department of Justice;

"(iii) a registered entity;

"(iv) a registered futures association;

"(v) a self–regulatory organization as defined in section 3(a) of the Securities Exchange Act of 1934 (15 U.S.C. 78c(a)); or

"(vi) a law enforcement organization;

"(B) to any whistleblower who is convicted of a criminal violation related to the judicial or administrative action for which the whistleblower otherwise could receive an award under this section;

"(C) to any whistleblower who submits information to the Commission that is based on the facts underlying the covered action submitted previously by another whistleblower;

"(D) to any whistleblower who fails to submit information to the Commission in such form as the Commission may, by rule or regulation, require.

"(d) REPRESENTATION. —

"(1) PERMITTED REPRESENTATION. — Any whistleblower who makes a claim for an award under subsection (b) may be represented by counsel.

"(2) REQUIRED REPRESENTATION. —

"(A)IN GENERAL. — Any whistleblower who anonymously makes a claim for an award under subsection (b) shall be represented by counsel if the whistleblower submits the information upon which the claim is based.

"(B)DISCLOSURE OF IDENTITY. — Prior to the payment of an award, a whistleblower shall disclose the identity of the whistleblower and provide such other information as the Commission may require, directly or through counsel for the whistleblower.

"(e) NO CONTRACT NECESSARY. — No contract with the Commission is necessary for any whistleblower to receive an award under subsection (b), unless otherwise required by the Commission, by rule or regulation.

"(f) APPEALS. —

"(1) IN GENERAL. — Any determination made under this section, including whether, to whom, or in what amount to make awards, shall be in the discretion of the Commission.

"(2) APPEALS. — Any determination described in paragraph (1) may be appealed to the appropriate court of appeals of the United States not more than 30 days after the determination is issued by the Commission.

"(3) REVIEW. — The court shall review the determination made by the Commission in accordance with section 7064 of title 5, United States Code.

"(g) COMMODITY FUTURES TRADING COMMISSION CUSTOMER PROTECTION

官员或雇员——

(i)相应的监管机关;

(ii)司法部;

(iii)注册实体;

(iv)注册期货协会;

(v)自律组织{定义见《1934年证券交易法》第3(a)条[《美国法典》第十五编第78c(a)节]};或

(vi)执法组织;

(B)任何举报人本可以依据本条获得奖励,但在相关司法或行政诉讼中被判犯有刑事违法违规行为;

(C)任何举报人向商品期货交易委员会提交的信息系基于其他举报人先前所提供的与所涉诉讼有关的事实;

(D)任何举报人未按照商品期货交易委员会发布的规则或规章所要求的格式向商品期货交易委员会提交信息。

(d)**代理**。——

(1)**选择性代理**。——依第(b)子条索取奖励的任何举报人可选择聘请律师进行代理。

(2)**强制性代理**。——

(A)**一般规定**。——如任何举报人提交了其认为应获得奖励的信息,则其在根据第(b)子条匿名索取奖励时应由律师代理。

(B)**身份披露**。——在支付奖励之前,任何举报人应披露其身份,直接或通过其律师提供商品期货交易委员会要求的其他信息。

(e) **不必签订合同**。——除非商品期货交易委员会发布的规则或规章另有要求,否则举报人根据第(b)子条获得奖励的,不必与商品期货交易委员会签订合同。

(f)**司法审查请求**。——

(1)**一般规定**。——依据本条作出的任何判定,包括是否给予奖励、奖励对象、奖励金额,应由商品期货交易委员会依其自由裁量权作出。

(2)**司法审查请求**。——对于第(1)款所述的任何判定,均可在商品期货交易委员会颁发判定后30天内向相应的联邦上诉法院提请司法审查。

(3)**审查**。——法院应根据《美国法典》第五编第7064节对商品期货交易委员会的判定进行审查。

(g)**商品期货交易委员会客户保护基金**。——

FUND. —

"(1) ESTABLISHMENT. — There is established in the Treasury of the United States a revolving fund to be known as the 'Commodity Futures Trading Commission Customer Protection Fund'.

"(2) USE OF FUND. — The Fund shall be available to the Commission, without further appropriation or fiscal year limitation, for —

"(A) the payment of awards to whistleblowers as provided in subsection (a); and

"(B) the funding of customer education initiatives designed to help customers protect themselves against fraud or other violations of this Act, or the rules and regulations thereunder.

"(3) DEPOSITS AND CREDITS. — There shall be deposited into or credited to the Fund:

"(A) MONETARY SANCTIONS. — Any monetary sanctions collected by the Commission in any covered judicial or administrative action that is not otherwise distributed to victims of a violation of this Act or the rules and regulations thereunder underlying such action, unless the balance of the Fund at the time the monetary judgment is collected exceeds $100,000,000.

"(B) ADDITIONAL AMOUNTS. — If the amounts deposited into or credited to the Fund under subparagraph (A) are not sufficient to satisfy an award made under subsection (b), there shall be deposited into or credited to the Fund an amount equal to the unsatisfied portion of the award from any monetary sanction collected by the Commission in any judicial or administrative action brought by the Commission under this Act that is based on information provided by a whistleblower.

"(C) INVESTMENT INCOME. — All income from investments made under paragraph (4).

"(4) INVESTMENTS. —

"(A) AMOUNTS IN FUND MAY BE INVESTED. — The Commission may request the Secretary of the Treasury to invest the portion of the Fund that is not, in the Commission's judgment, required to meet the current needs of the Fund.

"(B) ELIGIBLE INVESTMENTS. — Investments shall be made by the Secretary of the Treasury in obligations of the United States or obligations that are guaranteed as to principal and interest by the United States, with maturities suitable to the needs of the Fund as determined by the Commission.

"(C) INTEREST AND PROCEEDS CREDITED. — The interest on, and the proceeds from the sale or redemption of, any obligations held in the Fund shall be credited to, and form a part of, the Fund.

"(5) REPORTS TO CONGRESS. — Not later than October 30 of each year, the

(1)**设立**。——美国财政部下设‘商品期货交易委员会客户保护基金’,其性质为循环基金。

(2)**基金的使用**。——商品期货交易委员会应当将基金用于如下目的,不受追加拨款限制或财政年度限制——

(A)按第(a)子条规定向举报人支付奖励;及

(B)为客户教育项目提供经费,帮助客户保护自身不受欺诈或者其他违反本法或依据本法制定的规则与规章的行为侵害。

(3)**存储和贷项**。——下述款项应存入基金或记入基金贷项:

(A)**金钱制裁**。——商品期货交易委员会在任何所涉司法或行政诉讼中收取的金钱制裁款项中,未向引发该诉讼的违法违规行为(即违反本法或依其发布的规则与规章的行为)的受害人分配的部分,但收取金钱制裁款项时基金余额已超过1亿美元的除外。

(B)**补充金额**。——根据第(A)子款存入基金或记入基金贷项的金额不足以支付第(b)子条规定的奖励的,应从商品期货交易委员会基于举报人提供的信息而依本法提起的任何司法或行政诉讼中收取的任何金钱制裁款项提取不足的金额存入或记入基金贷项。

(C)**投资收益**。——根据第(4)款获得的所有投资收益。

(4)**投资**。——

(A)**基金内可用于投资的款项**。——对于商品期货交易委员会判断不必用于满足基金当前需求的基金款项,商品期货交易委员会可要求财政部部长对其进行投资。

(B)**适格投资**。——投资应由财政部部长作出,投资标的应为联邦政府债券,或联邦政府担保本金和利息的债券,债券期限应为商品期货交易委员会基于基金需求确定为适当的期限。

(C)**记入贷项的利息和卖出或赎回债券所获资金**。——基金所持任何债券产生的利息及其卖出或赎回所获资金均应记入基金贷项,构成基金的一部分。

(5)**向国会报告**。——商品期货交易委员会最迟应于每年的10月30日,向参议院

Commission shall transmit to the Committee on Agriculture, Nutrition, and Forestry of the Senate, and the Committee on Agriculture of the House of Representatives a report on —

"(A) the Commission's whistleblower award program under this section, including a description of the number of awards granted and the types of cases in which awards were granted during the preceding fiscal year;

"(B) customer education initiatives described in paragraph (2)(B) that were funded by the Fund during the preceding fiscal year;

"(C) the balance of the Fund at the beginning of the preceding fiscal year;

"(D) the amounts deposited into or credited to the Fund during the preceding fiscal year;

"(E) the amount of earnings on investments of amounts in the Fund during the preceding fiscal year;

"(F) the amount paid from the Fund during the preceding fiscal year to whistleblowers pursuant to subsection (b);

"(G) the amount paid from the Fund during the preceding fiscal year for customer education initiatives described in paragraph (2)(B);

"(H) the balance of the Fund at the end of the preceding fiscal year; and

"(I) a complete set of audited financial statements, including a balance sheet, income statement, and cash flow analysis.

"(h) PROTECTION OF WHISTLEBLOWERS. —

"(1) PROHIBITION AGAINST RETALIATION. —

"(A) IN GENERAL. — No employer may discharge, demote, suspend, threaten, harass, directly or indirectly, or in any other manner discriminate against, a whistleblower in the terms and conditions of employment because of any lawful act done by the whistleblower —

"(i) in providing information to the Commission in accordance with subsection (b); or

"(ii) in assisting in any investigation or judicial or administrative action of the Commission based upon or related to such information.

"(B) ENFORCEMENT. —

"(i)CAUSE OF ACTION. — An individual who alleges discharge or other discrimination in violation of subparagraph (A) may bring an action under this subsection in the appropriate district court of the United States for the relief provided in subparagraph (C), unless the individual who is alleging discharge or other discrimination in violation of subparagraph (A) is an employee of the Federal Government, in which case the individual shall only bring an action under section 1221 of title 5, United States Code.

"(ii) SUBPOENAS. — A subpoena requiring the attendance of a witness at a trial or hearing conducted under this subsection may be served at any place in the United States.

"(iii) STATUTE OF LIMITATIONS. — An action under this subsection may not be

的农业、营养与林业委员会以及众议院的农业委员会提交一份报告,说明如下事项——

(A)商品期货交易委员会依据本条制定的举报人奖励计划,包括在前一财政年度授予的奖励案件数量,以及授予奖励的案件类型;

(B)前一财政年度由基金提供经费支持的第(2)(B)款所述客户教育项目;

(C)前一财政年度期初基金余额;

(D)前一财政年度存入基金或记入基金贷项的金额;

(E)前一财政年度基金投资收益金额;

(F)前一财政年度依照第(b)子条从基金拨付的向举报人支付的金额;

(G)前一财政年度从基金向第(2)(B)款所述客户教育项目拨付的金额;

(H)前一财政年度期末基金余额;及

(I)整套审计财务报表,包括资产负债表、损益表和现金流量分析。

(h)**举报人保护**。——

(1)**禁止报复**。——

(A)**一般规定**。——任何雇主均不得因举报人从事下列任何合法行为而对举报人进行直接或间接的解聘、降职、停职、威胁、骚扰,亦不得在雇佣条款和条件上对之进行任何其他歧视——

(i)按照第(b)子条向商品期货交易委员会提供信息;或

(ii)为商品期货交易委员会基于上述信息提起的或与上述信息相关的任何调查行动、司法或行政诉讼提供协助。

(B)**执行**。——

(i)**诉因**。——主张存在违反第(A)子款规定的解聘或其他歧视行为的个人,可以根据本子条向相应的联邦地区法院提起诉讼,请求第(C)子款规定的救济,但如提起上述主张的个人为联邦政府雇员,则其仅得根据《美国法典》第五编第1221节提起诉讼。

(ii)**传票**。——传唤证人出席根据本子条开展的审判或听审的传票,可向美国境内的任何地方送达。

(iii)**诉讼时效**。——在第(A)子款所报告的违法违规行为发生之日2年后,不得

brought more than 2 years after the date on which the violation reported in subparagraph (A) is committed.

"(C)RELIEF. — Relief for an individual prevailing in an action brought under subparagraph (B) shall include —

"(i) reinstatement with the same seniority status that the individual would have had, but for the discrimination;

"(ii) the amount of back pay otherwise owed to the individual, with interest; and

"(iii)compensation for any special damages sustained as a result of the discharge or discrimination, including litigation costs, expert witness fees, and reasonable attorney's fees.

"(2) CONFIDENTIALITY. —

"(A)IN GENERAL. — Except as provided in subparagraphs (B) and (C), the Commission, and any officer or employee of the Commission, shall not disclose any information, including information provided by a whistleblower to the Commission, which could reasonably be expected to reveal the identity of a whistleblower, except in accordance with the provisions of section 552a of title 5, United States Code, unless and until required to be disclosed to a defendant or respondent in connection with a public proceeding instituted by the Commission or any entity described in subparagraph (C). For purposes of section 552 of title 5, United States Code, this paragraph shall be considered a statute described in subsection (b)(3)(B) of such section 552.

"(B) EFFECT. — Nothing in this paragraph is intended to limit the ability of the Attorney General to present such evidence to a grand jury or to share such evidence with potential witnesses or defendants in the course of an ongoing criminal investigation.

"(C) AVAILABILITY TO GOVERNMENT AGENCIES. —

"(i) IN GENERAL. — Without the loss of its status as confidential in the hands of the Commission, all information referred to in subparagraph (A) may, in the discretion of the Commission, when determined by the Commission to be necessary or appropriate to accomplish the purposes of this Act and protect customers and in accordance with clause (ii), be made available to —

"(I) the Department of Justice;

"(II) an appropriate department or agency of the Federal Government, acting within the scope of its jurisdiction;

"(III) a registered entity, registered futures association, or self–regulatory organization as defined in section 3(a) of the Securities Exchange Act of 1934 (15 U.S.C. 78c(a));

"(IV) a State attorney general in connection with any criminal investigation;

"(V) an appropriate department or agency of any State, acting within the scope of its jurisdiction; and

"(VI) a foreign futures authority.

再根据本子条提起诉讼。

(C)**救济**。——在根据第(B)子款提起的诉讼中,胜诉方享有的救济应包括——

(i)恢复如未发生歧视其本应有的雇佣年资;

(ii)获得本应向其支付的欠付工资及利息;及

(iii)获得因解聘或歧视而遭受的任何特殊损害补偿,包括诉讼费用、专家证人费以及合理的律师费。

(2)**保密**。——

(A)**一般规定**。——除第(B)子款和第(C)子款规定的情形外,商品期货交易委员会及其任何官员或雇员,除非遵照《美国法典》第五编第552a节的规定,否则不得披露据合理预期将导致举报人身份泄露的任何信息(包括举报人向商品期货交易委员会提供的信息),但在商品期货交易委员会或第(C)子款所述任何实体发起的公开程序中按规定向被告或相对人进行披露的除外。就《美国法典》第五编第552节而言,本款规定应视为该第552节第(b)(3)(B)子节所述的制定法。

(B)**影响**。——本款任何内容均无意限制联邦总检察长在正在进行的刑事调查中将证据呈交给大陪审团或提供给潜在证人或被告。

(C)**向政府机关提供保密信息**。——

(i)**一般规定**。——在商品期货交易委员会维持第(A)子款提及的信息保密状态的前提下，如果商品期货交易委员会判定将该等信息提供给以下机构对实现本法宗旨和保护客户确属必要或适当,并且符合第(ii)项规定,商品期货交易委员会可以依其自由裁量权将该信息提供给——

(I)司法部;

(II)在自身管辖范围内行事的相关联邦政府部门或机关;

(III)注册实体、注册期货协会或《1934年证券交易法》第3(a)条[《美国法典》第十五编第78c(a)节]所定义的自律组织;

(IV)州总检察长(涉及任何刑事调查);

(V)在自身管辖范围内行事的任何相关州部门或机关;及

(VI)外国期货监管机构。

"(ii) MAINTENANCE OF INFORMATION. — Each of the entities, agencies, or persons described in clause (i) shall maintain information described in that clause as confidential, in accordance with the requirements in subparagraph (A).

"(iii) STUDY ON IMPACT OF FOIA EXEMPTION ON COMMODITY FUTURES TRADING COMMISSION. —

"(I) STUDY. — The Inspector General of the Commission shall conduct a study —

"(aa) on whether the exemption under section 552(b)(3) of title 5, United States Code (known as the Freedom of Information Act) established in paragraph (2)(A) aids whistleblowers in disclosing information to the Commission;

"(bb) on what impact the exemption has had on the public's ability to access information about the Commission's regulation of commodity futures and option markets; and

"(cc) to make any recommendations on whether the Commission should continue to use the exemption.

"(II) REPORT. — Not later than 30 months after the date of enactment of this clause, the Inspector General shall —

"(aa) submit a report on the findings of the study required under this clause to the Committee on Banking, Housing, and Urban Affairs of the Senate and the Committee on Financial Services of the House of Representatives; and

"(bb) make the report available to the public through publication of a report on the website of the Commission.

"(3) RIGHTS RETAINED. — Nothing in this section shall be deemed to diminish the rights, privileges, or remedies of any whistleblower under any Federal or State law, or under any collective bargaining agreement.

"(i) RULEMAKING AUTHORITY. — The Commission shall have the authority to issue such rules and regulations as may be necessary or appropriate to implement the provisions of this section consistent with the purposes of this section.

"(j) IMPLEMENTING RULES. — The Commission shall issue final rules or regulations implementing the provisions of this section not later than 270 days after the date of enactment of the Wall Street Transparency and Accountability Act of 2010.

"(k) ORIGINAL INFORMATION. — Information submitted to the Commission by a whistleblower in accordance with rules or regulations implementing this section shall not lose its status as original information solely because the whistleblower submitted such information prior to the effective date of such rules or regulations, provided such information was submitted after the date of enactment of the Wall Street Transparency and Accountability Act of 2010.

"(l) AWARDS. — A whistleblower may receive an award pursuant to this section regardless of whether any violation of a provision of this Act, or a rule or regulation thereunder, underlying the judicial or administrative action upon which the award is based

(ii)**维持信息保密性**。——第(i)项所述每一实体、机关或人均应遵守第(A)子款的要求对该项所述信息进行保密。

(iii)**关于《信息自由法》豁免对商品期货交易委员会的影响的研究**。——

(I)**研究**。——商品期货交易委员会的监察长应针对以下事项进行研究——

(aa)第2(A)款针对《美国法典》第五编第552(b)(3)节(即《信息自由法》)规定的豁免是否有助于举报人向商品期货交易委员会透露信息;

(bb)该项豁免对于公众获得商品期货交易委员会的商品期货和期权市场监管相关信息的能力有何影响;及

(cc)针对商品期货交易委员会是否应当继续使用该项豁免作出相关建议。

(II)**报告**。——本项颁布之日后30个月内,监察长应——

(aa)就按照本项规定开展的研究之结论向参议院银行、住房与城市事务委员会以及众议院金融服务委员会提交报告;并

(bb)在商品期货交易委员会网站发布并向公众提供该报告。

(3)**保留权利**。——本条任何内容均不得视为削弱任何联邦法律、州法律或任何集体劳动合同赋予任何举报人的权利、特殊待遇或救济。

(i)**规则制定权**。——商品期货交易委员会有权发布对实施本条规定和实现本条目的确属必要或适当的规则与规章。

(j)**实施规则**。——在《2010年华尔街透明度与问责法》颁布之日后270天内,商品期货交易委员会应发布实施本条规定的最终规则或规章。

(k)**原始信息**。——举报人根据本条的实施规则或规章向商品期货交易委员会提交的信息,不会仅因其提交时间早于该等实施规则或规章生效日而失去其原始信息的性质,但该等信息必须是在《2010年华尔街透明度与问责法》颁布之日后提交的。

(l)**奖励**。——对于基于司法或行政诉讼所授予的奖励,所涉之违反本法规定或者依据本法制定的规则或规章的任何行为无论是否在《2010年华尔街透明度与问责法》颁布之日前发生的,均不影响举报人依照本条规定获得奖励。

occurred prior to the date of enactment of the Wall Street Transparency and Accountability Act of 2010.

"(m) PROVISION OF FALSE INFORMATION. — A whistleblower who knowingly and willfully makes any false, fictitious, or fraudulent statement or representation, or who makes or uses any false writing or document knowing the same to contain any false, fictitious, or fraudulent statement or entry, shall not be entitled to an award under this section and shall be subject to prosecution under section 1001 of title 18, United States Code.

"(n) NONENFORCEABILITY OF CERTAIN PROVISIONS WAIVING RIGHTS AND REMEDIES OR REQUIRING ARBITRATION OF DISPUTES. —

"(1) WAIVER OF RIGHTS AND REMEDIES. — The rights and remedies provided for in this section may not be waived by any agreement, policy form, or condition of employment including by a predispute arbitration agreement.

"(2) PREDISPUTE ARBITRATION AGREEMENTS. — No predispute arbitration agreement shall be valid or enforceable, if the agreement requires arbitration of a dispute arising under this section.".

SEC.749. CONFORMING AMENDMENTS.

(a) Section 4d of the Commodity Exchange Act (7 U.S.C. 6d) (as amended by section 724) is amended —

(1) in subsection (a) —

(A) in the matter preceding paragraph (1) —

(i) by striking "engage as" and inserting "be a"; and

(ii) by striking "or introducing broker" and all that follows through "or derivatives transaction execution facility";

(B) in paragraph (1), by striking "or introducing broker"; and

(C) in paragraph (2), by striking "if a futures commission merchant,"; and

(2) by adding at the end the following:

"(g) It shall be unlawful for any person to be an introducing broker unless such person shall have registered under this Act with the Commission as an introducing broker and such registration shall not have expired nor been suspended nor revoked.".

(b) Section 4m(3) of the Commodity Exchange Act (7 U.S.C. 6m(3)) is amended —

(1) by striking "(3) Subsection (1) of this section" and inserting the following:

"(3) EXCEPTION. —

"(A) IN GENERAL. — Paragraph (1)"; and

(2) by striking "to any investment trust" and all that follows through the period at the end and inserting the following: "to any commodity pool that is engaged primarily in trading commodity interests.

(m)**提供虚假信息**。——如果举报人在知情的情况下故意作出任何虚假、虚构或欺诈声明或陈述,或者在明知书面资料或文件包含任何虚假、虚构或欺诈声明或内容的情况下制作或使用该等虚假书面资料或文件,则无权按照本条规定获得奖励,且将按《美国法典》第十八编第1001节被追诉。

(n)**放弃权利和救济的特定条款或要求通过仲裁解决争议的条款不具有强制执行力**。——

(1)**放弃权利和救济**。——本条赋予的权利和救济不得通过任何协议、政策、格式条款或雇佣条件(包括发生争议前缔结的仲裁协议)予以放弃。

(2)**争议前缔结的仲裁协议**。——如果争议前缔结的仲裁协议要求通过仲裁解决本条下产生的争议,此类协议一律无效,不具强制执行力。”

第749条　一致性修正

(a)《商品交易法》第4d条(《美国法典》第七编第6d节)(以经第724条修正后的版本为准)修正如下——

(1)在第(a)子条中——

(A)第(1)款之前的内容——

(i)删除“任何人除非满足下列条件,否则该人从事期货经纪商活动的行为当属违法”,替以“任何人除非满足下列条件,否则该人担任期货经纪商的行为当属违法”;及

(ii)删除“或介绍经纪商”以及其后直至“或者衍生品交易执行设施”的所有内容;

(B)第(1)款删除“或介绍经纪商”;及

(C)第(2)款删除“如果是期货经纪商,则该人无论是否”,替以“该人无论是否”;及

(2)在本条结尾处增加如下内容:

“(g)任何人除非已按本法规定在商品期货交易委员会注册为介绍经纪商,且该注册尚未过期也未被暂停或撤销,否则该人担任介绍经纪商的行为当属违法。”

(b)《商品交易法》第4m(3)条[《美国法典》第七编第6m(3)节]修正如下——

(1)删除“(3)本条第(1)子条”,替以:

“(3)**例外规定**。——

(A)**一般规定**。——第(1)款”;及

(2)删除“为交易商品权益之目的而经营的任何投资信托、辛迪加或类似形式的企业”,并替以“以交易商品权益为主营业务的任何商品基金。

"(B) ENGAGED PRIMARILY. — For purposes of subparagraph (A), a commodity trading advisor or a commodity pool shall be considered to be 'engaged primarily' in the business of being a commodity trading advisor or commodity pool if it is or holds itself out to the public as being engaged primarily, or proposes to engage primarily, in the business of advising on commodity interests or investing, reinvesting, owning, holding, or trading in commodity interests, respectively.

"(C) COMMODITY INTERESTS. — For purposes of this paragraph, commodity interests shall include contracts of sale of a commodity for future delivery, options on such contracts, security futures, swaps, leverage contracts, foreign exchange, spot and forward contracts on physical commodities, and any monies held in an account used for trading commodity interests.".

(c) Section 5c of the Commodity Exchange Act (7 U.S.C. 7a－2) is amended —

(1) in subsection (a)(1) —

(A) by striking ", 5a(d),"; and

(B) by striking "and section (2)(h)(7) with respect to significant price discovery contracts,"; and

(2) in subsection (f)(1), by striking "section 4d(c) of this Act" and inserting "section 4d(e)".

(d) Section 5e of the Commodity Exchange Act (7 U.S.C. 7b) is amended by striking "or revocation of the right of an electronic trading facility to rely on the exemption set forth in section 2(h)(3) with respect to a significant price discovery contract,".

(e) Section 6(b) of the Commodity Exchange Act (7 U.S.C. 8(b)) is amended in the first sentence by striking ", or to revoke the right of an electronic trading facility to rely on the exemption set forth in section 2(h)(3) with respect to a significant price discovery contract,".

(f) Section 12(e)(2)(B) of the Commodity Exchange Act (7 U.S.C. 16(e)(2)(B)) is amended —

(1) by striking "section 2(c), 2(d), 2(f), or 2(g) of this Act" and inserting "section 2(c) or 2(f) of this Act"; and

(2) by striking "2(h) or".

(g) Section 17(r)(1) of the Commodity Exchange Act (7 U.S.C. 21(r)(1)) is amended by striking "section 4d(c) of this Act" and inserting "section 4d(e)".

(h) Section 22 of the Commodity Exchange Act is amended —

(1) in subsection (a)(1)(B), by —

(A) inserting "or any swap" after "commodity)"; and

(B) inserting "or any swap" after "such contract";

(2) in subsection (a)(1)(C), by adding at the end the following:

"(iv) a swap; or"; and

(B)**主营业务**。——就第(A)子款而言,如果某商品交易顾问的主营业务或拟开展的主营业务为商品权益顾问业务,或者公开宣称其主营业务或拟开展的主营业务为商品权益顾问业务,则该商品交易顾问应视为以商品交易顾问业务为‘主营’业务;如果某商品基金的主营业务或拟开展的主营业务为商品权益投资、再投资、拥有、持有或交易,或者公开宣称其主营业务或拟开展的主营业务为商品权益投资、再投资、拥有、持有或交易,则该商品基金应视为以商品基金业务为‘主营’业务。

(C)**商品权益**。——就本款而言,商品权益包括:远期交割商品出售合约、该等合约的期权、证券期货、互换、杠杆合约、外汇、实物商品的即期和远期合约,以及商品权益交易账户中的任何资金。”

(c)《商品交易法》第5c条(《美国法典》第七编第7a-2节)修正如下——

(1)在第(a)(1)子条中——

(A)删除“,第5a(d)条,”;及

(B)删除“以及(针对重要价格发现合约而言)第2(h)(7)条,”;及

(2)第(f)(1)子条删除“本法第4d(c)条”并替以“第4d(e)条”。

(d)《商品交易法》第5e条(《美国法典》第七编第7b节)修正如下:删除“或者针对重要价格发现合约而言,电子交易设施将被撤销其依赖第2(h)(3)条规定之豁免的权利,”。

(e)《商品交易法》第6(b)条[《美国法典》第七编第8(b)节]第一句修正如下:删除“,或者针对重要价格发现合约而言,电子交易设施将被撤销其依赖第2(h)(3)条规定之豁免的权利,”。

(f)《商品交易法》第12(e)(2)(B)条[《美国法典》第七编第16(e)(2)(B)节]修正如下——

(1)删除“本法第2(c)条、第2(d)条、第2(f)条或2(g)条”,替以“本法第2(c)条或第2(f)条”;及

(2)删除“第2(h)条或”。

(g)《商品交易法》第17(r)(1)条[《美国法典》第七编第21(r)(1)节]修正如下:删除“本法第4d(c)条”,替以“第4d(e)条”。

(h)《商品交易法》第22条修正如下——

(1)在第(a)(1)(B)子条中——

(A)在“商品期权)”之后插入“或任何互换”;及

(B)在“(或该等合约的期权或任何商品期权)”之后插入“或任何互换”;

(2)在第(a)(1)(C)子条结尾处增加如下内容:

“(iv)互换;或”;及

(3) in subsection (b)(1)(A), by striking "section 2(h)(7) or sections 5 through 5c" and inserting "section 5, 5b, 5c, 5h, or 21".

(i) Section 408(2)(C) of the Federal Deposit Insurance Corporation Improvement Act of 1991 (12 U.S.C. 4421(2)(C)) is amended —

(1) by striking "section 2(c), 2(d), 2(f), or (2)(g) of such Act" and inserting "section 2(c), 2(f), or 2(i) of that Act"; and

(2) by striking "2(h) or".

SEC.750. STUDY ON OVERSIGHT OF CARBON MARKETS.

(a) INTERAGENCY WORKING GROUP. — There is established to carry out this section an interagency working group (referred to in this section as the "interagency group") composed of the following members or designees:

(1) The Chairman of the Commodity Futures Trading Commission (referred to in this section as the "Commission"), who shall serve as Chairman of the interagency group.

(2) The Secretary of Agriculture.

(3) The Secretary of the Treasury.

(4) The Chairman of the Securities and Exchange Commission.

(5) The Administrator of the Environmental Protection Agency.

(6) The Chairman of the Federal Energy Regulatory Commission.

(7) The Commissioner of the Federal Trade Commission.

(8) The Administrator of the Energy Information Administration.

(b) ADMINISTRATIVE SUPPORT. — The Commission shall provide the interagency group such administrative support services as are necessary to enable the interagency group to carry out the functions of the interagency group under this section.

(c) CONSULTATION. — In carrying out this section, the interagency group shall consult with representatives of exchanges, clearinghouses, self–regulatory bodies, major carbon market participants, consumers, and the general public, as the interagency group determines to be appropriate.

(d) STUDY. — The interagency group shall conduct a study on the oversight of existing and prospective carbon markets to ensure an efficient, secure, and transparent carbon market, including oversight of spot markets and derivative markets.

(e) REPORT. — Not later than 180 days after the date of enactment of this Act, the interagency group shall submit to Congress a report on the results of the study conducted under subsection (b), including recommendations for the oversight of existing and prospective carbon markets to ensure an efficient, secure, and transparent carbon market, including oversight of spot markets and derivative markets.

(3)在第(b)(1)(A)子条中,删除“第2(h)7条或第5条至第5c条”,替以“第5条、第5b条、第5c条、第5h条或第21条”。

(i)《1991年联邦存款保险公司改良法》第408(2)(C)条[《美国法典》第十二编第4421(2)(C)节]修正如下——

(1)删除“该法第2(c)条、第2(d)条、第2(f)条或第(2)(g)条”,替以“该法第2(c)条、第2(f)条或第2(i)条”;及

(2)删除“第2(h)条或”。

第750条　碳市场监管研究

(a)**跨机关工作组**。——本条规定由下列成员或指定人员组成的跨机关工作组(本条中简称工作组)负责实施:

(1)商品期货交易委员会(英文文本中简称为委员会,中文文本保留全称商品期货交易委员会)主席,任工作组主席。

(2)农业部部长。

(3)财政部部长。

(4)证券交易委员会主席。

(5)环保局局长。

(6)联邦能源监管委员会主席。

(7)联邦贸易委员会主席。

(8)能源信息署署长。

(b)**行政支持**。——商品期货交易委员会应向工作组提供必要的行政支持服务,协助工作组根据本条规定履行其职能。

(c)**咨询**。——工作组在实施本条规定时,应咨询其认为相应的交易所代表、结算所代表、自律组织机构代表、主要碳市场参与者代表、消费者代表及一般公众代表的意见。

(d)**研究**。——为确保碳市场的高效、安全和透明,工作组应对现有及潜在碳市场的监管(包括即期市场和衍生品市场的监管)进行研究。

(e)**报告**。——本法颁布之日起180天内,工作组应就其根据第(b)子条开展的研究之结论向国会提交报告,报告内容应包括为确保碳市场的高效、安全和透明,就现有和未来碳市场的监管(包括即期市场和衍生品市场的监管)提出的建议。

SEC.751. ENERGY AND ENVIRONMENTAL MARKETS ADVISORY COMMITTEE.

Section 2(a) of the Commodity Exchange Act (7 U.S.C. 2(a)) (as amended by section 727) is amended by adding at the end the following:

"(15) ENERGY AND ENVIRONMENTAL MARKETS ADVISORY COMMITTEE.—

"(A) ESTABLISHMENT.—

"(i) IN GENERAL.—An Energy and Environmental Markets Advisory Committee is hereby established.

"(ii) MEMBERSHIP.—The Committee shall have 9 members.

"(iii) ACTIVITIES.—The Committee's objectives and scope of activities shall be—

"(I) to conduct public meetings;

"(II) to submit reports and recommendations to the Commission (including dissenting or minority views, if any); and

"(III) otherwise to serve as a vehicle for discussion and communication on matters of concern to exchanges, firms, end users, and regulators regarding energy and environmental markets and their regulation by the Commission.

"(B) REQUIREMENTS.—

"(i) IN GENERAL.—The Committee shall hold public meetings at such intervals as are necessary to carry out the functions of the Committee, but not less frequently than 2 times per year.

"(ii) MEMBERS.—Members shall be appointed to 3–year terms, but may be removed for cause by vote of the Commission.

"(C) APPOINTMENT.—The Commission shall appoint members with a wide diversity of opinion and who represent a broad spectrum of interests, including hedgers and consumers.

"(D) REIMBURSEMENT.—Members shall be entitled to perdiem and travel expense reimbursement by the Commission.

"(E) FACA.—The Committee shall not be subject to the Federal Advisory Committee Act (5 U.S.C. App.).".

SEC.752. INTERNATIONAL HARMONIZATION.

(a) In order to promote effective and consistent global regulation of swaps and security–based swaps, the Commodity Futures Trading Commission, the Securities and Exchange Commission, and the prudential regulators (as that term is defined in section 1a (39) of the Commodity Exchange Act), as appropriate, shall consult and coordinate with foreign regulatory authorities on the establishment of consistent international standards with respect to the regulation (including fees) of swaps, security–based swaps, swap entities, and security–based swap entities and may agree to such information–sharing arrangements as may be deemed to be necessary or appropriate in the public interest or for the protection of

第751条　能源及环境市场顾问委员会

在《商品交易法》第2(a)条[《美国法典》第七编第2(a)节](以经第727条修正后的版本为准)结尾处增加如下内容,作为对该条的修正:

"(15)**能源及环境市场顾问委员会**。——

(A)**设立**。——

(i)**一般规定**。——兹设立能源及环境市场顾问委员会。

(ii)**成员**。——委员会应由9名成员组成。

(iii)**委员会工作**。——委员会目标及工作范围如下——

(I)召开公开会议;

(II)向商品期货交易委员会提交报告和建议[包括异议或少数意见(如有)];及

(III)以其他方式发挥平台作用,以便交易所、公司、最终用户及监管者就其所关切的能源及环境市场相关事宜,以及商品期货交易委员会对该等市场的监管的相关事宜展开讨论和沟通。

(B)**要求**。——

(i)**一般规定**。——能源及环境市场顾问委员会应定期召开公开会议,会议频率应足以保证委员会正常履行其职能,但至少应每年召开2次。

(ii)**成员**。——能源及环境市场顾问委员会的成员任期3年,但是,存在正当原因的,可由商品期货交易委员会表决免职。

(C)**任命**。——商品期货交易委员会应任命广泛代表各方面利益并持有各种不同意见的委员,包括套期保值者和消费者。

(D)**报销**。——能源及环境市场顾问委员会的成员有权获得商品期货交易委员会提供的出差津贴及差旅费报销。

(E)**《联邦顾问委员会法》**。——能源及环境市场顾问委员会不受制于《联邦顾问委员会法》(《美国法典》第五编附件)的规定。"

第752条　国际协作

(a)为促进对互换和证券类互换的有效和一致的全球监管,在适当情况下,商品期货交易委员会、证券交易委员会和审慎监管者[定义见《商品交易法》第1a(39)条]应就互换、证券类互换、互换实体及证券类互换实体的一致的全球监管标准(包括费用标准)之制定与外国监管部门进行磋商及协调,并可以就其判定对维护公共利益或保护投资者、互换对手方及证券类互换对手方确属必要或适当的信息共享安排作出约定。

investors, swap counterparties, and security–based swap counterparties.

(b) In order to promote effective and consistent global regulation of contracts of sale of a commodity for future delivery and options on such contracts, the Commodity Futures Trading Commission shall consult and coordinate with foreign regulatory authorities on the establishment of consistent international standards with respect to the regulation of contracts of sale of a commodity for future delivery and options on such contracts, and may agree to such information–sharing arrangements as may be deemed necessary or appropriate in the public interest for the protection of users of contracts of sale of a commodity for future delivery.

SEC.753. ANTI–MANIPULATION AUTHORITY.

(a)PROHIBITION REGARDING MANIPULATION AND FALSE INFORMATION. — Subsection (c) of section 6 of the Commodity Exchange Act (7 U.S.C. 9, 15) is amended to read as follows:

"(c) PROHIBITION REGARDING MANIPULATION AND FALSE INFORMATION.—

"(1)PROHIBITION AGAINST MANIPULATION. — It shall be unlawful for any person, directly or indirectly, to use or employ, or attempt to use or employ, in connection with any swap, or a contract of sale of any commodity in interstate commerce, or for future delivery on or subject to the rules of any registered entity, any manipulative or deceptive device or contrivance, in contravention of such rules and regulations as the Commission shall promulgate by not later than 1 year after the date of enactment of the Dodd–Frank Wall Street Reform and Consumer Protection Act, provided no rule or regulation promulgated by the Commission shall require any person to disclose to another person nonpublic information that may be material to the market price, rate, or level of the commodity transaction, except as necessary to make any statement made to the other person in or in connection with the transaction not misleading in any material respect.

"(A) SPECIAL PROVISION FOR MANIPULATION BY FALSE REPORTING. — Unlawful manipulation for purposes of this paragraph shall include, but not be limited to, delivering, or causing to be delivered for transmission through the mails or interstate commerce, by any means of communication whatsoever, a false or misleading or inaccurate report concerning crop or market information or conditions that affect or tend to affect the price of any commodity in interstate commerce, knowing, or acting in reckless disregard of the fact that such report is false, misleading or inaccurate.

"(B) EFFECT ON OTHER LAW. — Nothing in this paragraph shall affect, or be construed to affect, the applicability of section 9(a)(2).

"(C) GOOD FAITH MISTAKES. — Mistakenly transmitting, in good faith, false or misleading or inaccurate information to a price reporting service would not be sufficient to violate subsection (c)(1)(A).

(b)为促进对远期交割商品出售合约及该等合约的期权的有效和一致的全球监管,商品期货交易委员会应就远期交割商品出售合约及该等合约的期权一致的全球监管标准之制定与外国监管部门进行磋商及协调,并可以就其判定对维护公共利益或保护远期交割商品出售合约用户确属必要或适当的信息共享安排作出约定。

第753条 打击操纵行为的权力

(a)**禁止操纵和提供虚假信息**。——《商品交易法》第6条第(c)子条(《美国法典》第七编第9节和第15节)修正后全文如下:

"(c)**禁止操纵和提供虚假信息**。——

(1)**禁止操纵**。——任何人违反商品期货交易委员会在《多德—弗兰克华尔街改革与消费者保护法》颁布之日后1年内颁发的规则与规章,而对任何互换、州际商业中的任何商品出售合约或在注册实体或按其规则进行远期交割的商品的出售合约直接或间接使用、利用或试图直接或间接使用或者利用任何具有操纵性或欺骗性的手段或伎俩的行为,当属违法;但是,商品期货交易委员会颁发的任何规则或规章均不得要求任何人向其他人披露对商品交易的市场价格、费率或水平可能有重要意义的非公开信息,但是,为了使该人向该其他人作出的任何交易声明或与交易相关的声明在任何重大方面不致具有误导性,该人所应披露的必要信息除外。

(A)**关于利用虚假报告进行操纵的特殊规定**。——就本款而言,非法操纵行为包括但不限于,在明知或漠视某一关于农作物或市场信息或状况的报告属于虚假报告、具有误导性或不准确这一事实的情况下,通过邮件或通过以任何通信手段开展的州际商业传送或通过第三方传送该等报告,且该等报告中所含的信息或状况影响或易于影响州际商业中的任何商品市场价格。

(B)**对其他法律的影响**。——本款任何内容均不影响亦不得被解释为影响第9(a)(2)条的适用范围。

(C)**善意过失**。——在善意的情况下向价格报告服务机构误传虚假、具有误导性或不准确的信息的,不足以构成违反第(c)(1)(A)子条规定的行为。

"(2) PROHIBITION REGARDING FALSE INFORMATION. — It shall be unlawful for any person to make any false or misleading statement of a material fact to the Commission, including in any registration application or any report filed with the Commission under this Act, or any other information relating to a swap, or a contract of sale of a commodity, in interstate commerce, or for future delivery on or subject to the rules of any registered entity, or to omit to state in any such statement any material fact that is necessary to make any statement of a material fact made not misleading in any material respect, if the person knew, or reasonably should have known, the statement to be false or misleading.

"(3) OTHER MANIPULATION. — In addition to the prohibition in paragraph (1), it shall be unlawful for any person, directly or indirectly, to manipulate or attempt to manipulate the price of any swap, or of any commodity in interstate commerce, or for future delivery on or subject to the rules of any registered entity.

"(4) ENFORCEMENT. —

"(A) AUTHORITY OF COMMISSION. — If the Commission has reason to believe that any person (other than a registered entity) is violating or has violated this subsection, or any other provision of this Act (including any rule, regulation, or order of the Commission promulgated in accordance with this subsection or any other provision of this Act), the Commission may serve upon the person a complaint.

"(B) CONTENTS OF COMPLAINT. — A complaint under subparagraph (A) shall —

"(i) contain a description of the charges against the person that is the subject of the complaint; and

"(ii) have attached or contain a notice of hearing that specifies the date and location of the hearing regarding the complaint.

"(C) HEARING. — A hearing described in subparagraph (B)(ii) —

"(i) shall be held not later than 3 days after service of the complaint described in subparagraph (A);

"(ii) shall require the person to show cause regarding why —

"(I) an order should not be made —

"(aa) to prohibit the person from trading on, or subject to the rules of, any registered entity; and

"(bb) to direct all registered entities to refuse all privileges to the person until further notice of the Commission; and

"(II) the registration of the person, if registered with the Commission in any capacity, should not be suspended or revoked; and

"(iii) may be held before —

"(I) the Commission; or

"(II) an administrative law judge designated by the Commission, under which the

(2)**禁止提供虚假信息**。——对于任何重大事实声明(包括根据本法向商品期货交易委员会提交的任何注册申请或报告所载声明,或者关于任何互换、州际商业中的商品出售合约或在注册实体或按其规则进行远期交割的商品的出售合约的其他信息所载声明),如果任何人明知或合理应知该等声明属于虚假声明或具有误导性,但仍向商品期货交易委员会作出该等声明,或在该等声明中遗漏使所作出的某一重大事实声明在任何重大方面不致具有误导性而有必要载明的重大事实的,当属违法。

(3)**其他操纵行为**。——除第(1)款禁止的行为之外,对于任何互换、州际商业中的商品出售合约或在任何注册实体或按其规则进行远期交割的商品的出售合约,任何人也不得直接或间接操纵或试图操纵其价格,否则亦属违法。

(4)**执行**。——

(A)**商品期货交易委员会的权力**。——如果商品期货交易委员会有理由相信,任何人(但注册实体除外)正在违反或已经违反了本子条或本法的任何其他规定(包括商品期货交易委员会根据本子条或本法任何其他条款颁发的任何规则、规章或命令),则商品期货交易委员会可以向该人送达指控告知书。

(B)**告知书的内容**。——第(A)子款所述告知书应——

(i)包含对被指控人的指控说明;及

(ii)附带或包含听证通知书,注明与指控相关的听证日期和地点;

(C)**听证**。——第(B)(ii)子款所述听证——

(i)应于第(A)子款所述指控告知书送达后3天内举行;

(ii)应要求该人提供理由说明为何——

(I)商品期货交易委员会不应发出命令——

(aa)禁止该人在任何注册实体交易或按其规则交易;及

(bb)责令所有注册实体在未收到商品期货交易委员会进一步通知前拒绝给予该人任何会员权;且

(II)其注册不应暂停或撤销(如果其已在商品期货交易委员会以任何身份注册);并

(iii)可由以下主体主持——

(I)商品期货交易委员会;或

(II)商品期货交易委员会指定的行政法官;在该种情形下,行政法官应确保以书

administrative law judge shall ensure that all evidence is recorded in written form and submitted to the Commission.

"(5) SUBPOENA. — For the purpose of securing effective enforcement of the provisions of this Act, for the purpose of any investigation or proceeding under this Act, and for the purpose of any action taken under section 12(f), any member of the Commission or any Administrative Law Judge or other officer designated by the Commission (except as provided in paragraph (7)) may administer oaths and affirmations, subpoena witnesses, compel their attendance, take evidence, and require the production of any books, papers, correspondence, memoranda, or other records that the Commission deems relevant or material to the inquiry.

"(6) WITNESSES. — The attendance of witnesses and the production of any such records may be required from any place in the United States, any State, or any foreign country or jurisdiction at any designated place of hearing.

"(7) SERVICE. — A subpoena issued under this section may be served upon any person who is not to be found within the territorial jurisdiction of any court of the United States in such manner as the Federal Rules of Civil Procedure prescribe for service of process in a foreign country, except that a subpoena to be served on a person who is not to be found within the territorial jurisdiction of any court of the United States may be issued only on the prior approval of the Commission.

"(8) REFUSAL TO OBEY. — In case of contumacy by, or refusal to obey a subpoena issued to, any person, the Commission may invoke the aid of any court of the United States within the jurisdiction in which the investigation or proceeding is conducted, or where such person resides or transacts business, in requiring the attendance and testimony of witnesses and the production of books, papers, correspondence, memoranda, and other records. Such court may issue an order requiring such person to appear before the Commission or member or Administrative Law Judge or other officer designated by the Commission, there to produce records, if so ordered, or to give testimony touching the matter under investigation or in question.

"(9) FAILURE TO OBEY. — Any failure to obey such order of the court may be punished by the court as a contempt thereof. All process in any such case may be served in the judicial district wherein such person is an inhabitant or transacts business or wherever such person may be found.

"(10) EVIDENCE. — On the receipt of evidence under paragraph (4)(C)(iii), the Commission may —

"(A) prohibit the person that is the subject of the hearing from trading on, or subject to the rules of, any registered entity and require all registered entities to refuse the person all privileges on the registered entities for such period as the Commission may require in the

面形式记录所有证据,并将其呈交给商品期货交易委员会。

(5)**传票**。——为确保有效执行本法规定,在依本法开展任何调查或程序之时,以及在依第12(f)条采取任何行动之时,商品期货交易委员会的任何委员或商品期货交易委员会指定的任何行政法官或任何其他官员[本条第(7)款规定的官员除外]可以主持证词宣誓或声明程序、传唤证人、强制证人出席听证、取证,并要求出示任何账簿、文书、通信、备忘录或商品期货交易委员会认为具有相关性或实质意义的其他记录或材料以供调查。

(6)**证人和证据**。——商品期货交易委员会可以指定任何听证地点,要求证人从美国、任何州、任何外国或境外地区的任何地方到指定的听证地点出席听证,或要求证人从该等任何地方到指定的听证地点出示任何上述记录。

(7)**送达**。——根据本条规定签发的传票可以按照《联邦民事诉讼规则》规定的境外送达司法文书方式,向被发现地在任何联邦法院地域管辖范围之外的任何人送达,但是只有在事先征得商品期货交易委员会批准的情况下,方可向被发现地在任何联邦法院地域管辖范围之外的人签发传票。

(8)**拒绝服从**。——任何人藐视法庭或拒绝服从法庭向其签发的传票的,商品期货交易委员会可请求调查或程序开展地的任何联邦法院或者该等人员居住地或营业地的任何联邦法院提供协助,要求证人出席作证以及出示账簿、文书、通信、备忘录和其他记录。该等法院可签发命令要求该等人员出席商品期货交易委员会、商品期货交易委员会委员、商品期货交易委员会指定的行政法官或其他官员主持的程序,按商品期货交易委员会、商品期货交易委员会委员、商品期货交易委员会指定的行政法官或其他官员的命令(如有)向其出示记录,或就正在进行调查的事宜或有关事宜作证。

(9)**不服从命令的情形**。——任何人不服从上述法院命令的行为均可作为藐视法庭罪予以处罚。任何该等案件的一切司法文书均可送达至该人的居住地、营业地或被发现地所属的司法辖区。

(10)**证据**。——商品期货交易委员会收到第(4)(C)(iii)款规定的证据后——

(A)可以禁止听证程序当事人在任何注册实体交易或按其规则交易,并要求所有注册实体拒绝给予该人任何会员权,禁止期和拒绝期的期限应在商品期货交易委员会的命令中明确规定;

order;

"(B) if the person is registered with the Commission in any capacity, suspend, for a period not to exceed 180 days, or revoke, the registration of the person;

"(C) assess such person —

"(i) a civil penalty of not more than an amount equal to the greater of —

"(I) $140,000; or

"(II) triple the monetary gain to such person for each such violation; or

"(ii) in any case of manipulation or attempted manipulation in violation of this subsection or section 9(a)(2), a civil penalty of not more than an amount equal to the greater of —

"(I) $1,000,000; or

"(II) triple the monetary gain to the person for each such violation; and

"(D) require restitution to customers of damages proximately caused by violations of the person.

"(11) ORDERS. —

"(A) NOTICE. — The Commission shall provide to a person described in paragraph (10) and the appropriate governing board of the registered entity notice of the order described in paragraph (10) by —

"(i) registered mail;

"(ii) certified mail; or

"(iii) personal delivery.

"(B) REVIEW. —

"(i) IN GENERAL. — A person described in paragraph (10) may obtain a review of the order or such other equitable relief as determined to be appropriate by a court described in clause (ii).

"(ii) PETITION. — To obtain a review or other relief under clause (i), a person may, not later than 15 days after notice is given to the person under clause (i), file a written petition to set aside the order with the United States Court of Appeals —

"(I) for the circuit in which the petitioner carries out the business of the petitioner; or

"(II) in the case of an order denying registration, the circuit in which the principal place of business of the petitioner is located, as listed on the application for registration of the petitioner.

"(C) PROCEDURE. —

"(i) DUTY OF CLERK OF APPROPRIATE COURT. — The clerk of the appropriate court under subparagraph (B)(ii) shall transmit to the Commission a copy of a petition filed under subparagraph (B)(ii).

"(ii) DUTY OF COMMISSION. — In accordance with section 2112 of title 28, United

(B)如果该人已经以任何身份在商品期货交易委员会注册,则可暂停(期限不超过180天)或撤销其注册资格;

(C)按下述标准对该人计征罚款——

(i)对每宗违法违规行为处以不高于下列数额的民事罚款(以较高者为准)——

(I)14万美元;或

(II)其货币性收益的三倍金额;或

(ii)对于违反本子条或第9(a)(2)条的任何操纵或试图操纵行为,每宗违法违规行为可处以不高于下列数额的民事罚款(以较高者为准)——

(I)100万美元;或

(II)其货币性收益的三倍金额;并

(D)可以要求该人按其违法违规行为直接导致的损失向客户返还该等款项。

(11)**命令**。——

(A)**通知**。——对于第(10)款所述命令,商品期货交易委员会应以下列方式向第(10)款所述之人和注册实体相应的管理机构提供通知——

(i)挂号邮件;

(ii)带回执邮件;或

(iii)专人送达。

(B)**审查**。——

(i)**一般规定**。——第(10)款所述之人可以获得第(ii)项所述法院对商品期货交易委员会命令进行审查或获得该法院判定确属适当的衡平法救济。

(ii)**请求**。——请求人可在收到第(i)项所述通知后15天内向下列联邦上诉法院提交撤销商品期货交易委员会命令的书面请求书,以获得第(i)项所述审查或其他救济——

(I)请求人业务开展地所在巡回区的联邦上诉法院;或

(II)如果案件所涉命令为拒绝注册申请令,请求人注册申请书所示主要营业地所在巡回区的联邦上诉法院。

(C)**程序步骤**。——

(i)**相应法院的书记员职责**。——第(B)(ii)子款所述相应法院的书记员应将根据第(B)(ii)子款提交的请求书复本转发给商品期货交易委员会。

(ii)**商品期货交易委员会的职责**。——根据《美国法典》第二十八编第2112节的

States Code, the Commission shall file in the appropriate court described in subparagraph (B)(ii) the record theretofore made.

"(iii) JURISDICTION OF APPROPRIATE COURT. — Upon the filing of a petition under subparagraph (B)(ii), the appropriate court described in subparagraph (B)(ii) may affirm, set aside, or modify the order of the Commission.".

(b) CEASE AND DESIST ORDERS, FINES. — Section 6 (d) of the Commodity Exchange Act (7 U.S.C. 13b) is amended to read as follows:

"(d) If any person (other than a registered entity), is violating or has violated subsection (c) or any other provisions of this Act or of the rules, regulations, or orders of the Commission thereunder, the Commission may, upon notice and hearing, and subject to appeal as in other cases provided for in subsection (c), make and enter an order directing that such person shall cease and desist therefrom and, if such person thereafter and after the lapse of the period allowed for appeal of such order or after the affirmance of such order, shall knowingly fail or refuse to obey or comply with such order, such person, upon conviction thereof, shall be fined not more than the higher of $140,000 or triple the monetary gain to such person, or imprisoned for not more than 1 year, or both, except that if such knowing failure or refusal to obey or comply with such order involves any offense within subsection (a) or (b) of section 9, such person, upon conviction thereof, shall be subject to the penalties of said subsection (a) or (b): Provided, That any such cease and desist order under this subsection against any respondent in any case of manipulation shall be issued only in conjunction with an order issued against such respondent under subsection (c).".

(c) MANIPULATIONS; PRIVATE RIGHTS OF ACTION. — Section 22(a)(1) of the Commodity Exchange Act (7 U.S.C. 25(a)(1)) is amended by striking subparagraph (D) and inserting the following:

"(D) who purchased or sold a contract referred to in subparagraph (B) hereof or swap if the violation constitutes —

"(i) the use or employment of, or an attempt to use or employ, in connection with a swap, or a contract of sale of a commodity, in interstate commerce, or for future delivery on or subject to the rules of any registered entity, any manipulative device or contrivance in contravention of such rules and regulations as the Commission shall promulgate by not later than 1 year after the date of enactment of the Dodd–Frank Wall Street Reform and Consumer Protection Act; or

"(ii) a manipulation of the price of any such contract or swap or the price of the commodity underlying such contract or swap.".

(d) EFFECTIVE DATE. —

(1) The amendments made by this section shall take effect on the date on which the final rule promulgated by the Commodity Futures Trading Commission pursuant to this Act

规定,商品期货交易委员会收到请求书复本后应将其所收到的证人出示的所有记录提交至第(B)(ii)子款所述相应法院。

(iii)**相应法院的管辖权**。——收到根据第(B)(ii)子款提交的请求书后,第(B)(ii)子款所述相应法院可以维持、撤销或变更商品期货交易委员会的命令。"

(b)**制止令;罚款**。——《商品交易法》第6(d)条(《美国法典》第七编第13b节)修正后全文如下:

"(d)如果任何人(但注册实体除外)正在违反或已经违反第(c)子条或本法任何其他规定或商品期货交易委员会依据本法颁发的规则、规章或命令,商品期货交易委员会可以在发出通知并举行听证后,制定并发出命令,责令该人停止该等行为,但是对于该等命令,该人可比照第(c)子条针对其他情形所做规定提请司法审查。如果该人在该等命令签发之后并且在允许对该等命令提请司法审查的期限届满后或在法院维持该等命令后,仍故意不服从或不遵守该命令,或拒绝服从或拒绝遵守该等命令,经判决有罪后应单处或并处不高于14万美元或该人货币性收益三倍金额的罚款(以较高者为准)或者1年以下(含)监禁。但是,如果故意不服从或不遵守该等命令或者拒绝服从或拒绝遵守该等命令的行为牵涉第9条第(a)子条或第(b)子条规定的任何违法违规行为,则经判决有罪后,应按上述第(a)子条或第(b)子条的规定处罚;但是,根据本子条向任何操纵案件中的被告发出的任何临时制止令,仅得与根据第(c)子条向该等被告签发的命令联合发出。"

(c)**操纵;私人诉讼权利**。——《商品交易法》第22(a)(1)条[《美国法典》第七编第25(a)(1)节]修正如下:删除第(D)子款,替以:

"(D)买入或卖出本款第(B)子款提及的合约的人,或者买入或卖出互换的人,其前提是该等违法行为——

(i)构成违反商品期货交易委员会应在《多德—弗兰克华尔街改革与消费者保护法》颁布之日后1年内颁发的规则与规章,针对互换、州际商业中的商品出售合约或在任何注册实体或按其规则进行远期交割的商品出售合约,使用、利用或试图使用、利用任何具有操纵性或欺骗性的手段或伎俩的行为;或

(ii)构成对上述任何合约或互换价格的操纵或者对上述任何合约或互换基础商品价格的操纵。"

(d)**生效日**。——

(1)本条所做修正的生效日即为商品期货交易委员会根据本法颁发的最终规则生效之日。

takes effect.

(2) Paragraph (1) shall not preclude the Commission from undertaking prior to the effective date any rulemaking necessary to implement the amendments contained in this section.

SEC.754. EFFECTIVE DATE.

Unless otherwise provided in this title, the provisions of this subtitle shall take effect on the later of 360 days after the date of the enactment of this subtitle or, to the extent a provision of this subtitle requires a rulemaking, not less than 60 days after publication of the final rule or regulation implementing such provision of this subtitle.

Subtitle B — Regulation of Security–Based Swap Markets

SEC.761. DEFINITIONS UNDER THE SECURITIES EXCHANGE ACT OF 1934.

(a) DEFINITIONS. — Section 3(a) of the Securities Exchange Act of 1934 (15 U.S.C. 78c(a)) is amended —

(1) in subparagraphs (A) and (B) of paragraph (5), by inserting "(not including security–based swaps, other than security–based swaps with or for persons that are not eligible contract participants)" after "securities" each place that term appears;

(2) in paragraph (10), by inserting "security–based swap," after "security future,";

(3) in paragraph (13), by adding at the end the following: "For security–based swaps, such terms include the execution, termination (prior to its scheduled maturity date), assignment, exchange, or similar transfer or conveyance of, or extinguishing of rights or obligations under, a security–based swap, as the context may require.";

(4) in paragraph (14), by adding at the end the following: "For security–based swaps, such terms include the execution, termination (prior to its scheduled maturity date), assignment, exchange, or similar transfer or conveyance of, or extinguishing of rights or obligations under, a security–based swap, as the context may require.";

(5) in paragraph (39) —

(A) in subparagraph (B)(i) —

(i) in subclause (I), by striking "or government securities dealer" and inserting "government securities dealer, security–based swap dealer, or major security–based swap participant"; and

(ii) in subclause (II), by inserting "security–based swap dealer, major security–based

(2)第(1)款的规定不得禁止商品期货交易委员会在上述生效日前开展实施本条中修正所需的规则制定工作。

第754条　生效日

除非本编另有规定,否则本子编的规定应于下列日期(以较晚者为准)生效:本子编颁布之日后第360天,或者本子编规定需要制定实施规则的,不迟于该规定的最终实施规则或规章公布之日后第60天。

第B子编——证券类互换市场的监管

第761条　《1934年证券交易法》中的定义

(a)**定义**。——《1934年证券交易法》第3(a)条[《美国法典》第十五编第78c(a)节]修正如下——

(1)在第(5)款第(A)子款和第(B)子款中,在所有"证券"一词之后插入"(不包括证券类互换,但与非适格合约参与者达成的或为其达成的证券类互换除外)";

(2)在第(10)款中,在"证券期货、"之后插入"证券类互换、";

(3)在第(13)款结尾处增加如下内容:"根据上下文,'证券类互换'一词包括证券类互换项下的权利或义务的执行、终止(指在预定的到期日之前终止)、转让、交换或类似转移或让与,或者消灭。"

(4)在第(14)款结尾处增加如下内容:"根据上下文,'证券类互换'一词包括证券类互换项下的权利或义务的执行、终止(指在预定的到期日之前终止)、转让、交换或类似转移或让与,或者消灭。"

(5)在第(39)款中——

(A)第(B)(i)子款——

(i)第(I)子项删除"或政府证券自营商",替以"政府证券自营商、证券类互换交易商或主要的证券类互换参与者";及

(ii)第(II)子项在"政府证券自营商"之后插入"证券类互换交易商或主要的证券

swap participant," after "government securities dealer,";

(B) in subparagraph (C), by striking "or government securities dealer" and inserting "government securities dealer, security–based swap dealer, or major security–based swap participant"; and

(C) in subparagraph (D), by inserting "security–based swap dealer, major security–based swap participant," after "government securities dealer,"; and

(6) by adding at the end the following:

"(65) ELIGIBLE CONTRACT PARTICIPANT. — The term 'eligible contract participant' has the same meaning as in section 1a of the Commodity Exchange Act (7 U.S.C. 1a).

"(66) MAJOR SWAP PARTICIPANT. — The term 'major swap participant' has the same meaning as in section 1a of the Commodity Exchange Act (7 U.S.C. 1a).

"(67) MAJOR SECURITY–BASED SWAP PARTICIPANT. —

"(A) IN GENERAL. — The term 'major security–based swap participant' means any person —

"(i) who is not a security–based swap dealer; and

"(ii)(I) who maintains a substantial position in security–based swaps for any of the major security–based swap categories, as such categories are determined by the Commission, excluding both positions held for hedging or mitigating commercial risk and positions maintained by any employee benefit plan (or any contract held by such a plan) as defined in paragraphs (3) and (32) of section 3 of the Employee Retirement Income Security Act of 1974 (29 U.S.C. 1002) for the primary purpose of hedging or mitigating any risk directly associated with the operation of the plan;

"(II) whose outstanding security–based swaps create substantial counterparty exposure that could have serious adverse effects on the financial stability of the United States banking system or financial markets; or

"(III) that is a financial entity that —

"(aa) is highly leveraged relative to the amount of capital such entity holds and that is not subject to capital requirements established by an appropriate Federal banking agency; and

"(bb) maintains a substantial position in outstanding security–based swaps in any major security–based swap category, as such categories are determined by the Commission.

"(B) DEFINITION OF SUBSTANTIAL POSITION. — For purposes of subparagraph (A), the Commission shall define, by rule or regulation, the term 'substantial position' at the threshold that the Commission determines to be prudent for the effective monitoring, management, and oversight of entities that are systemically important or can significantly impact the financial system of the United States. In setting the definition under this

类互换参与者”;

(B)第(C)子款删除“或政府证券自营商”,替以“政府证券自营商、证券类互换交易商或主要的证券类互换参与者”;及

(C)第(D)子款在“政府证券自营商”之后插入“证券类互换交易商、主要的证券类互换参与者”;及

(6)在本条结尾处增加如下内容:

“(65)**适格合约参与者**。——‘适格合约参与者’一词的含义以《商品交易法》第1a条(《美国法典》第七编第1a节)的定义为准。

(66)**主要互换参与者**。——‘主要互换参与者’一词的含义以《商品交易法》第1a条(《美国法典》第七编第1a节)的定义为准。

(67)**主要的证券类互换参与者**。——

(A)**一般规定**。——‘主要的证券类互换参与者’一词系指符合下列条件的任何人——

(i)并非证券类互换交易商;且

(ii)(I)在证券交易委员会判定的任何类别的主要的证券类互换中维持有大额持仓,但该等持仓不包括为了对商业风险进行套期保值或缓释而持有的持仓,亦不包括任何员工福利计划[定义见《1974年员工退休收入保障法》第3条第(3)款和第(32)款(《美国法典》第29编第1002节)]维持的主要旨在对与该计划运作直接相关的任何风险进行套期保值或缓释的持仓(或该等计划持有的任何合约);

(II)其尚未了结的证券类互换形成重大对手方风险敞口,而该等敞口可能给美国银行体系或金融市场的金融稳定带来重大不利影响;或

(III)身为具有下列特征的金融实体——

(aa)杠杆率相对于其持有的资本额而言过高且不受制于相应的联邦银行业监管机关设定的资本要求;且

(bb)对商品期货交易委员会判定的任何类别的主要的证券类互换持有大额未了结的证券类互换持仓。

(B)**大额持仓的定义**。——就第(A)子款而言,商品期货交易委员会应当按照其判定确属审慎的门槛标准,发布规则或规章对‘大额持仓’一词作出定义,以便有效监控、管理和监督具有系统重要性的或可能对美国金融体系产生重大影响的实体。在按照本子款确定上述定义时,商品期货交易委员会应考虑该等主体非集中结算的证券类互换的持仓和集中结算的证券类互换的持仓之间的比例,并可将该等主体为了担

subparagraph, the Commission shall consider the person's relative position in uncleared as opposed to cleared security–based swaps and may take into consideration the value and quality of collateral held against counterparty exposures.

"(C) SCOPE OF DESIGNATION. — For purposes of subparagraph (A), a person may be designated as a major security–based swap participant for 1 or more categories of security–based swaps without being classified as a major security–based swap participant for all classes of security–based swaps.

"(68) SECURITY–BASED SWAP. —

"(A) IN GENERAL. — Except as provided in subparagraph (B), the term 'security–based swap' means any agreement, contract, or transaction that —

"(i) is a swap, as that term is defined under section 1a of the Commodity Exchange Act (without regard to paragraph (47)(B)(x) of such section); and

"(ii) is based on —

"(I) an index that is a narrow–based security index, including any interest therein or on the value thereof;

"(II) a single security or loan, including any interest therein or on the value thereof; or

"(III) the occurrence, nonoccurrence, or extent of the occurrence of an event relating to a single issuer of a security or the issuers of securities in a narrow–based security index, provided that such event directly affects the financial statements, financial condition, or financial obligations of the issuer.

"(B)RULE OF CONSTRUCTION REGARDING MASTER AGREEMENTS. — The term 'security–based swap' shall be construed to include a master agreement that provides for an agreement, contract, or transaction that is a security–based swap pursuant to subparagraph (A), together with all supplements to any such master agreement, without regard to whether the master agreement contains an agreement, contract, or transaction that is not a security–based swap pursuant to subparagraph (A), except that the master agreement shall be considered to be a security–based swap only with respect to each agreement, contract, or transaction under the master agreement that is a security–based swap pursuant to subparagraph (A).

"(C) EXCLUSIONS. — The term 'security–based swap' does not include any agreement, contract, or transaction that meets the definition of a security–based swap only because such agreement, contract, or transaction references, is based upon, or settles through the transfer, delivery, or receipt of an exempted security under paragraph (12), as in effect on the date of enactment of the Futures Trading Act of 1982 (other than any municipal security as defined in paragraph (29) as in effect on the date of enactment of the Futures Trading Act of 1982), unless such agreement, contract, or transaction is of the character of, or is

保对手方风险敞口所持有的担保品价值和质量纳入考虑。

(C)**指定范围**。——就第(A)子款而言,任何主体均可被指定为一类或一类以上证券类互换的主要的证券类互换参与者,而不必同时被指定为所有类别的证券类互换的主要的证券类互换参与者。

(68)**证券类互换**。——

(A)**一般规定**。——除第(B)子款另有规定外,'证券类互换'一词系指具有下列特征的任何协议、合约或交易——

(i)属于《商品交易法》第1a条[该条第(47)(B)(x)款的规定不予考虑]定义的互换;且

(ii)系基于——

(I)某一属于窄基证券指数的指数,包括该指数的任何权益或基于该指数价值的任何权益;

(II)单一证券或贷款,包括该证券或贷款的任何权益或者基于该证券或贷款价值的任何权益;或

(III)与某一窄基证券指数中某一证券的单一发行人或某些证券的若干发行人相关之事件的发生、不发生或发生的范围或程度,但前提是该事件对上述发行人的财务报表、财务状况或财务义务有直接影响。

(B)**关于主协议的解释规则**。——'证券类互换'一词应解释为包括具有如下特征的某一主协议及其全部补充协议:对属于第(A)子款定义的证券类互换的协议、合约或交易作出规定的主协议,不论该主协议是否含有不属于第(A)子款定义的证券类互换的协议、合约或交易,但是,只有对于属于第(A)子款定义的证券类互换之主协议项下每一协议、合约或交易而言,主协议始得视为证券类互换。

(C)**除外规定**。——如任何协议、合约或交易之所以符合证券类互换之定义,完全系因为其参考或建基于在《1982年期货交易法》颁布之日已生效的第(12)款项下某一豁免证券[在《1982年期货交易法》颁布之日已生效的第(29)款定义的市政证券除外]的转移或交收,或完全系因为通过上述豁免证券的转移或交收来完成结算,则该等协议、合约或交易不应包括在'证券类互换'一词的定义之内,除非上述协议、合约或交易具有'看跌期权'、'看涨期权'或其他期权特质或通常被业界冠以该等名称。

commonly known in the trade as, a put, call, or other option.

"(D) MIXED SWAP. — The term 'security–based swap' includes any agreement, contract, or transaction that is as described in subparagraph (A) and also is based on the value of 1 or more interest or other rates, currencies, commodities, instruments of indebtedness, indices, quantitative measures, other financial or economic interest or property of any kind (other than a single security or a narrow–based security index), or the occurrence, non–occurrence, or the extent of the occurrence of an event or contingency associated with a potential financial, economic, or commercial consequence (other than an event described in subparagraph (A)(ii)(III)).

"(E) RULE OF CONSTRUCTION REGARDING USE OF THE TERM INDEX. — The term 'index' means an index or group of securities, including any interest therein or based on the value thereof.

"(69) SWAP. — The term 'swap' has the same meaning as in section 1a of the Commodity Exchange Act (7 U.S.C. 1a).

"(70) PERSON ASSOCIATED WITH A SECURITY–BASED SWAP DEALER OR MAJOR SECURITY–BASED SWAP PARTICIPANT. —

"(A) IN GENERAL. — The term 'person associated with a security–based swap dealer or major security–based swap participant' or 'associated person of a security–based swap dealer or major security–based swap participant' means —

"(i) any partner, officer, director, or branch manager of such security–based swap dealer or major security–based swap participant (or any person occupying a similar status or performing similar functions);

"(ii) any person directly or indirectly controlling, controlled by, or under common control with such security–based swap dealer or major security–based swap participant; or

"(iii) any employee of such security–based swap dealer or major security–based swap participant.

"(B) EXCLUSION. — Other than for purposes of section 15F(l)(2), the term 'person associated with a security–based swap dealer or major security–based swap participant' or 'associated person of a security–based swap dealer or major security–based swap participant' does not include any person associated with a security–based swap dealer or major security–based swap participant whose functions are solely clerical or ministerial.

"(71) SECURITY–BASED SWAP DEALER. —

"(A) IN GENERAL. — The term 'security–based swap dealer' means any person who —

"(i) holds themself out as a dealer in security–based swaps;

"(ii) makes a market in security–based swaps;

"(iii) regularly enters into security–based swaps with counterparties as an ordinary

(D)**混合互换**。——'证券类互换'一词包括第(A)子款所述的并且同时基于一项或一项以上利率或其他比率、货币、商品、债务工具、指数、量化指标、任何其他种类的金融或经济权益或财产(但单一证券或窄基证券指数除外)的价值的任何协议、合约或交易或者第(A)子款所述的并且同时基于伴随有潜在金融、经济或商业后果的某一事件的发生、某一事件的不发生或某一事件发生的范围或程度的任何协议、合约或交易,或者同时基于伴随有潜在金融、经济或商业后果的或有事件发生的可能性[但第(A)(ii)(III)子款所述事件除外]的任何协议、合约或交易。

(E)**关于指数一词使用的解释规则**。——'指数'一词系指证券指数或证券集合,包括该等集合或指数的任何权益,或者基于该等集合或指数价值的任何权益。

(69)**互换**。——'互换'一词的含义以《商品交易法》第1a条(《美国法典》第七编第1a节)的定义为准。

(70)**证券类互换交易商或主要的证券类互换参与者的业务相关人**。——

(A)**一般规定**。——'与证券类互换交易商或主要的证券类互换参与者存在业务相关关系的人'或者'证券类互换交易商或主要的证券类互换参与者的业务相关人'一词系指——

(i)该证券类互换交易商或主要的证券类互换参与者的任何合伙人、管理人员、董事或分支机构经理(或担任类似职务或履行类似职能的任何人);

(ii)直接或间接控制该证券类互换交易商或主要的证券类互换参与者,由该交易商或参与者控制或与其受同一控制的任何人;或

(iii)该证券类互换交易商或主要的证券类互换参与者的任何员工。

(B)**除外规定**。——除用于第15F(1)(2)条之外,'与证券类互换交易商或主要的证券类互换参与者存在业务相关关系的人'或'证券类互换交易商或主要的证券类互换参与者的业务相关人'一词不包括仅因履行文员或行政职能而与该交易商或参与者产生关联的人。

(71)**证券类互换交易商**。——

(A)**一般规定**。——'证券类互换交易商'一词系指具有以下特征的任何人——

(i)以证券类互换交易商身份自居;

(ii)为证券类互换做市;

(iii)为其自身账户在正常业务运作中经常地与对手方达成证券类互换;或

course of business for its own account; or

"(iv) engages in any activity causing it to be commonly known in the trade as a dealer or market maker in security–based swaps.

"(B) DESIGNATION BY TYPE OR CLASS. — A person may be designated as a security–based swap dealer for a single type or single class or category of security–based swap or activities and considered not to be a security–based swap dealer for other types, classes, or categories of security–based swaps or activities.

"(C) EXCEPTION. — The term 'security–based swap dealer' does not include a person that enters into security–based swaps for such person's own account, either individually or in a fiduciary capacity, but not as a part of regular business.

"(D) DE MINIMIS EXCEPTION. — The Commission shall exempt from designation as a security–based swap dealer an entity that engages in a de minimis quantity of security–based swap dealing in connection with transactions with or on behalf of its customers. The Commission shall promulgate regulations to establish factors with respect to the making of any determination to exempt.

"(72) APPROPRIATE FEDERAL BANKING AGENCY. — The term 'appropriate Federal banking agency' has the same meaning as in section 3(q) of the Federal Deposit Insurance Act (12 U.S.C. 1813(q)).

"(73) BOARD. — The term 'Board' means the Board of Governors of the Federal Reserve System.

"(74) PRUDENTIAL REGULATOR. — The term 'prudential regulator' has the same meaning as in section 1a of the Commodity Exchange Act (7 U.S.C. 1a).

"(75)SECURITY–BASED SWAP DATA REPOSITORY. — The term 'security–based swap data repository' means any person that collects and maintains information or records with respect to transactions or positions in, or the terms and conditions of, security–based swaps entered into by third parties for the purpose of providing a centralized recordkeeping facility for security–based swaps.

"(76) SWAP DEALER. — The term 'swap dealer' has the same meaning as in section 1a of the Commodity Exchange Act (7 U.S.C. 1a).

"(77)SECURITY–BASED SWAP EXECUTION FACILITY. — The term 'security–based swap execution facility' means a trading system or platform in which multiple participants have the ability to execute or trade security–based swaps by accepting bids and offers made by multiple participants in the facility or system, through any means of interstate commerce, including any trading facility, that —

"(A) facilitates the execution of security–based swaps between persons; and

"(B) is not a national securities exchange.

"(78) SECURITY–BASED SWAP AGREEMENT. —

(iv)因其从事的活动导致其被业界通称为证券类互换交易商或做市商。

(B)**按照类型或类别的指定**。——任何主体均可在被指定为某单一类型、类别或种类的证券类互换或活动的证券类互换交易商的同时,而不被视为其他类型、类别或种类的证券类互换或活动的证券类互换交易商。

(C)**例外规定**。——'证券类互换交易商'一词不包括:虽以自身身份或受信义务人身份为自身账户达成证券类互换,但并不以此为常规业务的主体。

(D)**微量豁免**。——对于因为与其客户进行的交易或代表其客户进行的交易而从事微量证券类互换交易的实体,商品期货交易委员会应授予其豁免,使其不必被指定为证券类互换交易商。商品期货交易委员会应颁发规章,明确规定作出上述豁免判定时应予考虑的因素。

(72)**相应的联邦银行业监管机关**。——'相应的联邦银行业监管机关'一词的含义以《联邦存款保险法》第3(q)条[《美国法典》第十二编第1813(q)节]的定义为准。

(73)**联邦储备委员会**。——'联邦储备委员会'一词系指美国联邦储备系统管理委员会。

(74)**审慎监管者**。——'审慎监管者'一词的含义以《商品交易法》第1a条(《美国法典》第七编第1a节)的定义为准。

(75)**证券类互换数据存管机构**。——'证券类互换数据存管机构'一词系指为了给证券类互换提供集中的记录保存设施,就第三方达成的证券类互换交易或持仓的相关信息或记录以及与该等证券类互换的条款和条件相关的信息或记录,进行收集和保存的任何主体。

(76)**互换交易商**。——'互换交易商'一词的含义以《商品交易法》第1a条(《美国法典》第七编第1a节)的定义为准。

(77)**证券类互换执行设施**。——'证券类互换执行设施'一词系指具有如下特征的交易系统或平台:众多参与者可以通过任何州际商业手段接受设施内或系统内众多参与者的买卖报价以执行或交易证券类互换。该等系统或平台包括符合下述条件的任何交易设施——

(A)为不同主体之间的证券类互换执行提供便利;且

(B)并非全国性证券交易所。

(78)**证券类互换协议**。——

"(A) IN GENERAL. — For purposes of sections 9, 10, 16, 20, and 21A of this Act, and section 17 of the Securities Act of 1933 (15 U.S.C. 77q), the term 'security–based swap agreement' means a swap agreement as defined in section 206A of the Gramm–Leach–Bliley Act (15 U.S.C. 78c note) of which a material term is based on the price, yield, value, or volatility of any security or any group or index of securities, or any interest therein.

"(B) EXCLUSIONS. — The term 'security–based swap agreement' does not include any security–based swap.".

(b) AUTHORITY TO FURTHER DEFINE TERMS. — The Securities and Exchange Commission may, by rule, further define —

(1) the term "commercial risk";

(2) any other term included in an amendment to the Securities Exchange Act of 1934 (15 U.S.C. 78c(a)) made by this subtitle; and

(3) the terms "security–based swap", "security–based swap dealer", "major security–based swap participant", and "eligible contract participant", with regard to security–based swaps (as such terms are defined in the amendments made by subsection (a)) for the purpose of including transactions and entities that have been structured to evade this subtitle or the amendments made by this subtitle.

SEC.762. REPEAL OF PROHIBITION ON REGULATION OF SECURITY–BASED SWAP AGREEMENTS.

(a) REPEAL. — Sections 206B and 206C of the Gramm–Leach–Bliley Act (Public Law 106–102; 15 U.S.C. 78c note) are repealed.

(b) CONFORMING AMENDMENTS TO GRAMM–LEACH–BLILEY. — Section 206A(a) of the Gramm–Leach–Bliley Act (15 U.S.C. 78c note) is amended in the material preceding paragraph (1), by striking "Except as" and all that follows through "that — " and inserting the following: "Except as provided in subsection (b), as used in this section, the term 'swap agreement' means any agreement, contract, or transaction that — ".

(c) CONFORMING AMENDMENTS TO THE SECURITIES ACT OF 1933. —

(1) Section 2A of the Securities Act of 1933 (15 U.S.C. 77b – 1) is amended —

(A) by striking subsection (a) and reserving that subsection; and

(B) by striking "(as defined in section 206B of the Gramm–Leach–Bliley Act)" each place that such term appears and inserting "(as defined in section 3(a)(78) of the Securities Exchange Act of 1934)".

(2) Section 17 of the Securities Act of 1933 (15 U.S.C. 77q) is amended —

(A) in subsection (a) —

(i) by inserting "(including security–based swaps)" after "securities"; and

(ii) by striking "(as defined in section 206B of the Gramm–Leach–Bliley Act)" and inserting "(as defined in section 3(a)(78) of the Securities Exchange Act)"; and

(A)**一般规定**。——就本法第9条、第10条、第16条、第20条和第21A条以及《1933年证券法》第17条(《美国法典》第十五编第77q节)而言,‘证券类互换协议’一词系指《格雷姆—里奇—比利雷法》第206A条(《美国法典》第十五编第78c节注释)定义的互换协议,且该等互换协议的某项重大条款系基于任何证券、任何证券集合、证券指数或上述各者的任何权益之价格、收益率、价值或波动性。

(B)**除外规定**。——‘证券类互换协议’一词不包括任何证券类互换。”

(b)**进一步界定术语的权力**。——证券交易委员会可以发布规则进一步对下列术语进行界定——

(1)“商业风险”;

(2)本子编对《1934年证券交易法》[《美国法典》第十五编第78c(a)节]作出的修正中包含的任何其他术语;及

(3)第(a)子条所做修正中定义的与证券类互换相关的下列术语:“证券类互换”、“证券类互换交易商”、“主要的证券类互换参与者”、“适格合约参与者”,以便将出于规避本子编规定或本子编所做修正之目的而构建的交易和实体纳入本子编的管辖范围。

第762条　废止证券类互换的监管禁令

(a)**废止**。——兹废止《格雷姆—里奇—比利雷法》第206B条和第206C条(第106—102号公法;《美国法典》第十五编第78c节注释)。

(b)**对《格雷姆—里奇—比利雷法》的一致性修正**。——对《格雷姆—里奇—比利雷法》第206A(a)条(《美国法典》第十五编第78c节注释)第(1)款之前的内容修正如下:删除“除”至“——”的所有内容,替以:“除第(b)子条规定的情形外,在本条中,‘互换协议’一词系指具有下列特征的任何协议、合约或交易——”。

(c)**对《1933年证券法》第2A条的一致性修正如下**。——

(1)《1933年证券法》第2A条(《美国法典》第十五编第77b-1节)修正如下——

(A)删除第(a)子条规定但保留该子条序号;及

(B)删除所有“(定义见《格雷姆—里奇—比利雷法》第206B条)”,并替以“[定义见《1934年证券交易法》第3(a)(78)条]”。

(2)《1933年证券法》第17条(《美国法典》第十五编第77q节)修正如下——

(A)第(a)子条——

(i)在“证券”之后插入“(包括证券类互换)”;及

(ii)删除“(定义见《格雷姆—里奇—比利雷法》第206B条)”,并替以“[定义见《1934年证券交易法》第3(a)(78)条]”;及

(B) in subsection (d), by striking "206B of the Gramm–Leach–Bliley Act" and inserting "3(a)(78) of the Securities Exchange Act of 1934".

(d) CONFORMING AMENDMENTS TO THE SECURITIES EXCHANGE ACT OF 1934. — The Securities Exchange Act of 1934 (15 U.S.C. 78a et seq.) is amended —

(1) in section 3A (15 U.S.C. 78c – 1) —

(A) by striking subsection (a) and reserving that subsection; and

(B) by striking "(as defined in section 206B of the Gramm–Leach–Bliley Act)" each place that the term appears;

(2) in section 9 (15 U.S.C. 78i) —

(A) in subsection (a), by striking paragraphs (2) through (5) and inserting the following:

"(2) To effect, alone or with 1 or more other persons, a series of transactions in any security registered on a national securities exchange, any security not so registered, or in connection with any security–based swap or security–based swap agreement with respect to such security creating actual or apparent active trading in such security, or raising or depressing the price of such security, for the purpose of inducing the purchase or sale of such security by others.

"(3) If a dealer, broker, security–based swap dealer, major security–based swap participant, or other person selling or offering for sale or purchasing or offering to purchase the security, a security–based swap, or a security–based swap agreement with respect to such security, to induce the purchase or sale of any security registered on a national securities exchange, any security not so registered, any security–based swap, or any security–based swap agreement with respect to such security by the circulation or dissemination in the ordinary course of business of information to the effect that the price of any such security will or is likely to rise or fall because of market operations of any 1 or more persons conducted for the purpose of raising or depressing the price of such security.

"(4) If a dealer, broker, security–based swap dealer, major security–based swap participant, or other person selling or offering for sale or purchasing or offering to purchase the security, a security–based swap, or security–based swap agreement with respect to such security, to make, regarding any security registered on a national securities exchange, any security not so registered, any security–based swap, or any security–based swap agreement with respect to such security, for the purpose of inducing the purchase or sale of such security, such security–based swap, or such security–based swap agreement any statement which was at the time and in the light of the circumstances under which it was made, false or misleading with respect to any material fact, and which that person knew or had reasonable ground to believe was so false or misleading.

"(5) For a consideration, received directly or indirectly from a broker, dealer,

(B)第(d)子条删除“《格雷姆—里奇—比利雷法》第206B条”,并替以“《1934年证券交易法》第3(a)(78)条”。

(d)**对《1934年证券交易法》的一致性修正**。——《1934年证券交易法》(《美国法典》第十五编第78a节及其后条文)修正如下——

(1)在第3A条中(《美国法典》第十五编第78c-1节)——

(A)删除第(a)子条规定但保留该子条序号;及

(B)删除所有“(定义见《格雷姆—里奇—比利雷法》第206B条)”;

(2)在第9条(《美国法典》第十五编第78i节)中——

(A)第(a)子条删除第(2)款至第(5)款,替以如下内容:

“(2)为诱使他人买卖在全国性证券交易所注册的或未在全国性证券交易所注册的任何证券,单独或与其他人(一人或多人)共同就该等证券实施系列交易,或就与该等证券有关的任何证券类互换或证券类互换协议实施系列交易,造成该等证券交易实际或表面活跃,或抬高或抑制该等证券的价格。

(3)买卖或要约买卖该证券、与该证券有关的证券类互换或证券类互换协议的自营商、经纪商、证券类互换交易商、主要的证券类互换参与者或其他主体,通过在其正常业务运作中散布或传播信息,诱使他人买卖在全国性证券交易所注册的或未在全国性证券交易所注册的任何证券、与该等证券有关的任何证券类互换或任何证券类互换协议,使任何该等证券的价格因一人或多人抬高或抑制该等证券价格的市场操作而势将或可能上涨或下跌。

(4)买卖或要约买卖该证券、与该证券有关的证券类互换或证券类互换协议的自营商、经纪商、证券类互换交易商、主要的证券类互换参与者或其他主体,就在全国性证券交易所注册的或未在全国性证券交易所注册的任何证券或与该等证券有关的任何证券类互换或任何证券类互换协议,作出根据当时的具体情况在重大事实方面存在虚假或误导性的陈述,且其明知或有合理理由相信该陈述属于虚假陈述或具有误导性,以诱使他人买卖该等证券、该等证券类互换或该等证券类互换协议。

(5)从买卖或要约买卖该证券、与该证券有关的证券类互换或证券类互换协议的

security-based swap dealer, major security-based swap participant, or other person selling or offering for sale or purchasing or offering to purchase the security, a security-based swap, or security-based swap agreement with respect to such security, to induce the purchase of any security registered on a national securities exchange, any security not so registered, any security-based swap, or any security-based swap agreement with respect to such security by the circulation or dissemination of information to the effect that the price of any such security will or is likely to rise or fall because of the market operations of any 1 or more persons conducted for the purpose of raising or depressing the price of such security."; and

(B)in subsection (i), by striking "(as defined in section 206B of the Gramm-Leach-Bliley Act)";

(3) in section 10 (15 U.S.C. 78j) —

(A)in subsection (b), by striking "(as defined in section 206B of the Gramm-Leach-Bliley Act)," each place that term appears; and

(B) in the matter following subsection (b), by striking "(as defined in section 206B of the Gramm-Leach-Bliley Act), in each place that such terms appear";

(4) in section 15 (15 U.S.C. 78o) —

(A)in subsection (c) (1) (A), by striking "(as defined in section 206B of the Gramm-Leach-Bliley Act),";

(B) in subparagraphs (B) and (C) of subsection (c)(1), by striking "(as defined in section 206B of the Gramm-Leach-Bliley Act)" each place that term appears;

(C) by redesignating subsection (i), as added by section 303 (f) of the Commodity Futures Modernization Act of 2000 (Public Law 106 - 554; 114 Stat. 2763A - 455)), as subsection (j); and

(D) in subsection (j), as redesignated by subparagraph (C), by striking "(as defined in section 206Bof the Gramm-Leach-Bliley Act)";

(5) in section 16 (15 U.S.C. 78p) —

(A)in subsection (a) (2) (C), by striking "(as defined in section 206 (b) of the Gramm-Leach-Bliley Act (15 U.S.C. 78c note))";

(B)in subsection (a) (3) (B), by inserting "or security-based swaps" after "security-based swap agreement";

(C) in the first sentence of subsection (b), by striking "(as defined in section 206B of the Gramm-Leach-Bliley Act)";

(D) in the third sentence of subsection (b), by striking "(as defined in section 206B of the Gramm-Leach Bliley Act)" and inserting "or a security-based swap"; and

(E)in subsection (g), by striking "(as defined in section 206B of the Gramm-Leach-Bliley Act)";

(6) in section 20 (15 U.S.C. 78t),

自营商、经纪商、证券类互换交易商、主要的证券类互换参与者或其他主体处直接或间接收取对价,从而散布或传播信息以诱使他人购买在全国性证券交易所注册的或未在全国性证券交易所注册的任何证券、与该等证券有关的任何证券类互换或任何证券类互换协议,使任何该等证券的价格因一人或多人抬高或压制该等证券价格的市场操作而势将或可能上涨或下跌。”及

(B)第(i)子条删除“(定义见《格雷姆—里奇—比利雷法》第206B条)”;

(3)在第10条(《美国法典》第十五编第78j节)中——

(A)第(b)子条删除所有的“(定义见《格雷姆—里奇—比利雷法》第206B条),”;及

(B)第(b)子条之后的内容删除所有的“(定义见《格雷姆—里奇—比利雷法》第206B条)”;

(4)在第15条(《美国法典》第十五编第78o节)中——

(A)第(c)(1)(A)子条删除“(定义见《格雷姆—里奇—比利雷法》第206B条),”;

(B)第(c)(1)子条第(B)子款和第(C)子款删除所有的“(定义见《格雷姆—里奇—比利雷法》第206B条)”;

(C)《2000年商品期货现代化法》第303(f)条(第106—554号公法;《美国制定法汇编》第114卷第2763A—455页)增加的第(i)子条重新编号为第(j)子条;及

(D)第(j)子条[以第(C)子款重新编号后的序号为准]删除“(定义见《格雷姆—里奇—比利雷法》第206B条)”;

(5)在第16条(《美国法典》第十五编第78p节)中——

(A)第(a)(2)(C)子条删除“[定义见《格雷姆—里奇—比利雷法》第206(b)条(《美国法典》第十五编第78c节注释)]”;

(B)第(a)(3)(B)子条在“证券类互换协议”之后插入“或证券类互换”;

(C)第(b)子条第一句删除“(定义见《格雷姆—里奇—比利雷法》第206B条)”;

(D)第(b)子条第三句删除“(定义见《格雷姆—里奇—比利雷法》第206B条)”,并插入“或某一证券类互换”;及

(E)第(g)子条删除“(定义见《格雷姆—里奇—比利雷法》第206B条)”;

(6)在第20条(《美国法典》第十五编第78t节)中——

(A) in subsection (d), by striking "(as defined in section 206B of the Gramm-Leach-Bliley Act)"; and

(B) in subsection (f), by striking "(as defined in section 206B of the Gramm-Leach-Bliley Act)"; and

(7) in section 21A (15 U.S.C. 78u - 1) —

(A)in subsection (a) (1), by striking "(as defined in section 206B of the Gramm-Leach-Bliley Act)"; and

(B)in subsection (g), by striking "(as defined in section 206B of the Gramm-Leach-Bliley Act)".

SEC.763. AMENDMENTS TO THE SECURITIES EXCHANGE ACT OF 1934.

(a) CLEARING FOR SECURITY-BASED SWAPS. — The Securities Exchange Act of 1934 (15 U.S.C. 78a et seq.) is amended by inserting after section 3B (as added by section 717 of this Act):

"SEC.3C. CLEARING FOR SECURITY-BASED SWAPS.

"(a) IN GENERAL. —

"(1) STANDARD FOR CLEARING. — It shall be unlawful for any person to engage in a security-based swap unless that person submits such security-based swap for clearing to a clearing agency that is registered under this Act or a clearing agency that is exempt from registration under this Act if the security-based swap is required to be cleared.

"(2) OPEN ACCESS. — The rules of a clearing agency described in paragraph (1) shall —

"(A) prescribe that all security-based swaps submitted to the clearing agency with the same terms and conditions are economically equivalent within the clearing agency and may be offset with each other within the clearing agency; and

"(B) provide for non-discriminatory clearing of a security-based swap executed bilaterally or on or through the rules of an unaffiliated national securities exchange or security-based swap execution facility.

"(b) COMMISSION REVIEW. —

"(1) COMMISSION-INITIATED REVIEW. —

"(A) The Commission on an ongoing basis shall review each security-based swap, or any group, category, type, or class of security-based swaps to make a determination that such security-based swap, or group, category, type, or class of security-based swaps should be required to be cleared.

"(B) The Commission shall provide at least a 30-day public comment period regarding any determination under subparagraph (A).

"(2) SWAP SUBMISSIONS. —

(A)第(d)子条删除“(定义见《格雷姆—里奇—比利雷法》第206B条)”;及

(B)第(f)子条删除“(定义见《格雷姆—里奇—比利雷法》第206B条)”;及

(7)在第21A条(《美国法典》第十五编第78u-1节)中——
(A)第(a)(1)子条删除“(定义见《格雷姆—里奇—比利雷法》第206B条)”;及

(B)第(g)子条删除“(定义见《格雷姆—里奇—比利雷法》第206B条)”。

第763条　对《1934年证券交易法》的修正

(a)**证券类互换的集中结算**。——《1934年证券交易法》(《美国法典》第十五编第78a节及其后条文)修正如下:在本法第717条增加的第3B条之后插入:

“第3C条　证券类互换的集中结算
(a)**一般规定**。——
(1)**集中结算标准**。——对于必须进行集中结算的证券类互换,若非将该等证券类互换提交根据本法注册的或者根据本法豁免注册的结算机构进行集中结算, 任何人不得从事该等证券类互换,否则当属违法。

(2)**准入开放性**。——第(1)款所述的结算机构的规则应——

(A)规定提交给该结算机构的具有相同条款及条件的所有证券类互换在该结算机构内应具有同等经济意义,并可在该结算机构内相互对冲;且

(B)为双边执行的证券类互换,或在非关联全国性证券交易所或证券类互换执行设施执行的或通过其规则执行的证券类互换提供无差别对待的集中结算。

(b)**证券交易委员会审查**。——
(1)**证券交易委员会发起的审查**。——
(A)证券交易委员会应对每一证券类互换或者任何证券类互换集合、种类、类型或类别进行持续性审查,判定该等证券类互换或证券类互换集合、种类、类型或类别是否应进行集中结算。

(B)证券交易委员会按照第(A)子款作出任何判定的,至少应提供30天的公众意见征求期。
(2)**拟受理结算的证券类互换的呈报**。——

"(A) A clearing agency shall submit to the Commission each security–based swap, or any group, category, type, or class of security–based swaps that it plans to accept for clearing and provide notice to its members (in a manner to be determined by the Commission) of such submission.

"(B) Any security–based swap or group, category, type, or class of security–based swaps listed for clearing by a clearing agency as of the date of enactment of this subsection shall be considered submitted to the Commission.

"(C) The Commission shall —

"(i) make available to the public any submission received under subparagraphs (A) and (B);

"(ii) review each submission made under subparagraphs (A) and (B), and determine whether the security–based swap, or group, category, type, or class of security–based swaps, described in the submission is required to be cleared; and

"(iii) provide at least a 30–day public comment period regarding its determination whether the clearing requirement under subsection (a)(1) shall apply to the submission.

"(3) DEADLINE. — The Commission shall make its determination under paragraph (2)(C) not later than 90 days after receiving a submission made under paragraphs (2)(A) and (2)(B), unless the submitting clearing agency agrees to an extension for the time limitation established under this paragraph.

"(4) DETERMINATION. —

"(A) In reviewing a submission made under paragraph (2), the Commission shall review whether the submission is consistent with section 17A.

"(B) In reviewing a security–based swap, group of security–based swaps or class of security–based swaps pursuant to paragraph (1) or a submission made under paragraph (2), the Commission shall take into account the following factors:

"(i) The existence of significant outstanding notional exposures, trading liquidity and adequate pricing data.

"(ii) The availability of rule framework, capacity, operational expertise and resources, and credit support infrastructure to clear the contract on terms that are consistent with the material terms and trading conventions on which the contract is then traded.

"(iii) The effect on the mitigation of systemic risk, taking into account the size of the market for such contract and the resources of the clearing agency available to clear the contract.

"(iv) The effect on competition, including appropriate fees and charges applied to clearing.

"(v) The existence of reasonable legal certainty in the event of the insolvency of the relevant clearing agency or 1 or more of its clearing members with regard to the treatment of

(A)结算机构应将拟受理结算的每一证券类互换或者任何证券类互换集合、种类、类型或类别呈报给证券交易委员会,并按证券交易委员会确定的方式向其会员提供相应通知。

(B)截至本子条规定颁布之日,结算机构已挂牌结算的任何证券类互换或证券类互换集合、种类、类型或类别均应视为已呈报证券交易委员会。

(C)证券交易委员会应——

(i)向公众公开其根据第(A)子款和第(B)子款收到的呈报信息;

(ii)对按照第(A)子款和第(B)子款进行的每项呈报进行审查,判定呈报材料中所述的证券类互换或者证券类互换集合、种类、类型或类别是否应进行集中结算;并

(iii)在对呈报的证券类互换者或证券类互换集合、种类、类型或类别是否应按照第(a)(1)子条的规定进行集中结算作出判定前,提供至少30天的公众意见征求期。

(3)**最后期限**。——除非进行呈报的结算机构同意延长本款规定的期限,否则证券交易委员会应在收到依据第(2)(A)款和第(2)(B)款进行的呈报后90天内按照第(2)(C)款作出判定。

(4)**判定**。——

(A)在对根据第(2)款进行的呈报进行审查时,证券交易委员会应审查呈报的证券类互换或者证券类互换集合、种类、类型或类别是否符合第17A条的规定。

(B)证券交易委员会根据第(1)款规定审查某一证券类互换、证券类互换集合或证券类互换类别时,或者审查根据第(2)款进行的呈报时,应考虑下列因素:

(i)是否存在重大未平仓名义风险敞口、交易流动性和充分的定价数据。

(ii)是否具有充分的规则框架、能力、运营专长和资源以及信用支持基础设施,能够按照与合约届时交易所依据的重要条款及交易惯例一致的条款对合约进行结算。

(iii)对缓释系统性风险的作用(此时应考虑该合约的市场规模和结算机构可用的结算该合约所需的资源)。

(iv)对竞争(包括针对结算收取的适当的费用和收费)的影响。

(v)相关结算机构或其1个或1个以上结算会员出现资不抵债的情况下,对客户及证券类互换对手方的持仓、资金及财产的处理是否存在合理的法律确定性。

customer and security–based swap counterparty positions, funds, and property.

"(C) In making a determination under subsection (b)(1) or paragraph (2)(C) that the clearing requirement shall apply, the Commission may require such terms and conditions to the requirement as the Commission determines to be appropriate.

"(5) RULES. — Not later than 1 year after the date of the enactment of this section, the Commission shall adopt rules for a clearing agency's submission for review, pursuant to this subsection, of a security–based swap, or a group, category, type, or class of security–based swaps, that it seeks to accept for clearing. Nothing in this paragraph limits the Commission from making a determination under paragraph (2)(C) for security–based swaps described in paragraph (2)(B).

"(c) STAY OF CLEARING REQUIREMENT. —

"(1) IN GENERAL. — After making a determination pursuant to subsection (b)(2), the Commission, on application of a counterparty to a security–based swap or on its own initiative, may stay the clearing requirement of subsection (a)(1) until the Commission completes a review of the terms of the security–based swap (or the group, category, type, or class of security–based swaps) and the clearing arrangement.

"(2) DEADLINE. — The Commission shall complete a review undertaken pursuant to paragraph (1) not later than 90 days after issuance of the stay, unless the clearing agency that clears the security–based swap, or group, category, type, or class of security–based swaps, agrees to an extension of the time limitation established under this paragraph.

"(3) DETERMINATION. — Upon completion of the review undertaken pursuant to paragraph (1), the Commission may —

"(A) determine, unconditionally or subject to such terms and conditions as the Commission determines to be appropriate, that the security–based swap, or group, category, type, or class of security–based swaps, must be cleared pursuant to this subsection if it finds that such clearing is consistent with subsection (b)(4); or

"(B) determine that the clearing requirement of subsection (a)(1) shall not apply to the security–based swap, or group, category, type, or class of security–based swaps.

"(4) RULES. — Not later than 1 year after the date of the enactment of this section, the Commission shall adopt rules for reviewing, pursuant to this subsection, a clearing agency's clearing of a security–based swap, or a group, category, type, or class of security–based swaps, that it has accepted for clearing.

"(d) PREVENTION OF EVASION. —

"(1) IN GENERAL. — The Commission shall prescribe rules under this section (and issue interpretations of rules prescribed under this section), as determined by the Commission to be necessary to prevent evasions of the mandatory clearing requirements under this Act.

(C)证券交易委员会根据第(b)(1)子条或第(2)(C)款判定应进行集中结算时,可就该等要求的条款和条件作出其判定确属适当的规定。

(5)**规则**。——证券交易委员会应在本条规定颁布之日后1年内,针对结算机构就其拟受理进行集中结算的证券类互换或者证券类互换集合、种类、类型或类别呈报给证券交易委员会以供审查的事宜,制定相关规则。本款任何规定均不限制证券交易委员会依据第(2)(C)款规定就第(2)(B)款所述的证券类互换作出判定。

(c)**集中结算要求的中止**。——

(1)**一般规定**。——证券交易委员会在根据第(b)(2)子条作出判定后,可根据证券类互换的对手方提出的申请或主动中止第(a)(1)子条所述集中结算要求,直至其完成对证券类互换(或者证券类互换集合、种类、类型或类别)的条款及集中结算安排的审查。

(2)**最后期限**。——除非对证券类互换或者证券类互换集合、种类、类型或类别进行集中结算的结算机构同意延长本款规定的期限,否则证券交易委员会应在发出中止令后90天内完成按照第(1)款规定执行的审查。

(3)**判定**。——证券交易委员会完成按照第(1)款执行的审查后,可以——

(A)判定证券类互换或证券类互换集合、种类、类型或类别必须无条件地按照本子条的规定进行集中结算,或在不违反商品期货交易委员会判定确属适当的条款及条件的情况下按照本子条的规定进行集中结算,其前提是其判定该结算符合第(b)(4)子条的规定;或

(B)判定证券类互换或证券类互换集合、种类、类型或类别不适用第(a)(1)子条的集中结算要求。

(4)**规则**。——证券交易委员会应在本条规定颁布之日后1年内,就结算机构已受理进行集中结算的证券类互换或任何证券类互换集合、种类、类型或类别的结算情况根据本子条规定进行审查的事宜,制定相关规则。

(d)**防范规避**。——

(1)**一般规定**。——证券交易委员会应依据本条规定制定其判定确属必要的规则(并就该等规则发布必要的解释),以防范规避本法的强制集中结算要求的行为。

"(2) DUTY OF COMMISSION TO INVESTIGATE AND TAKE CERTAIN ACTIONS. — To the extent the Commission finds that a particular security-based swap or any group, category, type, or class of security-based swaps that would otherwise be subject to mandatory clearing but no clearing agency has listed the security-based swap or the group, category, type, or class of security-based swaps for clearing, the Commission shall —

"(A) investigate the relevant facts and circumstances;

"(B) within 30 days issue a public report containing the results of the investigation; and

"(C) take such actions as the Commission determines to be necessary and in the public interest, which may include requiring the retaining of adequate margin or capital by parties to the security-based swap or the group, category, type, or class of security-based swaps.

"(3) EFFECT ON AUTHORITY. — Nothing in this subsection —

"(A) authorizes the Commission to adopt rules requiring a clearing agency to list for clearing a security-based swap or any group, category, type, or class of security-based swaps if the clearing of the security-based swap or the group, category, type, or class of security-based swaps would threaten the financial integrity of the clearing agency; and

"(B) affects the authority of the Commission to enforce the open access provisions of subsection (a)(2) with respect to a security-based swap or the group, category, type, or class of security-based swaps that is listed for clearing by a clearing agency.

"(e) REPORTING TRANSITION RULES. — Rules adopted by the Commission under this section shall provide for the reporting of data, as follows:

"(1) Security-based swaps entered into before the date of the enactment of this section shall be reported to a registered security-based swap data repository or the Commission no later than 180 days after the effective date of this section.

"(2) Security-based swaps entered into on or after such date of enactment shall be reported to a registered security-based swap data repository or the Commission no later than the later of —

"(A) 90 days after such effective date; or

"(B) such other time after entering into the security-based swap as the Commission may prescribe by rule or regulation.

"(f) CLEARING TRANSITION RULES. —

"(1) Security-based swaps entered into before the date of the enactment of this section are exempt from the clearing requirements of this subsection if reported pursuant to subsection (e)(1).

"(2) Security-based swaps entered into before application of the clearing requirement pursuant to this section are exempt from the clearing requirements of this section if reported pursuant to subsection (e)(2).

"(g) EXCEPTIONS. —

(2)**证券交易委员会开展调查及采取特定行动的职责**。——若证券交易委员会认定某一特定的证券类互换或者证券类互换集合、种类、类型或类别本应受制于强制集中结算要求,但无任何结算机构对该证券类互换或者证券类互换集合、种类、类型或类别进行挂牌结算,则证券交易委员会应——

(A)对相关事实及情况进行调查;

(B)在30天内就调查结果发布公开报告;并

(C)采取其判定确属必要的且符合公共利益的行动,该等行动可包括:要求该证券类互换或者证券类互换集合、种类、类型或类别的交易方保留充足的保证金或资本。

(3)**对证券交易委员会权力的影响**。——本子条的任何规定——

(A)不授权证券交易委员会制定规则,要求结算机构在证券类互换或者证券类互换集合、种类、类型或类别的集中结算将可能威胁该结算机构财务完整性的情况下仍须对该证券类互换或者证券类互换集合、种类、类型或类别进行挂牌结算;且

(B)不影响证券交易委员会就结算机构挂牌结算的证券类互换或者证券类互换集合、种类、类型或类别执行第(a)(2)子条的准入开放性规定的权力。

(e)**过渡性报告规则**。——证券交易委员会依据本条制定的规则应对数据报告作出如下规定:

(1)本条规定颁布之日以前达成的证券类互换应在本条规定生效之日后180天内向注册的证券类互换数据存管机构或证券交易委员会报告。

(2)本条规定颁布之日或之后达成的证券类互换应向注册的证券类互换数据存管机构或证券交易委员会报告,报告日不得迟于下述日期(以较晚者为准)——

(A)本条规定生效之日后第90天;或

(B)证券交易委员会发布的规则或规章另行规定的证券类互换达成后的其他时间。

(f)**过渡性集中结算规则**。——

(1)本条规定颁布之日以前达成的证券类互换已按照第(e)(1)子条的规定报告的,可豁免本子条的集中结算要求。

(2)在集中结算要求按本条规定开始适用之前达成的互换,已按照第(e)(2)子条的规定报告的,可豁免本条的集中结算要求。

(g)**例外规定**。——

"(1) IN GENERAL. — The requirements of subsection (a)(1) shall not apply to a security–based swap if 1 of the counterparties to the security–based swap —

"(A) is not a financial entity;

"(B) is using security–based swaps to hedge or mitigate commercial risk; and

"(C) notifies the Commission, in a manner set forth by the Commission, how it generally meets its financial obligations associated with entering into non–cleared security–based swaps.

"(2) OPTION TO CLEAR. — The application of the clearing exception in paragraph (1) is solely at the discretion of the counterparty to the security–based swap that meets the conditions of subparagraphs (A) through (C) of paragraph (1).

"(3) FINANCIAL ENTITY DEFINITION. —

"(A) IN GENERAL. — For the purposes of this subsection, the term 'financial entity' means —

"(i) a swap dealer;

"(ii) a security–based swap dealer;

"(iii) a major swap participant;

"(iv) a major security–based swap participant;

"(v) a commodity pool as defined in section 1a(10) of the Commodity Exchange Act;

"(vi) a private fund as defined in section 202(a) of the Investment Advisers Act of 1940 (15 U.S.C. 80–b–2(a));

"(vii) an employee benefit plan as defined in paragraphs (3) and (32) of section 3 of the Employee Retirement Income Security Act of 1974 (29 U.S.C. 1002);

"(viii) a person predominantly engaged in activities that are in the business of banking or financial in nature, as defined in section 4(k) of the Bank Holding Company Act of 1956.

"(B) EXCLUSION. — The Commission shall consider whether to exempt small banks, savings associations, farm credit system institutions, and credit unions, including —

"(i) depository institutions with total assets of $10,000,000,000 or less;

"(ii) farm credit system institutions with total assets of $10,000,000,000 or less; or

"(iii) credit unions with total assets of $10,000,000,000 or less.

"(4) TREATMENT OF AFFILIATES. —

"(A) IN GENERAL. — An affiliate of a person that qualifies for an exception under this subsection (including affiliate entities predominantly engaged in providing financing for the purchase of the merchandise or manufactured goods of the person) may qualify for the exception only if the affiliate, acting on behalf of the person and as an agent, uses the security–based swap to hedge or mitigate the commercial risk of the person or other affiliate of the person that is not a financial entity.

"(B) PROHIBITION RELATING TO CERTAIN AFFILIATES. — The exception in

(1)**一般规定**。——在下述情形下,证券类互换不适用第(a)(1)子条规定的要求:该证券类互换对手方之一——

(A)并非金融实体;

(B)正在利用证券类互换对商业风险进行套期保值或缓释;且

(C)已按照证券交易委员会规定的方式告知证券交易委员会在通常情况下其履行与达成非集中结算的证券类互换相关的财务义务的方式。

(2)**选择进行集中结算的权利**。——符合第(1)款第(A)子款至第(C)子款各项条件的证券类互换对手方可完全依其自由裁量权决定是否适用第(1)款中关于集中结算的例外规定。

(3)**金融实体的定义**。——

(A)**一般规定**。——就本子条而言,'金融实体'一词系指——

(i)互换交易商;

(ii)证券类互换交易商;

(iii)主要互换参与者;

(iv)主要的证券类互换参与者;

(v)《商品交易法》第1a(10)条定义的商品基金;

(vi)《1940年投资顾问法》第202(a)条[《美国法典》第十五编第80-b-2(a)节]定义的私募基金;

(vii)《1974年员工退休收入保障法》第3条第(3)款和第(32)款(《美国法典》第二十九编第1002节)定义的员工福利计划;

(viii)主营业务为银行或金融性质活动的人[银行或金融业务定义见《1956年银行控股公司法》第4(k)条]。

(B)**除外规定**。——证券交易委员会应考虑是否将下列实体豁免于上述定义:小型银行、储蓄协会、农业信贷系统机构和信贷联盟,包括——

(i)总资产100亿美元(含)以下的存款机构;

(ii)总资产100亿美元(含)以下的农业信贷系统机构;或

(iii)总资产100亿美元(含)以下的信贷联盟。

(4)**关联方的处理**。——

(A)**一般规定**。——对于符合本子条例外资格之主体,只有以代理人身份代表该主体利用证券类互换对该主体或该主体另一非金融实体关联方之商业风险进行套期保值或缓释的关联方(包括以为该主体之商品或产成品的购买提供融资作为主营业务的关联实体),方可被认定为符合该例外规定。

(B)**关于特定关联方的禁止性规定**。——关联方具有下列身份的,不得适用第

subparagraph (A) shall not apply if the affiliate is —

"(i) a swap dealer;

"(ii) a security–based swap dealer;

"(iii) a major swap participant;

"(iv) a major security–based swap participant;

"(v) an issuer that would be an investment company, as defined in section 3 of the Investment Company Act of 1940 (15 U.S.C. 80a – 3), but for paragraph (1) or (7) of subsection (c) of that Act (15 U.S.C. 80a–3(c));

"(vi) a commodity pool; or

"(vii) a bank holding company with over $50,000,000,000 in consolidated assets.

"(C) TRANSITION RULE FOR AFFILIATES. — An affiliate, subsidiary, or a wholly owned entity of a person that qualifies for an exception under subparagraph (A) and is predominantly engaged in providing financing for the purchase or lease of merchandise or manufactured goods of the person shall be exempt from the margin requirement described in section 15F (e) and the clearing requirement described in subsection (a) with regard to security–based swaps entered into to mitigate the risk of the financing activities for not less than a 2–year period beginning on the date of enactment of this subparagraph.

"(5) ELECTION OF COUNTERPARTY. —

"(A) SECURITY–BASED SWAPS REQUIRED TO BE CLEARED. — With respect to any security–based swap that is subject to the mandatory clearing requirement under subsection (a) and entered into by a security–based swap dealer or a major security–based swap participant with a counterparty that is not a swap dealer, major swap participant, security–based swap dealer, or major security–based swap participant, the counterparty shall have the sole right to select the clearing agency at which the security–based swap will be cleared.

"(B) SECURITY–BASED SWAPS NOT REQUIRED TO BE CLEARED. — With respect to any security–based swap that is not subject to the mandatory clearing requirement under subsection (a) and entered into by a security–based swap dealer or a major security–based swap participant with a counterparty that is not a swap dealer, major swap participant, security–based swap dealer, or major security–based swap participant, the counterparty —

"(i) may elect to require clearing of the security–based swap; and

"(ii) shall have the sole right to select the clearing agency at which the security–based swap will be cleared.

"(6) ABUSE OF EXCEPTION. — The Commission may prescribe such rules or issue interpretations of the rules as the Commission determines to be necessary to prevent abuse of the exceptions described in this subsection. The Commission may also request information

(A)子款所述的例外规定——

(i)互换交易商

(ii)证券类互换交易商;

(iii)主要互换参与者;

(iv)主要的证券类互换参与者;

(v)若非适用了该法第(c)子条第(1)款或第(7)款[《美国法典》第十五编第80a-3(c)节]的规定,将会构成《1940年投资公司法》第3条(《美国法典》第十五编第80a-3节)定义之投资公司的发行人;

(vi)商品基金;或

(vii)并表资产超过500亿美元的银行控股公司。

(C)**过渡性关联方规则**。——某主体的关联方、子公司或全资拥有的实体符合第(A)子款所述例外规定资格,且主营业务是为该主体之商品或产成品的购买或承租提供融资的,则就为缓释融资活动风险而达成的证券类互换而言,该等关联方、子公司或全资拥有的实体应豁免于第15F(e)条的保证金要求和第(a)子条的集中结算要求,豁免期至少为2年,自本子款规定颁布之日起算。

(5)**对手方选择结算机构的权利**。——

(A)**要求进行集中结算的证券类互换**。——证券类互换交易商或主要的证券类互换参与者与对手方达成的任何证券类互换如受制于第(a)子条规定的强制集中结算要求,且该对手方并不具有互换交易商、主要互换参与者、证券类互换交易商或主要的证券类互换参与者身份,则该对手方应可以全权自行挑选在哪一结算机构进行该证券类互换的集中结算。

(B)**不要求进行集中结算的证券类互换**。——证券类互换交易商或主要的证券类互换参与者与对手方达成的任何证券类互换如不受制于第(a)子条规定的强制集中结算要求,且该对手方并不具有互换交易商、主要互换参与者、证券类互换交易商或主要的证券类互换参与者身份,则该对手方——

(i)可以自行选择要求对该证券类互换进行集中结算;及

(ii)应可以全权自行挑选在哪一结算机构进行该证券类互换的集中结算。

(6)**例外规定的滥用**。——证券交易委员会可以制定其判定确属必要的规则或针对该等规则发布必要的解释,防止本子条的例外规定被滥用。证券交易委员会亦可要求申请适用集中结算例外规定的主体提供相关信息,以防止本子条的例外规定被

from those persons claiming the clearing exception as necessary to prevent abuse of the exceptions described in this subsection.

"(h) TRADE EXECUTION.—

"(1) IN GENERAL. — With respect to transactions involving security-based swaps subject to the clearing requirement of subsection (a)(1), counterparties shall —

"(A) execute the transaction on an exchange; or

"(B) execute the transaction on a security-based swap execution facility registered under section 3D or a security-based swap execution facility that is exempt from registration under section 3D(e).

"(2) EXCEPTION. — The requirements of subparagraphs (A) and (B) of paragraph (1) shall not apply if no exchange or security-based swap execution facility makes the security-based swap available to trade or for security-based swap transactions subject to the clearing exception under subsection (g).

"(i) BOARD APPROVAL. — Exemptions from the requirements of this section to clear a security-based swap or execute a security-based swap through a national securities exchange or security-based swap execution facility shall be available to a counterparty that is an issuer of securities that are registered under section 12 or that is required to file reports pursuant to section 15(d), only if an appropriate committee of the issuer's board or governing body has reviewed and approved the issuer's decision to enter into security-based swaps that are subject to such exemptions.

"(j) DESIGNATION OF CHIEF COMPLIANCE OFFICER.—

"(1) IN GENERAL. — Each registered clearing agency shall designate an individual to serve as a chief compliance officer.

"(2) DUTIES. — The chief compliance officer shall —

"(A) report directly to the board or to the senior officer of the clearing agency;

"(B) in consultation with its board, a body performing a function similar thereto, or the senior officer of the registered clearing agency, resolve any conflicts of interest that may arise;

"(C) be responsible for administering each policy and procedure that is required to be established pursuant to this section;

"(D) ensure compliance with this title (including regulations issued under this title) relating to agreements, contracts, or transactions, including each rule prescribed by the Commission under this section;

"(E) establish procedures for the remediation of noncompliance issues identified by the compliance officer through any —

"(i) compliance office review;

"(ii) look-back;

"(iii) internal or external audit finding;

滥用。

(h)**交易执行**。——

(1)**一般规定**。——涉及证券类互换的交易受制于第(a)(1)子条的集中结算要求的,对手方应——

(A)在某一交易所执行该等交易;或

(B)在根据第3D条注册的证券类互换执行设施或根据第3D(e)条豁免注册的证券类互换执行设施执行该等交易。

(2)**例外规定**。——如果没有任何交易所或证券类互换执行设施提供证券类互换以供交易,则在不违反第(g)子条的集中结算例外规定的前提下,不应适用第(1)款第(A)子款和第(B)子款的要求。

(i)**董事会批准**。——如对手方具有根据第12条规定注册的证券的发行人身份,或有义务根据第15(d)条提交报告,则该对手方可以豁免于本条要求通过全国性证券交易所或者证券类互换执行设施进行集中结算或执行证券类互换的规定,其前提是该发行人的董事会或管理机构下属相应的委员会已审议并批准了该发行人作出的达成适用上述豁免的证券类互换之决定。

(j)**首席合规官的指定**。——

(1)**一般规定**。——每一注册结算机构均应指定1名个人担任首席合规官。

(2)**职责**。——首席合规官应——

(A)向结算机构的董事会或高级管理人员直接汇报工作;

(B)与注册结算机构的董事会、履行与董事会类似职能的机构或高级管理人员磋商,解决任何可能发生的利益冲突问题;

(C)负责实施应当依据本条制定的每一项政策和程序;

(D)确保本编(包括依据本编发布的规章)中与协议、合约或交易相关的规定(包括证券交易委员会依据本条制定的每项规则)均得到遵守;

(E)制定相关程序,据以对首席合规官通过以下任何方式识别的不合规问题采取补救措施——

(i)合规办公室的审查工作;

(ii)回顾工作;

(iii)内部或外部审计认定结论;

"(iv) self–reported error; or

"(v) validated complaint; and

"(F) establish and follow appropriate procedures for the handling, management response, remediation, retesting, and closing of noncompliance issues.

"(3) ANNUAL REPORTS.—

"(A) IN GENERAL.— In accordance with rules prescribed by the Commission, the chief compliance officer shall annually prepare and sign a report that contains a description of—

"(i) the compliance of the registered clearing agency or security–based swap execution facility of the compliance officer with respect to this title (including regulations under this title); and

"(ii) each policy and procedure of the registered clearing agency of the compliance officer (including the code of ethics and conflict of interest policies of the registered clearing agency).

"(B) REQUIREMENTS.— A compliance report under subparagraph (A) shall—

"(i) accompany each appropriate financial report of the registered clearing agency that is required to be furnished to the Commission pursuant to this section; and

"(ii) include a certification that, under penalty of law, the compliance report is accurate and complete.".

(b) CLEARING AGENCY REQUIREMENTS.— Section 17A of the Securities Exchange Act of 1934 (15 U.S.C. 78q–1) is amended by adding at the end the following:

"(g) REGISTRATION REQUIREMENT.— It shall be unlawful for a clearing agency, unless registered with the Commission, directly or indirectly to make use of the mails or any means or instrumentality of interstate commerce to perform the functions of a clearing agency with respect to a security–based swap.

"(h) VOLUNTARY REGISTRATION.— A person that clears agreements, contracts, or transactions that are not required to be cleared under this title may register with the Commission as a clearing agency.

"(i) STANDARDS FOR CLEARING AGENCIES CLEARING SECURITY–BASED SWAP TRANSACTIONS.— To be registered and to maintain registration as a clearing agency that clears security–based swap transactions, a clearing agency shall comply with such standards as the Commission may establish by rule. In establishing any such standards, and in the exercise of its oversight of such a clearing agency pursuant to this title, the Commission may conform such standards or oversight to reflect evolving United States and international standards. Except where the Commission determines otherwise by rule or regulation, a clearing agency shall have reasonable discretion in establishing the manner in which it complies with any such standards.

(iv)自报失误;或

(v)有效的投诉;及

(F)制定并遵守用以对不合规问题进行处理、管理回应、补救、重新测试和终结的适当程序。

(3)**年度报告**。——

(A)**一般规定**。——首席合规官应根据证券交易委员会制定的规则每年编制并签署一份报告,其中应包含以下内容——

(i)首席合规官所属的注册结算机构或证券类互换执行设施对本编(包括依据本编制定的规章)的合规情况;及

(ii)首席合规官所属的注册结算机构的每项政策和程序(包括该注册结算机构的职业道德准则和利益冲突处理政策)。

(B)**要求**。——按照第(A)子款编制的合规报告应——

(i)与按本条规定应向证券交易委员会提交的每份相应的注册结算机构财务报告一并提交;及

(ii)包含一份自查证明,证明该合规报告的准确性和完整性,并明确表示其知晓作伪证将招致法律惩罚。”

(b)**结算机构要求**。——在《1934年证券交易法》第17A条(《美国法典》第十五编第78q-1节)结尾处增加如下内容,作为对该条的修正:

“(g)**注册要求**。——除非已在证券交易委员会注册,否则,任何结算机构直接或间接使用邮件或任何州际商业手段或工具就证券类互换履行结算机构职能的行为,当属违法。

(h)**自愿注册**。——对不必根据本编进行集中结算的协议、合约或交易进行集中结算的主体,可在证券交易委员会注册为结算机构。

(i)**结算机构对证券类互换交易进行集中结算的标准**。——要获得并维持对证券类互换进行集中结算的结算机构的注册资格,结算机构应当遵守证券交易委员会通过发布规则而制定的标准。证券交易委员会根据本编制定上述标准实施对结算机构的监管时,可对该等标准或监督进行调整,以反映美国和国际标准的发展。除非证券交易委员会发布规则或规章另行作出判定,否则结算机构应依其合理的自由裁量权决定其遵守任何上述标准的方式。

"(j) RULES. — The Commission shall adopt rules governing persons that are registered as clearing agencies for security-based swaps under this title.

"(k) EXEMPTIONS. — The Commission may exempt, conditionally or unconditionally, a clearing agency from registration under this section for the clearing of security-based swaps if the Commission determines that the clearing agency is subject to comparable, comprehensive supervision and regulation by the Commodity Futures Trading Commission or the appropriate government authorities in the home country of the agency. Such conditions may include, but are not limited to, requiring that the clearing agency be available for inspection by the Commission and make available all information requested by the Commission.

"(l) EXISTING DEPOSITORY INSTITUTIONS AND DERIVATIVE CLEARING ORGANIZATIONS. —

"(1) IN GENERAL. — A depository institution or derivative clearing organization registered with the Commodity Futures Trading Commission under the Commodity Exchange Act that is required to be registered as a clearing agency under this section is deemed to be registered under this section solely for the purpose of clearing security-based swaps to the extent that, before the date of enactment of this subsection —

"(A) the depository institution cleared swaps as a multilateral clearing organization; or

"(B) the derivative clearing organization cleared swaps pursuant to an exemption from registration as a clearing agency.

"(2) CONVERSION OF DEPOSITORY INSTITUTIONS. — A depository institution to which this subsection applies may, by the vote of the shareholders owning not less than 51 percent of the voting interests of the depository institution, be converted into a State corporation, partnership, limited liability company, or similar legal form pursuant to a plan of conversion, if the conversion is not in contravention of applicable State law.

"(3) SHARING OF INFORMATION. — The Commodity Futures Trading Commission shall make available to the Commission, upon request, all information determined to be relevant by the Commodity Futures Trading Commission regarding a derivatives clearing organization deemed to be registered with the Commission under paragraph (1).

"(m) MODIFICATION OF CORE PRINCIPLES. — The Commission may conform the core principles established in this section to reflect evolving United States and international standards.".

(c) SECURITY-BASED SWAP EXECUTION FACILITIES. — The Securities Exchange Act of 1934 (15 U.S.C. 78a et seq.) is amended by inserting after section 3C (as added by subsection (a) of this section) the following:

"SEC.3D. SECURITY-BASED SWAP EXECUTION FACILITIES.

"(a) REGISTRATION. —

(j)**规则**。——对于注册为结算机构,对本编当中证券类互换进行集中结算的主体,证券交易委员会应根据本编的规定制定规范该等主体的规则。

(k)**豁免**。——如果证券交易委员会判定,某结算机构所受到的来自商品期货交易委员会或该结算机构母国相应的政府机关的监管和规制整体而言足够全面,与证券交易委员会的监管和规制具有可比性,则证券交易委员会可有条件或无条件地豁免该结算机构,使其不必依照本条规定针对证券类互换的集中结算活动进行注册。上述条件包括但不限于要求结算机构接受证券交易委员会检查并按证券交易委员会的要求提供全部信息。

(l)**现有存款机构和衍生品结算组织**。——

(1)**一般规定**。——本条要求注册为结算机构的机构或组织,如已按照《商品交易法》在商品期货交易委员会注册为存款机构或衍生品结算组织,视为已按照本条规定注册（仅就证券类互换之集中结算而言）,其前提是在本子条规定颁布日期之前——

(A)该存款机构曾作为多边结算组织提供互换集中结算服务;或

(B)该衍生品结算组织曾在获得结算机构注册豁免的基础上提供互换集中结算服务。

(2)**存款机构的形式变更**。——经拥有存款机构51%以上表决权益的股东表决同意,适用本子条规定的存款机构可根据形式变更计划变更为州公司、合伙、有限责任公司或与之类似的法律形式,但该等形式变更不得违反适用的州法律。

(3)**信息共享**。——对于根据第(1)款规定被视为已在证券交易委员会注册的衍生品结算组织而言,商品期货交易委员会应按照证券交易委员会要求,向其提供商品期货交易委员会判定与该等结算组织相关的全部信息。

(m)**核心原则修改**。——证券交易委员会可以调整本条确定的核心原则,以反映美国及国际标准的发展。”

(c)**证券类互换执行设施**。——在《1934年证券交易法》(《美国法典》第十五编第78a节及其后条文)经本条第(a)子条增加的第3C条之后插入如下内容,作为对该法的修正:

“第3D条　证券类互换执行设施

(a)**注册**。——

"(1) IN GENERAL. — No person may operate a facility for the trading or processing of security–based swaps, unless the facility is registered as a security–based swap execution facility or as a national securities exchange under this section.

"(2) DUAL REGISTRATION. — Any person that is registered as a security–based swap execution facility under this section shall register with the Commission regardless of whether the person also is registered with the Commodity Futures Trading Commission as a swap execution facility.

"(b) TRADING AND TRADE PROCESSING. — A security–based swap execution facility that is registered under subsection (a) may —

"(1) make available for trading any security–based swap; and

"(2) facilitate trade processing of any security–based swap.

"(c) IDENTIFICATION OF FACILITY USED TO TRADE SECURITY–BASED SWAPS BY NATIONAL SECURITIES EXCHANGES. — A national securities exchange shall, to the extent that the exchange also operates a security–based swap execution facility and uses the same electronic trade execution system for listing and executing trades of security–based swaps on or through the exchange and the facility, identify whether electronic trading of such security–based swaps is taking place on or through the national securities exchange or the security–based swap execution facility.

"(d)CORE PRINCIPLES FOR SECURITY–BASED SWAP EXECUTION FACILITIES. —

"(1) COMPLIANCE WITH CORE PRINCIPLES. —

"(A) IN GENERAL. — To be registered, and maintain registration, as a security–based swap execution facility, the security–based swap execution facility shall comply with —

"(i) the core principles described in this subsection; and

"(ii) any requirement that the Commission may impose by rule or regulation.

"(B) REASONABLE DISCRETION OF SECURITY–BASED SWAP EXECUTION FACILITY. — Unless otherwise determined by the Commission, by rule or regulation, a security–based swap execution facility described in subparagraph (A) shall have reasonable discretion in establishing the manner in which it complies with the core principles described in this subsection.

"(2) COMPLIANCE WITH RULES. — A security–based swap execution facility shall —

"(A) establish and enforce compliance with any rule established by such security–based swap execution facility, including —

"(i) the terms and conditions of the security–based swaps traded or processed on or through the facility; and

"(ii) any limitation on access to the facility;

"(B) establish and enforce trading, trade processing, and participation rules that will

(1)**一般规定**。——任何人不得出于交易或处理证券类互换之目的,运营未依据本条注册为证券类互换执行设施或全国性证券交易所的设施,否则当属违法。

(2)**双重注册**。——根据本条规定注册为证券类互换执行设施的任何主体,无论其是否已同时在商品期货交易委员会注册为互换执行设施,均应在证券交易委员会办理注册。

(b)**交易和交易处理**。——依第(a)子条注册的证券类互换执行设施可以——

(1)提供任何证券类互换以供交易;及

(2)为任何证券类互换的交易处理提供便利。

(c)**指明全国性证券交易所中用于交易证券类互换的设施**。——如果全国性证券交易所同时也运营证券类互换执行设施,并使用同一套电子交易执行系统在该交易所(或通过该交易所)进行证券类互换的上市和证券类互换的交易执行,则该全国性证券交易所应指明该等证券类互换的电子交易是在(或通过)该交易所还是在(或通过)该证券类互换执行设施进行的。

(d)**证券类互换执行设施的核心原则**。——

(1)**核心原则合规**。——

(A)**一般规定**。——要注册为证券类互换执行设施并维持该注册,证券类互换执行设施应遵守——

(i)本子条所述核心原则;及

(ii)证券交易委员会发布的规则或规章规定的任何要求。

(B)**证券类互换执行设施的合理的自由裁量权**。——除非证券交易委员会发布的规则或规章作出不同判定,否则第(A)子款所述证券类互换执行设施应依其合理的自由裁量权决定其遵守本子条核心原则的方式。

(2)**规则合规**。——证券类互换执行设施应——

(A)制定并执行包括如下各项在内的该证券类互换执行设施的任何规则——

(i)在该证券类互换执行设施或通过该证券类互换执行设施交易或处理的证券类互换的条款及条件;及

(ii)该证券类互换执行设施的任何接入限制;

(B)制定并执行对滥用行为具有威慑作用的交易规则、交易处理规则和参与规

deter abuses and have the capacity to detect, investigate, and enforce those rules, including means —

"(i) to provide market participants with impartial access to the market; and

"(ii) to capture information that may be used in establishing whether rule violations have occurred; and

"(C) establish rules governing the operation of the facility, including rules specifying trading procedures to be used in entering and executing orders traded or posted on the facility, including block trades.

"(3)SECURITY–BASED SWAPS NOT READILY SUSCEPTIBLE TO MANIPULATION. — The security–based swap execution facility shall permit trading only in security–based swaps that are not readily susceptible to manipulation.

"(4)MONITORING OF TRADING AND TRADE PROCESSING. — The security–based swap execution facility shall —

"(A) establish and enforce rules or terms and conditions defining, or specifications detailing —

"(i) trading procedures to be used in entering and executing orders traded on or through the facilities of the security–based swap execution facility; and

"(ii) procedures for trade processing of security–based swaps on or through the facilities of the security–based swap execution facility; and

"(B) monitor trading in security–based swaps to prevent manipulation, price distortion, and disruptions of the delivery or cash settlement process through surveillance, compliance, and disciplinary practices and procedures, including methods for conducting real–time monitoring of trading and comprehensive and accurate trade reconstructions.

"(5) ABILITY TO OBTAIN INFORMATION. — The security–based swap execution facility shall —

"(A) establish and enforce rules that will allow the facility to obtain any necessary information to perform any of the functions described in this subsection;

"(B) provide the information to the Commission on request; and

"(C) have the capacity to carry out such international information–sharing agreements as the Commission may require.

"(6) FINANCIAL INTEGRITY OF TRANSACTIONS. — The security–based swap execution facility shall establish and enforce rules and procedures for ensuring the financial integrity of security–based swaps entered on or through the facilities of the security–based swap execution facility, including the clearance and settlement of security–based swaps pursuant to section 3C(a)(1).

"(7) EMERGENCY AUTHORITY. — The security–based swap execution facility shall adopt rules to provide for the exercise of emergency authority, in consultation or cooperation

则,并有能力发现、调查和执行上述规则,包括拥有——

(i)向市场参与者提供公平的市场准入的手段;及
(ii)捕捉用以判定是否存在违规行为的信息的手段;及

(C)制定规范设施运行的规则,包括对如下交易程序作出具体规定的规则,即对于在该设施交易的或发布的指令(包括大宗交易)之录入和执行所采用的交易程序。

(3)**不易受操纵的证券类互换**。——证券类互换执行设施应仅允许对不易受操纵的证券类互换进行交易;

(4)**交易及交易处理的监控**。——证券类互换执行设施应——

(A)制定并执行界定下列程序的规则或条款和条件,或者制定并执行对以下程序作出具体规定的细则——
(i)对于在该证券类互换执行设施的设施上或通过该等设施交易的指令之录入和执行所采用的交易程序;及
(ii)对在该证券类互换执行设施的设施或通过该等设施实施的证券类互换进行交易处理的程序;及
(B)通过监测、合规、纪律处分实践和程序(包括进行交易实时监控和全面而准确的交易回溯的方法)来监控证券类互换交易,从而防范操纵、价格扭曲,并防范交割或现金结算过程受到扰乱。

(5)**获取信息的能力**。——证券类互换执行设施应——

(A)制定并执行相关规则,使该设施能够获取履行本子款所述任何职能确属必要的信息;
(B)经证券交易委员会提出要求即向其提供上述信息;且
(C)有能力按证券交易委员会的要求执行国际信息共享协议。

(6)**交易的财务完整性**。——证券类互换执行设施应制定并执行相关规则和程序,以确保在该证券类互换执行设施的设施或通过该等设施达成的证券类互换[包括根据第3C(a)(1)条对证券类互换进行的清算和结算]的财务完整性。

(7)**紧急权力**。——证券类互换执行设施应在与商品期货交易委员会磋商后制定相关规则,或与商品期货交易委员会合作制定相关规则,以对必要且适当的紧急权

with the Commission, as is necessary and appropriate, including the authority to liquidate or transfer open positions in any security-based swap or to suspend or curtail trading in a security-based swap.

"(8) TIMELY PUBLICATION OF TRADING INFORMATION. —

"(A) IN GENERAL. — The security-based swap execution facility shall make public timely information on price, trading volume, and other trading data on security-based swaps to the extent prescribed by the Commission.

"(B) CAPACITY OF SECURITY-BASED SWAP EXECUTION FACILITY. — The security-based swap execution facility shall be required to have the capacity to electronically capture and transmit and disseminate trade information with respect to transactions executed on or through the facility.

"(9) RECORDKEEPING AND REPORTING. —

"(A) IN GENERAL. — A security-based swap execution facility shall —

"(i) maintain records of all activities relating to the business of the facility, including a complete audit trail, in a form and manner acceptable to the Commission for a period of 5 years; and

"(ii) report to the Commission, in a form and manner acceptable to the Commission, such information as the Commission determines to be necessary or appropriate for the Commission to perform the duties of the Commission under this title.

"(B) REQUIREMENTS. — The Commission shall adopt data collection and reporting requirements for security-based swap execution facilities that are comparable to corresponding requirements for clearing agencies and security-based swap data repositories.

"(10) ANTITRUST CONSIDERATIONS. — Unless necessary or appropriate to achieve the purposes of this title, the security-based swap execution facility shall not —

"(A) adopt any rules or taking any actions that result in any unreasonable restraint of trade; or

"(B) impose any material anticompetitive burden on trading or clearing.

"(11) CONFLICTS OF INTEREST. —The security-based swap execution facility shall—

"(A) establish and enforce rules to minimize conflicts of interest in its decision-making process; and

"(B) establish a process for resolving the conflicts of interest.

"(12) FINANCIAL RESOURCES. —

"(A) IN GENERAL. — The security-based swap execution facility shall have adequate financial, operational, and managerial resources to discharge each responsibility of the security-based swap execution facility, as determined by the Commission.

"(B) DETERMINATION OF RESOURCE ADEQUACY. — The financial resources of a security-based swap execution facility shall be considered to be adequate if the value of the

力(包括对未平仓的任何证券类互换进行平仓或移仓的权力,或者暂停或停止证券类互换交易的权力)的行使作出规定。

(8)**及时公布交易信息**。——

(A)**一般规定**。——证券类互换执行设施应在证券交易委员会的规定范围内及时公布证券类互换的成交价格、成交量和其他交易数据信息。

(B)**证券类互换执行设施的能力**。——证券类互换执行设施应有能力通过电子方式捕获和传送在证券类互换执行设施上或通过该设施执行的交易的信息。

(9)**记录保存和报告**。——

(A)**一般规定**。——证券类互换执行设施应——

(i)按照证券交易委员会认可的格式和方式保存与该设施业务相关的所有活动记录,包括完整的审计留痕记录,记录保存期限为5年;且

(ii)按照证券交易委员会认可的格式和方式向其报告证券交易委员会判定对其履行本法规定的职责确属必要或适当的相关信息。

(B)**要求**。——证券交易委员会对证券类互换执行设施制定的数据收集和报告要求,应与其就结算机构和证券类互换数据存管机构制定的相应要求具有可比性。

(10)**反垄断考量**。——除非对实现本编宗旨确属必要或适当,否则证券类互换执行设施不得——

(A)制定对交易造成任何不合理限制的任何规则或采取对交易造成任何不合理限制的任何行动;或

(B)对交易或结算施加任何阻碍竞争的实质性负担。

(11)**利益冲突**。——证券类互换执行设施应——

(A)制定并执行相关规则,将其决策过程中的利益冲突减到最低限度;及

(B)制定解决利益冲突的程序。

(12)**财务资源**。——

(A)**一般规定**。——证券类互换执行设施应具备充足的财务、运营和管理资源,以履行证券类互换执行设施的每项责任,财务、运营和管理资源的充足性以商品期货交易委员会的判定为准。

(B)**对资源充足性的判定**。——如果证券类互换执行设施的财务资源价值符合如下条件,则该设施应视为拥有充足的财务资源——

financial resources —

"(i) enables the organization to meet its financial obligations to its members and participants notwithstanding a default by the member or participant creating the largest financial exposure for that organization in extreme but plausible market conditions; and

"(ii) exceeds the total amount that would enable the security–based swap execution facility to cover the operating costs of the security–based swap execution facility for a 1–year period, as calculated on a rolling basis.

"(13) SYSTEM SAFEGUARDS. — The security–based swap execution facility shall —

"(A) establish and maintain a program of risk analysis and oversight to identify and minimize sources of operational risk, through the development of appropriate controls and procedures, and automated systems, that —

"(i) are reliable and secure; and

"(ii) have adequate scalable capacity;

"(B) establish and maintain emergency procedures, backup facilities, and a plan for disaster recovery that allow for —

"(i) the timely recovery and resumption of operations; and

"(ii) the fulfillment of the responsibilities and obligations of the security–based swap execution facility; and

"(C) periodically conduct tests to verify that the backup resources of the security–based swap execution facility are sufficient to ensure continued —

"(i) order processing and trade matching;

"(ii) price reporting;

"(iii) market surveillance; and

"(iv) maintenance of a comprehensive and accurate audit trail.

"(14) DESIGNATION OF CHIEF COMPLIANCE OFFICER. —

"(A) IN GENERAL. — Each security–based swap execution facility shall designate an individual to serve as a chief compliance officer.

"(B) DUTIES. — The chief compliance officer shall —

"(i) report directly to the board or to the senior officer of the facility;

"(ii) review compliance with the core principles in this subsection;

"(iii) in consultation with the board of the facility, a body performing a function similar to that of a board, or the senior officer of the facility, resolve any conflicts of interest that may arise;

"(iv) be responsible for establishing and administering the policies and procedures required to be established pursuant to this section;

"(v) ensure compliance with this title and the rules and regulations issued under this title, including rules prescribed by the Commission pursuant to this section;

(i)足以使该设施[1]履行其对其会员和参与者承担的财务责任(即使在极端但可能发生的市场情况中,形成最大财务风险敞口的该设施成员或参与者发生违约的情况下,也不例外);并

(ii)超出足以使该证券类互换执行设施支付该证券类互换执行设施1年的运营成本(以滚动方式计算)。

(13)**系统保障**。——每一证券类互换执行设施均应——

(A)建立并维持风险分析和监控计划,以便通过设置具有以下特征的适当的控制措施和程序以及自动系统,识别运营风险源并将其减到最低限度——

(i)可靠、安全;及

(ii)具备充分的升级能力;

(B)制定并维持应急程序、备用设施和灾难恢复计划,以便——

(i)及时恢复和重启运营;并

(ii)履行该证券类互换执行设施承担的各项责任和义务;并

(C)定期开展测试,以核实该证券类互换执行设施的备用资源是否足以确保下列活动的持续进行——

(i)指令处理和交易匹配;

(ii)价格报告;

(iii)市场监测;及

(iv)保持全面且准确的审计留痕记录。

(14)**指定首席合规官**。——

(A)**一般规定**。——每一证券类互换执行设施均应指定1名个人担任首席合规官。

(B)**职责**。——首席合规官应——

(i)向该设施的董事会或高级管理人员直接汇报工作;

(ii)审查对本子条核心原则的遵守情况;

(iii)与该设施的董事会、履行与董事会类似职能的机构或高级管理人员磋商,解决任何可能发生的利益冲突问题;

(iv)负责制定并实施应当依据本条制定的每一项政策和程序;

(v)确保本编以及依据本编发布的规则与规章(包括证券交易委员会依据本条制

1 鉴于本处涉及的主体是基于互换的执行设施,原文的"organization"似应为"facility",译文中按"设施"处理。——译者注

"(vi) establish procedures for the remediation of noncompliance issues found during —

"(I) compliance office reviews;

"(II) look backs;

"(III) internal or external audit findings;

"(IV) self-reported errors; or

"(V) through validated complaints; and

"(vii)establish and follow appropriate procedures for the handling, management response, remediation, retesting, and closing of noncompliance issues.

"(C) ANNUAL REPORTS. —

"(i) IN GENERAL. — In accordance with rules prescribed by the Commission, the chief compliance officer shall annually prepare and sign a report that contains a description of —

"(I) the compliance of the security-based swap execution facility with this title; and

"(II) the policies and procedures, including the code of ethics and conflict of interest policies, of the security-based security-based swap execution facility.

"(ii) REQUIREMENTS. — The chief compliance officer shall —

"(I) submit each report described in clause (i) with the appropriate financial report of the security-based swap execution facility that is required to be submitted to the Commission pursuant to this section; and

"(II) include in the report a certification that, under penalty of law, the report is accurate and complete.

"(e) EXEMPTIONS. — The Commission may exempt, conditionally or unconditionally, a security-based swap execution facility from registration under this section if the Commission finds that the facility is subject to comparable, comprehensive supervision and regulation on a consolidated basis by the Commodity Futures Trading Commission.

"(f) RULES. — The Commission shall prescribe rules governing the regulation of security-based swap execution facilities under this section.".

(d) SEGREGATION OF ASSETS HELD AS COLLATERAL IN SECURITY-BASED SWAP TRANSACTIONS. — The Securities Exchange Act of 1934 (15 U.S.C. 78a et seq.) is amended by inserting after section 3D (as added by subsection (b)) the following:

"SEC.3E. SEGREGATION OF ASSETS HELD AS COLLATERAL IN SECURITY-BASED SWAP TRANSACTIONS.

"(a) REGISTRATION REQUIREMENT. — It shall be unlawful for any person to accept any money, securities, or property (or to extend any credit in lieu of money, securities, or property) from, for, or on behalf of a security-based swaps customer to margin, guarantee, or secure a security-based swap cleared by or through a clearing agency (including money,

定的规则)均得到遵守;

(vi)制定相关程序,据以对首席合规官通过以下任何方式识别的不合规问题采取补救措施——

(I)合规办公室的审查工作;

(II)回顾工作;

(III)内部或外部的审计认定结论;

(IV)自报失误;或

(V)有效的投诉;及

(vii)制定并遵守用以对不合规问题进行处理、管理回应、补救、重新测试和终结的适当程序。

(C)**年度报告**。——

(i)**一般规定**。——首席合规官应根据证券交易委员会的规则每年编制并签署一份报告,其中应包含以下内容——

(I)证券类互换执行设施对本法规定的合规情况;及

(II)证券类互换执行设施的政策和程序(包括职业道德准则和利益冲突处理政策)。

(ii)**要求**。——首席合规官应——

(I)将第(i)项所述的每份报告与按本条规定应向证券交易委员会提交的相应的证券类互换执行设施财务报告一并提交;并

(II)在报告中纳入一份自查证明,证明该合规报告的准确性和完整性,并明确表示其知晓作伪证将招致法律责任。

(e)**豁免**。——如证券交易委员会认定,某证券类互换执行设施所受到的来自商品期货交易委员会的监管和规制整体而言足够全面,与证券交易委员会的监管和规制具有可比性,则证券交易委员会可有条件或无条件地豁免该证券类互换执行设施,使其不必依照本条规定进行注册。

(f)**规则**。——证券交易委员会应制定相关规则,规范根据本条规定对证券类互换执行设施的监管。"

(d)**证券类互换交易中作为担保品持有的资产之分离**。——在《1934年证券交易法》(《美国法典》第十五编第78a节及其后条文)经第(b)子条增加的第3D条之后插入如下内容,作为对该法的修正:

"第3E条　证券类互换交易中作为担保品持有的资产之分离

(a)**注册要求**。——对于由结算机构集中结算的或通过其集中结算的证券类互换而言,任何人不得出于为该等证券类互换提供保证金、保证或担保之目的,而接受证券类互换客户的任何现金、证券或财产(包括因该等证券类互换而产生并归属于客户的现金、证券或财产)或者为证券类互换客户接受或者代表证券类互换客户接受该等

securities, or property accruing to the customer as the result of such a security-based swap), unless the person shall have registered under this title with the Commission as a broker, dealer, or security-based swap dealer, and the registration shall not have expired nor been suspended nor revoked.

"(b) CLEARED SECURITY-BASED SWAPS. —

"(1) SEGREGATION REQUIRED. — A broker, dealer, or security-based swap dealer shall treat and deal with all money, securities, and property of any security-based swaps customer received to margin, guarantee, or secure a security-based swap cleared by or though a clearing agency (including money, securities, or property accruing to the security-based swaps customer as the result of such a security-based swap) as belonging to the security-based swaps customer.

"(2)COMMINGLING PROHIBITED. — Money, securities, and property of a security-based swaps customer described in paragraph (1) shall be separately accounted for and shall not be commingled with the funds of the broker, dealer, or security-based swap dealer or be used to margin, secure, or guarantee any trades or contracts of any security-based swaps customer or person other than the person for whom the same are held.

"(c) EXCEPTIONS. —

"(1) USE OF FUNDS. —

"(A)IN GENERAL. — Notwithstanding subsection (b), money, securities, and property of a security-based swaps customer of a broker, dealer, or security-based swap dealer described in subsection (b) may, for convenience, be commingled and deposited in the same 1 or more accounts with any bank or trust company or with a clearing agency.

"(B) WITHDRAWAL. — Notwithstanding subsection (b), such share of the money, securities, and property described in subparagraph (A) as in the normal course of business shall be necessary to margin, guarantee, secure, transfer, adjust, or settle a cleared security-based swap with a clearing agency, or with any member of the clearing agency, may be withdrawn and applied to such purposes, including the payment of commissions, brokerage, interest, taxes, storage, and other charges, lawfully accruing in connection with the cleared security-based swap.

"(2) COMMISSION ACTION. — Notwithstanding subsection (b), in accordance with such terms and conditions as the Commission may prescribe by rule, regulation, or order, any money, securities, or property of the security-based swaps customer of a broker, dealer, or security-based swap dealer described in subsection (b) may be commingled and deposited as provided in this section with any other money, securities, or property received by the broker, dealer, or security-based swap dealer and required by the Commission to be separately accounted for and treated and dealt with as belonging to the security-based swaps customer of the broker, dealer, or security-based swap dealer.

现金、证券或财产,亦不得进行替代性授信,否则当属违法,除非该人已经根据本编在证券交易委员会注册为经纪商、自营商或证券类互换交易商,且该注册尚未过期,也未被暂停或撤销。

(b)**集中结算的证券类互换**。——

(1)**分离要求**。——对于由结算机构集中结算的或通过其集中结算的证券类互换而言,经纪商、自营商或证券类互换交易商应将其收到的用于为该等证券类互换提供保证金、保证或担保的任何证券类互换客户的所有现金、证券和财产(包括因该等证券类互换而产生并归属于该证券类互换客户的现金、证券或财产)当作属于该证券类互换客户的现金、证券或者财产来对待和处理。

(2)**禁止混合**。——第(1)款所述证券类互换客户的现金、证券和财产应单独核算,不得与该经纪商、自营商或证券类互换交易商的自有资金混合,亦不得用于为该等现金、证券和财产所属客户以外的任何证券类互换客户或者任何其他人的任何交易或合约提供保证金、担保或保证。

(c)**例外规定**。——

(1)**资金的使用**。——

(A)**一般规定**。——无论第(b)子条如何规定,第(b)子条所述经纪商、自营商或证券类互换交易商可以出于便利目的,将其证券类互换客户的现金、证券和财产混合存入任何银行、信托公司或者结算机构的1个或1个以上相同账户之中。

(B)**提取**。——无论第(b)子条如何规定,可以在正常业务运作中提取必要份额的第(A)子款所述现金、证券或财产,用于为结算机构或其任何会员结算的证券类互换提供保证金、保证、担保、进行移仓、调整或结算操作,包括支付因集中结算的证券类互换而合法产生的佣金、经纪费、利息、税费、存储费及其他收费。

(2)**证券交易委员会的行动**。——无论第(b)子条如何规定,根据证券交易委员会发布的规则、规章或命令所规定的条款和条件,以下二者可以按照本条规定混合存储,即第(b)子条所述经纪商、自营商或证券类互换交易商的证券类互换客户的任何现金、证券和财产,以及该经纪商、自营商或证券类互换交易商收到的按照证券交易委员会要求应单独核算并当作该等证券类互换客户所有的现金、证券和财产处理和对待的任何其他现金、证券和财产。

"(d) PERMITTED INVESTMENTS. — Money described in subsection (b) may be invested in obligations of the United States, in general obligations of any State or of any political subdivision of a State, and in obligations fully guaranteed as to principal and interest by the United States, or in any other investment that the Commission may by rule or regulation prescribe, and such investments shall be made in accordance with such rules and regulations and subject to such conditions as the Commission may prescribe.

"(e) PROHIBITION. — It shall be unlawful for any person, including any clearing agency and any depository institution, that has received any money, securities, or property for deposit in a separate account or accounts as provided in subsection (b) to hold, dispose of, or use any such money, securities, or property as belonging to the depositing broker, dealer, or security–based swap dealer or any person other than the swaps customer of the broker, dealer, or security–based swap dealer.

"(f) SEGREGATION REQUIREMENTS FOR UNCLEARED SECURITY–BASED SWAPS. —

"(1) SEGREGATION OF ASSETS HELD AS COLLATERAL IN UNCLEARED SECURITY–BASED SWAP TRANSACTIONS. —

"(A) NOTIFICATION. — A security–based swap dealer or major security–based swap participant shall be required to notify the counterparty of the security–based swap dealer or major security–based swap participant at the beginning of a security–based swap transaction that the counterparty has the right to require segregation of the funds of other property supplied to margin, guarantee, or secure the obligations of the counterparty.

"(B) SEGREGATION AND MAINTENANCE OF FUNDS. — At the request of a counterparty to a security–based swap that provides funds or other property to a security–based swap dealer or major security–based swap participant to margin, guarantee, or secure the obligations of the counterparty, the security–based swap dealer or major security–based swap participant shall —

"(i) segregate the funds or other property for the benefit of the counterparty; and

"(ii) in accordance with such rules and regulations as the Commission may promulgate, maintain the funds or other property in a segregated account separate from the assets and other interests of the security–based swap dealer or major security–based swap participant.

"(2) APPLICABILITY. — The requirements described in paragraph (1) shall —

"(A) apply only to a security–based swap between a counterparty and a security–based swap dealer or major security–based swap participant that is not submitted for clearing to a clearing agency; and

"(B)(i) not apply to variation margin payments; or

"(ii) not preclude any commercial arrangement regarding —

"(I) the investment of segregated funds or other property that may only be invested in

(d)**允许的投资**。——第(b)子条所述的现金可投资于美国国债、任何州或州下属任何行政区域的一般债券、联邦政府全额担保本金和利息的债券或者证券交易委员会在其发布的规则或规章中所规定的任何其他投资,但是该等投资应按照证券交易委员会制定的规则和规章作出,并受制于其规定的条件。

(e)**禁止性规定**。——已收到依据第(b)子条规定应存入独立账户的任何现金、证券或财产的任何人(包括任何结算机构和任何存款机构),不得将该等现金、证券或财产当作属于实施存储操作的经纪商、自营商或证券类互换交易商的现金、证券或财产,或属于该经纪商、自营商或证券类互换交易商的互换客户以外的任何人的现金、证券或财产进行持有、处置或使用,否则当属违法。

(f)**关于非集中结算的证券类互换的分离要求**。——

(1)**用作非集中结算的证券类互换交易担保品的资产应分离管理**。——

(A)**通知**。——证券类互换交易开始之时,证券类互换交易商或主要的证券类互换参与者即应通知其对手方,告知该对手方有权要求对用于为对手方债务提供保证金、保证或担保的资金或其他财产进行分离管理。

(B)**资金的分离与维护**。——证券类互换对手方向证券类互换交易商或主要证券类互换的参与者提供资金或其他财产用于为该对手方债务提供保证金、保证或担保的,经该互换对手方提出请求,证券类互换交易商或主要的证券类互换参与者应——

(i)为了对手方的利益对该等资金或其他财产进行分离管理;并

(ii)根据证券交易委员会颁发的规则与规章,将该等资金或其他财产存储在分离的账户中,与证券类互换交易商或主要的证券类互换参与者的自有资产和其他权益独立开来。

(2)**适用范围**。——第(1)款所述要求应——

(A)仅适用于在对手方和证券类互换交易商或主要的证券类互换参与者之间达成的不提交给结算机构进行集中结算的证券类互换;且

(B)(i)不适用于追加保证金款项;或

(ii)不排除以下任何商业安排——

(I)分离资金或其他财产的投资(仅能投资于证券交易委员会发布的规则或规章

such investments as the Commission may permit by rule or regulation; and

"(II) the related allocation of gains and losses resulting from any investment of the segregated funds or other property.

"(3) USE OF INDEPENDENT THIRD-PARTY CUSTODIANS. — The segregated account described in paragraph (1) shall be —

"(A) carried by an independent third-party custodian; and

"(B) designated as a segregated account for and on behalf of the counterparty.

"(4) REPORTING REQUIREMENT. — If the counterparty does not choose to require segregation of the funds or other property supplied to margin, guarantee, or secure the obligations of the counterparty, the security-based swap dealer or major security-based swap participant shall report to the counterparty of the security-based swap dealer or major security-based swap participant on a quarterly basis that the back office procedures of the security-based swap dealer or major security-based swap participant relating to margin and collateral requirements are in compliance with the agreement of the counterparties.

"(g) BANKRUPTCY. — A security-based swap, as defined in section 3(a)(68) shall be considered to be a security as such term is used in section 101(53A)(B) and subchapter III of title 11, United States Code. An account that holds a security-based swap, other than a portfolio margining account referred to in section 15(c)(3)(C) shall be considered to be a securities account, as that term is defined in section 741 of title 11, United States Code. The definitions of the terms 'purchase' and 'sale' in section 3(a)(13) and (14) shall be applied to the terms 'purchase' and 'sale', as used in section 741 of title 11, United States Code. The term 'customer', as defined in section 741 of title 11, United States Code, excludes any person, to the extent that such person has a claim based on any open repurchase agreement, open reverse repurchase agreement, stock borrowed agreement, non-cleared option, or non-cleared security-based swap except to the extent of any margin delivered to or by the customer with respect to which there is a customer protection requirement under section 15(c)(3) or a segregation requirement.".

(e) TRADING IN SECURITY-BASED SWAPS. — Section 6 of the Securities Exchange Act of 1934 (15 U.S.C. 78f) is amended by adding at the end the following:

"(l) SECURITY-BASED SWAPS. — It shall be unlawful for any person to effect a transaction in a security-based swap with or for a person that is not an eligible contract participant, unless such transaction is effected on a national securities exchange registered pursuant to subsection (b).".

(f) ADDITIONS OF SECURITY-BASED SWAPS TO CERTAIN ENFORCEMENT PROVISIONS. — Section 9(b) of the Securities Exchange Act of 1934 (15 U.S.C. 78i(b)) is amended by striking paragraphs (1) through (3) and inserting the following:

"(1) any transaction in connection with any security whereby any party to such

所允许的投资);及

(II)该分离的资金或其他财产进行任何投资产生的收益和损失的相关分配。

(3)**使用独立的第三方存管人**。——第(1)款所述分离账户应——

(A)由独立的第三方存管人持有;且

(B)被指明系为了并代表该对手方持有的分离账户。

(4)**报告要求**。——针对用于为对手方债务提供保证金、保证或担保的资金或其他财产,如果该对手方选择不要求进行分离管理,则证券类互换交易商或主要的证券类互换参与者应每季度向该对手方作出报告,表明该证券类互换交易商或主要的证券类互换参与者关于保证金和担保品要求的后台管理程序符合对手方协议。

(g)**破产**。——第3(a)(68)条定义的证券类互换应视为《美国法典》第十一编第101(53A)(B)节和第三子章所述证券。持有证券类互换的账户[但第15(c)(3)(C)条所述组合保证金账户除外]应视为《美国法典》第十一编第741节定义的证券账户。第3(a)(13)条和第3(a)(14)条对'买入'和'卖出'二词的定义应适用于《美国法典》第十一编第741节中使用的'买入'和'卖出'二词。《美国法典》第十一编第741节定义的'客户'一词不包括基于任何开放式回购协议、开放式逆回购协议、股票借入协议、非集中结算的期权或非集中结算的证券类互换而拥有权利主张的任何人,除非对于针对上述权利主张而向客户提供的或由客户提供的任何保证金,第(15)(c)(3)条规定了客户保护要求,或存在分离管理要求。"

(e)**证券类互换交易**。——在《1934年证券交易法》第6条(《美国法典》第十五编第78f节)结尾处增加如下内容,作为对该条的修正:

"(l)**证券类互换**。——任何人不得与非适格合约参与者或为了该等人实施证券类互换交易,否则当属违法,但在根据第(b)子条注册的全国性证券交易所实施的交易除外。"

(f)**在特定执行条款中加入关于证券类互换的内容**。——《1934年证券交易法》第9(b)条[《美国法典》第十五编第78i(b)节]修正如下:删除第(1)款至第(3)款,替以如下内容:

"(1)与任何证券有关的符合以下条件的交易:交易一方获得——

transaction acquires —

"(A) any put, call, straddle, or other option or privilege of buying the security from or selling the security to another without being bound to do so;

"(B) any security futures product on the security; or

"(C) any security-based swap involving the security or the issuer of the security;

"(2) any transaction in connection with any security with relation to which such person has, directly or indirectly, any interest in any —

"(A) such put, call, straddle, option, or privilege;

"(B) such security futures product; or

"(C) such security-based swap; or

"(3) any transaction in any security for the account of any person who such person has reason to believe has, and who actually has, directly or indirectly, any interest in any —

"(A) such put, call, straddle, option, or privilege;

"(B) such security futures product with relation to such security; or

"(C) any security-based swap involving such security or the issuer of such security.".

(g) RULEMAKING AUTHORITY TO PREVENT FRAUD, MANIPULATION AND DECEPTIVE CONDUCT IN SECURITY-BASED SWAPS. — Section 9 of the Securities Exchange Act of 1934 (15 U.S.C. 78i) is amended by adding at the end the following:

"(j) It shall be unlawful for any person, directly or indirectly, by the use of any means or instrumentality of interstate commerce or of the mails, or of any facility of any national securities exchange, to effect any transaction in, or to induce or attempt to induce the purchase or sale of, any security-based swap, in connection with which such person engages in any fraudulent, deceptive, or manipulative act or practice, makes any fictitious quotation, or engages in any transaction, practice, or course of business which operates as a fraud or deceit upon any person. The Commission shall, for the purposes of this subsection, by rules and regulations define, and prescribe means reasonably designed to prevent, such transactions, acts, practices, and courses of business as are fraudulent, deceptive, or manipulative, and such quotations as are fictitious.".

(h) POSITION LIMITS AND POSITION ACCOUNTABILITY FOR SECURITY-BASED SWAPS. — The Securities Exchange Act of 1934 is amended by inserting after section 10A (15 U.S.C. 78j-1) the following:

"SEC.10B. POSITION LIMITS AND POSITION ACCOUNTABILITY FOR SECURITY-BASED SWAPS AND LARGE TRADER REPORTING.

"(a) POSITION LIMITS. — As a means reasonably designed to prevent fraud and manipulation, the Commission shall, by rule or regulation, as necessary or appropriate in the public interest or for the protection of investors, establish limits (including related hedge exemption provisions) on the size of positions in any security-based swap that may be held by

(A)买入或卖出该等证券的任何看跌期权、看涨期权、跨式期权组合或其他期权或优先权,但无义务行权;

(B)该证券的任何证券期货产品;或

(C)涉及该证券或该证券发行人的任何证券类互换;

(2)与任何证券有关的符合以下条件的交易:上述交易方直接或间接对以下各项拥有任何权益——

(A)上述看跌期权、看涨期权、跨式期权组合、其他期权或优先权;或

(B)上述证券期货产品;或

(C)上述证券类互换;或

(3)以下交易:为任何人的账户进行的证券交易,且上述交易方有理由认为该人,且该人实际上直接或间接对任何下列各项拥有权益——

(A)上述看跌期权、看涨期权、跨式期权组合或其他期权或优先权;

(B)与上述证券有关的任何证券期货产品;或

(C)任何涉及上述证券或证券发行人的证券类互换。"

(g)**制定防范关于证券类互换的欺诈、操纵或欺骗行为的规则的权力**。——在《1934年证券交易法》第9条(《美国法典》第十五编第78i节)结尾处增加如下内容,作为对该条的修正:

"(j)任何人直接或间接使用邮件或任何州际商业手段或工具或任何全国性证券交易所的任何设施,从而实施任何证券类互换交易,或者诱使或试图诱使他人买卖任何证券类互换,而在上述行为中从事带有欺诈、欺骗或操纵性的行为或做法,作出虚假报价,或从事构成对他人的欺诈或欺骗的任何交易、做法或日常业务的,当属违法。就本子条而言,证券交易委员会应通过规则及规章界定并规定合理设计的措施,以防范该等具有欺诈性、欺骗性或操纵性的交易、行为、做法以及业务运作和虚假报价。"

(h)**证券类互换的持仓限额和持仓说明**。——在《1934年证券交易法》第10A条(《美国法典》第十五编第78j-1节)之后插入如下内容,作为对该法的修正:

"第10B条　证券类互换的持仓限额和持仓说明及大户报告

(a)**持仓限额**。——作为合理设计的旨在防范欺诈和操纵的手段,证券交易委员会应发布规则或规章,设定对维护公共利益或保护投资者所必要或适当的限额(包括相关的套值保期豁免条款),以限制任何人持有的证券类互换的持仓数额。在设定上述限额时,证券交易委员会可要求任何人合并计算对下列各项的持仓——

any person. In establishing such limits, the Commission may require any person to aggregate positions in —

"(1) any security-based swap and any security or loan or group of securities or loans on which such security-based swap is based, which such security-based swap references, or to which such security-based swap is related as described in paragraph (68) of section 3(a), and any other instrument relating to such security or loan or group or index of securities or loans; or

"(2) any security-based swap and —

"(A) any security or group or index of securities, the price, yield, value, or volatility of which, or of which any interest therein, is the basis for a material term of such security-based swap as described in paragraph (68) of section 3(a); and

"(B) any other instrument relating to the same security or group or index of securities described under subparagraph (A).

"(b) EXEMPTIONS. — The Commission, by rule, regulation, or order, may conditionally or unconditionally exempt any person or class of persons, any security-based swap or class of security-based swaps, or any transaction or class of transactions from any requirement the Commission may establish under this section with respect to position limits.

"(c) SRO RULES. —

"(1)IN GENERAL. — As a means reasonably designed to prevent fraud or manipulation, the Commission, by rule, regulation, or order, as necessary or appropriate in the public interest, for the protection of investors, or otherwise in furtherance of the purposes of this title, may direct a self-regulatory organization —

"(A) to adopt rules regarding the size of positions in any security-based swap that may be held by —

"(i) any member of such self-regulatory organization; or

"(ii)any person for whom a member of such self-regulatory organization effects transactions in such security-based swap; and

"(B) to adopt rules reasonably designed to ensure compliance with requirements prescribed by the Commission under this subsection.

"(2) REQUIREMENT TO AGGREGATE POSITIONS. — In estab lishing the limits under paragraph(1), the self-regulatory organization may require such member or person to aggregate positions in —

"(A) any security-based swap and any security or loan or group or narrow-based security index of securities or loans on which such security-based swap is based, which such security-based swap references, or to which such security-based swap is related as described in section 3(a)(68), and any other instrument relating to such security or loan or group or narrow-based security index of securities or loans; or

(1)任何证券类互换,作为该证券类互换基础的,或该证券类互换所参考的,或第3(a)条第(68)款所述与该等证券类互换关联的任何证券或贷款或证券或贷款集合,以及与该证券或贷款、证券或贷款集合或指数相关 的任何其他工具;或

(2)任何证券类互换,及——

(A)第3(a)条第(68)款所述任何证券、证券集合或证券指数,且该等证券、证券集合或证券指数的价格、收益、价值或波动性或任何权益构成该证券类互换的某项重要条款的基础;及

(B)与第(A)子款所述证券或证券集合或证券指数相关的任何其他工具。

(b)**豁免**。——证券交易委员会可以发布规则、规章或命令,有条件或无条件地向任何主体或任何类别的主体、任何证券类互换或任何类别的证券类互换、任何交易或任何类别的交易授予豁免,获得豁免的主体、互换及交易不必遵守证券交易委员会按本条规定设定的持仓限额。

(c)**自律组织规则**。——

(1)**一般规定**。——作为合理设计的旨在防范欺诈或操纵的手段,证券交易委员会可以出于保护公共利益和投资者或实现本编其他宗旨之目的颁布必要或适当的规则、规章或命令,指令某一自律组织——

(A)针对下列主体可能持有的任何证券类互换的持仓数额制定规则——

(i)该自律组织的任何成员;或

(ii)该自律组织某一成员代为实施该等证券类互换交易的任何人;及

(B)制定合理设计的规则,确保证券交易委员会根据本子条制定的规定得到遵守。

(2)**合并计算持仓要求**。——在根据第(1)款设定持仓限额时,自律组织可要求上述成员或主体合并计算对下列各项的持仓——

(A)第3(a)(68)条所述的任何证券类互换,以及作为该证券类互换基础的,或该证券类互换所参考的,或与该等证券类互换关联的任何证券或贷款、证券或贷款集合或证券或贷款的窄基证券指数,以及与证券或贷款、证券或贷款集合或证券或贷款的窄基证券指数相关的任何其他工具;或

"(B)(i) any security–based swap; and

"(ii) any security–based swap and any other instrument relating to the same security or group or narrow–based security index of securities.

"(d) LARGE TRADER REPORTING. — The Commission, by rule or regulation, may require any person that effects transactions for such person's own account or the account of others in any securities–based swap or uncleared security–based swap and any security or loan or group or narrow–based security index of securities or loans as set forth in paragraphs (1) and (2) of subsection (a) under this section to report such information as the Commission may prescribe regarding any position or positions in any security–based swap or uncleared security–based swap and any security or loan or group or narrow–based security index of securities or loans and any other instrument relating to such security or loan or group or narrow–based security index of securities or loans as set forth in paragraphs (1) and (2) of subsection (a) under this section.".

(i) PUBLIC REPORTING AND REPOSITORIES FOR SECURITY–BASED SWAPS. — Section 13 of the Securities Exchange Act of 1934 (15 U.S.C. 78m) is amended by adding at the end the following:

"(m)PUBLIC AVAILABILITY OF SECURITY–BASED SWAP TRANSACTION DATA. —

"(1) IN GENERAL. —

"(A) DEFINITION OF REAL–TIME PUBLIC REPORTING. — In this paragraph, the term 'real–time public reporting' means to report data relating to a security–based swap transaction, including price and volume, as soon as technologically practicable after the time at which the security–based swap transaction has been executed.

"(B) PURPOSE. — The purpose of this subsection is to authorize the Commission to make security–based swap transaction and pricing data available to the public in such form and at such times as the Commission determines appropriate to enhance price discovery.

"(C) GENERAL RULE. — The Commission is authorized to provide by rule for the public availability of security–based swap transaction, volume, and pricing data as follows:

"(i) With respect to those security–based swaps that are subject to the mandatory clearing requirement described in section 3C(a)(1) (including those security–based swaps that are excepted from the requirement pursuant to section 3C(g)), the Commission shall require real–time public reporting for such transactions.

"(ii) With respect to those security–based swaps that are not subject to the mandatory clearing requirement described in section 3C(a)(1), but are cleared at a registered clearing agency, the Commission shall require real–time public reporting for such transactions.

"(iii) With respect to security–based swaps that are not cleared at a registered clearing agency and which are reported to a security–based swap data repository or the Commission

(B)(i)任何证券类互换;及

(ii)与上述证券、证券集合或证券窄基证券指数相关的任何证券类互换以及任何其他工具。

(d)**大户报告**。——任何人为其自身账户或他人账户就本条第(a)子条第(1)款和第(2)款所述的证券类互换、不进行集中结算的证券类互换、任何证券或贷款、证券或贷款集合或证券或贷款窄基证券指数实施交易的,证券交易委员会可以发布规则或规章要求该人按照证券交易委员会的规定报告对本条第(a)子条第(1)款和第(2)款所述任何证券类互换、非集中结算的证券类互换、任何证券或贷款、证券或贷款集合、证券或贷款窄基证券指数以及与该等证券或贷款、证券或贷款集合或证券或贷款窄基证券指数相关的任何其他工具的持仓信息。”

(i)**证券类互换的公开报告和存管机构**。——在《1934年证券交易法》第13条(《美国法典》第十五编第78m节)结尾处增加如下内容,作为对该条的修正:

“(m)**证券类互换交易数据的公开提供**。——

(1)**一般规定**。——

(A)**实时公开报告的定义**。——就本款而言,‘实时公开报告’一词系指在证券类互换交易执行之后技术可行的第一时间报告与该证券类互换交易相关的数据,包括成交价格和成交量。

(B)**目的**。——本子条规定旨在授权证券交易委员会以其判定确属适当的格式和时间,向公众公开提供证券类互换交易和定价数据,以加强价格发现。

(C)**一般规则**。——证券交易委员会有权发布规则,就证券类互换交易、成交量及定价数据的公开提供作出如下规定:

(i)对于受制于第3C(a)(1)条所述强制集中结算要求的证券类互换[包括第3C(g)条作为例外不适用该等要求的证券类互换],证券交易委员会应要求对该等交易进行实时公开报告。

(ii)对于不受制于第3C(a)(1)条所述强制集中结算要求,但仍在注册结算机构进行集中结算的证券类互换,证券交易委员会应要求对该等交易进行实时公开报告。

(iii)对于不在注册结算机构进行集中结算,但根据第3C(a)(6)条的规定向证券类互换数据存管机构或证券交易委员会报告的证券类互换,证券交易委员会应要求以

under section 3C(a)(6), the Commission shall require real-time public reporting for such transactions, in a manner that does not disclose the business transactions and market positions of any person.

"(iv) With respect to security-based swaps that are determined to be required to be cleared under section 3C(b) but are not cleared, the Commission shall require real-time public reporting for such transactions.

"(D) REGISTERED ENTITIES AND PUBLIC REPORTING. — The Commission may require registered entities to publicly disseminate the security-based swap transaction and pricing data required to be reported under this paragraph.

"(E) RULEMAKING REQUIRED. — With respect to the rule providing for the public availability of transaction and pricing data for security-based swaps described in clauses (i) and (ii) of subparagraph (C), the rule promulgated by the Commission shall contain provisions —

"(i) to ensure such information does not identify the participants;

"(ii)to specify the criteria for determining what constitutes a large notional security-based swap transaction (block trade) for particular markets and contracts;

"(iii) to specify the appropriate time delay for reporting large notional security-based swap transactions (block trades) to the public; and

"(iv) that take into account whether the public disclosure will materially reduce market liquidity.

"(F) TIMELINESS OF REPORTING. — Parties to a security-based swap (including agents of the parties to a security-based swap) shall be responsible for reporting security-based swap transaction information to the appropriate registered entity in a timely manner as may be prescribed by the Commission.

"(G) REPORTING OF SWAPS TO REGISTERED SECURITY-BASED SWAP DATA REPOSITORIES. — Each security-based swap (whether cleared or uncleared) shall be reported to a registered security-based swap data repository.

"(H) REGISTRATION OF CLEARING AGENCIES. — A clearing agency may register as a security-based swap data reposi tory.

"(2) SEMIANNUAL AND ANNUAL PUBLIC REPORTING OF AGGREGATE SECURITY-BASED SWAP DATA. —

"(A) IN GENERAL. — In accordance with subparagraph (B), the Commission shall issue a written report on a semiannual and annual basis to make available to the public information relating to —

"(i) the trading and clearing in the major security-based swap categories; and

"(ii) the market participants and developments in new products.

"(B) USE; CONSULTATION. — In preparing a report under subparagraph (A), the

不披露任何人的业务交易及市场持仓量的方式,对该等交易进行实时公开报告。

(iv)对于被判定应根据第3C(b)条的规定进行集中结算但结果并未集中结算的证券类互换,证券交易委员会应要求对该等交易进行实时公开报告。

(D)**注册实体和公开报告**。——证券交易委员会可以要求注册实体公开发布本款要求报告的证券类互换交易和定价数据。

(E)**规则制定要求**。——证券交易委员会颁发关于第(C)子款第(i)项和第(ii)项所述证券类互换的交易和定价数据的公开提供规则时,应纳入相关规定,以——

(i)确保该等信息不会披露参与者的身份;

(ii)具体规定对于特定市场和合约而言,构成大额名义证券类互换交易(大宗交易)的判定标准;

(iii)具体规定对于大额名义证券类互换交易(大宗交易)而言,向公众报告时可以适度延迟的时间;及

(iv)考虑公开披露是否会严重降低市场流动性。

(F)**及时报告**。——证券类互换的交易方(包括证券类互换的交易方的代理人)有责任按照证券交易委员会规定的方式,及时向相应的注册机构报告证券类互换交易信息。

(G)**向注册的证券类互换数据存管机构进行互换报告**。——每一证券类互换(不论是否集中结算)均应向注册的证券类互换数据存管机构进行报告。

(H)**结算机构的注册**。——结算机构可以注册为证券类互换数据存管机构。

(2)**汇总的证券类互换数据的半年度公开报告和年度公开报告**。——

(A)**一般规定**。——证券交易委员会应根据第(B)子款的规定,发布书面的半年度和年度报告,向公众提供与如下各项相关的信息——

(i)主要的证券类互换类别的交易和集中结算情况;及

(ii)新产品的市场参与者和开发情况。

(B)**信息利用;磋商**。——在编制第(A)子款规定的报告时,证券交易委员会

Commission shall —

"(i) use information from security-based swap data repositories and clearing agencies; and

"(ii) consult with the Office of the Comptroller of the Currency, the Bank for International Settlements, and such other regulatory bodies as may be necessary.

"(C) AUTHORITY OF COMMISSION. — The Commission may, by rule, regulation, or order, delegate the public reporting responsibilities of the Commission under this paragraph in accordance with such terms and conditions as the Commission determines to be appropriate and in the public interest.

"(n) SECURITY-BASED SWAP DATA REPOSITORIES. —

"(1) REGISTRATION REQUIREMENT. — It shall be unlawful for any person, unless registered with the Commission, directly or indirectly, to make use of the mails or any means or instrumentality of interstate commerce to perform the functions of a security-based swap datarepository.

"(2) INSPECTION AND EXAMINATION. — Each registered security-based swap data repository shall be subject to inspection and examination by any representative of the Commission.

"(3) COMPLIANCE WITH CORE PRINCIPLES. —

"(A) IN GENERAL. — To be registered, and maintain registration, as a security-based swap data repository, the security-based swap data repository shall comply with —

"(i) the requirements and core principles described in this subsection; and

"(ii) any requirement that the Commission may impose by rule or regulation.

"(B)REASONABLE DISCRETION OF SECURITY-BASED SWAP DATA REPOSITORY. — Unless otherwise determined by the Commission, by rule or regulation, a security-based swap data repository described in subparagraph (A) shall have reasonable discretion in establishing the manner in which the security-based swap data repository complies with the core principles described in this subsection.

"(4) STANDARD SETTING. —

"(A) DATA IDENTIFICATION. —

"(i) IN GENERAL. — In accordance with clause (ii), the Commission shall prescribe standards that specify the data elements for each security-based swap that shall be collected and maintained by each registered security-based swap data repository.

"(ii) REQUIREMENT. — In carrying out clause (i), the Commission shall prescribe consistent data element standards applicable to registered entities and reporting counterparties.

"(B) DATA COLLECTION AND MAINTENANCE. — The Commission shall prescribe data collection and data maintenance standards for security-based swap data repositories.

应——

(i)使用证券类互换数据存管机构和结算机构提供的信息;及

(ii)与货币监理署、国际清算银行及其他必要的监管机关进行磋商。

(C)**证券交易委员会的权力**。——证券交易委员会可以发布规则、规章或命令,按其判定确属适当且符合公共利益的条款及条件,将根据本款承担的公开报告责任委托给其他主体履行。

(n)**证券类互换数据存管机构**。——

(1)**注册要求**。——除非已在证券交易委员会注册,否则任何人直接或间接使用邮件或任何州际商业手段或工具履行证券类互换数据存管机构职能的行为皆属违法。

(2)**检查和核查**。——每一注册的证券类互换数据存管机构均应接受证券交易委员会代表的检查和核查。

(3)**核心原则合规**。——

(A)**一般规定**。——要注册为证券类互换数据存管机构并维持该注册,证券类互换数据存管机构应当遵守——

(i)本子条所述的要求和核心原则;及

(ii)证券交易委员会发布的规则或规章所施加的任何要求。

(B)**证券类互换数据存管机构合理的自由裁量权**。——除非证券交易委员会发布的规则或规章作出不同判定,否则第(A)子款所述证券类互换数据存管机构应依其合理自由裁量权决定其遵守本子条核心原则的方式。

(4)**标准设定**。——

(A)**数据识别**。——

(i)**一般规定**。——根据第(ii)项,证券交易委员会应制定标准,具体规定各个注册的证券类互换数据存管机构应针对每一证券类互换品种应收集和保存的数据元素。

(ii)**要求**。——执行第(i)项规定时,证券交易委员会应制定适用于注册实体和报告对手方的统一数据元素标准。

(B)**数据的收集和保存**。——证券交易委员会应针对证券类互换数据存管机构制定数据收集和保存标准。

"(C) COMPARABILITY. — The standards prescribed by the Commission under this subsection shall be comparable to the data standards imposed by the Commission on clearing agencies in connection with their clearing of security–based swaps.

"(5) DUTIES. — A security–based swap data repository shall —

"(A) accept data prescribed by the Commission for each security–based swap under subsection (b);

"(B) confirm with both counterparties to the security–based swap the accuracy of the data that was submitted;

"(C) maintain the data described in subparagraph (A) in such form, in such manner, and for such period as may be required by the Commission;

"(D)(i) provide direct electronic access to the Commission (or any designee of the Commission, including another registered entity); and

"(ii) provide the information described in subparagraph (A) in such form and at such frequency as the Commission may require to comply with the public reporting requirements set forth in subsection (m);

"(E) at the direction of the Commission, establish automated systems for monitoring, screening, and analyzing security–based swap data;

"(F) maintain the privacy of any and all security–based swap transaction information that the security–based swap data repository receives from a security–based swap dealer, counterparty, or any other registered entity; and

"(G) on a confidential basis pursuant to section 24, upon request, and after notifying the Commission of the request, make available all data obtained by the security–based swap data repository, including individual counterparty trade and position data, to —

"(i) each appropriate prudential regulator;

"(ii) the Financial Stability Oversight Council;

"(iii) the Commodity Futures Trading Commission;

"(iv) the Department of Justice; and

"(v) any other person that the Commission determines to be appropriate, including —

"(I) foreign financial supervisors (including foreign futures authorities);

"(II) foreign central banks; and

"(III) foreign ministries.

"(H) CONFIDENTIALITY AND INDEMNIFICATION AGREEMENT. — Before the security–based swap data repository may share information with any entity described in subparagraph (G) —

"(i) the security–based swap data repository shall receive a written agreement from each entity stating that the entity shall abide by the confidentiality requirements described in section 24 relating to the information on security–based swap transactions that is provided;

（C）**可比性**。——证券交易委员会依据本子条制定的标准应与其对结算机构的证券类互换集中结算设定的数据标准具有可比性。

（5）**职责**。——证券类互换数据存管机构应——

（A）受理证券交易委员会针对第（b）子条的每一证券类互换品种所规定的数据；

（B）与证券类互换的对手双方确认提交的数据的准确性；

（C）按照证券交易委员会要求的格式、方式和期限保存第（A）子款所述数据；

（D）（i）向证券交易委员会（或证券交易委员会的任何指定人，包括其他注册实体）提供直接的电子接入；且

（ii）按照证券交易委员会要求的格式和频率提供第（A）子款规定的信息，以遵守本第（m）子条的公开报告要求。

（E）在证券交易委员会的指导下，建立自动系统用以监控、筛选和分析证券类互换数据；

（F）维护证券类互换数据存管机构从证券类互换交易商、对手方或任何其他注册实体处获取的所有证券类互换交易数据的隐私性；及

（G）在遵守第24条保密规定的基础上，在下列机构提出请求时并在向证券交易委员会通知该等请求后，向下列机构提供该证券类互换数据存管机构获取的所有数据，包括具体单个对手方的交易和持仓数据——

（i）每一相应审慎监管者；

（ii）金融稳定监督委员会；

（iii）商品期货交易委员会；

（iv）司法部；及

（v）证券交易委员会判定确属适当的任何其他主体，包括——

（I）外国金融监管者（包括外国期货监管机构）；

（II）外国中央银行；及

（III）外国部委。

（H）**保密和补偿协议**。——在证券类互换数据存管机构与第（G）子款所述任何实体共享信息之前——

（i）证券类互换数据存管机构应从每一实体处收到一份书面协议，说明该实体将遵守第24条关于所提供的证券类互换交易信息的保密要求；且

and

“(ii) each entity shall agree to indemnify the security–based swap data repository and the Commission for any expenses arising from litigation relating to the information provided under section 24.

“(6) DESIGNATION OF CHIEF COMPLIANCE OFFICER. —

“(A) IN GENERAL. — Each security–based swap data repository shall designate an individual to serve as a chief compliance officer.

“(B) DUTIES. — The chief compliance officer shall —

“(i) report directly to the board or to the senior officer of the security–based swap data repository;

“(ii) review the compliance of the security–based swap data repository with respect to the requirements and core principles described in this subsection;

“(iii) in consultation with the board of the security–based swap data repository, a body performing a function similar to the board of the security–based swap data repository, or the senior officer of the security–based swap data repository, resolve any conflicts of interest that may arise;

“(iv) be responsible for administering each policy and procedure that is required to be established pursuant to this section;

“(v) ensure compliance with this title (including regulations) relating to agreements, contracts, or transactions, including each rule prescribed by the Commission under this section;

“(vi) establish procedures for the remediation of noncompliance issues identified by the chief compliance officer through any —

“(I) compliance office review;

“(II) look–back;

“(III) internal or external audit finding;

“(IV) self–reported error; or

“(V) validated complaint; and

“(vii) establish and follow appropriate procedures for the handling, management response, remediation, retesting, and closing of noncompliance issues.

“(C) ANNUAL REPORTS. —

“(i) IN GENERAL. — In accordance with rules prescribed by the Commission, the chief compliance officer shall annually prepare and sign a report that contains a description of —

“(I) the compliance of the security–based swap data repository of the chief compliance officer with respect to this title (including regulations); and

“(II) each policy and procedure of the security–based swap data repository of the chief compliance officer (including the code of ethics and conflict of interest policies of the

(ii)每一实体均应同意,如果依照第24条提供的信息引发相关诉讼,其将补偿证券类互换数据存管机构和证券交易委员会由此发生的任何费用。

(6)**首席合规官的指定**。——

(A)**一般规定**。——每一证券类互换数据存管机构均应指定1名个人担任首席合规官。

(B)**职责**。——首席合规官应——

(i)向证券类互换数据存管机构的董事会或高级管理人员直接汇报工作;

(ii)审查证券类互换数据存管机构对本子条所述要求和核心原则的遵守情况;

(iii)与证券类互换数据存管机构的董事会、履行与董事会类似职能的机构或高级管理人员磋商,解决任何可能发生的利益冲突问题;

(iv)负责实施依据本条要求制定的每一项政策和程序;

(v)确保本编(包括规章)中与协议、合约或交易相关的规定(包括证券交易委员会依据本条制定的每项规则)均得到遵守;且

(vi)制定相关程序,据以对首席合规官通过以下任何方式识别的不合规问题采取补救措施——

(I)合规办公室的审查工作;

(II)回顾工作;

(III)内部或外部的审计认定结论;

(IV)自报失误;或

(V)有效的投诉;及

(vii)制定并遵守用以对不合规问题进行处理、管理回应、补救、重新测试和终结的适当程序。

(C)**年度报告**。——

(i)**一般规定**。——首席合规官应根据证券交易委员会的规则每年编制并签署一份报告,其中应包含以下内容——

(I)首席合规官所属的证券类互换数据存管机构对本编(包括规章)规定的合规情况;及

(II)首席合规官所属的证券类互换数据存管机构的每项政策和程序(包括该互换数据存管机构的职业道德准则和利益冲突处理政策)。

security–based swap data repository).

"(ii) REQUIREMENTS. — A compliance report under clause (i) shall —

"(I) accompany each appropriate financial report of the security–based swap data repository that is required to be furnished to the Commission pursuant to this section; and

"(II) include a certification that, under penalty of law, the compliance report is accurate and complete.

"(7) CORE PRINCIPLES APPLICABLE TO SECURITY–BASED SWAP DATA REPOSITORIES. —

"(A) ANTITRUST CONSIDERATIONS. — Unless necessary or appropriate to achieve the purposes of this title, the swap data repository shall not —

"(i) adopt any rule or take any action that results in any unreasonable restraint of trade; or

"(ii) impose any material anticompetitive burden on the trading, clearing, or reporting of transactions.

"(B) GOVERNANCE ARRANGEMENTS. — Each security–based swap data repository shall establish governance arrangements that are transparent —

"(i) to fulfill public interest requirements; and

"(ii) to support the objectives of the Federal Government, owners, and participants.

"(C) CONFLICTS OF INTEREST. — Each security–based swap data repository shall —

"(i) establish and enforce rules to minimize conflicts of interest in the decision–making process of the security–based swap data repository; and

"(ii) establish a process for resolving any conflicts of interest described in clause (i).

"(D) ADDITIONAL DUTIES DEVELOPED BY COMMISSION. —

"(i) IN GENERAL. — The Commission may develop 1 or more additional duties applicable to security–based swap data repositories.

"(ii) CONSIDERATION OF EVOLVING STANDARDS. — In developing additional duties under subparagraph (A), the Commission may take into consideration any evolving standard of the United States or the international community.

"(iii) ADDITIONAL DUTIES FOR COMMISSION DESIGNEES. — The Commission shall establish additional duties for any registrant described in section 13(m)(2)(C) in order to minimize conflicts of interest, protect data, ensure compliance, and guarantee the safety and security of the security–based swap data repository.

"(8) REQUIRED REGISTRATION FOR SECURITY–BASED SWAP DATA REPOSITORIES. — Any person that is required to be registered as a security–based swap data repository under this subsection shall register with the Commission, regardless of whether that person is also licensed under the Commodity Exchange Act as a swap data repository.

(ii)**要求**。——按照第(i)项编制的合规报告应——

(I)与按本条规定应向证券交易委员会提交的证券类互换数据存管机构每份相应的财务报告一并提交;及

(II)包含一份自查证明,证明该合规报告的准确性和完整性,并明确表示其知晓作伪证将招致法律惩罚。

(7)**适用于证券类互换数据存管机构的核心原则**。——

(A)**反垄断考量**。——除非对本法宗旨的实现确属必要或适当,否则证券类互换数据存管机构不得——

(i)制定对交易造成任何不合理限制的任何规则或采取对交易造成任何不合理限制的任何行动;或

(ii)对交易、结算或交易报告施加任何阻碍竞争的实质性负担。

(B)**治理安排**。——每一证券类互换数据存管机构均应建立透明的治理安排,以——

(i)满足公共利益的要求;及

(ii)支持联邦政府、所有者和参与者实现其各自的目标。

(C)**利益冲突**。——每一证券类互换数据存管机构均应——

(i)制定并执行相关规则,将其决策过程中的利益冲突减到最低限度;及

(ii)制定解决第(i)项所述利益冲突的程序。

(D)**证券交易委员会设定的新增职责**。——

(i)**一般规定**。——证券交易委员会可以针对证券类互换数据存管机构规定一项或一项以上新增职责。

(ii)**对标准产生的变化的考虑**。——在根据第(A)子款设定新增职责时,商品期货交易委员会可以考虑美国或者国际标准的任何变化。

(iii)**证券交易委员会指定人的新增职责**。——证券交易委员会应设定本编第13(m)(2)(C)条所述任何注册人的新增职责,以期将利益冲突减到最低限度、保护数据、确保证券类互换数据存管机构合规并保证其安全和安保。

(8)**证券类互换数据存管机构的注册要求**。——按照本子条规定应注册为证券类互换数据存管机构的任何主体,无论其是否同时根据《商品交易法》获得互换数据存管机构执照,均应在证券交易委员会注册。

"(9) RULES. — The Commission shall adopt rules governing persons that are registered under this subsection.".

SEC.764. REGISTRATION AND REGULATION OF SECURITY-BASED SWAP DEALERS AND MAJOR SECURITY-BASED SWAP PARTICIPANTS.

(a) IN GENERAL. — The Securities Exchange Act of 1934 (15 U.S.C. 78a et seq.) is amended by inserting after section 15E (15 U.S.C. 78o-7) the following:

"SEC.15F. REGISTRATION AND REGULATION OF SECURITY-BASED SWAP DEALERS AND MAJOR SECURITY-BASED SWAP PARTICIPANTS.

"(a) REGISTRATION. —

"(1) SECURITY-BASED SWAP DEALERS. — It shall be unlawful for any person to act as a security-based swap dealer unless the person is registered as a security-based swap dealer with the Commission.

"(2) MAJOR SECURITY-BASED SWAP PARTICIPANTS. — It shall be unlawful for any person to act as a major security-based swap participant unless the person is registered as a major security-based swap participant with the Commission.

"(b) REQUIREMENTS. —

"(1) IN GENERAL. — A person shall register as a security-based swap dealer or major security-based swap participant by filing a registration application with the Commission.

"(2) CONTENTS. —

"(A) IN GENERAL. — The application shall be made in such form and manner as prescribed by the Commission, and shall contain such information, as the Commission considers necessary concerning the business in which the applicant is or will be engaged.

"(B) CONTINUAL REPORTING. — A person that is registered as a security-based swap dealer or major security-based swap participant shall continue to submit to the Commission reports that contain such information pertaining to the business of the person as the Commission may require.

"(3) EXPIRATION. — Each registration under this section shall expire at such time as the Commission may prescribe by rule or regulation.

"(4) RULES. — Except as provided in subsections (d) and (e), the Commission may prescribe rules applicable to security-based swap dealers and major security-based swap participants, including rules that limit the activities of non-bank security-based swap dealers and major security-based swap participants.

"(5) TRANSITION. — Not later than 1 year after the date of enactment of the Wall Street Transparency and Accountability Act of 2010, the Commission shall issue rules under this section to provide for the registration of security-based swap dealers and major security-based swap participants.

(9)**规则**。——证券交易委员会应针对依据本条规定注册的人制定相关规则。”

第764条 证券类互换交易商和主要的证券类互换参与者的注册和监管

(a)**一般规定**。——在《1934年证券交易法》(《美国法典》第十五编第78a节及其后条文)第15E条(《美国法典》第十五编第78o—7节)之后插入如下内容,作为对该法的修正:

“第15F条 证券类互换交易商和主要的证券类互换参与者的注册和监管

(a)**注册**。——

(1)**证券类互换交易商**。——任何人除非已在证券交易委员会注册为证券类互换交易商,否则该人以证券类互换交易商的身份行事当属违法。

(2)**主要的证券类互换参与者**。——任何人除非已在证券交易委员会注册为主要的证券类互换参与者,否则该人以主要的证券类互换参与者的身份行事当属违法。

(b)**要求**。——

(1)**一般规定**。——任何人如欲注册为互换交易商或主要的证券类互换参与者,应向证券交易委员会提交注册申请。

(2)**内容**。——

(A)**一般规定**。——注册申请应当按照证券交易委员会规定的格式和方式提交,并应包含证券交易委员会认为对于申请人目前从事或将要从事的业务确属必要的信息。

(B)**持续报告**。——注册为证券类互换交易商或主要的证券类互换参与者的任何人应持续地向证券交易委员会提交证券交易委员会要求的与其业务有关的信息报告。

(3)**注册到期**。——依据本条完成的注册于证券交易委员会发布的规则或规章所规定的时间到期。

(4)**规则**。——除第(d)子条和第(e)子条规定的情形外,证券交易委员会可以制定适用于证券类互换交易商和主要的证券类互换参与者的规则,包括制定限制非银行的证券类互换交易商和主要的证券类互换参与者的活动的规则。

(5)**过渡**。——证券交易委员会根据本条制定的规则应要求证券类互换交易商和主要的证券类互换参与者在《2010年华尔街透明度与问责法》颁布之日后1年内注册。

"(6) STATUTORY DISQUALIFICATION. — Except to the extent otherwise specifically provided by rule, regulation, or order of the Commission, it shall be unlawful for a security–based swap dealer or a major security–based swap participant to permit any person associated with a security–based swap dealer or a major security–based swap participant who is subject to a statutory disqualification to effect or be involved in effecting security–based swaps on behalf of the security–based swap dealer or major security–based swap participant, if the security–based swap dealer or major security–based swap participant knew, or in the exercise of reasonable care should have known, of the statutory disqualification.

"(c) DUAL REGISTRATION. —

"(1) SECURITY–BASED SWAP DEALER. — Any person that is required to be registered as a security–based swap dealer under this section shall register with the Commission, regardless of whether the person also is registered with the Commodity Futures Trading Commission as a swap dealer.

"(2) MAJOR SECURITY–BASED SWAP PARTICIPANT. — Any person that is required to be registered as a major security–based swap participant under this section shall register with the Commission, regardless of whether the person also is registered with the Commodity Futures Trading Commission as a major swap participant.

"(d) RULEMAKING. —

"(1) IN GENERAL. — The Commission shall adopt rules for persons that are registered as security–based swap dealers or major security–based swap participants under this section.

"(2) EXCEPTION FOR PRUDENTIAL REQUIREMENTS. —

"(A) IN GENERAL. — The Commission may not prescribe rules imposing prudential requirements on security–based swap dealers or major security–based swap participants for which there is a prudential regulator.

"(B) APPLICABILITY. — Subparagraph (A) does not limit the authority of the Commission to prescribe rules as directed under this section.

"(e) CAPITAL AND MARGIN REQUIREMENTS. —

"(1) IN GENERAL. —

"(A) SECURITY–BASED SWAP DEALERS AND MAJOR SECURITY–BASED SWAP PARTICIPANTS THAT ARE BANKS. — Each registered security–based swap dealer and major security–based swap participant for which there is not a prudential regulator shall meet such minimum capital requirements and minimum initial and variation margin requirements as the prudential regulator shall by rule or regulation prescribe under paragraph (2)(A).

"(B) SECURITY–BASED SWAP DEALERS AND MAJOR SECURITY–BASED SWAP PARTICIPANTS THAT ARE NOT BANKS. — Each registered security–based swap dealer and major security–based swap participant for which there is not a prudential regulator

(6)**法定失格**。——除非证券交易委员会发布规则、规章或命令另做具体规定,否则,如果证券类互换交易商或主要的证券类互换参与者明知或尽合理注意后应知其任何业务相关人处于法定失格状态的,则该证券类互换交易商或主要的证券类互换参与者不得允许该等业务相关人代表其实施证券类互换交易或参与证券类互换交易的实施工作,否则当属违法。

(c)**双重注册**。——

(1)**证券类互换交易商**。——根据本条规定应注册为互换交易商的任何主体,无论其是否已同时在商品期货交易委员会注册为互换交易商,均应在证券交易委员会办理注册。

(2)**主要的证券类互换参与者**。——根据本条规定应注册为主要的证券类互换参与者的任何主体,无论其是否已同时在商品期货交易委员会注册为主要的证券类互换参与者,均应在证券交易委员会办理注册。

(d)**规则制定**。——

(1)**一般规定**。——证券交易委员会应就依本条注册为证券类互换交易商或主要的证券类互换参与者的人制定规则。

(2)**关于审慎要求的例外规定**。——

(A)**一般规定**。——证券交易委员会不得针对受审慎监管者监管的证券类互换交易商或主要的证券类互换参与者制定施加审慎要求的规则。

(B)**适用范围**。——第(A)子款并不限制证券交易委员会制定本条要求的规则的权力。

(e)**资本和保证金要求**。——

(1)**一般规定**。——

(A)**证券类互换交易商和主要的证券类互换参与者为银行的情形**。——受审慎监管者监管的每一注册的证券类互换交易商和主要的证券类互换参与者均应达到该审慎监管者依据第(2)(A)款发布的规则或规章所规定的最低资本要求、最低初始保证金要求和追加保证金要求。

(B)**证券类互换交易商和主要的证券类互换参与者并非银行的情形**。——不受审慎监管者监管的每一注册的证券类互换交易商和主要的证券类互换参与者均应达到证券交易委员会依据第(2)(B)款发布的规则或规章所规定的最低资本要求、最低初始

shall meet such minimum capital requirements and minimum initial and variation margin requirements as the Commission shall by rule or regulation prescribe under paragraph (2)(B).

"(2) RULES. —

"(A) SECURITY-BASED SWAP DEALERS AND MAJOR SECURITY-BASED SWAP PARTICIPANTS THAT ARE BANKS. — The prudential regulators, in consultation with the Commission and the Commodity Futures Trading Commission, shall adopt rules for security-based swap dealers and major security-based swap participants, with respect to their activities as a swap dealer or major swap participant, for which there is a prudential regulator imposing —

"(i) capital requirements; and

"(ii) both initial and variation margin requirements on all security-based swaps that are not cleared by a registered clearing agency.

"(B) SECURITY-BASED SWAP DEALERS AND MAJOR SECURITY-BASED SWAP PARTICIPANTS THAT ARE NOT BANKS. — The Commission shall adopt rules for security-based swap dealers and major security-based swap participants, with respect to their activities as a swap dealer or major swap participant, for which there is not a prudential regulator imposing —

"(i) capital requirements; and

"(ii) both initial and variation margin requirements on all swaps that are not cleared by a registered clearing agency.

"(C) CAPITAL. — In setting capital requirements for a person that is designated as a security-based swap dealer or a major security-based swap participant for a single type or single class or category of security-based swap or activities, the prudential regulator and the Commission shall take into account the risks associated with other types of security-based swaps or classes of security-based swaps or categories of security-based swaps engaged in and the other activities conducted by that person that are not otherwise subject to regulation applicable to that person by virtue of the status of the person.

"(3) STANDARDS FOR CAPITAL AND MARGIN. —

"(A) IN GENERAL. — To offset the greater risk to the security-based swap dealer or major security-based swap participant and the financial system arising from the use of security-based swaps that are not cleared, the requirements imposed under paragraph (2) shall —

"(i) help ensure the safety and soundness of the security-based swap dealer or major security-based swap participant; and

"(ii) be appropriate for the risk associated with the non-cleared security-based swaps held as a security-based swap dealer or major security-based swap participant.

保证金要求和追加保证金要求。

(2)**规则**。——

(A)**证券类互换交易商和主要的证券类互换参与者为银行的情形**。——审慎监管者应与证券交易委员会和商品期货交易委员会进行磋商,针对受审慎监管者监管的证券类互换交易商和主要的证券类互换参与者以互换交易商或主要互换参与者身份开展的活动,联合制定施加如下要求的规则——

(i)资本要求;及

(ii)不在注册结算机构进行集中结算的所有证券类互换施加初始保证金要求和追加保证金要求。

(B)**证券类互换交易商和主要的证券类互换参与者并非银行的情形**。——证券交易委员会应针对不受任何审慎监管者监管的证券类互换交易商和主要的证券类互换参与者以互换交易商或主要互换参与者身份开展的活动,制定施加如下要求的规则——

(i)资本要求;及

(ii)不在注册结算机构进行集中结算的所有互换的初始保证金要求和追加保证金要求。

(C)**资本**。——如果某人因某单一类型、某单一类别或某单一种类的证券类互换或活动被指定为证券类互换交易商或主要的证券类互换参与者,审慎监管者和证券交易委员会在对其设定资本要求时,应考虑其从事的其他类型或者其他类别或其他种类的证券类互换和开展的其他活动(该等证券类互换或活动并不受该人以证券类互换交易商或主要的证券类互换参与者身份所受到的监管约束)所产生的风险。

(3)**资本和保证金标准**。——

(A)**一般规定**。——为了吸收由于使用非集中结算的证券类互换给证券类互换交易商或主要的证券类互换参与者及金融体系带来的额外风险,依据第(2)款施加的要求应——

(i)有助于确保证券类互换交易商或主要的证券类互换参与者的安全性和稳健性;且

(ii)对于以证券类互换交易商或主要的证券类互换参与者身份持有的非集中结算的证券类互换产生的风险而言,确属适当。

"(B) RULE OF CONSTRUCTION. —

"(i) IN GENERAL. — Nothing in this section shall limit, or be construed to limit, the authority —

"(I) of the Commission to set financial responsibility rules for a broker or dealer registered pursuant to section 15(b) (except for section 15(b)(11) thereof) in accordance with section 15(c)(3); or

"(II) of the Commodity Futures Trading Commission to set financial responsibility rules for a futures commission merchant or introducing broker registered pursuant to section 4f(a) of the Commodity Exchange Act (except for section 4f(a)(3) thereof) in accordance with section 4f(b) of the Commodity Exchange Act.

"(ii) FUTURES COMMISSION MERCHANTS AND OTHER DEALERS. — A futures commission merchant, introducing broker, broker, or dealer shall maintain sufficient capital to comply with the stricter of any applicable capital requirements to which such futures commission merchant, introducing broker, broker, or dealer is subject to under this title or the Commodity Exchange Act.

"(C) MARGIN REQUIREMENTS. — In prescribing margin requirements under this subsection, the prudential regulator with respect to security-based swap dealers and major security-based swap participants that are depository institutions, and the Commission with respect to security-based swap dealers and major security-based swap participants that are not depository institutions shall permit the use of noncash collateral, as the regulator or the Commission determines to be consistent with —

"(i) preserving the financial integrity of markets trading security-based swaps; and

"(ii) preserving the stability of the United States financial system.

"(D) COMPARABILITY OF CAPITAL AND MARGIN REQUIREMENTS. —

"(i) IN GENERAL. — The prudential regulators, the Commission, and the Securities and Exchange Commission shall periodically (but not less frequently than annually) consult on minimum capital requirements and minimum initial and variation margin requirements.

"(ii) COMPARABILITY. — The entities described in clause (i) shall, to the maximum extent practicable, establish and maintain comparable minimum capital requirements and minimum initial and variation margin requirements, including the use of noncash collateral, for —

"(I) security-based swap dealers; and

"(II) major security-based swap participants.

"(f) REPORTING AND RECORDKEEPING. —

"(1) IN GENERAL. — Each registered security-based swap dealer and major security-based swap participant —

"(A) shall make such reports as are required by the Commission, by rule or regulation,

(B)**解释规则**。——

(i)**一般规定**。——本条任何内容均不限制以下权力，亦不得被解释为构成对以下权力的限制——

(I)证券交易委员会根据第15(c)(3)条对依第15(b)条[但该法第15(b)(11)条除外]注册的经纪商或自营商制定财务责任规则的权力；或

(II)商品期货交易委员会根据《商品交易法》第4f(b)条针对依《商品交易法》第4f(a)条[但该法第4f(a)(3)条除外]注册的期货经纪商或介绍经纪商制定财务责任规则的权力。

(ii)**期货经纪商和其他交易商**。——期货经纪商、介绍经纪商、经纪商或自营商应根据本编或《商品交易法》要求其遵守的任何适用的资本要求中最严格的一项维持充足的资本。

(C)**保证金要求**。——依据本子条对保证金要求作出规定时，审慎监管者应允许具有存款机构身份的证券类互换交易商和主要的证券类互换参与者使用非现金担保品，证券交易委员会则应允许并非存款机构的证券类互换交易商和主要的证券类互换参与者使用非现金担保品，其前提是该监管者或证券交易委员会判定非现金担保品有利于——

(i)维护证券类互换交易市场的财务完整性；及

(ii)维护美国金融体系的稳定性。

(D)**具有可比性的资本和保证金要求**。——

(i)**一般规定**。——审慎监管者、证券交易委员会和商品期货交易委员会应定期(频率不得低于每年一次)就最低资本要求、最低初始保证金及追加保证金要求进行磋商。

(ii)**可比性**。——第(i)项所述实体在对以下各者分别设定最低资本要求、最低初始保证金及追加保证金要求时(包括就非现金担保品的使用设定要求时)，应尽最大可能维持其水平具有可比性——

(I)证券类互换交易商；及

(II)主要的证券类互换参与者。

(f)**报告和记录保存**。——

(1)**一般规定**。——每一注册的证券类互换交易商和主要的证券类互换参与者——

(A)均应按照证券交易委员会发布的规则或规章的要求，制作关于其交易及持仓

regarding the transactions and positions and financial condition of the registered security-based swap dealer or major security-based swap participant;

"(B)(i) for which there is a prudential regulator, shall keep books and records of all activities related to the business as a security-based swap dealer or major security-based swap participant in such form and manner and for such period as may be prescribed by the Commission by rule or regulation; and

"(ii) for which there is no prudential regulator, shall keep books and records in such form and manner and for such period as may be prescribed by the Commission by rule or regulation; and

"(C) shall keep books and records described in subparagraph (B) open to inspection and examination by any representative of the Commission.

"(2) RULES. — The Commission shall adopt rules governing reporting and recordkeeping for security-based swap dealers and major security-based swap participants.

"(g) DAILY TRADING RECORDS. —

"(1) IN GENERAL. — Each registered security-based swap dealer and major security-based swap participant shall maintain daily trading records of the security-based swaps of the registered security-based swap dealer and major security-based swap participant and all related records (including related cash or forward transactions) and recorded communications, including electronic mail, instant messages, and recordings of telephone calls, for such period as may be required by the Commission by rule or regulation.

"(2) INFORMATION REQUIREMENTS. — The daily trading records shall include such information as the Commission shall require by rule or regulation.

"(3) COUNTERPARTY RECORDS. — Each registered security-based swap dealer and major security-based swap participant shall maintain daily trading records for each counterparty in a manner and form that is identifiable with each security-based swap transaction.

"(4) AUDIT TRAIL. — Each registered security-based swap dealer and major security-based swap participant shall maintain a complete audit trail for conducting comprehensive and accurate trade reconstructions.

"(5) RULES. — The Commission shall adopt rules governing daily trading records for security-based swap dealers and major security-based swap participants.

"(h) BUSINESS CONDUCT STANDARDS. —

"(1) IN GENERAL. — Each registered security-based swap dealer and major security-based swap participant shall conform with such business conduct standards as prescribed in paragraph (3) and as may be prescribed by the Commission by rule or regulation that relate to —

"(A) fraud, manipulation, and other abusive practices involving security-based swaps

和财务状况的报告;

(B)(i)如受审慎监管者监管,则均应按证券交易委员会发布的规则或规章所规定的格式、方式和期限,就其以证券类互换交易商或主要的证券类互换参与者身份从事的所有业务活动保存相关账簿和记录;且

(ii)如不受审慎监管者监管,则均应按证券交易委员会在其发布的规则或规章中所规定的格式、方式和期限保存账簿和记录;及

(C)均应将按照第(B)子款保存的账簿和记录提供给证券交易委员会任何代表检查和核查。

(2)**规则**。——证券交易委员会应针对证券类互换交易商和主要的证券类互换参与者制定报告规则和记录保存规则。

(g)**每日交易记录**。——

(1)**一般规定**。——每一注册的证券类互换交易商和主要的证券类互换参与者均应按照证券交易委员会发布的规则或规章所规定的期限,就其证券类互换保存每日交易记录以及所有相关的记录(包括相关的现货交易或远期交易)和通讯记录(包括电子邮件、即时信息、电话录音等)。

(2)**信息要求**。——每日交易记录应包含证券交易委员会发布的规则或规章所规定的信息。

(3)**对手方记录**。——每一注册的证券类互换交易商和主要的证券类互换参与者均应为每一对手方留存每日交易记录,方式和格式应能够使人识别与每笔证券类互换交易相对应的交易记录。

(4)**审计留痕**。——每一注册的证券类互换交易商和主要的证券类互换参与者均应保持完整的审计留痕记录,以便进行全面而准确的交易回溯。

(5)**规则**。——证券交易委员会应制定规范证券类互换交易商和主要的证券类互换参与者的每日交易记录的规则。

(h)**业务行为准则**。——

(1)**一般规定**。——每一注册的证券类互换交易商和主要的证券类互换参与者均应遵守第(3)款规定的业务行为准则,并应遵守证券交易委员会发布的规则或规章对以下行为所规定的业务行为准则——

(A)涉及证券类互换(包括已要约但未达成的证券类互换)的欺诈、操纵和其他滥

(including security–based swaps that are offered but not entered into);

"(B) diligent supervision of the business of the registered security–based swap dealer and major security–based swap participant;

"(C) adherence to all applicable position limits; and

"(D) such other matters as the Commission determines to be appropriate.

"(2) RESPONSIBILITIES WITH RESPECT TO SPECIAL ENTITIES. —

"(A) ADVISING SPECIAL ENTITIES. — A security–based swap dealer or major security–based swap participant that acts as an advisor to special entity regarding a security–based swap shall comply with the requirements of paragraph (4) with respect to such special entity.

"(B) ENTERING OF SECURITY–BASED SWAPS WITH RESPECT TO SPECIAL ENTITIES. — A security–based swap dealer that enters into or offers to enter into security–based swap with a special entity shall comply with the requirements of paragraph (5) with respect to such special entity.

"(C) SPECIAL ENTITY DEFINED. — For purposes of this subsection, the term 'special entity' means —

"(i) a Federal agency;

"(ii) a State, State agency, city, county, municipality, or other political subdivision of a State or;

"(iii) any employee benefit plan, as defined in section 3 of the Employee Retirement Income Security Act of 1974 (29 U.S.C. 1002);

"(iv) any governmental plan, as defined in section 3 of the Employee Retirement Income Security Act of 1974 (29 U.S.C. 1002); or

"(v) any endowment, including an endowment that is an organization described in section 501(c)(3) of the Internal Revenue Code of 1986.

"(3) BUSINESS CONDUCT REQUIREMENTS. — Business conduct requirements adopted by the Commission shall —

"(A) establish a duty for a security–based swap dealer or major security–based swap participant to verify that any counterparty meets the eligibility standards for an eligible contract participant;

"(B) require disclosure by the security–based swap dealer or major security–based swap participant to any counterparty to the transaction (other than a security–based swap dealer, major security–based swap participant, security–based swap dealer, or major security–based swap participant) of —

"(i) information about the material risks and characteristics of the security–based swap;

"(ii) any material incentives or conflicts of interest that the security–based swap dealer or major security–based swap participant may have in connection with the security–based

用行为；

(B)对该注册的证券类互换交易商和主要的证券类互换参与者业务的尽职监管；

(C)对所有适用持仓限额要求的遵守；及

(D)证券交易委员会判定确属适当的任何其他事项。

(2)**与特殊实体相关的责任**。——

(A)**充当特殊实体的顾问**。——证券类互换交易商或主要的证券类互换参与者如果就某一证券类互换品种充当特殊实体的顾问，则应遵守第(4)款就该等特殊实体规定的相关要求。

(B)**与特殊实体达成证券类互换**。——与特殊实体达成或要约达成证券类互换的证券类互换交易商应遵守第(5)款规定的关于该等特殊实体的要求。

(C)**特殊实体的定义**。——就本子条而言，'特殊实体'一词系指——

(i)联邦机关；

(ii)州、州机关、州级市、郡、郡级市或其他州属下级行政区域；

(iii)任何员工福利计划(定义见《1974年员工退休收入保障法》第3条(《美国法典》第二十九编第1002节))；

(iv)任何政府计划[定义见《1974年员工退休收入保障法》第3条(《美国法典》第二十九编第1002节)]；或

(v)任何捐赠基金，包括性质属于《1986年国内税收法典》第501(c)(3)条所述组织的捐赠基金。

(3)**业务行为要求**。——证券交易委员会制定的业务行为要求应——

(A)规定证券类互换交易商或主要的证券类互换参与者有义务就每一对手方核实其是否符合适格合约参与者的适格性标准；

(B)要求该等证券类互换交易商或主要的证券类互换参与者向任何交易对手方(指并非证券类互换交易商、主要的证券类互换参与者、证券类互换交易商或主要的证券类互换参与者的对手方)披露以下信息——

(i)关于该等证券类互换的重大风险和特征的信息；

(ii)证券类互换交易商或主要的证券类互换参与者可能有的与该证券类互换相关的任何重大激励或利益冲突；及

swap; and

"(iii)(I) for cleared security-based swaps, upon the request of the counterparty, receipt of the daily mark of the transaction from the appropriate derivatives clearing organization; and

"(II) for uncleared security-based swaps, receipt of the daily mark of the transaction from the security-based swap dealer or the major security-based swap participant;

"(C) establish a duty for a security-based swap dealer or major security-based swap participant to communicate in a fair and balanced manner based on principles of fair dealing and good faith; and

"(D) establish such other standards and requirements as the Commission may determine are appropriate in the public interest, for the protection of investors, or otherwise in furtherance of the purposes of this Act.

"(4) SPECIAL REQUIREMENTS FOR SECURITY-BASED SWAP DEALERS ACTING AS ADVISORS. —

"(A) IN GENERAL. — It shall be unlawful for a security-based swap dealer or major security-based swap participant —

"(i) to employ any device, scheme, or artifice to defraud any special entity or prospective customer who is a special entity;

"(ii) to engage in any transaction, practice, or course of business that operates as a fraud or deceit on any special entity or prospective customer who is a special entity; or

"(iii) to engage in any act, practice, or course of business that is fraudulent, deceptive, or manipulative.

"(B) DUTY. — Any security-based swap dealer that acts as an advisor to a special entity shall have a duty to act in the best interests of the special entity.

"(C) REASONABLE EFFORTS. — Any security-based swap dealer that acts as an advisor to a special entity shall make reasonable efforts to obtain such information as is necessary to make a reasonable determination that any security-based swap recommended by the security-based swap dealer is in the best interests of the special entity, including information relating to —

"(i) the financial status of the special entity;

"(ii) the tax status of the special entity;

"(iii) the investment or financing objectives of the special entity; and

"(iv) any other information that the Commission may prescribe by rule or regulation.

"(5) SPECIAL REQUIREMENTS FOR SECURITY-BASED SWAP DEALERS AS COUNTERPARTIES TO SPECIAL ENTITIES. —

"(A) IN GENERAL. — Any security-based swap dealer or major security-based swap participant that offers to or enters into a security-based swap with a special entity shall —

"(i) comply with any duty established by the Commission for a security-based swap

(iii)(I)对集中结算的证券类互换而言,经对手方提出请求,应披露从相应的衍生品结算组织处收到的交易逐日盯市信息;及

(II)对非集中结算的证券类互换而言,应披露从证券类互换交易商或主要的证券类互换参与者处收到的交易逐日盯市信息。

(C)规定证券类互换交易商或主要的证券类互换参与者有责任基于公平交易原则和善意原则开展公平、公正的沟通;及

(D)设定证券交易委员会判定确属适当的其他标准和要求,以维护公共利益、保护投资者或促进本法其他宗旨的实现。

(4)**充当顾问的证券类互换交易商应遵守的特殊要求**。——

(A)**一般规定**。——证券类互换交易商或主要的证券类互换参与者不得从事以下活动,否则当属违法——

(i)使用任何手段、计谋或诡计欺诈任何特殊实体或具有特殊实体身份的潜在客户;

(ii)从事对任何特殊实体或具有特殊实体身份的潜在客户构成欺诈或欺骗的交易、做法或业务运作;或

(iii)从事具有欺诈性、欺骗性或操纵性的任何行为、做法或业务运作。

(B)**职责**。——充当特殊实体顾问的证券类互换交易商有责任以符合特殊实体最佳利益的方式行事。

(C)**合理努力**。——充当特殊实体顾问的证券类互换交易商应尽合理努力获取必要信息,以合理判定其推荐的任何证券类互换是否符合特殊实体的最佳利益,该等必要信息包括——

(i)特殊实体的财务状况信息;

(ii)特殊实体的税务状况信息;

(iii)特殊实体的投融资目标信息;及

(iv)证券交易委员会发布的规则或规章所规定的任何其他信息。

(5)**充当特殊实体对手方的证券类互换交易商应遵守的特殊要求**。——

(A)**一般规定**。——任何证券类互换交易商或主要的证券类互换参与者如要约与特殊实体达成证券类互换或与特殊实体达成证券类互换,均应——

(i)遵守证券交易委员会设定的作为适格合约参与者对手方的证券类互换交易商

dealer or major security–based swap participant, with respect to a counterparty that is an eligible contract participant within the meaning of subclause (Ⅰ) or (Ⅱ) of clause (vii) of section 1a(18) of the Commodity Exchange Act, that requires the security–based swap dealer or major security–based swap participant to have a reasonable basis to believe that the counterparty that is a special entity has an independent representative that —

"(Ⅰ) has sufficient knowledge to evaluate the transaction and risks;

"(Ⅱ) is not subject to a statutory disqualification;

"(Ⅲ) is independent of the security–based swap dealer or major security–based swap participant;

"(Ⅳ) undertakes a duty to act in the best interests of the counterparty it represents;

"(Ⅴ) makes appropriate disclosures;

"(Ⅵ) will provide written representations to the special entity regarding fair pricing and the appropriateness of the transaction; and

"(Ⅶ) in the case of employee benefit plans subject to the Employee Retirement Income Security act of 1974, is a fiduciary as defined in section 3 of that Act (29 U.S.C. 1002); and

"(ii) before the initiation of the transaction, disclose to the special entity in writing the capacity in which the security–based swap dealer is acting.

"(B) COMMISSION AUTHORITY. — The Commission may establish such other standards and requirements under this paragraph as the Commission may determine are appropriate in the public interest, for the protection of investors, or otherwise in furtherance of the purposes of this Act.

"(6) RULES. — The Commission shall prescribe rules under this subsection governing business conduct standards for security–based swap dealers and major security–based swap participants.

"(7) APPLICABILITY. — This subsection shall not apply with respect to a transaction that is —

"(A) initiated by a special entity on an exchange or security–based swaps execution facility; and

"(B) the security–based swap dealer or major security–based swap participant does not know the identity of the counterparty to the transaction."

"(i) DOCUMENTATION STANDARDS. —

"(1) IN GENERAL. — Each registered security–based swap dealer and major security–based swap participant shall conform with such standards as may be prescribed by the Commission, by rule or regulation, that relate to timely and accurate confirmation, processing, netting, documentation, and valuation of all security–based swaps.

"(2) RULES. — The Commission shall adopt rules governing documentation standards

或主要的证券类互换参与者的职责[适格合约参与者的定义见《商品交易法》第1a(18)条第(vii)项第(I)子项或第(II)子项],该等职责指,在交易对手方具有特殊实体身份的情况下,证券类互换交易商或主要的证券类互换参与者应有合理的依据确信该对手方有一名符合下述条件的独立代表:

(I)拥有评估交易和风险的充分知识;

(II)不存在法定失格情形;

(III)独立于证券类互换交易商或主要的证券类互换参与者;

(IV)负有为其所代表的对手方最佳利益行事的职责;

(V)进行适当披露;

(VI)将就交易公平定价和交易的适当性向特殊实体提供书面声明;且

(VII)就受制于《1974年员工退休收入保障法》规定的员工福利计划而言,身为该法第3条(《美国法典》第二十九编第1002节)所定义的受信义务人;且

(ii)在发起交易之前,向特殊实体书面披露证券类互换交易商行事的身份;及

(B)**证券交易委员会的权限**。——为了维护公共利益、保护投资者或促进本法其他宗旨的实现,证券交易委员会可以根据本款设定其判定确属适当的其他标准和要求。

(6)**规则**。——证券交易委员会应根据本子条制定规则,规范证券类互换交易商和主要的证券类互换参与者的业务行为准则。

(7)**适用范围**。——本子条不适用于如下交易——

(A)由特殊实体在交易所或证券类互换执行设施发起的交易;及

(B)证券类互换交易商或主要的证券类互换参与者不知道交易对手方身份的交易。”

“(i)**文档记录标准**。——

(1)**一般规定**。——每一注册的证券类互换交易商和主要的证券类互换参与者均应遵照执行证券交易委员会发布的规则或规章所规定的关于对所有证券类互换进行及时准确的确认、处理、净额结算、文档记录和估值的标准。

(2)**规则**。——证券交易委员会应制定规则,规范证券类互换交易商和主要的基

for security–based swap dealers and major security–based swap participants.

"(j) DUTIES. — Each registered security–based swap dealer and major security–based swap participant shall, at all times, comply with the following requirements:

"(1) MONITORING OF TRADING. — The security–based swap dealer or major security–based swap participant shall monitor its trading in security–based swaps to prevent violations of applicable position limits.

"(2) RISK MANAGEMENT PROCEDURES. — The security–based swap dealer or major security–based swap participant shall establish robust and professional risk management systems adequate for managing the day–to–day business of the security–based swap dealer or major security–based swap participant.

"(3) DISCLOSURE OF GENERAL INFORMATION. — The security–based swap dealer or major security–based swap participant shall disclose to the Commission and to the prudential regulator for the security–based swap dealer or major security–based swap participant, as applicable, information concerning —

"(A) terms and conditions of its security–based swaps;

"(B) security–based swap trading operations, mechanisms, and practices;

"(C) financial integrity protections relating to security–based swaps; and

"(D) other information relevant to its trading in security–based swaps.

"(4) ABILITY TO OBTAIN INFORMATION. — The security–based swap dealer or major security–based swap participant shall —

"(A) establish and enforce internal systems and procedures to obtain any necessary information to perform any of the functions described in this section; and

"(B) provide the information to the Commission and to the prudential regulator for the security–based swap dealer or major security–based swap participant, as applicable, on request.

"(5) CONFLICTS OF INTEREST. — The security–based swap dealer and major security–based swap participant shall implement conflict–of–interest systems and procedures that —

"(A) establish structural and institutional safeguards to ensure that the activities of any person within the firm relating to research or analysis of the price or market for any security–based swap or acting in a role of providing clearing activities or making determinations as to accepting clearing customers are separated by appropriate informational partitions within the firm from the review, pressure, or oversight of persons whose involvement in pricing, trading, or clearing activities might potentially bias their judgment or supervision and contravene the core principles of open access and the business conduct standards described in this title; and

"(B) address such other issues as the Commission determines to be appropriate.

于证券的互换参与者的文档记录标准。

(j)**职责**。——每一注册的证券类互换交易商和主要的证券类互换参与者均应始终遵守如下要求:

(1)**交易监控**。——证券类互换交易商或主要的证券类互换参与者应监控其证券类互换交易,从而防范违反适用的持仓限额的行为。

(2)**风险管理程序**。——证券类互换交易商或主要的证券类互换参与者应建立健全的、专业的风险管理制度,充分管理证券类互换交易商或主要的证券类互换参与者的日常业务。

(3)**一般信息披露**。——证券类互换交易商或主要的证券类互换参与者应向证券交易委员会和其审慎监管者(视具体情况而定)披露如下信息——

(A)证券类互换的条款和条件;

(B)证券类互换交易的运作、机制和惯例;

(C)与证券类互换相关的财务完整性保护措施;及

(D)与证券类互换交易相关的其他信息。

(4)**获取信息的能力**。——证券类互换交易商或主要的证券类互换参与者应——

(A)建立并执行内部制度和流程,以获取履行本条所述职能所需的任何必要信息;及

(B)按照证券交易委员会及其审慎监管者要求,向其提供证券类互换交易商或主要的证券类互换参与者(视具体情况而定)的信息。

(5)**利益冲突**。——证券类互换交易商和主要的证券类互换参与者应实施利益冲突处理制度和程序,该等制度和程序应——

(A)设立结构性和制度性保障,确保通过该等机构内部适当的信息隔离,将下列两类活动分开,即该等机构内部与任何证券类互换之价格或市场研究或分析相关的任何人的活动,或者负责提供结算活动或负责判断是否受理结算客户的人的活动,以及具有以下特征的人员开展的审查、施压或监督工作,即该等人员若参与定价、交易或结算活动,该等人员的判断或领导监管工作即可能产生偏差并违反准入开放性的核心原则及本编所述业务行为准则;且

(B)处理证券交易委员会判定确属适当的其他事项。

"(6) ANTITRUST CONSIDERATIONS. — Unless necessary or appropriate to achieve the purposes of this title, the security-based swap dealer or major security-based swap participant shall not —

"(A) adopt any process or take any action that results in any unreasonable restraint of trade; or

"(B) impose any material anticompetitive burden on trading or clearing.

"(7) RULES. — The Commission shall prescribe rules under this subsection governing duties of security-based swap dealers and major security-based swap participants.

"(k) DESIGNATION OF CHIEF COMPLIANCE OFFICER. —

"(1) IN GENERAL. — Each security-based swap dealer and major security-based swap participant shall designate an individual to serve as a chief compliance officer.

"(2) DUTIES. — The chief compliance officer shall —

"(A) report directly to the board or to the senior officer of the security-based swap dealer or major security-based swap participant;

"(B) review the compliance of the security-based swap dealer or major security-based swap participant with respect to the security-based swap dealer and major security-based swap participant requirements described in this section;

"(C) in consultation with the board of directors, a body performing a function similar to the board, or the senior officer of the organization, resolve any conflicts of interest that may arise;

"(D) be responsible for administering each policy and procedure that is required to beestablished pursuant to this section;

"(E) ensure compliance with this title (including regulations) relating to security-based swaps,including each rule prescribed by the Commission under this section;

"(F) establish procedures for the remediation of noncompliance issues identified by the chief compliance officer through any —

"(i) compliance office review;

"(ii) look-back;

"(iii) internal or external audit finding;

"(iv) self-reported error; or

"(v) validated complaint; and

"(G) establish and follow appropriate procedures for the handling, management response, remediation, retesting, and closing of noncompliance issues.

"(3) ANNUAL REPORTS. —

"(A) IN GENERAL. — In accordance with rules prescribed by the Commission, the chief compliance officer shall annually prepare and sign a report that contains a description of —

"(i) the compliance of the security-based swap dealer or major swap participant with

(6)**反垄断考量**。——除非为实现本编宗旨所必要或适当,否则证券类互换交易商或主要的证券类互换参与者不得——

(A)制定对交易造成任何不合理限制的任何程序或采取对交易造成任何不合理限制的任何行动;或

(B)对交易或结算施加任何阻碍竞争的实质性负担。

(7)**规则**。——证券交易委员会应根据本子条针对证券类互换交易商和主要的证券类互换参与者的职责制定规则。

(k)**首席合规官的指定**。——

(1)**一般规定**。——每一证券类互换交易商和主要的证券类互换参与者均应指定1名个人担任首席合规官。

(2)**职责**。——首席合规官应——

(A)向证券类互换交易商或主要的证券类互换参与者的董事会或高级管理人员直接汇报工作;

(B)审查证券类互换交易商或主要的证券类互换参与者对本条针对证券类互换交易商和主要的证券类互换参与者规定的要求的遵守情况;

(C)与董事会、履行与董事会类似职能的机构或高级管理人员磋商,解决任何可能发生的利益冲突问题;

(D)负责实施依据本条要求制定的每一项政策和程序;

(E)确保本编(包括规章)中与证券类互换相关的规定(包括证券交易委员会依据本条制定的每项规则)均得到遵守;

(F)制定相关程序,据以对首席合规官通过以下任何方式识别的不合规问题采取补救措——

(i)合规办公室的审查工作;

(ii)回顾工作;

(iii)内部或外部审计认定结论;

(iv)自报失误;或

(v)有效的投诉;及

(G)制定并遵守用以对不合规问题进行处理、管理回应、补救、重新测试和终结的适当程序。

(3)**年度报告**。——

(A)**一般规定**。——首席合规官应根据证券交易委员会制定的规则每年编制并签署一份报告,其中应包含以下内容——

(i)证券类互换交易商或主要的证券类互换参与者对本编(包括规章)的合规情

respect to this title (including regulations); and

"(ii) each policy and procedure of the security-based swap dealer or major security-based swap participant of the chief compliance officer (including the code of ethics and conflict of interest policies).

"(B) REQUIREMENTS. — A compliance report under subparagraph (A) shall —

"(i) accompany each appropriate financial report of the security-based swap dealer or major security-based swap participant that is required to be furnished to the Commission pursuant to this section; and

"(ii) include a certification that, under penalty of law, the compliance report is accurate and complete.

"(l) ENFORCEMENT AND ADMINISTRATIVE PROCEEDING AUTHORITY. —

"(1) PRIMARY ENFORCEMENT AUTHORITY. —

"(A) SECURITIES AND EXCHANGE COMMISSION. — Except as provided in subparagraph (B), (C), or (D), the Commission shall have primary authority to enforce subtitle B, and the amendments made by subtitle B of the Wall Street Transparency and Accountability Act of 2010, with respect to any person.

"(B) PRUDENTIAL REGULATORS. — The prudential regulators shall have exclusive authority to enforce the provisions of subsection (e) and other prudential requirements of this title (including risk management standards), with respect to security-based swap dealers or major security-based swap participants for which they are the prudential regulator.

"(C) REFERRAL. —

"(i) VIOLATIONS OF NONPRUDENTIAL REQUIREMENTS. — If the appropriate Federal banking agency for security-based swap dealers or major security-based swap participants that are depository institutions has cause to believe that such security-based swap dealer or major security-based swap participant may have engaged in conduct that constitutes a violation of the nonprudential requirements of this section or rules adopted by the Commission thereunder, the agency may recommend in writing to the Commission that the Commission initiate an enforcement proceeding as authorized under this title. The recommendation shall be accompanied by a written explanation of the concerns giving rise to the recommendation.

"(ii) VIOLATIONS OF PRUDENTIAL REQUIREMENTS. — If the Commission has cause to believe that a securities-based swap dealer or major securities-based swap participant that has a prudential regulator may have engaged in conduct that constitute a violation of the prudential requirements of subsection (e) or rules adopted thereunder, the Commission may recommend in writing to the prudential regulator that the prudential regulator initiate an enforcement proceeding as authorized under this title. The recommendation shall be accompanied by a written explanation of the concerns giving rise to

况;及

(ii)首席合规官所属的证券类互换交易商或主要的证券类互换参与者的每项政策和程序(包括职业道德准则和利益冲突处理政策)。

(B)**要求**。——按照第(A)子款编制的合规报告应——

(i)与按本条规定应向证券交易委员会提交的证券类互换交易商或主要的证券类互换参与者每份相应的财务报告一并提交;及

(ii)包含一份自查证明,证明该合规报告的准确性和完整性,并明确表示其知晓作伪证将招致法律惩罚。

(l)**执法和开展行政处理程序的权限**。——

(1)**优先执法权**。——

(A)**证券交易委员会**。——除第(B)子款、第(C)子款或第(D)子款规定的情形外,证券交易委员会应对《2010年华尔街透明度与问责法》第B子编及第B子编作出的修正享有优先执法权,有权对任何主体执行该等规定。

(B)**审慎监管者**。——审慎监管者应对第(e)子条以及本编其他审慎性要求(包括风险管理标准)享有排他执法权,有权对受其审慎监管的证券类互换交易商或主要的证券类互换参与者执行该等规定。

(C)**移交**。——

(i)**对非审慎性要求的违反**。——对于具有存款机构身份的证券类互换交易商或主要的证券类互换参与者而言,如果其相应的联邦银行业监管机关有理由相信,该证券类互换交易商或主要的证券类互换参与者可能作出了违反本条非审慎性要求或证券交易委员会根据本条制定的规则的行为,则该监管机关可书面建议证券交易委员会根据本编授权启动执法程序。在提出上述书面建议时,应附上一份书面说明,解释该监管机关提出该项建议时所关切的问题。

(ii)**对审慎性要求的违反**。——如果证券交易委员会有理由相信,受其审慎监管的证券类互换交易商或主要的证券类互换参与者可能作出了违反第(e)子条的审慎性要求或证券交易委员会根据该条制定的规则的行为,则证券交易委员会可书面建议审慎监管者根据本编授权启动执法程序。在提出上述书面建议时,应附上一份书面说明,解释证券交易委员会提出该项建议时所关切的问题。

the recommendation.

"(D) BACKSTOP ENFORCEMENT AUTHORITY.—

"(i) INITIATION OF ENFORCEMENT PROCEEDING BY PRUDENTIAL REGULATOR.—If the Commission does not initiate an enforcement proceeding before the end of the 90–day period beginning on the date on which the Commission receives a written report under subsection (C)(i), the prudential regulator may initiate an enforcement proceeding.

"(ii) INITIATION OF ENFORCEMENT PROCEEDING BY COMMISSION.—If the prudential regulator does not initiate an enforcement proceeding before the end of the 90–day period beginning on the date on which the prudential regulator receives a written report under subsection (C)(ii), the Commission may initiate an enforcement proceeding.

"(2) CENSURE, DENIAL, SUSPENSION; NOTICE AND HEARING.—The Commission, by order, shall censure, place limitations on the activities, functions, or operations of, or revoke the registration of any security–based swap dealer or major security–based swap participant that has registered with the Commission pursuant to subsection (b) if the Commission finds, on the record after notice and opportunity for hearing, that such censure, placing of limitations, or revocation is in the public interest and that such security–based swap dealer or major security–based swap participant, or any person associated with such security–based swap dealer or major security–based swap participant effecting or involved in effecting transactions in security–based swaps on behalf of such security–based swap dealer or major security–based swap participant, whether prior or subsequent to becoming so associated—

"(A) has committed or omitted any act, or is subject to an order or finding, enumerated in subparagraph (A), (D), or (E) of paragraph (4) of section 15(b);

"(B) has been convicted of any offense specified in subparagraph (B) of such paragraph (4) within 10 years of the commencement of the proceedings under this subsection;

"(C) is enjoined from any action, conduct, or practice specified in subparagraph (C) of such paragraph (4);

"(D) is subject to an order or a final order specified in subparagraph (F) or (H), respectively, of such paragraph (4); or

"(E) has been found by a foreign financial regulatory authority to have committed or omitted any act, or violated any foreign statute or regulation, enumerated in subparagraph (G) of such paragraph (4).

"(3) ASSOCIATED PERSONS.—With respect to any person who is associated, who is seeking to become associated, or, at the time of the alleged misconduct, who was associated or was seeking to become associated with a security–based swap dealer or major security–based

(D)**后备执法权**。——

(i)**由审慎监管者启动执法程序**。——如果证券交易委员会未在收到根据第(C)(i)子条提交的书面报告后90天期限届满前启动执法程序,则审慎监管者可以自行启动执法程序。

(ii)**证券交易委员会启动执法程序**。——如果审慎监管者未在收到根据第(C)(ii)子条提交的书面报告后90天期限届满前启动执法程序,则证券交易委员会可以自行启动执法程序。

(2)**谴责、驳回、暂停;通知和听证**。——证券交易委员会应签发命令,谴责或限制根据第(b)子条在证券交易委员会注册的证券类互换交易商或主要的证券类互换参与者的活动、职能或运营或者撤销其注册资格,前提是证券交易委员会在记录在案的基础上,发出通知并提供听证机会后,认定该项谴责、限制或资格撤销符合公共利益,且该证券类互换交易商或主要的证券类互换参与者或其任何业务相关人(该业务相关人在成为其业务相关人之前或之后,代表该证券类互换交易商或主要的证券类互换参与者实施证券类互换或参与证券类互换的实施工作)——

(A)从事了第15(b)条第(4)款第(A)子款、第(D)子款或第(E)子款列明的作为或不作为,或受制于上述条款所列命令或认定;

(B)在根据本子条启动程序后10年内被判犯有该第(4)款第(B)子款所列罪行;

(C)被禁止从事该第(4)款第(C)子款所列行动、行为或做法;

(D)受制于该第(4)款第(F)子款或第(H)子款所列命令或最终命令;或

(E)被外国金融监管机构认定从事了该第(4)款第(G)子款所列作为或不作为或违反了该子款指明的任何外国法律或法规。

(3)**业务相关人**。——证券交易委员会应签发命令,对以下人员进行谴责,或限制其活动或职能,或者暂停或禁止其与证券类互换交易商或主要的证券类互换参与者的业务相关关系(暂停时间不超过12个月):证券类互换交易商或主要的证券类互

swap participant for the purpose of effecting or being involved in effecting security–based swaps on behalf of such security–based swap dealer or major security–based swap participant, the Commission, by order, shall censure, place limitations on the activities or functions of such person, or suspend for a period not exceeding 12 months, or bar such person from being associated with a security–based swap dealer or major security–based swap participant, if the Commission finds, on the record after notice and opportunity for a hearing, that such censure, placing of limitations, suspension, or bar is in the public interest and that such person —

"(A) has committed or omitted any act, or is subject to an order or finding, enumerated in subparagraph (A), (D), or (E) of paragraph (4) of section 15(b);

"(B) has been convicted of any offense specified in subparagraph (B) of such paragraph (4) within 10 years of the commencement of the proceedings under this subsection;

"(C) is enjoined from any action, conduct, or practice specified in subparagraph (C) of such paragraph (4);

"(D) is subject to an order or a final order specified in subparagraph (F) or (H), respectively, of such paragraph (4); or

"(E) has been found by a foreign financial regulatory authority to have committed or omitted any act, or violated any foreign statute or regulation, enumerated in subparagraph (G) of such paragraph (4).

"(4) UNLAWFUL CONDUCT. — It shall be unlawful —

"(A) for any person as to whom an order under paragraph (3) is in effect, without the consent of the Commission, willfully to become, or to be, associated with a security–based swap dealer or major security–based swap participant in contravention of such order; or

"(B) for any security–based swap dealer or major security–based swap participant to permit such a person, without the consent of the Commission, to become or remain a person associated with the security–based swap dealer or major security–based swap participant in contravention of such order, if such security–based swap dealer or major security–based swap participant knew, or in the exercise of reasonable care should have known, of such order.".

(b) SAVINGS CLAUSE. — Notwithstanding any other provision of this title, nothing in this subtitle shall be construed as divesting any appropriate Federal banking agency of any authority it may have to establish or enforce, with respect to a person for which such agency is the appropriate Federal banking agency, prudential or other standards pursuant to authority by Federal law other than this title.

SEC.765. RULEMAKING ON CONFLICT OF INTEREST.

(a) IN GENERAL. — In order to mitigate conflicts of interest, not later than 180 days after the date of enactment of the Wall Street Transparency and Accountability Act of 2010,

换参与者的业务相关人、寻求成为该等业务相关人的人,或在被指控的不当行为发生时,为了代表证券类互换交易商或主要的证券类互换参与者实施证券类互换或参与证券类互换的实施工作而已成为证券类互换交易商或主要的证券类互换参与者的业务相关人或寻求成为该等业务相关人的人,前提是证券交易委员会在记录在案的基础上,发出通知并提供听证机会后,认定该项谴责、限制、暂停或禁止符合公共利益,且该人——

(A)从事了第15(b)条第(4)款第(A)子款、第(D)子款或第(E)子款所列作为或不作为,或受制于上述条款所列命令或认定;

(B)在根据本子条启动程序后10年内被判犯有该第(4)款第(B)子款所列罪行;

(C)被禁止从事该第(4)款第(C)子款所列行动、行为或做法;

(D)受制于该第(4)款第(F)子款或第(H)子款所列命令或最终命令;或

(E)被外国金融监管机构认定从事了该第(4)款第(G)子款所列作为或不作为或违反了该子款指明的外国法律或法规。

(4)**非法行为**。——下述行为当属违法——

(A)被签发第(3)款规定的命令的人,在命令有效期内,未经证券交易委员会同意,故意违反该命令成为或充当该证券类互换交易商或主要的证券类互换参与者的业务相关人;或

(B)证券类互换交易商或主要的证券类互换参与者未经证券交易委员会同意,允许上述人员违反上述命令成为或继续充当该证券类互换交易商或主要的证券类互换参与者的业务相关人(前提是该证券类互换交易商或主要的证券类互换参与者明知或尽合理注意后应知该命令)。”

(b)**保留条款**。——无论本编是否存在任何不同规定,如任何相应的联邦银行业监管机关根据本编之外的联邦法律规定的授权,可以对受其相应的联邦银行业监管的主体制定或执行审慎性标准或其他标准,则本子编的任何规定均不得被解释为解除该等监管机关所享有的上述权力。

第765条　利益冲突规则的制定

(a)**一般规定**。——在《2010年华尔街透明度与问责法》颁布之日起180天内,证券交易委员会应为减少利益冲突之目的制定相关规则,包括控制权或表决权的数量限

the Securities and Exchange Commission shall adopt rules which may include numerical limits on the control of, or the voting rights with respect to, any clearing agency that clears security–based swaps, or on the control of any security–based swap execution facility or national securities exchange that posts or makes available for trading security–based swaps, by a bank holding company (as defined in section 2 of the Bank Holding Company Act of 1956 (12 U.S.C. 1841)) with total consolidated assets of $50,000,000,000 or more, a nonbank financial company (as defined in section 102) supervised by the Board of Governors of the Federal Reserve System, affiliate of such a bank holding company or nonbank financial company, a security–based swap dealer, major security–based swap participant, or person associated with a security–based swap dealer or major security–based swap participant.

(b) PURPOSES. — The Securities and Exchange Commission shall adopt rules if the Commission determines, after the review described in subsection (a), that such rules are necessary or appropriate to improve the governance of, or to mitigate systemic risk, promote competition, or mitigate conflicts of interest in connection with a security–based swap dealer or major security–based swap participant's conduct of business with, a clearing agency, national securities exchange, or security–based swap execution facility that clears, posts, or makes available for trading security–based swaps and in which such security–based swap dealer or major security–based swap participant has a material debt or equity investment.

(c) CONSIDERATIONS. — In adopting rules pursuant to this section, the Securities and Exchange Commission shall consider any conflicts of interest arising from the amount of equity owned by a single investor, the ability to vote, cause the vote of, or withhold votes entitled to be cast on any matters by the holders of the ownership interest, and the governance arrangements of any derivatives clearing organization that clears swaps, or swap execution facility or board of trade designated as a contract market that posts swaps or makes swaps available for trading.

SEC.766. REPORTING AND RECORDKEEPING.

(a) IN GENERAL. — The Securities Exchange Act of 1934 (15 U.S.C. 78a et seq.) is amended by inserting after section 13 the following:

"SEC.13A. REPORTING AND RECORDKEEPING FOR CERTAIN SECURITY–BASED SWAPS.

"(a) REQUIRED REPORTING OF SECURITY–BASED SWAPS NOT ACCEPTED BY ANY CLEARING AGENCY OR DERIVATIVES CLEARING ORGANIZATION. —

"(1) IN GENERAL. — Each security–based swap that is not accepted for clearing by any clearing agency or derivatives clearing organization shall be reported to —

"(A) a security–based swap data repository described in section 13(n); or

"(B) in the case in which there is no security–based swap data repository that would accept the security–based swap, to the Commission pursuant to this section within such time

制规则,以限制以下实体对提供证券类互换的集中结算服务之任何结算机构拥有的控制权或表决权,或对发布证券类互换或提供证券类互换以供交易的任何证券类互换执行设施或全国性证券交易所拥有的控制权:并表资产总额达500亿美元(含)以上的银行控股公司[定义见《1956年银行控股公司法》第2条(《美国法典》第十二编第1841节)]、受联邦储备委员会监管的非银行金融公司(定义见第102条)、上述银行控股公司或非银行金融公司的关联方、证券类互换交易商、主要的证券类互换参与者或该等证券类互换交易商或主要的证券类互换参与者的业务相关人。

(b)**目的**。——证券交易委员会应在开展第(a)子条所述审查后,制定其判定确属必要或适当的规则,以改善证券类互换交易商或主要的证券类互换参与者的治理,缓释其系统性风险,促进竞争或减少其开展业务时与下述主体之间的利益冲突:由证券类互换交易商或主要的证券类互换参与者拥有重大债务或股权投资的,结算、发布证券类互换或提供证券类互换以供交易的结算机构、全国性证券交易所或证券类互换执行设施。

(c)**考虑因素**。——根据本条制定规则时,证券交易委员会应考虑以下因素:因单个投资者拥有的股权金额产生的利益冲突;直接表决能力、促使所有权权益持有人就其有权表决的任何事项进行表决或放弃表决的能力;以及对提供互换集中结算的任何衍生品结算组织,或被指定为合约市场的发布互换或提供互换以供交易的互换执行设施或交易场所的治理安排。

第766条　报告和记录保存

(a)**一般规定**。——在《1934年证券交易法》(《美国法典》第十五编第78a节及其后条文)第13条之后插入如下内容,作为对该法的修正:

"第13A条　报告特定的证券类互换并保存相关记录

(a)**未被任何结算机构或衍生品结算组织受理进行集中结算的证券类互换的报告要求**。——

(1)**一般规定**。——未被任何结算机构或衍生品结算组织受理进行集中结算的每一证券类互换均——

(A)应向第13(n)条所述证券类互换数据存管机构报告;或

(B)无任何互换数据存管机构受理该证券类互换报告的,应在证券交易委员会发布的规则或规章所规定的期限内依照本条规定向证券交易委员会报告。

period as the Commission may by rule or regulation prescribe.

"(2) TRANSITION RULE FOR PREENACTMENT SECURITY–BASED SWAPS. —

"(A) SECURITY–BASED SWAPS ENTERED INTO BEFORE THE DATE OF ENACTMENT OF THE WALL STREET TRANSPARENCY AND ACCOUNTABILITY ACT OF 2010. — Each security–based swap entered into before the date of enactment of the Wall Street Transparency and Accountability Act of 2010, the terms of which have not expired as of the date of enactment of that Act, shall be reported to a registered security–based swap data repository or the Commission by a date that is not later than —

"(i) 30 days after issuance of the interim final rule; or

"(ii) such other period as the Commission determines to be appropriate.

"(B) COMMISSION RULEMAKING. — The Commission shall promulgate an interim final rule within 90 days of the date of enactment of this section providing for the reporting of each security–based swap entered into before the date of enactment as referenced in subparagraph (A).

"(C) EFFECTIVE DATE. — The reporting provisions described in this section shall be effective upon the date of the enactment of this section.

"(3) REPORTING OBLIGATIONS. —

"(A) SECURITY–BASED SWAPS IN WHICH ONLY 1 COUNTERPARTY IS A SECURITY–BASED SWAP DEALER OR MAJOR SECURITY–BASED SWAP PARTICIPANT. — With respect to a security–based swap in which only 1 counterparty is a security–based swap dealer or major security–based swap participant, the security–based swap dealer or major security–based swap participant shall report the security–based swap as required under paragraphs (1) and (2).

"(B) SECURITY–BASED SWAPS IN WHICH 1 COUNTERPARTY IS A SECURITY–BASED SWAP DEALER AND THE OTHER A MAJOR SECURITY–BASED SWAP PARTICIPANT. — With respect to a security–based swap in which 1 counterparty is a security–based swap dealer and the other a major security–based swap participant, the security–based swap dealer shall report the security–based swap as required under paragraphs (1) and (2).

"(C) OTHER SECURITY–BASED SWAPS. — With respect to any other security–based swap not described in subparagraph (A) or (B), the counterparties to the security–based swap shall select a counterparty to report the security–based swap as required under paragraphs (1) and (2).

"(b) DUTIES OF CERTAIN INDIVIDUALS. — Any individual or entity that enters into a security–based swap shall meet each requirement described in subsection (c) if the individual or entity did not —

(2)**《2010年华尔街透明度与问责法》颁布之日前达成的证券类互换的过渡规则**。——

(A)《2010年华尔街透明度与问责法》颁布之日以前达成的证券类互换。——《2010年华尔街透明度与问责法》颁布之日前达成的每一证券类互换,其条款截至该法颁布之日尚未到期的,应不迟于以下期限向注册的证券类互换数据存管机构或证券交易委员会报告——

(i)最终规则(暂行版)发布后第30天;或

(ii)证券交易委员会判定确属适当的任何其他期限。

(B)**证券交易委员会的规则制定**。——证券交易委员会应于本条规定颁布之日起90天内颁发最终规则(暂行版),规定对第(A)子款提及的《2010年华尔街透明度与问责法》颁布之日以前达成的每一证券类互换进行报告。

(C)**生效日**。——本条规定颁布后,其关于报告的规定当即生效。

(3)**报告义务**。——

(A)**证券类互换中只有一个对手方是证券类互换交易商或主要的证券类互换参与者的情形**。——如果证券类互换中只有一个对手方是证券类互换交易商或主要的证券类互换参与者,则该证券类互换交易商或主要的证券类互换参与者应按第(1)款和第(2)款的规定对证券类互换进行报告。

(B)**证券类互换中一个对手方是证券类互换交易商而另一个对手方是主要的证券类互换参与者的情形**。——如果证券类互换中有一个对手方是证券类互换交易商而另一个对手方是主要的证券类互换参与者,则该证券类互换交易商应按第(1)款和第(2)款的规定对证券类互换进行报告。

(C)**其他证券类互换**。——就不属于第(A)子款或第(B)子款所述的任何其他证券类互换而言,证券类互换对手方应从双方之中选定一方,由其按第(1)款和第(2)款的规定对证券类互换进行报告。

(b)**特定个人的职责**。——达成证券类互换的任何个人或实体在下列情形下应遵守第(c)子条的每项要求——

"(1) clear the security–based swap in accordance with section 3C(a)(1); or

"(2) have the data regarding the security–based swap accepted by a security–based swap data repository in accordance with rules (including timeframes) adopted by the Commission under this title.

"(c) REQUIREMENTS.—An individual or entity described in subsection (b) shall—

"(1) upon written request from the Commission, provide reports regarding the security–based swaps held by the individual or entity to the Commission in such form and in such manner as the Commission may request; and

"(2) maintain books and records pertaining to the security–based swaps held by the individual or entity in such form, in such manner, and for such period as the Commission may require, which shall be open to inspection by—

"(A) any representative of the Commission;

"(B) an appropriate prudential regulator;

"(C) the Commodity Futures Trading Commission;

"(D) the Financial Stability Oversight Council; and

"(E) the Department of Justice.

"(d) IDENTICAL DATA. — In prescribing rules under this section, the Commission shall require individuals and entities described in subsection (b) to submit to the Commission a report that contains data that is not less comprehensive than the data required to be collected by security–based swap data repositories under this title.".

(b) BENEFICIAL OWNERSHIP REPORTING. — Section 13 of the Securities Exchange Act of 1934 (15 U.S.C. 78m) is amended—

(1) in subsection (d)(1), by inserting "or otherwise becomes or is deemed to become a beneficial owner of any of the foregoing upon the purchase or sale of a security–based swap that the Commission may define by rule, and" after "Alaska Native Claims Settlement Act,"; and

(2) in subsection (g)(1), by inserting "or otherwise becomes or is deemed to become a beneficial owner of any security of a class described in subsection (d)(1) upon the purchase or sale of a security–based swap that the Commission may define by rule" after "subsection (d)(1) of this section".

(c) REPORTS BY INSTITUTIONAL INVESTMENT MANAGERS. — Section 13(f)(1) of the Securities Exchange Act of 1934 (15 U.S.C. 78m(f)(1)) is amended by inserting "or otherwise becomes or is deemed to become a beneficial owner of any security of a class described in subsection (d)(1) upon the purchase or sale of a security–based swap that the Commission may define by rule," after "subsection (d)(1) of this section".

(d) ADMINISTRATIVE PROCEEDING AUTHORITY. — Section 15(b)(4) of the

(1)该个人或实体并未按本编第3C(a)(1)条的规定对该证券类互换进行集中结算;或

(2)该个人或实体不掌握与如下证券类互换相关的数据,即证券类互换数据存管机构按照证券交易委员会根据本编制定的规则(包括期限方面的规则)受理的互换。

(c)**要求**。——第(b)子条所述个人或实体——

(1)经证券交易委员会提出书面要求,应按照证券交易委员会要求的格式和方式,对其持有的证券类互换向证券交易委员会提交报告;且

(2)应对其持有的证券类互换保存账簿和记录,保存格式、方式和期限应符合证券交易委员会的相关要求,并可供以下机构检查——

(A)证券交易委员会的任何代表;

(B)相应的审慎监管者;

(C)商品期货交易委员会;

(D)金融稳定监督委员会;及

(E)司法部。

(d)**相同的数据**。——依据本条制定规则时,证券交易委员会应要求第(b)子条所述的个人和实体向证券交易委员会提交全面的数据报告,且其所含数据的全面程度应不亚于本编要求证券类互换数据存管机构收集的数据。"

(b)**受益所有权报告**。——《1934年证券交易法》第13条(《美国法典》第十五编第78m节)修正如下——

(1)在第(d)(1)子条中,在"或获得《阿拉斯加原住民土地权处理法》第37(d)(6)条[《美国法典》第四十三编第1629c(d)(6)节]规定的原住民公司的权益证券的受益所有权之后"之后插入"或在买卖证券类互换后成为或被视为成为任何上述权益证券的受益所有权人(证券交易委员会可发布规则对此作出定义),并且";及

(2)在第(g)(1)子条中,在"本条第(d)(1)子条所述任何类别证券5%以上受益所有权人时"之后插入"或在买卖证券类互换后成为或被视为成为第(d)(1)子条所述任何类别证券的受益所有权人(证券交易委员会可发布规则对此作出定义)时"。

(c)**机构投资管理人的报告**。——在《1934年证券交易法》第13(f)(1)条[《美国法典》第十五编第78m(f)(1)节]中,在"对持有本条(d)(1)款所述类别权益证券的账户行使投资决定权的"之后插入"或在买卖证券类互换后成为或被视为成为第(d)(1)子条所述任何类别证券的受益所有权人(证券交易委员会可发布规则对此作出定义)",作为对该条的修正。

(d)**开展行政处理程序的权力**。——《1934年证券交易法》第15(b)(4)条[《美国

Securities Exchange Act of 1934 (15 U.S.C. 78o(b)(4)) is amended—

(1) in subparagraph (C), by inserting "security–based swap dealer, major security–based swap participant," after "government securities dealer,"; and

(2) in subparagraph (F), by striking "broker or dealer" and inserting "broker, dealer, security–based swap dealer, or a major security–based swap participant".

(e) SECURITY–BASED SWAP BENEFICIAL OWNERSHIP. — Section 13 of the Securities Exchange Act of 1934 (15 U.S.C. 78m) is amended by adding at the end the following:

"(o) BENEFICIAL OWNERSHIP. — For purposes of this section and section 16, a person shall be deemed to acquire beneficial ownership of an equity security based on the purchase or sale of a security–based swap, only to the extent that the Commission, by rule, determines after consultation with the prudential regulators and the Secretary of the Treasury, that the purchase or sale of the security–based swap, or class of security–based swap, provides incidents of ownership comparable to direct ownership of the equity security, and that it is necessary to achieve the purposes of this section that the purchase or sale of the security–based swaps, or class of security–based swap, be deemed the acquisition of beneficial ownership of the equity security.".

SEC.767. STATE GAMING AND BUCKET SHOP LAWS.

Section 28(a) of the Securities Exchange Act of 1934 (15 U.S.C. 78bb(a)) is amended to read as follows:

"(a) LIMITATION ON JUDGMENTS. —

"(1) IN GENERAL. — No person permitted to maintain a suit for damages under the provisions of this title shall recover, through satisfaction of judgment in 1 or more actions, a total amount in excess of the actual damages to that person on account of the act complained of. Except as otherwise specifically provided in this title, nothing in this title shall affect the jurisdiction of the securities commission (or any agency or officer performing like functions) of any State over any security or any person insofar as it does not conflict with the provisions of this title or the rules and regulations under this title.

"(2) RULE OF CONSTRUCTION. — Except as provided in subsection (f), the rights and remedies provided by this title shall be in addition to any and all other rights and remedies that may exist at law or in equity.

"(3) STATE BUCKET SHOP LAWS. — No State law which prohibits or regulates the making or promoting of wagering or gaming contracts, or the operation of 'bucket shops' or other similar or related activities, shall invalidate —

"(A) any put, call, straddle, option, privilege, or other security subject to this title (except any security that has a pari–mutuel payout or otherwise is determined by the Commission, acting by rule, regulation, or order, to be appropriately subject to such laws), or

法典》第十五编第78o(b)(4)节]修正如下:

(1)在第(C)子款“政府证券自营商”之后插入“证券类互换交易商、主要的证券类互换参与者,”;及

(2)删去第(F)子款中的“经纪商或自营商”,插入“经纪商、自营商、证券类互换交易商或主要的证券类互换参与者”。

(e)**证券类互换受益所有权**。——在《1934年证券交易法》第13条(《美国法典》第十五编第78m节)结尾处增加如下内容,作为对该条的修正:

“(o)**受益所有权**。——就本条以及第16条而言,只有在满足以下条件时,相关主体始得视为因买卖证券类互换而获得股权证券的受益所有权:证券交易委员会在与审慎监管者及财政部磋商后发布规则,确定证券类互换或任何类别的证券类互换的买入或卖出提供了与该股权证券的直接所有权具有可比性的所有权附属权,并且为实现本条目的,有必要将买入或卖出该证券类互换或该类别证券类互换视为获得该股权证券的受益所有权。”

第767条　关于博彩和投机商号的州法律

《1934年证券交易法》第28(a)条[《美国法典》第十五编第78bb(a)节]修正后全文如下:

“(a)**判决的限制**。——

(1)**一般规定**。——任何获许根据本编规定提起赔偿金诉讼的人,均不得借由一项或一项以上诉讼判决的执行,获得超过该人因被起诉的行为而遭受的实际损失。除本编另有规定的情形外,本编的任何内容均不影响任何州证券委员会(或履行类似职能的任何机关或官员)对任何证券或任何人的管辖权,前提是该管辖权与本编规定或根据本编制定的规则与规章不相冲突。

(2)**解释规则**。——除第(f)子条规定的情形外,本编规定的权利和救济应与普通法或衡平法可能赋予的权利和救济具有并存性,前者不限制后者。

(3)**关于投机商号的州法律**。——禁止赌博或博彩合约的订立或推介或对该等订立或推广进行监管的任何州法律,或禁止或监管‘投机商号’的经营或其他类似或相关活动的州法律均不得——

(A)导致受本编管辖的任何看跌期权、看涨期权、跨式期权组合、期权、优先权或其他证券(有彩金支出的证券或由证券交易委员会发布的规则、规章或命令中判定应受该等法律相应管辖的证券除外)失效,或适用于任何该等证券的要约、买入、卖出、

apply to any activity which is incidental or related to the offer, purchase, sale, exercise, settlement, or closeout of any such security;

"(B) any security–based swap between eligible contract participants; or

"(C) any security–based swap effected on a national securities exchange registered pursuant to section 6(b).

"(4) OTHER STATE PROVISIONS. — No provision of State law regarding the offer, sale, or distribution of securities shall apply to any transaction in a security–based swap or a security futures product, except that this paragraph may not be construed as limiting any State antifraud law of general applicability. A security–based swap may not be regulated as an insurance contract under any provision of State law.".

SEC.768. AMENDMENTS TO THE SECURITIES ACT OF 1933; TREATMENT OF SECURITY–BASED SWAPS.

(a) DEFINITIONS. — Section 2(a) of the Securities Act of 1933 (15 U.S.C. 77b(a)) is amended —

(1) in paragraph (1), by inserting "security–based swap," after "security future,";

(2) in paragraph (3), by adding at the end the following: "Any offer or sale of a security–based swap by or on behalf of the issuer of the securities upon which such security–based swap is based or is referenced, an affiliate of the issuer, or an underwriter, shall constitute a contract for sale of, sale of, offer for sale, or offer to sell such securities."; and

(3) by adding at the end the following:

"(17) The terms 'swap' and 'security–based swap' have the same meanings as in section 1a of the Commodity Exchange Act (7 U.S.C. 1a).

"(18) The terms 'purchase' or 'sale' of a security–based swap shall be deemed to mean the execution, termination (prior to its scheduled maturity date), assignment, exchange, or similar transfer or conveyance of, or extinguishing of rights or obligations under, a security–based swap, as the context may require.".

(b) REGISTRATION OF SECURITY–BASED SWAPS. — Section 5 of the Securities Act of 1933 (15 U.S.C. 77e) is amended by adding at the end the following:

"(d) Notwithstanding the provisions of section 3 or 4, unless a registration statement meeting the requirements of section 10(a) is in effect as to a security–based swap, it shall be unlawful for any person, directly or indirectly, to make use of any means or instruments of transportation or communication in interstate commerce or of the mails to offer to sell, offer to buy or purchase or sell a security–based swap to any person who is not an eligible contract participant as defined in section 1a(18) of the Commodity Exchange Act (7 U.S.C. 1a(18)).".

行权、结算或了结所附带或与之相关的活动;

(B)导致适格合约参与者之间的任何证券类互换失效;或

(C)导致在根据第6(b)条注册的全国性证券交易所所实施的证券类互换失效。

(4)**其他州规定**。——州法律中关于证券的要约、销售或分销的规定均不适用于证券类互换或证券期货产品的交易,但本款不得被解释为限制任何州反欺诈法律的一般适用性。证券类互换不得作为根据任何州法律缔结的保险合同受到监管。”

第768条　对《1933年证券法》的修正;证券类互换的处理

(a)**定义**。——《1933年证券法》第2(a)条[《美国法典》第十五编第77b(a)节]修正如下——

(1)在第(1)款的“证券期货、”之后插入“证券类互换、”;

(2)在第(3)款的结尾处增加如下内容:“证券类互换如果由以下人员或其代表要约或卖出,则应构成该等证券的出售合约、出售行为、出售要约或约定卖出的要约:作为该证券类互换的基础或参考的证券的发行人、该发行人的关联方或承销商。”及

(3)在结尾处增加如下内容:

“(17)‘互换’和‘证券类互换’的含义以《商品交易法》第1a条(《美国法典》第七编第1a节)的定义为准。

(18)证券类互换的‘买入’或‘卖出’应根据上下文,视为指证券类互换的执行、终止(指在预定的到期日之前终止)、转让、交换或该等证券类互换规定的权利和义务的类似转移、让与或消灭。”

(b)**证券类互换的注册**。——在《1933年证券法》第5条(《美国法典》第十五编第77e节)结尾处增加如下内容,作为对该条的修正:

“(d)无论第3条或第4条如何规定,除非证券类互换具备符合第10(a)条要求的有效注册说明书,否则任何人直接或间接地使用任何州际商业中的运输或通信手段或工具或通过邮件向非适格合约参与者{定义见《商品交易法》第1a(18)条[《美国法典》第七编第1a(18)节]}要约买卖或买卖证券类互换的行为,当属违法。”

SEC.769. DEFINITIONS UNDER THE INVESTMENT COMPANY ACT OF 1940.

Section 2(a) of the Investment Company Act of 1940 (15 U.S.C. 80a-2) is amended by adding at the end the following: "(54) The terms 'commodity pool', 'commodity pool operator', 'commodity trading advisor', 'major swap participant', 'swap', 'swap dealer', and 'swap execution facility' have the same meanings as in section 1a of the Commodity Exchange Act (7 U.S.C. 1a).".

SEC.770. DEFINITIONS UNDER THE INVESTMENT ADVISERS ACT OF 1940.

Section 202(a) of the Investment Advisers Act of 1940 (15 U.S.C. 80b-2) is amended by adding at the end the following: "(29) The terms 'commodity pool', 'commodity pool operator', 'commodity trading advisor', 'major swap participant', 'swap', 'swap dealer', and 'swap execution facility' have the same meanings as in section 1a of the Commodity Exchange Act (7 U.S.C. 1a).".

SEC.771. OTHER AUTHORITY.

Unless otherwise provided by its terms, this subtitle does not divest any appropriate Federal banking agency, the Securities and Exchange Commission, the Commodity Futures Trading Commission, or any other Federal or State agency, of any authority derived from any other provision of applicable law.

SEC.772. JURISDICTION.

(a) IN GENERAL. — Section 36 of the Securities Exchange Act of 1934 (15 U.S.C. 78mm) is amended by adding at the end the following:

"(c) DERIVATIVES. — Unless the Commission is expressly authorized by any provision described in this subsection to grant exemptions, the Commission shall not grant exemptions, with respect to amendments made by subtitle B of the Wall Street Transparency and Accountability Act of 2010, with respect to paragraphs (65), (66), (68), (69), (70), (71), (72), (73), (74), (75), (76), and (79) of section 3(a), and sections 10B(a), 10B(b), 10B(c), 13A, 15F, 17A(g), 17A(h), 17A(i), 17A(j), 17A(k), and 17A(l); provided that the Commission shall have exemptive authority under this title with respect to security-based swaps as to the same matters that the Commodity Futures Trading Commission has under the Wall Street Transparency and Accountability Act of 2010 with respect to swaps, including under section 4(c) of the Commodity Exchange Act.".

(b) RULE OF CONSTRUCTION. — Section 30 of the Securities Exchange Act of 1934 (15 U.S.C. 78dd) is amended by adding at the end the following:

"(c) RULE OF CONSTRUCTION. — No provision of this title that was added by the Wall Street Transparency and Accountability Act of 2010, or any rule or regulation thereunder, shall apply to any person insofar as such person transacts a business in

第769条　《1940年投资公司法》中的定义

在《1940年投资公司法》第2(a)条(《美国法典》第十五编第80a—2节)结尾处增加如下内容,作为对该条的修正:"(54)'商品基金'、'商品基金管理人'、'商品交易顾问'、'主要互换参与者'、'互换'、'互换交易商'以及'互换执行设施'的含义以《商品交易法》第1a条(《美国法典》第七编第1a节)的定义为准。"

第770条　《1940年投资顾问法》中的定义

在《1940年投资顾问法》第202(a)条(《美国法典》第十五编第80b—2节)结尾处增加如下内容,作为对该条的修正:"(29)'商品基金'、'商品基金管理人'、'商品交易顾问'、'主要互换参与者'、'互换'、'互换交易商'以及'互换执行设施'的含义以《商品交易法》第1a条(《美国法典》第七编第1a节)的定义为准。"

第771条　其他权力

除非本子编另有规定,否则,本子编并不解除任何相应的联邦银行业监管机关、证券交易委员会、商品期货交易委员会或者任何其他联邦机关或州机关根据适用的法律之任何其他规定所享有的任何权力。

第772条　管辖权

(a)**一般规定**。——在《1934年证券交易法》第36条(《美国法典》第十五编第78mm节)结尾处增加如下内容,作为对该条的修正:

"(c)**衍生品**。——非经本子条的任何规定明确授权,证券交易委员会不得授予豁免《2010年华尔街透明度与问责法》第B子编对以下条款所做的修正:第3(a)条第(65)款、第(66)款、第(68)款、第(69)款、第(70)款、第(71)款、第(72)款、第(73)款、第(74)款、第(75)款、第(76)款和第(79)款,以及第10B(a)条、第10B(b)条、第10B(c)条、第13A条、第15F条、第17A(g)条、第17A(h)条、第17A(i)条、第17A(j)条、第17A(k)条和第17A(l)条;但是,对于商品期货交易委员会根据《2010年华尔街透明度与问责法》[包括根据《商品交易法》第4(c)条]就互换享有授予豁免的权力之事宜,证券交易委员会同样应根据本编就证券类互换享有授予豁免的权力。"

(b)**解释规则**。——在《1934年证券交易法》第30条(《美国法典》第十五编第78dd节)结尾处增加如下内容,作为对该条的修正:

"(c)**解释规则**。——《2010年华尔街透明度与问责法》在本编中增加的任何规定或者根据该等规定制定的任何规则或规章,均不得适用于在美国管辖权范围之外从事证券类互换业务的人,除非该人从事的上述业务违反了证券交易委员会为防范规

security–based swaps without the jurisdiction of the United States, unless such person transacts such business in contravention of such rules and regulations as the Commission may prescribe as necessary or appropriate to prevent the evasion of any provision of this title that was added by the Wall Street Transparency and Accountability Act of 2010. This subsection shall not be construed to limit the jurisdiction of the Commission under any provision of this title, as in effect prior to the date of enactment of the Wall Street Transparency and Accountability Act of 2010.".

SEC.773. CIVIL PENALTIES.

Section 21B of the Securities Exchange Act of 1934 （15 U.S.C. 78p–2）is amended by adding at the end the following:

"(f) SECURITY–BASED SWAPS. —

"(1) CLEARING AGENCY. — Any clearing agency that knowingly or recklessly evades or participates in or facilitates an evasion of the requirements of section 3C shall be liable for a civil money penalty in twice the amount otherwise available for a violation of section 3C.

"(2) SECURITY–BASED SWAP DEALER OR MAJOR SECURITY–BASED SWAP PARTICIPANT. — Any security–based swap dealer or major security–based swap participant that knowingly or recklessly evades or participates in or facilitates an evasion of the requirements of section 3C shall be liable for a civil money penalty in twice the amount otherwise available for a violation of section 3C.".

SEC.774. EFFECTIVE DATE.

Unless otherwise provided, the provisions of this subtitle shall take effect on the later of 360 days after the date of the enactment of this subtitle or, to the extent a provision of this subtitle requires a rulemaking, not less than 60 days after publication of the final rule or regulation implementing such provision of this subtitle.

避《2010年华尔街透明度与问责法》在本编中增加的任何规定而制定的必要或适当的规则和规章。本子条不得被解释为限制证券交易委员会根据本编任何规定享有的在《2010年华尔街透明度与问责法》颁布之日以前已生效的管辖权。”

第773条　民事罚款

在《1934年证券交易法》第21B条(《美国法典》第十五编第78p-2节)结尾处增加如下内容,作为对该条的修正:

“(f)**证券类互换**。——

(1)**结算机构**。——因故意或漠视而规避或参与规避第3C条规定或为该等规避行为提供便利的任何结算机构,均应处以民事罚款,罚款金额按违反第3C条行为的罚款金额的两倍计算。

(2)**证券类互换交易商或主要的证券类互换参与者**。——因故意或漠视而规避或参与规避第3C条规定或为该等规避行为提供便利的任何证券类互换交易商或主要的证券类互换参与者,均应处以民事罚款,罚款金额按违反第3C条行为的罚款金额的两倍计算。”

第774条　生效日

除非另有规定,否则本子编的规定应于下列日期(以较晚者为准)生效:在本子编颁布之日后第360天,或者本子编规定需要制定实施规则的,不迟于本子编规定的最终实施规则或规章公布之日后第60天。

TITLE VIII — PAYMENT, CLEARING, AND SETTLEMENT SUPERVISION

SEC.801. SHORT TITLE.

This title may be cited as the "Payment, Clearing, and Settlement Supervision Act of 2010".

SEC.802. FINDINGS AND PURPOSES.

(a) FINDINGS. — Congress finds the following:

(1) The proper functioning of the financial markets is dependent upon safe and efficient arrangements for the clearing and settlement of payment, securities, and other financial transactions.

(2) Financial market utilities that conduct or support multilateral payment, clearing, or settlement activities may reduce risks for their participants and the broader financial system, but such utilities may also concentrate and create new risks and thus must be well designed and operated in a safe and sound manner.

(3) Payment, clearing, and settlement activities conducted by financial institutions also present important risks to the participating financial institutions and to the financial system.

(4) Enhancements to the regulation and supervision of systemically important financial market utilities and the conduct of systemically important payment, clearing, and settlement activities by financial institutions are necessary —

(A) to provide consistency;

(B) to promote robust risk management and safety and soundness;

(C) to reduce systemic risks; and

(D) to support the stability of the broader financial system.

(b) PURPOSE. — The purpose of this title is to mitigate systemic risk in the financial system and promote financial stability by —

(1) authorizing the Board of Governors to promote uniform standards for the —

(A) management of risks by systemically important financial market utilities; and

(B) conduct of systemically important payment, clearing, and settlement activities by

第八编——支付、清算和结算监管

第801条　简称

引述本编时,可简称为《2010年支付、清算和结算监管法》。

第802条　事实认定和立法目的

(a)**事实认定**。——国会兹作出如下事实认定:

(1)金融市场的良好运行有赖于对支付、证券和其他金融交易的清算和结算作出安全而高效的安排。

(2)开展多边支付、清算或结算活动或为上述活动提供支持的金融市场服务平台可以减少该等平台参与者的风险和金融体系的整体风险,但也可能产生风险集中和新风险,因此,必须确保此类服务平台设计和运行的安全与稳健。

(3)金融机构所从事的支付、清算和结算活动也导致参与该等活动的金融机构和金融体系面临重大风险。

(4)为实现以下目标,必须加强对具有系统重要性的金融市场服务平台的监管与规制,以及对金融机构开展的具有系统重要性的支付、清算和结算活动的监管与规制——

(A)确保连贯性和一致性;

(B)加强风险管理水平,进一步提高安全性和稳健性;

(C)减少系统性风险;及

(D)加强金融体系的整体稳定性。

(b)**立法目的**。——本编的立法目的是通过采取以下措施减少金融体系的系统性风险和提高金融稳定性——

(1)授权联邦储备委员会推进以下活动的标准的统一——

(A)具有系统重要性的金融市场服务平台开展的风险管理活动;及

(B)金融机构开展的具有系统重要性的支付、清算和结算活动;

financial institutions;

(2) providing the Board of Governors an enhanced role in the supervision of risk management standards for systemically important financial market utilities;

(3) strengthening the liquidity of systemically important financial market utilities; and

(4) providing the Board of Governors an enhanced role in the supervision of risk management standards for systemically important payment, clearing, and settlement activities by financial institutions.

SEC.803. DEFINITIONS.

In this title, the following definitions shall apply:

(1) APPROPRIATE FINANCIAL REGULATOR. The term "appropriate financial regulator" means —

(A) the primary financial regulatory agency, as defined in section 2 of this Act;

(B) the National Credit Union Administration, with respect to any insured credit union under the Federal Credit Union Act (12 U.S.C. 1751 et seq.); and

(C) the Board of Governors, with respect to organizations operating under section 25A of the Federal Reserve Act (12 U.S.C. 611), and any other financial institution engaged in a designated activity.

(2) DESIGNATED ACTIVITY. — The term "designated activity" means a payment, clearing, or settlement activity that the Council has designated as systemically important under section 804.

(3) DESIGNATED CLEARING ENTITY. — The term "designated clearing entity" means a designated financial market utility that is a derivatives clearing organization registered under section 5b of the Commodity Exchange Act (7 U.S.C. 7a-1) or a clearing agency registered with the Securities and Exchange Commission under section 17A of the Securities Exchange Act of 1934 (15 U.S.C. 78q-1).

(4) DESIGNATED FINANCIAL MARKET UTILITY. — The term "designated financial market utility" means a financial market utility that the Council has designated as systemically important under section 804.

(5) FINANCIAL INSTITUTION. —

(A) IN GENERAL. — The term "financial institution" means —

(i) a depository institution, as defined in section 3 of the Federal Deposit Insurance Act (12 U.S.C. 1813);

(ii) a branch or agency of a foreign bank, as defined in section 1(b) of the International Banking Act of 1978 (12 U.S.C. 3101);

(iii) an organization operating under section 25 or 25A of the Federal Reserve Act (12 U.S.C. 601-604a and 611 through 631);

(iv) a credit union, as defined in section 101 of the Federal Credit Union Act (12 U.S.

(2)强化联邦储备委员会对具有系统重要性的金融市场服务平台的风险管理标准进行监管的职能;

(3)加强具有系统重要性的金融市场服务平台的流动性;及

(4)强化联邦储备委员会针对金融机构开展的具有系统重要性的支付、清算和结算活动的风险管理标准进行监管的职能。

第803条　定义

就本编而言,应适用如下定义:

(1)**相应的金融监管者**。"相应的金融监管者"一词——

(A)系指优先金融监管机关(定义见本法第2条);

(B)对于《联邦信贷联盟法》(《美国法典》第十二编第1751节及其后条文)中的任何参保信贷联盟而言,系指国家信贷联盟署;及

(C)对于根据《联邦储备法》第25A条(《美国法典》第十二编第611节)运营的组织和从事指定活动的任何其他金融机构而言,系指联邦储备委员会。

(2)**指定活动**。——"指定活动"一词系指金融稳定监督员会按照第804条规定指定的具有系统重要性的支付、清算或结算活动。

(3)**指定结算实体**。——"指定结算实体"一词系指具有如下身份的指定金融市场服务平台:按照《商品交易法》第5b条(《美国法典》第七编第7a–1节)注册的衍生品结算组织,或者按照《1934年证券交易法》第17A条(《美国法典》第十五编第78q–1节)在证券交易委员会注册的结算机构。

(4)**指定金融市场服务平台**。——"指定金融市场服务平台"一词系指金融稳定监督委员会根据第804条规定指定的具有系统重要性的金融市场服务平台。

(5)**金融机构**。——

(A)**一般规定**。——"金融机构"一词系指——

(i)存款机构[定义见《联邦存款保险法》第3条(《美国法典》第十二编第1813节)];

(ii)外国银行的分行或代理行[定义见《1978年国际银行法》第1(b)条(《美国法典》第十二编第3101节)];

(iii)根据《联邦储备法》第25条或第25A条[《美国法典》第十二编第601节至第604a节和第611节至第631节]运营的组织;

(iv)信贷联盟[定义见《联邦信贷联盟法》第101条(《美国法典》第十二编第

C. 1752);

(v) a broker or dealer, as defined in section 3 of the Securities Exchange Act of 1934 (15 U.S.C. 78c);

(vi) an investment company, as defined in section 3 of the Investment Company Act of 1940 (15 U.S.C. 80a-3);

(vii) an insurance company, as defined in section 2 of the Investment Company Act of 1940 (15 U.S.C. 80a-2);

(viii) an investment adviser, as defined in section 202 of the Investment Advisers Act of 1940 (15 U.S.C. 80b-2);

(ix) a futures commission merchant, commodity trading advisor, or commodity pool operator, as defined in section 1a of the Commodity Exchange Act (7 U.S.C. 1a); and

(x) any company engaged in activities that are financial in nature or incidental to a financial activity, as described in section 4 of the Bank Holding Company Act of 1956 (12 U.S.C. 1843(k)).

(B) EXCLUSIONS. — The term "financial institution" does not include designated contract markets, registered futures associations, swap data repositories, and swap execution facilities registered under the Commodity Exchange Act (7 U.S.C. 1 et seq.), or national securities exchanges, national securities associations, alternative trading systems, securities information processors solely with respect to the activities of the entity as a securities information processor, security-based swap data repositories, and swap execution facilities registered under the Securities Exchange Act of 1934 (15 U.S.C. 78a et seq.), or designated clearing entities, provided that the exclusions in this subparagraph apply only with respect to the activities that require the entity to be so registered.

(6) FINANCIAL MARKET UTILITY. —

(A) INCLUSION. — The term "financial market utility" means any person that manages or operates a multilateral system for the purpose of transferring, clearing, or settling payments, securities, or other financial transactions among financial institutions or between financial institutions and the person.

(B) EXCLUSIONS. — The term "financial market utility" does not include —

(i) designated contract markets, registered futures associations, swap data repositories, and swap execution facilities registered under the Commodity Exchange Act (7 U.S.C. 1 et seq.), or national securities exchanges, national securities associations, alternative trading systems, security-based swap data repositories, and swap execution facilities registered under the Securities Exchange Act of 1934 (15 U.S.C. 78a et seq.), solely by reason of their providing facilities for comparison of data respecting the terms of settlement of securities or futures transactions effected on such exchange or by means of any electronic system operated or controlled by such entities, provided that the exclusions in this clause apply only with

1752节）]；

（v）经纪商或自营商[定义见《1934年证券交易法》第3条（《美国法典》第十五编第78c节）]；

（vi）投资公司[（定义见《1940年投资公司法》第3条《美国法典》第十五编第80a-3节）]；

（vii）保险公司[定义见《1940年投资公司法》第2条（《美国法典》第十五编第80a-2节）]；

（viii）投资顾问[定义见《1940年投资顾问法》第202条（《美国法典》第十五编第80b-2节）]；

（ix）期货经纪商、商品交易顾问或商品基金管理人（定义见《商品交易法》第1a条（《美国法典》第七编第1a节））；及

（x）从事的活动性质属于《1956年银行控股公司法》第4条[《美国法典》第十二编第1843（k）节]所述金融活动或该等金融活动的附属活动的公司。

（B）**除外规定**。——"金融机构"一词不包括按照《商品交易法》（《美国法典》第七编第1节及其后条文）注册的指定合约市场、注册期货协会、互换数据存管机构和互换执行设施，亦不包括按照《1934年证券交易法》（《美国法典》第十五编第78a节及其后条文）注册的全国性证券交易所、全国性证券协会、另类交易系统、证券信息处理机构（对于证券信息处理机构而言，本除外规定仅针对其开展的证券信息处理机构活动适用）以及证券类互换数据存管机构和互换执行设施，也不包括指定结算实体，但是，本子款的除外规定仅针对上述类别实体从事按规定应注册为上述类别实体才能从事的活动适用。

（6）**金融市场服务平台**。——

（A）**包含的主体**。——"金融市场服务平台"一词系指为其自身与金融机构之间或不同金融机构之间的支付、证券或其他金融交易而管理或运营一个多边的转移、清算或结算系统的主体。

（B）**除外规定**。——"金融市场服务平台"一词不包括——

（i）按照《商品交易法》（《美国法典》第七编第1节及其后条文）注册的指定合约市场、注册期货协会、互换数据存管机构和互换执行设施，也不包括按照《1934年证券交易法》（《美国法典》第十五编第78a节及其后条文）注册的全国性证券交易所、全国性证券协会、另类交易系统、证券类互换数据存管机构以及互换执行设施。上述实体只要具备如下理由即可被排除在"金融市场服务平台"一词范围之外：针对在上述交易所进行的证券或期货交易或通过上类实体运营或控制的任何电子系统进行的证券或期货交易，提供用于对交易结算条款数据进行比较的设施。但是，本项除外规定仅针对上述类别实体从事按规定应注册为上述类别实体才能从事的活动适用；及

respect to the activities that require the entity to be so registered; and

(ii) any broker, dealer, transfer agent, or investment company, or any futures commission merchant, introducing broker, commodity trading advisor, or commodity pool operator, solely by reason of functions performed by such institution as part of brokerage, dealing, transfer agency, or investment company activities, or solely by reason of acting on behalf of a financial market utility or a participant therein in connection with the furnishing by the financial market utility of services to its participants or the use of services of the financial market utility by its participants, provided that services performed by such institution do not constitute critical risk management or processing functions of the financial market utility.

(7) PAYMENT, CLEARING, OR SETTLEMENT ACTIVITY. —

(A) IN GENERAL. — The term "payment, clearing, or settlement activity" means an activity carried out by 1 or more financial institutions to facilitate the completion of financial transactions, but shall not include any offer or sale of a security under the Securities Act of 1933 (15 U.S.C. 77a et seq.), or any quotation, order entry, negotiation, or other pre–trade activity or execution activity.

(B) FINANCIAL TRANSACTION. — For the purposes of subparagraph (A), the term "financial transaction" includes —

(i) funds transfers;

(ii) securities contracts;

(iii) contracts of sale of a commodity for future delivery;

(iv) forward contracts;

(v) repurchase agreements;

(vi) swaps;

(vii) security–based swaps;

(viii) swap agreements;

(ix) security–based swap agreements;

(x) foreign exchange contracts;

(xi) financial derivatives contracts; and

(xii) any similar transaction that the Council determines to be a financial transaction for purposes of this title.

(C) INCLUDED ACTIVITIES. — When conducted with respect to a financial transaction, payment, clearing, and settlement activities may include —

(i) the calculation and communication of unsettled financial transactions between counterparties;

(ii) the netting of transactions;

(iii) provision and maintenance of trade, contract, or instrument information;

(iv) the management of risks and activities associated with continuing financial

(ii)任何经纪商、自营商、过户代理人、投资公司、任何期货经纪商、介绍经纪商、商品交易顾问或商品基金管理人。上述实体只要具备如下理由即可被排除在“金融市场服务平台”一词范围之外:上述实体履行的职能系经纪、自营、过户代理或投资公司活动的一部分;或者就金融市场服务平台向其参与者提供的服务或就参与者对该等服务的使用,代表金融市场服务平台行事或代表其参与者行事。但是,本项除外规定适用的前提是,上述机构开展的服务不构成金融市场服务平台的关键风险管理职能或处理职能。

(7)**支付、清算或结算活动**。——

(A)**一般规定**。——“支付、清算或结算活动”一词系指1个或1个以上金融机构为促进金融交易的完成而开展的活动,但不包括依据《1933年证券法》(《美国法典》第十五编第77a节及其后条文)作出的证券要约或出售,也不包括报价、指令录入、谈判或其他交易前的活动或执行活动。

(B)**金融交易**。——就第(A)子款而言,“金融交易”一词包括——

(i)资金转移;
(ii)证券合约;
(iii)远期交割商品出售合约;
(iv)远期合约;
(v)回购协议;
(vi)互换;
(vii)证券类互换;
(viii)互换协议;
(ix)证券类互换协议;
(x)外汇合约;
(xi)金融衍生品合约;及
(xii)金融稳定监督委员会判定属于本编定义的金融交易的任何类似交易。

(C)**包含的活动**。——就一笔金融交易开展的支付、清算和结算活动可包括——

(i)对手方之间尚未结算的金融交易的计算和通信;

(ii)交易的净额结算;
(iii)交易、合约或文书信息的提供和保存;
(iv)与持续的金融交易相关的风险和活动之管理;

transactions;

(v) transmittal and storage of payment instructions;

(vi) the movement of funds;

(vii) the final settlement of financial transactions; and

(viii) other similar functions that the Council may determine.

(D) EXCLUSION. — Payment, clearing, and settlement activities shall not include public reporting of swap transaction data under section 727 or 763 (i) of the Wall Street Transparency and Accountability Act of 2010.

(8) SUPERVISORY AGENCY. —

(A) IN GENERAL. — The term "Supervisory Agency" means the Federal agency that has primary jurisdiction over a designated financial market utility under Federal banking, securities, or commodity futures laws, as follows:

(i) The Securities and Exchange Commission, with respect to a designated financial market utility that is a clearing agency registered with the Securities and Exchange Commission.

(ii) The Commodity Futures Trading Commission, with respect to a designated financial market utility that is a derivatives clearing organization registered with the Commodity Futures Trading Commission.

(iii) The appropriate Federal banking agency, with respect to a designated financial market utility that is an institution described in section 3(q) of the Federal Deposit Insurance Act.

(iv) The Board of Governors, with respect to a designated financial market utility that is otherwise not subject to the jurisdiction of any agency listed in clauses (i), (ii), and (iii).

(B) MULTIPLE AGENCY JURISDICTION. — If a designated financial market utility is subject to the jurisdictional supervision of more than 1 agency listed in subparagraph (A), then such agencies should agree on 1 agency to act as the Supervisory Agency, and if such agencies cannot agree on which agency has primary jurisdiction, the Council shall decide which agency is the Supervisory Agency for purposes of this title.

(9) SYSTEMICALLY IMPORTANT AND SYSTEMIC IMPORTANCE. — The terms "systemically important" and "systemic importance" mean a situation where the failure of or a disruption to the functioning of a financial market utility or the conduct of a payment, clearing, or settlement activity could create, or increase, the risk of significant liquidity or credit problems spreading among financial institutions or markets and thereby threaten the stability of the financial system of the United States.

SEC.804. DESIGNATION OF SYSTEMIC IMPORTANCE.

(a) DESIGNATION. —

(1) FINANCIAL STABILITY OVERSIGHT COUNCIL. — The Council, on a

(v)支付指令的传送和储存;

(vi)资金的运动;

(vii)金融交易的最终结算;及

(viii)金融稳定监督委员会判定的其他类似职能。

(D)**除外规定**。——支付、清算和结算活动不包括按照《2010年华尔街透明度与问责法》第727条或第763(i)条对互换交易数据进行的公开报告。

(8)**监管机关**。——

(A)**一般规定**。——"监管机关"一词系指根据联邦银行、证券或商品期货法律对指定金融市场服务平台拥有优先管辖权的联邦机关,具体指:

(i)证券交易委员会:对在证券交易委员会处注册为结算机构的指定金融市场服务平台拥有优先管辖权。

(ii)商品期货交易委员会:对在商品期货交易委员会处注册为衍生品结算组织的指定金融市场服务平台拥有优先管辖权。

(iii)相应的联邦银行业监管机关:对具有《联邦存款保险法》第3(q)条所述机构身份的指定金融市场服务平台拥有优先管辖权。

(iv)联邦储备委员会:对不受上述第(i)项、第(ii)项和第(iii)项所列联邦机关管辖的指定金融市场服务平台拥有优先管辖权。

(B)**多个联邦机关均有管辖权的情形**。——如果2个或2个以上第(A)子款所列的联邦机关对某一指定金融市场服务平台拥有管辖权,则该等机关之间应达成共识,由其中一个负责行使监管机关职能;如果彼此之间无法达成共识,应由金融稳定监督委员会决定由何者充当本编规定的监管机关。

(9)**"具有系统重要性"和"系统重要性"**。——"具有系统重要性"一词和"系统重要性"一词系指,如果某一金融市场服务平台运行失灵或受到扰乱,或者如果某一支付、清算或结算活动失灵或受到扰乱,将导致重大流动性或信用问题的风险在金融机构之间或市场之间相互传播的风险或加剧该等风险,并因此威胁到美国金融体系的稳定性。

第804条　关于系统重要性的指定

(a)**指定**。——

(1)**金融稳定监督委员会**。——如果金融稳定监督委员会判定特定金融市场服

nondelegable basis and by a vote of not fewer than 2/3 of members then serving, including an affirmative vote by the Chairperson of the Council, shall designate those financial market utilities or payment, clearing, or settlement activities that the Council determines are, or are likely to become, systemically important.

(2) CONSIDERATIONS. — In determining whether a financial market utility or payment, clearing, or settlement activity is, or is likely to become, systemically important, the Council shall take into consideration the following:

(A) The aggregate monetary value of transactions processed by the financial market utility or carried out through the payment, clearing, or settlement activity.

(B) The aggregate exposure of the financial market utility or a financial institution engaged in payment, clearing, or settlement activities to its counterparties.

(C) The relationship, interdependencies, or other interactions of the financial market utility or payment, clearing, or settlement activity with other financial market utilities or payment, clearing, or settlement activities.

(D) The effect that the failure of or a disruption to the financial market utility or payment, clearing, or settlement activity would have on critical markets, financial institutions, or the broader financial system.

(E) Any other factors that the Council deems appropriate.

(b) RESCISSION OF DESIGNATION. —

(1) IN GENERAL. — The Council, on a nondelegable basis and by a vote of not fewer than 2/3 of members then serving, including an affirmative vote by the Chairperson of the Council, shall rescind a designation of systemic importance for a designated financial market utility or designated activity if the Council determines that the utility or activity no longer meets the standards for systemic importance.

(2) EFFECT OF RESCISSION. — Upon rescission, the financial market utility or financial institutions conducting the activity will no longer be subject to the provisions of this title or any rules or orders prescribed under this title.

(c) CONSULTATION AND NOTICE AND OPPORTUNITY FOR HEARING. —

(1) CONSULTATION. — Before making any determination under subsection (a) or (b), the Council shall consult with the relevant Supervisory Agency and the Board of Governors.

(2) ADVANCE NOTICE AND OPPORTUNITY FOR HEARING. —

(A) IN GENERAL. — Before making any determination under subsection (a) or (b), the Council shall provide the financial market utility or, in the case of a payment, clearing, or settlement activity, financial institutions with advance notice of the proposed determination of the Council.

(B) NOTICE IN FEDERAL REGISTER. — The Council shall provide such advance

务平台或支付、清算或结算活动具有或可能具有系统重要性,则金融稳定监督委员会应作出相应的指定;金融稳定监督委员会不得将此权力委托给任何其他机构,并且,相关的指定须获得至少2/3届时在任成员的赞成票方能生效,且其中必须包括金融稳定监督委员会主席所投的赞成票。

(2)**考虑因素**。——在判定某金融市场服务平台或某支付、清算或结算活动是否具有或是否可能具有系统重要性时,金融稳定监督委员会应考虑以下因素:

(A)该金融市场服务平台处理的交易总金额,或者通过该支付、清算或结算活动开展的交易的总金额。

(B)该金融市场服务平台对其所有对手方的总风险敞口,或者从事支付、清算或结算活动的某金融机构对其所有对手方的总风险敞口。

(C)该金融市场服务平台或支付、清算或结算活动与其他金融市场服务平台或其他支付、清算或结算活动之间的关系、相互依存性或者其他互动关系。

(D)该金融市场服务平台或支付、清算或结算活动失灵或受到扰乱时将对关键市场、金融机构或金融体系产生的整体影响。

(E)金融稳定监督委员会认为应予考虑的任何其他适当因素。

(b)**指定的撤销**。——

(1)**一般规定**。——如果金融稳定监督委员会判定,某一指定金融市场服务平台或指定活动不再符合系统重要性标准,则金融稳定监督委员会应撤销之前的指定;金融稳定监督委员会不得将此权力委托给任何其他机构,并且,相关的撤销决定须获得至少2/3届时在任成员的赞成票方能生效,且其中必须包括金融稳定监督委员会主席所投的赞成票。

(2)**撤销的影响**。——之前所做的指定在按照上述规定撤销后,所涉及的金融市场服务平台或开展所涉活动的金融机构即不再受制于本编规定或按照本编规定颁布或签发的任何规则或命令。

(c)**磋商、通知和听证机会**。——

(1)**磋商**。——在按照第(a)子条或第(b)子条作出任何判定之前,金融稳定监督委员会应先与相关监管机关和联邦储备委员会磋商。

(2)**事先通知和听证机会**。——

(A)**一般规定**。——在按照第(a)子条或第(b)子条作出任何判定之前,金融稳定监督委员会应先向所涉及的金融市场服务平台或开展所涉及的支付、清算或结算活动的金融机构发布通知,说明其拟作出的判定之内容。

(B)**在《联邦公报》发布通知**。——金融稳定监督委员会应通过在《联邦公报》发

notice to financial institutions by publishing a notice in the Federal Register.

(C) REQUESTS FOR HEARING. — Within 30 days from the date of any notice of the proposed determination of the Council, the financial market utility or, in the case of a payment, clearing, or settlement activity, a financial institution engaged in the designated activity may request, in writing, an opportunity for a written or oral hearing before the Council to demonstrate that the proposed designation or rescission of designation is not supported by substantial evidence.

(D) WRITTEN SUBMISSIONS. — Upon receipt of a timely request, the Council shall fix a time, not more than 30 days after receipt of the request, unless extended at the request of the financial market utility or financial institution, and place at which the financial market utility or financial institution may appear, personally or through counsel, to submit written materials, or, at the sole discretion of the Council, oral testimony or oral argument.

(3) EMERGENCY EXCEPTION. —

(A) WAIVER OR MODIFICATION BY VOTE OF THE COUNCIL. — The Council may waive or modify the requirements of paragraph (2) if the Council determines, by an affirmative vote of not fewer than 2/3 of members then serving, including an affirmative vote by the Chairperson of the Council, that the waiver or modification is necessary to prevent or mitigate an immediate threat to the financial system posed by the financial market utility or the payment, clearing, or settlement activity.

(B) NOTICE OF WAIVER OR MODIFICATION. — The Council shall provide notice of the waiver or modification to the financial market utility concerned or, in the case of a payment, clearing, or settlement activity, to financial institutions, as soon as practicable, which shall be no later than 24 hours after the waiver or modification in the case of a financial market utility and 3 business days in the case of financial institutions. The Council shall provide the notice to financial institutions by posting a notice on the website of the Council and by publishing a notice in the Federal Register.

(d) NOTIFICATION OF FINAL DETERMINATION. —

(1) AFTER HEARING. — Within 60 days of any hearing under subsection (c)(2), the Council shall notify the financial market utility or financial institutions of the final determination of the Council in writing, which shall include findings of fact upon which the determination of the Council is based.

(2) WHEN NO HEARING REQUESTED. — If the Council does not receive a timely request for a hearing under subsection (c)(2), the Council shall notify the financial market utility or financial institutions of the final determination of the Council in writing not later than 30 days after the expiration of the date by which a financial market utility or a financial institution could have requested a hearing. All notices to financial institutions under this subsection shall be published in the Federal Register.

布通知的方式向金融机构提供事先通知。

(C)**听证请求**。——在金融稳定监督委员会就拟作出的判定内容发布通知后30天内,所涉及的金融市场服务平台或从事指定支付、清算或结算活动的金融机构可以通过书面形式请求获得在金融稳定监督委员会进行书面或口头听证的机会，以证明金融稳定监督委员会拟作出的指定判定或撤销指定的判定缺乏实质证据支持。

(D)**提交书面材料**。——在收到及时提交的听证请求后,金融稳定监督委员会应指定相关时间和地点，以便所涉及的金融市场服务平台或金融机构亲自或通过律师提交书面材料，或者金融稳定监督委员会亦可完全依其自由裁量权决定向该等机构提供提供口头证词或进行口头辩护的机会；上述时间不得迟于请求书收到后第30天(除非所涉及的金融市场服务平台或金融机构请求延期并获批准)。

(3)**紧急例外规定**。——

(A)**金融稳定监督委员会投票进行的豁免或修改**。——如果金融稳定监督委员会判定,为了防范所涉及的金融市场服务平台或支付、清算或结算活动对金融体系造成紧迫威胁或为缓解该等威胁,必须豁免或修改第(2)款的规定,则金融稳定监督委员会可以豁免或修改该等规定,但须获得至少2/3届时在任成员的赞成票方能生效,且其中必须包括金融稳定监督委员会主席所投的赞成票。

(B)**豁免或修改通知**。——在作出上述豁免或修改判定后,金融稳定监督委员会应尽快通知所涉及的金融市场服务平台或从事所涉及的支付、清算或结算活动的金融机构该等判定;就金融市场服务平台而言,必须在判定作出后24小时内发出通知,就金融机构而言,必须在判定作出后3个营业日内发出通知。金融稳定监督委员会应采取在其网站和《联邦公报》发布通知的方式作出给金融机构的通知。

(d)**最终判定通知**。——

(1)**已举行听证的情形**。——在按照第(c)(2)子条举行听证后60天内,金融稳定监督委员会应将其最终判定以书面形式通知所涉及的金融市场服务平台或金融机构,并在通知中说明该判定所依据的事实认定。

(2)**未收到听证请求的情形**。——如果金融稳定监督委员会并未收到按照第(c)(2)子条及时提出的听证请求,则应在金融市场服务平台或金融机构本可请求听证的期限结束后30天内，以书面形式将其最终判定通知所涉及的金融市场服务平台或金融机构。按照本子条向金融机构作出的所有通知均应在《联邦公报》发布。

(e) EXTENSION OF TIME PERIODS. — The Council may extend the time periods established in subsections (c) and (d) as the Council determines to be necessary or appropriate.

SEC.805. STANDARDS FOR SYSTEMICALLY IMPORTANT FINANCIAL MARKET UTILITIES AND PAYMENT, CLEARING, OR SETTLEMENT ACTIVITIES.

(a) AUTHORITY TO PRESCRIBE STANDARDS. —

(1) BOARD OF GOVERNORS. — Except as provided in paragraph (2), the Board of Governors, by rule or order, and in consultation with the Council and the Supervisory Agencies, shall prescribe risk management standards, taking into consideration relevant international standards and existing prudential requirements, governing —

(A) the operations related to the payment, clearing, and settlement activities of designated financial market utilities; and

(B) the conduct of designated activities by financial institutions.

(2) SPECIAL PROCEDURES FOR DESIGNATED CLEARING ENTITIES AND DESIGNATED ACTIVITIES OF CERTAIN FINANCIAL INSTITUTIONS. —

(A) CFTC AND COMMISSION. — The Commodity Futures Trading Commission and the Commission may each prescribe regulations, in consultation with the Council and the Board of Governors, containing risk management standards, taking into consideration relevant international standards and existing prudential requirements, for those designated clearing entities and financial institutions engaged in designated activities for which each is the Supervisory Agency or the appropriate financial regulator, governing —

(i) the operations related to payment, clearing, and settlement activities of such designated clearing entities; and

(ii) the conduct of designated activities by such financial institutions.

(B) REVIEW AND DETERMINATION. — The Board of Governors may determine that existing prudential requirements of the Commodity Futures Trading Commission, the Commission, or both (including requirements prescribed pursuant to subparagraph (A)) with respect to designated clearing entities and financial institutions engaged in designated activities for which the Commission or the Commodity Futures Trading Commission is the Supervisory Agency or the appropriate financial regulator are insufficient to prevent or mitigate significant liquidity, credit, operational, or other risks to the financial markets or to the financial stability of the United States.

(C) WRITTEN DETERMINATION. — Any determination by the Board of Governors under subparagraph (B) shall be provided in writing to the Commodity Futures Trading Commission or the Commission, as applicable, and the Council, and shall explain why existing prudential requirements, considered as a whole, are insufficient to ensure that the

(e)**延期**。——金融稳定监督委员会判定确属必要或适当之时,可以适当延长第(c)子条和第(d)子条规定的期限。

第805条 具有系统重要性的金融市场服务平台以及支付、清算和结算活动适用的标准

(a)**制定标准的权限**。——

(1)**联邦储备委员会**。——除第(2)款规定的情形外,联邦储备委员会应与金融稳定监督委员会和监管机关磋商,对相关国际标准和现行审慎要求作出考量之后,发布规则或命令制定规范以下活动的风险管理标准——

(A)与指定金融市场服务平台的支付、清算和结算活动相关的运营;及

(B)金融机构开展的指定活动。

(2)**指定结算实体以及特定金融机构的指定活动适用的特殊程序**。——

(A)**商品期货交易委员会与证券交易委员会**。——对于商品期货交易委员会和证券交易委员会各自以监管机关或者相应的金融监管者身份监管的指定结算实体和从事指定活动的金融机构,商品期货交易委员会和证券交易委员会在与金融稳定监督委员会和联邦储备委员会磋商后并在对相关国际标准和现行审慎要求作出考量之后,可以分别就以下活动制定含有风险管理标准的规章——

(i)与上述指定结算实体的支付、清算和结算活动相关的运营;及

(ii)上述金融机构开展的指定活动。

(B)**审查和判定**。——联邦储备委员会可以作出如下判定,即针对由商品期货交易委员会与证券交易委员会各自以监管机关或者相应的金融监管者身份监管的指定结算实体和从事指定活动的金融机构,商品期货交易委员会或证券交易委员会或二者所确定的现行审慎要求[包括按照第(A)子款制定的要求]不足以防范或缓释金融市场或美国金融稳定所面临的重大流动性、信用、运营或其他方面的风险。

(C)**书面判定**。——联邦储备委员会按照第(B)子款所做的任何判定均应以书面形式提供给商品期货交易委员会或证券交易委员会(视具体情况而定)以及金融稳定监督委员会,并说明现行各种审慎要求整体而言为何不足以防范指定结算实体的运营和活动或第(B)子款所述的金融机构的活动对金融市场或美国的金融稳定造成的

operations and activities of the designated clearing entities or the activities of financial institutions described in subparagraph (B) will not pose significant liquidity, credit, operational, or other risks to the financial markets or to the financial stability of the United States. The Board of Governors' determination shall contain a detailed analysis supporting its findings and identify the specific prudential requirements that are insufficient.

(D) CFTC AND COMMISSION RESPONSE. — The Commodity Futures Trading Commission or the Commission, as applicable, shall within 60 days either object to the Board of Governors' determination with a detailed analysis as to why existing prudential requirements are sufficient, or submit an explanation to the Council and the Board of Governors describing the actions to be taken in response to the Board of Governors' determination.

(E) AUTHORIZATION. — Upon an affirmative vote by not fewer than 2/3 of members then serving on the Council, the Council shall either find that the response submitted under subparagraph (D) is sufficient, or require the Commodity Futures Trading Commission, or the Commission, as applicable, to prescribe such risk management standards as the Council determines is necessary to address the specific prudential requirements that are determined to be insufficient."

(b) OBJECTIVES AND PRINCIPLES. — The objectives and principles for the risk management standards prescribed under subsection (a) shall be to —

(1) promote robust risk management;

(2) promote safety and soundness;

(3) reduce systemic risks; and

(4) support the stability of the broader financial system.

(c) SCOPE. — The standards prescribed under subsection (a) may address areas such as —

(1) risk management policies and procedures;

(2) margin and collateral requirements;

(3) participant or counterparty default policies and procedures;

(4) the ability to complete timely clearing and settlement of financial transactions;

(5) capital and financial resource requirements for designated financial market utilities; and

(6) other areas that are necessary to achieve the objectives and principles in subsection (b).

(d) LIMITATION ON SCOPE. — Except as provided in subsections (e) and (f) of section 807, nothing in this title shall be construed to permit the Council or the Board of Governors to take any action or exercise any authority granted to the Commodity Futures Trading Commission under section 2(h) of the Commodity Exchange Act or the Securities

重大流动性、信用、运营或其他方面的风险。联邦储备委员会的书面判定应就其得出该事实认定的理由进行详细分析,并具体指出存在不足的审慎要求。

(D)**商品期货交易委员会和证券交易委员会的答复**。——商品期货交易委员会或证券交易委员会(视具体情况而定)应在60天的期限内作出答复,其可就联邦储备委员会的判定提出异议并详细分析现行审慎要求足以防范相关风险的原因,或向金融稳定监督委员会和联邦储备委员会提交一份说明阐述将根据联邦储备委员会所做判定采取的行动。

(E)**核准**。——如获得金融稳定监督委员会至少2/3届时在任成员的赞成票,金融稳定监督委员会应认定按照第(D)子款所做的答复理由充分,或者要求商品期货交易委员会或证券交易委员会(视具体情况而定)制定金融稳定监督委员会判定确属必要的风险管理标准,以解决被判定存在不足的审慎要求问题。

(b)**目标和原则**。——按照第(a)子条制定的风险管理标准的目标和原则应旨在——

(1)加强风险管理水平;

(2)提高安全性和稳健性;

(3)减少系统性风险;及

(4)加强金融体系的整体稳定性。

(c)**范围**。——按照第(a)子条制定的标准可涉及以下领域——

(1)风险管理政策和程序;

(2)保证金和担保品要求;

(3)参与者或对手方违约处理政策和程序;

(4)对金融交易及时开展清算和结算的能力;

(5)指定金融市场服务平台的资本和财务资源要求;及

(6)为实现第(b)子条所述目标和原则而必须制定相应标准的其他领域。

(d)**范围限制**。——除了在第807条第(e)子条和第(f)子条规定的情形下,本编的任何规定均不得被解释为允许金融稳定监督委员会或联邦储备委员会采取《商品交易法》第2(h)条授权商品期货交易委员会采取的行动或者《1934年证券交易法》第3C(a)授权证券交易委员会采取的行动,亦不得被解释为允许金融稳定监督委员会或联

and Exchange Commission under section 3C(a) of the Securities Exchange Act of 1934, including—

(1) the approval of, disapproval of, or stay of the clearing requirement for any group, category, type, or class of swaps that a designated clearing entity may accept for clearing;

(2) the determination that any group, category, type, or class of swaps shall be subject to the mandatory clearing requirement of section 2(h)(1) of the Commodity Exchange Act or section 3C(a)(1) of the Securities Exchange Act of 1934;

(3) the determination that any person is exempt from the mandatory clearing requirement of section 2(h)(1) of the Commodity Exchange Act or section 3C(a)(1) of the Securities Exchange Act of 1934; or

(4) any authority granted to the Commodity Futures Trading Commission or the Securities and Exchange Commission with respect to transaction reporting or trade execution.

(e) THRESHOLD LEVEL. — The standards prescribed under subsection (a) governing the conduct of designated activities by financial institutions shall, where appropriate, establish a threshold as to the level or significance of engagement in the activity at which a financial institution will become subject to the standards with respect to that activity.

(f) COMPLIANCE REQUIRED. — Designated financial market utilities and financial institutions subject to the standards prescribed under subsection (a) for a designated activity shall conduct their operations in compliance with the applicable risk management standards.

SEC.806. OPERATIONS OF DESIGNATED FINANCIAL MARKET UTILITIES.

(a) FEDERAL RESERVE ACCOUNT AND SERVICES. — The Board of Governors may authorize a Federal Reserve Bank to establish and maintain an account for a designated financial market utility and provide the services listed in section 11A(b) of the Federal Reserve Act (12 U.S.C. 248a(b)) and deposit accounts under the first undesignated paragraph of section 13 of the Federal Reserve Act (12 U.S.C. 342) to the designated financial market utility that the Federal Reserve Bank is authorized under the Federal Reserve Act to provide to a depository institution, subject to any applicable rules, orders, standards, or guidelines prescribed by the Board of Governors.

(b) ADVANCES. — The Board of Governors may authorize a Federal Reserve bank under section 10B of the Federal Reserve Act (12 U.S.C. 347b) to provide to a designated financial market utility discount and borrowing privileges only in unusual or exigent circumstances, upon the affirmative vote of a majority of the Board of Governors then serving (or such other number in accordance with the provisions of section 11(r)(2) of the Federal Reserve Act (12 U.S.C. 248(r)(2)) after consultation with the Secretary, and upon a showing by the designated financial market utility that it is unable to secure adequate credit

邦储备委员会行使该等法律分别对商品期货交易委员会或证券交易委员会授予的权力,包括下述行动或权力——

(1)针对指定结算实体可以受理集中结算的任何互换集合、种类、类型或类别,批准、否决或中止其集中结算要求;

(2)判定任何互换集合、种类、类型或类别应受制于《商品交易法》第2(h)(1)条或《1934年证券交易法》第3C(a)(1)条的强制集中结算要求;

(3)判定可获得豁免的主体,使其不必受制于《商品交易法》第2(h)(1)条或《1934年证券交易法》第3C(a)(1)条的强制集中结算要求;或

(4)商品期货交易委员会或证券交易委员会获授的关于交易报告或交易执行的任何权力。

(e)**适用标准的最低门槛**。——按第(a)子条制定标准规范金融机构指定活动之开展时,应确立适当的最低适用门槛,以界定金融机构所从事的该等活动达到何等程度或重要性时即应受制于该等标准。

(f)**合规要求**。——指定金融市场服务平台以及受制于按第(a)子条制定的关于指定活动的标准的金融机构,在开展运营的过程中应遵守适用的风险管理标准。

第806条　指定金融市场服务平台的运营

(a)**联邦储备账户和服务**。——联邦储备委员会可授权一家联邦储备银行为指定金融市场服务平台开立并维持一个账户,并授权该联邦储备银行在不违反联邦储备委员会制定的任何规则、命令、标准或指引的前提下,向指定金融市场服务平台提供《联邦储备法》授权联邦储备银行向存款机构提供的《联邦储备法》第11A(b)条[《美国法典》第十二编第248a(b)节]所列服务以及《联邦储备法》第13条(《美国法典》第十二编第342节)第一个无编号段落所述储蓄账户。

(b)**预支款**。——在获得联邦储备委员会过半数在任委员的赞成票{或《联邦储备法》第11(r)(2)条[《美国法典》第十二编第248(r)(2)节]规定的其他票数要求}的前提下,联邦储备委员会可以在与财政部部长磋商后,并在指定金融市场服务平台证明其无法从其他银行机构获得充足信用融通的情况下,按照《联邦储备法》第10B条(《美国法典》第十二编第347b节)的规定授权一家联邦储备银行在非常或紧急情况下(且仅得在该等情况下)向上述指定金融市场服务平台提供贴现和借款权。所有该等贴现和借款权均应受制于联邦储备委员会制定或设定的其他限制、约束和规章。根据本条

accommodations from other banking institutions. All such discounts and borrowing privileges shall be subject to such other limitations, restrictions, and regulations as the Board of Governors may prescribe. Access to discount and borrowing privileges under section 10B of the Federal Reserve Act as authorized in this section does not require a designated financial market utility to be or become a bank or bank holding company.

(c) EARNINGS ON FEDERAL RESERVE BALANCES. — A Federal Reserve Bank may pay earnings on balances maintained by or on behalf of a designated financial market utility in the same manner and to the same extent as the Federal Reserve Bank may pay earnings to a depository institution under the Federal Reserve Act, subject to any applicable rules, orders, standards, or guidelines prescribed by the Board of Governors.

(d) RESERVE REQUIREMENTS. — The Board of Governors may exempt a designated financial market utility from, or modify any, reserve requirements under section 19 of the Federal Reserve Act (12 U.S.C. 461) applicable to a designated financial market utility.

(e) CHANGES TO RULES, PROCEDURES, OR OPERATIONS. —

(1) ADVANCE NOTICE. —

(A) ADVANCE NOTICE OF PROPOSED CHANGES REQUIRED. — A designated financial market utility shall provide notice 60 days in advance notice to its Supervisory Agency of any proposed change to its rules, procedures, or operations that could, as defined in rules of each Supervisory Agency, materially affect, the nature or level of risks presented by the designated financial market utility.

(B) TERMS AND STANDARDS PRESCRIBED BY THE SUPERVISORY AGENCIES. — Each Supervisory Agency, in consultation with the Board of Governors, shall prescribe regulations that define and describe the standards for determining when notice is required to be provided under subparagraph (A).

(C) CONTENTS OF NOTICE. — The notice of a proposed change shall describe —

(i) the nature of the change and expected effects on risks to the designated financial market utility, its participants, or the market; and

(ii) how the designated financial market utility plans to manage any identified risks.

(D) ADDITIONAL INFORMATION. — The Supervisory Agency may require a designated financial market utility to provide any information necessary to assess the effect the proposed change would have on the nature or level of risks associated with the designated financial market utility's payment, clearing, or settlement activities and the sufficiency of any proposed risk management techniques.

(E) NOTICE OF OBJECTION. — The Supervisory Agency shall notify the designated financial market utility of any objection regarding the proposed change within 60 days from the later of —

授权获得《联邦储备法》第10B条规定的贴现和借款权,并不以指定金融市场服务平台具有或获得银行或银行控股公司身份为前提。

(c)**联邦储备银行账户存款的收益**。——在不违反联邦储备委员会制定的任何适用规则、命令、标准或指引的前提下,联邦储备银行可按照其在《联邦储备法》下向存款机构支付收益的方式以及程度和范围,就指定金融市场服务平台或其代表在该银行维持的银行账户的存款余额支付收益。

(d)**准备金要求**。——联邦储备委员会可以豁免或修改《联邦储备法》第19条(《美国法典》第十二编第461节)规定的准备金要求对指定金融市场服务平台的适用。

(e)**规则、程序或运营方面的变更**。——

(1)**事先通知**。——

(A)**关于就拟议变更发出事先通知的要求**。——如果指定金融市场服务平台拟变更其规则、程序或运营,且根据各监管机关的规则,该等变更可能对该指定金融市场服务平台的风险水平或性质造成重大影响,则该指定金融市场服务平台应提前60天将拟议变更的内容通知其所属监管机关。

(B)**监管机关规定的条件和标准**。——各监管机关应在与联邦储备委员会磋商后制定相应规章,以界定并说明据以判定何时必须按照第(A)子款发出事先通知的标准。

(C)**通知的内容**。——关于拟议变更的通知应说明——

(i)变更的性质及该变更预期将对该指定金融市场服务平台及其参与者或市场造成的风险;及

(ii)该指定金融市场服务平台计划如何管理任何识别出的风险。

(D)**补充信息**。——监管机关可以要求指定金融市场服务平台提供任何必要信息,以评估拟议变更将会对该指定金融市场服务平台的支付、清算或结算活动的风险性质和水平造成的影响,并评估拟议风险管理措施是否充分。

(E)**反对意见通知**。——监管机关对拟议变更有任何反对意见的,应在以下日期(以较晚者为准)后60天内将反对意见通知该指定金融市场服务平台——

(i) the date that the notice of the proposed change is received; or

(ii) the date any further information requested for consideration of the notice is received.

(F) CHANGE NOT ALLOWED IF OBJECTION. — A designated financial market utility shall not implement a change to which the Supervisory Agency has an objection.

(G) CHANGE ALLOWED IF NO OBJECTION WITHIN 60 DAYS. — A designated financial market utility may implement a change if it has not received an objection to the proposed change within 60 days of the later of —

(i) the date that the Supervisory Agency receives the notice of proposed change; or

(ii) the date the Supervisory Agency receives any further information it requests for consideration of the notice.

(H) REVIEW EXTENSION FOR NOVEL OR COMPLEX ISSUES. — The Supervisory Agency may, during the 60-day review period, extend the review period for an additional 60 days for proposed changes that raise novel or complex issues, subject to the Supervisory Agency providing the designated financial market utility with prompt written notice of the extension. Any extension under this subparagraph will extend the time periods under subparagraphs (E) and (G).

(I) CHANGE ALLOWED EARLIER IF NOTIFIED OF NO OBJECTION. — A designated financial market utility may implement a change in less than 60 days from the date of receipt of the notice of proposed change by the Supervisory Agency, or the date the Supervisory Agency receives any further information it requested, if the Supervisory Agency notifies the designated financial market utility in writing that it does not object to the proposed change and authorizes the designated financial market utility to implement the change on an earlier date, subject to any conditions imposed by the Supervisory Agency.

(2) EMERGENCY CHANGES. —

(A) IN GENERAL. — A designated financial market utility may implement a change that would otherwise require advance notice under this subsection if it determines that —

(i) an emergency exists; and

(ii) immediate implementation of the change is necessary for the designated financial market utility to continue to provide its services in a safe and sound manner.

(B) NOTICE REQUIRED WITHIN 24 HOURS. — The designated financial market utility shall provide notice of any such emergency change to its Supervisory Agency, as soon as practicable, which shall be no later than 24 hours after implementation of the change.

(C) CONTENTS OF EMERGENCY NOTICE. — In addition to the information required for changes requiring advance notice, the notice of an emergency change shall describe —

(i) the nature of the emergency; and

(ii) the reason the change was necessary for the designated financial market utility to

(i)拟议变更通知收到之日;或

(ii)监管机关为对通知进行审议而要求提供的补充信息收到之日。

(F)**监管机关提出反对的,不得实施变更**。——监管机关对某项拟议变更提出反对意见的,指定金融市场服务平台不得予以实施。

(G)**监管机关60天内未提出反对意见的,可实施变更**。——指定金融市场服务平台未在以下日期(以较晚者为准)后60天内收到监管机关对其拟议变更提出的反对意见的,即可实施该变更——

(i)监管机关收到拟议变更通知之日;或

(ii)监管机关为对通知进行审议而要求提供的补充信息收到之日。

(H)**无先例可循问题或复杂问题审查期限的延长**。——如果拟议变更提出的问题无先例可循或异常复杂,监管机关可以在60天的审查期内将审查期限另行延长60天,但该监管机关必须及时以书面形式将延期决定通知指定金融市场服务平台。按照本子款延长期限的,第(E)子款和第(G)子款规定的期限也应相应顺延。

(I)**如收到无反对意见的通知,可提前实施变更**。——如果监管机关以书面形式通知指定金融市场服务平台,说明其不反对拟议变更,并授权该指定金融市场服务平台提前实施变更,则,在监管机关收到拟议变更通知后60天期限届满之前,或者如该监管机关曾要求提交补充信息,则在补充信息收到后60天届满之前,该指定金融市场服务平台可提前实施拟议变更,但以遵守监管机关规定的任何条件为前提。

(2)**紧急变更**。——

(A)**一般规定**。——尽管本子条要求在作出变更之前先发出通知,但是,指定金融市场服务平台作出以下判定的,可以在不事先发出通知的情况下实施该变更——

(i)存在紧急情况;且

(ii)为确保指定金融市场服务平台继续安全而稳健地提供服务,有必要及时实施相关变更。

(B)**24小时内发出通知的要求**。——指定金融市场服务平台应尽快将任何上述紧急变更通知其监管机关,通知时间不得迟于变更实施后24小时。

(C)**紧急通知的内容**。——除了就须提供事先通知的变更所应提供的信息外,紧急变更通知书还应说明——

(i)紧急情况的性质;及

(ii)为确保指定金融市场服务平台继续安全而稳健地提供服务,而有必要实施相

continue to provide its services in a safe and sound manner.

(D) MODIFICATION OR RESCISSION OF CHANGE MAY BE REQUIRED. — The Supervisory Agency may require modification or rescission of the change if it finds that the change is not consistent with the purposes of this Act or any applicable rules, orders, or standards prescribed under section 805(a).

(3) COPYING THE BOARD OF GOVERNORS. — The Supervisory Agency shall provide the Board of Governors concurrently with a complete copy of any notice, request, or other information it issues, submits, or receives under this subsection.

(4) CONSULTATION WITH BOARD OF GOVERNORS. — Before taking any action on, or completing its review of, a change proposed by a designated financial market utility, the Supervisory Agency shall consult with the Board of Governors.

SEC.807. EXAMINATION OF AND ENFORCEMENT ACTIONS AGAINST DESIGNATED FINANCIAL MARKET UTILITIES.

(a) EXAMINATION. — Notwithstanding any other provision of law and subject to subsection (d), the Supervisory Agency shall conduct examinations of a designated financial market utility at least once annually in order to determine the following:

(1) The nature of the operations of, and the risks borne by, the designated financial market utility.

(2) The financial and operational risks presented by the designated financial market utility to financial institutions, critical markets, or the broader financial system.

(3) The resources and capabilities of the designated financial market utility to monitor and control such risks.

(4) The safety and soundness of the designated financial market utility.

(5) The designated financial market utility's compliance with —

(A) this title; and

(B) the rules and orders prescribed under this title.

(b) SERVICE PROVIDERS. — Whenever a service integral to the operation of a designated financial market utility is performed for the designated financial market utility by another entity, whether an affiliate or non-affiliate and whether on or off the premises of the designated financial market utility, the Supervisory Agency may examine whether the provision of that service is in compliance with applicable law, rules, orders, and standards to the same extent as if the designated financial market utility were performing the service on its own premises.

(c) ENFORCEMENT. — For purposes of enforcing the provisions of this title, a designated financial market utility shall be subject to, and the appropriate Supervisory Agency shall have authority under the provisions of subsections (b) through (n) of section 8 of the Federal Deposit Insurance Act (12 U.S.C. 1818) in the same manner and to the same

关变更的原因。

(D)**监管机关可以要求修改或撤销变更**。——监管机关认定紧急变更有悖本法宗旨或违反按照第805(a)条制定或发布的任何规则、命令或标准的,可以要求修改或撤销紧急变更。

(3)**抄送联邦储备委员会**。——监管机关根据本子条发出、提交或收到的任何通知、请求或其他信息,均应同时向联邦储备委员会提供完整复本。

(4)**与联邦储备委员会进行磋商**。——在针对指定金融市场服务平台的拟议变更采取任何行动或完成对该等变更的审查之前,监管机关应先与联邦储备委员会磋商。

第807条　对指定金融市场服务平台实施的检查和执法行动

(a)**检查**。——无论是否存在任何不同法律规定,在不违反第(d)子条的前提下,监管机关至少应每年对指定金融市场服务平台进行一次检查,以便对以下内容作出认定:

(1)该指定金融市场服务平台的运营性质及其承担的风险。

(2)该指定金融市场服务平台对金融机构、关键市场或整体金融体系造成的财务和运营风险。

(3)该指定金融市场服务平台监控和控制上述风险的资源和能力。

(4)该指定金融市场服务平台的安全性和稳健性。

(5)该指定金融市场服务平台对以下二者的合规情况——

(A)本编规定;及

(B)按照本编制定的规则和命令。

(b)**服务提供商**。——如指定金融市场服务平台在开展运营的过程中,如另外一个实体为指定金融市场服务平台开展的服务系后者运营不可分割的组成部分,则不论该服务提供商是否为该指定金融市场服务平台的关联方,也不论该服务是否在该指定金融市场服务平台的场所内提供,监管机关均可以开展检查工作,查明上述服务的提供是否符合适用的法律、规则、命令和标准,且该等合规水平是否与该指定金融市场服务平台若在其场所内自行开展该服务所能达到的合规水平相当。

(c)**执法**。——执行本编规定时,指定金融市场服务平台应受制于《联邦存款保险法》第8条(《美国法典》第十二编第1818节)第(b)子条至第(n)子条的规定,且相应的监管机关应拥有上述条款规定的权力,其方式和范围或程度均如同该指定金融机构是一家参保存款机构,而该等相应的监管机关身为该等参保存款机构的相应的联邦

extent as if the designated financial market utility was an insured depository institution and the Supervisory Agency was the appropriate Federal banking agency for such insured depository institution.

(d) BOARD OF GOVERNORS INVOLVEMENT IN EXAMINATIONS.—

(1) BOARD OF GOVERNORS CONSULTATION ON EXAMINATION PLANNING.—The Supervisory Agency shall consult annually with the Board of Governors regarding the scope and methodology of any examination conducted under subsections (a) and (b). The Supervisory Agency shall lead all examinations conducted under subsections (a) and (b)

(2) BOARD OF GOVERNORS PARTICIPATION IN EXAMINATION.— The Board of Governors may, in its discretion, participate in any examination led by a Supervisory Agency and conducted under subsections (a) and (b).

(e) BOARD OF GOVERNORS ENFORCEMENT RECOMMENDATIONS.—

(1) RECOMMENDATION.— The Board of Governors may, after consulting with the Council and the Supervisory Agency, at any time recommend to the Supervisory Agency that such agency take enforcement action against a designated financial market utility in order to prevent or mitigate significant liquidity, credit, operational, or other risks to the financial markets or to the financial stability of the United States. Any such recommendation for enforcement action shall provide a detailed analysis supporting the recommendation of the Board of Governors.

(2) CONSIDERATION.—The Supervisory Agency shall consider the recommendation of the Board of Governors and submit a response to the Board of Governors within 60 days.

(3) BINDING ARBITRATION.— If the Supervisory Agency rejects, in whole or in part, the recommendation of the Board of Governors, the Board of Governors may refer the recommendation to the Council for a binding decision on whether an enforcement action is warranted.

(4) ENFORCEMENT ACTION.— Upon an affirmative vote by a majority of the Council in favor of the Board of Governors' recommendation under paragraph (3), the Council may require the Supervisory Agency to—

(A) exercise the enforcement authority referenced in subsection (c); and

(B) take enforcement action against the designated financial market utility.

(f) EMERGENCY ENFORCEMENT ACTIONS BY THE BOARD OF GOVERNORS.—

(1) IMMINENT RISK OF SUBSTANTIAL HARM.— The Board of Governors may, after consulting with the Supervisory Agency and upon an affirmative vote by a majority the Council, take enforcement action against a designated financial market utility if the Board of Governors has reasonable cause to conclude that—

(A) either—

(i) an action engaged in, or contemplated by, a designated financial market utility

银行业监管机关。

(d)**联邦储备委员会对检查工作的参与**。——

(1)**就检查工作的规划与联邦储备委员会磋商**。——监管机关每年应与联邦储备委员会就按照第(a)子条和第(b)子条开展检查工作的范围和方法进行磋商。按照第(a)子条和第(b)子条开展的所有检查工作,均应由监管机关领导开展。

(2)**联邦储备委员会参加检查工作**。——联邦储备委员会可依其自由裁量权自行决定参加监管机关按照第(a)子条和第(b)子条领导开展的检查工作。

(e)**联邦储备委员会关于执法行动的建议**。——

(1)**建议**。——在与金融稳定监督委员会和监管机关磋商后,联邦储备委员会可以随时建议监管机关针对某指定金融市场服务平台采取执法行动,以防范或缓释对金融市场或美国金融稳定造成的重大流动性、信用、运营或其他方面的风险。联邦储备委员会在作出任何执法建议时,均应提供详细分析,说明提出该建议的理由。

(2)**考虑**。——监管机关应考虑联邦储备委员会的建议,并在60天内向联邦储备委员会作出答复。

(3)**具有约束力的仲裁**。——如果监管机关部分或全部反对联邦储备委员会所做的建议,则联邦储备委员会可以将建议移交金融稳定监督委员会,由金融稳定监督委员会就该执法行动的正当性作出具有约束力的决定。

(4)**执法行动**。——如果金融稳定监督委员会以过半数赞成票批准联邦储备委员会按照第(3)款提出的建议,则金融稳定监督委员会可以要求监管机关——

(A)行使第(c)子条所述执法权;及

(B)针对该指定金融市场服务平台采取执法行动。

(f)**联邦储备委员会的紧急执法行动**。——

(1)**迫切的重大危害风险**。——在与监管机关磋商后,并在获得金融稳定监督委员会过半数赞成票支持的前提下,联邦储备委员会可以针对指定金融市场服务平台采取执法行动,前提是联邦储备委员会有合理理由——

(A)得出下列其中一项结论——

(i)指定金融市场服务平台作出的或拟作出的行动[包括将受制于第806(e)条规

(including any change proposed by the designated financial market utility to its rules, procedures, or operations that would otherwise be subject to section 806 (e)) poses an imminent risk of substantial harm to financial institutions, critical markets, or the broader financial system of the United States; or

(ii) the condition of a designated financial market utility poses an imminent risk of substantial harm to financial institutions, critical markets, or the broader financial system; and

(B) the imminent risk of substantial harm precludes the Board of Governors' use of the procedures in subsection (e).

(2) ENFORCEMENT AUTHORITY. — For purposes of taking enforcement action under paragraph (1), a designated financial market utility shall be subject to, and the Board of Governors shall have authority under the provisions of subsections (b) through (n) of section 8 of the Federal Deposit Insurance Act (12 U.S.C. 1818) in the same manner and to the same extent as if the designated financial market utility was an insured depository institution and the Board of Governors was the appropriate Federal banking agency for such insured depository institution.

SEC.808. EXAMINATION OF AND ENFORCEMENT ACTIONS AGAINST FINANCIAL INSTITUTIONS SUBJECT TO STANDARDS FOR DESIGNATED ACTIVITIES.

(a) EXAMINATION. — The appropriate financial regulator is authorized to examine a financial institution subject to the standards prescribed under section 805(a) for a designated activity in order to determine the following:

(1) The nature and scope of the designated activities engaged in by the financial institution.

(2) The financial and operational risks the designated activities engaged in by the financial institution may pose to the safety and soundness of the financial institution.

(3) The financial and operational risks the designated activities engaged in by the financial institution may pose to other financial institutions, critical markets, or the broader financial system.

(4) The resources available to and the capabilities of the financial institution to monitor and control the risks described in paragraphs (2) and (3).

(5) The financial institution's compliance with this title and the rules and orders prescribed under section 805(a).

(b) ENFORCEMENT. — For purposes of enforcing the provisions of this title, and the rules and orders prescribed under this section, a financial institution subject to the standards prescribed under section 805 (a) for a designated activity shall be subject to, and the appropriate financial regulator shall have authority under the provisions of subsections (b) through (n) of section 8 of the Federal Deposit Insurance Act (12 U.S.C. 1818) in the same

定的该指定金融市场服务平台拟就其规则、程序或运营作出的变更〕存在对金融机构、关键市场或美国整体金融体系迫切的重大危害风险;或

(ii)指定金融市场服务平台的状态存在对金融机构、关键市场或美国整体金融体系迫切的重大危害风险;且

(B)该迫切的重大危害风险使联邦储备委员会不应采用第(e)子条规定的程序。

(2)**执法权**。——在根据第(1)款采取执法行动时,指定金融市场服务平台应受制于《联邦存款保险法》第8条(《美国法典》第十二编第1818节)第(b)子条至第(n)子条的规定,且适当的监管机关应拥有上述条款规定的权力,其方式和范围或程度均如同该指定金融机构是一家参保存款机构,而联邦储备委员会身为该等参保存款机构的相应的联邦银行业监管机关。

第808条　针对须遵守指定活动标准的金融机构实施的检查和执法行动

(a)**检查工作**。——对于须遵守第805(a)条规定的标准的金融机构,相应的金融监管者有权针对某项指定活动开展检查工作,以便对以下内容作出判定:

(1)该金融机构从事的指定活动的性质和范围。

(2)该金融机构从事的指定活动可能对该金融机构的安全性和稳健性造成的财务和运营风险。

(3)该金融机构从事的指定活动可能对其他金融机构、关键市场或整体金融体系造成的财务和运营风险。

(4)该金融机构监控和控制上文第(2)款和第(3)款所述风险的资源和能力。

(5)该金融机构对本编规定以及按照第805(a)条制定的规则和命令的合规情况。

(b)**执法**。——执行本编规定以及根据本条制定的规则和命令时,须遵守第805(a)条规定的指定活动标准的金融机构应受制于《联邦存款保险法》第8条(《美国法典》第十二编第1818节)第(b)子条至第(n)子条的规定,且相应的金融监管者应拥有上述条款规定的权力,其方式和范围或程度均如同该金融机构是一家参保存款机构,而相应的金融监管者身为该等参保存款机构的相应的联邦银行业监管机关。

manner and to the same extent as if the financial institution was an insured depository institution and the appropriate financial regulator was the appropriate Federal banking agency for such insured depository institution.

(c) TECHNICAL ASSISTANCE. — The Board of Governors shall consult with and provide such technical assistance as may be required by the appropriate financial regulators to ensure that the rules and orders prescribed under this title are interpreted and applied in as consistent and uniform a manner as practicable.

(d) DELEGATION. —

(1) EXAMINATION. —

(A) REQUEST TO BOARD OF GOVERNORS. — The appropriate financial regulator may request the Board of Governors to conduct or participate in an examination of a financial institution subject to the standards prescribed under section 805(a) for a designated activity in order to assess the compliance of such financial institution with —

(i) this title; or

(ii) the rules or orders prescribed under this title.

(B) EXAMINATION BY BOARD OF GOVERNORS. — Upon receipt of an appropriate written request, the Board of Governors will conduct the examination under such terms and conditions to which the Board of Governors and the appropriate financial regulator mutually agree.

(2) ENFORCEMENT. —

(A) REQUEST TO BOARD OF GOVERNORS. — The appropriate financial regulator may request the Board of Governors to enforce this title or the rules or orders prescribed under this title against a financial institution that is subject to the standards prescribed under section 805(a) for a designated activity.

(B) ENFORCEMENT BY BOARD OF GOVERNORS. — Upon receipt of an appropriate written request, the Board of Governors shall determine whether an enforcement action is warranted, and, if so, it shall enforce compliance with this title or the rules or orders prescribed under this title and, if so, the financial institution shall be subject to, and the Board of Governors shall have authority under the provisions of subsections (b) through (n) of section 8 of the Federal Deposit Insurance Act (12 U.S.C. 1818) in the same manner and to the same extent as if the financial institution was an insured depository institution and the Board of Governors was the appropriate Federal banking agency for such insured depository institution.

(e) BACK-UP AUTHORITY OF THE BOARD OF GOVERNORS. —

(1) EXAMINATION AND ENFORCEMENT. — Notwithstanding any other provision of law, the Board of Governors may —

(A) conduct an examination of the type described in subsection (a) of any financial

(c)**技术协助**。——联邦储备委员会应与相应的金融监管者磋商,并按金融监管者的要求向其提供技术协助,确保按本编制定的规则和命令尽可能实现连贯、统一的解释和适用。

(d)**委托授权**。——

(1)**检查工作**。——

(A)**向联邦储备委员会提出请求**。——对于须遵守第805(a)条规定的指定活动标准的金融机构,相应的金融监管者可请求联邦储备委员会开展或参加对该等金融机构的检查工作,评估该金融机构对以下二者的合规情况——

(i)本编规定;或

(ii)按照本编制定的规则或命令。

(B)**联邦储备委员会开展的检查工作**。——在收到适当的书面请求后,联邦储备委员会将按其与相应的金融监管者共同约定的条款和条件开展检查工作。

(2)**执法**。——

(A)**向联邦储备委员会提出请求**。——对于须遵守第805(a)条规定的指定活动标准的金融机构,相应的金融监管者可请求联邦储备委员会对该等金融机构执行本编规定或执行按照本编制定的规则或命令。

(B)**联邦储备委员会开展的执法工作**。——收到适当的书面请求后,联邦储备委员会应判定是否应该开展执法行动,如结论是肯定的,应强制执行本编规定或根据本编制定的规则或命令。在执行上述规定、规则或命令时,金融机构应受制于《联邦存款保险法》第8条(《美国法典》第十二编第1818节)第(b)子条至第(n)子条的规定,且联邦储备委员会应拥有上述条款规定的权力,其方式和范围或程度均如同该金融机构是一家参保存款机构,而联邦储备委员会身为该等参保存款机构的相应的联邦银行业监管机关。

(e)**联邦储备委员会的后备权力**。——

(1)**检查和执法工作**。——无论是否存在任何不同法律规定,联邦储备委员会均可以——

(A)针对须遵守第805(a)条规定的指定活动标准的任何金融机构,开展第(a)子

institution that is subject to the standards prescribed under section 805(a) for a designated activity; and

(B) enforce the provisions of this title or any rules or orders prescribed under this title against any financial institution that is subject to the standards prescribed under section 805(a) for a designated activity.

(2) LIMITATIONS. —

(A) EXAMINATION. — The Board of Governors may exercise the authority described in paragraph (1)(A) only if the Board of Governors has —

(i) reasonable cause to believe that a financial institution is not in compliance with this title or the rules or orders prescribed under this title with respect to a designated activity;

(ii) notified, in writing, the appropriate financial regulator and the Council of its belief under clause (i) with supporting documentation included;

(iii) requested the appropriate financial regulator to conduct a prompt examination of the financial institution;

(iv) either —

(I) not been afforded a reasonable opportunity to participate in an examination of the financial institution by the appropriate financial regulator within 30 days after the date of the Board's notification under clause (ii); or

(II) reasonable cause to believe that the financial institution's noncompliance with this title or the rules or orders prescribed under this title poses a substantial risk to other financial institutions, critical markets, or the broader financial system, subject to the Board of Governors affording the appropriate financial regulator a reasonable opportunity to participate in the examination; and

(v) obtained the approval of the Council upon an affirmative vote by a majority of the Council.

(B) ENFORCEMENT. — The Board of Governors may exercise the authority described in paragraph (1)(B) only if the Board of Governors has —

(i) reasonable cause to believe that a financial institution is not in compliance with this title or the rules or orders prescribed under this title with respect to a designated activity;

(ii) notified, in writing, the appropriate financial regulator and the Council of its belief under clause (i) with supporting documentation included and with a recommendation that the appropriate financial regulator take 1 or more specific enforcement actions against the financial institution;

(iii) either —

(I) not been notified, in writing, by the appropriate financial regulator of the commencement of an enforcement action recommended by the Board of Governors against the financial institution within 60 days from the date of the notification under clause (ii); or

条规定的类型的检查工作;及

(B)针对须遵守第805(a)条规定的指定活动标准的任何金融机构,执行本编规定或按照本编制定的任何规则或命令。

(2)**限制**。——

(A) **检查工作**。——联邦储备委员会仅得在符合以下条件的情况下行使第(1)(A)款所述权限——

(i)联邦储备委员会有合理理由认为该金融机构从事的某项指定活动违反本编规定,或违反按照本编制定的规则或命令;

(ii)联邦储备委员会已通过书面形式将其按照第(i)项作出的认定结论通知相应的金融监管者和金融稳定监督委员会,并附上相关支持文件;

(iii)联邦储备委员会已请求该相应的金融监管者立即对该金融机构开展检查工作;

(iv)联邦储备委员会——

(I)在按照第(ii)项规定发出通知后的30天内,并未获得合理机会参与相应的金融监管者对该金融机构开展的检查工作;或

(II)有合理理由认为该金融机构违反本编规定的行为或违反按照本编制定的规则或命令的行为对其他金融机构、关键市场或整体金融体系造成了重大风险,但联邦储备委员会必须向相应的金融监管者提供参与检查工作的合理机会;且

(v)联邦储备委员会已获得金融稳定监督委员会以过半数赞成票通过的批准。

(B)**执法工作**。——联邦储备委员会仅得在符合以下条件的情况下行使第(1)(B)款所述权力——

(i)联邦储备委员会有合理理由认为该金融机构从事的某项指定活动违反本编规定,或违反按照本编制定的规则或命令;

(ii)联邦储备委员会已通过书面形式将其按照第(i)项作出的认定结论通知相应的金融监管者和金融稳定监督委员会,并附上相关支持文件,同时建议该相应的金融监管者针对该金融机构采取一项或一项以上具体执法行动;

(iii)联邦储备委员会——

(I)在按照第(ii)项发出通知后60天内,并未收到相应的金融监管者发出的关于其已根据联邦储备委员会的建议对相关金融机构启动执法工作的书面通知;或

(II) reasonable cause to believe that the financial institution's noncompliance with this title or the rules or orders prescribed under this title poses significant liquidity, credit, operational, or other risks to the financial markets or to the financial stability of the United States, subject to the Board of Governors notifying the appropriate financial regulator of the Board's enforcement action; and

(iv) obtained the approval of the Council upon an affirmative vote by a majority of the Council.

(3) ENFORCEMENT PROVISIONS. — For purposes of taking enforcement action under paragraph (1), the financial institution shall be subject to, and the Board of Governors shall have authority under the provisions of subsections (b) through (n) of section 8 of the Federal Deposit Insurance Act (12 U.S.C. 1818) in the same manner and to the same extent as if the financial institution was an insured depository institution and the Board of Governors was the appropriate Federal banking agency for such insured depository institution.

SEC.809. REQUESTS FOR INFORMATION, REPORTS, OR RECORDS.

(a) INFORMATION TO ASSESS SYSTEMIC IMPORTANCE. —

(1) FINANCIAL MARKET UTILITIES. — The Council is authorized to require any financial market utility to submit such information as the Council may require for the sole purpose of assessing whether that financial market utility is systemically important, but only if the Council has reasonable cause to believe that the financial market utility meets the standards for systemic importance set forth in section 804.

(2) FINANCIAL INSTITUTIONS ENGAGED IN PAYMENT, CLEARING, OR SETTLEMENT ACTIVITIES. — The Council is authorized to require any financial institution to submit such information as the Council may require for the sole purpose of assessing whether any payment, clearing, or settlement activity engaged in or supported by a financial institution is systemically important, but only if the Council has reasonable cause to believe that the activity meets the standards for systemic importance set forth in section 804.

(b) REPORTING AFTER DESIGNATION. —

(1) DESIGNATED FINANCIAL MARKET UTILITIES. — The Board of Governors and the Council may each require a designated financial market utility to submit reports or data to the Board of Governors and the Council in such frequency and form as deemed necessary by the Board of Governors or the Council in order to assess the safety and soundness of the utility and the systemic risk that the utility's operations pose to the financial system.

(2) FINANCIAL INSTITUTIONS SUBJECT TO STANDARDS FOR DESIGNATED ACTIVITIES. — The Board of Governors and the Council may each require 1 or more financial institutions subject to the standards prescribed under section 805 (a) for a designated activity to submit, in such frequency and form as deemed necessary by the Board

(II)有合理理由认为该金融机构违反本编规定的行为或违反按照本编制定的规则或命令的行为对金融市场或美国的金融稳定造成了重大流动性、信用、运营或其他方面的风险,但联邦储备委员会必须将其开展的执法行动通知相应的金融监管者;且

(iv)联邦储备委员会已获得金融稳定监督委员会以过半数赞成票通过的批准。

(3)**执法规定**。——在根据第(1)款采取执法行动时,金融机构应受制于《联邦存款保险法》第8条(《美国法典》第十二编第1818节)第(b)子条至第(n)子条的规定,且联邦储备委员会应拥有上述条款规定的权力,其方式和范围或程度均如同该金融机构是一家参保存款机构,而联邦储备委员会身为该等参保存款机构的相应的联邦银行业监管机关。

第809条 信息、报告或记录请求

(a)**评估系统重要性的信息**——

(1)**金融市场服务平台**。——金融稳定监督委员会有合理理由认为某金融市场服务平台符合第804条规定的系统重要性标准的,有权要求该金融市场服务平台按其要求提供信息,但信息的使用目的应仅限于评估该金融市场服务平台是否具有系统重要性。

(2)**从事支付、清算或结算活动的金融机构**。——金融稳定监督委员会有合理理由认为某金融市场服务平台所从事的或支持的支付、清算或结算活动符合第804条规定的系统重要性标准的,有权要求该金融市场服务平台按其要求提供信息,但信息的使用目的应仅限于评估该项支付、清算或结算活动是否具有系统重要性。

(b)**指定后的报告要求**。——

(1)**指定金融市场服务平台**。——联邦储备委员会和金融稳定监督委员会分别可以要求某指定金融市场服务平台按联邦储备委员会或金融稳定监督委员会判定确属必要的频率和格式提交报告或数据,以评估该设施的安全性和稳健性,并评估该设施的运营对金融体系造成的系统性风险。

(2)**须遵守指定活动标准的金融机构**。——联邦储备委员会和金融稳定监督委员会分别可以要求一家或一家以上须遵守第805(a)条规定的指定活动标准的金融机构,按其判定确属必要的频率和格式提交仅关于该指定活动开展的报告和数据,但该等报告和数据的使用目的应仅限于对以下内容进行评估——

of Governors or the Council, reports and data to the Board of Governors and the Council solely with respect to the conduct of the designated activity and solely to assess whether —

(A) the rules, orders, or standards prescribed under section 805 (a) with respect to the designated activity appropriately address the risks to the financial system presented by such activity; and

(B) the financial institutions are in compliance with this title and the rules and orders prescribed under section 805(a) with respect to the designated activity.

(3) LIMITATION. — The Board of Governors may, upon an affirmative vote by a majority of the Council, prescribe regulations under this section that impose a recordkeeping or reporting requirement on designated clearing entities or financial institutions engaged in designated activities that are subject to standards that have been prescribed under section 805(a)(2).

(c) COORDINATION WITH APPROPRIATE FEDERAL SUPERVISORY AGENCY. —

(1) ADVANCE COORDINATION. — Before requesting any material information from, or imposing reporting or recordkeeping requirements on, any financial market utility or any financial institution engaged in a payment, clearing, or settlement activity, the Board of Governors or the Council shall coordinate with the Supervisory Agency for a financial market utility or the appropriate financial regulator for a financial institution to determine if the information is available from or may be obtained by the agency in the form, format, or detail required by the Board of Governors or the Council.

(2) SUPERVISORY REPORTS. — Notwithstanding any other provision of law, the Supervisory Agency, the appropriate financial regulator, and the Board of Governors are authorized to disclose to each other and the Council copies of its examination reports or similar reports regarding any financial market utility or any financial institution engaged in payment, clearing, or settlement activities.

(d) TIMING OF RESPONSE FROM APPROPRIATE FEDERAL SUPERVISORY AGENCY. — If the information, report, records, or data requested by the Board of Governors or the Council under subsection (c)(1) are not provided in full by the Supervisory Agency or the appropriate financial regulator in less than 15 days after the date on which the material is requested, the Board of Governors or the Council may request the information or impose recordkeeping or reporting requirements directly on such persons as provided in subsections (a) and (b) with notice to the agency.

(e) SHARING OF INFORMATION. —

(1) MATERIAL CONCERNS. — Notwithstanding any other provision of law, the Board of Governors, the Council, the appropriate financial regulator, and any Supervisory Agency are authorized to —

(A) promptly notify each other of material concerns about a designated financial market

(A)根据第805(a)条针对指定活动制定的规则、命令或标准是否适当地解决了该等活动对金融体系造成的风险;及

(B)该金融机构对本编规定以及根据第805(a)条针对该指定活动制定的规则和命令的合规情况。

(3)**限制**。——在获得金融稳定监督委员会过半数赞成票支持的情况下,联邦储备委员会可以按照本条制定规章,针对须遵守按照第805(a)(2)条制定的标准的指定结算实体或从事指定活动的金融机构施加记录保存或报告要求。

(c)**与相关联邦监管机关的协作**。——

(1)**事先协作**。——在请求任何金融市场服务平台或从事支付、清算或结算活动的任何金融机构提供任何重要信息之前,或在向其施加报告或记录保存要求之前,针对金融市场服务平台,联邦储备委员会或金融稳定监督委员会应先与监管机关进行协作,而针对金融机构,联邦储备委员会或金融稳定监督委员会则应先与相应的金融监管者进行协作,以判定该监管机关或监管者是否拥有或可获得该等信息,且信息的形式、格式或细节是否符合联邦储备委员会或金融稳定监督委员会的要求。

(2)**监管报告**。——无论是否存在任何不同法律规定,对于检查报告或关于任何金融市场服务平台或从事支付、清算或结算活动的任何金融机构的其他类似报告,监管机关、相应的金融监管者以及联邦储备委员会均有权向彼此披露该等报告的复本,也有权向金融稳定监督委员会进行披露。

(d)**相关联邦监管机关的答复时间**。——如果在联邦储备委员会或金融稳定监督委员会按照第(c)(1)条发出信息请求后15天内,监管机关或相应的金融监管者并未全面提供相关信息、报告、记录或数据,则联邦储备委员会或金融稳定监督委员会可以按照第(a)子条和第(b)子条的规定直接请求相关主体提供信息,或对其施加记录保存或报告要求,但应同时向该等监管机关或监管者发出相应通知。

(e)**信息共享**。——

(1)**重大关切问题**。——无论是否存在任何不同法律规定,联邦储备委员会、金融稳定监督委员会、相应的金融监管者以及任何监管机关均有权——

(A)立即相互通知关于指定金融市场服务平台或从事指定活动的金融机构的重

utility or any financial institution engaged in designated activities; and

(B) share appropriate reports, information, or data relating to such concerns.

(2) OTHER INFORMATION. — Notwithstanding any other provision of law, the Board of Governors, the Council, the appropriate financial regulator, or any Supervisory Agency may, under such terms and conditions as it deems appropriate, provide confidential supervisory information and other information obtained under this title to each other, and to the Secretary, Federal Reserve Banks, State financial institution supervisory agencies, foreign financial supervisors, foreign central banks, and foreign finance ministries, subject to reasonable assurances of confidentiality, provided, however, that no person or entity receiving information pursuant to this section may disseminate such information to entities or persons other than those listed in this paragraph without complying with applicable law, including section 8 of the Commodity Exchange Act (7 U.S.C. 12).

(f) PRIVILEGE MAINTAINED. — The Board of Governors, the Council, the appropriate financial regulator, and any Supervisory Agency providing reports or data under this section shall not be deemed to have waived any privilege applicable to those reports or data, or any portion thereof, by providing the reports or data to the other party or by permitting the reports or data, or any copies thereof, to be used by the other party.

(g) DISCLOSURE EXEMPTION. — Information obtained by the Board of Governors, the Supervisory Agencies, or the Council under this section and any materials prepared by the Board of Governors, the Supervisory Agencies, or the Council regarding their assessment of the systemic importance of financial market utilities or any payment, clearing, or settlement activities engaged in by financial institutions, and in connection with their supervision of designated financial market utilities and designated activities, shall be confidential supervisory information exempt from disclosure under section 552 of title 5, United States Code. For purposes of such section 552, this subsection shall be considered a statute described in subsection (b)(3) of such section 552.

SEC.810. RULEMAKING.

The Board of Governors, the Supervisory Agencies, and the Council are authorized to prescribe such rules and issue such orders as may be necessary to administer and carry out their respective authorities and duties granted under this title and prevent evasions thereof.

SEC.811. OTHER AUTHORITY.

Unless otherwise provided by its terms, this title does not divest any appropriate financial regulator, any Supervisory Agency, or any other Federal or State agency, of any authority derived from any other applicable law, except that any standards prescribed by the Board of Governors under section 805 shall supersede any less stringent requirements established under other authority to the extent of any conflict.

大关切问题;及

(B)针对上述关切问题共享相关报告、信息或数据。

(2)**其他信息**。——无论是否存在任何不同法律规定,联邦储备委员会、金融稳定监督委员会、相应的金融监管者或任何监管机关均可按照其认为适当的条款和条件,相互提供按照本编规定获得的保密监管信息以及其他信息,并向财政部部长、联邦储备银行、州金融机构监管机关、外国金融监管机关、外国中央银行以及外国财政部部长提供上述信息,前提是必须已采取合理措施保证信息的保密性,同时,按照本条规定接收信息的任何人或实体均不得在违反适用的法律[包括《商品交易法》第8条(《美国法典》第七编第12节)]的情况下向本款列举范围之外的人或实体提供该等信息。

(f)**维持保密特权**。——联邦储备委员会、金融稳定监督委员会、相应的金融监管者以及按照本条提供报告或数据的任何监管机关相互之间提供报告或数据,或者允许对方使用该等报告或数据或其复本的,不得视为因此放弃该等报告或数据(或报告或数据的任何一部分)的保密特权。

(g)**披露豁免**。——联邦储备委员会、监管机关或金融稳定监督委员会按照本条规定获得的信息,以及联邦储备委员会、监管机关或金融稳定监督委员会为评估金融市场服务平台或金融机构从事的支付、清算或结算活动的系统重要性编制的任何材料,以及就其对指定金融市场服务平台和指定活动的监管工作编制的任何材料,均属保密监管信息,可豁免于《美国法典》第五编第552节规定的披露。就该第552节而言,本子条应视为第552节第(b)(3)子节所述的制定法。

第810条 规则制定

联邦储备委员会、监管机关以及金融稳定监督委员会有权制定必要的规则并发布必要的命令,以实施并履行本编赋予和规定的权力和职责,防范规避行为。

第811条 其他权力

除非本编条款另有规定,否则,本编并不解除任何其他适用的法律赋予相应的金融监管者、任何监管机关或任何其他联邦机关或州机关享有的任何权力,但是,如果联邦储备委员会按照第805条制定的标准与按照其他法律依据制定的要求存在冲突,而前者要求更为严格,则应以前者为准。

SEC.812. CONSULTATION.

(a) CFTC. — The Commodity Futures Trading Commission shall consult with the Board of Governors —

(1) prior to exercising its authorities under sections 2(h)(2)(C), 2(h)(3)(A), 2(h)(3)(C), 2(h)(4)(A), and 2(h)(4)(B) of the Commodity Exchange Act, as amended by the Wall Street Transparency and Accountability Act of 2010;

(2) with respect to any rule or rule amendment of a derivatives clearing organization for which a stay of certification has been issued under section 745 (b)(3) of the Wall Street Transparency and Accountability Act of 2010; and

(3) prior to exercising its rulemaking authorities under section 728 of the Wall Street Transparency and Accountability Act of 2010.

(b) SEC. — The Commission shall consult with the Board of Governors —

(1) prior to exercising its authorities under sections 3C(a)(2)(C), 3C(a)(3)(A), 3C(a)(3)(C), 3C (a)(4)(A), and 3C (a)(4)(B) of the Securities Exchange Act of 1934, as amended by the Wall Street Transparency and Accountability Act of 2010;

(2) with respect to any proposed rule change of a clearing agency for which an extension of the time for review has been designated under section 19(b)(2) of the Securities Exchange Act of 1934; and

(3) prior to exercising its rulemaking authorities under section 13(n) of the Securities Exchange Act of 1934, as added by section 763 (i) of the Wall Street Transparency and Accountability Act of 2010.

SEC.813. COMMON FRAMEWORK FOR DESIGNATED CLEARING ENTITY RISK MANAGEMENT.

The Commodity Futures Trading Commission and the Commission shall coordinate with the Board of Governors to jointly develop risk management supervision programs for designated clearing entities. Not later than 1 year after the date of enactment of this Act, the Commodity Futures Trading Commission, the Commission, and the Board of Governors shall submit a joint report to the Committee on Banking, Housing, and Urban Affairs and the Committee on Agriculture, Nutrition, and Forestry of the Senate, and the Committee on Financial Services and the Committee on Agriculture of the House of Representatives recommendations for —

(1) improving consistency in the designated clearing entity oversight programs of the Commission and the Commodity Futures Trading Commission;

(2) promoting robust risk management by designated clearing entities;

(3) promoting robust risk management oversight by regulators of designated clearing entities; and

第812条　磋商

(a)**商品期货交易委员会**。——商品期货交易委员会应按如下规定与联邦储备委员会磋商——

(1)在行使经《2010年华尔街透明度与问责法》修正后的《商品交易法》第2(h)(2)(C)条、第2(h)(3)(A)条、第2(h)(3)(C)条、第2(h)(4)(A)条和第2(h)(4)(B)条赋予的权力之前,应与联邦储备委员会磋商;

(2)如果任何衍生品结算组织的规则或规则修正的自查证明按照《2010年华尔街透明度与问责法》第745(b)(3)条被签发中止令,应与联邦储备委员会磋商;且

(3)在行使《2010年华尔街透明度与问责法》第728条赋予的规则制定权之前,应与联邦储备委员会磋商。

(b)**证券交易委员会**。——证券交易委员会应按如下规定与联邦储备委员会磋商——

(1)在行使经《2010年华尔街透明度与问责法》修正后的《1934年证券交易法》第3C(a)(2)(C)条、第3C(a)(3)(A)条、第3C(a)(3)(C)条、第3C(a)(4)(A)条和第3C(a)(4)(B)条赋予的权力之前,应与联邦储备委员会磋商;

(2)对于按照《1934年证券交易法》第19(b)(2)条被指定延长审查期限的结算机构规则变更草案,应与联邦储备委员会磋商;且

(3)在行使《1934年证券交易法》第13(n)条[该条规定由《2010年华尔街透明度与问责法》第763(i)条增加]赋予的规则制定权之前,应与联邦储备委员会磋商。

第813条　指定结算实体的通用风险管理框架

商品期货交易委员会和证券交易委员会应与联邦储备委员会进行协作，共同针对指定结算实体制定风险管理监管计划。在本法颁布之日后1年之内,商品期货交易委员会、证券交易委员会以及联邦储备委员会应向参议院的银行、住房与城市事务委员会和农业、营养与林业委员会以及众议院的金融服务委员会和农业委员会提交一份联合报告,就以下内容作出建议——

(1)改善证券交易委员会和商品期货交易委员会的指定结算实体监管计划的连贯和一致性;

(2)加强指定结算实体的风险管理;

(3)提高指定结算实体的监管者对风险管理的监管水平;及

(4) improving regulators' ability to monitor the potential effects of designated clearing entity risk management on the stability of the financial system of the United States.

SEC.814. EFFECTIVE DATE.

This title is effective as of the date of enactment of this Act.

(4)提高监管者对指定结算实体风险管理对美国金融体系的稳定性的潜在影响的监控能力。

第814条　生效日

本编规定于本法颁布之日生效。

Glossary 词汇表

Abusive swap	滥用性互换
Accelerated filer	加速报告人
Acceptance of securities	证券承兑
Acceptances	承兑汇票
Accredited investor	获许投资者
Accreted original issue discount	原始发行折价增值
Actual direct compensatory damages	实际直接损害赔偿/实际直接损害赔偿金
Administrative hearing	行政听证
Affiliate	关联方
Affiliate transactions	关联交易
Affiliated group	关联集团
Affiliations	关联关系
Agency consultation	机关磋商
Agency ombudsman	机关监察专员
Agricultural swap	农产品互换
Alaska Native Claims Settlement Act	《阿拉斯加原住民土地权处理法》
Allocated transaction	分配交易
Alternating examinations	替代性检查
Alternative Mortgage Transaction Parity Act of 1982	《1982 年另类抵押贷款交易平价法》
Anti-deficiency law	禁止追索差额法律
Antievasion	反规避
Antitrust laws	反垄断法律
Appropriate congressional committees	相应的国会委员会
Appropriate Federal banking agency	相应的联邦银行业监管机关
Appropriate financial regulator	相应的金融监管者
Arbitrage	套利
Armed group	武装团体
Assessment	计征费/计征款项/评估
Assessment base	计征基数

续表

Asset-threshold	资产门槛
Associated person of a securities holding company	证券控股公司关联人
Associated person of a swap dealer or major swap participant	互换交易商或主要互换参与者的业务相关人
Assuming insurer	再保险分入公司
Attachment	扣押令/扣押
Attestation	鉴证/证明
Attorney General	总检察长
Authority to enforce contracts	合约的强制执行权
Automated clearinghouse system	自动结算所系统
Average prime offer rate	平均最优惠利率
Avoidable transfers	可撤销的转让
Backup authority	后备权力
Back-up examination	后备检查权
Balance sheet	资产负债表
Balanced Budget and Emergency Deficit Control Act of 1985	《1985 年平衡预算和紧急赤字控制法》
Balloon payments	大额尾付
Bank Enterprise Act of 1991	《1991 年银行企业法》
Bank holding company	银行控股公司
Bank Holding Company Act Amendments of 1970	《1970 年银行控股公司法修正案》
Bank Holding Company Act of 1956	《1956 年银行控股公司法》
Bank Merger Act	《银行兼并法》
Bank Service Company Act	《银行服务公司法》
Banking entity	银行实体
Banking supervisors	银行监督官
Bankruptcy Code	《破产法》
Baseline	基本情形/基准/基础
Basis swap	基差互换
Block trades	大宗交易
Board of Governors	联邦储备委员会

续表

Board of trade	交易场所
Bona fide hedge positions	真正的套期保值持仓
Bretton Woods Agreements Act	《布雷顿森林协定法》
Bridge financial company	过渡金融公司
Bridge loan	过桥贷款
Broker	经纪商/经纪人
Broker licensing	经纪人执照
Brokerage	经纪费/经纪/经纪业务
Bureau of Consumer Financial Protection	消费者金融保护局
Bureau of Economic Analysis	经济分析局
Call	看涨期权/召集/需求
Capital adequacy	资本充足性
Capital stock and surplus	股本和资本公积金
Casualty insurance	意外险
Catalog of finacial entities and instruments	金融实体和工具目录
Cause of action	诉因
Cease and desist order	制止令
Cease-and-desist proceeding	制止令程序
Ceding insurer	再保险分出公司
Census tract	人口普查区
Central Registration Depository	集中注册信息存管系统
Certificate of deposit	存单
Certified Risk Manager/CRM	注册风险管理经理
Chapter	章
Chartered Property and Casualty Underwriter/CPCU	特许财产及意外险核保人
Chief compliance officer	首席合规官
Child Nutrition Act Of 1966	《1966 年儿童营养法》
Claims for damages for repudiation	拒绝履约赔偿请求权
Clayton Act	《克莱顿法》
Clearing agency	结算机构
Cohort default rate	群体违约比率

续表

Commercial paper	商业票据
Commercial risk	商业风险
Committee on Banking, Housing, and Urban Affairs of the Senate	参议院银行、住房与城市事务委员会
Committee on Financial Services of the House of Representatives	众议院金融服务委员会
Committee on the Judiciary of the House of Representatives	众议院司法委员会
Committee on the Judiciary of the Senate	参议院司法委员会
Commodity broker	商品经纪商
Commodity Futures Trading Commission	商品期货交易委员会
Commodity pool	商品基金
Commodity pool operator	商品基金管理人
Commodity swap	商品互换
Commodity trading advisor	商品交易顾问
Common stock	普通股
Commonwealth	准州
Community Development Banking and Financial Institutions Act of 1994	《1994 年社区发展银行与金融机构法》
Community development financial institution	社区发展金融机构
Community Reinvestment Act of 1977	《1977 年社区再投资法》
Compensation Committee	薪酬委员会
Compliance examiners	合规检查员
Compliance office	合规办公室
Component of Tier 1 capital	一级资本构成要素
Components of capital	资本构成要素
Compromise of action	诉讼妥协
Comptroller General of the United States	政府问责办公室主任
Comptroller of the Currency	货币监理署署长
Concentration limit	集中度限制
Concentrations in assets	资产集中
Conflict minerals	冲突矿物

续表

Consolidated supervision	并表监管
Consumer Financial Protection Fund	消费者金融保护基金
Consumer Handbook on Adjustable Rate Mortgages	《可调利率抵押贷款消费者手册》
Consumer Leasing Act of 1976	《1976 年消费者租赁法》
Contingent capital	或有资本
Contract proposals	合同建议书
Contractor	承包商/缔约人
Contracts to extend credit	授信合同
Cost and availability of credit in the United States	美国信贷成本和可获得性
Coupon book	宣传册
Covered agreement	所涉协定
Covered assistance	所涉补助金
Covered employee	所涉员工
Covered financial company	所涉金融公司
Cranston-Gonzalez National Affordable Housing Act	《克兰斯顿—冈塞雷斯国家住房国家住房保障法》
Credit card	信用卡
Credit card bank	信用卡银行
Credit default swap	信用违约互换
Credit exposure	信用风险敞口
Credit facility	信贷安排
Credit for reinsurance	再保险信用
Credit market	信贷市场
Credit risk	信用风险
Credit risk retention	信用风险自留
Credit spread	信贷息差
Credit swap	信贷互换
Credit union	信贷联盟
Crime Control Act of 1990	《1990 年犯罪控制法》
Cross-currency rate swap	跨货币利率互换
Cross-guarantees	交叉担保

续表

Currency swap	货币互换
CUSIP number	库斯普编号
Customer name securities	客户名下证券
Damages for pain and suffering	疼痛和精神痛苦赔偿
Data Center	数据中心
De minimis investment	微量投资
Debit card	借记卡
Debt index swap	债务指数互换
Debt swap	债务互换
Default	违约
Defense to foreclosure	止赎抗辩
Defenses	抗辩
Deferred compensation	递延薪酬
Department of Housing and Urban Development	住房与城市发展部
Department of Justice	司法部
Deposit insurance	存款保险
Depository institution	存款机构
Depository institution holding company	存款机构控股公司
Depository Institutions Management Interlocks Act	《禁止存款机构管理层交叉任职法》
Deposit-taking activity	吸收存款活动
Derivative transaction	衍生品交易
Derivative transactions in lending	衍生品交易借贷
Derivatives clearing organization	衍生品结算组织
Designated automated teller machine network	指定自动取款机网络
Designated clearing entity	指定结算实体
Designated financial market utility	指定金融市场服务平台
Designated transfer date	指定转移日
Director of the Federal Insurance Office	联邦保险办公室主任
Director of the Office of Thrift Supervision	储蓄机构监理局局长
Disclosure exemption	披露豁免
Discount window	贴现窗口

续表

Disruptive practices	扰乱性做法
District of Columbia savings and loan association	哥伦比亚特区储贷协会
Divestiture order	资产剥离令
Dual registration	双重注册
Dual service	双重任职
Electronic conduit services	电子渠道服务
Electronic debit transaction	电子借记交易
Electronic Fund Transfer Act	《电子资金划拨法》
Electronic Signatures in Global and National Commerce Act	《全球暨全美商业电子签章法》
Eligible bankers' acceptances	适格银行承兑汇票
Eligible contract participant	适格合约参与者
Emergency Economic Stabilization Act of 2008	《2008 年紧急经济稳定法》
Emergency Exception	紧急例外规定
Emergency Homeowners' Relief Act	《紧急业主救济法》
Emissions swap	排放互换
Employer's contribution	雇主缴款
Endorsement	背书
Energy Information Administration	能源信息署
Energy swap	能源互换
Enhancing Financial Institution Safety and Soundness Act of 2010	《2010 年金融机构安全性与稳健性改良法》
Equal Credit Opportunity Act	《信贷机会平等法》
Equitable remedies	衡平救济
Equity index swap	股指互换
Equity swap	股权互换
Event contract	事件合约
Excess funds	过剩资金
Exchange facilitator	交易中介
Executive Schedule	高级公务员序列
Exempt commercial purchaser	豁免商业购买人

续表

Exempt tax status	税收豁免地位
Existing retirement plan	既存退休计划
Expedited Funds Availability Act	《加速资金到位法》
Expedition	加急处理
Externally audited financial statement	经外部审计的财务报表
Failure to deliver shares sold short	卖空股份交割失信
Fair And Accurate Credit Transactions Act of 2003	《2003 年公平准确信用交易法》
Fair Credit Billing Act	《公平信用结账法》
Fair Credit Reporting Act	《公平信用报告法》
Fair Debt Collection Practices Act	《公平债务催收作业法》
Fair Housing Act	《公平住房法》
False Claims Act	《反欺骗政府法》
Family office	家族理财室
Fannie Mae	房利美
Farm Credit Act of 1971	《1971 年农业信贷法》
Farm Credit Administration	农业信贷管理局
Farm Credit System institution	农业信贷系统机构
Federal Advisory Committee Act/FACA	《联邦顾问委员会法》
Federal Agricultural Mortgage Corporation	联邦农业抵押贷款公司
Federal Aviation Act of 1958	《1958 年联邦民航法》
Federal Banking Agency	联邦银行业监管机关
Federal Deposit Insurance Act	《联邦存款保险法》
Federal Deposit Insurance Corporation	联邦存款保险公司
Federal Deposit Insurance Corporation Improvement Act of 1991	《1991 年联邦存款保险公司改良法》
Federal depository institution	联邦存款机构
Federal Employee Retirement Program	联邦雇员退休计划
Federal Energy Regulatory Commission	联邦能源监管委员会
Federal financial regulatory agency	联邦金融监管机关
Federal Home Loan Bank	联邦住房贷款银行
Federal Home Loan Bank Act	《联邦住房贷款银行法》

续表

Federal Home Loan Mortgage Corporation	联邦住房贷款抵押公司
Federal Housing Enterprises Financial Safety and Soundness Act of 1992	《1992 年联邦住房企业财务安全和稳健法》
Federal Housing Finance Agency	联邦住房金融局
Federal Insurance Office	联邦保险办公室
Federal Insurance Office Act of 2010	《2010 年联邦保险办公室法》
Federal National Mortgage Association	联邦国民抵押贷款协会
Federal Power Act	《联邦电力法》
Federal Property and Administrative Services Act of 1949	《1949 年联邦财产和行政服务法》
Federal Register	《联邦公报》
Federal Reserve Act	《联邦储备法》
Federal Reserve System Retirement Plan	联邦储备系统退休计划
Federal Reserve System Thrift Plan	联邦储备系统节俭计划
Federal Rules of Civil Procedure	《联邦民事诉讼规则》
Federal savings association	联邦储蓄协会
Federal Sentencing Guidelines	《联邦量刑指引》
Federal Trade Commission Act	《联邦贸易委员会法》
Federally Recognized Indian Tribe List Act of 1994	《1994 年联邦政府承认的印第安人部落清单法》
Fellowship program	英才计划
Fiduciary duty	受信义务
Filing date	破产申请日/报批日期/申报日期
Finance Board	金融委员会
Financial Accounting Statements	《财务会计准则公告》
Financial company	金融公司
Financial company reference database	金融公司参考数据库
Financial contract	金融合约
Financial decline	财务困境
Financial guarantee	金融担保
Financial holding company	金融控股公司
Financial Industry Regulatory Authority, FINRA	金融业监管局

续表

Financial Institutions Reform, Recovery, and Enforcement Act of 1989	《1989 年金融机构改革、复兴与实施法》
Financial Institutions Retirement Fund	金融机构退休基金
Financial Institutions Supervisory Act of 1966	《1966 年金融机构监管法》
Financial instrument	金融工具
Financial integrity	财务完整性
Financial literacy	金融扫盲/金融素养
Financial Literacy and Education Commission	金融扫盲和教育委员会
Financial Literacy and Education Improvement Act	《金融素养和教育改进法》
Financial market utilities	金融市场服务平台
Financial planners	金融理财师
Financial Privacy Act of 1978	《1978 年金融隐私权法》
Financial Research Fund	金融研究基金
Financial Stability Act of 2010	《2010 年金融稳定法》
Financial Stability Oversight Council	金融稳定监督委员会
Financial statement	财务报表
Financial transaction data	金融交易数据
Financing Corporation, and the Resolution Funding Corporation	融资公司以及清盘融资公司
Financing priority	融资优先性
Flood Disaster Protection Act of 1973	《1973 年洪水灾害防御法》
Floor broker	场内经纪商
Floor trader	场内交易商
Food and Nutrition Act Of 2008	《2008 年食品和营养法》
Foreign bank	外国银行
Foreign exchange forward	外汇远期
Foreign exchange swap	外汇互换
Foreign nonbank financial company	外国非银行金融公司
Foreign private adviser	外国私人顾问
Forward contract	远期合约
Forward-looking indicator	前瞻性指标

续表

Fraudulent transfers	欺诈性转让
Freddie Mac	房地美
Freedom of Information Act	《信息自由法》
Fully indexed rate	完全指数利率
Functionally regulated subsidiary	受制于功能监管的子公司
Futures	期货
Futures and options contracts	期货和期权合约
Futures commission merchant	期货经纪商
General Accounting Office; / GAO	政府问责办公室
Global Analyst Research Settlements	《全球分析师研究协议》
Global and National Commerce Act	《全球暨全美商业电子签章法》
Global Risk Management Institute	全球风险管理学会
Golden parachute benefits	金色降落伞福利
Government bond	政府债券
Government National Mortgage Association	美国政府国民抵押贷款协会
Graduated assessment rate	计征费分级费率
Gramm-Leach-Bliley Act	《格雷姆—里奇—比利雷法》
Grandfather Provision	不溯及既往条款
Guarantee	保函/担保/保证
Guaranteed investment contract	担保投资合约
Hart-Scott-Rodino Filing Requirement	《哈特—斯科—罗迪诺反垄断改进法》
Hazard insurance	灾害险
Hedge fund	对冲基金
Hedge transaction	套期保值交易
Helping Families Save Their Homes Act of 2009	《2009 年协助家庭保全房屋法》
Higher Education Act of 1965	《1965 年高等教育法》
High-frequency trading	高频交易
Home Affordable Modification Program Guidlines	《可负担房贷修改计划》
Home Mortgage Disclosure Act of 1975	《1975 年住房抵押贷款披露法》
Home Owners Protection Act of 1998	《1998 年业主保护法》
Home Owners' Loan Act	《业主贷款法》

续表

Home Ownership and Equity Protection Act of 1994	《1994 年住房所有权和房屋权益保护法》
Home Valuation Code of Conduct	《住房估值行为守则》
Homeowner's insurance	业主险
Housing Act of 1948	《1948 年住房法》
Housing and Community Development Act of 1992	《1992 年住房与社区发展法》
Housing and Urban-Rural Recovery Act of 1983	《1983 年住房与城乡复苏法》
HUD-approved counseling agency	住房与城市发展部批准的咨询机构
Hybrid capital instrument	混合资本工具
Illiquid fund	非流动性基金
Implementation expenses	实施费用
Independent director	独立董事
Independently procured insurance	独立购买的保险
Industrial bank	产业银行
Inflation swap	通货膨胀互换
Insider	内幕人士
Insolvency	资不抵债
Inspector General Act of 1978	《1978 年监察长法》
Institution of higher education	高等教育机构
Insurance commissioner	保险监督官
Insurance for Noninterest-Bearing Transaction Accounts	无息交易账户保险
Insurance Institute of America	美国保险学会
Insurance of transaction accounts	交易账户保险
Insured bank	参保银行
Insured branch	参保分支机构/参保分行
Insured depository institution	参保存款机构
Interactive data format	交互式数据格式
Interactive data standard	交互式数据标准
Interchange transaction fee	跨行手续费
Interest rate swap	利率互换
Interested parties	利害关系人

续表

Intermediate Holding Company	中间控股公司
Internal Revenue Code of 1986	《1986 年国内税收法典》
International Banking Act of 1978	《1978 年国际银行法》
International Lending Supervision Act of 1983	《1983 年国际贷款监管法》
International Swap Regulation	国际互换监管
Interstate Land Sales Full Disclosure Act	《州际土地销售完全披露法》
Introducing broker	介绍经纪商
Invalid dividends	无效股息
Investment adviser	投资顾问
Investment Adviser Registration Depository system	投资顾问注册信息存管系统
Investment Advisers Act of 1940	《1940 年投资顾问法》
Investment company	投资公司
Investment Company Act of 1940	《1940 年投资公司法》
Ipso Facto Clauses	破产约定条款
Irrevocable	不可撤销
Judicial discretion	司法自由裁量权
Judicial review	司法审查
Judicial stay	司法中止
Junior lien	次位留置权
Jury	陪审团
Large financial institution	大型金融机构
Large swap trader reporting	互换大户报告
Late fee	滞纳金
Leasehold interest	承租权益
Legal Certainty for Bank Products Act of 2000	《2000 年银行产品法律确定性法》
Letters of credit	信用证
Leverage	杠杆/杠杆率
Leverage capital	杠杆资本
Leverage transaction merchant	杠杆交易商
Lien	留置权
Life insurance program	寿险计划

续表

Line of credit	信用额度
Liquidation or rehabilitation	清算或整顿
Liquidity	流动性
Liquidity event	流动性事件
Liquidity measures	流动性指标
Loan-transaction coupled with a securities collar transaction	证券封顶保底交易附随的贷款交易
Long term care	长期医疗保险
Major swap participant	主要互换参与者
Mandatory regulations	强制性规章
Manufactured home	预制房
Margin loan	保证金贷款
Market discipline	市场约束
Material financial distress	重大财务困境
Maximum amount of liability	最高责任金额
McKinney-Vento Homeless Assistance Act	《麦金尼—文托无房者援助法》
Measures of the financial condition	财务状况计量指标
Member agency	成员机关
Memorandum	备忘录
Metal swap	金属互换
Minimum capital requirements	最低资本要求
Minimum leverage capital requirement	最低杠杆资本要求
Minimum reserve ratio	最低准备金率
Minimum risk-based capital requirement	最低风险基础资本要求
Minority	少数族裔/少数党
Minority-owned business	少数族裔拥有的企业
Misleading designation	误导性称号
Misleading or fraudulent marketing	误导性或欺诈性营销
Missing security holder	失去联络的证券持有人
Mitigation of risk	风险的缓释
Mixed swap	混合互换

续表

Model Regulations on the Use of Senior-Specific Certifications and Professional Designations in the Sale of Life Insurance and Annuities, Model Regulation on the Use of Senior-Specific Certifications and Professional Designations in the Sale of Life Insurance and Annuities	《美国保险监督官协会关于在人寿保险和年金销售中面向老年人的认证和专业称号的使用示范管理办法》
Model Rule on the Use of Senior-Specific Certifications and Professional Designations	《北美证券管理者协会关于面向老年人的认证和专业称号的使用示范规则》
Modular home	模块化房屋
Money damages	金钱损害赔偿
Mortgage loan	抵押贷款
Municipal advisor	市政顾问
Municipal securities dealer	市政证券自营商
Mutual Fund	共同基金
Narrow-based security index	窄基证券指数
NASAA Model Rule on the Use of Senior-Specific Certifications and Professional Designations	《北美证券管理者协会关于面向老年人的认证和专业称号的使用示范规则》
National Alliance for Insurance Education & Research	全国保险教育和研究联盟
national banking association	国民银行协会
National Credit Union Administration Board	国家信贷联盟署委员会
National Credit Union Share Insurance Fund	国家信贷联盟股份保险基金
National Endowment for the Humanities	全国人文基金会
National Endowment of the Arts	全国艺术基金会
National Housing Act	《国民住房法》
National member bank	国民成员银行
National nonmember bank	国民非成员银行
National securities exchange	全国性证券交易所
National Strategy for Financial Literacy	《全国金融扫盲战略》
National treatment	国民待遇
Nationally recognized statistical rating organization	全国公认统计评级组织
Natural Gas Act	《天然气法》
Negative amortization	负值摊还本金

续表

Neighborhood Reinvestment Corporation Act	《社区再投资公司法》
Net amount of insurance payable	应付保险净额
Net equity	权益净额
Net present value	净现值
Network fee	网络费用
Nonadmitted and Reinsurance Reform Act of 2010	《2010 年非本州监管保险和再保险改革法》
Non-Admitted Insurance Model Act	《非本州监管保险示范法》
Nonadmitted premium taxes	非本州监管保险的保费税金
Nonbank financial company	非银行金融公司
Nonbank financial company supervised by the Board of Governors	受联邦储备委员会监管的非银行金融公司
Non-cleared option	非集中结算的期权
Non-cleared security-based swap	非集中结算的基于证券的互换
Noninterest-bearing transaction account	无息交易账户
Nonprofit organization	非营利组织
Non-United States insurer	非美国保险公司
North American Securities Administrators Association/NASAA	北美证券管理者协会
Notice of deficiencies	缺陷通知
Off-balance-sheet activities	表外活动
Off-balance-sheet exposures	表外风险敞口/表外风险
Off-balance-sheet item	表外项目
Office of Credit Ratings	信用评级办公室
Office of Financial Protection for Older Americans	老年美国人金融保护办公室
Office of Financial Research	金融研究办公室
Office of Personnel Management	人事管理局
Office of Service Member Affairs	现役军人事务办公室
Office of the Comptroller of the Currency	货币监理署
Office of the Investor Advocate	投资者维权办公室
Office of Thrift Supervision	储蓄机构监理局
Officer of the United States	联邦官员

续表

Ombudsman	监察专员
Omnibus Appropriations Act, 2009	《2009 年综合拨款法》
Open repurchase agreement	开放式回购协议
Open reverse repurchase agreement	开放式逆回购协议
Option	期权
Options contract	期权合约
Orderly liquidation	有序清算
Orderly Liquidation Fund	有序清算基金
Overall risk management	整体风险管理
Packers and Stockyards Act, 1921	《1921 年包装食品生产厂及牲畜围栏法》
Paperwork Reduction Act	《文书削减法》
Paragraph	款
Pay It Back Act	《还款法》
Paying agent	付款代理人
Payment card network	支付卡网络
Payment, Clearing, and Settlement Supervision Act of 2010	《2010 年支付、清算和结算监管法》
Permissive Regulation	选择性规章
Person regulated by the Farm Credit Administration	受农业信贷管理局监管的主体
Phased retirement	阶段性退休
Points and fees	点数和费用
Portfolio margining account of a customer	客户投资组合保证金
Position accountability	持仓说明制度
Position data	持仓数据
Position limitations	持仓限额/限仓制度
Preferential transfers	偏颇性转让
Premium tax	保费税金
Prepaid securities forward transaction	预付证券远期交易
Prepaid variable forward contract	预付可变远期合约
Prepayment penalties	提前还款违约金
Primary financial regulatory agency	优先金融监管机关

续表

Primary Financial Regulatory Agency Inspector General	优先金融监管机关监察长
Prime brokerage transaction	大宗经纪交易
Principal office	主要办公场所
Principal place of business	主要营业地
Prior review	事先审查
Privacy Act of 1974	《1974 年隐私权法》
Private Education Loan Ombudsman	个人教育贷款监察官
Private Equity Fund	私募股权基金
Private Fund Investment Advisers Registration Act of 2010	《2010 年私募基金投资顾问注册法》
Private right of action	私人诉讼权利
Private Securities Litigation Act of 1995	《1995 年私人证券诉讼法》
Privilege	优先权/特权/会员权/保密特权
Procedure for expedited relief	加速救济程序
Procyclical assessments	顺周期计征费
Property interest	房产权益
Proprietary trading	自营交易
Proprietary trading in derivatives	衍生品自营交易
Protecting Tenants at Foreclosure Act	《止赎时承租人权益保护法》
Prudential standards	审慎性标准
Public Company Accounting Over sight Board	公众公司会计监督委员会
Public debt transactions	公共债务交易
Public disclosure	公开披露
Public Utility Holding Company Act of 1935	《1935 年公用事业控股公司法》
Punitive or exemplary damages	惩罚性赔偿金
Put	看跌期权
Qualified risk manager	合格风险经理
Rate cap	利率上限期权
Rate collar	保护性封顶保底利率期权
Rate floor	利率下限期权

续表

Real Estate Settlement Procedures	《1974 年房地产结算程序法》
Real Estate Settlement Procedures Act of 1974	《1974 年房地产结算程序法》
ReaL-time public reporting	实时公开报告
Recording tax	登记税
Reemployed annuitants	返聘年金受益人
Regulation	管理办法/规章/监管/法规
Regulatory capital	监管资本
Reinsurance	再保险
Related action	关联诉讼
Related person	关联主体
Reporting systems for risks to the financial stability of the United States	美国金融稳定的风险指标和报告系统
Repudiate contracts	拒绝履约
Repurchase agreement	回购协议
Rescission	撤销
Research and Analysis Center	研究分析中心
Reserve ratio	准备金率
Resolution mechanisms	清盘机制
Resolution plan	清盘计划
Resolution Trust Corporation	清盘信托公司
Resource extraction issuer	资源采掘发行人
Restitution remedies	恢复原状救济
Retail foreign exchange transactions	零售外汇交易
Retail transactions	零售交易
Retention of records	记录留存
Reverse mortgage	反向抵押贷款
Reverse repurchase agreement	逆回购协议
Revesting of assets	资产的重新占有
Revised Statutes of the United States	《美国制定法汇编》(修订版)
Richard B. Russell National School Lunch Act	《理查·B. 罗素全国学校午餐法》
Right to Financial Privacy Act of 1978	《1978 年金融隐私权法》

续表

Risk Committee	风险委员会
Risk management expert	风险管理专家
Risk participations in bankers' acceptance	银行承兑汇票的风险参与
Risk profile	风险特征
Risk-based capital	风险基础资本
Safe harbor	安全港
Sale and repurchase agreement	出售和回购协议
Sale or securitization of loan	贷款的出售或证券化
Sarbanes-Oxley Act of 2002	《2002 年萨班斯—奥克斯法》
Savings and loan holding company	储贷控股公司
Savings association	储蓄协会
Savings clause	保留条款
Savings provisions	保留条款
Secretary of Health and Human Services	卫生及公共服务部部长
Secretary of the Treasury	财政部部长
Section	条
Secure and Fair Enforcement/S. A. F. E. for Mortgage Licensing Act of 2008	《2008 年安全和公平执行抵押贷款发起人许可法》
Secured creditor haircuts	有担保债权人本金折价
Securities and Exchange Commission	证券交易委员会
Securities borrowing and lending transaction	融券交易
Securities contract	证券合约
Securities Exchange Act of 1934	《1934 年证券交易法》
Securities fraud offense	证券欺诈犯罪
Securities holding company	证券控股公司
Securities Investor Protection Act of 1970	《1970 年证券投资者保护法》
Securities Investor Protection Corporation/SIPC	证券投资者保护公司
Securities laws	证券法/证券法律
Securitized product	证券化产品
Security-based swap	证券类互换
Security-based swap data repository	证券类互换数据存管机构

续表

Security-based swap dealer	证券类互换交易商
Security-based swap execution facility	证券类互换执行设施
Self-regulatory organizations	自律组织
Self-reported error	自报失误
Senior executives	高级公务员/高级管理人员/高管
Senior liability	优先债务
Separate resolution	单独清盘/单独决议
Separately accounted	单独核算
Service periods	工龄
Setoff	抵销
Share insurance	股份保险
Short-swing profit reporting	短线收益报告
Short-term debt	短期债务
Significant bank holding company	重要非银行金融公司
Significant nonbank financial company	重要银行控股公司
Significant price discovery	重要价格发现
Single security	单一证券
Small Bank Holding Company Policy Statement of the Board of Governors	《联邦储备委员会关于小型银行控股公司的政策声明》
Small Business Act	《小型企业法》
Small Business Investment Act of 1958	《1958 年小型企业投资法》
Small business loan	小型企业贷款
Source of strength	财务后盾
Special Committee on Aging of the Senate	参议院老龄问题特别委员会
Special financial resolution court	特殊金融清盘法庭
Spoofing	电子欺诈
Stable value contract	稳定价值合约
Standard maximum cash advance amount	最高预付标准现金额
Standby letters of credit	备用信用证
State bank	州银行
State depository institution	州存款机构

续表

State housing finance agency	州住房融资机构
State insurance regulator	州保险监管者
State member bank	州成员银行
State nonmember bank	州非成员银行
State savings association	州储蓄协会
State -chartered corporation	特许注册公司
Statutory disqualification	法定失格
Statute of limitations	诉讼时效
Statutory Pay-As-You-Go-Act of 2010	《法定 2010 年财政收支平衡法》
Stock borrowed agreement	股票借入协议
Stockbroker	股票经纪商
Straddle	跨式期权组合
Stress test	压力测试
Subcontractor	分包商
Subparagraph	子款
Subpoena	传票
Subsection	子条
Subsidiary	子公司
Substantial position	大额持仓
Subtilte	子编
Suitability in Annuity Transactions Model Regulation of the National Association of Insurance Commissioners	《美国保险监督官协会关于在人寿保险和年金销售中面向老年人的认证和专业称号的使用示范管理办法》
Sunset	日落条款
Supervised securities holding company	受监管证券控股公司
Surplus lines broker	非本州监管保险的经纪人
Swap	互换
Swap agreement	互换协议
Swap data repository	互换数据存管机构
Swap dealer	互换交易商
Swap execution facility	互换执行设施
Swaps entity	互换实体

续表

Systemic risk	系统性风险
Systemic risk regulators	系统性风险监管者
Systemically important	系统重要性
Systemwide risk levels and patterns	系统性风险水平和模式
Tax qualified status	税惠资格
Tax-exempt securities	免税证券
Technical and Professional Advisory Committee	技术与专业顾问委员会
Telemarketing and Consumer Fraud and Abuse Prevention Act	《电话营销与消费者欺诈及滥用防范法》
Territory	属地
Terrorism Risk Insurance Act of 2002	《2002 年恐怖主义风险保险法》
Testimony by the chairperson	主席证词
The Bank Service Company Act	《银行服务公司法》
The Office of Financial Education	金融教育办公室
Title	编
Total consolidated assets	并表资产总额
Total return swap	总回报互换
Trading account	交易账户
Transactions in municipal securities	市政证券交易
Transfer agent	过户代理人
Transfer date	转移日
Transferor agency	职能转出机关
Transferred employee	转移雇员
Transition period	过渡期
Transition reserve ratio	过渡准备金率
Transitional provisions	过渡条款
Trust bank	信托银行
Trust Indenture Act of 1939	《1939 年信托契约法》
Trust preferred share	信托优先股份
Truth in Lending Act	《诚实信贷法》
Truth in Savings Act	《诚实储蓄法》

续表

Underwriters	承销商/贷款审核人
Uniform Standards of Professional Appraisal Practice	《专业评估执业统一标准》
Unit of general local government	一般地方政府行政分区
Unitary savings and loan holding company	单一储贷控股公司
United States Code	《美国法典》
United States District Court for the District of Columbia	哥伦比亚特区联邦地区法院
Valuation	估值
Valuation models	估值模型
Walkaway clause	走避条款
Wall Street Transparency and Accountability Act of 2010	《2010 年华尔街透明度与问责法》
Ways and Means of the House of Representatives	众议院筹款委员会
Weather swap	气候互换
Wells notification	韦尔斯通知
Whistleblower	举报人
Work papers	工作底稿
Workforce flexibility plan	弹性工作计划
Writ of Certiorari	调案复审令
Yield spread premium	利差溢价

图书在版编目(CIP)数据

美国多德—弗兰克华尔街改革与消费者保护法:全2册/中国证券监督管理委员会组织编译.—北京:法律出版社,2014.1
(境外资本市场重要法律文献译丛)
ISBN 978-7-5118-5312-7

Ⅰ.①美… Ⅱ.①中… Ⅲ.①金融法—法案—研究—美国 Ⅳ.①D971.222.8

中国版本图书馆CIP数据核字(2013)第201781号

责任编辑/陈 妮　　**装帧设计**/贾丹丹

出版/法律出版社　　**编辑统筹**/财税出版分社
总发行/中国法律图书有限公司　　**经销**/新华书店
印刷/北京中科印刷有限公司　　**责任印制**/吕亚莉

开本/787毫米×1092毫米 1/16　　**印张**/64.25　**字数**/1439千
版本/2014年1月第1版　　**印次**/2014年1月第1次印刷

法律出版社/北京市丰台区莲花池西里7号(100073)
电子邮件/info@lawpress.com.cn　　**销售热线**/010-63939792/9779
网址/www.lawpress.com.cn　　**咨询电话**/010-63939796

中国法律图书有限公司/北京市丰台区莲花池西里7号(100073)
全国各地中法图分、子公司电话:
第一法律书店/010-63939781/9782　**西安分公司**/029-85388843　**重庆公司**/023-65382816/2908
上海公司/021-62071010/1636　**北京分公司**/010-62534456　**深圳公司**/0755-83072995

书号:ISBN 978-7-5118-5312-7　　**定价(上、下册)**:780.00元